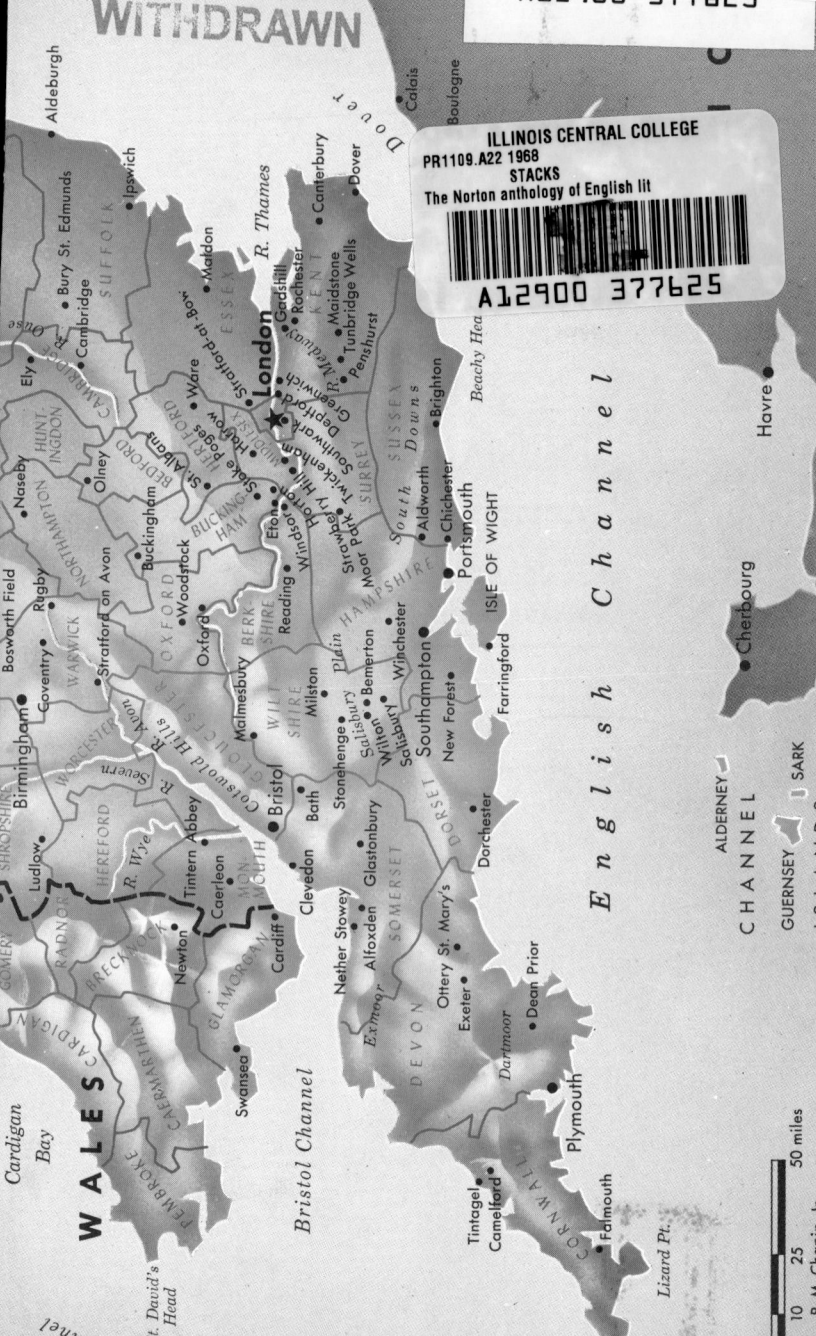

R. M. Chapin, Jr.

0   10   25   50 miles

The Norton Anthology
of English Literature
REVISED

M. H. Abrams, *General Editor*
Professor of English, Cornell University

E. Talbot Donaldson
Professor of English, University of California at Los Angeles

Hallett Smith
Professor of English and Chairman, Division of the Humanities,
California Institute of Technology

Robert M. Adams
Professor of English, Cornell University

Samuel Holt Monk
Professor of English, University of Minnesota

George H. Ford
Professor of English and Chairman, Department of English,
University of Rochester

David Daiches
Professor of English and Dean of the School of English and American Studies,
University of Sussex

MAJOR AUTHORS EDITION

W · W · NORTON & COMPANY · INC · *New York*

COPYRIGHT © 1968, 1962 BY

W. W. NORTON & COMPANY, INC.

Since this page cannot legibly accommodate
all the copyright notices, the page following
constitutes an extension of the copyright page.

Library of Congress Catalog Card No. 68–20833

Book design by John Woodlock

PRINTED IN THE UNITED STATES OF AMERICA

2 3 4 5 6 7 8 9 0

Contents

Preface to the Revised Edition   xxviii

The Middle Ages   1

BEOWULF   1

GEOFFREY CHAUCER (ca. 1343–1400)   61

THE CANTERBURY TALES   71
The General Prologue   73
The Wife of Bath's Prologue and Tale   95
The Pardoner's Prologue and Tale   125
    The Introduction   125
    The Prologue   127
    The Tale   130
    The Epilogue   140
The Nun's Priest's Tale   141
The Miller's Tale   156
    The Introduction   156
    The Tale   158
The Parson's Tale   173
    The Introduction   173
    [The Remedy Against Lechery]   175
    Chaucer's Retraction   178
LYRICS AND OCCASIONAL VERSE   179
To Rosamond   179
To His Scribe Adam   180
Complaint to His Purse   180
Merciless Beauty   181
Gentilesse   182
Truth   183

The Sixteenth Century (1485–1603) 184

EDMUND SPENSER (1552–1599) 204

The Shepheardes Calendar 207
  October 207
The Faerie Queene 212
  A Letter of the Authors 215
  Book I 218
  Book II, Canto XII [The Bower of Bliss] 354
  Book III, Canto VI [The Garden of Adonis] 365
  Book VII, Canto VIII 370
Amoretti 370
  Sonnet 1 ("Happy ye leaves when as those lilly hands") 370
  Sonnet 34 ("Lyke as a ship that through the ocean wyde") 371
  Sonnet 35 ("My hungry eyes through greedy covetize") 371
  Sonnet 37 ("What guyle is this, that those her golden tresses") 371
  Sonnet 54 ("Of this worlds theatre in which we stay") 372
  Sonnet 59 ("Thrise happie she, that is so well assured") 372
  Sonnet 68 ("Most glorious Lord of lyfe, that on this day") 372
  Sonnet 70 ("Fresh spring the herald of loves mighty king") 373
  Sonnet 75 ("One day I wrote her name upon the strand") 373
  Sonnet 79 ("Men call you fayre, and you doe credit it") 373
Epithalamion 374

WILLIAM SHAKESPEARE (1564–1616) 384
  SONGS FROM THE PLAYS 386
When Daisies Pied 386
The Woosel Cock So Black of Hue 387
Tell Me Where Is Fancy Bred 388
Sigh No More, Ladies 388
Under the Greenwood Tree 388
Blow, Blow, Thou Winter Wind 389
Oh Mistress Mine 389
Take, Oh, Take Those Lips Away 390
Fear No More the Heat o' the Sun 390
When Daffodils Begin to Peer 390
Full Fathom Five 391
Where the Bee Sucks, There Suck I 391

SONNETS   391

3 ("Look in thy glass, and tell the face thou viewest")   391
12 ("When I do count the clock that tells the time")   392
18 ("Shall I compare thee to a summer's day?")   392
29 ("When, in disgrace with fortune and men's eyes")   393
30 ("When to the sessions of sweet silent thought")   393
55 ("Not marble, nor the gilded monuments")   393
56 ("Sweet love, renew thy force; be it not said")   394
60 ("Like as the waves make towards the pebbled shore")   394
71 ("No longer mourn for me when I am dead")   394
73 ("That time of year thou mayst in me behold")   395
87 ("Farewell: thou art too dear for my possessing")   395
94 ("They that have power to hurt and will do none")   395
97 ("How like a winter hath my absence been")   396
98 ("From you have I been absent in the spring")   396
104 ("To me, fair friend, you never can be old")   397
106 ("When in the chronicle of wasted time")   397
107 ("Not mine own fears, nor the prophetic soul")   397
110 ("Alas, 'tis true I have gone here and there")   398
116 ("Let me not to the marriage of true minds")   398
118 ("Like as, to make our appetites more keen")   398
121 ("'Tis better to be vile than vile esteemed")   399
129 ("Th' expense of spirit in a waste of shame")   399
130 ("My mistress' eyes are nothing like the sun")   400
138 ("When my love swears that she is made of truth")   400
144 ("Two loves I have of comfort and despair")   400
146 ("Poor soul, the center of my sinful earth")   401

The Phoenix and the Turtle   401
Henry IV, Part I   403

The Seventeenth Century (1603–1660)   474

JOHN DONNE (1572–1631)   490

The Good-Morrow   494
Song ("Go and catch a falling star")   494
The Undertaking   495
The Indifferent   496
The Canonization   497
Twicknam Garden   498
The Apparition   499

Love's Alchemy	499
The Flea	500
The Bait	501
A Valediction: Forbidding Mourning	502
The Ecstasy	503
Lovers' Infiniteness	505
The Sun Rising	506
Air and Angels	507
Break of Day	507
A Valediction: Of Weeping	508
The Funeral	509
The Relic	509
To the Countess of Bedford	510
Elegy IV. The Perfume	512
Satire III, Religion	514
Good Friday, 1613. Riding Westward	517
Holy Sonnets	518
1 ("Thou hast made me, and shall Thy work decay?")	518
5 ("I am a little world made cunningly")	519
7 ("At the round earth's imagined corners, blow")	519
10 ("Death, be not proud, though some have called thee")	520
14 ("Batter my heart, three-personed God")	520
18 ("Show me, dear Christ, Thy spouse so bright and clear")	521
A Hymn to Christ, at the Author's Last Going into Germany	521
Hymn to God My God, in My Sickness	522
A Hymn to God the Father	523
Paradoxes and Problems	524
Paradox VI. That It Is Possible to Find Some Virtue in Women	524
Problem II. Why Puritans Make Long Sermons	525
Problem VI. Why Hath the Common Opinion Afforded Women Souls?	525
Devotions upon Emergent Occasions	526
Meditation XIV	526
Meditation XVII	527
Sermon LXXVI	529
[On Falling Out of God's Hand]	529
BEN JONSON (1572–1637)	530
To Penshurst	532

To the Memory of My Beloved Master William Shakespeare 535
To William Camden 537
On My First Daughter 537
On My First Son 538
To John Donne 538
It Was a Beauty That I Saw 538
Epitaph on Elizabeth, L. H. 539
An Elegy 539
Slow, Slow, Fresh Fount 540
Queen and Huntress 541
Gypsy Songs 541
Though I Am Young and Cannot Tell 542
Song: To Celia 542
Come, My Celia 543
The Triumph of Charis 543
Still to Be Neat 544
Ode to Himself 545
The Vision of Delight 546

JOHN MILTON (1608–1674) 553

L'Allegro 555
Il Penseroso 559
At a Solemn Music 563
Comus 564
    Sweet Echo 564
    Sabrina Fair 564
    By the Rushy-fringed Bank 564
Lycidas 565
How Soon Hath Time 571
When the Assault Was Intended to the City 572
A Book Was Writ of Late Called *Tetrachordon* 572
On the New Forcers of Conscience Under the Long
    Parliament 573
On the Late Massacre in Piedmont 574
Lawrence, of Virtuous Father Virtuous Son 574
When I Consider How My Light Is Spent 575
Methought I Saw My Late Espoused Saint 575
Of Education 576
Areopagitica 584
Paradise Lost 594
    Book I 597
    Book II 617

Book III   642
[The Consult in Heaven]   642
Book IV   652
[Satan's Entry into Paradise]   652
[Book V. Summary]   659
[Book VI. Summary]   660
Book VII   660
[The Invocation]   660
[Book VIII. Summary]   661
Book IX   661
Book X   690
[Consequences of the Fall]   690
[Book XI. Summary]   696
Book XII   696
[The Departure from Eden]   696
Samson Agonistes   701

FRANCIS BACON (1561–1626)   745

ESSAYS   746
Of Truth   746
Of Marriage and Single Life   748
Of Great Place   750
Of Studies   752

Novum Organum   753
[The Idols]   753
The New Atlantis   760
[Solomon's House]   760

The Restoration and the Eighteenth Century
(1660–1798)   769

JOHN DRYDEN (1631–1700)   784
Prologue to *The Tempest*   788
Epilogue to *Tyrannic Love*   789
Epilogue to *The Conquest of Granada, II*   790
Song from *The Indian Emperor*   791
Song from *An Evening's Love*   791
Song from *Marriage à la Mode*   792
Absalom and Achitophel: A Poem   792
Mac Flecknoe   817

To the Memory of Mr. Oldham 824
To the Pious Memory of the Accomplished Young Lady
    Mrs. Anne Killigrew 825
A Song for St. Cecilia's Day 831
Epigram on Milton 833
Alexander's Feast 833
The Secular Masque 838
An Essay of Dramatic Poesy 842
The Author's Apology for Heroic Poetry and Heroic License 847
A Discourse Concerning the Original and Progress of Satire 849
The Preface to *Fables Ancient and Modern* 850

JONATHAN SWIFT (1667–1745) 852

A Description of a City Shower 855
Verses on the Death of Dr. Swift 857
An Argument against the Abolishing of Christianity
    in England 868
Gulliver's Travels 878
  A Letter from Captain Gulliver to his Cousin Sympson 878
  The Publisher to the Reader 882
  Part II. A Voyage to Brobdingnag 883
  Part IV. A Voyage to the Country of the Houyhnhnms 933
A Modest Proposal 988

ALEXANDER POPE (1688–1744) 995

An Essay on Criticism 1001
  Part I 1001
  Part II 1006
The Rape of the Lock 1014
Ode on Solitude 1033
Epistle to Miss Blount 1034
Elegy to the Memory of an Unfortunate Lady 1035
Epistle to Robert, Earl of Oxford and Mortimer 1037
An Essay on Man 1038
  Epistle I. Of the Nature and State of Man, with
    Respect to the Universe 1039
  Epistle II. Of the Nature and State of Man with
    Respect to Himself, as an Individual 1046
The Universal Prayer 1046
The First Satire of the Second Book of Horace Imitated 1048
Epistle II. To a Lady 1052
Epistle to Dr. Arbuthnot 1060

SAMUEL JOHNSON (1709–1784)   1072

The Vanity of Human Wishes   1076
To Miss ———   1084
Prologue Spoken by Mr. Garrick   1085
On the Death of Dr. Robert Levet   1087
A Short Song of Congratulation   1088
Rambler No. 5 [On Spring]   1089
Idler No. 31 [On Idleness]   1092
The History of Rasselas, Prince of Abyssinia   1094
Prayers and Meditations   1120
    Easter Eve, 1761   1120
    Good Friday, 1779, 11 P.M.   1120
Rambler No. 4 [On Fiction]   1121
The Preface to Shakespeare   1125
    [Shakespeare and General Nature]   1125
    [Shakespeare's Faults. The Three Dramatic Unities]   1128
    [Henry IV]   1135

    LIVES OF THE POETS   1136
Cowley   1136
    [Metaphysical Wit]   1136
Milton   1138
    [Lycidas]   1138
    [L'Allegro. Il Penseroso]   1140
    [Paradise Lost]   1141
Pope   1147
    [Pope's Intellectual Character. Pope and Dryden
        Compared]   1147

JAMES BOSWELL (1740–1795)   1151

Boswell on the Grand Tour   1154
    [Boswell Interviews Voltaire]   1154
The Life of Samuel Johnson, LL.D.   1156
    [Plan of the *Life*]   1156
    [Johnson's Early Years. Marriage and London]
        [1709–52]   1158
    [The Letter to Chesterfield] [1754–62]   1164
    [A Memorable Year: Boswell Meets Johnson] [1763]   1168
    [Goldsmith. Sundry Opinions. Johnson Meets His
        King] [1763–67]   1171
    [Fear of Death] [1769]   1176
    [Ossian. "Talking for Victory"] [1775–76]   1177

[Dinner with Wilkes] [1776]   1179

[Dread of Solitude] [1777]   1185

["A Bottom of Good Sense." Bet Flint. "Clear Your
    Mind of Cant"] [1781–83]   1186

[Johnson Prepares for Death] [1783–84]   1187

[Johnson Faces Death] [1784]   1189

The Romantic Period (1798–1832)   1193

WILLIAM BLAKE (1757–1827)   1210

POETICAL SKETCHES   1215

Song ("How sweet I roamed from field to field")   1215

To the Evening Star   1215

Song ("Memory, hither come")   1216

Mad Song   1216

To the Muses   1217

SONGS OF INNOCENCE   1218

Introduction   1218

The Lamb   1219

The Divine Image   1219

The Chimney Sweeper   1220

Nurse's Song   1220

Holy Thursday   1221

The Little Black Boy   1221

SONGS OF EXPERIENCE   1222

Introduction   1222

Earth's Answer   1223

The Clod & the Pebble   1224

Holy Thursday   1224

The Chimney Sweeper   1224

Nurse's Song   1225

The Sick Rose   1225

The Tyger   1225

Ah Sun-Flower   1226

The Garden of Love   1226

London   1227

The Human Abstract   1227

Infant Sorrow   1228

A Poison Tree   1228

To Tirzah   1229

A Divine Image   1229

The Book of Thel   1230
The Marriage of Heaven and Hell   1234
For the Sexes: The Gates of Paradise   1248
  [Prologue] "Mutual Forgiveness of each Vice"   1248
  [Epilogue] To the Accuser who is The God of This World 1249

FROM BLAKE'S NOTEBOOK   1249
Never Pain to Tell Thy Love   1249
I Askéd a Thief   1249
Mock on, Mock on, Voltaire, Rousseau   1250
Morning   1250

And Did Those Feet   1250
[A Vision of The Last Judgment]   1251

WILLIAM WORDSWORTH (1770–1850)   1255

LYRICAL BALLADS   1258
We Are Seven   1258
Lines Written in Early Spring   1260
Expostulation and Reply   1261
The Tables Turned   1262
To My Sister   1262
Lines Composed a Few Miles Above Tintern Abbey   1264
Preface to the Second Edition   1268
Strange Fits of Passion Have I Known   1280
She Dwelt Among the Untrodden Ways   1281
Three Years She Grew   1282
A Slumber Did My Spirit Seal   1283
I Traveled Among Unknown Men   1283
Lucy Gray   1283
The Ruined Cottage   1285
Michael   1298
Written in March   1308
Resolution and Independence   1309
The Green Linnet   1313
Yew Trees   1314
I Wandered Lonely as a Cloud   1314
My Heart Leaps Up   1315
Ode: Intimations of Immortality   1315
Ode to Duty   1322
The Solitary Reaper   1324
Elegiac Stanzas   1325

SONNETS   1327
Composed upon Westminster Bridge, September 3, 1802 1327

It Is a Beauteous Evening   1327
Composed in the Valley near Dover, on the Day of Landing   1328
London, 1802   1328
The World Is Too Much with Us   1328
Surprised by Joy   1329
Composed by the Side of Grasmere Lake   1329
Afterthought   1330
Mutability   1330
Steamboats, Viaducts, and Railways   1331

Extempore Effusion upon the Death of James Hogg   1331
The Recluse   1333
  ["Prospectus"]   1333
The Prelude, or Growth of a Poet's Mind   1336
  Book I. Introduction—Childhood and Schooltime   1337
  Book II. Schooltime (continued)   1344
  Book III. Residence at Cambridge   1346
  Book IV. Summer Vacation   1348
  Book V. Books   1349
  Book VI. Cambridge and the Alps   1352
  Book VII. Residence in London   1355
  Book VIII. Retrospect—Love of Nature Leading to Love
    of Man   1357
  Book IX. Residence in France   1359
  Book X. Residence in France (continued)   1363
  Book XI. France (concluded)   1365
  Book XII. Imagination and Taste, How Impaired and
    Restored   1369
  Book XIII. Imagination and Taste, How Impaired and
    Restored (concluded)   1371
  Book XIV. Conclusion   1373

SAMUEL TAYLOR COLERIDGE (1772–1834)   1378

The Eolian Harp   1381
The Rime of the Ancient Mariner   1383
Kubla Khan   1399
Christabel   1401
Frost at Midnight   1417
Dejection: An Ode   1419
What Is Life?   1423
Phantom   1423
To William Wordsworth   1423
Recollections of Love   1426
On Donne's Poetry   1427

Work Without Hope 1427
Constancy to an Ideal Object 1428
Phantom or Fact 1428
Epitaph 1429
Biographia Literaria 1429
    Chapter I 1429
    Chapter IV 1437
    Chapter XIII 1440
    Chapter XIV 1441
    Chapter XVII 1447
Lectures on Shakespeare 1450
    [Fancy and Imagination in Shakespeare's Poetry] 1450
    [Mechanic vs. Organic Form] 1452

GEORGE GORDON, LORD BYRON (1788–1824) 1454

Written After Swimming from Sestos to Abydos 1460
When We Two Parted 1460
She Walks in Beauty 1461
Stanzas for Music 1462
    There Be None of Beauty's Daughters 1462
    They Say That Hope Is Happiness 1462
Darkness 1463
Childe Harold's Pilgrimage 1465
    Canto I 1465
    Canto III 1467
    Canto IV 1482
So We'll Go No More A-Roving 1485
Don Juan 1485
    Canto I 1487
    Canto II 1512
    Canto III 1530
    Canto IV 1536
The Vision of Judgment 1544
Stanzas to the Po 1566
When a Man Hath No Freedom to Fight for at Home 1567
Stanzas Written on the Road Between Florence and Pisa 1567

PERCY BYSSHE SHELLEY (1792–1822) 1568

Mutability 1573
Mont Blanc 1573
Hymn to Intellectual Beauty 1577
Ozymandias 1579
Sonnet ("Lift not the painted veil which those who live") 1580

Stanzas Written in Dejection, Near Naples 1580
Song to the Men of England 1582
England in 1819 1583
The Indian Serenade 1583
Ode to the West Wind 1584
Prometheus Unbound 1586
The Cloud 1608
To a Skylark 1610
Hymn of Apollo 1613
Hymn of Pan 1614
The Two Spirits: An Allegory 1615
The Tower of Famine 1616
To Night 1617
To ——— 1618
A Lament 1618
When Passion's Trance Is Overpast 1619
Hellas 1619
   Worlds on Worlds 1619
   The World's Great Age 1620
Adonais 1622
Lines: When the Lamp Is Shattered 1635
A Dirge 1636
To Jane: The Invitation 1636
To Jane: The Keen Stars Were Twinkling 1638
Lines Written in the Bay of Lerici 1638
The Triumph of Life 1640
A Defense of Poetry 1656

JOHN KEATS (1795–1821) 1669

On First Looking into Chapman's Homer 1672
Sleep and Poetry 1673
On Seeing the Elgin Marbles for the First Time 1675
On the Sea 1675
Endymion 1675
   Preface 1675
   Book I [A Thing of Beauty] 1676
   Book I [The "Pleasure Thermometer"] 1677
   Book IV [The Cave of Quietude] 1680
In Drear-Nighted December 1681
On Sitting Down to Read King Lear Once Again 1682
When I Have Fears 1682
To Homer 1683

The Eve of St. Agnes   1683
Bright Star   1693
Why Did I Laugh Tonight?   1693
La Belle Dame sans Merci   1694
On the Sonnet   1695
To Sleep   1695
On Fame   1696
Ode to Psyche   1696
Ode on a Grecian Urn   1698
Ode to a Nightingale   1700
Ode on Melancholy   1702
Lamia   1704
The Fall of Hyperion   1720
To Autumn   1735
This Living Hand   1736

LETTERS   1736
To Benjamin Bailey (Nov. 22, 1817) [The Authenticity of
    the Imagination]   1736
To George and Thomas Keats (Dec. 21, 27(?), 1817)
    [Negative Capability]   1738
To John Hamilton Reynolds (Feb. 3, 1818) [Wordsworth's
    Poetry]   1740
To John Taylor (Feb. 27, 1818) [Keats's Axioms in
    Poetry]   1741
To John Hamilton Reynolds (May 3, 1818) [Milton,
    Wordsworth, and the Chambers of Human Life]   1742
To Richard Woodhouse (Oct. 27, 1818) [A Poet Has No
    Identity]   1745
To George and Georgiana Keats (Feb. 14–May 3, 1819)
    ["The Vale of Soul-Making"]   1746
To Percy Bysshe Shelley (Aug. 16, 1820) ["Load Every
    Rift with Ore"]   1750

The Victorian Age (1832–1901)   1752

THOMAS CARLYLE (1795–1881)   1768

[Carlyle's Portraits of His Contemporaries]   1774
    [King William IV at 69]   1774
    [Queen Victoria at 18]   1774
    [Charles Lamb at 56]   1775

[Samuel Taylor Coleridge at 53] 1775
[William Wordsworth in His Seventies] 1780
[Alfred Tennyson at 34] 1783
[William Makepeace Thackeray at 42] 1783
Characteristics 1784
Sartor Resartus 1795
 Chapter VII. The Everlasting No 1795
 Chapter VIII. Centre of Indifference 1801
 Chapter IX. The Everlasting Yea 1810
The French Revolution 1818
 September in Paris 1818
 Place de la Révolution 1822
 Cause and Effect 1826
Past and Present 1828
 Democracy 1828
 Captains of Industry 1833

ALFRED, LORD TENNYSON (1809–1892) 1839

The Kraken 1843
Mariana 1844
Sonnet ("She took the dappled partridge flecked with
 blood") 1846
The Lady of Shalott 1846
The Lotos-Eaters 1850
You Ask Me, Why, Though Ill at Ease 1855
Morte d'Arthur 1855
 The Epic 1855
 Morte d'Arthur 1857
Ulysses 1863
Tithonus 1865
Break, Break, Break 1867
Locksley Hall 1867
Move Eastward, Happy Earth 1873
Lines ("Here often, when a child I lay reclined") 1874
The Eagle: A Fragment 1874

 THE PRINCESS 1874
Sweet and Low 1874
The Splendor Falls 1875
Tears, Idle Tears 1875
Ask Me No More 1876
Now Sleeps the Crimson Petal 1876
Come Down, O Maid 1877

In Memoriam A. H. H.   1878
The Charge of the Light Brigade   1920
Maud   1921
   VIII   ("She came to the village church")   1921
   XVI   ("Catch not my breath, O clamorous heart")   1922
   XVIII ("I have led her home, my love, my only friend") 1922
In the Valley of Cauteretz   1924
Idylls of the King   1924
   Dedication   1924
   In Love, If Love Be Love   1926
Northern Farmer: New Style   1926
Flower in the Crannied Wall   1928
The Revenge   1928
To Virgil   1931
"Frater Ave atque Vale"   1933
To E. FitzGerald   1933
Locksley Hall Sixty Years After   1934
By an Evolutionist   1944
June Bracken and Heather   1945
The Dawn   1945
The Silent Voices   1946
Crossing the Bar   1946

ROBERT BROWNING (1812–1889)   1947

Porphyria's Lover   1953
Soliloquy of the Spanish Cloister   1954
My Last Duchess   1956
The Laboratory   1957
The Lost Leader   1959
How They Brought the Good News from Ghent to Aix   1960
Home-Thoughts, from Abroad   1961
Home-Thoughts, from the Sea   1962
The Bishop Orders His Tomb at Saint Praxed's Church   1962
Meeting at Night   1965
Parting at Morning   1966
A Toccata of Galuppi's   1966
Memorabilia   1968
Love Among the Ruins   1969
Women and Roses   1971
"Childe Roland to the Dark Tower Came"   1972
Up at a Villa—Down in the City   1978
Respectability   1980

Fra Lippo Lippi 1981
In a Year 1989
The Last Ride Together 1991
Andrea del Sarto 1994
Two in the Campagna 2000
A Grammarian's Funeral 2002
Confessions 2005
Youth and Art 2006
Caliban upon Setebos 2008
Prospice 2016
Abt Vogler 2016
Rabbi Ben Ezra 2020
Apparent Failure 2025
O Lyric Love 2026
The Householder 2027
House 2028
To Edward FitzGerald 2029
Epilogue to *Asolando* 2030

MATTHEW ARNOLD (1822-1888) 2030

Shakespeare 2036
In Harmony with Nature 2036
To a Friend 2037
The Forsaken Merman 2037
Isolation. To Marguerite 2040
To Marguerite—Continued 2041
The Buried Life 2042
Stanzas in Memory of the Author of *Obermann* 2044
Memorial Verses 2049
Longing 2051
Lines Written in Kensington Gardens 2051
Philomela 2052
Requiescat 2053
The Scholar Gypsy 2054
Dover Beach 2061
Stanzas from the Grande Chartreuse 2062
Thyrsis 2067
Palladium 2073
The Better Part 2074
Growing Old 2074
The Last Word 2075
Preface to *Poems* (1853) 2076

The Function of Criticism at the Present Time 2088
Maurice de Guérin 2107
[Definition of Poetry] 2107
Culture and Anarchy 2109
Chapter I. Sweetness and Light 2109
Chapter II. Doing As One Likes 2111
Chapter V. Porro Unum Est Necessarium 2114
Wordsworth 2118
The Study of Poetry 2130
Literature and Science 2152

JOHN STUART MILL (1806–1873) 2168

What Is Poetry? 2170
Coleridge 2178
On Liberty 2181
Chapter III. Of Individuality As One of the Elements
of Well-Being 2181
Autobiography 2192
Chapter V. A Crisis in My Mental History. One Stage
Onward 2192

The Twentieth Century 2201

THOMAS HARDY (1840-1928) 2210
Hap 2212
The Impercipient 2212
Neutral Tones 2213
I Look into My Glass 2214
A Broken Appointment 2214
Drummer Hodge 2215
Lausanne 2215
The Darkling Thrush 2216
A Trampwoman's Tragedy 2217
Let Me Enjoy 2220
The Rash Bride 2220
One We Knew 2222
She Hears the Storm 2223
Channel Firing 2224
The Convergence of the Twain 2225
Ah, Are You Digging on My Grave? 2226

Under the Waterfall   2227
The Walk   2228
During Wind and Rain   2229
In Time of "The Breaking of Nations"   2229

GERARD MANLEY HOPKINS (1844–1889)   2230

God's Grandeur   2234
The Starlight Night   2234
Spring   2235
The Lantern Out of Doors   2235
The Windhover   2236
Pied Beauty   2236
Hurrahing in Harvest   2237
Binsey Poplars   2237
Duns Scotus's Oxford   2238
Felix Randal   2239
Spring and Fall   2239
Inversnaid   2240
[Carrion Comfort]   2240
[No Worst, There Is None]   2241
[Thou Art Indeed Just, Lord]   2241

GEORGE BERNARD SHAW (1856–1950)   2242

Preface to *Plays Pleasant*   2246
Arms and the Man   2248

JOSEPH CONRAD (1857–1924)   2297

Preface to *The Nigger of the "Narcissus"*   2299
[The Task of the Artist]   2299
Youth   2302
The Secret Sharer   2329

WILLIAM BUTLER YEATS (1865–1939)   2362

The Madness of King Goll   2367
The Stolen Child   2368
Down by the Salley Gardens   2370
The Rose of the World   2370
The Lake Isle of Innisfree   2371
The Sorrow of Love   2371
When You Are Old   2371
Who Goes with Fergus?   2372
The Man Who Dreamed of Faeryland   2372
The Secret Rose   2373
The Folly of Being Comforted   2375

Adam's Curse 2375
The Old Men Admiring Themselves in the Water 2376
No Second Troy 2376
The Fascination of What's Difficult 2377
September 1913 2377
To a Shade 2378
The Cold Heaven 2379
The Wild Swans at Coole 2379
Easter 1916 2380
On a Political Prisoner 2382
The Second Coming 2383
A Prayer for My Daughter 2384
Sailing to Byzantium 2386
Leda and the Swan 2387
Among School Children 2388
A Dialogue of Self and Soul 2390
For Anne Gregory 2391
Byzantium 2392
Crazy Jane Talks with the Bishop 2394
After Long Silence 2394
Lapis Lazuli 2395
Long-legged Fly 2396
The Circus Animals' Desertion 2397
Under Ben Bulben 2398
Reveries over Childhood and Youth 2401
[The Yeats Family] 2401
[An Irish Literature] 2404
The Trembling of the Veil 2405
[London and Pre-Raphaelitism] 2405
[Oscar Wilde] 2407
[The Handiwork of Art] 2408
[The Origin of *The Lake Isle of Innisfree*] 2410
[The Rhymers' Club] 2411

JAMES JOYCE (1882–1941) 2412

Araby 2418
A Portrait of the Artist as a Young Man 2424
[The Interview with the Director] 2424
[The Walk on the Shore] 2431
Ulysses 2438
[Proteus] 2438
[Lestrygonians] 2456

Finnegans Wake   2488
  Anna Livia Plurabelle   2488
D. H. LAWRENCE (1885–1930)   2493
Odor of Chrysanthemums   2498
The Horse Dealer's Daughter   2515
The Rainbow   2530
  Chapter II. They Live at the Marsh   2530
Women in Love   2536
  Chapter XVIII. Rabbit   2536
Etruscan Places   2545
  Tarquinia   2545
Why the Novel Matters   2558
Piano   2563
Bavarian Gentians   2564
Snake   2565
The Ship of Death   2567
T. S. ELIOT (1888–1965)   2569
The Love Song of J. Alfred Prufrock   2574
Landscapes   2577
  Rannoch, by Glencoe   2577
  Cape Ann   2578
Sweeney Among the Nightingales   2578
Whispers of Immortality   2580
The Waste Land   2581
Journey of the Magi   2598
Marina   2599
Four Quartets   2601
  Little Gidding   2601
Tradition and the Individual Talent   2608
The Metaphysical Poets   2615
Ulysses, Order, and Myth   2623
Yeats   2626

SELECTED BIBLIOGRAPHIES   2637
INDEX   2649

Preface
to the Revised Edition

This volume presents a selection of the best and most characteristic writings of thirty-two authors, reprinted from the second edition of the two-volume *Norton Anthology of English Literature*. It contains many more writers than other major-author anthologies and represents most of them in sufficient quantity to allow the instructor considerable latitude of choice. It also includes, in addition to introductory headnotes for individual authors, an extensive introduction to each literary period, designed to set the major writers in a historical context and to clarify the relations of their work to the literary and intellectual currents of their age.

Many of the teachers who used the first edition of this anthology volunteered suggestions and corrections, and many other teachers and scholars answered requests about their procedures and preferences generously and in detail. As a result of this information, the editors are able to provide in this revised edition a substantial enlargement and improvement of the first. To the twenty-eight original writers we have added the poem *Beowulf*, printed in its entirety, and three authors, Thomas Hardy, Joseph Conrad, and D. H. Lawrence. A number of works earlier represented only in part are now complete, among them Book I of *The Faerie Queene*, *Absalom and Achitophel*, and *The Marriage of Heaven and Hell*. New titles have been added for all the authors in the first edition, many of them long works reprinted *in toto*: Milton's *Samson Agonistes* (in addition to an expanded representation of *Paradise Lost*), Swift's *Argument against Abolishing Christianity*, and Part IV (in addition to Part II) of *Gulliver's Travels*, Blake's *Book of Thel*, Wordsworth's *Ruined Cottage*, Coleridge's *Eolian Harp*, Byron's *Vision of Judgment*, Shelley's *Mont Blanc* and *Triumph of Life*, and Keats's *Fall of Hyperion*. Other important additions have been made to many poets, especially to Spenser, Shakespeare, Tennyson, Browning, Arnold, Hopkins, and Yeats; and new selections of prose have been included for Johnson, Carlyle, Mill, and Eliot.

By an improvement in the quality of the paper, these and other items have been added without impairing the visibility and open layout of the texts. Poetry in this anthology can still be read as it was written to be read: in a single column, in a comfortable type, and with ample margins.

We continue faithful to the principle that texts for undergraduates should be no less scrupulously edited than texts for the scholar. Accordingly, we have printed a new translation of *Beowulf* by Talbot Donaldson and have reset the text of Blake from the new edition by David Erdman and Harold Bloom. Shelley's *Triumph of Life* is in the revised form recently published by Donald H. Reiman, and Wordsworth's great but neglected narrative poem, *The Ruined Cottage*, is a new and superior version edited from an unpublished manuscript by Jonathan Wordsworth.

Each editor has reconsidered all his introductory essays and footnotes and has rewritten many of them in the light of recent scholarship and criticism. The comprehensive introductions, the full glossing of archaisms and allusions, and suggestions (in carefully selected instances where the student is apt to go astray) about possibilities in interpretation free the student from dependence on a reference library and enable him to carry and read the book anywhere—in class, in his own room, or under a tree. The experience of many teachers has confirmed our expectation that these editorial aids would not displace the teacher but would open up possibilities to the student's own judgment and suggest points of departure for commentary and dialogue in the classroom. The bibliographical guides at the end of the volume, designed to encourage the student to read further on his own, have all been brought up to date. As a convenience to the student wishing to develop his own library, the symbol of a dagger indicates the titles currently available in paperback.

We have continued the editorial procedures which proved their utility in the earlier edition. In each of the historical and biographical introductions we list and identify the dates of crucial importance at the beginning and limit further chronological references to those the student needs to orient himself. In order, however, to specify the interrelations of individual works, we place after each selection, where the facts are known, the date of composition on the left and the date of first publication in book form on the right; the latter is sometimes preceded by the date of first appearance in a periodical publication. The writings of Chaucer and Spenser, which contain a high proportion of unfamiliar words, have been glossed in the margin, where the translation can be assimilated with least impediment to the flow of the reading. Whenever a portion of the text has been omitted, the omission is indicated by three asterisks. Titles supplied by the editors are enclosed in brackets.

All texts are printed in the form that makes them most immediately available to their particular audience. We have normalized spellings and capitalization according to modern American usage, but only in those instances in which the change does not alter semantic, phonological, or metric qualities. The verse of Spenser and Hopkins and the prose of Joyce, Shaw, Carlyle, and Keats (in his letters) have been reproduced in their original form; only the minimal changes necessary for ready intelligibility have been made in the writings of William Blake; and in all writers, significant deviations from the norm (Keats's "faery," for example) have been left unaltered. The writings of Chaucer have also been left in the original language, but each word is consistently spelled in that variant of its scribal forms which is closest to modern English. When we have altered punctuation, it has been on the conservative principle that a change should be made only when the old punctuation would mislead a modern reader.

In the process of compiling and revising this anthology, the editors incurred obligations to scores of teachers throughout the country who volunteered useful suggestions or gave essential information when asked. To each of these—too numerous to list here— we owe our thanks. We wish especially to acknowledge the wise counsel, in preparing the first edition, of W. R. Keast, now president of Wayne State University, and the detailed and helpful critiques toward revising that edition provided by a number of teacher-scholars: William Alfred (Harvard University); Harold Bloom (Yale University); Jack M. Davis (University of Connecticut); Peter Elbow (University of California, Berkeley); James Gindin (University of Michigan); David D. Harvey (State University of New York at Albany); Robert W. Hill, Jr. (Middlebury College); Arthur Hoffman (Syracuse University); David Kalstone (Rutgers, The State University); Robert Kimbrough (University of Wisconsin); R. M. Lumiansky (University of Pennsylvania); Hugh Maclean (State University of New York at Albany); Thomas Moser (Stanford University); Stephen M. Parrish (Cornell University); S. P. Rosenbaum (University of Toronto); and Clarence Tracy (University of British Columbia). Howard L. Anderson (Michigan State University) was of special assistance on the bibliography for the Eighteenth Century, and Richard L. Greene (Wesleyan University, Connecticut) provided the editors with a comprehensive and most helpful list of corrections and suggestions. George P. Brockway and John Benedict, of W. W. Norton & Company, Inc. —assisted ably by Eleanor Brooks, Kathleen Calkins, and S. H. Dammacco—have contributed immensely, by encouragement, caveats, and hard editorial work, to mitigate the chronic dilemmas in the endeavor to represent, justly and accurately, the work of all the major English writers in a single volume.

M. H. ABRAMS

The Middle Ages

(To 1485)

BEOWULF

Beowulf, the oldest of the great long poems written in English, was probably composed more than twelve hundred years ago, in the first half of the eighth century. Its author may have been a native of what was then West Mercia, the West Midlands of England today, though the late tenth-century manuscript, which alone preserves the poem, originated in the south in the kingdom of the West Saxons. In 1731, before any modern transcription of the text had been made, the manuscript was seriously damaged in the fire that destroyed the building in London which housed the extraordinary collection of medieval English manuscripts made by Sir Robert Bruce Cotton (1571–1631). As a result of the fire and of subsequent deterioration of the manuscript, a number of lines and words have been lost from the poem, but even if the manuscript had not been damaged, the poem would still have been difficult, because the poetic Old English (or Anglo-Saxon) in which it was written is itself hard, the style is allusive, the ideas often seem remote and strange to modern perceptions, and because the text was inevitably corrupted during the many transcriptions which must have intervened in the two and a half centuries between the poem's composition and the copying of the extant manuscript. Yet despite its difficulty, the somber grandeur of *Beowulf* is still capable of stirring the hearts of readers, and because of its excellence as well as its antiquity, the poem merits the high position that it is generally assigned in the study of English poetry.

While the poem itself is English in language and origin, it deals not with native Englishmen, but with their Germanic forebears, especially with two south Scandinavian tribes, the Danes and the Geats, who lived on the Danish island of Zealand and in southern Sweden, respectively. Thus, the historical period it concerns—insofar as it may be said to refer to history at all—is some two centuries before the poem was written; that is, it concerns a time following the initial invasion of England by Germanic tribes in 449, but before the Anglo-Saxon migration was completed, and perhaps before the arrival of the ancestors of the audience to whom the poem was sung: this audience may have considered itself to be of the same Geatish stock as the hero, Beowulf. The one datable fact of history mentioned in the poem

1

is a raid on the Franks made by Hygelac, the king of the Geats at the time Beowulf was a young man, and this raid occurred in the year 520. Yet despite their antiquity, the poet's materials must have been very much alive to his audience, for the elliptical way in which he alludes to events not directly concerned with his plot demands of the listener a wide knowledge of traditional Germanic history. This knowledge was probably kept alive by other heroic poetry, of which little has been preserved in English, though much must once have existed. As it stands, *Beowulf* is not only unique as an example of the Old English epic, but is also the greatest of the surviving epics composed by the Germanic peoples.

It is generally agreed that the poet who put the old materials into their present form was a Christian, and that his poem reflects a Christian tradition: the conversion of the Germanic settlers in England had largely been completed during the century preceding the one in which the poet wrote. But there is little general agreement as to how clearly *Beowulf* reflects a Christian tradition or, conversely, the actual nature of the Christian tradition that it is held to reflect. Many specifically Christian references occur, especially to the Old Testament: God is said to be the Creator of all things and His will seems recognized (sporadically if not systematically) as being identical with Fate (*wyrd*); Grendel is described as a descendant of Cain, and the sword that Beowulf finds in Grendel's mother's lair has engraved on it the story of the race of giants and their destruction by flood; the dead await God's judgment, and Hell and the Devil are ready to receive the souls of Grendel and his mother, while believers will find the Father's embrace; Hrothgar's speech of advice to Beowulf (section XXV) seems to reflect patristic doctrine in its emphasis on conscience and the Devil's lying in wait for the unwary. Yet there is no reference to the New Testament—to Christ and His Sacrifice which are the real bases of Christianity in any intelligible sense of the term. Furthermore, readers may well feel that the poem achieves rather little of its emotional power through invocation of Christian values or of values that are consonant with Christian doctrine as we know it. Perhaps the sense of tragic waste which pervades the Finnsburg episode (section XVI) springs from a Christian perception of the insane futility of the primitive Germanic thirst for vengeance; and the facts that Beowulf's chief adversaries are not men but monsters and that before his death he is able to boast that as king of the Geats he did not seek wars with neighboring tribes may reflect a Christian's appreciation for peace among men. But while admitting such values, the poet also invokes many others of a very different order, values that seem to belong to an ancient, pagan, warrior society of the kind described by the Roman historian Tacitus at the end of the first century. It should be noted that even Hrothgar's speech about conscience is directed more toward making Beowulf a good Germanic leader of men than a good Christian. One must, indeed, draw the conclusion from the poem itself that while Christian is a correct term for the religion of the poet and of his audience, it was a Christianity that had not yet by any means succeeded in obliterating an older pagan tradition, which still called forth powerful responses from men's hearts, despite the fact that many aspects of this tradition must be abhorrent to a sophisticated Christian. In this connection it is well to recall that the missionaries from Rome who initiated the con-

version of the English proceeded in a conciliatory manner, not so much up-
rooting paganism in order to plant Christianity as planting Christianity in
the faith that it would ultimately choke out the weeds of paganism. And the
English clung long to some of their ancient traditions: for instance, the
legal principle of the payment of *wergild* (defined below) remained in
force until the Norman Conquest, four centuries after the conversion of the
English.

In the warrior society whose values the poem constantly invokes, the most
important of human relationships was that which existed between the warrior—the thane—and his lord, a relationship based less on subordination of
one man's will to another's than on mutual trust and respect. When a
warrior vowed loyalty to his lord, he became not so much his servant as his
voluntary companion, one who would take pride in defending him and
fighting in his wars. In return, the lord was expected to take affectionate care
of his thanes and to reward them richly for their valor: a good king, one like
Hrothgar or Beowulf, is referred to by such poetic epithets as "protector of
warriors" and "dispenser of treasure" or "ring-giver," and the failure of bad
kings is ascribed to their ill-temper and avarice, both of which alienate them
from their retainers. The material benefit of this arrangement between lord
and thane is obvious, yet under a good king the relationship seems to have
had a significance more spiritual than material. Thus the treasure that an
ideal Germanic king seizes from his enemies and rewards his retainers with
is regarded as something more than mere wealth that will serve the well-
being of its possessor; rather, it is a kind of visible proof that all parties are
realizing themselves to the full in a spiritual sense—that the men of this
band are congenially and successfully united with one another. The symbolic
importance of treasure is illustrated by the poet's remark that the gift Beowulf gave the Danish coast-guard brought the latter honor among his
companions, and even more by the fact that although Beowulf dies while
obtaining a great treasure for his people, such objects as are removed from
the dragon's hoard are actually buried with him as a fitting sign of his ultimate achievement.

The relationship between kinsmen was also of deep significance to this
society and provides another emotional value for Old English heroic poetry.
If one of his kinsmen had been slain, a man had the special duty of either
killing the slayer or exacting from him the payment of *wergild* ("man-
price"): each rank of society was evaluated at a definite price, which had
to be paid to the dead man's kinsmen by the killer who wished to avoid
their vengeance—even if the killing had been accidental. Again, the money
itself had less significance as wealth than as a proof that the kinsmen had
done what was right. Relatives who failed either to exact *wergild* or to take
vengeance could never be happy, having found no practical way of satisfying
their grief for their kinsmen's death. "It is better for a man to avenge his
friend than much mourn," Beowulf says to the old Hrothgar, who is bewailing Aeschere's killing by Grendel's mother. And one of the most poignant
passages in the poem describes the sorrow of King Hrethel after one of his
sons had accidentally killed another: by the code of kinship Hrethel was
forbidden to kill or to exact compensation from a kinsman, yet by the same
code he was required to do one or the other in order to avenge the dead.

Caught in this curious dilemma, Hrethel became so disconsolate that he could no longer face life.

It is evident that the need to take vengeance would create never-ending feuds, which the practice of marrying royal princesses to the kings or princes of hostile tribes did little to mitigate, though the purpose of such marriages was to replace hostility by alliance. Hrothgar wishes to make peace with the Heatho-Bards by marrying his daughter to their king, Ingeld, whose father was killed by the Danes; but as Beowulf predicts, sooner or later the Heatho-Bards' desire for vengeance on the Danes will erupt, and there will be more bloodshed. And the Danish princess Hildeburh, married to Finn of the Jutes, will see her son and her brother both killed while fighting on opposite sides in a battle at her own home, and ultimately will see her husband killed by the Danes in revenge for her brother's death. Beowulf himself is, for a Germanic hero, curiously free of involvement in feuds of this sort, though he does boast that he avenged the death of his king, Heardred, on his slayer Onela. Yet the potentiality—or inevitability—of sudden attack, sudden change, swift death is omnipresent in *Beowulf*: men seen to be caught in a vast web of reprisals and counterreprisals from which there is little hope of escape. This is the aspect of the poem which is apt to make the most powerful impression on the reader—its strong sense of doom.

Beowulf himself is chiefly concerned not with tribal feuds but with fatal evil both less and more complex. Grendel and the dragon are threats to the security of the lands they infest just as human enemies would be, but they are not part of the social order and presumably have no one to avenge their deaths (that Grendel's mother appeared as an avenger seems to have been a surprise both to Beowulf and to the Danes). On the other hand, because they are outside the normal order of things, they require of their conqueror something greater than normal warfare requires. In each case, it is the clear duty of the king and his companions to put down the evil. But the Danish Hrothgar is old and his companions unenterprising, and excellent though Hrothgar has been in the kingship, he nevertheless lacks the quality that later impels the old Beowulf to fight the dragon that threatens his people. The poem makes no criticism of Hrothgar for this lack; he merely seems not to be the kind of man—one might almost say he was not fated—to develop his human potential to the fullest extent that Fate would permit: that is Beowulf's role. In undertaking to slay Grendel, and later Grendel's mother, Beowulf is testing his relationship with unknowable destiny. At any time, as he is fully aware, his luck may abandon him and he may be killed, as, indeed, he is in the otherwise successful encounter with the dragon. But whether he lives or dies, he will have done all that any man could do to develop his character heroically. It is this consciousness of testing Fate that probably explains the boasting that modern readers of heroic poetry often find offensive. When he boasts, Beowulf is not only demonstrating that he has chosen the heroic way of life, but is also choosing it, for when he invokes his former courage as pledge of his future courage, his boast becomes a vow; the hero has put himself in a position from which he cannot withdraw.

Courage is the instrument by which the hero realizes himself. "Fate often saves an undoomed man when his courage is good," says Beowulf in his account of his swimming match: that is, if Fate has not entirely doomed a man in advance, courage is the quality that can perhaps influence Fate

against its natural tendency to doom him now. It is this complex statement
(in which it is hard to read the will of God for Fate) that Beowulf's life
explores: he will use his great strength in the most courageous way by going
alone, even unarmed, against monsters. Doom, of course, ultimately claims
him, but not until he has fulfilled to its limits the pagan ideal of a heroic
life. And despite the desire he often shows to Christianize pagan virtues, the
Christian poet remains true to the older tradition when, at the end of his
poem, he leaves us with the impression that Beowulf's chief reward is pagan
immortality: the memory in the minds of later men of a hero's heroic actions. The poem itself is, indeed, a noble expression of that immortality.

OLD ENGLISH PROSODY

All the poetry of Old English is in the same verse form. The verse unit
is the single line, since rhyme was not used to link one line to another,
except very occasionally in late Old English. The organizing device of the
line is alliteration, the beginning of several words with the same sound
("Foemen fled"). The Old English alliterative line contains four principal
stresses, and is divided into two half-lines of two stresses each by a strong
medial caesura, or pause. These two half-lines are linked to each other by
the alliteration: at least one of the two stressed words in the first half-line,
and usually both of them, begin with the same sound as the first stressed
word of the second half-line (the second stressed word is generally non-
alliterative). The fourth line of *Beowulf* is an example:

> Oft Scyld Scefing   *sceaþena þreatum.*

For further examples, see the passage from *Beowulf* printed below. It
will be noticed that any vowel alliterates with any other vowel. In addition to the alliteration, the length of the unstressed syllables and their
number and pattern is governed by a highly complex set of rules. When
sung or intoned—as it was—to the rhythmic strumming of a harp, Old
English poetry must have been wonderfully impressive in the dignified,
highly formalized way which aptly fits both its subject matter and tone.

In Old English spelling, æ (line 1) is a vowel symbol that has not
survived; it represented both a short *a* sound and a long open *e* sound. þ
(line 2) and ð (line 3) both represented the sound *th*. The large space
in the middle of the line indicates the caesura.

> Hwæt! we Gar-Dena   in geardagum,
> þeodcyninga   þrym gefrunon—
> hu ða æþelingas   ellen fremedon!
> oft Scyld Scefing   sceaþena þreatum,
> monegum mægþum   meodosetla ofteah.
> egsode eorlas,   syððan ærest wearð
> feasceaft funden;   he þæs frofre gebad,
> weox under wolcnum,   weorðmyndum þah,
> oð þæt him æghwylc   þara ymbsittendra,
> ofer hronrade,   hyran scolde,
> gomban gyldan.   þæt was god cyning!

TRIBES AND GENEALOGIES

I. The Danes (Bright-, Half-, Ring-, Spear-, North-, East-, South-, West-Danes; Scyldings, Honor-, Victor-, War-Scyldings; Ing's friends).

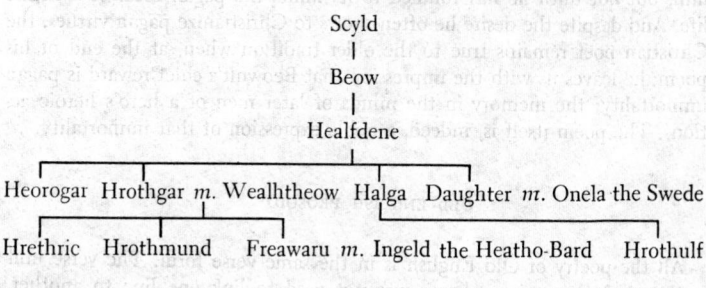

Scyld
|
Beow
|
Healfdene
|
Heorogar   Hrothgar *m.* Wealhtheow   Halga   Daughter *m.* Onela the Swede

Hrethric   Hrothmund   Freawaru *m.* Ingeld the Heatho-Bard   Hrothulf

II. The Geats (Sea-, War-, Weather-Geats)

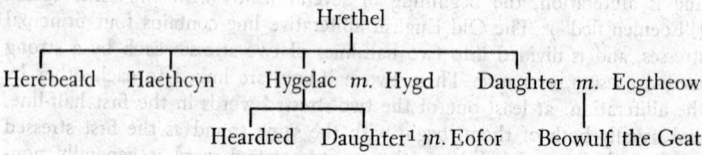

Hrethel

Herebeald   Haethcyn   Hygelac *m.* Hygd   Daughter *m.* Ecgtheow

Heardred   Daughter[1] *m.* Eofor   Beowulf the Geat

III. The Swedes.

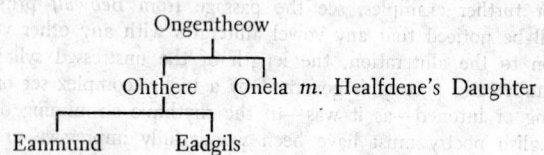

Ongentheow

Ohthere   Onela *m.* Healfdene's Daughter

Eanmund   Eadgils

IV. Miscellaneous.

A. The Half-Danes (also called Scyldings) involved in the fight at Finnsburg may represent a different tribe from the Danes of paragraph I, above. Their king Hoc had a son, Hnaef, who succeeded him, and a daughter Hildeburh, who married Finn, king of the Jutes.

B. The Jutes or Frisians are represented as enemies of the Danes in the fight at Finnsburg and as allies of the Franks or Hugas at the time Hygelac the Geat made the attack in which he lost his life and from which Beowulf swam home. Also allied with the Franks at this time were the Hetware.

C. The Heatho-Bards (i.e., "Battle-Bards") are represented as inveterate enemies of the Danes. Their king Froda had been killed in an attack on the Danes, and Hrothgar's attempt to make peace with them by marrying his daughter Freawaru to Froda's son Ingeld failed when the latter attacked Heorot. The attack was repulsed, though Heorot was burned.

1. The daughter of Hygelac who was   him by a former wife, older than
given to Eofor may have been born to   Hygd.

Beowulf [1]

[Prologue: The Earlier History of the Danes]

Yes, we have heard of the glory of the Spear-Danes' kings in the old days—how the princes of that people did brave deeds.

Often Scyld Scefing [2] took mead-benches away from enemy bands, from many tribes, terrified their nobles—after the time that he was first found helpless. [3] He lived to find comfort for that, became great under the skies, prospered in honors until every one of those who lived about him, across the whale-road, had to obey him, pay him tribute. That was a good king.

Afterwards a son was born to him, a young boy in his house, whom God sent to comfort the people: He had seen the sore need they had suffered during the long time they lacked a king. Therefore the Lord of Life, the Ruler of Heaven, gave him honor in the world: Beow [4] was famous, the glory of the son of Scyld spread widely in the Northlands. In this way a young man ought by his good deeds, by giving splendid gifts while still in his father's house, to make sure that later in life beloved companions will stand by him, that people will serve him when war comes. Through deeds that bring praise, a man shall prosper in every country.

Then at the fated time Scyld the courageous went away into the protection of the Lord. His dear companions carried him down to the sea-currents, just as he himself had bidden them do when, as protector of the Scyldings, [5] he had ruled them with his words —long had the beloved prince governed the land. There in the harbor stood the ring-prowed ship, ice-covered and ready to sail, a prince's vessel. Then they laid down the ruler they had loved, the ring-giver, in the hollow of the ship, the glorious man beside the mast. There was brought great store of treasure, wealth from lands far away. I have not heard of a ship more splendidly furnished with war-weapons and battle-dress, swords and mail-shirts. On his breast lay a great many treasures that should voyage with him far out into the sea's possession. They provided him with no lesser gifts, treasure of the people, than those had done who at his beginning first sent him forth on the waves, a child alone. Then also they set a golden standard high over his head, let the water take him, gave him to the sea. Sad was

1. The translation into modern English, by the editor (1966), is based on F. Klaeber's third edition of the poem (1950); in general, the emendations suggested by J. C. Pope, *The Rhythm of Beowulf*, second edition (1966), have been adopted. The division into sections headed by roman numerals is that of the manuscript, which makes, however, no provision for Section XXX. 2. The meaning is probably "son of Scyld").

Sceaf," although Scyld's origins are mysterious. 3. As is made clear shortly below, Scyld arrived in Denmark as a child alone in a ship loaded with treasures. 4. Although the manuscript reads "Beowulf," most scholars now agree that it should read "Beow." Beo was the grandfather of the Danish king Hrothgar. 5. I.e., the Danes ("descendants of Scyld").

their spirit, mournful their mind. Men cannot truthfully say who
received that cargo, neither counsellors in the hall nor warriors
under the skies.

(I) Then in the cities was Beo of the Scyldings beloved
king of the people, long famous among nations (his father
had gone elsewhere, the king from his land), until later great
Healfdene was born to him. As long as he lived, old and fierce
in battle, he upheld the glorious Scyldings. To him all told were
four children born into the world, to the leader of the armies:
Heorogar and Hrothgar and the good Halga. I have heard tell
that [. . . was On]ela's queen,[6] beloved bed-companion of the
Battle-Scylfing.

[*Beowulf and Grendel*]

[THE HALL HEOROT IS ATTACKED BY GRENDEL]

Then Hrothgar was given success in warfare, glory in battle,
so that his retainers gladly obeyed him and their company grew
into a great band of warriors. It came to his mind that he
would command men to construct a hall, a mead-building large[r]
than the children of men had ever heard of, and therein he
would give to young and old all that God had given him, except
for common land and men's bodies.[7] Then I have heard that
the work was laid upon many nations, wide through this middle-
earth, that they should adorn the folk-hall. In time it came to
pass—quickly, as men count it—that it was finished, the largest
of hall-dwellings. He gave it the name of Heorot,[8] he who ruled
wide with his words. He did not forget his promise: at the feast
he gave out rings, treasure. The hall stood tall, high and wide-
gabled: it would wait for the fierce flames of vengeful fire; [9]
the time was not yet at hand for sword-hate between son-in-law
and father-in-law to awaken after murderous rage.

Then the fierce spirit [1] painfully endured hardship for a time,
he who dwelt in the darkness, for every day he heard loud
mirth in the hall; there was the sound of the harp, the clear
song of the scop.[2] There he spoke who could relate the beginning of men far back in time, said that the Almighty made
earth, a bright field fair in the water that surrounds it, set up in
triumph the lights of the sun and the moon to lighten land-
dwellers, and adorned the surfaces of the earth with branches

---

6. The text is faulty, so that the name
of Healfdene's daughter has been lost;
her husband Onela was a Swedish
(Scylfing) king.
7. Or "men's lives." Apparently slaves,
along with public land, were not in the
king's power to give away.
8. I.e., "Hart."
9. The destruction by fire of Heorot
occurred at a later time than that of

the poem's action, probably during the
otherwise unsuccessful attack of the
Heatho-Bard Ingeld on his father-in-
law Hrothgar, mentioned in the next
clause.
1. I.e., Grendel.
2. The "scop" was the Anglo-Saxon
minstrel, who recited poetic stories to
the accompaniment of a harp.

and leaves, created also life for each of the kinds that move and breathe.—Thus these warriors lived in joy, blessed, until one began to do evil deeds, a hellish enemy. The grim spirit was called Grendel, known as a rover of the borders, one who held the moors, fen and fastness. Unhappy creature, he lived for a time in the home of the monsters' race, after God had condemned them as kin of Cain. The Eternal Lord avenged the murder in which he slew Abel. Cain had no pleasure in that feud, but He banished him far from mankind, the Ruler, for that misdeed. From him sprang all bad breeds, trolls and elves and monsters—likewise the giants who for a long time strove with God: He paid them their reward for that.

(II.) Then, after night came, Grendel went to survey the tall house—how, after their beer-drinking, the Ring-Danes had disposed themselves in it. Then he found therein a band of nobles asleep after the feast: they felt no sorrow, no misery of men. The creature of evil, grim and fierce, was quickly ready, savage and cruel, and seized from their rest thirty thanes. From there he turned to go back to his home, proud of his plunder, sought his dwelling with that store of slaughter.

Then in the first light of dawning day Grendel's war-strength was revealed to men: then after the feast weeping arose, great cry in the morning. The famous king, hero of old days, sat joyless; the mighty one suffered, felt sorrow for his thanes, when they saw the track of the foe, of the cursed spirit: that hardship was too strong, too loathsome and long-lasting. Nor was there a longer interval, but after one night Grendel again did greater slaughter—and had no remorse for it—vengeful acts and wicked: he was too intent on them. Thereafter it was easy to find the man who sought rest for himself elsewhere, farther away, a bed among the outlying buildings—after it was made clear to him, told by clear proof, the hatred of him who now controlled the hall.[3] Whoever escaped the foe held himself afterwards farther off and more safely. Thus Grendel held sway and fought against right, one against all, until the best of houses stood empty. It was a long time, the length of twelve winters, that the lord of the Scyldings suffered grief, all woes, great sorrows. Therefore, sadly in songs, it became well-known to the children of men that Grendel had fought a long time with Hrothgar, for many half-years maintained mortal spite, feud, and enmity—constant war. He wanted no peace with any of the men of the Danish host, would not withdraw his deadly rancor, or pay compensation: no counselor there had any reason to expect splendid repayment at the hands of the slayer.[4] For the monster was relentless, the dark

3. I.e., Grendel.
4. According to old Germanic law, a slayer could achieve peace with his victim's kinsmen only by paying them *wergild*, i.e., compensation for the life of the slain man.

death-shadow, against warriors old and young, lay in wait and ambushed them. In the perpetual darkness he held to the misty moors: men do not know where hell-demons direct their footsteps.

Thus many crimes the enemy of mankind committed, the terrible walker-alone, cruel injuries one after another. In the dark nights he dwelt in Heorot, the richly adorned hall. He might not approach the throne, [receive] treasure, because of the Lord; He had no love for him.[5]

This was great misery to the lord of the Scyldings, a breaking of spirit. Many a noble sat often in council, sought a plan, what would be best for strong-hearted men to do against the awful attacks. At times they vowed sacrifices at heathen temples, with their words prayed that the soul-slayer [6] would give help for the distress of the people. Such was their custom, the hope of heathens; in their spirits they thought of Hell, they knew not the Ruler, the Judge of Deeds, they recognized not the Lord God, nor indeed did they know how to praise the Protector of Heaven, the glorious King. Woe is him who in terrible trouble must thrust his soul into the fire's embrace, hope for no comfort, not expect change. Well is the man who after his death-day may seek the Lord and find peace in the embrace of the Father.

[THE COMING OF BEOWULF TO HEOROT]

(III.) So in the cares of his times the son of Healfdene constantly brooded, nor might the wise warrior set aside his woe. Too harsh, hateful and long-lasting was the hardship that had come upon the people, distress dire and inexorable, worst of night-horrors.

A thane of Hygelac,[7] a good man among the Geats, heard in his homeland of Grendel's deeds: of mankind he was the strongest of might in the time of this life, noble and great. He bade that a good ship be made ready for him, said he would seek the war-king over the swan's road, the famous prince, since he had need of men. Very little did wise men blame him for that adventure, though he was dear to them; they urged the brave one on, examined the omens. From the folk of the Geats the good man had chosen warriors of the bravest that he could find; one of fifteen he led the way, the warrior sought the wooden ship, the sea-skilled one the land's edge. The time had come: the ship was on the waves, the boat under the cliff. The warriors eagerly climbed on the prow—the sea-currents eddied, sea

---

5. Behind this obscure passage seems to lie the idea that Grendel, unlike Hrothgar's thanes, could not approach the throne to receive gifts from the king, having been condemned by God as an outlaw.

6. I.e., the Devil. Despite this assertion that the Danes were heathen, their king, Hrothgar, speaks consistently as a Christian.

7. I.e., Beowulf the Geat, whose king was Hygelac.

against sand; men bore bright weapons into the ship's bosom, splendid armor. Men pushed the well-braced ship from shore, warriors on a well-wished voyage. Then over the sea-waves, blown by the wind, the foam-necked boat traveled, most like a bird, until at good time on the second day the curved prow had come to where the seafarers could see land, the sea-cliffs shine, towering hills, great headlands. Then was the sea crossed, the journey at end. Then quickly the men of the Geats climbed upon the shore, moored the wooden ship; mail-shirts rattled, dress for battle. They thanked God that the wave-way had been easy for them.

Then from the wall the Scyldings' guard who should watch over the sea-cliffs saw bright shields borne over the gangway, armor ready for battle; strong desire stirred him in mind to learn what the men were. He went riding on his horse to the shore, thane of Hrothgar, forcefully brandished a great spear in his hands, with formal words questioned them: "What are you, bearers of armor, dressed in mail-coats, who thus have come bringing a tall ship over the sea-road, over the water to this place? Lo, for a long time I have been guard of the coast, held watch by the sea so that no foe with a force of ships might work harm on the Danes' land: never have shield-bearers more openly undertaken to come ashore here; nor did you know for sure of a word of leave from our warriors, consent from my kinsmen. I have never seen a mightier warrior on earth than is one of you, a man in battle-dress. That is no re-tainer made to seem good by his weapons—unless his appearance belies him, his unequalled form. Now I must learn your lineage before you go any farther from here, spies on the Danes' land. Now you far-dwellers, sea-voyagers, hear what I think: you must straightway say where you have come from."

(IV.) To him replied the leader, the chief of the band un-locked his word-hoard: "We are men of the Geatish nation and Hygelac's hearth-companions. My father was well-known among the tribes, a noble leader named Ecgtheow. He lived many winters before he went on his way, an old man, from men's dwellings. Every wise man wide over the earth readily remembers him. Through friendly heart we have come to seek your lord, the son of Healfdene, protector of the people. Be good to us and tell us what to do: we have a great errand to the famous one, the king of the Danes. And I too do not think that anything ought to be kept secret: you know whether it is so, as we have indeed heard, that among the Scyldings I know not what foe, what dark doer of hateful deeds in the black nights, shows in terrible manner strange malice, injury and slaughter. In openness of heart I may teach Hrothgar remedy for that, how he, wise and good, shall overpower the foe—if change is ever to come to him, relief from evil's distress—and how **his surging** cares may be made to cool. Or else ever after he will suffer tribulations, constraint, while the best of houses remains there on its high place."

The guard spoke from where he sat on his horse, brave officer: "A sharp-witted shield-warrior who thinks well must be able to judge each of the two things, words and works. I understand this: that here is a troop friendly to the Scyldings' king. Go forward, bearing weapons and war-gear. I will show you the way; I shall also bid my fellow-thanes honorably to hold your boat against all enemies, your new-tarred ship on the sand, until again over the sea-streams it bears its beloved men to the Geatish shore, the wooden vessel with curved prow. May it be granted by fate that one who behaves so bravely pass whole through the battle-storm."

Then they set off. The boat lay fixed, rested on the rope, the deep-bosomed ship, fast at anchor. Boar-images [8] shone over cheek-guards gold-adorned, gleaming and fire-hardened—the war-minded boar held guard over fierce men. The warriors hastened, marched together until they might see the timbered hall, stately and shining with gold; for earth-dwellers under the skies that was the most famous of buildings in which the mighty one waited—its light gleamed over many lands. The battle-brave guide pointed out to them the shining house of the brave ones so that they might go straight to it. Warrior-like he turned his horse, then spoke words: "It is time for me to go back. The All-Wielding Father in His grace keep you safe in your undertakings. I shall go back to the sea to keep watch against hostile hosts."

(V.) The road was stone-paved, the path showed the way to the men in ranks. War-corselet shone, hard and hand-wrought, bright iron rings sang on their armor when they first came walking to the hall in their grim gear. Sea-weary they set down their broad shields, marvelously strong protections, against the wall of the building. Then they sat down on the bench—mail-shirts, warrior's clothing, rang out. Spears stood together, sea-men's weapons, ash steel-gray at the top. The armed band was worthy of its weapons.

Then a proud-spirited man [9] asked the warriors there about their lineage: "Where do you bring those gold-covered shields from, gray mail-shirts and visored helmets, this multitude of battle-shafts? I am Hrothgar's herald and officer. I have not seen strangers—so many men—more bold. I think that it is for daring—not for refuge, but for greatness of heart—that you have sought Hrothgar." The man known for his courage replied to him; the proud man of the Geats, hardy under helmet, spoke

8. Carved images of boars (sometimes represented as clothed like human warriors) were placed on helmets in the belief that they would protect the wearer in battle.
9. Identified below as Wulfgar.

words in return: "We are Hygelac's table-companions. Beowulf is my name. I will tell my errand to Healfdene's son, the great prince your lord, if, good as he is, he will grant that we might address him." Wulfgar spoke—he was a man of the Wendels, his bold spirit known to many, his valor and wisdom: "I will ask the lord of the Danes about this, the Scyldings' king, the ring-giver, just as you request—will ask the glorious ruler about your voyage, and will quickly make known to you the answer the good man thinks best to give me."

He returned at once to where Hrothgar sat, old and hoary, with his company of earls. The man known for his valor went forward till he stood squarely before the Danes' king: he knew the custom of tried retainers. Wulfgar spoke to his lord and friend: "Here have journeyed men of the Geats, come far over the sea's expanse. The warriors call their chief Beowulf. They ask that they, my prince, might exchange words with you. Do not refuse them your answer, gracious Hrothgar. From their war-gear they seem worthy of earls' esteem. Strong indeed is the chief who has led the warriors here."

(VI.) Hrothgar spoke, protector of the Scyldings: "I knew him when he was a boy. His father was called Ecgtheow: Hrethel of the Geats [1] gave him his only daughter for his home. Now has his hardy offspring come here, sought a fast friend. Then, too, seafarers who took gifts there to please the Geats used to say that he has in his handgrip the strength of thirty men, a man famous in battle. Holy God of His grace has sent him to us West-Danes, as I hope, against the terror of Grendel. I shall offer the good man treasures for his daring. Now make haste, bid them come in together to see my company of kinsmen. In your speech say to them also that they are welcome to the Danish people."

Then Wulfgar went to the hall's door, gave the message from within: "The lord of the East-Danes, my victorious prince, has bidden me say to you that he knows your noble ancestry, and that you brave-hearted men are welcome to him over the sea-swells. Now you may come in your war-dress, under your battle helmets, to see Hrothgar. Let your war-shields, your wooden spears, await here the outcome of the talk."

Then the mighty one rose, many a warrior about him, a company of strong thanes. Some waited there, kept watch over the weapons as the brave one bade them. Together they hastened, as the warrior directed them, under Heorot's roof. The war-leader, hardy under helmet, advanced till he stood on the hearth. Beowulf spoke, his mail-shirt glistened, armor-net woven by the blacksmith's

---

1. Hrethel was the father of Hygelac and Beowulf's grandfather and guardian.

skill: "Hail, Hrothgar! I am kinsman and thane of Hygelac. In my youth I have set about many brave deeds. The affair of Grendel was made known to me on my native soil: sea-travelers say that this hall, best of buildings, stands empty and useless to all warriors after the evening-light becomes hidden beneath the cover of the sky. Therefore my people, the best wise earls, advised me thus, lord Hrothgar, that I should seek you because they know what my strength can accomplish. They themselves looked on when, bloody from my foes, I came from the fight where I had bound five, destroyed a family of giants, and at night in the waves slain water-monsters, suffered great pain, avenged an affliction of the Weather-Geats on those who had asked for trouble—ground enemies to bits. And now alone I shall settle affairs with Grendel, the monster, the demon. Therefore, lord of the Bright-Danes, protector of the Scyldings, I will make a request of you, refuge of warriors, fair friend of nations, that you refuse me not, now that I have come so far, that alone with my company of earls, this band of hardy men, I may cleanse Heorot. I have also heard say that the monster in his recklessness cares not for weapons. Therefore, so that my liege lord Hygelac may be glad of me in his heart, I scorn to bear sword or broad shield, yellow wood, to the battle, but with my grasp I shall grapple with the enemy and fight for life, foe against foe. The one whom death takes can trust the Lord's judgment. I think that if he may accomplish it, unafraid he will feed on the folk of the Geats in the war-hall as he has often done on the flower of men. You will not need to hide my head [2] if death takes me, for he will have me blood-smeared; he will bear away my bloody flesh meaning to savor it, he will eat ruthlessly, the walker alone, will stain his retreat in the moor; no longer will you need trouble yourself to take care of my body. If battle takes me, send to Hygelac the best of war-clothes that protects my breast, finest of mail-shirts. It is a legacy of Hrethel, the work of Weland.[3] Fate always goes as it must."

(VII.) Hrothgar spoke, protector of the Scyldings: "For deeds done, my friend Beowulf, and for past favors you have sought us. A fight of your father's brought on the greatest of feuds. With his own hands he became the slayer of Heatholaf among the Wylfings. After that the country of the Weather-Geats might not keep him, for fear of war. From there he sought the folk of the South-Danes, the Honor-Scyldings, over the sea-swell. At that time I was first ruling the Danish people and, still in my youth, held the wide kingdom, hoard-city of heroes. Heorogar had died then, gone from life, my older brother, son of Healfdene—he was better than I. Afterwards I paid blood-money to end the feud;

2. I.e., "bury my body."   3. The blacksmith of the Norse gods.

over the sea's back I sent to the Wylfings old treasures; he [4] swore oaths to me.

"It is a sorrow to me in spirit to say to any man what Grendel has brought me with his hatred—humiliation in Heorot, terrible violence. My hall-troop, warrior-band, has shrunk; fate has swept them away into Grendel's horror. (God may easily put an end to the wild ravager's deeds!) Full often over the ale-cups warriors made bold with beer have boasted that they would await with grim swords Grendel's attack in the beer-hall. Then in the morning this mead-hall was a hall shining with blood, when the day lightened, all the bench-floor blood-wet, a gore-hall. I had fewer faithful men, beloved retainers, for death had destroyed them. Now sit down to the feast and unbind your thoughts, your famous victories, as heart inclines."

[THE FEAST AT HEOROT]

Then was a bench cleared in the beer-hall for the men of the Geats all together. Then the stout-hearted ones went to sit down, proud in their might. A thane did his work who bore in his hands an embellished ale-cup, poured the bright drink. At times a scop sang, clear-voiced in Heorot. There was joy of brave men, no little company of Danes and Weather-Geats.

(VIII.) Unferth spoke, son of Ecglaf, who sat at the feet of the king of the Scyldings, unbound words of contention—to him was Beowulf's undertaking, the brave seafarer, a great vexation, for he would not allow that any other man of middle-earth should ever achieve more glory under the heavens than himself: "Are you that Beowulf who contended with Breca, competed in swimming on the broad sea, where for pride you explored the water, and for foolish boast ventured your lives in the deep? Nor might any man, friend nor enemy, keep you from the perilous venture of swimming in the sea. There you embraced the sea-streams with your arms, measured the sea-ways, flung forward your hands, glided over the ocean; the sea boiled with waves, with winter's swell. Seven nights you toiled in the water's power. He overcame you at swimming, had more strength. Then in the morning the sea bore him up among the Heathoraemas; from there he sought his own home, dear to his people, the land of the Brondings, the fair stronghold, where he had folk, castle, and treasures. All his boast against you the son of Beanstan carried out in deed. Therefore I expect the worse results for you—though you have prevailed everywhere in battles, in grim war—if you dare wait near Grendel a night-long space."

Beowulf spoke, the son of Ecgtheow: "Well, my friend Unferth, drunk with beer you have spoken a great many things

4. Ecgtheow, whose feud with the Wylfings Hrothgar had settled.

about Breca—told about his adventures. I maintain the truth that I had more strength in the sea, hardship on the waves, than any other man. Like boys we agreed together and boasted—we were both in our first youth—that we would risk our lives in the salt sea, and that we did even so. We had naked swords, strong in our hands, when we went swimming; we thought to guard ourselves against whale-fishes. He could not swim at all far from me in the flood-waves, be quicker in the water, nor would I move away from him. Thus we were together on the sea for the time of five nights until the flood drove us apart, the swelling sea, coldest of weathers, darkening night, and the north wind battle-grim turned against us: rough were the waves. The anger of the sea-fishes was roused. Then my body-mail, hard and hand-linked, gave me help against my foes; the woven war-garment, gold-adorned, covered my breast. A fierce cruel attacker dragged me to the bottom, held me grim in his grasp, but it was granted me to reach the monster with my sword-point, my battle-blade. The war-stroke destroyed the mighty sea-beast—through my hand.

(IX.) "Thus often loathsome assailants pressed me hard. I served them with my good sword, as the right was. They had no joy at all of the feast, the malice-workers, that they should eat me, sit around a banquet near the sea-bottom. But in the morning, sword-wounded they lay on the shore, left behind by the waves, put to sleep by the blade, so that thereafter they would never hinder the passage of sea-voyagers over the deep water. Light came from the east, bright signal of God, the sea became still so that I might see the headlands, the windy walls of the sea. Fate often saves an undoomed man when his courage is good. In any case it befell me that I slew with my sword nine sea-monsters. I have not heard tell of a harder fight by night under heaven's arch, nor of a man more hard-pressed in the sea-streams. Yet I came out of the enemies' grasp alive, weary of my adventure. Then the sea bore me onto the lands of the Finns, the flood with its current, the surging waters.

"I have not heard say of you any such hard matching of might, such sword-terror. Breca never yet in the games of war—neither he nor you—achieved so bold a deed with bright swords (I do not much boast of it), though you became your brothers' slayer, your close kin; for that you will suffer punishment in hell, even though your wit is keen. I tell you truly, son of Ecglaf, that Grendel, awful monster, would never have performed so many terrible deeds against your chief, humiliation in Heorot, if your spirit, your heart, were so fierce in fight as you claim. But he has noticed that he need not much fear the hostility, not much dread the terrible sword-storm of your people, the Victory-Scyldings.

He exacts forced levy, shows mercy to none of the Danish people; but he is glad, kills, carves for feasting, expects no fight from the Spear-Danes. But I shall show him soon now the strength and courage of the Geats, their warfare. Afterwards he will walk who may, glad to the mead, when the morning light of another day, the bright-clothed sun, shines from the south on the children of men."

Then was the giver of treasure in gladness, gray-haired and battle-brave. The lord of the Bright-Danes could count on help. The folk's guardian had heard from Beowulf a fast-resolved thought.

There was laughter of warriors, voices rang pleasant, words were cheerful. Wealhtheow came forth, Hrothgar's queen, mindful of customs, gold-adorned, greeted the men in the hall; and the noble woman offered the cup first to the keeper of the land of the East-Danes, bade him be glad at the beer-drinking, beloved of the people. In joy he partook of feast and hall-cup, king famous for victories. Then the woman of the Helmings went about to each one of the retainers, young and old, offered them the costly cup, until the time came that she brought the mead-bowl to Beowulf, the ring-adorned queen, mature of mind. Sure of speech she greeted the man of the Geats, thanked God that her wish was fulfilled, that she might trust in some man for help against deadly deeds. He took the cup, the warrior fierce in battle, from Wealhtheow, and then spoke, one ready for fight— Beowulf spoke, the son of Ecgtheow: "I resolved, when I set out on the sea, sat down in the sea-boat with my band of men, that I should altogether fulfill the will of your people or else fall in slaughter, fast in the foe's grasp. I shall achieve a deed of manly courage or else have lived to see in this mead-hall my ending day." These words were well-pleasing to the woman, the boast of the Geat. Gold-adorned, the noble folk-queen went to sit by her lord.

Then there were again as at first strong words spoken in the hall, the people in gladness, the sound of a victorious folk, until, in a little while, the son of Healfdene wished to seek his evening rest. He knew of the battle in the high hall that had been plotted by the monster, plotted from the time that they might see the light of the sun until the night, growing dark over all things, the shadowy shapes of darkness, should come gliding, black under the clouds. The company all arose. Then they saluted each other, Hrothgar and Beowulf, and Hrothgar wished him good luck, control of the wine-hall, and spoke these words: "Never before, since I could raise hand and shield, have I entrusted to any man the great hall of the Danes, except now to you. Hold now and guard the best of houses: remember your fame, show your great courage, keep watch against the fierce foe. You will not lack what you wish if you survive that deed of valor."

[THE FIGHT WITH GRENDEL]

(X.) Then Hrothgar went out of the hall with his company of warriors, the protector of the Scyldings. The war-chief would seek the bed of Wealhtheow the queen. The King of Glory—as men had learned—had appointed a hall-guard against Grendel; he had a special mission to the prince of the Danes: he kept watch against monsters.

And the man of the Geats had sure trust in his great might, the favor of the Ruler. Then he took off his shirt of armor, the helmet from his head, handed his embellished sword, best of irons, to an attendant, bade him keep guard over his war-gear. Then the good warrior spoke some boast-words before he went to his bed, Beowulf of the Geats: "I claim myself no poorer in war-strength, war works, than Grendel claims himself. Therefore I will not put him to sleep with a sword, so take away his life, though surely I might. He knows no good tools with which he might strike against me, cut my shield in pieces, though he is strong in fight. But we shall forgo the sword in the night—if he dare seek war without weapon—and then may wise God, Holy Lord, assign glory on whichever hand seems good to Him."

The battle-brave one laid himself down, the pillow received the earl's head, and about him many a brave seaman lay down to hall-rest. None of them thought that he would ever again seek from there his dear home, people or town where he had been brought up; for they knew that bloody death had carried off far too many men in the wine-hall, folk of the Danes. But the Lord granted to weave for them good fortune in war, for the folk of the Weather-Geats, comfort and help that they should quite overcome their foe through the might of one man, through his sole strength: the truth has been made known that mighty God has always ruled mankind.

There came gliding in the black night the walker in darkness. The warriors slept who should hold the horned house—all but one. It was known to men that when the Ruler did not wish it the hostile creature might not drag them away beneath the shadows. But he, lying awake for the fierce foe, with heart swollen in anger awaited the outcome of the fight.

(XI.) Then from the moor under the mist-hills Grendel came walking, wearing God's anger. The foul ravager thought to catch some one of mankind there in the high hall. Under the clouds he moved until he could see most clearly the wine-hall, treasure-house of men, shining with gold. That was not the first time that he had sought Hrothgar's home. Never before or since in his life-days did he find harder luck, hardier hall-thanes. The creature deprived of joy came walking to the hall. Quickly the door gave way, fastened with fire-forged bands, when he touched it with his hands. Driven by evil desire, swollen with rage, he tore it open, the hall's mouth. After that the foe at once stepped onto the shining floor, advanced angrily. From his eyes came a light not fair, most like a flame. He saw many men in the hall, a band of kinsmen all asleep together, a company of war-men. Then his heart laughed: dreadful monster, he thought that before the day came he would divide the life from the body of every one of them, for there had come to him a hope of full-feasting. It was not his fate that when that night was over he should feast on more of mankind.

The kinsman of Hygelac, mighty man, watched how the evil-doer would make his quick onslaught. Nor did the monster mean to delay it, but, starting his work, he suddenly seized a sleeping man, tore at him ravenously, bit into his bone-locks, drank the blood from his veins, swallowed huge morsels; quickly he had eaten all of the lifeless one, feet and hands. He stepped closer, then felt with his arm for the brave-hearted man on the bed, reached out towards him, the foe with his hand; at once in fierce response Beowulf seized it and sat up, leaning on his own arm. Straightway the fosterer of crimes knew that he had not en-countered on middle-earth, anywhere in this world, a harder hand-grip from another man. In mind he became frightened, in his spirit: not for that might he escape the sooner. His heart was eager to get away, he would flee to his hiding-place, seek his rabble of devils. What he met there was not such as he had ever before met in the days of his life. Then the kinsman of Hygelac, the good man, thought of his evening's speech, stood upright and laid firm hold on him: his fingers cracked. The giant was pulling away, the earl stepped forward. The notorious one thought to move farther away, wherever he could, and flee his way from there to his fen-retreat; he knew his fingers' power to be in a hateful grip. That was a painful journey that the loathsome de-spoiler had made to Heorot. The retainers' hall rang with the noise—terrible drink [5] for all the Danes, the house-dwellers, every brave man, the earls. Both were enraged, fury-filled, the two who meant to control the hall. The building resounded. Then was it much wonder that the wine-hall withstood them joined in fierce

5. The metaphor reflects the idea that the chief purpose of a hall such as Heorot was as a place for men to feast in.

fight, that it did not fall to the ground, the fair earth-dwelling; but it was so firmly made fast with iron bands, both inside and outside, joined by skillful smith-craft. There started from the floor—as I have heard say—many a mead-bench, gold-adorned, when the furious ones fought. No wise men of the Scyldings ever before thought that any men in any manner might break it down, splendid with bright horns, have skill to destroy it, unless flame should embrace it, swallow it in fire. Noise rose up, sound strange enough. Horrible fear came upon the North-Danes, upon every one of those who heard the weeping from the wall, God's enemy sing his terrible song, song without triumph—the hell-slave bewail his pain. There held him fast he who of men was strongest of might in the days of this life.

(XII.) Not for anything would the protector of warriors let the murderous guest go off alive: he did not consider his life-days of use to any of the nations. There more than enough of Beowulf's earls drew swords, old heirlooms, wished to protect the life of their dear lord, famous prince, however they might. They did not know when they entered the fight, hardy-spirited warriors, and when they thought to hew him on every side, to seek his soul, that not any of the best of irons on earth, no war-sword, would touch the evil-doer: for with a charm he had made victory-weapons useless, every sword-edge. His departure to death from the time of this life was to be wretched; and the alien spirit was to travel far off into the power of fiends. Then he who before had brought trouble of heart to mankind, committed many crimes—he was at war with God—found that his body would do him no good, for the great-hearted kinsman of Hygelac had him by the hand. Each was hateful to the other alive. The awful monster had lived to feel pain in his body, a huge wound in his shoulder was exposed, his sinews sprang apart, his bone-locks broke. Glory in battle was given to Beowulf. Grendel must flee from there, mortally sick, seek his joyless home in the fen-slopes. He knew the more surely that his life's end had come, the full number of his days. For all the Danes was their wish fulfilled after the bloody fight. Thus he who had lately come from far off, wise and stout-hearted, had purged Heorot, saved Hrothgar's house from affliction. He rejoiced in his night's work, a deed to make famous his courage. The man of the Geats had fulfilled his boast to the East-Danes; so too he had remedied all the grief, the malice-caused sorrow that they had endured before, and had had to suffer from harsh necessity, no small distress. That was clearly proved when the battle-brave man set the hand up under the curved roof—the arm and the shoulder: there all together was Grendel's grasp.

[CELEBRATION AT HEOROT]

(XIII.) Then in the morning, as I have heard, there was many a warrior about the gift-hall. Folk-chiefs came from far and near over the wide-stretching ways to look on the wonder, the footprints of the foe. Nor did his going from life seem sad to any of the men who saw the tracks of the one without glory—how, weary-hearted, overcome with injuries, he moved on his way from there to the mere [6] of the water-monsters with life-failing footsteps, death-doomed and in flight. There the water was boiling with blood, the horrid surge of waves swirling, all mixed with hot gore, sword-blood. Doomed to die he had hidden, then, bereft of joys, had laid down his life in his fen-refuge, his heathen soul: there hell took him.

From there old retainers—and many a young man, too—turned back in their glad journey to ride from the mere, high-spirited on horseback, warriors on steeds. There was Beowulf's fame spoken of; many a man said—and not only once—that, south nor north, between the seas, over the wide earth, no other man under the sky's expanse was better of those who bear shields, more worthy of ruling. Yet they found no fault with their own dear lord, gracious Hrothgar, for he was a good king. At times battle-famed men let their brown horses gallop, let them race where the paths seemed fair, known for their excellence. At times a thane of the king, a man skilled at telling adventures, songs stored in his memory, who could recall many of the stories of the old days, wrought a new tale in well-joined words; this man undertook with his art to recite in turn Beowulf's exploit, and skillfully to tell an apt tale, to lend words to it.

He spoke everything that he had heard tell of Sigemund's valorous deeds, many a strange thing, the strife of Waels's son,[7] his far journeys, feuds and crimes, of which the children of men knew nothing—except for Fitela with him, to whom he would tell everything, the uncle to his nephew, for they were always friends in need in every fight. Many were the tribes of giants that they had laid low with their swords. For Sigemund there sprang up after his death-day no little glory—after he, hardy in war, had killed the dragon, keeper of the treasure-hoard: under the hoary stone the prince's son had ventured alone, a daring deed, nor was Fitela with him. Yet it turned out well for him, so that his sword went through the gleaming worm and stood fixed in the wall, splendid weapon: the dragon lay dead of the murdering stroke. Through his courage the great warrior had brought it about that he might at his own wish enjoy the ring-hoard. He

6. Lake.   7. Waels was Sigemund's father.

loaded the sea-boat, bore into the ship's bosom the bright treasure, offspring of Waels. The hot dragon melted.

He was adventurer most famous, far and wide through the nations, for deeds of courage—he had prospered from that before, the protector of warriors—after the war-making of Heremod had come to an end, his strength and his courage.[8] Among the Jutes Heremod came into the power of his enemies, was betrayed, quickly dispatched. Surging sorrows had oppressed him too long: he had become a great care to his people, to all his princes; for many a wise man in former times had bewailed the journey of the fierce-hearted one—people who had counted on him as a relief from affliction—that that king's son should prosper, take the rank of his father, keep guard over the folk, the treasure and strong-hold, the kindgom of heroes, the home of the Scyldings. The kinsman of Hygelac became dearer to his friends, to all man-kind: crime took possession of Heremod.

Sometimes racing their horses they passed over the sand-covered ways. By then the morning light was far advanced, hastening on. Many a stout-hearted warrior went to the high hall to see the strange wonder. The king himself walked forth from the women's apart-ment, the guardian of the ring-hoards, secure in his fame, known for his excellence, with much company; and his queen with him passed over the path to the mead-hall with a troop of attendant women.

(XIV.) Hrothgar spoke—he had gone to the hall, taken his stand on the steps, looked at the high roof shining with gold, and at Grendel's hand: "For this sight may thanks be made quickly to the Almighty: I endured much from the foe, many griefs from Grendel: God may always work wonder upon wonder, the Guardian of Heaven. It was not long ago that I did not expect ever to live to see relief from any of my woes—when the best of houses stood shining with blood, stained with slaughter, a far-reaching woe for each of my counselors, for every one, since none thought he could ever defend the people's stronghold from its enemies, from demons and evil spirits. Now through the Lord's might a warrior has accomplished the deed that all of us with our skill could not perform. Yes, she may say, whatever woman brought forth this son among mankind—if she still lives —that the God of Old was kind to her in her child-bearing. Now, Beowulf, best of men, in my heart I will love you as a son: keep well this new kinship. To you will there be no lack

---

8. Heremod was an unsuccessful king of the Danes, one who began brilliantly but became cruel and avaricious, ul-timately having to take refuge among the Jutes, who put him to death. His reputation was thus overshadowed by that of Sigemund.

of the good things of the world that I have in my possession. Full often I have made reward for less, done honor with gifts to a lesser warrior, weaker in fighting. With your deeds you yourself have made sure that your glory will be ever alive. May the Almighty reward you with good—as just now he has done."

Beowulf spoke, the son of Ecgtheow: "With much good will we have achieved this work of courage, that fight, have ventured boldly against the strength of the unknown one. I should have wished rather that you might have seen him, your enemy brought low among your furnishings. I thought quickly to bind him on his deathbed with hard grasp, so that because of my hand-grip he should lie struggling for life—unless his body should escape. I could not stop his going, since the Lord did not wish it, nor did I hold him firmly enough for that, my life-enemy: he was too strong, the foe in his going. Yet to save his life he has left his hand behind to show that he was here—his arm and shoulder; nor by that has the wretched creature bought any comfort; none the longer will the loathsome ravager live, hard-pressed by his crimes, for a wound has clutched him hard in its strong grip, in deadly bonds. There, like a man outlawed for guilt, he shall await the great judgment, how the bright Lord will decree for him."

Then was the warrior more silent in boasting speech of warlike deeds, the son of Ecglaf,[9] after the nobles had looked at the hand, now high on the roof through the strength of a man, the foe's fingers. The end of each one, each of the nail-places, was most like steel; the hand-spurs of the heathen warrior were monstrous spikes. Everyone said that no hard thing would hurt him, no iron good from old times would harm the bloody battle-hand of the monster.

(XV.) Then was it ordered that Heorot be within quickly adorned by hands. Many there were, both men and women, who made ready the wine-hall, the guest-building. The hangings on the walls shone with gold, many a wondrous sight for each man who looks on such things. That bright building was much damaged, though made fast within by iron bonds, and its door-hinges sprung; the roof alone came through unharmed when the monster, outlawed for his crimes, turned in flight, in despair of his life. That is not easy to flee from—let him try it who will—but driven by need one must seek the place prepared for earth-dwellers, soul-bearers, the sons of men, the place where, after its feasting, one's body will sleep fast in its death-bed.

Then had the proper time come that Healfdene's son should go to the hall; the king himself would share in the feast. I have

---

9. I.e., Unferth, who had taunted Beowulf the night before.

never heard that a people in a larger company bore themselves better about their treasure-giver. Men who were known for courage sat at the benches, rejoiced in the feast. Their kinsmen, stout-hearted Hrothgar and Hrothulf, partook fairly of many a mead-cup in the high hall. Heorot within was filled with friends: the Scylding-people had not then known treason's web.[1]

Then the son of Healfdene gave Beowulf a golden standard to reward his victory—a decorated battle-banner—a helmet and mail-shirt: many saw the glorious, costly sword borne before the warrior. Beowulf drank of the cup in the mead-hall. He had no need to be ashamed before fighting men of those rich gifts. I have not heard of many men who gave four precious, gold-adorned things to another on the ale-bench in a more friendly way. The rim around the helmet's crown had a head-protection, wound of wire, so that no battle-hard sharp sword might badly hurt him when the shield-warrior should go against his foe. Then the people's protector commanded eight horses with golden bridles to be led into the hall, within the walls. The saddle of one of them stood shining with hand-ornaments, adorned with jewels: that had been the war-seat of the high king when the son of Healfdene would join sword-play: never did the warfare of the wide-known one fail when men died in battle. And then the prince of Ing's friends [2] yielded possession of both, horses and weapons, to Beowulf: he bade him use them well. So generously the famous prince, guardian of the hoard, repaid the warrior's battle-deeds with horses and treasure that no man will ever find fault with them—not he that will speak truth according to what is right.

(XVI.) Then further the lord gave treasure to each of the men on the mead-bench who had made the sea-voyage with Beowulf, gave heirlooms; and he commanded that gold be paid for the one whom in his malice Grendel had killed—as he would have killed more if wise God and the man's courage had not forestalled that fate. The Lord guided all the race of men then, as he does now. Yet is discernment everywhere best, fore-thought of mind. Many a thing dear and loath he shall live to see who here in the days of trouble long makes use of the world.

There was song and music together before Healfdene's battle-leader, the wooden harp touched, tale oft told, when Hrothgar's scop should speak hall-pastime among the mead-benches . . . [of] Finn's retainers when the sudden disaster fell upon them. . . .[3]

1. A reference to the later history of the Danes, when, after Hrothgar's death, his nephew Hrothulf apparently drove his son and successor Hrethric from the throne.
2. Ing was a legendary Danish king, and his "friends" are the Danes.
3. The lines introducing the scop's song seem faulty. The story itself is recounted in a highly allusive way, and many of its details are obscure, though some help is offered by an independent version of the story given in a fragmentary Old English lay called *The Fight at Finnsburg*.

The hero of the Half-Danes, Hnaef of the Scyldings, was fated to fall on Frisian battlefield. And no need had Hildeburh [4] to praise the good faith of the Jutes: blameless she was deprived of her dear ones at the shield-play, of son and brother; wounded by spears they fell to their fate. That was a mournful woman. Not without cause did Hoc's daughter lament the decree of destiny when morning came and she might see, under the sky, the slaughter of kinsmen—where before she had the greatest of world's joy. The fight took away all Finn's thanes except for only a few, so that he could in no way continue the battle on the field against Hengest, nor protect the survivors by fighting against the prince's thane. But they offered them peace-terms,[5] that they should clear another building for them, hall and high seat, that they might have control of half of it with the sons of the Jutes; and at givings of treasure the son of Folcwalda [6] should honor the Danes each day, should give Hengest's company rings, such gold-plated treasure as that with which he would cheer the Frisians' kin in the high hall. Then on both sides they confirmed the fast peace-compact. Finn declared to Hengest, with oaths deep-sworn, unfeigned, that he would hold those who were left from the battle in honor in accordance with the judgment of his counselors, so that by words or by works no man should break the treaty nor because of malice should ever mention that, princeless, the Danes followed the slayer of their own ring-giver, since necessity forced them. If with rash speech any of the Frisians should insist upon calling to mind the cause of murderous hate, then the sword's edge should settle it.

The funeral pyre was made ready and gold brought up from the hoard. The best of the warriors of the War-Scyldings [7] was ready on the pyre. At the fire it was easy to see many a blood-stained battle-shirt, boar-image all golden—iron-hard swine—many a noble destroyed by wounds: more than one had died in battle. Then Hildeburh bade give her own son to the flames on Hnaef's pyre, burn his blood vessels, put him in the fire at the shoulder of

4. Hildeburh, daughter of the former Danish king Hoc and sister of the ruling Danish king Hnaef, was married to Finn, king of the Jutes (Frisians). Hnaef with a party of Danes made what was presumably a friendly visit to Hildeburh and Finn at their home Finnsburg, but during a feast a quarrel broke out between the Jutes and the Danes (since the scop's sympathies are with the Danes, he ascribes the cause to the bad faith of the Jutes), and in the ensuing fight Hnaef and his nephew, the son of Finn and Hildeburh, were killed, along with many other Danes and Jutes.

5. It is not clear who proposed the peace terms, but in view of the teller's Danish sympathies, it was probably the Jutes that sought the uneasy truce from Hengest, who became the Danes' leader after Hnaef's death. The truce imposed upon Hengest and the Danes the intolerable condition of having to dwell in peace with the Jutish king who was responsible for the death of their own king.

6. I.e., Finn.

7. I.e., Hnaef.

his uncle. The woman mourned, sang her lament. The warrior took his place.[8] The greatest of death-fires wound to the skies, roared before the barrow. Heads melted as blood sprang out—wounds opened wide, hate-bites of the body. Fire swallowed them—greediest of spirits—all of those whom war had taken away from both peoples: their strength had departed.

(XVII.) Then warriors went to seek their dwellings, bereft of friends, to behold Friesland, their homes and high city.[9] Yet Hengest stayed on with Finn for a winter darkened with the thought of slaughter, all desolate. He thought of his land, though he might not drive his ring-prowed ship over the water—the sea boiled with storms, strove with the wind, winter locked the waves in ice-bonds—until another year came to men's dwellings, just as it does still, glorious bright weather always watching for its time. Then winter was gone, earth's lap fair, the exile was eager to go, the guest from the dwelling: [yet] more he thought of revenge for his wrongs than of the sea-journey—if he might bring about a fight where he could take account of the sons of the Jutes with his iron. So he made no refusal of the world's custom when the son of Hunlaf [1] placed on his lap Battle-Bright, best of swords: its edges were known to the Jutes. Thus also to war-minded Finn in his turn cruel sword-evil came in his own home, after Guthlaf and Oslaf complained of the grim attack, the injury after the sea-journey, assigned blame for their lot of woes: breast might not contain the restless heart. Then was the hall reddened from foes' bodies, and thus Finn slain, the king in his company, and the queen taken. The warriors of the Scyldings bore to ship all the hall-furnishings of the land's king, whatever of necklaces, skillfully wrought treasures, they might find at Finn's home. They brought the noble woman on the sea-journey to the Danes, led her to her people.

The lay was sung to the end, the song of the scop. Joy mounted again, bench-noise brightened; cup-bearers poured wine from wonderful vessels. Then Wealhtheow came forth to walk under gold crown to where the good men sat, nephew and uncle: their friendship was then still unbroken, each true to the other.[2] There too Unferth the spokesman sat at the feet of the prince

8. The line is obscure, but it perhaps means that the body of Hildeburh's son was placed on the pyre.

9. This seems to refer to the few survivors on the Jutish side.

1. The text is open to various interpretations. The one adopted here assumes that the Dane Hunlaf, brother of Guthlaf and Oslaf, had been killed in the fight, and that ultimately Hunlaf's son demanded vengeance by the sym-bolical act of placing his father's sword in Hengest's lap, while at the same time Guthlaf and Oslaf reminded Hengest of the Jutes' treachery. It is not clear whether the subsequent fight in which Finn was killed was waged by the Danish survivors alone, or whether the party first went back to Denmark and then returned to Finnsburg with reinforcements.

2. See section XV, note 1, above.

of the Scyldings: each of them trusted his spirit, that he had much courage, though he was not honorable to his kinsmen at sword-play. Then the woman of the Scyldings spoke:

"Take this cup my noble lord, giver of treasure. Be glad, gold-friend of warriors, and speak to the Geats with mild words, as a man ought to do. Be gracious to the Geats, mindful of gifts [which] [3] you now have from near and far. They have told me that you would have the warrior for your son. Heorot is purged, the bright ring-hall. Enjoy while you may many rewards, and leave to your kinsmen folk and kingdom when you must go forth to look on the Ruler's decree. I know my gracious Hrothulf, that he will hold the young warriors in honor if you, friend of the Scyldings, leave the world before him. I think he will repay our sons with good if he remembers all the favors we did to his pleasure and honor when he was a child."

Then she turned to the bench where her sons were, Hrethric and Hrothmund, and the sons of the warriors, young men together. There sat the good man Beowulf of the Geats beside the two brothers.

(XVIII.) The cup was borne to him and welcome offered in friendly words to him, and twisted gold courteously bestowed on him, two arm-ornaments, a mail-shirt and rings, the largest of necklaces of those that I have heard spoken of on earth. I have heard of no better hoard-treasure under the heavens since Hama carried away to his bright city the necklace of the Brosings, [4] chain and rich setting: he fled the treacherous hatred of Eormenric, got eternal favor. This ring Hygelac of the Geats, [5] grandson of Swerting, had on his last venture, when beneath his battle-banner he defended his treasure, protected the spoils of war: fate took him when for pride he sought trouble, feud with the Frisians. Over the cup of the waves the mighty prince wore that treasure, precious stone. He fell beneath his shield; the body of the king came into the grasp of the Franks, his breast-armor and the neck-ring together. Lesser warriors plundered the fallen after the war-harvest: people of the Geats held the place of corpses.

The hall was filled with noise. Wealhtheow spoke, before the company she said to him: "Wear this ring, beloved Beowulf, young man, with good luck, and make use of this mail-shirt from

---

3. The text seems corrupt.

4. The Brisings' (Brosings') necklace had been worn by the goddess Freya. Nothing more is known of this story of Hama, who seems to have stolen the necklace from the famous Gothic king Eormenric.

5. Beowulf is later said to have presented the necklace to Hygelac's queen, Hygd, though here Hygelac is said to have been wearing it on his ill-fated expedition against the Franks and Frisians, into whose hands it fell at his death.

the people's treasure, and prosper well; make yourself known with your might, and be kind of counsel to these boys: I shall remember to reward you for that. You have brought it about that, far and near, for a long time all men shall praise you, as wide as the sea surrounds the shores, home of the winds. While you live, prince, be prosperous. I wish you well of your treasure. Much favored one, be kind of deeds to my son. Here is each earl true to other, mild of heart, loyal to his lord; the thanes are at one, the people obedient, the retainers cheered with drink do as I bid."

Then she walked to her seat. There was the best of feasts, men drank wine. They did not know the fate, the grim decree made long before, as it came to pass to many of the earls after evening had come and Hrothgar had gone to his chambers, the noble one to his rest. A great number of men remained in the hall, just as they had often done before. They cleared the benches from the floor. It was spread over with beds and pillows. One of the beer-drinkers, ripe and fated to die, lay down to his hall-rest. They set at their heads their battle-shields, bright wood; there on the bench it was easy to see above each man his helmet that towered in battle, his ringed mail-shirt, his great spear-wood. It was their custom to be always ready for war whether at home or in the field, in any case at any time that need should befall their liege lord: that was a good nation.

[GRENDEL'S MOTHER'S ATTACK]

(XIX.) Then they sank to sleep. One paid sorely for his evening rest, just as had often befallen them when Grendel guarded the gold-hall, wrought wrong until the end came, death after misdeeds. It came to be seen, wide-known to men, that after the bitter battle an avenger still lived for an evil space: Grendel's mother, woman, monster-wife, was mindful of her misery, she who had to dwell in the terrible water, the cold currents, after Cain became sword-slayer of his only brother, his own father's son. Then Cain went as an outlaw to flee the cheerful life of men, marked for his murder, held to the wasteland. From him sprang many a devil sent by fate. Grendel was one of them, hateful outcast who at Heorot found a waking man waiting his warfare. There the monster had laid hold upon him, but he was mindful of the great strength, the large gift God had given him, and relied on the Almighty for favor, comfort and help. By that he overcame the foe, subdued the hell-spirit. Then he went off wretched, bereft of joy, to seek his dying-place, enemy of mankind. And his mother, still greedy and gallows-grim, would go on a sorrowful venture, avenge her son's death.

Then she came to Heorot where the Ring-Danes slept throughout the hall. Then change came quickly to the earls there, when Grendel's mother made her way in. The attack was the less terrible by just so much as is the strength of women, the war-terror of a wife, less than an armed man's when a hard blade, forge-hammered, a sword shining with blood, good of its edges, cuts the stout boar on a helmet opposite. Then in the hall was hard-edged sword raised from the seat, many a broad shield lifted firmly in hand: none thought of helmet, of wide mail-shirt, when the terror seized him. She was in haste, would be gone out from there, protect her life after she was discovered. Swiftly she had taken fast hold on one of the nobles, then she went to the fen. He was one of the men between the seas most beloved of Hrothgar in the rank of retainer, a noble shield-warrior whom she destroyed at his rest, a man of great repute. Beowulf was not there, for earlier, after the treasure-giving, another lodging had been appointed for the renowned Geat. Outcry arose in Heorot: she had taken, in its gore, the famed hand. Care was renewed, come again on the dwelling. That was not a good bargain, that on both sides they had to pay with the lives of friends.

Then was the old king, the hoary warrior, of bitter mind when he learned that his chief thane was lifeless, his dearest man dead. Quickly Beowulf was fetched to the bed-chamber, man happy in victory. At daybreak together with his earls he went, the noble champion himself with his retainers, to where the wise one was, waiting to know whether after tidings of woe the All-Wielder would ever bring about change for him. The worthy warrior walked over the floor with his retainers—hall-wood resounded —that he might address words to the wise prince of Ing's friends, asked if the night had been pleasant according to his desires.

(XX.) Hrothgar spoke, protector of the Scyldings: "Ask not about pleasure. Sorrow is renewed to the people of the Danes: Aeschere is dead, Yrmenlaf's elder brother, my speaker of wisdom and my bearer of counsel, my shoulder-companion when we used to defend our heads in battle, when troops clashed, beat on boar-images. Whatever an earl should be, a man good from old times, such was Aeschere. Now a wandering murderous spirit has slain him with its hands in Heorot. I do not know by what way the awful creature, glorying in its prey, has made its retreat, gladdened by its feast. She has avenged the feud—that last night you killed Grendel with hard hand-grips, savagely, because too long he had diminished and destroyed my people. He fell in the fight, his life forfeited, and now the other has come, a mighty worker of wrong, would avenge her kinsman, and has carried far her revenge—as many a thane may think who weeps in his spirit for his treasure-giver, bitter sorrow in heart. Now the hand lies lifeless that was strong in support of all your desires.

"I have heard landsmen, my people, hall-counselors, say this, that they have seen two such huge walkers in the wasteland holding to the moors, alien spirits. One of them, so far as they could clearly discern, was the likeness of a woman. The other wretched shape trod the tracks of exile in the form of a man, except that he was bigger than any other man. Land-dwellers in the old days named him Grendel. They know of no father, whether in earlier times any was begotten for them among the dark spirits. They hold to the secret land, the wolf-slopes, the windy headlands, the dangerous fen-paths where the mountain stream goes down under the darkness of the hills, the flood under the earth. It is not far from here, measured in miles, that the mere stands; over it hang frost-covered woods, trees fast of root close over the water. There each night may be seen fire on the flood, a fearful wonder. Of the sons of men there lives none, old of wisdom, who knows the bottom. Though the heath-stalker, the strong-horned hart, harassed by hounds makes for the forest after long flight, rather will he give his life, his being, on the bank than save his head by entering. That is no pleasant place. From it the surging waves rise up black to the heavens when the wind stirs up awful storms, until the air becomes gloomy, the skies weep. Now once again is the cure in you alone. You do not yet know the land, the perilous place, where you might find the seldom-seen creature: seek if you dare. I will give you wealth for the feud, old treasure, as I did before, twisted gold—if you come away."

(XXI.) Beowulf spoke, the son of Ecgtheow: "Sorrow not, wise warrior. It is better for a man to avenge his friend than much mourn. Each of us must await his end of the world's life. Let him who may get glory before death: that is best for the warrior after he has gone from life. Arise, guardian of the kingdom, let us go at once to look on the track of Grendel's kin. I promise you this: she will not be lost under cover, not in the earth's bosom nor in the mountain woods nor at the bottom of the sea, go where she will. This day have patience in every woe—as I expect you to."

Then the old man leapt up, thanked God, the mighty Lord, that the man had so spoken. Then was a horse bridled for Hrothgar, a curly-maned mount. The wise king moved in state; the band of shield-bearers marched on foot. The tracks were seen wide over the wood-paths where she had gone on the ground, made her way forward over the dark moor, borne lifeless the best of retainers of those who watched over their home with Hrothgar. The son of noble forebears [6] moved over the steep

6. I.e., **Hrothgar.**

rocky slopes, narrow paths where only one could go at a time, an unfamiliar trail, steep hills, many a lair of water-monsters. He went before with a few wise men to spy out the country, until suddenly he found mountain trees leaning out over hoary stone, a joyless wood: water lay beneath, bloody and troubled. It was pain of heart for all the Danes to suffer, for the friends of the Scyldings, for many a thane, grief to each earl when on the cliff over the water they came upon Aeschere's head. The flood boiled with blood—the men looked upon it—with hot gore. Again and again the horn sang its urgent war-song. The whole troop sat down to rest. Then they saw on the water many a snake-shape, strong sea-serpents exploring the mere, and water-monsters lying on the slopes of the shore such as those that in the morning often attend a perilous journey on the paths of the sea, serpents and wild beasts.

These fell away from the shore, fierce and rage-swollen: they had heard the bright sound, the war-horn sing. One of them a man of the Geats with his bow cut off from his life, his water-warring, after the hard war-arrow stuck in his heart: he was weaker in swimming the lake when death took him. Straightway he was hard beset on the waves with barbed boar-spears, strongly surrounded, pulled up on the shore, strange spawn of the waves. The men looked on the terrible alien thing.

Beowulf put on his warrior's dress, had no fear for his life. His war-shirt, hand-fashioned, broad and well-worked, was to explore the mere: it knew how to cover his body-cave so that foe's grip might not harm his heart, or grasp of angry enemy his life. But the bright helmet guarded his head, one which was to stir up the lake-bottom, seek out the troubled water—made rich with gold, surrounded with splendid bands, as the weapon-smith had made it in far-off days, fashioned it wonderfully, set it about with boar-images so that thereafter no sword or battle-blade might bite into it. And of his strong supports that was not the least which Hrothgar's spokesman [7] lent to his need: Hrunting was the name of the hilted sword; it was one of the oldest of ancient treasures; its edge was iron, decorated with poison-stripes, hardened with battle-sweat. Never had it failed in war any man of those who grasped it in their hands, who dared enter on danger-ous enterprises, onto the common meeting place of foes: this was not the first time that it should do work of courage. Surely the son of Ecglaf, great of strength, did not have in mind what, drunk with wine, he had spoken, when he lent that weapon to a better sword-fighter. He did not himself dare to risk his life under the warring waves, to engage his courage: there he lost his glory,

7. I.e., Unferth.

his name for valor. It was not so with the other when he had armed himself for battle.

[BEOWULF ATTACKS GRENDEL'S MOTHER]

(XXII.) Beowulf spoke, the son of Ecgtheow: "Think now, renowned son of Healfdene, wise king, now that I am ready for the venture, gold-friend of warriors, of what we said before, that, if at your need I should go from life, you would always be in a father's place for me when I am gone: be guardian of my young retainers, my companions, if battle should take me. The treasure you gave me, beloved Hrothgar, send to Hygelac. The lord of the Geats may know from the gold, the son of Hrethel may see when he looks on that wealth, that I found a ring-giver good in his gifts, enjoyed him while I might. And let Unferth have the old heirloom, the wide-known man my splendid-waved sword, hard-edged: with Hrunting I shall get glory, or death will take me."

After these words the man of the Weather-Geats turned away boldly, would wait for no answer: the surging water took the warrior. Then was it a part of a day before he might see the bottom's floor. Straightway that which had held the flood's tract a hundred half-years, ravenous for prey, grim and greedy, saw that some man from above was exploring the dwelling of monsters. Then she groped toward him, took the warrior in her awful grip. Yet not the more for that did she hurt his hale body within: his ring-armor shielded him about on the outside so that she could not pierce the war-dress, the linked body-mail, with hateful fingers. Then as she came to the bottom the sea-wolf bore the ring-prince to her house so that—no matter how brave he was —he might not wield weapons; but many monsters attacked him in the water, many a sea-beast tore at his mail-shirt with war-tusks, strange creatures afflicted him. Then the earl saw that he was in some hostile hall where no water harmed him at all, and the flood's onrush might not touch him because of the hall-roof. He saw firelight, a clear blaze shine bright.

Then the good man saw the accursed dweller in the deep, the mighty mere-woman. He gave a great thrust to his sword—his hand did not withhold the stroke—so that the etched blade sang at her head a fierce war-song. Then the stranger found that the battle-lightning would not bite, harm her life, but the edge failed the prince in his need: many a hand-battle had it endured before, often sheared helmet, war-coat of man fated to die: this was the first time for the rare treasure that its glory had failed.

But still he was resolute, not slow of his courage, mindful of fame, the kinsman of Hygelac. Then, angry warrior, he threw away the sword, wavy-patterned, bound with ornaments, so that it lay on the ground, hard and steel-edged: he trusted in his strength, his mighty hand-grip. So ought a man to do when he thinks to get long-lasting praise in battle: he cares not for his life. Then he seized by the hair Grendel's mother—the man of the War-Geats did not shrink from the fight. Battle-hardened, now swollen with rage, he pulled his deadly foe so that she fell to the floor. Quickly in her turn she repaid him his gift with her grim claws and clutched at him: then weary-hearted, the strongest of warriors, of foot-soldiers, stumbled so that he fell. Then she sat upon the hall-guest and drew her knife, broad and bright-edged. She would avenge her child, her only son. The woven breast-armor lay on his shoulder: that protected his life, with-stood entry of point or of edge. Then the son of Ecgtheow would have fared amiss under the wide ground, the champion of the Geats, if the battle-shirt had not brought help, the hard war-net—and holy God brought about victory in war; the wise Lord, Ruler of the Heavens, decided it with right, easily, when Beowulf had stood up again.

XXIII. Then he saw among the armor a victory-blessed blade, an old sword made by the giants, strong of its edges, glory of warriors: it was the best of weapons, except that it was larger than any other man might bear to war-sport, good and adorned, the work of giants. He seized the linked hilt, he who fought for the Scyldings, savage and slaughter-bent, drew the patterned-blade; desperate of life, he struck angrily so that it bit her hard on the neck, broke the bone-rings. The blade went through all the doomed body. She fell to the floor, the sword was sweating, the man rejoiced in his work.

The blaze brightened, light shone within, just as from the sky heaven's candle shines clear. He looked about the building; then he moved along the wall, raised his weapon hard by the hilt, Hygelac's thane, angry and resolute: the edge was not useless to the warrior, for he would quickly repay Grendel for the many attacks he had made on the West-Danes—many more than the one time when he slew in their sleep fifteen hearth-companions of Hrothgar, devoured men of the Danish people while they slept, and another such number bore away, a hateful prey. He had paid him his reward for that, the fierce champion, for there he saw Grendel, weary of war, lying at rest, lifeless with the wounds he had got in the fight at Heorot. The body bounded wide when it suffered the blow after death, the hard sword-swing; and thus he cut off his head.

At once the wise men who were watching the water with Hrothgar saw that the surging waves were troubled, the lake stained with blood. Gray-haired, old, they spoke together of the good warrior, that they did not again expect of the chief that he would come victorious to seek their great king; for many agreed on it, that the sea-wolf had destroyed him.

Then came the ninth hour of the day. The brave Scyldings left the hill. The gold-friend of warriors went back to his home. The strangers sat sick at heart and stared at the mere. They wished—and did not expect—that they would see their beloved lord himself.

Then the blade began to waste away from the battle-sweat, the war-sword into battle-icicles. That was a wondrous thing, that it should all melt, most like the ice when the Father loosens the frost's fetters, undoes the water-bonds—He Who has power over seasons and times: He is the true Ruler. Beowulf did not take from the dwelling, the man of the Weather-Geats, more treasures —though he saw many there—but only the head and the hilt, bright with jewels. The sword itself had already melted, its patterned blade burned away: the blood was too hot for it, the spirit that had died there too poisonous. Quickly he was swimming, he who had lived to see the fall of his foes; he plunged up through the water. The currents were all cleansed, the great tracts of the water, when the dire spirit left her life-days and this loaned world.

Then the protector of seafarers came toward the land, swimming stout-hearted; he had joy of his sea-booty, the great burden he had with him. They went to meet him, thanked God, the strong band of thanes, rejoiced in their chief that they might see him again sound. Then the helmet and war-shirt of the mighty one were quickly loosened. The lake drowsed, the water beneath the skies, stained with blood. They went forth on the foot-tracks, glad in their hearts, measured the path back, the known ways, men bold as kings. They bore the head from the mere's cliff, toilsomely for each of the great-hearted ones: four of them had trouble in carrying Grendel's head on spear-shafts to the gold-hall —until at last they came striding to the hall, fourteen bold warriors of the Geats; their lord, high-spirited, walked in their company over the fields to the mead-hall.

Then the chief of the thanes, man daring in deeds, enriched by new glory, warrior dear to battle, came in to greet Hrothgar. Then Grendel's head was dragged by the hair over the floor to where men drank, a terrible thing to the earls and the woman with them, an awful sight: the men looked upon it.

[FURTHER CELEBRATION AT HEOROT]

(XXIV.) Beowulf spoke, the son of Ecgtheow: "Yes, we have brought you this sea-booty, son of Healfdene, man of the Scyldings, gladly, as evidence of glory—what you look on here. Not easily did I come through it with my life, the war under water, not without trouble carried out the task. The fight would have been ended straightway if God had not guarded me. With Hrunting I might not do anything in the fight, though that is a good weapon. But the Wielder of Men granted me that I should see hanging on the wall a fair, ancient great-sword—most often He has guided the man without friends—that I should wield the weapon. Then in the fight when the time became right for me I hewed the house-guardians. Then that war-sword, wavy-patterned, burnt away as their blood sprang forth, hottest of battle-sweats. I have brought the hilt away from the foes. I have avenged the evil deeds, the slaughter of Danes, as it was right to do. I promise you that you may sleep in Heorot without care with your band of retainers, and that for none of the thanes of your people, old or young, need you have fear, prince of the Scyldings—for no life-injury to your men on that account, as you did before."

Then the golden hilt was given into the hand of the old man, the hoary war-chief—the ancient work of giants. There came into the possession of the prince of the Danes, after the fall of devils, the work of wonder-smiths. And when the hostile-hearted creature, God's enemy, guilty of murder, gave up this world, and his mother too, it passed into the control of the best of worldly kings between the seas, of those who gave treasure in the Northlands.

Hrothgar spoke—he looked on the hilt, the old heirloom, on which was written the origin of ancient strife, when the flood, rushing water, slew the race of giants—they suffered terribly: that was a people alien to the Everlasting Lord. The Ruler made them a last payment through water's welling. On the sword-guard of bright gold there was also rightly marked through rune-staves, set down and told, for whom that sword, best of irons, had first been made, its hilt twisted and ornamented with snakes. Then the wise man spoke, the son of Healfdene—all were silent: "Lo, this may one say who works truth and right for the folk, recalls all things far distant, an old guardian of the land: that this earl was born the better man. Glory is raised up over the far ways—your glory over every people, Beowulf my friend. All of it, all your strength, you govern steadily in the wisdom of your heart. I shall fulfill my friendship to you, just as we spoke before. You shall become a comfort, whole and long-lasting, to your people, a help to warriors.

"So was not Heremod to the sons of Ecgwela, the Honor-Scyldings. He grew great not for their joy, but for their slaughter, for the destruction of Danish people. With swollen heart he killed his table-companions, shoulder-comrades, until he turned away from the joys of men, alone, notorious king, although mighty God had raised him in power, in the joys of strength, had set him up over all men. Yet in his breast his heart's thought grew blood-thirsty: no rings did he give to the Danes for glory. He lived joyless to suffer the pain of that strife, the long-lasting harm of the people. Teach yourself by him, be mindful of munificence. Old of winters, I tell this tale for you.

"It is a wonder to say how in His great spirit mighty God gives wisdom to mankind, land and earlship—He possesses power over all things. At times He lets the thought of a man of high lineage move in delight, gives him joy of earth in his homeland, a stronghold of men to rule over, makes regions of the world so subject to him, wide kingdoms, that in his unwisdom he may not himself have mind of his end. He lives in plenty; illness and age in no way grieve him, neither does dread care darken his heart, nor does enmity bare sword-hate, for the whole world turns to his will—he knows nothing worse—(XXV.) until his portion of pride increases and flourishes within him; then the watcher sleeps, the soul's guardian; that sleep is too sound, bound in its own cares, and the slayer most near whose bow shoots treacherously. Then is he hit in the heart, beneath his armor, with the bitter arrow—he cannot protect himself—with the crooked dark commands of the accursed spirit. What he has long held seems to him too little, angry-hearted he covets, no plated rings does he give in men's honor, and then he forgets and regards not his destiny because of what God, Wielder of Heaven, has given him before, his portion of glories. In the end it happens in turn that the loaned body weakens, falls doomed; another takes the earl's ancient treasure, one who recklessly gives precious gifts, does not fearfully guard them.

"Keep yourself against that wickedness, beloved Beowulf, best of men, and choose better—eternal gains. Have no care for pride, great warrior. Now for a time there is glory in your might: yet soon it shall be that sickness or sword will diminish your strength, or fire's fangs, or flood's surge, or sword's swing, or spear's flight, or appalling age; brightness of eyes will fail and grow dark; then it shall be that death will overcome you, warrior.

"Thus I ruled the Ring-Danes for a hundred half-years under the skies, and protected them in war with spear and sword against many nations over middle-earth, so that I counted no one as my adversary underneath the sky's expanse. Well, disproof of that came to me in my own land, grief after my joys, when Grendel, ancient adversary, came to invade my home. Great sorrow of heart I have always suffered for his persecution. Thanks be to the Ruler, the Eternal Lord, that after old strife I have come to see in my lifetime, with my own eyes, his blood-stained head. Go now to your seat, have joy of the glad feast, made famous in battle. Many of our treasures will be shared when morning comes."

The Geat was glad at heart, went at once to seek his seat as the wise one bade. Then was a feast fairly served again, for a second time, just as before, for those famed for courage, sitting about the hall.

Night's cover lowered, dark over the warriors. The retainers all arose. The gray-haired one would seek his bed, the old Scylding. It pleased the Geat, the brave shield-warrior, immensely that he should have rest. Straightway a hall-thane led the way on for the weary one, come from far country, and showed every courtesy to the thane's need, such as in those days seafarers might expect as their due.

Then the great-hearted one rested; the hall stood high, vaulted and gold-adorned; the guest slept within until the black raven, blithe-hearted, announced heaven's joy. Then the bright light came passing over the shadows. The warriors hastened, the nobles were eager to set out again for their people. Bold of spirit, the visitor would seek his ship far thence.

Then the hardy one bade that Hrunting be brought to the son of Ecglaf,[8] that he take back his sword, precious iron. He spoke thanks for that loan, said that he accounted it a good war-friend, strong in battle; in his words he found no fault at all with the sword's edge: he was a thoughtful man. And then they were eager to depart, the warriors ready in their armor. The prince who had earned honor of the Danes went to the high seat where the other was: the man dear to war greeted Hrothgar.

[Beowulf Returns Home]

(XXVI.) Beowulf spoke, the son of Ecgtheow: "Now we sea-travelers come from afar wish to say that we desire to seek Hygelac. Here we have been entertained splendidly according to our desire: you have dealt well with us. If on earth I might in any way earn more of your heart's love, prince of warriors, than I have done before with warlike deeds, I should be ready at once. If beyond the sea's expanse I hear that men dwelling near threaten you with terrors, as those who hated you did before, I shall bring you a thousand thanes, warriors to your aid. I know of Hygelac, lord of the Geats, though he is young as a guardian of the people, that he will further me with words and works so that I may do you honor and bring spears to help you, strong support where you have need of men. If Hrethric, king's son, decides to come to the court of the Geats, he can find many friends there;

8. I.e., Unferth.

far countries are well sought by him who is himself strong."

Hrothgar spoke to him in answer: "The All-Knowing Lord sent those words into your mind: I have not heard a man of so young age speak more wisely. You are great of strength, mature of mind, wise of words. I think it likely if the spear, sword-grim war, takes the son of Hrethel, sickness or weapon your prince, the people's ruler, and you have your life, that the Sea-Geats will not have a better to choose as their king, as guardian of their treasure, if you wish to hold the kingdom of your kinsmen. So well your heart's temper has long pleased me, beloved Beowulf. You have brought it about that peace shall be shared by the peoples, the folk of the Geats and the Spear-Danes, and enmity shall sleep, acts of malice which they practiced before; and there shall be, as long as I rule the wide kingdom, sharing of treasures, many a man shall greet his fellow with good gifts over the sea-bird's baths; the ring-prowed ship will bring gifts and tokens of friendship over the sea. I know your people, blameless in every respect, set firm after the old way both as to foe and to friend."

Then the protector of earls, the kinsman of Healfdene, gave him there in the hall twelve precious things; he bade him with these gifts seek his own dear people in safety, quickly come back. Then the king noble of race, the prince of the Scyldings, kissed the best of thanes and took him by his ncek: tears fell from the gray-haired one. He had two thoughts of the future, the old and wise man, one more strongly than the other—that they would not see each other again, bold men at council. The man was so dear to him that he might not restrain his breast's welling, for fixed in his heartstrings a deep-felt longing for the beloved man burned in his blood. Away from him Beowulf, warrior glorious with gold, walked over the grassy ground, proud of his treasure. The sea-goer awaited its owner, riding at anchor. Then on the journey the gift of Hrothgar was oft-praised: that was a king blameless in all things until age took from him the joys of his strength—old age that has often harmed many.

(XXVII.) There came to the flood the band of brave-hearted ones, of young men. They wore mail-coats, locked limb-shirts. The guard of the coast saw the coming of the earls, just as he had done before. He did not greet the guests with taunts from the cliff's top, but rode to meet them, said that the return of the warriors in bright armor in their ship would be welcome to the people of the Weather-Geats. There on the sand the broad sea-boat was loaded with armor, the ring-prowed ship with horses and rich things. The mast stood high over Hrothgar's hoard-gifts. He gave the boat-guard a sword wound with gold, so that thereafter on the mead-bench he was held the worthier for the treasure, the heirloom. The boat moved out to furrow the deep water, left the land of the Danes. Then on the mast a sea-cloth, a sail, was made fast by a rope. The boat's beams creaked: wind did not keep the sea-floater from its way over the waves. The sea-goer moved, foamy-necked floated forth over the swell, the ship with bound prow over the sea-currents until they might see the cliffs of the Geats, the well-known headlands. The ship pressed ahead, borne by the wind, stood still at the land. Quickly the harbor-guard was at the sea-side, he who had gazed for a long time far out over the currents, eager to see the beloved men. He [9] moored the deep ship in the sand, fast by its anchor ropes, lest the force of the waves should drive away the fair wooden vessel. Then he bade that the prince's wealth be borne ashore, armor and plated gold. It was not far for them to seek the giver of treasure, Hygelac son of Hrethel, where he dwelt at home near the sea-wall, himself with his retainers.

The building was splendid, its king most valiant, set high in the hall, Hygd [1] most youthful, wise and well-taught, though she had lived within the castle walls few winters, daughter of Haereth. For she was not niggardly, nor too sparing of gifts to the men of the Geats, of treasures. Modthryth,[2] good folk-queen, did dreadful deeds [in her youth]: no bold one among her retainers dared venture—except her great lord—to set his eyes on her in daylight, but [if he did] he should reckon deadly bonds prepared for him, arresting hands: that straightway after his seizure the sword awaited him, that the patterned blade must settle it, make known its death-evil. Such is no queenly custom for a woman to practice, though she is peerless—that one who weaves peace [3] should take away the life of a beloved man after pretended injury. However the kinsman of Hemming stopped that: [4] ale-drinkers gave another account, said that she did less harm to the people, fewer injuries, after she was given, gold-adorned, to the young warrior, the beloved noble, when by her father's teaching she sought Offa's hall in a voyage over the pale sea. There on the throne she was afterwards famous for generosity, while living made use of her life, held high love toward the lord of

9. Beowulf.
1. Hygd is Hygelac's young queen. The suddenness of her introduction here is perhaps due to a faulty text.
2. A transitional passage introducing the contrast between Hygd's good behavior and Modthryth's bad behavior as young women of royal blood seems to have been lost. Modthryth's practice of having those who looked into her face put to death may reflect the folk-motif of the princess whose unsuccessful suitors are executed, though the text does not say that Modthryth's victims were suitors. Modthryth's "great lord" was probably her father.
3. Daughters of kings were frequently given in marriage to the king of a hostile nation in order to bring about peace; hence Modthryth may be called "one who weaves peace."
4. Offa, an Angle king who according to legend ruled Mercia in England; who Hemming was—besides being Offa's forebear—is not known.

warriors, [who was] of all mankind the best, as I have heard, between the seas of the races of men. Since Offa was a man brave of wars and gifts, wide-honored, he held his native land in wisdom. From him sprang Eomer to the help of warriors, kinsman of Hemming, grandson of Garmund, strong in battle.[5]

(XXVIII.) Then the hardy one came walking with his troop over the sand on the sea-plain, the wide shores. The world-candle shone, the sun moved quickly from the south. They made their way, strode swiftly to where they heard that the protector of earls, the slayer of Ongentheow,[6] the good young war-king, was dispensing rings in the stronghold. The coming of Beowulf was straightway made known to Hygelac, that there in his home the defender of warriors, his comrade in battle, came walking alive to the court, sound from the battle-play. Quickly the way within was made clear for the foot-guests, as the mighty one bade.

Then he sat down with him, he who had come safe through the fight, kinsman with kinsman, after he had greeted his liege lord with formal speech, loyal, with vigorous words. Haereth's daughter moved through the hall-building with mead-cups, cared lovingly for the people, bore the cup of strong drink to the hands of the warriors. Hygelac began fairly to question his companion in the high hall, curiosity pressed him, what the adventures of the Sea-Geats had been. "How did you fare on your journey, beloved Beowulf, when you suddenly resolved to seek distant combat over the salt water, battle in Heorot? Did you at all help the wide-known woes of Hrothgar, the famous prince? Because of you I burned with seething sorrows, care of heart—had no trust in the venture of my beloved man. I entreated you long that you should in no way approach the murderous spirit, should let the South-Danes themselves settle the war with Grendel. I say thanks to God that I may see you sound."

Beowulf spoke, the son of Ecgtheow: "To many among men it is not hidden, lord Hygelac, the great encounter—what a fight we had, Grendel and I, in the place where he made many sorrows for the Victory-Scyldings, constant misery. All that I avenged, so that none of Grendel's kin over the earth need boast of that clash at night—whoever lives longest of the loathsome kind, wrapped in malice. There I went forth to the ring-hall to greet Hrothgar. At once the famous son of Healfdene, when he knew my purpose, gave me a seat with his own sons. The company was in joy:

---

5. Offa, the only person that may be identified as English in this English poem, receives high praise; apparently the names of his father Garmund and son Eomer would strike a responsive chord in the poet's audience.

6. Ongentheow was a Scylfing (Swedish) king, whose story is fully told below, sections XL and XLI. In fact Hygelac was not his slayer, but is called so because he led the attack on the Scylfings in which Ongentheow was killed.

I have not seen in the time of my life under heaven's arch more mead-mirth of hall-sitters. At times the famous queen, peace-pledge of the people, went through all the hall, cheered the young men; often she would give a man a ring-band before she went to her seat. At times Hrothgar's daughter bore the ale-cup to the retainers, to the earls throughout the hall. I heard hall-sitters name her Freawaru when she offered the studded cup to warriors. Young and gold-adorned, she is promised to the fair son of Froda.[7] That has seemed good to the lord of the Scyldings, the guardian of the kingdom, and he believes of this plan that he may, with this woman, settle their portion of deadly feuds, of quarrels.[8] Yet most often after the fall of a prince in any nation the deadly spear rests but a little while, even though the bride is good.

"It may displease the lord of the Heatho-Bards and each thane of that people when he goes in the hall with the woman, [that while] the noble sons of the Danes, her retainers, [are] feasted,[9] the heirlooms of their ancestors will be shining on them [1]—the hard and wave-adorned treasure of the Heatho-Bards, [which was theirs] so long as they might wield those weapons, (XXIX.) until they led to the shield-play, to destruction, their dear companions and their own lives. Then at the beer he[2] who sees the treasure, an old ash-warrior who remembers it all, the spear-death of warriors—grim is his heart—begins, sad of mind, to tempt a young fighter in the thoughts of his spirit, to awaken war-evil, and speaks this word:

"'Can you, my friend, recognize that sword, the rare iron-blade, that your father, beloved man, bore to battle his last time in armor, where the Danes slew him, the fierce Scyldings, got possession of the battle-field, when Withergeld[3] lay dead, after the fall of warriors? Now here some son of his murderers walks in the hall, proud of the weapon, boasts of the murder, and wears the treasure that you should rightly possess.' So he will provoke and remind at every chance with wounding words until that moment comes that the woman's thane,[4] forfeiting life, shall lie dead, blood-smeared from the sword-bite, for his father's deeds. The other escapes with his life, knows the land well. Then on both sides the oath of the earls will be broken;

7. I.e., Ingeld, who succeeded his father a king of the Heatho-Bards.
8. I.e., the feud between the Danes and Heatho-Bards.
9. The text is faulty here.
1. I.e., the weapons and armor which had once belonged to the Heatho-Bards and were captured by the Danes will be worn by the Danish attendants of Hrothgar's daughter Freawaru when she goes to the Heatho-Bards to marry king Ingeld.
2. I.e., some old Heatho-Bard warrior.
3. Apparently a leader of the Heatho-Bards in their unsuccessful war with the Danes.
4. I.e., the Danish attendant of Freawaru who is wearing the sword of his Heatho-Bard attacker's father.

then deadly hate will well up in Ingeld, and his wife-love after the surging of sorrows will become cooler. Therefore I do not think the loyalty of the Heatho-Bards, their part in the alliance with the Danes, to be without deceit—do not think their friendship fast.

"I shall speak still more of Grendel, that you may readily know, giver of treasure, what the hand-fight of warriors came to in the end. After heaven's jewel had glided over the earth, the angry spirit came, awful in the evening, to visit us where, unharmed, we watched over the hall. There the fight was fatal to Hondscioh, deadly to one who was doomed. He was dead first of all, armed warrior. Grendel came to devour him, good young retainer, swallowed all the body of the beloved men. Yet not for this would the bloody-toothed slayer, bent on destruction, go from the gold-hall empty-handed; but, strong of might, he made trial of me, grasped me with eager hand. His glove⁵ hung huge and wonderful, made fast with cunning clasps: it had been made all with craft, with devil's devices and dragon's skins. The fell doer of evils would put me therein, guiltless, one of many. He might not do so after I had stood up in anger. It is too long to tell how I repaid the people's foe his due for every crime. My prince, there with my deeds I did honor to your people. He slipped away, for a little while had use of life's joy. Yet his right hand remained as his spoor in Heorot, and he went from there abject, mournful of heart sank to the mere's bottom.

"The lord of the Scyldings repaid me for that bloody combat with much plated gold, many treasures, after morning came and we sat down to the feast. There was song and mirth. The old Scylding, who has learned many things, spoke of times far-off. At times a brave one in battle touched the glad wood, the harp's joy; at times he told tales, true and sad; at times he related strange stories according to right custom; at times, again, the great-hearted king, bound with age, the old warrior, would begin to speak of his youth, his battle-strength. His heart welled within when, old and wise, he thought of his many winters. Thus we took pleasure there the livelong day until another night came to men.

"Then in her turn Grendel's mother swiftly made ready to take revenge for his injuries, made a sorrowful journey. Death had taken her son, war-hate of the Weather-Geats. The direful woman avenged her son, fiercely killed a warrior: there the life of Aeschere departed, a wise old counselor. And when morning came the folk of the Danes might not burn him, death-weary, in the fire, nor place him on the pyre, beloved man: she had borne

---

5. Apparently a large glove that could be used as a pouch.

his body away in fiend's embrace beneath the mountain stream.
That was the bitterest of Hrothgar's sorrows, of those that had
long come upon the people's prince. Then the king, sore-hearted,
implored me by your life [6] that I should do a man's work in the
tumult of the waters, venture my life, finish a glorious deed. He
promised me reward. Then I found the guardian of the deep pool,
the grim horror, as is now known wide. For a time there we
were locked hand in hand. Then the flood boiled with blood, and
in the war-hall I cut off the head of Grendel's mother with a
mighty sword. Not without trouble I came from there with my
life. I was not fated to die then, but the protector of earls again
gave me many treasures, the son of Healfdene.

(XXXI.) "Thus the king of that people lived with good customs.
I had lost none of the rewards, the meed of my might, but he
gave me treasures, the son of Healfdene, at my own choice. I
will bring these to you, great king, show my good will. On your
kindnesses all still depends: I have few close kinsmen besides you,
Hygelac."

Then he bade bring in the boar-banner—the head-sign—the
helmet towering in battle, the gray battle-shirt, the splendid sword
—afterwards spoke words: "Hrothgar, wise king, gave me this
armor; in his words he bade that I should first tell you about his
gift: he said that king Heorogar,[7] lord of the Scyldings, had
had it for a long time; not for that would he give it, the
breast-armor, to his son, bold Heoroweard, though he was loyal
to him. Use it all well!"

I have heard that four horses, swift and alike, followed that
treasure, fallow as apples. He gave him the gift of both horses
and treasure. So ought kinsmen do, not weave malice-nets for
each other with secret craft, prepare death for comrades. To
Hygelac his nephew was most true in hard fights, and each one
mindful of helping the other. I have heard that he gave Hygd
the neck-ring, the wonderfully wrought treasure, that Wealhtheow
had given him—gave to the king's daughter as well three horses,
supple and saddle-bright. After the gift of the necklace, her
breast was adorned with it.

Thus Beowulf showed himself brave, a man known in battles,
of good deeds, bore himself according to discretion. Drunk, he
slew no hearth-companions. His heart was not savage, but he held
the great gift that God had given him, the most strength of all
mankind, like one brave in battle. He had long been despised,[8]
so that the sons of the Geats did not reckon him brave, nor

---

6. I.e., "in your name."
7. Hrothgar's elder brother, whom
Hrothgar succeeded as king.

8. Beowulf's poor reputation as a young
man is mentioned only here.

would the lord of the Weather-Geats do him much gift-honor on the mead-bench. They strongly suspected that he was slack, a young man unbold. Change came to the famous man for each of his troubles.

Then the protector of earls bade fetch in the heirloom of Hrethel,[9] king famed in battle, adorned with gold. There was not then among the Geats a better treasure in sword's kind. He laid that in Beowulf's lap, and gave him seven thousand [hides of land], a hall and a throne. To both of them alike land had been left in the nation, home and native soil: to the other more especially wide was the realm, to him who was higher in rank.

[Beowulf and the Dragon]

Afterwards it happened, in later days, in the crashes of battle, when Hygelac lay dead and war-swords came to slay Heardred[1] behind the shield-cover, when the Battle-Scylfings, hard fighters, sought him among his victorious nation, attacked bitterly the nephew of Hereric—then the broad kingdom came into Beowulf's hand. He held it well fifty winters—he was a wise king, an old guardian of the land—until in the dark nights a certain one, a dragon, began to hold sway, which on the high heath kept watch over a hoard, a steep stone-barrow. Beneath lay a path unknown to men. By this there went inside a certain man [who made his way near to the heathen hoard; his hand took a cup, large, a shining treasure. The dragon did not afterwards conceal it though in his sleep he was tricked by the craft of the thief. That the people discovered, the neighboring folk—that he was swollen with rage].[2]

(XXXII.) Not of his own accord did he who had sorely harmed him[3] break into the worm's hoard, not by his own desire, but for hard constraint; the slave of some son of men fled hostile blows, lacking a shelter, and came there, a man guilty of wrong-doing. As soon as he saw him,[4] great horror arose in the stranger; [yet the wretched fugitive escaped the terrible worm . . . When the sudden shock came upon him, he carried off a precious cup.][5] There were many such ancient treasures in the earth-house, as in the old days some one of mankind had prudently hidden there the huge legacy of a noble race, rare treasures. Death had taken them all in earlier times, and the only one of the nation of people who still survived, who walked

9. Hygelac's father.
1. Hygelac's son Heardred, who succeeded Hygelac as king, was killed by the Swedes (Heatho-Scylfings) in his own land, as is explained more fully below, section XXXIII. His uncle Hereric was perhaps Hygd's brother.

2. This part of the manuscript is badly damaged, and the text within brackets is highly conjectural.
3. The dragon.
4. The dragon.
5. Several lines of the text have been lost.

there longest, a guardian mourning his friends, supposed the same of himself as of them—that he might little while enjoy the long-got treasure. A barrow stood all ready on the shore near the sea-waves, newly placed on the headland, made fast by having its entrances skillfully hidden. The keeper of the rings carried in the part of his riches worthy of hoarding, plated gold; he spoke few words:

"Hold now, you earth, now that men may not, the possession of earls. What, from you good men got it first! War-death has taken each man of my people, evil dreadful and deadly, each of those who has given up this life, the hall-joys of men. I have none who wears sword or cleans the plated cup, rich drinking vessel. The company of retainers has gone elsewhere. The hard helmet must be stripped of its fair-wrought gold, of its plating. The polishers are asleep who should make the war-mask shine. And even so the coat of mail, which withstood the bite of swords after the crashing of the shields, decays like its warrior. Nor may the ring-mail travel wide on the war-chief beside his warriors. There is no harp-delight, no mirth of the singing wood, no good hawk flies through the hall, no swift horse stamps in the castle court. Baleful death has sent away many races of men."

So, sad of mind, he spoke his sorrow, alone of them all, moved joyless through day and night until death's flood reached his heart. The ancient night-ravager found the hoard-joy standing open, he who burning seeks barrows, the smooth hateful dragon who flies at night wrapped in flame. Earth-dwellers much dread him. He it is who must seek a hoard in the earth where he will guard heathen gold, wise for his winters: he is none the better for it.

So for three hundred winters the harmer of folk held in the earth one of its treasure-houses, huge and mighty, until one man angered his heart. He bore to his master a plated cup, asked his lord for a compact of peace: thus was the hoard searched, the store of treasures diminished. His requests were granted the wretched man: the lord for the first time looked on the ancient work of men. Then the worm woke; cause of strife was renewed: for then he moved over the stones, hard-hearted beheld his foe's footprints—with secret stealth he had stepped forth too near the dragon's head. (So may an undoomed man who holds favor from the Ruler easily come through his woes and misery.) The hoard-guard sought him eagerly over the ground, would find the man who had done him injury while he slept. Hot and fierce-hearted, often he moved all about the outside of the barrow. No man at all was in the emptiness. Yet he took joy in the thought of war, in the work of fighting. At times he turned back into the barrow, sought his rich cup. Straightway he found that some man had tampered with his gold, his splendid treasure. The hoard-guard waited restless until evening came; then the barrow-keeper was in rage: he would requite that precious drinking cup with vengeful fire. Then the day was gone—to the joy of the worm. He would not wait long on the sea-wall, but set out with fire, ready with flame. The beginning was terrible to the folk on the land, as the ending was soon to be sore to their giver of treasure.

(XXXIII.) Then the evil spirit began to vomit flames, burn bright dwellings; blaze of fire rose, to the horror of men; there the deadly flying thing would leave nothing alive. The worm's warfare was wide-seen, his cruel malice, near and far—how the destroyer hated and hurt the people of the Geats. He winged back to the hoard, his hidden hall, before the time of day. He had circled the land-dwellers with flame, with fire and burning. He had trust in his barrow, in his war and his wall: his expectation deceived him.

Then the terror was made known to Beowulf, quickly in its truth, that his own home, best of buildings, had melted in surging flames, the throne-seat of the Geats. That was anguish of spirit to the good man, the greatest of heart-sorrows. The wise one supposed that he had bitterly offended the Ruler, the Eternal Lord, against old law. His breast within boiled with dark thoughts—as was not for him customary. The fiery dragon with his flames had destroyed the people's stronghold, the land along the sea, the heart of the country. Because of that the war-king, the lord of the Weather-Geats, devised punishment for him. The protector of fighting men, lord of earls, commanded that a wonderful battle-shield be made all of iron. Well he knew that the wood of the forest might not help him—linden against flame. The prince good from old times was to come to the end of the days that had been lent him, life in the world, and the worm with him, though he had long held the hoarded wealth. Then the ring-prince scorned to seek the far-flier with a troop, a large army. He had no fear for himself of the combat, nor did he think the worm's war-power anything great, his strength and his courage, because he himself had come through many battles before, dared perilous straits, clashes of war, after he had purged Hrothgar's hall, victorious warrior, and in combat crushed to death Grendel's kin, loathsome race.

Nor was that the least of his hand-combats where Hygelac was slain, when the king of the Geats, the noble lord of the people, the son of Hrethel, died of sword-strokes in the war-storm among the Frisians, laid low by the blade. From there Beowulf came away by means of his own strength, performed a feat of swimming; he had on his arm the armor of thirty earls when he turned back to the sea. There was no need for the Hetware [6] to exult in the foot-battle when they bore their shields against him: few came again from that warrior to seek their homes. Then the son of Ecgtheow swam over the water's expanse, forlorn and alone, back to his people. There Hygd offered him hoard and kingdom, rings and a prince's throne. She had no trust in her son, that he could hold his native throne against foreigners now that Hygelac was dead. By no means the sooner might the lordless ones get consent from the noble that he would become lord of Heardred or that he would accept royal power. [7] Yet he held him up among the people by friendly counsel, kindly with honor, until he became older, [8] ruled the Weather-Geats.

Outcasts from over the sea sought him, sons of Ohthere. [9] They had rebelled against the protector of the Scylfings, the best of the sea-kings of those who gave treasure in Sweden, a famous lord. For Heardred that became his life's limit: because of his hospitality there the son of Hygelac got his life's wound from the strokes of a sword. And the son of Ongentheow went back to seek his home after Heardred lay dead, let Beowulf hold the royal throne, rule the Geats: that was a good king.

(XXXIV.) In later days he was mindful of repaying the prince's fall, became the friend of the destitute Eadgils; [1] with folk he supported the son of Ohthere over the wide sea, with warriors and weapons. Afterwards he got vengeance by forays that brought with them cold care: he took the king's life.

Thus he had survived every combat, every dangerous battle, every deed of courage, the son of Ecgtheow, until that one day when he should fight with the worm. Then, one of twelve, the lord of the Geats, swollen with anger, went to look on the dragon. He had learned then from what the feud arose, the fierce malice to men: the glorious cup had come to his possession from the hand of the finder: he was the thirteenth of that company, the man who had brought on the beginning of the war, the sad-hearted slave—wretched, he must direct them to the place. Against his will he went to where he knew of an earth-hall, a barrow beneath the ground close to the sea-surge, to the strug-

6. I.e., a tribe, with whom the Frisians were allied.
7. I.e., Beowulf refused to take the throne from the rightful heir Heardred.
8. I.e., Beowulf supported the young Heardred.
9. Ohthere succeeded his father Ongentheow as king of the Scylfings (Swedes), but after his death his brother Onela seized the throne, driving out Ohthere's sons Eanmund and Eadgils. They were given refuge at the Geatish court by Heardred, whom Onela attacked for this act of hospitality. In the fight Eanmund and Heardred were killed, and Onela left the kingdom in Beowulf's charge.
1. The surviving son of Ohthere was befriended by Beowulf, who supported him in his successful attempt to gain the Swedish throne and who killed the usurper Onela.

gling waves: within, it was full of ornaments and gold chains. The terrible guardian, ready for combat, held the gold treasure, old under the earth. It was no easy bargain for any man to obtain. Then the king, hardy in fight, sat down on the headland; there he saluted his hearth-companions, gold-friend of the Geats. His mind was mournful, restless and ripe for death: very close was the fate which should come to the old man, seek his soul's hoard, divide life from his body; not for long then was the life of the noble one wound in his flesh.

Beowulf spoke, the son of Ecgtheow: "In youth I lived through many battle-storms, times of war. I remember all that. I was seven winters old when the lord of treasure, the beloved king of the folk, received me from my father: King Hrethel had me and kept me, gave me treasure and feast, mindful of kinship. During his life I was no more hated by him as a man in his castle than any of his own sons, Herebeald and Haethcyn, or my own Hygelac. For the eldest a murder-bed was wrongfully spread through the deed of a kinsman, when Haethcyn struck him down with an arrow from his horned bow—his friend and his lord—missed the mark and shot his kinsman dead, one brother the other, with the bloody arrowhead. That was a fatal fight, without hope of recompense, a deed wrongly done, baffling to the heart; yet it had happened that a prince had to lose life unavenged.

"So it is sad for an old man to endure that his son should ride young on the gallows. Then he may speak a story, a sorrowful song, when his son hangs for the joy of the raven, and, old in years and knowing, he can find no help for him. Always with every morning he is reminded of his son's journey elsewhere. He cares not to wait for another heir in his hall, when the first through death's force has come to the end of his deeds. Sorrowful he sees in his son's dwelling the empty wine-hall, the windy resting place without joy—the riders sleep, the warriors in the grave. There is no sound of the harp, no joy in the dwelling, as there was of old. (XXXV.) Then he goes to his couch, sings a song of sorrow, one alone for one gone. To him all too wide has seemed the land and the dwelling.

"So the protector of the Weather-Geats bore in his heart swelling sorrow for Herebeald. In no way could he settle his feud with the life-slayer; not the sooner could he wound the warrior with deeds of hatred, though he was not dear to him. Then for the sorrow that had too bitterly befallen him he gave up the joys of men, chose God's light. To his sons he left—as a happy man does—his land and his town when he went from life.

"Then there was battle and strife of Swedes and Geats, over

the wide water a quarrel shared, hatred between hardy ones, after Hrethel died. And the sons of Ongentheow [2] were bold and active in war, wanted to have no peace over the seas, but about Hreosnabeorh often devised awful slaughter. That my friends and kinsmen avenged, both the feud and the crime, as is well-known, though one of them bought it with his life, a hard bargain: the war was mortal to Haethcyn, lord of the Geats.[3] Then in the morning, I have heard, one kinsman avenged the other on his slayer with the sword's edge, when Ongentheow attacked Eofor: the war-helm split, the old Scylfing fell mortally wounded: his hand remembered feuds enough, did not withstand the life-blow.

"I repaid in war the treasures that he [4] gave me—with my bright sword, as was granted me by fate: he had given me land, a pleasant dwelling. There was not any need for him, any reason, that he should have to seek among the Gifthas or the Spear-Danes or in Sweden in order to buy with treasure a worse warrior. I would always go before him in the troop, alone in the front. And so all my life I shall wage battle while this sword endures that has served me early and late ever since I became Daeghrefn's slayer in the press—the warrior of the Hugas.[5] He could not bring armor to the king of the Frisians, breast ornament, but fell in the fight, keeper of the standard, a noble man. Nor was my sword's edge his slayer, but my warlike grip broke open his heart-streams, his bone-house. Now shall the sword's edge, the hand and hard blade, fight for the hoard."

[BEOWULF ATTACKS THE DRAGON]

Beowulf spoke, for the last time spoke words in boast: "In my youth I engaged in many wars. Old guardian of the people, I shall still seek battle, perform a deed of fame, if the evil-doer will come to me out of the earth-hall."

Then he saluted each of the warriors, the bold helmet-bearers, for the last time—his own dear companions. "I would not bear sword, weapon, to the worm, if I knew how else according to my boast I might grapple with the monster, as I did of old with Grendel. But I expect here hot battle-fire, steam and poison. Therefore I have on me shield and mail-shirt. I will not flee a foot-step from the barrow-ward, but it shall be with us at the wall as fate allots, the ruler of every man. I am confident in

2. I.e., the Swedes Onela and Ohthere: the reference is, of course, to a time earlier than that referred to in section XXXIII, note 9.
3. Haethcyn had succeeded his father Hrethel as king of the Geats after his accidental killing of his brother Herebeald. When Haethcyn was killed while attacking the Swedes, he was succeeded by Hygelac, who, as the next sentence relates, avenged Haethcyn's death on Ongentheow. The death of Ongentheow is described below, sections XL and XLI.
4. Hygelac.
5. I.e., the Franks.

heart, so I forgo help against the war-flier. Wait on the barrow, safe in your mail-shirts, men in armor—which of us two may better bear wounds after our bloody meeting. This is not your venture, nor is it right for any man except me alone that he should spend his strength against the monster, do this man's deed. By my courage I shall get gold, or war will take your king, dire life-evil."

Then the brave warrior arose by his shield; hardy under helmet he went in his mail-shirt beneath the stone-cliffs, had trust in his strength—that of one man: such is not the way of the cowardly. Then he saw by the wall—he who had come through many wars, good in his great-heartedness, many clashes in battle when troops meet together—a stone arch standing, through it a stream bursting out of the barrow: there was welling of a current hot with killing fires, and he might not endure any while unburnt by the dragon's flame the hollow near the hoard. Then the man of the Weather-Geats, enraged as he was, let a word break from his breast. Stout-hearted he shouted; his voice went roaring, clear in battle, in under the gray stone. Hate was stirred up, the hoard's guard knew the voice of a man. No more time was there to ask for peace. First the monster's breath came out of the stone, the hot war-steam. The earth resounded. The man below the barrow, the lord of the Geats, swung his shield against the dreadful visitor. Then the heart of the coiled thing aroused to seek combat. The good war-king had drawn his sword, the old heirloom, not blunt of edge. To each of them as they threatened destruction there was terror of the other. Firm-hearted he stood with his shield high, the lord of friends, while quickly the worm coiled itself; he waited in his armor. Then, coiling in flames, he came gliding on, hastening to his fate. The good shield protected the life and body of the famous prince, but for a shorter while than his wish was. There for the first time, the first day in his life, he might not prevail, since fate did not assign him such glory in battle. The lord of the Geats raised his hand, struck the shining horror so with his forged blade that the edge failed, bright on the bone, bit less surely than its folk-king had need, hard-pressed in perils. Then because of the battle-stroke the barrow-ward's heart was savage, he exhaled death-fire—the war-flames sprang wide. The gold-friend of the Geats boasted of no great victories: the war blade had failed, naked at need, as it ought not to have done, iron good from old times. That was no pleasant journey, not one on which the famous son of Ecgtheow would wish to leave his land; against his will he must take up a dwelling-place elsewhere—as every man must give up the days that are lent him.

It was not long until they came together again, dreadful foes. The hoard-guard took heart, once more his breast swelled with his breathing. Encircled with flames, he who before had ruled a folk felt harsh pain. Nor did his companions, sons of nobles, take up their stand in a troop about him with the courage of fighting men, but they crept to the wood, protected their lives. In only one of them the heart surged with sorrows: nothing can ever set aside kinship in him who means well.

(XXXVI.) He was called Wiglaf, son of Weohstan, a rare shield-warrior, a man of the Scylfings,[6] kinsman of Aelfhere. He saw his liege lord under his war-mask suffer the heat. Then he was mindful of the honors he had given him before, the rich dwelling-place of the Waegmundings, every folk-right such as his father possessed. He might not then hold back, his hand seized his shield, the yellow linden-wood; he drew his ancient sword. Among men it was the heirloom of Eanmund, the son of Ohthere:[7] Weohstan had become his slayer in battle with sword's edge—an exile without friends; and he bore off to his kin the bright-shining helmet, the ringed mail-armor, the old sword made by giants that Onela had given him,[8] his kinsman's war-armor, ready battle-gear: he did not speak of the feud, though he had killed his brother's son.[9] He[1] held the armor many half-years, the blade and the battle-dress, until his son might do manly deeds like his old father. Then he gave him among the Geats war-armor of every kind, numberless, when, old, he went forth on the way from life. For the young warrior this was the first time that he should enter the war-storm with his dear lord. His heart's courage did not slacken, nor did the heirloom of his kinsman fail in the battle. That the worm found when they had come together.

Wiglaf spoke, said many fit words to his companions—his mind was mournful: "I remember that time we drank mead, when we

---

6. Though in the next sentence Wiglaf is said to belong to the family of the Waegmundings, the Geatish family to which Beowulf belonged, he is here called a Scylfing (Swede), and immediately below his father Weohstan is represented as having fought for the Swede Onela in his attack on the Geats. But for a man to change his nation was not unusual, and Weohstan, who may have had both Swedish and Geatish blood, had evidently become a Geat long enough before to have brought up his son Wiglaf as one. The identity of Aelfhere is not known.

7. See above, section XXXIII, note 9. Not only did Weohstan support Onela's attack on the Geat king Heardred, but

actually killed Eanmund whom Heardred was supporting, and it is Eanmund's sword that Wiglaf is now wielding.

8. The spoils of war belonged to the victorious king, who apportioned them among his fighters: thus Onela gave Weohstan the armor of Eanmund, whom Weohstan had killed.

9. This ironic remark points out that Onela did not claim *wergild* or seek vengeance from Weohstan, as in other circumstances he ought to have done inasmuch as Weohstan had killed Onela's close kinsman, his nephew Eanmund: but Onela was himself trying to kill Eanmund.

1. Weohstan.

promised our lord in the beer-hall—him who gave us these rings—
that we would repay him for the war-arms if a need like this
befell him—the helmets and the hard swords. Of his own will
he chose us among the host for this venture, thought us worthy
of fame—and gave me these treasures—because he counted us
good war-makers, brave helm-bearers, though our lord intended
to do this work of courage alone, as keeper of the folk, because
among men he had performed the greatest deeds of glory, daring
actions. Now the day has come that our liege lord has need of
the strength of good fighters. Let us go to him, help our war-
chief while the grim terrible fire persists. God knows of me that
I should rather that the flame enfold my body with my gold-
giver. It does not seem right to me for us to bear our shields
home again unless we can first fell the foe, defend the life of
the prince of the Weather-Geats. I know well that it would be
no recompense for past deeds that he alone of the company of
the Geats should suffer pain, fall in the fight. For us both shall
there be a part in the work of sword and helmet, of battle-shirt
and war-clothing."

Then he waded through the deadly smoke, bore his war-helmet
to the aid of his king, spoke in few words: "Beloved Beowulf,
do all well, for, long since in your youth, you said that you
would not let your glory fail while you lived. Now, great-
spirited noble, brave of deeds, you must protect your life with
all your might. I shall help you."

After these words, the worm came on, angry, the terrible
malice-filled foe, shining with surging flames, to seek for the second
time his enemies, hated men. Fire advanced in waves; shield burned
to the boss; mail-shirt might give no help to the young spear-warrior;
but the young man went quickly under his kinsman's shield when
his own was consumed with flames. Then the war-king was again
mindful of fame, struck with his war-sword with great strength so
that it stuck in the head-bone, driven with force: Naegling broke,
the sword of Beowulf failed in the fight, old and steel-gray. It was
not ordained for him that iron edges might help in the combat. Too
strong was the hand that I have heard strained every sword with its
stroke, when he bore wound-hardened weapon to battle: he was
none the better for it.

Then for the third time the folk-harmer, the fearful fire-
dragon, was mindful of feuds, set upon the brave one when the
chance came, hot and battle-grim seized all his neck with his
sharp fangs: he was smeared with life-blood, gore welled out
in waves.

(XXXVII.) Then, I have heard, at the need of the folk-king
the earl at his side made his courage known, his might and his

keenness—as was natural to him. He took no heed for that head,[2] but the hand of the brave man was burned as he helped his kinsman, as the man in armor struck the hateful foe a little lower down, so that the sword sank in, shining and engraved; and then the fire began to subside. The king himself then still controlled his senses, drew the battle-knife, biting and war-sharp, that he wore on his mail-shirt: the protector of the Weather-Geats cut the worm through the middle. They felled the foe, courage drove his life out, and they had destroyed him together, the two noble kinsmen. So ought a man be, a thane at need. To the prince that was the last moment of victory for his own deeds, of work in the world.

Then the wound that the earth-dragon had caused began to burn and to swell; at once he felt dire evil boil in his breast, poison within him. Then the prince, wise of thought, went to where he might sit on a seat near the wall. He looked on the work of giants, how the timeless earth-hall held within it stone-arches fast on pillars. Then with his hands the thane, good without limit, washed him with water, blood-besmeared, the famous prince, his beloved lord, sated with battle; and he unfastened his helmet.

Beowulf spoke—despite his wounds spoke, his mortal hurts. He knew well he had lived out his days' time, joy on earth; all passed was the number of his days, death very near. "Now I would wish to give my son my war-clothing, if any heir after me, part of my flesh, were granted. I held this people fifty winters. There was no folk-king of those dwelling about who dared approach me with swords, threaten me with fears. In my land I awaited what fate brought me, held my own well, sought no treacherous quarrels, nor did I swear many oaths unrightfully. Sick with life-wounds, I may have joy of all this, for the Ruler of Men need not blame me for the slaughter of kinsmen when life goes from my body. Now quickly go to look at the hoard under the gray stone, beloved Wiglaf, now that the worm lies sleeping from sore wounds, bereft of his treasure. Be quick now, so that I may see the ancient wealth, the golden things, may clearly look on the bright curious gems, so that for that, because of the treasure's richness, I may the more easily leave life and nation I have long held."

(XXXVIII.) Then I have heard that the son of Weohstan straightway obeyed his lord, sick with battle-wounds, according to the words he had spoken, went wearing his ring-armor, woven battle-shirt, under the barrow's roof. Then he saw, as he went

---

2. I.e., the dragon's flame-breathing head.

by the seat, the brave young retainer, triumphant in heart, many precious jewels, glittering gold lying on the ground, wonders on the wall, and the worm's lair, the old night-flier's—cups standing there, vessels of men of old, with none to polish them, stripped of their ornaments. There was many a helmet old and rusty, many an arm-ring skillfully twisted. (Easily may treasure, gold in the ground, betray each one of the race of men, hide it who will.) Also he saw a standard all gold hang high over the hoard, the greatest of hand-wonders, linked with fingers' skill. From it came a light so that he might see the ground, look on the works of craft. There was no trace of the worm, for the blade had taken him. Then I have heard that one man in the mound pillaged the hoard, the old work of giants, loaded in his bosom cups and plates at his own desire. He took also the standard, brightest of banners. The sword of the old lord—its edge was iron—had already wounded the one who for a long time had been guardian of the treasure, waged his fire-terror, hot for the hoard, rising up fiercely at midnight, till he died in the slaughter.

The messenger was in haste, eager to return, urged on by the treasures. Curiosity tormented him, whether eagerly seeking he should find the lord of the Weather-Geats, strength gone, alive in the place where he had left him before. Then with the treasures he found the great prince, his lord, bleeding, at the end of his life. Again he began to sprinkle him with water until this word's point broke through his breast-hoard—he spoke, the king, old man in sorrow, looked on the gold: "I speak with my words thanks to the Lord of All for these treasures, to the King of Glory, Eternal Prince, for what I gaze on here, that I might get such for my people before my death-day. Now that I have bought the hoard of treasures with my old life, you attend to the people's needs hereafter: I can be here no longer. Bid the battle-renowned make a mound, bright after the funeral fire, on the sea's cape. It shall stand high on Hronesness as a reminder to my people, so that sea-travelers later will call it Beowulf's barrow, when they drive their ships far over the darkness of the seas."

He took off his neck the golden necklace, bold-hearted prince, gave it to the thane, to the young spear-warrior—gold-gleaming helmet, ring, and mail-shirt, bade him use them well. "You are the last left of our race, of the Waegmundings. Fate has swept away all my kinsmen, earls in their strength, to destined death. I have to go after." That was the last word of the old man, of the thoughts of his heart, before he should taste the funeral pyre, hot hostile flames. The soul went from his breast to seek the doom of those fast in truth.

[*Beowulf's Funeral*]

(XXXIX.) Then sorrow came to the young man that he saw him whom he most loved on the earth, at the end of his life, suffering piteously. His slayer likewise lay dead, the awful earth-dragon bereft of life, overtaken by evil. No longer should the coiled worm rule the ring-hoard, for iron edges had taken him, hard and battle-sharp work of the hammers, so that the wide-flier, stilled by wounds, had fallen on the earth near the treasure-house. He did not go flying through the air at midnight, proud of his property, showing his aspect, but he fell to earth through the work of the chief's hands. Yet I have heard of no man of might on land, though he was bold of every deed, whom it should prosper to rush against the breath of the venomous foe or disturb with hands the ring-hall, if he found the guard awake who lived in the barrow. The share of the rich treasures became Beowulf's, paid for by death: each of the two had journeyed to the end of life's loan.

Then it was not long before the battle-slack ones left the woods, ten weak troth-breakers together, who had not dared fight with their spears in their liege lord's great need. But they bore their shields, ashamed, their war-clothes, to where the old man lay, looked on Wiglaf. He sat wearied, the foot-soldier near the shoulders of his lord, would waken him with water: it gained him nothing. He might not, though he much wished it, hold life in his chieftain on earth nor change anything of the Ruler's: the judgment of God would control the deeds of every man, just as it still does now. Then it was easy to get from the young man a grim answer to him who before had lost courage. Wiglaf spoke, the son of Weohstan, a man sad at heart, looked on the unloved ones:

"Yes, he who will speak truth may say that the liege lord who gave you treasure, the war-gear that you stand in there, when he used often to hand out to hall-sitters on the ale-benches, a prince to his thanes, helmets and war-shirts such as he could find mightiest anywhere, both far and near—that he quite threw away the war-gear, to his distress when war came upon him. The folk-king had no need to boast of his war-comrades. Yet God, Ruler of Victories, granted him that he might avenge himself, alone with his sword, when there was need for his courage. I was able to give him little life-protection in the fight, and yet beyond my power I did begin to help my kinsman. The deadly foe was ever the weaker after I struck him with my sword, fire poured less strongly from his head. Too few defenders thronged about the prince when the hard time came upon him. Now there shall cease for your race the receiving of treasure and the giving of swords, all enjoyment of pleasant homes, comfort. Each man of your kindred must go deprived of his land-right when nobles from afar learn of your flight, your inglorious deed. Death is better for any earl than a life of blame."

(XL.) Then he bade that the battle-deed be announced in the city, up over the cliff-edge, where the band of warriors sat the whole morning of the day, sad-hearted, shield-bearers in doubt whether it was the beloved man's last day or whether he would come again. Little did he fail to speak of new tidings, he who rode up the hill, but spoke to them all truthfully: "Now the joy-giver of the people of the Weathers, the lord of the Geats, is fast on his death-bed, lies on his slaughter-couch through deeds of the worm. Beside him lies his life-enemy, struck down with dagger-wounds—with his sword he might not work wounds of any kind on the monster. Wiglaf son of Weohstan sits over Beowulf, one earl by the lifeless other, in weariness of heart holds death-watch over the loved and the hated.

"Now may the people expect a time of war, when the king's fall becomes wide-known to the Franks and the Frisians. A harsh quarrel was begun with the Hugas when Hygelac came traveling with his sea-army to the land of the Frisians, where the Hetware assailed him in battle, quickly, with stronger forces, made the mailed warrior bow; he fell in the ranks: that chief gave no treasure to his retainers. Ever since then the good will of the Merewioing king has been denied us.

"Nor do I expect any peace or trust from the Swedish people, for it is wide-known that Ongentheow took the life of Haethcyn, Hrethel's son, near Ravenswood when in their over-pride the people of the Geats first went against the War-Scylfings. Straightway the wary father of Ohthere,[3] old and terrible, gave a blow in return, cut down the sea-king,[4] rescued his wife, old woman of times past, bereft of her gold, mother of Onela and Ohthere, and then he followed his life-foes until they escaped, lordless, painfully, to Ravenswood. Then with a great army he besieged those whom the sword had left, weary with wounds, often vowed woes to the wretched band the livelong night, said that in the morning he would cut them apart with sword-blades, [hang] some on gallows-trees as sport for birds. Relief came in turn to the sorry-hearted together with dawn when they heard Hygelac's horn and trumpet, his sound as the good man came on their track with a body of retainers. (XLI.) Wide-seen was the bloody track of Swedes and

3. I.e., Ongentheow.
4. I.e., Haethcyn, king of the Geats. Haethcyn's brother Hygelac, who succeeded him, was not present at this battle, but arrived after the death of Haethcyn with reinforcements to relieve the survivors and to pursue Ongentheow in his retreat to his city.

Geats, the slaughter-strife of men, how the peoples stirred up the feud between them. Then the good man went with his kinsmen, old and much-mourning, to seek his stronghold: the earl Ongentheow moved further away. He had heard of the warring of Hygelac, of the war-power of the proud one. He did not trust in resistance, that he might fight off the sea-men, defend his hoard against the war-sailors, his children and wife. Instead he drew back, the old man behind his earth-wall.

"Then pursuit was offered to the people of the Swedes, the standards of Hygelac overran the stronghold as Hrethel's people pressed forward to the citadel. There Ongentheow the gray-haired was brought to bay by sword-blades, and the people's king had to submit to the judgment of Eofor alone. Wulf [5] son of Wonred had struck him angrily with his weapon so that for the blow the blood sprang forth in streams beneath his hair. Yet not for that was he afraid, the old Scylfing, but he quickly repaid the assault with worse exchange, the folk-king, when he turned toward him. The strong son of Wonred could not give the old man a return blow, for Ongentheow had first cut through the helmet of his head so that he had to sink down, smeared with blood—fell on the earth: he was not yet doomed, for he recovered, though the wound hurt him. The hardy thane of Hygelac,[6] when his brother lay low, let his broad sword, old blade made by giants, break the great helmet across the shield-wall; then the king bowed, the keeper of the folk was hit to the quick.

"Then there were many who bound up the brother, quickly raised him up after it was granted them to control the battle-field. Then one warrior stripped the other, took from Ongentheow his iron-mail, hard-hilted sword, and his helmet, too; he bore the arms of the hoary one to Hygelac. He accepted that treasure and fairly promised him rewards among the people, and he stood by it thus: the lord of the Geats, the son of Hrethel, when he came home, repaid Wulf and Eofor for their battle-assault with much treasure, gave each of them a hundred thousand [units] of land and linked rings: there was no need for any man on middle-earth to blame him for the rewards, since they had performed great deeds. And then he gave Eofor his only daughter as a pledge of friendship—a fair thing for his home.

"That is the feud and the enmity, the death-hatred of men, for which I expect that the people of the Swedes, bold shield-warriors after the fall of princes, will set upon us after they learn that our prince has gone from life, he who before held hoard and

---

5. The two sons of Wonred, Wulf and Eofor, attacked Ongentheow in turn. Wulf was struck down but not killed by the old Swedish king, who was then slain by Eofor.
6. I.e., Eofor.

kingdom against our enemies, did good to the people, and further still, did what a man should. Now haste is best, that we look on the people's king there and bring him who gave us rings on his way to the funeral pyre. Nor shall only a small share melt with the great-hearted one, but there is a hoard of treasure, gold uncounted, grimly purchased, and rings bought at the last now with his own life. These shall the fire devour, flames enfold—no earl to wear ornament in remembrance, nor any bright maiden add to her beauty with neck-ring; but mournful-hearted, stripped of gold, they shall walk, often, not once, in strange countries— now that the army-leader has laid aside laughter, his game and his mirth. Therefore many a spear, cold in the morning, shall be grasped with fingers, raised by hands; no sound of harp shall waken the warriors, but the dark raven, low over the doomed, shall tell many tales, say to the eagle how he fared at the feast when with the wolf he spoiled the slain bodies."

Thus the bold man was a speaker of hateful news, nor did he much lie in his words or his prophecies. The company all arose. Without joy they went below Earnaness [7] to look on the wonder with welling tears. Then they found on the sand, soulless, keeping his bed of rest, him who in former times had given them rings. Then the last day of the good man had come, when the war-king, prince of the Weather-Geats, died a wonderful death. First they saw the stranger creature, the worm lying loathsome, opposite him in the place. The fire-dragon was grimly terrible with his many colors, burned by the flames; he was fifty feet long in the place where he lay. Once he had joy of the air at night, came back down to seek his den. Then he was made fast by death, had made use of the last of his earth-caves. Beside him stood cups and pitchers, plates and rich swords lay eaten through by rust, just as they had been there in the bosom of the earth for a thousand winters. Then that huge heritage, gold of men of old, was wound in a spell, so that no one of men must touch the ring-hall unless God himself, the True King of Victories—He is men's protection—should grant to whom He wished to open the hoard—whatever man seemed fit to Him.

(XLII.) Then it was seen that the act did not profit him who wrongly kept hidden the handiworks under the wall. The keeper had first slain a man like few others, then the feud had been fiercely avenged. It is a wonder where an earl famed for courage may reach the end of his allotted life—then may dwell no longer in the mead-hall, man with his kin. So it was with Beowulf when he sought quarrels, the barrow's ward: he himself did not then know in what way his parting with the world should come. The

7. The headland near where Beowulf had fought the dragon.

great princes who had put it [8] there had laid on it so deep a
curse until doomsday that the man who should plunder the place
should be guilty of sins, imprisoned in idol-shrines, fixed with
hell-bonds, punished with evils—unless the Possessor's favor were
first shown the more clearly to him who desired the gold.

Wiglaf spoke, the son of Weohstan: "Often many a man must
suffer distress for the will of one man, as has happened to us.
We might by no counsel persuade our dear prince, keeper of the
kingdom, not to approach the gold-guardian, let him lie where
he long was, live in his dwelling to the world's end. He held to
his high destiny. The hoard has been made visible, grimly got.
What drove the folk-king thither was too powerfully fated. I have
been therein and looked at it all, the rare things of the chamber,
when it was granted me—not at all friendly was the journey that
I was permitted beneath the earth-wall. In haste I seized with
my hands a huge burden of hoard-treasures, of great size, bore
it out here to my king. He was then still alive, sound-minded and
aware. He spoke many things, old man in sorrow, and bade greet
you, commanded that for your lord's deeds you make a high
barrow in the place of his pyre, large and conspicuous, since
he was of men the worthiest warrior through the wide earth,
while he might enjoy wealth in his castle.

"Let us now hasten to see and visit for the second time the
heap of precious jewels, the wonder under the walls. I shall
direct you so that you may look on enough of them from near
at hand—rings and broad gold. Let the bier be made ready,
speedily prepared, when we come out, and then let us carry our
prince, beloved man, where he shall long dwell in the Ruler's
protection."

Then the son of Weohstan, man brave in battle, bade command
many warriors, men who owned houses, leaders of the people,
that they carry wood from afar for the pyre for the good man.
"Now shall flame eat the chief of warriors—the fire shall grow
dark—who often survived the iron-shower when the storm of
arrows driven from bow-strings passed over the shield-wall—
the shaft did its task, made eager by feather-gear served the
arrowhead."

And then the wise son of Weohstan summoned from the host
thanes of the king, seven together, the best; one of eight warriors,
he went beneath the evil roof. One who walked before bore a
torch in his hands. Then there was no lot to decide who should
plunder that hoard, since the men could see that every part of
it rested in the hall without guardian, lay wasting. Little did any
man mourn that hastily they should bear out the rare treasure.

8. The treasure.

Also they pushed the dragon, the worm, over the cliff-wall, let the wave take him, the flood enfold the keeper of the treasure. Then twisted gold was loaded on a wagon, an uncounted number of things, and the prince, hoary warrior, borne to Hronesness.

(XLIII.) Then the people of the Geats made ready for him a funeral pyre on the earth, no small one, hung with helmets, battle-shields, bright mail-shirts, just as he had asked. Then in the midst they laid the great prince, lamenting their hero, their beloved lord. Then warriors began to awaken on the barrow the greatest of funeral-fires; the wood-smoke climbed, black over the fire; the roaring flame mixed with weeping—the wind-surge died down—until it had broken the bone-house, hot at its heart. Sad in spirit they lamented their heart-care, the death of their liege lord. [And the Geatish woman, wavy-haired, sang a sorrowful song about Beowulf, said] [9] again and again that she sorely feared for herself invasions of armies, many slaughters, terror of troops, humiliation, and captivity. Heaven swallowed the smoke.

Then the people of the Weather-Geats built a mound on the promontory, one that was high and broad, wide-seen by seafarers, and in ten days completed a monument for the bold in battle, surrounded the remains of the fire with a wall, the most splendid that men most skilled might devise. In the barrow they placed rings and jewels, all such ornaments as troubled men had earlier taken from the hoard. They let the earth hold the wealth of earls, gold in the ground, where now it still dwells, as useless to men as it was before. Then the brave in battle rode round the mound, children of nobles, twelve in all, would bewail their sorrow and mourn their king, recite dirges and speak of the man. They praised his great deeds and his acts of courage, judged well of his prowess. So it is fitting that man honor his liege lord with words, love him in heart when he must be led forth from the body. Thus the people of the Geats, his hearth-companions, lamented the death of their lord. They said that he was of world-kings the mildest of men and the gentlest, kindest to his people, and most eager for fame.

9. The manuscript is badly damaged and the interpretation conjectural.

GEOFFREY CHAUCER
(ca. 1343–1400)

1370: The *Book of the Duchess* (first important extant poem).
1372: First Italian journey: contact with Italian literature.
1385: *Troilus and Criseide.*
1386: *Canterbury Tales* begun.

Social thought in the Middle Ages lagged far behind social realities. Medieval England did not recognize the existence of any class between the aristocracy, a relatively small group that attained its position by birth alone, and the commons, which included everyone not of high birth. There was, theoretically, no way by which one might advance from the commons to the aristocracy. But in actual fact there existed a large and increasingly important middle class that was constantly infiltrating the aristocracy, and it was into this middle class that Chaucer was born. He was the son of a well-to-do wine merchant, and probably spent his boyhood in the down-to-earth atmosphere of London's Vintry, the wine-merchandising area; here, despite the privileges, especially in the way of education, that his father's wealth secured for him, he must have mixed daily with other commoners of all sorts. He might well have passed his whole life there, counting casks and money; but in his early teens he was sent to serve as a page in one of the great aristocratic households of England, that of Lionel of Antwerp, a son of the reigning monarch, Edward III. The rest of his life Chaucer spent in close association with the ruling nobility of the kingdom, not only with Lionel, but with his more powerful brother John of Gaunt; with their father King Edward; with their nephew Richard II, who succeeded to the throne in 1377; and finally with John's son Henry IV, who deposed his cousin and became king in 1399. Chaucer's wife Philippa was a member of the households of Edward's queen and of John of Gaunt's second wife, Constance of Castile, and she was doubtless of higher birth than the poet. A Thomas Chaucer, who was probably their son, was an eminent man in the next generation, and an Alice Chaucer, quite possibly Chaucer's granddaughter, was sufficiently important in her day to have been married successively to the Earl of Salisbury and the Duke of Norfolk. The theoretically unbridgeable gap between the commons and the aristocracy was thus ably bridged by the poet.

In order to accomplish this, Chaucer must have been able in other ways than as a poet, though doubtless his extraordinary poetic ability was of great service to his advancement. Yet if one were to rely merely on the preserved historical records, one would have little reason to suspect that the Geoffrey Chaucer they keep mentioning ever wrote a line of verse. We catch glimpses of him serving as a page in Lionel's household (1357); as a soldier getting himself captured by the French in one of Edward III's many sallies to the continent (1359); of his being the well-beloved *vallectus* of Edward III (1367)—despite the term, which means "valet," Chaucer's duties were hardly menial—and the well-beloved servant of John of Gaunt (1374), and of receiving substantial rewards for his services; of his being sent to Italy to assist in arranging a trade agreement with the Genoese (1372), and to France, perhaps to assist in getting a royal bride for young Prince Richard (1377); of his receiving a rent-free house on the city wall of London (1374); of his keeping, "in his own hand," the accounts for which he was responsible as Controller of the Customs and Subsidies on Wool for the port of London (1374–86)—and the wool trade was England's largest trade; of other trips abroad on official business; of his becoming Justice of the Peace and Knight of the Shire (Member of Parliament) for the county of Kent (1385–86); of his erecting grandstands, inventorying pots and pans, and getting himself robbed as Clerk of the King's Works (1389–91); of his being appointed deputy forester of one of the royal preserves in Somerset (1391); and—throughout his life—of his receiving grants and annuities, or having them confirmed by royal act when a new king took the throne, or asking that butts of wine given him by the crown be transformed into cash, or merely asking for money or more money. We last glimpse him, in the final months of his life, renting a house in the garden of Westminster Abbey, within a stone's throw of Westminster Hall, the ancient seat of English government.

CHAUCER'S LITERARY CAREER

It might seem that a man so busy would have had little time to write poetry, but Chaucer seems to have been an assiduous versifier all his adult life. Unfortunately, few of his poems can be precisely dated, and some have not been preserved. Probably among his earliest works was a translation of the *Roman de la Rose*, a 13th-century French poem that exercised a profound influence on Chaucer's work. The first part of the *Roman* is an allegory, written by Guillaume de Lorris, which tells, in the form of a dream, the progress of a youthful love affair. Guillaume left the poem unfinished, but an enormous sequel was added to it after Guillaume's death by Jean de Meun: in this sequel the young courtier finally wins his lady (the rose), but not until Jean has discussed at great length many of the issues considered important by medieval intellectuals. The poem is a mixture of highly diverse elements, and it is characteristic of Chaucer's love of variety that he was able to assimilate into his own work both the courtly emotionalism of Guillaume and the philosophical, often satiric, detachment of Jean. Of a 14th-century English translation of the French poem only a fragment has come down to us, and that without any mention of the translator's name; scholars are generally agreed that the first 1700 lines of this fragment are Chaucer's.

Chaucer's work on the *Roman* is thought to have been done during the 60's. During this decade he probably made other translations from the French, and kept on sharpening his rhetorical tools. At the end of the decade he produced his first major work (and the only one of his poems that can be accurately dated): the *Book of the Duchess*, probably completed in early 1370, an elegy for John of Gaunt's first wife, the lovely Blanche of Lancaster, who died in 1369. This is at once one of Chaucer's most derivative and most original poems: many of its octosyllabic lines are translated directly from various works by Jean Froissart, a French poet contemporary with Chaucer, and from his countryman Guillaume de Machaut as well as from other Frenchmen; yet the plan of the work is imaginative and daring, and as a whole the elegy is on a level of excellence never attained by the poets from whom Chaucer is borrowing. It is also interesting to observe how that tact which was later to earn Chaucer his status as a minor diplomat controls the direction of the poem and gives it artistic form.

In the first period of his literary activity Chaucer's specific poetic models were French, but a knowledge of writings in Latin lies behind virtually everything he wrote—although the Latin writers Chaucer read were not the same as those which we should study today. He probably had a more than adequate knowledge of the *Aeneid* and of Ovid in the original, but it is likely that he knew the other classical authors mostly through French translations and paraphrases. He was directly familiar with a number of (to us) cumbersome medieval Latin poems. Certainly his favorite Latin writer was Boethius, the 6th-century Roman whose *Consolation of Philosophy*, written while its author was in prison awaiting his execution, became one of the most valued of books for the whole Middle Ages, which never failed to find inspiration and comfort in its nobly stoic doctrine. Chaucer's own philosophical attitude, that of living wholeheartedly in the world while remaining spiritually detached from it, is at least partially a legacy from Boethius. His wooden but painstaking prose translation of the *Consolation*, probably made during the 70's, is only one of innumerable indications of Chaucer's reverence for the Roman writer.

The journey that Chaucer made to Italy in 1372 was in all likelihood a milestone in his literary development. Hitherto the influences upon him had been largely French and Latin, and while he may have read Italian before, it is likely that it was his Italian journey that immersed him in the works of Dante, Petrarch, and Boccaccio—the last two still alive at the time of Chaucer's visit, though he probably did not meet them. Between Chaucer and the greatest of the Italian writers, Dante, there was a large dissimilarity of temperament; yet if Chaucer could not assimilate *The Divine Comedy*, he nevertheless appreciated its austere moral grandeur, and his work shows its influences in subtle, oblique ways. Moreover, one of his funniest poems, the *House of Fame*, written sometime while he was in the customs (1374–86), may be read as a lighthearted imitation of the *Comedy*, though not a wholly successful one. From the works of Petrarch, also a writer of alien temperament, Chaucer obtained less, though he accords him respect on the several occasions when he mentions him. It was Boccaccio, whose cast of mind was far more congenial to Chaucer than the more sober Dante and Petrarch, who was to provide the source for some of Chaucer's finest poems—though his name is never mentioned in Chaucer's works. Many of the *Canterbury Tales* are indebted to one or another of Boccaccio's works, as is his lovely, cryptic love vision, the *Parliament of Fowls* (between 1375 and 1385). And his longest poem, *Troilus and Criseide*, probably completed about 1385, is an adaptation of Boccaccio's *Il Filostrato* ("The

Love-Stricken"). The Italian work is one of considerable stature, which Chaucer reworked into one of the greatest love poems in any language. Even if he had never written the *Canterbury Tales*, *Troilus* would have secured Chaucer a place among the great English poets.

Chaucer probably began work on the *Canterbury Tales* in 1386, and this was his chief literary interest until his death. The old tripartite division of Chaucer's literary career which assigns him a French period (to 1372), and an Italian period (1372–85), calls this last period of his life "English." But it was not English in the same sense as the earlier periods were French and Italian (i.e., dominated by French and Italian models), for the fact is that Chaucer from the beginning to the end stands apart from the mainstream of English literature. In the Rhyme of Sir Thopas, which he assigns himself in the *Canterbury Tales*, the wonderful fun he makes of popular Middle English romances shows his intimate knowledge of them; and undoubtedly he had read much English writing of all kinds. Yet his notion of literary art seems to have excluded many of the common characteristics—and the characteristic vices—of what had been and was being written in English, so that it is difficult to relate his work to that of his fellow English writers. His friend John Gower is a case in point: like Chaucer, he wrote a collection of English narrative poems in his *Confessio Amantis* ("The Lover's Confession"), and Chaucer tells some of the same stories in the *Canterbury Tales* and in the *Legend of Good Women*. The last, which may have interrupted Chaucer's work on the *Canterbury Tales* in the late 80's, was apparently assigned him by some eminent person; in order to make amends for his portrait of the unfaithful Criseide, he had to write a series of short poems celebrating famous faithful women. To make each story prove exactly the same point and nothing more is something that the conventional Gower had no trouble in doing. Yet Chaucer was able to complete the tales of only nine solemnly steadfast ladies before giving up in something like despair, and the most amusing thing about his narratives is his evident exasperation with having to make everything accord to a single formula. He could not bring himself to use the simple moralistic technique of conventional English poetry, and what Gower treats seriously appears in Chaucer often to be bordering on burlesque. Every comparison between Chaucer and run-of-the-mill English poetry either so exalts him as to make the act of comparison ludicrous or else, when Chaucer is trying to behave conventionally, shows him writing with his left hand. Chaucer had no really "English" period; English poetry had little to teach the first great English poet.

CHAUCER'S ART

The extraordinary variety of the *Canterbury Tales* as well as their number might well have demanded their author's full energy and attention during the last fourteen years of his life, but while he was at work on them he continued, almost to the end, to perform what seem to have been full-time jobs having nothing to do with literaure. Doubtless this practical business prevented him from achieving more than the 22 tales he finished; and it probably made him search his old papers for tales that he could work in without substantial revision. Yet if it reduced his liter-

ary output—which, even so, is enormous—this lifelong involvement with
the practical is one of the chief reasons for his greatness as a poet. From
his birth to his death he dealt continually with all sorts of people, the
highest and the lowest, and his wonderfully observant mind made the most
of this ever-present opportunity. His wide reading gave him plots and ideas,
but his experience gave him people. As a commoner himself he had a
sympathy with and understanding of the lower classes that few men who
attained his ultimate station might boast of—and the lower classes must
have accepted him. Similarly, he seems to have won full acceptance from
the proud and important personages with whom he associated at court,
and this he could not have won if he had not understood them perfectly.
He understands both the high and the low, but he remains curiously detached from both, and it is detachment, perfectly balanced in his poetry
by sympathy, which distinguishes Chaucer's art. Although he was born
a commoner, he did not live as a commoner; and although he was accepted by the aristocracy, he must always have been conscious of the fact
that he did not really belong to that society of which birth alone could
make one a true member. Medieval aristocratic society arrogated to itself all idealism, and Chaucer characteristically regards life in terms of
aristocratic ideals; but he never lost the ability, which for the poorer class
was also a positive necessity, of regarding life as a purely practical matter.
The art of being at once involved in and detached from a given situation
is peculiarly Chaucer's.

In the physical realm, double vision results in a blurred image, but not
so in Chaucer's poetic world, where images have often an extraordinary
clarity, as if reality itself were made more real. His Prioress in the *Canterbury Tales* is an example of the basic human paradox which places what
people are in opposition to what they think they are or pretend to be:
Chaucer shows us clearly her inability to be what she professes to be, a
nun; shows also the inadequacy of what she thinks a nun ought to be, a
lady; and shows the great human charm of what she is, a woman. The
elements of the portrait are divided between the critical and the admiring:
a heavily satiric poet might well enhance the critical comment, so that
our ultimate impression would be of the Prioress' weakness, while a sentimental one might enhance her amiable side so as to make that the aspect
which we should remember. But in Chaucer's handling the reality comprehends both sides of the Prioress, expresses the paradox without attempting to resolve it. He appears to have been a man who had no illusions
about the world or its inhabitants, but was nevertheless deeply fond of
them both, and thought it worth while to keep the world spinning as well
as possible, either by telling stories of high artistic truth or by counting
pots and pans.

The text given here is from the present editor's *Chaucer's Poetry: An
Anthology for the Modern Reader* (1958). For the *Canterbury Tales* the
Hengwrt Manuscript has provided the textual basis. The spelling has been
altered to improve consistency, and has been modernized in so far as
is possible without distorting the phonological values of the Middle English.

CHAUCER'S LANGUAGE AND VERSIFICATION

Chaucer wrote in the East Midland dialect of Middle English, as the language spoken in England between 1100 and 1500 is called. The earliest records of Middle English date from the early 12th century; it gave way to Modern English shortly after the introduction of printing at the end of the 15th century. It included a number of differing regional dialects, each with its own peculiarities of sound and its own systems for representing sounds in writing. Middle English was a somewhat more heavily inflected language than our own (that is, the words often changed form to indicate changes in usage, such as person, number, tense, case, mood, etc. Even Modern English, despite its tendency to weaken inflections, is still an inflected language—for example, its personal pronouns change their forms when used as possessives or objects). Chaucer's Midland dialect—the dialect of his London and the ancestor of our standard speech—is the easiest of the Middle English dialects for us to read, but it is nevertheless not without difficulty. This is caused chiefly by its spelling, which may be described as a rough-and-ready phonetic system that lacks consistency. In order to meet this difficulty, the selections from Chaucer given here have been respelled by the editor.

I. THE SOUNDS OF MIDDLE ENGLISH: GENERAL RULES

The following general analysis of the sounds of Middle English will enable the reader who has not time for detailed study to read Middle English aloud so as to preserve some of its most essential characteristics, without, however, giving heed to many important details. Section II, Detailed Analysis, is designed for the reader who wishes to go more deeply into the pronunciation of Middle English.

Middle English differs from Modern English in three principal respects: 1. the pronunciation of the long vowels *a, e, i* (or *y*), *o,* and *u* (spelled *ou, ow*); 2. the fact that Middle English final *e* is often sounded; 3. the fact that all Middle English consonants are sounded.

1. Long Vowels

Middle English vowels are long when they are doubled (*aa, ee, oo*) or when they are terminal (*he, to, holy*); *a, e,* and *o* are long when followed by a single consonant plus a vowel (*name, mete, note*). Middle English vowels are short when they are followed by two consonants.

Long *a* is sounded like the *a* in Modern English "father": *maken, maad*.

Long *e* may be sounded like the *a* in Modern English "name" (ignoring the distinction between the close and open vowel): *be, sweete*.

Long *i* (or *y*) is sounded like the *i* in Modern English "machine": *lif, whit; myn, holy*.

Long *o* may be sounded like the *o* in Modern English "note" (again ignoring the distinction between the close and open vowel): *do, soone*.

Long *u* (spelled *ou, ow*) is sounded like the *oo* in Modern English "goose": *hous, flowr*.

Note that in general Middle English long vowels are pronounced like long vowels in modern languages other than English. Short vowels and diphthongs, however, may be pronounced as in Modern English.

The nonphonetic Middle English spelling of *o* for short *u* has been preserved in a number of Modern English words ("love," "son," "come"), but in others *u* has been restored: "sun" (*sonne*), "run" (*ronne*).

For the treatment of final *e*, see above, General Rules, section 2.

2. Diphthongs

Sound	Pronunciation	Example
ai, ay, ei, ay	between *ai* in "aisle" and *ay* in "day"	*saide, day, veine, preye*
au, aw	*ou* in "out"	*chaunge, bawdy*
eu, ew	*ew* in "few"	*newe*
oi, oy	*oy* in "joy"	*joye, point*
ou, ow	*ou* in "thought"	*thought, lowe*

Note that in words with *ou, ow* which in Modern English are sounded with the *ou* of "about," the combination indicates not the diphthong but the simple vowel long *u* (see above, Simple Vowels).

3. Consonants

In general, all consonants except *h* were always sounded in Middle English, including consonants that have become silent in Modern English, such as the *g* in *gnaw*, the *k* in *knight*, the *l* in *folk*, and the *w* in *write*. In noninitial *gn*, however, the *g* was silent as in Modern English "sign." Initial *h* was silent in short common English words and in words borrowed from French, and may have been almost silent in all words. The combination *gh* as in *night* or *thought* was sounded like the *ch* of German *ich* or *nach*. Note that Middle English *gg* represents both the hard sound of "dagger" and the soft sound of "bridge."

III. PARTS OF SPEECH AND GRAMMAR

1. Nouns

The plural and possessive of nouns end in *es*, formed by adding *s* or *es* to the singular: *knight, knightes; roote, rootes;* a final consonant is frequently doubled before *es: bed, beddes.* A common irregular plural is *yën*, from *yë*, eye.

2. Pronouns

The chief differences from Modern English are as follows:

Modern English	Middle English
I	*I, ich* (*ik* is a northern form)
you (singular)	*thou* (subjective); *thee* (objective)
her	*hir(e), her(e)*
its	*his*
you (plural)	*ye* (subjective); *you* (objective)
their	*hir*
them	*hem*

In formal speech, the second person plural is often used for the singular. The possessive adjectives *my, thy* take *n* before a word beginning with a vowel or *h: thyn yë, myn host.*

3. Adjectives

Adjectives ending in a consonant add final *e* when they stand before the noun they modify and after another modifying word such as *the, this,*

2. *Final e*

In Middle English syllabic verse, final *e* is sounded like the *a* in "sofa" to provide a needed unstressed syllable: *Another Nonnë with hire haddë she*. But (cf. *hire* in the example) final *e* is suppressed when not needed for the meter. It is commonly silent before words beginning with a vowel or *h*.

3. *Consonants*

Middle English consonants are pronounced separately in all combinations—*gnat: g-nat; knave: k-nave; write: w-rite; folk: fol-k*. In a simplified system of pronunciation the combination *gh* as in *night* or *thought* may be treated as if it were silent.

II. THE SOUNDS OF MIDDLE ENGLISH: DETAILED ANALYSIS

1. *Simple Vowels*

Sound	Pronunciation	Example
long *a* (spelled *a, aa*)	*a* in "father"	*maken, maad*
short *a*	*o* in "hot"	*cappe*
long *e* close (spelled *e, ee*)	*a* in "name"	*be, sweete*
long *e* open (spelled *e, ee*)	*e* in "there"	*mete, heeth*
short *e*	*e* in "set"	*setten*
final *e*	*a* in "sofa"	*large*
long *i* (spelled *i, y*)	*i* in "machine"	*lif, myn*
short *i*	*i* in "wit"	*wit*
long *o* close (spelled *o, oo*)	*o* in "note"	*do, soone*
long *o* open (spelled *o, oo*)	*oa* in "broad"	*go, goon*
short *o*	*o* in "oft"	*pot*
long *u* when spelled *ou, ow*	*oo* in "goose"	*hous, flowr*
long *u* when spelled *u*	*u* in "pure"	*vertu*
short *u* (spelled *u, o*)	*u* in "full"	*ful, love*

Doubled vowels and terminal vowels are always long, while single vowels before two consonants other than *th, ch* are always short. The vowels *a, e,* and *o* are long before a single consonant followed by a vowel: *nāmë, sēkë* (sick), *hōly*. In general, words that have descended into Modern English reflect their original Middle English quantity: *liven* (to live), but *līf* (life).

The close and open sounds of long *e* and long *o* may often be identified by the Modern English spellings of the words in which they appear. Original long close *e* is generally represented in Modern English by *ee*: "sweet," "knee," "teeth," "see" have close *e* in Middle English, but so does "be"; original long open *e* is generally represented in Modern English by *ea*: "meat," "heath," "sea," "great," "breath" have open *e* in Middle English. Similarly, original long close *o* is now generally represented by *oo*: "soon," "food," "good," but also "do," "to"; original long open *o* is represented either by *oa* or by *o*: "coat," "boat," "moan," but also "go," "bone," "foe," "home." Notice that original close *o* is now almost always pronounced like the *oo* in "goose," but that original open *o* is almost never so pronounced; thus it is often possible to identify the Middle English vowels through Modern English sounds.

The imperative singular of most weak verbs is *e*: (*thou*) *love*, but of some weak verbs and all strong verbs, the imperative singular is without termination: (*thou*) *heer, taak, gin*. The imperative plural of all verbs is either *e* or *eth*: (*ye*) *love*(*th*), *heere*(*th*), *take*(*th*), *ginne*(*th*).

The infinitive of verbs is *e* or *en*: *love*(*n*), *heere*(*n*), *take*(*n*), *ginne*(*n*).

The past participle of weak verbs is the same as the preterite without inflectional ending: *loved, herd*. In strong verbs the ending is either *e* or *en*: *take*(*n*), *gonne*(*n*). The prefix *y* often appears on past participles: *yloved, yherd, ytake*(*n*).

IV. CHAUCER'S VERSIFICATION

In general, the *Canterbury Tales* are written in rhymed couplets, the line containing five stresses with regular alternation—technically known as iambic pentameter, the standard English poetic line, perhaps introduced into English by Chaucer. In reading Chaucer and much pre-Chaucerian verse one must remember that the final *e*, which is silent in Modern English, was pronounced at any time in order to provide a needed unstressed syllable. Evidence seems to indicate that it was also pronounced at the end of the line, even though it thus produced a line with eleven syllables. Although he was a very regular metricist, Chaucer used various conventional devices which are apt to make the reader stumble until he understands them. Final *e* is often not pronounced before a word beginning with a vowel or *h*, and may be suppressed whenever metrically convenient. The same medial and terminal syllables that are slurred in Modern English are apt to be suppressed in Chaucer's English: *Canterb'ry* for *Canterbury*; *ev'r* (perhaps *e'er*) for *evere*. The plural in *es* may either be syllabic or reduced to *s* as in Modern English. Despite these seeming irregularities, Chaucer's verse is not difficult to read if one constantly bears in mind the basic pattern of the iambic pentameter line.

that, or nouns or pronouns in the possessive: *a good hors,* but *the* (*this, my, the kinges*) *goode hors.* They also generally add *e* when standing before and modifying a plural noun, a noun in the vocative, or any proper noun: *goode men, oh goode man, faire Venus.*

Adjectives are compared by adding *er*(*e*) for the comparative, *est*(*e*) for the superlative. Sometimes the stem vowel is shortened or altered in the process: *sweete, swettere, swettest; long, lenger, lengest.*

4. Adverbs

Adverbs are formed from adjectives by adding *e, ly,* or *liche*; the adjective *fair* thus yields *faire, fairly, fairliche.*

5. Verbs

Middle English verbs, like Modern English verbs, are either "weak" or "strong." Weak verbs form their preterites and past participles with a *t* or *d* suffix and preserve the same stem vowel throughout their systems, though it is sometimes shortened in the preterite and past participle: *love, loved; bend, bent; hear, heard; meet, met.* Strong verbs do not use the *t* or *d* suffix, but vary their stem vowel in the preterite and past participle: *take, took, taken; begin, began, begun; find, found, found.*

The inflectional endings are the same for Middle English strong verbs and weak verbs except in the preterite singular and the imperative singular. In the following paradigms, the weak verbs *loven* (to love) and *heeren* (to hear), and the strong verbs *taken* (to take) and *ginnen* (to begin) serve as models.

	Present Indicative	Preterite Indicative
I	*love, heere*	*loved*(*e*), *herde*
	take, ginne	*took, gan*
thou	*lovest, heerest*	*lovedest, herdest*
	takest, ginnest	*tooke, gonne*
he, she, it	*loveth, heereth*	*loved*(*e*), *herde*
	taketh, ginneth	*took, gan*
we, ye, they	*love*(*n*) (*th*), *heere*(*n*) (*th*)	*loved*(*e*) (*en*), *herde*(*n*)
	take(*n*) (*th*), *ginne*(*n*) (*th*)	*tooke*(*n*), *gonne*(*n*)

The present plural ending *eth* is southern, while the *e*(*n*) ending is Midland and characteristic of Chaucer. In the north, *s* may appear as the ending of all persons of the present. In the weak preterite, when the ending *e* gave a verb three or more syllables, it was frequently dropped. Note that in certain strong verbs like *ginnen* there are two distinct stem vowels in the preterite: even in Chaucer's time, however, one of these had begun to replace the other, and Chaucer occasionally writes *gan* for all persons of the preterite.

	Present Subjunctive	Preterite Subjunctive
Singular	*love, heere*	*lovede, herde*
	take, ginne	*tooke, gonne*
Plural	*love*(*n*), *heere*(*n*)	*lovede*(*n*), *herde*(*n*)
	take(*n*), *ginne*(*n*)	*tooke*(*n*), *gonne*(*n*)

In verbs like *ginnen,* which have two stem vowels in the indicative preterite, it is the vowel of the plural and of the second person singular that is used for the preterite subjunctive.

the succeeding tales. Indeed, so powerful are these resonances that some see in them a thematic unifying device: the question of marriage that the Wife introduces is further treated from two opposing points of view by the Clerk and the Merchant, and is finally settled by the common sense of the Franklin. In addition to such artistic stratagems as these, the personality and mind of the reporter—a half-burlesque version of Chaucer himself—permeates the poem and enriches its meaning.

The composition of none of the tales can be accurately dated; most of them were written during the last fourteen years of Chaucer's life, though some which fail to fit their tellers may be much earlier. The popularity of the poem in late medieval England is attested by the number of surviving manuscripts: more than 80, mostly from the 15th century. It was also twice printed by Caxton, and often reprinted by Caxton's early successors. The manuscripts reflect the unfinished state of the poem—the fact that when he died Chaucer had not made up his mind about a number of details, and hence left many inconsistencies. The poem appears in the manuscripts as nine or ten "fragments" or blocks of tales; the order of the poems within each fragment is generally the same, but the order of the fragments themselves varies widely. The fragment containing the General Prologue, the Knight's, Miller's and Reeve's Tales, and the Cook's unfinished tale, always comes first, and the fragment consisting of the Parson's Tale and the Retraction always comes last; but the others, such as that containing the Wife of Bath, the Friar, and the Summoner, or that consisting of the Physician and Pardoner, or the longest fragment consisting of six tales concluding with the Nun's Priest's, are by no means stable in relation to one another. Either of two orders seems as satisfactory a solution as the unfinished state of the poem will allow. According to these, the selections in this book would run: General Prologue, Miller, Wife of Bath, Pardoner, Nun's Priest (or Nun's Priest, Wife of Bath, Pardoner), Parson. For pedagogical reasons—since it represents a certain extreme of Chaucer's art—the Miller's Tale has here been placed out of order.

THE GENERAL PROLOGUE

Chaucer did not need to make a pilgrimage himself in order to meet the types of people that his fictitious pilgrimage includes, for most of them had long inhabited literature as well as life: the ideal Knight, who had fought against the pagans in all the great battles of the last half-century; his son the Squire, a lover out of any love poem; the Prioress without a vocation but with the dogs and jewelry that satirical literature was always condemning nuns for; the hunting Monk and flattering Friar, chief butts of medieval satirists; the too-busy and too-rich lawyer; the prosperous Franklin; the fraudulent Doctor; the Wife—or Archwife—of Bath; the austere Parson; and so on down through the lower orders to that flamboyant hypocrite, the Pardoner, a living vice. One meets all these types in medieval literature, and, since literature imitates life, one might have met them also in medieval society, as Chaucer, with his wide experience, undoubtedly did. Indeed, it has been argued that in some of his portraits he is drawing real people; but the appearance of doing so is actually a function of his art, which is able to endow types with a reality we generally

The Canterbury Tales Chaucer's original plan for the *Canterbury Tales* projected about 120 stories, two for each pilgrim to tell on the way to Canterbury and two more on the way back. Chaucer actually completed only 22, though two more exist in fragments; a modification of the original plan is seen in the assignment of one of the completed tales to a pilgrim who was not a member of the group that assembled at Southwark. The work was probably first conceived in 1386, when Chaucer was living in Greenwich, some miles east of London. From his house he might have been able to see the pilgrim road that led toward the shrine of the famous English saint, Thomas à Becket, the Archbishop of Canterbury who was murdered in his cathedral in 1170. Medieval pilgrims were notorious taletellers (liars, according to the austere Langland), and the sight and sound of the bands riding toward Canterbury may well have suggested to Chaucer the idea of using a fictitious pilgrimage as a "framing" device for a number of stories. Collections of stories linked by such a device were common in the later Middle Ages. Chaucer's contemporary John Gower had used one in his *Confessio Amantis*; earlier in the century Boccaccio had placed the hundred tales of his *Decameron* in the mouths of ten characters, each of whom told a tale a day for ten days; and another Italian, Giovanni Sercambi, had placed a series of stories in the mouth of the leader of a group of persons journeying on horseback. Even if, as seems likely, Chaucer was unaware of the Italian precedents, the device of the framing fiction was in the air.

Chaucer's artistic exploitation of the device is, however, altogether his own. In Gower and Sercambi, one speaker relates all the stories; and in Boccaccio, the relationship between any one of the ten speakers and the story he tells is haphazard, so that reassignment of all the stories to different speakers would not materially change the effect. But in the best of the *Canterbury Tales* there is a fascinating accord between the narrator and his story, so that the story takes on rich overtones from what we have learned of its teller in the General Prologue and elsewhere, and the character himself grows and is revealed by his story. Chaucer conducts two fictions simultaneously—that of the individual tale and that of the pilgrim to whom he has assigned it. He develops the second fiction not only through the General Prologue but also through the "links," the interchanges among the pilgrims between stories. These interchanges sometimes lead to animosities. Thus the Miller's Tale offends the Reeve, who, formerly a carpenter, sees himself slandered in the figure of the Miller's silly, cuckolded carpenter; and the Reeve replies with a story that scores a miller who seems very like the pilgrim Miller. Similarly the Friar and the Summoner quarrel at the end of the Wife of Bath's Prologue, so that when the Friar is called upon he tells a tale most offensive to the Summoner, who in turn retaliates with an even more offensive story about a friar. The effect of each of these tales is enhanced by the animus of its teller, while the description of the animus in the links is exciting in itself: we are given at once a story and a drama. Furthermore, the Wife of Bath's monstrous feminism sets up resonances that are felt through all

Thanne longen folk to goon° on pilgrimages,   *go*
And palmeres[6] for to seeken straunge strondes
To ferne halwes, couthe° in sondry londes;   *known*
15 And specially from every shires ende
Of Engelond to Canterbury they wende,
The holy blisful martyr[7] for to seeke
That hem hath holpen° whan that they were seke.° *helped / sick*
   Bifel that in that seson on a day,
20 In Southwerk[8] at the Tabard as I lay,
Redy to wenden on my pilgrimage
To Canterbury with ful° devout corage,   *very*
At night was come into that hostelrye
Wel nine and twenty in a compaignye
25 Of sondry folk, by aventure° yfalle   *chance*
In felaweshipe, and pilgrimes were they alle
That toward Canterbury wolden° ride.   *would*
The chambres and the stables weren wide,
And wel we weren esed° at the beste.[9]   *accommodated*
30 And shortly, whan the sonne was to reste,[1]
So hadde I spoken with hem everichoon°   *every one*
That I was of hir felaweshipe anoon,°   *at once*
And made forward[2] erly for to rise,
To take oure way ther as[3] I you devise.°   *describe*
35   But nathelees,° whil I have time and space,[4] *nevertheless*
Er° that I ferther in this tale pace,°   *before / pass*
Me thinketh it accordant to resoun[5]
To telle you al the condicioun
Of eech of hem, so as it seemed me,
40 And whiche they were, and of what degree,
And eek in what array that they were inne:
And at a knight thanne° wol I first biginne.   *then*
   A Knight ther was, and that a worthy man,
That fro the time that he first bigan
45 To riden out, he loved chivalrye,
Trouthe[6] and honour, freedom and curteisye.
Ful worthy was he in his lordes werre,°   *war*
And therto hadde he riden, no man ferre,°   *further*
As wel in Cristendom as hethenesse,°   *heathen lands*
50 And[7] evere honoured for his worthinesse.
   At Alisandre[8] he was whan it was wonne;

6. Palmers, wide-ranging pilgrims—especially those who sought out the "straunge strondes" (foreign shores) of the Holy Land. "Ferne halwes": far-off shrines.
7. St. Thomas à Becket, murdered in Canterbury Cathedral in 1170.
8. Southwark, site of the Tabard Inn, was then a suburb of London, south of the Thames River.
9. In the best possible way.
1. Had set.

2. I.e., (we) made an agreement.
3. "Ther as": where.
4. I.e., opportunity.
5. It seems to me according to reason.
6. Integrity. "Freedom" is here generosity of spirit, while "curteisye" is courtesy.
7. I.e., and he was.
8. The Knight has taken part in campaigns fought against all three groups of pagans who threatened Europe during the 14th century: the Moslems in

associate only with people we know. Chaucer achieves this effect largely by persuading us that his own interest lies only in the visible, in what actually met his eye on the pilgrimage. He pretends to let the salient features of each pilgrim leap out directly at the reader, and does not seem to mind if some of his descriptions are from top to toe, others all toe and no top. This imitation of the way our minds actually perceive reality may make us fail to notice the care with which Chaucer has selected his details in order to give an integrated sketch of the person being described. While they are generally not full-blown literary symbols, most of these details give something more than mere verisimilitude to the description; actually, they mediate between the world of types and the world of real people. Independent bourgeois women of the time were often makers of cloth, so that the Wife of Bath's proficiency at the trade is, in one way, merely part of her historical reality; yet the first weaver of cloth was the unparadised Eve, and her descendant is an unregenerate member of the distaff side. The Franklin's red face and white beard are in the same way merely individualizing factors in the portrait; yet the red face and white beard seem always to associate themselves with a man of good will who likes good living, and since Chaucer's time they have become the distinguishing marks of a kind of mythic Franklin, Santa Claus.

The rich suggestiveness of the details is what makes the portraits worth reading again and again. One may begin by enjoying the bright if flat photographic image of reality that the reporter creates, but one will find that the initial appearance of flatness is deceptive, and that the more one rereads the more complex and significant the portraits become. Here, as elsewhere in his work, Chaucer shows himself to be a rival to Shakespeare in the art of providing entertainment on the most primitive level, and at the same time, of significantly increasing the reader's ability to comprehend reality.

From THE CANTERBURY TALES
The General Prologue

Whan that April with his° showres soote°	*its / sweet*
The droughte of March hath perced to the roote,	
And bathed every veine[1] in swich° licour,°	*such / liquid*
Of which vertu[2] engendred is the flowr;	
5 Whan Zephyrus[3] eek° with his sweete breeth	*also*
Inspired hath in every holt° and heeth°	*grove / field*
The tendre croppes,° and the yonge sonne[4]	*shoots*
Hath in the Ram his halve cours yronne,	
And smale fowles maken melodye	
10 That sleepen al the night with open yë°—	*eye*
So priketh hem° Nature in hir corages[5]—	*them*

1. I.e., in plants.
2. By the power of which.
3. The west wind.
4. The sun is young because it has run only halfway through its course in Aries, the Ram—the first sign of the zodiac in the solar year.
5. Their hearts.

In hope to stonden in his lady° grace.   lady's
  Embrouded° was he as it were a mede,[3]   embroidered
90 Al ful of fresshe flowres, white and rede;°   red
Singing he was, or floiting,° al the day: whistling
He was as fressh as is the month of May.
Short was his gowne, with sleeves longe and wide.
Wel coude he sitte on hors, and faire ride;
95 He coude songes make, and wel endite,°   compose verse
Juste[4] and eek daunce, and wel portraye° and write.   sketch
So hote° he loved that by nightertale[5]   hotly
He slepte namore than dooth a nightingale.
Curteis he was, lowely,° and servisable,   humble
100 And carf biforn his fader at the table.[6]

  A Yeman[7] hadde he and servants namo°   no more
At that time, for him liste[8] ride so;
And he[9] was clad in cote and hood of greene.
A sheef of pecok arwes,° bright and keene,   arrows
105 Under his belt he bar° ful thriftily;°   bore / properly
Wel coude he dresse° his takel° yemanly:[1]   tend to / gear
His arwes drouped nought with fetheres lowe.
And in his hand he bar a mighty bowe.
A not-heed° hadde he with a brown visage.   close-cut head
110 Of wodecraft wel coude° he al the usage.   knew
Upon his arm he bar a gay bracer,[2]
And by his side a swerd° and a bokeler,[3]   sword
And on that other side a gay daggere,
Harneised° wel and sharp as point of spere;   mounted
115 A Cristophre[4] on his brest of silver sheene;°   bright
An horn he bar, the baudrik[5] was of greene.
A forster° was he soothly,° as I gesse.   forester / truly

  Ther was also a Nonne, a Prioresse,[6]
That of hir smiling was ful simple and coy.
120 Hir gretteste ooth was but by sainte Loy!°   Eloi
And she was cleped° Madame Eglantine.   named
Ful wel she soong° the service divine,   sang
Entuned° in hir nose ful semely;[7]   chanted
And Frenssh she spak ful faire and fetisly,°   elegantly
125 After the scole° of Stratford at the Bowe[8]—   school
For Frenssh of Paris was to hire unknowe.
At mete° wel ytaught was she withalle:°   meals / besides

3. Mead, meadow.
4. Joust, fight in a tournament.
5. At night.
6. It was a squire's duty to carve his lord's meat.
7. The "Yeman" (Yeoman) is an independent commoner who acts as the Knight's military servant; "he" is the Knight.
8. "Him liste": it pleased him to.
9. I.e., the Yeoman.
1. In a workmanlike way.

2. Wristguard for archers.
3. Buckler (a small shield).
4. St. Christopher medal.
5. Baldric (a supporting strap).
6. The Prioress is the mother superior of her nunnery. "Simple and coy": sincere and mild.
7. In a seemly manner.
8. The French learned in a convent school in Stratford-at-the-Bow, a suburb of London, was evidently not up to the Parisian standard.

Ful ofte time he hadde the boord bigonne[9]
Aboven alle nacions in Pruce;
In Lettou had he reised,° and in Ruce,   *campaigned*
₅₅ No Cristen man so ofte of his degree;
In Gernade at the sege eek hadde he be
Of Algezir, and riden in Belmarye;
At Lyeis was he, and at Satalye,
Whan they were wonne; and in the Grete See[1]
₆₀ At many a noble armee° hadde he be.   *assembly of forces*
      At mortal batailes[2] hadde he been fifteene,
And foughten for oure faith at Tramissene
In listes[3] thries,° and ay° slain his fo.   *thrice / always*
      This ilke° worthy Knight hadde been also   *same*
₆₅ Somtime with the lord of Palatye[4]
Again° another hethen in Turkye;   *against*
And everemore he hadde a soverein pris.°   *reputation*
And though that he were worthy,[5] he was wis,
And of his port° as meeke as is a maide.   *demeanor*
₇₀ He nevere yit no vilainye° ne saide   *rudeness*
In al his lif unto no manere wight:[6]
He was a verray,° parfit,° gentil knight.   *true / perfect*
But for to tellen you of his array,
His hors° were goode, but he was nat gay.   *horses*
₇₅ Of fustian° he wered° a gipoun[7]   *thick cloth / wore*
Al bismotered with his haubergeoun,[8]
For he was late come from his viage,°   *expedition*
And wente for to doon his pilgrimage.
      With him ther was his sone, a yong Squier,[9]
₈₀ A lovere and a lusty bacheler,
With lokkes crulle° as they were laid in presse.   *curly*
Of twenty yeer of age he was, I gesse.
Of his stature he was of evene° lengthe,   *moderate*
And wonderly delivere,° and of greet° strengthe.   *agile / great*
₈₅ And he hadde been som time in chivachye[1]
In Flandres, in Artois, and Picardye,
And born him wel as of so litel space,[2]

the Near East, from whom Alexandria was seized after a famous siege; the northern barbarians in Prussia, Lithuania, and Russia; and the Moors in North Africa. The place names in the following lines refer to battlegrounds in these continuing wars.
9. Sat in the seat of honor at military feasts.
1. The Mediterranean.
2. Tournaments fought to the death.
3. Lists, tournament grounds.
4. "The lord of Palatye" was a pagan: alliances of convenience were often made during the Crusades between Christians and pagans.
5. I.e., a valiant knight.
6. "No manere wight": any sort of person. In Middle English, negatives are multiplied for emphasis, as in these two lines: "nevere," "no," "ne," "no."
7. Tunic worn underneath the coat of mail.
8. All rust-stained from his hauberk (coat of mail).
9. The vague term "Squier" (Squire) here seems to be the equivalent of "bacheler," a young knight still in the service of an older one.
1. On cavalry expeditions. The places in the next line are sites of skirmishes in the constant warfare between the English and the French.
2. I.e., considering the little time he had been in service.

Ful many a daintee° hors hadde he in stable,   *fine*
And whan he rood,° men mighte his bridel heere   *rode*
170 Ginglen° in a whistling wind as clere   *jingle*
And eek as loude as dooth the chapel belle
Ther as this lord was kepere of the cclle.[4]
The rule of Saint Maure or of Saint Beneit,[5]
By cause that it was old and somdeel strait—
175 This ilke Monk leet olde thinges pace,°   *pass away*
And heeld° after the newe world the space.[6]   *held*
He yaf nought of that text a pulled hen[7]
That saith that hunteres been° nought holy men,   *are*
Ne that a monk, whan he is recchelees,[8]
180 Is likned til° a fissh that is waterlees—   *to*
This is to sayn, a monk out of his cloistre;
But thilke° text heeld he nat worth an oystre.   *that same*
And I saide his opinion was good:
What° sholde he studye and make himselven wood°   *why / crazy*
185 Upon a book in cloistre alway to poure,
Or swinke° with his handes and laboure,   *work*
As Austin bit?[9] How shal the world be served?
Lat Austin have his swink to him reserved!
Therfore he was a prikasour° aright.   *hard rider*
190 Grehoundes he hadde as swift as fowl in flight.
Of priking° and of hunting for the hare   *riding*
Was al his lust,° for no cost wolde he spare.   *pleasure*
I sawgh his sleeves purfiled° at the hand   *fur-lined*
With gris,° and that the fineste of a land;   *gray fur*
195 And for to festne his hood under his chin
He hadde of gold wrought a ful curious[1] pin:
A love-knotte in the grettere° ende ther was.   *greater*
His heed was balled,° that shoon as any glas,   *bald*
And eek his face, as he hadde been anoint:
200 He was a lord ful fat and in good point;[2]
His yën steepe,° and rolling in his heed,   *protruding*
That stemed as a furnais of a leed,[3]
His bootes souple,° his hors in greet estat°—   *supple / condition*
Now certainly he was a fair prelat.[4]
205 He was nat pale as a forpined° gost: *wasted away*
A fat swan loved he best of any rost.
His palfrey° was as brown as is a berye.   *saddle horse*
    A Frere[5] ther was, a wantoune and a merye,

---

4. Keeper of an outlying cell (branch) of the monastery.
5. St. Maurus and St. Benedict, authors of monastic rules. "Somdeel strait": somewhat strict.
6. I.e., in his own lifetime (?).
7. He didn't give a plucked hen for that text.
8. Reckless, careless of rule.
9. I.e., as St. Augustine bids. St. Augus-

tine had written that monks should perform manual labor.
1. Of careful workmanship.
2. In good shape, plump.
3. That glowed like a furnace with a pot in it.
4. Prelate (an important churchman).
5. The "Frere" (Friar) is a member of one of the four religious orders whose members live by begging; as a "limi-

She leet° no morsel from hir lippes falle,   *let*
Ne wette hir fingres in hir sauce deepe;
130 Wel coude she carye a morsel, and wel keepe°   *take care*
That no drope ne fille° upon hir brest.   *should fall*
In curteisye was set ful muchel hir lest.[9]
Hir over-lippe wiped she so clene
That in hir coppe° ther was no ferthing° seene *cup / bit*
135 Of grece,° whan she dronken hadde hir draughte; *grease*
Ful semely after hir mete she raughte.°   *reached*
And sikerly° she was of greet disport,[1]   *certainly*
And ful plesant, and amiable of port,°   *mien*
And pained hire to countrefete cheere[2]
140 Of court, and to been statlich° of manere,   *dignified*
And to been holden digne[3] of reverence.
But, for to speken of hir conscience,
She was so charitable and so pitous°   *merciful*
She wolde weepe if that she saw a mous
145 Caught in a trappe, if it were deed° or bledde. *dead*
Of[4] smale houndes hadde she that she fedde
With rosted flessh, or milk and wastelbreed;° *fine white bread*
But sore wepte she if oon of hem were deed,
Or if men smoot it with a yerde smerte;[5]
150 And al was conscience and tendre herte.
Ful semely hir wimpel° pinched° was,   *headdress / pleated*
Hir nose tretis,° hir yën° greye as glas,   *well-formed / eyes*
Hir mouth ful smal, and therto° softe and reed,° *moreover / red*
But sikerly° she hadde a fair forheed: *certainly*
155 It was almost a spanne brood,[6] I trowe,° *believe*
For hardily,° she was nat undergrowe.   *assuredly*
Ful fetis° was hir cloke, as I was war;° *becoming / aware*
Of smal° coral aboute hir arm she bar   *dainty*
A paire[7] of bedes, gauded al with greene,
160 And theron heeng° a brooch of gold ful sheene,° *hung / bright*
On which ther was first writen a crowned A,[8]
And after, *Amor vincit omnia.*[9]

   Another Nonne with hire hadde she
That was hir chapelaine,° and preestes three.[1] *secretary*
165 A Monk ther was, a fair for the maistrye,[2]
An outridere[3] that loved venerye,°   *hunting*
A manly man, to been an abbot able.°   *worthy*

---

9. I.e., her chief delight lay in good manners.
1. Of great good cheer.
2. And took pains to imitate the behavior.
3. And to be considered worthy.
4. I.e., some.
5. If someone struck it with a rod sharply.
6. A handsbreadth wide.
7. String (i.e., a rosary); "gauded al with greene": provided with green

beads to mark certain prayers.
8. An *A* with an ornamental crown on it.
9. A Latin motto meaning "Love conquers all."
1. Although he here awards this charming lady three priests, Chaucer later reduces the number to one.
2. I.e., a superlatively fine one.
3. A monk charged with supervising property distant from the monastery.

But al with riche, and selleres of vitaile;°   *foodstuffs*
And over al ther as profit sholde arise,
250 Curteis he was, and lowely of servise.
Ther was no man nowher so vertuous:°   *efficient*
He was the beste beggere in his hous.°   *friary*
And yaf a certain ferme for the graunt:[8]
Noon of his bretheren cam ther in his haunt.[9]
255 For though a widwe° hadde nought a sho,°   *widow / shoe*
So plesant was his *In principio*[1]
Yit wolde he have a ferthing° er he wente;   *small coin*
His purchas was wel bettre than his rente.[2]
And rage he coude as it were right a whelpe;[3]
260 In love-dayes[4] ther coude he muchel° helpe,   *much*
For ther he was nat lik a cloisterer,
With a thredbare cope, as is a poore scoler,
But he was lik a maister[5] or a pope.
Of double worstede was his semicope,°   *short robe*
265 And rounded as a belle out of the presse.°   *bell-mold*
Somwhat he lipsed° for his wantounesse°   *lisped / affectation*
To make his Englissh sweete upon his tonge;
And in his harping, whan he hadde songe,°   *sung*
His yën twinkled in his heed aright
270 As doon the sterres° in the frosty night.   *stars*
This worthy limitour was cleped Huberd.

     A Marchant was ther with a forked beerd,
In motelee,[6] and hye on hors he sat,
Upon his heed a Flandrissh° bevere hat,   *Flemish*
275 His bootes clasped faire and fetisly.°   *elegantly*
His resons° he spak ful solempnely,   *opinions*
Souning° alway th'encrees of his winning.   *sounding*
He wolde the see were kept for any thing[7]
Bitwixen Middelburgh and Orewelle.
280 Wel coude he in eschaunge sheeldes[8] selle.
This worthy man ful wel his wit bisette:°   *employed*
Ther wiste° no wight that he was in dette,   *knew*
So statly° was he of his governaunce,[9]   *dignified*
With his bargaines,[1] and with his chevissaunce.
285 Forsoothe he was a worthy man withalle;
But, sooth to sayn, I noot° how men him calle.   *don't know*

8. And he paid a certain rent for the privilege of begging.
9. Assigned territory.
1. A friar's usual salutation (John i.1): "In the beginning (was the Word)."
2. I.e., the money he got through such activity was more than his regular income.
3. And he could flirt wantonly, as if he were a puppy.
4. Days appointed for the settlement of lawsuits out of court.
5. A man of recognized learning.

6. Motley, a cloth of mixed color.
7. I.e., he wished the sea to be guarded at all costs. The sea route between Middelburgh (in the Netherlands) and Orwell (in Suffolk) was vital to the Merchant's export and import of wool—the basis of England's chief trade at the time.
8. Shields, *ecus* (French coins): he could speculate profitably (if illegally) in foreign exchange.
9. The management of his affairs.
1. Bargainings; "chevissaunce": borrowing.

A limitour, a ful solempne° man.　　　　　　　*pompous*
210 In alle the ordres foure is noon that can°　　　*knows*
So muche of daliaunce° and fair langage:　　　*flirtation*
He hadde maad ful many a mariage
Of yonge wommen at his owene cost;
Unto his ordre he was a noble post.[6]
215 Ful wel biloved and familier was he
With frankelains over al[7] in his contree,
And with worthy wommen of the town—
For he hadde power of confessioun,
As saide himself, more than a curat,°　　　　*parish priest*
220 For of° his ordre he was licenciat.[8]　　　　　*by*
Ful swetely herde he confessioun,
And plesant was his absolucioun.
He was an esy man to yive penaunce
Ther as he wiste to have[9] a good pitaunce;°　　*donation*
225 For unto a poore ordre for to yive
Is signe that a man is wel yshrive;[1]
For if he yaf, he dorste make avaunt°　　　　　*boast*
He wiste that a man was repentaunt;
For many a man so hard is of his herte
230 He may nat weepe though him sore smerte:[2]
Therfore, in stede of weeping and prayeres,
Men mote° yive silver to the poore freres.[3]　　*may*
　　His tipet° was ay farsed° ful of knives　　*scarf / packed*
And pinnes, for to yiven faire wives;
235 And certainly he hadde a merye note;
Wel coude he singe and playen on a rote;°　　*fiddle*
Of yeddinges he bar outrely the pris.[4]
His nekke whit was as the flowr-de-lis;°　　　*lily*
Therto he strong was as a champioun.
240 He knew the tavernes wel in every town,
And every hostiler° and tappestere,°　　*innkeeper / barmaid*
Bet° than a lazar[5] or a beggestere.　　　　　　*better*
For unto swich a worthy man as he
Accorded nat, as by his facultee,[6]
245 To have with sike° lazars aquaintaunce:　　　*sick*
It is nat honeste,° it may nought avaunce,°　*dignified / profit*
For to delen with no swich poraile,[7]

tour" (line 209) he has been granted
exclusive begging rights within a certain limited area.
6. I.e., pillar.
7. I.e., with franklins everywhere.
Franklins were well-to-do country men.
8. I.e., licensed to hear confessions.
9. Where he knew he would have.
1. Shriven, absolved.
2. Though he is sorely grieved.
3. Before granting absolution, the confessor must be sure the sinner is contrite; moreover, the absolution is contingent upon the sinner's performance

of an act of satisfaction. In the case of
Chaucer's Friar, a liberal contribution
served both as proof of contrition and
as satisfaction.
4. He absolutely took the prize for
ballads.
5. Leper; "beggestere": female beggar.
6. It was not suitable because of his
position.
7. I.e., poor people. The oldest order of
friars had been founded by St. Francis
to administer to the spiritual needs of
precisely those classes the Friar avoids.

That from the time of King William[7] were falle.
Therto he coude endite and make a thing,[8]
Ther coude no wight pinchen° at his writing; *cavil*
And every statut coude° he plein° by rote.[9] *knew / entire*
330 He rood but hoomly ° in a medlee cote,[1] *unpretentiously*
Girt with a ceint of silk, with barres smale.
Of his array telle I no lenger tale.
 A Frankelain[2] was in his compaignye:
Whit was his beerd as is the dayesye;° *daisy*
335 Of his complexion he was sanguin.[3]
Wel loved he by the morwe a sop in win.[4]
To liven in delit° was evere his wone,° *sensual delight / wont*
For he was Epicurus[5] owene sone,
That heeld opinion that plein° delit *full*
340 Was verray felicitee parfit.
An housholdere and that a greet was he:
Saint Julian[6] he was in his contree.
His breed, his ale, was always after oon;[7]
A bettre envined° man was nevere noon. *wine-stocked*
345 Withouten bake mete was nevere his hous,
Of fissh and flessh, and that so plentevous° *plenteous*
It snewed° in his hous of mete and drinke, *snowed*
Of alle daintees that men coude thinke.
After° the sondry sesons of the yeer *according to*
350 So chaunged he his mete[8] and his soper.
Ful many a fat partrich hadde he in mewe,° *cage*
And many a breem,° and many a luce° in stewe.[9] *carp / pike*
Wo was his cook but if his sauce were
Poinant° and sharp, and redy all his gere. *pungent*
355 His table dormant in his halle alway
Stood redy covered all the longe day.[1]
At sessions[2] ther was he lord and sire.
Ful ofte time he was Knight of the Shire.
An anlaas° and a gipser° al of silk *dagger / purse*
360 Heeng at his girdel,[3] whit as morne° milk. *morning*
A shirreve° hadde he been, and countour.[4] *sheriff*
Was nowher swich a worthy vavasour.[5]

7. I.e., the Conqueror (reigned 1066–87).
8. Compose and draw up a deed.
9. By heart.
1. A coat of mixed color. "Ceint": belt; "barres": transverse stripes.
2. The "Frankelain" (Franklin) is a prosperous country man, whose lower-class ancestry is no impediment to the importance he has attained in his county.
3. A reference to the fact that the Franklin's temperament is dominated by blood as well as to his red face.
4. I.e., in the morning he was very fond of a piece of bread soaked in wine.
5. The Greek philosopher whose teach-ing is popularly believed to make pleasure the chief goal of life.
6. The patron saint of hospitality.
7. Always of the same high quality.
8. Dinner; "soper": supper.
9. Fishpond.
1. Tables were usually dismounted when not in use, but the Franklin kept his mounted and set ("covered"), hence "dormant."
2. I.e., sessions of the justices of the peace. "Knight of the Shire": county representative in Parliament.
3. Hung at his belt.
4. Auditor of county finances.
5. Member of an upper, but not an aristocratic, feudal class.

A Clerk[2] ther was of Oxenforde also
That unto logik hadde longe ygo.[3]
As lene was his hors as is a rake,
290 And he was nought right fat, I undertake,
But looked holwe,° and therto sobrely.   hollow
Ful thredbare was his overeste courtepy,[4]
For he hadde geten him yit no benefice,
Ne was so worldly for to have office.°   secular employment
295 For him was levere[5] have at his beddes heed
Twenty bookes, clad in blak or reed,
Of Aristotle and his philosophye,
Than robes riche, or fithele,° or gay sautrye.[6]   fiddle
But al be that he was a philosophre[7]
300 Yit hadde he but litel gold in cofre;°   coffer
But al that he mighte of his freendes hente,°   take
On bookes and on lerning he it spente,
And bisily gan for the soules praye
Of hem that yaf him wherwith to scoleye.°   study
305 Of studye took he most cure° and most heede.   care
Nought oo° word spak he more than was neede,   one
And that was said in forme[8] and reverence,
And short and quik,° and ful of heigh sentence:[9]   lively
Souninge° in moral vertu was his speeche,   resounding
310 And gladly wolde he lerne, and gladly teche.

    A Sergeant of the Lawe,[1] war and wis,
That often hadde been at the Parvis[2]
Ther was also, ful riche of excellence.
Discreet he was, and of greet reverence—
315 He seemed swich, his wordes weren so wise.
Justice he was ful often in assise°   circuit courts
By patente[3] and by plein° commissioun   full
For his science° and for his heigh renown   knowledge
Of fees and robes hadde he many oon.
320 So greet a purchasour° was nowher noon;   speculator in land
Al was fee simple[4] to him in effect—
His purchasing mighte nat been infect.[5]
Nowher so bisy a man as he ther nas;°   was not
And yit he seemed bisier than he was.
325 In termes[6] hadde he caas and doomes alle

2. The Clerk is a student at Oxford; in order to become a student, he would have had to signify his intention of becoming a cleric, but he was not bound to proceed to a position of responsibility in the church.
3. Who had long since matriculated in philosophy.
4. Outer cloak. "Benefice": ecclesiastical living.
5. He would rather.
6. Psaltery (a kind of harp).
7. The word may also mean "alchemist."

8. With decorum.
9. Elevated thought.
1. The Sergeant is not only a practicing lawyer, but one of the high justices of the nation. "War and wis": wary and wise.
2. The "Paradise," a meeting place for lawyers and their clients.
3. Royal warrant.
4. "Fee simple": owned outright without legal impediments.
5. Invalidated on a legal technicality.
6. I.e., by heart. "Caas and doomes": lawcases and decisions.

His stremes° and his daungers° him bisides,[8]   *currents / hazards*
405 His herberwe° and his moone, his lodemenage,[9]   *anchorage*
There was noon swich from Hulle to Cartage.[1]
Hardy he was and wis to undertake;
With many a tempest hadde his beerd been shake;
He knew alle the havenes° as they were   *harbors*
410 Fro Gotlond to the Cape of Finistere,[2]
And every crike° in Britaine° and in Spaine.   *inlet / Brittany*
His barge ycleped was the Maudelaine.°   *Magdalene*

With us ther was a Doctour of Physik:°   *medicine*
In al this world ne was ther noon him lik
415 To speken of physik and of surgerye.
For° he was grounded in astronomye,°   *because / astrology*
He kepte° his pacient a ful greet deel[3]   *tended to*
In houres[4] by his magik naturel.
Wel coude he fortunen the ascendent
420 Of his images[5] for his pacient.
He knew the cause of every maladye,
Were it of hoot or cold or moiste or drye,
And where engendred and of what humour:[6]
He was a verray parfit praktisour.[7]
425 The cause yknowe,° and of his harm the roote,   *known*
Anoon he yaf the sike man his boote.°   *remedy*
Ful redy hadde he his apothecaries
To senden him drogges° and his letuaries,°   *drugs / medicines*
For eech of hem made other for to winne:
430 Hir frendshipe was nought newe to biginne.
Wel knew he the olde Esculapius,[8]
And Deiscorides and eek Rufus,
Olde Ipocras, Hali, and Galien,
Serapion, Razis, and Avicen,

8. Around him.
9. Pilotage.
1. From Hull (in northern England) to Cartagena (in Spain).
2. From Gotland (an island in the Baltic) to Finisterre (the westernmost point in Spain).
3. Closely.
4. I.e., the astrologically important hours (when conjunctions of the planets might help his recovery). "Magik naturel": natural—as opposed to black—magic.
5. Assign the propitious time, according to the position of stars, for using talismanic images. Such images, representing either the patient himself or points in the zodiac, were thought to be influential on the course of the disease.
6. Diseases were thought to be caused by a disturbance of one or another of the four bodily "humors," each of which, like the four elements, was a compound of two of the elementary

qualities mentioned in line 422: the melancholy humor, seated in the black bile was cold and dry (like earth); the sanguine, seated in the blood, hot and moist (like air); the choleric, seated in the yellow bile, hot and dry (like fire); the phlegmatic, seated in the phlegm, cold and moist (like water).
7. True perfect practitioner.
8. The Doctor is familiar with the treatises that the Middle Ages attributed to the "great names" of medical history, whom Chaucer names in lines 431–36: the purely legendary Greek demigod Aesculapius; the Greeks Dioscorides, Rufus, Hippocrates, Galen, and Serapion; the Persians Hali and Rhazes; the Arabians Avicenna and Averroës; the early Christians John (?) of Damascus and Constantine Afer; the Scotsman Bernard Gordon; the Englishmen John of Gatesden and Gilbert, the former an early contemporary of Chaucer.

An Haberdasshere and a Carpenter,
A Webbe,° a Dyere, and a Tapicer°—   *weaver / tapestry-maker*
365 And they were clothed alle in oo liveree[6]
Of a solempne and greet fraternitee.
Ful fresshe and newe hir gere apiked° was;   *polished*
Hir knives were chaped° nought with bras,   *mounted*
But al with silver; wrought ful clene and weel
370 Hir girdles and hir pouches everydeel.°   *altogether*
Wel seemed eech of hem a fair burgeis°   *burgher*
To sitten in a yeldehalle° on a dais.   *guildhall*
Everich, for the wisdom that he can,[7]
Was shaply° for to been an alderman.   *suitable*
375 For catel° hadde they ynough and rente,°   *property / income*
And eek hir wives wolde it wel assente—
And elles certain were they to blame:
It is ful fair to been ycleped "Madame,"
And goon to vigilies[8] all bifore,
380 And have a mantel royalliche ybore.[9]
    A Cook they hadde with hem for the nones,[1]
To boile the chiknes with the marybones,°   *marrowbones*
And powdre-marchant tart and galingale.[2]
Wel coude he knowe° a draughte of London ale.   *recognize*
385 He coude roste, and seethe,° and broile, and frye,   *boil*
Maken mortreux,° and wel bake a pie.   *stews*
But greet harm was it, as it thoughte° me,   *seemed to*
That on his shine a mormal° hadde he.   *ulcer*
For blankmanger,[3] that made he with the beste.
390   A Shipman was ther, woning° fer by weste—   *dwelling*
For ought I woot,° he was of Dertemouthe.[4]   *know*
He rood upon a rouncy° as he couthe,[5]   *large nag*
In a gowne of falding° to the knee.   *heavy wool*
A daggere hanging on a laas° hadde he   *strap*
395 Aboute his nekke, under his arm adown.
The hote somer hadde maad his hewe° al brown;   *color*
And certainly he was a good felawe.
Ful many a draughte of win hadde he drawe[6]
Fro Burdeuxward,[7] whil that the chapman sleep:
400 Of nice° conscience took he no keep;°   *fastidious / heed*
If that he faught and hadde the hyer hand,
By water he sente hem hoom to every land.
But of his craft, to rekene wel his tides,

6. In one livery, i.e., the uniform of their "fraternitee" or guild, a partly religious, partly social organization.
7. Was capable of.
8. Feasts held on the eve of saints' days. "Al bifore": i.e., at the head of the procession.
9. Royally carried.
1. For the occasion.
2. "Powdre-marchant" and "galingale" are flavoring materials.
3. An elaborate stew.
4. Dartmouth, a port in the southwest of England.
5. As best he could.
6. Drawn, i.e., stolen.
7. From Bordeaux; i.e., while carrying wine from Bordeaux (the wine center of France). "Chapman sleep": merchant slept.

Of remedies of love she knew parchaunce,°   *as it happened*
For she coude of that art the olde daunce.⁹

   A good man was ther of religioun,
480 And was a poore Person° of a town,   *parson*
But riche he was of holy thought and werk.
He was also a lerned man, a clerk,
That Cristes gospel trewely° wolde preche;   *faithfully*
His parisshens° devoutly wolde he teche.   *parishioners*
485 Benigne he was, and wonder° diligent,   *wonderfully*
And in adversitee ful pacient,
And swich he was preved° ofte sithes.°   *proved / times*
Ful loth were him to cursen for his tithes,¹
But rather wolde he yiven, out of doute,²
490 Unto his poore parisshens aboute
Of his offring³ and eek of his substaunce:°   *property*
He coude in litel thing have suffisaunce.°   *sufficiency*
Wid was his parissh, and houses fer asonder,
But he ne lafte° nought for rain ne thonder,   *neglected*
495 In siknesse nor in meschief,° to visite   *misfortune*
The ferreste° in his parissh, muche and lite,⁴   *farthest*
Upon his feet, and in his hand a staf.
This noble ensample° to his sheep he yaf   *example*
That first he wroughte,⁵ and afterward he taughte.
500 Out of the Gospel he tho° wordes caughte,°   *those / took*
And this figure he added eek therto:
That if gold ruste, what shal iren do?
For if a preest be foul, on whom we truste,
No wonder is a lewed° man to ruste.   *uneducated*
505 And shame it is, if a preest take keep,°   *heed*
A shiten° shepherde and a clene sheep.   *befouled*
Wel oughte a preest ensample for to yive
By his clennesse how that his sheep sholde live.
He sette nought his benefice⁶ to hire
510 And leet his sheep encombred in the mire
And ran to London, unto Sainte Poules,⁷
To seeken him a chaunterye⁸ for soules,
Or with a bretherhede to been withholde,⁹
But dwelte at hoom and kepte wel his folde,
515 So that the wolf ne made it nought miscarye:
He was a shepherde and nought a mercenarye.

---

9. I.e., she knew all the tricks of that trade.
1. He would be most reluctant to invoke excommunication in order to collect his tithes.
2. Without doubt.
3. The offering made by the congregation of his church was at the Parson's disposal.
4. Great and small.
5. I.e., he practiced what he preached.
6. I.e., his parish. A priest might rent his parish to another and take a more profitable position. "Leet": i.e., he did not leave.
7. St. Paul's Cathedral.
8. Chantry, i.e., a foundation that employed priests for the sole duty of saying masses for the souls of certain persons. St. Paul's had many of them.
9. Or to be employed by a brotherhood; i.e., to take a lucrative and fairly easy position as chaplain with a parish guild.

435 Averrois, Damascien, and Constantin,
    Bernard, and Gatesden, and Gilbertin.
    Of his diete mesurable° was he,   *moderate*
    For it was of no superfluitee,
    But of greet norissing° and digestible.   *nourishment*
440 His studye was but litel on the Bible.
    In sanguin° and in pers° he clad was al, *blood-red / blue*
    Lined with taffata and with sendal;°   *silk*
    And yit he was but esy of dispence;°   *expenditure*
    He kepte that he wan in pestilence.[9]
445 For° gold in physik is a cordial,[1]   *because*
    Therfore he loved gold in special.
      A good Wif was ther of biside Bathe,
    But she was somdeel deef, and that was scathe.°   *a pity*
    Of cloth-making she hadde swich an haunt,°   *practice*
450 She passed° hem of Ypres and of Gaunt.[2]   *surpassed*
    In al the parissh wif ne was ther noon
    That to the offring[3] bifore hire sholde goon,
    And if ther dide, certain so wroth° was she   *angry*
    That she was out of alle charitee.
455 Hir coverchiefs ful fine were of ground°—   *texture*
    I dorste° swere they weyeden° ten pound   *dare / weighed*
    That on a Sonday weren° upon hir heed.   *were*
    Hir hosen weren of fin scarlet reed,°   *red*
    Ful straite yteyd,[4] and shoes ful moiste° and newe. *unworn*
460 Bold was hir face and fair and reed of hewe.
    She was a worthy womman al hir live:
    Housbondes at chirche dore[5] she hadde five,
    Withouten other compaignye in youthe—
    But therof needeth nought to speke as nouthe.°   *now*
465 And thries hadde she been at Jerusalem;
    She hadde passed many a straunge° streem;   *foreign*
    At Rome she hadde been, and at Boloigne,
    In Galice at Saint Jame, and at Coloigne:[6]
    She coude° muchel of wandring by the waye.   *knew*
470 Gat-toothed° was she, soothly for to saye.   *gap-toothed*
    Upon an amblere[7] esily she sat,
    Ywimpled° wel, and on hir heed an hat   *veiled*
    As brood as is a bokeler or a targe,[8]
    A foot-mantel° aboute hir hipes large,   *riding skirt*
475 And on hir feet a paire of spores° sharpe.   *spurs*
    In felaweshipe wel coude she laughe and carpe:°   *talk*

9. He saved the money he made during
the plague time.
1. A stimulant. Gold was thought to
have some medicinal properties.
2. Ypres and Ghent ("Gaunt") were
Flemish cloth-making centers.
3. The offering in church, when the congregation brought its gifts forward.
4. Tightly laced.

5. In medieval times, weddings were
performed at the church door.
6. Rome; Boulogne (in France); St.
James (of Compostella) in Galicia
(Spain); Cologne (in Germany): all
sites of shrines much visited by pilgrims.
7. Horse with an easy gait.
8. "Bokeler" and "targe": small shields.

560 A swerd and a bokeler° bar° he by his side.   *shield / bore*
His mouth as greet was as a greet furnais.°   *furnace*
He was a janglere° and a Goliardais,[2]   *chatterer*
And that was most of sinne and harlotries.°   *obscenities*
Wel coude he stelen corn and tollen thries[3]—
565 And yit he hadde a thombe[4] of gold, pardee.°   *by heaven*
A whit cote and a blew hood wered° he.   *wore*
A baggepipe wel coude he blowe and soune,°   *sound*
And therwithal° he broughte us out of towne.   *therewith*

A gentil Manciple[5] was ther of a temple,
570 Of which achatours° mighte take exemple   *buyers of food*
For to been wise in bying of vitaile;°   *victuals*
For wheither that he paide or took by taile,[6]
Algate he waited so in his achat[7]
That he was ay biforn[8] and in good stat.
575 Now is nat that of God a ful fair grace
That swich a lewed° mannes wit shal pace°   *ignorant / surpass*
The wisdom of an heep of lerned men?
Of maistres° hadde he mo than thries ten   *masters*
That weren of lawe expert and curious,°   *cunning*
580 Of whiche ther were a dozeine in that hous
Worthy to been stiwardes of rente° and lond   *income*
Of any lord that is in Engelond,
To make him live by his propre good[9]
In honour dettelees but if[1] he were wood,°   *insane*
585 Or live as scarsly° as him list° desire,   *sparely / it pleases*
And able for to helpen al a shire
In any caas° that mighte falle° or happe,   *event / befall*
And yit this Manciple sette hir aller cappe![2]

The Reeve[3] was a sclendre° colerik man;   *slender*
590 His beerd was shave as neigh° as evere he can;   *close*
His heer was by his eres ful round yshorn;
His top was dokked[4] lik a preest biforn;
Ful longe were his legges and ful lene,
Ylik a staf, ther was no calf yseene.°   *visible*
595 Wel coude he keepe° a gerner° and a binne—   *guard / granary*
Ther was noon auditour coude on him winne.[5]
Wel wiste° he by the droughte and by the rain   *knew*
The yeelding of his seed and of his grain.

2. Goliard, teller of ribald stories.
3. Take toll thrice—i.e., deduct from the grain far more than the lawful percentage.
4. Thumb. The narrator seems to be questioning the validity of the adage that (only) an honest miller has a golden thumb.
5. The Manciple is the steward of a community of lawyers in London (a "temple").
6. By talley, i.e., on credit.
7. Always he was on the watch in his purchasing.

8. I.e., ahead of the game. "Stat": financial condition.
9. His own money.
1. Out of debt unless.
2. This Manciple made fools of them all.
3. The Reeve is the superintendent of a large farming estate; "colerik" (choleric) describes a man whose dominant humor is yellow bile (choler)—i.e., a hot-tempered man.
4. Cut short: the clergy wore the head partially shaved.
5. I.e., find him in default.

And though he holy were and vertuous,
He was to sinful men nought despitous,°   *scornful*
Ne of his speeche daungerous° ne digne,°   *disdainful / haughty*
520 But in his teching discreet and benigne,
To drawen folk to hevene by fairnesse
By good ensample—this was his bisinesse.
But it° were any persone obstinat,   *if there*
What so he were, of heigh or lowe estat,
525 Him wolde he snibben° sharply for the nones:[1]   *scold*
A bettre preest I trowe° ther nowher noon is.   *believe*
He waited after[2] no pompe and reverence,
Ne maked him a spiced conscience,[3]
But Cristes lore° and his Apostles twelve   *teaching*
530 He taughte, but first he folwed it himselve.
     With him ther was a Plowman, was his brother,
That hadde ylad° of dong° ful many a fother.[4]   *carried / dung*
A trewe swinkere° and a good was he,   *worker*
Living in pees° and parfit charitee.   *peace*
535 God loved he best with al his hoole° herte   *whole*
At alle times, though him gamed or smerte,[5]
And thanne his neighebor right as himselve.
He wolde thresshe, and therto dike° and delve,   *dig ditches*
For Cristes sake, for every poore wight,
540 Withouten hire, if it laye in his might.
His tithes payed he ful faire and wel,
Bothe of his propre swink[6] and his catel.°   *property*
In a tabard° he rood upon a mere.°   *short coat / mare*
     Ther was also a Reeve° and a Millere,   *estate manager*
545 A Somnour, and a Pardoner[7] also,
A Manciple,° and myself—ther were namo.   *steward*
     The Millere was a stout carl° for the nones.   *fellow*
Ful big he was of brawn° and eek of bones—   *muscle*
That preved[8] wel, for overal ther he cam
550 At wrastling he wolde have alway the ram.[9]
He was short-shuldred, brood,° a thikke knarre.° *broad / bully*
Ther was no dore that he nolde heve of harre,[1]
Or breke it at a renning° with his heed.°   *running / head*
His beerd as any sowe or fox was reed,°   *red*
555 And therto brood, as though it were a spade;
Upon the cop° right of his nose he hade   *ridge*
A werte,° and theron stood a tuft of heres,   *wart*
Rede as the bristles of a sowes eres;
His nosethirles° blake were and wide.   *nostrils*

---

1. On any occasion.
2. I.e., expected.
3. Nor did he assume an overfastidious
conscience.
4. Load.
5. Whether he was pleased or grieved.
6. His own work.
7. "Somnour" (Summoner): server of

summonses to the ecclesiastical court;
Pardoner: dispenser of papal pardons.
See lines 625 and 671, and notes, below.
8. Proved, i.e., was evident.
9. A ram was frequently offered as the
prize in wrestling.
1. He would not heave off (its) hinge.

And whan that he wel dronken hadde the win,
640 Thanne wolde he speke no word but Latin:
A fewe termes hadde he, two or three,
That he hadde lerned out of som decree;
No wonder is—he herde it al the day,
And eek ye knowe wel that a jay°   *parrot*
645 Can clepen "Watte"[7] as wel as can the Pope—
But whoso coude in other thing him grope,°   *examine*
Thanne hadde he spent all his philosophye;[8]
Ay *Questio quid juris*[9] wolde he crye.

He was a gentil harlot° and a kinde;   *rascal*
650 A bettre felawe sholde men nought finde:
He wolde suffre,° for a quart of win,   *permit*
A good felawe to have his concubin
A twelfmonth, and excusen him at the fulle;[1]
Ful prively a finch eek coude he pulle.[2]
655 And if he foond° owher° a good felawe   *found / anywhere*
He wolde techen him to have noon awe
In swich caas of the Ercedekenes curs,[3]
But if[4] a mannes soule were in his purs,
For in his purs he sholde ypunisshed be.
660 "Purs is the Ercedekenes helle," saide he.
But wel I woot he lied right in deede:
Of cursing° oughte eech gilty man drede,   *excommunication*
For curs wol slee° right as assoiling° savith—   *slay / absolution*
And also war him of a *significavit*.[5]
665 In daunger[6] hadde he at his owene gise°   *disposal*
The yonge girles of the diocise,
And knew hir conseil,° and was al hir reed.[7]   *secrets*
A gerland hadde he set upon his heed
As greet as it were for an ale-stake;[8]
670 A bokeler hadde he maad him of a cake.
With him ther rood a gentil Pardoner[9]
Of Rouncival, his freend and his compeer,°   *comrade*
That straight was comen fro the Court of Rome.
Ful loude he soong,° "Com hider, love, to me."   *sang*
675 This Somnour bar to him a stif burdoun:[1]

7. Call out: "Walter"—like modern parrots' "Polly."
8. I.e., learning.
9. "What point of law does this investigation involve?": a phrase frequently used in ecclesiastical courts.
1. "At the fulle": fully. Ecclesiastical courts had jurisdiction over many offenses which today would come under civil law, including sexual offenses.
2. "To pull a finch" is to have carnal dealings with a woman.
3. Archdeacon's sentence of excommunication.
4. "But if": unless.
5. And also one should be careful of a *significavit* (the writ which transferred the guilty offender from the ecclesiastical to the civil arm for punishment).
6. Under his domination.
7. Was their chief source of advice.
8. A tavern was signalized by a pole ("ale-stake"), rather like a modern flagpole, projecting from its front wall; on this hung a garland, or "bush."
9. A Pardoner dispensed papal pardon for sins to those who contributed to the charitable institution that he was licensed to represent; this Pardoner purported to be collecting for the hospital of Roncesvalles ("Rouncival") in Spain, which had a London branch.
1. I.e., provided him with a strong vocal accompaniment.

His lordes sheep, his neet,° his dayerye,   cattle
600 His swin, his hors, his stoor,° and his pultrye   stock
Was hoolly° in this Reeves governinge,   wholly
And by his covenant yaf⁶ the rekeninge,
Sin° that his lord was twenty yeer of age.   since
There coude no man bringe him in arrerage.⁷
605 Ther nas baillif, hierde, nor other hine,
That he ne knew his sleighte and his covine⁸—
They were adrad° of him as of the deeth.°   afraid / plague
His woning° was ful faire upon an heeth;°   dwelling / meadow
With greene trees shadwed was his place.
610 He coude bettre than his lord purchace.°   acquire goods
Ful riche he was astored° prively.°   stocked / secretly
His lord wel coude he plesen subtilly,
To yive and lene° him of his owene good,°   lend / property
And have a thank, and yit a cote and hood.
615 In youthe he hadde lerned a good mister:°   occupation
He was a wel good wrighte, a carpenter.
This Reeve sat upon a ful good stot°   stallion
That was a pomely° grey and highte° Scot. dapple / was named
A long surcote° of pers° upon he hade,⁹   overcoat / blue
620 And by his side he bar° a rusty blade.   bore
Of Northfolk was this Reeve of which I telle,
Biside a town men clepen Baldeswelle.°   Bawdswell
Tukked¹ he was as is a frere aboute,
And evere he rood the hindreste of oure route.²
625   A Somnour³ was ther with us in that place
That hadde a fir-reed° cherubinnes⁴ face,   fire-red
For saucefleem° he was, with yën narwe,   pimply
And hoot° he was, and lecherous as a sparwe,°   hot / sparrow
With scaled° browes blake and piled⁵ beerd: scabby
630 Of his visage children were aferd.°   afraid
Ther nas quiksilver, litarge, ne brimstoon,
Boras, ceruce, ne oile of tartre noon,⁶
Ne oinement that wolde clense and bite,
That him mighte helpen of his whelkes° white,   blotches
635 Nor of the knobbes° sitting on his cheekes.   lumps
Wel loved he garlek, oinons, and eek leekes,
And for to drinke strong win reed as blood.
Thanne wolde he speke and crye as he were wood;°   mad

6. And according to his contract he gave.
7. Convict him of being in arrears financially.
8. There was no bailiff (i.e., foreman), shepherd, nor other farm laborer whose craftiness and plots he didn't know.
9. "Upon he hade": he had on.
1. With clothing tucked up.
2. Hindmost of our group.
3. The "Somnour" (Summoner) is an employee of the ecclesiastical court, whose defined duty is to bring to court persons whom the archdeacon—the justice of the court—suspects of offenses against canon law. By this time, however, summoners had generally transformed themselves into corrupt detectives who spied out offenders and blackmailed them by threats of summonses.
4. Cherub's, often depicted in art with a red face.
5. Uneven, partly hairless.
6. These are all ointments for diseases affecting the skin, probably diseases of venereal origin.

And if ye vouche sauf that it be so,
810 Telle me anoon, withouten wordes mo,°   *more*
And I wol erly shape me[6] therfore."
    This thing was graunted and oure othes swore
With ful glad herte, and prayden[7] him also
That he wolde vouche sauf for to do so,
815 And that he wolde been oure governour,
And of oure tales juge and reportour,°   *accountant*
And sette a soper at a certain pris,°   *price*
And we wol ruled been at his devis,°   *disposal*
In heigh and lowe; and thus by oon assent
820 We been accorded to his juggement.
And therupon the win was fet° anoon;   *fetched*
We dronken and to reste wente eechoon
Withouten any lenger° taryinge.   *longer*
Amorwe° whan that day bigan to springe   *in the morning*
825 Up roos oure Host and was oure aller cok,[8]
And gadred us togidres in a flok,
And forth we riden, a litel more than pas,°   *a step*
Unto the watering of Saint Thomas;[9]
And ther oure Host bigan his hors arreste,°   *halt*
830 And saide, "Lordes, herkneth if you leste:°   *it please*
Ye woot youre forward° and it you recorde:[1]   *agreement*
If evensong and morwesong° accorde,°   *morningsong / agree*
Lat see now who shal telle the firste tale
As evere mote I drinken win or ale,
835 Who so be rebel to my juggement
Shal paye for al that by the way is spent.
Now draweth cut[2] er that we ferrer twinne:
He which that hath the shorteste shal biginne.
    "Sire Knight," quod he, "my maister and my lord,
840 Now draweth cut, for that is myn accord.°   *will*
Cometh neer," quod he, "my lady Prioresse,
And ye, sire Clerk, lat be youre shamefastnesse°—   *modesty*
Ne studieth nought. Lay hand to, every man!"
    Anoon to drawen every wight bigan,
845 And shortly for to tellen as it was,
Were it by aventure, or sort, or cas,[3]
The soothe° is this, the cut fil° to the Knight;   *truth / fell*
Of which ful blithe and glad was every wight,
And telle he moste° his tale, as was resoun,   *must*
850 By forward and by composicioun,[4]
As ye han herd. What needeth wordes mo?
And whan this goode man sawgh that it was so,
As he that wis was and obedient

6. Prepare myself.
7. I.e., we prayed.
8. Was rooster for us all.
9. A watering place near Southwark.
1. You recall it.

2. I.e., draw lots; "ferrer twinne": go
farther.
3. Whether it was luck, fate, or chance.
4. By agreement and compact.

And saide thus, "Now, lordinges, trewely,
Ye been to me right welcome, hertely.°   *heartily*
765 For by my trouthe, if that I shal nat lie,
I sawgh nat this yeer so merye a compaignye
At ones in this herberwe° as is now.   *inn*
Fain° wolde I doon you mirthe, wiste I⁸ how.   *gladly*
And of a mirthe I am right now bithought,
770 To doon you ese, and it shal coste nought.
     "Ye goon to Canterbury—God you speede;
The blisful martyr quite you youre meede.⁹
And wel I woot as ye goon by the waye
Ye shapen you¹ to talen° and to playe,   *converse*
775 For trewely, confort ne mirthe is noon
To ride by the waye domb as stoon;°   *stone*
And therfore wol I maken you disport
As I saide erst,° and doon you som confort;   *before*
And if you liketh alle, by oon assent,
780 For to stonden at² my juggement,
And for to werken as I shal you saye,
Tomorwe whan ye riden by the waye—
Now by my fader° soule that is deed,   *father's*
But° ye be merye I wol yive you myn heed!°   *unless / head*
785 Holde up youre handes withouten more speeche."
     Oure counseil was nat longe for to seeche;°   *seek*
Us thoughte it was nat worth to make it wis,³
And graunted him withouten more avis,°   *deliberation*
And bade him saye his voirdit° as him leste.⁴   *verdict*
790 "Lordinges," quod he, "now herkneth for the beste;
But taketh it nought, I praye you, in desdain.
This is the point, to speken short and plain,
That eech of you, to shorte with oure waye
In this viage, shal tellen tales twaye°—   *two*
795 To Canterburyward, I mene it so,
And hoomward he shal tellen othere two,
Of aventures that whilom° have bifalle;   *once upon a time*
And which of you that bereth him best of alle—
That is to sayn, that telleth in this cas
800 Tales of best sentence° and most solas°—   *purport / delight*
Shal have a soper at oure aller cost,⁵
Here in this place, sitting by this post,
Whan that we come again fro Canterbury.
And for to make you the more mury°   *merry*
805 I wol myself goodly° with you ride—   *kindly*
Right at myn owene cost—and be youre gide.
And who so wol my juggement withsaye°   *contradict*
Shal paye al that we spende by the waye.

8. If I knew.
9. Pay you your reward.
1. "Shapen you": intend.
2. Abide by.

3. We didn't think it worthwhile to make it an issue of it.
4. It pleased.
5. At the cost of us all.

Why that assembled was this compaignye
720 In Southwerk at this gentil hostelrye
That highte the Tabard, faste° by the Belle;[8]   close
But now is time to you for to telle
How that we baren us[9] that ilke° night   same
Whan we were in that hostelrye alight;
725 And after wol I telle of oure viage,°   trip
And al the remenant of oure pilgrimage.
But first I praye you of youre curteisye
That ye n'arette it nought my vilainye[1]
Though that I plainly speke in this matere
730 To telle you hir wordes and hir cheere,°   behavior
Ne though I speke hir wordes proprely;°   accurately
For this ye knowen also wel as I:
Who so shal telle a tale after a man
He moot° reherce,° as neigh as evere he can,   nust / repeat
735 Everich a word, if it be in his charge,°   responsibility
Al speke he[2] nevere so rudeliche and large,°   broadly
Or elles he moot telle his tale untrewe,
Or feine° thing, or finde° wordes newe;   falsify / devise
He may nought spare[3] although he were his brother:
740 He moot as wel saye oo word as another.
Crist spak himself ful brode° in Holy Writ,   broadly
And wel ye woot no vilainye is it;
Eek Plato saith, who so can him rede,
The wordes mote be cosin to the deede.
745   Also I praye you to foryive it me
Al° have I nat set folk in hir degree   although
Here in this tale as that they sholde stonde:
My wit is short, ye may wel understonde.
    Greet cheere made oure Host[4] us everichoon;
750 And to the soper sette he us anoon.°   at once
He served us with vitaile° at the beste.   food
Strong was the win, and wel to drinke us leste.°   it pleased
A semely man oure Hoste was withalle
For to been a marchal[5] in an halle;
755 A large man he was, with yën steepe,°   prominent
A fairer burgeis° was ther noon in Chepe[6]—   burgher
Bold of his speeche, and wis, and wel ytaught,
And of manhood him lakkede right naught.
Eek therto he was right a merye man,
760 And after soper playen he bigan,
And spak of mirthe amonges othere thinges—
Whan that we hadde maad oure rekeninges[7]—

8. Another tavern in Southwark.
9. Bore ourselves.
1. That you do not charge it to my lack of decorum.
2. Although he speak.
3. I.e., spare anyone.
4. The Host is the landlord of the Tabard Inn.
5. Marshal, one who was in charge of feasts.
6. Cheapside, bourgeois center of London.
7. Had paid our bills.

Was nevere trompe° of half so greet a soun.   *trumpet*
   This Pardoner hadde heer as yelow as wex,
But smoothe it heeng° as dooth a strike° of
   flex;°   *hung / hank / flax*
By ounces² heenge his lokkes that he hadde,
680 And therwith he his shuldres overspradde,°   *overspread*
But thinne it lay, by colpons,° oon by oon;   *strands*
But hood for jolitee° wered° he noon,   *nonchalance / wore*
For it was trussed up in his walet:°   *pack*
Him thoughte he rood al of the newe jet.°   *fashion*
685 Dischevelee° save his cappe he rood al bare.   *with hair down*
Swiche glaring yën hadde he as an hare.
A vernicle³ hadde he sowed upon his cappe,
His walet biforn him in his lappe,
Bretful° of pardon, comen from Rome al hoot.°   *brimful / hot*
690 A vois he hadde as smal° as hath a goot;°   *fine / goat*
No beerd hadde he, ne nevere sholde have;
As smoothe it was as it were late yshave:
I trowe° he were a gelding or a mare.   *believe*
But of his craft, fro Berwik into Ware;⁴
695 Ne was ther swich another pardoner;
For in his male° he hadde a pilwe-beer°   *bag / pillowcase*
Which that he saide was Oure Lady veil;
He saide he hadde a gobet° of the sail   *piece*
That Sainte Peter hadde whan that he wente
700 Upon the see, til Jesu Crist him hente.°   *seized*
He hadde a crois° of laton,° ful of stones,   *cross / brassy metal*
And in a glas he hadde pigges bones,
But with thise relikes⁵ whan that he foond°   *found*
A poore person° dwelling upon lond,⁶   *parson*
705 Upon° a day he gat° him more moneye   *in / got*
Than that the person gat in monthes twaye;
And thus with feined° flaterye and japes°   *false / tricks*
He made the person and the peple his apes.°   *dupes*
But trewely to tellen at the laste,
710 He was in chirche a noble ecclesiaste;
Wel coude he rede a lesson and a storye,°   *liturgical narrative*
But alderbest° he soong an offertorye,   *best of all*
For wel he wiste° whan that song was songe,   *knew*
He moste° preche and wel affile° his tonge   *must / sharpen*
715 To winne silver, as he ful wel coude—
Therfore he soong the merierly° and loude.   *more merrily*
   Now have I told you soothly in a clause⁷
Th'estaat, th'array, the nombre, and eek the cause

---

2. I.e., thin strands.
3. Portrait of Christ's face as it was said to have been impressed on St. Veronica's handkerchief.
4. Probably towns south and north of London.

5. Relics—i.e., the pigs' bones which the Pardoner represented as saints' bones.
6. "Upon lond": upcountry.
7. I.e., in a short space.

To keepe his forward by his free assent,
855 He saide, "Sin I shal biginne the game,
What, welcome be the cut, in Goddes name!
Now lat us ride, and herkneth what I saye."
And with that word we riden forth oure waye,
And he bigan with right a merye cheere°   countenance
860 His tale anoon, and saide as ye heere.

The Wife of Bath's Prologue and Tale

The Prologue [1]

Experience, though noon auctoritee
Were in this world, is right ynough for me
To speke of wo that is in mariage:
For lordinges,° sith I twelf yeer was of age—   gentlemen
5 Thanked be God that is eterne on live—
Housbondes at chirche dore[2] I have had five
(If I so ofte mighte han wedded be),
And alle were worthy men in hir degree.
But me was told, certain, nat longe agoon is,
10 That sith that Crist ne wente nevere but ones

1. The Wife of Bath is the remarkable culmination of many centuries of an antifeminism that was particularly nurtured by the medieval church. In their eagerness to exalt the spiritual ideal of chastity, certain theologians developed an idea of womankind that was nothing less than monstrous. According to these, insatiable lecherousness and indomitable shrewishness (plus a host of attendant vices) were characteristic of women. This notion was given most eloquent expression by St. Jerome in his attack (written about A.D. 400) on the monk Jovinian, who had uttered some good words for matrimony, and it is Jerome that the Wife of Bath comes forward not, curiously enough, to refute, but to confirm. The first part of her Prologue is a mass of quotations from that part of Jerome's tract where he is appealing to St. Paul's Epistle (I Corinthians vii) for antimatrimonial authority. On the narrow issue of her right to remarry, to be sure, the Wife finds fault—rather mildly—with Jerome, but on the more central issue of why she wishes to marry and remarry she expresses no disagreement with him. Yet in the failure to defend herself and refute the saint, she somehow manages to make the latter's point of view look a good deal sillier than she looks herself; and instead of embodying the satire on womanhood that one would ex-

pect because of her origins in antifeminist literature, she becomes instead a satirist of the grotesquely woman-hating men who had first defined her personality.

More important, because of the extraordinary vitality that Chaucer has imparted to her, the Wife of Bath by the end of her Prologue comes to bear a less significant relation to satire than she does to reality itself. Making the best of the world in which they have arbitrarily been placed is the occupation of both the Wife of Bath and the reader, and it is in doing this that the Wife ceases to be a monstrosity of fiction and becomes alive—wonderfully alive, both to the potentialities of which she and her world are capable and to the limitations that even in her world time and age place upon her. It is especially in the attitude with which she regards these limitations that her fiction becomes most true to life, since they are also the limitations imposed by the real world. Despite the loss of youth and beauty, her best weapons, she faces her future not only with a woman's ability to endure and enjoy what she cannot reshape, but also with a zest for life on its own terms that is almost more than human.
2. The actual wedding ceremony was celebrated at the church door, not in the chancel.

To wedding in the Cane[3] of Galilee,
That by the same ensample° taughte he me   *example*
That I ne sholde wedded be but ones.
Herke eek,° lo, which° a sharp word for the nones,[4] *also / what*
15 Biside a welle, Jesus, God and man,
Spak in repreve° of the Samaritan: *reproof*
"Thou hast yhad five housbondes," quod he,
"And that ilke° man that now hath thee   *same*
Is nat thyn housbonde." Thus saide he certain.
20 What that he mente therby I can nat sayn,
But that I axe° why the fifthe man   *ask*
Was noon housbonde to the Samaritan?[5]
How manye mighte she han in mariage?
Yit herde I nevere tellen in myn age
25 Upon this nombre diffinicioun.°   *definition*
Men may divine° and glosen° up and down,   *guess / interpret*
But wel I woot,° expres,° withouten lie,   *know / expressly*
God bad us for to wexe[6] and multiplye:
That gentil text can I wel understonde.
30   Eek wel I woot° he saide that myn housbonde   *know*
Sholde lete° fader and moder and take to me,[7]   *leave*
But of no nombre mencion made he—
Of bigamye or of octogamye:[8]
Why sholde men thanne speke of it vilainye?
35   Lo, here the wise king daun° Salomon: *master*
I trowe° he hadde wives many oon,[9]   *believe*
As wolde God it leveful° were to me   *permissible*
To be refresshed half so ofte as he.
Which yifte[1] of God hadde he for alle his wives!
40 No man hath swich that in this world alive is.
God woot this noble king, as to my wit,°   *knowledge*
The firste night hadde many a merye fit°   *bout*
With eech of hem, so wel was him on live.[2]
Blessed be God that I have wedded five,
45 Of whiche I have piked out the beste,[3]
Bothe of hir nether° purs and of hir cheste.° *lower / moneybox*
Diverse scoles maken parfit° clerkes,   *perfect*
And diverse practikes[4] in sondry werkes
Maken the werkman parfit sikerly:°   *certainly*
50 Of five housbondes scoleying° am I.   *schooling*
Welcome the sixte whan that evere he shal![5]

3. Cana (see John ii.1).
4. To the purpose.
5. Christ was actually referring to a sixth man who was not married to the Samaritan woman (cf. John iv.6 ff.).
6. I.e., increase. See Genesis i.28.
7. See Matthew xix.5.
8. I.e., of two or even eight marriages. The Wife is referring to successive, rather than simultaneous marriages.
9. Solomon had 700 wives and 300 concubines (I Kings xi.3).
1. What a gift.
2. I.e., so pleasant a life he had.
3. Whom I have cleaned out of everything worthwhile.
4. Practical experiences.
5. I.e., shall come along.

For sith I wol nat kepe me chast in al,
Whan my housbonde is fro the world agoon,
Som Cristen man shal wedde me anoon.°   *right away*
55 For thanne th'Apostle[6] saith that I am free
To wedde, a Goddes half,[7] where it liketh me.
He said that to be wedded is no sinne:
Bet° is to be wedded than to brinne.°   *better / burn*
What rekketh me[8] though folk saye vilainye
60 Of shrewed° Lamech[9] and his bigamye?   *cursed*
I woot wel Abraham was an holy man,
And Jacob eek, as fer as evere I can,°   *know*
And eech of hem hadde wives mo than two,
And many another holy man also.
65   Where can ye saye in any manere age
That hye God defended° mariage   *prohibited*
By expres word? I praye you, telleth me.
Or where comanded he virginitee?
I woot as wel as ye, it is no drede,°   *doubt*
70 Th'Apostle, whan he speketh of maidenhede,°   *maidenhood*
He saide that precept therof hadde he noon:
Men may conseile a womman to be oon,°   *single*
But conseiling nis no comandement.
He putte it in oure owene juggement.
75 For hadde God comanded maidenhede,
Thanne hadde he dampned° wedding with the
    deede;[1]   *condemned*
And certes, if there were no seed ysowe,
Virginitee, thanne wherof sholde it growe?
Paul dorste nat comanden at the leeste
80 A thing of which his maister yaf° no heeste.°   *gave / command*
The dart[2] is set up for virginitee:
Cacche whoso may, who renneth° best lat see.   *runs*
But this word is nought take of[3] every wight,
But ther as[4] God list° yive it of his might.   *it pleases*
85 I woot wel that th'Apostle was a maide,°   *virgin*
But nathelees, though that he wroot and saide
He wolde that every wight were swich° as he,   *such*
Al nis but conseil to virginitee;
And for to been a wif he yaf me leve
90 Of indulgence; so nis it no repreve°   *disgrace*
To wedde me[5] if that my make° die,   *mate*
Withouten excepcion of bigamye[6]—

---

6. St. Paul.
7. On God's behalf; "it liketh me": I please.
8. What do I care.
9. The first man whom the Bible mentions as having two wives (Genesis iv.19–24).

1. i.e., at the same time.
2. I.e., prize in a race.
3. Understood for, i.e., applicable to.
4. Where.
5. For me to marry.
6. I.e., without there being any legal objection on the score of remarriage.

Al° were it good no womman for to touche   *although*
(He mente as in his bed or in his couche,
95 For peril is bothe fir° and tow° t'assemble—   *fire / flax*
Ye knowe what this ensample may resemble).[7]
This al and som,[8] he heeld virginitee
More parfit than wedding in freletee.°   *frailty*
(Freletee clepe I but if[9] that he and she
100 Wolde leden al hir lif in chastitee.)
I graunte it wel, I have noon envye
Though maidenhede preferre° bigamye:°   *excel / remarriage*
It liketh hem to be clene in body and gost.°   *spirit*
Of myn estaat ne wol I make no boost;
105 For wel ye knowe, a lord in his houshold
Ne hath nat every vessel al of gold:
Some been of tree,° and doon hir lord servise.   *wood*
God clepeth folk to him in sondry wise,
And everich hath of God a propre[1] yifte,
110 Som this, som that, as him liketh shifte.°   *ordain*
Virginitee is greet perfeccioun,
And continence eek with devocioun,
But Crist, that of perfeccion is welle,°   *source*
Bad nat every wight he sholde go selle
115 Al that he hadde and yive it to the poore,
And in swich wise folwe him and his fore:[2]
He spak to hem that wolde live parfitly°—   *perfectly*
And lordinges, by youre leve, that am nat I.
I wol bistowe the flour of al myn age
120 In th'actes and in fruit of mariage.
    Telle me also, to what conclusioun°   *end*
Were membres maad of generacioun
And of so parfit wis a wrighte ywrought?[3]
Trusteth right wel, they were nat maad for nought.
125 Glose° whoso wol, and saye bothe up and down   *interpret*
That they were maked for purgacioun
Of urine, and oure bothe thinges smale
Was eek to knowe a femele from a male,
And for noon other cause—saye ye no?
130 Th'experience woot it is nought so.
So that the clerkes be nat with me wrothe,
I saye this, that they been maad for bothe—
That is to sayn, for office° and for ese   *excretion*
Of engendrure, ther we nat God displese.
135 Why sholde men elles in hir bookes sette
That man shal yeelde[4] to his wif hir dette?

---

7. I.e., what this metaphor may apply to.
8. This is all there is to it.
9. Frailty I call it unless.
1. I.e., his own.

2. Matthew xix.21. "Fore": footsteps.
3. And wrought by so perfectly wise a maker.
4. I.e., pay.

Now wherwith sholde he make his payement
If he ne used his sely° instrument?   *innocent*
Thanne were they maad upon a creature
140 To purge urine, and eek for engendrure.
    But I saye nought that every wight is holde,°   *bound*
That hath swich harneis° as I to you tolde,   *equipment*
To goon and usen hem in engendrure:
Thanne sholde men take of chastitee no cure.°   *heed*
145 Crist was a maide° and shapen as a man,   *virgin*
And many a saint sith that the world bigan,
Yit lived they evere in parfit chastitee.
I nil envye no virginitee:
Lat hem be breed° of pured° whete seed,   *bread / refined*
150 And lat us wives hote° barly breed—   *be called*
And yit with barly breed, Mark telle can,
Oure Lord Jesu refresshed many a man.[5]
In swich estaat as God hath cleped us
I wol persevere: I nam nat precious.°   *fastidious*
155 In wifhood wol I use myn instrument
As freely° as my Makere hath it sent.   *generously*
If I be daungerous,° God yive me sorwe: *stand-offish*
Myn housbonde shal it han bothe eve and morwe,°   *morning*
Whan that him list[6] come forth and paye his dette.
160 An housbonde wol I have, I wol nat lette,[7]
Which shal be bothe my dettour° and my thral,°   *debtor / slave*
And have his tribulacion withal
Upon his flessh whil that I am his wif.
I have the power during al my lif
165 Upon his propre° body, and nat he: *own*
Right thus th'Apostle tolde it unto me,
And bad oure housbondes for to love us weel.
Al this sentence° me liketh everydeel.°   *purport / entirely*

[AN INTERLUDE]

    Up sterte° the Pardoner and that anoon: *started*
170 "Now dame," quod he, "by God and by Saint John,
Ye been a noble prechour in this cas.
I was aboute to wedde a wif: allas,
What° sholde I bye° it on my flessh so dere?   *why / purchase*
Yit hadde I levere wedde no wif toyere."°   *this year*
175   "Abid," quod she, "my tale is nat bigonne.
Nay, thou shalt drinken of another tonne,°   *tun*
Er that I go, shal savoure wors than ale.
And whan that I have told thee forth my tale
Of tribulacion in mariage,
180 Of which I am expert in al myn age—

5. In the descriptions of the miracle of the loaves and fishes, it is actually John, not Mark, who mentions barley bread (vi.9).
6. When he wishes to.
7. I will make no difficulty.

This is to saye, myself hath been the whippe—
Thanne maistou chese° wheither thou wolt sippe   *choose*
Of thilke° tonne that I shal abroche:°   *this same / broach*
Be war of it, er thou too neigh approche,
185 For I shal telle ensamples mo than ten.
'Whoso that nile° be war by othere men,   *would not*
By him shal othere men corrected be.'
Thise same wordes writeth Ptolomee:
Rede in his *Almageste* and take it there."[8]
190 "Dame, I wolde praye you if youre wil it were,"
Saide this Pardoner, "as ye bigan,
Telle forth youre tale; spareth for no man,
And teche us yonge men of youre practike."°   *mode of operation*
 "Gladly," quod she, "sith it may you like;°   *please*
195 But that I praye to al this compaignye,
If that I speke after my fantasye,[9]
As taketh nat agrief° of that I saye,   *amiss*
For myn entente nis but for to playe."

    [THE WIFE CONTINUES]

 Now sire, thanne wol I telle you forth my tale.
200 As evere mote I drinke win or ale,
I shal saye sooth: tho° housbondes that I hadde,   *those*
As three of hem were goode, and two were badde.
The three men were goode, and riche, and olde;
Unnethe° mighte they the statut holde   *with difficulty*
205 In which they were bounden unto me—
Ye woot wel what I mene of this, pardee.
As help me God, I laughe whan I thinke
How pitously anight I made hem swinke;°   *work*
And by my fay,° I tolde of it no stoor:[1]   *faith*
210 They hadde me yiven hir land and hir tresor;
Me needed nat do lenger diligence
To winne hir love or doon hem reverence.
They loved me so wel, by God above,
That I ne tolde no daintee of[2] hir love.
215 A wis womman wol bisye hire evere in oon[3]
To gete hire love, ye, ther as she hath noon.
But sith I hadde hem hoolly in myn hand,
And sith that they hadde yiven me al hir land,
What° sholde I take keep° hem for to plese,   *why / care*
220 But it were for my profit and myn ese?
I sette hem so awerke,° by my fay,°   *awork / faith*
That many a night they songen° wailaway.   *sang*

8. The *Almagest*, an astronomical work
by the Greek astronomer and mathematician Ptolemy (second century A.D.),
contains no such aphorism. The aphorism does, however, appear in a collection
ascribed to him.
9. If I speak according to my whim.
1. I set no store by it.
2. Set no value on.
3. Busy herself constantly.

The bacon was nat fet° for hem, I trowe, *brought back*
That some men han in Essexe at Dunmowe.⁴
225 I governed hem so wel after° my lawe *according to*
That eech of hem ful blisful was and fawe° *glad*
To bringe me gaye thinges fro the faire;
They were ful glade whan I spak hem faire,
For God it woot, I chidde° hem spitously.° *chided / cruelly*
230 Now herkneth how I bar me⁵ properly:
Ye wise wives, that conne understonde,
Thus sholde ye speke and bere him wrong on honde⁶—
For half so boldely can ther no man
Swere and lie as a woman can.
235 I saye nat this by wives that been wise,
But if it be whan they hem misavise.⁷
A wis wif, if that she can hir good,⁸
Shal bere him on hande the cow is wood,⁹
And take witnesse of hir owene maide
240 Of hir assent.¹ But herkneth how I saide:
 "Sire olde cainard,° is this thyn array?² *sluggard*
Why is my neighebores wif so gay?
She is honoured overal ther she gooth:
I sitte at hoom; I have no thrifty° cloth. *decent*
245 What doostou at my neighebores hous?
Is she so fair? Artou so amorous?
What roune° ye with oure maide, benedicite?³ *whisper*
Sire olde lechour, lat thy japes° be. *tricks, intrigues*
And if I have a gossib° or a freend, *confidant*
250 Withouten gilt ye chiden as a feend,
If that I walke or playe unto his hous.
Thou comest hoom as dronken as a mous,
And prechest on thy bench, with yvel preef.⁴
Thou saist to me, it is a greet meschief° *misfortune*
255 To wedde a poore womman for costage.⁵
And if that she be riche, of heigh parage,° *descent*
Thanne saistou that it is a tormentrye
To suffre hir pride and hir malencolye.
And if that she be fair, thou verray knave,
260 Thou saist that every holour° wol hire have: *whoremonger*
She may no while in chastitee abide
That is assailed upon eech a side.
 "Thou saist som folk desiren us for richesse,

---

4. The Dunmow flitch was awarded to the couple who after a year of marriage could claim no quarrels, no regrets, and the desire, if freed, to remarry one another.
5. Bore myself, behaved.
6. Accuse him falsely.
7. When they make a mistake.
8. If she knows what's good for her.
9. Shall persuade him the chough has gone crazy. The chough, or jackdaw, was popularly supposed to tell husbands of their wives' infidelity.
1. And call as a witness her maid, who is on her side.
2. I.e., is this how you behave?
3. Bless me.
4. I.e., (may you have) bad luck.
5. Because of the expense.

Som[6] for oure shap, and som for oure fairnesse,
265 And som for she can outher° singe or daunce,   *either*
And som for gentilesse and daliaunce,°   *flirtatiousness*
Som for hir handes and hir armes smale°—   *slender*
Thus gooth al to the devel by thy tale![7]
Thou saist men may nat keepe[8] a castel wal,
270 It may so longe assailed been overal.°   *everywhere*
And if that she be foul, thou saist that she
Coveiteth° every man that she may see;   *desires*
For as a spaniel she wol on him lepe,
Til that she finde som man hire to chepe.°   *buy*
275 Ne noon so grey goos gooth ther in the lake,
As, saistou, wol be withoute make;°   *mate*
And saist it is an hard thing for to weelde°   *possess*
A thing that no man wol, his thankes, heelde.[9]
Thus saistou, lorel,° whan thou goost to bedde,   *loafer*
280 And that no wis man needeth for to wedde,
Ne no man that entendeth° unto hevene—   *aims*
With wilde thonder-dint[1] and firy levene
Mote thy welked nekke be tobroke![2]
Thou saist that dropping° houses and eek smoke   *leaking*
285 And chiding wives maken men to flee
Out of hir owene hous: a, benedicite,
What aileth swich an old man for to chide?
Thou saist we wives wil oure vices hide
Til we be fast,[3] and thanne we wol hem shewe—
290 Wel may that be a proverbe of a shrewe!°   *villain*
Thou saist that oxen, asses, hors,° and houndes,   *horses*
They been assayed at diverse stoundes;°   *times*
Bacins, lavours,° er that men hem bye,   *washbowls*
Spoones, stooles, and al swich housbondrye,°   *household goods*
295 And so be° pottes, clothes, and array°—   *are / clothing*
But folk of wives maken noon assay
Til they be wedded—olde dotard shrewe!
And thanne, saistou, we wil oure vices shewe.
Thou saist also that it displeseth me
300 But if that thou wolt praise my beautee,
And but thou poure alway upon my face,
And clepe me 'Faire Dame' in every place,
And but thou make a feeste on thilke day
That I was born, and make me fressh and gay,
305 And but thou do to my norice° honour,   *nurse*
And to my chamberere within my bowr,[4]
And to my fadres folk, and his allies[5]—

6. "Som," in this and the following lines, means "one."
7. I.e., according to your story.
8. I.e., keep safe.
9. No man would willingly hold.
1. Thunderbolt; "levene": lightning.
2. May thy withered neck be broken!
3. I.e., married.
4. And to my chambermaid within my bedroom.
5. Relatives by marriage.

Thus saistou, olde barel-ful of lies.
And yit of our apprentice Janekin,
310 For his crispe° heer, shining as gold so fin,   *curly*
And for he squiereth me bothe up and down,
Yit hastou caught a fals suspecioun;
I wil° him nat though thou were deed° tomorwe.   *want / dead*
   "But tel me this, why hidestou with sorwe⁶
315 The keyes of thy cheste away fro me?
It is my good° as wel as thyn, pardee.   *property*
What, weenestou° make an idiot of oure dame?   *do you think to*
Now by that lord that called is Saint Jame,
Thou shalt nought bothe, though thou were wood,°   *furious*
320 Be maister of my body and of my good:
That oon thou shalt forgo, maugree thine yën.⁷
   "What helpeth it of me enquere° and spyen?   *inquire*
I trowe thou woldest loke° me in thy cheste.   *lock*
Thou sholdest saye, 'Wif, go wher thee leste.°   *it may please*
325 Taak youre disport. I nil leve° no tales: *believe*
I knowe you for a trewe wif, dame Alis.'
We love no man that taketh keep or charge⁸
Wher that we goon: we wol been at oure large.⁹
Of alle men yblessed mote he be
330 The wise astrologen° daun Ptolomee,   *astronomer*
That saith this proverbe in his *Almageste*:
'Of alle men his wisdom is the hyeste
That rekketh° nat who hath the world in honde.'   *cares*
By this proverbe thou shalt understonde,
335 Have thou¹ ynough, what thar° thee rekke or care   *need*
How merily that othere folkes fare?
For certes, olde dotard, by youre leve,
Ye shal han queinte° right ynough at eve: *pudendum*
He is too greet a nigard that wil werne°   *refuse*
340 A man to lighte a candle at his lanterne;
He shal han nevere the lasse° lighte, pardee.   *less*
Have thou ynough, thee thar nat plaine thee.²
   "Thou saist also that if we make us gay
With clothing and with precious array,
345 That it is peril of oure chastitee,
And yit with sorwe thou moste enforce thee,³
And saye thise wordes in th'Apostles name:
'In habit° maad with chastitee and shame   *clothing*
Ye wommen shal apparaile you,' quod he,
350 'And nat in tressed heer⁴ and gay perree,°   *jewelry*
As perles ne with gold ne clothes riche.'⁵
After thy text, ne after thy rubriche,⁶

6. I.e., with sorrow to you.
7. Despite your eyes—i.e., despite anything you can do about it.
8. Notice or interest.
9. I.e., liberty.
1. If you have.

2. I.e., you need not complain.
3. Strengthen your position.
4. I.e., elaborate hairdo.
5. See I Timothy ii.9.
6. Rubric, i.e., direction.

I wol nat werke as muchel as a gnat.
Thou saidest this, that I was lik a cat:
355 For whoso wolde senge° a cattes skin,　　　　　　　　*singe*
Thanne wolde the cat wel dwellen in his in;°　　　　*lodging*
And if the cattes skin be slik° and gay,　　　　　　*sleek*
She wol nat dwelle in house half a day,
But forth she wol, er any day be dawed,[7]
360 To shewe her skin and goon a-caterwawed.°　　　　*caterwauling*
This is to saye, if I be gay, sire shrewe,
I wol renne° out, my borel° for to shewe.　　　　*run / clothing*
Sire olde fool, what helpeth[8] thee t'espyen?
Though thou praye Argus with his hundred yën
365 To be my wardecors,° as he can best,　　　　　　*bodyguard*
In faith, he shal nat keepe° me but me lest:[9]　　　*guard*
Yit coude I make his beerd,[1] so mote I thee.°　　　*thrive*
　　"Thou saidest eek that ther been thinges three,
The whiche thinges troublen al this erthe,
370 And that no wight may endure the ferthe.°　　　　*fourth*
O leve° sire shrewe, Jesu shorte° thy lif!　　　　*dear / shorten*
Yit prechestou and saist an hateful wif
Yrekened is for oon of thise meschaunces.
Been ther nat none othere resemblaunces
375 That ye may likne youre parables to,[2]
But if[3] a sely° wif be oon of tho?　　　　　　　*innocent*
　　"Thou liknest eek wommanes love to helle,
To bareine° land ther water may nat dwelle;　　　　*barren*
Thou liknest it also to wilde fir—
380 The more it brenneth,° the more it hath desir　　　*burns*
To consumen every thing that brent° wol be;　　　　*burned*
Thou saist right° as wormes shende° a tree,　　*just / destroy*
Right so a wif destroyeth hir housbonde—
This knowen they that been to wives bonde."°　　　　*bound*
385 　　Lordinges, right thus, as ye han understonde,
Bar I stifly mine olde housbondes on honde[4]
That thus they saiden in hir dronkenesse—
And al was fals, but that I took witnesse
On Janekin and on my nece also.
390 O Lord, the paine I dide hem and the wo,
Ful giltelees, by Goddes sweete pine!°　　　　　　*suffering*
For as an hors I coude bite and whine;°　　　　　　*whinny*
I coude plaine° and° I was in the gilt,　　　　*complain / if*
Or elles often time I hadde been spilt.°　　　　　*ruined*
395 Whoso that first to mille comth first grint.°　　　*grinds*

---

7. Has dawned.
8. What does it help.
9. Unless I please.
1. I.e., deceive him.
2. Isn't there something else appropriate that you can apply your metaphors to?
3. Unless.
4. I rigorously accused my old husbands.

I plained first: so was oure werre stint.[5]
They were ful glade to excusen hem ful blive°   *quickly*
Of thing of which they nevere agilte hir live.[6]
Of wenches wolde I beren hem on honde,
400 Whan that for sik[7] they mighte unnethe° stonde,   *scarcely*
Yit tikled I his herte for that he
Wende° I hadde had of him so greet cheertee.[8]   *thought*
I swoor that al my walking out by nighte
Was for to espye wenches that he dighte.[9]
405 Under that colour[1] hadde I many a mirthe.
For al swich wit is yiven us in oure birthe:
Deceite, weeping, spinning God hath yive
To wommen kindely° whil they may live.   *naturally*
And thus of oo thing I avaunte me:[2]
410 At ende I hadde the bet° in eech degree,   *better*
By sleighte or force, or by som manere thing,
As by continuel murmur° or grucching;°   *complaint / grumbling*
Namely° abedde hadden they meschaunce: *especially*
Ther wolde I chide and do hem no plesaunce;[3]
415 I wolde no lenger in the bed abide
If that I felte his arm over my side,
Til he hadde maad his raunson° unto me;   *ransom*
Thanne wolde I suffre him do his nicetee.°   *lust*
And therfore every man this tale I telle:
420 Winne whoso may, for al is for to selle;
With empty hand men may no hawkes lure.
For winning° wolde I al his lust endure,   *profit*
And make me a feined appetit—
And yit in bacon[4] hadde I nevere delit.
425 That made me that evere I wolde hem chide;
For though the Pope hadde seten° hem biside,   *sat*
I wolde nought spare hem at hir owene boord.
For by my trouthe, I quitte° hem word for word.   *repaid*
As help me verray God omnipotent,
430 Though I right now sholde make my testament,
I ne owe hem nat a word that it nis quit.
I broughte it so aboute by my wit
That they moste yive it up as for the beste,
Or elles hadde we nevere been in reste;
435 For though he looked as a wood° leoun,   *furious*
Yit sholde he faile of his conclusioun.°   *object*
    Thanne wolde I saye, "Goodelief, taak keep,[5]
How mekely looketh Wilekin, oure sheep!

5. Our war brought to an end.
6. Of a thing in which they never offended in their lives.
7. I.e., sickness.
8. Affection.
9. Had intercourse with.

1. I.e., excuse.
2. Boast.
3. Show them no affection.
4. I.e., old meat.
5. Good friend, take notice.

Com neer my spouse, lat me ba° thy cheeke——   *kiss*
440 Ye sholden be al pacient and meeke,
And han a sweete-spiced⁶ conscience,
Sith ye so preche of Jobes pacience;
Suffreth alway, sin ye so wel can preche;
And but ye do, certain, we shal you teche
445 That it is fair to han a wif in pees.
Oon of us two moste bowen, doutelees,
And sith a man is more resonable
Than womman is, ye mosten been suffrable.°   *patient*
What aileth you to grucche° thus and grone?   *grumble*
450 Is it for ye wolde have my queinte° allone?   *pudendum*
Why, taak it al—lo, have it everydeel.°   *altogether*
Peter, I shrewe° you but ye love it weel.   *curse*
For if I wolde selle my bele chose,⁷
I coude walke as fressh as is a rose;
455 But I wol keepe it for youre owene tooth.°   *taste*
Ye be to blame. By God, I saye you sooth!"
Swiche manere° wordes hadde we on honde.   *kind of*
Now wol I speke of my ferthe° housbonde.   *fourth*
    My ferthe housbonde was a revelour—
460 This is to sayn, he hadde a paramour°——   *mistress*
And I was yong and ful of ragerye,°   *wantonness*
Stibourne° and strong and joly as a pie:°   *untamable / magpie*
How coude I daunce to an harpe smale,°   *gracefully*
And singe, ywis,° as any nightingale,   *indeed*
465 Whan I hadde dronke a draughte of sweete win.
Metellius, the foule cherl, the swin,
That with a staf birafte° his wif hir lif   *deprived*
For° she drank win, though I hadde been his wif,   *because*
Ne sholde nat han daunted me fro drinke;
470 And after win on Venus moste° I thinke,   *must*
For also siker° as cold engendreth hail,   *sure*
A likerous° mouth moste han a likerous° tail: *greedy / lecherous*
In womman vinolent° is no defence——   *bibulous*
This knowen lechours by experience.
475   But Lord Crist, whan that it remembreth me⁸
Upon my youthe and on my jolitee,
It tikleth me aboute myn herte roote——
Unto this day it dooth myn herte boote°   *good*
That I have had my world as in my time.
480 But age, allas, that al wol envenime,°   *poison*
Hath me biraft⁹ my beautee and my pith——
Lat go, farewel, the devel go therwith!
The flour is goon, ther is namore to telle:
The bren° as I best can now moste I selle;   *husks*
485 But yit to be right merye wol I fonde.°   *strive*

6. I.e., delicate.   8. When I look back.
7. Fair thing.   9. Has taken away from me.

Now wol I tellen of my ferthe housbonde.
   I saye I hadde in herte greet despit
That he of any other hadde delit,
But he was quit,° by God and by Saint Joce: *paid back*
490 I made him of the same wode a croce[1]—
Nat of my body in no foul manere—
But, certainly, I made folk swich cheere
That in his owene grece I made him frye,
For angre and for verray jalousye.
495 By God, in erthe I was his purgatorye,
For which I hope his soule be in glorye.
For God it woot, he sat ful ofte and soong°   *sang*
Whan that his sho ful bitterly him wroong.°   *pinched*
Ther was no wight save God and he that wiste°   *knew*
500 In many wise how sore I him twiste.
He deide whan I cam fro Jerusalem,
And lith ygrave under the roode-beem,[2]
Al° is his tombe nought so curious[3]   *although*
As was the sepulcre of him Darius,
505 Which that Apelles wroughte subtilly:[4]
It nis but wast to burye him preciously.°   *expensively*
Lat him fare wel, God yive his soule reste;
He is now in his grave and in his cheste.
   Now of my fifthe housbonde wol I telle—
510 God lete his soule nevere come in helle—
And yit he was to me the moste shrewe:[5]
That feele I on my ribbes al by rewe,[6]
And evere shal unto myn ending day.
But in oure bed he was so fressh and gay,
515 And therwithal so wel coulde he me glose°   *wheedle*
Whan that he wolde han my bele chose,
That though he hadde me bet° on every boon,° *beaten / bone*
He coude winne again my love anoon.°   *immediately*
I trowe I loved him best for that he
520 Was of his love daungerous[7] to me.
We wommen han, if that I shal nat lie,
In this matere a quainte fantasye:
Waite what[8] thing we may nat lightly° have,   *easily*
Therafter wol we crye al day and crave;
525 Forbede us thing, and that desiren we;
Preesse on us faste, and thanne wol we flee.
With daunger oute we al oure chaffare:[9]
   Greet prees° at market maketh dere° ware, *crowd / expensive*

---

1. I made him a cross of the same wood.
The proverb has much the same sense
as the one quoted in line 493.
2. And lies buried under the rood beam
(the crucifix beam running between nave
and chancel).
3. Carefully wrought.
4. According to medieval legend, the

artist Apelles decorated the tomb of
Darius, king of the Persians.
5. Worst rascal.
6. In a row.
7. I.e., he played hard to get.
8. "Waite what": whatever.
9. With coyness, we spread out our
merchandise.

And too greet chepe is holden at litel pris.[1]
530 This knoweth every womman that is wis.
　　My fifthe housbonde—God his soule blesse!—
Which that I took for love and no richesse,
He somtime was a clerk at Oxenforde,
And hadde laft° scole and wente at hoom to boorde　　　*left*
535 With my gossib,° dwelling in oure town—　　　*confidante*
God have hir soule!—hir name was Alisoun;
She knew myn herte and eek my privetee°　　　*secrets*
Bet° than oure parissh preest, as mote I thee.°　　*better / thrive*
To hire biwrayed° I my conseil° al,　　　*disclosed / secrets*
540 For hadde myn housbonde pissed on a wal,
Or doon a thing that sholde han cost his lif,
To hire,° and to another worthy wif,　　　*her*
And to my nece which I loved weel,
I wolde han told his conseil everydeel;°　　　*entirely*
545 And so I dide ful often, God it woot,
That made his face often reed° and hoot°　　　*red / hot*
For verray shame, and blamed himself for he
Hadde told to me so greet a privetee.
　　And so bifel that ones in a Lente—
550 So often times I to my gossib wente,
For evere yit I loved to be gay,
And for to walke in March, Averil, and May,
From hous to hous, to heere sondry tales—
That Janekin clerk and my gossib dame Alis
555 And I myself into the feeldes wente.
Myn housbonde was at London al that Lente:
I hadde the better leiser for to playe,
And for to see, and eek for to be seye°　　　*seen*
Of lusty folk—what wiste I wher my grace°　　　*luck*
560 Was shapen° for to be, or in what place?　　　*destined*
Therfore I made my visitaciouns
To vigilies[2] and to processiouns,
To preching eek, and to thise pilgrimages,
To playes of miracles and to mariages,
565 And wered upon[3] my gaye scarlet gites°—　　　*dress*
Thise wormes ne thise motthes ne thise mites,
Upon my peril, frete° hem neveradeel:　　　*ate*
And woostou why? For they were used weel.
　　Now wol I tellen forth what happed me.
570 I saye that in the feeldes walked we,
Til trewely we hadde swich daliaunce,°　　　*flirtation*
This clerk and I, that of my purveyaunce°　　　*foresight*
I spak to him and saide him how that he,
If I were widwe, sholde wedde me.

1. Too good a bargain is held at little　　　2. Feasts preceding a saint's day.
value.　　　3. Wore.

575 For certainly, I saye for no bobaunce,°   *boast*
   Yit was I nevere withouten purveyaunce
   Of mariage n'of othere thinges eek:
   I holde a mouses herte nought worth a leek
   That hath but oon hole for to sterte° to,   *run*
580 And if that faile thanne is al ydo.[4]
   I bar him on hand[5] he hadde enchaunted me
   (My dame taughte me that subtiltee);
   And eek I saide I mette° of him al night: *dreamed*
   He wolde han slain me as I lay upright,°   *supine*
585 And al my bed was ful of verray blood—
   "But yit I hope that ye shul do me good;
   For blood bitokeneth gold, as me was taught."
   And al was fals, I dremed of it right naught,
   But as I folwed ay my dames° lore°   *mother's / teaching*
590 As wel of that as othere thinges more.
   But now sire—lat me see, what shal I sayn?
   Aha, by God, I have my tale again.
     Whan that my ferthe housbonde was on beere,°   *bier*
   I weep° algate,° and made sory cheere,   *wept / anyhow*
595 As wives moten,° for it is usage,°   *must / custom*
   And with my coverchief covered my visage;
   But for I was purveyed° of a make.°   *provided / mate*
   I wepte but smale, and that I undertake.°   *guarantee*
     To chirche was myn housbonde born amorwe[6]
600 With neighebores that for him maden sorwe,
   And Janekin oure clerk was oon of tho.
   As help me God, whan that I saw him go
   After the beere, me thoughte he hadde a paire
   Of legges and of feet so clene[7] and faire,
605 That al myn herte I yaf unto his hold.°   *possession*
   He was, I trowe,° twenty winter old,   *believe*
   And I was fourty, if I shal saye sooth—
   But yit I hadde alway a coltes tooth:[8]
   Gat-toothed° was I, and that bicam me weel;   *gap-toothed*
610 I hadde the prente[9] of Sainte Venus seel.
   As help me God, I was a lusty oon,
   And fair and riche and yong and wel-bigoon,°   *well-situated*
   And trewely, as mine housbondes tolde me,
   I hadde the beste quoniam° mighte be.   *pudendum*
615 For certes I am al Venerien[1]
   In feeling, and myn herte is Marcien:
   Venus me yaf my lust, my likerousnesse,°   *lecherousness*
   And Mars yaf me my sturdy hardinesse.

---

4. I.e., the game is up.
5. I pretended to him.
6. In the morning.
7. I.e., neat.

8. I.e., youthful appetites.
9. Print, i.e., a birthmark; "seel": seal.
1. Astrologically influenced by Venus;
"Marcien": influenced by Mars.

Myn ascendent was Taur[2] and Mars therinne—
620 Allas, allas, that evere love was sinne!
I folwed ay° my inclinacioun   *ever*
By vertu of my constellacioun;[3]
That made me I coude nought withdrawe
My chambre of Venus from a good felawe.
625 Yit have I Martes° merk upon my face,   *Mars'*
And also in another privee place.
For God so wis° be my savacioun,°   *surely / salvation*
I loved nevere by no discrecioun,
But evere folwede myn appetit,
630 Al were he short or long or blak or whit;
I took no keep,° so that he liked° me,   *heed / pleased*
How poore he was, ne eek of what degree.
    What sholde I saye but at the monthes ende
This joly clerk Janekin that was so hende°   *nice*
635 Hath wedded me with greet solempnitee,°   *splendor*
And to him yaf I al the land and fee°   *property*
That evere was me yiven therbifore—
But afterward repented me ful sore:
He nolde suffre no thing of my list.°   *pleasure*
640 By God, he smoot° me ones on the list°   *struck / ear*
For that I rente° out of his book a leef,   *tore*
That of the strook° myn ere weex° al deef.   *blow / grew*
Stibourne° I was as is a leonesse,   *stubborn*
And of my tonge a verray jangleresse,°   *blabbermouth*
645 And walke I wolde, as I hadde doon biforn,
From hous to hous, although he hadde it[4] sworn;
For which he often times wolde preche,
And me of olde Romain geestes° teche,   *stories*
How he Simplicius Gallus lafte° his wif,   *left*
650 And hire forsook for terme of al his lif,
Nought but for open-heveded he hire sey[5]
Looking out at his dore upon a day.
    Another Romain tolde he me by name
That, for his wif was at a someres° game   *summer's*
655 Withouten his witing,° he forsook hire eke;   *knowledge*
And thanne wolde he upon his Bible seeke
That ilke proverbe of Ecclesiaste[6]
Where he comandeth and forbedeth faste°   *strictly*
Man shal nat suffre his wif go roule° aboute;   *roam*
660 Thanne wolde he saye right thus withouten doute:
"Whoso that buildeth his hous al of salwes,°   *willow sticks*
And priketh° his blinde hors over the falwes,[7]   *rides*

2. My birth sign was the constellation   5. Just because he saw her bareheaded.
Taurus.   6. Ecclesiasticus (xxv.25).
3. I.e., horoscope.   7. Plowed land.
4. I.e., the contrary.

And suffreth his wif to go seeken halwes,°   *shrines*
Is worthy to be hanged on the galwes."°   *gallows*
665 But al for nought—I sette nought an hawe[8]
Of his proverbes n'of his olde sawe;
N'I wolde nat of him corrected be:
I hate him that my vices telleth me,
And so doon mo, God woot, of us than I.
670 This made him with me wood al outrely:[9]
I nolde nought forbere° him in no cas.   *submit to*
    Now wol I saye you sooth, by Saint Thomas,
Why that I rente° out of his book a leef,   *tore*
For which he smoot me so that I was deef.
675 He hadde a book that gladly night and day
For his disport he wolde rede alway.
He cleped it *Valerie*[1] *and Theofraste*,
At which book he lough° alway ful faste;   *laughed*
And eek ther was somtime a clerk at Rome,
680 A cardinal, that highte Saint Jerome,
That made a book[2] again Jovinian;
In which book eek ther was Tertulan,[3]
Crysippus, Trotula, and Helouis,
That was abbesse nat fer fro Paris;
685 And eek the Parables of Salomon,[4]
Ovides *Art*, and bookes many oon—
And alle thise were bounden in oo volume.
And every night and day was his custume,
Whan he hadde leiser and vacacioun
690 From other worldly occupacioun,
To reden in this book of wikked wives.
He knew of hem mo legendes and lives
Than been of goode wives in the Bible.
For trusteth wel, it is an impossible°   *impossibility*
695 That any clerk wol speke good of wives,
But if it be of holy saintes lives,
N'of noon other womman nevere the mo—
Who painted the leon, tel me who?[5]
By God, if wommen hadden writen stories,
700 As clerkes han within hir oratories,

8. I did not rate at the value of a haw-thorn berry.
9. Entirely.
1. I.e., the *Letter of Valerius Concerning Not Marrying*, by Walter Map; "*Theofraste*": Theophrastus' *Book Concerning Marriage*. Medieval manu-scripts often contained a number of different works, sometimes, as here, dealing with the same subject.
2. St. Jerome's antifeminist *Reply to Jovinian*; "again": against.
3. Tertullian, author of treatises on sexual modesty. Crysippus (or Chrysip-pus), in the next line, is mentioned by Jerome as an antifeminist; Trotula was a female doctor whose presence here is unexplained; "Helouis" is Eloise, whose love affair with the great scholar Abe-lard was a medieval scandal.
4. The Biblical Book of Proverbs; "Ovides *Art*": Ovid's *Art of Love*.
5. In one of Aesop's fables, the lion, shown a picture of a man killing a lion, asked who painted the picture. Had a lion been the artist, of course, the roles would have been reversed.

They wolde han writen of men more wikkednesse
Than al the merk[6] of Adam may redresse.
The children of Mercurye and Venus[7]
    Been in hir werking° ful contrarious:°   *operation / opposed*
705 Mercurye loveth wisdom and science,
And Venus loveth riot° and dispence;°   *parties / expenditures*
And for hir diverse disposicioun
Each falleth in otheres exaltacioun,[8]
And thus, God woot, Mercurye is desolat
710 In Pisces wher Venus is exaltat,[9]
And Venus falleth ther Mercurye is raised:
Therfore no womman of no clerk is praised.
The clerk, whan he is old and may nought do
Of Venus werkes worth his olde sho,°   *shoe*
715 Thanne sit° he down and writ° in his dotage   *sits / writes*
That wommen can nat keepe hir mariage.
    But now to purpose why I tolde thee
That I was beten for a book, pardee:
Upon a night Janekin, that was oure sire,[1]
720 Redde on his book as he sat by the fire
Of Eva first, that for hir wikkednesse
Was al mankinde brought to wrecchednesse,
For which that Jesu Crist himself was slain
That boughte° us with his herte blood again——   *redeemed*
725 Lo, heer expres of wommen may ye finde
That womman was the los° of al mankinde.[2]   *ruin*
    Tho° redde he me how Sampson loste his heres: *then*
Sleeping his lemman° kitte° it with hir sheres,   *mistress / cut*
Thurgh which treson loste he both his yën.
730   Tho redde he me, if that I shal nat lien,
Of Ercules and of his Dianire,[3]
That caused him to sette himself afire.
    No thing forgat he the sorwe and wo
That Socrates hadde with his wives two——
735 How Xantippa caste pisse upon his heed:
This sely° man sat stille as he were deed;   *silly*
He wiped his heed, namore dorste he sayn
But "Er that thonder stinte,° comth a rain."   *stops*
    Of Pasipha[4] that was the queene of Crete——
740 For shrewednesse° him thoughte the tale sweete——   *malice*

6. Mark, sex.
7. I.e., clerks and women, astrologically ruled by Mercury and Venus respectively.
8. Because of their contrary positions (as planets), each one descends (in the belt of the zodiac) as the other rises; hence one loses its power as the other becomes dominant.
9. I.e., Mercury is deprived of power in Pisces (the sign of the Fish), where Venus is most powerful.
1. My husband.
2. The stories of wicked women Chaucer drew mainly from St. Jerome and Walter Map.
3. Dejanira unwittingly gave Hercules a poisoned shirt, which hurt him so much that he committed suicide by fire.
4. Pasiphaë, who fell in love with a bull.

Fy, speek namore, it is a grisly thing
Of hir horrible lust and hir liking.°   *pleasure*
    Of Clytermistra[5] for hir lecherye
That falsly made hir housbonde for to die,
745 He redde it with ful good devocioun.
    He tolde me eek for what occasioun
Amphiorax[6] at Thebes loste his lif:
Myn housbonde hadde a legende of his wif
Eriphylem, that for an ouche° of gold   *trinket*
750 Hath prively unto the Greekes told
Wher that hir housbonde hidde him in a place,
For which he hadde at Thebes sory grace.
Of Livia[7] tolde he me and of Lucie:
They bothe made hir housbondes for to die,
755 That oon for love, that other was for hate;
Livia hir housbonde on an even late
Empoisoned hath for that she was his fo;
Lucia likerous° loved hir housbonde so   *lecherous*
That for° he sholde alway upon hire thinke,   *in order that*
760 She yaf him swich a manere love-drinke
That he was deed er it were by the morwe.[8]
And thus algates° housbondes han sorwe.   *constantly*
    Thanne tolde he me how oon Latumius
Complained unto his felawe Arrius
765 That in his gardin growed swich a tree,
On which he saide how that his wives three
Hanged hemself for herte despitous.[9]
    "O leve° brother," quod this Arrius,   *dear*
"Yif me a plante of thilke blessed tree,
770 And in my gardin planted shal it be."
    Of latter date of wives hath he red
That some han slain hir housbondes in hir bed
And lete hir lechour dighte[1] hire al the night,
Whan that the cors° lay in the floor upright;°   *corpse / supine*
775 And some han driven nailes in hir brain
Whil that they sleepe, and thus they han hem slain;
Some han hem yiven poison in hir drinke.
He spak more harm than herte may bithinke,°   *imagine*
And therwithal he knew of mo proverbes
780 Than in this world ther growen gras or herbes:
"Bet is," quod he, "thyn habitacioun
Be with a leon or a foul dragoun

5. Clytemnestra, who, with her lover Aegisthus, slew her husband Agamemnon.
6. Amphiaraus, betrayed by his wife Eriphyle and forced to go to the war against Thebes.
7. Livia murdered her husband in behalf of her lover Sejanus. "Lucie": Lucilla, who was said to have poisoned her husband, the poet Lucretius, with a potion designed to keep him faithful.
8. He was dead before it was near morning.
9. For malice of heart.
1. Have intercourse with.

Than with a womman using° for to chide."   *accustomed*
"Bet is," quod he, "hye in the roof abide
785 Than with an angry wif down in the hous:
They been so wikked° and contrarious,   *perverse*
They haten that hir housbondes loveth ay."
He saide, "A womman cast° hir shame away   *casts*
Whan she cast of° hir smok,"[2] and ferthermo,   *off*
790 "A fair womman, but she be chast also,
Is like a gold ring in a sowes nose."
Who wolde weene,° or who wolde suppose   *think*
The wo that in myn herte was and pine?°   *suffering*
   And whan I sawgh he wolde nevere fine°   *end*
795 To reden on this cursed book al night,
Al sodeinly three leves have I plight°   *snatched*
Out of his book right as he redde, and eke
I with my fist so took[3] him on the cheeke
That in oure fir he fil° bakward adown.   *fell*
800 And up he sterte as dooth a wood° leoun,   *raging*
And with his fist he smoot me on the heed°   *head*
That in the floor I lay as I were deed.
And whan he sawgh how stille that I lay,
He was agast, and wolde have fled his way,
805 Til atte laste out of my swough° I braide:°   *swoon / started*
"O hastou slain me, false thief?" I saide,
"And for my land thus hastou mordred° me?   *murdered*
Er I be deed° yit wol I kisse thee."   *dead*
And neer he cam and kneeled faire adown,
810 And saide, "Dere suster Alisoun,
As help me God, I shal thee nevere smite.
That I have doon, it is thyself to wite.°   *blame*
Foryif it me, and that I thee biseeke."
And yit eftsoones° I hitte him on the cheeke,   *again*
815 And saide, "Thief, thus muchel am I wreke.°   *avenged*
Now wol I die: I may no lenger speke."
   But at the laste with muchel care and wo
We fille[4] accorded by us selven two.
He yaf me al the bridel° in myn hand,   *bridle*
820 To han the governance of hous and land,
And of his tonge and his hand also;
And made[5] him brenne° his book anoonright tho.   *burn*
And whan that I hadde geten unto me
By maistrye° al the sovereinetee,°   *skill / dominion*
825 And that he saide, "Myn owene trewe wif,
Do as thee lust° the terme of al thy lif;   *it pleases*
Keep thyn honour, and keep eek myn estat,"
After that day we hadde nevere debat.

2. Undergarment.   4. I.e., became.
3. I.e., hit.   5. I.e., I made.

God help me so, I was to him as kinde
830 As any wif from Denmark unto Inde,
And also trewe, and so was he to me.
I praye to God that sit° in majestee,   *sits*
So blesse his soule for his mercy dere.
Now wol I saye my tale if ye wol heere.

[ANOTHER INTERRUPTION]

835   The Frere lough° whan he hadde herd al this: *laughed*
"Now dame," quod he, "so have I joye or blis,
This is a long preamble of a tale."
And whan the Somnour herde the Frere gale,°   *exclaim*
"Lo," quod the Somnour, "Goddes armes two,
840 A frere wol entremette him[6] everemo!
Lo, goode men, a flye and eek a frere
Wol falle in every dissh and eek matere.
What spekestou of preambulacioun?
What, amble or trotte or pisse or go sitte down!
845 Thou lettest° oure disport in this manere."   *hinder*
   "Ye, woltou so, sire Somnour?" quod the Frere.
"Now by my faith, I shal er that I go
Telle of a somnour swich a tale or two
That al the folk shal laughen in this place."
850   "Now elles, Frere, I wol bishrewe° thy face,"   *curse*
Quod this Somnour, "and I bishrewe me,
But if I telle tales two or three
Of freres, er I come to Sidingborne,[7]
That I shal make thyn herte for to moorne—
855 For wel I woot thy pacience is goon."
   Oure Hoste cride, "Pees, and that anoon!"
And saide, "Lat the womman telle hir tale:
Ye fare as folk that dronken been of ale.
Do, dame, tel forth youre tale, and that is best."
860   "Al redy, sire," quod she, "right as you lest°—   *it pleases*
If I have licence of this worthy Frere."
"Yis, dame," quod he, "tel forth and I wol heere."

6. Intrude himself.
7. Sittingbourne (a town forty miles from London).

The Tale[1]

In th'olde dayes of the King Arthour,
Of which that Britouns° speken greet honour, *Bretons*
865 Al was this land fulfild of faïrye:[2]
The elf-queene with hir joly compaignye
Daunced ful ofte in many a greene mede°— *meadow*
This was the olde opinion as I rede;
I speke of many hundred yeres ago.
870 But now can no man see none elves mo,
For now the grete charitee and prayeres
Of limitours,[3] and othere holy freres,
That serchen every land and every streem,
As thikke as motes in the sonne-beem,
875 Blessing halles, chambres, kichenes, bowres,
Citees, burghes,° castels, hye towres, *townships*
Thropes, bernes, shipnes,[4] dayeries—
This maketh that ther been no faïries.
For ther as wont to walken was an elf
880 Ther walketh now the limitour himself,
In undermeles° and in morweninges,° *afternoons / mornings*
And saith his Matins and his holy thinges,
As he gooth in his limitacioun.[5]
Wommen may go saufly° up and down: *safely*
885 In every bussh or under every tree
Ther is noon other incubus[6] but he,
And he ne wol doon hem but dishonour.

And so bifel it that this King Arthour
Hadde in his hous a lusty bacheler,
890 That on a day cam riding fro river,[7]
And happed° that, allone as he was born, *it happened*

1. The story of the knight who fully realizes what women most desire only after having been told it in a number of ways was popular in Chaucer's time and a natural one for him to assign to the Wife of Bath, whose well-loved fifth husband had also been slow to learn. But Chaucer reshaped the tale in such a way as to make it fit the Wife and her thesis even more closely. In the other medieval versions of the story the knight is guiltless of any offense to womanhood, and in several of them he is Sir Gawain, traditional model of chivalric courtesy, who weds the hideous hag to save not his own life but that of his lord, King Arthur. Chaucer has made the knight a most ill-behaved and ill-mannered man who needs to learn what women most desire as much in order to redeem his disagreeably virile character as to save his neck. Because within her story he is the sole male in a world of women, Dame Alice is able not only to prove conclusively the value of woman's sovereignty, but also to pay her respects to a world of men that had preached antifeminism, a world here represented by a single rapist.

The story is suited to the Wife's own character psychologically as well as dramatically, for she, like the old hag, had wedded a young man—though unlike the hag she could not restore her former beauty. But if there is a touch of melancholy in the incompleteness of this similarity, it is sharply dispelled by the Wife's final comments, which reassert the sturdy fighting spirit that permeates her Prologue.
2. I.e., filled full of supernatural creatures.
3. Friars licenced to beg in a certain territory.
4. Thorps (villages), barns, stables.
5. I.e., the friar's assigned area. His "holy thinges" are prayers.
6. A spirit that lies with mortal women. "Ne * * * but" in the next line means "only."
7. Hawking, usually carried out on the banks of a stream.

He sawgh a maide walking him biforn;
Of which maide anoon, maugree hir heed,[8]
By verray force he rafte° hir maidenheed;   *deprived her of*
895 For which oppression° was swich clamour,   *rape*
And swich pursuite° unto the King Arthour,   *petitioning*
That dampned was this knight for to be deed[9]
By cours of lawe, and sholde han lost his heed—
Paraventure° swich was the statut tho—   *perhaps*
900 But that the queene and othere ladies mo
So longe prayeden the king of grace,
Til he his lif him graunted in the place,
And yaf him to the queene, al at hir wille,
To chese° wheither she wolde him save or spille.[1]   *choose*
905 The queene thanked the king with al hir might,
And after this thus spak she to the knight,
Whan that she saw hir time upon a day:
"Thou standest yit," quod she, "in swich array°   *condition*
That of thy lif yit hastou no suretee.°   *guarantee*
910 I graunte thee lif if thou canst tellen me
What thing it is that wommen most desiren:
Be war and keep thy nekke boon° from iren.   *bone*
And if thou canst nat tellen me anoon,
Yit wol I yive thee leve for to goon
915 A twelfmonth and a day to seeche° and lere°   *search / learn*
An answere suffisant° in this matere,   *satisfactory*
And suretee wol I han er that thou pace,°   *pass*
Thy body for to yeelden in this place."
    Wo was this knight, and sorwefully he siketh.°   *sighs*
920 But what, he may nat doon al as him liketh,
And atte laste he chees° him for to wende,   *chose*
And come again right at the yeres ende,
With swich answere as God wolde him purveye,°   *provide*
And taketh his leve and wendeth forth his waye.
925 He seeketh every hous and every place
Wher as he hopeth for to finde grace,
To lerne what thing wommen love most.
But he ne coude arriven in no coost[2]
Wher as he mighte finde in this matere
930 Two creatures according in fere.[3]
    Some saiden wommen loven best richesse;
Some saide honour, some saide jolinesse;°   *wantonness*
Some riche array, some saiden lust° abedde,   *pleasure*
And ofte time to be widwe and wedde.
935 Some saide that oure herte is most esed
Whan that we been yflatered and yplesed—
He gooth ful neigh the soothe, I wol nat lie:
A man shal winne us best with flaterye,

---

8. Despite her head, i.e., despite anything she could do.
9. This knight was condemned to death.

1. Put to death.
2. I.e., country.
3. Agreeing together.

And with attendance and with bisinesse°   *assiduousness*
940 Been we ylimed,° bothe more and lesse.   *ensnared*
    And some sayen that we loven best
For to be free, and do right as us lest,°   *it pleases*
And that no man repreve° us of oure vice,   *reprove*
But saye that we be wise and no thing nice.°   *foolish*
945 For trewely, ther is noon of us alle,
If any wight wol clawe us on the galle,°   *sore spot*
That we nil kike° for° he saith us sooth: *kick / because*
Assaye and he shal finde it that so dooth.
For be we nevere so vicious withinne,
950 We wol be holden° wise and clene of sinne.   *considered*
    And some sayn that greet delit han we
For to be holden stable and eek secree,[1]
And in oo purpos stedefastly to dwelle,
And nat biwraye° thing that men us telle—   *disclose*
955 But that tale is nat worth a rake-stele.°   *rake handle*
Pardee, we wommen conne no thing hele:°   *conceal*
Witnesse on Mida.° Wol ye heere the tale?   *Midas*
    Ovide, amonges othere thinges smale,
Saide Mida hadde under his longe heres,
960 Growing upon his heed, two asses eres,
The whiche vice° he hidde as he best mighte   *defect*
Ful subtilly from every mannes sighte,
That save his wif ther wiste° of it namo.   *knew*
He loved hire most and trusted hire also.
965 He prayed hire that to no creature
She sholde tellen of his disfigure.°   *deformity*
    She swoor him nay, for al this world to winne,
She nolde do that vilainye or sinne
To make hir housbonde han so foul a name:
970 She nolde nat telle it for hir owene shame.
But nathelees, hir thoughte that she dyde°   *would die*
That she so longe sholde a conseil° hide;   *secret*
Hire thoughte it swal° so sore aboute hir herte   *swelled*
That nedely som word hire moste asterte,[5]
975 And sith she dorste nat telle it to no man,
Down to a mareis° faste° by she ran—   *marsh / close*
Til she cam there hir herte was afire—
And as a bitore[6] bombleth in the mire,
She laide hir mouth unto the water down:
980 "Biwray° me nat, thou water, with thy soun,"°   *betray / sound*
Quod she. "To thee I telle it and namo:°   *to no one else*
Myn housbonde hath longe asses eres two.
Now is myn herte al hool,[7] now is it oute.
I mighte no lenger keepe it, out of doute."
985 Here may ye see, though we a time abide,

---

4. Reliable and also close-mouthed.   6. Bittern, a heron. "Bombleth": makes
5. Of necessity some word must escape   a booming noise.
her.   7. I.e., sound.

Yit oute it moot:° we can no conseil hide.   must
The remenant of the tale if ye wol heere,
Redeth Ovide, and ther ye may it lere.[8]
    This knight of which my tale is specially,
990 Whan that he sawgh he mighte nat come therby—
This is to saye what wommen loven most—
Within his brest ful sorweful was his gost,°   spirit
But hoom he gooth, he mighte nat sojurne:°   delay
The day was come that hoomward moste° he turne.   must
995 And in his way it happed him to ride
In al this care under a forest side,
Wher as he sawgh upon a daunce go
Of ladies foure and twenty and yit mo;
Toward the whiche daunce he drow ful yerne,[9]
1000 In hope that som wisdom sholde he lerne.
But certainly, er he cam fully there,
Vanisshed was this daunce, he niste° where.   knew not
No creature sawgh he that bar° lif,   bore
Save on the greene he sawgh sitting a wif—
1005 A fouler wight ther may no man devise.°   imagine
Again[1] the knight this olde wif gan rise,
And saide, "Sire knight, heer forth lith° no way.°   lies / road
Telle me what ye seeken, by youre fay.°   faith
Paraventure it may the better be:
1010 Thise olde folk conne° muchel thing," quod she.   know
    "My leve moder,"° quod this knight, "certain,   mother
I nam but deed but if that I can sayn
What thing it is that wommen most desire.
Coude ye me wisse,° I wolde wel quite youre hire."[2]   teach
1015   "Plight me thy trouthe here in myn hand," quod she,
"The nexte thing that I requere° thee,   require of
Thou shalt it do, if it lie in thy might,
And I wol telle it you er it be night."
    "Have heer my trouthe," quod the knight. "I graunte."
1020   "Thanne," quod she, "I dar me wel avaunte°   boast
Thy lif is sauf,° for I wol stande therby.   safe
Upon my lif the queene wol saye as I.
Lat see which is the pruddeste° of hem alle   proudest
That wereth on[3] a coverchief or a calle°   headdress
1025 That dar saye nay of that I shal thee teche.
Lat us go forth withouten lenger speeche."
Tho rouned° she a pistel° in his ere,   whispered / sentence
And bad him to be glad and have no fere.
    Whan they be comen to the court, this knight
1030 Saide he hadde holde his day as he hadde hight,°   promised
And redy was his answere, as he saide.
Ful many a noble wif, and many a maide,

8. Learn. The reeds disclosed the secret
by whispering *"aures asinelli"* (asses'
ears).
9. **Drew very quickly.**

1. I.e., to meet.
2. Repay your trouble.
3. That wears.

And many a widwe—for that they been wise—
The queene hirself sitting as justise,
1035 Assembled been this answere for to heere,
And afterward this knight was bode° appere.   *bidden to*
To every wight comanded was silence,
And that the knight sholde telle in audience°   *open hearing*
What thing that worldly wommen loven best.
1040 This knight ne stood nat stille as dooth a best,°   *beast*
But to his question anoon answerde
With manly vois that al the court it herde.
    "My lige° lady, generally," quod he,   *liege*
"Wommen desire to have sovereinetee°   *dominion*
1045 As wel over hir housbonde as hir love,
And for to been in maistrye him above.
This is youre moste desir though ye me kille.
Dooth as you list:° I am here at youre wille."   *please*
    In al the court ne was ther wif ne maide
1050 Ne widwe that contraried° that he saide,   *contradicted*
But saiden he was worthy han° his lif.   *to have*
    And with that word up sterte° that olde wif,   *started*
Which that the knight sawgh sitting on the greene;
"Mercy," quod she, "my soverein lady queene,
1055 Er that youre court departe, do me right.
I taughte this answere unto the knight,
For which he plighte me his trouthe there
The firste thing I wolde him requere°   *require*
He wolde it do, if it laye in his might.
1060 Bifore the court thanne praye I thee, sire knight,"
Quod she, "that thou me take unto thy wif,
For wel thou woost that I have kept° thy lif.   *saved*
If I saye fals, say nay, upon thy fay."
    This knight answerde, "Allas and wailaway,
1065 I woot right wel that swich was my biheeste.°   *promise*
For Goddes love, as chees° a newe requeste: *choose*
Taak al my good and lat my body go."
    "Nay thanne," quod she, "I shrewe° us bothe two.   *curse*
For though that I be foul and old and poore,
1070 I nolde for al the metal ne for ore
That under erthe is grave° or lith° above,   *buried / lies*
But if thy wif I were and eek thy love."
    "My love," quod he. "Nay, my dampnacioun!°   *damnation*
Allas, that any of my nacioun[4]
1075 Sholde evere so foule disparaged° be."   *disgraced*
But al for nought, th'ende is this, that he
Constrained was: he needes moste hire wedde,
And taketh his olde wif and gooth to bedde.
    Now wolden some men saye, paraventure,
1080 That for my necligence I do no cure[5]
To tellen you the joy and al th'array

---

4. I.e., family.   5. I do not take the trouble.

That at the feeste was that ilke day.
To which thing shortly answere I shal:
I saye ther nas no joye ne feeste at al;
1085 Ther nas but hevinesse and muche sorwe.
For prively he wedded hire on morwe,[6]
And al day after hidde him as an owle,
So wo was him, his wif looked so foule.
    Greet was the wo the knight hadde in his thought:
1090 Whan he was with his wif abedde brought,
He walweth° and he turneth to and fro.   *tosses*
His olde wif lay smiling everemo,
And saide, "O dere housbonde, benedicite,°   *bless me*
Fareth° every knight thus with his wif as ye?   *behaves*
1095 Is this the lawe of King Arthures hous?
Is every knight of his thus daungerous?°   *stand-offish*
I am youre owene love and youre wif;
I am she which that saved hath youre lif;
And certes yit ne dide I you nevere unright.
1100 Why fare ye thus with me this firste night?
Ye faren like a man hadde lost his wit.
What is my gilt? For Goddes love, telle it,
And it shal been amended if I may."
    "Amended!" quod this knight. "Allas, nay, nay,
1105 It wol nat been amended neveremo.
Thou art so lothly° and so old also,   *loathsome*
And therto comen of so lowe a kinde,°   *race*
That litel wonder is though I walwe and winde.°   *turn*
So wolde God myn herte wolde breste!"°   *break*
1110   "Is this," quod she, "the cause of youre unreste?"
"Ye, certainly," quod he. "No wonder is."
    "Now sire," quod she, "I coude amende al this,
If that me liste, er it were dayes three,
So° wel ye mighte bere you[7] unto me.   *provided that*
1115   "But for ye speken of swich gentilesse
As is descended out of old richesse—
That therfore sholden ye be gentilmen—
Swich arrogance is nat worth an hen.
Looke who that is most vertuous alway,
1120 Privee and apert,[8] and most entendeth ay
To do the gentil deedes that he can,
Taak him for the gretteste° gentilman.   *greatest*
Crist wol° we claime of him oure gentilesse,   *desires that*
Nat of oure eldres for hir 'old richesse.'[9]
1125 For though they yive us al hir heritage,
For which we claime to been of heigh parage,°   *descent*
Yit may they nat biquethe for no thing
To noon of us hir vertuous living,
That made hem gentilmen ycalled be,

6. In the morning.
7. Behave.
8. Privately and publicly.
9. See Chaucer's *Gentilesse*, line 16.

1130 And bad[1] us folwen hem in swich degree.
    "Wel can the wise poete of Florence,
That highte Dant,[2] speken in this sentence;°   *topic*
Lo, in swich manere rym is Dantes tale:
'Ful selde° up riseth by his braunches[3] smale   *seldom*
1135 Prowesse° of man, for God of his prowesse   *excellence*
Wol that of him we claime oure gentilesse.'
For of oure eldres may we no thing claime
But temporel thing that man may hurte and maime.
Eek every wight woot this as wel as I,
1140 If gentilesse were planted natureelly
Unto a certain linage down the line,
Privee and apert, thanne wolde they nevere fine°   *cease*
To doon of gentilesse the faire office°—   *function*
They mighte do no vilainye or vice.
1145   "Taak fir and beer° it in the derkeste hous   *bear*
Bitwixe this and the Mount of Caucasus,
And lat men shette° the dores and go thenne,°   *shut / thence*
Yit wol the fir as faire lie[4] and brenne°   *burn*
As twenty thousand men mighte it biholde:
1150 His° office natureel ay wol it holde,   *its*
Up° peril of my lif, til that it die.   *upon*
Heer may ye see wel how that genterye°   *gentility*
Is nat annexed° to possessioun,[5]   *related*
Sith folk ne doon hir operacioun
1155 Alway, as dooth the fir, lo, in his kinde.°   *nature*
For God it woot, men may wel often finde
A lordes sone do shame and vilainye;
And he that wol han pris of his gentrye,[6]
For he was boren° of a gentil hous,   *born*
1160 And hadde his eldres noble and vertuous,
And nil himselven do no gentil deedes,
Ne folwen his gentil auncestre that deed° is,   *dead*
He nis nat gentil, be he duc or erl—
For vilaines sinful deedes maken a cherl.
1165 Thy gentilesse[7] nis but renomee°   *renown*
Of thine auncestres for hir heigh bountee,°   *magnanimity*
Which is a straunge° thing for thy persone.   *alien*
For gentilesse[8] cometh fro God allone.
Thanne comth oure verray gentilesse of grace:
1170 It was no thing biquethe us with oure place.
Thenketh how noble, as saith Valerius,[9]
Was thilke Tullius Hostilius
That out of poverte° roos to heigh noblesse.   *poverty*
Redeth Senek,° and redeth eek Boece:°   *Seneca / Boethius*
1175 Ther shul ye seen expres that no drede° is   *doubt*

---

1. I.e., they bade.
2. Dante; see his *Convivio*.
3. I.e., by its own efforts.
4. I.e., remain.
5. I.e., inheritable property.

6. Have credit for his noble birth.
7. I.e., the gentility you claim.
8. I.e., true gentility.
9. A Roman historian.

That he is gentil that dooth gentil deedes.
And therfore, leve housbonde, I thus conclude:
Al were it that mine auncestres weren rude,[1]
Yit may the hye God—and so hope I—
1180 Graunte me grace to liven vertuously.
Thanne am I gentil whan that I biginne
To liven vertuously and waive° sinne.   avoid
        "And ther as ye of poverte me repreve,°   reprove
The hye God, on whom that we bileve,
1185 In wilful° poverte chees° to live his lif;   voluntary / chose
And certes every man, maiden, or wif
May understonde that Jesus, hevene king,
Ne wolde nat chese° a vicious living.   choose
Glad poverte is an honeste° thing, certain;   honorable
1190 This wol Senek and othere clerkes sayn.
Whoso that halt him paid of[2] his poverte,
I holde him riche al hadde he nat a sherte.°   shirt
He that coveiteth[3] is a poore wight,
For he wolde han that is nat in his might;
1195 But he that nought hath, ne coveiteth° have,   desires to
Is riche, although we holde him but a knave.
Verray poverte it singeth proprely.°   appropriately
Juvenal saith of poverte, 'Merily
 The poore man, whan he gooth by the waye,
1200 Biforn the theves he may singe and playe.'
Poverte is hateful good, and as I gesse,
A ful greet bringere out of bisinesse;[4]
A greet amendere eek of sapience
To him that taketh it in pacience;
1205 Poverte is thing, although it seeme elenge,°   wretched
Possession that no wight wol chalenge;[5]
Poverte ful often, whan a man is lowe,
Maketh[6] his God and eek himself to knowe;
Poverte a spectacle° is, as thinketh me,   pair of spectacles
1210 Thurgh which he may his verray freendes see.
And therfore, sire, sin that I nought you greve,
Of my poverte namore ye me repreve.°   reproach
        "Now sire, of elde° ye repreve me: old age
And certes sire, though noon auctoritee
1215 Were in no book, ye gentils of honour
Sayn that men sholde an old wight doon favour,
And clepe him fader for youre gentilesse—
And auctours[7] shal I finden, as I gesse.
        "Now ther ye saye that I am foul and old:
1220 Thanne drede you nought to been a cokewold,°   cuckold
For filthe and elde, also mote I thee,[8]
Been grete wardeins° upon chastitee.   guardians

1. I.e., low born.
2. Considers himself satisfied with.
3. I.e., suffers desires.
4. I.e., cares.
5. Claim as his property.
6. I.e., makes him.
7. I.e., authorities.
8. So may I thrive.

But nathelees, sin I knowe your delit,
I shal fulfille youre worldly appetit.

1225 "Chees now," quod she, "oon of thise thinges twaye:
To han me foul and old til that I deye
And be to you a trewe humble wif,
And nevere you displese in al my lif,
Or elles ye wol han me yong and fair,
1230 And take youre aventure° of the repair⁹   *chance*
That shal be to youre hous by cause of me—
Or in som other place, wel may be.
Now chees youreselven wheither° that you liketh."   *whichever*
This knight aviseth him¹ and sore siketh;°   *sighs*
1235 But atte laste he saide in this manere:
"My lady and my love, and wif so dere,
I putte me in youre wise governaunce:
Cheseth° youreself which may be most plesaunce²   *choose*
And most honour to you and me also.
1240 I do no fors the wheither³ of the two,
For as you liketh it suffiseth° me."   *satisfies*
"Thanne have I gete° of you maistrye," quod she,   *got*
"Sin I may chese and governe as me lest?"°   *it pleases*
"Ye, certes, wif," quod he. "I holde it best."
1245 "Kisse me," quod she. "We be no lenger wrothe.
For by my trouthe, I wol be to you bothe—
This is to sayn, ye, bothe fair and good.
I praye to God that I mote sterven wood,⁴
But° I to you be al so good and trewe   *unless*
1250 As evere was wif sin that the world was newe.
And but I be tomorn° as fair to seene   *tomorrow morning*
As any lady, emperisse, or queene,
That is bitwixe the eest and eek the west,
Do with my lif and deeth right as you lest:
1255 Caste up the curtin, looke how that it is."
And whan the knight sawgh verraily al this,
That she so fair was and so yong therto,
For joye he hente° hire in his armes two;   *took*
His herte bathed in a bath of blisse;
1260 A thousand time arewe° he gan hire kisse,   *in a row*
And she obeyed him in every thing
That mighte do him plesance or liking.°   *pleasure*
And thus they live unto hir lives ende
In parfit° joye. And Jesu Crist us sende   *perfect*
1265 Housbondes meeke, yonge, and fresshe abedde—
And grace t'overbide° hem that we wedde.   *outlive*
And eek I praye Jesu shorte° hir lives   *shorten*
That nought wol be governed by hir wives,
And olde and angry nigardes of dispence°—   *expenditure*
1270 God sende hem soone a verray° pestilence!   *veritable*

9. I.e., visits.   3. I do not care whichever.
1. Considers.   4. Die mad.
2. Pleasure.

The Pardoner's Prologue and Tale[1]

The Introduction

Oure Hoste gan to swere as he were wood;°   *insane*
"Harrow,"° quod he, "by nailes[2] and by blood,   *help*

1. The Pardoner is the chief actor in a grim comedy which shows how a clever hypocrite exploits Christian principles in order to enrich himself—and which, in the Epilogue, suggests that the exploiter of Christian principles is not immune to their operation. The medieval pardoner's function was to collect money for charitable enterprises supported by branches of the church and to act as the Pope's agent in rewarding donors with some temporal remission of their sins. According to theological doctrine, St. Peter—and through him his papal successors—received from Christ the power to make a gift of mercy from God's infinite treasury to those of the faithful that had earned special favor, such as contributors to charity. The charitable enterprises themselves—generally hospitals—hired pardoners to raise money, but the pardoners had also to be licensed by the Pope to pass on to contributors the papal indulgence. By canon law pardoners were permitted to work only in a prescribed area; within that area they might visit churches during Sunday service, briefly explain their mission, receive contributions, and, in the Pope's name, issue indulgence, which was considered not a sale, but a free gift made in return for a free gift. In actual fact pardoners seem seldom to have behaved as the law required them. Since a parish priest was forbidden to exclude properly licensed pardoners, they made their way into churches at will, and once there did not confine themselves to a mere statement of their business, but rather, in order to make the congregation free of its gifts, preached highly emotive sermons and boasted of the extraordinary efficacy of their own particular pardon, claiming for it powers that not even the Pope could have invested it with. An honest pardoner, if such existed, was entitled to a percentage of his collections; dishonest pardoners took more than their share, and some took everything; indeed, some were complete frauds, bearing forged credentials which, in an age when even clerical illiteracy was common, were no less impressive than if they had been real.

While Chaucer's Pardoner belongs, as he boastfully tells us, to the most dishonest class of fund-gatherers, he is an extremely able one. His text is always the same: *Radix malorum est cupiditas*, "The love of money is the root of all evil," and he uses it most effectively in order to frighten his hearers into a generosity that will fulfill his own cupidity. The Pardoner's audacious description of his behavior in a parish church is followed by a sample sermon on his invariable text. Aware that his audience is more interested in narrative than in the moralization one expects of a sermon he first introduces the three dissolute young men of his *exemplum*, that is, of the story which is to illustrate concretely the sermon's point. Having titillated his hearers with the promise of a lurid story, he proceeds to the moralization; curiously enough, this does not concern the sin of avarice, but drunkenness, gluttony, lechery, gambling, and cursing. Yet the apparent lack of logic serves the Pardoner's deeper purpose, for these are the sins people find it exciting to hear about. When his audience has thus been emotionally prepared by a discussion of the debauchees' more flamboyant sins, the Pardoner tells his *exemplum* of the destructiveness of avarice, shutting it off at the moment of highest interest, and concluding with a demand to the congregation for money in return for his pardon.

The story of the young men who seek Death only to find him in a treasure that had made them forget him is a masterpiece of irony, and indeed the Pardoner is in all ways a master ironist. So highly developed is his own sense of irony that it enables him to feel superior not only to other men but to God, for he dares to exempt himself from the effect of his Christian text. Yet the brief Epilogue seems to show that God's irony, like His other attributes, is supreme. The one fact that the Pardoner's candid confession has concealed—that it was perhaps spoken in order to conceal—is that he is a eunuch. When in the Epilogue his proud avarice leads him to see if he can get money from the pilgrims to whom he has revealed his hypocrisy, the Pardoner's secret is revealed by the Host's coarse response, and the verbal facility by which he maintains his superiority fails him.

2. I.e., God's nails.

This was a fals cherl and a fals justise.[3]
As shameful deeth as herte may devise
5 Come to thise juges and hir advocats.
Algate° this sely° maide is slain, allas!   *at an rate / innocent*
Allas, too dere boughte she beautee!
Wherfore I saye alday° that men may see   *always*
The yiftes of Fortune and of Nature
10 Been cause of deeth to many a creature.
As bothe yiftes that I speke of now,
Men han ful ofte more for harm than prow.°   *benefit*
   "But trewely, myn owene maister dere,
This is a pitous tale for to heere.
15 But nathelees, passe over, is no fors:[4]
I praye to God so save thy gentil cors,°   *body*
And eek thine urinals and thy jurdones,[5]
Thyn ipocras[6] and eek thy galiones,
And every boiste° ful of thy letuarye°—   *box / medicine*
20 God blesse hem, and oure lady Sainte Marye.
So mote I theen,[7] thou art a propre man,
And lik a prelat, by Saint Ronian![8]
Saide I nat wel? I can nat speke in terme.[9]
But wel I woot, thou doost° myn herte to erme°   *make / grieve*
25 That I almost have caught a cardinacle.[1]
By corpus bones,[2] but if I have triacle,°   *medicine*
Or elles a draughte of moiste° and corny° ale,   *fresh / malty*
Or but I heere anoon° a merye tale,   *at once*
Myn herte is lost for pitee of this maide.
30   "Thou bel ami,[3] thou Pardoner," he saide,
"Tel us som mirthe or japes° right anoon."   *joke*
   "It shal be doon," quod he, "by Saint Ronion.
But first," quod he, "here at this ale-stake[4]
I wol bothe drinke and eten of a cake."
35   And right anoon thise gentils gan to crye,
"Nay, lat him telle us of no ribaudye.°   *ribaldry*
Tel us som moral thing that we may lere,°   *learn*
Som wit,[5] and thanne wol we gladly heere."
   "I graunte, ywis," quod he, "but I moot thinke
40 Upon som honeste° thing whil that I drinke."   *decent*

3. The Host has been affected by the Physician's sad tale of the Roman maiden Virginia, whose great beauty caused a judge to attempt to obtain her person by means of a trumped-up lawsuit in which he connived with a "churl" who claimed her as his slave; in order to preserve her chastity, her father killed her.
4. I.e., never mind.
5. Jordans (chamber pots): the Host is somewhat confused in his endeavor to use technical medical terms.
6. A medicinal drink named after Hippocrates; "galiones": a medicine, prob-

ably invented on the spot by the Host, named after Galen.
7. So might I thrive.
8. St. Ronan or St. Ninian, with a possible play on "runnion" (sexual organ).
9. Speak in technical idiom.
1. Apparently a cardiac condition, confused in the Host's mind with a cardinal.
2. An illiterate oath, mixing "God's bones" with *corpus dei*. "But if": unless.
3. Fair friend.
4. Sign of a tavern.
5. I.e., something with significance.

The Prologue

Lordinges—quod he—in chirches whan I preche,
I paine me⁶ to han an hautein° speeche,   *loud*
And ringe it out as round as gooth a belle,
For I can al by rote⁷ that I telle.

45 My theme is alway oon,⁸ and evere was:
*Radix malorum est cupiditas.*⁹
First I pronounce whennes° that I come,   *whence*
And thanne my bulles¹ shewe I alle and some:
Oure lige lordes seel on my patente,²

50 That shewe I first, my body to warente,°   *keep safe*
That no man be so bold, ne preest ne clerk,
Me to destourbe of Cristes holy werk.
And after that thanne telle I forth my tales³—
Bulles of popes and of cardinales,

55 Of patriarkes and bisshopes I shewe,
And in Latin I speke a wordes fewe,
To saffron with⁴ my predicacioun,°   *preaching*
And for to stire hem to devocioun.

Thanne shewe I forth my longe crystal stones,°   *jars*
60 Ycrammed ful of cloutes° and of bones—   *rags*
Relikes been they, as weenen° they eechoon.   *suppose*
Thanne have I in laton° a shulder-boon   *zinc*
Which that was of an holy Jewes sheep.
"Goode men," I saye, "take of my wordes keep:°   *notice*

65 If that this boon be wasshe in any welle,
If cow, or calf, or sheep, or oxe swelle,
That any worm hath ete or worm ystonge,⁵
Take water of that welle and wassh his tonge,
And it is hool⁶ anoon. And ferthermoor,

70 Of pokkes° and of scabbe and every soor°   *pox / sore*
Shal every sheep be hool that of this welle
Drinketh a draughte. Take keep eek° that I telle: *also*
If that the goode man that the beestes oweth°   *owns*
Wol every wike,° er that the cok him croweth,   *week*

75 Fasting drinken of this welle a draughte—
As thilke° holy Jew oure eldres taughte—   *that same*
His beestes and his stoor° shal multiplye.   *stock*
"And sire, also it heleth jalousye:
For though a man be falle in jalous rage,

80 Lat maken with this water his potage,°   *soup*
And nevere shal he more his wif mistriste,°   *mistrust*

---

6. Take pains.
7. I know all by heart.
8. I.e., the same.
9. Avarice is the root of evil (I Timothy vi.10).
1. Episcopal mandates; "alle and some": each and every one.

2. I.e., the Pope's seal on my papal license.
3. I go on with my yarn.
4. To add spice to.
5. That has eaten or been bitten by any worm.
6. I.e., sound.

Though he the soothe of hir defaute wiste,[7]
Al hadde she[8] taken preestes two or three.
    "Here is a mitein° eek that ye may see: *mitten*
85 He that his hand wol putte in this mitein
He shal have multiplying of his grain,
Whan he hath sowen, be it whete or otes—
So that he offre pens or elles grotes.[9]
    "Goode men and wommen, oo thing warne I you:
90 If any wight be in this chirche now
That hath doon sinne horrible, that he
Dar nat for shame of it yshriven° be,   *absolved*
Or any womman, be she yong or old,
That hath ymaked hir housbonde cokewold,°   *cuckold*
95 Swich folk shal have no power ne no grace
To offren to[1] my relikes in this place;
And whoso findeth him out of swich blame,
He wol come up and offre in Goddes name,
And I assoile° him by the auctoritee   *absolve*
100 Which that by bulle ygraunted was to me."
    By this gaude° have I wonne, yeer by yeer,   *trick*
An hundred mark[2] sith° I was pardoner.   *since*
I stonde lik a clerk in my pulpet,
And whan the lewed° peple is down yset,   *ignorant*
105 I preche so as ye han herd bifore,
And telle an hundred false japes° more.   *tricks*
Thanne paine I me[3] to strecche forth the nekke,
And eest and west upon the peple I bekke[4]
As dooth a douve,° sitting on a berne;°   *dove / barn*
110 Mine handes and my tonge goon so yerne°   *fast*
That it is joye to see my bisinesse.
Of avarice and of swich cursednesse°   *sin*
Is al my preching, for to make hem free°   *generous*
To yiven hir pens, and namely° unto me,   *especially*
115 For myn entente is nat but for to winne,[5]
And no thing for correccion of sinne:
I rekke° nevere whan that they been beried°   *care / buried*
Though that hir soules goon a-blakeberied.[6]
For certes, many a predicacioun°   *sermon*
120 Comth ofte time of yvel entencioun:
Som for plesance of folk and flaterye,
To been avaunced° by ypocrisye,   *promoted*
And som for vaine glorye, and som for hate;
For whan I dar noon otherways debate,°   *fight*
125 Thanne wol I stinge him with my tonge smerte
In preching, so that he shal nat asterte°   *escape*

7. Knew the truth of her infidelity.
8. Even if she had.
9. Pennies, groats, coins.
1. To make gifts in reverence of.
2. Marks (pecuniary units).
3. I take pains.
4. I.e., I shake my head.
5. Only to gain.
6. Go blackberrying, i.e., go to hell.

To been defamed falsly, if that he
Hath trespassed to[7] my bretheren or to me.
For though I telle nought his propre name,
130 Men shal wel knowe that it is the same
By signes and by othere circumstaunces.
Thus quite° I folk that doon us displesaunces;[8]   *pay back*
Thus spete° I out my venim under hewe°   *spit / color*
Of holinesse, to seeme holy and trewe.
135 But shortly myn entente I wol devise:°   *describe*
I preche of no thing but for coveitise;
Therfore my theme is yit and evere was
Radix malorum est cupiditas.
    Thus can I preche again that same vice
140 Which that I use, and that is avarice.
But though myself be gilty in that sinne,
Yit can I make other folk to twinne°   *separate*
From avarice, and sore to repente—
But that is nat my principal entente:
145 I preche no thing but for coveitise.
Of this matere it oughte ynough suffise.
    Thanne telle I hem ensamples[9] many oon
Of olde stories longe time agoon,
For lewed° peple loven tales olde—   *ignorant*
150 Swiche thinges can they wel reporte and holde.[1]
What, trowe° ye that whiles I may preche,   *believe*
And winne gold and silver for° I teche,   *because*
That I wol live in poverte wilfully?
Nay, nay, I thoughte° it nevere, trewely,   *intended*
155 For I wol preche and begge in sondry landes;
I wol nat do no labour with mine handes,
Ne make baskettes and live therby,
By cause I wol nat beggen idelly.[2]
I wol none of the Apostles countrefete:°   *imitate*
160 I wol have moneye, wolle,° cheese, and whete,   *wool*
Al were it[3] yiven of the pooreste page,
Or of the pooreste widwe in a village—
Al sholde hir children sterve[4] for famine.
Nay, I wol drinke licour of the vine
165 And have a joly wenche in every town.
But herkneth, lordinges, in conclusioun,
Youre liking° is that I shal telle a tale: *pleasure*
Now have I dronke a draughte of corny ale,
By God, I hope I shal you telle a thing
170 That shal by reson been at youre liking;
For though myself be a ful vicious man,
A moral tale yit I you telle can,

7. Injured.
8. Do us discourtesies.
9. *Exempla* (stories illustrating moral principles).

1. Repeat and remember.
2. I.e., without profit.
3. Even though it were.
4. Even though her children should die.

Which I am wont to preche for to winne.
Now holde youre pees, my tale I wol biginne.

The Tale

175	In Flandres whilom° was a compaignye	once
	Of yonge folk that haunteden° folye—	practiced
	As riot, hasard, stewes,[5] and tavernes,	
	Wher as with harpes, lutes, and giternes°	guitars
	They daunce and playen at dees° bothe day and night,	dice
180	And ete also and drinke over hir might,[6]	
	Thurgh which they doon the devel sacrifise	
	Within that develes temple in cursed wise	
	By superfluitee° abhominable.	overindulgence
	Hir othes been so grete and so dampnable	
185	That it is grisly for to heere hem swere:	
	Oure blessed Lordes body they totere[7]—	
	Hem thoughte that Jewes rente° him nought ynough.	tore
	And eech of hem at otheres sinne lough.°	laughed
	And right anoon thanne comen tombesteres,°	dancing girls
190	Fetis° and smale,° and yonge frutesteres,[8]	shapely / neat
	Singeres with harpes, bawdes,° wafereres[9]—	pimps
	Whiche been the verray develes officeres,	
	To kindle and blowe the fir of lecherye	
	That is annexed unto glotonye:[1]	
195	The Holy Writ take I to my witnesse	
	That luxure° is in win and dronkenesse.	lechery
	Lo, how that dronken Lot[2] unkindely°	unnaturally
	Lay by his doughtres two unwitingly:	
	So dronke he was he niste° what he wroughte.	didn't know
200	Herodes, who so wel the stories soughte,[3]	
	Whan he of win was repleet at his feeste,	
	Right at his owene table he yaf his heeste°	command
	To sleen° the Baptist John, ful giltelees.	slay
	Senek[4] saith a good word doutelees:	
205	He saith he can no difference finde	
	Bitwixe a man that is out of his minde	
	And a man which that is dronkelewe,°	drunken
	But that woodnesse, yfallen in a shrewe,[5]	
	Persevereth lenger than dooth dronkenesse.	
210	O glotonye, ful of cursednesse!°	wickedness
	O cause first of oure confusioun!°	downfall
	O original of oure dampnacioun,°	damnation
	Til Crist hadde bought° us with his blood again!	redeemed

5. Wild parties, gambling, brothels.
6. Beyond their capacity.
7. Tear apart (a reference to oaths sworn by parts of His body, such as "God's bones!" or "God's teeth!").
8. Fruit-selling girls.
9. Girl cake-vendors.
1. I.e., closely related to gluttony.

2. For Lot, see Genesis xix.30–36.
3. For the story of Herod and St. John the Baptist, see Mark vi.17–29. "Who so * * * soughte": i.e., whoever looked it up in the Gospel would find.
4. Seneca, the Roman Stoic philosopher.
5. But that madness, occurring in a wicked man.

Lo, how dere, shortly for to sayn,

215 Abought° was thilke° cursed vilainye;   *paid for / that same*
Corrupt was al this world for glotonye:
Adam oure fader and his wif also
Fro Paradis to labour and to wo
Were driven for that vice, it is no drede.°   *doubt*

220 For whil that Adam fasted, as I rede,
He was in Paradis; and whan that he
Eet° of the fruit defended° on a tree,   *ate / forbidden*
Anoon he was out cast to wo and paine.
O glotonye, on thee wel oughte us plaine!°   *complain*

225 O, wiste a man[6] how manye maladies
Folwen of excesse and of glotonies,
He wolde been the more mesurable°   *moderate*
Of his diete, sitting at his table.
Allas, the shorte throte, the tendre mouth,

230 Maketh that eest and west and north and south,
In erthe, in air, in water, men to swinke,°   *work*
To gete a gloton daintee mete and drinke.
Of this matere, O Paul, wel canstou trete:
"Mete unto wombe,° and wombe eek unto mete,   *belly*

235 Shal God destroyen bothe," as Paulus saith.[7]
Allas, a foul thing is it, by my faith,
To saye this word, and fouler is the deede
Whan man so drinketh of the white and rede[8]
That of his throte he maketh his privee°   *privy*

240 Thurgh thilke cursed superfluitee.°   *overindulgence*
  The Apostle[9] weeping saith ful pitously,
"Ther walken manye of which you told have I—
I saye it now weeping with pitous vois—
They been enemies of Cristes crois,°   *cross*

245 Of whiche the ende is deeth—wombe is hir god!"[1]
O wombe, O bely, O stinking cod,°   *bag*
Fulfilled° of dong° and of corrupcioun!   *filled full / dung*
At either ende of thee foul is the soun.°   *sound*
How greet labour and cost is thee to finde!°   *provide for*

250 Thise cookes, how they stampe[2] and straine and grinde,
And turnen substance into accident[3]
To fulfillen al thy likerous° talent!°   *dainty / appetite*
Out of the harde bones knokke they
The mary,° for they caste nought away   *marrow*

255 That may go thurgh the golet[4] softe and soote.°   *sweetly*
Of spicerye° of leef and bark and roote   *spices*
Shal been his sauce ymaked by delit,

6. If a man knew.
7. See I Corinthians vi.13.
8. I.e., white and red wines.
9. I.e., St. Paul.
1. See Philippians iii.18.
2. Pound.

3. A philosophic joke, depending on the distinction between inner reality (substance) and outward appearance (accident).
4. Through the gullet.

To make him yit a newer appetit.
But certes, he that haunteth swiche delices°   *pleasures*
260 Is deed° whil that he liveth in tho° vices.   *dead / those*
   A lecherous thing is win, and dronkenesse
Is ful of striving° and of wrecchednesse.   *quarreling*
O dronke man, disfigured is thy face!
Sour is thy breeth, foul artou to embrace!
265 And thurgh thy dronke nose seemeth the soun
As though thou saidest ay,° "Sampsoun, Sampsoun."   *always*
And yit, God woot,° Sampson drank nevere win.[5]   *knows*
Thou fallest as it were a stiked swin;[6]
Thy tonge is lost, and al thyn honeste cure,
270 For dronkenesse is verray sepulture°   *burial*
Of mannes wit° and his discrecioun.   *intelligence*
In whom that drinke hath dominacioun
He can no conseil° keepe, it is no drede.°   *secrets / doubt*
Now keepe you fro the white and fro the rede—
275 And namely° fro the white win of Lepe[7]   *particularly*
That is to selle in Fisshstreete or in Chepe:[8]
The win of Spaine creepeth subtilly
In othere wines growing faste° by,   *close*
Of which ther riseth swich fumositee°   *heady fumes*
280 That whan a man hath dronken draughtes three
And weeneth° that he be at hoom in Chepe,   *supposes*
He is in Spaine, right at the town of Lepe,
Nat at The Rochele ne at Burdeux town;[9]
And thanne wol he sayn, "Sampsoun, Sampsoun."
285   But herkneth, lordinges, oo° word I you praye,   *one*
That alle the s<nowiki>overein actes,[1] dar I saye,
Of victories in the Olde Testament,
Thurgh verray God that is omnipotent,
Were doon in abstinence and in prayere:
290 Looketh° the Bible and ther ye may it lere.°   *behold / learn*
   Looke Attila, the grete conquerour,[2]
Deide° in his sleep with shame and dishonour,   *died*
Bleeding at his nose in dronkenesse:
A capitain sholde live in sobrenesse.
295 And overal this, aviseth you[3] right wel
What was comanded unto Lamuel[4]—
Nat Samuel, but Lamuel, saye I—
Redeth the Bible and finde it expresly,
Of win-yiving° to hem that han[5] justise: *wine-serving*

---

5. Before Samson's birth an angel told his mother that he would be a Nazarite throughout his life; members of this sect took no strong drink.
6. Stuck pig. "Honeste cure": care for self-respect.
7. A town in Spain.
8. Fishstreet and Cheapside in the London market district.
9. The Pardoner is joking about the illegal custom of adulterating fine wines of Bordeaux and La Rochelle with strong Spanish wine.
1. Distinguished deeds.
2. Attila was the leader of the Huns who captured Rome in the 5th century.
3. Consider.
4. Lemuel's mother told him that kings should not drink (Proverbs xxxi.4–5).
5. I.e., administer.

300 Namore of this, for it may wel suffise.
        And now that I have spoken of glotonye,
    Now wol I you defende° hasardrye:°   *prohibit / gambling*
    Hasard is verray moder° of lesinges,°   *mother / lies*
    And of deceite and cursed forsweringes,
305 Blaspheme of Crist, manslaughtre, and wast° also   *waste*
    Of catel° and of time; and ferthermo,   *property*
    It is repreve° and contrarye of honour   *disgrace*
    For to been holden a commune hasardour,°   *gambler*
    And evere the hyer he is of estat
310 The more is he holden desolat.[6]
    If that a prince useth hasardrye,
    In alle governance and policye
    He is, as by commune opinioun,
    Yholde the lasse° in reputacioun.   *less*
315   Stilbon, that was a wis embassadour,
    Was sent to Corinthe in ful greet honour
    Fro Lacedomye° to make hir alliaunce,   *Sparta*
    And whan he cam him happede° parchaunce   *it happened*
    That alle the gretteste° that were of that lond   *greatest*
320 Playing at the hasard he hem foond,   *found*
    For which as soone as it mighte be
    He stal him[7] hoom again to his contree,
    And saide, "Ther wol I nat lese° my name,   *lose*
    N'I wol nat take on me so greet defame°   *dishonor*
325 You to allye unto none hasardours:
    Sendeth othere wise embassadours,
    For by my trouthe, me were levere[8] die
    Than I you sholde to hasardours allye.
    For ye that been so glorious in honours
330 Shal nat allye you with hasardours
    As by my wil, ne as by my tretee."°   *treaty*
    This wise philosophre, thus saide he.
        Looke eek that to the king Demetrius
    The King of Parthes,° as the book[9] saith us,   *Parthians*
335 Sente him a paire of dees° of gold in scorn,   *dice*
    For he hadde used hasard therbiforn,
    For which he heeld his glorye or his renown
    At no value or reputacioun.
    Lordes may finden other manere play
340 Honeste° ynough to drive the day away.   *honorable*
        Now wol I speke of othes false and grete
    A word or two, as olde bookes trete:
        Greet swering is a thing abhominable,
    And fals swering is yit more reprevable.°   *reprehensible*
345 The hye God forbad swering at al—

6. I.e., dissolute.
7. He stole away.
8. I had rather.
9. The book that relates this and the

previous incident is the *Policraticus* of
the 12th-century Latin writer, John of
Salisbury.

Witnesse on Mathew.[1] But in special
Of swering saith the holy Jeremie,[2]
"Thou shalt swere sooth thine othes and nat lie,
And swere in doom[3] and eek in rightwisnesse,
350 But idel swering is a cursednesse."°   *wickedness*
    Biholde and see that in the firste Table[4]
Of hye Goddes heestes° honorable   *commandments*
How that the seconde heeste of him is this:
"Take nat my name in idel or amis."
355 Lo, rather° he forbedeth swich swering   *sooner*
Than homicide, or many a cursed thing.
I saye that as by ordre thus it stondeth—
This knoweth that[5] his heestes understondeth
How that the seconde heeste of God is that.
360 And fertherover,° I wol thee telle al plat°   *moreover / flat*
That vengeance shal nat parten° from his hous   *depart*
That of his othes is too outrageous.
"By Goddes precious herte!" and "By his nailes!"°   *fingernails*
And "By the blood of Crist that is in Hailes,[6]
365 Sevene is my chaunce, and thyn is cink and traye!"[7]
"By Goddes armes, if thou falsly playe
This daggere shal thurghout thyn herte go!"
This fruit cometh of the bicche bones[8] two—
Forswering, ire, falsnesse, homicide.
370 Now for the love of Crist that for us dyde,
Lete° youre othes bothe grete and smale.   *leave*
But sires, now wol I telle forth my tale.
    Thise riotoures° three of whiche I telle,   *revelers*
Longe erst er prime[9] ronge of any belle,
375 Were set hem in a taverne to drinke,
And as they sat they herde a belle clinke
Biforn a cors° was caried to his grave.   *corpse*
That oon of hem gan callen to his knave:°   *servant*
"Go bet,"[1] quod he, "and axe° redily°   *ask / promptly*
380 What cors is this that passeth heer forby,
And looke° that thou reporte his name weel."°   *be sure / well*
    "Sire," quod this boy, "it needeth neveradeel:[2]
It was me told er ye cam heer two houres.
He was, pardee, an old felawe of youres.
385 And sodeinly he was yslain tonight,°   *last night*
Fordronke° as he sat on his bench upright;   *very drunk*
Ther cam a privee° thief men clepeth° Deeth,   *stealthy / call*
That in this contree al the peple sleeth,°   *slays*

1. "But I say unto you, Swear not at all" (Matthew v.34).
2. Jeremiah (iv.2).
3. Equity; "rightwisnesse": righteousness.
4. I.e., the first four of the Ten Commandments.
5. I.e., he that.

6. An abbey in Gloucestershire supposed to possess some of Christ's blood.
7. Five and three.
8. I.e., damned dice.
9. Long before 9 A.M.
1. Better, i.e., quick.
2. It isn't a bit necessary.

And with his spere he smoot his herte atwo,
390 And wente his way withouten wordes mo.
He hath a thousand slain this° pestilence.   *during this*
And maister, er ye come in his presence,
Me thinketh that it were necessarye
For to be war of swich an adversarye;
395 Beeth redy for to meete him everemore:
Thus taughte me my dame.° I saye namore."   *mother*
    "By Sainte Marye," saide this taverner,
"The child saith sooth, for he hath slain this yeer,
Henne° over a mile, within a greet village,   *hence*
400 Bothe man and womman, child and hine³ and page.
I trowe° his habitacion be there.   *believe*
To been avised° greet wisdom it were   *wary*
Er that he dide a man a dishonour."
    "Ye, Goddes armes," quod this riotour,
405 "Is it swich peril with him for to meete?
I shal him seeke by way and eek by streete,⁴
I make avow to Goddes digne° bones.   *worthy*
Herkneth, felawes, we three been alle ones:°   *of one mind*
Lat eech of us holde up his hand to other
410 And eech of us bicome otheres brother,
And we wol sleen this false traitour Deeth.
He shal be slain, he that so manye sleeth,
By Goddes dignitee, er it be night."
    Togidres han thise three hir trouthes plight⁵
415 To live and dien eech of hem with other,
As though he were his owene ybore° brother.   *born*
And up they sterte,° al dronken in this rage,   *started*
And forth they goon towardes that village
Of which the taverner hadde spoke biforn.
420 And many a grisly ooth thanne han they sworn,
And Cristes blessed body they torente:°   *tore apart*
Deeth shal be deed° if that they may him hente.°   *dead / catch*
    Whan they han goon nat fully half a mile,
Right as they wolde han treden° over a stile,   *stepped*
425 An old man and a poore with hem mette;
This olde man ful mekely hem grette,°   *greeted*
And saide thus, "Now lordes, God you see."⁶
    The pruddeste° of thise riotoures three   *proudest*
Answerde again, "What, carl° with sory grace,   *churl*
430 Why artou al forwrapped save thy face?
Why livestou so longe in so greet age?"
    This olde man gan looke in his visage,
And saide thus, "For° I ne can nat finde   *because*
A man, though that I walked into Inde,
435 Neither in citee ne in no village,

---

3. Farm laborer.   5. Pledged their words of honor.
4. By highway and byway.   6. May God protect you.

That wolde chaunge his youthe for myn age;
And therfore moot I han myn age stille,
As longe time as it is Goddes wille.
"Ne Deeth, allas, ne wol nat have my lif.
440 Thus walke I lik a restelees caitif,°   *captive*
And on the ground which is my modres° gate   *mother's*
I knokke with my staf bothe erly and late,
And saye, 'Leve° moder, leet me in: *dear*
Lo, how I vanisshe, flessh and blood and skin.
445 Allas, whan shal my bones been at reste?
Moder, with you wolde I chaunge° my cheste[7]   *exchange*
That in my chambre longe time hath be,
Ye, for an haire-clout[8] to wrappe me.'
But yit to me she wol nat do that grace,
450 For which ful pale and welked° is my face.   *withered*
But sires, to you it is no curteisye
To speken to an old man vilainye,°   *rudeness*
But° he trespasse° in word or elles in deede.   *unless / offend*
In Holy Writ ye may yourself wel rede,
455 'Agains[9] an old man, hoor° upon his heed,   *hoar*
Ye shal arise.'[1] Wherfore I yive you reed,°   *advice*
Ne dooth unto an old man noon harm now,
Namore than that ye wolde men dide to you
In age, if that ye so longe abide.
460 And God be with you wher ye go° or ride: *walk*
I moot go thider as I have to go."
    "Nay, olde cherl, by God thou shalt nat so,"
Saide this other hasardour anoon.
"Thou partest nat so lightly,° by Saint John!   *easily*
465 Thou speke° right now of thilke traitour Deeth,   *spoke*
That in this contree alle oure freendes sleeth:
Have here my trouthe, as thou art his espye,
Tel wher he is, or thou shalt it abye,°   *pay for*
By God and by the holy sacrament!
470 For soothly thou art oon of his assent[2]
To sleen us yonge folk, thou false thief."
    "Now sires," quod he, "if that ye be so lief°   *anxious*
To finde Deeth, turne up this crooked way,
For in that grove I lafte° him, by my fay,°   *left / faith*
475 Under a tree, and ther he wol abide:
Nat for youre boost° he wol him no thing hide.   *boast*
See ye that ook?° Right ther ye shal him finde.   *oak*
God save you, that boughte again[3] mankinde,
And you amende." Thus saide this olde man.
480   And everich of thise riotoures ran
Til he cam to that tree, and ther they founde

---

7. Chest for one's belongings, used here as the symbol for life—or perhaps a coffin.
8. Haircloth, for a winding sheet.
9. In the presence of.
1. Cf. Leviticus xix.32.
2. I.e., one of his party.
3. Redeemed.

Of florins° fine of gold ycoined rounde   *coins*
Wel neigh an eighte busshels as hem thoughte—
Ne lenger thanne after Deeth they soughte,
485 But eech of hem so glad was of the sighte,
For that the florins been so faire and brighte,
That down they sette hem by this precious hoord.
The worste of hem he spak the firste word:
    "Bretheren," quod he, "take keep° what that I saye: *heed*
490 My wit is greet though that I bourde° and playe.   *joke*
This tresor hath Fortune unto us yiven
In mirthe and jolitee oure lif to liven,
And lightly° as it cometh so wol we spende.   *easily*
Ey, Goddes precious dignitee, who wende[4]
495 Today that we sholde han so fair a grace?
But mighte this gold be caried fro this place
Hoom to myn hous—or elles unto youres—
For wel ye woot that al this gold is oures—
Thanne were we in heigh felicitee.
500 But trewely, by daye it mighte nat be:
Men wolde sayn that we were theves stronge,°   *flagrant*
And for oure owene tresor doon us honge.[5]
This tresor moste ycaried be by nighte,
As wisely and as slyly as it mighte.
505 Therfore I rede° that cut° amonges us alle   *advise / lots*
Be drawe, and lat see wher the cut wol falle;
And he that hath the cut with herte blithe
Shal renne° to the town, and that ful swithe,°   *run / quickly*
And bringe us breed and win ful prively;
510 And two of us shal keepen° subtilly   *guard*
This tresor wel, and if he wol nat tarye,
Whan it is night we wol this tresor carye
By oon assent wher as us thinketh best."
That oon of hem the cut broughte in his fest°   *fist*
515 And bad hem drawe and looke wher it wol falle;
And it fil° on the yongeste of hem alle,   *fell*
And forth toward the town he wente anoon.
And also° soone as that he was agoon,°   *as / gone away*
That oon of hem spak thus unto that other:
520 "Thou knowest wel thou art my sworen brother,
Thy profit wol I telle thee anoon:
Thou woost wel that oure felawe is agoon,
And here is gold, and that ful greet plentee,
That shal departed° been among us three.   *divided*
525 But nathelees, if I can shape° it so   *arrange*
That it departed were among us two,
Hadde I nat doon a freendes turn to thee?"
    That other answerde, "I noot[6] how that may be:

---

4. Who would have supposed.   6. Don't know.
5. Have us hanged.

He woot that the gold is with us twaye.
530 What shal we doon? What shal we to him saye?"
    "Shal it be conseil?"[7] saide the firste shrewe.°   villain
"And I shal telle in a wordes fewe
What we shul doon, and bringe it wel aboute."
    "I graunte," quod that other, "out of doute,
535 That by my trouthe I wol thee nat biwraye."°   expose
    "Now," quod the firste, "thou woost wel we be twaye,
And two of us shal strenger° be than oon: stronger
Looke whan that he is set that right anoon
Aris as though thou woldest with him playe,
540 And I shal rive° him thurgh the sides twaye,   pierce
Whil that thou strugelest with him as in game,
And with thy daggere looke thou do the same:
And thanne shal al this gold departed be,
My dere freend, bitwixe thee and me.
545 Thanne we may bothe oure lustes° al fulfille,   desires
And playe at dees° right at oure owene wille."   dice
And thus accorded been thise shrewes twaye
To sleen the thridde, as ye han herd me saye.
    This yongeste, which that wente to the town,
550 Ful ofte in herte he rolleth up and down
The beautee of thise florins newe and brighte.
"O Lord," quod he, "if so were that I mighte
Have al this tresor to myself allone,
Ther is no man that liveth under the trone°   throne
555 Of God that sholde live so merye as I."
And at the laste the feend oure enemy
Putte in his thought that he sholde poison beye,°   buy
With which he mighte sleen his felawes twaye—
Forwhy° the feend foond him in swich livinge   because
560 That he hadde leve° him to sorwe bringe:[8]   permission
For this was outrely° his fulle entente,   plainly
To sleen hem bothe, and nevere to repente.
    And forth he gooth—no lenger wolde he tarye—
Into the town unto a pothecarye,°   apothecary
565 And prayed him that he him wolde selle
Som poison that he mighte his rattes quelle,°   kill
And eek ther was a polcat[9] in his hawe°   yard
That, as he saide, his capons hadde yslawe,°   slain
And fain he wolde wreke him[1] if he mighte
570 On vermin that destroyed him[2] by nighte.
    The pothecarye answerde, "And thou shalt have
A thing that, also° God my soule save,   as
In al this world there is no creature
That ete or dronke hath of this confiture°—   mixture

7. A secret.
8. Christian doctrine teaches that the devil may not tempt men except with God's permission.
9. A weasel-like animal.
1. He would gladly avenge himself.
2. I.e., were ruining his farming.

575 Nat but the mountance° of a corn° of whete—   amount / grain
    That he ne shal his lif anoon forlete.°   lose
    Ye, sterve° he shal, and that in lasse° while   die / less
    Than thou wolt goon a paas³ nat but a mile,
    The poison is so strong and violent."
580 This cursed man hath in his hand yhent°   taken
    This poison in a box and sith° he ran   then
    Into the nexte streete unto a man
    And borwed of him large botels three,
    And in the two his poison poured he—
585 The thridde he kepte clene for his drinke,
    For al the night he shoop him⁴ for to swinke°   work
    In carying of the gold out of that place.
    And whan this riotour with sory grace
    Hadde filled with win his grete botels three,
590 To his felawes again repaireth he.
      What needeth it to sermone of it more?
    For right as they had cast° his deeth bifore,   plotted
    Right so they han him slain, and that anoon.
    And whan that this was doon, thus spak that oon:
595 "Now lat us sitte and drinke and make us merye,
    And afterward we wol his body berye."°   bury
    And with that word it happed him par cas⁵
    To take the botel ther the poison was,
    And drank, and yaf his felawe drinke also,
600 For which anoon they storven° bothe two.   died
      But certes I suppose that Avicen
    Wroot nevere in no canon ne in no *fen*⁶
    Mo wonder signes⁷ of empoisoning
    Than hadde thise wrecches two er hir ending:
605 Thus ended been thise homicides two,
    And eek the false empoisonere also.
      O cursed sinne of alle cursednesse!
    O traitours homicide, O wikkednesse!
    O glotonye, luxure,° and hasardrye!   lechery
610 Thou blasphemour of Crist with vilainye
    And othes grete of usage° and of pride!   habit
    Allas, mankinde, how may it bitide
    That to thy Creatour which that thee wroughte,
    And with his precious herte blood thee boughte,°   redeemed
615 Thou art so fals and so unkinde,° allas?   unnatural
      Now goode men, God foryive you youre trespas,
    And ware° you fro the sinne of avarice: guard
    Myn holy pardon may you alle warice°—   save
    So that ye offre nobles or sterlinges,⁸

---

3. Take a walk.
4. He was preparing.
5. By chance.
6. The *Canon of Medicine*, by Avicenna, an 11th-century Arabic philosopher, was divided into sections called *"fens."*
7. More wonderful symptoms.
8. "Nobles" and "sterlinges" were valuable coins.

620 Or elles silver brooches, spoones, ringes.
Boweth your heed under this holy bulle!
Cometh up, ye wives, offreth of youre wolle!°   *wool*
Youre name I entre here in my rolle: anoon
Into the blisse of hevene shul ye goon.
625 I you assoile° by myn heigh power—   *absolve*
Ye that wol offre—as clene and eek as cleer
As ye were born.—And lo, sires, thus I preche.
And Jesu Crist that is oure soules leeche°   *physician*
So graunte you his pardon to receive,
630 For that is best—I wol you nat deceive.

The Epilogue

"But sires, oo word forgat I in my tale:
I have relikes and pardon in my male°   *bag*
As faire as any man in Engelond,
Whiche were me yiven by the Popes hond.
635 If any of you wol of devocioun
Offren and han myn absolucioun,
Come forth anoon, and kneeleth here adown,
And mekely receiveth my pardoun,
Or elles taketh pardon as ye wende,
640 Al newe and fressh at every miles ende—
So that ye offre alway newe and newe⁹
Nobles or pens whiche that be goode and trewe.
It is an honour to everich that is heer
That ye have a suffisant° pardoner   *competent*
645 T'assoile you in contrees as ye ride,
For aventures whiche that may bitide:
Paraventure ther may falle oon or two
Down of his hors and breke his nekke atwo;
Looke which a suretee° is it to you alle   *safeguard*
650 That I am in youre felaweshipe yfalle
That may assoile you, bothe more and lasse,¹
Whan that the soule shal fro the body passe.
I rede° that oure Hoste shal biginne,   *advise*
For he is most envoluped° in sinne.   *involved*
655 Com forth, sire Host, and offre first anoon,
And thou shalt kisse the relikes everichoon,°   *each one*
Ye, for a grote: unbokele° anoon thy purs."   *unbuckle*
"Nay, nay," quod he, "thanne have I Cristes curs!
Lat be," quod he, "it shal nat be, so theech!°   *may I thrive*
660 Thou woldest make me kisse thyn olde breech°   *breeches*
And swere it were a relik of a saint,
Though it were with thy fundament depeint.°   *stained*
But, by the crois which that Sainte Elaine foond,²

9. Over and over.
1. Both high and low (i.e., everybody).
2. I.e., by the cross that St. Helena

found. Helena, mother of Constantine
the Great, was reputed to have found
the True Cross.

I wolde I hadde thy coilons° in myn hond,   *testicles*
665 In stede of relikes or of saintuarye.°   *relic-box*
Lat cutte hem of: I wol thee helpe hem carye.
They shal be shrined in an hogges tord."°   *turd*
    This Pardoner answerde nat a word:
So wroth he was no word ne wolde he saye.
670 "Now," quod oure Host, "I wol no lenger playe
With thee, ne with noon other angry man."
    But right anoon the worthy Knight bigan,
Whan that he sawgh that al the peple lough,°   *laughed*
"Namore of this, for it is right ynough.
675 Sire Pardoner, be glad and merye of cheere,
And ye, sire Host that been to me so dere,
I praye you that ye kisse the Pardoner,
And Pardoner, I praye thee, draw thee neer,
And as we diden lat us laughe and playe."
680 Anoon they kiste and riden forth hir waye.

The Nun's Priest's Tale[1]

A poore widwe somdeel stape° in age   *advanced*
Was whilom° dwelling in a narwe[2] cotage,   *once upon a time*
Biside a grove, stonding in a dale:
This widwe of which I telle you my tale,
5 Sin thilke° day that she was last a wif,   *that same*
In pacience ladde° a ful simple lif.   *led*

1. The Nun's Priest's Tale is an example of the literary genre known as the "beast fable," in which animals behave like human beings. The beast fable is inevitably injurious to man's dignity, since to pretend that animals behave like men is to suggest that men behave like animals, for a pig cannot look like a man unless a man in some way looks like a pig. In the Nun's Priest's Tale, as in its French source, the history of Reynard the Fox, the beast fable is combined with the mock heroic, and the result is doubly injurious to man's dignity. The elevated language of true heroic poetry means to enhance the splendid deeds of men of great stature, while the elevated language of mock heroic, by treating the trivial as if it were sublime, reveals man's lack of dignity in the awful gulf that separates the idealized language from the petty action it describes; and when the petty action is carried on not even by men, but by animals masquerading as men (that is, by men reduced to the status of animals), the loss of human dignity is even greater.

The nominal hero of the Tale is Chauntecleer, a fowl of courtly bearing, profound learning, and superior crowing. This rooster is, like Achilles or Aeneas, made the center of a "great" action—which, however, takes up a relatively small portion of the total number of lines in the poem. The hero of the larger portion, and the real hero of the poem, is rhetoric, which is responsible for all Chauntecleer's importance, though it almost drowns his story in its vast tumid flow. Rhetoric as employed by the Nun's Priest includes not only elevated speech, but proverbs, saws, conventional similes—all the clichés of formal language and thought. Epic mannerisms abound; proverbs fly thick and fast and contradict one another with impunity; sententious generalizations about the tragic inevitability of certain events, the bad counsel given by women, and the folly of heeding flattery are successively used to account for Chauntecleer's near-fall; and throughout the tale learned pedantry invokes rhetorical tradition to footnote the least original of ideas. All rhetoric's ordering devices achieve a fine disorder.
2. I.e., small.

For litel was hir catel° and hir rente,°   *property / income*
By housbondrye° of swich as God hire scnte   *economy*
She foond° hirself and eek hir doughtren two.   *provided for*
10 Three large sowes hadde she and namo,
Three kin,° and eek a sheep that highte Malle.   *cows*
Ful sooty was hir bowr° and eek hir halle,   *bedroom*
In which she eet ful many a sclendre° mcel;   *scanty*
Of poinant° sauce hire needed neveradeel: *pungent*
15 No daintee morsel passed thurgh hir throte—
Hir diete was accordant to hir cote.°   *cottage*
Repleccioun° ne made hire nevere sik: *overeating*
Attempre° diete was al hir physik,°   *moderate / medicine*
And exercise and hertes suffisaunce.°   *contentment*
20 The goute lette hire nothing for to daunce,[3]
N'apoplexye shente° **nat hir** heed.°   *nurt / head*
No win ne drank she, **neither** whit ne reed:°   *red*
Hir boord° was **served most** with whit and blak,[4]   *table*
Milk and brown **breed, in which** she foond no lak;[5]
25 Seind bacon, and **somtime** an ey° or twaye,   *egg*
For she was as it were **a manere daye.**[6]
A yeerd° she hadde, enclosed al withoute   *yard*
With stikkes, and a drye dich aboute,
In which she hadde a cok heet° Chauntecleer: *named*
30 In al the land of crowing nas° his peer.   *was not*
His vois was merier than the merye orgon
On massedayes that in the chirche goon;[7]
Wel sikerer[8] was his crowing in his logge°   *dwelling*
Than is a clok or an abbeye orlogge;°   *timepiece*
35 By nature he knew eech ascensioun
Of th'equinoxial[9] in thilke town:
For whan degrees fifteene were ascended,
Thanne crew[1] he that it mighte nat been amended
His comb was redder than the fin coral,
40 And batailed° as it were a castel wal;   *battlemented*
His bile° was blak, and as the jeet° it shoon;   *bill / jet*
Like asure[2] were his legges and his toon;°   *toes*
His nailes whitter° than the lilye flowr,   *whiter*
And lik the burned° gold was his colour.   *burnished*
45 This gentil cok hadde in his governaunce
Sevene hennes for to doon al his plesaunce,°   *pleasure*
Whiche were his sustres and his paramours,[3]
And wonder like to him as of colours;

---

3. The gout didn't hinder her at all from dancing.
4. I.e., milk and bread.
5. Found no fault. "Seind": scorched (i.e., broiled).
6. I.e., a kind of dairymaid.
7. I.e., is played.
8. More reliable.
9. I.e., he knew by instinct each step in the progression of the celestial equator. The celestial equator was thought to make a 360-degree rotation around the earth every 24 hours; therefore a progression of 15 degrees would be equal to the passage of an hour (line 37).
1. Crowed; "amended": improved.
2. Lapis lazuli.
3. His sisters and his mistresses.

Of whiche the faireste hewed° on hir throte   *colored*
50   Was cleped faire damoisele Pertelote:
Curteis she was, discreet, and debonaire,°   *meek*
And compaignable,[4] and bar° hirself so faire,   *bore*
Sin thilke day that she was seven night old,
That trewely she hath the herte in hold
55   Of Chauntecleer, loken° in every lith.°   *locked / limb*
He loved hire so that wel was him therwith.[5]
But swich a joye was it to heere hem singe,
Whan that the brighte sonne gan to springe,
In sweete accord *My Lief is Faren in Londe*[6]—
60   For thilke time, as I have understonde,
Beestes and briddes couden speke and singe.
    And so bifel that in a daweninge,
As Chauntecleer among his wives alle
Sat on his perche that was in the halle,
65   And next him sat this faire Pertelote,
This Chauntecleer gan gronen in his throte,
As man that in his dreem is drecched° sore.   *troubled*
    And whan that Pertelote thus herde him rore,
She was agast, and saide, "Herte dere,
70   What aileth you to grone in this manere?
Ye been a verray slepere,[7] fy, for shame!"
    And he answerde and saide thus, "Madame,
I praye you that ye take it nat agrief.°   *amiss*
By God, me mette I was in swich meschief[8]
75   Right now, that yit myn herte is sore afright.
Now God," quod he, "my swevene recche aright,[9]
And keepe my body out of foul prisoun!
Me mette how that I romed up and down
Within oure yeerd, wher as I sawgh a beest,
80   Was lik an hound and wolde han maad arrest[1]
Upon my body, and han had me deed.[2]
His colour was bitwixe yelow and reed,
And tipped was his tail and bothe his eres
With blak, unlik the remenant° of his heres;°   *rest / hairs*
85   His snoute smal, with glowing yën twaye.
Yit of his look for fere almost I deye:°   *die*
This caused me my groning, doutelees."
    "Avoi,"° quod she, "fy on you, hertelees!°   *fie / coward*
Allas," quod she, "for by that God above,
90   Now han ye lost myn herte and al my love!
I can nat love a coward, by my faith.
For certes, what so any womman saith,
We alle desiren, if it mighte be,

---

4. Companionable.
5. That he was well contented.
6. A popular song of the time.
7. Sound sleeper.
8. I dreamed that I was in such mis-

fortune.
9. Interpret my dream correctly (i.e., in an auspicious manner).
1. Would have laid hold.
2. I.e., killed me.

To han housbondes hardy, wise, and free,°   *generous*
95 And secree,° and no nigard, ne no fool,   *discreet*
Ne him that is agast of every tool,°   *weapon*
Ne noon avauntour.° By that God above,   *boaster*
How dorste ye sayn for shame unto youre love
That any thing mighte make you aferd?
100 Have ye no mannes herte and han a beerd?
Allas, and conne° ye been agast of swevenes?°   *can / dreams*
No thing, God woot, but vanitee³ in swevene is!
Swevenes engendren of replexiouns,⁴
And ofte of fume° and of complexiouns,°   *gas / bodily humors*
105 Whan humours been too habundant in a wight.⁵
Certes, this dreem which ye han met° tonight   *dreamed*
Comth of the grete superfluitee
Of youre rede colera,⁶ pardee,
Which causeth folk to dreden° in hir dremes   *fear*
110 Of arwes,° and of fir with rede lemes,°   *arrows / flames*
Of rede beestes, that they wol hem bite,
Of contek,° and of whelpes grete and lite⁷—   *strife*
Right° as the humour of malencolye⁸   *just*
Causeth ful many a man in sleep to crye
115 For fere of blake beres° or boles° blake,   *bears / bulls*
Or elles blake develes wol hem take.
Of othere humours coude I tell also
That werken many a man in sleep ful wo,
But I wol passe as lightly° as I can.   *quickly*
120 Lo, Caton,⁹ which that was so wis a man,
Saide he nat thus? 'Ne do no fors of¹ dremes.'
Now, sire," quod she, "whan we flee fro the bemes,²
For Goddes love, as take som laxatif.
Up° peril of my soule and of my lif,   *upon*
125 I conseile you the beste, I wol nat lie,
That bothe of colere and of malencolye
Ye purge you; and for° ye shal nat tarye,   *in order that*
Though in this town is noon apothecarye,
I shal myself to herbes techen you,
130 That shal been for youre hele³ and for youre prow,
And in oure yeerd tho herbes shal I finde,
The whiche han of hir propretee by kinde°   *nature*
To purge you binethe and eek above.
Foryet° nat this, for Goddes owene love.   *forget*
135 Ye been ful colerik° of complexioun;   *bilious*

3. I.e., empty illusion.
4. Dreams have their origin in over-eating.
5. I.e., when humors are too abundant in a person. Pertelote's diagnosis is based on the familiar concept that an overabundance of one of the bodily humors in a person affected his temperament.

6. Red bile.
7. And of big and little dogs.
8. I.e., black bile.
9. Dionysius Cato, supposed author of a book of maxims used in elementary education.
1. Pay no attention to.
2. Fly down from the rafters.
3. Health; "prow": benefit.

Ware° the sonne in his ascencioun   *beware that*
Ne finde you nat repleet° of humours hote;°   *filled / hot*
And if it do, I dar wel laye° a grote   *bet*
That ye shul have a fevere terciane,[4]
140 Or an agu that may be youre bane.°   *death*
A day or two ye shul han digestives
Of wormes, er ye take youre laxatives
Of lauriol, centaure, and fumetere,[5]
Or elles of ellebor° that groweth there,   *hellebore*
145 Of catapuce, or of gaitres beries,[6]
Of herbe-ive° growing in oure yeerd ther merye is.[7] *herb ivy*
Pekke hem right up as they growe and ete hem in.
Be merye, housbonde, for youre fader kin!
Dredeth no dreem: I can saye you namore."

150   "Madame," quod he, "graunt mercy of youre lore.[8]
But nathelees, as touching daun° Catoun,   *master*
That hath of wisdom swich a greet renown,
Though that he bad no dremes for to drede,
By God, men may in olde bookes rede
155 Of many a man more of auctoritee°   *authority*
Than evere Caton was, so mote I thee,°   *thrive*
That al the revers sayn of his sentence,°   *opinion*
And han wel founden by experience
That dremes been significaciouns
160 As wel of joye as tribulaciouns
That folk enduren in this lif present.
Ther needeth make of this noon argument:
The verray preve[9] sheweth it in deede.
   "Oon of the gretteste auctour[1] that men rede
165 Saith thus, that whilom two felawes wente
On pilgrimage in a ful good entente,
And happed so they comen in a town,
Wher as ther was swich congregacioun
Of peple, and eek so strait of herbergage,[2]
170 That they ne founde as muche as oo cotage
In which they bothe mighte ylogged° be;   *lodged*
Wherfore they mosten° of necessitee   *must*
As for that night departe° compaignye.   *part*
And eech of hem gooth to his hostelrye,
175 And took his logging as it wolde falle.°   *befall*
That oon of hem was logged in a stalle,
Fer° in a yeerd, with oxen of the plough;   *far away*
That other man was logged wel ynough,
As was his aventure° or his fortune,   *lot*

4. Tertian (recurring every other day).
5. Of laureole, centaury, and fumitory.
These, and the herbs mentioned in the
next lines, were all common medieval
medicines used as cathartics.
6. Of caper berry or of gaiter berry.
7. Where it is pleasant.
8. Many thanks for your instruction.
9. Actual experience.
1. I.e., one of the greatest authors (perhaps Cicero).
2. And also such a shortage of lodging.

₁₈₀ That us governeth alle as in commune.
And so bifel that longe er it were day,
This man mette° in his bed, ther as he lay,   *dreamed*
How that his felawe gan upon him calle,
And saide, 'Allas, for in an oxes stalle
₁₈₅ This night I shal be mordred° ther I lie!   *murdered*
Now help me, dere brother, or I die!
In alle haste com to me,' he saide.
    "This man out of his sleep for fere abraide,°   *started up*
But whan that he was wakened of his sleep,
₁₉₀ He turned him and took of this no keep:°   *heed*
Him thoughte his dreem nas but a vanitee.
Thus twies in his sleeping dremed he,
And atte thridde time yit his felawe
Cam, as him thoughte, and saide, 'I am now slawe:°   *slain*
₁₉₅ Bihold my bloody woundes deepe and wide.
Aris up erly in the morwe tide[3]
And atte west gate of the town,' quod he,
'A carte ful of dong° ther shaltou see,   *dung*
In which my body is hid ful prively:
₂₀₀ Do thilke carte arresten boldely.[4]
My gold caused my mordre, sooth to sayn'—
And tolde him every point how he was slain,
With a ful pitous face, pale of hewe.
And truste wel, his dreem he foond° ful trewe,   *found*
₂₀₅ For on the morwe° as soone as it was day,   *morning*
To his felawes in° he took the way,   *lodging*
And whan that he cam to this oxes stalle,
After his felawe he bigan to calle.
    "The hostiler° answerde him anoon,   *innkeeper*
₂₁₀ And saide, 'Sire, youre felawe is agoon:°   *gone away*
As soone as day he wente out of the town.'
    "This man gan fallen in suspecioun,
Remembring on his dremes that he mette;°   *dreamed*
And forth he gooth, no lenger wolde he lette,°   *tarry*
₂₁₅ Unto the west gate of the town, and foond
A dong carte, wente as it were to donge° lond,   *put manure on*
That was arrayed in that same wise
As ye han herd the dede° man devise;   *dead*
And with an hardy herte he gan to crye,
₂₂₀ 'Vengeance and justice of this felonye!
My felawe mordred is this same night,
And in this carte he lith° gaping upright!°   *lies / supine*
I crye out on the ministres,' quod he,
'That sholde keepe and rulen this citee.
₂₂₅ Harrow,° allas, here lith my felawe slain!'   *help*
What sholde I more unto this tale sayn?
The peple up sterte° and caste the carte to grounde,   *started*

3. In the morning.   4. Boldly have this same cart stopped.

And in the middel of the dong they founde
The dede man that mordred was al newe.[5]

230 "O blisful God that art so just and trewe,
Lo, how that thou biwrayest° mordre alway!   *disclose*
Mordre wol out, that see we day by day:
Mordre is so wlatsom° and abhominable   *loathsome*
To God that is so just and resonable,

235 That he ne wol nat suffre it heled° be,   *concealed*
Though it abide a yeer or two or three.
Mordre wol out: this my conclusioun.
And right anoon ministres of that town
Han hent° the cartere and so sore him pined,[6]   *seized*

240 And eek the hostiler so sore engined,°   *racked*
That they biknewe° hir wikkednesse anoon,   *confessed*
And were anhanged° by the nekke boon.   *hanged*
Here may men seen that dremes been to drede.[7]

"And certes, in the same book I rede—
245 Right in the nexte chapitre after this—
I gabbe° nat, so have I joye or blis—   *lie*
Two men that wolde han passed over see
For certain cause into a fer contree,
If that the wind ne hadde been contrarye

250 That made hem in a citee for to tarye,
That stood ful merye upon an haven° side—   *harbor's*
But on a day again° the even tide   *toward*
The wind gan chaunge, and blewe right as hem leste:[8]
Jolif° and glad they wenten unto reste,   *merry*

255 And casten hem[9] ful erly for to saile.
"But to that oo man fil° a greet mervaile;   *befell*
That oon of hem, in sleeping as he lay,
Him mette[1] a wonder dreem again the day:
Him thoughte a man stood by his beddes side,

260 And him comanded that he sholde abide,
And saide him thus, 'If thou tomorwe wende,
Thou shalt be dreint:° my tale is at an ende.'   *drowned*
"He wook and tolde his felawe what he mette,
And prayed him his viage° to lette;°   *voyage / delay*

265 As for that day he prayed him to bide.
"His felawe that lay by his beddes side
Gan for to laughe, and scorned him ful faste.°   *hard*
'No dreem,' quod he, 'may so myn herte agaste°   *terrify*
That I wol lette° for to do my thinges.°   *delay / business*

270 I sette nat a straw by thy dreminges,[2]
For swevenes been but vanitees and japes:[3]
Men dreme alday° of owles or of apes,[4]   *constantly*

5. Recently.
6. Tortured.
7. Worthy of being feared.
8. Just as they wished.
9. Determined.

1. He dreamed.
2. I don't care a straw for your dreamings.
3. Dreams are but illusions and frauds.
4. I.e., of absurdities.

And of many a maze° therwithal—   *delusion*
Men dreme of thing that nevere was ne shal.[5]
275 But sith I see that thou wolt here abide,
And thus forsleuthen° wilfully thy tide,°   *waste / time*
Good woot, it reweth me;[6] and have good day.'
And thus he took his leve and wente his way.
But er that he hadde half his cours ysailed—
280 Noot I nat why ne what meschaunce it ailed—
But casuelly the shippes botme rente,[7]
And ship and man under the water wente,
In sighte of othere shippes it biside,
That with hem sailed at the same tide.
285 And therfore, faire Pertelote so dere,
By swiche ensamples olde maistou lere°   *learn*
That no man sholde been too recchelees°   *careless*
Of dremes, for I saye thee doutelees
That many a dreem ful sore is for to drede.
290   "Lo, in the lif of Saint Kenelm[8] I rede—
That was Kenulphus sone, the noble king
Of Mercenrike°—how Kenelm mette a thing   *Mercia*
A lite° er he was mordred on a day.   *little*
His mordre in his avision° he sey.°   *dream / saw*
295 His norice° him expounded everydeel°   *nurse / entirely*
His swevene, and bad him for to keepe him[9] weel
For traison, but he nas but seven yeer old,
And therfore litel tale hath he told
Of any dreem,[1] so holy was his herte.
300 By God, I hadde levere than my sherte[2]
That ye hadde rad° his legende as have I.   *read*
    "Dame Pertelote, I saye you trewely,
Macrobeus,[3] that writ the *Avisioun*
In Affrike of the worthy Scipioun,
305 Affermeth° dremes, and saith that they been   *confirms*
Warning of thinges that men after seen.
    "And ferthermore, I praye you looketh wel
In the Olde Testament of Daniel,
If he heeld° dremes any vanitee.[4]   *considered*
310   "Rede eek of Joseph[5] and ther shul ye see
Wher° dremes be somtime—I saye nat alle—   *whether*
Warning of thinges that shul after falle.
    "Looke of Egypte the king daun Pharao,
His bakere and his botelere° also,   *butler*

5. I.e., shall be.
6. I'm sorry.
7. I don't know why nor what was the
trouble with it—but accidentally the
ship's bottom split.
8. Kenelm succeeded his father as king
of Mercia at the age of 7, but was
slain by his aunt (in 821).
9. Guard himself.
1. Therefore he has set little store by

any dream.
2. I.e., I'd give my shirt.
3. Macrobius wrote a famous commentary on Cicero's account in *De
Republica* of the dream of Scipio
Africanus Minor; the commentary came
to be regarded as a standard authority
on dream lore.
4. See Daniel vii.
5. See Genesis xxxvii.

315: Wher they ne felte noon effect in dremes.[6]
　　Whoso wol seeke actes of sondry remes°　　　　*realms*
　　May rede of dremes many a wonder thing.
　　　"Lo Cresus, which that was of Lyde° king,　　*Lydia*
　　Mette° he nat that he sat upon a tree,　　　　*dreamed*
320　Which signified he sholde anhanged° be?　　　*hanged*
　　　"Lo here Andromacha, Ectores° wif,　　　　*Hector's*
　　That day that Ector sholde lese° his lif,　　　*lose*
　　She dremed on the same night biforn
　　How that the lif of Ector sholde be lorn,°　　　*lost*
325　If thilke° day he wente into bataile;　　　　*that same*
　　She warned him, but it mighte nat availe:°　　*do any good*
　　He wente for to fighte nathelees,
　　But he was slain anoon° of Achilles.　　　　*right away*
　　But thilke tale is al too long to telle,
330　And eek it is neigh day, I may nat dwelle.
　　Shortly I saye, as for conclusioun,
　　That I shal han of this avisioun[7]
　　Adversitee, and I saye ferthermoor
　　That I ne telle of[8] laxatives no stoor,
335　For they been venimes,° I woot it weel:　　　*poisons*
　　I hem defye, I love hem neveradeel.°　　　　*not a bit*
　　　"Now lat us speke of mirthe and stinte° al this.　　*stop*
　　Madame Pertelote, so have I blis,
　　Of oo thing God hath sente me large grace:
340　For whan I see the beautee of youre face—
　　Ye been so scarlet reed° aboute youre yën—　　*red*
　　It maketh al my drede for to dien.
　　For also siker° as *In principio*,[9]　　　　*certain*
　　Mulier est hominis confusio.[1]
345　Madame, the sentence° of this Latin is,　　　*meaning*
　　'Womman is mannes joye and al his blis.'
　　For whan I feele anight youre softe side—
　　Al be it that I may nat on you ride,
　　For that oure perche is maad so narwe, allas—
350　I am so ful of joye and of solas°　　　　　*delight*
　　That I defye bothe swevene and dreem."
　　And with that word he fleigh° down fro the beem,　*flew*
　　For it was day, and eek his hennes alle,
　　And with a "chuk" he gan hem for to calle,
355　For he hadde founde a corn lay in the yeerd.
　　Real° he was, he was namore aferd:°　　*regal / afraid*
　　He fethered[2] Pertelote twenty time,
　　And trad[3] hire as ofte er it was prime.

6. See Genesis xxxix–xli.
7. Divinely inspired dream (as opposed to the more ordinary "swevene" or "dreem").
8. Set by.
9. A tag from the Gospel of St. John which gives the essential premises of

Christianity: "In the beginning was the Word."
1. Woman is man's ruination.
2. I.e., embraced.
3. Trod, copulated with; "prime": 9 A.M.

He looketh as it were a grim leoun,
360 And on his toes he rometh up and down:
Him deined[4] nat to sette his foot to grounde.
He chukketh whan he hath a corn yfounde,
And to him rennen° thanne his wives alle.   *run*
Thus royal, as a prince is in his halle,
365 Leve I this Chauntecleer in his pasture,
And after wol I telle his aventure.
    Whan that the month in which the world bigan,
That highte March, whan God first maked man,
Was compleet, and passed were also,
370 Sin March bigan, thritty dayes and two,[5]
Bifel that Chauntecleer in al his pride,
His sevene wives walking him biside,
Caste up his yën to the brighte sonne,
That in the signe of Taurus hadde yronne
375 Twenty degrees and oon and somwhat more,
And knew by kinde,° and by noon other lore,   *nature*
That it was prime, and crew with blisful stevene.   *voice*
"The sonne," he saide, "is clomben[6] up on hevene
Fourty degrees and oon and more, ywis.
380 Madame Pertelote, my worldes blis,
Herkneth thise blisful briddes° how they singe,   *birds*
And see the fresshe flowres how they springe:
Ful is myn herte of revel and solas."
But sodeinly him fil° a sorweful cas,°   *befell / chance*
385 For evere the latter ende of joye is wo—
God woot that worldly joye is soone ago,
And if a rethor° coude faire endite,   *rhetorician*
He in a cronicle saufly° mighte it write,   *safely*
As for a soverein notabilitee.[7]
390 Now every wis man lat him herkne me:
This storye is also° trewe, I undertake,   *as*
As is the book of *Launcelot de Lake*,[8]
That wommen holde in ful greet reverence.
Now wol I turne again to my sentence.°   *main point*
395   A colfox[9] ful of sly iniquitee,
That in the grove hadde woned° yeres three,   *dwelled*
By heigh imaginacion forncast,[1]
The same night thurghout the hegges° brast°   *hedges / burst*
Into the yeerd ther Chauntecleer the faire
400 Was wont, and eek his wives, to repaire;

4. He deigned.
5. The rhetorical time-telling is perhaps burlesque; it can be read as yielding the date April 3, though May 3
seems intended from lines 374–75: on
May 3 the sun would have passed some
twenty degrees through Taurus (the
Bull), the second sign of the zodiac;
the sun would be forty degrees from the
horizon at 9 o'clock in the morning.
6. Has climbed.
7. Indisputable fact.
8. Romances of the courteous knight
Lancelot of the Lake were very popular.
9. Fox with black markings.
1. Predestined by divine planning.

And in a bed of wortes° stille he lay   *cabbages*
Til it was passed undren° of the day,   *midmorning*
Waiting his time on Chauntecleer to falle,
As gladly doon thise homicides alle,
405 That in await liggen to mordre[2] men.
O false mordrour, lurking in thy den!
O newe Scariot![3] Newe Geniloun!
False dissimilour!° O Greek Sinoun,[4]   *dissembler*
That broughtest Troye al outrely° to sorwe!   *utterly*
410 O Chauntecleer, accursed be that morwe°   *morning*
That thou into the yeerd flaugh° fro the bemes!   *flew*
Thou were ful wel ywarned by thy dremes
That thilke day was perilous to thee;
But what that God forwoot° moot° needes be,   *foreknows / must*
415 After° the opinion of certain clerkes: *according to*
Witnesse on him that any parfit° clerk is   *perfect*
That in scole is greet altercacioun
In this matere, and greet disputisoun,°   *disputation*
And hath been of an hundred thousand men.
420 But I ne can nat bulte° it to the bren,°   *sift / husks*
As can the holy doctour Augustin,
Or Boece, or the bisshop Bradwardin[5]—
Wheither that Goddes worthy forwiting°   *foreknowledge*
Straineth me nedely[6] for to doon a thing
425 ("Nedely" clepe I simple necessitee),
Or elles if free chois be graunted me
To do that same thing or do it nought,
Though God forwoot° it er that I was wrought;   *foreknew*
Or if his witing° straineth neveradeel,   *knowledge*
430 But by necessitee condicionel[7]—
I wol nat han to do of swich matere:
My tale is of a cok, as ye may heere,
That took his conseil of his wif with sorwe,
To walken in the yeerd upon that morwe
435 That he hadde met° the dreem that I you tolde.   *dreamed*
Wommenes conseils been ful ofte colde,[8]
Wommanes conseil broughte us first to wo,
And made Adam fro Paradis to go,
Ther as he was ful merye and wel at ese.
440 But for I noot° to whom it mighte displese   *don't know*
If I conseil of wommen wolde blame,

2. That lie in ambush to murder.
3. Judas Iscariot. "Geniloun" is Ganelon, who betrayed Roland to the Saracens (in the medieval French epic *The Song of Roland*).
4. Sinon, who persuaded the Trojans to take the Greeks' wooden horse into their city—with, of course, the result that the city was destroyed.
5. St. Augustine, Boethius (6th-century Roman philosopher, whose *Consolation of Philosophy* was translated by Chaucer), and Thomas Bradwardine (Archbishop of Canterbury, d. 1349) were all concerned with the interrelationship between man's free will and God's foreknowledge.
6. Constrains me necessarily.
7. Boethius' "conditional necessity" permitted a large measure of free will.
8. I.e., baneful.

Passe over, for I saide it in my game°——   *sport*
Rede auctours where they trete of swich matere,
And what they sayn of wommen ye may heere——
₄₄₅ Thise been the cokkes wordes and nat mine:
I can noon harm of no womman divine.°   *guess*
  Faire in the sond° to bathe hire merily   *sand*
Lith° Pertelote, and alle hir sustres by,   *lies*
Again° the sonne, and Chauntecleer so free°   *in / noble*
₄₅₀ Soong° merier than the mermaide in the see——   *sang*
For Physiologus⁹ saith sikerly
How that they singen wel and merily.
  And so bifel that as he caste his yë
Among the wortes on a boterflye,°   *butterfly*
₄₅₅ He was war of this fox that lay ful lowe.
No thing ne liste him¹ thanne for to crowe,
But cride anoon "Cok cok!" and up he sterte,°   *started*
As man that² was affrayed in his herte——
For naturelly a beest desireth flee
₄₆₀ Fro his contrarye³ if he may it see,
Though he nevere erst° hadde seen it with his yë.   *before*
This Chauntecleer, whan he gan him espye,
He wolde han fled, but that the fox anoon
Saide, "Gentil sire, allas, wher wol ye goon?
₄₆₅ Be ye afraid of me that am youre freend?
Now certes, I were worse than a feend
If I to you wolde° harm or vilainye.   *meant*
I am nat come youre conseil° for t'espye,   *secrets*
But trewely the cause of my cominge
₄₇₀ Was only for to herkne how that ye singe:
For trewely, ye han as merye a stevene°   *voice*
As any angel hath that is in hevene.
Therwith ye han in musik more feelinge
Than hadde Boece,⁴ or any that can singe.
₄₇₅ My lord your fader—God his soule blesse!——
And eek youre moder, of hir gentilesse,°   *gentility*
Han in myn hous ybeen, to my grete ese.
And certes sire, ful fain° wolde I you plese.   *gladly*
  "But for men speke of singing, I wol saye,
₄₈₀ So mote I brouke⁵ wel mine yën twaye,
Save ye, I herde nevere man so singe
As dide youre fader in the morweninge.
Certes, it was of herte⁶ al that he soong.°   *sang*
And for to make his vois the more strong,
₄₈₅ He wolde so paine him⁷ that with bothe his yën

9. Supposed author of a bestiary, a book of moralized zoology describing both natural and supernatural animals (including mermaids).
1. He wished.
2. Like one who.
3. I.e., his natural enemy.
4. Boethius also wrote a treatise on music.
5. So might I enjoy the use of.
6. Heartfelt.
7. Take pains.

He moste winke,[8] so loude wolde he cryen;
And stonden on his tiptoon therwithal,
And strecche forth his nekke long and smal;
And eek he was of swich discrecioun
490 That ther nas no man in no regioun
That him in song or wisdom mighte passe.
I have wel rad° in *Daun Burnel the Asse*[9]   *read*
Among his vers how that ther was a cok,
For a preestes sone yaf him a knok[1]
495 Upon his leg whil he was yong and nice,°   *foolish*
He made him for to lese° his benefice.[2]   *lose*
But certain, ther nis no comparisoun
Bitwixe the wisdom and discrecioun
Of youre fader and of his subtiltee.
500 Now singeth, sire, for sainte° charitee!   *holy*
Lat see, conne° ye youre fader countrefete?"° *can / imitate*
  This Chauntecleer his winges gan to bete,
As man that coude his traison nat espye,
So was he ravisshed with his flaterye.
505 Allas, ye lordes, many a fals flatour°   *flatterer*
Is in youre court, and many a losengeour,° *deceiver*
That plesen you wel more, by my faith,
Than he that soothfastnesse° unto you saith! *truth*
Redeth Ecclesiaste[3] of flaterye.
510 Beeth war, ye lordes, of hir trecherye.
  This Chauntecleer stood hye upon his toos,
Strecching his nekke, and heeld his yën cloos,
And gan to crowe loude for the nones;°   *occasion*
And daun Russel the fox sterte° up atones, *jumped*
515 And by the gargat° hente° Chauntecleer, *throat / seized*
And on his bak toward the wode him beer,° *bore*
For yit ne was ther no man that him sued.° *followed*
  O destinee that maist nat been eschued!° *eschewed*
Allas that Chauntecleer fleigh° fro the bemes! *flew*
520 Allas his wif ne roughte nat of[4] dremes!
And on a Friday fil° al this meschaunce!   *befell*
  O Venus that art goddesse of plesaunce,
Sin that thy servant was this Chauntecleer,
And in thy service dide al his power—
525 More for delit than world[5] to multiplye—
Why woldestou suffre him on thy day[6] to die?
  O Gaufred,[7] dere maister soverein,

---

8. He had to shut his eyes.
9. Master Brunellus, a discontented donkey, was the hero of a 12th-century satirical poem by Nigel Wireker.
1. Because a priest's son gave him a knock.
2. The offended cock neglected to crow so that his master, now grown to manhood, overslept, missing his ordination and losing his benefice.
3. The Book of Ecclesiasticus, in the Apocrypha.
4. Didn't care for.
5. I.e., population.
6. Friday is Venus' day.
7. Geoffrey of Vinsauf, a famous medieval rhetorician, who wrote a lament on the death of Richard I in which he

That, whan thy worthy king Richard was slain
With shot,[8] complainedest his deeth so sore,
530 Why ne hadde I now thy sentence and thy lore,[9]
The Friday for to chide as diden ye?
For on a Friday soothly slain was he.
Thanne wolde I shewe you how that I coude plaine[1]
For Chauntecleres drede and for his paine.
535   Certes, swich cry ne lamentacioun
Was nevere of ladies maad whan Ilioun°   Ilium, Troy
Was wonne, and Pyrrus[2] with his straite swerd,
Whan he hadde hent° King Priam by the beerd   seized
And slain him, as saith us *Eneidos*,[3]
540 As maden alle the hennes in the cloos,°   yard
Whan they hadde seen of Chauntecleer the sighte.
But sovereinly[4] Dame Pertelote shrighte°   shrieked
Ful louder than dide Hasdrubales[5] wif
Whan that hir housbonde hadde lost his lif,
545 And that the Romains hadden brend° Cartage: burned
She was so ful of torment and of rage°   madness
That wilfully unto the fir she sterte,°   jumped
And brende hirselven with a stedefast herte.
O woful hennes, right so criden ye
550 As, whan that Nero brende the citee
Of Rome, criden senatoures wives
For that hir housbondes losten alle hir lives:[6]
Withouten gilt this Nero hath hem slain.
Now wol I turne to my tale again.
555   The sely° widwe and eek hir doughtres two   innocent
Herden thise hennes crye and maken wo,
And out at dores sterten° they anoon,   leaped
And sien° the fox toward the grove goon,   saw
And bar upon his bak the cok away,
560 And criden, "Out, harrow,° and wailaway,   help
Ha, ha, the fox," and after him they ran,
And eek with staves many another man;
Ran Colle oure dogge, and Talbot and Gerland,[7]
And Malkin with a distaf in hir hand,
565 Ran cow and calf, and eek the verray hogges,
Sore aferd° for berking of the dogges   frightened
And shouting of the men and wommen eke
They ronne° so hem thoughte hir herte breke;[8]   ran
They yelleden as feendes doon in helle;

scolded Friday, the day on which the
king died.
8. I.e., a missile.
9. Thy wisdom and thy learning.
1. Lament.
2. Pyrrhus was the Greek who slew
Priam, king of Troy. "Straite": rigorous, unsparing.
3. As the *Aeneid* tells us.

4. Splendidly.
5. Hasdrubal was king of Carthage
when it was destroyed by the Romans.
6. According to the legend, Nero not
only set fire to Rome (in A.D. 64) but
also put many senators to death.
7. Two other dogs.
8. Would break.

570 The dokes° criden as men wolde hem quelle;°   ducks / kill
    The gees for fere flowen° over the trees;   flew
    Out of the hive cam the swarm of bees;
    So hidous was the noise, a, benedicite,°   bless me
    Certes, he Jakke Straw⁹ and his meinee°   company
575 Ne made nevere shoutes half so shrille
    Whan that they wolden any Fleming kille,
    As thilke day was maad upon the fox:
    Of bras they broughten bemes° and of box,° trumpets / boxwood
    Of horn, of boon,° in whiche they blewe and pouped,¹ bone
580 And therwithal they skriked² and they houped—
    It seemed as that hevene sholde falle.
        Now goode men, I praye you herkneth alle:
    Lo, how Fortune turneth° sodeinly   reverses, overturns
    The hope and pride eek of hir enemy.
585 This cok that lay upon the foxes bak,
    In al his drede unto the fox he spak,
    And saide, "Sire, if that I were as ye,
    Yit sholde I sayn, as wis° God helpe me,   surely
    'Turneth ayain, ye proude cherles alle!
590 A verray pestilence upon you falle!
    Now am I come unto this wodes side,
    Maugree your heed,³ the cok shal here abide.
    I wol him ete, in faith, and that anoon.'"
        The fox answerde, "In faith, it shal be doon."
595 And as he spak that word, al sodeinly
    The cok brak from his mouth deliverly,°   nimbly
    And hye upon a tree he fleigh° anoon.   flew
        And whan the fox sawgh that he was agoon,
    "Allas," quod he, "O Chauntecleer, allas!
600 I have to you," quod he, "ydoon trespas,
    In as muche as I maked you aferd
    Whan I you hente° and broughte out of the yeerd.   seized
    But sire, I dide it in no wikke° entente: wicked
    Come down, and I shal telle you what I mente.
605 I shal saye sooth to you, God help me so."
        "Nay thanne," quod he, "I shrewe° us bothe two: curse
    But first I shrewe myself, bothe blood and bones,
    If thou bigile me ofter than ones;
    Thou shalt namore thurgh thy flaterye
610 Do° me to singe and winken with myn yë.   cause
    For he that winketh whan he sholde see,
    Al wilfully, God lat him nevere thee."°   thrive
        "Nay," quod the fox, "but God yive him meschaunce
    That is so undiscreet of governaunce°   self-control
615 That jangleth° whan he sholde holde his pees."   chatters

9. One of the leaders of the Peasant's   1. Tooted.
Revolt in 1381, which was partially di-   2. Shrieked; "houped": whooped.
rected against the Flemings living in   3. Despite your head—i.e., despite any-
London.   thing you can do.

Lo, swich it is for to be recchelees°   *careless*
And necligent and truste on flaterye.
But ye that holden this tale a folye
As of a fox, or of a cok and hen,
620 Taketh the moralitee, goode men.
For Saint Paul saith that al that writen is
To oure doctrine it is ywrit, ywis:[4]
Taketh the fruit, and lat the chaf be stille.
Now goode God, if that it be thy wille,
625 As saith my lord, so make us alle goode men,
And bringe us to his hye blisse. Amen.

The Miller's Tale[1]

The Introduction

Whan that the Knight hadde thus his tale ytold,[2]
In al the route° nas ther yong ne old   *group*
That he ne saide it was a noble storye,
And worthy for to drawen° to memorye,   *recall*
5 And namely° the gentils everichoon.   *especially*
Oure Hoste lough° and swoor, "So mote I goon,[3]   *laughed*
This gooth aright: unbokeled is the male.°   *pouch*
Lat see now who shal telle another tale.
For trewely the game is wel bigonne.
10 Now telleth ye, sire Monk, if that ye conne,°   *can*
Somwhat to quite° with the Knightes tale."   *repay*
The Millere, that for dronken[4] was al pale,
So that unnethe° upon his hors he sat,   *with difficulty*
He nolde avalen° neither hood ne hat,   *doff*
15 Ne abiden no man for his curteisye,
But in Pilates vois[5] he gan to crye,

4. See Romans xv.4.
1. The Miller's Tale belongs to the literary genre known as the "fabliau," a short story in verse that generally involves bourgeois or lower-class characters in an outrageous, often obscene plot, which is, however, realistically handled by the narrator. The fabliau is peculiarly French, and aside from the three or four examples in Chaucer there are few representatives of it in English. Yet Chaucer was supreme in this kind of tale as in many others, and the Miller's Tale is generally considered the best-told fabliau in any language.

Two originally separate plots are the basis of the Miller's Tale, both of them probably already old in Chaucer's time. In the first, a student—students are often the heroes of fabliaux and were probably often their authors—creates an opportunity to sleep with a woman by persuading her husband that Noah's flood is about to be repeated; and in the second, a lover who has been tricked into a humiliatingly misdirected kiss takes a dreadful vengeance on his tormentor. Whether or not Chaucer first united these traditional plots is not clear, but in any case their union, culminating in the scorched student's cry of "Water!" is a brilliant stroke, and brilliantly handled by Chaucer.
2. The Knight's Tale is actually the first one told on the Canterbury pilgrimage, immediately following the General Prologue.
3. So might I walk.
4. I.e., drunkenness.
5. The harsh voice usually associated with the character of Pontius Pilate in the mystery plays.

And swoor, "By armes[6] and by blood and bones,
I can° a noble tale for the nones,   *know*
With which I wol now quite the Knightes tale."
20   Oure Hoste sawgh that he was dronke of ale,
And saide, "Abide, Robin, leve° brother,   *dear*
Som bettre man shal telle us first another.
Abide, and lat us werken thriftily."°   *with propriety*
    "By Goddes soule," quod he, "that wol nat I,
25 For I wol speke or elles go my way."
    Oure Host answerde, "Tel on, a devele way![7]
Thou art a fool; thy wit is overcome."
    "Now herkneth," quod the Millere, "alle and some.[8]
But first I make a protestacioun°   *public affirmation*
30 That I am dronke: I knowe it by my soun.°   *tone of voice*
And therfore if that I mis° speke or saye,   *amiss*
Wite it[9] the ale of Southwerk, I you praye;
For I wol telle a legende and a lif
Bothe of a carpenter and of his wif,
35 How that a clerk hath set the wrightes cappe."[1]
    The Reeve answerde and saide, "Stint thy clappe![2]
Lat be thy lewed° dronken harlotrye.°   *ignorant / obscenity*
It is a sinne and eek° a greet folye   *also*
To apairen° any man or him defame,   *injure*
40 And eek to bringen wives in swich fame.°   *report*
Thou maist ynough of othere thinges sayn."
    This dronken Millere spak ful soone again,
And saide, "Leve° brother Osewold,   *dear*
Who hath no wif, he is no cokewold.°   *cuckold*
45 But I saye nat therfore that thou art oon.
Ther ben ful goode wives many oon,°   *a one*
And evere a thousand goode ayains oon badde.
That knowestou wel thyself but if thou madde.°   *rave*
Why artou angry with my tale now?
50 I have a wif, pardee, as wel as thou,
Yit nolde° I, for the oxen in my plough,   *would not*
Take upon me more than ynough
As deemen of myself that I were oon:
I wol bileve wel that I am noon.
55 An housbonde shal nought been inquisitif
Of Goddes privetee,° nor of his wif.   *secrets*
So[3] he may finde Goddes foison° there,   *plenty*
Of the remenant° needeth nought enquere."°   *rest / inquire*
    What sholde I more sayn but this Millere
60 He nolde his wordes for no man forbere,
But tolde his cherles tale in his manere,
M'athinketh° that I shal reherce° it here,   *I regret / repeat*

6. I.e., by God's arms.
7. I.e., in the devil's name.
8. Each and every one.
9. Blame it on.

1. I.e., how a clerk made a fool of a carpenter.
2. Stop your chatter.
3. Provided that.

And therfore every gentil wight I praye,
Deemeth nought, for Goddes love, that I saye
65 Of yvel entente, but for° I moot reherse   *because*
Hir tales alle, be they bet° or werse,   *better*
Or elles falsen° som of my matere.   *falsify*
And therfore, whoso list it nought yheere
Turne over the leef, and chese° another tale,   *choose*
70 For he shal finde ynowe,° grete and smale,   *enough*
Of storial[4] thing that toucheth gentilesse,°   *gentility*
And eek moralitee and holinesse:
Blameth nought me if that ye chese amis.
The Millere is a cherl, ye knowe wel this,
75 So was the Reeve eek, and othere mo,
And harlotrye° they tolden bothe two.   *ribaldry*
Aviseth you,[5] and putte me out of blame:
And eek men shal nought maken ernest of game.

The Tale

Whilom° ther was dwelling at Oxenforde   *once upon a time*
80 A riche gnof° that gestes heeld to boorde,[6]   *boor*
And of his craft he was a carpenter.
With him ther was dwelling a poore scoler,
Hadde lerned art,[7] but al his fantasye°   *interest*
Was turned for to lere° astrologye,   *learn*
85 And coude a certain of conclusiouns,
To deemen by interrogaciouns,[8]
If that men axed° him in certain houres   *asked*
Whan that men sholde have droughte or elles showres,
Or if men axed him what shal bifalle
90 Of every thing—I may nat rekene hem alle.
This clerk was cleped° hende[9] Nicholas.   *called*
Of derne love he coude, and of solas,[1]
And therto he was sly and ful privee,°   *secretive*
And lik a maide meeke for to see.
95 A chambre hadde he in that hostelrye
Allone, withouten any compaignye,
Ful fetisly ydight[2] with herbes swoote,°   *sweet*
And he himself as sweete as is the roote
Of licoris or any setewale.[3]
100 His *Almageste*[4] and bookes grete and smale,
His astrelabye,[5] longing for his art,
His augrim stones,[6] layen faire apart

4. Historical, i.e., true.
5. Take heed.
6. I.e., took in boarders.
7. Who had completed the first stage of university education (the trivium).
8. I.e., and he knew a number of propositions on which to base astrological analyses (which would reveal the matters in ll. 87–90).
9. Handy, sly, attractive.

1. I.e., he knew about secret love and pleasurable practices.
2. Elegantly furnished.
3. Setwall, a spice.
4. 2nd-century treatise by Ptolemy, still the standard astronomy textbook.
5. Astrolabe, an astronomical instrument. "Longing for": belonging to.
6. Counters used in arithmetic.

On shelves couched° at his beddes heed;   set
His presse° ycovered with a falding reed;[7]   storage chest
105 And al above ther lay a gay sautrye,°   psaltery
On which he made a-nightes melodye
So swetely that al the chambre roong,°   rang
And *Angelus ad Virginem*[8] he soong,
And after that he soong the *Kinges Note:*
110 Ful often blessed was his merye throte.
And thus this sweete clerk his time spente
After his freendes finding and his rente.[9]
    This carpenter hadde wedded newe° a wif   lately
Which that he loved more than his lif.
115 Of eighteteene yeer she was of age;
Jalous he was, and heeld hire narwe in cage,
For she was wilde and yong, and he was old,
And deemed himself been lik a cokewold.[1]
He knew nat Caton,[2] for his wit was rude,
120 That bad men sholde wedde his similitude:[3]
Men sholde wedden after hir estat,[4]
For youthe and elde° is often at debat.   age
But sith that he was fallen in the snare,
He moste endure, as other folk, his care.
125   Fair was this yonge wif, and therwithal
As any wesele° hir body gent and smal.[5]   weasel
A ceint she wered, barred[6] al of silk;
A barmcloth° as whit as morne milk   apron
Upon hir lendes,° ful of many a gore;°   loins / strip of cloth
130 Whit was hir smok,° and broiden[7] al bifore   undergarment
And eek bihinde, on hir coler° aboute,   collar
Of° col-blak silk, withinne and eek withoute;   with
The tapes° of hir white voluper°   ribbons / cap
Were of the same suite of[8] hir coler;
135 Hir filet° brood° of silk and set ful hye;   headband / broad
And sikerly° she hadde a likerous° yë;   certainly / wanton
Ful smale ypulled[9] were hir browes two,
And tho were bent,° and blake as any slo.°   arching / sloeberry
She was ful more blisful on to see
140 Than is the newe perejonette° tree,   pear
And softer than the wolle° is of a wether;°   wool / ram
And by hir girdel° heeng° a purs of lether,   belt / hung
Tasseled with silk and perled with latoun.[1]

7. Red coarse wool.
8. "The Angel's Address to the Virgin,"
a hymn; *"Kinges Note":* probably a
popular song of the time.
9. In accordance with his friends' provision and his own income.
1. I.e., suspected of himself that he was
like a cuckold.
2. Dionysius Cato, the supposed author
of a book of maxims used in elementary
education.
3. Commanded that one should wed his
equal.
4. Men should marry according to their
condition.
5. Slender and delicate.
6. A belt she wore, with transverse
stripes.
7. Embroidered.
8. I.e., the same pattern as.
9. Delicately plucked.
1. I.e., with brassy spangles on it.

In al this world, to seeken up and down,
145 Ther nis no man so wis that coude thenche°   *imagine*
So gay a popelote° or swich° a wenche.   *doll / such*
Ful brighter was the shining of hir hewe
Than in the Towr[2] the noble° yforged newe.   *gold coin*
But of hir song, it was as loud and yerne°   *lively*
150 As any swalwe sitting on a berne.°   *barn*
Therto she coude skippe and make game[3]
As any kide or calf folwing his dame.°   *mother*
Hir mouth was sweete as bragot or the meeth,[4]
Or hoord of apples laid in hay or heeth.°   *heather*
155 Winsing° she was as is a joly° colt,   *skittish / high-spirited*
Long as a mast, and upright° as a bolt.°   *straight / arrow*
A brooch she bar upon hir lowe coler
As brood as is the boos° of a bokeler;°   *boss / shield*
Hir shoes were laced on hir legges hye.
160 She was a primerole,° a piggesnye,°   *cowslip / pig's eye*
For any lord to leggen° in his bedde,   *lay*
Or yit for any good yeman to wedde.

  Now sire, and eft° sire, so bifel the cas   *again*
That on a day this hende Nicholas
165 Fil° with this yonge wif to rage° and playe,   *happened / flirt*
Whil that hir housbonde was at Oseneye[5]
(As clerkes been ful subtil and ful quainte),°   *clever*
And prively he caughte hire by the queinte;°   *pudendum*
And saide, "Ywis, but if ich° have my wille,   *I*
170 For derne° love of thee, lemman, I spille,"°   *secret / die*
And heeld hire harde by the haunche-bones,
And saide, "Lemman,° love me al atones,[6]   *mistress*
Or I wol dien, also° God me save."   *so*
And she sproong° as a colt dooth in a trave,[7]   *sprang*
175 And with hir heed she wried° faste away;   *twisted*
She saide, "I wol nat kisse thee, by my fay.°   *faith*
Why, lat be," quod she, "lat be, Nicholas!
Or I wol crye 'Out, harrow,° and allas!'   *help*
Do way youre handes, for your curteisye!"
180 This Nicholas gan mercy for to crye,
And spak so faire, and profred him so faste,[8]
That she hir love him graunted atte laste,
And swoor hir ooth by Saint Thomas of Kent[9]
That she wolde been at his comandement,
185 Whan that she may hir leiser[1] wel espye.
"Myn housbonde is so ful of jalousye
That but ye waite° wel and been privee,   *be on guard*
I woot right wel I nam but deed," quod she.

---

2. The Tower of London.
3. Play.
4. "Bragot" and "meeth" are honey drinks.
5. A town near Oxford.

6. Right now.
7. Frame for a restive horse.
8. I.e., pushed himself so vigorously.
9. Thomas à Becket.
1. I.e., opportunity.

"Ye moste been ful derne as in this cas."
190   "Nay, therof care thee nought," quod Nicholas.
"A clerk hadde litherly biset his while,[2]
But if he coude a carpenter bigile."
And thus they been accorded and ysworn
To waite° a time, as I have told biforn.   *watch for*
195 Whan Nicholas hadde doon this everydeel,
And thakked° hire upon the lendes° weel,   *patted / loins*
He kiste hire sweete, and taketh his sautrye,
And playeth faste, and maketh melodye.
    Thanne fil° it thus, that to the parissh chirche,   *befell*
200 Cristes owene werkes for to wirche,°   *perform*
This goode wif wente on an haliday:°   *holy day*
Hir forheed shoon as bright as any day,
So was it wasshen whan she leet° hir werk.   *left*
    Now was ther of that chirche a parissh clerk,
205 The which that was ycleped° Absolon: *called*
Crul° was his heer, and as the gold it shoon,   *curly*
And strouted° as a fanne[3] large and brode;   *spread out*
Ful straight and evene lay his joly shode.[4]
His rode° was reed, his yën greye as goos.°   *complexion / goose*
210 With Poules window corven[5] on his shoos,
In hoses° rede he wente fetisly.°   *stockings / elegantly*
Yclad he was ful smale° and proprely,   *finely*
Al in a kirtel° of a light waget°—   *tunic / blue*
Ful faire and thikke been the pointes[6] set—
215 And therupon he hadde a gay surplis,°   *surplice*
As whit as is the blosme upon the ris.°   *bough*
A merye child° he was, so God me save.   *lad*
Wel coude he laten° blood, and clippe, and shave,   *let*
And maken a chartre of land, or acquitaunce;[7]
220 In twenty manere° coude he trippe and daunce   *ways*
After the scole of Oxenforde tho,
And with his legges casten° to and fro,   *prance*
And playen songes on a smal rubible;°   *fiddle*
Therto he soong somtime a loud quinible.[8]
225 And as wel coude he playe on a giterne:°   *guitar*
In al the town nas brewhous ne taverne
That he ne visited with his solas,°   *entertainment*
Ther any gailard tappestere[9] was.
    But sooth to sayn, he was somdeel squaimous°   *squeamish*
230 Of farting, and of speeche daungerous,°   *fastidious*
    This Absolon, that joly° was and gay,   *pretty, amorous*
Gooth with a cencer° on the haliday,   *incense-burner*

---

2. Poorly employed his time.
3. Wide-mouthed basket for separating grain from chaff.
4. Parting of the hair.
5. Carved with intricate designs, like the tracery in the windows of St. Paul's.
6. Laces for fastening the tunic and holding up the hose.
7. Legal release.
8. Part requiring a very high voice.
9. Gay barmaid.

Cencing the wives of the parissh faste,
And many a lovely look on hem he caste,
235 And namely° on this carpenteres wif: *especially*
To looke on hire him thoughte a merye lif.
She was so propre° and sweete and likerous,[1]   *neat*
I dar wel sayn, if she hadde been a mous,
And he a cat, he wolde hire hente° anoon.   *pounce on*
240 This parissh clerk, this joly Absolon,
Hath in his herte swich a love-longinge°   *lovesickness*
That of no wif ne took he noon offringe—
For curteisye he saide he wolde noon.
The moone, whan it was night, ful brighte shoon,°   *shone*
245 And Absolon his giterne° hath ytake—   *guitar*
For paramours° he thoughte for to wake—   *love*
And forth he gooth, jolif° and amorous,   *pretty*
Til he cam to the carpenteres hous,
A litel after cokkes hadde ycrowe,
250 And dressed him up by a shot-windowe[2]
That was upon the carpenteres wal.
He singeth in his vois gentil and smal,°   *dainty*
"Now dere lady, if thy wille be,
I praye you that ye wol rewe° on me,"   *have pity*
255 Ful wel accordant to his giterninge.[3]
This carpenter awook and herde him singe,
And spak unto his wif, and saide anoon,
"What, Alison, heerestou nought Absolon
That chaunteth thus under oure bowres° wal?"   *bedroom's*
260 And she answerde hir housbonde therwithal,
"Yis, God woot, John, I heere it everydeel."
    This passeth forth. What wol ye bet than weel?[4]
Fro day to day this joly Absolon
So woweth° hire that him is wo-bigoon: *woos*
265 He waketh° al the night and al the day;   *stays awake*
He kembed° his lokkes brode[5] and made him gay;   *combed*
He woweth hire by menes and brocage,[6]
And swoor he wolde been hir owene page;°   *personal servant*
He singeth, brokking° as a nightingale;   *trilling*
270 He sente hire piment,[7] meeth, and spiced ale,
And wafres° piping hoot out of the gleede;°   *pastries / coals*
And for she was of towne,[8] he profred meede°—   *bribe*
For som folk wol be wonnen for richesse,
And som for strokes,° and som for gentilesse.   *blows*
275 Somtime to shewe his lightnesse and maistrye,[9]
He playeth Herodes[1] upon a scaffold° hye.   *platform, stage*

1. Wanton, appetizing.
2. Took his position by a hinged window.
3. In harmony with his guitar-playing.
4. Better than well.
5. I.e., wide-spreading.
6. By intermediaries and mediation.
7. Spiced wine; "meeth": mead.
8. Since she was a town woman.
9. Facility and virtuosity.
1. Herod, a role traditionally played as a bully in the mystery plays.

But what availeth him as in this cas?
She loveth so this hende Nicholas
That Absolon may blowe the bukkes horn;[2]
280 He ne hadde for his labour but a scorn.
And thus she maketh Absolon hir ape,[3]
And al his ernest turneth til a jape.°   *joke*
Ful sooth is this proverbe, it is no lie;
Men saith right thus: "Alway the nye slye
285 Maketh the ferre leve to be loth."[4]
For though that Absolon be wood° or wroth,   *furious*
By cause that he fer was from hir sighte,
This nye° Nicholas stood in his lighte.   *nearby*
     Now beer° thee wel, thou hende Nicholas,   *bear*
290 For Absolon may waile and singe allas.
     And so bifel it on a Saterday
This carpenter was goon til Oseney,
And hende Nicholas and Alisoun
Accorded been to this conclusioun,
295 That Nicholas shal shapen° hem a wile°   *arrange / trick*
This sely[5] jalous housbonde to bigile,
And if so be this game wente aright,
She sholden sleepen in his arm al night—
For this was his desir and hire° also.   *hers*
300 And right anoon, withouten wordes mo,
This Nicholas no lenger wolde tarye,
But dooth ful softe unto his chambre carye
Bothe mete and drinke for a day or twaye,
And to hir housbonde bad hire for to saye,
305 If that he axed after Nicholas,
She sholde saye she niste° wher he was—   *didn't know*
Of al that day she sawgh him nought with yë:
She trowed° that he was in maladye,   *believed*
For for no cry hir maide coude him calle,
310 He nolde answere for no thing that mighte falle.°   *happen*
     This passeth forth al thilke° Saterday   *this*
That Nicholas stille in his chambre lay,
And eet,° and sleep,° or dide what him leste,[6]   *ate / slept*
Til Sonday that the sonne gooth to reste.
315   This sely carpenter hath greet mervaile
Of Nicholas, or what thing mighte him aile,
And saide, "I am adrad,° by Saint Thomas,   *afraid*
It stondeth nat aright with Nicholas.
God shilde° that he deide sodeinly!   *forbid*
320 This world is now ful tikel,° sikerly: *changeable*
I sawgh today a corps yborn to chirche
That now a° Monday last I sawgh him wirche.°   *on / work*

2. Blow the buck's horn, i.e., go without reward.
3. I.e., thus she makes a fool of Absolon.
4. Always the sly man at hand makes the distant dear one hated.
5. "Poor innocent."
6. He wanted.

Go up," quod he unto his knave° anoon,   *manservant*
"Clepe° at his dore or knokke with a stoon.°   *call / stone*
325 Looke how it is and tel me boldely."
  This knave gooth him up ful sturdily,
And at the chambre dore whil that he stood
He cride and knokked as that he were wood,°   *mad*
"What? How? What do ye, maister Nicholay?
330 How may ye sleepen al the longe day?"
But al for nought: he herde nat a word.
An hole he foond ful lowe upon a boord,
Ther as the cat was wont in for to creepe,
And at that hole he looked in ful deepe,
335 And atte laste he hadde of him a sighte.
  This Nicholas sat evere caping° uprighte   *gaping*
As he hadde kiked° on the newe moone.   *gazed*
Adown he gooth and tolde his maister soone
In what array° he saw this ilke° man. *condition / same*
340 This carpenter to blessen him[7] bigan,
And saide, "Help us, Sainte Frideswide!
A man woot litel what him shal bitide.
This man is falle, with his astromye,[8]
In som woodnesse° or in som agonye.   *madness*
345 I thoughte ay° wel how that it sholde be: *always*
Men sholde nought knowe of Goddes privetee.
Ye, blessed be alway a lewed° man   *ignorant*
That nought but only his bileve° can.° *creed / knows*
So ferde° another clerk with astromye: *fared*
350 He walked in the feeldes for to prye
Upon the sterres,° what ther sholde bifalle,   *stars*
Til he was in a marle-pit[9] yfalle—
He saw nat that. But yit, by Saint Thomas,
Me reweth sore[1] for hende Nicholas.
355 He shal be rated of[2] his studying,
If that I may, by Jesus, hevene king!
Get me a staf that I may underspore,°   *pry up*
Whil that thou, Robin, hevest° up the dore.   *heave*
He shal[3] out of his studying, as I gesse."
360 And to the chambre dore he gan him dresse.[4]
His knave was a strong carl° for the nones,° *fellow / purpose*
And by the haspe he haaf° it up atones: *heaved*
Into° the floor the dore fil° anoon.   *on / fell*
This Nicholas sat ay as stille as stoon,
365 And evere caped up into the air.
This carpenter wende° he were in despair,   *thought*
And hente° him by the shuldres mightily,   *seized*
And shook him harde, and cride spitously,°   *roughly*

7. Cross himself.
8. Illiterate form of "astronomye."
9. Pit from which a fertilizing clay is dug.

1. I sorely pity.
2. Scolded for.
3. I.e., shall come.
4. Took his stand.

"What, Nicholay, what, how! What! Looke adown!
370 Awaak and thenk on Cristes passioun![5]
I crouche[6] thee from elves and fro wightes."
Therwith the nightspel saide he anoonrightes[7]
On foure halves° of the hous aboute,   *sides*
And on the threshfold° on the dore withoute: *threshold*
375 "Jesu Crist and Sainte Benedight,°   *Benedict*
Blesse this hous from every wikked wight!
For nightes nerye the White Pater Noster.[8]
Where wentestou, Sainte Petres soster?"°   *sister*
And at the laste this hende Nicholas
380 Gan for to sike° sore, and saide, "Allas,   *sigh*
Shal al the world be lost eftsoones° now?"   *again*
        This carpenter answerde, "What saistou?
What, thenk on God as we doon, men that swinke."[9]
        This Nicholas answerde, "Fecche me drinke,
385 And after wol I speke in privetee
Of certain thing that toucheth me and thee.
I wol telle it noon other man, certain."
        This carpenter gooth down and comth again,
And broughte of mighty ale a large quart,
390 And when that eech of hem hadde dronke his part,
This Nicholas his dore faste shette,°   *shut*
And down the carpenter by him he sette,
And saide, "John, myn hoste lief° and dere,   *beloved*
Thou shalt upon thy trouthe° swere me here   *word of honor*
395 That to no wight thou shalt this conseil° wraye;°   *secret / disclose*
For it is Cristes conseil that I saye,
And if thou telle it man,[1] thou art forlore,°   *lost*
For this vengeance thou shalt have therfore,
That if thou wraye me, thou shalt be wood." [2]
400   "Nay, Crist forbede it, for his holy blood,"
Quod tho this sely° man. "I nam no labbe,[3]   *innocent*
And though I saye, I nam nat lief to gabbe.[4]
Say what thou wilt, I shal it nevere telle
To child ne wif, by him that harwed helle."[5]
405   "Now John," quod Nicholas, "I wol nought lie.
I have yfounde in myn astrologye,
As I have looked in the moone bright,
That now a Monday next, at quarter night,[6]
Shal falle a rain, and that so wilde and wood,°   *furious*
410 That half so greet was nevere Noees° flood.   *Noah's*
This world," he saide, "in lasse° than an hour   *less*

5. I.e., the Crucifixion.
6. Make the sign of the cross on;
"wightes": wicked creatures.
7. The night-charm he said right away.
8. I.e., the White Lord's Prayer defend
(us). This personification was considered a powerful beneficent spirit.
9. Work.

1. To anyone.
2. Go mad.
3. Blabbermouth.
4. And though I say it myself, I don't
like to gossip.
5. By Him that despoiled hell—i.e.,
Christ.
6. I.e., shortly before dawn.

Shal al be dreint,° so hidous is the showr. *drowned*
Thus shal mankinde drenche° and lese° hir lif." *drown / lose*
  This carpenter answerde, "Allas, my wif!
415 And shal she drenche? Allas, myn Alisoun!"
For sorwe of this he fil almost[7] adown,
And saide, "Is there no remedye in this cas?"
  "Why yis, for[8] Gode," quod hende Nicholas,
"If thou wolt werken after lore and reed[9]—
420 Thou maist nought werken after thyn owene heed;° *head*
For thus saith Salomon that was ful trewe,
'Werk al by conseil and thou shalt nought rewe.'° *be sorry*
And if thou werken wolt by good conseil,
I undertake, withouten mast or sail,
425 Yit shal I save hire and thee and me.
Hastou nat herd how saved was Noee
Whan that oure Lord hadde warned him biforn
That al the world with water sholde be lorn?"° *lost*
  "Yis," quod this carpenter, "ful yore ago."
430   "Hastou nat herd," quod Nicholas, "also
The sorwe of Noee with his felaweshipe?
Er that he mighte gete his wif to shipe,
Him hadde levere,[1] I dar wel undertake,
At thilke time than alle his wetheres blake
435 That she hadde had a ship hirself allone.[2]
And therfore woostou° what is best to doone? *do you know*
This axeth° haste, and of an hastif° thing *requires / urgent*
Men may nought preche or maken tarying.
Anoon go gete us faste into this in° *lodging*
440 A kneeding trough or elles a kimelin° *brewing tub*
For eech of us, but looke that they be large,° *wide*
In whiche we mowen swimme as in a barge,[3]
And han therinne vitaile suffisaunt[4]
But for a day—fy° on the remenaunt! *fie*
445 The water shal aslake° and goon away *diminish*
Aboute prime[5] upon the nexte day.
But Robin may nat wite° of this, thy knave, *know*
Ne eek thy maide Gille I may nat save.
Axe nought why, for though thou axe me,
450 I wol nought tellen Goddes privetee.° *secrets*
Suffiseth thee, but if thy wittes madde,° *go mad*
To han° as greet a grace as Noee hadde. *have*
Thy wif shal I wel saven, out of doute.
Go now thy way, and speed thee heraboute.
455 But whan thou hast for hire° and thee and me *her*

---

7. Almost fell.
8. I.e., by.
9. Act according to learning and advice.
1. He had rather. "Wetheres": rams. I.e., he'd have given all the rams he had.

2. The reluctance of Noah's wife to board the ark is a traditional comic theme in the mystery plays.
3. In which we can float as in a vessel.
4. Sufficient food.
5. 9 A.M.

Ygeten us thise kneeding-tubbes three,
Thanne shaltou hangen hem in the roof ful hye,
That no man of oure purveyance° espye.   *foresight*
And whan thou thus hast doon as I have said,
460 And hast oure vitaile faire in hem ylaid,
And eek an ax to smite the corde atwo,
Whan that the water comth that we may go,
And broke an hole an heigh[6] upon the gable
Unto the gardinward,[7] over the stable,
465 That we may freely passen forth oure way,
Whan that the grete showr is goon away,
Thanne shaltou swimme as merye, I undertake,
As dooth the white doke° after hir drake.   *duck*
Thanne wol I clepe,° 'How, Alison? How, John?   *call*
470 Be merye, for the flood wol passe anoon.'
And thou wolt sayn, 'Hail, maister Nicholay!
Good morwe, I see thee wel, for it is day!'
And thanne shal we be lordes al oure lif
Of al the world, as Noee and his wif.
475 But of oo thing I warne thee ful right:
Be wel avised on that ilke night
That we been entred into shippes boord
That noon of us ne speke nought a word,
Ne clepe, ne crye, but been in his prayere,
480 For it is Goddes owene heeste dere.[8]
Thy wif and thou mote hange fer atwinne,[9]
For that bitwixe you shal be no sinne—
Namore in looking than ther shal in deede.
This ordinance is said: go, God thee speede.
485 Tomorwe at night whan men been alle asleepe,
Into oure kneeding-tubbes wol we creepe,
And sitten there, abiding Goddes grace.
Go now thy way, I have no lenger space°   *time*
To make of this no lenger sermoning.
490 Men sayn thus: 'Send the wise and say no thing.'
Thou art so wis it needeth thee nat teche:
Go save oure lif, and that I thee biseeche."
    This sely carpenter gooth forth his way:
Ful ofte he saide allas and wailaway,
495 And to his wif he tolde his privetee,
And she was war,° and knew it bet° than he,   *aware / better*
What al this quainte cast° was for to saye.°   *trick / mean*
But nathelees she ferde° as she wolde deye,   *acted*
And saide, "Allas, go forth thy way anoon.
500 Help us to scape,° or we been dede eechoon.   *escape*
I am thy trewe verray wedded wif:
Go, dere spouse, and help to save oure lif."

6. On high.   8. Precious commandment.
7. Toward the garden.   9. Far apart.

Lo, which a greet thing is affeccioun!°   *emotion*
Men may dien of imaginacioun,
505 So deepe° may impression be take.   *deeply*
This sely carpenter biginneth quake;
Him thinketh verrailiche° that he may see   *truly*
Noees flood come walwing° as the see   *rolling*
To drenchen° Alison, his hony dere.   *drown*
510 He weepeth, waileth, maketh sory cheere;
He siketh° with ful many a sory swough,°   *sighs / breath*
And gooth and geteth him a kneeding-trough,
And after a tubbe and a kimelin,
And prively he sente hem to his in,°   *dwelling*
515 And heeng° hem in the roof in privetee;   *hung*
His owene hand he made laddres three,
To climben by the ronges° and the stalkes°   *rungs / uprights*
Unto the tubbes hanging in the balkes,°   *rafters*
And hem vitailed,° bothe trough and tubbe,   *victualed*
520 With breed and cheese and good ale in a jubbe,°   *jug*
Suffising right ynough as for a day.
But er that he hadde maad al this array,
He sente his knave, and eek his wenche also,
Upon his neede[1] to London for to go.
525 And on the Monday whan it drow to[2] nighte,
He shette° his dore withouten candel-lighte,   *shut*
And dressed° alle thing as it sholde be,   *arranged*
And shortly up they clomben° alle three.   *climbed*
They seten° stille wel a furlong way.[3]   *sat*
530 "Now, Pater Noster, clum,"[4] saide Nicholay,
And "Clum" quod John, and "Clum" saide Alisoun.
This carpenter saide his devocioun,
And stille he sit° and biddeth his prayere,   *sits*
Awaiting on the rain, if he it heere.°   *might hear*
535 The dede sleep, for wery bisinesse,
Fil° on this carpenter right as I gesse   *fell*
Aboute corfew time,[5] or litel more.
For travailing of his gost[6] he groneth sore,
And eft° he routeth,° for his heed mislay.[7]   *then / snores*
540 Down of the laddre stalketh Nicholay,
And Alison ful softe adown she spedde:
Withouten wordes mo they goon to bedde
Ther as the carpenter is wont to lie.
Ther was the revel and the melodye,
545 And thus lith° Alison and Nicholas   *lies*
In bisinesse of mirthe and of solas,°   *pleasure*
Til that the belle of Laudes[8] gan to ringe,

---

1. On an errand for him.
2. Drew toward.
3. The time it takes to go a furlong (i.e., a few minutes).
4. Hush (?).
5. Probably about 8 p.m.
6. Affliction of his spirit.
7. Lay in the wrong position.
8. The first church service of the day.

And freres in the chauncel° gonne singe.   *chancel*
　This parissh clerk, this amorous Absolon,
550 That is for love alway so wo-bigoon,
Upon the Monday was at Oseneye,
With compaignye him to disporte and playe,
And axed upon caas⁹ a cloisterer
Ful prively after John the carpenter;
555 And he drow him apart out of the chirche,
And saide, "I noot:¹ I sawgh him here nought wirche
Sith Saterday. I trowe that he be went
For timber ther oure abbot hath him sent.
For he is wont for timber for to go,
560 And dwellen atte grange² a day or two.
Or elles he is at his hous, certain.
Where that he be I can nought soothly sayn."
　This Absolon ful jolif was and light,³
And thoughte, "Now is time to wake al night,
565 For sikerly,° I sawgh him nought stiringe   *certainly*
Aboute his dore sin day bigan to springe.
So mote° I thrive, I shal at cokkes crowe   *may*
Ful prively knokken at his windowe
That stant° ful lowe upon his bowres⁴ wal.   *stands*
570 To Alison now wol I tellen al
My love-longing,° for yet I shal nat misse   *lovesickness*
That at the leeste way⁵ I shal hire kisse.
Som manere confort shal I have, parfay.   *in faith*
My mouth hath icched al this longe day:
575 That is a signe of kissing at the leeste.
Al night me mette⁶ eek I was at a feeste.
Therfore I wol go sleepe an hour or twaye,
And al the night thanne wol I wake and playe."
　Whan that the firste cok hath crowe, anoon
580 Up rist° this joly lovere Absolon,   *rises*
And him arrayeth gay at point devis.⁷
But first he cheweth grain⁸ and licoris,
To smellen sweete, er he hadde kembd° his heer.   *combed*
Under his tonge a trewe-love⁹ he beer,°   *bore*
585 For therby wende° he to be gracious.°   *supposed / pleasing*
He rometh° to the carpenteres hous,   *strolls*
And stille he stant° under the shot-windowe—   *stands*
Unto his brest it raughte,° it was so lowe—   *reached*
And ofte he cougheth with a semisoun.°   *small sound*
590 "What do ye, hony-comb, sweete Alisoun,
My faire brid,¹ my sweete cinamome?
Awaketh, lemman° myn, and speketh to me.   *mistress*

9. By chance; "cloisterer": here, a
member of the religious order of Osney
Abbey.
1. Don't know; "wirche": work.
2. The outlying farm belonging to the
abbey.
3. Was very amorous and gay.

4. Bower's, bedroom's.
5. I.e., at least.
6. I dreamed.
7. To perfection.
8. Grain of paradise (a spice).
9. Sprig of a clover-like plant.
1. Bird or bride.

Wel litel thinken ye upon my wo
That for your love I swete° ther I go.　　*sweat*
595 No wonder is though that I swelte° and swete:　*melt*
I moorne as doth a lamb after the tete.°　　*tit*
Ywis, lemman, I have swich love-longinge,
That lik a turtle° trewe is my moorninge:　　*dove*
I may nat ete namore than a maide."
600 "Go fro the windowe, Jakke fool," she saide.
"As help me God, it wol nat be com-pa-me.°　*come-kiss-me*
I love another, and elles I were to blame,
Wel bet° than thee, by Jesu, Absolon.　　*better*
Go forth thy way or I wol caste a stoon,
605 And lat me sleepe, a twenty devele way."[2]
　　"Allas," quod Absolon, "and wailaway,
That trewe love was evere so yvele biset.[3]
Thanne kis me, sin that it may be no bet,
For Jesus love and for the love of me."
610 "Woltou thanne go thy way therwith?" quod she.
"Ye, certes, lemman," quod this Absolon.
"Thanne maak thee redy," quod she. "I come anoon."
And unto Nicholas she saide stille,°　　*quietly*
"Now hust,° and thou shalt laughen al thy fille."　*hush*
615 This Absolon down sette him on his knees,
And said, "I am a lord at alle degrees,[4]
For after this I hope ther cometh more.
Lemman, thy grace, and sweete brid, thyn ore!"°　*mercy*
The windowe she undooth, and that in haste.
620 "Have do," quod she, "come of and speed thee faste,
Lest that oure neighebores thee espye."
　　This Absolon gan wipe his mouth ful drye:
Derk was the night as pich or as the cole,
And at the windowe out she putte hir hole,
625 And Absolon, him fil no bet ne wers,[5]
But with his mouth he kiste hir naked ers,
Ful savourly,° er he were war of this.　　*with relish*
Abak he sterte,° and thoughte it was amis,　*started*
For wel he wiste a womman hath no beerd.
630 He felte a thing al rough and longe yherd,°　*haired*
And saide, "Fy, allas, what have I do?"
　　"Teehee," quod she, and clapte the windowe to.
And Absolon gooth forth a sory pas.[6]
　　"A beerd, a beerd!" quod hende Nicholas,
635 "By Goddes corpus,° this gooth faire and weel."　*body*
　　This sely Absolon herde everydeel,
And on his lippe he gan for anger bite,
And to himself he saide, "I shal thee quite."°　*repay*
　　Who rubbeth now, who froteth° now his lippes　*wipes*
640 With dust, with sond,[7] with straw, with cloth, with chippes,

2. In the name of twenty devils.　　5. It befell him neither better nor worse
3. Ill-used.　　6. I.e., walking sadly.
4. In every way.　　7. Sand.

But Absolon, that saith ful ofte allas?
"My soule bitake° I unto Satanas,°   *commit / Satan*
But me were levere[8] than all this town," quod he,
"Of this despit° awroken° for to be.   *insult / avenged*
645 Allas," quod he, "allas I ne hadde ybleint!"°   *turned aside*
His hote love was cold and al yqueint,°   *quenched*
For fro that time that he hadde kist hir ers
Of paramours he sette nought a kers,[9]
For he was heled° of his maladye.   *cured*
650 Ful ofte paramours he gan defye,°   *renounce*
And weep° as dooth a child that is ybete.   *wept*
A softe paas[1] he wente over the streete
Until° a smith men clepen daun Gervais,[2]   *to*
That in his forge smithed plough harneis:°   *equipment*
655 He sharpeth shaar and cultour[3] bisily.
This Absolon knokketh al esily,°   *quietly*
And saide, "Undo, Gervais, and that anoon."°   *at once*
"What, who artou?" "It am I, Absolon."
"What, Absolon? What, Cristes sweete tree!
660 Why rise ye so rathe?° Ey, benedicite,°   *early / bless me*
What aileth you? Som gay girl, God it woot,
Hath brought you thus upon the viritoot.[4]
By Sainte Note, ye woot wel what I mene."
    This Absolon ne roughte nat a bene[5]
665 Of al his play. No word again he yaf:
He hadde more tow on his distaf[6]
Than Gervais knew, and saide, "Freend so dere,
This hote coultour in the chimenee° here,   *fireplace*
As lene[7] it me: I have therwith to doone."
670 I wol bringe it thee again ful soone."
    Gervais answerde, "Certes, were it gold,
Or in a poke nobles alle untold,[8]
Thou sholdest have, as I am trewe smith.
Ey, Cristes fo,[9] what wol ye do therwith?"
675   "Therof," quod Absolon, "be as be may.
I shal wel telle it thee another day,"
And caughte the cultour by the colde stele.°   *handle*
Ful softe out at the dore he gan to stele,
And wente unto the carpenteres wal:
680 He cougheth first and knokketh therwithal
Upon the windowe, right as he dide er.°   *before*
    This Alison answerde, "Who is ther
That knokketh so? I warante[1] it a thief."
    "Why, nay," quod he, "God woot, my sweete lief,° *dear*

8. I had rather.
9. He didn't care a piece of cress for woman's love.
1. I.e., quiet walk.
2. Master Gervais.
3. He sharpens plowshare and coulter (the turf-cutter on a plow).

4. I.e., on the prowl.
5. Didn't care a bean.
6. I.e., more on his mind.
7. I.e., please lend.
8. Or gold coins all uncounted in a bag.
9. Foe, i.e., Satan.
1. I.e., wager.

685 I am thyn Absolon, my dereling.
Of gold," quod he, "I have thee brought a ring—
My moder yaf it me, so God me save;
Ful fin it is and therto wel ygrave:°   *engraved*
This wol I yiven thee if thou me kisse."

690   This Nicholas was risen for to pisse,
And thoughte he wolde amenden[2] al the jape:°   *joke*
He sholde kisse his ers er that he scape.
And up the windowe dide he hastily,
And out his ers he putteth prively,

695 Over the buttok to the haunche-boon.
    And therwith spak this clerk, this Absolon,
"Speek, sweete brid, I noot nought wher thou art."
This Nicholas anoon leet flee[3] a fart
As greet as it hadde been a thonder-dent°   *thunderbolt*

700 That with the strook he was almost yblent,°   *blinded*
And he was redy with his iren hoot,°   *hot*
And Nicholas amidde the ers he smoot:°   *smote*
Of gooth the skin an hande-brede° aboute;   *handsbreadth*
The hote cultour brende so his toute°   *buttocks*

705 That for the smert he wende for to[4] die;
As he were wood° for wo he gan to crye,   *crazy*
"Help! Water! Water! Help, for Goddes herte!"
    This carpenter out of his slomber sterte,
And herde oon cryen "Water!" as he were wood,

710 And thoughte, "Allas, now cometh Noweles[5] flood!"
He sette him up withoute wordes mo,
And with his ax he smoot the corde atwo,
And down gooth al: he foond neither to selle
Ne breed ne ale til he cam to the celle,[6]

715 Upon the floor, and ther aswoune° he lay.   *in a faint*
    Up sterte hire[7] Alison and Nicholay,
And criden "Out" and "Harrow" in the streete.
The neighebores, bothe smale and grete,
In ronnen for to gauren° on this man   *gape*

720 That aswoune lay bothe pale and wan,
For with the fal he brosten° hadde his arm;   *broken*
But stonde he moste° unto his owene harm,   *must*
For whan he spak he was anoon bore down[8]
With° hende Nicholas and Alisoun: *by*

725 They tolden every man that he was wood—
He was agast so of Noweles flood,
Thurgh fantasye, that of his vanitee°   *folly*
He hadde ybought him kneeding-tubbes three,
And hadde hem hanged in the roof above,

730 And that he prayed hem, for Goddes love,

---

2. Improve on.
3. Let fly.
4. Thought he would.
5. The carpenter is confusing Noah and Noel (Christmas).
6. He found time to sell neither bread nor ale until he arrived at the foundation.
7. Started.
8. Refuted.

To sitten in the roof, *par compaignye*.[9]
 The folk gan laughen at his fantasye.
Into the roof they kiken° and they cape,°   *peer / gape*
And turned al his harm unto a jape,°   *joke*
735 For what so that this carpenter answerde,
 It was for nought: no man his reson° herde;   *argument*
With othes grete he was so sworn adown,
That he was holden° wood in al the town,   *considered*
For every clerk anoonright heeld with other:
740 They saide, "The man was wood, my leve brother,"
 And every wight gan laughen at this strif.°   *fuss*
Thus swived° was the carpenteres wif   *slept with*
For al his keeping° and his jalousye,   *guarding*
And Absolon hath kist hir nether° yë,   *lower*
745 And Nicholas is scalded in the toute:
 This tale is doon, and God save al the route!° *company*

From The Parson's Tale[1]

The Introduction

By that[2] the Manciple hadde his tale al ended,
The sonne fro the south line[3] was decended

9. For company's sake.
1. Among the moral writers of the later Middle Ages the pilgrimage was so commonly treated as an allegory of man's life that Chaucer's audience must have been surprised to find the *Canterbury Tales* so little allegorical. At the end of his life, however, and at the end of his work, Chaucer seems to have been caught up in the venerable allegory. Some ten months before his death he rented a house in the garden of Westminster Abbey, and it is possible that during these months—perhaps when he felt his death approaching—he fell under the influence of the monks of Westminster. In any case, in the Parson's Tale, and in its short Introduction and in the Retraction that follows it, Chaucer seems to be making an end for two pilgrimages that had become one, that of his fiction and that of his life.

In the Introduction to the tale we find the 29 pilgrims moving through a nameless little village as the sun sinks to within 29 degrees of the horizon. The atmosphere contains something of both the chill and the urgency of a late autumn afternoon, and we are surprised to find that the pilgrimage is almost over, that there is need for haste in order to make that "good end" that every medieval Christian hoped for. This delicately suggestive passage, rich with allegorical overtones, introduces an extremely long sermon on penitence and the seven deadly sins, probably

translated by Chaucer from French or Latin some years earlier, before he had begun the *Canterbury Tales*. The other stories have many echoes of it: for instance, in the selection printed here one sees the germ of ideas that reappear—in highly altered form—in the Wife of Bath. The sermon is at times not without animation, but in general Chaucer provides no exception to the statement that Middle English prose is inferior to Middle English verse. But then the intent of the sermon is didactic, not artistic, and according to the more rigorous theologians of the time, didactic intent is infinitely more important than artistic expression.

It is to this doctrine that Chaucer yielded at the end of his life. The Retraction which follows and concludes the Parson's Tale offers Chaucer's apology for having written all the works on which his reputation as a great poet depends, not only such stories as the Miller's Tale, but also his loveliest and seemingly most harmless poems. Yet a readiness to deny his own reality before the reality of his God is implicit in many of Chaucer's works, and the placement of the Retraction within the artistic structure of the *Canterbury Tales* suggests that while Chaucer denied his art, he seems to have recognized that he and it were inseparable.
2. By the time that.
3. I.e., the line that runs some 28 de-

So lowe, that he nas nat to my sighte
Degrees nine and twenty as in highte.
5 Four of the clokke it was, so as I gesse,
For elevene foot, or litel more or lesse,
My shadwe was at thilke time as there,
Of swich feet as° my lengthe parted° were   *as if / divided*
In sixe feet equal of proporcioun.⁴
10 Therwith the moones exaltacioun⁵—
I mene Libra—alway gan ascende,
As we were entring at a thropes° ende.   *village's*
For which oure Host, as he was wont to gie°   *lead*
As in this caas oure joly compaignye,
15 Saide in this wise, "Lordinges everichoon,
Now lakketh us no tales mo than oon:
Fulfild is my sentence° and my decree;   *purpose*
I trowe° that we han herd of eech degree;   *believe*
Almost fulfild is al myn ordinaunce.
20 I praye to God, so yive him right good chaunce
That telleth this tale to us lustily.
Sire preest," quod he, "artou a vicary,°   *vicar*
Or arte a Person? Say sooth, by thy fay.°   *faith*
Be what thou be, ne breek° thou nat oure play,   *break*
25 For every man save thou hath told his tale.
Unbokele and shew us what is in thy male!°   *bag*
For trewely, me thinketh by thy cheere°   *expression*
Thou sholdest knitte up wel a greet matere.
Tel us a fable anoon, for cokkes bones!"
30   This Person answerde al atones,⁶
"Thou getest fable noon ytold for me,
For Paul, that writeth unto Timothee,
Repreveth° hem that waiven soothfastnesse,⁷   *reproves*
And tellen fables and swich wrecchednesse.
35 Why sholde I sowen draf° out of my fest,°   *chaff / fist*
Whan I may sowen whete if that me lest?⁸
For which I saye that if you list to heere
Moralitee and vertuous matere,
And thanne that ye wol yive me audience,
40 I wol ful fain,° at Cristes reverence,   *gladly*
Do you plesance leveful° as I can.   *lawful*
But trusteth wel, I am a southren man:
I can nat geeste Rum-Ram-Ruf by lettre⁹—
Ne, God woot, rym holde° I but litel bettre.   *consider*
45 And therfore, if you list, I wol nat glose;¹

grees to the south of the celestial equator and parallel to it.
4. This detailed analysis merely says
that the shadows are lengthening.
5. I.e., the astrological sign in which
the moon's influence was dominant.
"Libra": the constellation of the
Scales.
6. Immediately.

7. Depart from truth. See I Timothy
i.4.
8. It pleases me.
9. I.e., I cannot tell stories in the
alliterative measure (without rhyme):
this form of poetry was not common
in southeastern England.
1. I.e., speak in order to please.

I wol you telle a merye tale in prose,
To knitte up al this feeste and make an ende.
And Jesu for his grace wit me sende
To shewe you the way in this viage°   *iourney*
50 Of thilke parfit glorious pilgrimage
That highte Jerusalem celestial.
And if ye vouche sauf, anoon I shal
Biginne upon my tale, for which I praye
Telle youre avis:° I can no bettre saye.   *opinion*
55 But nathelees, this meditacioun
I putte it ay under correccioun
Of clerkes, for I am nat textuel:[2]
I take but the sentence,° trusteth wel.   *meaning*
Therfore I make protestacioun°   *public acknowledgment*
60 That I wol stonde to correccioun."
        Upon this word we han assented soone,
For, as it seemed, it was for to doone
To enden in som vertuous sentence,°   *doctrine*
And for to yive him space and audience;
65 And bede[3] oure Host he sholde to him saye
That alle we to telle his tale him praye.
        Oure Hoste hadde the wordes for us alle:
"Sire preest," quod he, "now faire you bifalle:
Telleth," quod he, "youre meditacioun.
70 But hasteth you; the sonne wol adown.
Beeth fructuous,° and that in litel space,°   *fruitful / time*
And to do wel God sende you his grace.
Saye what you list, and we wol gladly heere."
And with that word he saide in this manere.

[The Remedy Against Lechery]

Now cometh the remedye agains leccherye, and that is generally chastitee and continence that restraineth alle the desordeinee mevinges[4] that comen of flesshly talentes. And evere the grettere merite shal he han that most restraineth the wikkede eschaufinges of the ardor[5] of this sinne. And this is in two maneres, that is to sayn, chastitee in mariage and chastitee of widwehood. Now shaltou understonde that matrimoine is leveful[6] assembling of man and of woman that receiven by vertu of the sacrement the bond thurgh which they may nat be departed[7] in al hir lif—that is to sayn, whil that they liven bothe. This, as saith the book, is a ful greet sacrement. God maked it, as I have said, in Paradis, and wolde himself be born in mariage. And for to halwen[8] mariage he was at a wedding wheras he turned water into win, which was the firste miracle that

2. Literal, faithful to the letter.
3. I.e., we bade.
4. Inordinate urges. "Talentes": desires.
5. The wicked blazings up of the fire.
6. Permissible.
7. Separated.
8. Sanctify.

he wroughte in erthe biforn his disciples. Trewe effect of mariage clenseth fornicacion and replenissheth holy chirche of[9] good linage, for that is the ende of mariage. And it chaungeth deedly[1] sinne into venial sinne bitwixe hem that been ywedded, and maketh the hertes al oon[2] of hem that been ywedded, as wel as the bodies. This is verray[3] mariage that was establisshed by God er that sinne bigan, whan naturel lawe was in his righte point[4] in Paradis. And it was ordained that oo[5] man sholde have but oo womman, and oo womman but oo man, as saith Saint Augustin, by manye reasons.

First, for mariage is figured[6] bitwixe Crist and holy chirche. And that other[7] is for a man is heed of a womman—algate, by ordinance[8] it sholde be so. For if a womman hadde mo[9] men than oon, thanne sholde she have mo hedes than oon, and that were an horrible thing bifore God. And eek a womman ne mighte nat plese too many folk atones. And also ther ne sholde nevere be pees ne reste amonges hem, for everich[1] wolde asken his owene thing. And fertherover,[2] no man ne sholde knowe his owne engendrure,[3] ne who sholde have his heritage. And the womman sholde been the lesse biloved fro the time that she were conjoint[4] to manye men.

Now cometh how that a man sholde bere him[5] with his wif, and namely in two thinges, that is to sayn, in suffrance[6] and in reverence, as shewed Crist whan he made first womman. For he ne made hire nat of the heed of Adam for[7] she sholde nat claime too greet lordshipe. For theras the womman hath the maistrye[8] she maketh too muche desray. Ther needen none ensamples of this: the experience of day by day oughte suffise. Also certes God ne made nat womman of the foot of Adam for she ne sholde nat been holden too lowe: for she can nat paciently suffre. But God made womman of the rib of Adam for womman sholde be felawe unto man. Man sholde bere him to his wif in faith, in trouthe, and in love, as saith Saint Paul[9] that a man sholde loven his wif as Crist loved holy chirche, that loved it so wel that he deide for it: so sholde a man for his wif, if it were neede.

Now how that a womman sholde be subjet to hir housbonde, that telleth Saint Peter.[1] First, in obedience; and eek, as saith the decree, a woman that is wif, as longe as she is a wif, she hath noon auctoritee to swere ne to bere witnesse withoute leve[2] of hir hous-

---

9. With.
1. Deadly.
2. I.e., in union.
3. True.
4. I.e., in its natural working order.
5. One.
6. I.e., symbolizes the relationship.
7. Second; "heed": head.
8. At any rate, by proper management.
9. More.
1. Each.

2. Moreover.
3. Children.
4. Joined.
5. Behave. "Namely": especially.
6. Patience.
7. In order that.
8. Domination; "desray": disturbance.
9. In Ephesians v.25.
1. See I Peter iii.1.
2. Permission.

bonde that is hir lord—algate, he sholde be so by reson. She sholde eek serven him in alle honestee, and been attempree[3] of hir array. I woot wel that they sholde setten hir entente[4] to plesen hir housbondes, but nat by hir quaintise[5] of array. Saint Jerome saith that wives that been appareiled in silk and in precious purpre[6] ne mowe nat clothen hem in Jesu Crist. Loke what saith Saint John eek in this matere. Saint Gregorye eek saith that no wight seeketh precious array but only for vaineglorye, to been honoured the more bifore the peple. It is a greet folye a womman to have a fair array outward and in hireself be foul inward. A wif sholde eek be mesurable[7] in looking and in bering and in laughing, and discreet in alle hir wordes and hir deedes. And aboven alle worldly thing she sholde loven hir housbonde with al hir herte and to him be trewe of hir body. So sholde an housbonde eek be to his wif. For sith[8] that al the body is the housbondes, so sholde hir herte been, or elles ther is bitwixe hem two as in that no parfit[9] mariage. Thanne shal men understonde that for three thinges a man and his wif flesshly mowen[1] assemble. The firste is in entente of engendrure of[2] children to the service of God: for certes that is the cause final of matrimoine. Another cause is to yeelden everich[3] of hem to other the dette of hir bodies, for neither of hem hath power of his owene body. The thridde[4] is for to eschewe leccherye and vilainye. The ferthe[5] is forsoothe deedly sinne. As to the firste, it is meritorye;[6] the seconde also for, as saith the decree, that she hath merite of chastitee that yeeldeth to hir housbonde the dette of hir body, ye, though it be again hir liking and the lust[7] of hir herte. The thridde manere is venial sinne: and trewely, scarsly may ther any of thise be withoute venial sinne, for the corrupcion and the delit.[8] The ferthe manere is for to understonde, as if they assemble only for amorous love and for noon of the foresaide causes, but for to accomplisshe thilke brenning[9] delit, they rekke nevere how ofte. Soothly it is deedly sinne. And yit, with sorwe, some folk wol painen hem[1] more to doon than to hir appetit suffiseth. * * *

Another remedye agayns leccherye is specially to withdrawen swiche[2] thinges as yive occasion to thilke vilainye, as ese, eting, and drinking. For certes whan the pot boileth strongly, the beste remedye is to withdrawe the fir. Sleeping longe in greet quiete is eek a greet norice[3] to leccherye.

3. Modest.
4. Do their best.
5. Extravagance.
6. Royal scarlet; "mowe": may.
7. Modest; "bering": behavior.
8. Since.
9. Perfect.
1. May.
2. With desire to beget.
3. Pay each.
4. Third.
5. Fourth.
6. Meritorious.
7. Desire.
8. On account of the impurity and bodily delight.
9. That burning.
1. Exert themselves.
2. Such.
3. Nurse.

Another remedye agains leccherye is that a man or a womman eschewe the compaignye of hem by whiche he douteth[4] to be tempted. For albeit so that the deede be withstonden, yit is ther greet temptacion. Soothly, a whit wal, although it brenne[5] nought fully by stiking of a candele, yit is the wal blak of the leit.[6] Ful ofte time I rede that no man truste in his owene perfeccion but[7] he be stronger than Sampson and holier than David and wiser than Salomon. * * *

Chaucer's Retraction

Now praye I to hem alle that herkne this litel tretis[8] or rede, that if ther be any thing in it that liketh[9] hem, that therof they thanken oure Lord Jesu Crist, of whom proccedeth al wit[1] and al goodnesse. And if ther be any thing that displese him, I praye hem also that they arrette it to the defaute of myn unconning,[2] and nat to my wil, that wolde ful fain have said bettre if I hadde had conning. For oure book saith, "Al that is writen is writen for oure doctrine,"[3] and that is myn entente. Wherfore I biseeke[4] you mekely, for the mercy of God, that ye praye for me that Crist have mercy on me and foryive me my giltes, and namely[5] of my translacions and enditinges of worldly vanitees, the whiche I revoke in my retraccions: as is the *Book of Troilus*; the *Book* also *of Fame*; the *Book of the Five and Twenty Ladies*;[6] the *Book of the Duchesse*; the *Book of Saint Valentines Day of the Parlement of Briddes*; the *Tales of Canterbury*, thilke that sounen into[7] sinne; the *Book of the Leon*;[8] and many another book, if they were in my remembrance, and many a song and many a leccherous lay: that Crist for his grete mercy foryive me the sinne. But of the translacion of Boece[9] *De Consolatione*, and othere bookes of legendes of saintes, and omelies,[1] and moralitee, and devocion, that thanke I oure Lord Jesu Crist and his blisful Moder and alle the saintes of hevene, biseeking hem that they from hennes[2] forth unto my lives ende sende me grace to biwaile my giltes and to studye to the salvacion of my soule, and graunte me grace of verray penitence, confession, and satisfaccion to doon in this present lif, thurgh the benigne grace of him that is king of kinges and preest over alle preestes, that boughte[3] us with the precious blood of his herte, so that I may

4. Fears.
5. Burn; "stiking": application.
6. Flame.
7. Unless.
8. Hear this little treatise.
9. Pleases.
1. Understanding.
2. Ascribe it to the defect of my lack of skill.
3. Romans xv.4.
4. Beseech.

5. Especially. "Enditinges": compositions.
6. I.e., the *Legend of Good Women*.
7. Those that tend toward.
8. The *Book of the Lion* has not been preserved.
9. Boethius.
1. Homilies.
2. Hence.
3. Redeemed.

been oon of hem at the day of doom that shulle be saved. *Qui cum patre et Spiritu Sancto vivis et regnas Deus per omnia saecula.*[4] Amen.

1386–1400

LYRICS AND OCCASIONAL VERSE[1]
To Rosamond[2]

Madame, ye been of alle beautee shrine
As fer as cercled is the mapemounde:[3]
For as the crystal glorious ye shine,
And like ruby been youre cheekes rounde.
5 Therwith ye been so merye and so jocounde
That at a revel whan that I see you daunce
It is an oinement unto my wounde,
Though ye to me ne do no daliaunce.[4]

For though I weepe of teres ful a tine,°   *tub*
10 Yit may that wo myn herte nat confounde;
Youre semy° vois, that ye so smale outtwine,[5]   *small*
Maketh my thought in joye and blis habounde:°   *abound*
So curteisly I go with love bounde
That to myself I saye in my penaunce,[6]
15 "Suffiseth me to love you, Rosemounde,
Though ye to me ne do no daliaunce."

Was nevere pik walwed in galauntine[7]
As I in love am walwed and vwounde,
For which ful ofte I of myself divine
20 That I am trewe Tristam[8] the secounde;

4. Who with the Father and the Holy Spirit livest and reignest God forever.
1. As a man of accomplishments who was often at court, Chaucer must, like other courtiers, have been called upon to write both occasional verses and lyrics. Of the handful of these shorter poems that have survived, several of the best are included here: they reveal the ways in which Chaucer handled some of the poetic modes and attitudes of his time. These modes—particularly the lyric strain, which seeks expression in a brief form—seem to have been uncongenial to his temperament. Some, in fact, might well be termed "anti-lyrics"; these are the poems where the extreme conventions of the courtly-love lyric become a framework in which Chaucer's irony and indirection may be brought into immediate play. Chaucer's best work, however, is in his longer poems, for irony and indirection are qualities

which can be given proper development only if the poet has ample room to work in.
2. This lyric extends the extravagant images of the stylized courtly-love lyric to outrageous lengths: a lover might well weep a flood of tears but would hardly measure them by the tubful (line 9), and he might be overwhelmed with love—but not like a fish buried in sauce (line 17). The general imperturbability of tone contrasts ironically with the grotesque metaphors.
3. I.e., to the farthest circumference of the map of the world.
4. I.e., show me no encouragement.
5. That you so delicately spin out.
6. I.e., pangs of unrequited love.
7. Pike rolled in galantine sauce.
8. The famous lover of Isolt (Iseult, Isolde) in medieval legend, renowned for his constancy.

My love may not refreide nor affounde;[9]
I brenne° ay in amorous plesaunce: burn
Do what you list, I wol youre thral° be founde,   slave
Though ye to me ne do no daliaunce.

To His Scribe Adam[1]

Adam scrivain,° if evere it thee bifalle   scribe
Boece[2] or *Troilus* for to writen newe,
Under thy longe lokkes thou moste[3] have the scalle,° scurf
But after my making thou write more trewe.[4]
5 So ofte a day I moot° thy werk renewe,   must
It to correcte, and eek to rubbe and scrape:
And al is thurgh thy necligence and rape.°   haste

Complaint to His Purse[5]

To you, my purs, and to noon other wight,
Complaine I, for ye be my lady dere.
I am so sory, now that ye be light,
For certes, but if[6] ye make me hevy cheere,
5 Me were as lief[7] be laid upon my beere;°   bier
For which unto youre mercy thus I crye:
Beeth hevy again, or elles moot° I die.   must

Now voucheth sauf this day er it be night
That I of you the blisful soun may heere,
10 Or see youre colour, lik the sonne bright,
That of yelownesse hadde nevere peere.
Ye be my life, ye be myn hertes steere,°   rudder, guide
Queene of confort and of good compaignye:
Beeth hevy again, or elles moot I die.

15 Ye purs, that been to me my lives light
And saviour, as in this world down here,

9. Cool nor chill.
1. This *jeu d'esprit*, called forth by the inefficiency of his amanuensis, is written in the verse form of Chaucer's great poem *Troilus and Criseide*.
2. I.e., Chaucer's translation of Boethius' *De Consolatione*. "Troilus": *Troilus and Criseide*.
3. I.e., may you.
4. Unless you write more accurately what I've composed.
5. In this variation on the courtly-love lyric the conventional language of love is both used and misused to express love of cash. Ladies, like coins, should be golden, and like purses they should not be "light" (i.e., fickle). On the other hand, they should not be heavy, as purses should be. The poem is in the characteristic three-stanza *ballade* form, with the usual "envoy" addressed to a noble patron. In this case the patron apparently heard the complaint, for, three days after his accession (in 1399), King Henry IV renewed and increased the pension Chaucer had received from Richard II.
6. Unless.
7. I'd just as soon.

Out of this tonne[8] helpe me thurgh your might,
Sith that ye wol nat be my tresorere;°   *disburser*
For I am shave as neigh° as any frere.°   *close / friar*
20 But yit I praye unto youre curteisye:
Beeth hevy again, or elles moot I die.

Envoy to Henry IV

O conquerour of Brutus Albioun,[9]
Which that by line and free eleccioun
Been verray king, this song to you I sende:
25 And ye, that mowen° alle oure harmes amende,   *may*
Have minde upon my supplicacioun.

Merciless Beauty[1]

1

Youre yën two wol slee° me sodeinly: *slay*
I may the beautee of hem nat sustene,°   *withstand*
So woundeth it thurghout myn herte keene.°   *keenly*

And but° youre word wol helen hastily   *unless*
5 Myn hertes wounde, whil that it is greene,[2]
    Youre yën two wol slee me sodeinly:
    I may the beautee of hem nat sustene.

Upon my trouthe, I saye you faithfully
That ye been of my lif and deeth the queene,
10 For with my deeth the trouthe shal be seene.
    Youre yën two wol slee me sodeinly:
    I may the beautee of hem nat sustene,
    So woundeth it thurghout myn herte keene.

2

So hath youre beautee fro youre herte chaced
15 Pitee, that me ne availeth nought to plaine:°   *complain*
For Daunger halt[3] youre mercy in his chaine.

Giltelees my deeth thus han ye me purchaced;°   *procured*
I saye you sooth, me needeth nought to feine:°   *dissemble*
    So hath youre beautee fro youre herte chaced
20   Pitee, that me ne availeth nought to plaine.

---

8. Tun, meaning "predicament."
9. Britain (Albion) was supposed to have been founded by Brutus, the grandson of Aeneas, the founder of Rome.
1. The first two sections of this poem employ the typical imagery and extravagant emotion of courtly-love lyrics—the power of the lady's eyes to slay the lover, for instance, and the struggle between her native pity and her "daunger" (haughtiness). But it ends where a real lyric could never end: the poet's self-congratulation, at the failure of his affair, on his unimpaired health.
2. I.e., fresh.
3. Haughtiness holds.

Allas, that nature hath in you compaced°   *enclosed*
So greet beautee that no man may attaine
To mercy, though he sterve° for the paine.   *die*
    So hath youre beautee fro youre herte chaced
25   Pitee, that me ne availeth nought to plaine:
    For Daunger halt youre mercy in his chaine.

3

Sin I fro Love escaped am so fat,
I nevere thenke° to been in his prison lene: *intend*
Sin I am free, I counte him nat a bene.[4]

30 He may answere and saye right this and that;
    I do no fors,[5] I speke right as I mene:
    Sin I fro Love escaped am so fat,
    I nevere thenke to been in his prison lene.

Love hath my name ystrike° out of his sclat,°   *struck / slate*
35 And he is strike out of my bookes clene
For everemo; ther is noon other mene.°   *solution*
    Sin I fro Love escaped am so fat,
    I nevere thenke to been in his prison lene:
    Sin I am free, I counte him nat a bene.

Gentilesse[6]

The firste fader and findere° of gentilesse,   *founder*
What° man desireth gentil for to be   *whatever*
Moste folwe his traas,° and alle his wittes dresse[7]   *path*
Vertu to sue,° and vices for to flee: *follow*
5 For unto vertu longeth° dignitee,   *belongs*
And nought the revers, saufly° dar I deeme,   *safely*
Al were he[8] mitre, crowne, or diademe.

This firste stok was ground of rightwisnesse,°   *righteousness*
Trewe of his word, sobre, pietous,[9] and free,
10 Clene of his gost,° and loved bisinesse   *spirit*
Against the vice of slouthe,° in honestee;   *sloth*
And but his heir love vertu as dide he,
He is nat gentil, though he riche° seeme,   *noble*
Al were he mitre, crowne, or diademe.

15 Vice may wel be heir to old richesse,
But ther may no man, as ye may wel see,
Biquethe his heir his vertuous noblesse:

---

4. I don't consider him worth a bean.
5. I don't care.
6. The virtue of "gentilesse" combined a courtesy of manner with a courtesy of mind. That it is not the inevitable adjunct of aristocratic birth (though most appropriate to it) was a medieval commonplace, to which Chaucer here gives succinct—if conventional—expression. It is important to observe, however,

that the moral democracy implied by this doctrine was never transferred by the Middle Ages to the political or even the social realm.
7. I.e., must follow his (the first father's) path and dispose all his (own) wits.
8. Even if he wear.
9. Merciful; "free": generous.

That is appropred° unto no degree   *exclusively assigned*
But to the firste fader in majestee,
20 That maketh his heir him that wol him queme,°   *please*
Al were he mitre, crowne, or diademe.

Truth[1]

Flee fro the prees° and dwelle with soothfastnesse;   *crowd*
Suffise unto° thy thing, though it be smal;   *to be content with*
For hoord hath[2] hate, and climbing tikelnesse;°   *insecurity*
Prees hath envye, and wele° blent° overal.   *prosperity / blinds*
5 Savoure° no more than thee bihoove shal;   *relish*
Rule wel thyself that other folk canst rede:°   *advise*
And Trouthe shal delivere,[3] it is no drede.°   *doubt*

Tempest thee nought al crooked to redresse[4]
In trust of hire[5] that turneth as a bal;
10 Muche wele stant in litel bisinesse;[6]
Be war therfore to spurne ayains an al.[7]
Strive nat as dooth the crokke° with the wal.   *pot*
Daunte° thyself that dauntest otheres deede: *master*
And Trouthe shal delivere, it is no drede.

15 That thee is sent, receive in buxomnesse;°   *obedience*
The wrastling for the world axeth° a fal;   *asks for*
Here is noon hoom, here nis but wildernesse:
Forth, pilgrim, forth! Forth, beest, out of thy stal!
Know thy countree, looke up, thank God of al.
20 Hold the heigh way and lat thy gost° thee lede: *spirit*
And Trouthe shal delivere, it is no drede.

Therfore, thou Vache,[8] leve thyn olde wrecchednesse
Unto the world; leve[9] now to be thral.
Crye him mercy that of his heigh goodnesse
25 Made thee of nought, and in especial
Draw unto him, and pray in general,
For thee and eek for othere, hevenelich meede:°   *reward*
And Trouthe shal delivere, it is no drede.

1. Taking as his theme Christ's words to his disciples (in John viii.32), "And ye shall know the truth, and the truth shall make you free," Chaucer plays upon the triple meaning that the Middle English word "trouthe" seems to have had for him: the religious truth of Christianity, the moral virtue of integrity, and the philosophical idea of reality. By maintaining one's faith and one's integrity, one rises superior to the vicissitudes of this world and comes eventually to know reality—which is not, however, of this world.

2. Hoarding causes.
3. I.e., truth shall make you free.
4. Do not disturb yourself to straighten all that's crooked.
5. Fortune, who turns like a ball in that she is always presenting a different aspect to men.
6. Peace of mind stands in little anxiety.
7. I.e. to kick against the pricks.
8. Probably Sir Philip de la Vache, with a pun on the French for "cow."
9. I.e. cease.

The Sixteenth Century

(1485-1603)

1485: Accession of Henry VII inaugurates age of the Tudor sovereigns.

1509: Accession of Henry VIII.

1517: Martin Luther's Wittenberg Theses; beginning of the Reformation.

1535: Henry VIII acknowledged "Supreme Head on Earth" of the English church.

1557: Publication of *Tottel's Miscellany*, containing poems by Sir Thomas Wyatt, Henry Howard Earl of Surrey, and others.

1558: Accession of Queen Elizabeth I.

1576: The Theatre, the first permanent structure in England for the presentation of plays, is built.

1588: Defeat of the Spanish Armada.

1603: Death of Elizabeth I; accession of James I, first of the Stuart line.

ENGLAND UNDER HENRY VII

The 16th century in England is the age of the Tudor sovereigns. There were three generations of them; they ruled England from 1485 to 1603. Before the first Tudor, the Earl of Richmond who became Henry VII, won his crown by defeating Richard III at Bosworth field, the country had for more than thirty years been torn by a dynastic strife between the houses of York and Lancaster. Henry VII was Lancastrian, but he married Elizabeth of the house of York, sister of Edward V and neice of the Yorkist king he defeated, Richard III. The barons, impoverished and divided by the dynastic wars, could not effectively oppose the power of the crown, and the church, the other great force in society, was closer to alliance with royal power than to opposition. So Tudor government meant, in comparison with what had gone before and with other conceivable alternatives, a government of strong central authority, of order, and of practical solutions to problems.

About a decade before Henry VII won his throne, the art of printing from movable type, a German invention, had been introduced into England by William Caxton (ca. 1422-91), who had learned and practiced it in the Low Countries. Literacy had been increasing during the 15th century, so that many more people could read than in Chaucer's time. It is estimated that some 30 per cent of the people could read English in the early 15th century and some 60 per cent by 1530. Printing of course made books cheaper and more plentiful, and accordingly there were more opportunities to read and more incentive to learn to read.

Seven years after Henry VII became king, Columbus discovered America, and a few years later Vasco da Gama reached the Orient by sailing around the Cape of Good Hope. The English were not pioneers in the discovery and exploration of the western hemisphere, but the consequences of new discoveries were to affect their place in the world profoundly, for in the next century they became great colonizers and merchants.

Significant changes in trade and in the arts of war also marked the early years of the Tudor regime. Henry VII made commercial treaties with European countries; England, which had always been a sheep-raising country, began to manufacture and export significant amounts of cloth. As lands were enclosed to permit grazing on a larger scale, people were driven off the land to the cities, London grew into a metropolitan market, and business in the modern sense began to develop. At the same time the old feudal structure began to break down, partly because the introduction of firearms had made obsolete the old armored knight on horseback, as well as the English bowman who had won such famous victories in France under King Henry V. The "new men" who supported the Tudors and profited from their favor could adapt themselves more easily to a changed society than could the survivors of the great families of the feudal 15th century.

Yet it would be a mistake to visualize these changes as sudden and dramatic. Although Caxton introduced printed books, and was an author and translator as well as a printer, his publications consisted of long prose romances translated from the French, collections of moral sayings, and other works—such as Malory's *Morte Darthur*—that were medieval rather than modern. And even though the armored knight was obsolete, for a century jousts and tournaments took place at court and the approved code of behavior was the traditional code of chivalry. As often in an age of spectacular novelty, full of significance for the future, men's minds looked back instead of forward. Confronted with innovation, they dreamed of an idealized past instead of looking forward to an uncertain future. The best writers of the time of Henry VII were imitators of Chaucer, who had died about a century before. They were Scottish rather than English: William Dunbar (ca. 1460–ca. 1520), Gavin Douglas (1475–1522), and Sir David Lindsay (1485–1555). Even the English writers looked back; a typical one is Stephen Hawes (1474–1523), who imitated not Chaucer but John Lydgate, monk of Bury.

HUMANISM

During the 15th century a few English clerics and government officials had journeyed to Italy and had seen something of the extraordinary cultural and intellectual movement flourishing in the city-states there. But it was only near the end of the century that Italian influence came to be important, and it was not until the accession of Henry VIII to the throne in 1509 that a notable renaissance took place in England.

Humanism was a revolt against the other-worldly orientation of medieval philosophy and religion. The humanists turned to newly recovered Greek manuscripts for inspiration and enlightenment; they saw in the ancient classics a more "modern" and more desirable world than the one they lived in. They proposed to reform education in the direction of Ciceronian *humanitas*, to make men realize their human capabilities as individuals, to free them from the shackles of Scholasticism and the view that, as Chaucer had expressed it, "this world nis but a thurghfare ful of wo."

The thesis of humanism was that man's proper role in the world was action, not contemplation. Wealth and power were not necessarily evil, since they might provide the means of achieving good. The mind and the will had to be properly disciplined, but they were to be used positively, not renounced for the sake of the salvation of the soul. Passion, striving for glory, the aspiring mind were to be encouraged when the motives were noble, and becoming the master of the earth and thereby achieving benefits for mankind was a noble motive. The Italian humanists studied the Greek text of the new Testament (St. Jerome's Latin text, the Vulgate, was the official text of the church). In Florence, under the patronage of Lorenzo de Medici, such scholars of Plato as Marsilio Ficino (1433–99) and Pico della Mirandola (1463–94) created the liveliest intellectual atmosphere in Europe.

The humanist influence began to reach England slightly before the beginning of the 16th century. The Dutch scholar Desiderius Erasmus (ca. 1466–1536) wrote in 1499 about his first visit to England,

I have met with so much kindness and so much learning, not backward and trivial, but deep, accurate, ancient, Latin and Greek, that but for the curiosity of seeing it, I do not so much care for Italy. When I hear my Colet [John Colet, 1467–1519, Lecturer on the New Testament at Oxford and founder of St. Paul's School], I seem to be listening to Plato himself. In Grocyn [William Grocyn, 1446–1519, Lecturer in Greek at Oxford], who does not marvel at such a perfect round of learning? What can be more acute, profound, and delicate than the judgment of Linacre? [Thomas Linacre, physician and scholar, tutor to princes] What has nature ever created more gentle, more sweet, more happy than the genius of Thomas More?

The masterpiece of English humanism was More's *Utopia*, written in Latin, though More's English prose, his *Richard III* and his controversial pamphlets, is more important for the period. (It was easier, one must remember, for a scholar of this time to write in Latin than in English.) The *History of Richard III*, which drew upon what he had learned from Cardinal Morton as a young page in Morton's household, was a justification of the Tudor dynasty by blackening its immediate predecessor. Another important humanist historian was the naturalized Italian, Polydore Vergil (ca. 1470–1555), who, like More, defended Henry VII's right to the throne but also attacked the medieval legends of Brutus, the mythical founder of Britain, and the stories of King Arthur and his Round Table. Humanism was to have a profound effect upon English intellectual life, education, and writing all through the 16th century. Queen Elizabeth herself, with her command of languages and her practical sense of the problems of government, was a typical product of a humanistic education.

Elizabethan education was based upon the medieval *trivium* (grammar, logic, and rhetoric) and *quadrivium* (arithmetic, geometry, astronomy, and music). Grammar was of course Latin grammar, and the rhetoric that went with it was a rigorous discipline in all the stylistic devices used by classical authors. The purpose was a utilitarian one—to train the student to speak and write good Latin, the language of diplomacy, of the professions, and of all higher learning. But the books read and studied rhetorically were not considered mere exhibitions of literary style; from the *Sententiae Pueriles* for beginners, on up through Terence, Virgil, Horace, and Cicero's *De Officiis*, the works were studied for the moral, political, and philosophical content they offered. Elizabethan schoolmasters might use the system of double translation, from English into Latin and then from Latin back into English, to develop facility and rhetorical elegance, but they well knew that the rapid development from child into man (so much more rapid than we consider either feasible or desirable) required moral instruction, and this was to be found in the Latin classics. It was a mission of the English humanists like Colet, Elyot, and Ascham to persuade the English gentry that their sons should be bred to this kind of learning as the most suitable preparation for public service.

Although Sir Thomas More had turned naturally to Latin in writing his *Utopia*, the choice was not as easy for succeeding generations. In fact, the question of whether to write in English or in Latin became a question of great seriousness. The vernaculars seemed relatively new and unstable to learned men, and with their great desire for eternal fame it was natural that they should concern themselves about the durability of their medium. Furthermore, the age of the humanists had emphasized the value of the classical languages; Cicero and the other masters of rhetoric were imitated in their own tongues. But in Italy, France, and England alike, there came to be a revolt against this sterile and slavish imitation of the classics. It is the contention of Joachim Du Bellay's *Défense et Illustration de la Langue Française* (1549) that the value of a language is not inherent in the language itself, but depends upon what great and fine works are written in that language; furthermore, and this is even more important, the feeling of nationality itself dictates that the vernacular should be used. If the tongue of the people is not so refined and polished as the Greek or Latin, all the more reason why men of learning should improve it by studying it and writing their most ambitious works in it. Roger Ascham (1515–68), tutor to Princess Elizabeth, included in his book on archery called *Toxophilus* (1545) a defense of writing in English, though he said it would be easier for him to write in Latin or Greek. He dedicated the book to King Henry, and his patriotic motives are expressed in verses addressed to England:

> Stick to the truth, and evermore thou shall
> Through Christ, King Henry, the book and the bow,
> All manner of enemies quite overthrow.

Richard Mulcaster (ca. 1530–1611), principal of the Merchant Taylors' School and teacher of Edmund Spenser, said:

I do write in my natural English tongue, because though I make the learned my judges, which understand Latin, yet I mean good to the unlearned, which understand but English. * * * For is it not indeed a marvelous bondage, to become servants to one tongue for learning's sake the most of our time, with loss of most time, whereas we may have the very same treasure in our own tongue, with the gain of most time? our own bearing the joyful title of our liberty and freedom, the Latin tongue remembering us of our thralldom and bondage? I love Rome, but London better; I favor Italy, but England more; I honor the Latin, but I worship the English.

THE REFORMATION—HENRY VIII, EDWARD VI, AND MARY

Humanists like Erasmus advocated and practiced a scholarly and critical study of the Scriptures; humanists like More were opposed to corrupt and ignorant clergy and such abuses as the sale of papal indulgences and pardons. But when, after Martin Luther nailed his famous Theses to the church door in Wittenberg in 1517, the Reformation itself gathered force, Erasmus and More drew back. Humanism and Reformation for a while seemed to be hostile forces.

What was the Reformation? From the point of view of those who supported it, it was a return to pure Christianity—cleansing the church of all the filth and idolatry that had accumulated over the centuries. From a less partisan point of view it was the break-up of western Christendom, the secularization of society, the establishment of princely ascendancy over the church, and consequently the identification of religious feelings with patriotic, nationalistic ones. From the point of view of the Catholic Church it was, of course, damnable heresy.

In England, one cannot say that the Reformation had an ideological basis. There had been John Wycliffe and the Lollard movement, a popular protest in the time of Chaucer, but little of this survived in the second decade of the 16th century. The split with the Church of Rome was caused by a man who considered himself a Catholic champion against Luther and his opinions: Henry VIII, who for writing a book against Luther had been given the title "Defender of the Faith" by Pope Leo X. Henry's motives were dynastic, not religious; he needed a legitimate son and he could not get one without the divorce which Rome refused him. He insisted upon being Supreme Head of the English church and requiring oaths of allegiance to him in that role; Sir Thomas More, his Lord Chancellor, resigned and finally gave up his life rather than sign such an oath. More's successor, Thomas Cromwell, dissolved the monasteries and distributed the property to a group of people who thereafter would not side with Rome. And though under Henry the great English translator of the Bible, William Tyndale, was persecuted, driven out of England, and finally martyred in 1536, it was also in Henry's reign that the Scriptures in English were made available in The Great Bible of 1539 to anyone who could read.

Under Henry's son, the child king Edward VI (b. 1537; reigned 1547–53), the English Reformation, which had taken place for political reasons, acquired a strong religious and spiritual force. Protestant theologians from the Continent swarmed to England, the Book of Common Prayer was published in 1549 and 1552, and by 1553, the year of the boy king's death, the 42 Articles which officially defined the beliefs of the English church were thoroughly Protestant.

The successor to the young Protestant king was his older sister Mary, half-Spanish and devoutly Catholic, who married her cousin, Philip II of Spain. The leading Protestants either fled to the Continent or were burned at the stake as heretics; ideologically the Reformation could be reversed, but some of its practical consequences, like the distribution of monastery lands, could not. A Spaniard on the throne of England was not popular, and Mary, whose accession had been opposed by the Council which had proclaimed Lady Jane Grey queen, and whose throne was challenged by a rebellion led by Sir Thomas Wyatt the Younger, son of the poet, dared not press her people too far. She could herself return to Roman allegiance but she could not undo the work of her father and brother. The most necessary thing to do was something she could not do—produce an heir. (Had she done so, England and the United States would probably be Catholic countries today.) Her reign was short, and the Protestant exiles swarmed back at her death to be a potent force in English society during the long reign of Mary's half sister, Elizabeth.

NATIONALISM—ELIZABETH I

Elizabeth Tudor, who ascended the throne in 1558 and ruled until 1603, was one of the most remarkable political geniuses ever produced by a people which has not been barren of political geniuses. Vain, difficult, and head-strong, she nevertheless had a very shrewd instinct about her country's strengths and weaknesses, and she identified herself with her country as no previous ruler had done. Although she was susceptible to the flattery of her courtiers and favorites, she nevertheless entrusted power to such solid men as William Cecil and Francis Walsingham. Cecil (1520–98) was her chief and most trusted Secretary. He devoted his great talents with unswerving loyalty to preserving a balance of forces in England, maintaining the queen's supremacy over ambitious nobles, and extracting money from the Commons to run the government. Walsingham (ca. 1530–90), a gifted diplomat and administrator, was her principal architect of foreign policy.

England's weakness was its politico-religious division. The Catholics, who had never been reformed and who adhered to the pro-Spanish faction of the previous reign, and the Protestant exiles, whose sojourn on the Continent had only sharpened their zeal for the eradication of papistry everywhere in Europe, were the extremes. Between them were the majority of Englishmen whose main desire was for order (remembering the civil conflicts of the previous century), and for these Englishmen Elizabeth, in her person and her policy, became the symbol and the cause.

England's strength lay in its middle position in the balance of power in Europe—it could throw its weight either way in the power contest between Spain and France; it could support or fail to support the Protestant uprising in the Low Countries. Moreover the queen was unmarried, and the general assumption was that of course she would marry, since as her father had undoubtedly taught her, one of a monarch's major duties is to provide an unquestioned, strong, legitimate heir to the throne. As long as she was capable of bearing children, Elizabeth's possible marriage was an important factor in European diplomacy. By the time it was too late to marry, England was strong and united, capable of shaking off (in 1588) the attempt of the Spanish king, Philip II, to invade the country. What unified England more than anything else was the papal bull of 1570, ex-communicating Elizabeth and relieving her subjects of their loyalty to her. This bull, had it taken effect, would have brought to the throne Mary Queen of Scots, Catholic by faith and French by culture—an insupportable thought; Englishmen rallied to their queen and she became a symbol of Englishness and nationalism. The adulation of her, in the face of trouble on the Scottish border, near-chaos in Ireland, and varying threats from the Continent, grew to almost religious heights; her beauty (which was exaggerated), her wisdom (which generally did not need exaggeration), and her divine mission to guide England became articles of faith. In 1588 the defeat of the great Spanish Armada, the mightiest invasion fleet ever mounted against England, seemed to justify that faith.

In matters of religion Elizabeth chose a middle way which satisfied neither the Catholics nor the Puritans. She imposed a form of service, compelled her subjects to attend it, and left their consciences to themselves. The effect was again nationalistic; in the settled and established Elizabethan church, Christians looked toward neither Rome nor Geneva as the prime source of authority, but to the throne of their own sovereign.

The desire for commercial profit also strengthened nationalistic feelings. In 1493 the Pope had divided the new world between the Spanish and the Portuguese by drawing a line from pole to pole (hence Brazil speaks Portuguese today and the rest of Latin America speaks Spanish): the English were not in the picture. But by the end of Edward VI's reign the Company of Merchant Adventurers was founded and Englishmen had become interested in Asia and North America. As Protestantism progressed, many fishing fleets lacked work, for the sale of fish depended in great part upon the Catholic practice of eating no meat on Fridays and other fast days. So they turned to piracy, preying on Spanish ships which were returning laden with wealth from the New World. This business soon became a private undeclared war, with the queen and her courtiers investing in these raids privately but accepting no responsibility for them. The greatest of many dazzling exploits was the voyage of Francis Drake in 1577–80: he sailed through the Straits of Magellan, pillaged Spanish towns on the Pacific, reached as far north as San Francisco, crossed to the Philippines and returned around the Cape of Good Hope; he came back with £1,000,000 in treasure, and his investors earned a dividend of 5,000 per cent. Queen Elizabeth knighted him on the deck of his ship, *The Golden Hind*.

More than anything else, the mere survival of Elizabeth for so long provided the opportunity for nationalistic consciousness and feeling to become established. When she came to the throne in 1558 she was 25 years old; her sister had reigned only five years and her brother only six, but she would remain queen for almost 45 years. The second half of the 16th century is very appropriately called the Elizabethan age.

DRAMATIC LITERATURE

The dramatic literature of the age of Elizabeth is the greatest cultural achievement of the period. It grew out of the drama of the medieval church, but it was more directly influenced by the popular morality plays which continued to be performed on down to 1600. The emphasis in the moralities—as in the earlier mystery and miracle plays—was, of course, religious, and the plays were usually presented on church festival days. But by the end of the 15th century, plays with secular plots and characters began to be written, usually for presentation after a courtly dinner—or, if they were short enough, between the courses. Plays of this nature are now called "interludes"; the earliest known is *Fulgens and Lucrece*, by Henry

Medwall, produced in 1497 at Lambeth Palace. Several members of Sir Thomas More's circle wrote interludes, especially his brother-in-law John Rastell (1475–1536) and his nephew John Heywood (ca. 1497–ca. 1580). Heywood in particular made his interludes "merry" by introducing broad comic scenes on the model of contemporary French farce. The interlude was essentially courtly entertainment; it reached its height under Henry VIII, and remained popular down into the reign of Elizabeth. As it decayed, the Devils and other vicious characters of the old morality plays were fused into a single "Vice," who became essentially a comic character. Some late interludes, like John Bale's *King John* (ca. 1561), had political themes, a development that was to be important later in Elizabethan tragedies and chronicle history plays.

Classical Latin drama, particularly the tragedies of Seneca and the comedies of Plautus and Terence, began to influence English drama in the 60's. Students at schools and universities read and sometimes acted Latin plays, and it was an easy step from that to writing and producing imitations in English. Seneca's tragedies were constructed in five acts and were characterized by violent and bloody plots, resounding rhetorical speeches, and the presence of ghosts among the cast of characters; the first English tragedy based on these models was *Gorboduc, or Ferrex and Porrex*, by two lawyers, Thomas Sackville and Thomas Norton, produced at the Inner Temple in 1561 and later before the queen. Like Bale's *King John*, it has a political theme—the ruinous consequences of leaving a country without an heir to the throne.

Even earlier (ca. 1550), a schoolmaster, Nicholas Udall, had written a classical comedy in English, called *Ralph Roister Doister*, for his students to act. About the same time a play called *Gammer Gurton's Needle*, classical in form but thoroughly English in content, with much knockabout horseplay and native English provincial humor, was being acted before the scholars of Christ's College, Cambridge. In the first of these comedies the classical *miles gloriosus* (cowardly braggart soldier) makes his appearance in English; the type was to have its supreme fulfillment in Sir John Falstaff of Shakespeare's 1 and 2 *Henry IV*.

The fusion of classical form with English content brought about the possibility of a mature and artistic drama. But such drama must have an audience, a theater, and professional actors, or it will remain only a possibility. The earliest English drama had been acted by members of the clergy in the church; the mystery and miracle plays had been acted by amateurs —members of the local trade guilds—ordinarily on wagons in the streets of the towns. Moralities and interludes were produced by semi-amateur groups who traveled about, or by the servants of a lord in the hall of his castle. (See *The Second Shepherds' Play* and *Everyman* in this volume.) By 1450 one professional group was on tour. But there was no guild of actors, and they tended to be classed with jugglers, acrobats, mountebanks, and other traveling entertainers of dubious character; in 1545 actors were classified by statute as idle rogues and vagabonds and, as such, subject to arrest. Some noblemen maintained a company of actors as their personal servants, wearing livery and the badge of their masters. They could travel and practice their craft when not needed by their lords, and they were of course exempt from the statute. So it came about that the professional acting companies of Shakespeare's time, including Shakespeare's own, attached themselves to a nobleman and were technically his servants, even though virtually all of their time was devoted to, and their income came from, the public.

To reach a public audience they set up a platform in the courtyard of an enclosed inn, so the spectators could watch them from the ground of the courtyard or from the windows of the inn. The most profitable audiences could of course be collected in London innyards, particularly on Sundays. Their behavior was perhaps not very orderly; at any rate the City authorities, Puritans as they were, argued that such crowds contributed to riot, fire, accidents, ungodliness (especially on Sunday), absence from work (on weekdays), and the spread of the plague. The Puritans generally thought the drama vain and wicked: plays sometimes contained oaths and blasphemy, and it was morally shocking that men and boys put on female clothes to enact the roles of women.

To escape from the London authorities and to avoid sharing their profits with innkeepers, the Earl of Leicester's Men built in 1576 their own building outside the City limits in Shoreditch, and called it The Theatre. In general structure it resembled the innyards in which the plays had earlier been performed: it was open to the sky (except for sheltered galleries on three sides), and the stage very probably consisted of a large raised platform jutting out into the middle of the arena. A structure of this kind would place different requirements on actors than would our more intimate indoor theaters of today, and the style of acting was probably more declamatory and rhetorical. Other theaters followed, in Shoreditch and also in Southwark across the Thames, close to the pits where bull-baiting and bear-baiting satisfied the public taste for a more primitive kind of entertainment.

The companies were what would now be called "repertory companies" —that is, they filled the roles of each play from members of their own group, not employing outsiders, and they performed a number of different plays on consecutive days, not continuing a single play for a "run." Actors were shareholders in the profits of the company. Boys were apprenticed to actors just as they would be apprenticed to master craftsmen in a guild, and they took the women's parts in the plays until their voices changed. The plays might be bought for the company from a hack-writer or groups of hack-writers; or, as in Shakespeare's company, the Lord Chamberlain's Men, the company might have one of its members who could supply it with some (but by no means all) of its plays. The text remained the property of the company, but a popular play was eagerly sought by the printers, and the company sometimes had trouble achieving effective control over its rights in the play.

Public performance, though profitable, was not the only goal of the acting companies. The queen and the court must be entertained, especially at the holiday season or when foreign dignitaries paid a visit, and the rewards, both in money and prestige, of being selected to perform at court were great. There is a legend that Shakespeare wrote *The Merry Wives of Windsor* at the specific command of the queen, who found Falstaff amusing and wanted to see him in love, and it is quite clear that he wrote *Macbeth* with the Scottish interests of King James I in mind. The court audience was important in other ways. The best plays of the 1580's, a series of prose comedies by John Lyly, were written for the court circle and performed by a boys' company from one of the schools for choristers. Such performances, and others, could be put on in "private" theaters, indoors under a roof, with artificial lighting, like the "private" theater in Blackfriars which Shakespeare's company used. Lyly's comedies, such as *Endymion* and *Sapho and Phao*, were sophisticated, witty, and topical, masking under mythological or historical names actual persons of the queen's court.

It was for the courtly audience, also, that the first strain of real poetry was introduced into English drama. What Marlowe scornfully called the "jigging veins of rhyming mother wits / And such conceits as clownage keeps in pay" prevailed until George Peele's *Arraignment of Paris* (before 1584), an extravagantly flattering tribute to the queen in lovely verse, was acted by the Children of the Chapel. The 80's and 90's were to see such mighty poets as Marlowe and Shakespeare devote their genius to the stage.

Thomas Kyd, a friend of Marlowe, wrote a Senecan revenge play called *The Spanish Tragedy* which was popular for years, and probably also an early version of *Hamlet*, now lost. At the turn of the century Ben Jonson was beginning his great series of satirical comedies, such as *Every Man in His Humor* (1598), *Volpone* (1609), and *The Alchemist* (1610), and his less popular classical tragedies. Thomas Dekker (*The Shoemaker's Holiday*, 1599) and Thomas Heywood (*A Woman Killed With Kindness*, 1603) were successful playwrights who appealed to a middle-class audience. After James I came to the throne in 1603 the split between the tastes of the aristocratic audiences and the common people became more marked. Francis Beaumont and John Fletcher collaborated in comedies (*The Knight of the Burning Pestle*, ca. 1607) and tragedies (*The Maid's Tragedy*, ca. 1609) appealing to the taste of the court. Sensational plots set in the decadent courts of Italy provided material for John Webster (*The Duchess of Malfi*, ca. 1613) and Thomas Middleton (*Women Beware Women*, ca. 1621), and the same violence of action and morbidity of sentiment may be found in John Ford (*The Broken Heart*, ca. 1633) and James Shirley (*The Cardinal*, 1641) not long before the closing of the theaters and the beginning of the Civil Wars in 1642.

POET, PATRON, AND PUBLISHER

In the court the greatest opportunities existed, but there also were the greatest disappointments to be found. "It was overrun with place-seekers," writes M. St. Clare Byrne in *Elizabethan Life in Town and Country*, "but it was also undeniably the focus of the national life. It drew to it the clever mountebanks, but also the real vigor and talent. It captured and stimulated men's imaginations, even if eventually it disheartened and disgusted them." Men like Sir Christopher Hatton and Sir Walter Ralegh leaped from obscurity to great power and prominence as a result of their success as courtiers, but it must not be forgotten that they had other abilities than the gallantry and dancing which have made them famous in anecdote. The security of the courtier was always precarious, and there was scarcely one of Queen Elizabeth's courtiers who did not know, at some time or other, the harshness of the sovereign's disapproval. The great guide and conduct book for the courtier was Castiglione's *Il Cortegiano* (1528, translated into English by Sir Thomas Hoby in 1561), and according to its theses the function of the courtier was to give good and honest advice to the prince. But, as Sir Philip Sidney found out when he tried to advise the queen against a French marriage, advice is not always relished by a monarch whose powers over any individual subject are almost absolute. As a result there was a long tradition of literature against court life, comparing it unfavorably to the country life of the retired and obscure man. Sir Thomas Wyatt's verse epistles to Sir Francis Bryan and John Poins are early examples of this attitude, and it runs all through the period. Of course the fact that there was a "tradition" means that everything unfavorable said about the court should not be taken at its face value. But enough evidence exists to show that there was a definite feeling that court life was too precarious, too superficial, too corrupt, too hypocritical. From the time of Wyatt to the time of Ralegh the bitter tone is consistent.

For literary men like Edmund Spenser and Lyly, men who by birth were not in a position to be real courtiers, the court offered a faint hope of livelihood, notice, and encouragement. But for these two, at any rate, it was a source of bitter disappointment. Lyly's long wait for the office of the Revels and Spenser's disillusionment after hoping for court favor (reflected in *Mother Hubberds Tale* and *Colin Clouts Come Home Againe*) tell the story. Much of the satire of the period is directed against the superficiality and treachery of the court atmosphere. "A thousand hopes, but all nothing," wailed Lyly, "a hundred promises, but yet nothing."

Although most of the literature which is still considered worth reading shows the predominant influences of the court, it would be a mistake to underestimate the influence of the City of London on the literary taste and production of the period. London had grown tremendously since the time of Chaucer. Instead of a population of about 50,000 it had 93,276 in 1563 and 224,275 in 1605. It was by far the most important city in the realm, and the political history of the 17th century is understandable only if one recognizes the great power the City had, even as against the Crown. The printing presses were located in London, the publishers were located in London, and the mass of the middle-class population which set the style for literature written for the ordinary man lived in London. The middle class found among the university men some writers who catered to them: Thomas Heywood is a good example. And although Thomas Nashe scornfully rejects the claim of the bourgeois to have any literary taste at all or to have any ability at producing literature, still the class had its own writers, like Thomas Deloney, and it knew what it liked—books of instruction, romances, religious tracts, and sensational ballads. Whether the aristocrats admitted it or not, the standards and tastes of the middle class affected all writing, all publishing, and all literary success. For finally the writer saw his work exhibited on the stalls of St. Paul's churchyard, and the customers who frequented that center of the book trade were more often members of the middle class than of the court circle. Louis B. Wright has shown (in his *Middle-Class Culture in Elizabethan England*) how extensive and profound was the influence of the citizenry upon the writing and publication of books, and how bourgeois standards of edification and utility dictated to most of the authors of the time.

Next to the court and the City, the most important sources of literature were of course the two universities. In Elizabeth's reign they were old-fashioned in their curriculum, poor in discipline, and undistinguished in learning, in comparison with what they had been a generation before. There was a great shortage of ministers in the country, partly because of the poor living standard provided for members of the clergy and partly because of the loss of ministers through the religious changes of the middle of the century. Hence the universities were attempting to train ministers exclusively. The university man had either to get a fellowship and remain in academic life (which almost always meant taking holy orders), to enter the church and get a poor living, or to go into law or medicine. The career of a professional man of letters as such did not exist: literature was regarded as an adjunct, not a primary occupation.

The university graduate who came to London to make a literary career for himself faced a very difficult situation. It is best pictured, perhaps, in the Cambridge trilogy of *Parnassus* plays, performed at the end of the century but fairly faithfully reflecting conditions which held good during the whole period. It was the university wits, to be sure, who gave to the drama some of the classical form it needed, and who inaugurated the great literary vogue of the 90's. But the lives of Nashe and Marlowe, of Robert Greene and George Peele, do not suggest that the path was easy. The diary of Philip Henslowe, a leading theatrical manager, has entry after entry showing university graduates in prison or in debt or even at best miserably eking out an existence patching plays.

Financial rewards for writing and publishing prose or poetry came mostly in the form of gifts from patrons—in reality the old system of master and servant which had come down from the Middle Ages and had not changed much with the invention of printing. The writer by a dedication hoped for a suitable reward, and in an age when honor and vanity were motives much more sharply defined or observed than they are today, this procedure sometimes worked. Yet the patron whose vanity was amply satisfied by his own conceit and would not reward an author for a dedication remained a constant irritation to the writers of the time, and we hear many complaints that the age is degenerate because patrons are not more munificent. There were some generous and literary-minded patrons, notably Sir Philip Sidney and his sister Mary, the Countess of Pembroke. Shakespeare's relations with his patron, the Earl of Southampton, little as we know about them, were apparently satisfactory, as the dedication to *The Rape of Lucrece* (1594) is much warmer and more personal than the earlier one, to *Venus and Adonis* (1593). But the experience of Robert Greene is perhaps more typical than that of Shakespeare in this respect. He had sixteen different patrons for seventeen books; this suggests that he was not fortunate in finding favor or support from any one. A fraudulent practice grew up of printing the book and then printing off separate dedications, so that an impecunious author could deceive several patrons each into thinking that he was the one to be honored by the volume. Two or three pounds seems to have been the usual reward for the dedication of a pamphlet or small volume of verse. Ben Jonson, who fared much better than most of his contemporaries, sums up the matter, for poets at least, when he says: "Poetry in this latter age hath proved but a mean mistress to such as have wholly addicted themselves to her, or given their names up to her family. Those who have but saluted her on the way, and now and then tendered their visits, she hath done much for, and advanced in the way of their own professions (both the law and the gospel) beyond all they could have hoped or done for themselves without her favor."

The other possible source of reward, besides the patron, was the publisher. And rewards from the publisher in the 16th century were nothing at all like the rewards from that source now. In the first place there was no such thing as copyright, and no such thing, in the ordinary way, as royalties paid according to the sale of the book. An author sold his manuscript to the publisher outright, for what seems now like a ridiculously low price—for a pamphlet or small book of poetry, usually forty shillings.

The writer's troubles were not over when he had written his book, gone through the difficulty of finding a publisher, and finally come to terms with him for the sale of it. He still had to face the many and stringent regulations of the press by political and ecclesiastical authorities, and the fact that he had sold the manuscript did not exempt him from responsibility for what was in it. The authorities were, first, the Privy Council and the Court of Star Chamber, the highest political authority in the realm below the queen; then the Court of High Commission, the supreme ecclesiastical authority, which sometimes supervised matters which had only the slightest connection with religion; then the Stationers' Company, with whom a book had to be registered but who supervised and protected the publisher and printer rather than the author.

The principal rules governing the publication of books were that the number of printers (not publishers) was strictly limited; that nothing could be printed except in the City of London and the Universities of Oxford and Cambridge; that everything printed must receive the imprimatur of the Archbishop of Canterbury and the Bishop of London or their representatives; and that everything published in London must be entered in the registers of the Stationers' Company, if any kind of property protection were desired for it. An example of the regulation which reached back of the publisher to the author himself can be seen in the history of John Stubbs, who protested against Elizabeth's projected French marriage in a pamphlet called *The Discovery of a Gaping Gulf* (1579). For writing this pamphlet, Stubbs was condemned to have his right hand cut off with one stroke of a butcher's cleaver. When the execution had taken place, Stubbs took off his hat with his left hand and cried "God save the queen!"

Almost every writer of the period got into some sort of trouble for publishing a book. It might be prison, it might be merely a reprimand, it might be an investigation by the Star Chamber. It was dangerous to put pen to paper, and it was so unprofitable that it is a wonder that any original writing was published at all. Yet the Elizabethan age is an extremely prolific one in writing and publishing. The *Short Title Catalogue* of the Bibliographical Society, which lists works and editions published between 1475 and 1640, includes over 26,000 items, and it does not include all that were published.

To suppose that poetry, or even prose, circulated only in printed form would be a mistake. The 16th century was the first century of the printed book, and the older way, of circulating in manuscript, lingered on into the 17th century. This was particularly true of poets of gentle or noble rank.

Sidney is the most prominent example. Sir John Harington, in his translation of Ariosto's *Orlando Furioso* in 1591, mentions a sonnet of Sidney's "which many I am sure have read"; that particular sonnet was not published until seven years later. Many people kept commonplace books in which they would copy down poems from borrowed manuscript copies. Professional scribes made a living by copying manuscripts, for authors or for readers. There are even complaints by printers of the hoarding of literary manuscripts by "their grand possessors." There is a difference, which has not always been appreciated, between the poetry of the professional poets who wrote for print and the gentle or noble poets who wrote for circulation in manuscript among their cultivated friends.

ART, NATURE, AND POETRY

Elizabethan taste had some very definite and particular characteristics of its own, and the student who wishes to read Elizabethan literature in the spirit of its own time must adjust his mind to the differences between the aesthetic principles of the 16th century and those of our own day. In the 16th century there still remained much of the medieval awareness of the arts as *crafts*, and every writer of the period shows an amazing knowledge of the techniques of many crafts or "mysteries" now unfamiliar. Shakespeare is not an isolated example, and it has been often noticed that his works show an intimate knowledge of such matters as gardening, hawking, dressmaking, archery, building, and so on. Managing the great horse in the tournament was an art. Sailing was an art. Planting a kitchen garden was an art. What they had in common was that they all used the materials of nature but exploited the ingenuity of man's mind. The same fundamental characteristic was thought to apply to the art or craft of writing.

We have been taught by the Romantic movement to glorify nature and to regard the works of art as attempts, usually unsuccessful, to emulate nature. This conception would have seemed strange indeed to the Elizabethans. They recognized, of course, that nature was the cause and basis of all; but that seemed to them no reason why the ingenuity of man should not be used in enabling nature to outdo herself. In *The Winter's Tale* Polixenes is amused at the naïveté of Perdita, who protests that she will have no streaked carnations or gillyflowers in her garden because

> I have heard it said
> There is an art which in their piedness shares
> With great creating nature.

"Say there be," replies Polixenes,

> Yet nature is made better by no mean
> But nature makes that mean. So, over that art
> Which you say adds to nature, is an art
> That nature makes. You see, sweet maid, we marry
> A gentler scion to the wildest stock
> And make conceive a bark of baser kind
> By bud of nobler race. This is an art
> Which does mend nature—change it rather; but
> The art itself is nature.

There was no uneasiness in the Elizabethan mind about a possible conflict between art and nature, for the reason that Polixenes gives. And the improvement by device, by arrangement, by art, of something naturally beautiful extended to all aspects of life, so that there was felt to be no great gulf between literature and the sports of the field or the arts of the kitchen. George Puttenham, in discussing ornament in his *Art of English Poesy* (1589), compares poetry to dress and to jewelry:

And as we see in these great Madames of honor, be they for personage or otherwise never so comely and beautiful, yet if they want their courtly habiliments or at leastwise such other apparel as custom and civility have ordained to cover their naked bodies, would be half ashamed or greatly out of countenance to be seen in that sort, and perchance do then think themselves more amiable in every man's eye when they be in their richest attire, suppose of silks or tissues and costly embroideries, than when they go in cloth or in any other plain and simple apparel. Even so cannot our vulgar Poesy show itself either gallant or gorgeous, if any limb be left naked and bare and not clad in his kindly clothes and colors, such as may convey them somewhat out of sight, that is, from the common course of ordinary speech and capacity of the vulgar judgment, and yet being artificially handled must needs yield it much more beauty and commendation. This ornament we speak of is given to it by figures and figurative speeches, which be the flowers, as it were, and colors that a poet setteth upon his language by art, as the embroiderer doth his stone and pearl or passements of gold upon the stuff of a princely garment, or as th' excellent painter bestoweth the rich Orient colors upon his table of portrait.

"Artificially" is used by Puttenham, and by the other Elizabethans, as a word of praise. It means "done with artifice, with skill, with art." And the word "curious" meant to the Elizabethans "skillfully, elaborately, or beautifully wrought" or, in a more general sense, "excellent or fine."

The Elizabethan garden was designed as a square, filled with elaborate and intricate, but perfectly regular, design. Francis Bacon protests at gardens which include plots of different colored earths, so arranged as to form a design even without the flowers planted in them; he says he sees enough of this kind of thing in confections and tarts. Yet the very protest shows that his taste was perhaps not typical, and a contemporary might well have asked him why a garden should not look like a confection from the baker's—they were both samples of the art of design. Some Elizabethans had their houses built in the shape of an E, out of honor to the queen, and one man, John Thorpe, designed his house in the form of his own initials. These instances were extreme, of course, but they show the tendency.

Contrapuntal music (composed of several independent melodies joined together), which was sung by the Elizabethans in an accomplished amateur manner, was an intricate kind of music, with elaborate patterns and complex harmonies. The composer Thomas Morley (ca. 1557–1603) says of the madrigal:

As for the music, it is, next unto the motet, the most artificial and to men of understanding most delightful. If therefore you will compose in this kind you must possess yourself with an amorous humor * * * so that you must in your music be wavering like the wind, sometime wanton, sometime grave and staid, otherwhile effeminate; you may maintain points and revert them, use triplaes and show the very uttermost of your variety, and the more variety you show the better shall you please.

But a rigid form was to control all of this extravagance, just as the square border of a garden and the regularity of the pattern controlled the exuberance of the curves in the "knot" or design.

All of this has its counterpart in poetry. The geometrical design is present in such poems as the one by Arthur Gorges which begins

Your face	Your tongue	Your wit
Your face	Your tongue	Your wit
So fair	So sweet	So sharp
First bent	Then drew	So hit
Mine eye	Mine ear	My heart * * *

(It can be read both ways, across and down.) The balance and antithesis in Lyly's prose style is an example of the same kind of literary interest. The sestina, a poem in which the last words of each line in the first stanza are repeated in a different order in each of the following stanzas, was a form used by Sidney and other craftsmen in poetry.

The verse forms used by the Elizabethans range from the extremely simple four-line ballad stanza through the rather complicated form of the sonnet to the elaborate and beautiful 18-line stanza of Spenser's *Epithalamion*. A stanza such as

> The man of life upright
> Whose guileless heart is free
> From all dishonest deeds
> Or thought of vanity

might have been written by any one of many poets at almost any time in the 16th century; it happened to have been written by a fine craftsman, Thomas Campion, near the end of it. Henry Howard, Earl of Surrey, who introduced blank verse into English and helped introduce the sonnet in the reign of Henry VIII, was also a practitioner of a form of iambic couplet in which the first line had twelve syllables and the second fourteen:

> The young man eke that feels his bones with pains oppressed,
> How he would be a rich old man, to live and lie at rest.

This verse form, called "poulter's measure" (because a poulter's dozen was supposed to be sometimes twelve and sometimes fourteen), was the most common verse form in the 60's and 70's. Its dreary monotony in long stretches is matched only by the "fourteener" couplet of fourteen syllables in a line. We still have examples of these forms in our hymnbooks; when each line of poulter's measure is printed as two lines, the hymnbooks call it "short meter"; when they so divide fourteeners they call it "common meter."

Sonnets, which the Elizabethans often called "quatorzains," using the term "sonnet" loosely for any short poem, are fourteen-line poems in iambic pentameter with elaborate rhyme schemes. The most common Italian form, which Wyatt, Sidney, and others imitated, was divided structurally into the octave (first eight lines) and the sestet (last six). A typical rhyme scheme was *abba abba cdc dee*. The so-called English sonnet, introduced by Surrey and practiced by Shakespeare, is structurally three quatrains and a couplet: *abab cdcd efef gg*. Spenser, the most experimental and the most gifted prosodist of the century, preferred a form that is harder to write and richer in rhymes: *abab bcbc cdcd ee*.

The six-line "Troilus stanza" and the seven-line rhyme royal stanza, both practiced by Chaucer, survived into the 16th century. Shakespeare used the former in *Venus and Adonis* and the latter in *The Rape of Lucrece*; that popular collection of historical poems, *The Mirror for Magistrates*, features rhyme royal.

An innovation was Spenser's nine-line stanza, called after him the "Spenserian stanza," which added to the Italian ottava rima (*abab bc bc*) an additional line of twelve syllables, an Alexandrine, rhyming with the preceding line. This is the stanza form which serves so well the large descriptive and narrative requirements of *The Faerie Queene*. The elaborate scheme of the stanza Spenser devised for his *Epithalamion* perhaps illustrates the height of Elizabethan craftsmanship in verse. Its eighteen lines rhyme *ababcc*, then various combinations in the second six, and finally three couplets. Lines 6, 11, and 16 are short, having only six syllables contrasted to the pentameter's ten, and the last line is an Alexandrine, as in the Spenserian stanza.

GENRES AND CONVENTIONS IN POETRY

A literary convention is a pattern that has become habitual and arouses certain expectations in the reader. For the Elizabethan poet available conventions enabled him to assume particular responses from his audience and to show his learning by his exploitation of these well-known patterns and his virtuosity by his ingenious elaborations of them. It must not be supposed that these conventions were lifeless forms, so stale with use that they no longer carried meaning or conviction. They were charged with values, with associations. They related writer and reader to other times, other languages, other cultures.

The pastoral convention presented a simple and idealized world, inhabited by shepherds and shepherdesses, concerned not at all with war or politics or commerce. Its business consisted of tending the flocks, friendly poetic contests among shepherds, love, and the pursuit of contentment rather than fame or fortune.

Pastoral lyrics expressed the joys of pastoral life or disappointment in love. Pastoral eclogues were dialogues between shepherds in which a poetic contest was staged, or there was serious, satirical comment on abuses in the great world concealed in the disguise of the homely local concerns of country folk. There were also, of course, pastoral dramas and pastoral romances (prose fiction) which embodied the same values of *otium* (leisure), freedom from pride and ambition, and the pursuit of humble contentment.

Another popular convention was that of the mythological-erotic poem, derived from Ovid mainly but influenced by Italian imitations of him. In the middle ages Ovid's poetry had been allegorized and interpreted morally —the same process that has overtaken the love songs in the Song of Solomon in the Old Testament. This process continued on into the 17th century, but a newer treatment of the convention returned to the frank sensuality of the Latin amatory poets and allowed for elaborate mythological decoration of the narrative without worrying about moral propriety or allegorical interpretation. Such poems appealed to a courtly taste; they validated the senses and they asserted the primacy of physical beauty and the imagination. Shakespeare in *Venus and Adonis* and Marlowe in *Hero and Leander* were among the poets who practiced in this convention.

Sometimes related to the Ovidian tradition but separate from it in origin was the convention of the complaint poem. This goes back to a medieval genre represented by works of the Italian Boccaccio and his English imitators, Lydgate and the authors of *The Mirror for Magistrates*. The complaint poem is essentially tragic and moral. In it the ghost of someone who fell from high place bemoans his fate and warns others. If the ghost is a woman, like Daniel's Rosamund, her fall was caused by the frailty of her sex and the poem may be related to the Ovidian tradition. Another kind of poem, which came both from Ovid and the *Mirror for Magistrates* tradition, was the heroical epistle, practised notably by Drayton.

The Elizabethan sonnet, which reached the height of its vogue in the last decade of the 16th century, depended upon a convention established by Petrarch and followed by his many imitators in Italy and France. In this tradition the poet complains of his lady's coldness; he describes the contrary states of feeling the lover experiences; and he writes sonnets on the conventional themes of sleep, absence, originality, renunciation, and others. The purposes of the love sonneteers differed, of course, but what they had in common might be described as an ambition to give dignity and power to the theme of love by the elaborate rhetorical and stylistic devices available in the Petrarchan tradition. Lesser poets often produced nothing but standard conceits served up in fourteen-line helpings, but major poets such as Sidney, Spenser, and Shakespeare wrote sonnets of power and originality that stand out as major poetic products of the Elizabethan Age.

The conventional forms for satire were less well fixed in the 16th century than in some later periods, though there is a good deal of Elizabethan satirical verse. Some examples belong to a medieval tradition coming down from *Piers Plowman*, which was believed to be the only English masterpiece in satire until satires by the "university wits" in the tradition of the Latin satirists Persius and Juvenal began to appear, and some were written by young John Donne and circulated only in manuscript until after the poet's death in 1631. The epigram was a form that flourished, both in the classical tradition of Martial and in the lyric form of words for a madrigal; the famous *The Silver Swan* (p. 847) is an example.

Poetry for music also followed some conventions: the dance song of course had its definite rhythms and refrains, and many well-known tunes provided the formula by which poet after poet composed new words. In the polyphonic madrigal, the same phrases tend to be repeated again and again, while the words often get lost in the music because various voices sing different words at the same time. As a result, the poem written as a madrigal is usually short and simple both in language and ideas. The "ayre," however, is a song written for a single voice to a lute accompaniment and is usually sung straight through. Since the words are much more intelligible, the thought can be more complex. While the poem is often a good deal longer than the madrigal (since the same melody is repeated over and over), the poem is divided into repetitive stanzas.

There were conventions as well for the heroic poem, of which Spenser's *Faerie Queene* is the prime example. The classical epics of Homer and Virgil had their influence, but so did the romantic Italian epics of Ariosto and Tasso. Chapman's Homer and Harington's Ariosto were regarded by contemporaries as something more than translation, having much of the interest and significance of original poems.

The major conventions in poetry did not stifle originality; they served as both an ordering device and a challenge that stimulated the poet to something fresh and new. When these conventions were alive for writers and readers, they had significance in themselves, which was an essential part of the total significance of the poem. Knowledge of the more important Elizabethan conventions is not simply of scholarly interest; it is essential to the experience of the poem as a poem.

ELIZABETHAN MOODS AND ATTITUDES

The English Renaissance was no sharp break with the past. Attitudes and feelings which had been characteristic of the 15th or 14th centuries persisted well down into the era of humanism and Reformation. George Gascoigne, the leading writer of the 1570's, has in many ways a medieval point of view, and the popular collection of verse tales of the fall of princes called *The Mirror for Magistrates* (first published in 1559, and reprinted with additions in 1563, 1587, and 1610) derives from Lydgate and Boccaccio. Even a lyric by that flamboyant and "modern" Elizabethan, Sir Walter Ralegh, may embody a sentiment of the vanity and transitoriness of all earthly ambitions and achievements. The Dance of Death and related images were still living symbols to the Elizabethan imagination; witness Shakespeare's *Richard II* (III.ii.152–70):

> And nothing can we call our own but death
> And that small model of the barren earth
> Which serves as paste and cover to our bones.
> For God's sake let us sit upon the ground
> And tell sad stories of the death of kings!
> How some have been deposed; some slain in war;
> Some haunted by the ghosts they have deposed;
> Some poisoned by their wives; some sleeping killed—
> All murthered; for within the hollow crown
> That rounds the mortal temples of a king
> Keeps Death his court, and there the antic sits,
> Scoffing his state and grinning at his pomp;
> Allowing him a breath, a little scene,
> To monarchize, be feared, and kill with looks;
> Infusing him with self and vain conceit,
> As if this flesh which walls about our life
> Were brass impregnable: and humored thus,
> Comes at the last, and with a little pin
> Bores through the castle wall, and farewell king!

Yet there was at the same time a spirit of joy and gaiety, of innocence and lightheartedness, that future ages were to look back on as "merry England." This spirit is popular, it comes from the folk and from the persistent love of Englishmen for their countryside; it is spontaneous, yet it seems somehow stable and permanent. Perhaps its best expression is in the songs of Shakespeare's plays:

> When daffodils begin to peer,
> With heigh! the doxy over the dale,
> Why, then comes in the sweet o' the year;
> For the red blood reigns in the winter's pale.

or

> When daisies pied and violets blue
> And ladysmocks all silver-white
> And cuckoobuds of yellow hue
> Do paint the meadows with delight.

The mood of pastoral, as we have already seen in our notice of that convention, is generally one of quiet contentment, of reflective leisure, of the enjoyment of a simple, idealized world. Marlowe's *Passionate Shepherd to His Love* beautifully invokes this world.

There was of course also among the Elizabethans the opposite mood: the burning desire for conquest, for achievement, for surmounting all obstacles. The Elizabethans called it "the aspiring mind." The great projector of this mood is Christopher Marlowe, who has his heroes fling themselves into the pursuit of power—

> Is it not passing brave to be a king
> And ride in triumph through Persepolis?—

or into the lust for gold—

> Infinite riches in a little room—

or into the search for knowledge—

> All things that move between the quiet poles
> Shall be at my command; emperors and kings
> Are but obeyed in their several provinces,
> Nor can they raise the wind or rend the clouds;
> But his dominion that excels in this
> Stretcheth as far as doth the mind of man.

Marlowe's heroes are defeated finally, all of them, but their fiery spirit in assaulting the limits of the possible echoes after they are gone.

The Elizabethan spirit has been described as "sensuous, comprehensive, extravagant, disorderly, thirsty for beauty, abounding in the zest for life." This is part of the truth, but not all of it. Fundamentally, the thought and feeling of Shakespeare's contemporaries was far more deeply affected by Christian humanism than by the extravagances of Marlowe. We need to remember Ben Jonson, with his classical principles of structure and decorum and his ideal of the balanced man. Jonson was in every respect more typical of his age than Shakespeare. His emphasis upon learning, his reconciliation of ancient models and English content, and his critical responsibility truly represent the ideal English poet of his time, as Sidney would have visualized him. Because his major work was done after 1603, he is represented in the 17th-century section of this anthology.

The second generation of English humanists—men like Roger Ascham (1515–68, tutor to Queen Elizabeth), Sir John Cheke (1514–57, professor of Greek at Cambridge), and Thomas Wilson (1525–81, rhetorician and translator)—combined an earnest Protestant Christianity with their classical learning, and Ascham vigorously opposed the more secular, pagan humanism that was coming out of Italy. These men shaped the University of Cambridge, which in turn shaped many men. It was an Oxford man, however—Richard Hooker—who provided in his great work, *The Laws of Ecclesiastical Polity* (1593 and later), the supreme masterpiece of English Christian humanism. In so far as his doctrine is concerned, Spenser is a Christian humanist, and the label can justly be applied to John Milton, both in content and in form.

If the beginning of the Tudor era showed more links with the past than with the future, it is equally true that the end of Elizabeth's reign prefigured some of the conflict and uncertainty of the time to come. "The disenchantment of the Elizabethans" is a phrase that has been used to describe it. In 1599, the year of Spenser's death, occurred the abortive revolt of the Earl of Essex. Elizabeth was old, a peaceful succession was by no means assured, and the rifts in society which were to mean civil war in the midcentury were already present. An outbreak of satire and epigrams had to be stopped by the authorities. Some of the cynical undercurrent in Shakespeare's *Hamlet* and *Troilus and Cressida* reflects the spirit of the time. John Donne was already writing his poems, and a very different age, the 17th century, was in the offing. In 1603 Elizabeth, the last of the Tudors, died, and to the immense relief of anxious Englishmen, the succession took place peacefully. The new monarch was the Protestant James VI of Scotland, who became James I of England.

EDMUND SPENSER
(1552–1599)

1579: Publication of *The Shepheardes Calender*.
1580: In Ireland, where he remains for the rest of his life.
1590: First three books of *The Faerie Queene* published.

The greatest nondramatic poet of the English Renaissance, Edmund Spenser, was born in London, probably in 1552, and attended the Merchant Taylors' School under its famous headmaster Richard Mulcaster. In 1569 he went to Cambridge as a "sizar" or poor scholar. His Cambridge experience strongly colored the rest of his life; it was at the university that Spenser began as a poet by translating some poems for a volume of anti-Catholic propaganda. His work, then and later, reflects the strong Puritanical environment of Cambridge where the popular preacher Thomas Cartwright was beginning to make the authorities uneasy. Spenser's friendship with Gabriel Harvey, a Cambridge don, humanist, pamphleteer, and eccentric, also began at the university. Some correspondence between Harvey and Spenser, published in 1580, shows that they were interested in theories of poetry and in experiments in quantitative versification in English; it also shows that Spenser had ambitious plans as a poet.

He proceeded through the university, receiving the degree of B.A. in 1573 and M.A. in 1576. He then entered upon a series of positions in the retinues of prominent men, including Dr. John Young, Bishop of Rochester; the Earl of Leicester, the queen's favorite; and finally, Lord Grey of Wilton, Lord Deputy of Ireland. During his employment in Leicester's household he came to know Sir Philip Sidney and his friend Sir Edward Dyer, courtiers who were interested in promoting a new English poetry. Spenser's own contribution to the movement is *The Shepheardes Calender*, published in 1579 and dedicated to Sidney in the verses:

> **To His Booke**
> Goe little booke: thy selfe present,
> As child whose parent is unkent,
> To him that is the president
> Of noblesse and of chevalree.
> And if that Envie barke at thee,
> As sure it will, for succoure flee
> Under the shadow of his wing
> And, asked who thee forth did bring,
> A shepheardes swaine saye did thee sing,
> All as his straying flocke he fedde;
> And when his honor has thee redde,
> Crave pardon for my hardy hedde.
> But if that any aske thy name,
> Say thou wert base begot with blame,
> For thy thereof thou takest shame.
> And when thou art past jeopardee,
> Come tell me what was said of mee
> And I will send more after thee.

Immerito [Unworthy].

The *Calender* consists of twelve pastoral eclogues, one for each month of the year. Each is prefaced by an illustrative woodcut representing the characters or theme of the poem and picturing the appropriate sign of the zodiac for that month in the clouds above. The eclogue was a classical form, practiced by Virgil and others; it presents, usually in dialogue between shepherds, the moods and feelings and attitudes of the simple life. But often the pastoral eclogue criticizes the world as it is by reflection from the world as it might be, and in Spenser, as in other Renaissance poets, the eclogue at times becomes didactic or satirical. Though it pretends to represent simple shepherds, it is really commenting on contemporary affairs. The eclogues of the *Calender* are divided by its commentator, "E. K.," into three groups—plaintive, recreative, and moral. Of the moral eclogues, the final and climactic one is *October*, which deals with the problem of poetry in modern life and the responsibility of the poet in time—in an important way, the theme of the whole *Calender*. It looks forward to related themes in Milton's *Lycidas*.

Spenser used a deliberately archaic language, partly out of homage to Chaucer, whom he refers to as Tityrus, the god of shepherds, "who taught me, homely as I can, to make." But Spenser also used this language to get a rustic effect. The patron to whom the *Calender* is dedicated did not approve; Sidney wrote in his *Apology for Poetry*, "The Shepheardes Calendar hath much poetry in his Eclogues, indeed worthy the reading, if I be not deceived. That same framing of his style to an old rustic language I dare not allow, since neither Theocritus in Greek, Virgil in Latin, nor Sannazaro in Italian did affect it." Another classical purist, Ben Jonson, growled that Spenser "writ no language," but that he would have him read for his matter. It would be a pity to follow Jonson's advice too literally, for Spenser's skillful use of many verse forms and his extraordinary musical effects indicate that here indeed is a poet to inaugurate the "new poetry" of the Elizabethan age.

There are thirteen different meters in *The Shepheardes Calender:* three kinds of couplet; three kinds of four-line stanza; three kinds of six-line stanza; stanzas of eight, nine, and ten lines; and a sestina. Some of these Spenser invented, some he adapted, but most of them were novel: only three or four were at all common in 1579. Spenser was a prolific experimenter: of the thirteen different meters in the *Calender* he used only three in his later poems. He went on to make further innovations—the special rhyme scheme of the Spenserian sonnet, richer than any other; the remarkably beautiful adaptation of Italian *canzone* forms for the *Epithalamion* and *Prothalamion*, and the nine-line stanza of *The Faerie Queene*, with its extraordinary six-foot line at the end, are only the most famous. Spenser is sometimes called the "poet's poet" because so many later English poets have learned the art of versification from him. In the 19th century alone his influence may be seen in Shelley's *Revolt of Islam*, Byron's *Childe Harold's Pilgrimage*, Keats's *Eve of St. Agnes*, and Tennyson's *The Lotos Eaters*.

The year after the publication of *The Shepheardes Calender* Spenser went to Ireland to serve Lord Grey; he spent the rest of his life there, except for two visits to England. He was at work on his great romantic epic, *The Faerie Queene*, when Sir Walter Ralegh visited him at Kilcolman Castle; the result was a trip to England and the publication, in 1590, of the first three books of *The Faerie Queene*. After that there was no question that Edmund Spenser was "the prince of poets in his time." He published a volume of poems called *Complaints*; a pastoral sequel to some of the eclogues in *The Shepheardes Calender* called *Colin Clouts Come Home Againe* (1595), which gave his views of the English court on his visit there in 1590; a sonnet cycle, *Amoretti*, and two marriage poems, *Epithalamion* and *Prothalamion*, but he completed only six of his projected twelve books of *The Faerie Queene:* in 1596 the first three books appeared again, with alterations, together with Books IV, V, and VI; the so-called "Mutability Cantos" first appeared in the edition of 1609.

In the second half of the decade, Ireland was torn by revolt and civil war; Spenser's castle was destroyed, and the poet was sent to England with messages from the besieged garrison in Ireland. He died in Westminster on January 13, 1599, and was buried near his beloved Chaucer in what is now called the Poets' Corner of Westminster Abbey.

Spenser is a complex genius who cannot be put into neatly labeled categories. He is, for instance, strongly influenced by Renaissance Neoplatonism, but remains always firmly grounded in earthiness and practicality. In *The Faerie Queene* he reaches toward the highest ideals of the Renaissance but knows, at the same time, what it is to want to remain an animal. He is a lover and celebrator of physical beauty, and he is sternly moral. His "morality" is, however, not of the repressive sort; it arises from his understanding of right action and of the temptations that entrap men as they try to achieve such action. Spenser was strongly influenced by Puritanism in his early days; he always remained a thoroughgoing Protestant; the Roman Catholic Church is made a villain in *The Faerie Queene*—and yet his understanding of faith and of sin has its roots in the great Catholic thinkers. He is profoundly English and patriotic; in him nationality and religion were inextricably joined. In the Proem to Book V of *The Faerie Queene* he characteristically looks back to the antique world and compares his own time with it most unfavorably. Yet his strongest links are not with the past, despite his love of Chaucer and his deliberately antique language: his closest affinity is with Milton, who was born nine years after Spenser's death. Milton called Spenser a better teacher than Scotus or Aquinas. He recognized Spenser, his great predecessor, as, like himself, a Christian humanist and British poet-prophet.

Spenser's poetry is always printed in the original spelling and punctuation (although a few of the most confusing punctuation marks have been altered in the present text), since it was a deliberate choice on Spenser's part that his language should seem antique. (A modern reader who read Shakespeare or the King James version of the Bible in the original spelling would not find as much difference in Spenser, but he would find some.) Furthermore, Spenser uses his spelling to suggest rhymes to the eye, sometimes to suggest etymologies, often incorrectly. The fact that Spenser's spelling is inconsistent is simply typical of his time; in the 16th century a man varied the spelling of even his name to suit convenience or a whim.

From THE SHEPHEARDES CALENDER[1]

October

Argument

In Cuddie[2] is set out the perfecte paterne of a Poete, whiche finding no maintenaunce of his state and studies, complayneth of

---

1. When *The Shepheardes Calender* was published in 1579, each of the twelve eclogues was followed by a "Glosse," which contained explications of difficult or archaic words, together with learned discussions of—and disagreements with —Spenser's ideas, imagery, and poetics. The Glosses are by one "E. K.," whose identity has never been satisfactorily ascertained. Although certain scholars have suggested that E. K. was Spenser himself, it is equally possible that he was a friend.

E. K.'s editorial apparatus is usually printed along with the poems from the *Calender*. In the text that follows, the present editor has incorporated the glosses into the footnotes, abridging only some of E. K.'s longer exegeses, anecdotes, and tags from classical and contemporary authors; the original spelling has also been retained. E. K. first discusses the poem's sources: "This Aeglogue is made in imitation of Theocritus his xvi. Idilion, wherein hee reproved the Tyranne Hiero of Syracuse for his nigardise towarde Poetes, in whome is the power to make men immortall for theyr good dedes, or shameful for their naughty lyfe. And the lyke also is in Mantuane. The style hereof as also that in Theocritus, is more loftye then the rest, and applyed to the heighte of Poeticall witte." Actually Spenser's eclogue owes very little to Theocritus, but it does draw heavily upon the fifth eclogue of Baptista Spagnuoli, called Mantuan.

2. "I doubte whether by Cuddie be specified the authour selfe, or some

the contempte of Poetrie, and the causes thereof: Specially having
bene in all ages, and even amongst the most barbarous alwayes of
singular accounpt[3] and honor, and being indede so worthy and
commendable an arte: or rather no arte, but a divine gift and heavenly instinct not to bee gotten by laboure and learning, but adorned
with both: and poured into the witte by a certaine ἐνθουσιασμὸς[4]
and celestiall inspiration, as the Author hereof els where at large
discourseth, in his booke called the *English Poete*, which booke
being lately come to my hands, I mynde also by Gods grace upon
further advisement to publish.

PIERS

Cuddie, for shame hold up thy heavye head,
And let us cast with what delight to chace,
And weary thys long lingring Phoebus race.[5]
Whilome° thou wont the shepheards laddes to leade,   *formerly*
5 In rymes, in ridles, and in bydding base:[6]
Now they in thee, and thou in sleepe art dead.

CUDDIE

Piers, I have pyped erst° so long with payne,   *up to now*
That all mine Oten reedes[7] bene rent and wore:
And my poore Muse hath spent her sparéd store,
10 Yet little good hath got, and much lesse gayne.
Such pleasaunce makes the Grashopper so poore,
And ligge so layd,[8] when Winter doth her straine:

The dapper[9] ditties, that I wont devise,
To feede youthes fancie, and the flocking fry,[1]
15 Delighten much: what I the bett forthy?
They han the pleasure, I a sclender prise.
I beate the bush, the byrds to them doe flye:
What good thereof to Cuddie can arise?

PIERS

Cuddie, the prayse is better, then the price,
20 The glory eke much greater then the gayne:
O what an honor is it, to restraine
The lust of lawlesse youth with good advice:[2]

other. For in the eyght Aeglogue the
same person was brought in, singing a
Cantion of Colins making, as he sayth.
So that some doubt, that the persons be
different" [E. K.'s Glosse].
3. Account, reputation.
4. The Greek word from which "enthusiasm" derives; it means inspiration. The *"English Poete"* is a lost work
by Spenser, apparently never published.
5. I.e., let us see how we may pass the
day pleasantly.
6. A popular game, here probably a
poetry contest.
7. "Avena" [E. K.'s Glosse]. Avena
means "stalks" and was used by Virgil
(*Eclogues* I.2) to signify the shepherd's
pipe. E. K. thinks Spenser's "oten

reeds" translates Avena.
8. "Lye so faynt and unlustie" [E. K.'s
Glosse]. The reference is to the fable
of the industrious ant and the carefree
grasshopper.
9. "Pretye" [E. K.'s Glosse].
1. "Frye is a bold Metaphore, forced
from the spawning fishes. For the multitude of young fish be called the frye"
[E. K.'s Glosse]. In the next line,
"what * * * for thy?" means, "what
better am I for this reason?"
2. "This place seemeth to conspyre with
Plato, who in his first booke *de Legibus*
sayth, that the first invention of Poetry
was of very vertuous intent * * * "
[E. K.'s Glosse].

Or pricke° them forth with pleasaunce of thy vaine,   *stimulate*
Whereto thou list their traynéd° willes entice.   *ensnared*

25 Soone as thou gynst to sette thy notes in frame,
O how the rurall routes° to thee doe cleave: *crowds*
Seemeth thou dost their soule of sence bereave,[3]
All as the shepheard, that did fetch his dame
From Plutoes balefull bowre withouten leave:
30 His musicks might the hellish hound did tame.

CUDDIE

So praysen babes the Peacoks spotted traine,
And wondren at bright Argus blazing eye:[4]
But who rewards him ere the more forthy?
Or feedes him once the fuller by a graine?
35 Sike° prayse is smoke, that sheddeth in the skye,   *such*
Sike words bene wynd, and wasten soone in vayne.

PIERS

Abandon then the base and viler clowne,°   *rustic*
Lyft up thy selfe out of the lowly dust:
And sing of bloody Mars, of wars, of giusts,°   *jousts*
40 Turne thee to those, that weld° the awful crowne.   *wield*
To doubted[5] Knights, whose woundlesse armour rusts,
And helmes unbruzéd wexen dayly browne.

There may thy Muse display her fluttryng wing,[6]
And stretch herselfe at large from East to West:
45 Whither thou list in fayre Elisa rest,
Or if thee please in bigger notes to sing,
Advaunce the worthy whome shee loveth best,
That first the white beare to the stake did bring.[7]

3. "What the secrete working of Musick is in the myndes of men, as well appeareth, hereby, that some of the auncient Philosophers, and those the moste wise, as Plato and Pythagoras held for opinion, that the mynd was made of a certaine harmonie and musicall nombers, for the great compassion and likenes of affection in thone and in the other * * * So that it is not incredible which the Poete here sayth, that Musick can bereave the soule of sence" [E. K.'s Glosse]. The "shepheard" in the next line is "Orpheus: of whom is sayd, that by his excellent skil in Musick and Poetry, he recovered his wife Eurydice from hell" [E. K.'s Glosse].

4. "Of Argus is before said, that Juno to him committed hir husband Jupiter his Paragon Iô, bicause he had an hundred eyes: but afterwarde Mercury wyth hys Musick lulling Argus aslepe, slew him and brought Iô away, whose eyes it is sayd that Juno for his eternall memory placed in her byrd the Pea-

cocks tayle. For those coloured spots indeede resemble eyes" [E. K.'s Glosse].

5. Redoubted, dreaded. The knights' "armour" is "woundlesse" because "unwounded in warre, [they] doe rust through long peace" [E. K.'s Glosse].

6. "A poeticall metaphore: whereof the meaning is, that if the Poet list showe his skill in matter of more dignitie, then is the homely Aeglogue, good occasion is him offered of higher veyne and more Heroicall argument, in the person of our most gratious soveraign, whom (as before) he calleth Elisa. Or if mater of knighthoode and chevalrie please him better, that there be many Noble and valiaunt men, that are both worthy of his payne in theyr deserved prayses, and also favourers of hys skil and faculty" [E. K.'s Glosse].

7. "He meaneth (as I guesse) the most honorable and renowmed the Erle of Leycester * * * " [E. K.'s Glosse]. Leicester's device was the bear and ragged staff.

And when the stubborne stroke of stronger stounds,°   *efforts*
50 Has somewhat slackt the tenor of thy string:[8]
Of love and lustihead tho mayst thou sing,
And carrol lowde, and leade the Myllers rownde,[9]
All° were Elisa one of thilke same ring.   *although*
So mought our Cuddies name to Heaven sownde.

CUDDIE

55 Indeede the Romish Tityrus,[1] I heare,
Through his Mecaenas left his Oaten reede,
Whereon he earst° had taught his flocks to feede,   *before*
And laboured lands to yield the timely eare,
And eft did sing of warres and deadly drede,[2]
60 So as the Heavens did quake his verse to here.

But ah Mecaenas is yclad in claye,
And great Augustus long ygoe is dead:
And all the worthies liggen wrapt in leade,
That matter made for Poets on to play:
65 For ever, who in derring doe[3] were dreade,
The loftie verse of hem was lovéd aye.[4]

But after vertue gan for age to stoupe,
And mighty manhode brought a bedde of ease:[5]
The vaunting Poets found nought worth a pease,
70 To put in preace[6] emong the learned troupe.
Tho gan the streames of flowing wittes to cease,
And sonnebright honour pend in shamefull coupe.[7]

And if that any buddes of Poesie,
Yet of the old stocke gan to shoote agayne:

8. "That is when thou chaungest thy verse from stately discourse, to matter of more pleasaunce and delight" [E. K.'s Glosse].
9. "A kind of daunce" [E. K.'s Glosse]. "Ring," in the next line, E. K. explains as a "company of dauncers."
1. "Well knowen to be Virgile, who by Mecaenas means was brought into the favour of the Emperor Augustus, and by him moved to write in loftier kinde, then he erst had doen" [E. K.'s Glosse].
2. "In these three verses are the three severall workes of Virgile intended. For in teaching his flocks to feede, is meant his Aeglogues. In labouring of lands, is hys Bucoliques. In singing of wars and deadly dreade, is his divine Aeneis figured" [E. K.'s Glosse].
3. "In manhoode and chevalrie" [E. K.'s Glosse].
4. "He sheweth the cause, why Poetes were wont be had in such honor of noble men; that is, that by them their worthines and valor shold through

theyr famous Posies be commended to al posterities. Wherefore it is sayd, that Achilles had never bene so famous, as he is, but for Homeres immortal verses. Which is the only advantage, which he had of Hector. * * * As also that Alexander destroying Thebes, when he was enformed that the famous Lyrick Poet Pindarus was borne in that citie, not onely commaunded streightly, that no man should upon payne of death do any violence to that house by fire or otherwise: but also specially spared most, and some highly rewarded, that were of hys kinne. * * * Such honor have Poetes alwayes found in the sight of princes and noble men. Which this author here very well sheweth, as els where more notably" [E. K.'s Glosse].
5. "He sheweth the cause of contempt of Poetry to be idlenesse and basenesse of mynd" [E. K.'s Glosse].
6. Put in press, crowd in among.
7. Coop. E. K. explains the phrase as "shut up in slouth, as in a coope or cage."

75 Or it mens follies mote be forst to fayne,
And rolle with rest in rymes of rybaudrye:
Or as it sprong, it wither must agayne:
Tom Piper makes us better melodie.[8]

PIERS

O pierlesse Poesye, where is then thy place?
80 If nor in Princes pallace thou doe sitt:
(And yet is Princes pallace the most fitt)
Ne brest of baser birth[9] doth thee embrace.
Then make thee winges of thine aspyring wit,
And, whence thou camst, flye backe to heaven apace.

CUDDIE

85 Ah Percy it is all to weake and wanne,
So high to sore, and make so large a flight:
Her peecéd pyneons[1] bene not so in plight,
For Colin fittes such famous flight to scanne:
He, were he not with love so ill bedight,
90 Would mount as high, and sing as soote as Swanne.[2]

PIERS

Ah fon,° for love does teach him climbe so hie,   *fool*
And lyftes him up out of the loathsome myre:
Such immortall mirrhor,[3] as he doth admire,
Would rayse ones mynd above the starry skie.
95 And cause a caytive corage[4] to aspire,
For lofty love doth loath a lowly eye.

CUDDIE

All otherwise the state of Poet stands,
For lordly love is such a Tyranne fell:
That where he rules, all power he doth expell.
100 The vaunted verse a vacant head demaundes,
Ne wont with crabbéd care the Muses dwell.
Unwisely weaves, that takes two webbes in hand.

Who ever casts to compasse weightye prise,
And thinks to throwe out thondring words of threate:
105 Let powre in lavish cups and thriftie bitts of meate,[5]
For Bacchus fruite is frend to Phoebus wise.

8. "An Ironicall Sarcasmus, spoken in derision of these rude wits, whych make more account of a ryming rybaud, then of skill grounded upon learning and judgment" [E. K.'s Glosse].
9. "The meaner sort of men" [E. K.'s Glosse].
1. Patched-up wings. "Unperfect skil. Spoken wyth humble modestie" [E. K.'s Glosse]. "Colin fittes": it is appropriate for Colin (Spenser).
2. "The comparison seemeth to be strange: for the swanne hath ever wonne small commendation for her swete singing: but it is sayd of the learned that the swan a little before hir death, singeth most pleasantly, as prophecying by a secrete instinct her neere destinie * * * " [E. K.'s Glosse].
3. "Beauty, which is an excellent object of Poeticall spirites * * * " [E. K.'s Glosse].
4. "A base and abject minde" [E. K.'s Glosse].
5. I.e., let him pour lavish drink and nourishing ("thrifty") food.

And when with Wine the braine begins to sweate,
The nombers flowe as fast as spring doth ryse.

Thou kenst not Percie howe the ryme should rage.
110 O if my temples were distaind° with wine,[6]   *distended*
And girt in girlonds of wild Yvie twine,
How I could reare the Muse on stately stage,
And teache her tread aloft in bus-kin[7] fine,
With queint Bellona[8] in her equipage.

115 But ah my corage cooles ere it be warme,
For thy, content us in thys humble shade:
Where no such troublous tydes° han us assayde,   *seasons*
Here we our slender pipes may safely charme.[9]

PIERS

And when my Gates shall han their bellies layd:[1]
120 Cuddie shall have a Kidde to store his farme.

Cuddies Embleme.[2]
Agitante calescimus illo &c.

                                                        1579

6. "He seemeth here to be ravished with a Poetical furie. For (if one rightly mark) the numbers rise so ful, and the verse groweth so big, that it seemeth he hath forgot the meanenesse of shepheards state and stile" [E. K.'s Glosse]. E. K. adds an explanation of "wild Yvie" in the next line: "For it is dedicated to Bacchus and therefore it is sayd that the Maenades (that is Bacchus franticke priestes) used in theyr sacrifice to carry *Thyrsos*, which were pointed staves or Javelins, wrapped about with yvie."
7. "It was the maner of Poetes and plaiers in tragedies to were buskins, as also in Comedies to use stockes and light shoes. So that the buskin in Poetry is used for tragical matter * * * " [E. K.'s Glosse].
8. "Strange Bellona; the goddesse of battaile, that is Pallas, which may therefore wel be called queint for that (as Lucian saith) when Jupiter hir father was in traveile of her, he caused his sonne Vulcane with his axe to hew his head. Out of which leaped forth lustely a valiant damsell armed at all poyntes, whom seeing Vulcane so faire

and comely, lightly leaping to her, proferred her some cortesie, which the Lady disdeigning, shaked her speare at him, and threatned his saucinesse. Therefore such straungenesse is well applyed to her" [E. K.'s Glosse]. E. K. also glosses "equipage": order.
9. "Temper and order. For Charmes were wont to be made by verses as Ovid sayth, *Aut si carminibus*" [E. K.'s Glosse]. E. K. had a slip of memory: the fragment is not in Ovid.
1. I.e., when my goats bear their young.
2. An "embleme" is a motto or relevant quotation. The Latin line, of which Spenser gives the first three words here, is from Ovid, *Fasti* vi.5: "There is a god within us; it is from his stirring that we feel warm." E. K. comments on the quotation: "Hereby is meant, as also in the whole course of this Aeglogue, that Poetry is a divine instinct and unnatural rage passing the reache of comen reason. Whom Piers answereth *Epiphonematicos* [by way of summary] as admiring the excellencye of the skyll whereof in Cuddie hee hadde alreadye hadde a taste."

The Faerie Queene Spenser's masterpiece is a poem peculiarly characteristic of its age. It is a "courtesy book," like Castiglione's *Courtier,* intended to "fashion a gentleman or noble person" by exhibiting the traits such a person should have. Only six of the twelve projected books were finished. These exhibit the virtues of Holiness, Temperance, Chastity, Friendship, Justice, and Courtesy. A fragment of another book, the cantos on Mutability, also survives. But whereas the ordinary courtesy book was a piece of explanation and exhortation, *The Faerie Queene* is also a poem, and, as Elizabethans all believed, a poem teaches by delighting. Spenser's great work is full of adventures and marvels, dragons, witches, enchanted trees, giants, jousting knights, and castles; a romantic epic, like Ariosto's *Orlando Furioso* (1516). But it is also an allegory, like Tasso's *Gerusalemme Liberata* (1575); the heroes of the several books represent the virtues portrayed in those books. The Redcrosse Knight in Book I is of course St. George, the patron saint of England, but he also represents Holiness, as Sir Guyon in Book II represents Temperance (not simply abstinence in drinking but self-control under all the temptations of the senses). The heroes do not have the virtues they represent at the beginning of their adventures—they acquire them in the course of the book. Spenser explains his allegorical method in a preliminary letter to Sir Walter Ralegh; however he does not explain what would be obvious to every contemporary reader, the many conventional symbols and attributes which would identify his characters. For example, when a woman appears who has a miter, wears scarlet clothes, and comes from the river Tiber, the reader is supposed to know immediately that she represents the Roman Catholic Church, which had been so often identified by Protestant preachers with the Whore of Babylon in the Book of Revelation.

Book I of *The Faerie Queene* is in a way an epitome of the whole poem, or the part of it Spenser completed. It is almost entirely self-contained; it has been called a miniature epic in itself. It consists of twelve cantos, as Virgil's *Aeneid* consists of twelve books. The introductory lines are intended to remind the reader of Virgil, who began with pastoral poetry and moved on to the epic, as Spenser is now doing.

The theme is not arms and the man, however, but something more romantic—"Fierce warres and faithfull loves." The scenery, too, is not classical but romantic. There are plains and forests and caves and castles and magical trees and springs; one meets dwarfs and giants and lions and pilgrims and magicians and Saracens or "paynims" (with French names). An accurate map of Faerie Land is impossible but unnecessary; if you are going somewhere you just start out and, after many adventures, get there. A clear, pleasant stream may be dangerous to drink because it produces loss of strength. Any stranger you meet is more than likely to be a villain and to be in disguise.

The good people are subject to the Faerie Queene and are called Faeries or Elves. They are human beings, though not much individualized. They undergo the trials and tribulations men undergo in the ordinary world, but these events are told in a romantic, fantastic way in order to arouse wonder. The bad creatures, people and monsters, are various vices, evils, and temptations, often revealed to the reader by their names or by the short verse summaries at the beginning of each canto but not revealed to the hero until he has conquered them. Houses, castles, and animals also stand for abstract virtues or vices. The world of Faerie Land is a visual world in which the meaning of something is made fully evident by its appearance when stripped of all disguise.

Read as romantic narrative, the plot of Book I is a series of chivalric adventures undertaken by the Redcrosse Knight culminating in his killing the dragon, rescuing Una's parents, and winning her as his bride. Read as spiritual allegory, the book tells the story of the Christian's struggle for salvation—his wandering between the evil extremes of pride and despair, his encounter with the seven deadly sins, his separation from and reunion with the one true faith, the purgation of his sinfulness, and his final salvation by divine grace added to heroic effort.

The poem can be enjoyed on many levels, and it may, in fact, work on several of these levels at a time. In addition to being—most especially— a heroic poem and a spiritual allegory, it also embodies many religious and political aspects of Spenser's own England; a "political allegory" runs all through Book I. This is a romantic, "medieval," heroic, religious, political, magical world, and the reader entering it must be prepared to move as the story moves, taking the meanings on whatever level seems most viable at the moment. Spenser is not a great explainer; more usually, he gives the reader a scene or a surface, and lets the full allegorical import work its way out.

Moreover, that scene or surface may draw on the riches of literary and pictorial traditions. Entire episodes may be adopted from the Italian romantic epics of Ariosto and Tasso and, either through them or independently, from Homer, Virgil, or Ovid (this was an age when borrowing and reworking earlier materials was praiseworthy in a poet). Places, such as Lucifera's castle; individual attributes, such as Una's lamb or Speranza's anchor; even names or colors came to Spenser from the classics, from theologians, from liturgical tradition, from the village pulpit, from folk tales and pageants, from tapestries, paintings, and emblem books. In our notes we have attempted to show what some of the sources were—but more important is the understanding that these traditions had a life for Spenser and his readers; they could flow together, separate, recombine.

The strangeness of *The Faerie Queene* becomes, on closer acquaintance, a source of delight. No work of the English Renaissance is more exuberant, more fertile, more full.

From THE FAERIE QUEENE
A Letter of the Authors

EXPOUNDING HIS WHOLE INTENTION IN THE COURSE OF THIS WORKE:
WHICH FOR THAT IT GIVETH GREAT LIGHT TO THE READER, FOR THE
BETTER UNDERSTANDING IS HEREUNTO ANNEXED

*To the Right noble, and Valorous, Sir Walter Raleigh knight,
Lo. Wardein of the Stanneryes, and her Majesties liefetenaunt
of the County of Cornewayll*

Sir knowing how doubtfully all Allegories may be construed, and
this booke of mine, which I have entituled the *Faery Queene*, being a continued Allegory, or darke conceit, I have thought good as
well for avoyding of gealous opinions and misconstructions, as also
for your better light in reading thereof, (being so by you commanded,) to discover unto you the general intention and meaning,
which in the whole course thereof I have fashioned, without expressing of any particular purposes or by-accidents [1] therein occasioned. The generall end therefore of all the booke is to fashion [2] a
gentleman or noble person in vertuous and gentle discipline:
Which for that I conceived shoulde be most plausible and pleasing,
being coloured with an historicall fiction, the which the most part
of men delight to read, rather for variety of matter, then for profite
of the ensample: I chose the historye of King Arthure, as most fitte
for the excellency of his person, being made famous by many mens
former workes, and also furthest from the daunger of envy, and
suspition of present time.[3] In which I have followed all the antique
Poets historicall, first Homere, who in the Persons of Agamemnon
and Ulysses hath ensampled a good governour and a vertuous man,
the one in his *Ilias*, the other in his *Odysseis*: then Virgil, whose
like intention was to doe in the person of Aeneas: after him Ariosto
comprised them both in his Orlando: and lately Tasso dissevered
them againe, and formed both parts in two persons, namely that
part which they in Philosophy call Ethice, or vertues of a private
man, coloured in his Rinaldo: The other named Politice in his
Godfredo.[4] By ensample of which excellente Poets, I labour to
pourtraict in Arthure, before he was king, the image of a brave
knight, perfected in the twelve private morall vertues, as Aristotle

1. Secondary matters.
2. I.e., to represent (secondarily, to educate).
3. I.e., free from current political controversy.
4. Lodovico Ariosto (1474–1533) was
author of the epic-romance *Orlando Fu-*
rioso, first published in complete form
in 1532; Torquato Tasso (1544–95)
published his chivalric romance *Rinaldo*
in 1562 and the epic *Gerusalemme Lib-*
erata (centered on the heroic figure of
Count Godfredo) in 1581.

hath devised,[5] the which is the purpose of these first twelve bookes: which if I finde to be well accepted, I may be perhaps encouraged, to frame the other part of polliticke vertues in his person, after that hee came to be king. To some I know this Methode will seeme displeasaunt, which had rather have good discipline delivered plainly in way of precepts, or sermoned at large, as they use, then thus clowdily enwrapped in Allegoricall devises. But such, me seeme, should be satisfide with the use of these dayes, seeing all things accounted by their showes, and nothing esteemed of, that is not delightfull and pleasing to commune sence. For this cause is Xenophon preferred before Plato, for that the one in the exquisite depth of his judgment, formed a Commune welth [6] such as it should be, but the other in the person of Cyrus and the Persians fashioned a governement such as might best be: So much more profitable and gratious is doctrine by ensample, then by rule. So have I laboured to doe in the person of Arthure: whome I conceive after his long education by Timon, to whom he was by Merlin delivered to be brought up, so soone as he was borne of the Lady Igrayne, to have seene in a dream or vision the Faery Queen, with whose excellent beauty ravished, he awaking resolved to seeke her out, and so being by Merlin armed, and by Timon throughly instructed, he went to seeke her forth in Faerye land. In that Faery Queene I meane glory in my generall intention, but in my particular I conceive the most excellent and glorious person of our soveraine the Queene, and her kingdome in Faery land. And yet in some places els, I doe otherwise shadow [7] her. For considering she beareth two persons, the one of a most royall Queene or Empresse, the other of a most vertuous and beautifull Lady, this latter part in some places I doe express in Belphoebe, fashioning her name according to your owne excellent conceipt of Cynthia,[8] (Phoebe and Cynthia being both names of Diana.) So in the person of Prince Arthure I sette forth magnificence in particular, which vertue for that (according to Aristotle and the rest) it is the perfection of all the rest, and conteineth in it them all, therefore in the whole course I mention the deedes of Arthure applyable to that vertue, which I write of in that booke. But of the xii. other vertues, I make xii. other knights the patrones, for the more variety of the history. Of which these three bookes contayn three, The first of the knight of the Redcrosse, in whome I expresse Holynes: The seconde of Sir Guyon, in whome I sette forth Temperaunce: The third of Brito-

5. Aristotle did not devise twelve private moral virtues: Spenser was in fact relying upon more modern philosophers— his friend Lodowick Bryskett and the Italian Piccolomini. That Spenser actually planned a poem four times as long as the six books we now have rather staggers the imagination, but his language is plain.
6. The allusion is to Plato's *Republic* and Xenophon's *Cyropaedia*.
7. Picture, portray.
8. Ralegh's poem *Cynthia* praised Queen Elizabeth.

martis a Lady knight, in whome I picture Chastity. But because the
beginning of the whole worke seemeth abrupte and as depending
upon other antecedents, it needs that ye know the occasion of these
three knights severall adventures. For the Methode of a Poet historical is not such, as of an Historiographer. For an Historiographer
discourseth of affayres orderly as they were donne, accounting as
well the times as the actions, but a Poet thrusteth into the middest, even where it most concerneth him, and there recoursing to
the thinges forepaste, and divining of thinges to come, maketh a
pleasing Analysis of all. The beginning therefore of my history, if
it were to be told by an Historiographer, should be the twelfth
booke, which is the last, where I devise that the Faery Queene
kept her Annuall feaste xii. dayes, uppon which xii. severall dayes,
the occasions of the xii. severall adventures hapned, which being
undertaken by xii. severall knights, are in these xii books severally
handled and discoursed. The first was this. In the beginning of the
feaste, there presented him selfe a tall clownishe [9] younge man,
who falling before the Queen of Faeries desired a boone (as the
manner then was) which during that feast she might not refuse:
which was that hee might have the atchievement of any adventure,
which during that feaste should happen, that being graunted, he
rested him on the floore, unfitte through his rusticity for a better
place. Soone after entred a faire Ladye in mourning weedes, riding
on a white Asse, with a dwarfe behind her leading a warlike steed,
that bore the Armes of a knight, and his speare in the dwarfes
hand. Shee falling before the Queene of Faeries, complayned that
her father and mother an ancient King and Queene, had bene by
an huge dragon many years shut up in a brasen Castle, who thence
suffred them not to yssew: and therefore besought the Faery
Queene to assygne her some one of her knights to take on him that
exployt. Presently that clownish person upstarting, desired that adventure: whereat the Queene much wondering, and the Lady much
gainesaying, yet he earnestly importuned his desire. In the end the
Lady told him that unlesse that armour which she brought, would
serve him (that is the armour of a Christian man specified by Saint
Paul v. Ephes.) that he could not succeed in that enterprise, which
being forthwith put upon him with dewe furnitures [1] thereunto,
he seemed the goodliest man in al that company, and was well
liked of the Lady. And eftesoones taking on him knighthood, and
mounting on that straunge Courser, he went forth with her on that
adventure: where beginneth the first booke, vz.

A gentle knight was pricking on the playne. &c.

The second day ther came in a Palmer bearing an Infant with

bloody hands, whose Parents he complained to have bene slayn by an Enchaunteresse called Acrasia: and therfore craved of the Faery Queene, to appoint him some knight, to performe that adventure, which being assigned to Sir Guyon, he presently went forth with that same Palmer: which is the beginning of the second booke and the whole subject thereof. The third day there came in, a Groome who complained before the Faery Queene, that a vile Enchaunter called Busirane had in hand a most faire Lady called Amoretta, whom he kept in most grievous torment, because she would not yield him the pleasure of her body. Whereupon Sir Scudamour the lover of that Lady presently tooke on him that adventure. But being unable to performe it by reason of the hard Enchauntments, after long sorrow, in the end met with Britomartis, who succoured him, and reskewed his love.

But by occasion hereof, many other adventures are intermedled, but rather as Accidents,² then intendments.² As the love of Britomart, the overthrow of Marinell, the misery of Florimell, the vertuousnes of Belphoebe, the lasciviousnes of Hellenora, and many the like.

Thus much Sir, I have briefly overronne to direct your understanding to the wel-head of the History, that from thence gathering the whole intention of the conceit, ye may as in a handfull gripe al the discourse, which otherwise may happily³ seeme tedious and confused. So humbly craving the continuaunce of your honorable favour towards me, and th'eternall establishment of your happines, I humbly take leave.

23. January, 1589
Yours most humbly affectionate.
ED. SPENSER.

The First Booke of the Faerie Queene

CONTAYNING
*The Legende of the
Knight of the Red Crosse,*
OR
OF HOLINESSE

1

Lo I the man, whose Muse whilome did maske,
As time her taught, in lowly Shepheards weeds,⁴

2. That is, there are episodes that are merely romantic and not specifically allegorical. Characters are often types, not symbols.
3. By chance.
4. I.e., behold me, the poet who ap-

propriately appeared before ("whilome") as a writer of humble pastoral (i.e., *The Shepheardes Calender*). These lines are imitated from the verses prefixed to Virgil's *Aeneid*.

Am now enforst a far unfitter taske,
  For trumpets sterne to chaunge mine Oaten reeds,[5]
5 And sing of Knights and Ladies gentle deeds;
  Whose prayses having slept in silence long,[6]
  Me, all too meane, the sacred Muse areeds °   *appoints*
  To blazon broad emongst her learned throng:
Fierce warres and faithfull loves shall moralize my song.

2

10 Helpe then, O holy Virgin chiefe of nine,[7]
  Thy weaker Novice to performe thy will,
  Lay forth out of thine everlasting scryne [8]
  The antique rolles, which there lye hidden still,
  Of Faerie knights and fairest Tanaquill,[9]
15 Whom that most noble Briton Prince [1] so long
  Sought through the world, and suffered so much ill,
  That I must rue his undeservéd wrong:
O helpe thou my weake wit, and sharpen my dull tong.

3

And thou most dreaded impe [2] of highest Jove,
20 Faire Venus sonne, that with thy cruell dart
  At that good knight so cunningly didst rove,°   *shoot*
  That glorious fire it kindled in his hart,
  Lay now thy deadly Heben ° bow apart,   *ebony*
  And with thy mother milde come to mine ayde:
25 Come both, and with you bring triumphant Mart,[3]
  In loves and gentle jollities arrayd,
After his murdrous spoiles and bloudy rage allayd.

4

And with them eke,° O Goddesse heavenly bright,   *also*
  Mirrour of grace and Majestie divine,
30 Great Lady of the greatest Isle, whose light
  Like Phoebus lampe throughout the world doth shine,
  Shed thy faire beames into my feeble eyne,
  And raise my thoughts too humble and too vile,°   *lowly*
  To thinke of that true glorious type ° of thine,   *pattern*
35 The argument of mine afflicted stile:
The which to heare, vouchsafe, O dearest dred [4] a-while.

Canto I

The Patron of true Holinesse,
Foule Errour doth defeate:
Hypocrisie him to entrappe,
Doth to his home entreate.

5. To write heroic poetry, of which the trumpet is a symbol, instead of pastoral poetry like *The Shepheardes Calender*, symbolized by the humble shepherd's pipe ("Oaten reeds").
6. Lines 5 and 6 are imitated from the opening lines of Ariosto's *Orlando Furioso*.
7. Clio, the Muse of history; "weaker": too weak.
8. A chest for papers.
9. I.e., Gloriana.
1. I.e., Arthur.
2. Child, i.e., Cupid.
3. Mars, god of war and lover of Venus.
4. Object of awe.

1

A Gentle Knight was pricking ° on the plaine,   cantering
    Ycladd in mightie armes and silver shielde,
    Wherein old dints of deepe wounds did remaine,
    The cruell markes of many a bloudy fielde;
5   Yet armes till that time did he never wield: ⁵
    His angry steede did chide his foming bitt,
    As much disdayning to the curbe to yield:
    Full jolly ° knight he seemd, and faire did sitt,   courageous
As one for knightly giusts ° and fierce encounters   tourneys, jousts
    fitt.

2

10 But on his brest a bloudie Crosse he bore,
    The deare remembrance of his dying Lord,
    For whose sweete sake that glorious badge he wore,
    And dead as living ever him adored:
    Upon his shield the like was also scored,
15 For soveraine hope, which in his helpe he had:
    Right faithfull true he was in deede and word,
    But of his cheere ⁶ did seeme too solemne sad; °   serious
Yet nothing did he dread, but ever was ydrad.°   dreaded, feared

3

Upon a great adventure he was bond,
20 That greatest Gloriana to him gave,
    That greatest Glorious Queene of Faerie Lond,
    To winne him worship, and her grace to have,
    Which of all earthly things he most did crave;
    And ever as he rode, his hart did earne °   yearn
25 To prove his puissance in battell brave
    Upon his foe, and his new force to learne;
Upon his foe, a Dragon horrible and stearne.

4

A lovely Ladie rode him faire beside,
    Upon a lowly Asse more white then snow,
30 Yet she much whiter, but the same did hide
    Under a vele, that wimpled ° was full low,   folded
    And over all a blacke stole she did throw,
    As one that inly mournd: so was she sad,
    And heavie sat upon her palfrey slow:
35 Seeméd in heart some hidden care she had,
And by her in a line a milke white lambe she lad.⁷

---

5. Redcrosse wears the armor of the Christian man, as Spenser explained in the letter to Ralegh: "put on the whole armor of God, that ye may be able to stand against the wiles of the devil" (Ephesians vi.10–22). The armor bears the dents of every Christian's fight against evil; Redcrosse himself is as yet untried.
6. Facial expression.

7. The lady will be called by name in line 405; she is Una, short for *Una Vera Fides*, "The One True Faith" (if it is true it can only be *one*). But, like other figures, she may bear other roles and attributes. Therefore she may also be the Church of England, with whom Redcrosse, in his role as Britain (St. George) will be united. Her parents typify all mankind—originally lords of

5

So pure an innocent, as that same lambe,
　She was in life and every vertuous lore,
　And by descent from Royall lynage came
40　Of ancient Kings and Queenes, that had of yore
　Their scepters stretcht from East to Westerne shore,
　And all the world in their subjection held;
　Till that infernall feend with foule uprore
　Forwasted all their land, and them expeld:
45　Whom to avenge, she had this Knight from far compeld.° *summoned*

6

Behind her farre away a Dwarfe did lag,
　That lasie seemd in being ever last,
　Or wearied with bearing of her bag
　Of needments at his backe.[8] Thus as they past,
50　The day with cloudes was suddeine overcast,
　And angry Jove an hideous storme of raine
　Did poure into his Lemans[9] lap so fast,
　That every wight° to shrowd° it did constrain, *creature/cover*
And this faire couple eke ° to shroud themselves were fain. *also*

7

55　Enforst to seeke some covert nigh at hand,
　A shadie grove not far away they spide,
　That promist ayde the tempest to withstand:
　Whose loftie trees yclad with sommers pride,
　Did spred so broad, that heavens light did hide,
60　Not perceable with power of any starre:
　And all within were pathes and alleies wide,
　With footing worne, and leading inward farre:
Faire harbour that them seemes; so in they entred arre.

8

And foorth they passe, with pleasure forward led,
65　Joying to heare the birdes sweete harmony,
　Which therein shrouded from the tempest dred,
　Seemd in their song to scorne the cruell sky.
　Much can° they prayse the trees, so straight and hy, *did*
　The sayling Pine, the Cedar proud and tall,

Eden, now fallen. She is veiled because fallen man cannot see the one truth but only fragments thereof, and she is sad because man is fallen. It is a characteristic Spenserian subtlety that Una enters the poem under a veil and only appears to the Redcrosse Knight, unveiled and radiant, in Canto vii. The "lowly Asse" she rides (line 29) is a figure of humility (cf. Christ's entry into Jerusalem), and the "lambe" is that of innocence. Having filled its symbolic function, the lamb does not appear in the poem again. C. S. Lewis, in *The Allegory of Love* (pp. 310–11) discusses another aspect of Spenser's alle-

gorical imagination that this passage reveals: "the lady was commonly represented leading her lamb in the pageants [local religious dramas] of St. George and the dragon." That is, many of the associations evoked in *The Faerie Queene* are not merely literary but "popular, homely, patriotic."
8. The Dwarfe is sometimes taken as Redcrosse's conscience—useful in emergencies, otherwise forgotten or lost. In addition, or alternatively, the Dwarfe may represent common sense or common prudence.
9. His lover, i.e., the earth.

70   The vine-prop Elme, the Poplar never dry,
       The builder Oake, sole king of forrests all,
   The Aspine good for staves, the Cypresse funerall.

              9

   The Laurell, meed° of mightie Conquerours   *reward*
       And Poets sage, the Firre that weepeth still,
75   The Willow worne of forlorne Paramours,
       The Eugh obedient to the benders will,
       The Birch for shaftes, the Sallow for the mill,
       The Mirrhe sweete bleeding in the bitter wound,
       The warlike Beech, the Ash for nothing ill,
80   The fruitfull Olive, and the Platane round,
   The carver Holme, the Maple seeldom inward sound.[1]

             10

   Led with delight, they thus beguile the way,
       Untill the blustring storme is overblowne;
       When weening° to returne, whence they did stray,   *supposing*
85   They cannot finde that path, which first was showne,
       But wander too and fro in wayes unknowne,
       Furthest from end then, when they neerest weene,
       That makes them doubt, their wits be not their owne:
       So many pathes, so many turnings seene,
90   That which of them to take, in diverse doubt they been.

             11

   At last resolving forward still to fare,
       Till that some end they finde or° in or out,   *either*
       That path they take, that beaten seemd most bare,
       Which when by tract[2] they hunted had throughout,
95   And like to lead the labyrinth about;°   *out of*
       At length it brought them to a hollow cave,
       Amid the thickest woods. The Champion stout
       Eftsoones° dismounted from his courser brave,   *forthwith*
   And to the Dwarfe a while his needlesse spere he gave.

             12

100   "Be well aware," quoth then that Ladie milde,
       "Least suddaine mischiefe ye too rash provoke:
       The danger hid, the place unknowne and wilde,
       Breedes dreadfull doubts: Oft fire is without smoke,
       And perill without show: therefore your stroke
105   Sir knight with-hold, till further triall made."
       "Ah Ladie," said he, "shame were to revoke
       The forward footing for° an hidden shade: *because of*
   Vertue gives her selfe light, through darkenesse for to wade."

             13

   "Yea but," quoth she, "the perill of this place
110   I better wot then you, though now too late

---

1. In these lines, Spenser has been imitating Chaucer's catalogue of trees in
the *Parliament of Fowls;* the convention goes back to Ovid.
2. By following the track.

To wish you backe returne with foule disgrace,
Yet wisedome warnes, whilest foot is in the gate,
To stay the steepe, ere forcéd to retrate.
This is the wandring wood, this Errours den,
115 A monster vile, whom God and man does hate:
Therefore I read° beware." "Fly fly," quoth then   *advise*
The fearefull Dwarfe: "this is no place for living men."

14

But full of fire and greedy hardiment,°   *boldness*
The youthfull knight could not for ought be staide,
120 But forth unto the darksome hole he went,
And lookéd in: his glistring armor made
A litle glooming light, much like a shade,
By which he saw the ugly monster plaine,
Halfe like a serpent horribly displaide,[3]
125 But th' other halfe did womans shape retaine,
Most lothsom, filthie, foule, and full of vile disdaine.

15

And as she lay upon the durtie ground,
Her huge long taile her den all overspred,
Yet was in knots and many boughtes° upwound,   *coils*
130 Pointed with mortall sting. Of her there bred
A thousand yong ones, which she dayly fed,
Sucking upon her poisonous dugs, eachone
Of sundry shapes, yet all ill favoréd:
Soone as that uncouth° light upon them shone,   *unfamiliar*
135 Into her mouth they crept, and suddain all were gone.

16

Their dam upstart, out of her den effraide,
And rushéd forth, hurling her hideous taile
About her curséd head, whose folds displaid
Were stretcht now forth at length without
140   entraile.°   *winding, coiling*
She lookt about, and seeing one in mayle
Arméd to point, sought backe to turne againe;
For light she hated as the deadly bale,°   *evil*
Ay wont in desert darknesse to remaine,
145 Where plaine none might her see, nor she see any plaine.

17

Which when the valiant Elfe[4] pereived, he lept
As Lyon fierce upon the flying pray,
And with his trenchand° blade her boldly kept   *cutting*
From turning backe, and forcéd her to stay:
150 Therewith enraged she loudly gan to bray,

3. That Errour (or theological, doctrinal heresy) is half serpent reminds us of the primal error in Eden, which the serpent instigated. "Errour," at first glance, may not seem an important demon; here Lewis is helpful in reminding us that "Spenser is writing in an age of religious doubt and controversy when the avoidance of error is a problem as pressing as, and in a sense prior to, the conquest of sin" (*Allegory of Love*, p. 334). The description echoes both classical and Biblical monsters (cf. Revelation ix.7–10).
4. Knight of Faerie Land.

150 And turning fierce, her speckled taile advaunst,
Threatning her angry sting, him to dismay:
Who nough aghast, his mightie hand enhaunst:°   *lifted up*
The stroke down from her head unto her shoulder glaunst.

18

Much daunted with that dint, her sence was dazd,
155 Yet kindling rage, her selfe she gathered round,
And all attonce her beastly body raizd
With doubled forces high above the ground:
Tho° wrapping up her wrethéd sterne arownd,   *then*
Lept fierce upon his shield, and her huge traine°   *tail*
160 All suddenly about his body wound,
That hand or foot to stirre he strove in vaine:
God helpe the man so wrapt in Errours endlesse traine.

19

His Lady sad to see his sore constraint,
Cride out, "Now now Sir knight, shew what ye bee,
165 Add faith unto your force, and be not faint:
Strangle her, else she sure will strangle thee."
That when he heard, in great perplexitie,
His gall did grate for griefe° and high disdaine,   *wrath*
And knitting all his force got one hand free,
170 Wherewith he grypt her gorge° with so great paine,   *neck*
That soone to loose her wicked bands did her constraine.

20

Therewith she spewd out of her filthy maw
A floud of poyson horrible and blacke,
Full of great lumpes of flesh and gobbets raw,
175 Which stunck so vildly, that it forst him slacke
His grasping hold, and from her turne him backe:
Her vomit full of bookes and papers[5] was,
With loathly frogs and toades, which eyes did lacke,
And creeping sought way in the weedy gras:
180 Her filthy parbreake° all the place defiléd has.[6]   *vomit*

21

As when old father Nilus gins to swell
With timely pride above the Aegyptian vale,
His fattie° waves do fertile slime outwell,   *rich*
And overflow each plaine and lowly dale:
185 But when his later spring gins to avale,°   *subside*
Huge heapes of mudd he leaves, wherein there breed
Ten thousand kindes of creatures, partly male
And partly female of his fruitfull seed;
Such ugly monstrous shapes elswhere may no man reed.°   *see*

---

5. The reference is to books and pamphlets of Catholic propaganda, particularly attacks on Queen Elizabeth in 1588—and, indeed, to violent religious controversy of any kind.

6. Revelation xvi.13: "And I saw three unclean spirits like frogs come out of the mouth of the dragon, and out of the mouth of the beast, and out of the mouth of the false prophet."

22

190 The same so sore annoyéd has the knight,
    That welnigh chokéd with the deadly stinke,
    His forces faile, ne can no longer fight.
    Whose corage when the feend perceived to shrinke,
    She pouréd forth out of her hellish sinke
195   Her fruitfull curséd spawne of serpents small,
    Deforméd monsters, fowle, and blacke as inke,
    Which swarming all about his legs did crall,
And him encombred sore, but could not hurt at all.

23

As gentle Shepheard in sweete even-tide,
200   When ruddy Phoebus gins to welke° in west,   *sink*
    High on an hill, his flocke to vewen wide,
    Markes which do byte their hasty supper best;
    A cloud of combrous gnattes do him molest,
    All striving to infixe their feeble stings,
205   That from their noyance he no where can rest,
    But with his clownish° hands their tender wings   *rustic*
He brusheth oft, and oft doth mar their murmurings.

24

Thus ill bestedd,° and fearfull more of shame,   *situated*
    Then of the certaine perill he stood in,
210   Halfe furious unto his foe he came,
    Resolved in minde all suddenly to win,
    Or soone to lose, before he once would lin;°   *cease, stop*
    And strooke at her with more then manly force,
    That from her body full of filthie sin
215   He raft° her hatefull head without remorse;   *cut away*
A streame of cole black bloud forth gushéd from her corse.

25

Her scattred brood, soone as their Parent deare
    They saw so rudely falling to the ground,
    Groning full deadly, all with troublous feare,
220   Gathred themselves about her body round,
    Weening their wonted entrance to have found
    At her wide mouth: but being there withstood
    They flockéd all about her bleeding wound,
    And suckéd up their dying mothers blood,
225 Making her death their life, and eke° her hurt their good.   *also*

26

That detestable sight him much amazde,
    To see th' unkindly Impes of heaven accurst,
    Devoure their dam; on whom while so he gazd,
    Having all satisfide their bloudy thurst,
230   Their bellies swolne he saw with fulnesse burst,
    And bowels gushing forth: well worthy end
    Of such as drunke her life, the which them nurst;
    Now needeth him no lenger labour spend,
His foes have slaine themselves, with whom he should contend.

27

235 His Ladie seeing all, that chaunst, from farre
  Approcht in hast to greet his victorie,
  And said, "Faire knight, borne under happy starre,
  Who see your vanquisht foes before you lye;
  Well worthy be you of that Armorie,[7]
240 Wherein ye have great glory wonne this day,
  And prooved your strength on a strong enimie,
  Your first adventure: many such I pray,
And henceforth ever wish, that like succeed it may."

28

 Then mounted he upon his Steede againe,
245 And with the Lady backward sought to wend;
  That path he kept, which beaten was most plaine,
  Ne ever would to any by-way bend,
  But still did follow one unto the end,
  The which at last out of the wood them brought.
250 So forward on his way (with God to frend[8])
  He passéd forth, and new adventure sought;
Long way he travelléd, before he heard of ought.

29

 At length they chaunst to meet upon the way
  An aged Sire, in long blacke weedes yclad,[9]
255 His feete all bare, his beard all hoarie gray,
  And by his belt his booke he hanging had;
  Sober he seemde, and very sagely sad,°   *pensive*
  And to the ground his eyes were lowly bent,
  Simple in shew, and voyde of malice bad,
260 And all the way he prayéd, as he went,
And often knockt his brest, as one that did repent.[1]

30

 He faire the knight saluted, louting° low,   *bowing*
  Who faire him quited,° as that courteous was: *answered*
  And after askéd him, if he did know
265 Of straunge adventures, which abroad did pas.
  "Ah my deare Sonne," quoth he, "how should, alas,
  Silly° old man, that lives in hidden cell,   *innocent*
  Bidding° his beades all day for his trespas, *telling*
  Tydings of warre and worldly trouble tell?
270 With holy father sits not with such things to mell.° *meddle*

---

7. I.e., Christian armor.
8. With God as friend.
9. Dressed in long black garments.
1. The Sire is in reality Archimago (arch, or head, magician)—i.e., hypocrisy, the archdeceiver, Satan, idolatry of the Roman Catholic Church. He is disguised as a holy man, as evil is so often under the guise of good in Christian thought and legend. Note (especially in lines 312–15) that his "holiness" is in talking, not in doing, and that he is far too reminiscent of the Catholic monasteries to be trustworthy. The black magician in hermit's disguise often appears in medieval romance and in Italian romance epics.

31

"But if of daunger which hereby doth dwell,
       And homebred evill ye desire to heare,
       Of a straunge man I can you tidings tell,
       That wasteth all this countrey farre and neare."
275   "Of such," said he, "I chiefly do inquere,
       And shall you well reward to shew the place,
       In which that wicked wight his dayes doth weare:
       For to all knighthood it is foule disgrace,
That such a cursed creature lives so long a space."

32

280   "Far hence," quoth he; "in wastfull° wildernesse   *desolate*
       His dwelling is, by which no living wight
       May ever passe, but thorough great distresse."
       "Now," sayd the Lady, "draweth toward night,
       And well I wote, that of your later° fight   *recent*
285   Ye all forwearied be: for what so strong,
       But wanting rest will also want of might?
       The Sunne that measures heaven all day long,
At night doth baite° his steedes the Ocean waves emong. *feed, refresh*

33

"Then with the Sunne take Sir, your timely rest,
290   And with new day new worke at once begin:
       Untroubled night they say gives counsell best."
       "Right well Sir knight ye have adviséd bin,"
       Quoth then that aged man; "the way to win
       Is wisely to advise: now day is spent;
295   Therefore with me ye may take up your In°   *lodging*
       For this same night." The knight was well content:
So with that godly father to his home they went.

34

A little lowly Hermitage it was,
       Downe in a dale, hard by a forests side,
300   Far from resort of people, that did pas
       In travell to and froe: a little wyde°   *apart*
       There was an holy Chappell edifyde,°   *built*
       Wherein the Hermite dewly wont° to say   *was wont*
       His holy things each morne and eventyde:
305   Thereby a Christall streame did gently play,
Which from a sacred fountaine welléd forth alway.

35

Arrivéd there, the little house they fill,
       Ne looke for entertainement, where none was:
       Rest is their feast, and all things at their will;
310   The noblest mind the best contentment has.
       With faire discourse the evening so they pas:
       For that old man of pleasing wordes had store,
       And well could file his tongue as smooth as glas;
       He told of Saintes and Popes, and evermore
315   He strowd an *Ave-Mary* after and before.

36

The drouping Night thus creepeth on them fast,
   And the sad humour[2] loading their eye liddes,
   As messenger of Morpheus[3] on them cast
   Sweet slombring deaw, the which to sleepe them biddes.
320   Unto their lodgings then his guestes he riddes:°   *leads*
   Where when all drownd in deadly sleepe he findes,
   He to his study goes, and there amiddes
   His Magick bookes and artes of sundry kindes,
He seekes out mighty charmes, to trouble sleepy mindes.

37

325 Then choosing out few wordes most horrible
   (Let none them read), thereof did verses frame,
   With which and other spelles like terrible,
   He bade awake blacke Plutoes griesly Dame,[4]
   And curséd heaven, and spake reprochfull shame
330   Of highest God, the Lord of life and light;
   A bold bad man, that dared to call by name
   Great Gorgon, Prince of darknesse and dead night,
At which Cocytus quakes, and Styx[5] is put to flight.

38

And forth he cald out of deepe darknesse dred
335   Legions of Sprights, the which like little flyes
   Fluttring about his ever damnéd hed,
   A-waite whereto their service he applyes,
   To aide his friends, or fray° his enimies: *frighten*
   Of those he chose out two, the falsest twoo,
340   And fittest for to forge true-seeming lyes;
   The one of them he gave a message too,
The other by him selfe staide other worke to doo.

39

He making speedy way through sperséd° ayre,   *dispersed*
   And through the world of waters wide and deepe,
345   To Morpheus house doth hastily repaire.
   Amid the bowels of the earth full steepe,
   And low, where dawning day doth never peepe,
   His dwelling is; there Tethys[6] his wet bed
   Doth ever wash, and Cynthia[7] still doth steepe
350   In silver deaw his ever-drouping hed,
Whiles sad Night over him her mantle black doth spred.

40

Whose double gates he findeth lockéd fast,
   The one faire framed of burnisht Yvory,
   The other all with silver overcast;
355   And wakefull dogges before them farre do lye,

2. Heavy moisture.
3. The god of sleep.
4. I.e., Proserpine.

5. Rivers of hell.
6. The wife of Ocean.
7. I.e., Diana, the goddess of the moon.

Watching to banish Care their enimy,
Who oft is wont to trouble gentle Sleepe.
By them the Sprite doth passe in quietly,
And unto Morpheus comes, whom drownéd deepe
360 In drowsie fit he findes: of nothing he takes keepe.°   *notice*

41

And more, to lulle him in his slumber soft,
A trickling streame from high rocke tumbling downe
And ever-drizling raine upon the loft,
Mixt with a murmuring winde, much like the sowne
365 Of swarming Bees, did cast him in a swowne:°   *faint*
No other noyse, nor peoples troublous cryes,
As still° are wont t'annoy the walléd towne,   *always*
Might there be heard: but carelesse Quiet lyes,
Wrapt in eternall silence farre from enemyes.[8]

42

370 The messenger approching to him spake,
But his wast° wordes returnd to him in vaine: *wasted*
So sound he slept, that nought mought him awake.
Then rudely he him thrust, and pusht with paine,
Whereat he gan to stretch: but he againe
375 Shooke him so hard, that forced him to speake.
As one then in a dreame, whose dryer braine[9]
Is tost with troubled sights and fancies weake,
He mumbled soft, but would not all his silence breake.

43

The Sprite then gan more boldly him to wake,
380 And threatned unto him the dreaded name
Of Hecate:[1] whereat he gan to quake,
And lifting up his lumpish head, with blame
Halfe angry askéd him, for what he came.
"Hither," quoth he, "me Archimago sent,
385 He that the stubborne Sprites can wisely tame,
He bids thee to him send for his intent
A fit false dreame, that can delude the sleepers sent."°   *senses*

44

The God obayde, and calling forth straight way
A diverse° dreame out of his prison darke,   *misleading*
390 Delivered it to him, and downe did lay
His heavie head, devoide of carefull carke,[2]
Whose sences all were straight benumbd and starke.
He backe returning by the Yvorie dore,[3]

8. Spenser is imitating descriptions of the house of Morpheus in Chaucer, Ovid, and other ancient writers, but he achieves originality, particularly by means of the sound effects in stanza 41.
9. According to the old physiology, old people and other light sleepers had too little moisture in the brain.
1. Queen of Hades.
2. Anxious concerns.
3. False dreams came through the ivory door, true dreams through the gate of horn (Homer, *Odyssey* XIX.562–67; Virgil, *Aeneid* VI.893–96).

Remounted up as light as chearefull Larke,
And on his litle winges the dreame he bore
In hast unto his Lord, where he him left afore.

45

Who all this while with charmes and hidden artes,
Had made a Lady of that other Spright,
And framed of liquid ayre her tender partes
So lively,° and so like in all mens sight,   *lifelike*
That weaker° sence it could have ravisht quight   *too weak*
The maker selfe for all his wondrous witt,
Was nigh beguiléd with so goodly sight:
Her all in white he clad, and over it
Cast a blacke stole, most like to seeme for Una⁴ fit.

46

Now when that ydle dreame was to him brought
Unto that Elfin knight he bad him fly,
Where he slept soundly void of evill thought
And with false shewes abuse his fantasy,°   *imagination*
In sort as⁵ he him schooléd privily:
And that new creature borne without her dew⁶
Full of the makers guile, with usage sly
He taught to imitate that Lady trew,
Whose semblance she did carrie under feignéd hew.°   *form*

47

Thus well instructed, to their worke they hast
And comming where the knight in slomber lay
The one upon his hardy head him plast,
And made him dreame of loves and lustfull play
That nigh his manly hart did melt away,
Bathéd in wanton blis and wicked joy:
Then seeméd him his Lady by him lay,
And to him playnd,° how that false wingéd boy   *complained*
Her chast hart had subdewd, to learne Dame pleasures toy.

48

And she her selfe of beautie soveraigne Queene
Faire Venus seemde unto his bed to bring
Her, whom he waking evermore did weene
To be the chastest flowre, that ay° did spring   *ever*
On earthly braunch, the daughter of a king,
Now a loose Leman° to vile service bound: *paramour*
And eke the Graces seeméd all to sing,
Hymen iô Hymen, dauncing all around,
Whilst freshest Flora her with Yvie girlond crownd.⁷

4. The lady is now given her name.
5. In the way.
6. Unnaturally.
7. The three graces of classical mythology were personifications of grace and beauty, yet here they sing a call to the pleasures of the marriage bed (Hymen was god of marriage). On Flora, cf. E.K.'s Glosse to the March eclogue: "the Goddesse of flowres, but indede (as saith Tacitus) a famous harlot."

49

In this great passion of unwonted lust,
  Or wonted feare of doing ought amis,
435 He started up, as seeming to mistrust
  Some secret ill, or hidden foe of his:
  Lo there before his face his Lady is,
  Under blake stole hyding her bayted hooke,
  And as halfe blushing offred him to kis,
440 With gentle blandishment and lovely looke,
Most like that virgin true, which for her knight him took.

50

All cleane dismayd to see so uncouth sight,
  And halfe enragéd at her shamelesse guise,
  He thought have slaine her in his fierce despight:°   *indignation*
445 But hasty heat tempring with sufferance wise,
  He stayde his hand, and gan himselfe advise
  To prove his sense, and tempt her faignéd truth.
  Wringing her hands in wemens pitteous wise,
  Tho can she[8] weepe, to stirre up gentle ruth,°   *pity*
450 Both for her noble bloud, and for her tender youth.

51

And said, "Ah Sir, my liege Lord and my love,
  Shall I accuse the hidden cruell fate,
  And mightie causes wrought in heaven above,
  Or the blind God, that doth me thus amate,°   *dismay*
455 For° hopéd love to winne me certaine hate?   *instead of*
  Yet thus perforce he bids me do, or die.
  Die is my dew: yet rew my wretched state
  You, whom my hard avenging destinie
Hath made judge of my life or death indifferently.

52

460 "Your owne deare sake forst me at first to leave
  My Fathers kingdome," There she stopt with teares;
  Her swollen hart her speach seemd to bereave,
  And then againe begun, "My weaker yeares
  Captived to fortune and frayle worldly feares,
465 Fly to your faith for succour and sure ayde:
  Let me not dye in languor and long teares.
  "Why Dame," quoth he, "what hath ye thus dismayd?
What frayes ye, that were wont to comfort me affrayd?"

53

"Love of your selfe," she said, "and deare° constraint   *dire*
470 Lets me not sleepe, but wast the wearie night
  In secret anguish and unpittied plaint,
  Whiles you in carelesse sleepe are drownéd quight."
  Her doubtfull words made that redoubted knight
Suspect her truth: yet since no untruth he knew,

8. Then she began to.

475   Her fawning love with foule disdainefull spight
     He would not shend,° but said, "Deare dame I rew,   *reject*
  That for my sake unknowne such griefe unto you grew.

54

  "Assure your selfe, it fell not all to ground;
     For all so deare as life is to my hart,
480   I deeme your love, and hold me to you bound;
     Ne let vaine feares procure your needlesse smart,
     Where cause is none, but to your rest depart."
     Not all content, yet seemd she to appease°   *cease*
     Her mournefull plaintes, beguiléd of her art,
485   And fed with words, that could not chuse but please,
  So slyding softly forth, she turnd as to her ease.

55

  Long after lay he musing at her mood,
     Much grieved to thinke that gentle Dame so light,
     For whose defence he was to shed his blood.
490   At last dull wearinesse of former fight
     Having yrockt a sleepe his irkesome spright,°   *spirit*
     That troublous dreame gan freshly tosse his braine,
     With bowres, and beds, and Ladies deare delight:[9]
     But when he saw his labour all was vaine,
495   With that misforméd spright he backe returnd againe.

Canto II

The guilefull great Enchaunter parts
The Redcrosse Knight from Truth:
Into whose stead faire falshood steps,
And workes him wofull ruth.

1

  By this the Northerne wagoner had set
     His seven fold teame behind the stedfast starre,[1]
     That was in Ocean waves yet never wet,
     But firme is fixt, and sendeth light from farre
5   To all, that in the wide deepe wandring arre.
     And chearefull Chaunticlere with his note shrill
     Had warnéd once, that Phoebus fiery carre[2]
     In hast was climbing up the Easterne hill,
  Full envious that night so long his roome did fill.

2

10   When those accurséd messengers of hell,
     That feigning dreame, and that faire-forgéd Spright
     Came to their wicked maister, and gan tell
     Their bootelesse° paines, and ill succeeding night: *useless*
     Who all in rage to see his skilfull might

9. Redcrosse has been unable to distinguish the false Una from the true because his reason has been clouded by desire (see I.ii.6).

1. I.e., by this time the Big Dipper had set behind the North Star.
2. The chariot of the sun.

15 Deluded so, gan threaten hellish paine
    And sad Prosérpines wrath, them to affright.
    But when he saw his threatning was but vaine,
    He cast about, and searcht his balefull° bookes againe.   *deadly*

3

    Eftsoones he tooke that miscreated faire,
20   And that false other Spright, on whom he spred
    A seeming body of the subtile aire,
    Like a young Squire, in loves and lusty-hed
    His wanton dayes that ever loosely led,
    Without regard of armes and dreaded fight:
25 Those two he tooke, and in a secret bed,
    Covered with darknesse and misdeeming° night,   *misleading*
    Them both together laid, to joy in vaine delight.

4

    Forthwith he runnes with feignéd faithfull hast
    Unto his guest, who after troublous sights
30   And dreames, gan now to take more sound repast,°   *rest*
    Whom suddenly he wakes with fearefull frights,
    As one aghast with feends or damnéd sprights,
    And to him cals, "Rise rise unhappy Swaine,
    That here wex old in sleepe, whiles wicked wights
35.   Have knit themselves in Venus shamefull chaine;
    Come see, where your false Lady doth her honour staine."

5

    All in amaze he suddenly up start
    With sword in hand, and with the old man went;
    Who soone him brought into a secret part,
40   Where that false couple were full closely ment°   *mingled*
    In wanton lust and lewd embracément:
    Which when he saw, he burnt with gealous fire,
    The eye of reason was with rage yblent,°   *blinded*
    And would have slaine them in his furious ire,
45 But hardly was restreinéd of that aged sire.

6

    Returning to his bed in torment great,
    And bitter anguish of his guiltie sight,
    He could not rest, but did his stout heart eat,
    And wast his inward gall with deepe despight,
50   Yrkesome of life, and too long lingring night.
    At last faire Hesperus[3] in highest skie
    Had spent his lampe, and brought forth dawning light
    Then up he rose, and clad him hastily;
    The Dwarfe him brought his steed: so both away do fly.[4]

7

55 Now when the rosy-fingred Morning faire,
    Weary of aged Tithones[5] saffron bed,

3. The evening star.
4. Reason and discrimination are defeated, and so "Holiness" is separated
from the one true faith.
5. The husband of Aurora, goddess of
the dawn.

Had spred her purple robe through deawy aire,
And the high hils Titan° discoveréd,   *the sun*
The royall virgin shooke off drowsy-hed,
60   And rising forth out of her baser° bowre,   *humbler*
Lookt for her knight, who far away was fled,
And for her Dwarfe, that wont to wait each houre;
Then gan she waile and weepe, to see that woefull stowre.°   *affliction*

8

And after him she rode with so much speede
65   As her slow beast could make; but all in vaine:
For him so far had borne his light-foot steede,
Prickéd with wrath and fiery fierce disdaine,
That him to follow was but fruitlesse paine;
Yet she her weary limbes would never rest,
70   But every hill and dale, each wood and plaine
Did search, sore grievéd in her gentle brest,
He so ungently left her, whom she lovéd best.

9

But subtill Archimago, when his guests
He saw divided into double parts,
75   And Una wandring in woods and forrests,
Th' end of his drift, he praisd his divelish arts
That had such might over true meaning harts;
Yet rests not so, but other meanes doth make,
How he may worke unto her further smarts:
80   For her he hated as the hissing snake,
And in her many troubles did most pleasure take.

10

He then devisde himselfe how to disguise;
For by his mightie science° he could take   *knowledge*
As many formes and shapes in seeming wise,
85   As ever Proteus to himselfe could make:
Sometime a fowle, sometime a fish in lake,
Now like a foxe, now like a dragon fell,°   *fierce*
That of himselfe he oft for feare would quake,
And oft would flie away. O who can tell
90   The hidden power of herbes, and might of Magicke spell?

11

But now seemde best, the person to put on
Of that good knight, his late beguiléd guest:
In mighty armes he was yclad anon,
And silver shield: upon his coward brest
95   A bloudy crosse, and on his craven crest
A bounch of haires discolourd diversly:
Full jolly knight he seemde, and well addrest,
And when he sate upon his courser free,
Saint George himself ye would have deeméd him to be.[6]

6. Archimago, in disguising himself as Holiness, takes on the role of the Anti-Christ.

12

But he the knight, whose semblaunt° he did beare,   *likness*
   The true Saint George was wandred far away,
   Still flying from his thoughts and gealous feare;
   Will was his guide,[7] and griefe led him astray.
   At last him chaunst to meete upon the way
   A faithlesse Sarazin° all armed to point,   *Saracen*
   In whose great shield was writ with letters gay
Sans foy:[8] full large of limbe and every joint
He was, and caréd not for God or man a point.

13

He had a faire companion of his way,
   A goodly Lady clad in scarlot red,
   Purfled° with gold and pearle of rich assay,   *decorated*
   And like a Persian mitre on her hed
   She wore, with crownes and owches° garnishéd,   *brooches*
   The which her lavish lovers to her gave;
   Her wanton palfrey all was overspred
With tinsell trappings, woven like a wave,
Whose bridle rung with golden bels and bosses brave.

14

With faire disport° and courting dalliaunce   *diversion*
   She intertainde her lover all the way:
   But when she saw the knight his speare advaunce,
   She soone left off her mirth and wanton play,
   And bad her knight addresse him to the fray:
   His foe was nigh at hand. He prickt° with pride   *pranced*
   And hope to winne his Ladies heart that day,
   Forth spurréd fast: adowne his coursers side
The red bloud trickling staind the way, as he did ride.

15

The knight of the Redcrosse when him he spide,
   Spurring so hote with rage dispiteous,
   Gan fairely couch° his speare, and towards ride: *lower*
   Soone meete they both, both fell and furious,
   That daunted with their forces hideous,
   Their steeds do stagger, and amazéd stand,
   And eke themselves too rudely rigorous,
   Astonied° with the stroke of their owne hand,   *stunned*
Do backe rebut,° and each to other yeeldeth land.   *recoil*

16

As when two rams stird with ambitious pride,
   Fight for the rule of the rich fleecéd flocke,
   Their hornéd fronts so fierce on either side
   Do meete, that with the terrour of the shocke

---

7. Will was his guide; but will, of all the human faculties, is least fitted to be one's guide; it should itself be under the guidance of intelligence or truth.
8. Redcrosse's victory over the monster Errour did not give him the discrimination to pierce the deceptions of either Archimago or the false Una. His second trial will be against Sans foy—"without faith," atheism.

140   Astonied both, stand sencelesse as a blocke,
          Forgetfull of the hanging victory:
          So stood these twaine, unmovéd as a rocke,
          Both staring fierce, and holding idely
    The broken reliques of their former cruelty.

                 17

145 The Sarazin sore daunted with the buffe
          Snatcheth his sword, and fiercely to him flies;
          Who well it wards, and quyteth° cuff with cuff: *requites*
          Each others equall puissaunce envies,
          And through their iron sides with cruell spies°   *looks*
150   Does seeke to perce: repining courage yields
          No foote to foe. The flashing fier flies
          As from a forge out of their burning shields,
    And streames of purple bloud new dies the verdant fields.

                 18

    "Curse on that Crosse," quoth then the Sarazin,
155   "That keepes thy body from the bitter fit;°   *stroke*
          Dead long ygoe I wote thou haddest bin,
          Had not that charme from thee forwarnéd it:
          But yet I warne thee now assuréd sitt,
          And hide thy head." Therewith upon his crest
160   With rigour so outrageous he smitt,
          That a large share it hewd out of the rest,
    And glauncing downe his shield, from blame him fairely blest.[9]

                 19

    Who thereat wondrous wroth, the sleeping spark
          Of native vertue gan eftsoones revive,
165   And at his haughtie helmet making mark,
          So hugely stroke, that it the steele did rive,
          And cleft his head. He tumbling downe alive,
          With bloudy mouth his mother earth did kis,
          Greeting his grave: his grudging ghost did strive
170   With the fraile flesh; at last it flitted is,
    Whither the soules do fly of men, that live amis.

                 20

    The Lady when she saw her champion fall,
          Like the old ruines of a broken towre,
          Staid not to waile his woefull funerall,
175   But from him fled away with all her powre;
          Who after her as hastily gan scowre,°   *scurry*
          Bidding the Dwarfe with him to bring away
          The Sarazins shield, signe of the conqueroure.
          Her soone he overtooke, and bad to stay,
180 For present cause was none of dread her to dismay.

                 21

    She turning backe with ruefull countenaunce,
          Cride, "Mercy mercy Sir vouchsafe to show
          On silly° Dame, subject to hard mischaunce,   *innocent*

9. Preserved him from harm.

And to your mighty will." Her humblesse low
185 In so ritch weedes and seeming glorious show,
Did much emmove his stout heroicke heart,
And said, "Deare dame, your suddein overthrow
Much rueth° me; but now put feare apart,   *grieves*
And tell, both who ye be, and who that tooke your part."

22

190 Melting in teares, then gan she thus lament;
"The wretched woman, whom unhappy howre
Hath now made thrall to your commandément,
Before that angry heavens list to lowre,
And fortune false betraide me to your powre
195 Was (O what now availeth that I was!)
Borne the sole daughter of an Emperour,
He that the wide West under his rule has,
And high hath set his throne, where Tiberis doth pas.[1]

23

"He in the first flowre of my freshest age,
200 Betrothéd me unto the onely haire°   *heir*
Of a most mighty king, most rich and sage;
Was never Prince so faithfull and so faire,
Was never Prince so meeke and debonaire;°   *gracious*
But ere my hopéd day of spousall shone,
205 My dearest Lord fell from high honours staire,
Into the hands of his accursed fone,°   *foes*
And cruelly was slaine, that shall I ever mone.

24

"His blessed body spoild of lively breath,
Was afterward, I know not how, convaid
210 And fro me hid: of whose most innocent death
When tidings came to me unhappy maid,
O how great sorrow my sad soule assaid.°   *afflicted*
Then forth I went his woefull corse to find,
And many yeares throughout the world I straid,

1. The Tiber River runs through Rome. The lady's admission that she is the daughter of Rome (and hence the Roman Catholic Church) is an immediate clue to the fact that she is evil. Her appearance, as described in stanza 13, was, however, also full of clues. She resembles the Whore of Babylon (Revelation xvii.3–4): "and I saw a woman sit upon a scarlet coloured beast, full of names of blasphemy, having seven heads and ten horns. And the woman was arrayed in purple and scarlet colour, and decked with gold and precious stones and pearls, having a golden cup in her hand full of abominations and filthiness of her fornication." Her father, she says, is ruler of the West—but Una's father had the rule of both East *and* West (I.i.5): on the historical plane, the true church once embraced east and west whereas the false rules only the west; truth is universal and comprehends falsehood, which is partial. As the false church, she wears the pope's miter. The Roman church is an embodiment of villainy and evil in *The Faerie Queene* because this was a time of violent Protestant-Catholic controversy in both Europe and England, which had led to exchanges of Protestant and Catholic monarchs, bloodshed, and burnings; England had only recently emerged from its own religious strife. Popular fear of Catholicism was very real, and Spenser draws partly on the "bogey" images of this fear in erecting his figures of evil.

215 A virgin widow, whose deepe wounded mind
With love, long time did languish as the striken hind.[2]

25

"At last it chauncéd this proud Sarazin
    To meete me wandring, who perforce me led
    With him away, but yet could never win
220 The fort, that Ladies hold in soveraigne dread.
    There lies he now with foule dishonour dead,
    Who whiles he livde, was calléd proud Sans foy,
    The eldest of three brethren, all three bred
    Of one bad sire, whose youngest is Sans joy,
225 And twixt them both was borne the bloudy bold Sans loy.[3]

26

"In this sad plight, friendlesse, unfortunate,
    Now miserable I Fidessa dwell,
    Craving of you in pitty of my state,
    To do none° ill, if please ye not do well."   *no*
230 He in great passion all this while did dwell,
    More busying his quicke eyes, her face to view,
    Then his dull eares, to heare what she did tell;
    And said, "Faire Lady hart of flint would rew
The undeservéd woes and sorrowes, which ye shew.

27

235 "Henceforth in safe assuraunce may ye rest,
    Having both found a new friend you to aid,
    And lost an old foe, that did you molest:
    Better new friend than an old foe is[4] said."
    With chaunge of cheare the seeming simple maid
240 Let fall her eyen, as shamefast to the earth,
    And yeelding soft, in that she nought gain-said,
    So forth they rode, he feining seemely merth,
And she coy lookes: so dainty they say maketh derth.[5]

28

Long time they thus together traveiléd,
245 Till weary of their way, they came at last,
    Where grew two goodly trees, that faire did spred
    Their armes abroad, with gray mosse overcast,
    And their greene leaves trembling with every blast,°   *breeze*
    Made a calme shadow far in compasse round:

2. Her story is full of lies, inasmuch as she is not a "virgin widow," while Christ, the "Prince," is not "hid"; she is unaware that he has risen from the dead.
3. Literally, "without law." Sans foy means "without faith"; Sans joy, "without joy." *The Faerie Queene* is full of characters who come in sets—opposing principles or double and triple incarnations of the same principle. Una and this lady (falsely named Fidessa, or "faith"), for example, are in opposition; the three Saracens form a triad of degenerative qualities that Holiness must defeat. For Holiness, even untried, to defeat atheism ("without faith") was comparatively easy.
4. I.e., it is.
5. Proverbial: "what's dear is rare." Here, "coyness creates unsatisfied desire." Redcrosse is unaware of the falsehoods in the lady's story—as England was seduced again to the false church during the reign of Mary.

250 The fearefull Shepheard often there aghast
    Under them never sat, ne wont there sound
His mery oaten pipe, but shund th' unlucky ground.

29

But this good knight soone as he them can spie,
    For the coole shade him thither hastly got:
255   For golden Phoebus now ymounted hie,
    From fiery wheeles of his faire chariot
    Hurléd his beame so scorching cruell hot,
    That living creature mote it not abide;
    And his new Lady it enduréd not.
260   There they alight, in hope themselves to hide
From the fierce heat, and rest their weary limbs a tide.°   *time*

30

Faire seemely pleasaunce each to other makes,
    With goodly purposes there as they sit:
    And in his falséd fancy he her takes
265   To be the fairest wight that livéd yit;
    Which to expresse, he bends his gentle wit,
    And thinking of those braunches greene to frame
    A girlond for her dainty forehead fit,
    He pluckt a bough; out of whose rift there came
270 Small drops of gory bloud, that trickled downe the same.

31

Therewith a piteous yelling voyce was heard,
    Crying, "O spare with guilty hands to teare
    My tender sides in this rough rynd embard,°   *imprisoned*
    But fly, ah fly far hence away, for feare
275   Least to you hap, that happened to me heare,
    And to this wretched Lady, my deare love,
    O too deare love, love bought with death too deare."
    Astond he stood, and up his haire did hove°   *heave, raise*
And with that suddein horror could no member move.

32

280 At last whenas the dreadfull passion
    Was overpast, and manhood well awake,
    Yet musing at the straunge occasion,
    And doubting much his sence, he thus bespake;
    "What voyce of damnéd Ghost from Limbo[6] lake,
285   Or guilefull spright wandring in empty aire,
    Both which fraile men do oftentimes mistake,°   *mislead*
    Sends to my doubtfull eares these speaches rare,
And ruefull plaints, me bidding guiltlesse bloud to spare?"

33

Then groning deepe, "Nor damned Ghost," quoth he,
290   "Nor guilefull sprite to thee these wordes doth speake,
    But once a man Fradubio,° now a tree,   *Doubt*
    Wretched man, wretched tree; whose nature weake,

---

6. The abode of lost spirits.

A cruell witch her curséd will to wreake,
Hath thus transformed, and plast in open plaines,
295   Where Boreas° doth blow full bitter bleake,   *the North Wind*
And scorching Sunne does dry my secret vaines:
For though a tree I seeme, yet cold and heat me paines."

34

"Say on Fradubio then, or° man, or tree,"   *whether*
Quoth then the knight, "by whose mischievous arts
300   Art thou misshapéd thus, as now I see?
He oft finds med'cine, who his griefe imparts;
But double griefs afflict concealing harts,
As raging flames who striveth to suppresse."
"The author then," said he, "of all my smarts,
305   Is one Duessa[7] a false sorceresse,
That many errant° knights hath brought to wretchednesse. *wandering*

35

"In prime of youthly yeares, when corage hot
The fire of love and joy of chevalree
First kindled in my brest, it was my lot
310   To love this gentle Lady, whom ye see,
Now not a Lady, but a seeming tree;
With whom as once I rode accompanyde,
Me chauncéd of a knight encountred bee,
That had a like faire Lady by his syde,
315 Like a faire Lady, but did fowle Duessa hyde.

36

"Whose forgéd beauty he did take in hand,[8]
All other Dames to have exceeded farre;
I in defence of mine did likewise stand,
Mine, that did then shine as the Morning starre:
320   So both to battell fierce arraungéd arre,
In which his harder fortune was to fall
Under my speare: such is the dye° of warre: *hazard*
His Lady left as a prise martiall,[9]
Did yield her comely person, to be at my call.

37

325 "So doubly loved of Ladies unlike faire,
Th' one seeming such, the other such indeede,
One day in doubt I cast for to compare,
Whether° in beauties glorie did exceede;   *which one (of two)*
A Rosy girlond was the victors meede:°   *reward*
330   Both seemde to win, and both seemde won to bee,
So hard the discord was to be agreede.
Fraelissa° was as faire, as faire mote bee,   *Frailty*
And ever false Duessa seemde as faire as shee.

38

"The wicked witch now seeing all this while
335   The doubtfull ballaunce equally to sway,

---

7. Duessa means "two," of double na-   8. He maintained.
ture.   9. Spoil of battle.

What not by right, she cast to win by guile,
And by her hellish science raisd streight way
A foggy mist, that overcast the day,
And a dull blast, that breathing on her face,
340   Dimmed her former beauties shining ray,
And with foule ugly forme did her disgrace:
Then was she faire alone, when none was faire in place.[1]

39

"Then cride she out, 'Fye, fye, deforméd wight,
Whose borrowed beautie now appeareth plaine
345   To have before bewitchéd all mens sight;
O leave her soone, or let her soone be slaine.'
Her lothly visage viewing with disdaine,
Eftsoones I thought her such, as she me told,
And would have kild her; but with faignéd paine,
350   The false witch did my wrathfull hand withhold;
So left her, where she now is turnd to trëen mould.[2]

40

"Thens forth I tooke Duessa for my Dame,
And in the witch unweeting° joyd long time,   *unknowingly*
Ne ever wist, but that she was the same,
355   Till on a day (that day is every Prime,[3]
When Witches wont do penance for their crime)
I chaunst to see her in her proper hew,
Bathing her selfe in origane and thyme:[4]
A filthy foule old woman I did vew,
360   That ever to have toucht her, I did deadly rew.

41

"Her neather partes misshapen, monstruous,
Were hidd in water, that I could not see,
But they did seeme more foule and hideous,
Then womans shape man would beleeve to bee.
365   Thens forth from her most beastly companie
I gan refraine, in minde to slip away,
Soone as appeard safe opportunitie:
For danger great, if not assured decay°   *destruction*
I saw before mine eyes, if I were knowne to stray.

42

370   "The divelish hag by chaunges of my cheare°   *countenance*
Perceived my thought, and drownd in sleepie night,
With wicked herbes and ointments did besmeare
My bodie all, through charmes and magicke might,
That all my senses were bereavéd quight:
375   Then brought she me into this desert waste,
And by my wretched lovers side me pight,°   *pitched*
Where now enclosd in wooden wals full faste,
Banisht from living wights, our wearie dayes we waste."

1. Perhaps, "when nobody else was fair."
2. The form of a tree.
3. The first appearance of the new moon.
4. Two kinds of herbs; they were associated, in classical tradition, with witches like Scylla, Circe, and Medea.

43

"But how long time," said then the Elfin knight,
380   "Are you in this misforméd house to dwell?"
    "We may not chaunge," quoth he, "this evil plight,
    Till we be bathéd in a living well;
    That is the terme prescribéd by the spell."
    "O how," said he, "mote I that well out find,
385   That may restore you to your wonted well?"°   *well-being*
    "Time and sufficéd fates to former kynd
Shall us restore, none else from hence may us unbynd."[5]

44

The false Duessa, now Fidessa hight,°   *called*
    Heard how in vaine Fradubio did lament,
390   And knew well all was true. But the good knight
    Full of sad feare and ghastly dreriment,°   *gloom*
    When all this speech the living tree had spent,
    The bleeding bough did thrust into the ground,
    That from the bloud he might be innocent,
395   And with fresh clay did close the wooden wound:
Then turning to his Lady, dead with feare her found.

45

Her seeming dead he found with feignéd feare,
    As all unweeting of that well she knew,[6]
    And paynd himselfe with busie care to reare
400   Her out of carelesse° swowne. Her eylids blew   *unconscious*
    And dimméd sight with pale and deadly hew
    At last she up gan lift: with trembling cheare
    Her up he tooke, too simple and too trew,
    And oft her kist. At length all passéd feare,[7]
405 He set her on her steede, and forward forth did beare.

Canto III

Forsaken Truth long seekes her love,
    And makes the Lyon mylde,
Marres° blind Devotions mart,° and fals   *spoils / business*
    In hand of leachour vylde.

1

Nought is there under heav'ns wide hollownesse,
    That moves more deare compassion of mind,

5. The tale of a man imprisoned in a tree is paralleled by Virgil's *Aeneid* III. 27–42 and Ariosto's *Orlando Furioso* VI.26–53. His hesitation between Fraelissa and Duessa parallels Redcrosse's own spiritual state between Una and Duessa (the real name of "Fidessa," as line 388 casually informs us). The very name "Duessa" (two) reveals her falsity next to Una ("one"). Note that Fra-dubio ("father doubt") cannot warn Redcrosse against Duessa, who is present at the whole recital: doubt is not, perhaps, a trustworthy help to Holiness. Doubt and frailty can only be helped by baptism (lines 381–82).
6. I.e., pretending ignorance of what she knew well.
7. I.e., having passed all fear.

Then beautie brought t'unworthy° wretchednesse   *undeserved*
Through envies snares or fortunes freakes unkind:
5   I, whether lately through her brightnesse blind,
Or through alleageance and fast fealtie,
Which I do owe unto all woman kind,
Feele my heart perst° with so great agonie,   *pierced*
When such I see, that all for pittie I could die.

2

10   And now it is empassionéd so deepe,
For fairest Unas sake, of whom I sing,
That my fraile eyes these lines with teares do steepe,
To thinke how she through guilefull handeling,
Though true as touch,° though daughter of a king,   *touchstone*
15   Though faire as ever living wight was faire,
Though nor in word nor deede ill meriting,
Is from her knight divorcéd in despaire
And her due loves derivéd° to that vile witches share.   *diverted*

3

Yet she most faithfull Ladie all this while
20   Forsaken, wofull, solitarie mayd
Farre from all peoples prease,° as in exile,   *press, crowd*
In wildernesse and wastfull deserts strayd,
To seeke her knight; who subtilly betrayd
Through that late vision, which th' Enchaunter wrought,
25   Had her abandond. She of nought affrayd,
Through woods and wastnesse wide him daily sought;
Yet wishéd tydings none of him unto her brought.

4

One day nigh wearie of the yrkesome way,
From her unhastie beast she did alight,
30   And on the grasse her daintie limbes did lay
In secret shadow,° farre from all mens sight: *shade*
From her faire head her fillet she undight,[8]
And laid her stole aside. Her angels face
As the great eye of heaven shynéd bright,
35   And made a sunshine in the shadie place;
Did never mortall eye behold such heavenly grace.

5

It fortunéd out of the thickest wood
A ramping Lyon rushéd suddainly,
Hunting full greedie after salvage blood;[9]
40   Soone as the royall virgin he did spy,
With gaping mouth at her ran greedily,
To have attonce devoured her tender corse:
But to the pray when as he drew more ny,
His bloudie rage asswagéd with remorse,
45   And with the sight amazd, forgat his furious forse.

---

8. She took off her headband.   9. Wild game.

6

In stead thereof he kist her wearie feet,
  And lickt her lilly hands with fawning tong,
  As[1] he her wrongéd innocence did weet.° understand
  O how can beautie maister the most strong,
50 And simple truth subdue avenging wrong?
  Whose yeelded pride and proud submission,
  Still dreading death, when she had markéd long,
  Her hart gan melt in great compassion,
And drizling teares did shed for pure affection.

7

55 "The Lyon Lord of everie beast in field,"
  Quoth she, "his princely puissance° doth abate power
  And mightie proud to humble weake does yield,
  Forgetfull of the hungry rage, which late
  Him prickt, in pittie of my sad estate:° condition
60 But he my Lyon, and my noble Lord,
  How does he find in cruell hart to hate
  Her that him loved, and ever most adord,
As the God of my life? why hath he me abhord?"

8

Redounding teares did choke th'end of her plaint,
65 Which softly ecchoed from the neighbour wood;
  And sad to see her sorrowfull constraint° affliction
  The kingly beast upon her gazing stood;
  With pittie calmd, downe fell his angry mood.
  At last in close hart shutting up her paine,
70 Arose the virgin borne of heavenly brood,° parentage
  And to her snowy Palfrey got againe,
To seeke her strayéd Champion, if she might attaine.° overtake

9

The Lyon would not leave her desolate,
  But with her went along, as a strong gard
75 Of her chast person, and a faithfull mate
  Of her sad troubles and misfortunes hard:
  Still when she slept, he kept both watch and ward,
  And when she wakt, he waited diligent,
  With humble service to her will prepard:
80 From her faire eyes he tooke commaundement,
And ever by her lookes conceivéd her intent.[2]

10

Long she thus traveiléd through deserts wyde,
  By which she thought her wandring knight shold pas,
  Yet never shew of living wight espyde;
85 Till that at length she found the troden gras,

1. As though.
2. Whereas Redcrosse, the man, has confusedly abandoned truth, the lion, king of beasts, an animal under nature's law, follows truth instinctively. Lions revere the heroine in the romance *Sir Bevis of Hamptoun* and accompany the heroes of other medieval romances; they have long been associated with the British crown.

In which the tract° of peoples footing was,   *track*
    Under the steepe foot of a mountaine hore;°   *gray*
    The same she followes, till at last she has
    A damzell spyde slow footing her before,
90 That on her shoulders sad° a pot of water bore.   *heavy*

11

To whom approching she to her gan call,
    To weet, if dwelling place were nigh at hand;
    But the rude° wench her answered nought at all,   *ignorant*
    She could not heare, nor speake, nor understand;
95 Till seeing by her side the Lyon stand,
    With suddaine feare her pitcher downe she threw,
    And fled away: for never in that land
    Face of faire Ladie she before did vew,
And that dread Lyons looke her cast in deadly° hew.   *deathlike*

12

100 Full fast she fled, ne ever lookt behynd,
    As if her life upon the wager lay,
    And home she came, whereas her mother blynd
    Sate in eternall night: nought could she say,
    But suddaine catching hold, did her dismay
105 With quaking hands, and other signes of feare:
    Who full of ghastly fright and cold affray,
    Gan shut the dore. By this arrivéd there
Dame Una, wearie Dame, and entrance did requere.°   *request*

13

Which when none yeelded, her unruly Page
110 With his rude clawes the wicket° open rent,   *door*
    And let her in; where of his cruell rage
    Nigh dead with feare, and faint astonishment,
    She found them both in darkesome corner pent;°   *huddled*
    Where that old woman day and night did pray
115 Upon her beades devoutly penitent;
    Nine hundred *Pater nosters* every day,
And thrise nine hundred *Aves* she was wont to say.[3]

14

And to augment her painefull pennance more,
    Thrise every weeke in ashes she did sit,
120 And next her wrinkled skin rough sackcloth wore,
    And thrise three times did fast from any bit:°   *food*
    But now for feare her beads she did forget.
    Whose needlesse dread for to remove away,
    Faire Una framéd words and count'nance fit:
125 Which hardly doen, at length she gan them pray,
That in their cotage small, that night she rest her may.

3. "Them both" will be named in line 157. The old lady's name, Corceca, means "blind devotion." The (obviously Catholic) prayers that the two mouthe are motivated by fear, not faith. Her daughter's name, "Abessa," suggests the monastic orders (i.e., "abbess") and (from *ab esse*, "non-being," "withdrawal") that she is superstition. Her timorous reaction to the Lyon was typically excessive, and her pitcher of water was perhaps emblematic of her fickle state.

15

The day is spent, and commeth drowsie night,
  When every creature shrowded is in sleepe;
  Sad Una downe her laies in wearie plight,
130   And at her feet the Lyon watch doth keepe:
  In stead of rest, she does lament, and weepe
  For the late losse of her deare lovéd knight,
  And sighes, and grones, and evermore does steepe
  Her tender brest in bitter teares all night,
135 All night she thinks too long, and often lookes for light.

16

Now when Aldeboran was mounted hie
Above the shynie Cassiopeias chaire,[4]
  And all in deadly sleepe did drownéd lie,
  One knockéd at the dore, and in would fare;
140   He knockéd fast,° and often curst, and sware,   *insistently*
  That readie entrance was not at his call:
  For on his backe a heavy load he bare
  Of nightly stelths and pillage severall,
Which he had got abroad by purchase° criminall.   *acquisition*

17

145 He was to weete[5] a stout and sturdie thiefe,
  Wont to robbe Churches of their ornaments,
  And poore mens boxes[6] of their due reliefe,
  Which given was to them for good intents;
  The holy Saints of their rich vestments
150   He did disrobe, when all men carelesse slept,
  And spoild the Priests of their habiliments,°   *vestments*
  Whiles none the holy things in safety kept;
Then he by cunning sleights in at the window crept.

18

And all that he by right or wrong could find,
155   Unto this house he brought, and did bestow
  Upon the daughter of this woman blind,
  Abessa daughter of Corceca slow,
  With whom he whoredome usd, that few did know,
  And fed her fat with feast of offerings,
160   And plentie, which in all the land did grow;
  Ne sparéd he to give her gold and rings:
And now he to her brought part of his stolen things.

19

Thus long the dore with rage and threats he bet,°   *beat*
  Yet of those fearefull women none durst rize,
165   The Lyon frayéd° them, him in to let: *terrify*
  He would no longer stay him to advize,
  But open breakes the dore in furious wize,

---

4. Aldebaran, in the constellation Taurus, mounts over the constellation Cassiopeia.
5. In fact.

6. A box for alms for the poor, especially one placed near the door of a church.

And entring is; when that disdainfull beast
Encountring fierce, him suddaine doth surprize,
170 And seizing° cruell clawes on trembling brest,   *fastening*
Under his Lordly foot him proudly hath supprest.[7]

20

Him booteth not resist,[8] nor succour call,
His bleeding hart is in the vengers hand,
Who streight him rent in thousand peeces small,
175 And quite dismembred hath: the thirstie land
Drunke up his life; his corse left on the strand.°   *ground*
His fearefull friends weare out the wofull night,
Ne dare to weepe, nor seeme to understand
The heavie hap,° which on them is alight,   *lot*
180 Affraid, least to themselves the like mishappen might.

21

Now when broad day the world discovered° has,   *revealed*
Up Una rose, up rose the Lyon eke,
And on their former journey forward pas,
In wayes unknowne, her wandring knight to seeke,
185 With paines farre passing that long wandring Greeke,
That for his love refuséd deitie;[9]
Such were the labours of this Lady meeke,
Still seeking him, that from her still did flie,
Then furthest from her hope, when most she weenéd nie.[1]

22

190 Soone as she parted thence, the fearefull twaine,
That blind old woman and her daughter deare
Came forth, and finding Kirkrapine there slaine,
For anguish great they gan to rend their heare,
And beat their brests, and naked flesh to teare.
195 And when they both had wept and wayld their fill,
Then forth they ranne like two amazéd deare,
Halfe mad through malice, and revenging will,[2]
To follow her, that was the causer of their ill.

23

Whom overtaking, they gan loudly bray,
200 With hollow howling, and lamenting cry,
Shamefully at her rayling all the way,
And her accusing of dishonesty,°   *unchastity*
That was the flowre of faith and chastity;
And still amidst her rayling, she[3] did pray,
205 That plagues, and mischiefs, and long misery

7. The thief is named Kirkrapine (in line 192), which means "church robbery." That he brings illgotten gains to the house of superstition may represent the accumulation of the monastic estates and their sheltering under the privileges of the Roman church. By this interpretation, the lion becomes Henry VIII, who expropriated the monasteries.
8. It does no good to resist.
9. Odysseus, who renounced immortality and the love of the nymph Calypso for his wife Penelope.
1. Believed near.
2. Desire of revenge.
3. I.e., Corceca.

Might fall on her, and follow all the way,
And that in endlesse error° she might ever stray.   *wandering*

24

But when she saw her prayers nought prevaile,
    She backe returnéd with some labour lost;
210   And in the way as she did weepe and waile,
    A knight her met in mighty armes embost,°   *encased*
    Yet knight was not for all his bragging bost,
    But subtill Archimag, that Una sought
    By traynes° into new troubles to have tost: *tricks*
215   Of that old woman tydings he besought,
If that of such a Ladie she could tellen ought.

25

Therewith she gan her passion to renew,
    And cry, and curse, and raile, and rend her heare,
    Saying, that harlot she too lately knew,
220   That causd her shed so many a bitter teare,
    And so forth told the story of her feare:
    Much seeméd he to mone her haplesse chaunce,
    And after for that Ladie did inquere;
    Which being taught, he forward gan advaunce
225 His fair enchaunted steed, and eke his charméd launce.

26

Ere long he came, where Una traveild slow,
    And that wilde Champion wayting° her besyde: *attending*
    Whom seeing such, for dread he durst not show
    Himselfe too nigh at hand, but turnéd wyde
230   Unto an hill; from whence when she him spyde,
    By his like seeming shield, her knight by name
    She weend it was, and towards him gan ryde:
    Approching nigh, she wist° it was the same,   *believed*
And with faire fearefull humblesse towards him shee came.

27

235 And weeping said, "Ah my long lackéd Lord,
    Where have ye bene thus long out of my sight?
    Much fearéd I to have bene quite abhord,
    Or ought° have done, that ye displeasen might,   *aught*
    That should as death unto my deare hart light:[4]
240   For since mine eye your joyous sight did mis,
    My chearefull day is turnd to chearelesse night,
    And eke my night of death the shadow is;
But welcome now my light, and shining lampe of blis."

28

He thereto meeting[5] said, "My dearest Dame,
245   Farre be it from your thought, and fro my will,
    To thinke that knighthood I so much should shame,
    As you to leave, that have me lovéd still,
    And chose in Faery court of meere° goodwill,   *pure*
    Where noblest knights were to be found on earth:

4. I.e., be as a death-blow to my sad   5. Answering in like manner.
heart.

250 　The earth shall sooner leave her kindly° skill 　　　　　*natural*
　　　To bring forth fruit, and make eternall derth,° 　　　　*desert*
　　Then I leave you, my liefe, yborne of heavenly berth.

29

　　"And sooth to say, why I left you so long,
　　　Was for to seeke adventure in strange place,
255 　Where Archimago said a felon strong
　　　To many knights did daily worke disgrace;
　　　But knight he now shall never more deface:
　　　Good cause of mine excuse; that mote° ye please 　　　*may*
　　　Well to accept, and evermore embrace
260 　My faithfull service, that by land and seas
　　Have vowd you to defend, now then your plaint appease."

30

　　His lovely° words her seemd due recompence 　　　　　*loving*
　　　Of all her passéd paines: one loving howre
　　　For many yeares of sorrow can dispence:° 　　　　*make amends*
265 　A dram of sweet is worth a pound of sowre:
　　　She has forgot, how many a wofull stowre° 　　　　*trouble*
　　　For him she late endured; she speakes no more
　　　Of past: true is, that true love hath no powre
　　　To looken backe; his eyes be fixt before.
270 Before her stands her knight, for whom she toyld so sore.

31

　　Much like, as when the beaten marinere,
　　　That long hath wandred in the Ocean wide,
　　　Oft soust° in swelling Tethys[6] saltish teare, 　　　　*soaked*
　　　And long time having tand his tawney hide
275 　With blustring breath of heaven, that none can bide,
　　　And scorching flames of fierce Orions hound,[7]
　　　Soone as the port from farre he has espide,
　　　His chearefull whistle merrily doth sound,
　　And Nereus crownes with cups;[8] his mates him
　　　　pledg° around. 　　　　　　　　　　　　*toast*

32

280 　Such joy made Una, when her knight she found;
　　　And eke th'enchaunter joyous seemd no lesse,
　　　Then the glad marchant, that does vew from ground.
　　　His ship farre come from watrie wildernesse,
　　　He hurles out vowes, and Neptune oft doth blesse:
285 　So forth they past, and all the way they spent
　　　Discoursing of her dreadfull late distresse,
　　　In which he askt her, what the Lyon ment:
　　Who told her all that fell° in journey as she went. 　　*befell*

33

　　They had not ridden farre, when they might see
290 　One pricking towards them with hastie heat,

---

6. The wife of Ocean; here, Ocean.
7. Sirius, the dog star, symbolizing hot weather (the "dog days").
8. Nereus is god of the Mediterranean, to whom the mariner in gratitude makes libations.

Full strongly armd, and on a courser free,
That through his fiercenesse fomed all with sweat,
And the sharpe yron° did for anger eat,   bit
  When his hot ryder spurd his chaufféd° side;   heated
295 His looke was sterne, and seeméd still to threat
  Cruell revenge, which he in hart did hyde,
And on his shield Sans loy[9] in bloudie lines was dyde.

34

When nigh he drew unto this gentle payre
  And saw the Red-crosse, which the knight did beare,
300 He burnt in fire, and gan eftsoones prepare
  Himselfe to battell with his couchéd speare.
  Loth was that other, and did faint through feare,
  To taste th'untryed dint of deadly steele;
  But yet his Lady did so well him cheare,
305 That hope of new good hap he gan to feele;
So bent° his speare, and spurnd his horse with yron heele.   lowered

35

But that proud Paynim° forward came so fierce,   pagan
  And full of wrath, that with his sharp-head speare
  Through vainely crosséd shield[1] he quite did pierce,
310 And had his staggering steede not shrunke for feare,
  Through shield and bodie eke he should him beare:°   thrust
  Yet so great was the puissance of his push,
  That from his saddle quite he did him beare:
  He tombling rudely downe to ground did rush,
315 And from his goréd wound a well of bloud did gush.[2]

36

Dismounting lightly from his loftie steed,
  He to him lept, in mind to reave° his life,   take
  And proudly said, "Lo there the worthie meed
  Of him, that slew Sans foy with bloudie knife;
320 Henceforth his ghost freed from repining strife,
  In peace may passen over Lethe[3] lake,
  When mourning altars purgd° with enemies life,   cleansed
  The blacke infernall Furies[4] doen aslake:°   appease
Life from Sans foy thou tookst, Sans loy shall from thee take."

37

325 Therewith in haste his helmet gan unlace,
  Till Una cride, "O hold that heavie hand,
  Deare Sir, what ever that thou be in place:[5]
  Enough is, that thy foe doth vanquisht stand
  Now at thy mercy: Mercie not withstand:

9. The name means "without law." Law here is not, of course, merely state law, but the law of the cosmos, of nature, of civil government, and of man—the law that holds all life, both above the earth and on it, together. Hence "Sans loy" stands for the loss of all order, or chaos.
1. The cross on Archimago's shield was false and did not give him the protection the Redcrosse knight received in his fight with Sans foy; see I.ii.18.
2. This is true poetic justice: lawlessness defeats the devil.
3. A river in Hades whose water when drunk caused forgetfulness.
4. Spirits of discord and revenge.
5. Whoever you are.

330　　For he is one the truest knight alive,
　　　　Though conquered now he lie on lowly land,
　　　　And whilest him fortune favourd, faire did thrive
　　In bloudie field: therefore of life him not deprive."

38

　　Her piteous words might not abate his rage,
335　　But rudely rending up his helmet, would
　　　　Have slaine him straight: but when he sees his age,
　　　　And hoarie head of Archimago old,
　　　　His hastie hand he doth amazéd hold,
　　　　And halfe ashaméd, wondred at the sight:
340　　For the old man well knew he, though untold,
　　　　In charmes and magicke to have wondrous might,
　　Ne ever wont in field, ne in round lists[6] to fight.

39

　　And said, "Why Archimago, lucklesse syre,
　　　　What doe I see? what hard mishap is this,
345　　That hath thee hither brought to taste mine yre?
　　　　Or thine the fault, or mine the error is,
　　　　In stead of foe to wound my friend amis?"
　　　　He answered nought, but in a traunce still lay,
　　　　And on those guilefull dazéd eyes of his
350　　The cloud of death did sit. Which doen away,[7]
　　He left him lying so, ne would no lenger stay.

40

　　But to the virgin comes, who all this while
　　　　Amaséd stands, her selfe so mockt° to see　　　　　　*deceived*
　　　　By him, who has the guerdon° of his guile,　　　　　*reward*
355　　For so misfeigning her true knight to bee:
　　　　Yet is she now in more perplexitie,
　　　　Left in the hand of that same Paynim bold,
　　　　From whom her booteth not at all to flie;
　　　　Who by her cleanly garment catching hold,
360　　Her from her Palfrey pluckt, her visage to behold.

41

　　But her fierce servant full of kingly awe
　　　　And high disdaine, whenas his soveraine Dame
　　　　So rudely handled by her foe he sawe,
　　　　With gaping jawes full greedy at him came,
365　　And ramping on his shield, did weene° the same　　　*intend*
　　　　Have reft away with his sharpe rending clawes
　　　　But he was stout, and lust did now inflame
　　　　His corage more, that from his griping pawes
　　He hath his shield redeemed, and foorth his swerd he drawes.

42

370　　O then too weake and feeble was the forse
　　　　Of salvage beast, his puissance to withstand:
　　　　For he was strong, and of so mightie corse,

6. Enclosures for fighting tournaments.　　7. When he recovered from the swoon.

As ever wielded speare in warlike hand,
And feates of armes did wisely understand.
Eftsoones he perced through his chaufed chest
With thrilling° point of deadly yron brand,°   *penetrating / sword*
And launcht° his Lordly hart: with death opprest   *pierced*
He roared aloud, whiles life forsooke his stubborne brest.[8]

43

Who now is left to keepe the forlorne maid
From raging spoile of lawlesse victors will?
Her faithfull gard removed, her hope dismaid,
Her selfe a yeelded pray to save or spill.°   *destroy*
He now Lord of the field, his pride to fill,
With foule reproches, and disdainfull spight
Her vildly entertaines, and will or nill,
Beares her away upon his courser light:
Her prayers nought prevaile; his rage is more of might.

44

And all the way, with great lamenting paine,
And piteous plaints she filleth his dull° eares,   *deaf*
That stony hart could riven have in twaine,
And all the way she wets with flowing teares:
But he enraged with rancor, nothing heares.
Her servile beast yet would not leave her so,
But followes her farre off, ne ought he feares,
To be partaker of her wandring woe,
More mild in beastly kind,° then that her beastly foe.   *nature*

Canto IV

To sinfull house of Pride, Duessa
guides the faithfull knight,
Where brothers death to wreak° Sansjoy   *avenge*
doth chalenge him to fight.

1

Young knight, what ever that dost armes professe,
And through long labours huntest after fame,
Beware of fraud, beware of ficklenesse,
In choice, and change of thy deare lovéd Dame,
Least thou of her beleeve too lightly blame,
And rash misweening doe thy hart remove:
For unto knight there is no greater shame,
Then lightnesse and inconstancie in love;
That doth this Redcrosse knights ensample° plainly prove.   *example*

2

Who after that he had faire Una lorne,°   *lost*
Through light misdeeming of her loialtie,   *misjudging*
And false Duessa in her sted had borne,

---

8. Nature's law is, perhaps, defenseless against human lawlessness. Sans loy's killing of the lion might also be taken as the momentary triumph of Catholicism under Mary Tudor.

Called Fidess', and so supposd to bee;
Long with her traveild, till at last they see
A goodly building, bravely garnishéd,°   *adorned*
The house of mightie Prince it seemd to bee:
And towards it a broad high way[9] that led,
All bare through peoples feet, which thither traveiléd.

15

3

Great troupes of people traveild thitherward
Both day and night, of each degree and place,°   *rank*
But few returnéd, having scapéd hard,
With balefull beggerie, or foule disgrace,
Which ever after in most wretched case,
Like loathsome lazars,° by the hedges lay.   *lepers*
Thither Duessa bad him bend his pace:
For she is wearie of the toilesome way,
And also nigh consuméd is the lingring day.

20

25

4

A stately Pallace built of squaréd bricke,
Which cunningly was without morter laid,
Whose wals were high, but nothing strong, nor thick,
And golden foile° all over them displaid,   *thin layer*
That purest skye with brightnesse they dismaid°:   *outdid*
High lifted up were many loftie towres,
And goodly galleries farre over laid,[1]
Full of faire windowes, and delightfull bowres;
And on the top a Diall told the timely howres.[2]

30

35

5

It was a goodly heape° for to behould,   *building*
And spake the praises of the workmans wit;
But full great pittie, that so faire a mould°   *structure*
Did on so weake foundation ever sit:
For on a sandie hill, that still did flit,°   *give way*
And fall away, it mounted was full hie,
That every breath of heaven shakéd it:
And all the hinder parts, that few could spie,
Were ruinous and old, but painted cunningly.

40

45

6

Arrivéd there they passéd in forth right;
For still to all the gates stood open wide,
Yet charge of them was to a Porter hight°   *committed*
Cald Malvenù,[3] who entrance none denide:
Thence to the hall, which was on every side
With rich array and costly arras dight:[4]
Infinite sorts of people did abide

50

9. "Broad is the way that leadeth to destruction" (Matthew vii.13).
1. Placed above.
2. The clock ("Diall") is illustrative of the power of time over the life of this world, as it is lived in the House of Pride. This proud elegant castle is remi-niscent of Alcina's palace in *Orlando Furioso* VI.
3. The name means "unwelcome." In courtly-love allegories, the porter is often called "Bienvenu" or "Bel-accueil" ("welcome").
4. Decorated with costly wall hangings.

There waiting long, to win the wishéd sight
Of her, that was the Lady of that Pallace bright.

7

55   By them they passe, all gazing on them round,
    And to the Presence° mount; whose glorious vew   *reception hall*
    Their frayle amazéd senses did confound:
    In living Princes court none ever knew
    Such endlesse richesse, and so sumptuous shew;
60   Ne Persia selfe, the nourse of pompous pride
    Like ever saw. And there a noble crew
    Of Lordes and Ladies stood on every side,
Which with their presence faire, the place much beautifide.

8

High above all a cloth of State[5] was spred,
65   And a rich throne, as bright as sunny day,
    On which there sate most brave embellishéd[6]
    With royall robes and gorgeous array,
    A mayden Queene, that shone as Titans° ray,   *the sun's*
    In glistring gold, and peerelesse pretious stone:
70   Yet her bright blazing beautie did assay°   *attempt*
    To dim the brightnesse of her glorious throne,
As envying her selfe, that too exceeding shone.

9

Exceeding shone, like Phoebus fairest childe,
    That did presume his fathers firie wayne,°   *chariot*
75   And flaming mouthes of steedes unwonted wilde
    Through highest heaven with weaker° hand to rayne;   *too weak*
    Proud of such glory and advancement vaine,
    While flashing beames do daze his feeble eyen,
    He leaves the welkin° way most beaten plaine,   *skyey*
80   And rapt° with whirling wheeles, inflames the skyen,   *carried away*
With fire not made to burne, but fairely for to shyne.[7]

10

So proud she shynéd in her Princely state,°   *throne*
    Looking to heaven; for earth she did disdayne,
    And sitting high; for lowly° she did hate: *lowliness*
85   Lo underneath her scornefull feete, was layne
    A dreadfull Dragon with an hideous trayne,°   *tail*
    And in her hand she held a mirrhour bright,[8]
    Wherein her face she often vewéd fayne,
    And in her selfe-loved semblance tooke delight;
90   For she was wondrous faire, as any living wight.

---

5. Canopy.
6. Handsomely clad.
7. Phaëton tried to drive the chariot of Phoebus, his father, but set the skies on fire and fell, as Lucifer (Satan) fell from heaven. Lucifera (Pride) shines like Phaëton (line 82), which suggests a similar fate. Although her House does not fall, it is seen first as glorious, then for what it really is.
8. Pride, and figures associated with her in Renaissance literature and art, often hold a mirror, emblematic of self-love.

11

Of griesly Pluto she the daughter was,
  And sad Proserpina the Queene of hell;
  Yet did she thinke her pearelesse worth to pas
  That parentage, with pride so did she swell,
95   And thundring Jove, that high in heaven doth dwell,
  And wield° the world, she clayméd for her syre,   *govern*
  Or if that any else did Jove excell:
  For to the highest she did still aspyre,
Or if ought higher were then that, did it desyre.

12

100 And proud Lucifera men did her call,
  That made her selfe a Queene, and crownd to be,
  Yet rightfull kingdome she had none at all,
  Ne heritage of native soveraintie,
  But did usurpe with wrong and tyrannie
105   Upon the scepter, which she now did hold:
  Ne ruld her Realmes with lawes, but pollicie,°   *conspiracy*
  And strong advizement of six wisards old,
That with their counsels bad her kingdome did uphold.

13

Soone as the Elfin knight in presence came,
110   And false Duessa seeming Lady faire,
  A gentle Husher,° Vanitie by name   *usher*
  Made rowme, and passage for them did prepaire:
  So goodly brought them to the lowest staire
  Of her high throne, where they on humble knee
115   Making obeyssance, did the cause declare,
  Why they were come, her royall state to see,
To prove° the wide report of her great Majestee.   *verify*

14

With loftie eyes, halfe loth to looke so low,
  She thankéd them in her disdainefull wise,
120   Ne other grace vouchsaféd them to show
  Of Princesse worthy, scarse them bad arise
  Her Lordes and Ladies all this while devise
  Themselves to setten forth to straungers sight:
  Some frounce° their curléd haire in courtly guise,   *frizzle*
125   Some prancke° their ruffes, and others trimly dight°   *display/adjust*
Their gay attire: each others greater pride does spight.

15

Goodly they all that knight do entertaine,
  Right glad with him to have increast their crew:
  But to Duess' each one himselfe did paine
130   All kindnesse and faire courtesie to shew;
  For in that court whylome° her well they knew: *formerly*
  Yet the stout Faerie mongst the middest° crowd   *thickest*
  Thought all their glorie vaine in knightly vew,
  And that great Princesse too exceeding prowd,
135 That to strange knight no better countenance allowd.

16

Suddein upriseth from her stately place
  The royall Dame, and for her coche doth call:

All hurtlen° forth, and she with Princely pace,   rush
As faire Aurora in her purple pall,°   robe
140   Out of the East the dawning day doth call:
So forth she comes: her brightnesse brode° doth blaze;   abroad
The heapes of people thronging in the hall,
Do ride° each other, upon her to gaze: crowd
Her glorious glitterand° light doth all mens eyes amaze.   glittering

17

145   So forth she comes, and to her coche does clyme,
Adornéd all with gold, and girlonds gay,
That seefnd as fresh as Flora in her prime,
And strove to match, in royall rich array,
Great Junos golden chaire,° the which they say   chariot
150   The Gods stand gazing on, when she does ride
To Joves high house through heavens bras-pavéd way
Drawne of faire Pecocks, that excell in pride,
And full of Argus eyes their tailes dispredden wide.[9]

18

But this was drawne of six unequall beasts,
155   On which her six sage Counsellours did ryde,
Taught to obay their bestiall beheasts,
With like conditions to their kinds applyde:[1]
Of which the first, that all the rest did guyde,
Was sluggish Idlenesse the nourse of sin;
160   Upon a slouthfull Asse he chose to ryde,
Arayd in habit blacke, and amis° thin,   hood, cape
Like to an holy Monck, the service to begin.

19

And in his hand his Portesse° still he bare,   breviary
That much was worne, but therein little red,
165   For of devotion he had little care,
Still drownd in sleepe, and most of his dayes ded;
Scarse could he once uphold his heavie hed,
To looken, whether it were night or day:
May seeme the wayne° was very evill led,   chariot
170   When such an one had guiding of the way,
That knew not, whether right he went, or else astray.

20

From worldly cares himselfe he did esloyne,°   withdraw
And greatly shunnéd manly exercise,
From every worke he chalengéd essoyne,°   excuse
175   For contemplation sake: yet otherwise,
His life he led in lawlesse riotise;
By which he grew to grievous malady;
For in his lustlesse° limbs through evill guise°   feeble/living

---

9. The many-eyed monster Argus was
set by Juno to watch Jupiter's love Io.
When Mercury killed Argus, his eyes
were put in the peacock's tail feathers.
1. The "sage Counsellours" do not guide
their beasts, but are guided by them

(i.e., by their bestial "kinds," or natures). This procession of the seven
deadly sins—of which Pride is the queen,
the chief sin—had a long tradition in
medieval art and literature. And see
Marlowe's *Dr. Faustus* (II.ii.111–64).

A shaking fever raignd continually:
180 Such one was Idlenesse, first of this company.

21

And by his side rode loathsome Gluttony,
    Deforméd creature, on a filthie swyne,
    His belly was up-blowne with luxury,
    And eke with fatnesse swollen were his eyne,
185 And like a Crane his necke was long and fyne,°   *thin*
    With which he swallowd up excessive feast,
    For want whereof poore people oft did pyne;°   *starve*
    And all the way, most like a brutish beast,
He spuéd up his gorge, that all did him deteast.

22

190 In greene vine leaves he was right fitly clad;
    For other clothes he could not weare for heat,
    And on his head an yvie girland had,
    From under which fast trickled downe the sweat:
    Still as he rode, he somewhat° still did eat,   *something*
195 And in his hand did beare a bouzing can,
    Of which he supt so oft, that on his seat
    His dronken corse he scarse upholden can,
In shape and life more like a monster, then a man.[2]

23

Unfit he was for any worldly thing,
200 And eke unhable once° to stirre or go,°   *at all/walk*
    Not meet to be of counsell to a king,
    Whose mind in meat and drinke was drownéd so,
    That from his friend he seldome knew his fo:
    Full of diseases was his carcas blew,°   *livid*
205 And a dry dropsie through his flesh did flow:
    Which by misdiet daily greater grew:
Such one was Gluttony, the second of that crew.

24

And next to him rode lustfull Lechery,
    Upon a bearded Goat, whose rugged haire,
210 And whally° eyes (the signe of gelosy,)   *greenish*
    Was like the person selfe, whom he did beare:
    Who rough, and blacke, and filthy did appeare,
    Unseemely man to please faire Ladies eye;
    Yet he of Ladies oft was lovéd deare,
215 When fairer faces were bid standenby:°   *away*
O who does know the bent of womens fantasy?

25

In a greene gowne he clothéd was full faire,
    Which underneath did hide his filthinesse,
    And in his hand a burning hart he bare,
220 Full of vaine follies, and new fanglenesse:°   *fickleness*
    For he was false, and fraught with ficklenesse,

---

2. The drunken old Silenus of Greek mythology (see Ovid's *Metamorphoses*) is echoed here.

And learnéd had to love with secret lookes,
And well could daunce, and sing with ruefulnesse,
And fortunes tell, and read in loving° bookes,   *erotic*
225 And thousand other wayes, to bait his fleshly hookes.

26

Inconstant man, that lovéd all he saw,
And lusted after all, that he did love,
Ne would his looser life be tide to law,
But joyd weake wemens hearts to tempt and prove°   *try*
230 If from their loyall loves he might then move;
Which lewdnesse fild him with reprochfull paine
Of that fowle evill,[3] which all men reprove,
That rots the marrow, and consumes the braine:
Such one was Lecherie, the third of all this traine.

27

235 And greedy Avarice by him did ride,
Upon a Camell loaden all with gold;
Two iron coffers hong on either side,
With precious mettall full, as they might hold,
And in his lap an heape of coine he told;°   *counted*
240 For of his wicked pelfe his God he made,
And unto hell him selfe for money sold;
Accursed usurie was all his trade,
And right and wrong ylike in equall ballaunce waide.[4]

28

His life was nigh unto deaths doore yplast,
245 And thread-bare cote, and cobled shoes he ware,
Ne scarse good morsell all his life did tast,
But both from backe and belly still did spare,
To fill his bags, and richesse to compare;°   *acquire*
Yet chylde ne kinsman living had he none
250 To leave them to; but thorough daily care
To get, and nightly feare to lose his owne,
He led a wretched life unto him selfe unknowne.

29

Most wretchéd wight, whom nothing might suffise,
Whose greedy lust did lacke in greatest store,°   *plenty*
255 Whose need had end, but no end covetise,
Whose wealth was want, whose plenty made him pore,
Who had enough, yet wishéd ever more;
A vile disease, and eke in foote and hand
A grievous gout tormented him full sore,
260 That well he could not touch, nor go, nor stand:
Such one was Avarice, the fourth of this faire band.

30

And next to him malicious Envie rode,
Upon a ravenous wolfe, and still did chaw

---

3. I.e., syphilis.   4. I.e., made no distinction between right
and wrong.

Betweene his cankred teeth a venemous tode,
265　That all the poison ran about his chaw;°　　　　　*jaw*
But inwardly he chawéd his owne maw°　　　　　　*entrails*
At neighbours wealth, that made him ever sad;
For death it was, when any good he saw,
And wept, that cause of weeping none he had,
270　But when he heard of harme, he wexéd wondrous glad.

31

All in a kirtle of discolourd say⁵
He clothéd was, ypainted full of eyes;
And in his bosome secretly there lay
An hatefull Snake, the which his taile uptyes
275　In many folds, and mortall sting implyes.°　　　　*enfolds*
Still as he rode, he gnasht his teeth, to see
Those heapes of gold with griple° Covetyse,　　　*grasping*
And grudgéd at the great felicitie
Of proud Lucifera, and his owne companie.

32

280　He hated all good workes and vertuous deeds,
And him no lesse, that any like did use;
And who with gracious bread the hungry feeds,
His almes for want of faith he doth accuse;
So every good to bad he doth abuse:°　　　　　　*twist*
285　And eke the verse of famous Poets witt
He does backebite, and spightfull poison spues
From leprous mouth on all, that ever writt:
Such one vile Envie was, that fifte in row did sitt.

33

And him beside rides fierce revenging Wrath,
290　Upon a Lion, loth for to be led;
And in his hand a burning brond° he hath,　　　　*sword*
The which he brandisheth about his hed;
His eyes did hurle forth sparkles fiery red,
And staréd sterne on all, that him beheld,
295　As ashes pale of hew and seeming ded;
And on his dagger still his hand he held,
Trembling through hasty rage, when choler° in him sweld.　*anger*

34

His ruffin° raiment all was staind with blood,　　　*disarranged*
Which he had spilt, and all to rags yrent,°　　　　*torn*
300　Through unadviséd rashnesse woxen wood,⁶
For of his hands he had no governement,°　　　　　*control*
Ne cared for bloud in his avengement:
But when the furious fit was overpast,
His cruell facts° he often would repent;　　　　　*actions*
305　Yet wilfull man he never would forecast,
How many mischieves should ensue his heedlesse hast.

---

5. Jacket of many-colored wool.　　　　6. Grown insane.

35

Full many mischiefes follow cruell Wrath;
    Abhorréd bloudshed, and tumultuous strife,
    Unmanly° murder, and unthrifty scath,°   *inhuman/damage*
310   Bitter despight, with rancours rusty knife,
    And fretting griefe the enemy of life;
    All these, and many evils moe° haunt ire,   *more*
    The swelling Splene,° and Frenzy raging rife,   *malice*
    The shaking Palsey, and Saint Fraunces fire:[7]
315 Such one was Wrath, the last of this ungodly tire.°   *train*

36

And after all, upon the wagon beame
    Rode Sathan, with a smarting whip in hand,
    With which he forward lasht the laesie teme,
    So oft as Slowth still in the mire did stand.
320   Huge routs of people did about them band,
    Showting for joy, and still before their way
    A foggy mist had covered all the land;
    And underneath their feet, all scattered lay
Dead sculs and bones of men, whose life had gone astray.

37

325 So forth they marchen in this goodly sort,
    To take the solace° of the open aire,   *recreation*
    And in fresh flowring fields themselves to sport;
    Emongst the rest rode that false Lady faire,
    The fowle Duessa, next unto the chaire
330   Of proud Lucifera, as one of the traine:
    But that good knight would not so nigh repaire,°   *approach*
    Him selfe estrounging from their joyaunce vaine,
Whose fellowship seemd far unfit for warlike swaine.

38

So having solacéd themselves a space
335   With pleasaunce of the breathing° fields yfed,   *fragrant*
    They backe returnéd to the Princely Place;
    Whereas an errant knight in armes ycled,°   *clad*
    And heathnish shield, wherein with letters red
    Was writ Sans joy, they new arrivéd find:
340   Enflamed with fury and fiers hardy-hed,°   *audacity*
    He seemd in hart to harbour thoughts unkind,
And nourish bloudy vengeaunce in his bitter mind.[8]

39

Who when the shaméd shield[9] of slaine Sans foy
    He spied with that same Faery champions page,
345   Bewraying° him, that did of late destroy   *revealing*

---

7. St. Anthony's fire, erysipelas, or the flaming itch; appropriate to Wrath.
8. Sans joy ("without joy") stands, not simply for gloom or "no fun," but for *accidie*, loss of heart. Redcrosse's high-minded rejection of the seven deadly sins (lines 331–33) does not protect him from this darkness of the spirit.
9. With the arms reversed. See below, line 369.

His eldest brother, burning all with rage
He to him leapt, and that same envious gage[1]
Of victors glory from him snatcht away:
But th'Elfin knight, which ought° that warlike   *owned/trophy*
    wage,°
350 Disdaind to loose the meed he wonne in fray,
And him rencountring fierce, reskewd the noble pray.

40
Therewith they gan to hurtlen° greedily,   *skirmish*
    Redoubted battaile ready to darrayne,°   *contest*
And clash their shields, and shake their swords on hy,
355 That with their sturre they troubled all the traine;
Till that great Queene upon eternall paine
Of high displeasure, that ensewen might,
Commaunded them their fury to refraine,
And if that either to that shield had right,
360 In equall lists they should the morrow next it fight.

41
"Ah dearest Dame," quoth then the Paynim bold,
    "Pardon the errour of enragéd wight,
Whom great griefe made forget the raines to hold
Of reasons rule, to see this recreant knight,
365 No knight, but treachour full of false despight
And shamefull treason, who through guile hath slayn
The prowest° knight, that ever field did fight,   *bravest*
Even stout Sans foy (O who can then refrayn?)
Whose shield he beares renverst, the more to heape disdayn.

42
370 "And to augment the glorie of his guile,
    His dearest love[2] the faire Fidessa loe
Is there possessed of° the traytour vile,   *by*
Who reapes the harvest sowen by his foe,
Sowen in bloudy field, and bought with woe:
375 That brothers hand shall dearely well requight
So be, O Queene, you equall favour showe."
Him litle answerd th'angry Elfin knight:
He never meant with words, but swords to plead his right.

43
But threw his gauntlet as a sacred pledge,
380 His cause in combat the next day to try:
So been they parted both, with harts on edge,
To be avenged each on his enimy.
That night they pas in joy and jollity,
Feasting and courting both in bowre and hall;
385 For Steward was excessive Gluttonie,
That of his plenty pouréd forth to all;
Which doen,° the Chamberlain Slowth did to rest them call.   *done*

1. Envied prize.   2. I.e. Sans foy's.

44

Now whenas darkesome night had all displayd
Her coleblacke curtein over brightest skye,
390 The warlike youthes on dayntie couches layd,
Did chace away sweet sleepe from sluggish eye,
To muse on meanes of hopéd victory.
But whenas Morpheus³ had with leaden mace
Arrested all that courtly company,
395 Up-rose Duessa from her resting place,
And to the Paynims lodging comes with silent pace.

45

Whom broad awake she finds, in troublous fit,°   mood
Forecasting, how his foe he might annoy,
And him amoves with speaches seeming fit:
400 "Ah deare Sans joy, next dearest to Sans foy,
Cause of my new griefe, cause of my new joy,
Joyous, to see his ymage in mine eye,
And greeved, to thinke how foe did him destroy,
That was the flowre of grace and chevalrye;
405 Lo his Fidessa to thy secret faith I flye."

46

With gentle wordes he can° her fairely greet,   did
And bad say on the secret of her hart.
Then sighing soft, "I learne that litle sweet
Oft tempred is," quoth she, "with muchell smart:
410 For since my brest was launcht° with lovely dart   pierced
Of deare Sans foy, I never joyéd howre,
But in eternall woes my weaker hart
Have wasted, loving him with all my powre,
And for his sake have felt full many an heavie stowre.°   grief

47

415 "At last when perils all I weenéd past,
And hoped to reape the crop of all my care,
Into new woes unweeting° I was cast,   unknowing
By this false faytor,° who unworthy ware   deceiver
His worthy shield, whom he with guilefull snare
420 Entrappéd slew, and brought to shamefull grave.
Me silly° maid away with him he bare,   innocent
And ever since hath kept in darksome cave,
For that I would not yeeld, that° to Sans foy I gave.   what

48

"But since faire Sunne hath sperst° that lowring clowd,   dispersed
425 And to my loathéd life now shewes some light,
Under your beames I will me safely shrowd,
From dreaded storme of his disdainfull spight:
To you th'inheritance belongs by right
Of brothers prayse, to you eke longs° his love.   belongs
430 Let not his love, let not his restlesse spright°   ghost
Be unrevenged, that calles to you above
From wandring Stygian⁴ shores, where it doth endlesse move."

---

3. The god of sleep.   4. Of the river Styx, in the underworld.

49

Thereto said he, "Faire Dame be nought dismaid
For sorrowes past; their griefe is with them gone:
435 Ne yet of present perill be affraid;
For needlesse feare did never vantage° none,   *aid*
And helplesse hap it booteth not to mone.
Dead is Sans-foy, his vitall paines are past,
Though greevéd ghost for vengeance deepe do grone:
440 He lives, that shall him pay his dewties° last,   *rites*
And guiltie Elfin bloud shall sacrifice in hast."

50

"O but I feare the fickle freakes,"⁵ quoth shee,
"Of fortune false, and oddes of armes in field."
"Why dame," quoth he, "what oddes can ever bee,
445 Where both do fight alike, to win or yield?"
"Yea but," quoth she, "he beares a charméd shield,
And eke enchaunted armes, that none can perce,
Ne none can wound the man, that does them wield."
"Charmd or enchaunted," answerd he then ferce,°   *fiercely*
450 "I no whit reck, ne you the like need to reherce.°   *recount*

51

"But faire Fidessa, sithens° fortunes guile,   *since*
Or enimies powre hath now captivéd you,
Returne from whence ye came, and rest a while
Till morrow next, that I the Elfe subdew,
455 And with Sans foyes dead dowry you endew."⁶
"Ay me, that is a double death," she said,
"With proud foes sight my sorrow to renew:
Where ever yet I be, my secrete aid
Shall follow you." So passing forth she him obaid.

Canto V

The faithfull knight in equall field
subdewes his faithlesse foe,
Whom false Duessa saves, and for
his cure to hell does goe.

1

The noble hart, that harbours vertuous thought,
And is with child of glorious great intent,
Can never rest, untill it forth have brought
Th'eternall brood of glorie excellent:⁷
5 Such restlesse passion did all night torment
The flaming corage of that Faery knight,
Devizing, how that doughtie turnament
With greatest honour he atchieven might;
Still did he wake, and still did watch for dawning light.

5. Unpredictable tricks.
6. I.e., endow you with the dowry of the dead Sans foy.
7. That good is manifested only in action, not in mere intent, is an important commonplace of Renaissance thinking.

2

10 At last the golden Orientall gate
   Of greatest heaven gan to open faire,
   And Phoebus fresh, as bridegrome to his mate,
   Came dauncing forth, shaking his deawie haire:
   And hurld his glistring beames through gloomy aire.
15 Which when the wakeful Elfe perceived, streight way
   He started up, and did him selfe prepaire,
   In sun-bright armes, and battailous array:
For with that Pagan proud he combat will that day.

3

And forth he comes into the commune hall,
20 Where earely waite him many a gazing eye,
   To weet what end to straunger knights may fall.
   There many Minstrales maken melody,
   To drive away the dull melancholy,
   And many Bardes, that to the trembling chord
25 Can tune their timely° voyces cunningly,   *measured*
   And many Chroniclers, that can record
Old loves, and warres for ladies doen by many a Lord.

4

Soone after comes the cruell Sarazin,
   In woven maile all arméd warily,
30 And sternly lookes at him, who not a pin
   Does care for looke of living creatures eye.
   They bring them wines of Greece and Araby,
   And daintie spices fetcht from furthest Ynd,°   *India*
   To kindle heat of courage privily:°   *within*
35 And in the wine a solemne oth they bynd
T'observe the sacred lawes of armes, that are assynd.

5

At last forth comes that far renowméd Queene,
   With royall pomp and Princely majestie;
   She is ybrought unto a paléd° greene,   *fenced*
40 And placéd under stately canapee,°   *canopy*
   The warlike feates of both those knights to see.
   On th'other side in all mens open vew
   Duessa placéd is, and on a tree
   Sans-foy his shield is hangd with bloudy hew:
45 Both those the lawrell girlonds to the victor dew.

6

A shrilling trompet sownded from on hye,
   And unto battaill bad them selves addresse:
   Their shining shieldes about their wrestes° they tye,   *wrists*
   And burning blades about their heads do blesse,°   *brandish*
50 The instruments of wrath and heavinesse:
   With greedy force each other doth assayle,
   And strike so fiercely, that they do impresse

Deepe dinted furrowes in the battred mayle;
The yron walles to ward their blowes are weake and fraile.

7

55 The Sarazin was stout, and wondrous strong,
    And heapéd blowes like yron hammers great:
    For after bloud and vengeance he did long.
    The knight was fiers, and full of youthly heat:
    And doubled strokes, like dreaded thunders threat:
60 For all for prayse and honour he did fight.
    Both stricken strike, and beaten both do beat,
    That from their shields forth flyeth firie light,
And helmets hewen deepe, shew marks of eithers might.

8

So th'one for wrong, the other strives for right:
65 As when a Gryfon⁸ seizéd of his pray,
    A Dragon fiers encountreth in his flight,
    Through widest ayre making his ydle way,
    That would his rightfull ravine° rend away: *prey*
    With hideous horrour both together smight,
70 And souce° so sore, that they the heavens affray: *strike*
    The wise Southsayer° seeing so sad sight,   *soothsayer*
Th'amazéd vulgar tels of warres and mortall fight.

9

So th'one for wrong, the other strives for right,
    And each to deadly shame would drive his foe:
75 The cruell steele so greedily doth bight
    In tender flesh, that streames of bloud down flow,
    With which the armes, that earst so bright did show,
    Into a pure vermillion now are dyde:
    Great ruth in all the gazers harts did grow,
80 Seeing the goréd woundes to gape so wyde,
That victory they dare not wish to either side.

10

At last the Paynim chaunst to cast his eye,
    His suddein° eye, flaming with wrathfull fyre,   *darting*
    Upon his brothers shield, which hong thereby:
85 Therewith redoubled was his raging yre,
    And said, "Ah wretched sonne of wofull syre,
    Doest thou sit wayling by black Stygian lake,
    Whilest here thy shield is hangd for victors hyre,° *reward*
    And sluggish german⁹ doest thy forces slake,
90 To after-send his foe, that him may overtake?

11

"Goe caytive° Elfe, him quickly overtake,   *wretched*
    And soone redeeme from his long wandring woe;
    Goe guiltie ghost, to him my message make,
    That I his shield have quit° from dying foe."   *rescued*

8. A legendary monster, half eagle, half   9. I.e., his brother (Sans foy).
lion.

95 Therewith upon his crest he stroke him so,
  That twise he reeléd, readie twise to fall;
  End of the doubtfull battell deeméd tho°   *then*
  The lookers on, and lowd to him gan call
The false Duessa, "Thine the shield, and I, and all."[1]

12

100 Soone as the Faerie heard his Ladie speake,
  Out of his swowning dreame he gan awake,
  And quickning° faith, that earst was woxen weake, *vitalizing*
  The creeping deadly cold away did shake:
  Tho moved with wrath, and shame, and Ladies sake,
105 Of all attonce he cast° avengd to bee,   *determined*
  And with so'exceeding furie at him strake,
  That forcéd him to stoupe upon his knee;
Had he not stoupéd so, he should have cloven bee,

13

 And to him said, "Goe now proud Miscreant,
110 Thy selfe thy message doe° to german deare, *give*
  Alone he wandring thee too long doth want:
  Goe say, his foe thy shield with his doth beare."
  Therewith his heavie hand he high gan reare,
  Him to have slaine; when loe a darkesome clowd
115 Upon him fell: he no where doth appeare,
  But vanisht is. The Elfe him cals alowd,
But answer none receives: the darknes him does shrowd.[2]

14

 In haste Duessa from her place arose,
  And to him running said, "O prowest° knight, *bravest*
120 That ever Ladie to her love did chose,
  Let now abate the terror of your might,
  And quench the flame of furious despight,
  And bloudie vengeance; lo th'infernall powres
  Covering your foe with cloud of deadly night,
125 Have borne him hence to Plutoes balefull bowres.
The conquest yours, I yours, the shield, and glory yours."

15

 Not all so satisfide, with greedie eye
  He sought all round about, his thirstie blade
  To bath in bloud of faithlesse enemy;
130 Who all that while lay hid in secret shade:
  He standes amazéd, how he thence should fade.
  At last the trumpets Triumph sound on hie,
  And running Heralds humble homage made,
  Greeting him goodly with new victorie,
135 And to him brought the shield, the cause of enmitie.

1. Duessa is, of course, calling to Sans joy, but Redcrosse (lines 100 ff.) hears her as "Fidessa."
2. This inconclusive ending to the fight is a traditional epic device. Cf., in *Iliad* III, the battle between Menelaus and Paris and *Paradise Lost* IV. In Tasso's *Gerusalemme Liberata* (VII.44–45) the enchantress Armida protects Rambaldo in like manner.

16

Wherewith he goeth to that soveraine Queene,
  And falling her before on lowly knee,
  To her makes present of his service seene:[3]
  Which she accepts, with thankes, and goodly gree,°   *favor*
140 Greatly advauncing° his gay chevalree.   *extolling*
  So marcheth home, and by her takes the knight,
  Whom all the people follow with great glee,
  Shouting, and clapping all their hands on hight,
That all the aire it fils, and flyes to heaven bright.

17

145 Home is he brought, and laid in sumptuous bed:
  Where many skilfull leaches° him abide,°   *doctors/attend*
  To salve his hurts, that yet still freshly bled.
  In wine and oyle they wash his woundes wide,
  And softly can embalme° on every side.   *anoint*
150 And all the while, most heavenly melody
  About the bed sweet musicke did divide,[4]
  Him to beguile of griefe and agony:
And all the while Duessa wept full bitterly.

18

As when a wearie traveller that strayes
155 By muddy shore of broad seven-mouthéd Nile,
  Unweeting of the perillous wandring wayes,
  Doth meet a cruell craftie Crocodile,
  Which in false griefe hyding his harmefull guile,
  Doth weepe full sore, and sheddeth tender teares:
160 The foolish man, that pitties all this while
  His mournefull plight, is swallowed up unwares,
Forgetfull of his owne, that mindes anothers cares.

19

So wept Duessa untill eventide,
  That° shyning lampes in Joves high house were light: *when*
165 Then forth she rose, ne lenger would abide,
  But comes unto the place, where th'Hethen knight
  In slombring swownd nigh voyd of vitall spright,
  Lay covered with inchaunted cloud all day:
  Whom when she found, as she him left in plight,
170 To wayle his woefull case she would not stay,
But to the easterne coast of heaven makes speedy way.

20

Where griesly Night, with visage deadly sad,
  That Phoebus chearefull face durst never vew,
  And in a foule blacke pitchie mantle clad,
175 She findes forth comming from her darkesome mew,°   *den*
  Where she all day did hide her hated hew.
  Before the dore her yron charet stood,

3. Proved. Redcrosse's act of idolatrous   itual health.
worship to Lucifera bodes ill for his spir-   4. Played variations.

Alreadie harnesséd for journey new;
And cole blacke steedes yborne of hellish brood,
180 That on their rustie bits did champ, as they were wood.[5]

21

Who when she saw Duessa sunny bright,
Adornd with gold and jewels shining cleare,
She greatly grew amazéd at the sight,
And th'unacquainted light began to feare:
185 For never did such brightnesse there appeare,
And would have backe retyred to her cave,
Untill the witches speech she gan to heare,
Saying, "Yet O thou dreaded Dame, I crave
Abide, till I have told the message, which I have."

22

190 She stayd, and foorth Duessa gan proceede,
"O thou most auncient Grandmother of all,
More old then Jove, whom thou at first didst breede,
Or that great house of Gods caelestiall,
Which wast begot in Daemogorgons hall,[6]
195 And sawst the secrets of the world unmade,[7]
Why suffredst thou thy Nephewes° deare to fall   grandsons
With Elfin sword, most shamefully betrade?
Lo where the stout Sans joy doth sleepe in deadly shade.

23

"And him before, I saw with bitter eyes
200 The bold Sans foy shrinke underneath his speare;
And now the pray of fowles in field he lyes,
Nor wayld of friends, nor laid on groning beare,°   bier
That whylome was to me too dearely deare.
O what of Gods then boots it to be borne,
205 If old Aveugles sonnes so evill heare?[8]
Or who shall not great Nightes children scorne,
When two of three her Nephews are so fowle forlorne.

24

"Up then, up dreary Dame, of darknesse Queene,
Go gather up the reliques of thy race,
210 Or else goe them avenge, and let be seene,
That dreaded Night in brightest day hath place,
And can the children of faire light deface."°   destroy
Her feeling speeches some compassion moved
In hart, and chaunge in that great mothers face:
215 Yet pittie in her hart was never proved
Till then: for evermore she hated, never loved.

25

And said, "Deare daughter rightly may I rew
The fall of famous children borne of mee,

5. Mad. The description of night echoes
not only descriptions in classical poetry
but also the world of popular superstition in the English countryside.
6. I.e., in Chaos.

7. Before it was made.
8. I.e., are so badly thought of. "Aveu-
gle" means "blind"; he is son of Night
and father of Sans foy, Sans joy, and
Sans loy.

And good successes, which their foes ensew:°   *attend*
220 But who can turne the streame of destinee,
Or breake the chayne of strong necessitee,
Which fast is tyde to Joves eternall seat?[9]
The sonnes of Day he favoureth, I see,
And by my ruines thinkes to make them great:
225 To make one great by others losse, is bad excheat.°   *profit*

26

"Yet shall they not escape so freely all;
For some shall pay the price of others guilt:
And he the man that made Sans foy to fall,
Shall with his owne bloud price that[1] he hath spilt.
230 But what art thou, that telst of Nephews kilt?"
"I that do seeme not I, Duessa am,"
Quoth she, "how ever now in garments gilt,
And gorgeous gold arayd I to thee came;
Duessa I, the daughter of Deceipt and Shame."

27

235 Then bowing downe her agéd backe, she kist
The wicked witch, saying; "In that faire face
The false resemblance of Deceipt, I wist°   *knew*
Did closely lurke; yet so true-seeming grace
It carried, that I scarse in darkesome place
240 Could it discerne, though I the mother bee
Of falshood, and root of Duessaes race.
O welcome child, whom I have longd to see,
And now have seene unwares. Lo now I go with thee."

28

Then to her yron wagon she betakes,
245 And with her beares the fowle welfavourd witch:
Through mirkesome aire her readie way she makes.
Her twyfold° Teme, of which two blacke as pitch,   *twofold*
And two were browne, yet each to each unlich,°   *unlike*
Did softly swim away, ne ever stampe,
250 Unlesse she chaunst their stubborne mouths to twitch;
Then foming tarre, their bridles they would champe,
And trampling the fine element,[2] would fiercely rampe.°   *rear*

29

So well they sped, that they be come at length
Unto the place, whereas the Paynim lay,
255 Devoid of outward sense, and native strength,
Coverd with charméd cloud from vew of day,
And sight of men, since his late luckelesse fray.
His cruell wounds with cruddy° bloud congealed,   *clotted*
They binden up so wisely, as they may,

9. The golden chain of concord or design that binds the entire universe; the image goes back as far as Homer (*Iliad* VIII.18–27) and was given classic statement by Boethius (*Consolation of Philosophy* II.8). Cf. ix.1.
1. I.e., pay for what.
2. The air.

260 And handle softly, till they can be healed:
So lay him in her charet, close in night concealed.

30

And all the while she stood upon the ground,
  The wakefull dogs did never cease to bay,
  As giving warning of th'unwonted sound,
265 With which her yron wheeles did them affray,
  And her darke griesly looke them much dismay;
  The messenger of death, the ghastly Owle
  With drearie shriekes did also her bewray;°   *reveal*
  And hungry Wolves continually did howle,
270 At her abhorréd face, so filthy and so fowle.

31

Thence turning backe in silence soft they stole,
  And brought the heavie corse with easie pace
  To yawning gulfe of deepe Avernus hole.[3]
  By that same hole an entrance darke and bace
275 With smoake and sulphure hiding all the place,
  Descends to hell: there creature never past,
  That backe returnéd without heavenly grace;
  But dreadfull Furies, which their chaines have brast,° *burst*
And damnéd sprights sent forth to make ill° men aghast. *evil*

32

280 By that same way the direfull dames doe drive
  Their mournefull charet, fild with rusty blood,
  And downe to Plutoes house are come bilive:°   *quickly*
  Which passing through, on every side them stood
  The trembling ghosts with sad amazéd mood,
285 Chattring their yron teeth, and staring wide
  With stonie eyes; and all the hellish brood
  Of feends infernall flockt on every side,
To gaze on earthly wight, that with the Night durst ride.

33

They pas the bitter waves of Acheron,
290 Where many soules sit wailing woefully,
  And come to fiery flood of Phlegeton,
  Whereas the damnéd ghosts in torments fry,
  And with sharpe shrilling shriekes doe bootlesse cry,
  Cursing high Jove, the which them thither sent.
295 The house of endlesse paine is built thereby,
  In which ten thousand sorts of punishment
The curséd creatures doe eternally torment.

34

Before the threshold dreadfull Cerberus
  His three deforméd heads did lay along,°   *down*

---

3. In classical mythology, Avernus is
Hell, where Pluto reigns (line 282).
Acheron (line 289) and Phlegeton (line
291) are rivers in Hell. Cerberus (line
298), the three-headed dog, is guardian
there. Stanzas 31–35 recall much of
Aeneas's descent into Hell (Virgil, *Aeneid* VI.200, 239–40).

300 Curled with thousands adders venemous,
  And lilléd° forth his bloudie flaming tong: *lolled*
  At them he gan to reare his bristles strong,
  And felly gnarre,[4] untill dayes enemy
  Did him appease; then downe his taile he hong
305 And suffered them to passen quietly:
For she in hell and heaven had power equally.

35

 There was Ixion turnéd on a wheele,
  For daring tempt the Queene of heaven to sin;
  And Sisyphus an huge round stone did reele°   *roll*
310 Against an hill, ne might from labour lin;°   *cease*
  There thirstie Tantalus hong by the chin;
  And Tityus fed a vulture on his maw;°   *liver*
  Typhoeus joynts were stretchéd on a gin,°   *rack*
  Theseus condemned to endlesse slouth° by law,   *sloth*
315 And fifty sisters water in leake° vessels draw.[5]   *leaky*

36

 They all beholding worldly wights in place,
  Leave off their worke, unmindfull of their smart,
  To gaze on them; who forth by them doe pace,
  Till they be come unto the furthest part:
320 Where was a Cave ywrought by wondrous art,
  Deepe, darke, uneasie, dolefull, comfortlesse,
  In which sad Aesculapius farre a part
  Emprisond was in chaines remedilesse,
For that Hippolytus rent corse he did redresse.[6]

37

325 Hippolytus a jolly° huntsman was,   *fine*
  That wont in charet chace the foming Bore;
  He all his Peeres in beautie did surpas,
  But Ladies love as losse of time forbore:
  His wanton stepdame[7] lovéd him the more,
330 But when she saw her offred sweets refused
  Her love she turnd to hate, and him before
  His father fierce of treason false accused,
And with her gealous termes his open eares abused.

38

 Who all in rage his Sea-god syre[8] besought,
335 Some curséd vengeance on his sonne to cast:

---

4. Savagely growl.
5. Ixion was being punished for attempting to seduce Juno; Sisyphus for refusing to pray to the gods; Tantalus for stealing the gods' nectar; Tityus for having tried to seduce Apollo's mother; the monster Typhoeus for creating unfavorable winds; Theseus for stealing Persephone from Hades; and the daughters of King Danaus for having killed their husbands on the wedding night.

Ovid, Virgil, and Homer are Spenser's sources here.
6. Aesculapius was god of medicine. Spenser draws most closely for the story of Hippolytus upon Boccaccio's *De Genealogica* (X.50), although Ovid and Virgil also tell the story.
7. Phaedra, the wife of his father, Theseus.
8. Poseidon (Neptune).

From surging gulf two monsters straight were brought,
With dread whereof his chasing steedes aghast,
Both charet swift and huntsman overcast.
His goodly corps on ragged cliffs yrent,
340 Was quite dismembred, and his members chast
Scattered on every mountaine, as he went,
That of Hippolytus was left no moniment.[9]

39

His cruell stepdame seeing what was donne,
Her wicked dayes with wretched knife did end,
345 In death avowing th'innocence of her sonne.
Which hearing his rash Syre, began to rend
His haire, and hastie tongue, that did offend:
Tho gathering up the relicks of his smart[1]
By Dianes meanes, who was Hippolyts frend,
350 Them brought to Aesculape, that by his art
Did heale them all againe, and joynéd every part.

40

Such wondrous science in mans wit to raine
When Jove avizd,° that could the dead revive,   discovered
And fates expiréd could renew againe,
355 Of endlesse life he might him not deprive,
But unto hell did thrust him downe alive,
With flashing thunderbolt ywounded sore:
Where long remaining, he did alwaies strive
Himselfe with salves to health for to restore,
360 And slake the heavenly fire, that raged evermore.

41

There auncient Night arriving, did alight
From her nigh wearie waine, and in her armes
To Aesculapius brought the wounded knight:
Whom having softly disarayd of armes,
365 Tho gan to him discover all his harmes,
Beseeching him with prayer, and with praise,
If either salves, or oyles, or herbes, or charmes
A fordonne° wight from dore of death mote raise,   undone
He would at her request prolong her nephews daies.

42

370 "Ah Dame," quoth he, "thou temptest me in vaine,
To dare the thing, which daily yet I rew,
And the old cause of my continued paine
With like attempt to like end to renew.
Is not enough, that thrust from heaven dew°   fitting
375 Here endlesse penance for one fault I pay,
But that redoubled crime with vengeance new
Thou biddest me to eeke?° Can Night defray°   increase/appease
The wrath of thundring Jove, that rules both night and day?"

9. I.e., no trace of identity.   1. I.e., his remains.

43

"Not so," quoth she; "but sith that heavens king
380   From hope of heaven hath thee excluded quight,
      Why fearest thou, that canst not hope for thing,
      And fearest not, that more thee hurten might,
      Now in the powre of everlasting Night?
      Goe to then, O thou farre renowméd sonne
385   Of great Apollo, shew thy famous might
      In medicine, that else° hath to thee wonne   *already*
Great paines, and greater praise, both never to be donne."° *ended*

44

Her words prevaild: And then the learnéd leach°   *doctor*
      His cunning hand gan to his wounds to lay,
390   And all things else, the which his art did teach:
      Which having seene, from thence arose away
      The mother of dread darknesse, and let stay
      Aveugles sonne there in the leaches cure,
      And backe returning tooke her wonted way,
395   To runne her timely race,[2] whilst Phoebus pure
In westerne waves his wearie wagon did recure.°   *refresh*

45

The false Duessa leaving noyous° Night,   *harmful*
      Returnd to stately pallace of dame Pride;
      Where when she came, she found the Faery knight
400   Departed thence, albe° his woundes wide   *although*
      Not throughly heald, unreadie were to ride.
      Good cause he had to hasten thence away;
      For on a day his wary Dwarfe had spide,
      Where in a dongeon deepe huge numbers lay
405   Of caytive° wretched thrals,° that wayléd night   *captive/slaves*
      and day.[3]

46

A ruefull sight, as could be seene with eie;
      Of whom he learnéd had in secret wise
      The hidden cause of their captivitie,
      How mortgaging their lives to Covetise,
410   Through wastfull Pride, and wanton Riotise,
      They were by law of that proud Tyrannesse[4]
      Provokt with Wrath, and Envies false surmise,
      Condemnéd to that Dongeon mercilesse,
Where they should live in woe, and die in wretchednesse.

47

415   There was that great proud king of Babylon,[5]
      That would compell all nations to adore,
      And him as onely God to call upon,
      Till through celestiall doome° throwne out of dore, *judgment*
      Into an Oxe he was transformed of yore:
420   There also was king Croesus,[6] that enhaunst°   *exalted*

2. Her measured (nightly) journey.
3. The Dwarfe here acts as a "wary" conscience.
4. I.e., Lucifera, whose "law" is that of destruction by sin. The noble sinners named in stanzas 47–50 exemplify a theme common to Renaissance morality, the fall of princes.
5. Nebuchadnezzar (Daniel iii–iv).
6. King of Lydia, famous for his riches.

His heart too high through his great riches store;
And proud Antiochus,[7] the which advaunst
His curséd hand gainst God, and on his altars daunst.

48

And them long time before, great Nimrod[8] was,
425   That first the world with sword and fire warrayd;°   *ravaged*
And after him old Ninus farre did pas°   *surpass*
In princely pompe, of all the world obayd;
There also was that mightie Monarch layd
Low under all, yet above all in pride,
430   That name of native° syre did fowle upbrayd,   *natural*
And would as Ammons sonne[8a] be magnifide,
Till scornd of God and man a shamefull death he dide.

49

All these together in one heape were throwne,
Like carkases of beasts in butchers stall.
435   And in another corner wide were strowne
The antique ruines of the Romaines fall:[9]
Great Romulus the Grandsyre of them all,
Proud Tarquin, and too lordly Lentulus,
Stout Scipio, and stubborne Hanniball,
440   Ambitious Sylla, and sterne Marius,
High Caesar, great Pompey, and fierce Antonius.

50

Amongst these mighty men were wemen mixt,
Proud wemen, vaine, forgetfull of their yoke:
The bold Semiramis,[1] whose sides transfixt
445   With sonnes owne blade, her fowle reproches spoke;
Faire Sthenoboea,[2] that her selfe did choke
With wilfull cord, for wanting° of her will;   *lacking*
High minded Cleopatra, that with stroke
Of Aspes sting her selfe did stoutly kill:
450   And thousands moe the like, that did that dongeon fill.

51

Besides the endlesse routs of wretched thralles,
Which thither were assembled day by day,
From all the world after their wofull falles,
Through wicked pride, and wasted wealthes decay.
455   But most of all, which in that Dongeon lay
Fell from high Princes courts, or Ladies bowres,
Where they in idle pompe, or wanton play,
Consuméd had their goods, and thriftlesse howres,
And lastly throwne themselves into these heavy stowres.°   *disasters*

7. King of Syria, who tried to stamp out the Jewish religion (I Maccabees i.20–24).
8. A mighty hunter, associated with the Tower of Babel (Genesis x.9). Founder of Nineveh.
8a. Alexander the Great, occasionally worshiped as the son of Jupiter Ammon.
9. Romulus, founder of Rome; Tarquin, Roman tyrant; Lentulus, a conspirator with Catiline; Scipio, Roman general, conqueror of Carthage; Hannibal, Carthaginian general; Sulla, Roman civil war general; Marius, Sulla's rival; Julius Caesar; Pompey the Great; and Mark Anthony. All are memorialized in Plutarch's *Lives*.
1. Wife of Ninus.
2. Queen of King Proetus of Argos, who fell vainly in love with Bellerophon.

52

460 Whose case whenas the carefull Dwarfe had tould,
    And made ensample of their mournefull sight
    Unto his maister, he no lenger would
    There dwell in perill of like painefull plight,
    But early rose, and ere that dawning light
465 Discovered had the world to heaven wyde,
    He by a privie Posterne° tooke his flight,   *gate*
    That of no envious eyes he mote be spyde:[3]
For doubtlesse death ensewd, if any him descryde.

53

    Scarse could he footing find in that fowle way,
470 For many corses, like a great Lay-stall°   *rubbish heap*
    Of murdred men which therein strowéd lay,
    Without remorse, or decent funerall:
    Which all through that great Princesse pride did fall
    And came to shamefull end. And them beside
475 Forth ryding underneath the castell wall,
    A donghill of dead carkases he spide,
The dreadfull spectacle° of that sad house of Pride.   *example*

Canto VI

From lawlesse lust by wondrous grace
    fayre Una is release:
Whom salvage nation does adore,
    and learnes her wise beheast.°   *bidding*

1

As when a ship, that flyes faire under saile,
    An hidden rocke escapéd hath unwares,
    That lay in waite her wrack for to bewaile,
    The Marriner yet halfe amazéd stares
5 At perill past, and yet in doubt ne dares
    To joy at his foole-happie oversight:
    So doubly is distrest twixt joy and cares
    The dreadlesse courage° of this Elfin knight,   *heart*
Having escapt so sad ensamples in his sight.

2

10 Yet sad he was that his too hastie speed
    The faire Duess' had forst him leave behind;
    And yet more sad, that Una his deare dreed°   *object of reverence*
    Her truth had staind with treason so unkind;°   *unnatural*
    Yet crime in her could never creature find,
15 But for his love, and for her owne selfe sake,
    She wandred had° from one to other Ynd,   *would have*
    Him for to seeke, ne ever would forsake,
Till her unwares the fierce Sansloy did overtake.

---

3. Redcrosse entered the House of Pride from above; he leaves it from below.

3

Who after Archimagoes fowle defeat,
20   Led her away into a forrest wilde,
        And turning wrathfull fire to lustfull heat,
        With beastly sin thought her to have defilde,
        And made the vassall of his pleasures vilde.°   *vile*
        Yet first he cast by treatie,° and by traynes,°   *persuasion/tricks*
25   Her to perswade, that stubborne fort to yilde:
        For greater conquest of hard love he gaynes,
That workes it to his will, then he that it constraines.°   *forces*

4

With fawning wordes he courted her a while,
        And looking lovely,° and oft sighing sore,   *lovingly*
30   Her constant hart did tempt with diverse guile:
        But wordes, and lookes, and sighes she did abhore,
        As rocke of Diamond stedfast evermore.[4]
        Yet for to feed his fyrie lustfull eye,
        He snatcht the vele, that hong her face before;
35   Then gan her beautie shine, as brightest skye,
And burnt his beastly hart t'efforce° her chastitye.   *violate*

5

So when he saw his flatt'ring arts to fayle,
        And subtile engines bet° from batteree,   *beaten*
        With greedy force he gan the fort assayle,
40   Whereof he weend possesséd soone to bee,
        And win rich spoile of ransackt chastetee.
        Ah heavens, that do this hideous act behold,
        And heavenly virgin thus outragéd see,
        How can ye vengeance just so long withhold,
45   And hurle not flashing flames upon that Paynim bold?

6

The pitteous maden carefull° comfortlesse,   *full of cares*
        Does throw out thrilling shriekes, and shrieking cryes,
        The last vaine helpe of womens great distresse,
        And with loud plaints importuneth the skyes,
50   That molten starres do drop like weeping eyes;
        And Phoebus flying so most shamefull sight,
        His blushing face in foggy cloud implyes,°   *buries*
        And hides for shame. What wit of mortall wight
Can now devise to quit a thrall[5] from such a plight?

7

55 Eternall providence exceeding thought,
        Where none appeares can make her selfe a way:
        A wondrous way it for this Lady wrought,
        From Lyons clawes to pluck the gripéd pray.
        Her shrill outcryes and shriekes so loud did bray,
60   That all the woodes and forestes did resownd;

4. The diamond was traditionally per-   made of diamond.
fect; Arthur's shield (I.vii.33) is also   5. Release a victim.

A troupe of Faunes and Satyres far away
Within the wood were dauncing in a rownd,
Whiles old Sylvanus slept in shady arber sownd.[6]
8

Who when they heard that pitteous strainéd voice,
65   In hast forsooke their rurall meriment,
And ran towards the far rebownded noyce,
To weet, what wight so loudly did lament.
Unto the place they come incontinent:°   *immediately*
Whom when the raging Sarazin espide,
70   A rude, misshapen, monstrous rablement,
Whose like he never saw, he durst not bide,
But got his ready steed, and fast away gan ride.[7]
9

The wyld woodgods arrivéd in the place,
There find the virgin dolefull desolate,
75   With ruffled rayments, and faire blubbred face,
As her outrageous foe had left her late,
And trembling yet through feare of former hate;
All stand amazéd at so uncouth° sight,   *strange*
And gin to pittie her unhappie state,
80   All stand astonied at her beautie bright,
In their rude eyes unworthie° of so wofull plight.   *undeserving*
10

She more amazed, in double dread doth dwell;
And every tender part for feare does shake:
As when a greedie Wolfe through hunger fell
85   A seely° Lambe farre from the flocke does take,   *innocent*
Of whom he meanes his bloudie feast to make,
A Lyon spyes fast running towards him,
The innocent pray in hast he does forsake,
Which quit from death yet quakes in every lim
90   With chaunge of feare, to see the Lyon looke so grim.
11

Such fearefull fit assaid° her trembling hart,   *afflicted*
Ne word to speake, ne joynt to move she had:
The salvage nation feele her secret smart,
And read her sorrow in her count'nance sad;
95   Their frowning forheads with rough hornes yclad,
And rusticke horror[8] all a side doe lay,
And gently grenning, shew a semblance glad
To comfort her, and feare to put away,
Their backward bent knees teach[9] her humbly to obay.

---

6. Fauns and satyrs, creatures with men's bodies above the waist and goats' bodies below, noted in classical mythology for their sensuality, engage here in "rurall meriment"; Sylvanus, Roman god of the woods, is traditionally associated with fauns.

7. The "woodgods," like the Lyon of Canto iii, bear some natural goodness— unlike Sans loy, who is alien to nature. They perhaps represent religious belief and practice before Christianity.

8. Rough manner.

9. I.e., teach them.

12

100 The doubtfull Damzell dare not yet commit
    Her single° person to their barbarous truth,°   *solitary/honesty*
    But still twixt feare and hope amazd does sit,
    Late learnd what harme to hastie trust ensu'th,
    They in compassion of her tender youth,
105 And wonder of her beautie soveraine,
    Are wonne with pitty and unwonted ruth,
    And all prostrate upon the lowly plaine,
Do kisse her feete, and fawne on her with count'nance faine.° *pleasant*

13

Their harts she ghesseth by their humble guise,
110   And yieldes her to extremitie of time;[1]
    So from the ground she fearelesse doth arise,
    And walketh forth without suspect of crime:
    They all as glad, as birdes of joyous Prime,°   *springtime*
    Thence lead her forth, about her dauncing round,
115 Shouting, and singing all a shepheards ryme,
    And with greene braunches strowing all the ground,
Do worship her, as Queene, with olive girlond cround.

14

And all the way their merry pipes they sound,
    That all the woods with doubled Eccho ring,
120 And with their hornéd feet do weare the ground,
    Leaping like wanton kids in pleasant Spring.
    So towards old Sylvanus they her bring;
    Who with the noyse awakéd, commeth out,
    To weet the cause, his weake steps governing
125 An agéd limbs on Cypresse stadle° stout,   *staff*
And with an yvie twyne his wast is girt about.

15

Far off he wonders, what them makes so glad,
    Or° Bacchus merry fruit[2] they did invent,°   *whether/find*
    Or Cybeles franticke rites[3] have made them mad;
130 They drawing nigh, unto their God present
    That flowre of faith and beautie excellent.
    The God himselfe vewing that mirrhour rare,
    Stood long amazd, and burnt in his intent;[4]
    His owne faire Dryope now he thinkes not faire,
135 And Pholoe fowle, when her to this he doth compare.[5]

16

The woodborne people fall before her flat,
    And worship her as Goddesse of the wood;
    And old Sylvanus selfe bethinkes not, what
    To thinke of wight so faire, but gazing stood,

---

1. I.e., necessity of the time.
2. Wine grapes.
3. Orgiastic dances in worship of Cybele, goddess of the powers of Nature.
4. Glowed with intense concentration. Una is a "mirrhour rare" in that she reflects heavenly beauty.
5. Dryope and Pholoe were nymphs loved by Faunus and Pan; for Spenser, the names "Faunus," "Pan," and "Sylvanus" were apparently interchangeable.

140 In doubt to deeme her borne of earthly brood;
   Sometimes Dame Venus selfe he seemes to see,
   But Venus never had so sober mood;
   Sometimes Diana he her takes to bee,
 But misseth bow, and shaftes, and buskins° to her knee. *soft boots*

17

145 By vew of her he ginneth to revive
   His ancient love, and dearest Cyparisse,[6]
   And calles to mind his pourtraiture alive,[7]
   How faire he was, and yet not faire to this,
   And how he slew with glauncing dart amisse
150 A gentle Hynd, the which the lovely boy
   Did love as life, above all worldly blisse;
   For griefe whereof the lad n'ould° after joy, *would not*
 But pynd away in anguish and selfe-wild annoy.° *suffering*

18

  The wooddy Nymphes, faire Hamadryades[8]
155 Her to behold do thither runne apace,
   And all the troupe of light-foot Naiades,[9]
   Flocke all about to see her lovely face:
   But when they vewéd have her heavenly grace,
   They envie her in their malitious mind,
160 And fly away for feare of fowle disgrace:
   But all the Satyres scorne their woody kind,
 And henceforth nothing faire, but her on earth they find.

19

  Glad of such lucke, the luckelesse lucky maid,
   Did her content to please their feeble eyes,
165 And long time with that salvage people staid,
   To gather breath in many miseries.
   During which time her gentle wit she plyes,
   To teach them truth, which worshipt her in vaine,
   And made her th'Image of Idolatryes;
170 But when their bootlesse zeale she did restraine
 From her own worship, they her Asse would worship fayn.[1]

20

  It fortunéd a noble warlike knight
   By just occasion to that forrest came,
   To seeke his kindred, and the lignage right,° *true*
175 From whence he tooke his well deservéd name:
   He had in armes abroad wonne muchell fame,
   And fild far landes with glorie of his might,
   Plaine, faithfull, true, and enimy of shame,
   And ever loved to fight for Ladies right,
180 But in vaine glorious frayes he litle did delight.

---

6. A fair youth, beloved of Sylvanus, turned into a cypress tree.
7. I.e., his appearance when alive.
8. Nymphs whose life depended upon the trees with which they were associated.
9. Water nymphs.
1. I.e., willingly. Natural goodness can give some recognition, albeit only externally, to Una. Though Una does her best to teach the satyrs true religion, they are idolaters even in the truth.

21

A Satyres sonne yborne in forrest wyld,
  By straunge adventure as it did betyde,
  And there begotten of a Lady myld,
  Faire Thyamis the daughter of Labryde,
185 That was in sacred bands of wedlocke tyde
  To Therion, a loose unruly swayne:[2]
  Who had more joy to raunge the forrest wyde,
  And chase the salvage beast with busie payne,[3]
Then serve his Ladies love, and wast in pleasures vayne.

22

190 The forlorne mayd did with loves longing burne,
  And could not lacke° her lovers company,   *be without*
  But to the wood she goes, to serve her turne,
  And seeke her spouse, that from her still does fly,
  And followes other game and venery:[4]
195 A Satyre chaunst her wandring for to find,
  And kindling coles of lust in brutish eye,
  The loyall links of wedlocke did unbind,
And made her person thrall unto his beastly kind.

23

So long in secret cabin there he held
200 Her captive to his sensuall desire,
  Till that with timely fruit her belly sweld,
  And bore a boy unto that salvage sire:
  Then home he suffred her for to retire,
  For ransome leaving him the late borne childe;
205 Whom till to ryper yeares he gan aspire,°   *grow up*
  He noursled up in life and manners wilde,
Emongst wild beasts and woods, from lawes of men exilde.

24

For all he taught the tender ymp,° was but   *child*
  To banish cowardize and bastard° feare;   *base*
210 His trembling hand he would him force to put
  Upon the Lyon and the rugged Beare,
  And from the she Beares teats her whelps to teare;
  And eke wyld roring Buls he would him make
  To tame, and ryde their backes not made to beare;
215 And the Robuckes in flight to overtake,
That every beast for feare of him did fly and quake.

25

Thereby so fearelesse, and so fell° he grew,   *fierce*
  That his owne sire and maister of his guise[5]

2. "Thyamis" means "passion," "Therion," "wild beast." Their child Satyrane
(he is named in line 249) ought to be
a savage creature, but instead his natural
goodness welcomes and reveres truth and
grace in Una with a higher understanding than the lion or the woodgods can
give.
3. Painstaking care.
4. The word means both "hunting" and
"sexual play."
5. Teacher of his manners.

Did often tremble at his horrid° vew,   *rough*
220 And oft for dread of hurt would him advise,
The angry beasts not rashly to despise,
Nor too much to provoke; for he would learne°   *teach*
The Lyon stoup to him in lowly wise,
(A lesson hard) and make the Libbard° sterne   *leopard*
225 Leave roaring, when in rage he for revenge did earne.° *yearn*

26

And for to make his powre approvéd° more,   *extended*
Wyld beasts in yron yokes he would compell;
The spotted Panther, and the tuskéd Bore,
The Pardale° swift, and the Tigre cruell;   *panther*
230 The Antelope, and Wolfe both fierce and fell;
And them constraine in equall teme to draw.
Such joy he had, their stubborne harts to quell,
And sturdie courage tame with dreadfull aw,
That his beheast they fearéd, as a tyrans law.

27

235 His loving mother came upon a day
Unto the woods, to see her little sonne;
And chaunst unwares to meet him in the way,
After his sportes, and cruell pastime donne,
When after him a Lyonesse did runne,
240 That roaring all with rage, did lowd requere°   *demand*
Her children deare, whom he away had wonne:
The Lyon whelpes she saw how he did beare,
And lull in rugged armes, withouten childish feare.

28

The fearefull Dame all quakéd at the sight,
245 And turning backe, gan fast to fly away,
Untill with love revokt° from vaine affright,   *restrained*
She hardly yet perswaded was to stay,
And then to him these womanish words gan say;
"Ah Satyrane, my dearling, and my joy,
250 For love of me leave off this dreadfull play;
To dally thus with death, is no fit toy,
Go find some other play-fellowes, mine own sweet boy."

29

In these and like delights of bloudy game
He traynéd was, till ryper yeares he raught,°   *reached*
255 And there abode, whilst any beast of name
Walkt in that forest, whom he had not taught
To feare his force: and then his courage haught°   *high*
Desird of forreine foemen to be knowne,
And far abroad for straunge adventures sought:
260 In which his might was never overthrowne,
But through all Faery lond his famous worth was blown.

30

Yet evermore it was his manner faire,
.After long labours and adventures spent,
. Unto those native woods for to repaire,
265 To see his sire and ofspring° auncient.   origin
And now he thither came for like intent;
'Where he unwares the fairest Una found,
Straunge Lady, in so straunge habiliment,
Teaching the Satyres, which her sat around,
270 Trew sacred lore, which from her sweet lips did redound.

31

He wondred at her wisedome heavenly rare,
. Whose like in womens wit he never knew;
And when her curteous deeds he did compare,
Gan her admire, and her sad sorrowes rew,
275 Blaming of Fortune, which such troubles threw,
And joyd to make proofe of her crueltie
. On gentle Dame, so hurtlesse,° and so trew: harmless
Thenceforth he kept her goodly company,
And learnd her discipline of faith and veritie.

32

280 But she all vowd unto the Redcrosse knight,
His wandring perill closely° did lament,   secretly
Ne in this new acquaintaunce could delight,
But her deare heart with anguish did torment,
'And all her wit in secret counsels spent,
285 How to escape. At last in privie wise
To Satyrane she shewéd her intent;
Who glad to gain such favour, gan devise,
How with that pensive Maid he best might thence arise.°   depart

33

So on a day when Satyres all were gone,
290 To do their service to Sylvanus old,
The gentle virgin left behind alone
He led away with courage stout and bold.
Too late it was, to Satyres to be told,
Or ever hope recover her againe:
295 In vaine he seekes that having cannot hold.
So fast he carried her with carefull paine,[6]
That they the woods are past, and come now to the plaine.

34

The better part now of the lingring day,
. They traveild had, when as they farre espide
300 A wearie wight forwandring° by the way,   wandering along
And towards him they gan in hast to ride,
To weet of newes, that did abroad betide,
Or tydings of her knight of the Redcrosse.
But he them spying, gan to turne aside,

6. Painstaking care.

305 For feare as seemd, or for some feignéd losse;
More greedy they of newes, fast towards him do crosse.

35

A silly° man, in simple weedes forworne,°   *simple/worn out*
And solid with dust of the long dried way;
His sandales were with toilesome travell torne,
310 And face all tand with scorching sunny ray,
As he had traveild many a sommers day,
Through boyling sands of Arabie and Ynde;
And in his hand a Jacobs staffe,⁷ to stay
His wearie limbes upon: and eke behind,
315 His scrip° did hang, in which his needments he did bind.   *bag*

36

The knight approching nigh, of him inquerd
Tydings of warre, and of adventures new;
But warres, nor new adventures none he herd.
Then Una gan to aske, if ought he knew,
320 Or heard abroad of that her champion trew,
That in his armour bare a croslet° red.   *small cross*
"Aye me, Deare dame," quoth he, "well may I rew
To tell the sad sight, which mine eies have red:°   *beheld*
These eyes did see that knight both living and eke ded."

37

325 That cruell word her tender hart so thrild,°   *pierced*
That suddein cold did runne through every vaine,
And stony horrour all her sences fild
With dying fit, that downe she fell for paine.
The knight her lightly rearéd up againe,
330 And comforted with curteous kind reliefe:
Then wonne from death, she bad him tellen plaine
The further processe° of her hidden griefe;   *account*
The lesser pangs can beare, who hath endured the chiefe.

38

Then gan the Pilgrim thus, "I chaunst this day,
335 This fatall day, that shall I ever rew,
To see two knights in travell on my way
(A sory sight) arraungéd in battell new,
Both breathing vengeaunce, both of wrathfull hew:
My fearefull flesh did tremble at their strife,
340 To see their blades so greedily imbrew,°   *thrust*
That drunke with bloud, yet thristed after life:
What more? the Redcrosse knight was slaine with Paynim knife."

39

"Ah dearest Lord," quoth she, "how might that bee,
And he the stoutest knight, that ever wonne?"°   *fought*
345 "Ah dearest dame," quoth he, "how might I see
The thing, that might not be, and yet was donne?"
"Where is," said Satyrane, "that Paynims sonne,
That him of life, and us of joy hath reft?"

7. I.e., pilgrim's staff.

"Not far away," quoth he, "he hence doth wonne°   *stay*
350   Foreby a fountaine, where I late him left
Washing his bloudy wounds, that through° the steele were cleft."   *by*

40

Therewith the knight thence marchéd forth in hast,
    Whiles Una with huge heavinesse opprest,
    Could not for sorrow follow him so fast;
355   And soone he came, as he the place had ghest,
    Whereas that Pagan proud him selfe did rest,
    In secret shadow by a fountaine side:
    Even he it was, that earst would have supprest°   *violated*
    Faire Una: whom when Satyrane espide,
360 With fowle reprochfull words he boldly him defide.

41

And said, "Arise thou cursed Miscreaunt,
    That hast with knightlesse guile and trecherous train°   *deceit*
    Faire knighthood fowly shamed, and doest vaunt
    That good knight of the Redcrosse to have slain:
365   Arise, and with like treason now maintain
    Thy guilty wrong, or else thee guilty yield."
    The Sarazin this hearing, rose amain,°   *at once*
    And catching up in hast his three square[8] shield,
And shining helmet, soone him buckled to the field.

42

370 And drawing nigh him said, "Ah misborne° Elfe,   *base-born*
    In evill houre thy foes thee hither sent,
    Anothers wrongs to wreake upon thy selfe:
    Yet ill thou blamest me, for having blent°   *stained*
    My name with guile and traiterous intent;
375   That Redcrosse knight, perdie, I never slew,
    But had he beene, where earst his armes were lent,
    Th' enchaunter vaine his errour should not rew:
But thou his errour shalt, I hope now proven trew."[9]

43

Therewith they gan, both furious and fell,
380   To thunder blowes, and fiersly to assaile
    Each other bent his enimy to quell,°   *kill*
    That with their force they perst both plate and maile,
    And made wide furrowes in their fleshes fraile,
    That it would pitty° any living eie.   *bring pity to*
385   Large floods of bloud adowne their sides did raile:°   *flow*
    But floods of bloud could not them satisfie:
Both hungred after death: both chose to win, or die.

---

8. Triangular.
9. I.e., had Redcrosse been where his
arms were, the enchanter Archimago
would not have to regret his error in
fighting me. But you will now repeat his
error in fighting me and demonstrate
what an error it is.

44

So long they fight, and fell revenge pursue,
  That fainting each, themselves to breathen let,
  And oft refreshéd, battell oft renue:
  As when two Bores with rancling malice met,
  Their gory sides fresh bleeding fiercely fret,°   *tear*
  Til breathlesse both them selves aside retire,
  Where foming wrath, their cruell tuskes they whet,
  And trample th'earth, the whiles they may respire
Then backe to fight againe, new breathéd and entire.°   *refreshed*

45

So fiersly, when these knights had breathéd once,
  They gan to fight returne, increasing more
  Their puissant force, and cruell rage attonce,
  With heapéd strokes more hugely, then before,
  That with their drerie° wounds and bloudy gore   *dreadful*
  They both deforméd, scarsely could be known.
  By this sad Una fraught with anguish sore,
  Led with their noise, which through the aire was thrown,
Arrived, where they in erth their fruitles bloud had sown.

46

Whom all so soone as that proud Sarazin
  Espide, he gan revive the memory
  Of his lewd lusts, and late attempted sin,
  And left the doubtfull battell hastily,
  To catch her, newly offred to his eie:
  But Satyrane with strokes him turning, staid,
  And sternely bad him other businesse plie,
  Then hunt the steps of pure unspotted Maid:
Wherewith he all enraged, these bitter speaches said.

47

"O foolish faeries sonne, what furie mad
  Hath thee incenst, to hast thy dolefull fate?
  Were it not better, I that Lady had,
  Then that thou hadst repented it too late?
  Most sencelesse man he, that himselfe doth hate,
  To love another. Lo then for thine ayd
  Here take thy lovers token on thy pate."
  So they to fight; the whiles the royall Mayd
Fled farre away, of that proud Paynim sore afrayd.

48

But that false Pilgrim, which that leasing° told,   *lying*
  Being in deed old Archimage, did stay
  In secret shadow, all this to behold,
  And much rejoycéd in their bloudy fray:
  But when he saw the Damsell passe away
  He left his stond,° and her pursewd apace,   *place*

430   In hope to bring her to her last decay.°   *destruction*
        But for to tell her lamentable cace,
And eke this battels end, will need another place.

Canto VII

The Redcrosse knight is captive made
By Gyaunt proud opprest,
Prince Arthur meets with Una great-
ly with those newes distrest.

1

What man so wise, what earthly wit so ware,°   *wary*
    As to descry° the crafty cunning traine,   *perceive*
    By which deceipt doth maske in visour faire,
    And cast her colours dyéd deepe in graine,
5   To seeme like Truth, whose shape she well can faine,
    And fitting gestures to her purpose frame,
    The guiltlesse man with guile to entertaine?°   *receive*
    Great maistresse of her art was that false Dame,
The false Duessa, clokéd with Fidessaes name.

2

10 Who when returning from the drery Night,
    She fownd not in that perilous house of Pryde,
    Where she had left, the noble Redcrosse knight,
    Her hopéd pray, she would no lenger bide,
    But forth she went, to seeke him far and wide.
15   Ere long she fownd, whereas° he wearie sate,   *where*
    To rest him selfe, foreby° a fountaine side,   *beside*
    Disarméd all of yron-coted Plate,
And by his side his steed the grassy forage ate.

3

He feedes upon the cooling shade, and bayes°   *bathes*
20   His sweatie forehead in the breathing wind,
    Which through the trembling leaves full gently playes
    Wherein the cherefull birds of sundry kind
    Do chaunt sweet musick, to delight his mind:
    The Witch approaching gan him fairely greet,
25   And with reproch of carelesnesse unkind
    Upbrayd, for leaving her in place unmeet,°   *unfitting*
With fowle words tempring faire, soure gall with hony sweet.

4

Unkindnesse past, they gan of solace treat,
    And bathe in pleasaunce of the joyous shade,
30   Which shielded them against the boyling heat,
    And with greene boughes decking a gloomy glade,
    About the fountaine like a girlond made;
    Whose bubbling wave did ever freshly well,
    Ne ever would through fervent° sommer fade: *hot*
35   The sacred Nymph, which therein wont to dwell,
Was out of Dianes favour, as it then befell.

5

The cause was this: one day when Phoebe[1] fayre
  With all her band was following the chace,
  This Nymph, quite tyred with heat of scorching ayre
40 Sat downe to rest in middest of the race:
  The goddesse wroth gan fowly her disgrace,°   *scold*
  And bad the waters, which from her did flow,
  Be such as she her selfe was then in place.[2]
  Thenceforth her waters waxéd dull and slow,
45 And all that drunke thereof, did faint and feeble grow.

6

Hereof this gentle knight unweeting was,
  And lying downe upon the sandie graile,°   *gravel*
  Drunke of the streame, as cleare as cristall glas;
  Eftsoones his manly forces gan to faile,
50 And mightie strong was turnd to feeble fraile.
  His chaunged powres at first themselves not felt,
  Till crudled° cold his corage° gan assaile,   *curdled/vigor*
  And chearefull bloud in faintnesse chill did melt,
Which like a fever fit through all his body swelt.°   *raged*

7

55 Yet goodly court he made still to his Dame,
  Pourd out in loosnesse on the grassy grownd,
  Both carelesse of his health, and of his fame:
  Till at the last he heard a dreadfull sownd,
  Which through the wood loud bellowing, did rebownd,
60 That all the earth for terrour seemed to shake,
  And trees did tremble. Th'Elfe therewith astownd,°   *amazed*
  Upstarted lightly from his looser make,°   *companion*
And his unready weapons gan in hand to take.[3]

8

But ere he could his armour on him dight,
65 Or get his shield, his monstrous enimy
  With sturdie steps came stalking in his sight,
  An hideous Geant horrible and hye,
  That with his talnesse seemd to threat the skye,
  The ground eke groned under him for dreed;
70 His living like saw never living eye,
  Ne durst behold: his stature did exceed
The hight of three the tallest sonnes of mortall seed.

9

The greatest Earth his uncouth mother was,
  And blustring Aeolus his boasted sire,[4]
75 Who with his breath, which through the world doth pas,
  Her hollow womb did secretly inspire,°   *breathe into*

1. I.e., Diana, goddess of the moon.
2. At that time.
3. Redcrosse is weakened by his encounter with the despair of Sans joy; he has been seduced by falsehood, Duessa; he has drunk of the waters of spiritual sloth: he is thus, now, an easy victim.

4. Aeolus was keeper of the winds. His son, the giant, is Orgoglio (named in line 122), which means "pride." That this sin, pride of the flesh, unchristian and unreasonable, should be the son of the gross earth and the "blustring" wind seems appropriate.

And fild her hidden caves with stormie yre,
That she conceived; and trebling the dew time,
In which the wombes of women do expire,°   *bring forth*
80   Brought forth this monstrous masse of earthly slime,
Puft up with emptie wind, and fild with sinfull crime.

10

So growen great through arrogant delight
Of th'high descent, whereof he was yborne,
And through presumption of his matchlesse might,
85   All other powres and knighthood he did scorne.
Such now he marcheth to this man forlorne,
And left to losse:° his stalking steps are stayde   *destruction*
Upon a snaggy Oke, which he had torne
Out of his mothers bowelles, and it made
90   His mortall mace, wherewith his foemen he dismayde.

11

That when the knight he spide, he gan advance
With huge force and insupportable mayne,[5]
And towardes him with dreadfull fury praunce;
Who haplesse, and eke hopelesse, all in vaine
95   Did to him pace, sad battaile to darrayne,°   *contest*
Disarmd, disgrast, and inwardly dismayde,[6]
And eke so faint in every joynt and vaine,
Through that fraile° fountaine, which him feeble made,   *enfeebling*
That scarsely could he weeld his bootlesse° single blade.   *futile*

12

100   The Geaunt strooke so maynly° mercilesse,   *mightily*
That could have overthrowne a stony towre,
And were not heavenly grace, that him did blesse,
He had beene pouldred° all, as thin as flowre: *powdered*
But he was wary of that deadly stowre,
105   And lightly lept from underneath the blow:
Yet so exceeding was the villeins powre,
That with the wind it did him overthrow,
And all his sences stound,° that still he lay full low.   *stunned*

13

As when that divelish yron Engin[7] wrought
110   In deepest Hell, and framd by Furies skill,   *explosive*
With windy Nitre and quick° Sulphur fraught,
And ramd with bullet round, ordaind to kill,
Conceiveth fire, the heavens it doth fill
With thundring noyse, and all the ayre doth choke,
115   That none can breath, nor see, nor heare at will,
Through smouldry cloud of duskish stincking smoke,
That th'onely breath[8] him daunts, who hath escapt the stroke.

---

5. Irresistable power.   7. I.e., cannon.
6. Dis-made, dissolved.   8. I.e., the blast alone.

14

So daunted when the Geaunt saw the knight,
His heavie hand he heavéd up on hye,
120 And him to dust thought to have battred quight,
Untill Duessa loud to him gan crye;
"O great Orgoglio, greatest under skye,
O hold thy mortall hand for Ladies sake,
125 Hold for my sake, and do him not to dye,
But vanquisht thine eternall bondslave make,
And me thy worthy meed unto thy Leman take."[9]

15

He hearkned, and did stay from further harmes,
To gayne so goodly guerdon,° as she spake: reward
So willingly she came into his armes,
130 Who her as willingly to grace° did take,   favor
And was posseséd of his new found make.°   mate
Then up he tooke the slombred sencelesse corse,
And ere he could out of his swowne awake,
Him to his castle brought with hastie forse,
135 And in a Dongeon deepe him threw without remorse.

16

From that day forth Duessa was his deare,
And highly honourd in his haughtie eye,
He gave her gold and purple pall° to weare,   robe
And triple crowne set on her head full hye,[1]
140 And her endowd with royall majestye:
Then for to make her dreaded more of men,
And peoples harts with awfull terrour tye,
A monstrous beast ybred in filthy fen
He chose, which he had kept long time in darksome den.

17

145 Such one it was, as that renowméd Snake
Which great Alcides in Stremona slew,
Long fostred in the filth of Lerna lake,
Whose many heads out budding ever new,
Did breed him endlesse labour to subdew:[2]
150 But this same Monster much more ugly was;
For seven great heads out of his body grew,
An yron brest, and backe of scaly bras,
And all embrewd° in bloud, his eyes did shine as glas.   stained

9. I.e., take me, your worthy reward, as your mistress.
1. Duessa is attired like the Whore of Babylon in Revelation xvii.3–4; the triple crown is that of the papacy. See i.13, also i.22 and note.
2. The nine-headed Lernean hydra slain by Hercules (Alcides). The seven-headed monster is the red dragon of Revelation: "behold a great red dragon, having seven heads and ten horns, and seven crowns upon his heads * * * [whose] tail drew the third part of the stars of heaven, and did cast them to the earth * * * [he is] that old serpent, called the Devil, and Satan, which deceiveith the whole world" (xii.3–4,9). Pictures of the Beast of the Apocalypse illustrate medieval literature on the vices. On the historical plane, Spenser associates it with the Roman church.

18

His tayle was strechéd out in wondrous length,
155   That to the house of heavenly gods it raught,°   *reached*
   And with extorted powre, and borrowed strength,
   The ever-burning lamps from thence it brought,
   And prowdly threw to ground, as things of nought;
   And underneath his filthy feet did tread
160   The sacred things, and holy heasts° foretaught.   *commandments*
   Upon this dreadfull Beast with sevenfold head
He set the false Duessa, for more aw and dread.

19

The wofull Dwarfe, which saw his maisters fall,
   Whiles he had keeping of his grasing steed,
165   And valiant knight become a caytive thrall,
   When all was past, tooke up his forlorne weed,[3]
   His mightie armour, missing most at need;
   His silver shield, now idle maisterlesse;
   His poynant° speare, that many made to bleed,   *piercing*
170   The ruefull moniments of heavinesse,
And with them all departes, to tell his great distresse.

20

He had not travaild long, when on the way
   He wofull Ladie, wofull Una met,[4]
   Fast flying from the Paynims greedy pray,°   *clutch*
175   Whilest Satyrane him from pursuit did let:°   *prevent*
   Who when her eyes she on the Dwarfe had set,
   And saw the signes, that deadly tydings spake,
   She fell to ground for sorrowfull regret,
   And lively breath her sad brest did forsake,
180 Yet might her pitteous hart be seene to pant and quake.

21

The messenger of so unhappie newes
   Would faine have dyde: dead was his hart within,
   Yet outwardly some little comfort shewes:
   At last recovering hart, he does begin
185   To rub her temples, and to chaufe her chin,
   And every tender part does tosse and turne:
   So hardly he the flitted life does win,
   Unto her native prison[5] to retourne:
Then gins her grievéd ghost° thus to lament and mourne.   *spirit*

22

190 "Ye dreary instruments of dolefull sight,
   That doe this deadly spectacle behold,
   Why do ye lenger feed on loathéd light,
   Or liking find to gaze on earthly mould,°   *form*
   Sith cruell fates the carefull° threeds unfould,   *anguished*
195   The which my life and love together tyde?

---

3. Abandoned garment.
4. Only in Faerie Land could the Dwarfe
find Una so soon after Redcrosse's for-

tunes are at their lowest.
5. I.e., the body.

Now let the stony dart of senselesse cold
Perce to my hart, and pas through every side,
And let eternall night so sad sight fro me hide.

23

"O lightsome day, the lampe of highest Jove,
200 First made by him, mens wandring wayes to guyde,
When darknesse he in deepest dongeon drove,
Henceforth thy hated face for ever hyde,
And shut up heavens windowes shyning wyde:
For earthly sight can nought but sorrow breed,
205 And late repentance, which shall long abyde.
Mine eyes no more on vanitie shall feed,
But seeléd up with death, shall have their deadly meed."[6]

24

Then downe againe she fell unto the ground;
But he her quickly rearéd up againe:
210 Thrise did she sinke adowne in deadly swownd,
And thrise he her revived with busie paine:
At last when life recovered had the raine,°   *rein*
And over-wrestled his strong enemie,
With foltring tong, and trembling every vaine,
215 "Tell on," quoth she, "the wofull Tragedie,
The which these reliques sad present unto mine eie.

25

"Tempestuous fortune hath spent all her spight,
And thrilling sorrow throwne his utmost dart;
Thy sad tongue cannot tell more heavy plight,
220 Then that I feele, and habour in mine hart:
Who hath endured the whole, can beare each part.
If death it be, it is not the first wound,
That launchéd° hath my brest with bleeding smart.   *pierced*
Begin, and end the bitter balefull stound;°   *disaster*
225 If lesse, then that I feare, more favour I have found."

26

Then gan the Dwarfe the whole discourse declare,
The subtill traines of Archimago old;
The wanton loves of false Fidessa faire,
Bought with the bloud of vanquisht Paynim bold:
230 The wretched payre transformed to treen mould;[7]
The house of Pride, and perils round about;
The combat, which he with Sans joy did hould;
The lucklesse conflict with the Gyant stout,
Wherein captived, of life or death he stood in doubt.

27

235 She heard with patience all unto the end,
And strove to maister sorrowfull assay,[8]
Which greater grew, the more she did contend,
And almost rent her tender hart in tway;

6. Reward of death.   8. I.e., attack of sorrow.
7. Shape of a tree.

And love fresh coles unto her fire did lay:

240   For greater love, the greater is the losse.

Was never Ladie lovéd dearer° day,   *more dearly*

Then she did love the knight of the Redcrosse;

For whose deare sake so many troubles her did tosse.

28

At last when fervent sorrow slakéd was,

245   She up arose, resolving him to find

Alive or dead: and forward forth doth pas,

All as the Dwarfe the way to her assynd:°   *showed*

And evermore in constant carefull mind

She fed her wound with fresh renewéd bale;°   *anguish*

250   Long tost with stormes, and bet° with bitter wind,   *beat*

High over hils, and low adowne the dale,

She wandred many a wood, and measurd many a vale.

29

At last she chauncéd by good hap to meet

A goodly knight,[9] faire marching by the way

255   Together with his Squire, arayéd meet:

His glitterand° armour shinéd farre away,   *glittering*

Like glauncing light of Phoebus brightest ray;

From top to toe no place appeeréd bare,

That deadly dint of steele endanger may:

260   Athwart his brest a bauldrick° brave he ware,   *sash*

That shynd, like twinkling stars, with stons most pretious rare.

30

And in the midst thereof one pretious stone

Of wondrous worth, and eke of wondrous mights,

Shapt like a Ladies head,[1] exceeding shone,

265   Like Hesperus° emongst the lesser lights,   *evening star*

And strove for to amaze the weaker sights;

Thereby his mortall blade full comely hong

In yvory sheath, ycarved with curious slights;°   *patterns*

Whose hilts were burnisht gold, and handle strong

270   Of mother pearle, and buckled with a golden tong.°   *pin*

31

His haughtie helmet, horrid° all with gold,   *bristling*

Both glorious brightnesse, and great terrour bred;

For all the crest a Dragon did enfold

With greedie pawes, and over all did spred

9. Prince Arthur, the supreme hero of the entire *Faerie Queene*. As Spenser explained to Ralegh, "So in the person of Prince Arthure I sette forth magnificence in particular, which vertue for that (according to Aristotle and the rest) it is the perfection of all the rest, and conteineth in it them all." Since, he says, "I mention [in each book] the deeds of Arthur appliable to that vertue which I write of in that book," and since the "virtue" in Book I is Holiness, Arthur will be not unlike Christ, or the power of Christian grace, in the ensuing episodes.

1. I.e., that of the Faerie Queene, Gloriana.

275   His golden wings: his dreadfull hideous hed
       Close couchéd on the bever,° seemed to throw   *visor*
       From flaming mouth bright sparkles fierie red,
       That suddeine horror to faint harts did show;
    And scaly tayle was stretcht adowne his backe full low.

32

280   Upon the top of all his loftie crest,
       A bunch of haires discolourd° diversly,   *dyed*
       With sprincled pearle, and gold full richly drest,
       Did shake, and seemed to daunce for jollity,
       Like to an Almond tree ymounted hye
285   On top of greene Selinis all alone,
       With blossomes brave bedeckéd daintily;
       Whose tender locks do tremble every one
    At every little breath, that under heaven is blowne.

33

    His warlike shield all closely covered was,
290   Ne might of mortall eye be ever seene;
       Not made of steele, nor of enduring bras,
       Such earthly mettals soone consuméd bene:
       But all of Diamond perfect pure and cleene°   *clear*
       It framéd was, one massie entire mould,
295   Hewen out of Adamant rocke with engines keene,
       That point of speare it never percen could,
    Ne dint of direfull sword divide the substance would.[2]

34

    The same to wight he never wont disclose,
      But° when as monsters huge he would dismay,   *except*
300   Or daunt unequall armies of his foes,
       Or when the flying heavens he would affray;
       For so exceeding shone his glistring ray,
       That Phoebus golden face it did attaint,°   *dim*
       As when a cloud his beames doth over-lay;
305   And silver Cynthia° wexéd pale and faint,   *the moon*
    As when her face is staynd with magicke arts constraint.°   *force*

35

    No magicke arts hereof had any might,
      Nor bloudie wordes of bold Enchaunters call,
       But all that was not such, as seemd in sight,
310   Before that shield did fade, and suddeine fall:
       And when him list the raskall routes[3] appall,
       Men into stones therewith he could transmew,°   *change*
       And stones to dust, and dust to nought at all;
       And when him list the prouder lookes subdew,
315   He would them gazing blind, or turne to other hew.°   *form*

---

2. The diamond—unflawed, unpierce-able, translucent—is emblematic of the perfect faith which is Arthur's shield. Cf. Ephesians vi.16: "Above all, taking the shield of faith, wherewith ye shall be able to quench all the fiery darts of the wicked."

3. Unruly mobs.

36

Ne let it seeme, that credence this exceedes,
    For he that made the same, was knowne right well
    To have done much more admirable deedes.
    It Merlin was, which whylome° did excell   *formerly*
320   All living wightes in might of magicke spell:
    Both shield, and sword, and armour all he wrought
    For this young Prince, when first to armes he fell;
    But when he dyde, the Faerie Queene it brought
To Faerie lond, where yet it may be seene, if sought.[4]

37

325 A gentle youth, his dearely lovéd Squire
    His speare of heben° wood behind him bare,   *ebony*
    Whose harmefull head, thrice heated in the fire,
    Had riven many a brest with pikehead square;
    A goodly person, and could menage° faire   *control*
330   His stubborne steed with curbéd canon bit,[5]
    Who under him did trample as the aire,
    And chauft,° that any on his backe should sit;   *fretted*
The yron rowels into frothy fome he bit.

38

When as this knight nigh to the Ladie drew,
335   With lovely court he gan her entertaine;
    But when he heard her answers loth, he knew
    Some secret sorrow did her heart distraine:°   *oppress*
    Which to allay, and calme her storming paine,
    Faire feeling words he wisely gan display,
340   And for her humour fitting purpose faine,[6]
    To tempt the cause it selfe for to bewray;
Wherewith emmoved, these bleeding words she gan to say.

39

"What worlds delight, or joy of living speach
    Can heart, so plunged in sea of sorrowes deepe,
345   And heapéd with so huge misfortunes, reach?
    The carefull° cold beginneth for to creepe,   *afflicting*
    And in my heart his yron arrow steepe,
    Soone as I thinke upon my bitter bale:
    Such helplesse harmes yts better hidden keepe,
350   Then rip up griefe, where it may not availe,
My last left comfort is, my woes to weepe and waile."

40

"Ah Ladie deare," quoth then the gentle knight,
    "Well may I weene, your griefe is wondrous great;
    For wondrous great griefe groneth in my spright,°   *spirit*
355   Whiles thus I heare you of your sorrowes treat.
    But wofull Ladie let me you intrete,
    For to unfold the anguish of your hart:
    Mishaps are maistred by advice discrete,

---

4. I.e., Arthur's virtues may be seen
still in Queen Elizabeth's England.

5. Cannon-bit; a smooth, round bit.

6. I.e., suited his manner to her mood.

And counsell mittigates the greatest smart;
360 Found never helpe, who never would his hurts impart."

41

"O but," quoth she, "great griefe will not be tould,
And can more easily be thought, then said."
"Right so"; quoth he, "but he, that never would,
Could never: will to might gives greatest aid."
365 "But grief," quoth she, "does greater grow displaid,
If then it find not helpe, and breedes despaire."
"Despaire breedes not," quoth he, "where faith is staid."°   *firm*
"No faith so fast," quoth she, "but flesh does paire."°   *impair*
"Flesh may empaire," quoth he, "but reason can repaire."

42

370 His goodly reason, and well guided speach
So deepe did settle in her gratious thought,
That her perswaded to disclose the breach,
Which love and fortune in her heart had wrought,
And said; "Faire Sir, I hope good hap hath brought
375 You to inquire the secrets of my griefe,
Or that your wisedome will direct my thought,
Or that your prowesse can me yield reliefe:
Then heare the storie sad, which I shall tell you briefe.

43

"The forlorne Maiden, whom your eyes have seene
380 The laughing stocke of fortunes mockeries,
Am th'only daughter of a King and Queene,
Whose parents deare, whilest equall destinies
Did runne about,[7] and their felicities
The favourable heavens did not envy,
385 Did spread their rule through all the territories,
Which Phison and Euphrates floweth by,
And Gehons golden waves doe wash continually.[8]

44

"Till that their cruell curséd enemy,
An huge great Dragon horrible in sight,
390 Bred in the loathly lakes of Tartary,°   *Tartarus (Hell)*
With murdrous ravine,° and devouring might   *destruction*
Their kingdome spoild, and countrey wasted quight:
Themselves, for feare into his jawes to fall,
He forst to castle strong to take their flight,
395 Where fast embard in mightie brasen wall,
He has them now foure yeres besiegd to make them thrall.

45

"Full many knights adventurous and stout
Have enterprizd that Monster to subdew;
From every coast that heaven walks about,
400 Have thither come the noble Martiall crew,
That famous hard atchievements still pursew,

---

7. I.e., while impartial destinies surrounded them.

8. These three rivers flow in the Garden
of Eden (Genesis ii.11–14).

Yet never any could that girlond win,
But all still shronke,° and still he greater grew: quailed
All they for want of faith, or guilt of sin,
405 The pitteous pray of his fierce crueltie have bin.

46

"At last yledd° with farre reported praise,   led
Which flying fame throughout the world had spread,
Of doughtie knights, whom Faery land did raise,
That noble order hight° of Maidenhed,[9]   called
410 Forthwith to court of Gloriane I sped,
Of Gloriane great Queene of glory bright,
Whose kingdomes seat Cleopolis is red,[1]
There to obtaine some such redoubted knight,
That Parents deare from tyrants powre deliver might.

47

415 "It was my chance (my chance was faire and good)
There for to find a fresh unprovéd knight,
Whose manly hands imbrewed in guiltie blood
Had never bene, ne ever by his might
Had throwne to ground the unregarded right:
420 Yet of his prowesse proofe he since hath made
(I witnesse am) in many a cruell fight;
The groning ghosts of many one dismaide
Have felt the bitter dint of his avenging blade.

48

"And ye the forlorne reliques of his powre,
425 His byting sword, and his devouring speare,
Which have enduréd many a dreadfull stowre,°   conflict
Can speake his prowesse, that did earst you beare,
And well could rule: now he hath left you heare,
To be the record of his ruefull losse,
430 And of my dolefull disaventurous deare:[2]
O heavie record of the good Redcrosse,
Where have you left your Lord, that could so well you tosse?

49

"Well hopéd I, and faire beginnings had,
That he my captive langour should redeeme,[3]
435 Till all unweeting, an Enchaunter bad
His sence abusd, and made him to misdeeme
My loyalty, not such as it did seeme;
That° rather death desire, then such despight.   I, who
Be judge ye heavens, that all things right esteeme,
440 How I him loved, and love with all my might,
So thought I eke of him, and thinke I thought aright.

---

9. Historically, the Order of the Garter. Its emblem shows St. George killing the dragon.
1. Named. "Cleopolis" means "famous city." In the historical allegory, it is London, as Gloriana is Elizabeth. In other contexts, however, it may be Camelot or the earthly counterpart of the New Jerusalem.
2. Unfortunate lover.
3. I.e., relieve my state, captive to sadness.

50

"Thenceforth me desolate he quite forsooke,
　To wander, where wilde fortune would me lead,
　And other bywaies he himselfe betooke,
445　Where never foot of living wight did tread,
　That brought not backe the balefull body dead;[4]
　In which him chauncéd false Duessa meete,
　Mine onely foe, mine onely deadly dread,
　Who with her witchcraft and misseeming° sweete,　*deception*
450　Inveigled him to follow her desires unmeete.°　*improper*

51

"At last by subtill sleights she him betraid
　Unto his foe, a Gyant huge and tall,
　Who him disarméd, dissolute,° dismaid,　*enfeebled*
　Unwares surpriséd, and with mightie mall°　*club*
455　The monster mercilesse him made to fall,
　Whose fall did never foe before behold;
　And now in darkesome dungeon, wretched thrall,
　Remedilesse, for aie° he doth him hold;　*ever*
This is my cause of griefe, more great, then may be told."

52

460　Ere she had ended all, she gan to faint:
　But he her comforted and faire bespake,
　"Certes, Madame, ye have great cause of plaint,
　That stoutest heart, I weene, could cause to quake.
　But be of cheare, and comfort to you take:
465　For till I have acquit° your captive knight,　*freed*
　Assure your selfe, I will you not forsake."
　His chearefull words revived her chearelesse spright,
So forth they went, the Dwarfe them guiding ever right.

Canto VIII

Faire virgin to redeeme her deare
brings Arthur to the fight:
Who slayes the Gyant, wounds the beast,
and strips Duessa quight.

1

Ay me, how many perils doe enfold
　The righteous man, to make him daily fall?
　Were not, that heavenly grace doth him uphold,
　And stedfast truth acquite him out of all.
5　Her love is firme, her care continuall,
　So oft as he through his owne foolish pride,
　Or weaknesse is to sinfull bands° made thrall:　*bonds*
　Else should this Redcrosse knight in bands have dyde,
For whose deliverance she this Prince doth thither guide.

4. I.e., who returned alive.

2

10 They sadly traveild thus, untill they came
    Nigh to a castle builded strong and hie:
    Then cryde the Dwarfe, "lo yonder is the same,
    In which my Lord my liege doth lucklesse lie,
    Thrall to that Gyants hatefull tyrannie:
15   Therefore, deare Sir, your mightie powres assay."
    The noble knight alighted by and by[5]
    From loftie steede, and bad the Ladie stay,
To see what end of fight should him befall that day.

3

    So with the Squire, th'admirer of his might,
20   He marchéd forth towards that castle wall;
    Whose gates he found fast shut, ne living wight
    To ward° the same, nor answere commers call.   *guard*
    Then tooke that Squire an horne of bugle small,[6]
    Which hong adowne his side in twisted gold,
25   And tassels gay. Wyde wonders over all
    Of that same hornes great vertues weren told,
Which had approvéd° bene in uses manifold.   *demonstrated*

4

    Was never wight, that heard that shrilling sound,
    But trembling feare did feele in every vaine;
30   Three miles it might be easie heard around,
    And Ecchoes three answered it selfe againe:
    No false enchauntment, nor deceiptfull traine
    Might once abide the terror of that blast,
    But presently was voide and wholly vaine:
35   No gate so strong, no locke so firme and fast,
But with that percing noise flew open quite, or brast.°   *burst*

5

    The same before the Geants gate he blew,
    That all the castle quakéd from the ground,
    And every dore of freewill open flew.
40   The Gyant selfe dismaiéd with that sownd,
    Where he with his Duessa dalliance° fownd,   *amorous play*
    In hast came rushing forth from inner bowre,
    With staring countenance sterne, as one astownd,
    And staggering steps, to weet, what suddein stowre°   *disturbance*
45 Had wrought that horror strange, and dared his dreaded powre.

6

    And after him the proud Duessa came,
    High mounted on her manyheaded beast,
    And every head with fyrie tongue did flame,
    And every head was crownéd on his creast,
50   And bloudie mouthéd with late cruell feast.[7]
    That when the knight beheld, his mightie shild

5. Immediately.
6. A "bugle" is a wild ox; the "wide wonders" (marvelous tales) told of the horn connect it with the horn of Roland and the ram's horn of Joshua, with which he razed the walls of Jericho

(Joshua vi.5).
7. Evidently the St. Bartholomew's Day Massacre of 1572, in which the French Huguenots (Protestants) were slaughtered.

Upon his manly arme he soone addrest,°   *adjusted*
And at him fiercely flew, with courage fild,°   *filled*
And eger greedinesse° through every member thrild.   *desire*

7

55 Therewith the Gyant buckled him to fight,
    Inflamed with scornefull wrath and high disdaine,
    And lifting up his dreadfull club on hight,
    All armed with ragged snubbes° and knottie graine,   *snags*
    Him thought at first encounter to have slaine.
60 But wise and warie was that noble Pere,°   *peer*
    And lightly leaping from so monstrous maine,°   *force*
    Did faire avoide the violence him nere;
It booted nought, to thinke, such thunderbolts to beare.[8]

8

Ne shame he thought to shunne so hideous might:
65 The idle° stroke, enforcing furious way,   *inaccurate*
    Missing the marke of his misayméd sight
    Did fall to ground, and with his° heavie sway°   *its/force*
    So deepely dinted in the driven clay,
    That three yardes deepe a furrow up did throw:
70 The sad earth wounded with so sore assay,°   *assault*
    Did grone full grievous underneath the blow,
And trembling with strange feare, did like an earthquake show.

9

As when almightie Jove in wrathfull mood,
    To wreake° the guilt of mortall sins is bent,   *punish*
75 Hurles forth his thundring dart with deadly food,[9]
    Enrold in flames, and smouldring dreriment,
    Through riven cloudes and molten firmament;
    The fierce threeforkéd engin° making way,   *weapon*
    Both loftie towres and highest trees hath rent,
80 And all that might his angrie passage stay,
And shooting in the earth, casts up a mount of clay.

10

His boystrous° club, so buried in the ground,   *huge*
    He could not rearen up againe so light,
    But that the knight him at avantage found,
85 And whiles he strove his combred clubbe to quight°   *release*
    Out of the earth, with blade all burning bright
    He smote off his left arme, which like a blocke
    Did fall to ground, deprived of native might;
    Large streames of bloud out of the trunckéd stocke
90 Forth gushéd, like fresh water streame from riven rocke.[1]

11

Dismaiéd with so desperate deadly wound,
    And eke impatient of[2] unwonted paine,
    He loudly brayd with beastly yelling sound,
    That all the fields rebellowéd againe;

---

8. The ensuing battle may be taken as the struggle of the Protestant against the Roman church—or that of Christian grace against evil, the Antichrist.

9. Hatred (feud).
1. Cf. Exodus xvii.6, where Moses smites the rock and water flows forth.
2. Agonized by.

95 As great a noyse, as when in Cymbrian plaine
    An heard of Bulles, whom kindly° rage doth sting,   *natural*
    Do for the milkie mothers want complaine,[3]
    And fill the fields with troublous bellowing,
The neighbour woods around with hollow murmur ring.

12

100 That when his deare Duessa heard, and saw
    The evill stownd,° that daungerd her estate,   *blow*
    Unto his aide she hastily did draw
    Her dreadfull beast, who swolne with bloud of late
    Came ramping forth with proud presumpteous gate,
105 And threatned all his heads like flaming brands.°   *torches*
    But him the Squire made quickly to retrate,
    Encountring fierce with single° sword in hand,   *only*
And twixt him and his Lord did like a bulwarke stand,

13

The proud Duessa full of wrathfull spight,
110 And fierce disdaine, to be affronted so,
    Enforst her purple beast with all her might
    That stop° out of the way to overthroe,   *obstacle*
    Scorning the let° of so unequall foe: *obstruction*
    But nathemore° would that courageous swayne   *never the more*
115 To her yeeld passage, gainst his Lord to goe,
    But with outrageous strokes did him restraine,
And with his bodie bard the way atwixt them twaine.

14

Then tooke the angrie witch her golden cup,
    Which still she bore, replete with magick artes;[4]
120 Death and despeyre did many thereof sup,
    And secret poyson through their inner parts,
    Th' eternall bale of heavie wounded harts;
    Which after charmes and some enchauntments said,
    She lightly sprinkled on his weaker° parts;   *too weak*
125 Therewith his sturdie courage soone was quayd,°   *quelled*
And all his senses were with suddeine dread dismayd.

15

So downe he fell before the cruell beast,
    Who on his necke his bloudie clawes did seize,
    That life nigh crusht out of his panting brest:
130 No powre he had to stirre, nor will to rize.
    That when the carefull° knight gan well avise,   *watchful*
    He lightly left the foe, with whom he fought,
    And to the beast gan turne his enterprise;
    For wondrous anguish in his hart it wrought,
135 To see his lovéd Squire into such thraldome brought.

16

And high advauncing his bloud-thirstie blade,

---

3. I.e., mourn the cows' absence.
4. Cf. the golden cup of the woman in
Revelation, which is "full of abominations" (xvii.4), the chalice of the Roman
church, and the cup of Circe (in *Odyssey* X).

Stroke one of those deforméd heads so sore,[5]
That of his puissance proud ensample made;
His monstrous scalpe° downe to his teeth it tore   *skull*
140 And that misforméd shape mis-shapéd more:
A sea of bloud gusht from the gaping wound,
That her gay garments staynd with filthy gore,
And overflowéd all the field around;
That over shoes in bloud he waded on the ground.

17

145 Thereat he roaréd for exceeding paine,
That to have heard, great horror would have bred,
And scourging th' emptie ayre with his long traine,
Through great impatience° of his grievéd hed   *agony*
His gorgeous ryder from her loftie sted
150 Would have cast downe, and trod in durtie myre,
Had not the Gyant soone her succouréd;
Who all enraged with smart and franticke yre,
Came hurtling in full fierce, and forst the knight retyre.

18

The force, which wont in two to be disperst,
155 In one alone left hand he now unites,
Which is through rage more strong then both were erst;
With which his hideous club aloft he dites,°   *raises*
And at his foe with furious rigour smites,
That strongest Oake might seeme to overthrow:
160 The stroke upon his shield so heavie lites,
That to the ground it doubleth him full low:
What mortall wight could ever beare so monstrous blow?

19

And in his fall his shield, that covered was,
Did loose his vele° by chaunce, and open flew: *veil*
165 The light whereof, that heavens light did pas,°   *surpass*
Such blazing brightnesse through the aier threw,
That eye mote not the same endure to vew.
Which when the Gyaunt spyde with staring° eye,   *awed*
He downe let fall his arme, and soft withdrew
170 His weapon huge, that heavéd was on hye
For to have slaine the man, that on the ground did lye.

20

And eke the fruitfull-headed° beast, amazed   *many-headed*
At flashing beames of that sunshiny shield,
Became starke blind, and all his senses dazed,
175 That downe he tumbled on the durtie field,
And seemed himselfe as conqueréd to yield.
Whom when his maistresse proud perceived to fall,
Whiles yet his feeble feet for faintnesse reeld,
Unto the Gyant loudly she gan call,
180 "O helpe Orgoglio, helpe, or else we perish all."

5. "I saw one of [the beast's] heads as it were wounded to death" (Revelation xiii.3).

21

At her so pitteous cry was much amooved
 Her champion stout, and for to ayde his frend,
 Againe his wonted angry weapon prooved:°   *tried*
 But all in vaine: for he has read his end
185 In that bright shield, and all their forces spend
 Themselves in vaine: for since that glauncing° sight, *flashing*
 He hath no powre to hurt, nor to defend;
 As where th' Almighties lightning brond does light,
It dimmes the dazéd eyen, and daunts the senses quight.

22

190 Whom when the Prince, to battell new addrest,
 And threatning high his dreadfull stroke did see,
 His sparkling blade about his head he blest,°   *waved*
 And smote off quite his right leg by the knee,
 That downe he tombled; 6 as an aged tree,
195 High growing on the top of rocky clift,
 Whose hartstrings with keene steele nigh hewen be,
 The mightie trunck halfe rent, with ragged rift
Doth roll adowne the rocks, and fall with fearefull drift.° *impact*

23

Or as a Castle rearéd high and round,
200 By subtile engins and malitious slight°   *magic*
 Is underminéd from the lowest ground,
 And her foundation forst,° and feebled quight, *shattered*
 At last downe falles, and with her heapéd hight
 Her hastie ruine does more heavie make,
205 And yields it selfe unto the victours might;
 Such was this Gyaunts fall, that seemed to shake
The stedfast globe of earth, as it for feare did quake.

24

The knight then lightly leaping to the pray,
 With mortall steele him smot againe so sore,
210 That headlesse his unweldy bodie lay,
 All wallowd in his owne fowle bloudy gore,
 Which flowéd from his wounds in wondrous store.
 But soone as breath out of his breast did pas,
 That huge great body, which the Gyaunt bore,
215 Was vanisht quite, and of that monstrous mas
Was nothing left, but like an emptie bladder was.

25

Whose grievous fall, when false Duessa spide,
 Her golden cup she cast unto the ground,
 And crownéd mitre rudely threw aside;
220 Such percing griefe her stubborne hart did wound,
 That she could not endure that dolefull stound,° *sorrow*
 But leaving all behind her, fled away:
 The light-foot Squire her quickly turned around,
 And by hard meanes enforcing her to stay,
225 So brought unto his Lord, as his deservéd pray.

6. Pride is not defeated all at once, but step by step; for the image of the tree,
cf. *Aeneid* II.626–31, among other sources.

26

The royall Virgin, which beheld from farre,
In pensive plight, and sad perplexitie,
The whole atchievement° of this doubtfull warre, *course*
Came running fast to greet his victorie,
230 With sober gladnesse, and myld modestie,
And with sweet joyous cheare him thus bespake;
"Faire braunch of noblesse, flowre of chevalrie,
That with your worth the world amazéd make,
How shall I quite° the paines, ye suffer for my sake? *requite*

27

235 "And you [7] fresh bud of vertue springing fast,
Whom these sad eyes saw nigh unto deaths dore,
What hath poore Virgin for such perill past,
Wherewith you to reward? Accept therefore
My simple selfe, and service evermore;
240 And he that high does sit, and all things see
With equall° eyes, their merites to restore,° *impartial/reward*
Behold what ye this day have done for mee,
And what I cannot quite, requite with usuree.

28

"But sith the heavens, and your faire handeling° *conduct*
245 Have made you maister of the field this day,
Your fortune maister eke with governing,[8]
And well begun end all so well, I pray,
Ne let that wicked woman scape away;
For she it is, that did my Lord bethrall,
250 My dearest Lord, and deepe in dongeon lay,
Where he his better dayes hath wasted all.
O heare, how piteous he to you for ayd does call."

29

Forthwith he gave in charge unto his Squire,
That scarlot whore to keepen carefully;
255 Whiles he himselfe with greedie ° great desire *eager*
Into the Castle entred forcibly,
Where living creature none he did espye;
Then gan he lowdly through the house to call:
But no man cared to answere to his crye.
260 There raignd a solemne silence over all,
Nor voice was heard, nor wight was seene in bowre or hall.

30

At last with creeping crooked pace forth came
An old old man, with beard as white as snow,
That on a staffe his feeble steps did frame,
265 And guide his wearie gate both too and fro:
For his eye sight him failéd long ygo,
And on his arme a bounch of keyes he bore,
The which unuséd rust did overgrow:
Those were the keyes of every inner dore,
270 But he could not them use, but kept them still in store.

7. I.e., the Squire. Una's reward to the Squire who has done such faithful service in the war against Pride is itself an exemplary act of humility.
8. Secure your good fortune also by prudent management.

31

But very uncouth sight was to behold,
    How he did fashion his untoward° pace,   *awkward*
    For as he forward mooved his footing old,
    So backward still was turned his wrincled face,
275   Unlike to men, who ever as they trace,
    Both feet and face one way are wont to lead.
    This was the auncient keeper of that place,
    And foster father of the Gyant dead;
His name Ignaro did his nature right aread.[9]

32

280 His reverend haires and holy gravitie
    The knight much honord, as beseeméd well,[1]
    And gently askt, where all the people bee,
    Which in that stately building wont to dwell.
    Who answerd him full soft, he could not tell.
285   Againe he askt, where that same knight was layd,
    Whom great Orgoglio with his puissaunce fell
    Had made his caytive thrall; againe he sayde,
He could not tell: ne ever other answere made.

33

Then askéd he, which way he in might pas:
290   He could not tell, againe he answeréd.
    Thereat the curteous knight displeaséd was,
    And said, "Old sire, it seemes thou hast not red °   *recognized*
    How ill it sits with [2] that same silver hed
    In vaine to mocke, or mockt in vaine to bee:
295   But if thou be, as thou art pourtrahéd
    With natures pen, in ages grave degree,[3]
Aread in graver wise, what I demaund of thee."

34

His answere likewise was, he could not tell.
    Whose sencelesse speach, and doted ignorance
300   When as the noble Prince had markéd well,
    He ghest his nature by his countenance,
    And calmd his wrath with goodly temperance.
    Then to him stepping, from his arme did reach
    Those keyes, and made himselfe free enterance.
305   Each dore he openéd without any breach;°   *forcing*
There was no barre to stop, nor foe him to empeach.°   *hinder*

35

There all within full rich arayd he found,
    With royall arras and resplendent gold.
    And did with store of every thing abound,
310   That greatest Princes presence might behold.
    But all the floore (too filthy to be told)
    With bloud of guiltlesse babes, and innocents trew,

---

9. Make known. Doting ignorance ("Ignaro") is a fit servant for pride and the
false church; he has his counterparts in
Abessa and Corceca.

1. Seemed proper.
2. I.e., suits.
3. I.e., dignity.

Which there were slaine, as sheepe out of the fold,
Defiléd was, that dreadfull was to vew,
315   And sacred° ashes over it was strowéd new.   accursed

36

And there beside of marble stone was built
    An Altare, carved with cunning imagery,
    On which true Christians bloud was often spilt,
    And holy Martyrs often doen to dye,[4]
320   With cruell malice and strong tyranny:
    Whose blessed sprites from underneath the stone
    To God for vengeance cryde continually,[5]
    And with great griefe were often heard to grone,
That hardest heart would bleede, to heare their piteous mone.

37

325 Through every rowme he sought, and every bowr,
    But no where could he find that wofull thrall:
    At last he came unto an yron doore,
    That fast was lockt, but key found not at all
    Emongst that bounch, to open it withall;
330   But in the same a little grate was pight,°   placed
    Through which he sent his voyce, and lowd did call
    With all his powre, to weet, if living wight
Were houséd therewithin, whom he enlargen° might.   release

38

Therewith an hollow, dreary, murmuring voyce
335   These piteous plaints and dolours did resound;
    "O who is that, which brings me happy choyce°   chance
    Of death, that here lye dying every stound,°   moment
    Yet live perforce in balefull darkenesse bound?
    For now three Moones have changéd thrice their hew,°   shape
340   And have beene thrice hid underneath the ground,
    Since I the heavens chearefull face did vew,
O welcome thou, that doest of death bring tydings trew."

39

Which when that Champion heard, with percing point
    Of pitty deare° his hart was thrilléd sore,   extreme
345   And trembling horrour ran through every joynt,
    For ruth of gentle knight so fowle forlore:
    Which shaking off, he rent that yron dore,
    With furious force, and indignation fell;°   fierce
    Where entred in, his foot could find no flore,
350   But all a deepe descent, as darke as hell,
That breathéd ever forth a filthie banefull smell.

40

But neither darkenesse fowle, nor filthy bands,
    Nor noyous smell his purpose could withhold,
    (Entire affection hateth nicer° hands)   too fastidious

4. Put to death.
5. "And when he had opened the fifth seal, I saw under the altar the souls of them that were slain for the word of God, and for the testimony which they held: And they cried with a loud voice, saying, How long, O Lord, holy and true, dost thou not judge and avenge our blood on them that dwell on the earth?" (Revelation vi.9–10).

355 But that with constant zeale, and courage bold,
After long paines and labours manifold,
He found the meanes that Prisoner up to reare;
Whose feeble thighes, unhable to uphold
His pinéd° corse, him scarse to light could beare,   *wasted*
360 A ruefull spectacle of deathe and ghastly drere.°   *wretchedness*

41

His sad dull eyes deepe sunck in hollow pits,
Could not endure th' unwonted sunne to view;
His bare thin cheekes for want of better bits,°   *food*
And empty sides deceivéd° of their dew,   *cheated*
365 Could make a stony hart his hap to rew;
His rawbone armes, whose mighty brawnéd bowrs°   *muscles*
Were wont to rive steele plates, and helmets hew,
Were cleane consumed, and all his vitall powres
Decayd, and all his flesh shronk up like withered flowres.

42

370 Whom when his Lady saw, to him she ran
With hasty joy: to see him made her glad,
And sad to view his visage pale and wan,
Who earst in flowres of freshest youth was clad.
Tho° when her well of teares she wasted had,   *then*
375 She said, "Ah dearest Lord, what evill starre
On you hath fround, and pourd his influence bad,
That of your selfe ye thus berobbéd arre,
And this misseeming hew⁶ your manly looks doth marre?

43

"But welcome now my Lord, in wele or woe,
380 Whose presence I have lackt to long a day;
And fie on Fortune mine avowéd foe,
Whose wrathfull wreakes° them selves do now alay.   *punishments*
And for these wrongs shall treble penaunce pay
Of treble good: good growes of evils priefe."⁷
385 The chearelesse man, whom sorrow did dismay,°   *unnerve*
Had no delight to treaten° of his griefe;   *speak*
His long enduréd famine needed more reliefe.

44

"Faire Lady," then said that victorious knight,⁸
"The things, that grievous were to do, or beare,
390 Them to renew, I wote, breeds no delight;
Best musicke breeds delight in loathing eare:
But th'onely good, that growes of passéd feare,
Is to be wise, and ware° of like agein.   *wary*
This dayes ensample hath this lesson deare
395 Deepe written in my heart with yron pen,
That blisse may not abide in state of mortall men.

45

"Henceforth sir knight, take to you wonted strength,
And maister these mishaps with patient might;

6. Unseemly shape.   8. I.e., Arthur.
7. Endurance of evil.

Loe where your foe lyes stretcht in monstrous length,
400 And loe that wicked woman in your sight,[9]
The roote of all your care, and wretched plight,
Now in your powre, to let her live, or dye."
"To do her dye," quoth Una, "were despight,°   *spiteful*
And shame t'avenge so weake an enimy;
405 But spoile her of her scarlot robe, and let her fly."

46

So as she bad, that witch they disaraid,
And robd of royall robes, and purple pall,
And ornaments that richly were displaid;
Ne sparéd they to strip her naked all.
410 Then when they had despoild her tire° and call,°   *robe/headdress*
Such as she was, their eyes might her behold,
That her misshapéd parts did them appall,
A loathly, wrinckled hag, ill favoured, old,
Whose secret filth good manners biddeth not be told.

47

415 Her craftie head was altogether bald,
And as in hate of honorable eld,°   *age*
Was overgrowne with scurfe and filthy scald;°   *scabs*
Her teeth out of her rotten gummes were feld,°   *fallen*
And her sowre breath abhominably smeld;
420 Her dried dugs, like bladders lacking wind,
Hong downe, and filthy matter from them weld;
Her wrizled skin as rough, as maple rind,
So scabby was, that would have loathd all womankind.

48

Her neather parts, the shame of all her kind,[1]
425 My chaster Muse for shame doth blush to write;
But at her rompe she growing had behind
A foxes taile, with dong all fowly dight;°   *covered*
And eke her feete most monstrous were in sight;
For one of them was like an Eagles claw,
430 With griping talaunts armd to greedy fight,
The other like a Beares uneven° paw;   *rough*
More ugly shape yet never living creature saw.[2]

49

Which when the knights beheld, amazd they were,
And wondred at so fowle deforméd wight.
435 "Such then," said Una, "as she seemeth here,
Such is the face of falshood, such the sight
Of fowle Duessa, when her borrowed light
Is laid away, and counterfesaunce° knowne."   *disguise*
Thus when they had the witch disrobéd quight,
440 And all her filthy feature° open showne,   *form*
They let her goe at will, and wander wayes unknowne.

9. Over there.
1. I.e., womankind.
2. Cf. Duessa with the House of Pride: fair above, foul below. Her filthiness is like that of Alcina in Ariosto's *Orlando Furioso*, VII.71–73. Cf. also Revelation xvii.16: "these shall hate the whore, and shall make her desolate and naked." Foxes (cf. line 427) were noted for cunning; eagles and bears (lines 429, 431) for rapacity, cruelty, and brutality.

50

She flying fast from heavens hated face,
And from the world that her discovered wide,
Fled to the wastfull wildernesse apace,
445   From living eyes her open shame to hide,
And lurkt in rocks and caves long unespide.
But that faire crew of knights, and Una faire
Did in that castle afterwards abide,
To rest them selves, and weary powres repaire,
450 Where store they found of all, that dainty was and rare.

Canto IX

His loves and lignage Arthur tells:
The knights knit friendly bands:
Sir Trevisan flies from Despayre,
Whom Redcrosse knight withstands.

1

O goodly golden chaine,[3] wherewith yfere°   *together*
The vertues linkéd are in lovely wize:
And noble minds of yore allyéd were,
In brave poursuit of chevalrous emprize,°   *adventure*
5   That none did others safety despize,
Nor aid envy° to him, in need that stands,   *begrudge*
But friendly each did others prayse devize
How to advaunce with favourable hands,
As this good Prince redeemd the Redcrosse knight from bands.°*bonds*

2

10 Who when their powres, empaird through labour long,
With dew repast they had recuréd° well,   *restored*
And that weake captive wight now wexéd strong,
Them list no lenger there at leasure dwell,
But forward fare, as their adventures fell,
15   But ere they parted, Una faire besought
That straunger knight his name and nation tell;
Least so great good, as he for her had wrought,
Should die unknown, and buried be in thanklesse thought.

3

"Faire virgin," said the Prince, "ye me require
20   A thing without the compas[4] of my wit:
For both the lignage and the certain Sire,
From which I sprong, from me are hidden yit.
For all so soone as life did me admit
Into this world, and shewéd heavens light,
25   From mothers pap I taken was unfit:°   *unsuitably*
And streight delivered to a Faery knight,
To be upbrought in gentle thewes° and martiall might. *manners*

---

3. Stanza 1 opens with an invocation of the golden chain of love or concord which binds the world and the human race together (cf. v.25 and note). It will be reaffirmed in stanza 19 when the two knights exchange symbolic gifts and shake hands in token of fellowship.
4. I.e., beyond the reach of.

4

"Unto old Timon[5] he me brought bylive,°   *immediately*
   Old Timon, who in youthly yeares hath beene
30 In warlike feates th'expertest man alive,
   And is the wisest now on earth I weene;
   His dwelling is low in a valley greene,
   Under the foot of Rauran mossy hore,°   *gray*
   From whence the river Dee as silver cleene°   *pure*
35 His tombling billowes rolls with gentle rore:[6]
There all my dayes he traind me up in vertuous lore.

5

"Thither the great Magicien Merlin came,
   As was his use, ofttimes to visit me:
   For he had charge my discipline to frame,
40 And Tutours nouriture° to oversee.   *training*
   Him oft and oft I askt in privitie,
   Of what loines and what lignage I did spring:
   Whose aunswere bad me still assuréd bee,
   That I was sonne and heire unto a king,
45 As time in her just terme[7] the truth to light should bring."

6

"Well worthy impe,"° said then the Lady gent,°   *offspring/gentle*
   "And Pupill fit for such a Tutours hand.
   But what adventure, or what high intent
   Hath brought you hither into Faery land,
50 Aread° Prince Arthur, crowne of Martiall band?"   *declare*
   "Full hard it is," quoth he, "to read aright
   The course of heavenly cause, or understand
   The secret meaning of th'eternall might,
That rules mens wayes, and rules the thoughts of living wight.

7

55 "For whither he through fatall° deepe foresight   *prophetic*
   Me hither sent, for cause to me unghest,
   Or that fresh bleeding wound, which day and night
   Whilome° doth rancle in my riven brest,   *incessantly*
   With forcéd fury following his° behest,   *its*
60 Me hither brought by wayes yet never found,
   You to have helpt I hold my selfe yet blest."
   "Ah curteous knight," quoth she, "what secret wound
Could ever find,° to grieve the gentlest hart on ground?"   *succeed*

8

"Deare Dame," quoth he, "you sleeping sparkes awake,
65 Which trubled once, into huge flames will grow,
   Ne ever will their fervent fury slake
   Till living moysture into smoke do flow,
   And wasted° life do lye in ashes low.   *consumed*
   Yet sithens° silence lesseneth not my fire,   *since*

5. The name means "Honor."
6. The hill Rauran is in Wales; the river Dee also flows in, and forms part of the boundary of Wales. The Tudors (Queen Elizabeth's family) were origi- nally Welsh, and the legends of Arthur had their beginnings in the Celtic mythology of early Wales.
7. Due course.

70 But told it flames, and hidden it does glow,
I will revele, what ye so much desire:
Ah Love, lay downe thy bow, the whiles I may respire.°   breathe

9

"It was in freshest flowre of youthly yeares,
When courage first does creepe in manly chest,
75 Then first the coale of kindly° heat appeares   of nature
To kindle love in every living brest;
But me had warnd old Timons wise behest,
Those creeping flames by reason to subdew,
Before their rage grew to so great unrest,
80 As miserable lovers use to rew,
Which still wex old in woe, whiles woe still wexeth new.

10

"That idle name of love, and lovers life,
As losse of time, and vertues enimy
I ever scornd, and joyd to stirre up strife,
85 In middest of their mournfull Tragedy,
Ay wont to laugh, when them I heard to cry,
And blow the fire, which them to ashes brent:°   burned
Their God himselfe, grieved at my libertie,
Shot many a dart at me with fiers intent,
90 But I them warded all with wary government.⁸

11

"But all in vaine: no fort can be so strong,
Ne fleshly brest can arméd be so sound,
But will at last be wonne with battrie° long,   siege
Or unawares at disavantage found;
95 Nothing is sure, that growes on earthly ground:
And who most trustes in arme of fleshly might,
And boasts, in beauties chaine not to be bound,
Doth soonest fall in disaventrous° fight.   disastrous
And yeeldes his caytive neck to victours most° despight.   greatest

12

100 "Ensample make of him your haplesse joy,
And of my selfe now mated,° as ye see;   overcome
Whose prouder° vaunt that proud avenging boy   too proud
Did soone pluck downe, and curbd my libertie.
For on a day prickt° forth with jollitie   rode
105 Of looser life, and heat of hardiment,°   boldness
Raunging the forest wide on courser free,
The fields, the floods, the heavens with one consent
Did seeme to laugh° on me, and favour mine intent.   smile

13

"For-wearied with my sports, I did alight
110 From loftie steed, and downe to sleepe me layd;
The verdant gras my couch did goodly dight,°   make
And pillow was my helmet faire displayd:

---

8. I.e., self-control. The descriptions here of Cupid's archery and of the siege of the castle of chastity (in the next stanza) have many echoes from the courtly-love traditions.

Whiles every sence the humour sweet embayd,°   *pervaded*
And slombring soft my hart did steale away,
Me seeméd, by my side a royall Mayd
Her daintie limbes full softly down did lay:
So faire a creature yet saw never sunny day.

14

"Most goodly glee° and lovely blandishment°   *pleasure/compliment*
She to me made, and bad me love here deare,
For dearely sure her love was to me bent,
As when just time expiréd[9] should appeare.
But whether dreames delude, or true it were,
Was never hart so ravisht with delight,
Ne living man like words did ever heare,
As she to me delivered all that night;
And at her parting said, She Queene of Faeries hight.[1]

15

"When I awoke, and found her place devoyd,°   *empty*
And nought but presséd gras, where she had lyen,
I sorrowed all so much, as earst I joyd,
And washéd all her place with watry eyen.
From that day forth I loved that face divine;
From that day forth I cast in carefull mind,
To seeke her out with labour, and long tyne,°   *hardship*
And never vow to rest, till her I find,
Nine monethes I seeke in vaine yet ni'll° that vow unbind."   *will not*

16

Thus as he spake, his visage wexéd pale,
And chaunge of hew great passion did bewray;
Yet still he strove to cloke his inward bale,°   *grief*
And hide the smoke, that did his fire display,
Till gentle Una thus to him gan say;
"Oh happy Queene of Faeries, that hast found
Mongst many, one that with his prowesse may
Defend thine honour, and thy foes confound:
True Loves are often sown, but seldom grow on ground."

17

"Thine, O then," said the gentle Redcrosse knight,
"Next to that Ladies love, shalbe the place,
O fairest virgin, full of heavenly light,
Whose wondrous faith, exceeding earthly race,
Was firmest fixt in mine extremest case.
And you, my Lord, the Patrone° of my life,   *protector*
Of that great Queene may well gaine worthy grace:
For onely worthy you through prowes priefe[2]
Yf living man mote worthy be, to be her liefe."°   *love*

---

9. The right occasion having arisen.
1. Was called. Gloriana is also, in the two principal allegories, Queen Elizabeth and Heavenly Grace. This is one of the passages where the "faery" nature of *The Faerie Queene* makes itself strongly felt. In the background are many folk-tales and ballads of a hero bewitched by the Queen of Faery. Note further the complex layering, by which Arthur, who is a character in Faery, has entered this world through a vision in a dream.
2. Demonstration of prowess.

18

So diversly discoursing of their loves,
155   The golden Sunne his glistring head gan shew,
   And sad remembraunce now the Prince amoves,
   With fresh desire his voyage to pursew:
   Als° Una earnd° her traveill to renew.   *so/yearned*
   Then those two knights, fast friendship for to bynd,
160   And love establish each to other trew,
    Gave goodly gifts, the signes of gratefull mynd,
And eke as pledges firme, right hands together joynd.

19

Prince Arthur gave a boxe of Diamond sure,°   *flawless*
   Embowd° with gold and gorgeous ornament,   *bound*
165   Wherein were closd few drops of liquor pure,
   Of wondrous worth, and vertue excellent,
   That any wound could heale incontinent:°   *immediately*
   Which to requite, the Redcrosse knight him gave
   A booke, wherein his Saveours testament
170   Was writ with golden letters rich and brave;
A worke of wondrous grace, and able soules to save.

20

Thus beene they parted, Arthur on his way
   To seeke his love, and th'other for to fight
   With Unas foe, that all her realme did pray.°   *prey upon*
175   But she now weighing the decayéd plight,
   And shrunken synewes of her chosen knight,
   Would not a while her forward course pursew,
   Ne bring him forth in face of dreadfull fight,
   Till he recovered had his former hew:
180 For him to be yet weake and wearie well she knew.

21

So as they traveild, lo they gan espy
   An arméd knight towards them gallop fast,
   That seeméd from some fearéd foe to fly,
   Or other griesly thing, that him agast.°   *scared*
185   Still as he fled, his eye was backward cast,
   As if his feare still followed him behind;
   Als flew his steed, as he his bands had brast,
   And with his wingéd heeles did tread the wind,
As he had beene a fole of Pegasus his kind.[3]

22

190 Nigh as he drew, they might perceive his head
   To be unarmd, and curld uncombéd heares
   Upstaring stiffe, dismayd with uncouth dread;
   Nor drop of bloud in all his face appeares
   Nor life in limbe: and to increase his feares,
195   In fowle reproch° of knighthoods faire degree,°   *disgrace/position*
   About his neck an hempen rope he weares,
   That with his glistring armes does ill agree;[4]
But he of rope or armes has now no memoree.

---

3. I.e., like Pegasus (a flying horse).
4. The rope around his neck suggests attempts (past and future) at suicide— the reason for which becomes clear a few stanzas later.

23

The Redcrosse knight toward him crosséd fast,
  To weet, what mister° wight was so dismayd: *kind of*
There him he finds all sencelesse and aghast,
That of him selfe he seemd to be afrayd;
Whom hardly he from flying forward stayd,
Till he these wordes to him deliver might;
  "Sir knight, aread who hath ye thus arayd,
  And eke from whom make ye this hasty flight:
For never knight I saw in such misseeming° plight." *unseemly*

24

He answerd nought at all, but adding new
  Feare to his first amazment, staring wide
With stony eyes, and hartlesse hollow hew,
Astonisht stood, as one that had aspide
Infernall furies, with their chaines untide.
Him yet againe, and yet againe bespake
  The gentle knight; who nought to him replide,
  But trembling every joynt did inly quake,
And foltring tongue at last these words seemd forth to shake.

25

"For Gods deare love, Sir knight, do me not stay;
  For loe he comes, he comes fast after mee."
Eft° looking backe would faine have runne away;   *again*
  But he him forst to stay, and tellen free
  The secret cause of his perplexitie:
Yet nathemore° by his bold hartie speach,   *not at all*
  Could his bloud-frosen hart emboldned bee,
  But through his boldnesse rather feare did reach,
Yet forst, at last he made through silence suddein breach.

26

"And am I now in safetie sure," quoth he,
  "From him, that would have forcéd me to dye?
And is the point of death now turnd fro mee,
That I may tell this haplesse history?"
"Feare nought:" quoth he, "no daunger now is nye."
  "Then shall I you recount a ruefull cace,"
  Said he, "the which with this unlucky eye
I late beheld, and had not greater grace
Me reft from it, had bene partaker of the place.⁵

27

"I lately chaunst (Would I had never chaunst)
  With a faire knight to keepen companee,
Sir Terwin hight, that well himselfe advaunst
In all affaires, and was both bold and free,
But not so happie as mote happie bee:
  He loved, as was his lot, a Ladie gent,°   *noble*
  That him againe° loved in the least degree: *in return*
For she was proud, and of too high intent,° *ambition*
And joyd to see her lover languish and lament.

5. I.e., shared the same fate.

28

"From whom returning sad and comfortlesse,
245 As on the way together we did fare,
We met that villen (God from him me blesse°)   defend
That curséd wight, from whom I scapt why leare,°   recently
A man of hell, that cals himselfe Despaire;[6]
Who first us greets, and after faire areedes°   tells
250 Of tydings strange, and of adventures rare:
So creeping close, as Snake in hidden weedes,
Inquireth of our states, and of our knightly deedes.

29

"Which when he knew, and felt our feeble harts
Embost° with bale,° and bitter byting griefe,   exhausted/sorrow
255 Which love had launchéd with his deadly darts,
With wounding words and termes of foule repriefe°   insult
He pluckt from us all hope of due reliefe,
That earst us held in love of lingring life;
Then hopelesse hartlesse, gan the cunning thiefe
260 Perswade us die, to stint° all further strife: end
To me he lent this rope, to him a rustie knife.

30

"With which sad instrument of hastie death,
That wofull lover, loathing lenger° light,   longer
A wide way made to let forth living breath.
265 But I more fearefull, or more luckie wight,
Dismayd with that deforméd dismall sight,
Fled fast away, halfe dead with dying feare:[7]
Ne yet assured of life by you, Sir knight,
Whose like infirmitie like chaunce may beare:
270 But God you never let his charméd speeches heare."

31

"How may a man," said he, "with idle speach
Be wonne, to spoyle the Castle of his health?"
"I wote," quoth he, "whom triall° late did teach,   experience
That like would not[8] for all this worldes wealth:
275 His subtill tongue, like dropping honny, mealt'th° melts
Into the hart, and searcheth every vaine,
That ere one be aware, by secret stealth
His powre is reft, and weaknesse doth remaine.
O never Sir desire to try° his guilefull traine."   test

32

280 "Certes," said he, "hence shall I never rest,
Till I that treachours art have heard and tride;
And you Sir knight, whose name mote° I request,   might
Of grace do me unto his cabin guide."

6. Redcrosse has hitherto been the victim of pride and rashness; here, another spiritual vice, directly contrary, is met —the temptation to the ultimate Christian sin, the despair of God's grace. Such despair was a concern to Renaissance writers of religious and medical works. Robert Burton, in his *Anatomy of Melancholy* (1621), wrote that the despair "which concerns God * * * [is] opposite to hope, and a most pernicious sin * * * The part affected is the whole soul" ("Religious Melancholy," II.i.2).
7. Fear of death.
8. I.e., would not do the like again.

"I that hight Trevisan," quoth he, "will ride
285   Against my liking backe, to doe you grace:
But nor for gold nor glee° will I abide   *glitter*
By you, when ye arrive in that same place;
For lever° had I die, then see his deadly face."   *rather*

33

Ere long they come, where that same wicked wight
290   His dwelling has, low in an hollow cave,
Farre underneath a craggie clift ypight,°   *placed*
Darke, dolefull, drearie, like a greedie grave,
That still for carrion carcases doth crave:
On top whereof aye dwelt the ghastly Owle,
295   Shrieking his balefull note, which ever drave
Farre from that haunt all other chearefull fowle;
And all about it wandring ghostes did waile and howle.

34

And all about old stockes and stubs of trees,
Whereon nor fruit, nor leafe was ever seene,
300   Did hang upon the ragged rocky knees;°   *crags*
On which had many wretches hangéd beene,
Whose carcases were scattered on the greene,
And throwne about the cliffs. Arrivéd there,
That bare-head knight for dread and dolefull teene,° *grief*
305   Would faine have fled, ne durst approachen neare,
But th'other forst him stay, and comforted in feare.

35

That darkesome cave they enter, where they find
That curséd man, low sitting on the ground,
Musing full sadly in his sullein mind;
310   His griesie° lockes, long growen, and unbound,   *gray*
Disordred hong about his shoulders round,
And hid his face; through which his hollow eyne
Lookt deadly dull, and staréd as astound;
His raw-bone cheekes through penurie and pine,° *starvation*
315   Were shronke into his jawes, as° he did never dine. *as if*

36

His garment nought but many ragged clouts,°   *cloths*
With thornes together pind and patchéd was,
The which his naked sides he wrapt abouts;
And him beside there lay upon the gras
320   A drearie corse, whose life away did pas,
All wallowd in his owne yet luke-warme blood,
That from his wound yet welléd fresh alas;
In which a rustie knife fast fixéd stood,
And made an open passage for the gushing flood.

37

325   Which piteous spectacle, approving trew
The wofull tale that Trevisan had told,
When as the gentle Redcrosse knight did vew,
With firie zeale he burnt in courage bold,

Him to avenge, before his bloud were cold,
330 And to the villein said, "Thou damnéd wight,
The author of this fact,° we here behold,   *deed*
What justice can but judge against thee right,
With thine owne bloud to price° his bloud, here   *pay for*
    shed in sight?"

38

"What franticke fit," quoth he,[9] "hath thus distraught
335 Thee, foolish man, so rash a doome° to give?   *judgment*
What justice ever other judgement taught,
But he should die, who merites not to live?
None else to death this man despayring drive,°   *drove*
But his owne guiltie mind deserving death.
340 Is then unjust to each his due to give?
Or let him die, that loatheth living breath?
Or let him die at ease, that liveth here uneath°?   *uneasily*

39

"Who travels by the wearie wandring way,
    To come unto his wishéd home in haste,
345 And meetes a flood, that doth his passage stay,
Is not great grace to helpe him over past,
Or free his feet, that in the myre sticke fast?
Most envious man, that grieves at neighbours good,
And fond,° that joyest in the woe thou hast,   *foolish*
350 Why wilt not let him passe, that long hath stood
Upon the banke, yet wilt thy selfe not passe the flood?

40

"He there does now enjoy eternall rest
    And happie ease, which thou doest want and crave,
And further from it daily wanderest:
355 What if some litle paine the passage have,
That makes fraile flesh to feare the bitter wave?
Is not short paine well borne, that brings long ease,
And layes the soule to sleepe in quiet grave?
Sleepe after toyle, port after stormie seas,
360 Ease after warre, death after life does greatly please."[1]

41

The knight much wondred at his suddeine° wit,   *quick*
And said, "The terme of life is limited,
Ne may a man prolong, nor shorten it;
The souldier may not move from watchfull sted,°   *position*
365 Nor leave his stand, untill his Captaine bed."°   *commands*
"Who life did limit by almightie doome,"
Quoth he,[2] "knowes best the termes establishéd;
And he, that points the Centonell his roome,°   *station*
Doth license him depart at sound of morning droome."

---

9. I.e., Despaire.
1. Despaire's arguments on behalf of suicide as against a painful life are derived, like those of Hamlet in his third soliloquy (*Hamlet* III.i.56–88), princi-

pally from Seneca, Marcus Aurelius, and the ancient stoics, and from Old Testament utterings on divine justice.
2. I.e., Despaire.

42

370 "Is not his deed, what ever thing is donne,
　　　In heaven and earth? did not he all create
　　　To die againe? all ends that was begonne.
　　　Their times in his eternall booke of fate
　　　Are written sure, and have their certaine date.
375　Who then can strive with strong necessitie,　　　　　　　　*its*
　　　That holds the world in his° still chaunging state,
　　　Or shunne the death ordaynd by destinie?
When houre of death is come, let none aske whence, nor why.

43

"The lenger life, I wote° the greater sin,　　　　　　　　　*know*
380　The greater sin, the greater punishment:
　　　All those great battels, which thou boasts to win,
　　　Through strife, and bloud-shed, and avengement,
　　　Now praysd, hereafter deare thou shalt repent:
　　　For life must life, and bloud must bloud repay.
385　Is not enough thy evill life forespent?
　　　For he, that once hath miss'd the right way,
The further he doth goe, the further he doth stray.

44

"Then do no further goe, no further stray,
　　　But here lie downe, and to thy rest betake,
390　Th'ill to prevent, that life ensewen may.[3]
　　　For what hath life, that may it lov'd make,
　　　And gives not rather cause it to forsake?
　　　Feare, sicknesse, age, losse, labour, sorrow, strife,
　　　Paine, hunger, cold, that makes the hart to quake;
395　And ever fickle fortune rageth rife,
All which, and thousands mo° do make a loathsome life.　　　*more*

45

"Thou wretched man, of death hast greatest need,
　　　If in true ballance thou wilt weigh thy state:
　　　For never knight, that dar'd warlike deede,
400　More lucklesse disaventures did amate:°　　　　　　　　*appall*
　　　Witnesse the dongeon deepe, wherein of late
　　　Thy life shut up, for death so oft did call;
　　　And though good lucke prolong'd hath thy date,°　　　*span of life*
　　　Yet death then, would the like mishaps forestall,
405　Into the which hereafter thou maiest happen fall.

46

"Why then doest thou, O man of sin, desire
　　　To draw thy dayes forth to their last degree?
　　　Is not the measure of thy sinfull hire[4]
　　　High heapéd up with huge iniquitie,
410　Against the day of wrath,[5] to burden thee?
　　　Is not enough that to this Ladie milde
　　　Thou fals'd hast thy faith with perjurie,
　　　And sold thy selfe to serve Duessa vilde,°　　　　　　　*vile*
With whom in all abuse thou hast thy selfe defilde?

3. I.e., to prevent the evil that will en-　　4. Service to sin.
sue in the rest of your life.　　　　　　　　5. Judgment Day.

47

415 "Is not he just, that all this doth behold
From highest heaven, and beares an equall° eye?   *impartial*
Shall he thy sins up in his knowledge fold,
And guiltie be of thine impietie?
Is not his law, Let every sinner die:
420 Die shall all flesh? what then must needs be donne,
Is it not better to doe willinglie,
Then linger, till the glasse be all out ronne?
Death is the end of woes: die soone, O faeries sonne."

48

The knight was much enmovéd with his speach,
425 That as a swords point through his hart did perse,
And in his conscience made a secret breach,
Well knowing true all, that he did reherse°   *recount*
And to his fresh remembrance did reverse°   *bring back*
The ugly vew of his deforméd crimes,
430 That all his manly powres it did disperse,
As he were charméd with inchaunted rimes,
That oftentimes he quakt, and fainted oftentimes.

49

In which amazement, when the Miscreant
Perceivéd him to waver weake and fraile,
435 Whiles trembling horror did his conscience dant,°   *daunt*
And hellish anguish did his soule assaile,
To drive him to despaire, and quite to quaile,°   *be dismayed*
He shewed him painted in a table° plaine,   *picture*
The damnéd ghosts, that doe in torments waile,
440 And thousand feends that doe them endlesse paine
With fire and brimstone, which for ever shall remaine.

50

The sight whereof so throughly him dismaid,
That nought but death before his eyes he saw,
And ever burning wrath before him laid,
445 By righteous sentence of th'Almighties law:
Then gan the villein him to overcraw,°   *exult over*
And brought unto him swords, ropes, poison, fire,
And all that might him to perdition draw;
And bad him choose, what death he would desire:
450 For death was due to him, that had provokt Gods ire.[6]

51

But when as none of them he saw him take,
He to him raught° a dagger sharpe and keene,   *reached*
And gave it him in hand: his hand did quake,
And tremble like a leafe of Aspin greene,
455 And troubled bloud through his pale face was seene
To come, and goe with tydings from the hart,
As it a running messenger had beene.
At last resolved to worke his finall smart,
He lifted up his hand, that backe againe did start.

6. Hamlet turned aside from suicide because of fear of the unknown; here, however, Redcrosse is tempted by the powerfully exciting allurement of death.

52

460 Which when as Una saw, through every vaine
    The crudled cold ran to her well of life,
    As in a swowne: but soone relived° againe,   *revived*
    Out of his hand she snatcht the curséd knife,
    And threw it to the ground, enragéd rife,°   *deeply*
465 And to him said, "Fie, fie, faint harted knight,
    What meanest thou by this reprochfull strife?
    Is this the battell, which thou vauntst to fight
With the fire-mouthéd Dragon, horrible and bright?

53

"Come, come away, fraile, feeble, fleshly wight,
470 Ne let vaine words bewitch thy manly hart,
    Ne divelish thoughts dismay thy constant spright.
    In heavenly mercies hast thou not a part?
    Why shouldst thou then despeire, that chosen art?
    Where justice growes, there grows eke greater grace,
475 The which doth quench the brond of hellish smart,
    And that accurst hand-writing doth deface.°   *blot out*
Arise, Sir knight arise, and leave this curséd place."[7]

54

So up he rose, and thence amounted streight.
    Which when the carle° beheld, and saw his guest   *churl*
480 Would safe depart, for all his subtill sleight,
    He chose an halter from among the rest,
    And with it hung himselfe, unbid unblest.
    But death he could not worke himselfe thereby;
    For thousand times he so himselfe had drest,°   *made ready*
485 Yet nathelesse it could not doe him die,
Till he should die his last, that is eternally.[8]

Canto X

Her faithfull knight faire Una brings
to house of Holinesse,
Where he is taught repentance, and
the way to heavenly blesse.°   *bliss*

1

What man is he, that boasts of fleshly might,
    And vaine assurance of mortality,°   *immortality*
    Which all so soone, as it doth come to fight,
    Against spirituall foes, yeelds by and by,[1]
5   Or from the field most cowardly doth fly?
    Ne let the man ascribe it to his skill,
    That thorough grace hath gainéd victory.
    If any strength we have, it is to ill,

7. Una reminds Redcrosse of God's mercy, the "greater grace" conspicuously missing from Despaire's eloquent speeches.
8. Despaire cannot kill himself. Compare his fruitless suicide attempts with Aesculapius's equally fruitless attempts "himself with salves to health for to restore" (I.v.40).
1. Immediately.

But all the good is Gods, both power and eke will.[2]

2

10 By that, which lately hapned, Una saw,
  That this her knight was feeble, and too faint;
  And all his sinews woxen weake and raw,°   *unready*
  Through long enprisonment, and hard constraint,
  Which he enduréd in his late restraint,
15 That yet he was unfit for bloudie fight:
  Therefore to cherish him with diets daint,°   *dainty*
  She cast to bring him, where he chearen° might, *be cheered*
Till he recovered had his[3] late decayéd plight.

3

 There was an auntient house not farre away,
20 Renowmd throughout the world for sacred lore,
  And pure unspotted life: so well they say
  It governd was, and guided evermore,
  Through wisedome of a matrone grave and hore;° *gray-haired*
  Whose onely joy was to relieve the needes
25 Of wretched soules, and helpe the helpelesse pore:
  All night she spent in bidding of her bedes,[4]
And all the day in doing good and godly deedes.

4

 Dame Caelia[5] men did her call, as thought
  From heaven to come, or thither to arise,
30 The mother of three daughters, well upbrought
  In goodly thewes,° and godly exercise: *habits*
  The eldest two most sober, chast, and wise,
  Fidelia and Speranza virgins were,
  Though spousd,° yet wanting wedlocks solemnize; *bethrothed*
35 But faire Charissa to a lovely fere°   *mate*
Was linckéd, and by him had many pledges dere.[6]

5

 Arrivéd there, the dore they find fast lockt;
  For it was warely watchéd night and day,
  For feare of many foes: but when they knockt,
40 The Porter opened unto them streight way:
  He was an agéd syre, all hory gray,
  With lookes full lowly cast, and gate full slow,
  Wont on a staffe his feeble steps to stay,
  Hight Humilta.° They passe in stouping low; *humility*
45 For streight and narrow was the way, which he did show.[7]

---

2. "For by grace are ye saved through faith; and that not of yourselves: it is the gift of God: Not of works, lest any men should boast" (Ephesians ii.8–9).
3. I.e., from his.
4. Saying prayers.
5. The name means "heavenly."
6. I.e., many children. The daughters' names mean "faith," "hope," and "charity." Cf. with them the three Saracens, Sans foy, Sans joy, and Sans loy: "faith" is the answer to atheism; "hope," the answer to empty despair; and "charity" (the highest law that embraces all other laws) the answer to chaos. "And now abideth faith, hope, charity, these three; but the greatest of these is charity" (I Corinthians xiii.13). Canto x, in which Spenser's didactic purpose is expressed with particular directness, is especially rich in scriptural references and echoes. Many aspects of the House of Holiness oppose their counterparts in the House of Pride (Canto iv).
7. "Strait is the gate, and narrow is the way, which leadeth unto life, and few there be that find it" (Matthew vii.14).

6

Each goodly thing is hardest to begin,
 But entred in a spacious court they see,
 Both plaine, and pleasant to be walkéd in,
 Where them does meete a francklin° faire and free, *freeholder*
50 And entertaines with comely courteous glee,
 His name was Zele, that him right well became,
 For in his speeches and behaviour hee
 Did labour lively to expresse the same,
And gladly did them guide, till to the Hall they came.

7

55 There fairely them receives a gentle Squire,
 Of milde demeanure, and rare courtesie,
 Right cleanly clad in comely sad° attire; *sober*
 In word and deede that shewed great modestie,
 And knew his good° to all of each degree, *proper respect*
60 Hight Reverence. He them with speeches meet
 Does faire entreat; no courting nicetie,° *affectation*
 But simple true, and eke unfainéd sweet,
As might become a Squire so great persons to greet.

8

And afterwards them to his Dame he leades,
65 That agéd Dame, the Ladie of the place:
 Who all this while was busie at her beades:
 Which doen, she up arose with seemely grace,
 And toward them full matronely did pace.
 Where when that fairest Una she beheld,
70 Whom well she knew to spring from heavenly race,
 Her hart with joy unwonted inly sweld,
As feeling wondrous comfort in her weaker eld.° *older age*

9

And her embracing said, "O happie earth,
 Whereon thy innocent feet doe ever tread,
75 Most vertuous virgin borne of heavenly berth,
 That to redeeme thy woefull parents head,
 From tyrans rage, and ever-dying dread,[8]
 Hast wandred through the world now long a day;
 Yet ceasest not thy wearie soles to lead,
80 What grace hath thee now hither brought this way?
Or doen thy feeble feet unweeting hither stray?

10

"Strange thing it is an errant° knight to see *wandering*
 Here in this place, or any other wight,
 That hither turnes his steps. So few there bee,
85 That chose the narrow path, or seeke the right:
 All keepe the broad high way, and take delight
 With many rather for to go astray,
 And be partakers of their evill plight,
 Then with a few to walke the rightest way;
90 O foolish men, why haste ye to your owne decay?"

8. Continuing fear of death.

11

"Thy selfe to see, and tyred limbs to rest,
O matrone sage," quoth she, "I hither came,
And this good knight his way with me addrest,
Led with thy prayses and broad-blazéd fame,
95   That up to heaven is blowne." The auncient Dame
Him goodly greeted in her modest guise,
And entertaynd them both, as best became,
With all the court'sies, that she could devise,
Ne wanted ought, to shew her bounteous or wise.

12

100 Thus as they gan of sundry things devise,°   *talk*
Loe two most goodly virgins came in place,
Ylinkéd arme in arme in lovely° wise,   *loving*
With countenance demure, and modest grace,
They numbred even steps and equall pace:
105   Of which the eldest, that Fidelia hight,
Like sunny beames threw from her Christall face,
That could have dazd the rash beholders sight,
And round about her head did shine like heavens light.[9]

13

She was araiéd all in lilly white,
110   And in her right hand bore a cup of gold,
With wine and water fild up to the hight,
In which a Serpent did himselfe enfold,
That horrour made to all, that did behold;
But she no whit did chaunge her constant mood:[1]
115   And in her other hand she fast did hold
A booke, that was both signd and seald with blood,
Wherein darke things were writ, hard to be understood.[2]

14

Her younger sister, that Speranza hight,
Was clad in blew, that her beseeméd well;
120   Not all so chearefull seeméd she of sight,[3]
As was her sister; whether dread did dwell,
Or anguish in her hart, is hard to tell:
Upon her arme a silver anchor[4] lay,
Whereon she leanéd ever, as befell:
125   And ever up to heaven, as she did pray,
Her stedfast eyes were bent, ne swarvéd other way.

15

They seeing Una, towards her gan wend,

9. Cf. the brightness of Arthur's shield, unveiled (viii.19).
1. Expression. The serpent in the cup is a symbol of St. John the Evangelist, whose faith was so great he could drink venom without harm. Contrast Duessa's cup (viii.14). The symbolic details in these portraits appear also in the allegorical figures in other works of Renaissance literature and art—particularly the emblem books.
2. The New Testament. See II Peter iii.16: "in which are some things hard to be understood, which they that are unlearned and unstable wrest, as they do also the other scriptures, unto their own destruction." Peter says this of St. Paul's writings, but it could also be said of many other parts of the New Testament—which is "signed and sealed with [the] blood" of Christ and the martyrs.
3. In appearance.
4. The iconographic symbol of hope.

Who them encounters with like courtesie;
Many kind speeches they betwene them spend,
130 And greatly joy each other well to see:
Then to the knight with shamefast° modestie   *humble*
They turne themselves, at Unas meeke request,
And him salute with well beseeming glee;
Who faire them quites,° as him beseeméd best,   *returns the salute*
135 And goodly gan discourse of many a noble gest.°   *achievement*

16

Then Una thus; "But she your sister deare;
The deare Charissa where is she become?
Or wants she health, or busie is elsewhere?"
"Ah no," said they, "but forth she may not come:
140 For she of late is lightned of her wombe,
And hath encreast the world with one sonne more,[5]
That her to see should be but troublesome."
"Indeede," quoth she, "that should her trouble sore,
But thankt be God, that her encrease so° evermore."   *truly*

17

145 Then said the aged Caelia, "Deare dame,
And you good Sir, I wote that of your toyle,
And labours long, through which ye hither came,
Ye both forwearied be: therefore a whyle
I read° you rest, and to your bowres recoyle."[6]   *suggest*
150 Then calléd she a Groome, that forth him led
Into a goodly lodge, and gan despoile°   *disrobe*
Of puissant armes, and laid in easie bed;
His name was meeke Obedience rightfully' aréd.°   *understood*

18

Now when their wearie limbes with kindly° rest,   *natural*
155 And bodies were refresht with due repast,
Faire Una gan Fidelia faire request,
To have her knight into her schoolehouse plaste,
That of her heavenly learning he might taste,
And heare the wisedome of her words divine.
160 She graunted, and that knight so much agraste,°   *favored*
That she him taught celestiall discipline,
And opened his dull eyes, that light mote in them shine.

19

And that her sacred Booke, with bloud[7] ywrit,
That none could read, except she did them teach,
165 She unto him discloséd every whit,
And heavenly documents° thereout did preach,   *doctrines*
That weaker whit of man could never reach,
Of God, of grace, of justice, of free will,
That wonder was to heare her goodly speach:
170 For she was able, with her words to kill,
And raise againe to life the hart, that she did thrill.°   *pierce*

5. Charity, the fruitful virtue, is often depicted pictorially as a mother with children.
6. Retire to your rooms.
7. I.e., the blood of Christ.

20

And when she list poure out her larger spright,[8]
  She would commaund the hastie Sunne to stay,
  Or backward turne his course from heavens hight;
175 Sometimes great hostes of men she could dismay,
  Dry-shod to passe, she parts the flouds in tway;
  And eke huge mountaines from their native seat
  She would commaund, themselves to beare away,
  And throw in raging sea with roaring threat.
180 Almightie God her gave such powre, and puissance great.[9]

21

The faithfull knight now grew in litle space,
  By hearing her, and by her sisters lore,
  To such perfection of all heavenly grace,
  That wretched world he gan for to abhore,
185 And mortall life gan loath, as thing forelore,
  Greeved with remembrance of his wicked wayes,
  And prickt with anguish of his sinnes so sore,
  That he desirde to end his wretched dayes:
So much the dart of sinfull guilt the soule dismayes.

22

190 But wise Speranza gave him comfort sweet,
  And taught him how to take assuréd hold
  Upon her silver anchor, as was meet;
  Else had his sinnes so great, and manifold
  Made him forget all that Fidelia told.
195 In this distresséd doubtfull agonie,
  When him his dearest Una did behold,
  Disdeining life, desiring leave to die,
She found her selfe assayld with great perplexitie.

23

And came to Caelia to declare her smart,
200 Who well acquainted with that commune plight,
  Which sinfull horror[1] workes in wounded hart,
  Her wisely comforted all that she might,
  With goodly counsell and advisement right;
  And streightway sent with carefull diligence,
205 To fetch a Leach,° the which had great insight   *doctor*
  In that disease of grievéd conscience,
And well could cure the same; His name was Patience.

24

Who comming to that soule-diseaséd knight,
  Could hardly him intreat, to tell his griefe:
210 Which knowne, and all that noyd° his heavie spright   *troubled*
  Well searcht, eftsoones he gan apply reliefe
  Of salves and med'cines, which had passing priefe,[2]

---

8. Full spiritual power.
9. Joshua made the sun stand still
(Joshua x.12); Hezekiah made it turn
backwards (II Kings xx.10); Gideon
was victorious over the Midianites
(Judges vii.7); Moses led the Israelites

through the parted waters of the Red
Sea (Exodus xiv.21–31); faith, said
Christ, can move mountains (Matthew
xxi.21). All these are miracles of faith.
1. Horror of sin.
2. Which had extraordinary power.

And thereto added words of wondrous might:[3]
By which to ease he him recuréd briefe,°   *speedily*
215   And much asswaged the passion° of his plight,   *suffering*
That he his paine endured, as seeming now more light.

25

But yet the cause and root of all his ill,
Inward corruption, and infected sin,
Not purged nor heald, behind remainéd still,
220   And festring sore did rankle yet within,
Close° creeping twixt the marrow and the skin.   *secretly*
Which to extirpe,° he laid him privily   *extirpate*
Downe in a darkesome lowly place farre in,
Whereas he meant his corrosives to apply,
225   And with streight° diet tame his stubborne malady.   *strict*

26

In ashes and sackcloth he did array
His daintie corse, proud humors[4] to abate,
And dieted with fasting every day,
The swelling of his wounds to mitigate,
230   And made him pray both earely and eke late:
And ever as superfluous flesh did rot
Amendment readie still at hand did wayt,
To pluck it out wth pincers firie whot,°   *hot*
That soone in him was left no one corrupted jot.

27

235   And bitter Penance with an yron whip,
Was wont him once to disple° every day: *discipline*
And sharpe Remorse his hart did pricke and nip,
That drops of bloud thence like a well did play;
And sad Repentance uséd to embay°   *bathe*
240   His bodie in salt water smarting sore,
The filthy blots of sinne to wash away.[5]
So in short space they did to health restore
The man that would not live, but earst° lay at deathes dore.   *before*

28

In which his torment often was so great,
245   That like a Lyon he would cry and rore,
And rend his flesh, and his owne synewes eat.
His own deare Una hearing evermore
His ruefull shriekes and gronings, often tore
Her guiltlesse garments, and her golden heare,
250   For pitty of his paine and anguish sore;
Yet all with patience wisely she did beare;
For well she wist, his crime could else be never cleare.

29

Whom thus recovered by wise Patience,
And trew Repentance they to Una brought:
255   Who joyous of his curéd conscience,
Him dearely kist, and fairely eke besought

3. I.e., absolution, or spiritual counseling generally.
4. Passions—i.e., pride.

5. "Wash me throughly from mine iniquity, and cleanse me from my sin"
(Psalms li.2).

Himselfe to chearish,° and consuming thought   *cheer*
To put away out of his carefull brest.
By this Charissa, late in child-bed brought,
260 Was woxen strong, and left her fruitfull nest;
To her faire Una brought this unacquainted guest.

30

She was a woman in her freshest age,
 Of wondrous beauty, and of bountie° rare,   *virtue*
 With goodly grace and comely personage,
265 That was on earth not easie to compare;
 Full of great love, but Cupids wanton snare
 As hell she hated, chast in worke and will;
 Her necke and breasts were ever open bare,
 That ay thereof her babes might sucke their fill;
270 The rest was all in yellow robes arayéd still.[6]

31

A multitude of babes about her hong,
 Playing their sports, that joyd her to behold,
 Whom still she fed, whiles they were weake and young,
 But thrust them forth still, as they wexéd old:
275 And on her head she wore a tyre° of gold,   *headdress*
 Adornd with gemmes and owches° wondrous faire, *jewels*
 Whose passing° price uneath° was to be told; *surpassing/scarcely*
 And by her side there sate a gentle paire
Of turtle doves, she sitting in an yvorie chaire.

32

280 The knight and Una entring, faire her greet,
 And bid her joy of that her happie brood;
 Who them requites with court'sies seeming meet,° *appropriate*
 And entertaines with friendly chearefull mood.
 Then Una her besought, to be so good,
285 As in her vertuous rules to schoole her knight,
 Now after all his torment well withstood,
 In that sad° house of Penaunce, where his spright *solemn*
Had past the paines of hell, and long enduring night.

33

She was right joyous of her just request,
290 And taking by the hand that Faeries sonne,
 Gan him instruct in every good behest,
 Of love, and righteousness, and well to donne,[7]
 And wrath, and hatred warely to shonne,
 That drew on men Gods hatred, and his wrath,
295 And many soules in dolours° had fordonne:° *misery/destroyed*
 In which when him she well instructed hath,
From thence to heaven she teacheth him the ready path.

34

Wherein his weaker° wandring steps to guide,   *too weak*
 An auncient matrone she to her does call,

---

6. Her yellow (saffron) robe is the emblem of fruitfulness. That she is "chast in work and will" and hates "Cupids wanton snare" does not contradict her "multitude of babes"; Spenser is distinguishing between *eros* and *agape*, sexual love and Christian love.
7. I.e., right action.

300 Whose sober lookes her wisedome well describe:°   *made known*
     Her name was Mercie, well knowne over all,
     To be both gratious, and eke liberall:
     To whom the carefull charge of him she gave,
     To lead aright, that he should never fall
305 In all his wayes through this wide worldés wave,°   *expanse*
That Mercy in the end his righteous soule might save.

35

The godly Matrone by the hand him beares
     Forth from her presence, by a narrow way,
     Scattred with bushy thornes, and ragged breares,°   *briers*
310 Which still before him she removed away,
     That nothing might his ready passage stay:
     And ever when his feet encombred were,
     Or gan to shrinke, or from the right to stray,
     She held him fast, and firmely did upbeare,
315 As carefull Nourse her child from falling oft does reare.

36

Eftsoones unto an holy Hospitall,°   *retreat*
     That was fore°by the way, she did him bring,   *close*
     In which seven Bead-men[8] that had vowéd all
     Their life to service of high heavens king
320 Did spend their dayes in doing godly thing:
     Their gates to all were open evermore,
     That by the wearie way were traveiling,
     And one sate wayting ever them before,
To call in commers-by, that needy were and pore.

37

325 The first of them that eldest was, and best,°   *chief*
     Of all the house had charge and governement,
     As Guardian and Steward of the rest:
     His office was to give entertainement
     And lodging, unto all that came, and went:
330 Not unto such, as could him feast againe,
     And double quite,° for that he on them spent,   *repay*
     But such, as want of harbour° did constraine: *shelter*
Those for Gods sake his dewty was to entertaine.

38

The second was as Almner° of the place,   *almoner*
335 His office was, the hungry for to feed,
     And thristy give to drinke, a worke of grace:
     He feard not once him selfe to be in need,
     Ne cared to hoord for those, whom he did breede:[9]
     The grace of God he layd up still in store,
340 Which as a stocke he left unto his seede;
     He had enough, what need him care for more?
And had he lesse, yet some he would give to the pore.

39

The third had of their wardrobe custodie,
     In which were not rich tyres,° nor garments gay,   *robes*

---

8. Men of prayer.   9. I.e., his children.

345   The plumes of pride, and wings of vanitie,
      But clothes meet to keepe keene could° away,   cold
      And naked nature seemely to aray;
      With which bare wretched wights he dayly clad,
      The images of God in earthly clay;
350   And if that no spare clothes to give he had,
His owne coate he would cut, and it distribute glad.

40

The fourth appointed by his office was,
      Poore prisoners to relieve with gratious ayd,
      And captives to redeeme with price of bras,°   money
355   From Turkes and Sarazins, which them had stayd;°   held captive
      And though they faultie were, yet well he wayd,
      That God to us forgiveth every howre
      Much more then that, why° they in bands were layd,   for which
      And he that harrowd hell[1] with heavie stowre,
360   The faultie soules from thence brought to his heavenly bowre.

41

The fift had charge sicke persons to attend,
      And comfort those, in point of death which lay;
      For them most needeth comfort in the end,
      When sin, and hell, and death do most dismay
365   The feeble soule departing hence away.
      All is but lost, that living we bestow,°   store up
      If not well ended at our dying day.
      O man have mind of that last bitter throw;°   throe
For as the tree does fall, so lyes it ever low.

42

370   The sixt had charge of them now being dead,
      In seemely sort their courses to engrave,°   bury
      And deck with dainty flowres their bridall bed,
      That to their heavenly spouse both sweet and brave
      They might appeare, when he their soules shall save.
375   The wondrous workemanship of Gods owne mould,°   image
      Whose face he made, all beasts to feare, and gave
      All in his hand, even dead we honour should.
Ah dearest God me graunt, I dead be not defould.°   abused

43

The seventh now after death and buriall done,
380   Had charge the tender Orphans of the dead
      And widowes ayd, least they should be undone:
      In face of judgement[2] he their right would plead,
      Ne ought the powre of mighty men did dread
      In their defence, nor would for gold or fee
385   Be wonne their rightfull causes downe to tread:

---

1. I.e., Christ, who journeyed to hell to deliver those good people who lived before his time, according to a popular story in the Middle Ages. It originated in the apocryphal gospel of Nicodemus.
2. I.e., in court.
3. Always freely. The seven Bead-men here correspond to, and perform, the seven works of charity, or corporal mercy: lodging the homeless, feeding the hungry, clothing the naked, redeeming the captive, comforting the sick, honoring the dead, and succoring the orphan. Cf. the seven deadly sins in the House of Pride.

And when they stood in most necessitee,
He did supply their want, and gave them ever free.[3]

44

There when the Elfin knight arrivéd was,
   The first and chiefest of the seven, whose care
390   Was guests to welcome, towardes him did pas:
   Where seeing Mercie, that his steps up bare,°   *supported*
   And alwayes led, to her with reverence rare
   He humbly louted° in meeke lowlinesse,   *bowed*
   And seemely welcome for her did prepare:
395   For of their order she was Patronesse,
Albe° Charissa were their chiefest founderesse.   *although*

45

There she awhile him stayes, him selfe to rest,
   That to the rest more able he might bee:
   During which time, in every good behest
400   And godly worke of Almes and charitee
   She him instructed with great industree;
   Shortly therein so perfect he became,
   That from the first unto the last degree,
   His mortall life he learnéd had to frame
405 In holy righteousnesse, without rebuke or blame.

46

Thence forward by that painfull way they pas,
   Forth to an hill, that was both steepe and hy;
   On top whereof a sacred chappell was,
   And eke a litle Hermitage thereby,
410   Wherein an agéd holy man did lye,
   That day and night said his devotion,
   Ne other worldly busines did apply;
   His name was heavenly Contemplation;
Of God and goodnesse was his meditation.

47

415 Great grace that old man to him given had;
   For God he often saw from heavens hight,
   All° were his earthly eyen both blunt° and bad,   *although/dim*
   And through great age had lost their kindly° sight,   *natural*
   Yet wondrous quick and persant° was his spright,   *piercing*
420   As Eagles eye, that can behold the Sunne:
   That hill they scale with all their powre and might,
   That his frayle thighes nigh wearie and fordonne°   *exhausted*
Gan faile, but by her helpe the top at last he wonne.

48

There they do finde that godly agéd Sire,
425   With snowy lockes adowne his shoulders shed,
   As hoarie frost with spangles doth attire
   The mossy braunches of an Oke halfe ded.
   Each bone might through his body well be red,°   *observed*
   And every sinew seene through his long fast:
430   For nought he cared his carcas long unfed;
   His mind was full of spirituall repast,
And pynéd° his flesh, to keepe his body low and chast.   *starved*

49

Who when these two approching he aspide,
    At their first presence grew agrievéd sore,
435   That forst him lay his heavenly thoughts aside;
    And had he not that Dame respected more,°   *greatly*
    Whom highly he did reverence and adore,
    He would not once have movéd for the knight.
    They him saluted standing far afore;°   *away*
440   Who well them greeting, humbly did requight,
And asked, to what end they clomb° that tedious height. *had climbed*

50

"What end," quoth she, "should cause us take such paine,
    But that same end, which every living wight
    Should make his marke, high heaven to attaine?
445   Is not from hence the way, that leadeth right
    To that most glorious house, that glistreth bright
    With burning starres, and everliving fire,
    Whereof the keyes are to thy hand behight°   *entrusted*
    By wise Fidelia? she doth thee require,
450   To shew it to this knight, according his desire."

51

"Thrise happy man," said then the father grave,
    "Whose staggering steps thy steady hand doth lead,
    And shewes the way, his sinfull soule to save.
    Who better can the way to heaven aread,
455   Then thou thy selfe, that was both borne and bred
    In heavenly throne, where thousand Angels shine?
    Thou doest the prayers of the righteous sead°   *offspring*
    Present before the majestie divine,
    And his avenging wrath to clemencie incline.

52

460   "Yet since thou bidst, thy pleasure shalbe donne.
    Then come thou man of earth, and see the way,
    That never yet was seene of Faeries sonne,
    That never leads the traveiler astray,
    But after labours long, and sad delay,
465   Brings them to joyous rest and endlesse blis.
    But first thou must a season fast and pray,
    Till from her bands the spright assoiléd° is,   *released*
And have her strength recured° from fraile infirmitis."   *recovered*

53

That done, he leads him to the highest Mount;
470   Such one, as that same mighty man of God,
    The bloud-red billowes like a walléd front
    On either side disparted with his rod,
    Till that his army dry-foot through them yod,°   *went*
    Dwelt fortie dayes upon; where writ in stone
475   With bloudy letters by the hand of God,
    The bitter doome° of death and balefull mone   *judgment*
He did receive, whiles flashing fire about him shone.

54

Or like that sacred hill, whose head full hie,

Adornd with fruitfull Olives all arownd,
480 Is, as it were for endlesse memory
Of that deare Lord, who oft thereon was fownd,
For ever with a flowring girlond crownd:
Or like that pleasaunt Mount, that is for ay
Through famous Poets verse each where° renownd,   *everywhere*
485 On which the thrise three learned Ladies play
Their heavenly notes, and make full many a lovely lay.[4]

55

From thence, far off he unto him did shew
A litle path, that was both steepe and long,
Which to a goodly Citie led his vew;
490 Whose wals and towres were builded high and strong
Of perle and precious stone, that earthly tong
Cannot describe, nor wit of man can tell;
Too high a ditty° for my simple song;   *subject*
The Citie of the great king hight it well,
495 Wherein eternall peace and happinesse doth dwell.

56

As he thereon stood gazing, he might see
The blessed Angels to and fro descend
From highest heaven, in gladsome companee,
And with great joy into that Citie wend,
500 As commonly° as friend does with his frend.[5]   *generally*
Whereat he wondred much, and gan enquere,
What stately building durst so high extend
Her loftie towres unto the starry sphere,
And what unknowen nation there empeopled were.

57

505 "Faire knight," quoth he, "Hierusalem that is,
The new Hierusalem, that God has built
For those to dwell in, that are chosen his,
His chosen people purged from sinfull guilt,
With pretious bloud, which cruelly was spilt
510 On curséd tree, of that unspotted lam,
That for the sinnes of all the world was kilt:
Now are they Saints all in that Citie sam,°   *together*
More deare unto their God, then younglings to their dam."[6]

58

"Till now," said then the knight, "I weenéd well,
515 That great Cleopolis,[7] where I have beene,

4. The mountain is successively compared to Mount Sinai (lines 469-77), where Moses, after parting the "bloud-red billowes" of the Red Sea, received the tablets of the laws of Judaism; to the Mount of Olives (lines 478-82), associated with Christ; and to Mount Parnassus (lines 483-86), where dwelled the nine muses of art and poetry. This last has the effect of equating poetry with the profoundest religious experience —a tradition that Sidney's *Apology* also incorporates.

5. Cf. Jacob's ladder: "And he dreamed, and behold a ladder set up on the earth, and the top of it reached to heaven; and behold the angels of God ascending and descending on it" (Genesis xxviii.12).
6. The New Jerusalem is described in Revelation xxi-xxii; "the nations of them which are saved shall walk in the light of it" (xxi.24).
7. London, Camelot—and here, the earthly counterpart of the Heavenly Kingdom.

In which that fairest Faerie Queene doth dwell,
The fairest Citie was, that might be seene;
And that bright towre all built of christall cleene,°   clear
Panthea,[8] seemd the brightest thing, that was:
520   But now by proofe all otherwise I weene;
For this great Citie that does far surpas,
And this bright Angels towre quite dims that towre of glas."

59

"Most trew," then said the holy aged man;
"Yet is Cleopolis for earthly frame,°   structure
525   The fairest peece, that eye beholden can:
And well beseemes all knights of noble name,
That covet in th'immortall booke of fame
To be eternizéd, that same to haunt,°   frequent
And doen their service to that soveraigne Dame,
530   That glorie does to them for guerdon° graunt: reward
For she is heavenly borne, and heaven may justly vaunt.°   claim

60

"And thou faire ymp, sprong out from English race,
How ever now accompted° Elfins sonne,   accounted
Well worthy doest thy service for her grace,°   favor
535   To aide a virgin desolate foredonne.
But when thou famous victorie hast wonne,
And high emongst all knights has hong thy shield,
Thenceforth the suit° of earthly conquest shonne,   pursuit
And wash thy hands from guilt of bloudy field:
540   For bloud can nought but sin, and wars but sorrowes yield.

61

"Then seeke this path, that I to thee presage,°   point out
Which after all to heaven shall thee send;
Then peaceably thy painefull pilgrimage
To yonder same Hierusalem do bend,
545   Where is for thee ordaind a blessed end:
For thou emongst those Saints, whom thou doest see,
Shalt be a Saint, and thine owne nations frend
And Patrone: thou Saint George shalt calléd bee,
Saint George of mery England, the signe of victoree."[9]

62

550   "Unworthy wretch," quoth he, "of so great grace,
How dare I thinke such glory to attaine?"
"These that have it attaind, were in like cace,"
Quoth he, "as wretched, and lived in like paine."
"But deeds of armes must I at last be faine,
555   And Ladies love to leave so dearely bought?"
"What need of armes, where peace doth ay remaine,"
Said he, "and battailes none are to be fought?
As for loose loves are vaine, and vanish into nought."

---

8. Reminiscent of the temple of glass in Chaucer's *Hous of Fame;* perhaps intended to represent Richmond Palace or Westminster Abbey.
9. Spenser's conception of St. George, patron saint of England, draws on the *Legenda Aurea* (translated by Caxton in 1487); on pictures, tapestries, and pageants; and on folklore.

63

"O let me not," quoth he, "then turne againe
560 Backe to the world, whose joyes so fruitlesse are;
But let me here for aye in peace remaine,
Or streight way on that last long voyage fare,
That nothing may my present hope empare."°   *impair*
"That may not be," said he, "ne maist thou yit
565 Forgo that royall maides bequeathéd care,°   *charge*
Who did her cause into thy hand commit,
Till from her curséd foe thou have her freely quit."°   *released*

64

"Then shall I soone," quoth he, "so God me grace,
Abet° that virgins cause disconsolate,   *support*
570 And shortly backe returne unto this place
To walke this way in Pilgrims poore estate.
But now aread, old father, why of late
Didst thou behight me borne of English blood,
Whom all a Faeries sonne doen nominate?"°   *name*
575 "That word shall I," said he, "avouchen° good,   *prove*
Sith to thee is unknowne the cradle of thy brood.

65

"For well I wote, thou springst from ancient race
Of Saxon kings, that have with mightie hand
And many bloudie battailes fought in place°   *there*
580 High reard their royall throne in Britane land,
And vanquisht them, unable to withstand:
From thence a Faerie thee unweeting reft,[1]
There as thou slepst in tender swadling band,
And her base Elfin brood there for thee left.
585 Such men do Chaungelings call, so chaungd by Faeries theft.

66

"Thence she thee brought into this Faerie lond,
And in an heapéd furrow did thee hyde,
Where thee a Ploughman all unweeting fond,
As he his toylesome teme that way did guyde,
590 And brought thee up in ploughmans state to byde,
Whereof Georgos he thee gave to name;[2]
Till prickt with courage, and thy forces pryde,
To Faery court thou cam'st to seeke for fame,
And prove thy puissaunt armes, as seemes thee best became."°   *suited*

67

595 "O holy Sire," quoth he, "how shall I quight
The many favours I with thee have found,
That has my name and nation red aright,
And taught the way that does to heaven bound?"°   *go*
This said, adowne he lookéd to the ground,
600 To have returnd, but dazéd were his eyne,
Through passing° brightnesse, which did quite confound *surpassing*
His feeble sence, and too exceeding shyne.
So darke are earthly things compard to things divine.

1. Secretly stole.
2. *Georgos* is Greek for "farmer" (cf. Virgil's *Georgics*, on farming).

68

At last whenas himselfe he gan to find,
To Una back he cast him to retire;
Who him awaited still with pensive mind.
Great thankes and goodly meed° to that good syre,   *gift*
He thence departing gave for his paines hyre.°   *reward*
So came to Una, who him joyd to see,
And after litle rest, gan him desire,
Of her adventure mindfull for to bee.
So leave they take of Caelia, and her daughters three.

Canto XI

The knight with that old Dragon fights
two dayes incessantly:
The third him overthrowes, and gayns
most glorious victory.

1

High time now gan it wex° for Una faire,   *develop*
To thinke of those her captive Parents deare,
And their forwasted kingdome to repaire:[3]
Whereto whenas they now approachéd neare,
With hartie words her knight she gan to cheare,
And in her modest manner thus bespake;
"Deare knight, as deare, as ever knight was deare,
That all these sorrowes suffer for my sake,
High heaven behold the tedious toyle, ye for me take.

2

"Now are we come unto my native soyle,
And to the place, where all our perils dwell;
Here haunts that feend, and does his dayly spoyle,
Therefore henceforth be at your keeping well,[4]
And ever ready for your foeman fell.
The sparke of noble courage now awake,
And strive your excellent selfe to excell;
That shall ye evermore renowméd make,
Above all knights on earth, that batteill undertake."

3

And pointing forth, "lo yonder is," said she,
"The brasen towre in which my parents deare
For dread of that huge feend emprisond be,
Whom I from far see on the walles appeare,
Whose sight my feeble° soule doth greatly cheare: *melancholy*
And on the top of all I do espye
The watchman wayting tydings glad to heare,
That O my parents might I happily
Unto you bring, to ease you of your misery."

4

With that they heard a roaring hideous sound,

---

3. I.e., to restore their kingdom, laid   4. I.e., be alert to your responsibilities.
waste (by the dragon) to health.

That all the ayre with terrour filléd wide,
30 And seemd uneath° to shake the stedfast ground.   *almost*
Eftsoones that dreadfull Dragon they espide,
Where stretcht he lay upon the sunny side
Of a great hill, himselfe like a great hill.
But all so soone, as he from far descride
35 Those glistring armes, that heaven with light did fill,
He rousd himselfe full blith,° and hastned them   *eagerly/*
  untill.°   *toward*

5

Then bad the knight his Lady yede° aloofe,   *step*
And to an hill her selfe withdraw aside,
From whence she might behold that battailles proof°   *outcome*
40 And eke be safe from daunger far descryde:
She him obayd, and turnd a little wyde.°   *aside*
Now I thou sacred Muse,[5] most learned Dame,
Faire ympe° of Phoebus, and his aged bride,[6]   *child*
The Nourse of time, and everlasting fame,
45 That warlike hands ennoblest with immortall name;

6

O gently come into my feeble brest,
Come gently, but not with that mighty rage,
Wherewith the martiall troupes thou doest infest,°   *arouse*
And harts of great Heroës doest enrage,
50 That nought their kindled courage may aswage,
Soone as thy dreadfull trompe begins to sownd;
The God of warre with his fiers equipage
Thou doest awake, sleepe never he so sownd,
And scaréd nations doest with horrour sterne astown.°   *appall*

7

55 Faire Goddesse lay that furious fit° aside,   *mood*
Till I of warres and bloudy Mars do sing[7]
And Briton fields with Sarazin bloud bedyde,
Twixt that great faery Queene and Paynim king,
That with their horrour heaven and earth did ring,
60 A worke of labour long, and endlesse prayse:
But now a while let downe that haughtie string,
And to my tunes thy second tenor rayse,[8]
That I this man of God his godly armes may blaze.°   *describe*

8

By this the dreadfull Beast drew nigh to hand,
65 Halfe flying, and halfe footing in his hast,
That with his largenesse measuréd much land,
And made wide shadow under his huge wast;°   *girth*
As mountaine doth the valley overcast.
Approching nigh, he rearéd high afore
70 His body monstrous, horrible, and vast,
Which to increase his wondrous greatnesse more,
Was swolne with wrath, and poyson, and with bloudy gore.

---

5. Calliope, muse of epic poetry, or Clio, muse of history.
6. I.e., Mnemosyne (memory).
7. Spenser refers to a projected book of *The Faerie Queene* which he never wrote.

8. The "haughtie" (high-pitched) mode would be appropriate to a large-scale epic war; the "second tenor" (lower in pitch) to this present battle.

9

And over, all with brasen scales was armd,
    Like plated coate of steele, so couchéd neare,[9]
75 That nought mote perce, ne might his corse be harmd
    With dint of sword, nor push of pointed speare;
    Which as an Eagle, seeing pray appeare,
    His aery Plumes doth rouze,° full rudely dight,   shake
    So shakéd he, that horrour was to heare,
80 For as the clashing of an Armour bright,
Such noyse his rouzéd scales did send unto the knight.

10

His flaggy° wings when forth he did display,   drooping
    Were like two sayles, in which the hollow wynd
    Is gathered full, and worketh speedy way:
85 And eke the pennes,° that did his pineons bynd,   quills
    Were like mayne-yards, with flying canvas lynd,
    With which whenas him list the ayre to beat,
    And there by force unwonted passage find,
    The cloudes before him fled for terrour great,
90 And all the heavens stood still amazéd with his threat.

11

His huge long tayle wound up in hundred foldes,
    Does overspred his long bras-scaly backe,
    Whose wreathéd boughts° when ever he unfoldes,   coils
    And thicke entangled knots adown does slacke,
95 Bespotted as with shields of red and blacke,
    It sweepeth all the land behind him farre,
    And of three furlongs does but litle lacke;
    And at the point two stings in-fixéd arre,
Both deadly sharpe, that sharpest steele exceeden farre.

12

100 But stings and sharpest steele did far exceed[1]
    The sharpnesse of his cruell rending clawes;
    Dead was it sure, as sure as death in deed,
    What ever thing does touch his ravenous pawes,
    Or what within his reach he ever drawes.
105 But his most hideous head my toung to tell
    Does tremble: for his deepe devouring jawes
    Wide gapéd, like the griesly mouth of hell,
Through which into his darke abisse all ravin° fell.[2]   prey, booty

13

And that more wondrous was, in either jaw
110   Threeranckes of yron teeth enraungéd were,
    In which yet trickling bloud and gobbets raw
    Of late devouréd bodies did appeare,
    That sight thereof bred cold congealéd feare:
    Which to increase, and all at once to kill,
115 A cloud of smoothering smoke and sulphur seare°   burning

9. Closely overlaid.
1. I.e., were far exceeded by.
2. In emphasizing the deathly, hellish aspects of the dragon, this stanza reveals the stakes of the battle: holiness vs. sin, the Protestant vs. the Catholic churches, life vs. death.

Out of his stinking gorge° forth steeméd still,   *maw*
That all the ayre about with smoke and stench did fill.

14

His blazing eyes, like two bright shining shields,
    Did burne with wrath, and sparkled living fyre;
120   As two broad Beacons, set in open fields,
    Send forth their flames farre off to every shyre,
    And warning give, that enemies conspyre,
    With fire and sword the region to invade;
    So flamed his eyne with rage and rancorous yre:
125   But farre within, as in a hollow glade,
Those glaring lampes were set, that made a dreadfull shade.[3]

15

So dreadfully he towards him did pas,
    Forelifting up aloft his speckled brest,
    And often bounding on the bruséd gras,
130   As for great joyance of his newcome guest.
    Eftsoones he gan advance his haughtie crest,
    As chaufféd° Bore his bristles doth upreare,   *vexed*
    And shoke his scales to battell readie drest;
    That made the Redcrosse knight nigh quake for feare,
135 As bidding bold defiance to his foeman neare.

16

The knight gan fairely couch° his steadie speare,   *rest, aim*
    And fiercely ran at him with rigorous might:
    The pointed steele arriving rudely theare,
    His harder hide would neither perce, nor bight,
140   But glauncing by forth passéd forward right;
    Yet sore amovéd with so puissant push,
    The wrathfull beast about him turnéd light,°   *quickly*
    And him so rudely passing by, did brush
With his long tayle, that horse and man to ground did rush.

17

145 Both horse and man up lightly rose againe,
    And fresh encounter towards him addrest:
    But th' idle stroke yet backe recoyld in vaine,
    And found no place his° deadly point to rest.   *its*
    Exceeding rage enflamed the furious beast,
150   To be avengéd of so great despight;°   *outrage*
    For never felt his imperceable brest
    So wondrous force, from hand of living wight;
Yet had he proved° the powre of many a puissant knight.   *tested*

18

Then with his waving wings displayéd wyde,
155   Himselfe up high he lifted from the ground,
    And with strong flight did forcibly divide
    The yielding aire, which nigh too feeble found
    Her flitting partes, and element unsound,

---

3. Cf. among other echoes, the great beast of Revelation (xiii.2): "And the beast which I saw was like unto a leopard, and his feet were as the feet of a bear, and his mouth as the mouth of a lion: and the dragon gave him his power, and his seat, and great authority."

To beare so great a weight: he cutting way
160   With his broad sayles, about him soaréd round:
  At last low stouping with unweldie sway,[4]
Snatcht up both horse and man, to beare them quite away.

19

Long he them bore above the subject plaine,[5]
  So farre as Ewghen[6] bow a shaft may send,
165   Till struggling strong did him at last constraine,
  To let them downe before his flightés end:
  As hagard° hauke presuming to contend   *untrained*
  With hardie fowle, above his hable might,[7]
  His wearie pounces° all in vaine doth spend,   *claws*
170   To trusse° the pray too heavie for his flight;   *seize*
Which comming downe to ground, does free it selfe by fight.

20

He so disseizéd of his gryping grosse,[8]
  The knight his thrillant° speare againe assayd   *piercing*
  In his bras-plated body to embosse,°   *plunge*
175   And three mens strength unto the stroke he layd;
  Wherewith the stiffe beame quakéd, as affrayd,
  And glauncing from his scaly necke, did glyde
  Close under his left wing, then broad displayd.
  The percing steele there wrought a wound full wyde,
180 That with the uncouth smart the Monster lowdly cryde.

21

He cryde, as raging seas are wont to rore,
  When wintry storme his wrathfull wreck does threat,
  The rolling billowes beat the ragged shore,
  As they the earth would shoulder from her seat,
185   And greedie gulfe does gape, as he would eat
  His neighbour element[9] in his revenge:
  Then gin the blustring brethren[1] boldly threat,
  To move the world from off his stedfast henge,°   *hinge*
And boystrous battell make, each other to avenge.

22

190 The steely head stucke fast still in his flesh,
  Till with his cruell clawes he snatcht the wood,
  And quite a sunder broke. Forth flowéd fresh
  A gushing river of blacke goarie blood,
  That drownéd all the land, whereon he stood;
195   The stream thereof would drive a water-mill.
  Trebly augmented was his furious mood
  With bitter sense of his deepe rooted ill,
That flames of fire he threw forth from his large noséthrill.

23

His hideous tayle then hurléd he about,
200   And therewith all enwrapt the nimble thyes

---

4. Ponderous force.   8. Freed from his formidable grip.
5. I.e., the ground below.   9. I.e., earth.
6. Yewen, of yew.   1. I.e., the winds.
7. Able power.

Of his froth-fomy steed, whose courage stout
Striving to loose the knot, that fast him tyes,
Himselfe in streighter bandes too rash implyes,
That to the ground he is perforce constraynd
205 To throw his rider: who can° quickly ryse   *began to*
From off the earth, with durty bloud distaynd,
For that reprochfull fall right fowly he disdaynd.

24

And fiercely tooke his trenchand° blade in hand,   *sharp*
With which he stroke so furious and so fell,
210 That nothing seemd the puissance could withstand:
Upon his crest the hardned yron fell,
But his more hardned crest was armd so well,
That deeper dint therein it would not make;
Yet so extremely did the buffe him quell,°   *dismay*
215 That from thenceforth he shund the like to take,
But when he saw them come, he did them still forsake.°   *avoid*

25

The knight was wrath to see his stroke beguyld,
And smote againe with more outrageous might;
But backe againe the sparckling steele recoyld,
220 And left not any marke, where it did light;
As if in Adamant rocke it had bene pight.°   *struck against*
The beast impatient of his smarting wound,
And of so fierce and forcible despight,
Thought with his wings to stye° above the ground;   *mount*
225 But his late wounded wing unserviceable found.

26

Then full of griefe and anguish vehement,
He lowdly brayd, that like was never heard,
And from his wide devouring oven sent
A flake° of fire, that flashing in his beard,   *flash*
230 Him all amazd, and almost made affeard;
The scorching flame sore swingéd° all his face,   *singed*
And through his armour all his bodie seard,
That he could not endure so cruell cace,
But thought his armes to leave, and helmet to unlace.

27

235 Not that great Champion of the antique world,
Whom famous Poetes verse so much doth vaunt,
And hath for twelve huge labours high extold,
So many furies and sharpe fits did haunt,
When him the poysoned garment did enchaunt
240 With Centaures bloud, and bloudie verses charmed,
As did this knight twelve thousand dolours daunt,
Whom fyrie steele now burnt, that earst him armed,
That erst him goodly armed, now most of all him harmed.[2]

2. Redcrosse's fire-baptism is compared to the burning shirt of Nessus, which killed Hercules, "that great Champion of the antique world" (line 235); the meta-phor of warfare and battle is here supplemented, as often in Spenser, by a metaphor of healing and purgation.

28

Faint, wearie, sore, emboyléd, grievéd, brent°   *burned*
245   With heat, toyle, wounds, armes, smart, and inward fire
      That never man such mischiefes did torment;
      Death better were, death did he oft desire,
      But death will never come, when needes require.
      Whom so dismayd when that his foe beheld,
250   He cast to suffer him no more respire,°   *rest*
      But gan his sturdie sterne° about to weld,°   *tail/lash*
And him so strongly stroke, that to the ground him feld.

29

It fortunéd (as faire it then befell)
      Behind his backe unweeting, where he stood,
255   Of auncient time there was a springing well,
      From which fast trickled forth a silver flood,
      Full of great vertues, and for med'cine good.
      Whylome,° before that curséd Dragon got   *formerly*
      That happie land, and all with innocent blood
260   Defyld those sacred waves, it rightly hot°   *was called*
The Well of Life, ne yet his° vertues had forgot.   *its*

30

For unto life the dead it could restore,
      And guilt of sinfull crimes cleane wash away,
      Those that with sicknesse were infected sore,
265   It could recure, and aged long decay
      Renew, as one were borne that very day.
      Both Silo this, and Jordan did excell,
      And th' English Bath, and eke the german Spau,
      Ne can Cephise, nor Hebrus match this well:
270   Into the same the knight backe overthrowen, fell.[3]

31

Now gan the golden Phoebus for to steepe
      His fierie face in billowes of the west,
      And his faint steedes watred in Ocean deepe,
      Whiles from their journall° labours they did rest,   *daily*
275   When that infernall Monster, having kest°   *cast*
      His wearie foe into that living well,
      Can° high advaunce his broad discoloured brest,   *did*
      Above his wonted pitch,° with countenance fell,   *height*
And clapt his yron wings, as victor he did dwell.°   *remain*

32

280   Which when his pensive Ladie saw from farre,
      Great woe and sorrow did her soule assay,°   *attack*
      As weening that the sad end of the warre,
      And gan to highest God entirely° pray,   *earnestly*
      That fearéd chaunce° from her to turne away;   *fate*

3. In the old English metrical romance *Sir Bevis of Hampton,* the hero is saved in his fight with a dragon by a healing well; "a pure river of water of life" is also described in Revelation xxii.1–2. The Well of Life, with its baptismal powers of renewal, is successively compared to waters of the Bible, of England and Europe, and of classical antiquity. In Siloam (Silo) a blind man was cured by Christ (John ix.7); the crossing of the river Jordan saved the Jews (Deuteronomy xxvii.2–9), and Christ was baptized therein (Matthew iii.16); "Bath" and "Spau" (Spa) were famed for their medicinal waters; "Cephise" and "Hebrus" in Greece were noted for their clear streams.

²⁸⁵   With folded hands and knees full lowly bent
    All night she watcht, ne once adowne would lay
    Her daintie limbs in her sad dreriment,
But praying still did wake, and waking did lament.

33

    The morrow next gan early to appeare,
²⁹⁰   That Titan⁴ rose to runne his daily race;
    But early ere the morrow next gan reare
    Out of the sea faire Titans deawy face,
    Up rose the gentle virgin from her place,
    And lookéd all about, if she might spy
²⁹⁵   Her loved knight to move his manly pace:
For she had great doubt of his safety,
Since late she saw him fall before his enemy.

34

    At last she saw, where he upstarted brave
    Out of the well, wherein he drenchéd lay;
³⁰⁰   As Eagle fresh out of the Ocean wave,
    Where he hath left his plumes all hoary gray,
    And deckt himselfe with feathers youthly gay,
    Like Eyas° hauke up mounts unto the skies,   *young*
    His newly budded pineons to assay,
³⁰⁵   And marveiles at himselfe, still as he flies:
So new this new-borne knight to battell new did rise.

35

    Whom when the damnéd feend so fresh did spy,
    No wonder if he wondred at the sight,
    And doubted, whether his late enemy
³¹⁰   It were, or other new suppliéd knight.
    He, now to prove his late renewéd might,
    High brandishing his bright deaw-burning blade,
    Upon his crested scalpe so sore did smite,
    That to the scull a yawning wound it made:
³¹⁵   The deadly dint his dulléd senses all dismaid.

36

    I wote not, whether the revenging steele
    Were hardnéd with that holy water dew,
    Wherein he fell, or sharper edge did feele,
    Or his baptizéd hands now greater° grew;   *stronger*
³²⁰   Or other secret vertue did ensew;
    Else never could the force of fleshly arme,
    Ne molten mettall in his bloud embrew:°   *plunge*
    For till that stownd° could never wight him harme,   *stunning blow*
By subtilty, nor slight,° nor might, nor mighty charme.   *trickery*

37

³²⁵   The cruell wound enragéd him so sore,
    That loud he yelléd for exceeding paine;
    As hundred ramping Lyons seemed to rore,
    Whom ravenous hunger did there to constraine:
    Then gan he tosse aloft his stretchéd traine,
³³⁰   And therewith scourge the buxome° aire so sore,   *yielding*

4. When the sun.

That to his force to yeelden it was faine;
Ne ought° his sturdie strokes might stand afore,   *anything*
That high trees overthrew, and rocks in peeces tore.

38

The same advauncing high above his head,
335   With sharpe intended° sting so rude him smot,   *shot out*
That to the earth him drove, as stricken dead,
Ne living wight would have him life behot:°   *granted*
The mortall sting his angry needle shot
Quite through his shield, and in his shoulder seasd,
340   Where fast it stucke, ne would there out be got:
The griefe thereof him wondrous sore diseasd,°   *afflicted*
Ne might his ranckling paine with patience be appeasd.[5]

39

But yet more mindfull of his honour deare,
Then of the grievous smart, which him did wring,°   *torment*
345   From loathéd soile he can° him lightly reare,   *began to*
And strove to loose the farre infixéd sting:
Which when in vaine he tryde with struggeling,
Inflamed with wrath, his raging blade he heft,
And strooke so strongly, that the knotty string
350   Of his huge taile he quite a sunder cleft,
Five joynts thereof he hewd, and but the stump him left.

40

Hart cannot thinke, what outrage, and what cryes,
With foule enfouldred[6] smoake and flashing fire,
The hell-bred beast threw forth unto the skyes,
355   That all was coveréd with darknesse dire:
Then fraught with rancour, and engorgéd° ire,   *choking*
He cast at once him to avenge for all,
And gathering up himselfe out of the mire,
With his uneven wings did fiercely fall
360   Upon his sunne-bright shield, and gript it fast withall.

41

Much was the man encombred with his hold,
In feare to lose his weapon in his paw,
Ne wist yet, how his talents° to unfold;   *talons*
Nor harder was from Cerberus greedie jaw
365   To plucke a bone, then from his cruell claw
To reave° by strength the gripéd gage° away: *seize/prize*
Thrise he assayd it from his foot to draw,
And thrise in vaine to draw it did assay,
It booted nought to thinke, to robbe him of his pray.

42

370   Tho when he saw no power might prevaile,
His trustie sword he cald to his last aid,
Wherewith he fiercely did his foe assaile,
And double blowes about him stoutly laid,
That glauncing fire out of the yron plaid;
375   As sparkles from the Andvile use to fly,

5. Redcrosse's wound suggests Christ's   6. Hurled out like thunder.
wounded side.

When heavie hammers on the wedge are swaid;°   *struck*
Therewith at last he forst him to unty°   *loosen*
One of his grasping feete, him to defend thereby.

43

The other foot, fast fixéd on his shield,
380   Whenas no strength, nor stroks mote him constraine
To loose, ne yet the warlike pledge to yield,
He smot thereat with all his might and maine,
That nought so wondrous puissance might sustaine;
Upon the joynt the lucky steele did light,
385   And made such way, that hewd it quite in twaine;
The paw yet misséd not his minisht° might,   *lessened*
But hong still on the shield, as it at first was pight.

44

For griefe thereof, and divelish despight,
From his infernall fournace forth he threw
390   Huge flames, that dimméd all the heavens light,
Enrold in duskish smoke and brimstone blew;
As burning Aetna from his boyling stew°   *cauldron*
Doth belch out flames, and rockes in peeces broke,
And ragged ribs of mountaines molten new
395   Enwrapt in coleblacke clouds and filthy smoke,
That all the land with stench, and heaven with horror choke.

45

The heate whereof, and harmefull pestilence
So sore him noyd,° that forst him to retire   *troubled*
A little backward for his best defence,
400   To save his bodie from the scorching fire,
Which he from hellish entrailes did expire.°   *breathe out*
It chaunst (eternall God that chaunce did guide)
As he recoyléd backward, in the mire
His nigh forwearied feeble feet did slide,
405   And downe he fell, with dread of shame sore terrifide.

46

There grew a goodly tree him faire beside,
Loaden with fruit and apples rosie red,
As they in pure vermilion had beene dide,
Whereof great vertues over all were red:°   *declared*
410   For happie life to all, which thereon fed,
And life eke everlasting did befall:
Great God it planted in that blessed sted°   *place*
With his almightie hand, and did it call
The Tree of Life, the crime of our first fathers fall.[7]

47

415 In all the world like was not to be found,
Save in that soile, where all good things did grow,
And freely sprong out of the fruitfull ground,
As incorrupted Nature did them sow,

---

7. In Genesis ii.9 appears the Tree of Life which God planted in the Garden of Eden. The "crime of our first fathers fall" is that Adam, in being banished from Eden, separated himself—and us—from the tree. The tree appears again in the New Jerusalem (Revelation xxii.2).

Till that dread Dragon all did overthrow.
420 Another like faire tree eke grew thereby,
Whereof who so did eat, eftsoones did know
Both good and ill: O mornefull memory:
That tree through one mans fault hath doen us all to dy.[8]

48

From that first tree forth flowd, as from a well,
425 A trickling streame of Balme, most soveraine
And daintie deare,[9] which on the ground still fell,
And overflowéd all the fertill plaine,
As it had deawéd bene with timely° raine: seasonable
Life and long health that gratious° ointment gave,   full of grace
430 And deadly woundes could heale, and reare againe
The senselesse corse appointed° for the grave.   made ready
Into that same he fell: which did from death him save.[1]

49

For nigh thereto the ever damnéd beast
Durst not approch, for he was deadly made,[2]
435 And all that life preservéd, did detest:
Yet he it oft adventured to invade.
By this the drouping day-light gan to fade,
And yeeld his roome to sad succeeding night,
Who with her sable mantle gan to shade
440 The face of earth, and wayes of living wight,
And high her burning torch set up in heaven bright.

50

When gentle Una saw the second fall
Of her deare knight, who wearie of long fight,
And faint through losse of bloud, moved not at all,
445 But lay as in a dreame of deepe delight,
Besmeard with pretious Balme, whose vertuous might
Did heale his wounds, and scorching heat alay,
Againe she stricken was with sore affright,
And for his safetie gan devoutly pray;
450 And watch the noyous° night, and wait for joyous day.   afflicting

51

The joyous day gan early to appeare,
And faire Aurora from the deawy bed
Of aged Tithone gan her selfe to reare,[3]
With rosie cheekes, for shame as blushing red;
455 Her golden lockes for haste were loosely shed
About her eares, when Una her did marke
Clymbe to her charet, all with flowers spred,
From heaven high to chase the chearelesse darke;
With merry note her loud salutes the mounting larke.

---

8. I.e., killed us. The tree described here is the Tree of Knowledge of Good and Evil in the Garden of Eden.
9. Precious.
1. A healing balm flowing from the tree of mercy is used by Seth to anoint Adam in the apocryphal Gospel of Nicodemus. This same balm is used later by Christ and is understood to be His blood. Christ's blood was shed to redeem mankind from eternal damnation.
2. I.e., a child of death.
3. Aurora is goddess of the dawn, Tithonus her husband ("aged" because he was granted everlasting life without everlasting youth).

52

460 Then freshly up arose the doughtie knight,
     All healéd of his hurts and woundés wide,
     And did himselfe to battell readie dight;
     Whose early foe awaiting him beside
     To have devourd, so soone as day he spyde,
465 When now he saw himselfe so freshly reare,
     As if late fight had nought him damnifyde,°   *injured*
     He woxe dismayd, and gan his fate to feare;
Nathlesse° with wonted rage he him advauncéd neare.   *nevertheless*

53

And in his first encounter, gaping wide,
470 He thought attonce him to have swallowed quight,
     And rusht upon him with outragious pride;
     Who him r'encountring fierce, as hauke in flight,
     Perforce rebutted° backe. The weapon bright   *drove*
     Taking advantage of his open jaw,
475 Ran through his mouth with so importune° might,   *violent*
     That deepe emperst his darksome hollow maw,
And back retyrd, his life bloud forth with all did draw.

54

So downe he fell, and forth his life did breath,
     That vanisht into smoke and cloudés swift;
480 So downe he fell, that th' earth him underneath
     Did grone, as feeble so great load to lift;
     So downe he fell, as an huge rockie clift,
     Whose false° foundation waves have washt away,   *insecure*
     With dreadfull poyse° is from the mayneland rift,   *falling weight*
485 And rolling downe, great Neptune doth dismay;
So downe he fell, and like an heapéd mountaine lay.

55

The knight himselfe even trembled at his fall,
     So huge and horrible a masse it seemed;
     And his deare Ladie, that beheld it all,
490 Durst not approch for dread, which she misdeemed,°   *misjudged*
     But yet at last, when as the direfull feend
     She saw not stirre, off-shaking vaine affright,
     She nigher drew, and saw that joyous end:
     Then God she praysd, and thankt her faithfull knight,
495 That had atchieved so great a conquest by his might.

Canto XII

*Faire Una to the Redcrosse knight
betrouthéd is with joy:
Though false Duessa it to barre
her false sleights doe imploy.*

1

Behold I see the haven nigh at hand,
     To which I meane my wearie course to bend;

Vere the maine shete, and beare up with the land,[4]
The which afore is fairely to be kend,°   *recognized*
5 And seemeth safe from stormes, that may offend;
There this faire virgin wearie of her way
Must landed be, now at her journeyes end:
There eke my feeble barke° a while may stay,   *ship*
Till merry wind and weather call her thence away.

2

10 Scarsely had Phoebus in the glooming East
Yet harnesséd his firie-footed teeme,
Ne reard above the earth his flaming creast,
When the last deadly smoke aloft did steeme,
That signe of last outbreathéd life did seeme
15 Unto the watchman on the castle wall;
Who thereby dead that balefull Beast did deeme,
And to his Lord and Ladie lowd gan call,
To tell, how he had seene the Dragons fatall fall.

3

Uprose with hastie joy, and feeble speed
20 That aged Sire, the Lord of all that land,
And lookéd forth, to weet, if true indeede
Those tydings were, as he did understand,
Which whenas true by tryall he out fond,
He bad to open wyde his brazen gate,
25 Which long time had bene shut, and out of hond[5]
Proclayméd joy and peace through all his state;
For dead now was their foe, which them forrayéd late.[6]

4

Then gan triumphant Trompets sound on hie,
That sent to heaven the ecchoéd report
30 Of their new joy, and happie victorie
Gainst him, that had them long opprest with tort,°   *wrong*
And fast imprisonéd in siegéd fort.
Then all the people, as in solemne feast,
To him assembled with one full consort,[7]
35 Rejoycing at the fall of that great beast,
From whose eternall bondage now they were releast.

5

Forth came that auncient Lord and aged Queene,
Arayd in antique robes downe to the ground,
And sad° habiliments right well beseene;°   *dignified/proper*
40 A noble crew about them waited round
Of sage and sober Peres, all gravely gownd;
Whom farre before did march a goodly band
Of tall young men, all hable armes to sownd,[8]
But now they laurell braunches bore in hand;
45 Glad signe of victorie and peace in all their land.

---

4. Release the mainsail line and sail toward the land. The metaphor in this
stanza echoes many classical authors and
Chaucer's *Troilus and Criseyde* (II.1–7).

5. Straightway.
6. Had recently ravaged.
7. All together.
8. Able to fight with weapons.

6

Unto that doughtie Conquerour they came,
  And him before themselves prostrating low,
  Their Lord and Patrone loud did him proclame,
  And at his feet their laurell boughes did throw.
50   Soone after them all dauncing on a row
  The comely virgins came, with girlands dight,
  As fresh as flowres in medow greene do grow,
  When morning deaw upon their leaves doth light:
And in their hands sweet Timbrels° all upheld   *tambourines*
    on hight.

7

55 And them before, the fry° of children young   *crowd*
  Their wanton° sports and childish mirth did play,   *playful*
  And to the Maydens sounding tymbrels sung
  In well attunéd notes, a joyous lay,
  And made delightfull musicke all the way,
60   Untill they came, where that faire virgin stood;
  As faire Diana in fresh sommers day
  Beholds her Nymphes, enraunged in shadie wood,
Some wrestle, some do run, some bathe in christall flood.

8

  So she beheld those maydens meriment
65   With chearefull vew; who when to her they came,
  Themselves to ground with gratious humblesse bent,
  And her adored by honorable name,
  Lifting to heaven her everlasting fame:
  Then on her head they set a girland greene,
70   And crownéd her twixt earnest and twixt game; [9]
  Who in her selfe-resemblance well beseene,[1]
Did seeme such, as she was, a goodly maiden Queene.

9

And after all, the raskall many° ran,   *mob*
  Heapéd together in rude rablement,
75   To see the face of that victorious man:
  Whom all admired, as from heaven sent,
  And gazd upon with gaping wonderment.
  But when they came, where that dead Dragon lay,
  Stretcht on the ground in monstrous large extent,
80   The sight with idle° feare did them dismay,   *baseless*
Ne durst approch him nigh, to touch, or once assay.

10

Some feard, and fled; some feard and well it faynd;
  One that would wiser seeme, then all the rest,
  Warnd him not touch, for yet perhaps remaynd
85   Some lingring life within his hollow brest,
  Or in his wombe might lurke some hidden nest
  Of many Dragonets, his fruitfull seed;
  Another said, that in his eyes did rest
  Yet sparckling fire, and bad thereof take heed;
90 Another said, he saw him move his eyes indeed.

9. I.e., half in fun.   1. I.e., looking appropriately like herself.

11

One mother, when as her foolehardie chyld
   Did come too neare, and with his talants play,
   Halfe dead through feare, her litle babe revyld,°   *scolded*
   And to her gossips° gan in counsell say;   *women friends*
95   "How can I tell, but that his talants may
   Yet scratch my sonne, or rend his tender hand?"
   So diversly themselves in vaine they fray;°   *scare*
   Whiles some more bold, to measure him nigh stand,
To prove° how many acres he did spread of land.   *determine*

12

100 Thus flockéd all the folke him round about,
   The whiles that hoarie king, with all his traine,
   Being arrivéd, where that champion stout
   After his foes defeasance° did remaine,   *defeat*
   Him goodly greetes, and faire does entertaine,
105   With princely gifts of yvorie and gold,
   And thousand thankes him yeelds for all his paine.
   Then when his daughter deare he does behold,
Her dearely doth imbrace, and kisseth manifold.°   *many times*

13

And after to his Pallace he them brings,
110   With shaumes,[2] and trompets, and with Clarions sweet;
   And all the way the joyous people sings,
   And with their garments strowes the pavéd street:
   Whence mounting up, they find purveyance° meet   *provisions*
   Of all, that royall Princes court became,°   *suited*
115   And all the floore was underneath their feet
   Bespred with costly scarlot of great name,[3]
On which they lowly sit, and fitting purpose frame.

14

What needs me tell their feast and goodly guize,°   *mode of life*
   In which was nothing riotous nor vaine?
120 What needs of daintie dishes to devize,°   *talk*
   Of comely services, or courtly trayne?
   My narrow leaves cannot in them containe
   The large discourse[4] of royall Princes state.
   Yet was their manner then but bare and plaine:
125   For th' antique world excesse and pride did hate;[5]
Such proud luxurious pompe is swollen up but late.

15

Then when with meates and drinkes of every kinde
   Their fervent appetites they quenchéd had,
   That auncient Lord gan fit occasion finde,
130   Of straunge adventures, and of perils sad,
   Which in his travell him befallen had,
   For to demaund of his renowméd guest:
   Who then with utt'rance grave, and count'nance sad,
   From point to point, as is before exprest,
135 Discourst his voyage long, according his request.

2. Ancient wind instrument like an oboe.
3. I.e., famous scarlet cloth.
4. I.e., full description.

5. The question of "excesse" will be paramount in Book II, "The Legend of Sir Guyon, or of Temperance."

16

Great pleasure mixt with pittifull° regard,   *sympathetic*
  That godly King and Queene did passionate,[6]
  Whiles they his pittifull adventures heard,
  That oft they did lament his lucklesse state,
140 And often blame the too importune fate,
  That heapd on him so many wrathfull wreakes:°   *injuries*
  For never gentle knight, as he of late,
    So tosséd was in fortunes cruell freakes;
And all the while salt teares bedeawd the hearers cheaks.

17

145 Then said that royall Pere in sober wise:
  "Deare Sonne, great beene the evils, which ye bore
  From first to last in your late enterprise,
  That I note,° whether prayse, or pitty more: *know not*
  For never living man, I weene, so sore
150 In sea of deadly daungers was distrest;
  But since now safe ye seiséd° have the shore,   *reached*
    And well arrivéd are (high God be blest),
Let us devize of ease and everlasting rest."

18

"Ah dearest Lord," said then that doughty knight,
155   "Of ease or rest I may not yet devize;
  For by the faith, which I to armes have plight,
  I bounden am streight after this emprize,°   *enterprise*
  As that your daughter can ye well advize,
  Backe to returne to that great Faerie Queene,
160 And her to serve six yeares in warlike wize,
  Gainst that proud Paynim king, that workes her teene:°   *sorrow*
Therefore I ought crave pardon, till I there have beene."[7]

19

"Unhappie falles that hard necessitie,"
  Quoth he, "the troubler of my happie peace,
165 And vowéd foe of my felicitie;
  Ne I against the same can justly preace:°   *press*
  But since that band° ye cannot now release,   *obligation*
  Nor doen undo (for vowes may not be vaine),
  Soone as the terme of those six yeares shall cease,
170 Ye then shall hither backe returne againe,
The marriage to accomplish vowd betwixt you twain.

20

"Which for my part I covet to performe,
  In sort as through the world I did proclame,
  That who so kild that monster most deforme,
175 And him in hardy battaile overcame,
  Should have mine onely daughter to his Dame,°   *wife*

6. I.e., did feel and express.
7. That the marriage of Redcrosse and Una cannot be made final here and now signifies primarily that the final Christian triumph, the marriage of Christ and the true church will be achieved only at the end of time, the Day of Judgment. Meanwhile, the struggle against evil (and the Roman Church) continues.

And of my kingdome heire apparaunt bee:
  Therefore since now to thee perteines the same,
  By dew desert of noble chevalree,
180 Both daughter and eke kingdome, lo I yield to thee."

21

Then forth he calléd that his daughter faire,
  The fairest Un' his onely daughter deare,
  His onely daughter, and his onely heyre;
  Who forth proceeding with sad° sober cheare,°   *grave/countenance*
185 As bright as doth the morning starre appeare
  Out of the East, with flaming lockes bedight,°   *bedecked*
  To tell that dawning day is drawing neare,
  And to the world does bring long wishéd light;
So faire and fresh that Lady shewd her selfe in sight.

22

190 So faire and fresh, as freshest flowre in May;
  For she had layd her mournefull stole aside,
  And widow-like sad wimple° throwne away,   *veil*
  Wherewith her heavenly beautie she did hide,
  Whiles on her wearie journey she did ride;
195 And on her now a garment she did weare,
  All lilly white, withoutten spot, or pride,°   *ornament*
  That seemed like silke and silver woven neare,°   *tightly*
But neither silke nor silver therein did appeare.[8]

23

The blazing brightnesse of her beauties beame,
200 And glorious light of her sunshyny face[9]
  To tell, were as to strive against the streame.
  My ragged rimes are all too rude and bace,
  Her heavenly lineaments for to enchace.°   *adorn*
  Ne wonder; for her owne deare lovéd knight,
205 All° were she dayly with himselfe in place,   *although*
  Did wonder much at her celestiall sight:
Oft had he seene her faire, but never so faire dight.

24

So fairely dight, when she in presence came,
  She to her Sire made humble reverence,
210 And bowéd low, that her right well became,
  And added grace unto her excellence:
  Who with great wisdome, and grave eloquence
  Thus gan to say. But eare° he thus had said,   *ere*
  With flying speede, and seeming great pretence,°   *importance*
215 Came running in, much like a man dismaid,
A Messenger with letters, which his message said.

8. "The marriage of the Lamb is come, and his wife hath made herself ready. And to her was granted that she shou.d be arrayed in fine linen, clean and white: for the fine linen is the righteousness of saints" (Revelation xix.7–8).
9. Revelation xxi.9, 11 describes the New Jerusalem as "the bride, the Lamb's wife * * * her light was like unto a store most precious." Contemplation showed Redcrosse the "real New Jerusalem" (xi.505–13); by these allusions, Spenser associates it with Una and her father's kingdom, Eden (now restored).

25

All in the open hall amazéd stood,
    At suddeinnesse of that unwarie° sight,   *unexpected*
    And wondred at his breathlesse hastie mood.
220 But he for nought would stay his passage right°   *direct*
    Till fast° before the king he did alight;   *close*
    Where falling flat, great humblesse he did make,
    And kist the ground, whereon his foot was pight;°   *placed*
    Then to his hands that writ° he did betake,   *document*
225 Which he disclosing, red thus, as the paper spake.

26

"To thee, most mighty king of Eden faire,
    Her greeting sends in these sad lines addrest,
    The wofull daughter, and forsaken heire
    Of that great Emperour of all the West;
230 And bids thee be advizéd for the best,
    Ere thou thy daughter linck in holy band
    Of wedlocke to that new unknowen guest:
    For he already plighted his right hand
Unto another love, and to another land.

27

235 "To me sad mayd, or rather widow sad,
    He was affiauncéd long time before,
    And sacred pledges he both gave, and had,
    False erraunt knight, infamous, and forswore:
    Witnesse the burning Altars, which° he swore,   *by which*
240 And guiltie heavens of[1] his bold perjury,
    Which though he hath polluted oft of yore,
    Yet I to them for judgement just do fly,
And them conjure t' avenge this shamefull injury.

28

"Therefore since mine he is, or° free or bond,   *whether*
245 Or false or trew, or living or else dead,
    Withhold, O soveraine Prince, your hasty hond
    From knitting league with him, I you aread;°   *advise*
    Ne wene° my right with strength adowne to tread,   *think*
    Through weakenesse of my widowhed, or woe:
250 For truth is strong, her rightfull cause to plead,
    And shall find friends, if need requireth soe,
So bids thee well to fare, Thy neither friend, nor foe, Fidessa."

29

When he these bitter byting words had red,
    The tydings straunge did him abashéd make,
255 That still he sate long time astonishéd
    As in great muse, ne word to creature spake.
    At last his solemne silence thus he brake,
    With doubtfull eyes fast fixéd on his guest:
    "Redoubted knight, that for mine onely sake
260 Thy life and honour late adventurest,
Let nought be hid from me, that ought to be exprest.

1. I.e., and heavens polluted by.

30

"What meane these bloudy vowes, and idle threats,
   Throwne out from womanish impatient mind?
   What heavens? what altars? what enragéd heates
265   Here heapéd up with termes of love unkind,°   *unnatural*
   My conscience cleare with guilty bands[2] would bind?
   High God be witnesse, that I guiltlesse ame.
   But if your selfe, Sir knight, ye faultie find,
   Or wrappéd be in loves of former Dame,
270 With crime do not it cover, but disclose the same."

31

To whom the Redcrosse knight this answere sent,
   "My Lord, my King, be nought hereat dismayd,
   Till well ye wote by grave intendiment,[3]
   What woman, and wherefore doth me upbrayd
275   With breach of love, and loyalty betrayd.
   It was in my mishaps, as hitherward
   I lately traveild, that unwares I strayd
   Out of my way, through perils straunge and hard;
That day should faile me, ere I had them all declard.

32

280 "There did I find, or rather I was found
   Of this false woman, that Fidessa hight,
   Fidessa hight the falsest Dame on ground,
   Most false Duessa, royall richly dight,
   That easie was t' invegle° weaker sight: *deceive*
285   Who by her wicked arts, and wylie skill,
   Too fasle and strong for earthly skill or might,
   Unwares me wrought unto her wicked will,
And to my foe betrayd, when least I fearéd ill."

33

Then steppéd forth the goodly royall Mayd,
290   And on the ground her selfe prostrating low,
   With sober countenaunce thus to him sayd:
   "O pardon me, my soveraigne Lord, to show
   The secret treasons, which of late I know
   To have bene wroght by that false sorceresse.
295   She onely she it is, that earst did throw
   This gentle knight into so great distresse,
That death him did awaite in dayly wretchednesse.

34

"And now it seemes, that she subornéd hath
   This craftie messenger with letters vaine,
300   To worke new woe and improvided scath,[4]
   By breaking of the band betwixt us twaine;
   Wherein she uséd hath the practicke paine[5]
   Of this false footman, clokt with simplenesse,
   Whom if ye please for to discover plaine,
305   Ye shall him Archimago find, I ghesse,
The falsest man alive; who tries shall find no lesse."

2. I.e., bonds of guilt.   4. Unexpected harm.
3. I.e., serious investigation.   5. Treacherous skill.

35

The king was greatly movéd at her speach,
    And all with suddein indignation fraight,°   *laden*
    Bad° on that Messenger rude hands to reach.   *bade*
310 Eftsoones the Gard, which on his state did wait,
    Attacht that faitor° false, and bound him strait: *impostor*
    Who seeming sorely chafféd° at his band,   *angered*
    As chainéd Beare, whom cruell dogs do bait,
    With idle force did faine them to withstand,
315 And often semblaunce made to scape out of their hand.

36

But they him layd full low in dungeon deepe,
    And bound him hand and foote with yron chains.
    And with continaull watch did warely keepe;
    Who then would thinke, that by his subtile trains
320 He could escape fowle death or deadly paines?[6]
    Thus when that Princes wrath was pacifide,
    He gan renew the late forbidden banes,[7]
    And to the knight his daughter deare he tyde,
With sacred rites and vowes for ever to abyde.

37

325 His owne two hands the holy knots did knit,
    That none but death for ever can devide;
    His owne two hands, for such a turne most fit,
    The housling° fire did kindle and provide,   *sacramental*
    And holy water thereon sprinckled wide;[8]
330 At which the bushy Teade° a groome did light,   *marriage torch*
    And sacred lampe in secret chamber hide,
    Where it should not be quenchéd day nor night,
For feare of evill fates, but burnen ever bright.

38

Then gan they sprinckle all the posts with wine,
335 And made great feast to solemnize that day;
    They all perfumde with frankensense divine,
    And precious odours fetcht from far away,
    That all the house did sweat with great aray:
    And all the while sweete Musicke did apply
340 Her curious° skill, the warbling notes to play,   *intricate*
    To drive away the dull Melancholy;
The whiles one sung a song of love and jollity.

39

During the which there was an heavenly noise
    Heard sound through all the Pallace pleasantly,

---

6. "And he laid hold on the dragon, that old serpent, which is the Devil, and Satan, and bound him a thousand years, And cast him into the bottomless pit, and shut him up, and set a seal upon him, that he should deceive the nations no more, till the thousand years should be fulfilled: and after that he must be loosed a little season" (Revelation xx.2–3).
7. Banns, i.e., announcements of marriage.

8. So marriages in ancient times were solemnized with sacramental fire and water. Plutarch (*Roman Questions* 1) explains the practice on four counts, of which two may especially have interested Spenser: (a) fire is masculine and active, water feminine and relatively passive; (b) as fire and water are most usefully productive in combination, so the joining of male and female in marriage appropriately completes society.

345   Like as it had bene many an Angels voice,
        Singing before th' eternall majesty,
        In their trinall triplicities[9] on hye;
        Yet wist no creature, whence that heavenly sweet°   *delight*
        Proceeded, yet each one felt secretly°   *inwardly*
350   Himselfe thereby reft of his sences meet,°   *proper*
    And ravishéd with rare impression in his sprite.[10]

40

    Great joy was made that day of young and old,
        And solemne feast proclaimd throughout the land,
        That their exceeding merth may not be told:
355   Suffice it heare by signes to understand
        The usuall joyes at knitting of loves band.
        Thrise happy man the knight himselfe did hold,
        Possesséd of his Ladies hart and hand,
        And ever, when his eye did her behold,
360   His heart did seeme to melt in pleasures manifold.

41

    Her joyous presence and sweet company
        In full content he there did long enjoy,
        Ne wicked envie, ne vile gealosy
        His deare delights were able to annoy:
365   Yet swimming in that sea of blisfull joy,
        He nought forgot, how he whilome had sworne,
        In case he could that monstrous beast destroy,
        Unto his Faerie Queene backe to returne:
    The which he shortly did, and Una left to mourne.

42

370   Now strike your sailes ye jolly Mariners,
        For we be come unto a quiet rode,°   *harbor*
        Where we must land some of our passengers,
        And light this wearie vessell of her lode.
        Here she a while may make her safe abode,
375   Till she repairéd have her tackles spent,°   *worn out*
        And wants supplide. And then againe abroad
        On the long voyage whereto she is bent:
    Well may she speede and fairely finish her intent.

From Book II, Canto XII[1]

[*The Bower of Bliss*]

42

370   Thence passing forth, they shortly do arrive,
        Whereas the Bowre of Blisse was situate;

9. The "trinall triplicities" are the nine angelic orders, divided, according to the pseudo-Areopagite, into three groups of three, the whole hierarchy corresponding to the nine spheres of the universe; what is heard in this stanza is, therefore, the music of the spheres.
10. Spirit. "Let us be glad and rejoice, and give honor to him: for the marriage of the Lamb is come" (Revelation xix.6).

In Revelation, the marriage of Christ and the New Jerusalem signalizes the general redemption.
1. Book II is the story of Sir Guyon, who represents and becomes the virtue of Temperance (or moderation, self-control) as Redcrosse represented, and became, Holiness; his companion is a "palmer," a "sage and sober" pilgrim. In the present selection from the last

A place pickt out by choice of best alive,[2]
That natures worke by art can imitate:
In which what ever in this worldly state
375 Is sweet, and pleasing unto living sense,
Or that may dayntiest fantasie aggrate,°   *please, satisfy*
Was pouréd forth with plentifull dispence,°   *liberality*
And made there to abound with lavish affluence.

43

Goodly it was encloséd round about,
380 Aswell their entred guestes to keepe within,
As those unruly beasts to hold without;
Yet was the fence thereof but weake and thin;
Nought feard their force, that fortilage° to win,   *fortalice, fort*
But wisedomes powre, and temperaunces might,[3]
385 By which the mightiest things efforcéd bin:°   *were*
And eke the gate was wrought of substaunce light,
Rather for pleasure, then for battery or fight.

44

Yt framéd was of precious yvory,
That seemd a worke of admirable wit;
390 And therein all the famous history
Of Jason and Medaea was ywrit;
Her mighty charmes, her furious loving fit,
His goodly conquest of the golden fleece,
His falséd faith, and love too lightly flit,
395 The wondred° Argo, which in venturous peece   *admired*
First through the Euxine seas bore all the flowr of Greece.

45

Ye might have seene the frothy billowes fry°   *foam*
Under the ship, as thorough them she went,

Canto, they visit and destroy the Bower of Bliss. The Bower functions, much as Lucifera's palace or Orgoglio's dungeon did in Book I, as an allegorical locale where a symbolic action takes place. Spenser had first shown his readers the Bower in Canto v; there Cymochles is found reclining "amidst a flock of Damzelles"; they are half-naked, wantonly flirtatious, while he, "like an Adder lurking in the weedes, / His wandring thought in deep desire does steepe." That was, however, only a preliminary glimpse.

The "Bower of Bliss," perhaps the most famous of Spenser's "set pieces," has been variously interpreted. In *The Allegory of Love*, C. S. Lewis argues convincingly that the Bower "is not a picture of lawless, that is, unwedded love as opposed to lawful love. It is a picture, one of the most powerful ever painted, of the whole sexual nature in disease. There is not a kiss or an embrace in the island: only male prurience and female provocation" (p. 332). This is especially true of Acrasia, the mistress of the Bower, whose name means both "excess" and "impotence"; she is

seen (stanzas 77–79) statically posed, doing nothing, only *appearing* as the archetypal seductress. The Bower is certainly a place where sexuality is sterile, as the Garden of Adonis (in the following selection) is a place where it is fertile. Some readers may find, however, that imagery partly overflows moral intention. For example, the two girls bathing in a pool (stanzas 63–68) are assuredly pin-ups out of a man's magazine of the mid-20th century—and yet Spenser compares them to the morning star and to the Venus of Cyprus (lines 577–80).

2. I.e., the best living artists. The imitating of nature by art had been foreshadowed in Canto v, where "art, striving to compare / with nature, did an Arber greene dispred" (II.v.272–73). Nature is important to Sir Guyon, as it was not to Redcrosse, because temperance is attainable by unaided nature, whereas holiness requires the help of grace.

3. The fear is not of the physical force of Guyon and the Palmer but of the virtuous power of their temperance and wisdom.

That seemd the waves were into yvory,
Or yvory into the waves were sent;
And other where the snowy substaunce sprent
With vermell,° like the boyes bloud therein shed,   *vermilion*
A piteous spectacle did represent,
And otherwhiles° with gold besprinkeléd;   *elsewhere*
Yt seemd th' enchaunted flame, which did Creüsa wed.[4]

46

All this, and more might in that goodly gate
Be red; that ever open stood to all,[5]
Which thither came: but in the Porch there sate
A comely personage of stature tall,
And semblaunce° pleasing, more than naturall,   *appearance*
That travellers to him seemd to entize;
His looser° garment to the ground did fall,   *too loose*
And flew about his heeles in wanton wize,
Not fit for speedy pace, or manly exercize.

47

They in that place him Genius° did call: *guiding spirit*
Not that celestiall powre, to whom the care
Of life, and generation of all
That lives, pertaines in charge particulare,
Who wondrous things concerning our welfare,
And straunge phantomes doth let us oft forsee,
And oft of secret ill bids us beware:
That is our Selfe, whom though we do not see,
Yet each doth in him selfe it well perceive to bee.

48

Therefore a God him sage Antiquity
Did wisely make, and good Agdistes call:
But this same was to that quite contrary,
The foe of life, that good envyes° to all,   *grudges*
That secretly doth us procure to fall,
Through guilefull semblaunts,° which he makes us see.   *illusions*
He of this Gardin had the governall,
And Pleasures porter was devizd° to bee,   *considered*
Holding a staffe in hand for more formalitee.

49

With diverse flowres he daintily was deckt,
And strowéd round about, and by his side
A mighty mazer° bowle of wine was set,   *drinking*
As if it had to him bene sacrifide;
Wherewith all new-come guests he gratifide:

4. Jason, in his ship the *Argo*, sought the Golden Fleece of the king of Colchis; the witch Medea, the king's daughter, fell in love with him and used "her mighty charmes" to help him obtain it (lines 392–93). The "boyes bloud" (line 402) refers to Absyrtus, Medea's younger brother, whose body she cut into pieces and scattered, to delay her father's pursuit by making him stop to collect the fragments. Later, Jason deserted Medea for Creüsa; in revenge, Medea gave the girl a dress which burst into fire when she put it on; the flame consumed and thus "wed" her (line 405). This tales of unnatural "furious loving," with all its attendant violence, is appropriate to the Bower.
5. "Wide is the gate, and broad is the way, that leadeth to destruction, and many there be which go in thereat" (Matthew vii.13).

So did he eke Sir Guyon passing by:
But he his idle curtesie defide,
440 And overthrew his bowle disdainfully;
And broke his staffe, with which he charméd semblants sly.[6]

50

Thus being entred, they behold around
A large and spacious plaine, on every side
Strowed with pleasauns,° whose faire grassy ground   *gardens*
445 Mantled with greene, and goodly beautifide
With all the ornaments of Floraes pride,
Wherewith her mother Art, as halfe in scorne
Of niggard Nature, like a pompous bride
Did decke her, and too lavishly adorne,
450 When forth from virgin bowre she comes in th' early morne.[7]

51

Thereto the Heavens always Joviall,°   *propitious*
Lookt on them lovely,° still in stedfast state,   *lovingly*
Ne suffred storme nor frost on them to fall,
Their tender buds or leaves to violate,
455 Nor scorching heat, nor cold intemperate
T' afflict the creatures, which therein did dwell,
But the milde aire with season moderate
Gently attempred, and disposd so well,
That still it breathéd forth sweet spirit and holesome smell.

52

460 More sweet and holesome, then the pleasaunt hill
Of Rhodope, on which the Nimphe, that bore
A gyaunt babe, her selfe for griefe did kill;
Or the Thessalian Tempe, where of yore
Faire Daphne Phoebus hart with love did gore;
465 Or Ida, where the Gods loved to repaire,
When ever they their heavenly bowres forlore;[8]
Or sweet Parnasse, the haunt of Muses faire;
Or Eden selfe, if ought with Eden mote compaire.

53

Much wondred Guyon at the faire aspect
470 Of that sweet place, yet suffred no delight
To sincke into his sence, nor mind affect,
But passéd forth, and lookt still forward right,°   *straight ahead*
Bridling his will, and maistering his might:
Till that he came unto another gate;
475 No gate, but like one, being goodly dight
With boughes and braunches, which did broad dilate°   *spread out*
Their clasping armes, in wanton wreathings intricate.

6. I.e., raised deceitful apparitions. The rod and bowl are traditional emblems of enchantment (cf. for example, Duessa's cup, in I.viii.14).

7. Art no longer merely imitates nature but undertakes to supplant it, by excess.

8. Deserted. The nymph Rhodope, who had a "gyaunt babe," Athos, by Neptune (lines 460–62), was turned into a mountain; Daphne, another nymph, charmed Apollo so that he pursued her until she prayed for aid and was turned into a laurel tree; Mount Ida was the scene of the rape of Ganymede and the judgment of Paris, and the gods watched the Trojan War from its heights. These are all allusions to violent and unhappy passion—and yet the Bower is also compared to Mt. Parnassus, home of the Muses, and to the Garden of Eden.

54

So fashionéd a Porch with rare device,
    Archt over head with an embracing vine,
480   Whose bounches hanging downe, seemed to entice
    All passers by, to tast their lushious wine
    And did themselves into their hands incline,
    As freely offering to be gatheréd:
    Some deepe empurpled as the Hyacint,
485   Some as the Rubine, laughing sweetly red,
Some like faire Emeraudes, not yet well ripenéd.

55

And them amongst, some were of burnisht gold,
    So made by art, to beautifie the rest,
    Which did themselves emongst the leaves enfold,
490   As lurking from the vew of covetous guest,
    That the weake bowes, with so rich load opprest,
    Did bowe adowne, as over-burdenéd.
    Under that Porch a comely dame did rest,
    Clad in faire weedes,° but fowle disorderéd,   *garments*
495 And garments loose, that seemd unmeet for womanhed.° *womanhood*

56

In her left hand a Cup of gold she held,
    And with her right the riper° fruit did reach,   *overripe*
    Whose sappy liquor, that with fulnesse sweld,
    Into her cup she scruzd,° with daintie breach   *crushed*
500   Of her fine fingers, without fowle empeach,°   *hindrance*
    That so faire wine-presse made the wine more sweet:
    Thereof she usd to give to drinke to each,
    Whom passing by she happenéd to meet:
It was her guise,° all Straungers goodly so to greet.   *custom*

57

505 So she to Guyon offred it to tast;
    Who taking it out of her tender hond,
    The cup to ground did violently cast,
    That all in peeces it was broken fond,°   *found*
    And with the liquor stainéd all the lond.°   *land*
510   Whereat Excesse exceedingly was wroth,
    Yet no'te° the same amend, ne yet withstond,   *knew not how to*
    But suffered him to passe, all° were she loth;   *although*
Who nought regarding her displeasure forward goth.

58

There the most daintie Paradise on ground,
515   It selfe doth offer to his sober eye,
    In which all pleasures plenteously abound,
    And none does others happinesse envye:
    The painted flowres, the trees upshooting hye,
    The dales for shade, the hilles for breathing space,
520   The trembling groves, the Christall running by;
    And that, which all faire workes doth most aggrace,°   *add grace to*
The art, which all that wrought, appearéd in no place.

59

One would have thought (so cunningly, the rude,
    And scornéd parts were mingled with the fine)
525 That nature had for wantonesse ensude°   *imitated*
    Art, and that Art at nature did repine;°   *complain*
    So striving each th' other to undermine,
    Each did the others worke more beautifie;
    So diff'ring both in willes, agreed in fine:[9]
530 So all agreed through sweete diversitie,
This Gardin to adorne with all varietie.

60

And in the midst of all, a fountaine stood,
    Of richest substaunce, that on earth might bee,
    So pure and shiny, that the silver flood
535 Through every channell running one might see;
    Most goodly it with curious imageree
    Was over-wrought, and shapes of naked boyes,
    Of which some seemd with lively jollitee,
    To fly about, playing their wanton toyes,°   *sports*
540 Whilest others did them selves embay° in liquid joyes.   *drench*

61

And over all, of purest gold was spred,
    A trayle of yvie in his native hew:
    For the rich metall was so colouréd,
    That wight, who did not well avised it vew,
545 Would surely deeme it to be yvie trew:[1]
    Low his lascivious armes adown did creepe,
    That themselves dipping in the silver dew,
    Their fleecy flowres they tenderly did steepe,
Which° drops of Christall seemd for wantones°   *on which/wantonness*
        to weepe.

62

550 Infinit streames continually did well
    Out of this fountaine, sweet and faire to see,
    The which into an ample laver° fell,   *basin*
    And shortly grew to so great quantitie,
    That like a little lake it seemd to bee;
555 Whose depth exceeded not three cubits hight,
    That through the waves one might the bottom see,
    All pavéd beneath with Jasper shining bright,
That seemd the fountaine in that sea did sayle upright.

63

And all the margent round about was set,
560 With shady Laurell trees, thence to defend°   *ward off*
    The sunny beames, which on the billowes bet,
    And those which therein bathéd, mote offend.
    As Guyon hapned by the same to wend,
    Two naked Damzelles he therein espyde,

9. I.e., at the end. Art and nature har-
monize with each other in effect, although antagonistic in intention.

1. The golden ivy has attracted much
critical comment as an image of artifice
with a touch of the repellent about it.

565   Which therein bathing, seeméd to contend,
      And wrestle wantonly, ne cared to hyde,
  Their dainty parts from vew of any, which them eyde.

64

  Sometimes the one would lift the other quight
      Above the waters, and then downe againe
570   Her plong, as over maisteréd by might,
      Where both awhile would coveréd remaine,
      And each the other from to rise restraine;
      The whiles their snowy limbes, as through a vele,
      So through the Christall waves appearéd plaine:
575   Then suddeinly both would themselves unhele,°   *uncover*
  And th' amarous sweet spoiles to greedy eyes revele.

65

  As that faire Starre, the messenger of morne,
      His deawy face out of the sea doth reare:
      Or as the Cyprian goddesse,[2] newly borne
580   Of th' Oceans fruitfull froth, did first appeare:
      Such seeméd they, and so their yellow heare
      Christalline humour[3] droppéd downe apace.
      Whom such when Guyon saw, he drew him neare,
      And somewhat gan relent his earnest pace,
585   His stubborne brest gan secret pleasaunce to embrace.

66

  The wanton Maidens him espying, stood
      Gazing a while at his unwonted guise;°   *manner*
      Then th' one her selfe low duckéd in the flood,
      Abasht, that her a straunger did avise:°   *see*
590   But th' other rather higher did arise,
      And her two lilly paps aloft displayd,
      And all, that might his melting hart entise
      To her delights, she unto him bewrayed:°   *revealed*
  The rest hid underneath, him more desirous made.

67

595   With that, the other likewise up arose,
      And her faire lockes, which formerly were bownd
      Up in one knot, she low adowne did lose: °   *loosen*
      Which flowing long and thick, her clothed arownd,
      And th' yvorie in golden mantle gownd:
600   So that faire spectacle from him was reft,
      Yet that, which reft it, no lesse faire was fownd:
      So hid in lockes and waves from lookers theft,
  Nought but her lovely face she for his looking left.

68

  Withall she laughéd, and she blusht withall,
605   That blushing to her laughter gave more grace,
      And laughter to her blushing, as did fall:
      Now when they spide the knight to slacke his pace,
      Them to behold, and in his sparkling face

2. Venus (one of whose principal   3. Clear liquid.
shrines was on the island of Cyprus).

The secret signes of kindled lust appeare,
610   Their wanton meriments they did encreace,
   And to him beckned, to approach more neare,
And shewd him many sights, that courage cold could reare.[4]

69

On which when gazing him the Palmer saw,
   He much rebukt those wandring eyes of his,
615   And counseld well, him forward thence did draw.
   Now are they come nigh to the Bowre of blis
   Of her fond favorites so named amis:
   When thus the Palmer: "Now Sir, well avise;°   *take care*
   For here the end of all our travell is:
620 Here wonnes° Acrasia, whom we must surprise,   *dwells*
Else she will slip away, and all our drift° despise."   *plan, effort*

70

Eftsoones they heard a most melodious sound,
   Of all that mote delight a daintie eare,
   Such as attonce might not on living ground,
625   Save in this Paradise, be heard elswhere:
   Right hard it was, for wight, which did it heare,
   To read, what manner musicke that mote bee:
   For all that pleasing is to living eare,
   Was there consorted in one harmonee,
630 Birdes, voyces, instruments, windes, waters, all agree.

71

The joyous birdes shrouded in chearefull shade,
   Their notes unto the voyce attempred° sweet;   *attuned*
   Th' Angelicall soft trembling voyces made
   To th' instruments divine respondence meet:°   *fitting*
635   The silver sounding instruments did meet°   *join*
   With the base murmure of the waters fall:
   The waters fall with difference discreet,°   *suitable*
   Now soft, now loud, unto the wind did call:
The gentle warbling wind low answered to all.[5]

72

640 There, whence that Musick seeméd heard to bee,
   Was the faire Witch her selfe now solacing,
   With a new Lover, whom through sorceree
   And witchcraft, she from farre did thither bring:
   There she had him now layd a slombering,
645   In secret shade, after long wanton joyes:
   Whilst round about them pleasauntly did sing
   Many faire Ladies, and lascivious boyes,
That ever mixt their song with light licentious toyes.

---

4. That could arouse a cold spirit.
5. Taste, sight, smell, and sound are all titillated here; little is said, however, of touching. Acrasia, whom we are about to see, bears many resemblances to Circe (not only the cool figure of *Odyssey* X, but the much more witchlike and seductive creature painted by Ovid) and to the enchantresses of Italian romance who derive from Circe, such as Acratia in Trissino's *L'Italia Liberata* and Armida in Tasso's *Gerusalemme Liberata*. In fact, much of the description in Canto xii is imitated from Armida's garden in that poem, and the rose song of stanzas 74 and 75 (a classic statement of the *carpe-diem* theme) is a direct translation.

73

And all that while, right over him she hong,
  With her false eyes fast fixéd in his sight,
  As seeking medicine, whence she was stong,
  Or greedily depasturing° delight: *feeding on*
  And oft inclining downe with kisses light,
  For feare of waking him, his lips bedewd,
  And through his humid eyes did sucke his spright,
  Quite molten into lust and pleasure lewd;
Wherewith she sighéd soft, as if his case she rewd.°   *pitied*

74

The whiles some one did chaunt this lovely lay:
  "Ah see, who so faire thing doest faine° to see   *delight*
  In springing flowre the image of thy day;
  Ah see the Virgin Rose, how sweetly shee
  Doth first peepe forth with bashfull modestee
  That fairer seemes, the lesse ye see her may
  Lo see soone after, how more bold and free
  Her baréd bosome she doth broad display;
Loe see soone after, how she fades, and falles away.

75

"So passeth, in the passing of a day,
  Of mortall life the leafe, the bud, the flowre,
  Ne more doth flourish after first decay,
  That earst was sought to decke both bed and bowre,
  Of many a Ladie, and many a Paramowre: °   *lover*
  Gather therefore the Rose, whilest yet is prime
  For soone comes age, that will her pride deflowre:
  Gather the Rose of love, whilest yet is time,
Whilest loving thou mayst lovéd be with equal crime."

76

He ceast, and then gan all the quire of birdes
  Their diverse notes t' attune unto his lay,
  As in approvance of his pleasing words.
  The constant paire heard all, that he did say,
  Yet swarved not, but kept their forward way,
  Through many covert groves, and thickets close,
  In which they creeping did at last display°   *discover*
  That wanton Ladie, with her lover lose,°   *loose*
Whose sleepie head she in her lap did soft dispose.

77

Upon a bed of Roses she was layd,[6]
  As faint through heat, or dight to pleasant sin,
  And was arayd, or rather disarayd,
  All in a vele of silke and silver thin,
  That hid no whit her alablaster skin,
  But rather shewd more white, if more might bee:
  More subtile web Arachne° cannot spin,   *the spider*
  Nor the fine nets, which oft we woven see
Of scorched deaw, do not in th' aire more lightly flee.°   *float*

6. Prepared for.

78

Her snowy brest was bare to readie spoyle
Of hungry eies, which n'ote° therewith be fild,   *could not*
And yet through languor of her late sweet toyle,
Few drops, more cleare than Nectar, forth distild,
That like pure Orient perles adowne it trild,°   *trickled*
And her faire eyes sweet smyling in delight,
Moystened their fierie beames, with which she thrild
Fraile harts, yet quenchéd not; like starry light
Which sparckling on the silent waves, does seeme more bright.

79

The young man sleeping by her, seemd to bee
Some goodly swayne of honorable place,°   *rank*
That certés it great pittie was to see
Him his nobilitie so foule deface;°   *disgrace*
A sweet regard, and amiable grace,
Mixed with manly sternnesse did appeare
Yet sleeping, in his well proportioned face,
And on his tender lips the downy heare
Did now but freshly spring, and silken blossomes beare.

80

His warlike armes, the idle instruments
Of sleeping praise, were hong upon a tree,
And his brave shield, full of old moniments,
Was fowly ra'st,[7] that none the signes might see;
Ne for them, ne for honour caréd hee,
Ne ought, that did to his advauncement tend,
But in lewd loves, and wastfull luxuree,
His dayes, his goods, his bodie he did spend:
O horrible enchantment, that him so did blend.°   *blind*

81

The noble Elfe,[8] and carefull Palmer drew
So nigh them, minding nought, but lustfull game,
That suddein forth they on them rusht, and threw
A subtile net, which onely for the same
The skilfull Palmer formally° did frame.   *scientifically*
So held them under fast, the whiles the rest
Fled all away for feare of fowler shame.
The faire Enchauntresse, so unwares opprest,
Tryde all her arts, and all her sleights, thence out to wrest.

82

And eke her lover strove: but all in vaine;
For that same net so cunningly was wound,
That neither guile, nor force might it distraine.°   *tear*
They tooke them both, and both them strongly bound
In captive bandes, which there they readie found:
But her in chaines of adamant he tyde;
For nothing else might keepe her safe and sound;

7. Erased. The removal of the emblems   a knight.
from his shield was the last disgrace of   8. Knight of fairyland.

But Verdant[9] (so he hight) he soone untyde,
And counsell sage in steed thereof to him applyde.

83

But all those pleasant bowres and Pallace brave,
740   Guyon broke downe, with rigour pittilesse;
  Ne ought their goodly workmanship might save
  Them from the tempest of his wrathfulnesse,
  But that their blisse he turned to balefulnesse:
  Their groves he feld, their gardins did deface,
745   Their arbers spoyle, their Cabinets° suppresse,   *summerhouses*
  Their banket houses burne, their buildings race,°   *raze*
And of the fairest late, now made the fowlest place.

84

Then led they her away, and eke that knight
  They with them led, both sorrowfull and sad:
750   The way they came, the same retourned they right,
  Till they arrivéd, where they lately had
  Charmed those wild-beasts, that raged with furie mad.
  Which now awaking, fierce at them gan fly,
  As in their mistresse reskew, whom they lad;°   *lead*
755   But them the Palmer soone did pacify.
Then Guyon askt, what meant those beastes, which there did ly.

85

Said he, "These seeming beasts are men indeed,
  Whom this Enchauntresse hath transforméd thus,
  Whylome her lovers, which her lusts did feed,
760   Now turned into figures hideous,
  According to their mindes like monstruous."[1]
  "Sad end," quoth he, "of life intemperate,
  And mournefull meed of joyes delicious:
  But Palmer, if it mote thee so aggrate,°   *please*
765 Let them returnéd be unto their former state."

86

Streight way he with his vertuous staffe them strooke,
  And streight of beasts they comely men became;
  Yet being men they did unmanly looke,
  And staréd ghastly, some for inward shame,
770   And some for wrath, to see their captive Dame:
  But one above the rest in speciall,
  That had an hog beene late, hight Grille by name,
  Repinéd greatly, and did him miscall,°   *abuse*
That had from hoggish forme him brought to naturall.

87

775 Said Guyon, "See the mind of beastly man,
  That hath so soone forgot the excellence
  Of his creation, when his life began,
  That now he chooseth, with vile difference,°   *change*
  To be a beast, and lacke intelligence."

9. The name means "green" and may
refer, therefore, to a young man in the
springtime of his sensuality.
1. Circe had changed Odysseus' companions into swine, but Odysseus was
empowered to release them. Cf. also the
animals upon which the sins rode in I.v.

780　To whom the Palmer thus, "The donghill kind
　　　Delights in filth and foule incontinence:
　　　Let Grill be Grill, and have his hoggish mind,
But let us hence depart, whilest wether serves and wind."

From Book III, Canto VI[1]

[The Garden of Adonis]

30

In that same Gardin all the goodly flowres,
　　Wherewith dame Nature doth her beautifie,
　　And decks the girlonds of her paramoures,
265　Are fetcht: there is the first seminarie°　　　　　*genetic source*
　　Of all things, that are borne to live and die,
　　According to their kindes. Long worke it were,
　　Here to account the endlesse progenie
　　Of all the weedes,° that bud and blossome there;　*plants*
270　But so much as doth need, must needs be counted here.

31

It sited was in fruitfull soyle of old,
　　And girt in with two walles on either side;
　　The one of yron, the other of bright gold,
　　That none might thorough breake, nor overstride:
275　And double gates it had, which opened wide,
　　By which both in and out men moten° pas;　　　*could*
　　Th' one faire and fresh, the other old and dride:
　　Old Genius the porter of them was,
Old Genius, the which a double nature has.

32

280　He letteth in, he letteth out to wend,°　　　　　*go*
　　All that to come into the world desire;
　　A thousand thousand naked babes attend
　　About him day and night, which doe require,
　　That he with fleshly weedes would them attire:[2]
285　Such as him list, such as eternall fate
　　Ordainéd hath, he clothes with sinfull mire,[3]
　　And sendeth forth to live in mortall state,
Till they againe returne backe by the hinder gate.

1. The "hero" of Book III is the lady Britomart, the representative of Chastity. By "chastity" is meant, however, not abstinence but a love that is devoted and active. The "Garden of Adonis" passage here reprinted is the "allegorical core" of the book, but unlike Orgoglio's castle or the Bower of Bliss, the knight does not enter upon any symbolic action therein; in fact, Britomart does not even appear.
　　The Garden of Adonis is part of a long literary tradition of earthly paradises, among them Homer's Garden of Alcinous (*Odyssey* VII) and Chaucer's Garden of Nature in the *Parliament of Fowls* (lines 120–308), and of gardens in courtly-love allegories. The broadly Neoplatonic ideas in stanzas 30–50 parallel classical and later sources such as the Myth of Er in Plato's *Republic*, the *Enneads* of Plotinus, and Arthur Golding's translation of Ovid's *Metamorphoses*. In Spenser's Garden all living things are formed and re-formed; as the center of generation and regeneration, it is the axis upon which the idea of love, as the life-producing power, turns. The Garden exhibits a picture of what love would be if man were not what he is.
2. The "naked babes" may be taken as the "seeds" from which all life springs, or as souls in the pre-existent state. "Weedes" are clothes, so "fleshly weedes" are, here, the body.
3. I.e., the flesh.

33

After that they againe returnéd beene,
290   They in that Gardin planted be againe;
       And grow afresh, as they had never seene
       Fleshly corruption, nor mortall paine.
       Some thousand yeares so doen they there remaine;
       And then of him are clad with other hew,°   *form*
295   Or sent into the chaungefull world againe,
       Till thither they returne, where first they grew:
So like a wheele around they runne from old to new.

34

Ne needs there Gardiner to set, or sow,
       To plant or prune: for of their owne accord
300   All things, as they created were, doe grow,
       And yet remember well the mightie word,
       Which first was spoken by th' Almightie lord,
       That bad them to increase and multiply:
       Ne doe they need with water of the ford,°   *stream*
305   Or of the clouds to moysten their roots dry;
For in themselves eternall moisture they imply.°   *contain*

35

Infinite shapes of creatures there are bred,
       And uncouth° formes, which none yet ever knew,   *strange*
       And every sort is in a sundry° bed   *separate*
310   Set by it selfe, and ranckt in comely rew:°   *row, rank*
       Some fit for reasonable soules t' indew,°   *put on*
       Some made for beasts, some made for birds to weare,
       And all the fruitfull spawne of fishes hew
       In endlesse rancks along enraungéd were,
315 That seemed the Ocean could not containe them there.

36

Daily they grow, and daily forth are sent
       Into the world, it to replenish more;
       Yet is the stocke not lessenéd, nor spent,
       But still remaines in everlasting store,
320   As it at first created was of yore.
       For in the wide wombe of the world there lyes,
       In hatefull darkenesse and in deepe horrore,
       An huge eternall Chaos, which supplyes
The substances of natures fruitfull progenyes.

37

325 All things from thence doe their first being fetch,
       And borrow matter, whereof they are made,
       Which when as forme and feature it does ketch,[4]
       Becomes a bodie, and doth then invade°   *enter*
       The state of life, out of the griesly shade.
330   That substance is eterne, and bideth so,
       Ne when the life decayes, and forme does fade,
       Doth it consume, and into nothing go,
But chaungéd is, and often altred to and fro.

---

4. I.e., when it takes shape and outline.

38

335

The substance is not chaunged, nor alteréd,
But th' only forme and outward fashion;°   *appearance*
For every substance is conditionéd
To change her hew, and sundry formes to don,
Meet for her temper and complexion:
For formes are variable and decay,

340

By course of kind,° and by occasion;   *nature*
And that faire flowre of beautie fades away,
As doth the lilly fresh before the sunny ray.[5]

39

Great enimy to it, and to all the rest,
That in the Gardin of Adonis springs,

345

Is wicked Time, who with his scyth addrest,°   *armed*
Does mow the flowring herbes and goodly things,
And all their glory to the ground downe flings,
Where they doe wither, and are fowly mard:
He flyes about, and with his flaggy° wings   *drooping*

350

Beates downe both leaves and buds without regard,
Ne ever pittie may relent his malice hard.

40

Yet pittie often did the gods relent,
To see so faire things mard, and spoyléd quight:
And their great mother Venus did lament

355

The losse of her deare brood, her deare delight:
Her hart was pierst with pittie at the sight,
When walking through the Gardin, them she spyde,
Yet no'te[6] she find redresse for such despight.
For all that lives, is subject to that law:

360

All things decay in time, and to their end do draw.

41

But were it not, that Time their troubler is,
All that in this delightfull Gardin growes,
Should happie be, and have immortall blis,
For here all plentie, and all pleasure flowes,

365

For sweet love gentle fits° emongst them throwes,   *impulses*
Without fell rancor, or fond gealosie;
Franckly each paramour° his leman° knowes,   *lover / sweetheart*
Each bird his mate, ne any does envie
Their goodly meriment, and gay felicite.

42

370

There is continuall spring, and harvest there
Continuall, both meeting at one time:[7]
For both the boughes doe laughing blossomes beare,
And with fresh colours decke the wanton Prime,°   *Spring*
And eke attonce the heavy trees they clime,

375

Which seeme to labour under their fruits lode:

5. While stanzas 30–35 emphasized the
cyclical process of all life, stanzas 36–
38 describe the indestructible substance
that persists through the cycles.
6. Did not know how to.
7. The sexuality of the Garden is life-
giving—unlike the sexuality of the
Bower of Bliss, which was life-destroy-
ing. The Garden is untroubled by sea-
sonal change, like other perfect gardens
in Renaissance and medieval literature,
which are types of an ideal world.

The whiles the joyous birdes make their pastime
Emongst the shadie leaves, their sweet abode,
And their true loves without suspition tell abrode.

43

Right in the middest of that Paradise,
380   There stood a stately Mount, on whose round top
     A gloomy grove of mirtle trees did rise,
     Whose shadie boughes sharpe steele did never lop,
     Nor wicked beasts their tender buds did crop,
     But like a girlond compasséd the hight,
385   And from their fruitfull sides sweet gum did drop,
     That all the ground with precious deaw bedight,
Threw forth most dainty odours, and most sweet delight.

44

And in the thickest covert of that shade,
     There was a pleasant arbour, not by art,
390   But of the trees owne inclination made,[8]
     Which knitting their rancke° braunches part to part,   *dense*
     With wanton yvie twyne entrayld athwart,
     And Eglantine, and Caprifole[9] emong,
     Fashiond above within their inmost part,
395   That nether Phoebus beams could through them throng,
Nor Aeolus sharp blast could worke them any wrong.

45

And all about grew every sort of flowre,
     To which sad lovers were transformed of yore;
     Fresh Hyacinthus, Phoebus paramoure,
400   And dearest love,
     Foolish Narcisse, that likes the watry shore,
     Sad Amaranthus, made a flowre but late,
     Sad Amaranthus, in whose purple gore
     Me seemes I see Amintas wretched fate,
405 To whom sweet Poets verse hath given endlesse date.[1]

46

There wont faire Venus often to enjoy
     Her deare Adonis joyous company,
     And reape sweet pleasure of the wanton boy;
     There yet, some say, in secret he does ly,
410   Lappéd in flowres and pretious spycery,
     By her hid from the world, and from the skill°   *knowledge*
     Of Stygian Gods, which doe her love envy;

8. Unlike the Bower of Bliss, where art rivaled or supplanted nature, Venus's bower is entirely natural.
9. Honeysuckle or woodbine.
1. Hyacinthus was a youth loved by Apollo and Zephyrus; returning the love of the former, he was killed out of jealousy by the latter, and the flower known by his name sprang from his blood. Narcissus, enamored of his own reflection in a pool, died and was also transformed into a flower. "Amintas" is Spenser's name for Sir Philip Sidney, on whose death Spenser, like all the other poets of his day, produced a poem. All these young men, turned into flowers after being cut off in the flower of their lives, suggest the quality of Adonis's garden; it is the place where unfulfilled potentialities are renewed, and spiritual vitality is restored to wounded ideals. "Amaranthus" completes this idea, for its name means, in Greek, the "undying, unfading flower"; it symbolizes spiritual immortality for Adonis and his group of handsome, unfulfilled young men.

But she her selfe, when ever that she will,
Possesseth him, and of his sweetnesse takes her fill.

47

415 And sooth it seemes they say: for he may not
For ever die, and ever buried bee
In balefull night, where all things are forgot;
All° be he subject to mortalitie,   *although*
Yet is eterne in mutabilitie,
420 And by succession made perpetuall,
Transforméd oft, and chaungéd diverslie:
For him the Father of all formes they call;
Therefore needs mote he live, that living gives to all.[2]

48

There now he liveth in eternall blis,
425 Joying his goddesse, and of her enjoyd:
Ne feareth he hence forth that foe of his,
Which with his cruell tuske him deadly cloyd:°   *pierced*
For that wilde Bore, the which him once annoyd,°   *injured*
She firmely hath emprisonéd for ay,
430 That her sweet love his malice mote avoyd,
In a strong rocky Cave, which is they say,
Hewen underneath that Mount, that none him losen may.[3]

49

There now he lives in everlasting joy,
With many of the Gods in company,
435 Which thither haunt, and with the wingéd boy[4]
Sporting himselfe in safe felicity:
Who when he hath with spoiles and cruelty
Ransackt the world, and in the wofull harts
Of many wretches set his triumphes hye,
440 Thither resorts, and laying his sad darts
Aside, with faire Adonis playes his wanton parts.

50

And his true love faire Psyche with him playes,
Faire Psyche to him lately reconcyld,
After long troubles and unmeet upbrayes,°   *reproaches*
445 With which his mother Venus her revyld,°   *scolded*
And eke himselfe her cruelly exyld:[5]
But now in stedfast love and happy state
She with him lives, and hath him borne a chyld,
Pleasure, that doth both gods and men aggrate,°   *gratify*
450 Pleasure, the daughter of Cupid and Psyche late.

2. Adonis might be taken to symbolize the changing forms of matter, which cannot be destroyed but remain "eterne in mutabilitie," line 419.

3. "Losen": set free. This stanza retells the myth of Venus and Adonis. The boar may stand for animal passion, violence, and disorder.

4. I.e., Cupid—who, it should be noted, never appeared in the Bower of Bliss.

5. Psyche, a beautiful princess, was visited by her lover Cupid only at night. Curious to see him, she lighted a lamp while he was asleep accidentally dropped some hot oil on him, and awakened him. He was angry at her lack of trust and left her; she wandered in search of him and endured many hardships imposed by Venus, who was jealous of her beauty. She was finally reunited with Cupid and made immortal. Her story has been taken to represent the arduous purification, by trial and misfortune, of the human soul.

From Book VII, Mutabilitie[1]

The VIII *Canto, Unperfite*

When I bethinke me on that speech whyleare,
  Of Mutability,[2] and well it way:
Me seemes, that though she all unworthy were
  Of the Heav'ns Rule; yet very sooth to say,
5 In all things else she beares the greatest sway.
  Which makes me loath this state of life so tickle,°   *precarious*
  And love of things so vaine to cast away;
  Whose flowring pride, so fading and so fickle,
Short Time shall soon cut down with his consuming sickle.

                    2

10 Then gin I thinke on that which Nature sayd,
  Of that same time when no more Change shall be,
  But stedfast rest of all things firmely stayd
  Upon the pillours of Eternity,
  That is contrayr to Mutabilitie:
15 For, all that moveth, doth in Change delight:
  But thence-forth all shall rest eternally
  With Him that is the God of Sabbaoth hight:
O that great Sabbaoth God, graunt me that Sabaoths sight.[3]

                                1590, 1596, 1609

From Amoretti[4]

Sonnet 1

Happy ye leaves when as those lilly hands,
  Which hold my life in their dead doing[5] might,
  Shall handle you and hold in loves soft bands,
  Lyke captives trembling at the victors sight.
5 And happy lines, on which with starry light,
  Those lamping eyes will deigne sometimes to look
  And reade the sorrowes of my dying spright,°   *spirit*
  Written with teares in harts close° bleeding book.   *secret*
  And happy rymes bathed in the sacred brooke,

1. Cantos VI and VII and two stanzas of Canto VIII, called the "Mutability Cantos," were first published in 1609, ten years after Spenser's death. According to the title page, they "appear to be parcel of some following book of *The Faerie Queene*, under the legend of Constancie." These cantos give Spenser's reflections, influenced perhaps by Lucretius, on change and permanence in the world—a subject enthralling to the Elizabethan imagination.
2. Before an assembly of the gods the Titaness Mutability had pleaded that since all things are subject to change, she should be goddess over all.
3. A play on *sabaoth* (Hebrew: "hosts," "armies") and "Sabbath," day of rest.

4. I.e., "little loves" or "little love poems." They are sonnets to a woman named Elizabeth—probably Elizabeth Boyle, who became Spenser's second wife. The sequence, or cycle, tells of a courtship (*Epithalamion*, with which they were published, is a song for a wedding). The *Amoretti* draws, like other sonnet cycles, upon characteristic and conventional themes and conceits; what is characteristically Spenserian about them is his understanding, and yoking, of the spirit and the flesh; see, for example, lines 9–12 of Sonnet 1. The rhyme scheme is *abab bcbc cdcd ee*, a difficult pattern requiring four words for two of the rhymes.
5. I.e., killing.

10 Of Helicon[6] whence she derivéd is,
When ye behold that Angels blessed looke,
My soules long lackéd foode, my heavens blis.
Leaves, lines, and rymes, seeke her to please alone,
Whom if ye please, I care for other none.

Sonnet 34

Lyke as a ship that through the ocean wyde,
By conduct of some star doth make her way,
Whenas a storme hath dimd her trusty guyde,
Out of her course doth wander far astray.
5 So I whose star, that wont with her bright ray,
Me to direct, with cloudes is overcast,
Doe wander now in darknesse and dismay,
Through hidden perils round about me plast.°   *placed*
Yet hope I well, that when this storme is past
10 My Helice[7] the lodestar of my lyfe
Will shine again, and looke on me at last,
With lovely light to cleare my cloudy grief.
Till then I wander carefull° comfortlesse,   *full of cares*
In secret sorow and sad pensivenesse.

Sonnet 35

My hungry eyes through greedy covetize,
Still to behold the object of their paine,
With no contentment can themselves suffize:
But having pine° and having not complaine.   *starve*
5 For lacking it they cannot lyfe sustayne,
And having it they gaze on it the more:
In their amazement lyke Narcissus[8] vaine
Whose eyes him starved: so plenty makes me poore.
Yet are mine eyes so filled with the store°   *abundance*
10 Of that faire sight, that nothing else they brooke,
But lothe the things which they did like before,
And can no more endure on them to looke.
All this worlds glory seemeth vayne to me,
And all their showes but shadowes, saving she.

Sonnet 37

What guyle is this, that those her golden tresses,
She doth attyre under a net of gold:
And with sly° skill so cunningly them dresses,   *clever*
That which is gold or heare, may scarse be told?
5 Is it that mens frayle eyes, which gaze too bold,
She may entangle in that golden snare:
And being caught may craftily enfold,
Theyr weaker harts, which are not wel aware?
Take heed therefore, myne eyes, how ye doe stare
10 Henceforth too rashly on that guilefull net,

6. The "sacred brooke" is the Hippocrene, which flows from Mount Helicon,
the mountain sacred to the Muses. It
not only inspires the poet but here represents heaven, where his belovéd originated.
7. The Big Dipper or North Star.
8. The beautiful youth in mythology
who fell in love with his own reflection.

In which if ever ye entrappéd are,
Out of her bands ye by no means shall get.
Fondnesse° it were for any being free,   *foolishness*
To covet fetters, though they golden bee.

Sonnet 54

Of this worlds theatre in which we stay,
My love like the spectator ydly sits
Beholding me that all the pageants play,
Disguysing diversly my troubled wits.
5   Sometimes I joy when glad occasion fits,
And mask in myrth lyke to a comedy:
Soone after when my joy to sorrow flits,
I waile and make my woes a tragedy.
Yet she, beholding me with constant eye,
10   Delights not in my merth nor rues my smart:
But when I laugh she mocks, and when I cry
She laughs and hardens evermore her heart.
What then can move her? if nor merth nor mone,°   *moan*
She is no woman, but a sencelesse stone.

Sonnet 59

Thrise happie she, that is so well assured
Unto her selfe and setled so in hart:
That nether will for better be allured,
Ne feard with worse to any chaunce to start:
5   But like a steddy ship doth strongly part
The raging waves and keepes her course aright:
Ne ought ° for tempest doth from it depart,   *at all*
Ne ought for fayrer weathers false delight.
Such selfe assurance need not feare the spight
10   Of grudging foes, ne favour seek of friends:
But in the stay of her owne stedfast might,
Nether to one her self nor other bends.
Most happy she that most assured doth rest,
But he most happy who such one loves best.

Sonnet 68

Most glorious Lord of lyfe, that on this day,[9]
Didst make thy triumph over death and sin:
And having harrowed hell,[1] didst bring away
Captivity thence captive us to win:
5   This joyous day, deare Lord, with joy begin,
And grant that we for whom thou diddest dye
Being with thy deare blood clene washt from sin,
May live for ever in felicity.
And that thy love we weighing worthily,
10   May likewise love thee for the same againe:

9. Easter Day.
1. In the apocryphal gospels, Christ
descended into hell and led out those
who had lived before his time that deserved to be saved. "Captivity thence
captive" is a Biblical phrase, as in
Judges v.12 and Ephesians iv.8.

And for thy sake that all lyke deare didst buy,
With love may one another entertayne.
So let us love, deare love, lyke as we ought,
Love is the lesson which the Lord us taught.[2]

Sonnet 70

Fresh spring the herald of loves mighty king,
In whose cote armour[3] richly are displayd
All sorts of flowers the which on earth do spring
In goodly colours gloriously arrayd.
5 Goe to my love, where she is carelesse layd,
Yet in her winters bowre not well awake:
Tell her the joyous time wil not be staid
Unlesse she doe him by the forelock take.
Bid her therefore her selfe soone ready make,
10 To wayt on love amongst his lovely crew:
Where every one that misseth then her make,°   *mate, lover*
Shall be by him amearest with penance dew.[4]
Make hast therefore sweet love, whilest it is prime,°*early morning*
For none can call againe the passéd time.

Sonnet 75[5]

One day I wrote her name upon the strand,
But came the waves and washéd it away:
Agayne I wrote it with a second hand,
But came the tyde, and made my paynes his pray.
5 "Vayne man," sayd she, "that doest in vaine assay,
A mortall thing so to immortalize,
For I my selve shall lyke to this decay,
And eek my name bee wypéd out lykewize."
"Not so," quod° I, "let baser things devize   *quoth*
10 To dy in dust, but you shall live by fame:
My verse your vertues rare shall eternize,
And in the heavens wryte your glorious name.
Where whenas death shall all the world subdew,
Our love shall live, and later life renew."

Sonnet 79

Men call you fayre, and you doe credit° it,   *believe*
For that your selfe ye dayly such doe see:
But the trew fayre, that is the gentle wit,
And vertuous mind, is much more praysd of me.
5 For all the rest, how ever fayre it be,
Shall turne to nought and loose that glorious hew:
But onely that is permanent and free
From frayle corruption, that doth flesh ensew.°   *outlast*
That is true beautie: that doth argue you

---

2. Cf. John xv.12: "This is my commandment, That ye love one another, as I have loved you."
3. Coat of arms.
4. I.e., have suitable penance imposed upon him.
5. The theme here expressed is an ancient and traditional one. Cf. Shakespeare's Sonnet 55, "Not marble, nor the gilded monuments."

10 To be divine and borne of heavenly seed:
Derived from that fayre Spirit, from whom al true
And perfect beauty did at first proceed.
He onely fayre, and what he fayre hath made:
All other fayre, lyke flowres, untymely fade.

1595

Epithalamion[1]

Ye learned sisters which have oftentimes
Beene to me ayding, others to adorne:[2]
Whom ye thought worthy of your gracefull rymes,
That even the greatest did not greatly scorne
5 To heare theyr names sung in your simple layes,
But joyéd in theyr prayse.
And when ye list your owne mishaps to mourne,
Which death, or love, or fortunes wreck did rayse,
Your string could soone to sadder tenor° turne,   *mood*
10 And teach the woods and waters to lament
Your dolefull dreriment.°   *sorrow*
Now lay those sorrowfull complaints aside,
And having all your heads with girland crownd,
Helpe me mine owne loves prayses to resound,
15 Ne let the same of° any be envide: *by*
So Orpheus did for his owne bride,[3]
So I unto my selfe alone will sing,
The woods shall to me answer and my Eccho ring.

Early before the worlds light giving lampe,
20 His golden beame upon the hils doth spred,

1. An epithalamion is a wedding song or poem; its Greek name conveys that it was sung on the threshold of the bridal chamber. The genre was widely practiced by the Latin poets, particularly Catullus. Catullus wrote two kinds of epithalamion: one in an elevated ceremonial style, the other in a more private, lyric style; it is the latter style that Spenser follows. Common elements are the invocation to the Muses, the bringing home of the bride, the singing and dancing at the wedding party, and the preparations for the wedding night. The reader should be aware that the poem's merit is not in its "originality" but in its evocative, many-layered commingling of the conventions. Spenser blends with these conventional elements his own Irish setting and native folklore.
In addition, the *Epithalamion* is highly structured. First there is an introductory stanza, then two 10-stanza sections on each side of the two central stanzas about the church ceremony itself. Each of the 10-stanza sections is divided into units of 3-4-3. As A. Kent Hieatt has pointed out in his book, *Short Time's Endless Monument* (1960), the poem also has a surprising and complex numerical structure that reinforces the motif of the passage of time. For example, the poem has exactly 365 long lines (composed of five or more metrical feet) matching the number of days in the year. There are 24 stanzas, counting the envoy, matching the hours of one day and night. Of these stanzas, the first 16 describe the course of the day, in which the woods echo the various sounds; the last 8 describe the night, a time of silence in which the woods no longer echo. At the summer solstice (cf. line 266 and note) in the latitude of Ireland, night in fact falls after 16 hours of daylight.
To point to these elements of high artistry is not, of course, to explain why the *Epithalamion* is one of the great poems of the language. The subtle time structure serves to reinforce the idea implicit throughout the poem that this marriage has reference to all marriages; it emphasizes the endless cycle of time, measured by the passing of the hours and the years—as against which marriage, as a Christian sacrament, stands firm, "eterne in mutabilitie."
2. I.e., to write poems in praise of others (e.g., Queen Elizabeth in *The Faerie Queene*). The "learned sisters" are the Muses.
3. Orpheus, the most famous musician of classical antiquity, was equally famous for his love for his wife Eurydice.

Having disperst the nights unchearefull dampe,
Doe ye awake, and with fresh lustyhed°   *vigor*
Go to the bowre° of my belovéd love,   *bedchamber*
My truest turtle dove,
25 Bid her awake; for Hymen[4] is awake,
And long since ready forth his maske to move,
With his bright Tead[5] that flames with many a flake,°   *spark*
And many a bachelor to waite on him,
In theyr fresh garments trim.
30 Bid her awake therefore and soone her dight,°   *dress*
For lo the wishéd day is come at last,
That shall for al the paynes and sorrowes past,
Pay to her usury of long delight:
And whylest she doth her dight,
35 Doe ye to her of joy and solace sing,
That all the woods may answer and your eccho ring.

Bring with you all the Nymphes that you can heare[6]
Both of the rivers and the forrests greene:
And of the sea that neighbours to her neare,
40 Al with gay girlands goodly wel beseene.[7]
And let them also with them bring in hand,
Another gay girland
For my fayre love of lillyes and of roses,
Bound truelove wize[8] with a blew silke riband.
45 And let them make great store of bridale poses,°   *posies*
And let them eeke bring store of other flowers
To deck the bridale bowers.
And let the ground whereas her foot shall tread,
For feare the stones her tender foot should wrong
50 Be strewed with fragrant flowers all along,
And diapred lyke the discolored mead. [9]
Which done, doe at her chamber dore awayt,
For she will waken strayt, °   *straightway*
The whiles doe ye this song unto her sing,
55 The woods shall to you answer and your Eccho ring.

Ye Nymphes of Mulla[1] which with careful heed,
The silver scaly trouts doe tend full well,
And greedy pikes which use therein to feed,
(Those trouts and pikes all others doo excell)
60 And ye likewise, which keepe the rushy lake,
Where none doo fishes take,
Bynd up the locks the which hang scatterd light,
And in his waters which your mirror make,
Behold your faces as the christall bright,
65 That when you come whereas my love doth lie,
No blemish she may spie.

4. The god of marriage, who leads a "maske" or procession at weddings.
5. A ceremonial torch, associated with marriages since classical times.
6. I.e., that can hear you.
7. I.e., beautified.
8. I.e., in a love knot.
9. I.e., ornamented like the many-colored meadow.
1. The vale of Mulla, near Spenser's home in Ireland.

And eke ye lightfoot mayds which keepe the deere.[2]
That on the hoary mountayne use to towre,
And the wylde wolves which seeke them to devoure,
70 With your steele darts doo chace from comming neer
Be also present heere,
To helpe to decke her and to help to sing,
That all the woods may answer and your eccho ring.

Wake, now my love, awake; for it is time,
75 The Rosy Morne long since left Tithones bed,
All ready to her silver coche to clyme,
And Phoebus gins to shew his glorious hed.
Hark how the cheerefull birds do chaunt theyr laies
And carroll of loves praise.
80 The merry Larke hir mattins° sing aloft,   morning prayers
The thrust replyes, the Mavis descant[3] playes,
The Ouzell shrills, the Ruddock warbles soft,
So goodly all agree with sweet consent,
To this dayes merriment.
85 Ah my deere love why doe ye sleepe thus long,
When meeter were that ye should now awake,
T' awayt the comming of your joyous make,°   mate
And hearken to the birds lovelearnéd song,
The deawy leaves among.
90 For they of joy and pleasance to you sing,
That all the woods them answer and theyr eccho ring.

My love is now awake out of her dreame,
And her fayre eyes like stars that dimméd were
With darksome cloud, now shew theyr goodly beams
95 More bright then Hesperus° his head doth rere.   evening star
Come now ye damzels, daughters of delight,
Helpe quickly her to dight,
But first come ye fayre houres which were begot
In Joves sweet paradice, of Day and Night,
100 Which doe the seasons of the yeare allot,
And al that ever in this world is fayre
Doe make and still repayre.[4]
And ye three handmayds of the Cyprian Queene,[5]
The which doe still adorne her beauties pride,
105 Helpe to addorne my beautifullest bride:
And as ye her array, still throw betweene°   now and then
Some graces to be seene,
And as ye use to Venus, to her sing,
The whiles the woods shal answer and your eccho ring.

110 Now is my love all ready forth to come,
Let all the virgins therefore well awayt,

2. I.e., all wild animals, kept by the forest nymphs. To "towre" (a falconry term) is to occupy heights.
3. A melody or counterpoint written above a musical theme—a soprano ob-bligato. The "Mavis" is the thrush. The "Ouzell" is the blackbird (which sings in England); the "Ruddock," the European robin. The birds' concert is a convention of medieval love poetry.
4. In the passage of the hours, all things on earth change. "Still": continuously.
5. The Graces attending on Venus ("Cyprian Queene"), representing bright-ness, joy, and bloom.

And ye fresh boyes that tend upon her groome
Prepare your selves; for he is comming strayt.
Set all your things in seemely good aray°   *order*
115   Fit for so joyfull day,
The joyfulst day that ever sunne did see.
Faire Sun, shew forth thy favourable ray,
And let thy lifull° heat not fervent be   *lifegiving*
For feare of burning her sunshyny face,
120   Her beauty to disgrace.
O fayrest Phoebus, father of the Muse,
If ever I did honour thee aright,
Or sing the thing, that mote° they mind delight,   *might*
Doe not thy servants simple boone refuse,
125   But let this day let this one day be myne,
Let all the rest be thine.
Then I thy soverayne prayses loud wil sing,
That all the woods shal answer and theyr eccho ring.

Harke how the Minstrels gin to shrill aloud
130   Their merry Musick that resounds from far,
The pipe, the tabor, and the trembling Croud,[6]
That well agree withouten breach or jar.°   *discord*
But most of all the Damzels doe delite,
When they their tymbrels° smyte,   *tambourines*
135   And thereunto doe daunce and carrol sweet,
That all the sences they doe ravish quite,
The whyles the boyes run up and downe the street,
Crying aloud with strong confuséd noyce,
As if it were once voyce.
140   *Hymen iô Hymen, Hymen*[7] they do shout,
That even to the heavens theyr shouting shrill
Doth reach, and all the firmament doth fill,
To which the people standing all about,
As in approvance doe thereto applaud
145   And loud advaunce her laud,°   *praise*
And evermore they *Hymen Hymen* sing,
That al the woods them answer and theyr eccho ring.

Loe where she comes along with portly° pace   *stately*
Lyke Phoebe from her chamber of the East,
150   Arysing forth to run her mighty race,[8]
Clad all in white, that seemes° a virgin best.   *suits*
So well it her beseems that ye would weene
Some angell she had beene.
Her long loose yellow locks lyke golden wyre,
155   Sprinckled with perle, and perling° flowres a tweene,   *winding*
Doe lyke a golden mantle her attyre,

---

6. Primitive fiddle; the "tabor" is a small drum. Spenser here designates Irish, not classical, instruments and music for the classical masque or ballet.
7. The name of the god of marriage, used as a conventional exclamation at weddings.
8. Phoebe is the moon, a virgin like the bride; the reference to her antici-pates the night.

And being crownéd with girland greene,
Seeme lyke some mayden Queene.
Her modest eyes abashéd to behold
160 So many gazers, as on her do stare,
Upon the lowly ground affixéd are.
Ne dare lift up her countenance too bold,
But blush to heare her prayses sung so loud,
So farre from being proud.
165 Nathlesse doe ye still loud her prayses sing.
That all the woods may answer and your eccho ring.

Tell me ye merchants daughters did ye see
So fayre a creature in your towne before,
So sweet, so lovely, and so mild as she,
170 Adornd with beautyes grace and vertues store,
Her goodly eyes lyke Saphyres shining bright,
Her forehead yvory white,
Her cheekes lyke apples which the sun hath rudded,°   made red
Her lips lyke cherryes charming men to byte,
175 Her brest like to a bowle of creame uncrudded,°   uncurdled
Her paps lyke lyllies budded,
Her snowie necke lyke to a marble towre,
And all her body like a pallace fayre,
Ascending uppe with many a stately stayre,
180 To honors seat and chastities sweet bowre.[9]
Why stand ye still ye virgins in amaze,
Upon her so to gaze,
Whiles ye forget your former lay to sing,
To which the woods did answer and your eccho ring.

185 But if ye saw that which no eyes can see,
The inward beauty of her lively spright,°   soul
Garnisht with heavenly guifts of high degree,
Much more then would ye wonder at that sight,
And stand astonisht lyke to those which red°   discern
190 Medusaes mazeful hed.[1]
There dwels sweet love and constant chastity,
Unspotted fayth and comely womanhood,
Regard of honour and mild modesty,
There vertue raynes as Queene in royal throne,
195 And giveth lawes alone.
The which the base° affections doe obay,   lower
And yeeld theyr services unto her will,
Ne thought of thing uncomely ever may
Thereto approch to tempt her mind to ill.
200 Had ye once seene these her celestial threasures,
And unreveaéd pleasures,
Then would ye wonder and her prayses sing,
That al the woods should answer and your echo ring.

---

9. The head, where the higher faculties
are. The catalogue of qualities is a convention in love poetry. Cf. also The Song
of Solomon iv–viii.

1. Medusa, one of the Gorgons, had
serpents instead of hair (hence a "mazeful hed"): the effect on a beholder was
to turn him to stone.

Open the temple gates unto my love,
205 Open them wide that she may enter in,
And all the postes adorne as doth behove,[2]
And all the pillours deck with girlands trim,
For to recyve this Saynt with honour dew,
That commeth in to you.
210 With trembling steps and humble reverence,
She commeth in, before th' almighties vew,
Of her ye virgins learne obedience,
When so ye come into those holy places,
To humble your proud faces:
215 Bring her up to th' high altar, that she may
The sacred ceremonies there partake,
The which do endless matrimony make,
And let the roring Organs loudly play
The praises of the Lord in lively notes,
220 The whiles with hollow throates
The Choristers the joyous Antheme sing,
That al the woods may answere and their eccho ring.

Behold whiles she before the altar stands
Hearing the holy priest that to her speakes
225 And blesseth her with his two happy hands,
How the red roses flush up in her cheekes,
And the pure snow with goodly vermill stayne,
Like crimsin dyde in grayne,°   fast color
That even th' Angels which continually,
230 About the sacred Altare doe remaine,
Forget their service and about her fly,
Ofte peeping in her face that seemes more fayre,
The more they on it stare.
But her sad° eyes still fastened on the ground,   modest
235 Are governéd with goodly modesty,
That suffers not one looke to glaunce awry,
Which may let in a little thought unsownd.
Why blush ye love to give to me your hand,
The pledge of all our band?°   bond, tie
240 Sing ye sweet Angels, Alleluya sing,
That all the woods may answere and your eccho ring.

Now al is done; bring home the bride againe,
Bring home the triumph of our victory,
Bring home with you the glory of her gaine,[3]
245 With joyance bring her and with jollity.
Never had man more joyfull day then this,
Whom heaven would heape with blis.
Make feast therefore now all this live long day,
This day for ever to me holy is,
250 Poure out the wine without restraint or stay,
Poure not by cups, but by the belly full,

2. As is proper. The doorposts were trimmed for weddings in classical times, and the custom was often referred to in classical and medieval love poetry.
3. I.e., the glory of gaining her.

Poure out to all that wull,°   *want it*
And sprinkle all the postes and wals with wine,
That they may sweat, and drunken be withall.

255 Crowne ye God Bacchus with a coronall,°   *flower garland*
And Hymen also crowne with wreathes of vine,
And let the Graces daunce unto the rest;
For they can doo it best:
The whiles the maydens doe theyr carroll sing,

260 To which the woods shal answer and theyr eccho ring.

Ring ye the bels, ye young men of the towne,
And leave your wonted labors for this day:
This day is holy; doe ye write it downe,
That ye for ever it remember may.

265 This day the sunne is in his chiefest hight,
With Barnaby the bright,[4]
From whence declining daily by degrees,
He somewhat loseth of his heat and light,
When once the Crab[5] behind his back he sees.

270 But for this time it ill ordainéd was,
To chose the longest day in all the yeare,
And shortest night, when longest fitter weare:
Yet never day so long, but late° would passe.   *at last*
Ring ye the bels, to make it weare away,

275 And bonefiers make all day,
And daunce about them, and about them sing:
That all the woods may answer, and your eccho ring.

Ah when will this long weary day have end,
And lende me leave to come unto my love?

280 How slowly do the houres theyr numbers spend?
How slowly does sad Time his feathers move?
Hast thee O fayrest Planet to thy home
Within the Westerne fome:
Thy tyred steedes long since have need of rest.

285 Long though it be, at last I see it gloome,
And the bright evening star with golden creast
Appeare out of the East.
Fayre childe of beauty, glorious lampe of love
That all the host of heaven in rankes doost lead,

290 And guydest lovers through the nightés dread,
How chearefully thou lookest from above,
And seemst to laugh atweene thy twinkling light
As joying in the sight
Of these glad many which for joy doe sing,

295 That all the woods them answer and their echo ring.

Now ceasse ye damsels your delights forepast;
Enough is it, that all the day was youres:
Now day is doen, and night is nighing fast:
Now bring the Bryde into the brydall boures.

---

4. St. Barnabas' Day, at the time of the summer solstice.
5. The constellation Cancer between Gemini and Leo. The sun, passing through the zodiac, leaves the Crab behind toward the end of July.

300 Now night is come, now soone her disaray,
　　And in her bed her lay;
　　Lay her in lillies and in violets,
　　And silken courteins over her display,°   *spread*
　　And odourd sheetes, and Arras° coverlets.   *tapestry*
305 Behold how goodly my faire love does ly
　　In proud humility;
　　Like unto Maia,[6] when as Jove her tooke,
　　In Tempe, lying on the flowry gras,
　　Twixt sleepe and wake, after she weary was,
310 With bathing in the Acidalian brooke.
　　Now it is night, ye damsels may be gon,
　　And leave my love alone,
　　And leave likewise your former lay to sing:
　　The woods no more shal answere, nor your echo ring.

315 Now welcome night, thou night so long expected,
　　That long daies labour doest at last defray,°   *pay*
　　And all my cares, which cruell love collected,
　　Hast sumd in one, and cancelléd for aye:
　　Spread thy broad wing over my love and me,
320 That no man may us see,
　　And in thy sable mantle us enwrap,
　　From feare of perrill and foule horror free.
　　Let no false treason seeke us to entrap,
　　Nor any dread disquiet once annoy
325 The safety of our joy:
　　But let the night be calme and quietsome,
　　Without tempestuous storms or sad afray:
　　Lyke as when Jove with fayre Alcmena[7] lay,
　　When he begot the great Tirynthian groome:
330 Or lyke as when he with thy selfe[8] did lie,
　　And begot Majesty.
　　And let the mayds and yongmen cease to sing:
　　Ne let the woods them answer, nor theyr eccho ring.

　　Let no lamenting cryes, nor dolefull teares,
335 Be heard all night within nor yet without.
　　Ne let false whispers, breeding hidden feares,
　　Breake gentle sleepe with misconceivéd dout.
　　Let no deluding dreames, nor dreadful sights
　　Make sudden sad affrights;
340 Ne let housefyres, nor lightnings helpelesse harmes,
　　Ne let the Pouke,[9] nor other evill sprights,
　　Ne let mischivous witches with theyr charmes,
　　Ne let hob Goblins, names whose sence we see not,
　　Fray us with things that be not.
345 Let not the shriech Oule, nor the Storke be heard:

6. The eldest and most beautiful of the Pleiades.
7. The mother of Hercules ("the great Tirynthian groome").
8. I.e., night.
9. Puck, Robin Goodfellow—here more powerful and evil than Shakespeare made him.

Nor the night Raven that still deadly yels,[1]
Nor damnéd ghosts cald up with mighty spels,
Nor griesly vultures make us once affeard:
Ne let th'unpleasant Quyre of Frogs still croking
350 Make us to wish theyr choking.
Let none of these theyr drery accents sing;
Ne let the woods them answer, nor theyr eccho ring.

But let stil Silence trew night watches keepe,
That sacred peace may in assurance rayne,
355 And tymely sleep, when it is tyme to sleepe,
May poure his limbs forth on your[2] pleasant playne,
The whiles an hundred little wingéd loves,[3]
Like divers fethered doves,
Shall fly and flutter round about your bed,
360 And in the secret darke, that none reproves,
Their prety stealthes shal worke, and snares shal spread
To filch away sweet snatches of delight,
Conceald through covert night.
Ye sonnes of Venus, play your sports at will,
365 For greedy pleasure, carelesse of your toyes,°   *frivolities*
Thinks more upon her paradise of joyes,
Then what ye do, albe it good or ill.
All night therefore attend your merry play,
For it will soone be day:
370 Now none doth hinder you, that say or sing,
Ne will the woods now answer, nor your Eccho ring.

Who is the same, which at my window peepes?
Or whose is that faire face, that shines so bright,
Is it not Cinthia,[4] she that never sleepes,
375 But walkes about high heaven al the night?
O fayrest goddesse, do thou not envy
My love with me to spy:
For thou likewise didst love, though now unthought,° *unsuspected*
And for a fleece of woll,° which privily,   *wool*
380 The Latmian shephard[5] once unto thee brought,
His pleasures with thee wrought,
Therefore to us be favorable now;
And sith of wemens labours thou hast charge,[6]
And generation goodly dost enlarge,
385 Encline thy will t' effect our wishfull vow,
And the chast wombe informe with timely seed,
That may our comfort breed:
Till which we cease our hopefull hap to sing,
Ne let the woods us answere, nor our Eccho ring.

1. The owl and the night raven were
birds of ill omen; the stork, in Chaucer's
Parliament of Fowls, is called an avenger
of adultery. "Still": always.
2. I.e., Night's.
3. Cupids (or amoretti).
4. I.e., the moon.
5. Endymion, beloved by the moon.

The "fleece of woll," however, comes
from another story—that of Pan's en-
ticement of the moon.
6. Diana (the moon, "Cinthia") is,
as Lucina, patroness of births; the "labours" are, of course, those of childbirth.

390 And thou great Juno, which with awful might
     The lawes of wedlock still dost patronize,
     And the religion of the faith first plight
     With sacred rites hast taught to solemnize:
     And eeke for comfort often callèd art
395 Of women in their smart,°   *labor*
     Eternally bind thou this lovely band,
     And all thy blessings unto us impart.
     And thou glad Genius,[7] in whose gentle hand,
     The bridale bowre and geniall bed remaine,
400 Without blemish or staine,
     And the sweet pleasures of theyr loves delight
     With secret ayde doest succour and supply,
     Till they bring forth the fruitfull progeny,
     Send us the timely fruit of this same night.
405 And thou fayre Hebe,[8] and thou Hymen free,
     Grant that it may be so.
     Til which we cease your further prayse to sing,
     Ne any woods shal answer, nor your Eccho ring.

     And ye high heavens, the temple of the gods,
410 In which a thousand torches flaming bright
     Doe burne, that to us wretched earthly clods,
     In dreadful darknesse lend desired light;
     And all ye powers which in the same remayne,
     More than we men can fayne,
415 Poure out your blessing on us plentiously,
     And happy influence upon us raine,
     That we may raise a large posterity,
     Which from the earth, which they may long possesse,
     With lasting happinesse,
420 Up to your haughty pallaces may mount,
     And for the guerdon of theyr glorious merit
     May heavenly tabernacles there inherit,
     Of blessed Saints for to increase the count.
     So let us rest, sweet love, in hope of this,
425 And cease till then our tymely joyes to sing,
     The woods no more us answer, nor our eccho ring.

     Song made in lieu of many ornaments,
     With which my love should duly have bene dect,
     Which cutting off through hasty accidents,
430 Ye would not stay your dew time to expect,
     But promist both to recompens,
     Be unto her a goodly ornament,
     And for short time an endlesse moniment.[9]

                                                              1595

---

7. Patron of sex, pregnancy, reproduction. Cf. Genius in the Garden of Adonis (*The Faerie Queene* III.vi.31).
8. Patron of youth and freedom.
9. The envoy is traditionally apologetic in tone: the poem is offered as a substitute for wedding presents ("ornaments") that did not arrive in time for the wedding. But this elaborate poem is itself a "goodly ornament," for (in a final reference to the theme of time and eternity) it stands as a timeless monument of art to the passing day which it celebrates.

WILLIAM SHAKESPEARE
(1564–1616)

ca. 1588–92: In London as actor and playwright.
ca. 1592–98: Devotes himself mainly to chronicle histories and comedies.
ca. 1601–9: Period of the great tragedies and romantic comedies.
ca. 1610: Retires to Stratford.

William Shakespeare was born in Stratford-on-Avon in April (probably April 23), 1564. His father was a citizen of some prominence who became an alderman and bailiff, but who later suffered financial reverses. Shakespeare presumably attended the Stratford grammar school, where he could have acquired a respectable knowledge of Latin, but he did not proceed to Oxford or Cambridge. There are legends about Shakespeare's youth but no documented facts. The first record we have of his life after his christening is that of his marriage in 1582 to Anne Hathaway. A daughter was born to the young Shakespeares in 1583 and twins, a boy and a girl, in 1585. We possess no information about his activities for the next seven years, but by 1592 he was in London as an actor and apparently well-known as a playwright, for Robert Greene refers to him resentfully in *A Groatsworth of Wit* as "an upstart crow, beautified with our feathers," who, "being an absolute *Johannes Factotum*, is in his own conceit the only Shake-scene in a country."

At this time, there were several companies of actors in London and in the provinces. What connection Shakespeare had with one or more of them before 1592 is conjectural, but we do know of his long and fruitful connection with the most successful troupe, the Lord Chamberlain's Men, who later, when James I came to the throne, became the King's Men. Shakespeare not only acted with this company, but eventually became a leading shareholder and the principal playwright. The company included some of the most famous actors of the day, such as Richard Burbage, who no doubt created the roles of Hamlet, Lear, and Othello, and Will Kempe and Robert Armin, who acted Shakespeare's clowns and fools. In 1599 the Chamberlain's Men built and occupied that best known of Elizabethan theaters, the Globe.

Shakespeare did not, in his early years, confine himself to the theater. In 1593 he published a mythological-erotic poem, *Venus and Adonis*, dedicated to the Earl of Southampton; in the next year he dedicated a "graver labor," *The Rape of Lucrece*, to the same noble patron. By 1597 Shakespeare had so prospered that he was able to purchase New Place, a handsome house in Stratford; he could now call himself a gentleman, as his father had been granted a coat of arms in the previous year.

Our first record of the playwright's actual work occurs in Francis Meres' *Palladis Tamia: Wit's Treasury* (1598), in which Meres compared English poets with the ancients; of Shakespeare he says, "As Plautus and Seneca are accounted the best for Comedy and Tragedy among the Latins, so Shakespeare among the English is the most excellent in both kinds for the stage." He goes on to list *Richard II, Richard III, Henry IV, King John, Titus Andronicus,* and *Romeo and Juliet* for tragedy and *Two Gentlemen of Verona, The Comedy of Errors, A Midsummer Night's Dream, The Merchant of Venice, Love's Labor's Lost,* and the unknown (or perhaps retitled) *Love's Labor's Won* as comedy. All of the plays Meres lists as tragedy (except for *Romeo and Juliet* and the very early *Titus Andronicus*) we would call chronicle history plays, a popular kind of drama based upon history books like Raphael Holinshed's *Chronicle* and presenting dramatically the events in the reigns of various English kings. About the turn of the century Shakespeare wrote his great romantic comedies, *As You Like It, Twelfth Night,* and *Much Ado About Nothing,* and his concluding history play in the Prince Hal series, *Henry V.* The next decade was the period of the great tragedies: *Hamlet, Macbeth, Othello, King Lear,* and *Antony and Cleopatra.*

About 1610 Shakespeare apparently retired to Stratford, though he continued to write, both by himself (*The Tempest*) and in collaboration (*Henry VIII*). This is the period of the "romances" or "tragicomedies," which include, besides *The Tempest, Cymbeline* and *The Winter's Tale.* Aside from his two early nondramatic poems, Shakespeare devoted his genius primarily to the stage. Meres mentioned in 1598, however, that he was known for "his sugared sonnets among his private friends"; the sonnets were published in 1609, apparently without his authorization. He contributed the strange and beautiful poem, *The Phoenix and the Turtle,* to an anthology in 1601.

The plays contain some of the finest songs ever written. They are of various types: the aubade, or morning song, the gay pastoral invitation, love songs of various kinds, the ballad sung by wandering minstrels, and the funeral dirge. They illustrate many sides of Shakespeare's genius—his incomparable lyric gift, his ready humor, and his marvelous sensitivity to the sights and sounds of English life, especially the life of the country.

The sonnets are Shakespeare's contribution to a popular vogue, but his cycle is quite unlike the other sonnet sequences of his day. Shakespeare's cycle suggests a story, though the details are vague, and there is doubt even whether the sonnets as published in 1609 are in the correct order. Certain motifs are clear: a series celebrating the beauty of a young man and urging him to marry; some sonnets to a lady; some sonnets (like 144) about a strange triangle of love involving two men and a woman; sonnets on the destructive power of time and the permanence of poetry; sonnets about a rival poet; and incidental sonnets of moral insight, like 129 and 146. The biographical background of the sonnets has aroused much speculation, but very little of it is convincing. The poems themselves are what is important. Though the vocabulary is often simple, the metaphorical style of the sonnets is rich. "Shall I compare thee to a summer's day" is a question which might lead to a very ordinary conceit; instead it introduces a profound meditation on time, change, and beauty.

The structure of the sonnet frequently reinforces the power of the metaphors; each quatrain in 73 develops an image of lateness, of approaching extinction—of a season, of a day, and of a fire, but they also apply to a life. The three quatrains may be equally and successively at work preparing for the conclusion in the couplet, or the first eight lines may contain a catalogue and the last six turn in quite a different direction, as in sonnet

29. The rhetorical strategy of the sonnets is also worth careful attention. Some begin with a purported reminiscence; some are imperative; others make an almost proverbial statement, then elaborate it. The imagery comes from a wide variety of sources: gardening, navigation, law, farming, business, pictorial art, astrology, domestic affairs. The moods are also not confined to what the Renaissance thought were those of the despairing Petrarchan lover; they include delight, pride, melancholy, shame, disgust, fear. It is evident that the poet of the sonnets is also the author of the great plays.

When Shakespeare died, in Stratford in 1616, no collected edition of his plays had been published. Some of them had been printed in separate editions ("quartos") without his editorial supervision, sometimes from his manuscripts, sometimes from playhouse prompt books, sometimes from pirated texts secured by shorthand reports of a performance or from reconstruction from memory by an actor or spectator.

In 1623, two members of Shakespeare's company, John Heminges and Henry Condell, published the great collection of all the plays they considered authentic; it is called the First Folio. They printed the best texts they had, according to their lights. The Folio contains an epistle "to the great variety of readers" which urges us to read Shakespeare again and again; if we do not like him, say Heminges and Condell, it is evident that we do not understand him. Another preliminary document in the First Folio is a poem by Shakespeare's great rival, critic, and opposite, Ben Jonson. In it he asserts the superiority of Shakespeare not only to other English playwrights but to the Greek and Latin masters. Jonson first states what has come to be a universal opinion:

> Triumph, my Britain, thou hast one to show
> To whom all scenes of Europe homage owe.
> He was not of an age, but for all time!

SONGS FROM THE PLAYS
When Daisies Pied[1]

SPRING

When daisies pied and violets blue
  And ladysmocks all silver-white
And cuckoobuds of yellow hue
  Do paint the meadows with delight,
The cuckoo then, on every tree,
Mocks married men;[2] for thus sings he,
          Cuckoo;
Cuckoo, cuckoo: Oh word of fear,
Unpleasing to a married ear!   5

1. This song concludes *Love's Labour's Lost* (1594–95), one of Shakespeare's earliest comedies. Announced as a "Dialogue * * * in praise of the Owl and the Cuckoo," it provides a lyric commentary on the bittersweet mood that dominates the play's last scene. "Pied": variegated.
2. The cuckoo's song—"Cuckoo!"— is taken to mean "Cuckold!"

When shepherds pipe on oaten straws,[3]   10
  And merry larks are plowmen's clocks,
When turtles tread,[4] and rooks, and daws,
  And maidens bleach their summer smocks,
The cuckoo then, on every tree,
Mocks married men; for thus sings he,   15
          Cuckoo;
Cuckoo, cuckoo: Oh word of fear,
Unpleasing to a married ear!

WINTER

When icicles hang by the wall
  And Dick the shepherd blows his nail [5]   20
And Tom bears logs into the hall,
  And milk comes frozen home in pail,
When blood is nipped and ways be foul,
Then nightly sings the staring owl,
          Tu-who;   25
Tu-whit, tu-who: a merry note,
While greasy Joan doth keel[6] the pot.

When all aloud the wind doth blow,
  And coughing drowns the parson's saw,[7]
And birds sit brooding in the snow,   30
  And Marian's nose looks red and raw,
When roasted crabs[8] hiss in the bowl,
Then nightly sings the staring owl,
          Tu-who;
Tu-whit, tu-who: a merry note   35
While greasy Joan doth keel the pot.

The Woosel Cock So Black of Hue[1]

The woosel cock so black of hue,
  With orange-tawny bill,
The throstle[2] with his note so true,
  The wren with little quill—
The finch, the sparrow, and the lark,   5
  The plain-song cuckoo[3] gray,
Whose note full many a man doth mark,
  And dares not answer nay.

3. The reed pipes played by shepherds.
4. Turtledoves mate. The "larks" are "plowmen's clocks" because they sing at sunrise.
5. Warms his fingers by blowing on them.
6. Stir, to prevent boiling over.
7. Wise saying.
8. Crabapples.
1. *A Midsummer Night's Dream* (1596) III.i.128.ff.; Bottom, the rustic weaver, sings this song to keep his spirits up when he is alone in the wood, unaware that his head has been changed for that of an ass. "Woosel" is Bottom's mispronunciation of "ousel," a blackbird.
2. Song thrush.
3. Plain-song was the thematic melody or regular tune to which variations or "descant" were sung. To the cuckoo's monotonous theme, no one can make variations.

Tell Me Where Is Fancy Bred[9]

Tell me where is fancy bred,
Or in the heart or in the head?
How begeot, how nourishéd?
    Reply, reply.
It is engendered in the eyes,   5
With gazing fed; and fancy dies
In the cradle where it lies.
    Let us all ring fancy's knell:
I'll begin it—Ding, dong, bell.
Ding, dong, bell.   10

Sigh No More, Ladies[1]

Sigh no more, ladies, sigh no more,
    Men were deceivers ever;
One foot in sea, and one on shore,
    To one thing constant never.
        Then sigh not so,   5
        But let them go,
    And be you blithe and bonny,
Converting all your sounds of woe
    Into Hey nonny, nonny.

Sing no more ditties, sing no mo   10
    Of dumps [2] so dull and heavy;
The fraud of men was ever so,
    Since summer first was leavy.
        Then sigh not so,
        But let them go,   15
    And be you blithe and bonny,
Converting all your sounds of woe
    Into Hey nonny, nonny.

Under the Greenwood Tree[3]

    Under the greenwood tree
    Who loves to lie with me,

9. *The Merchant of Venice* (1596–97) III.ii.63 ff.; sung while Bassanio is trying to choose between the caskets of gold, silver, and lead—one of which contains the token that will enable him to gain Portia as his wife. The song is perhaps intended to help Bassanio's choice: notice the number of words that rhyme with "lead." "Fancy" is a superficial love or liking for something attractive.
1. *Much Ado About Nothing* (1598–99) II.iii.64 ff.
2. Sad songs.
3. *As You Like It* (1599–1600) II.v.1 ff.; this song provides a comment on the happy existence of the banished Duke and his followers in the Forest of Arden, where life is "more sweet / Than that of painted pomp."

And turn his merry note
Unto the sweet bird's throat,[4]
Come hither, come hither, come hither: 5
    Here shall he see
    No enemy
But winter and rough weather.

    Who doth ambition shun
    And loves to live i' the sun,   10
    Seeking the food he eats,
    And pleased with what he gets,
Come hither, come hither, come hither:
    Here shall he see
    No enemy   15
But winter and rough weather.

Blow, Blow, Thou Winter Wind[5]

Blow, blow, thou winter wind,
Thou art not so unkind
    As man's ingratitude;
Thy tooth is not so keen,
Because thou art not seen,   5
    Although thy breath be rude.
Heigh-ho! sing, heigh-ho! unto the green holly:
Most friendship is feigning, most loving mere folly:
    Then, heigh-ho, the holly!
    This life is most jolly.   10

Freeze, freeze, thou bitter sky,
That dost not bite so nigh
    As benefits forgot:
Though thou the waters warp,[6]
Thy sting is not so sharp   15
    As friend remembered not.
Heigh-ho! sing, etc.

Oh Mistress Mine[7]

Oh mistress mine! where are you roaming?
Oh! stay and hear; your true love's coming,
    That can sing both high and low.
Trip no further, pretty sweeting;
Journeys end in lovers meeting,   5
    Every wise man's son doth know.

What is love? 'tis not hereafter;
Present mirth hath present laughter;
    What's to come is still unsure:

---

4. I.e., improvise his song in harmony with the bird's.
5. Also from *As You Like It* II.vii. 174 ff. The contrast here between na-ture and man's willful behavior is one of the continuing themes of the play.
6. I.e., roughen by freezing.
7. *Twelfth Night* (1601–2) II.iii.40 ff.

In delay there lies no plenty;   10
  Then come kiss me, sweet and twenty,
    Youth's a stuff will not endure.

Take, Oh, Take Those Lips Away[8]

Take, Oh, take those lips away,
  That so sweetly were forsworn;
And those eyes, the break of day,
  Lights that do mislead the morn:
But my kisses bring again, bring again;   5
Seals of love, but sealed in vain, sealed in vain.

Fear No More the Heat o' the Sun[9]

Fear no more the heat o' the sun,
  Nor the furious winter's rages;
Thou thy worldly task hast done,
  Home art gone, and ta'en thy wages:
Golden lads and girls all must,   5
As [1] chimney-sweepers, come to dust.

Fear no more the frown o' the great;
  Thou art past the tyrant's stroke;
Care no more to clothe and eat;
  To thee the reed is as the oak: 10
The scepter, learning, physic, must
All follow this, and come to dust.

Fear no more the lightning flash,
  Nor the all-dreaded thunder stone;[2]
Fear not slander, censure rash;   15
  Thou hast finished joy and moan:
All lovers young, all lovers must
Consign to thee, and come to dust.

No exorciser harm thee!
Nor no witchcraft charm thee!   20
Ghost unlaid forbear thee!
Nothing ill come near thee!
Quiet consummation have;
And renownéd be thy grave!

When Daffodils Begin to Peer[3]

When daffodils begin to peer,
  With heigh! the doxy[4] over the dale,

8. *Measure for Measure* (1604) IV.i.
1 ff.; Mariana's desolation at being
jilted by her lover Angelo is poignantly
conveyed in this song, which is sung
at her first entrance.
9. A lament for the supposedly dead
Imogen, sung in *Cymbeline* IV.ii.258 ff.
1. Like.
2. The sound of thunder was commonly
thought to be caused by the falling of
stones or meteorites.
3. *The Winter's Tale* (1610–11) IV.
iii.1 ff. Autolycus, ballad-singer, peddler, and rogue, makes his entrance
singing this song, which not only effectively establishes his character but
also helps to move the play from the
wintry mood of the earlier scenes to
the spring mood of the later scenes.
4. Girl or mistress (thieves' slang).

Why, then comes in the sweet o' the year;
   For the red blood reigns in the winter's pale.[5]

The white sheet bleaching on the hedge,[6]   5
   With heigh! the sweet birds, Oh, how they sing!
Doth set my pugging[7] tooth on edge;
   For a quart of ale is a dish for a king.

The lark, that tirra-lirra chants,
   With heigh! with heigh! the thrush and the jay,   10
Are summer songs for me and my aunts,[8]
   While we lie tumbling in the hay.

Full Fathom Five[9]

Full fathom five thy father lies;
   Of his bones are coral made;
Those are pearls that were his eyes:
   Nothing of him that doth fade,
But doth suffer a sea change   5
Into something rich and strange.
Sea nymphs hourly ring his knell:
   Ding-dong.
Hark! now I hear them—Ding-dong, bell.

Where the Bee Sucks, There Suck I[1]

Where the bee sucks, there suck I:
In a cowslip's bell I lie;
There I couch when owls do cry.
On the bat's back I do fly
After summer merrily.   5
Merrily, merrily shall I live now
Under the blossom that hangs on the bough.

Sonnets

3

Look in thy glass, and tell the face thou viewest
Now is the time that face should form another,
Whose fresh repair if now thou not renewest,

5. A pun on (1) a territory over which one has jurisdiction (2) lacking in color.
6. Laundry, dried or bleached on hedges, was sometimes stolen by passing vagabonds like Autolycus.
7. Thieving.
8. Girls or mistresses.
9. *The Tempest* (1611–12) I.ii.396 ff. Ariel, the airy spirit of the enchanted isle, sings this song to Ferdinand, prince of Naples. Ferdinand wonders at it: "The ditty does remember my drowned father. / This is no mortal business, nor no sound/ That the earth owes [owns]."
1. Also from *The Tempest* V.i.88 ff.: Ariel is happily anticipating the freedom of his future life.

Thou dost beguile the world, unbless some mother.
For where is she so fair whose uneared[2] womb   5
Disdains the tillage of thy husbandry?
Or who is he so fond[3] will be the tomb
Of his self-love, to stop posterity?
Thou art thy mother's glass,[4] and she in thee
Calls back the lovely April of her prime;   10
So thou through windows of thine age shalt see,
Despite of wrinkles, this thy golden time.
But if thou live rememb'red not to be,
Die single, and thine image dies with thee.

12

When I do count the clock that tells the time
And see the brave[5] day sunk in hideous night,
When I behold the violet past prime
And sable curls all silver'd o'er with white,
When lofty trees I see barren of leaves,   5
Which erst[6] from heat did canopy the herd,
And summer's green all girded up in sheaves
Borne on the bier with white and bristly beard—
Then of thy beauty do I question make
That thou among the wastes of time must go,   10
Since sweets and beauties do themselves forsake
And die as fast as they see others grow,
And nothing 'gainst Time's scythe can make defense
Save breed,[7] to brave him when he takes thee hence.

18

Shall I compare thee to a summer's day?
Thou art more lovely and more temperate:
Rough winds do shake the darling buds of May,
And summer's lease hath all too short a date:
Sometime too hot the eye of heaven shines   5
And often is his gold complexion dimmed;
And every fair from fair sometimes declines,
By chance or nature's changing course untrimmed;[8]
But thy eternal summer shall not fade,
Nor lose possession of that fair thou ow'st;[9]   10
Nor shall death brag thou wander'st in his shade,
When in eternal lines to time thou grow'st:
So long as men can breathe, or eyes can see,
So long lives this, and this gives life to thee.[1]

2. Unplowed.
3. Foolish.
4. Mirror.
5. Splendid.
6. Formerly.
7. Offspring; "to brave": to defy.
8. Stripped of gay apparel.

9. Ownest.
1. The boast of immortality for one's verse was a Renaissance convention and goes back to the classics. It implies, not egotism on the part of the poet, but a faith in the permanence of poetry.

29

When, in disgrace with fortune and men's eyes,
I all alone beweep my outcast state,
And trouble deaf heaven with my bootless[2] cries,
And look upon myself, and curse my fate,
Wishing me like to one more rich in hope,   5
Featured like him, like him with friends possessed,
Desiring this man's art and that man's scope,
With what I most enjoy contented least;
Yet in these thoughts myself almost despising,
Haply I think on thee—and then my state,[3]   10
Like to the lark at break of day arising
From sullen earth, sings hymns at heaven's gate;
For thy sweet love remembered such wealth brings
That then I scorn to change my state with kings.[4]

30

When to the sessions[5] of sweet silent thought
I summon up remembrance of things past,
I sigh the lack of many a thing I sought,
And with old woes new wail[6] my dear time's waste:
Then can I drown an eye, unused to flow,   5
For precious friends hid in death's dateless[7] night,
And weep afresh love's long since canceled woe,
And moan the expense[8] of many a vanished sight:
Then can I grieve at grievances foregone,[9]
And heavily from woe to woe tell o'er   10
The sad account of fore-bemoanèd moan,
Which I new pay as if not paid before.
But if the while I think on thee, dear friend,
All losses are restored and sorrows end.

55

Not marble, nor the gilded monuments
Of princes, shall outlive this powerful rhyme;
But you shall shine more bright in these contents
Than unswept stone, besmeared with sluttish time.[1]
When wasteful war shall statues overturn,   5
And broils root out the work of masonry,
Nor Mars his[2] sword nor war's quick fire shall burn
The living record of your memory.
'Gainst death and all-oblivious enmity[3]

---

2. Futile.
3. Condition, state of mind; but in line 14 there is a pun on "state" meaning chair of state, throne.
4. This sonnet and the next are companion pieces, one dealing with present troubles, the other with those past.
5. Sittings of court; "summon up" (line 2) continues the metaphor.
6. Bewail anew.

7. Endless.
8. Loss.
9. Old subjects for grief. "Tell": count.
1. I.e., than in a stone tomb or effigy which time wears away and covers with dust.
2. Mars's.
3. The enmity of oblivion, of being forgotten.

Shall you pace forth; your praise shall still find room   10
Even in the eyes of all posterity
That wear this world out to the ending doom.[4]
So, till the judgment that yourself arise,
You live in this, and dwell in lovers' eyes.

56

Sweet love, renew thy force; be it not said
Thy edge should blunter be than appetite,
Which but today by feeding is allayed,
Tomorrow sharpened in his former might.
So, love, be thou: although today thou fill   5
Thy hungry eyes even till they wink[5] with fullness,
Tomorrow see again, and do not kill
The spirit of love with a perpetual dullness.
Let this sad int'rim like the ocean be
Which parts the shore where two contracted new[6]   10
Come daily to the banks, that, when they see
Return of love, more blest may be the view;
Or call it winter, which, being full of care,
Makes summer's welcome thrice more wished, more rare.

60

Like as the waves make towards the pebbled shore,
So do our minutes hasten to their end;
Each changing place with that which goes before,
In sequent toil all forwards do contend.[7]
Nativity, once in the main[8] of light,   5
Crawls to maturity, wherewith being crowned,
Crooked eclipses 'gainst his glory fight,
And time that gave doth now his gift confound.
Time doth transfix the flourish[9] set on youth
And delves the parallels in beauty's brow,   10
Feeds on the rarities of nature's truth,
And nothing stands but for his scythe to mow.
And yet to times in hope[1] my verse shall stand,
Praising thy worth, despite his cruel hand.

71

No longer mourn for me when I am dead
Than you shall hear the surly sullen bell[2]
Give warning to the world that I am fled
From this vile world, with vilest worms to dwell:

4. Judgment Day. The next line is paraphrased, "Until you rise from the dead on Judgment Day."
5. Close (not momentarily).
6. A newly engaged couple.
7. Toiling and following each other, the waves struggle to press forward.
8. Broad expanse.

9. Remove the embellishment. "Delves the parallels": digs the parallel furrows (wrinkles). To "flourish" is also to blossom.
1. Future times.
2. The bell was tolled to announce the death of a member of the parish— one stroke for each year of his life.

Nay, if you read this line, remember not   5
The hand that writ it; for I love you so,
That I in your sweet thoughts would be forgot,
If thinking on me then should make you woe.
Oh, if, I say, you look upon this verse
When I perhaps compounded am with clay,   10
Do not so much as my poor name rehearse,
But let your love even with my life decay;
Lest the wise world should look into your moan,
And mock you with me after I am gone.

73

That time of year thou mayst in me behold
When yellow leaves, or none, or few, do hang
Upon those boughs which shake against the cold,
Bare ruined choirs, where late the sweet birds sang.
In me thou see'st the twilight of such day   5
As after sunset fadeth in the west;
Which by and by black night doth take away,
Death's second self that seals up all in rest.
In me thou see'st the glowing of such fire,
That on the ashes of his youth doth lie,   10
As the deathbed whereon it must expire,
Consumed with that which it was nourished by.[3]
This thou perceiv'st, which makes thy love more strong,
To love that well which thou must leave ere long.

87

Farewell: thou art too dear[4] for my possessing,
And like enough thou know'st thy estimate.[5]
The charter[6] of thy worth gives thee releasing;
My bonds in thee are all determinate.[7]
For how do I hold thee but by thy granting,   5
And for that riches where is my deserving?
The cause of this fair gift in me is wanting,
And so my patent [8] back again is swerving.
Thyself thou gav'st, thy own worth then not knowing,
Or me, to whom thou gav'st it, else mistaking;   10
So thy great gift, upon misprision[9] growing,
Comes home again, on better judgment making.
Thus have I had thee as a dream doth flatter,
In sleep a king, but waking no such matter.

94

They that have power to hurt and will do none,
That do not do the thing they most do show,[1]

3. Choked by the ashes of that which
once nourished its flame.
4. "Expensive," "beloved."
5. Value.
6. Deed, contract for property.

7. Expired.
8. Title.
9. Mistake, oversight.
1. Seem to do.

Who, moving others, are themselves as stone,
Unmovéd, cold, and to temptation slow;
They rightly do inherit heaven's graces   5
And husband nature's riches from expense; [2]
They are the lords and owners of their faces,
Others but stewards of their excellence.
The summer's flower is to the summer sweet,
Though to itself it only live and die,   10
But if that flower with base infection meet,
The basest weed outbraves his dignity:
For sweetest things turn sourest by their deeds;
Lilies that fester smell far worse than weeds. [3]

97

How like a winter hath my absence been
From thee, the pleasure of the fleeting year!
What freezings have I felt, what dark days seen!
What old December's bareness everywhere!
And yet this time removed was summer's time,   5
The teeming autumn big with rich increase,
Bearing the wanton burthen of the prime, [4]
Like widowed wombs after their lords' decease;
Yet this abundant issue seemed to me
But hope of orphans and unfathered fruit;   10
For summer and his pleasures wait on thee,
And, thou away, the very birds are mute;
Or, if they sing, 'tis with so dull a cheer
That leaves look pale, dreading the winter's near.

98

From you have I been absent in the spring,
When proud-pied [5] April, dressed in all his trim,
Hath put a spirit of youth in everything,
That heavy Saturn [6] laughed and leaped with him.
Yet nor the lays of birds, nor the sweet smell   5
Of different flowers in odor and in hue,
Could make me any summer's story tell,
Or from their proud lap pluck them where they grew;
Nor did I wonder at [7] the lily's white,
Nor praise the deep vermilion in the rose;   10
They were but sweet, but figures of delight,
Drawn after you, you pattern of all those.
Yet seemed it winter still, and, you away,
As with your shadow I with these did play.

2. I.e., they do not squander nature's gifts.
3. This line appears in *Edward III* (II. i.451), an apocryphal Shakespearean play licensed December 1, 1595.
4. Spring, which has engendered the lavish crop ("wanton burthen") that autumn is now left to bear.
5. Magnificent in many colors.
6. God of meloncholy.
7. Admire.

104

To me, fair friend, you never can be old,
For as you were when first your eye I eyed
Such seems your beauty still. Three winters cold
Have from the forests shook three summer's pride,
Three beauteous springs to yellow autumn turned   5
In process [8] of the seasons have I seen,
Three April perfumes in three hot Junes burned,
Since first I saw you fresh, which yet are green.
Ah, yet doth beauty, like a dial-hand,[9]
Steal from his figure, and no pace perceived;   10
So your sweet hue, which methinks still doth stand,
Hath motion, and mine eye may be deceived:
For fear of which, hear this, thou age unbred:[1]
Ere you were born was beauty's summer dead.

106

When in the chronicle of wasted [2] time
I see descriptions of the fairest wights,
And beauty making beautiful old rhyme
In praise of ladies dead and lovely knights,
Then, in the blazon[3] of sweet beauty's best,   5
Of hand, of foot, of lip, of eye, of brow,
I see their antique pen would have expressed
Even such a beauty as you master now.
So all their praises are but prophecies
Of this our time, all you prefiguring;   10
And, for they looked but with divining eyes,
They had not skill enough your worth to sing:[4]
For we, which now behold these present days,
Have eyes to wonder, but lack tongues to praise.

107

Not mine own fears, nor the prophetic soul
Of the wide world dreaming on things to come,[5]
Can yet the lease of my true love control,
Supposed as forfeit to a confinéd doom.[6]
The mortal moon hath her eclipse endured,   5
And the sad augurs mock their own presage;[7]
Incertainties now crown themselves assured,
And peace[8] proclaims olives of endless age.

8. Procession.
9. Hand of a watch.
1. Unborn generation.
2. Past.
3. Display.
4. Because ("for") they were able *only* ("but") to foresee prophetically.
5. This sonnet refers to contemporary events and the prophecies, common in Elizabethan almanacs, of disaster.
6. I.e., can yet put an end to my love, which I thought doomed to early forfeiture.

7. The "mortal moon" is Queen Elizabeth; her "eclipse" is probably her climacteric year, her 63rd (thought significant because the product of two "significant" numbers, 7 and 9), which ended in September, 1596. The sober astrologers ("sad augurs") now ridicule their own predictions ("presage") of catastrophe, since they turned out to be false.
8. Probably an agreement between Henry IV of France and Elizabeth.

Now with the drops of this most balmy time
My love looks fresh, and death to me subscribes,[9]   10
Since, spite of him, I'll live in this poor rhyme,
While he insults o'er dull and speechless tribes:
And thou in this shalt find thy monument,
When tyrants' crests and tombs of brass are spent.

110[1]

Alas, 'tis true I have gone here and there
And made myself a motley[2] to the view,
Gored[3] mine own thoughts, sold cheap what is most dear,
Made old offenses of affections new;[4]
Most true it is that I have looked on truth   5
Askance and strangely; but, by all above,
These blenches[5] gave my heart another youth,
And worse essays[6] proved thee my best of love.
Now all is done, have what shall have no end:
Mine appetite I never more will grind[7]   10
On newer proof, to try an older friend,
A god in love, to whom I am confined.
Then give me welcome, next my heaven the best,
Even to thy pure and most most loving breast.

116

Let me not to the marriage of true minds
Admit impediments.[8] Love is not love
Which alters when it alteration finds,
Or bends with the remover to remove:
Oh, no! it is an ever-fixéd mark,   5
That looks on tempests and is never shaken;
It is the star to every wandering bark,
Whose worth's unknown, although his height[9] be taken.
Love's not Time's fool, though rosy lips and cheeks
Within his[1] bending sickle's compass come;   10
Love alters not with his brief hours and weeks,
But bears it out even to the edge of doom.[2]
If this be error and upon me proved,
   I never writ, nor no man ever loved.

118

Like as, to make our appetites more keen,
With eager[3] compounds we our palate urge;

---

9. Submits.
1. This is the second in a group of sonnets that deal with the poet's absence from the friend and an unfaithfulness to him. The first three lines may refer to Shakespeare's career as an actor.
2. A clown (with a varicolored costume).
3. Wounded.
4. Offended by changing old friends for new.
5. Offenses.
6. Trials of what is worse.

7. Whet.
8. From the Marriage Service: "If any of you know cause or just impediment why these persons should not be joined together * * * "
9. The star's value is not known, though the star's "height" (altitude) may be known and used for practical navigation.
1. I.e., Time's (as also in line 11).
2. Brink of the Last Judgment.
3. Bitter.

As, to prevent our maladies unseen,
We sicken to shun sickness when we purge:[4]
Even so, being full of your ne'er-cloying sweetness,   5
To bitter sauces did I frame my feeding;
And, sick of welfare,[5] found a kind of meetness
To be diseased ere that there was true needing.
Thus policy in love, t' anticipate
The ills that were not, grew to faults assuréd,   10
And brought to medicine a healthful state,
Which, rank of goodness, would by ill be curéd.
But thence I learn, and find the lesson true,
Drugs poison him that so fell sick of you.

121

'Tis better to be vile than vile esteemed
When not to be receives reproach of being,[6]
And the just pleasure lost, which is so deemed
Not by our feeling but by others' seeing.
For why should others' false adulterate eyes   5
Give salutation to my sportive blood?[7]
Or on my frailties why are frailer spies,[8]
Which in their wills count bad what I think good?
No, I am that I am; and they that level[9]
At my abuses reckon up their own: 10
I may be straight though they themselves be bevel;[1]
By their rank thoughts my deeds must not be shown,
Unless this general evil they maintain:
All men are bad and in their badness reign.

129

Th' expense of spirit in a waste of shame
Is lust in action;[2] and till action, lust
Is perjured, murderous, bloody, full of blame,
Savage, extreme, rude, cruel, not to trust;
Enjoyed no sooner but despiséd straight: 5
Past reason hunted; and no sooner had,
Past reason hated, as a swallowed bait,
On purpose laid to make the taker mad:
Mad in pursuit, and in possession so;
Had, having, and in quest to have, extreme;   10
A bliss in proof[3] and proved, a very woe;

---

4. Take cathartics.
5. Replete with well-being; as in "rank of goodness" (line 12). "Sick of" does not have the modern meaning "tired of"; it rather means "sick with," here and in line 14.
6. I.e., it is better to be vicious than to be thought vicious when the innocent are thought vicious.
7. Others' falsified, lewdly corrupt eyes tempt me.

8. Men with more frailties.
9. Aim.
1. Crooked, slanting.
2. The word order here is inverted and slightly obscures the meaning. Lust, when put into action, expends "spirit" (life, vitality) in a "waste" (desert, with a possible pun on "waist," also) of shame.
3. A bliss during the experience.

Before, a joy proposed; behind, a dream.
All this the world well knows; yet none knows well
To shun the heaven that leads men to this hell.

130

My mistress' eyes are nothing like the sun;[4]
Coral is far more red than her lips' red;
If snow be white, why then her breasts are dun;
If hairs be wires, black wires grow on her head.
I have seen roses damasked,[5] red and white,   5
But no such roses see I in her cheeks;
And in some perfumes is there more delight
Than in the breath that from my mistress reeks.
I love to hear her speak, yet well I know
That music hath a far more pleasing sound;   10
I grant I never saw a goddess go;[6]
My mistress, when she walks, treads on the ground.
And yet, by heaven, I think my love as rare
As any she belied with false compare.

138

When my love swears that she is made of truth,
I do believe her, though I know she lies,
That she might think me some untutored youth,
Unlearned in the world's false subtleties.
Thus vainly thinking that she thinks me young,   5
Although she knows my days are past the best,[7]
Simply I credit her false-speaking tongue:
On both sides thus is simple truth suppressed.
But wherefore says she not she is unjust?[8]
And wherefore say not I that I am old?   10
Oh, love's best habit[9] is in seeming trust,
And age in love loves not to have years told.
Therefore I lie with her and she with me,
And in our faults by lies we flattered be.

144

Two loves I have of comfort and despair,
Which like two spirits do suggest me still:[1]
The better angel is a man right fair,
The worser spirit a woman, colored ill.[2]
To win me soon to hell, my female evil   5
Tempteth my better angel from my side,
And would corrupt my saint to be a devil,

---

4. An anti-Petrarchan sonnet. All of the details commonly attributed by other Elizabethan sonneteers to their ladies are here denied to the poet's mistress.
5. Variegated. The damask rose (supposedly from Damascus, originally) is pink.
6. Walk.

7. Shakespeare was 35 or younger when he wrote this sonnet (it first appeared in *The Passionate Pilgrim*, 1599). "Simply": like a simpleton.
8. Unfaithful.
9. Appearance, deportment.
1. Tempt me constantly.
2. Dark.

Wooing his purity with her foul pride.
And whether that my angel be turned fiend
Suspect I may, yet not directly tell;   10
But being both from[3] me, both to each friend,
I guess one angel in another's hell.
Yet this shall I ne'er know, but live in doubt,
Till my bad angel fire[4] my good one out.

146

Poor soul, the center of my sinful earth,
Lord of[5] these rebel powers that thee array,[6]
Why dost thou pine within and suffer dearth,
Painting thy outward walls so costly gay?
Why so large cost, having so short a lease,   5
Dost thou upon thy fading mansion spend?
Shall worms, inheritors of this excess,
Eat up thy charge? Is this thy body's end?
Then, soul, live thou upon thy servant's loss,
And let that pine to aggravate thy store;[7]   10
Buy terms[8] divine in selling hours of dross;
Within be fed, without be rich no more.
So shalt thou feed on death, that feeds on men,
And death once dead, there's no more dying then.

The Phoenix and the Turtle[1]

Let the bird of loudest lay,[2]
On the sole Arabian tree,
Herald sad and trumpet be,
To whose sound chaste wings obey.

3. Away from; "each": each other.
4. Drive out by fire.
5. An emendation. The Quarto repeats the last three words of line 1. Other suggestions are "Thrall to," "Starv'd by," "Press'd by," and leaving the repetition but dropping "that'thee" in line 2
6. Dress out, often used in a military sense.
7. Let "that" (i.e., the body) deteriorate to increase ("aggravate") the soul's riches ("thy store").
8. Long periods; "dross": refuse, rubbish.
1. First published in Robert Chester's *Love's Martyr, or Rosalin's Complaint* (1601). It is part of an appendix containing "divers poetical essays" by other poets, all supposedly dealing with the same subject. This subject has something to do with a Welsh knight, Sir John Salusbury, and his lady. But Shakespeare's poem is not consistent with the other poems in the volume, for some of them celebrate the birth of offspring to the phoenix and the turtle, whereas Shakespeare says the birds died leaving no posterity. The phoenix is a legendary bird of Arabia: it perishes in flames and a new one arises from the ashes; only one is alive at a time. Queen Elizabeth, the Virgin Queen, was sometimes symbolized by the unique and virginal phoenix. The "turtle" (turtledove) is common in Elizabethan imagery as the most loving of birds. Bird poems were traditionally allegorical, from Chaucer's time on down, but the key to this allegory (if it is one) has been lost.
2. Cry or song. This stanza might be paraphrased, "Let the bird with the loudest voice proclaim from the perch of the phoenix ('Arabian tree'); all gentle birds ('chaste wings') will respond to the summons."

But thou shrieking harbinger,
Foul precurrer of the fiend,[3]
Augur of the fever's end,
To this troop come thou not near!   5

From this session interdict
Every fowl of tyrant wing,
Save the eagle, feathered king: 10
Keep the obsequy so strict.

Let the priest in surplice white,
That defunctive music can,[4]
Be the death-divining swan,   15
Lest the requiem lack his right.

And thou treble-dated[5] crow,
That thy sable gender mak'st
With the breath thou giv'st and tak'st,[6]
'Mongst our mourners shalt thou go.   20

Here the anthem doth commence:
Love and constancy is dead,
Phoenix and the turtle fled
In a mutual flame from hence.

So they loved as love in twain   25
Had the essence but in one;[7]
Two distincts, division none:
Number there in love was slain.

Hearts remote, yet not asunder;
Distance, and no space was seen   30
'Twixt this turtle and his queen;
But in them[8] it were a wonder.

So between them love did shine
That the turtle saw his right[9]
Flaming in the phoenix' sight: 35
Either was the other's mine.[1]

Property[2] was thus appalled,
That the self was not the same;
Single nature's double name
Neither two nor one was called.   40

3. Forerunner of the devil. "Harbinger"; precursor. The screech owl is probably meant.
4. I.e., skilled in funeral ("defunctive") music. The swan was supposed to sing only once, just before its death.
5. Living three lifetimes.
6. "Sable gender": black offspring. The crow was supposed to conceive and lay its eggs through the bill.
7. They were originally two, but by love were united into one. Since one is singular, and not a number, "Number there in love was slain."
8. In any other case than theirs.
9. What was due him, love returned.
1. Rich source of wealth or treasure.
2. Peculiar or essential quality. "Property" is "appalled" to find that personality ("self") is obliterated in the union of the two. Accordingly it is impossible to say whether they were two or one.

Reason, in itself confounded,
Saw division grow together,[3]
To themselves yet either neither,
Simple were so well compounded;

That it cried, "How true a twain   45
Seemeth this concordant one!
Love hath reason, reason none,
If what parts can so remain."[4]

Whereupon it made this threne[5]
To the phoenix and the dove,   50
Co-supremes and stars of love,
As chorus to their tragic scene.

Threnos

Beauty, truth, and rarity,
Grace in all simplicity,
Here enclosed in cinders lie.   55

Death is now the phoenix' nest;
And the turtle's loyal breast
To eternity doth rest,

Leaving no posterity:
'Twas not their infirmity,   60
It was married chastity.

Truth may seem, but cannot be;
Beauty brag, but 'tis not she:[6]
Truth and Beauty buried be.

To this urn let those repair   65
That are either true or fair;
For these dead birds sigh a prayer.

1601

1 Henry IV   The title page of the first quarto edition of Shakespeare's 1 *Henry IV*, published in 1598, reads: "THE HISTORY OF HENRIE THE FOURTH; With the the battell at Shrewsburie, *betweene the King and Lord* Henry Percy, surnamed Henrie Hotspur of the North. *With the humorous conceits of Sir* John Falstalffe." It had been performed on the stage and at court before publication, and from that time to this it has remained one of Shakespeare's most popular plays.

Shakespeare had already inaugurated a new dramatic type by writing

---

3. Reason, which discriminates parts of a thing, is here confounded because the two parts are merged. Each element lost its identity in being fused with the other.
4. Love is more reasonable than reason, because it has proved that the

separateness of entities (one of reason's laws) does not always hold true.
5. Threnody, funeral song.
6. Whatever may appear hereafter as truth or beauty will be only illusion. Real truth and beauty lie buried here.

four plays dealing with fairly recent English history, and had then gone back to a period two centuries earlier to portray, in *Richard II*, the downfall of the weak, effeminate and poetic young King Richard ("that sweet lovely rose," as he is called in this play) at the hands of the hard, efficient Bolingbroke, who came to the throne as Henry IV. Before this seizure of the crown there had been a prophecy, put by Shakespeare into the mouth of the Bishop of Carlisle in *Richard II* (IV.i.136–44), of the dire consequences to follow:

> And if you crown him, let me prophesy,
> The blood of English shall manure the ground
> And future ages groan for this foul act;
> Peace shall go sleep with Turks and infidels,
> And in this seat of peace tumultuous wars
> Shall kin with kin and kind with kind confound;
> Disorder, horror, fear, and mutiny
> Shall here inhabit, and this land be called
> The field of Golgotha and dead men's skulls.

Shakespeare drew his historical material from the prose chronicle histories, specifically Raphael Holinshed's *Chronicles of England, Scotland, and Ireland*, Samuel Daniel's historical poem *Civil Wars*, and an earlier play, either the popular farcical piece called *The Famous Victories of Henry V* or a lost play which was its source. His sources gave him the portrait of a gay and reckless Prince of Wales and his roistering companions. Chief of these was a fat knight, Sir John Oldcastle; Shakespeare at first used this name, but later, because of protests from the descendants of that Protestant martyr, changed the name to Sir John Falstaff. This character, whose "humorous conceits" are advertised on the title page, is one of the greatest comic creations in all literature. Shakespeare continued to exploit his inexhaustible exuberance through a sequel, *The Second Part of Henry IV*, and a comedy of middle-class life, supposed to have been written at Queen Elizabeth's command, *The Merry Wives of Windsor*.

The ominous wars of Carlisle's prophecy could thus be mixed with hilarious fooling, but *1 Henry IV* succeeds, not only as a comedy, but as a serious play about character and history. The real hero is not King Henry IV, nor the fat Falstaff, but Prince Hal, the handsome playboy who in time of crisis reforms and saves his father's throne. He is the prince who later became Henry V, the English national hero who reconquered France.

Shakespeare's theme in all his history plays is the importance of order and degree, of the disruptive effects of civil strife and rebellion. But as he matured as a dramatist (and *1 Henry IV* stands at the beginning of his great period of maturity), he found character to be more interesting than the philosophy or events of history. How to demonstrate the kind of character that would make the English national hero was his problem, and he solved it by a method of comparison and contrast, utilizing four men of different types. At one extreme is Falstaff, who loves to eat, drink, joke, and dramatize himself, and to whom anything as intangible as honor is a mere word, a breath of air. Opposite in every way is Hotspur, fiery and impatient, completely ambitious for honor and fame, scornful of the soft, civilized arts of poetry and music, a hardheaded fanatic. A third type is the wild Welshman Glendower, a believer in magic and a practitioner of it, an accomplished poet yet a valiant, if superstitious, warrior, and an egotist like his ally Hotspur. Finally there is Prince Hal, whose sense of humor rivals Falstaff's, but who turns out to be the match for Hotspur in valor and his superior in knightly courtesy. It is worth noting that Shakespeare changed history in order to make this dramatic contrast: in Holinshed's *Chronicle* Hotspur is older than Prince Hal's father, but Shakespeare makes them contemporaries. It is in the excesses of the other three that we see the merits of the Prince's character illuminated. The four characters represent not only men but ways of life. And these ways of life are all relevant to fundamental questions about social and political responsibility, honor, and loyalty to a cause.

Some background in 15th-century English history, as Shakespeare understood it, is needed if we are to respond readily to the play. Henry Hereford, called Bolingbroke, was in exile in France when his father, John of Gaunt, died. He returned to England to claim his inheritance, and profited from the aid of the Percy family, powerful nobles in the north. The two brothers, Henry Percy, Earl of Northumberland, and Thomas Percy, Earl of Worcester, together with Northumberland's son Henry (called Hotspur) received Bolingbroke's oath at Doncaster (see V.i.32–58) to seize only his inheritance. But King Richard II was in Ireland fighting, having named Edmund Mortimer, Earl of March, his successor if he did not return. In the confused situation in England, Bolingbroke was able to collect enough power so that on Richard's return he could force him to abdicate and then have him killed in prison. Various troubles on the borders made the throne of the new king (Henry IV) insecure. Hotspur managed to defeat the Scots under Douglas at Holmedon (see I.i.62–75) and took many important prisoners. But Mortimer, in fighting against Glendower in Wales, was taken captive and married Glendower's daughter. Henry IV refused to ransom Mortimer, and the indignation of Mortimer's brother-in-law, Hotspur, led him to refuse to turn over his prisoners to the king. So came the conspiracy into being—and such a formidable opposition as that of the Percies, Douglas, Glendower, and certain disaffected churchmen like the Archbishop of York meant a critical danger to Henry's throne. The Battle of Shrewsbury, the climax of this play, decides the conflict.

Much critical comment has been devoted to the character of Falstaff. He has certain resemblances to the traditional *miles gloriosus* (braggart soldier) of Latin comedy, but he far transcends the type; he sometimes resembles the Vice, a comic character in the old morality plays, who is usually an allegorical personification of extreme self-indulgence or of a particular sin; and he often uses, or parodies, the language of the Puritans. Critics differ on whether Falstaff is really a coward or not, and on the question of how much he expects his lies to be believed. But everyone agrees about his inexhaustible vitality and resiliency. It is not surprising that he, like other immortal characters in literature, remains something of a mystery.

The First Part of
King Henry the Fourth

Dramatis Personae

KING HENRY THE FOURTH
HENRY, *Prince of Wales*
PRINCE JOHN OF LANCASTER } *Sons to the* KING
EARL OF WESTMORELAND
SIR WALTER BLUNT
THOMAS PERCY, *Earl of Worcester*
HENRY PERCY, *Earl of Northumberland*
HENRY PERCY, *surnamed* HOTSPUR, *his son*
EDMUND MORTIMER, *Earl of March*
RICHARD SCROOP, *Archbishop of York*
ARCHIBALD, *Earl of Douglas*
OWEN GLENDOWER
SIR RICHARD VERNON
SIR MICHAEL, *a friend to the* ARCHBISHOP OF YORK
SIR JOHN FALSTAFF
POINS
GADSHILL
PETO
BARDOLPH
LADY PERCY, *wife to* HOTSPUR, *and sister to* MORTIMER
LADY MORTIMER, *daughter to* GLENDOWER, *and wife to* MORTIMER
MISTRESS QUICKLY, *hostess of a tavern in Eastcheap*
LORDS, OFFICERS, SHERIFF, VINTNER, CHAMBERLAIN, DRAWERS, *two*
    CARRIERS, TRAVELERS, *and* ATTENDANTS

Act I

SCENE 1

[*Enter the* KING, PRINCE JOHN OF LANCASTER, THE EARL OF
    WESTMORELAND, SIR WALTER BLUNT, *with others.*]

KING. So shaken as we are, so wan with care,
    Find we a time for frighted peace to pant,[1]
    And breathe short-winded accents of new broils[2]
    To be commenced in stronds afar remote.
    No more the thirsty entrance[3] of this soil   5
    Shall daub her lips with her own children's blood;
    No more shall trenching war channel her fields,
    Nor bruise her flowerets with the arméd hoofs
    Of hostile paces:[4] those opposéd eyes,
    Which, like the meteors of a troubled heaven,   10
    All of one nature, of one substance bred,
    Did lately meet in the intestine shock[5]
    And furious close of civil butchery,
    Shall now, in mutual well-beseeming ranks,

1. I.e., let us allow peace to catch her
breath.
2. I.e., news of new wars; "stronds":
strands, regions.
3. Surface.
4. The tread of war horses.
5. Internal violence; "close": encounter.

March all one way and be no more opposed 15
Against acquaintance, kindred, and allies.
The edge of war, like an ill-sheathéd knife,
No more shall cut his master: therefore, friends,
As far as to the sepulcher of Christ,
Whose soldier now, under whose blessed cross 20
We are impresséd and engaged to fight,
Forthwith a power[6] of English shall we levy,
Whose arms were molded in their mother's womb
To chase these pagans in those holy fields
Over whose acres walked those blessed feet 25
Which fourteen hundred years ago were nailed
For our advantage on the bitter cross.
But this our purpose now is twelve month old,
And bootless[7] 'tis to tell you we will go.
Therefore we meet not now:[8] then let me hear 30
Of you, my gentle cousin Westmoreland,
What yesternight our council did decree
In forwarding this dear expedience.[9]

WEST. My liege, this haste was hot in question,[1]
And many limits of the charge set down 35
But yesternight, when all athwart[2] there came
A post from Wales loaden with heavy news,
Whose worst was that the noble Mortimer,
Leading the men of Herefordshire to fight
Against the irregular[3] and wild Glendower, 40
Was by the rude hands of that Welshman taken,
A thousand of his people butcheréd,
Upon whose dead corpse[4] there was such misuse,
Such beastly shameless transformatión,
By those Welshwomen done as may not be 45
Without much shame retold or spoken of.

KING. It seems then that the tidings of this broil
Brake off our business for the Holy Land.

WEST. This matched with other did, my gracious lord,
For more uneven and unwelcome news 50
Came from the north, and thus it did import:
On Holyrood Day[5] the gallant Hotspur there,
Young Harry Percy, and brave Archibald,
That ever-valiant and approvéd Scot,
At Holmedon met, 55
Where they did spend a sad and bloody hour;
As by discharge of their artillery,
And shape of likelihood,[6] the news was told;
For he that brought them[7] in the very heat

6. Army. He is planning a crusade, in expiation of his guilt for the death of Richard II.
7. Useless.
8. I.e., that is not the reason for our present meeting. "Cousin": kinsman.
9. Important, urgent matter.
1. Actively discussed. "Limits of the charge": assignment of commands.

2. Interrupting, crossing our purpose. "Post": messenger.
3. Guerilla.
4. Bodies.
5. Holy Cross Day (Sept. 14).
6. Probable inference. "As": since.
7. I.e., the news (usually a plural in Shakespeare). "Pride": height; literally, the top of a falcon's flight.

And pride of their contention did take horse,   60
Uncertain of the issue any way.
KING. Here is a dear, a true industrious friend,
   Sir Walter Blunt, new lighted from his horse,
   Stained with the variation of each soil
   Betwixt that Holmedon and this seat of ours;   65
   And he hath brought us smooth and welcome news.
   The Earl of Douglas is discomfited;
   Ten thousand bold Scots, two and twenty knights
   Balked[8] in their own blood did Sir Walter see
   On Holmedon's plains. Of prisoners Hotspur took   70
   Mordake Earl of Fife, and eldest son
   To beaten Douglas, and the Earl of Athol,
   Of Murray, Angus, and Menteith;
   And is not this an honorable spoil,
   A gallant prize? ha, cousin, is it not?   75
WEST. In faith,
   It is a conquest for a prince to boast of.
KING. Yea, there thou mak'st me sad and mak'st me sin
   In envy that my Lord Northumberland
   Should be the father to so blest a son,   80
   A son who is the theme of honor's tongue,
   Amongst a grove the very straightest plant,
   Who is sweet Fortune's minion[9] and her pride;
   Whilst I, by looking on the praise of him,
   See riot and dishonor stain the brow   85
   Of my young Harry. O that it could be proved
   That some night-tripping fairy had exchanged
   In cradle-clothes our children where they lay,
   And called mine Percy, his Plantagenet!
   Then would I have his Harry, and he mine.   90
   But let him from my thoughts. What think you, coz,
   Of this young Percy's pride? The prisoners
   Which he in this adventure hath surprised
   To his own use he keeps, and sends me word
   I shall have none but Mordake Earl of Fife.   95
WEST. This is his uncle's teaching, this is Worcester,
   Malevolent to you in all aspects,[1]
   Which makes him prune himself,[2] and bristle up
   The crest of youth against your dignity.
KING. But I have sent for him to answer this;   100
   And for this cause awhile we must neglect
   Our holy purpose to Jerusalem.
   Cousin, on Wednesday next our council we
   Will hold at Windsor, so inform the lords;
   But come yourself with speed to us again,   105
   For more is to be said and to be done
   Than out of anger can be utteréd.
WEST. I will, my liege.   [*Exeunt.*]

8. Heaped.
9. Favorite.
1. Hostile in every way. The figure is
from astrology.

2. Plume himself. "Bristle up" and
"crest" continue the image, which is
that of a fighting cock.

SCENE 2

[*Enter* HENRY, PRINCE OF WALES, *and* SIR JOHN FALSTAFF.]

FAL. Now Hal, what time of day is it, lad?

PRINCE. Thou art so fat-witted with drinking of old sack,[3] and un-
buttoning thee after supper, and sleeping upon benches after
noon, that thou hast forgotten to demand that truly which
thou wouldst truly know. What a devil hast thou to do with   5
the time of the day? Unless hours were cups of sack, and minutes capons, and clocks the tongues of bawds, and dials the
signs of leaping-houses,[4] and the blessed sun himself a fair hot
wench in flame-colored taffeta, I see no reason why thou
shouldst be so superfluous to demand the time of the day.   10

FAL. Indeed you come near me now, Hal, for we that take purses
go by the moon and the seven stars, and not by Phoebus,[5] he,
"that wandering knight so fair." And I prithee, sweet wag,
when thou art king, as, God save thy grace—majesty I should
say, for grace[6] thou wilt have none—   15

PRINCE. What, none?

FAL. No, by my troth, not so much as will serve to be prologue
to an egg and butter.

PRINCE. Well, how then? come, roundly, roundly.[7]

FAL. Marry then, sweet wag, when thou art king, let not us that   20
are squires of the night's body[8] be called thieves of the day's
beauty; let us be Diana's foresters, gentlemen of the shade,
minions of the moon; and let men say we be men of good
government, being governed as the sea is, by our noble and
chaste mistress the moon, under whose countenance we steal.   25

PRINCE. Thou sayest well, and it holds well too, for the fortune
of us that are the moon's men doth ebb and flow like the sea,
being governed as the sea is by the moon. As for proof now:
a purse of gold most resolutely snatched on Monday night and
most dissolutely spent on Tuesday morning, got with swearing   30
"Lay by" and spent with crying "Bring in," now in as low an
ebb as the foot of the ladder and by and by in as high a flow
as the ridge of the gallows.[9]

FAL. By the Lord thou sayest true, lad. And is not my hostess of
the tavern a most sweet wench?   35

PRINCE. As the honey of Hybla,[1] my old lad of the castle. And is
not a buff jerkin a most sweet robe of durance?[2]

3. Sherry.
4. Whorehouses.
5. The sun. Falstaff then quotes from
a popular ballad.
6. A triple pun: (1) "your Grace,"
the correct manner of addressing a
prince or duke; (2) the divine influence
which produces sanctity; and (3) a
short prayer before a meal—hence
Falstaff's allusion to "egg and butter,"
a common hasty breakfast.
7. Plainly.
8. Two puns are involved: a "squire
of the body" was an attendant on a
knight, and "body" would be pronounced *bawdy*. "Beauty" also puns
with "booty" (which thieves take);

Diana is, of course, the moon goddess.
9. "Lay by": i.e., hand over (a robber's command to his victim); "bring
in": a customer's command for more
drink at a tavern. The "foot of the
ladder" is at the bottom of the gallows
(robbery was a hanging offense);
the "ridge" is the crosspiece at the
top.
1. A town in Sicily, famous for honey;
"old lad of the castle" is a reference
to Falstaff's original name, Oldcastle.
2. A "buff jerkin" was the leather
jacket worn by a sheriff's sergeant;
"durance" is a pun: (1) lasting quality
and (2) imprisonment.

FAL. How now, how now, mad wag! what, in thy quips and thy quiddities?[3] what a plague have I to do with a buff jerkin?

PRINCE. Why, what a pox have I to do with my hostess of the tavern? 40

FAL. Well, thou hast called her to a reckoning many a time and oft.

· PRINCE. Did I ever call for thee to pay thy part?

FAL. No, I'll give thee thy due, thou hast paid all there. 45

PRINCE. Yea, and elsewhere, so far as my coin would stretch, and where it would not I have used my credit.

FAL. Yea, and so used it that were it not here apparent that thou art heir apparent[4]—but I prithee, sweet wag, shall there be gallows standing in England when thou art king? and resolu- 50
tion thus fobbed as it is with the rusty curb of old father antic the law?[5] Do not thou, when thou art king, hang a thief.

PRINCE. No, thou shalt.

FAL. Shall I? O rare! By the Lord, I'll be a brave judge.

PRINCE. Thou judgest false already; I mean thou shalt have the 55
hanging of the thieves and so become a rare hangman.

FAL. Well, Hal, well; and in some sort it jumps with my humor[6] as well as waiting in the court, I can tell you.

PRINCE. For obtaining of suits?[7]

FAL. Yea, for obtaining of suits, whereof the hangman hath no 60
lean wardrobe. 'Sblood,[8] I am as melancholy as a gib cat or a lugged bear.

PRINCE. Or an old lion, or a lover's lute.

FAL. Yea, or the drone of a Lincolnshire bagpipe.

PRINCE. What sayest thou to a hare, or the melancholy of Moor- 65
ditch?[9]

FAL. Thou hast the most unsavory similes and art indeed the most comparative,[1] rascalliest, sweet young prince. But Hal, I prithee, trouble me no more with vanity. I would to God thou and I knew where a commodity of good names were to be 70
bought. An old lord of the council rated[2] me the other day in the street about you, sir, but I marked him not; and yet he talked very wisely, but I regarded him not; and yet he talked wisely, and in the street too.

PRINCE. Thou didst well, for wisdom cries out in the streets and 75
no man regards it.[3]

FAL. O, thou hast damnable iteration[4] and art indeed able to corrupt a saint. Thou hast done much harm upon me, Hal, God forgive thee for it! Before I knew thee, Hal, I knew noth-

3. Quibbles.
4. "Here" and "heir" would pun in Elizabethan pronunciation.
5. "Resolution": bravery; "fobbed": cheated; "antic": a clown.
6. I.e., agrees with my disposition.
7. Special favors, but "clothing" in the next line. The hangman was given the clothes of his victims.
8. God's blood, a common oath. "Gib cat": tomcat; "lugged": baited (in the bear-baiting pits a bear was attacked by

dogs as a public amusement).
9. The "hare" was traditionally associated with melancholy; Moorditch was a foul-smelling ditch on the outskirts of London.
1. Affecting wit, dealing in comparisons.
2. Scolded, berated.
3. Prince Hal is quoting Proverbs i. 20 and 24.
4. Repetition, especially of sacred texts.

ing, and now am I, if a man should speak truly, little better 80
than one of the wicked. I must give over this life, and I will
give it over; by the Lord, an⁵ I do not, I am a villain; I'll be
damned for never a king's son in Christendom.

PRINCE. Where shall we take a purse tomorrow, Jack?

FAL. Zounds, where thou wilt, lad; I'll make one; an I do not, 85
call me villain and baffle⁶ me.

PRINCE. I see a good amendment of life in thee—from praying
to purse-taking.

FAL. Why, Hal, 'tis my vocation,⁷ Hal; 'tis no sin for a man to
labor in his vocation. 90

[*Enter* POINS.]

Poins! Now shall we know if Gadshill⁸ have set a match. O, if
men were to be saved by merit, what hole in hell were hot
enough for him? This is the most omnipotent villain that ever
cried "stand" to a true man.

PRINCE. Good morrow, Ned. 95

POINS. Good morrow, sweet Hal. What says Monsieur Remorse?
what says Sir John Sack and Sugar? Jack! how agrees the devil
and thee about thy soul, that thou soldest him on Good Friday last for a cup of Madeira and a cold capon's leg?

PRINCE. Sir John stands to his word; the devil shall have his bar- 100
gain, for he was never yet a breaker of proverbs; he will give
the devil his due.

POINS. Then art thou damned for keeping thy word with the
devil.

PRINCE. Else he had been damned for cozening⁹ the devil. 105

POINS. But my lads, my lads, tomorrow morning by four o'clock,
early at Gadshill, there are pilgrims going to Canterbury with
rich offerings, and traders riding to London with fat purses.
I have vizards¹ for you all, you have horses for yourselves; Gadshill lies tonight in Rochester; I have bespoke supper tomorrow 110
night in Eastcheap; we may do it as secure as sleep. If you will
go, I will stuff your purses full of crowns; if you will not, tarry
at home and be hanged.

FAL. Hear ye, Yedward, if I tarry at home and go not, I'll hang
you for going. 115

POINS. You will, chops?²

FAL. Hal, wilt thou make one?

PRINCE. Who, I rob? I a thief? not I, by my faith.

FAL. There's neither honesty, manhood, nor good fellowship in
thee, nor thou camest not of the blood royal,³ if thou darest 120

---

5. If.
6. A knight in the days of chivalry was "baffled" or disgraced by having his shield hung upside down. Falstaff may mean "hang me up by the heels."
"Zounds": a common oath, a contraction of "by God's wounds" (i.e., Jesus' wounds on the Cross).
7. Falstaff is here making fun of the Puritan doctrine of "calling" or vocation, based on the parable of the talents (see Matthew xxv.25 ff.).
8. Gadshill is both a man and a place: the place is a hill 27 miles from London on the road to Rochester; it was notorious for robberies. The man, so called from the place, is the thieves' "setter," who arranges when and where the robbery will occur.
9. Cheating.
1. Masks.
2. Fat face.
3. A pun: the coin called a "royal" was worth ten shillings. "Stand for" also puns: it means both "represent" and "fight for."

not stand for ten shillings.

PRINCE. Well then, once in my days I'll be a madcap.

FAL. Why, that's well said.

PRINCE. Well, come what will, I'll tarry at home.

FAL. By the Lord, I'll be a traitor then, when thou art king. 125

PRINCE. I care not.

POINS. Sir John, I prithee leave the prince and me alone; I will lay him down such reasons for this adventure that he shall go.

FAL. Well, God give thee the spirit of persuasion and him the ears of profiting, that what thou speakest may move and what 130 he hears may be believed, that the true prince may, for recreation sake, prove a false thief; for the poor abuses of the time want countenance.[4] Farewell; you shall find me in Eastcheap.

PRINCE. Farewell, thou latter spring, farewell, Allhallown summer![5]

[⟨*Exit* FALSTAFF.⟩][6]

POINS. Now, my good sweet honey lord, ride with us tomorrow; 135 I have a jest to execute that I cannot manage alone. Falstaff, Bardolph, Peto, and Gadshill shall rob those men that we have already waylaid; yourself and I will not be there, and when they have the booty, if you and I do not rob them, cut this head off from my shoulders. 140

PRINCE. How shall we part with them in setting forth?

POINS. Why, we will set forth before or after them, and appoint them a place of meeting, wherein it is at our pleasure to fail, and then will they adventure upon the exploit themselves, which they shall have no sooner achieved but we'll set upon 145 them.

PRINCE. Yea, but 'tis like that they will know us by our horses, by our habits,[7] and by every other appointment to be ourselves.

POINS. Tut, our horses they shall not see—I'll tie them in the wood; our vizards we will change after we leave them: and, 150 sirrah, I have cases of buckram for the nonce,[8] to immask our noted outward garments.

PRINCE. Yea, but I doubt they will be too hard for us.

POINS. Well, for two of them, I know them to be as true-bred cowards as ever turned back; and for the third, if he fight 155 longer than he sees reason, I'll forswear arms. The virtue of this jest will be the incomprehensible lies that this same fat rogue will tell us when we meet at supper: how thirty at least he fought with; what wards,[9] what blows, what extremities he endured; and in the reproof of this lies the jest. 160

PRINCE. Well, I'll go with thee. Provide us all things necessary

---

4. A satirical reference to the common complaint that the nobility did not properly give "countenance" to (i.e., encourage) good causes, and to the Puritan habit of attacking the "abuses of the time." This entire speech parodies the language of the Puritans.

5. I.e., Indian summer. The two epithets are intended to suggest how unseasonable it is for Falstaff, an old man, to be engaged in youthful, hood-

lum exploits.

6. This stage direction, like some others in the play, does not appear in the earliest editions; it was added by a later editor. All such interpolated directions are indicated in our text by the special brackets used here.

7. Clothes.

8. I.e., outer clothes (of a coarse, stiff cloth) for the occasion.

9. Guards in fencing.

and meet me tomorrow night[1] in Eastcheap; there I'll sup.
Farewell.

POINS. Farewell, my lord. [*Exit* POINS.]

PRINCE. I know you all, and will awhile uphold   165
    The unyoked humor[2] of your idleness;
    Yet herein will I imitate the sun,
    Who doth permit the base contagious clouds
    To smother up his beauty from the world,
    That, when he please again to be himself,   170
    Being wanted, he may be more wondered at
    By breaking through the foul and ugly mists
    Of vapors that did seem to strangle him.
    If all the year were playing holidays,
    To sport would be as tedious as to work;   175
    But when they seldom come, they wished for come,
    And nothing pleaseth but rare accidents.
    So, when this loose behavior I throw off
    And pay the debt I never promiséd,
    By how much better than my word I am,   180
    By so much shall I falsify men's hopes,
    And like bright metal on a sullen ground,[3]
    My reformation, glittering o'er my fault,
    Shall show more goodly and attract more eyes
    Than that which hath no foil[4] to set it off.   185
    I'll so offend to make offense a skill,[5]
    Redeeming time when men think least I will.   [*Exit.*]

SCENE 3

[*Enter the* KING, NORTHUMBERLAND, WORCESTER, HOT-
SPUR, SIR WALTER BLUNT, *with others.*]

KING. My blood hath been too cold and temperate,
    Unapt to stir at these indignities,
    And you have found me,[6] for accordingly
    You tread upon my patience; but be sure
    I will from henceforth rather be myself,   5
    Mighty and to be feared, than my condition,[7]
    Which hath been smooth as oil, soft as young down,
    And therefore lost that title of respect
    Which the proud soul ne'er pays but to the proud.

WOR. Our house, my sovereign liege, little deserves   10
    The scourge of greatness to be used on it,

1. Either the text should read "to-night" (before the robbery) or else Shakespeare intends to show Prince Hal's mind intent, not on the robbery, but on its aftermath. The soliloquy of the Prince that follows has provoked much critical discussion. Read psychologically, it makes Hal seem like a prig and a self-conscious schemer, but this surely was not Shakespeare's intention. Rather, the speech belongs to the old dramatic convention in which the speaker steps out of character for a moment to deliver a message from the playwright to the audience.
2. Undisciplined whim.
3. Dull background.
4. I.e., contrast.
5. Piece of good policy. "Redeeming time": making good use of time, following the advice given to Christians in a non-Christian world. See Ephesians v.16.
6. Discovered this to be true.
7. Disposition.

And that same greatness too which our own hands
Have holp[8] to make so portly.
NORTH. My lord—
KING. Worcester, get thee gone, for I do see   15
    Danger and disobedience in thine eye;
    O, sir, your presence is too bold and peremptory,
    And majesty might never yet endure
    The moody frontier of a servant brow.[9]
    You have good leave to leave us; when we need   20
    Your use and counsel we shall send for you.   [*Exit* WOR.]
    You were about to speak.   [⟨*to* NORTH.⟩]
NORTH.   Yea, my good lord.
    Those prisoners in your highness' name demanded,
    Which Harry Percy here at Holmedon took,
    Were, as he says, not with such strength denied   25
    As is delivered to your majesty.
    Either envy therefore or misprisión[1]
    Is guilty of this fault, and not my son.
HOT. My liege, I did deny no prisoners.
    But I remember, when the fight was done,   30
    When I was dry with rage and extreme toil,
    Breathless and faint, leaning upon my sword,
    Came there a certain lord, neat and trimly dressed,
    Fresh as a bridegroom, and his chin new reaped
    Showed like a stubble-land at harvest-home;   35
    He was perfuméd like a milliner,[2]
    And 'twixt his finger and his thumb he held
    A pouncet box,[3] which ever and anon
    He gave his nose and took 't away again;
    Who therewith angry, when it next came there,   40
    Took it in snuff;[4] and still he smiled and talked,
    And as the soldiers bore dead bodies by,
    He called them untaught knaves, unmannerly,
    To bring a slovenly[5] unhandsome corse
    Betwixt the wind and his nobility.   45
    With many holiday and lady terms[6]
    He questioned me; amongst the rest, demanded
    My prisoners in your majesty's behalf.
    I then, all smarting with my wounds being cold,
    To be so pestered with a popinjay,[7]   50
    Out of my grief and my impatience
    Answered neglectingly I know not what,
    He should, or he should not; for he made me mad
    To see him shine so brisk and smell so sweet

---

8. Helped; "portly": stately.
9. I.e., a servant's brow showing defiance, like a fortification ("frontier").
1. "Envy": malice; "misprision": mistake.
2. Not a maker of hats, but a dealer in perfumes, women's gloves, etc.
3. Perfume box.

4. I.e., was annoyed at it, with a pun on "snuffing it up."
5. Nasty, disgusting; "corse": corpse, body.
6. Affected and effeminate language (not "everyday" English).
7. Parrot.

And talk so like a waiting-gentlewoman 55
Of guns and drums and wounds—God save the mark!—
And telling me the sovereign'st thing on earth
Was parmaceti[8] for an inward bruise,
And that it was great pity, so it was,
This villanous saltpeter[9] should be digged 60
Out of the bowels of the harmless earth,
Which many a good tall[1] fellow had destroyed
So cowardly, and but for these vile guns
He would himself have been a soldier.
This bald[2] unjointed chat of his, my lord, 65
I answered indirectly as I said,
And I beseech you, let not his report
Come current[3] for an accusation
Betwixt my love and your high majesty.

BLUNT. The circumstance considered, good my lord, 70
Whate'er Lord Harry Percy then had said
To such a person and in such a place,
At such a time, with all the rest retold,
May reasonably die and never rise
To do him wrong or any way impeach 75
What then he said, so he unsay it now.

KING. Why, yet[4] he doth deny his prisoners,
But with proviso and exceptión,
That we at our own charge shall ransom straight
His brother-in-law, the foolish Mortimer, 80
Who, on my soul, hath willfully betrayed
The lives of those that he did lead to fight
Against that great magician, damned Glendower,
Whose daughter, as we hear, the Earl of March
Hath lately married. Shall our coffers then 85
Be emptied to redeem a traitor home?
Shall we buy treason? and indent with fears,[5]
When they have lost and forfeited themselves?
No, on the barren mountains let him starve;
For I shall never hold that man my friend 90
Whose tongue shall ask me for one penny cost
To ransom home revolted Mortimer.

HOT. Revolted Mortimer!
He never did fall off, my sovereign liege,
But by the chance of war. To prove that true 95
Needs no more but one tongue for all those wounds,
Those mouthéd wounds[6] which valiantly he took
When on the gentle Severn's sedgy bank
In single opposition, hand to hand,

8. Spermaceti, whale oil used as an ointment.
9. Used in gunpowder.
1. Brave.
2. Trivial. "Indirectly": negligently.
3. Be considered valid.
4. I.e., even after all this (the strong use of "yet"). "But": except.

5. Enter into a contract with cowards.
6. Wounds are often likened to mouths in Shakespeare. The image may derive from their appearance and from the idea that they could speak as witnesses to what caused them. Cf. *Julius Caesar* III.ii.229–31 and *Richard III* I.ii. 55–56.

He did confound the best part of an hour
In changing hardiment[7] with great Glendower;
Three times they breathed[8] and three times did they drink
Upon agreement of swift Severn's flood,
Who then, affrighted with their bloody looks,
Ran fearfully among the trembling reeds,
And hid his crisp[9] head in the hollow bank
Bloodstainéd with these valiant combatants.
Never did bare and rotten policy[1]
Color her working with such deadly wounds,
Nor never could the noble Mortimer
Receive so many, and all willingly;
Then let not him be slandered with revolt.

KING. Thou dost belie him, Percy, thou dost belie him;
  He never did encounter with Glendower.
  I tell thee,
  He durst as well have met the devil alone
  As Owen Glendower for an enemy.
  Art thou not ashamed? But, sirrah,[2] henceforth
  Let me not hear you speak of Mortimer;
  Send me your prisoners with the speediest means,
  Or you shall hear in such a kind from me
  As will displease you. My Lord Northumberland,
  We license your departure with your son.
  Send us your prisoners, or you will hear of it.
    [*Exeunt* KING, ⟨BLUNT, *and train.*⟩]

HOT. An if the devil come and roar for them
  I will not send them; I will after straight
  And tell him so, for I will ease my heart
  Albeit I make a hazard of my head.

NORTH. What, drunk with choler?[3] stay and pause awhile.
  Here comes your uncle.
    [*Enter* WORCESTER.]

HOT.   Speak of Mortimer!
  Zounds, I will speak of him, and let my soul
  Want mercy if I do not join with him;
  Yea, on his part[4] I'll empty all these veins,
  And shed my dear blood drop by drop in the dust,
  But I will lift the downtrod Mortimer
  As high in the air as this unthankful king,
  As this ingrate and cankered[5] Bolingbroke.

NORTH. Brother, the king hath made your nephew mad.

WOR. Who struck this heat up after I was gone?

HOT. He will, forsooth, have all my prisoners;
  And when I urged the ransom once again
  Of my wife's brother, then his cheek looked pale,
  And on my face he turned an eye of death,

7. Testing prowess and exchanging blows. "Confound": spend.
8. Paused for breath.
9. I.e., curly (because of the waves).
1. Craftiness or conspiracy; "color": disguise.
2. A form of "Sir," but used familiarly, and sometimes, as here, with a tone of contempt. "Speak of": i.e., even mention (an emphatic sense of "speak").
3. Anger.
4. Behalf.
5. Ungrateful and malignant.

Trembling even at the name of Mortimer.

WOR. I cannot blame him; was not he proclaimed   145
    By Richard, that dead is, the next of blood?

NORTH. He was—I heard the proclamatión;
    And then it was when the unhappy king
    (Whose wrongs in us God pardon![6]) did set forth
    Upon his Irish expeditión;   150
    From whence he intercepted did return
    To be deposed and shortly murderéd.

WOR. And for whose death we in the world's wide mouth
    Live scandalized and foully spoken of.

HOT. But soft, I pray you; did King Richard then   155
    Proclaim my brother[7] Edmund Mortimer
    Heir to the crown?

NORTH.   He did; myself did hear it.

HOT. Nay, then I cannot blame his cousin king
    That wished him on the barren mountains starve.
    But shall it be that you, that set the crown   160
    Upon the head of this forgetful man
    And for his sake wear the detested blot
    Of murderous subornation[8]—shall it be
    That you a world of curses undergo,
    Being the agents, or base second means,[9]   165
    The cords, the ladder, or the hangman rather?
    O pardon me that I descend so low
    To show the line and the predicament
    Wherein you range[1] under this subtle king!
    Shall it for shame be spoken in these days,   170
    Or fill up chronicles in time to come,
    That men of your nobility and power
    Did gage[2] them both in an unjust behalf,
    As both of you—God pardon it!—have done,
    To put down Richard, that sweet lovely rose,   175
    And plant this thorn, this canker,[3] Bolingbroke?
    And shall it in more shame be further spoken,
    That you are fooled, discarded, and shook off
    By him for whom these shames ye underwent?
    No; yet time serves wherein you may redeem   180
    Your banished honors and restore yourselves
    Into the good thoughts of the world again,
    Revenge the jeering and disdained[4] contempt
    Of this proud king, who studies day and night
    To answer all the debt he owes to you   185
    Even with the bloody payment of your deaths:
    Therefore, I say—

WOR.   Peace, cousin, say no more;
    And now I will unclasp a secret book,

6. I.e., God pardon in us the wrongs we did to him.
7. Brother-in-law.
8. I.e., the stain of aiding and abetting murder.
9. Tools, helpers.
1. I.e., to show the position and the category (or class) in which you are placed.
2. Pledge; "behalf": cause.
3. "Canker" meant not only a wild rose but also a diseased spot (a cancer).
4. Disdainful.

And to your quick-conceiving discontents
I'll read you matter deep and dangerous,   190
As full of peril and adventurous spirit
As to o'er-walk a current roaring loud
On the unsteadfast footing of a spear.

HOT. If he fall in, good night, or sink or swim;[5]
Send danger from the east unto the west,   195
So honor cross it from the north to south,
And let them grapple; O, the blood more stirs
To rouse a lion than to start[6] a hare!

NORTH. Imagination of some great exploit
Drives him beyond the bounds of patience.   200

HOT. By heaven, methinks it were an easy leap
To pluck bright honor from the pale-faced moon,
Or dive into the bottom of the deep,
Where fathom line could never touch the ground,
And pluck up drownéd honor by the locks,   205
So he that doth redeem her thence might wear
Without corrival[7] all her dignities;
But out upon this half-faced fellowship![8]

WOR. He apprehends a world of figures[9] here,
But not the form of what he should attend.   210
Good cousin, give me audience for a while.

HOT. I cry you mercy.

WOR.   Those same noble Scots
That I have prisoners—

HOT.   I'll keep them all;
By God, he shall not have a Scot of them;
No, if a Scot would save his soul he shall not.   215
I'll keep them, by this hand.

WOR.   You start away
And lend no ear unto my purposes.
Those prisoners you shall keep.

HOT.   Nay, I will; that's flat.
He said he would not ransom Mortimer,
Forbade my tongue to speak of Mortimer,   220
But I will find him when he lies asleep,
And in his ear I'll holla "Mortimer!"
Nay,
I'll have a starling shall be taught to speak[1]
Nothing but "Mortimer," and give it him   225
To keep his anger still in motion.

WOR. Hear you, cousin, a word.

HOT. All studies here I solemnly defy,
Save how to gall[2] and pinch this Bolingbroke;
And that same sword-and-buckler[3] Prince of Wales,   230
But that I think his father loves him not

5. I.e., either sink or swim.
6. Arouse, in hunting.
7. Rival.
8. Miserable sharing (of honor) with someone else.
9. Rhetorical figures of speech.

1. Starlings used to be taught to speak, as parrots are now.
2. Irritate.
3. Weapons used not by gentlemen but by servants or rustic clowns.

And would be glad he met with some mischance,
I would have him poisoned with a pot of ale.[4]

WOR. Farewell, kinsman; I'll talk to you
When you are better tempered to attend.   235

NORTH. Why, what a wasp-stung and impatient fool
Art thou to break into this woman's mood,
Tying thine ear to no tongue but thine own!

HOT. Why, look you, I am whipped and scourged with rods,
Nettled and stung with pismires,[5] when I hear   240
Of this vile politician Bolingbroke.
In Richard's time—what do you call the place?—
A plague upon it, it is in Gloucestershire—
'Twas where the madcap duke his uncle kept,[6]
His uncle York, where I first bowed my knee   245
Unto this king of smiles, this Bolingbroke—
'Sblood!—
When you and he came back from Ravenspurgh.

NORTH. At Berkeley castle.

HOT. You say true.   250
Why, what a candy deal of courtesy
This fawning greyhound[7] then did proffer me!
"Look when his infant fortune came to age,"
And "gentle Harry Percy," and "kind cousin";
O, the devil take such cozeners![8] God forgive me!   255
Good uncle, tell your tale; I have done.

WOR. Nay, if you have not, to it again;
We will stay your leisure.

HOT.   I have done, i' faith.

WOR. Then once more to your Scottish prisoners.
Deliver them up without their ransom straight,   260
And make the Douglas' son your only mean
For powers in Scotland, which, for divers reasons
Which I shall send you written, be assured
Will easily be granted. You, my lord,   [⟨*to* NORTHUMBERLAND⟩]
Your son in Scotland being thus employed,   265
Shall secretly into the bosom creep
Of that same noble prelate well beloved,
The archbishop.

HOT. Of York, is it not?

WOR. True; who bears hard   270
His brother's death at Bristol, the Lord Scroop.
I speak not this in estimation,[9]
As what I think might be, but what I know
Is ruminated, plotted, and set down,
And only stays but to behold the face   275
Of that occasion that shall bring it on.

---

4. The drink of the lower classes.
5. Ants.
6. Lived.
7. A complex image which occurs in Shakespeare several times (cf. *Hamlet* III.ii.65–67 and *Antony and Cleopatra* IV.xii.20–23). The idea of fawning or flattery called up to Shakespeare's mind the image of a dog begging for sweetmeats ("candy").
8. Cheaters, with of course a pun on the word "cousin."
9. I.e., guessing.

HOT. I smell it; upon my life, it will do well.

NORTH. Before the game is afoot, thou still let'st slip.[1]

HOT. Why, it cannot choose but be a noble plot;
And then the power of Scotland and of York 280
To join with Mortimer, ha?

WOR.   And so they shall.

HOT. In faith, it is exceedingly well aimed.

WOR. And 'tis no little reason bids us speed,
To save our heads by raising of a head;[2]
For, bear ourselves as even as we can, 285
The king will always think him in our debt,
And think we think ourselves unsatisfied,
Till he hath found a time to pay us home;
And see already how he doth begin
To make us strangers to his looks of love. 290

HOT. He does, he does; we'll be revenged on him.

WOR. Cousin, farewell. No further go in this
Than I by letters shall direct your course.
When time is ripe, which will be suddenly,
I'll steal to Glendower and Lord Mortimer, 295
Where you and Douglas and our powers at once,
As I will fashion it, shall happily meet,
To bear our fortunes in our own strong arms,
Which now we hold at much uncertainty.

NORTH. Farewell, good brother; we shall thrive, I trust. 300

HOT. Uncle, adieu; O, let the hours be short
Till fields and blows and groans applaud our sport! [*Exeunt.*]

Act II

SCENE 1

[*Enter a* CARRIER *with a lantern in his hand.*]

FIRST CAR. Heigh-ho! an it be not four by the day, I'll be hanged;
Charles' wain[3] is over the new chimney, and yet our horse not
packed. What, ostler!

OST. [*within*] Anon, anon.

FIRST CAR. I prithee, Tom, beat Cut's saddle,[4] put a few flocks 5
in the point; poor jade, is wrung in the withers out of all cess.[5]
[*Enter another* CARRIER.]

SEC. CAR. Peas and beans are as dank here as a dog, and that is the
next way to give poor jades the bots;[6] this house is turned upside down since Robin Ostler died.

FIRST CAR. Poor fellow, never joyed since the price of oats rose; 10
it was the death of him.

SEC. CAR. I think this be the most villainous house in all London

1. An image from hunting. The meaning is: "You always ('still') release the
dogs before we are ready to pursue the
game."
2. Raising an army.
3. The constellation of the Great Bear
or Big Dipper.
4. The saddle was beaten to make it

soft; "Cut" is a name for a horse with
a docked tail. "Flocks in the point":
pieces of wool under the point of the
saddle.
5. I.e., is sore in the shoulders excessively.
6. I.e., that is the easiest way to give
poor nags worms in the stomach.

road for fleas; I am stung like a tench.[7]

FIRST CAR. Like a tench! by the mass, there is ne'er a king christen[8] could be better bit than I have been since the first cock. 15

SEC. CAR. Why, they will allow us ne'er a jordan, and then we leak in your chimney, and your chamber-lye breeds fleas like a loach.[9]

FIRST CAR. What, ostler! come away and be hanged, come away! 20

SEC. CAR. I have a gammon[1] of bacon and two razes of ginger, to be delivered as far as Charing Cross.

FIRST CAR. God's body! the turkeys in my pannier[2] are quite starved. What, ostler! A plague on thee, hast thou never an eye in thy head? canst not hear? An 'twere not as good deed as 25 drink to break the pate on thee, I am a very villain. Come and be hanged! hast no faith in thee?

　　　[*Enter* GADSHILL.]

GADS. Good morrow, carriers. What's o'clock?

FIRST CAR. I think it be two o'clock.

GADS. I prithee lend me thy lantern to see my gelding in the 30 stable.

FIRST CAR. Nay, by God, soft; I know a trick worth two of that, i' faith.

GADS. I pray thee lend me thine.

SEC. CAR. Aye, when? canst tell?[3] Lend me thy lantern, quoth 35 he? marry, I'll see thee hanged first.

GADS. Sirrah carrier, what time do you mean to come to London?

SEC. CAR. Time enough to go to bed with a candle, I warrant thee. Come, neighbor Mugs, we'll call up the gentlemen; they will along with company, for they have great charge.[4] 40

　　　[*Exeunt* ⟨CARRIERS.⟩]

GADS. What ho! chamberlain!

CHAM. [*within*] At hand, quoth pickpurse.

GADS. That's even as fair as At hand, quoth the chamberlain, for thou variest no more from picking of purses than giving direction[5] doth from laboring; thou layest the plot how. 45

　　　[*Enter* CHAMBERLAIN.]

CHAM. Good morrow, Master Gadshill. It holds current[6] that I told you yesternight; there's a franklin[7] in the weald of Kent hath brought three hundred marks with him in gold—I heard him tell it to one of his company last night at supper—a kind of auditor,[8] one that hath abundance of charge too, God 50 knows what. They are up already and call for eggs and butter;

---

7. A fish covered with red spots, like fleabites.
8. Christian king.
9. "Jordan": chamber pot; "chamber-lye": urine. The "loach" is a fish which breeds prolifically.
1. Haunch; "razes": roots.
2. Basket.
3. A colloquial expression of contemptuous refusal.
4. Valuable cargo.
5. A pun: "giving direction" means

supervising, as contrasted with "laboring," but it was also the name for informing thieves about the journeys of prospective victims (laying "the plot how").
6. Remains true.
7. A freeholder, just below a gentleman in rank. "Weald of Kent": a section of that county, formerly wooded.
8. Revenue officer; "abundance of charge": considerable property.

they will away presently.[9]

GADS. Sirrah, if they meet not with Saint Nicholas' clerks,[1] I'll give thee this neck.

CHAM. No, I'll none of it; I pray thee, keep that for the hang- man, for I know thou worshipest Saint Nicholas as truly as a man of falsehood may.

GADS. What talkest thou to me of the hangman? if I hang, I'll make a fat pair of gallows; for if I hang, old Sir John hangs with me, and thou knowest he is no starveling. Tut! there are other Trojans[2] that thou dreamest not of, the which for sport sake are content to do the profession some grace, that would, if matters should be looked into, for their own credit sake make all whole. I am joined with no foot land-rakers,[3] no long- staff sixpenny strikers, none of these mad mustachio purple- hued maltworms,[4] but with nobility and tranquility, burgo- masters and great oneyers, such as can hold in, such as will strike sooner than speak, and speak sooner than drink, and drink sooner than pray; and yet, zounds, I lie, for they pray continually to their saint, the commonwealth, or rather, not pray to her but prey on her, for they ride up and down on her and make her their boots.[5]

CHAM. What, the commonwealth their boots? will she hold out water in foul way?

GADS. She will, she will; justice hath liquored her. We steal as in a castle, cocksure; we have the receipt of fern seed,[6] we walk in- visible.

CHAM. Nay, by my faith, I think you are more beholding to the night than to fern seed for your walking invisible.

GADS. Give me thy hand; thou shalt have a share in our purchase,[7] as I am a true man.

CHAM. Nay, rather let me have it, as you are a false thief.

GADS. Go to; *homo* is a common name to all men. Bid the ostler bring my gelding out of the stable. Farewell, you muddy[8] knave.

[*Exeunt.*]

SCENE 2

[*Enter* PRINCE *and* POINS.]

POINS. Come shelter, shelter; I have removed Falstaff's horse, and he frets like a gummed velvet.[9]

PRINCE. Stand close.

[*Enter* FALSTAFF.]

FAL. Poins! Poins, and be hanged! Poins!

PRINCE. Peace, ye fat-kidneyed rascal! what a brawling dost thou keep!

FAL. Where's Poins, Hal?

9. At once.
1. Highwaymen.
2. Roisterers, good fellows.
3. Footpads; "sixpenny strikers": small-time thieves.
4. Flushed, swaggering barflies. "Oney- ers": dignitaries; "hold in": keep se- cret.
5. Booty.

6. I.e., we have the recipe for fern seed (supposed to make one invisible). "Liquored": greased.
7. Takings.
8. Muddle-headed.
9. Cheap velvet was treated with gum to make the pile stiff; as a result it soon fretted or wore away. "Stand close": hide.

PRINCE. He is walked up to the top of the hill; I'll go seek him.
[⟨*He pretends to go, but hides onstage with* POINS.⟩]

FAL. I am accursed to rob in that thief's company; the rascal
hath removed my horse, and tied him I know not where. If
I travel but four foot by the squier[1] further afoot, I shall break
my wind. Well, I doubt not but to die a fair death for all this,
if I 'scape hanging for killing that rogue. I have forsworn his
company hourly any time this two and twenty years, and yet
I am bewitched with the rogue's company. If the rascal have
not given me medicines to make me love him, I'll be hanged;
it could not be else; I have drunk medicines. Poins! Hal! a
plague upon you both! Bardolph! Peto! I'll starve ere I'll rob
a foot further. An 'twere not as good a deed as drink to turn
true man and to leave these rogues, I am the veriest varlet
that ever chewed with a tooth. Eight yards of uneven ground
is threescore and ten miles afoot with me, and the stony-hearted
villains know it well enough; a plague upon it when thieves
cannot be true one to another! [*They whistle.*] Whew! A
plague upon you all! Give me my horse, you rogues; give me
my horse, and be hanged!

PRINCE. Peace, ye fat-guts! lie down; lay thine ear close to the
ground and list if thou canst hear the tread of travelers.

FAL. Have you any levers to lift me up again, being down?
'Sblood, I'll not bear my own flesh so far afoot again for all
the coin in thy father's exchequer. What a plague mean ye to
colt[2] me thus?

PRINCE. Thou liest; thou art not colted, thou art uncolted.

FAL. I prithee, good Prince, Hal, help me to my horse, good king's
son.

PRINCE. Out, ye rogue! shall I be your ostler?

FAL. Go hang thyself in thine own heir-apparent garters! If I be
ta'en, I'll peach for this. An I have not ballads made on you
all and sung to filthy tunes, let a cup of sack be my poison;
when a jest is so forward, and afoot too! I hate it.

[*Enter* GADSHILL, ⟨BARDOLPH *and* PETO *with him.*⟩]

GADS. Stand.

FAL. So I do, against my will.

POINS. O, 'tis our setter; I know his voice. Bardolph, what news?

BARD. Case[3] ye, case ye, on with your vizards; there's money of
the king's coming down the hill; 'tis going to the king's exchequer.

FAL. You lie, you rogue; 'tis going to the king's tavern.

GADS. There's enough to make us all.

FAL. To be hanged.

PRINCE. Sirs, you four shall front them in the narrow lane; Ned
Poins and I will walk lower; if they 'scape from your encounter,
then they light on us.

PETO. How many be there of them?

GADS. Some eight or ten.

FAL. Zounds, will they not rob us?

1. Ruler, yardstick.   3. Mask.
2. Trick.

PRINCE. What, a coward, Sir John Paunch?

FAL. Indeed, I am not John of Gaunt your grandfather, but yet no coward, Hal.

PRINCE. Well, we leave that to the proof.

POINS. Sirrah Jack, thy horse stands behind the hedge; when thou 60
needest him, there thou shalt find him. Farewell, and stand fast.

FAL. Now cannot I strike him, if I should be hanged.

PRINCE. [⟨*aside to* POINS⟩] Ned, where are our disguises?

POINS. [⟨*aside*⟩] Here, hard by; stand close. 65
　　　　[⟨*Exeunt* PRINCE *and* POINS.⟩]

FAL. Now, my masters, happy man be his dole,⁴ say I; every man to his business.
　　　　[*Enter the* TRAVELERS.]

FIRST TRAV. Come, neighbor, the boy shall lead our horses down the hill; we'll walk afoot awhile, and ease our legs.

THIEVES. Stand! 70

TRAVELERS. Jesus bless us!

FAL. Strike; down with them; cut the villains' throats. Ah, whoreson caterpillars,⁵ bacon-fed knaves, they hate us youth! Down with them, fleece them.

TRAVELERS. O, we are undone, both we and ours forever! 75

FAL. Hang ye, gorbellied⁶ knaves, are ye undone? No, ye fat chuffs, I would your store were here! On, bacons, on! What, ye knaves, young men must live! You are grand jurors, are ye? we'll jure ye, faith.
　　　　[*Here they rob them and bind them. Exeunt.*]
　　　　[*Enter the* PRINCE *and* POINS.]

PRINCE. The thieves have bound the true men. Now could thou 80
and I rob the thieves and go merrily to London; it would be argument⁷ for a week, laughter for a month, and a good jest forever.

POINS. Stand close; I hear them coming.
　　　　[*Enter the* THIEVES *again.*]

FAL. Come, my masters, let us share, and then to horse before 85
day. An the Prince and Poins be not two arrant cowards, there's no equity stirring;⁸ there's no more valor in that Poins than in a wild duck.

PRINCE. Your money!

POINS. Villains! 90
　　　　[*As they are sharing, the* PRINCE *and* POINS *set upon them; they all run away; and* FALSTAFF, *after a blow or two, runs away too, leaving the booty behind them.*]

PRINCE. Got with much ease. Now merrily to horse;
　　The thieves are all scattered and possessed with fear
　　So strongly that they dare not meet each other;
　　Each takes his fellow for an officer.
　　Away, good Ned. Falstaff sweats to death, 95

---

4. I.e., good luck!
5. "Caterpillars of the commonwealth" was a common phrase, referring to rogues. Falstaff here applies ridiculously inappropriate terms to the travelers

and to himself (e.g., "youth").
6. Fat; "chuffs": misers.
7. Subject of stories.
8. There's no justice.

And lards the lean earth as he walks along;
Were 't not for laughing, I should pity him.

POINS. How the rogue roared! [*Exeunt.*]

SCENE 3

[*Enter* HOTSPUR, *alone, reading a letter.*]

HOT. "But for mine own part, my lord, I could be well contented
to be there, in respect of the love I bear your house." "He
could be contented"; why is he not, then? "In respect of the
love he bears our house," he shows in this, he loves his own
barn better than he loves our house. Let me see some more. 5
"The purpose you undertake is dangerous." Why, that's certain. 'Tis dangerous to take a cold, to sleep, to drink; but I tell
you, my lord fool, out of this nettle, danger, we pluck this
flower, safety. "The purpose you undertake is dangerous, the
friends you have named uncertain, the time itself unsorted,[9] 10
and your whole plot too light for the counterpoise of so great
an opposition." Say you so, say you so? I say unto you again,
you are a shallow cowardly hind,[1] and you lie. What a lack-
brain is this! By the Lord, our plot is a good plot as ever was
laid, our friends true and constant; a good plot, good friends, 15
and full of expectation; an excellent plot, very good friends.
What a frosty-spirited rogue is this! Why, my lord of York[2]
commends the plot and the general course of the action.
Zounds, an I were now by this rascal I could brain him with
his lady's fan. Is there not my father, my uncle, and myself? 20
Lord Edmund Mortimer, my lord of York, and Owen Glendower? is there not besides the Douglas? have I not all their
letters to meet me in arms by the ninth of the next month, and
are they not some of them set forward already? What a pagan
rascal is this, an infidel! Ha! you shall see now in very sincerity 25
of fear and cold heart, will he to the king and lay open all our
proceedings. O, I could divide myself and go to buffets,[3] for
moving such a dish of skim milk with so honorable an action!
Hang him! let him tell the king. We are prepared; I will set
forward tonight. 30

[*Enter his* LADY.]

How now, Kate! I must leave you within these two hours.

LADY. O, my good lord, why are you thus alone?
For what offense have I this fortnight been
A banished woman from my Harry's bed?
Tell me, sweet lord, what is 't that takes from thee 35
Thy stomach,[4] pleasure, and thy golden sleep?
Why dost thou bend thine eyes upon the earth,
And start so often when thou sit'st alone?
Why hast thou lost the fresh blood in thy cheeks,
And given my treasures and my rights of thee 40
To thick-eyed musing and cursed melancholy?
In thy faint slumbers I by thee have watched
And heard thee murmur tales of iron wars,

9. Unsuitable.
1. Peasant.
2. The Archbishop of York.

3. Split myself in two and let the parts
fight each other; "moving": urging.
4. Appetite.

Speak terms of manage⁵ to thy bounding steed,
Cry "Courage! to the field!" And thou hast talked   45
Of sallies and retires, of trenches, tents,
Of palisadoes, frontiers, parapets,
Of basilisks, of cannon, culverin,⁶
Of prisoners' ransom and of soldiers slain,
And all the currents of a heady fight.   50
Thy spirit within thee hath been so at war
And thus hath so bestirred thee in thy sleep
That beads of sweat have stood upon thy brow
Like bubbles in a late-disturbèd stream,
And in thy face strange motions have appeared   55
Such as we see when men restrain their breath
On some great sudden hest.⁷ O, what portents are these?
Some heavy business hath my lord in hand
And I must know it, else he loves me not.

HOT. What, ho!
      [⟨*Enter* SERVANT.⟩]
              Is Gilliams with the packet gone?   60
SERV. He is, my lord, an hour ago.
HOT. Hath Butler brought those horses from the sheriff?
SERV. One horse, my lord, he brought even now.
HOT. What horse? a roan, a crop-ear, is it not?
SERV. It is, my lord.
HOT.   That roan shall be my throne.   65
   Well, I will back⁷ᵃ him straight; O Esperance!⁸
   Bid Butler lead him forth into the park.   [⟨*Exit* SERVANT.⟩]
LADY. But hear you, my lord.
HOT. What say'st thou, my lady?
LADY. What is it carries you away?   70
HOT. Why, my horse, my love, my horse.
LADY. Out, you mad-headed ape!
   A weasel hath not such a deal of spleen⁹
   As you are tossed with. In faith
   I'll know your business, Harry, that I will.   75
   I fear my brother Mortimer doth stir
   About his title, and hath sent for you
   To line¹ his enterprise; but if you go—
HOT. So far afoot, I shall be weary, love.
LADY. Come, come, you paraquito, answer me   80
   Directly unto this question that I ask;
   In faith, I'll break thy little finger, Harry,
   An if thou wilt not tell me all things true.
HOT. Away,
   Away, you trifler! Love! I love thee not,   85

---

5. Horsemanship.
6. Three kinds of artillery (named here in decreasing order of weight).
7. Command.
7a. Mount.
8. The battle cry of the Percies:
"Hope!"
9. The spleen was supposed to be the source of sudden and violent emotions; the weasel was considered a very impetuous animal.
1. Support.

I care not for thee, Kate; this is no world
To play with mammets and to tilt with lips;
We must have bloody noses and cracked crowns,[2]
And pass them current too. God's me, my horse!
What say'st thou, Kate? what wouldst thou have with me?   90
LADY. Do you not love me? do you not, indeed?
Well, do not then, for since you love me not
I will not love myself. Do you not love me?
Nay, tell me if you speak in jest or no.
HOT. Come, wilt thou see me ride?   95
And when I am o' horseback, I will swear
I love thee infinitely. But hark you, Kate,
I must not have you henceforth question me
Whither I go, nor reason whereabout;
Whither I must, I must; and, to conclude,   100
This evening must I leave you, gentle Kate.
I know you wise, but yet no farther wise
Than Harry Percy's wife; constant you are,
But yet a woman, and for secrecy
No lady closer; for I well believe   105
Thou wilt not utter what thou dost not know,
And so far will I trust thee, gentle Kate.
LADY. How! so far?
HOT. Not an inch further. But hark you, Kate,
Whither I go, thither shall you go too;   110
Today will I set forth, tomorrow you.
Will this content you, Kate?
LADY.   It must of force.   [*Exeunt.*]

SCENE 4

[*Enter the* PRINCE *and* POINS.]

PRINCE. Ned, prithee come out of that fat[3] room, and lend me
thy hand to laugh a little.
POINS. Where hast been, Hal?
PRINCE. With three or four loggerheads[4] amongst three or fourscore hogsheads. I have sounded the very bass string of humil-   5
ity. Sirrah, I am sworn brother to a leash of drawers,[5] and can
call them all by their christen names, as Tom, Dick, and Francis. They take it already upon their salvation, that though I be
but Prince of Wales, yet I am the king of courtesy, and tell me
flatly I am no proud Jack, like Falstaff, but a Corinthian,[6] a lad   10
of mettle, a good boy—by the Lord, so they call me—and when
I am king of England I shall command all the good lads in
Eastcheap. They call drinking deep, dyeing scarlet, and when
you breathe in your watering[7] they cry "hem!" and bid you
play it off. To conclude, I am so good a proficient in one quar-   15
ter of an hour that I can drink with any tinker in his own lan-

2. Broken heads, with a pun on
"crowns" as coins. "Mammets": breasts.
3. Vat. This establishes that the scene is
a tavern.
4. Blockheads.
5. Group of tapsters, waiters.
6. Good fellow.
7. Drinking.

guage during my life. I tell thee, Ned, thou hast lost much
honor, that thou wert not with me in this action. But, sweet
Ned—to sweeten which name of Ned, I give thee this pennyworth of sugar, clapped even now into my hand by an under- 20
skinker,[8] one that never spake other English in his life than
"Eight shillings and sixpence," and "You are welcome," with
this shrill addition, "Anon, anon, sir! Score a pint of bastard
in the Half-Moon,"[9] or so. But, Ned, to drive away the time
till Falstaff come, I prithee do thou stand in some by-room, 25
while I question my puny drawer to what end he gave me the
sugar, and do thou never leave calling "Francis," that his tale
to me may be nothing but "Anon." Step aside, and I'll show
thee a precedent.

POINS. Francis! 30

PRINCE. Thou art perfect.

POINS. Francis! [⟨*Exit* POINS.⟩]

[*Enter* DRAWER.]

FRAN. Anon, anon, sir. Look down into the Pomgarnet,[1] Ralph.

PRINCE. Come hither, Francis.

FRAN. My lord? 35

PRINCE. How long hast thou to serve,[2] Francis?

FRAN. Forsooth, five years, and as much as to—

POINS. [*within*] Francis!

FRAN. Anon, anon, sir.

PRINCE. Five year! by'r Lady, a long lease for the clinking of 40
pewter. But, Francis, darest thou be so valiant as to play the
coward with thy indenture and show it a fair pair of heels and
run from it?

FRAN. O Lord, sir, I'll be sworn upon all the books in England, I
could find in my heart— 45

POINS. [*within*] Francis!

FRAN. Anon, sir.

PRINCE. How old art thou, Francis?

FRAN. Let me see—about Michaelmas next I shall be—

POINS. [*within*] Francis! 50

FRAN. Anon, sir. Pray stay a little, my lord.

PRINCE. Nay, but hark you, Francis: for the sugar thou gavest
me, 'twas a pennyworth, was't not?

FRAN. O Lord, I would it had been two!

PRINCE. I will give thee for it a thousand pound; ask me when 55
thou wilt, and thou shalt have it.

POINS. [*within*] Francis!

FRAN. Anon, anon.

PRINCE. Anon, Francis? No, Francis, but tomorrow, Francis; or
Francis, o' Thursday, or indeed, Francis, when thou wilt. But, 60

---

8. Assistant waiter.
9. I.e., charge a pint of "bastard" (a
sweet Spanish wine) to a customer in
the room called "Half-Moon." "Anon":
immediately (the reply of a servant
when called, equivalent to "Coming!").

1. Pomegranate (another room in the
tavern).
2. I.e., to finish out his apprenticeship,
usually a seven-year period under an
"indenture" or agreement.

Francis!

FRAN. My lord?

PRINCE. Wilt thou rob this leathern-jerkin,[3] crystal-button, not-pated, agate-ring, puke-stocking, caddis-garter, smooth-tongue, Spanish-pouch—   65

FRAN. O Lord, sir, who do you mean?

PRINCE. Why, then, your brown bastard is your only drink, for look you, Francis, your white canvas doublet will sully. In Barbary, sir, it cannot come to so much.[4]

FRAN. What, sir?   70

POINS. [*within*] Francis!

PRINCE. Away, you rogue, dost thou not hear them call?
  [*Here they both call him; the drawer stands amazed,
  not knowing which way to go.*]
  [*Enter* VINTNER.]

VINT. What, stand'st thou still, and hear'st such a calling? Look to the guests within. [*Exit* FRANCIS.] My lord, old Sir John with half-a-dozen more are at the door; shall I let them in?   75

PRINCE. Let them alone awhile, and then open the door. [*Exit* VINTNER.] Poins!
  [*Enter* POINS.]

POINS. Anon, anon, sir.

PRINCE. Sirrah, Falstaff and the rest of the thieves are at the door; shall we be merry?   80

POINS. As merry as crickets, my lad. But hark ye, what cunning match have you made with this jest of the drawer? come, what's the issue?

PRINCE. I am now of all humors[5] that have showed themselves humors since the old days of goodman Adam to the pupil[6] age   85 of this present twelve o'clock at midnight.
  [⟨*Enter* FRANCIS.⟩]
  What's o'clock, Francis?

FRAN. Anon, anon, sir.   [⟨*Exit.*⟩]

PRINCE. That ever this fellow should have fewer words than a parrot, and yet the son of a woman! His industry is upstairs   90 and downstairs, his eloquence the parcel[7] of a reckoning. I am not yet of Percy's mind, the Hotspur of the north, he that kills me some six or seven dozen of Scots at a breakfast, washes his hands, and says to his wife "Fie upon this quiet life! I want work." "O my sweet Harry," says she, "how many hast thou   95 killed today?" "Give my roan horse a drench," says he, and answers "Some fourteen," an hour after, "a trifle, a trifle." I prithee, call in Falstaff; I'll play Percy, and that damned brawn shall play Dame Mortimer his wife. "Rivo!"[8] says the drunkard. Call in ribs, call in tallow.   100
  [*Enter* FALSTAFF, ⟨GADSHILL, BARDOLPH, *and* PETO, FRAN-

---

3. Leather-jacketed; "not-pated": with short hair; "puke": dark gray; "caddis": worsted tape.
4. Deliberate nonsense to confuse Francis.
5. Temperaments, dispositions.
6. Youthful.
7. Item.
8. Drink up!

CIS *following with wine.*)]

POINS. Welcome, Jack; where hast thou been?

FAL. A plague of all cowards, I say, and a vengeance too, marry and amen! Give me a cup of sack, boy. Ere I lead this life long, I'll sew nether stocks[9] and mend them and foot them too. A plague of all cowards! Give me a cup of sack, rogue. Is there no 105 virtue extant?   [*He drinks.*]

PRINCE. Didst thou ever see Titan[1] kiss a dish of butter, pitiful-hearted butter that melted at the sweet tale of the sun's? If thou didst, then behold that compound.

FAL. You rogue, here's lime in this sack too;[2] there is nothing but 110 roguery to be found in villainous man, yet a coward is worse than a cup of sack with lime in it. A villainous coward! Go thy ways, old Jack, die when thou wilt; if manhood, good manhood, be not forgot upon the face of the earth, then am I a shotten herring.[3] There lives not three good men unhanged in Eng- 115 land, and one of them is fat and grows old. God help the while; a bad world, I say. I would I were a weaver; I could sing psalms[4] or anything. A plague of all cowards, I say still.

PRINCE. How now, woolsack, what mutter you?

FAL. A king's son! If I do not beat thee out of thy kingdom with 120 a dagger of lath, and drive all thy subjects afore thee like a flock of wild geese, I'll never wear hair on my face more. You Prince of Wales!

PRINCE. Why, you whoreson round man, what's the matter?

FAL. Are not you a coward? answer me to that; and Poins there? 125

POINS. Zounds, ye fat paunch, an ye call me coward, by the Lord I'll stab thee.

FAL. I call thee coward! I'll see thee damned ere I call thee cow-ard; but I would give a thousand pound I could run as fast as thou canst. You are straight enough in the shoulders, you 130 care not who sees your back; call you that backing of your friends? A plague upon such backing! give me them that will face me. Give me a cup of sack; I am a rogue if I drunk today.

PRINCE. O villain! thy lips are scarce wiped since thou drunkest last.   135

FAL. All's one for that. [*He drinks.*] A plague of all cowards, still say I.

PRINCE. What's the matter?

FAL. What's the matter! there be four of us here have ta'en a thousand pound this day morning.   140

PRINCE. Where is it, Jack? where is it?

FAL. Where is it? taken from us it is—a hundred upon poor four of us.

PRINCE. What, a hundred, man?

FAL. I am a rogue if I were not at half-sword[5] with a dozen of 145 them two hours together. I have 'scaped by miracle. I am

9. Stockings.
1. The sun.
2. Lime was used to adulterate wine.
3. A herring that has cast its spawn
and is lean.
4. Protestant weavers from Flanders were notorious for singing psalms.
5. At half a sword's length.

eight times thrust through the doublet, four through the hose,
my buckler cut through and through, my sword hacked like a
handsaw—*ecce signum!*[6] I never dealt better since I was a
man; all would not do. A plague of all cowards! Let them
speak; if they speak more or less than truth, they are villains
and the sons of darkness.

PRINCE. Speak, sirs; how was it?

GADS. We four set upon some dozen—

FAL. Sixteen at least, my lord.

GADS. And bound them.

PETO. No, no, they were not bound.

FAL. You rogue, they were bound, every man of them, or I am a
Jew else, an Ebrew Jew

GADS. As we were sharing, some six or seven fresh men set upon
us—

FAL. And unbound the rest, and then come in the other.

PRINCE. What, fought you with them all?

FAL. All! I know not what you call all, but if I fought not with
fifty of them, I am a bunch of radish; if there were not two
or three and fifty upon poor old Jack, then am I no two-legged
creature.

PRINCE. Pray God you have not murdered some of them.

FAL. Nay, that's past praying for; I have peppered two of them.
Two I am sure I have paid, two rogues in buckram suits. I
tell thee what, Hal, if I tell thee a lie, spit in my face, call me
horse. Thou knowest my old ward;[7] here I lay, and thus I bore
my point. Four rogues in buckram let drive at me—

PRINCE. What, four? thou saidst but two even now.

FAL. Four, Hal; I told thee four.

POINS. Aye, aye, he said four.

FAL. These four came all a-front, and mainly[8] thrust at me. I
made me no more ado but took all their seven points in my
target,[9] thus.

PRINCE. Seven? why, there were but four even now.

FAL. In buckram.

POINS. Aye, four, in buckram suits.

FAL. Seven, by these hilts, or I am a villain else.

PRINCE. Prithee, let him alone; we shall have more anon.

FAL. Dost thou hear me, Hal?

PRINCE. Aye, and mark thee too, Jack.

FAL. Do so, for it is worth the listening to. These nine in buckram that I told thee of—

PRINCE. So, two more already.

FAL. Their points being broken—

POINS. Down fell their hose.[1]

FAL. Began to give me ground; but I followed me close, came in
foot and hand, and with a thought seven of the eleven I paid.

6. Here's the proof!
7. Defense; "here I lay": this was my
stance.
8. Strongly.

9. Shield.
1. Poins puns on the other meaning
of "points": the laces used to tie up
trousers ("hose").

PRINCE. O monstrous! eleven buckram men grown out of two!

FAL. But, as the devil would have it, three misbegotten knaves 195
in Kendal green came at my back and let drive at me, for it
was so dark, Hal, that thou couldst not see thy hand.

PRINCE. These lies are like their father that begets them—gross
as a mountain, open, palpable. Why, thou clay-brained guts,
thou knotty-pated fool, thou whoreson, obscene, greasy tallow- 200
catch²—

FAL. What, art thou mad? art thou mad? is not the truth the
truth?

PRINCE. Why, how couldst thou know these men in Kendal green,
when it was so dark thou couldst not see thy hand? come, tell 205
us your reason. What sayest thou to this?

POINS. Come, your reason, Jack, your reason.

FAL. What, upon compulsion? Zounds, an I were at the strap-
pado,³ or all the racks in the world, I would not tell you on
compulsion. Give you a reason on compulsion! if reasons⁴ 210
were as plentiful as blackberries, I would give no man a reason
upon compulsion, I.

PRINCE. I'll be no longer guilty of this sin; this sanguine coward,
this bed-presser, this horseback-breaker, this huge hill of
flesh— 215

FAL. 'Sblood, you starveling, you eelskin, you dried neat's tongue,
you bull's pizzle, you stockfish!⁵ O for breath to utter what is
like thee! you tailor's yard, you sheath, you bow case, you vile
standing-tuck⁶—

PRINCE. Well, breathe awhile, and then to it again; and when 220
thou hast tired thyself in base comparisons, hear me speak
but this.

POINS. Mark, Jack.

PRINCE. We two saw you four set on four and bound them, and
were masters of their wealth. Mark now, how a plain tale shall 225
put you down. Then did we two set on you four; and, with a
word, outfaced you from your prize, and have it, yea, and can
show it you here in the house; and, Falstaff, you carried your
guts away as nimbly, with as quick dexterity, and roared for
mercy and still run and roared, as ever I heard bullcalf. What a 230
slave art thou, to hack thy sword as thou hast done, and then
say it was in fight! What trick, what device, what starting-
hole,⁷ canst thou now find out to hide thee from this open
and apparent shame?

POINS. Come, let's hear, Jack; what trick hast thou now? 235

FAL. By the Lord, I knew ye as well as he that made ye. Why,
hear you, my masters: was it for me to kill the heir apparent?
should I turn upon the true prince? why, thou knowest I am

2. Piece of tallow from which chandlers made candles.
3. A method of torture; "racks": another method.
4. A pun on the word "raisin," which was spelled and pronounced like "rea-son" in Elizabethan England.
5. I.e., you ox tongue, you bull's penis, you dried cod!
6. Stiff rapier.
7. Evasion.

as valiant as Hercules; but beware instinct; the lion will not
touch the true prince.[8] Instinct is a great matter; I was now 240
a coward on instinct. I shall think the better of myself and
thee during my life; I for a valiant lion, and thou for a true
prince. But, by the Lord, lads, I am glad you have the money.
Hostess, clap to the doors; watch tonight, pray tomorrow.
Gallants, lads, boys, hearts of gold, all the titles of good fellow- 245
ship come to you! What, shall we be merry? shall we have a
play extempore?

PRINCE. Content; and the argument[9] shall be thy running away.

FAL. Ah, no more of that, Hal, an thou lovest me!

[*Enter* HOSTESS.]

HOST. O Jesu, my lord the prince! 250

PRINCE. How now, my lady the hostess! what sayest thou to me?

HOST. Marry, my lord, there is a nobleman of the court at door
would speak with you; he says he comes from your father.

PRINCE. Give him as much as will make him a royal[1] man, and
send him back again to my mother. 255

FAL. What manner of man is he?

HOST. An old man.

FAL. What doth gravity out of his bed at midnight? Shall I give
him his answer?

PRINCE. Prithee, do, Jack. 260

FAL. Faith, and I'll send him packing. [*Exit.*]

PRINCE. Now, sirs. By 'r Lady, you fought fair; so did you, Peto;
so did you, Bardolph; you are lions too, you ran away upon
instinct, you will not touch the true prince; no, fie!

BARD. Faith, I ran when I saw others run. 265

PRINCE. Faith, tell me now in earnest, how came Falstaff's sword
so hacked?

PETO. Why, he hacked it with his dagger, and said he would
swear truth out of England but he would make you believe it
was done in fight, and persuaded us to do the like. 270

BARD. Yea, and to tickle our noses with speargrass to make them
bleed, and then to beslubber our garments with it and swear
it was the blood of true men. I did that I did not this seven
year before, I blushed to hear his monstrous devices.

PRINCE. O villain, thou stolest a cup of sack eighteen years ago, 275
and wert taken with the manner,[2] and ever since thou hast
blushed fire[3] and sword on thy side, and yet thou rannest away; what instinct hadst thou for it?

BARD. My lord, do you see these meteors? do you behold these
exhalations? 280

PRINCE. I do.

BARD. What think you they portend?

PRINCE. Hot livers and cold purses.[4]

8. In many medieval romances the lion, as king of beasts, shows respect for royalty.
9. Plot or story.
1. A "royal" was half of a pound sterling, a "noble" was a third.
2. In the act.
3. "Fire" and the allusions to "meteors" and "exhalations" (shooting stars) refer to Bardolph's red nose.
4. I.e., drunkenness and poverty.

BARD. Choler, my lord, if rightly taken.

PRINCE. No, if rightly taken, halter.   285

    [*Enter* FALSTAFF.]

    Here comes lean Jack, here comes bare-bone. How now, my
sweet creature of bombast,[5] how long is 't ago, Jack, since thou
sawest thine own knee?

FAL. My own knee! when I was about thy years, Hal, I was not
an eagle's talon in the waist; I could have crept into any alder-   290
man's thumb ring. A plague of sighing and grief—it blows a
man up·like a bladder. There's villainous news abroad; here
was Sir John Bracy from your father; you must to the court
in the morning. That same mad fellow of the north, Percy, and
he of Wales, that gave Amamon[6] the bastinado and made   295
Lucifer cuckold and swore the devil his true liegeman upon the
cross of a Welsh hook[7]—what a plague call you him?

POINS. O, Glendower.

FAL. Owen, Owen, the same; and his son-in-law Mortimer, and
old Northumberland, and that sprightly Scot of Scots, Doug-   300
las, that runs o' horseback up a hill perpendicular—

PRINCE. He that rides at high speed and with his pistol kills a
sparrow flying.

FAL. You have hit it.

PRINCE. So did he never the sparrow.   305

FAL. Well, that rascal hath good mettle in him; he will not run.

PRINCE. Why, what a rascal art thou then, to praise him so for
running!

FAL. O' horseback, ye cuckoo; but afoot he will not budge a foot.

PRINCE. Yes, Jack, upon instinct.   310

FAL. I grant ye, upon instinct. Well, he is there too, and one
Mordake, and a thousand blue-caps[8] more. Worcester is stolen
away tonight; thy father's beard is turned white with the news;
you may buy land now as cheap as stinking mackerel.

PRINCE. Why then, it is like, if there come a hot June, and this   315
civil buffeting hold, we shall buy maidenheads as they buy
hobnails, by the hundreds.

FAL. By the mass, lad, thou sayest true; it is like we shall have
good trading that way. But tell me, Hal, art not thou horrible
afeard? thou being heir apparent, could the world pick thee   320
out three such enemies again as that fiend Douglas, that spirit
Percy, and that devil Glendower? Art thou not horribly afraid?
doth not thy blood thrill at it?

PRINCE. Not a whit, i' faith; I lack some of thy instinct.

FAL. Well, thou wilt be horribly chid tomorrow when thou com-   325
est to thy father; if thou love me, practice an answer.

PRINCE. Do thou stand for[9] my father and examine me upon the
particulars of my life.

FAL. Shall I? Content. This chair shall be my state,[1] this dagger

5. Padding, stuffing.
6. A devil. "Bastinado": a beating, cudgelling.
7. A long spear with a hook on it.

8. Scots.
9. Represent.
1. Throne.

my scepter, and this cushion my crown. 330

PRINCE. Thy state is taken for a joint-stool,[2] thy golden scepter
for a leaden dagger, and thy precious rich crown for a pitiful
bald crown!

FAL. Well, an the fire of grace be not quite out of thee, now
shalt thou be moved. Give me a cup of sack to make my eyes 335
look red, that it may be thought I have wept, for I must speak
in passion, and I will do it in King Cambyses'[3] vein.

PRINCE. Well, here is my leg.[4]

FAL. And here is my speech. Stand aside, nobility.

HOST. O Jesu, this is excellent sport, i' faith! 340

FAL. Weep not, sweet queen, for trickling tears are vain.

HOST. O, the father, how he holds his countenance!

FAL. For God's sake, lords, convey my tristful queen,
For tears do stop the floodgates of her eyes.

HOST. O Jesu, he doth it as like one of these harlotry players as 345
ever I see!

FAL. Peace, good pint pot, peace, good ticklebrain. Harry, I do
not only marvel where thou spendest thy time, but also how
thou art accompanied, for though the camomile,[5] the more it
is trodden on the faster it grows, so youth, the more it is 350
wasted the sooner it wears. That thou art my son, I have partly
thy mother's word, partly my own opinion, but chiefly a villainous trick of thine eye and a foolish hanging of thy nether
lip that doth warrant[6] me. If then thou be son to me, here lies
the point; why, being son to me, art thou so pointed at? Shall 355
the blessed sun of heaven prove a micher[7] and eat blackberries?
a question not to be asked. Shall the son of England prove
a thief and take purses? a question to be asked. There is a
thing, Harry, which thou hast often heard of and it is known
to many in our land by the name of pitch. This pitch, as an- 360
cient writers do report, doth defile; so doth the company thou
keepest: for, Harry, now I do not speak to thee in drink but
in tears, not in pleasure but in passion, not in words only, but
in woes also: and yet there is a virtuous man whom I have
often noted in thy company, but I know not his name. 365

PRINCE. What manner of man, an it like your majesty?

FAL. A goodly portly man, i' faith, and a corpulent; of a cheerful
look, a pleasing eye and a most noble carriage; and, as I think,
his age some fifty, or, by 'r Lady, inclining to threescore; and
now I remember me, his name is Falstaff. If that man should 370
be lewdly given, he deceiveth me, for, Harry, I see virtue in
his looks. If then the tree may be known by the fruit, as the
fruit by the tree, then, peremptorily I speak it, there is virtue
in that Falstaff; him keep with, the rest banish. And tell me

2. An ordinary stool, made by a joiner
(carpenter).
3. Like the bombastic hero of the old
play *Cambyses*.
4. I.e., he bows, makes an obeisance.
5. An aromatic herb. The style in this

speech is a parody of Euphuism, the
ornate, elaborate, balanced style made
popular by Lyly's *Euphues*.
6. Assure.
7. Truant.

now, thou naughty varlet, tell me, where hast thou been this [375] month?

PRINCE. Dost thou speak like a king? Do thou stand for me, and I'll play my father.

FAL. Depose me? if thou dost it half so gravely, so majestically, both in word and matter, hang me up by the heels for a [380] rabbit-sucker[8] or a poulter's hare.

PRINCE. Well, here I am set.[9]

FAL. And here I stand; judge, my masters.

PRINCE. Now, Harry, whence come you?

FAL. My noble lord, from Eastcheap. [385]

PRINCE. The complaints I hear of thee are grievous.

FAL. 'Sblood, my lord, they are false: nay, I'll tickle ye for a young prince, i' faith.

PRINCE. Swearest thou, ungracious boy? thenceforth ne'er look on me. Thou art violently carried away from grace; there is a [390] devil haunts thee in the likeness of an old fat man; a tun[1] of man is thy companion. Why dost thou converse with that trunk of humors, that bolting-hutch[2] of beastliness, that swollen parcel of dropsies, that huge bombard of sack, that stuffed cloak-bag of guts, that roasted Manningtree[3] ox with the pud- [395] ding in his belly, that reverend vice, that gray iniquity, that father ruffian, that vanity in years? Wherein is he good, but to taste sack and drink it? wherein neat and cleanly, but to carve a capon and eat it? wherein cunning, but in craft? wherein crafty, but in villainy? wherein villainous, but in all things? [400] wherein worthy, but in nothing?

FAL. I would your grace would take me with you; whom means your grace?

PRINCE. That villainous abominable misleader of youth, Falstaff, that old white-bearded Satan. [405]

FAL. My lord, the man I know.

PRINCE. I know thou dost.

FAL. But to say I know more harm in him than in myself were to say more than I know. That he is old (the more the pity, his white hairs do witness it; but that he is, saving your reverence, [410] a whoremaster, that I utterly deny. If sack and sugar be a fault, God help the wicked! if to be old and merry be a sin, then many an old host that I know is damned; if to be fat be to be hated, then Pharaoh's lean kine[4] are to be loved. No, my good lord, banish Peto, banish Bardolph, banish Poins, [415] but for sweet Jack Falstaff, kind Jack Falstaff, true Jack Falstaff, valiant Jack Falstaff, and therefore more valiant, being as he is old Jack Falstaff, banish not him thy Harry's company, banish not him thy Harry's company; banish plump Jack, and ban-

8. Suckling rabbit.
9. Seated.
1. Large barrel.
2. Trough; "bombard": leather wine vessel.
3. Town in Essex, noted for barbecues;

"pudding": sausage. The "vice" was a comic character in the old morality plays. Falstaff is in some respects a descendant of this type-character.
4. In the dream Joseph interpreted. See Genesis xli.19–21.

ish all the world.   420
PRINCE. I do, I will.   [⟨*A knocking heard.*⟩]
                                          [⟨*Exeunt* HOSTESS *and* BARDOLPH.⟩]
          [*Enter* BARDOLPH, *running.*]
BARD. O, my lord, my lord, the sheriff with a most monstrous
     watch is at the door.
FAL. Out, ye rogue! Play out the play; I have much to say in the
     behalf of that Falstaff.   425
          [*Enter the* HOSTESS.]
HOST. O Jesu, my lord, my lord!
FAL. Heigh, heigh! the devil rides upon a fiddlestick;[5] what's the
     matter?
HOST. The sheriff and all the watch are at the door; they are come
     to search the house. Shall I let them in?   430
FAL. Dost thou hear, Hal? never call a true piece of gold a coun-
     terfeit; thou art essentially mad, without seeming so.[6]
PRINCE. And thou a natural coward, without instinct.
FAL. I deny your major;[7] if you will deny the sheriff, so; if not,
     let him enter. If I become not a cart as well as another man,   435
     a plague on my bringing up! I hope I shall as soon be strangled
     with a halter as another.[8]
PRINCE. Go hide thee behind the arras;[9] the rest walk up above.
     Now, my masters, for a true face and good conscience.
FAL. Both which I have had; but their date is out,[1] and therefore   440
     I'll hide me.
PRINCE. Call in the sheriff.
                    [*Exeunt* ⟨*all except the* PRINCE *and* POINS.⟩]
          [*Enter* SHERIFF *and the* CARRIER.]
     Now, master sheriff, what is your will with me?
SHER. First pardon me, my lord. A hue and cry
     Hath followed certain men unto this house.   445
PRINCE. What men?
SHER. One of them is well known, my gracious lord,
     A gross fat man.
CAR.   As fat as butter.
PRINCE. The man, I do assure you, is not here,
     For I myself at this time have employed him,   450
     And, sheriff, I will engage my word to thee
     That I will by tomorrow dinnertime
     Send him to answer thee or any man
     For anything he shall be charged withal;
     And so let me entreat you leave the house.   455
SHER. I will, my lord. There are two gentlemen

5. I.e., there's a commotion.
6. I.e., don't give a true man (me, Falstaff) away as a thief. He goes on to accuse the prince, in his reversal of values in the play scene, of being out of his mind, though he appears rational.
7. Your major premise (that I, Falstaff, am a coward).
8. I.e., I hope my fat neck will not make the process of strangling on the gallows longer for me than for the rest of you. The "cart" is the wagon on which criminals were taken to be hanged.
9. The hangings or draperies. On the Elizabethan stage these would conceal the inner stage. "Up above": on the balcony.
1. Lease has expired.

Have in this robbery lost three hundred marks.
PRINCE. It may be so; if he have robbed these men
He shall be answerable; and so farewell.
SHER. Good night, my noble lord.   460
PRINCE. I think it is good morrow, is it not?
SHER. Indeed, my lord, I think it be two o'clock.
    [*Exeunt* ⟨SHERIFF *and* CARRIER.⟩]
PRINCE. This oily rascal is known as well as Paul's.[2] Go call him
  forth.
POINS. Falstaff!—Fast asleep behind the arras, and snorting like   465
  a horse.
PRINCE. Hark, how hard he fetches breath. Search his pockets.
  [*He searcheth his pockets, and findeth certain papers.*] What
  hast thou found?
POINS. Nothing but papers, my lord.   470
PRINCE. Let's see what they be: read them.
POINS. [*reads*] "Item, a capon. . . . . . 2s. 2d.
           Item, sauce. . . . . . .   4d.
           Item, sack, two gallons. . 5s. 8d.
           Item, anchovies and sack   475
              after supper. . . . . 2s. 6d.
           Item, bread. . . . . . .   ob."[3]
PRINCE. O monstrous! but one halfpennyworth of bread to this
  intolerable deal of sack! What there is else, keep close; we'll
  read it at more advantage; there let him sleep till day. I'll to   480
  the court in the morning. We must all to the wars, and thy
  place shall be honorable. I'll procure this fat rogue a charge
  of foot,[4] and I know his death will be a march of twelvescore.
  The money shall be paid back again with advantage. Be with
  me betimes[5] in the morning, and so good morrow, Poins.   485
POINS. Good morrow, good my lord.   [*Exeunt.*]

Act III

SCENE 1

[*Enter* HOTSPUR, WORCESTER, LORD MORTIMER, *and* OWEN
  GLENDOWER.]
MORT. These promises are fair, the parties sure,
  And our induction[6] full of prosperous hope.
HOT. Lord Mortimer, and cousin Glendower,
  Will you sit down?
  And uncle Worcester; a plague upon it,   5
  I have forgot the map.
GLEND.   No, here it is.
  Sit, cousin Percy, sit, good cousin Hotspur,
  For by that name as oft as Lancaster
  Doth speak of you, his cheek looks pale and with

---

2. St. Paul's Cathedral.
3. Oble, a halfpenny.
4. Company of infantry. "Twelve-

score": i.e., 240 yards.
5. Early.
6. Initial step.

A rising sigh he wisheth you in heaven. 10
HOT. And you in hell as often as he hears Owen Glendower spoke
of.
GLEND. I cannot blame him; at my nativity
The front[7] of heaven was full of fiery shapes,
Of burning cressets, and at my birth 15
The frame and huge foundation of the earth
Shaked like a coward.
HOT. Why, so it would have done at the same season if your
mother's cat had but kittened, though yourself had never been
born. 20
GLEND. I say the earth did shake when I was born.
HOT. And I say the earth was not of my mind,
If you suppose as fearing you it shook.
GLEND. The heavens were all on fire, the earth did tremble.
HOT. O then the earth shook to see the heavens on fire, 25
And not in fear of your nativity.
Diseaséd nature oftentimes breaks forth
In strange eruptions; oft the teeming earth
Is with a kind of colic pinched and vexed
By the imprisoning of unruly wind 30
Within her womb, which for enlargement striving
Shakes the old beldam[8] earth and topples down
Steeples and moss-grown towers. At your birth
Our grandam earth, having this distemperature,[9]
In passion shook.
GLEND.   Cousin, of many men 35
I do not bear these crossings. Give me leave
To tell you once again that at my birth
The front of heaven was full of fiery shapes,
The goats ran from the mountains, and the herds
Were strangely clamorous to the frighted fields. 40
These signs have marked me extraordinary,
And all the courses of my life do show
I am not in the roll of common men.
Where is he living, clipped in with[1] the sea
That chides the banks of England, Scotland, Wales, 45
Which calls me pupil or hath read to me?
And bring him out that is but woman's son
Can trace me in the tedious ways of art[2]
And hold me pace in deep experiments.
HOT. I think there's no man speaks better Welsh. I'll to dinner. 50
MORT. Peace, cousin Percy; you will make him mad.
GLEND. I can call spirits from the vasty deep.
HOT. Why, so can I, or so can any man;
But will they come when you do call for them?
GLEND. Why, I can teach you, cousin, to command 55
The devil.

7. The forehead. "Cressets": lamps.   1. Within the limits of.
8. Old woman.   2. Follow me in practicing difficult
9. Ailment.   magic.

HOT. And I can teach thee, coz, to shame the devil
  By telling truth; tell truth and shame the devil.[3]
  If thou have power to raise him, bring him hither,
  And I'll be sworn I have power to shame him hence. 60
  O, while you live, tell truth and shame the devil!
MORT. Come, come, no more of this unprofitable chat.
GLEND. Three times hath Henry Bolingbroke made head
  Against my power, thrice from the banks of Wye
  And sandy-bottomed Severn have I sent him 65
  Bootless[4] home and weather-beaten back.
HOT. Home without boots, and in foul weather too!
  How 'scapes he agues,[5] in the devil's name?
GLEND. Come, here is the map; shall we divide our right
  According to our threefold order ta'en?[6] 70
MORT. The archdeacon hath divided it
  Into three limits very equally:
  England, from Trent and Severn hitherto,
  By south and east is to my part assigned;
  All westward, Wales beyond the Severn shore, 75
  And all the fertile land within that bound,
  To Owen Glendower; and, dear coz, to you
  The remnant northward lying off from Trent;
  And our indentures tripartite are drawn,
  Which being sealéd interchangeably, 80
  A business that this night may execute,
  Tomorrow, cousin Percy, you and I
  And my good Lord of Worcester will set forth
  To meet your father[7] and the Scottish power,
  As is appointed us, at Shrewsbury. 85
  My father Glendower is not ready yet,
  Nor shall we need his help these fourteen days.
  Within that space you may have drawn together
  Your tenants, friends, and neighboring gentlemen.
GLEND. A shorter time shall send me to you, lords, 90
  And in my conduct shall your ladies come,
  From whom you now must steal and take no leave,
  For there will be a world of water shed
  Upon the parting of your wives and you.
HOT. Methinks my moiety,[8] north from Burton here, 95
  In quantity equals not one of yours;
  See how this river comes me cranking[9] in,
  And cuts me from the best of all my land
  A huge half-moon, a monstrous cantle[1] out.
  I'll have the current in this place dammed up; 100
  And here the smug[1a] and silver Trent shall run

---

3. A proverb.
4. Unsuccessful; but Hotspur takes it in the other sense.
5. Fevers and chills.
6. Divide our property according to the arrangement for division into three parts.
7. Father-in-law.
8. Part, share.
9. Curving.
1. Corner.
1a. Smooth.

In a new channel, fair and evenly;
It shall not wind with such a deep indent
To rob me of so rich a bottom[2] here.

GLEND. Not wind? it shall, it must; you see it doth. 105

MORT. Yea, but
Mark how he bears his course, and runs me up
With like advantage on the other side;
Gelding the opposéd continent[3] as much
As on the other side it takes from you. 110

WOR. Yea, but a little charge will trench him here
And on this north side win this cape of land,
And then he runs straight and even.

HOT. I'll have it so; a little charge will do it.

GLEND. I'll not have it altered.

HOT.   Will not you? 115

GLEND. No, nor you shall not.

HOT.   Who shall say me nay?

GLEND. Why, that will I.

HOT. Let me not understand you then; speak it in Welsh.

GLEND. I can speak English, lord, as well as you,
For I was trained up in the English court,
Where, being but young, I framéd to the harp 120
Many an English ditty lovely well
And gave the tongue a helpful ornament,
A virtue that was never seen in you.

HOT. Marry, 125
And I am glad of it with all my heart;
I had rather be a kitten and cry mew
Than one of these same meter ballad-mongers;
I had rather hear a brazen canstick turned,[4]
Or a dry wheel grate on the axletree, 130
And that would set my teeth nothing on edge,
Nothing so much as mincing[5] poetry;
'Tis like the forced gait of a shuffling nag.

GLEND. Come, you shall have Trent turned.

HOT. I do not care; I'll give thrice so much land 135
To any well-deserving friend;
But in the way of bargain, mark ye me,
I'll cavil[6] on the ninth part of a hair.
Are the indentures drawn? shall we be gone?

GLEND. The moon shines fair; you may be away by night. 140
I'll haste the writer, and withal
Break with[7] your wives of your departure hence.
I am afraid my daughter will run mad,
So much she doteth on her Mortimer. [*Exit.*]

MORT. Fie, cousin Percy, how you cross my father! 145

HOT. I cannot choose; sometime he angers me

2. Valley.
3. I.e., cutting off from the opposite side.
4. A brass candlestick turned on a lathe.
5. Affected.
6. Quibble.
7. Inform.

With telling me of the moldwarp[8] and the ant,
Of the dreamer Merlin and his prophecies,
And of a dragon and a finless fish,
A clip-winged griffin and a molten raven,   150
A couching lion and a ramping[9] cat,
And such a deal of skimble-skamble stuff
As puts me from my faith. I tell you what;
He held me last night at least nine hours
In reckoning up the several devils' names   155
That were his lackeys. I cried "hum" and "well, go to,"
But marked him not a word. O, he is as tedious
As a tired horse, a railing[1] wife,
Worse than a smoky house. I had rather live
With cheese and garlic in a windmill,[2] far,   160
Than feed on cates and have him talk to me
In any summer house in Christendom.

MORT. In faith, he is a worthy gentleman,
Exceedingly well read, and profited
In strange concealments,[3] valiant as a lion   165
And wondrous affable and as bountiful
As mines of India. Shall I tell you, cousin?
He holds your temper[4] in a high respect
And curbs himself even of his natural scope
When you come 'cross his humor; faith, he does.   170
I warrant you that man is not alive
Might so have tempted him as you have done
Without the taste of danger and reproof;
But do not use it oft, let me entreat you.

WOR. In faith, my lord, you are too willful-blame,   175
And since your coming hither have done enough
To put him quite beside his patience.
You must needs learn, lord, to amend this fault.
Though sometimes it show greatness, courage, blood[5]—
And that's the dearest grace it renders you—   180
Yet oftentimes it doth present harsh rage,
Defect of manners, want of government,[6]
Pride, haughtiness, opinion, and disdain;
The least of which haunting a nobleman
Loseth men's hearts and leaves behind a stain   185
Upon the beauty of all parts besides,
Beguiling them of commendation.

HOT. Well, I am schooled; good manners be your speed!
Here come our wives, and let us take our leave.

8. Mole. According to the chronicler Holinshed there were prophecies in which Henry IV was referred to as "a moldwarp, cursed of God." Merlin was the famous prophet of King Arthur's court; many later prophecies were attributed to him.
9. "Couching" and "ramping" are Hotspur's versions of the heraldic terms "couchant" (lying down) and "ramp-
ant" (erect, on hind feet).
1. Nagging.
2. Cheese and garlic would be smelly, and the living quarters in a mill would be noisy. "Cates": delicacies.
3. Experienced in secret mysteries.
4. Character.
5. Passion.
6. Self-control. "Opinion": arrogance.

[Enter GLENDOWER *with the ladies.]*

MORT. This is the deadly spite that angers me; 160
 My wife can speak no English, I no Welsh.

GLEND. My daughter weeps; she will not part with you,
 She'll be a soldier too, she'll to the wars.

MORT. Good father, tell her that she and my aunt Percy
 Shall follow in your conduct speedily. 195

  *[*GLENDOWER SPEAKS *to her in Welsh, and she answers*
  him in the same.]

GLEND. She is desperate here; a peevish self-willed harlotry,[7] one
 that no persuasion can do good upon.

  [The lady speaks in Welsh.]

MORT. I understand thy looks; that pretty Welsh
 Which thou pour'st down from these swelling heavens[8]
 I am too perfect in; and, but for shame, 200
 In such a parley should I answer thee.

  [The lady speaks again in Welsh.]

 I understand thy kisses and thou mine,
 And that's a feeling disputation,
 But I will never be a truant, love,
 Till I have learned thy language, for thy tongue 205
 Makes Welsh as sweet as ditties highly penned,
 Sung by a fair queen in a summer's bower,
 With ravishing division,[9] to her lute.

GLEND. Nay, if you melt, then will she run mad.

  [The lady speaks again in Welsh.]

MORT. O, I am ignorance itself in this! 210

GLEND. She bids you on the wanton rushes[1] lay you down
 And rest your gentle head upon her lap,
 And she will sing the song that pleaseth you
 And on your eyelids crown the god of sleep,
 Charming your blood with pleasing heaviness, 215
 Making such difference 'twixt wake and sleep
 As is the difference betwixt day and night
 The hour before the heavenly-harnessed team[2]
 Begins his golden progress in the east.

MORT. With all my heart I'll sit and hear her sing; 220
 By that time will our book,[3] I think, be drawn.

GLEND. Do so;
 And those musicians that shall play to you
 Hang in the air a thousand leagues from hence,
 And straight they shall be here; sit, and attend. 225

HOT. Come, Kate, thou art perfect in lying down; come, quick,
 quick, that I may lay my head in thy lap.

LADY P. Go, ye giddy goose.

---

7. Wench; used affectionately, not
seriously (Juliet's father applies the
same phrase to her in *Romeo and
Juliet*).
8. I.e., tears from her eyes. "Answer
thee": cry likewise.

9. Musical variation.
1. The dry reeds used a floor covering
in Elizabethan England.
2. The horses of the sun.
3. The indenture.

[*The music plays.*]

HOT. Now I perceive the devil understands Welsh,
    And 'tis no marvel, he is so humorous.[4]   230
    By 'r Lady, he is a good musician.

LADY P. Then should you be nothing but musical, for you are al-
    together governed by humors. Lie still, ye thief, and hear the
    lady sing in Welsh.

HOT. I had rather hear Lady, my brach,[5] howl in Irish.   235

LADY P. Wouldst thou have thy head broken?

HOT. No.

LADY P. Then be still.

HOT. Neither; 'tis a woman's fault.[6]

LADY P. Now God help thee.   240

HOT. To the Welsh lady's bed.

LADY P. What's that?

HOT. Peace! she sings.

       [*Here the lady sings a Welsh song.*]

HOT. Come, Kate, I'll have your song too.

LADY P. Not mine, in good sooth.   245

HOT. Not yours, in good sooth! Heart! you swear like a comfit-
    maker's[7] wife. "Not you, in good sooth," and "as true as I
    live," and "as God shall mend me," and "as sure as day,"
    And givest such sarcenet[8] surety for thy oaths
    As if thou never walk'st further than Finsbury.   250
    Swear me, Kate, like a lady as thou art,
    A good mouth-filling oath, and leave "in sooth,"
    And such protest of pepper-gingerbread,[9]
    To velvet-guards and Sunday citizens.
    Come, sing.   255

LADY P. I will not sing.

HOT. 'Tis the next way to turn tailor, or be redbreast teacher.[1]
    An the indentures be drawn, I'll away within these two hours;
    and so, come in when ye will.   [*Exit.*]

GLEND. Come, come, Lord Mortimer, you are as slow   260
    As hot Lord Percy is on fire to go.
    By this our book is drawn; we will but seal,
    And then to horse immediately.

MORT.   With all my heart.   [*Exeunt.*]

SCENE 2

[*Enter the* KING, PRINCE OF WALES, *and others.*]

KING. Lords, give us leave; the Prince of Wales and I

4. Capricious, governed by humors.
5. My bitch hound, Lady.
6. Hotspur sarcastically reverses the usual saying about women and talkativeness.
7. Confectioner's.
8. Thin silk. Finsbury: a recreation ground outside London, frequented by citizens and their wives on Sundays, but not by ladies of Lady Percy's class.
9. I.e., such tame oaths, as crumbly and unsubstantial as gingerbread. "Velvet-guards": respectable people of the middle class, who wore velvet stripes on their clothes; "Sunday citizens": city folk out for a stroll on Sunday.
1. I.e., it is the easiest way to become a tailor (supposedly tailors sang at their work) or a person who teaches birds to sing. Hotspur is equally scornful of music and of people who work for a living.

Must have some private conference; but be near at hand,
For we shall presently have need of you.   [*Exeunt* LORDS.]
I know not whether God will have it so
For some displeasing service I have done,
That, in his secret doom, out of my blood[2]   5
He'll breed revengement and a scourge for me;
But thou dost in thy passages[3] of life
Make me believe that thou art only marked
For the hot vengeance and the rod of heaven
To punish my mistreadings.[4] Tell me else,   10
Could such inordinate and low desires,
Such poor, such bare, such lewd,[5] such mean attempts,
Such barren pleasures, rude society
As thou art matched withal and grafted to
Accompany the greatness of thy blood   15
And hold their level with thy princely heart?
PRINCE. So please your majesty, I would I could
Quit[6] all offenses with as clear excuse
As well as I am doubtless I can purge
Myself of many I am charged withal;   20
Yet such extenuation let me beg,
As, in reproof of many tales devised
(Which oft the ear of greatness needs must hear)
By smiling pickthanks[7] and base newsmongers,
I may, for some things true, wherein my youth   25
Hath faulty wandered and irregular,
Find pardon on my true submission.
KING. God pardon thee; yet let me wonder, Harry,
At thy affections, which doth hold a wing   30
Quite from the flight of all thy ancestors.
Thy place in council thou hast rudely lost,
Which by thy younger brother is supplied,
And art almost an alien to the hearts
Of all the court and princes of my blood.   35
The hope and expectation of thy time[8]
Is ruined, and the soul of every man
Prophetically do forethink thy fall.
Had I so lavish of my presence been,
So common-hackneyed in the eyes of men,   40
So stale and cheap to vulgar company,
Opinion,[9] that did help me to the crown,
Had still kept loyal to possession
And left me in reputeless banishment,
A fellow of no mark nor likelihood.   45
By being seldom seen, I could not stir

2. Through my son.
3. Actions.
4. False steps, misdeeds.
5. Low.
6. Acquit myself of. "Doubtless": sure.
7. Flatterers; "newsmongers": tattle-
tales.
8. Lifetime.
9. Popularity, public opinion. "Possession": i.e., the possessor, Richard II.

But like a comet I was wondered at,
That men would tell their children "This is he";
Others would say "Where, which is Bolingbroke?"
And then I stole all courtesy from heaven,   50
And dressed myself in such humility
That I did pluck allegiance from men's hearts,
Loud shouts and salutations from their mouths,
Even in the presence of the crownéd king.
Thus did I keep my person fresh and new,   55
My presence like a robe pontifical,
Ne'er seen but wondered at; and so my state,[1]
Seldom but sumptuous, showed like a feast
And wan[2] by rareness such solemnity.
The skipping king, he ambled up and down   60
With shallow jesters and rash bavin wits,[3]
Soon kindled and soon burnt, carded his state,
Mingled his royalty with capering fools,
Had his great name profanéd with their scorns
And gave his countenance[4] against his name   65
To laugh at gibing boys and stand the push
Of every beardless vain comparative,[5]
Grew a companion to the common streets,
Enfeoffed himself to popularity,[6]
That, being daily swallowed by men's eyes,   70
They surfeited with honey and began
To loathe the taste of sweetness, whereof a little
More than a little is by much too much.
So when he had occasion to be seen
He was but as the cuckoo is in June,[7]   75
Heard, not regarded, seen, but with such eyes
As, sick and blunted with community,[8]
Afford no extraordinary gaze
Such as is bent on sunlike majesty
When it shines seldom in admiring eyes,   80
But rather drowsed and hung their eyelids down,
Slept in his face[9] and rendered such aspéct
As cloudy men use to their adversaries,
Being with his presence glutted, gorged, and full.
And in that very line, Harry, standest thou,   85
For thou hast lost thy princely privilege
With vile participation.[1] Not an eye
But is a-weary of thy common sight,

1. Public ceremonial appearances.
2. Won. "Such solemnity": i.e., the greatest possible majestic effect (an intensive use of "such"). King Henry's theory of public relations is of course not based upon the assumption of a democratic society.
3. "Rash": quick; "bavin": brushwood; the image is explained in the next line. "Carded his state": degraded his royal dignity.

4. Authority; "name": reputation.
5. Shallow satirical pretender to wit.
6. Made himself the common property of the public.
7. The cuckoo is noticed in April, when its song is first heard; by June it is commonplace.
8. Commonness.
9. I.e., yawned in his face. "Aspect": looks; "cloudy": sullen.
1. Association with vile companions.

Save mine, which hath desired to see thee more,
Which now doth that I would not have it do,   90
Make blind itself with foolish tenderness.
PRINCE. I shall hereafter, my thrice gracious lord,
  Be more myself.
KING.   For all the world
  As thou art to this hour was Richard then
  When I from France set foot at Ravenspurgh,   95
  And even as I was then is Percy now.
  Now, by my scepter and my soul to boot,
  He hath more worthy interest to the state
  Than thou the shadow of succession;[2]
  For of no right, nor color like to right,   100
  He doth fill fields with harness in the realm,
  Turns head against the lion's arméd jaws,[3]
  And, being no more in debt to years than thou,
  Leads ancient lords and reverend bishops on
  To bloody battles and to bruising arms.   105
  What never-dying honor hath he got
  Against renownéd Douglas! whose high deeds,
  Whose hot incursions and great name in arms
  Holds from all soldiers chief majority
  And military title capital[4]   110
  Through all the kingdoms that acknowledge Christ.
  Thrice hath this Hotspur, Mars in swaddling clothes,
  This infant warrior, in his enterprises
  Discomfited great Douglas, ta'en him once,
  Enlargéd[5] him and made a friend of him,   115
  To fill the mouth of deep defiance up[6]
  And shake the peace and safety of our throne.
  And what say you to this? Percy, Northumberland,
  The Archbishop's grace of York, Douglas, Mortimer,
  Capitulate[7] against us and are up.   120
  But wherefore do I tell these news to thee?
  Why, Harry, do I tell thee of my foes,
  Which art my nearest and dearest enemy?
  Thou that art like enough through vassal fear,
  Base inclination and the start of spleen,[8]   125
  To fight against me under Percy's pay,
  To dog his heels and curtsy at his frowns,
  To show how much thou art degenerate.
PRINCE. Do not think so; you shall not find it so;
  And God forgive them that so much have swayed   130
  Your majesty's good thoughts away from me.

2. I.e., Hotspur's claim to the throne
is more solid, because of his achievements, than is Hal's, which rests only
on shadowy rights of succession by
birth. "Color": false pretense.
3. I.e., takes military action against
the king's army. "Harness": armor.
4. Has the greatest reputation among
soldiers. "Incursions": raids; "majority": superiority.
5. Freed.
6. I.e., to make the voice of defiance
full in volume.
7. Make agreements; "up": in arms.
8. Unreasoning impulse.

I will redeem all this on Percy's head
And in the closing of some glorious day
Be bold to tell you that I am your son,
When I will wear a garment all of blood   135
And stain my favors[9] in a bloody mask,
Which, washed away, shall scour my shame with it;
And that shall be the day, whene'er it lights,
That this same child of honor and renown,
This gallant Hotspur, this all-praiséd knight,   140
And your unthought-of Harry chance to meet.
For every honor sitting on his helm—
Would they were multitudes, and on my head
My shames redoubled!—for the time will come
That I shall make this northern youth exchange   145
His glorious deeds for my indignities.
Percy is but my factor,[1] good my lord,
To engross up glorious deeds on my behalf,
And I will call him to so strict account,
That he shall render every glory up,   150
Yea, even the slightest worship[2] of his time,
Or I will tear the reckoning from his heart.
This in the name of God I promise here,
The which if He be pleased I shall perform,
I do beseech your majesty, may salve   155
The long-grown wounds of my intemperance;
If not, the end of life cancels all bands,[3]
And I will die a hundred thousand deaths
Ere break the smallest parcel of this vow.
KING. A hundred thousand rebels die in this;   160
Thou shalt have charge and sovereign trust herein.
          [*Enter* BLUNT.]
How now, good Blunt? thy looks are full of speed.
BLUNT. So hath the business that I come to speak of.
Lord Mortimer of Scotland hath sent word
That Douglas and the English rebels met   165
The eleventh of this month at Shrewsbury;
A mighty and a fearful head[4] they are,
If promises be kept on every hand,
As ever offered foul play in a state.
KING. The Earl of Westmoreland set forth today,   170
With him my son, Lord John of Lancaster,
For this advertisement[5] is five days old.
On Wednesday next, Harry, you shall set forward;
On Thursday we ourselves will march. Our meeting
Is Bridgenorth and, Harry, you shall march   175
Through Gloucestershire, by which account,[6]

9. Features.   4. Power.
1. Agent; "engross up": collect, ac-   5. News.
quire.   6. Method. "Our business valued": ac-
2. Honor.   cording to estimates.
3. Bonds, debts.

Our business valued, some twelve days hence
Our general forces at Bridgenorth shall meet.
Our hands are full of business: let's away;
Advantage feeds him fat while men delay.[7]   [*Exeunt.*] 180

SCENE 3

[*Enter* FALSTAFF *and* BARDOLPH.]

FAL. Bardolph, am I not fallen away vilely since this last action?[8]
   do I not bate? do I not dwindle? Why, my skin hangs about
   me like an old lady's loose gown; I am withered like an old
   applejohn.[9] Well, I'll repent, and that suddenly, while I am
   in some liking; I shall be out of heart shortly, and then I shall   5
   have no strength to repent. An I have not forgotten what the
   inside of a church is made of, I am a peppercorn, a brewer's
   horse. The inside of a church! Company, villainous company,
   hath been the spoil of me.

BARD. Sir John, you are so fretful you cannot live long.   10

FAL. Why, there is it; come sing me a bawdy song, make me
   merry. I was as virtuously given as a gentleman need to be:
   virtuous enough, swore little, diced not above seven times a
   week, went to a bawdyhouse not above once in a quarter—of an
   hour, paid money that I borrowed three or four times, lived   15
   well and in good compass; and now I live out of all order, out
   of all compass.

BARD. Why, you are so fat, Sir John, that you must needs be out
   of all compass, out of all reasonable compass, Sir John.

FAL. Do thou amend thy face, and I'll amend my life; thou art   20
   our admiral,[1] thou bearest the lantern in the poop, but 'tis in
   the nose of thee; thou art the Knight of the Burning Lamp.

BARD. Why, Sir John, my face does you no harm.

FAL. No, I'll be sworn; I make as good use of it as many a man
   doth of a death's-head or a *memento mori*.[2] I never see thy   25
   face but I think upon hell-fire and Dives[3] that lived in purple,
   for there he is in his robes, burning, burning. If thou wert any
   way given to virtue, I would swear by thy face; my oath should
   be "By this fire, that's God's angel"; but thou art altogether
   given over, and wert indeed, but for the light in thy face, the   30
   son of utter darkness. When thou rannest up Gadshill in the
   night to catch my horse, if I did not think thou hadst been an
   ignis fatuus[4] or a ball of wildfire, there's no purchase in money.
   O, thou art a perpetual triumph,[5] an everlasting bonfire light!
   Thou hast saved me a thousand marks in links[6] and torches,   35
   walking with thee in the night betwixt tavern and tavern, but

---

7. I.e., the rebels' "advantage" (opportunity) grows as the king's men delay.
8. I.e., the Gadshill robbery; "bate":
lose weight.
9. A keeping apple with a wrinkled
skin. "In some liking": in good condition.
1. Flagship.

2. I.e., a skull or some other reminder
of death.
3. The rich man who would not give
food to Lazarus and was punished in
hell for it. See Luke xvi.19–31.
4. Will-o'-the-wisp; "wildfire": a fire-
work used for military purposes.
5. Illumination at a public festival.
6. Small torches carried at night.

the sack that thou hast drunk me would have bought me lights
as good cheap at the dearest chandler's[7] in Europe. I have maintained that salamander of yours with fire any time this two and
thirty years, God reward me for it.   40

BARD. 'Sblood, I would my face were in your belly!

FAL. God-a-mercy! so should I be sure to be heartburned.

    [*Enter* HOSTESS.]

How now, Dame Partlet[8] the hen! have you inquired yet who
picked my pocket?

HOST. Why, Sir John, what do you think, Sir John? do you think   45
I keep thieves in my house? I have searched, I have inquired,
so has my husband, man by man, boy by boy, servant by servant; the tithe[9] of a hair was never lost in my house before.

FAL. Ye lie, hostess; Bardolph was shaved and lost many a hair,
and I'll be sworn my pocket was picked. Go to, you are a   50
woman, go.

HOST. Who, I? no, I defy thee; God's light, I was never called
so in mine own house before.

FAL. Go to, I know you well enough.

HOST. No, Sir John; you do not know me, Sir John. I know   55
you, Sir John; you owe me money, Sir John, and now you
pick a quarrel to beguile me of it; I bought you a dozen of
shirts to your back.

FAL. Dowlas,[1] filthy dowlas; I have given them away to bakers'
wives, and they have made bolters of them.   60

HOST. Now, as I am a true woman, holland[2] of eight shillings an
ell. You owe money here besides, Sir John, for your diet and
by-drinkings,[3] and money lent you, four and twenty pound.

FAL. He had his part of it; let him pay.

HOST. He? alas, he is poor; he hath nothing.   65

FAL. How! poor? look upon his face; what call you rich? let them
coin his nose, let them coin his cheeks; I'll not pay a denier.[4]
What, will you make a younker of me? shall I not take mine
ease in mine inn but I shall have my pocket picked? I have lost
a seal ring of my grandfather's worth forty mark.[5]   70

HOST. O Jesu, I have heard the prince tell him I know not how
oft that that ring was copper.

FAL. How! the prince is a Jack,[6] a sneak-up; 'sblood, an he were
here, I would cudgel him like a dog if he would say so.

    [*Enter the* PRINCE ⟨*and* POINS⟩, *marching, and* FALSTAFF
    meets them playing upon his truncheon like a fife.]

How now, lad, is the wind in that door, i' faith? must we all   75
march?

---

7. Candlemaker's. "Salamanders" were
lizards that supposedly lived in fire
and ate it.
8. A nickname from the hen in Chaucer's Nun's Priest's Tale; in Shakespeare's time a conventional name for
a scolding woman.
9. Tenth part.
1. A coarse cloth. "Bolters": sieves for

flour.
2. Fine linen; "ell": 45 inches.
3. Drinks between meals.
4. French penny, worth a tenth of an
English penny. "Younker": youngster,
novice.
5. A mark was worth two-thirds of a
pound.
6. Rascal; "sneak-up": a sneak.

BARD. Yea, two and two, Newgate fashion.[7]

HOST. My lord, I pray you hear me.

PRINCE. What sayest thou, Mistress Quickly? How doth thy husband? I love him well; he is an honest man. 80

HOST. Good my lord, hear me.

FAL. Prithee let her alone, and list to me.

PRINCE. What sayest thou, Jack?

FAL. The other night I fell asleep here behind the arras and had my pocket picked; this house is turned bawdyhouse, they pick 85 pockets.

PRINCE. What didst thou lose, Jack?

FAL. Wilt thou believe me, Hal? three or four bonds of forty pound apiece, and a seal ring of my grandfather's.

PRINCE. A trifle, some eightpenny matter. 90

HOST. So I told him, my lord, and I said I heard your grace say so; and, my lord, he speaks most vilely of you, like a foulmouthed man as he is, and said he would cudgel you.

PRINCE. What, he did not?

HOST. There's neither faith, truth, nor womanhood in me else. 95

FAL. There's no more faith in thee than in a stewed prune,[8] nor no more truth in thee than in a drawn fox, and for womanhood Maid Marian may be the deputy's wife of the ward to thee.[9] Go, you thing, go.

HOST. Say, what thing, what thing? 100

FAL. What thing! why, a thing to thank God on.

HOST. I am no thing to thank God on, I would thou shouldst know it; I am an honest man's wife, and, setting thy knighthood aside,[1] thou art a knave to call me so.

FAL. Setting thy womanhood aside, thou art a beast to say other- 105 wise.

HOST. Say, what beast, thou knave, thou?

FAL. What beast? why, an otter.

PRINCE. An otter, Sir John, why an otter?

FAL. Why, she's neither fish nor flesh, a man knows not where 110 to have her.[2]

HOST. Thou art an unjust man in saying so; thou or any man knows where to have me, thou knave, thou!

PRINCE. Thou sayest true, hostess, and he slanders thee most grossly. 115

HOST. So he doth you, my lord, and said this other day you ought[3] him a thousand pound.

PRINCE. Sirrah, do I owe you a thousand pound?

FAL. A thousand pound, Hal! A million. Thy love is worth a mil-

7. Chained together, like prisoners at Newgate.
8. Stewed prunes were commonly served in bawdyhouses, as a supposed protection against venereal disease. "Drawn": hunted.
9. "Maid Marian" was a female character of low morals in the popular Robin Hood plays; a "deputy's wife of the ward" would be a respectable

woman.
1. I.e., ignoring, or intending no disrespect to, the rank of knighthood. Falstaff intentionally misunderstands the phrase.
2. I.e., how to understand her. But the Hostess' retort is, unconsciously, equivalent to saying that she is completely promiscuous.
3. Owed.

lion; thou owest me thy love.   120

HOST. Nay, my lord, he called you Jack, and said he would cudgel
you.

FAL. Did I, Bardolph?

BARD. Indeed, Sir John, you said so.

FAL. Yea, if he said my ring was copper.   125

PRINCE. I say 'tis copper; darest thou be as good as thy word now?

FAL. Why, Hal, thou knowest, as thou art but man, I dare; but
as thou art prince, I fear thee as I fear the roaring of the lion's
whelp.

PRINCE. And why not as the lion?   130

FAL. The king himself is to be feared as the lion; dost thou think
I'll fear thee as I fear thy father? Nay, an I do, I pray God my
girdle[4] break.

PRINCE. O, if it should, how would thy guts fall about thy knees!
But, sirrah, there's no room for faith, truth, nor honesty in this 135
bosom of thine; it is all filled up with guts and midriff. Charge
an honest woman with picking thy pocket! Why, thou whoreson, impudent, embossed rascal,[5] if there were anything in thy
pocket but tavern-reckonings, memorandums of bawdyhouses,
and one poor pennyworth of sugar candy to make thee long- 140
winded, if thy pocket were enriched with any other injuries but
these, I am a villain. And yet you will stand to it, you will not
pocket up wrong; art thou not ashamed?

FAL. Dost thou hear, Hal? thou knowest in the state of innocency
Adam fell, and what should poor Jack Falstaff do in the days 145
of villainy? Thou seest I have more flesh than another man,
and therefore more frailty. You confess then, you picked my
pocket?

PRINCE. It appears so by the story.

FAL. Hostess, I forgive thee; go make ready breakfast, love thy 150
husband, look to thy servants, cherish thy guests; thou shalt
find me tractable to any honest reason; thou seest I am pacified
still. Nay, prithee begone. [*Exit* HOSTESS.] Now, Hal, to the
news at court; for the robbery, lad, how is that answered?

PRINCE. O, my sweet beef, I must still be good angel to thee; the 155
money is paid back again.

FAL. O, I do not like that paying back; 'tis a double labor.

PRINCE. I am good friends with my father and may do anything.

FAL. Rob me the exchequer the first thing thou doest, and do it
with unwashed hands too.   160

BARD. Do, my lord.

PRINCE. I have procured thee, Jack, a charge of foot.[6]

FAL. I would it had been of horse. Where shall I find one that
can steal well? O for a fine thief, of the age of two and twenty
or thereabouts! I am heinously unprovided. Well, God be 165
thanked for these rebels, they offend none but the virtuous; I

4. Belt.
5. Swollen rascal; "embossed" was also
a technical term in hunting, applied to
a deer which was exhausted and foaming at the mouth.
6. Command of a company of foot-
soldiers. "Horse": cavalry.

laud them, I praise them.
PRINCE. Bardolph!
BARD. My lord?
PRINCE. Go bear this letter to Lord John of Lancaster, to my 170
brother John; this to my Lord of Westmoreland. [*Exit* BAR-
DOLPH.] Go, Poins, to horse, to horse; for thou and I have
thirty miles to ride yet ere dinnertime. [*Exit* POINS.] Jack, meet
me tomorrow in the Temple Hall at two o'clock in the after-
noon.   175
There shalt thou know thy charge, and there receive
Money and order for their furniture.[7]
The land is burning, Percy stands on high,
And either we or they must lower lie.   [⟨*Exit.*⟩]
FAL. Rare words, brave world! Hostess, my breakfast, come.   180
O, I could wish this tavern were my drum![7a]   [*Exit.*]

Act IV

SCENE 1

[*Enter* HOTSPUR, WORCESTER, *and* DOUGLAS.]
HOT. Well said, my noble Scot. If speaking truth
In this fine age were not thought flattery,
Such attribution should the Douglas have
As not a soldier of this season's stamp
Should go so general current[8] through the world.   5
By God, I cannot flatter; I do defy
The tongues of soothers,[9] but a braver place
In my heart's love hath no man than yourself;
Nay, task me to my word,[1] approve me, lord.
DOUG.   Thou art the king of honor;   10
No man so potent breathes upon the ground
But I will beard him.[2]
HOT.   Do so, and 'tis well.
[*Enter a* MESSENGER *with letters.*]
What letters hast thou there?—I can but thank you.
MESS. These letters come from your father.
HOT. Letters from him! why comes he not himself?   15
MESS. He cannot come, my lord; he is grievous sick.
HOT. Zounds! how has he the leisure to be sick
In such a justling[3] time? Who leads his power?
Under whose government come they along?
MESS. His letters bears his mind, not I, my lord.   20
WOR. I prithee tell me, doth he keep his bed?
MESS. He did, my lord, four days ere I set forth,
And at the time of my departure thence

7. Furnishings, equipment.
7a. Headquarters.
8. I.e., that not a soldier of this year's coinage should achieve such currency. "Attribution": praise.
9. Flatterers; "braver": more distin-
guished.
1. Compare my actions with my speech. "Approve": prove, test.
2. I.e., I will take on anybody, however powerful.
3. Turbulent.

He was much feared by[4] his physiciáns.

WOR. I would the state of time had first been whole   25
    Ere he by sickness had been visited;
    His health was never better worth than now.

HOT. Sick now! droop now! this sickness doth infect
    The very lifeblood of our enterprise;
    'Tis catching hither, even to our camp.   30
    He writes me here that inward sickness—
    And that his friends by deputation could not
    So soon be drawn,[5] nor did he think it meet
    To lay so dangerous and dear a trust
    On any soul removed but on his own.   35
    Yet doth he give us bold advertisement
    That with our small conjunction[6] we should on
    To see how fortune is disposed to us;
    For, as he writes, there is no quailing now,
    Because the king is certainly possessed[7]   40
    Of all our purposes. What say you to it?

WOR. Your father's sickness is a maim to us.

HOT. A perilous gash, a very limb lopped off;
    And yet in faith it is not; his present want[8]
    Seems more than we shall find it. Were it good   45
    To set the exact wealth of all our states
    All at one cast, to set so rich a main[9]
    On the nice hazard of one doubtful hour?
    It were not good, for therein should we read
    The very bottom and the soul of hope,[1]
    The very list, the very utmost bound   50
    Of all our fortunes.

DOUG.   Faith, and so we should,
    Where now remains a sweet reversion.[2]
    We may boldly spend upon the hope of what
    Is to come in;
    A comfort of retirement[3] lives in this.   55

HOT. A rendezvous, a home to fly unto,
    If that the devil and mischance look big
    Upon the maidenhead of our affairs.[4]

WOR. But yet I would your father had been here.   60
    The quality and hair[5] of our attempt
    Brooks no division; it will be thought
    By some that know not why he is away
    That wisdom, loyalty, and mere dislike
    Of our proceedings kept the earl from hence.   65

4. Feared for by. "State of time": public affairs.
5. Could not quickly be organized under a deputy. "Soul removed": other person.
6. Unified forces.
7. Informed.
8. Our present awareness of his absence.

9. Stake, in betting; "nice hazard": risky chance.
1. Foundation and essence of our expectations. "List": limit.
2. A fund to be inherited in the future.
3. Sustaining place to fall back on.
4. I.e., threaten the beginning of our affairs.
5. Character; "brooks": allows.

And think how such an apprehensión
May turn the tide of fearful factión[6]
And breed a kind of question in our cause,
For well you know we of the offering[7] side
Must keep aloof from strict arbitrement,   70
And stop all sight-holes, every loop[8] from whence
The eye of reason may pry in upon us.
This absence of your father's draws a curtain,
That shows the ignorant a kind of fear
Before not dreamt of.

HOT.   You strain too far.   75
    I rather of his absence make this use:
    It lends a luster and more great opinion,
    A larger dare to our great enterprise,
    Than if the earl were here, for men must think,
    If we without his help can make a head   80
    To push against a kingdom, with his help
    We shall o'erturn it topsy-turvy down.
    Yet all goes well, yet all our joints are whole.

DOUG. As heart can think; there is not such a word
    Spoke of in Scotland as this term of fear.   85

        [*Enter* SIR RICHARD VERNON.]

HOT. My cousin Vernon, welcome, by my soul!
VER. Pray God my news be worth a welcome, lord.
    The Earl of Westmoreland, seven thousand strong,
    Is marching hitherwards; with him Prince John.
HOT. No harm; what more?
VER.   And further I have learned   90
    The king himself in person is set forth,
    Or hitherwards intended speedily,
    With strong and mighty preparatión.
HOT. He shall be welcome too. Where is his son,
    The nimble-footed madcap Prince of Wales,   95
    And his comrades that daft[9] the world aside
    And bid it pass?
VER.   All furnished, all in arms,
    All plumed like estridges[1] that with the wind
    Bated, like eagles having lately bathed,
    Glittering in golden coats like images,   100
    As full of spirit as the month of May,
    And gorgeous as the sun at midsummer,
    Wanton as youthful goats, wild as young bulls.
    I saw young Harry, with his beaver[2] on,
    His cushes on his thighs, gallantly armed,   105
    Rise from the ground like feathered Mercury,
    And vaulted with such ease into his seat,

---

6. Conspiracy.
7. Challenging. "Arbitrement": investigation.
8. Loophole.
9. Push.

1. Ostriches; "bated": fluttering their wings.
2. Helmet. "Cushes": cuisses, armor for the thighs.

As if an angel dropped down from the clouds,
To turn and wind[3] a fiery Pegasus
And witch the world with noble horsemanship.   110
HOT. No more, no more. Worse than the sun in March
  This praise doth nourish agues.[4] Let them come;
  They come like sacrifices in their trim,
  And to the fire-eyed maid of smoky war
  All hot and bleeding will we offer them;   115
  The mailéd Mars shall on his altar sit
  Up to the ears in blood. I am on fire
  To hear this rich reprisal[5] is so nigh
  And yet not ours. Come, let me taste my horse,
  Who is to bear me like a thunderbolt   120
  Against the bosom of the Prince of Wales;
  Harry to Harry shall, hot horse to horse,
  Meet and ne'er part till one drop down a corse.
  O that Glendower were come!
VER.   There is more news;
  I learned in Worcester, as I rode along,   125
  He cannot draw his power this fourteen days.
DOUG. That's the worst tidings that I hear of yet.
WOR. Aye, by my faith, that bears a frosty sound.
HOT. What may the king's whole battle[6] reach unto?
VER. To thirty thousand.
HOT.   Forty let it be;   130
  My father and Glendower being both away,
  The powers of us may serve so great a day.
  Come, let us take a muster speedily;
  Doomsday is near; die all, die merrily.
DOUG. Talk not of dying; I am out out of fear   135
  Of death or death's hand for this one-half year.   [*Exeunt.*]

SCENE 2

[*Enter* FALSTAFF *and* BARDOLPH.]
FAL. Bardolph, get thee before to Coventry; fill me a bottle of
  sack, our soldiers shall march through. We'll to Sutton Co'fil'
  tonight.
BARD. Will you give me money, captain?
FAL. Lay out, lay out.
BARD. This bottle makes an angel.[7]   5
FAL. An if it do, take it for thy labor; and if it make twenty, take
  them all; I'll answer the coinage. Bid my lieutenant Peto
  meet me at town's end.
BARD. I will, captain; farewell.   [*Exit.*] 10
FAL. If I be not ashamed of my soldiers, I am a soused gurnet.[8]
  I have misused the king's press damnably. I have got in ex-

3. Direct. "Pegasus": winged horse.
4. Fevers. Malaria was thought to be caused by vapors from the marshes, drawn up by the sun in spring.
5. Prize.
6. Army.
7. Ten shillings' worth.
8. Pickled anchovy. "Press": the draft or impressment of soldiers into service.

change of a hundred and fifty soldiers three hundred and odd pounds. I press me none but good householders, yeomen's sons, inquire me out contracted bachelors, such as had been asked twice on the banns,[9] such a commodity[1] of warm slaves as had as lieve hear the devil as a drum, such as fear the report of a caliver worse than a struck fowl or a hurt wild duck. I pressed me none but such toasts-and-butter[2] with hearts in their bellies no bigger than pins' heads, and they have bought out their services, and now my whole charge consists of ancients,[3] corporals, lieutenants, gentlemen of companies, slaves as ragged as Lazarus in the painted cloth where the glutton's dogs licked his sores, and such as indeed were never soldiers, but discarded unjust serving-men, younger sons to younger brothers, revolted tapsters and ostlers trade-fallen,[4] the cankers of a calm world and a long peace, ten times more dishonorable ragged than an old-fac'd ancient,[5] and such have I to fill up the rooms of them that have bought out their services, that you would think that I had a hundred and fifty tattered prodigals lately come from swine-keeping, from eating draff[6] and husks. A mad fellow met me on the way and told me I had unloaded all the gibbets and pressed the dead bodies. No eye hath seen such scarecrows. I'll not march through Coventry with them, that's flat; nay, and the villains march wide betwixt the legs, as if they had gyves[7] on, for indeed I had the most of them out of prison. There's but a shirt and a half in all my company, and the half shirt is two napkins tacked together and thrown over the shoulders like a herald's coat without sleeves, and the shirt, to say the truth, stolen from my host at Saint Alban's, or the red-nose innkeeper of Daventry. But that's all one; they'll find linen enough on every hedge.[8]

[*Enter the* PRINCE *and the Lord of* WESTMORELAND.]

PRINCE. How now, blown Jack! how now, quilt!

FAL. What, Hal, how now, mad wag! what a devil dost thou in Warwickshire? My good Lord of Westmoreland, I cry you mercy; I thought your honor had already been at Shrewsbury.

WEST. Faith, Sir John, 'tis more than time that I were there, and you too; but my powers are there already. The king, I can tell you, looks for us all; we must away all night.

FAL. Tut, never fear me; I am as vigilant as a cat to steal cream.

PRINCE. I think, to steal cream indeed, for thy theft hath already made thee butter. But tell me, Jack, whose fellows are these that come after?

FAL. Mine, Hal, mine.

PRINCE. I did never see such pitiful rascals.

---

9. Notice of approaching marriage, announced three times publicly in church before the marriage could take place.
1. "Commodity": collection; "warm": well-to-do; "caliver": musket.
2. Sissies.
3. Ensigns.
4. Hostlers out of work; "cankers":

canker worms.
5. Frayed flag.
6. Garbage. The prodigal son, in the Bible, fed on husks before returning to the paternal board.
7. Leg-irons.
8. Laundry was customarily hung on hedges to dry.

FAL. Tut, tut, good enough to toss,[9] food for powder, food for powder; they'll fill a pit as well as better; tush, man, mortal men, mortal men.

WEST. Aye, but, Sir John, methinks they are exceeding poor and bare, too beggarly.   60

FAL. Faith, for their poverty I know not where they had that, and for their bareness I am sure they never learned that of me.

PRINCE. No, I'll be sworn, unless you call three fingers on the ribs bare. But, sirrah, make haste; Percy is already in the field.

FAL. What, is the king encamped?   65

WEST. He is, Sir John; I fear we shall stay too long.

FAL. Well,
  To the latter end of a fray and the beginning of a feast
  Fits a dull fighter and a keen guest.   [*Exeunt.*]

SCENE 3

[*Enter* HOTSPUR, WORCESTER, DOUGLAS, *and* VERNON.]

HOT. We'll fight with him tonight.

WOR.   It may not be.

DOUG. You give him then advantage.

VER.   Not a whit.

HOT. Why say you so? looks he not for supply?

VER. So do we.

HOT.   His is certain, ours is doubtful.

WOR. Good cousin, be advised; stir not tonight.   5

VER. Do not, my lord.

DOUG.   You do not counsel well;
  You speak it out of fear and cold heart.

VER. Do me no slander, Douglas; by my life,
  And I dare well maintain it with my life,
  If well-respected honor bid me on,
  I hold as little counsel with weak fear   10
  As you, my lord, or any Scot that this day lives.
  Let it be seen tomorrow in the battle
  Which of us fears.

DOUG.   Yea, or tonight.

VER.   Content.

HOT. Tonight, say I.   15

VER. Come, come, it may not be. I wonder much,
  Being men of such great leading as you are,
  That you foresee not what impediments
  Drag back our expedition;[1] certain horse
  Of my cousin Vernon's are not yet come up,   20
  Your uncle Worcester's horse came but today,
  And now their pride and mettle is asleep,
  Their courage with hard labor tame and dull,
  That not a horse is half the half of himself.

HOT. So are the horses of the enemy   25

9. I.e., on a pike, or long spear.   1. Retard our speed.

In general, journey-bated[2] and brought low;
The better part of ours are full of rest.

WOR. The number of the king exceedeth ours;
For God's sake, cousin, stay till all come in.

[*The trumpet sounds a parley. Enter* SIR WALTER BLUNT.]

BLUNT. I come with gracious offers from the king,   30
If you vouchsafe me hearing and respect.

HOT. Welcome, Sir Walter Blunt; and would to God
You were of our determinatión!
Some of us love you well, and even those some
Envy your great deservings and good name   35
Because you are not of our quality,[3]
But stand against us like an enemy.

BLUNT. And God defend[4] but still I should stand so,
So long as out of limit and true rule
You stand against anointed majesty.   40
But to my charge. The king hath sent to know
The nature of your griefs, and whereupon
You conjure from the breast of civil peace
Such bold hostility, teaching his duteous land
Audacious cruelty. If that the king   45
Have any way your good deserts forgot,
Which he confesseth to be manifold,
He bids you name your griefs, and with all speed
You shall have your desires with interest
And pardon absolute for yourself and these   50
Herein misled by your suggestión.

HOT. The king is kind, and well we know the king
Knows at what time to promise, when to pay.
My father and my uncle and myself
Did give him that same royalty he wears;   55
And when he was not six and twenty strong,
Sick in the world's regard, wretched and low,
A poor unminded outlaw sneaking home,
My father gave him welcome to the shore;
And when he heard him swear and vow to God   60
He came but to be Duke of Lancaster,
To sue his livery[5] and beg his peace,
With tears of innocency and terms of zeal,
My father, in kind heart and pity moved,
Swore him assistance and performed it too.   65
Now when the lords and barons of the realm
Perceived Northumberland did lean to him,
The more and less came in with cap and knee,
Met him in boroughs, cities, villages,
Attended him on bridges, stood in lanes,   70
Laid gifts before him, proffered him their oaths,

2. Tired from travel.
3. Fellowship, party.
4. Forbid; "still": always.

5. I.e., claim title to his late father's
lands (held by King Richard II).

Gave him their heirs as pages, followed him
Even at the heels in golden multitudes.
He presently, as greatness knows itself,
Steps me a little higher than his vow, 75
Made to my father while his blood was poor
Upon the naked shore at Ravenspurgh,
And now, forsooth, takes on him to reform
Some certain edicts and some strait⁶ decrees
That lie too heavy on the commonwealth, 80
Cries out upon abuses, seems to weep
Over his country's wrongs, and by this face,
This seeming brow of justice, did he win
The hearts of all that he did angle for;
Proceeded further, cut me off the heads 85
Of all the favorites that the absent king
In deputation left behind him here,
When he was personal⁷ in the Irish war.
BLUNT. Tut, I came not to hear this.
HOT.   Then to the point.
In short time after he deposed the king, 90
Soon after that deprived him of his life,
And in the neck of that tasked⁸ the whole state;
To make that worse, suffered his kinsman March
(Who is, if every owner were well placed,
Indeed his king) to be engaged⁹ in Wales, 95
There without ransom to lie forfeited;
Disgraced¹ me in my happy victories,
Sought to entrap me by intelligence,²
Rated mine uncle from the council board,
In rage dismissed my father from the court, 100
Broke oath on oath, committed wrong on wrong,
And in conclusion drove us to seek out
This head of safety,³ and withal to pry
Into his title, the which we find
Too indirect for long continuance. 105
BLUNT. Shall I return this answer to the king?
HOT. Not so, Sir Walter; we'll withdraw awhile.
Go to the king, and let there be impawned⁴
Some surety for a safe return again,
And in the morning early shall mine uncle 110
Bring him our purposes; and so farewell.
BLUNT. I would you would accept of grace and love.
HOT. And may be so we shall.
BLUNT.   Pray God you do.   [*Exeunt.*]

6. Strict.
7. Actively participating in person.
8. I.e., immediately after that, (he) taxed.
9. Pawned as a hostage.

1. I.e., did not favor.
2. Spying; "rated": angrily dismissed.
3. Army for our safety.
4. Pledged; "surety": guarantee.

SCENE 4

[*Enter the* ARCHBISHOP OF YORK *and* SIR MICHAEL.]

ARCH. Hie, good Sir Michael; bear this sealéd brief[5]
  With wingéd haste to the lord marshal,
  This to my cousin Scroop, and all the rest
  To whom they are directed. If you knew
  How much they do import you would make haste.   5
SIR M. My good lord,
  I guess their tenor.
ARCH.   Like enough you do.
  Tomorrow, good Sir Michael, is a day
  Wherein the fortune of ten thousand men
  Must bide the touch;[6] for, sir, at Shrewsbury,   10
  As I am truly given to understand,
  The king with mighty and quick-raiséd power
  Meets with Lord Harry; and I fear, Sir Michael,
  What with the sickness of Northumberland,
  Whose power was in the first proportión,[7]   15
  And what with Owen Glendower's absence thence,
  Who with them was a rated[8] sinew too
  And comes not in, o'er-ruled by prophecies—
  I fear the power of Percy is too weak
  To wage an instant trial with the king.   20
SIR M. Why, my good lord, you need not fear;
  There is Douglas and Lord Mortimer.
ARCH. No, Mortimer is not there.
SIR M. But there is Mordake, Vernon, Lord Harry Percy,
  And there is my Lord of Worcester and a head   25
  Of gallant warriors, noble gentlemen.
ARCH. And so there is; but yet the king hath drawn
  The special head[9] of all the land together:
  The Prince of Wales, Lord John of Lancaster,
  The noble Westmoreland, and warlike Blunt,   30
  And many more corrivals[1] and dear men
  Of estimation and command in arms.
SIR M. Doubt not, my lord, they shall be well opposed.
ARCH. I hope no less, yet needful 'tis to fear,
  And to prevent the worst, Sir Michael, speed;   35
  For if Lord Percy thrive not, ere the king
  Dismiss his power, he means to visit[2] us,
  For he hath heard of our confederacy,
  And 'tis but wisdom to make strong against him;
  Therefore make haste. I must go write again   40
  To other friends; and so farewell, Sir Michael.   [*Exeunt.*]

5. Letter.
6. Stand the test.
7. The largest part.
8. Highly regarded.

9. Principal army.
1. Associates; "dear": noble.
2. Attack.

Act V

SCENE 1

[*Enter the* KING, PRINCE OF WALES, PRINCE JOHN OF
LANCASTER, SIR WALTER BLUNT, *and* FALSTAFF.]

KING. How bloodily the sun begins to peer
  Above yon busky³ hill! The day looks pale
  At his distemperature.⁴

PRINCE.   The southern wind
  Doth play the trumpet to his purposes,⁵
  And by his hollow whistling in the leaves   5
  Foretells a tempest and a blustering day.

KING. Then with the losers let it sympathize,
  For nothing can seem foul to those that win.

    [*The trumpet sounds. Enter* WORCESTER ⟨*and* VERNON.⟩]

  How now, my lord of Worcester! 'Tis not well
  That you and I should meet upon such terms   10
  As now we meet. You have deceived our trust
  And made us doff our easy robes of peace,
  To crush⁶ our old limbs in ungentle steel;
  This is not well, my lord, this is not well.
  What say you to it? will you again unknit   15
  This churlish knot of all-abhorréd war
  And move in that obedient orb⁷ again
  Where you did give a fair and natural light,
  And be no more an exhaled meteor,⁸
  A prodigy of fear and a portent   20
  Of broachéd mischief to the unborn times?⁹

WOR. Hear me, my liege:
  For mine own part I could be well content
  To entertain the lag end of my life
  With quiet hours, for I do protest   25
  I have not sought the day of this dislike.

KING. You have not sought it! how comes it then?

FAL. Rebellion lay in his way, and he found it.

PRINCE. Peace, chewet,¹ peace!

WOR. It pleased your majesty to turn your looks
  Of favor from myself and all our house,   30
  And yet I must remember² you, my lord,
  We were the first and dearest of your friends.
  For you my staff of office did I break
  In Richard's time, and posted day and night   35
  To meet you on the way and kiss your hand

---

3. Wooded.
4. I.e., the sun's illness or malevolence.
5. I.e., the sun's intentions; the southern wind supports them.
6. Enfold, cramp.
7. Regular orbit, as of a planet.
8. Meteors were thought to be made of gas exhaled by a planet and were commonly associated with civil commotion.
9. I.e., of harm or disaster opened up ("broached") to plague the future. Note that "mischief" conveyed a stronger meaning to Shakespeare than it does to us.
1. Chattering bird.
2. Remind.

When yet you were in place and in account
Nothing so strong and fortunate as I.
It was myself, my brother, and his son
That brought you home and boldly did outdare   40
The dangers of the time. You swore to us,
And you did swear that oath at Doncaster,
That you did nothing purpose 'gainst the state
Nor claim no further than your new-fall'n right,
The seat of Gaunt, dukedom of Lancaster.   45
To this we swore our aid. But in short space
It rained down fortune showering on your head
And such a flood of greatness fell on you,
What with our help, what with the absent king,
What with the injuries of a wanton time,   50
The seeming sufferances³ that you had borne,
And the contrarious winds that held the king
So long in his unlucky Irish wars
That all in England did repute him dead;
And from this swarm of fair advantages   55
You took occasion to be quickly wooed
To gripe the general sway⁴ into your hand,
Forgot your oath to us at Doncaster,
And being fed by us you used us so
As that ungentle gull⁵ the cuckoo's bird   60
Useth the sparrow, did oppress our nest,
Grew by our feeding to so great a bulk
That even our love durst not come near your sight
For fear of swallowing;⁶ but with nimble wing
We were enforced for safety sake to fly   65
Out of your sight and raise this present head,
Whereby we stand oppos'd by such means
As you yourself have forged against yourself
By unkind usage, dangerous countenance,⁷
And violation of all faith and troth   70
Sworn to us in your younger enterprise.
KING. These things indeed you have articulate,⁸
    Proclaimed at market crosses, read in churches,
    To face the garment of rebellión
    With some fine color that may please the eye   75
    Of fickle changelings and poor discontents,
    Which gape and rub the elbow at the news
    Of hurlyburly innovatión;
    And never yet did insurrection want
    Such water colors to impaint his cause,   80
    Nor moody beggars starving for a time
    Of pellmell havoc and confusión.
PRINCE. In both our armies there is many a soul

---

3. Sufferings.
4. Seize power over the whole state.
5. Rude nestling; the cuckoo hatches
its young in other birds' nests.

6. Being swallowed.
7. Threatening looks.
8. Drawn up in detail.

Shall pay full dearly for this encounter,
If once they join in trial. Tell your nephew   85
The Prince of Wales doth join with all the world
In praise of Henry Percy; by my hopes,
This present enterprise set off his head,[9]
I do not think a braver gentleman,
More active-valiant or more valiant-young,   90
More daring or more bold, is now alive
To grace this latter age with noble deeds.
For my part, I may speak it to my shame,
I have a truant been to chivalry—
And so I hear he doth account me too—   95
Yet this before my father's majesty:
I am content that he shall take the odds
Of his great name and estimátion,
And will, to save the blood on either side,
Try fortune with him in a single fight.   100

KING. And, Prince of Wales, so dare we venture thee,
Albeit considerations infinite
Do make[1] against it. No, good Worcester, no,
We love our people well; even those we love
That are misled upon your cousin's part;   105
And, will they take the offer of our grace,
Both he and they and you, yea, every man
Shall be my friend again and I'll be his.
So tell your cousin, and bring me word
What he will do; but if he will not yield,   110
Rebuke and dread correction wait on[2] us
And they shall do their office. So, be gone;
We will not now be troubled with reply.
We offer fair; take it advisedly.
        [*Exit* WORCESTER ⟨*and* VERNON.⟩]

PRINCE. It will not be accepted, on my life;   115
The Douglas and the Hotspur both together
Are confident against the world in arms.

KING. Hence, therefore, every leader to his charge,
For on their answer will we set on them,
And God befriend us, as our cause is just!   120
        [*Exeunt all but the* PRINCE *and* FALSTAFF.]

FAL. Hal, if thou see me down in the battle and bestride me, so;
    'tis a point of friendship.

PRINCE. Nothing but a colossus can do thee that friendship. Say
    thy prayers, and farewell.

FAL. I would 'twere bedtime, Hal, and all well.   125

PRINCE. Why, thou owest God a death.   [⟨*Exit.*⟩]

FAL. 'Tis not due yet; I would be loath to pay him before his day.
    What need I be so forward with him that calls not on me?
    Well, 'tis no matter; honor pricks me on. Yea, but how if honor

9. Deducted from his account.   2. Accompany.
1. Weigh.

prick me off when I come on? How then? can honor set to a ¹³⁰
leg? No. Or an arm? No. Or take away the grief of a wound?
No. Honor hath no skill in surgery, then? No. What is honor?
A word. What is in that word honor? what is that honor? Air.
A trim reckoning![3] Who hath it? He that died o' Wednesday.
Doth he feel it? No. Doth he hear it? No. 'Tis insensible,[4] ¹³⁵
then? Yea, to the dead. But will it not live with the living? No.
Why? Detraction will not suffer it. Therefore I'll none of it;
Honor is a mere scutcheon.[5] And so ends my catechism. [*Exit.*]

SCENE 2

[*Enter* WORCESTER *and* SIR RICHARD VERNON.]

WOR. O no, my nephew must not know, Sir Richard,
  The liberal and kind offer of the king.
VER. 'Twere best he did.
WOR.   Then are we all undone
  It is not possible, it cannot be,
  The king should keep his word in loving us;   5
  He will suspect us still and find a time
  To punish this offense in other faults.
  Suspicion all our lives shall be stuck full of eyes,
  For treason is but trusted like the fox
  Who, ne'er so tame, so cherished and locked up,   10
  Will have a wild trick of his ancestors;
  Look how we can, or sad or merrily,
  Interpretation will misquote our looks,
  And we shall feed like oxen at a stall,
  The better cherished, still the nearer death.   15
  My nephew's trespass may be well forgot;
  It hath the excuse of youth and heat of blood
  And an adopted name of privilege,[6]
  A harebrained Hotspur, governed by a spleen.
  All his offenses live upon my head   20
  And on his father's; we did train him on,
  And, his corruption being ta'en from us,[7]
  We, as the spring of all, shall pay for all.
  Therefore, good cousin, let not Harry know
  In any case the offer of the king.   25
VER. Deliver what you will; I'll say 'tis so.
  Here comes your cousin.
        [*Enter* HOTSPUR ⟨*and* DOUGLAS.⟩]
HOT. My uncle is returned;
  Deliver up my Lord of Westmoreland.
  Uncle, what news?   30
WOR. The king will bid you battle presently.[8]
DOUG. Defy him by the Lord of Westmoreland.

3. A fine totaling of the bill.
4. Not capable of being felt.
5. A coat of arms, as often put on a tombstone.
6. A nickname which gives him priv-ileges. "Spleen": impetuous temperament.
7. Being attributed to. "Train": entice.
8. Immediately.

HOT. Lord Douglas, go you and tell him so.

DOUG. Marry, and shall, and very willingly.   [*Exit.*]

WOR. There is no seeming mercy in the king.   35

HOT. Did you beg any? God forbid!

WOR. I told him gently of our grievances,
     Of his oath-breaking, which he mended thus,
     By now forswearing⁹ that he is forsworn;
     He calls us rebels, traitors, and will scourge   40
     With haughty arms this hateful name in us.
            [*Enter* DOUGLAS.]

DOUG. Arm, gentlemen, to arms! for I have thrown
     A brave defiance in King Henry's teeth,
     And Westmoreland, that was engaged,¹ did hear it,
     Which cannot choose but bring him quickly on.   45

WOR. The Prince of Wales stepped forth before the king,
     And, nephew, challenged you to single fight.

HOT. O, would the quarrel lay upon our heads,
     And that no man might draw short breath today
     But I and Harry Monmouth! Tell me, tell me,   50
     How showed his tasking?² seemed it in contempt?

VER. No, by my soul; I never in my life
     Did hear a challenge urged more modestly,
     Unless a brother should a brother dare
     To gentle exercise and proof of arms.   55
     He gave you all the duties of a man,
     Trimmed up your praises with a princely tongue,
     Spoke your deservings like a chronicle,
     Making you ever better than his praise
     By still dispraising praise valued with you;   60
     And, which became him like a prince indeed,
     He made a blushing cital³ of himself,
     And chid his truant youth with such a grace
     As if he mastered there a double spirit
     Of teaching and of learning instantly.   65
     There did he pause; but let me tell the world,
     If he outlive the envy of this day,
     England did never owe⁴ so sweet a hope,
     So much misconstrued in his wantonness.

HOT. Cousin, I think thou art enamoured   70
     On his follies; never did I hear
     Of any prince so wild a libertine.
     But be he as he will, yet once ere night
     I will embrace him with a soldier's arm,
     That he shall shrink under my courtesy.   75
     Arm, arm with speed; and, fellows, soldiers, friends,
     Better consider what you have to do
     Than I, that have not well the gift of tongue,

9. Swearing falsely.   3. Mention, recital.
1. Held as a hostage.   4. Own. "Wantonness": frivolity.
2. Challenge.

Can lift your blood up with persuasión.
    [*Enter a* MESSENGER.]
MESS. My lord, here are letters for you.   80
HOT. I cannot read them now.
  O gentlemen, the time of life is short!
  To spend that shortness basely were too long,
  If life did ride upon a dial's point,[5]
  Still ending at the arrival of an hour;   85
  And if we live, we live to tread on kings,
  If die, brave death when princes die with us!
  Now, for our consciences, the arms are fair,
  When the intent of bearing them is just.
      [*Enter another* MESSENGER.]
MESS. My lord, prepare; the king comes on apace.   90
HOT. I thank him that he cuts me from my tale,
  For I profess not talking; only this—
  Let each man do his best; and here draw I
  A sword whose temper I intend to stain
  With the best blood that I can meet withal   95
  In the adventure of this perilous day.
  Now, Esperance! Percy![6] and set on.
  Sound all the lofty instruments of war,
  And by that music let us all embrace;
  For, heaven to earth,[7] some of us never shall   100
  A second time do such a courtesy.
    [*The trumpets sound. They embrace and exeunt.*]

SCENE 3

[*The* KING *enters with his power. Alarum*[8] *to the battle.*
Then enter DOUGLAS *and* SIR WALTER BLUNT.]
BLUNT. What is thy name, that in the battle thus
  Thou crossest me? what honor dost thou seek
  Upon my head?
DOUG.   Know then, my name is Douglas,
  And I do haunt thee in the battle thus
  Because some tell me that thou art a king.[9]   5
BLUNT. They tell thee true.
DOUG. The Lord of Stafford dear[1] today hath bought
  Thy likeness, for instead of thee, King Harry,
  This sword hath ended him; so shall it thee,
  Unless thou yield thee as my prisoner.   10
BLUNT. I was not born a yielder, thou proud Scot,
  And thou shalt find a king that will revenge
  Lord Stafford's death.   [*They fight.* DOUGLAS *kills* BLUNT.]
    [*Enter* HOTSPUR.]

5. Hand of a clock; "still": always.
Hotspur's meaning (in lines 83–85)
is that a base life would be too long
even if it lasted only an hour.
6. Hope, Percy! (the family motto).
7. I.e., the odds are heaven to earth

that.
8. Trumpet signal.
9. Blunt and others are dressed to look
like the king.
1. Expensively.

HOT. O Douglas, hadst thou fought at Holmedon thus,
 I never had triumphed upon a Scot.   15
DOUG. All's done, all's won; here breathless lies the king.
HOT. Where?
DOUG. Here.
HOT. This, Douglas? No, I know this face full well;
 A gallant knight he was, his name was Blunt; 20
 Semblably furnished like the king himself.
DOUG. Ah fool, go with thy soul whither it goes!
 A borrowed title hast thou bought too dear;
 Why didst thou tell me that thou wert a king?
HOT. The king hath many marching in his coats. 25
DOUG. Now, by my sword, I will kill all his coats;
 I'll murder all his wardrobe, piece by piece,
 Until I meet the king.
HOT.   Up and away!
 Our soldiers stand full fairly for the day. [*Exeunt.*]
 [*Alarum. Enter* FALSTAFF *alone.*]
FAL. Though I could 'scape shot-free² at London, I fear the shot 30
here; here's no scoring but upon the pate. Soft, who are you?
Sir Walter Blunt; there's honor for you, here's no vanity! I
am as hot as molten lead, and as heavy too; God keep lead out
of me! I need no more weight than mine own bowels. I have
led my ragamuffins where they are peppered; there's not three 35
of my hundred and fifty left alive, and they are for the town's
end, to beg during life. But who comes here?
 [*Enter the* PRINCE.]
PRINCE. What, stand'st thou idle here? lend me thy sword;
 Many a nobleman lies stark and stiff
 Under the hoofs of vaunting enemies, 40
 Whose deaths are yet unrevenged; I prithee, lend me thy sword.
FAL. O Hal, I prithee give me leave to breathe awhile. Turk Greg-
ory³ never did such deeds in arms as I have done this day. I
have paid Percy, I have made him sure.
PRINCE. He is indeed, and living to kill thee. I prithee, lend me 45
 thy sword.
FAL. Nay, before God, Hal, if Percy be alive, thou get'st not
my sword; but take my pistol if thou wilt.
PRINCE. Give it me; what, is it in the case?
FAL. Aye, Hal; 'tis hot, 'tis hot; there's that will sack a city. 50
 [*The* PRINCE *draws it out, and finds it to be a bottle of
 sack.*]
PRINCE. What, is it a time to jest and dally now?
 [*He throws the bottle at him. Exit.*]
FAL. Well, if Percy be alive, I'll pierce him. If he do come in my
way, so; if he do not, if I come in his willingly, let him make a

---

2. Scot-free, without paying the bill at
a tavern; "scoring" continues the pun;
it means (1) marking up a charge;
(2) cutting with a sword.

3. Falstaff combines Pope Gregory
VII, of whom fantastic stories were
told, with "Turk" (the Turks were
noted for ferocity).

carbonado[4] of me. I like not such grinning honor as Sir Walter
hath; give me life, which if I can save, so; if not, honor comes ₅₅
unlooked for, and there's an end.   [*Exit.*]

SCENE 4

[*Alarum. Excursions.*[5] *Enter the* KING, *the* PRINCE, PRINCE
JOHN OF LANCASTER, *and* EARL OF WESTMORELAND.]

KING. I prithee,
    Harry, withdraw thyself; thou bleed'st too much.
    Lord John of Lancaster, go you with him.
LAN. Not I, my lord, unless I did bleed too.
PRINCE. I beseech your majesty, make up,[6]   ₅
    Lest your retirement do amaze your friends.
KING. I will do so.
    My Lord of Westmoreland, lead him to his tent.
WEST. Come, my lord, I'll lead you to your tent.
PRINCE. Lead me, my lord? I do not need your help,   ₁₀
    And God forbid a shallow scratch should drive
    The Prince of Wales from such a field as this,
    Where stained nobility lies trodden on,
    And rebels' arms triumph in massacres!
LAN. We breathe too long; come, cousin Westmoreland,   ₁₅
    Our duty this way lies; for God's sake, come.
        [⟨*Exeunt* PRINCE JOHN *and* WESTMORELAND.⟩]
PRINCE. By God, thou hast deceived me, Lancaster;
    I did not think thee lord of such a spirit.
    Before, I loved thee as a brother, John,
    But now I do respect thee as my soul.   ₂₀
KING. I saw him hold Lord Percy at the point
    With lustier maintenance than I did look for
    Of such an ungrown warrior.
PRINCE.   O, this boy
    Lends mettle to us all!   [*Exit.*]
        [*Enter* DOUGLAS.]
DOUG. Another king! they grow like Hydra's heads.[7]   ₂₅
    I am the Douglas, fatal to all those
    That wear those colors on them; what art thou,
    That counterfeit'st the person of a king?
KING. The king himself, who, Douglas, grieves at heart
    So many of his shadows thou hast met   ₃₀
    And not the very king. I have two boys
    Seek Percy and thyself about the field,
    But seeing thou fall'st on me so luckily
    I will assay thee; so defend thyself.
DOUG. I fear thou art another counterfeit,   ₃₅
    And yet, in faith, thou bearest thee like a king;
    But mine I am sure thou art, whoe'er thou be,

4. A cubed steak.
5. Brief appearances and exits of soldiers fighting.
6. Advance; "amaze": dismay.

7. The heads of this fabulous monster
grew back faster than they could be
cut off.

And thus I win thee.

    [*They fight; the* KING *being in danger, enter* PRINCE OF
    WALES.]

PRINCE. Hold up thy head, vile Scot, or thou art like

   Never to hold it up again! the spirits   40

   Of valiant Shirley, Stafford, Blunt, are in my arms;

   It is the Prince of Wales that threatens thee,

   Who never promiseth but he means to pay.

      [*They fight;* DOUGLAS *flieth.*]

   Cheerly, my lord; how fares your grace?

   Sir Nicholas Gawsey hath for succor sent,   45

   And so hath Clifton; I'll to Clifton straight.

KING. Stay, and breathe awhile.

   Thou hast redeemed thy lost opinión,

   And showed thou makest some tender of[8] my life

   In this fair rescue thou hast brought to me.   50

PRINCE. O God, they did me too much injury

   That ever said I hearkened for your death.

   If it were so, I might have let alone

   The insulting hand of Douglas over you,

   Which would have been as speedy in your end   55

   As all the poisonous potions in the world

   And saved the treacherous labor of your son.

KING. Make up to Clifton; I'll to Sir Nicholas Gawsey.   [*Exit.*]

     [*Enter* HOTSPUR.]

HOT. If I mistake not, thou art Harry Monmouth.

PRINCE. Thou speak'st as if I would deny my name.   60

HOT. My name is Harry Percy.

PRINCE.   Why then I see

   A very valiant rebel of the name.

   I am the Prince of Wales, and think not, Percy,

   To share with me in glory any more:

   Two stars keep not their motion in one sphere,[9]   65

   Nor can one England brook a double reign

   Of Harry Percy and the Prince of Wales.

HOT. Nor shall it, Harry, for the hour is come

   To end the one of us; and would to God

   Thy name in arms were now as great as mine!   70

PRINCE. I'll make it greater ere I part from thee,

   And all the budding honors on thy crest

   I'll crop to make a garland for my head.

HOT. I can no longer brook thy vanities.   [*They fight.*]

     [*Enter* FALSTAFF.]

FAL. Well said, Hal, to it, Hal! Nay, you shall find no boy's play   75

  here, I can tell you.

     [*Enter* DOUGLAS; *he fighteth with* FALSTAFF, *who falls
     down as if he were dead.* ⟨*Exit* DOUGLAS.⟩ *The* PRINCE
     killeth* PERCY.]

---

8. I.e., you have some concern for.   9. Orbit. "Brook": endure.
"Opinion": reputation.

HOT. O Harry, thou hast robbed me of my youth!
  I better brook the loss of brittle life
  Than those proud titles thou hast won of me;
  They wound my thoughts worse than thy sword my flesh;   80
  But thought's the slave of life, and life time's fool,
  And time, that takes survey of all the world,
  Must have a stop. O, I could prophesy,
  But that the earthy and cold hand of death
  Lies on my tongue; no, Percy, thou art dust,   85
  And food for—   [⟨*Dies.*⟩]
PRINCE. For worms, brave Percy; fare thee well, great heart!
  Ill-weaved ambition, how much art thou shrunk!
  When that this body did contain a spirit
  A kingdom for it was too small a bound,   90
  But now two paces of the vilest earth
  Is room enough; this earth that bears thee dead
  Bears not alive so stout[1] a gentleman.
  If thou wert sensible of courtesy,
  I should not make so dear[2] a show of zeal;   95
  But let my favors hide thy mangled face[3]
  And, even in thy behalf, I'll thank myself
  For doing these fair rites of tenderness.
  Adieu, and take thy praise with thee to heaven;
  Thy ignominy sleep with thee in the grave,   100
  But not remembered in thy epitaph!
    [*He spieth* FALSTAFF *on the ground.*]
  What, old acquaintance, could not all this flesh
  Keep in a little life? Poor Jack, farewell;
  I could have better spared a better man.
  O, I should have a heavy miss of thee,   105
  If I were much in love with vanity!
  Death hath not struck so fat a deer today,
  Though many dearer,[4] in this bloody fray.
  Emboweled will I see thee by and by;
  Till then in blood by noble Percy lie.   [*Exit.*]   110
FAL. [*rising up*] Emboweled! if thou embowel me today, I'll give
  you leave to powder[5] me and eat me tomorrow. 'Sblood, 'twas
  time to counterfeit, or that hot termagant[6] Scot had paid me
  scot and lot too. Counterfeit? I lie, I am no counterfeit; to die
  is to be a counterfeit, for he is but the counterfeit of a man   115
  who hath not the life of a man; but to counterfeit dying when
  a man thereby liveth is to be no counterfeit, but the true and
  perfect image of life indeed. The better part[7] of valor is discretion, in the which better part I have saved my life. Zounds, I
  am afraid of this gunpowder Percy, though he be dead; how if   120
  he should counterfeit too and rise? By my faith, I am afraid he
  would prove the better counterfeit. Therefore I'll make him

1. Valiant.
2. Open.
3. Prince Hal here covers Hotspur's face with a scarf.
4. Nobler. "Emboweled": embalmed.
5. Pickle.
6. Violent; "scot and lot": completely.
7. Quality, not "portion."

sure; yea, and I'll swear I killed him. Why may not he rise as
well as I? Nothing confutes me but eyes, and nobody sees me.
Therefore, sirrah [*stabbing him*], with a new wound in your 125
thigh, come you along with me.

[*He takes up* HOTSPUR *on his back.*]
[*Enter the* PRINCE *and* JOHN OF LANCASTER.]

PRINCE. Come, brother John, full bravely hast thou fleshed[8]
Thy maiden sword.

LAN.   But soft, whom have we here?
Did you not tell me this fat man was dead?

PRINCE. I did; I saw him dead,   130
Breathless and bleeding on the ground. Art thou alive?
Or is it fantasy[9] that plays upon our eyesight?
I prithee speak; we will not trust our eyes
Without our ears; thou art not what thou seem'st.

FAL. No, that's certain, I am not a double man; but if I be not 135
Jack Falstaff, then am I a Jack.[1] There is Percy [*throwing the
body down*]; if your father will do me any honor, so; if not, let
him kill the next Percy himself. I look to be either earl or duke,
I can assure you.

PRINCE. Why, Percy I killed myself and saw thee dead.   140

FAL. Didst thou? Lord, Lord, how this world is given to lying! I
grant you I was down and out of breath, and so was he; but we
rose both at an instant and fought a long hour by Shrewsbury
clock. If I may be believed, so; if not, let them that should reward valor bear the sin upon their own heads. I'll take it upon 145
my death, I gave him this wound in the thigh; if the man were
alive and would deny it, zounds, I would make him eat a piece
of my sword.

LAN. This is the strangest tale that ever I heard.

PRINCE. This is the strangest fellow, brother John.   150
Come, bring your luggage nobly on your back;
For my part, if a lie may do thee grace,
I'll gild it with the happiest terms I have.

[*A retreat is sounded.*]
The trumpet sounds retreat;[2] the day is ours.
Come, brother, let us to the highest[3] of the field,   155
To see what friends are living, who are dead.

[*Exeunt* ⟨PRINCE OF WALES *and* LANCASTER.⟩]

FAL. I'll follow, as they say, for reward. He that rewards me, God
reward him! If I do grow great,[4] I'll grow less, for I'll purge and
leave sack, and live cleanly as a nobleman should do. [*Exit.*]

SCENE 5

[*The trumpets sound. Enter the* KING, PRINCE OF WALES,
PRINCE JOHN OF LANCASTER, EARL OF WESTMORELAND,
with WORCESTER *and* VERNON *prisoners.*]

8. Initiated.
9. Illusion.
1. I.e., a worthless fellow.
2. The signal to stop pursuit of the
defeated enemy.
3. Highest part.
4. I.e., become "either earl or duke."
"Purge": take cleansing medicines.

KING. Thus ever did rebellion find rebuke.
  Ill-spirited Worcester, did not we send grace,
  Pardon, and terms of love to all of you?
  And wouldst thou turn our offers contrary,
  Misuse the tenor of thy kinsman's trust?   5
  Three knights upon our party slain today,
  A noble earl and many a creature else
  Had been alive this hour,
  If like a Christian thou hadst truly borne
  Betwixt our armies true intelligence.   10
WOR. What I have done my safety urged me to,
  And I embrace this fortune patiently,
  Since not to be avoided it falls on me.
KING. Bear Worcester to the death and Vernon too;
  Other offenders we will pause upon.   15
     [*Exeunt* WORCESTER *and* VERNON ⟨*guarded.*⟩]
  How goes the field?
PRINCE. The noble Scot, Lord Douglas, when he saw
  The fortune of the day quite turned from him,
  The noble Percy slain, and all his men
  Upon the foot of fear,[5] fled with the rest,   20
  And falling from a hill he was so bruised
  That the pursuers took him. At my tent
  The Douglas is, and I beseech your grace
  I may dispose of him.
KING.   With all my heart.
PRINCE. Then, brother John of Lancaster, to you   25
  This honorable bounty shall belong;
  Go to the Douglas and deliver him
  Up to his pleasure, ransomless and free;
  His valor shown upon our crests today
  Hath taught us how to cherish such high deeds   30
  Even in the bosom of our adversaries.
LAN. I thank your grace for this high courtesy,
  Which I shall give away immediately.
KING. Then this remains, that we divide our power.
  You, son John and my cousin Westmoreland,   35
  Towards York shall bend you with your dearest[6] speed
  To meet Northumberland and the prelate Scroop,
  Who, as we hear, are busily in arms;
  Myself and you, son Harry, will towards Wales
  To fight with Glendower and the Earl of March.   40
  Rebellion in this land shall lose his sway,
  Meeting the check of such another day;
  And since this business so fair is done,
  Let us not leave till all our own be won.   [*Exeunt.*]

1598

5. Fleeing in panic.   6. Greatest.

The Seventeenth Century

(1603-1660)

1603: Death of Elizabeth Tudor, accession of James Stuart.
1605: Gunpowder Plot: Guy Fawkes and the last desperate effort of Catholic extremists.
1620: First emigration of Pilgrims to the New World.
1625: Death of James I, accession of Charles I.
1642: Outbreak of the English Civil War; closing of the theaters.
1649: Execution of Charles I, beginning of Cromwellian Protectorate.
1660: End of the Protectorate, Restoration of Charles II.

"THIS OTHER EDEN"

An unnaturally farsighted Englishman who surveyed his circumstances in 1605 (looking backward and projecting forward in time, casting his eye outward through space) might well have congratulated himself and his nation on their peculiarly favored position. England had escaped early and relatively undamaged from the medieval turbulence of dynastic and regional feuds. The Wars of the Roses had been for the most part noblemen's squabbles, fought by little bands of knights and retainers in the semi-privacy of back fields; they were not wars of populations, with large-scale burning, looting, and cattle-killing, such as were commonplace on the Continent. And in 1485 the Tudor settlement had imposed the "king's peace" upon England so successfully that civil strife on any large scale did not occur in the 16th century. Under Henry VIII, the church too had undergone a relatively peaceful reformation, imposed from above and carried out below, with docility, if not always with enthusiasm, by populace and clergy. Thus the English church had entered on its historic "middle way," between Catholicism as practiced in Rome and Presbyterianism as practiced in Scotland; and this way it took, not violently or divisively, but through the typical English arts of compromise and consensus. Pacification had been, over the past hundred years, a notable tendency throughout England, in both church and state. In 1588 the social order was put to the test of the Spanish Armada, a test which it passed triumphantly, almost (it appeared to contemporaries) miraculously. Finally, in 1603, the peaceful and even popular accession of James Stuart, Elizabeth Tudor's

Scottish cousin, had seemed to assure the continuance of the same practical compromises and domestic discipline which had been so successful in the past.

Looking over at the Continent, our Englishman might shudder at visible evidence of the disasters which his country had happily escaped. Climaxing generations of religious strife, which was invariably bloody, fanatical, and destructive, the Thirty Years' War (1618–48) was about to break out in Germany, and it would shortly involve most other Continental countries. The French Protestants, known as Huguenots, were struggling desperately and dangerously for their existence. By fire and flood, the Dutch had just won a precarious independence from Spain; and the fragile prosperity of the Spanish golden age itself was just collapsing under the impact of an exploding inflation. Italy was prostrate and fragmented, Portugal in political and social decadence. Everywhere abroad political strife, religious dissension, and economic distress clouded the horizon. In England alone peace, harmony, and prosperity seemed to prevail, and their prevailing bore visible fruit. The English yeoman ate good beef, drank stout ale, and wore leather shoes, while his Continental counterpart ate black bread, drank sour wine, and wore wooden sabots. Such prosperity could not be undeserved. How could one doubt that God was preparing His Englishmen for some great and special destiny?

The island nation from which our speculative Englishman surveyed Europe with so much complacency was tightly organized into two coextensive and almost completely comprehensive bodies, the church and the state. Neither was threatened by visible enemies of any magnitude. A few dissenting voices might, indeed, be heard within the church; a certain number of English subjects even dared to exist outside the English church, maintaining their ancient allegiance to Rome. But the old Catholic families, though socially powerful, were politically torpid; and rash, radical Catholics, like Guy Fawkes (who formed the Gunpowder Plot, to blow up Parliament, in 1605), were without any popular support at all. There were also, within the church, a certain number of hyper-Protestant critics who wished to make the Reformation more thorough; they were first called "Presbyterians" and were just now coming to be called "Puritans" because of their desire to "purify" Anglican church discipline. But their numbers were small, their influence uncertain, and their energies largely devoted to reforming, not to replacing or rivaling the English church. Those who felt bitterly enough about the inadequacies of the Anglican discipline were free to go to Holland or America; and in 1620, the search for religious freedom actually began to lead men to the New World, though in negligible numbers. But by and large the English church, during the first part of the 17th century, was in reputable if not flourishing estate. It included some of the most learned scholars in the world; its faults of discipline and fabric were relatively venial; and its stability, under the Crown, must have seemed beyond challenge.

As for the political strength of the regime, it too must have seemed unshakable. For if there were a few Puritans in the church and an uncertain number of Catholics outside of it, there was no Englishman of the early 17th century who challenged the root idea of monarchy. Democracy was an idea as terrible as communism, from which it seemed to be only a stage removed. Nobody believed in liberalism, progress, or social change; in fact, the reformers of the age were vociferous in demanding a return to the original foundation of things. All the progress of this revolutionary age was to take place under the paradoxical battle cry of "back, back to the good old days." But this paradox was only latent in 1605, and the staunch, provincial conservatism of the English country gentleman must have seemed like a bulwark against radical social change of any sort.

To be sure, a few signs of truculent independence had appeared in the House of Commons during the last years of Elizabeth's reign. The Commons had shown an increasing tendency to take the order of business into their own hands, and to put off the government demands for "supply," i.e., fresh taxes, until certain grievances had been investigated. But these grievances did not seem, in 1605, like momentous matters. Various petty domestic monopolies, granted by the government to the detriment of local interests; a foreign policy rather too lenient toward Catholic Spain and not sufficiently vigorous in behalf of the Continental Protestants; an occasional greedy minister, a conniving churchman—who could suppose a revolt would some day spring from causes like these? Who could suppose that by midcentury the fabric of both church and state would be furiously rent? What possible reason could be found for anticipating that a kingdom, peaceable and settled for a century and a half, would suddenly depose a lawful monarch, cut off his head and his succession, set up a new tyranny and tear it down again in order to call back the murdered monarch's wandering son, and then finally eject the whole line for a second time less than thirty years after calling it back? Toward the end of the century Dryden remarked half-humorously that Englishmen were naturally crazy; once every twenty years, by natural instinct, they were bound to have a revolution. But this was true only in the 17th century; the 18th and 19th centuries were to be even more placid, dynastically, than the 16th.

CHURCH AND CONSTITUTION

The turmoil into which 17th-century England was so unexpectedly plunged involved basic issues of religious and political authority. The English church and the English state as they existed at the turn of the century were essentially authoritarian institutions, modified by the discretion of the Tudor monarchs. In an effort to disturb her subjects' religious consciences as little as possible, Queen Elizabeth and her bishops had tolerated a wide variety of opinions and even practices within the English church. In the state, too, authoritarianism concealed itself. The royal prerogative (that is, essentially, the royal privilege of taking independent action) had never been clearly defined, and it continued to be exercised, but Queen Elizabeth was careful not to alarm her subjects by acting in any serious matter without the advice and opinion of her council and of her predominantly loyal and obedient parliaments. The system in both church and state could be described as absolutism tempered by political discretion and deliberate vagueness.

But James and Charles Stuart possessed none of Elizabeth Tudor's tact and flexibility; James especially had a pedantic need for clarity, which was in the highest degree inexpedient politically. Both the Stuart kings tried to stamp out Presbyterianism, Puritanism, and all forms of dissent and organized protest within the church. They tried to impose new restrictions on a parliament already restive under the restraints which had become traditional under Elizabeth. Being consistent men, and devoid of political sense, they tended to see every minor grievance as an incipient case of treachery or heresy, to be vigorously repressed. But they did not have the machinery to carry out a policy of wholesale repression. The Puritans, forbidden to organize directly for the reform of the church, undertook a long-term program of indirect propaganda. They used the pulpit to preach, not the overthrow of the English church, but a new way of life, a life of godly, disciplined endeavor, of sober yet dedicated activity. Under strict Presbyterian discipline as Calvin had conceived it, this way of life would have been imposed on the entire population, by a potent mixture of lay and clerical authority, acting through individual church synods and local councils. Such a rigid system had in fact been installed in Geneva and in parts of Scotland. But in England, where the discipline could not be imposed from above (although the preachers were free to talk about it in a general way), it became the subject of popular agitation from below; and so each man formed his own idea of what the godly discipline would be like. While every man could see that the existing institution was faulty as compared with his private ideal, not very many reformers could appreciate that their own ultimate ideals were wildly incompatible with one another.

Thus the Puritan movement developed into a powerful destructive force, so far as its original enemy, the Anglican Church, was concerned; but as soon as that enemy was defeated (ca. 1642), the inner disagreements of Puritanism came to the surface. A national convention was called, known as the Westminster Assembly from its place of sitting in Westminster Hall. Convoked in 1643 to reform the national church of England, it sat for nearly six years; and the longer its members sat, the less they could agree upon. Meanwhile, in the country at large, sects, segments, and schisms multiplied. Arians, Baptists, Anabaptists, Shakers, Quakers, Diggers, Levelers, Fifth Monarchy Men, and many other groups of true believers proliferated. About 1643, a conservative Presbyterian named Thomas Edwards started to list them all in a book which he called, picturesquely, *Gangraena*. But history outran the historian. Even while the first volume of *Gangraena* was passing through the press, enough new sects sprang up to call for a second volume; and after a third volume, Edwards gave up in despair. Men who believed in a single unified national church were naturally distressed by the sects. But it would be a mistake to ignore the existence of a sizable body of Englishmen who rejoiced in the sectarian squabbles and even helped provoke them, because they frankly preferred either no church government at all or a very weak and docile one. These "Erastians" (so called from Thomas Erastus, a 16th-century Swiss theologian who advocated the supremacy of the state in ecclesiastical matters) were not a very vocal, or highly organized, or even a very active group. But of all parties, they were that for which the Puritan revolutionary movement held fewest heartaches. John Selden typified their cool unconcern. He often stopped by the Westminster Assembly to watch the assembled parsons quoting texts at one another; like the Persian princes, he said, he liked to see the wild asses fight.

From the beginning of the century, political opposition to the Stuart regime was concentrated among the lawyers and the gentry, that class of rural landlords which contributed so largely to the membership of Elizabeth's augmented House of Commons. Sporadic moves were made in the parliaments of James I to investigate particular abuses, and a determined fight was waged by lawyers and judges to maintain the supremacy of the common law against the aggressions of the ecclesiastical lawyers. But these were piecemeal and essentially defensive maneuvers; and gradually a concerted strategy was evolved for putting pressure on the king. The House of Commons simply refused to vote any taxes unless the king took steps toward a general reform of abuses in church and state. It is never hard or even unpleasant to refuse taxes. The last parliaments of James voted him less and less money. And almost from the day his son Charles I ascended the throne, the parliaments cut the king's income (not merely his personal income, but the whole budget of executive government) to a trickle. About 1630, Charles resolved to do without parliaments altogether, and for the next eleven years, he managed to govern through his own personal agencies. The two arms of his policy were the church, under Archbishop William Laud (1573–1645), and the army, under Thomas Wentworth, Earl of Strafford (1593–1641). Between themselves these two agents of the king's power referred laconically to the royal program as "Thorough." "Thorough" was royal absolutism, government without Parliament.

Lacking a regular income, which only Parliament could vote, Charles I and his aides were bound to improvise ways of levying money. Various medieval taxes, long since obsolete, were revived during the 1630's and put into effect because they did not require parliamentary approval. "Ship money" and "tonnage and poundage," two levies imposed by prerogative power, did something to fill the king's empty coffers; they also roused widespread fears that men's estates might be taken from them arbitrarily. Adding to these fears was the act of the administration in fostering the swift growth of ecclesiastical and prerogative courts. These courts, notably Archbishop Laud's revived and expanded Star Chamber, dispensed a speedier justice than the old courts of common law, a more arbitrary justice, and one more concerned with equity than with precedent. Any property owner looks with dismay upon a legal system which elevates equity above precedent. Thus disaffection grew throughout the land like a festering sore, though on the surface all remained placid.

The structure of "Thorough" was shaky at best, depending as it did on the almost unaided vigilance and energy of two highly placed men; in 1639 it was rocked by a rash effort to impose episcopal discipline on the strongly Presbyterian Scots. They reacted angrily by raising an army and invading England. Their aim was not to conquer; but they were well aware that they would have good friends in Parliament, if that were ever called into session. Charles had to call it; it was convened, refused to vote supplies, and was dissolved three weeks later, having earned the name of the Short Parliament. Its successor was convened within a year and sat for twenty years—earning the name of the Long Parliament. Strongly Puritan in feeling, it first acted to call Laud and Strafford to account. Both men were imprisoned and ultimately executed; the prerogative courts were abolished forever, "Thorough" was wiped from the face of the earth, and

Parliament began reforming the abuses in church and state about which many of its members had long been clamoring. As the reformers set enthusiastically to work, the king, despairing of his future with men so radical, left London and raised his banner at Nottingham. In August, 1642, open civil war broke out.

From a military point of view, the wars between the king and his Parliament were no equal contest. After a few preliminary successes, the king's forces were steadily ground down by the Parliament's superior money, manpower, and supplies. Actually, the greatest obstacle to Parliamentary victory was the divided loyalty of its military commanders. To most Englishmen there was something profoundly shocking in the idea of fighting against an anointed king to whom one had sworn eternal allegiance. What would one do if one met him on the battlefield—fire or kneel down and beg his pardon? But as always in civil wars, the more resolved and desperate men moved quickly to the fore. On the Parliamentary side, these shortly came to consist of soldiers the like of whom had never before been seen in English warfare. The Puritan regiments were no band of starveling cutthroats, out for plunder, pay, and drink; they carried Bibles in their pockets, and sang psalms before entering battle. But they were terrible agents of the Lord's will, who feared neither king nor bishop nor cavalry; and they defeated the royal armies with brutal ease. Before long the king himself was prisoner. But it was one thing to beat the king on the field and another thing to make peace with him. A treaty between the king and his Parliament was legally unthinkable, and in practice very difficult. Neither side really trusted the other, and after protracted negotiations, the Parliamentary leaders resolved to rid themselves of Charles Stuart, once and for all. Expelling its moderate members, the House of Commons reduced itself to a small minority of hard-core radicals (about 50 out of an original 325 members). This remainder, known derisively to its enemies as the Rump, constituted itself a court of justice, tried its sovereign as an enemy of the English people, and on January 30, 1649, had him beheaded. In a very direct way, this solved the problem of making peace with the king; but it left no clear or effective source of political power in England. For a short time, the Rump tried to govern on its own; but it proved incapable, and Cromwell took the power in his own hands, establishing what was, in effect, a military dictatorship—the Protectorate.

Thus the Puritan Revolution failed in its two major aims, of establishing responsible civil government and achieving a purified, uniform religious discipline. So long as Cromwell stayed in power, gaining military and diplomatic triumphs abroad, there was no changing the government. But as soon as Cromwell died in 1658, his regime started to weaken. Powerful forces in the community began secret negotiations with the government of Charles II, who had been in exile at Paris. Finally, in 1660, the new monarch and his court returned to take up the government of England. Out of retirement came the bishops, archbishops, deacons, and other Anglican officials. Parliamentary elections were called for and a new parliament convened. Charles II was crowned king of England in the ancient ritual. Evidently the *form* of Restoration government would be pretty much the same as before the wars. Time would show, however, that the Revolution and Civil Wars had altered the course of history very considerably. Neither church nor state could be returned to the pre-revolutionary condition. There remained a sizable body of Dissenters, who refused to return to the Anglican church. And the new Parliament, though loyal to the point of fanaticism, had no intention of allowing Charles II to think himself independent, as Charles I had done.

SOCIAL AND INTELLECTUAL TRENDS

The political and religious conflicts of the 17th century began as a search for certainty, and though often distracted from it, reverted at their finest moments to a conflict of intellectual principles. Terrifying as this conflict must have been, especially for men accustomed to the leisurely security of the Elizabethan state, it was responsible for the enormous intellectual vitality of the early 17th century. One can trace its impact in many fields of study. This was the great age of English polemical divinity. The art is lost today, but in its time it called forth vast learning, acuteness, and complexity of mind. In Hooker, Andrewes, Laud, Ussher, and Chillingworth, the English church boasted a group of controversialists before whom the greatest Catholic apologists of the age, Baronius and Bellarmine, might have paused in respect. And 17th-century learning was not confined to the clergy. A lawyer like Sir Edward Coke was more than a great lawyer, a great judge, even a great legal scholar; as a result of his studies he was able to recast the common law of England into a shape which it holds to this day. His friend John Selden was very likely the most learned man of his day; he was an Orientalist, a lawyer and legal historian, a rabbinical student, an editor, a scholar of heraldry, and an able parliamentarian. Other students of the past, famous in their day throughout Europe, were Sir Robert Cotton and William Camden. But the mind of the 17th century reached forward as well as backward, it was capacious as well as subtle. The most noted exponent of scientific method in the century was Francis Bacon. Edward Herbert, Thomas Hobbes, and James Harrington were philosophers of originality, whose thought exercised powerful influence on ages to come. Robert Boyle and William Harvey represent names well known in physical and medical research. William Gilbert laid open the principles of magnetism in a scientific classic published during the first year of the century; and in the last years of the Protectorate, John Wallis laid the foundations of the differential calculus. In most fields of intellectual activity, the first half of the 17th century was an age of reaching and grasping, of intellectual strain and fresh discovery.

For all its complexity of detail, the general development of English society during the period 1603–60 is simple enough to be described in a few phrases. A strict, inclusive, hierarchical, and authoritarian pattern of life was shattered. After a period of uncertainty and experiment, the old system was restored in a looser version, more spacious than any of the individual parties considered ideal, yet still rigid enough to preserve the fundamentals of private property, social order, and Christian control.

Politically and socially, the change accomplished by the Puritan Revolution was one of *degree*; government after the Restoration was like Elizabethan government, only more tolerant of differences. But culturally and intellectually, the change was one of *kind*, as far-reaching as any in the history of thought. The English community changed from one founded on the concepts of uniformity, hierarchy, and relation to one founded on the concepts of multiplicity, disparity, and toleration. Intellectually and imaginatively, the Commonwealth and Protectorate are a vast dividing line. Dryden spoke of the Elizabethans as "the giant race before the flood"; and he was right. In the quality of his imagination, in the structure of the world he took for granted, Dryden was farther removed from Shakespeare than Shakespeare was from Chaucer.

For the Elizabethan, when he looked at the world about him, viewed it (as had many a medieval philosopher before him) through the veil of a great nostalgia for order. In the Elizabethan view, every creature, from the highest archangel to the lowest worm, had his place in the great order of divine appointments; and by being a worm or an archangel to the height of his powers, he echoed forth the supreme goodness of the Almighty. Man was not only united to every other creature in the cosmos by a "great Chain of Being," which assigned to him a middle position, subordinate to some creatures and superior to others; within his own nature, some elements were superior to others. Reason, which ruled in man, made him natural lord over passion, which ruled—for example—in woman. The king was "head" of the body politic; in him reason ruled, as it ought, over the passionate and tumultuous multitude. Whether one looked high or low on the great Chain of Being, one found that the universal principle of analogy rendered all modes and levels of existence systematically correspondent to one another. The king was to his subjects as Michael was to the other archangels, as the bishop was to his pastors, as the Archbishop of Canterbury was to his bishops, as the lion was to other beasts, as the eagle was to other birds, as the diamond was to other stones, as gold was to other metals. Within every category and species, there was an order of excellence; and though the noblest lion was less than the lowest man, yet he was a monarch of his species. That the king was "father of his country" was a metaphor, to be sure; but that a father was "king of his family" was also a metaphor, and both were metaphors derived from the central fact that God the Father was King of Kings.

Now a world view like this, insubstantial as it appears to modern reason, offered many securities and assurances. In Elizabethan minds, it seems to have existed halfway between a fact and a hope. Shakespeare caused Ulysses to expound it dramatically but inconclusively in that puzzling, bitter tragicomedy, *Troilus and Cressida*. Raphael explained it to Adam in Milton's *Paradise Lost* (V.469–505), but of course he was speaking of the universe before the Fall. It was less a description of fact than an ideal.

During the 17th century, this world view came under attack from two main directions and was substantially demolished. The Puritans seized on the ancient doctrine of the Christian calling, and with their usual emphasis on a direct relation between God and the individual soul, declared that every man must decide for himself what God intended him to have as his "calling" on earth. If he thought the squire, or the constable, or King Charles I was a sinner, the Puritan's calling required him to oppose that sinner with might and main. Across the fine strands of analogy and hierarchy which bound together an earlier cosmos, the Puritan brushed a rougher, simpler division, a division between saints and sinners, between those who are of God's party and those who are of Satan's. The older social creed was shattered by that of an individual seeker, a fighter.

The other enemy of the Elizabethan world view, less hostile by intent, but more deadly in its ultimate effects, was scientific method. Most 17th-century scientists were pious men, who shrank from the idea that their work might harm religion. And yet Galileo's validation of Copernicus' theory—that the sun, the other stars, and the planets did not all revolve around the earth—wrought havoc in the analogical universe. It rendered conceivable a plurality, perhaps even an infinity of worlds; and so destroyed the symmetry of this one. Conversely, men came to think it most improbable that the God who created the universe of intergalactic space was so fanciful as to make this world along the intricate ingenious lines envisaged by the Elizabethans.

The analogical universe, informed with moral meaning, largely disappeared, then, in the course of the 17th century; and though God did not forthwith disappear from the universe, He withdrew behind it. He had been constantly at man's elbow, issuing (through His signatures in the natural world) veiled warnings, encouragements, demands; He was to become personally remote, yet powerful in His established laws, like the architect of an ancient house.

The tendency of 17th-century thought was to dissociate God increasingly from the intimate texture of the world, its day-to-day functioning. The growing scientism of the age tended also to dissociate the world of man's thought from that of his feeling. Astrology gave way to astronomy, alchemy to chemistry, and the immense corpus of "curious learning," accumulated from generation to generation, and cherished less because it was presumed true than because it was thought instructive, was subjected to the cruel test of fact. The new science enabled the scientist to understand the world better, and to manipulate it more accurately, than ever before; but it deprived the ordinary man of a structure, a framework, a set of ordered directives for his life. The test of truth gradually changed, under the double impulsion of scientific method and prolonged, inconclusive sectarian conflict, from conformity with a large-scale view, philosophical or religious, to conformity with experimental data, manipulative fact. "The truth" became something objective, public, general, impersonal; a man's private insights, the feelings of a poet, an "enthusiast," an individual, were something secondary. T. S. Eliot has described the sort of divorce between thought and feeling which he feels the 17th century inaugurated as the work of Dryden and Milton; but in fact the names of these poets are mere symbols for vast processes, anonymous and ill-defined, which affected the intellectual weather of the age. The pursuit of the heavenly kingdom gave way to the pursuit of earthly prosperity; the ideal of strenuous intellectual and spiritual effort gave way to the ideal of gentlemanly good taste; the rule of the saints gave way to the rule of the well-to-do and respectable. Truth, instead of standing on a rough, high hill up which each man must find his own difficult way (cf. Donne, *Satire III*, lines 79–82), became plain, natural, easy, and common to all. Wit, instead of being serious intellectual work, became the pointed enunciation of commonplaces.

For, tied in with all these intellectual and spiritual changes, and very likely underlying them, is a single social shift of immense import. England in the course of the 17th century became increasingly bourgeois. The City tradesman, who was a figure of ridicule and contempt for Ben Jonson and Shakespeare (in different manifestations he is Bottom the Weaver in *A Midsummer Night's Dream* and Corbaccio the Crow in *Volpone*), became by the century's end a respectable member of the cultured community. During the last half of the 17th century, chivalry faded as an ideal, and pragmatic common sense flourished. The courtier, like Sir Philip Sidney (1554–86) gave way, as the characteristic leader of his society, to an 18th-century Whig landlord with good commercial connections in the City. The word "Whig," which first came into prominence in the last years of the 17th century, connotes all sorts of particulars, both as to creed and social position. Broadly, it implies a landed oligarchy, closely allied with the money power; jealous of the royal prerogative and hostile to popular democracy; strong for property rights and gradual social evolution; Low-Church or latitudinarian in religion, and protectionist in its economic policies. But to be ruled by Whigs is to be ruled frankly by an interest, not a principle.

As it advanced toward the 18th century, England changed markedly its social tone. The ancient and indigenous art of madrigal-singing died out. Henry Purcell, England's last composer of note before Sir Edward Elgar, died in 1695; and the English musical tradition was replaced by professionals imported from Germany and Italy, and by the hymns of Isaac Watts and John Wesley. The Maypoles were torn down throughout England, the fairy legends were dismissed as idle or sinful, the folk culture fell under blighting disapproval. Middle-class antipathy for the stage, though deeply rooted and of long standing, was less immediate in its destructive effects; yet by 1700, as a regular way for a writer to make a reputable living, the stage had all but ceased to exist. During the great age of English drama, the stage and the court (closely allied as they were) had represented the main sources from which a writer could anticipate reward for his work. (Jonson and Dryden, the two professional authors of the 17th century, wrote primarily for the stage and the court; a man like Milton, who could appeal to neither, went substantially unrewarded.) But after the exile of the house of Stuart, in 1688, England was governed for better than a century by monarchs who spoke English only as a second language. Thus royal patronage for literature dried up. Lacking court patronage and a dependable source of theatrical income, authors betook themselves to hack work or hired out to political parties. The immediate result of either choice was a definite lowering of literary tone.

The suppression of "pagan superstitions" like Maypoles and folk songs, the cold hand of morality laid on the stage, the instituting of the glum English Nonconformist Sunday, all suggest a new if rather grim power in religion as a repressive force. No doubt it was so. But in matters of money, in their power to censure or direct economic matters, the clergy had lost ground. The advent of large-scale banking and joint-stock enterprise removed much economic conduct from the realm of personal behavior; in addition, the idea of clerical interference in the nation's economic life called forth hateful memories of Laud and "Thorough." Thus the power of clergymen to adjudicate economic matters shrank, as their power over personal life, of the lower orders in particular, grew. On balance, this was no gain for the men of the cloth. There was much more talk at the end of the century regarding "contempt of the clergy" than there had been in 1600.

The alliance of physical science and the money interest was a supreme social fact at the end of the century. Material improvements, like street-lighting, canals, water supplies, coal mines, banking facilities, and good roads, were matters of general concern in 1700, as dynastic diplomacy, the rise and fall of royal favorites, and ecclesiastical intrigues had been the characteristic concerns of 1600. Behind the dramatic clash of Anglican and Puritan, behind the comings and goings of the house of Stuart, behind the slogans and heroisms associated with the rise and fall of Cromwell, one notes the steady growth in influence of the power of money as against the power of land. (This process is never clearcut, because money is always transforming itself into land by the simple process of purchase; but the struggle can usefully be thought of as new money and new land asserting themselves against old land and the authority that goes with it.) What the 17th century was busy consolidating was that Whig oligarchy which was to rule England almost uninterruptedly from the Glorious Revolution of 1688 till the Reform Bill of 1832.

THE ELIZABETHAN LITERARY HERITAGE

The 17th century naturally inherited a full quota of literary genres and traditions from the previous age. No clearcut line separates the drama produced under James and Charles Stuart from that produced under Elizabeth Tudor, though during the first thirty years of the century, tragicomedy, pastoral romance, and the masque grew steadily in popularity. The trage-dies of John Ford, John Webster, and Cyril Tourneur are dark and horrify-ing productions, shot through with moments of powerful poetic statement. The great comic artist of the age was of course Ben Jonson, though many of his later plays were described unkindly as his "dotages." After the the-aters were closed (by the Puritans in 1642) and reopened (by Charles II in 1660), taste turned to broad sexual comedy (William Wycherley, *The Country Wife*) or to the comedy of manners (George Etherege, *The Man of Mode, or Sir Fopling Flutter*); while tragedy assumed the pompous, in-flated manner known as "heroic tragedy."

The Elizabethans had rung most of the available changes on the sonnet of courtly or romantic love, and 17th-century sonneteers tuned their in-struments to new pitches—devotion for Donne, politics for Milton. After undergoing a number of interesting vocational variations (fishermen's eclogues, shoemakers' eclogues, and the like), the pastoral reached high-water mark in *Lycidas* (1637); and throughout the middle years of the century, religious and meditative lyrics expanded sharply in importance. The Elizabethan lyric, generally gay and musical, grew graver though no less melodious under the Stuarts; the ode, the elegy, and the epigram, forms deliberately modeled on classical originals, enjoyed the periodic re-vivals one would anticipate in an age of great classical scholarship, and underwent interesting adaptations by Ben Jonson, John Donne, and Abraham Cowley. As the lyric impulse gradually faded, discursive and social modes of poetry came to the fore. A major development in verse genres was the advent of formal satire, which began about 1590 and de-veloped steadily until it became the literary mode most characteristic of the Restoration and early 18th century. Though exploited with complete success only by Milton, the epic retained its traditional position as the supreme literary form. But Milton's use of blank verse for nondramatic poems was a major technical innovation, which would be emulated, not only in future epics, but in discursive and narrative poems of many different sorts. Another major technical development was the gradual emergence, after many hesitant and uncoordinated steps, of the heroic couplet, that razor-sharp, double-edged weapon which Dryden handled with such cool assurance.

In prose, though the 17th century inherited a number of traditional forms, it had to invent several more; for prose, in the early stages of a culture, generally develops more slowly and with greater difficulty than verse. Long before 1600 the design and pattern of a sermon had been pretty thoroughly worked out; so had some techniques of religious controversy and various modes of devotional and meditative prose. Elsewhere relatively little had been accomplished in English prose. Setting aside chronicles and other such compilations, there were few distinguished histories in English before Edward Hyde, first Earl of Clarendon, began his *History of the Rebellion* in 1650; even fewer full-length English biographies before Izaak Walton began his biography of John Donne in 1640; no informal English essays before Francis Bacon began his in 1597; no character sketches before Joseph Hall produced his in 1608. In all these genres, the 17th century had by 1660 produced, not simply examples, but masterpieces. Yet the 17th century was not, in prose any more than in verse, an age of startling novelties. Most of the genres which it introduced into English had a history in other languages. Even in the matter of prose style, the 17th century built on foundations solidly laid by the craftsmen of two centuries. The great work of the 17th-century prose writers was to enrich, diversify, perhaps even to individualize English style. They applied their native tongue to science and philosophy, and made of it an instrument as precise as Latin; they applied it to meditative and speculative themes, and found it richly expressive. They applied it to the work of political and social persuasion, and created a practical common-sense prose idiom. In only two major areas is the period substantially barren. Perhaps feeling that "mere fables" failed to meet the urgent needs of the age, the early 17th century created next to no prose fiction. And, apparently not needing to do so, the writers of the age created no literary criticism of significance. Jonson is the only notable critic in the early century; and he writes no essays, only notebook entries. Milton's criticism, often suggestive, is more often a simple rationalization of his own practice; and Thomas Hobbes belongs, by influence and affinity, to the Restoration. In both fiction and criticism, then, the writers of the 17th century inherited more from the age of Elizabeth than they transmitted to that of Charles II.

But if they did not expound very much original criticism, the writers of the early 17th century clung all the more earnestly to critical standards which they had inherited; and in reading their poetry, it is important to bear in mind some of the ideals which helped to shape it. However contradictory they seem, the age took them seriously and knew how to reconcile them artfully. One major ideal was that of *copia* or fullness; a poet was expected to have a full supply of imagery, based on traditional knowledge, with which to render his subject graphic and vivid. The epic poet, particularly, was expected to be a man of universal learning; he must know all the arts and sciences of war and peace, in order to display the ideal man in action. In addition to this discursive knowledge, the poet was expected also to show individual ingenuity and acuteness of mind. The word "originality" did not yet exist in criticism; but all men agreed that the poet's imagery must be fresh and unhackneyed—some even thought that it might be his proper function to surprise. Yet an ideal of stylistic chastity also prevailed; not only were many 17th-century poems notably restrained in the matter of decoration, those which fell into the trap of over-ingenuity were often subjected to cruel mockery. Even with regard to a matter as simple as harmony, contradictory standards stood side by side. Poets like Spenser and Shakespeare were praised enthusiastically for writing smooth and mellifluous verse; other poets, like Donne and George Chapman, were praised with equal enthusiasm for writing deliberately rough and difficult lines.

The key to these apparent contradictions lies in the important 17th-century concept of decorum. Socially, "decorum" is propriety or sedateness. But in its critical context the word was used in the 17th century to describe what was fitting, seemly, or in keeping with the particular poetic kind, or genre. Thus rough lines were decorous in a satire, because the satire was supposed to be spoken by a rough, discontented person, intent on telling rough truths. But these same lines would be thoroughly indecorous in a traditional love poem. Some of Donne's roughest and bawdiest poems may thus be described as perfect examples of decorum—style, subject, imagery, occasion, and imagined speaker are all of a piece. One need not think the concept of decorum an ultimate answer to all questions of literary tone, style, and structure to see that because of the great variety of recognized poetic kinds, it granted the poets of the 17th century a remarkable range of literary freedoms only vaguely tempered by responsibility. More elaborate critical doctrines have sometimes accomplished less.

METAPHYSICAL, CAVALIER, AND SPENSERIAN POETRY

The early 17th century was an age of intellectual conflict. Men sought for certainty, not just because it was pleasant to have, but because on it they could build structures of compulsion; they exploded other men's certainties to event them from erecting other structures. It was an age of intellectual mine and countermine.

The poetry of the age represents several distinct responses to this universal search for certainty. "Metaphysical" poetry, that written by John Donne and his followers, is so called for a curious complex of irrelevant reasons; the adjective was not even invented until Samuel Johnson published his *Life of Cowley* in 1779, many years after all the metaphysical poets were dead. But it has caught on, because it implies what no reader of John Donne can fail to recognize in an instant—that his is a sinewy, searching style, rooted in the conception of a "difficult" image often derived from Scholastic concepts. Its larger structure is that of an argument; its tone is frequently paradoxical. It tries to reach through conventional ideas, beyond the mere surface of things, by sheer force of intellectual energy. This is characteristic of the whole metaphysical school. The basic idiom of metaphysical poetry is daring, colloquial, and passionate; its meter is often deliberately rough, with many short syllables irregularly spaced, as in the rhythms of everyday speech. This poetry delights in ingenious, knotty, many-sided metaphors, which the age itself referred to as "conceits."

The word "conceit" derives, not from the notion of egotism in the author, but from the Italian *concetto*; it is most closely allied to the English "concept." In this sense, it is an almost separable unit of intellectual or verbal ingenuity, which occurs in a poem but can be detached from it and appreciated separately. A frequent early form was the conventional physical comparison of the Petrarchan sonnet (one's mistress has eyes like diamonds, lips like cherries, hair like golden wire, and so forth). The most famous conceit in English verse is doubtless the comparison of two separated lovers to the legs of a compass, which occurs at the end of Donne's *Valediction: Forbidding Mourning*. Even bolder is the conceit by Richard Crashaw which describes Christ as clad in the garment of his own blood, which has been taken from the purple wardrobe on his side (*On Our Crucified Lord, Naked and Bloody*). These are extreme examples of the conceit—the latter example is grotesque. Metaphysical poetry, with its restless intellectual manner, found the witty, exaggerated conceit particularly useful as a means of making complex, compressed assertions about a world which appeared divided if not fragmented, and of displaying at the same time the individuality of the poet. The metaphysical conceit is often consciously odd and far-fetched; hence it takes some getting used to. But its ultimate effect is one of highly compressed, sharply angled perspectives on an object of contemplation, glittering and intellectually provocative.

The second major poetic school was conservative rather than extravagant. Poets who had no taste for exploding the Elizabethan decorative image into a metaphysical conceit tended to chasten it, under classical influence, into a correct and restrained mode of verse quite new to English literary experience. Pruning off the redundant modifiers and subordinate grammatical clauses, eliminating the Spenserian surplus of expletives ("doth run," "do eat," and the like), and cutting down on a profusion of unaccented syllables and run-on lines, Ben Jonson and his followers produced verse which had the special Latin quality of being "lapidary." At its best their poetry gave the impression of being written to be carved in marble. Restrained in feeling, deliberately limited in its subject matter, intellectually thin but meticulously clear and incisive in expression, the poems of Jonson are models of this style. A song like *Queen and Huntress*, or *Still To Be Neat*, or *Drink to Me Only* is unadorned to the point of plainness, chaste in its diction, and silvery-pure in its feeling. It is strong syntactically—i.e., closely knit in its grammar—as a poem by Donne is strong metaphorically. One of the few critical terms in which the age had any confidence was "strong lines." On the whole, the early 17th century liked strong lines; and though it did not distinguish them clearly, liked them strong in two very different ways. Jonson's poems were strong in their compressed and muscular syntax; Donne's through the energy of their startling and far-reaching conceits.

Influential as it has proved in the 20th century, the metaphysical school of Donne by no means overpowered the 17th century. It had something of a vogue in what we would call the "intellectual circles" of the early century; but being at its best subtle and allusive, it was almost always a private and, one might almost say, unsocial poetry. Between 1600 and 1900, it is only a rare and unusually catholic critic like Coleridge, who will be found suggesting that its virtues outweighed its defects.

The severe, restrained style of Ben Jonson, on the other hand, proved one of the root inspirations for poets of the later 17th and 18th centuries. To be sure, the sort of beautifully phrased but social and conventional poem which Jonson wrote had a tendency in the hands of lesser practitioners to reduce itself to the elegant verbal trifle. Many of the "Sons of Ben," disciples who gathered round Jonson during the 1620's and early 1630's, spent their energies on these gallant, fluffy compliments; and a certain group of them (Lovelace, Herrick, Carew, Waller, Suckling) have been memorialized by literary historians under the name of "the Cavalier poets." Still, if gentlemen had less and less to express as the century advanced, the polished Jonsonian style offered them more and more elegant ways to express it. At their best, the Cavalier poets wrote poems of unexampled neatness. And the "reforming of our numbers" (that is, the polishing of English metrics) accomplished by Cavalier poets like Edmund Waller and Sir John Denham paved the way for many of the achievements of Dryden and his followers during the Restoration and 18th century.

The metaphysical style of Donne and the neoclassical style of Jonson are two characteristically 17th-century developments of poetic art; and most poets of the early century wrote in one (or occasionally both) of these styles. But a third strain persists well into the century, of Spenserian or post-Spenserian style. Most of the post-Spenserians are not distinguished poets at all. William Browne of Tavistock produces something very close to doggerel, and the brothers Fletcher (Giles and Phineas) are scarcely more important than he as literary artists. But this relatively old-fashioned Spenserian manner, surviving past its time into the 17th century, bore fruit when Milton grafted onto it his own highly individual style. Allegorical romance, imbued with moral feeling and narrated in ornate verse, was the essence of the Spenserian manner. Milton may have adopted it as a flexible vehicle, capable of absorbing the immense burden of his classical learning; or he may have thought it the best model for a narrative poet, who must work to a large scale, in a steady and uniform style. In any event, he enriched the manner with formal diction and rhetorical patterns, stiffened it with strict Latin syntax, and, liberating it from rhyme and stanza, taught it to branch out boldly into verse paragraphs. All these developments were to have an enormous and permanent influence on English poetry.

PROSE: GORGEOUS, DIGNIFIED, AND PLAIN

As it became steadily less ornate in the course of the century, prose became steadily more practical, popular, and common-sense. A spectacular development of the age of Elizabeth was the use of gorgeous and gallant devices in prose. Writers were fascinated by old saws and wise adages, by puns, parallels, alliterations; they rejoiced in new and fancy coinages. This highly adorned and artificial prose style, called "Euphuism," was not much more than a courtier's freak. But it had more enduring analogues in the witty and conceited style of pulpit oratory which prevailed for a while at the beginning of the century. Men like Lancelot Andrewes and John Donne preached to sophisticated and learned auditories, who were quick to catch a Greek, Latin, or Hebrew allusion, avid after ingenious puns, and delighted by a display of metaphorical fireworks or intellectual gymnastics. The preachers responded with fantastic shows of verbal virtuosity. Long, rolling periods, complex metaphors, Latinate construction, formal balance, and florid, deliberate flights of rhetorical fancy are found in the prose of Jeremy Taylor, even after the Restoration, when a chaster diction and more conversational tone had come into general use.

A great master of gorgeous, learned prose in English was John Milton. Much of his prose work is devoted to controversy, and this material cannot be read today without profound discomfort. Heavily armored with Latin and learning, Milton did not have a mind or a style flexible enough for controversy. In the field of polemical journalism lesser men, with a shrewder sense of how to appeal to the popular mind, could write rings around him. But when he fancied himself mounted upon such a rostrum as the ancient Athenian Areopagus, a free citizen of a free nation, delivering his mind freely to the citizens at large on a matter of public moment, his style and his thought took on a nobility for which his own age, and ours, do not furnish many parallels. When he is worthy of himself, Milton the prose-writer pours forth an impetuous, complicated rhetoric, in which the complexity and learning of the mind do not seem like irrelevant distractions, far less like hampering armor; they are marks of genuine authority.

But gorgeous prose, with its emphasis on rhetorical figures and external decoration, stood clearly apart from the main intellectual concern of the 17th century—the search for grounds of certainty. The real work of forging intellectual tools for use in the everyday work of exposition and persuasion demanded a less elaborate, a less distracting diction. Repeated experiments in simple prose, throughout the century, testify to the need for clear, accurate, persuasive communication. Bacon was particularly conscious of the need for a natural, informal style, and made the *Essays* into examples of it. The root inspiration here is the condensed, aphoristic manner characteristic of Seneca, the Roman philosopher. Bacon does not really succeed in molding a smooth or consecutive prose style out of his successive aphorisms. Each individual sentence has the air of starting afresh and ending abruptly before it is really under way. But it is forceful, and above all it is clear writing.

All varieties of English prose met their supreme test in the Civil War. The powerful poetic metaphors of Biblical style stirred the hearts and souls of men to great imaginings. Their plain English common sense, on the other hand, tested these dreams against considerations of homely, down-to-earth realism. One outcome of the popular discussion of public issues was the rise of periodical journalism—communication reduced to the lowest common denominator. A happier result was a certain lustiness and amplitude about the post-Restoration English prose styles. Never pruned, clipped, or formalized by an official academy, English prose grew by taking over metaphors from farm and forge, from shop and barn. It grew too by adapting itself to the casual rhythms and unpretentious periods of colloquial speech. This **extraordinary** fusion of elements—the colloquial with the elegant, the learned with the vulgar, the taut with the casual—distinguishes the prose style of Jonathan Swift, and marks the end toward which 17th century prose is moving.

JOHN DONNE
(1572–1631)

1601: Secret marriage to Ann More.
1615: Sacred orders.
1633: First publication of *Songs and Sonnets*.

There are two distinct but related authors known as John Donne. First is the scandalous young spark, who wrote bawdy and cynical verses—Jack Donne, the rake. Then there is the gravely witty, passionately religious divine, who wrote verses to his God as ardent as those he had once addressed to his mistresses. This is Dr. John Donne, the Dean of St. Paul's. Yet the key to both men is the same; it is a kind of restless, searching energy, which scorns the easy platitude and the smooth, empty phrase; which is vivid, immediate, troubling; and which makes the reading of Donne's poetry an imaginative and intellectual struggle and an all-absorbing experience.

Donne was born into an old Roman Catholic family, at a time when anti-Catholic feeling in England was near its height. His faith barred him from many of the usual avenues of success, and his point of view was always that of an insecure outsider. Though he attended both Oxford and Cambridge Universities, as well as Lincoln's Inn (where barristers got their training), he never took any academic degrees and never practiced law. After quietly abandoning Catholicism some time during the 1590's, he had scruples about becoming an Anglican. He had no gift for commerce, and though he inherited money from his father (who died when Donne was only 4), it was far from enough to render him independent. Hence he had to make his way in the world indirectly—by wit, charm, learning, valor, and above all, favor. Partly from sheer intellectual curiosity, he read enormously in divinity, medicine, law, and the classics; he wrote to display his learning and wit. He traveled on the Continent, especially, it would seem, to Spain; even in later years, he was an inveterate voyager. With Ralegh and Essex he took part in two hit-and-run expeditions against Cadiz and the Azores. He put himself in the way of court employment, danced attendance on great court ladies, and generally lived the life of a brilliant young man hopeful of preferment.

When in 1598 Donne was appointed private secretary to Sir Thomas Egerton, the Lord Keeper, his prospects for worldly advancement seemed good. He sat in Elizabeth's last parliament and moved in court circles. But in 1601 he secretly married Lady Egerton's niece, 16-year-old Ann More, and thereby ruined his own worldly hopes. The marriage turned out happily, but Donne's imprudence was never forgiven. Sir George More had Donne imprisoned and dismissed from his post; and for the next dozen years, the poet had to struggle at a series of makeshift employments to support his growing family. As a man of 35, Donne was no longer the brilliant young gallant of the 1590's; sick, poor, and unhappy, he was composing, but not publishing, a treatise on the lawfulness of suicide (*Biathanatos*). As he approached 40, he was engaged with Thomas Morton, Dean of Gloucester, in composing anti-Catholic polemics (*Pseudo-Martyr*, 1610; *Ignatius his Conclave*, 1611). In return for patronage from Sir Robert Drury, he wrote in 1611 and 1612 a pair of long poems, *The Anniversaries*, on the death of Sir Robert's daughter Elizabeth. None of these activities represent a full employment of Donne's volcanic intellectual energy. To be sure, Donne's social position need not be painted too blackly. He had friends among the courtiers, politicians, poets, and clergy—Mrs. Magdalen Herbert and her sons George and Edward, Ben Jonson, Sir Henry Goodyere, and Sir Henry Wotton among them. He was never quite without resources. Yet, broadly speaking, the middle years of Donne's life were a period of searching, uncertainty, and unhappiness.

Though Donne had flatly refused in 1607 to take Anglican orders, King James was certain that he would some day make a great Anglican preacher. Hence he declared that Donne could have no preferment or employment from him, except in the church. Finally, in 1615, Donne overcame his scruples, not the least of which was the fear of seeming ambitious, and entered the ministry. He was promptly appointed Reader in Divinity at Lincoln's Inn. In the 17th century, among court circles and at the Inns of Court where lawyers congregated, preaching was at once a form of spiritual devotion, an intellectual exercise, and a dramatic entertainment. Donne's metaphorical style, bold erudition, and dramatic wit at once established him as a great preacher in an age of great preachers. Fully 160 of his sermons survive. In 1621 he was made Dean of St. Paul's, where he preached to great congregations of "City" lawyers, courtiers, merchants, and tradesmen. In addition, his private devotions were published in 1624, and he continued to write sacred poetry till the very end of his life. Obsessed with the idea of death, Donne preached what was called his own funeral sermon just a few weeks before he died, and is supposed to have written the last, and one of the greatest, of his poems on his deathbed. He even had his portrait painted in his shroud.

The poetry of Donne represents a sharp break with that written by his predecessors and most of his contemporaries. Much Elizabethan verse is decorative and flowery in its quality. Its images adorn, its meter is mellifluous. Image harmonizes with image, and line swells almost predictably into line. Donne's poetry, on the other hand, is written very largely in *conceits*—concentrated images which involve an element of dramatic contrast, of strain, or of intellectual difficulty. Most of the traditional "flowers of rhetoric" disappear completely. For instance, in his love poetry one never encounters bleeding hearts, cheeks like roses, lips like cherries, teeth like pearls, or Cupid shooting the arrows of love. The tears which flow in *A Valediction: of Weeping* are different from, and more complex than, the ordinary saline fluid of unhappy lovers; they are ciphers, naughts, symbols of the world's emptiness without the beloved; or else, suddenly reflecting her image, they are globes, worlds, they contain the sum of things. The poet who plays with conceits not only displays his own ingenuity; he may see into the nature of the world as deeply as the philosopher. Donne's conceits in particular leap continually in a restless orbit from the personal to the cosmic and back again.

Donne's rhythms are colloquial and various. He likes to twist and distort not only ideas, but metrical patterns and grammar itself. In the satires, which Renaissance writers understood to be "harsh" and "crabbed" as a genre, Donne's distortions often threaten to choke off the stream of expression entirely. But in the lyrics (both those which are worldly and those which are religious in theme), as in the elegies and sonnets, the verse never fails of a complex and memorable melody. Donne had an unusual gift, rather like that of a modern poet, T. S. Eliot, for striking off phrases which ring in the mind like a silver coin. They are two masters of the colloquial style, removed alike from the dignified, weighty manner of Milton and the sugared sweetness of the Elizabethans.

Donne and his followers are known to literary history as the "metaphysical school" of poets. Strictly speaking, this is a misnomer; there was no organized group of poets who imitated Donne, and if there had been, they would not have called themselves "metaphysical" poets. That term was invented by Dryden and Dr. Johnson. But the influence of Donne's poetic style was widely felt, especially by men whose taste was formed before 1660. George Herbert, Richard Crashaw, Henry Vaughan, Andrew Marvell, and Abraham Cowley are only the best known of those on whom Donne's influence is recognizable. The great change of taste which took place in 1660 threw Donne and the "conceited" style out of fashion; during the 18th and 19th centuries both he and his followers were rarely read and still more rarely appreciated. Finally, in the late 19th and early 20th centuries, three new editions of Donne appeared, of which Sir H. J. C. Grierson's, published in 1912, was quickly accepted as standard. By clarifying and purifying the often-garbled text, Grierson did a great deal to make Donne's poetry more available to the modern reader. Almost at once it started to exert an influence on modern poetic practice, the modern poets being hungry for a "tough" style which would free them from the worn-out rhetoric of late 19th-century romanticism. And Donne's status among the English poets quickly climbed from that of a curiosity to that of an acknowledged master.

Modern criticism, particularly, has rejoiced in the revival of Donne and the metaphysicals. Endlessly patient of subtle paradoxes and ambiguities, the new critics have succeeded in bringing out the rich sensibility and subtly intellectual music which underlie Donne's abrupt and muscular manner. Whether he writes of love or devotion, Donne's peculiar blend of wit and seriousness—of intense feeling, darting thought, and vast erudition—creates a fascination quite beyond the reach of easier styles and less strenuous minds. His poems, like his mind, are overwhelmingly mobile. Some of his poems are burlesques of traditional poetic modes. Platonic love places woman on a pedestal where she is to be worshiped spiritually; *Love's Alchemy* tears her down. Petrarch and his followers assured their readers that love was immutable, immortal, infinite; *The Indifferent* proclaims that it is a trifling game. Yet Donne can take the old forms seriously still. *The Undertaking* is in the spirit of serious Platonic love, and *The Good-Morrow* is an extravagant Petrarchan compliment. Indeed, Donne's mind is so mobile that a single poem may change points of view, and, beginning in passion, end in defiance (*The Funeral*).

The poems of Donne occasionally appear willful or shocking because they mention unconventional topics under unconventional circumstances. Corpses rotting in graves turn up in love poems, alongside geometrical compasses and astronomical data. The soul's union with God is described under the image of rape. The shock value of these images is sometimes exploited for its own sake. But just as often, Donne has a perfectly serious point to make. In *The Relic* that "bracelet of bright hair about the bone" is more than a macabre touch; the image of a spiritual marriage, it is shown triumphing by a miracle over death. In *The Sun Rising* the poet addresses the sun itself as a "busy old fool"; and this is audacious cleverness, but it also defines a psychological situation. The speaker, as he lies in bed with his mistress, feels himself exalted far above the sun—he looks down from an immense psychological height. Thus the wit is dramatically revealing as well as just shocking.

The first editors of Donne's poetry divided his work into about a dozen groupings, sometimes including only a single longer poem in a group. The *Songs and Sonnets*, which open the volume, are generally amorous in theme; the *Divine Poems*, which close it, are described in their title. In between, and harder to categorize, fall such sizable groups as the five satires, eighteen epigrams, twenty elegies, and 34 verse letters. There are also four epithalamia, or marriage songs, seven epicedes (i.e., mortuary poems) and obsequies on the death of sundry personages, and about a dozen epigrams. In short, Donne, whom Grierson shrewdly characterized as one of the great talkers in English verse, wrote in almost all the customary forms and on all the customary occasions of his day.

With three or four exceptions (the two *Anniversaries*, an *Elegy on Prince Henry*, and a trifle on Coryat's *Crudities*), none of the poetry on which Donne's reputation stands today appeared in print during his lifetime. Yet his poems were widely read and well known. The explanation of this paradox lies in the custom of circulating little clusters of manuscript poems among the witty and cultured circles of Elizabethan and Jacobean society. Hard poems imply small audiences. When one could hope for no more than a thousand or so readers, at best, and when most of them were concentrated in London and the two universities, publication became an unnecessary luxury. Copied out by hand, and gathered together in little bundles, the poems of Donne enjoyed a subterranean popularity, in the boudoir and in the law library, where they were doubtless hidden behind heavier and more respectable volumes. Donne himself had little reason to quarrel with this arrangement. Many of the poems for which he was admired would have constituted black marks on his reputation as an earnest and godly divine. Hence they were deliberately kept out of print during his later years.

Of the poems which follow, the *Hymn to God, My God, in my Sickness* and *Holy Sonnet 5* first appeared in 1635; while *Holy Sonnet 18* saw the light of day only in 1899, when Sir Edmund Gosse published his *Life of John Donne*. All the other poems bear a publication date of 1633; and as for date of composition, almost all of them might be assigned a question mark. We must guess at their dates from the scanty marks of internal evidence. Early scholars took for granted that all the bawdy, cynical, and lecherous poems were written by young Jack Donne, while all the somber, penitent, devotional poems were written by the godly divine. The more

we learn about the matter (and progress is astonishingly slow), the less
this easy division seems to stand up. But then, the less we believe John
Donne underwent a tremendous conversion experience, the less important
problems of exact dating become. It is one mind throughout, whatever
different facet happens to be showing.

The basic text which follows is that of Sir Herbert Grierson (1912), but
it has been modified, wherever sensible improvement seemed possible, and
sometimes supplemented, by that of Miss Helen Gardner (*Divine Poems*,
1952, and *The Elegies and the Songs and Sonnets*, 1964).

The Good-Morrow

I wonder, by my troth, what thou and I
Did, till we loved? Were we not weaned till then,
But sucked on country pleasures, childishly?
Or snorted we in the seven sleepers' den?[1]
'Twas so; But this, all pleasures fancies be.　　　　　5
If ever any beauty I did see,
Which I desired, and got, 'twas but a dream of thee.

And now good morrow to our waking souls,
Which watch not one another out of fear;
For love all love of other sights controls,　　　　　10
And makes one little room an everywhere.
Let sea-discoverers to new worlds have gone,
Let maps to other,[2] worlds on worlds have shown,
Let us possess one world; each hath one, and is one.

My face in thine eye, thine in mine appears,[3]　　　　　15
And true plain hearts do in the faces rest;
Where can we find two better hemispheres
Without sharp North, without declining West?
Whatever dies was not mixed equally;[4]
If our two loves be one, or thou and I　　　　　20
Love so alike that none do slacken, none can die.

1633

Song

Go and catch a falling star,
Get with child a mandrake root,[5]

1. Both Christian and Mohammedan
authors recite the legend of seven youths
of Ephesus, who hid in a cave from the
persecutions of Decius, and slept there
for 187 years. "Sucked" and "snorted"
are words carefully chosen for their impact on the love poem.
2. I.e., let us concede that maps to
other investigators have shown, etc.
("other" is an archaic plural form). In
line 14 an alternative reading is "Let us
possess *our* world" (from Miss Gardner).
3. Reflected in the pupils of one another's eyes, the lovers are, and possess,
worlds of their own.
4. Scholastic philosophy taught that
when the elements were imperfectly
("not equally") mixed, matter was
mortal and mutable; but when they
were perfectly mixed, it was undying
and unchanging. The dividing line between these two natures was the sphere
of the moon.
5. The mandrake root, or mandragora,
forked like the lower part of the human
body, was highly reputed as an aphro-
disiac; to get one with child is a supreme impossibility.

Tell me where all past years are,
   Or who cleft the Devil's foot,
Teach me to hear mermaids[6] singing,   5
Or to keep off envy's stinging,
      And find
      What wind
Serves to advance an honest mind.

If thou beest born to strange sights,   10
   Things invisible to see,
Ride ten thousand days and nights,
   Till age snow white hairs on thee,
Thou, when thou return'st, wilt tell me
All strange wonders that befell thee,   15
      And swear
      No where
Lives a woman true, and fair.

If thou find'st one, let me know,
   Such a pilgrimage were sweet;   20
Yet do not, I would not go,
   Though at next door we might meet;
Though she were true when you met her.
And last till you write your letter,
      Yet she   25
      Will be
False, ere I come, to two, or three.

                  1633

The Undertaking

I have done one braver thing
   Than all the Worthies[1] did,
And yet a braver thence doth spring,
   Which is, to keep that hid.

It were but madness now t' impart   5
   The skill of specular stone,[2]
When he which can have learned the art
   To cut it, can find none.

So, if I now should utter this,
   Others (because no more   10

6. Identified with the sirens, whose song only the wily Odysseus survived.
1. According to medieval legend, the Nine Worthies, or supreme heroes of history, included three Jews (Joshua, David, Judas Maccabeus), three pagans (Hector, Alexander, Julius Caesar), and three Christians (Arthur, Charlemagne, Godfrey of Bouillon).
2. A transparent or translucent material, reputed to have been used in antiquity for mirrors (in Latin, *speculae*), but no longer known.

Such stuff to work upon, there is)
    Would love but as before.

But he who loveliness within
    Hath found, all outward loathes,
For he who color loves, and skin,   15
    Loves but their oldest clothes.

If, as I have, you also do
    Virtue attired in woman see,
And dare love that, and say so too,
    And forget the He and She;   20

And if this love, though placéd so,
    From profane men you hide,
Which will no faith on this bestow,
    Or, if they do, deride;

Then you have done a braver thing   25
    Than all the Worthies did;
And a braver thence will spring,
    Which is, to keep that hid.

                                        1633

The Indifferent

I can love both fair and brown,[1]
Her whom abundance melts, and her whom want betrays,
Her who loves loneness best, and her who masks and plays,
Her whom the country formed, and whom the town,
Her who believes, and her who tries,[2]   5
Her who still weeps with spongy eyes,
And her who is dry cork, and never cries;
I can love her, and her, and you, and you,
I can love any, so she be not true.

Will no other vice content you?   10
Will it not serve your turn to do as did your mothers?
Or have you all old vices spent, and now would find out others?
Or doth a fear that men are true torment you?
O we are not, be not you so;
Let me, and do you, twenty know.   15
Rob me, but bind me not, and let me go.
Must I, who came to travail[3] thorough you
Grow your fixed subject, because you are true?

Venus heard me sigh this song,
And by love's sweetest part, variety, she swore,   20
She heard not this till now; and that it should be so no more.

1. Both blonde and brunette.   3. "Grief, sorrow," but also "journey,
2. "Attempts to believe" and "tries   travel."
things out."

She went, examined, and returned ere long,
And said, Alas, some two or three
Poor heretics in love there be,
Which think to 'stablish dangerous constancy.   25
But I have told them, Since you will be true,
You shall be true to them who are false to you.

1633

The Canonization

For God's sake hold your tongue, and let me love,
   Or chide my palsy, or my gout,
My five gray hairs, or ruined fortune, flout,
     With wealth your state, your mind with arts improve,
      Take you a course, get you a place,[1]   5
      Observe His Honor, or His Grace,
   Or the King's real, or his stamped face[2]
     Contemplate; what you will, approve,[3]
     So you will let me love.

Alas, alas, who's injured by my love?   10
   What merchant's ships have my sighs drowned?
Who says my tears have overflowed his ground?
     When did my colds a forward spring remove?[4]
      When did the heats which my veins fill
      Add one man to the plaguy bill?[5]   15
Soldiers find wars, and lawyers find out still
   Litigious men, which quarrels move,
     Though she and I do love.

Call us what you will, we are made such by love;
   Call her one, me another fly,   20
We're tapers too, and at our own cost die,[6]
     And we in us find the eagle and the dove.[7]
     The phoenix riddle hath more wit

1. "Take you a course": not necessarily of physic or instruction, but in the general sense of "settling yourself in life." A "place" is an appointment, at court or elsewhere.
2. On coins.
3. Put to proof, find by experience.
4. By freezing it up.
5. Deaths from the hot-weather plague were recorded, by parish, in weekly lists.
6. Like the "fly," a symbol of transitory life, we are burned up in "tapers," which consume themselves. There is a hint here of the old superstition that every act of intercourse subtracts a day from one's life. (To "die," in the punning terminology of the 17th century, was to consummate the act of sex.)
7. The eagle and the dove are symbols of earthly wisdom (strength) and heavenly meekness (purity), the latter paradoxically more powerful than the former. The phoenix, in general mythology, was a fabulous Arabian bird, only one of which existed at any one time. After living a thousand years, it lit its own funeral pyre, jumped in, and sang its funeral song as it was consumed—then rose triumphantly from its ashes, a new bird. Thus it was a symbol of immortality, as well as of desire rising from its own exhaustion. "Eagle" and "dove" are also alchemical terms for processes leading to the rise of "phoenix," a stage in the transmutation of metals.

By us: we two being one, are it.
So, to one neutral thing both sexes fit. 25
We die and rise the same, and prove
Mysterious by this love.

We can die by it, if not live by love,
And if unfit for tombs and hearse
Our legend be, it will be fit for verse; 30
And if no piece of chronicle we prove,
We'll build in sonnets pretty rooms;
As well a well-wrought urn becomes
The greatest ashes, as half-acre tombs,
And by these hymns,[8] all shall approve 35
Us canonized for love:

And thus invoke us: You whom reverend love
Made one another's hermitage;
You, to whom love was peace, that now is rage;
Who did the whole world's soul contract,[8a] and drove 40
Into the glasses of your eyes
(So made such mirrors, and such spies,
That they did all to you epitomize)
Countries, towns, courts: Beg from above
A pattern of your love![9] 45

1633

Twicknam Garden[1]

Blasted with sighs, and surrounded with tears,
Hither I come to seek the spring,
And at mine eyes, and at mine ears,
Receive such balms as else cure everything;
But oh, self traitor, I do bring 5
The spider love, which transubstantiates all,
And can convert manna to gall;[2]
And that this place may thoroughly be thought
True paradise, I have the serpent brought.

'Twere wholesomer for me that winter did 10
Benight the glory of this place,
And that a grave frost did forbid

8. Donne's own poems, transformed into hymns in a new love-religion; "all": posterity.
8a. In line 40 Miss Gardner reads "extract" for "contract."
9. The poet and his mistress, turned to saints, are implored by the rest of the population to get from heaven ("above") a pattern of their love for general distribution. "Countries, towns, courts" are objects of the verb "drove"; the notion that eyes both see and reflect the outside world, and so "contain" it doubly, was very delightful to Donne.
1. The poem takes its title from the country house at Twickenham Park, of Lucy, Countess of Bedford; she was one of Donne's patrons.
2. Love is a spider because it infuses its poison into every experience, turning one substance into another ("transubstantiates all"), and converting "manna," the essence of sweetness, to "gall," the essence of bitterness.

These trees to laugh and mock me to my face;
    But that I may not this disgrace
Endure, nor leave this garden, Love, let me   15
    Some senseless piece of this place be;
Make me a mandrake, so I may groan here,[3]
    Or a stone fountain weeping out my year.

Hither with crystal vials, lovers, come
    And take my tears, which are love's wine,   20
    And try your mistress' tears at home,
For all are false that taste not just like mine;
    Alas, hearts do not in eyes shine,
Nor can you more judge woman's thoughts by tears,
    Than by her shadow what she wears.   25
O perverse sex, where none is true but she,
    Who's therefore true, because her truth kills me.

                            1633

The Apparition

When by thy scorn, O murderess, I am dead,
And that thou thinkst thee free
From all solicitation from me,
Then shall my ghost come to thy bed,
And thee, feigned vestal,[4] in worse arms shall see;   5
Then thy sick taper will begin to wink,
And he whose thou art then, being tired before,
Will, if thou stir, or pinch to wake him, think
    Thou call'st for more,
And in false sleep will from thee shrink,   10
And then, poor aspen wretch,[5] neglected thou
Bathed in a cold quicksilver sweat[6] wilt lie
    A verier ghost than I;
What I will say, I will not tell thee now,
Lest that preserve thee; and since my love is spent,   15
I had rather thou shouldst painfully repent,
Than by my threatenings rest still innocent.

                            1633

Love's Alchemy

Some that have deeper digged love's mine than I,
    Say where his centric happiness doth lie;

3. The mandrake, also called mandragora, was popularly thought to shriek when uprooted.
4. In Roman history the "vestals" were sacred virgins.
5. Aspen leaves flutter in the slightest breeze.
6. Sweating in terror; with an added innuendo from the circumstance that quicksilver (mercury) was a stock prescription for venereal disease.

I have loved, and got, and told,
But should I love, get, tell, till I were old,
I should not find that hidden mystery;
    O, 'tis imposture all:
And as no chemic yet the elixir got,[1]
    But glorifies his pregnant pot,[2]
    If by the way to him befall
Some odoriferous thing, or medicinal;   10
    So lovers dream a rich and long delight,
    But get a winter-seeming summer's night.

Our ease, our thrift, our honor, and our day,
Shall we for this vain bubble's shadow pay?
    Ends love in this, that my man   15
Can be as happy as I can if he can
Endure the short scorn of a bridegroom's play?
    That loving wretch that swears,
'Tis not the bodies marry, but the minds,
    Which he in her angelic finds,
    Would swear as justly that he hears,   20
In that day's rude hoarse minstrelsy, the spheres.[3]
    Hope not for mind in women; at their best
    Sweetness and wit they are, but mummy, possessed.[4]

1633

The Flea

Mark but this flea, and mark in this,
How little that which thou deniest me is;
Me it sucked first, and now sucks thee,
And in this flea our two bloods mingled be;
Thou know'st that this cannot be said
A sin, or shame, or loss of maidenhead,
    Yet this enjoys before it woo,   5
    And pampered swells with one blood made of two,
    And this, alas, is more than we would do.[1]

Oh stay, three lives in one flea spare,
Where we almost, nay more than married, are.   10
    This flea is you and I, and this

---

1. "Chemic": alchemist; "the elixir": a magic medicine sought by alchemists and reputed to heal all ills.
2. Praises his fertile (and womb-shaped) retort.
3. The perfect harmony of the planets, moving in concentric crystalline spheres, is contrasted with the charivari, a boisterous serenade for pots, pans, and trumpets, performed on the wedding night.
4. Almost all punctuation for the last two lines represents conjectures by modern editors. There might equally well be commas after "best" and "wit." The last word, "possessed," may modify "mummy," meaning "mummy with a demon in it," or else "they," meaning "women who, when you have possessed them, are nothing but dried mummy."

1. I.e., we, alas, don't dare hope for this consummation of our love, which the flea freely accepts. The idea of swelling suggests that of pregnancy.

Our marriage bed and marriage temple is;
Though parents grudge, and you, we are met,
And cloistered in these living walls of jet,   15
　　Though use[2] make you apt to kill me
　　Let not to that, self-murder added be,
　　And sacrilege, three sins in killing three.

Cruel and sudden, hast thou since
Purpled thy nail, in blood of innocence?[3]   20
Wherein could this flea guilty be,
Except in that drop which it sucked from thee?
Yet thou triumph'st, and say'st that thou
Find'st not thy self nor me the weaker now;
　　'Tis true, then learn how false fears be;   25
　　Just so much honor, when thou yield'st to me,
　　Will waste, as this flea's death took life from thee.

1633

The Bait[4]

　　Come live with me and be my love,
　　And we will some new pleasures prove,
　　Of golden sands and crystal brooks,
　　With silken lines and silver hooks.

　　There will the river whispering run,   5
　　Warmed by thine eyes more than the sun.
　　And there th' enamored fish will stay,
　　Begging themselves they may betray.

　　When thou wilt swim in that live bath,
　　Each fish, which every channel hath,   10
　　Will amorously to thee swim,
　　Gladder to catch thee, than thou him.

　　If thou, to be so seen, beest loath,
　　By sun or moon, thou darkenest both;
　　And if myself have leave to see,   15
　　I need not their light, having thee.

　　Let others freeze with angling reeds,
　　And cut their legs with shells and weeds,
　　Or treacherously poor fish beset
　　With strangling snare, or windowy net.   20

　　Let coarse bold hands from slimy nest
　　The bedded fish in banks out-wrest,

2. Custom.
3. Like Herod, Donne's mistress has slaughtered the innocents, and is now clothed in imperial purple.
4. This poem is Donne's response to Marlowe's *Passionate Shepherd to His Love*. Another of the many replies was Ralegh's *Nymph's Reply to the Shepherd*.

Or curious traitors, sleave-silk flies,[5]
Bewitch poor fishes' wandering eyes.

For thee, thou needest no such deceit,   25
For thou thyself art thine own bait;
That fish that is not catched thereby,
Alas, is wiser far than I.

                                                          1633

A Valediction: Forbidding Mourning[1]

As virtuous men pass mildly away,
  And whisper to their souls to go,
Whilst some of their sad friends do say
  The breath goes now, and some say, No;

So let us melt, and make no noise,   5
  No tear-floods, nor sigh-tempests move,
'Twere profanation of our joys
  To tell the laity our love.

Moving of th' earth brings harms and fears,
  Men reckon what it did and meant;   10
But trepidation of the spheres,
  Though greater far, is innocent.[2]

Dull sublunary[3] lovers' love
  (Whose soul[4] is sense) cannot admit
Absence, because it doth remove   15
  Those things which elemented[5] it.

But we by a love so much refined
  That our selves know not what it is,
Inter-assuréd of the mind,
  Care less, eyes, lips, and hands to miss.   20

Our two souls therefore, which are one,
  Though I must go, endure not yet
A breach, but an expansion,
  Like gold to airy thinness beat.

5. Flies of unraveled silk, floss-silk.

1. The particularly serious and steady tone of this poem may be due to the circumstances of its composition. Izaak Walton tells us it was addressed to Donne's wife on the occasion of his trip to the Continent in 1612. Donne had many forebodings of misfortune, which were verified when his wife gave birth to a stillborn child during his absence.

2. I.e., earthquakes are thought to threaten evil consequences, but the variations of the spheres from true circularity, though they involve greater motions, are not considered sinister. "Trepidation of the spheres" (literally, "shuddering") was an additional arbitrary motion of the eighth sphere, introduced into the Ptolemaic system about the year 950 to account for certain celestial phenomena which were really due to the wobbling of the earth on its axis.

3. Beneath the moon, therefore mundane and subject to change.

4. Essence.

5. Composed.

If they be two, they are two so   25
   As stiff twin compasses are two;
Thy soul, the fixed foot, makes no show
   To move, but doth, if th' other do.

And though it in the center sit,
   Yet when the other far doth roam,   30
It leans and hearkens after it,
   And grows erect, as it comes home.

Such wilt thou be to me, who must
   Like th' other foot, obliquely run;
Thy firmness makes my circle just,   35
   And makes me end where I begun.[6]

1633

The Ecstasy

Where, like a pillow on a bed,
   A pregnant bank swelled up to rest
The violet's reclining head,
   Sat we two, one another's best.
Our hands were firmly cemented   5
   With a fast balm, which thence did spring.
Our eye-beams twisted, and did thread
   Our eyes upon one double string;[1]
So to intergraft our hands, as yet
   Was all our means to make us one;   10
And pictures in our eyes to get
   Was all our propagation.
As 'twixt two equal armies, Fate
   Suspends uncertain victory,
Our souls (which to advance their state,   15
   Were gone out) hung 'twixt her and me.
And whilst our souls negotiate there,
   We like sepulchral statues lay;
All day the same our postures were,
   And we said nothing all the day.   20
If any, so by love refined
   That he soul's language understood,
And by good love were grown all mind,
   Within convenient distance stood,
He (though he know not which soul spake,   25
   Because both meant, both spake the same)
Might thence a new concoction[2] take,

6. The circle is an emblem of perfection; cf. also the motto of Mary, Queen of Scots, "In my end is my beginning." An excitingly complex, if perhaps overly medieval, reading of the poem is offered by John Freccero in *ELH*, XXX (December, 1963), 335–376.

1. Joining hands and eyes is the only intercourse of the two lovers: "eye-beams" are invisible shafts of light, thought of as going out of the eyes and so enabling one to see things.
2. Purified mixture.

And part far purer than he came.
    This ecstasy doth unperplex,[3]
We said, and tell us what we love;   30
    We see by this it was not sex;
We see we saw not what did move;[4]
But as all several souls contain
    Mixture of things, they know not what,
Love these mixed souls doth mix again,   35
    And makes both one, each this and that.
A single violet transplant,
    The strength, the colour, and the size
(All which before was poor, and scant)
    Redoubles still, and multiplies.   40
When love, with one another so
    Interinanimates two souls,
That abler soul, which thence doth flow,
    Defects of loneliness controls.[5]
We then, who are this new soul, know,   45
    Of what we are composed, and made,
For, th' atomies[6] of which we grow,
    Are souls, whom no change can invade.
But O alas, so long, so far
    Our bodies why do we forbear?   50
They are ours, though they are not we; we are
    The intelligences, they the sphere.[7]
We owe them thanks because they thus,
    Did us to us at first convey,
Yielded their forces, sense, to us,   55
    Nor are dross to us, but allay.[8]
On man heaven's influence works not so
    But that it first imprints the air,[9]
So soul into the soul may flow,
    Though it to body first repair.   60
As our blood labors to beget
    Spirits as like souls as it can,[1]
Because such fingers need to knit
    That subtle knot which makes us man:
So must pure lovers' souls descend   65
    T' affections, and to faculties
Which sense may reach and apprehend;

---

3. I.e., separate and clarify.
4. I.e., we see that we did not understand before what motivated ("did move") us.
5. The "abler soul" which derives from the union of two lesser ones can eliminate the loneliness with which each in itself is afflicted.
6. Atoms.
7. Medieval astronomers believed that the planets, set in crystalline spheres, were inhabited by "intelligences" which guided and controlled them. Similarly, Donne says, our bodies are guided and controlled by our selves.
8. "Dross" is an impurity which weakens metal, "allay" (alloy) an impurity which strengthens it. Our bodies contribute sensation ("sense") to the soul, and so reinforce it.
9. Astrological influences were thought to work on man through the surrounding air.
1. "Animal spirits" were thought to be begotten by the blood, to serve as intermediaries between body and soul.

Else a great Prince in prison lies.
To our bodies turn we then, that so
Weak men on love revealed may look;   70
Love's mysteries in souls do grow,
But yet the body is his book.[2]
And if some lover, such as we,
Have heard this dialogue of one,[3]
Let him still mark us; he shall see   75
Small change when we are to bodies gone.

1633

Lovers' Infiniteness

If yet I have not all[4] thy love,
Dear, I shall never have it all;
I cannot breathe one other sigh to move,
Nor can entreat one other tear to fall;
All my treasure, which should purchase thee,   5
Sighs, tears, and oaths, and letters, I have spent.
Yet no more can be due to me
Than at the bargain made was meant;
If then thy gift of love were partial,
That some to me, some should to others fall,   10
  Dear, I shall never have thee all.

Or if then thou gavest me all,
All was but all which thou hadst then;
But if in thy heart since there be or shall
New love created be by other men,   15
Which have their stocks entire, and can in tears,
In sighs, in oaths, and letters outbid me,
This new love may beget new fears,
For this love was not vowed by thee.
And yet it was, thy gift being general;   20
The ground, thy heart, is mine; whatever shall
  Grow there, dear, I should have it all.

Yet I would not have all yet.
He that hath all can have no more;
And since my love doth every day admit   25
New growth, thou shouldst have new rewards in store.
Thou canst not every day give me thy heart,
If thou canst give it, then thou never gavest it.
Love's riddles are, that though thy heart depart,

2. I.e., love, a god within man, puts forth in the body a book where his mysteries may be read (as God the Creator put forth the book of Nature and the book of Scripture).
3. The characteristic Donne poem might be described as a "dialogue of one."
4. The influence of Donne's legal training is very clear here; the poem is a series of technical verbal quibbles on the word "all."

It stays at home, and thou with losing savest it.   30
But we will have a way more liberal
Than changing hearts, to join them;[5] so we shall
    Be one, and one another's all.

1633

The Sun Rising

    Busy old fool, unruly sun,
      Why dost thou thus,
Through windows and through curtains call on us?
Must to thy motions lovers' seasons run?
    Saucy pedantic wretch, go chide   5
    Late school boys and sour prentices,
  Go tell court huntsmen that the King will ride,
  Call country ants to harvest offices;[1]
Love, all alike, no season knows nor clime,
Nor hours, days, months, which are the rags of time.   10

    Thy beams, so reverend and strong
      Why shouldst thou think?
I could eclipse and cloud them with a wink,
But that I would not lose her sight so long;
    If her eyes have not blinded thine,
    Look, and tomorrow late, tell me,   15
  Whether both th' Indias of spice and mine[2]
  Be where thou leftst them, or lie here with me.
Ask for those kings whom thou saw'st yesterday,
And thou shalt hear, All here in one bed lay.   20

    She is all states, and all princes, I,
      Nothing else is.
Princes do but play us; compared to this,
All honor's mimic, all wealth alchemy.[3]
    Thou, sun, art half as happy as we,   25
    In that the world's contracted thus;
  Thine age asks ease, and since thy duties be
  To warm the world, that's done in warming us.
Shine here to us, and thou art everywhere;
This bed thy center is,[4] these walls, thy sphere.   30

1633

---

5. To join hearts is more liberal than to "change" (exchange) them; "liberal" implies amorous generosity, also relief from legal hairsplitting.
1. Harvest chores, duties.

2. The India of "spice" is East India, that of "mine" (gold), the West Indies.
3. I.e., metaphorically, fraudulent.
4. The "center" of the sun's orbit.

Air and Angels

Twice or thrice had I loved thee,
Before I knew thy face or name;
So in a voice, so in a shapeless flame,
Angels affect us oft, and worshiped be;
    Still when, to where thou wert, I came,   5
Some lovely glorious nothing I did see.
    But since my soul, whose child love is,
Takes limbs of flesh, and else could nothing do,
    More subtle than the parent is
Love must not be, but take a body too;   10
    And therefore what thou wert, and who,
        I bid love ask, and now
That it assume thy body I allow,
And fix itself in thy lip, eye, and brow.

Whilst thus to ballast love I thought,   15
And so more steadily to have gone,
With wares which would sink admiration,
I saw I had love's pinnace overfraught;[1]
    Every thy hair[2] for love to work upon
Is much too much, some fitter must be sought;   20
    For, nor in nothing, nor in things
Extreme and scatt'ring[3] bright, can love inhere.
    Then as an angel, face and wings
Of air, not pure as it, yet pure doth wear,
    So thy love may be my love's sphere.[4]   25
        Just such disparity
As is 'twixt air and angels' purity,
'Twixt women's love and men's will ever be.

                  1633

Break of Day[5]

'Tis true, 'tis day; what though it be?
O wilt thou therefore rise from me?

1. Her physical beauty (his "wares") would sink admiration—i.e., overwhelm wonder itself. This is too much ballast for love's "pinnace" (a small boat).
2. I.e., each hair of thine.
3. Diffused, dazzling.
4. Some Scholastic philosophers held that angels, when they appeared to men, assumed a body of air. Such a body, though pure, was less so than the angel's spiritual being. Similarly, women's love, which Donne thinks *less* pure than that of men, may still serve as the receptacle ("sphere") for the love of men.
5. Modeled on the Provençal aubade, or song of the lovers' parting at dawn, this poem is a departure for Donne in that it assumes a feminine point of view. As a rule, he is among the most consistently masculine of poets.

Why should we rise, because 'tis light?
Did we lie down, because 'twas night?
Love, which in spite of darkness brought us hither,   5
Should in despite of light keep us together.

Light hath no tongue, but is all eye;
If it could speak as well as spy,
This were the worst that it could say,
That being well, I fain would stay,   10
And that I loved my heart and honor so,
That I would not from him, that had them, go.

Must business thee from hence remove?
O, that's the worst disease of love.
The poor, the foul, the false, love can   15
Admit, but not the busied man.
He which hath business, and makes love, doth do
Such wrong, as when a married man doth woo.

1633

A Valediction: Of Weeping

    Let me pour forth
My tears before thy face whilst I stay here,
For thy face coins them, and thy stamp they bear,
And by this mintage they are something worth,
    For thus they be   5
    Pregnant of thee;
Fruits of much grief they are, emblems of more—
When a tear falls, that Thou falls which it bore,
So thou and I are nothing then, when on a diverse shore.[1]

    On a round ball   10
A workman that hath copies by, can lay
An Europe, Afric, and an Asia,
And quickly make that, which was nothing, all;[2]
    So doth each tear
    Which thee doth wear,   15
A globe, yea world, by that impression grow,
Till thy tears mixed with mine do overflow
This world; by waters sent from thee, my heaven dissolvéd so.[3]

    O more than moon,
Draw not up seas to drown me in thy sphere;   20

1. The loss of the lovers in their separation is figured in the fall of a tear which contains the image of the mistress.
2. I.e., on a blank globe an artist can draw the world, and so convert a cipher, the image of nothingness, to the whole world.
3. In describing Creation, Genesis i.6–7 makes mention of certain heavenly waters, some above and some below the firmament. Their existence and function has been much debated by Bible scholars.

Weep me not dead, in thine arms, but forbear
To teach the sea what it may do too soon.
      Let not the wind
      Example find
To do me more harm than it purposeth;   25
Since thou and I sigh one another's breath,
Whoe'er sighs most is cruelest, and hastes the other's death.[4]

                                        1633

The Funeral

Whoever comes to shroud me, do not harm
      Nor question much
That subtle wreath of hair which crowns my arm;
The mystery, the sign you must not touch,
      For 'tis my outward soul,   5
Viceroy to that, which then to heaven being gone,
      Will leave this to control,
And keep these limbs, her provinces, from dissolution.

For if the sinewy thread[1] my brain lets fall
      Through every part   10
Can tie those parts and make me one of all;
These hairs, which upward grew, and strength and art
      Have from a better brain,
Can better do it; except she meant that I
      By this should know my pain,   15
As prisoners then are manacled, when they're condemned to die.

Whate'er she meant by it, bury it with me,
      For since I am
Love's martyr, it might breed idolatry,
If into others' hands these relics came;   20
      As 'twas humility[2]
To afford to it all that a soul can do,
      So 'tis some bravery,
That since you would save none of me, I bury some of you.

                                        1633

The Relic

      When my grave is broke up again
      Some second guest to entertain
      (For graves have learned that woman-head[1]
      To be to more than one a bed),

4. The breath of life has been interchanged between the lovers.
1. The spinal cord and nervous system.
2. It was humility to grant, in the first thirteen and a half lines of the poem, that her hair could act as a soul; it is also "bravery" (defiance) to bury a part of the mistress in revenge for her cruelty.
1. I.e., characteristic of women. On the re-use of graves, see Sir Thomas Browne's *Urn-Burial* and *Hamlet* V.i.

And he that digs it, spies   5
A bracelet of bright hair about the bone,
    Will he not let us alone,
And think that there a loving couple lies,
Who thought that this device might be some way
To make their souls, at the last busy day,   10
Meet at this grave, and make a little stay?

    If this fall in a time, or land,
    Where mis-devotion² doth command,
    Then he that digs us up, will bring
    Us to the Bishop and the King,   15
      To make us relics; then
Thou shalt be a Mary Magdalen, and I
    A something else thereby;³
All women shall adore us, and some men;
And since at such time, miracles are sought,   20
I would have that age by this paper taught
What miracles we harmless lovers wrought.

    First, we loved well and faithfully,
    Yet knew not what we loved, nor why,
    Difference of sex no more we knew,   25
    Than our guardian angels do;
      Coming and going, we
Perchance might kiss, but not between those meals;⁴
    Our hands ne'er touched the seals,
Which nature, injured by late law, sets free:
These miracles we did; but now, alas,   30
All measure and all language I should pass,
Should I tell what a miracle she was.

                      1633

To the Countess of Bedford¹

MADAM,
Reason is our soul's left hand, faith her right,
By these we reach divinity, that's you;

---

2. False devotion, superstition. Donne seems to have in mind Roman Catholicism.
3. The rhythm of "something else" suggests the complete but blasphemous parallel, "Jesus Christ."
4. The kiss of salutation and parting was, in the 17th century, a peculiarly English custom; the passage that follows seems to suggest some greater intimacy, permitted by nature, but unjustly abridged by "late law." It is hard to imagine what Donne had in mind here; he was not opposed to the sacrament of matrimony, and the laws of marriage could not be called "late," i.e., recent.

1. The social relations implied in this verse letter offer an interesting puzzle. Lucy, Countess of Bedford, was a gay, rich, clever, and decorative lady in a very worldly court; Donne was an eager, clever climber, not yet in holy or-

Their loves, who have the blessings of your light,
Grew from their reason, mine from fair faith grew.

But as, although a squint left-handedness   5
Be ungracious, yet we cannot want[2] that hand,
So would I, not to increase, but to express
My faith, as I believe, so understand.[3]

Therefore I study you first in your saints,
Those friends whom your election glorifies,   10
Then in your deeds, accesses, and restraints,
And what you read, and what yourself devise.

But soon the reasons why you are loved by all
Grow infinite, and so pass reason's reach,
Then back again to implicit faith I fall,   15
And rest on what the catholic[4] voice doth teach;

That you are good: and not one heretic
Denies it: if he did, yet you are so.
For, rocks which high-topped and deep-rooted stick,
Waves wash, not undermine, nor overthrow.   20

In every thing there naturally grows
A balsamum,[5] to keep it fresh and new,
If 'twere not injured by extrinsic blows;
Your birth and beauty are this balm in you.

But you of learning and religion,   25
And virtue, and such ingredients, have made
A mithridate,[6] whose operation
Keeps off, or cures, what can be done or said.

Yet, this is not your physic[7] but your food,
A diet fit for you; for you are here   30
The first good angel, since the world's frame stood,
That ever did in woman's shape appear.

Since you are then God's masterpiece, and so
His factor[8] for our loves; do as you do,

ders, disgraced by his rash marriage,
and, as he clearly says in the poem,
altogether unknown to the lady. His
poem is in the audacious, semi-blas-
phemous tone of courtly adulation;
would her response have taken the
form of an invitation to dinner, an
assignation, a religious homily, or a
bank note? Donne wrote numerous verse
letters, including several later ones to
the Countess of Bedford.
2. Do without, lack.
3. He requests the pleasure of her acquaintance.
4. Universal.
5. Paracelsus and other early physicians have much to say of a natural

balsam, or balm, which preserves life
and cures all human ailments.
6. From Mithridates, the Persian king,
who (it is related) ate poisons in small
doses to render himself immune from
large ones; hence, an immunizing dose.
7. Medicine.
8. A factor is one who does business for
another, an agent. The sense of the last
stanza is dark. "Home" (line 35) and
"there" (line 37) certainly refer to
heaven; he is, then, asking her to become a saint and intervene with God
in his behalf, rather than help him in a
worldly sense, the shape of which remains rather ill-defined.

Make your return home gracious; and bestow   35
This life on that; so make one life of two.
For so God help me, I would not miss you there
For all the good which you can do me here.

1633

Elegy IV. The Perfume[1]

Once, and but once found in thy company,
All thy supposed escapes are laid on me;
And as a thief at bar is questioned there
By all the men that have been robbed that year,
So am I (by this traitorous means surprised),   5
By thy hydroptic[2] father catechized.
Though he had wont to search with glazéd eyes,
As though he came to kill a cockatrice,[3]
Though he hath often sworn that he would remove
Thy beauty's beauty, and food of our love,   10
Hope of his goods, if I with thee were seen,
Yet close and secret as our souls we have been.
Though thy immortal mother, which doth lie
Still buried in her bed, yet will not die,
Takes this advantage to sleep out day light,   15
And watch thy entries and returns all night,
And when she takes thy hand, and would seem kind,
Doth search what rings and armlets she can find,
And, kissing, notes the color of thy face,
And, fearing lest thou art swollen, doth thee embrace;   20

1. In Latin poetry, an elegy is not necessarily a funeral lament, but may be simply a discursive or reflective poem written in elegiac meter (alternating dactylic pentameters and hexameters). In English, the genre has been even vaguer, partly because this metrical pattern is unusual; and many early poems in pentameter couplets have been classified as elegies simply because they discussed some matter more or less consecutively and seriously. Twenty poems by Donne are customarily grouped together as elegies; they are not so rough as the satires nor so clearly musical as many of the *Songs and Sonnets,* but to find any other common denominator will not be easy. They include dramatic sketches and monologues, short stories in verse, satires, jokes, epigrams, and simple love lyrics. Apparently they were written over a considerable period of time, and with no single purpose or unifying theme in mind.

Elegy IV is rowdy and cynical, with a "low" point of view and a sour, suspicious eye for everyone's worst motives—including the poet's own. The poem is addressed to the speaker's mistress, a girl living with her parents. (Others of the elegies are to married women, court ladies, or to nobody in particular.) The circumstances of the poem suggest a middle-class family, probably of merchant status; the poet assumes the part of an adventurer, ruthless and greedy. Clearly Donne is playing here with a situation. Hence the word "escapes," meaning "sexual lapses," is not really an insult, for the whole situation is that of a comic story of sexual misadventure.
2. Thirsty for information, curious; with the additional overtone of "dropsical," i.e., swollen with disease and money, flabby.
3. The cockatrice, or basilisk, was a fabulous beast, reputed to kill its enemies by its very glance; the girl's father is so suspicious of the speaker that he scarcely looks at him. In this situation of unmasked social warfare, the speaker can admit that for him the beauty of the girl's beauty (i.e., its essence) is hope of her father's goods.

And to try if thou long, doth name strange meats,
And notes thy paleness, blushing, sighs, and sweats;[4]
And politicly[5] will to thee confess
The sins of her own youth's rank lustiness;
Yet Love these sorceries did remove, and move   25
Thee to gull[6] thine own mother for my love.
Thy little brethren, which like fairy sprites
Oft skipped into our chamber, those sweet nights,
And kissed and ingled[7] on thy father's knee,
Were bribed next day to tell what they did see: 30
The grim, eight-foot-high, iron-bound serving-man,
That oft names God in oaths, and only then,
He that to bar the first gate doth as wide
As the great Rhodian Colossus[8] stride,
Which, if in hell no other pains there were,   35
Makes me fear hell, because he must be there:
Though by thy father he were hired to this,
Could never witness any touch or kiss.
But O, too common ill, I brought with me
That which betrayed me to my enemy,   40
A loud perfume, which at my entrance cried
Even at thy father's nose, so we were spied.
When, like a tyrant king that in his bed
Smelt gunpowder, the pale wretch shiveréd.[9]
Had it been some bad smell, he would have thought   45
That his own feet, or breath, that smell had wrought.
But as we, in our isle imprisonéd,
Where cattle only, and divers dogs are bred,
The precious unicorns strange monsters call,
So thought he good, strange, that had none at all.[1]   50
I taught my silks their whistling to forbear,
Even my oppressed shoes dumb and speechless were,
Only thou bitter-sweet, whom I had laid
Next me, me traitorously hast betrayed,
And unsuspected hast invisibly   55
At once fled unto him, and stayed with me.
Base excrement of earth, which dost confound
Sense from distinguishing the sick from sound;
By thee the silly amorous sucks his death
By drawing in a leprous harlot's breath;   60
By thee the greatest stain to man's estate
Falls on us, to be called effeminate;

4. All the stock tests for pregnancy are being applied.
5. With policy (in order to provoke a counter-confession from her daughter).
6. Fool, deceive.
7. Fondled, caressed.
8. The giant statue of Apollo at Rhodes was one of the seven wonders of the ancient world.
9. The reference may be to James I and the Gunpowder Plot, which would date the poem sometime after 1605.
1. I.e., knowing only local cattle, we think unicorns strange, even though they are precious; so he, who had no proper sense of smell, thought even a good odor strange. Only in Donne's poetry do we find rarefied reflections like this rising from the smell of a man's feet.

Though you be much loved in the prince's hall,
There, things that seem exceed substantial;[2]
Gods, when ye fumed on altars,[3] were pleased well   65
Because you were burnt, not that they liked your smell;
You are loathsome all, being taken simply alone;
Shall we love ill things joined, and hate each one?[4]
If you were good, your good doth soon decay;
And you are rare, that takes the good away.[5]   70
All my perfumes I give most willingly
To embalm thy father's corpse; What? will he die?[6]

1633

2. I.e., at court more attention is paid to empty appearances than to matters of substance.
3. Incense.
4. The ingredients in perfume are often unpleasant individually; why should we like the end product?
5. I.e., that (your rarity) spoils any good you may possess.
6. The word "corpse" gives the speaker sudden hope.

Satire III, Religion For the first time in English literary history, the mode of satire flourished in the last decade of Elizabeth's reign and under the first two Stuarts. Many social circumstances contributed to its popularity: a surplus of clever young men without jobs, bitter antipathies between social classes and groups, and a general spirit of disillusion and doubt which has been characterized as "Jacobean melancholy."

Out of this mood of prolonged doubt, search, and obstinate questioning came the five satires of John Donne. *Satire III, Religion* is not a satire in the customary sense of a mocking attack on some person or custom. It is a strenuous, inconclusive discussion of an acute theological problem: How may a man recognize the true church, to which all Christians claim to belong? The person to whom it is addressed is evidently a man without specific religious commitment, but with a great and anxious interest in religion, and a specially nervous feeling that the claims of Roman Catholicism may be justified. He has been a sailor, a soldier, a bit of a rake, a bit of a theologian; he has more than a smattering of law. In many small ways, he reminds us of young Jack Donne himself. But the most characteristic thing about this poem on the search for certainty is the toughness of mind which it evinces throughout. Donne's images have a raw, contemptuous force, his phrasing is clipped, his grammar and his meter are twisted by the energy of his argument. He has no easy answer for the question raised, and makes no effort to charm or lull the reader. His poem is sheer display of intellectual force, a pointed, inconclusive game of mind.

Satire III, Religion

Kind pity chokes my spleen; brave scorn forbids
Those tears to issue which swell my eyelids;
I must not laugh, nor weep sins, and be wise,

Can railing then cure these worn maladies?
Is not our mistress, fair Religion,   5
As worthy of all our souls' devotion,
As virtue was to the first blinded age?[1]
Are not heaven's joys as valiant to assuage
Lusts, as earth's honor was to them?[2] Alas,
As we do them in means, shall they surpass   10
Us in the end, and shall thy father's spirit
Meet blind philosophers in heaven, whose merit
Of strict life may be imputed faith,[3] and hear
Thee, whom he taught so easy ways and near
To follow, damned? O, if thou dar'st, fear this;   15
This fear great courage and high valor is.
Dar'st thou aid mutinous Dutch,[4] and dar'st thou lay
Thee in ships, wooden sepulchers, a prey
To leaders' rage, to storms, to shot, to dearth?
Dar'st thou dive seas and dungeons of the earth?   20
Hast thou courageous fire to thaw the ice
Of frozen North discoveries? and thrice
Colder than salamanders,[5] like divine
Children in the oven,[6] fires of Spain, and the line,
Whose countries limbecks to our bodies be,   25
Canst thou for gain bear?[7] And must every he
Which cries not, "Goddess!" to thy mistress, draw,[8]
Or eat thy poisonous words? Courage of straw!
O desperate coward, wilt thou seem bold, and
To thy foes and his[9] (who made thee to stand   30
Sentinel in his world's garrison) thus yield,
And for forbidden wars, leave th' appointed field?
Know thy foes: The foul Devil (whom thou
Strivest to please) for hate, not love, would allow
Thee fain his whole realm to be quit;[1] and as   35
The world's all parts[2] wither away and pass,
So the world's self, thy other loved foe, is
In her decrepit wane, and thou, loving this,
Dost love a withered and worn strumpet; last,

1. The age of paganism, blind to the light of Christianity, but capable of following natural morality ("virtue").
2. I.e., hope of heaven should be as powerful ("valiant") an antidote to sin in us as earthly honor was to "them"—the pagans.
3. Even without Christian faith, pagan philosophers may achieve heaven (see *The Divine Comedy, Paradiso* XX) by an extraordinary display of virtue which causes faith to be imputed to them.
4. The Dutch continually enlisted English volunteers in their rebellious wars against the Spaniards. Donne had never fought in Flanders, though he had sailed twice against the Spaniards, to Cadiz and the Azores.
5. The salamander was traditionally so cold-blooded that it could live even in a fire.
6. The "divine children in the oven" are Shadrach, Meshach, and Abednego, rescued from the fiery furnace in Daniel iii.
7. The object of "bear" is "fires of Spain, and the line"—Inquisitorial and equatorial heats, which roast men as chemists heat materials in "limbecks" (alembics, or retorts for distilling).
8. I.e., fight a duel.
9. God's.
1. I.e., the Devil would gladly give you a free hand with his whole kingdom.
2. All parts of the world. It was a common belief in the 17th century that the world was getting old and decrepit.

Flesh (itself's death) and joys which flesh can taste,   40
Thou lovest; and thy fair goodly soul, which doth
Give this flesh power to taste joy, thou dost loathe.
Seek true religion. O, where? Mirreus,[3]
Thinking her unhoused here, and fled from us,
Seeks her at Rome; there, because he doth know   45
That she was there a thousand years ago.
He loves her rags so, as we here obey
The statecloth[4] where the Prince sat yesterday.
Crantz to such brave loves will not be enthralled,
But loves her only, who at Geneva is called   50
Religion—plain, simple, sullen, young,
Contemptuous, yet unhandsome; as among
Lecherous humors,[5] there is one that judges
No wenches wholesome but coarse country drudges.
Graius stays still at home here, and because   55
Some preachers, vile ambitious bawds, and laws
Still new, like fashions, bid him think that she
Which dwells with us, is only perfect, he
Embraceth her whom his Godfathers will
Tender to him, being tender, as wards still   60
Take such wives as their guardians offer, or
Pay values.[6] Careless Phrygius doth abhor
All, because all cannot be good, as one
Knowing some women whores, dares marry none.
Graccus loves all as one, and thinks that so   65
As women do in divers countries go
In divers habits, yet are still one kind,
So doth, so is religion; and this blind-
ness too much light breeds; but unmoved thou
Of force must one, and forced but one allow;   70
And the right;[7] ask thy father which is she,
Let him ask his; though truth and falsehood be
Near twins, yet truth a little elder is;
Be busy to seek her, believe me this,
He's not of none, nor worst, that seeks the best.[8]   75
To adore, or scorn an image, or protest,
May all be bad; doubt wisely; in strange way
To stand inquiring right, is not to stray;
To sleep, or run wrong, is. On a huge hill,
Cragged and steep, Truth stands, and he that will   80

3. The imaginary characters in this passage represent different creeds. "Mirreus" is a Roman Catholic, "Crantz" a Geneva Presbyterian, "Graius" an Erastian (i.e., believing in any religion sponsored by the state), "Phrygius" a skeptic, and "Graccus" a Universalist.
4. The royal canopy, a symbol of kingly power.
5. Tempers, temperaments.
6. Young men (of "tender" years) might reject the wives offered ("tendered") them by their guardians; but, if they did so, had to pay "values," i.e. fines.
7. I.e., being blind to the differences between religions, Graccus has too much light to see anything (lines 68–69). But the poet insists that without being swayed by human pressures, we must find just one true religion, "the right" true religion.
8. The man who seeks the best church is neither an unbeliever nor the worst sort of believer.

Reach her, about must, and about must go,
And what the hill's suddenness resists, win so;
Yet strive so, that before age, death's twilight,
Thy soul rest, for none can work in that night.
To will⁹ implies delay, therefore now do.   85
Hard deeds, the body's pains; hard knowledge too
The mind's endeavors reach,¹ and mysteries
Are like the sun, dazzling, yet plain to all eyes.
Keep the truth which thou hast found; men do not stand
In so ill case here, that God hath with his hand   90
Signed kings' blank charters to kill whom they hate,
Nor are they vicars, but hangmen to fate.²
Fool and wretch, wilt thou let thy soul be tied
To man's laws, by which she shall not be tried
At the last day? O, will it then boot thee   95
To say a Philip, or a Gregory,
A Harry, or a Martin taught thee this?³
Is not this excuse for mere contraries
Equally strong? Cannot both sides say so?
That thou mayest rightly obey power, her bounds know;   100
Those passed, her nature and name is changed; to be
Then humble to her is idolatry.⁴
As streams are, power is; those blest flowers that dwell
At the rough stream's calm head, thrive and do well,
But having left their roots, and themselves given   105
To the stream's tyrannous rage, alas, are driven
Through mills, and rocks, and woods, and at last, almost
Consumed in going, in the sea are lost.
So perish souls, which more choose men's unjust
Power from God claimed, than God himself to trust.   110

                                                            1633

Good Friday, 1613. Riding Westward

Let man's soul be a sphere, and then, in this,
The intelligence that moves, devotion is,¹
And as the other spheres, by being grown
Subject to foreign motions, lose their own,
And being by others hurried every day,   5

9. To intend a future action.
1. I.e., the body's pains achieve ("reach") hard deeds; the mind's endeavors will reach hard knowledge.
2. Human authority does not represent divine justice on earth; men are not God's vicars on earth (the hit here is at both the Pope and the secular monarch), but his hangmen at best—agents through whom his justice is fulfilled without carte blanche ("blank charters") to use their own judgments.
3. "Philip" is Philip II of Spain, and

"Gregory" any one of several Pope Gregories (VII, XIII, XIV); "Harry" is England's Henry VIII, and "Martin" is Martin Luther. Laymen and clergy, Protestants and Catholics, all are covered. "Boot": profit.
4. I.e., when the true limits of ecclesiastical power have been passed, obedience becomes idolatry.
1. As intelligences guide the visible planets, devotion is or should be the guiding principle of man's life.

Scarce in a year their natural form obey;
Pleasure or business, so, our souls admit
For their first mover, and are whirled by it.[2]
Hence is 't, that I am carried towards the West
This day, when my soul's form bends towards the East.   10
There I should see a Sun,[3] by rising, set,
And by that setting endless day beget:
But that Christ on this cross did rise and fall,
Sin had eternally benighted all.
Yet dare I almost be glad I do not see   15
That spectacle, of too much weight for me.
Who sees God's face, that is self-life, must die;
What a death were it then to see God die?
It made his own lieutenant, Nature, shrink;
It made his footstool crack, and the sun wink.[4]   20
Could I behold those hands which span the poles,
And tune all spheres at once, pierced with those holes?
Could I behold that endless height which is
Zenith to us, and our antipodes,[5]
Humbled below us? Or that blood which is   25
The seat of all our souls, if not of His,
Make dirt of dust, or that flesh which was worn
By God, for his apparel, ragg'd and torn?
If on these things I durst not look, durst I
Upon his miserable mother cast mine eye,   30
Who was God's partner here, and furnished thus
Half of that sacrifice which ransomed us?
Though these things, as I ride, be from mine eye,
They are present yet unto my memory,
For that looks towards them; and Thou look'st towards me,   35
O Saviour, as Thou hang'st upon the tree.
I turn my back to Thee but to receive
Corrections, till Thy mercies bid Thee leave.
O think me worth Thine anger; punish me;
Burn off my rusts and my deformity;   40
Restore Thine image so much, by Thy grace,
That Thou may'st know me, and I'll turn my face.

1633

From Holy Sonnets[1]

1

Thou hast made me, and shall Thy work decay?
Repair me now, for now mine end doth haste;

2. I.e., spheres are deflected from their true orbits by outside influences; so our souls are deflected by business or pleasure.
3. The sun-Son pun was an ancient one. Christ, the Son of God, set when he rose on the Cross, and his setting

(death) gave rise to the Christian era.
4. An earthquake and eclipse supposedly accompanied the Crucifixion.
5. "Zenith" and "antipodes" are the highest and farthest reach of heaven.
1. Several of the *Holy Sonnets* contain specific indications of date; number 17

I run to death, and death meets me as fast,
And all my pleasures are like yesterday.
I dare not move my dim eyes any way,   5
Despair behind, and death before doth cast
Such terror, and my feeble flesh doth waste
By sin in it, which it towards hell doth weigh.
Only Thou art above, and when towards Thee
By Thy leave I can look, I rise again;   10
But our old subtle foe so tempteth me
That not one hour myself I can sustain.
Thy grace may wing me to prevent his art,
And Thou like adamant draw mine iron heart.[2]

1633

5

I am a little world made cunningly
Of elements, and an angelic sprite;[3]
But black sin hath betrayed to endless night
My world's both parts, and O, both parts must die.
You which beyond that heaven which was most high   5
Have found new spheres, and of new lands can write,[4]
Pour new seas in mine eyes, that so I might
Drown my world with my weeping earnestly,
Or wash it if it must be drowned no more.[5]
But O, it must be burnt! Alas, the fire   10
Of lust and envy have burnt it heretofore,
And made it fouler; let their flames retire,
And burn me, O Lord, with a fiery zeal
Of Thee and Thy house, which doth in eating heal.[6]

1635

7

At the round earth's imagined corners,[7] blow
Your trumpets, angels; and arise, arise

makes reference to the recent death of
Donne's wife (August 15, 1617) and
number 18 may have been inspired by
the Elector Palatine's defeat (October
29, 1620). But most are considerably
earlier (1609–10). They are nineteen in
number, conventional in their rhyme
scheme and broad metrical pattern, but
rhythmically bold, powerful in their
imagery, and marked by deep emotional
coloring. Donne's religion was never a
secure or comfortable experience; his
Holy Sonnets are documents which mingle anguished despair with no less anguished hope. And in a sonnet like *Holy
Sonnet 14*, his faith rises to a series of
knotted paradoxes involving coercion
and submission, which would be revolting were it not for the full and evident
sincerity of the mind to which they were
inevitable.
2. "Wing": strengthen; "prevent":

counteract; "adamant": loadstone. Note
throughout the sonnets a combination
of strong imperatives and protestations
of abject helplessness which determines
the tone of Donne's religious feeling.
3. Both body and soul—the former
made of "elements," the latter "angelic
sprite" (spirit).
4. Donne asks the astronomers and explorers to find new oceans for tears to
weep or waters to wash away his sins.
5. God promised (Genesis ix.11) after
Noah's experience that the earth would
never again be flooded.
6. See Psalm lxix.9: "For the zeal of
thine house hath eaten me up." The
passage involves three sorts of flame—
those of the Last Judgment; those of
lust and envy; and those of zeal, which
alone heal.
7. Donne may have been thinking of

From death, you numberless infinities
Of souls, and to your scattered bodies go;
All whom the flood did, and fire shall, o'erthrow,   5
All whom war, dearth, age, agues, tyrannies,
Despair, law, chance hath slain, and you whose eyes
Shall behold God, and never taste death's woe.[8]
But let them sleep, Lord, and me mourn a space;
For, if above all these, my sins abound,   10
'Tis late to ask abundance of Thy grace
When we are there. Here on this lowly ground,
Teach me how to repent; for that's as good
As if Thou hadst sealed my pardon with Thy blood.

1633

10

Death, be not proud, though some have calléd thee
Mighty and dreadful, for thou art not so;
For those whom thou think'st thou dost overthrow
Die not, poor Death, nor yet canst thou kill me.
From rest and sleep, which but thy pictures be,   5
Much pleasure; then from thee much more must flow,
And soonest our best men with thee do go,
Rest of their bones, and soul's delivery.[9]
Thou art slave to fate, chance, kings, and desperate men,
And dost with poison, war, and sickness dwell,   10
And poppy or charms can make us sleep as well
And better than thy stroke; why swell'st[1] thou then?
One short sleep past, we wake eternally
And death shall be no more; Death, thou shalt die.

1633

14

Batter my heart, three-personed God; for You
As yet but knock, breathe, shine, and seek to mend;
That I may rise and stand, o'erthrow me, and bend
Your force to break, blow, burn, and make me new.
I, like an usurped town, to another due,   5
Labor to admit You, but O, to no end;
Reason, Your viceroy in me, me should defend,
But is captived, and proves weak or untrue.
Yet dearly I love You, and would be loved fain,
But am bethrothed unto Your enemy.   10
Divorce me, untie or break that knot again;
Take me to You, imprison me, for I,

---

the angels on old maps, who blow their trumpets to the four points of the compass. See also Revelation vii.1.
8. See Matthew xvi.28, Mark ix.1, and Luke ix.27, where the worthies are described who ascended directly to heaven from this life.
9. I.e., our best men go with you to find rest for their bones and freedom ("delivery") for their souls.
1. Puff up with pride.

Except You enthrall me, never shall be free,
Nor ever chaste, except You ravish me.

1633

18

Show me, dear Christ, Thy spouse so bright and clear.[2]
What! is it she which on the other shore
Goes richly painted? or which, robbed and tore,
Laments and mourns in Germany and here?[3]
Sleeps she a thousand, then peeps up one year?   5
Is she self-truth, and errs? now new, now outwore?
Doth she, and did she, and shall she evermore
On one, on seven, or on no hill appear?[4]
Dwells she with us, or like adventuring knights
First travel[5] we to seek, and then make love?   10
Betray, kind husband, Thy spouse to our sights,
And let mine amorous soul court Thy mild dove,
Who is most true and pleasing to Thee then
When she is embraced and open to most men.

1899

A Hymn to Christ, at the Author's Last Going into Germany[6]

In what torn ship soever I embark,
That ship shall be my emblem of Thy ark;
What sea soever swallow me, that flood
Shall be to me an emblem of Thy blood;
Though Thou with clouds of anger do disguise   5
Thy face, yet through that mask I know those eyes,
      Which, though they turn away sometimes,
            They never will despise.

I sacrifice this island unto Thee,
And all whom I loved there, and who loved me;   10
When I have put our seas twixt them and me,
Put Thou Thy seas betwixt my sins and Thee.
As the tree's sap doth seek the root below
In winter, in my winter now I go

2. "What are the marks of a true church?" was a deeply fought field of interdenominational debate in the 17th century. Few Anglican clergymen would have expressed an indecision as universal as Donne's in this sonnet. Its skepticism, and a sense that versifying did not beseem a clergyman, kept the sonnet out of all 17th-century editions.
3. The Church of Rome is "she which goes richly painted on the other shore"; she is contrasted with the reformed churches "in Germany and here."
4. The Mount of Olives, the seven hills of Rome, and (perhaps) by Lake Geneva or in the town of Canterbury.
5. The 17th-century spelling, *travaile*, includes the idea of labor.
6. Donne went to Germany as chaplain to the Earl of Doncaster in 1619; the mission was a diplomatic one, to the King and Queen of Bohemia.

Where none but Thee, th' eternal root   15
    Of true love, I may know.

Nor Thou nor Thy religion dost control
The amorousness of an harmonious soul,
But Thou would'st have that love Thyself; as Thou
Art jealous, Lord, so I am jealous now;   20
Thou lov'st not, till from loving more,[7] Thou free
My soul; whoever gives, takes liberty;
    Oh, if Thou car'st not whom I love,
        Alas, Thou lov'st not me.

Seal then this bill of my divorce to all   25
On whom those fainter beams of love did fall;
Marry those loves, which in youth scattered be
On fame, wit, hopes (false mistresses), to Thee.
Churches are best for prayer that have least light:
To see God only, I go out of sight;   30
    And to 'scape stormy days, I choose
        An everlasting night.

                                                    1633

Hymn to God My God, in My Sickness[1]

Since I am coming to that holy room
    Where, with Thy choir of saints for evermore,
I shall be made Thy music; as I come
    I tune the instrument here at the door,
    And what I must do then, think here before.   5

Whilst my physicians by their love are grown
    Cosmographers, and I their map, who lie
Flat on this bed, that by them may be shown
    That this is my southwest discovery[2]
    Per fretum febris,[3] by these straits to die,   10

I joy, that in these straits, I see my West;[4]
    For, though their currents yield return to none,
What shall my West hurt me? As West and East
    In all flat maps (and I am one) are one,
    So death doth touch the resurrection.   15

Is the Pacific Sea my home? Or are
    The Eastern riches? Is Jerusalem?

---

7. From loving elsewhere. Donne is playing with the idea, "To give me true love you must take away my freedom to love elsewhere."
1. Izaak Walton, Donne's first biographer, says this poem was written March 23, 1631, eight days before Donne's death.
2. The Straits of Magellan, or something spiritual which is analogous to them.
3. I.e., through the straits of fever.
4. Where the sun sets, hence where life ends.

Anyan,[5] and Magellan, and Gibraltar,
  All straits, and none but straits, are ways to them,
Whether where Japhet dwelt, or Cham, or Shem.[6]   20

We think that Paradise and Calvary,
  Christ's cross, and Adam's tree, stood in one place;
Look, Lord, and find both Adams met in me;
  As the first Adam's sweat surrounds my face,
  May the last Adam's blood my soul embrace.   25

So, in his purple wrapped,[7] receive me, Lord;
  By these his thorns give me his other crown;
And, as to others' souls I preached Thy word,
  Be this my text, my sermon to mine own;
  Therefore that he may raise the Lord throws down.   30

1635

A Hymn to God the Father[1]

Wilt Thou forgive that sin where I begun,
  Which is my sin, though it were done before?
Wilt Thou forgive that sin through which I run,
  And do run still, though still I do deplore?
    When Thou hast done, Thou hast not done,   5
    For I have more.

Wilt Thou forgive that sin which I have won
  Others to sin? and made my sin their door?
Wilt Thou forgive that sin which I did shun
  A year or two, but wallowed in a score?
    When Thou hast done, Thou hast not done,   10
    For I have more.

I have a sin of fear, that when I have spun
  My last thread, I shall perish on the shore;
Swear by Thy self, that at my death Thy Son   15
  Shall shine as he shines now and heretofore;
    And, having done that, Thou hast done,
    I fear no more.

1633

---

5. The Bering Straits.
6. Japhet, Cham (Ham), and Shem
were the three sons of Noah by whom
the world was repopulated after the
Flood (Genesis x). The descendants
of Japhet were thought to inhabit Europe, those of Ham Africa, and those
of Shem Asia.

7. The purple of Christ is his blood;
also a royal garment.
1. Even in poetry of unquestioned seriousness, Donne's mind expressed itself
naturally in puns; there are several in
this short hymn, which Walton tells us
was written during Donne's illness of
1623.

Prose   One volume of average size contains handily the complete poetical works of John Donne; his prose works would fill out at least fifteen such.
Of this prose material, much will seem to the modern reader intolerably

heavy going. Donne's formal preaching was tailored to the tastes of his age. He divides and subdivides his text, and regularly cites ancient ecclesiastical authorities in their original Latin. Sermons in the 17th century were expected to be vigorous intellectual exercises, and Donne's auditors obviously relished the rigor of the game. This was a game at which Donne had been practicing since youth—like most of his contemporaries, he read the Bible as a lawyer reads a contract—but its exhilarations are largely reserved for specialists.

Donne's most viable prose performances remain those which reveal his character as a poet. Thoughts of disease, death, and damnation rarely failed to stir in him a penitential fervor in which he became, as it were, representative of his audience and of humanity at large. His genius was irresistibly dramatic, even self-dramatizing; his prose contains a frequent confessional strain. At his most characteristic, he is the spokesman before God of a virile, vulnerable, unconquerable humanity.

From Paradoxes and Problems[1]

Paradox VI. *That It Is Possible to Find Some Virtue in Women*

I am not of that seared[2] impudence that I dare defend women, or pronounce them good; yet we see physicians allow some virtue in every poison. Alas! why should we except women? since certainly they are good for physic[3] at least, so as some wine is good for a fever. And though they be the occasioners of many sins, they are also the punishers and revengers of the same sins: for I have seldom seen one which consumes his substance and body upon them, escapes diseases or beggary; and this is their justice. And if *suum cuique dare*[4] be the fulfilling of all civil justice, they are most just; for they deny that which is theirs to no man.

Tanquam non liceat nulla puella negat.[5]

And who may doubt of great wisdom in them, that doth but observe with how much labor and cunning our justicers and other dispensers of the laws study to embrace them: and how zealously our preachers dehort[6] men from them, only by urging their subtleties and policies and wisdom, which are in them? Or who can deny them a good measure of fortitude, if he consider how valiant men they have overthrown, and being themselves overthrown, how much and how patiently they bear? And though they be most

1. In 1633, two years after Donne's death, a volume of his *Juvenilia*, or youthful productions, appeared. The "Paradoxes and Problems," as they are subtitled, are bits of logical horseplay, loaded with legal aphorisms perversely misapplied, and perfectly impudent in their cheerful, brassy assurance. This is the mood, and sometimes the mode, of many of the *Songs and Sonnets; Go and Catch a Falling Star* involves a playful misuse of logic akin to that of Paradox VI.
2. Insensitive, unfeeling.
3. As a medicine, to cure a morbid condition.
4. "To give each his own."
5. "So long as it's forbidden, no girl will deny it."
6. Discourage, draw away.

intemperate, I care not, for I undertook to furnish them with some virtue, not with all. Necessity, which makes even bad things good, prevails also for them, for we must say of them, as of some sharp pinching laws: If men were free from infirmities, they were needless. These or none must serve for reasons, and it is my great happiness that examples prove not rules, for to confirm this opinion, the world yields not one example.

Problem II. Why Puritans Make Long Sermons?

It needs not for perspicuousness, for God knows they are plain enough: nor do all of them use sem-brief accents, for some of them have crotchets enough.[7] It may be they intend not to rise like glorious tapers and torches, but like thin-wretched-sick-watching-candles, which languish and are in a divine consumption from the first minute, yea in their snuff, and stink when others are in their more profitable glory. I have thought sometimes that out of conscience they allow "Long measure to coarse ware."[8] And sometimes that, usurping in that place a liberty to speak freely of kings, they would reign as long as they could. But now I think they do it out of a zealous imagination that it is their duty to preach on till their auditory wake.

Problem VI. Why Hath the Common Opinion Afforded Women Souls?

It is agreed that we have not so much from them as any part of either our mortal souls of sense or growth;[9] and we deny souls to others equal to them in all but in speech, for which they are beholding to their bodily instruments: for perchance an ox's heart, or a goat's, or a fox's, or a serpent's would speak just so, if it were in the breast, and could move that tongue and jaws. Have they so many advantages and means to hurt us (for, ever their loving destroyed us) that we dare not displease them, but give them what they will? And so when some call them Angels, some Goddesses, and the Palpulian heretics make them bishops,[1] we descend so much with the stream to allow them souls? Or do we somewhat (in this dignifying of them) flatter princes and great personages, that are so much governed by them? Or do we in that easiness and

7. The sem-brief (now spelled *semi-breve*) is, in modern music, the longest note in ordinary use, a whole note; the crotchet is a note with half the value of a minim, a very short note indeed. But Donne is also playing with another meaning of "crotchet": a cranky idea on an unimportant point.
8. I.e., extra quantity to atone for poor quality.
9. 17th-century anatomy imputed to man several vital principles in addi-

tion to his immortal soul. The "animal spirits" and "vital spirits" which governed man's senses and his growth might be referred to freely as "souls."
1. "Palpulians," a nonsense word, is probably a misprint for "Pepulians." The Montanist sect, which centered at Pepuza in Phrygia, admitted women to the offices of deacon and sometimes of priest; Donne exaggerates when he mentions bishops.

prodigality, wherein we daily lose our own souls to we care not whom, so labor to persuade ourselves, that sith a woman hath a soul, a soul is no great matter? Or do we lend them souls but for use,[2] since they for our sakes give their souls again, and their bodies to boot? Or perchance because the devil (who is all soul) doth most mischief, and for convenience and proportion, because they would come nearer him, we allow them some souls, and so as the Romans naturalized some provinces in revenge, and made them Romans only for the burden of the commonwealth; so we have given women souls only to make them capable of damnation?

1633

From Devotions upon Emergent Occasions[1]

Meditation XIV

Idque notant criticis medici evenisse diebus.[2]

The physicians observe these accidents to have fallen upon the critical days.

I would not make man worse than he is, nor his condition more miserable than it is. But could I though I would? As a man cannot flatter God nor overpraise him, so a man cannot injure man nor undervalue him. Thus much must necessarily be presented to his remembrance, that those false happinesses which he hath in this world have their times and their seasons and their critical days; and they are judged and denominated according to the times when they befall us. What poor elements are our happinesses made of if time, time which we can scarce consider to be anything, be an essential part of our happiness! All things are done in some place; but if we consider place to be no more but the next hollow superficies[3] of the air, alas! how thin and fluid a thing is air, and how thin a film is a superficies, and a superficies of air! All things are done in time too; but if we consider time to be but the measure of motion, and howsoever it may seem to have three stations, past, present, and future, yet the first and last of these are not (one is not now, and the other is not yet) and that which you call *present* is not now the same that it was when you began to call it so in this line (before you sound that word *present* or that monosyllable

2. I.e., usury. Donne is suggesting that women's souls are only rented, to yield a profit to men.

1. The *Private Devotions* were written during an attack of illness in the winter of 1623. They describe in detail the stages of Donne's disease and recovery; each stage comprises a meditation on the human condition, an expostulation and debate with God, and a prayer to Him. The book was published almost immediately it was written, and to

great effect—the blend of private feeling and public moralizing rendering it particularly accessible to 17th-century readers. And its eloquent periods have provided a title for at least one major modern novel (see Meditation XVII). "Emergent" occasions are those which arise casually or unexpectedly.

2. Donne's Latin epigraphs are followed by his English translations, some of them very free ones indeed.

3. Surface.

now, the present and the now is past). If this imaginary half-nothing, time, be of the essence of our happinesses, how can they be thought durable? Time is not so; how can they be thought to be? Time is not so; not so considered in any of the parts thereof. If we consider eternity, into that time never entered; eternity is not an everlasting flux of time, but time is a short parenthesis in a long period; and eternity had been the same as it is, though time had never been. If we consider, not eternity, but perpetuity; not that which had no time to begin in, but which shall outlive time and be, when time shall be no more, what a minute is the life of the durablest creature compared to that! and what a minute is man's life in respect of the sun's or of a tree! and yet how little of our life is occasion, opportunity to receive good in; and how little of that occasion do we apprehend and lay hold of! How busy and perplexed a cobweb is the happiness of man here, that must be made up with a watchfulness to lay hold upon occasion, which is but a little piece of that which is nothing, time! And yet the best things are nothing without that. Honors, pleasures, possessions presented to us out of time, in our decrepit and distasted[4] and unapprehensive age, lose their office and lose their name; they are not honors to us that shall never appear nor come abroad into the eyes of the people to receive honor from them who give it; nor pleasures to us who have lost our sense to taste them; nor possessions to us who are departing from the possession of them. Youth is their critical day; that judges them, that denominates them, that inanimates and informs them, and makes them honors and pleasures and possessions; and when they come in an unapprehensive age, they come as a cordial when the bell rings out,[5] as a pardon when the head is off. We rejoice in the comfort of fire, but does any man cleave to it at midsummer? We are glad of the freshness and coolness of a vault, but does any man keep his Christmas there? or are the pleasures of the spring acceptable in autumn? If happiness be in the season or in the climate, how much happier then are birds than men, who can change the climate and accompany and enjoy the same season ever.

Meditation XVII

Nunc lento sonitu dicunt, morieris.

Now this bell tolling softly for another, says to me, Thou must die.

Perchance he for whom this bell tolls may be so ill as that he knows not it tolls for him; and perchance I may think myself so much better than I am, as that they who are about me and see my state may have caused it to toll for me, and I know not that. The church is catholic, universal, so are all her actions; all that she does

4. Having lost the sense of taste.
5. A "cordial" (medicine) which arrives when the parish bell is already tolling is a bit too late.

belongs to all. When she baptizes a child, that action concerns me; for that child is thereby connected to that body which is my head too,[6] and ingrafted into that body whereof I am a member. And when she buries a man, that action concerns me: all mankind is of one author and is one volume; when one man dies, one chapter is not torn out of the book, but translated[7] into a better language; and every chapter must be so translated. God employs several translators; some pieces are translated by age, some by sickness, some by war, some by justice; but God's hand is in every translation, and his hand shall bind up all our scattered leaves again for that library where every book shall lie open to one another. As therefore the bell that rings to a sermon calls not upon the preacher only, but upon the congregation to come, so this bell calls us all; but how much more me, who am brought so near the door by this sickness. There was a contention as far as a suit[8] (in which piety and dignity, religion and estimation,[9] were mingled) which of the religious orders should ring to prayers first in the morning; and it was determined that they should ring first that rose earliest. If we understand aright the dignity of this bell that tolls for our evening prayer, we would be glad to make it ours by rising early, in that application, that it might be ours as well as his whose indeed it is. The bell doth toll for him that thinks it doth; and though it intermit again, yet from that minute that that occasion wrought upon him, he is united to God. Who casts not up his eye to the sun when it rises? but who takes off his eye from a comet when that breaks out? Who bends not his ear to any bell which upon any occasion rings? but who can remove it from that bell which is passing a piece of himself out of this world? No man is an island, entire of itself; every man is a piece of the continent, a part of the main.[1] If a clod be washed away by the sea, Europe is the less, as well as if a promontory were, as well as if a manor of thy friend's or of thine own were. Any man's death diminishes me because I am involved in mankind, and therefore never send to know for whom the bell tolls; it tolls for thee. Neither can we call this a begging of misery or a borrowing of misery, as though we were not miserable enough of ourselves but must fetch in more from the next house, in taking upon us the misery of our neighbors. Truly it were an excusable covetousness if we did; for affliction is a treasure, and scarce any man hath enough of it. No man hath affliction enough that is not matured and ripened by it and made fit for God by that affliction. If a man carry treasure in bullion, or in a wedge of gold, and have none coined

6. I.e., the Christian church is the head of all men, as well as a body composed of its members.
7. Literally, "carried across"; hence, on the spiritual level, exalted from one sphere to another.
8. Controversy which went as far as a lawsuit.
9. Self-esteem.
1. Mainland.

into current money, his treasure will not defray² him as he travels. Tribulation is treasure in the nature of it, but it is not current money in the use of it, except we get nearer and nearer our home, heaven, by it. Another man may be sick too, and sick to death, and this affliction may lie in his bowels as gold in a mine and be of no use to him; but this bell that tells me of his affliction digs out and applies that gold to me, if by this consideration of another's danger I take mine own into contemplation and so secure myself by making my recourse to my God, who is our only security.

1623   1624

From Sermon LXXVI³

[*On Falling out of God's Hand*]

* * * When God's hand is bent to strike, "it is a fearful thing to fall into the hands of the living God";⁴ but to fall out of the hands of the living God is a horror beyond our expression, beyond our imagination. That God should let my soul fall out of his hand into a bottomless pit and roll an unremovable stone upon it and leave it to that which it finds there (and it shall find that there which it never imagined till it came thither) and never think more of that soul, never have more to do with it; that of that providence of God that studies the life of every weed and worm and ant and spider and toad and viper there should never, never any beam flow out upon me; that that God who looked upon me when I was nothing and called me when I was not, as though I had been, out of the womb and depth of darkness, will not look upon me now, when though a miserable and a banished and a damned creature, yet I am his creature still and contribute something to his glory even in my damnation; that that God who hath often looked upon me in my foulest uncleanness and when I had shut out the eye of the day, the sun, and the eye of the night, the taper, and the eyes of all the world with curtains and windows and doors, did yet see me and see me in mercy by making me see that he saw me and sometimes brought me to a present remorse and (for that time) to a

---

2. Pay his expenses.
3. Of Donne's estimated 180 sermons, the extraordinary total of 160 survive —monumental evidence that he was both a prolific and a popular preacher. The reasons for his popularity are clear: the sermons are not only rich in learning and curious lore; they are characteristically personal and powerful in their phrasing. Concepts which Donne used in his poems continually recur in the sermons, and the fuller context of

the prose often sheds useful light on the meaning of the poetry. Our present selection comes from the concluding part of a sermon preached "to the Earl of Carlisle and his company, at Sion" on the text, Mark xvi.16: "He that believeth not, shall be damned." The date is some time after 1623, when Sion College was founded in London by Dr. Thomas White.

4. Hebrews x.31.

forbearing of that sin, should so turn himself from me to his glorious saints and angels as that no saint nor angel nor Christ Jesus himself should ever pray him to look towards me, never remember[5] him that such a soul there is; that that God who hath so often said to my soul, *Quare morieris?* why wilt thou die? and so often sworn to my soul, *Vivit Dominus,* as the Lord liveth, I would not have thee die but live, will neither let me die nor let me live, but die an everlasting life and live an everlasting death; that that God who, when he could not get into me by standing and knocking, by his ordinary means of entering, by his word, his mercies, hath applied his judgments and hath shaked the house, this body, with agues and palsies, and set this house on fire with fevers and calentures,[6] and frighted the master of the house, my soul, with horrors and heavy apprehensions and so made an entrance into me; that that God should frustrate all his own purposes and practices upon me and leave me and cast me away as though I had cost him nothing; that this God at last should let this soul go away as a smoke, as a vapor, as a bubble; and that then this soul cannot be a smoke, a vapor, nor a bubble, but must lie in darkness as long as the Lord of light is light itself, and never spark of that light reach to my soul; what Tophet is not paradise, what brimstone is not amber, what gnashing is not a comfort, what gnawing of the worm is not a tickling, what torment is not a marriage bed to this damnation, to be secluded eternally, eternally, eternally from the sight of God? * * *

1640

5. Remind.   6. Fever with delirium.

BEN JONSON
(1572–1637)

1598:   *Every Man in His Humor,* Jonson's first play.
1616:   Jonson appointed poet laureate; publishes his
           Works.
1618–19: Journey to Scotland; conversations with Drummond
           of Hawthornden.

Ben Jonson played a vast part in the literary life of the 17th century. His special blend of satiric realism, romantic sentiment, and classical correctness was a root inspiration for nearly 200 years; his impact was felt on the stage, as well as in poetry, criticism, and standards of literary taste generally. He was in effect the precursor of English neoclassicism.

Jonson's father, a clergyman, died shortly after his son was born. Adopted in infancy by a bricklayer, Ben was educated for several years by William

Camden, the great Elizabethan antiquary, at Westminster School. He learned a great deal from Camden, and picked up much more of his splendid erudition on his own; for though he later received honorary degrees from both Oxford and Cambridge, he never attended either university. Instead, after leaving Westminster School, he seems to have worked for a while at the trade of bricklaying, and then to have entered the army. In Flanders, where the Dutch, allies of England, were warring for their liberty against the Spaniards, he fought singlehanded with one of the enemy before the massed armies, and killed his man. Returning to England about 1595, he began to work as an actor and playwright, and conquered the stage as vigorously as he had done the foreign foe. Hot of head and quick of hand, he was jailed for killing a fellow actor in a duel, jailed for insulting the Scotch at a time when King James was newly arrived on the throne from Scotland, and furiously embroiled in a series of literary wars with his fellow playwrights. But as he grew older, he grew mellower; and he succeeded in becoming literary dictator of London, not by the length of his sword or the sharpness of his pen, but by gaining the friendship of men like Donne, Shakespeare, Francis Beaumont, John Selden, John Fletcher, and Bacon. In addition, he engaged the affection of younger men (poets like Robert Herrick, Thomas Carew, and Sir John Suckling, speculative thinkers like Lord Falkland and Sir Kenelm Digby), who delighted to christen themselves "Sons of Ben." Sons of Ben provided the nucleus of the entire "Cavalier school" of English lyric poets.

The first of Jonson's great plays was *Every Man in His Humor*, in which Shakespeare acted a leading role. It was also the first of the so-called "comedies of humors," in which the prevailing eccentricities and ruling passions (i.e., "humors") of characters were exposed to satiric deflation. Though Jonson's classical tragedy *Sejanus* (1603) has been generally discounted as overloaded with antiquarian lore, *Volpone* (1606) and *The Alchemist* (1610) are two supreme satiric comedies of the English stage. Meanwhile, starting in 1605, Jonson began to write for the court a series of masques—elaborate and very expensive spectacles involving music, song, and dance, built around a moral allegory, and culminating in a compliment to the king or queen. Thus he became closely involved with the life of the court, a connection which was formalized in 1616, when he was appointed poet laureate with a substantial pension from the king. In 1618 he made a walking tour to Scotland, where he was entertained by William Drummond of Hawthornden, who recorded a good deal of his rather opinionated conversation. Perhaps because his later plays were generally unsuccessful on the stage, Jonson developed a tendency to vilify the taste of the age while applauding his own integrity, in a way that laid him open to satire. Yet even those who mocked him, admired; and he vindicated himself by leaving among his posthumous papers poetry as fine and delicate as any he had ever written—for example, the lovely *Sad Shepherd*, a pastoral drama. His death was universally mourned as the end of an era, for he was the last of the great Elizabethans as well as the first precursor of neoclassicism. His body lies in Westminster Abbey under the laconic, ambiguous inscription, "O Rare Ben Jonson."

In lyric poetry, as elsewhere, Jonson's primary debt was to the classics. His epigrams and satires have the tart and crackling energy of Martial's;

his songs and lyrical productions move with an elegant softness reminiscent of Catullus; he can turn a compliment or grace a playful little occasion with all the suavity of Horace. In all these qualities, as in the terse, masculine rhythms of his verse and the strong energy of his syntax, Jonson drew upon the Latin tongue for the advantage of his native English. He is one of the great discipliners of our speech; he reformed a diction overrun with sprawling, florid, intertangled metaphors into one capable of the chiseled phrase. His best work is always chaste and clear of outline, specific and strong in its language, bold in its effects. *Queen and Huntress* has a trochaic severity of meter which contrasts finely with the silver purity of its images. The tribute *To Penshurst* manages to describe, not just a building, but a way of life, an image of the great society which combines simplicity and elegance as Jonson himself combined them. This is done with complex, though unobtrusive, art. Note, for instance, how the description rises through the scale of creatures, from vegetables to animals to pretty girls— who carry emblems of themselves in the form of ripe fruit—to the lord of the manor, and finally to the king himself. Each person is in his place, each is in harmony with general nature, all things are ordered according to an architecture of full proportion; so that a kind of heroic image of the just society rises out of a simple description of a country house.

There is, indeed, a kind of Roman splendor about Jonson's writing, to which the typographers themselves have generally responded. When he published his *Works* in 1616 (the word is a translation of Latin *Opera*, a title previously applied only to the complete works of classical poets), the folio was one of the most elegant ever printed; and he has continued to appear in volumes of ripe, imperial dignity ever since.

To Penshurst[1]

Thou art not, Penshurst, built to envious show,
Of touch[2] or marble; nor canst boast a row
Of polished pillars, or a roof of gold;
Thou hast no lantern, whereof tales are told,
Or stair, or courts; but stand'st an ancient pile,   5
And, these[3] grudged at, art reverenced the while.
Thou joy'st in better marks, of soil, of air,
Of wood, of water; therein thou art fair.
Thou hast thy walks for health, as well as sport;
Thy mount, to which the dryads[4] do resort,   10
Where Pan and Bacchus their high feasts have made,
Beneath the broad beech and the chestnut shade;
That taller tree, which of a nut was set
At his great birth where all the Muses met.[5]

1. The country seat of the Sidney family (famous for Sir Philip) in Kent; Jonson's is one of the first English poems celebrating a specific place (later examples are *Cooper's Hill* by John Denham and *Windsor Castle* by Alexander Pope).

2. Touchstone, i.e., basanite, a pure black, finely grained, and therefore expensive variety of basalt.
3. More pretentious houses.
4. Wood nymphs.
5. Sir Philip Sidney was born at Penshurst; an oak tree, planted the day of

There in the writhéd bark are cut the names 15
Of many a sylvan,[6] taken with his flames;
And thence the ruddy satyrs oft provoke
The lighter fauns to reach thy Lady's Oak.[7]
Thy copse too, named of Gamage,[8] thou hast there,
That never fails to serve thee seasoned deer 20
When thou wouldst feast or exercise thy friends.
The lower land, that to the river bends,
Thy sheep, thy bullocks, kine, and calves do feed;
The middle grounds thy mares and horses breed.
Each bank doth yield thee conies;[9] and the tops, 25
Fertile of wood, Ashore and Sidney's copse,[1]
To crown thy open table, doth provide
The purpled pheasant with the speckled side;
The painted partridge lies in every field,
And for thy mess is willing to be killed. 30
And if the high-swollen Medway[2] fail thy dish,
Thou hast thy ponds, that pay thee tribute fish,
Fat aged carps that run into thy net,
And pikes, now weary their own kind to eat,
As loath the second draught or cast to stay, 35
Officiously at first themselves betray;
Bright eels that emulate them, and leap on land
Before the fisher, or into his hand.
Then hath thy orchard fruit, thy garden flowers,
Fresh as the air, and new as are the hours. 40
The early cherry, with the later plum,
Fig, grape, and quince, each in his time doth come;
The blushing apricot and woolly peach
Hang on thy walls, that every child may reach.
And though thy walls be of the country stone, 45
They are reared with no man's ruin, no man's groan;
There's none that dwell about them wish them down;
But all come in, the farmer and the clown,[3]
And no one empty-handed, to salute
Thy lord and lady, though they have no suit. 50
Some bring a capon, some a rural cake,
Some nuts, some apples; some that think they make
The better cheeses bring them, or else send
By their ripe daughters, whom they would commend
This way to husbands, and whose baskets bear 55
An emblem of themselves in plum or pear.
But what can this (more than express their love)

his birth, is still shown as "Sidney's oak."
6. Woodsman.
7. Lady Leicester's oak, named after a lady of the house who once entered into labor under its branches. "Provoke": challenge to a race.
8. Lady Barbara Gamage gave her name to a grove near the entrance of the park.
9. Rabbits.
1. "Ashore and Sidney's copse" are little woods and spinneys, lovingly enumerated by Jonson. They still survive, under their ancient names.
2. The local river.
3. Yokel.

Add to thy free provisions, far above
The need of such? whose liberal board doth flow
With all that hospitality doth know;   60
Where comes no guest but is allowed to eat,
Without his fear, and of thy lord's own meat;
Where the same beer and bread, and selfsame wine,
That is his lordship's shall be also mine,
And I not fain to sit (as some this day   65
At great men's tables), and yet dine away.[4]
Here no man tells[5] my cups; nor, standing by,
A waiter doth my gluttony envy,
But gives me what I call, and lets me eat;
He knows below he shall find plenty of meat.   70
Thy tables hoard not up for the next day;
Nor, when I take my lodging, need I pray
For fire, or lights, or livery;[6] all is there,
As if thou then wert mine, or I reigned here:
There's nothing I can wish, for which I stay.[7]   75
That found King James when, hunting late this way
With his brave son, the prince, they saw thy fires
Shine bright on every hearth, as the desires
Of thy Penates[8] had been set on flame
To entertain them; or the country came   80
With all their zeal to warm their welcome here.
What (great I will not say, but) sudden cheer
Didst thou then make 'em! and what praise was heaped
On thy good lady then, who therein reaped
The just reward of her high housewifery;   85
To have her linen, plate, and all things nigh,
When she was far; and not a room but dressed
As if it had expected such a guest!
These, Penshurst, are thy praise, and yet not all.
Thy lady's noble, fruitful, chaste withal.   90
His children thy great lord may call his own,
A fortune in this age but rarely known.
They are, and have been, taught religion; thence
Their gentler spirits have sucked innocence.
Each morn and even they are taught to pray,   95
With the whole household, and may, every day,
Read in their virtuous parents' noble parts
The mysteries of manners, arms, and arts.
Now, Penshurst, they that will proportion[9] thee
With other edifices, when they see   100
Those proud, ambitious heaps, and nothing else,
May say their lords have built, but thy lord dwells.

                                                    1616

4. Because the tables were so large, different courses might be served at different ends—hence the possibility of sitting at a man's table, yet dining away.
5. Counts.
6. Rations, food.
7. Wait.
8. Roman household gods. A room in the house is still known as "King James's room."
9. Compare.

To the Memory of My Beloved Master William Shakespeare

AND WHAT HE HATH LEFT US[1]

To draw no envy, Shakespeare, on thy name,
Am I thus ample to thy book and fame,
While I confess thy writings to be such
As neither man nor Muse can praise too much.
'Tis true, and all men's suffrage.[2] But these ways   5
Were not the paths I meant unto thy praise:
For silliest ignorance on these may light,
Which, when it sounds at best, but echoes right;
Or blind affection,[3] which doth ne'er advance
The truth, but gropes, and urgeth all by chance;   10
Or crafty malice might pretend this praise,
And think to ruin where it seemed to raise.
These are as some infamous bawd or whore
Should praise a matron. What could hurt her more?
But thou art proof against them, and, indeed,   15
Above th' ill fortune of them, or the need.
I therefore will begin. Soul of the age!
The applause! delight! the wonder of our stage!
My Shakespeare, rise; I will not lodge thee by
Chaucer or Spenser, or bid Beaumont lie   20
A little further to make thee a room:[4]
Thou art a monument without a tomb,
And art alive still while thy book doth live,
And we have wits to read and praise to give.
That I not mix thee so, my brain excuses,   25
I mean with great, but disproportioned[5] Muses;
For, if I thought my judgment were of years,
I should commit thee surely with thy peers,
And tell how far thou didst our Lyly outshine,
Or sporting Kyd, or Marlowe's mighty line.[6]   30
And though thou hadst small Latin and less Greek,[7]
From thence to honor thee I would not seek
For names, but call forth thund'ring Aeschylus,
Euripides, and Sophocles to us,

1. This poem was prefixed to the first folio of Shakespeare's plays, published in 1623.
2. Agreement, consent.
3. Prejudice.
4. Chaucer, Spenser, and Francis Beaumont were buried in Westminster Abbey; Shakespeare, of course, in Stratford. Jonson endorses the separation; Shakespeare should not be crowded.
5. Not comparable.
6. John Lyly, Thomas Kyd, and Christopher Marlowe, Elizabethan dramatists put in the shade by Shakespeare.
7. Shakespeare had, by modern standards, a very adequate command of Latin; Jonson is speaking from the lofty height of his own remarkable scholarship. Shakespeare's French and Italian (he was competent in both tongues) Jonson does not think worthy of mention.

Pacuvius, Accius, him of Cordova dead,[8]   35
To life again, to hear thy buskin[9] tread
And shake a stage; or, when thy socks were on,
Leave thee alone for the comparison
Of all that insolent Greece or haughty Rome
Sent forth, or since did from their ashes come.   40
Triumph, my Britain; thou hast one to show
To whom all scenes[1] of Europe homage owe.
He was not of an age, but for all time!
And all the Muses still were in their prime
When like Apollo he came forth to warm   45
Our ears, or like a Mercury to charm
Nature herself was proud of his designs,
And joyed to wear the dressing of his lines,
Which were so richly spun, and woven so fit,
As, since, she will vouchsafe no other wit: 50
The merry Greek, tart Aristophanes,
Neat Terence, witty Plautus[2] now not please,
But antiquated and deserted lie,
As they were not of Nature's family.
Yet must I not give Nature all; thy Art,   55
My gentle Shakespeare, must enjoy a part.
For though the poet's matter Nature be,
His Art doth give the fashion; and that he
Who casts to write a living line must sweat
(Such as thine are) and strike the second heat   60
Upon the muses' anvil; turn the same,
And himself with it, that he thinks to frame,
Or for the laurel he may gain a scorn;
For a good poet's made as well as born.
And such wert thou! Look how the father's face   65
Lives in his issue; even so the race
Of Shakespeare's mind and manners brightly shines
In his well-turned and true-filed lines,
In each of which he seems to shake a lance,[3]
As brandished at the eyes of ignorance.   70
Sweet swan of Avon, what a sight it were
To see thee in our waters yet appear,
And make those flights upon the banks of Thames
That so did take Eliza and our James![4]
But stay; I see thee in the hemisphere   75
Advanced and made a constellation there![5]
Shine forth, thou star of poets, and with rage

8. Marcus Pacuvius and Lucius Accius (2nd century B.C.) and "him of Cordova," Seneca the Younger (1st century A.D.), the greatest of the Latin tragedians. Only fragments survive of the plays of Pacuvius and Accius; Jonson's comparisons are more pedantic, in these instances, than relevant.
9. The symbol of tragedy, as contrasted with "socks" (in the next line), symbols of comedy.

1. Stages.
2. Aristophanes, the great Greek satirist and comic writer; Terence and Plautus (3rd and 2nd centuries B.C.), Roman writers of comedy.
3. Pun on Shake-speare.
4. Queen Elizabeth and King James.
5. Heroes and demigods were typically exalted after death to a place among the stars.

Or influence[6] chide or cheer the drooping stage,
Which, since thy flight from hence, hath mourned like night,
And despairs day, but for thy volume's light.   80

1623

To William Camden[1]

Camden, most reverend head, to whom I owe
All that I am in arts, all that I know
(How nothing's that!), to whom my country owes
The great renown and name wherewith she goes;[2]
Than thee the age sees not that thing more grave,   5
More high, more holy, that she more would crave.
What name, what skill, what faith hast thou in things!
What sight in searching the most antique springs!
What weight and what authority in thy speech!
Man scarce can make that doubt, but thou canst teach.[3]   10
Pardon free truth and let thy modesty,
Which conquers all, be once overcome by thee.
Many of thine, this better could than I;
But for[4] their powers, accept my piety.

1616

On My First Daughter

Here lies, to each her parents' ruth,[5]
Mary, the daughter of their youth;
Yet all heaven's gifts being heaven's due,
It makes the father less to rue.
At six months' end she parted hence   5
With safety of her innocence;
Whose soul heaven's queen, whose name she bears,
In comfort of her mother's tears,
Hath placed amongst her virgin-train:
Where, while that severed doth remain,   10
This grave partakes the fleshly birth;
Which cover lightly, gentle earth!

1616

6. "Rage" and "influence" describe the supposed effects of the planets on earthly affairs. "Rage" also implies poetic inspiration.
1. Camden (1551–1623), a famous antiquary and historical scholar, had been Jonson's schoolmaster.
2. Camden's antiquarian studies in *Britannia* (1586) and *Remains of a* *Greater Work Concerning Britain* (1605) ran into several editions and were translated abroad.
3. I.e., man can scarcely ask a question to which you don't know the answer.
4. But in lieu of.
5. Grief. There is no sure identification of Jonson's daughter, nor a positive date of composition for the poem.

On My First Son

Farewell, thou child of my right hand,[6] and joy;
My sin was too much hope of thee, loved boy:
Seven years thou wert lent to me, and I thee pay,
Exacted by thy fate, on the just day.
O could I lose all father[7] now! for why   5
Will man lament the state he should envy,
To have so soon 'scaped world's and flesh's rage,
And, if no other misery, yet age?
Rest in soft peace, and asked, say, "Here doth lie
Ben Jonson his best piece of poetry."   10
For whose sake henceforth all his vows be such
As what he loves may never like too much.[8]

1616

To John Donne

Donne, the delight of Phoebus and each Muse,
Who, to thy one, all other brains refuse;[9]
Whose every work, of thy most early wit,
Came forth example and remains so yet;
Longer a-knowing than most wits do live,   5
And which no affection praise enough can give.
To it[1] thy language, letters, arts, best life,
Which might with half mankind maintain a strife.
All which I meant to praise, and yet I would,
But leave, because I cannot as I should.   10

1616

It Was a Beauty That I Saw[2]

It was a beauty that I saw,
So pure, so perfect, as the frame

6. "Child of the right hand" is a literal translation of the Hebrew name "Benjamin," which implies the meanings "dexterous" or "fortunate." The boy was born in 1596, and died on his birthday in 1603.
7. Relinquish all thoughts of being a father.
8. The obscure grammar of the last lines seems to refer back to the feeling in line 2, that too much affection

is fatal to the loved one.
9. The word "refuse" could imply a reproach against Donne's obscurity, a notion of egotism ("refusal" involving preference of one over others), or the idea of welding (re-fusing) lesser minds to a greater.
1. The verb "add" is understood.
2. In *The New Inn* IV.4, this song is sung by Lovel.

Of all the universe was lame
To that one figure, could I draw
Or give least line of it a law.   5
A skein of silk without a knot,
A fair march made without a halt,
A curious[3] form without a fault,
A printed book without a blot:
All beauty, and without a spot.   10

1629

Epitaph on Elizabeth, L. H.[4]

Wouldst thou hear what man can say
In a little? Reader, stay.
Underneath this stone doth lie
As much beauty as could die;
Which in life did harbor give   5
To more virtue than doth live.
If at all she had a fault,
Leave it buried in this vault.
One name was Elizabeth;
Th' other, let it sleep with death: 10
Fitter, where it died, to tell,
Than that it lived at all. Farewell!

1616

An Elegy

Though beauty be the mark of praise,
   And yours of whom I sing be such
   As not the world can praise too much,
Yet is 't your virtue now I raise.

A virtue, like allay,[5] so gone   5
   Throughout your form as, though that move
   And draw and conquer all men's love,
This subjects you to love of one.

Wherein you triumph yet; because
   'Tis of yourself, and that you use   10
   The noblest freedom, not to choose
Against or faith or honor's laws.

3. Elaborate.
4. The subject of this epitaph may have been Elizabeth, Lady Hatton; but, in fact, her name has slept with death.
5. Alloy. The thought is that her beauty makes her loved by all, while her virtue confines her to a single lover (her husband?). Jonson here is in an unusually metaphysical mood.

But who should less expect from you,
   In whom alone Love lives again?
   By whom he is restored to men,   15
And kept, and bred, and brought up true.

His falling temples you have reared,
   The withered garlands ta'en away;
   His altars kept from the decay
That envy wished, and nature feared;   20

And on them burn so chaste a flame,
   With so much loyalties' expense,
   As Love, t' acquit such excellence,
Is gone himself into your name.[6]

And you are he; the deity   25
   To whom all lovers are designed
   That would their better objects find;
Among which faithful troop am I.

Who, as an offspring[7] at your shrine,
   Have sung this hymn, and here entreat   30
   One spark of your diviner heat
To light upon a love of mine.

Which, if it kindle not, but scant
   Appear, and that to shortest view,
   Yet give me leave t' adore in you   35
What I in her am grieved to want.[8]

                           1640

Slow, Slow, Fresh Fount[9]

Slow, slow, fresh fount, keep time with my salt tears;
Yet slower, yet, O faintly, gentle springs!
List to the heavy part the music bears,
Woe weeps out her division,[1] when she sings.
    Droop herbs and flowers;
    Fall grief in showers;   5
Our beauties are not ours. O, I could still,
Like melting snow upon some craggy hill,

6. To repay the lady's devotion, Love himself has entered her name; from these lines it has been conjectured that the poem was addressed to Lady Covell.
7. Perhaps "descendant," more likely a wandering offshoot of the "faithful troop."
8. Can Jonson possibly be saying here that his own mistress is a poor copy of the lady to whom this poem is addressed? This hardly seems complimentary to either lady, though it is in the Donne tradition of bold, witty truth-telling.
9. From the satiric comedy *Cynthia's Revels* (1600). It deals with the sin of self-love, and this famous lyric is a lament sung by Echo for Narcissus, who was entranced by his own image and ultimately transformed into a flower.
1. Grief, but also a rapid, melodic passage of music.

Drop, drop, drop, drop,[2]   10
Since nature's pride is now a withered daffodil.

1600

Queen and Huntress[3]

Queen and huntress, chaste and fair,
Now the sun is laid to sleep,
Seated in thy silver chair,
State in wonted manner keep;
Hesperus entreats thy light,   5
Goddess excellently bright.

Earth, let not thy envious shade
Dare itself to interpose;
Cynthia's shining orb was made
Heaven to clear, when day did close.   10
Bless us then with wishèd sight,
Goddess excellently bright.

Lay thy bow of pearl apart,
And thy crystal-shining quiver;
Give unto the flying hart   15
Space to breathe, how short soever.
Thou that mak'st a day of night,
Goddess excellently bright.

1600

Gypsy Songs[4]

1

The faery beam upon you,
The stars to glister on you;
    A moon of light
    In the noon of night,
Till the fire-drake[5] hath o'ergone you!   5
The wheel of fortune guide you,
The boy with the bow[6] beside you;
    Run ay in the way
    Till the bird of day,
And the luckier lot betide you!   10

2. This line shows how far Jonson could go in adapting his verse to the needs of a composer.
3. Also from *Cynthia's Revels*, this song is sung by Hesperus, the evening star, to Cynthia, or Diana, goddess of chastity and the moon—with whom Queen Elizabeth was, almost automatically, equated.
4. From one of Jonson's masques, *The Gypsies Metamorphosed*.
5. I.e., till the will-o'-the-wisp has passed you by.
6. Cupid.

2

To the old, long life and treasure!
To the young, all health and pleasure!
  To the fair, their face
  With eternal grace
And the soul to be loved at leisure!   5
To the witty, all clear mirrors;
To the foolish, their dark errors;
  To the loving sprite,
  A secure delight;
To the jealous, his own false terrors!   10

1621

Though I Am Young and Cannot Tell[7]

Though I am young, and cannot tell
  Either what Death or Love is well,
Yet I have heard they both bear darts,
  And both do aim at human hearts.
And then again, I have been told   5
  Love wounds with heat, as Death with cold;
So that I fear they do but bring
  Extremes to touch, and mean one thing.

As in a ruin[8] we it call
  One thing to be blown up, or fall;   10
Or to our end like way may have
  By a flash of lightning, or a wave;
So Love's inflaméd shaft or brand
  May kill as soon as Death's cold hand;
Except Love's fires the virtue have   15
  To fright the frost out of the grave.

1641

Song: To Celia[9]

Drink to me only with thine eyes,
  And I will pledge with mine;
Or leave a kiss but in the cup,
  And I'll not look for wine.

7. This song is sung in *The Sad Shepherd* by Caroline; the pastoral simplicity of her character is caught in the naïve monosyllables of the poem.
8. Demolition, explosion.
9. These famous lines are a patchwork of five separate passages in the *Epistles* of Philostratus, a Greek sophist of the 3rd century A.D. Jonson very carefully reworded the phrases (there are several early MS. versions of the poem) into this classic lyric.

The thirst that from the soul doth rise,   5
Doth ask a drink divine:
But might I of Jove's nectar sup,
I would not change for thine.

I sent thee late a rosy wreath,
Not so much honoring thee,   10
As giving it a hope, that there
It could not withered be.
But thou thereon did'st only breathe,
And sent'st it back to me;
Since when it grows and smells, I swear,   15
Not of itself, but thee.

                                         1616

Come, My Celia[1]

Come, my Celia, let us prove,[2]
While we can, the sports of love;
Time will not be ours forever;
He at length our good will sever.
Spend not then his gifts in vain.   5
Suns that set may rise again;
But if once we lose this light,
'Tis with us perpetual night.
Why should we defer our joys?
Fame and rumor are but toys.   10
Cannot we delude the eyes
Of a few poor household spies,
Or his easier ears beguile,
So removéd by our wile?
'Tis no sin love's fruit to steal;   15
But the sweet thefts to reveal,
To be taken, to be seen,
These have crimes accounted been.

                                         1606

The Triumph of Charis[3]

See the chariot at hand here of Love,
  Wherein my lady rideth!
Each that draws is a swan or a dove,

1. This song is sung by Volpone, in the comedy of the same name. It paraphrases a poem by Catullus.
2. Experience.
3. *A Celebration of Charis* consists of ten loosely connected lyrics, which were printed as a unit, amid a posthumous collection of Jonson's lyric poetry. The *Triumph* is the fourth of the ten poems.

And well the car Love guideth.
As she goes, all hearts do duty
    Unto her beauty;   5
And, enamored, do wish, so they might
    But enjoy such a sight,
That they still were to run by her side,
Through swords, through seas, whither she would ride.   10

Do but look on her eyes; they do light
    All that Love's world compriseth!
Do but look on her hair; it is bright
    As Love's star when it riseth!
Do but mark, her forehead's smoother   15
    Than words that soothe her!
And from her arched brows, such a grace
    Sheds itself through the face,
As alone there triumphs to the life
All the gain, all the good, of the elements' strife.   20

Have you seen but a bright lily grow,
    Before rude hands have touched it?
Ha' you marked but the fall o' the snow
    Before the soil hath smutched it?
Ha' you felt the wool o' the beaver?   25
    Or swan's down ever?
Or have smelt o' the bud o' the brier?
    Or the nard[4] in the fire?
Or have tasted the bag o' the bee?
O so white, O so soft, O so sweet is she![5]

                    30
                  1640

Still to Be Neat[6]

Still to be neat, still to be dressed,
As you were going to a feast;
Still to be powdered, still perfumed;
Lady, it is to be presumed,
Though art's hid causes are not found,   5
All is not sweet, all is not sound.

Give me a look, give me a face
That makes simplicity a grace;
Robes loosely flowing, hair as free;
Such sweet neglect more taketh me   10
Then all th' adulteries of art.
They strike mine eyes, but not my heart.

                    1609

4. I.e., spikenard, an aromatic Oriental bush.
5. This last stanza, expanded from the Latin epigrammatist Martial, was so pleasing to Jonson that he used it in several different poems.
6. In *Epicoene, or The Silent Woman,* this song is sung by Clerimont.

Ode to Himself[7]

Come leave the loathéd stage,
  And the more loathsome age,
Where pride and impudence, in faction knit,
    Usurp the chair of wit!
Indicting and arraigning every day   5
    Something they call a play.
  Let their fastidious, vain
  Commission of the brain
Run on and rage, sweat, censure, and condemn;
They were not made for thee, less thou for them.   10

Say that thou pour'st them wheat,
  And they will acorns eat;
'Twere simple fury still thyself to waste
    On such as have no taste!
To offer them a surfeit of pure bread,   15
    Whose appetites are dead!
  No, give them grains their fill,
  Husks, draff to drink and swill:[8]
If they love lees, and leave the lusty wine,
Envy them not; their palate's with the swine.   20

No doubt some moldy tale,
  Like *Pericles*,[9] and stale
As the shrieve's crusts, and nasty as his fish—
    Scraps, out every dish
Thrown forth and raked into the common tub,   25
    May keep up the Play-club:
  There, sweepings do as well
  As the best-ordered meal;
For who the relish of these guests will fit
Needs set them but the alms basket of wit.   30

And much good do 't you then:
  Brave plush and velvet men
Can feed on orts;[1] and, safe in your stage clothes,
    Dare quit, upon your oaths,
The stagers and the stage-wrights too, your peers,[2]   35
    Of larding your large ears
  With their foul comic socks,

7. The failure of Jonson's *The New Inn* (1629) inspired this heroic assault on criticism and the public taste.
8. Jonson gets into one line three words which suggest pig-food.
9. Shakespeare's play, at least in part (printed 1609), which Jonson compares to poorhouse fare.

1. Scraps.
2. This fourth stanza turns toward an attack on the players and playwrights themselves, whom Jonson holds responsible for the low state of public taste. His anger here comes close to incoherence, and the plain sense of the stanza is most unclear.

Wrought upon twenty blocks;
Which, if they are torn, and turned, and patched enough,
The gamesters share your guilt, and·you their stuff.   40

Leave things so prostitute
And take th' Alcaic lute;[3]
Or thine own Horace, or Anacreon's lyre;
    Warm thee by Pindar's fire:
And though thy nerves be shrunk, and blood be cold,   45
    Ere years have made thee old,
Strike that disdainful heat
Throughout, to their defeat,
As curious fools, and envious of thy strain,
May, blushing, swear no palsy's in thy brain.   50

But when they hear thee sing
The glories of thy king,
His zeal to God and his just awe o'er men,
    They may, blood-shaken then,
Feel such a flesh-quake to possess their powers   55
    As they shall cry, "Like ours,
In sound of peace or wars,
No harp e'er hit the stars
In tuning forth the acts of his sweet reign,
And raising Charles his chariot 'bove his Wain."[4]   60

1629   1640

The Vision of Delight[1]
Presented at Court in Christmas, 1617

THE SCENE—A *Street in Perspective of Fair Building Discovered.*

DELIGHT *is seen to come as afar off, accompanied with* GRACE, LOVE,
HARMONY, REVEL, SPORT, LAUGHTER. WONDER *following.*

    DELIGHT *spake in song (stylo recitativo)*:
Let us play, and dance, and sing,
    Let us now turn every sort

3. That of Alcaeus, who lived ca. 600
B.C., and became famous, along with
Horace, Anacreon, and Pindar, among
the greatest lyric poets.
4. Jonson's poetry will elevate the
chariot of Charles I (symbol of his
royal power) above Charles's Wain
(the seven bright stars of Ursa Major)
among the constellations.
1. The sort of extravagant allegorical
entertainment represented by *The Vision
of Delight* was enormously popular at
the court of James I. The parts were
taken by courtiers, there was usually
only a single representation of each
masque, and enormous sums of money
were expended on the *décor.* The three

traditional elements of the masque are
spectacle, allegory, and compliment; it
is of the essence that the mythological-
allegorical world of the masque should
finally be converted into the "actual"
world of the court, just as Delight
promises to do in the first four lines of
her first speech.
    Jonson's stage directions, being partly
descriptive (for the reader), partly instructive (for the performer), are rather
casual about observing consistency of
tense. The chief actor in *The Vision of
Delight* was George Villiers, newly
created Marquis of Buckingham;
among the audience was an American
visitor, Pocahontas.

Of the pleasures of the spring
To the graces of a court.

From air, from cloud, from dreams, from toys,[2]   5
To sounds, to sense, to love, to joys;
Let your shows[3] be new, as strange,
Let them oft and sweetly vary;
Let them haste so to their change,
As the seers may not tarry;   10
Too long to expect the pleasingest sight
Doth take away from the delight.

Here the first ANTIMASQUE[4] *entered.*
A she-monster *delivered of six* BURRATINES, *that dance with six*
PANTALOONS; *which done,*
                    DELIGHT *spoke again:*

Yet hear what your Delight doth pray:
All sour and sullen looks away,
That are the servants of the day;   15
Our sports are of the humorous[5] Night,
Who feeds the stars that give her light,
And useth (than her wont) more bright,[6]
To help the vision of DELIGHT.

Here the NIGHT *rises, and took her chariot bespangled with stars.*
                    DELIGHT *proceeds:*

See, see her scepter and her crown   20
Are all of flame, and from her gown
A train of light comes waving down.
This night in dew she will not steep
The brain, nor lock the sense in sleep;
But all awake with Phantoms keep,   25
And those to make DELIGHT more deep.

By this time the NIGHT *and* MOON *being both risen,* NIGHT, *hovering*
over the place, sang:

Break, Fancy, from thy cave of cloud,
And spread thy purple wings;
Now all thy figures are allowed,
And various shapes of things;   30
Create of airy forms a stream;
It must have blood, and naught of fleam,[7]
And though it be a waking dream;
THE CHOIR: Yet let it like an odor rise
                    To all the senses here,   35

2. Trifles.
3. Displays.
4. The "good" characters—Delight and her following—are the "masque"; the "antimasque" comprises grotesques who threaten and oppose them. "Burratines" are puppet-figures; "pantaloons" are clowns. Both names come from the Italian, and there is a possibility that Jonson modeled this masque in its entirety on an Italian original.
5. Whimsical.
6. I.e., and remains (is accustomed to be, "useth") brighter than usual.
7. Phlegm, the dull, muddy humor. Fancy (fantasy) must be of a hot, sanguine humor ("must have blood") to present lively pictures.

And fall like sleep upon their eyes,
Or music in their ear.

The scene here changed to cloud, and FANCY, *breaking forth, spake:*[8]

Bright Night, I obey thee, and am come at thy call,
But it is no one dream that can please these all;
Wherefore I would know what dreams would delight 'em;   40
For never was Fancy more loath to affright 'em.
And Fancy, I tell you, has dreams that have wings,
And dreams that have honey, and dreams that have stings;
Dreams of the maker, and dreams of the teller,
Dreams of the kitchen, and dreams of the cellar: 45
Some that are tall, and some that are dwarfs,
Some that are haltered, and some that wear scarfs;
Some that are proper, and signify o' thing,
And some another, and some that are nothing:
For say the French verdingale and the French hood   50
Were here to dispute; must it be understood,
A feather, for a wisp, were a fit moderator?[9]
Your ostrich, believe it, is no faithful translator
Of perfect Utopian; and then, 'twere an odd piece
To see the conclusion peep forth at a codpiece.[1]   55
    The political pudding hath still his two ends,
Though the bellows and the bagpipe were ne'er so good friends;
And who can report what offense it would be
For the squirrel to see a dog climb a tree?
If a dream should come in now, to make you afeard,   60
With a windmill on 's head, and bells at his beard,
Would you straight wear your spectacles here at your toes,
And your boots on your brows, and your spurs on your nose?[2]
Your whale he will swallow a hogshead for a pill;
But the maker o' the mouse-trap is he that hath skill.   65
And the nature of the onion is to draw tears,
As well as the mustard; peace, pitchers have ears,
And shuttlecocks wings; these things, do not mind 'em.
If the bell have any sides, the clapper will find 'em;
There's twice so much music in beating the tabor   70
As in the stockfish,[3] and somewhat less labor.
Yet all this while, no proportion is boasted
'Twixt an egg and an ox, though both have been roasted,
For grant the most barbers can play o' the cittern,[4]
Is it requisite a lawyer should plead to a gittern?   75

8. Fancy's speech is almost a parody of metaphysical poetry, a series of glaring, brilliant metaphors, jumbled together without making much sense.
9. I.e., the vast hooped petticoat and the full French hood would overwhelm a wispy feather which tried to mediate their quarrel.
1. A flap, often ornamented, concealing an opening in the front of men's breeches; fashionable in the 15th and 16th centuries.
2. Fancy's mind runs on dreams with fantastic consequences, dreams which might scare an audience "out of its wits."
3. Dried codfish, which had to be pounded into a pulp before it was edible. "Tabor": drum. The logic of Fancy is purposely erratic and obscure.
4. Zither. "Gittern" (in the next line) is a guitar.

You will say now, the morris-bells[5] were but bribes
To make the heel forget that ever it had kibes;[6]
I say, let the wine make never so good jelly,
The conscience of the bottle is much in the belly.
For why? do but take common council in your way,   80
And tell me who'll then set a bottle of hay
Before the old usurer, and to his horse
A slice of salt-butter, perverting the course
Of civil society?[7] Open that gap,
And out skip your fleas, four and twenty at a clap,   85
With a chain and a trundle-bed following at the heels,
And will they not cry then, the world runs a wheels:
As for example, a belly and no face,
With the bill of a shoveler,[8] may here come in place;
The haunches of a drum, with the feet of a pot,   90
And the tail of a Kentishman to it; why not?
Yet would I take the stars to be cruel,
If the crab and the ropemaker ever fight duel,[9]
On any dependence, be it right, be it wrong.
But mum; a thread may be drawn out too long.   95

Here the second ANTIMASQUE *of* FANTASMS *came forth, which danced.*

FANCY *proceeded:*
Why, this, you will say, was fantastical now,
As the cock and the bull, the whale and the cow;
   But vanish away, I have change to present you,
And such as (I hope) will more truly content you:
   Behold the gold-haired Hour[1] descending here,   100
That keeps the gate of heaven, and turns the year,
   Already with her sight, how she doth cheer,
And makes another face of things appear.

Here one of the HOURS *descending, the whole scene changed to the Bower of* ZEPHYRUS, *whilst* PEACE *sang, as followeth:*

Why look you so, and all turn dumb
   To see the opener of the New Year come?   105
My presence rather should invite
   And aid and urge and call to your delight.
The many pleasures that I bring
   Are all of youth, of heat, of life, of spring,
And were prepared to warm your blood,   110
   Not fix it thus, as if you statues stood.

5. Bells worn by morris-dancers.
6. Sores.
7. Fancy's argument has vaguely to do with the proper uses of things; if it weren't for the arrangements of civil society, everything would be topsy-turvy, and we would get all sorts of monstrous combinations.
8. A bird with a wide, flat beak.
9. A crab is a tool used by ropemakers to twist yarn; the point is that no man should fall out with the tools of his trade.
1. Fancy has shown, as in dreams, the decay and disintegration of things which takes places under the aegis of Night and the old year; the Hour now brings forth spring, dawn, and a new era for everyone.

THE CHOIR: We see, we hear, we feel, we taste,
We smell the change in every flower,
We only wish that all could last,
And be as new still as the hour.   115

The song ended, WONDER *spake:*

WONDER must speak or break. What is this? Grows
The wealth of Nature here, or Art? It shows
As if Favonius,[2] father of the spring,
Who, in the verdant meads, doth reign sole king,
Had roused him here, and shook his feathers, wet   120
With purple-swelling nectar; and had let
The sweet and fruitful dew fall on the ground
To force out all the flowers that might be found.
   Or a Minerva with her needle had
Th' enamoured earth with all her riches clad,   125
And made the downy Zephyr as he flew
Still to be followed with the spring's best hue.[3]
   The gaudy peacock boasts not in his train
So many lights and shadows, nor the rain-
Resolving Iris,[4] when the sun doth court her,   130
Nor purple pheasant while his aunt[5] doth sport her
To hear him crow; and with a perchéd[6] pride
Wave his discolored neck and purple side.
   I have not seen the place could more surprise;
It looks (methinks) like one of nature's eyes,   135
Or her whole body set in art. Behold!
How the blue bind-weed doth itself enfold
With honeysuckle, and both these entwine
Themselves with bryony[7] and jessamine
To cast a kind and odoriferous shade!   140

FANCY:

How better than they are are all things made
By WONDER![8] But a while refresh thine eye,
I'll put thee to thy oftener What and Why?

Here (to a loud music) the Bower opens, and the MASQUERS *discovered,[9] as the glories of the spring.*

WONDER *again spake:*

Thou wilt indeed; what better change appears?
Whence is it that the air so sudden clears   145
And all things in a moment turn so mild?

2. Sometimes called Zephyrus, a god of the west wind and hence of spring.
3. Athena or Minerva, though often represented with spear and shield, was a famous needlewoman (witness the story of Arachne), and is here imagined as embroidering the spring.
4. I.e., the rainbow.
5. Doxy, mistress; a term from thieve's slang.
6. Lofty.
7. A wild vine, often credited with magic powers.
8. The allegorical meaning of Jonson's characters comes out in a speech like this, which at the same time paves the way for the masque's climactic compliment.
9. Unmasked.

Whose breath or beams have got proud earth with child
Of all the treasures that great Nature's worth,
And makes her every minute to bring forth?
How comes it winter is so quite forced hence,   150
And locked up under ground? that every sense
Hath several objects? trees have got their heads,
The fields their coats? that now the shining meads
Do boast the paunce,[1] the lily, and the rose;
And every flower doth laugh as Zephyr blows?   155
That seas are now more even than the land?
The rivers run as smoothéd by his hand;
Only their heads are crispéd[2] by his stroke.
How plays the yearling with his brow scarce broke[3]
Now in the open grass? and frisking lambs   160
Make wanton salts[4] about their dry-sucked dams,
Who to repair their bags do rob the fields?
    How is 't each bough a several[5] music yields?
The lusty throstle, early nightingale
Accord in tune, though vary in their tale?   165
The chirping swallow, called forth by the sun,
And crested lark doth his division run?
The yellow bees the air with murmur fill?
The finches carol, and the turtles bill?
Whose power is this? What God?

FANCY:
                    Behold a king   170
Whose presence maketh this perpetual spring,
The glories of which spring grow in that bower,
And are the marks and beauties of his power.

To which the CHOIR *answered:*

'Tis he, 'tis he, and no power else,
That makes all this what Fancy tells;   175
    The founts, the flowers, the birds, the bees,
The herds, the flocks, the grass, the trees,
Do all confess him; but most these
Who call him lord of the four seas,
King of the less and greater isles,[6]   180
And all those happy when he smiles.
    Advance, his favor calls you to advance,
And do your (this night's) homage in a dance.

Here they danced their ENTRY, *after which they sung again:*

Again, again; you cannot be
Of such a true delight too free,   185

1. Pansy.
2. Curled.
3. By budding horns.
4. Leaps.
5. Separate.

6. James was king of Ireland ("the less") and England ("the greater isle"), and laid claim to sovereignty over the "four seas" surrounding England.

Which who once saw would ever sea;
And if they could the object prize,
Would while it lasts not think to rise,
　But wish their bodies were all eyes.

They danced their MAIN DANCE, *after which they sung:*

In curious knots and mazes so　　　　　　　　　　　190
The spring at first was taught to go;
And Zephyr when he came to woo
His Flora had their motions too,
　And thence did Venus learn to lead
　Th' Idalian brawls,[7] and so to tread,　　　　　195
As if the wind, not she, did walk;
Nor pressed a flower, nor bowed a stalk.

They danced with LADIES, *and the whole* REVELS[8] *followed; after*
which AURORA *appeared (the* NIGHT *and* MOON *descended) and this*
EPILOGUE *followed:*

AURORA:

I was not wearier where I lay
By frozen Tithon's side tonight[9]
Than I am willing now to stay　　　　　　　　　　200
And be a part of your delight.
　But I am urgéd by the day,
Against my will, to bid you come away.

THE CHOIR:

　They yield to Time, and so must all.
As Night to sport, Day doth to action call,　　　　205
　Which they the rather do obey,
Because the Morn with roses strews the way.

Here they danced their going off, and ended.

1631

7. The dances of Venus on Mt. Ida were
legendary in antiquity. "Brawls" had a
less rowdy connotation in the 17th century than the word bears today.
8. Procession of masquers.
9. Aurora was the unwilling bride of
chilly old Tithonus (who was granted
eternal life without the privilege of eternal youth); hence she was eager to
come to the morning's entertainment,
and now is reluctant to leave it.

JOHN MILTON
(1608–1674)

1637:	*Lycidas.*
1640–60:	The pamphlet wars.
1651:	Blindness.
1667:	*Paradise Lost.*

The life of John Milton falls conveniently into three divisions. There is a period of youthful education and apprenticeship, which culminates in the writing of *Lycidas* (1637) and Milton's foreign travels (1638–39). There is a period of prose and controversy (1640–60), when almost all his verse was occasional, and when his major preoccupations were political and social; and finally, there are the last fourteen years of his life, when he returned to literature, a mature and somewhat embittered figure, to publish his three great poems, *Paradise Lost* (1667), *Paradise Regained* (1671), and *Samson Agonistes* (1671).

Milton was born at Bread Street in Cheapside, the elder son of what we would nowadays probably call a real-estate man. From the beginning, Milton showed prodigious gifts as a student of languages. At St. Paul's School he mastered Latin and Greek, and before long he was adept in most modern European tongues, as well as Hebrew. Sent to Christ's College, Cambridge, he proceeded B.A. in 1629 and M.A. in 1632, meanwhile continuing to read voraciously and writing (too infrequently for his own satisfaction) an occasional poem. In the normal course of events, a career like this would have culminated in ordination to the ministry and a position in the church. Both Milton and his parents seem to have anticipated this. But after taking his M.A., Milton, who disliked the trend of civil and religious affairs in England, did not take orders; instead, he retired to his father's country house at Horton in Buckinghamshire, and for five more years, under his own direction, read day and night. It seems likely that Milton, in his time, read just about everything that was ever written in English, Latin, Greek, and Italian. (Of course, he had the Bible by heart.) In 1634 he wrote, at the invitation of a nearby noble family, the masque known as *Comus*; and in 1637 he contributed to a volume memorializing a college classmate the elegy of *Lycidas*. Finally, in 1638, his most indulgent father sent this most voracious of students abroad, to put the finishing touches on an already splendid education. For two years, Milton traveled on the Continent, visiting famous literary figures and scenes; then, hearing rumors of impending troubles in England, he returned home in 1639.

Of Milton's complex and troubled career in controversy we need not say much. It too is divided in three phases. He began by publishing anti-prelatical tracts, against the government of the church by bishops. These are rough, knockabout, name-calling tracts in the style of the times, which take a popular position on a relatively popular issue. But Milton's next venture procured him a reputation as a radical. In June, 1642, he married Mary Powell. Within six weeks, she left him, to return to her parents' house; and from 1643 to 1645, Milton published a series of pamphlets advocating that divorce be granted on the grounds of incompatibility. Clearly his personal situation had influenced his social judgment; just as clearly, respectable Englishmen, who were disturbed by the troubles of the time, were bound to feel that "divorce at pleasure" represented the end of all social order, the coming of complete anarchy. Milton not only effected no change in the divorce laws, he largely discredited himself by his divorce pamphlets. His last undertaking was more worthy of his gifts. After the execution of Charles I, in 1649, he published a series of Latin disputations against Continental critics of the regime, defending the actions of Parliament in executing Charles. In the middle of this work, he went blind, as the result of eyestrain continued over many years. By the use of secretaries and amanuenses, however, he was able to fulfill his duties as Latin Secretary to Cromwell's Council of State, and to contribute very substantially to the diplomatic dignity of the new government.

Meanwhile, his first wife returned to him, and having born him three daughters, died in 1652. In 1656 Milton married Katharine Woodcock, who died in childbirth, in 1658. Finally, in 1660, the whole political movement for which Milton had sacrificed so much, went to smash. Though Milton boldly published pamphlets in its support to the very last minute, the Good Old Cause was defeated, and Charles II recalled from his travels. For a time under the Restoration, Milton was imprisoned and in danger of his life; but friends intervened, and he escaped with a fine and the loss of most of his property.

In 1663 Milton married his third wife, Elizabeth Minshull; and in blindness, poverty, defeat, and relative isolation, he set about completing a poem "justifying the ways of God to men," which he had first envisaged many years before. It was published in 1667, as *Paradise Lost;* and despite the many difficulties which it presented, despite its unfamiliar meter (blank verse was rare outside drama), despite the unpopularity of its attitudes and Milton's reputation as a dangerous man, it was recognized at once as a supreme epic achievement. In 1671 Milton published *Paradise Regained*, an epic poem in four books describing Christ's temptation in the wilderness, and *Samson Agonistes*, a "closet" tragedy (i.e., not intended for the stage). He died, of complications arising from gout, in 1674.

In the writings of Milton, the work of two tremendous intellectual and social movements comes to a head. The Renaissance is responsible for the rich and complex texture of Milton's style, the multiplicity of its classical references, its wealth of ornament and decoration. *Paradise Lost*, being an epic, not only challenges comparison with Homer and Virgil, it undertakes to encompass the whole life of mankind—war, love, religion, Hell, Heaven, the cosmos. It is a poem vastly capacious of worldly experience. On the other hand, the Reformation speaks with equal, if not greater, authority in Milton's earnest and individually-minded Christianity. The great epic, which resounds with the grandeur and multiplicity of the world, is also a poem the central actions of which take place inwardly, at the core of man's conscience. Adam's fate culminates in an act of passive suffering, not of active heroism. He does not kill Hector or Turnus, much less Satan, he picks up the burden of worldly existence, and triumphs over his guilt by admitting it and repenting of it.

These two contrasting aspects of Milton's life and thought place him among the Christian humanists. His literary art places him in the small circle of great epic writers.

L'Allegro[1]

Hence loathéd Melancholy
    Of Cerberus[2] and blackest midnight born,
In Stygian[3] cave forlorn
    'Mongst horrid shapes, and shrieks, and sights unholy,
Find out some uncouth cell,   5
    Where brooding Darkness spreads his jealous wings,
And the night-raven sings;
    There under ebon shades, and low-browed rocks,
As ragged as thy locks,
    In dark Cimmerian[4] desert ever dwell.   10
But come thou goddess fair and free,
    In Heaven yclept Euphrosyne,[5]
And by men, heart-easing Mirth,
    Whom lovely Venus at a birth
With two sister Graces more   15
    To ivy-crownéd Bacchus bore;[6]
Or whether (as some sager sing)[7]
    The frolic wind that breathes the spring,
Zephyr with Aurora playing,
    As he met her once a-Maying,   20
There on beds of violets blue,
    And fresh-blown[8] roses washed in dew,

1. *L'Allegro* and *Il Penseroso* are a pair of companion-poems, probably written around 1630 or 1631, in those dancing tetrameter couplets which are so hard to keep from degenerating into singsong, and so delightful when controlled. Milton's handling of this difficult meter may be compared with those of Marvell (*To His Coy Mistress*), Keats (*Lines on the Mermaid Tavern*) and A. E. Housman (*Terence, This Is Stupid Stuff*).

The titles are almost untranslatable, which is why Milton did not translate them. But within the framework of two contrasted days, we see the cheerful, sociable man, and the melancholy, contemplative man in their typical spiritual attitudes. Milton's interest in the typical accounts for the striking generality of the pictures: "And every shepherd tells his tale / Under the hawthorn in the dale"—there is no effort to create an individual shepherd in a particular setting. All the shepherds in all the dales for miles around are telling one story or another, each under his own hawthorn bush. But Milton's focus is on the mind that sees, and on the tone which it casts over a landscape. The cheerful man infuses his world with contagious cheerfulness; the melancholy man casts over the events of his day (which, as events, are not very different) a pervasive veil of melancholy. The backgrounds of this complex contemplative mood may be explored in Burton's famous *Anatomy of Melancholy;* in a more recent book, Erwin Panofsky's study, *Albrecht Dürer*, where it occurs in connection with Dürer's magnificent engraving of Melancholia; or in Saxl, Panofsky, and Klibansky's immense study, *Saturn and Melancholy* (1964). There is a history of literary cheerfulness, too—*The Happy Man*, by Maren Sofie Røstvig (1954).

Milton's poems stand in contrast to one another, but the contrasts are shaded, not glaring; there is no effort to "decide" the conflict, or to make melancholy black and cheerfulness convivial. Both poems exist in a reflective half-light, as little idyls of description which for sheer elegance and charm have rarely been equaled.

2. The three-headed hell-hound of classical mythology.
3. I.e., near the river Styx, the river of the underworld.
4. The Cimmerians, who gave their name to Crimea, were supposed to live on the outer edge of the world, in perpetual twilight.
5. Euphrosyne, Aglaia, and Thalia were the Graces, daughters (according to one story) of Zeus himself, and goddesses of beauty and delight. "Yclept": called.
6. Bacchus is god of wine.
7. The "sager" (poets) who describe the Graces as born of Zephyr and Aurora are in fact John Milton himself; he invented this version of the myth.
8. Newly opened.

Filled her with thee a daughter fair,
So buxom,[9] blithe, and debonair.
Haste thee nymph, and bring with thee   25
Jest and youthful Jollity,
Quips and Cranks,[1] and wanton Wiles,
Nods, and Becks, and wreathéd Smiles,
Such as hang on Hebe's[2] cheek,
And love to live in dimple sleek;   30
Sport that wrinkled Care derides,
And Laughter, holding both his sides.
Come, and trip it as ye go
On the light fantastic toe,
And in thy right hand lead with thee,   35
The mountain nymph, sweet Liberty;
And if I give thee honor due,
Mirth, admit me of thy crew
To live with her and live with thee,
In unreprovéd pleasures free;   40
To hear the lark begin his flight,
And, singing, startle the dull night,
From his watch-tower in the skies,
Till the dappled dawn doth rise;
Then to come[3] in spite of sorrow,   45
And at my window bid good morrow,
Through the sweetbriar, or the vine,
Or the twisted eglantine.
While the cock with lively din,
Scatters the rear of darkness thin,   50
And to the stack, or the barn door,
Stoutly struts his dames before;
Oft listening how the hounds and horn
Cheerly rouse the slumbering morn,
From the side of some hoar hill,   55
Through the high wood echoing shrill.
Sometime walking not unseen
By hedgerow elms, on hillocks green,
Right against the eastern gate,
Where the great sun begins his state,[4]   60
Robed in flames, and amber light,
The clouds in thousand liveries dight;[5]
While the plowman near at hand,
Whistles o'er the furrowed land,
And the milkmaid singeth blithe,   65
And the mower whets his scythe,
And every shepherd tells his tale,
Under the hawthorn in the dale.
Straight mine eye hath caught new pleasures
Whilst the landscape round it measures,   70

9. Lively.   3. I.e., then admit me to come.
1. Jokes. "Becks": curtseys.   4. Procession.
2. Goddess of youth and cupbearer to   5. Dressed.
the other gods.

Russet lawns and fallows gray,
Where the nibbling flocks do stray,
Mountains on whose barren breast
The laboring clouds do often rest;
Meadows trim with daisies pied,[6]   75
Shallow brooks, and rivers wide.
Towers and battlements it sees
Bosomed high in tufted trees,
Where perhaps some beauty lies,
The cynosure[7] of neighboring eyes.   80
Hard by, a cottage chimney smokes,
From betwixt two aged oaks,
Where Corydon and Thyrsis[8] met,
Are at their savory dinner set
Of herbs, and other country messes,   85
Which the neat-handed Phyllis dresses;
And then in haste her bower she leaves,
With Thestylis to bind the sheaves;
Or if the earlier season lead
To the tanned haycock in the mead.   90
Sometimes with secure delight
The upland hamlets will invite,
When the merry bells ring round
And the jocund rebecks[9] sound
To many a youth and many a maid,   95
Dancing in the checkered shade;
And young and old come forth to play
On a sunshine holiday,
Till the livelong daylight fail;
Then to the spicy nut-brown ale,   100
With stories told of many a feat,
How fairy Mab[1] the junkets eat;
She was pinched and pulled, she said,
And he, by Friar's lantern led,
Tells how the drudging goblin[2] sweat   105
To earn his cream-bowl, duly set,
When in one night, ere glimpse of morn,
His shadowy flail hath threshed the corn
That ten day-laborers could not end;
Then lies him down the lubber fiend,[3]   110
And, stretched out all the chimney's length,
Basks at the fire his hairy strength;
And crop-full out of doors he flings
Ere the first cock his matin rings.

6. Dappled.
7. Literally, the bright polestar, by which mariners steer; here, a splendid, eminent object, much gazed at.
8. Since the days of Theocritus, the names "Corydon," "Thyrsis," "Phyllis," and "Thestylis" have been traditional shepherds' names.
9. A rebeck is a small three-stringed fiddle; "jocund" implies a festive oc-casion.
1. Queen Mab, wife of Oberon, the fairy king. "She" and "he" in the next two lines are country folk, telling of their experiences with the fairies.
2. Robin Goodfellow, alias Puck, Pook, or Hobgoblin. "Friar's lantern": will-o'-the-wisp.
3. Oafish spirit.

Thus done the tales, to bed they creep,   115
By whispering winds soon lulled asleep.
Towered cities please us then,
And the busy hum of men,
Where throngs of knights and barons bold,
In weeds[4] of peace high triumphs hold,   120
With store of ladies, whose bright eyes
Rain influence,[5] and judge the prize
Of wit, or arms, while both contend
To win her grace, whom all commend.
There let Hymen[6] oft appear   125
In saffron robe, with taper clear,
And pomp, and feast, and revelry,
With masque, and antique pageantry;
Such sights as youthful poets dream
On summer eves by haunted stream.   130
Then to the well-trod stage anon,
If Jonson's learned sock[7] be on,
Or sweetest Shakespeare, fancy's child,
Warble his native wood-notes wild.
And ever against eating cares[8]   135
Lap me in soft Lydian airs,[9]
Married to immortal verse
Such as the meeting soul may pierce
In notes, with many a winding bout[1]
Of linkéd sweetness long drawn out,   140
With wanton heed, and giddy cunning,
The melting voice through mazes running;
Untwisting all the chains that tie
The hidden soul of harmony;
That Orpheus' self[2] may heave his head   145
From golden slumber on a bed
Of heaped Elysian flowers, and hear
Such strains as would have won the ear
Of Pluto, to have quite set free
His half-regained Eurydice.   150
These delights if thou canst give,
Mirth, with thee I mean to live.

ca. 1631   1645

4. Garments. "Triumphs": festive ceremonies.
5. The ladies' eyes are stars, and so
have astrological influence over the
men.
6. Roman god of marriage, wearing a
yellow ("saffron") robe.
7. A low-heeled slipper, worn by actors
in classical comedy, and often contrasted
with the buskin (high-heeled boot) appropriate to tragedy. The contrast of
Jonson as a "learned" poet with Shakespeare as a "natural" one was conventional.
8. "Eating cares" is but one of many
classical phrases in the poem; it is
from Horace, *Odes* II.xi.18 (*curas
edaces*).
9. "Lydian" airs in music would be
soft, languishing, sensual—unlike the
chaste Dorian and brisk Ionian.
1. A musical "run" passage.
2. Orpheus went to the underworld to
regain his wife Eurydice, and by his
music dissolved the guardians of Hades
in tears. But as they left, he violated
the condition of her release by looking
back at her, and so lost her again.
Milton uses the Orpheus story again
in *Il Penseroso, Lycidas,* and *Paradise
Lost* VII.32 ff.

Il Penseroso

Hence vain deluding Joys,
    The brood of Folly without father bred.
How little you bestead,[3]
    Or fill the fixéd mind with all your toys;[4]
Dwell in some idle brain,   5
    And fancies fond[5] with gaudy shapes possess,
As thick and numberless
    As the gay motes that people the sunbeams,
Or likest hovering dreams,
    The fickle pensioners[6] of Morpheus' train.   10
But hail thou Goddess, sage and holy,
Hail, divinest Melancholy,
Whose saintly visage is too bright
To hit[7] the sense of human sight;
And therefore to our weaker view,   15
O'erlaid with black, staid Wisdom's hue.
Black, but such as in esteem,
Prince Memnon's sister[8] might beseem,
Or that starred Ethiope queen[9] that strove
To set her beauty's praise above   20
The sea nymphs, and their powers offended.
Yet thou art higher far descended;
Thee bright-haired Vesta long of yore
To solitary Saturn bore;[1]
His daughter she (in Saturn's reign   25
Such mixture was not held a stain).
Oft in glimmering bowers and glades
He met her, and in secret shades
Of woody Ida's inmost grove,
While yet there was no fear of Jove.   30
Come pensive nun, devout and pure,
Sober, steadfast, and demure,
All in a robe of darkest grain,[2]
Flowing with majestic train,
And sable stole of cypress lawn[3]   35
Over thy decent shoulders drawn.
Come, but keep thy wonted state,

3. Avail, help.
4. Trifles.
5. Foolish.
6. Followers. Morpheus is the god of sleep; the melancholy man feels the cheerful man lives in a dream.
7. Suit, agree with.
8. Memnon in *Odyssey* XI was a handsome Ethiopian prince who fought for Troy; his sister, mentioned not by Homer but by later commentators, was Hemera.
9. Cassiopeia, who was "starred" (i.e., turned into a constellation) for bragging that her daughter Andromeda or she herself (Milton follows this second version) was more beautiful than the sea nymphs.

1. Vesta was a goddess of purity; Milton invented the story of her connection with Saturn on Mt. Ida in Crete, and of her giving birth to Melancholy. But Saturn helps out the poem because he was a primitive deity (hence melancholy is "natural") and because a saturnine complexion is said to show a dark and melancholy disposition.
2. Color.
3. "Cypress": a dark, delicate cloth (originally Cyprus, from the island; but the cypress is also the tree of death). "Lawn": a transparent, gauzy material, much like crape. "Decent": comely, proper.

With even step and musing gait,
And looks commercing with the skies,
Thy rapt soul sitting in thine eyes: 40
There held in holy passion still,
Forget thyself to marble, till
With a sad leaden downward cast,
Thou fix them on the earth as fast.
And join with thee calm Peace and Quiet,   45
Spare Fast, that oft with gods doth diet.
And hears the Muses in a ring
Aye round about Jove's altar sing.
And add to these retired Leisure,
That in trim gardens takes his pleasure;   50
But first, and chiefest, with thee bring,
Him that yon soars on golden wing,
Guiding the fiery-wheeléd throne,
The cherub Contemplation;[4]
And the mute Silence hist along   55
'Less Philomel[5] will deign a song,
In her sweetest, saddest plight,
Smoothing the rugged brow of night,
While Cynthia[6] checks her dragon yoke
Gently o'er th' accustomed oak;   60
Sweet bird that shunn'st the noise of folly,
Most musical, most melancholy!
Thee chantress oft the woods among,
I woo to hear thy evensong;
And missing thee, I walk unseen   65
On the dry smooth-shaven green,
To behold the wandering moon,
Riding near her highest noon,
Like one that had been led astray
Through the Heaven's wide pathless way;   70
And oft as if her head she bowed,
Stooping through a fleecy cloud.
Oft on a plat[7] of rising ground,
I hear the far-off curfew sound,
Over some wide-watered shore,   75
Swinging slow with sullen roar;
Or if the air will not permit,
Some still removéd place will fit,
Where glowing embers through the room
Teach light to counterfeit a gloom   80
Far from all resort of mirth,
Save the cricket on the hearth,
Or the bellman's[8] drowsy charm,

4. The cherub Contemplation is suggested by the Biblical vision of Ezekiel.
5. The nightingale, whose song is traditionally one of grief. "Hist": summon.
6. Goddess of the moon, and of the underworld as well, she drives a pair of sleepless dragons.
7. Plot, flat open space.
8. The night watchman in little villages rang a bell to call the hours.

To bless the doors from nightly harm;
Or let my lamp at midnight hour   85
Be seen in some high lonely tower,
Where I may oft outwatch the Bear,[9]
With thrice great Hermes,[1] or unsphere
The spirit of Plato to unfold
What worlds, or what vast regions hold   90
The immortal mind that hath forsook
Her mansion in this fleshly nook;
And of those demons[2] that are found
In fire, air, flood, or underground,
Whose power hath a true consent[3]   95
With planet, or with element.
Some time let gorgeous Tragedy
In sceptered pall[4] come sweeping by,
Presenting Thebes', or Pelops' line,
Or the tale of Troy divine.[5]   100
Or what (though rare) of later age
Ennobled hath the buskined[6] stage.
But, O sad virgin, that thy power
Might raise Musaeus[7] from his bower,
Or bid the soul of Orpheus[8] sing   105
Such notes as, warbled to the string,
Drew iron tears down Pluto's cheek,
And made Hell grant what Love did seek.
Or call up him[9] that left half told
The story of Cambuscan bold,   110
Of Camball, and of Algarsife,
And who had Canacee to wife,
That owned the virtuous[1] ring and glass,
And of the wondrous horse of brass,
On which the Tartar king did ride;   115
And if aught else great bards beside
In sage and solemn tunes have sung,
Of tourneys and of trophies hung,
Of forests and enchantments drear,
Where more is meant than meets the ear.[2]   120

9. Since the Great Bear never sets, outwatching it is a major enterprise.
1. The Egyptian god Thoth or Hermes, to whom were attributed various esoteric books of the 3rd and 4th centuries A.D.; under the name of Hermes Trismegistus he later became a patron of magicians and alchemists. To "unsphere" Plato is to call Plato by magical means back to earth from the sphere he now inhabits.
2. Not devils, but classical beings akin to heroes, halfway between gods and men. There were four sorts of demons, corresponding to the four elements, each with a corresponding planet.
3. Mysterious agreement.
4. Royal robe (from Latin *palla*, the robe of tragic actors).
5. Tragedies about the royal line of Thebes would include Sophocles' Oedipus cycle; those about the line of Pelops, Aeschylus' *Oresteia;* and those about Troy, Euripides' *Trojan Women.*
6. The buskin of tragedy, contrasted with the sock of comedy.
7. A mythical poet-priest of the pre-Homeric age, supposedly son or pupil of the equally mythical Orpheus.
8. For the story of Orpheus, see *L'Allegro,* line 145, and note.
9. I.e., Chaucer, who in the Squire's Tale left the tale of Cambuscan half told.
1. Having special power.
2. A capsule description of allegory.

Thus, Night, oft see me in thy pale career,
Till civil-suited morn appear,[3]
Not tricked and frounced as she was wont,
With the Attic boy to hunt,
But kerchiefed in a comely cloud,   125
While rocking winds are piping loud,
Or ushered with a shower still,
When the gust hath blown his fill,
Ending on the rustling leaves,
With minute-drops from off the eaves.   130
And when the sun begins to fling
His flaring beams, me, Goddess, bring
To archéd walks of twilight groves,
And shadows brown that Sylvan[4] loves
Of pine or monumental oak,   135
Where the rude ax with heavéd stroke,
Was never heard the nymphs to daunt,
Or fright them from their hallowed haunt.
There in close covert by some brook,
Where no profaner eye may look,   140
Hide me from day's garish eye,
While the bee with honeyed thigh,
That at her flowery work doth sing,
And the waters murmuring
With such consort[5] as they keep,   145
Entice the dewy-feathered sleep;
And let some strange mysterious dream,
Wave at his wings in airy stream,
Of lively portraiture displayed,
Softly on my eyelids laid.[6]   150
And as I wake, sweet music breathe
Above, about, or underneath,
Sent by some spirit to mortals good,
Or th' unseen genius[7] of the wood.
But let my due feet never fail   155
To walk the studious cloister's pale,[8]
And love the high embowéd roof,
With antic[9] pillars massy proof,
And storied windows[1] richly dight,
Casting a dim religious light.   160
There let the pealing organ blow,
To the full-voiced choir below,

3. The goddess Aurora, who once fell in love with Cephalus ("the Attic boy," line 124), and used to go hunting with him. "Tricked and frounced": adorned and frizzled.
4. Roman god of the woodlands.
5. Accompaniment.
6. Milton's syntax gets loose and dreamy too, here. He means, "Let some strange dream wave at the wings of sleep, while a stream of vivid pictures passes softly over my eyelids."
7. Guardian angel.
8. Enclosure.
9. I.e., covered with quaint, grotesque, or antic carvings; but "antique," which derives from the same Latin root, was not excluded from the sense. "Massy proof": massive and strong.
1. I.e., with stories told by stained-glass images. "Dight": dressed.

In service high, and anthems clear,
As may with sweetness, through mine ear,
Dissolve me into ecstasies,   165
And bring all heaven before mine eyes.
And may at last my weary age
Find out the peaceful hermitage,
The hairy gown and mossy cell,
Where I may sit and rightly spell[2]   170
Of every star that Heaven doth show,
And every herb that sips the dew
Till old experience do attain
To something like prophetic strain.
These pleasures, Melancholy, give,   175
And I with thee will choose to live.

ca. 1631   1645

At a Solemn Music

Blest pair of Sirens,[3] pledges of Heaven's joy,
Sphere-born harmonious sisters, Voice and Verse,
Wed your divine sounds, and mixed power employ
Dead things with inbreathed sense able to pierce,
And to our high-raised fantasy[4] present   5
That undisturbed song of pure consent,[5]
Aye sung before the sapphire-colored throne
To him that sits thereon
With saintly shout and solemn jubilee,
Where the bright seraphim in burning row   10
Their loud uplifted angel-trumpets blow,
And the cherubic host in thousand choirs
Touch their immortal harps of golden wires,
With those just spirits that wear victorious palms,[6]
Hymns devout and holy psalms   15
Singing everlastingly;[7]
That we on earth with undiscording voice
May rightly answer that melodious noise;
As once we did, till disproportioned sin
Jarred against nature's chime, and with harsh din   20
Broke the fair music that all creatures made
To their great Lord, whose love their motion swayed
In perfect diapason, whilst they stood
In first obedience, and their state of good.[8]

2. Study. The melancholy man wants to think his way into the cosmos until he becomes a prophet.
3. The Sirens, enticing mermaids who lured men to destruction (*Odyssey* XII), were traditionally sweet but evilly intentioned singers; Milton's Sirens are "blest," i.e., not only "happy" but "of good omen."
4. Imagination.
5. Harmony, agreement.
6. The saints wear palms in token of their victory over sin.
7. "Singing" modifies "spirits" (line 14), and takes as an object "hymns devout and holy psalms" (line 15). Milton is practicing at balancing the masses of his long sentences on a Latin grammar and word order.
8. Before man fell, the whole cosmos was in moral and intellectual concord ("diapason"), hence the music of the spheres could be heard on earth.

O may we soon again renew that song,   25
And keep in tune with Heaven, till God ere long
To his celestial consort us unite,
To live with him, and sing in endless morn of light.

1632   1645

Songs from Comus

Sweet Echo[1]

Sweet Echo, sweetest nymph that liv'st unseen
  Within thy airy shell
    By slow Meander's[2] margent green,
And in the violet-embroidered vale
  Where the lovelorn nightingale
Nightly to thee her sad song mourneth well.   5
Canst thou not tell me of a gentle pair
  That likest thy Narcissus[3] are?
    O if thou have
  Hid them in some flowery cave,   10
    · Tell me but where
Sweet queen of parley, daughter of the sphere,[4]
  So mayest thou be translated to the skies,
  And give resounding grace to all Heaven's harmonies.

Sabrina Fair[5]

Sabrina fair
  Listen where thou art sitting
Under the glassy, cool, translucent wave,
  In twisted braids of lilies knitting
The loose train of thy amber-dropping hair;   5
  Listen for dear honor's sake,
  Goddess of the silver lake,
    Listen and save.

By the Rushy-fringed Bank

[*Sabrina rises, attended by water nymphs, and sings*]
  By the rushy-fringéd bank,
  Where grows the willow and the osier[6] dank,
    My sliding chariot stays,
  Thick set with agate, and the azurn sheen
  Of turquoise blue, and emerald green   5
    That in the channel strays;
    Whilst from off the waters fleet

1. To keep up her courage, the Lady in Milton's masque, *Comus*, sings this song to Echo when she is alone and benighted in a dark forest.
2. A Near-Eastern river, famous for its many twistings and turnings.
3. The lady is looking for her two brothers ("a gentle pair"); they are like Narcissus (with whom Echo fell in love and because of whom she pined away to an empty voice) in being handsome, not in admiring themselves.
4. Echo is "queen of parley," i.e., of speech, because she talked so much. The flaw for which she was punished becomes a ground for compliment. She is "daughter of the sphere" because her "airy shell" is the arch of the sky.
5. The song is sung by the Attendant Spirit, to invoke the aid of Sabrina (goddess of the river Severn and patroness of chastity) in freeing the Lady from Comus' magic charms.
6. Osier is actually a variety of willow; but the name sounds much danker and moister than willow alone.

Thus I set my printless feet
O'er the cowslip's velvet head,
That bends not as I tread;   10
Gentle swain, at thy request
    I am here.
1634   1637

Lycidas   This poem is a pastoral elegy; that is, it uses the sometimes
artificial imagery supplied by an idyllic shepherd's existence to bewail the
loss of a friend. Among its many predecessors in the Renaissance and in
classical antiquity are poems by Spenser, Ronsard, Castiglione, Mantuan,
Petrarch, Virgil, Theocritus, Moschus, and Bion; its successors include
poems like *Adonais* by Shelley and *Thyrsis* by Matthew Arnold. T. P.
Harrison and H. J. Leon have collected in *The Pastoral Elegy* (1939) a
selection of poems from the tradition.

All pastoral poems enjoy the privilege of saying something about the
world as a whole while seeming to talk simply of an artificial play-society;
they are irresistibly allegorical. They have certain conventions—the swain
(i.e., the shepherd) is ignorant but unspoiled, naturally virtuous, in-
herently poetic; life is pleasant and easy, yet just for this reason the
basic human preoccupations stand out. The pastoral elegy has a further
list of conventions—a history of past friendship, a questioning of destiny,
a procession of mourners, a laying-on of flowers, a consolation, and usually a refrain. Milton adapted all but the last of these to *Lycidas*.

Edward King, who was the occasion of the poem if not its subject,
was a fellow student of Milton's at Cambridge. Milton says he was a
poet, and he was in the church. While proceeding to his new parish in
Ireland, he was drowned, in 1637; and Milton joined with his schoolfellows, the following year, to produce a little memorial volume. *Justa
Edouardo King* includes 35 poems, mostly in Latin; only *Lycidas* is of
literary consequence.

It is written in a flowing, extended manner, with many run-on lines
and great impetus, predominantly in pentameter, but with many variations
of line length, and an irregular rhyme scheme including ten unrhymed
lines and two perfectly formed stanzas of ottava rima. Many of these
technical qualities are reminiscent of the Italian *canzone* or song, but
most of them had been exemplified previously in Spenser's *Epithalamion*.

There are usually taken to be three explicit climaxes in *Lycidas*, each
having to do with an aspect of the shepherd's life and with a problem
which Milton wished to pose regarding the meaning of existence. Apollo
answers his first question about the reward of poetry; St. Peter answers
a second question, about the spiritual shepherd who betrays his flock; and
finally Lycidas is translated into the Christian Paradise, to be at one with
the Lamb of God, the Good Shepherd, the supreme giver of poetic fame,
and the proper subject of all song. Subordinate patterns of imagery include vegetation and nature deities, water and water gods, who serve an
immense variety of purposes.

Lycidas

IN THIS MONODY[1] THE AUTHOR BEWAILS A LEARNED FRIEND,
UNFORTUNATELY DROWNED IN HIS PASSAGE FROM CHESTER
ON THE IRISH SEAS, 1637. AND BY OCCASION FORETELLS
THE RUIN OF OUR CORRUPTED CLERGY,
THEN IN THEIR HEIGHT.

Yet once more, O ye laurels, and once more
Ye myrtles brown, with ivy never sere,[2]
I come to pluck your berries harsh and crude,[3]
And with forced fingers rude,
Shatter your leaves before the mellowing year.   5
Bitter constraint, and sad occasion dear,[4]
Compels me to disturb your season due;
For Lycidas is dead, dead ere his prime,
Young Lycidas, and hath not left his peer.
Who would not sing for Lycidas? He knew   10
Himself to sing, and build the lofty rhyme.
He must not float upon his watery bier
Unwept, and welter to the parching wind,
Without the meed[5] of some melodious tear.
    Begin then, sisters of the sacred well[6]   15
That from beneath the seat of Jove doth spring,
Begin, and somewhat loudly sweep the string.
Hence with denial vain, and coy excuse;
So may some gentle Muse
With lucky words favor my destined urn,[7]   20
And as he passes turn,
And bid fair peace be to my sable shroud.
For we were nursed upon the selfsame hill,
Fed the same flock, by fountain, shade, and rill.
    Together both, ere the high lawns[8] appeared   25
Under the opening eyelids of the morn,
We drove afield, and both together heard
What time the grayfly winds her sultry horn,[9]
Battening our flocks with the fresh dews of night,
Oft till the star that rose at evening bright   30
Toward Heaven's descent had sloped his westering wheel.

1. A song sung in Greek drama by a single voice.
2. "Laurels" for the crown of poetry given by Apollo; "myrtles" for the undying love granted by Venus; "ivy," the plant of Bacchus. All three plants are evergreens associated with poetic inspiration.
3. Unripe.
4. Heartfelt, profoundly moving; but also, in the 17th century, with overtones of "dire."
5. Reward.
6. The nine sister Muses were reported to dwell by various springs or "wells"; most likely Milton had in mind that of Aganippe near Mt. Helicon.
7. The speaker suggests that if he sings for Lycidas, "some gentle Muse" (i.e., poet) may some day sing for him.
8. Upland pastures.
9. I.e., heard the grayfly when she buzzes ("winds her sultry horn"). "Battening": feeding.

Meanwhile the rural ditties were not mute,
Tempered to th' oaten flute,[1]
Rough satyrs danced, and fauns with cloven heel
From the glad sound would not be absent long,   35
And old Damoetas[2] loved to hear our song.

    But O the heavy change, now thou art gone,
Now thou art gone, and never must return!
Thee, shepherd, thee the woods and desert caves,
With wild thyme and the gadding[3] vine o'ergrown,   40
And all their echoes mourn.
The willows and the hazel copses green
Shall now no more be seen,
Fanning their joyous leaves to thy soft lays.
As killing as the canker[4] to the rose,   45
Or taint-worm to the weanling herds that graze,
Or frost to flowers that their gay wardrobe wear,
When first the white thorn blows;[5]
Such, Lycidas, thy loss to shepherd's ear.

    Where were ye, nymphs,[6] when the remorseless deep   50
Closed o'er the head of your loved Lycidas?
For neither were ye playing on the steep,
Where your old Bards, the famous Druids[7] lie,
Nor on the shaggy top of Mona high,[8]
Nor yet where Deva spreads her wizard stream: 55
Ay me! I fondly dream—
Had ye been there—for what could that have done?
What could the Muse[9] herself that Orpheus bore,
The Muse herself, for her inchanting[1] son
Whom universal Nature did lament,   60
When by the rout[2] that made the hideous roar,
His gory visage down the stream was sent,
Down the swift Hebrus to the Lesbian shore?

    Alas! What boots[3] it with incessant care
To tend the homely slighted shepherd's trade,   65
And strictly meditate the thankless Muse?[4]

1. Traditional Panpipes, played by shepherds.
2. A type name from pastoral poetry, possibly referring to some specific tutor at Cambridge.
3. Straggling.
4. Cankerworm.
5. Blossoms (as in the surviving expression, "full-blown").
6. Nature deities.
7. The Druids, priestly poet-kings of Celtic Britain, worshiped the forces of nature. They lie dead in their burying ground on the mountain ("steep") Kerig-y-Druidion in Wales.
8. "Mona" is the island of Anglesey. "Deva" is the river Dee in Cheshire. The Dee is magic ("wizard") because the size and position of its shifting stream foretold prosperity or dearth for the land. All the places mentioned in lines 52–55 are in the West Country, near where King drowned.
9. Calliope, Muse of epic poetry, was the mother of Orpheus.
1. "Inchanting" implies both song and magic; the root word survives as "incantation."
2. Orpheus was torn to pieces by a mob ("rout") of screaming Thracian women, who threw his gory head into the river Hebrus, down which it floated, still singing, and out to Lesbos in the Aegean. The fate of Orpheus and the Druids suggests that nature everywhere is indifferent to the destruction of the poet.
3. Profits.
4. Study to write poetry (the phrase is Virgil's).

Were it not better done as others use,
To sport with Amaryllis in the shade,
Or with the tangles of Neaera's hair?[5]
Fame is the spur that the clear spirit doth raise   70
(That last infirmity of noble mind)
To scorn delights, and live laborious days;
But the fair guerdon[6] when we hope to find,
And think to burst out into sudden blaze,
Comes the blind Fury[7] with th' abhorréd shears,   75
And slits the thin spun life. "But not the praise,"
Phoebus[8] replied, and touched my trembling ears;
"Fame is no plant that grows on mortal soil,
Not in the glistering foil[9]
Set off to th' world, nor in broad rumor lies,   80
But lives and spreads aloft by those pure eyes,
And perfect witness of all-judging Jove;
As he pronounces lastly on each deed,
Of so much fame in Heaven expect thy meed."

O fountain Arethuse,[1] and thou honored flood,   85
Smooth-sliding Mincius, crowned with vocal reeds,
That strain I heard was of a higher mood.
But now my oat[2] proceeds,
And listens to the herald of the sea[3]
That came in Neptune's plea.   90
He asked the waves, and asked the felon winds,
"What hard mishap hath doomed this gentle swain?"
And questioned every gust of rugged wings
That blows from off each beakéd promontory;
They knew not of his story,   95
And sage Hippotades[4] their answer brings,
That not a blast was from his dungeon strayed,
The air was calm, and on the level brine,
Sleek Panope[5] with all her sisters played.
It was that fatal and perfidious bark   100
Built in th' eclipse,[6] and rigged with curses dark,

5. "Amaryllis" and "Neaera," conventional names for pretty nymphs, a passing hour's diversion for idle shepherds.
6. Reward.
7. Atropos, one of the three Fates, bearing scissors with which she cuts the thread of human life. Milton, to suggest the bitterness of death, makes her an avenging Fury.
8. Phoebus Apollo, god of poetic inspiration. Touching the ears of one's hearers was a traditional Roman way of asking them to remember something that had been said (Virgil, *Eclogues* VI; Horace, *Satires* I.ix.77).
9. Cheap, flashy metal, used to add glitter to glass gems.
1. Arethusa was a fountain in Sicily, Mincius a river in Lombardy, the former associated with the pastorals of Theocritus, the latter with those of Virgil. Arethusa was originally a nymph who went bathing in the river Alpheus, in Arcadian Greece. The river god grew enamored, and gave chase; she dove into the ocean and fled undersea to Sicily, where she came up as a fountain. Milton plays here with the idea of his pastoral going underground while the "strain of a higher mood" (line 87) is heard.
2. Pipe, hence song.
3. Neptune's "herald" is Triton, pleading his master's innocence in the death of Lycidas.
4. Aeolus, god of winds, and son of Hippotas.
5. The chief Nereid or sea nymph.
6. I.e., time of the worst possible luck.

That sunk so low that sacred head of thine.
  Next Camus,[7] reverend sire, went footing slow,
His mantle hairy, and his bonnet sedge,
Inwrought with figures dim, and on the edge   105
Like to that sanguine flower inscribed with woe.[8]
"Ah! who hath reft," quoth he, "my dearest pledge?"
Last came and last did go
The pilot of the Galilean lake,[9]
Two massy keys he bore of metals twain   110
(The golden opes, the iron shuts amain[1]).
He shook his mitered locks,[2] and stern bespake:
"How well could I have spared for thee, young swain,
Enow[3] of such as for their bellies' sake,
Creep and intrude, and climb into the fold!   115
Of other care they little reckoning make,
Than how to scramble at the shearers' feast,
And shove away the worthy bidden guest.
Blind mouths![4] That scarce themselves know how to hold
A sheep-hook,[5] or have learned aught else the least 120
That to the faithful herdsman's art belongs!
What recks it them?[6] What need they? They are sped;
And when they list,[7] their lean and flashy songs
Grate on their scrannel[8] pipes of wretched straw.
The hungry sheep look up, and are not fed,   125
But swoln with wind, and the rank mist they draw,
Rot inwardly, and foul contagion spread,
Besides what the grim wolf with privy paw[9]
Daily devours apace, and nothing said.
But that two-handed engine at the door[1]   130
Stands ready to smite once, and smite no more."
  Return, Alpheus,[2] the dread voice is past,

7. God of the river Cam (properly, Granta), representing the ancient University of Cambridge, but slow and shaggy like the stream.
8. The bonnet and mantle of Camus have marks of woe on the edge like the *AI AI* supposedly found on the hyacinth, a "sanguine flower" sprung from the blood of a youth killed accidentally by Apollo.
9. St. Peter, originally a fisherman on Lake Tiberias in Galilee, was first founder and bishop of the Christian church; his keys open and shut the gates to heaven.
1. Literally "in full force," "exceedingly"; in this context, "for good," "once and for all."
2. He wears the bishop's miter.
3. An old plural form of "enough," used here with contemptuous intensification, as if to say, "enough and more than enough."
4. This audacious metaphor, as of tapeworms, takes on new depth when one notes that the word *episcopus* (bishop)
originally meant "over-seer" and a "pastor" is properly one who feeds his flock.
5. The bishop's staff, or crozier, is made in the form of a shepherd's crook.
6. What do they care? "They are sped": i.e., they have prospered in a worldly sense; but also, "their doom is sealed."
7. Choose (that is, choose to play on their pipes, as shepherds should); but with the secondary meaning of "listen."
8. Harsh, meager. Milton's is the first recorded literary use of the word in English; it existed previously only in a North-Country dialect.
9. I.e., Roman Catholicism, whose agents operated in secret.
1. Many guesses as to the specific meaning of the "two-handed engine" are on record; it may be St. Peter's keys, the two houses of Parliament, or a big sword, but there is no harm in letting it remain an indistinct, apocalyptic instrument of revenge.
2. With the return of Alpheus, the pastoral mode of the poem revives (see

That shrunk thy streams; return, Sicilian muse,
And call the vales, and bid them hither cast
Their bells and flowerets of a thousand hues. 135
Ye valleys low where the mild whispers use,[3]
Of shades and wanton winds, and gushing brooks,
On whose fresh lap the swart star[4] sparely looks,
Throw hither all your quaint enameled eyes,
That on the green turf suck the honeyed showers, 140
And purple all the ground with vernal flowers.
Bring the rathe[5] primrose that forsaken dies.
The tufted crow-toe, and pale jessamine,
The white pink, and the pansy freaked[6] with jet,
The glowing violet, 145
The musk-rose, and the well attired woodbine.
With cowslips wan that hang the pensive head,
And every flower that sad embroidery wears:
Bid amaranthus[7] all his beauty shed,
And daffadillies fill their cups with tears, 150
To strew the laureate hearse[8] where Lycid lies.
For so to interpose a little ease,
Let our frail thoughts dally with false surmise.[9]
Ay me! Whilst thee the shores and sounding seas
Wash far away, where'er thy bones are hurled, 155
Whether beyond the stormy Hebrides,[1]
Where thou perhaps under the whelming tide
Visit'st the bottom of the monstrous world;
Or whether thou, to our moist vows denied,
Sleep'st by the fable of Bellerus old,[2] 160
Where the great vision of the guarded mount
Looks toward Namancos and Bayona's hold:[3]
Look homeward angel now, and melt with ruth:[4]
And, O ye dolphins,[5] waft the hapless youth.
      Weep no more, woeful shepherds, weep no more, 165
For Lycidas your sorrow is not dead,

above, lines 85–87), and a catalogue of
flowers serves, as in Castiglione's *Alcon*,
to "interpose a little ease."
3. I.e., are used or accustomed to be
heard.
4. The Dog Star, Sirius, which during
the heats of late summer "looks
sparely" (witheringly) on the vegetation.
5. Early.
6. Flecked (the early verb survives in
our word "freckle").
7. The amaranth is an imaginary
flower that never fades; but for Lycidas
it will.
8. Bier decked with laurels (see line
1).
9. The "false surmise" is that the
body of Lycidas has been recovered
and can receive Christian burial.
1. Islands off the coast of Scotland,
representing the northern terminus of
the Irish Sea.
2. The fabulous giant Bellerus is supposed to lie buried on Land's End in
Cornwall.
3. St. Michael's Mount, in Cornwall,
from which the archangel is envisioned
as looking south, over miles of open
Atlantic, across the Bay of Biscay, to
Bayona and the stronghold of Namancos in northern Spain, where the historical Catholic enemy of Protestant England lay entrenched.
4. Michael is implored to look homeward, relaxing his stern guard for a
moment of grief and pity ("ruth").
5. Dolphins, admirable sea beasts,
brought the Greek poet Arion safely
ashore for love of his verses, and also
wafted the dead body of Melicertes to
land, where he was promptly transformed to a sea god, Palaemon.

Sunk though he be beneath the watery floor,
So sinks the day-star[6] in the ocean bed,
And yet anon repairs his drooping head,
And tricks[7] his beams, and with new-spangled ore,   170
Flames in the forehead of the morning sky:
So Lycidas sunk low, but mounted high,
Through the dear might of him that walked the waves,
Where other groves, and other streams along,
With nectar pure his oozy locks he laves,   175
And hears the unexpressive nuptial song,[8]
In the blest kingdoms meek of joy and love.
There entertain him all the saints above,
In solemn troops and sweet societies
That sing, and singing in their glory move,   180
And wipe the tears forever from his eyes.
Now, Lycidas, the shepherds weep no more;
Henceforth thou art the genius[9] of the shore,
In thy large recompense, and shalt be good
To all that wander in that perilous flood.   185
    Thus sang the uncouth swain[1] to th' oaks and rills,
While the still morn went out with sandals gray;
He touched the tender stops of various quills,[2]
With eager thought warbling his Doric[3] lay:
And now the sun had stretched out all the hills,   190
And now was dropped into the western bay;
At last he rose, and twitched his mantle blue:
Tomorrow to fresh woods, and pastures new.

                                                        1637

How Soon Hath Time

How soon hath Time, the subtle thief of youth,
    Stoln on his wing my three and twentieth year!
    My hasting days fly on with full career,
    But my late spring no bud or blossom show'th.
Perhaps my semblance might deceive the truth,   5
    That I to manhood am arrived so near,
    And inward ripeness doth much less appear,
    That some more timely-happy spirits endu'th.[1]
Yet be it less or more, or soon or slow,
    It shall be still in strictest measure even[2]   10

6. The sun.
7. Dresses.
8. Inexpressible hymn of joy, sung at "the marriage supper of the Lamb" (Revelation xix).
9. One who by divine appointment haunts a locality (in this case, "the shore") where he suffered and died, protecting others who might undergo a fate like his own.
1. Unlettered shepherd (a stock convention of this supremely literary form).
2. The oaten stalks of Panpipes.
3. Rustic, simple.
1. Endoweth.
2. Equal, adequate. Whenever it appears and however much it amounts

To that same lot, however mean or high,
    Toward which Time leads me, and the will of Heaven;
      All is, if I have grace to use it so,
      As ever in my great Taskmaster's eye.[3]

1631   1645

When the Assault Was Intended to the City[4]

Captain or Colonel,[5] or Knight in Arms,
    Whose chance on these defenseless doors may seize,
    If deed of honor did thee ever please,
    Guard them, and him within protect from harms.
He can requite thee; for he knows the charms   5
    That call fame on such gentle acts as these,
    And he can spread thy name o'er lands and seas,
    Whatever clime the sun's bright circle warms.
Lift not thy spear against the Muses' bower:
    The great Emathian conqueror bid spare   10
    The house of Pindarus, when temple and tower
Went to the ground;[6] and the repeated air
    Of sad Electra's poet had the power
    To save th' Athenian walls from ruin bare.[7]

1642   1645

A Book Was Writ of Late Called *Tetrachordon*

A book was writ of late called *Tetrachordon*,[8]
    And woven close, both matter, form, and style;
    The subject new: it walked the town a while,
    Numb'ring good intellects; now seldom pored on.
Cries the stall-reader, "Bless us! what a word on   5
    A title-page is this!"; and some in file
    Stand spelling false,[9] while one might walk to Mile-
End Green. Why is it harder, sirs, than Gordon,

to, Milton's inner growth will be adequate to the destiny which time and
heaven are preparing.
3. The last two lines are enigmatic;
their sense depends on whether one
reads the "all" of line 13 as referring
to time or talent.
4. During the campaign of 1642, the
king's forces seemed at one point in a
position to assault London. This sonnet
is a half-humorous plea that the poet's
house be spared; though the idea that
the Muse might and should protect her
spokesman was thoroughly congenial to
Milton (cf. *Lycidas*). Fortunately the
king's armies turned back without a battle, and the poem's persuasive powers
were never tested.
5. Colonel: pronounced with three syllables.

6. Alexander the Great gave orders that
Pindar's house be spared when Thebes
was captured. Emathian: Macedonian.
7. Plutarch is authority for the story
that when the Spartans had defeated
Athens and were about to raze the walls
of the city, they were stopped by an
Athenian officer, who recited the opening chorus of Euripides' *Electra*.
8. The title of Milton's third tract
on divorce (published with the fourth,
Colasterion, in 1645). It was called
"Tetrachordon," a Greek term for the
four-tone scale in music, because the
tract expounded and sought to harmo-
nize the four chief biblical passages on
marriage and divorce.
9. Misinterpreting. Mile-End Green was
at the East End of London.

Colkitto, or Macdonnel, or Galasp?[1]
    Those rugged names to our like mouths grow sleek   10
    That would have made Quintilian[2] stare and gasp.
Thy age, like ours, O soul of Sir John Cheke,
    Hated not learning worse than toad or asp,
    When thou taught'st Cambridge and King Edward Greek.[3]

1645–46   1673

On the New Forcers of Conscience Under the Long Parliament[1]

Because you have thrown off your prelate lord,[2]
    And with stiff vows renounced his liturgy,
    To seize the widowed whore Plurality[3]
    From them whose sin ye envied, not abhorred,
Dare ye for this adjure the civil sword   5
    To force our consciences that Christ set free,
    And ride us with a classic hierarchy[4]
    Taught ye by mere A. S. and Rutherford?[5]
Men whose life, learning, faith, and pure intent
    Would have been held in high esteem with Paul   10
    Must now be named and printed heretics
By shallow Edwards and Scotch what d'ye call:[6]
    But we do hope to find out all your tricks,
    Your plots and packing worse than those of Trent,[7]
        That so the Parliament   15
May with their wholesome and preventive shears
Clip your phylacteries,[8] though balk your ears,
    And succor our just fears

1. Scottish names made familiar through Scotland's involvement in the Civil War.
2. The great 1st-century Roman authority on rhetoric, who disapproved of barbarous words.
3. Sir John Cheke (1514–57) was the first to teach Greek at Cambridge; he was also tutor to Edward VI. In *Tetrachordon* Milton praises Edward's reign (1547–53) as the "best and purest" age of the English Reformation, and he commends Cheke's learning and piety. But even then, Milton is saying, a man of learning had to contend with much ignorant hostility and suspicion.
1. "The new forcers of conscience" are Presbyterians, whom Milton at first supported against the Episcopalians (Church-of-England men). Now, under the Puritan-dominated Long Parliament, he finds them as bad as their predecessors ("whose sin ye envied, not abhorred"). The sonnet proper has 14 lines followed by two "tails" of three lines each; in Italy, where it was common, this was called a *sonnetto caudato*, or "tailed sonnet."
2. Bishop.
3. I.e., the comfortable, and sometimes necessary, practice of one priest's holding several livings at once.
4. A church discipline made up on the Presbyterian model of synods or classes, ecclesiastical governing boards with strong powers over the laity.
5. Adam Stuart and Samuel Rutherford, Presbyterian pamphleteers, whose full names Milton does not deign to give.
6. Thomas Edwards, alarmed by the spread of heresies, began to describe them in a book picturesquely titled *Gangraena* (1645–46). Before giving up in despair, he wrote three fat volumes, including a denunciation of Milton, whom he described unjustly as an advocate of "divorce at pleasure." "Scotch what d'ye call" is Milton's humanistic sneer at the unpronounceability of Scottish names.
7. I.e., of the Council of Trent, held by the Papacy in consequence of the Reformation; it was widely reported to have been the scene of political jockeying.
8. Little scrolls, containing texts from the Pentateuch, worn by orthodox Jews to remind them of the Law. Milton uses them here as symbols of superstition.

When they shall read this clearly in your charge:
New presbyter is but *old priest* writ large.   20
ca. 1646   1673

On the Late Massacre in Piedmont[1]

Avenge, O Lord, thy slaughtered saints, whose bones
    Lie scattered on the Alpine mountains cold,
    Even them who kept thy truth so pure of old
    When all our fathers worshiped stocks and stones,
Forget not: in thy book record their groans   5
    Who were thy sheep and in their ancient fold
    Slain by the bloody Piemontese that rolled
    Mother with infant down the rocks. Their moans
The vales redoubled to the hills, and they
    To Heaven. Their martyred blood and ashes sow   10
    O'er all th' Italian fields where still doth sway
The triple tyrant:[2] that from these may grow
    A hundredfold, who having learnt thy way
    Early may fly the Babylonian woe.[3]
1655   1673

Lawrence, of Virtuous Father Virtuous Son[1]

Lawrence, of virtuous father virtuous son,
    Now that the fields are dank and ways are mire,
    Where shall we sometimes meet, and by the fire
    Help waste a sullen day, what may be won
From the hard season gaining? Time will run   5
    On smoother, till Favonius[2] reinspire
    The frozen earth, and clothe in fresh attire
The lily and rose, that neither sowed nor spun.
What neat repast shall feast us, light and choice,
    Of Attic taste,[3] with wine, whence we may rise   10

Mutilation by having one's ears cut off was a common punishment for sedition, and several Presbyterian leaders had suffered it. Milton's MS. read, "Clip ye as close as marginal P——'s ears," but the jeer was too brutal. William Prynne, whose books had many footnotes in the margins, and whose ears had twice been cropped, had suffered for a cause in which Milton at the time believed; and his final version of the line is gentler.
1. The Waldenses were a heretical sect, probably of Eastern origin by way of Venice; they lived in the valleys of northern Italy ("the Piedmont") and southern France, professing a creed which was particularly akin to Protestantism in its avoidance of graven images ("stocks and stones"). The understanding which had allowed them freedom of worship was terminated in 1655, and the massacre which ensued was widely protested by the Protestant powers of Europe. Milton, as Latin secretary to Cromwell, wrote several indignant letters.
2. I.e., the Pope, wearing his tiara with three crowns.
3. Protestants in Milton's day frequently identified the Roman Church with the "whore of Babylon" (Revelation xvii, xviii).
1. The "virtuous father" was Henry Lawrence, author of theological tracts and Lord President of Cromwell's Council for a time; his son, Edward Lawrence, became a member of parliament but died at the age of 24.
2. The west wind of spring.
3. I.e., "light and choice" (line 9), also flavored with wit.

To hear the lute well touched, or artful voice
Warble immortal notes and Tuscan⁴ air?
He who of those delights can judge, and spare⁵
To interpose them oft, is not unwise.

1655   1673

When I Consider How My Light Is Spent¹

When I consider how my light is spent
   Ere half my days, in this dark world and wide,
   And that one talent which is death to hide,
   Lodged with me useless, though my soul more bent
To serve therewith my Maker, and present   5
   My true account, lest he returning chide;
   "Doth God exact day-labor, light denied?"
   I fondly² ask; but Patience to prevent
That murmur, soon replies, "God doth not need
   Either man's work or his own gifts; who best   10
   Bear his mild yoke, they serve him best. His state
Is kingly. Thousands at his bidding speed
   And post o'er land and ocean without rest:
   They also serve who only stand and wait."

1655   1673

Methought I Saw My Late Espoused Saint

Methought I saw my late espoуséd saint
   Brought to me like Alcestis¹ from the grave,
   Whom Jove's great son to her glad husband gave,
   Rescued from death by force though pale and faint.
Mine, as whom washed from spot of childbed taint,   5
   Purification in the old law did save,²
   And such, as yet once more I trust to have
Full sight of her in Heaven without restraint,
   Came vested all in white, pure as her mind.
   Her face was veiled, yet to my fancied sight,   10

---

4. Italian, and specifically Florentine, calling to mind the carnival songs composed by such men as Lorenzo the Magnificent.
5. "Spare": in one possible sense, afford, spare time; in another, refrain, limit oneself (from too frequent interposing). The poem contains quite as many reinings-in of appetite as invitations to indulgence; it balances out to a very sober festivity or festive sobriety.
1. Milton's sonnet on his blindness is very close, in theme, to that on his 23rd birthday. But the absolute repose of the latter sonnet's final line is beyond anything in the earlier one.
2. Foolishly. "Prevent": forestall.
1. Alcestis, wife of Admetus, was rescued from the underworld by Hercules ("Jove's great son").
2. The old law, prescribing periods for the purification of women after childbirth, is found in Leviticus xii. The compression of line 5 is perhaps extreme; expanded, it would read, "My wife, like the woman whom when washed from spot of childbed taint," etc.

Love, sweetness, goodness, in her person shined
So clear, as in no face with more delight.
But O, as to embrace me she inclined,
I waked, she fled, and day brought back my night.

1658   1673

From Of Education[1]

* * * I shall detain you no longer in the demonstration of what we should not do, but straight conduct ye to a hillside, where I will point ye out the right path of a virtuous and noble education; laborious indeed at the first ascent, but else so smooth, so green, so full of goodly prospect and melodious sounds on every side, that the harp of Orpheus was not more charming. I doubt not but ye shall have more ado to drive our dullest and laziest youth, our stocks and stubs,[2] from the infinite desire of such a happy nurture, than we have now to haul and drag our choicest and hopefulest wits to that asinine[3] feast of sow-thistles and brambles which is commonly set before them, as all the food and entertainment of their tenderest and most docible[4] age. I call, therefore, a complete and generous education, that which fits a man to perform justly, skillfully, and magnanimously all the offices, both private and public, of peace and war. And how all this may be done between twelve and one-and-twenty, less time than is now bestowed in pure trifling at grammar and sophistry, is to be thus ordered.

First, to find out a spacious house and ground about it fit for an academy, and big enough to lodge a hundred and fifty persons, whereof twenty or thereabout may be attendants, all under the government of one who shall be thought of desert sufficient, and ability either to do all or wisely to direct and oversee it done. This place should be at once both school and university, not needing a remove to any other house of scholarship, except it be some peculiar[5]

1. Written in the form of an open letter to Samuel Hartlib (a noted educational reformer of the 17th century), *Of Education* was the product of Milton's leisure hours, and of an occasion. Hartlib had published in 1642 a book called *A Reformation of Schools*, putting forward some ideas derived from the Bohemian pedagogue John Comenius. On the whole, Hartlib, like Comenius, was interested in simple, easy schemes of education for everyone. Milton's proposal, which appeared as a tract on June 5, 1644, was courteous enough but definitely modeled on different lines. Characteristically, Milton called for a limited and intensive educational operation aimed at training a few distinguished leaders. But for them it was necessary to know nothing less than everything. Milton's aim was the humanistic one of producing a complete man who could design a building, storm a city, write an epic, or cure a lame knee. To the noble confidence of this program one can still respond, even though the details of the program itself appear antiquated.
2. Backward students.
3. Stupid; and, of course (reinforcing the metaphor), fit for donkeys.
4. Docile, teachable.
5. Set apart for particular studies.

college of law or physic, where they mean to be practitioners; but as for those general studies which take up all our time from Lily[6] to the commencing, as they term it, Master of Art, it should be absolute. After this pattern, as many edifices may be converted to this use as shall be needful in every city throughout this land, which would tend much to the increase of learning and civility everywhere. This number, less or more, thus collected, to the convenience of a foot-company or interchangeably two troops of cavalry, should divide their day's work into three parts, as it lies orderly: their studies, their exercise, and their diet.

For their studies: first, they should begin with the chief and necessary rules of some good grammar, either that now used, or any better; and while this is doing, their speech is to be fashioned to a distinct and clear pronunciation, as near as may be to the Italian, especially in the vowels. For we Englishmen, being far northerly, do not open our mouths in the cold air wide enough to grace a southern tongue; but are observed by all other nations to speak exceeding close and inward, so that to smatter Latin with an English mouth is as ill a hearing as law French.[7] Next, to make them expert in the usefulest points of grammar, and withal to season them and win them early to the love of virtue and true labor, ere any flattering seducement or vain principle seize them wandering, some easy and delightful book of education would be read to them, whereof the Greeks have store, as Cebes, Plutarch, and other Socratic discourses;[8] but in Latin we have none of classic authority extant, except the two or three first books of Quintilian[9] and some select pieces elsewhere. But here the main skill and groundwork will be to temper[1] them such lectures and explanations upon every opportunity, as may lead and draw them in willing obedience, inflamed with the study of learning and the admiration of virtue, stirred up with high hopes of living to be brave men and worthy patriots, dear to God and famous to all ages: that they may despise and scorn all their childish and ill-taught qualities, to delight in manly and liberal exercises; which he who hath the art and proper eloquence to catch them with, what with mild and effectual persua-

---

6. William Lily, first headmaster of St. Paul's School, was responsible for the elementary Latin grammar one encountered as a schoolboy beginning Latin. Milton is describing education from the level we should call the beginning of junior high school through college.
7. Norman French terms in English law-courts grated harshly on Milton's humanistic ear.
8. *The Picture* by Cebes describes and recommends the path to virtue and learning (its author's dates are highly uncertain). The book of Plutarch which Milton has in mind might be his essay on *The Education of Children* or perhaps the biographies; his moral essays are reserved for a later stage in the student's education. By "other Socratic discourses" Milton may mean either discourses using the Socratic method of question and answer or discourses teaching Socratic (i.e., Platonic) doctrine.
9. Quintilian wrote a famous book of instructions in oratory (1st century A.D.) which greatly influenced Milton's ideas on education.
1. Afford.

sions, and what with the intimation of some fear, if need be, but chiefly by his own example, might in a short space gain them to an incredible diligence and courage, infusing into their young breasts such an ingenuous and noble ardor as would not fail to make many of them renowned and matchless men. At the same time, some other hour of the day might be taught them the rules of arithmetic; and, soon after, the elements of geometry, even playing, as the old manner was. After evening repast till bedtime their thoughts would be best taken up in the easy grounds of religion and the story of Scripture. The next step would be to the authors of agriculture, Cato, Varro, and Columella,[2] for the matter is most easy; and if the language be difficult, so much the better; it is not a difficulty above their years. And here will be an occasion of inciting and enabling them hereafter to improve the tillage of their country, to recover the bad soil, and to remedy the waste that is made of good; for this was one of Hercules' praises. Ere half these authors be read, which will soon be with plying hard and daily, they cannot choose but be masters of any ordinary prose: so that it will be then seasonable for them to learn in any modern author the use of the globes and all the maps, first with the old names and then with the new; or they might be then capable to read any compendious method of natural philosophy: and, at the same time, might be entering into the Greek tongue, after the same manner as was before prescribed in the Latin; whereby the difficulties of grammar being soon overcome, all the historical physiology of Aristotle and Theophrastus [3] are open before them and, as I may say, under contribution. The like access will be to Vitruvius, to Seneca's *Natural Questions,* to Mela, Celsus, Pliny, or Solinus.[4] And having thus passed the principles of arithmetic, geometry, astronomy, and geography, with a general compact[5] of physics, they may descend in mathematics to the instrumental science of trigonometry, and from thence to fortification, architecture, enginery,[6] or navigation. And in natural philosophy they may proceed leisurely from the history of meteors, minerals, plants, and living creatures, as far as anatomy. Then also in course might be read to them out of some not tedious writer the institution of physic;[7] that they may

2. In the 2nd and 1st centuries B.C. and the 1st century A.D., all three wrote books about farming; during the Renaissance these treatises were customarily bound together.
3. Aristotle's *Natural History of Animals* would naturally be supplemented by his pupil Theophrastus' *Inquiry into Plants.*
4. Vitruvius wrote not only of architecture, but of engineering problems; Celsus was famous for a book on medicine; Seneca and Pliny were natural historians; Mela and Solinus wrote

general descriptions of the world. All these authors were of the 1st century A.D. except Solinus, who was of the 3rd.
5. Digest.
6. I.e., mechanics.
7. Instruction in medicine. Milton's pupils must learn the four "humors" (blood, phlegm, choler, and melancholy or black choler) and their "tempers" and "seasons" (i.e., mixtures and timings), in order to avoid a "crudity" (an upset stomach resulting from an ill mixture of humors).

know the tempers, the humors, the seasons, and how to manage a crudity; which he who can wisely and timely do is not only a great physician to himself and to his friends, but also may at some time or other save an army by this frugal and expenseless means only, and not let the healthy and stout bodies of young men rot away under him for want of this discipline; which is a great pity, and no less a shame to the commander. To set forward all these proceedings in nature and mathematics, what hinders but that they may procure, as oft as shall be needful, the helpful experiences of hunters, fowlers, fishermen, shepherds, gardeners, apothecaries; and in the other sciences, architects, engineers, mariners, anatomists; who, doubtless, would be ready, some for reward and some to favor such a hopeful seminary. And this will give them such a real tincture of natural knowledge as they shall never forget, but daily augment with delight. Then also those poets which are now counted most hard will be both facile and pleasant: Orpheus, Hesiod, Theocritus, Aratus, Nicander, Oppian, Dionysius; and, in Latin, Lucretius, Manilius, and the rural part of Virgil.[8]

By this time, years and good general precepts will have furnished them more distinctly with that act of reason which in ethics is called *proairesis*,[9] that they may with some judgment contemplate upon moral good and evil. Then will be required a special reinforcement of constant and sound indoctrinating to set them right and firm, instructing them more amply in the knowledge of virtue and the hatred of vice; while their young and pliant affections are led through all the moral works of Plato, Xenophon, Cicero, Plutarch, Laertius, and those Locrian remnants;[1] but still to be reduced in their nightward studies, wherewith they close the day's work, under the determinate sentence of David or Solomon, or the evangels and apostolic Scriptures.[2] Being perfect in the knowledge of personal duty, they may then begin the study of economics.[3] And either now or before this they may have easily learned at any odd hour the Italian tongue. And soon after, but with wariness and good antidote, it would be wholesome enough to let them taste some choice comedies, Greek, Latin, or Italian; those tragedies also that treat of household matters, as *Trachiniae*, *Alcestis*, and the

8. All these poets were didactic in character; for instance, the Hellenistic cultists who wrote under the mythical name of Orpheus created a poem called *Lithica* on the magic properties of precious stones; Oppian and Dionysius of Alexandria (2nd century A.D.) wrote on fishes and geography, Manilius (1st century A.D.) on astrology.
9. An Aristotelian term transliterated by Milton from the *Nicomachean Ethics* (II.iv.3) to suggest the idea of reason as choice.
1. Plato's dialogues, Plutarch's *Moralia*, and Cicero's moral essays all prescribe the principles of ethical behavior. Diogenes Laertius (ca. 150 A.D.) and Xenophon, the disciple of Socrates, are authorities on the lives of the philosophers. The "Locrian remnants" are a forgery, supposed to be by Plato's teacher, Timaeus of Locri, and titled *On the Soul of the World*.
2. In the evening all this pagan learning is shown to be subsumed in the Bible, the last word ("determinate sentence") of the Proverbs, Psalms, and apostolic Epistles.
3. Not the dismal science, but household management.

like. The next remove must be to the study of politics; to know the beginning, end, and reasons of political societies, that they may not, in a dangerous fit of the commonwealth, be such poor, shaken, uncertain reeds, of such a tottering conscience as many of our great counselors have lately shown themselves, but steadfast pillars of the state. After this they are to dive into the grounds of law and legal justice, delivered first and with best warrant by Moses; and, as far as human prudence can be trusted, in those extolled remains of Grecian law-givers, Lycurgus, Solon, Zaleucus, Charondas; and thence to all the Roman edicts and tables, with their Justinian; and so down to the Saxon and common laws of England and the statutes. Sundays also and every evening may be now understandingly spent in the highest matters of theology and church history, ancient and modern; and ere this time the Hebrew tongue at a set hour might have been gained, that the Scriptures may be read in their own original; whereto it would be no impossibility to add the Chaldee and the Syrian dialect.[4] When all these employments are well conquered, then will the choice histories, heroic poems, and Attic tragedies of stateliest and most regal argument, with all the famous political orations, offer themselves; which, if they were not only read, but some of them got by memory, and solemnly pronounced with right accent and grace, as might be taught, would endue them even with the spirit and vigor of Demosthenes or Cicero, Euripides or Sophocles. And now, lastly, will be the time to read with them those organic arts which enable men to discourse and write perspicuously, elegantly, and according to the fitted style of lofty, mean, or lowly. Logic, therefore, so much as is useful, is to be referred to this due place, with all her well-couched heads and topics, until it be time to open her contracted palm into a graceful and ornate rhetoric taught out of the rule of Plato, Aristotle, Phalereus, Cicero, Hermogenes, Longinus.[5] To which poetry would be made subsequent, or, indeed, rather precedent, as being less subtle and fine, but more simple, sensuous, and passionate; I mean not here the prosody of a verse, which they could not but have hit on before among the rudiments of grammar, but that sublime art which in Aristotle's *Poetics*, in Horace, and the Italian commentaries of Castelvetro, Tasso, Mazzoni,[6] and others, teaches what the laws are of a true epic poem, what of a dramatic, what of a lyric, what decorum is, which is the grand masterpiece to observe. This would make them soon perceive

4. Many passages of the Bible are more thoroughly understood by the man who can compare the Hebrew text with its Aramaic and Syriac versions.
5. Logic is a closed fist, say Aristotle and Cicero; rhetoric is an open palm. Phalereus and Hermogenes (2nd centuries B.C. and A.D. respectively) wrote

treatises on rhetoric.
6. Only Castelvetro wrote what is properly speaking a commentary on Aristotle; but Tasso's *Discourse on Epic Poetry* and Mazzoni's *Defense of the "Divine Comedy" of Dante* were important critical documents for Milton the poet.

what despicable creatures our common rhymers and play-writers be; and show them what religious, what glorious and magnificent use might be made of poetry, both in divine and human things. From hence, and not till now, will be the right season of forming them to be able writers and composers in every excellent matter, when they shall be thus fraught with an universal insight into things.[7] Or whether they be to speak in Parliament or Council, honor and attention would be waiting on their lips. There would then also appear in pulpits other visages, other gestures, and stuff otherwise wrought than what we now sit under, ofttimes to as great a trial of our patience as any other that they preach to us. These are the studies wherein our noble and our gentle youth ought to bestow their time in a disciplinary way from twelve to one-and-twenty, unless they rely more upon their ancestors dead than upon themselves living. In which methodical course it is so supposed they must proceed by the steady pace of learning onward, as at convenient times for memory's sake to retire back into the middle ward,[8] and sometimes into the rear of what they have been taught, until they have confirmed and solidly united the whole body of their perfected knowledge, like the last embattling of a Roman legion. Now will be worth the seeing what exercises and what recreations may best agree and become these studies.

Their Exercise

The course of study hitherto briefly described is, what I can guess by reading, likest to those ancient and famous schools of Pythagoras, Plato, Isocrates, Aristotle, and such others, out of which were bred such a number of renowned philosophers, orators, historians, poets, and princes all over Greece, Italy, and Asia, besides the flourishing studies of Cyrene and Alexandria. But herein it shall exceed them, and supply a defect as great as that which Plato noted in the commonwealth of Sparta; whereas that city trained up their youth most for war, and these in their academies and Lyceum all for the gown,[9] this institution of breeding which I here delineate shall be equally good both for peace and war. Therefore, about an hour and a half ere they eat at noon should be allowed them for exercise, and due rest afterwards; but the time for this may be enlarged at pleasure, according as their rising in the morning shall be early. The exercise which I commend first is the exact use of their weapon, to guard, and to strike safely with edge or point; this will keep them healthy, nimble, strong, and well in breath, is also the likeliest means to make them grow large and

---

7. Note how late the art of composition occurs in Milton's curriculum. He felt that students should not be asked, or even allowed, to write about anything till they had mastered the subject.

8. Milton's metaphor comes from the sport of fencing; the various "wards" represent so many postures of attack or defense.

9. The academic gown, i.e., study.

tall, and to inspire them with a gallant and fearless courage, which, being tempered with seasonable lectures and precepts to them of true fortitude and patience, will turn into a native and heroic valor, and make them hate the cowardice of doing wrong. They must be also practiced in all the locks and grips of wrestling, wherein Englishmen were wont to excel, as need may often be in fight to tug, to grapple, and to close. And this, perhaps, will be enough wherein to prove and heat their single strength. The interim of unsweating themselves regularly, and convenient rest before meat, may both with profit and delight be taken up in recreating and composing their travailed spirits with the solemn and divine harmonies of music heard or learned; either while the skillful organist plies his grave and fancied descant in lofty fugues,[1] or the whole symphony with artful and unimaginable touches adorn and grace the well-studied chords of some choice composer; sometimes the lute or soft organ-stop, waiting on[2] elegant voices, either to religious, martial, or civil ditties; which, if wise men and prophets be not extremely out,[3] have a great power over dispositions and manners, to smooth and make them gentle from rustic harshness and distempered passions. The like also would not be inexpedient after meat, to assist and cherish nature in her first concoction, and send their minds back to study in good tune and satisfaction. Where having followed it close under vigilant eyes until about two hours before supper, they are, by a sudden alarum or watchword, to be called out to their military motions, under sky or covert, according to the season, as was the Roman wont; first on foot, then, as their age permits, on horseback, to all the art of cavalry; that having in sport, but with much exactness and daily muster, served out the rudiments of their soldiership in all the skill of embattling, marching, encamping, fortifying, besieging, and battering, with all the helps of ancient and modern stratagems, tactics, and warlike maxims, they may, as it were out of a long war, come forth renowned and perfect commanders in the service of their country. They would not then, if they were trusted with fair and hopeful armies, suffer them for want of just and wise discipline to shed away from about them like sick feathers, though they be never so oft supplied; they would not suffer their empty and unrecruitable colonels of twenty men in a company to quaff out or convey into secret hoards, the wages of a delusive list and a miserable remnant;[4] yet in the meanwhile to be overmastered with a score or two of drunkards, the only soldiery left about them, or else to comply with all rapines and violences. No, certainly, if they knew aught of that

1. I.e., while the organist plays variations on a theme in the form of a fugue. "Symphony": orchestra.
2. Accompanying.
3. Mistaken.
4. Milton is indignant with colonels who cannot recruit more than twenty men to a company, or who deliberately hold down the rosters so they can collect (and drink up) the pay of the absentees.

knowledge that belongs to good men or good governors, they would not suffer these things. But to return to our own institute: besides these constant exercises at home, there is another opportunity of gaining experience to be won from pleasure itself abroad; in those vernal seasons of the year, when the air is calm and pleasant, it were an injury and sullenness against nature not to go out and see her riches and partake in her rejoicing with heaven and earth. I should not, therefore, be a persuader to them of studying much then, after two or three years that they have well laid their grounds, but to ride out in companies with prudent and staid guides to all quarters of the land, learning and observing all places of strength, all commodities of building and of soil, for towns and tillage, harbors, and ports for trade. Sometimes taking sea as far as to our navy, to learn there also what they can in the practical knowledge of sailing and of sea fight. These ways would try all their peculiar gifts of nature; and if there were any secret excellence among them, would fetch it out and give it fair opportunities to advance itself by, which could not but mightily redound to the good of this nation, and bring into fashion again those old admired virtues and excellencies, with far more advantage now in this purity of Christian knowledge. Nor shall we then need the monsieurs of Paris to take our hopeful youth into their slight and prodigal custodies, and send them over back again transformed into mimics, apes, and kickshaws.[5] But if they desire to see other countries at three or four and twenty years of age, not to learn principles, but to enlarge experience and make wise observation, they will by that time be such as shall deserve the regard and honor of all men where they pass, and the society and friendship of those in all places who are best and most eminent. And perhaps then other nations will be glad to visit us for their breeding, or else to imitate us in their own country.

Now, lastly, for their diet there cannot be much to say, save only that it would be best in the same house; for much time else would be lost abroad, and many ill habits got; and that it should be plain, healthful, and moderate, I suppose is out of controversy. Thus, Mr. Hartlib, you have a general view in writing, as your desire was, of that which at several times I had discoursed with you concerning the best and noblest way of education; not beginning, as some have done, from the cradle, which yet might be worth many considerations, if brevity had not been my scope. Many other circumstances also I could have mentioned; but this, to such as have the worth in them to make trial, for light and direction may be enough. Only I believe that this is not a bow for every man to shoot in that counts himself a teacher, but will require sinews almost equal to

5. A corruption of *quelque chose,* a thing of no real value, hence a trifling person.

those which Homer gave Ulysses; yet I am withal persuaded that it may prove much more easy in the assay[6] than it now seems at distance, and much more illustrious: howbeit not more difficult than I imagine, and that imagination presents me with nothing but very happy and very possible according to best wishes; if God have so decreed, and this age have spirit and capacity enough to apprehend.

1644

From Areopagitica[1]

* * * In Athens, where books and wits were ever busier than in any other part of Greece, I find but only two sorts of writings which the magistrate cared to take notice of: those either blasphemous and atheistical, or libelous. Thus the books of Protagoras were by the judges of Areopagus commanded to be burnt, and himself banished the territory for a discourse begun with his confessing not to know *whether there were gods, or whether not*.[2] And against defaming, it was decreed that none should be traduced by name, as was the manner of Vetus Comoedia,[3] whereby we may guess how they censured libeling: and this course was quick enough, as Cicero writes, to quell both the desperate wits of other atheists, and the open way of defaming, as the event showed. Of other sects and

6. In experience.
1. *Areopagitica* appeared on November 24, 1644. The title means "things to be said before the Areopagus." The Areopagus was an ancient, powerful, and much-respected tribunal in Athens, before which Isocrates, in 355 B.C., delivered a famous speech. Milton's title implies a comparison between the Areopagus and the English Parliament, and this comparison may be thought to validate, in some degree, the florid, oratorical tone of the tract.

Areopagitica is a plea for the liberty of unlicensed printing; its occasion was a severe ordinance for the control of printing which had been passed by Parliament on June 14, 1643. This ordinance, however disagreeable at the moment, was no striking novelty in English history. On the contrary, control of the press had been actively exercised by all the Tudors and both the early Stuarts. The aim of this government regulation was traditionally defined as the preservation of order and uniformity in church and state; but it also had an economic motive. Unlicensed printers threatened a monopoly enjoyed by the twenty licensed printers of London. Thus the censorship laws familiar to Englishmen had generally been strictly defined and had bristled with penalties. But to enforce them

was another matter entirely. Tudor and Stuart police forces being what they were, few printers or authors had to worry about the consequences of going to print without a license. As a matter of fact, *Areopagitica* was itself unlicensed, Milton's third unlicensed pamphlet since the passage of the Ordinance for Printing only seventeen months before.

Thus the practical effects of the Ordinance for Printing were less important (particularly, we may be sure, in Milton's eyes) than the principle involved. Having taken the lead in destroying the licensing system of the Stuarts, Parliament was now setting up a censorship of its own. After a long prologue, Milton's first approach to his subject was to undertake a condensed history of censorship, intended to discredit the institution by showing that only degenerate cultures ever made use of it.

2. It was in the 5th century B.C. that the sophist Protagoras of Abdera was censured in the manner described; Cicero wrote approvingly of this action in his treatise *On the Nature of the Gods* I.xxiii.

3. The "Old Comedy" of Aristophanes dealt with individuals, unlike the "New Comedy" of Menander, which dealt with types.

opinions, though tending to voluptuousness and the denying of
Divine Providence, they took no heed. Therefore we do not read
that either Epicurus, or that libertine school of Cyrene, or what
the Cynic impudence uttered, was ever questioned by the laws.[4]
Neither is it recorded that the writings of those old comedians were
suppressed, though the acting of them were forbid; and that Plato
commended the reading of Aristophanes, the loosest of them all, to
his royal scholar Dionysius,[5] is commonly known, and may be
excused, if holy Chrysostom, as is reported, nightly studied so
much the same author and had the art to cleanse a scurrilous
vehemence into the style of a rousing sermon.[6] * * *

And that the primitive councils and bishops were wont only to
declare what books were not commendable, passing no further, but
leaving it to each one's conscience to read or to lay by, till after
the year 800, is observed already by Padre Paolo, the great un-
masker of the Trentine Council.[7] After which time the Popes of
Rome, engrossing what they pleased of political rule into their own
hands, extended their dominion over men's eyes, as they had before
over their judgments, burning and prohibiting to be read what
they fancied not; yet sparing in their censures, and the books not
many which they so dealt with: till Martin the Fifth, by his bull,
not only prohibited, but was the first that excommunicated the
reading of heretical books; for about that time Wycliffe and Huss[8]
growing terrible, were they who first drove the papal court to a
stricter policy of prohibiting. Which course Leo the Tenth and his
successors followed, until the Council of Trent and the Spanish
Inquisition engendering together brought forth, or perfected, those
catalogues and expurging indexes,[9] that rake through the entrails
of many an old good author with a violation worse than any could

4. Epicurus (4th and 3rd centuries
B.C.) thought the gods had no influence
on human affairs, but he did not deny
their existence; therefore he was free
of censorship. Aristippus of Cyrene,
the pupil of Socrates, was like Epicurus
in making pleasure the end of life. His
school was known, from the Greek word
for "pleasure," as the school of He-
donism; but, like Epicurus, he is misunderstood as a sensualist. Diogenes
was the most famous of the Cynics,
who often affected a rude and truculent
disposition ("Cynic impudence"). All
these philosophers flourished in and
about the 4th century B.C.
5. That Plato told Dionysius, tyrant
of Syracuse, to read Aristophanes is
an ancient tradition. St. John Chrysostom, archbishop of Constantinople in
the 4th century, is said to have hated
the stage plays of his own day but
profited from a constant perusal of
Aristophanes.
6. After working his way through the
various cities of Greece and the meager

records of Roman censorship, Milton
takes his readers to the ages of primitive Christianity, where he finds no
positive censorship, merely an occasional recommendation of certain books
to be read or not to be read.
7. Father Paolo Sarpi (d. 1623) was
a Venetian historian who opposed papal
claims to secular authority. His *History of the Council of Trent* was
favorite reading matter for Protestants,
since it described in graphic detail the
"plots and packing" which went on
behind the scenes of the Counter-
Reformation. See Milton's sonnet *On
the New Forcers of Conscience*, line
14.
8. John Wycliffe (d. 1384) was an
English church reformer and translator
of the Bible; John Huss (burned at the
stake in 1415) was a Bohemian reformer of similar tendencies.
9. Literally from the Latin, *indices
expurgatorii*, lists of books forbidden to
Catholics.

be offered to his tomb.

Nor did they stay in matters heretical, but any subject that was not to their palate, they either condemned in a Prohibition, or had it straight into the new purgatory of an Index. To fill up the measure of encroachment, their last invention was to ordain that no book, pamphlet, or paper should be printed (as if St. Peter had bequeathed them the keys of the press also out of paradise) unless it were approved and licensed under the hands of two or three glutton friars. For example:[1]

Let the Chancellor Cini be pleased to see if in this present work be contained aught that may withstand the printing.
                    Vincent Rabatta, Vicar of Florence.

I have seen this present work, and find nothing athwart the Catholic faith and good manners: in witness whereof I have given, etc.
                    Nicolò Cini, Chancellor of Florence.

Attending the precedent relation, it is allowed that this present work of Davanzati may be printed.
                    Vincent Rabatta, etc.

It may be printed, July 15.
                    Friar Simon Mompei d'Amelia, Chancellor
                        of the holy office in Florence.

Sure they have a conceit,[2] if he of the bottomless pit had not long since broke prison, that this quadruple exorcism would bar him down. I fear their next design will be to get into their custody the licensing of that which they say Claudius intended,[3] but went not through with. Vouchsafe to see another of their forms, the Roman stamp:

Imprimatur, If it seem good to the reverend master of the holy palace.
                    Belcastro, Vicegerent.

Imprimatur, Friar Nicolò Rodolphi, Master of the holy palace.

Sometimes five Imprimaturs are seen together dialogue-wise in the piazza of one title page, complimenting and ducking each to other with their shaven reverences, whether the author, who stands by in perplexity at the foot of his epistle, shall to the press or to the sponge.[4] These are the pretty responsories, these are the dear antiphonies, that so bewitched of late our prelates and their chaplains

---

1. Milton's examples come from a book on *The English Schism*, translated by Bernardo Davanzati from the original of an English Jesuit.
2. Notion.
3. The Roman historian Suetonius says that Claudius once planned to tax the act of breaking wind. Milton's note refers to this impractical scheme in the decent obscurity of a learned language.
4. I.e., the eraser. In the next sentence, "responsories" and "antiphonies" are ecclesiastical services after the pattern of a dialogue.

with the goodly echo they made; and besotted us to the gay imitation of a lordly Imprimatur, one from Lambeth House, another from the west end of Paul's;[5] so apishly Romanizing, that the word of command still was set down in Latin; as if the learned grammatical pen that wrote it would cast no ink without Latin; or perhaps, as they thought, because no vulgar tongue was worthy to express the pure conceit of an Imprimatur; but rather, as I hope, for that our English, the language of men ever famous and foremost in the achievements of liberty, will not easily find servile letters enow to spell such a dictatory presumption English.[6] * * *

Good and evil we know in the field of this world grow up together almost inseparably; and the knowledge of good is so involved and interwoven with the knowledge of evil, and in so many cunning resemblances hardly to be discerned, that those confused seeds which were imposed on Psyche as an incessant labor to cull out and sort asunder,[7] were not more intermixed. It was from out the rind of one apple tasted, that the knowledge of good and evil, as two twins cleaving together, leaped forth into the world. And perhaps this is that doom which Adam fell into of knowing good and evil, that is to say of knowing good by evil.

As therefore the state of man now is, what wisdom can there be to choose, what continence to forbear without the knowledge of evil? He that can apprehend and consider vice with all her baits and seeming pleasures, and yet abstain, and yet distinguish, and yet prefer that which is truly better, he is the true wayfaring[8] Christian. I cannot praise a fugitive and cloistered virtue, unexercised and unbreathed, that never sallies out and sees her adversary, but slinks out of the race where that immortal garland[9] is to be run for, not without dust and heat. Assuredly we bring not innocence into the world, we bring impurity much rather; that which purifies us is trial, and trial is by what is contrary. That virtue therefore which is but a youngling in the contemplation of evil, and knows not the utmost that vice promises to her followers, and rejects it, is but a blank virtue, not a pure; her whiteness is but an excremental[1] whiteness; which was the reason why our sage and serious poet Spenser (whom I dare be known to think a better teacher than Scotus or Aquinas),[2]

<hr/>

5. Lambeth House is the Archbishop of Canterbury's London home. "Paul's" is St. Paul's Cathedral, headquarters of the Bishop of London. Under the prerogative government of Charles, these were the two chief censors.

6. Having finished with the history of censorship, Milton proceeds to argue more generally that the institution itself is evil and unchristian. As God left man free to choose among the many physical foods of this world, urging only temperance, so he left him free to pick and choose among ideas.

7. Angry at her son Cupid's love for Psyche, Venus set Psyche to sorting out a vast mound of mixed seeds; but the ants took pity on her, and did the work. See Apuleius, *The Golden Ass*.

8. There has been debate whether this word should be read "wayfaring" or "warfaring," but in the image of Christian life as a pilgrimage, a crusade, the two ideas are united.

9. The crown of righteousness, the garland of virtue.

1. Exterior (like a whited sepulcher, covering corruption within).

2. Duns Scotus and Thomas Aquinas, taken as types of the Scholastic theo-

describing true temperance under the person of Guyon, brings him in with his palmer through the cave of Mammon and the bower of earthly bliss, that he might see and know, and yet abstain.

Since therefore the knowledge and survey of vice is in this world so necessary to the constituting of human virtue, and the scanning of error to the confirmation of truth, how can we more safely, and with less danger, scout into the regions of sin and falsity than by reading all manner of tractates and hearing all manner of reason? And this is the benefit which may be had of books promiscuously read.

But of the harm that may result hence, three kinds are usually reckoned. First, is feared the infection that may spread; but then all human learning and controversy in religious points must remove out of the world, yea, the Bible itself; for that ofttimes relates blasphemy not nicely,[3] it describes the carnal sense of wicked men not unelegantly, it brings in holiest men passionately murmuring against Providence through all the arguments of Epicurus:[4] in other great disputes it answers dubiously and darkly to the common reader: and ask a Talmudist what ails the modesty of his marginal Keri, that Moses and all the prophets cannot persuade him to pronounce the textual Chetiv.[5] For these causes we all know the Bible itself put by the papist into the first rank of prohibited books. The ancientest Fathers must be next removed, as Clement of Alexandria, and that Eusebian book of evangelic preparation, transmitting our ears through a hoard of heathenish obscenities to receive the Gospel.[6] Who finds not that Irenaeus, Epiphanius, Jerome, and others discover[7] more heresies than they well confute, and that oft for heresy which is the truer opinion?[8] * * *

Impunity and remissness, for certain, are the bane of a commonwealth; but here the great art lies, to discern in what the law is to bid restraint and punishment, and in what things persuasion only is to work. If every action which is good or evil in man at ripe years were to be under pittance[9] and prescription and compulsion, what were virtue but a name, what praise could be then due to

---

logian. The passage of Spenser referred to is *Faerie Queene* II.vii.

3. Daintily.

4. See the Book of Ecclesiastes.

5. "Keri" are the marginal comments of rabbinical scholars on the "Chetiv" of the Bible, the text itself. When the text was too free-spoken for later commentators, Keri was sometimes read in place of Chetiv.

6. Eusebius' *Preparatio Evangelica*, like many early Christian books of polemic, describes heathen wickedness in fascinating detail, as an encouragement to Christan faith. St. Irenaeus, St. Epiphanius, St. Jerome, and even that ancient and edifying convert, Clement

of Alexandria, are all subject to this charge.

7. Describe (and so preserve, report).

8. Milton now argues that books cannot pervert men unless they are given force and vitality by a teacher, who, if he is a good teacher, needs no books. A fool, he urges, can find material for his folly in the best books, and a wise man material for his wisdom in the worst. Plato, indeed, recommended censorship in his *Republic;* but in real life one cannot censor books without censoring ballads, fiddlers, clothing, conversation, and social life as a whole.

9. Rationing.

well-doing, what gramercy[1] to be sober, just, or continent?

Many there be that complain of Divine Providence for suffering Adam to transgress; foolish tongues! when God gave him reason, he gave him freedom to choose, for reason is but choosing; he had been else a mere artificial Adam, such an Adam as he is in the motions.[2] We ourselves esteem not of that obedience, or love, or gift, which is of force: God therefore left him free, set before him a provoking object, ever almost in his eyes; herein consisted his merit, herein the right of his reward, the praise of his abstinence. Wherefore did he create passions within us, pleasures round about us, but that these rightly tempered are the very ingredients of virtue? They are not skillful considerers of human things, who imagine to remove sin by removing the matter of sin; for, besides that it is a huge heap increasing under the very act of diminishing, though some part of it may for a time be withdrawn from some persons, it cannot from all, in such a universal thing as books are; and when this is done, yet the sin remains entire. Though ye take from a covetous man all his treasure, he has yet one jewel left, ye cannot bereave him of his covetousness. Banish all objects of lust, shut up all youth into the severest discipline that can be exercised in any hermitage, ye cannot make them chaste that came not thither so: such great care and wisdom is required to the right managing of this point.

Suppose we could expel sin by this means; look how much we thus expel of sin, so much we expel of virtue: for the matter of them both is the same; remove that, and ye remove them both alike. This justifies the high providence of God, who, though he commands us temperance, justice, continence, yet pours out before us, even to a profuseness, all desirable things, and gives us minds that can wander beyond all limit and satiety. Why should we then affect a rigor contrary to the manner of God and of nature, by abridging or scanting those means, which books freely permitted are, both to the trial of virtue and the exercise of truth?[3] * * *

Well knows he who uses to consider, that our faith and knowledge thrives by exercise, as well as our limbs and complexion.[4] Truth is compared in Scripture to a streaming fountain; if her waters flow not in a perpetual progression, they sicken into a muddy pool of conformity and tradition. A man may be a heretic in the truth; and if he believe things only because his pastor says so, or the Assembly so determines, without knowing other reason, though his

1. Reward, thanks.
2. Puppet shows.
3. Censorship, Milton urges, is a vulgar, mechanical job; no man of intelligence will undertake it, and a dunderhead will make serious blunders. Finally, to put stupid men in authority over intelligent ones will discourage the pursuit of learning on every hand, except so far as censorship, by giving authority to banned books, will encourage men to seek out and cling to perverse opinions.
4. Constitution, regarded as the proper mingling of certain qualities in one's body.

belief be true, yet the very truth he holds becomes his heresy. There is not any burden that some would gladlier post off to another than the charge and care of their religion. There be, who knows not that there be, of Protestants and professors[5] who live and die in as arrant an implicit faith as any lay papist of Loretto.[6] A wealthy man, addicted to his pleasure and to his profits, finds religion to be a traffic so entangled, and of so many piddling accounts, that of all mysteries he cannot skill[7] to keep a stock going upon that trade. What should he do? Fain he would have the name to be religious, fain he would bear up with his neighbors in that. What does he therefore, but resolves to give over toiling, and to find himself out some factor,[8] to whose care and credit he may commit the whole managing of his religious affairs; some divine of note and estimation that must be. To him he adheres, resigns the whole warehouse of his religion, with all the locks and keys, into his custody; and indeed makes the very person of that man his religion; esteems his associating with him a sufficient evidence and commendatory of his own piety. So that a man may say his religion is now no more within himself, but is become a dividual[9] movable, and goes and comes near him, according as that good man frequents the house. He entertains him, gives him gifts, feasts him, lodges him; his religion comes home at night, prays, is liberally supped, and sumptuously laid to sleep, rises, is saluted, and after the malmsey, or some well-spiced brewage, and better breakfasted than He whose morning appetite would have gladly fed on green figs between Bethany and Jerusalem,[1] his religion walks abroad at eight, and leaves his kind entertainer in the shop trading all day without his religion.

Another sort there be who, when they hear that all things shall be ordered, all things regulated and settled, nothing written but what passes through the custom-house of certain publicans that have the tonnaging and poundaging[2] of all free-spoken truth, will straight give themselves up into your hands, make 'em and cut 'em out what religion ye please: there be delights, there be recreations and jolly pastimes that will fetch the day about from sun to sun, and rock the tedious year as in a delightful dream. What need they torture their heads with that which others have taken so strictly and so unalterably into their own purveying? These are the fruits which a dull ease and cessation of our knowledge will bring forth among the people. How goodly and how to be wished were

5. "Professors" in this context are people professing the Protestant faith.
6. A famous Catholic shrine.
7. Trades he cannot manage.
8. Agent.
9. I.e., separate or separable. Milton is describing the common institution of the household chaplain.

1. Mark xi.12–13. Jesus, hungry, found nothing but leaves on the fig tree, for the time of the figs was not yet.
2. "Publicans": tax collectors. Tonnage and poundage were excise taxes levied illegally by the king before 1641, and therefore specially odious to Milton's readers.

such an obedient unanimity as this, what a fine conformity would it starch us all into! Doubtless a staunch and solid piece of framework, as any January could freeze together.[3] * * *

Truth indeed came once into the world with her Divine Master, and was a perfect shape most glorious to look on: but when he ascended, and his apostles after him were laid asleep, then straight arose a wicked race of deceivers, who, as that story goes of the Egyptian Typhon with his conspirators, how they dealt with the good Osiris,[4] took the virgin Truth, hewed her lovely form into a thousand pieces, and scattered them to the four winds. From that time ever since, the sad friends of Truth, such as durst appear, imitating the careful search that Isis made for the mangled body of Osiris, went up and down gathering up limb by limb, still as they could find them. We have not yet found them all, Lords and Commons, nor ever shall do, till her Master's second coming; he shall bring together every joint and member, and shall mold them into an immortal feature of loveliness and perfection. Suffer not these licensing prohibitions to stand at every place of opportunity, forbidding and disturbing them that continue seeking, that continue to do our obsequies to the torn body of our martyred saint. We boast our light; but if we look not wisely on the sun itself, it smites us into darkness. Who can discern those planets that are oft combust,[5] and those stars of brightest magnitude that rise and set with the sun, until the opposite motion of their orbs bring them to such a place in the firmament where they may be seen evening or morning? The light which we have gained was given us, not to be ever staring on, but by it to discover onward things more remote from our knowledge. It is not the unfrocking of a priest, the unmitering of a bishop, and the removing him from off the Presbyterian shoulders, that will make us a happy nation. No, if other things as great in the church, and in the rule of life both economical[6] and political, be not looked into and reformed, we have looked so long upon the blaze that Zwinglius[7] and Calvin hath beaconed up to us, that we are stark blind.

There be who perpetually complain of schisms and sects, and make it such a calamity that any man dissents from their maxims. 'Tis their own pride and ignorance which causes the disturbing, who neither will hear with meekness, nor can convince; yet all must be suppressed which is not found in their syntagma.[8] They are the

3. To set barriers in the way of fresh truths implies that a nation has all the truth it needs; but this, Milton argues, is far from the case. England has no grounds for smugness; the nation needs every bit of truth it can discover.

4. Plutarch tells, in his *Isis and Osiris*, of Typhon's scattering the fragments of his brother Osiris, and of Isis' efforts to recover them.

5. Literally, burned up; in astrology, so close to the sun as not to be visible.

6. Domestic.

7. Zwingli and Calvin, both radical Swiss reformers, were mainstays of the Presbyterian cause, which Milton was already feeling to be a little narrow.

8. Compilation of beliefs, creed.

troublers, they are the dividers of unity, who neglect and permit not others to unite those dissevered pieces which are yet wanting to the body of Truth. To be still searching what we know not by what we know, still closing up truth to truth as we find it (for all her body is homogeneal and proportional), this is the golden rule in theology as well as in arithmetic, and makes up the best harmony in a church; not the forced and outward union of cold and neutral and inwardly divided minds.

Lords and Commons of England, consider what nation it is whereof ye are, and whereof ye are the governors: a nation not slow and dull, but of a quick, ingenious and piercing spirit, acute to invent, subtle and sinewy to discourse, not beneath the reach of any point, the highest that human capacity can soar to. Therefore the studies of learning in her deepest sciences have been so ancient and so eminent among us, that writers of good antiquity and ablest judgment have been persuaded that even the school of Pythagoras and the Persian wisdom took beginning from the old philosophy of this island.[9] And that wise and civil Roman, Julius Agricola, who governed once here for Caesar, preferred the natural wits of Britain before the labored studies of the French. Nor is it for nothing that the grave and frugal Transylvanian sends out yearly from as far as the mountainous borders of Russia, and beyond the Hercynian wilderness, not their youth, but their staid men, to learn our language and our theologic arts.

Yet that which is above all this, the favor and the love of heaven, we have great argument[1] to think in a peculiar manner propitious and propending towards us. Why else was this nation chosen before any other, that out of her, as out of Zion,[2] should be proclaimed and sounded forth the first tidings and trumpet of Reformation to all Europe? And had it not been the obstinate perverseness of our prelates against the divine and admirable spirit of Wycliffe, to suppress him as a schismatic and innovator, perhaps neither the Bohemian Huss and Jerome,[3] no, nor the name of Luther or of Calvin, had been ever known: the glory of reforming all our neighbors had been completely ours. But now, as our obdurate clergy have with violence demeaned[4] the matter, we are become hitherto the latest and backwardest scholars of whom God offered to have made us the teachers. Now once again by all concurrence of signs, and by the general instinct of holy and devout men, as they daily

9. So far as it concerns Pythagoras and the Persians, this sentence is better patriotism than it is intellectual history. Agricola's opinion of the British intellect (referred to next), is found in Tacitus' *Life of Agricola;* "civil" means "cultured, civilized." The Transylvanians, being Protestants. did sometimes come to England from "beyond the Hercynian wilderness" (the Harz mountains) to study.
1. Reason. "Propending": inclining, favorable.
2. Mt. Zion, in Jerusalem, the site of the temple, the holy of holies.
3. Jerome of Prague (martyred in 1416) was a follower of Huss and so of Wycliffe.
4. Conducted.

and solemnly express their thoughts, God is decreeing to begin some new and great period in his church, even to the reforming of Reformation itself; what does he then but reveal himself to his servants, and as his manner is, first to his Englishmen? I say, as his manner is, first to us, though we mark not the method of his counsels, and are unworthy. Behold now this vast city: a city of refuge, the mansion house of liberty, encompassed and surrounded with his protection; the shop of war hath not there more anvils and hammers waking, to fashion out the plates[5] and instruments of armed justice in defense of beleaguered truth, than there be pens and heads there, sitting by their studious lamps, musing, searching, revolving new notions and ideas wherewith to present, as with their homage and their fealty, the approaching Reformation: others as fast reading, trying all things, assenting to the force of reason and convincement.

What could a man require more from a nation so pliant and so prone to seek after knowledge? What wants there to such a towardly[6] and pregnant soil, but wise and faithful laborers, to make a knowing people, a nation of prophets, of sages, and of worthies? We reckon more than five months yet to harvest; there need not be five weeks; had we but eyes to lift up, the fields are white already.[7] Where there is much desire to learn, there of necessity will be much arguing, much writing, many opinions; for opinion in good men is but knowledge in the making. Under these fantastic terrors of sect and schism we wrong the earnest and zealous thirst after knowledge and understanding which God hath stirred up in this city.

What some lament of, we rather should rejoice at, should rather praise this pious forwardness among men, to reassume the ill-deputed care of their religion into their own hands again. A little generous prudence, a little forbearance of one another, and some grain of charity might win all these diligences to join, and unite into one general and brotherly search after truth; could we but forgo this prelatical tradition of crowding free consciences and Christian liberties into canons and precepts of men. I doubt not, if some great and worthy stranger should come among us, wise to discern the mold and temper of a people, and how to govern it, observing the high hopes and aims, the diligent alacrity of our extended thoughts and reasonings in the pursuance of truth and freedom, but that he would cry out as Pyrrhus did, admiring the Roman docility and courage: "If such were my Epirots, I would not despair the greatest design that could be attempted, to make a church or kingdom happy."[8] Yet these are the men cried out against for schismat-

---

5. Plate mail, armor plate.
6. Favorable.
7. Milton is paraphrasing Christ's words to the disciples (John iv.35).

8. Though King Pyrrhus of Epirus beat the Roman armies at Heraclea in 280 B.C., he was much impressed by their discipline.

ics and sectaries;[9] as if, while the temple of the Lord was building, some cutting, some squaring the marble, others hewing the cedars, there should be a sort of irrational men, who could not consider there must be many schisms and many dissections[1] made in the quarry and in the timber, ere the house of God can be built. And when every stone is laid artfully together, it cannot be united into a continuity, it can but be contiguous in this world; neither can every piece of the building be of one form; nay rather the perfection consists in this, that out of many moderate varieties and brotherly dissimilitudes that are not vastly disproportional, arises the goodly and the graceful symmetry that commends the whole pile and structure. Let us therefore be more considerate builders, more wise in spiritual architecture, when great reformation is expected. For now the time seems come, wherein Moses the great prophet may sit in heaven rejoicing to see that memorable and glorious wish of his fulfilled, when not only our seventy elders, but all the Lord's people, are become prophets.[2] * * *

Methinks I see in my mind a noble and puissant nation rousing herself like a strong man after sleep, and shaking her invincible locks: methinks I see her as an eagle mewing[3] her mighty youth, and kindling her undazzled eyes at the full midday beam; purging and unscaling her long-abused sight at the fountain itself of heavenly radiance; while the whole noise of timorous and flocking birds, with those also that love the twilight, flutter about, amazed at what she means, and in their envious gabble would prognosticate a year of sects and schisms.[4] * * *

1644

9. Sectarians, dividers of the church.
1. Milton puns on the literal meanings of "schisms" and "dissections" ("split" and "cut up") to press the image of the church as a temple built of believers.
2. In Numbers xi.29, Moses expressed the wish that all the Lord's people (not just the council of "seventy," or Sanhedrin) were prophets.
3. Molting, shaking off. Or the word may be "newing," i.e., renewing.
4. With this vigorous expression of idealistic optimism, Milton's argument subsides into a few last repetitions and afterthoughts. In practical terms, it was not a successful argument; the ordinance against which it protested was not repealed, though it was never effectively enforced, being, in effect, unenforceable. In time, Milton himself became, temporarily, a licenser of news sheets under Cromwell. But this biographical fact need not and must not be taken as a retraction or limitation of the position assumed in *Areopagitica*, which moves throughout on a plane of policy far removed from mundane considerations of practical politics.

Paradise Lost   The entry into *Paradise Lost* is easy—deceptively so. Carried along by the impetus of Satan's tremendous adventures, readers are apt to forget there is any other part to the poem. Indeed, while we are getting acclimated to the Miltonic world, there is no reason to hold back our sympathy with Satan, our admiration for his heroic energy. It is energy in a bad cause, clearly; but it is energy, it is heroically exercised, and there is as yet no source of virtuous power to oppose or offset it. With the appearance of Christ the Son, at the opening of Book III, we begin to see in heavenly Love the counterpoise of Satan's hellish Hate; and in Book IV, as we are introduced not only to Adam and Eve but to Paradise, our sympathies gradually shift. Satan is no longer a glamorous underdog, fighting his adventurous way through the universe against enormous odds; he is a menacing vulture, a cormorant, a toad, a snake. He is not only dangerous, he is dull; whatever richness and variety he discovers in the universe serve only to produce in him envious hatred and destructiveness. His sin is incestuous, as the allegory of Sin and Death points out; it breeds out of itself ever fresh occasions of sin. Adam and Eve, who are weaker, less active, and less spectacular in every way, finally outweigh Satan in our interest and sympathy simply because they can respond to life, and to the terrifying experience of guilt, more vigorously than Satan can.

Seen overall—from above, as it were—*Paradise Lost* is a vast but delicately balanced structure. The adventure of Satan in Books I–III balances the history of mankind in Books X–XII. Book IV, the entry of Satan (and the reader) into Paradise, balances Book IX, describing the loss of Paradise. Books V and VI, describing the destructive war in Heaven, balance as on a fulcrum against Books VII and VIII, which describe the Creation and deal with the problems of understanding it.

Within the poem's larger structure, there are all sorts of secondary balances which the knowing reader will recognize for himself. The consult in Hell (Book II) is paralleled by a consult in Heaven (Book III); the Heavenly Trinity of Father, Son, and Holy Ghost is paralleled by a diabolic trinity of Satan, Sin, and Death. Satan's fall parallels Adam's fall, and the parallel is prolonged into that extended series of falls and recoveries which is the history of mankind. Moloch contrasts with Mammon; the Son's mercy with the Father's justice; Raphael's affability with Michael's severity; and so on, almost without limit.

The structure of the poem is at once massive and delicate; its language is also both rich and strong. Milton's range of classical reference and gift for epithet are undoubtedly staggering at first view, and his long, complexly subordinated sentences are sometimes hard to follow. Footnotes, alas, provide the only proper solution to this problem. But one need not equal, or even follow, all Milton's learning in order to appreciate his poem, especially at a first reading. The poem progresses as through a garden of metaphor and reference which stretches away on either side of one, as far as the eye can see; on a first tour, it is enough to get the general prospect clear, without learning the name of each particular blossom. Ultimately, the reader who is experienced in the poem comes to appreciate its details—epic similes like Leviathan the seabeast (I.201), no less than the one-eyed Arimaspians and the gryphon (II.944)—its epithets and circumlocutions like Mulciber (I.740), who is Vulcan, and Amram's son (I.339) who is Moses—without sense of strain or strangeness. Milton himself moved securely through the literatures of half a dozen languages and as many cultures; it is one of the supreme rewards of literary study to be able to follow him with an equivalent security.

Paradise Lost is at once a deeply traditional and a boldly original poem. Milton takes pains to fulfill the traditional prescriptions of the epic form; he gives us love, war, supernatural characters, a descent into Hell, a catalogue of warriors, all the conventional items of epic machinery. Yet no poem in which the climax of the central action is a woman eating a piece of fruit can be a conventional epic. Similarly, Milton himself defined his own moral purpose as being to "justify the ways of God to men." This seems no more than conventionally meek. Yet we cannot even think of equating the message of Milton's poem with Pope's injunction to "submit" because "whatever is is right." The way of life which Adam and Eve take up as the poem ends is that of the Christian pilgrimage through this world. Paradise was no place or condition in which to exercise Christian heroism as Milton conceives it. Expelled from Eden, our first "grand parents" pick up the burdens of humanity as we know them, sustained by a faith which we also know, and go forth to seek a blessing which we do not know yet. They are to become wayfaring, warfaring Christians, like John Milton; and in this condition, with its weaknesses and strivings and inevitable defeats, there is a glory that no devil can ever understand. Thus Milton strikes, humanly as well as artistically, a grand resolving chord. It is the careful, triumphant balancing and tempering of this conclusion which makes Milton's poem the noble architecture it is; and which makes of the end a richer, if not a more exciting, experience than the beginning.

From Paradise Lost

Book I

The Argument[1]

This first book proposes, first in brief, the whole subject, man's disobedience, and the loss thereupon of Paradise, wherein he was placed: then touches the prime cause of his fall, the serpent, or rather Satan in the serpent; who, revolting from God, and drawing to his side many legions of angels, was, by the command of God, driven out of Heaven, with all his crew, into the great deep. Which action passed over, the poem hastens into the midst of things;[2] presenting Satan, with his angels, now fallen into Hell—described here not in the center (for heaven and earth may be supposed as yet not made, certainly not yet accursed), but in a place of utter darkness, fitliest called Chaos. Here Satan with his angels lying on the burning lake, thunderstruck and astonished, after a certain space recovers, as from confusion; calls up him who, next in order and dignity, lay by him: they confer of their miserable fall. Satan awakens all his legions, who lay till then in the same manner confounded. They rise: their numbers; array of battle; their

1. *Paradise Lost* appeared originally without any sort of prose aid to the reader; but, since many readers found the poem hard going, the printer asked Milton for some prose "Arguments" or summary explanations of the action in the various books, and prefixed them to later issues of the poem. We reprint those for the first two books and the ninth.

2. Adapted from Horace's prescription that the epic poet should start *"in medias res."*

chief leaders named, according to the idols known afterwards in Canaan and the countries adjoining. To these Satan directs his speech; comforts them with hope yet of regaining Heaven; but tells them, lastly, of a new world and new kind of creature to be created, according to an ancient prophecy, or report, in Heaven; for that angels were long before this visible creation was the opinion of many ancient fathers.[3] To find out the truth of this prophecy, and what to determine[4] thereon, he refers to a full council. What his associates thence attempt. Pandemonium, the palace of Satan, rises, suddenly built out of the deep: the infernal peers there sit in council.

Of man's first disobedience, and the fruit[5]
Of that forbidden tree whose mortal[6] taste
Brought death into the world, and all our woe,
With loss of Eden, till one greater Man[7]
Restore us, and regain the blissful seat,   5
Sing, Heavenly Muse,[8] that, on the secret top
Of Oreb, or of Sinai, didst inspire
That shepherd who first taught the chosen seed
In the beginning how the Heavens and Earth
Rose out of Chaos: or, if Sion hill[9]   10
Delight thee more, and Siloa's brook that flowed
Fast[1] by the oracle of God, I thence
Invoke thy aid to my adventurous song,
That with no middle flight intends to soar
Above th' Aonian mount,[2] while it pursues   15
Things unattempted yet in prose or rhyme.
And chiefly thou, O Spirit,[3] that dost prefer
Before all temples th' upright heart and pure,
Instruct me, for thou know'st; thou from the first
Wast present, and, with mighty wings outspread,   20
Dovelike sat'st brooding[4] on the vast abyss,

3. I.e., Church Fathers, the Christian writers of the first three centuries of the church.
4. I.e., what action to take upon their information.
5. Eve's apple, of course; but also all the consequences of eating it.
6. Deadly; but also "to mortals" (i.e., human beings).
7. Christ, the second Adam.
8. In Greek mythology, Urania, Muse of astronomy and epic poetry; but here identified, by references to Oreb and Sinai, with the Holy Spirit of the Bible, which inspired Moses ("that shepherd") to write Genesis and the other four books of the Pentateuch for the instruction of the Jews ("the chosen seed").
9. The hill of Sion and the brook of Siloa are two features of the landscape around Jerusalem likely to appeal to a Muse, whose natural haunts are springs and mountains (see *Lycidas*,

line 15). Milton's aim is to show that poetry is everywhere recognized as an inspiration close to that of religion.
1. Close.
2. Helicon, home of the classical Muses; Milton is deliberately courting comparison with Homer and Virgil.
3. The Spirit is an impulse or voice of God, by which the Hebrew prophets were directly inspired.
4. A composite of phrases and ideas from Genesis i.2 ("And the earth was without form, and void; and darkness was upon the face of the deep. And the Spirit of God moved upon the face of the waters"); Matthew iii.16 ("and he saw the Spirit of God descending like a dove, and lighting upon him"); and Luke iii.22 ("and the Holy Ghost descended in a bodily shape like a dove upon him"). Milton's mind as he wrote was impregnated with expressions from the King James Bible, only a few of which can be indicated in the notes.

And mad'st it pregnant: what in me is dark
Illumine; what is low, raise and support;
That, to the height of this great argument,[5]
I may assert Eternal Providence,   25
And justify the ways of God to men.

Say first (for Heaven hides nothing from thy view,
Nor the deep tract of Hell), say first what cause
Moved our grand[6] parents, in that happy state,
Favored of Heaven so highly, to fall off   30
From their Creator, and transgress his will
For[7] one restraint, lords of the world besides?[8]
Who first seduced them to that foul revolt?

Th' infernal serpent; he it was, whose guile,
Stirred up with envy and revenge, deceived   35
The mother of mankind, what time[9] his pride
Had cast him out from Heaven, with all his host
Of rebel angels, by whose aid, aspiring
To set himself in glory above his peers,[1]
He trusted to have equaled the Most High,   40
If he opposed; and with ambitious aim
Against the throne and monarchy of God,
Raised impious war in Heaven and battle proud,
With vain attempt. Him the Almighty Power
Hurled headlong flaming from th' ethereal sky,   45
With hideous ruin and combustion, down
To bottomless perdition, there to dwell
In adamantine chains and penal fire,
Who durst defy th' Omnipotent to arms.

Nine times the space that measures day and night   50
To mortal men, he with his horrid crew,
Lay vanquished, rolling in the fiery gulf,
Confounded though immortal. But his doom
Reserved him to more wrath; for now the thought
Both of lost happiness and lasting pain   55
Torments him; round he throws his baleful[2] eyes,
That witnessed huge affliction and dismay,
Mixed with obdúrate pride and steadfast hate.
At once, as far as angels ken,[3] he views
The dismal situation waste and wild: 60
A dungeon horrible, on all sides round,
As one great furnace flamed; yet from those flames
No light,[4] but rather darkness visible

5. Theme.
6. First in importance; by implication, in time also.
7. Because of.
8. In every other respect.
9. I.e., at the time when.
1. His equals. The sentence mimics Satan's action, piling clause loosely upon clause, and building ever higher, till "with vain attempt" (line 44) brings the whole structure crashing

down. It is a dramatic entry into "the midst of things," where epics begin. Book VI will recount more largely the war in Heaven, in the full narrative form which Aeneas used to tell Dido of the last days of Troy.
2. Malignant, as well as suffering.
3. As far as angels can see.
4. Omitting the verb conveys abruptly the paradox: fire-without-light.

Served only to discover sights of woe,
Regions of sorrow, doleful shades, where peace 65
And rest can never dwell, hope never comes
That comes to all,[5] but torture without end
Still urges,[6] and a fiery deluge, fed
With ever-burning sulphur unconsumed.
Such place Eternal Justice had prepared 70
For those rebellious; here their prison ordained
In utter[7] darkness, and their portion set,
As far removed from God and light of Heaven
As from the center[8] thrice to th' utmost pole.
O how unlike the place from whence they fell! 75
There the companions of his fall, o'erwhelmed
With floods and whirlwinds of tempestuous fire,
He soon discerns; and, weltering by his side,
One next himself in power, and next in crime,
Long after known in Palestine, and named 80
Beëlzebub.[9] To whom th' arch-enemy,
And thence in Heaven called Satan,[1] with bold words
Breaking the horrid silence, thus began:
    "If thou beëst he—but O how fallen! how changed
From him who, in the happy realms of light 85
Clothed with transcendent brightness, didst outshine
Myriads, though bright! if he whom mutual league,
United thoughts and counsels, equal hope
And hazard in the glorious enterprise,
Joined with me once, now misery hath joined 90
In equal ruin; into what pit thou seest[2]
From what height fallen, so much the stronger proved
He with his thunder:[3] and till then who knew
The force of those dire arms? Yet not for those,
Nor what the potent Victor in his rage 95
Can else inflict, do I repent, or change,
Though changed in outward luster, that fixed mind,
And high disdain from sense of injured merit,

5. The phrase echoes an expression in Dante ("All hope abandon, ye who enter here"), but Milton expresses it as a logical absurdity. Hope comes to "all" but not to Helldwellers; they are not included in "all."
6. Afflicts.
7. "Complete" but also "outer."
8. The earth. Milton makes use in *Paradise Lost* of two images of the cosmos: (1) the earth is the center of the *created* (Ptolemaic) cosmos of nine concentric spheres; but (2) the earth and the whole created cosmos are a mere appendage, hanging from Heaven by a golden chain, in the larger, aboriginal, and less shapely cosmos. In the present passage, the fall from Heaven to Hell (through the aboriginal universe) is described as thrice as far as the distance (in the created universe) from the center (earth) to the outermost sphere.

9. A Phoenician deity, or Baal (the name means "Lord of flies"); traditionally, a prince of devils and enemy of Jehovah. The Phoenician Baal, a sun god, had many aspects and so many names; most Baals were nature deities. But in the poem's time scheme all this lies in the future; Beelzebub's angelic name, whatever it was, has been erased from the Book of Life, and as he has not yet got another one, he must be called by the name he will have later on.
1. In Hebrew, the name means "Adversary."
2. Satan's syntax, like that of a man recovering from a stunning blow, is not of the clearest.
3. God with his thunderbolts.

That with the Mightiest raised me to contend,
And to the fierce contentions brought along   100
Innumerable force of spirits armed,
That durst dislike his reign, and, me preferring,
His utmost power with adverse power opposed
In dubious battle on the plains of Heaven,
And shook his throne. What though the field be lost?   105
All is not lost: the unconquerable will,
And study[4] of revenge, immortal hate,
And courage never to submit or yield:
And what is else not to be overcome?[5]
That glory never shall his wrath or might   110
Extort from me. To bow and sue for grace
With suppliant knee, and deify his power[6]
Who, from the terror of this arm, so late
Doubted his empire[7]—that were low indeed;
That were an ignominy and shame beneath   115
This downfall; since, by fate, the strength of gods,[8]
And this empyreal substance, cannot fail;
Since, through experience of this great event,
In arms not worse, in foresight much advanced,
We may with more successful hope resolve   120
To wage by force or guile eternal war,
Irreconcilable to our grand Foe,
Who now triúmphs, and in th' excess of joy
Sole reigning holds the tyranny[9] of Heaven."
      So spake th' apostate angel, though in pain,   125
Vaunting aloud, but racked with deep despair;
And him thus answered soon his bold compeer:[1]
      "O prince, O chief of many thronéd powers,
That led th' embattled seraphim[2] to war
Under thy conduct, and, in dreadful deeds   130
Fearless, endangered Heaven's perpetual King,
And put to proof his high supremacy,
Whether upheld by strength, or chance, or fate![3]
Too well I see and rue the dire event[4]

4. Pursuit.
5. I.e., what else does it mean not to
be beaten? "That glory" is the glory
of hearing Satan confess himself overcome.
6. I.e., deify the power of him who.
Milton sometimes writes English as if
it were an inflected language.
7. I.e., doubted whether he could maintain his empire.
8. The essence of Satan's fault is his
claim to the position of a god, subject
to fate but to nothing else. His substance is "empyreal" (heavenly, from
the empyrean), and cannot be destroyed; but, as he learns in the poem,
it can be confounded by God's greater
power and weakened by its own corruption and self-contradictions. "Fail":

cease to exist.
9. The accusation is bold, but one of
the aims of the poem is to show that
Satan is a tyrant and God is not. The
next two lines start this dramatic
process by suggesting that Satan's
brave exterior is merely a front.
1. Comrade and equal.
2. According to tradition, there were
nine orders of angels—seraphim, cherubim, thrones, dominions, virtues, powers, principalities, archangels, and angels; but Milton does not use these
systematic categories systematically.
3. The devils can conceive of any reason for God's continuing rule, except
goodness and justice.
4. Outcome.

That with sad overthrow and foul defeat 135
Hath lost us Heaven, and all this mighty host
In horrible destruction laid thus low,
As far as gods and heavenly essences
Can perish: for the mind and spirit remains
Invincible, and vigor soon returns, 140
Though all our glory extinct, and happy state
Here swallowed up in endless misery.
But what if he our Conqueror (whom I now
Of force[5] believe almighty, since no less
Than such could have o'erpowered such force as ours) 145
Have left us this our spirit and strength entire,
Strongly to suffer and support our pains,
That we may so suffice[6] his vengeful ire,
Or do him mightier service as his thralls
By right of war, whate'er his business be, 150
Here in the heart of Hell to work in fire,
Or do his errands in the gloomy deep?
What can it then avail though yet we feel
Strength undiminished, or eternal being
To undergo eternal punishment?" 155
　　Whereto with speedy words th' arch-fiend[7] replied:
"Fallen cherub, to be weak is miserable,
Doing or suffering:[8] but of this be sure,
To do aught good never will be our task,
But ever to do ill our sole delight, 160
As being the contrary to his high will
Whom we resist. If then his providence
Out of our evil seek to bring forth good,
Our labor must be to pervert that end,
And out of good still to find means of evil; 165
Which oft times may succeed, so as perhaps
Shall grieve him, if I fail not,[9] and disturb
His inmost counsels from their destined aim.
But see! the angry Victor hath recalled
His ministers of vengeance and pursuit 170
Back to the gates of Heaven; the sulphurous hail,
Shot after us in storm, o'erblown hath laid
The fiery surge that from the precipice
Of Heaven received us falling; and the thunder,
Winged with red lightning and impetuous rage, 175.
Perhaps hath spent his shafts, and ceases now
To bellow through the vast and boundless deep.
Let us not slip[1] th' occasion, whether scorn
Or satiate fury yield it from our Foe.
Seest thou yon dreary plain, forlorn and wild, 180
The seat of desolation, void of light;

---

5. Perforce, necessarily.
6. Satisfy.
7. A fiend is an enemy, one who hates; the word is an antonym of "friend."
8. Whether one is active or passive.
9. "Unless I'm mistaken" (direct from the Latin, *ne fallor*).
1. I.e., let slip.

Save what the glimmering of these livid flames
Casts pale and dreadful? Thither let us tend
From off the tossing of these fiery waves;
There rest, if any rest can harbor there;   185
And, reassembling our afflicted powers,[2]
Consult how we may henceforth most offend
Our enemy, our own loss how repair,
How overcome this dire calamity,
What reinforcement we may gain from hope,   190
If not, what resolution from despair."[3]
     Thus Satan, talking to his nearest mate,
With head uplift above the wave, and eyes
That sparkling blazed; his other parts besides,
Prone on the flood, extended long and large,   195
Lay floating many a rood,[4] in bulk as huge
As whom[5] the fables name of monstrous size,
Titanian or Earth-born, that warred on Jove,
Briareos or Typhon,[6] whom the den
By ancient Tarsus held, or that sea beast   200
Leviathan,[7] which God of all his works
Created hugest that swim th' ocean-stream.
Him, haply, slumbering on the Norway foam,
The pilot of some small night-foundered[8] skiff,
Deeming some island, oft, as seamen tell,   205
With fixéd anchor in his scaly rind,
Moors by his side under the lee, while night
Invests[9] the sea, and wishéd morn delays.
So stretched out huge in length the arch-fiend lay,
Chained on the burning lake; nor ever thence   210
Had risen or heaved his head, but that the will
And high permission of all-ruling Heaven
Left him at large to his own dark designs,
That with reiterated crimes he might
Heap on himself damnation, while he sought   215
Evil to others, and enraged might see
How all his malice served but to bring forth
Infinite goodness, grace, and mercy shown
On man by him seduced, but on himself

2. Stricken armies.
3. Of the last nine lines of Satan's speech, no less than five rhyme. Milton may have felt the need for something like the couplet with which blank-verse dramatists cut off their scenes.
4. An old unit of measure, between six and eight yards.
5. I.e., as those whom.
6. Both the Titans, led by Briareos, and the earth-born Giants, represented by Typhon (who lived in Cilicia near Tarsus), fought with Jove. Briareos was said to have a hundred hands, and Typhon a hundred heads; and both were said, by different authors, to have

been punished for their rebellion (like Satan for his) by being thrown into the underworld. Briareos and Typhon are still heard grumbling from time to time under Mt. Etna.
7. The great sea monster of Isaiah xxvii.1 or Job xli; for Milton and us, simply a whale, but scaly (line 206).
8. Overtaken by darkness.
9. Wraps, covers. The story of sailors mooring to whales was an old one, but the reference to Norway suggests that Milton was thinking of a recently translated version by Olaus Magnus, the Swedish historian.

Treble confusion, wrath, and vengeance poured.   220
   Forthwith upright he rears from off the pool
His mighty stature; on each hand the flames
Driven backward slope their pointing spires,[1] and, rolled
In billows, leave i' th' midst a horrid[2] vale.
Then with expanded wings he steers his flight   225
Aloft, incumbent on[3] the dusky air,
That felt unusual weight; till on dry land
He lights, if it were land that ever burned
With solid, as the lake with liquid fire,
And such appeared in hue; as when the force   230
Of subterranean wind transports a hill
Torn from Pelorus,[4] or the shattered side
Of thundering Etna, whose combustible
And fueled entrails, thence conceiving fire,
Sublimed[5] with mineral fury, aid the winds,   235
And leave a singéd bottom all involved[6]
With stench and smoke. Such resting found the sole
Of unblest feet. Him followed his next mate,
Both glorying to have 'scaped the Stygian[7] flood
As gods, and by their own recovered strength,   240
Not by the sufferance[8] of supernal power.
   "Is this the region, this the soil, the clime,"
Said then the lost archangel, "this the seat
That we must change[9] for Heaven? this mournful gloom
For that celestial light? Be it so, since he   245
Who now is sovereign can dispose and bid
What shall be right: farthest from him is best,
Whom reason hath equaled, force hath made supreme
Above his equals.[1] Farewell, happy fields,
Where joy forever dwells! Hail, horrors! hail,   250
Infernal world! and thou, profoundest Hell,
Receive thy new possessor, one who brings
A mind not to be changed by place or time.
The mind is its own place, and in itself
Can make a Heaven of Hell, a Hell of Heaven.   255
What matter where, if I be still the same,
And what I should be, all but less[2] than he
Whom thunder hath made greater? Here at least
We shall be free; th' Almighty hath not built
Here for his envy, will not drive us hence: 260
Here we may reign secure; and, in my choice,
To reign is worth ambition, though in Hell:

1. Points of flame.
2. Not simply "ghastly," but in the Latin sense, "bristling."
3. Resting upon.
4. Pelorus and Etna are volcanic mountains in Sicily, which Milton pictures as exploding under pressure of underground winds.
5. Kindled.
6. Wrapped.

7. Of the river Styx, i.e., demonic, hellish.
8. Permission.
9. Exchange.
1. Satan likes to think that by "reason" he is God's equal; this only shows how far he is from "right reason."
2. Second only to. The expression "all but less than" telescopes "all but equal to" and "only less than."

Better to reign in Hell than serve in Heaven.
But wherefore let we then our faithful friends,
Th' associates and copartners of our loss,   265
Lie thus astonished[3] on th' oblivious pool,
And call them not to share with us their part
In this unhappy mansion, or once more
With rallied arms to try what may be yet
Regained in Heaven, or what more lost in Hell?"   270
    So Satan spake; and him Beëlzebub
Thus answered: "Leader of those armies bright
Which, but th' Omnipotent, none could have foiled!
If once they hear that voice, their liveliest pledge
Of hope in fears and dangers, heard so oft   275
In worst extremes, and on the perilous edge[4]
Of battle, when it raged, in all assaults
Their surest signal, they will soon resume
New courage and revive, though now they lie
Groveling and prostrate on yon lake of fire,   280
As we erewhile, astounded and amazed;
No wonder, fallen such a pernicious height!"
    He scarce had ceased when the superior fiend
Was moving toward the shore; his ponderous shield,
Ethereal temper,[5] massy, large, and round,   285
Behind him cast. The broad circumference
Hung on his shoulders like the moon, whose orb
Through optic glass the Tuscan artist[6] views
At evening, from the top of Fesolè,
Or in Valdarno, to descry new lands,   290
Rivers, or mountains, in her spotty globe.
His spear, to equal which the tallest pine
Hewn on Norwegian hills, to be the mast
Of some great admiral,[7] were but a wand,
He walked with, to support uneasy steps   295
Over the burning marl,[8] not like those steps
On Heaven's azure; and the torrid clime
Smote on him sore besides, vaulted with fire.
Nathless[9] he so endured, till on the beach
Of that inflaméd[1] sea he stood, and called   300
His legions, angel forms, who lay entranced,
Thick as autumnal leaves that strow the brooks
In Vallombrosa,[2] where th' Etrurian shades

---

3. Stunned. The epithet "oblivious" is transferred from the fallen angels to the pool in which they have fallen.
4. Not the fringe of battle but the front line (Latin *acies*).
5. With the qualities of ether, which, being the fifth element, is not subject to change, corruption, or decay.
6. Galileo, who looked through a telescope ("optic glass") from the hill town of Fiesole outside Florence in the Val

d'Arno, is the only contemporary mentioned by Milton in *Paradise Lost*.
7. Not the naval commander, but his flagship, usually the biggest of the fleet.
8. Soil.
9. A compressed, archaic form of "not the less."
1. Flaming, of course, but also fevered.
2. Literally, "Shady Valley," a few miles from Florence.

High over-arched embower;[3] or scattered sedge
Afloat, when with fierce winds Orion armed   305
Hath vexed the Red-Sea coast, whose waves o'erthrew
Busiris and his Memphian chivalry,
While with perfidious hatred they pursued
The sojourners of Goshen, who beheld
From the safe shore their floating carcasses   310
And broken chariot wheels.[4] So thick bestrown,
Abject and lost, lay these, covering the flood,
Under amazement of their hideous change.
He called so loud that all the hollow deep
Of Hell resounded: "Princes, potentates,   315
Warriors, the flower of Heaven, once yours, now lost,
If such astonishment as this can seize
Eternal spirits! or have ye chosen this place
After the toil of battle to repose
Your wearied virtue,[5] for the ease you find   320
To slumber here, as in the vales of Heaven?
Or in this abject posture have ye sworn
To adore the Conqueror, who now beholds
Cherub and seraph rolling in the flood
With scattered arms and ensigns,[6] till anon   325
His swift pursuers from Heaven-gates discern
Th' advantage, and descending tread us down
Thus drooping, or with linkéd thunderbolts
Transfix us to the bottom of this gulf?
Awake, arise, or be forever fallen!"   330
   They heard, and were abashed, and up they sprung
Upon the wing, as when men wont to watch
On duty, sleeping found by whom they dread,
Rouse and bestir themselves ere well awake.
Nor did they not perceive[7] the evil plight   335
In which they were, or the fierce pains not feel;
Yet to their general's voice they soon obeyed
Innumerable. As when the potent rod
Of Amram's son,[8] in Egypt's evil day,
Waved round the coast, up called a pitchy cloud   340
Of locusts, warping[9] on the eastern wind,
That o'er the realm of impious Pharaoh hung
Like night, and darkened all the land of Nile;

3. I.e., form bowers by enclosing space.
4. Orion is a constellation, visible chiefly in late summer and autumn, hence associated with storms; in the Red Sea, where sedge grows thick, these storms result in much floating seaweed. This reminds Milton of how the sea must have looked after the Israelites ("sojourners of Goshen") passed through it while escaping from Egypt, when it was covered with the littered corpses of Pharaoh ("Busiris") and his pursuing horsemen ("Memphian chivalry").
5. Strength, but Satan's sarcasm makes use of the other connotation too.
6. Standards, battle flags.
7. The double negatives make a positive: they did indeed perceive both plight and pains. (Latin, *neque non*, "nor . . . not," "and.")
8. Moses, who drew down a plague of locusts on Egypt (Exodus x.12–15). Milton's learned locution is designed to keep Moses out of Hell, as well as from appearing too often in the poem (cf. above, 307–11).
9. Floating.

So numberless were those bad angels seen
Hovering on wing under the cope[1] of Hell,   345
'Twixt upper, nether, and surrounding fires;
Till, as a signal given, th' uplifted spear
Of their great sultan[2] waving to direct
Their course, in even balance down they light
On the firm brimstone, and fill all the plain: 350
A multitude like which the populous North[3]
Poured never from her frozen loins to pass
Rhene or the Danaw, when her barbarous sons
Came like a deluge on the South, and spread
Beneath Gibraltar to the Libyan sands.   355
Forthwith, from every squadron and each band,
The heads and leaders thither haste where stood
Their great commander; godlike shapes, and forms
Excelling human; princely dignities,
And powers that erst in Heaven sat on thrones,   360
Though of their names in Heavenly records now
Be no memorial, blotted out and rased[4]
By their rebellion from the Books of Life.
Nor had they yet among the sons of Eve
Got them new names, till, wandering o'er the Earth,   365
Through God's high sufferance for the trial of man,
By falsities and lies the greatest part
Of mankind they corrupted to forsake
God their Creator, and th' invisible
Glory of him that made them to transform   370
Oft to the image of a brute, adorned
With gay religions[5] full of pomp and gold,
And devils to adore for deities.
Then were they known to men by various names,
And various idols through the heathen world.   375
    Say, Muse, their names then known, who first, who last,[6]
Roused from the slumber on that fiery couch,
At their great emperor's call, as next in worth
Came singly[7] where he stood on the bare strand,
While the promiscuous crowd stood yet aloof.   380
    The chief were those who, from the pit of Hell
Roaming to seek their prey on Earth, durst fix
Their seats, long after, next the seat of God,[8]

---

1. Roof.
2. A first use of the image, which will be reinforced later, of Satan as an Oriental despot.
3. The barbarian invasions of falling Rome began with crossings of the Rhine ("Rhene") and Danube ("Danaw") Rivers, and spread across Spain, via Gibraltar, to North Africa.
4. Erased. See above, line 81. Though reluctant to state the view strongly, Milton believed all the pagan deities had been devils in disguise.

5. Ceremonies.
6. The catalogue of gods here is an epic convention; Homer catalogues ships, Virgil warriors.
7. One at a time. The diabolical aristocrats rally round Satan, while the "promiscuous crowd," the vulgar gods, stand apart.
8. The first group of devils come from the Near East, close neighbors and intimate enemies of Jehovah at Jerusalem.

Their altars by his altar, gods adored
Among the nations round, and durst abide   385
Jehovah thundering out of Sion, throned
Between the cherubim; yea, often placed
Within his sanctuary itself their shrines,
Abominations; and with curséd things
His holy rites and solemn feasts profaned,   390
And with their darkness durst affront his light.
First, Moloch,[9] horrid king, besmeared with blood
Of human sacrifice, and parents' tears;
Though, for the noise of drums and timbrels loud,
Their children's cries unheard, that passed through fire   395
To his grim idol. Him the Ammonite[1]
Worshiped in Rabba and her watery plain,
In Argob and in Basan, to the stream
Of utmost Arnon. Nor content with such
Audacious neighborhood, the wisest heart   400
Of Solomon he led by fraud to build
His temple right against the temple of God
On that opprobrious hill,[2] and made his grove
The pleasant valley of Hinnom, Tophet thence
And black Gehenna called, the type of Hell.   405
Next Chemos,[3] th' obscene dread of Moab's sons,
From Aroar to Nebo and the wild
Of southmost Abarim; in Hesebon
And Horonaim, Seon's realm, beyond
The flowery dale of Sibma clad with vines,   410
And Elealè to th' Asphaltic pool:
Peor[4] his other name, when he enticed
Israel in Sittim, on their march from Nile,
To do him wanton rites, which cost them woe.
Yet thence his lustful orgies he enlarged   415
Even to that hill of scandal, by the grove
Of Moloch homicide,[5] lust hard by hate,
Till good Josiah drove them thence to Hell.
With these came they who, from the bordering flood
Of old Euphrates to the brook that parts   420

9. A sun god, sometimes represented as a roaring bull or with a calf's head, within whose brazen image living children were often burned as sacrifices (for a lurid fictional account, see Flaubert's *Salammbô*). "Timbrels": tambourines.
1. The Ammonites lived east of the Jordan, and Milton uses uncouth place names ("Rabba," "Argob," "Basan," "utmost Arnon") to suggest wildness.
2. The rites of Moloch on "that opprobrious hill" (the Mount of Olives) right opposite the Jewish temple, and in the valley of Hinnom, so polluted these places that they were turned into the refuse dump of Jerusalem. Thus they became "types" (analogies) of

Hell, under the names "Tophet" and "Gehenna."
3. Chemos or Chemosh was another name for Moloch, used in Moab, a nation lying south and east of the Dead Sea ("th' Asphaltic pool"). Many of the geographical names clustered here come from Isaiah xv–xvi.
4. For the story of how Peor seduced "Israel in Sittim," see Numbers xxv.
5. An epithet was often joined to a god's name as a surname (e.g., *Jupiter Tonans*, Jove the Thunderer); Milton's epithet involves almost a parody, Moloch the Mankiller. The story of "good Josiah" and his campaign against pagan gods is told in II Kings xxiii.

Egypt from Syrian ground,[6] had general names
Of Baalim and Ashtaroth, those male,
These feminine.[7] For spirits, when they please,
Can either sex assume, or both; so soft
And uncompounded is their essence pure,   425
Not tied or manacled with joint or limb,
Nor founded on the brittle strength of bones,
Like cumbrous flesh; but, in what shape they choose,
Dilated or condensed, bright or obscure,
Can execute their airy purposes,   430
And works of love or enmity fulfill.
For those the race of Israel oft forsook
Their Living Strength,[8] and unfrequented left
His righteous altar, bowing lowly down
To bestial gods; for which their heads as low   435
Bowed down in battle, sunk before the spear
Of despicable foes. With these in troop
Came Astoreth, whom the Phoenicians called
Astartè, queen of heaven, with crescent horns;
To whose bright image nightly by the moon   440
Sidonian virgins[9] paid their vows and songs;
In Sion also not unsung, where stood
Her temple on th' offensive mountain,[1] built
By that uxorious king[2] whose heart, though large,
Beguiled by fair idolatresses, fell   445
To idols foul. Thammuz[3] came next behind,
Whose annual wound in Lebanon allured
The Syrian damsels to lament his fate
In amorous ditties all a summer's day,
While smooth Adonis[4] from his native rock   450
Ran purple to the sea, supposed with blood
Of Thammuz yearly wounded: the love tale
Infected Sion's daughters with like heat,
Whose wanton passions in the sacred porch
Ezekiel[5] saw, when, by the vision led,   455
His eye surveyed the dark idolatries
Of alienated Judah. Next came one
Who mourned in earnest, when the captive ark

6. Palestine lies between the Euphrates and "the brook Besor" (I Samuel xxx.10).
7. I.e., plural forms, masculine and feminine respectively, for Baal and Astarte. As Baals were aspects of the sun god, Astartes (Ishtars) were manifestations of the moon goddess.
8. The Jews lost battles, Milton says, when they neglected Jehovah.
9. Sidon and Tyre were the chief cities of Phoenicia.
1. The Mount of Olives again (see above, lines 403 and 416).
2. Solomon, who "loved many strange women" (I Kings xi.1–8).
3. A Syrian god, who was supposed to have been killed by a boar in Lebanon; annual festivals mourned his death and celebrated his revival, imitating the cycle of vegetable life. In his Greek form he was Adonis, god of the solar year.
4. A Lebanese river, named after the deity because every spring it turned blood-red with sedimentary mud.
5. Ezekiel complained that the Jewish women of his day were worshiping Thammuz (Ezekiel viii.14).

Maimed his brute image, head and hands lopped off,
In his own temple, on the grunsel-edge,[6]   460
Where he fell flat, and shamed his worshipers:
Dagon his name, sea monster, upward man
And downward fish; yet had his temple high
Reared in Azotus, dreaded through the coast
Of Palestine, in Gath and Ascalon,   465
And Accaron and Gaza's frontier bounds.[7]
Him followed Rimmon, whose delightful seat
Was fair Damascus, on the fertile banks
Of Abbana and Pharphar, lucid streams.
He also 'gainst the house of God was bold: 470
A leper once he lost, and gained a king,
Ahaz,[8] his sottish conqueror, whom he drew
God's altar to disparage and displace
For one of Syrian mode, whereon to burn
His odious offerings, and adore the gods   475
Whom he had vanquished. After these appeared
A crew who, under names of old renown,
Osiris, Isis, Orus,[9] and their train,
With monstrous shapes[1] and sorceries abused
Fanatic Egypt and her priests to seek   480
Their wandering gods disguised in brutish forms
Rather than human. Nor did Israel 'scape
Th' infection, when their borrowed gold composed
The calf in Oreb;[2] and the rebel king
Doubled that sin in Bethel and in Dan,   485
Likening his Maker to the grazéd ox[3]—
Jehovah, who, in one night, when he passed
From Egypt marching, equaled[4] with one stroke
Both her first-born and all her bleating gods.
Belial[5] came last; than whom a spirit more lewd   490
Fell not from Heaven, or more gross to love
Vice for itself. To him no temple stood
Or altar smoked; yet who more oft than he
In temples and at altars, when the priest

6. When the Philistines stole the ark of God, they tried to store it in the temple of their sea god, Dagon; but in the morning the mutilated statue of Dagon was found on the threshold ("grunsel-edge"). See I Samuel v.1–5.
7. Milton names the five chief cities of the Philistines as places where Dagon was worshiped.
8. A Syrian general, Naaman, was cured of leprosy and converted from worship of Rimmon by the waters of the Jordan (II Kings v). King Ahaz "turned from the house of the Lord for the king of Assyria" (II Kings xvi).
9. The second group of devils includes those from Egypt.
1. Monstrous, because often represented with animals' heads.

2. Aaron made a golden calf in the wilderness (Exodus xxxii); Milton thought it an idol of the Egyptian god Apis because the gold of which it was made had been borrowed from the Egyptians.
3. Jeroboam, "the rebel king," doubled Aaron's sin by making *two* golden calves (I Kings xii.28–30).
4. Leveled. See Exodus xii.12 for Jehovah's vengeance on the first-born of Egypt and their gods.
5. Belial was never worshiped as a god; his name was originally an abstract noun meaning "wickedness"; hence used mainly in set phrases like "sons of Belial." He comes last, because weak and slothful.

Turns atheist, as did Eli's sons,[6] who filled   495
With lust and violence the house of God?
In courts and palaces he also reigns,
And in luxurious cities, where the noise
Of riot ascends above their loftiest towers,
And injury and outrage; and, when night   500
Darkens the streets, then wander forth the sons
Of Belial, flown[7] with insolence and wine.
Witness the streets of Sodom,[8] and that night
In Gibeah, when the hospitable door
Exposed a matron, to avoid worse rape.   505
   These were the prime in order and in might;
The rest were long to tell, though far renowned,
Th' Ionian gods, of Javan's issue held
Gods, yet confessed later than Heaven and Earth,
Their boasted parents;[9] Titan, Heaven's first-born,   510
With his enormous brood, and birthright seized
By younger Saturn; he from mightier Jove,
His own and Rhea's son, like measure found;
So Jove usurping reigned.[1] These, first in Crete
And Ida known, thence on the snowy top   515
Of cold Olympus ruled the middle air,
Their highest heaven; or on the Delphian cliff,
Or in Dodona, and through all the bounds
Of Doric land; or who with Saturn old
Fled over Adria to th' Hesperian fields,   520
And o'er the Celtic roamed the utmost isles.
   All these and more came flocking; but with looks
Downcast and damp,[2] yet such wherein appeared
Obscure some glimpse of joy, to have found their chief
Not in despair, to have found themselves not lost   525
In loss itself; which on his countenance cast
Like doubtful hue.[3] But he, his wonted pride
Soon recollecting, with high words, that bore
Semblance of worth, not substance, gently raised
Their fainting courage, and dispelled their fears: 530
Then straight commands that, at the warlike sound

6. The misdeeds of Eli's sons, and the epithet "sons of Belial" applied to them, will be found in I Samuel ii. 12–17.
7. Flushed.
8. In Sodom and Gibeah ancient outrages befell, described in Genesis xix and Judges xix.
9. Though considered ancient by the Greeks ("Javan's issue," i.e., offspring of Javan, son of Japhet, son of Noah) and worshiped as the first children of "Heaven" (Uranus) and "Earth" (Ge), the Titans, Milton says, were actually confessed to be of a later age.
1. Cronos or Saturn, one of the Titans, deposed his elder brother, married his

sister Rhea, and ruled until Zeus, who had been reared in secret on Mt. Ida in Crete, overthrew his own father and came to rule on Mt. Olympus. Zeus was also worshiped in Delphos, Dodona, and throughout the "Doric (Grecian) land." Meanwhile Saturn (lines 519–21), after his downfall, fled across the Adriatic Sea ("Adria") to Italy ("th' Hesperian fields"), crossed "the Celtic" (fields) of France, and finally reached Britain ("the utmost isles").
2. Depressed.
3. Their comfort is the chilly one of finding themselves not completely annihilated; and at first it is reflected in Satan's face.

Of trumpets loud and clarions,[4] be upreared
His mighty standard. That proud honor claimed
Azazel[5] as his right, a cherub tall:
Who forthwith from the glittering staff unfurled   535
Th' imperial ensign; which, full high advanced,
Shone like a meteor streaming to the wind,
With gems and golden luster rich emblazed,
Seraphic arms and trophies; all the while
Sonorous metal[6] blowing martial sounds: 540
At which the universal host up sent
A shout that tore Hell's concave,[7] and beyond
Frighted the reign of Chaos and old Night.[8]
All in a moment through the gloom were seen
Ten thousand banners rise into the air,   545
With orient[9] colors waving: with them rose
A forest huge of spears; and thronging helms
Appeared, and serried[1] shields in thick array
Of depth immeasurable. Anon they move
In perfect phalanx to the Dorian[2] mood   550
Of flutes and soft recorders; such as raised
To height of noblest temper heroes old
Arming to battle, and instead of rage
Deliberate valor breathed, firm, and unmoved
With dread of death to flight or foul retreat;   555
Nor wanting power to mitigate and swage[3]
With solemn touches troubled thoughts, and chase
Anguish and doubt and fear and sorrow and pain
From mortal or immortal minds. Thus they,
Breathing united force with fixéd thought,   560
Moved on in silence to soft pipes that charmed
Their painful steps o'er the burnt soil. And now
Advanced in view they stand, a horrid[4] front
Of dreadful length and dazzling arms, in guise
Of warriors old, with ordered spear and shield,   565
Awaiting what command their mighty chief
Had to impose. He through the arméd files
Darts his experienced eye, and soon traverse[5]
The whole battalion views, their order due,
Their visages and stature as of gods;   570
Their number last he sums. And now his heart
Distends with pride, and hardening in his strength
Glories; for never, since created man,[6]
Met such embodied force as, named with these,

4. Small, shrill, treble trumpets.
5. Among the historians of angels and devils, a traditional diabolic leader.
6. Reverberant trumpets.
7. Vault.
8. Disorder and darkness, the first materials of the cosmos, still maintain a kingdom between Heaven and Hell.
9. Lustrous, like the colors of a pearl.
1. Locked together.

2. Severe, simple. The shrill trumpet, which first roused the courage of the devils, now gives way to firm, martial tones, played on instruments of softer timbre, in the Spartan manner.
3. Assuage.
4. Bristling.
5. Across. Satan glances, like a reviewing officer, down the files and columns.
6. I.e., since the creation of man.

Could merit more than that small infantry   575
Warred on by cranes:[7] though all the giant brood
Of Phlegra with th' heroic race were joined
That fought at Thebes and Ilium, on each side
Mixed with auxiliar[8] gods; and what resounds
In fable or romance of Uther's son,   580
Begirt with British and Armoric knights;
And all who since, baptized or infidel,
Jousted in Aspramont, or Montalban,
Damasco, or Marocco, or Trebisond;
Or whom Biserta sent from Afric shore   585
When Charlemagne with all his peerage fell
By Fontarabbia.[9] Thus far these beyond
Compare of mortal prowess, yet observed[1]
Their dread commander. He, above the rest
In shape and gesture proudly eminent,   590
Stood like a tower. His form had yet not lost
All her[2] original brightness, nor appeared
Less than archangel ruined, and th' excess
Of glory obscured: as when the sun new-risen
Looks through the horizontal[3] misty air   595
Shorn of his beams, or from behind the moon,
In dim eclipse,[4] disastrous twilight sheds
On half the nations, and with fear of change
Perplexes monarchs. Darkened so, yet shone
Above them all th' archangel; but his face   600
Deep scars of thunder had entrenched, and care
Sat on his faded cheek, but under brows
Of dauntless courage, and considerate[5] pride
Waiting revenge. Cruel his eye, but cast
Signs of remorse and passion,[6] to behold   605
The fellows of his crime, the followers rather
(Far other once beheld in bliss), condemned
Forever now to have their lot in pain;
Millions of spirits for his fault amerced[7]
Of Heaven, and from eternal splendors flung   610

7. The pygmies had periodic fights with the cranes, which (according to Pliny) they won by riding to battle on pigs and goats. This would make them cavalry; but Milton wanted the pun on "infants." His idea is that, compared with the devils, all other armies that ever were would look puny.
8. Allied.
9. The Giants of Greek mythology were born at Phlegra (line 577); Milton imagines them joined with the Seven who fought against Thebes, and the whole Greek host that besieged Troy ("Ilium"), plus the various gods who helped on both sides. He even adds the knights "British or Armoric" (from Brittany) who fought with King Arthur ("Uther's son"), and includes a list of proper names taken from the cycles of romance and suggesting vast, remote armies. Fontarabbia, the best known, was reputed to be the scene of Roland's last stand in the *Chanson de Roland*; Milton thus mingles the fall of Charlemagne with that of his best-known knight.
1. Obeyed.
2. *Forma*, in Latin, is feminine; hence "her."
3. The rays of the sun, as it first rises over the horizon, are almost horizontal.
4. Time of ill omen. "Disastrous": threatening disaster.
5. Thoughtful, conscious.
6. Compassion.
7. Deprived.

For his revolt; yet faithful how they stood,
Their glory withered; as, when Heaven's fire
Hath scathed the forest oaks or mountain pines,
With singéd top their stately growth, though bare,
Stands on the blasted heath. He now prepared   615
To speak; whereat their doubled ranks they bend
From wing to wing, and half enclose him round
With all his peers: attention held them mute.
Thrice he essayed, and thrice, in spite of scorn,
Tears, such as angels weep, burst forth: at last   620
Words interwove with sighs found out their way:
    "O myriads of immortal spirits! O powers
Matchless, but with th' Almighty!—and that strife
Was not inglorious, though th' event[8] was dire,
As this place testifies, and this dire change,   625
Hateful to utter. But what power of mind,
Foreseeing or presaging, from the depth
Of knowledge past or present, could have feared
How such united force of gods, how such
As stood like these, could ever know repulse?   630
For who can yet believe, though after loss,
That all these puissant[9] legions, whose exile
Hath emptied Heaven, shall fail to reascend,
Self-raised, and repossess their native seat?
For me, be witness all the host of Heaven,   635
If counsels different,[1] or danger shunned
By me, have lost our hopes. But he who reigns
Monarch in Heaven, till then as one secure
Sat on his throne, upheld by old repute,
Consent or custom, and his regal state   640
Put forth at full, but still his strength concealed,
Which tempted our attempt,[2] and wrought our fall.
Henceforth his might we know, and know our own,
So as not either to provoke, or dread
New war provoked: our better part remains   645
To work in close design,[3] by fraud or guile,
What force effected not; that he no less
At length from us may find, who overcomes
By force hath overcome but half his foe.
Space may produce new worlds; whereof so rife   650
There went a fame[4] in Heaven that he ere long
Intended to create, and therein plant
A generation whom his choice regard
Should favor equal to the sons of Heaven.
Thither, if but to pry, shall be perhaps   655
Our first eruption—thither, or elsewhere;

8. Outcome, result.
9. Potent, powerful.
1. Contradictory or even selfish, but also, in an obsolete sense, delaying.
2. Satan is an inveterate punster and player on words.
3. I.e., our best choice is to achieve by secret schemes.
4. Rumor. "Rife": common.

For this infernal pit shall never hold
Celestial spirits in bondage, nor th' abyss
Long under darkness cover. But these thoughts
Full counsel must mature. Peace is despaired,   660
For who can think submission? War, then, war
Open or understood,[5] must be resolved."
    He spake; and, to confirm his words, outflew
Millions of flaming swords, drawn from the thighs
Of mighty cherubim; the sudden blaze   665
Far round illumined Hell. Highly they raged
Against the Highest, and fierce with graspéd arms
Clashed on their sounding shields the din of war,[6]
Hurling defiance toward the vault of Heaven.
    There stood a hill not far, whose grisly[7] top   670
Belched fire and rolling smoke; the rest entire
Shone with a glossy scurf,[8] undoubted sign
That in his womb was hid metallic ore,
The work of sulphur.[9] Thither, winged with speed,
A numerous brigade hastened: as when bands   675
Of pioneers,[1] with spade and pickax armed,
Forerun the royal camp, to trench a field,
Or cast a rampart. Mammon led them on,
Mammon, the least erected[2] spirit that fell
From Heaven; for even in Heaven his looks and thoughts   680
Were always downward bent, admiring more
The riches of Heaven's pavement, trodden gold,
Than aught divine or holy else enjoyed
In vision beatific. By him first
Men also, and by his suggestion taught,   685
Ransacked the center, and with impious hands
Rifled the bowels of their mother Earth
For treasures better hid. Soon had his crew
Opened into the hill a spacious wound,
And digged out ribs[3] of gold. Let none admire   690
That riches grow in Hell; that soil may best
Deserve the precious bane. And here let those
Who boast in mortal things, and wondering tell
Of Babel, and the works of Memphian kings,
Learn how their greatest monuments of fame   695
And strength, and art, are easily outdone
By spirits reprobate,[4] and in an hour
What in an age they, with incessant toil
And hands innumerable, scarce perform.

5. Agreed-upon, tacit, hence secret.
6. Like Roman legionaries, the fallen
angels applaud by beating swords on
shields.
7. Horrible.
8. Crust.
9. Sulphur and mercury were considered the basic substances of all metals.
1. Sappers, engineers.
2. Elevated. Mammon is not a god but
an abstract word meaning "wealth"; cf.
Belial.
3. Bars, of course, but also with a hit
at Eve, who was a "precious bane"
(sweet poison) dug out of Adam's side.
"Admire": wonder.
4. The tower of Babel and the Pyramids of Egypt ("works of Memphian
kings") are easily outdone by the
devils ("spirits reprobate").

Nigh on the plain, in many cells prepared,   700
That underneath had veins of liquid fire
Sluiced from the lake, a second multitude
With wondrous art founded the massy ore,
Severing each kind, and scummed the bullion-dross.
A third as soon had formed within the ground   705
A various mold, and from the boiling cells
By strange conveyance filled each hollow nook;[5]
As in an organ, from one blast of wind,
To many a row of pipes the soundboard breathes.
Anon out of the earth a fabric huge   710
Rose like an exhalation, with the sound
Of dulcet symphonies and voices sweet,
Built like a temple, where pilasters[6] round
Were set, and Doric pillars[7] overlaid
With golden architrave; nor did there want   715
Cornice or frieze, with bossy[8] sculptures graven;
The roof was fretted[9] gold. Not Babylon
Nor great Alcairo such magnificence
Equaled in all their glories,[1] to enshrine
Belus or Serapis their gods, or seat   720
Their kings, when Egypt with Assyria strove
In wealth and luxury. Th' ascending pile
Stood fixed[2] her stately height; and straight the doors,
Opening their brazen folds, discover, wide
Within, her ample spaces o'er the smooth   725
And level pavement: from the archéd roof,
Pendent by subtle magic, many a row
Of starry lamps and blazing cressets,[3] fed
With naphtha and asphaltus, yielded light
As from a sky. The hasty multitude   730
Admiring entered; and the work some praise,
And some the architect. His hand was known
In Heaven by many a towered structure high,
Where sceptered angels held their residence,
And sat as princes, whom the súpreme King   735
Exalted to such power, and gave to rule,
Each in his hierarchy, the orders bright.
Nor was his name unheard or unadored
In ancient Greece; and in Ausonian land
Men called him Mulciber;[4] and how he fell   740

5. After melting the gold with fire from the lake and pouring it into molds, the devils cause their building to rise by a sort of spiritual-musical magic.
6. Columns set in a wall.
7. Doric pillars are severe and plain.
8. Embossed.
9. Patterned.
1. At Babylon in Assyria there were temples to "Belus" or Baal; at Alcairo (modern Cairo, ancient Memphis) in Egypt, they were to Osiris, one of whose names was Serapis (here, but not ordi-narily, accented on the first syllable).
2. Complete; "straight": straightway.
3. Basketlike lamps, hung from the ceiling.
4. Hephaestus, or Vulcan, was some-times known in "Ausonian land" (Italy) by the secondary epithet of "Mulciber." The story of Jove's tossing him out of Heaven is told, to the accompaniment of much Homeric laughter, in *Iliad* I. Milton calls him by a secondary name because he is a little uneasy at having to put a "good" Greek deity in Hell.

From Heaven they fabled, thrown by angry Jove
Sheer o'er the crystal battlements: from morn
To noon he fell, from noon to dewy eve,
A summer's day, and with the setting sun
Dropped from the zenith, like a falling star,   745
On Lemnos, th' Aegean isle. Thus they relate,
Erring;[5] for he with this rebellious rout
Fell long before; nor aught availed him now
To have built in Heaven high towers; nor did he 'scape
By all his engines, but was headlong sent,   750
With his industrious crew, to build in Hell.
    Meanwhile the wingéd heralds, by command
Of sovereign power, with awful ceremony
And trumpet's sound, throughout the host proclaim
A solemn council forthwith to be held   755
At Pandemonium,[6] the high capital
Of Satan and his peers.[7] Their summons called
From every band and squaréd regiment
By place or choice the worthiest; they anon
With hundreds and with thousands trooping came   760
Attended. All access was thronged, the gates
And porches wide, but chief the spacious hall
(Though like a covered field, where champions bold
Wont ride in armed, and at the soldan's[8] chair
Defied the best of paynim chivalry   765
To mortal combat, or career with lance),
Thick swarmed, both on the ground and in the air,
Brushed with the hiss of rustling wings. As bees
In springtime, when the sun with Taurus[9] rides,
Pour forth their populous youth about the hive   770
In clusters; they among fresh dews and flowers
Fly to and fro, or on the smoothéd plank,
The suburb of their straw-built citadel,
New rubbed with balm, expatiate, and confer[1]
Their state-affairs: so thick the airy crowd   775
Swarmed and were straitened; till, the signal given,
Behold a wonder! They but now who seemed
In bigness to surpass Earth's giant sons,
Now less than smallest dwarfs, in narrow room
Throng numberless—like that pygmean race   780
Beyond the Indian mount;[2] or faery elves,
Whose midnight revels, by a forest side
Or fountain, some belated peasant sees,

5. Milton tells the story, and gives it six lines of splendid poetry (740–46), but in the end condemns it as a corrupt version of the Biblical truth.
6. "Pandemonium" means literally "All-Demons"; an inversion of Pantheon, "All-Gods."
7. Nobility.
8. Sultan's. "Paynim": pagan.

9. The sun is in the Zodiacal sign of Taurus from April 19 to May 20.
1. Spread out and discuss, bring together. The simile of bees prepares for the sudden contraction of the devils' size; they can shrink or dilate at will.
2. The pygmies were supposed to live beyond the Himalayas, "the Indian mount."

Or dreams he sees, while overhead the Moon
Sits arbitress,[3] and nearer to the Earth   785
Wheels her pale course; they, on their mirth and dance
Intent, with jocund[4] music charm his ear;
At once with joy and fear his heart rebounds.
Thus incorporeal spirits to smallest forms
Reduced their shapes immense, and were at large,   790
Though without number still, amidst the hall
Of that infernal court. But far within,
And in their own dimensions like themselves,
The great seraphic lords and cherubim
In close recess and secret conclave sat,   795
A thousand demigods on golden seats,
Frequent and full.[5] After short silence then,
And summons read, the great consult began.

Book II

The Argument

The consultation begun, Satan debates whether another battle be
to be hazarded for the recovery of Heaven: some advise it, others
dissuade. A third proposal is preferred, mentioned before by Satan
—to search the truth of that prophecy or tradition in Heaven concerning another world, and another kind of creature, equal or not
much inferior to themselves, about this time to be created. Their
doubt who shall be sent on this difficult search: Satan, their chief,
undertakes alone the voyage; is honored and applauded. The council thus ended, the rest betake them several ways and to several
employments, as their inclinations lead them, to entertain[1] the
time till Satan return. He passes on his journey to Hell-gates; finds
them shut, and who sat there to guard them; by whom at length
they are opened, and discover[2] to him the great gulf between Hell
and Heaven. With what difficulty he passes through, directed by
Chaos, the power of that place, to the sight of this new world
which he sought.

High on a throne of royal state, which far
Outshone the wealth of Ormus[3] and of Ind,
Or where the gorgeous East with richest hand
Showers on her kings barbaric pearl and gold,
Satan exalted sat, by merit raised   5
To that bad eminence; and, from despair

---

3. Witness.
4. Merry.
5. Crowded ("frequent") and in full
complement ("full"); all present and
accounted for.

1. Pass.
2. Disclose.
3. An island in the Persian Gulf, modern Hormuz, famous for pearls. "Ind":
India

Thus high uplifted beyond hope, aspires
Beyond thus high, insatiate to pursue
Vain war with Heaven; and, by success[4] untaught,
His proud imaginations thus displayed: 10
   "Powers and dominions, deities of Heaven!
For since no deep within her gulf can hold
Immortal vigor, though oppressed and fallen,
I give not Heaven for lost: from this descent
Celestial virtues rising will appear   15
More glorious and more dread than from no fall,
And trust themselves to fear no second fate.
Me though just right, and the fixed laws of Heaven
Did first create your leader, next, free choice,
With what besides, in council or in fight,   20
Hath been achieved of merit, yet this loss
Thus far at least recovered, hath much more
Established in a safe unenvied throne
Yielded with full consent.[5] The happier state
In Heaven, which follows dignity, might draw   25
Envy from each inferior; but who here
Will envy whom the highest place exposes
Foremost to stand against the Thunderer's aim,
Your bulwark, and condemns to greatest share
Of endless pain? Where there is then no good   30
For which to strive, no strife can grow up there
From faction; for none sure will claim in Hell
Precédence, none, whose portion is so small
Of present pain, that with ambitious mind
Will covet more. With this advantage then   35
To union, and firm faith, and firm accord,
More than can be in Heaven, we now return
To claim our just inheritance of old,
Surer to prosper than prosperity
Could have assured us;[6] and by what best way,   40
Whether of open war or covert guile,
We now debate; who can advise, may speak."
   He ceased, and next him Moloch, sceptered king,
Stood up, the strongest and the fiercest spirit
That fought in Heaven; now fiercer by despair.   45
His trust was with th' Eternal to be deemed
Equal in strength, and rather than be less
Cared not to be at all; with that care lost
Went all his fear: of God, or Hell, or worse
He recked[7] not, and these words thereafter spake: 50

"My sentence[8] is for open war: of wiles,
More unexpert,[9] I boast not: them let those
Contrive who need, or when they need, not now.
For while they sit contriving, shall the rest,
Millions that stand in arms, and longing wait   55
The signal to ascend, sit lingering here
Heaven's fugitives, and for their dwelling place
Accept this dark opprobrious den of shame,
The prison of his tyranny who reigns
By our delay? No! let us rather choose,   60
Armed with Hell-flames and fury, all at once
O'er Heaven's high towers to force resistless way,
Turning our tortures into horrid arms
Against the Torturer; when to meet the noise
Of his almighty engine[1] he shall hear   65
Infernal thunder, and for lightning see
Black fire and horror shot with equal rage
Among his angels, and his throne itself
Mixed with Tartarean[2] sulphur, and strange fire,
His own invented torments. But perhaps   70
The way seems difficult and steep to scale
With upright wing against a higher foe.
Let such bethink them, if the sleepy drench[3]
Of that forgetful lake benumb not still,
That in our proper motion[4] we ascend   75
Up to our native seat; descent and fall
To us is adverse. Who but felt of late,
When the fierce foe hung on our broken rear
Insulting,[5] and pursued us through the deep,
With what compulsion and laborious flight   80
We sunk thus low? Th' ascent is easy then;
Th' event[6] is feared: should we again provoke
Our stronger,[7] some worse way his wrath may find
To our destruction; if there be in Hell
Fear to be worse destroyed! What can be worse   85
Than to dwell here, driven out from bliss, condemned
In this abhorréd deep to utter woe;
Where pain of unextinguishable fire
Must exercise us without hope of end,
The vassals[8] of his anger, when the scourge   90
Inexorably, and the torturing hour,
Calls us to penance? More destroyed than thus,
We should be quite abolished, and expire.
What fear we then? what[9] doubt we to incense

---

8. Judgment.
9. Inexperienced. Moloch never had to be clever, and is proud of it.
1. The thunderbolt.
2. Tartarus is a classical name for Hell.
3. A draught of physic, as for animals; hence. used contemptuously here.
4. Natural impulse.

5. With the Latin sense of stamping or dancing on.
6. Outcome.
7. The word "enemy" is understood.
8. Servants, underlings; but perhaps also—or alternatively—"vessels."
9. Why.

His utmost ire? Which, to the height enraged,   95
Will either quite consume us, and reduce
To nothing this essential,[1] happier far
Than miserable to have eternal being!
Or if our substance be indeed divine,
And cannot cease to be, we are at worst   100
On this side nothing;[2] and by proof we feel
Our power sufficient to disturb his Heaven,
And with perpetual inroads to alarm,
Though inaccessible, his fatal throne:
Which, if not victory, is yet revenge."   105
    He ended frowning, and his look denounced
Desperate revenge, and battle dangerous
To less than gods.[3] On th' other side up rose
Belial, in act more graceful and humane;
A fairer person lost not Heaven; he seemed   110
For dignity composed, and high exploit.
But all was false and hollow; though his tongue
Dropped manna,[4] and could make the worse appear
The better reason, to perplex and dash
Maturest counsels: for his thoughts were low,   115
To vice industrious, but to nobler deeds
Timorous and slothful: yet he pleased the ear,
And with persuasive accent thus began:
    "I should be much for open war, O peers,
As not behind in hate, if what was urged   120
Main reason to persuade immediate war,
Did not dissuade me most, and seem to cast
Ominous conjecture on the whole success;[5]
When he who most excels in fact of arms,
In what he counsels, and in what excels   125
Mistrustful, grounds his courage on despair
And utter dissolution, as the scope
Of all his aim, after some dire revenge.
First, what revenge? The towers of Heaven are filled
With arméd watch, that render all access   130
Impregnable; oft on the bordering deep
Encamp their legions, or with óbscure wing
Scout far and wide into the realm of Night,
Scorning surprise. Or could we break our way
By force, and at our heels all Hell should rise   135
With blackest insurrection, to confound
Heaven's purest light, yet our great enemy
All incorruptible would on his throne

---

1. Essence.
2. I.e., we are now as badly off as we can be without being nothing, and so need have no fear.
3. Only gods could have withstood Moloch.
4. His tongue was honeyed. To "make the worse appear / The better reason" was characteristic of Sophists—hollow, mercenary logic-choppers of ancient Greece. "Dash": confuse.
5. As above, line 9, outcome. "Fact": feat.

Sit unpolluted, and th' ethereal mold[6]
Incapable of stain would soon expel   140
Her mischief, and purge off the baser fire,
Victorious. Thus repulsed, our final hope
Is flat despair: we must exasperate
Th' almighty Victor to spend all his rage,
And that must end us, that must be our cure,   145
To be no more. Sad cure! for who would lose,
Though full of pain, this intellectual being,
Those thoughts that wander through eternity,
To perish rather, swallowed up and lost
In the wide womb of uncreated Night,   150
Devoid of sense and motion? And who knows,
Let this be good,[7] whether our angry Foe
Can give it, or will ever? How he can
Is doubtful; that he never will is sure.
Will he, so wise, let loose at once his ire,   155
Belike[8] through impotence, or unaware,
To give his enemies their wish, and end
Them in his anger, whom his anger saves
To punish endless? 'Wherefore cease we then?'
Say they who counsel war, 'we are decreed,   160
Reserved and destined to eternal woe;
Whatever doing, what can we suffer more,
What can we suffer worse?' Is this then worst,
Thus sitting, thus consulting, thus in arms?
What when we fled amain,[9] pursued and strook   165
With Heaven's afflicting thunder, and besought
The deep to shelter us? this Hell then seemed
A refuge from those wounds. Or when we lay
Chained on the burning lake? that sure was worse.
What if the breath that kindled those grim fires,   170
Awaked, should blow them into sevenfold rage,
And plunge us in the flames? or from above
Should intermitted[1] vengeance arm again
His red right hand to plague us? What if all
Her[2] stores were opened, and this firmament   175
Of Hell should spout her cataracts of fire,
Impendent[3] horrors, threatening hideous fall
One day upon our heads; while we perhaps
Designing or exhorting glorious war,
Caught in a fiery tempest shall be hurled,   180
Each on his rock transfixed, the sport and prey
Of racking whirlwinds, or forever sunk
Under yon boiling ocean, wrapped in chains;

---

6. Substance. "Ethereal" substance, derived from "ether," is thought to be incorruptible.
7. I.e., suppose it is good to be destroyed.
8. Ironically, in the sense of "I dare say."
9. Headlong. "Strook": struck.
1. Momentarily suspended.
2. Those of Hell.
3. In the Latin sense, hanging down, threatening.

There to converse with everlasting groans,
Unrespited, unpitied, unreprieved,   185
Ages of hopeless end! This would be worse.
War therefore, open or concealed, alike
My voice dissuades; for what can force or guile[4]
With him, or who deceive his mind, whose eye
Views all things at one view? He from Heaven's height   190
All these our motions[5] vain, sees and derides,
Not more almighty to resist our might
Than wise to frustrate all our plots and wiles.
Shall we then live thus vile, the race of Heaven
Thus trampled, thus expelled to suffer here   195
Chains and these torments? Better these than worse,
By my advice; since fate inevitable
Subdues us, and omnipotent decree,
The Victor's will. To suffer, as to do,
Our strength is equal,[6] nor the law unjust   200
That so ordains: this was at first resolved,
If we were wise, against so great a foe
Contending, and so doubtful what might fall.
I laugh, when those who at the spear are bold
And venturous, if that fail them, shrink and fear   205
What yet they know must follow, to endure
Exile, or ignominy, or bonds, or pain,
The sentence of their Conqueror. This is now
Our doom; which if we can sustain and bear,
Our súpreme Foe in time may much remit   210
His anger, and perhaps, thus far removed,
Not mind us not offending, satisfied
With what is punished;[7] whence these raging fires
Will slacken, if his breath stir not their flames.
Our purer essence then will overcome   215
Their noxious vapor, or inured[8] not feel,
Or changed at length, and to the place conformed
In temper and in nature, will receive
Familiar the fierce heat, and void of pain;
This horror will grow mild, this darkness light;   220
Besides what hope the never-ending flight
Of future days may bring, what chance, what change
Worth waiting, since our present lot appears
For happy though but ill, for ill not worst,[9]
If we procure not to ourselves more woe."   225
        Thus Belial, with words clothed in reason's garb,

4. The verb "accomplish" or "achieve" is omitted.
5. Proposals, plots.
6. I.e., passive endurance and active energy are both in the devils' power. Belial points out, with dangerous good sense, that they must have known from the beginning that they might have to exercise both (lines 201–3).
7. A Latinism, *quod punitum est;* God will be satisfied with the punishment that has been inflicted.
8. Accustomed.
9. I.e., from the point of view of happiness, the devils are but ill off; from the point of view of evil, they could be worse. This is diabolic relativism.

Counseled ignoble ease and peaceful sloth,
Not peace; and after him thus Mammon spake:
"Either to disenthrone the King of Heaven
We war, if war be best, or to regain   230
Our own right lost: him to unthrone we then
May hope, when everlasting Fate shall yield
To fickle Chance, and Chaos judge the strife.
The former, vain to hope, argues[1] as vain
The latter; for what place can be for us   235
Within Heaven's bound, unless Heaven's Lord supreme
We overpower? Suppose he should relent
And publish grace to all, on promise made
Of new subjection; with what eyes could we
Stand in his presence humble, and receive   240
Strict laws imposed, to celebrate his throne
With warbled hymns, and to his Godhead sing
Forced Halleluiahs; while he lordly sits
Our envied Sovereign, and his altar breathes
Ambrosial odors and ambrosial flowers,   245
Our servile offerings? This must be our task
In Heaven, this our delight; how wearisome
Eternity so spent in worship paid
To whom we hate! Let us not then pursue,
By force impossible, by leave obtained   250
Unacceptable, though in Heaven, our state
Of spendid vassalage;[2] but rather seek
Our own good from ourselves, and from our own
Live to ourselves, though in this vast recess,
Free, and to none accountable, preferring   255
Hard liberty before the easy yoke
Of servile pomp. Our greatness will appear
Then most conspicuous, when great things of small,
Useful of hurtful, prosperous of adverse,
We can create, and in what place soe'er   260
Thrive under evil, and work ease out of pain
Through labor and endurance. This deep world
Of darkness do we dread? How oft amidst
Thick clouds and dark doth Heaven's all-ruling Sire
Choose to reside, his glory unobscured,   265
And with the majesty of darkness round
Covers his throne; from whence deep thunders roar,
Mustering their rage, and Heaven resembles Hell!
As he our darkness, cannot we his light
Imitate when we please? This desert soil   270
Wants[3] not her hidden luster, gems, and gold;
Nor want we skill or art, from whence to raise
Magnificence; and what can Heaven show more?

1. Proves.
2. Servitude.
3. Lacks. Mammon proposes a tawdry
imitation-Heaven in Hell; this is the
ultimate in diabolic degradation.

Our torments also may in length of time
Become our elements, these piercing fires   275
As soft as now severe, our temper changed
Into their temper; which must needs remove
The sensible[4] of pain. All things invite
To peaceful counsels, and the settled state
Of order, how in safety best we may   280
Compose our present evils, with regard
Of what we are and where, dismissing quite
All thoughts of war. Ye have what I advise."
   He scarce had finished, when such murmur filled
Th' assembly, as when hollow rocks retain   285
The sound of blustering winds, which all night long
Had roused the sea, now with hoarse cadence lull
Seafaring men o'erwatched,[5] whose bark by chance,
Or pinnace, anchors in a craggy bay
After the tempest: such applause was heard   290
As Mammon ended, and his sentence pleased,
Advising peace; for such another field
They dreaded worse than Hell; so much the fear
Of thunder and the sword of Michaël[6]
Wrought still within them; and no less desire   295
To found this nether empire, which might rise
By policy, and long process of time,
In emulation opposite to Heaven.
Which when Beëlzebub perceived, than whom,
Satan except, none higher sat, with grave   300
Aspect he rose, and in his rising seemed
A pillar of state; deep on his front[7] engraven
Deliberation sat and public care;
And princely counsel in his face yet shone,
Majestic though in ruin. Sage he stood   305
With Atlantean[8] shoulders fit to bear
The weight of mightiest monarchies; his look
Drew audience and attention still as night
Or summer's noontide air, while thus he spake:
   "Thrones and imperial powers, offspring of Heaven, 310
Ethereal virtues; or these titles now
Must we renounce, and, changing style, be called
Princes of Hell? For so the popular vote
Inclines, here to continue, and build up here
A growing empire—Doubtless! while we dream,   315
And know not that the King of Heaven hath doomed
This place our dungeon, not our safe retreat
Beyond his potent arm, to live exempt
From Heaven's high jurisdiction, in new league

---

4. Sense, sensation.
5. Tired out with watching.
6. The warrior angel, chief stay of the angelic armies.
7. Forehead, brow.

8. Worthy of Atlas, one of the Titans, who as a punishment for rebellion was condemned to stand in North Africa and hold up the heavens.

Banded against his throne, but to remain 320
In strictest bondage, though thus far removed,
Under th' inevitable curb, reserved
His captive multitude. For he, be sure,
In height or depth, still first and last will reign
Sole King, and of his kingdom lose no part 325
By our revolt, but over Hell extend
His empire, and with iron scepter rule
Us here, as with his golden those in Heaven.
What[9] sit we then projecting peace and war?
War hath determined us,[1] and foiled with loss 330
Irreparable; terms of peace yet none
Vouchsafed or sought; for what peace will be given
To us enslaved, but custody severe,
And stripes, and arbitrary punishment
Inflicted? and what peace can we return, 335
But, to our power,[2] hostility and hate,
Untamed reluctance,[3] and revenge, though slow,
Yet ever plotting how the Conqueror least
May reap his conquest, and may least rejoice
In doing what we most in suffering feel?[4] 340
Nor will occasion want, nor shall we need
With dangerous expedition to invade
Heaven, whose high walls fear no assault or siege,
Or ambush from the deep. What if we find
Some easier enterprise? There is a place 345
(If ancient and prophetic fame[5] in Heaven
Err not), another world, the happy seat
Of some new race called *Man*, about this time
To be created like to us,[6] though less
In power and excellence, but favored more 350
Of him who rules above; so was his will
Pronounced among the gods, and by an oath,
That shook Heaven's whole circumference, confirmed.
Thither let us bend all our thoughts, to learn
What creatures there inhabit, of what mold, 355
Or substance, how endued,[7] and what their power,
And where their weakness, how attempted[8] best,
By force or subtlety. Though Heaven be shut,
And Heaven's high Arbitrator sit secure
In his own strength, this place may lie exposed, 360
The utmost border of his kingdom, left
To their defense who hold it;[9] here, perhaps,

9. Why.
1. I.e., war has decided the question for (but also, limited) us.
2. I.e., to the best of our power.
3. Resistance (in the Latin sense, struggling back).
4. How God may get least pleasure from our pain—a devil's view of the deity.

5. Report, rumor.
6. The created (Ptolemaic) cosmos only came into existence after the fall of Satan, and the fallen angels, being otherwise occupied, could not know of it.
7. Endowed.
8. Attacked, but also "tempted."
9. To be defended by the occupants.

Some advantageous act may be achieved
By sudden onset: either with Hell-fire
To waste[1] his whole creation, or possess   365
All as our own, and drive, as we were driven,
The puny habitants; or if not drive,
Seduce them to our party, that their God
May prove their foe, and with repenting hand
Abolish his own works. This would surpass   370
Common revenge, and interrupt his joy
In our confusion, and our joy upraise
In his disturbance; when his darling sons,
Hurled headlong to partake with us, shall curse
Their frail original,[2] and faded bliss,   375
Faded so soon! Advise if this be worth
Attempting, or to sit in darkness here
Hatching vain empires." Thus Beëlzebub
Pleaded his devilish counsel, first devised
By Satan, and in part proposed; for whence,   380
But from the author of all ill could spring
So deep a malice, to confound[3] the race
Of mankind in one root, and Earth with Hell
To mingle and involve, done all to spite
The great Creator? But their spite still serves   385
His glory to augment. The bold design
Pleased highly those infernal states, and joy
Sparkled in all their eyes; with full assent
They vote: whereat his speech he thus renews:
    "Well have ye judged, well ended long debate,   390
Synod of gods, and, like to what ye are,
Great things resolved; which from the lowest deep
Will once more lift us up, in spite of Fate,
Nearer our ancient seat; perhaps in view
Of those bright confines, whence with neighboring arms   395
And opportune excursion we may chance
Re-enter Heaven; or else in some mild zone
Dwell not unvisited of Heaven's fair light,
Secure, and at the brightening orient beam
Purge off this gloom; the soft delicious air,   400
To heal the scar of these corrosive fires,
Shall breathe her balm. But first, whom shall we send
In search of this new world? whom shall we find
Sufficient? who shall tempt[4] with wandering feet
The dark, unbottomed, infinite abyss,   405
And through the palpable obscure[5] find out
His uncouth way, or spread his airy flight
Upborn with indefatigable wings

1. Lay waste.
2. Originator, parent; or, perhaps, "their original condition."
3. Destroy, ruin. Adam, the first man, is the "root" of mankind.
4. Try, attempt (from Latin *temptare*).
5. Darkness so thick it can be felt. "Uncouth": strange, new.

Over the vast abrupt,[6] ere he arrive
The happy isle?[7] What strength, what art, can then   410
Suffice, or what evasion bear him safe
Through the strict senteries[8] and stations thick
Of angels watching round? Here he had need
All circumspection, and we now no less
Choice in our suffrage;[9] for on whom we send   415
The weight of all, and our last hope, relies."
    This said, he sat; and expectation held
His look suspense,[1] awaiting who appeared
To second, or oppose, or undertake
The perilous attempt; but all sat mute,   420
Pondering the danger with deep thoughts; and each
In others' countenance read his own dismay,
Astonished. None among the choice and prime
Of those Heaven-warring champions could be found
So hardy as to proffer or accept   425
Alone the dreadful voyage; till at last
Satan, whom now transcendent glory raised
Above his fellows, with monarchal pride
Conscious of highest worth, unmoved thus spake:
    "O progeny of Heaven, empyreal thrones!   430
With reason hath deep silence and demur[2]
Seized us, though undismayed. Long is the way
And hard, that out of Hell leads up to light;
Our prison strong, this huge convex[3] of fire,
Outrageous to devour, immures us round   435
Ninefold,[4] and gates of burning adamant,
Barred over us, prohibit all egress.
These passed, if any pass, the void profound
Of unessential[5] Night receives him next,
Wide gaping, and with utter loss of being   440
Threatens him, plunged in that abortive gulf.
If thence he 'scape into whatever world,
Or unknown region, what remains him less[6]
Than unknown dangers and as hard escape?
But I should ill become this throne, O peers,   445
And this imperial sovereignty, adorned
With splendor, armed with power, if aught proposed
And judged of public moment,[7] in the shape
Of difficulty or danger, could deter
Me from attempting. Wherefore do I assume   450

6. Chaos; a striking example of sound imitating sense.
7. Wherever man is (for the fallen angels do not yet know of Earth).
8. Old spelling of *sentries*, necessary here for the meter.
9. Care in our voting.
1. I.e., everyone sat waiting in suspense.
2. Delay.
3. Vault.

4. Walls us in with nine thicknesses. See below, lines 645 ff.
5. Without real being, darkness being merely the absence of light. The "abortive gulf" expresses again this completely negative quality of Chaos and Night.
6. I.e., what awaits him except.
7. Importance.

These royalties,[8] and not refuse to reign,
Refusing to accept as great a share
Of hazard as of honor, due alike
To him who reigns, and so much to him due
Of hazard more, as he above the rest   455
High honored sits?[9] Go therefore, mighty powers,
Terror of Heaven, though fallen; intend[1] at home,
While here shall be our home, what best may ease
The present misery, and render Hell
More tolerable; if there be cure or charm   460
To respite, or deceive, or slack the pain
Of this ill mansion; intermit no watch
Against a wakeful foe, while I abroad
Through all the coasts of dark destruction seek
Deliverance for us all: this enterprise   465
None shall partake with me." Thus saying, rose
The monarch, and prevented[2] all reply;
Prudent, lest, from his resolution raised,[3]
Others among the chief might offer now
(Certain to be refused) what erst they feared,   470
And, so refused, might in opinion stand
His rivals, winning cheap the high repute
Which he through hazard huge must earn. But they
Dreaded not more th' adventure than his voice
Forbidding; and at once with him they rose;   475
Their rising all at once was as the sound
Of thunder heard remote. Towards him they bend
With awful[4] reverence prone; and as a god
Extol him equal to the Highest in Heaven.
Nor failed they to express how much they praised,   480
That for the general safety he despised
His own; for neither do the spirits damned
Lose all their virtue; lest bad men should boast
Their specious deeds on Earth, which glory excites,
Or close ambition varnished o'er with zeal.[5]   485
    Thus they their doubtful consultations dark
Ended, rejoicing in their matchless chief:
As when from mountain tops the dusky clouds
Ascending, while the north wind sleeps, o'erspread
Heaven's cheerful face, the lowering element   490
Scowls o'er the darkened landscape snow or shower;
If chance the radiant sun with farewell sweet
Extend his evening beam, the fields revive,

8. Insignia of royalty. "Refusing": i.e., if I refuse.
9. Satan's argument, simple though entangled in rhetoric, is that rulers must share in the dangers as well as the rewards of an enterprise.
1. Undertake, endeavor.
2. Forestalled, anticipated.
3. After their courage had been raised by his resolution.
4. Full of respect and awe.
5. The sense is that damned spirits still retain some virtues; lest bad men boast of good deeds they have done out of glory and ambition, Milton has shown us that devils do just as much. "Specious": pretending virtue. "Close": secret.

The birds their notes renew, and bleating herds
Attest their joy, that hill and valley rings.   495
O shame to men! Devil with devil damned
Firm concord holds, men only disagree
Of creatures rational, though under hope
Of heavenly grace; and, God proclaiming peace,[6]
Yet live in hatred, enmity, and strife   500
Among themselves, and levy cruel wars,
Wasting the earth, each other to destroy:
As if (which might induce us to accord)
Man had not hellish foes enow[7] besides,
That day and night for his destruction wait!   505
    The Stygian council thus dissolved; and forth
In order came the grand infernal peers.
Midst came their mighty paramount,[8] and seemed
Alone th' antagonist of Heaven, nor less
Than Hell's dread emperor, with pomp supreme,   510
And godlike imitated state; him round
A globe[9] of fiery seraphim enclosed
With bright emblazonry,[1] and horrent arms.
Then of their session ended they bid cry
With trumpets' regal sound the great result: 515
Toward the four winds four speedy cherubim
Put to their mouths the sounding alchemy[2]
By herald's voice explained; the hollow abyss
Heard far and wide, and all the host of Hell
With deafening shout, returned them loud acclaim.   520
Thence more at ease their minds and somewhat raised
By false presumptuous hope, the rangéd[3] powers
Disband; and, wandering, each his several way
Pursues, as inclination or sad choice
Leads him perplexed where he may likeliest find   525
Truce to his restless thoughts, and entertain
The irksome hours, till his great chief return.
Part on the plain, or in the air sublime,[4]
Upon the wing, or in swift race contend,
As at th' Olympian games or Pythian fields;[5]   530
Part curb their fiery steeds, or shun the goal
With rapid wheels, or fronted brígades form.
As when, to warn proud cities, war appears
Waged in the troubled sky, and armies rush
To battle in the clouds;[6] before each van   535
Prick forth the airy knights, and couch their spears

6. I.e., though God proclaims peace.
7. I.e., enough; the old plural emphatic form.
8. Champion, chief.
9. Band or crowd.
1. Decorated shields. "Horrent": bristling.
2. I.e., resonant trumpets (made of the alloy brass by a marriage of metals which Milton associates with alchemy).
3. Arrayed in ranks.
4. Aloft, uplifted (the adjective modifies the flyer, not the air).
5. The Olympic games were held at Olympia, the Pythian games at Delphi. To "shun the goal" is to drive a chariot as close as possible around a column without hitting it.
6. Warfare in the skies at night, portending trouble on earth. "Prick": spur.

Till thickest legions close; with feats of arms
From either end of Heaven the welkin[7] burns.
Others with vast Typhoean[8] rage more fell
Rend up both rocks and hills, and ride the air   540
In whirlwind; Hell scarce holds the wild uproar.
As when Alcides, from Oechalia crowned
With conquest, felt th' envenomed robe, and tore
Through pain up by the roots Thessalian pines,
And Lichas from the top of Oeta threw   545
Into th' Euboic sea.[9] Others more mild,
Retreated in a silent valley, sing
With notes angelical to many a harp
Their own heroic deeds and hapless fall
By doom of battle; and complain that Fate   550
Free Virtue should enthrall to Force or Chance.
Their song was partial,[1] but the harmony
(What could it less when spirits immortal sing?)
Suspended[2] Hell, and took with ravishment
The thronging audience. In discourse more sweet   555
(For eloquence the soul, song charms the sense)
Others apart sat on a hill retired,
In thoughts more elevate, and reasoned high
Of providence, foreknowledge, will, and fate,
Fixed fate, free will, foreknowledge absolute,   560
And found no end, in wandering mazes lost.
Of good and evil much they argued then,
Of happiness and final misery,
Passion and apathy,[3] and glory and shame,
Vain wisdom all, and false philosophy![4]   565
Yet with a pleasing sorcery could charm
Pain for a while or anguish, and excite
Fallacious hope, or arm th' obduréd[5] breast
With stubborn patience as with triple steel.
Another part, in squadrons and gross[6] bands,   570
On bold adventure to discover wide
That dismal world, if any clime perhaps
Might yield them easier habitation, bend
Four ways their flying march, along the banks
Of four infernal rivers that disgorge   575

7. Sky.
8. Like that of Typhon, the hundred-headed Titan. See above, I.199.
9. Hercules, returning in triumph from Oechalia, prepared to sacrifice to the gods on top of Mt. Oeta, and sent to his wife Dejanira for a new robe. She had been told by the dying Nessus, a centaur whom Hercules had killed, that centaur's blood would preserve her husband's love. So she sent Hercules a robe anointed with the blood of Nessus. The "envenomed robe" tortured him into a frenzy, and before he died, he threw Lichas, who had brought it, together with a good part of Mt. Oeta itself, into the sea of Euboea.
1. Prejudiced.
2. Held in suspense.
3. Feeling and lack of feeling; the angels are dabbling in Stoicism.
4. Milton means, not that the subjects themselves are vain (he himself, in the present poem, has a good deal to say on these topics), but that the very premises with which devils start are bound to land them in error.
5. Hardened.
6. Solid, dense.

Into the burning lake their baleful streams:[7]
Abhorréd Styx, the flood of deadly hate;
Sad Acheron of sorrow, black and deep;
Cocytus, named of lamentation loud
Heard on the rueful stream; fierce Phlegethon   580
Whose waves of torrent fire inflame with rage.
Far off from these a slow and silent stream,
Lethe, the river of oblivion, rolls
Her watery labyrinth, whereof who drinks
Forthwith his former state and being forgets,   585
Forgets both joy and grief, pleasure and pain.
Beyond this flood a frozen continent
Lies dark and wild, beat with perpetual storms
Of whirlwind and dire hail, which on firm land
Thaws not, but gathers heap,[8] and ruin seems   590
Of ancient pile; all else deep snow and ice,
A gulf profound as that Serbonian bog[9]
Betwixt Damiata and Mount Casius old,
Where armies whole have sunk: the parching air
Burns frore,[1] and cold performs th' effect of fire.   595
Thither by harpy-footed[2] Furies haled,
At certain revolutions[3] all the damned
Are brought; and feel by turns the bitter change
Of fierce extremes, extremes by change more fierce,
From beds of raging fire to starve[4] in ice   600
Their soft ethereal warmth, and there to pine
Immovable, infixed, and frozen round
Periods of time; thence hurried back to fire.
They ferry over this Lethean sound
Both to and fro, their sorrow to augment,   605
And wish and struggle, as they pass, to reach
The tempting stream, with one small drop to lose
In sweet forgetfulness all pain and woe,
All in one moment, and so near the brink;
But Fate withstands, and to oppose th' attempt   610
Medusa[5] with Gorgonian terror guards
The ford, and of itself the water flies
All taste of living wight, as once it fled
The lips of Tantalus.[6] Thus roving on
In confused march forlorn, th' adventurous bands   615

7. The four rivers are traditional in hellish geography; Milton takes pains to distinguish them by the original meanings of their Greek names (Styx means "hateful," Acheron "woeful," etc.).
8. In a heap, so that it looks like the ruin of an old building ("ancient pile").
9. Lake Serbonis, once famous for its quicksands but today dried up, used to lie on the coast of Egypt, just east of the Nile, between Damiata and Mt. Cassius.

1. Frosty.
2. With hooked claws.
3. I.e., of time.
4. Benumb.
5. One of the three Gorgons, women with snaky hair, scaly bodies, and boar's tusks, the very sight of whose faces changed men to stone.
6. Tantalus, afflicted with a raging thirst, stood in the middle of a lake, the water of which always eluded his grasp (hence, "tantalize").

With shuddering horror pale, and eyes aghast
Viewed first their lamentable lot, and found
No rest. Through many a dark and dreary vale
They passed, and many a region dolorous,
O'er many a frozen, many a fiery alp,[7]   620
Rocks, caves, lakes, fens, bogs, dens, and shades of death,
A universe of death, which God by curse
Created evil, for evil only good,
Where all life dies, death lives, and Nature breeds,
Perverse, all monstrous, all prodigious things,   625
Abominable, unutterable, and worse
Than fables yet have feigned, or fear conceived,
Gorgons, and Hydras, and Chimeras[8] dire.
    Meanwhile the adversary of God and man,
Satan with thoughts inflamed of highest design,   630
Puts on swift wings,[9] and toward the gates of Hell
Explores his solitary flight; sometimes
He scours the right hand coast, sometimes the left;
Now shaves with level wing the deep, then soars
Up to the fiery concave[1] towering high.   635
As when far off at sea a fleet descried
Hangs in the clouds, by equinoctial winds
Close sailing from Bengala,[2] or the isles
Of Ternate and Tidore,[3] whence merchants bring
Their spicy drugs; they on the trading flood   640
Through the wide Ethiopian[4] to the Cape
Ply stemming nightly toward the pole: so seemed
Far off the flying fiend. At last appear
Hell bounds, high reaching to the horrid roof,
And thrice threefold the gates; three folds were brass,   645
Three iron, three of adamantine rock,
Impenetrable, impaled with circling fire,
Yet unconsumed. Before the gates there sat
On either side a formidable shape;[5]
The one seemed woman to the waist, and fair,   650
But ended foul in many a scaly fold
Voluminous and vast, a serpent armed
With mortal sting. About her middle round
A cry[6] of Hellhounds never-ceasing barked

---

7. A "fiery alp" is a volcano.
8. The Hydra was a serpent with nine heads, which was slain by Hercules; the Chimera was a fire-breathing creature, part lion, part dragon, part goat. They exemplify abominations of nature.
9. Satan does not fasten on his wings; he takes swiftly to wing.
1. Vault.
2. An old form of "Bengal."
3. Two of the Molucca or "Spice" Islands, modern Indonesia.
4. The Indian Ocean, east of Africa. "The Cape" is of course the Cape of

Good Hope; "the pole," the South Pole.
5. The allegorical figures of Sin and Death are founded on James i.15: "Then when lust hath conceived, it bringeth forth sin: and sin, when it is finished, bringeth forth death." But the incestuous relations of Sin and Death are Milton's own invention. Physically, Sin is modeled on Homer's Scylla, with some touches adopted from Spenser's Error; Death is a traditional figure, vague and vast.
6. Pack.

With wide Cerberean[7] mouths full loud, and rung   655
A hideous peal; yet, when they list, would creep,
If aught disturbed their noise, into her womb,
And kennel there, yet there still barked and howled
Within unseen. Far less abhorred than these
Vexed Scylla,[8] bathing in the sea that parts   660
Calabria from the hoarse Trinacrian shore;
Nor uglier follow the night-hag,[9] when, called
In secret, riding through the air she comes,
Lured with the smell of infant blood, to dance
With Lapland witches, while the laboring moon   665
Eclipses at their charms. The other shape,
If shape it might be called that shape had none
Distinguishable in member, joint, or limb,
Or substance might be called that shadow seemed,
For each seemed either; black it stood as night,   670
Fierce as ten Furies, terrible as Hell,
And shook a dreadful dart; what seemed his head
The likeness of a kingly crown had on.
Satan was now at hand, and from his seat
The monster moving onward came as fast,   675
With horrid strides; Hell trembled as he strode.
Th' undaunted fiend what this might be admired,[1]
Admired, not feared; God and his Son except,
Created thing nought valued he nor shunned;
And with disdainful look thus first began: 680
   "Whence and what art thou, execrable shape,
That dar'st, though grim and terrible, advance
Thy miscreated front[2] athwart my way
To yonder gates? Through them I mean to pass,
That be assured, without leave asked of thee.   685
Retire, or taste thy folly, and learn by proof,
Hell-born, not to contend with spirits of Heaven."
   To whom the goblin, full of wrath, replied:
"Art thou that traitor angel, art thou he,
Who first broke peace in Heaven, and faith, till then   690
Unbroken, and in proud rebellious arms
Drew after him the third part of Heaven's sons
Conjured[3] against the Highest, for which both thou
And they, outcast from God, are here condemned
To waste eternal days in woe and pain?   695
And reckon'st thou thyself with spirits of Heaven,
Hell-doomed, and breath'st defiance here and scorn,
Where I reign king, and, to enrage thee more,

---

7. Like Cerberus, the traditional hound of Hell.
8. Circe out of jealousy threw poison into the water where Scylla bathed, in the straits between Calabria and Sicily ("Trinacria"); as a result of the poisons, Scylla developed a ring of barking, snapping dogs around her waist.

9. Hecate, goddess of sorcery. She attends the orgies of witches in the home of all witchcraft, Lapland, whither she is drawn by the blood of babies sacrificed for the occasion.
1. Wondered.
2. Misshapen forehead, or face.
3. Sworn together by an oath.

Thy king and lord? Back to thy punishment,
False fugitive, and to thy speed add wings,   700
Lest with a whip of scorpions I pursue
Thy ling'ring, or with one stroke of this dart
Strange horror seize thee, and pangs unfelt before."
    So spake the grisly terror, and in shape,
So speaking and so threatening, grew tenfold   705
More dreadful and deform. On th' other side,
Incensed with indignation, Satan stood
Unterrified, and like a comet burned
That fires the length of Ophiucus[4] huge
In th' Arctic sky, and from his horrid hair   710
Shakes pestilence and war. Each at the head
Leveled his deadly aim; their fatal hands
No second stroke intend,[5] and such a frown
Each cast at th' other, as when two black clouds,
With Heaven's artillery fraught,[6] come rattling on   715
Over the Caspian,[7] then stand front to front
Hovering a space, till winds the signal blow
To join their dark encounter in mid-air:
So frowned the mighty combatants, that Hell
Grew darker at their frown; so matched they stood;   720
For never but once more was either like
To meet so great a foe.[8] And now great deeds
Had been achieved, whereof all Hell had rung,
Had not the snaky sorceress that sat
Fast by Hell-gate, and kept the fatal key,   725
Ris'n, and with hideous outcry rushed between.
    "O father, what intends thy hand," she cried,
"Against thy only son?[9] What fury, O son,
Possesses thee to bend that mortal dart
Against thy father's head? and know'st for whom?   730
For Him who sits above and laughs the while
At thee ordained his drudge, to execute
Whate'er his wrath, which he calls Justice, bids;
His wrath which one day will destroy ye both!"
    She spake, and at her words the hellish pest   735
Forbore, then these to her Satan returned:
    "So strange thy outcry, and thy words so strange
Thou interposest, that my sudden hand,
Prevented,[1] spares to tell thee yet by deeds
What it intends, till first I know of thee,   740
What thing thou art, thus double-formed, and why,
In this infernal vale first met, thou call'st

4. A vast Northern constellation, "The Serpent-Holder" (also called "Serpentarius"). Satan will soon appear as a snake; and, like a comet, he portends "pestilence and war."
5. I.e., the first stroke will do the business.
6. Loaded with thunderbolts.

7. The Caspian is a particularly stormy area.
8. I.e., the Son of God.
9. Sin, Death, and Satan, in their various interrelations, parody obscenely the relations between God and the Son, Adam and Eve.
1. Forestalled.

Me father, and that phantasm call'st my son?
I know thee not, nor ever saw till now
Sight more detestable than him and thee."   745
    T' whom thus the portress of Hell-gate replied:
"Hast thou forgot me then, and do I seem
Now in thine eye so foul? once deemed so fair
In Heaven, when at th' assembly, and in sight
Of all the seraphim with thee combined   750
In bold conspiracy against Heaven's King,
All on a sudden miserable pain
Surprised thee; dim thine eyes, and dizzy swum
In darkness, while thy head flames thick and fast
Threw forth, till on the left side opening wide,   755
Likest to thee in shape and countenance bright,
Then shining heavenly-fair, a goddess armed
Out of thy head I sprung.² Amazement seized
All th' host of Heaven; back they recoiled afraid
At first, and called me *Sin*, and for a sign   760
Portentous held me; but, familiar grown,
I pleased, and with attractive graces won
The most averse, thee chiefly, who full oft
Thyself in me thy perfect image viewing
Becam'st enamored;³ and such joy thou took'st   765
With me in secret, that my womb conceived
A growing burden. Meanwhile war arose,
And fields were fought in Heaven; wherein remained
(For what could else?) to our almighty Foe
Clear victory, to our part loss and rout   770
Through all the empyrean. Down they fell,
Driven headlong from the pitch⁴ of Heaven, **down**
Into this deep, and in the general fall
I also; at which time this powerful key
Into my hand was given, with charge to keep   775
These gates forever shut, which none can pass
Without my opening. Pensive here I sat
Alone, but long I sat not, till my womb
Pregnant by thee, and now excessive grown,
Prodigious motion felt and rueful throes.   780
At last this odious offspring whom thou seest,
Thine own begotten, breaking violent way,
Tore through my entrails, that, with fear and **pain**
Distorted, all my nether shape thus grew
Transformed; but he, my inbred enemy,   785
Forth issued, brandishing his fatal dart,
Made to destroy. I fled, and cried out *Death!*
Hell trembled at the hideous name, and sighed
From all her caves, and back resounded *Death!*

---

2. As Athena sprang full-grown from the head of Zeus.
3. Sin looks attractive at first, being a lovely woman at the top of her body; but she is a serpent below, and ends in a "mortal sting," i.e., death.
4. Peak.

I fled; but he pursued (though more, it seems,   790
Inflamed with lust than rage) and, swifter far,
Me overtook, his mother, all dismayed,
And in embraces forcible and foul
Engendering with me, of that rape begot
These yelling monsters, that with ceaseless cry   795
Surround me, as thou sawest, hourly conceived
And hourly born, with sorrow infinite
To me; for when they list, into the womb
That bred them they return, and howl, and gnaw
My bowels, their repast; then, bursting forth   800
Afresh, with conscious terrors vex me round,
That rest or intermission none I find.
Before mine eyes in opposition sits
Grim Death, my son and foe, who sets them on,
And me his parent would full soon devour   805
For want of other prey, but that he knows
His end with mine involved; and knows that I
Should prove a bitter morsel, and his bane,
Whenever that shall be; so Fate pronounced.
But thou, O father, I forewarn thee, shun   810
His deadly arrow; neither vainly hope
To be invulnerable in those bright arms,
Though tempered heavenly; for that mortal dint,
Save he who reigns above, none can resist."[5]
     She finished, and the subtle fiend his lore   815
Soon learned, now milder, and thus answered smooth:
"Dear daughter, since thou claimest me for thy sire,
And my fair son here show'st me, the dear pledge
Of dalliance had with thee in Heaven, and joys
Then sweet, now sad to mention, through dire change   820
Befallen us unforeseen, unthought of; know
I come no enemy, but to set free
From out this dark and dismal house of pain,
Both him and thee, and all the Heavenly host
Of spirits that, in our just pretenses[6] armed,   825
Fell with us from on high. From them I go
This uncouth errand sole,[7] and one for all
Myself expose, with lonely steps to tread
Th' unfounded deep, and through the void immense
To search with wandering quest a place foretold   830
Should be, and, by concurring signs, ere now
Created vast and round, a place of bliss
In the purlieus[8] of Heaven, and therein placed
A race of upstart creatures, to supply
Perhaps our vacant room, though more removed,   835
Lest Heaven, surcharged[9] with potent multitude,

---

5. I.e., only God is immune to death.   8. Outskirts, suburbs.
6. Grievances.   9. Too full. "Broils": controversies.
7. Alone on a desolate journey.

Might hap to move new broils. Be this, or aught
Than this more secret, now designed, I haste
To know; and, this once known, shall soon return,
And bring ye to the place where thou and Death   840
Shall dwell at ease, and up and down unseen
Wing silently the buxom[1] air, embalmed
With odors: there ye shall be fed and filled
Immeasurably; all things shall be your prey."
He ceased, for both seemed highly pleased, and Death   845
Grinned horrible a ghastly smile, to hear
His famine[2] should be filled, and blessed his maw
Destined to that good hour. No less rejoiced
His mother bad, and thus bespake her sire:
   "The key of this infernal pit, by due   850
And by command of Heaven's all-powerful King
I keep, by him forbidden to unlock
These adamantine gates; against all force
Death ready stands to interpose his dart,
Fearless to be o'ermatched by living might.   855
But what owe I to his commands above
Who hates me, and hath hither thrust me down
Into this gloom of Tartarus profound,
To sit in hateful office here confined,
Inhabitant of Heaven and heavenly-born,   860
Here in perpetual agony and pain,
With terrors and with clamors compassed round
Of mine own brood that on my bowels feed?
Thou art my father, thou my author, thou
My being gav'st me; whom should I obey   865
But thee? whom follow? Thou wilt bring me soon
To that new world of light and bliss, among
The gods who live at ease, where I shall reign
At thy right hand voluptuous,[3] as beseems
Thy daughter and thy darling, without end."   870
   Thus saying, from her side the fatal key,
Sad instrument of all our woe, she took;
And, towards the gate rolling her bestial train,[4]
Forthwith the huge portcullis high up-drew,
Which but herself not all the Stygian powers[5]   875
Could once have moved; then in the keyhole turns
Th' intricate wards, and every bolt and bar
Of massy iron or solid rock with ease
Unfastens: on a sudden open fly
With impetuous recoil and jarring sound   880
Th' infernal doors, and on their hinges grate

---

1. Yielding. "Embalmed": made fragrant, but also with a thought of the process associated with death.
2. Hunger, belly.
3. As the Son sits at God's right hand, Sin will sit at Satan's; a blasphemous parody, showed up by the word "voluptuous."
4. I.e., accompanied by her yelping offspring.
5. The powers of Hell.

Harsh thunder, that the lowest bottom shook
Of Erebus.[6] She opened, but to shut
Excelled[7] her power; the gates wide open stood,
That with extended wings a bannered host,   885
Under spread ensigns[8] marching, might pass through
With horse and chariots ranked in loose array;
So wide they stood, and like a furnace-mouth
Cast forth redounding[9] smoke and ruddy flame.
Before their eyes in sudden view appear   890
The secrets of the hoary deep, a dark
Illimitable ocean, without bound,
Without dimension; where length, breadth, and height,
And time and place are lost; where eldest Night
And Chaos, ancestors of Nature, hold   895
Eternal anarchy, amidst the noise
Of endless wars, and by confusion stand.
For Hot, Cold, Moist, and Dry, four champions fierce
Strive here for mastery, and to battle bring
Their embryon atoms;[1] they around the flag   900
Of each his faction, in their several clans,
Light-armed or heavy, sharp, smooth, swift, or slow,
Swarm populous, unnumbered as the sands
Of Barca or Cyrene's torrid soil,[2]
Levied to side with warring winds, and poise[3]   905
Their lighter wings. To whom these most adhere,
He rules a moment; Chaos[4] umpire sits,
And by decision more embroils the fray
By which he reigns: next him, high arbiter,
Chance governs all. Into this wild abyss,   910
The womb of Nature and perhaps her grave,
Of neither sea, nor shore, nor air, nor fire,
But all these in their pregnant causes[5] mixed
Confusedly, and which thus must ever fight,
Unless th' Almighty Maker them ordain   915
His dark materials to create more worlds,[6]
Into this wild abyss the wary fiend
Stood on the brink of Hell and looked awhile,
Pondering his voyage; for no narrow frith[7]
He had to cross. Nor was his ear less pealed[8]   920
With noises loud and ruinous (to compare
Great things with small) than when Bellona[9] storms,

6. Another classical name for Hell.
7. Exceeded. That Sin cannot shut Hell
gate, though she can open it, is sym-
bolical.
8. Standards, flags.
9. Billowing.
1. The four elements, fire, earth, water,
and air, struggle endlessly in Chaos.
"Embryon": embryo, unformed.
2. Barca and Cyrene were cities built
on the shifting sands of North Africa.
3. Give weight to.

4. Chaos is both the place where confusion reigns and personified confusion
itself.
5. Chaos is not organized to the point
of being matter; it is the seeds of all
forms of matter.
6. God must impose order on Chaos to
create worlds from it.
7. Channel, firth.
8. Rung.
9. Goddess of war.

With all her battering engines bent to raze
Some capital city; or less than if this frame
Of Heaven were falling, and these elements 925
In mutiny had from her axle torn
The steadfast Earth. At last his sail-broad vans[1]
He spreads for flight, and in the surging smoke
Uplifted spurns the ground; thence many a league,
As in a cloudy chair ascending, rides 930
Audacious; but that seat soon failing, meets
A vast vacuity: all unawares,
Fluttering his pennons[2] vain, plumb down he drops
Ten thousand fathom deep, and to this hour
Down had been falling, had not by ill chance 935
The strong rebuff[3] of some tumultuous cloud,
Instinct[4] with fire and niter, hurried him
As many miles aloft; that fury stayed,
Quenched in a boggy Syrtis,[5] neither sea,
Nor good dry land, nigh foundered on he fares, 940
Treading the crude consistence, half on foot,
Half flying; behoves[6] him now both oar and sail.
As when a gryphon through the wilderness
With wingèd course o'er hill or moory dale,
Pursues the Arimaspian, who by stealth 945
Had from his wakeful custody purloined
The guarded gold:[7] so eagerly the fiend
O'er bog or steep, through strait, rough, dense, or rare,
With head, hands, wings, or feet pursues his way,
And swims, or sinks, or wades, or creeps, or flies. 950
At length a universal hubbub wild
Of stunning sounds and voices all confused
Borne through the hollow dark, assaults his ear
With loudest vehemence. Thither he plies
Undaunted, to meet there whatever power 955
Or spirit of the nethermost abyss
Might in that noise reside, of whom to ask
Which way the nearest coast of darkness lies
Bordering on light; when straight behold the throne
Of Chaos, and his dark pavilion spread 960
Wide on the wasteful deep! With him enthroned
Sat sable-vested Night, eldest of things,
The consort of his reign; and by them stood
Orcus and Ades,[8] and the dreaded name

---

1. Wings.
2. Pinions, from Latin *pennae*, "wings."
3. Puff or blast.
4. Filled. "Niter": saltpeter.
5. Quicksand, from the North African gulfs, famous for their shifting sandbars.
6. Befits.
7. Gryphons, fabulous creatures, half-eagle, half-dragon, lived in northern Europe, and were said to hoard gold. When it was stolen from them by the one-eyed Arimaspians, they pursued these curious malefactors, hopping, flapping, and squawking. The story is a piece of moralized medieval natural history, directed against the love of money.
8. Latin and Greek names of Pluto, god of Hell.

Of Demogorgon;[9] Rumor next and Chance, 965
And Tumult and Confusion all embroiled,
And Discord with a thousand various mouths.
    T' whom Satan, turning boldly, thus: "Ye powers
And spirits of this nethermost abyss,
Chaos and ancient Night, I come no spy, 970
With purpose to explore or to disturb
The secrets of your realm; but by constraint
Wandering this darksome desert, as my way
Lies through your spacious empire up to light,
Alone and without guide, half lost, I seek 975
What readiest path leads where your gloomy bounds
Confine with[1] Heaven; or if some other place
From your dominion won, th' Ethereal King
Possesses lately, thither to arrive
I travel this profound.[2] Direct my course: 980
Directed, no mean recompense it brings
To your behoof,[3] if I that region lost,
All usurpation thence expelled, reduce
To their original darkness and your sway
(Which is my present journey[4]), and once more 985
Erect the standard there of ancient Night.
Yours be th' advantage all, mine the revenge!"
    Thus Satan; and him thus the anarch[5] old,
With faltering speech and visage incomposed,[6]
Answered: "I know thee, stranger, who thou art, 990
That mighty leading angel, who of late
Made head against Heaven's King, though overthrown.
I saw and heard; for such a numerous host
Fled not in silence through the frighted deep
With ruin upon ruin, rout on rout, 995
Confusion worse confounded; and Heaven-gates
Poured out by millions her victorious bands,
Pursuing. I upon my frontiers here
Keep residence; if all I can will serve,
That little which is left so to defend 1000
Encroached on still through our intestine broils[7]
Weakening the scepter of old Night: first Hell,
Your dungeon, stretching far and wide beneath;
Now lately Heaven and Earth,[8] another world
Hung o'er my realm, linked in a golden chain 1005
To that side Heaven from whence your legions fell.
If that way be your walk, you have not far;

9. A mysterious subdeity, stronger than Fate itself, first invented by Boccaccio. Cf. Shelley's *Prometheus Unbound*.
1. Border on.
2. Deep pit.
3. On your behalf.
4. I.e., the purpose of my present journey.
5. Chaos is not "monarch" of his realm, but "anarch," i.e., nonruler.
6. Disturbed.
7. I.e., our territory is continually shrinking because of our civil wars ("intestine broils").
8. Our human world and its sky have been carved out of Chaos. The sky is distinguished from "Heaven" as used in line 1006, meaning the abode of the blessed, the Empyrean.

So much the nearer danger. Go, and speed!
Havoc and spoil and ruin are my gain."
    He ceased; and Satan stayed not to reply,   1010
But, glad that now his sea should find a shore,
With fresh alacrity and force renewed
Springs upward, like a pyramid of fire,
Into the wild expanse, and through the shock
Of fighting elements, on all sides round   1015
Environed, wins his way; harder beset
And more endangered, than when Argo[9] passed
Through Bosporus betwixt the jostling rocks;
Or when Ulysses on the larboard shunned
Charybdis, and by th' other whirlpool steered: 1020
So he with difficulty and labor hard
Moved on: with difficulty and labor he;
But, he once past, soon after when man fell,
Strange alteration! Sin and Death amain,[1]
Following his track (such was the will of Heaven),   1025
Paved after him a broad and beaten way
Over the dark abyss, whose boiling gulf
Tamely endured a bridge of wondrous length
From Hell continued reaching th' utmost orb[2]
Of this frail world; by which the spirits perverse   1030
With easy intercourse pass to and fro
To tempt or punish mortals, except whom
God and good angels guard by special grace.
But now at last the sacred influence
Of light appears, and from the walls of Heaven   1035
Shoots far into the bosom of dim Night
A glimmering dawn. Here Nature first begins
Her farthest verge,[3] and Chaos to retire,
As from her outmost works a broken foe
With tumult less and with less hostile din;   1040
That[4] Satan with less toil, and now with ease
Wafts on the calmer wave by dubious light,
And, like a weather-beaten vessel, holds[5]
Gladly the port, though shrouds and tackle torn;
Or in the emptier waste, resembling air,   1045
Weighs his spread wings, at leisure to behold
Far off th' empyreal Heaven, extended wide
In circuit, undetermined[6] square or round,

9. Jason and his fifty Argonauts, sailing through the Bosporus to the Black Sea in pursuit of the Golden Fleece, had to pass through the Symplegades, or clashing rocks. Ulysses also had a tight squeeze to pass between Scylla and Charybdis, where Italy almost touches Sicily. Charybdis was a whirlpool, but Scylla, the dog-monster who ate alive six of Ulysses' best men, is called by Milton "th' other whirlpool."
1. At full speed, vigorously.
2. The world is surrounded by nine spheres, the whole construction comprising the created universe. The bridge built by Sin and Death ends on the outermost of these spheres.
3. Threshold. The end of Chaos is the beginning of (created) Nature.
4. So that.
5. Makes for.
6. Heaven is so vast that simply by looking at it one cannot tell its shape. Of course it is really round, the circle being an emblem of perfection.

With opal towers and battlements adorned
Of living sapphire, once his native seat;   1050
And fast by, hanging in a golden chain,
This pendant world,[7] in bigness as a star
Of smallest magnitude close by the moon.
Thither, full fraught with mischievous revenge,
Accursed, and in a cursèd hour, he hies.   1055

From Book III

[The Consult in Heaven]

Hail, holy Light, offspring of Heaven first-born!
Or of th' Eternal coeternal beam,
May I express thee unblamed?[1] since God is light,
And never but in unapproachèd light
Dwelt from eternity, dwelt then in thee,   5
Bright effluence of bright essence increate![2]
Or hear'st thou rather[3] pure ethereal stream,
Whose fountain who shall tell? Before the sun,
Before the heavens, thou wert, and at the voice
Of God, as with a mantle, didst invest[4]   10
The rising world of waters dark and deep,
Won from the void and formless infinite!
Thee I revisit now with bolder wing,
Escaped the Stygian pool, though long detained
In that obscure sojourn, while in my flight,   15
Through utter and through middle darkness[5] borne,
With other notes than to th' Orphean lyre[6]
I sung of Chaos and eternal Night;
Taught by the Heavenly Muse[7] to venture down
The dark descent, and up to reascend,   20
Though hard and rare. Thee I revisit safe,
And feel thy sovereign vital lamp; but thou
Revisit'st not these eyes, that roll in vain
To find thy piercing ray, and find no dawn;
So thick a drop serene[8] hath quenched their orbs,   25
Or dim suffusion veiled. Yet not the more
Cease I to wander where the Muses haunt
Clear spring, or shady grove, or sunny hill,

7. Homer first showed the world as hanging from Heaven by a golden chain (*Iliad* VIII). As Milton uses the image, it has a symbolic meaning as well; earth is dependent on Heaven. The world which hangs from Heaven is not just our earth, but earth and all its nine spheres, the created cosmos, as described by Ptolemy.
1. Milton feels some hesitation at calling Light coeternal with God himself; his reasons follow.

2. Uncreated, i.e., eternal.
3. I.e., would you rather be called. The construction is a Latinism.
4. Occupy.
5. Hell and Chaos.
6. One of the so-called Orphean Hymns is *To Night*. But Milton's darkness, being Christian, is deeper and wider.
7. Urania.
8. One medical theory about blindness attributed it to a *gutta serena*, another to a *suffusio nigra*.

Smit with the love of sacred song;[9] but chief
Thee, Sion,[1] and the flowery brooks beneath,   30
That wash thy hallowed feet, and warbling flow,
Nightly I visit: nor sometimes forget[2]
Those other two equaled with me in fate,[3]
So were I equaled with them in renown,
Blind Thamyris and blind Maeonides,   35
And Tiresias and Phineus, prophets old:[4]
Then feed on thoughts that voluntary move
Harmonious numbers; as the wakeful bird[5]
Sings darkling, and, in shadiest covert hid,
Tunes her nocturnal note. Thus with the year   40
Seasons return; but not to me returns
Day, or the sweet approach of even or morn,
Or sight of vernal bloom, or summer's rose,
Or flocks, or herds, or human face divine;
But cloud instead and ever-during dark   45
Surrounds me, from the cheerful ways of men
Cut off, and, for the book of knowledge fair,
Presented with a universal blank
Of Nature's works, to me expunged and rased,[6]
And wisdom at one entrance quite shut out.   50
So much the rather thou, Celestial Light,
Shine inward, and the mind through all her powers
Irradiate; there plant eyes; all mist from thence
Purge and disperse, that I may see and tell
Of things invisible to mortal sight.   55
    Now had th' Almighty Father from above,
From the pure empyrean where he sits
High throned above all height, bent down his eye,
His own works and their works at once to view:
About him all the sanctities of Heaven   60
Stood thick as stars, and from his sight[7] received
Beatitude past utterance; on his right
The radiant image of his glory sat,
His only Son. On Earth he first beheld
Our two first parents, yet the only two   65
Of mankind, in the happy garden placed,
Reaping immortal fruits of joy and love,
Uninterrupted joy, unrivaled love,

9. The phrase is Virgilian, *"ingenti percussus amore"* (*Georgics* II.476), but the adjective "sacred" is Milton's own reservation.
1. The mountain of Scriptural inspiration, with its brooks Siloa and Kidron.
2. I.e., and never forget: therefore always remember.
3. Blind like me.
4. Thamyris was a blind Thracian poet, who lived before Homer. "Maeonides" is an epithet of Homer, either as a son of Maeon or as a native of Maeonia. Tiresias was the blind prophet of

Thebes (cf. *Oedipus Rex*); Phineus was another blind prophet and soothsayer (*Aeneid* III). For Milton poetry and prophesy were intimately joined; blindness of the outer eye rendered more acute the sight of the inner eye; and the very thought of these matters moved him, as he says, spontaneously to verse.
5. The nightingale. "Darkling": at night.
6. Shaved off (like a Roman tablet), erased.
7. From sight of him.

In blissful solitude. He then surveyed
Hell and the gulf between, and Satan there 70
Coasting the wall of Heaven on this side Night,
In the dun air sublime,[8] and ready now
To stoop, with wearied wings and willing feet,
On the bare outside of this world, that seemed
Firm land embosomed without firmament, 75
Uncertain which, in ocean or in air.
Him God beholding from his prospect high,
Wherein past, present, future, he beholds,
Thus to his only Son foreseeing spake:
    "Only-begotten Son, seest thou what rage 80
Transports our adversary? whom no bounds
Prescribed, no bars of Hell, nor all the chains
Heaped on him there, nor yet the main abyss
Wide interrupt,[9] can hold; so bent he seems
On desperate revenge, that shall redound 85
Upon his own rebellious head. And now,
Through all restraint broke loose, he wings his way
Not far off Heaven, in the precincts of light,
Directly towards the new-created world,
And man there placed, with purpose to essay 90
If him by force he can destroy, or, worse,
By some false guile pervert: and shall pervert;
For man will hearken to his glozing lies,
And easily transgress the sole command,
Sole pledge of his obedience; so will fall 95
He and his faithless progeny. Whose fault?
Whose but his own? Ingrate, he had of me
All he could have; I made him just and right,
Sufficient to have stood, though free to fall.
Such I created all th' ethereal powers 100
And spirits, both them who stood and them who failed:
Freely they stood who stood, and fell who fell.
Not free, what proof could they have given sincere[1]
Of true allegiance, constant faith, or love,
Where only what they needs must do appeared, 105
Not what they would? What praise could they receive,
What pleasure I, from such obedience paid,
When Will and Reason (Reason also is Choice),
Useless and vain, of freedom both despoiled,
Made passive both, had served Necessity, 110
Not me? They, therefore, as to right belonged,
So were created, nor can justly accuse
Their Maker, or their making, or their fate,

8. From the aspect of God's radiance the air is "dun," i.e., dusky; Satan is literally "sublime" in it, i.e., lifted up, aloft. But from where Satan hangs, outside the world's outer shell, he cannot be sure the world and its nine concentric spheres are not a single solid (line 75). The points of view are precisely distinguished.
9. Dividing, in between.
1. The delayed modifier is a favorite stylistic device of Milton's. "Sincere" goes with "proof."

As if predestination overruled
Their will, disposed by absolute decree   115
Or high foreknowledge. They themselves decreed
Their own revolt, not I. If I foreknew,
Foreknowledge had no influence on their fault,
Which had no less proved certain unforeknown.[2]
So without least impulse or shadow of fate,   120
Or aught by me immutably foreseen,
They trespass, authors to themselves in all,
Both what they judge and what they choose; for so
I formed them free, and free they must remain
Till they enthrall themselves: I else must change   125
Their nature, and revoke the high decree
Unchangeable, eternal, which ordained
Their freedom; they themselves ordained their fall.
The first sort[3] by their own suggestion fell,
Self-tempted, self-depraved; man falls, deceived   130
By the other first: man, therefore, shall find grace;
The other, none. In mercy and justice both,[4]
Through Heaven and Earth, so shall my glory excel;
But mercy, first and last, shall brightest shine."
        Thus while God spake ambrosial fragrance filled   135
All Heaven, and in the blessed spirits elect
Sense of new joy ineffable diffused.
Beyond compare the Son of God was seen
Most glorious; in him all his Father shone
Substantially expressed;[5] and in his face   140
Divine compassion visibly appeared,
Love without end, and without measure grace;
Which uttering, thus he to his Father spake:
        "O Father, gracious was that word which closed
Thy sovereign sentence, that man should find grace;   145
For which both Heaven and Earth shall high extol
Thy praises, with th' innumerable sound
Of hymns and sacred songs, wherewith thy throne
Encompassed shall resound thee ever blest.
For, should man finally be lost, should man,   150
Thy creature late so loved, thy youngest son,
Fall circumvented thus by fraud, though joined
With his own folly? That be from thee far,
That far be from thee, Father, who art judge
Of all things made, and judgest only right!   155
Or shall the adversary[6] thus obtain
His end, and frustrate thine? shall he fulfill
His malice, and thy goodness bring to naught

2. I.e., if I had not foreknown it.
3. The bad angels, Satan and his crew.
4. Mercy and justice are two key terms in the poem. Their personifications here are separate: God is justice (he claims to be merciful, but his speech does not have this tone at all), the Son is mercy; but by Book XII Milton intends to show their identity.
5. God himself cannot be directly apprehended, except through the Son.
6. "Satan" in Hebrew means "Adversary."

Or proud return, though to his heavier doom,
Yet with revenge accomplished, and to Hell 160
Draw after him the whole race of mankind,
By him corrupted? Or wilt thou thyself
Abolish thy creation, and unmake,
For him, what for thy glory thou hast made?
So should thy goodness and thy greatness both 165
Be questioned and blasphemed without defense."
　　To whom the great Creator thus replied:
"O Son, in whom my soul hath chief delight,
Son of my bosom, Son who art alone
My word, my wisdom, and effectual might, 170
All hast thou spoken as my thoughts are, all
As my eternal purpose hath decreed.[7]
Man shall not quite be lost, but saved who will;
Yet not of will in him, but grace in me
Freely vouchsafed. Once more I will renew 175
His lapséd powers, though forfeit, and enthralled
By sin to foul exorbitant desires:
Upheld by me, yet once more he shall stand
On even ground against his mortal foe,
By me upheld,[8] that he may know how frail 180
His fallen condition is, and to me owe
All his deliverance, and to none but me.
Some I have chosen of peculiar grace,
Elect above the rest; so is my will:
The rest shall hear me call, and oft be warned 185
Their sinful state,[9] and to appease betimes
Th' incenséd Deity, while offered grace
Invites; for I will clear their senses dark
What may suffice,[1] and soften stony hearts
To pray, repent, and bring obedience due. 190
To prayer, repentance, and obedience due,
Though but endeavored with sincere intent,
Mine ear shall not be slow, mine eye not shut.
And I will place within them as a guide
My umpire Conscience; whom if they will hear, 195
Light after light well used they shall attain,[2]
And to the end persisting, safe arrive.
This my long sufferance, and my day of grace,
They who neglect and scorn shall never taste;
But hard be hardened, blind be blinded more, 200
That they may stumble on, and deeper fall;
And none but such from mercy I exclude.
But yet all is not done. Man, disobeying,

---

7. The Lord's speech is notably rhythmic and even rhymed.
8. Note the ambiguity: the second "by
me upheld" (line 180) may modify
either "he" (line 178) or "his mortal
foe" (line 179). Both divine and hellish energy are ultimately divine.
9. I.e., warned about their sinful state.
1. I.e., as much as need be.
2. By using light well, they will reach
even more light, and, in the end, salvation.

Disloyal, breaks his fealty, and sins
Against the high supremacy of Heaven,   205
Affecting[3] godhead, and so, losing all,
To expiate his treason hath naught left,
But, to destruction sacred and devote,[4]
He with his whole posterity must die;
Die he or Justice must; unless for him   210
Some other, able and as willing,[5] pay
The rigid satisfaction, death for death.
Say, heavenly powers, where shall we find such love?
Which of ye will be mortal, to redeem
Man's mortal crime,[6] and just, th' unjust to save?   215
Dwells in all Heaven charity so dear?"
        He asked, but all the heavenly choir stood mute,[7]
And silence was in Heaven: on man's behalf
Patron or intercessor none appeared,
Much less that durst upon his own head draw   220
The deadly forfeiture, and ransom set.
And now without redemption all mankind
Must have been lost, adjudged to Death and Hell
By doom severe, had not the Son of God,
In whom the fullness dwells of love divine,   225
His dearest mediation[8] thus renewed:
    "Father, thy word is passed, man shall find grace;
And shall Grace not find means, that finds her way,
The speediest of thy wingéd messengers,
To visit all thy creatures, and to all   230
Comes unprevented,[9] unimplored, unsought?
Happy for man, so coming! He her aid
Can never seek, once dead in sins and lost;
Atonement for himself, or offering meet,
Indebted and undone, hath none to bring.   235
Behold me, then: me for him, life for life,
I offer; on me let thine anger fall;
Account me man: I for his sake will leave
Thy bosom, and this glory next to thee
Freely put off, and for him lastly die   240
Well pleased; on me let Death wreak all his rage.
Under his gloomy power I shall not long
Lie vanquished. Thou hast given me to possess
Life in myself forever; by thee I live;
Though now to Death I yield, and am his due,   245
All that of me can die, yet, that debt paid,
Thou wilt not leave me in the loathsome grave
His prey, nor suffer my unspotted soul

3. Pretending to.
4. Dedicated, given up to.
5. I.e., able to pay, and as willing as
he is able.
6. Note that "mortal" means "human"
(line 214) but "deadly" (line 215).

7. The silence of the good angels in
face of a difficult task parallels that of
the devils in the "great consult" (II.
420–26).
8. Intercession.
9. Unforestalled.

Forever with corruption there to dwell;
But I shall rise victorious, and subdue   250
My vanquisher, spoiled of his vaunted spoil.
Death his death's wound shall then receive, and stoop[1]
Inglorious, of his mortal sting disarmed;
I through the ample air in triumph high
Shall lead Hell captive maugre[2] Hell, and show   255
The powers of darkness bound. Thou, at the sight
Pleased, out of Heaven shalt look down and smile,
While, by thee raised, I ruin[3] all my foes,
Death last, and with his carcass glut the grave;
Then, with the multitude of my redeemed,   260
Shall enter Heaven, long absent, and return,
Father, to see thy face, wherein no cloud
Of anger shall remain, but peace assured
And reconcilement: wrath shall be no more
Thenceforth, but in thy presence joy entire."   265
     His words here ended; but his meek aspéct
Silent yet spake, and breathed immortal love
To mortal men, above which only shone
Filial obedience: as a sacrifice
Glad to be offered, he attends the will   270
Of his great Father. Admiration[4] seized
All Heaven, what this might mean, and whither tend,
Wondering; but soon th' Almighty thus replied:
     "O thou in Heaven and Earth the only peace
Found out for mankind under wrath,[5] O thou   275
My sole complacence![6] well thou know'st how dear
To me are all my works; nor man the least,
Though last created, that for him I spare
Thee from my bosom and right hand, to save,
By losing thee a while, the whole race lost!   280
Thou, therefore, whom thou only canst redeem,
Their nature also to thy nature join;[7]
And be thyself man among men on Earth,
Made flesh, when time shall be, of virgin seed,
By wondrous birth; be thou in Adam's room   285
The head of all mankind, though Adam's son.[8]
As in him perish all men, so in thee,
As from a second root, shall be restored

1. Be humbled, fall.
2. In spite of (French, *malgré*). The Son's triumph is represented in a series of fantastic paradoxes—a vanquisher vanquished, a spoiler spoiled, death dead, Hell captured in all Hell's despite.
3. In the Latin sense, throw down.
4. Wonder, curiosity.
5. The Lord is looking to the future, when mankind will be under his wrath.
6. Contentment.
7. I.e., join the nature of those people (mankind) whom you alone can save to your own nature; in other words,

"Become a man and suffer the pains of mortality." The antecedent of "whom" is, loosely construed, the "their" which follows it.
8. Adam is, properly, the "Old Adam"; Christ is the Second Adam (there was an old tradition that the Forbidden Tree and the Cross of Christ stood on the same spot). The Son of God, who long antedates the creation of Adam, and who is actually the first created being (III.383), is historical Jesus Christ in one sense, an eternal spiritual principle in another.

As many as are restored; without thee, none.
His crime makes guilty all his sons;[9] thy merit,   290
Imputed, shall absolve them who renounce
Their own both righteous and unrighteous deeds,[1]
And live in thee transplanted, and from thee
Receive new life. So man, as is most just,
Shall satisfy for man, be judged and die,   295
And dying rise, and, rising, with him raise
His brethren, ransomed with his own dear life.
So heavenly love shall outdo hellish hate,
Giving to death, and dying to redeem,
So dearly to redeem, what hellish hate   300
So easily destroyed, and still destroys
In those who, when they may, accept not grace.
Nor shalt thou, by descending to assume
Man's nature, lessen or degrade thine own.
Because thou hast, though throned in highest bliss   305
Equal to God, and equally enjoying
Godlike fruition,[2] quitted all to save
A world from utter loss, and hast been found
By merit more than birthright Son of God,[3]
Found worthiest to be so by being good,   310
Far more than great or high; because in thee
Love hath abounded more than glory abounds;
Therefore thy humiliation shall exalt
With thee thy manhood also to this throne:
Here shalt thou sit incarnate, here shalt reign   315
Both God and man, Son both of God and man,
Anointed[4] universal King. All power
I give thee; reign forever, and assume
Thy merits; under thee, as Head Supreme,
Thrones, princedoms, powers, dominions, I reduce: 320
All knees to thee shall bow of them that bide
In Heaven, or Earth, or under Earth in Hell.
When thou, attended gloriously from Heaven,
Shalt in the sky appear, and from thee send
The summoning archangels to proclaim   325
Thy dread tribunal, forthwith from all winds[5]
The living, and forthwith the cited dead
Of all past ages, to the general doom
Shall hasten; such a peal shall rouse their sleep.
Then, all thy saints assembled, thou shalt judge   330
Bad men and angels; they arraigned shall sink
Beneath thy sentence; Hell, her numbers full,

9. The intense legalism of the Deity is
apparent.
1. I.e., the merit of Christ, imputed to
men, frees from original sin those who
renounce their own deeds both good and
bad and hoped to be saved by faith.
2. Godlike pleasures, rewards.
3. An audacious doctrine, that Christ

was Son of God by merit. Satan, one
notes, was sultan of Hell on the same
principle.
4. "The Anointed," in Hebrew, is the
Messiah.
5. From all directions. "Cited": summoned.

Thenceforth shall be forever shut. Meanwhile
The world shall burn, and from her ashes spring
New Heaven and Earth, wherein the just shall dwell,[6]   335
And, after all their tribulations long,
See golden days, fruitful of golden deeds,
With Joy and Love triúmphing, and fair Truth.
Then thou thy regal scepter shalt lay by;
For regal scepter then no more shall need;[7]   340
God shall be all in all. But all ye gods,[8]
Adore him who, to compass all this, dies;
Adore the Son, and honor him as me."
   No sooner had th' Almighty ceased, but all
The multitude of angels, with a shout   345
Loud as from numbers without number, sweet
As from blest voices, uttering joy, Heaven rung[9]
With jubilee, and loud hosannas filled
Th' eternal regions. Lowly reverent
Towards either throne[1] they bow, and to the ground   350
With solemn adoration down they cast
Their crowns, inwove with amarant[2] and gold;
Immortal amarant, a flower which once
In Paradise, fast by the Tree of Life,
Began to bloom, but soon for man's offense   355
To Heaven removed, where first it grew, there grows
And flowers aloft, shading the Fount of Life,
And where the River of Bliss through midst of Heaven
Rolls o'er Elysian[3] flowers her amber stream.
With these, that never fade, the spirits elect   360
Bind their resplendent locks, enwreathed with beams.
Now in loose garlands thick thrown off, the bright
Pavement, that like a sea of jasper shone,
Empurpled with celestial roses smiled.
Then, crowned again, their golden harps they took,   365
Harps ever tuned, that glittering by their side
Like quivers hung; and with preamble sweet
Of charming symphony they introduce
Their sacred song, and waken raptures high:
No voice exempt,[4] no voice but well could join   370
Melodious part; such concord is in Heaven.
   Thee, Father, first they sung, Omnipotent,
Immutable, Immortal, Infinite,[5]

---

6. The burning of the earth is based on II Peter iii.12, 13.
7. Be needed.
8. In addressing the angels as gods, the Lord is merely indicating their share in his divinity; the word is not literal.
9. "Multitude" (line 345) is subject of the sentence, "rung" the verb, and "Heaven" the object.
1. Those of God and the Son.
2. Or "amaranth"; in Greek, "unwithering"—an unfading flower and hence a

type of immortality, which could not continue on earth after man became subject to death.
3. Milton draws freely, and with no sense of incongruity, on pagan properties for his Christian Heaven. "Amber": not "yellow," but "clear." Milton's epithets are not always visually strong.
4. Abstaining.
5. Joshua Sylvester, in translating the long, pedestrian poem of Du Bartas on the creation, makes use of this line. It

Eternal King; thee, Author of all being,
Fountain of light, thyself invisible   375
Amidst the glorious brightness where thou sitt'st
Throned inaccessible, but when thou shad'st
The full blaze of thy beams, and through a cloud
Drawn round about thee like a radiant shrine
Dark with excessive bright thy skirts appear,[6]   380
Yet dazzle Heaven, that brightest seraphim
Approach not, but with both wings veil their eyes.
Thee next they sang, of all creation first,
Begotten Son, divine similitude,
In whose conspicuous countenance, without cloud   385
Made visible, th' Almighty Father shines,
Whom else[7] no creature can behold: on thee
Impressed th' effulgence of his glory abides;
Transfused on thee his ample spirit rests.
He Heaven of Heavens, and all the powers therein,   390
By thee created; and by thee threw down
Th' aspiring dominations.[8] Thou that day
Thy Father's dreadful thunder didst not spare,
Nor stop thy flaming chariot wheels, that shook
Heaven's everlasting frame, while o'er the necks   395
Thou drov'st of warring angels disarrayed.
Back from pursuit, thy powers with loud acclaim
Thee only extolled, Son of thy Father's might,
To execute fierce vengeance on his foes.
Not so on man: him, through their malice fallen,   400
Father of mercy and grace, thou didst not doom
So strictly, but much more to pity incline.
No sooner did thy dear and only Son
Perceive thee purposed not to doom frail man
So strictly, but much more to pity inclined,[9]   405
He, to appease thy wrath, and end the strife
Of mercy and justice in thy face discerned,
Regardless of the bliss wherein he sat
Second to thee, offered himself to die
For man's offense. O unexampled love!   410
Love nowhere to be found less than divine!
Hail, Son of God, Savior of men! Thy name
Shall be the copious matter of my[1] song
Henceforth, and never shall my harp thy praise
Forget, nor from thy Father's praise disjoin!   415

is the only example, and not a very
striking one, of Milton's paralleling an
English predecessor for ten consecutive
syllables.
6. In this hymn, for the first time, we
get a sense of the majesty and mystery
of the Godhead; hitherto, he has been
rather querulous and legalistic.
7. Except for whom (if it were not for
the Son, no creature could see God).
8. I.e., the rebel angels.

9. A "than" or "but" is understood at
the end of line 405. The repetition
(lines 402, 405) suggests the choral
nature of the psalm. Note in 407 the
re-emphasis on a conflict of mercy and
justice.
1. Either the angels are singing as a
single chorus, or Milton wishes to associate himself with them; possibly both.
The change of pronoun is deliberate and
striking.

Summary   The consult in Heaven, which occupies the first half of Book III, has momentarily interrupted Milton's account of Satan's journey. During the latter half of Book III, he continues to describe this journey. Satan, passing through the dim air outside the firmament, lights on the outer shell of the created cosmos, in a barren, windy place later to be known as the Paradise of Fools. He finds a passageway leading down through the concentric crystal spheres in which the planets are set, and spirals down toward Earth, at the center of this smaller cosmos, hung on a chain in the midst of the larger cosmos. But to find Eden he needs directions, and so, disguising himself as an inquisitive but virtuous angel, he imposes on Uriel, the archangel of the sun. Uriel gives him instructions, and Satan stops near Mt. Niphates, in Armenia.

From Book IV

Summary   On the point of entering Paradise, Satan is momentarily overcome by remorse, fear, envy, and despair; but in a dramatic soliloquy, he reasons himself back into resolution, and pushes forward.

[*Satan's Entry into Paradise*]

So on he fares, and to the border comes
Of Eden, where delicious Paradise,
Now nearer, crowns with her enclosure green,
As with a rural mound, the champaign[1] head
Of a steep wilderness, whose hairy sides   135
With thicket overgrown, grotesque[2] and wild,
Access denied; and overhead up grew
Insuperable height of loftiest shade,
Cedar, and pine, and fir, and branching palm,
A sylvan scene, and, as the ranks ascend   140
Shade above shade, a woody theater[3]
Of stateliest view. Yet higher than their tops
The verdurous wall of Paradise up sprung;
Which to our general sire[4] gave prospect large
Into his nether empire neighboring round.   145
And higher than that wall a circling row
Of goodliest trees, laden with fairest fruit,
Blossoms and fruits at once of golden hue,
Appeared, with gay enameled colors mixed;
On which the sun more glad impressed his beams   150
Than in fair evening cloud, or humid bow,[5]

1. From French *champs*, open country-side. Paradise is an open garden on top of a hill straddling a river in the east of Eden.
2. One of the earliest uses of the word in English to mean "romantic" or "picturesque."
3. As if in a Greek amphitheater, the trees are set row on row.
4. Adam.
5. The rainbow. There is a thick wall of trees around Paradise, which "access denied"; then above them, the shaggy sides of Paradise itself ("the verdurous wall"), and above it the garden of fruit trees.

When God hath showered the earth: so lovely seemed
That landscape. And of pure now purer air[6]
Meets his approach, and to the heart inspires
Vernal delight and joy, able to drive[7]   155
All sadness but despair. Now gentle gales,
Fanning their odoriferous wings, dispense
Native perfumes, and whisper whence they stole
Those balmy spoils. As when to them who sail
Beyond the Cape of Hope, and now are past   160
Mozambic, off at sea northeast winds blow
Sabean odors from the spicy shore
Of Araby the Blest,[8] with such delay
Well pleased they slack their course, and many a league
Cheered with the grateful smell old Ocean smiles;   165
So entertained those odorous sweets the fiend
Who came their bane, though with them better pleased
Than Asmodëus with the fishy fume
That drove him, though enamored, from the spouse
Of Tobit's son,[9] and with a vengeance sent   170
From Media post to Egypt, there fast bound.
　　Now to th' ascent of that steep savage[1] hill
Satan had journeyed on, pensive and slow;
But further way found none; so thick entwined,
As one continued brake, the undergrowth   175
Of shrubs and tangling bushes had perplexed
All path of man or beast that passed that way.
One gate there only was, and that looked east
On th' other side. Which when th' arch-felon saw,
Due entrance he disdained, and, in contempt,   180
At one slight bound high overleaped all bound[2]
Of hill or highest wall, and sheer within
Lights on his feet. As when a prowling wolf,
Whom hunger drives to seek new haunt for prey,
Watching where shepherds pen their flocks at eve,   185
In hurdled cotes[3] amid the field secure,
Leaps o'er the fence with ease into the fold;
Or as a thief, bent to unhoard the cash
Of some rich burgher, whose substantial doors,
Cross-barred and bolted fast, fear no assault,   190
In at the window climbs, or o'er the tiles;

6. After breathing pure air, Satan now breathes even purer.
7. Scatter.
8. Coasting up East Africa after doubling the Cape of Good Hope, Milton supposes off "Mozambic" (Mozambique) one might meet "Sabean" (i.e., as from Sheba) odors coming from "Araby the Blest" (Arabia Felix). This is the fantasy of a man who learned his geography from medieval atlases and Diodorus Siculus, for the distance between Mozambique and Arabia is close to 2,000 miles.

9. Milton retells briefly here the story of Tobias, Tobit's son, who married Sara and was saved from the fate of her seven previous husbands by the advice of Raphael, who showed him how to make a fishy smell that would drive away the devil Asmodeus. See the Book of Tobit among the Apocrypha.
1. Wooded, entangled (from Latin, *silvaticus*, through Italian *selvaggio*, and French *sauvage*).
2. Satan enters Paradise, not only illegally, but with a contemptuous pun.
3. Pens made of woven reeds.

So clomb[4] this first grand thief into God's fold:
So since into his church lewd[5] hirelings climb.
Thence up he flew, and on the Tree of Life,
The middle tree and highest there that grew,   195
Sat like a cormorant; yet not true life
Thereby regained, but sat devising death
To them who lived; nor on the virtue thought
Of that life-giving plant, but only used
For prospect,[6] what, well used, had been the pledge   200
Of immortality. So little knows
Any, but God alone, to value right
The good before him, but perverts best things
To worst abuse, or to their meanest use.
    Beneath him, with new wonder, now he views,   205
To all delight of human sense exposed,
In narrow room Nature's whole wealth; yea, more,
A Heaven on Earth; for blissful Paradise
Of God the garden was, by him in the east
Of Eden planted. Eden stretched her line   210
From Auran eastward to the royal towers
Of great Seleucia, built by Grecian kings,
Or where the sons of Eden long before
Dwelt in Telassar.[7] In this pleasant soil
His far more pleasant garden God ordained.   215
Out of the fertile ground he caused to grow
All trees of noblest kind for sight, smell, taste;
And all amid them stood the Tree of Life,
High eminent, blooming ambrosial fruit
Of vegetable gold; and next to life,   220
Our death, the Tree of Knowledge, grew fast by—
Knowledge of good, bought dear by knowing ill.
Southward through Eden went a river large,
Nor changed his course, but through the shaggy hill
Passed underneath engulfed; for God had thrown   225
That mountain, as his garden-mold,[8] high raised
Upon the rapid current, which, through veins
Of porous earth with kindly[9] thirst up drawn,
Rose a fresh fountain, and with many a rill
Watered the garden; thence united fell   230
Down the steep glade, and met the nether flood,
Which from his darksome passage now appears,

4. Old past tense of "climb," but used with a special feeling of ungainly energy. The whole metaphor, of God· as a rich citizen hoarding Adam and Eve from Satan the second-story-man, is instinct with comic feeling. On the devil as a thief, see John x.1.
5. Base.
6. Perspective, lookout.
7. By suggesting alternate boundaries of Eden, Milton invokes a hazy sense of the richness, vastness, and antiquity of the Middle East. "Auran" is an area in Syria, to the south of Damascus; "Seleucia" lies near modern Bagdad, a powerful city founded by one of Alexander's generals (hence, "built by Grecian kings"); and "Telassar" is another Near Eastern kingdom, this one probably on the east bank of the Euphrates.
8. The mountain is God's topsoil, out of which grows Paradise. The river (traditionally Tigris) flowed under the hill.
9. Natural.

And now, divided into four main streams,
Runs diverse, wandering many a famous realm
And country, whereof here needs no account;[1]   235
But rather to tell how, if art could tell,
How, from that sapphire fount the crispéd[2] brooks,
Rolling on orient pearl and sands of gold,
With mazy error[3] under pendant shades
Ran nectar, visiting each plant, and fed   240
Flowers worthy of Paradise; which not nice[4] art
In beds and curious knots, but Nature boon[5]
Poured forth profuse on hill, and dale, and plain,
Both where the morning sun first warmly smote
The open field, and where the unpierced shade   245
Embrowned[6] the noontide bowers. Thus was this place,
A happy rural seat of various view:[7]
Groves whose rich trees wept odorous gums and balm;
Others whose fruit, burnished with golden rind,
Hung amiable[8]—Hesperian fables true,   250
If true, here only—and of delicious taste.
Betwixt them lawns, or level downs, and flocks
Grazing the tender herb, were interposed,
Or palmy hillock; or the flowery lap
Of some irriguous[9] valley spread her store,   255
Flowers of all hue, and without thorn the rose.[1]
Another side, umbrageous[2] grots and caves
Of cool recess, o'er which the mantling vine
Lays forth her purple grape, and gently creeps
Luxuriant; meanwhile murmuring waters fall   260
Down the slope hills dispersed, or in a lake,
That to the fringéd bank with myrtle crowned
Her crystal mirror holds, unite their streams.
The birds their choir apply;[3] airs, vernal airs,
Breathing the smell of field and grove, attune   265
The trembling leaves, while universal Pan,[4]
Knit with the Graces and the Hours in dance,
Led on th' eternal spring.[5] Not that fair field
Of Enna, where Proserpin gathering flowers,
Herself a fairer flower, by gloomy Dis   270
Was gathered, which cost Ceres all that pain

1. Milton has in mind Genesis ii.10; but the expression "whereof here needs no account" dodges many questions about the correct translation of this passage.
2. Wavy, ruffled.
3. From Latin *errare*, "wandering."
4. Particular, careful.
5. Liberal, bounteous.
6. Darkened.
7. Aspect.
8. Lovely. These were real golden apples like those said to have existed in the Hesperides, fabulous islands of the Western Ocean; Paradise was the only place where the fable of the Hesperides was literally true.
9. Well-watered.
1. Figuratively and literally, there was no need for thorns in Paradise.
2. Shady.
3. Practice their song. "Airs" may be either "breezes" or "melodies," and probably are both.
4. The god of all nature. "Pan" in Greek means "all" but it is also the name of the goat-legged nature god.
5. The god of nature dances with the Graces and Hours, an image of perfect harmony.

To seek her through the world; nor **that sweet grove**
Of Daphne,[6] by Orontes and th' inspired
Castalian spring, might with this Paradise
Of Eden strive; nor that Nyseian isle,   275
Girt with the river Triton, where old Cham,
Whom Gentiles Ammon call and Libyan Jove,
Hid Amalthea, and her florid son,
Young Bacchus, from his stepdame Rhea's eye;[7]
Nor, where Abassin kings their issue guard,   280
Mount Amara[8] (though this by some supposed
True Paradise) under the Ethiop line
By Nilus' head, enclosed with shining rock,
A whole day's journey high, but wide remote
From this Assyrian garden, where the fiend   285
Saw undelighted all delight, all kind
Of living creatures, new to sight and strange.
Two of far nobler shape, erect and tall,
Godlike erect,[9] with native honor clad
In naked majesty, seemed lords of all,   290
And worthy seemed; for in their looks divine,
The image of their glorious Maker, shone
Truth, wisdom, sanctitude severe and pure—
Severe, but in true filial freedom[1] placed,
Whence true authority in men; though both   295
Not equal, as their sex not equal seemed.
For contemplation he and valor formed,
For softness she and sweet attractive grace;
He for God only, she for God in him.[2]
His fair large front[3] and eye sublime declared   300
Absolute rule; and hyacinthine[4] locks
Round from his parted forelock manly hung

---

6. Milton is comparing Paradise with the famous beauty spots of antiquity. Enna in Sicily was a lovely meadow from which "Proserpin" was kidnapped by "gloomy Dis" (i.e., Pluto); her mother Ceres sought her throughout the world. The grove of Daphne, near Antioch and the Orontes river in the Near East, had a spring called "Castalia" in imitation of the Muses' fountain near Delphi.

7. The isle of Nysa in the river Triton in Tunisia was where Ammon hid Bacchus, his bastard child by Amalthea, from the eye of his wife Rhea. "Florid" (wine-flushed) Bacchus, when he grew up, received the name of Dionysus in honor of his birthplace. The identification of the Egyptian god Ammon or Hammon with Cham or Ham, the son of Noah, is a piece of comparative anthropology on Milton's part.

8. Finally, Paradise ("this Assyrian garden," line 285) is finer than the palaces atop Mt. Amara, where the "Abassin" (Abyssinian) kings had a splendid palace. Milton's authority for this exotic scene was Peter Heylyn (*Cosmographie* IV.lxiv), from whom he took several phrases direct. His passage then had a continuing influence on the names and phrasings of Coleridge's *Kubla Khan*.

9. By emphasizing the word "erect," Milton means to distinguish man from the beasts of the field, who went "prone."

1. Though almost a paradox, the phrase suggests Milton's idea that true freedom always involves respect for authority and hierarchy. Cf. Eve's foolish question, "For, inferior, who is free?" (IX.825).

2. Milton's ideas on the relations between the sexes were strict for his day, though not as strict as they now appear.

3. Forehead.

4. A classical metaphor, often applied to hair, and implying "brown" or perhaps "flowing," but actually not very definite in its import.

Clustering, but not beneath his shoulders broad:
She, as a veil down to the slender waist,
Her unadornéd golden tresses wore   305
Disheveled, but in wanton ringlets waved
As the vine curls her tendrils,[5] which implied
Subjection, but required with gentle sway,
And by her yielded, by him best received,
Yielded with coy[6] submission, modest pride,   310
And sweet, reluctant, amorous delay.
Nor those mysterious parts were then concealed;
Then was not guilty shame. Dishonest shame
Of Nature's works, honor dishonorable,
Sin-bred, how have ye troubled all mankind   315
With shows instead, mere shows of seeming pure,
And banished from man's life his happiest life,
Simplicity and spotless innocence!
So passed they naked on, nor shunned the sight
Of God or angel; for they thought no ill;   320
So hand in hand they passed, the loveliest pair
That ever since in love's embraces met:
Adam the goodliest man of men since born
His sons; the fairest of her daughters Eve.[7]
Under a tuft of shade that on a green   325
Stood whispering soft, by a fresh fountain-side,
They sat them down; and, after no more toil
Of their sweet gardening labor than sufficed
To recommend cool Zephyr,[8] and make ease
More easy, wholesome thirst and appetite   330
More grateful, to their supper fruits they fell,
Nectarine fruits, which the compliant boughs
Yielded them, sidelong as they sat recline
On the soft downy bank damasked with flowers.
The savory pulp they chew, and in the rind,   335
Still as they thirsted scoop the brimming stream;
Nor gentle purpose,[9] nor endearing smiles
Wanted, nor youthful dalliance, as beseems
Fair couple linked in happy nuptial league,
Alone as they. About them frisking played   340
All beasts of th' earth, since wild, and of all chase[1]
In wood or wilderness, forest or den.
Sporting the lion ramped,[2] and in his paw
Dandled the kid; bears, tigers, ounces, pards,[3]
Gamboled before them; th' unwieldly elephant,   345
To make them mirth, used all his might, and wreathed

5. Eve's hair is curly, abundant, un-
controlled; like the vegetation in Paradise, it clings seductively about a severe
and masculine virtue.
6. Shy.
7. Logically these constructions are absurd; Adam was not born since his day,
Eve was not one of her own daughters.

Milton combines comparative with superlative forms for emphatic effect.
8. I.e., to make a cool breeze welcome.
9. Conversation. "Wanted": lacked.
1. Who lurk in every sort of cover.
2. Reared up.
3. Lynxes and leopards.

His lithe proboscis; close the serpent sly,
Insinuating,[4] wove with Gordian twine
His braided train,[5] and of his fatal guile
Gave proof unheeded. Others on the grass   350
Couched and now filled with pasture, gazing sat,
Or bedward ruminating;[6] for the sun,
Declined, was hasting now with prone career
To th' ocean isles,[7] and in th' ascending scale
Of Heaven the stars that usher evening rose: 355
When Satan, still in gaze as first he stood,
Scarce thus at length failed speech recovered sad:[8]
    "O Hell! what do mine eyes with grief behold?
Into our room of bliss thus high advanced
Creatures of other mold, Earth-born perhaps,   360
Not spirits, yet to heavenly spirits bright
Little inferior; whom my thoughts pursue
With wonder, and could love; so lively shines
In them divine resemblance, and such grace
The hand that formed them on their shape hath poured.[9]   365
Ah! gentle pair, ye little think how nigh
Your change approaches, when all these delights
Will vanish, and deliver ye to woe,
More woe, the more your taste is now of joy:
Happy, but for so happy[1] ill secured   370
Long to continue, and this high seat, your Heaven,
Ill fenced for Heaven to keep out such a foe
As now is entered; yet no purposed foe
To you, whom I could pity thus forlorn,
Though I unpitied. League with you I seek,   375
And mutual amity, so strait, so close,
That I with you must dwell, or you with me,
Henceforth.[2] My dwelling, haply, may not please,
Like this fair Paradise, your sense; yet such
Accept your Maker's work; he gave it me,   380
Which I as freely give. Hell shall unfold,
To entertain you two, her widest gates,
And send forth all her kings; there will be room,
Not like these narrow limits, to receive
Your numerous offspring; if no better place,   385
Thank him who puts me, loath, to this revenge
On you, who wrong me not, for him who wronged.[3]

4. Writhing and twisting, but with a glance at the Tempter's rhetorical techniques.
5. Checkered body. "Gordian twine": knots, like the Gordian knot, cut by Alexander the Great.
6. The animals are chewing their cuds before bedtime; in Paradise, where the animal kingdom is not yet subject to death, they are perforce vegetarians.
7. The Azores.
8. The choked, laborious line mirrors Satan's heavy, congested mind.
9. Though Satan's moral values are topsy-turvy ("Evil, be thou my Good," he has said in the first part of Book IV), his aesthetic values are strictly orthodox.
1. Such happiness.
2. Though it starts in simple admiration, Satan's friendship for mankind is, at the end, rather grisly and sardonic. The turning point seems to be "though I unpitied" (line 375)—the reaction of a spoiled child.
3. I.e., it is not my fault; Satan's favorite phrase.

And, should I at your harmless innocence
Melt, as I do, yet public reason just—
Honor and empire with revenge enlarged   390
By conquering this new world—compels me now
To do what else, though damned, I should abhor."[4]
    So spake the fiend, and with necessity,
The tyrant's plea, excused his devilish deeds.
Then from his lofty stand on that high tree   395
Down he alights among the sportful herd
Of those four-footed kinds, himself now one,
Now other, as their shape served best his end
Nearer to view his prey, and unespied,
To mark what of their state he more might learn   400
By word or action marked. About them round
A lion now he stalks with fiery glare;
Then as a tiger, who by chance hath spied
In some purlieu[5] two gentle fawns at play,
Straight couches close; then, rising, changes oft   405
His couchant watch, as one who chose his ground,
Whence rushing he might surest seize them both
Griped in each paw * * *

4. Satan's final reason for destroying Adam and Eve is thoroughly Satanic; it is *ragione di stato*, reason of state, the public interest.
5. The outskirt of a forest. Note that Satan can and does enter any animal he wants; it is only for the special purposes of the temptation that he finds the serpent specially convenient.

Summary   By eavesdropping on Adam and Eve, Satan learns of the prohibited Tree of Knowledge; this weakness he resolves to exploit. Meanwhile Uriel, rendered suspicious by Satan's fierce demeanor outside Paradise, reports to Gabriel, the angel specially assigned to guard mankind, that a diabolic intruder may be near. Gabriel promises to search him out. After Adam and Eve say their evening prayers and retire, Gabriel divides his night watch into groups, assigning Ithuriel and Zephon to guard closely the bower of Adam and Eve. They find Satan whispering in the ear of the sleeping Eve, and bring him before Gabriel. A battle impends, but is averted by a heavenly signal, and Satan flees out of Paradise.

Book V. Summary   In the morning Eve is distressed by her dreams of the previous night, which she relates to Adam; he comforts her. Meanwhile God dispatches Raphael to warn man of the approaching danger. Raphael arrives about noon, and dines with Adam and Eve. He then warns his hosts of the need to remain obedient, and, to explain the risks they run, recounts the story of Satan's revolt and fall. He describes how Satan, pretending that God's creation of the Son was an offense to angelic dignity, persuaded a host of his fellow angels to withdraw their allegiance to God and set up a camp in the north. When open war on God was announced, however, one of these angels was able to repent. The seraph Abdiel, though scorned by his fellows, denounced the rebellion and returned, heroically alone, to the camp of God's followers.

Book VI. Summary   Continuing the story of the war in Heaven, Raphael describes the assembling of the armies and a first skirmish in which Satan is both insulted and wounded by Abdiel. After the first day's battle, the evil angels retire discomfited; but overnight Satan invents cannon with which, on the second day, the good angels are put to some disorder. In the fury of the fight, however, they pull up mountains by the roots and bury the cannon beneath them; thus the issue remains inconclusive. On the third day, God withdraws all his armies and sends the Son alone into battle; the Son drives his enemies irresistibly over the wall of Heaven, and after falling nine days through Chaos they are swallowed up in Hell.

From Book VII

[*The Invocation*][1]

Descend from Heaven, Urania, by that name
If rightly thou art called,[2] whose voice divine
Following, above th' Olympian hill I soar,
Above the flight of Pegasean wing![3]
The meaning, not the name I call: for thou   5
Nor of the Muses nine, nor on the top
Of old Olympus dwell'st, but heavenly born,
Before the hills appeared, or fountain flowed,
Thou with eternal Wisdom didst converse,
Wisdom thy sister, and with her didst play   10
In presence of th' Almighty Father,[4] pleased
With thy celestial song. Up led by thee
Into the Heaven of Heavens I have presumed,
An earthly guest, and drawn empyreal air,
Thy tempering;[5] with like safety guided down,   15
Return me to my native element:
Lest from this flying steed unreined (as once
Bellerophon,[6] though from a lower clime),
Dismounted, on th' Aleian field I fall,
Erroneous[7] there to wander and forlorn.   20

---

1. To start the second half of his poem, Milton must counterbalance the destruction of the war in Heaven with the creation by God of a new universe, centering on the Earth. Book VII is devoted to this topic; and to approach so vast a subject, Milton once more invokes his Muse.

2. Milton has only the names of classical Muses with which to invoke the spiritual principles of Christian theology. Properly the Muse of astronomy, Urania is also the symbol of heavenly love and of divine wisdom; Milton here renews the invocation he made in Book I.

3. Pegasus, the flying horse of poetry, suggests (in connection with Bellero-

phon, line 18) Milton's sense of his own perilous audacity in writing so vast a poem.

4. In Proverbs viii.30, Wisdom is made to speak of "playing always before God" previous even to the Creation. Milton makes his Muse coeval with divine wisdom.

5. Tempered by thee.

6. Bellerophon tried to explore the stars astride Pegasus the flying horse; but Zeus sent a gadfly to sting Pegasus, and his rider, after falling onto the Aleian plain in Lycia, wandered about there till he died.

7. From Latin *errare*, "to wander," as well as "to be mistaken."

Half yet remains unsung, but narrower bound
Within the visible diurnal sphere;
Standing on Earth, not rapt above the pole,
More safe I sing with mortal voice, unchanged
To hoarse or mute, though fall'n on evil days,   25
On evil days though fall'n, and evil tongues;
In darkness, and with dangers compassed round,
And solitude; yet not alone, while thou
Visit'st my slumbers nightly, or when morn
Purples the east:[8] still govern thou my song,   30
Urania, and fit audience find, though few.
But drive far off the barbarous dissonance
Of Bacchus and his revelers, the race
Of that wild rout that tore the Thracian bard[9]
In Rhodope, where woods and rocks had ears   35
To rapture, till the savage clamor drowned
Both harp and voice; nor could the Muse defend
Her son. So fail not thou, who thee implores:
For thou art heavenly, she an empty dream.

8. Milton composed mostly at night or very early in the morning.
9. The Thracian Bacchantes, female worshipers of Bacchus, tore Orpheus to pieces in Rhodope, though even the rocks and trees were so impressed with his music that they refused to be used against the poet. See *Lycidas*, lines 58–63. Orpheus was son of Calliope, the epic Muse.

Summary At Adam's request, Raphael continues his narration and describes how God, to replace the fallen angels, created the world, its creatures, and finally man, in the course of six days; the story of the creation concludes, on the seventh day, with a chorus of thanksgiving by the angels.

Book VIII. Summary Adam asks Raphael why so many and such splendid stars seem to be at the service of the earth, which appears smaller and less noble than they; at this point Eve leaves her husband and his guest to continue the discussion alone. Raphael proposes various astronomical possibilities but gives no conclusive answer to Adam's question, urging him instead to confine his curiosity to more practical matters. Adam now, at Raphael's request, describes his own recollections of his creation, as well as his first meeting and marriage with Eve. In the course of the story, he shows a somewhat exaggerated deference for Eve, which the angel rebukes; Adam is to be the head of the family, and follow his own judgment, not his wife's. Repeating his admonitions to beware of temptation, Raphael departs.

Book IX

The Argument

Satan, having compassed the Earth, with meditated guile returns as a mist by night into Paradise; enters into the serpent sleeping. Adam and Eve in the morning go forth to their labors, which Eve proposes to divide in several places, each laboring apart: Adam consents not, alleging the danger lest that enemy of whom they were forewarned should attempt her found alone. Eve, loath to be thought not circumspect or firm enough, urges her going apart, the rather desirous to make trial of her strength; Adam at last yields. The serpent finds her alone: his subtle approach, first gazing, then speaking, with much flattery extolling Eve above all other creatures. Eve, wondering to hear the serpent speak, asks how he attained to human speech and such understanding not till now; the serpent answers that by tasting of a certain tree in the garden he attained both to speech and reason, till then void of both. Eve requires him to bring her to that tree, and finds it to be the Tree of Knowledge forbidden: the serpent, now grown bolder, with many wiles and arguments induces her at length to eat. She, pleased with the taste, deliberates a while whether to impart thereof to Adam or not; at last brings him of the fruit; relates what persuaded her to eat thereof. Adam, at first amazed, but perceiving her lost, resolves, through vehemence of love, to perish with her, and, extenuating[1] the trespass, eats also of the fruit. The effects thereof in them both; they seek to cover their nakedness; then fall to variance and accusation of one another.

No more of talk where God[2] or angel guest
With man, as with his friend, familiar used
To sit indulgent, and with him partake
Rural repast, permitting him the while
Venial[3] discourse unblamed. I now must change   5
Those notes to tragic; foul distrust, and breach
Disloyal, on the part of man, revolt
And disobedience; on the part of Heaven,
Now alienated, distance and distaste,
Anger and just rebuke, and judgment given,   10
That brought into this world a world of woe,
Sin and her shadow Death, and Misery,
Death's harbinger. Sad task! yet argument
Not less but more heroic than the wrath
Of stern Achilles on his foe pursued   15
Thrice fugitive about Troy wall; or rage
Of Turnus for Lavinia disespoused;
Or Neptune's ire, or Juno's, that so long
Perplexed the Greek, and Cytherea's son:[4]

1. Not "diminishing" or "excusing" as in customary English usage, but carrying further, drawing out.
2. God, of course, has not been lunching with Adam; but since man is about to fall, the age is now over when such an occasion could be contemplated.
3. Permissible.
4. In the *Iliad* (XXII), Achilles pur-

sues Hector three times around Troy wall before catching him. In the *Aeneid*, Aeneas must fight with Turnus for the hand of Lavinia. Neptune (or Poseidon) was unfriendly to Odysseus (the Greek); Juno (or Hera) to Aeneas, who was Cytherea's, i.e., Aphrodite's, son by Anchises.

If answerable style I can obtain   20
Of my celestial Patroness,[5] who deigns
Her nightly visitation unimplored,
And dictates to me slumbering, or inspires
Easy my unpremeditated verse,[6]
Since first this subject for heroic song   25
Pleased me, long choosing and beginning late,[7]
Not sedulous by nature to indite
Wars, hitherto the only argument
Heroic deemed, chief mastery to dissect[8]
With long and tedious havoc fabled knights   30
In battles feigned (the better fortitude
Of patience and heroic martyrdom
Unsung), or to describe races and games,
Or tilting furniture,[9] emblazoned shields,
Impresses quaint, caparisons and steeds,   35
Bases and tinsel trappings, gorgeous knights
At joust and tournament; then marshaled feast
Served up in hall with sewers and seneschals:[1]
The skill of artifice or office mean;
Not that which justly gives heroic name   40
To person or to poem. Me, of these
Nor skilled nor studious, higher argument
Remains,[2] sufficient of itself to raise
That name,[3] unless an age too late, or cold
Climate, or years, damp my intended wing   45
Depressed; and much they may if all be mine,
Not hers who brings it nightly to my ear.
     The sun was sunk, and after him the star
Of Hesperus, whose office is to bring
Twilight upon the Earth, short arbiter   50
'Twixt day and night, and now from end to end
Night's hemisphere had veiled the horizon round,
When Satan, who late fled before the threats
Of Gabriel out of Eden,[4] now improved
In meditated fraud and malice, bent   55
On man's destruction, mauger what might hap
Of heavier on himself,[5] fearless returned.

---

5. The muse, Urania.
6. Milton, we are told by his nephew Edward Philips, used to wake up in the morning with lines of poetry full-formed in his head; he would then dictate them to an amanuensis.
7. Milton's early plans for epics, preserved in manuscript, did center on national heroes; his choice of a sacred subject is a novelty within the epic tradition. "Sedulous": eager.
8. I.e., in describing wars one's chief task is to dissect; dissect, in its strict Latin sense of "cut apart," but perhaps also with a comic overtone from the anatomy table.

9. The equipment of tournaments; "impresses quaint": elaborate devices on shields; "bases": trappings for horses.
1. Waiters and stewards.
2. I.e., for me, when these things are set aside which I neither can nor want to do, there remains a higher argument.
3. I.e., the name heroic poet. "Age too late": not Milton's age, but the age of the world. Milton felt a "cold climate," by forcing people to keep their mouths shut and mumble, was inimical to epic poetry. "Damp": stupefy, benumb.
4. At the end of Book IV.
5. Despite the peril of heavier (punishments).

By night he fled, and at midnight returned
From compassing the Earth—cautious of day
Since Uriel, regent of the sun, descried   60
His entrance, and forewarned the Cherubim
That kept their watch.[6] Thence, full of anguish, driven,
The space of seven continued nights he rode
With darkness; thrice the equinoctial line[7]
He circled, four times crossed the car of Night   65
From pole to pole, traversing each colure;
On the eighth returned, and on the coast averse
From entrance or cherubic watch by stealth
Found unsuspected way. There was a place   70
(Now not, though sin, not time, first wrought the change)
Where Tigris, at the foot of Paradise,
Into a gulf shot under ground, till part
Rose up a fountain by the Tree of Life.
In with the river sunk, and with it rose,   75
Satan, involved in rising mist; then sought
Where to lie hid. Sea he had searched and land
From Eden over Pontus, and the pool
Maeotis, up beyond the river Ob;[8]
Downward as far antarctic; and, in length,   80
West from Orontes to the ocean barred
At Darien, thence to the land where flows
Ganges and Indus.[9] Thus the orb he roamed
With narrow search, and with inspection deep
Considered every creature, which of all   85
Most opportune might serve his wiles, and found
The serpent subtlest beast of all the field.[1]
Him, after long debate, irresolute
Of thoughts revolved,[2] his final sentence chose
Fit vessel, fittest imp[3] of fraud, in whom   90
To enter, and his dark suggestions hide
From sharpest sight; for in the wily snake
Whatever sleights none would suspicious mark,
As from his wit and native subtlety
Proceeding, which, in other beasts observed,   95
Doubt[4] might beget of diabolic power
Active within beyond the sense of brute.

6. At the beginning of Book IV. These connections with Book IV not only bridge the intervening narration, but emphasize a balancing of the whole epic; see the headnote.
7. The equator. The colures are the two great circles of the celestial sphere which intersect at the poles. By circling the globe, either from east to west or over the north and south poles, Satan can remain continually hidden in darkness.
8. Pontus is the Black Sea, the pool Maeotis the swamps of the Sea of Azov; the river Ob flows north through Siberia into the Arctic Ocean.
9. Flying west from Orontes in Syria, Satan now crosses the Atlantic to the Isthmus of Panama (Darien), then crosses the Pacific and southeast Asia to India.
1. Genesis iii.1 describes the serpent as the subtlest beast of the field.
2. I.e., unable to decide among his revolving thoughts. "Sentence": decision.
3. Graft, offshoot.
4. Suspicion.

Thus he resolved, but first from inward grief
His bursting passion into plaints thus poured:
   "O Earth, how like to Heaven, if not preferred
More justly, seat worthier of Gods, as built   100
With second thought, reforming what was old!
For what God, after better, worse would build?
Terrestrial Heaven, danced round by other Heavens,
That shine, yet bear their bright officious lamps,
Light above light, for thee alone, as seems,   105
In thee concent'ring all their precious beams
Of sacred influence![5] As God in Heaven
Is center, yet extends to all, so thou
Cent'ring receiv'st from all those orbs; in thee,
Not in themselves, all their known virtue appears,   110
Productive in herb, plant, and nobler birth
Of creatures animate with gradual life
Of growth, sense, reason,[6] all summed up in man.
With what delight could I have walked thee round,
If I could joy in aught; sweet interchange   115
Of hill and valley, rivers, woods, and plains,
Now land, now sea, and shores with forest crowned,
Rocks, dens, and caves! But I in none of these
Find place or refuge; and the more I see
Pleasures about me, so much more I feel   120
Torment within me, as from the hateful siege[7]
Of contraries; all good to me becomes
Bane,[8] and in Heaven much worse would be my state.
But neither here seek I, no, nor in Heaven,
To dwell, unless by mastering Heaven's Supreme;   125
Nor hope to be myself less miserable
By what I seek, but others to make such
As I, though thereby worse to me redound.
For only in destroying I find ease
To my relentless thoughts, and him [9] destroyed,   130
Or won to what may work his utter loss,
For whom all this was made, all this [1] will soon
Follow, as to him linked in weal or woe:
In woe then, that destruction wide may range!
To me shall be the glory sole among   135
The infernal Powers, in one day to have marred
What he, Almighty styled, six nights and days
Continued making, and who knows how long
Before had been contriving? though perhaps
Not longer than since I in one night freed   140

5. Satan, like Adam in Book VIII, is impressed that so many heavenly bodies center on (and "serve") the earth—as the old Ptolemaic astronomy taught that they did. "Officious": dutiful.
6. The sacred influence of the stars was thought to generate and foster life within the earth.
7. Conflict.
8. Poison.
9. I.e., man.
1. I.e., the created cosmos.

From servitude inglorious well-nigh half
Th' angelic name, and thinner left the throng
Of his adorers. He, to be avenged,
And to repair his numbers thus impaired,
Whether such virtue,[2] spent of old, now failed   145
More angels to create (if they at least
Are his created),[3] or to spite us more,
Determined to advance into our room
A creature formed of earth, and him endow,
Exalted from so base original,   150
With heavenly spoils, our spoils. What he decreed
He effected; man he made, and for him built
Magnificent this World, and Earth his seat,
Him lord pronounced, and, O indignity!
Subjected to his service angel-wings   155
And flaming ministers, to watch and tend
Their earthy charge. Of these the vigilance
I dread, and to elude, thus wrapt in mist
Of midnight vapor, glide obscure, and pry
In every bush and brake, where hap may find   160
The serpent sleeping, in whose mazy folds
To hide me, and the dark intent I bring.
O foul descent! that I, who erst contended
With Gods to sit the highest, am now constrained
Into a beast, and, mixed with bestial slime,   165
This essence to incarnate and imbrute,[4]
That to the height of deity aspired!
But what will not ambition and revenge
Descend to? Who aspires must down as low
As high he soared, obnoxious,[5] first or last,   170
To basest things. Revenge, at first though sweet,
Bitter ere long, back on itself recoils.
Let it; I reck not, so it light well aimed,
Since higher I fall short, on him who next
Provokes my envy, this new favorite   175
Of Heaven, this man of clay, son of despite,
Whom, us the more to spite,[6] his Maker raised
From dust: spite then with spite is best repaid."
      So saying, through each thicket, dank or dry,
Like a black mist low-creeping, he held on   180
His midnight search, where soonest he might find
The serpent. Him fast sleeping soon he found,
In labyrinth of many a round self-rolled,
His head the midst, well stored with subtle wiles:
Not yet in horrid shade or dismal den,   185

2. Strength, energy.
3. Satan never raises this question, whether angels are created or independent beings, without hesitating over it.
4. Satan's incarnation in a snake is a grotesque parody of the Son of God's incarnation in Christ.
5. Subject to.
6. Satan sees God in his own image, as a spiteful creature.

Nor nocent [7] yet, but on the grassy herb,
Fearless, unfeared, he slept. In at his mouth
The devil entered, and his brutal sense,
In heart or head, possessing soon inspired
With act intelligential; but his sleep   190
Disturbed not, waiting close[8] th' approach of morn.
  Now, whenas sacred light began to dawn
In Eden on the humid flowers, that breathed
Their morning incense, when all things that breathe
From th' Earth's great altar send up silent praise   195
To the Creator, and his nostrils fill
With grateful smell, forth came the human pair,
And joined their vocal worship to the choir
Of creatures wanting voice; that done, partake
The season,[9] prime for sweetest scents and airs;   200
Then commune how that day they best may ply
Their growing work; for much their work outgrew
The hands' dispatch of two gardening so wide:
And Eve first to her husband thus began:
  "Adam, well may we labor still [1] to dress   205
This garden, still to tend plant, herb, and flower,
Our pleasant task enjoined; but, till more hands
Aid us, the work under our labor grows,
Luxurious by restraint: what we by day
Lop overgrown, or prune, or prop, or bind,   210
One night or two with wanton growth derides,
Tending to wild. Thou, therefore, now advise,
Or hear what to my mind first thoughts present.
Let us divide our labors; thou where choice
Leads thee, or where most needs, whether to wind   215
The woodbine round this arbor, or direct
The clasping ivy where to climb; while I
In yonder spring [2] of roses intermixed
With myrtle find what to redress till noon.
For, while so near each other thus all day   220
Our task we choose, what wonder if so near
Looks intervene and smiles, or objects new
Casual discourse draw on, which intermits
Our day's work, brought to little, though begun
Early, and th' hour of supper comes unearned!"   225
  To whom mild answer Adam thus returned:
"Sole Eve, associate sole, to me beyond
Compare above all living creatures dear!
Well hast thou motioned,[3] well thy thoughts employed
How we might best fulfil the work which here   230
God hath assigned us, nor of me shalt pass

7. Harmful.   1. Continually.
8. In secret.   2. Growth.
9. I.e., go forth into the morning air.   3. Suggested.
"Prime": the best.

Unpraised; for nothing lovelier can be found
In woman than to study household good,
And good works in her husband to promote.[4]
Yet not so strictly hath our Lord imposed   235
Labor as to debar us when we need
Refreshment, whether food or talk between,
Food of the mind, or this sweet intercourse
Of looks and smiles; for smiles from reason flow,
To brute denied, and are of love the food,   240
Love, not the lowest end of human life.
For not to irksome toil, but to delight,
He made us, and delight to reason joined.
These paths and bowers doubt not but our joint hands
Will keep from wilderness with ease, as wide   245
As we need walk, till younger hands ere long
Assist us. But, if much converse perhaps
Thee satiate, to short absence I could yield;
For solitude sometimes is best society,
And short retirement urges sweet return.   250
But other doubt possesses me, lest harm
Befall thee, severed from me; for thou know'st
What hath been warned us, what malicious foe,
Envying our happiness, and of his own
Despairing, seeks to work us woe and shame   255
By sly assault, and somewhere nigh at hand
Watches, no doubt, with greedy hope to find
His wish and best advantage, us asunder,[5]
Hopeless to circumvent us joined, where each
To other speedy aid might lend at need.   260
Whether his first design be to withdraw
Our fealty from God, or to disturb
Conjugal love, than which perhaps no bliss
Enjoyed by us excites his envy more;
Or this, or worse,[6] leave not the faithful side   265
That gave thee being, still shades thee and protects.
The wife, where danger or dishonor lurks,
Safest and seemliest by her husband stays,
Who guards her, or with her the worst endures."
   To whom the virgin [7] majesty of Eve,   270
As one who loves, and some unkindness meets,
With sweet austere composure thus replied:
   "Offspring of Heaven and Earth, and all Earth's lord!
That such an enemy we have, who seeks
Our ruin, both by thee informed I learn,   275
And from the parting angel overheard,

4. Proverbs xxxi is devoted to the praise
of a good wife, and Milton doubtless
had it in mind here.
5. I.e., to find us apart; which will answer his wishes and serve his advantage.
6. I.e., whether this or something worse
be his intent.
7. Unspotted.

As in a shady nook I stood behind,
Just then returned at shut of evening flowers.
But that thou shouldst my firmness therefore doubt
To God or thee, because we have a foe   280
May tempt it, I expected not to hear.
His violence thou fear'st not, being such
As we, not capable of death or pain,
Can either not receive, or can repel.
His fraud is, then, thy fear; which plain infers   285
Thy equal fear that my firm faith and love
Can by his fraud be shaken or seduced:
Thoughts, which how found they harbor in thy breast,
Adam, misthought of her to thee so dear?" [8]
      To whom, with healing words, Adam replied: 290
"Daughter of God and man, immortal Eve,
For such thou art, from sin and blame entire; [9]
Not diffident of thee do I dissuade
Thy absence from my sight, but to avoid
Th' attempt itself, intended by our foe.   295
For he who tempts, though in vain, at least asperses [1]
The tempted with dishonor foul, supposed
Not incorruptible of faith, not proof
Against temptation. Thou thyself with scorn
And anger wouldst resent the offered wrong,   300
Though ineffectual found; misdeem not, then,
If such affront I labor to avert
From thee alone, which on us both at once
The enemy, though bold, will hardly dare;
Or, daring, first on me th' assault shall light.   305
Nor thou his malice and false guile contemn—
Subtle he needs must be who could seduce
Angels—nor think superfluous others' aid.
I from the influence of thy looks receive
Access in every virtue; [2] in thy sight   310
More wise, more watchful, stronger, if need were
Of outward strength; while shame, thou looking on,
Shame to be overcome or overreached,[3]
Would utmost vigor raise, and raised unite.
Why shouldst not thou like sense within thee feel   315
When I am present, and thy trial choose
With me, best witness of thy virtue tried?"
      So spake domestic Adam in his care
And matrimonial love; but Eve, who thought
Less[4] attributed to her faith sincere,   320

---

8. I.e., these thoughts were misthought of (misapplied to) her to thee so dear (me).
9. "Entire" is from Latin *integer*, untouched. "Diffident": the usual English meaning is "shy," "timid"; Milton emphasizes the Latin roots, *dis* + *fides* = mistrustful.
1. The word is from Latin *spargere*, to sprinkle, with overtones from English "aspersion," an ugly insinuation.
2. Extra strength.
3. Overpowered or outwitted.
4. Too little.

Thus her reply with accent sweet renewed:
　"If this be our condition, thus to dwell
In narrow circuit straitened by a foe,
Subtle or violent, we not endued
Single with like defence wherever met,　　　　　325
How are we happy, still in fear of harm?
But harm precedes not sin: only our foe
Tempting affronts us with his foul esteem
Of our integrity: his foul esteem
Sticks no dishonor on our front,[5] but turns　　330
Foul on himself; then wherefore shunned or feared
By us, who rather double honor gain
From his surmise proved false, find peace within,
Favor from Heaven, our witness, from th' event?
And what is faith, love, virtue, unassayed　　　335
Alone, without exterior help sustained?
Let us not then suspect our happy state
Left so imperfect by the Maker wise
As not secure to single or combined.
Frail is our happiness, if this be so;　　　　　340
And Eden were no Eden, thus exposed."
　　To whom thus Adam fervently replied:
"O woman, best are all things as the will
Of God ordained them; his creating hand
Nothing imperfect or deficient left　　　　　345
Of all that he created, much less man,
Or aught that might his happy state secure,
Secure from outward force. Within himself
The danger lies, yet lies within his power;
Against his will he can receive no harm.　　　350
But God left free the will; for what obeys
Reason is free; and reason he made right,
But bid her well beware, and still erect,[6]
Lest, by some fair appearing good surprised,
She dictate false, and misinform the will　　355
To do what God expressly hath forbid.
Not then mistrust, but tender love, enjoins
That I should mind [7] thee oft; and mind thou me.
Firm we subsist, yet possible to swerve,
Since reason not impossibly may meet　　　360
Some specious object by the foe suborned,
And fall into deception unaware,
Not keeping strictest watch, as she was warned.
Seek not temptation, then, which to avoid
Were better, and most likely if from me　　　365

5. Forehead.
6. Remain alert.

7. Remind; in the next phrase, "mind"
means "obey."

Thou sever not: trial will come unsought.
Wouldst thou approve thy constancy, approve [8]
First thy obedience; th' other who can know,
Not seeing thee attempted, who attest?
But if thou think trial unsought may find   370
Us both securer than thus warned thou seem'st,
Go; for thy stay, not free, absents thee more.
Go in thy native innocence; rely
On what thou hast of virtue; summon all;
For God towards thee hath done his part: do thine.'   375
      So spake the patriarch of mankind; but Eve
Persisted; yet submiss, though last, replied:
      "With thy permission,[9] then, and thus forewarned,
Chiefly by what thy own last reasoning words
Touched only, that our trial, when least sought,   380
May find us both perhaps far less prepared,
The willinger I go, nor much expect
A foe so proud will first the weaker seek;
So bent, the more shall shame him his repulse."
Thus saying, from her husband's hand her hand   385
Soft she withdrew, and like a wood nymph light,
Oread or dryad, or of Delia's train,[1]
Betook her to the groves, but Delia's self
In gait surpassed and goddesslike deport,
Though not as she with bow and quiver armed,   390
But with such gardening tools as art yet rude,
Guiltless of fire[2] had formed, or angels brought.
To Pales, or Pomona, thus adorned,
Likest she seemed, Pomona when she fled
Vertumnus, or to Ceres in her prime,   395
Yet virgin of Proserpina from Jove.[3]
Her long with ardent look his eye pursued
Delighted, but desiring more her stay.
Oft he to her his charge of quick return
Repeated; she to him as oft engaged   400
To be returned by noon amid the bower,
And all things in best order to invite
Noontide repast, or afternoon's repose.
O much deceived, much failing, hapless Eve,

8. Prove, give evidence of.
9. Eve takes a reluctant and extorted permission as free leave to do what she wants. Though apparently submissive, she gets the last word.
1. An "oread" is a nymph of the mountain, a "dryad" one of the wood. "Delia" is Diana or Artemis, goddess of the chase, who when she hunted was accompanied by a train of nymphs.
2. There was no need of fire in Paradise; but that fire is a possession which renders one guilty suggests an overtone of the Prometheus myth.
3. Pales is a Roman goddess of flocks, Pomona a Roman divinity of fruits and orchards. Pomona was wooed by Vertumnus, god of spring, who assumed all sorts of shapes to win her. Ceres, the Mother Nature of the ancients (hence, the word "cereal"), bore Proserpina to Jupiter. All three goddesses are patrons of agriculture, like Eve.

Of thy presumed return!⁴ Event perverse! 405
Thou never from that hour in Paradise
Found'st either sweet repast, or sound repose;
Such ambush hid among sweet flowers and shades
Waited with hellish rancor imminent⁵
To intercept thy way, or send thee back 410
Despoiled of innocence, of faith, of bliss.
For now, and since first break of dawn, the fiend,
Mere serpent in appearance, forth was come,
And on his quest, where likeliest he might find
The only two of mankind, but in them 415
The whole included race, his purposed prey.
In bower and field he sought, where any tuft
Of grove or garden-plot more pleasant lay,
Their tendance⁶ or plantation for delight;
By fountain or by shady rivulet 420
He sought them both, but wished his hap might find
Eve separate; he wished, but not with hope
Of what so seldom chanced; when to his wish,
Beyond his hope, Eve separate he spies,
Veiled in a cloud of fragrance, where she stood, 425
Half spied, so thick the roses bushing round
About her glowed, oft stooping to support
Each flower of slender stalk, whose head though gay
Carnation, purple, azure, or specked with gold,
Hung drooping unsustained, them she upstays 430
Gently with myrtle band, mindless the while
Herself, though fairest unsupported flower,
From her best prop so far, and storm so nigh.⁷
Nearer he drew, and many a walk traversed
Of stateliest covert, cedar, pine, or palm; 435
Then voluble⁸ and bold, now hid, now seen
Among thick-woven arborets⁹ and flowers
Embordered on each bank, the hand of Eve:
Spot more delicious than those gardens feigned
Or of revived Adonis,¹ or renowned 440
Alcinous, host of old Laertes' son,
Or that, not mystic, where the sapient king²
Held dalliance with his fair Egyptian spouse.
Much he the place admired, the person more.
As one who long in populous city pent, 445

4. "Much deceived" carries over; Eve was "much deceived of" (about) her "presumed return."
5. Threatening.
6. Object of their tending.
7. The conceit of the flower-gatherer who is herself gathered is repeated here from IV.270, where it was applied to Proserpina.
8. Rolling (a Latinism).
9. Bushes. "Hand": handiwork.
1. The garden of Adonis was a heavenly bower where Venus' lover was supposed still to lie in secret, recovering from his wound received on earth (Venus would not allow him to die). Alcinous was king of the Phaeacians. His garden, visited by Odysseus ("old Laertes' son"), is described in the *Odyssey*.
2. Solomon; his "fair Egyptian spouse" is Pharaoh's daughter: Milton is referring to the Song of Solomon vi.2. The fact that it is "not mystic" (i.e., not mythical) distinguishes the Scriptural garden from the "feigned" (line 439) ones of classical legend.

Where houses thick and sewers annoy[3] the air,
Forth issuing on a summer's morn to breathe
Among the pleasant villages and farms
Adjoined, from each thing met conceives delight,
The smell of grain, or tedded[4] grass, or kine,   450
Or dairy, each rural sight, each rural sound:
If chance with nymphlike step fair virgin pass,[5]
What pleasing seemed, for her now pleases more,
She most, and in her look sums all delight.[6]
Such pleasure took the serpent to behold   455
This flowery plat,[7] the sweet recess of Eve
Thus early, thus alone; her heavenly form
Angelic, but more soft, and feminine,
Her graceful innocence, her every air
Of gesture or least action overawed   460
His malice, and with rapine[8] sweet bereaved
His fierceness of the fierce intent it brought:
That space the evil one abstracted stood
From his own evil, and for the time remained
Stupidly good,[9] of enmity disarmed,   465
Of guile, of hate, of envy, of revenge.
But the hot Hell that always in him burns,
Though in mid Heaven, soon ended his delight,
And tortures him now more, the more he sees
Of pleasure not for him ordained: then soon   470
Fierce hate he recollects, and all his thoughts
Of mischief, gratulating,[1] thus excites:
  "Thoughts, whither have ye led me? with what sweet
Compulsion thus transported to forget
What hither brought us? hate, not love, nor hope   475
Of Paradise for Hell, hope here to taste
Of pleasure, but all pleasure to destroy,
Save what is in destroying;[2] other joy
To me is lost. Then let me not let pass
Occasion which now smiles; behold alone   480
The woman, opportune to all attempts,
Her husband, for I view far round, not nigh,
Whose higher intellectual more I shun,
And strength, of courage haughty, and of limb
Heroic built, though of terrestrial mold;[3]   485
Foe not informidable, exempt from wound,[4]
I not; so much hath Hell debased, and pain

3. Make noisome, befoul.
4. Tossed and drying in the sun.
5. I.e., if it chance that with nymph-like step a fair virgin should pass.
6. I.e., in her look sums up, or epitomizes, all delight.
7. Plot.
8. It is a deliberate paradox that her sweetness can ravish his malice; the word is deliberately overviolent.
9. Without his evil, Satan (like many

wicked people) is quite dull and ordinary. But at the moment he is stunned.
1. Exulting.
2. What brought Satan to Paradise was not hope of pleasure, but the wish to destroy all pleasure except the pleasure of destruction itself.
3. Made of earth.
4. Adam in the state of innocence is invulnerable.

Enfeebled me, to what I was in Heaven.
She fair, divinely fair, fit love for gods,
Not terrible, though terror be in love   490
And beauty, not approached by stronger hate,
Hate stronger, under show of love well feigned,
The way which to her ruin now I tend."[5]
        So spake the enemy of mankind, enclosed
In serpent, inmate bad, and toward Eve   495
Addressed his way, not with indented wave,
Prone on the ground, as since, but on his rear,
Circular base of rising folds, that towered
Fold above fold a surging maze; his head
Crested aloft, and carbuncle[6] his eyes;   500
With burnished neck of verdant gold, erect
Amidst his circling spires,[7] that on the grass
Floated redundant. Pleasing was his shape,
And lovely; never since of serpent kind
Lovelier, not those that in Illyria changed   505
Hermione and Cadmus,[8] or the god
In Epidaurus;[9] nor to which transformed
Ammonian Jove, or Capitoline was seen,
He with Olympias, this with her who bore
Scipio, the height of Rome.[1] With tract oblique   510
At first, as one who sought access, but feared
To interrupt, sidelong he works his way.
As when a ship by skillful steersman wrought
Nigh river's mouth or foreland, where the wind
Veers oft, as oft so steers, and shifts her sail: 515
So varied he, and of his tortuous train
Curled many a wanton wreath in sight of Eve,
To lure her eye: she busied heard the sound
Of rustling leaves, but minded not, as used
To such disport before her through the field,   520
From every beast, more duteous at her call,
Than at Circean call the herd disguised.[2]
He bolder now, uncalled before her stood:
But as in gaze admiring; oft he bowed
His turret crest, and sleek enameled neck,   525
Fawning, and licked the ground whereon she trod.
His gentle dumb expression turned at length

5. I.e., love and beauty are terrible un-less counteracted by hate—as they are being counteracted in Satan, to the ruin of Eve.
6. Deep red, inflamed.
7. Coils. "Redundant": abundantly, to excess.
8. Ovid tells how Cadmus and Harmonia (Milton's "Hermione") were changed to serpents after they retired (in despair at the misfortunes of their children) to Illyria.
9. Aesculapius, god of medicine, had a temple at Epidaurus, from which he

sometimes emerged in the form of a serpent.
1. Jupiter Ammon ("Ammonian Jove"), in the form of a snake, was said to have consorted with Olympias to beget Alexander the Great; and in the same way, the Jupiter of the Roman capitol (Jove "Capitoline") was thought to have begotten Scipio Africanus, the savior and leader ("height") of Rome.
2. Circe, who enchanted men into the shape of swine, was attended by an obedient herd in the *Odyssey*.

The eye of Eve to mark his play: he, glad
Of her attention gained, with serpent tongue
Organic, or impulse of vocal air,[3]   530
His fraudulent temptation thus began.
    "Wonder not, sovereign mistress, if perhaps
Thou canst, who art sole wonder; much less arm
Thy looks, the heaven of mildness, with disdain,
Displeased that I approach thee thus, and gaze   535
Insatiate, I thus single, nor have feared
Thy awful brow, more awful thus retired.
Fairest resemblance of thy Maker fair,
Thee all things living gaze on, all things thine
By gift, and thy celestial beauty adore   540
With ravishment beheld, there best beheld
Where universally admired: but here
In this enclosure wild, these beasts among,
Beholders rude, and shallow to discern
Half what in thee is fair, one man except,   545
Who sees thee?[4] (and what is one?) who shouldst be seen
A goddess among gods, adored and served
By angels numberless, thy daily train."
    So glozed[5] the tempter, and his proem tuned;
Into the heart of Eve his words made way,   550
Though at the voice much marveling: at length,
Not unamazed, she thus in answer spake.
    "What may this mean? Language of man pronounced
By tongue of brute, and human sense expressed?
The first at least of these I thought denied   555
To beasts, whom God on their creation-day
Created mute to all articulate sound;
The latter I demur,[6] for in their looks
Much reason, and in their actions oft appears.
Thee, serpent, subtlest beast of all the field   560
I knew, but not with human voice endued:[7]
Redouble then this miracle, and say,
How cam'st thou speakable of mute,[8] and how
To me so friendly grown above the rest
Of brutal kind, that daily are in sight?   565
Say, for such wonder claims attention due."
    To whom the guileful tempter thus replied:
"Empress of this fair world, resplendent Eve!
Easy to me it is to tell thee all
What thou command'st and right thou shouldst be obeyed: 570
I was at first as other beasts that graze
The trodden herb, of abject thoughts and low,

---

3. I.e., Satan either used the actual tongue of the serpent or himself impressed the air with speech.
4. The beasts cannot see the beauty of Eve's soul, only Adam can. Satan's entire speech is couched in the extravagant phrases of the Petrarchan love conven-tion.
5. Flattered. "Proem": introduction.
6. I.e., as to whether rational sense was denied to brutes, I am doubtful.
7. Endowed.
8. To have speech after being dumb.

As was my food, nor aught but food discerned
Or sex, and apprehended nothing high:
Till on a day, roving the field, I chanced   575
A goodly tree far distant to behold
Loaden with fruit of fairest colors mixed,
Ruddy and gold; I nearer drew to gaze;
When from the boughs a savory odor blown,
Grateful to appetite, more pleased my sense   580
Than smell of sweetest fennel,[9] or the teats
Of ewe or goat dropping with milk at even,
Unsucked of lamb or kid, that tend their play.
To satisfy the sharp desire I had
Of tasting those fair apples, I resolved   585
Not to defer: hunger and thirst at once,
Powerful persuaders, quickened at the scent
Of that alluring fruit, urged me so keen.
About the mossy trunk I wound me soon,
For, high from ground, the branches would require   590
Thy utmost reach, or Adam's: round the tree
All other beasts that saw, with like desire
Longing and envying stood, but could not reach.
Amid the tree now got, where plenty hung
Tempting so nigh, to pluck and eat my fill   595
I spared not;[1] for such pleasure till that hour
At feed or fountain never had I found.
Sated at length, ere long I might perceive
Strange alteration in me, to degree
Of reason in my inward powers, and speech   600
Wanted not long, though to this shape retained.[2]
Thenceforth to speculations high or deep
I turned my thoughts, and with capacious mind
Considered all things visible in Heaven,
Or Earth, or middle, all things fair and good: 605
But all that fair and good in thy divine
Semblance, and in thy beauty's heavenly ray
United I beheld: no fair[3] to thine
Equivalent or second, which compelled
Me thus, though importune perhaps, to come   610
And gaze, and worship thee of right declared
Sovereign of creatures, universal dame."
     So talked the spirited[4] sly snake: and Eve
Yet more amazed, unwary thus replied:
     "Serpent, thy overpraising leaves in doubt   615
The virtue of that fruit, in thee first proved.
But say, where grows the tree, from hence how far?

---

9. Milton learned probably from Pliny,
the natural historian, that serpents were
fond of fennel; popular superstition had
it that they drank the milk of sheep and
goats.
1. Refrained not.

2. His inward powers, his mental constitution and gift of speech, were
changed; but he retained his exterior
shape as before.
3. Beauty.
4. Possessed by a spirit, inspired.

For many are the trees of God that grow
In Paradise, and various, yet unknown
To us; in such abundance lies our choice,   620
As leaves a greater store of fruit untouched,
Still hanging incorruptible, till men
Grow up to their provision, and more hands
Help to disburden Nature of her bearth."[5]
    To whom the wily adder, blithe and glad: 625
"Empress, the way is ready, and not long,
Beyond a row of myrtles, on a flat,
Fast by a fountain, one small thicket past
Of blowing[6] myrrh and balm: if thou accept
My conduct, I can bring thee thither soon."   630
    "Lead then," said Eve. He leading swiftly rolled
In tangles, and made intricate seem straight,
To mischief swift.[7] Hope elevates, and joy
Brightens his crest; as when a wandering fire
Compact of unctuous vapor,[8] which the night   635
Condenses, and the cold environs round,
Kindled through agitation to a flame
(Which oft, they say, some evil spirit attends),
Hovering and blazing with delusive light,
Misleads th' amazed night-wanderer from his way   640
To bogs and mires, and oft through pond or pool,
There swallowed up and lost, from succor far:
So glistered the dire snake, and into fraud
Led Eve our credulous mother, to the tree
Of prohibition,[9] root of all our woe: 645
Which when she saw, thus to her guide she spake:
    "Serpent, we might have spared our coming hither,
Fruitless to me, though fruit be here to excess,
The credit of whose virtue rest with thee;[1]
Wondrous indeed, if cause of such effects!   650
But of this tree we may not taste nor touch:
God so commanded, and left that command
Sole daughter of his voice;[2] the rest, we live
Law to ourselves; our reason is our law."
    To whom the Tempter guilefully replied: 655
"Indeed? Hath God then said that of the fruit
Of all these garden trees ye shall not eat,
Yet lords declared of all in Earth or air?"
    To whom thus Eve, yet sinless: "Of the fruit
Of each tree in the garden we may eat,   660
But of the fruit of this fair tree amidst

---

5. So spelled to pun on the idea of trees bearing fruit and thus in a way giving birth to young.
6. Blooming.
7. Milton's physical descriptions of the serpent often have distinct moral overtones, as here.
8. Composed of oily vapor; Milton's theory of the *ignis fatuus*, or will-o'-the-wisp, is strikingly material and "scientific."
9. Prohibited tree (a Hebraism).
1. I.e., you must remain the only evidence of the fruit's power.
2. His one injunction (a literal Hebraism). "The rest": in everything else.

The garden, God hath said, 'Ye shall not eat
Thereof, nor shall ye touch it, lest ye die.' "
　　She scarce had said, though brief, when now more bold,
The tempter, but with show of zeal and love　　　　　　665
To man, and indignation at his wrong,
New part puts on, and as to passion moved,
Fluctuates disturbed, yet comely, and in act
Raised,³ as of some great matter to begin.
As when of old some orator renowned　　　　　　　　670
In Athens or free Rome, where eloquence
Flourished, since mute, to some great cause addressed,
Stood in himself collected, while each part,
Motion, each act, won audience ere the tongue,
Sometimes in height began, as no delay　　　　　　　675
Of preface brooking,⁴ through his zeal of right.
So standing, moving, or to height upgrown
The tempter all impassioned thus began:
　　"O sacred, wise, and wisdom-giving plant,
Mother of science!⁵ now I feel thy power　　　　　　680
Within me clear, not only to discern
Things in their causes, but to trace the ways
Of highest agents, deemed however wise.
Queen of this universe! do not believe
Those rigid threats of death. Ye shall not die;　　　685
How should ye? By the fruit? it gives you life
To knowledge;⁶ by the Threatener? look on me,
Me who have touched and tasted, yet both live,
And life more perfect have attained than Fate
Meant me, by venturing higher than my lot.　　　　　690
Shall that be shut to man, which to the beast
Is open? Or will God incense his ire
For such a petty trespass, and not praise
Rather your dauntless virtue, whom the pain
Of death denounced, whatever thing death be,　　　695
Deterred not from achieving what might lead
To happier life, knowledge of good and evil?
Of good, how just!⁷ Of evil, if what is evil
Be real, why not known, since easier shunned?
God therefore cannot hurt ye, and be just;　　　　　700
Not just, not God; not feared then, nor obeyed:
Your fear itself of death removes the fear.⁸
Why then was this forbid? Why but to awe,
Why but to keep ye low and ignorant,
His worshipers? He knows that in the day　　　　　　705
Ye eat thereof, your eyes that seem so clear,

3. Poised in posture.
4. The orator, as if too much moved to be bothered with a preface, bursts into the middle of his speech.
5. Knowledge.
6. Life in addition to knowledge; or, life with which to enlarge your knowledge.
7. I.e., how just to have knowledge of good!
8. I.e., your fear of death removes your fear of God; since if God inflicts death, he will not be just and hence not God. The serpent's sophism is visible.

Yet are but dim, shall perfectly be then
Opened and cleared, and ye shall be as gods,
Knowing both good and evil, as they know.
That ye should be as gods, since I as man,   710
Internal man,[9] is but proportion meet,
I, of brute, human; ye, of human, gods.
So ye shall die perhaps, by putting off
Human, to put on gods: death to be wished,
Though threatened, which no worse than this can bring.   715
And what are gods that man may not become
As they, participating[1] godlike food?
The gods are first, and that advantage use
On our belief, that all from them proceeds.
I question it; for this fair Earth I see,   720
Warmed by the sun, producing every kind,
Them nothing: If they all things,[2] who enclosed
Knowledge of good and evil in this tree,
That whoso eats thereof forthwith attains
Wisdom without their leave? And wherein lies   725
Th' offense, that man should thus attain to know?
What can your knowledge hurt him, or this tree
Impart against his will if all be his?
Or is it envy, and can envy dwell
In heavenly breasts?[3] These, these, and many more   730
Causes import your need of this fair fruit.
Goddess humane,[4] reach then, and freely taste!"
    He ended, and his words, replete with guile,
Into her heart too easy entrance won:
Fixed on the fruit she gazed, which to behold   735
Might tempt alone, and in her ears the sound
Yet rung of his persuasive words, impregned[5]
With reason, to her seeming, and with truth;
Meanwhile the hour of noon drew on, and waked
An eager appetite, raised by the smell   740
So savory of that fruit, which with desire,
Inclinable now grown to touch or taste,
Solicited her longing eye;[6] yet first
Pausing a while, thus to herself she mused:
    "Great are thy virtues, doubtless, best of fruits,   745
Though kept from man, and worthy to be admired,
Whose taste, too long forborn, at first essay
Gave elocution to the mute, and taught
The tongue not made for speech to speak thy praise:
Thy praise he also who forbids thy use,   750

9. Man in intellectual powers.
1. Sharing.
2. The verb "produced" is understood.
Satan is telling now, not about "God,"
but "the gods."
3. Adapted from Virgil, *Aeneid* I.15.
"Import": imply, suggest.

4. Not so much "human goddess" (a
Satanic paradox) as "kindly," "gracious" goddess.
5. Impregnated.
6. The five senses of Eve—sight, hearing, smell, taste, and touch—are all
solicited by the fruit.

Conceals not from us,[7] naming thee the Tree
Of Knowledge, knowledge both of good and evil;
Forbids us then to taste; but his forbidding
Commends thee more, while it infers the good
By thee communicated, and our want: 755
For good unknown, sure is not had, or had
And yet unknown, is as not had at all.[8]
In plain then, what forbids he but to know?
Forbids us good, forbids us to be wise!
Such prohibitions bind not. But if Death   760
Bind us with after-bands, what profits then
Our inward freedom? In the day we eat
Of this fair fruit, our doom is, we shall die.
How dies the serpent? He hath eaten and lives,
And knows, and speaks, and reasons, and discerns,   765
Irrational till then. For us alone
Was death invented? Or to us denied
This intellectual food, for beasts reserved?
For beasts it seems: yet that one beast which first
Hath tasted, envies not, but brings with joy   770
The good befallen him, author unsuspect,[9]
Friendly to man, far from deceit or guile.
What fear I then, rather what know to fear[1]
Under this ignorance of good and evil,
Of God or death, of law or penalty?   775
Here grows the cure of all, this fruit divine,
Fair to the eye, inviting to the taste,
Of virtue[2] to make wise: what hinders then
To reach, and feed at once both body and mind?"
  So saying, her rash hand in evil hour,   780
Forth reaching to the fruit, she plucked, she eat.[3]
Earth felt the wound, and Nature from her seat[4]
Sighing through all her works gave signs of woe,
That all was lost. Back to the thicket slunk
The guilty serpent, and well might, for Eve   785
Intent now wholly on her taste, naught else
Regarded; such delight till then, as seemed,
In fruit she never tasted, whether true
Or fancied so, through expectation high
Of knowledge; nor was godhead from her thought.[5]   790
Greedily she engorged without restraint,
And knew not eating death:[6] satiate at length,
And heightened as with wine, jocund and boon,[7]

---

7. God himself, by naming it, has called
attention to the tree's magic powers.
8. An unknown good is like no good at
all. "In plain": i.e., in plain language.
9. A witness beyond suspicion.
1. In her ignorance, Eve does not really
know what to fear and what not to
fear.
2. Power.
3. In the 17th century, an accepted

past tense of "eat."
4. Wherever Nature is hidden, in the
heart of things, she sighs.
5. She expected to achieve godhead immediately.
6. A grim pun. She is eating death and
does not know it; but death is eating
her too. Compare "eating cares" (*L'Allegro*, line 135).
7. Joyous and liberal.

Thus to herself she pleasingly began:
   "O sovereign, virtuous, precious of all trees   795
In Paradise! of operation blest
To sapience,[8] hitherto obscured, infamed,
And thy fair fruit let hang, as to no end
Created; but henceforth my early care,
Not without song each morning, and due praise   800
Shall tend thee, and the fertile burden ease
Of thy full branches offered free to all;
Till dieted by thee I grow mature
In knowledge, as the gods who all things know;
Though others[9] envy what they cannot give: 805
For had the gift been theirs, it had not here
Thus grown. Experience, next to thee I owe,
Best guide; not following thee I had remained
In ignorance; thou open'st Wisdom's way,
And giv'st access, though secret she retire.   810
And I perhaps am secret; Heaven is high,
High and remote to see from thence distinct
Each thing on Earth; and other care perhaps
May have diverted from continual watch
Our great Forbidder,[1] safe with all his spies   815
About him. But to Adam in what sort[2]
Shall I appear? Shall I to him make known
As yet my change, and give him to partake
Full happiness with me, or rather not,
But keep the odds[3] of knowledge in my power   820
Without copartner? so to add what wants
In female sex, the more to draw his love,
And render me more equal, and perhaps,
A thing not undesirable, sometime
Superior: for, inferior, who is free?[4]   825
This may be well: but what if God have seen
And death ensue? Then I shall be no more,
And Adam, wedded to another Eve,
Shall live with her enjoying, I extinct;
A death to think. Confirmed then I resolve,   830
Adam shall share with me in bliss or woe:
So dear I love him, that with him all deaths
I could endure, without him live no life."[5]
   So saying, from the tree her step she turned,
But first low reverence done,[6] as to the power   835
That dwelt within, whose presence had infused

8. To the point of wisdom, but also for wise people. "Infamed": without fame, but also, defamed.
9. The gods, i.e., other gods. In saying that God did not give the tree, Eve is merely echoing a lesson learned from the serpent.
1. Now that Eve has fallen, God is a "great Forbidder," and all his gifts in Paradise are forgotten.
2. Guise.
3. Balance.
4. Eve's fatal foolishness implies that the only person in the world who can ever be free is an absolute tyrant.
5. Her affection is not unlike Satan's (IV.374–385) in its destructiveness.
6. Eve's first physical act after falling is idolatry.

Into the plant sciental[7] sap, derived
From nectar, drink of gods. Adam the while
Waiting desirous her return, had wove
Of choicest flowers a garland to adorn   840
Her tresses, and her rural labors crown,
As reapers oft are wont their harvest queen.
Great joy he promised to his thoughts, and new
Solace in her return, so long delayed:
Yet oft his heart, divine[8] of something ill,   845
Misgave him; he the faltering measure[9] felt;
And forth to meet her went, the way she took
That morn when first they parted. By the Tree
Of Knowledge he must pass; there he her met,
Scarce from the tree returning; in her hand   850
A bough of fairest fruit that downy smiled,
New gathered, and ambrosial smell diffused.
To him she hastened, in her face excuse
Came prologue, and apology to prompt,[1]
Which with bland words at will she thus addressed: 855
    "Hast thou not wondered, Adam, at my stay?
Thee I have missed, and thought it long, deprived
Thy presence, agony of love till now
Not felt, nor shall be twice; for never more
Mean I to try, what rash untried I sought,   860
The pain of absence from thy sight. But strange
Hath been the cause, and wonderful to hear:
This tree is not as we are told, a tree
Of danger tasted,[2] nor to evil unknown
Opening the way, but of divine effect   865
To open eyes, and make them gods who taste;
And hath been tasted such. The serpent wise,
Or not restrained as we, or not obeying,
Hath eaten of the fruit, and is become,
Not dead, as we are threatened, but thenceforth   870
Endued with human voice and human sense,
Reasoning to admiration,[3] and with me
Persuasively hath so prevailed, that I
Have also tasted, and have also found
Th' effects to correspond, opener mine eyes   875
Dim erst, dilated spirits, ampler heart,
And growing up to godhead;[4] which for thee
Chiefly I sought, without thee can despise.
For bliss, as thou hast part, to me is bliss,
Tedious, unshared with thee, and odious soon.   880
Thou therefore also taste, that equal lot

---

7. Knowledge-giving.
8. Foreboding, suspicious.
9. I.e., of his pulse.
1. Her face had an excuse in it, as prologue to an apology which followed after.

2. If tasted.
3. Admirably. "Persuasively": by persuasion.
4. Everything that Eve says she feels is what Satan has told her she will feel.

May join us, equal joy, as equal love;
Lest, thou not tasting, different degree[5]
Disjoin us, and I then too late renounce
Deity for thee, when Fate will not permit."[6]   885
   Thus Eve with countenance blithe her story told;
But in her cheek distemper[7] flushing glowed.
On th' other side, Adam, soon as he heard
The fatal trespass done by Eve, amazed,
Astonied[8] stood and blank, while horror chill   890
Ran through his veins, and all his joints relaxed;
From his slack hand the garland wreathed for Eve
Down dropped, and all the faded roses shed.
Speechless he stood and pale, till thus at length
First to himself he inward silence broke: 895
   "O fairest of creation, last and best
Of all God's works, creature in whom excelled
Whatever can to sight or thought be formed,
Holy, divine, good, amiable, or sweet!
How art thou lost, how on a sudden lost,   900
Defaced, deflowered, and now to death devote?[9]
Rather how hast thou yielded to transgress
The strict forbiddance, how to violate
The sacred fruit forbidden! Some cursèd fraud
Of enemy hath beguiled thee, yet unknown,[1]   905
And me with thee hath ruined, for with thee
Certain my resolution is to die.
How can I live without thee, how forgo
Thy sweet converse and love so dearly joined,
To live again in these wild woods forlorn?[2]   910
Should God create another Eve, and I
Another rib afford, yet loss of thee
Would never from my heart; no, no! I feel
The link of nature draw me: flesh of flesh,
Bone of my bone thou art, and from thy state   915
Mine never shall be parted, bliss or woe."
   So having said, as one from sad dismay
Recomforted, and after thoughts disturbed
Submitting to what seemed remediless,
Thus in calm mood his words to Eve he turned: 920
   "Bold deed thou hast presumed, adventurous Eve
And peril great provoked, who thus hath dared
Had it been only coveting to eye
That sacred fruit, sacred[3] to abstinence,
Much more to taste it, under ban to touch.   925

5. Differing rank in the hierarchy of creatures.
6. Contrast Eve's logic when she is alone (lines 817–825).
7. The proportion of Eve's humors—which, in the state of innocence, gave her perfect health—has been disturbed, and she is running a fever.
8. Astonished, perhaps even "petrified." "Blank": empty of mind.
9. Doomed.
1. "Yet unknown" modifies "enemy."
2. Without Eve, Paradise itself is wild and forlorn.
3. Devoted.

But past who can recall, or done undo?
Not God omnipotent, nor Fate! Yet so
Perhaps thou shalt not die, perhaps the fact[4]
Is not so heinous now, foretasted fruit,
Profaned first by the serpent, by him first   930
Made common and unhallowed ere our taste,
Nor yet on him found deadly; he yet lives,
Lives, as thou saidst, and gains to live as man
Higher degree of life: inducement strong
To us, as likely, tasting, to attain   935
Proportional ascent, which cannot be
But to be gods, or angels, demigods.[5]
Nor can I think that God, Creator wise,
Though threatening, will in earnest so destroy
Us his prime creatures, dignified so high,   940
Set over all his works, which in our fall,
For us created, needs with us must fail,
Dependent made; so God shall uncreate,
Be frustrate, do, undo, and labor lose;
Not well conceived of God,[6] who, though his power 945
Creation could repeat, yet would be loath
Us to abolish, lest the adversary
Triumph and say: 'Fickle their state whom God
Most favors; who can please him long? Me first
He ruined, now mankind; whom will he next?'   950
Matter of scorn, not to be given the foe.
However, I with thee have fixed my lot,
Certain to undergo like doom: if death
Consort with thee, death is to me as life;
So forcible within my heart I feel   955
The bond of nature draw me to my own,
My own in thee, for what thou art is mine;
Our state cannot be severed; we are one,
One flesh; to lose thee were to lose myself."

     So Adam, and thus Eve to him replied: 960
"O glorious trial of exceeding love,
Illustrious evidence, example high!
Engaging me to emulate; but short
Of thy perfection, how shall I attain,
Adam? from whose dear side I boast me sprung,   965
And gladly of our union hear thee speak,
One heart, one soul in both; whereof good proof
This day affords, declaring thee resolved,
Rather than death or aught than death more dread
Shall separate us, linked in love so dear,   970
To undergo with me one guilt, one crime,
If any be, of tasting this fair fruit;

---

4. Act.
5. Note how Adam agrees first in Eve's harmless errors about the serpent, then in her sinful ambition to achieve

a higher form of life.
6. I.e., not a proper conception of God (as making his actions dependent on those of an inferior).

Whose virtue (for of good still good proceeds,
Direct, or by occasion[7]) hath presented
This happy trial of thy love, which else   975
So eminently never had been known.
Were it I thought death menaced would ensue[8]
This my attempt, I would sustain alone
The worst, and not persuade thee, rather die
Deserted, than oblige[9] thee with a fact   980
Pernicious to thy peace, chiefly assured
Remarkably so late of thy so true,
So faithful love unequaled;[1] but I feel
Far otherwise th' event;[2] not death, but life
Augmented, opened eyes, new hopes, new joys,   985
Taste so divine, that what of sweet before
Hath touched my sense, flat seems to this, and harsh.
On my experience, Adam, freely taste,
And fear of death deliver to the winds."
　　So saying, she embraced him, and for joy   990
Tenderly wept, much won that he his love
Had so ennobled, as of choice to incur
Divine displeasure for her sake, or death.
In recompense (for such compliance bad
Such recompense best merits), from the bough   995
She gave him of that fair enticing fruit
With liberal hand; he scrupled not to eat,
Against his better knowledge, not deceived,
But fondly overcome with female charm.[3]
Earth trembled from her entrails, as again   1000
In pangs, and Nature gave a second groan,
Sky lowered, and muttering thunder, some sad drops
Wept at completing of the mortal sin
Original; while Adam took no thought,
Eating his fill, nor Eve to iterate   1005
Her former trespass feared, the more to soothe
Him with her loved society; that now
As with new wine intoxicated both,
They swim in mirth, and fancy that they feel
Divinity within them breeding wings   1010
Wherewith to scorn the Earth. But that false fruit
Far other operation first displayed,
Carnal desire inflaming; he on Eve
Began to cast lascivious eyes, she him
As wantonly repaid; in lust they burn,   1015
Till Adam thus 'gan Eve to dalliance move:
　　"Eve, now I see thou art exact[4] of taste,

7. Indirectly.
8. Result from.
9. Render liable, involve.
1. Now that she knows Adam loves her, Eve has more misgivings than ever about involving him in her crime.

2. Result (of eating the apple).
3. See I Timothy ii.14: "And Adam was not deceived, but the woman being deceived was in the transgression."
4. Exacting, demanding.

And elegant, of sapience[5] no small part,
Since to each meaning savor we apply,
And palate call judicious. I the praise   1020
Yield thee, so well this day thou hast purveyed.[6]
Much pleasure we have lost, while we abstained
From this delightful fruit, nor known till now
True relish, tasting; if such pleasure be
In things to us forbidden, it might be wished,   1025
For this one tree had been forbidden ten.
But come; so well refreshed, now let us play,
As meet is, after such delicious fare;
For never did thy beauty, since the day
I saw thee first and wedded thee, adorned   1030
With all perfections, so enflame my sense
With ardor to enjoy thee, fairer now
Than ever, bounty of this virtuous tree."
        So said he, and forbore not glance or toy[7]
Of amorous intent, well understood   1035
Of[8] Eve, whose eye darted contagious fire.
Her hand he seized, and to a shady bank,
Thick overhead with verdant roof embowered
He led her, nothing loath; flowers were the couch,
Pansies, and violets, and asphodel,   1040
And hyacinth, Earth's freshest, softest lap.
There they their fill of love and love's disport
Took largely, of their mutual guilt the seal,
The solace of their sin, till dewy sleep
Oppressed them, wearied with their amorous play. 1045
        Soon as the force of that fallacious fruit,
That with exhilarating vapor bland
About their spirits had played, and inmost powers
Made err, was now exhaled, and grosser sleep
Bred of unkindly fumes,[9] with conscious dreams 1050
Encumbered, now had left them, up they rose
As from unrest, and each the other viewing,
Soon found their eyes how opened, and their minds
How darkened. Innocence, that as a veil
Had shadowed them from knowing ill, was gone;   1055
Just confidence, and native righteousness,
And honor from about them, naked left
To guilty Shame; he covered, but his robe
Uncovered more.[1] So rose the Danite strong,
Herculean Samson, from the harlot-lap   1060
Of Philistean Dalilah, and waked
Shorn of his strength;[2] they destitute and bare

5. Wisdom, but the word comes from Latin *sapere*, "to taste," which gives rise, via another etymology, to the word "savor." Adam's sentence plays rather heavily on these two meanings of *sapere*.
6. Provided for us, provisioned us.
7. Caress.
8. By.

9. Unnatural vapors.
1. They were covered with shame, which made them conscious of their nakedness as they had never been before.
2. See the story of Samson and Delilah, Judges xvi.4–20.

Of all their virtue. Silent, and in face
Confounded, long they sat, as strucken mute;
Till Adam, though not less than Eve abashed,   1065
At length gave utterance to these words constrained:
   "O Eve, in evil hour[3] thou didst give ear
To that false worm,[4] of whomsoever taught
To counterfeit man's voice, true in our fall,
False in our promised rising; since our eyes   1070
Opened we find indeed, and find we know
Both good and evil, good lost, and evil got:
Bad fruit of knowledge, if this be to know,
Which leaves us naked thus, of honor void,
Of innocence, of faith, of purity,   1075
Our wonted ornaments now soiled and stained,
And in our faces evident the signs
Of foul concupiscence; whence evil store,[5]
Even shame, the last of evils; of the first
Be sure then.[6] How shall I behold the face   1080
Henceforth of God or angel, erst with joy
And rapture so oft beheld? Those heavenly shapes
Will dazzle now this earthly[7] with their blaze
Insufferably bright. O might I here
In solitude live savage, in some glade   1085
Obscured, where highest woods, impenetrable
To star or sunlight, spread their umbrage broad,
And brown[8] as evening! Cover me, ye pines,
Ye cedars, with innumerable boughs
Hide me, where I may never see them more![9]   1090
But let us now, as in bad plight, devise
What best may for the present serve to hide
The parts of each from other, that seem most
To shame obnoxious,[1] and unseemliest seen;
Some tree whose broad smooth leaves together sewed,   1095
And girded on our loins, may cover round
Those middle parts, that this newcomer, Shame,
There sit not, and reproach us as unclean."
   So counseled he, and both together went
Into the thickest wood; there soon they chose   1100
The figtree,[2] not that kind for fruit renowned,
But such as at this day, to Indians known,
In Malabar or Deccan[3] spreads her arms

---

3. Even in his misery, Adam cannot resist the word-play on Eve-evil.
4. Serpent, with a connotation of disgust. "Of": by.
5. A store of evil.
6. I.e., since we now feel shame, the last and worst of evils, we shall soon experience the first and lesser ones.
7. The noun "nature" or "vision" is understood.
8. Dark.
9. Cf. Revelation vi.16: "And said to the mountains and rocks, Fall on us, and hide us from the face of him that sitteth on the throne, and from the wrath of the Lamb."
1. Vulnerable, liable.
2. The banyan, or Indian fig. It has, in fact, small leaves, but Milton's knowledge of it came from Gerard's *Herball*, where all the details of lines 1104-10 may be found.
3. Sections of southern India.

Branching so broad and long, that in the ground
The bended twigs take root, and daughters grow   1105
About the mother tree, a pillared shade
High overarched, and echoing walks between;
There oft the Indian herdsman, shunning heat,
Shelters in cool, and tends his pasturing herds
At loopholes cut through thickest shade. Those leaves   1110
They gathered, broad as Amazonian targe,[4]
And with what skill they had, together sewed,
To gird their waist; vain covering, if to hide
Their guilt and dreaded shame! O how unlike
To that first naked glory! Such of late   1115
Columbus found th' American, so girt
With feathered cincture,[5] naked else and wild
Among the trees on isles and woody shores.
Thus fenced, and, as they thought, their shame in part
Covered, but not at rest or ease of mind,   1120
They sat them down to weep; nor only tears
Rained at their eyes, but high winds worse within
Began to rise, high passions, anger, hate,
Mistrust, suspicion, discord, and shook sore
Their inward state of mind, calm region once   1125
And full of peace, now tossed and turbulent:
For Understanding ruled not, and the Will
Heard not her lore, both in subjection now
To sensual Appetite, who, from beneath
Usurping over sovereign Reason, claimed   1130
Superior sway.[6] From thus distempered breast,
Adam, estranged in look and altered style,
Speech intermitted thus to Eve renewed:
   "Would thou hadst hearkened to my words, and stayed
With me, as I besought thee, when that strange   1135
Desire of wandering, this unhappy morn,
I know not whence possessed thee! we had then
Remained still happy, not as now, despoiled
Of all our good, shamed, naked, miserable.
Let none henceforth seek needless cause to approve[7]   1140
The faith they owe; when earnestly they seek
Such proof, conclude, they then begin to fail."
   To whom, soon moved with touch of blame, thus Eve:
"What words have passed thy lips, Adam severe?
Imput'st thou that to my default, or will   1145
Of wandering, as thou call'st it, which who knows
But might as ill have happened, thou being by,
Or to thyself perhaps? Hadst thou been there,
Or here th' attempt, thou couldst not have discerned

4. Shield. The Amazons. mythical female warriors, carried large crescent-shaped shields.
5. Belt.
6. The psychology of the Fall is made explicit here. The higher faculties of reason, represented by the brain, are in subjection to the lower faculties of appetite, represented by sensuality. Moreover, Adam has lost his superiority over Eve.
7. Test. prove. "Owe": own.

Fraud in the serpent, speaking as he spake;   1150
No ground of enmity between us known,
Why he should mean me ill, or seek to harm?
Was I to have never parted from thy side?
As good have grown there still a lifeless rib.
Being as I am, why didst not thou, the head,[8]   1155
Command me absolutely not to go,
Going into such danger, as thou saidst?
Too facile[9] then, thou didst not much gainsay,
Nay, didst permit, approve, and fair dismiss.
Hadst thou been firm and fixed in thy dissent,   1160
Neither had I transgressed, nor thou with me."

    To whom, then first incensed, Adam replied:
"Is this the love, is this the recompense
Of mine to thee, ingrateful Eve, expressed
Immutable[1] when thou were lost, not I,   1165
Who might have lived and joyed immortal bliss,
Yet willingly chose rather death with thee?
And am I now upbraided as the cause
Of thy transgressing? not enough severe,
It seems, in thy restraint! What could I more?   1170
I warned thee, I admonished thee, foretold
The danger, and the lurking enemy
That lay in wait; beyond this had been force,
And force upon free will hath here no place.
But confidence then bore thee on, secure   1175
Either to meet no danger, or to find
Matter of glorious trial; and perhaps
I also erred in overmuch admiring
What seemed in thee so perfect, that I thought
No evil durst attempt thee! but I rue   1180
That error now, which is become my crime,
And thou th' accuser. Thus it shall befall
Him who, to worth in women overtrusting,
Lets her will rule; restraint she will not brook,[2]
And, left to herself, if evil thence ensue,   1185
She first his weak indulgence will accuse."

    Thus they in mutual accusation spent
The fruitless hours, but neither self-condemning;
And of their vain contést appeared no end.

8. Head of the family, but also the rational director, as the head is to the
rest of the body. Cf. I Corinthians xi.3,
"the head of the woman is the man."

9. Easy, permissive.
1. Shown to be unchangeable.
2. Accept.

From Book X

Summary When it is known in Heaven that man has fallen, God sends the Son to pass judgment on the sinners. He receives the confession of Adam and Eve and passes sentence on the sinners—cursing the serpent, condemning Eve to the pains of childbirth, and Adam to those of daily labor; but in mercy he clothes the human couple, both outwardly with the skins of animals and inwardly with his righteousness. Meanwhile Sin and Death, sitting by Hell-gate, feel new strength, and pass across Chaos, leaving a great bridge behind them. On their way, they meet their parent, Satan, returning in triumph. Satan reappears in Pandemonium, and describes to the assembly the success of his venture, but instead of the expected applause is received with a vast hiss—he and all the other devils have been transformed to snakes, in which shape they are tormented with humiliating delusions.

Sin and Death now invest the earth; but God prophesies their ultimate defeat. Now the earth and the elements are rearranged, to replace the previous temperate climate with extremes of heat and cold; and discord enters the animal kingdom too, where hitherto all the creatures have dwelt in peace.

[Consequences of the Fall]

<pre>
                          * * * Thus began
Outrage from lifeless things; but Discord, first
Daughter of Sin, among th' irrational,
Death introduced through fierce antipathy:[1]
Beast now with beast 'gan war, and fowl with fowl,
And fish with fish: to graze the herb[2] all leaving,
Devoured each other; nor stood much in awe
Of man, but fled him, or with countenance grim
Glared on him passing. These were from without
The growing miseries, which Adam saw   715
Already in part, though hid in gloomiest shade,
To sorrow abandoned, but worse felt within,
And in a troubled sea of passion tossed,
Thus to disburden sought with sad complaint:
    "O miserable of happy![3] Is this the end   720
Of this new glorious world, and me so late
The glory of that glory? who now, become
Accursed of blessed, hide me from the face
Of God, whom to behold was then my height
Of happiness! Yet well, if here would end   725
The misery; I deserved it, and would bear
My own deservings; but this will not serve.
</pre>

---

1. "Discord" is the subject of the sentence, "Death" the object. "Th' irrational" are the beasts.

2. Grass.

3. I.e., change, to misery from happiness.

All that I eat or drink, or shall beget,
Is propagated curse.[4] O voice, once heard
Delightfully, 'Increase and multiply,'   730
Now death to hear! for what can I increase
Or multiply, but curses on my head?
Who, of all ages to succeed, but, feeling
The evil on him brought by me, will curse
My head: "Ill fare our ancestor impure!   735
For this we may thank Adam!' but his thanks
Shall be the execration;[5] so, besides
Mine own that bide upon me, all from me
Shall with a fierce reflux on me redound,
On me, as on their natural center, light   740
Heavy, though in their place.[6] O fleeting joys
Of Paradise, dear bought with lasting woes!
Did I request thee, Maker, from my clay
To mold me man? Did I solicit thee
From darkness to promote me, or here place   745
In this delicious garden? As my will
Concurred not to my being, it were but right
And equal[7] to reduce me to my dust,
Desirous to resign and render back
All I received, unable to perform   750
Thy terms too hard, by which I was to hold
The good I sought not. To the loss of that,
Sufficient penalty, why hast thou added
The sense of endless woes? Inexplicable
Thy justice seems; yet, to say truth, too late   755
I thus contest; then should have been refused
Those terms whatever, when they were proposed.
Thou[8] didst accept them; wilt thou enjoy the good,
Then cavil the conditions? And though God
Made thee without thy leave, what if thy son   760
Prove disobedient, and reproved, retort,
'Wherefore didst thou beget me? I sought it not.'
Wouldst thou admit for his contempt of thee
That proud excuse? Yet him not thy election,[9]
But natural necessity begot.   765
God made thee of choice his own, and of his own
To serve him; thy reward was of his grace;
Thy punishment then justly is at his will.
Be it so, for I submit; his doom is fair,
That dust I am and shall to dust return.   770
O welcome hour whenever! Why delays

---

4. Whatever prolongs life extends the curse.
5. The only thanks for Adam will be mankind's curses.
6. Adam plays with the notion that natural objects have weight only as long as they are above their "natural" positions; so all curses will flow natu-

rally to him, but they will still be heavy when they have lighted.
7. Just.
8. "Thou," which referred to God in lines 753 and 755, here shifts as Adam suddenly addresses himself.
9. Choice.

His hand to execute what his decree
Fixed on this day? Why do I overlive?
Why am I mocked with death, and lengthened out
To deathless pain? How gladly would I meet   775
Mortality, my sentence, and be earth
Insensible! how glad would lay me down
As in my mother's lap![1] There I should rest
And sleep secure; his dreadful voice no more
Would thunder in my ears; no fear of worse   780
To me and to my offspring would torment me
With cruel expectation. Yet one doubt
Pursues me still, lest all I cannot die;[2]
Lest that pure breath of life, the spirit of man
Which God inspired, cannot together perish   785
With this corporeal clod; then, in the grave,
Or in some other dismal place, who knows
But I shall die a living death? O thought
Horrid, if true! Yet why? It was but breath
Of life that sinned; what dies but what had life   790
And sin? the body properly hath neither.
All of me then shall die: let this appease
The doubt, since human reach no further knows.[3]
For though the Lord of all be infinite,
Is his wrath also? Be it, man is not so,   795
But mortal doomed. How can he exercise
Wrath without end on man whom death must end?
Can he make deathless death? That were to make
Strange contradiction, which to God himself
Impossible is held, as argument   800
Of weakness, not of power.[4] Will he draw out,
For anger's sake, finite to infinite
In punished man, to satisfy his rigor
Satisfied never? That were to extend
His sentence beyond dust and Nature's law;   805
By which all causes else according still
To the reception of their matter act,
Not to th' extent of their own sphere.[5] But say
That death be not one stroke, as I supposed,
Bereaving[6] sense, but endless misery   810
From this day onward, which I feel begun
Both in me and without me, and so last
To perpetuity—Ay me! that fear
Comes thundering back with dreadful revolution

---

1. Adam's lamentations owe a good deal to the Book of Job iii.
2. Direct from Horace, *Odes* III.xxx.6: *non omnis moriar.*
3. Adam convinces himself, as Milton was apparently convinced, that both soul and body die at death; the corollary is that they are resurrected together.
4. For a man in a state of nature, Adam displays a fine command of medieval theology. He holds that if God contradicts himself, it is a sign of weakness.
5. A maxim of 17th-century physics; all agents (other than God) act according to the capacity of the object, not to the extent of their inherent powers.
6. Taking away.

On my defenseless head! Both death and I   815
Am found eternal, and incorporate[7] both:
Nor I on my part single; in me all
Posterity stands cursed. Fair patrimony
That I must leave ye, sons! O, were I able
To waste it all myself, and leave ye none!   820
So disinherited, how would ye bless
Me, now your curse! Ah, why should all mankind
For one man's fault thus guiltless be condemned,
If guiltless? But from me what can proceed,
But all corrupt, both mind and will depraved,   825
Not to do only, but to will the same
With me?[8] How can they then acquitted stand
In sight of God? Him, after all disputes,
Forced[9] I absolve. All my evasions vain
And reasonings, though through mazes, lead me still   830
But to my own conviction: first and last
On me, me only, as the source and spring
Of all corruption, all the blame lights due;[1]
So might the wrath! Fond[2] wish! Couldst thou support
That burden, heavier than the earth to bear;   835
Than all the world much heavier, though divided
With that bad woman? Thus, what thou desir'st,
And what thou fear'st, alike destroys all hope
Of refuge, and concludes thee miserable[3]
Beyond all past example and future;   840
To Satan only like, both crime and doom.
O Conscience! into what abyss of fears
And horrors hast thou driven me; out of which
I find no way, from deep to deeper plunged!"

   Thus Adam to himself lamented loud   845
Through the still night, not now, as ere man fell,
Wholesome and cool and mild, but with black air
Accompanied, with damps and dreadful gloom;
Which to his evil conscience represented
All things with double terror. On the ground   850
Outstretched he lay, on the cold ground, and oft
Cursed his creation; Death as oft accused
Of tardy execution, since denounced
The day of his offense. "Why comes not Death,"
Said he, "with one thrice-acceptable stroke   855
To end me? Shall Truth fail to keep her word,
Justice divine not hasten to be just?
But Death comes not at call; Justice divine

---

7. In the same body. Adam is appalled
to find that he has become death incarnate; the grammar ("both dead and
I / Am") displays his shock.
8. Not only will men repeat Adam's
sin; their will is corrupted and they
will *want* to be fallen like Adam.
9. Perforce.

1. In this discovery that he alone must
accept the guilt of mankind, Adam has
chosen crucially to be like Christ and
unlike Satan—at the very moment
when he feels exactly the opposite.
2. Foolish.
3. Shows thee to be miserable.

Mends not her slowest pace for prayers or cries.
O woods, O fountains, hillocks, dales, and bowers!   860
With other echo late I taught your shades
To answer, and resound far other song."
Whom thus afflicted when sad Eve beheld,
Desolate where she sat, approaching nigh,
Soft words to his fierce passion she essayed;   865
But her with stern regard he thus repelled:
    "Out of my sight, thou serpent! that name best
Befits thee, with him leagued, thyself as false
And hateful: nothing wants, but that thy shape,
Like his, and color serpentine, may show   870
Thy inward fraud, to warn all creatures from thee
Henceforth; lest that too heavenly form, pretended[4]
To hellish falsehood, snare them. But for thee
I had persisted happy, had not thy pride
And wandering vanity, when least was safe,   875
Rejected my forewarning, and disdained
Not to be trusted, longing to be seen
Though by the devil himself, him overweening[5]
To overreach, but, with the serpent meeting,
Fooled and beguiled; by him thou, I by thee,   880
To trust thee from my side, imagined wise,
Constant, mature, proof against all assaults;
And understood not all was but a show
Rather than solid virtue, all but a rib
Crooked by nature—bent, as now appears,   885
More to the part sinister[6]—from me drawn;
Well if thrown out, as supernumerary
To my just number found![7] Oh, why did God,
Creator wise, that peopled highest Heaven
With spirits masculine, create at last   890
This novelty on earth, this fair defect
Of nature, and not fill the world at once
With men, as angels, without feminine;
Or find some other way to generate
Mankind?[8] This mischief had not then befallen,   895
And more that shall befall—innumerable
Disturbances on earth through female snares,
And strait conjunction[9] with this sex. For either
He never shall find out fit mate, but such
As some misfortune brings him, or mistake;   900
Or whom he wishes most shall seldom gain,
Through her perverseness, but shall see her gained
By a far worse, or, if she love, withheld

4. Serving as a mask.
5. Overconfident.
6. "On the left hand," as in Latin; also "unlucky."
7. Since men visibly have twelve ribs on both sides, it was supposed that Adam originally had thirteen ribs on his left side, so that he could give up one and still have twelve, an even ("just") number.
8. Ancient traditions of antifeminist thought lie behind these ungenerous speculations.
9. Close connections, i.e., matrimony.

By parents, or his happiest choice too late
Shall meet, already linked and wedlock-bound   905
To a fell[1] adversary, his hate or shame:
Which infinite calamity shall cause
To human life, and household peace confound."
     He added not, and from her turned; but Eve,
Not so repulsed, with tears that ceased not flowing,   910
And tresses all disordered, at his feet
Fell humble, and, embracing them, besought
His peace, and thus proceeded in her plaint:
     "Forsake me not thus, Adam! witness Heaven
What love sincere and reverence in my heart   915
I bear thee, and unweeting[2] have offended,
Unhappily deceived! Thy suppliant[3]
I beg, and clasp thy knees; bereave me not,
Whereon I live, thy gentle looks, thy aid,
Thy counsel in this uttermost distress,   920
My only strength and stay: forlorn of thee,
Whither shall I betake me, where subsist?
While yet we live, scarce one short hour perhaps,
Between us two let there be peace; both joining,
As joined in injuries, one enmity   925
Against a foe by doom express assigned us,
That cruel serpent. On me exercise not
Thy hatred for this misery befallen;
On me already lost, me than thyself
More miserable. Both have sinned, but thou   930
Against God only; I against God and thee,
And to the place of judgement will return,
There with my cries importune Heaven, that all
The sentence, from thy head removed, may light
On me, sole cause to thee of all this woe,   935
Me, me only, just object of his ire."[4]
     She ended weeping; and her lowly plight,
Immovable till peace obtained from fault
Acknowledged and deplored,[5] in Adam wrought
Commiseration. Soon his heart relented   940
Towards her, his life so late and sole delight,
Now at his feet submissive in distress,
Creature so fair his reconcilement seeking,
His counsel, whom she had displeased, his aid;
As one disarmed, his anger all he lost,   945
And thus with peaceful words upraised her soon:
     "Unwary, and too desirous, as before,
So now, of what thou know'st not,[6] who desir'st

1. Bitter.
2. Unintentionally.
3. As a suppliant to thee.
4. Eve too now offers to accept the blame for the Fall; and the moral regeneration of man is henceforth possible.
5. Her suppliant posture ("lowly plight") would not be changed till she obtained forgiveness ("peace") from her admission of her fault, and repentance for it.
6. Adam's remark is rueful but affectionate; Eve is still looking for more trouble than she knows how to handle.

The punishment all on thyself! Alas!
Bear thine own first, ill able to sustain   950
His full wrath, whose thou feel'st as yet least part,[7]
And my displeasure bear'st so ill. If prayers
Could alter high decrees, I to that place
Would speed before thee, and be louder heard,
That on my head all might be visited,   955
Thy frailty and infirmer sex forgiven,
To me committed, and by me exposed.
But rise; let us no more contend, nor blame
Each other, blamed enough elsewhere, but strive
In offices of love, how we may lighten   960
Each other's burden in our share of woe;
Since this day's death denounced, if aught I see,
Will prove no sudden, but a slow-paced evil,
A long day's dying to augment our pain,
And to our seed (O hapless seed!) derived."[8]   965

7. I.e., ill able to sustain the full wrath   have felt only the least part.
of God—of whose wrath, so far, you   8. Handed down.

Summary   In her despair, Eve proposes to Adam that they refrain from having children, or commit suicide, in order to frustrate Sin and Death, but Adam persuades her to a better resolution. Book X ends with Adam and Eve reconciled to one another, partially reconciled to their fate, and praying forgiveness for their sins.

Book XI. Summary   The prayers of Adam and Eve prove acceptable to God. But while man may now hope for ultimate redemption, he may no longer dwell in Paradise; and Michael, the warrior archangel, is dispatched to explain the sentence, offer some hope for the future, and dismiss mankind from the happy garden. Adam is at first overcome with grief; but the angel encourages him, and while Eve is put in a trance, Adam is raised to the peak of a high hill and shown in a vision the future of the human race as far as the flood of Noah.

From Book XII

Summary   Continuing his instruction of Adam, Michael relates the history of the world from the time of Noah through the coming of Christ, whose ascent into Heaven and triumph over Death after the Crucifixion he describes. The Church which Christ and his apostles leave behind, however, will not be free from troubles caused by greedy and ambitious men; it will require reform. But the reformers will be persecuted and their road will be hard, until at length, in the Last Judgment, Satan and his kingdom will be dissolved, and new heavens and new earths created to exist in eternal bliss.

[The Departure from Eden]

So spake th' archangel Michaël; then paused,
As at the world's great period;[1] and our sire,
Replete with joy and wonder, thus replied:
"O goodness infinite, goodness immense!
That all this good of evil shall produce,   470
And evil turn to good; more wonderful
Than that which by creation first brought forth
Light out of darkness! Full of doubt I stand,
Whether I should repent me now of sin
By me done and occasioned, or rejoice   475
Much more that much more good thereof shall spring;
To God more glory, more good will to men
From God, and over wrath grace shall abound.
But say, if our Deliverer up to Heaven
Must reascend, what will betide the few,   480
His faithful, left among th' unfaithful herd,
The enemies of truth? Who then shall guide
His people, who defend? Will they not deal
Worse with his followers than with him they dealt?"
"Be sure they will," said th' angel; "but from Heaven   485
He to his own a Comforter will send,
The promise of the Father, who shall dwell,
His Spirit, within them, and the law of faith,
Working through love, upon their hearts shall write,
To guide them in all truth, and also arm   490
With spiritual armor, able to resist
Satan's assaults, and quench his fiery darts,
What[2] man can do against them, not afraid,
Though to the death; against such cruelties
With inward consolations recompensed,   495
And oft supported so as shall amaze
Their proudest persecutors.[3] For the Spirit,
Poured first on his Apostles, whom he sends
To evangelize the nations, then on all
Baptized, shall them with wondrous gifts endue[4]   500
To speak all tongues, and do all miracles,
As did their Lord before them. Thus they win
Great numbers of each nation to receive
With joy the tidings brought from Heaven: at length,
Their ministry performed, and race well run,   505
Their doctrine and their story written left,

---

1. Conclusion.
2. As much as.
3. Milton briefly summarizes here the
story of the Christian martyrs.
4. Endow.

They die; but in their room, as they forewarn,
Wolves shall succeed for teachers, grievous wolves,[5]
Who all the sacred mysteries of Heaven
To their own vile advantages shall turn   510
Of lucre and ambition, and the truth
With superstitions and traditions taint,
Left only in those written records pure,
Though not but by the Spirit understood.
Then shall they seek to avail themselves of names,   515
Places, and titles,[6] and with these to join
Secular power, though feigning still to act
By spiritual; to themselves appropriating
The Spirit of God, promised alike and given
To all believers; and, from that pretense,   520
Spiritual laws by carnal[7] power shall force
On every conscience, laws which none shall find
Left them enrolled, or what the Spirit within
Shall on the heart engrave.[8] What will they then,
But force the Spirit of Grace itself, and bind   525
His consort, Liberty? what but unbuild
His living temples,[9] built by faith to stand,
Their own faith, not another's? for, on Earth,
Who against faith and conscience can be heard
Infallible? Yet many will presume: 530
Whence heavy persecution shall arise
On all who in the worship persevere
Of Spirit and Truth; the rest, far greater part,
Will deem in outward rites and specious[1] forms
Religion satisfied; Truth shall retire   535
Bestuck with slanderous darts, and works of faith
Rarely be found. So shall the world go on,
To good malignant, to bad men benign,
Under her own weight groaning,[2] till the day
Appear of respiration[3] to the just   540
And vengeance to the wicked, at return
Of Him so lately promised to thy aid,
The Woman's Seed,[4] obscurely then foretold,
Now amplier known thy Savior and thy Lord;
Last in the clouds from Heaven to be revealed   545

5. To profit by religion was for Milton the lowest of crimes; he felt that priests should serve without pay. In addition, he regularly uses the wolf as an emblem of the Papacy; see *Lycidas*, line 128.
6. The name "Catholic," the place of court preacher, and the title of "bishop," for example.
7. Fleshly, i.e., secular, of this world.
8. I.e., the wolves will enforce laws which have no ancient authority or appeal to the conscience.
9. Individual believers. Milton's strict Protestant individualism speaks throughout this passage of protest against persecution.
1. Fair-seeming.
2. This passage, which in isolation appears to offer some justification for viewing the end of the poem as essentially pessimistic, should be set against Adam's earlier statement (lines 470–78) that the Fall was really a fortunate event, and gave rise to more good than evil.
3. Relief, refreshment.
4. Christ, whose Second Coming is here foreseen.

In glory of the Father, to dissolve
Satan with his perverted world; then raise
From the conflagrant mass,[5] purged and refined,
New Heavens, new Earth, ages of endless date
Founded in righteousness and peace and love,   550
To bring forth fruits, joy and eternal bliss."
    He ended, and thus Adam last replied:
"How soon hath thy prediction, seer blest,
Measured this transient world, the race of Time,
Till Time stand fixed! Beyond is all abyss,   555
Eternity, whose end no eye can reach.
Greatly instructed I shall hence depart,
Greatly in peace of thought, and have my fill
Of knowledge, what[6] this vessel can contain;
Beyond which was my folly to aspire.   560
Henceforth I learn that to obey is best,
And love with fear the only God, to walk
As in his presence, ever to observe
His providence, and on him sole depend,
Merciful over all his works, with good   565
Still overcoming evil, and by small
Accomplishing great things, by things deemed weak
Subverting worldly-strong, and worldly-wise
By simply meek; that suffering for truth's sake
Is fortitude to highest victory,   570
And to the faithful, death the gate of life;
Taught this by his example whom I now
Acknowledge my Redeemer ever blest."
    To whom thus also th' angel last replied:
"This having learned, thou hast attained the sum[7]   575
Of wisdom; hope no higher, though all the stars
Thou knew'st by name,[8] and all th' ethereal powers,
All secrets of the deep, all Nature's works,
Or works of God in heaven, air, earth, or sea,
And all the riches of this world enjoy'dst,   580
And all the rule, one empire. Only add
Deeds to thy knowledge answerable;[9] add faith,
Add virtue, patience, temperance; add love,
By name to come called charity, the soul
Of all the rest: then wilt thou not be loath   585
To leave this Paradise, but shalt possess
A Paradise within thee, happier far.
Let us descend now, therefore, from this top
Of speculation;[1] for the hour precise
Exacts[2] our parting hence; and, see! the guards,   590
By me encamped on yonder hill, expect

---

5. The burning world.
6. As much as.
7. Total.
8. Michael glances back at the rebuke administered by Raphael in Book VIII

to Adam's astronomical curiosity.
9. Corresponding.
1. Hill of vision.
2. Requires.

Their motion, at whose front[3] a flaming sword,
In signal of remove, waves fiercely round.
We may no longer stay. Go, waken Eve;
Her also I with gentle dreams have calmed,   595
Portending good, and all her spirits composed
To meek submission: thou, at season fit,
Let her with thee partake what thou hast heard;
Chiefly what may concern her faith to know,
The great deliverance by her seed to come   600
(For by the Woman's Seed) on all mankind;
That ye may live, which will be many days,[4]
Both in one faith unanimous; though sad
With cause for evils past, yet much more cheered
With meditation on the happy end."   605
   He ended, and they both descend the hill.
Descended, Adam to the bower where Eve
Lay sleeping ran before, but found her waked;
And thus with words not sad she him received:
   "Whence thou return'st and whither went'st, I know;   610
For God is also in sleep, and dreams advise,
Which he hath sent propitious, some great good
Presaging, since, with sorrow and heart's distress
Wearied, I fell asleep. But now lead on;
In me is no delay; with thee to go   615
Is to stay here; without thee here to stay
Is to go hence unwilling; thou to me
Art all things under Heaven, all places thou,
Who for my willful crime art banished hence.
This further consolation yet secure   620
I carry hence: though all by me is lost,
Such favor I unworthy am vouchsafed,
By me the Promised Seed shall all restore."
   So spake our mother Eve; and Adam heard
Well pleased, but answered not; for now too nigh   625
Th' archangel stood, and from the other hill
To their fixed station, all in bright array,
The cherubim descended; on the ground
Gliding meteorous, as evening mist
Risen from a river o'er the marish[5] glides,   630
And gathers ground fast at the laborer's heel
Homeward returning. High in front advanced,
The brandished sword of God before them blazed,
Fierce as a comet; which with torrid heat,
And vapor as the Libyan air adust,[6]   635
Began to parch that temperate clime; whereat
In either hand the hastening angel caught
Our lingering parents, and to th' eastern gate
Led them direct, and down the cliff as fast

3. Before whom.
4. Adam lived to be 930 (Genesis v.5).
5. Marsh (an old form).
6. The scorched climate of Libya, in North Africa, was proverbial.

To the subjected[7] plain; then disappeared.   640
They, looking back, all th' eastern side beheld
Of Paradise, so late their happy seat,[8]
Waved over by that flaming brand;[9] the gate
With dreadful faces thronged and fiery arms.
Some natural tears they dropped, but wiped them soon;   645
The world was all before them, where to choose
Their place of rest, and Providence their guide.
They, hand in hand, with wandering steps and slow,
Through Eden took their solitary way.

1662–67   1667, 1674

7. Low-lying.   9. "Sword," with the extra overtone
8. Home.   of "burning."

Samson Agonistes The figure of Samson, as one finds him in the
Book of Judges, does not seem at first glance particularly adaptable to the
elevated mode of tragedy. He is a promiscuous, violent fellow, given to riddles and practical jokes—the last of which puts a gruesome end to himself
and his enemies. His long shaggy hair, his name (Samson, in Hebrew
Shimshun), which includes the Hebrew word for "sun," and a persistent
association with fire, all suggest a connection with some primitive solar
cult, such as can be seen behind the equivalent figure of Hercules. A burly,
truculent, and not-very-clever giant, in short; one would not easily see in
him the dignified and purifying figure of the tragic sufferer.

But though Samson's rude vigor and vengeful nature appealed to Milton
on one level; the story of his fall through the treachery of a woman on
another; and the fact of his blindness on still another; there was a last
level on which he could in fact be represented as the type and precursor
of the Christian hero. He suffered for his people; in the very pit of despair
he was rendered suddenly capable of God's revivifying grace; long exercised
in physical warfare, he gave evidence in his last heroic action of having
learned the principles of spiritual warfare.

Milton approached the idea of tragedy with hesitations and misgivings;
for a Puritan of his day, the very idea of a stage play was instinct with
moral danger. But the example of the Greeks and of his much-admired
Tasso prevailed; he wrote a "closet drama," a drama intended not for the
actual stage but for reading. As a play, Dr. Johnson proclaimed it deficient;
it had, he said, a beginning and an end but no proper middle. Modern
criticism, dissenting as usual from Dr. Johnson and stimulated as usual by
his judgment, has exercised itself to find in Samson's spiritual progression
during the successive visits of Manoa, Dalila, and Harapha ample psychological movement to sustain both action and interest. This is beyond doubt
a useful exercise; but it is useful also to reflect that Samson acts in the end
by direction of an inward spirit, a private, intimate inspiration; and that
for the coming of this spirit there is no sufficient preparation. "The wind
bloweth where it listeth, and thou hearest the sound thereof, but canst not
tell whence it cometh, and whither it goeth: so is every one that is born
of the Spirit" (John iii.8).

The story of Samson is told in Judges xiii-xvi. "Agonistes" means "in struggle" or "under trial"; it is a term derived from the Greek word for a wrestler and suggests not only that Samson is an athlete of the Lord but that he will wrestle with the pillars.

Samson Agonistes

A DRAMATIC POEM

Of That Sort of Dramatic Poem Which Is Called Tragedy

Tragedy, as it was anciently composed, hath been ever held the gravest, moralest, and most profitable of all other poems: therefore said by Aristotle to be of power, by raising pity and fear, or terror, to purge the mind of those and such-like passions, that is, to temper and reduce them to just measure with a kind of delight, stirred up by reading or seeing those passions well imitated.[1] Nor is Nature wanting in her own effects to make good his assertion; for so, in physic, things of melancholic hue and quality are used against melancholy, sour against sour, salt to remove salt humors.[2] Hence philosophers and other gravest writers, as Cicero, Plutarch, and others, frequently cite out of tragic poets, both to adorn and illustrate their discourse. The Apostle Paul himself thought it not unworthy to insert a verse of Euripides into the text of Holy Scripture, I Cor. xv. 33; and Paraeus, commenting on the Revelation, divides the whole book, as a tragedy, into acts, distinguished each by a chorus of heavenly harpings and song between.[3] Heretofore men in highest dignity have labored not a little to be thought able to compose a tragedy. Of that honor Dionysius the elder was no less ambitious than before of his attaining to the tyranny.[4] Augustus Caesar also had begun his *Ajax*, but unable to please his own judgment with what he had begun, left it unfinished. Seneca the philosopher is by some thought the author of those tragedies (at least the best of them) that go under that name. Gregory Nazianzen, a Father of the Church, thought it not unbeseeming the sanctity of his person to write a tragedy, which he entitled *Christ Suffering*.[5] This is mentioned to vindicate tragedy from the small esteem, or rather infamy, which in the account of many it undergoes at this

1. Milton is paraphrasing Aristotle's *Poetics* 6.
2. Italian critics like Minturno had applied notions of homeopathic medicine (like cures like) to tragedy; the idea is not Aristotelean. "Physic": medicine.
3. David Paraeus, a 17th-century German Calvinist.
4. Dionysius (4th century B.C.) won a prize at Athens for tragedy, after becoming tyrant of Syracuse.
5. Seneca the philosopher was indeed the author of tragedies; but Gregory Nazianzen, a Greek ecclesiastic of the 4th century, did not write the tragedy *Christ Suffering*, which scholarly opinion of Milton's day attributed to him.

day, with other common interludes—happening through the poet's error of intermixing comic stuff with tragic sadness and gravity, or introducing trivial and vulgar persons—which by all judicious hath been counted absurd, and brought in without discretion, corruptly to gratify the people. And, though ancient tragedy use no prologue,[6] yet using sometimes, in case of self-defense or explanation, that which Martial calls an epistle,[7] in behalf of this tragedy, coming forth after the ancient manner, much different from what among us passes for best, thus much beforehand may be epistled, that chorus is here introduced after the Greek manner, not ancient only, but modern, and still in use among the Italians.[8] In the modeling therefore of this poem, with good reason, the ancients and Italians are rather followed, as of much more authority and fame. The measure of verse used in the chorus is of all sorts, called by the Greeks *Monostrophic*,[9] or rather *Apolelymenon*,[1] without regard had to strophe, antistrophe, or epode, which were a kind of stanzas framed only for the music, then used with the chorus that sung; not essential to the poem, and therefore not material; or, being divided into stanzas or pauses, they may be called *alloeostropha*.[2] Division into act and scene, referring chiefly to the stage (to which this work never was intended), is here omitted.[3]

It suffices if the whole drama be found not produced [4] beyond the fifth act. Of the style and uniformity, and that commonly called the plot, whether intricate or explicit—which is nothing indeed but such economy, or disposition of the fable, as may stand best with verisimilitude and decorum[5]—they only will best judge who are not unacquainted with Aeschylus, Sophocles, and Euripides, the three tragic poets unequaled yet by any, and the best rule to all who endeavor to write tragedy. The circumscription of time wherein the whole drama begins and ends is, according to ancient rule and best example, within the space of twenty-four hours.[6]

6. Prologues and epilogues were frequent on the Restoration stage; Milton sets himself apart from contemporary styles. ·
7. Martial, the Roman epigrammatist of the 1st century A.D., prefixed an epistle to his book of epigrams.
8. Tasso's tragedy *Re Torrismondo* was modeled closely on classical examples.
9. Not divided into strophe, antistrophe, and epode.
1. Free from stanzaic patterns altogether.
2. With various forms of strophe, irregular.
3. The reader who cares will not find Milton's drama hard to divide into the

customary five acts, each ending with a chorus: Act I (Samson and chorus) lines 1–325; II (Samson and Manoa) 326–709; III (Samson and Dalila) 710–1060; IV (Samson and Harapha) 1061–1296; V (Catastrophe) 1297–the end.
4. Led along, drawn out.
5. Decorum, for a Renaissance writer, is not simply solemn or sedate behavior but the use of appropriate and suitable style, depending on speaker, subject, setting, genre, and so on.
6. The so-called "unity of time," limiting dramatic action to 24 hours, was derived from Aristotle's *Poetics* by the Renaissance critic Castelvetro.

The Argument

Samson, made captive, blind, and now in the prison at Gaza,[7] there to labor as in a common workhouse, on a festival day, in the general cessation from labor, comes forth into the open air, to a place nigh, somewhat retired, there to sit a while and bemoan his condition. Where he happens at length to be visited by certain friends and equals of his tribe, which make the chorus, who seek to comfort him what they can; then by his old father, Manoa, who endeavors the like, and withal tells him his purpose to procure his liberty by ransom; lastly, that this feast was proclaimed by the Philistines as a day of thanksgiving for their deliverance from the hands of Samson—which yet more troubles him. Manoa then departs to prosecute his endeavor with the Philistian lords for Samson's redemption; who, in the meanwhile, is visited by other persons, and, lastly, by a public officer to require his coming to the feast before the lords and people, to play or show his strength in their presence. He at first refuses, dismissing the public officer with absolute denial to come; at length persuaded inwardly that this was from God, he yields to go along with him, who came now the second time with great threatenings to fetch him. The chorus yet remaining on the place, Manoa returns full of joyful hope to procure ere long his son's deliverance: in the midst of which discourse an Ebrew[8] comes in haste, confusedly at first, and afterwards more distinctly, relating the catastrophe—what Samson had done to the Philistines, and by accident to himself; wherewith the tragedy ends.

The Persons

SAMSON	HARAPHA *of Gath*
MANOA, *the father of* Samson	*Public Officer*
	Messenger
DALILA, *his wife*	*Chorus of Danites*[9]

The Scene, before the Prison in Gaza.

SAMSON. A little onward lend thy guiding hand
  To these dark steps, a little further on;
  For yonder bank hath choice of sun or shade.
  There I am wont to sit, when any chance
  Relieves me from my task of servile toil,   5
  Daily in the common prison else enjoined me,[1]

---

7. The Philistines, warlike and commercial, lived in Southwest Palestine (the southern coast of modern Israel between, approximately, Tel Aviv and Gaza) in five great cities splendidly named Ashdod, Eshkol, Gaza, Gath, and Ashkalon. They were a wholly urban people as against the largely rural Israelites.

8. Milton follows an old English tradition in transliterating the name "Ebrew."

9. Hebrews of the tribe of Dan, Samson's tribe. When the land of Canaan was divided among the twelve tribes, they received the southern portion, adjacent to the Philistines.

1. The metrical pattern of this line, with its many unaccented syllables and careful placement of the strong word "else," merits careful study.

Where I, a prisoner chained, scarce freely draw
The air, imprisoned also, close and damp,
Unwholesome draught. But here I feel amends—
The breath of heaven fresh blowing, pure and sweet,   10
With day-spring[2] born; here leave me to respire.
This day a solemn feast the people hold
To Dagon,[3] their sea-idol, and forbid
Laborious works. Unwillingly this rest
Their superstition yields me; hence, with leave   15
Retiring from the popular noise, I seek
This unfrequented place, to find some ease—
Ease to the body some, none to the mind
From restless thoughts, that, like a deadly swarm
Of hornets armed, no sooner found alone   20
But rush upon me thronging, and present
Times past, what once I was, and what am now.
Oh, wherefore was my birth from Heaven foretold
Twice by an angel,[4] who at last, in sight
Of both my parents, all in flames ascended   25
From off the altar where an offering burned,
As in a fiery column charioting
His godlike presence, and from some great act
Or benefit revealed to Abraham's race?
Why was my breeding ordered and prescribed   30
As of a person separate to God,
Designed for great exploits,[5] if I must die
Betrayed, captived, and both my eyes put out,
Made of my enemies the scorn and gaze,
To grind in brazen fetters under task   35
With this heaven-gifted strength? O glorious strength,
Put to the labor of a beast, debased
Lower than bondslave! Promise was that I
Should Israel from Philistian yoke deliver;
Ask for this great deliverer now, and find him   40
Eyeless in Gaza, at the mill with slaves,
Himself in bonds under Philistian yoke.
Yet stay; let me not rashly call in doubt
Divine prediction. What if all foretold
Had been fulfilled but through mine own default?   45
Whom have I to complain of but myself,
Who this high gift of strength committed to me,
In what part lodged, how easily bereft me,
Under the seal of silence could not keep,[6]

2. Break of day.
3. Dagon's name comes from *dag*, fish, and he seems to have had a fishy shape. His would thus be a marine cult to correspond with that of the many Baals, or land gods of the Philistines. See *Paradise Lost* I.457–66.
4. Before Samson was born an angel foretold that he would begin the delivery of Israel from the Philistines (Judges xiii.5).
5. Samson was a Nazarite, member of an ascetic group specially dedicated to the service of God. See Numbers vi.
6. I.e., who could not keep silent about the high gift of strength committed to me, or about where it was located, or about how easily it could be taken from me.

But weakly to a woman must reveal it, 50
O'ercome with importunity and tears?
O impotence of mind in body strong!
But what is strength without a double share
Of wisdom? Vast, unwieldy, burdensome,
Proudly secure,[7] yet liable to fall 55
By weakest subtleties; not made to rule,
But to subserve where wisdom bears command.
God, when he gave me strength, to show withal,
How slight the gift was, hung it in my hair.
But peace! I must not quarrel with the will 60
Of highest dispensation,[8] which herein
Haply had ends above my reach to know.
Suffices that to me strength is my bane,
And proves the source of all my miseries—
So many, and so huge, that each apart 65
Would ask a life to wail. But, chief of all,
O loss of sight, of thee I most complain!
Blind among enemies! O worse than chains,
Dungeon, or beggary, or decrepit age!
Light, the prime work of God,[9] to me is extinct, 70
And all her various objects of delight
Annulled, which might in part my grief have eased.
Inferior to the vilest now become
Of man or worm, the vilest here excel me:
They creep, yet see; I, dark in light, exposed 75
To daily fraud, contempt, abuse, and wrong,
Within doors, or without, still as a fool,
In power of others, never in my own—
Scarce half I seem to live, dead more than half.
O dark, dark, dark, amid the blaze of noon, 80
Irrecoverably dark, total eclipse
Without all hope of day!
O first-created beam, and thou great Word,
"Let there be light, and light was over all,"
Why am I thus bereaved thy prime decree?[1] 85
The sun to me is dark
And silent[2] as the moon,
When she deserts the night,
Hid in her vacant interlunar cave.[3]
Since light so necessary is to life, 90
And almost life itself, if it be true
That light is in the soul,
She all in every part,[4] why was the sight

---

7. Confident, free from care (Latin, *cura*).
8. Providence.
9. God's first ("prime") act in creating the world was to say "Let there be light" (Genesis i.3), a phrase Milton paraphrases below.
1. I.e., why am I thus deprived of the first-created (and most important) thing?
2. Unperceived.
3. Ancient astronomers supposed that during the daytime the moon hid in a cave.
4. A famous formula of Plotinus (*Ennead* IV.ii.1) describes the soul as "all in all and all in every part."

To such a tender ball as th' eye confined,
So obvious[5] and so easy to be quenched,   95
And not, as feeling, through all parts diffused,
That she might look at will through every pore?
Then had I not been thus exiled from light,
As in the land of darkness, yet in light,
To live a life half dead, a living death,   100
And buried; but, O yet more miserable!
Myself my sepulcher, a moving grave;
Buried, yet not exempt,
By privilege of death and burial,
From worst of other evils, pains, and wrongs;   105
But made hereby obnoxious[6] more
To all the miseries of life,
Life in captivity
Among inhuman foes.
But who are these? for with joint pace I hear   110
The tread of many feet steering this way;
Perhaps my enemies, who come to stare
At my affliction, and perhaps to insult,
Their daily practice to afflict me more.

CHORUS. This, this is he; softly a while;   115
Let us not break in upon him.
O change beyond report, thought, or belief!
See how he lies at random, carelessly diffused,[7]
With languished head unpropped,
As one past hope, abandoned,   120
And by himself given over,
In slavish habit, ill-fitted weeds [8]
O'er-worn and soiled.
Or do my eyes misrepresent? Can this be he,
That heroic, that renowned,   125
Irresistible Samson? whom, unarmed,
No strength of man, or fiercest wild beast, could withstand: [9]
Who tore the lion as the lion tears the kid;
Ran on embattled armies clad in iron,
And, weaponless himself,   130
Made arms ridiculous, useless the forgery[1]
Of brazen shield and spear, the hammered cuirass,
Chalybean-tempered[2] steel, and frock of mail
Adamantean proof;
But safest he who stood aloof,   135
When insupportably[3] his foot advanced,
In scorn of their proud arms and warlike tools,

---

5. Exposed.
6. Vulnerable, subject.
7. Literally, "poured forth," out-stretched.
8. Rags.
9. Judges xiv.5–6 tells the story of Samson ripping apart a lion with his bare hands.

1. Weapons of forged steel, but also fraudulent, exterior protections.
2. The Chalybes lived on the Black Sea and were famous ironworkers. "Adamantean proof": hard as adamant, i.e., diamond.
3. Irresistibly.

Spurned them to death by troops. The bold Ascalonite[4]
Fled from his lion ramp; old warriors turned
Their plated backs under his heel,   140
Or groveling soiled their crested helmets in the dust.
Then with what trivial weapon came to hand,
The jaw of a dead ass, his sword of bone,
A thousand foreskins fell, the flower of Palestine,
In Ramath-lechi, famous to this day; [5]   145
Then by main force pulled up, and on his shoulders bore,
The gates of Azza, post and massy bar,
Up to the hill by Hebron, seat of giants old,
No journey of a Sabbath day, and loaded so,
Like whom the Gentiles feign to bear up Heaven.[6]   150
Which shall I first bewail,
Thy bondage or lost sight,
Prison within prison
Inseparably dark?
Thou art become (O worst imprisonment!)   155
The dungeon of thyself; thy soul
(Which men enjoying sight oft without cause complain),
Imprisoned now indeed,
In real darkness of the body dwells,
Shut up from outward light   160
To incorporate with gloomy night;
For inward light, alas!
Puts forth no visual beam.[7]
O mirror of our fickle state,
Since man on earth unparalleled! [8]   165
The rarer thy example stands,
By how much from the top of wondrous glory,
Strongest of mortal men,
To lowest pitch of abject fortune thou art fallen!
For him I reckon not in high estate   170
Whom long descent of birth,
Or the sphere[9] of fortune, raises;
But thee, whose strength, while virtue was her mate,
Might have subdued the Earth,

4. A man from Ascalon, or Ashkalon, one of the five great Philistine cities. "Lion ramp": a lion in the act of attacking its prey, rampant.
5. On one occasion Samson killed a thousand Philistines (i.e., "foreskins", uncircumcised warriors), using the jawbone of an ass (Judges xv.15–17). Judges xvi.3 tells how Samson, to escape his enemies, picked up and carried off the gates of Gaza (Azza).
6. In Greek (or, as Milton calls it, Gentile) mythology, Atlas supports the heavens. From Gaza to Hebron would be about forty miles—no journey for the day of rest.

7. Renaissance physiologists supposed the eye saw by sending forth a "visual beam" which it directed at various objects.
8. I.e., no such example (has been seen) since man (was) on earth. "Fickle": changeable.
9. "Sphere": wheel. Fortune was described as possessing a wheel which merely by rotating automatically interchanged the highest and lowest social positions. Milton's definition of "high estate" is interior and spiritual; he has no interest in the old "Fall of Princes" theme. In fact, the play exactly reverses that theme.

Universally crowned with highest praises.   175
SAMSON. I hear the sound of words; their sense the air
  Dissolves unjointed ere it reach my ear.
CHORUS. He speaks: let us draw nigh. Matchless in might,
  The glory late of Israel, now the grief!
  We come, thy friends and neighbors not unknown,   180
  From Eshtaol and Zora's fruitful vale,
  To visit or bewail thee; or, if better,
  Counsel or consolation we may bring,
  Salve to thy sores: apt words have power to swage[1]
  The tumors of a troubled mind,   185
  And are as balm to festered wounds.
SAMSON. Your coming, friends, revives me; for I learn
  Now of my own experience, not by talk,
  How counterfeit a coin they are who "friends"
  Bear in their superscription (of the most   190
  I would be understood). In prosperous days
  They swarm, but in adverse withdraw their head,
  Not to be found, though sought. Ye see, O friends,
  How many evils have enclosed me round;
  Yet that which was the worst now least afflicts me,   195
  Blindness; for, had I sight, confused with shame,
  How could I once look up, or heave[2] the head,
  Who, like a foolish pilot, have shipwrecked
  My vessel trusted to me from above,
  Gloriously rigged, and for a word, a tear,   200
  Fool! have divulged the secret gift of God
  To a deceitful woman? Tell me, friends,
  Am I not sung and proverbed for a fool
  In every street? Do they not say, "How well
  Are come upon him his deserts"? Yet why?   205
  Immeasurable strength they might behold
  In me; of wisdom nothing more than mean.[3]
  This with the other should at least have paired;[4]
  These two, proportioned ill, drove me transverse.[5]
CHORUS. Tax not divine disposal. Wisest men   210
  Have erred, and by bad women been deceived;
  And shall again, pretend they ne'er so wise.[6]
  Deject not, then, so overmuch thyself,
  Who hast of sorrow thy full load besides.
  Yet, truth to say, I oft have heard men wonder   215
  Why thou should'st wed Philistian women rather
  Than of thine own tribe fairer, or as fair,
  At least of thy own nation, and as noble.
SAMSON. The first I saw at Timna, and she pleased
  Me, not my parents, that I sought to wed   220

---

1. Assuage.
2. Lift.
3. Average.
4. Been equal.
5. Off the true course.
6. I.e., intend they never so wisely.

The daughter of an infidel.[7] They knew not
That what I motioned[8] was of God; I knew
From intimate impulse, and therefore urged
The marriage on, that, by occasion hence,[9]
I might begin Israel's deliverance—   225
The work to which I was divinely called.
She proving false, the next I took to wife
(O that I never had! fond wish too late!)
Was in the vale of Sorec, Dálila,[1]
That specious monster, my accomplished snare.   230
I thought it lawful from my former act
And the same end, still watching to oppress
Israel's oppressors. Of what now I suffer
She was not the prime cause, but I myself,
Who, vanquished with a peal of words (O weakness!),   235
Gave up my fort of silence to a woman.
CHORUS. In seeking just occasion to provoke
The Philistine, thy country's enemy,
Thou never wast remiss, I bear thee witness;
Yet Israel still serves with all his sons.[2]   240
SAMSON. That fault I take not on me, but transfer
On Israel's governors and heads of tribes,
Who, seeing those great acts which God had done
Singly by me against their conquerors,
Acknowledged not, or not at all considered   245
Deliverance offered. I, on th' other side,
Used no ambition to commend my deeds;[3]
The deeds themselves, though mute, spoke loud the doer.
But they persisted deaf, and would not seem
To count them things worth notice, till at length   250
Their lords, the Philistines, with gathered powers,
Entered Judea seeking me, who then
Safe to the rock of Etham was retired,
Not flying, but forecasting in what place
To set upon them, what advantaged best.   255
Meanwhile the men of Judah, to prevent
The harass of their land, beset me round;
I willingly on some conditions came
Into their hands, and they as gladly yield me
To the uncircumcised[4] a welcome prey,   260
Bound with two cords. But cords to me were threads
Touched with the flame: on their whole host I flew
Unarmed, and with a trivial weapon felled
Their choicest youth; they only lived who fled.[5]

7. Judges xiv.1–4 tells the story of
Samson's first decision to marry outside
his own tribe and nation.
8. Intended.
9. I.e., so that it might provide an occasion for me to begin Israel's deliverance.
1. Judges xvi.4.
2. I.e., Israel and the children of Israel

are still in servitude.
3. I.e., sought for no testimonials to my actions.
4. Foreigners, the people outside the covenant of Abraham.
5. Judges xv.8–17 tells the tale of Samson's single-handed victory, using a "trivial weapon," the jawbone of an ass.

Had Judah that day joined, or one whole tribe,   ₂₆₅
They had by this[6] possessed the towers of Gath,
And lorded over them whom now they serve.
But what more oft, in nations grown corrupt,
And by their vices brought to servitude,
Than to love bondage more than liberty,   ₂₇₀
Bondage with ease than strenuous liberty,[7]
And to despise, or envy, or suspect,
Whom God hath of his special favor raised
As their deliverer? If he aught begin,
How frequent to desert him, and at last   ₂₇₅
To heap ingratitude on worthiest deeds!

CHORUS. Thy words to my remembrance bring
How Succoth and the fort of Penuel
Their great deliverer contemned,
The matchless Gideon, in pursuit   ₂₈₀
Of Madian, and her vanquished kings; [8]
And how ingrateful Ephraim
Had dealt with Jephtha, who by argument,
Not worse than by his shield and spear,
Defended Israel from the Ammonite,   ₂₈₅
Had not his prowess quelled their pride
In that sore battle when so many died
Without reprieve, adjudged to death
For want of well pronouncing *Shibboleth*.[9]

SAMSON. Of such examples add me to the roll.   ₂₉₀
Me easily indeed mine[1] may neglect,
But God's proposed deliverance not so.

CHORUS. Just are the ways of God,
And justifiable to men,
Unless there be who think not God at all.   ₂₉₅
If any be, they walk obscure;
For of such doctrine never was there school,
But the heart of the fool,
And no man therein doctor but himself.[2]
    Yet more there be who doubt his ways not just,
As to his own edicts found contradicting;   ₃₀₀
Then give the reins to wandering thought,
Regardless of his glory's diminution,
Till, by their own perplexities involved,
They ravel [3] more, still less resolved,
But never find self-satisfying solution.   ₃₀₅
As if they would confine th' Interminable,[4]
And tie him to his own prescript,

---

6. By this time.
7. Milton obviously has in mind, not only early Israel, but also contemporary England.
8. Judges viii: Succoth and Penuel refused aid to Gideon when he was pursuing the common foe, and he punished them.

9. Judges xi and xii.
1. My people.
2. Psalm xiv deals with the fool who says in his heart there is no God. "Doctor": teacher.
3. Become entangled.
4. Infinite.

Who made our laws to bind us, not himself,
And hath full right to exempt   310
Whomso it pleases him by choice
From national obstriction,[5] without taint
Of sin, or legal debt;
For with his own laws he can best dispense.
    He would not else, who never wanted means,   315
Nor in respect of the enemy just cause,
To set his people free,
Have prompted this heroic Nazarite,
Against his vow of strictest purity,
To seek in marriage that fallacious bride,   320
Unclean, unchaste.
    Down, Reason, then; at least, vain reasonings down;
Though Reason here aver
That moral verdict quits her of unclean:
Unchaste was subsequent; her stain, not his.[6]   325
But see! here comes thy reverend sire,
With careful step, locks white as down,[7]
Old Manoa: advise [8]
Forthwith how thou ought'st to receive him.

SAMSON. Ay me! another inward grief, awaked   330
    With mention of that name, renews th' assault.

MANOA. Brethren and men of Dan (for such ye seem,
    Though in this uncouth[9] place), if old respect,
As I suppose, towards your once gloried friend,
My son, now captive, hither hath informed[1]   335
Your younger feet, while mine, cast back with age,
Came lagging after, say if he be here.

CHORUS. As signal[2] now in low dejected state
    As erst in highest, behold him where he lies.

MANOA. O miserable change! Is this the man,   340
    That ínvincible Samson, far renowned,
The dread of Israel's foes, who with a strength
Equivalent to angels' walked their streets,
None offering fight; who, single combatant,
Dueled their armies ranked in proud array,   345
Himself an army—now unequal match
To save himself against a coward armed
At one spear's length? O ever-failing trust
In mortal strength! and, oh, what not in man
Deceivable and vain? [3] Nay, what thing good   350

5. Obligation, i.e., the law against marrying Gentiles (Deuteronomy vii.3). The chorus here accepts Samson's argument that God had prompted him inexplicably to marry the woman of Timna.
6. The chorus, having accused the woman of Timna of being unclean (i.e., Gentile and taboo) and unchaste, now admits that since Samson married her at God's instigation she was not unclean to him; and that she was unchaste only after Samson left her. Reason is therefore puzzled.
7. "Careful": full of care; "down": swan's down.
8. Reflect, consider inwardly.
9. Unknown, unfamiliar.
1. Directed.
2. Notable, eminent.
3. I.e., what is there in man that is not deceivable and vain?

Prayed for, but often proves our woe, our bane?
I prayed for children, and thought barrenness
In wedlock a reproach; I gained a son,
And such a son as all men hailed me happy:
Who would be now a father in my stead? 355
Oh, wherefore did God grant me my request,
And as a blessing with such pomp adorned?
Why are his gifts desirable, to tempt
Our earnest prayers, then, given with solemn hand
As graces, draw a scorpion's tail behind? 360
For this did the angel twice descend?[4] for this
Ordained thy nurture holy, as of a plant
Select and sacred? glorious for a while,
The miracle of men; then in an hour
Ensnared, assaulted, overcome, led bound, 365
Thy foes' derision, captive, poor and blind,
Into a dungeon thrust, to work with slaves!
Alas! methinks whom God hath chosen once
To worthiest deeds, if he through frailty err,
He should not so o'erwhelm, and as a thrall 370
Subject him to so foul indignities,
Be it but for honor's sake of former deeds.
SAMSON. Appoint not heavenly disposition,[5] father.
Nothing of all these evils hath befallen me
But justly; I myself have brought them on, 375
Sole author I, sole cause.[6] If aught seem vile,
As vile hath been my folly, who have profaned
The mystery of God, given me under pledge
Of vow, and have betrayed it to a woman,
A Canaanite, my faithless enemy. 380
This well I knew, nor was at all surprised,
But warned by oft experience. Did not she
Of Timna first betray me, and reveal
The secret wrested from me in her height
Of nuptial love professed, carrying it straight 385
To them who had corrupted her, my spies
And rivals?[7] In this other was there found
More faith, who, also in her prime of love,
Spousal embraces, vitiated with gold,
Though offered only, by the scent conceived, 390
Her spurious first-born, treason against me?[8]
Thrice she assayed, with flattering prayers and sighs,
And amorous reproaches, to win from me

4. The angel who announced Samson's
birth was sent a second time, in answer
to Manoa's request, to give instructions
concerning his education and training.
5. I.e., do not presume to control heaven's decisions.
6. Like Adam, *Paradise Lost* X, Samson proves his own resurgent virtue by

accepting responsibility for his own
faults.
7. Samson's first wife, the woman of
Timna, revealed Samson's riddle to his
enemies (Judges xiv.8–19).
8. At the mere scent of gold, Dalila
conceived a bastard ("spurious") offspring for Samson—treason.

My capital secret,[9] in what part my strength
Lay stored, in what part summed, that she might know;   395
Thrice I deluded her, and turned to sport
Her importunity, each time perceiving
How openly and with what impudence
She purposed to betray me, and (which was worse
Than undissembled hate) with what contempt   400
She sought to make me traitor to myself.[1]
Yet, the fourth time, when, mustering all her wiles,
With blandished parleys, feminine assaults,
Tongue-batteries, she surceased[2] not day nor night
To storm me, over-watched and wearied out,   405
At times when men seek most repose and rest,
I yielded, and unlocked her all my heart,
Who, with a grain of manhood well resolved,
Might easily have shook off all her snares;
But foul effeminacy [3] held me yoked   410
Her bondslave. O indignity, O blot
To honor and religion! servile mind
Rewarded well with servile punishment!
The base degree to which I now am fallen,
These rags, this grinding, is not yet so base   415
As was my former servitude, ignoble,
Unmanly, ignominious, infamous,
True slavery; and that blindness worse than this,
That saw not how degenerately I served.
MANOA. I cannot praise thy marriage-choices, son,   420
Rather approved them not; but thou didst plead
Divine impulsion[4] prompting how thou might'st
Find some occasion to infest our foes.
I state not that; this I am sure, our foes
Found soon occasion thereby to make thee   425
Their captive, and their triumph; thou the sooner
Temptation found'st, or over-potent charms,
To violate the sacred trust of silence
Deposited within thee; which to have kept
Tacit was in thy power. True; and thou bear'st   430
Enough, and more, the burden of that fault;
Bitterly hast thou paid, and still art paying,
That rigid score.[5] A worse thing yet remains:
This day the Philistines a popular feast
Here celebrate in Gaza, and proclaim   435
Great pomp, and sacrifice, and praises loud,
To Dagon, as their god who hath delivered
Thee, Samson, bound and blind, into their hands—

9. The secret Dalila learned was of capital importance; also, it involved the hair on Samson's head (*caput*).
1. Judges xvi.5–20.
2. Forbore.
3. "Effeminacy": uxoriousness, over-

fondness, the fault of Adam.
4. Prudent Manoa mistrusts the inner impulse which is Samson's conscience and the first principle of his life. "Infest": attack.
5. Debt.

Them out of thine, who slew'st them many a slain.[6]
So Dagon shall be magnified,[7] and God,   440
Besides whom is no god, compared with idols,
Disglorified, blasphemed, and had in scorn
By th' idolatrous rout amidst their wine;
Which to have come to pass by means of thee,
Samson, of all thy sufferings think the heaviest,   445
Of all reproach the most with shame that ever
Could have befallen thee and thy father's house.
SAMSON. Father, I do acknowledge and confess
  That I this honor, I this pomp, have brought
  To Dagon, and advanced his praises high   450
  Among the heathen round; to God have brought
  Dishonor, obloquy, and oped the mouths
  Of idolists and atheists; have brought scandal
  To Israel, diffidence[8] of God, and doubt
  In feeble hearts, propense[9] enough before   455
  To waver, or fall off and join with idols:
  Which is my chief affliction, shame and sorrow,
  The anguish of my soul, that suffers not
  Mine eye to harbor sleep, or thoughts to rest.
  This only hope relieves me, that the strife   460
  With me hath end. All the contést is now
  'Twixt God and Dagon. Dagon hath presumed,
  Me overthrown, to enter lists[1] with God,
  His deity comparing and preferring
  Before the God of Abraham. He, be sure,   465
  Will not connive,[2] or linger, thus provoked,
  But will arise, and his great name assert.
  Dagon must stoop, and shall ere long receive
  Such a discomfit as shall quite despoil him
  Of all these boasted trophies won on me,   470
  And with confusion blank[3] his worshipers.
MANOA. With cause this hope relieves thee; and these words
  I as a prophecy receive; for God
  (Nothing more certain) will not long defer
  To vindicate the glory of his name   475
  Against all competition, nor will long
  Endure it doubtful whether God be Lord
  Or Dagon. But for thee what shall be done?
  Thou must not in the meanwhile, here forgot,
  Lie in this miserable loathsome plight   480
  Neglected. I already have made way
  To some Philistian lords, with whom to treat
  About thy ransom. Well they may by this [4]
  Have satisfied their utmost of revenge,

6. I.e., who slew many a one for them.
7. Glorified.
8. Mistrust.
9. Inclined.
1. Jousting courts as in medieval tourneys.
2. Hesitate, palter.
3. Confound, turn pale.
4. By this time.

By pains and slaveries, worse than death, inflicted   485
On thee, who now no more canst do them harm.
SAMSON. Spare that proposal, father; spare the trouble
  Of that solicitation. Let me here,
  As I deserve, pay on my punishment,
  And expiate, if possible, my crime,   490
  Shameful garrulity. To have revealed
  Secrets of men, the secrets of a friend,
  How heinous had the fact been, how deserving
  Contempt and scorn of all; to be excluded
  All friendship, and avoided as a blab,   495
  The mark of fool set on his front! [5] But I
  God's counsel have not kept, his holy secret
  Presumptuously have published, impiously,
  Weakly at least and shamefully: a sin
  That Gentiles in their parables condemn   500
  To their abyss and horrid pains confined.[6]
MANOA. Be penitent, and for thy fault contrite;
  But act not in thy own affliction, son.
  Repent the sin; but, if the punishment
  Thou canst avoid, self-preservation bids;   505
  Or th' execution leave to high disposal,
  And let another hand, not thine, exact
  Thy penal forfeit from thyself. Perhaps
  God will relent, and quit [7] thee all his debt;
  Who ever more approves and more accepts   510
  (Best pleased with humble and filial submission)
  Him who, imploring mercy, sues for life,
  Than who, self-rigorous, chooses death as due; [8]
  Which argues over-just, and self-displeased
  For self-offense more than for God offended.   515
  Reject not, then, what offered means who knows
  But God hath set before us to return thee
  Home to thy country and his sacred house,
  Where thou may'st bring thy offerings, to avert
  His further ire, with prayers and vows renewed.   520
SAMSON. His pardon I implore; but, as for life,
  To what end should I seek it? When in strength
  All mortals I excelled, and great in hopes,
  With youthful courage, and magnanimous thoughts
  Of birth from Heaven foretold and high exploits,   525
  Full of divine instinct, after some proof
  Of acts indeed heroic, far beyond
  The sons of Anak,[9] famous now and blazed,
  Fearless of danger, like a petty god

---

5. Forehead.
6. In classical legend, Tantalus was confined to hell and torment because he betrayed the secrets of the gods, and Prometheus was savagely punished for giving to mankind the secret of fire.

7. Cancel.
8. This is very similar to Adam's argument against suicide in *Paradise Lost* X.1013–30.
9. Giants, described in Numbers xiii.

I walked about, admired of all, and dreaded   530
On hostile ground, none daring my affront.
Then, swoll'n with pride, into the snare I fell
Of fair fallacious looks, venereal trains,[1]
Softened with pleasure and voluptuous life;
At length to lay my head and hallowed pledge   535
Of all my strength in the lascivious lap
Of a deceitful concubine, who shore me,
Like a tame wether,[2] all my precious fleece,
Then turned me out ridiculous, despoiled,
Shaven, and disarmed among my enemies.   540
CHORUS. Desire of wine and all delicious drinks,
Which many a famous warrior overturns,
Thou could'st repress; nor did the dancing ruby,
Sparkling out-poured, the flavor or the smell,
Or taste, that cheers the heart of gods and men,   545
Allure thee from the cool crystalline stream.
SAMSON. Wherever fountain or fresh current flowed
Against the eastern ray, translucent, pure
With touch ethereal of Heaven's fiery rod,[3]
I drank, from the clear milky juice allaying   550
Thirst, and refreshed; nor envied them the grape
Whose heads that turbulent liquor fills with fumes.
CHORUS. O madness! to think use of strongest wines
And strongest drinks our chief support of health,
When God with these forbidden made choice to rear   555
His mighty champion, strong above compare,
Whose drink was only from the liquid brook![4]
SAMSON. But what availed this temperance, not complete
Against another object more enticing?
What boots it at one gate to make defence,   560
And at another to let in the foe,
Effeminately vanquished? by which means,
Now blind, disheartened, shamed, dishonored, quelled,
To what can I be useful? wherein serve
My nation, and the work from Heaven imposed?   565
But to sit idle on the household hearth,
A burdenous drone; to visitance a gaze,[5]
Or pitied object; these redundant [6] locks,
Robustious to no purpose, clustering down,
Vain monument of strength; till length of years   570
And sedentary numbness craze [7] my limbs
To a contemptible old age obscure.

1. **Sensual, sexual lures.**
2. **A castrated male sheep.**
3. **The rays of the sun.** Samson is saying that wherever water was purest and cleanest, he drank of it—never of wine; "rod" intimates a parallel with Moses, who like Samson brought forth a spring in the middle of the desert.
4. Samson's calling as a Nazarite forbade him the use of wine.
5. A spectacle for visitors.
6. In its Latin sense, "redundant" means "flowing," in the English sense "unnecessary," "unemployed." "Robustious": strong.
7. Weaken, twist.

Here rather let me drudge, and earn my bread,
Till vermin, or the draff of servile food,[8]
Consume me, and oft-invocated death   575
Hasten the welcome end of all my pains.
MANOA. Wilt thou then serve the Philistines with that gift
  Which was expressly given thee to annoy them?
  Better at home lie bed-rid, not only idle,
  Inglorious, unemployed, with age outworn.   580
  But God, who caused a fountain at thy prayer
  From the dry ground to spring, thy thirst to allay
  After the brunt of battle,[9] can as easy
  Cause light again within thy eyes to spring,
  Wherewith to serve him better than thou hast.   585
  And I persuade me so. Why else this strength
  Miraculous yet remaining in those locks?
  His might continues in thee not for naught,
  Nor shall his wondrous gifts be frustrate thus.
SAMSON. All otherwise to me my thoughts portend,   590
  That these dark orbs no more shall treat with light,
  Nor th' other light of life continue long,
  But yield to double darkness nigh at hand;
  So much I feel my genial spirits [1] droop,
  My hopes all flat: Nature within me seems   595
  In all her functions weary of herself;
  My race of glory run, and race of shame,
  And I shall shortly be with them that rest.
MANOA. Believe not these suggestions, which proceed
  From anguish of the mind, and humors black   600
  That mingle with thy fancy.[2] I, however,
  Must not omit a father's timely care
  To prosecute the means of thy deliverance
  By ransom or how else: meanwhile be calm,
  And healing words from these thy friends admit.   605
SAMSON. Oh, that torment should not be confined
  To the body's wounds and sores,
  With maladies innumerable
  In heart, head, breast, and reins,
  But must secret passage find   610
  To th' inmost mind,
  There exercise all his fierce accidents,[3]
  And on her purest spirits prey,
  As on entrails, joints, and limbs,
  With answerable pains, but more intense,   615
  Though void of corporal sense!

8. Garbage given to slaves as food.
9. The story of how Samson, with divine aid, created a spring in the desert after the battle with the ass's jawbone, is told in Judges xv.18–19.
1. Life forces, vital energy.

2. Black bile, the melancholy humor, was supposed to have specially ill effects on the imagination.
3. I.e., there put into effect all the fierce qualities (of torment).

My griefs not only pain me
As a lingering disease,
But, finding no redress, ferment and rage;
Nor less than wounds immedicable   620
Rankle, and fester, and gangrene,
To black mortification.[4]
Thoughts, my tormentors, armed with daily stings,
Mangle my apprehensive tenderest parts,
Exasperate, exulcerate, and raise   625
Dire inflammation, which no cooling herb
Or med'cinal liquor can assuage,
Nor breath of vernal air from snowy Alp.
Sleep hath forsook and given me o'er
To death's benumbing opium as my only cure;   630
Thence faintings, swoonings of despair,
And sense of Heaven's desertion.[5]
    I was his nursling once and choice delight,
His destined from the womb,
Promised by heavenly message [6] twice descending. 635
Under his special eye
Abstemious I grew up and thrived amain;
He led me on to mightiest deeds,
Above the nerve [7] of mortal arm,
Against the uncircumcised, our enemies: 640
But now hath cast me off as never known,
And to those cruel enemies,
Whom I by his appointment had provoked,
Left me, all helpless with th' irreparable loss
Of sight, reserved alive to be repeated [8]   645
The subject of their cruelty or scorn.
Nor am I in the list of them that hope;
Hopeless are all my evils, all remediless.
This one prayer yet remains, might I be heard,
No long petition—speedy death,   650
The close of all my miseries and the balm.
CHORUS. Many are the sayings of the wise,
In ancient and in modern books enrolled,
Extolling patience as the truest fortitude,
And to the bearing well of all calamities,   655
All chances incident to man's frail life,
Consolatories writ
With studied argument, and much persuasion sought,
Lenient [9] of grief and anxious thought.
But with th' afflicted in his pangs their sound   660
Little prevails, or rather seems a tune

4. A medical term for decay.
5. Samson comes close here to suggesting that religious despair is the symptom of a physical condition; cf. Burton's *Anatomy of Melancholy*.
6. Messenger.
7. Sinew, hence, strength.
8. Repeatedly, continually.
9. Soothing (from Latin, *leniens*).

Harsh, and of dissonant mood [1] from his complaint,
Unless he feel within
Some source of consolation from above,
Secret refreshings that repair his strength   665
And fainting spirits uphold. [2]
        God of our fathers! what is man,
That thou towards him with hand so various—
Or might I say contrarious?—
Temper'st thy providence through his short course: 670
Not evenly, as thou rul'st
The angelic orders, and inferior creatures mute,
Irrational and brute? [3]
Nor do I name of men the common rout,
That, wandering loose about,   675
Grow up and perish as the summer fly,
Heads without name, no more remembered;
But such as thou hast solemnly elected,
With gifts and graces eminently adorned,
To some great work, thy glory,   680
And people's safety, which in part they effect.
Yet toward these, thus dignified, thou oft,
Amidst their height of noon,
Changest thy countenance and thy hand, with no regard
Of highest favors past   685
From thee on them, or them to thee of service. [4]
        Nor only dost degrade them, or remit
To life obscured, which were a fair dismission,
But throw'st them lower than thou didst exalt them high,
Unseemly falls in human eye,   690
Too grievous for the trespass or omission;
Oft leav'st them to the hostile sword
Of heathen and profane, their carcasses
To dogs and fowls a prey, or else captíved,
Or to the unjust tribunals, under change of times,   695
And condemnation of the ingrateful multitude. [5]
If these they 'scape, perhaps in poverty
With sickness and disease thou bow'st them down,
Painful diseases and deformed,
In crude [6] old age;   700
Though not disordinate, [7] yet causeless suffering
The punishment of dissolute days. In fine,

1. The musical mode, or psychological mood, of the comforter jars on that of the sufferer.
2. Compare Job's answers to his comforters, especially xiv.
3. The chorus feels that the beings above and below man on the Great Chain of Being (the nine orders of angels above, the many mute beasts below) are ruled by a less capricious code than is man.
4. Manoa has already voiced this plaint, lines 368–72.

5. After the Restoration, many Puritan leaders were executed, jailed, or exiled, while even the corpses of some who were dead were exhumed, beheaded, and publicly exhibited.
6. Literally, "raw," but, figuratively, "premature."
7. I.e., though they have not been dissipated (disordinate). Milton resented having the gout, supposed to be a disease of the luxurious.

Just or unjust alike seem miserable,
For oft alike both come to evil end.
    So deal not with this once thy glorious champion,   705
The image of thy strength, and mighty minister.[8]
What do I beg? how hast thou dealt already!
Behold him in this state calamitous, and turn
His labors, for thou canst, to peaceful end.
    But who is this? what thing of sea or land—   710
Female of sex it seems—
That, so bedecked, ornate, and gay,
Comes this way sailing,
Like a stately ship
Of Tarsus, bound for th' isles   715
Of Javan or Gadire,[9]
With all her bravery on, and tackle trim,
Sails filled, and streamers waving,
Courted by all the winds that hold them play;
An amber [1] scent of odorous perfume   720
Her harbinger, a damsel train behind?
Some rich Philistian matron she may seem;
And now, at nearer view, no other certain
Than Dálila thy wife.[2]
SAMSON. My wife! my traitress! let her not come near me.   725
CHORUS. Yet on she moves; now stands and eyes thee fixed,
    About t'have spoke; but now, with head declined,
    Like a fair flower surcharged with dew, she weeps,
    And words addressed seem into tears dissolved,
    Wetting the borders of her silken veil.   730
    But now again she makes address to speak.
DALILA. With doubtful feet and wavering resolution
    I came, still dreading thy displeasure, Samson;
    Which to have merited, without excuse,
    I cannot but acknowledge. Yet, if tears   735
    May expiate (though the fact more evil drew
    In the perverse event than I foresaw),[3]
    My penance hath not slackened, though my pardon
    No way assured. But conjugal affection,
    Prevailing over fear and timorous doubt,   740
    Hath led me on, desirous to behold
    Once more thy face, and know of thy estate,[4]
    If aught in my ability may serve
    To lighten what thou suffer'st, and appease
    Thy mind with what amends is in my power—   745

8. Agent, but with a religious connotation as well.
9. Tarsus (the birthplace of St. Paul) is a trading city in modern Turkey; the isles of Javan are the isles of Greece, supposed to be populated by descendants of Javan, son of Noah's son Japhet. Gadire is modern Cadiz in Spain. Many of these geographical details are to be found an Isaiah II.lxvi, etc.
1. Ambergris.
2. The circling, mocking, derisive description of the chorus carefully holds Samson in suspense till the last minute.
3. I.e., my action turned out worse than I intended.
4. Condition.

Though late, yet in some part to recompense
My rash but more unfortunate misdeed.

SAMSON.   Out, out, hyena! [5] These are thy wonted arts,
And arts of every woman false like thee,
To break all faith, all vows, deceive, betray;   750
Then, as repentant, to submit, beseech,
And reconcilement move with feigned remorse,
Confess, and promise wonders in her change—
Not truly penitent, but chief to try
Her husband, how far urged his patience bears,   755
His virtue or weakness which way to assail:
Then, with more cautious and instructed skill,
Again transgresses, and again submits;
That wisest and best men, full oft beguiled,
With goodness principled not to reject   760
The penitent, but ever to forgive,
Are drawn to wear out miserable days,
Entangled with a poisonous bosom-snake,
If not by quick destruction soon cut off,
As I by thee, to ages an example.   765

DALILA.   Yet hear me, Samson, not that I endeavor
To lessen or extenuate my offense,
But that, on th' other side, if it be weighed
By itself, with aggravations not surcharged,
Or else with just allowance counterpoised,   770
I may, if possible, thy pardon find
The easier towards me, or thy hatred less.
First granting, as I do, it was a weakness
In me, but incident to all our sex,
Curiosity, inquisitive, importune   775
Of secrets, then with like infirmity
To publish them, both common female faults,
Was it not weakness also to make known,
For importunity, that is for naught,
Wherein consisted all thy strength and safety?   780
To what I did thou show'dst me first the way.
But I to enemies revealed, and should not!
Nor should'st thou have trusted that to woman's frailty: [6]
Ere I to thee, thou to thyself wast cruel.
Let weakness, then, with weakness come to parle,[7]   785
So near related, or the same of kind;
Thine forgive mine, that men may censure thine
The gentler, if severely thou exact not
More strength from me than in thyself was found.

---

5. Apart from being an animal of odious habits and appearance, the hyena was a traditional beast of hypocrisy, supposed to entice men to destruction by its power of imitating the human voice.
6. Like Eve, who wore down Adam with importunity, then blamed him for giving in (*Paradise Lost* IX.1155–61). Dalila blames Samson for doing what she herself has demanded.
7. Parley, agreement.

And what if love, which thou interpret'st hate,   790
The jealousy of love, powerful of sway
In human hearts, nor less in mine towards thee,
Caused what I did? I saw thee mutable
Of fancy; feared lest one day thou would'st leave me,
As her at Timna; sought by all means, therefore,   795
How to endear, and hold thee to me firmest:
No better way I saw than by importuning
To learn thy secrets, get into my power
Thy key of strength and safety. Thou wilt say,
"Why, then, revealed?" I was assured by those   800
Who tempted me that nothing was designed
Against thee but safe custody and hold.
That made for me; I knew that liberty
Would draw thee forth to perilous enterprises,
While I at home sat full of cares and fears,   805
Wailing thy absence in my widowed bed;
Here I should still enjoy thee, day and night,
Mine and love's prisoner, not the Philistines',
Whole to myself, unhazarded abroad,
Fearless at home of partners in my love.   810
These reasons in love's law have passed for good,
Though fond [8] and reasonless to some perhaps;
And love hath oft, well meaning, wrought much woe,
Yet always pity or pardon hath obtained.
Be not unlike all others, not austere   815
As thou art strong, inflexible as steel.
If thou in strength all mortals dost exceed,
In uncompassionate anger do not so.

SAMSON. How cunningly the sorceress displays
Her own transgressions, to upbraid me mine!   820
That malice, not repentance, brought thee hither,
By this appears. I gave, thou say'st, th' example,
I led the way—bitter reproach, but true;
I to myself was false ere thou to me.
Such pardon, therefore, as I give my folly   825
Take to thy wicked deed; which when thou seest
Impartial, self-severe, inexorable,
Thou wilt renounce thy seeking, and much rather
Confess it feigned. Weakness is thy excuse,
And I believe it, weakness to resist   830
Philistian gold. If weakness may excuse,
What murderer, what traitor, parricide,
Incestuous, sacrilegious, but may plead it?
All wickedness is weakness; that plea, therefore,
With God or man will gain thee no remission.   835
But love constrained thee! Call it furious rage
To satisfy thy lust. Love seeks to have love;

8. Foolish.

My love how could'st thou hope, who took'st the way
To raise in me inexpiable [9] hate,
Knowing, as needs I must, by thee betrayed?   840
In vain thou striv'st to cover shame with shame,
Or by evasions thy crime uncover'st more.
DALILA. Since thou determin'st weakness for no plea
In man or woman, though to thy own condemning,
Hear what assaults I had, what snares besides,   845
What sieges girt me round, ere I consented;
Which might have awed the best resolved of men,
The constantest, to have yielded without blame.
It was not gold, as to my charge thou lay'st,
That wrought with me.[1] Thou know'st the magistrates   850
And princes of my country came in person,
Solicited, commanded, threatened, urged,
Adjured by all the bonds of civil duty
And of religion—pressed how just it was,
How honorable, how glorious, to entrap   855
A common enemy, who had destroyed
Such numbers of our nation: and the priest
Was not behind, but ever at my ear,
Preaching how meritorious with the gods
It would be to ensnare an irreligious   860
Dishonorer of Dagon. What had I
To oppose against such powerful arguments?
Only my love of thee held long debate,
And combated in silence all these reasons
With hard contest. At length, that grounded maxim,   865
So rife and celebrated in the mouths
Of wisest men, that to the public good
Private respects must yield,[2] with grave authority
Took full possession of me, and prevailed;
Virtue, as I thought, truth, duty, so enjoining.   870
SAMSON. I thought where all thy circling wiles would end,
In feigned religion, smooth hypocrisy!
But, had thy love, still odiously pretended,
Been, as it ought, sincere, it would have taught thee
Far other reasonings, brought forth other deeds.   875
I, before all the daughters of my tribe
And of my nation, chose thee from among
My enemies, loved thee, as too well thou knew'st;
Too well; unbosomed all my secrets to thee,
Not out of levity, but overpowered   880
By thy request, who could deny thee nothing;
Yet now am judged an enemy. Why, then,

9. Inextinguishable.
1. Judges xvi is very explicit that Dalila betrayed Samson for money—eleven hundred pieces of silver offered her by each one of the Philistine lords.

2. Reason of state, political expediency, was in Milton's eyes the worst of all possible motives for an action. Cf. *Paradise Lost* IV. 393–94.

Didst thou at first receive me for thy husband,
Then, as since then, thy country's foe professed?
Being once a wife, for me thou wast to leave   885
Parents and country; nor was I their subject,
Nor under their protection, but my own;
Thou mine, not theirs.³ If aught against my life
Thy country sought of thee, it sought unjustly,
Against the law of nature, law of nations;   890
No more thy country, but an impious crew
Of men conspiring to uphold their state
By worse than hostile deeds, violating the ends
For which our country is a name so dear;
Not therefore to be obeyed. But zeal moved thee;   895
To please thy gods thou didst it! Gods unable
To acquit themselves and prosecute their foes
But by ungodly deeds, the contradiction
Of their own deity, gods cannot be;
Less therefore to be pleased, obeyed, or feared.   900
These false pretexts and varnished colors failing,
Bare in thy guilt, how foul must thou appear!

DALILA. In argument with men a woman ever
Goes by the worse,⁴ whatever be her cause.

SAMSON. For want of words, no doubt, or lack of breath!   905
Witness when I was worried with thy peals.

DALILA. I was a fool, too rash, and quite mistaken
In what I thought would have succeeded best.
Let me obtain forgiveness of thee, Samson;
Afford me place to show what recompense   910
Towards thee I intend for what I have misdone,
Misguided. Only what remains past cure
Bear not too sensibly,⁵ nor still insist
To afflict thyself in vain. Though sight be lost,
Life yet hath many solaces, enjoyed   915
Where other senses want not their delights—
At home, in leisure and domestic ease,
Exempt from many a care and chance to which
Eyesight exposes, daily, men abroad.
I to the lords will intercede, not doubting   920
Their favorable ear, that I may fetch thee
From forth this loathsome prison house, to abide
With me, where my redoubled love and care,
With nursing diligence, to me glad office,
May ever tend about thee to old age,   925
With all things grateful cheered, and so supplied
That what by me thou hast lost thou least shalt miss.

SAMSON. No, no; of my condition take no care;

---

3. I.e., you were under my protection, not theirs.
4. Comes off second best.

5. "Too sensibly": with too great sensitivity.

It fits not; thou and I long since are twain;
Nor think me so unwary or accursed [6]   930
To bring my feet again into the snare
Where once I have been caught. I know thy trains,
Though dearly to my cost, thy gins, and toils.[7]
Thy fair enchanted cup, and warbling charms,
No more on me have power; their force is nulled;   935
So much of adder's wisdom I have learned,
To fence my ear against thy sorceries.[8]
If in my flower of youth and strength, when all men
Loved, honored, feared me, thou alone could hate me,
Thy husband, slight me, sell me, and forgo me,   940
How would'st thou use me now, blind, and thereby
Deceivable, in most things as a child
Helpless, thence easily contemned and scorned,
And last neglected! How would'st thou insult,
When I must live uxorious to thy will   945
In perfect thraldom! how again betray me,
Bearing my words and doings to the lords
To gloss upon, and, censuring, frown or smile! [9]
This jail I count the house of liberty
To thine, whose doors my feet shall never enter.   950

DALILA. Let me approach at least, and touch thy hand.

SAMSON. Not for thy life, lest fierce remembrance wake
My sudden rage to tear thee joint by joint.[1]
At distance I forgive thee, go with that;
Bewail thy falsehood, and the pious works   955
It hath brought forth to make thee memorable
Among illustrious women, faithful wives;
Cherish thy hastened widowhood with the gold
Of matrimonial treason: so farewell.

DALILA. I see thou art implacable, more deaf   960
To prayers than winds and seas. Yet winds to seas
Are reconciled at length, and sea to shore:
Thy anger, unappeasable, still rages,
Eternal tempest never to be calmed.
Why do I humble thus myself, and, suing   965
For peace, reap nothing but repulse and hate,
Bid go with evil omen,[2] and the brand
Of infamy upon my name denounced?
To mix with thy concernments I desist
Henceforth, nor too much disapprove my own.   970

---

6. I.e., so neglectful or bewitched.
7. "Trains": tricks; "gins": snares; "toils": nets. The traditional images for female wiles are heightened by reference to an enchanting cup and warbled charms reminiscent of Homer's Circe (*Odyssey*, X).
8. Psalm lviii verses 4 and 5 describes the "deaf adder that stoppeth her ear; which will not hearken to the voice of

charmers, charming never so wisely."
9. Milton's libertarian hatred of censorship and managed liberty is very apparent.
1. What Samson might remember, at the touch of Dalila, which would lead him to tear her to pieces, is a problem in domestic psychology.
2. I.e., dismissed with threats of ill fame.

Fame, if not double-faced, is double-mouthed,
And with contrary blast proclaims most deeds; [3]
On both his wings, one black, th' other white,
Bears greatest names in his wild airy flight.
My name, perhaps, among the circumcised   975
In Dan, in Judah, and the bordering tribes,
To all posterity may stand defamed,
With malediction mentioned, and the blot
Of falsehood most unconjugal traduced.
But in my country, where I most desire,   980
In Ecron, Gaza, Asdod, and in Gath,
I shall be named among the famousest
Of women, sung at solemn festivals,
Living and dead recorded, who to save
Her country from a fierce destroyer chose   985
Above the faith of wedlock bands; my tomb
With odors [4] visited and annual flowers;
Not less renowned than in Mount Ephraim
Jael, who, with inhospitable guile,
Smote Sisera sleeping,[5] through the temples nailed.   990
Nor shall I count it heinous to enjoy
The public marks of honor and reward
Conferred upon me for the piety
Which to my country I was judged to have shown.
At this whoever envies or repines,   995
I leave him to his lot, and like my own.
CHORUS. She's gone, a manifest serpent by her sting
Discovered in the end, till now concealed.
SAMSON. So let her go. God sent her to debase me,
And aggravate my folly, who committed   1000
To such a viper his most sacred trust
Of secrecy, my safety, and my life.
CHORUS. Yet beauty, though injurious, hath strange power,
After offense returning, to regain
Love once possessed, nor can be easily   1005
Repulsed, without much inward passion [6] felt,
And secret sting of amorous remorse.
SAMSON. Love-quarrels oft in pleasing concord end;
Not wedlock-treachery, endangering life.
CHORUS. It is not virtue, wisdom, valor, wit,   1010
Strength, comeliness of shape, or amplest merit.
That woman's love can win, or long inherit; [7]
But what it is hard is to say,
Harder to hit,

---

3. The figure of Fame, in Milton's youthful poem *On the Fifth of November*, does indeed have a double tongue, one for truth and one for lies. Fame or Rumor was a favorite grotesque allegorical figure in classical poets like Ovid (*Metamorphoses* XII.43 ff.) and Virgil (*Aeneid* IV.173 ff.).

4. Perfumes.
5. Jael lured Sisera, who saw in her the wife of his ally and friend, into a tent, and there drove a large nail into his head (Judges iv.17–21).
6. Suffering.
7. Possess.

Which way soever men refer it   1015
(Much like thy riddle, Samson),[8] in one day
Or seven though one should musing sit.
    If any of these, or all, the Timnian bride
Had not so soon preferred
Thy paranymph, worthless to thee compared,   1020
Successor in thy bed,[9]
Nor both so loosely disallied
Their nuptials,[1] nor this last so treacherously
Had shorn the fatal harvest of thy head.
Is it for that [2] such outward ornament   1025
Was lavished on their sex, that inward gifts
Were left for haste unfinished, judgment scant,
Capacity not raised to apprehend
Or value what is best
In choice, but oftest to affect [3] the wrong?   1030
Or was too much of self-love mixed,
Of constancy no root infixed,
That either they love nothing, or not long?
    Whate'er it be, to wisest men and best,
Seeming at first all heavenly under virgin veil,   1035
Soft, modest, meek, demure,
Once joined, the contrary she proves, a thorn
Intestine,[4] far within defensive arms
A cleaving [5] mischief, in his way to virtue
Adverse and turbulent; or by her charms   1040
Draws him awry, enslaved
With dotage, and his sense depraved
To folly and shameful deeds, which ruin ends.
What pilot so expert but needs must wreck,
Embarked with such a steers-mate at the helm?   1045
    Favored of Heaven who finds
One virtuous, rarely found,
That in domestic good combines:
Happy that house! his way to peace is smooth:
But virtue which breaks through all opposition,   1050
And all temptation can remove,
Most shines and most is acceptable above.
    Therefore God's universal law
Gave to the man despotic power
Over his female in due awe,   1055
Nor from that right to part an hour,
Smile she or lour:
So shall he least confusion draw
On his whole life, not swayed

8. Samson's riddle is propounded and answered in Judges xiv, verses 14 and 18.
9. I.e., if any of these ("virtue, . . . ," lines 1010–11) sufficed, Samson's first wife (the Timnian bride) would not have preferred to marry his "paranymph" (best man). See Judges xiv.
1. I.e., nor would both your wives have been so careless about their marriage vows.
2. Because.
3. Desire.
4. An inward thorn, a viper in the bosom.
5. Clinging; a traditional emblem of marriage was the elm and the vine.

By female usurpation, nor dismayed.   1060
    But had we best retire? I see a storm.
SAMSON. Fair days have oft contracted [6] wind and rain.
CHORUS. But this another kind of tempest brings.
SAMSON. Be less abstruse; my riddling days are past.
CHORUS. Look now for no enchanting voice, nor fear   1065
    The bait of honeyed words; a rougher tongue
    Draws hitherward, I know him by his stride,
    The giant Harapha [7] of Gath, his look
    Haughty, as is his pile [8] high-built and proud.
    Comes he in peace? What wind hath blown him hither   1070
    I less conjecture than when first I saw
    The sumptuous Dalila floating this way: [9]
    His habit carries peace, his brow defiance.
SAMSON. Or peace or not, alike to me he comes.
CHORUS. His fraught [1] we soon shall know: he now arrives.   1075
HARAPHA. I come not, Samson, to condole thy chance,
    As these [2] perhaps, yet wish it had not been,
    Though for no friendly intent. I am of Gath;
    Men call me Harapha, of stock renowned
    As Og, or Anak, and the Emims old   1080
    That Kiriathaim held.[3] Thou know'st me now,
    If thou at all art known.[4] Much I have heard
    Of thy prodigious might and feats performed,
    Incredible to me, in this displeased,
    That I was never present on the place   1085
    Of those encounters, where we might have tried
    Each other's force in camp or listed field; [5]
    And now am come to see of whom such noise
    Hath walked about, and each limb to survey,
    If thy appearance answer loud report.   1090
SAMSON. The way to know were not to see, but taste.[6]
HARAPHA. Dost thou already single [7] me? I thought
    Gyves and the mill had tamed thee. O that fortune
    Had brought me to the field where thou art famed
    To have wrought such wonders with an ass's jaw!   1095
    I should have forced thee soon wish [8] other arms,

6. Drawn after them.
7. Harapha does not appear at all within the story told in the Book of Judges; Milton invented him with the help of some hints from the image of Goliath in I Samuel xvii and some other giants in II Samuel xxi. *Rapha* means giant in Hebrew.
8. Body; with the suggestion that he is tall as a tower.
9. That the various visitors of Samson are blown hither and yon by the winds of occasion serves to emphasize the deep steadiness of Samson's final resolution.
1. Intent.
2. The chorus of Danites, naturally sympathetic to Samson.
3. Og was a giant King of Bashan in Deuteronomy iii.11; Anak and his sons were giants in Numbers xiii.33; the Emims were giants in Deuteronomy ii. 10–11 and Genesis xiv.5.
4. I.e., you know me now if you know anything; but also "if you are anyone worth knowing." Compare Satan's brag to Zephon and Ithuriel, "Not to know me argues yourselves unknown." *Paradise Lost* IV.830.
5. "Camp": field of battle (from Latin, *campus*); "listed field": lists, tourney-ground.
6. Make a trial of.
7. Challenge; "gyves": chains.
8. Eighteenth-century editors changed "wish" to "with", easing the grammar at the expense of the sense.

Or left thy carcass where the ass lay thrown;
So had the glory of prowess been recovered
To Palestine, won by a Philistine
From the unforeskinned race, of whom thou bear'st   1100
The highest name for valiant acts. That honor,
Certain to have won by mortal duel from thee,
I lose, prevented by thy eyes put out.

SAMSON. Boast not of what thou would'st have done, but do
    What then thou would'st; thou seest it in thy hand.   1105

HARAPHA. To combat with a blind man I disdain,
    And thou hast need much washing to be touched.

SAMSON. Such usage as your honorable lords
    Afford me, assassinated [9] and betrayed;
    Who durst not with their whole united powers   1110
    In fight withstand me single and unarmed,
    Nor in the house with chamber ambushes [1]
    Close-banded durst attack me, no, not sleeping,
    Till they had hired a woman with their gold,
    Breaking her marriage-faith, to circumvent me.   1115
    Therefore, without feigned shifts, let be assigned
    Some narrow place enclosed, where sight may give thee,
    Or rather flight, no great advantage on me;
    Then put on all thy gorgeous arms, thy helmet
    And brigandine of brass, thy broad habergeon,   1120
    Vant-brace and greaves and gauntlet; [2] add thy spear,
    A weaver's beam, and seven-times-folded shield:
    I only with an oaken staff will meet thee,
    And raise such outcries on thy clattered iron,
    Which long shall not withhold me from thy head,   1125
    That in a little time, while breath remains thee,
    Thou oft shalt wish thyself at Gath, to boast
    Again in safety what thou would'st have done
    To Samson, but shalt never see Gath more.

HARAPHA. Thou durst not thus disparage glorious arms,   1130
    Which greatest heroes have in battle worn,
    Their ornament and safety, had not spells
    And black enchantments, some magician's art,
    Armed thee or charmed thee strong, which thou from Heaven
    Feign'dst at thy birth was given thee in thy hair,   1135
    Where strength can least abide, though all thy hairs
    Were bristles ranged like those that ridge the back
    Of chafed wild boars or ruffled porcupines.

SAMSON. I know no spells, use no forbidden arts;
    My trust is in the Living God, who gave me,   1140

9. Treacherously assailed.
1. Samson refers to the four occasions on which Philistines hid in his bedroom while Dalila tried unsuccessfully to betray him to them.
2. "Brigandine": a padded chest-protector, covered with iron scales or rings; "habergeon": a coat of mail, a hauberk;

"vant-brace": a steel cuff for the forearm; greaves protect the shins and thighs, and gauntlets the hands. A weaver's beam, emblem of weightiness, is used to keep threads hanging tautly in a loom. All these military details are from the description of Goliath, I Samuel xvii.4–7.

At my nativity, this strength, diffused
No less through all my sinews, joints, and bones,
Than thine, while I preserved these locks unshorn,
The pledge of my unviolated vow.
For proof hereof, if Dagon be thy god,   1145
Go to his temple, invocate his aid
With solemnest devotion, spread before him
How highly it concerns his glory now
To frustrate and dissolve these magic spells,
Which I to be the power of Israel's God   1150
Avow, and challenge Dagon to the test,
Offering to combat thee, his champion bold,
With th' utmost of his godhead seconded:
Then thou shalt see, or rather to thy sorrow
Soon feel, whose God is strongest, thine or mine.   1155
HARAPHA. Presume not on thy God. Whate'er he be,
Thee he regards not, owns not, hath cut off
Quite from his people, and delivered up
Into thy enemies' hand; permitted them
To put out both thine eyes, and fettered send thee   1160
Into the common prison, there to grind
Among the slaves and asses, thy comrádes,
As good for nothing else, no better service
With those thy boisterous locks; no worthy match
For valor to assail, nor by the sword   1165
Of noble warrior, so to stain his honor,
But by the barber's razor best subdued.
SAMSON. All these indignities, for such they are
From thine,[3] these evils I deserve and more,
Acknowledge them from God inflicted on me   1170
Justly, yet despair not of his final pardon,
Whose ear is ever open, and his eye
Gracious to re-admit the suppliant;
In confidence whereof I once again
Defy thee to the trial of mortal fight,   1175
By combat to decide whose god is God,
Thine, or whom I with Israel's sons adore.
HARAPHA. Fair honor that thou dost thy God, in trusting
He will accept thee to defend his cause,
A murderer, a revolter, and a robber!   1180
SAMSON. Tongue-doughty giant, how dost thou prove me these?
HARAPHA. Is not thy nation subject to our lords?
Their magistrates confessed it when they took thee
As a league-breaker, and delivered bound
Into our hands;[4] for hadst not committed   1185

3. Thy people.
4. Judges xiv.8–20 and xv.9–15 describe the episode. Samson when he came to Timna to be married proposed a riddle and a bet to the marriage guests; they got his intended bride to reveal the riddle, and in revenge he killed thirty of their people and left the lady to the "paranymph," or best man. Old Testament Samson is indeed a rude and savage figure; Milton, with characteristic confidence, undertakes his legal defense in everything.

Notorious murder on those thirty men
At Ascalon, who never did thee harm,
Then, like a robber, stripp'dst them of their robes?
The Philistines, when thou hadst broke the league,
Went up with arméd powers thee only seeking,   1190
To others did no violence nor spoil.
SAMSON. Among the daughters of the Philistines
I chose a wife, which argued me no foe,
And in your city held my nuptial feast;
But your ill-meaning politician lords,   1195
Under pretense of bridal friends and guests,
Appointed to await me thirty spies,
Who, threatening cruel death, constrained the bride
To wring from me, and tell to them, my secret,
That solved the riddle which I had proposed.   1200
When I perceived all set on enmity,
As on my enemies, wherever chanced,
I used hostility, and took their spoil,
To pay my underminers in their coin.
My nation was subjected to your lords! [5]   1205
It was the force of conquest; force with force
Is well ejected when the conquered can.
But I, a private person, whom my country
As a league-breaker gave up bound, presumed
Single rebellion, and did hostile acts!   1210
I was no private,[6] but a person raised,
With strength sufficient, and command from Heaven,
To free my country. If their servile minds
Me, their deliverer sent, would not receive,
But to their masters gave me up for nought,   1215
Th' unworthier they; whence to this day they serve.
I was to do my part from Heaven assigned,
And had performed it if my known offense
Had not disabled me, not all your force.
These shifts refuted, answer thy appellant,[7]   1220
Though by his blindness maimed for high attempts,
Who now defies thee thrice to single fight,
As a petty enterprise of small enforce.[8]
HARAPHA. With thee, a man condemned, a slave enrolled,
Due by the law to capital punishment?   1225
To fight with thee no man of arms will deign.
SAMSON. Cam'st thou for this, vain boaster, to survey me,
To descant on my strength, and give thy verdict?
Come nearer; part not hence so slight informed;
But take good heed my hand survey not thee.   1230
HARAPHA. O Baal-zebub! [9] can my ears unused

5. I.e., you argue that my nation was
subjected to your lords.
6. Outlaw.
7. I.e., now that we've disposed of these
dodges, answer your challenger. "Apel-
lant": literally, caller, one who calls
you out.
8. Difficulty.
9. Baal-zebub is Beelzebub, god of the
flies.

Hear these dishonors, and not render death?

SAMSON. No man withholds thee; nothing from thy hand
    Fear I incurable; bring up thy van; [1]
    My heels are fettered, but my fist is free.   1235

HARAPHA. This insolence other kind of answer fits.

SAMSON. Go, baffled coward, lest I run upon thee,
    Though in these chains, bulk without spirit vast,
    And with one buffet lay thy structure low,
    Or swing thee in the air, then dash thee down,   1240
    To the hazard of thy brains and shattered sides.

HARAPHA. By Astaroth, [2] ere long thou shalt lament
    These braveries, [3] in irons loaden on thee.

CHORUS. His giantship is gone somewhat crestfallen,
    Stalking with less unconscionable [4] strides,   1245
    And lower looks, but in a sultry chafe.

SAMSON. I dread him not, nor all his giant brood,
    Though fame divulge him father of five sons,
    All of gigantic size, Goliath chief. [5]

CHORUS. He will directly to the lords, I fear,   1250
    And with malicious counsel stir them up
    Some way or other yet further to afflict thee.

SAMSON. He must allege some cause, and offered fight
    Will not dare mention, lest a question rise
    Whether he durst accept the offer or not;   1255
    And that he durst not plain enough appeared.
    Much more affliction than already felt
    They cannot well impose, nor I sustain,
    If they intend advantage of my labors,
    The work of many hands, which earns my keeping,   1260
    With no small profit daily to my owners.
    But come what will; my deadliest foe will prove
    My speediest friend, by death to rid me hence;
    The worst that he can give to me the best.
    Yet so it may fall out, because their end   1265
    Is hate, not help to me, it may with mine
    Draw their own ruin who attempt the deed.

CHORUS. O, how comely it is, and how reviving
    To the spirits of just men long oppressed,
    When God into the hands of their deliverer   1270
    Puts invincible might,
    To quell the mighty of the earth, th' oppressor,
    The brute and boisterous force of violent men,
    Hardy and industrious to support
    Tyrannic power, but raging to pursue   1275
    The righteous, and all such as honor truth!

1. The vanguard of an army was, naturally, the first group engaged. Samson invites Harapha to start the fight.
2. Moon-goddess of the Philistines, consort of Dagon. See *Paradise Lost* I.437–46.
3. Boasts.
4. Excessive.
5. II Samuel xxi describes four giants "born to the giant in Gath" and slain by David; Milton makes the identification with Harapha on his own.

He all their ammunition
And feats of war defeats,[6]
With plain heroic magnitude of mind
And celestial vigor armed;   1280
Their armories and magazines contemns,
Renders them useless, while
With wingéd expedition [7]
Swift as the lightning glance he executes
His errand on the wicked, who, surprised,   1285
Lose their defense, distracted and amazed.
   But patience is more oft the exercise
Of saints, the trial of their fortitude,
Making them each his own deliverer,
And victor over all   1290
That tyranny or fortune can inflict.
Either of these is in thy lot,[8]
Samson, with might endued
Above the sons of men; but sight bereaved
May chance to number thee with those   1295
Whom patience finally must crown.[9]
   This Idol's day hath been to thee no day of rest,
Laboring thy mind
More than the working day thy hands.
And yet, perhaps, more trouble is behind;   1300
For I descry this way
Some other tending; in his hand
A scepter or quaint [1] staff he bears,
Comes on amain, speed in his look.
By his habit I discern him now   1305
A public officer, and now at hand.
His message will be short and voluble.[2]
OFFICER. Ebrews, the prisoner Samson here I seek.
CHORUS. His manacles remark [3] him; there he sits.
OFFICER. Samson, to thee our lords thus bid me say: 1310
This day to Dagon is a solemn feast,
With sacrifices, triumph, pomp, and games;
Thy strength they know surpassing human rate,
And now some public proof thereof require
To honor this great feast, and great assembly.   1315
Rise, therefore, with all speed, and come along,
Where I will see thee heartened and fresh clad,
To appear as fits before th' illustrious lords.
SAMSON. Thou know'st I am an Ebrew; therefore tell them
Our law forbids at their religious rites   1320
My presence; for that cause I cannot come.

6. A touch of the pervasive Miltonic
punning.
7. Haste.
8. Fate.
9. The Christian tragedy, like the Christian epic, must center ultimately on an
act of passive, not active, fortitude. It
is the special achievement of Samson to
combine in a single action both qualities.
1. Ornamented.
2. To the point.
3. Distinguish.

OFFICER. This answer, be assured, will not content them.
SAMSON. Have they not sword-players, and every sort
　Of gymnic artists, wrestlers, riders, runners,
　Jugglers and dancers, antics, mummers, mimics,[4]　1325
　But they must pick me out, with shackles tired,
　And over-labored at their public mill,
　To make them sport with blind activity?
　Do they not seek occasion of new quarrels,
　On my refusal, to distress me more,　1330
　Or make a game of my calamities?
　Return the way thou cam'st; I will not come.
OFFICER. Regard thyself; this will offend them highly.
SAMSON. Myself? my conscience, and internal peace.
　Can they think me so broken, so debased　1335
　With corporal servitude, that my mind ever
　Will condescend to such absurd commands?
　Although their drudge, to be their fool or jester,
　And, in my midst of sorrow and heart-grief,
　To show them feats, and play before their god,　1340
　The worst of all indignities, yet on me
　Joined [5] with supreme contempt! I will not come.
OFFICER. My message was imposed on me with speed,
　Brooks no delay: is this thy resolution?
SAMSON. So take it with what speed thy message needs.　1345
OFFICER. I am sorry what this stoutness [6] will produce.
SAMSON. Perhaps thou shalt have cause to sorrow indeed.
CHORUS. Consider, Samson; matters now are strained
　Up to the height, whether to hold or break.
　He's gone, and who knows how he may report　1350
　Thy words by adding fuel to the flame?
　Expect another message, more imperious,
　More lordly thundering than thou well wilt bear.
SAMSON. Shall I abuse this consecrated gift
　Of strength, again returning with my hair　1355
　After my great transgression, so requite
　Favor renewed, and add a greater sin
　By prostituting holy things to idols,
　A Nazarite, in place abominable,
　Vaunting my strength in honor to their Dagon?　1360
　Besides how vile, contemptible, ridiculous,
　What act more execrably unclean,[7] profane?
CHORUS. Where the heart joins not, outward acts defile not.
　Idolatrous, uncircumcised, unclean.
SAMSON. Not in their idol-worship, but by labor　1365
　Honest and lawful to deserve my food
　Of those who have me in their civil power.
CHORUS. Where the heart joins not, outward acts defile not.

---

4. "Gymnic artists": gymnasts; "antics": clowns; "mummers": actors.
5. Enjoined, ordered.

6. Defiance.
7. Taboo.

SAMSON. Where outward force constrains, the sentence holds: [8]
  But who constrains me to the temple of Dagon,   1370
  Not dragging? The Philistian lords command:
  Commands are no constraints. If I obey them,
  I do it freely, venturing to displease
  God for the fear of man, and man prefer,
  Set God behind; which, in his jealousy,   1375
  Shall never, unrepented, find forgiveness.
  Yet that he may dispense with me, or thee,
  Present in temples at idolatrous rites
  For some important cause,[9] thou need'st not doubt.
CHORUS. How thou wilt here come off surmounts my reach.   1380
SAMSON. Be of good courage; I begin to feel
  Some rousing motions in me, which dispose
  To something extraordinary my thoughts.
  I with this messenger will go along—
  Nothing to do, be sure, that may dishonor   1385
  Our Law, or stain my vow of Nazarite.
  If there be aught of presage in the mind,
  This day will be remarkable in my life
  By some great act, or of my days the last.[1]
CHORUS. In time thou hast resolved: the man returns.   1390
OFFICER. Samson, this second message from our lords
  To thee I am bid say: Art thou our slave,
  Our captive, at the public mill our drudge,
  And dar'st thou, at our sending and command,
  Dispute thy coming? Come without delay;   1395
  Or we shall find such engines to assail
  And hamper thee, as thou shalt come of force,
  Though thou wert firmlier fastened than a rock.
SAMSON. I could be well content to try their art,
  Which to no few of them would prove pernicious;   1400
  Yet, knowing their advantages too many,
  Because [2] they shall not trail me through their streets
  Like a wild beast, I am content to go.
  Masters' commands come with a power resistless
  To such as owe them absolute subjection;   1405
  And for a life who will not change his purpose?
  (So mutable are all the ways of men!)
  Yet this be sure, in nothing to comply
  Scandalous or forbidden in our Law.
OFFICER. I praise thy resolution.[3] Doff these links: 1410
  By this compliance thou wilt win the lords
  To favor, and perhaps to set thee free.

8. I.e., where outward force constrains, your motto may be right.
9. God will make a special dispensation for Samson to attend idolatrous ceremonies "for some important cause," which Samson cannot yet define but which he intuits.
1. By a classic device of dramatic irony, Samson proposes as alternatives two events which will both simultaneously come true. "Presage": premonition, presight.
2. So that.
3. Decision. "Doff these links": take off these chains.

SAMSON. Brethren, farewell. Your company along
  I will not wish, lest it perhaps offend them
  To see me girt with friends; and how the sight   1415
  Of me, as of a common enemy,
  So dreaded once, may now exasperate them
  I know not. Lords are lordliest in their wine;
  And the well-feasted priest then soonest fired
  With zeal, if aught religion seem concerned; [4]   1420
  No less the people, on their holy-days,
  Impetuous, insolent, unquenchable.
  Happen what may, of me expect to hear
  Nothing dishonorable, impure, unworthy
  Our God, our Law, my nation, or myself;   1425
  The last of me or no I cannot warrant.
CHORUS. Go, and the Holy One
  Of Israel be thy guide
  To what may serve his glory best, and spread his name
  Great among the heathen round;   1430
  Send thee the angel of thy birth, to stand
  Fast by thy side, who from thy father's field
  Rode up in flames after his message told
  Of thy conception, and be now a shield
  Of fire; that Spirit that first rushed on thee   1435
  In the camp of Dan,
  Be efficacious in thee now at need! [5]
  For never was from Heaven imparted
  Measure of strength so great to mortal seed
  As in thy wondrous actions hath been seen.   1440
  But wherefore comes old Manoa in such haste
  With youthful steps? Much livelier than erewhile
  He seems: supposing here to find his son,
  Or of him bringing to us some glad news?
MANOA. Peace with you, brethren! My inducement hither   1445
  Was not at present here to find my son,
  By order of the lords new parted hence
  To come and play before them at their feast.
  I heard all as I came; the city rings,
  And numbers thither flock: I had no will,   1450
  Lest I should see him forced to things unseemly.
  But that which moved my coming now was chiefly
  To give ye part with me [6] what hope I have
  With good success to work his liberty.
CHORUS. That hope would much rejoice us to partake   1455
  With thee. Say, reverend sire; we thirst to hear.
MANOA. I have attempted, one by one, the lords,

---

4. Milton's animus against paid priests, whom he considers particularly likely to contaminate the Word of God with their own private interests and worldly desires, comes out plainly here.
5. Samson's angel, appearing before his birth and at various crises during his life (Judges xiv.6,19; xv.14) is here invoked almost as a tutelary spirit or guardian angel.
6. I.e., to impart to you.

Either at home, or through the high street passing,
With supplication prone and father's tears,
To accept of ransom for my son, their prisoner.   1460
Some much averse I found, and wondrous harsh,
Contemptuous, proud, set on revenge and spite;
That part most reverenced Dagon and his priests:
Others more moderate seeming, but their aim
Private reward, for which both God and State   1465
They easily would set to sale: a third
More generous far and civil, who confessed
They had enough revenged, having reduced
Their foe to misery beneath their fears;
The rest was magnanimity to remit,   1470
If some convenient ransom were proposed.[7]
What noise or shout was that? It tore the sky.
CHORUS. Doubtless the people shouting to behold
Their once great dread, captive and blind before them,
Or at some proof of strength before them shown.   1475
MANOA. His ransom, if my whole inheritance
May compass it, shall willingly be paid
And numbered down. Much rather I shall choose
To live the poorest in my tribe, than richest
And he in that calamitous prison left.   1480
No, I am fixed not to part hence without him.
For his redemption all my patrimony,
If need be, I am ready to forgo
And quit. Not wanting him, I shall want nothing.
CHORUS. Fathers are wont to lay up for their sons;   1485
Thou for thy son art bent to lay out all:
Sons wont to nurse their parents in old age;
Thou in old age car'st how to nurse thy son,
Made older than thy age through eyesight lost.
MANOA. It shall be my delight to tend his eyes,   1490
And view him sitting in his house, ennobled
With all those high exploits by him achieved,
And on his shoulders waving down those locks
That of a nation armed the strength contained.
And I persuade me God hath not permitted   1495
His strength again to grow up with his hair
Garrisoned round about him like a camp
Of faithful soldiery, were not his purpose
To use him further yet in some great service—
Not to sit idle with so great a gift   1500
Useless, and thence ridiculous, about him.[8]
And, since his strength with eyesight was not lost,

7. The three parties are in effect bigots, swinders, and gentlemen—three types common enough in Restoration England, with whom Milton and the defeated Puritans must have had frequently to deal.
8. A good deal of the play deals with the concept of relevance and irrelevance; outward weapons and outward strength are often beside the point ("ridiculous") in the face of inward and spiritual powers.

God will restore him eyesight to [9] his strength.
CHORUS. Thy hopes are not ill founded, nor seem vain,
Of his delivery, and thy joy thereon   1505
Conceived, agreeable to a father's love;
In both which we, as next,[1] participate.
MANOA. I know your friendly minds, and—O, what noise!
Mercy of Heaven! what hideous noise was that?
Horribly loud, unlike the former shout.   1510
CHORUS. Noise call you it, or universal groan,
As if the whole inhabitation perished?
Blood, death, and deathful deeds, are in that noise,
Ruin,[2] destruction at the utmost point.
MANOA. Of ruin indeed methought I heard the noise.   1515
Oh! it continues; they have slain my son.
CHORUS. Thy son is rather slaying them; that outcry
From slaughter of one foe could not ascend.
MANOA. Some dismal accident it needs must be.
What shall we do, stay here, or run and see?   1520
CHORUS. Best keep together here, lest, running thither,
We unawares run into danger's mouth.
This evil on the Philistines is fallen:
From whom could else a general cry be heard?
The sufferers then will scarce molest us here;   1525
From other hands we need not much to fear.
What if, his eyesight (for to Israel's God
Nothing is hard) by miracle restored,
He now be dealing dole [3] among his foes,
And over heaps of slaughtered walk his way?   1530
MANOA. That were a joy presumptuous to be thought.
CHORUS. Yet God hath wrought things as incredible
For his people of old; what hinders now?
MANOA. He can, I know, but doubt to think he will;
Yet hope would fain subscribe, and tempts belief.   1535
A little stay will bring some notice hither.
CHORUS. Of good or bad so great, of bad the sooner;
For evil news rides post, while good news baits.[4]
And to our wish I see one hither speeding—
An Ebrew, as I guess, and of our tribe.   1540
MESSENGER.[5] O, whither shall I run, or which way fly
The sight of this so horrid spectacle,
Which erst [6] my eyes beheld, and yet behold?
For dire imagination still pursues me.
But providence or instinct of nature seems,   1545
Or reason, though disturbed, and scarce consulted,
To have guided me aright, I know not how,

9. To accompany.
1. "As next": as kinsmen.
2. From Latin *ruina*, downfall.
3. Wreaking havoc.
4. Pauses to renew (bait) the horses.
5. Greek tragedy forbade the representation on stage of actual bloodshed; a
messenger is therefore a frequent figure at the end of the Greek tragedy, arriving posthaste from the scene of the final catastrophe, to deliver in a long set speech a descriptive report.
6. A moment ago.

To thee first, reverend Manoa, and to these
My countrymen, whom here I knew remaining,
As [7] at some distance from the place of horror,   1550
So in the sad event too much concerned.
MANOA. The accident was loud, and here before thee
With rueful cry; yet what it was we hear not.
No preface needs; thou seest we long to know.
MESSENGER. It would burst forth; but I recover breath,   1555
And sense distract, to know well what I utter.
MANOA. Tell us the sum; the circumstance defer.
MESSENGER. Gaza yet stands; but all her sons are fallen,
All in a moment overwhelmed and fallen.
MANOA. Sad, but thou know'st to Israelites not saddest   1560
The desolation of a hostile city.
MESSENGER. Feed on that first; there may in grief be surfeit.[8]
MANOA. Relate by whom.
MESSENGER.   By Samson.
MANOA.   That still lessens
The sorrow, and coverts it nigh to joy.
MESSENGER. Ah! Manoa, I refrain too suddenly   1565
To utter what will come at last too soon,
Lest evil tidings, with too rude irruption
Hitting thy agéd ear, should pierce too deep.
MANOA. Suspense in news is torture; speak them out.
MESSENGER. Then take the worst in brief: Samson is dead.   1570
MANOA. The worst indeed! O, all my hopes defeated
To free him hence! but Death, who sets all free,
Hath paid his ransom now and full discharge.
What windy [9] joy this day had I conceived,
Hopeful of his delivery, which now proves   1575
Abortive as the first-born bloom of spring
Nipped with the lagging rear of winter's frost!
Yet, ere I give the reins to grief, say first
How died he; death to life is crown or shame.
All by him fell, thou say'st; by whom fell he?   1580
What glorious hand gave Samson his death's wound?
MESSENGER. Unwounded of his enemies he fell.
MANOA. Wearied with slaughter, then, or how? explain.
MESSENGER. By his own hands.
MANOA.   Self-violence! What cause
Brought him so soon at variance with himself   1585
Among his foes?
MESSENGER.   Inevitable cause
At once both to destroy and be destroyed.
The edifice, where all were met to see him,
Upon their heads and on his own he pulled.
MANOA. O lastly over-strong against thyself!   1590
A dreadful way thou took'st to thy revenge.

7. The construction "As . . . So . . ." is   to follow.
equivalent to a "Though . . . Yet . . .".   9. Empty and talky.
8. I.e., there may be all too much grief

More than enough we know; but, while things yet
Are in confusion, give us, if thou canst,
Eyewitness of what first or last was done,
Relation more particular and distinct.   1595
MESSENGER. Occasions drew me early to this city;
    And, as the gates I entered with sunrise,
    The morning trumpets festival proclaimed
    Through each high street. Little I had dispatched,
    When all abroad was rumored that this day   1600
    Samson should be brought forth, to show the people
    Proof of his mighty strength in feats and games.
    I sorrowed at his captive state, but minded
    Not to be absent at that spectacle.
    The building was a spacious theater,   1605
    Half round on two main pillars vaulted high,
    With seats where all the lords, and each degree
    Of sort,[1] might sit in order to behold;
    The other side was open, where the throng
    On banks and scaffolds under sky might stand:[2]   1610
    I among these aloof obscurely stood.
    The feast and noon grew high, and sacrifice
    Had filled their hearts with mirth, high cheer, and wine,
    When to their sports they turned. Immediately
    Was Samson as a public servant brought,   1615
    In their state livery clad: before him pipes
    And timbrels;[3] on each side went arméd guards;
    Both horse and foot before him and behind,
    Archers and slingers, cataphracts[4] and spears.
    At sight of him the people with a shout   1620
    Rifted the air, clamoring their god with praise,
    Who had made their dreadful enemy their thrall.
    He patient, but undaunted, where they led him,
    Came to the place; and what was set before him,
    Which without help of eye might be assayed,[5]   1625
    To heave, pull, draw, or break, he still performed
    All with incredible, stupendious force,
    None daring to appear antagonist.
    At length, for intermission sake, they led him
    Between the pillars; he his guide requested   1630
    (For so from such as nearer stood we heard),
    As over-tired, to let him lean a while
    With both his arms on those two massy pillars,
    That to the archéd roof gave main support.
    He unsuspicious led him; which when Samson   1635
    Felt in his arms, with head a while inclined,

---

1. Of rank.
2. The temple at Gaza comprised a covered pavilion or shell for the gentry, semi-circular in shape and supported at the center of the semi-circle by two pillars; on the open side, under the hot sun, and behind the stage, as it were, sat the common people.
3. Tambourines.
4. Armored horsemen on armored horses.
5. Attempted.

And eyes fast fixed, he stood, as one who prayed,
Or some great matter in his mind revolved:
At last, with head erect, thus cried aloud:
"Hitherto, Lords, what your commands imposed   1640
I have performed, as reason was, obeying,
Not without wonder or delight beheld;
Now, of my own accord,[6] such other trial
I mean to show you of my strength yet greater
As with amaze shall strike all who behold."   1645
This uttered, straining all his nerves,[7] he bowed;
As with the force of winds and waters pent
When mountains tremble,[8] those two massy pillars
With horrible convulsion to and fro
He tugged, he shook, till down they came, and drew   1650
The whole roof after them with burst of thunder
Upon the heads of all who sat beneath,
Lords, ladies, captains, counselors, or priests,
Their choice nobility and flower, not only
Of this, but each Philistian city round,   1655
Met from all parts to solemnize this feast.
Samson, with these immixed, inevitably
Pulled down the same destruction on himself;
The vulgar [9] only 'scaped, who stood without.

CHORUS. O dearly bought revenge, yet glorious!   1660
Living or dying thou hast fulfilled
The work for which thou wast foretold
To Israel, and now li'st victorious
Among thy slain self-killed;
Not willingly, but tangled in the fold   1665
Of dire Necessity,[1] whose law in death conjoined
Thee with thy slaughtered foes, in number more
Than all thy life had slain before.

SEMICHORUS. While their hearts were jocund and sublime,[2]
Drunk with idolatry, drunk with wine   1670
And fat regorged [3] of bulls and goats,
Chaunting their idol, and preferring
Before our living Dread, who dwells
In Silo, his bright sanctuary,[4]
Among them he a spirit of frenzy sent,   1675
Who hurt their minds,
And urged them on with mad desire
To call in haste for their destroyer.
They, only set on sport and play,

---

6. Latin, *mea sponte,* on spontaneous impulse of conscience.
7. Muscles.
8. Earthquakes in Milton's day were supposed to be the effect of escaping winds and waters imprisoned (pent) beneath the earth.

9. The common people.
1. Samson must not be supposed guilty of suicide. See above, lines 1586–87.
2. Joyous and exalted.
3. Greedily devoured.
4. Shiloh, where the Israelites established their tabernacle (Joshua xviii.1).

Unweetingly [5] importuned   1680
Their own destruction to come speedy upon them.
So fond are mortal men,
Fallen into wrath divine,
As their own ruin on themselves to invite,
Insensate left, or to sense reprobate,   1685
And with blindness internal [6] struck.

SEMICHORUS. But he, though blind of sight,
  Despised, and thought extinguished quite,
  With inward eyes illuminated,
  His fiery virtue roused   1690
  From under ashes into sudden flame,
  And as an evening dragon [7] came,
  Assailant on the perchéd roosts
  And nests in order ranged
  Of tame villatic [8] fowl, but as an eagle   1695
  His cloudless thunder bolted on their heads.
  So Virtue, given for lost,[9]
  Depressed and overthrown, as seemed,
  Like that self-begotten bird,[1]
  In the Arabian woods embossed,[2]   1700
  That no second knows nor third,
  And lay erewhile a holocaust,[3]
  From out her ashy womb now teemed,
  Revives, reflourishes, then vigorous most
  When most unactive deemed;   1705
  And, though her body die, her fame survives,
  A secular [4] bird, ages of lives.

MANOA. Come, come; no time for lamentation now,
  Nor much more cause. Samson hath quit [5] himself
  Like Samson, and heroicly hath finished   1710
  A life heroic, on his enemies
  Fully revenged; hath left them years of mourning
  And lamentation to the sons of Caphtor [6]
  Through all Philistian bounds; to Israel
  Honor hath left and freedom, let but them   1715
  Find courage to lay hold on this occasion;
  To himself and father's house eternal fame;
  And, which is best and happiest yet, all this
  With God not parted from him, as was feared,
  But favoring and assisting to the end.   1720
  Nothing is here for tears, nothing to wail

5. Unwittingly.
6. The play accomplishes itself by showing the internal blindness of the Philistines at the very moment of Samson's spiritual illumination.
7. Serpent (from Latin, *draco*).
8. Farmyard (from Latin, *villaticus*); "bolted": cast as a thunderbolt.
9. "Given up for lost."
1. The mythical phoenix begets itself out of its own ashes; it is unique, that is, there is only one phoenix alive at any one time, and it lives in the deserts of Arabia.
2. Enclosed, hidden.
3. A sacrifice burned whole on the altar.
4. Living through the centuries (Latin, *saecula*).
5. Acquitted.
6. In Amos ix.7 the Philistines are described as immigrants from Caphtor, i.e. Crete.

Or knock the breast; no weakness, no contempt,
Dispraise, or blame; nothing but well and fair,
And what may quiet us in a death so noble.
Let us go find the body where it lies   1725
Soaked in his enemies' blood, and from the stream
With lavers [7] pure, and cleansing herbs, wash off
The clotted gore. I, with what speed the while [8]
(Gaza is not in plight to say us nay),
Will send for all my kindred, all my friends,   1730
To fetch him hence, and solemnly attend,
With silent obsequy and funeral train,
Home to his father's house. There will I build him
A monument, and plant it round with shade
Of laurel ever green and branching palm,[9]   1735
With all his trophies hung, and acts enrolled
In copious legend, or sweet lyric song.
Thither shall all the valiant youth resort,
And from his memory inflame their breasts
To matchless valor and adventures high;   1740
The virgins also shall, on feastful days,
Visit his tomb with flowers, only bewailing
His lot unfortunate in nuptial choice,
From whence captivity and loss of eyes.

CHORUS.[1] All is best, though we oft doubt   1745
What th' unsearchable dispose [2]
Of Highest Wisdom brings about,
And ever best found in the close.
Oft he seems to hide his face,
But unexpectedly returns,   1750
And to his faithful champion hath in place [3]
Bore witness gloriously; whence Gaza mourns,
And all that band them to resist
His uncontrollable intent.
His servants he, with new acquist [4]   1755
Of true experience from this great event,
With peace and consolation hath dismissed,
And calm of mind, all passion spent.   1671

7. Basins.
8. I.e., with what speed (I may) in the meanwhile.
9. Leaves of laurel were worn by civic conquerors on triumphal occasions; wreaths of palm were given to victors in the Olympic games. Samson, as both

an athletic victor in his *agon* and the favored of Heaven, gets both.
1. The final chorus of the play is cast in the form of a sonnet.
2. Appointment, disposition.
3. On this very spot, at this very instant.
4. Increase, acquisition.

FRANCIS BACON
(1561–1626)

1597: First edition of the *Essays* (augmented and revised editions in 1612 and 1625).
1605: *The Advancement of Learning.*
1620: *Novum Organum.*
1621: Bacon's disgrace and retirement.

"The wisest, brightest, meanest of mankind"—in these words Pope described the character of Francis Bacon; and the adjectives have clung to his reputation like an evil odor. Nor are they entirely unjust. Bacon was one of those cool, controlled spirits who seem to have such empire over themselves, and over the world, that we are secretly a bit glad when they fail in some shameful and humiliating way. The younger son of a high Elizabethan official, Bacon studied law at Cambridge and Gray's Inn. He then rose steadily and securely through the legal bureaucracy of Elizabeth and James until he stood at the head of his profession, as Lord Chancellor of England. In passing, he sprinkled his career with magisterial essays on human conduct and lordly surveys of human learning. In 1618 he was created Baron Verulam; in 1621, he became Viscount St. Albans. Two months later, he fell from grace with a crash, accused of taking bribes in office, and confessing himself guilty of corruption and neglect. The last five years of his life were spent in retirement. His name has stood since as that of a man a little inhuman in his brilliance but all too human in his frailties.

Informal prose discourse was familiar to the classic writers, but it usually took the form of the epistle, the dialogue, or the impersonal treatise; the essay is essentially a modern form, of Renaissance invention. A series of tentative and often individual formulations, it offers a fluid and casual way of exploring one's relations to the world; it implies an interest in the self which Renaissance men were probably the first to feel. Bacon, who published in 1597, was the first English essayist; indeed, the very first essayist of all, Michel de Montaigne, antedated him by only seventeen years. But Bacon's essays are so different from Montaigne's as to constitute almost a fresh and separate act of creation.

Bacon's essays make little effort to follow the Montaigne pattern of leisurely self-exploration and discursive self-revelation; their sententious clarity compresses complex angles of speculation into a phrase. Bacon gives us a Lord Chancellor's view of the world; he sees it shrewdly, from the outside and from above, and delivers his judgment in sentences. Talking on a topic like *Marriage and Single Life*, he is cold common sense personified; one could not possibly tell from the essay itself whether he was married or not when he wrote it. (He waited, actually, to the prudent age of 45 before yielding a hostage to fortune, and he never had any children.)

Montaigne, writing on this topic, would have told us on the first page about his marriage, its pleasures, its problems, his hopes, his fears, his children. The Baconian essay is more formal, more philosophical; it owes more to Seneca. And Bacon's general position in the history of the English essay is fittingly one of solitary eminence. Cowley, his only rival in the 17th century, did not publish till 1661, and then in the vein of Montaigne. It was not till the age of Joseph Addison and Sir Richard Steele, the early 18th century, that Bacon, the founder of the formal essay, acquired his first followers.

But Bacon's greatest achievement is not his *Essays*; rather, it is his scientific writing, all of which he contemplated arranging in one gigantic structure to be known as "The Great Instauration." The "new instrument of learning" announced in *Novum Organum* was to be the second part of this great project; the book represents a preliminary arrangement of the actual field of human learning in relation to man's potential knowledge. The simple audacity of this subject is enough to make one gasp; and the fact is that Bacon shared too many of the mistaken views of the age ever to be able to discriminate truth from falsehood in a wholesale way. Yet this is not the impression with which a reading of *Novum Organum* ultimately leaves us. Though he may have been mistaken in a hundred particulars, the general rightness of Bacon's intellectual method is not open to dispute; and the confidence with which he pointed a new direction for the human mind encouraged and enlightened experimenters in a hundred different disciplines.

The third section of the Great Instauration was to be a natural history of formidable proportions. One fragment which Bacon wrote in connection with this project (probably as early as 1617) is the little fantasy known as *The New Atlantis*. Bacon never finished this sketch, and never published it; it is less pretentious than his other works, and perhaps less polished. Yet it has proved one of the most popular and stimulating things he ever wrote. His idea of a "Solomon's House" devoted to study and research in the natural sciences was certainly responsible for the chartering of the Royal Society, more than thirty years after Bacon's death.

Bacon himself died a martyr to the scientific spirit, though perhaps not as dramatically as one would like: while collecting snow to refrigerate a chicken, he caught a cold and died of bronchitis. Yet of him, more than of any other 17th-century figure, it can be said that if you seek his monument, you have only to look at the world about you. Modern science would have existed without Bacon, but it certainly would not have been modern science as we know it.

From Essays
Of Truth

"What is truth?" said jesting Pilate; and would not stay for an answer.[1] Certainly there be that delight in giddiness,[2] and count it

1. See John xviii.38 for Pilate's idle query to Jesus.

2. Changeability, insecurity of ideas. "That": those who.

a bondage to fix a belief; affecting free-will in thinking, as well as in acting. And though the sects of philosophers of that kind[3] be gone, yet there remain certain discoursing wits, which are of the same veins, though there be not so much blood in them as was in those of the ancients. But it is not only the difficulty and labor which men take in finding out of truth; nor again, that when it is found, it imposeth upon[4] men's thoughts, that doth bring lies in favor; but a natural though corrupt love of the lie itself. One of the later school of the Grecians examineth the matter, and is at a stand to think what should be in it, that men should love lies; where neither they make for pleasure, as with poets; nor for advantage, as with the merchant, but for the lie's sake. But I cannot tell:[5] this same truth is a naked and open daylight, that doth not show the masks and mummeries and triumphs of the world half so stately and daintily as candle lights. Truth may perhaps come to the price of a pearl, that showeth best by day, but it will not rise to the price of a diamond or carbuncle,[6] that showeth best in varied lights. A mixture of a lie doth ever add pleasure. Doth any man doubt that if there were taken out of men's minds vain opinions, flattering hopes, false valuations, imaginations as one would, and the like, but it would leave the minds of a number of men poor shrunken things, full of melancholy and indisposition, and unpleasing to themselves? One of the fathers, in great severity, called poesy *vinum daemonum*,[7] because it filleth the imagination, and yet it is but with the shadow of a lie. But it is not the lie that passeth through the mind, but the lie that sinketh in, and settleth in it, that doth the hurt, such as we spake of before. But howsoever these things are thus in men's depraved judgments and affections, yet truth, which only doth judge itself, teacheth that the inquiry of truth, which is the love-making, or wooing of it, the knowledge of truth, which is the presence of it, and the belief of truth, which is the enjoying of it, is the sovereign good of human nature. The first creature[8] of God, in the works of the days, was the light of the sense; the last was the light of reason; and His sabbath work ever since is the illumination of His Spirit. First, He breathed light upon the face of the matter, or chaos; then He breathed light into the face of man; and still He breatheth and inspireth light into the face of His chosen. The poet that beautified the sect that was otherwise inferior to the rest[9] saith yet excellently well: "It is a pleasure to stand upon the shore, and to see ships tossed upon the sea: a pleasure to stand in the window of a castle,

3. The Greek Skeptics, who taught the uncertainty of all knowledge. "Discoursing wits": discursive minds.
4. Restricts, limits.
5. "I cannot tell," says Bacon, and tells.
6. Ruby.
7. The wine of devils; St. Augustine is probably being cited.
8. Creation.
9. Lucretius' *On the Nature of Things* expressed the Epicurean creed, which Bacon thought inferior because it emphasized pleasure. The passage cited comprises the first words of Book I.

and to see a battle, and the adventures thereof below: but no pleasure is comparable to the standing upon the vantage ground of truth" (a hill not to be commanded,[1] and where the air is always clear and serene), "and to see the errors, and wanderings, and mists, and tempests, in the vale below": so always that this prospect[2] be with pity, and not with swelling or pride. Certainly, it is heaven upon earth to have a man's mind move in charity, rest in providence, and turn upon the poles of truth.

To pass from theological and philosophical truth to the truth of civil business; it will be acknowledged even by those that practice it not, that clear and round dealing[3] is the honor of man's nature, and that mixture of falsehood is like alloy in coin of gold and silver, which may make the metal work the better, but it embaseth[4] it. For these winding and crooked courses are the goings of the serpent; which goeth basely upon the belly, and not upon the feet. There is no vice that doth so cover a man with shame as to be found false and perfidious; and therefore Montaigne saith prettily, when he inquired the reason why the word of the lie should be such a disgrace, and such an odious charge, saith he, "If it be well weighed, to say that a man lieth is as much as to say that he is brave towards God and a coward towards men."[5] For a lie faces God, and shrinks from man. Surely the wickedness of falsehood and breach of faith cannot possibly be so highly expressed, as in that it shall be the last peal to call the judgments of God upon the generations of men, it being foretold that when Christ cometh, he shall not "find faith upon the earth."[6]

1625

Of Marriage and Single Life[1]

He that hath wife and children hath given hostages to fortune; for they are impediments to great enterprises, either of virtue or mischief. Certainly the best works, and of greatest merit for the public, have proceeded from the unmarried or childless men, which both in affection and means have married and endowed the public. Yet it were great reason that those that have children should have greatest care of future times, unto which they know they must transmit their dearest pledges. Some there are who, though they lead a single life, yet their thoughts do end with themselves, and account future times impertinences.[2] Nay, there are some other that account wife and children but as bills of charges. Nay more, there

1. Dominated.
2. I.e., provided always that this contemplation.
3. The dealing that Bacon calls "round" we should describe as "square."
4. Debases.
5. *Essays* II.18.
6. Luke xviii.8.
1. The text is that of the 1625 edition.
2. Irrelevant concerns.

are some foolish rich covetous men that take a pride in having no children, because they may be thought so much the richer. For perhaps they have heard some talk, "Such an one is a great rich man," and another except to it, "Yea, but he hath a great charge of children"; as if it were an abatement to his riches. But the most ordinary cause of a single life is liberty, especially in certain self-pleasing and humorous[3] minds, which are so sensible of every restraint, as they will go near to think their girdles and garters to be bonds and shackles. Unmarried men are best friends, best masters, best servants, but not always best subjects, for they are light to run away, and almost all fugitives are of that condition. A single life doth well with churchmen, for charity will hardly water the ground where it must first fill a pool. It is indifferent for judges and magistrates, for if they be facile[4] and corrupt, you shall have a servant five times worse than a wife. For soldiers, I find the generals commonly in their hortatives[5] put men in mind of their wives and children; and I think the despising of marriage amongst the Turks maketh the vulgar soldier more base. Certainly wife and children are a kind of discipline of humanity; and single men, though they be many times more charitable, because their means are less exhaust,[6] yet, on the other side, they are more cruel and hard-hearted (good to make severe inquisitors), because their tenderness is not so oft called upon. Grave natures, led by custom, and therefore constant, are commonly loving husbands, as was said of Ulysses, *Vetulam suam praetulit immortalitati.*[7] Chaste women are often proud and froward, as presuming upon the merit of their chastity. It is one of the best bonds, both of chastity and obedience, in the wife if she think her husband wise, which she will never do if she find him jealous. Wives are young men's mistresses, companions for middle age, and old men's nurses, so as a man may have a quarrel[8] to marry when he will. But yet he was reputed one of the wise men that made answer to the question when a man should marry: "A young man not yet, an elder man not at all."[9] It is often seen that bad husbands have very good wives; whether it be that it raiseth the price of their husbands' kindness when it comes, or that the wives take a pride in their patience. But this never fails, if the bad husbands were of their own choosing, against their friends' consent; for then they will be sure to make good their own folly.

1612, 1625

3. Unbalanced, whimsical.
4. Pliable.
5. Exhortations.
6. Exhausted, drained.
7. "He preferred his old wife to immortality." Ulysses might have had immortality in the company of the nymph Calypso, but preferred to go back to Penelope.
8. Pretext.
9. Thales (6th century B.C.) was the confirmed bachelor who made this remark. He was one of the Seven Sages of Greece.

Of Great Place[1]

Men in great place are thrice servants: servants of the sovereign or state, servants of fame, and servants of business. So as they have no freedom, neither in their persons, nor in their actions, nor in their times. It is a strange desire, to seek power and lose liberty, or to seek power over others and to lose power over a man's self. The rising unto place is laborious, and by pains men come to greater pains; and it is sometimes base, and by indignities men come to dignities. The standing is slippery, and the regress is either a downfall or at least an eclipse, which is a melancholy thing: *Cum non sis qui fueris, non esse cur velis vivere.*[2] Nay, retire men cannot when they would, neither will they when it were reason; but are impatient of privateness,[3] even in age and sickness, which require the shadow; like old townsmen, that will be still sitting at their street door, though thereby they offer age to scorn. Certainly, great persons had need to borrow other men's opinions to think themselves happy; for if they judge by their own feeling, they cannot find it; but if they think with themselves what other men think of them, and that other men would fain be as they are, then they are happy, as it were by report; when perhaps they find the contrary within. For they are the first that find their own griefs, though they be the last that find their own faults. Certainly, men in great fortunes are strangers to themselves, and while they are in the puzzle of business they have no time to tend their health, either of body or mind. *Illi mors gravis incubat, qui notus nimis omnibus, ignotus moritur sibi.*[4] In place there is license to do good and evil, whereof the latter is a curse; for in evil the best condition is not to will, the second not to can.[5] But power to do good is the true and lawful end of aspiring; for good thoughts (though God accept them) yet towards men are little better than good dreams, except they be put in act; and that cannot be without power and place, as the vantage and commanding ground. Merit and good works is the end of man's motion, and conscience[6] of the same is the accomplishment of man's rest; for if a man can be partaker of God's theater,[7] he shall likewise be partaker of God's rest. *Et conversus Deus, ut aspiceret opera quae fecerunt manus suae, vidit quod omnia essent bona nimis;*[8] and then the sabbath.

1. The text is that of the 1625 edition.
2. "When you aren't what you were, there's no reason to live" (Cicero, *Familiar Letters* vii.3).
3. I.e., they object to retirement. "The shadow" is that of retirement, out of the glare of public life.
4. "Death lies heavily on him who, while too well known to everyone else, dies unknown to himself" (Seneca, *Thyestes*).
5. Be able.
6. Consciousness.
7. The world.
8. "And God saw every thing that he had made, and, behold, it was very good" (Genesis i.31).

In the discharge of thy place set before thee the best examples, for imitation is a globe[9] of precepts. And after a time set before thee thine own example; and examine thyself strictly, whether thou didst not best at first. Neglect not also the examples of those that have carried themselves ill in the same place; not to set off thyself by taxing[1] their memory, but to direct thyself what to avoid. Reform, therefore, without bravery, or scandal[2] of former times and persons; but yet set it down to thyself, as well to create good precedents as to follow them. Reduce things to the first institution,[3] and observe wherein and how they have degenerate; but yet ask counsel of both times; of the ancient time what is best, and of the latter time what is fittest. Seek to make thy course regular, that men may know beforehand what they may expect; but be not too positive and peremptory, and express thyself well when thou digressest from thy rule. Preserve the right of thy place, but stir not questions of jurisdiction; and rather assume thy right in silence and *de facto*,[4] than voice it with claims and challenges. Preserve likewise the rights of inferior places, and think it more honor to direct in chief than to be busy in all. Embrace and invite helps and advices touching the execution of thy place, and do not drive away such as bring thee information as meddlers, but accept of them in good part. The vices of authority are chiefly four: delays, corruption, roughness, and facility.[5] For delays, give easy access, keep times appointed, go through with that which is in hand, and interlace not business[6] but of necessity. For corruption, do not only bind thine own hands or thy servants' hands from taking, but bind the hands of suitors also from offering. For integrity used doth the one; but integrity professed and with a manifest detestation of bribery, doth the other. And avoid not only the fault, but the suspicion. Whosoever is found variable and changeth manifestly, without manifest cause, giveth suspicion of corruption. Therefore, always when thou changest thine opinion or course, profess it plainly and declare it, together with the reasons that move thee to change; and do not think to steal it.[7] A servant or a favorite, if he be inward,[8] and no other apparent cause of esteem, is commonly thought but a by-way to close[9] corruption. For roughness, it is a needless cause of discontent; severity breedeth fear, but roughness breedeth hate. Even reproofs from authority ought to be grave, and not taunting. As for facility, it is worse than bribery; for bribes come but now and then; but if importunity or idle respects[1] lead a man, he shall never be without. As Solomon saith, "To respect persons is not good, for such a man will transgress for a piece of bread."[2]

9. World.
1. Blaming.
2. Defaming, imputing evil to. "Bravery": ostentation.
3. I.e., go back to first principles.
4. Without debate as to right and wrong, as a matter of course.
5. Docility, too great obligingness.

6. I.e., do not carry on different businesses at the same time.
7. Change your mind without its being noticed.
8. In his master's confidence.
9. Secret.
1. Irrelevant considerations.
2. Cf. Proverbs xxviii.21.

It is most true that was anciently spoken, "A place showeth the man"; and it showeth some to the better and some to the worse. *Omnium consensu capax imperii, nisi imperasset,*[3] saith Tacitus of Galba; but of Vespasian he saith, *Solus imperantium Vespasianus mutatus in melius:*[4] though the one was meant of sufficiency, the other of manners and affection. It is an assured sign of a worthy and generous spirit, whom honor amends.[5] For honor is, or should be, the place of virtue; and as in nature things move violently to their place and calmly in their place, so virtue in ambition is violent, in authority settled and calm. All rising to great place is by a winding stair; and if there be factions, it is good to side a man's self[6] whilst he is in the rising, and to balance himself when he is placed. Use the memory of thy predecessor fairly and tenderly; for if thou dost not, it is a debt will sure be paid when thou art gone. If thou have colleagues, respect them, and rather call them when they look not for it, than exclude them when they have reason to look to be called. Be not too sensible[7] or too remembering of thy place in conversation and private answers to suitors; but let it rather be said, "When he sits in place he is another man."

1612, 1625

Of Studies[1]

Studies serve for delight, for ornament, and for ability. Their chief use for delight is in privateness[2] and retiring; for ornament, is in discourse; and for ability, is in the judgment and disposition of business. For expert men[3] can execute, and perhaps judge of particulars, one by one; but the general counsels, and the plots and marshaling of affairs, come best from those that are learned. To spend too much time in studies is sloth; to use them too much for ornament is affectation; to make judgment wholly by their rules is the humor[4] of a scholar. They perfect nature, and are perfected by experience; for natural abilities are like natural plants, that need pruning by study; and studies themselves do give forth directions too much at large, except they be bounded in by experience. Crafty men contemn studies, simple men admire them, and wise men use them, for they teach not their own use; but that is a wisdom without them, and above them, won by observation. Read not to contradict and confute, nor to believe and take for granted, nor to find talk and discourse, but to weigh and consider. Some books are to be tasted,

3. "Everyone would have thought him a good ruler, if he had not ruled."
4. "Of all the emperors, only Vespasian changed for the better." "Sufficiency": abilities. "Affection": disposition.
5. I.e., whom promotion improves.
6. For a man to take sides.

7. Sensitive.
1. The text is that of the 1625 edition.
2. Private life.
3. Men of experience, the English adjective being used in its Latin sense, *experti*.
4. Mannerism, implying absurd error.

others to be swallowed, and some few to be chewed and digested; that is, some books are to be read only in parts; others to be read, but not curiously;[5] and some few to be read wholly, and with diligence and attention. Some books also may be read by deputy and extracts made of them by others, but that would be only in the less important arguments and the meaner sort of books; else distilled books are like common distilled waters,[6] flashy things. Reading maketh a full man, conference[7] a ready man, and writing an exact man. And therefore, if a man write little, he had need have a great memory; if he confer little, he had need have a present wit;[8] and if he read little, he had need have more cunning, to seem to know that[9] he doth not. Histories make men wise; poets, witty;[1] the mathematics, subtle; natural philosophy, deep; moral, grave; logic and rhetoric, able to contend. *Abeunt studia in mores*.[2] Nay, there is no stond or impediment in the wit but may be wrought out by fit studies, like as diseases of the body may have appropriate exercises. Bowling is good for the stone and reins,[3] shooting for the lungs and breast, gentle walking for the stomach, riding for the head, and the like. So if a man's wit be wandering, let him study the mathematics; for in demonstrations, if his wit be called away never so little, he must begin again. If his wit be not apt to distinguish or find differences, let him study the schoolmen,[4] for they are *Cymini sectores*. If he be not apt to beat over matters[5] and to call up one thing to prove and illustrate another, let him study the lawyer's cases. So every defect of the mind may have a special receipt.[6]

1597, 1625

From Novum Organum[1]

[*The Idols*]

50

But by far the greatest hindrance and aberration of the human understanding proceeds from the dullness, incompetency, and de-

5. Not with care.
6. Infusions of herbs, etc., used as home remedies.
7. Conversation, meetings.
8. Lively intelligence.
9. That which.
1. Imaginative, inventive.
2. "Studies culminate in manners" (Ovid, *Heroides*). "Stond": difficulty.
3. Gall bladder and kidneys.
4. Medieval theologians. The Latin means "dividers of cuminseed," i.e., hairsplitters.
5. Discuss a subject thoroughly.
6. Cure, prescription.
1. *Novum Organum*, or "The New In-

strument of Learning," does not properly represent a work of English literature, since it was written in Latin, for an international scholarly audience. (Bacon rather mistrusted the modern languages, thinking they would "wear away" in time; but Latin was safe.) Still, no history of English ideas can afford to ignore this book; for it was the keystone of Bacon's vast project to renovate the structure of human learning from the ground up. The translation is that of Spedding, Ellis, and Heath, from their edition of the *Works* (1860–64).

Observation was the essential process

ceptions of the senses; in that things which strike the sense out-weigh things which do not immediately strike it, though they[2] be more important. Hence it is that speculation commonly ceases where sight ceases; insomuch that of things invisible there is little or no observation. Hence all the working of the spirits enclosed in tangible bodies lies hid and unobserved of men.[3] So also all the more subtle changes of form in the parts of coarser substances (which they commonly call alteration, though it is in truth local motion through exceedingly small spaces) is in like manner unob-served. And yet unless these two things just mentioned be searched out and brought to light, nothing great can be achieved in nature, as far as the production of works is concerned. So again the essential nature of our common air, and of all bodies less dense than air (which are very many), is almost unknown. For the sense by itself is a thing infirm and erring; neither can instruments for enlarging or sharpening the senses do much; but all the truer kind of interpre-tation of nature is effected by instances and experiments fit and apposite; wherein the sense decides touching the experiment only, and the experiment touching the point in nature and the thing itself.

51

The human understanding is of its own nature prone to abstrac-tions and gives a substance and reality to things which are fleeting. But to resolve nature into abstractions is less to our purpose than to dissect her into parts; as did the school of Democritus,[4] which went further into nature than the rest. Matter rather than forms should be the object of our attention, its configurations and changes of configuration, and simple action, and law of action or motion; for forms are figments of the human mind, unless you will call those laws of action forms.

52

Such then are the idols which I call *Idols of the Tribe;*[5] and which take their rise either from the homogeneity of the substance of the human spirit, or from its preoccupation, or from its narrowness, or

of Bacon's new method; he felt that only observation, long continued and carefully directed, was capable of pro-ducing certainty about the operations of nature. As against the true intel-lectual mean produced by careful ob-servation and controlled experiment, he set the frivolity of the skeptics and the unwarranted confidence of the dog-matists. This argument rises to its height about halfway through the first (destructive) part of the book, in an extended account of the various Idols, or delusive ideas, which mislead and bewilder the human understanding.
2. The latter.
3. Though his views on scientific method were amazingly modern, Bacon's ideas about physical phenomena were those

of his age; he believed in subtle spirit-ual principles which might lie concealed in physical objects, unobserved by men.
4. The school of Democritus, the "laughing philosopher" of ancient Greece (5th century B.C.), held that the world was composed of atoms. Democritus developed the atomic theory, of which Leucippus was the originator; Lucretius (four centuries later) became the great literary ex-ponent of this school.
5. By "Idols" Bacon means delusive images of truth, leading men away from the exact knowledge of science. By "Idols of the Tribe" he denotes par-ticularly generalizations based on in-adequate facts—a fault to which all men are prone.

from its restless motion, or from an infusion of the affections, or from the incompetency of the senses, or from the mode of impression.

53

The *Idols of the Cave* take their rise in the peculiar constitution, mental or bodily, of each individual; and also in education, habit, and accident. Of this kind there is a great number and variety; but I will instance those the pointing out of which contains the most important caution, and which have most effect in disturbing the clearness of the understanding.

54

Men become attached to certain particular sciences[6] and speculations, either because they fancy themselves the authors and inventors thereof, or because they have bestowed the greatest pains upon them and become most habituated to them. But men of this kind, if they betake themselves to philosophy and contemplations of a general character, distort and color them in obedience to their former fancies; a thing especially to be noticed in Aristotle, who made his natural philosophy a mere bondservant to his logic, thereby rendering it contentious and well nigh useless. The race of chemists[7] again out of a few experiments of the furnace have built up a fantastic philosophy, framed with reference to a few things; and Gilbert also, after he had employed himself most laboriously in the study and observation of the loadstone, proceeded at once to construct an entire system in accordance with his favorite subject.[8]

55

There is one principal and, as it were, radical distinction between different minds, in respect of philosophy and the sciences, which is this: that some minds are stronger and apter to mark the differences of things, others to mark their resemblances. The steady and acute mind can fix its contemplations and dwell and fasten on the subtlest distinctions: the lofty and discursive mind recognizes and puts together the finest and most general resemblances. Both kinds however easily err in excess, by catching the one at gradations, the other at shadows.

56

There are found some minds given to an extreme admiration of antiquity, others to an extreme love and appetite for novelty; but few so duly tempered that they can hold the mean, neither carping at what has been well laid down by the ancients, nor despising what is well introduced by the moderns. This however turns to the great injury of the sciences and philosophy; since these affectations of antiquity and novelty are the humors of partisans rather than judg-

---

6. Ideas, bits of information.
7. Alchemists.
8. William Gilbert, author of a famous treatise on the magnet (1600), serves Bacon (rather unfairly) as an example of dogmatism founded on a few limited experiments.

ments; and truth is to be sought for not in the felicity of any age, which is an unstable thing, but in the light of nature and experience, which is eternal. These factions therefore must be abjured, and care must be taken that the intellect be not hurried by them into assent.

57

Contemplations of nature and of bodies in their simple form break up and distract the understanding, while contemplations of nature and bodies in their composition and configuration overpower and dissolve the understanding:[9] a distinction well seen in the school of Leucippus and Democritus as compared with the other philosophies. For that school is so busied with the particles that it hardly attends to the structure; while the others are so lost in admiration of the structure that they do not penetrate to the simplicity of nature. These kinds of contemplation should therefore be alternated and taken by turns; that so the understanding may be rendered at once penetrating and comprehensive, and the inconveniences above mentioned, with the idols which proceed from them, may be avoided.

58

Let such then be our provision and contemplative prudence for keeping off and dislodging the *Idols of the Cave*, which grow for the most part either out of the predominance of a favorite subject, or out of an excessive tendency to compare or to distinguish, or out of partiality for particular ages, or out of the largeness or minuteness of the objects contemplated. And generally let every student of nature take this as a rule—that whatever his mind seizes and dwells upon with peculiar satisfaction is to be held in suspicion, and that so much the more care is to be taken in dealing with such questions to keep the understanding even and clear.

59

But the *Idols of the Market-place* are the most troublesome of all: idols which have crept into the understanding through the alliances of words and names. For men believe that their reason governs words; but it is also true that words react on the understanding; and this it is that has rendered philosophy and the sciences sophistical and inactive. Now words, being commonly framed and applied according to the capacity of the vulgar, follow those lines of division which are most obvious to the vulgar understanding. And whenever an understanding of greater acuteness or a more diligent observation would alter those lines to suit the true divisions of nature, words stand in the way and resist the change. Whence it comes to pass that the high and formal discussions of learned men end oftentimes in disputes about words and names; with which (according to the use[1] and wisdom of the mathematicians) it would be more prudent to begin, and so by means of definitions reduce them to order. Yet

9. I.e., reducing nature to first principles is, intellectually, as dangerous as trying to observe all its particulars.
1. Custom.

even definitions cannot cure this evil in dealing with natural and material things; since the definitions themselves consist of words, and those words beget others: so that it is necessary to recur to individual instances, and those in due series and order; as I shall say presently when I come to the method and scheme for the formation of notions and axioms.[2]

60

The idols imposed by words on the understanding are of two kinds. They are either names of things which do not exist (for as there are things left unnamed through lack of observation, so likewise are there names which result from fantastic suppositions and to which nothing in reality responds), or they are names of things which exist, but yet confused and ill-defined, and hastily and irregularly derived from realities. Of the former kind are Fortune, the Prime Mover, Planetary Orbits, Element of Fire, and like fictions which owe their origin to false and idle theories.[3] And this class of idols is more easily expelled, because to get rid of them it is only necessary that all theories should be steadily rejected and dismissed as obsolete.[4]

But the other class, which springs out of a faulty and unskillful abstraction, is intricate and deeply rooted. Let us take for example such a word as *humid*; and see how far the several things which the word is used to signify agree with each other; and we shall find the word *humid* to be nothing else than a mark loosely and confusedly applied to denote a variety of actions which will not bear to be reduced to any constant meaning. For it both signifies that which easily spreads itself round any other body; and that which in itself is indeterminate and cannot solidize; and that which readily yields in every direction; and that which easily divides and scatters itself; and that which easily unites and collects itself; and that which readily flows and is put in motion; and that which readily clings to another body and wets it; and that which is easily reduced to a liquid, or being solid easily melts. Accordingly when you come to apply the word—if you take it in one sense, flame is humid; if in another, air is not humid; if in another, fine dust is humid; if in another, glass is humid. So that it is easy to see that the notion is taken by abstraction only from water and common and ordinary liquids,

2. Bacon's mistrust of words, evident here, led the Royal Society to cultivate a plain, stripped prose style for purposes of scientific communication.
3. The "Prime Mover" was a transparent sphere on the outside of the universe, supposed to move all the other spheres; the "Element of Fire" was an area of pure, invisible fire, supposed to exist above the atmosphere. In the nature of things, these concepts could be based on no observation. "Planetary Orbits," on the other hand,

are very real; Bacon may be referring to the old notion of crystalline spheres in which the planets were supposed to be set.
4. Bacon does not really mean "theories" in the inclusive modern sense, but "abstractions loosely invoked to explain particular facts." He is actually restating William of Occam's famous 14th-century principle, known as "Occam's razor," to the effect that "essences must not be multiplied beyond necessity."

without any due verification.

There are however in words certain degrees of distortion and error. One of the least faulty kinds is that of names of substances, especially of lowest species and well-deduced (for the notion of *chalk* and of *mud* is good, of *earth* bad); a more faulty kind is that of actions, as *to generate, to corrupt, to alter;* the most faulty is of qualities (except such as are the immediate objects of the sense), as *heavy, light, rare, dense,* and the like. Yet in all these cases some notions are of necessity a little better than others, in proportion to the greater variety of subjects that fall within the range of the human sense.

61

But the *Idols of the Theater*[5] are not innate, nor do they steal into the understanding secretly, but are plainly impressed and received into the mind from the play-books of philosophical systems and the perverted rules of demonstration. To attempt refutations in this case would be merely inconsistent with what I have already said: for since we agree neither upon principles nor upon demonstrations, there is no place for argument. And this is so far well, inasmuch as it leaves the honor of the ancients untouched. For they are no wise disparaged—the question between them and me being only as to the way. For as the saying is, the lame man who keeps the right road outstrips the runner who takes a wrong one. Nay, it is obvious that when a man runs the wrong way, the more active and swift he is the further he will go astray.

But the course I propose for the discovery of sciences is such as leaves but little to the acuteness and strength of wits, but places all wits and understandings nearly on a level. For as in the drawing of a straight line or a perfect circle, much depends on the steadiness and practice of the hand, if it be done by aim of hand only, but if with the aid of rule or compass, little or nothing; so is it exactly with my plan. But though particular confutations would be of no avail, yet touching the sects and general divisions of such systems I must say something; something also touching the external signs which show that they are unsound; and finally something touching the causes of such great infelicity and of such lasting and general agreement in error; that so the access to truth may be made less difficult, and the human understanding may the more willingly submit to its purgation and dismiss its idols.

62

Idols of the Theater, or of systems, are many, and there can be and perhaps will be yet many more. For were it not that now for many ages men's minds have been busied with religion and theology; and were it not that civil governments, especially monarchies, have

5. I.e., those derived from previous philosophical systems, which misrepresent life by overdramatizing it and mislead men by pretending to show them reality itself.

been averse to such novelties, even in matters speculative; so that men labor therein to the peril and harming of their fortunes—not only unrewarded, but exposed also to contempt and envy; doubtless there would have arisen many other philosophical sects like to those which in great variety flourished once among the Greeks. For as on the phenomena of the heavens many hypotheses may be constructed, so likewise (and more also) many various dogmas may be set up and established on the phenomena of philosophy. And in the plays of this philosophical theater you may observe the same thing which is found in the theater of the poets, that stories invented for the stage are more compact and elegant, and more as one would wish them to be, than true stories out of history.

In general, however, there is taken for the material of philosophy either a great deal out of a few things, or a very little out of many things; so that on both sides philosophy is based on too narrow a foundation of experiment and natural history, and decides on the authority of too few cases. For the rational school of philosophers snatches from experience a variety of common instances, neither duly ascertained nor diligently examined and weighed, and leaves all the rest to meditation and agitation of wit.[6]

There is also another class of philosophers, who having bestowed much diligent and careful labor on a few experiments, have thence made bold to educe and construct systems; wresting all other facts in a strange fashion to conformity therewith.

And there is yet a third class, consisting of those who out of faith and veneration mix their philosophy with theology and traditions; among whom the vanity of some has gone so far aside as to seek the origin of sciences among spirits and genii. So that this parent stock of errors—this false philosophy—is of three kinds; the sophistical, the empirical, and the superstitious. * * *

68

So much concerning the several classes of idols, and their equipage: all of which must be renounced and put away with a fixed and solemn determination, and the understanding thoroughly freed and cleansed; the entrance into the kingdom of man, founded on the sciences, being not much other than the entrance into the kingdom of heaven, whereinto none may enter except as a little child.

1620

6. Bacon's thought contained a concealed element of anti-intellectualism: his enthusiasm for experiment led him to denigrate the value of reason, as very few modern scientists would feel it necessary to do. What he is opposing here is an excessive concern with the forms of logic, as exemplified, he would say, in "the schoolmen."

From The New Atlantis[1]
[*Solomon's House*]

We came at our day and hour, and I was chosen by my fellows for the private access.[2] We found him in a fair chamber, richly hanged, and carpeted under foot, without any degrees to the state.[3] He was set upon a low throne richly adorned, and a rich cloth of state over his head, of blue satin embroidered. He was alone, save that he had two pages of honor, on either hand one, finely attired in white. His undergarments were the like that we saw him wear in the chariot; but instead of his gown, he had on him a mantle with a cape of the same fine black, fastened about him. When we came in, as we were taught, we bowed low at our first entrance, and when we were come near his chair, he stood up, holding forth his hand ungloved and in posture of blessing; and we every one of us stooped down, and kissed the hem of his tippet.[4] That done, the rest departed, and I remained. Then he warned the pages forth of the room, and caused me to sit down beside him, and spake to me thus in the Spanish tongue:

"God bless thee, my son; I will give thee the greatest jewel I have. For I will impart unto thee, for the love of God and men, a relation of the true state of Solomon's House. Son, to make you know the true state of Solomon's House, I will keep this order. First, I will set forth unto you the end of our foundation. Secondly, the preparations and instruments we have for our works. Thirdly, the several employments and functions whereto our fellows are assigned. And fourthly, the ordinances and rites which we observe.

"The end of our foundation is the knowledge of causes, and secret motions of things; and the enlarging of the bounds of human empire, to the effecting of all things possible.

"The preparations and instruments are these. We have large and deep caves of several depths: the deepest are sunk six hundred

1. Sir Thomas More's *Utopia* (1516) set a fashion for imaginary communities with ideal forms of government which was suddenly taken up in the early 17th century. The German Johann Andreae published in 1619 his *Christianopolis;* Thomas Campanella, languishing in a Neapolitan jail, wrote his *City of the Sun* in 1623. Bacon's contribution to the discussion, perhaps because he never completed it, is really tangential to the concept of an ideal commonwealth. His *New Atlantis* is in effect a research establishment which could exist in any society that would tolerate it. Perhaps for that reason, it had an immediate influence beyond that of most full-fledged Utopias; and was largely realized, within thirty years of its publication, in the shape of the Philosophical Society which in 1662 became the Royal Society. Bacon begins by describing an imaginary voyage to the island of Bensalem, supposed to lie in the vicinity of the Bering Straits. Here, after learning about the miraculous diffusion of Christianity to the island, he is invited to visit their most interesting institution, Solomon's House.

2. Audience.

3. I.e., without stairs leading up to the dais.

4. Scarf.

fathoms; and some of them are digged and made under great hills
and mountains; so that if you reckon together the depth of the hill,
and the depth of the cave, they are, some of them, above three miles
deep. For we find that the depth of a hill, and the depth of a cave
from the flat, is the same thing; both remote alike from the sun and
heaven's beams, and from the open air. These caves we call the
lower region, and we use them for all coagulations, indurations,[5]
refrigerations, and conservations of bodies. We use them likewise
for the imitation of natural mines, and the producing also of new
artificial metals, by compositions and materials which we use, and
lay there for many years. We use them also sometimes (which may
seem strange) for curing of some diseases, and for prolongation of
life in some hermits that choose to live there, well accommodated
of[6] all things necessary, and indeed live very long; by whom also we
learn many things.

"We have burials in several earths, where we put divers cements,[7]
as the Chinese do their porcelain. But we have them in greater
variety, and some of them more fine. We also have great variety of
composts[8] and soils, for the making of the earth fruitful.

"We have high towers, the highest about half a mile in height,
and some of them likewise set upon high mountains, so that the
vantage of the hill, with the tower, is in the highest of them three
miles at least. And these places we call the upper region, accounting
the air between the high places and the low as a middle region. We
use these towers, according to their several heights and situations,
for insolation,[9] refrigeration, conservation, and for the view of divers meteors—as winds, rain, snow, hail;[1] and some of the fiery meteors also. And upon them, in some places, are dwellings of hermits,
whom we visit sometimes, and instruct what to observe.

"We have great lakes, both salt and fresh, whereof we have use
for the fish and fowl. We use them also for burials of some natural
bodies, for we find a difference in things buried in earth, or in air
below the earth, and things buried in water. We have also pools, of
which some do strain fresh water out of salt, and others by art do
turn fresh water into salt. We have also some rocks in the midst of
the sea, and some bays upon the shore, for some works wherein is
required the air and vapor of the sea. We have likewise violent
streams and cataracts, which serve us for many motions; and likewise
engines for multiplying and enforcing[2] of winds to set also on going
divers motions.

"We have also a number of artificial wells and fountains, made
in imitation of the natural sources and baths, as tincted upon[3]

5. Hardenings.
6. Provided with.
7. Clays and pottery mixtures.
8. Manures.
9. Exposure to the sun.

1. Anything that fell from the sky was,
in Renaissance terminology, a meteor.
2. Re-enforcing, strengthening.
3. Tinctured with.

vitriol, sulphur, steel, brass, lead, nitre, and other minerals; and again, we have little wells for infusions of many things, where the waters take the virtue[4] quicker and better than in vessels or basins. And amongst them we have a water, which we call Water of Paradise, being by that we do to it, made very sovereign[5] for health and prolongation of life.

"We have also great and spacious houses, where we imitate and demonstrate meteors—as snow, hail, rain, some artificial rains of bodies, and not of water, thunders, lightnings; also generations of bodies in air—as frogs, flies, and divers others.

"We have also certain chambers, which we call chambers of health, where we qualify[6] the air as we think good and proper for the cure of divers diseases, and preservation of health.

"We have also fair and large baths, of several mixtures, for the cure of diseases, and the restoring of a man's body from arefaction;[7] and others for the confirming of it in strength of sinews, vital parts, and the very juice and substance of the body.

"We have also large and various orchards and gardens, wherein we do not so much respect beauty as variety of ground and soil, proper for divers trees and herbs, and some very spacious, where trees and berries are set, whereof we make divers kinds of drinks, besides the vineyards. In these we practice likewise all conclusions[8] of grafting and inoculating, as well of wild-trees as fruit-trees, which produceth many effects. And we make (by art) in the same orchards and gardens trees and flowers to come earlier or later than their seasons, and to come up and bear more speedily than by their natural course they do. We make them also by art greater much than their nature; and their fruit greater and sweeter, and of differing taste, smell, color, and figure, from their nature. And many of them we so order as they become of medicinal use.

"We have also means to make divers plants rise by mixtures of earths without seeds, and likewise to make divers new plants, differing from the vulgar,[9] and to make one tree or plant turn into another.

"We have also parks, and enclosures of all sorts, of beasts and birds; which we use not only for view or rareness, but likewise for dissections and trials,[1] that thereby we may take light what may be wrought upon the body of man. Wherein we find many strange effects: as continuing life in them, though divers parts, which you account vital, be perished and taken forth; resuscitating of some that seem dead in appearance, and the like. We try also all poisons, and other medicines upon them, as well of chirurgery[2] as physic. By art

4. Property (of the substances put into water).
5. Efficacious.
6. Modify.
7. Drying up.

8. Theories.
9. Ordinary.
1. Experiments.
2. Surgery.

likewise, we make them greater or taller than their kind is, and contrariwise dwarf them and stay their growth; we make them more fruitful and bearing than their kind is, and contrariwise barren and not generative. Also we make them differ in color, shape, activity, many ways. We find means to make commixtures and copulations of divers kind, which have produced many new kinds,[3] and them not barren, as the general opinion is. We make a number of kinds of serpents, worms, fishes, flies, of putrefaction, whereof some are advanced (in effect) to be perfect creatures, like beasts or birds, and have sexes, and do propagate. Neither do we this by chance, but we know beforehand of what matter and commixture what kind of those creatures will arise.

"We have also particular pools where we make trials upon fishes, as we have said before of beasts and birds.

"We have also places for breed and generation of those kinds of worms and flies which are of special use; such as are with you your silkworms and bees.

"I will not hold you long with recounting of our brew-houses, bake-houses, and kitchens, where are made divers drinks, breads, and meats, rare and of special effects. Wines we have of grapes, and drinks of other juice of fruits, of grains, and of roots, and of mixtures with honey, sugar, manna, and fruits dried and decocted;[4] also of the tears or woundings of trees, and of the pulp of canes. And these drinks are of several ages, some to the age or last[5] of forty years. We have drinks also brewed with several herbs, and roots and spices; yea, with several fleshes and whitemeats;[6] whereof some of the drinks are such as they are in effect meat and drink both, so that divers, especially in age, do desire to live with them, with little or no meat or bread. And above all, we strive to have drinks of extreme thin parts, to insinuate into the body, and yet without all biting, sharpness, or fretting; insomuch as some of them, put upon the back of your hand, will with a little stay[7] pass through to the palm, and yet taste mild to the mouth. We have also waters, which we ripen in that fashion, as they become nourishing, so that they are indeed excellent drink, and many will use no other. Bread we have of several grains, roots, and kernels; yea, and some of flesh, and fish, dried; with divers kinds of leavenings and seasonings; so that some do extremely move appetites; some do nourish so, as divers do live of them, without any other meat, who live very long. So for meats, we have some of them so beaten, and made tender, and mortified,[8] yet without all corrupting, as a weak heat of the stomach will turn them into good chylus,[9] as well as a strong heat would meat other-

3. Species.
4. Dissolved in water, by boiling.
5. Duration.
6. Breast of chicken, fish, sometimes cheese.
7. Delay.

8. Softened.
9. Chyle, food in its emulsified and digestible form. Bacon thinks of the stomach as a furnace, which softens food by heat.

wise prepared. We have some meats also, and breads, and drinks, which taken by men, enable them to fast long after; and some other, that used[1] make the very flesh of men's bodies sensibly more hard and tough, and their strength far greater than otherwise it would be.

"We have dispensatories, or shops of medicines; wherein you may easily think, if we have such variety of plants and living creatures more than you have in Europe (for we know what you have), the simples,[2] drugs, and ingredients of medicines, must likewise be in so much the greater variety. We have them likewise of divers ages, and long fermentations. And for their preparations, we have not only all manner of exquisite distillations and separations, and especially by gentle heats, and percolations through divers strainers, yea, and substances; but also exact forms of composition,[3] whereby they incorporate almost as they were natural simples.

"We have also divers mechanical arts, which you have not; and stuffs made by them, as papers, linen, silks, tissues, dainty works of feathers of wonderful luster, excellent dyes, and many others: and shops likewise, as well for such as are not brought into vulgar use amongst us, as for those that are. For you must know, that of the things before recited, many of them are grown into use throughout the kingdom, but yet, if they did flow from our invention, we have of them also for patterns and principals.[4]

"We have also furnaces of great diversities, and that keep great diversity of heats: fierce and quick, strong and constant, soft and mild; blown, quiet; dry, moist; and the like. But above all we have heats, in imitations of the sun's and heavenly bodies' heats, that pass divers inequalities, and (as it were) orbs, progresses, and returns,[5] whereby we produce admirable effects. Besides, we have heats of dungs, and of bellies and maws of living creatures and of their bloods and bodies, and of hays and herbs laid up moist, of lime unquenched, and such like. Instruments also which generate heat only by motion. And farther, places for strong insolations; and again, places under the earth, which by nature or art yield heat. These divers heats we use as the nature of the operation which we intend requireth.

"We have also perspective houses,[6] where we make demonstrations of all lights and radiations, and of all colors; and out of things uncolored and transparent we can represent unto you all several colors, not in rainbows (as it is in gems and prisms), but of themselves single. We represent also all multiplications of light, which we carry to great distance, and make so sharp, as to discern small

---

1. The word "when" is understood here.
2. Herbs.
3. Ways of putting the ingredients of medicines together, making compounds.

4. Models.
5. I.e., the furnaces produce various heats at will.
6. For optical experiments.

points and lines. Also all colorations of light; all delusions and deceits of the sight, in figures, magnitudes, motions, colors; all demonstrations of shadows. We find also divers means, yet unknown to you, of producing of light originally from divers bodies. We procure means of seeing objects afar off, as in the heaven and remote places; and represent things near as afar off, and things afar off as near, making feigned distances. We have also helps for the sight, far above spectacles and glasses in use. We have also glasses and means to see small and minute bodies, perfectly and distinctly; as the shapes and colors of small flies and worms, grains and flaws in gems which cannot otherwise be seen, observations in urine and blood not otherwise to be seen. We make artificial rainbows, halos, and circles about light. We represent also all manner of reflections, refractions, and multiplications of visual beams of objects.

"We have also precious stones of all kinds, many of them of great beauty and to you unknown; crystals likewise; and glasses of divers kinds; and amongst them some of metals vitrificated,[7] and other materials besides those of which you make glass. Also a number of fossils and imperfect minerals, which you have not. Likewise loadstones of prodigious virtue:[8] and other rare stones, both natural and artificial.

"We have also sound-houses, where we practice and demonstrate all sounds and their generation. We have harmonies which you have not, of quarter sounds and lesser slides of sounds. Divers instruments of music likewise to you unknown, some sweeter than any you have; together with bells and rings that are dainty and sweet. We represent small sounds as great and deep; likewise great sounds, extenuate[9] and sharp; we make divers tremblings and warblings of sounds, which in their original are entire.[1] We represent and imitate all articulate sounds and letters, and the voices and notes of beasts and birds. We have certain helps, which set to the ear do further the hearing greatly. We have also divers strange and artificial echoes, reflecting the voice many times, and as it were tossing it; and some that give back the voice louder than it came, some shriller and some deeper; yea, some rendering[2] the voice, differing in the letters or articulate sound from that they receive. We have also means to convey sounds in trunks[3] and pipes, in strange lines and distances.

"We have also perfume-houses, wherewith we join also practices of taste. We multiply smells, which may seem strange: we imitate smells, making all smells to breathe out of other mixtures than those that give them. We make divers imitations of taste likewise, so that they will deceive any man's taste. And in this house we contain also

7. Turned to glass.
8. Strength.
9. Drawn out thin.
1. I.e., we can vary notes which in nature are single.
2. Transforming.
3. Tubes.

a confiture-house, where we make all sweetmeats, dry and moist, and divers pleasant wines, milks, broths, and salads, far in greater variety than you have.

"We have also engine-houses, where are prepared engines and instruments for all sorts of motions. There we imitate and practice to make swifter motions than any you have, either out of your muskets or any engine that you have; and to make them and multiply them more easily and with small force, by wheels and other means, and to make them stronger and more violent than yours are, exceeding your greatest cannons and basilisks.[4] We represent also ordnance and instruments of war and engines of all kinds; and likewise new mixtures and compositions of gunpowder, wildfires burning in water and unquenchable; also fireworks of all variety, both for pleasure and use. We imitate also flights of birds; we have some degrees of flying[5] in the air. We have ships and boats for going under water and brooking[6] of seas, also swimming girdles and supporters. We have divers curious clocks, and other like motions of return, and some perpetual motions. We imitate also motions of living creatures by images of men, beasts, birds, fishes, and serpents; we have also a great number of other various motions, strange for equality,[7] fineness, and subtlety.

"We have also a mathematical-house, where are represented all instruments, as well of geometry as astronomy, exquisitely made.

"We have also houses of deceits of the senses, where we represent all manners of feats of juggling, false apparitions, impostures and illusions, and their fallacies. And surely you will easily believe that we, that have so many things truly natural which induce admiration, could in a world of particulars deceive the senses if we would disguise those things, and labor to make them seem more miraculous. But we do hate all impostures and lies, insomuch as we have severely forbidden it to all our fellows, under pain of ignominy and fines, that they do not show any natural work or thing adorned or swelling, but only pure as it is, and without all affectation of strangeness.

"These are, my son, the riches of Solomon's House.

"For the several employments and offices of our fellows, we have twelve that sail into foreign countries under the names of other nations (for our own we conceal), who bring us the books and abstracts and patterns of experiments of all other parts. These we call Merchants of Light.

"We have three that collect the experiments which are in all books. These we call Depredators.

"We have three that collect the experiments of all mechanical arts, and also of liberal sciences, and also of practices which are not brought into arts. These we call Mystery-men.

4. Cannon, named after the fabulous beast that killed by a beam from its eye.

5. I.e., rudimentary forms of flying.
6. Withstanding.
7. Unusual for their evenness.

"We have three that try new experiments, such as themselves think good. These we call Pioneers or Miners.

"We have three that draw the experiments of the former four into titles and tables, to give the better light for the drawing of observations and axioms out of them. These we call Compilers.

"We have three that bend themselves, looking into the experiments of their fellows, and cast about how to draw out of them things of use and practice for man's life and knowledge, as well for works as for plain demonstration of causes, means of natural divinations, and the easy and clear discovery of the virtues and parts of bodies. These we call Dowry-men or Benefactors.

"Then after divers meetings and consults of our whole number, to consider of the former labors and collections, we have three that take care out of them to direct new experiments, of a higher light, more penetrating into Nature than the former. These we call Lamps.

"We have three others that do execute the experiments so directed, and report them. These we call Inoculators.

"Lastly, we have three that raise the former discoveries by experiments into greater observations, axioms, and aphorisms. These we call Interpreters of Nature.[8]

"We have also, as you must think, novices and apprentices, that the succession of the former employed men do not fail; besides a great number of servants and attendants, men and women. And this we do also: we have consultations, which of the inventions and experiences which we have discovered shall be published, and which not; and take all an oath of secrecy for the concealing of those which we think fit to keep secret; though some of those we do reveal sometimes to the State, and some not.[9]

"For our ordinances and rites, we have two very long and fair galleries: in one of these we place patterns and samples of all manner of the more rare and excellent inventions; in the other we place the statues of all principal inventors. There we have the statue of your Columbus, that discovered the West Indies; also the inventor of ships; your monk that was the inventor of ordnance and of gunpowder;[1] the inventor of music; the inventor of letters; the inventor of printing; the inventor of observations of astronomy; the inventor of works in metal; the inventor of glass; the inventor of silk of the worm; the inventor of wine; the inventor of corn and bread; the inventor of sugars; and all these by more certain tradition than you have. Then we have divers inventors of our own, of excellent works, which since you have not seen, it were too long to

8. The total staff of Solomon's House is 36; a generous allowance, by Bacon's estimate, for the project of understanding the natural cosmos. Modern researchers would want a little more staff.
9. Observe Bacon's suspicion of the body politic, and the freedom which he allows to Solomon's House from political pressure.
1. Tradition credits Roger Bacon, a 13th-century monk, with the discovery of gunpowder. Bacon tactfully avoids his name

make descriptions of them; and besides, in the right understanding of those descriptions you might easily err. For upon every invention of value we erect a statue to the inventor, and give him a liberal and honorable reward. These statues are some of brass, some of marble and touchstone,[2] some of cedar and other special woods gilt and adorned; some of iron, some of silver, some of gold.

"We have certain hymns and services, which we say daily of laud and thanks to God for His marvelous works. And forms of prayer, imploring His aid and blessing for the illumination of our labors, and the turning of them into good and holy uses.

"Lastly, we have circuits or visits, of divers principal cities of the kingdom; where, as it cometh to pass, we do publish such new profitable inventions as we think good. And we do also declare natural divinations of diseases, plagues, swarms of hurtful creatures, scarcity, tempests, earthquakes, great inundations, comets, temperature of the year, and divers other things; and we give counsel thereupon, what the people shall do for the prevention and remedy of them."

And when he had said this he stood up; and I, as I had been taught, kneeled down; and he laid his right hand upon my head, and said, "God bless thee, my son, and God bless this relation which I have made. I give thee leave to publish it, for the good of other nations; for we here are in God's bosom, a land unknown." And so he left me; having assigned a value of about two thousand ducats for a bounty to me and my fellows. For they give great largesses, where they come, upon all occasions.

The rest was not perfected.

1627

2. A hard basaltic-type rock.

The Restoration and the Eighteenth Century

(1660-1798)

1660:   Charles II restored to the English throne.
1688–89: The Glorious Revolution: deposition of James II
            and accession of William of Orange.
1700:   Death of John Dryden.
1707:   Act of Union unites Scotland and England, which
            thus become "Great Britain."
1714:   Rule by house of Hanover begins with accession of
            George I.
1744–45: Deaths of Pope and Swift.
1784:   Death of Samuel Johnson.
1789:   The French Revolution begins.

The years between the restoration of Charles Stuart to the English throne in 1660 and the outbreak of the Revolution in France in 1789 can conveniently be thought of as a single period in the political (and, as we shall see, in the literary) history of England. The kingdom to which Charles returned had just passed through twenty years of civil war and a radical political and religious revolution that would have left a less virile people exhausted. Early in Charles's reign, the people were visited by two frightful calamities that seemed to the superstitious to be the work of a Divine Providence outraged by rebellion and regicide: the plague visited England in 1665, carrying off over 70,000 people in London alone; and in September, 1666, a fire which raged for five days destroyed a large part of the City, burning more than 13,000 houses and leaving about two-thirds of the population homeless. Yet, within two decades of the king's return, the Royal Navy had defeated the navy of Holland, England's greatest maritime and commercial rival; and, in a series of wars fought between 1689 and 1763 against France, the British acquired an empire which included Canada in the west and India in the east. Despite the loss of her thirteen North American colonies, Great Britain was able to enter the final struggle with Revolutionary and Napoleonic France as a world power.

769

RELIGION AND POLITICS

Religion and politics were generally inseparable during the 17th century, for until the religious issues of the age were resolved no stable political settlement was possible. Extremes of belief in religion and of opinions in politics had driven to violent and open conflict Crown and Parliament, Anglican and Puritan, during the twenty years preceding the Restoration. Charles came home to the almost universal satisfaction of his subjects, for after the abdication of Richard Cromwell in 1659 had seemed to bring the country to the brink of chaos, Britons were eager to believe that the king would bring order, peace, freedom under law, and a spirit of mildness back into the national life. But the Restoration itself actually postponed rather than solved the nation's problems. Another thirty years had to pass before any sort of adjustment was possible among antagonistic parties which had made the 17th century so turbulent an age in England.

The restoration of the monarchy meant, inevitably, the restoration of the Established Church; and though Charles had promised mildness toward all but a few of his late father's enemies, the bishops and Anglican clergy felt anything but Christian charity toward their Dissenting brothers. In 1662 Parliament reimposed the Book of Common Prayer on all ministers and congregations, and in 1664 religious meetings in which the forms of the Established Church were not followed were declared illegal. Thousands of clergymen resigned their livings, and the jails were filled with Nonconformist preachers who, like John Bunyan, refused to be silenced. In 1673 the triumph of the Establishment was completed by the Test Act, which required all holders of civil and military offices to receive the sacrament according to the Anglican rite and to declare their disbelief in transubstantiation. Thus the two adversaries of the Anglican Church, Protestant Dissenters and Roman Catholics, were alike excluded from public life, though the practice of occasional conformity (i.e., receiving the sacrament in an Anglican church at rare intervals) enabled many Dissenters to comply with the law. Throughout the closing decades of the 17th century, Anglicans associated Nonconformity with revolution, regicide, republicanism, and the rule of the Puritan Saints—hence, with subversion; and with excessive zeal, "enthusiasm" (i.e., belief in private revelation), and irrationality—hence, with absurdity. The scorn and detestation in which Dissenters were held may be measured by the delight that readers took in Samuel Butler's caricature of Presbyterians and Independents in *Hudibras* (1663), an attitude that persisted unchanged for the rest of the century, as Jonathan Swift's *Tale of a Tub*, written about 1697, makes clear. As for the English Catholics, they appeared always as potential traitors of whom anything evil could be believed. Few doubted, for example, that the Great Fire of 1666 had been set by Catholics.

Although ecclesiastical problems seemed to have been quickly and effectively solved, the constitutional issues which had divided Charles I and Parliament were not so readily settled. Charles II had promised to govern through Parliament, but like other members of his family he held strong views on the power and prerogatives of the Crown. Nevertheless, he was content to avoid crises whenever he could, and since he was an astute politician he frequently could. He concealed from his subjects his Catholic sympathies (on his deathbed he received the last rites of the Roman

Church), for he had no wish "to go on his travels" again. The one great religious and constitutional crisis of his reign was the Popish Plot and its political consequences (1678–81)—the unsuccessful attempt of a faction in Parliament to force Charles to accept a bill excluding his Catholic brother, James, Duke of York, from the succession. Except in this instance, where he was successful because of his courage, duplicity, and political skill, Charles allowed no opportunity for a test of strength between Crown and Parliament.

One important result of the political and religious turmoils of the decade following the Popish Plot was the emergence of two clearly defined political parties, Whig and Tory. The party of the court, which supported the king in 1681, came to be called Tories; the king's opponents, Whigs. By the end of the century the two parties had developed opposed attitudes on other important issues. The Tories drew their strength largely from the landed gentry and the country clergy. They were the conservatives of the period: strong supporters of the Crown and of the Established Church as the two great sources of political and social stability, they bitterly (though futilely) opposed toleration of Dissenters and successfully supported the Test Act. They were hostile to the new moneyed interests, whether among the newer nobility or the increasingly well-to-do middle class, for they held that landed wealth is the only responsible wealth. The Whigs were a less homogeneous group: many powerful nobles, jealous of the powers of the Crown, the merchants and financiers of London, a number of bishops and Low Church clergymen, and the Dissenters; these varied groups were united by their policies of toleration and support of commerce.

After James II came to the throne in 1685, an atmosphere of crisis rapidly developed. He was a most maladroit politician and was afflicted with the stubbornness that characterized all Stuart rulers. Determined to relieve Catholics of civil disabilities and to advance the cause of the Roman Church in England, he began a course of action that soon earned him the distrust and opposition of the great majority of his subjects. Claiming the right to set aside laws and to overrule Parliament, he issued in 1687 a Declaration of Indulgence, suspending the Tests and penal laws against both Catholics and Dissenters, and he began to fill the army and the government—not to mention the universities—with his coreligionists. Matters came to a crisis in the summer of 1688, when a son was born to the queen and the prospect of a succession of Catholic monarchs confronted the nation. Secret negotiations paved the way for the arrival in England of the Dutchman William of Orange at the head of a small armed force. He was the leading champion of Protestantism on the Continent and the husband of James's Protestant daughter Mary. Finding resistance to his hostile subjects impossible, James, after sending his wife and the infant prince out of the country, fled to France on December 11. There he was cordially received by Louis XIV, granted a subsidy, and established with his court at St. Germain. For over half a century the possibility of invasion and the forcible restoration first of James, later of his son "the Old Pretender," and finally of his grandson Prince Charles Edward, was a source of anxiety to the English government. Adherents of the exiled family are called Jacobites (from the Latin *Jacobus*, James).

Many Englishmen and a great many more Scots remained loyal to the house of Stuart until there was nothing left of the Jacobite cause but a pleasant sentiment. Two serious Jacobite rebellions actually occurred: in 1715, when the Old Pretender arrived in Scotland to support an uprising against the newly crowned Hanoverian, George I, and more threateningly in 1745, when Prince Charles Edward (the "Bonnie Prince Charlie" of romantic story) came dangerously close to success in his invasion of England, an event which affects the fortunes of the hero in Henry Fielding's novel *Tom Jones.*

It was only with the flight of James that England could begin to bury the past and to turn toward her destiny in the next age. The coming in of William and Mary and the settlement achieved in 1689 were known as the Glorious or Bloodless Revolution, all the more glorious for being bloodless. A more tolerant era was opening, as was made apparent in important acts passed by Parliament in the first year of the new reign. Since the Revolution had been largely achieved by Whigs, Whig principles prevailed during William's reign. In 1689 the Bill of Rights limited the powers of the Crown, reaffirmed the supremacy of Parliament, and guaranteed important legal rights to individuals. Moreover, the Toleration Act, although it did not repeal the Test, did grant freedom of worship to Dissenters. A number of the conflicting elements in the national life were thus reconciled through what proved to be a workable compromise; and with the passage of the Act of Settlement in 1701, settling the succession to the throne upon Sophia, Electress of Hanover, and her descendants (as the granddaughter of James I, she was the closest Protestant relative of the Princess Anne, James II's younger daughter, whose sole surviving child died in that year), the difficult problems that had so long divided England seemed resolved. The principles established in 1689 brought stability and order into English life and endured unaltered in essentials until the Reform Bill of 1832.

During the reign of Anne, the last Stuart monarch (1702–14), a renewal of tension embittered the political atmosphere. On the Continent England led her allies, Holland, Austria, and Bavaria, to victory in the War of the Spanish Succession against France and Spain (1702–13). The hero of the war was the brilliant Captain-General John Churchill, Duke of Marlborough, who, with his duchess, dominated the queen until 1710. The war was a Whig war, supported by powerful Whig lords and the Whig merchants of London, who grew increasingly rich on war profits and who stood to gain by any weakening of the power of France and Spain. The Whigs were anxious to reward the Dissenters for their loyalty by removing the Test. Unfortunately for them, Anne was especially devoted to the church, and when, in 1710, they were made to appear to threaten the health of the Establishment, she dismissed her Whig ministers and called in Robert Harley as Lord Treasurer and the brilliant young Henry St. John as Secretary of State (in charge of foreign relations) to form the Tory ministry which governed England during the last four years of her reign. The Marlboroughs were dismissed, the duke even losing his command in 1711, but not before the royal favor and a grateful nation had made him immensely rich and had given him the land on which he built his famous palace, Blenheim (pronounced *Blen'm*) in memory of the most brilliant victory (pronounced *Blén-hime*) of the war.

It was these Tory ministers whom Defoe and Swift served in their different ways; it was for them that Matthew Prior negotiated the Peace of Utrecht, ratified in 1713. To Swift's despair, a bitter rivalry developed between Harley (then Earl of Oxford) and St. John (then Viscount Bolingbroke) during 1713–14, and as the queen's life faded in the summer of 1714, Bolingbroke succeeded in ousting Oxford, only to have his own ambitions thwarted by the death of Anne and the return to power of the vindictive Whigs with the accession of George I, son of the late Sophia, Electress of Hanover. For a moment it seemed as if this event might not occur without bloodshed, but the crisis quickly passed, the Protestant succession was not immediately opposed by Jacobites, and the Whigs turned happily to investigating the conduct of the former ministers. Harley was imprisoned in the Tower of London (where he remained until 1717), and Bolingbroke, charged with treasonable correspondence with the Pretender, fled to France, where he actually became, for a while, Secretary of State to the Jacobite court. Pardoned in 1723 but denied his seat in the House of Lords, he returned to England and directed the opposition to Robert Walpole, while seeing much of Pope and playing the gentleman-farmer-philosopher at Dawley Farm.

The three Georges who occupied the throne during the rest of the century presided over a nation that grew increasingly prosperous through war, trade, and the beginnings of industrialism. George I (reigned 1714–27) and George II (reigned 1727–60) spoke broken English, had little interest in the affairs of the country. In their hearts they remained petty German princelings even when they were kings of Great Britain, spending as much time as possible in Hanover. Under such circumstances it was inevitable that ministers should become more important and more independent of the Crown than they had been under stronger and more intelligent monarchs. Through the indifference of two kings and the ambition and great abilities of the Whig Prime Minister Sir Robert Walpole, the modern system of ministerial government began to develop. This was the last important contribution of the age to British political institutions. Walpole's long ascendency (1721–42) brought a period of peace and prosperity and of capable government based, paradoxically, on flagrant political corruption. Although Walpole strengthened the importance of the House of Commons in British politics, he nonetheless continued, if he did not increase, the corruption of its members through bribery. He was a practical man and cared little for literature, preferring to spend money on useful journalists and voting Members of Parliament rather than on poets. Thus with two kings who knew nothing of literature and a prime minister who was indifferent to it, English writers could not expect the shower of offices and government sinecures that had made the age of Anne the great age of patronage: Congreve, Steele, Addison, Prior, Swift had expected and obtained such rewards both for their literary eminence and for their service to party. But after 1715, as patronage declined, authors found that they must turn to the publishers, who could pay them well because of the growing reading public. Indeed, Johnson was accustomed to declare that the booksellers of the midcentury had become the patrons of literature.

The long reign of George III (1760–1820), the first Hanoverian monarch born in England, somewhat retarded the development of government through parties and responsible ministers, for the king was determined to rule personally, and he succeeded in doing so to a remarkable degree. This was a dangerous policy for a man who, as a politician, was neither wise nor liberal. He brought the Tories back into power after they had been excluded from office for 46 years, and he did all that he could to crush the long-powerful Whig oligarchy.

INTELLECTUAL BACKGROUND

The political turbulence of the 17th century subsided only gradually during the last decades of the century, and the "peace of the Augustans" did not settle over England until the Protestant succession had been safely accomplished. Analogously, the literature of the Restoration period (1660–1700) did not at once attain the measured pace and disciplined order that we associate with "classic" art. John Dryden himself, the principal writer of the period, retained much of the characteristic boldness and extravagant wit of the literature of the earlier part of the century, delighting, as Johnson remarked, "in wild and daring sallies of sentiment, in the irregular and excentric violence of wit." The period is remarkable for variety: Milton's major poems, relics of an earlier age, appeared in 1667 (*Paradise Lost*) and 1671 (*Paradise Regained* and *Samson Agonistes*). The age that produced Bunyan's *Pilgrim's Progress*, perhaps the greatest literary expression of the Nonconformist conscience, produced also the libertine poems of such court wits as Rochester, Sedley, and Etherege, savage satire like Butler's, the brilliant depiction of the dissolute but elegant manners of the upper classes in the comedies of Etherege, Wycherley, and Congreve, and the rant and bombast of Dryden's rhymed heroic plays. But the general drift was toward classic restraint and good sense; and both Dryden's example, in the works of his maturity, and his numerous critical essays helped to formulate standards and to make the period the foundation on which the neoclassical art of the next century was erected. His literary theories, the poetic language that he shaped, and his metrics determined the dominant literary tendencies of the 18th century.

Perhaps most people think of the Restoration as a period wholly given over to frivolity and debauchery. It is true that Puritan rigidities (never enforced quite as rigorously as sometimes has been made out) were quickly repudiated by the upper classes and that the Saints were rendered impotent by harsh prohibitive laws. It is true that the king was easy-going, pleasure-loving, and amorous, more fond of the society of boon companions than he was of business of state, and lavishly extravagant in squandering public funds on his mistresses. It is true that the court itself was luxurious, immoral, full of intrigue. It is true that all this is vividly reflected in lampoons, satires, and comedies. But the ordinary life of the nation did not radically change. Rural manners, then as now, were conservative and old-fashioned. The London citizens, middle-class and respectable, cherishing much of the independence and piety of Dissent, were scandalized by the behavior of such lewd young men as Rochester and Etherege, who regarded them with contempt and considered their wives and daughters fair game. Even good royalists like John Evelyn and Samuel Pepys often speak anxiously in their diaries of the moral laxness of the court and the danger to the country of the king's example.

Charles himself had serious intellectual interests and was a patron of the arts. He dabbled in chemistry and was interested in the progress of science. A characteristic act was his chartering in 1662 the Royal Society of London for the Improving of Natural Knowledge, thus giving official approval to the scientific movement that Francis Bacon had initiated early in the century and that was just then coming to maturity. The king's love of music and painting led him to import from the Continent composers, musicians, new musical instruments, the French and Italian opera, and painting and painters largely from the Low Countries. His interest in the theater was demonstrated by the chartering of two companies of actors in 1660, both under royal patronage, the King's Players, and the Duke's— the Duke being James, Duke of York.

It is natural, therefore, that the most characteristic art of the period reflected the interests and tastes of those who supported it, as is the case today. Artists addressed themselves to court and "town," the western sub-urbs which were the center of fashion. The middle-class tradesmen who lodged over their shops in the City (i.e., that part of greater London which was once within the city walls and which was then thickly popu-lated—not, as it is today, almost wholly given over to business and fi-nance) were scorned as tasteless barbarians. Except in the theater, litera-ture was not in itself a gainful profession (as it was to become in the 18th century), and writers looked for patronage from the court and the great nobles. Milton, for example, received only £10 for the first edition of *Para-dise Lost*. By the end of the century, however, thanks to the enterprise of the bookseller Jacob Tonson and the new device of publishing books through subscription (i.e., soliciting payment in advance for de luxe copies of a work, in addition to publishing a regular trade edition), Dryden was able to earn between £1000 and £1200 by his translation of the works of Virgil (1697). And Pope's Homer, similarly published between 1715 and 1726, was to prove even more profitable.

Perhaps the most important aspect of the Restoration period is the in-creasing challenge of various forms of secular thought to the old religious orthodoxies which had been matters of life and death since the Reforma-tion. We can observe most clearly in this period the beginnings of the secularization of values and thought that characterizes Western society to-day. As the contentious voices of Roman, Anglican, and Dissenter grew more and more subdued, other interests attracted adventurous minds. Thomas Hobbes in a bold and, to many, shocking book, *Leviathan* (1651), had taught a philosophic materialism and advocated an absolute government as the most efficacious check to human nature, which he described as wholly driven by egoistic and predatory passions. Detested by the church and attacked on all sides, these ideas nonetheless played their role in the lives and writings of some of the more advanced young men, and they provoked by way of reaction in the next century an opti-mistic insistence on the natural goodness of man. A soberer and more ancient tradition was philosophic skepticism. Originating in ancient Greece, skepticism had found its most persuasive recent statement in the essays of the Frenchman Michel de Montaigne (1533–92), whose influence was widespread throughout 17th-century Europe. The skeptic argued that all our knowledge is derived from our senses, but that our senses do not report the world around us accurately, and that therefore reliable knowledge is an impossibility. The safest course is to affirm nothing as absolutely true, to remember that most beliefs are mere opinions, and, where possible, to be guided by the traditional in matters intellectual, political, and ethical. Butler, Dryden, and Rochester, among others, more or less adhered to this doctrine. But though the skeptic remained in doubt about the results of human reasoning, he was not precluded from religious beliefs, for he could assert (as did Dryden after his conversion to Catholicism) that faith alone is necessary for accepting the mysteries of the Christian religion.

The new science, already self-confident if not quite triumphant, was rapidly altering men's view of nature. The members of the Royal Society were all good theists and would have been perplexed had they been told that, in the 19th century, science and religion would come to seem incompatible. Science in the 17th century was principally concerned with the physical sciences—with astronomy, physics, and to a lesser degree, chemistry; and the discoveries in these sciences were reassuring in their revelation of universal and immutable law and order, clear revelations of the wisdom and goodness of God in His creation. Such laws of nature as Boyle's law of the behavior of gases under pressure or Newton's law of gravitation seemed obviously to support the idea that a beneficent, divine intelligence created and directs the universe: they could be reduced to simple mathematical terms and were demonstrably universal and unchanging. The whole creation appeared a revelation of the mind, intent, and nature of the Creator. The truest truths proved to be the clearest, the simplest, the most general. Such truths, while they confirmed the existence of a Deity, seemed at the same time to render unnecessary, even preposterous, the intricate a priori reasoning of Scholastic philosophy, and to promise a time, not remote, when mystery would be banished entirely from nature. Indeed the new religion, Deism or Natural Religion, which had an increasingly wide appeal to "enlightened" minds, deduced its simple rationalistic creed from the Book of Nature, God's first and to many 18th-century men, only valid revelation. The Deists deduced the existence of a Supreme Being or First Cause from the existence of the universe: a creature presupposes a Creator. The laws of nature, the structure of the universe—its regularity, order, and purposefulness—sufficiently proved the reasonableness, goodness, and wisdom of this Creator. Him we can and must revere; but, good though He is, it is demonstrable that He does not punish vice and reward virtue in this life; and therefore, being good and just, He must do so in some future life: hence, we must believe in immortality. Meanwhile, here on earth, it is our duty to co-operate with Nature and the Deity, cultivating as best we can wisdom, virtue, and benevolence. This creed is as simple and as rational as one of Newton's laws; but its complete omission of the "second revelation" of the Scriptures, the scheme of salvation through the vicarious atonement, made it unacceptable to many Christians, although many were attracted by its reasonableness and found it possible to accept both Natural Religion and revealed Christianity.

As the 17th century drew to a close, its temper became more secular, tolerant, and moderate. If it is not quite possible to talk sensibly of an "Age of Reason" in England, it is possible to think of the early decades of the 18th century as a period of good sense, restraint, and reasonableness. "Enthusiasm," that state of mind which asserted the validity of private inspiration and which had fostered a dangerous zeal among the Saints of Dissent, was decried. The new age was willing to settle for the possible within the limits of human intelligence and of the material world. Its temper was expressed by its most influential philosopher, John Locke (1632–1704), in his *Essay Concerning Human Understanding* (1690):

If by this inquiry into the nature of the understanding, I can discover the powers thereof; how far they reach; to what things they are in any degree proportionate; and where they fail us, I suppose it may be of use to prevail with the busy mind of man to be more cautious in meddling with things exceeding its comprehension; to stop when it is at the utmost extent of its tether; and to sit down in a quiet ignorance of those things which, upon examination, are found to be beyond the reach of our capacities. We should not then perhaps be so forward, out of an affectation of an universal knowledge, to raise questions, and perplex ourselves and others with disputes about things to which our understandings are not suited; and of which we cannot frame in our minds any clear and distinct perceptions, or whereof * * * we have not any notions at all. If we can find out how far the understanding can extend its view; how far it has faculties to attain certainty; and in what cases it can only judge and guess, we may learn to content ourselves with what is attainable by us in this state. * * * Our business here is not to know all things, but those which concern our conduct.

These words might be taken as the creed of 18th-century England. Such a position is Swift's, when he inveighs against metaphysics, abstract logical deductions, and theoretical science; it is similar to Pope's in the *Essay on Man*; it prompts Dr. Johnson to talk of "the business of living"; it helps to account for the emphasis that the Anglican clergy put on good works, rather than faith, as the way to salvation, and for their dislike of emotion and "enthusiasm" in religion.

But if the 18th century brought a recognition of the limitations of man, it also took an optimistic view of his moral nature. Rejecting Hobbes's view of man as in essence a selfish and predatory creature and ignoring politely the Christian doctrine of original sin, 18th-century philosophers asserted that man is naturally good and that he finds his highest happiness in the exercise of virtue and benevolence. Such a view of human nature we describe as "sentimental." It found the source of virtue in men's instinctive and social impulses rather than in a code of conduct sanctioned by divine law. And men began to feel—or to fancy that they felt—exquisite pleasure in the exercise of benevolent impulses. Sentimentalism fostered a benevolism that led to social reforms seldom envisioned in earlier times—to the improvement of jails, to the relief of imprisoned debtors, to the establishment of foundling hospitals and of homes for penitent prostitutes, and ultimately to the abolition of the slave trade; but it also encouraged a ready flow of feeling and tears and a capacity to respond to the joys and sorrows of others which suggests that the period was much more an Age of Feeling than an Age of Reason. The doctrine of the natural goodness of man seemed to many to suggest that it is civilization which corrupts us and that primitive men, "noble savages" who live according to nature, are models of innocence and virtue. Such notions encouraged an interest in primitive societies and even helped to prepare for the enthusiastic reception given the peasant poet Robert Burns, an "original genius," as well as for William Wordsworth's interest in children and in simple, rural people.

As the wave of sentimentalism mounted, a parallel rise of religious feeling occurred after about 1740. The great religious revival known as Methodism was led by John Wesley (1703–91), his brother Charles (1707–88), and George Whitefield (1714–70), all Oxford graduates. The Methodists took their gospel to the common people, preaching the necessity of a conviction of sin, and of conversion, and the joy of the "blessed assurance" of being saved. Often denied the privilege of preaching in village churches, they preached to thousands in the open fields and in barns. The somnolent Anglican Church and the self-assured upper classes were repelled by the emotionalism aroused by Methodist preachers among the lower orders. It seemed as if the irrationality, zeal, and enthusiasm of the Puritan sects were being revived. But the religious awakening persisted, and affected many clergymen and laymen within the Establishment, who, as "Evangelicals," reanimated the church and promoted unworldliness and piety. And yet the insistence of Methodists on faith over works as the way to salvation did not prevent them or their Anglican counterparts from playing important roles in many of the social reforms of the time, especially in helping to abolish slavery and the slave trade.

NEOCLASSICAL LITERARY THEORY

The literature of the period between 1660 and 1785 can conveniently, though perhaps too schematically, be considered as falling into three lesser periods of about forty years each: the first, extending to the death of Dryden in 1700, may be thought of as the period in which English "neoclassical" literature came into being and its critical principles were formulated; the second, ending with the death of Pope in 1744 and of Swift in 1745, brought to its culmination the literary movement initiated by Dryden and his generation; the third, concluding with the death of Johnson in 1784 and the publication of William Cowper's *The Task* in 1785, was a period in which neoclassical principles were confronted by new ideas which contained within themselves the origins of the Romantic movement of the early 19th century.

Seldom in the course of English literature can we find so radical and apparently sudden a change of taste as took place about 1660. But actually the change was not so sudden as it appears. Like the English Renaissance, it was part of a general movement in European culture, seen perhaps at its most impressive in 17th-century France. Described most simply, it was a reaction against the intricacy and occasional obscurity, boldness, and extravagance of European literature of the late Renaissance, in favor of greater simplicity, clarity, restraint, regularity, and good sense in all sorts of writing. This tendency is most readily to be observed in the preference of Dryden and his contemporaries for "easy, natural" wit, which aims to surprise rather than to shock, as did much metaphysical wit. It accompanied, though it was not necessarily caused by, the development of certain rationalistic philosophies and the rise of experimental science, as well as a desire for peace and order after an era of violent extremism.

This movement produced in France the impressive body of classical literature that distinguished the age of Louis XIV. In England it produced a literature that we term "neoclassical," or "Augustan," because it was strongly influenced by the writers of the reign of the first Roman Emperor, Augustus Caesar, just before the beginning of the Christian era. Rome's Augustan Age was a period of stability and peace after the civil war that followed the death of Julius Caesar. Its chief poets, Virgil, Horace, and Ovid, addressed their carefully ordered, disciplined, and polished works to a sophisticated aristocracy, among whom they found generous patrons. Dryden's generation was aware of an analogy between the situations of post-Civil War England and Augustan Rome. Charles seemed in 1660 a kind of Augustus, bringing to England civilized order and enlightened patronage of the arts, which, as in ancient Rome, reflected the interests and taste of the aristocracy. The English Augustans, in fact, were self-consciously Augustan in a way that Wordsworth and Coleridge could not have been self-consciously "Romantic." The image of Augustan Rome and the example of her writers play an active role in the literature of the age.

Charles and his followers, who had spent many years of their exile in France, inevitably brought back to England an admiration of contemporary French literature as well as of French fashions and elegance. But it is a mistake to regard the Restoration, as many historians have done, as a period in which the court and its poets betrayed English genius to French rules and taste. The French critics were of course known and studied in England, and the theories of such writers as Pierre Corneille, René Rapin, and Nicolas Boileau were influential in helping Dryden and his fellows to formulate their own standards. But as, during the period of Italian influence in the 16th century, English literature remained stubbornly English, so now: English writers took what they required from France, but used it for their own ends. It was not Dryden's aim merely to imitate the French poets or for that matter the Latin, but to produce in England works that would be worthy to stand beside theirs. He knew that this could be done only if English literature remained true to its living tradition: Chaucer, Spenser, Shakespeare, Jonson, Donne entered into his literary consciousness as well as Virgil, Horace, Longinus, or Corneille.

It is likely that, had Charles never lived abroad, the English neoclassical period would have come into existence pretty much in the form that it actually assumed. Ben Jonson's classicism (manifested in his poems and comedies and in the critical observations gathered from ancient and Renaissance writers which make up his *Discoveries*) brought to a focus by both example and precept the classicizing tendencies of the English Renaissance. His closed heroic couplets are the model for those of Edmund Waller and Sir John Denham, whom Dryden considered the principal "refiners" of English metrics. One of the lesser "Sons of Ben," Sir John Beaumont, at least as early as 1625—and incidentally in couplets that might have been the very pattern of those of Dryden and Pope—proposed critical standards that became dominant after 1660:

> Pure phrase, fit epithets, a sober care
> Of metaphors, descriptions clear, yet rare,
> Similitudes contracted, smooth and round,
> Not vexed by learning, but with Nature crowned:
> Strong figures drawn from deep invention's springs,
> Consisting less in words, and more in things:
> A language not affecting ancient times,
> Nor Latin shreds, by which the pedant climbs.
>
> [*To His Late Majesty, Concerning the True Form
> of English Poetry*]

Such standards are alien to the poetry of Donne, Crashaw, or Milton; on the other hand they prefigure the poetry of the Augustans, and make evident the fact that a native "classicism" existed side by side with metaphysical poetry. The emphasis on the correct ("pure"), the appropriate ("fit"), restraint and discipline ("sober care"), clarity, the fresh and surprising ("rare"), Nature, strength, freedom from pedantry—these indicate exactly the direction English literature was to take after the Restoration.

What was the prevalent idea of the nature of the poet? He must, of course, be a genius, for all agreed with Horace that the poet is born, not made. But even genius must be trained and disciplined if it is to produce art. The word *poet* is derived from a Greek word meaning "maker," and it is this notion that dominated the Augustans' idea of the poet: he is not a prophet, a visionary, a seer, but the maker of an object, a poem. He must have "invention," the gift of finding materials for his poems—fictional, but representative, images of human actions and of the world in which those actions take place; and he must so vivify, heighten, and order those materials that they seem true pictures of what is, or might or ought to be, or of the evil and folly that we should avoid. For the poet makes this image of life in order to teach, not so much by precept and moral sentences as by examples that move our love and admiration or evoke our fear and detestation. And to teach effectively he must please us by his fictions and by all the ornaments of language, metrics, and rhetoric that belong to his craft.

The materials of poetry must derive from, conform to, and recognizably represent "Nature," a word of many meanings in the neoclassic or any age. The Augustans were especially conscious of one meaning: Nature as the universal, permanent, and representative elements in the moral and intellectual experience of men. External nature—the landscape—both as a source of aesthetic pleasure and as an object of scientific inquiry or religious contemplation attracted the attention of Englishmen throughout the 18th century. But Pope's injunction to the critic, "First follow Nature," has primarily *human* nature and *human* experience in view. Nature is truth in the sense that it includes the permanent, enduring, general truths which have been, are, and will be true for all men, in all times, everywhere. The poet exists not to take us on long voyages to discover the new and unique ("We were the first that ever burst / Into that silent sea") but to reveal the permanent and the representative in human experience through what becomes for us an act of recognition. As Pope says of "true wit" or poetry, it "gives us back an image of our minds."

So Johnson, in Chapter X of *Rasselas*, says that the poet is to examine "not the individual, but the species; to remark general properties and large appearances * * * to exhibit in his portraits of nature such prominent and striking features as recall the original to every mind." Historians during this period studied the particulars of history in order to observe the uinversal human nature which those particulars reveal; and scientists formulated, after experiment and observation of particulars, universal and permanent laws of nature. Indeed, Sir Isaac Newton's *Principia* (1687) did much to reinforce scientifically the idea of Nature as order, which underlies such a typical 18th-century work as Pope's *Essay on Man*.

But it would be erroneous to assume that this emphasis on the general and the representative excluded the particular from the arts and reduced their material to the merely obvious, typical, and familiar. No art—and no theory of art—can be so simple. Originality, novelty, accuracy of observation were desired in neoclassical as well as in Romantic art. If human nature was held to be uniform, men were known to be infinitely varied; and the task of the artist was so to treat the particular as to render it representative. Thus Pope, after praising the characters of Shakespeare because they are "Nature herself," continued: "But every single character in Shakespeare is as much an individual as those in life itself; it is * * * impossible to find any two alike * * * " And Johnson praised the poet James Thomson because he looked on external nature "with a mind that at once comprehends the vast, and attends to the minute."

But although Nature was "at once the source, and end, and test of art," the poet could learn much from the ancients—the great writers, philosophers, critics, sculptors, and architects of Greece and especially of Rome. They were useful guides not because they were ancient or because they were thought to have some prescriptive authority to command attention and respect, but because they had so truly expressed Nature that, despite changes as radical as those wrought by the establishment of Christianity in Europe, they had lost none of their relevance to the experience of modern men. As Pope said, Homer and Nature were the same; and both Pope and his readers found Horace's satires on Roman society thoroughly applicable to their own world, for Horace had followed Nature, "one clear, unchanged, and universal light."

And how did a poet come to know Nature? Not, certainly, by a life of solitude or rural retirement, or by the intermittent light of visionary gleams. The poet was to be a man living among men and speaking to men, a member of society, an important and functional part of a civilized community that would not be civilized without his presence. Only by living among men and by ceaseless and sympathetic observation of them could he gain the knowledge of Nature required of him as a poet. He was also to supplement his own inevitably limited experience by the wisdom of the past, by studying Nature wherever truthfully represented: in Homer, Virgil, Horace, or Shakespeare.

He could learn also from the ancients how to practice his craft. If a poem is an object to be made, the maker, like an architect or a cabinet-maker, must follow sound principles or botch the job. The ancients—Aristotle in his *Poetics*, Horace in his *Ars Poetica*, Quintilian in his *Institutio Oratoria*, for instance—had left more or less systematized principles (or to use the word current among the Augustans, "rules") by which to order "Nature"—the material of art—into an epic, a tragedy, a dramatic character, an oration. They had deduced these rules from the practice of earlier masters—Homer, Sophocles, the Greek and Roman orators. Italian and French critics during the 16th and 17th centuries invented new rules of their own and refined on and further codified those of the ancients. The rules directed the planning and executing of one or another of the literary "kinds," or genres: epic, tragedy, comedy, pastoral, satire, ode; the choice of language, which must differ from genre to genre; the use of figures and tropes; tone, style, characters. They could serve as a short cut to Nature, for as Pope said, they "are Nature methodized."

In England, actually, the rules were followed in rather a casual way. Most readers were prepared to admit that mere correctness could not recommend a poem which was commonplace in thought and sentiment and unanimated by the vital force of genius. Almost everyone acknowledged that Shakespeare had written the greatest body of drama in modern literature without following the rules of the ancients or the moderns. Indeed, the presence of Shakespeare and the native English suspicion of mere theory prevented English neoclassical literature from being shackled by pedantic critics. In 1765 Samuel Johnson was to brush aside in the name of Shakespeare and good sense two hundred years of critical reverence for the three unities of action, place, and time, a reverence which had not, however, much affected the plotting of English plays during that period.

The idea that each of the literary kinds is distinct and has its own proper material, characters, language, and style, was influential throughout our period. Epic and tragedy, the loftiest and most serious of the kinds, demand noble English, stately verse, heightened diction, splendor of figures and ornaments. (This can be readily understood by examining a few pages of *Paradise Lost.*) Comedy, on the other hand, since it deals not with ideal heroes or great kings and generals as do epic and tragedy, but with ordinary people in daily life, calls for a lower style and natural, unadorned language. This principle was known as the principle of "decorum" or the appropriate; it determined Dryden's definition of wit as "a propriety of thoughts and words; or, in other terms, thoughts and words elegantly adapted to the subject."

Examining the psychological faculties that distinguish the artist from other men, critics fixed upon "wit" as his most important and characteristic endowment. "Wit," like "Nature," is a complicated word of many meanings. Here it implies quickness and liveliness of mind, inventiveness, a readiness to perceive resemblances between things apparently unlike and so to enliven literary discourse with appropriate images, similes, and metaphors. This faculty was often identified with "fancy" or "imagination," and was thought to be irregular, wayward, extravagant, unless curbed and disciplined by another and soberer faculty, "judgment." An excess of imagination was considered dangerous to sanity, and in literature to lead away from Nature and truth to falsehood and such violent and farfetched conceits as we find in the poetry of Donne or Crashaw at their boldest. One task of the age was to tame what seemed the wildness of metaphysical wit into the more reasonable and decorous wit that Dryden described in the passage quoted above. So Pope insists in the *Essay on Criticism*, lines 80–83, on the necessity of a harmonious union of judgment and fancy (which he calls "wit") in a work of literature. Though judgment was to tame, it was not to suppress passion, energy, or originality, but to make them more effective through discipline. Pope expresses the aesthetic ideal of the age succinctly in a traditional image: "The wingèd courser, like a generous horse, / Shows most true mettle when you check his course." Only that literature is true which remains true to universal human experience; and for it to do so, wayward wit or fancy must be firmly guided.

Two more general observations must be made. When Wordsworth, in the Preface to *Lyrical Ballads* (1800), declared that the poems were written "in a selection of the language really used by men," he went on to attack 18th-century poets for their use of an artificial and stock "diction" and to illustrate it by Thomas Gray's sonnet, *On the Death of Richard West*. Coleridge, in *Biographia Literaria* (1817), also had a good deal to say on the subject. Although the bulk of good poetry in the 18th century, as in other times, is written in "a selection of the language really used by men," the special and stylized diction to which the two early Romantics objected did exist, especially in heroic, descriptive, pastoral, and lyric poetry. It is characterized by periphrasis (a roundabout and elegant way of avoiding homely words: "finny tribe" for "fish," or "household feathery people" for "chickens"); frequently used stock phrases, such as "shining sword," "verdant mead," "bounding main," "checkered shade"; words used in their original Latin sense, such as "genial," "gelid," "horrid"; and a fondness for adjectives ending in *y*. This language is much older than the 18th century. It originated in the attempt of Renaissance poets all over Europe to rival the elegant and golden diction of Virgil and other Roman writers. Milton depended on it to help him obtain "answerable style" for the lofty theme of *Paradise Lost*. Dryden used it in his translation of Virgil. Thomson found it suitable in passages of generalized description in *The Seasons*, and Pope employed it, not always happily, in his versions of Homer. Used with discretion it could be both subtle and expressive; but when it became a mannerism as it did with Gray (see stanzas 3 and 4 of his *Eton* ode), or a dead and conventional language used mechanically, as it did with scores of mere versifiers, it properly became an object of contempt. An extreme example of a desire to attain dignity by periphrasis is this absurd translation into poetic diction of the simple sentence, "Hay and straw were burned in the fields of Thessaly":

> There at his words devouring Vulcan feasts
> On all the tribute which Thessalian meads
> Yield to the scythe, and riots on the heaps
> Of Ceres, emptied of the ripened grain.
> [Glover's *Leonidas*, 1737]

But such extremes of mannerism are seldom to be found in the works of the good poets of the century.

Finally, there is the matter of versification. Everyone associates the neoclassical period with the "closed" heroic couplet—i.e., a pentameter couplet which more often than not contains within itself a complete statement and so is closed by a semicolon, period, question mark, or exclamation point. Within these two lines it was possible, but neither imperative nor habitual, to attain certain rhetorical or witty effects by the use of parallelism, balance, or antithesis within the couplet as a whole or the individual line. The second line of the couplet might be made closely parallel in structure and meaning to the first, or the two could be played off against each other in antithesis; taking advantage of the fact that normally a pentameter line of English verse contains at some point a slight pause called a "caesura," one part of a line so divided can be made parallel with or antithetical to the other or even to one of the two parts of the following line. This can be illustrated by a passage from Sir John Denham's *Cooper's Hill* (1642), which was quoted and parodied *ad nauseam* for many years. The poem addresses the Thames and builds up a witty comparison between the flow of a river and the flow of verse (italics are the present editor's, to illustrate the rhetorical effects):

> O could I flow like thee, || and make thy stream
>
> Parallelism: My great *example*, || as it is *my theme!*
>
> Double balance: *Though deep*, yet *clear*, || *though gentle*, yet not *dull*,
>
> Double balance: *Strong* without *rage*, || without o'er*flowing, full*.

Shortly after the beginning of the 18th century began the vogue of blank verse—the other metrical form most favored by the age. Philosophical poems, descriptive poems, meditative poems, and original or translated epics employed blank verse of one sort or another from Thomson's *Seasons* (1726–30) to Cowper's *The Task* (1785); and the tradition determined Wordsworth's use of the form in *Tintern Abbey* and *The Prelude*. The two chief patterns of blank verse available to the age were the blank verse of Milton in *Paradise Lost* and the dramatic blank verse of Dryden and other Restoration tragic poets. The influence of Milton is easily detected, not by the success with which his manner was imitated, but by the amateur performance of most of those who tried to play on his instrument. The dramatic blank verse of the Restoration too often led in 18th-century poetry to a rather disagreeably declamatory and rhetorical manner. But gradually a more lyrical blank verse developed, of which William Cowper is the master; and this more plastic metrical line had a formative influence on the blank verse of William Wordsworth.

JOHN DRYDEN
(1631–1700)

1668:   Made poet laureate.
1681:   *Absalom and Achitophel*.
ca. 1686: Conversion to Catholicism.
1689:   Loss of court offices upon accession of William and Mary.
1697:   Translation of Virgil.

Although John Dryden's parents seem to have sided with Parliament against the king, there is no evidence that the poet grew up in a strict

Puritan family. His father, a country gentleman of moderate fortune, gave his son a gentleman's education at Westminster School, under the renowned Dr. Richard Busby, who used the rod as a pedagogical aid in imparting a sound knowledge of the learned languages and literatures to his charges (among others John Locke and Matthew Prior). From Westminster, Dryden went to Trinity College, Cambridge, where he took his A.B. in 1654. He probably held a minor post in Cromwell's government, and if he did so, it was obtained through the influence of his cousin Sir Gilbert Pickering, a member of the Protector's Council. His first important and impressive poem, *Heroic Stanzas* (1659), was written to commemorate the death of Cromwell. It was followed in the next year by *Astraea Redux*, celebrating the return of Charles II to his throne. Years later Dryden's political and religious enemies taunted him with this sudden change of position, as if he had been a political turncoat, ready to change sides whenever he could serve his own interests. The charge has often been repeated, but it is both malicious and stupid: as Dr. Johnson long ago said, "if he changed, he changed with the nation," for in 1660 most Englishmen enthusiastically welcomed the Restoration. During the rest of his life Dryden was to remain entirely loyal to Charles and to his successor James II.

Dryden is the commanding literary figure of the last four decades of the 17th century. He is that rare phenomenon, the man of letters in whose work the image of an age can be discerned. Every important aspect of the life of his times—political, religious, philosophical, artistic—finds expression somewhere in his writings. Dryden is the least personal of our poets. He is not at all the solitary, subjective poet listening to the murmur of his own voice and preoccupied with his own personal view of experience, but rather a citizen of the world commenting publicly on matters of public concern.

From the beginning to the end of his literary career, Dryden's original nondramatic poems are most typically occasional poems, i.e., poems which celebrate particular events of a public character—a coronation, a military victory, a death, a political crisis. Such poems are social and ceremonial, and they demand of the writer tact as well as talent. They are public and formal, blending poetry with rhetoric and oratory, and their tone is that of the forum, not of intimate conversation or private meditation. In varying degrees Dryden's occasional poems have these qualities. His earliest published poem, to be sure, *Upon the Death of Lord Hastings* (1649), belongs stylistically to the tradition of metaphysical poetry, but ten years later, when his next ambitious poem appeared, the *Heroic Stanzas* on the death of Cromwell, he had mastered the tone, language, and manner of grave public speech. His principal achievements in this form are the two poems on the king's return and his coronation; *Annus Mirabilis* (1667), which celebrates the English naval victory over the Dutch and the fortitude of the people of London and the king during the Great Fire, both events of that "wonderful year," 1666; the political poems, the lines on the death of Oldham (1684), the odes, and the masque printed below.

Between 1664 and 1681, however, Dryden was mainly and most seri-

ously a playwright. The newly chartered theaters needed a modern repertory, and Dryden was foremost among those who set vigorously about
supplying the need. As his *Essay of Dramatic Poesy* (1668) shows, he
studied the works of the great playwrights of Greece and Rome, of the
English Renaissance, and of contemporary France, seeking sound theoretical principles on which to construct the new drama that the age demanded. Indeed his fine critical intelligence always supported his creative
powers, and because he took literature seriously and enjoyed discussing it,
he became, it appears almost casually, what Dr. Johnson called him: "the
father of English criticism." His abilities as both poet and dramatist
brought him to the attention of the king, who in 1668 made him poet
laureate. Two years later the post of Historiographer Royal was added
to the laureateship at a combined stipend of £200, well over £2000 in
modern money.

Dryden is not a great playwright, but he was influential in his own time.
He wrote his plays, as he frankly confessed, to please his audiences, which
were not heterogeneous, like Shakespeare's, but were largely drawn from
the court and from the fashionable world that took its standard from the
court. He followed rather than formed the taste of his audiences, producing rhymed heroic plays, in which incredibly noble heroes and heroines
face incredibly difficult choices between their mutual love and the claims
of honor, and the dialogue is conducted in a boldly rhetorical style; comedies of busy intrigue and bright, witty repartee, especially between a male
and female rake; and, later, libretti for the newly introduced dramatic
form, the opera. His one great tragedy—on Antony and Cleopatra—is
All for Love (1677), in blank verse, written more in emulation than in
imitation of Shakespeare.

Between 1678 and 1681, when he was nearing 50, Dryden discovered his
great gift for writing formal verse satire. A quarrel with Thomas Shadwell,
a playwright of some talent, prompted the mock-heroic episode *Mac
Flecknoe*, which was probably written about 1678 but which was not published until 1682. Out of the stresses occasioned by the Popish Plot
(1678) and its political aftermath came his major political satires, *Absalom and Achitophel* (1681), and *The Medal* (1682), his final attack
on the villain of *Absalom and Achitophel*, the Earl of Shaftesbury. Twenty
years' experience as poet and playwright had prepared him technically
for the triumphant achievement that *Absalom and Achitophel* undoubtedly
is. He had completely mastered the heroic couplet, having fashioned it
into an instrument suitable in his hands for every sort of discourse from
the thrust and parry of quick logical argument, to lyric feeling, rapid narrative, or forensic declamation. And he had fashioned a noble, resonant,
and malleable language as well. Thanks to this long discipline, he was
able in one stride to assume his proper place beside the masters of verse
satire: Horace, Juvenal, Persius, in ancient Rome, and Boileau, his French
contemporary.

The consideration of religious and political questions that the events of
1678–81 forced on Dryden brought a new seriousness to his mind and
works. In 1682 he published *Religio Laici*, a poem in which he examined
the grounds of his religious faith and defended the *via media* of the Angli-

can Church against the rationalism of Deism on the one hand and the authoritarianism of Rome on the other. But he had moved closer to Rome than he perhaps realized when he wrote the poem. Charles II died in 1685 and was succeeded by his Catholic brother, James II. Within less than a year Dryden and his two sons were converted to Catholicism. Just when, by whom, and under what circumstances the poet was converted we do not know, but once again his enemies were loud in denouncing his apparent venality. Again the accusation does not survive serious scrutiny. Dryden's court appointments had been renewed promptly on the accession of James, certainly before his conversion. Moreover, as Louis Bredvold has shown, Dryden's early philosophic skepticism (the conviction that the human reason cannot arrive at truth) gave way to fideism (the acceptance by faith alone of Christian mysteries as interpreted by some valid tradition). The development was slow and consistent, and his sincerity is borne out by his steadfast loyalty to the Roman Church after James abdicated and the Protestant William and Mary came in; as a result he was to lose his offices and their much-needed stipends. From his new position as a Roman Catholic, Dryden wrote in 1687 *The Hind and the Panther*, in which he defended the doctrines of his church and the policies (which he knew to be ruinous for the king and his coreligionists) that James was pursuing. Though full of splendid passages, this poem is a rather odd performance. The various religious sects of England are represented by appropriate animals, and, surprisingly enough, we listen to a prolonged theological debate between two of them, the milk-white Hind (the Roman Church) and the spotted Panther (the Anglican Church).

Dryden was now nearing 60, with a family to support on a much-diminished income. With quiet dignity he once more undertook to earn his living. He easily resumed his career as a playwright, producing five more plays before his death. He had occasionally practiced translation in the past and to this minor but, in his time, highly esteemed art he now returned. In 1693 appeared his translations from Juvenal and Persius, with the long dedicatory epistle on satire; and in 1697, his greatest achievement in this mode, the magnificent folio, illustrated, of the works of Virgil. At the very end, two months before his death, came the *Fables Ancient and Modern*, prefaced by one of the finest of his critical essays and made up of superb translations from Ovid, Boccaccio, and Chaucer.

What was the nature of Dryden's achievement? His drama, by and large, belongs entirely to his age, though its influence persisted into the next century. His critical writings established canons of taste and theoretical principles that determined the character of neoclassic literature in the next century. He helped establish a new sort of prose—easy, lucid, plain, and shaped to the cadences of natural speech. This is the prose that we like to think of as "modern," although it is not everywhere evident in our modern age. Johnson praised it for its informality and apparent artlessness:

* * * every word seems to drop by chance, though it falls into its proper place. Nothing is cold or languid; the whole is airy, animated, and vigorous * * * though all is easy, nothing is feeble; though all seems careless, there is nothing harsh * * *

His satire, as vital today as it was nearly 300 years ago, exerted a fruitful influence on the most brilliant verse satirist of the next century, Alexander Pope. The vigor and variety of his metrics made inevitable the long-enduring vogue of the heroic couplet among his successors. At the same time, he created a poetic language that remained the basic language of poetry until the early 19th century and that even the Romantic movement did not wholly destroy. This is not to say that he created the stock "poetic diction" to which Wordsworth and Coleridge justly objected later on, though he added to it and used it judiciously. His language is the superbly civilized language of the Augustan style at its best: dignified, unaffected, precise and always musical—a noble instrument of public speech. Johnson's final estimate remains valid:

By him we were taught *sapere et fari*, to think naturally and express forcibly * * * What was said of Rome, adorned by Augustus, may be applied by an easy metaphor to English poetry embellished by Dryden, *lateritiam invenit, marmoream reliquit*, he found it brick, and he left it marble.

Prologue to *The Tempest*[1]

OR THE ENCHANTED ISLAND

As, when a tree's cut down, the secret root
Lives underground, and thence new branches shoot;
So from old Shakespeare's honored dust, this day
Springs up and buds a new reviving play:
Shakespeare, who (taught by none)[2] did first impart   5
To Fletcher[3] wit, to laboring Jonson art.
He, monarch-like, gave those, his subjects, law;
And is that nature which they paint and draw.
Fletcher reached that which on his heights did grow,
Whilst Jonson crept, and gathered all below.   10
This did his love, and this his mirth digest:
One imitates him most, the other best.
If they have since outwrit all other men,
'Tis with the drops which fell from Shakespeare's pen.
The storm which vanished on the neighboring shore,   15
Was taught by Shakespeare's *Tempest* first to roar.[4]
That innocence and beauty which did smile
In Fletcher, grew on this *Enchanted Isle.*
But Shakespeare's magic could not copied be;
Within that circle none durst walk but he.   20
I must confess 'twas bold, nor would you now

1. In 1667 Dryden collaborated with the poet laureate, Sir William Davenant, in adapting Shakespeare's *Tempest* to the Restoration stage and the tastes of Restoration audiences.
2. The view of Shakespeare as a natural genius, writing without the advantages of classical learning, was a critical commonplace. Compare Jonson's *To the Memory of * * * Shakespeare*, line 31, Milton's *L'Allegro*,

lines 131–34, and Dryden's *Essay of Dramatic Poesy.*
3. John Fletcher (1579–1625), who collaborated with Francis Beaumont (ca. 1584–1616) in writing plays. During the early years of the Restoration period, their dramas were the most frequently revived plays "of the last age."
4. Details of the plot of *The Sea-Voyage* (1622), by Fletcher and Philip Massinger, suggest *The Tempest.*

That liberty to vulgar wits[5] allow,
Which works by magic supernatural things;
But Shakespeare's power is sacred as a king's.
Those legends from old priesthood were received,   25
And he then writ, as people then believed.
But if for Shakespeare we your grace implore,
We for our theater shall want it more:
Who by our dearth of youths are forced to employ
One of our women to present a boy;   30
And that's a transformation, you will say,
Exceeding all the magic in the play.
Let none expect in the last act to find
Her sex transformed from man to womankind.
Whate'er she was before the play began,   35
All you shall see of her is perfect man.
Or if your fancy will be farther led
To find her woman, it must be abed.

1667   1670

Epilogue to *Tyrannic Love*

SPOKEN BY MRS. ELLEN,[1] WHEN SHE WAS TO BE
CARRIED OFF DEAD BY THE BEARERS

[*To the Bearer.*] Hold, are you mad? you damned confounded
  dog,
I am to rise, and speak the epilogue.
  [*To the Audience.*] I come, kind gentlemen, strange news to tell
  ye,
I am the ghost of poor departed Nelly.
Sweet ladies, be not frighted, I'll be civil;   5
I'm what I was, a little harmless devil:
For after death, we sprites have just such natures
We had for all the world, when human creatures;[2]
And therefore, I that was an actress here,
Play all my tricks in hell, a goblin there.   10
Gallants, look to it, you say there are no sprites;
But I'll come dance about your beds at nights.
And faith you'll be in a sweet kind of taking,
When I surprise you between sleep and waking.
To tell you true, I walk because I die   15
Out of my calling in a tragedy.
O poet, damned dull poet, who could prove
So senseless! to make Nelly die for love!
Nay, what's yet worse, to kill me in the prime

5. The common run of poets.
1. The famous actress Nell Gwynn ("Mrs."—i.e., "Mistress"—was the title given all young unmarried women); her beauty and wit made her not only a favorite of London audiences, but eventually a mistress of Charles II. As he lay dying he was heard to say, "Don't let poor Nelly starve." Her great roles were comic parts, but in *Tyrannic Love* she acted Valeria, the daughter of the wicked Roman Emperor Maximin, who puts to death St. Catharine of Alexandria. Valeria is killed in the general slaughter which ends the play.
2. Pope develops this idea brilliantly in the sylphs and gnomes of *The Rape of the Lock.*

Of Easter term,[3] in tart and cheese-cake time!   20
I'll fit[4] the fop, for I'll not one word say
To excuse his godly out-of-fashion play:
A play, which if you dare but twice sit out,
You'll all be slandered, and be thought devout.
But farewell, gentlemen, make haste to me;   25
I'm sure ere long to have your company.
As for my epitaph, when I am gone,
I'll trust no poet, but will write my own:

Here Nelly lies, who, though she lived a slattern,
Yet died a princess, acting in St. Cathar'n.[5]   30
1669   1670

Epilogue to *The Conquest of Granada*, II[1]

They who have best succeeded on the stage
Have still conformed their genius to their age.
Thus Jonson did mechanic humor[2] show,
When men were dull, and conversation low.
Then comedy was faultless, but 'twas coarse: 5
Cob's[3] tankard was a jest, and Otter's horse.
And, as their comedy, their love was mean;
Except, by chance, in some one labored scene
Which must atone for an ill-written play.
They rose, but at their height could seldom stay.   10
Fame then was cheap, and the first comer sped;
And they have kept it since, by being dead.
But, were they now to write, when critics weigh
Each line, and every word, throughout a play,
None of 'em, no, not Jonson in his height,   15
Could pass, without allowing grains for weight.[4]
Think it not envy, that these truths are told;
Our poet's not malicious, though he's bold.
'Tis not to brand 'em, that their faults are shown,
But, by their errors, to excuse his own.   20
If love and honor[5] now are higher raised,
'Tis not the poet, but the age is praised.
Wit's now arrived to a more high degree;
Our native language more refined and free.
Our ladies and our men now speak more wit   25
In conversation, than those poets writ.

3. One of the four periods of the year when the law courts sit.
4. Punish.
5. The normal pronunciation of *Catharine* at the time.
1. This epilogue, in which Dryden compared unfavorably the manners, the conversation, and the drama of the earlier 17th century with those of his own time, had provoked such hostile criticism that, when he published the· play in 1672, he included a long prose defense of his position.

2. The eccentricities of artisans, as opposed to people of the middle and upper classes.
3. A character in Jonson's play *Every Man in His Humor;* "Otter" appears in Jonson's *Epicoene, or the Silent Woman.*
4. Without weighting the scale in his favor. A "grain" is the smallest unit of weight.
5. The two themes of the rhymed heroic play, of which *The Conquest of Granada* is the most distinguished example.

Then, one of these is, consequently, true;
That what this poet writes comes short of you,
And imitates you ill (which most he fears),
Or else his writing is not worse than theirs.   30
Yet, though you judge (as sure the critics will)
That some before him writ with greater skill,
In this one praise he has their fame surpassed,
To please an age more gallant than the last.

1671   1672

Song from The Indian Emperor

Ah, fading joy, how quickly art thou past!
   Yet we thy ruin haste.
As if the cares of human life were few,
   We seek out new:
And follow fate, which would too fast pursue.[1]   5

See how on every bough the birds express
   In their sweet notes their happiness.
   They all enjoy and nothing spare;
But on their mother nature lay their care:
Why then should man, the lord of all below,   10
   Such troubles choose to know
As none of all his subjects undergo?

Hark, hark, the waters fall, fall, fall,
   And with a murmuring sound
   Dash, dash upon the ground.   15
    To gentle slumber's call.

1665   1667

Song from An Evening's Love

1

Calm was the even, and clear was the sky,
   And the new-budding flowers did spring,
When all alone went Amyntas and I
   To hear the sweet nightingale sing.
I sate, and he laid him down by me,   5
   But scarcely his breath he could draw;
For when with a fear, he began to draw near,
   He was dashed with: "A ha ha ha ha!"

2

He blushed to himself, and lay still for a while,
   And his modesty curbed his desire;   10
But straight I convinced [2] all his fear with a smile,

1. Dryden's enemies ridiculed this line   2. Overcame.
as nonsense.

Which added new flames to his fire.
"O Sylvia," said he, "you are cruel,
    To keep your poor lover in awe";
Then once more he pressed with his hand to my breast,   15
    But was dashed with: "A ha ha ha ha!"

3
I knew 'twas his passion that caused all his fear,
    And therefore I pitied his case;
I whispered him softly: "There's nobody near,"
    And laid my cheek close to his face: 20
But as he grew bolder and bolder,
    A shepherd came by us and saw,
And just as our bliss we began with a kiss,
    He laughed out with: "A ha ha ha ha!"

1668   1671

Song *from* Marriage à la Mode

1
Why should a foolish marriage vow,
    Which long ago was made,
Oblige us to each other now,
    When passion is decayed?
We loved, and we loved, as long as we could,   5
    Till our love was loved out in us both;
But our marriage is dead when the pleasure is fled:
    'Twas pleasure first made it an oath.

2
If I have pleasures for a friend,
    And farther love in store,
What wrong has he whose joys did end,   10
    And who could give no more?
'Tis a madness that he should be jealous of me,
    Or that I should bar him of another:
For all we can gain is to give ourselves pain,   15
    When neither can hinder the other.

ca. 1672   1673

Absalom and Achitophel   In 1678 a dangerous crisis, both religious and political, threatened to undo the Restoration settlement and to precipitate England once again into civil war. The Popish Plot and its aftermath not only whipped up extreme anti-Catholic passions, but led between 1679 and 1681 to a bitter political struggle between Charles II (whose adherents came to be called Tories) and the Earl of Shaftesbury (whose followers were termed Whigs). The issues were nothing less than the prerogatives of the Crown and the possible exclusion of the king's Catholic brother, James, Duke of York, from his rightful position as heir-presumptive to the throne. Charles's cool courage and brilliant, if unscrupulous, political genius saved the throne for his brother and gave at least temporary peace to his people.

Charles was a Catholic at heart—he received the last rites of that Church on his deathbed—and was eager to do what he could do discreetly for the relief of his Catholic subjects, who suffered severe civil and religious disabilities imposed by their numerically superior Protestant countrymen. James openly professed the Catholic religion, an awkward fact politically, for he was next in line of succession since Charles had no legitimate children. The household of the duke, as well as that of Charles's neglected queen, Catherine of Braganza, inevitably became the center of Catholic life and intrigue at court and consequently of Protestant prejudice and suspicion.

No one understood, however, that the situation was explosive until 1678, when Titus Oates (a renegade Catholic convert and a man of the most infamous character) offered sworn testimony of the existence of a Jesuit plot to assassinate the king, burn London, massacre Protestants, and re-establish the Roman Church.

The country might have kept its head and come to realize (what no historian has doubted) that Oates and his confederates were perjured rascals, as Charles himself quickly perceived. But panic was created by the discovery of the murdered body of a prominent London Justice of the Peace, Sir Edmund Berry Godfrey, who a few days before had received for safekeeping a copy of Oates's testimony. The crime, immediately ascribed to the Catholics, has never been solved. Fear and indignation reached a hysterical pitch when the seizure of the papers of the Duke of York's secretary revealed that he had been in correspondence with the confessor of Louis XIV regarding the re-establishment of the Roman Church in England. Before the terror subsided many innocent men were executed on the increasingly bold and always false evidence of Oates and his fellows.

The Earl of Shaftesbury, the Duke of Buckingham, and others quickly took advantage of the situation. With the support of the Commons and the City of London, they moved to exclude the Duke of York from the succession. Between 1679 and 1681 Charles and Shaftesbury were engaged in a mighty struggle. The Whigs found a candidate of their own in the king's favorite illegitimate son, the handsome and engaging Duke of Monmouth, whom they advanced as a proper successor to his father. They urged Charles to legitimize him, and when he refused they whispered that there was proof that the king had secretly married Monmouth's mother. The young man allowed himself to be used against his father. He was sent on a triumphant progress through western England, where he was enthusiastically received. Twice an Exclusion Bill nearly passed both Houses. But by early 1681 Charles had secured his own position by secretly accepting from Louis XIV a three-year subsidy that made him independent of Parliament, which had tried to force his hand by refusing to vote him funds. He summoned Parliament to meet at Oxford in the spring of 1681, and, a few moments after the Commons had passed the Exclusion Bill, in a bold stroke he abruptly dissolved Parliament, which never met again during his reign. Already, as Charles was aware, a reaction had set in against the violence of the Whigs. In midsummer, when he felt it safe to move against his enemies, Shaftesbury was sent to the Tower, charged with high treason. In November the Grand Jury, packed with Whigs, threw out the indictment, and the earl was free; but his power was broken, and he lived only two more years.

Shortly before the Grand Jury acted, Dryden published anonymously the first part of *Absalom and Achitophel*, apparently hoping to influence their verdict. It is worthy of the occasion which produced it. The issues in question were grave; the chief actors, the most important men in the realm. Dryden, therefore, could not use burlesque and caricature as had Butler, or the mock-heroic as he himself had done in *Mac Flecknoe*. Only a heroic style and manner were appropriate to his weighty material, and the poem is most original in its blending of the heroic and the satiric. Dryden's task called for all his tact and literary skill; he had to mention, but to gloss over, the king's faults: his indolence and love of pleasure; his neglect of his wife and his devotion to his mistresses—conduct which had left him with many children, but no heir except his Catholic brother. He had to deal gently with Monmouth, whom Charles still loved. And he had to present, or appear to present, the king's case objectively.

The remarkable parallels between the rebellion of Absalom against his father King David (II Samuel xiii–xviii) had already been remarked in sermons, satires, and pamphlets. Dryden took the hint and gave contemporary events a due distance and additional dignity by approaching them indirectly through their Biblical analogues. The poem is famous for its brilliant portraits of the king's enemies and friends; but equally admirable are the temptation scene (which, like other passages, is indebted to *Paradise Lost*) and the remarkably astute analysis of the Popish Plot itself.

A second part of *Absalom and Achitophel* appeared in 1682. Most of it is the work of Nahum Tate, but lines 310–509, which include the devastating portraits of Doeg and Og (two Whig poets, Elkanah Settle and Thomas Shadwell) are certainly by Dryden.

Absalom and Achitophel: A Poem

In pious times, ere priestcraft did begin,
Before polygamy was made a sin;
When man on many multiplied his kind,
Ere one to one was cursedly confined;
When nature prompted and no law denied   5
Promiscuous use of concubine and bride;
Then Israel's monarch after Heaven's own heart,[1]
His vigorous warmth did variously impart
To wives and slaves; and, wide as his command,
Scattered his Maker's image through the land.   10
Michal,[2] of royal blood, the crown did wear,
A soil ungrateful to the tiller's care:
Not so the rest; for several mothers bore
To godlike David several sons before.
But since like slaves his bed they did ascend,   15
No true succession could their seed attend.

1. David ("a man after [God's] own heart," according to Acts xiii.22) represents Charles II.

2. "Michal," one of David's wives, represents the childless queen, Catherine of Braganza.

Of all this numerous progeny was none
So beautiful, so brave, as Absalom:[3]
Whether, inspired by some diviner lust,
His father got him with a greater gust,[4]   20
Or that his conscious destiny made way,
By manly beauty, to imperial sway.
Early in foreign fields he won renown,
With kings and states allied to Israel's crown:[5]
In peace the thoughts of war he could remove,   25
And seemed as he were only born for love.
Whate'er he did, was done with so much ease,
In him alone 'twas natural to please;
His motions all accompanied with grace;
And paradise was opened in his face.   30
With secret joy indulgent David viewed
His youthful image in his son renewed:
To all his wishes nothing he denied;
And made the charming Annabel[6] his bride.
What faults he had (for who from faults is free?)   35
His father could not, or he would not see.
Some warm excesses which the law forbore,
Were construed youth that purged by boiling o'er:
And Amnon's murther,[7] by a specious name,
Was called a just revenge for injured fame.   40
Thus praised and loved the noble youth remained,
While David, undisturbed, in Sion[8] reigned.
But life can never be sincerely[9] blest;
Heaven punishes the bad, and proves[1] the best.
The Jews,[2] a headstrong, moody, murmuring race,   45
As ever tried the extent and stretch of grace;
God's pampered people, whom, debauched with ease,
No king could govern, nor no God could please
(Gods they had tried of every shape and size
That god-smiths could produce, or priests devise);[3]   50
These Adam-wits,[4] too fortunately free,
Began to dream they wanted liberty;
And when no rule, no precedent was found,
Of men by laws less circumscribed and bound,
They led their wild desires to woods and caves,   55
And thought that all but savages were slaves.
They who, when Saul[5] was dead, without a blow,

3. James Scott, Duke of Monmouth (1649–85).
4. Relish, pleasure.
5. Monmouth had won repute as a soldier fighting for France against Holland and for Holland against France.
6. Anne Scott, Duchess of Buccleuch (pronounced *Bue-cloo*), a beauty and a great heiress.
7. Absalom killed his half-brother Amnon, who had raped Absalom's sister Tamar (II Samuel xiii.28–29). The parallel with Monmouth is vague. He is known to have committed acts of violence in his youth, but certainly not fratricide.
8. London.
9. Wholly.
1. Tests.
2. The English.
3. Dryden recalls the political and religious controversies which, since the Reformation, had divided England and finally caused civil war.
4. Adam rebelled because he felt that he lacked ("wanted") liberty, since he was forbidden to eat the fruit of one tree.
5. Oliver Cromwell. "Ishbosheth": Saul's son; he stands for Richard Cromwell, who succeeded his father as Lord Protector.

Made foolish Ishbosheth the crown forgo;
Who banished David did from Hebron[6] bring,
And with a general shout proclaimed him king: 60
Those very Jews, who, at their very best,
Their humor[7] more than loyalty expressed,
Now wondered why so long they had obeyed
An idol monarch, which their hands had made;
Thought they might ruin him they could create,   65
Or melt him to that golden calf,[8] a state.
But these were random bolts;[9] no formed design
Nor interest made the factious crowd to join:
The sober part of Israel, free from stain,
Well knew the value of a peaceful reign;   70
And, looking backward with a wise affright,
Saw seams of wounds, dishonest[1] to the sight:
In contemplation of whose ugly scars
They cursed the memory of civil wars.
The moderate sort of men, thus qualified,[2]   75
Inclined the balance to the better side;
And David's mildness managed it so well,
The bad found no occasion to rebel.
But when to sin our biased[3] nature leans,
The careful Devil is still at hand with means;   80
And providently pimps for ill desires:
The Good Old Cause[4] revived, a plot requires.
Plots, true or false, are necessary things,
To raise up commonwealths and ruin kings.
    The inhabitants of old Jerusalem   85
Were Jebusites;[5] the town so called from them;
And theirs the native right.
But when the chosen people[6] grew more strong,
The rightful cause at length became the wrong;
And every loss the men of Jebus bore,   90
They still were thought God's enemies the more.
Thus worn and weakened, well or ill content,
Submit they must to David's government:
Impoverished and deprived of all command,
Their taxes doubled as they lost their land;   95
And, what was harder yet to flesh and blood,
Their gods disgraced, and burnt like common wood.[7]
This set the heathen priesthood[8] in a flame;
For priests of all religions are the same:
Of whatsoe'er descent their godhead be,   100

6. Where David reigned over Judah after the death of Saul and before he became king of Israel (II Samuel i–v).
Charles had been crowned in Scotland
in 1651.
7. Caprice.
8. The image worshiped by the Children
of Israel during the period that Moses
spent on Mt. Sinai, receiving the law
from God. "A state": a republic.
9. Shots.
1. Disgraceful.
2. Assuaged.

3. Inclined. Cf. *Mac Flecknoe*, line 189
and note.
4. The Commonwealth. Dryden stig-
matizes the Whigs by associating them
with subversion.
5. Roman Catholics. The original name
of Jerusalem (here, London) was Jebus.
6. Protestants.
7. Such oppressive laws against Roman
Catholics date from the time of Elizabeth I.
8. Roman Catholic clergy.

Stock, stone, or other homely pedigree,
In his defense his servants are as bold,
As if he had been born of beaten gold.
The Jewish rabbins,⁹ though their enemies,
In this conclude them honest men and wise: 105
For 'twas their duty, all the learned think,
To espouse his cause, by whom they eat and drink.
From hence began that Plot, the nation's curse,
Bad in itself, but represented worse;
Raised in extremes, and in extremes decried;   110
With oaths affirmed, with dying vows denied;
Not weighed or winnowed by the multitude;
But swallowed in the mass, unchewed and crude.
Some truth there was, but dashed¹ and brewed with lies,
To please the fools, and puzzle all the wise.   115
Succeeding times did equal folly call,
Believing nothing, or believing all.
The Egyptian² rites the Jebusites embraced,
Where gods were recommended by their taste.
Such savory deities must needs be good,   120
As served at once for worship and for food.
By force they could not introduce these gods,
For ten to one in former days was odds;
So fraud was used (the sacrificer's trade):
Fools are more hard to conquer than persuade.   125
Their busy teachers mingled with the Jews,
And raked for converts even the court and stews:³
Which Hebrew priests the more unkindly took,
Because the fleece accompanies the flock.⁴
Some thought they God's anointed ⁴ᵃ meant to slay   130
By guns, invented since full many a day:
Our author swears it not; but who can know
How far the Devil and Jebusites may go?
This Plot, which failed for want of common sense,
Had yet a deep and dangerous consequence: 135
For, as when raging fevers boil the blood,
The standing lake soon floats into a flood,
And every hostile humor, which before
Slept quiet in its channels, bubbles o'er;
So several factions from this first ferment   140
Work up to foam, and threat the government.
Some by their friends, more by themselves thought wise,
Opposed the power to which they could not rise.
Some had in courts been great, and thrown from thence,
Like fiends were hardened in impenitence;   145
Some, by their monarch's fatal mercy, grown
From pardoned rebels kinsmen to the throne,
Were raised in power and public office high;

9. Anglican clergy.
1. Adulterated.
2. French, therefore Catholic. In the next line Dryden sneers at the doctrine of transubstantiation.
3. Brothels.

4. Dryden charges that the Anglican clergy ("Hebrew priests") resented proselytizing by Catholics chiefly because they stood to lose their tithes ("fleece").
4a. The King.

Strong bands, if bands ungrateful men could tie.
Of these the false Achitophel[5] was first;   150
A name to all succeeding ages cursed:
For close designs, and crooked counsels fit;
Sagacious, bold, and turbulent of wit;[6]
Restless, unfixed in principles and place;
In power unpleased, impatient of disgrace: 155
A fiery soul, which, working out its way,   ⎱
Fretted the pygmy body to decay,   ⎰
And o'er-informed the tenement of clay.[7]
A daring pilot in extremity;
Pleased with the danger, when the waves went high,   160
He sought the storms; but, for a calm unfit,
Would steer too nigh the sands, to boast his wit.
Great wits[8] are sure to madness near allied,
And thin partitions do their bounds divide;
Else why should he, with wealth and honor blest,   165
Refuse his age the needful hours of rest?
Punish a body which he could not please;
Bankrupt of life, yet prodigal of ease?
And all to leave what with his toil he won,
To that unfeathered two-legged thing,[9] a son;   170
Got, while his soul did huddled[1] notions try;
And born a shapeless lump, like anarchy.
In friendship false, implacable in hate,
Resolved to ruin or to rule the state.
To compass this the triple bond[2] he broke,   ⎱   175
The pillars of the public safety shook,   ⎰
And fitted Israel for a foreign yoke;
Then seized with fear, yet still affecting fame,
Usurped a patriot's all-atoning name.
So easy still it proves in factious times,   180
With public zeal to cancel private crimes.
How safe is treason, and how sacred ill,
Where none can sin against the people's will!
Where crowds can wink, and no offense be known,
Since in another's guilt they find their own!   185
Yet fame deserved, no enemy can grudge;
The statesman we abhor, but praise the judge.
In Israel's courts ne'er sat an Abbethdin[3]

5. Anthony Ashley Cooper, 1st Earl of Shaftesbury (1621–83). He had served in the Parliamentary army and been a member of Cromwell's Council of State. He later helped bring back Charles, and in 1670 was made a member of the notorious Cabal Ministry, which formed an alliance with Louis XIV in which England betrayed her ally, Holland, and joined France in war against that country. In 1672 he became Lord Chancellor, but with the dissolution of the Cabal in 1673 he was removed from office. Lines 146–49 apply perfectly to him.
6. Unruly imagination.
7. The soul is thought of as the animat-ing principle, the force that puts the body in motion. Shaftesbury's body seemed too small to house his fiery, energetic soul.
8. Men of genius. That genius and mad-ness are akin is a very old idea.
9. Cf. Plato's definition of man: "a featherless biped."
1. Confused, hurried.
2. The Triple Alliance of England, Sweden, and Holland against France, 1668. Shaftesbury helped to bring about the war against Holland in 1672.
3. The chief of the seventy elders who composed the Jewish supreme court. The allusion is to Shaftesbury's serving as Lord Chancellor in 1672–73. Dry-

With more discerning eyes, or hands more clean;
Unbribed, unsought, the wretched to redress;   190
Swift of dispatch, and easy of access.
Oh, had he been content to serve the crown,
With virtues only proper to the gown;
Or had the rankness of the soil been freed
From cockle, that oppressed the noble seed;   195
David for him his tuneful harp had strung,
And Heaven had wanted one immortal song.[4]
But wild Ambition loves to slide, not stand,
And Fortune's ice prefers to Virtue's land.
Achitophel, grown weary to possess   200
A lawful fame, and lazy happiness,
Disdained the golden fruit to gather free,
And lent the crowd his arm to shake the tree.
Now, manifest of[5] crimes contrived long since,
He stood at bold defiance with his prince;   205
Held up the buckler of the people's cause
Against the crown, and skulked behind the laws.
The wished occasion of the Plot he takes;
Some circumstances finds, but more he makes.
By buzzing emissaries fills the ears   210
Of listening crowds with jealousies[6] and fears
Of arbitrary counsels brought to light,
And proves the king himself a Jebusite.
Weak arguments! which yet he knew full well
Were strong with people easy to rebel.   215
For, governed by the moon, the giddy Jews
Tread the same track when she the prime renews;[7]
And once in twenty years, their scribes record,
By natural instinct they change their lord.
Achitophel still wants a chief, and none   220
Was found so fit as warlike Absalom:
Not that he wished his greatness to create
(For politicians neither love nor hate),
But, for he knew his title not allowed,
Would keep him still depending on the crowd,   225
That kingly power, thus ebbing out, might be
Drawn to the dregs of a democracy.[8]
Him he attempts with studied arts to please,
And sheds his venom in such words as these:
    "Auspicious prince, at whose nativity   230
Some royal planet[9] ruled the southern sky;
Thy longing country's darling and desire;

den's praise of Shaftesbury's integrity in this office, by suggesting a balanced judgment, makes his condemnation of the statesman more effective than it might otherwise have been.
4. I.e., David would have had occasion to write one less song of praise to Heaven. The reference may be to II Samuel xxii or to Psalm iv.
5. Detected in.
6. Suspicions.
7. The moon "renews her prime" when her several phases recur on the same day of the solar calendar—i.e., complete a cycle—as happens approximately every twenty years. The crisis between Charles I and Parliament began to grow acute about 1640; Charles II returned in 1660; it is now 1680 and a full cycle has been completed.
8. To Dryden, "democracy" meant popular government. The "dregs of a democracy" would be mob rule.
9. A planet whose influence destines him to kingship.

Their cloudy pillar and their guardian fire:[1]
Their second Moses, whose extended wand
Divides the seas, and shows the promised land;   235
Whose dawning day in every distant age
Has exercised the sacred prophet's rage:
The people's prayer, the glad diviners' theme,
The young men's vision, and the old men's dream![2]
Thee, savior, thee, the nation's vows[3] confess,   240
And, never satisfied with seeing, bless:
Swift unbespoken pomps thy steps proclaim,
And stammering babes are taught to lisp thy name.
How long wilt thou the general joy detain,
Starve and defraud the people of thy reign?   245
Content ingloriously to pass thy days
Like one of Virtue's fools that feeds on praise;
Till thy fresh glories, which now shine so bright,
Grow stale and tarnish with our daily sight.
Believe me, royal youth, thy fruit must be   250
Or gathered ripe, or rot upon the tree.
Heaven has to all allotted, soon or late,
Some lucky revolution of their fate;
Whose motions if we watch and guide with skill
(For human good depends on human will),   255
Our Fortune rolls as from a smooth descent,
And from the first impression takes the bent;
But, if unseized, she glides away like wind,
And leaves repenting Folly far behind.
Now, now she meets you with a glorious prize,   260
And spreads her locks before her as she flies.[4]
Had thus old David, from whose loins you spring,
Not dared, when Fortune called him, to be king,
At Gath[5] an exile he might still remain,
And heaven's anointing[6] oil had been in vain.   265
Let his successful youth your hopes engage;
But shun the example of declining age;
Behold him setting in his western skies,
The shadows lengthening as the vapors rise.
He is not now, as when on Jordan's sand[7]   270
The joyful people thronged to see him land,
Covering the beach, and blackening all the strand;
But, like the Prince of Angels, from his height
Comes tumbling downward with diminished light;[8]

1. After their exodus from Egypt under
the leadership of Moses, whose "extended wand" separated the waters of
the Red Sea so that they crossed over
on dry land, the Israelites were led in
their forty-year wandering in the wilderness by a pillar of cloud by day and
a pillar of fire by night. See Exodus
xiii–xiv.
2. Cf. Joel ii.28.
3. Solemn promises of fidelity.
4. Achitophel gives to Fortune the traditional attributes of the allegorical
personification of Opportunity: bald except for a forelock, she can be seized
only as she approaches.
5. Brussels, where Charles spent his
last years in exile. David took refuge
from Saul in Gath (I Samuel xxvii.4).
6. After God rejected Saul, He sent
Samuel to anoint the boy David, as a
token that he should finally come to
the throne (I Samuel xvi.1–13).
7. The seashore at Dover, where Charles
landed (May 25, 1660).
8. Cf. the fall of Satan in *Paradise
Lost*, which dims the brightness of the
archangel. The choice of the undigni-
fied word "tumbling" is deliberate.

Betrayed by one poor plot to public scorn 275
(Our only blessing since his cursed return),
Those heaps of people which one sheaf did bind,
Blown off and scattered by a puff of wind.
What strength can he to your designs oppose,
Naked of friends, and round beset with foes? 280
If Pharaoh's⁹ doubtful succor he should use,
A foreign aid would more incense the Jews;
Proud Egypt would dissembled friendship bring;
Foment the war, but not support the king:
Nor would the royal party e'er unite 285
With Pharaoh's arms to assist the Jebusite;
Or if they should, their interest soon would break,
And with such odious aid make David weak.
All sorts of men by my successful arts,
Abhorring kings, estrange their altered hearts 290
From David's rule: and 'tis the general cry,
'Religion, commonwealth, and liberty.'¹
If you, as champion of the public good,
Add to their arms a chief of royal blood,
What may not Israel hope, and what applause 295
Might such a general gain by such a cause?
Not barren praise alone, that gaudy flower
Fair only to the sight, but solid power;
And nobler is a limited command,
Given by the love of all your native land, 300
Than a successive title,² long and dark,
Drawn from the moldy rolls of Noah's ark."
    What cannot praise effect in mighty minds,
When flattery soothes, and when ambition blinds!
Desire of power, on earth a vicious weed, 305
Yet, sprung from high, is of celestial seed:
In God 'tis glory; and when men aspire,
'Tis but a spark too much of heavenly fire.
The ambitious youth, too covetous of fame,
Too full of angels' metal³ in his frame, 310
Unwarily was led from virtue's ways,
Made drunk with honor, and debauched with praise.
Half loath, and half consenting to the ill
(For loyal blood within him struggled still),
He thus replied: "And what pretense have I 315
To take up arms for public liberty?
My father governs with unquestioned right;
The faith's defender, and mankind's delight,
Good, gracious, just, observant of the laws:
And heaven by wonders has espoused his cause. 320
Whom has he wronged in all his peaceful reign?
Who sues for justice to his throne in vain?
What millions has he pardoned of his foes,

---

9. Louis XIV of France.
1. Cf. line 82 and note.
2. A title to the crown based on succession.
3. An alternative spelling of *mettle*, (i.e., spirit). But a pun on "metal" is intended, as is obvious from the pun "angel" (a purely intellectual being and a coin). Ambition caused the revolt of the angels in heaven.

Whom just revenge did to his wrath expose?
Mild, easy, humble, studious of our good,   325
Inclined to mercy, and averse from blood;
If mildness ill with stubborn Israel suit,
His crime is God's beloved attribute.
What could he gain, his people to betray,
Or change his right for arbitrary sway?   330
Let haughty Pharaoh curse with such a reign
His fruitful Nile, and yoke a servile train.
If David's rule Jerusalem displease,
The Dog Star[4] heats their brains to this disease.
Why then should I, encouraging the bad,   335
Turn rebel and run popularly mad?
Were he a tyrant, who, by lawless might
Oppressed the Jews, and raised the Jebusite,
Well might I mourn; but nature's holy bands
Would curb my spirits and restrain my hands: 340
The people might assert[5] their liberty,
But what was right in them were crime in me.
His favor leaves me nothing to require,
Prevents my wishes, and outruns desire.
What more can I expect while David lives?   345
All but his kingly diadem he gives:
And that"— But there he paused; then sighing, said—
"Is justly destined for a worthier head.
For when my father from his toils shall rest
And late augment the number of the blest,   350
His lawful issue shall the throne ascend,
Or the collateral line,[6] where that shall end.
His brother, though oppressed with vulgar spite,
Yet dauntless, and secure of native right,
Of every royal virtue stands possessed;   355
Still dear to all the bravest and the best.
His courage foes, his friends his truth proclaim;
His loyalty the king, the world his fame.
His mercy even the offending crowd will find,
For sure he comes of a forgiving kind.[7]   360
Why should I then repine at heaven's decree,
Which gives me no pretense to royalty?
Yet O that fate, propitiously inclined,
Had raised my birth, or had debased my mind;
To my large soul not all her treasure lent,   365
And then betrayed it to a mean descent!
I find, I find my mounting spirits bold,
And David's part disdains my mother's mold.
Why am I scanted by a niggard birth?[8]

4. Sirius, which in midsummer rises and sets with the sun and is thus associated with the maddening heat of the "dog days."
5. Claim.
6. In the event of Charles's dying without legitimate issue, the throne would constitutionally pass to his brother James, or his descendants, the "collateral line."
7. Race, in the sense of family.
8. I.e., why am I limited by a sordid birth?

My soul disclaims the kindred of her earth;   370
And, made for empire, whispers me within,
'Desire of greatness is a godlike sin.' "
   Him staggering so when hell's dire agent found,[9]
While fainting Virtue scarce maintained her ground,
He pours fresh forces in, and thus replies: 375
   "The eternal God, supremely good and wise,
Imparts not these prodigious gifts in vain:
What wonders are reserved to bless your reign!
Against your will, your arguments have shown,
Such virtue's only given to guide a throne.   380
Not that your father's mildness I contemn,
But manly force becomes the diadem.
'Tis true he grants the people all they crave;
And more, perhaps, than subjects ought to have:
For lavish grants suppose a monarch tame,   385
And more his goodness than his wit[1] proclaim.
But when should people strive their bonds to break,
If not when kings are negligent or weak?
Let him give on till he can give no more,
The thrifty Sanhedrin[2] shall keep him poor;   390
And every shekel which he can receive,
Shall cost a limb of his prerogative.[3]
To ply him with new plots shall be my care;
Or plunge him deep in some expensive war;
Which when his treasure can no more supply,   395
He must, with the remains of kingship, buy.
His faithful friends our jealousies and fears
Call Jebusites, and Pharaoh's pensioners;
Whom when our fury from his aid has torn,
He shall be naked left to public scorn.   400
The next successor, whom I fear and hate,
My arts have made obnoxious to the state;
Turned all his virtues to his overthrow,
And gained our elders[4] to pronounce a foe.
His right, for sums of necessary gold,   405
Shall first be pawned, and afterward be sold;
Till time shall ever-wanting David draw,
To pass your doubtful title into law:
If not, the people have a right supreme
To make their kings; for kings are made for them.   410
All empire is no more than power in trust,
Which, when resumed, can be no longer just.
Succession, for the general good designed,
In its own wrong a nation cannot bind;
If altering that the people can relieve,   415
Better one suffer than a nation grieve.

9. Observe the Miltonic inversion, which helps to maintain the epic tone.
1. Intelligence.
2. The highest judicial counsel of the Jews; here, Parliament.
3. The Whigs hoped to limit the special privileges of the Crown (the royal "prerogative") by refusing to vote money to Charles. He circumvented them by living on French subsidies and refusing to summon Parliament.
4. The chief magistrates and rulers of the Jews. Shaftesbury had won over ("gained") country gentlemen and nobles to his hostile view of James.

The Jews well know their power: ere Saul they chose,[5]
God was their king, and God they durst depose.
Urge now your piety,[6] your filial name,
A father's right, and fear of future fame;   420
The public good, that universal call,
To which even heaven submitted, answers all.
Nor let his love enchant your generous mind;
'Tis Nature's trick to propagate her kind.
Our fond begetters, who would never die,   425
Love but themselves in their posterity.
Or let his kindness by the effects be tried,
Or let him lay his vain pretense aside.
God said he loved your father; could he bring
A better proof than to anoint him king?   430
It surely showed he loved the shepherd well,
Who gave so fair a flock as Israel.
Would David have you thought his darling son?
What means he then, to alienate[7] the crown?
The name of godly he may blush to bear: 435
'Tis after God's own heart[8] to cheat his heir.
He to his brother gives supreme command;
To you a legacy of barren land,[7a]
Perhaps the old harp, on which he thrums his lays,
Or some dull Hebrew ballad in your praise.   440
Then the next heir, a prince severe and wise,
Already looks on you with jealous eyes;
Sees through the thin disguises of your arts,
And marks your progress in the people's hearts.
Though now his mighty soul its grief contains,   445
He meditates revenge who least complains;
And, like a lion, slumbering in the way,
Or sleep dissembling, while he waits his prey,
His fearless foes within his distance draws,
Constrains his roaring, and contracts his paws;   450
Till at the last, his time for fury found,
He shoots with sudden vengeance from the ground;
The prostrate vulgar[9] passes o'er and spares,
But with a lordly rage his hunters tears.
Your case no tame expedients will afford: 455
Resolve on death, or conquest by the sword,
Which for no less a stake than life you draw;
And self-defense is nature's eldest law.
Leave the warm people no considering time;
For then rebellion may be thought a crime.   460
Prevail yourself of what occasion gives,
But try your title while your father lives;
And that your arms may have a fair pretense,[1]

---

5. Before Saul, the first king of Israel, came to the throne, the Jews were governed by judges. Similarly Oliver Cromwell ("Saul") as Lord Protector took over the reins of government, after he had dissolved the Rump Parliament in 1653.
6. Dutifulness to a parent.

7. In law, to convey the title to property to another person.
7a. James was given the title of generalissimo in 1678. In 1679 Monmouth was banished and withdrew to Holland.
8. An irony: cf. line 7, note.
9. Common people.
1. Pretext.

Proclaim you take them in the king's defense;
Whose sacred life each minute would expose   465
To plots, from seeming friends, and secret foes.
And who can sound the depth of David's soul?
Perhaps his fear his kindness may control.
He fears his brother, though he loves his son,
For plighted vows too late to be undone.   470
If so, by force he wishes to be gained,
Like women's lechery, to seem constrained.[2]
Doubt not; but when he most affects the frown,
Commit a pleasing rape upon the crown.
Secure his person to secure your cause: 475
They who possess the prince, possess the laws."
    He said, and this advice above the rest
With Absalom's mild nature suited best:
Unblamed of life (ambition set aside),
Not stained with cruelty, nor puffed with pride,   480
How happy had he been, if destiny
Had higher placed his birth, or not so high!
His kingly virtues might have claimed a throne,
And blest all other countries but his own.
But charming greatness since so few refuse,   485
'Tis juster to lament him than accuse.
Strong were his hopes a rival to remove,
With blandishments to gain the public love;
To head the faction while their zeal was hot,
And popularly prosecute the Plot.   490
To further this, Achitophel unites
The malcontents of all the Israelites;
Whose differing parties he could wisely join,
For several ends, to serve the same design:
The best (and of the princes some were such),   495
Who thought the power of monarchy too much;
Mistaken men, and patriots in their hearts;
Not wicked, but seduced by impious arts.
By these the springs of property were bent,
And wound so high, they cracked the government.   500
The next for interest sought to embroil the state,
To sell their duty at a dearer rate;
And make their Jewish markets of the throne,
Pretending public good, to serve their own.
Others thought kings an useless heavy load,   505
Who cost too much, and did too little good.
These were for laying honest David by,
On principles of pure good husbandry.[3]
With them joined all the haranguers of the throng,
That thought to get preferment by the tongue.   510
Who follow next, a double danger bring,
Not only hating David, but the king:
The Solymaean rout,[4] well-versed of old
In godly faction, and in treason bold;

2. Forced.
3. Economy.
4. I.e., London rabble. Solyma was a name for Jerusalem.

Cowering and quaking at a conqueror's sword,   515
But lofty to a lawful prince restored;
Saw with disdain an ethnic[5] plot begun,
And scorned by Jebusites to be outdone.
Hot Levites[6] headed these; who, pulled before
From the ark, which in the Judges' days they bore,   520
Resumed their cant, and with a zealous cry
Pursued their old beloved theocracy:
Where Sanhedrin and priest enslaved the nation,
And justified their spoils by inspiration:[7]
For who so fit for reign as Aaron's race,[8]   525
If once dominion they could found in grace?
These led the pack; though not of surest scent,
Yet deepest-mouthed[9] against the government.
A numerous host of dreaming saints[1] succeed,
Of the true old enthusiastic breed: 530
'Gainst form and order they their power employ,
Nothing to build, and all things to destroy.
But far more numerous was the herd of such,
Who think too little, and who talk too much.
These out of mere instinct, they knew not why,   535
Adored their fathers' God and property;
And, by the same blind benefit of fate,
The Devil and the Jebusite did hate:
Born to be saved, even in their own despite,
Because they could not help believing right.   540
Such were the tools; but a whole Hydra more
Remains, of sprouting heads too long to score.
Some of their chiefs were princes of the land:
In the first rank of these did Zimri[2] stand;
A man so various, that he seemed to be   545
Not one, but all mankind's epitome:
Stiff in opinions, always in the wrong;

5. Gentile; here, Roman Catholic.
6. I.e., Presbyterian clergymen. The tribe of Levi, assigned to duties in the tabernacle, carried the ark of the covenant during the forty-year sojourn in the wilderness (Numbers iv). Under the Commonwealth ("in the Judges' days") Presbyterianism became the state religion, and its clergy therefore "bore the ark." The Act of Uniformity (1662) forced the Presbyterian clergy out of their livings: in short, before the Popish Plot, they had been "pulled from the ark." They are represented here as joining the Whigs in the hope of restoring the Commonwealth, "their old beloved theocracy."
7. Observe in these lines the cluster of disparaging words: "cant," "zealous," "inspiration." Dryden shared Samuel Butler's contempt for the irrationality of Dissenters.
8. Priests had to be descendants of Aaron (Exodus xxviii.1; Numbers xviii.7).
9. Loudest. The phrase is applied to hunting dogs. "Pack" and "scent" sustain the image.

1. A term used by certain Dissenters for those elected to salvation. The extreme fanaticism of the "saints" and their claims to inspiration are characterized as a form of religious madness ("enthusiastic").
2. George Villiers, 2nd Duke of Buckingham (1628–87), wealthy, brilliant, dissolute, unstable. He had been an influential member of the Cabal, but after 1673 had joined Shaftesbury in opposition to the Court party. This is the least political of the satirical portraits in the poem. Buckingham had been the chief author of *The Rehearsal* (1671), the play which satirized the heroic play and ridiculed Dryden in the character of Mr. Bayes. Politics gave Dryden an opportunity to retaliate. He comments on this portrait in his *Discourse Concerning the Original and Progress of Satire*. Dryden had two Biblical Zimris in mind: the Zimri destroyed for his lustfulness and blasphemy (Numbers xxv) and the conspirator and regicide of I Kings xvi.8–20 and II Kings ix.31.

Was everything by starts, and nothing long;
But, in the course of one revolving moon,
Was chymist,[3] fiddler, statesman, and buffoon: 550
Then all for women, painting, rhyming, drinking,
Besides ten thousand freaks that died in thinking.
Blest madman, who could every hour employ,
With something new to wish, or to enjoy!
Railing[4] and praising were his usual themes; 555
And both (to show his judgment) in extremes:
So over-violent, or over-civil,
That every man, with him, was God or Devil.
In squandering wealth was his peculiar art:
Nothing went unrewarded but desert. 560
Beggared by fools, whom still he found[5] too late,
He had his jest, and they had his estate.
He laughed himself from court; then sought relief
By forming parties, but could ne'er be chief;
For, spite of him, the weight of business fell 565
On Absalom and wise Achitophel:
Thus, wicked but in will, of means bereft,
He left not faction, but of that was left.

　　Titles and names 'twere tedious to rehearse
Of lords, below the dignity of verse. 570
Wits, warriors, Commonwealth's men, were the best;
Kind husbands, and mere nobles, all the rest.
And therefore, in the name of dullness, be
The well-hung Balaam and cold Caleb, free;
And canting Nadab[6] let oblivion damn, 575
Who made new porridge for the paschal lamb.
Let friendship's holy band some names assure;
Some their own worth, and some let scorn secure.
Nor shall the rascal rabble here have place,
Whom kings no titles gave, and God no grace: 580
Not bull-faced Jonas,[7] who could statutes draw
To mean rebellion, and make treason law.
But he, though bad, is followed by a worse,
The wretch who heaven's anointed dared to curse:
Shimei,[8] whose youth did early promise bring 585
Of zeal to God and hatred to his king,
Did wisely from expensive sins refrain,

3. Chemist.
4. Reviling, abusing.
5. **Found out; "still": constantly.**
6. The identities of Balaam, Caleb, and Nadab have not been certainly established, although various Whig nobles have been suggested. For Balaam see Numbers xxii–xxiv; for Caleb, Numbers xiii–xiv; for Nadab, Leviticus x.1–2. "Well-hung" may mean "fluent of speech" or "sexually potent" or both; "cold" would contrast with the second meaning of "well-hung." "Canting" points to a Nonconformist, as does the obscure line 576, for Dissenters referred to the Book of Common Prayer contemptuously as "porridge," a hodgepodge, unsubstantial stuff. The "paschal

lamb," the lamb slain at the Passover, is Christ.
7. Sir William Jones, Attorney General, had been largely responsible for the passage of the first Exclusion Bill by the House of Commons. He prosecuted the accused in the Popish Plot.
8. Shimei cursed and stoned David when he fled into the wilderness during Absalom's revolt (II Samuel xvi.5–14); his name is used here for one of the two sheriffs of London, Slingsby Bethel, a Whig, former republican, and virulent enemy of Charles. He packed juries with Whigs and so secured the acquittal of enemies of the court, among them Shaftesbury himself.

And never broke the Sabbath, but for gain;
Nor ever was he known an oath to vent,
Or curse, unless against the government. 590
Thus heaping wealth, by the most ready way
Among the Jews, which was to cheat and pray,
The city, to reward his pious hate
Against his master, chose him magistrate.
His hand a vare[9] of justice did uphold; 595
His neck was loaded with a chain of gold.
During his office, treason was no crime;
The sons of Belial[1] had a glorious time;
For Shimei, though not prodigal of pelf,
Yet loved his wicked neighbor as himself. 600
When two or three were gathered to declaim ⎫
Against the monarch of Jerusalem, ⎬
Shimei was always in the midst of them; ⎭
And if they cursed the king when he was by,
Would rather curse than break good company. 605
If any durst his factious friends accuse,
He packed a jury of dissenting Jews;
Whose fellow-feeling in the godly cause
Would free the suffering saint from human laws.
For laws are only made to punish those 610
Who serve the king, and to protect his foes.
If any leisure time he had from power
(Because 'tis sin to misemploy an hour),
His business was, by writing, to persuade
That kings were useless, and a clog to trade; 615
And, that his noble style he might refine,
No Rechabite[2] more shunned the fumes of wine.
Chaste were his cellars, and his shrieval board[3]
The grossness of a city feast abhorred:
His cooks, with long disuse, their trade forgot; 620
Cool was his kitchen, though his brains were hot.
Such frugal virtue malice may accuse,
But sure 'twas necessary to the Jews;
For towns once burnt[4] such magistrates require
As dare not tempt God's providence by fire. 625
With spiritual food he fed his servants well,
But free from flesh that made the Jews rebel;
And Moses' laws he held in more account,
For forty days of fasting in the mount.[5]
To speak the rest, who better are forgot, 630
Would tire a well-breathed witness of the Plot.
Yet, Corah,[6] thou shalt from oblivion pass:

9. Staff.
1. Sons of wickedness. Cf. Milton, *Paradise Lost* I.490–505. Dryden probably intended a pun on Balliol, the Oxford college in which leading Whigs stayed during the brief and fateful meeting of Parliament at Oxford in 1681.
2. An austere Jewish sect that drank

no wine (Jeremiah xxxv.2–19).
3. Sheriff's dinner table.
4. London burned in 1666.
5. Mt. Sinai, where, during a fast of forty days, Moses received the law (Exodus xxxiv.28).
6. Or Korah, a rebellious Levite, swallowed up by the earth because of his

Erect thyself, thou monumental brass,
High as the serpent of thy metal made,[7]
While nations stand secure beneath thy shade.   635
What though his birth were base, yet comets rise
From earthy vapors, ere they shine in skies.
Prodigious actions may as well be done
By weaver's issue,[8] as by prince's son.
This arch-attestor for the public good   640
By that one deed ennobles all his blood.
Who ever asked the witnesses' high race
Whose oath with martyrdom did Stephen grace?[9]
Ours was a Levite, and as times went then,
His tribe were God Almighty's gentlemen.   645
Sunk were his eyes, his voice was harsh and loud,
Sure signs he neither choleric[1] was nor proud:
His long chin proved his wit; his saintlike grace
A church vermilion, and a Moses' face.[2]
His memory, miraculously great,   650
Could plots, exceeding man's belief, repeat;
Which therefore cannot be accounted lies,
For human wit could never such devise.
Some future truths are mingled in his book;
But where the witness failed, the prophet spoke: 655
Some things like visionary flights appear;
The spirit caught him up, the Lord knows where,
And gave him his rabbinical degree,
Unknown to foreign university.[3]
His judgment yet his memory did excel;   660
Which pieced his wondrous evidence so well,
And suited to the temper of the times,
Then groaning under Jebusitic crimes.
Let Israel's foes suspect his heavenly call,
And rashly judge his writ apocryphal;[4]   665
Our laws for such affronts have forfeits made:
He takes his life, who takes away his trade.
Were I myself in witness Corah's place,
The wretch who did me such a dire disgrace
Should whet my memory, though once forgot,   670
To make him an appendix of my plot.
His zeal to heaven made him his prince despise,
And load his person with indignities;

crimes (Numbers xvi). Corah is Titus
Oates, the self-appointed, perjured, and
"well-breathed" (long-winded) witness
of the Plot.
7. Moses erected a brazen serpent to
heal the Jews bitten by fiery serpents
(Numbers xxi.4–9). "Brass" also means
"impudence" or "shamelessness."
8. Oates's father, a clergyman, belonged
to an obscure family of ribbon weavers.
9. The first Christian martyr, accused
by false witnesses (Acts vi–vii).

1. Prone to anger.
2. Moses' face shone when he came
down from Mt. Sinai with the tables of
the law (Exodus xxxiv.29–30). Oates's
face suggests high living, not spiritual
illumination.
3. Oates falsely claimed to be a Doctor
of Divinity in the University of Sala-
manca.
4. Not inspired, and hence excluded
from Holy Writ.

But zeal peculiar privilege affords,
Indulging latitude to deeds and words; 675
And Corah might for Agag's murder [5] call,
In terms as coarse as Samuel used to Saul.
What others in his evidence did join
(The best that could be had for love or coin),
In Corah's own predicament will fall; 680
For *witness* is a common name to all.
    Surrounded thus with friends of every sort,
Deluded Absalom forsakes the court:
Impatient of high hopes, urged with renown,
And fired with near possession of a crown. 685
The admiring crowd are dazzled with surprise,
And on his goodly person feed their eyes:
His joy concealed, he sets himself to show,
On each side bowing popularly [6] low;
His looks, his gestures, and his words he frames, 690
And with familiar ease repeats their names.
Thus formed by nature, furnished out with arts,
He glides unfelt into their secret hearts.
Then, with a kind compassionating look,
And sighs, bespeaking pity ere he spoke, 695
Few words he said; but easy those and fit,
More slow than Hybla-drops,[7] and far more sweet.
    "I mourn, my countrymen, your lost estate;
Though far unable to prevent your fate:
Behold a banished man, for your dear cause 700
Exposed a prey to arbitrary laws!
Yet oh! that I alone could be undone,
Cut off from empire, and no more a son!
Now all your liberties a spoil are made; ⎱
Egypt and Tyrus [8] intercept your trade, ⎰ 705
And Jebusites your sacred rites invade. ⎰
My father, whom with reverence yet I name,
Charmed into ease, is careless of his fame;
And, bribed with petty sums of foreign gold,
Is grown in Bathsheba's [9] embraces old; 710
Exalts his enemies, his friends destroys;
And all his power against himself employs.
He gives, and let him give, my right away;
But why should he his own, and yours betray?
He only, he can make the nation bleed, 715
And he alone from my revenge is freed.
Take then my tears (with that he wiped his eyes),

5. Agag is probably one of the five Catholic peers executed for the Popish Plot in 1680, most likely Lord Stafford, against whom Oates fabricated testimony; almost certainly not, as is usually suggested, Sir Edmund Berry Godfrey (cf. title note). For "Agag's murder" and Samuel's coarse terms to Saul, see I Samuel xv.

6. "So as to please the crowd" (Johnson's *Dictionary*).
7. The famous honey of Hybla in Sicily.
8. France and Holland.
9. With whom David committed adultery (II Samuel xi); here, Charles II's French mistress, Louise de Keroualle, Duchess of Portsmouth.

'Tis all the aid my present power supplies:
No court-informer can these arms accuse;
These arms may sons against their fathers use: 720
And 'tis my wish, the next successor's reign
May make no other Israelite complain."
　　Youth, beauty, graceful action seldom fail;
But common interest always will prevail;
And pity never ceases to be shown 725
To him who makes the people's wrongs his own.
The crowd (that still believe their kings oppress),
With lifted hands their young Messiah bless:
Who now begins his progress to ordain
With chariots, horsemen, and a numerous train; 730
From east to west his glories he displays,[1]
And, like the sun, the promised land surveys.
Fame runs before him as the morning star,
And shouts of joy salute him from afar:
Each house receives him as a guardian god, 735
And consecrates the place of his abode:
But hospitable treats did most commend
Wise Issachar,[2] his wealthy western friend.
This moving court, that caught the people's eyes,
And seemed but pomp, did other ends disguise: 740
Achitophel had formed it, with intent
To sound the depths, and fathom where it went,
The people's hearts; distinguish friends from foes,
And try their strength, before they came to blows.
Yet all was colored with a smooth pretense 745
Of specious love, and duty to their prince.
Religion, and redress of grievances,
Two names that always cheat and always please,
Are often urged; and good King David's life
Endangered by a brother and a wife.[3] 750
Thus, in a pageant show, a plot is made,
And peace itself is war in masquerade.
O foolish Israel! never warned by ill,
Still the same bait, and circumvented still!
Did ever men forsake their present ease, 755
In midst of health imagine a disease;
Take pains contingent mischiefs to foresee,
Make heirs for monarchs, and for God decree?
What shall we think![4] Can people give away
Both for themselves and sons, their native sway? 760
Then they are left defenseless to the sword
Of each unbounded, arbitrary lord:

1. In 1680 Monmouth made a progress through the west of England, seeking popular support for his cause.
2. Thomas Thynne of Longleat. He entertained Monmouth on his journey in the west. "Wise" is, of course, ironic.
3. Titus Oates had sworn that both James, Duke of York, and the Queen were involved in a plot to poison Charles II.
4. In the passage that follows, Dryden states his political philosophy. He bases the royal authority on a covenant entered into by the governor and the governed.

And laws are vain, by which we right enjoy,
If kings unquestioned can those laws destroy.
Yet if the crowd be judge of fit and just,   765
And kings are only officers in trust,
Then this resuming covenant was declared
When kings were made, or is forever barred.
If those who gave the scepter could not tie
By their own deed their own posterity,   770
How then could Adam bind his future race?
How could his forfeit on mankind take place?
Or how could heavenly justice damn us all,
Who ne'er consented to our father's fall?
Then kings are slaves to those whom they command,   775
And tenants to their people's pleasure stand.
Add, that the power for property allowed
Is mischievously seated in the crowd;
For who can be secure of private right,
If sovereign sway may be dissolved by might?   780
Nor is the people's judgment always true:
The most may err as grossly as the few;
And faultless kings run down, by common cry,
For vice, oppression, and for tyranny.
What standard is there in a fickle rout,   785
Which, flowing to the mark,[5] runs faster out?
Nor only crowds, but Sanhedrins may be
Infected with this public lunacy,
And share the madness of rebellious times,
To murder monarchs for imagined crimes.[6]   790
If they may give and take whene'er they please,
Not kings alone (the Godhead's images),
But government itself at length must fall
To nature's state, where all have right to all.
Yet, grant our lords the people kings can make,   795
What prudent men a settled throne would shake?
For whatsoe'er their sufferings were before,
That change they covet makes them suffer more.
All other errors but disturb a state,
But innovation is the blow of fate.   800
If ancient fabrics nod, and threat to fall,
To patch the flaws, and buttress up the wall,
Thus far 'tis duty; but here fix the mark;
For all beyond it is to touch our ark.[7]
To change foundations, cast the frame anew,   805
Is work for rebels, who base ends pursue,
At once divine and human laws control,
And mend the parts by ruin of the whole.

---

5. An obscure couplet, rare in Dryden. George R. Noyes paraphrases it thus: "The fickle crowd is apparently compared to water, which, after rising to the *mark*, or boundary, it was intended to reach, overflows all the faster."

6. An allusion to the execution of Charles I.

7. Uzzah was struck dead because he sacrilegiously touched the Ark of the Covenant. II Samuel vi. 6–7.

The tampering world is subject to this curse,
To physic their disease into a worse.   810
    Now what relief can righteous David bring?
How fatal 'tis to be too good a king!
Friends he has few, so high the madness grows:
Who dare be such, must be the people's foes:
Yet some there were, even in the worst of days;   815
Some let me name, and naming is to praise.
    In this short file Barzillai [8] first appears;
Barzillai, crowned with honor and with years:
'Long since, the rising rebels he withstood
In regions waste, beyond the Jordan's flood: 820
Unfortunately brave to buoy the State;
But sinking underneath his master's fate:
In exile with his godlike prince he mourned;
For him he suffered, and with him returned.
The court he practiced, not the courtier's art: 825
Large was his wealth, but larger was his heart:
Which well the noblest objects knew to choose,
The fighting warrior, and recording Muse.
His bed could once a fruitful issue boast;
Now more than half a father's name is lost.   830
His eldest hope,[9] with every grace adorned,
By me (so Heaven will have it) always mourned,
And always honored, snatched in manhood's prime
By unequal fates, and Providence's crime:
Yet not before the goal of honor won,   835
All parts fulfilled of subject and of son;
Swift was the race, but short the time to run.
O narrow circle, but of power divine,
Scanted in space, but perfect in thy line!
By sea, by land, thy matchless worth was known,   840
Arms thy delight, and war was all thy own:
Thy force, infused, the fainting Tyrians [1] propped;
And haughty Pharaoh found his fortune stopped.
Oh ancient honor! Oh unconquered hand,
Whom foes unpunished never could withstand!   845
But Israel was unworthy of thy name:
Short is the date of all immoderate fame.
It looks as Heaven our ruin had designed,
And durst not trust thy fortune and thy mind.
Now, free from earth, thy disencumbered soul   850
Mounts up, and leaves behind the clouds and starry pole:
From thence thy kindred legions mayst thou bring,
To aid the guardian angel of thy king.
Here stop my Muse, here cease thy painful flight;

---

8. James Butler, Duke of Ormond (1610–88). He was famous for his loyalty to the Stuart cause. He fought for Charles I in Ireland, and when that cause was hopeless, he joined Charles II in his exile abroad. He spent a large fortune in behalf of the King and continued to serve him loyally after the Restoration.
9. Ormond's son, Thomas, Earl of Ossory (1634–80), a famous soldier, and like his father devoted to Charles II.
1. The Dutch.

No pinions can pursue immortal height: 855
Tell good Barzillai thou canst sing no more,
And tell thy soul she should have fled before.
Or fled she with his life, and left this verse
To hang on her departed patron's hearse?
Now take thy steepy flight from heaven, and see 860
If thou canst find on earth another *he*:
Another *he* would be too hard to find;
See then whom thou canst see not far behind.
Zadoc the priest,[2] whom, shunning power and place,
His lowly mind advanced to David's grace: 865
With him the Sagan of Jerusalem,
Of hospitable soul, and noble stem;
Him of the western dome, whose weighty sense
Flows in fit words and heavenly eloquence.
The prophets' sons, by such example led, 870
To learning and to loyalty were bred:
For colleges on bounteous kinds depend,
And never rebel was to arts a friend.
To these succeed the pillars of the laws,
Who best could plead, and best can judge a cause. 875
Next them a train of loyal peers ascend;
Sharp-judging Adriel, the Muses' friend,
Himself a Muse—in Sanhedrin's debate
True to his prince, but not a slave of state:
Whom David's love with honors did adorn, 880
That from his disobedient son were torn.
Jotham of piercing wit, and pregnant thought,
Indued by nature, and by learning taught
To move assemblies, who but onely tried
The worse a while, then chose the better side; 885
Nor chose alone, but turned the balance too;
So much the weight of one brave man can do.
Hushai, the friend of David in distress,
In public storms, of manly steadfastness:
By foreign treaties he informed his youth, 890
And joined experience to his native truth.
His frugal care supplied the wanting throne,
Frugal for that, but bounteous of his own:
'Tis easy conduct when exchequers flow,
But hard the task to manage well the low; 895
For sovereign power is too depressed or high,
When kings are forced to sell, or crowds to buy.
Indulge one labor more, my weary Muse,
For Amiel: who can Amiel's praise refuse?
Of ancient race by birth, but nobler yet 900

2. William Sancroft, Archbishop of Canterbury; the Sagan is Henry Compton, Bishop of London; "Him of the western dome" is John Dolben, Dean of Westminster; "The prophets' sons" are the boys of Westminster School, which Dryden had attended; Adriel is John Sheffield, Earl of Mulgrave; Jotham, George Savile, Marquis of Halifax; Hushai, Laurence Hyde, Earl of Rochester; and Amiel is Edward Seymour, Speaker of the House of Commons.

In his own worth, and without title great:
The Sanhedrin long time as chief he ruled,
Their reason guided, and their passion cooled:
So dexterous was he in the crown's defence,
So formed to speak a loyal nation's sense,   905
That, as their band was Israel's tribes in small,
So fit was he to represent them all.
Now rasher charioteers the seat ascend,
Whose loose careers his steady skill commend:
They like the unequal ruler of the day,   910
Misguide the seasons, and mistake the way;
While he withdrawn at their mad labor smiles,
And safe enjoys the sabbath of his toils.
    These were the chief, a small but faithful band ⎤
Of worthies, in the breach who dared to stand, ⎬   915
And tempt the united fury of the land. ⎦
With grief they viewed such powerful engines bent,
To batter down the lawful government:
A numerous faction, with pretended frights,
In Sanhedrins to plume the regal rights;   920
The true successor from the court removed: [3]
The Plot, by hireling witnesses, improved.
These ills they saw, and, as their duty bound,
They showed the king the danger of the wound:
That no concessions from the throne would please,   925
But lenitives [4] fomented the disease;
That Absalom, ambitious of the crown,
Was made the lure to draw the people down;
That false Achitophel's pernicious hate
Had turned the Plot to ruin Church and State: 930
The council violent, the rabble worse;
That Shimei taught Jerusalem to curse.
    With all these loads of injuries oppressed,
And long revolving in his careful breast,
The event of things, at last, his patience tired,   935
Thus from his royal throne, by Heaven inspired,
The godlike David spoke: with awful fear
His train their Maker in their master hear.
    "Thus long have I, by native mercy swayed,
My wrongs dissembled, my revenge delayed: 940
So willing to forgive the offending age,
So much the father did the king assuage.
But now so far my clemency they slight,
The offenders question my forgiving right.
That one was made for many, they contend;   945
But 'tis to rule; for that's a monarch's end.
They call my tenderness of blood, my fear;
Though manly tempers can the longest bear.
Yet, since they will divert my native course,

---

3. The Duke of York had been banished   4. Any medicine that relieves pain.
from England.

'Tis time to show I am not good by force.   950
Those heaped affronts that haughty subjects bring,
Are burdens for a camel, not a king:
Kings are the public pillars of the State,
Born to sustain and prop the nation's weight:
If my young Samson will pretend a call   955
To shake the column, let him share the fall: 5
But, oh, that yet he would repent and live!
How easy 'tis for parents to forgive!
With how few tears a pardon might be won
From nature, pleading for a darling son!   960
Poor pitied youth, by my paternal care
Raised up to all the height his frame could bear:
Had God ordained his fate for empire born,
He would have given his soul another turn:
Gulled 6 with a patriot's name, whose modern sense
Is one that would by law supplant his prince: 965
The people's brave, the politician's tool;
Never was patriot yet, but was a fool.
Whence comes it that religion and the laws
Should more be Absalom's than David's cause?   970
His old instructor, ere he lost his place,
Was never thought indued with so much grace.7
Good heavens, how faction can a patriot paint!
My rebel ever proves my people's saint:
Would *they* impose an heir upon the throne?   975
Let Sanhedrins be taught to give their own.
A king's at least a part of government,
And mine as requisite as their consent;
Without my leave a future king to choose,
Infers a right the present to depose: 980
True, they petition me to approve their choice;
But Esau's hands suit ill with Jacob's voice.8
My pious subjects for my safety pray,
Which to secure, they take my power away.
From plots and treasons Heaven preserve my years,   985
But save me most from my petitioners.
Unsatiate as the barren womb or grave;
God cannot grant so much as they can crave.
What then is left but with a jealous eye
To guard the small remains of royalty?   990
The law shall still direct my peaceful sway,
And the same law teach rebels to obey:
Votes shall no more established power control—
Such votes as make a part exceed the whole:
No groundless clamors shall my friends remove,   995
Nor crowds have power to punish ere they prove:
For gods and godlike kings, their care express,
Still to defend their servants in distress.

---

5. Judges xvi.   7. The Earl of Shaftesbury.
6. Deceived.   8. Genesis xxvii. 22.

O that my power to saving were confined:
Why am I forced, like Heaven, against my mind,
To make examples of another kind?
Must I at length the sword of justice draw?
O curst effects of necessary law!
How ill my fear they by my mercy scan!
Beware the fury of a patient man.   1005
Law they require, let Law then show her face;
They could not be content to look on Grace,
Her hinder parts, but with a daring eye
To tempt the terror of her front and die.[9]
By their own arts, 'tis righteously decreed,   1010
Those dire artificers of death shall bleed.
Against themselves their witnesses will swear,
Till viper-like their mother Plot they tear:
And suck for nutriment that bloody gore,
Which was their principle of life before.   1015
Their Belial with their Belzebub [10] will fight;
Thus on my foes, my foes shall do me right:
Nor doubt the event; for factious crowds engage,
In their first onset, all their brutal rage.
Then let 'em take an unresisted course,   1020
Retire and traverse, and delude their force:
But when they stand all breathless, urge the fight,
And rise upon 'em with redoubled might:
For lawful power is still superior found,
When long driven back, at length it stands the ground."   1025
    He said. The Almighty, nodding, gave consent;
And peals of thunder shook the firmament.
Henceforth a series of new time began,
The mighty years in long procession ran:
Once more the godlike David was restored,   1030
And willing nations knew their lawful lord.

1681

Mac Flecknoe[1]

OR A SATIRE UPON THE TRUE-BLUE-PROTESTANT POET, T. S.

    All human things are subject to decay,
    And when fate summons, monarchs must obey.

9. Moses was not allowed to see the countenance of Jehovah. Exodus xxxiii. 20–23.

10. Belial, the incarnation of all evil; Beelzebub, a god of the Philistines.

1. The victim of this superb satire, which is cast in the form of a mock-heroic episode, is Thomas Shadwell (1640–92), the playwright, with whom Dryden had been on good terms for a number of years, certainly as late as March, 1678. Shadwell considered himself the successor of Ben Jonson and the champion of the type of comedy that Jonson had written, the "comedy of humors," in which each character is presented under the domination of a single psychological trait or eccentricity, his humor. His plays are not without merit, but they are often clumsy and prolix, and certainly much inferior to Jonson's. For many years he had conducted a public argument with Dryden on the merits of Jonson's comedies, which he thought Dryden undervalued. Exactly what moved Dry-

This Flecknoe found, who, like Augustus,[2] young
Was called to empire, and had governed long;
In prose and verse, was owned, without dispute,   5
Through all the realms of Nonsense, absolute.
This aged prince, now flourishing in peace,
And blest with issue of a large increase,
Worn out with business, did at length debate
To settle the succession of the state;   10
And, pondering which of all his sons was fit
To reign, and wage immortal war with wit,
Cried: " 'Tis resolved; for nature pleads that he
Should only rule, who most resembles me.
Sh——[3] alone my perfect image bears,   15
Mature in dullness from his tender years:
Sh—— alone, of all my sons, is he
Who stands confirmed in full stupidity.
The rest to some faint meaning make pretense,
But Sh—— never deviates into sense.   20
Some beams of wit on other souls may fall,
Strike through, and make a lucid interval;
But Sh——'s genuine night admits no ray,
His rising fogs prevail upon the day.
Besides, his goodly fabric[4] fills the eye,   25
And seems designed for thoughtless majesty:
Thoughtless as monarch oaks that shade the plain,
And, spread in solemn state, supinely reign.

den to attack him is a matter of conjecture: he may simply have grown progressively bored or irritated by Shadwell and his tedious argument. The poem seems to have been written in late 1678 or 1679 and to have circulated only in manuscript, until it was printed in 1682 in a pirated edition by an obscure publisher. By that time, the two playwrights were alienated by politics as well as by literary quarrels. Shadwell was a violent Whig and the reputed author of a sharp attack on Dryden as the Tory author of *Absalom and Achitophel* and *The Medal*. It was probably for this reason that the printer added the subtitle referring to Shadwell's Whiggism in the phrase "true-blue-Protestant poet." Political passions were running high and sales would be helped if the poem seemed to refer to the events of the day.

Whereas Butler had debased and degraded his victims by using burlesque, caricature, and the grotesque, Dryden exposed Shadwell to ridicule by using the devices of mock-epic, which treats the low, mean, or absurd in the grand language, lofty style, and solemn tone of epic poetry. The obvious disparity between subject and style makes the satiric point. In 1678 an execrable Irish poet and playwright, Richard Flecknoe, died. Dryden conceived the idea of presenting Shadwell (the self-proclaimed heir of Ben Jonson, the laureate) as the son and successor of Flecknoe—hence *Mac* (i.e., son of) *Flecknoe*—from whom he interits the throne of dullness. Flecknoe in the triple role of king, priest, and poet hails his successor, pronounces a panegyric on his perfect fitness for the throne, anoints and crowns him, foretells his glorious reign, and, as he sinks (leaden dullness cannot soar), leaves his mantle to fall symbolically upon Shadwell's shoulders. The poem abounds in literary allusions—to Roman legend and history and to the *Aeneid;* to Cowley's fragmentary epic, *The Davideis,* and to *Paradise Lost;* and to Shadwell's own plays. Biblical allusions add an unexpected dimension of incongruous dignity to the low scene. The coronation takes place in the City, to the plaudits of the citizens, who are fit to admire only what is dull. In 217 lines Dryden created an image of Shadwell which has fixed his reputation to this day.

2. In 31 B.C. Octavian became the first Roman emperor at the age of 32. He assumed the title Augustus in 27 B.C.

3. Thomas Shadwell. The initial and second letter of the name followed by a dash give the appearance, but only the appearance, of protecting Dryden's victim by concealing his name. A common device in the satire of the period.

4. His body. Shadwell was a corpulent man.

Heywood and Shirley[5] were but types of thee,
Thou last great prophet of tautology.[6]   30
Even I, a dunce of more renown than they,
Was sent before but to prepare thy way;
And, coarsely clad in Norwich drugget,[7] came
To teach the nations in thy greater name.[8]
My warbling lute, the lute I whilom[9] strung,   35
When to King John of Portugal I sung,
Was but the prelude to that glorious day,
When thou on silver Thames didst cut thy way,
With well-timed oars before the royal barge,
Swelled with the pride of thy celestial charge;   40
And big with hymn, commander of a host,
The like was ne'er in Epsom blankets tossed.[1]
Methinks I see the new Arion[2] sail,
The lute still trembling underneath thy nail.
At thy well-sharpened thumb from shore to shore   45
The treble squeaks for fear, the basses roar;
Echoes from Pissing Alley Sh—— call,
And Sh—— they resound from Aston Hall.
About thy boat the little fishes throng,
As at the morning toast[3] that floats along.   50
Sometimes, as prince of thy harmonious band,
Thou wield'st thy papers in thy threshing hand.
St. André's[4] feet ne'er kept more equal time,
Not ev'n the feet of thy own *Psyche's* rhyme;
Though they in number as in sense excel: 55
So just, so like tautology, they fell,
That, pale with envy, Singleton[5] forswore
The lute and sword, which he in triumph bore,
And vowed he ne'er would act Villerius[6] more."
Here stopped the good old sire, and wept for joy   60
In silent raptures of the hopeful boy.
All arguments, but most his plays, persuade,
That for anointed[7] dullness he was made.

5. Thomas Heywood (ca. 1570–1641) and James Shirley (1596–1666), playwrights popular before the closing of the theaters in 1642 but now out of fashion. They are introduced here as "types" (i.e., prefigurings) of Shadwell, in the sense that Solomon was regarded as an Old Testament prefiguring of Christ, the "last [final] great prophet."
6. Unnecessary repetition of meaning in different words.
7. A coarse woolen cloth.
8. The parallel between Flecknoe, as forerunner of Shadwell, and John the Baptist, as forerunner of Jesus, is made plain in lines 32–34 by the use of details and even words taken from Matthew iii.3–4 and John i.23.
9. Formerly. Flecknoe boasted of the patronage of the Portuguese king.
1. A reference to Shadwell's comedy *Epsom Wells* and to the farcical scene

in his *Virtuoso*, in which Sir Samuel Hearty is tossed in a blanket.
2. A legendary Greek poet. Returning home by sea, he was robbed and thrown overboard by the sailors, but was saved by a dolphin which had been charmed by his music.
3. Sewage.
4. A French dancer who designed the choreography of Shadwell's opera *Psyche* (1675). Dryden's sneer in the next line at the mechanical metrics of the songs in *Psyche* is justified.
5. John Singleton (d. 1686), a musician at the Theatre Royal.
6. A character in Sir William Davenant's *Siege of Rhodes* (1656), the first English opera.
7. The anticipated phrase is "anointed *majesty*." English kings are anointed with oil at their coronations.

Close to the walls which fair Augusta[8] bind
(The fair Augusta much to fears inclined),   65
An ancient fabric[9] raised to inform the sight,
There stood of yore, and Barbican it hight:
A watchtower once; but now, so fate ordains,
Of all the pile an empty name remains.
From its old ruins brothel houses rise,   70
Scenes of lewd loves, and of polluted joys,
Where their vast courts the mother-strumpets keep,
And, undisturbed by watch, in silence sleep.
Near these a Nursery[1] erects its head,
Where queens are formed, and future heroes bred;   75
Where unfledged actors learn to laugh and cry,   ⎫
Where infant punks[2] their tender voices try,   ⎬
And little Maximins[3] the gods defy.   ⎭
Great Fletcher[4] never treads in buskins here,
Nor greater Jonson dares in socks appear;   80
But gentle Simkin[5] just reception finds
Amidst this monument of vanished minds:
Pure clinches[6] the suburbian Muse affords,
And Panton[7] waging harmless war with words.
Here Flecknoe, as a place to fame well known,   85
Ambitiously design'd his Sh——'s throne;
For ancient Dekker[8] prophesied long since,   ⎫
That in this pile would reign a mighty prince,   ⎬
Born for a scourge of wit, and flail of sense;   ⎭
To whom true dullness should some *Psyches* owe,   90
But worlds of *Misers* from his pen should flow;
Humorists and *Hypocrites*[9] it should produce,
Whole *Raymond* families, and tribes of *Bruce*.
Now Empress Fame had published the renown
Of Sh——'s coronation through the town.   95
Roused by report of Fame, the nations meet,
From near Bunhill, and distant Watling Street.[1]
No Persian carpets spread the imperial way,
But scattered limbs of mangled poets lay;
From dusty shops neglected authors come,   100
Martyrs of pies, and relics of the bum.[2]

8. London. The next line alludes to
the fears excited by the Popish Plot
(cf. *Absalom and Achitophel*).
9. Building.
1. The name of a training school for
young actors.
2. Prostitutes.
3. Maximin is the cruel emperor in
Dryden's *Tyrannic Love* (1669), notorious for his bombast.
4. John Fletcher (1579–1625), the
playwright and collaborator with Francis Beaumont (ca. 1584–1616). "Buskins" and "socks" were the symbols of
tragedy and comedy.
5. A popular character in low farces.
6. Puns.
7. Said to have been a celebrated punster.

8. Thomas Dekker (ca. 1572–1632),
the playwright, whom Jonson had satirized in *The Poetaster*.
9. Three of Shadwell's plays; *The Hypocrite*, a failure, was not published.
"Raymond" and "Bruce" (line 94) are
characters in *The Humorists* and *The
Virtuoso* respectively.
1. Since Bunhill is about a quarter of
a mile and Watling Street little more
than half a mile from the site of the
Nursery, where the coronation is held,
Shadwell's fame is narrowly circumscribed. Moreover, his subjects live in
the heart of the City, regarded by men
of wit and fashion as the abode of bad
taste and middle-class vulgarity.
2. Unsold books eventually went to
bakers' shops and privies.

Much Heywood, Shirley, Ogilby[3] there lay,
But loads of Sh—— almost choked the way.
Bilked stationers[4] for yeomen stood prepared,
And Herringman was captain of the guard.   105
The hoary prince in majesty appeared,
High on a throne of his own labors reared.
At his right hand our young Ascanius[5] sate,
Rome's other hope, and pillar of the state.
His brows thick fogs, instead of glories, grace,   110
And lambent dullness played around his face.
As Hannibal did to the altars come,
Sworn by his sire a mortal foe to Rome,[6]
So Sh—— swore, nor should his vow be vain,
That he till death true dullness would maintain;   115
And, in his father's right, and realm's defense,
Ne'er to have peace with wit, nor truce with sense.
The king himself the sacred unction[7] made,
As king by office, and as priest by trade.
In his sinister[8] hand, instead of ball,   120
He placed a mighty mug of potent ale;
Love's Kingdom to his right he did convey,
At once his scepter, and his rule of sway;
Whose righteous lore the prince had practiced young,
And from whose loins recorded *Psyche* sprung.   125
His temples, last, with poppies were o'erspread,
That nodding seemed to consecrate his head.
Just at that point of time, if fame not lie,
On his left hand twelve reverend owls did fly.[9]
So Romulus, 'tis sung, by Tiber's brook,   130
Presage of sway from twice six vultures took.
The admiring throng loud acclamations make,
And omens of his future empire take.
The sire then shook the honors[1] of his head,
And from his brows damps of oblivion shed   135
Full on the filial dullness: long he stood,
Repelling from his breast the raging god;
At length burst out in this prophetic mood:

3. John Ogilby, a translator of Homer and Virgil, ridiculed by both Dryden and Pope as a bad poet.
4. Cheated publishers, who acted as "yeomen" of the guard, led by Henry Herringman, who until 1679 was the publisher of both Shadwell and Dryden.
5. Or Iulus, son of Aeneas; Virgil referred to him as *"spes altera Romae"* ("Rome's other hope"; *Aeneid* XII. 168). As Troy fell, he was marked as favored by the gods when a flickering ("lambent") flame played round his head (*Aeneid* II.680–84).
6. Hannibal, who almost conquered Rome in 216 B.C., during the 2nd Punic War, took this oath at the age of 9 (Livy xxi.1).
7. The sacramental oil, used in the coronation.
8. Left. During his coronation a British monarch holds two symbols of kingship: a globe ("ball") representing the world in his left hand, a scepter in his right. In lines 121–27, Shadwell's symbols of monarchy—a mug of ale; Flecknoe's dreary play, *Love's Kingdom;* a crown of poppies—suggest heaviness, dullness, drowsiness. The poppies also refer obliquely to Shadwell's addiction to opium.
9. Birds of night, appropriate substitutes for the twelve vultures whose flight confirmed to Romulus the destined site of Rome, of which he was founder and king.
1. Ornaments, hence locks.

"Heavens bless my son, from Ireland let him reign
To far Barbadoes on the western main;[2]   140
Of his dominion may no end be known,
And greater than his father's be his throne;
Beyond *Love's Kingdom* let him stretch his pen!"
He paused, and all the people cried, "Amen."
Then thus continued he: "My son, advance   145
Still in new impudence, new ignorance.
Success let others teach, learn thou from me
Pangs without birth, and fruitless industry.
Let *Virtuosos* in five years be writ;
Yet not one thought accuse thy toil of wit.   150
Let gentle George[3] in triumph tread the stage,
Make Dorimant betray, and Loveit rage;
Let Cully, Cockwood, Fopling, charm the pit,
And in their folly show the writer's wit.
Yet still thy fools shall stand in thy defense,   155
And justify their author's want of sense.
Let 'em be all by thy own model made
Of dullness, and desire no foreign aid;
That they to future ages may be known,
Not copies drawn, but issue of thy own.   160
Nay, let thy men of wit too be the same,
All full of thee, and differing but in name.
But let no alien S—dl—y[4] interpose,
To lard with wit[5] thy hungry *Epsom* prose.
And when false flowers of rhetoric thou wouldst cull,   165
Trust nature, do not labor to be dull;
But write thy best, and top; and, in each line,
Sir Formal's[6] oratory will be thine:
Sir Formal, though unsought, attends thy quill,
And does thy northern dedications[7] fill.   170
Nor let false friends seduce thy mind to fame,
By arrogating Jonson's hostile name.
Let father Flecknoe fire thy mind with praise,
And uncle Ogilby thy envy raise.
Thou art my blood, where Jonson has no part: 175
What share have we in nature, or in art?
Where did his wit on learning fix a brand,
And rail at arts he did not understand?
Where made he love in Prince Nicander's vein,[8]
Or swept the dust in *Psyche's* humble strain?   180

2. Shadwell's empire is vast but empty.
3. Sir George Etherege (ca. 1635–91),
a writer of brilliant comedies. In the
next couplet Dryden names characters
from his plays.
4. Sir Charles Sedley (1638–1701),
wit, rake, poet, playwright. Dryden
hints that he contributed more than the
prologue to Shadwell's *Epsom Wells*.
5. The phrase "lard with wit" recalls
a sentence in Burton's *Anatomy of Melancholy*: "They lard their lean books
with the fat of others' works * * * "
6. Sir Formal Trifle, the ridiculous and
vapid orator in *The Virtuoso*.
7. Shadwell frequently dedicated his
works to the Duke of Newcastle and
members of his family.
8. In *Psyche*.

Where sold he bargains,[9] 'whip-stitch, kiss my arse,'
Promised a play and dwindled to a farce?[1]
When did his Muse from Fletcher scenes purloin,
As thou whole Eth'rege dost transfuse to thine?
But so transfused, as oil on water's flow,   185
His always floats above, thine sinks below.
This is thy province, this thy wondrous way,
New humors to invent for each new play:
This is that boasted bias[2] of thy mind,
By which one way, to dullness, 'tis inclined;   190
Which makes thy writings lean on one side still,
And, in all changes, that way bends thy will.
Nor let thy mountain-belly make pretense
Of likeness; thine's a tympany[3] of sense.
A tun[4] of man in thy large bulk is writ,   195
But sure thou'rt but a kilderkin of wit.
Like mine, thy gentle numbers feebly creep;
Thy tragic Muse gives smiles, thy comic sleep.
With whate'er gall thou sett'st thyself to write,
Thy inoffensive satires never bite.   200
In thy felonious heart though venom lies,
It does but touch thy Irish pen,[5] and dies.
Thy genius calls thee not to purchase fame
In keen iambics,[6] but mild anagram.
Leave writing plays, and choose for thy command   205
Some peaceful province in acrostic land.
There thou may'st wings display and altars raise,
And torture one poor word ten thousand ways.[7]
Or, if thou wouldst thy different talent suit,
Set thy own songs, and sing them to thy lute."   210
    He said: but his last words were scarcely heard
For Bruce and Longville had a trap prepared,
And down they sent the yet declaiming bard.[8]
Sinking he left his drugget robe behind,
Borne upwards by a subterranean wind.   215

9. To "sell bargains" is to answer an innocent question with a coarse or indecent phrase as in this line. "Whipstitch" is a nonsense word frequently used by Sir Samuel Hearty in *The Virtuoso*.
1. Low comedy which depends largely on situation rather than wit, consistently condemned by Dryden and other serious playwrights.
2. In bowling, the spin given to the bowl that causes it to swerve. Dryden closely parodies a passage in Shadwell's epilogue to *The Humorists*.
3. A swelling in some part of the body caused by wind.
4. A large wine cask. "Kilderkin": a very small cask.
5. Flecknoe was Irish, and so his son must be Irish. Ireland suggested only poverty, superstition, and barbarity to 17th-century Londoners.
6. Sharp satire.
7. "Anagram": the transposition of letters in a word so as to make a new one; "acrostic": a poem in which the first letter of each line, read downward, makes up the name of the person or thing that is the subject of the poem; "wings" and "altars" refer to poems in the shape of these objects as in George Herbert's *Easter Wings* and *The Altar*. Dryden is citing instances of triviality and overingenuity in literature.
8. In *The Virtuoso*, Bruce and Longville play this trick on Sir Formal Trifle while he makes a speech.

The mantle fell to the young prophet's part,[9]
With double portion of his father's art.

ca. 1679   1682

To the Memory of Mr. Oldham[1]

Farewell, too little, and too lately known,
Whom I began to think and call my own:
For sure our souls were near allied, and thine
Cast in the same poetic mold with mine.
One common note on either lyre did strike,
And knaves and fools[2] we both abhorred alike.   5
To the same goal did both our studies drive;
The last set out the soonest did arrive.
Thus Nisus[3] fell upon the slippery place,
While his young friend performed and won the race.   10
O early ripe! to thy abundant store
What could advancing age have added more?
It might (what nature never gives the young)
Have taught the numbers[4] of thy native tongue.
But satire needs not those, and wit will shine   15
Through the harsh cadence of a rugged line:[5]
A noble error, and but seldom made,
When poets are by too much force betrayed.
Thy generous fruits, though gathered ere their prime, ⎱
Still showed a quickness;[6] and maturing time   ⎰ 20
But mellows what we write to the dull sweets of rhyme. ⎰
Once more, hail and farewell;[7] farewell, thou young,
But ah too short, Marcellus[8] of our tongue;
Thy brows with ivy, and with laurels bound;[9]
But fate and gloomy night encompass thee around.   25

1684

9. When the prophet Elijah was carried to heaven in a chariot of fire borne on a whirlwind, his mantle fell on his successor, the younger prophet Elisha (II Kings.ii.8–14). Flecknoe, prophet of dullness, naturally cannot ascend, but must sink.
1. John Oldham (1653–83), the young poet whose *Satires upon the Jesuits* (1681) won Dryden's admiration. This elegy was published in Oldham's *Remains in Verse and Prose* (1684).
2. The objects of satire.
3. Nisus, on the point of winning a foot race, slipped in a pool of blood; his "young friend" was Euryalus (Virgil, *Aeneid* V.315–39).
4. Metrics, verse.
5. Dryden repeats the Renaissance idea

that the satirist should avoid smoothness and affect rough meters ("harsh cadence").
6. Sharpness of flavor.
7. Dryden echoes the famous words that conclude Catullus' elegy to his brother: "*Atque in perpetuum, frater, ave atque vale*" ("And forever, brother, hail and farewell!").
8. The nephew of Augustus, adopted by him as his successor. After winning military fame as a youth, he died at the age of 20. Virgil celebrated him in the *Aeneid* VI.854–86; the last line of Dryden's poem is a reminiscence of *Aeneid* VI.866.
9. The poet's wreath. Cf. Milton's *Lycidas*, lines 1–2.

To the Pious Memory of the Accomplished Young Lady Mrs.[1] Anne Killigrew

EXCELLENT IN THE TWO SISTER ARTS OF POESY AND PAINTING.

An Ode [1a]

1

Thou youngest virgin-daughter of the skies,
Made in the last promotion of the blest,
Whose palms,[2] new plucked from paradise,

1. "Mrs." means "Mistress," used at this time for our "Miss."

1a. Like Milton's *Lycidas,* Dryden's ode to Anne Killigrew is not so much the expression of private grief as it is a decorous ceremonial gesture dignifying a public occasion. In both poems the death of an individual becomes the point of departure for the treatment of larger topics. The fact that Mrs. Killigrew was not a distinguished poet or painter is irrelevant: her death prompted the poet to consider the arts themselves, their present state in a corrupt age, their central role in civilization, their service to virtue and religion. In the course of the poem, the dead woman is transformed into a symbol of the sister arts themselves, what they are, and what, on earth, they might become. *Lycidas* is an elegy; Dryden's ode combines the elegiac with the lyric and the heroic. Although *Lycidas* is cast in the traditional mode of the pastoral lament, and *Anne Killigrew* in the form of a eulogistic memorial, both poems develop classical and Christian themes which had become conventions of the funeral poem: the death of the young and promising, the praise of his genius and virtues, a lament for the times which suffer such loss, and a consolation, offered by describing the reception of the soul of the dead into heaven.

Dryden's poem, in form, is an irregular ode, a lyric poem which develops a serious theme in a dignified or exalted manner. Two kinds of ode were recognized during the 18th century. To quote Johnson: " * * * the ode is either of the greater or less kind. The less is characterized by sweetness and ease; the greater by sublimity, rapture, and quickness of transition." The greater ode, of which this is the finest example in 17th-century poetry, was associated with the odes of Pindar, the lyric poet of 5th-century Greece, whose intricate metrics, bold imagery, and intense and energetic power were aspired to (seldom with success) by English poets throughout our period. Pindar's odes were rigorously constructed: each

was divided into long stanzas, which in turn were subdivided into three parts —called in Greek strophe, antistrophe, and epode—whose metrical structure was repeated throughout the whole poem. Strophes and antistrophes were identical but the epodes followed a different metrical pattern. Such symmetry is not easily attained in English verse because of the paucity of rhymes in our language, but Ben Jonson's *To the Immortal Memory * * * of * * * Sir Lucius Cary and Sir Henry Morison* is strictly Pindaric, as are Thomas Gray's *The Progress of Poesy* and *The Bard* (1757).

In 1656 Abraham Cowley published loose paraphrases of two of Pindar's odes in which he abandoned the formal structure of the originals in favor of irregular meters and irregularly constructed stanzas, while trying to preserve Pindar's rapture, boldness, and sublimity. Thanks to Cowley's popularity, his irregular Pindarics became the standard of what the age considered the loftiest sort of lyric poetry. It was a tempting form for poets who wished to achieve (or to simulate) the loftiest lyric rapture, for the apparent structural disorder could suggest inspired improvisation. The result was a plague of turgid rhetoric in uninteresting irregular meter.

Dryden declared that Cowley's Pindarics lacked "somewhat of a finer turn and more lyrical verse" and that such odes should consist in "the warmth and vigor of fancy, the masterly figures, and the copiousness of imagination" (Ker, *Essays* I.267–268). His superb ear and gift for melodious eloquence enabled him in this poem to raise the greater ode to heights not to be equaled again until Wordsworth wrote his *Ode: Intimations of Immortality.*

The lesser ode, often in this period associated with the odes of Horace, is more quiet and contemplative, more lyrical in mood, and it usually employs an uncomplicated, rather short stanza.

2. The symbol of victory (cf. Revelation vii.9).

In spreading branches more sublimely rise,
Rich with immortal green above the rest;   5
Whether, adopted to some neighboring star,
Thou roll'st above us in thy wandering race,
 Or in procession fixed and regular,
 Moved with the heavens' majestic pace,
 Or called to more superior bliss,   10
Thou tread'st with seraphims the vast abyss:[3]
Whatever happy region is thy place,
Cease thy celestial song a little space;
Thou wilt have time enough for hymns divine,
 Since heaven's eternal year is thine.   15
Hear then a mortal Muse thy praise rehearse,
  In no ignoble verse;
But such as thy own voice did practice here,
When thy first fruits of poesy were given,
To make thyself a welcome inmate there,   20
  While yet a young probationer,
  And candidate of heaven.

2

  If by traduction came thy mind,
  Our wonder is the less to find
A soul so charming from a stock so good;   25
Thy father was transfused into thy blood:[4]
So wert thou born into the tuneful strain
(An early, rich, and inexhausted vein).
  But if thy pre-existing soul
  Was formed at first with myriads more,   30
It did through all the mighty poets roll
  Who Greek or Latin laurels wore,
And was that Sappho last, which once it was before.[5]
 If so, then cease thy flight, O heaven-born mind!
 Thou hast no dross to purge from thy rich ore;   35
 Nor can thy soul a fairer mansion find   ⎫
 Than was the beauteous frame she left behind: ⎬
Return, to fill or mend the choir of thy celestial kind. ⎭

3

 May we presume to say that at thy birth
New joy was sprung in heaven, as well as here on earth?   40
  For sure the milder planets did combine ⎱

3. Dryden is speculating on where the soul of the dead poetess has come to rest: is she the tutelary deity of a planet ("neighboring star")? or of one of the remote "fixed" stars? or does she enjoy the higher ("superior") bliss of having joined the "seraphim," the guardians of the throne of God? (cf. Isaiah vi). Like Milton, Dryden makes use of the Ptolemaic universe of concentric spheres moving around the earth "in procession fixed and regular."
4. The idea that the soul is transmitted by the father at the moment of conception. Since Henry Killigrew

had written a tragedy, his daughter is said to have inherited a poet's soul from him. In lines 29–32, Dryden proposes the theory that the soul exists before birth, and less seriously that through the ages it transmigrates from body to body.
5. Mrs. Killigrew is said to have been Sappho (the Greek lyric poetess of the 7th century B.C.) twice: "once before," when her soul transmigrated into Sappho's body, and most recently ("last"), when it inhabited the body of the modern Sappho, Anne Killigrew.

On thy auspicious horoscope to shine,[6]
And even the most malicious were in trine.
Thy brother-angels at thy birth
    Strung each his lyre, and tuned it high,   45
    That all the people of the sky
Might know a poetess was born on earth.
    And then, if ever, mortal ears
Had heard the music of the spheres!
    And if no clustering swarm of bees   50
On thy sweet mouth distilled their golden dew,[7]
    'Twas that such vulgar miracles
    Heaven had not leisure to renew:
For all the blest fraternity of love
Solemnized there thy birth, and kept thy holiday above.   55

4

    O gracious God! how far have we
Profaned thy heavenly gift of poesy!
Made prostitute and profligate the Muse,
Debased to each obscene and impious use,
Whose harmony was first ordained above   60
For tongues of angels, and for hymns of love!
O wretched we! why were we hurried down
    This lubric and adulterate[8] age
(Nay, added fat pollutions of our own)
    To increase the steaming ordures of the stage?   65
What can we say to excuse our second fall?
Let this thy vestal,[9] Heaven, atone for all:
Her Arethusan stream remains unsoiled,
Unmixed with foreign filth, and undefiled;
Her wit was more than man, her innocence a child!   70

5

    Art she had none, yet wanted none,
    For nature did that want supply;
    So rich in treasures of her own,
    She might our boasted stores defy:
Such noble vigor did her verse adorn   75
That it seemed borrowed where 'twas only born.
Her morals too were in her bosom bred,
  By great examples daily fed,
What in the best of books, her father's life, she read.
And to be read herself she need not fear;   80
Each test and every light her Muse will bear,

6. The familiar idea that character and destiny are determined by the position of the planets at the moment of birth ("horoscope"). Mrs. Killigrew's horoscope was fortunate ("auspicious"): even those planets that are usually baleful ("malicious") were "in trine" —120 degrees apart and hence favorable in their influence.

7. It was said that bees clustered on the lips of the infant Pindar, thus foretelling his greatness as a lyric poet.

8. Lewd and corrupted.

9. I.e., thy virgin. The Roman "vestal" virgins guarded the fire in the Temple of Vesta, goddess of the hearth. For "Arethusan stream," cf. Milton's *Lycidas*, line 85.

Though Epictetus with his lamp were there.[1]
Even love (for love sometimes her Muse expressed)
Was but a lambent flame[2] which played about her breast,
Light as the vapors of a morning dream;   85
So cold herself, whilst she such warmth expressed,
'Twas Cupid bathing in Diana's stream.

6

Born to the spacious empire of the Nine,[3]
One would have thought she should have been content
To manage well that mighty government;   90
But what can young ambitious souls confine?
   To the next realm she stretched her sway,
   For Painture[4] near adjoining lay,
A plenteous province, and alluring prey.
   A chamber of dependences[5] was framed   95
(As conquerors will never want pretense,
   When armed, to justify the offense)
And the whole fief in right of Poetry she claimed.
The country open lay without defense;
For poets frequent inroads there had made,   100
   And perfectly could represent
   The shape, the face, with every lineament;
And all the large demains[6] which the dumb Sister swayed,
   All bowed beneath her government,
   Received in triumph wheresoe'er she went.   105
Her pencil[7] drew whate'er her soul designed,
And oft the happy draft surpassed the image in her mind.
   The sylvan scenes[8] of herds and flocks
   And fruitful plains and barren rocks;
   Of shallow brooks that flowed so clear   110
   The bottom did the top appear;
   Of deeper too and ampler floods,
   Which, as in mirrors, showed the woods;
   Of lofty trees, with sacred shades
   And perspectives[9] of pleasant glades,   115
   Where nymphs of brightest form appear,
   And shaggy satyrs standing near,
   Which them at once admire and fear;

1. A collector is said to have paid a large sum for the lamp of the philosopher Epictetus in the faith that owning it would make him wise. Dryden merely means that Anne Killigrew's poems would appear pure even if judged in the light of the most severe Stoic ethical standards.
2. I.e., "a flickering flame." Cf. Dryden's *Mac Flecknoe*, line 111 and note on line 108.
3. The nine Muses, who preside over the arts of literature, the dance, music, and astronomy.
4. The art of painting (a Gallicism).
5. In the elaborate figure that dominates lines 95–98, Dryden alludes to recent peaceful annexations by Louis XIV of France, who in 1679 added most of Alsace, Lorraine, and Luxembourg to his realm through his policy of *"réunions,"* by setting up *"Chambres de Réunions."* These chambers by quasi-legal means awarded to Louis, as overlord, towns, cities, and estates with all their "dependences" or fiefs, i.e., estates held under the feudal system from overlords, to whom the holders owed services and rents.
6. I.e., an estate held in one's own right, as opposed to "fief" (line 98) The "dumb Sister" is the Muse of painting.
7. Painter's brush.
8. Cf. Milton, *Paradise Lost* IV.140.
9. Vistas.

The ruins, too, of some majestic piece,
Boasting the power of ancient Rome or Greece,
Whose statues, friezes, columns broken lie,
And, though defaced, the wonder of the eye:[1]
What nature, art, bold fiction e'er durst frame,
Her forming hand gave feature to the name.
So strange a concourse ne'er was seen before
But when the peopled ark the whole creation bore.[2]

7

The scene then changed: with bold erected look
Our martial king[3] the sight with reverence strook;
For, not content to express his outward part,
Her hand called out the image of his heart:
His warlike mind, his soul devoid of fear,
His high-designing thoughts were figured there,
As when by magic, ghosts are made appear.
Our phoenix queen[4] was portrayed, too, so bright,
Beauty alone could beauty take[5] so right:
Her dress, her shape, her matchless grace
Were all observed, as well as heavenly face.
With such a peerless majesty she stands
As in that day she took the crown from sacred hands;[6]
Before a train of heroines was seen,
In beauty foremost, as in rank the queen.
Thus nothing to her genius was denied,
    But like a ball of fire, the further thrown,
    Still with a greater blaze she shone,
And her bright soul broke out on every side.
What next she had designed, heaven only knows;[7]
To such immoderate growth her conquest rose
That fate alone its progress could oppose.

8

Now all those charms, that blooming grace,
The well-proportioned shape, and beauteous face,
Shall never more be seen by mortal eyes:
In earth the much-lamented virgin lies!
    Not wit nor piety could fate prevent;
    Nor was the cruel destiny content
    To finish all the murder at a blow,
    To sweep at once her life and beauty too;
But, like a hardened felon, took a pride

---

1. Mrs. Killigrew's landscapes are typical of the ideal classical landscape of 17th-century Italian painters: contrasts of fruitful plains and barren rocks, water that reflects trees, vistas, classical ruins, and mythological figures.
2. Noah's ark, which contained all that survived of created beings.
3. James II, who, as Duke of York, had won a reputation for courage and skill while fighting as a soldier with the French armies in the 1650's and serving as an admiral during the English-Dutch wars of the 1660's.
4. Mary of Modena, wife of James II, whose unique beauty is expressed by the reference to the "phoenix," the fabulous bird, only one of which exists during each thousand years.
5. I.e., take the likeness of.
6. The queen was crowned by the "sacred hands" of the Archbishop of Canterbury.
7. God alone knows.

To work more mischievously slow,
And plundered first, and then destroyed.
O double sacrilege on things divine,   160
To rob the relic, and deface the shrine!
        But thus Orinda died:[8]
Heaven, by the same disease, did both translate;
As equal were their souls, so equal was their fate.

                                9

        Meantime her warlike brother[9] on the seas   165
        His waving streamers to the winds displays,
And vows for his return with vain devotion pays.
        Ah, generous youth, that wish forbear;
        The winds too soon will waft thee here!
        Slack all thy sails, and fear to come,   170
Alas, thou know'st not thou art wrecked at home!
No more shalt thou behold thy sister's face;
Thou hast already had her last embrace.
But look aloft, and if thou kenn'st[1] from far,
Among the Pleiads,[2] a new-kindled star,   175
If any sparkles than the rest more bright,
'Tis she that shines in that propitious light.

                               10

        When in mid-air the golden trump shall sound,
        To raise the nations under ground;
        When in the Valley of Jehosaphat[3]   180
The judging God shall close the book of fate,
        And there the last assizes[4] keep
        For those who wake and those who sleep;
        When rattling bones together fly
        From the four corners of the sky;   185
When sinews o'er the skeletons are spread,
Those clothed with flesh, and life inspires the dead;
The sacred poets first shall hear the sound,   ⎤
And foremost from the tomb shall bound,   ⎬
For they are covered with the lightest ground,   ⎦   190
And straight, with inborn vigor, on the wing,
Like mounting larks, to the new morning sing.
There thou, sweet saint, before the choir shalt go, ⎤
As harbinger[5] of heaven, the way to show,   ⎬
The way which thou so well hast learned below.   ⎦   195

                                                        1686

---

8. The poetess Katharine Philips (1631–64), fancifully referred to by her admirers as "the matchless Orinda," who, like Anne Killigrew, died of the disfiguring disease, smallpox.
9. Henry Killigrew, an officer in the Royal Navy. Pennons ("streamers") fly from the mast of his ship.
1. Perceivest.
2. The Pleiades, a cluster of stars (six are visible to the unaided eye) in the constellation Taurus.
3. Joel iii.12; Ezekial xxxvii.
4. Periodical sessions of superior courts held in each county in England; here, of course, the Last Judgment—at which some will be alive on earth ("wake") and many will have already died ("sleep").
5. One who goes ahead to provide a lodging.

A Song for St. Cecilia's Day[1]

1

From harmony, from heavenly harmony
   This universal frame began:
When Nature[2] underneath a heap
   Of jarring atoms lay,
   And could not heave her head,   5
The tuneful voice was heard from high:
   "Arise, ye more than dead."
Then cold, and hot, and moist, and dry,
In order to their stations leap,
      And Music's power obey.   10
From harmony, from heavenly harmony
   This universal frame began:
   From harmony to harmony
Through all the compass of the notes it ran,
The diapason[3] closing full in man.   15

2

What passion cannot Music raise and quell![4]
   When Jubal[5] struck the corded shell,
   His listening brethren stood around,
   And, wondering, on their faces fell
   To worship that celestial sound.   20
Less than a god they thought there could not dwell
   Within the hollow of that shell
   That spoke so sweetly and so well.
What passion cannot Music raise and quell!

1. St. Cecilia, a Roman lady, was an early Christian martyr. She has long been regarded as the patroness of music and the supposed inventor of the organ. Celebrations of her festival day (November 22) in England were usually devoted to music and the praise of music, and from about 1683 to 1703 a "Musical Society" in London annually commemorated it with a religious service and a public concert. This concert always included an ode written and set to music for the occasion, of which the two by Dryden (*A Song for St. Cecilia's Day*, 1687, and *Alexander's Feast*, 1697) are the most distinguished. G. B. Draghi, an Italian brought to England by Charles II, set this ode to music, but Handel's fine score, composed in 1739, has completely obscured the original setting. Like the ode to Mrs. Killigrew, this is an irregular ode in the manner of Cowley. In stanzas 3–6 Dryden boldly attempted to suggest in the sounds of his words the characteristic tones of the instruments mentioned.
2. Created nature, ordered by the Divine Wisdom out of chaos, which Dryden, adopting the physics of the Greek philosopher Epicurus, describes as composed of the warring and discordant ("jarring") atoms of the four elements: earth, fire, water, air ("cold," "hot," "moist," "dry").
3. The entire compass of tones in the scale. Dryden is thinking of the Chain of Being, the ordered creation from inanimate nature up to man, God's latest and final work. The just gradations of notes in a scale is analogous to the equally just gradations in the ascending scale of created beings. Both are the result of harmony.
4. The power of music to describe, evoke, or subdue emotion ("passion") is a frequent theme in 17th-century literature. In stanzas 2–6 the poet considers music as awakening religious awe, warlike courage, sorrow for unrequited love, jealousy and fury, and the impulse to worship God.
5. According to Genesis iv.21, the inventor of the harp and the organ. Dryden imagines Jubal's harp to have been made of a tortoise shell ("corded shell").

3

The trumpet's loud clangor   25
    Excites us to arms,
With shrill notes of anger,
    And mortal alarms.
The double double double beat
    Of the thundering drum   30
Cries: "Hark! the foes come;
Charge, charge, 'tis too late to retreat."

4

The soft complaining flute
In dying notes discovers
The woes of hopeless lovers,   35
Whose dirge is whispered by the warbling lute.

5

Sharp violins[6] proclaim
Their jealous pangs, and desperation,
Fury, frantic indignation,
Depth of pains, and height of passion,   40
    For the fair, disdainful dame.

6

    But O! what art can teach,
    What human voice can reach,
The sacred organ's praise?
    Notes inspiring holy love,   45
Notes that wing their heavenly ways
    To mend the choirs above.

7

Orpheus[7] could lead the savage race;
And trees unrooted left their place,
    Sequacious of the lyre;   50
But bright Cecilia raised the wonder higher:
When to her organ vocal breath was given,
An angel heard, and straight appeared,[8]
    Mistaking earth for heaven.

GRAND CHORUS

As from the power of sacred lays
    The spheres began to move,[9]   55
And sung the great Creator's praise
    To all the blest above;
So, when the last and dreadful hour

5. A reference to the bright tone of the modern violin, introduced into England at the Restoration. The tone of the old-fashioned viol is much duller (Bronson).

7. A legendary poet, son of one of the Muses, who played so wonderfully on the lyre that wild beasts ("the savage race") grew tame and followed him, as did even rocks and trees. "Sequacious of": following.

8. According to the legend, it was Cecilia's piety, not her music, that brought an angel to visit her.

9. As it was harmony which ordered the universe, so it was angelic song ("sacred lays") which put the celestial bodies ("spheres") in motion. The harmonious chord which results from the traditional "music of the spheres" is a hymn of "praise" sung by created nature to its "Creator."

This crumbling pageant[1] shall devour,   60
The trumpet shall be heard on high,[2]
The dead shall live, the living die,
And Music shall untune the sky.

1687

Epigram on Milton[3]

Three poets, in three distant ages born,
Greece, Italy, and England did adorn.
The first in loftiness of thought surpassed,
The next in majesty, in both the last:
The force of Nature could no farther go;   5
To make a third, she joined the former two.

1688

Alexander's Feast[1]

OR THE POWER OF MUSIC; AN ODE IN HONOR OF
ST. CECILIA'S DAY

1

'Twas at the royal feast, for Persia won
    By Philip's[2] warlike son:
Aloft in awful state
The godlike hero sate
    On his imperial throne;   5
His valiant peers were placed around;
Their brows with roses and with myrtles[3] bound:
    (So should desert in arms be crowned).
The lovely Thaïs, by his side,
Sate like a blooming Eastern bride   10
In flower of youth and beauty's pride.
    Happy, happy, happy pair!
      None but the brave,
      None but the brave,
    None but the brave deserves the fair.   15

1. The universe: the stage on which the drama of man's salvation has been acted out.
2. The "last trump" of I Corinthians xv.52, which will announce the Resurrection and the Last Judgment. Dryden develops his theme of harmony as order in such a way as to give full emphasis of the splendid paradox ("Music shall *untune*") in the final line of the ode.
3. Engraved beneath the portrait of Milton in Jacob Tonson's edition of *Paradise Lost* (1688). The "three poets" are Homer, Virgil, Milton.
1. In Dryden's earlier poem for St. Cecilia's Day, music was celebrated primarily as harmony and order, though its power over the passions was also praised. *Alexander's Feast* is devoted entirely to the second theme. It is based upon a well-known episode in the life of Alexander the Great. After the de-

feat of the Persian Emperor Darius III and the fall of the Persian capital, Persepolis (331 B.C.), Alexander held a great feast for his officers. Thaïs, his Athenian mistress, persuaded him to set fire to the palace in revenge for the burning of Athens by the Persians under Xerxes in 480 B.C. According to Plutarch, Alexander was moved by love and wine, not by music; but Dryden, perhaps altering an old tradition that Alexander's musician Timotheus once caused the hero by his flute-playing to start up and arm himself, attributes the burning of Persepolis to the power of music. The original music was by Jeremiah Clarke, but Handel's score of 1736 is better known.
2. King Philip II of Macedonia, father of Alexander the Great.
3. The Greeks and Romans wore wreaths of flowers at banquets. Roses and myrtles are emblems of love.

CHORUS

Happy, happy, happy pair!
None but the brave,
None but the brave,
None but the brave deserves the fair.

2

Timotheus, placed on high   20
  Amid the tuneful choir,
    With flying fingers touched the lyre:
The trembling notes ascend the sky,
              And heavenly joys inspire.
The song began from Jove,   25
Who left his blissful seats above
(Such is the power of mighty love).[4]
A dragon's fiery form belied the god:
Sublime on radiant spires[5] he rode,
      When he to fair Olympia pressed;   30
      And while he sought her snowy breast:
Then, round her slender waist he curled,
And stamped an image of himself, a sovereign of the world.
The listening crowd admire[6] the lofty sound:
"A present deity," they shout around;   35
"A present deity," the vaulted roofs rebound.
          With ravished ears
          The monarch hears,
          Assumes the god,
          Affects to nod,
And seems to shake the spheres.[7]   40

CHORUS

    With ravished ears
    The monarch hears,
    Assumes the god,
    Affects to nod,
  And seems to shake the spheres.   45

3

The praise of Bacchus[8] then the sweet musician sung,
  Of Bacchus ever fair and ever young:
    The jolly god in triumph comes;
    Sound the trumpets; beat the drums;   50
      Flushed with a purple grace
      He shows his honest face:
Now give the hautboys[9] breath; he comes, he comes!
    Bacchus, ever fair and young
      Drinking joys did first ordain;   55

4. An oracle had declared that Alexander was the son of Zeus ("Jove") by Philip's wife Olympias (not, as Dryden calls her in line 30, "Olympia"), thus conferring on him that semi-divinity often claimed by heroes. Zeus habitually conducted his amours with mortals in the guise of an animal: in this case a dragon.
5. High on shining coils ("radiant spires"). "Spires" for the coils of a serpent is derived from the Latin word *spira*, which Virgil uses in this sense, *Aeneid* II.217. Cf. *Paradise Lost* IX.502.
6. Wonder at.
7. According to Virgil (*Aeneid* X.115) the nod of Jove causes earthquakes.
8. The god of wine.
9. Oboes.

Bacchus' blessings are a treasure,
Drinking is a soldier's pleasure;
    Rich the treasure,
    Sweet the pleasure,
Sweet is pleasure after pain.   60

CHORUS

Bacchus' blessings are a treasure,
Drinking is the soldier's pleasure;
    Rich the treasure,
    Sweet the pleasure,
Sweet is pleasure after pain.   65

4

Soothed with the sound, the king grew vain;
    Fought all his battles o'er again,
And thrice he routed all his foes, and thrice he slew the slain.
The master saw the madness rise,
His glowing cheeks, his ardent eyes;   70
And, while he[1] heaven and earth defied,
Changed his hand, and checked his pride.
    He chose a mournful Muse,
        Soft pity to infuse:
He sung Darius great and good,   75
        By too severe a fate
Fallen, fallen, fallen, fallen,
        Fallen from his high estate,
           And weltering in his blood;
Deserted at his utmost need   80
By those his former bounty fed;
On the bare earth exposed he lies,
With not a friend to close his eyes.[2]
With downcast looks the joyless victor sate,
    Revolving[3] in his altered soul   85
        The various turns of chance below;
And, now and then, a sigh he stole,
    And tears began to flow.

CHORUS

Revolving in his altered soul
    The various turns of chance below;
And, now and then, a sigh he stole,   90
    And tears began to flow.

5

The mighty master smiled to see
That love was in the next degree;
'Twas but[4] a kindred sound to move,   95
For pity melts the mind to love.
    Softly sweet, in Lydian[5] measures,

---

1. Alexander; in line 72, "his hand" is the hand of Timotheus, "his pride," the pride of Alexander.
2. After his final defeat by Alexander, Darius was assassinated by his own followers.
3. Pondering.
4. I.e., it was necessary only.
5. In Greek music the Lydian mode expressed the plaintive and the sad.

Soon he soothed his soul to pleasures.
"War," he sung, "is toil and trouble;
Honor, but an empty bubble. 100
 Never ending, still beginning,
Fighting still, and still destroying:
 If the world be worth thy winning,
Think, O think it worth enjoying.
  Lovely Thaïs sits beside thee, 105
  Take the good the gods provide thee."
The many[6] rend the skies with loud applause;
So Love was crowned, but Music won the cause.
 The prince, unable to conceal his pain,
   Gazed on the fair 110
   Who caused his care,
  And sighed and looked, sighed and looked,
 Sighed and looked, and sighed again:
At length, with love and wine at once oppressed,
The vanquished victor sunk upon her breast. 115

CHORUS

* The prince, unable to conceal his pain,*
*   Gazed on the fair*
*   Who caused his care,*
* And sighed and looked, sighed and looked,*
* Sighed and looked, and sighed again:* 120
At length, with love and wine at once oppressed,
The vanquished victor sunk upon her breast.

6

Now strike the golden lyre again:
A louder yet, and yet a louder strain.
Break his bands of sleep asunder, 125
And rouse him, like a rattling peal of thunder.
  Hark, hark, the horrid[7] sound
   Has raised up his head:
  As waked from the dead,
  And amazed, he stares around. 130
"Revenge, revenge!" Timotheus cries,
  "See the Furies[8] arise!
  See the snakes that they rear,
  How they hiss in their hair,
And the sparkles that flash from their eyes! 135
  Behold a ghastly band,
  Each a torch in his hand!
Those are Grecian ghosts, that in battle were slain,
  And unburied remain[9]
  Inglorious on the plain: 140

6. As G. R. Noyes points out, "many" means *meiny*, "a retinue," a spelling that Dryden used elsewhere in his work.
7. Rough, from Latin *horridus*.
8. The Erinyes of the Greeks, avengers of crimes against the natural and the social orders. They are described as women with snakes in their hair and around their waists and arms.
9. According to Greek beliefs, the shades of the dead could not rest until their bodies were buried.

Give the vengeance due
To the valiant crew.
Behold how they toss their torches on high,
    How they point to the Persian abodes,
And glittering temples of their hostile gods!"   145
The princes applaud, with a furious joy;
And the king seized a flambeau[1] with zeal to destroy;
    Thaïs led the way,
    To light him to his prey,
And, like another Helen, fired another Troy.[2]   150

CHORUS

And the king seized a flambeau with zeal to destroy;
    Thaïs led the way,
    To light him to his prey,
And, like another Helen, fired another Troy.

7

    Thus long ago,   155
    Ere heaving bellows learned to blow,
      While organs yet were mute;
    Timotheus, to his breathing flute,
      And sounding lyre,
Could swell the soul to rage, or kindle soft desire.   160
    At last, divine Cecilia came,
    Inventress of the vocal frame;[3]
The sweet enthusiast,[4] from her sacred store,
    Enlarged the former narrow bounds,
    And added length to solemn sounds,   165
With nature's mother wit, and arts unknown before.
    Let old Timotheus yield the prize,
    Or both divide the crown:
    He raised a mortal to the skies;
    She drew an angel down.   170

GRAND CHORUS

    At last, divine Cecilia came,
    Inventress of the vocal frame;
The sweet enthusiast, from her sacred store,
    Enlarged the former narrow bounds,
    And added length to solemn sounds,   175
With nature's mother wit, and arts unknown before
    Let old Timotheus yield the prize,
    Or both divide the crown:
    He raised a mortal to the skies;
    She drew an angel down.   180

1697

1. Torch.
2. Helen's elopement to Troy with Paris brought on the Trojan War and the ultimate destruction of the city by the Greeks.
3. Organ.
4. Usually at this time a disparaging word, frequently, though not always, applied to a religious zealot or fanatic. Here it is used approvingly and in its literal sense, "possessed by a god," an allusion to Cecilia's angelic companion referred to in line 170. But see note on *Song for St. Cecilia's Day*, line 53.

The Secular Masque[1]

[Enter JANUS.[2]]

JANUS.   Chronos,[3] Chronos, mend thy pace;
          An hundred times the rolling sun
          Around the radiant belt[4] has run
          In his revolving race.
          Behold, behold, the goal in sight;   5
          Spread thy fans,[5] and wing thy flight.

[Enter CHRONOS, with a scythe in his hand, and a great globe on his back, which he sets down at his entrance.]

CHRONOS.   Weary, weary of my weight,
          Let me, let me drop my freight,
          And leave the world behind.
          I could not bear   10
          Another year
          The load of humankind.

[Enter MOMUS,[6] laughing.]

MOMUS.   Ha! ha! ha! ha! ha! ha! well hast thou done
          To lay down thy pack,
          And lighten thy back;   15
          The world was a fool, e'er since it begun,
          And since neither Janus, nor Chronos, nor I
          Can hinder the crimes,
          Or mend the bad times,
          'Tis better to laugh than to cry.   20

CHORUS OF ALL THREE.
          'Tis better to laugh than to cry.

JANUS.   Since Momus comes to laugh below,
          Old Time, begin the show,
          That he may see, in every scene,
          What changes in this age have been.   25

CHRONOS.   Then, goddess of the silver bow,[7] begin.

[Horns, or hunting music within.]
[Enter DIANA.]

DIANA.   With horns and with hounds I waken the day,

---

1. A masque is a dramatic performance, usually mythological in character, that combines poetry, music, dance, and spectacle. Distinctly a courtly form of art, it flourished at the courts of James I and Charles I. This masque, however, was written for public performance as an afterpiece to the revival of Fletcher's *The Pilgrim*, revised by Sir John Vanbrugh, and produced for the financial benefit of Dryden himself. It is a "secular masque" because it celebrates the end of the century, "secular" being derived from the Latin *saeculares*, applied to the games, plays, and shows celebrated in Rome once an "age," a period of 120 years. It is not certain that Dryden lived to see his masque performed.

2. The god of beginnings, who here presides over the opening of the new century.

3. God of time.

4. The sun, in the course of a year, passes through all twelve signs of the zodiac ("the radiant belt").

5. Wings.

6. God of mockery and faultfinding.

7. Diana, the virgin goddess of the moon, a huntress. She symbolizes England before the Civil War, an allusion to James I's passion for the chase.

And hie to my woodland walks away;
I tuck up my robe, and am buskined[8] soon,
And tie to my forehead a wexing[9] moon. 30
I course the fleet stag, unkennel the fox,
And chase the wild goats o'er summits of rocks;
With shouting and hooting we pierce through the sky,
And Echo turns hunter, and doubles the cry.

CHORUS OF ALL.
With shouting and hooting we pierce through the sky, 35
And Echo turns hunter, and doubles the cry.

JANUS. Then our age was in its prime:
CHRONOS. Free from rage:
DIANA. And free from crime:
MOMUS. A very merry, dancing, drinking,
Laughing, quaffing, and unthinking time. 40

CHORUS OF ALL.
Then our age was in its prime,
Free from rage, and free from crime;
A very merry, dancing, drinking,
Laughing, quaffing, and unthinking time.
[*Dance of* DIANA's *attendants.*]
[*Enter* MARS.[1]]

MARS. Inspire[2] the vocal brass, inspire; 45
The world is past its infant age:
Arms and honor,
Arms and honor,
Set the martial mind on fire,
And kindle manly rage. 50
Mars has looked the sky to red;
And Peace, the lazy good, is fled.
Plenty, Peace, and Pleasure fly;
The sprightly green
In woodland walks no more is seen; 55
The sprightly green has drunk the Tyrian dye.[3]

CHORUS OF ALL.
Plenty, Peace, etc.

MARS. Sound the trumpet, beat the drum;
Through all the world around,
Sound a reveille, sound, sound, 60
The warrior god is come.

CHORUS OF ALL.
Sound the trumpet, etc.

MOMUS. Thy sword within the scabbard keep,
And let mankind agree;
Better the world were fast asleep, 65

---

8. Wearing hunting boots.
9. Waxing (i.e., increasing, because in the first quarter).
1. God of war, who represents the period of the Civil War and the Commonwealth.

2. Breathe into.
3. I.e., the costume has changed from the green of the hunter to the crimson of the soldier (at once the color of blood and of "Tyrian dye," known to the ancients as "purple").

Than kept awake by thee.
The fools are only thinner,
    With all our cost and care;
But neither side a winner,
    For things are as they were.   70

CHORUS OF ALL.
    The fools are only, etc.
        [*Enter* VENUS.[4]]

VENUS.   Calms appear when storms are past,
Love will have his hour at last:
Nature is my kindly care;
Mars destroys, and I repair;   75
Take me, take me, while you may;
Venus comes not every day.

CHORUS OF ALL.
    Take her, take her, etc.

CHRONOS.   The world was then so light,
I scarcely felt the weight;   80
Joy ruled the day, and Love the night.
But since the Queen of Pleasure left the ground,[5]
    I faint, I lag,
    And feebly drag
The ponderous orb around.   85

MOMUS.   All, all of a piece throughout:
        [*Pointing to* DIANA.]
Thy chase had a beast in view;
        [*To* MARS.]
Thy wars brought nothing about;
        [*To* VENUS.]
Thy lovers were all untrue.

JANUS.   'Tis well an old age is out: 90
CHRONOS.   And time to begin a new.

CHORUS OF ALL.
    All, all of a piece throughout:
    Thy chase had a beast in view;
    Thy wars brought nothing about;
    Thy lovers were all untrue.   95
    'Tis well an old age is out,
    And time to begin a new.

[*Dance of huntsmen, nymphs, warriors, and lovers.*]

                                      1700

4. Goddess of love and beauty, representing the licentious reigns of Charles II and James II.

5. Sir Walter Scott suggested that this line refers to the exiled Queen Mary of Modena, wife of James II.

Criticism   Because Dryden liked to talk about literature, he became a critic, indeed the first comprehensive critic in England. The Elizabethans, largely impelled by the example of Italian humanists, had produced an interesting and unsystematic body of critical writings. Dryden could look back to such pioneer works as George Puttenham's *Art of English Poesy* (1589), Sir Philip Sidney's *Apology for Poetry* (1595), Samuel Daniel's *Defense of Rhyme* (ca. 1603), and Ben Jonson's *Timber, or Discoveries* (1641), which is more Jonson's commonplace book than a collection of critical essays. These and later writings Dryden knew, as he knew the ancient critics, especially Aristotle, Horace, Quintilian, and Longinus, and the important contemporary French critics, notably Corneille, Rapin, and Boileau. Taken as a whole, his critical prefaces and dedications, which appeared between 1664 and 1700, are the work of a man of independent mind who has made his own synthesis of critical canons from wide reading, a great deal of thinking, and the constant practice of the art of writing. As a critic he is no man's disciple, and he has the saving grace of being always willing to change his mind. This unwillingness to construct a rigid and dogmatic critical system has been regarded by many as mere inconsistency, but recent students of Dryden have held that it is actually the sign of a lively mind, always capable of growth.

All but a very few of Dryden's critical works (most notably the *Essay of Dramatic Poesy*) grew out of the works to which they served as prefaces: comedies, heroic plays, tragedies, translations, poems of various sorts. Each work posed problems which Dryden was eager to discuss with his readers, and the topics that he treated proved to be important in the development of the new literature of which he was the principal apologist. Little that was pertinent escaped his attention: the processes of literary creation fascinated him and led him to talk of wit, fancy, imagination, and judgment; the question of the relation of the poet to tradition prompted him to explore earlier literatures in search of safe guides and models; the problems posed by the new theater and the new drama made it desirable that he, as a playwright, should reassess the achievement of Shakespeare's generation and should theorize about the nature of the forms of modern drama from tragedy down to farce; his interest in poetry as a craft started discussions of metrics, language, imagery, metaphors, poetic license, methods of translation, the literary kinds, the decorum of styles; and always his ready enthusiasm for great writers evoked warm and generous characterizations of the genius of other poets: Shakespeare, Jonson, Chaucer, Juvenal, Horace, Homer, Virgil. For nearly forty years this voice was heard in the land, and when it was finally silenced, a set of critical standards had come into existence and the Augustan age was approaching maturity. The representative selections below may give some insight into how Dryden helped to order taste and critical standards, while he sacrificed nothing of that freedom without which the English literary genius could not function.

From An Essay of Dramatic Poesy[1]
[*Two Sorts of Bad Poetry*]

" * * * I have a mortal apprehension of two poets,[2] whom this victory, with the help of both her wings, will never be able to escape." " 'Tis easy to guess whom you intend," said Lisideius; "and without naming them, I ask you if one of them does not perpetually pay us with clenches[3] upon words, and a certain clownish kind of raillery?[4] if now and then he does not offer at a catachresis[5] or Clevelandism, wresting and torturing a word into another meaning: in fine, if he be not one of those whom the French would call *un mauvais buffon*;[6] one who is so much a well-willer to the satire, that he spares no man; and though he cannot strike a blow to hurt any, yet ought to be punished for the malice of the action, as our witches are justly hanged, because they think themselves so, and suffer deservedly for believing they did mischief, because they meant it." "You have described him," said Crites, "so exactly that I am afraid to come after you with my other extremity of poetry. He is one of those who, having had some advantage of education and converse, knows better than the other what a poet should be,

1. With the reopening of the theaters in 1660, older plays were revived, but, despite their power and charm, they seemed old-fashioned. Although new playwrights, ambitious to create a modern English drama, soon appeared, they were uncertain of their direction. What, if anything, useful could they learn from the dramatic practice of the ancients? Should they ignore the English dramatists of the late 16th and early 17th centuries? Should they make their example the vigorous contemporary drama of France? Dryden addresses himself to these and other problems in this essay, his first extended piece of criticism. Its purpose, he tells us, was "chiefly to vindicate the honor of our English writers from the censure of those who unjustly prefer the French before them." Its method is skeptical: Dryden presents several points of view, but imposes none. The form is a dialogue among friends, like the *Tusculan Disputations* or the *Brutus* of Cicero. Crites praises the drama of the ancients; Eugenius protests against their authority and argues for the idea of progress in the arts; Lisideius urges the excellence of French plays; Neander, speaking in the climactic position, defends the native tradition and the greatness of Shakespeare, Fletcher, and Jonson. The dialogue takes place on June 3, 1665, in a boat on the Thames. The four friends are rowed downstream to listen to the cannonading of the English and Dutch fleets, engaged in battle off the Suffolk coast. As the gunfire recedes they are assured of victory and order their boatman to return to London, and naturally enough they fall to discussing the number of bad poems that the victory will evoke.

2. Probably Robert Wilde and possibly Richard Flecknoe, whom Dryden later ridiculed in *Mac Flecknoe*. Their actual identity is unimportant, for they merely represent two extremes in poetry, both deplorable: the fantastic and extravagant manner of decadent metaphysical wit and its opposite, the flat and the dull. The new poetry was to seek a mean between these extremes. Cf. Pope, *Essay on Criticism* II.239–42 and 289–300.

3. Puns.

4. Boorish banter.

5. The use of a word in a sense remote from its normal meaning: a legitimate figure of speech used by all poets, it had been abused by John Cleveland (1613–58), who was at first admired for his ingenuity, but whose reputation declined rapidly after the Restoration. A Clevelandism: "The marigold, whose courtier's face / *Echoes* the sun * * * "

6. A malicious jester.

but puts it into practice more unluckily than any man; his style and matter are everywhere alike: he is the most calm, peaceable writer you ever read: he never disquiets your passions[7] with the least concernment, but still[8] leaves you in as even a temper as he found you; he is a very Leveler[9] in poetry: he creeps along with ten little words in every line, and helps out his numbers with *for to*, and *unto*, and all the pretty expletives[1] he can find, till he drags them to the end of another line; while the sense is left tired halfway behind it: he doubly starves all his verses, first for want of thought, and then of expression; his poetry neither has wit in it, nor seems to have it; like him in Martial:

> *Pauper videri Cinna vult, et est pauper.*[2]

"He affects plainness, to cover his want of imagination: when he writes the serious way, the highest flight of his fancy is some miserable antithesis, or seeming contradiction; and in the comic he is still reaching at some thin conceit, the ghost of a jest, and that too flies before him, never to be caught; these swallows which we see before us on the Thames are the just resemblance of his wit: you may observe how near the water they stoop, how many proffers they make to dip, and yet how seldom they touch it; and when they do, it is but the surface: they skim over it but to catch a gnat, and then mount into the air and leave it."

[*The Wit of the Ancients: The Universal*]

" * * * A thing well said will be wit in all languages; and though it may lose something in the translation, yet to him who reads it in the original, 'tis still the same: he has an idea of its excellency, though it cannot pass from his mind into any other expression or words than those in which he finds it. When Phaedria, in the *Eunuch*,[3] had a command from his mistress to be absent two days, and, encouraging himself to go through with it, said, '*Tandem ego non illa caream, si sit opus, vel totum triduum?*'[4]—Parmeno, to mock the softness of his master, lifting up his hands and eyes, cries out, as it were in admiration,[5] '*Hui! universum triduum!*' the elegancy of which *universum*, though it cannot be rendered in our language, yet leaves an impression on our souls: but this happens seldom in him; in Plautus[6] oftener, who is infinitely too bold

7. Emotions.
8. Always.
9. The Levelers were radical egalitarians and republicans, a powerful political force in the Puritan Army about 1648. They were suppressed by Cromwell.
1. Words used merely to fill out a line of verse. Cf. Pope, *Essay on Criticism* II.346–47.
2. "Cinna wishes to seem poor, and he is poor" (*Epigrams* VIII.xix).

3. A comedy by the Roman poet Terence (ca. 185–159 B.C.).
4. "Shall I not then do without her, if need be, for three whole days?"
5. Wonder. The wit of Parmeno's exclamation, "Oh, three entire days," depends on *universum*, which suggests that a lover may regard three days as an eternity.
6. Titus Maccus Plautus, Roman comic poet (ca. 254–184 B.C.).

in his metaphors and coining words, out of which many times his wit is nothing; which questionless was one reason why Horace falls upon him so severely in those verses:

> *Sed proavi nostri Plautinos et numeros et*
> *Laudavere sales, nimium patienter utrumque,*
> *Ne dicam stolide.*[7]

For Horace himself was cautious to obtrude a new word on his readers, and makes custom and common use the best measure of receiving it into our writings:

> *Multa renascentur quae nunc cecidere, cadentque*
> *Quae nunc sunt in honore vocabula, si volet usus,*
> *Quem penes arbitrium est, et jus, et norma loquendi.*[8]

"The not observing this rule is that which the world has blamed in our satirist, Cleveland: to express a thing hard and unnaturally is his new way of elocution. 'Tis true no poet but may sometimes use a catachresis: Virgil does it—

> *Mistaque ridenti colocasia fundet acantho*[9]—

in his eclogue of Pollio; and in his seventh *Aeneid:*

> *mirantur et undae,*
> *Miratur nemus insuetum fulgentia longe*
> *Scuta virum fluvio pictasque innare carinas.*[1]

And Ovid once so modestly that he asks leave to do it:

> *quem, si verbo audacia detur,*
> *Haud metuam summi dixisse Palatia caeli.*[2]

calling the court of Jupiter by the name of Augustus his palace; though in another place he is more bold, where he says, '*et longas visent Capitolia pompas.*'[3] But to do this always, and never be able to write a line without it, though it may be admired by some few pedants, will not pass upon those who know that wit is best conveyed to us in the most easy language; and is most to be admired when a great thought comes dressed in words so commonly received that it is understood by the meanest apprehensions, as the

---

7. "But our ancestors too tolerantly (I do not say foolishly) praised both the verse and the wit of Plautus" (*Ars Poetica*, lines 270–72). Dryden misquotes slightly.
8. "Many words that have perished will be born again, and those shall perish that are now esteemed, if usage wills it, in whose power are the judgment, the law, and the pattern of speech" (*Ars Poetica*, lines 70–72).
9. "[The earth] shall give forth the Egyptian bean, mingled with the smiling acanthus" (*Eclogues* IV.20). "Smil-

ing acanthus" is a catachresis.
1. Actually *Aeneid* VIII.91–93. Dryden's paraphrase makes the point clearly: "The woods and waters wonder at the gleam / Of shields and painted ships that stem the stream" (*Aeneis* VIII.125–26). "Wonder" is a catachresis.
2. "[This is the place] which, if boldness of expression be permitted, I shall not hesitate to call the Palace of high heaven" (*Metamorphoses* I.175–76).
3. "And the Capitol shall see the long processions" (*Metamorphoses* I.561).

best meat is the most easily digested: but we cannot read a verse of Cleveland's without making a face at it, as if every word were a pill to swallow: he gives us many times a hard nut to break our teeth, without a kernel for our pains. So that there is this difference betwixt his satires and Doctor Donne's; that the one gives us deep thoughts in common language, though rough cadence; the other gives us common thoughts in abstruse words: 'tis true in some places his wit is independent of his words, as in that of the *Rebel Scot*:

> Had Cain been Scot, God would have changed his doom;
> Not forced him wander, but confined him home.[4]

"*Si sic omnia dixisset!*[5] This is wit in all languages: it is like mercury, never to be lost or killed:[6] and so that other—

> For beauty, like white powder, makes no noise,
> And yet the silent hypocrite destroys.

You see the last line is highly metaphorical, but it is so soft and gentle that it does not shock us as we read it."

[Shakespeare and Ben Jonson Compared]

"To begin, then, with Shakespeare. He was the man who of all modern, and perhaps ancient poets, had the largest and most comprehensive soul. All the images of Nature were still present to him, and he drew them, not laboriously, but luckily; when he describes anything, you more than see it, you feel it too. Those who accuse him to have wanted learning, give him the greater commendation: he was naturally learned; he needed not the spectacles of books to read Nature; he looked inwards, and found her there. I cannot say he is everywhere alike; were he so, I should do him injury to compare him with the greatest of mankind. He is many times flat, insipid; his comic wit degenerating into clenches, his serious swelling into bombast. But he is always great when some great occasion is presented to him; no man can say he ever had a fit subject for his wit and did not then raise himself as high above the rest of poets,

Quantum lenta solent inter viburna cupressi[7]

The consideration of this made Mr. Hales of Eton[8] say that there was no subject of which any poet ever writ, but he would produce it much better treated of in Shakespeare; and however others are now generally preferred before him, yet the age wherein he lived,

---

4. Lines 63–64.
5. "Had he said everything thus!" (Juvenal, *Satires* X.123–24).
6. Mercury is said to be "killed" if its fluidity is destroyed. The couplet quoted below is from *Rupertismus*,
lines 39–40.
7. "As do cypresses among the bending shrubs" (Virgil, *Eclogues* I.25).
8. The learned John Hales (1584–1656), provost of Eton. He is reputed to have said this to Jonson himself.

which had contemporaries with him Fletcher and Jonson, never equaled them to him in their esteem: and in the last king's[9] court, when Ben's reputation was at highest, Sir John Suckling,[1] and with him the greater part of the courtiers, set our Shakespeare far above him. * * *

"As for Jonson, to whose character I am now arrived, if we look upon him while he was himself (for his last plays were but his dotages), I think him the most learned and judicious writer which any theater ever had. He was a most severe judge of himself, as well as others. One cannot say he wanted wit, but rather that he was frugal of it. In his works you find little to retrench[2] or alter. Wit, and language, and humor also in some measure, we had before him; but something of art[3] was wanting to the drama till he came. He managed his strength to more advantage than any who preceded him. You seldom find him making love in any of his scenes or endeavoring to move the passions; his genius was too sullen and saturnine[4] to do it gracefully, especially when he knew he came after those who had performed both to such an height. Humor was his proper sphere:[5] and in that he delighted most to represent mechanic people.[6] He was deeply conversant in the ancients, both Greek and Latin, and he borrowed boldly from them: there is scarce a poet or historian among the Roman authors of those times whom he has not translated in *Sejanus* and *Catiline*.[7] But he has done his robberies so openly, that one may see he fears not to be taxed by any law. He invades authors like a monarch; and what would be theft in other poets is only victory in him. With the spoils of these writers he so represents old Rome to us, in its rites, ceremonies, and customs, that if one of their poets had written either of his tragedies, we had seen less of it than in him. If there was any fault in his language, 'twas that he weaved it too closely and laboriously, in his serious plays:[8] perhaps, too, he did a little too much Romanize our tongue, leaving the words which he translated almost as much Latin as he found them: wherein, though he learnedly followed the idiom of their language, he did not enough comply with the idiom of ours. If I would compare him with Shakespeare, I must acknowledge him the more correct poet, but Shakespeare the greater wit.[9] Shakespeare was the Homer, or father of our dramatic poets; Jonson was the Virgil, the pattern of elaborate writing; I admire him, but I love Shakespeare. To

9. Charles I.
1. Courtier, poet, playwright, much admired in Dryden's time for his wit and the easy naturalness of his style.
2. Delete.
3. Craftsmanship.
4. Heavy.
5. In Jonson's comedies the characters are seen under the domination of some psychological trait, ruling passion, or

affectation—i.e., some "humor"—which makes them unique and ridiculous.
6. I.e., artisans.
7. Jonson's two Roman plays, dated 1605 and 1611 respectively.
8. This is the reading of the first edition. Curiously enough, in the second edition Dryden altered the phrase to "in his comedies especially."
9. Genius.

conclude of him; as he has given us the most correct plays, so in the precepts which he has laid down in his *Discoveries,* we have as many and profitable rules for perfecting the stage, as any wherewith the French can furnish us."

1668

From The Author's Apology for Heroic Poetry and Heroic License[1]

["*Boldness*" *of Figures and Tropes Defended: The Appeal to* "*Nature*"]

* * * They, who would combat general authority with particular opinion, must first establish themselves a reputation of understanding better than other men. Are all the flights of heroic poetry to be concluded bombast, unnatural, and mere madness, because they are not affected with their excellencies? It is just as reasonable as to conclude there is no day, because a blind man cannot distinguish of light and colors. Ought they not rather, in modesty, to doubt of their own judgments, when they think this or that expression in Homer, Virgil, Tasso, or Milton's *Paradise* to be too far strained, than positively to conclude that 'tis all fustian and mere nonsense? 'Tis true there are limits to be set betwixt the boldness and rashness of a poet; but he must understand those limits who pretends to judge as well as he who undertakes to write: and he who has no liking to the whole ought, in reason, to be excluded from censuring of the parts. He must be a lawyer before he mounts the tribunal; and the judicature of one court, too, does not qualify a man to preside in another. He may be an excellent pleader in the Chancery, who is not fit to rule the Common Pleas. But I will presume for once to tell them that the boldest strokes of poetry, when they are managed artfully, are those which most delight the reader.

Virgil and Horace, the severest writers of the severest age, have made frequent use of the hardest metaphors and of the strongest hyperboles; and in this case the best authority is the best argument, for generally to have pleased, and through all ages, must bear the force of universal tradition. And if you would appeal from thence to right reason, you will gain no more by it in effect than,

---

1. This essay was prefixed to Dryden's *State of Innocence,* the libretto for an opera (never produced), based on *Paradise Lost.* Dryden had been ridiculed for the extravagant and bold imagery and rhetorical figures that are typical of the style of his rhymed heroic plays. This preface is a defense not only of his own predilection for what Samuel Johnson described as "wild and daring sallies of sentiment, in the irregular and eccentric violence of wit," but also of the theory that heroic and idealized materials should be treated in lofty and boldly metaphorical style; hence his definition of "wit" as propriety.

first, to set up your reason against those authors, and, secondly, against all those who have admired them. You must prove why that ought not to have pleased which has pleased the most learned and the most judicious; and, to be thought knowing, you must first put the fool upon all mankind. If you can enter more deeply than they have done into the causes and resorts[2] of that which moves pleasure in a reader, the field is open, you may be heard: but those springs of human nature are not so easily discovered by every superficial judge: it requires philosophy, as well as poetry, to sound the depth of all the passions, what they are in themselves, and how they are to be provoked; and in this science the best poets have excelled. * * * From hence have sprung the tropes[3] and figures, for which they wanted a name who first practiced them and succeeded in them. Thus I grant you that the knowledge of Nature was the original rule, and that all poets ought to study her, as well as Aristotle and Horace, her interpreters.[4] But then this also undeniably follows, that those things which delight all ages must have been an imitation of Nature—which is all I contend. Therefore is rhetoric made an art; therefore the names of so many tropes and figures were invented, because it was observed they had such and such effect upon the audience. Therefore catachreses and hyperboles[5] have found their place amongst them; not that they were to be avoided, but to be used judiciously and placed in poetry as heightenings and shadows are in painting, to make the figure bolder, and cause it to stand off to sight. * * *

[Wit as "Propriety"]

* * * [Wit] is a propriety of thoughts and words; or, in other terms, thought and words elegantly adapted to the subject. If our critics will join issue on this definition, that we may *convenire in aliquo tertio;*[6] if they will take it as a granted principle, it will be easy to put an end to this dispute. No man will disagree from another's judgment concerning the dignity of style in heroic poetry; but all reasonable men will conclude it necessary that sublime subjects ought to be adorned with the sublimest, and, consequently, often with the most figurative expressions. * * *

1677

2. Mechanical springs which set something in motion.
3. The use of a word in a figurative sense; "figures," in this phrase, means such figures of speech as metaphors and similes.
4. In the words of the French critic René Rapin, the rules (largely derived from Aristotle's *Poetics* and Horace's *Ars Poetica*) were made in order to "reduce Nature to method." Cf. Pope, *Essay on Criticism* I.88–89.
5. "Catachresis" is the use of a word in a sense remote from its normal meaning; "hyperbole," deliberate overstatement or exaggeration.
6. "To find some means of agreement, in a third term, between the two opposites" [W. P. Ker's note].

From A Discourse Concerning the Original and Progress of Satire[1]
[*The Art of Satire*]

* * * How easy is it to call rogue and villain, and that wittily! But how hard to make a man appear a fool, a blockhead, or a knave without using any of those opprobrious terms! To spare the grossness of the names, and to do the thing yet more severely, is to draw a full face, and to make the nose and cheeks stand out, and yet not to employ any depth of shadowing.[2] This is the mystery of that noble trade, which yet no master can teach to his apprentice; he may give the rules, but the scholar is never the nearer in his practice. Neither is it true that this fineness of raillery[3] is offensive. A witty man is tickled while he is hurt in this manner, and a fool feels it not. The occasion of an offense may possibly be given, but he cannot take it. If it be granted that in effect this way does more mischief; that a man is secretly wounded, and though he be not sensible himself, yet the malicious world will find it out for him; yet there is still a vast difference betwixt the slovenly butchering of a man, and the fineness of a stroke that separates the head from the body, and leaves it standing in its place. A man may be capable, as Jack Ketch's[4] wife said of his servant, of a plain piece of work, a bare hanging; but to make a malefactor die sweetly was only belonging to her husband. I wish I could apply it to myself, if the reader would be kind enough to think it belongs to me. The character of Zimri in my *Absalom*[5] is, in my opinion, worth the whole poem: it is not bloody, but it is ridiculous enough; and he, for whom it was intended, was too witty to resent it as an injury. If I had railed,[6] I might have suffered for it justly; but I managed my own work more happily, perhaps more dexterously. I avoided the mention of great crimes, and applied myself to the representing of blindsides, and little extravagancies; to which, the wittier a man is, he is generally the more obnoxious.[7] It succeeded as I

1. This passage is an excerpt from the long and rambling preface which served as the dedication of a translation of the satires of the Roman satirists Juvenal and Persius to Charles Sackville, 6th Earl of Dorset. The translations were made by Dryden and other writers, among them William Congreve. Dryden traces the origin and development of verse satire in Rome, and in a very fine passage contrasts Horace and Juvenal as satiric poets. It is plain that he prefers the "tragic" satire of Juvenal to the urbane and laughing satire of Horace. But in the passage printed here he praises his own satiric character of Zimri (the Duke of Buckingham) in *Absalom and Achitophel* for the very

reason that it is modeled on Horatian "raillery," not Juvenalian invective.
2. Early English miniaturists prided themselves on the art of giving roundness to the full face without painting in shadows.
3. Satirical mirth, good-natured satire.
4. A notorious public executioner of Dryden's time (d. 1686). His name later became a generic term for all members of his profession.
5. See *Absalom and Achitophel* I.544–68.
6. Reviled, abused. Observe that the verb differed in meaning from its noun, defined above.
7. Liable.

wished; the jest went round, and he was laughed at in his turn who began the frolic. * * *

1693

From The Preface to *Fables Ancient and Modern*[1]
[In Praise of Chaucer]

In the first place, as he is the father of English poetry, I hold him in the same degree of veneration as the Grecians held Homer, or the Romans Virgil. He is a perpetual fountain of good sense; learned in all sciences;[2] and, therefore, speaks properly on all subjects. As he knew what to say, so he knows also when to leave off; a continence which is practiced by few writers, and scarcely by any of the ancients, excepting Virgil and Horace. * * *

Chaucer followed Nature everywhere, but was never so bold to go beyond her; and there is a great difference of being *poeta* and *nimis poeta*,[3] if we may believe Catullus, as much as betwixt a modest behavior and affectation. The verse of Chaucer, I confess, is not harmonious to us; but 'tis like the eloquence of one whom Tacitus commends, it was *auribus istius temporis accommodata:*[4] they who lived with him, and some time after him, thought it musical; and it continues so, even in our judgment, if compared with the numbers[5] of Lydgate and Gower, his contemporaries; there is the rude sweetness of a Scotch tune in it, which is natural and pleasing, though not perfect. 'Tis true I cannot go so far as he who published the last edition of him;[6] for he would make us believe the fault is in our ears, and that there were really ten syllables in a verse where we find but nine; but this opinion is not worth confuting; 'tis so gross and obvious an error that common sense (which is a rule in everything but matters of faith and revelation) must convince the reader that equality of numbers in every verse which we call heroic[7] was either not known, or not always practiced in

1. Dryden's final work, published in the year of his death, was a collection of translations from Homer, Ovid, Boccaccio, and Chaucer, and one or two other pieces. The Preface, in many ways, is Dryden's ripest and finest critical essay. In it, he is not concerned with critical theory or with a formalistic approach to literature; he is simply a man, grown old in the reading and writing of poetry, who is eager to talk informally with his readers about some of his favorite authors. His praise of Chaucer (unusually sympathetic and perceptive for 1700) is animated by that love of great literature which is manifest in everything that Dryden wrote.
2. Branches of learning.
3. A poet ("*poeta*") and too much of

a poet ("*nimis poeta*"). The phrase is not from Catullus but from Martial (*Epigrams* III.44).
4. "Suitable to the ears of that time." Tacitus was a Roman historian and writer on oratory (A.D. ca. 55–ca. 117).
5. Versification. John Lydgate (ca. 1370–ca. 1449) wrote poetry which shows the influence of Chaucer. John Gower (d. 1408), poet and friend of Chaucer.
6. Thomas Speght's Chaucer, which Dryden used, was first published in 1598; the second edition, published in 1602, was reprinted in 1687.
7. The pentameter line. In Dryden's time few readers knew how to pronounce Middle English, especially the syllabic *e*. Moreover, Chaucer's works were

Chaucer's age. It were an easy matter to produce some thousands of his verses which are lame for want of half a foot, and sometimes a whole one, and which no pronunciation can make otherwise. We can only say that he lived in the infancy of our poetry, and that nothing is brought to perfection at the first. * * *

He must have been a man of a most wonderful comprehensive nature, because, as it has been truly observed of him, he has taken into the compass of his *Canterbury Tales* the various manners and humors (as we now call them) of the whole English nation in his age. Not a single character has escaped him. All his pilgrims are severally distinguished from each other; and not only in their inclinations but in their very physiognomies and persons. Baptista Porta[8] could not have described their natures better than by the marks which the poet gives them. The matter and manner of their tales, and of their telling, are so suited to their different educations, humors, and callings that each of them would be improper in any other mouth. Even the grave and serious characters are distinguished by their several sorts of gravity: their discourses are such as belong to their age, their calling, and their breeding; such as are becoming of them, and of them only. Some of his persons are vicious, and some virtuous; some are unlearned, or (as Chaucer calls them) lewd, and some are learned. Even the ribaldry of the low characters is different: the Reeve, the Miller, and the Cook are several[9] men, and distinguished from each other as much as the mincing Lady Prioress and the broad-speaking, gap-toothed Wife of Bath. But enough of this; there is such a variety of game springing up before me that I am distracted in my choice, and know not which to follow. 'Tis sufficient to say, according to the proverb, that here is God's plenty. * * *

1700

known only in corrupt printed texts. As a consequence Chaucer's verse seemed rough and irregular.
8. Giambattista della Porta (ca. 1535– 1615), author of a Latin treatise on physiognomy.
9. Different.

JONATHAN SWIFT
(1667–1745)

1704:   A *Tale of a Tub* and *The Battle of the Books*.
1710–14: Alignment with Tories; political writings in defense
          of the Tory ministry.
1713:   Made Dean of St. Patrick's Cathedral, Dublin.
1726:   Publication of *Gulliver's Travels*.

Swift—a posthumous child—was born of English parents in Dublin. Through the generosity of an uncle he was educated at Kilkenny School and Trinity College, Dublin; but before he could fix on a career, the troubles that followed upon James II's abdication and his subsequent invasion of Ireland drove him along with other Anglo-Irish to England. Between 1689 and 1699 he was more or less continuously a member of the household of his kinsman Sir William Temple, an urbane, civilized man, a retired diplomat, and a friend of King William. During these years Swift read widely; rather reluctantly decided on the church as a career and so took orders; and discovered his astonishing gifts as a satirist. About 1696–97 he wrote his powerful satires on corruptions in religion and learning, A *Tale of a Tub* and *The Battle of the Books*, which were published in 1704 and reached their final form only in the fifth edition of 1710. These were the years in which he slowly came to maturity. When at the age of 32, he returned to Ireland as chaplain to the Lord Justice, the Earl of Berkeley, he had a clear sense of his genius.

It was at Temple's that Swift met and learned to love the woman whose role in his life has been the cause of much conjecture. Esther Johnson (Swift's "Stella") was the daughter of Temple's steward, and when Swift first knew her she was little more than a child. He educated her, formed her character, and came to love her as he was to love no other person. After Temple's death she removed (at Swift's suggestion) with her lifelong companion, Rebecca Dingley, to Dublin, where she and Swift met constantly, but never alone. To her he wrote the famous journal-letters, later published (1766) as *The Journal to Stella*, during his four-year residence in London when he was working with the Tories; and to her he wrote charming poems. Whether they were secretly married or whether they never married—and in either case why—has been often debated. A marriage of any sort seems most unlikely; and however perplexing their relationship was to others, it was obviously satisfying to each of them. Not even the violent passion that Swift awakened, no doubt unwittingly, in a much younger woman, Hester Vanhomrigh (pronounced V*an-úm-mer-y*), her pleadings and reproaches and early death, could unsettle his devotion to Stella. An enigmatic account of his relations with "Vanessa," as he called Miss Vanhomrigh, is given in his poem *Cadenus and Vanessa*.

The man who gained the lifelong devotion of Stella and evoked the romantic passion of Vanessa was also admired and loved by many of the distinguished men of his time. His friendships with Addison, Pope, Dr. Arbuthnot, John Gay, Prior, Oxford, Bolingbroke, not to mention those with his less brilliant, but pleasant, Irish circle, bear witness to his moral integrity and social charm. The dark side of Swift's nature has been exaggerated at the cost of neglecting the wit and gaiety, the playful humor, and the consciously assumed eccentricities which marked his social behavior. Nor is it tenable that his satires are the product of a diseased mind which was gradually disintegrating throughout his life. Swift suffered most of his adult life from what we now recognize as Ménière's syndrome, which affects the inner ear, causing dizziness, nausea, and deafness. By all these ills he was greatly afflicted, but he was never in any sense insane. After 1739, when he was 72 years old, his infirmities and deafness cut him off from social life and his duties as Dean, and from then on senility advanced inexorably. In 1742 guardians were appointed to administer his affairs, and his last three years were spent in gloom and lethargy. But the writer of the satires was a man in full control of very great intellectual powers.

Because Swift was a clergyman, a spirited controversialist, and a devoted supporter of the Anglican Church as an institution no less important than the Crown itself, he was drawn into politics in both England and Ireland. He was hostile to all who seemed to threaten the Established Church— Deists, freethinkers, Roman Catholics, Nonconformists, or merely Whig politicians. In 1710 he abandoned his old party, the Whig, because he disapproved of its indifference to the welfare of the Anglican Church in Ireland and of its desire to repeal the Test Act, which required all holders of offices of state to take the Sacrament according to the Anglican rites, thus excluding Roman Catholics and Dissenters. Welcomed by the Tories, he became the most brilliant political journalist of the day, serving the government of Oxford and Bolingbroke as editor of the party organ, the *Examiner*, and as author of its most powerful articles, as well as writing longer pamphlets in support of important policies, such as that favoring the Peace of Utrecht (1713). He was greatly valued by the two ministers, who admitted him to social intimacy, though never to their counsels. The reward of his services was not the English bishopric which he had a right to expect, but the Deanship of St. Patrick's Cathedral in Dublin, which came to him in 1713, a year before the death of Queen Anne and the fall of the Tories put an end to all his hopes of preferment in England.

In Ireland, where he lived unwillingly, he became not only an efficient ecclesiastical administrator, but also, in 1724, the leader of Irish resistance to English oppression. Under the pseudonym of "M. B., Drapier," he published the famous series of public letters that aroused the country to refuse to accept £100,000 in new copper coins (minted in England by William Wood, who had obtained his patent through court corruption) which, it was feared, would further debase the coinage of the already poverty-stricken kingdom. Although his authorship of the letters was known to all Dublin, no one could be found to earn the £300 offered by the government for information as to the identity of the Drapier. Swift is still venerated in Ireland as a national hero. He earned the right to refer to himself in the epitaph that he wrote for his tomb as a vigorous defender of liberty.

For all his involvement in public affairs, Swift seems to stand apart from his contemporaries—a striking figure even among the statesmen of the time, a man who towered above other writers by reason of his more profound imagination, mordant wit, and emotional intensity. He has been called a misanthrope, a hater of mankind; and *Gulliver's Travels* has been considered an expression of savage misanthropy. It is true that Swift proclaimed himself a misanthrope in a letter to Pope, declaring that though he loved individuals, he hated mankind in general, and offering a new definition of man as not *animal rationale* ("a rational animal"), but as merely *animal rationis capax* ("an animal *capable* of reason"). This, he declared, is the "great foundation" upon which his "misanthropy" was erected. Swift was stating not his hatred of his fellowmen, but his antagonism to the current optimistic view that human nature is essentially good. To the "philanthropic" flattery that sentimentalism and Deistic rationalism were paying to human nature, Swift opposed a more ancient and plausible view: that human nature is deeply and permanently flawed, and that we can do nothing with or for the human race until we recognize its moral and intellectual limitations. This attitude he was pleased to call "misanthropy." In his epitaph he spoke of the "fierce indignation" which had torn his heart, an indignation that found superb expression in his greatest satires. It was provoked by the constant spectacle of creatures capable of reason, and therefore of reasonable conduct, steadfastly refusing to live up to their capabilities.

Gulliver's Travels is Swift's most universal satire. Although it is full of allusions to recent and contemporary historical events, it is as valid today as it was in 1726, for its objects are man's moral nature and the defective political, economic, and social institutions which, because of his imperfections, he creates. Swift adopts an ancient satirical device: the imaginary voyage. Lemuel Gulliver, the narrator, is a ship's surgeon, a reasonably well-educated man, kindly, resourceful, cheerful, inquiring, patriotic, truthful, and rather unimaginative. He is, in short, a reasonably decent example of humanity, with whom we identify ourselves readily enough. He undertakes four voyages, all of which end disastrously among "several remote nations of the world." In the first, Gulliver is shipwrecked in the empire of Lilliput, where he finds himself a giant among a diminutive people, charmed by their miniature city and amused by their toylike prettiness. But in the end they prove to be treacherous, malicious, ambitious, vengeful, and cruel. As we read we grow disenchanted with the inhabitants of this fanciful kingdom, and then gradually we begin to recognize our likeness to them, especially in the disproportion between our natural pettiness and our boundless and destructive passions. In the second voyage (printed below), Gulliver is abandoned by his shipmates in Brobdingnag, a land of giants, creatures ten times as large as Europeans, as Gulliver had been twelve times as large as the Lilliputians. Naturally enough, he assumes that such monsters must be brutes, but the reverse proves to be the case. Brobdingnag is something of a utopia, governed by a humane and enlightened prince who is the embodiment of moral and political wisdom. In the long interview in which Gulliver pridefully enlarges on the glories of England and her political institutions, the King reduces him to resentful silence by asking questions which reveal the difference between what is and what ought to be in human, especially British, institutions. In Brobdingnag, Gulliver finds himself a Lilliputian, his pride humbled by his helpless state and his human vanity diminished by the realization that his body must have seemed as disgusting to the Lilliputians as do the bodies of the Brobdingnagians to him.

In the third voyage, to Laputa, Swift is chiefly concerned with attacking extremes of theoretical and speculative reasoning, whether in science, politics, or economics. Much of this voyage is an allegory of political life under the administration of the Whig minister, Sir Robert Walpole. The final voyage sets Gulliver between a race of horses, Houyhnhnms (pronounced *Hwin-ims*), who live entirely by reason except for a few well-controlled and muted social affections, and their slaves, the Yahoos, whose bodies are obscene caricatures of the human body, and who have no glimmer of reason, but are mere creatures of appetite and passion.

Swift is one of our greatest writers of prose. He defined a good style as "proper words in proper places," a more complex and difficult saying than at first appears. Clear, simple, concrete diction, uncomplicated syntax, economy and conciseness of language mark all of his writings. His is a style that shuns ornaments and singularity of all kinds, a style that grows more tense and controlled the more fierce the indignation that it is called upon to express. The virtues of his prose are those of his poetry, which only lately has come to be much valued. It is unpoetic poetry, devoid of, indeed as often as not mocking at, inspiration, romantic love, easily assumed literary attitudes, and conventional poetic language. Like the prose it is predominantly satiric in purpose, but not without its moments of comedy and light-heartedness, though written most often not so much to divert as to reform mankind.

A Description of a City Shower

Careful observers may foretell the hour
(By sure prognostics) when to dread a shower:
While rain depends,[1] the pensive cat gives o'er
Her frolics, and pursues her tail no more.
Returning home at night, you'll find the sink[2] 5
Strike your offended sense with double stink.
If you be wise, then go not far to dine;
You'll spend in coach hire more than save in wine.
A coming shower your shooting corns presage,
Old aches throb, your hollow tooth will rage. 10
Sauntering in coffeehouse is Dulman[3] seen;

1. Impends, is imminent. An example of elevated diction used frequently throughout the poem in order to gain a mock dignity, comically inappropriate to the homely and realistic subject.
2. Sewer.

3. A type name (from "dull man"), like Congreve's "Petulant" or "Witwoud." It was commonly believed at this time that the Englishman's tendency to melancholy ("the spleen") was attributable to the rainy climate.

He damns the climate and complains of spleen.
   Meanwhile the South, rising with dabbled wings,
A sable cloud athwart the welkin flings,
That swilled more liquor than it could contain,   15
And, like a drunkard, gives it up again.
Brisk Susan whips her linen from the rope,
While the first drizzling shower is borne aslope:
Such is that sprinkling which some careless quean[4]
Flirts on you from her mop, but not so clean: 20
You fly, invoke the gods; then turning, stop
To rail; she singing, still whirls on her mop.
Not yet the dust had shunned the unequal strife,
But, aided by the wind, fought still for life,
And wafted with its foe by violent gust,   25
'Twas doubtful which was rain and which was dust.
Ah! where must needy poet seek for aid,
When dust and rain at once his coat invade?
Sole coat, where dust cemented by the rain
Erects the nap, and leaves a mingled stain.   30
   Now in contiguous drops the flood comes down,
Threatening with deluge this devoted town.
To shops in crowds the daggled[5] females fly,
Pretend to cheapen goods, but nothing buy.
The Templar[6] spruce, while every spout's abroach,   35
Stays till 'tis fair, yet seems to call a coach.
The tucked-up sempstress walks with hasty strides,
While streams run down her oiled umbrella's sides.
Here various kinds, by various fortunes led,
Commence acquaintance underneath a shed.   40
Triumphant Tories and desponding Whigs
Forget their feuds,[7] and join to save their wigs.
Boxed in a chair[8] the beau impatient sits,
While spouts run clattering o'er the roof by fits,
And ever and anon with frightful din   45
The leather sounds;[9] he trembles from within.
So when Troy chairmen bore the wooden steed,
Pregnant with Greeks impatient to be freed
(Those bully Greeks, who, as the moderns do,
Instead of paying chairmen, run them through[1]),   50
Laocoön struck the outside with his spear,
And each imprisoned hero quaked for fear.[2]

4. Wench, slut.
5. Spattered with mud. "To cheapen": to bargain for.
6. A young man engaged in studying law. In the literature of the period the Templar is usually depicted as neglecting his professional studies for the sake of dissipation and the pursuit of literature. Cf. the Member of the Inner Temple in *Spectator* 2. "Abroach": pouring out water.
7. The Whig ministry had just fallen and the Tories, led by Harley and St. John, were forming the government with which Swift was to be closely associated until the death of the Queen in 1714.
8. Sedan chair.
9. The roof of the sedan chair was made of leather.
1. Run them through with their swords. The bully, always prone to violence, was a familiar figure in London streets and places of amusement.
2. *Aeneid* II.40–53.

Now from all parts the swelling kennels[3] flow,
And bear their trophies with them as they go:
Filth of all hues and odors seem to tell   55
What street they sailed from, by their sight and smell.
They, as each torrent drives with rapid force,
From Smithfield or St. Pulchre's shape their course,
And in huge confluence joined at Snow Hill ridge,
Fall from the conduit prone to Holborn Bridge.[4]   60
Sweepings from butchers' stalls, dung, guts, and blood,
Drowned puppies, stinking sprats,[5] all drenched in mud,
Dead cats, and turnip tops, come tumbling down the flood.[6]

1710

Verses on the Death of Dr. Swift

OCCASIONED BY READING A MAXIM IN ROCHEFOUCAULD [1]

*Dans l'adversité de nos meilleurs amis nous trouvons toujours quelque chose,
qui ne nous déplaît pas.*[2]

As Rochefoucauld his maxims drew
From nature, I believe 'em true:
They argue no corrupted mind
In him; the fault is in mankind.
This maxim more than all the rest   5
Is thought too base for human breast:
"In all distresses of our friends
We first consult our private ends,
While Nature, kindly bent to ease us,
Points out some circumstance to please us."   10
If this perhaps your patience move,
Let reason and experience prove.
We all behold with envious eyes
Our equal raised above our size.
Who would not at a crowded show   15
Stand high himself, keep others low?
I love my friend as well as you,

3. The open gutters in the middle of the street.
4. An accurate description of the drainage system of this part of London—the eastern edge of Holborn and West Smithfield, which lie outside the old walls west and east of Newgate. The great cattle and sheep markets were in Smithfield. The church of St. Sepulchre ("St. Pulchre's") stood opposite Newgate Prison. Holborn Conduit was at the foot of Snow Hill. It drained into Fleet Ditch, an evil-smelling open sewer, at Holborn Bridge.
5. Small herrings.
6. In Falkner's edition of Swift's *Works* (Dublin, 1735) a note almost certainly suggested by Swift points to the con-cluding triplet, with its resonant final Alexandrine, as a burlesque of a mannerism of Dryden and other Restoration poets, and claims that Swift's ridicule banished the triplet from contemporary poetry.
1. François de La Rochefoucauld (1613–80), writer of witty, cynical maxims. Writing to Pope (November 26, 1725), Swift, opposing the optimistic philosophy that Pope and Bolingbroke were at that time developing, professed to have founded his whole character on these maxims.
2. "In the misfortune of our best friends we always find something that does not displease us."

But why should he obstruct my view?
Then let me have the higher post;
Suppose it but an inch at most.   20
     If in a battle you should find
One, whom you love of all mankind,
Had some heroic action done,
A champion killed, or trophy won;
Rather than thus be overtopped,   25
Would you not wish his laurels cropped?
     Dear honest Ned is in the gout,
Lies racked with pain, and you without:
How patiently you hear him groan!
How glad the case is not your own!   30
     What poet would not grieve to see
His brethren write as well as he?
But rather than they should excel,
He'd wish his rivals all in hell.
     Her end when Emulation misses,   35
She turns to envy, stings, and hisses:
The strongest friendship yields to pride,
Unless the odds be on our side.
     Vain humankind! fantastic race!
Thy various follies who can trace?   40
Self-love, ambition, envy, pride,
Their empire in our hearts divide.
Give others riches, power, and station;
'Tis all on me an usurpation;
I have no title to aspire,   45
Yet, when you sink, I seem the higher.
In Pope I cannot read a line,
But with a sigh I wish it mine:
When he can in one couplet fix
More sense than I can do in six,   50
It gives me such a jealous fit,
I cry, "Pox take him and his wit!"
     I grieve to be outdone by Gay [3]
In my own humorous biting way.
Arbuthnot [4] is no more my friend,   55
Who dares to irony pretend,
Which I was born to introduce,
Refined it first, and showed its use.
St. John,[5] as well as Pulteney, knows

---

3. John Gay (1685–1732), author of
the famous *Beggar's Opera* (1728), intimate friend of Swift and Pope. His
*Trivia, or the Art of Walking the
Streets of London* (1716) owes something to Swift's *City Shower*.
4. Dr. John Arbuthnot, physician and
wit, friend of Swift and Pope. See
Pope's *Epistle to Dr. Arbuthnot*.
5. Henry St. John, Lord Bolingbroke
(see note, Pope's *Essay on Man*. I.1),

though debarred from the House of
Lords and from public office, had become the center of a group of Tories
and discontented young Whigs (of
whom William Pulteney was one) who
united in opposing Sir Robert Walpole,
the chief minister. They published a
political periodical, the *Craftsman*, thus
rivaling Swift in his role of political
pamphleteer and enemy of Sir Robert.

That I had some repute for prose; 60
And, till they drove me out of date,
Could maul a minister of state.
If they have mortified my pride,
And made me throw my pen aside;
If with such talents Heaven hath blessed 'em, 65
Have I not reason to detest 'em?
    To all my foes, dear Fortune, send
Thy gifts, but never to my friend:
I tamely can endure the first,
But this with envy makes me burst. 70
    Thus much may serve by way of proem;
Proceed we therefore to our poem.
    The time is not remote, when I
Must by the course of nature die;
When, I foresee, my special friends 75
Will try to find their private ends:
Though it is hardly understood
Which way my death can do them good;
Yet thus, methinks, I hear 'em speak:
"See how the Dean begins to break! 80
Poor gentleman! he droops apace!
You plainly find it in his face.
That old vertigo [6] in his head
Will never leave him till he's dead.
Besides, his memory decays; 85
He recollects not what he says;
He cannot call his friends to mind;
Forgets the place where last he dined;
Plies you with stories o'er and o'er;
He told them fifty times before. 90
How does he fancy we can sit
To hear his out-of-fashion wit?
But he takes up with younger folks,
Who for his wine will bear his jokes.
Faith, he must make his stories shorter, 95
Or change his comrades once a quarter;
In half the time he talks them round,
There must another set be found.
    "For poetry, he's past his prime;
He takes an hour to find a rhyme; 100
His fire is out, his wit decayed,
His fancy sunk, his Muse a jade.[7]
I'd have him throw away his pen—
But there's no talking to some men."
    And then their tenderness appears 105
By adding largely to my years:
"He's older than he would be reckoned,

6. Johnson in his *Dictionary* authorizes Swift's pronunciation: *ver-ti-go*.
7. A worn-out horse, in contrast to Pegasus, the winged horse of Greek mythology, emblem of poetic inspiration.

And well remembers Charles the Second.
He hardly drinks a pint of wine;
And that, I doubt, is no good sign.   110
His stomach, too, begins to fail;
Last year we thought him strong and hale;
But now he's quite another thing;
I wish he may hold out till spring."
They hug themselves, and reason thus: 115
"It is not yet so bad with us."
    In such a case they talk in tropes,[8]
And by their fears express their hopes.
Some great misfortune to portend
No enemy can match a friend.   120
With all the kindness they profess,
The merit of a lucky guess
(When daily how-d'ye's come of course,
And servants answer, "Worse and worse!")
Would please 'em better, than to tell   125
That God be praised! the Dean is well.
Then he who prophesied the best,
Approves his foresight to the rest:
"You know I always feared the worst,
And often told you so at first."   130
He'd rather choose that I should die,
Than his prediction prove a lie.
Not one foretells I shall recover,
But all agree to give me over.
    Yet, should some neighbor feel a pain   135
Just in the parts where I complain,
How many a message would he send!
What hearty prayers that I should mend!
Inquire what regimen I kept;
What gave me ease, and how I slept,   140
And more lament, when I was dead,
Then all the snivelers round my bed.
    My good companions, never fear;
For though you may mistake a year,
Though your prognostics run too fast,   145
They must be verified at last.
    Behold the fatal day arrive!
    "How is the Dean?"—"He's just alive."
Now the departing prayer is read.
"He hardly breathes"—"The Dean is dead."   150
Before the passing bell begun,
The news through half the town has run.
"Oh! may we all for death prepare!
What has he left? and who's his heir?"
"I know no more than what the news is;   155
'Tis all bequeathed to public uses."
"To public use! a perfect whim!

8. Figures of speech.

What had the public done for him?
Mere envy, avarice, and pride:
He gave it all—but first he died.   160
And had the Dean in all the nation
No worthy friend, no poor relation?
So ready to do strangers good,
Forgetting his own flesh and blood?"
Now Grub Street [9] wits are all employed;   165
With elegies the town is cloyed;
Some paragraph in every paper
To curse the Dean, or bless the Drapier.[1]
    The doctors, tender of their fame,
Wisely on me lay all the blame.   170
"We must confess his case was nice; [2]
But he would never take advice.
Had he been ruled, for aught appears,
He might have lived these twenty years:
For, when we opened him, we found,   175
That all his vital parts were sound."
    From Dublin soon to London spread,
'Tis told at court, "The Dean is dead."
Kind Lady Suffolk,[3] in the spleen,
Runs laughing up to tell the Queen.   180
The Queen, so gracious, mild and good,
Cries, "Is he gone? 'tis time he should.
He's dead, you say; why, let him rot:
I'm glad the medals were forgot.[4]
I promised him, I own; but when?   185
I only was the Princess then;
But now, as consort of the King,
You know, 'tis quite a different thing."
    Now Chartres,[5] at Sir Robert's levee,
Tells with a sneer the tidings heavy: 190
"Why, is he dead without his shoes?"
Cries Bob, "I'm sorry for the news:
Oh, were the wretch but living still,
And in his place my good friend Will! [6]
Or had a miter on his head,   195
Provided Bolingbroke were dead!"
    Now Curll his shop from rubbish drains: [7]

---

9. Originally a street in London largely inhabited by hack writers; later, a generic term applied to all such writers.
1. It was in the character of "M. B.," a Dublin drapier, that Swift aroused the Irish people to resistance against the importation of Wood's halfpence. See biographical introduction.
2. Delicate; hence demanding careful diagnosis and treatment.
3. George II's mistress, with whom Swift became friendly during his visit to Pope in 1726. "In the spleen": in low spirits. The phrase is ironic, as "laughing" in the next line makes clear.
4. Queen Caroline had promised Swift some medals when she was Princess of Wales during the same year.
5. Col. Francis Chartres, a debauchee often satirized by Pope; Sir Robert Walpole.
6. William Pulteney (see line 59 and its note.)
7. Edmund Curll, shrewd and disreputable bookseller, published pirated works, scandalous biographies, and works falsely ascribed to notable writers of the time.

Three genuine tomes of Swift's remains!
And then, to make them pass the glibber,
Revised by Tibbalds, Moore, and Cibber.[8]   200
He'll treat me as he does my betters,
Publish my will, my life, my letters;
Revive the libels born to die,
Which Pope must bear, as well as I.
   Here shift the scene, to represent   205
How those I love my death lament.
Poor Pope will grieve a month, and Gay
A week, and Arbuthnot a day.
   St. John himself will scarce forbear
To bite his pen, and drop a tear.   210
The rest will give a shrug, and cry,
"I'm sorry—but we all must die!"
   Indifference clad in wisdom's guise
All fortitude of mind supplies:
For how can stony bowels melt   215
In those who never pity felt?
When *we* are lashed, *they* kiss the rod,
Resigning to the will of God.
   The fools, my juniors by a year,
Are tortured with suspense and fear;   220
Who wisely thought my age a screen,
When death approached, to stand between:
The screen removed, their hearts are trembling;
They mourn for me without dissembling.
   My female friends, whose tender hearts   225
Have better learned to act their parts,
Receive the news in doleful dumps:
"The Dean is dead (and what is trumps?)
Then, Lord have mercy on his soul!
(Ladies, I'll venture for the vole.[9])   230
Six deans, they say, must bear the pall.
(I wish I knew what king to call.)
Madam, your husband will attend
The funeral of so good a friend?"
"No, madam, 'tis a shocking sight;   235
And he's engaged tomorrow night:
My Lady Club would take it ill,
If he should fail her at quadrille.
He loved the Dean—(I lead a heart)
But dearest friends, they say, must part.   240
His time was come; he ran his race;
We hope he's in a better place."
   Why do we grieve that friends should die?

---

8. Lewis Theobald (1688–1744), Shakespeare scholar and editor, already enthroned as King of the Dunces in Pope's *Dunciad* (1728). Like Pope, Swift spells the name phonetically. James Moore-Smyth, poetaster and playwright, an enemy of Pope. Colley Cibber (1671–1757), comic actor, playwright, and supremely untalented poet laureate. He succeeded Theobald as King of the Dunces in the *Dunciad* of 1743.
9. The equivalent in the card game quadrille of bidding a grand slam in bridge.

No loss more easy to supply.
One year is past; a different scene! 245
No further mention of the Dean,
Who now, alas! no more is missed,
Than if he never did exist.
Where's now this favorite of Apollo?
Departed—and his works must follow, 250
Must undergo the common fate;
His kind of wit is out of date.

    Some country squire to Lintot [1] goes,
Inquires for Swift in verse and prose.
Says Lintot, "I have heard the name; 255
He died a year ago."—"The same."
He searches all the shop in vain.
"Sir, you my find them in Duck Lane: [2]
I sent them, with a load of books,
Last Monday to the pastry-cook's. [3] 260
To fancy they could live a year!
I find you're but a stranger here.
The Dean was famous in his time,
And had a kind of knack at rhyme.
His way of writing now is past: 265
The town has got a better taste.
I keep no antiquated stuff;
But spick and span I have enough.
Pray do but give me leave to show 'em:
Here's Colley Cibber's birthday poem. 270
This ode you never yet have seen
By Stephen Duck [4] upon the Queen.
Then here's a letter finely penned
Against the *Craftsman* [5] and his friend;
It clearly shows that all reflection 275
On ministers is disaffection.
Next, here's Sir Robert's vindication, [6]
    And Mr. Henley's last oration. [7]
The hawkers have not got them yet:
Your honor please to buy a set? 280
    "Here's Woolston's tracts, [8] the twelfth edition;
'Tis read by every politician:
The country members, when in town,
To all their boroughs send them down;
You never met a thing so smart; 285

1. Bernard Lintot, the publisher of Pope's Homer and some of his early poems.
2. London street where second-hand books and publishers' "remainders" were sold.
3. To be used as waste paper for lining baking dishes and wrapping parcels.
4. Stephen Duck, "the thresher poet," an agricultural laborer, whose mild poetic gifts brought him to the notice and patronage of Queen Caroline.
5. See line 59 and its note.
6. "Walpole hires a string of party scribblers who do nothing else but write in his defense" [Swift's note].
7. "Orator" John Henley, an Independent preacher, who dazzled unlearned audiences with his oratory and who wrote treatises on elocution.
8. Thomas Woolston (1670–1733), a freethinker, whose *Discourses on the Miracles of Our Saviour* had recently earned him notoriety.

The courtiers have them all by heart;
Those maids of honor (who can read)
Are taught to use them for their creed.
The reverend author's good intention
Has been rewarded with a pension.   290
He does an honor to his gown,
By bravely running priestcraft down;
He shows, as sure as God's in Gloucester,
That Jesus was a grand impostor;
That all his miracles were cheats,   295
Performed as jugglers do their feats:
The Church had never such a writer;
A shame he has not got a miter!"
   Suppose me dead; and then suppose
A club assembled at the Rose;   300
Where, from discourse of this and that,
I grow the subject of their chat.
And while they toss my name about,
With favor some, and some without,
One, quite indifferent in the cause,   305
My character impartial draws:
   "The Dean, if we believe report,
Was never ill received at court.
As for his works in verse and prose,
I own myself no judge of those;   310
Nor can I tell what critics thought 'em:
But this I know, all people bought 'em,
As with a moral view designed
To cure the vices of mankind.
   "His vein, ironically grave,   315
Exposed the fool and lashed the knave,
To steal a hint was never known,
But what he writ was all his own.
   "He never thought an honor done him,
Because a duke was proud to own him,   320
Would rather slip aside and choose
To talk with wits in dirty shoes;
Despised the fools with stars and garters,
So often seen caressing Chartres.
He never courted men in station,   325
Nor persons held in admiration;
Of no man's greatness was afraid,
Because he sought for no man's aid.
Though trusted long in great affairs,
He gave himself no haughty airs;   330
Without regarding private ends,
Spent all his credit for his friends;
And only chose the wise and good;
No flatterers, no allies in blood;
But succored virtue in distress,   335
And seldom failed of good success;

As numbers in their hearts must own,
Who, but for him, had been unknown.
　　"With princes kept a due decorum,
But never stood in awe before 'em.　　　　　　340
He followed David's lesson just;
In princes never put thy trust:[9]
And would you make him truly sour,
Provoke him with a slave in power.
The Irish senate if you named,　　　　　　345
With what impatience he declaimed!
Fair Liberty was all his cry,
For her he stood prepared to die;
For her he boldly stood alone;
For her he oft exposed his own.　　　　　　350
Two kingdoms, just as faction led,
Had set a price upon his head,
But not a traitor could be found,
To sell him for six hundred pound.[1]
　　"Had he but spared his tongue and pen,　　355
He might have rose like other men;
But power was never in his thought,
And wealth he valued not a groat:
Ingratitude he often found,
And pitied those who meant the wound;　　　　360
But kept the tenor of his mind,
To merit well of human kind:
Nor made a sacrifice of those
Who still were true, to please his foes.
He labored many a fruitless hour,　　　　　365
To reconcile his friends in power;
Saw mischief by a faction brewing,
While they pursued each other's ruin.
But finding vain was all his care,
He left the court in mere despair.[2]　　　　370
　　"And, oh! how short are human schemes!
Here ended all our golden dreams.
What St. John's skill in state affairs,
What Ormonde's [3] valor, Oxford's cares,
To save their sinking country lent,　　　　375
Was all destroyed by one event.[4]

9. Psalm cxlvi.3.
1. In 1714 the government offered £300 for the discovery of the author of Swift's *Public Spirit of the Whigs,* and in 1724 the Irish government offered a similar amount for the discovery of the author of the fourth of Swift's *Drapier's Letters.*
2. The antagonism between the two chief ministers (his dear friends), Robert Harley, Earl of Oxford, and Bolingbroke paralyzed the Tory ministry in the crucial last months of Queen Anne's life and drove Swift to retirement in Ireland, whence he returned in 1714 to make a final effort to heal the breach and save the government. He failed and retired to the country in despair. There he received the news of Anne's death on August 1. The Hanoverian succession brought the Whigs back in triumph, ruined Swift's friends, and brought Swift's public life to a close.
3. James Butler, Duke of Ormonde, who succeeded to the command of the English armies on the Continent, when, in 1711, the Duke of Marlborough was stripped of his offices by Anne. He went into exile in 1714 and was active in Jacobite intrigue.
4. The death of Queen Anne.

Too soon that precious life was ended,
On which alone our weal depended.
When up a dangerous faction starts,[5]
With wrath and vengeance in their hearts;   380
By solemn League and Covenant bound,
To ruin, slaughter, and confound;
To turn religion to a fable,
And make the government a Babel;
Pervert the laws, disgrace the gown,   385
Corrupt the senate, rob the crown;
To sacrifice old England's glory,
And make her infamous in story:
When such a tempest shook the land,
How could unguarded Virtue stand?   390
With horror, grief, despair, the Dean
Beheld the dire destructive scene:
His friends in exile, or the Tower,[6]
Himself within the frown of power,
Pursued by base envenomed pens,   395
Far to the land of slaves and fens;[7]
A servile race in folly nursed,
Who truckle most, when treated worst.
    "By innocence and resolution,
He bore continual persecution;   400
While numbers to preferment rose,
Whose merits were to be his foes;
When even his own familiar friends,
Intent upon their private ends,
Like renegadoes now he feels,   405
Against him lifting up their heels.
    "The Dean did, by his pen, defeat
An infamous destructive cheat;[8]
Taught fools their interest how to know,
And gave them arms to ward the blow.   410
Envy has owned it was his doing,
To save that hapless land from ruin;
While they who at the steerage [9] stood,
And reaped the profit, sought his blood.
    "To save them from their evil fate,   415
In him was held a crime of state.
A wicked monster on the bench,[1]

5. Swift's view of the policies of the "dangerous faction" (the Whig party) is hardly impartial. He feared it especially because of its toleration of Dissenters, and so as an enemy of the Church of England.
6. Bolingbroke was in exile; Oxford was sent to the Tower by the Whigs.
7. Ireland.
8. The scheme to introduce Wood's copper halfpence into Ireland in 1723–24.
9. Literally the steering of a ship. Here the direction and management of public affairs in Ireland.
1. William Whitshed, Lord Chief Justice of the King's Bench of Ireland. In 1720, when the jury refused to find Swift's anonymous pamphlet *Proposal for the Universal Use of Irish Manufacture* wicked and seditious, Whitshed sent them back nine times, hoping to force them to another verdict. In 1724 he presided over the trial of Harding, the printer of Swift's fourth *Drapier's Letter*, but again was unable, despite bullying, to force a verdict of guilty.

Whose fury blood could never quench;
As vile and profligate a villain,
As modern Scroggs, or old Tresilian;[2]   420
Who long all justice had discarded,
Nor feared he God, nor man regarded;
Vowed on the Dean his rage to vent,
And make him of his zeal repent:
But Heaven his innocence defends,   425
The grateful people stand his friends;
Not strains of law, nor judge's frown,
Nor topics brought to please the crown,
Nor witness hired, nor jury picked,
Prevail to bring him in convict.   430
    "In exile, with a steady heart,
He spent his life's declining part;
Where folly, pride, and faction sway
Remote from St. John, Pope, and Gay.
    "His friendships there, to few confined,   435
Were always of the middling kind;
No fools of rank, a mongrel breed,
Who fain would pass for lords indeed:
Where titles give no right or power,
And peerage is a withered flower;   440
He would have held it a disgrace,
If such a wretch had known his face.
On rural squires, that kingdom's bane,
He vented oft his wrath in vain;
Biennial squires [3] to market brought: 445
Who sell their souls, and votes for naught;
The nation stripped, go joyful back,
To rob the church, their tenants rack,
Go snacks with rogues and rapparees;[4]
And keep the peace to pick up fees;   450
In every job to have a share,
A jail or barrack to repair;
And turn the tax for public roads,
Commodious to their own abodes.
    "Perhaps I may allow the Dean   455
Had too much satire in his vein;
And seemed determined not to starve it,
Because no age could more deserve it.
Yet malice never was his aim;
He lashed the vice, but spared the name;   460
No individual could resent,
Where thousands equally were meant;
His satire points at no defect,

2. Sir William Scroggs, Lord Chief Justice of England at the time of the Popish Plot, 1678 (see Dryden's *Absalom and Achitophel*), was impeached for his misdemeanors in office in 1680. Sir Robert Tresilian punished with great severity in 1381 men who had participated in the Peasants' Revolt; he was impeached and in 1387 was hanged.
3. Members of the Irish Parliament.
4. Highwaymen.

But what all mortals may correct;
For he abhorred that senseless tribe   465
Who call it humor when they gibe:
He spared a hump, or crooked nose,
Whose owners set not up for beaux.
True genuine dullness moved his pity,
Unless it offered to be witty.   470
Those who their ignorance confessed,
He ne'er offended with a jest;
But laughed to hear an idiot quote
A verse from Horace learned by rote.
    "He knew an hundred pleasant stories,   475
With all the turns of Whigs and Tories:
Was cheerful to his dying day;
And friends would let him have his way.
    "He gave the little wealth he had
To build a house for fools and mad;[5]   480
And showed by one satiric touch,
No nation wanted it so much.
That kingdom he hath left his debtor,
I wish it soon may have a better."

1731   1739

AN ARGUMENT TO PROVE THAT THE

Abolishing of Christianity in England

MAY, AS THINGS NOW STAND, BE ATTENDED WITH
SOME INCONVENIENCES, AND PERHAPS NOT
PRODUCE THOSE MANY GOOD EFFECTS PRO-
POSED THEREBY.[1]

I am very sensible what a weakness and presumption it is, to reason against the general humor and disposition of the world. I remember it was with great justice, and a due regard to the freedom both of the public and the press, forbidden upon several penalties to write, or discourse, or lay wagers against the Union,[2] even before it was confirmed by Parliament, because that was looked upon as a design to oppose the current of the people, which, besides the folly of it, is a manifest breach of the fundamental law that makes this

---

5. Swift left funds to endow a hospital for the insane.

1. The Test Act of 1673 required all holders of public office to take the sacrament of the Lord's Supper according to the usage of the Church of England; it was directed against Dissenters and Roman Catholics. In 1708 the Whigs (with whom Swift was then allied) were seeking to repeal the Test in Ireland and eventually in England, in an effort to consolidate the support of the dissenters. Swift believed that repeal would do

great harm to the Established Church, and as a good Anglican priest he opposed it with this essay.

Swift's technique is to assume blandly that to argue against the Test Act is to argue against Christianity and the Church, and he constructs his essay accordingly. The basic satiric principle is therefore that of the *reductio ad absurdum*, but this device is surrounded by a host of other ironies.

2. The union of Scotland and England under one crown in 1707.

majority of opinion the voice of God. In like manner, and for the very same reasons, it may perhaps be neither safe nor prudent to argue against the abolishing of Christianity at a juncture when all parties appear so unanimously determined upon the point, as we cannot but allow from their actions, their discourses, and their writings. However, I know not how, whether from the affectation of singularity, or the perverseness of human nature, but so it unhappily falls out that I cannot be entirely of this opinion. Nay, though I were sure an order were issued for my immediate prosecution by the attorney-general, I should still confess that in the present posture of our affairs at home or abroad, I do not yet see the absolute necessity of extirpating the Christian religion from among us.

This perhaps may appear too great a paradox even for our wise and paradoxical age to endure: therefore I shall handle it with all tenderness, and with the utmost deference to that great and profound majority which is of another sentiment.

And yet the curious may please to observe how much the genius of a nation is liable to alter in half an age: I have heard it affirmed for certain by some very old people that the contrary opinion was even in their memories as much in vogue as the other is now; and that a project for the abolishing of Christianity would then have appeared as singular, and been thought as absurd, as it would be at this time to write or discourse in its defense.

Therefore I freely own that all appearances are against me. The system of the Gospel, after the fate of other systems, is generally antiquated and exploded; and the mass or body of the common people, among whom it seems to have had its latest credit, are now grown as much ashamed of it as their betters; opinions, like fashions, always descending from those of quality to the middle sort, and thence to the vulgar, where at length they are dropped and vanish.

But here I would not be mistaken, and must therefore be so bold as to borrow a distinction from the writers on the other side, when they make a difference between nominal and real Trinitarians. I hope no reader imagines me so weak to stand up in the defense of real Christianity, such as used in primitive times (if we may believe the authors of those ages) to have an influence upon men's belief and actions: to offer at the restoring of that would indeed be a wild project; it would be to dig up foundations; to destroy at one blow all the wit, and half the learning of the kingdom; to break the entire frame and constitution of things; to ruin trade, extinguish arts and sciences with the professors of them; in short, to turn our courts, exchanges, and shops into deserts; and would be full as absurd as the proposal of Horace,[3] where he advises the Romans all in a body to

3. *Epode* xvi.

leave their city and seek a new seat in some remote part of the world, by way of cure for the corruption of their manners.

Therefore I think this caution was in itself altogether unnecessary (which I have inserted only to prevent all possibility of caviling), since every candid reader will easily understand my discourse to be intended only in defense of nominal Christianity, the other having been for some time wholly laid aside by general consent as utterly inconsistent with all other present schemes of wealth and power.

But why we should therefore cast off the name and title of Christians, although the general opinion and resolution be so violent for it, I confess I cannot (with submission) apprehend the consequence necessary. However, since the undertakers propose such wonderful advantages to the nation by this project, and advance many plausible objections against the system of Christianity, I shall briefly consider the strength of both, fairly allow them their greatest weight, and offer such answers as I think most reasonable. After which I will beg leave to show what inconveniences may possibly happen by such an innovation, in the present posture of our affairs.

First, one great advantage proposed by the abolishing of Christianity is that it would very much enlarge and establish liberty of conscience, that great bulwark of our nation, and of the protestant religion, which is still too much limited by priestcraft, notwithstanding all the good intentions of the legislature, as we have lately found by a severe instance. For it is confidently reported that two young gentlemen of real hopes, bright wit, and profound judgment, who upon a thorough examination of causes and effects, and by the mere force of natural abilities, without the least tincture of learning, having made a discovery that there was no God, and generously communicating their thoughts for the good of the public, were some time ago, by an unparalleled severity, and upon I know not what obsolete law, broke only for blasphemy. And as it hath been wisely observed, if persecution once begins, no man alive knows how far it may reach, or where it will end.

In answer to all which, with deference to wiser judgments, I think this rather shows the necessity of a nominal religion among us. Great wits love to be free with the highest objects; and if they cannot be allowed a God to revile or renounce, they will speak evil of dignities, abuse the government, and reflect upon the ministry; which I am sure few will deny to be of much more pernicious consequence, according to the saying of Tiberius, *Deorum offensa diis curae*.[4] As to the particular fact related, I think it is not fair to argue from one instance; perhaps another cannot be produced; yet (to the comfort of all those who may be apprehensive of persecution) blasphemy we know is freely spoken a million of times in every

---

4. "Offenses against the gods are the concern of the gods" (Tacitus, *Annals* I.lxxiii).

coffeehouse and tavern, or wherever else good company meet. It must be allowed indeed, that to break an English freeborn officer only for blasphemy, was, to speak the gentlest of such an action, a very high strain of absolute power. Little can be said in excuse for the general; perhaps he was afraid it might give offense to the allies [5] among whom, for aught we know, it may be the custom of the country to believe a God. But if he argued, as some have done, upon a mistaken principle, that an officer who is guilty of speaking blasphemy may some time or other proceed so far as to raise a mutiny, the consequence is by no means to be admitted: for, surely the commander of an English army is likely to be but ill obeyed whose soldiers fear and reverence him as little as they do a deity.

It is further objected against the gospel system that it obliges men to the belief of things too difficult for freethinkers, and such who have shaken off the prejudices that usually cling to a confined education. To which I answer that men should be cautious how they raise objections which reflect upon the wisdom of the nation. Is not everybody freely allowed to believe whatever he pleases, and to publish his belief to the world whenever he thinks fit, especially if it serves to strengthen the party which is in the right? Would any indifferent foreigner who should read the trumpery lately written by Asgil, Tindal, Toland, Coward,[6] and forty more, imagine the Gospel to be our rule of faith, and confirmed by parliaments? Does any man either believe, or say he believes, or desire to have it thought that he says he believes one syllable of the matter? And is any man worse received upon that score, or does he find his want of nominal faith a disadvantage to him in the pursuit of any civil or military employment? What if there be an old dormant statute or two against him? Are they not now obsolete to a degree that Empson and Dudley [7] themselves, if they were now alive, would find it impossible to put them in execution?

It is likewise urged that there are by computation in this kingdom above ten thousand parsons whose revenues, added to those of my lords the bishops, would suffice to maintain at least two hundred young gentlemen of wit and pleasure, and freethinking enemies to priestcraft, narrow principles, pedantry, and prejudices; who might be an ornament to the court and town. And then again, so great a number of able (-bodied) divines might be a recruit to our fleet and armies. This indeed appears to be a consideration of some weight; but then, on the other side, several things deserve to be considered likewise: as, first, whether it may not be thought necessary that in certain tracts of country, like what we call parishes, there shall be one man at least of abilities to read and write. Then it

5. England's principal allies against France in the War of the Spanish Succession were Holland, Austria, Prussia, Portugal, and Savoy.

6. Deistic writers.
7. Two corrupt ministers of Henry VII, notorious for reviving obsolete statutes in subservience to that king's greed.

seems a wrong computation that the revenues of the Church throughout this island would be large enough to maintain two hundred young gentlemen, or even half that number, after the present refined way of living; that is, to allow each of them such a rent [8] as, in the modern form of speech, would make them easy. But still there is in this project a greater mischief behind; and we ought to beware of the woman's folly who killed the hen that every morning laid her a golden egg. For, pray, what would become of the race of men in the next age if we had nothing to trust to beside the scrofulous, consumptive productions, furnished by our men of wit and pleasure, when, having squandered away their vigor, health, and estates, they are forced by some disagreeable marriage to piece up their broken fortunes, and entail rottenness and politeness on their posterity? Now here are ten thousand persons reduced by the wise regulations of Henry the Eighth to the necessity of a low diet and moderate exercise,[9] who are the only great restorers of our breed, without which the nation would in an age or two become one great hospital.

Another advantage proposed by the abolishing of Christianity is the clear gain of one day in seven, which is now entirely lost, and consequently the kingdom one-seventh less considerable in trade, business, and pleasure; besides the loss to the public of so many stately structures now in the hands of the clergy, which might be converted into playhouses, exchanges, markethouses, common dormitories, and other public edifices.

I hope I shall be forgiven a hard word, if I call this a perfect cavil. I readily own there hath been an old custom, time out of mind, for people to assemble in the churches every Sunday, and that shops are still frequently shut, in order, as it is conceived, to preserve the memory of that ancient practice; but how this can prove a hindrance to business or pleasure is hard to imagine. What if the men of pleasure are forced, one day in the week, to game at home instead of the chocolatehouse? Are not the taverns and coffeehouses open? Can there be a more convenient season for taking a dose of physic? Are fewer claps got upon Sundays than other days? Is not that the chief day for traders to sum up the accounts of the week and for lawyers to prepare their briefs? But I would fain know how it can be pretended that the churches are misapplied? Where are more appointments and rendezvouses of gallantry? Where more care to appear in the foremost box with greater advantage of dress? Where more meetings for business? Where more bargains driven of all sorts? And where so many conveniences or incitements to sleep?

<hr/>

8. Income.

9. Swift refers ironically to Henry VIII's expropriation of church lands at the time of the Reformation. Instead of giving them to the church for the support of the clergy, as Swift thought he should have done, he bestowed them on laymen, thus impoverishing the lower clergy, who were deprived of the tithes that would otherwise have been their due.

There is one advantage greater than any of the foregoing proposed by the abolishing of Christianity: that it will utterly extinguish parties among us by removing those factious distinctions of High and Low Church, of Whig and Tory, Presbyterian and Church of England, which are now so many mutual clogs upon public proceedings, and dispose men to prefer the gratifying themselves, or depressing their adversaries, before the most important interest of the state.

I confess, if it were certain that so great an advantage would redound to the nation by this expedient, I would submit and be silent: but will any man say that if the words *whoring, drinking, cheating, lying, stealing,* were by act of Parliament ejected out of the English tongue and dictionaries, we should all awake next morning chaste and temperate, honest and just, and lovers of truth? Is this a fair consequence? Or, if the physicians would forbid us to pronounce the words *pox, gout, rheumatism,* and *stone,* would that expedient serve like so many talismans to destroy the diseases themselves? Are party and faction rooted in men's hearts no deeper than phrases borrowed from religion, or founded upon no firmer principles? And is our language so poor that we cannot find other terms to express them? Are *envy, pride, avarice,* and *ambition* such ill nomenclators that they cannot furnish appellations for their owners? Will not *heydukes* and *mamalukes, mandarins* and *patshaws,* or any other words formed at pleasure, serve to distinguish those who are in the ministry from others who would be in it if they could? What, for instance, is easier than to vary the form of speech, and instead of the *church,* make it a question in politics whether the Monument [1] be in danger? Because religion was nearest at hand to furnish a few convenient phrases, is our invention so barren we can find no others? Suppose, for argument sake, that the Tories favored Margarita, the Whigs Mrs. Tofts, and the Trimmers Valentini,[2] would not *Margaritians, Toftians,* and *Valentinians* be very tolerable marks of distinction? The *Prasini* and *Veniti,*[3] two most virulent factions in Italy, began (if I remember right) by a distinction of colors in ribbons, which we might do with as good a grace about the dignity of the blue and the green, and would serve as properly to divide the court, the Parliament, and the kingdom between them, as any terms of art whatsoever borrowed from religion. Therefore I think there is little force in this objection against Christianity, or prospect of so great an advantage as is proposed in the abolishing of it.

'Tis again objected as a very absurd, ridiculous custom that a set of men should be suffered, much less employed and hired, to bawl one day in seven against the lawfulness of those methods most in use toward the pursuit of greatness, riches, and pleasure, which are

1. The column that commemorates the great fire of London, 1666.
2. Singers in the popular Italian opera.
3. Rival factions in the Roman chariot races, violently supported by the populace.

the constant practice of all men alive on the other six. But this objection is, I think, a little unworthy so refined an age as ours. Let us argue this matter calmly; I appeal to the breast of any polite freethinker whether in the pursuit of gratifying a predominant passion he hath not always felt a wonderful incitement, by reflecting it was a thing forbidden; and therefore we see, in order to cultivate this taste, the wisdom of the nation hath taken special care that the ladies should be furnished with prohibited silks and the men with prohibited wine. And indeed, it were to be wished that some other prohibitions were promoted in order to improve the pleasures of the town; which, for want of such expedients begin already, as I am told, to flag and grow languid, giving way daily to cruel inroads from the spleen.[4]

'Tis likewise proposed as a great advantage to the public that if we once discard the system of the Gospel, all religion will of course be banished for ever; and consequently, along with it, those grievous prejudices of education, which under the names of *virtue, conscience, honor, justice,* and the like, are so apt to disturb the peace of human minds, and the notions whereof are so hard to be eradicated by right reason or freethinking, sometimes during the whole course of our lives.

Here first I observe how difficult it is to get rid of a phrase which the world is once grown fond of, though the occasion that first produced it be entirely taken away. For several years past, if a man had but an ill-favored nose, the deep thinkers of the age would some way or other contrive to impute the cause to the prejudice of his education. From this fountain were said to be derived all our foolish notions of justice, piety, love of our country, all our opinions of God, or a future state, heaven, hell, and the like: and there might formerly perhaps have been some pretense for this charge. But so effectual care hath been since taken to remove those prejudices by an entire change in the methods of education that (with honor I mention it to our polite innovators) the young gentlemen who are now on the scene, seem to have not the least tincture of those infusions, or string of those weeds; and, by consequence, the reason for abolishing nominal Christianity upon that pretext is wholly ceased.

For the rest, it may perhaps admit a controversy whether the banishing of all notions of religion whatsoever would be convenient for the vulgar. Not that I am in the least of opinion with those who hold religion to have been the invention of politicians to keep the lower part of the world in awe by the fear of invisible powers; unless mankind were then very different from what it is now: for I look upon the mass or body of our people here in England to be as freethinkers, that is to say, as staunch unbelievers, as any of the highest

4. Melancholy; often a real affliction, but as often affected as a fashionable ailment.

rank. But I conceive some scattered notions about a superior power to be of singular use for the common people, as furnishing excellent materials to keep children quiet when they grow peevish, and providing topics of amusement in a tedious winter night.

Lastly, it is proposed as a singular advantage that the abolishing of Christianity will very much contribute to the uniting of Protestants, by enlarging the terms of communion so as to take in all sorts of Dissenters, who are now shut out of the pale upon account of a few ceremonies which all sides confess to be things indifferent; that this alone will effectually answer the great ends of a scheme for comprehension, by opening a large noble gate, at which all bodies may enter: whereas the chaffering with Dissenters, and dodging about this or t'other ceremony, is but like opening a few wickets [5] and leaving them at jar, by which no more than one can get in at a time, and that, not without stooping, and sideling, and squeezing his body.

To all this I answer that there is one darling inclination of mankind, which usually affects to be a retainer to religion, though she be neither its parent, its godmother, or its friend; I mean the spirit of opposition, that lived long before Christianity, and can easily subsist without it. Let us, for instance, examine wherein the opposition of sectaries [6] among us consists; we shall find Christianity to have no share in it at all. Does the Gospel any where prescribe a starched, squeezed countenance, a stiff, formal gait, a singularity of manners and habit, or any affected modes of speech different from the reasonable part of mankind? Yet, if Christianity did not lend its name to stand in the gap, and to employ or divert these humors, they must of necessity be spent in contraventions to the laws of the land, and disturbance of the public peace. There is a portion of enthusiasm assigned to every nation, which, if it hath not proper objects to work on, will burst out, and set all in a flame. If the quiet of state can be bought by only flinging men a few ceremonies to devour, it is a purchase no wise man would refuse. Let the mastiffs amuse themselves about a sheepskin stuffed with hay, provided it will keep them from worrying the flock. The institution of convents abroad seems in one point a strain of great wisdom, there being few irregularities in human passions that may not have recourse to vent themselves in some of those orders, which are so many retreats for the speculative, the melancholy, the proud, the silent, the politic and the morose, to spend themselves, and evaporate the noxious particles; for each of whom we in this island are forced to provide a several sect of religion, to keep them quiet. And whenever Christianity shall be abolished, the legislature must find some other expedient to employ and entertain them. For what imports it how large a gate you open if there will be always left a number who place a pride and merit in refusing to enter?

5. Small gates.   6. Adherents of one of the dissenting sects.

Having thus considered the most important objections against Christianity and the chief advantages proposed by the abolishing thereof, I shall now with equal deference and submission to wiser judgments as before, proceed to mention a few inconveniences that may happen if the Gospel should be repealed; which perhaps the projectors may not have sufficiently considered.

And first, I am very sensible how much the gentlemen of wit and pleasure are apt to murmur, and be choked at the sight of so many daggled-tail parsons who happen to fall in their way, and offend their eyes. But at the same time, these wise reformers do not consider what an advantage and felicity it is for great wits to be always provided with objects of scorn and contempt, in order to exercise and improve their talents, and divert their spleen from falling on each other or on themselves; especially when all this may be done without the least imaginable danger to their persons.

And to urge another argument of a parallel nature: if Christianity were once abolished, how could the freethinkers, the strong reasoners, and the men of profound learning, be able to find another subject so calculated in all points whereon to display their abilities? What wonderful productions of wit should we be deprived of from those whose genius by continual practice hath been wholly turned upon raillery and invectives against religion, and would therefore never be able to shine or distinguish themselves upon any other subject! We are daily complaining of the great decline of wit among us, and would we take away the greatest, perhaps the only, topic we have left? Who would ever have suspected Asgil for a wit, or Toland for a philosopher, if the inexhaustible stock of Christianity had not been at hand to provide them with materials? What other subject, through all art or nature, could have produced Tindal for a profound author, or furnished him with readers? It is the wise choice of the subject that alone adorns and distinguishes the writer. For had a hundred such pens as these been employed on the side of religion, they would have immediately sunk into silence and oblivion.

Nor do I think it wholly groundless, or my fears altogether imaginary, that the abolishing of Christianity may perhaps bring the Church in danger, or at least put the senate to the trouble of another securing vote. I desire I may not be mistaken; I am far from presuming to affirm or think that the Church is in danger at present, or as things now stand; but we know not how soon it may be so when the Christian religion is repealed. As plausible as this project seems, there may a dangerous design lurk under it. Nothing can be more notorious than that the atheists, deists, Socinians,[7] Antitrinitarians, and other subdivisions of freethinkers are persons of little zeal for the present ecclesiastical establishment: their declared opinion is for repealing the Sacramental Test; they are very

---

7. The Socinians denied the divinity of Jesus.

indifferent with regard to ceremonies; nor do they hold the *jus divinum* of Episcopacy.[8] Therefore this may be intended as one politic step toward altering the constitution of the Church established, and setting up Presbytery [9] in the stead, which I leave to be further considered by those at the helm.

In the last place, I think nothing can be more plain than that by this expedient, we shall run into the evil we chiefly pretend to avoid; and that the abolishment of the Christian religion will be the readiest course we can take to introduce popery. And I am the more inclined to this opinion because we know it has been the constant practice of the Jesuits to send over emissaries with instructions to personate themselves members of the several prevailing sects among us. So it is recorded that they have at sundry times appeared in the guise of Presbyterians, Anabaptists, Independents, and Quakers, according as any of these were most in credit; so, since the fashion hath been taken up of exploding religion, the popish missionaries have not been wanting to mix with the freethinkers; among whom, Toland, the great oracle of the Antichristians, is an Irish priest, the son of an Irish priest; and the most learned and ingenious author of a book called *The Rights of the Christian Church*, was in a proper juncture reconciled to the Romish faith, whose true son, as appears by an hundred passages in his treatise, he still continues. Perhaps I could add some others to the number; but the fact is beyond dispute, and the reasoning they proceed by is right: for, supposing Christianity to be extinguished, the people will never be at ease till they find out some other method of worship; which will as infallibly produce superstition as this will end in popery.

And therefore, if notwithstanding all I have said, it still be thought necessary to have a bill brought in for repealing Christianity, I would humbly offer an amendment; that instead of the word *Christianity* may be put *religion* in general; which I conceive will much better answer all the good ends proposed by the projectors of it. For, as long as we leave in being a God and his providence, with all the necessary consequences which curious and inquisitive men will be apt to draw from such premises, we do not strike at the root of the evil, though we should ever so effectually annihilate the present scheme of the Gospel. For of what use is freedom of thought, if it will not produce freedom of action, which is the sole end, how remote soever in appearance, of all objections against Christianity? And, therefore, the freethinkers consider it as a sort of edifice wherein all the parts have such a mutual dependence on each other that if you happen to pull out one single nail, the whole fabric must fall to the ground. This was happily expressed by him who had heard of a text brought for proof of the Trinity, which in an ancient manuscript was differently read; he thereupon immedi-

8. The divine authority of Anglican bishops, derived from apostolic succession.

9. The Presbyterians opposed episcopacy and set up a democratic form of church government.

ately took the hint, and by a sudden deduction of a long *sorites*,[10] most logically concluded, "Why, if it be as you say, I may safely whore and drink on, and defy the parson." From which, and many the like instances easy to be produced, I think nothing can be more manifest than that the quarrel is not against any particular points of hard digestion in the Christian system, but against religion in general; which, by laying restraints on human nature, is supposed the great enemy to the freedom of thought and action.

Upon the whole, if it shall still be thought for the benefit of Church and State that Christianity be abolished, I conceive, however, it may be more convenient to defer the execution to a time of peace, and not venture in this conjuncture to disoblige our allies, who, as it falls out, are all Christians; and many of them, by the prejudices of their education, so bigoted as to place a sort of pride in the appellation. If upon being rejected by them, we are to trust to an alliance with the Turk, we shall find ourselves much deceived: for, as he is too remote, and generally engaged in war with the Persian emperor, so his people would be more scandalized at our infidelity than our Christian neighbors. Because the Turks are not only strict observers of religious worship, but what is worse, believe a God; which is more than is required of us even while we preserve the name of Christians.

To conclude: whatever some may think of the great advantages to trade by this favorite scheme, I do very much apprehend that in six months time after the act is passed for the extirpation of the Gospel, the Bank and East-India Stock may fall at least one per cent. And since that is fifty times more than ever the wisdom of our age thought fit to venture for the preservation of Christianity, there is no reason we should be at so great a loss merely for the sake of destroying it.

1708   1711

From Gulliver's Travels[1]

A Letter from Captain Gulliver to His Cousin Sympson

I hope you will be ready to own publicly, whenever you shall be called to it, that by your great and frequent urgency you prevailed on me to publish a very loose and uncorrect account of my travels;

10. "An argument when one proposition is accumulated on another" (Johnson's *Dictionary*).

1. Swift's full title for this work was *Travels into Several Remote Nations of the World. In Four Parts. By Lemuel Gulliver, First a Surgeon, and then a Captain of several Ships.* In the first edition (1726), either the bookseller or Swift's friends Charles Ford, Pope, and others, who were concerned in getting the book anonymously into print, altered and omitted so much of the original manuscript (because of its dangerous political implications) that Swift was seriously annoyed. When, in 1735, the Dublin bookseller George Faulkner brought out an edition of Swift's works, the Dean seems to have taken pains, surreptitiously, to see that a more authen-

with direction to hire some young gentlemen of either University to put them in order, and correct the style, as my Cousin Dampier [2] did by my advice, in his book called *A Voyage round the World*. But I do not remember I gave you power to consent that anything should be omitted, and much less that anything should be inserted: therefore, as to the latter, I do here renounce everything of that kind; particularly a paragraph about her Majesty the late Queen Anne, of most pious and glorious memory; although I did reverence and esteem her more than any of human species. But you, or your interpolator, ought to have considered that as it was not my inclination, so was it not decent to praise any animal of our composition before my master Houyhnhnm; and besides, the fact was altogether false; for to my knowledge, being in England during some part of her Majesty's reign, she did govern by a chief Minister; nay, even by two successively; the first whereof was the Lord of Godolphin, and the second the Lord of Oxford; so that you have made me *say the thing that was not*. Likewise, in the account of the Academy of Projectors, and several passages of my discourse to my master Houyhnhnm, you have either omitted some material circumstances, or minced or changed them in such a manner, that I do hardly know mine own work. When I formerly hinted to you something of this in a letter, you were pleased to answer that you were afraid of giving offense; that people in power were very watchful over the press; and apt not only to interpret, but to punish everything which looked like an *inuendo* (as I think you called it). But pray, how could that which I spoke so many years ago, and at above five thousand leagues distance, in another reign, be applied to any of the Yahoos, who now are said to govern the herd; especially, at a time when I little thought on or feared the unhappiness of living under them. Have not I the most reason to complain, when I see these very Yahoos carried by Houyhnhnms in a vehicle, as if these were brutes, and those the rational creatures? And, indeed, to avoid so monstrous and detestable a sight was one principal motive of my retirement hither.[3]

Thus much I thought proper to tell you in relation to yourself, and to the trust I reposed in you.

I do in the next place complain of my own great want of judgment, in being prevailed upon by the intreaties and false reasonings of you and some others, very much against mine own opinion, to suffer my travels to be published. Pray bring to your mind how often I desired you to consider, when you insisted on the motive of

tic version of the work was published. This text is the basis of modern editions.

In this letter, first published in 1735, Swift complains, among other matters, of the alterations in his original text made by the publisher, Benjamin Motte, in the interest of what he considered political discretion.

2. William Dampier (1652–1715), the explorer, whose account of his circumnavigation of the globe Swift had read.

3. To Nottinghamshire.

public good, that the Yahoos were a species of animals utterly incapable of amendment by precepts or examples; and so it hath proved; for instead of seeing a full stop put to all abuses and corruptions, at least in this little island, as I had reason to expect, behold, after above six months warning. I cannot learn that my book hath produced one single effect according to mine intentions; I desired you would let me know by a letter, when party and faction were extinguished; judges learned and upright; pleaders honest and modest, with some tincture of common sense; and Smithfield[4] blazing with pyramids of law books; the young nobility's education entirely changed; the physicians banished; the female Yahoos abounding in virtue, honor, truth, and good sense; courts and levees of great ministers thoroughly weeded and swept; wit, merit, and learning rewarded; all disgracers of the press in prose and verse, condemned to eat nothing but their own cotton,[5] and quench their thirst with their own ink. These, and a thousand other reformations, I firmly counted upon by your encouragement; as indeed they were plainly deducible from the precepts delivered in my book. And, it must be owned that seven months were a sufficient time to correct every vice and folly to which Yahoos are subject; if their natures had been capable of the least disposition to virtue or wisdom; yet so far have you been from answering mine expectation in any of your letters, that on the contrary, you are loading our carrier every week with libels, and keys, and reflections, and memoirs, and second parts; wherein I see myself accused of reflecting upon great statesfolk; of degrading human nature (for so they have still the confidence to style it) and of abusing the female sex. I find likewise, that the writers of those bundles are not agreed among themselves; for some of them will not allow me to be author of mine own travels; and others make me author of books to which I am wholly a stranger.

I find likewise that your printer hath been so careless as to confound the times, and mistake the dates of my several voyages and returns; neither assigning the true year, or the true month, or day of the month; and I hear the original manuscript is all destroyed, since the publication of my book. Neither have I any copy left; however, I have sent you some corrections, which you may insert, if ever there should be a second edition; and yet I cannot stand to them, but shall leave that matter to my judicious and candid readers, to adjust it as they please.

I hear some of our sea Yahoos find fault with my sea language, as not proper in many parts, nor now in use. I cannot help it. In my first voyages, while I was young, I was instructed by the oldest mariners, and learned to speak as they did. But I have since found

---

4. A part of London containing many
bookshops.

5. Presumably their paper.

that the sea Yahoos are apt, like the land ones, to become new fangled in their words; which the latter change every year; insomuch, as I remember upon each return to mine own country, their old dialect was so altered, that I could hardly understand the new. And I observe, when any Yahoo comes from London out of curiosity to visit me at mine own house, we neither of us are able to deliver our conceptions in a manner intelligible to the other.[6]

If the censure of Yahoos could any way affect me, I should have great reason to complain that some of them are so bold as to think my book of travels a mere fiction out of mine own brain; and have gone so far as to drop hints that the Houyhnhnms, and Yahoos have no more existence than the inhabitants of Utopia.

Indeed I must confess that as to the people of Lilliput, Brobdingrag (for so the word should have been spelled, and not erroneously Brobdingnag) and Laputa, I have never yet heard of any Yahoo so presumptuous as to dispute their being, or the facts I have related concerning them; because the truth immediately strikes every reader with conviction. And, is there less probability in my account of the Houyhnhnms or Yahoos, when it is manifest as to the latter, there are so many thousands even in this city, who only differ from their brother brutes in Houyhnhnmland, because they use a sort of a jabber, and do not go naked. I wrote for their amendment, and not their approbation. The united praise of the whole race would be of less consequence to me, than the neighing of those two degenerate Houyhnhnms I keep in my stable; because, from these, degenerate as they are, I still improve in some virtues, without any mixture of vice.

Do these miserable animals presume to think that I am so far degenerated as to defend my veracity; Yahoo as I am, it is well known through all Houyhnhnmland, that by the instructions and example of my illustrious master, I was able in the compass of two years (although I confess with the utmost difficulty) to remove that infernal habit of lying, shuffling, deceiving, and equivocating, so deeply rooted in the very souls of all my species; especially the Europeans.

I have other complaints to make upon this vexatious occasion; but I forbear troubling myself or you any further. I must freely confess that since my last return, some corruptions of my Yahoo nature have revived in me by conversing with a few of your species, and particularly those of mine own family, by an unavoidable necessity; else I should never have attempted so absurd a project as that of reforming the Yahoo race in this kingdom; but I have now done with all such visionary schemes for ever.

1727?   1735

6. Swift was the inveterate enemy of slang.

The Publisher to the Reader

The author of these travels, Mr. Lemuel Gulliver, is my ancient and intimate friend; there is likewise some relation between us by the mother's side. About three years ago Mr. Gulliver, growing weary of the concourse of curious people coming to him at his house in Redriff,[1] made a small purchase of land, with a convenient house, near Newark, in Nottinghamshire, his native country; where he now lives retired, yet in good esteem among his neighbors.

Although Mr. Gulliver were born in Nottinghamshire, where his father dwelt, yet I have heard him say his family came from Oxfordshire; to confirm which, I have observed in the churchyard at Banbury, in that county, several tombs and monuments of the Gullivers.

Before he quitted Redriff, he left the custody of the following papers in my hands, with the liberty to dispose of them as I should think fit. I have carefully perused them three times; the style is very plain and simple; and the only fault I find is that the author, after the manner of travelers, is a little too circumstantial. There is an air of truth apparent through the whole; and indeed the author was so distinguished for his veracity, that it became a sort of proverb among his neighbors at Redriff, when anyone affirmed a thing, to say, it was as true as if Mr. Gulliver had spoke it.

By the advice of several worthy persons, to whom, with the author's permission, I communicated these papers, I now venture to send them into the world; hoping they may be, at least for some time, a better entertainment to our young noblemen, than the common scribbles of politics and party.

This volume would have been at least twice as large, if I had not made bold to strike out innumerable passages relating to the winds and tides, as well as to the variations and bearings in the several voyages; together with the minute descriptions of the management of the ship in storms, in the style of sailors; likewise the account of the longitudes and latitudes, wherein I have reason to apprehend that Mr. Gulliver may be a little dissatisfied; but I was resolved to fit the work as much as possible to the general capacity of readers. However, if my own ignorance in sea affairs shall have led me to commit some mistakes, I alone am answerable for them; and if any traveler hath a curiosity to see the whole work at large, as it came from the hand of the author, I will be ready to gratify him.

As for any further particulars relating to the author, the reader will receive satisfaction from the first pages of the book.

RICHARD SYMPSON

1. Rotherhithe, a district in southern London, below Tower Bridge, then frequented by sailors.

Part II. A Voyage to Brobdingnag

CHAPTER I. *A great storm described. The longboat sent to fetch water; the Author goes with it to discover the country. He is left on shore, is seized by one of the natives, and carried to a farmer's house. His reception there, with several accidents that happened there. A description of the inhabitants.*

Having been condemned by nature and fortune to an active and restless life, in ten months after my return I again left my native country, and took shipping in the Downs on the 20th day of June, 1702, in the *Adventure,* Captain John Nicholas, a Cornish man, Commander, bound for Surat.[2] We had a very prosperous gale till we arrived at the Cape of Good Hope, where we landed for fresh water, but discovering a leak we unshipped our goods and wintered there; for the Captain falling sick of an ague, we could not leave the Cape till the end of March. We then set sail, and had a good voyage till we passed the Straits of Madagascar; but having got northward of that island, and to about five degrees south latitude, the winds, which in those seas are observed to blow a constant equal gale between the north and west from the beginning of December to the beginning of May, on the 19th of April began to blow with much greater violence and more westerly than usual, continuing so for twenty days together, during which time we were driven a little to the east of the Molucca Islands and about three degrees northward of the Line, as our Captain found by an observation he took the 2nd of May, at which time the wind ceased, and it was a perfect calm, whereat I was not a little rejoiced. But he, being a man well experienced in the navigation of those seas, bid us all prepare against a storm, which accordingly happened the day following: for a southern wind, called the southern monsoon, began to set in.

Finding it was likely to overblow,[3] we took in our spritsail, and stood by to hand the foresail; but making foul weather, we looked the guns were all fast, and handed the mizzen. The ship lay very broad off, so we thought it better spooning before the sea, than trying or hulling. We reefed the foresail and set him, we hauled aft the foresheet; the helm was hard aweather. The ship wore bravely. We belayed the fore-downhaul; but the sail was split, and we hauled down the yard and got the sail into the ship, and unbound all the things clear of it. It was a very fierce storm; the sea broke

2. In India. The geography of the voyage is simple: The *Adventure,* after sailing up the east coast of Africa to about 5° south of the equator (the "Line"), is blown past India into the Malay Archipelago, north of the islands of Buru and Ceram. The storm then drives the ship northward and eastward, away from the coast of Siberia ("Great Tartary") into the northeast Pacific, at that time unexplored. Brobdingnag lies somewhere in the vicinity of Alaska.

3. This paragraph is taken almost literally from Samuel Sturmy's *Mariner's Magazine* (1669). Swift is ridiculing the use of technical terms by writers of popular voyages.

strange and dangerous. We hauled off upon the lanyard of the whip-staff, and helped the man at helm. We would not get down our topmast, but let all stand, because she scudded before the sea very well, and we knew that the topmast being aloft, the ship was the wholesomer, and made better way through the sea, seeing we had searoom. When the storm was over, we set foresail and mainsail, and brought the ship to. Then we set the mizzen, main topsail and the fore topsail. Our course was east-northeast, the wind was at southwest. We got the starboard tacks aboard, we cast off our weather braces and lifts; we set in the lee braces, and hauled forward by the weather bowlings, and hauled them tight, and belayed them, and hauled over the mizzen tack to windward, and kept her full and by as near as she would lie.

During this storm, which was followed by a strong wind west-southwest, we were carried by my computation about five hundred leagues to the east, so that the oldest sailor on board could not tell in what part of the world we were. Our provisions held out well, our ship was stanch, and our crew all in good health; but we lay in the utmost distress for water. We thought it best to hold on the same course rather than turn more northerly, which might have brought us to the northwest parts of Great Tartary, and into the frozen sea.

On the 16th day of June, 1703, a boy on the topmast discovered land. On the 17th we came in full view of a great island or continent (for we knew not whether) on the south side whereof was a small neck of land jutting out into the sea, and a creek[4] too shallow to hold a ship of above one hundred tons. We cast anchor within a league of this creek, and our Captain sent a dozen of his men well armed in the longboat, with vessels for water if any could be found. I desired his leave to go with them that I might see the country and make what discoveries I could. When we came to land we saw no river or spring, nor any sign of inhabitants. Our men therefore wandered on the shore to find out some fresh water near the sea, and I walked alone about a mile on the other side, where I observed the country all barren and rocky. I now began to be weary, and seeing nothing to entertain my curiosity, I returned gently down towards the creek; and the sea being full in my view, I saw our men already got into the boat, and rowing for life to the ship. I was going to hollow after them, although it had been to little purpose, when I observed a huge creature walking after them in the sea as fast as he could; he waded not much deeper than his knees and took prodigious strides, but our men had the start of him half a league, and the sea thereabouts being full of sharp-pointed rocks, the monster was not able to overtake the boat. This I was afterwards told, for I durst not stay to see the issue of that adventure, but ran as fast as I could the way I first went, and

4. A small bay or cove, affording anchorage.

then climbed up a steep hill, which gave me some prospect of the country. I found it fully cultivated; but that which first surprised me was the length of the grass, which, in those grounds that seemed to be kept for hay, was about twenty foot high.[5]

I fell into a highroad, for so I took it to be, although it served to the inhabitants only as a footpath through a field of barley. Here I walked on for some time, but could see little on either side, it being now near harvest, and the corn[6] rising at least forty foot. I was an hour walking to the end of this field, which was fenced in with a hedge of at least one hundred and twenty foot high, and the trees so lofty that I could make no computation of their altitude. There was a stile to pass from this field into the next: it had four steps, and a stone to cross over when you came to the utmost. It was impossible for me to climb this stile, because every step was six foot high, and the upper stone above twenty. I was endeavoring to find some gap in the hedge when I discovered one of the inhabitants in the next field advancing towards the stile, of the same size with him whom I saw in the sea pursuing our boat. He appeared as tall as an ordinary spire-steeple, and took about ten yards at every stride, as near as I could guess. I was struck with the utmost fear and astonishment, and ran to hide myself in the corn, from whence I saw him at the top of the stile, looking back into the next field on the right hand; and heard him call in a voice many degrees louder than a speaking trumpet; but the noise was so high in the air that at first I certainly thought it was thunder. Whereupon seven monsters like himself came towards him with reaping hooks in their hands, each hook about the largeness of six scythes. These people were not so well clad as the first, whose servants or laborers they seemed to be. For, upon some words he spoke, they went to reap the corn in the field where I lay. I kept from them at as great a distance as I could, but was forced to move with extreme difficulty, for the stalks of the corn were sometimes not above a foot distant, so that I could hardly squeeze my body betwixt them. However, I made a shift to go forward till I came to a part of the field where the corn had been laid by the rain and wind; here it was impossible for me to advance a step, for the stalks were so interwoven that I could not creep through, and the beards of the fallen ears so strong and pointed that they pierced through my clothes into my flesh. At the same time I heard the reapers not above an hundred yards behind me. Being quite dispirited with toil, and wholly overcome by grief and despair, I lay down between two ridges and heartily wished I might there end my days. I bemoaned my desolate widow and fatherless children; I lamented my own folly and willfulness in attempting a second voyage against the advice of all my friends and relations. In this terrible agitation of mind, I could not forbear thinking of Lilliput, whose inhabitants looked upon me as the

5. Swift's intention, not always carried out accurately, is that everything in Brobdingnag should be, in relation to our familiar world, on a scale of ten to one.

6. Wheat, not maize.

greatest prodigy that ever appeared in the world; where I was able to draw an imperial fleet in my hand, and perform those other actions which will be recorded forever in the chronicles of that empire, while posterity shall hardly believe them, although attested by millions. I reflected what a mortification it must prove to me to appear as inconsiderable in this nation as one single Lilliputian would be among us. But this I conceived was to be the least of my misfortunes; for as human creatures are observed to be more savage and cruel in proportion to their bulk, what could I expect but to be a morsel in the mouth of the first among these enormous barbarians who should happen to seize me? Undoubtedly philosophers are in the right when they tell us that nothing is great or little otherwise than by comparison. It might have pleased fortune to let the Lilliputians find some nation where the people were as diminutive with respect to them as they were to me. And who knows but that even this prodigious race of mortals might be equally overmatched in some distant part of the world, whereof we have yet no discovery?

Scared and confounded as I was, I could not forbear going on with these reflections; when one of the reapers approaching within ten yards of the ridge where I lay, made me apprehend that with the next step I should be squashed to death under his foot, or cut in two with his reaping hook. And therefore when he was again about to move, I screamed as loud as fear could make me. Whereupon the huge creature trod short, and looking round about under him for some time, at last espied me as I lay on the ground. He considered a while with the caution of one who endeavors to lay hold on a small dangerous animal in such a manner that it shall not be able either to scratch or to bite him, as I myself have sometimes done with a weasel in England. At length he ventured to take me up behind by the middle between his forefinger and thumb, and brought me within three yards of his eyes, that he might behold my shape more perfectly. I guessed his meaning, and my good fortune gave me so much presence of mind that I resolved not to struggle in the least as he held me in the air about sixty foot from the ground, although he grievously pinched my sides, for fear I should slip through his fingers. All I ventured was to raise mine eyes towards the sun, and place my hands together in a supplicating posture, and to speak some words in an humble melancholy tone, suitable to the condition I then was in. For I apprehended every moment that he would dash me against the ground, as we usually do any little hateful animal which we have a mind to destroy. But my good star would have it that he appeared pleased with my voice and gestures, and began to look upon me as a curiosity, much wondering to hear me pronounce articulate words, although he could not understand them. In the meantime I was not able to forbear groaning and shedding tears and turning my head towards my sides, letting him know, as well as I could, how cruelly I was hurt by the pressure of his thumb and finger. He seemed to apprehend my meaning; for, lifting up the lappet[7] of his coat, he put me gently into it, and immediately ran along with me to his master, who was a substantial farmer, and the same person I had first seen in the field.

The farmer having (as I supposed by their talk) received such an account of me as his servant could give him, took a piece of a small straw about the size of a walking staff, and therewith lifted up the lappets of my coat, which it seems he thought to be some kind of covering that nature had given me. He blew my hairs aside to take a better view of my face. He called his hinds[8] about him, and asked them (as I afterwards learned) whether they had ever seen in the fields any little creature that resembled me. He then placed me softly on the ground upon all four; but I got immediately up, and walked slowly backwards and forwards, to let those people see I had no intent to run away. They all sat down in a circle about me, the better to observe my motions. I pulled off my hat, and made a low bow towards the farmer; I fell on my knees, and lifted up my hands and eyes, and spoke several words as loud as I could; I took a purse of gold out of my pocket, and humbly presented it to him. He received it on the palm of his hand, then applied it close to his eye to see what it was, and afterwards turned it several times with the point of a pin (which he took out of his sleeve), but could make nothing of it. Whereupon I made a sign that he should place his hand on the ground; I then took the purse, and opening it, poured all the gold into his palm. There were six Spanish pieces of four pistoles each, beside twenty or thirty smaller coins. I saw him wet the tip of his little finger upon his tongue, and take up one of my largest pieces, and then another; but he seemed to be wholly ignorant what they were. He made me a sign to put them again into my purse, and the purse again into my pocket, which after offering to him several times, I thought it best to do.

The farmer by this time was convinced I must be a rational creature. He spoke often to me, but the sound of his voice pierced my ears like that of a water mill, yet his words were articulate enough. I answered as loud as I could in several languages, and he often laid his ear within two yards of me, but all in vain, for we were wholly unintelligible to each other. He then sent his servants to their work, and taking his handkerchief out of his pocket, he doubled and spread it on his hand, which he placed flat on the ground with the palm upwards, making me a sign to step into it, as I could easily do, for it was not above a foot in thickness. I thought it my part to obey, and for fear of falling, laid myself at full length upon the handkerchief, with the remainder of which

7. Flap or fold.   8. Farm servants.

he lapped me up to the head for further security, and in this manner carried me home to his house. There he called his wife, and showed me to her; but she screamed and ran back as women in England do at the sight of a toad or a spider. However, when she had a while seen my behavior, and how well I observed the signs her husband made, she was soon reconciled, and by degrees grew extremely tender of me.

It was about twelve at noon, and a servant brought in dinner. It was only one substantial dish of meat (fit for the plain condition of an husbandman) in a dish of about four-and-twenty foot diameter. The company were the farmer and his wife, three children, and an old grandmother. When they were sat down, the farmer placed me at some distance from him on the table, which was thirty foot high from the floor. I was in a terrible fright, and kept as far as I could from the edge, for fear of falling. The wife minced a bit of meat, then crumbled some bread on a trencher,[9] and placed it before me. I made her a low bow, took out my knife and fork, and fell to eat; which gave them exceeding delight. The mistress sent her maid for a small dram cup, which held about two gallons, and filled it with drink; I took up the vessel with much difficulty in both hands, and in a most respectful manner drank to her ladyship's health, expressing the words as loud as I could in English; which made the company laugh so heartily that I was almost deafened with the noise. This liquor tasted like a small cider,[1] and was not unpleasant. Then the master made me a sign to come to his trencher side; but as I walked on the table, being in great surprise all the time, as the indulgent reader will easily conceive and excuse, I happened to stumble against a crust, and fell flat on my face, but received no hurt. I got up immediately, and observing the good people to be in much concern, I took my hat (which I held under my arm out of good manners) and waving it over my head, made three huzzas to show I had got no mischief by my fall. But advancing forwards toward my master (as I shall henceforth call him), his youngest son who sat next him, an arch[2] boy of about ten years old, took me up by the legs, and held me so high in the air that I trembled every limb; but his father snatched me from him, and at the same time gave him such a box on the left ear as would have felled an European troop of horse to the earth, ordering him to be taken from the table. But being afraid the boy might owe me a spite, and well remembering how mischievous all children among us naturally are to sparrows, rabbits, young kittens, and puppy dogs, I fell on my knees, and pointing to the boy, made my master to understand, as well as I could, that I desired his son might be pardoned. The father complied, and the lad took his seat again; whereupon I went to him and kissed his hand, which my master took, and made him stroke me gently with it.

9. A platter.   2. Mischievous.
1. I.e., weak cider.

In the midst of dinner, my mistress's favorite cat leaped into her lap. I heard a noise behind me like that of a dozen stocking weavers at work; and turning my head, I found it proceeded from the purring of this animal, who seemed to be three times larger than an ox, as I computed by the view of her head and one of her paws, while her mistress was feeding and stroking her. The fierceness of this creature's countenance altogether discomposed me, although I stood at the farther end of the table, above fifty foot off, and although my mistress held her fast for fear she might give a spring and seize me in her talons. But it happened there was no danger, for the cat took not the least notice of me when my master placed me within three yards of her. And as I have been always told, and found true by experience in my travels, that flying or discovering[3] fear before a fierce animal is a certain way to make it pursue or attack you, so I resolved in this dangerous juncture to show no manner of concern. I walked with intrepidity five or six times before the very head of the cat, and came within half a yard of her; whereupon she drew herself back, as if she were more afraid of me; I had less apprehension concerning the dogs, whereof three or four came into the room, as it is usual in farmers' houses; one of which was a mastiff, equal in bulk to four elephants, and a greyhound, somewhat taller than the mastiff, but not so large.

When dinner was almost done, the nurse came in with a child of a year old in her arms, who immediately spied me, and began a squall that you might have heard from London Bridge to Chelsea, after the usual oratory of infants, to get me for a plaything. The mother out of pure indulgence took me up, and put me towards the child, who presently seized me by the middle, and got my head in his mouth, where I roared so loud that the urchin was frighted and let me drop; and I should infallibly have broke my neck if the mother had not held her apron under me. The nurse to quiet her babe made use of a rattle, which was a kind of hollow vessel filled with great stones, and fastened by a cable to the child's waist: but all in vain, so that she was forced to apply the last remedy by giving it suck. I must confess no object ever disgusted me so much as the sight of her monstrous breast, which I cannot tell what to compare with so as to give the curious reader an idea of its bulk, shape, and color. It stood prominent six foot, and could not be less than sixteen in circumference. The nipple was about half the bigness of my head, and the hue both of that and the dug so varified with spots, pimples, and freckles that nothing could appear more nauseous: for I had a near sight of her, she sitting down the more conveniently to give suck, and I standing on the table. This made me reflect upon the fair skins of our English ladies, who appear so beautiful to us, only because they are of our own size, and their defects not to be seen but through a magnifying glass, where

3. Revealing.

we find by experiment that the smoothest and whitest skins look rough and coarse and ill colored.

I remember when I was at Lilliput, the complexion of those diminutive people appeared to me the fairest in the world; and talking upon this subject with a person of learning there, who was an intimate friend of mine, he said that my face appeared much fairer and smoother when he looked on me from the ground than it did upon a nearer view when I took him up in my hand and brought him close, which he confessed was at first a very shocking sight. He said he could discover great holes in my skin; that the stumps of my beard were ten times stronger than the bristles of a boar, and my complexion made up of several colors altogether disagreeable: although I must beg leave to say for myself that I am as fair as most of my sex and country and very little sunburnt by all my travels. On the other side, discoursing of the ladies in that Emperor's court, he used to tell me one had freckles, another too wide a mouth, a third too large a nose; nothing of which I was able to distinguish. I confess this reflection was obvious enough; which however I could not forbear, lest the reader might think those vast creatures were actually deformed: for I must do them justice to say they are a comely race of people; and particularly the features of my master's countenance, although he were but a farmer, when I beheld him from the height of sixty foot, appeared very well proportioned.

When dinner was done, my master went out to his laborers; and as I could discover by his voice and gesture, gave his wife a strict charge to take care of me. I was very much tired and disposed to sleep, which my mistress perceiving, she put me on her own bed, and covered me with a clean white handkerchief, but larger and coarser than the mainsail of a man-of-war.

I slept about two hours, and dreamed I was at home with my wife and children, which aggravated my sorrows when I awaked and found myself alone in a vast room, between two and three hundred foot wide, and above two hundred high, lying in a bed twenty yards wide. My mistress was gone about her household affairs, and had locked me in. The bed was eight yards from the floor. Some natural necessities required me to get down; I durst not presume to call, and if I had, it would have been in vain with such a voice as mine at so great a distance from the room where I lay to the kitchen where the family kept. While I was under these circumstances, two rats crept up the curtains, and ran smelling backwards and forwards on the bed. One of them came up almost to my face; whereupon I rose in a fright, and drew out my hanger[4] to defend myself. These horrible animals had the boldness to attack me on both sides, and one of them held his forefeet at my collar; but I had the good fortune to rip up his belly before he

4. A short, broad sword.

could do me any mischief. He fell down at my feet; and the other seeing the fate of his comrade, made his escape, but not without one good wound on the back, which I gave him as he fled, and made the blood run trickling from him. After this exploit I walked gently to and fro on the bed, to recover my breath and loss of spirits. These creatures were of the size of a large mastiff, but infinitely more nimble and fierce; so that if I had taken off my belt before I went to sleep, I must have infallibly been torn to pieces and devoured. I measured the tail of the dead rat, and found it to be two yards long, wanting an inch; but it went against my stomach to drag the carcass off the bed, where it lay still bleeding; I observed it had yet some life, but with a strong slash cross the neck, I thoroughly dispatched it.

Soon after, my mistress came into the room, who seeing me all bloody, ran and took me up in her hand. I pointed to the dead rat, smiling and making other signs to show I was not hurt, whereat she was extremely rejoiced, calling the maid to take up the dead rat with a pair of tongs, and throw it out of the window. Then she set me on a table, where I showed her my hanger all bloody, and wiping it on the lappet of my coat, returned it to the scabbard. I was pressed to do more than one thing, which another could not do for me, and therefore endeavored to make my mistress understand that I desired to be set down on the floor; which after she had done, my bashfulness would not suffer me to express myself farther than by pointing to the door, and bowing several times. The good woman with much difficulty at last perceived what I would be at, and taking me up again in her hand, walked into the garden, where she set me down. I went on one side about two hundred yards; and beckoning to her not to look or to follow me, I hid myself between two leaves of sorrel, and there discharged the necessities of nature.

I hope the gentle reader will excuse me for dwelling on these and the like particulars, which however insignificant they may appear to groveling vulgar[5] minds, yet will certainly help a philosopher to enlarge his thoughts and imagination, and apply them to the benefit of public as well as private life, which was my sole design in presenting this and other accounts of my travels to the world; wherein I have been chiefly studious of truth, without affecting any ornaments of learning or of style. But the whole scene of this voyage made so strong an impression on my mind, and is so deeply fixed in my memory, that in committing it to paper I did not omit one material circumstance; however, upon a strict review, I blotted out several passages of less moment which were in my first copy, for fear of being censured as tedious and trifling, whereof travelers are often, perhaps not without justice, accused.

5. Commonplace, uncultivated, in contrast to the scientist ("philosopher"); an irony.

CHAPTER II. *A description of the farmer's daughter. The Author carried to a market town, and then to the metropolis. The particulars of his journey.*

My mistress had a daughter of nine years old, a child of towardly parts for her age, very dexterous at her needle, and skillful in dressing her baby.[6] Her mother and she contrived to fit up the baby's cradle for me against night: the cradle was put into a small drawer of a cabinet, and the drawer placed upon a hanging shelf for fear of the rats. This was my bed all the time I stayed with those people, although made more convenient by degrees as I began to learn their language, and make my wants known. This young girl was so handy, that after I had once or twice pulled off my clothes before her, she was able to dress and undress me, although I never gave her that trouble when she would let me do either myself. She made me seven shirts, and some other linen of as fine cloth as could be got, which indeed was coarser than sackcloth, and these she constantly washed for me with her own hands. She was likewise my schoolmistress to teach me the language: when I pointed to anything, she told me the name of it in her own tongue, so that in a few days I was able to call for whatever I had a mind to. She was very good-natured, and not above forty foot high, being little for her age. She gave me the name of *Grildrig,* which the family took up, and afterwards the whole kingdom. The word imports what the Latins call *nanunculus,* the Italian *homunceletino,*[7] and the English *mannikin.* To her I chiefly owe my preservation in that country: we never parted while I was there; I called her my *Glumdalclitch,* or little nurse: and I should be guilty of great ingratitude if I omitted this honorable mention of her care and affection towards me, which I heartily wish it lay in my power to requite as she deserves, instead of being the innocent but unhappy instrument of her disgrace, as I have too much reason to fear.

It now began to be known and talked of in the neighborhood that my master had found a strange animal in the field, about the bigness of a *splacknuck,* but exactly shaped in every part like a human creature, which it likewise imitated in all its actions: seemed to speak in a little language of its own, had already learned several words of theirs, went erect upon two legs, was tame and gentle, would come when it was called, do whatever it was bid, had the finest limbs in the world, and a complexion fairer than a nobleman's daughter of three years old. Another farmer who lived hard by, and was a particular friend of my master, came on a visit on purpose to inquire into the truth of this story. I was immediately produced, and placed upon a table, where I walked as I was commanded, drew my hanger, put it up again, made my reverence to my master's

6. Doll.
7. The Latin and Italian words are Swift's own coinages, as, of course, are the various words from the Brobdingnagian language.

guest, asked him in his own language how he did, and told him he was welcome, just as my little nurse had instructed me. This man, who was old and dimsighted, put on his spectacles to behold me better, at which I could not forbear laughing very heartily, for his eyes appeared like the full moon shining into a chamber at two windows. Our people, who discovered the cause of my mirth, bore me company in laughing, at which the old fellow was fool enough to be angry and out of countenance. He had the character of a great miser, and to my misfortune he well deserved it by the cursed advice he gave my master to show me as a sight upon a market day in the next town, which was half an hour's riding, about two and twenty miles from our house. I guessed there was some mischief contriving when I observed my master and his friend whispering long together, sometimes pointing at me; and my fears made me fancy that I overheard and understood some of their words. But the next morning Glumdalclitch, my little nurse, told me the whole matter, which she had cunningly picked out from her mother. The poor girl laid me on her bosom, and fell a weeping with shame and grief. She apprehended some mischief would happen to me from rude vulgar folks, who might squeeze me to death, or break one of my limbs by taking me in their hands. She had also observed how modest I was in my nature, how nicely I regarded my honor, and what an indignity I should conceive it to be exposed for money as a public spectacle to the meanest of the people. She said her papa and mamma had promised that Grildrig should be hers; but now she found they meant to serve her as they did last year, when they pretended to give her a lamb, and yet, as soon as it was fat, sold it to a butcher. For my own part, I may truly affirm that I was less concerned than my nurse. I had a strong hope, which never left me, that I should one day recover my liberty; and as to the ignominy of being carried about for a monster, I considered myself to be a perfect stranger in the country, and that such a misfortune could never be charged upon me as a reproach, if ever I should return to England; since the King of Great Britain himself, in my condition, must have undergone the same distress.

My master, pursuant to the advice of his friend, carried me in a box the next market day to the neighboring town, and took along with him his little daughter, my nurse, upon a pillion[8] behind him. The box was close on every side, with a little door for me to go in and out, and a few gimlet holes to let in air. The girl had been so careful to put the quilt of her baby's bed into it, for me to lie down on. However, I was terribly shaken and discomposed in this journey, although it were but of half an hour. For the horse went about forty foot at every step, and trotted so high that the agitation was equal to the rising and falling of a ship in a great storm, but much more frequent. Our journey was somewhat further than

8. A pad attached to the hinder part of a saddle, on which a second person, usually a woman, could ride.

from London to St. Albans. My master alighted at an inn which he used to frequent; and after consulting a while with the innkeeper, and making some necessary preparations, he hired the *Grultrud*, or crier, to give notice through the town of a strange creature to be seen at the Sign of the Green Eagle, not so big as a *splacknuck* (an animal in that country very finely shaped, about six foot long), and in every part of the body resembling an human creature, could speak several words and perform an hundred diverting tricks.

I was placed upon a table in the largest room of the inn, which might be near three hundred foot square. My little nurse stood on a low stool close to the table, to take care of me, and direct what I should do. My master, to avoid a crowd, would suffer only thirty people at a time to see me. I walked about on the table as the girl commanded; she asked me questions as far as she knew my understanding of the language reached, and I answered them as loud as I could. I turned about several times to the company, paid my humble respects, said they were welcome, and used some other speeches I had been taught. I took up a thimble filled with liquor, which Glumdalclitch had given me for a cup, and drank their health. I drew out my hanger, and flourished with it after the manner of fencers in England. My nurse gave me part of a straw, which I exercised as a pike, having learned the art in my youth. I was that day shown to twelve sets of company, and as often forced to go over again with the same fopperies, till I was half dead with weariness and vexation. For those who had seen me made such wonderful reports that the people were ready to break down the doors to come in. My master for his own interest would not suffer anyone to touch me except my nurse; and, to prevent danger, benches were set round the table at such a distance as put me out of everybody's reach. However, an unlucky schoolboy aimed a hazelnut directly at my head, which very narrowly missed me; otherwise, it came with so much violence that it would have infallibly knocked out my brains, for it was almost as large as a small pumpion:[9] but I had the satisfaction to see the young rogue well beaten, and turned out of the room.

My master gave public notice that he would show me again the next market day, and in the meantime he prepared a more convenient vehicle for me, which he had reason enough to do; for I was so tired with my first journey, and with entertaining company for eight hours together, that I could hardly stand upon my legs or speak a word. It was at least three days before I recovered my strength; and that I might have no rest at home, all the neighboring gentlemen from an hundred miles round, hearing of my fame, came to see me at my master's own house. There could not be fewer than thirty persons with their wives and children (for the country is very populous); and my master demanded the rate of a

9. Pumpkin.

full room whenever he showed me at home, although it were only to a single family. So that for some time I had but little ease every day of the week (except Wednesday, which is their Sabbath) although I were not carried to the town.

My master finding how profitable I was like to be, resolved to carry me to the most considerable cities of the kingdom. Having therefore provided himself with all things necessary for a long journey, and settled his affairs at home, he took leave of his wife; and upon the 17th of August, 1703, about two months after my arrival, we set out for the metropolis, situated near the middle of that empire, and about three thousand miles distance from our house. My master made his daughter Glumdalclitch ride behind him. She carried me on her lap in a box tied about her waist. The girl had lined it on all sides with the softest cloth she could get, well quilted underneath, furnished it with her baby's bed, provided me with linen and other necessaries, and made everything as convenient as she could. We had no other company but a boy of the house, who rode after us with the luggage.

My master's design was to show me in all the towns by the way, and to step out of the road for fifty or an hundred miles to any village or person of quality's house where he might expect custom. We made easy journeys of not above seven or eight score miles a day: for Glumdalclitch, on purpose to spare me, complained she was tired with the trotting of the horse. She often took me out of my box at my own desire, to give me air and show me the country, but always held me fast by leading strings. We passed over five or six rivers many degrees broader and deeper than the Nile or the Ganges; and there was hardly a rivulet so small as the Thames at London Bridge. We were ten weeks in our journey, and I was shown in eighteen large towns, besides many large villages and private families.

On the 26th day of October, we arrived at the metropolis, called in their language *Lorbrulgrud*, or Pride of the Universe. My master took a lodging in the principal street of the city, not far from the royal palace, and put out bills in the usual form, containing an exact description of my person and parts. He hired a large room between three and four hundred foot wide. He provided a table sixty foot in diameter, upon which I was to act my part, and palisadoed it round three foot from the edge, and as many high, to prevent my falling over. I was shown ten times a day to the wonder and satisfaction of all people. I could now speak the language tolerably well, and perfectly understood every word that was spoken to me. Besides, I had learned their alphabet, and could make a shift to explain a sentence here and there; for Glumdalclitch had been my instructor while we were at home, and at leisure hours during our journey. She carried a little book in her pocket, not much larger than a Sanson's *Atlas*;[1] it was a common treatise for the use of young girls, giving a short account of their religion: out of this she taught me my letters, and interpreted the words.

CHAPTER III. *The Author sent for to Court. The Queen buys him of his master, the farmer, and presents him to the King. He disputes with his Majesty's great scholars. An apartment at Court provided for the Author. He is in high favor with the Queen. He stands up for the honor of his own country. His quarrels with the Queen's dwarf.*

The frequent labors I underwent every day made in a few weeks a very considerable change in my health: the more my master got by me, the more unsatiable he grew. I had quite lost my stomach, and was almost reduced to a skeleton. The farmer observed it, and concluding I soon must die, resolved to make as good a hand of me as he could. While he was thus reasoning and resolving with himself, a *Slardral*, or Gentleman Usher, came from Court, commanding my master to carry me immediately thither for the diversion of the Queen and her ladies. Some of the latter had already been to see me and reported strange things of my beauty, behavior, and good sense. Her Majesty and those who attended her were beyond measure delighted with my demeanor. I fell on my knees and begged the honor of kissing her Imperial foot; but this gracious princess held out her little finger towards me (after I was set on a table), which I embraced in both my arms, and put the tip of it, with the utmost respect, to my lip. She made me some general questions about my country and my travels, which I answered as distinctly and in as few words as I could. She asked whether I would be content to live at Court. I bowed down to the board of the table, and humbly answered that I was my master's slave, but if I were at my own disposal, I should be proud to devote my life to her Majesty's service. She then asked my master whether he were willing to sell me at a good price. He, who apprehended I could not live a month, was ready enough to part with me, and demanded a thousand pieces of gold, which were ordered him on the spot, each piece being about the bigness of eight hundred moidores;[2] but, allowing for the proportion of all things between that country and Europe, and the high price of gold among them, was hardly so great a sum as a thousand guineas would be in England. I then said to the Queen, since I was now her Majesty's most humble creature and vassal, I must beg the favor that Glumdalclitch, who had always tended me with so much care and kindness, and understood to do it so well, might be admitted into her service, and continue to be my nurse and instructor. Her Majesty agreed to my petition, and easily got the farmer's consent, who was glad enough to have his daughter preferred at Court; and the poor girl herself was not able to hide her

1. I.e., over two feet long and about two feet wide.   2. Portuguese coins.

joy. My late master withdrew, bidding me farewell, and saying he had left me in a good service; to which I replied not a word, only making him a slight bow.

The Queen observed my coldness, and when the farmer was gone out of the apartment, asked me the reason. I made bold to tell her Majesty that I owed no other obligation to my late master than his not dashing out the brains of a poor harmless creature found by chance in his field; which obligation was amply recompensed by the gain he had made in showing me through half the kingdom, and the price he had now sold me for. That the life I had since led was laborious enough to kill an animal of ten times my strength. That my health was much impaired by the continual drudgery of entertaining the rabble every hour of the day; and that if my master had not thought my life in danger, her Majesty would not have got so cheap a bargain. But as I was out of all fear of being ill treated under the protection of so great and good an Empress, the Ornament of Nature, the Darling of the World, the Delight of her Subjects, the Phoenix of the Creation; so I hoped my late master's apprehensions would appear to be groundless, for I already found my spirits to revive by the influence of her most august presence.

This was the sum of my speech, delivered with great improprieties and hesitation; the latter part was altogether framed in the style peculiar to that people, whereof I learned some phrases from Glumdalclitch, while she was carrying me to Court.

The Queen, giving great allowance for my defectiveness in speaking, was however surprised at so much wit and good sense in so diminutive an animal. She took me in her own hand, and carried me to the King, who was then retired to his cabinet.[3] His Majesty, a prince of much gravity, and austere countenance, not well observing my shape at first view, asked the Queen after a cold manner how long it was since she grew fond of a *splacknuck*; for such it seems he took me to be, as I lay upon my breast in her Majesty's right hand. But this princess, who hath an infinite deal of wit and humor, set me gently on my feet upon the scrutore,[4] and commanded me to give his Majesty an account of myself, which I did in a very few words; and Glumdalclitch, who attended at the cabinet door, and could not endure I should be out of her sight, being admitted, confirmed all that had passed from my arrival at her father's house.

The King, although he be as learned a person as any in his dominions, had been educated in the study of philosophy and particularly mathematics; yet when he observed my shape exactly, and saw me walk erect, before I began to speak, conceived I might be a piece of clockwork (which is in that country arrived to a very great perfection) contrived by some ingenious artist. But when he heard my voice, and found what I delivered to be regular and ra-

3. A private apartment.   4. Writing desk.

tional, he could not conceal his astonishment. He was by no means satisfied with the relation I gave him of the manner I came into his kingdom, but thought it a story concerted between Glumdalclitch and her father, who had taught me a set of words to make me sell at a higher price. Upon this imagination he put several other questions to me, and still received rational answers, no otherwise defective than by a foreign accent, and an imperfect knowledge in the language, with some rustic phrases which I had learned at the farmer's house, and did not suit the polite style of a court.

His Majesty sent for three great scholars who were then in their weekly waiting (according to the custom in that country). These gentlemen, after they had a while examined my shape with much nicety, were of different opinions concerning me. They all agreed that I could not be produced according to the regular laws of nature, because I was not framed with a capacity of preserving my life, either by swiftness, or climbing of trees, or digging holes in the earth. They observed by my teeth, which they viewed with great exactness, that I was a carnivorous animal; yet most quadrupeds being an overmatch for me, and field mice, with some others, too nimble, they could not imagine how I should be able to support myself, unless I fed upon snails and other insects; which they offered, by many learned arguments, to evince that I could not possibly do. One of them seemed to think that I might be an embryo, or abortive birth. But this opinion was rejected by the other two, who observed my limbs to be perfect and finished, and that I had lived several years, as it was manifest from my beard, the stumps whereof they plainly discovered through a magnifying glass. They would not allow me to be a dwarf, because my littleness was beyond all degrees of comparison; for the Queen's favorite dwarf, the smallest ever known in that kingdom, was nearly thirty foot high. After much debate, they concluded unanimously that I was only *relplum scalcath*, which is interpreted literally, *lusus naturae*;[5] a determination exactly agreeable to the modern philosophy of Europe, whose professors, disdaining the old evasion of *occult causes*, whereby the followers of Aristotle endeavor in vain to disguise their ignorance, have invented this wonderful solution of all difficulties, to the unspeakable advancement of human knowledge.

After this decisive conclusion, I entreated to be heard a word or two. I applied myself to the King, and assured his Majesty that I came from a country which abounded with several millions of both sexes, and of my own stature, where the animals, trees, and houses were all in proportion, and where by consequence I might be as able to defend myself, and to find sustenance, as any of his Majesty's subjects could do here; which I took for a full answer to

5. One of nature's sports, or, roughly, freaks. Swift had contempt for both the medieval schoolmen, who discussed "occult causes," the unknown causes of observable effects, and modern scientists, who, he believed, often concealed their ignorance by using equally meaningless terms.

those gentlemen's arguments. To this they only replied with a smile of contempt, saying that the farmer had instructed me very well in my lesson. The King, who had a much better understanding, dismissing his learned men, sent for the farmer, who by good fortune was not yet gone out of town; having therefore first examined him privately, and then confronted him with me and the young girl, his Majesty began to think that what we told him might possibly be true. He desired the Queen to order that a particular care should be taken of me, and was of opinion that Glumdalclitch should still continue in her office of tending me, because he observed we had a great affection for each other. A convenient apartment was provided for her at Court; she had a sort of governess appointed to take care of her education, a maid to dress her, and two other servants for menial offices; but the care of me was wholly appropriated to herself. The Queen commanded her own cabinet-maker to contrive a box that might serve me for a bedchamber, after the model that Glumdalclitch and I should agree upon. This man was a most ingenious artist, and according to my directions, in three weeks finished for me a wooden chamber of sixteen foot square and twelve high, with sash windows, a door, and two closets, like a London bedchamber. The board that made the ceiling was to be lifted up and down by two hinges, to put in a bed ready furnished by her Majesty's upholsterer, which Glumdalclitch took out every day to air, made it with her own hands, and letting it down at night, locked up the roof over me. A nice[6] workman, who was famous for little curiosities, undertook to make me two chairs, with backs and frames, of a substance not unlike ivory, and two tables, with a cabinet to put my things in. The room was quilted on all sides, as well as the floor and the ceiling, to prevent any accident from the carelessness of those who carried me, and to break the force of a jolt when I went in a coach. I desired a lock for my door to prevent rats and mice from coming in: the smith, after several attempts, made the smallest that ever was seen among them, for I have known a larger at the gate of a gentleman's house in England. I made a shift[7] to keep the key in a pocket of my own, fearing Glumdalclitch might lose it. The Queen likewise ordered the thinnest silks that could be gotten, to make me clothes, not much thicker than an English blanket, very cumbersome till I was accustomed to them. They were after the fashion of the kingdom, partly resembling the Persian, and partly the Chinese, and are a very grave, decent habit.

The Queen became so fond of my company that she could not dine without me. I had a table placed upon the same at which her Majesty ate, just at her left elbow, and a chair to sit on. Glumdalclitch stood upon a stool on the floor, near my table, to assist and take care of me. I had an entire set of silver dishes and plates, and

6. **Exact.**   7. **Contrived.**

other necessaries, which, in proportion to those of the Queen, were not much bigger than what I have seen of the same kind in a London toyshop,[8] for the furniture of a baby-house: these my little nurse kept in her pocket in a silver box and gave me at meals as I wanted them, always cleaning them herself. No person dined with the Queen but the two Princesses Royal, the elder sixteen years old, and the younger at that time thirteen and a month. Her Majesty used to put a bit of meat upon one of my dishes, out of which I carved for myself; and her diversion was to see me eat in miniature. For the Queen (who had indeed but a weak stomach) took up at one mouthful as much as a dozen English farmers could eat at a meal, which to me was for some time a very nauseous sight. She would craunch the wing of a lark, bones and all, between her teeth, although it were nine times as large as that of a full-grown turkey; and put a bit of bread into her mouth as big as two twelve-penny loaves. She drank out of a golden cup, above a hogshead at a draught. Her knives were twice as long as a scythe set straight upon the handle. The spoons, forks, and other instruments were all in the same proportion. I remember when Glumdalclitch carried me out of curiosity to see some of the tables at Court, where ten or a dozen of these enormous knives and forks were lifted up together, I thought I had never till then beheld so terrible a sight.

It is the custom that every Wednesday (which, as I have before observed, was their Sabbath) the King and Queen, with the royal issue of both sexes, dine together in the apartment of his Majesty, to whom I was now become a favorite; and at these times my little chair and table were placed at his left hand, before one of the salt-cellars. This prince took a pleasure in conversing with me, inquiring into the manners, religion, laws, government, and learning of Europe; wherein I gave him the best account I was able. His apprehension was so clear, and his judgment so exact, that he made very wise reflections and observations upon all I said. But I confess that after I had been a little too copious in talking of my own beloved country, of our trade and wars by sea and land, of our schisms in religion and parties in the state, the prejudices of his education prevailed so far that he could not forbear taking me up in his right hand, and stroking me gently with the other, after an hearty fit of laughing, asked me whether I were a Whig or a Tory. Then turning to his first minister, who waited behind him with a white staff, near as tall as the mainmast of the *Royal Sovereign*,[9] he observed how contemptible a thing was human grandeur, which could be mimicked by such diminutive insects as I: "and yet," said he, "I dare engage, these creatures have their titles and distinctions of honor; they contrive little nests and burrows, that they call houses and cities; they make a figure in dress and equipage;[1] they love, they

8. A shop for selling knickknacks.
9. At the English court the Lord Treasurer bore a white staff as the symbol of his office. The *Royal Sover-*

eign was one of the largest ships in the Royal Navy.
1. A carriage and horses, with attendant footmen.

fight, they dispute, they cheat, they betray." And thus he continued on, while my color came and went several times with indignation to hear our noble country, the mistress of arts and arms, the scourge of France, the arbitress of Europe, the seat of virtue, piety, honor, and truth, the pride and envy of the world, so contemptuously treated.

But as I was not in a condition to resent injuries, so, upon mature thoughts, I began to doubt whether I were injured or no. For, after having been accustomed several months to the sight and converse of this people, and observed every object upon which I cast my eyes to be of proportionable magnitude, the horror I had first conceived from their bulk and aspect was so far worn off that if I had then beheld a company of English lords and ladies in their finery and birthday clothes,[2] acting their several parts in the most courtly manner of strutting and bowing and prating, to say the truth, I should have been strongly tempted to laugh as much at them as this King and his grandees did at me. Neither indeed could I forbear smiling at myself when the Queen used to place me upon her hand towards a looking glass, by which both our persons appeared before me in full view together; and there could be nothing more ridiculous than the comparison; so that I really began to imagine myself dwindled many degrees below my usual size.

Nothing angered and mortified me so much as the Queen's dwarf, who being of the lowest stature that was ever in that country (for I verily think he was not full thirty foot high) became so insolent at seeing a creature so much beneath him that he would always affect to swagger and look big as he passed by me in the Queen's antechamber, while I was standing on some table talking with the lords or ladies of the court; and he seldom failed of a smart word or two upon my littleness, against which I could only revenge myself by calling him brother, challenging him to wrestle, and such repartees as are usual in the mouths of Court pages. One day at dinner this malicious little cub was so nettled with something I had said to him that, raising himself upon the frame of Her Majesty's chair, he took me up by the middle, as I was sitting down, not thinking any harm, and let me drop into a large silver bowl of cream, and then ran away as fast as he could. I fell over head and ears, and if I had not been a good swimmer, it might have gone very hard with me; for Glumdalclitch in that instant happened to be at the other end of the room, and the Queen was in such a fright that she wanted presence of mind to assist me. But my little nurse ran to my relief, and took me out, after I had swallowed above a quart of cream. I was put to bed; however, I received no other damage than the loss of a suit of clothes, which was utterly spoiled. The dwarf was soundly whipped, and as a further punishment, forced to drink up the bowl of cream into which he had

2. Courtiers dressed with especial splendor on the monarch's birthday.

thrown me; neither was he ever restored to favor: for soon after the Queen bestowed him to a lady of high quality, so that I saw him no more, to my very great satisfaction; for I could not tell to what extremity such a malicious urchin might have carried his resentment.

He had before served me a scurvy trick, which set the Queen a laughing, although at the same time she were heartily vexed, and would have immediately cashiered him,[3] if I had not been so generous as to intercede. Her Majesty had taken a marrow bone upon her plate, and after knocking out the marrow, placed the bone again in the dish, erect as it stood before; the dwarf watching his opportunity, while Glumdalclitch was gone to the sideboard, mounted upon the stool she stood on to take care of me at meals, took me up in both hands, and squeezing my legs together, wedged them into the marrow bone above my waist, where I stuck for some time, and made a very ridiculous figure. I believe it was near a minute before anyone knew what was become of me, for I thought it below me to cry out. But, as princes seldom get their meat hot, my legs were not scalded, only my stockings and breeches in a sad condition. The dwarf at my entreaty had no other punishment than a sound whipping.

I was frequently rallied by the Queen upon account of my fearfulness, and she used to ask me whether the people of my country were as great cowards as myself. The occasion was this. The kingdom is much pestered with flies in summer, and these odious insects, each of them as big as a Dunstable lark, hardly gave me any rest while I sat at dinner, with their continual humming and buzzing about my ears. They would sometimes alight upon my victuals, and leave their loathsome excrement or spawn behind, which to me was very visible, although not to the natives of that country, whose large optics were not so acute as mine in viewing smaller objects. Sometimes they would fix upon my nose or forehead, where they stung me to the quick, smelling very offensively; and I could easily trace that viscous matter, which our naturalists tell us enables those creatures to walk with their feet upwards upon a ceiling. I had much ado to defend myself against these destable animals, and could not forbear starting when they came on my face. It was the common practice of the dwarf to catch a number of these insects in his hand, as schoolboys do among us, and let them out suddenly under my nose, on purpose to frighten me, and divert the Queen. My remedy was to cut them in pieces with my knife as they flew in the air, wherein my dexterity was much admired.

I remember one morning when Glumdalclitch had set me in my box upon a window, as she usually did in fair days to give me air (for I durst not venture to let the box be hung on a nail out of the window, as we do with cages in England), after I had lifted up one

3. Dismissed him.

of my sashes, and sat down at my table to eat a piece of sweet cake for my breakfast, above twenty wasps, allured by the smell, came flying into the room, humming louder than the drones of as many bagpipes. Some of them seized my cake, and carried it piecemeal away; others flew about my head and face, confounding me with the noise, and putting me in the utmost terror of their stings. However, I had the courage to rise and draw my hanger, and attack them in the air. I dispatched four of them, but the rest got away, and I presently shut my window. These insects were as large as partridges; I took out their stings, found them an inch and a half long, and as sharp as needles. I carefully preserved them all, and having since shown them with some other curiosities in several parts of Europe, upon my return to England I gave three of them to Gresham College,[4] and kept the fourth for myself.

CHAPTER IV. *The country described. A proposal for correcting modern maps. The King's palace, and some account of the metropolis. The Author's way of traveling. The chief temple described.*

I now intend to give the reader a short description of this country, as far as I have traveled in it, which was not above two thousand miles round Lorbrulgrud the metropolis. For the Queen, whom I always attended, never went further when she accompanied the King in his progresses, and there stayed till his Majesty returned from viewing his frontiers. The whole extent of this prince's dominions reacheth about six thousand miles in length, and from three to five in breadth. From whence I cannot but conclude that our geographers of Europe are in a great error by supposing nothing but sea between Japan and California: for it was ever my opinion that there must be a balance of earth to counterpoise the great continent of Tartary; and therefore they ought to correct their maps and charts by joining this vast tract of land to the northwest parts of America, wherein I shall be ready to lend them my assistance.

The kingdom is a peninsula, terminated to the northeast by a ridge of mountains thirty miles high, which are altogether impassable by reason of the volcanoes upon the tops. Neither do the most learned know what sort of mortals inhabit beyond those mountains, or whether they be inhabited at all. On the three other sides it is bounded by the ocean. There is not one seaport in the whole kingdom; and those parts of the coasts into which the rivers issue are so full of pointed rocks, and the sea generally so rough, that there is no venturing with the smallest of their boats; so that these people are wholly excluded from any commerce with the rest of the world. But the large rivers are full of vessels, and abound with excellent fish, for they seldom get any from the sea, because the sea fish are of the same size with those in Europe, and consequently

4. The Royal Society, in its earliest years, met in Gresham College.

not worth catching; whereby it is manifest that nature, in the production of plants and animals of so extraordinary a bulk, is wholly confined to this continent, of which I leave the reasons to be determined by philosophers. However, now and then they take a whale that happens to be dashed against the rocks, which the common people feed on heartily. These whales I have known so large that a man could hardly carry one upon his shoulders; and sometimes for curiosity they are brought in hampers to Lorbrulgrud: I saw one of them in a dish at the King's table, which passed for a rarity, but I did not observe he was fond of it; for I think indeed the bigness disgusted him, although I have seen one somewhat larger in Greenland.

The country is well inhabited, for it contains fifty-one cities, near an hundred walled towns, and a great number of villages. To satisfy my curious reader, it may be sufficient to describe Lorbrulgrud. This city stand upon almost two equal parts on each side the river that passes through. It contains above eighty thousand houses, and about six hundred thousand inhabitants. It is in length three *glongluns* (which make about fifty-four English miles) and two and a half in breadth, as I measured it myself in the royal map made by the King's order, which was laid on the ground on purpose for me, and extended an hundred feet; I paced the diameter and circumference several times barefoot, and computing by the scale, measured it pretty exactly.

The King's palace is no regular edifice, but an heap of buildings about seven miles round: the chief rooms are generally two hundred and forty foot high, and broad and long in proportion. A coach was allowed to Glumdalclitch and me, wherein her governess frequently took her out to see the town, or go among the shops; and I was always of the party, carried in my box, although the girl at my own desire would often take me out, and hold me in her hand, that I might more conveniently view the houses and the people as we passed along the streets. I reckoned our coach to be about a square of Westminster Hall,[5] but not altogether so high; however, I cannot be very exact. One day the governess ordered our coachman to stop at several shops, where the beggars, watching their opportunity, crowded to the sides of the coach, and gave me the most horrible spectacles that ever an English eye beheld. There was a woman with a cancer in her breast, swelled to a monstrous size, full of holes, in two or three of which I could have easily crept, and covered my whole body. There was a fellow with a wen in his neck, larger than five woolpacks, and another with a couple of wooden legs, each about twenty foot high. But the most hateful sight of all was the lice crawling on their clothes. I could see distinctly the limbs of these vermin with my naked eye, much better than those

5. The ancient hall, now incorporated into the Houses of Parliament, where the Law Courts then sat. Swift presum- ably means the square of its breadth (just under 68 feet).

of an European louse through a microscope, and their snouts with which they rooted like swine. They were the first I had ever beheld; and I should have been curious enough to dissect one of them if I had proper instruments (which I unluckily left behind me in the ship), although indeed the sight was so nauseous that it perfectly turned my stomach.

Besides the large box in which I was usually carried, the Queen ordered a smaller one to be made for me, of about twelve foot square and ten high, for the convenience of traveling, because the other was somewhat too large for Glumdalclitch's lap, and cumbersome in the coach; it was made by the same artist, whom I directed in the whole contrivance. This traveling closet was an exact square with a window in the middle of three of the squares, and each window was latticed with iron wire on the outside, to prevent accidents in long journeys. On the fourth side, which had no window, two strong staples were fixed, through which the person that carried me, when I had a mind to be on horseback, put in a leathern belt, and buckled it about his waist. This was always the office of some grave trusty servant in whom I could confide, whether I attended the King and Queen in their progresses, or were disposed to see the gardens, or pay a visit to some great lady or minister of state in the court, when Glumdalclitch happened to be out of order: for I soon began to be known and esteemed among the greatest officers, I suppose more upon account of their Majesties' favor than any merit of my own. In journeys, when I was weary of the coach, a servant on horseback would buckle my box, and place it on a cushion before him; and there I had a full prospect of the country on three sides from my three windows. I had in this closet a field bed and a hammock hung from the ceiling, two chairs and a table, neatly screwed to the floor to prevent being tossed about by the agitation of the horse or the coach. And having been long used to sea voyages, those motions, although sometimes very violent, did not much discompose me.

When I had a mind to see the town, it was always in my traveling closet, which Glumdalclitch held in her lap in a kind of open sedan, after the fashion of the country, borne by four men, and attended by two others in the Queen's livery. The people, who had often heard of me, were very curious to crowd about the sedan; and the girl was complaisant enough to make the bearers stop, and to take me in her hand that I might be more conveniently seen.

I was very desirous to see the chief temple, and particularly the tower belonging to it, which is reckoned the highest in the kingdom. Accordingly one day my nurse carried me thither, but I may truly say I came back disappointed; for the height is not above three thousand foot, reckoning from the ground to the highest pinnacle top; which, allowing for the difference between the size of those people and us in Europe, is no great matter for admiration, nor at all equal in proportion (if I rightly remember) to Salisbury steeple.[6] But, not to detract from a nation to which during my life I shall acknowledge myself extremely obliged, it must be allowed that whatever this famous tower wants in height is amply made up in beauty and strength. For the walls are near an hundred foot thick, built of hewn stone, whereof each is about forty foot square, and adorned on all sides with statues of gods and emperors cut in marble larger than the life, placed in their several niches. I measured a little finger which had fallen down from one of these statues, and lay unperceived among some rubbish, and found it exactly four foot and an inch in length. Glumdalclitch wrapped it up in a handkerchief, and carried it home in her pocket to keep among other trinkets, of which the girl was very fond, as children at her age usually are.

The King's kitchen is indeed a noble building, vaulted at top, and about six hundred foot high. The great oven is not so wide by ten paces as the cupola at St. Paul's:[7] for I measured the latter on purpose after my return. But if I should describe the kitchen grate, the prodigious pots and kettles, the joints of meat turning on the spits, with many other particulars, perhaps I should be hardly believed; at least a severe critic would be apt to think I enlarged a little, as travelers are often suspected to do. To avoid which censure, I fear I have run too much into the other extreme, and that if this treatise should happen to be translated into the language of Brobdingnag (which is the general name of that kingdom) and transmitted thither, the King and his people would have reason to complain that I had done them an injury by a false and diminutive representation.

His Majesty seldom keeps above six hundred horses in his stables: they are generally from fifty-four to sixty foot high. But when he goes abroad on solemn days, he is attended for state by a militia guard of five hundred horse, which indeed I thought was the most splendid sight that could be ever beheld, till I saw part of his army in battalia;[8] whereof I shall find another occasion to speak.

CHAPTER V. *Several adventures that happened to the Author. The execution of a criminal. The Author shows his skill in navigation.*

I should have lived happy enough in that country if my littleness had not exposed me to several ridiculous and troublesome accidents, some of which I shall venture to relate. Glumdalclitch often carried me into the gardens of the court in my smaller box, and would sometimes take me out of it and hold me in her hand, or set me down to walk. I remember, before the dwarf left the Queen, he followed us one day into those gardens; and my nurse having set me down, he and I being close together near some dwarf apple

6. One of the most beautiful Gothic steeples in England is that of Salisbury Cathedral, 404 feet high.

7. The cupola of St. Paul's Cathedral in London is 108 feet in diameter.

8. Battle array.

trees, I must needs show my wit by a silly allusion between him and the trees, which happens to hold in their language as it doth in ours. Whereupon, the malicious rogue watching his opportunity, when I was walking under one of them, shook it directly over my head, by which a dozen apples, each of them near as large as a Bristol barrel, came tumbling about my ears; one of them hit me on the back as I chanced to stoop, and knocked me down flat on my face, but I received no other hurt; and the dwarf was pardoned at my desire, because I had given the provocation.

Another day Glumdalclitch left me on a smooth grassplot to divert myself while she walked at some distance with her governess. In the meantime there suddenly fell such a violent shower of hail that I was immediately by the force of it struck to the ground: and when I was down, the hailstones gave me such cruel bangs all over the body as if I had been pelted with tennis balls;[9] however I made a shift to creep on all four, and shelter myself by lying on my face on the lee side of a border of lemon thyme, but so bruised from head to foot that I could not go abroad in ten days. Neither is this at all to be wondered at, because nature in that country observing the same proportion through all her operations, a hailstone is near eighteen hundred times as large as one in Europe; which I can assert upon experience, having been so curious to weigh and measure them.

But a more dangerous accident happened to me in the same garden when my little nurse, believing she had put me in a secure place, which I often entreated her to do that I might enjoy my own thoughts, and having left my box at home to avoid the trouble of carrying it, went to another part of the garden with her governess and some ladies of her acquaintance. While she was absent and out of hearing, a small white spaniel belonging to one of the chief gardeners, having got by accident into the garden, happened to range near the place where I lay. The dog following the scent, came directly up, and taking me in his mouth, ran straight to his master, wagging his tail, and set me gently on the ground. By good fortune he had been so well taught that I was carried between his teeth without the least hurt, or even tearing my clothes. But the poor gardener, who knew me well, and had a great kindness for me, was in a terrible fright. He gently took me up in both his hands, and asked me how I did; but I was so amazed and out of breath that I could not speak a word. In a few minutes I came to myself, and he carried me safe to my little nurse, who by this time had returned to the place where she left me, and was in cruel agonies when I did not appear nor answer when she called; she severely reprimanded the gardener on account of his dog. But the thing was hushed up and never known at court; for the girl was afraid of the Queen's anger; and truly, as to myself, I thought it

9. 18th-century tennis balls, unlike the modern, were very hard.

would not be for my reputation that such a story should go about.

This accident absolutely determined Glumdalclitch never to trust me abroad for the future out of her sight. I had been long afraid of this resolution, and therefore concealed from her some little unlucky adventures that happened in those times when I was left by myself. Once a kite[1] hovering over the garden made a swoop at me, and if I had not resolutely drawn my hanger, and run under a thick espalier,[2] he would have certainly carried me away in his talons. Another time walking to the top of a fresh molehill, I fell to my neck in the hole through which that animal had cast up the earth, and coined some lie, not worth remembering, to excuse myself for spoiling my clothes. I likewise broke my right shin against the shell of a snail, which I happened to stumble over, as I was walking alone, and thinking on poor England.

I cannot tell whether I were more pleased or mortified to observe in those solitary walks that the smaller birds did not appear to be at all afraid of me; but would hop about within a yard distance, looking for worms and other food with as much indifference and security as if no creature at all were near them. I remember a thrush had the confidence to snatch out of my hand with his bill a piece of cake that Glumdalclitch had just given me for my breakfast. When I attempted to catch any of these birds, they would boldly turn against me, endeavoring to pick my fingers, which I durst not venture within their reach; and then they would hop back unconcerned to hunt for worms or snails, as they did before. But one day I took a thick cudgel, and threw it with all my strength so luckily at a linnet that I knocked him down, and seizing him by the neck with both my hands, ran with him in triumph to my nurse. However, the bird, who had only been stunned, recovering himself, gave me so many boxes with his wings on both sides of my head and body, though I held him at arm's length, and was out of the reach of his claws, that I was twenty times thinking to let him go. But I was soon relieved by one of our servants, who wrung off the bird's neck, and I had him next day for dinner, by the Queen's command. This linnet, as near as I can remember, seemed to be somewhat larger than an English swan.

The Maids of Honor often invited Glumdalclitch to their apartments, and desired she would bring me along with her, on purpose to have the pleasure of seeing and touching me. They would often strip me naked from top to toe and lay me at full length in their bosoms; wherewith I was much disgusted, because, to say the truth, a very offensive smell came from their skins, which I do not mention or intend to the disadvantage of those excellent ladies, for whom I have all manner of respect; but I conceive that my sense was more acute in proportion to my littleness, and that those illus-

1. A bird of prey. 2. A trellis on which fruit trees are trained

trious persons were no more disagreeable to their lovers, or to each other, than people of the same quality are with us in England. And, after all, I found their natural smell was much more supportable than when they used perfumes, under which I immediately swooned away. I cannot forget that an intimate friend of mine in Lilliput took the freedom in a warm day, when I had used a good deal of exercise, to complain of a strong smell about me, although I am as little faulty that way as most of my sex: but I suppose his faculty of smelling was as nice with regard to me as mine was to that of this people. Upon this point, I cannot forbear doing justice to the Queen, my mistress, and Glumdalclitch, my nurse, whose persons were as sweet as those of any lady in England.

That which gave me most uneasiness among these Maids of Honor, when my nurse carried me to visit them, was to see them use me without any manner of ceremony, like a creature who had no sort of consequence. For they would strip themselves to the skin and put on their smocks in my presence, while I was placed on their toilet[3] directly before their naked bodies; which, I am sure, to me was very far from being a tempting sight, or from giving me any other emotions than those of horror and disgust. Their skins appeared so coarse and uneven, so variously colored, when I saw them near, with a mole here and there as broad as a trencher, and hairs hanging from it thicker than pack-threads, to say nothing further concerning the rest of their persons. Neither did they at all scruple, while I was by, to discharge what they had drunk, to the quantity of at least two hogsheads, in a vessel that held above three tuns. The handsomest among these Maids of Honor, a pleasant frolicsome girl of sixteen, would sometimes set me astride upon one of her nipples, with many other tricks, wherein the reader will excuse me for not being over particular. But I was so much displeased that I entreated Glumdalclitch to contrive some excuse for not seeing that young lady any more.

One day a young gentleman, who was nephew to my nurse's governess, came and pressed them both to see an execution. It was of a man who had murdered one of that gentleman's intimate acquaintance. Glumdalclitch was prevailed on to be of the company, very much against her inclination, for she was naturally tender-hearted: and as for myself, although I abhorred such kind of spectacles, yet my curiosity tempted me to see something that I thought must be extraordinary. The malefactor was fixed in a chair upon a scaffold erected for the purpose, and his head cut off at a blow with a sword of about forty foot long. The veins and arteries spouted up such a prodigious quantity of blood, and so high in the air, that the great *jet d'eau*[4] at Versailles was not equal for the time it lasted; and the head, when it fell on the scaffold floor, gave such a bounce,[5]

3. Toilet table.
4. This fountain rose over forty feet in
the air.
5. A sudden noise.

as made me start, although I were at least half an English mile distant.

The Queen, who often used to hear me talk of my sea voyages, and took all occasions to divert me when I was melancholy, asked me whether I understood how to handle a sail or an oar, and whether a little exercise of rowing might not be convenient for my health. I answered that I understood both very well. For although my proper employment had been to be surgeon or doctor to the ship, yet often, upon a pinch, I was forced to work like a common mariner. But I could not see how this could be done in their country, where the smallest wherry was equal to a first-rate man-of-war among us, and such a boat as I could manage would never live in any of their rivers. Her Majestry said, if I would contrive a boat, her own joiner[6] should make it, and she would provide a place for me to sail in. The fellow was an ingenious workman and, by my instructions, in ten days finished a pleasure boat with all its tackling, able conveniently to hold eight Europeans. When it was finished, the Queen was so delighted that she ran with it in her lap to the King, who ordered it to be put in a cistern full of water, with me in it, by way of trial; where I could not manage my two sculls, or little oars, for want of room. But the Queen had before contrived another project. She ordered the joiner to make a wooden trough of three hundred foot long, fifty broad, and eight deep; which being well pitched to prevent leaking, was placed on the floor along the wall in an outer room of the palace. It had a cock near the bottom to let out the water when it began to grow stale, and two servants could easily fill it in half an hour. Here I often used to row for my own diversion, as well as that of the Queen and her ladies, who thought themselves well entertained with my skill and agility. Sometimes I would put up my sail, and then my business was only to steer, while the ladies gave me a gale with their fans; and when they were weary, some of the pages would blow my sail forward with their breath, while I showed my art by steering starboard or larboard as I pleased. When I had done, Glumdalclitch always carried my boat into her closet, and hung it on a nail to dry.

In this exercise I once met an accident which had like to have cost me my life. For one of the pages having put my boat into the trough, the governess who attended Glumdalclitch very officiously[7] lifted me up to place me in the boat; but I happened to slip through her fingers, and should have infallibly fallen down forty feet upon the floor, if by the luckiest chance in the world I had not been stopped by a corking-pin[8] that stuck in the good gentlewoman's stomacher; the head of the pin passed between my shirt and the waistband of my breeches, and thus I was held by the middle in the air until Glumdalclitch ran to my relief.

6. A skilled woodworker.
7. Kindly, dutifully.
8. A pin of the largest size. "Stom-acher": an ornamental covering for the front and upper part of the body.

Another time, one of the servants, whose office it was to fill my trough every third day with fresh water, was so careless to let a huge frog (not perceiving it) slip out of his pail. The frog lay concealed till I was put into my boat, but then seeing a resting place, climbed up, and made it lean so much on one side that I was forced to balance it with all my weight on the other, to prevent overturning. When the frog was got in, it hopped at once half the length of the boat, and then over my head, backwards and forwards, daubing my face and clothes with its odious slime. The largeness of its features made it appear the most deformed animal that can be conceived. However, I desired Glumdalclitch to let me deal with it alone. I banged it a good while with one of my sculls, and at last forced it to leap out of the boat.

But the greatest danger I ever underwent in that kingdom was from a monkey, who belonged to one of the clerks of the kitchen. Glumdalclitch had locked me up in her closet, while she went somewhere upon business or a visit. The weather being very warm, the closet window was left open, as well as the windows in the door of my bigger box, in which I usually lived, because of its largeness and conveniency. As I sat quietly meditating at my table, I heard something bounce in at the closet window, and skip about from one side to the other, whereat, although I was much alarmed, yet I ventured to look out, but stirred not from my seat; and then I saw this frolicsome animal, frisking and leaping up and down, till at last he came to my box, which he seemed to view with great pleasure and curiosity, peeping in at the door and every window. I retreated to the farther corner of my room, or box, but the monkey looking in at every side, put me into such a fright that I wanted presence of mind to conceal myself under the bed, as I might easily have done. After some time spent in peeping, grinning, and chattering, he at last espied me, and reaching one of his paws in at the door, as a cat does when she plays with a mouse, although I often shifted place to avoid him, he at length seized the lappet of my coat (which, being made of that country cloth, was very thick and strong) and dragged me out. He took me up in his right forefoot, and held me as a nurse does a child she is going to suckle, just as I have seen the same sort of creature do with a kitten in Europe: and when I offered to struggle, he squeezed me so hard that I thought it more prudent to submit. I have good reason to believe that he took me for a young one of his own species, by his often stroking my face very gently with his other paw. In these diversions he was interrupted by a noise at the closet door, as if somebody were opening it, whereupon he suddenly leaped up to the window at which he had come in, and thence upon the leads and gutters, walking upon three legs, and holding me in the fourth, till he clambered up to a roof that was next to ours. I heard Glumdalclitch give a shriek at the moment he was carrying me out. The poor girl was almost distracted: that quarter of the palace was all in an uproar; the servants ran for ladders; the monkey was seen by hundreds in the court, sitting upon the ridge of a building, holding me like a baby in one of his forepaws and feeding me with the other, by cramming into my mouth some victuals he had squeezed out of the bag on one side of his chaps, and patting me when I would not eat; whereat many of the rabble below could not forbear laughing; neither do I think they justly ought to be blamed, for without question the sight was ridiculous enough to everybody but myself. Some of the people threw up stones, hoping to drive the monkey down; but this was strictly forbidden, or else very probably my brains had been dashed out.

The ladders were now applied, and mounted by several men; which the monkey observing, and finding himself almost encompassed, not being able to make speed enough with his three legs, let me drop on a ridge tile, and made his escape. Here I sat for some time three hundred yards from the ground, expecting every moment to be blown down by the wind, or to fall by my own giddiness, and come tumbling over and over from the ridge to the eaves. But an honest lad, one of my nurse's footmen, climbed up, and putting me into his breeches pocket, brought me down safe.

I was almost choked with the filthy stuff the monkey had crammed down my throat; but my dear little nurse picked it out of my mouth with a small needle, and then I fell a vomiting, which gave me great relief. Yet I was so weak and bruised in the sides with the squeezes given me by this odious animal that I was forced to keep my bed a fortnight. The King, Queen, and all the Court sent every day to inquire after my health, and her Majesty made me several visits during my sickness. The monkey was killed, and an order made that no such animal should be kept about the palace.

When I attended the King after my recovery, to return him thanks for his favors, he was pleased to rally me a good deal upon this adventure. He asked me what my thoughts and speculations were while I lay in the monkey's paw, how I liked the victuals he gave me, his manner of feeding, and whether the fresh air on the roof had sharpened my stomach. He desired to know what I would have done upon such an occasion in my own country. I told his Majesty that in Europe we had no monkeys, except such as were brought for curiosities from other places, and so small that I could deal with a dozen of them together, if they presumed to attack me. And as for that monstrous animal with whom I was so lately engaged (it was indeed as large as an elephant), if my fears had suffered me to think so far as to make use of my hanger (looking fiercely and clapping my hand upon the hilt as I spoke) when he poked his paw into my chamber, perhaps I should have given him such a wound as would have made him glad to withdraw it with more haste than he put it in. This I delivered in a firm tone, like a person who was jealous lest his courage should be called in question. However, my speech produced nothing else besides a loud laughter, which all the respect due to his Majesty from those about him could not make them contain. This made me reflect how vain an attempt it is for a man to endeavor doing himself honor among those who are out of all degree of equality or comparison with him. And yet I have seen the moral of my own behavior very frequent in England since my return, where a little contemptible varlet, without the least title to birth, person, wit, or common sense, shall presume to look with importance, and put himself upon a foot with the greatest persons of the kingdom.

I was every day furnishing the court with some ridiculous story; and Glumdalclitch, although she loved me to excess, yet was arch enough to inform the Queen whenever I committed any folly that she thought would be diverting to her Majesty. The girl, who had been out of order, was carried by her governess to take the air about an hour's distance, or thirty miles from town. They alighted out of the coach near a small footpath in a field, and Glumdalclitch setting down my traveling box, I went out of it to walk. There was a cow dung in the patch, and I must needs try my activity by attempting to leap over it. I took a run, but unfortunately jumped short, and found myself just in the middle up to my knees. I waded through with some difficulty, and one of the footmen wiped me as clean as he could with his handkerchief; for I was filthily bemired, and my nurse confined me to my box till we returned home, where the Queen was soon informed of what had passed and the footmen spread it about the Court, so that all the mirth, for some days, was at my expense.

CHAPTER VI. *Several contrivances of the Author to please the King and Queen. He shows his skill in music. The King inquires into the state of Europe, which the Author relates to him. The King's observations thereon.*

I used to attend the King's levee[9] once or twice a week, and had often seen him under the barber's hand, which indeed was at first very terrible to behold. For the razor was almost twice as long as an ordinary scythe. His Majesty, according to the custom of the country, was only shaved twice a week. I once prevailed on the barber to give me some of the suds or lather, out of which I picked forty or fifty of the strongest stumps of hair. I then took a piece of fine wood, and cut it like the back of a comb, making several holes in it at equal distance with as small a needle as I could get from Glumdalclitch. I fixed in the stumps so artificially,[1] scraping

---

9. A morning reception held by a prince or nobleman, sometimes while dressing for the day.

1. Skillfully.

and sloping them with my knife towards the points, that I made a very tolerable comb; which was a seasonable supply, my own being so much broken in the teeth that it was almost useless; neither did I know any artist in that country so nice and exact as would undertake to make me another.

And this puts me in mind of an amusement wherein I spent many of my leisure hours. I desired the Queen's woman to save for me the combings of her Majesty's hair, whereof in time I got a good quantity; and consulting with my friend the cabinetmaker, who had received general orders to do little jobs for me, I directed him to make two chair frames, no larger than those I had in my box, and then to bore little holes with a fine awl round those parts where I designed the backs and seats; through these holes I wove the strongest hairs I could pick out, just after the manner of cane chairs in England. When they were finished, I made a present of them to her Majesty, who kept them in her cabinet, and used to show them for curiosities, as indeed they were the wonder of every one that beheld them. The Queen would have made me sit upon one of these chairs, but I absolutely refused to obey her, protesting I would rather die a thousand deaths than place a dishonorable part of my body on those precious hairs that once adorned her Majesty's head. Of these hairs (as I had always a mechanical genius) I likewise made a neat little purse above five foot long, with her Majesty's name deciphered in gold letters, which I gave to Glumdalclitch by the Queen's consent. To say the truth, it was more for show than use, being not of strength to bear the weight of the larger coins; and therefore she kept nothing in it but some little toys[2] that girls are fond of.

The King, who delighted in music, had frequent consorts[3] at court, to which I was sometimes carried, and set in my box on a table to hear them; but the noise was so great that I could hardly distinguish the tunes. I am confident that all the drums and trumpets of a royal army, beating and sounding together just at your ears, could not equal it. My practice was to have my box removed from the places where the performers sat, as far as I could, then to shut the doors and windows of it, and draw the window curtains, after which I found their music not disagreeable.

I had learned in my youth to play a little upon the spinet. Glumdalclitch kept one in her chamber, and a master attended twice a week to teach her: I call it a spinet, because it somewhat resembled that instrument, and was played upon in the same manner. A fancy came into my head that I would entertain the King and Queen with an English tune upon this instrument. But this appeared extremely difficult: for the spinet was near sixty foot long, each key being almost a foot wide; so that, with my arms extended, I could

2. Trifles.   3. Concerts.

not reach to above five keys, and to press them down required a good smart stroke with my fist, which would be too great a labor and to no purpose. The method I contrived was this: I prepared two round sticks about the bigness of common cudgels; they were thicker at one end than the other, and I covered the thicker ends with a piece of a mouse's skin, that by rapping on them I might neither damage the tops of the keys, nor interrupt the sound. Before the spinet a bench was placed, about four foot below the keys, and I was put upon the bench. I ran sideling upon it that way and this, as fast as I could, banging the proper keys with my two sticks; and made a shift to play a jig, to the great satisfaction of both their Majesties: but it was the most violent exercise I ever underwent, and yet I could not strike above sixteen keys, nor, consequently, play the bass and treble together, as other artists do; which was a great disadvantage to my performance.

The King, who, as I before observed, was a prince of excellent understanding, would frequently order that I should be brought in my box and set upon the table in his closet. He would then command me to bring one of my chairs out of the box, and sit down within three yards distance upon the top of the cabinet, which brought me almost to a level with his face. In this manner I had several conversations with him. I one day took the freedom to tell his Majesty that the contempt he discovered towards Europe, and the rest of the world, did not seem answerable to those excellent qualities of mind that he was master of. That reason did not extend itself with the bulk of the body: on the contrary, we observed in our country that the tallest persons were usually least provided with it. That among other animals, bees and ants had the reputation of more industry, art, and sagacity than many of the larger kinds; and that, as inconsiderable as he took me to be, I hoped I might live to do his Majesty some signal service. The King heard me with attention, and began to conceive a much better opinion of me than he had before. He desired I would give him as exact an account of the government of England as I possibly could; because, as fond as princes commonly are of their own customs (for so he conjectured of other monarchs, by my former discourses), he should be glad to hear of anything that might deserve imitation.

Imagine with thyself, courteous reader, how often I then wished for the tongue of Demosthenes or Cicero, that might have enabled me to celebrate the praise of my own dear native country in a style equal to its merits and felicity.

I began my discourse by informing his Majesty that our dominions consisted of two islands, which composed three mighty kingdoms under one sovereign, beside our plantations in America. I dwelt long upon the fertility of our soil, and the temperature[4] of

4. Temperateness.

our climate. I then spoke at large upon the constitution of an English Parliament, partly made up of an illustrious body called the House of Peers, persons of the noblest blood, and of the most ancient and ample patrimonies. I described that extraordinary care always taken of their education in arts and arms, to qualify them for being counselors born to the king and kingdom; to have a share in the legislature, to be members of the highest Court of Judicature, from whence there could be no appeal; and to be champions always ready for the defense of their prince and country, by their valor, conduct, and fidelity. That these were the ornament and bulwark of the kingdom, worthy followers of their most renowned ancestors, whose honor had been the reward of their virtue, from which their posterity were never once known to degenerate. To these were joined several holy persons, as part of that assembly, under the title of Bishops, whose peculiar business it is to take care of religion, and of those who instruct the people therein. These were searched and sought out through the whole nation, by the prince and his wisest counselors, among such of the priesthood as were most deservedly distinguished by the sanctity of their lives and the depth of their erudition, who were indeed the spiritual fathers of the clergy and the people.

That the other part of the Parliament consisted of an assembly called the House of Commons, who were all principal gentlemen, freely picked and culled out by the people themselves, for their great abilities and love of their country, to represent the wisdom of the whole nation. And these two bodies make up the most august assembly in Europe, to whom, in conjunction with the prince, the whole legislature is committed.

I then descended to the Courts of Justice, over which the Judges, those venerable sages and interpreters of the law, presided, for determining the disputed rights and properties of men, as well as for the punishment of vice, and protection of innocence. I mentioned the prudent management of our treasury, the valor and achievements of our forces by sea and land. I computed the number of our people, by reckoning how many millions there might be of each religious sect, or political party among us. I did not omit even our sports and pastimes, or any other particular which I thought might redound to the honor of my country. And I finished all with a brief historical account of affairs and events in England for about an hundred years past.

This conversation was not ended under five audiences, each of several hours, and the King heard the whole with great attention, frequently taking notes of what I spoke, as well as memorandums of several questions he intended to ask me.

When I had put an end to these long discourses, his Majesty in a sixth audience consulting his notes, proposed many doubts, queries, and objections, upon every article. He asked what methods were used to cultivate the minds and bodies of our young nobility, and in what kind of business they commonly spent the first and teachable part of their lives. What course was taken to supply that assembly when any noble family became extinct. What qualifications were necessary in those who were to be created new lords. Whether the humor[5] of the prince, a sum of money to a Court lady or a prime minister, or a design of strengthening a party opposite to the public interest, ever happened to be motives in those advancements. What share of knowledge these lords had in the laws of their country, and how they came by it, so as to enable them to decide the properties of their fellow subjects in the last resort. Whether they were always so free from avarice, partialities, or want that a bribe or some other sinister view could have no place among them. Whether those holy lords I spoke of were constantly promoted to that rank upon account of their knowledge in religious matters, and the sanctity of their lives, had never been compliers with the times while they were common priests, or slavish prostitute chaplains to some nobleman, whose opinions they continued servilely to follow after they were admitted into that assembly.

He then desired to know what arts were practiced in electing those whom I called Commoners. Whether a stranger with a strong purse might not influence the vulgar voters to choose him before their own landlord or the most considerable gentleman in the neighborhood. How it came to pass that people were so violently bent upon getting into this assembly, which I allowed to be a great trouble and expense, often to the ruin of their families, without any salary or pension: because this appeared such an exalted strain of virtue and public spirit that his Majesty seemed to doubt it might possibly not be always sincere; and he desired to know whether such zealous gentlemen could have any views of refunding themselves for the charges and trouble they were at, by sacrificing the public good to the designs of a weak and vicious prince in conjunction with a corrupted ministry. He multiplied his questions, and sifted me thoroughly upon every part of this head, proposing numberless inquiries and objections, which I think it not prudent or convenient to repeat.

Upon what I said in relation to our Courts of Justice, his Majesty desired to be satisfied in several points: and this I was the better able to do, having been formerly almost ruined by a long suit in chancery, which was decreed for me with costs. He asked what time was usually spent in determining between right and wrong, and what degree of expense. Whether advocates and orators had liberty to plead in causes manifestly known to be unjust, vexatious, or oppressive. Whether party in religion or politics were observed

5. Whim.

to be of any weight in the scale of justice. Whether those pleading orators were persons educated in the general knowledge of equity, or only in provincial, national, and other local customs. Whether they or their judges had any part in penning those laws which they assumed the liberty of interpreting and glossing upon at their pleasure. Whether they had ever at different times pleaded for and against the same cause, and cited precedents to prove contrary opinions. Whether they were a rich or a poor corporation. Whether they received any pecuniary reward for pleading or delivering their opinions. And particularly whether they were ever admitted as members in the lower senate.

He fell next upon the management of our treasury, and said he thought my memory had failed me, because I computed our taxes at about five or six millions a year, and when I came to mention the issues,[6] he found they sometimes amounted to more than double, for the notes he had taken were very particular in this point; because he hoped, as he told me, that the knowledge of our conduct might be useful to him, and he could not be deceived in his calculations. But if what I told him were true, he was still at a loss how a kingdom could run out of its estate like a private person. He asked me, who were our creditors? and where we should find money to pay them? He wondered to hear me talk of such chargeable and extensive wars; that certainly we must be a quarrelsome people, or live among very bad neighbors, and that our generals must needs be richer than our kings.[7] He asked what business we had out of our own islands, unless upon the score of[8] trade or treaty or to defend the coasts with our fleet. Above all, he was amazed to hear me talk of a mercenary standing army[9] in the midst of peace, and among a free people. He said if we were governed by our own consent in the persons of our representatives, he could not imagine of whom we were afraid, or against whom we were to fight; and would hear my opinion whether a private man's house might not better be defended by himself, his children, and family, than by half a dozen rascals picked up at a venture[1] in the streets for small wages, who might get an hundred times more by cutting their throats.

He laughed at my odd kind of arithmetic (as he was pleased to call it) in reckoning the numbers of our people by a computation drawn from the several sects among us in religion and politics. He said he knew no reason why those who entertain opinions prejudicial to the public should be obliged to change, or should not be obliged

6. Expenditures.
7. An allusion to the enormous fortune gained by the Duke of Marlborough, formerly Captain-General of the army, whom Swift detested.
8. For the sake of.
9. Since the declaration of the Bill of Rights (1689), a standing army without authorization by Parliament had been illegal. Swift and the Tories in general were vigilant in their opposition to such an army.
1. By chance.

to conceal them. And as it was tyranny in any government to require the first, so it was weakness not to enforce the second: for a man may be allowed to keep poisons in his closet, but not to vend them about for cordials.[2]

He observed that among the diversions of our nobility and gentry I had mentioned gaming.[3] He desired to know at what age this entertainment was usually taken up, and when it was laid down; how much of their time it employed; whether it ever went so high as to affect their fortunes; whether mean, vicious people, by their dexterity in that art, might not arrive at great riches, and sometimes keep our very nobles in dependence, as well as habituate them to vile companions, wholly take them from the improvement of their minds, and force them, by the losses they have received, to learn and practice that infamous dexterity upon others.

He was perfectly astonished with the historical account I gave him of our affairs during the last century, protesting it was only an heap of conspiracies, rebellions, murders, massacres, revolutions, banishments, the very worst effects that avarice, faction, hypocrisy, perfidiousness, cruelty, rage, madness, hatred, envy, lust, malice, or ambition could produce.

His Majesty in another audience was at the pains to recapitulate the sum of all I had spoken; compared the questions he made with the answers I had given; then taking me into his hands, and stroking me gently, delivered himself in these words, which I shall never forget nor the manner he spoke them in. "My little friend Grildrig, you have made a most admirable panegyric[4] upon your country. You have clearly proved that ignorance, idleness, and vice are the proper ingredients for qualifying a legislator. That laws are best explained, interpreted, and applied by those whose interests and abilities lie in perverting, confounding, and eluding them. I observe among you some lines of an institution which in its original might have been tolerable; but these half erased, and the rest wholly blurred and blotted by corruptions. It doth not appear from all you have said how any one virtue is required towards the procurement of any one station among you; much less that men are ennobled on account of their virtue, that priests are advanced for their piety or learning, soldiers for their conduct or valor, judges for their integrity, senators for the love of their country, or counselors for their wisdom. As for yourself," continued the King, "who have spent the greatest part of your life in traveling, I am well disposed to hope you may hitherto have escaped many vices of your country. But by what I have gathered from your own relation, and the answers I have with much pains wringed and extorted from you, I cannot but conclude the bulk of your natives to be the most pernicious race

2. Medicines to stimulate the heart, or, equally commonly, liqueurs.
3. Gambling.
4. A formal oration in praise of someone or something.

of little odious vermin that nature ever suffered to crawl upon the surface of the earth."

CHAPTER VII. *The Author's love of his country. He makes a proposal of much advantage to the King; which is rejected. The King's great ignorance in politics. The learning of that country very imperfect and confined. Their laws, and military affairs, and parties in the State.*

Nothing but an extreme love of truth could have hindered me from concealing this part of my story. It was in vain to discover my resentments, which were always turned into ridicule: and I was forced to rest with patience while my noble and most beloved country was so injuriously treated. I am heartily sorry as any of my readers can possibly be that such an occasion was given, but this prince happened to be so curious and inquisitive upon every particular that it could not consist either with gratitude or good manners to refuse giving him what satisfaction I was able. Yet thus much I may be allowed to say in my own vindication: that I artfully eluded many of his questions, and gave to every point a more favorable turn by many degrees than the strictness of truth would allow. For I have always borne that laudable partiality to my own country, which Dionysius Halicarnassensis[5] with so much justice recommends to an historian. I would hide the frailties and deformities of my political mother, and place her virtues and beauties in the most advantageous light. This was my sincere endeavor in those many discourses I had with that mighty monarch, although it unfortunately failed of success.

But great allowances should be given to a King who lives wholly secluded from the rest of the world, and must therefore be altogether unacquainted with the manners and customs that most prevail in other nations: the want of which knowledge will ever produce many *prejudices*, and a certain *narrowness of thinking*, from which we and the politer countries of Europe are wholly exempted. And it would be hard indeed if so remote a prince's notions of virtue and vice were to be offered as a standard for all mankind.

To confirm what I have now said, and further, to show the miserable effects of a *confined education*, I shall here insert a passage which will hardly obtain belief. In hopes to ingratiate myself farther into his Majesty's favor, I told him of an invention discovered between three and four hundred years ago, to make a certain powder, into an heap of which the smallest spark of fire falling would kindle the whole in a moment, although it were as big as a mountain, and make it all fly up in the air together, with a noise and agitation

5. A Greek rhetorician and historian, who flourished ca. 25 B.C. His history of Rome was written to reconcile the Greeks to their Roman masters.

greater than thunder. That a proper quantity of this powder rammed into an hollow tube of brass or iron, according to its bigness, would drive a ball of iron or lead with such violence and speed as nothing was able to sustain its force. That the largest balls thus discharged would not only destroy whole ranks of an army at once, but batter the strongest walls to the ground; sink down ships with a thousand men in each, to the bottom of the sea; and, when linked together by a chain, would cut through masts and rigging; divide hundreds of bodies in the middle, and lay all waste before them. That we often put this powder into large hollow balls of iron, and discharged them by an engine into some city we were besieging; which would rip up the pavements, tear the houses to pieces, burst and throw splinters on every side, dashing out the brains of all who came near. That I knew the ingredients very well, which were cheap and common; I understood the manner of compounding them, and could direct his workmen how to make those tubes of a size proportionable to all other things in his Majesty's kingdom, and the largest need not be above two hundred foot long; twenty or thirty of which tubes, charged with the proper quantity of powder and balls, would batter down the walls of the strongest town in his dominions in a few hours; or destroy the whole metropolis, if ever it should pretend to dispute his absolute commands. This I humbly offered to his Majesty as a small tribute of acknowledgment in return of so many marks that I had received of his royal favor and protection.

The King was struck with horror at the description I had given of those terrible engines and the proposal I had made. He was amazed how so impotent and groveling an insect as I (these were his expressions) could entertain such inhuman ideas, and in so familiar a manner as to appear wholly unmoved at all the scenes of blood and desolation which I had painted as the common effects of those destructive machines; whereof he said some evil genius, enemy to mankind, must have been the first contriver. As for himself, he protested that although few things delighted him so much as new discoveries in art or in nature, yet he would rather lose half his kingdom than be privy[6] to such a secret, which he commanded me, as I valued my life, never to mention any more.

A strange effect of *narrow principles* and *short views!* that a prince possessed of every quality which procures veneration, love, and esteem; of strong parts, great wisdom, and profound learning; endued with admirable talents for government, and almost adored by his subjects; should from a *nice, unnecessary scruple*, whereof in Europe we can have no conception, let slip an opportunity put into his hands that would have made him absolute master of the lives, the liberties, and the fortunes of his people. Neither do I say this with the least intention to detract from the many virtues of that

6. To share secret knowledge.

excellent King, whose character I am sensible will on this account be very much lessened in the opinion of an English reader: but I take this defect among them to have risen from their ignorance; they not having hitherto reduced politics into a science, as the more acute wits of Europe have done. For I remember very well, in a discourse one day with the King, when I happened to say there were several thousand books among us written upon the art of government, it gave him (directly contrary to my intention) a very mean opinion of our understandings. He professed both to abominate and despise all *mystery, refinement,* and *intrigue,* either in a prince or a minister. He could not tell what I meant by *secrets of state,* where an enemy or some rival nation were not in the case. He confined the knowledge of governing within very *narrow bounds:* to common sense and reason, to justice and lenity,[7] to the speedy determination of civil and criminal causes, with some other obvious topics which are not worth considering. And he gave it for his opinion that whoever could make two ears of corn or two blades of grass to grow upon a spot of ground where only one grew before would deserve better of mankind and do more essential service to his country than the whole race of politicians [7a] put together.

The learning of this people is very defective, consisting only in morality, history, poetry, and mathematics; wherein they must be allowed to excel. But the last of these is wholly applied to what may be useful in life, to the improvement of agriculture and all mechanical arts; so that among us it would be little esteemed. And as to ideas, entities, abstractions, and transcendentals,[8] I could never drive the least conception into their heads.

No law of that country must exceed in words the number of letters in their alphabet, which consists only in two and twenty. But indeed few of them extend even to that length. They are expressed in the most plain and simple terms, wherein those people are not mercurial[9] enough to discover above one interpretation. And to write a comment upon any law is a capital crime. As to the decision of civil causes, or proceedings against criminals, their precedents[1] are so few that they have little reason to boast of any extraordinary skill in either.

They have had the art of printing as well as the Chinese, time out of mind. But their libraries are not very large; for that of the King's, which is reckoned the biggest, doth not amount to above a thousand volumes, placed in a gallery of twelve hundred foot long, from whence I had liberty to borrow what books I pleased. The

---

7. Mildness.
7a. By "politicians" Swift means something like our modern "political scientists"—theorists.
8. In Swift's time, "transcendental" was practically synonymous with "metaphysical."
9. Changeable.

1. A legal decision or a course of action which comes to serve as a rule in determining similar cases in the future. In the Fourth Voyage of *Gulliver's Travels,* Gulliver is made to say: "It is a maxim among these lawyers that whatever hath been done before may legally be done again. * * * "

Queen's joiner had contrived in one of the Glumdalclitch's rooms a kind of wooden machine five and twenty foot high, formed like a standing ladder; the steps were each fifty foot long. It was indeed a movable pair of stairs, the lowest end placed at ten foot distance from the wall of the chamber. The book I had a mind to read was put up leaning against the wall. I first mounted to the upper step of the ladder, and turning my face towards the book, began at the top of the page, and so walking to the right and left about eight or ten paces according to the length of the lines, till I had gotten a little below the level of mine eyes, and then descending gradually till I came to the bottom: after which I mounted again, and began the other page in the same manner, and so turned over the leaf, which I could easily do with both my hands, for it was as thick and stiff as a pasteboard, and in the largest folios[2] not above eighteen or twenty foot long.

Their style is clear, masculine, and smooth, but not florid; for they avoid nothing more than multiplying unnecessary words or using various expressions. I have perused many of their books, especially those in history and morality. Among the rest, I was much diverted with a little old treatise, which always lay in Glumdalclitch's bedchamber, and belonged to her governess, a grave elderly gentlewoman, who dealt in writings of morality and devotion. The book treats of the weakness of human kind, and is in little esteem, except among the women and the vulgar. However, I was curious to see what an author of that country could say upon such a subject. This writer went through all the usual topics of European moralists: showing how diminutive, contemptible, and helpless an animal was man in his own nature; how unable to defend himself from the inclemencies of the air, or the fury of wild beasts; how much he was excelled by one creature in strength, by another in speed, by a third in foresight, by a fourth in industry. He added that nature was degenerated in these latter declining ages of the world, and could now produce only small abortive births in comparison of those in ancient times. He said it was very reasonable to think, not only that the species of men were originally much larger, but also that there must have been giants in former ages; which, as it is asserted by history and tradition, so it hath been confirmed by huge bones and skulls casually dug up in several parts of the kingdom, far exceeding the common dwindled race of man in our days. He argued that the very laws of nature absolutely required we should have been made in the beginning of a size more large and robust, not so liable to destruction from every little accident of a tile falling from a house, or a stone cast from the hand of a boy, or of being drowned in a little brook. From this way of reasoning, the author drew several moral applications useful in the

2. A book of the largest size.

conduct of life, but needless here to repeat. For my own part, I could not avoid reflecting how universally this talent was spread, of drawing lectures in morality, or indeed rather matter of discontent and repining, from the quarrels we raise with nature. And I believe, upon a strict inquiry, those quarrels might be shown as ill grounded among us as they are among that people.

As to their military affairs, they boast that the King's army consists of an hundred and seventy-six thousand foot and thirty-two thousand horse: if that may be called an army which is made up of tradesmen in the several cities, and farmers in the country, whose commanders are only the nobility and gentry, without pay or reward. They are indeed perfect enough in their exercises, and under very good discipline, wherein I saw no great merit; for how should it be otherwise, where every farmer is under the command of his own landlord, and every citizen under that of the principal men in his own city, chosen after the manner of Venice by ballot?

I have often seen the militia of Lorbrulgrud drawn out to exercise in a great field near the city, of twenty miles square. They were in all not above twenty-five thousand foot, and six thousand horse; but it was impossible for me to compute their number, considering the space of ground they took up. A cavalier mounted on a large steed might be about an hundred foot high. I have seen this whole body of horse, upon a word of command, draw their swords at once, and brandish them in the air. Imagination can figure nothing so grand, so surprising, and so astonishing. It looked as if ten thousand flashes of lightning were darting at the same time from every quarter of the sky.

I was curious to know how this prince, to whose dominions there is no access from any other country, came to think of armies, or to teach his people the practice of military discipline. But I was soon informed, both by conversation and reading their histories. For in the course of many ages they have been troubled with the same disease to which the whole race of mankind is subject: the nobility often contending for power, the people for liberty, and the King for absolute dominion. All which, however happily tempered by the laws of the kingdom, have been sometimes violated by each of the three parties, and have more than once occasioned civil wars, the last whereof was happily put an end to by this prince's grandfather in a general composition;[3] and the militia, then settled with common consent, hath been ever since kept in the strictest duty.

CHAPTER VIII. *The King and Queen make a progress to the frontiers. The Author attends them. The manner in which he leaves the country very particularly related. He returns to England.*

3. A political settlement based upon general agreement of all parties.

I had always a strong impulse that I should some time recover my liberty, though it were impossible to conjecture by what means, or to form any project with the least hope of succeeding. The ship in which I sailed was the first ever known to be driven within sight of that coast; and the King had given strict orders that if at any time another appeared, it should be taken ashore, and with all its crew and passengers brought in a tumbrel[4] to Lorbrulgrud. He was strongly bent to get me a woman of my own size, by whom I might propagate the breed: but I think I should rather have died than undergone the disgrace of leaving a posterity to be kept in cages like tame canary birds, and perhaps in time sold about the kingdom to persons of quality for curiosities. I was indeed treated with much kindness: I was the favorite of a great King and Queen, and the delight of the whole Court, but it was upon such a foot as ill became the dignity of human kind. I could never forget those domestic pledges[5] I had left behind me. I wanted to be among people with whom I could converse upon even terms, and walk about the streets and fields without fear of being trod to death like a frog or a young puppy. But my deliverance came sooner than I expected, and in a manner not very common; the whole story and circumstances of which I shall faithfully relate.

I had now been two years in this country; and about the beginning of the third, Glumdalclitch and I attended the King and Queen in progress to the south coast of the kingdom. I was carried as usual in my traveling box, which, as I have already described, was a very convenient closet of twelve foot wide. I had ordered a hammock to be fixed by silken ropes from the four corners at the top, to break the jolts when a servant carried me before him on horseback, as I sometimes desired; and would often sleep in my hammock while we were upon the road. On the roof of my closet, set not directly over the middle of the hammock, I ordered the joiner to cut out a hole of a foot square to give me air in hot weather as I slept, which hole I shut at pleasure with a board that drew backwards and forwards through a groove.

When we came to our journey's end, the King thought proper to pass a few days at a palace he hath near Flanflasnic, a city within eighteen English miles of the seaside. Glumdalclitch and I were much fatigued; I had gotten a small cold, but the poor girl was so ill as to be confined to her chamber. I longed to see the ocean, which must be the only scene of my escape, if ever it should happen. I pretended to be worse than I really was, and desired leave to take the fresh air of the sea with a page whom I was very fond of, and who had sometimes been trusted with me. I shall never forget with what unwillingness Glumdalclitch consented, nor the strict charge she gave the page to be careful of me, bursting at the

---

4. A farm wagon.   5. His wife and children.

same time into a flood of tears, as if she had some foreboding of
what was to happen. The boy took me out in my box about half
an hour's walk from the palace, towards the rocks on the seashore.
I ordered him to set me down, and lifting up one of my sashes,
cast many a wistful melancholy look towards the sea. I found myself not very well, and told the page that I had a mind to take a
nap in my hammock, which I hoped would do me good. I got in,
and the boy shut the window close down, to keep out the cold. I
soon fell asleep: and all I can conjecture is that while I slept, the
page, thinking no danger could happen, went among the rocks to
look for birds' eggs; having before observed him from my window
searching about, and picking up one or two in the clefts. Be that
as it will, I found myself suddenly awaked with a violent pull upon
the ring which was fastened at the top of my box for the conveniency of carriage. I felt my box raised very high in the air, and then
borne forward with prodigious speed. The first jolt had like to have
shaken me out of my hammock, but afterwards the motion was
easy enough. I called out several times as loud as I could raise my
voice, but all to no purpose. I looked towards my windows, and
could see nothing but the clouds and sky. I heard a noise just over
my head like the clapping of wings, and then began to perceive the
woeful condition I was in; that some eagle had got the ring of my
box in his beak, with an intent to let it fall on a rock, like a tortoise
in a shell, and then pick out my body and devour it. For the sagacity
and smell of this bird enable him to discover his quarry at a great
distance, although better concealed than I could be within a two-
inch board.

In a little time I observed the noise and flutter of wings to increase very fast, and my box was tossed up and down like a sign-
post in a windy day. I heard several bangs or buffets, as I thought,
given to the eagle (for such I am certain it must have been that
held the ring of my box in his beak), and then all on a sudden felt
myself falling perpendicularly down for above a minute, but with
such incredible swiftness that I almost lost my breath. My fall was
topped by a terrible squash, that sounded louder to mine ears than
the cataract of Niagara; after which I was quite in the dark for another minute, and then my box began to rise so high that I could
see light from the tops of my windows. I now perceived that I was
fallen into the sea. My box, by the weight of my body, the goods
that were in, and the broad plates of iron fixed for strength at the
four corners of the top and bottom, floated about five foot deep in
water. I did then and do now suppose that the eagle which flew
away with my box was pursued by two or three others, and forced
to let me drop while he was defending himself against the rest, who
hoped to share in the prey. The plates of iron fastened at the bottom of the box (for those were the strongest) preserved the bal-

ance while it fell, and hindered it from being broken on the surface of the water. Every joint of it was well grooved, and the door did not move on hinges, but up and down like a sash; which kept my closet so tight that very little water came in. I got with much difficulty out of my hammock, having first ventured to draw back the slip-board on the roof already mentioned, contrived on purpose to let in air, for want of which I found myself almost stifled.

How often did I then wish myself with my dear Glumdalclitch, from whom one single hour had so far divided me! And I may say with truth that in the midst of my own misfortune, I could not forbear lamenting my poor nurse, the grief she would suffer for my loss, the displeasure of the Queen, and the ruin of her fortune. Perhaps many travelers have not been under greater difficulties and distress than I was at this juncture, expecting every moment to see my box dashed in pieces, or at least overset by the first violent blast or a rising wave. A breach in one single pane of glass would have been immediate death, nor could anything have preserved the windows but the strong lattice wires placed on the outside against accidents in traveling. I saw the water ooze in at several crannies, although the leaks were not considerable, and I endeavored to stop them as well as I could. I was not able to lift up the roof of my closet, which otherwise I certainly should have done, and sat on the top of it, where I might at least preserve myself from being shut up, as I may call it, in the hold. Or, if I escaped these dangers for a day or two, what could I expect but a miserable death of cold and hunger! I was four hours under these circumstances, expecting and indeed wishing every moment to be my last.

I have already told the reader that there were two strong staples fixed upon that side of my box which had no window and into which the servant, who used to carry me on horseback, would put a leathern belt, and buckle it about his waist. Being in this disconsolate state, I heard, or at least thought I heard, some kind of grating noise on that side of my box where the staples were fixed; and soon after I began to fancy that the box was pulled or towed along in the sea; for I now and then felt a sort of tugging, which made the waves rise near the tops of my windows, leaving me almost in the dark. This gave me some faint hopes of relief, although I was not able to imagine how it could be brought about. I ventured to unscrew one of my chairs, which were always fastened to the floor; and having made a hard shift to screw it down again directly under the slipping-board that I had lately opened, I mounted on the chair, and putting my mouth as near as I could to the hole, I called for help in a loud voice, and in all the languages I understood. I then fastened my handkerchief to a stick I usually carried, and thrusting it up the hole, waved it several times in the air, that if any boat or ship were near, the seamen might conjecture some unhappy mortal to be shut up in the box.

I found no effect from all I could do, but plainly perceived my closet to be moved along; and in the space of an hour or better, that side of the box where the staples were, and had no window, struck against something that was hard. I apprehended it to be a rock, and found myself tossed more than ever. I plainly heard a noise upon the cover of my closet, like that of a cable, and the grating of it as it passed through the ring. I then found myself hoisted up by degrees at least three foot higher than I was before. Whereupon I again thrust up my stick and handkerchief, calling for help till I was almost hoarse. In return to which, I heard a great shout repeated three time, giving me such transports of joy as are not to be conceived but by those who feel them. I now heard a trampling over my head, and somebody calling through the hole with a loud voice in the English tongue: "If there be anybody below, let them speak." I answered, I was an Englishman, drawn by ill fortune into the greatest calamity that ever any creature underwent, and begged, by all that was moving, to be delivered out of the dungeon I was in. The voice replied, I was safe, for my box was fastened to their ship; and the carpenter should immediately come and saw an hole in the cover, large enough to pull me out. I answered, that was needless and would take up too much time, for there was no more to be done but let one of the crew put his finger into the ring, and take the box out of the sea into the ship, and so into the captain's cabin. Some of them, upon hearing me talk so wildly, thought I was mad; others laughed; for indeed it never came into my head that I was now got among people of my own stature and strength. The carpenter came, and in a few minutes sawed a passage about four foot square; then let down a small ladder, upon which I mounted, and from thence was taken into the ship in a very weak condition.

The sailors were all in amazement, and asked me a thousand questions, which I had no inclination to answer. I was equally confounded at the sight of so many pygmies, for such I took them to be, after having so long accustomed my eyes to the monstrous objects I had left. But the Captain, Mr. Thomas Wilcocks, an honest, worthy Shropshire man, observing I was ready to faint, took me into his cabin, gave me a cordial to comfort me, and made me turn in upon his own bed, advising me to take a little rest, of which I had great need. Before I went to sleep I gave him to understand that I had some valuable furniture in my box, too good to be lost, a fine hammock, an handsome field bed, two chairs, a table, and a cabinet; that my closet was hung on all sides, or rather quilted with silk and cotton; that if he would let one of the crew bring my closet into his cabin, I would open it before him and show him my goods. The Captain, hearing me utter these absurdities, concluded I was

raving; however (I suppose to pacify me), he promised to give order as I desired, and going upon deck, sent some of his men down
into my closet, from whence (as I afterwards found) they drew
up all my goods and stripped off the quilting; but the chairs, cabinet, and bedstead, being screwed to the floor, were much damaged
by the ignorance of the seamen, who tore them up by force. Then
they knocked off some of the boards for the use of the ship; and
when they had got all they had a mind for, let the hulk drop into
the sea, which, by reason of many breaches made in the bottom
and sides, sunk to rights.[6] And indeed I was glad not to have been
a spectator of the havoc they made, because I am confident it would
have sensibly touched me, by bringing former passages into my
mind, which I had rather forget.

I slept some hours, but perpetually disturbed with dreams of the
place I had left, and the dangers I had escaped. However, upon
waking, I found myself much recovered. It was now about eight
o'clock at night, and the Captain ordered supper immediately,
thinking I had already fasted too long. He entertained me with
great kindness, observing me not to look wildly, or talk inconsist-
ently; and when we were left alone, desired I would give him a
relation of my travels, and by what accident I came to be set adrift
in that monstrous wooden chest. He said that about twelve o'clock
at noon, as he was looking through his glass, he spied it at a distance, and thought it was a sail, which he had a mind to make,[7]
being not much out of his course, in hopes of buying some biscuit,
his own beginning to fall short. That, upon coming nearer, and
finding his error, he sent out his longboat to discover what I was;
that his men came back in a fright, swearing they had seen a swimming house. That he laughed at their folly, and went himself in the
boat, ordering his men to take a strong cable along with them. That
the weather being calm, he rowed round me several times, observed
my windows, and the wire lattices that defended them. That he
discovered two staples upon one side, which was all of boards, without any passage for light. He then commanded his men to row up
to that side, and fastening a cable to one of the staples, ordered
his men to tow my chest (as he called it) towards the ship. When
it was there, he gave directions to fasten another cable to the ring
fixed in the cover, and to raise up my chest with pulleys, which all
the sailors were not able to do above two or three foot. He said
they saw my stick and handkerchief thrust out of the hole, and
concluded that some unhappy man must be shut up in the cavity.
I asked whether he or the crew had seen any prodigious birds in
the air about the time he first discovered me. To which he answered
that, discoursing this matter with the sailors while I was asleep,
one of them said he had observed three eagles flying towards the

6. **At once**; altogether.   7. Overtake.

north, but remarked nothing of their being larger than the usual size (which I suppose must be imputed to the great height they were at), and he could not guess the reason of my question. I then asked the Captain how far he reckoned we might be from land; he said, by the best computation he could make, we were at least an hundred leagues. I assured him that he must be mistaken by almost half; for I had not left the country from whence I came above two hours before I dropped into the sea. Whereupon he began again to think that my brain was disturbed, of which he gave me a hint, and advised me to go to bed in a cabin he had provided. I assured him I was well refreshed with his good entertainment and company, and as much in my senses as ever I was in my life. He then grew serious and desired to ask me freely whether I were not troubled in mind by the consciousness of some enormous crime, for which I was punished at the command of some prince, by exposing me in that chest, as great criminals in other countries have been forced to sea in a leaky vessel without provisions; for although he should be sorry to have taken so ill[8] a man into his ship, yet he would engage his word to set me safe on shore in the first port where we arrived. He added that his suspicions were much increased by some very absurd speeches I had delivered at first to the sailors, and afterwards to himself, in relation to my closet or chest, as well as by my odd looks and behavior while I was at supper.

I begged his patience to hear me tell my story, which I faithfully did from the last time I left England to the moment he first discovered me. And as truth always forceth its way into rational minds, so this honest, worthy gentleman, who had some tincture of learning, and very good sense, was immediately convinced of my candor and veracity. But further to confirm all I had said, I entreated him to give order that my cabinet should be brought, of which I kept the key in my pocket (for he had already informed me how the seamen disposed of my closet). I opened it in his presence and showed him the small collection of rarities I made in the country from whence I had been so strangely delivered. There was the comb I had contrived out of the stumps of the King's beard, and another of the same materials, but fixed into a paring of her Majesty's thumbnail, which served for the back. There was a collection of needles and pins from a foot to half a yard long; four wasp-stings, like joiners' tacks; some combings of the Queen's hair; a gold ring which one day she made me a present of in a most obliging manner, taking it from her little finger, and throwing it over my head like a collar. I desired the Captain would please to accept this ring in return for his civilities, which he absolutely refused. I showed him a corn that I had cut off with my own hand from a Maid of Honor's toe; it was about the bigness of a Kentish pippin,[9] and grown so

8. Evil.   9. Apple.

hard that, when I returned to England, I got it hollowed into a cup and set in silver. Lastly, I desired him to see the breeches I had then on, which were made of a mouse's skin.

I could force nothing on him. but a footman's tooth, which I observed him to examine with great curiosity, and found he had a fancy for it. He received it with abundance of thanks, more than such a trifle could deserve. It was drawn by an unskillful surgeon in a mistake from one of Glumdalclitch's men, who was afflicted with the toothache; but it was as sound as any in his head. I got it cleaned, and put it into my cabinet. It was about a foot long, and four inches in diameter.

The Captain was very well satisfied with this plain relation I had given him, and said he hoped when we returned to England I would oblige the world by putting it in paper and making it public. My answer was that I thought we were already overstocked with books of travels; that nothing could now pass which was not extraordinary; wherein I doubted some authors less consulted truth than their own vanity or interest, or the diversion of ignorant readers. That my story could contain little besides common events, without those ornamental descriptions of strange plants, trees, birds, and other animals, or the barbarous customs and idolatry of savage people, with which most writers abound. However, I thanked him for his good opinion, and promised to take the matter into my thoughts.

He said he wondered at one thing very much, which was to hear me speak so loud, asking me whether the King or Queen of that country were thick of hearing. I told him it was what I had been used to for above two years past, and that I admired[1] as much at the voices of him and his men, who seemed to me only to whisper, and yet I could hear them well enough. But, when I spoke in that country, it was like a man talking in the street to another looking out from the top of a steeple, unless when I was placed on a table, or held in any person's hand. I told him I had likewise observed another thing: that when I first got into the ship, and the sailors stood all about me, I thought they were the most little contemptible creatures I had ever beheld. For indeed while I was in that prince's country, I could never endure to look in a glass after mine eyes had been accustomed to such prodigious objects, because the comparison gave me so despicable a conceit[2] of myself. The Captain said that while we were at supper he observed me to look at everything with a sort of wonder, and that I often seemed hardly able to contain my laughter; which he knew not well how to take, but imputed it to some disorder in my brain. I answered, it was very true; and I wondered how I could forbear, when I saw his dishes of the size of a silver threepence, a leg of pork hardly a

1. Wondered at.   2. Notion.

mouthful, a cup not so big as a nutshell; and so I went on, describing the rest of his household stuff and provisions after the same manner. For, although the Queen had ordered a little equipage[3] of all things necessary for me while I was in her service, yet my ideas were wholly taken up with what I saw on every side of me, and I winked at my own littleness, as people do at their own faults. The Captain understood my raillery very well, and merrily replied with the old English proverb, that he doubted[4] mine eyes were bigger than my belly, for he did not observe my stomach so good, although I had fasted all day; and continuing in his mirth, protested he would have gladly given an hundred pounds to have seen my closet in the eagle's bill, and afterwards in its fall from so great an height into the sea; which would certainly have been a most astonishing object, worthy to have the description of it transmitted to future ages: and the comparison of Phaeton[5] was so obvious, that he could not forbear applying it, although I did not much admire the conceit.

The Captain having been at Tonquin,[6] was in his return to England driven northeastward to the latitude of 44 degrees, and of longitude 143. But meeting a trade wind two days after I came on board him, we sailed southward a long time, and coasting New Holland[7] kept our course west-southwest, and then south-southwest till we doubled the Cape of Good Hope. Our voyage was very prosperous, but I shall not trouble the reader with a journal of it. The Captain called in at one or two ports, and sent in his longboat for provisions and fresh water; but I never went out of the ship till we came into the Downs,[8] which was on the third day of June, 1706, about nine months after my escape. I offered to leave my goods in security for payment of my freight; but the Captain protested he would not receive one farthing. We took kind leave of each other, and I made him promise he would come to see me at my house in Redriff.[9] I hired a horse and guide for five shillings, which I borrowed of the Captain.

As I was on the road, observing the littleness of the houses, the trees, the cattle, and the people, I began to think myself in Lilliput. I was afraid of trampling on every traveler I met, and often called aloud to have them stand out of the way, so that I had like to have gotten one or two broken heads for my impertinence.

When I came to my own house, for which I was forced to inquire, one of the servants opening the door, I bent down to go in

---

3. Furnishings.
4. Feared.
5. The son of Apollo, whose unsuccessful attempt to drive the chariot of the sun god resulted in his death, when he was hurled by Zeus from the sky and fell into the river Eridanus, where he drowned.

6. Tonkin, in Indo-China.
7. Australia.
8. The sheltered anchorage between Goodwin Sands and the coast of Kent, near Deal.
9. Rotherhithe, on the south bank of the Thames, slightly below the City.

(like a goose under a gate) for fear of striking my head. My wife ran out to embrace me, but I stooped lower than her knees, thinking she could otherwise never be able to reach my mouth. My daughter kneeled to ask my blessing, but I could not see her till she arose, having been so long used to stand with my head and eyes erect to above sixty foot; and then I went to take her up with one hand by the waist. I looked down upon the servants and one or two friends who were in the house, as if they had been pygmies and I a giant. I told my wife she had been too thrifty; for I found she had starved herself and her daughter to nothing. In short, I behaved myself so unaccountably that they were all of the Captain's opinion when he first saw me, and concluded I had lost my wits. This I mention as an instance of the great power of habit and prejudice.

In a little time I and my family and friends came to a right understanding; but my wife protested I should never go to sea any more, although my evil destiny so ordered that she had not power to hinder me; as the reader may know hereafter. In the meantime I here conclude the second part of my unfortunate voyages.

                                                                1726, 1735

Part IV. A Voyage to the Country of the Houyhnhnms [1]

CHAPTER I. *The Author sets out as Captain of a ship. His men conspire against him, confine him a long time to his cabin, set him on shore in an unknown land. He travels up into the country. The Yahoos, a strange sort of animal, described. The Author meets two Houyhnhnms.*

I continued at home with my wife and children about five months in a very happy condition, if I could have learned the lesson of knowing when I was well. I left my poor wife big with child, and accepted an advantageous offer made me to be Captain of the *Adventure*, a stout merchantman of 350 tons; for I understood navigation well, and being grown weary of a surgeon's employment at sea, which however I could exercise upon occasion, I took a skillful young man of that calling, one Robert Purefoy, into my ship. We set sail from Portsmouth upon the 7th day of September, 1710; on the 14th we met with Captain Pocock of Bristol, at Tenariff,[2] who was going to the Bay of Campeachy [3] to cut logwood. On the 16th he was parted from us by a storm; I heard since my return that his ship foundered and none escaped, but one cabin boy. He was an honest man and a good sailor, but a little too positive in his own opinions, which was the cause of his destruction,

---

1. Pronounced Hwin-ims. The word suggests the neigh characteristic of a horse.

2. Teneriffe, one of the Canary Islands.
3. In the Gulf of Mexico.

as it hath been of several others. For if he had followed my advice, he might at this time have been safe at home with his family as well as myself.

I had several men died in my ship of calentures,[4] so that I was forced to get recruits out of Barbadoes and the Leeward Islands, where I touched by the direction of the merchants who employed me; which I had soon too much cause to repent, for I found afterwards that most of them had been buccaneers. I had fifty hands on board; and my orders were that I should trade with the Indians in the South Sea, and make what discoveries I could. These rogues whom I had picked up debauched my other men, and they all formed a conspiracy to seize the ship and secure me; which they did one morning, rushing into my cabin, and binding me hand and foot, threatening to throw me overboard, if I offered to stir. I told them I was their prisoner, and would submit. This they made me swear to do, and then unbound me, only fastening one of my legs with a chain near my bed, and placed a sentry at my door with his piece charged, who was commanded to shoot me dead if I attempted my liberty. They sent me down victuals and drink, and took the government of the ship to themselves. Their design was to turn pirates and plunder the Spaniards, which they could not do, till they got more men. But first they resolved to sell the goods in the ship, and then go to Madagascar for recruits, several among them having died since my confinement. They sailed many weeks, and traded with the Indians; but I knew not what course they took, being kept close prisoner in my cabin, and expecting nothing less than to be murdered, as they often threatened me.

Upon the 9th day of May, 1711, one James Welch came down to my cabin; and said he had orders from the Captain to set me ashore. I expostulated with him, but in vain; neither would he so much as tell me who their new Captain was. They forced me into the long-boat, letting me put on my best suit of clothes, which were as good as new, and a small bundle of linen, but no arms except my hanger; and they were so civil as not to search my pockets, into which I conveyed what money I had, with some other little necessaries. They rowed about a league, and then set me down on a strand. I desired them to tell me what country it was; they all swore, they knew no more than myself, but said that the Captain (as they called him) was resolved, after they had sold the lading, to get rid of me in the first place where they discovered land. They pushed off immediately, advising me to make haste, for fear of being overtaken by the tide, and bade me farewell.

In this desolate condition I advanced forward, and soon got upon firm ground, where I sat down on a bank to rest myself, and con-

---

4. "A distemper peculiar to sailors, in hot climates; wherein they imagine the sea to be green fields, and will throw themselves into it, if not restrained" (Johnson's *Dictionary*).

sider what I had best to do. When I was a little refreshed, I went up
into the country, resolving to deliver myself to the first savages I
should meet, and purchase my life from them by some bracelets,
glass rings, and other toys, which sailors usually provide themselves
with in those voyages, and whereof I had some about me. The land
was divided by long rows of trees, not regularly planted, but naturally growing; there was great plenty of grass, and several fields of
oats. I walked very circumspectly for fear of being surprised, or suddenly shot with an arrow from behind, or on either side. I fell into a
beaten road, where I saw many tracks of human feet, and some of
cows, but most of horses. At last I beheld several animals in a field,
and one or two of the same kind sitting in trees. Their shape was
very singular, and deformed, which a little discomposed me, so that
I lay down behind a thicket to observe them better. Some of them
coming forward near the place where I lay, gave me an opportunity
of distinctly marking their form. Their heads and breasts were
covered with a thick hair, some frizzled and others lank; they had
beards like goats, and a long ridge of hair down their backs, and the
fore parts of their legs and feet; but the rest of their bodies were
bare, so that I might see their skins, which were of a brown buff
color. They had no tails, nor any hair at all on their buttocks, except about the anus; which, I presume Nature had placed there to
defend them as they sat on the ground; for this posture they used,
as well as lying down, and often stood on their hind feet. They
climbed high trees, as nimbly as a squirrel, for they had strong extended claws before and behind, terminating in sharp points, and
hooked. They would often spring, and bound, and leap with prodigious agility. The females were not so large as the males; they had
long lank hair on their heads, and only a sort of down on the rest of
their bodies, except about the anus, and pudenda. Their dugs hung
between their forefeet, and often reached almost to the ground as
they walked. The hair of both sexes was of several colors, brown,
red, black, and yellow. Upon the whole, I never beheld in all my
travels so disagreeable an animal, or one against which I naturally
conceived so strong an antipathy. So that thinking I had seen
enough, full of contempt and aversion, I got up and pursued the
beaten road, hoping it might direct me to the cabin of some
Indian: I had not gone far when I met one of these creatures full in
my way, and coming up directly to me. The ugly monster, when he
saw me, distorted several ways every feature of his visage, and stared
as at an object he had never seen before; then approaching nearer,
lifted up his forepaw, whether out of curiosity or mischief, I could
not tell; but I drew my hanger, and gave him a good blow with the
flat side of it; for I durst not strike him with the edge, fearing the
inhabitants might be provoked against me, if they should come to
know that I had killed or maimed any of their cattle. When the
beast felt the smart, he drew back, and roared so loud, that a herd of

at least forty came flocking about me from the next field, howling and making odious faces; but I ran to the body of a tree, and leaning my back against it, kept them off, by waving my hanger. Several of this cursed brood getting hold of the branches behind, leaped up into the tree, from whence they began to discharge their excrements on my head; however, I escaped pretty well, by sticking close to the stem of the tree, but was almost stifled with the filth, which fell about me on every side.

In the midst of this distress, I observed them all to run away on a sudden as fast as they could; at which I ventured to leave the tree, and pursue the road, wondering what it was that could put them into this fright. But looking on my left hand, I saw a horse walking softly in the field; which my persecutors having sooner discovered, was the cause of their flight. The horse started a little when he came near me, but soon recovering himself, looked full in my face with manifest tokens of wonder; he viewed my hands and feet, walking round me several times. I would have pursued my journey, but he placed himself directly in the way, yet looking with a very mild aspect, never offering the least violence. We stood gazing at each other for some time; at last I took the boldness, to reach my hand towards his neck, with a design to stroke it; using the common style and whistle of jockies when they are going to handle a strange horse. But, this animal seeming to receive my civilities with disdain, shook his head, and bent his brows, softly raising up his left forefoot to remove my hand. Then he neighed three or four times, but in so different a cadence, that I almost began to think he was speaking to himself in some language of his own.

While he and I were thus employed, another horse came up; who applying himself to the first in a very formal manner, they gently struck each others right hoof before, neighing several times by turns, and varying the sound, which seemed to be almost articulate. They went some paces off, as if it were to confer together, walking side by side, backward and forward, like persons deliberating upon some affair of weight; but often turning their eyes towards me, as it were to watch that I might not escape. I was amazed to see such actions and behavior in brute beasts; and concluded with myself that if the inhabitants of this country were endued with a proportionable degree of reason, they must needs be the wisest people upon earth. This thought gave me so much comfort, that I resolved to go forward until I could discover some house or village, or meet with any of the natives, leaving the two horses to discourse together as they pleased. But the first, who was a dapple grey, observing me to steal off, neighed after me in so expressive a tone that I fancied myself to understand what he meant; whereupon I turned back, and came near him, to expect his farther commands; but concealing my fear as much as I could; for I began to be in some pain, how this adventure might terminate; and the reader will easily believe I did not much like my present situation.

The two horses came up close to me, looking with great earnestness upon my face and hands. The grey steed rubbed my hat all round with his right fore hoof, and discomposed it so much that I was forced to adjust it better, by taking it off, and settling it again; whereat both he and his companion (who was a brown bay) appeared to be much surprised; the latter felt the lappet of my coat, and finding it to hang loose about me, they both looked with new signs of wonder. He stroked my right hand, seeming to admire the softness, and color; but he squeezed it so hard between his hoof and his pastern, that I was forced to roar; after which they both touched me with all possible tenderness. They were under great perplexity about my shoes and stockings, which they felt very often, neighing to each other, and using various gestures, not unlike those of a philosopher, when he would attempt to solve some new and difficult phenomenon.

Upon the whole, the behavior of these animals was so orderly and rational, so acute and judicious, that I at last concluded, they must needs be magicians, who had thus metamorphosed themselves upon some design; and seeing a stranger in the way, were resolved to divert themselves with him; or perhaps were really amazed at the sight of a man so very different in habit, feature, and complexion from those who might probably live in so remote a climate. Upon the strength of this reasoning, I ventured to address them in the following manner: "Gentlemen, if you be conjurers, as I have good cause to believe, you can understand any language; therefore I make bold to let your worships know that I am a poor distressed Englishman, driven by his misfortunes upon your coast; and I entreat one of you, to let me ride upon his back, as if he were a real horse, to some house or village, where I can be relieved. In return of which favor, I will make you a present of this knife and bracelet" (taking them out of my pocket). The two creatures stood silent while I spoke, seeming to listen with great attention; and when I had ended, they neighed frequently towards each other, as if they were engaged in serious conversation. I plainly observed, that their language expressed the passions very well, and the words might with little pains be resolved into an alphabet more easily than the Chinese.

I could frequently distinguish the word *Yahoo*,[5] which was repeated by each of them several times; and although it were impossible for me to conjecture what it meant, yet while the two horses were busy in conversation, I endeavored to practice this word upon my tongue; and as soon as they were silent, I boldly pronounced "Yahoo" in a loud voice, imitating, at the same time, as near as I could, the neighing of a horse; at which they were both visibly sur-

5. Morley suggested that *Yahoo* was compounded from two expressions of dis- gust, *yah* and *ugh* (or *hoo*) common in the 18th century [Case's note].

prised, and the grey repeated the same word twice, as if he meant to teach me the right accent, wherein I spoke after him as well as I could, and found myself perceivably to improve every time, although very far from any degree of perfection. Then the bay tried me with a second word, much harder to be pronounced; but reducing it to the English orthography, may be spelt thus, *Houyhnhnm.* I did not succeed in this so well as the former, but after two or three farther trials, I had better fortune; and they both appeared amazed at my capacity.

After some farther discourse, which I then conjectured might relate to me, the two friends took their leaves, with the same compliment of striking each other's hoof; and the grey made me signs that I should walk before him; wherein I thought it prudent to comply, till I could find a better director. When I offered to slacken my pace, he would cry, "Hhuun, Hhuun"; I guessed his meaning, and gave him to understand, as well as I could that I was weary, and not able to walk faster; upon which, he would stand a while to let me rest.

CHAPTER II. *The Author conducted by a Houyhnhnm to his house. The house described. The Author's reception. The food of the Houyhnhnms. The Author in distress for want of meat is at last relieved. His manner of feeding in that country.*

Having traveled about three miles, we came to a long kind of building, made of timber, stuck in the ground, and wattled across; the roof was low, and covered with straw. I now began to be a little comforted, and took out some toys, which travelers usually carry for presents to the savage Indians of America and other parts, in hopes the people of the house would be thereby encouraged to receive me kindly. The horse made me a sign to go in first; it was a large room with a smooth clay floor, and a rack and manger extending the whole length on one side. There were three nags, and two mares, not eating, but some of them sitting down upon their hams, which I very much wondered at; but wondered more to see the rest employed in domestic business; the last seemed but ordinary cattle; however this confirmed my first opinion, that a people who could so far civilize brute animals must needs excel in wisdom all the nations of the world. The grey came in just after, and thereby prevented any ill treatment, which the others might have given me. He neighed to them several times in a style of authority, and received answers.

Beyond this room there were three others, reaching the length of the house, to which you passed through three doors, opposite to each other, in the manner of a vista; we went through the second room towards the third; here the grey walked in first, beckoning me to attend; [6] I waited in the second room, and got ready my presents,

6. To wait.

for the master and mistress of the house; they were two knives, three bracelets of false pearl, a small looking glass and a bead necklace. The horse neighed three or four times, and I waited to hear some answers in a human voice, but I heard no other returns than in the same dialect, only one or two a little shriller than his. I began to think that this house must belong to some person of great note among them, because there appeared so much ceremony before I could gain admittance. But, that a man of quality should be served all by horses, was beyond my comprehension. I feared my brain was disturbed by my sufferings and misfortunes; I roused myself, and looked about me in the room where I was left alone; this was furnished as the first, only after a more elegant manner. I rubbed my eyes often, but the same objects still occurred. I pinched my arms and sides, to awake myself, hoping I might be in a dream. I then absolutely concluded that all these appearances could be nothing else but necromancy and magic. But I had no time to pursue these reflections; for the grey horse came to the door, and made me a sign to follow him into the third room; where I saw a very comely mare, together with a colt and foal, sitting on their haunches, upon mats of straw, not unartfully made, and perfectly neat and clean.

The mare soon after my entrance, rose from her mat, and coming up close, after having nicely observed my hands and face, gave me a most contemptuous look; then turning to the horse, I heard the word Yahoo often repeated betwixt them; the meaning of which word I could not then comprehend, although it were the first I had learned to pronounce; but I was soon better informed, to my everlasting mortification: for the horse beckoning to me with his head, and repeating the word, "Hhuun, Hhuun," as he did upon the road, which I understood was to attend him, led me out into a kind of court, where was another building at some distance from the house. Here we entered, and I saw three of those detestable creatures, which I first met after my landing, feeding upon roots, and the flesh of some animals, which I afterwards found to be that of asses and dogs, and now and then a cow dead by accident or disease. They were all tied by the neck with strong withes, fastened to a beam; they held their food between the claws of their forefeet, and tore it with their teeth.

The master horse ordered a sorrel nag, one of his servants, to untie the largest of these animals, and take him into a yard. The beast and I were brought close together; and our countenances diligently compared, both by master and servant, who thereupon repeated several times the word "Yahoo." My horror and astonishment are not to be described, when I observed, in this abominable animal, a perfect human figure; the face of it indeed was flat and broad, the nose depressed, the lips large, and the mouth wide; but these differences are common to all savage nations, where the lineaments of the countenance are distorted by the natives suffering their infants to lie groveling on the earth, or by carrying them on their backs, nuzzling with their face against the mother's shoulders. The fore-feet of the Yahoo differed from my hands in nothing else but the length of the nails, the coarseness and brownness of the palms, and the hairiness on the backs. There was the same resemblance be-tween our feet, with the same differences, which I knew very well, although the horses did not, because of my shoes and stockings; the same in every part of our bodies, except as to hairiness and color, which I have already described.

The great difficulty that seemed to stick with the two horses was to see the rest of my body so very different from that of a Yahoo, for which I was obliged to my clothes, whereof they had no conception; the sorrel nag offered me a root, which he held (after their manner, as we shall describe in its proper place) between his hoof and pastern; I took it in my hand, and having smelled it, returned it to him again as civilly as I could. He brought out of the Yahoo's kennel a piece of ass's flesh, but it smelled so offensively that I turned from it with loathing; he then threw it to the Yahoo, by whom it was greedily devoured. He afterwards showed me a wisp of hay, and a fetlock full of oats; but I shook my head, to signify that neither of these were food for me. And indeed, I now apprehended that I must absolutely starve, if I did not get to some of my own species; for as to those filthy Yahoos, although there were few greater lovers of mankind, at that time, than myself, yet I confess I never saw any sensitive being so detestable on all accounts; and the more I came near them, the more hateful they grew, while I stayed in that coun-try. This the master horse observed by my behavior, and therefore sent the Yahoo back to his kennel. He then put his forehoof to his mouth, at which I was much surprised, although he did it with ease, and with a motion that appeared perfectly natural; and made other signs to know what I would eat; but I could not return him such an answer as he was able to apprehend; and if he had under-stood me, I did not see how it was possible to contrive any way for finding myself nourishment. While we were thus engaged, I ob-served a cow passing by; whereupon I pointed to her, and expressed a desire to let me go and milk her. This had its effect; for he led me back into the house, and ordered a mare-servant to open a room, where a good store of milk lay in earthen and wooden vessels, after a very orderly and cleanly manner. She gave me a large bowl full, of which I drank very heartily, and found myself well refreshed.

About noon I saw coming towards the house a kind of vehicle, drawn like a sledge by four Yahoos. There was in it an old steed, who seemed to be of quality; he alighted with his hind feet for-ward, having by accident got a hurt in his left forefoot. He came to dine with our horse, who received him with great civility. They dined in the best room, and had oats boiled in milk for the second course, which the old horse eat warm, but the rest cold. Their mangers were placed circular in the middle of the room, and divided into several partitions, round which they sat on their haunches upon bosses of straw. In the middle was a large rack with angles answering to every partition of the manger. So that each horse and mare eat their own hay, and their own mash of oats and milk, with much decency and regularity. The behavior of the young colt and foal appeared very modest; and that of the master and mistress extremely cheerful and complaisant to their guest. The grey ordered me to stand by him; and much discourse passed between him and his friend concerning me, as I found by the stranger's often looking on me, and the frequent repetition of the word Yahoo.

I happened to wear my gloves; which the master grey observing, seemed perplexed; discovering signs of wonder what I had done to my forefeet; he put his hoof three or four times to them, as if he would signify, that I should reduce them to their former shape, which I presently did, pulling off both my gloves, and putting them into my pocket. This occasioned farther talk, and I saw the company was pleased with my behavior, whereof I soon found the good effects. I was ordered to speak the few words I understood; and while they were at dinner, the master taught me the names for oats, milk, fire, water, and some others which I could readily pronounce after him, having from my youth a great facility in learning languages.

When dinner was done, the master horse took me aside, and by signs and words made me understand the concern he was in that I had nothing to eat. Oats in their tongue are called *hlunnh*. This word I pronounced two or three times; for although I had refused them at first, yet upon second thoughts, I considered that I could contrive to make a kind of bread, which might be sufficient with milk to keep me alive, till I could make my escape to some other country, and to creatures of my own species. The horse immediately ordered a white mare-servant of his family to bring me a good quantity of oats in a sort of wooden tray. These I heated before the fire as well as I could, and rubbed them till the husks came off, which I made a shift to winnow from the grain; I ground and beat them between two stones, then took water, and made them into a paste or cake, which I toasted at the fire, and eat warm with milk. It was at first a very insipid diet, although common enough in many parts of Europe, but grew tolerable by time; and having been often reduced to hard fare in my life, this was not the first experiment I had made how easily nature is satisfied. And I cannot but observe that I never had one hour's sickness, while I staid in this island. It is true, I sometimes made a shift to catch a rabbit, or bird, by springes [7] made of Yahoos' hairs; and I often gathered wholesome herbs, which I boiled, or eat as salads with my bread; and now and then, for a rarity, I made a little butter, and drank the whey. I was

7. Snares.

at first at a great loss for salt; but custom soon reconciled the want of it; and I am confident that the frequent use of salt among us is an effect of luxury, and was first introduced only as a provocative to drink; except where it is necessary for preserving of flesh in long voyages, or in places remote from great markets. For we observe no animal to be fond of it but man; [8] and as to myself, when I left this country, it was a great while before I could endure the taste of it in anything that I eat.

This is enough to say upon the subject of my diet, wherewith other travelers fill their books, as if the readers were personally concerned whether we fare well or ill. However, it was necessary to mention this matter, lest the world should think it impossible that I could find sustenance for three years in such a country, and among such inhabitants.

When it grew towards evening, the master horse ordered a place for me to lodge in; it was but six yards from the house, and separated from the stable of the Yahoos. Here I got some straw, and covering myself with my own clothes, slept very sound. But I was in a short time better accommodated, as the reader shall know hereafter, when I come to treat more particularly about my way of living.

CHAPTER III. *The Author studious to learn the language, the Houyhnhnm his master assists in teaching him. The language described. Several Houyhnhnms of quality come out of curiosity to see the Author. He gives his master a short account of his voyage.*

My principal endeavor was to learn the language, which my master (for so I shall henceforth call him) and his children, and every servant of his house were desirous to teach me. For they looked upon it as a prodigy, that a brute animal should discover such marks of a rational creature. I pointed to everything, and enquired the name of it, which I wrote down in my journal book when I was alone, and corrected my bad accent, by desiring those of the family to pronounce it often. In this employment, a sorrel nag, one of the under servants, was very ready to assist me.

In speaking, they pronounce through the nose and throat, and their language approaches nearest to the High Dutch or German, of any I know in Europe; but is much more graceful and significant. The Emperor Charles V made almost the same observation, when he said, that if he were to speak to his horse, it should be in High Dutch.[9]

The curiosity and impatience of my master were so great, that he spent many hours of his leisure to instruct me. He was convinced (as he afterwards told me) that I must be a Yahoo, but my

---

8. Gulliver is, of course, in error. Many animals require salt.
9. The Emperor is supposed to have said that he would speak to his God in Spanish, to his mistress in Italian, and to his horse in German.

teachableness, civility, and cleanliness astonished him; which were qualities altogether so opposite to those animals. He was most perplexed about my clothes, reasoning sometimes with himself whether they were a part of my body; for I never pulled them off till the family were asleep, and got them on before they waked in the morning. My master was eager to learn from whence I came; how I acquired those appearances of reason, which I discovered in all my actions; and to know my story from my own mouth, which he hoped he should soon do by the great proficiency I made in learning and pronouncing their words and sentences. To help my memory, I formed all I learned into the English alphabet, and writ the words down with the translations. This last, after some time, I ventured to do in my master's presence. It cost me much trouble to explain to him what I was doing; for the inhabitants have not the least idea of books or literature.

In about ten weeks time I was able to understand most of his questions; and in three months could give him some tolerable answers. He was extremely curious to know from what part of the country I came, and how I was taught to imitate a rational creature; because the Yahoos (whom he saw I exactly resembled in my head, hands, and face, that were only visible) with some appearance of cunning, and the strongest disposition to mischief, were observed to be the most unteachable of all brutes. I answered that I came over the sea, from a far place, with many others of my own kind, in a great hollow vessel made of the bodies of trees; that my companions forced me to land on this coast, and then left me to shift for myself. It was with some difficulty, and by the help of many signs, that I brought him to understand me. He replied that I must needs be mistaken, or that I *said the thing which was not*. (For they have no word in their language to express lying or falsehood.) He knew it was impossible that there could be a country beyond the sea, or that a parcel of brutes could move a wooden vessel whither they pleased upon water. He was sure no Houyhnhnm alive could make such a vessel, or would trust Yahoos to manage it.

The word Houyhnhnm, in their tongue, signifies a Horse; and in its etymology, the Perfection of Nature. I told my master that I was at a loss for expression, but would improve as fast as I could; and hoped in a short time I should be able to tell him wonders; he was pleased to direct his own mare, his colt, and foal, and the servants of the family to take all opportunities of instructing me; and every day for two or three hours, he was at the same pains himself; several horses and mares of quality in the neighborhood came often to our house, upon the report spread of a wonderful Yahoo, that could speak like a Houyhnhnm, and seemed in his words and actions to discover some glimmerings of reason. These delighted to converse with me; they put many questions, and received such answers as I was able to return. By all which advantages,

I made so great a progress, that in five months from my arrival, I understood whatever was spoke, and could express myself tolerably well.

The Houyhnhnms who came to visit my master, out of a design of seeing and talking with me, could hardly believe me to be a right Yahoo, because my body had a different covering from others of my kind. They were astonished to observe me without the usual hair or skin, except on my head, face, and hands; but I discovered that secret to my master, upon an accident, which happened about a fortnight before.

I have already told the reader, that every night when the family were gone to bed, it was my custom to strip and cover myself with my clothes; it happened one morning early, that my master sent for me, by the sorrel nag, who was his valet; when he came, I was fast asleep, my clothes fallen off on one side, and my shirt above my waist. I awaked at the noise he made, and observed him to deliver his message in some disorder; after which he went to my master, and in a great fright gave him a very confused account of what he had seen; this I presently discovered; for going as soon as I was dressed, to pay my attendance upon his honor, he asked me the meaning of what his servant had reported; that I was not the same thing when I slept as I appeared to be at other times; that his valet assured him, some part of me was white, some yellow, at least not so white, and some brown.

I had hitherto concealed the secret of my dress, in order to distinguish myself as much as possible, from that cursed race of Yahoos; but now I found it in vain to do so any longer. Besides, I considered that my clothes and shoes would soon wear out, which already were in a declining condition, and must be supplied by some contrivance from the hides of Yahoos, or other brutes; whereby the whole secret would be known. I therefore told my master, that in the country from whence I came, those of my kind always covered their bodies with the hairs of certain animals prepared by art, as well for decency, as to avoid inclemencies of air both hot and cold; of which, as to my own person I would give him immediate conviction, if he pleased to command me; only desiring his excuse, if I did not expose those parts that nature taught us to conceal. He said, my discourse was all very strange, but especially the last part; for he could not understand why Nature should teach us to conceal what Nature had given. That neither himself nor family were ashamed of any parts of their bodies; but however I might do as I pleased. Whereupon, I first unbuttoned my coat, and pulled it off. I did the same with my waistcoat; I drew off my shoes, stockings, and breeches. I let my shirt down to my waist, and drew up the bottom, fastening it like a girdle about my middle to hide my nakedness.

My master observed the whole performance with great signs of curiosity and admiration. He took up all my clothes in his pastern, one piece after another, and examined them diligently; he then stroked my body very gently, and looked round me several times; after which he said, it was plain I must be a perfect Yahoo; but that I differed very much from the rest of my species, in the whiteness and smoothness of my skin, my want of hair in several parts of my body, the shape and shortness of my claws behind and before, and my affectation of walking continually on my two hinder feet. He desired to see no more; and gave me leave to put on my clothes again, for I was shuddering with cold.

I expressed my uneasiness at his giving me so often the appellation of Yahoo, an odious animal, for which I had so utter an hatred and contempt. I begged he would forbear applying that word to me, and take the same order in his family, and among his friends whom he suffered to see me. I requested likewise, that the secret of my having a false covering to my body might be known to none but himself, at least as long as my present clothing should last; for as to what the sorrel nag his valet had observed, his honor might command him to conceal it.

All this my master very graciously consented to; and thus the secret was kept till my clothes began to wear out, which I was forced to supply by several contrivances, that shall hereafter be mentioned. In the meantime, he desired I would go on with my utmost diligence to learn their language, because he was more astonished at my capacity for speech and reason, than at the figure of my body, whether it were covered or no; adding that he waited with some impatience to hear the wonders which I promised to tell him.

From thenceforward he doubled the pains he had been at to instruct me; he brought me into all company, and made them treat me with civility, because, as he told them privately, this would put me into good humor, and make me more diverting.

Every day when I waited on him, beside the trouble he was at in teaching, he would ask me several questions concerning myself, which I answered as well as I could; and by those means he had already received some general ideas, although very imperfect. It would be tedious to relate the several steps, by which I advanced to a more regular conversation, but the first account I gave of myself in any order and length was to this purpose:

That, I came from a very far country, as I already had attempted to tell him, with about fifty more of my own species; that we traveled upon the seas, in a great hollow vessel made of wood, and larger than his honor's house. I described the ship to him in the best terms I could; and explained by the help of my handkerchief displayed, how it was driven forward by the wind. That, upon a quarrel among us, I was set on shore on this coast, where I walked forward without knowing whither, till he delivered me from the persecution of those execrable Yahoos. He asked me who made the ship, and how it was possible that the Houyhnhnms of my country would leave it to the management of brutes? My answer was that I durst proceed no farther in my relation, unless he would give me his word and honor that he would not be offended; and then I would tell him the wonders I had so often promised. He agreed; and I went on by assuring him, that the ship was made by creatures like myself, who in all the countries I had traveled, as well as in my own, were the only governing, rational animals; and that upon my arrival hither, I was as much astonished to see the Houyhnhnms act like rational beings, as he or his friends could be in finding some marks of reason in a creature he was pleased to call a Yahoo; to which I owned my resemblance in every part, but could not account for their degenerate and brutal nature. I said farther, that if good fortune ever restored me to my native country, to relate my travels hither, as I resolved to do; everybody would believe that I *said the thing which was not*; that I invented the story out of my own head; and with all possible respect to himself, his family, and friends, and under his promise of not being offended, our countrymen would hardly think it probable, that a Houyhnhnm should be the presiding creature of a nation, and a Yahoo the brute.

CHAPTER IV. *The Houyhnhnms' notion of truth and falsehood. The author's discourse disapproved by his master. The author gives a more particular account of himself, and the accidents of his voyage.*

My master heard me with great appearances of uneasiness in his countenance; because *doubting* or *not believing* are so little known in this country, that the inhabitants cannot tell how to behave themselves under such circumstances. And I remember in frequent discourses with my master concerning the nature of manhood, in other parts of the world, having occasion to talk of *lying* and *false representation*, it was with much difficulty that he comprehended what I meant; although he had otherwise a most acute judgment. For he argued thus: that the use of speech was to make us understand one another, and to receive information of facts; now if anyone *said the thing which was not*, these ends were defeated; because I cannot properly be said to understand him; and I am so far from receiving information, that he leaves me worse than in ignorance; for I am led to believe a thing *black* when it is *white*, and *short* when it is *long*. And these were all the notions he had concerning that faculty of *lying*, so perfectly well understood, and so universally practiced among human creatures.

To return from this digression; when I asserted that the Yahoos were the only governing animals in my country, which my master said was altogether past his conception, he desired to know, whether we had Houyhnhnms among us, and what was their employment; I told him we had great numbers; that in summer they grazed in the fields, and in winter were kept in houses, with hay and oats, where Yahoo servants were employed to rub their skins smooth, comb their manes, pick their feet, serve them with food, and make their beds. "I understand you well," said my master; "it is now very plain from all you have spoken, that whatever share of reason the Yahoos pretend to, the Houyhnhnms are your masters; I heartily wish our Yahoos would be so tractable." I begged his honor would please to excuse me from proceeding any farther, because I was very certain that the account he expected from me would be highly displeasing. But he insisted in commanding me to let him know the best and the worst; I told him he should be obeyed. I owned that the Houyhnhnms among us, whom we called Horses, were the most generous [1] and comely animal we had; that they excelled in strength and swiftness; and when they belonged to persons of quality, employed in traveling, racing, and drawing chariots, they were treated with much kindness and care, till they fell into diseases, or became foundered in the feet; but then they were sold, and used to all kind of drudgery till they died; after which their skins were stripped and sold for what they were worth, and their bodies left to be devoured by dogs and birds of prey. But the common race of horses had not so good fortune, being kept by farmers and carriers, and other mean people, who put them to greater labor, and feed them worse. I described as well as I could, our way of riding; the shape and use of a bridle, a saddle, a spur, and a whip; of harness and wheels. I added, that we fastened plates of a certain hard substance called iron at the bottom of their feet, to preserve their hoofs from being broken by the stony ways on which we often traveled.

My master, after some expressions of great indignation, wondered how we dared to venture upon a Houyhnhnm's back; for he was sure, that the weakest servant in his house would be able to shake off the strongest Yahoo; or by lying down, and rolling upon his back, squeeze the brute to death. I answered that our horses were trained up from three or four years old to the several uses we intended them for; that if any of them proved intolerably vicious, they were employed for carriages; that they were severely beaten while they were young for any mischievous tricks; that the males, designed for the common use of riding or draught, were generally castrated about two years after their birth, to take down their spirits, and make them more tame and gentle; that they were indeed sensible of rewards and punishments; but his honor would please to consider that they had not the least tincture of reason any more than the Yahoos in this country.

It put me to the pains of many circumlocutions to give my master a right idea of what I spoke; for their language doth not abound in variety of words, because their wants and passions are fewer than

1. Noble.

among us. But it is impossible to express his noble resentment at our savage treatment of the Houyhnhnm race; particularly after I had explained the manner and use of castrating horses among us, to hinder them from propagating their kind, and to render them more servile. He said, if it were possible there could be any country where Yahoos alone were endued with reason, they certainly must be the governing animal, because reason will in time always prevail against brutal strength. But, considering the frame of our bodies, and especially of mine, he thought no creature of equal bulk was so ill-contrived for employing that reason in the common offices of life; whereupon he desired to know whether those among whom I lived resembled me or the Yahoos of his country. I assured him that I was as well shaped as most of my age; but the younger and the females were much more soft and tender, and the skins of the latter generally as white as milk. He said I differed indeed from other Yahoos, being much more cleanly, and not altogether so deformed; but in point of real advantage, he thought I differed for the worse. That my nails were of no use either to my fore or hinder feet; as to my forefeet, he could not properly call them by that name, for he never observed me to walk upon them; that they were too soft to bear the ground; that I generally went with them uncovered, neither was the covering I sometimes wore on them of the same shape, or so strong as that on my feet behind. That I could not walk with any security; for if either of my hinder feet slipped, I must inevitably fall. He then began to find fault with other parts of my body; the flatness of my face, the prominence of my nose, my eyes placed directly in front, so that I could not look on either side without turning my head; that I was not able to feed myself without lifting one of my forefeet to my mouth; and therefore nature had placed those joints to answer that necessity. He knew not what could be the use of those several clefts and divisions in my feet behind; that these were too soft to bear the hardness and sharpness of stones without a covering made from the skin of some other brute; that my whole body wanted a fence against heat and cold, which I was forced to put on and off every day with tediousness and trouble. And lastly, that he observed every animal in his country naturally to abhor the Yahoos, whom the weaker avoided, and the stronger drove from them. So that supposing us to have the gift of reason, he could not see how it were possible to cure that natural antipathy which every creature discovered against us; nor consequently, how we could tame and render them serviceable. However, he would (as he said) debate the matter no farther, because he was more desirous to know my own story, the country where I was born, and the several actions and events of my life before I came hither.

I assured him how extremely desirous I was that he should be satisfied in every point; but I doubted much whether it would be possible for me to explain myself on several subjects whereof his honor could have no conception, because I saw nothing in his country to which I could resemble them. That however, I would do my best, and strive to express myself by similitudes, humbly desiring his assistance when I wanted proper words; which he was pleased to promise me.

I said, my birth was of honest parents, in an island called England, which was remote from this country, as many days journey as the strongest of his honor's servants could travel in the annual course of the sun. That I was bred a surgeon, whose trade it is to cure wounds and hurts in the body, got by accident or violence. That my country was governed by a female man, whom we called a queen. That I left it to get riches, whereby I might maintain myself and family when I should return. That in my last voyage, I was Commander of the ship and had about fifty Yahoos under me, many of which died at sea, and I was forced to supply them by others picked out from several nations. That our ship was twice in danger of being sunk; the first time by a great storm, and the second, by striking against a rock. Here my master interposed, by asking me, how I could persuade strangers out of different countries to venture with me, after the losses I had sustained, and the hazards I had run. I said, they were fellows of desperate fortunes, forced to fly from the places of their birth, on account of their poverty or their crimes. Some were undone by lawsuits; others spent all they had in drinking, whoring, and gaming; others fled for treason; many for murder, theft, poisoning, robbery, perjury, forgery, coining false money; for committing rapes or sodomy; for flying from their colors, or deserting to the enemy; and most of them had broken prison. None of these durst return to their native countries for fear of being hanged, or of starving in a jail; and therefore were under a necessity of seeking a livelihood in other places.

During this discourse, my master was pleased often to interrupt me. I had made use of many circumlocutions in describing to him the nature of the several crimes, for which most of our crew had been forced to fly their country. This labor took up several days conversation before he was able to comprehend me. He was wholly at a loss to know what could be the use or necessity of practicing those vices. To clear up which I endeavored to give him some ideas of the desire of power and riches; of the terrible effects of lust, intemperance, malice, and envy. All this I was forced to define and describe by putting of cases, and making suppositions. After which, like one whose imagination was struck with something never seen or heard of before, he would lift up his eyes with amazement and indignation. Power, government, war, law, punishment, and a thousand other things had no terms, wherein that language could express them; which made the difficulty almost insuperable to give my master any conception of what I meant; but being of an excellent understanding, much improved by contemplation and converse, he at last arrived at a competent knowledge of what human nature in our parts of the world is capable to perform; and desired I would give him some particular account of that land, which we call Europe, especially, of my own country.

CHAPTER V. *The Author, at his master's commands, informs him of the state of England. The causes of war among the princes of Europe. The Author begins to explain the English Constitution.*

The reader may please to observe that the following extract of many conversations I had with my master contains a summary of the most material points, which were discoursed at several times for above two years; his honor often desiring fuller satisfaction as I farther improved in the Houyhnhnm tongue. I laid before him, as well as I could, the whole state of Europe; I discoursed of trade and manufactures, of arts and sciences; and the answers I gave to all the questions he made, as they arose upon several subjects, were a fund of conversation not to be exhausted. But I shall here only set down the substance of what passed between us concerning my own country, reducing it into order as well as I can, without any regard to time or other circumstances, while I strictly adhere to truth. My only concern is that I shall hardly be able to do justice to my master's arguments and expressions; which must needs suffer by my want of capacity, as well as by a translation into our barbarous English.

In obedience therefore to his honor's commands, I related to him the Revolution under the Prince of Orange; the long war with France entered into by the said Prince, and renewed by his successor the present queen; wherein the greatest powers of Christendom were engaged, and which still continued. I computed at his request, that about a million of Yahoos might have been killed in the whole progress of it; and perhaps a hundred or more cities taken, and five times as many ships burned or sunk.[2]

He asked me what were the usual causes or motives that made one country to go to war with another. I answered, they were innumerable; but I should only mention a few of the chief. Sometimes the ambition of princes, who never think they have land or people enough to govern; sometimes the corruption of ministers, who engage their master in a war in order to stifle or divert the clamor of the subjects against their evil administration. Difference in opinions hath cost many millions of lives; for instance, whether flesh be bread, or bread be flesh; whether the juice of a certain berry be blood or wine; whether whistling be a vice or a virtue; whether it be better to kiss a post, or throw it into the fire; what is the best color for a coat, whether black, white, red, or grey; and

2. Gulliver relates recent English history: the Glorious Revolution of 1688 and the War of Spanish Succession (1703–13). He greatly exaggerates the casualties in the war.

whether it should be long or short, narrow or wide, dirty or clean;[3] with many more. Neither are any wars so furious and bloody, or of so long continuance, as those occasioned by difference in opinion, especially if it be in things indifferent.[4]

Sometimes the quarrel between two princes is to decide which of them shall dispossess a third of his dominions, where neither of them pretend to any right. Sometimes one prince quarreleth with another, for fear the other should quarrel with him. Sometimes a war is entered upon, because the enemy is too strong, and sometimes because he is too weak. Sometimes our neighbors want the things which we have, or have the things which we want; and we both fight, till they take ours or give us theirs. It is a very justifiable cause of war to invade a country after the people have been wasted by famine, destroyed by pestilence, or embroiled by factions amongst themselves. It is justifiable to enter into a war against our nearest ally, when one of his towns lies convenient for us, or a territory of land, that would render our dominions round and compact. If a prince send forces into a nation, where the people are poor and ignorant, he may lawfully put half of them to death, and make slaves of the rest, in order to civilize and reduce them from their barbarous way of living. It is a very kingly, honorable, and frequent practice, when one prince desires the assistance of another to secure him against an invasion, that the assistant, when he hath driven out the invader, should seize on the dominions himself, and kill, imprison, or banish the prince he came to relieve. Alliance by blood or marriage is a sufficient cause of war between princes; and the nearer the kindred is, the greater is their disposition to quarrel; poor nations are hungry, and rich nations are proud; and pride and hunger will ever be at variance. For these reasons, the trade of a soldier is held the most honorable of all others: because a soldier is a Yahoo hired to kill in cold blood as many of his own species, who have never offended him, as possibly he can.

There is likewise a kind of beggarly princes in Europe, not able to make war by themselves, who hire out their troops to richer nations for so much a day to each man; of which they keep three fourths to themselves, and it is the best part of their maintenance; such are those in many northern parts of Europe.[5]

"What you have told me," said my master, "upon the subject of war, doth indeed discover most admirably the effects of that reason you pretend to; however, it is happy that the shame is greater than the danger; and that Nature hath left you utterly uncapable of doing much mischief; for your mouths lying flat with your faces, you can hardly bite each other to any purpose, unless by

---

3. Gulliver refers to the religious controversies of the Reformation and Counter Reformation: the doctrine of transubstantiation, the use of music in church services, the veneration of the crucifix, and the wearing of priestly vestments.
4. Of little consequence.
5. A satiric glance at George I, who, as Elector of Hanover, had dealt in this trade.

consent. Then, as to the claws upon your feet before and behind, they are so short and tender, that one of our Yahoos would drive a dozen of yours before him. And therefore in recounting the numbers of those who have been killed in battle, I cannot but think that you have *said the thing which is not*."

I could not forbear shaking my head and smiling a little at his ignorance. And, being no stranger to the art of war, I gave him a description of cannons, culverins, muskets, carabines, pistols, bullets, powder, swords, bayonets, battles, sieges, retreats, attacks, undermines, countermines, bombardments, sea fights; ships sunk with a thousand men; twenty thousand killed on each side; dying groans, limbs flying in the air; smoke, noise, confusion, trampling to death under horses' feet; flight, pursuit, victory; fields strewed with carcasses left for food to dogs, and wolves, and birds of prey; plundering, stripping, ravishing, burning, and destroying. And, to set forth the valor of my own dear countrymen, I assured him that I had seen them blow up a hundred enemies at once in a siege, and as many in a ship; and beheld the dead bodies drop down in pieces from the clouds, to the great diversion of all the spectators.

I was going on to more particulars, when my master commanded me silence. He said, whoever understood the nature of Yahoos might easily believe it possible for so vile an animal, to be capable of every action I had named, if their strength and cunning equaled their malice. But, as my discourse had increased his abhorrence of the whole species, so he found it gave him a disturbance in his mind, to which he was wholly a stranger before. He thought his ears being used to such abominable words, might by degrees admit them with less detestation. That, although he hated the Yahoos of this country, yet he no more blamed them for their odious qualities, than he did a *gnnayh* (a bird of prey) for its cruelty, or a sharp stone for cutting his hoof. But, when a creature pretending to reason could be capable of such enormities, he dreaded lest the corruption of that faculty might be worse than brutality itself. He seemed therefore confident, that instead of reason, we were only possessed of some quality fitted to increase our natural vices; as the reflection from a troubled stream returns the image of an ill-shapen body, not only larger, but more distorted.

He added that he had heard too much upon the subject of war, both in this and some former discourses. There was another point which a little perplexed him at present. I had said that some of our crew left their country on account of being ruined by law: that I had already explained the meaning of the word; but he was at a loss how it should come to pass, that the law which was intended for every man's preservation, should be any man's ruin. Therefore he desired to be farther satisfied what I meant by law, and the dispensers thereof, according to the present practice in my own country; because he thought nature and reason were sufficient guides for a reasonable animal, as we pretended to be, in showing us what we ought to do, and what to avoid.

I assured his honor that law was a science wherein I had not much conversed, further than by employing advocates, in vain, upon some injustices that had been done me. However, I would give him all the satisfaction I was able.

I said there was a society of men among us, bred up from their youth in the art of proving by words multiplied for the purpose, that white is black, and black is white, according as they are paid. To this society all the rest of the people are slaves.

"For example. If my neighbor hath a mind to my cow, he hires a lawyer to prove that he ought to have my cow from me. I must then hire another to defend my right; it being against all rules of law that any man should be allowed to speak for himself. Now in this case, I who am the true owner lie under two great disadvantages. First, my lawyer being practiced almost from his cradle in defending falsehood is quite out of his element when he would be an advocate for justice, which as an office unnatural, he always attempts with great awkwardness, if not with ill-will. The second disadvantage is that my lawyer must proceed with great caution, or else he will be reprimanded by the judges, and abhorred by his brethren, as one who would lessen the practice of the law. And therefore I have but two methods to preserve my cow. The first is to gain over my adversary's lawyer with a double fee; who will then betray his client, by insinuating that he hath justice on his side. The second way is for my lawyer to make my cause appear as unjust as he can; by allowing the cow to belong to my adversary; and this if it be skillfully done, will certainly bespeak the favor of the bench.

"Now, your honor is to know that these judges are persons appointed to decide all controversies of property, as well as for the trial of criminals; and picked out from the most dextrous lawyers who are grown old or lazy; and having been biased all their lives against truth and equity, lie under such a fatal necessity of favoring fraud, perjury, and oppression, that I have known some of them to have refused a large bribe from the side where justice lay, rather than injure the faculty,[6] by doing anything unbecoming their nature or their office.

"It is a maxim among these lawyers, that whatever hath been done before may legally be done again; and therefore they take special care to record all the decisions formerly made against common justice and the general reason of mankind. These, under the name of *precedents*, they produce as authorities to justify the most iniquitous opinions; and the judges never fail of directing accordingly.

6. Profession.

"In pleading, they studiously avoid entering into the merits of the cause; but are loud, violent, and tedious in dwelling upon all circumstances which are not to the purpose. For instance, in the case already mentioned, they never desire to know what claim or title my adversary hath to my cow; but whether the said cow were red or black; her horns long or short; whether the field I graze her in be round or square; whether she were milked at home or abroad; what diseases she is subject to, and the like. After which they consult precedents, adjourn the cause, from time to time, and in ten, twenty, or thirty years come to an issue.

"It is likewise to be observed, that this society hath a peculiar cant and jargon of their own, that no other mortal can understand, and wherein all their laws are written, which they take special care to multiply; whereby they have wholly confounded the very essence of truth and falsehood, of right and wrong; so that it will take thirty years to decide whether the field, left me by my ancestors for six generations, belong to me, or to a stranger three hundred miles off.

"In the trial of persons accused for crimes against the state, the method is much more short and commendable: the judge first sends to sound the disposition of those in power; after which he can easily hang or save the criminal, strictly preserving all the forms of law."

Here my master interposing said it was a pity that creatures endowed with such prodigious abilities of mind as these lawyers, by the description I gave of them must certainly be, were not rather encouraged to be instructors of others in wisdom and knowledge. In answer to which, I assured his honor that in all points out of their own trade, they were usually the most ignorant and stupid generation among us, the most despicable in common conversation, avowed enemies to all knowledge and learning; and equally disposed to pervert the general reason of mankind, in every other subject of discourse as in that of their own profession.

CHAPTER VI. *A continuation of the state of England, under Queen Anne. The character of a first minister in the courts of Europe.*

My master was yet wholly at a loss to understand what motives could incite this race of lawyers to perplex, disquiet, and weary themselves by engaging in a confederacy of injustice, merely for the sake of injuring their fellow animals; neither could he comprehend what I meant in saying they did it for hire. Whereupon I was at much pains to describe to him the use of money, the materials it was made of, and the value of the metals; that when a Yahoo had got a great store of his precious substance, he was able to purchase whatever he had a mind to; the finest clothing, the noblest houses, great tracts of land, the most costly meats and drinks; and have his choice of the most beautiful females. Therefore since money alone was able to perform all these feats, our Yahoos thought they could never have enough of it to spend or to save, as they found themselves inclined from their natural bent either to profusion or avarice. That the rich man enjoyed the fruit of the poor man's labor, and the latter were a thousand to one in proportion to the former. That the bulk of our people was forced to live miserably, by laboring every day for small wages to make a few live plentifully. I enlarged myself much on these and many other particulars to the same purpose, but his honor was still to seek,[7] for he went upon a supposition that all animals had a title to their share in the productions of the earth; and especially those who presided over the rest. Therefore he desired I would let him know what these costly meats were, and how any of us happened to want[8] them. Whereupon I enumerated as many sorts as came into my head, with the various methods of dressing them, which could not be done without sending vessels by sea to every part of the world, as well for liquors to drink, as for sauces, and innumerable other conveniencies. I assured him, that this whole globe of earth must be at least three times gone round, before one of our better female Yahoos could get her breakfast, or a cup to put it in. He said, "That must needs be a miserable country which cannot furnish food for its own inhabitants." But what he chiefly wondered at, was how such vast tracts of ground as I described, should be wholly without fresh water, and the people put to the necessity of sending over the sea for drink. I replied that England (the dear place of my nativity) was computed to produce three times the quantity of food, more than its inhabitants are able to consume, as well as liquors extracted from grain, or pressed out of the fruit of certain trees, which made excellent drink; and the same proportion in every other convenience of life. But, in order to feed the luxury and intemperance of the males, and the vanity of the females, we sent away the greatest part of our necessary things to other countries, from whence in return we brought the materials of diseases, folly, and vice, to spend among ourselves. Hence it follows of necessity, that vast numbers of our people are compelled to seek their livelihood by begging, robbing, stealing, cheating, pimping, forswearing, flattering, suborning, forging, gaming, lying, fawning, hectoring, voting, scribbling, star gazing, poisoning, whoring, canting, libeling, freethinking, and the like occupations; every one of which terms, I was at much pains to make him understand.

That, wine was not imported among us from foreign countries, to supply the want of water or other drinks, but because it was a sort of liquid which made us merry, by putting us out of our senses; diverted all melancholy thoughts, begat wild extravagant imaginations in the brain, raised our hopes, and banished our

7. Still did not understand.   8. Lack.

fears; suspended every office of reason for a time, and deprived us of the use of our limbs, until we fell into a profound sleep; although it must be confessed, that we always awaked sick and dispirited; and that the use of this liquor filled us with diseases, which made our lives uncomfortable and short.

But beside all this, the bulk of our people supported themselves by furnishing the necessities or conveniencies of life to the rich, and to each other. For instance, when I am at home and dressed as I ought to be, I carry on my body the workmanship of an hundred tradesmen; the building and furniture of my house employ as many more; and five times the number to adorn my wife.

I was going on to tell him of another sort of people, who get their livelihood by attending the sick; having upon some occasions informed his honor that many of my crew had died of diseases. But here it was with the utmost difficulty that I brought him to apprehend what I meant. He could easily conceive that a Houyhnhnm grew weak and heavy a few days before his death; or by some accident might hurt a limb. But that nature, who worketh all things to perfection, should suffer any pains to breed in our bodies, he thought impossible; and desired to know the reason of so unaccountable an evil. I told him, we fed on a thousand things which operated contrary to each other; that we eat when we were not hungry, and drank without the provocation of thirst; that we sat whole nights drinking strong liquors without eating a bit, which disposed us to sloth, inflamed our bodies, and precipitated or prevented digestion. That, prostitute female Yahoos acquired a certain malady, which bred rottenness in the bones of those who fell into their embraces; that this and many other diseases were propagated from father to son; so that great numbers come into the world with complicated maladies upon them; that it would be endless to give him a catalogue of all diseases incident to human bodies; for they could not be fewer than five or six hundred, spread over every limb, and joint; in short, every part, external and intestine, having diseases appropriated to each. To remedy which, there was a sort of people bred up among us, in the profession or pretense of curing the sick. And because I had some skill in the faculty, I would in gratitude to his honor let him know the whole mystery and method by which they proceed.

Their fundamental is that all diseases arise from repletion; from whence they conclude, that a great evacuation of the body is necessary, either through the natural passage, or upwards at the mouth. Their next business is, from herbs, minerals, gums, oils, shells, salts, juices, seaweed, excrements, barks of trees, serpents, toads, frogs, spiders, dead men's flesh and bones, birds, beasts and fishes, to form a composition for smell and taste the most abominable, nauseous, and detestable, that they can possibly contrive, which the stomach immediately rejects with loathing, and this they call a vomit. Or else from the same storehouse, with some other poisonous additions, they command us to take in at the orifice above or below (just as the physician then happens to be disposed) a medicine equally annoying and disgustful to the bowels; which relaxing the belly, drives down all before it; and this they call a purge, or a clyster. For nature (as the physicians allege) having intended the superior anterior orifice only for the intromission of solids and liquids, and the inferior posterior for ejection, these artists ingeniously considering that in all diseases nature is forced out of her seat; therefore to replace her in it, the body must be treated in a manner directly contrary, but interchanging the use of each orifice; forcing solids and liquids in at the anus, and making evacuations at the mouth.

But, besides real diseases, we are subject to many that are only imaginary, for which the physicians have invented imaginary cures; these have their several names, and so have the drugs that are proper for them; and with these our female Yahoos are always infested.

One great excellency in this tribe is their skill at prognostics, wherein they seldom fail; their predictions in real diseases, when they rise to any degree of malignity, generally portending death, which is always in their power, when recovery is not, and therefore, upon any unexpected signs of amendment, after they have pronounced their sentence rather than be accused as false prophets, they know how to approve [9] their sagacity to the world by a seasonable dose.

They are likewise of special use to husbands and wives, who are grown weary of their mates; to eldest sons, to great ministers of state, and often to princes.

I had formerly upon occasion discoursed with my master upon the nature of government in general, and particularly of our own excellent constitution, deservedly the wonder and envy of the whole world. But having here accidently mentioned a minister of state, he commanded me some time after to inform him what species of Yahoo I particularly meant by that appellation.

I told him that a first or chief minister of state, whom I intended to describe, was a creature wholly exempt from joy and grief, love and hatred, pity and anger; at least makes use of no other passions but a violent desire of wealth, power, and titles; that he applies his words to all uses, except to the indication of his mind; that he never tells a truth, but with an intent that you should take it for a lie; nor a lie, but with a design that you should take it for a truth; that those he speaks worst of behind their backs are in the surest way to preferment; and whenever he begins to praise you to others or to yourself, you are from that day forlorn. The worst mark you can receive is a promise, especially when it is confirmed

9. Prove.

with an oath; after which every wise man retires, and gives over all hopes.

There are three methods by which a man may rise to be chief minister: the first is by knowing how with prudence to dispose of a wife, a daughter, or a sister; the second, by betraying or undermining his predecessor; and the third is by a furious zeal in public assemblies against the corruptions of the court. But a wise prince would rather choose to employ those who practice the last of these methods; because such zealots prove always the most obsequious and subservient to the will and passions of their master. That, these ministers having all employments at their disposal, preserve themselves in power by bribing the majority of a senate or great council; and at last by an expedient called an Act of Indemnity [1] (whereof I described the nature to him) they secure themselves from after reckonings, and retire from the public, laden with the spoils of the nation.

The palace of a chief minister is a seminary to breed up others in his own trade; the pages, lackies, and porter, by imitating their master, become ministers of state in their several districts, and learn to excel in the three principal ingredients, of insolence, lying, and bribery. Accordingly, they have a subaltern court paid to them by persons of the best rank; and sometimes by the force of dexterity and impudence, arrive through several gradations to be successors to their lord.

He is usually governed by a decayed wench, or favorite footman, who are the tunnels through which all graces are conveyed, and may properly be called, in the last resort, the governors of the kingdom.

One day, my master, having heard me mention the nobility of my country, was pleased to make me a compliment which I could not pretend to deserve: that, he was sure, I must have been born of some noble family, because I far exceeded in shape, color, and cleanliness, all the Yahoos of his nation, although I seemed to fail in strength, and agility, which must be imputed to my different way of living from those other brutes; and besides, I was not only endowed with the faculty of speech, but likewise with some rudiments of reason, to a degree, that with all his acquaintance I passed for a prodigy.

He made me observe, that among the Houyhnhnms, the white, the sorrel, and the iron grey were not so exactly shaped as the bay, the dapple grey, and the black; nor born with equal talents of mind, or a capacity to improve them; and therefore continued always in the condition of servants, without ever aspiring to match out of their own race, which in that country would be reckoned monstrous and unnatural.

1. An act passed at each session of Parliament to protect ministers of state who in good faith might have acted illegally.

I made his honor my most humble acknowledgments for the good opinion he was pleased to conceive of me; but assured him at the same time, that my birth was of the lower sort, having been born of plain, honest parents, who were just able to give me a tolerable education; that, nobility among us was altogether a different thing from the idea he had of it; that, our young noblemen are bred from their childhood in idleness and luxury; that, as soon as years will permit, they consume their vigor, and contract odious diseases among lewd females; and when their fortunes are almost ruined, they marry some woman of mean birth, disagreeable person, and unsound constitution, merely for the sake of money, whom they hate and despise. That, the productions of such marriages are generally scrofulous, rickety or deformed children; by which means the family seldom continues above three generations, unless the wife take care to provide a healthy father among her neighbors, or domestics, in order to improve and continue the breed. That a weak diseased body, a meager countenance, and sallow complexion are the true marks of noble blood; and a healthy robust appearance is so disgraceful in a man of quality, that the world concludes his real father to have been a groom or a coachman. The imperfections of his mind run parallel with those of his body; being a composition of spleen, dullness, ignorance, caprice, sensuality, and pride.

Without the consent of this illustrious body, no law can be enacted, repealed, or altered, and these nobles have likewise the decision of all our possessions without appeal.

CHAPTER VII. *The Author's great love of his native country. His master's observations upon the constitution and administration of England, as described by the Author, with parallel cases and comparisons. His master's observations upon human nature.*

The reader may be disposed to wonder how I could prevail on myself to give so free a representation of my own species, among a race of mortals who were already too apt to conceive the vilest opinion of humankind, from that entire congruity betwixt me and their Yahoos. But I must freely confess that the many virtues of those excellent quadrupeds placed in opposite view to human corruptions had so far opened my eyes, and enlarged my understanding, that I began to view the actions and passions of man in a very different light; and to think the honor of my own kind not worth managing; [2] which, besides, it was impossible for me to do before a person of so acute a judgment as my master, who daily convinced me of a thousand faults in myself, whereof I had not the least perception before, and which with us would never be numbered even among human infirmities. I had likewise learned from his example an utter detestation of all falsehood or disguise; and

2. Taking care of.

truth appeared so amiable to me, that I determined upon sacrificing everything to it.

Let me deal so candidly with the reader as to confess that there was yet a much stronger motive for the freedom I took in my representation of things. I had not been a year in this country, before I contracted such a love and veneration for the inhabitants, that I entered on a firm resolution never to return to humankind, but to pass the rest of my life among these admirable Houyhnhnms in the contemplation and practice of every virtue; where I could have no example or incitement to vice. But it was decreed by fortune, my perpetual enemy, that so great a felicity should not fall to my share. However, it is now some comfort to reflect that in what I said of my countrymen, I extenuated their faults as much as I durst before so strict an examiner; and upon every article, gave as favorable a turn as the matter would bear. For, indeed, who is there alive that will not be swayed by his bias and partiality to the place of his birth?

I have related the substance of several conversations I had with my master, during the greatest part of the time I had the honor to be in his service; but have indeed for brevity sake omitted much more than is here set down.

When I had answered all his questions, and his curiosity seemed to be fully satisfied; he sent for me one morning early, and commanding me to sit down at some distance (an honor which he had never before conferred upon me), he said he had been very seriously considering my whole story, as far as it related both to myself and my country; that, he looked upon us as a sort of animals to whose share, by what accident he could not conjecture, some small pittance of reason had fallen, whereof we made no other use than by its assistance to aggravate our natural corruptions, and to acquire new ones which nature had not given us. That we disarmed ourselves of the few abilities she had bestowed; had been very successful in multiplying our original wants, and seemed to spend our whole lives in vain endeavors to supply them by our own inventions. That, as to myself, it was manifest I had neither the strength or agility of a common Yahoo; that I walked infirmly on my hinder feet; had found out a contrivance to make my claws of no use or defense, and to remove the hair from my chin, which was intended as a shelter from the sun and the weather. Lastly, that I could neither run with speed, nor climb trees like my brethren (as he called them) the Yahoos in this country.

That our institutions of government and law were plainly owing to our gross defects in reason, and by consequence, in virtue; because reason alone is sufficient to govern a rational creature; which was therefore a character we had no pretense to challenge, even from the account I had given of my own people; although he manifestly perceived, that in order to favor them, I had concealed many particulars, and often *said the thing which was not*.

He was the more confirmed in this opinion, because he observed that I agreed in every feature of my body with other Yahoos, except where it was to my real disadvantage in point of strength, speed, and activity, the shortness of my claws, and some other particulars where nature had no part; so, from the representation I had given him of our lives, our manners, and our actions, he found as near a resemblance in the disposition of our minds. He said the Yahoos were known to hate one another more than they did any different species of animals; and the reason usually assigned was the odiousness of their own shapes, which all could see in the rest, but not in themselves. He had therefore begun to think it not unwise in us to cover our bodies, and by that invention, conceal many of our deformities from each other, which would else be hardly supportable. But he now found he had been mistaken; and that the dissentions of those brutes in his country were owing to the same cause with ours, as I had described them. For, if (said he) you throw among five Yahoos as much food as would be sufficient for fifty, they will, instead of eating peaceably, fall together by the ears, each single one impatient to have all to itself; and therefore a servant was usually employed to stand by while they were feeding abroad, and those kept at home were tied at a distance from each other. That, if a cow died of age or accident, before a Houyhnhnm could secure it for his own Yahoos, those in the neighborhood would come in herds to seize it, and then would ensue such a battle as I had described, with terrible wounds made by their claws on both sides, although they seldom were able to kill one another, for want of such convenient instruments of death as we had invented. At other times the like battles have been fought between the Yahoos of several neighborhoods without any visible cause; those of one district watching all opportunities to surprise the next before they are prepared. But if they find their project hath miscarried, they return home, and for want of enemies, engage in what I call a civil war among themselves.

That, in some fields of his country, there are certain shining stones of several colors, whereof the Yahoos are violently fond; and when part of these stones are fixed in the earth, as it sometimes happeneth, they will dig with their claws for whole days to get them out, and carry them away, and hide them by heaps in their kennels; but still looking round with great caution, for fear their comrades should find out their treasure. My master said he could never discover the reason of this unnatural appetite, or how these stones could be of any use to a Yahoo; but now he believed it might proceed from the same principle of avarice, which I had ascribed to mankind. That he had once, by way of experiment, privately removed a heap of these stones from the place where one of his Yahoos had buried it, whereupon, the sordid animal missing his treasure, by his loud lamenting brought the whole herd to the place, there miserably howled, then fell to biting and tearing the rest; began to pine away, would neither eat nor sleep, nor work, till he ordered a servant privately to convey the stones into the same hole, and hide them as before; which when his Yahoo had found, he presently recovered his spirits and good humor; but took care to remove them to a better hiding place; and hath ever since been a very serviceable brute.

My master farther assured me, which I also observed myself; that in the fields where these shining stones abound, the fiercest and most frequent battles are fought, occasioned by perpetual inroads of the neighboring Yahoos.

He said it was common when two Yahoos discovered such a stone in a field, and were contending which of them should be the proprietor, a third would take the advantage, and carry it away from them both; which my master would needs contend to have some resemblance with our suits at law; wherein I thought it for our credit not to undeceive him; since the decision he mentioned was much more equitable than many decrees among us; because the plaintiff and defendant there lost nothing beside the stone they contended for; whereas our courts of equity would never have dismissed the cause while either of them had anything left.

My master continuing his discourse said there was nothing that rendered the Yahoos more odious, than their undistinguished appetite to devour everything that came in their way, whether herbs, roots, berries, corrupted flesh of animals, or all mingled together; and it was peculiar in their temper, that they were fonder of what they could get by rapine or stealth at a greater distance, than much better food provided for them at home. If their prey held out, they would eat till they were ready to burst, after which nature had pointed out to them a certain root that gave them a general evacuation.

There was also another kind of root very juicy, but something rare and difficult to be found, which the Yahoos fought for with much eagerness, and would suck it with great delight; it produced the same effects that wine hath upon us. It would make them sometimes hug, and sometimes tear one another; they would howl and grin, and chatter, and reel, and tumble, and then fall asleep in the mud.

I did indeed observe that the Yahoos were the only animals in this country subject to any diseases; which however, were much fewer than horses have among us, and contracted not by any ill treatment they meet with, but by the nastiness and greediness of that sordid brute. Neither has their language any more than a general appellation for those maladies; which is borrowed from the name of the beast, and called *Hnea Yahoo*, or the Yahoo's Evil; and the cure prescribed is a mixture of their own dung and urine, forcibly put down the Yahoo's throat. This I have since often known to have been taken with success, and do here freely recommend it to my countrymen, for the public good, as an admirable specific against all diseases produced by repletion.

As to learning, government, arts, manufactures, and the like, my master confessed he could find little or no resemblance between the Yahoos of that country and those in ours. For he only meant to observe what parity there was in our natures. He had heard indeed some curious Houyhnhnms observe that in most herds there was a sort of ruling Yahoo (as among us there is generally some leading or principal stag in a park) who was always more deformed in body, and mischievous in disposition, than any of the rest. That this leader had usually a favorite as like himself as he could get, whose employment was to lick his master's feet and posteriors, and drive the female Yahoos to his kennel; for which he was now and then rewarded with a piece of ass's flesh. This favorite is hated by the whole herd; and therefore to protect himself, keeps always near the person of his leader. He usually continues in office till a worse can be found; but the very moment he is discarded, his successor, at the head of all the Yahoos in that district, young and old, male and female, come in a body, and discharge their excrements upon him from head to foot. But how far this might be applicable to our courts and favorites, and ministers of state, my master said I could best determine.

I durst make no return to this malicious insinuation, which debased human understanding below the sagacity of a common hound, who hath judgment enough to distinguish and follow the cry of the ablest dog in the pack, without being ever mistaken.

My master told me there were some qualities remarkable in the Yahoos, which he had not observed me to mention, or at least very slightly, in the accounts I had given him of humankind. He said, those animals, like other brutes, had their females in common; but in this they differed, that the she-Yahoo would admit the male while she was pregnant; and that the hes would quarrel and fight with the females as fiercely as with each other. Both which practices were such degrees of infamous brutality, that no other sensitive creature ever arrived at.

Another thing he wondered at in the Yahoos was their strange disposition to nastiness and dirt; whereas there appears to be a natural love of cleanliness in all other animals. As to the two former accusations, I was glad to let them pass without any reply, because I had not a word to offer upon them in defense of my species, which otherwise I certainly had done from my own inclinations. But I could have easily vindicated humankind from the imputation of singularity upon the last article, if there had been any swine in that country (as unluckily for me there were not) which although it may be a sweeter quadruped than a Yahoo, cannot I humbly conceive in justice pretend to more cleanliness; and so his honor himself must have owned, if he had seen their filthy way of feeding, and their custom of wallowing and sleeping in the mud.

My master likewise mentioned another quality, which his servants had discovered in several Yahoos, and to him was wholly unaccountable. He said, a fancy would sometimes take a Yahoo, to retire into a corner, to lie down and howl, and groan, and spurn away all that came near him, although he were young and fat, and wanted neither food nor water; nor did the servants imagine what could possibly ail him. And the only remedy they found was to set him to hard work, after which he would infallibly come to himself. To this I was silent out of partiality to my own kind; yet here I could plainly discover the true seeds of spleen,[3] which only seizeth on the lazy, the luxurious, and the rich; who, if they were forced to undergo the same regimen, I would undertake for the cure.

His Honor had farther observed, that a female Yahoo would often stand behind a bank or a bush, to gaze on the young males passing by, and then appear, and hide, using many antic gestures and grimaces; at which time it was observed, that she had a most offensive smell; and when any of the males advanced, would slowly retire, looking back, and with a counterfeit show of fear, run off into some convenient place where she knew the male would follow her.

At other times, if a female stranger came among them, three or four of her own sex would get about her, and stare and chatter, and grin, and smell her all over; and then turn off with gestures that seemed to express contempt and disdain.

Perhaps my master might refine a little in these speculations, which he had drawn from what he observed himself, or had been told by others; however, I could not reflect without some amazement, and much sorrow, that the rudiments of lewdness, coquetry, censure, and scandal, should have place by instinct in womankind.

I expected every moment that my master would accuse the Yahoos of those unnatural appetites in both sexes, so common among us. But nature it seems hath not been so expert a schoolmistress; and these politer pleasures are entirely the productions of art and reason, on our side of the globe.

CHAPTER VIII. *The Author relateth several particulars of the Yahoos. The great virtues of the Houyhnhnms. The education and exercises of their youth. Their general assembly.*

As I ought to have understood human nature much better than I supposed it possible for my master to do, so it was easy to apply

3. Hypochondria.

the character he gave of the Yahoos to myself and my countrymen; and I believed I could yet make farther discoveries from my own observation. I therefore often begged his honor to let me go among the herds of Yahoos in the neighborhood; to which he always very graciously consented, being perfectly convinced that the hatred I bore those brutes would never suffer me to be corrupted by them; and his honor ordered one of his servants, a strong sorrel nag, very honest and good-natured, to be my guard; without whose protection I durst not undertake such adventures. For I have already told the reader how much I was pestered by those odious animals upon my first arrival. I afterwards failed very narrowly three or four times of falling into their clutches, when I happened to stray at any distance without my hanger. And I have reason to believe, they had some imagination that I was of their own species, which I often assisted myself, by stripping up my sleeves, and shewing my naked arms and breast in their sight, when my protector was with me; at which times they would approach as near as they durst, and imitate my actions after the manner of monkeys, but ever with great signs of hatred; as a tame jackdaw with cap and stockings is always persecuted by the wild ones, when he happens to be got among them.

They are prodigiously nimble from their infancy; however, I once caught a young male of three years old, and endeavored by all marks of tenderness to make it quiet; but the little imp fell a squalling, scratching, and biting with such violence, that I was forced to let it go; and it was high time, for a whole troop of old ones came about us at the noise; but finding the cub was safe (for away it ran) and my sorrel nag being by, they durst not venture near us. I observed the young animal's flesh to smell very rank, and the stink was somewhat between a weasel and a fox, but much more disagreeable. I forgot another circumstance (and perhaps I might have the reader's pardon, if it were wholly omitted) that while I held the odious vermin in my hands, it voided its filthy excrements of a yellow liquid substance, all over my clothes; but by good fortune there was a small brook hard by, where I washed myself as clean as I could; although I durst not come into my master's presence until I were sufficiently aired.

By what I could discover, the Yahoos appear to be the most unteachable of all animals, their capacities never reaching higher than to draw or carry burdens. Yet I am of opinion, this defect ariseth chiefly from a perverse, restive disposition. For they are cunning, malicious, treacherous and revengeful. They are strong and hardy, but of a cowardly spirit, and by consequence insolent, abject, and cruel. It is observed that the red-haired of both sexes are more libidinous and mischievous than the rest, whom yet they much exceed in strength and activity.

The Houyhnhnms keep the Yahoos for present use in huts not far from the house; but the rest are sent abroad to certain fields, where they dig up roots, eat several kinds of herbs, and search about for carrion, or sometimes catch weasels and *luhimuhs* (a sort of wild rat) which they greedily devour. Nature hath taught them to dig deep holes with their nails on the side of a rising ground, wherein they lie by themselves; only the kennels of the females are larger, sufficient to hold two or three cubs.

They swim from their infancy like frogs, and are able to continue long under water, where they often take fish, which the females carry home to their young. And upon this occasion, I hope the reader will pardon my relating an odd adventure.

Being one day abroad with my protector the sorrel nag, and the weather exceeding hot, I entreated him to let me bathe in a river that was near. He consented, and I immediately stripped myself stark naked, and went down softly into the stream. It happened that a young female Yahoo standing behind a bank, saw the whole proceeding; and inflamed by desire, as the nag and I conjectured, came running with all speed, and leaped into the water within five yards of the place where I bathed. I was never in my life so terribly frighted; the nag was grazing at some distance, not suspecting any harm; she embraced me after a most fulsome manner; I roared as loud as I could, and the nag came galloping towards me, whereupon she quitted her grasp, with the utmost reluctancy, and leaped upon the opposite bank, where she stood gazing and howling all the time I was putting on my clothes.

This was matter of diversion to my master and his family, as well as of mortification to myself. For now I could no longer deny that I was a real Yahoo, in every limb and feature, since the females had a natural propensity to me as one of their own species; neither was the hair of this brute of a red color (which might have been some excuse for an appetite a little irregular) but black as a sloe, and her countenance did not make an appearance altogether so hideous as the rest of the kind; for I think, she could not be above eleven years old.

Having already lived three years in this country, the reader I suppose will expect that I should, like other travelers, give him some account of the manners and customs of its inhabitants, which it was indeed my principal study to learn.

As these noble Houyhnhnms are endowed by Nature with a general disposition to all virtues, and have no conceptions or ideas of what is evil in a rational creature; so their grand maxim is to cultivate reason, and to be wholly governed by it. Neither is reason among them a point problematical as with us, where men can argue with plausibility on both sides of a question; but strikes you with immediate conviction; as it must needs do where it is not mingled, obscured, or discolored by passion and interest. I remember it was with extreme difficulty that I could bring my master to understand the meaning of the word "opinion," or how a point could be disputable; because reason taught us to affirm or deny only where we are certain; and beyond our knowledge we cannot do either. So that controversies, wranglings, disputes, and positiveness in false or dubious propositions are evils unknown among the Houyhnhnms. In the like manner when I used to explain to him our several systems of natural philosophy, he would laugh that a creature pretending to reason should value itself upon the knowledge of other people's conjectures, and in things, where that knowledge, if it were certain, could be of no use. Wherein he agreed entirely with the sentiments of Socrates, as Plato delivers them, which I mention as the highest honor I can do that prince of philosophers. I have often since reflected what destruction such a doctrine would make in the libraries of Europe; and how many paths to fame would be then shut up in the learned world.

Friendship and benevolence are the two principal virtues among the Houyhnhnms; and these not confined to particular objects, but universal to the whole race. For a stranger from the remotest part is equally treated with the nearest neighbor, and wherever he goes, looks upon himself as at home. They preserve decency and civility in the highest degrees, but are altogether ignorant of ceremony. They have no fondness for their colts or foals; but the care they take in educating them proceedeth entirely from the dictates of reason. And I observed my master to show the same affection to his neighbor's issue that he had for his own. They will have it that nature teaches them to love the whole species, and it is reason only that maketh a distinction of persons, where there is a superior degree of virtue.

When the matron Houyhnhnms have produced one of each sex, they no longer accompany with their consorts, except they lose one of their issue by some casualty, which very seldom happens; but in such a case they meet again; or when the like accident befalls a person whose wife is past bearing, some other couple bestows on him one of their own colts, and then go together a second time, until the mother be pregnant. This caution is necessary to prevent the country from being overburdened with numbers. But the race of inferior Houyhnhnms bred up to be servants is not so strictly limited upon this article; these are allowed to produce three of each sex, to be domestics in the noble families.

In their marriages they are exactly careful to choose such colors as will not make any disagreeable mixture in the breed. Strength is chiefly valued in the male, and comeliness in the female; not upon the account of love, but to preserve the race from degenerating; for, where a female happens to excel in strength, a consort is chosen with regard to comeliness. Courtship, love, presents, join-tures, settlements, have no place in their thoughts, or terms whereby to express them in their language. The young couple meet and are joined, merely because it is the determination of their parents and friends; it is what they see done every day; and they look upon it as one of the necessary actions in a reasonable being. But the violation of marriage, or any other unchastity, was never heard of; and the married pair pass their lives with the same friendship and mutual benevolence that they bear to all others of the same species who come in their way, without jealousy, fond-ness, quarreling, or discontent.

In educating the youth of both sexes, their method is admirable, and highly deserveth our imitation. These are not suffered to taste a grain of oats, except upon certain days, till eighteen years old; nor milk, but very rarely; and in summer they graze two hours in the morning, and as many in the evening, which their parents likewise observe; but the servants are not allowed above half that time; and a great part of the grass is brought home, which they eat at the most convenient hours, when they can be best spared from work.

Temperance, industry, exercise, and cleanliness are the lessons equally enjoined to the young ones of both sexes; and my master thought it monstrous in us to give the females a different kind of education from the males, except in some articles of domestic management; whereby, as he truly observed, one half of our natives were good for nothing but bringing children into the world; and to trust the care of their children to such useless animals, he said was yet a greater instance of brutality.

But the Houyhnhnms train up their youth to strength, speed, and hardiness, by exercising them in running races up and down steep hills, or over hard stony grounds; and when they are all in a sweat, they are ordered to leap over head and ears into a pond or a river. Four times a year the youth of certain districts meet to show their proficiency in running, and leaping, and other feats of strength or agility; where the victor is rewarded with a song made in his or her praise. On this festival the servants drive a herd of Yahoos into the field, laden with hay, and oats, and milk for a repast to the Houyhnhnms; after which these brutes are immediately driven back again, for fear of being noisome to the assembly.

Every fourth year, at the vernal equinox, there is a representative council of the whole nation, which meets in a plain about twenty miles from our house, and continueth about five or six days. Here they inquire into the state and condition of the several districts; whether they abound or be deficient in hay or oats, or cows or Yahoos? And wherever there is any want (which is but seldom) it is immediately supplied by unanimous consent and contribution. Here likewise the regulation of children is settled: as for instance,

if a Houyhnhnm hath two males, he changeth one of them
with another who hath two females, and when a child hath been
lost by any casualty, where the mother is past breeding, it is
determined what family in the district shall breed another to
supply the loss.

CHAPTER IX. *A grand debate at the general assembly of the
Houyhnhnms, and how it was determined. The learning of the
Houyhnhnms. Their buildings. Their manner of burials. The de-
fectiveness of their language.*

One of these grand assemblies was held in my time, about three
months before my departure, whither my master went as the representative of our district. In this council was resumed their old debate, and indeed, the only debate that ever happened in their
country; whereof my master after his return gave me a very particular account.

The question to be debated was whether the Yahoos should be
exterminated from the face of the earth. One of the members for
the affirmative offered several arguments of great strength and
weight, alleging that, as the Yahoos were the most filthy, noisome,
and deformed animal which nature ever produced, so they were
the most restive and indocible, mischievous, and malicious; they
would privately suck the teats of the Houyhnhnms' cows; kill and
devour their cats, trample down their oats and grass, if they were
not continually watched; and commit a thousand other extravagancies. He took notice of a general tradition, that Yahoos had not
been always in their country, but that many ages ago, two of these
brutes appeared together upon a mountain; whether produced by
the heat of the sun upon corrupted mud and slime, or from the
ooze and froth of the sea, was never known. That these Yahoos engendered, and their brood in a short time grew so numerous as to
overrun and infest the whole nation. That the Houyhnhnms to get
rid of this evil, made a general hunting, and at last enclosed the
whole herd; and destroying the older, every Houyhnhnm kept two
young ones in a kennel, and brought them to such a degree of
tameness as an animal so savage by nature can be capable of acquiring, using them for draft and carriage. That there seemed to be
much truth in this tradition, and that those creatures could not be
ylnhniamshy (or aborigines of the land) because of the violent
hatred the Houyhnhnms as well as all other animals bore them;
which although their evil disposition sufficiently deserved, could
never have arrived at so high a degree, if they had been aborigines,
or else they would have long since been rooted out. That the
inhabitants taking a fancy to use the service of the Yahoos, had very
imprudently neglected to cultivate the breed of asses, which were
a comely animal, easily kept, more tame and orderly, without any
offensive smell, strong enough for labor, although they yield to the

other in agility of body; and if their braying be no agreeable sound, it is far preferable to the horrible howlings of the Yahoos.

Several others declared their sentiments to the same purpose, when my master proposed an expedient to the assembly, whereof he had indeed borrowed the hint from me. He approved of the tradition, mentioned by the honorable member, who spoke before; and affirmed, that the two Yahoos said to be first seen among them, had been driven thither over the sea; that coming to land, and being forsaken by their companions, they retired to the mountains, and degenerating by degrees, became in process of time much more savage than those of their own species in the country from whence these two originals came. The reason of his assertion was that he had now in his possession a certain wonderful Yahoo (meaning myself) which most of them had heard of, and many of them had seen. He then related to them how he first found me; that my body was all covered with an artificial composure of the skins and hairs of other animals; that I spoke in a language of my own, and had thoroughly learned theirs; that I had related to him the accidents which brought me thither; that when he saw me without my covering, I was an exact Yahoo in every part, only of a whiter color, less hairy and with shorter claws. He added how I had endeavored to persuade him that in my own and other countries the Yahoos acted as the governing, rational animal, and held the Houyhnhnms in servitude; that he observed in me all the qualities of a Yahoo, only a little more civilized by some tincture of reason, which however was in a degree as far inferior to the Houyhnhnm race as the Yahoos of their country were to me; that among other things, I mentioned a custom we had of castrating Houyhnhnms when they were young, in order to render them tame; that the operation was easy and safe; that it was no shame to learn wisdom from brutes, as industry is taught by the ant, and building by the swallow (for so I translate the world *lyhannh*, although it be a much larger fowl). That this invention might be practiced upon the younger Yahoos here, which, besides rendering them tractable and fitter for use, would in an age put an end to the whole species without destroying life. That in the meantime the Houyhnhnms should be exhorted to cultivate the breed of asses, which, as they are in all respects more valuable brutes, so they have this advantage, to be fit for service at five years old, which the others are not till twelve.

This was all my master thought fit to tell me at that time, of what passed in the grand council. But he was pleased to conceal one particular, which related personally to myself, whereof I soon felt the unhappy effect, as the reader will know in its proper place, and from whence I date all the succeeding misfortunes of my life.

The Houyhnhnms have no letters, and consequently, their knowledge is all traditional. But there happening few events of any moment among a people so well united, naturally disposed to every virtue, wholly governed by reason, and cut off from all commerce with other nations, the historical part is easily preserved without burdening their memories. I have already observed that they are subject to no diseases, and therefore can have no need of physicians. However, they have excellent medicines composed of herbs, to cure accidental bruises and cuts in the pastern or frog of the foot by sharp stones, as well as other maims and hurts in the several parts of the body.

They calculate the year by the revolution of the sun and the moon, but use no subdivisions into weeks. They are well enough acquainted with the motions of those two luminaries, and understand the nature of eclipses; and this is the utmost progress of their astronomy.

In poetry they must be allowed to excell all other mortals; wherein the justness of their similes, and the minuteness, as well as exactness of their descriptions, are indeed inimitable. Their verses abound very much in both of these, and usually contain either some exalted notions of friendship and benevolence, or the praises of those who were victors in races and other bodily exercises. Their buildings, although very rude and simple, are not inconvenient, but well contrived to defend them from all injuries of cold and heat. They have a kind of tree, which at forty years old loosens in the root, and falls with the first storm; it grows very straight, and being pointed like stakes with a sharp stone (for the Houyhnhnms know not the use of iron), they stick them erect in the ground about ten inches asunder, and then weave in oat straw, or sometimes wattles, betwixt them. The roof is made after the same manner, and so are the doors.

The Houyhnhnms use the hollow part between the pastern and the hoof of their forefeet as we do our hands, and this with greater dexterity than I could at first imagine. I have seen a white mare of our family thread a needle (which I lent her on purpose) with that joint. They milk their cows, reap their oats, and do all the work which requires hands in the same manner. They have a kind of hard flints, which by grinding against other stones they form into instruments that serve instead of wedges, axes, and hammers. With tools made of these flints, they likewise cut their hay, and reap their oats, which there groweth naturally in several fields; the Yahoos draw home the sheaves in carriages, and the servants tread them in certain covered huts, to get out the grain, which is kept in stores. They make a rude kind of earthen and wooden vessels, and bake the former in the sun.

If they can avoid casualties, they die only of old age, and are buried in the obscurest places that can be found, their friends and relations expressing neither joy nor grief at their departure; nor does the dying person discover the least regret that he is leaving the world, any more than if he were upon returning home from a visit to one of his neighbors; I remember my master having once made an appointment with a friend and his family to come to his house upon some affair of importance; on the day fixed, the mistress and her two children came very late; she made two excuses, first for her husband, who, as she said, happened that very morning to *lhnuwnh*. The word is strongly expressive in their language, but not easily rendered into English; it signifies, *to retire to his first Mother*. Her excuse for not coming sooner was that her husband dying late in the morning, she was a good while consulting her servants about a convenient place where his body should be laid; and I observed she behaved herself at our house, as cheerfully as the rest; she died about three months after.

They live generally to seventy or seventy-five years, very seldom to fourscore; some weeks before their death they feel a gradual decay, but without pain. During this time they are much visited by their friends, because they cannot go abroad with their usual ease and satisfaction. However, about ten days before their death, which they seldom fail in computing, they return the visits that have been made by those who are nearest in the neighborhood, being carried in a convenient sledge drawn by Yahoos; which vehicle they use, not only upon this occasion, but when they grow old, upon long journeys, or when they are lamed by any accident. And therefore when the dying Houyhnhnms return those visits, they take a solemn leave of their friends, as if they were going to some remote part of the country, where they designed to pass the rest of their lives.

I know not whether it may be worth observing, that the Houyhnhnms have no word in their language to express anything that is evil, except what they borrow from the deformities or ill qualities of the Yahoos. Thus they denote the folly of a servant, an omission of a child, a stone that cuts their feet, a continuance of foul or unseasonable weather, and the like, by adding to each the epithet of Yahoo. For instance, *hhnm Yahoo, whnaholm Yahoo, ynlhmndwihlma Yahoo*, and an ill-contrived house, *ynholmhnmrohlnw Yahoo*.

I could with great pleasure enlarge farther upon the manners and virtues of this excellent people; but intending in a short time to publish a volume by itself expressly upon that subject, I refer the reader thither. And in the meantime, proceed to relate my own sad catastrophe.

CHAPTER X. *The Author's economy, and happy life among the Houyhnhnms. His great improvement in virtue, by conversing with them. Their conversations. The Author hath notice given him by his master that he must depart from the country. He falls into a swoon for grief, but submits. He contrives and finishes a canoe, by the help of a fellow servant, and puts to sea at a venture.*

I had settled my little economy to my own heart's content. My master had ordered a room to be made for me after their manner, about six yards from the house; the sides and floors of which I plastered with clay, and covered with rush mats of my own contriving; I had beaten hemp, which there grows wild, and made of it a sort of ticking; this I filled with the feathers of several birds I had taken with springes made of Yahoos' hairs, and were excellent food. I had worked two chairs with my knife, the sorrel nag helping me in the grosser and more laborious part. When my clothes were worn to rags, I made myself others with the skins of rabbits, and of a certain beautiful animal about the same size, called *nnuhnoh*, the skin of which is covered with a fine down. Of these I likewise made very tolerable stockings. I soled my shoes with wood which I cut from a tree, and fitted to the upper leather, and when this was worn out, I supplied it with the skins of Yahoos, dried in the sun. I often got honey out of hollow trees, which I mingled with water, or eat it with my bread. No man could more verify the truth of these two maxims, that *Nature is very easily satisfied*; and, that *Necessity is the mother of invention*. I enjoyed perfect health of body, and tranquility of mind; I did not feel the treachery or inconstancy of a friend, nor the inquiries of a secret or open enemy. I had no occasion of bribing, flattering, or pimping to procure the favor of any great man, or of his minion. I wanted no fence against fraud or oppression; here was neither physician to destroy my body, nor lawyer to ruin my fortune; no informer to watch my words and actions, or forge accusations against me for hire; here were no gibers, censurers, backbiters, pickpockets, highwaymen, housebreakers, attorneys, bawds, buffoons, gamesters, politicians, wits, splenetics, tedious talkers, controvertists, ravishers, murderers, robbers, virtuosos; no leaders or followers of party and faction; no encouragers to vice, by seducement or examples; no dungeons, axes, gibbets, whipping posts, or pillories; no cheating shopkeepers or mechanics; no pride, vanity or affectation; no fops, bullies, drunkards, strolling whores, or poxes; no ranting, lewd, expensive wives; no stupid, proud pedants; no importunate, overbearing, quarrelsome, noisy, roaring, empty, conceited, swearing companions; no scoundrels raised from the dust upon the merit of their vices; or nobility thrown into it on account of their virtues; no lords, fiddlers, judges, or dancing masters.

I had the favor of being admitted to several Houyhnhnms, who came to visit or dine with my master; where his honor graciously suffered me to wait in the room, and listen to their discourse. Both he and his company would often descend to ask me questions, and receive my answers. I had also sometimes the honor of attending my master in his visits to others. I never presumed to speak, except in answer to a question; and then I did it with inward regret, because it was a loss of so much time for improving myself; but I was infinitely delighted with the station of an humble auditor in such conversations, where nothing passed but what was useful, expressed in the fewest and most significant words; where (as I have already said) the greatest decency was observed, without the least degree of ceremony; where no person spoke without being pleased himself, and pleasing his companions; where there was no interruption, tediousness, heat, or difference of sentiments. They have a notion, that when people are met together, a short silence doth much improve conversation; this I found to be true; for during those little intermissions of talk, new ideas would arise in their minds, which very much enlivened the discourse. Their subjects are generally on friendship and benevolence; on order and economy; sometimes upon the visible operations of nature, or ancient traditions; upon the bounds and limits of virtue; upon the unerring rules of reason; or upon some determinations, to be taken at the next great assembly; and often upon the various excellencies of poetry. I may add, without vanity, that my presence often gave them sufficient matter for discourse, because it afforded my master an occasion of letting his friends into the history of me and my country, upon which they were all pleased to discant in a manner not very advantageous to human kind; and for that reason I shall not repeat what they said; only I may be allowed to observe that his honor, to my great admiration, appeared to understand the nature of Yahoos much better than myself. He went through all our vices and follies, and discovered many which I had never mentioned to him; by only supposing what qualities a Yahoo of their country, with a small proportion of reason, might be capable of exerting; and concluded, with too much probability, how vile as well as miserable such a creature must be.

I freely confess, that all the little knowledge I have of any value was acquired by the lectures I received from my master, and from hearing the discourses of him and his friends; to which I should be prouder to listen, than to dictate to the greatest and wisest assembly in Europe. I admired the strength, comeliness, and speed of the inhabitants; and such a constellation of virtues in such amiable persons produced in me the highest veneration. At first, indeed, I did not feel that natural awe which the Yahoos and all other animals bear towards them; but it grew upon me by degrees, much sooner than I imagined, and was mingled with a respectful love and gratitude, that they would condescend to distinguish me from the rest of my species.

When I thought of my family, my friends, my countrymen, or human race in general, I considered them as they really were, Yahoos in shape and disposition, perhaps a little more civilized, and qualified with the gift of speech; but making no other use of reason than to improve and multiply those vices, whereof their brethren in this country had only the share that nature allotted them. When I happened to behold the reflection of my own form in a lake or fountain, I turned away my face in horror and detestation of myself, and could better endure the sight of a common Yahoo than of my own person. By conversing with the Houyhnhnms, and looking upon them with delight, I fell to imitate their gait and gesture, which is now grown into a habit; and my friends often tell me in a blunt way, that I trot like a horse; which, however, I take for a great compliment; neither shall I disown, that in speaking I am apt to fall into the voice and manner of the Houyhnhnms, and hear myself ridiculed on that account without the least mortification.

In the midst of this happiness, when I looked upon myself to be fully settled for life, my master sent for me one morning a little earlier than his usual hour. I observed by his countenance that he was in some perplexity, and at a loss how to begin what he had to speak. After a short silence, he told me, he did not know how I would take what he was going to say; that, in the last general assembly, when the affair of the Yahoos was entered upon, the representatives had taken offense at his keeping a Yahoo (meaning myself) in his family more like a Houyhnhnm than a brute animal. That he was known frequently to converse with me, as if he could receive some advantage of pleasure in my company; that such a practice was not agreeable to reason or nature, or a thing ever heard of before among them. The assembly did therefore exhort him, either to employ me like the rest of my species, or command me to swim back to the place from whence I came. That the first of these expedients was utterly rejected by all the Houyhnhnms who had ever seen me at his house or their own; for, they alleged, that because I had some rudiments of reason, added to the natural pravity of those animals, it was to be feared, I might be able to seduce them into the woody and mountainous parts of the country, and bring them in troops by night to destroy the Houyhnhnms' cattle, as being naturally of the ravenous kind, and averse from labor.

My master added that he was daily pressed by the Houyhnhnms of the neighborhood to have the assembly's exhortation executed, which he could not put off much longer. He doubted it would be impossible for me to swim to another country; and therefore wished I would contrive some sort of vehicle resembling those I had described to him, that might carry me on the sea; in which work I should have the assistance of his own servants, as well as those of his neighbors. He concluded that for his own part he could have been content to keep me in his service as long as I lived; because he found I had cured myself of some bad habits and dispositions, by endeavoring, as far as my inferior nature was capable, to imitate the Houyhnhnms.

I should here observe to the reader, that a decree of the general assembly in this country is expressed by the word *hnhloayn*, which signifies an exhortation, as near as I can render it; for they have no conception how a rational creature can be compelled, but only advised, or exhorted; because no person can disobey reason without giving up his claim to be a rational creature.

I was struck with the utmost grief and despair at my master's discourse; and being unable to support the agonies I was under, I fell into a swoon at his feet; when I came to myself, he told me that he concluded I had been dead (for these people are subject to no such imbecilities of nature). I answered, in a faint voice, that death would have been too great an happiness; that although I could not blame the assembly's exhortation, or the urgency of his friends; yet in my weak and corrupt judgment, I thought it might consist with reason to have been less rigorous. That I could not swim a league, and probably the nearest land to theirs might be distant above an hundred; that many materials, necessary for making a small vessel to carry me off, were wholly wanting in this country, which, however, I would attempt in obedience and gratitude to his honor, although I concluded the thing to be impossible, and therefore looked on myself as already devoted [4] to destruction. That the certain prospect of an unnatural death was the least of my evils; for, supposing I should escape with life by some strange adventure, how could I think with temper [5] of passing my days among Yahoos, and relapsing into my old corruptions, for want of examples to lead and keep me within the paths of virtue. That I knew too well upon what solid reasons all the determinations of the wise Houyhnhnms were founded, not to be shaken by arguments of mine, a miserable Yahoo; and therefore after presenting him with my humble thanks for the offer of his servants' assistance in making a vessel, and desiring a reasonable time for so difficult a work, I told him I would endeavor to preserve a wretched being; and, if ever I returned to England, was not without hopes of being useful to my own species by celebrating the praises of the renowned Houyhnhnms, and proposing their virtues to the imitation of mankind.

My master in a few words made me a very gracious reply, allowed me the space of two months to finish my boat, and ordered the sorrel nag, my fellow servant (for so at this distance I may presume to call him), to follow my instructions, because I told my master that his help would be sufficient, and I knew he had a tenderness for me.

In his company my first business was to go to that part of the coast where my rebellious crew had ordered me to be set on shore. I got upon a height, and looking on every side into the sea, fancied I saw a small island towards the northeast; I took out my pocket glass, and could then clearly distinguish it about five leagues off, as I computed; but it appeared to the sorrel nag to be only a blue cloud; for, as he had no conception of any country besides his own, so he

4. Doomed.   5. Equanimity.

could not be as expert in distinguishing remote objects at sea, as we who so much converse in that element.

After I had discovered this island, I considered no farther; but resolved, it should, if possible, be the first place of my banishment, leaving the consequence to fortune.

I returned home, and consulting with the sorrel nag, we went into a copse at some distance, where I with my knife, and he with a sharp flint fastened very artificially,[6] after their manner, to a wooden handle, cut down several oak wattles about the thickness of a walking staff, and some larger pieces. But I shall not trouble the reader with a particular description of my own mechanics; let it suffice to say, that in six weeks time, with the help of the sorrel nag, who performed the parts that required most labor, I finished a sort of Indian canoe; but much larger, covering it with the skins of Yahoos, well stitched together, with hempen threads of my own making. My sail was likewise composed of the skins of the same animal; but I made use of the youngest I could get, the older being too tough and thick; and I likewise provided myself with four paddles. I laid in a stock of boiled flesh, of rabbits and fowls; and took with me two vessels, one filled with milk, and the other with water.

I tried my canoe in a large pond near my master's house, and then corrected in it what was amiss, stopping all the chinks with Yahoo's tallow, till I found it staunch, and able to bear me and my freight. And when it was as complete as I could possibly make it, I had it drawn on a carriage very gently by Yahoos, to the seaside, under the conduct of the sorrel nag and another servant.

When all was ready, and the day came for my departure, I took leave of my master and lady, and the whole family, my eyes flowing with tears and my heart quite sunk with grief. But his honor, out of curiosity, and perhaps (if I may speak it without vanity) partly out of kindness, was determined to see me in my canoe; and got several of his neighboring friends to accompany him. I was forced to wait above an hour for the tide, and then observing the wind very fortunately bearing towards the island to which I intended to steer my course, I took a second leave of my master; but as I was going to prostrate myself to kiss his hoof, he did me the honor to raise it gently to my mouth. I am not ignorant how much I have been censured for mentioning this last particular. Detractors are pleased to think it improbable that so illustrious a person should descend to give so great a mark of distinction to a creature so inferior as I. Neither have I forgot how apt some travelers are to boast of extraordinary favors they have received. But, if these censurers were better acquainted with the noble and courteous disposition of the Houyhnhnms, they would soon change their opinion. I paid my respects to the rest of the Houyhnhnms in his honor's company; then getting into my canoe, I pushed off from shore.

6. Artfully.

CHAPTER XI. *The Author's dangerous voyage. He arrives at New Holland, hoping to settle there. Is wounded with an arrow by one of the natives. Is seized and carried by force into a Portuguese ship. The great civilities of the Captain. The Author arrives at England.*

I began this desperate voyage on February 15, 1714/5,[7] at 9 o'clock in the morning. The wind was very favorable; however, I made use at first only of my paddles; but considering I should soon be weary, and that the wind might probably chop about, I ventured to set up my little sail; and thus, with the help of the tide, I went at the rate of a league and a half an hour, as near as I could guess. My master and his friends continued on the shore, till I was almost out of sight; and I often heard the sorrel nag (who always loved me) crying out, "*Hnuy illa nyha maiah Yahoo*," ("Take care of thyself, gentle Yahoo").

My design was, if possible, to discover some small island uninhabited, yet sufficient by my labor to furnish me with necessaries of life, which I would have thought a greater happiness than to be first minister in the politest court of Europe, so horrible was the idea I conceived of returning to live in the society and under the government of Yahoos. For in such a solitude as I desired, I could at least enjoy my own thoughts, and reflect with delight on the virtues of those inimitable Houyhnhnms, without any opportunity of degenerating into the vices and corruptions of my own species.

The reader may remember what I related when my crew conspired against me, and confined me to my cabin, how I continued there several weeks, without knowing what course we took; and when I was put ashore in the longboat, how the sailors told me with oaths, whether true or false, that they knew not in what part of the world we were. However, I did then believe us to be about 10 degrees southward of the Cape of Good Hope, or about 45 degrees southern latitude, as I gathered from some general words I overheard among them, being I supposed to the southeast in their intended voyage to Madagascar. And although this were but little better than conjecture, yet I resolved to steer my course eastward, hoping to reach the southwest coast of New Holland, and perhaps some such island as I desired, lying westward of it. The wind was full west, and by six in the evening I computed I had gone eastward at least eighteen leagues; when I spied a very small island about half a league off, which I soon reached. It was nothing but a rock with one creek,[8] naturally arched by the force of tempests. Here I put in my canoe, and climbing a part of the rock, I could plainly discover land to the east, extending from south to north. I lay all night in my canoe; and repeating my voyage early in the morning, I arrived in seven hours to the southeast point of New Holland. This confirmed me in the opinion I have long entertained, that the maps and

7. I.e., 1714. The year began on March 25th.   8. A bay.

charts place this country at least three degrees more to the east than it really is; which thought I communicated many years ago to my worthy friend Mr. Herman Moll,[9] and gave him my reasons for it, although he hath rather chosen to follow other authors.

I saw no inhabitants in the place where I landed; and being unarmed, I was afraid of venturing far into the country. I found some shellfish on the shore, and eat them raw, not daring to kindle a fire, for fear of being discovered by the natives. I continued three days feeding on oysters and limpets, to save my own provisions; and I fortunately found a brook of excellent water, which gave me great relief.

On the fourth day, venturing out early a little too far, I saw twenty or thirty natives upon a height, not above five hundred yards from me. They were stark naked, men, women, and children round a fire, as I could discover by the smoke. One of them spied me, and gave notice to the rest; five of them advanced towards me, leaving the women and children at the fire. I made what haste I could to the shore, and getting into my canoe, shoved off; the savages observing me retreat, ran after me; and before I could get far enough into the sea, discharged an arrow, which wounded me deeply on the inside of my left knee. (I shall carry the mark to my grave.) I apprehended the arrow might be poisoned; and paddling out of the reach of their darts (being a calm day) I made a shift to suck the wound, and dress it as well as I could.

I was at a loss what to do, for I durst not return to the same landing place, but stood to the north, and was forced to paddle; for the wind, although very gentle, was against me, blowing northwest. As I was looking about for a secure landing place, I saw a sail to the north northeast, which appearing every minute more visible, I was in some doubt whether I should wait for them or no; but at last my detestation of the Yahoo race prevailed; and turning my canoe, I sailed and paddled together to the south, and got into the same creek from whence I set out in the morning, choosing rather to trust myself among these barbarians than live with European Yahoos. I drew up my canoe as close as I could to the shore, and hid myself behind a stone by the little brook, which, as I have already said, was excellent water.

The ship came within half a league of this creek, and sent out her longboat with vessels to take in fresh water (for the place it seems was very well known), but I did not observe it until the boat was almost on shore; and it was too late to seek another hiding place. The seamen at their landing observed my canoe, and rummaging it all over, easily conjectured that the owner could not be far off. Four of them well armed searched every cranny and lurking hole, till at last they found me flat on my face behind the stone. They gazed a while in admiration [1] at my strange uncouth dress;

9. A famous contemporary map maker.   1. Wonder.

my coat made of skins, my wooden-soled shoes, and my furred stock-ings; from whence, however, they concluded I was not a native of the place, who all go naked. One of the seamen in Portuguese bid me rise, and asked who I was. I understood that language very well, and getting upon my feet, said I was a poor Yahoo, banished from the Houyhnhnms, and desired they would please to let me depart. They admired to hear me answer them in their own tongue, and saw by my complexion I must be an European; but were at a loss to know what I meant by Yahoos and Houyhnhnms, and at the same time fell a laughing at my strange tone in speaking, which resembled the neighing of a horse. I trembled all the while betwixt fear and hatred; I again desired leave to depart, and was gently moving to my canoe; but they laid hold on me, desiring to know what country I was of? whence I came? with many other questions. I told them I was born in England, from whence I came about five years ago, and then their country and ours was at peace. I therefore hoped they would not treat me as an enemy, since I meant them no harm, but was a poor Yahoo, seeking some desolate place where to pass the remainder of his unfortunate life.

When they began to talk, I thought I never heard or saw any thing so unnatural; for it appeared to me as monstrous as if a dog or a cow should speak in England, or a Yahoo in Houyhnhnmland. The honest Portuguese were equally amazed at my strange dress, and the odd manner of delivering my words, which however they under-stood very well. They spoke to me with great humanity, and said they were sure their Captain would carry me *gratis* to Lisbon, from whence I might return to my own country; that two of the seamen would go back to the ship, to inform the Captain of what they had seen, and receive his orders; in the meantime, unless I would give my solemn oath not to fly, they would secure me by force. I thought it best to comply with their proposal. They were very curious to know my story, but I gave them very little satisfaction; and they all conjectured, that my misfortunes had impaired my reason. In two hours the boat, which went laden with vessels of water, returned with the Captain's commands to fetch me on board. I fell on my knees to preserve my liberty; but all was in vain, and the men having tied me with cords, heaved me into the boat, from whence I was taken into the ship, and from thence into the Captain's cabin.

His name was Pedro de Mendez; he was a very courteous and generous person; he entreated me to give some account of myself, and desired to know what I would eat or drink; said I should be used as well as himself, and spoke so many obliging things, that I wondered to find such civilities from a Yahoo. However, I remained silent and sullen; I was ready to faint at the very smell of him and his men. At last I desired something to eat out of my own canoe; but he ordered me a chicken and some excellent wine, and then di-rected that I should be put to bed in a very clean cabin. I would not undress myself, but lay on the bedclothes; and in half an hour stole out, when I thought the crew was at dinner; and getting to the side of the ship, was going to leap into the sea, and swim for my life, rather than continue among Yahoos. But one of the seamen prevented me, and having informed the Captain, I was chained to my cabin.

After dinner Don Pedro came to me, and desired to know my reason for so desperate an attempt; assured me he only meant to do me all the service he was able; and spoke so very movingly, that at last I descended to treat him like an animal which had some little portion of reason. I gave him a very short relation of my voyage; of the conspiracy against me by my own men; of the country where they set me on shore, and of my five years residence there. All which he looked upon as if it were a dream or a vision; whereat I took great offense; for I had quite forgot the faculty of lying, so peculiar to Yahoos in all countries where they preside, and consequently the disposition of suspecting truth in others of their own species. I asked him whether it were the custom of his country to *say the thing that was not?* I assured him I had almost forgot what he meant by falsehood; and if I had lived a thousand years in Houyhnhnmland, I should never have heard a lie from the meanest servant. That I was altogether indifferent whether he believed me or no; but however, in return for his favors, I would give so much allowance to the corruption of his nature, as to answer any objection he would please to make; and he might easily discover the truth.

The Captain, a wise man, after many endeavors to catch me tripping in some part of my story, at last began to have a better opinion of my veracity. But he added that since I professed so inviolable an attachment to truth, I must give him my word of honor to bear him company in this voyage without attempting anything against my life; or else he would continue me a prisoner till we arrived at Lisbon. I gave him the promise he required; but at the same time protested that I would suffer the greatest hardships rather than return to live among Yahoos.

Our voyage passed without any considerable accident. In gratitude to the Captain I sometimes sat with him at his earnest request, and strove to conceal my antipathy against humankind, although it often broke out; which he suffered to pass without observation. But the greatest part of the day, I confined myself to my cabin, to avoid seeing any of the crew. The Captain had often entreated me to strip myself of my savage dress, and offered to lend me the best suit of clothes he had. This I would not be prevailed on to accept, abhorring to cover myself with anything that had been on the back of a Yahoo. I only desired he would lend me two clean shirts, which having been washed since he wore them, I believed would not so much defile me. These I changed every second day, and washed them myself.

We arrived at Lisbon, Nov. 5, 1715. At our landing, the Captain forced me to cover myself with his cloak, to prevent the rabble from crowding about me. I was conveyed to his own house; and at my earnest request, he led me up to the highest room backwards.[2] I conjured him to conceal from all persons what I had told him of the Houyhnhnms; because the least hint of such a story would not only draw numbers of people to see me, but probably put me in danger of being imprisoned, or burned by the Inquisition. The Captain persuaded me to accept a suit of clothes newly made; but I would not suffer the tailor to take my measure; however, Don Pedro being almost of my size, they fitted me well enough. He accoutred me with other necessaries, all new, which I aired for twenty-four hours before I would use them.

The Captain had no wife, nor above three servants, none of which were suffered to attend at meals; and his whole deportment was so obliging, added to very good human understanding, that I really began to tolerate his company. He gained so far upon me, that I ventured to look out of the back window. By degrees I was brought into another room, from whence I peeped into the street, but drew my head back in a fright. In a week's time he seduced me down to the door. I found my terror gradually lessened, but my hatred and contempt seemed to increase. I was at last bold enough to walk the street in his company, but kept my nose well stopped with rue, or sometimes with tobacco.

In ten days, Don Pedro, to whom I had given some account of my domestic affairs, put it upon me as a point of honor and conscience that I ought to return to my native country, and live at home with my wife and children. He told me there was an English ship in the port just ready to sail, and he would furnish me with all things necessary. It would be tedious to repeat his arguments, and my contradictions. He said it was altogether impossible to find such a solitary island as I had desired to live in; but I might command in my own house, and pass my time in a manner as recluse as I pleased.

I complied at last, finding I could not do better. I left Lisbon the 24th day of November, in an English merchantman, but who was the Master I never inquired. Don Pedro accompanied me to the ship, and lent me twenty pounds. He took kind leave of me, and embraced me at parting; which I bore as well as I could. During this last voyage I had no commerce with the Master, or any of his men; but pretending I was sick kept close in my cabin. On the fifth of December, 1715, we cast anchor in the Downs about nine in the morning, and at three in the afternoon I got safe to my house at Redriff.

My wife and family received me with great surprise and joy, because they concluded me certainly dead; but I must freely confess, the sight of them filled me only with hatred, disgust, and con-

2. At the rear.

tempt; and the more, by reflecting on the near alliance I had to them. For, although since my unfortunate exile from the Houyhnhnm country, I had compelled myself to tolerate the sight of Yahoos, and to converse with Don Pedro de Mendez; yet my memory and imaginations were perpetually filled with the virtues and ideas of those exalted Houyhnhnms. And when I began to consider that by copulating with one of the Yahoo species, I had become a parent of more, it struck me with the utmost shame, confusion, and horror.

As soon as I entered the house, my wife took me in her arms, and kissed me; at which, having not been used to the touch of that odious animal for so many years, I fell in a swoon for almost an hour. At the time I am writing, it is five years since my last return to England; during the first year I could not endure my wife or children in my presence, the very smell of them was intolerable; much less could I suffer them to eat in the same room. To this hour they dare not presume to touch my bread, or drink out of the same cup; neither was I ever able to let one of them take me by the hand. The first money I laid out was to buy two young stone-horses,[3] which I keep in a good stable, and next to them the groom is my greatest favorite; for I feel my spirits revived by the smell he contracts in the stable. My horses understand me tolerably well; I converse with them at least four hours every day. They are strangers to bridle or saddle; they live in great amity with me, and friendship to each other.

CHAPTER XII. *The Author's veracity. His design in publishing this work. His censure of those travelers who swerve from the truth. The Author clears himself from any sinister ends in writing. An objection answered. The method of planting colonies. His native country commended. The right of the crown to those countries described by the Author is justified. The difficulty of conquering them. The Author takes his last leave of the reader; proposeth his manner of living for the future; gives good advice, and concludeth.*

Thus, gentle reader, I have given thee a faithful history of my travels for sixteen years, and above seven months; wherein I have not been so studious of ornament as of truth. I could perhaps like others have astonished thee with strange improbable tales; but I rather chose to relate plain matter of fact in the simplest manner and style; because my principal design was to inform, and not to amuse thee.

It is easy for us who travel into remote countries, which are seldom visited by Englishmen or other Europeans, to form descriptions of wonderful animals both at sea and land. Whereas a traveler's chief aim should be to make men wiser and better, and to improve their minds by the bad as well as good example of

3. Stallions.

what they deliver concerning foreign places.

I could heartily wish a law were enacted, that every traveler, before he were permitted to publish his voyages, should be obliged to make oath before the Lord High Chancellor that all he intended to print was absolutely true to the best of his knowledge; for then the world would no longer be deceived as it usually is, while some writers, to make their works pass the better upon the public, impose the grossest falsities on the unwary reader. I have perused several books of travels with great delight in my younger days; but, having since gone over most parts of the globe, and been able to contradict many fabulous accounts from my own observation, it hath given me a great disgust against this part of reading, and some indignation to see the credulity of mankind so impudently abused. Therefore, since my acquaintance were pleased to think my poor endeavors might not be unacceptable to my country; I imposed on myself as a maxim, never to be swerved from, that I would *strictly adhere to truth*; neither indeed can I be ever under the least temptation to vary from it, while I retain in my mind the lectures and example of my noble master, and the other illustrious Houyhnhnms, of whom I had so long the honor to be an humble hearer.

> ——*Nec si miserum Fortuna Sinonem*
> *Finxit, vanum etiam, mendacemque improba finget.*[4]

I know very well how little reputation is to be got by writings which require neither genius nor learning, nor indeed any other talent, except a good memory, or an exact *Journal*. I know likewise, that writers of travels, like dictionary-makers, are sunk into oblivion by the weight and bulk of those who come last, and therefore lie uppermost. And it is highly probable that such travelers who shall hereafter visit the countries described in this work of mine, may be detecting my errors (if there be any) and adding many new discoveries of their own, jostle me out of vogue, and stand in my place, making the world forget that ever I was an author. This indeed would be too great a mortification if I wrote for fame; but, as my sole intention was the PUBLIC GOOD, I cannot be altogether disappointed. For, who can read the virtues I have mentioned in the glorious Houyhnhnms, without being ashamed of his own vices, when he considers himself as the reasoning, governing animal of his country? I shall say nothing of those remote nations where Yahoos preside; amongst which the least corrupted are the Brobdingnagians, whose wise maxims in morality and government it would be our happiness to observe. But I forbear descanting further, and rather leave the judicious reader to his own remarks and applications.

---

4. Virgil, *Aeneid*, II, 79–80. "* * * nor if Fortune had moulded Sinon for misery, will she also in spite mould him as false and lying."

I am not a little pleased that this work of mine can possibly meet with no censurers; for what objections can be made against a writer who relates only plain facts that happened in such distant countries, where we have not the least interest with respect either to trade or negotiations? I have carefully avoided every fault with which common writers of travels are often too justly charged. Besides, I meddle not the least with any party, but write without passion, prejudice, or ill-will against any man or number of men whatsoever. I write for the noblest end, to inform and instruct mankind, over whom I may, without breach of modesty, pretend to some superiority, from the advantages I received by conversing so long among the most accomplished Houyhnhnms. I write without any view towards profit or praise. I never suffer a word to pass that may look like reflection, or possibly give the least offense even to those who are most ready to take it. So that, I hope, I may with justice pronounce myself an Author perfectly blameless; against whom the tribes of answerers, considerers, observers, reflectors, detecters, remarkers will never be able to find matter for exercising their talents.

I confess it was whispered to me that I was bound in duty as a subject of England, to have given in a memorial to a secretary of state, at my first coming over; because, whatever lands are discovered by a subject, belong to the Crown. But I doubt whether our conquests in the countries I treat of would be as easy as those of Ferdinando Cortez over the naked Americans. The Lilliputians, I think, are hardly worth the charge of a fleet and army to reduce them; and I question whether it might be prudent or safe to attempt the Brobdingnagians; or, whether an English army would be much at their ease with the Flying Island over their heads. The Houyhnhnms, indeed, appear not to be so well prepared for war, a science to which they are perfect strangers, and especially against missive weapons. However, supposing myself to be a minister of state, I could never give my advice for invading them. Their prudence, unanimity, unacquaintedness with fear, and their love of their country would amply supply all defects in the military art. Imagine twenty thousand of them breaking into the midst of an European army, confounding the ranks, overturning the carriages, battering the warriors' faces into mummy,[5] by terrible yerks[6] from their hinder hoofs: for they would well deserve the character given to Augustus, *Recalcitrat undique tutus*.[7] But instead of proposals for conquering that magnanimous nation, I rather wish they were in a capacity or disposition to send a sufficient number of their inhabitants for civilizing Europe; by teaching us the first principles of Honor, Justice, Truth, Temperance,

---

5. Pulp.
6. Kicks.
7. Horace, *Satires* II.i.20. "* * * he

kicks backward, at every point on his guard."

public Spirit, Fortitude, Chastity, Friendship, Benevolence, and Fidelity. The names of all which Virtues are still retained among us in most languages, and are to be met with in modern as well as ancient authors, which I am able to assert from my own small reading.

But I had another reason which made me less forward to enlarge his majesty's dominions by my discoveries: to say the truth, I had conceived a few scruples with relation to the distributive justice of princes upon those occasions. For instance, a crew of pirates are driven by a storm they know not whither; at length a boy discovers land from the topmast; they go on shore to rob and plunder; they see an harmless people, are entertained with kindness, they give the country a new name, they take formal possession of it for the king, they set up a rotton plank or a stone for a memorial, they murder two or three dozen of the natives, bring away a couple more by force for a sample, return home, and get their pardon. Here commences a new dominion acquired with a title by Divine Right. Ships are sent with the first opportunity; the natives driven out or destroyed, their princes tortured to discover their gold; a free license given to all acts of inhumanity and lust; the earth reeking with the blood of its inhabitants: and this execrable crew of butchers employed in so pious an expedition is a *modern colony* sent to convert and civilize an idolatrous and barbarous people.

But this description, I confess, doth by no means affect the British nation, who may be an example to the whole world for their wisdom, care, and justice in planting colonies; their liberal endowments for the advancement of religion and learning; their choice of devout and able pastors to propagate Christianity; their caution in stocking their provinces with people of sober lives and conversations from this the Mother Kingdom; their strict regard to the distribution of justice, in supplying the civil administration through all their colonies with officers of the greatest abilities, utter strangers to corruption: and to crown all, by sending the most vigilant and virtuous governors, who have no other views than the happiness of the people over whom they preside, and the honor of the king their master.

But, as those countries which I have described do not appear to have any desire of being conquered, and enslaved, murdered, or driven out by colonies, nor abound either in gold, silver, sugar, or tobacco, I did humbly conceive they were by no means proper objects of our zeal, our valor, or our interest. However, if those whom it may concern, think fit to be of another opinion, I am ready to depose, when I shall be lawfully called, that no European did ever visit these countries before me. I mean, if the inhabitants ought to be believed.

But, as to the formality of taking possession in my sovereign's name, it never came once into my thoughts; and if it had, yet as my affairs then stood, I should perhaps in point of prudence and self-preservation have put it off to a better opportunity.

Having thus answered the only objection that can be raised against me as a traveler, I here take a final leave of my courteous readers, and return to enjoy my own speculations in my little garden at Redriff; to apply those excellent lessons of virtue which I learned among the Houyhnhnms; to instruct the Yahoos of my own family as far as I shall find them docible animals; to behold my figure often in a glass, and thus if possible habituate myself by time to tolerate the sight of a human creature; to lament the brutality of Houyhnhnms in my own country, but always treat their persons with respect, for the sake of my noble master, his family, his friends, and the whole Houyhnhnm race, whom these of ours have the honor to resemble in all their lineaments, however their intellectuals came to degenerate.

I began last week to permit my wife to sit at dinner with me, at the farthest end of a long table; and to answer (but with the utmost brevity) the few questions I ask her. Yet the smell of a Yahoo continuing very offensive, I always keep my nose well stopped with rue, lavender, or tobacco leaves. And although it be hard for a man late in life to remove old habits, I am not altogether out of hopes in some time to suffer a neighbor Yahoo in my company, without the apprehensions I am yet under of his teeth or his claws.

My reconcilement to the Yahoo kind in general might not be so difficult, if they would be content with those vices and follies only which nature hath entitled them to. I am not in the least provoked at the sight of a lawyer, a pickpocket, a colonel, a fool, a lord, a gamester, a politician, a whoremonger, a physician, an evidence, a suborner, an attorney, a traitor, or the like: this is all according to the due course of things. But when I behold a lump of deformity, and diseases both in body and mind, smitten with pride, it immediately breaks all the measures of my patience; neither shall I be ever able to comprehend how such an animal and such a vice could tally together. The wise and virtuous Houyhnhnms, who abound in all excellencies that can adorn a rational creature, have no name for this vice in their language, which hath no terms to express anything that is evil, except those whereby they describe the detestable qualities of their Yahoos, among which they were not able to distinguish this of pride, for want of thoroughly understanding human nature, as it showeth itself in other countries, where that animal presides. But I, who had more experience, could plainly observe some rudiments of it among the wild Yahoos.

But the Houyhnhnms, who live under the government of reason, are no more proud of the good qualities they possess, than I should be for not wanting a leg or an arm, which no man in his wits would boast of, although he must be miserable without them. I dwell the longer upon this subject from the desire I have to make the society of an English Yahoo by any means not insupportable; and therefore I here entreat those who have any tincture of this absurd vice, that they will not presume to appear in my sight.

1726, 1735

A Modest Proposal[1]

FOR PREVENTING THE CHILDREN OF POOR PEOPLE IN IRELAND FROM BEING A BURDEN TO THEIR PARENTS OR COUNTRY, AND FOR MAKING THEM BENEFICIAL TO THE PUBLIC

It is a melancholy object to those who walk through this great town[2] or travel in the country, when they see the streets, the roads, and cabin doors, crowded with beggars of the female sex, followed by three, four, or six children, all in rags and importuning every passenger for an alms. These mothers, instead of being able to work for their honest livelihood, are forced to employ all their time in strolling to beg sustenance for their helpless infants, who, as they grow up, either turn thieves for want of work, or leave their dear native country to fight for the Pretender in Spain, or sell themselves to the Barbadoes.[3]

I think it is agreed by all parties that this prodigious number of children in the arms, or on the backs, or at the heels of their mothers, and frequently of their fathers, is in the present deplor-

1. *A Modest Proposal* is an example of Swift's favorite satiric devices used with superb effect. Irony (from the deceptive adjective "modest" in the title to the very last sentence) pervades the piece. A rigorous logic deduces ghastly arguments from a shocking premise so quietly assumed that the reader assents before he is aware of what his assent implies. Parody, at which Swift is adept, allows him to glance sardonically at the by then familiar figure of the benevolent humanitarian (forerunner of the modern sociologist, social worker, economic planner) concerned to correct a social evil by means of a theoretically conceived plan. The proposer, as naïve as he is apparently logical and kindly, ignores and therefore emphasizes for the reader the enormity of his plan. The whole is an elaboration of a rather trite metaphor: "The English are devouring the Irish." But there is nothing trite about the pamphlet, which ex-presses in Swift's most controlled style his pity for the oppressed, ignorant, populous, and hungry Catholic peasants of Ireland, and his anger at the rapacious English absentee landlords, who were bleeding the country white with the silent approbation of Parliament, ministers, and the Crown.
2. Dublin.
3. James Francis Edward Stuart (1688–1766), the son of James II, was claimant ("Pretender") to the throne of England from which the Glorious Revolution had barred his succession. Catholic Ireland was loyal to him, and Irishmen joined him in his exile on the Continent. Because of the poverty in Ireland, many Irishmen emigrated to the West Indies and other British colonies in America; they paid their passage by binding themselves to work for a stated period for one of the planters.

able state of the kingdom a very great additional grievance; and therefore whoever could find out a fair, cheap, and easy method of making these children sound, useful members of the commonwealth would deserve so well of the public as to have his statue set up for a preserver of the nation.

But my intention is very far from being confined to provide only for the children of professed beggars; it is of a much greater extent, and shall take in the whole number of infants at a certain age who are born of parents in effect as little able to support them as those who demand our charity in the streets.

As to my own part, having turned my thoughts for many years upon this important subject, and maturely weighed the several schemes of other projectors,[4] I have always found them grossly mistaken in their computation. It is true, a child just dropped from its dam may be supported by her milk for a solar year, with little other nourishment; at most not above the value of two shillings, which the mother may certainly get, or the value in scraps, by her lawful occupation of begging; and it is exactly at one year old that I propose to provide for them in such a manner as instead of being a charge upon their parents or the parish, or wanting food and raiment for the rest of their lives, they shall on the contrary contribute to the feeding, and partly to the clothing, of many thousands.

There is likewise another great advantage in my scheme, that it will prevent those voluntary abortions, and that horrid practice of women murdering their bastard children, alas, too frequent among us, sacrificing the poor innocent babes, I doubt, more to avoid the expense than the shame, which would move tears and pity in the most savage and inhuman breast.

The number of souls in this kingdom[5] being usually reckoned one million and a half, of these I calculate there may be about two hundred thousand couple whose wives are breeders; from which number I subtract thirty thousand couples who are able to maintain their own children, although I apprehend there cannot be so many under the present distresses of the kingdom; but this being granted, there will remain an hundred and seventy thousand breeders. I again subtract fifty thousand for those women who miscarry, or whose children die by accident or disease within the year. There only remain an hundred and twenty thousand children of poor parents annually born. The question therefore is, how this number shall be reared and provided for, which, as I have already said, under the present situation of affairs, is utterly impossible by all the methods hitherto proposed. For we can neither employ them in handicraft or agriculture; we neither build houses (I mean in the country) nor cultivate land. They can very seldom pick up a livelihood

4. Devisers of schemes.   5. Ireland.

by stealing till they arrive at six years old, except where they are of towardly[6] parts; although I confess they learn the rudiments much earlier, during which time they can however be looked upon only as probationers, as I have been informed by a principal gentleman in the county of Cavan, who protested to me that he never knew above one or two instances under the age of six, even in a part of the kingdom so renowned for the quickest proficiency in that art.

I am assured by our merchants that a boy or a girl before twelve years old is no salable commodity; and even when they come to this age they will not yield above three pounds, or three pounds and half a crown at most on the Exchange; which cannot turn to account either to the parents or the kingdom, the charge of nutriment and rags having been at least four times that value.

I shall now therefore humbly propose my own thoughts, which I hope will not be liable to the least objection.

I have been assured by a very knowing American of my acquaintance in London, that a young healthy child well nursed is at a year old a most delicious, nourishing, and wholesome food, whether stewed, roasted, baked, or boiled; and I make no doubt that it will equally serve in a fricassee or a ragout.[7]

I do therefore humbly offer it to public consideration that of the hundred and twenty thousand children, already computed, twenty thousand may be reserved for breed, whereof only one fourth part to be males, which is more than we allow to sheep, black cattle, or swine; and my reason is that these children are seldom the fruits of marriage, a circumstance not much regarded by our savages, therefore one male will be sufficient to serve four females. That the remaining hundred thousand may at a year old be offered in sale to the persons of quality and fortune through the kingdom, always advising the mother to let them suck plentifully in the last month, so as to render them plump and fat for a good table. A child will make two dishes at an entertainment for friends; and when the family dines alone, the fore or hind quarter will make a reasonable dish, and seasoned with a little pepper or salt will be very good boiled on the fourth day, especially in winter.

I have reckoned upon a medium that a child just born will weigh twelve pounds, and in a solar year if tolerably nursed increaseth to twenty-eight pounds.

I grant this food will be somewhat dear, and therefore very proper for landlords, who, as they have already devoured most of the parents, seem to have the best title to the children.

Infant's flesh will be in season throughout the year, but more plentiful in March, and a little before and after. For we are told by a grave author, an eminent French physician,[8] that fish being

---

6. Dutiful, tractable.
7. A highly seasoned meat stew.
8. François Rabelais (ca. 1494–1553),
a humorist and a satirist, by no means grave.

a prolific diet, there are more children born in Roman Catholic countries about nine months after Lent than at any other season; therefore, reckoning a year after Lent, the markets will be more glutted than usual, because the number of popish infants is at least three to one in this kingdom; and therefore it will have one other collateral advantage, by lessening the number of Papists among us.

I have already computed the charge of nursing a beggar's child (in which list I reckon all cottagers, laborers, and four fifths of the farmers) to be about two shillings per annum, rags included; and I believe no gentleman would repine to give ten shillings for the carcass of a good fat child, which, as I have said, will make four dishes of excellent nutritive meat, when he hath only some particular friend or his own family to dine with him. Thus the squire will learn to be a good landlord, and grow popular among the tenants; the mother will have eight shillings net profit, and be fit for work till she produces another child.

Those who are more thrifty (as I must confess the times require) may flay the carcass; the skin of which artificially[9] dressed will make admirable gloves for ladies, and summer boots for fine gentlemen.

As to our city of Dublin, shambles[1] may be appointed for this purpose in the most convenient parts of it, and butchers we may be assured will not be wanting; although I rather recommend buying the children alive, and dressing them hot from the knife as we do roasting pigs.

A very worthy person, a true lover of his country, and whose virtues I highly esteem, was lately pleased in discoursing on this matter to offer a refinement upon my scheme. He said that many gentlemen of this kingdom, having of late destroyed their deer, he conceived that the want of venison might be well supplied by the bodies of young lads and maidens, not exceeding fourteen years of age nor under twelve, so great a number of both sexes in every county being now ready to starve for want of work and service; and these to be disposed of by their parents, if alive, or otherwise by their nearest relations. But with due deference to so excellent a friend and so deserving a patriot, I cannot be altogether in his sentiments; for as to the males, my American acquaintance assured me from frequent experience that their flesh was generally tough and lean, like that of our schoolboys, by continual exercise, and their taste disagreeable; and to fatten them would not answer the charge. Then as to the females, it would, I think with humble submission, be a loss to the public, because they soon would become breeders themselves: and besides, it is not improbable that some scrupulous people might be apt to censure such a practice (although indeed very unjustly) as a little bordering upon cruelty;

9. Skillfully.   1. Slaughterhouses.

which, I confess, hath always been with me the strongest objection against any project, how well soever intended.

But in order to justify my friend, he confessed that this expedient was put into his head by the famous Psalmanazar,[2] a native of the island Formosa, who came from thence to London above twenty years ago, and in conversation told my friend that in his country when any young person happened to be put to death, the executioner sold the carcass to persons of quality as a prime dainty; and that in his time the body of a plump girl of fifteen, who was crucified for an attempt to poison the emperor, was sold to his Imperial Majesty's prime minister of state, and other great mandarins of the court, in joints from the gibbet, at four hundred crowns. Neither indeed can I deny that if the same use were made of several plump young girls in this town, who without one single groat to their fortunes cannot stir abroad without a chair, and appear at the playhouse and assemblies in foreign fineries which they never will pay for, the kingdom would not be the worse.

Some persons of a desponding spirit are in great concern about that vast number of poor people who are aged, diseased, or maimed, and I have been desired to employ my thoughts what course may be taken to ease the nation of so grievous an encumbrance. But I am not in the least pain upon that matter, because it is very well known that they are every day dying and rotting by cold and famine, and filth and vermin, as fast as can be reasonably expected. And as to the younger laborers, they are now in almost as hopeful a condition. They cannot get work, and consequently pine away for want of nourishment to a degree that if at any time they are accidentally hired to common labor, they have not strength to perform it; and thus the country and themselves are happily delivered from the evils to come.

I have too long digressed, and therefore shall return to my subject. I think the advantages by the proposal which I have made are obvious and many, as well as of the highest importance.

For first, as I have already observed, it would greatly lessen the number of Papists, with whom we are yearly overrun, being the principal breeders of the nation as well as our most dangerous enemies; and who stay at home on purpose to deliver the kingdom to the Pretender, hoping to take their advantage by the absence of so many good Protestants, who have chosen rather to leave their country than stay at home and pay tithes against their conscience to an Episcopal curate.

Secondly, the poorer tenants will have something valuable of their own, which by law may be made liable to distress,[3] and help

2. George Psalmanazar (ca. 1679–1763), a famous imposter. A Frenchman, he imposed himself on English bishops, noblemen, and scientists as a Formosan. He wrote an entirely fictitious account of Formosa, in which he described human sacrifices and cannibalism.

3. Distraint, i.e., the seizing, through legal action, of property for the payment of debts and other obligations.

to pay their landlord's rent, their corn and cattle being already seized and money a thing unknown.

Thirdly, whereas the maintenance of an hundred thousand children, from two years old and upwards, cannot be computed at less than ten shillings a piece per annum, the nation's stock will be thereby increased fifty thousand pounds per annum, besides the profit of a new dish introduced to the tables of all gentlemen of fortune in the kingdom who have any refinement in taste. And the money will circulate among ourselves, the goods being entirely of our own growth and manufacture.

Fourthly, the constant breeders, besides the gain of eight shillings sterling per annum by the sale of their children, will be rid of the charge of maintaining them after the first year.

Fifthly, this food would likewise bring great custom to taverns, where the vintners will certainly be so prudent as to procure the best receipts for dressing it to perfection, and consequently have their houses frequented by all the fine gentlemen, who justly value themselves upon their knowledge in good eating; and a skillful cook, who understands how to oblige his guests, will contrive to make it as expensive as they please.

Sixthly, this would be a great inducement to marriage, which all wise nations have either encouraged by rewards or enforced by laws and penalties. It would increase the care and tenderness of mothers toward their children, when they were sure of a settlement for life to the poor babes, provided in some sort by the public, to their annual profit instead of expense. We should see an honest emulation among the married women, which of them could bring the fattest child to the market. Men would become as fond of their wives during the time of their pregnancy as they are now of their mares in foal, their cows in calf, or sows when they are ready to farrow; nor offer to beat or kick them (as is too frequent a practice) for fear of a miscarriage.

Many other advantages might be enumerated. For instance, the addition of some thousand carcasses in our exportation of barreled beef, the propagation of swine's flesh, and improvement in the art of making good bacon, so much wanted among us by the great destruction of pigs, too frequent at our tables, which are no way comparable in taste or magnificence to a well-grown, fat, yearling child, which roasted whole will make a considerable figure at a lord mayor's feast or any other public entertainment. But this and many others I omit, being studious of brevity.

Supposing that one thousand families in this city would be constant customers for infants' flesh, besides others who might have it at merry meetings, particularly weddings and christenings, I compute that Dublin would take off annually about twenty thousand carcasses, and the rest of the kingdom (where probably they will be sold somewhat cheaper) the remaining eighty thousand.

I can think of no one objection that will possibly be raised against this proposal, unless it should be urged that the number of people will be thereby much lessened in the kingdom. This I freely own, and it was indeed one principal design in offering it to the world. I desire the reader will observe, that I calculate my remedy for this one individual kingdom of Ireland and for no other that ever was, is, or I think ever can be upon earth. Therefore let no man talk to me of other expedients: of taxing our absentees at five shillings a pound: of using neither clothes nor household furniture except what is of our own growth and manufacture: of utterly rejecting the materials and instruments that promote foreign luxury: of curing the expensiveness of pride, vanity, idleness, and gaming in our women: of introducing a vein of parsimony, prudence, and temperance: of learning to love our country, in the want of which we differ even from Laplanders and the inhabitants of Topinamboo:[4] of quitting our animosities and factions, nor acting any longer like the Jews, who were murdering one another at the very moment their city was taken:[5] of being a little cautious not to sell our country and conscience for nothing: of teaching landlords to have at least one degree of mercy toward their tenants: lastly, of putting a spirit of honesty, industry, and skill into our shopkeepers; who, if a resolution could now be taken to buy only our native goods, would immediately unite to cheat and exact upon us in the price, the measure, and the goodness, nor could ever yet be brought to make one fair proposal of just dealing, though often and earnestly invited to it.[6]

Therefore I repeat, let no man talk to me of these and the like expedients, till he hath at least some glimpse of hope that there will ever be some hearty and sincere attempt to put them in practice.

But as to myself, having been wearied out for many years with offering vain, idle, visionary thoughts, and at length utterly despairing of success, I fortunately fell upon this proposal, which, as it is wholly new, so it hath something solid and real, of no expense and little trouble, full in our own power, and whereby we can incur no danger in disobliging England. For this kind of commodity will not bear exportation, the flesh being of too tender a consistence to admit a long continuance in salt, although perhaps I could name a country which would be glad to eat up our whole nation without it.[7]

After all, I am not so violently bent upon my own opinion as

4. I.e., even Laplanders love their frozen, infertile country and the savage tribes of Brazil their jungle more than the Anglo-Irish love Ireland.

5. During the siege of Jerusalem by the Roman Emperor Titus, who captured and destroyed the city in A.D. 70, the city was torn by bloody fights between factions of fanatics.

6. Swift himself had made all these proposals in various pamphlets. In editions printed during his lifetime the various proposals were italicized to indicate that Swift is no longer being ironic.

7. I.e., England.

to reject any offer proposed by wise men, which shall be found equally innocent, cheap, easy, and effectual. But before something of that kind shall be advanced in contradiction to my scheme, and offering a better, I desire the author or authors will be pleased maturely to consider two points. First, as things now stand, how they will be able to find food and raiment for an hundred thousand useless mouths and backs. And secondly, there being a round million of creatures in human figure throughout this kingdom, whose sole subsistence put into a common stock would leave them in debt two millions of pounds sterling, adding those who are beggars by profession to the bulk of farmers, cottagers, and laborers, with their wives and children who are beggars in effect; I desire those politicians who dislike my overture, and may perhaps be so bold to attempt an answer, that they will first ask the parents of these mortals whether they would not at this day think it a great happiness to have been sold for food at a year old in the manner I prescribe, and thereby have avoided such a perpetual scene of misfortunes as they have since gone through by the oppression of landlords, the impossibility of paying rent without money or trade, the want of common sustenance, with neither house nor clothes to cover them from the inclemencies of the weather, and the most inevitable prospect of entailing the like or greater miseries upon their breed forever.

I profess, in the sincerity of my heart, that I have not the least personal interest in endeavoring to promote this necessary work, having no other motive than the public good of my country, by advancing our trade, providing for infants, relieving the poor, and giving some pleasure to the rich. I have no children by which I can propose to get a single penny; the youngest being nine years old, and my wife past childbearing.

1729

ALEXANDER POPE
(1688–1744)

1711:   *Essay on Criticism.*
1712:   First version of *The Rape of the Lock.*
1713–26: Translating Homer, editing Shakespeare.
1728:   The *Dunciad* begins Pope's career as major verse satirist.
1733–34: The *Essay on Man* begins Pope's career as ethical and philosophical poet.

Pope is the only important writer of his generation who was solely a man of letters. Since he could not, as a Roman Catholic, attend a university, vote, or hold public office, he was excluded from the sort of patronage which was freely bestowed by statesmen on most writers during the reign of Anne. This disadvantage he turned into a positive good, for the translation of Homer's *Iliad* and *Odyssey*, which he undertook for profit as well as for fame, gave him ample means to live the life of an independent suburban gentleman. After 1718 he lived hospitably in his villa by the Thames at Twickenham (then pronounced *Twit'nam*), entertaining his friends and converting his five acres of land into a diminutive landscape garden. Almost exactly a century earlier, Shakespeare had earned enough to retire to a country estate at Stratford—but he had been an actor-manager as well as a playwright; Pope, therefore, was the first writer to demonstrate that literature alone could be a gainful profession.

Ill health plagued Pope almost from birth. Delicate as a child, he was early stunted and deformed by tuberculosis of the spine. His father, a well-to-do London merchant, retired from business in the year of the poet's birth, and about 1700 acquired a small property at Binfield in Windsor Forest. In rural surroundings, as the boy's health improved, he early acquired his lifelong taste for natural beauty and for gardening. There he completed by wide reading the desultory schooling that both his ill health and his religion had made inevitable, and, encouraged by his father, he began also to develop his precocious talent for poetry. The removal to Binfield, then, was in every way advantageous. But Pope was never to enjoy good health: in later life he was troubled by violent head-aches, and he suffered from easily exacerbated nerves. This neurotic irritability was a price he had to pay for the sensitive and ardent temperament that helped make him one of our greatest poets. Because of it, he both hated and loved intensely; because of it his responsiveness to beauty in all its forms was unusually acute.

Pope's first striking success as a poet was the *Essay on Criticism* (1711), which earned him the fame of Addison's approval and the notoriety of an intemperate personal attack from the critic John Dennis, who was angered by a casual reference to himself in the poem. *The Rape of the Lock*, both in its original shorter version of 1712 and in its more elaborate version of 1714, established the author of the *Essay on Criticism* as a master not only of metrics and of language, but also of witty, urbane satire. In the earlier work, Pope had excelled all his predecessors in writing a didactic poem after the example of Horace; in the later, he had written the most brilliant mock epic in the language. But there was another vein in Pope's youthful poetry, much of which, concerned as it is with natural beauty and love, reveals a temperament that in a later poet might have been called "Romantic." The *Pastorals* (1709), Pope's first publication, and *Windsor Forest* (1713; much of it was written earlier) are essentially nature poems, abounding in visual imagery and descriptive passages of ideally ordered nature. They remind us that Pope was an amateur painter who delighted in the beauty of external nature, as well as in the artificial beauty of the world of *The Rape of the Lock*. The *Elegy to the Memory of an Unfortunate Lady*, published in the collected poems of 1717, presents the high heroics of romantic love. Looking back to his early poems, Pope said that he had wandered "in Fancy's maze." And even the long task of translating Homer, the "dull duty" of editing Shakespeare, and, in middle age, his preoccupation with ethical and satirical poetry did not extinguish this side of Pope's nature and art. He learned to subordinate, but he did not cease to use, this sensitive awareness of visual beauty in his later poetry.

Pope's early poetry brought him to the attention of literary men, with whom he began to associate in the masculine world of coffeehouse and tavern. His fragile health never permitted him to live the rakish life that he would have liked, but it did not prevent his enjoying the company of some of the most distinguished men of letters of the time. Between 1706 and 1711 he came to know, among many others, William Congreve, William Walsh, the critic and poet, and Richard Steele and Joseph Addison, who, after 1709, were two of the most admired writers of the day. As it happened, all these men were Whigs. Pope was probably indifferent to politics at this time, or at least he could readily ignore politics in the excitement of taking his place among the leading wits of the town. But after the fall of the Whigs in 1710, and the formation of the Tory government under Robert Harley (later Earl of Oxford) and Henry St. John (later Viscount Bolingbroke) party loyalties bred bitterness among the wits as among the politicians.

By 1712 Pope had made the acquaintance of another group of writers, all Tories, who soon became his intimate friends: Jonathan Swift, by then the close associate of Harley and St. John and the principal propagandist for their policies; Dr. John Arbuthnot, physician to the queen, a learned scientist, a wit of the first quality, and a man of deep humanity and utter integrity; John Gay, the poet, who in 1728 was to produce the *Beggar's Opera*, the greatest theatrical success of the century; and Thomas Parnell, a poet of some distinction, who died prematurely in 1718. It was among these men that Pope was to find his lifelong friends; and it was through them that he became the friend and admirer of Oxford, and later the intimate of Bolingbroke. As he grew more intimate with his new circle, he began to drift away from Addison and his earlier friends.

In 1714 this group, at the instigation of Pope, formed a club which was to cooperate in a scheme for satirizing all sorts of false learning and pedantry in philosophy, science, and other branches of knowledge. They were joined by the Earl of Oxford, who attended as often as business permitted. The friends proposed to write jointly the biography of a learned fool whom they named Martinus Scriblerus (Martin the Scribbler), whose life and opinions would be a running commentary on whatever they considered the abuses of learning and the follies of the learned. The death of the queen in August, 1714, brought the venture to a premature end, but not before some amusing episodes had been invented, as the published (probably very much rewritten) version of the *Memoirs of Martinus Scriblerus* (1741), makes plain. The real importance of the club, however, is that it fostered a satiric temper which was to find unexpected expression in such mature works of the friends as *Gulliver's Travels*, the *Dunciad*, and even, perhaps, the *Beggar's Opera*.

"The life of a wit is a warfare on earth," said Pope, generalizing from his own experience. His very success as a poet (and his astonishing precocity brought him success very early) made enemies among the less talented and consequently envious writers, who were to plague him in pamphlets, verse satires, and squibs in the journals throughout his entire literary career. He was to be attacked for his writings, his religion, and his physical deformity. Though he smarted under the jibes of his detractors, he was a fighter who struck back, always giving better than he got. The common notion that he was a malicious, treacherous, venomous man, motivated merely by personal vanity and malice, is the creation of his enemies, and can be accepted by no one who reads the vicious attacks on him published from 1711 to the end of his life. Usually he was not the aggressor, but he never forgot an insult or forgave an injury, and sooner or later he took his revenge—sometimes, it must be admitted, in rather un-savory ways. But he was loved and trusted by many of the most honorable, eminent, and gifted men of his time, and with only a few exceptions (aside from politicians), the objects of his satire are people who would be for-gotten today had they not been so humiliatingly preserved to posterity.

Pope's literary warfare began in 1713, when he announced his intention of translating the *Iliad* and sought, with the support of his friends, sub-scribers to a de luxe edition of the work. Subscribers came in droves, but Pope had enemies as well. The Whig writers who surrounded Addison at Button's Coffee House did all they could through anonymous attacks to hinder the success of the venture, and even (with Addison's knowledge and perhaps encouragement) announced a rival translation by Thomas Tickell, one of Addison's Oxford friends. The eventual success of the first published installment of his *Iliad* in 1715 did not obliterate Pope's just resentment against Addison and his "little senate"; and this resentment found expression in the damaging portrait of Addison (under the name of Atticus), which, years after it was written, was included in Pope's *Epistle to Dr. Arbuthnot* (1735), lines 193–214. The not unjustified attacks on Pope's edition of Shakespeare (1725), especially those by the learned Shakespeare scholar Lewis Theobald (Pope always spelled and pronounced the name "Tibbald" in his satires), led to Theobald's appearance as king of the dunces in the *Dunciad* (1728). In this impressive poem Pope stigmatized his literary enemies as agents of all that he disliked and feared in the literary tendencies of his time—the vulgarization of taste and the arts consequent on the rapid growth of the reading public, the develop-ment of journalism, magazines, and other popular and cheap publications, which spread scandal, sensationalism, and political partisanship—in short the new commercial spirit of the nation, which was corrupting not only the arts, but, as Pope saw it, the national life itself.

In the 1730's Pope moved on to philosophical, ethical, and political sub-jects in the *Essay on Man*, the *Epistles to Several Persons*, and the *Imita-tions of Horace*. The reigns of George I and George II appeared to him, as to Swift and other Tories, a period of rapid moral, political, and cultural deterioration. The agents of decay seemed in one way or another related to the spread of moneyed (as opposed to landed) wealth, which accounted for the political corruption encouraged by Sir Robert Walpole and the court party, and the increasing influence in all aspects of the national life of a vulgar class of *nouveaux riches*. Pope assumed the role of the cham-pion of traditional civilization: of right reason, humanistic learning, sound art, good taste, and public virtue. For him the supreme value was order

—cosmic, political, social, aesthetic—which he saw (or believed he saw) threatened on all sides. It was fortunate that most of his enemies seem to have been designed by nature to illustrate various degrees of unreason, pedantry, bad art, vulgar taste, and, at best, indifferent morals. Personal malice edged his satire, but his art elevated his unhappy victims into symbols of Georgian barbarism.

The principal obstacle between the modern reader and Pope's satires is that they seem to require a vast amount of particular knowledge about a long-vanished age. This is not entirely the case. Although a certain amount of social and political history is helpful, the whole body of Pope's satire can be read and enjoyed without much biographical information. The satirist traditionally deals in generally prevalent evils and generally observable human types, and this is true of Pope, even when he named actual individuals. Usually in the late satires, as in the earlier *Rape*, he used fictional or type names, although he most often had an individual in mind —Sappho, Atossa, Atticus, Sporus; and when he named individuals (as he consistently did in the *Dunciad* and occasionally elsewhere), his purpose was to raise his victims to the bad eminence of typifying some sort of obliquity. Nor need we be concerned with whether or not the moral character of the speaker of the satires is identical with that of Alexander Pope of Twickenham. Pope created a clearly defined person (the "I" of the satires) with the character and personality of one who could freely censure the age. This fictional or semi-fictional figure is the detached observer, somewhat removed from City, town, and court, the centers of corruption; he is the friend of virtuous men, whose friendship for him testifies to his integrity; he is fond of peace, country life, the arts, morality, and truth, and he detests their opposites which flourish in the great world. In such an age, Pope implies, it is impossible for such a man—honest, truthful, blunt—not to write satire. Where even political power and law are subject to the corruptor wealth, no weapon remains to the guardian of the public weal but the "sacred weapon" of satire. This is the satirist whom Pope creates, and to move from him to the private character of Pope is to move away from the poems.

Something must be said about Pope's versification, and the varied styles of his poems. It takes only a little familiarity with his writings to discover how wrong has been the conventional judgment that they are artificial, mechanical, and monotonous. From first to last, the permanent elements of Pope's poetic style are his remarkable rhythmic variety, despite the apparently rigid metrical unit—the heroic couplet—in which he wrote; the precision of meaning and the harmony (or the expressive disharmony, when necessary) of his language; and his superb discipline, which enables him at his characteristic best to achieve maximum conciseness together with maximum complexity. Something of Pope's metrical variety and verbal harmony can be observed in even so short a passage as lines 71–76 of the pastoral *Summer* (1709), lines so lyrical that Handel set them to music. In the passage quoted below (as also in the following quotation), only those rhetorical stresses which distort the normal iambic flow of the verse have been marked; internal pauses within the line are indicated by single and double bars, alliteration and assonance by italics.

Oh deign to visit our forsaken seats,
The mossy fountains || and the green retreats!
Where'er you walk || cool gales shall fan the glade,
Trees where you sit || shall crowd into a shade:
Where'er you tread || the blushing flowers shall rise,
And all things flourish where you turn your eyes.

Pope has attained metrical variety here by the free substitution of trochees and spondees for the normal iambs; he has achieved rhythmic variety by arranging phrases and clauses (units of syntax and logic) of different lengths within single lines and couplets, so that the passage moves with the sinuous fluency of thought and feeling, not the mechanical regularity of a metronome; and he has not only chosen musical combinations of words, but has also subtly modulated the harmony of the passage by unobtrusive patterns of alliteration and assonance.

Contrast with this pastoral passage lines 16–25 of the *Epilogue to the Satires, Dialogue II* (1738), in which Pope is not making music, but is imitating actual conversation so realistically that the metrical pattern and the integrity of the couplet and individual line seem to be destroyed (though in fact they are very much present). The poet-satirist is engaged in a dialogue with a friend who warns him that his satire is too personal, indeed mere libel. The poet is speaking:

Ye statesmen, | priests of one religion all!
Ye tradesmen vile || in army, court, or hall!
Ye reverend atheists. || F. Scandal! | name them, | Who?
  P. Why that's the thing you bid me not to do.
Who starved a sister, || who foreswore a debt,
I never named; || the town's inquiring yet.
The poisoning dame— | F. You mean— | P. I don't— | F. You do.
  P. See, now I keep the secret, || and not you!
The bribing statesman— | F. Hold, || too high you go.
  P. The bribed elector— || F. There you stoop too low.

In such a passage the language and rhythms of poetry merge with the language and rhythms of impassioned living speech.

But there is another sort of variety within Pope's work as a whole which derives from the poet's respect for the idea that the different kinds of literature have their different and appropriate styles. Thus the *Essay on Criticism*, an informal discussion of literary theory, is written, like Horace's *Ars Poetica*, a similarly didactic poem, in a plain style, relatively devoid of imagery and eloquence, and in the easy language of well-bred talk. *The Rape of the Lock*, being "a heroi-comical poem" (that is, a comic poem that treats trivial material in an epic style), employs the lofty heroic language that Dryden had perfected in his translation of Virgil, and introduces amusing parodies of passages in *Paradise Lost*. The grave epistles that make up the *Essay on Man*, a philosophical discussion of such majestic themes as the Creator and his creation, the universe, and the nature of man, of human society, and of happiness, are written in a stately forensic language and tone and constantly employ the traditional rhetorical figures. The *Imitations of Horace,* and, above all, the *Epistle to Dr. Arbuthnot,* his finest poem "in the Horatian way," reveal Pope's final mastery of the plain style of Horace's epistles and satires and justify his image of himself as the heir of the Roman poet. In short no other poet of the century can equal Pope in the range of his materials, the diversity of his poetic styles, and the sheer mastery of the poet's craft.

From An Essay on Criticism[1]

Part I

'Tis hard to say, if greater want of skill
Appear in writing or in judging ill;
But of the two less dangerous is the offense
To tire our patience than mislead our sense.
Some few in that, but numbers err in this,   5
Ten censure[1a] wrong for one who writes amiss;

---

1. There is no pleasanter introduction to the canons of taste in the English Augustan age than Pope's *Essay on Criticism.* As Addison said in his review in *Spectator* 253, it assembles the "most known and most received observations on the subject of literature and criticism." Pope was attempting to do for his time what Horace, in his *Ars Poetica,* and what Nicolas Boileau (French poet of the age of Louis XIV), in his *L'Art Poëtique,* had done for theirs. Horace is not only one of Pope's instructors in the principles of criticism; he is also Pope's model in this poem, especially in the simple, conversational language, the tone of well-bred ease, and the deliberately plain style of the *Ars Poetica*— all of which qualities Pope reproduces.

In framing his critical creed, Pope did not try for novelty: he drew from the standard writings of classical antiquity, especially from the *Ars Poetica,* and the *Institutio Oratoria* of the Roman rhetorician Quintilian; from French critical theory. of the preceding century; and from Ben Jonson's *Timber, or Discoveries* and the prefaces of John Dryden. He wished merely to give to generally accepted doctrines pleasing and memorable expression. Here one meets the key words of neoclassical criticism: *wit, Nature, ancients, rules, genius. Wit* in the poem is a word of many meanings—a clever remark, or the man who makes it; a conceit; liveliness of mind; inventiveness; fancy; genius; a genius; poetry itself, among

others. *Nature* is an equally ambiguous word, meaning not "things out there," or "the outdoors," but most importantly that which is representative, universal, permanent in human experience as opposed to the idiosyncratic, the individual, the temporary. In line 21, the word comes close to meaning "intuitive knowledge." In line 52, it means that half-personified power manifested in the cosmic order, which in its modes of working is a model for art. The reverence felt by most Augustans for the works of the great writers of ancient Greece and Rome raised the question how far the authority of these *ancients* extended. Were their works to be received as models to be conscientiously imitated? Were the *rules* received from them or deducible from their works to be accepted as prescriptive laws or merely convenient guides? Was individual *genius* to be bound by what has been conventionally held to be *Nature,* by the authority of the *ancients,* and by the legalistic pedantry of *rules?* Or could it go its own way?

In Part I of the *Essay* Pope constructs a harmonious system in which he effects a compromise among all these conflicting forces—a compromise which is typically 18th century in spirit. Part II analyzes the causes of faulty criticism. Part III (not printed here) characterizes the good critic and praises the great critics of the past.

1a. Judge.

A fool might once himself alone expose,
Now one in verse makes many more in prose.
'Tis with our judgments as our watches, none
Go just alike, yet each believes his own.   10
In poets as true genius is but rare,
True taste as seldom is the critic's share;
Both must alike from Heaven derive their light,
These born to judge, as well as those to write.
Let such teach others who themselves excel,   15
And censure freely who have written well.
Authors are partial to their wit, 'tis true,
But are not critics to their judgment too?
    Yet if we look more closely, we shall find
Most have the seeds of judgment in their mind: 20
Nature affords at least a glimmering light;
The lines, though touched but faintly, are drawn right.
But as the slightest sketch, if justly traced,
Is by ill coloring but the more disgraced,
So by false learning is good sense defaced: 25
Some are bewildered in the maze of schools,
And some made coxcombs[2] Nature meant but fools.
In search of wit these lose their common sense,
And then turn critics in their own defense:
Each burns alike, who can, or cannot write,   30
Or with a rival's or an eunuch's spite.
All fools have still an itching to deride,
And fain would be upon the laughing side.
If Maevius[3] scribble in Apollo's spite,
There are who judge still worse than he can write.   35
    Some have at first for wits, then poets passed,
Turned critics next, and proved plain fools at last.
Some neither can for wits nor critics pass,
As heavy mules are neither horse nor ass.
Those half-learn'd witlings, numerous in our isle,   40
As half-formed insects on the banks of Nile;[4]
Unfinished things, one knows not what to call,
Their generation's so equivocal:
To tell[5] them would a hundred tongues require,
Or one vain wit's, that might a hundred tire.   45
    But you who seek to give and merit fame,
And justly bear a critic's noble name,
Be sure yourself and your own reach to know,
How far your genius, taste, and learning go;
Launch not beyond your depth, but be discreet,   50
And mark that point where sense and dullness meet.
    Nature to all things fixed the limits fit,
And wisely curbed proud man's pretending wit.
As on the land while here the ocean gains,

2. Superficial pretenders to learning.
3. A silly poet alluded to contemptuously by Virgil in *Eclogue III* and by Horace in *Epode X*.
4. The ancients believed that many forms of life were spontaneously generated in the fertile mud of the Nile.
5. Reckon, count.

In other parts it leaves wide sandy plains; 55
Thus in the soul while memory prevails,
The solid power of understanding fails;
Where beams of warm imagination play,
The memory's soft figures melt away.
One science[6] only will one genius fit, 60
So vast is art, so narrow human wit.
Not only bounded to peculiar arts,
But oft in those confined to single parts.
Like kings we lose the conquests gained before,
By vain ambition still to make them more; 65
Each might his several province well command,
Would all but stoop to what they understand.
　　First follow Nature, and your judgment frame
By her just standard, which is still the same;
Unerring Nature, still divinely bright, 70
One clear, unchanged, and universal light,
Life, force, and beauty must to all impart,
At once the source, and end, and test of art.
Art from that fund each just supply provides,
Works without show, and without pomp presides. 75
In some fair body thus the informing soul
With spirits feeds, with vigor fills the whole,
Each motion guides, and every nerve sustains;
Itself unseen, but in the effects remains.
Some, to whom Heaven in wit has been profuse, 80
Want as much more to turn it to its use;
For wit and judgment often are at strife,
Though meant each other's aid, like man and wife.
'Tis more to guide than spur the Muse's steed,
Restrain his fury than provoke his speed; 85
The wingèd courser,[7] like a generous horse,
Shows most true mettle when you check his course.
　　Those rules of old discovered, not devised,
Are Nature still, but Nature methodized;
Nature, like liberty, is but restrained 90
By the same laws which first herself ordained.
　　Hear how learn'd Greece her useful rules indites,
When to repress and when indulge our flights:
High on Parnassus' top her sons she showed,
And pointed out those arduous paths they trod; 95
Held from afar, aloft, the immortal prize,
And urged the rest by equal steps to rise.
Just precepts thus from great examples given,
She drew from them what they derived from Heaven.
The generous critic fanned the poet's fire, 100
And taught the world with reason to admire.
Then criticism the Muse's handmaid proved,

6. Branch of learning.
7. Pegasus, associated with the Muses　—and poetic inspiration; "generous": spirited, highly bred.

To dress her charms, and make her more beloved:
But following wits from that intention strayed,
Who could not win the mistress, wooed the maid;   105
Against the poets their own arms they turned,
Sure to hate most the men from whom they learned.
So modern 'pothecaries, taught the art
By doctors' bills[8] to play the doctor's part,
Bold in the practice of mistaken rules,   110
Prescribe, apply, and call their masters fools.
Some on the leaves of ancient authors prey,
Nor time nor moths e'er spoiled so much as they.
Some dryly plain, without invention's aid,
Write dull receipts[9] how poems may be made.   115
These leave the sense their learning to display,
And those explain the meaning quite away.
    You then whose judgment the right course would steer,
Know well each ancient's proper character;
His fable,[1] subject, scope in every page;   120
Religion, country, genius of his age:
Without all these at once before your eyes,
Cavil you may, but never criticize.
Be Homer's works your study and delight,
Read them by day, and meditate by night;   125
Thence form your judgment, thence your maxims bring,
And trace the Muses upward to their spring.
Still with itself compared, his text peruse;
And let your comment be the Mantuan Muse.[2]
    When first young Maro in his boundless mind   130
A work to outlast immortal Rome designed,
Perhaps he seemed above the critic's law,
And but from Nature's fountains scorned to draw;
But when to examine every part he came,
Nature and Homer were, he found, the same.   135
Convinced, amazed, he checks the bold design, ⎫
And rules as strict his labored work confine ⎬
As if the Stagirite[3] o'erlooked each line. ⎭
Learn hence for ancient rules a just esteem;
To copy Nature is to copy them.   140
    Some beauties yet no precepts can declare,
For there's a happiness as well as care.[4]

---

8. Prescriptions.
9. Formulas for preparing a dish; recipes. Pope himself wrote an amusing burlesque *Receipt to Make an Epic Poem*, first published in the *Guardian* 78 (1713).
1. Plot or story of a play or poem.
2. Virgil, the "young Maro" of the following line, was born in a village adjacent to Mantua in Italy; hence "Mantuan Muse." His epic, the *Aeneid*, was modeled on Homer's *Iliad* and *Odyssey* and was considered to be a refinement on the Greek poems. Thus it could be thought of as a commentary ("comment") on Homer's poems.
3. Aristotle, native of Stagira, from whose *Poetics* later critics formulated strict rules for writing tragedy and the epic.
4. I.e., no rules ("precepts") can explain ("declare") some beautiful effects in a work of art which can be the result only of inspiration or good luck ("happiness"), not of painstaking labor ("care").

Music resembles poetry, in each

Are nameless graces which no methods teach,

And which a master hand alone can reach.   145

If, where the rules not far enough extend

(Since rules were made but to promote their end)

Some lucky license answer to the full

The intent proposed, that license is a rule.

Thus Pegasus, a nearer way to take,   150

May boldly deviate from the common track.

From vulgar bounds with brave disorder part,

And snatch a grace beyond the reach of art,

Which without passing through the judgment, gains

The heart, and all its end at once attains.   155

In prospects thus, some objects please our eyes,

Which out of Nature's common order rise,

The shapeless rock, or hanging precipice.

Great wits sometimes may gloriously offend,

And rise to faults true critics dare not mend;   160

But though the ancients thus their rules invade

(As kings dispense with laws themselves have made)

Moderns, beware! or if you must offend

Against the precept, ne'er transgress its end;

Let it be seldom, and compelled by need;   165

And have at least their precedent to plead.

The critic else proceeds without remorse,

Seizes your fame, and puts his laws in force.

    I know there are, to whose presumptuous thoughts

Those freer beauties, even in them, seem faults.[5]   170

Some figures monstrous and misshaped appear,

Considered singly, or beheld too near,

Which, but proportioned to their light or place,

Due distance reconciles to form and grace.

A prudent chief not always must display   175

His powers in equal ranks and fair array,

But with the occasion and the place comply,

Conceal his force, nay seem sometimes to fly.

Those oft are stratagems which errors seem,

Nor is it Homer nods, but we that dream.   180

    Still green with bays each ancient altar stands

Above the reach of sacrilegious hands,

Secure from flames, from envy's fiercer rage,

Destructive war, and all-involving age.

See, from each clime the learn'd their incense bring!   185

Here in all tongues consenting[6] paeans ring!

In praise so just let every voice be joined,[7]

And fill the general chorus of mankind.

Hail, bards triumphant! born in happier days,

Immortal heirs of universal praise!   190

5. Pronounced *fawts*.   7. Pronounced *jined*.

6. Agreeing, concurring.

Whose honors with increase of ages grow,
As streams roll down, enlarging as they flow;
Nations unborn your mighty names shall sound,
And worlds applaud that must not yet be found!
Oh, may some spark of your celestial fire,   195
The last, the meanest of your sons inspire
(That on weak wings, from far, pursues your flights,
Glows while he reads, but trembles as he writes)
To teach vain wits a science little known,
To admire superior sense, and doubt their own!   200

Part II

Of all the causes which conspire to blind
Man's erring judgment, and misguide the mind,
What the weak head with strongest bias rules,
Is pride, the never-failing vice of fools.
Whatever Nature has in worth denied,   205
She gives in large recruits[8] of needful pride;
For as in bodies, thus in souls, we find
What wants in blood and spirits swelled with wind:
Pride, where wit fails, steps in to our defense,
And fills up all the mighty void of sense.   210
If once right reason drives that cloud away,
Truth breaks upon us with resistless day.
Trust not yourself: but your defects to know,
Make use of every friend—and every foe.
A little learning is a dangerous thing;   215
Drink deep, or taste not the Pierian spring.[9]
There shallow draughts intoxicate the brain,
And drinking largely sobers us again.
Fired at first sight with what the Muse imparts,
In fearless youth we tempt[1] the heights of arts,   220
While from the bounded level of our mind
Short views we take, nor see the lengths behind;
But more advanced, behold with strange surprise
New distant scenes of endless science rise!
So pleased at first the towering Alps we try,   225
Mount o'er the vales, and seem to tread the sky,
The eternal snows appear already past,
And the first clouds and mountains seem the last;
But, those attained, we tremble to survey
The growing labors of the lengthened way,   230
The increasing prospect tires our wandering eyes,
Hills peep o'er hills, and Alps on Alps arise!
A perfect judge will read each work of wit
With the same spirit that its author writ:
Survey the whole, nor seek slight faults to find   235
Where Nature moves, and rapture warms the mind;

8. Supplies.
9. The spring in Pieria on Mt. Olympus, sacred to the Muses.
1. Attempt.

Nor lose, for that malignant dull delight,
The generous pleasure to be charmed with wit.
But in such lays as neither ebb nor flow,
Correctly cold, and regularly low,   240
That, shunning faults, one quiet tenor keep,
We cannot blame indeed—but we may sleep.
In wit, as nature, what affects our hearts
Is not the exactness of peculiar parts;
'Tis not a lip, or eye, we beauty call,   245
But the joint force and full result of all.
Thus when we view some well-proportioned dome
(The world's just wonder, and even thine, O Rome![2]),
No single parts unequally surprise,
All comes united to the admiring eyes: 250
No monstrous height, or breadth, or length appear;
The whole at once is bold and regular.
    Whoever thinks a faultless piece to see,
Thinks what ne'er was, nor is, nor e'er shall be.
In every work regard the writer's end,   255
Since none can compass more than they intend;
And if the means be just, the conduct true,
Applause, in spite of trivial faults, is due.
As men of breeding, sometimes men of wit,
To avoid great errors must the less commit,   260
Neglect the rules each verbal critic lays,
For not to know some trifles is a praise.
Most critics, fond of some subservient art,
Still make the whole depend upon a part:
They talk of principles, but notions prize,   265
And all to one loved folly sacrifice.
    Once on a time La Mancha's knight,[3] they say,
A certain bard encountering on the way,
Discoursed in terms as just, with looks as sage,
As e'er could Dennis,[4] of the Grecian stage;   270
Concluding all were desperate sots and fools
Who durst depart from Aristotle's rules.
Our author, happy in a judge so nice,
Produced his play, and begged the knight's advice;
Made him observe the subject and the plot,   275
The manners, passions, unities; what not?
All which exact to rule were brought about,
Were but a combat in the lists left out.
"What! leave the combat out?" exclaims the knight.
"Yes, or we must renounce the Stagirite."   280
"Not so, by Heaven!" he answers in a rage,

2. The dome of St. Peter's, designed by Michelangelo.
3. Don Quixote. The story comes not from Cervantes' novel, but from a spurious sequel to it by Don Alonzo Fernandez de Avellaneda.
4. John Dennis (1657–1734), though one of the leading critics of the time, was frequently ridiculed by the wits for his irascibility and his rather solemn pomposity. Pope apparently did not know Dennis personally, but his jibe at him in Part III of this poem incurred the critic's lasting animosity.

"Knights, squires, and steeds must enter on the stage."
"So vast a throng the stage can ne'er contain."
"Then build a new, or act it in a plain."
    Thus critics of less judgment than caprice,   285
Curious,[5] not knowing, not exact, but nice,
Form short ideas, and offend in arts
(As most in manners), by a love to parts.
    Some to conceit[6] alone their taste confine,
And glittering thoughts struck out at every line;   290
Pleased with a work where nothing's just or fit,
One glaring chaos and wild heap of wit.
Poets, like painters, thus unskilled to trace
The naked nature and the living grace,
With gold and jewels cover every part,   295
And hide with ornaments their want of art.
    True wit is Nature to advantage dressed,
What oft was thought, but ne'er so well expressed;
Something whose truth convinced at sight we find,
That gives us back the image of our mind.   300
As shades more sweetly recommend the light,
So modest plainness sets off sprightly wit;
For works may have more wit than does them good,
As bodies perish through excess of blood.
    Others for language all their care express,   305
And value books, as women men, for dress.
Their praise is still—the style is excellent;
The sense they humbly take upon content.[7]
Words are like leaves; and where they most abound,
Much fruit of sense beneath is rarely found.   310
False eloquence, like the prismatic glass,
Its gaudy colors spreads on every place;[8]
The face of Nature we no more survey,
All glares alike, without distinction gay.
But true expression, like the unchanging sun, ⎤   315
Clears and improves whate'er it shines upon;   ⎬
It gilds all objects, but it alters none.   ⎦
Expression is the dress of thought, and still
Appears more decent as more suitable.
    A vile conceit in pompous words expressed   320
Is like a clown[9] in regal purple dressed:
For different styles with different subjects sort,
As several garbs with country, town, and court.
Some by old words to fame have made pretense,
Ancients in phrase, mere moderns in their sense.   325
Such labored nothings, in so strange a style,
Amaze the unlearn'd, and make the learned smile;

5. Laboriously careful. "Nice": minutely accurate, over refined.
6. Pointed wit, ingenuity and extravagance, or affectation in the use of figures,
especially similes and metaphors.
7. Mere acquiescence.

8. A very up-to-date scientific reference. Newton's *Optics*, which treated of
the prism and the spectrum, had been
published in 1704, though his theories
had been known earlier.
9. Rustic, boor.

Unlucky as Fungoso[1] in the play,
These sparks with awkward vanity display
What the fine gentleman wore yesterday;   330
And but so mimic ancient wits at best,
As apes our grandsires in their doublets dressed.
In words as fashions the same rule will hold,
Alike fantastic if too new or old:
Be not the first by whom the new are tried,   335
Nor yet the last to lay the old aside.
　　But most by numbers[2] judge a poet's song,
And smooth or rough with them is right or wrong.
In the bright Muse though thousand charms conspire,
Her voice is all these tuneful fools admire,   340
Who haunt Parnassus but to please their ear,
Not mend their minds; as some to church repair,
Not for the doctrine, but the music there.
These equal syllables alone require,
Though oft the ear the open vowels tire,[3]   345
While expletives[4] their feeble aid do join,
And ten low words oft creep in one dull line:
While they ring round the same unvaried chimes,
With sure returns of still expected rhymes;
Where'er you find "the cooling western breeze,"   350
In the next line, it "whispers through the trees";
If crystal streams "with pleasing murmurs creep,"
The reader's threatened (not in vain) with "sleep";
Then, at the last and only couplet fraught
With some unmeaning thing they call a thought,   355
A needless Alexandrine[5] ends the song
That, like a wounded snake, drags its slow length along.
Leave such to tune their own dull rhymes, and know
What's roundly smooth or languishingly slow;
And praise the easy vigor of a line   360
Where Denham's strength and Waller's sweetness join.[6]
True ease in writing comes from art, not chance,
As those move easiest who have learned to dance.
'Tis not enough no harshness gives offense,
The sound must seem an echo to the sense.   365
Soft is the strain when Zephyr gently blows,
And the smooth stream in smoother numbers flows;
But when loud surges lash the sounding shore,
The hoarse, rough verse should like the torrent roar.
When Ajax strives some rock's vast weight to throw,   370

1. A character in Ben Jonson's comedy *Every Man out of His Humor* (1599).
2. Versification.
3. In lines 345–57 Pope cleverly contrives to make his own metrics or diction illustrate the faults that he is exposing.
4. Words used merely to achieve the necessary number of feet in a line of verse.

5. A line of verse containing six iambic feet; it is illustrated in the next line.
6. Dryden, whom Pope echoes here, considered Sir John Denham (1615–69) and Edmund Waller (1606–87) to have been the principal shapers of the closed pentameter couplet. He had distinguished the "strength" of the one and the "sweetness" of the other.

The line too labors, and the words move slow;
Not so when swift Camilla scours the plain,
Flies o'er the unbending corn, and skims along the main.
Hear how Timotheus'[7] varied lays surprise,
And bid alternate passions fall and rise!   375
While at each change the son of Libyan Jove[8]
Now burns with glory, and then melts with love;
Now his fierce eyes with sparkling fury glow,
Now sighs steal out, and tears begin to flow:
Persians and Greeks like turns of nature[9] found   380
And the world's victor stood subdued by sound!
The power of music all our hearts allow,
And what Timotheus was is Dryden now.

　　Avoid extremes; and shun the fault of such
Who still are pleased too little or too much.   385
At every trifle scorn to take offense:
That always shows great pride, or little sense.
Those heads, as stomachs, are not sure the best,
Which nauseate all, and nothing can digest.
Yet let not each gay turn thy rapture move;   390
For fools admire,[1] but men of sense approve:
As things seem large which we through mists descry,
Dullness is ever apt to magnify.

　　Some foreign writers, some our own despise;
The ancients only, or the moderns prize.   395
Thus wit, like faith, by each man is applied
To one small sect, and all are damned beside.
Meanly they seek the blessing to confine,
And force that sun but on a part to shine,
Which not alone the southern wit sublimes,   400
But ripens spirits in cold northern climes;
Which from the first has shone on ages past,
Enlights the present, and shall warm the last;
Though each may feel increases and decays,
And see now clearer and now darker days.   405
Regard not then if wit be old or new,
But blame the false and value still the true.

　　Some ne'er advance a judgment of their own,
But catch the spreading notion of the town;
They reason and conclude by precedent,   410
And own stale nonsense which they ne'er invent.
Some judge of authors' names, not works, and then
Nor praise nor blame the writings, but the men.
Of all this servile herd the worst is he
That in proud dullness joins with quality,   415
A constant critic at the great man's board,
To fetch and carry nonsense for my lord.

7. The musician in Dryden's *Alexander's Feast.* Pope retells the story of
that poem in the following lines.
8. Alexander the Great.

9. Alternations of feelings.
1. Wonder. "Approve": judge favorably
only after due deliberation.

What woeful stuff this madrigal would be
In some starved hackney sonneteer or me!
But let a lord once own the happy lines,   420
How the wit brightens! how the style refines!
Before his sacred name flies every fault,
And each exalted stanza teems with thought!
    The vulgar thus through imitation err;
As oft the learn'd by being singular;   425
So much they scorn the crowd, that if the throng
By chance go right, they purposely go wrong.
So schismatics[2] the plain believers quit,
And are but damned for having too much wit.
Some praise at morning what they blame at night,   430
But always think the last opinion right.
A Muse by these is like a mistress used,
This hour she's idolized, the next abused;
While their weak heads like towns unfortified,
'Twixt sense and nonsense daily change their side.   435
Ask them the cause; they're wiser still, they say;
And still tomorrow's wiser than today.
We think our fathers fools, so wise we grow;
Our wiser sons, no doubt, will think us so.
Once school divines[3] this zealous isle o'erspread;   440
Who knew most sentences was deepest read.
Faith, Gospel, all seemed made to be disputed,
And none had sense enough to be confuted.
Scotists and Thomists now in peace remain
Amidst their kindred cobwebs in Duck Lane.[4]   445
If faith itself has different dresses worn,
What wonder modes in wit should take their turn?
Oft, leaving what is natural and fit,
The current folly proves the ready wit;
And authors think their reputation safe,   450
Which lives as long as fools are pleased to laugh.
    Some valuing those of their own side or mind,
Still make themselves the measure of mankind:
Fondly[5] we think we honor merit then,
When we but praise ourselves in other men.   455
Parties in wit attend on those of state,
And public faction doubles private hate.
Pride, Malice, Folly against Dryden rose,
In various shapes of parsons, critics, beaux;
But sense survived, when merry jests were past;   460
For rising merit will buoy up at last.

2. Those who have divided the church on points of theology. Pope stressed the first syllable, the pronunciation approved by Johnson in his *Dictionary*.
3. The medieval theologians, such as the followers of Duns Scotus and St. Thomas Aquinas mentioned in line 444; "sentences" alludes to Peter Lombard's *Book of Sentences*, a book esteemed by Scholastic philosophers.
4. Street where publishers' remainders and second-hand books were sold.
5. Foolishly.

Might he return and bless once more our eyes,
New Blackmores and new Milbourns must arise.[6]
Nay, should great Homer lift his awful head,
Zoilus[7] again would start up from the dead.   465
Envy will merit, as its shade, pursue,
But like a shadow, proves the substance true;
For envied wit, like Sol eclipsed, makes known
The opposing body's grossness, not its own.
When first that sun too powerful beams displays,   470
It draws up vapors which obscure its rays;
But even those clouds at last adorn its way,
Reflect new glories, and augment the day.
   Be thou the first true merit to befriend;
His praise is lost who stays till all commend.   475
Short is the date, alas! of modern rhymes,
And 'tis but just to let them live betimes.
No longer now that golden age appears,
When patriarch wits survived a thousand years:
Now length of fame (our second life) is lost,   480
And bare threescore is all even that can boast;
Our sons their fathers' failing language see,
And such as Chaucer is shall Dryden be.[8]
So when the faithful pencil has designed
Some bright idea of the master's mind,   485
Where a new world leaps out at his command,
And ready Nature waits upon his hand;
When the ripe colors soften and unite,
And sweetly melt into just shade and light;
When mellowing years their full perfection give,   490
And each bold figure just begins to live,
The treacherous colors the fair art betray,
And all the bright creation fades away!
   Unhappy wit, like most mistaken things,
Atones not for that envy which it brings.   495
In youth alone its empty praise we boast,
But soon the short-lived vanity is lost;
Like some fair flower the early spring supplies,
That gaily blooms, but even in blooming dies,
What is this wit, which must our cares employ?   500
The owner's wife, that other men enjoy;
Then most our trouble still when most admired,
And still the more we give, the more required;
Whose fame with pains we guard, but lose with ease,
Sure some to vex, but never all to please;   505

---

6. Sir Richard Blackmore, physician
and poet, had attacked Dryden for the
immorality of his plays; the Rev. Luke
Milbourn had attacked his translation
of Virgil.
7. A Greek critic of the 4th century
B.C., who wrote a book of carping criticism of Homer.

8. The radical changes that took place
in the English language between the
death of Chaucer in 1400 and the death
of Dryden in 1700 suggested that in
another 300 years Dryden would be
unintelligible. Latin seemed the only
means of attaining enduring fame.

'Tis what the vicious fear, the virtuous shun,
By fools 'tis hated, and by knaves undone!
   If wit so much from ignorance undergo,
Ah, let not learning too commence its foe!
Of old those met rewards who could excel,   510
And such were praised who but endeavored well;
Though triumphs were to generals only due,
Crowns were reserved to grace the soldiers too.
Now they who reach Parnassus' lofty crown
Employ their pains to spurn some others down;   515
And while self-love each jealous writer rules,
Contending wits become the sport of fools;
But still the worst with most regret commend,
For each ill author is as bad a friend.
To what base ends, and by what abject ways,   520
Are morals urged through sacred[9] lust of praise!
Ah, ne'er so dire a thirst of glory boast,
Nor in the critic let the man be lost!
Good nature and good sense must ever join;
To err is human, to forgive divine.   525
   But if in noble minds some dregs remain
Nor yet purged off, of spleen and sour disdain,
Discharge that rage on more provoking crimes,
Nor fear a dearth in these flagitious[1] times.
No pardon vile obscenity should find,   530
Though wit and art conspire to move your mind;
But dullness with obscenity must prove
As shameful sure as impotence in love.
In the fat age of pleasure, wealth, and ease
Sprung the rank weed, and thrived with large increase: 535
When love was all an easy monarch's[2] care,
Seldom at council, never in a war;
Jilts ruled the state, and statesmen farces writ;
Nay, wits had pensions, and young lords had wit;
The fair sat panting at a courtier's play,   540
And not a mask[3] went unimproved away;
The modest fan was lifted up no more,
And virgins smiled at what they blushed before.
The following license of a foreign reign
Did all the dregs of bold Socinus drain;[4]   545
Then unbelieving priests reformed the nation,
And taught more pleasant methods of salvation;
Where Heaven's free subjects might their rights dispute,
Lest God himself should seem too absolute;
Pulpits their sacred satire learned to spare,   550

9. Accursed. The phrase imitates Virgil's *"auri sacra famis,"* "accursed hunger for gold" (*Aeneid* III.57).
1. Scandalously wicked.
2. Charles II. The concluding lines of Part II discuss the corruption of wit and poetry under this monarch.

3. A woman wearing a mask.
4. The "foreign reign" refers to William III, a Dutchman. Socinus was the name of two Italian theologians of the 16th century who denied the divinity of Jesus.

And Vice admired to find a flatterer there!
Encouraged thus, wit's Titans braved the skies,
And the press groaned with licensed blasphemies.
These monsters, critics! with your darts engage,
Here point your thunder, and exhaust your rage!
Yet shun their fault, who, scandalously nice,
Will needs mistake an author into vice;
All seems infected that the infected spy,
As all looks yellow to the jaundiced eye.

1709   1711

The Rape of the Lock[1]

AN HEROI-COMICAL POEM

Nolueram, Belinda, tuos violare capillos;
sed juvat hoc precibus me tribuisse tuis.
—MARTIAL

TO MRS. ARABELLA FERMOR

MADAM,

It will be in vain to deny that I have some regard for this piece,
since I dedicate it to you. Yet you may bear me witness, it was intended only to divert a few young ladies, who have good sense and

1. *The Rape of the Lock* is based upon
an actual episode that provoked a
quarrel between two prominent Catholic
families. Pope's friend John Caryll, to
whom the poem is addressed (line 3),
suggested that Pope write it, in the
hope that a little laughter might serve
to soothe ruffled tempers. Lord Petre had
cut off a lock of hair from the head of
the lovely Arabella Fermor (often
spelled "Farmer" and doubtless so pronounced), much to the indignation of
the lady and her relatives. In its
original version of two cantos and 334
lines, published in 1712, *The Rape of
the Lock* was a great success. In 1713
a new version was undertaken against
the advice of Addison, who considered
the poem perfect as it was first written.
Pope greatly expanded the earlier version, adding the delightful "machinery"
(i.e., the supernatural agents in epic
action) of the Sylphs, Belinda's toilet,
the card game, and the visit to the Cave
of Spleen in Canto IV, In 1717, with
the addition of Clarissa's speech on
good humor, the poem assumed its final
form.

With supreme tact, delicate fancy,
playful wit, and the gentlest satire, Pope
elaborated the trivial episode which occasioned the poem into the semblance of
an epic in miniature, the most nearly
perfect "heroi-comical poem" in English. The poem abounds in parodies
and echoes of the *Iliad*, the *Aeneid*, and
Paradise Lost, thus constantly forcing
the reader to compare small things with
great. The familiar devices of epic are
observed, but the incidents or characters are beautifully proportioned to
the scale of mock epic. The *Rape* tells

of war, but it is the drawing-room war
between the sexes; it has its heroes and
heroines, but they are beaux and belles;
it has its supernatural characters
("machinery") but they are Sylphs
(borrowed, as Pope tells us in his engaging dedicatory letter, from Rosi-
crucian lore)—creatures of the air, the
souls of dead coquettes, with tasks appropriate to their nature—or the Gnome
Umbriel, once a prude on earth; it has
its epic game, played on the "velvet
plain" of the card table, its feasting
heroes, who sip coffee and gossip, its
battle, fought with the clichés of compliment and conceits, with frowns and
angry glances, with snuff and a bodkin;
it has the traditional epic journey to
the underworld—here the Cave of Spleen,
emblematic of the peevish ill nature
of spoiled and hypochondriacal women.
And Pope creates a world in which these
actions take place, a world that is
dense with beautiful objects: brocades,
ivory and tortoise shell, cosmetics and
diamonds, lacquered furniture, silver
teapot, delicate chinaware. It is a world
that is constantly in motion and that
sparkles and glitters with light, whether
the light of the sun, or of Belinda's eyes,
or that light into which the "fluid"
bodies of the Sylphs seem to dissolve as
they flutter in the shrouds and around
the mast of Belinda's ship. Though Pope
laughs at this world and its creatures—
and remembers that a grimmer, darker
world surrounds it (III.19–24 and V.
145–48)—he makes us very much aware
of its beauty and its charm.

The epigraph may be translated, "I
was unwilling, Belinda, to ravish your
locks; but I rejoice to have conceded

good humor enough to laugh not only at their sex's little un-guarded follies, but at their own. But it was communicated with the air of a secret, it soon found its way into the world. An imperfect copy having been offered to a bookseller, you had the good nature for my sake to consent to the publication of one more correct; this I was forced to, before I had executed half my design, for the machinery was entirely wanting to complete it.

The machinery, Madam, is a term invented by the critics, to signify that part which the deities, angels, or demons are made to act in a poem; for the ancient poets are in one respect like many modern ladies: let an action be never so trivial in itself, they always make it appear of the utmost importance. These machines I determined to raise on a very new and odd foundation, the Rosi-crucian [1a] doctrine of spirits.

I know how disagreeable it is to make use of hard words before a lady; but 'tis so much the concern of a poet to have his works under-stood, and particularly by your sex, that you must give me leave to explain two or three difficult terms.

The Rosicrucians are a people I must bring you acquainted with. The best account I know of them is in a French book called *Le Comte de Gabalis*,[1b] which both in its title and size is so like a novel, that many of the fair sex have read it for one by mistake. According to these gentlemen, the four elements are inhabited by spirits, which they call Sylphs, Gnomes, Nymphs, and Salamanders. The Gnomes or Demons of earth delight in mischief; but the Sylphs, whose habitation is in the air, are the best-conditioned creatures imaginable. For they say, any mortals may enjoy the most intimate familiarities with these gentle spirits, upon a condition very easy to all true adepts, an inviolate preservation of chastity.

As to the following cantos, all the passages of them are as fabulous as the vision at the beginning, or the transformation at the end; (except the loss of your hair, which I always mention with reverence). The human persons are as fictitious as the airy ones; and the character of Belinda, as it is now managed, resembles you in nothing but in beauty.

If this poem had as many graces as there are in your person, or in your mind, yet I could never hope it should pass through the world half so uncensured as you have done. But let its fortune be what it will, mine is happy enough, to have given me this occasion of assuring you that I am, with the truest esteem,

MADAM,

Your most obedient, humble servant,

A. POPE

this to your prayers" (Martial, *Epigrams* XII.lxxxiv.1–2). Pope substituted his heroine for Martial's Polytimus. The epigraph is intended to suggest that the poem was published at Miss Fermor's request.

1a. A system of arcane philosophy introduced into England from Germany in the 17th century.
1b. By the Abbé de Montfaucon de Villars, published in 1670.

Canto I

What dire offense from amorous causes springs,
What mighty contests rise from trivial things,
I sing—This verse to Caryll, Muse! is due:
This, even Belinda may vouchsafe to view:
Slight is the subject, but not so the praise,   5
If she inspire, and he approve my lays.
  Say what strange motive, Goddess! could compel
A well-bred lord to assault a gentle belle?
Oh, say what stranger cause, yet unexplored,
Could make a gentle belle reject a lord?   10
In tasks so bold can little men engage,
And in soft bosoms dwells such mighty rage?
  Sol through white curtains shot a timorous ray,
And oped those eyes that must eclipse the day.
Now lapdogs give themselves the rousing shake,   15
And sleepless lovers just at twelve awake:
Thrice rung the bell, the slipper knocked the ground,[2]
And the pressed watch returned a silver sound.
Belinda still her downy pillow pressed,
Her guardian Sylph prolonged the balmy rest: 20
'Twas he had summoned to her silent bed
The morning dream that hovered o'er her head.
A youth more glittering than a birthnight beau[3]
(That even in slumber caused her cheek to glow)
Seemed to her ear his winning lips to lay,   25
And thus in whispers said, or seemed to say:
  "Fairest of mortals, thou distinguished care
Of thousand bright inhabitants of air!
If e'er one vision touched thy infant thought,
Of all the nurse and all the priest have taught,   30
Of airy elves by moonlight shadows seen,
The silver token, and the circled green,[4]
Or virgins visited by angel powers,
With golden crowns and wreaths of heavenly flowers,
Hear and believe! thy own importance know,   35
Nor bound thy narrow views to things below.
Some secret truths, from learned pride concealed,
To maids alone and children are revealed:
What though no credit doubting wits may give?
The fair and innocent shall still believe.   40
Know, then, unnumbered spirits round thee fly,
The light militia of the lower sky:

2. Belinda thus summons her maid. A "pressed watch" chimes the hour and the quarter-hour when the stem is pressed down.
3. Courtiers wore especially fine clothes on the sovereign's birthday.
4. According to popular belief fairies skim off the cream from jugs of milk left standing overnight and leave a coin ("silver token") in payment. Rings of bright green grass, which are common in England even in winter, were held to be due to the round dances of fairies.

These, though unseen, are ever on the wing,
Hang o'er the box, and hover round the Ring.[5]
Think what an equipage thou hast in air, 45
And view with scorn two pages and a chair.[6]
As now your own, our beings were of old,
And once enclosed in woman's beauteous mold;
Thence, by a soft transition, we repair
From earthly vehicles to these of air. 50
Think not, when woman's transient breath is fled,
That all her vanities at once are dead:
Succeeding vanities she still regards,
And though she plays no more, o'erlooks the cards.
Her joy in gilded chariots, when alive, 55
And love of ombre,[7] after death survive.
For when the Fair in all their pride expire,
To their first elements[8] their souls retire:
The sprites of fiery termagants in flame
Mount up, and take a Salamander's name.[9] 60
Soft yielding minds to water glide away,
And sip, with Nymphs, their elemental tea.[1]
The graver prude sinks downward to a Gnome,
In search of mischief still on earth to roam.
The light coquettes in Sylphs aloft repair, 65
And sport and flutter in the fields of air.
    "Know further yet; whoever fair and chaste
Rejects mankind, is by some Sylph embraced:
For spirits, freed from mortal laws, with ease
Assume what sexes and what shapes they please.[2] 70
What guards the purity of melting maids,
In courtly balls, and midnight masquerades,
Safe from the treacherous friend, the daring spark,
The glance by day, the whisper in the dark,
When kind occasion prompts their warm desires, 75
When music softens, and when dancing fires?
'Tis but their Sylph, the wise Celestials know,
Though Honor is the word with men below.
    "Some nymphs there are, too conscious of their face,
For life predestined to the Gnomes' embrace. 80
These swell their prospects and exalt their pride,
When offers are disdained, and love denied:
Then gay ideas[3] crowd the vacant brain,

5. The "box" in the theater and the
fashionable circular drive ("Ring") in
Hyde Park.
6. Sedan chair.
7. The popular card game. See III.27 ff.
and note.
8. The four elements out of which all
things were believed to have been made:
were fire, water, earth, and air. One or
another of these elements was supposed
to be predominant in both the physical
and psychological make-up of each
human being. In this context they are

spoken of as "humors."
9. Pope borrowed his supernatural beings from Rosicrucian mythology. Each
element was inhabited by a spirit, as
the following lines explain. The salamander is a lizardlike animal, in antiquity believed to live in fire.
1. Pronounce *tay.*
2. Cf. *Paradise Lost* I.427-31; this is
one of many allusions to that poem in
the *Rape.*
3. Images.

While peers, and dukes, and all their sweeping train,
And garters, stars, and coronets appear,   85
And in soft sounds, 'your Grace' salutes their ear.
'Tis these that early taint the female soul,
Instruct the eyes of young coquettes to roll,
Teach infant cheeks a bidden blush to know,
And little hearts to flutter at a beau.   90
    "Oft, when the world imagine women stray,
The Sylphs through mystic mazes guide their way,
Through all the giddy circle they pursue,
And old impertinence expel by new.
What tender maid but must a victim fall   95
To one man's treat, but for another's ball?
When Florio speaks what virgin could withstand,
If gentle Damon did not squeeze her hand?
With varying vanities, from every part,
They shift the moving toyshop⁴ of their heart;   100
Where wigs with wigs, with sword-knots sword-knots strive,
Beaux banish beaux, and coaches coaches drive.
This erring mortals levity may call;
Oh, blind to truth! the Sylphs contrive it all.
    "Of these am I, who thy protection claim,   105
A watchful sprite, and Ariel is my name.
Late, as I ranged the crystal wilds of air,
In the clear mirror of thy ruling star
I saw, alas! some dread event impend,
Ere to the main this morning sun descend,   110
But Heaven reveals not what, or how, or where:
Warned by the Sylph, O pious maid, beware!
This to disclose is all thy guardian can:
Beware of all, but most beware of Man!"
    He said; when Shock,⁵ who thought she slept too long, 115
Leaped up, and waked his mistress with his tongue.
'Twas then, Belinda, if report say true,
Thy eyes first opened on a billet-doux;
Wounds, charms, and ardors were no sooner read,
But all the vision vanished from thy head.   120
    And now, unveiled, the toilet stands displayed,
Each silver vase in mystic order laid.
First, robed in white, the nymph intent adores,
With head uncovered, the cosmetic powers.
A heavenly image in the glass appears;   125
To that she bends, to that her eyes she rears.
The inferior priestess, at her altar's side,
Trembling begins the sacred rites of Pride.
Unnumbered treasures ope at once, and here
The various offerings of the world appear;   130
From each she nicely culls with curious toil,

4. A shop stocked with baubles and   5. Belinda's lapdog.
trifles.

And decks the goddess with the glittering spoil.
This casket India's glowing gems unlocks,
And all Arabia breathes from yonder box.
The tortoise here and elephant unite,   135
Transformed to combs, the speckled and the white.
Here files of pins extend their shining rows,
Puffs, powders, patches, Bibles,[6] billet-doux.
Now awful Beauty puts on all its arms;
The fair each moment rises in her charms,   140
Repairs her smiles, awakens every grace,
And calls forth all the wonders of her face;
Sees by degrees a purer blush arise,
And keener lightnings quicken in her eyes.
The busy Sylphs surround their darling care,   145
These set the head, and those divide the hair,
Some fold the sleeve, whilst others plait the gown;
And Betty's[7] praised for labors not her own.

Canto II

Not with more glories, in the ethereal plain,
The sun first rises o'er the purpled main,
Than, issuing forth, the rival of his beams
Launched on the bosom of the silver Thames.
Fair nymphs and well-dressed youths around her shone,   5
But every eye was fixed on her alone.
On her white breast a sparkling cross she wore,
Which Jews might kiss, and infidels adore.
Her lively looks a sprightly mind disclose,
Quick as her eyes, and as unfixed as those: 10
Favors to none, to all she smiles extends;
Oft she rejects, but never once offends.
Bright as the sun, her eyes the gazers strike,
And, like the sun, they shine on all alike.
Yet graceful ease, and sweetness void of pride,   15
Might hide her faults, if belles had faults to hide:
If to her share some female errors fall,
Look on her face, and you'll forget 'em all.
This nymph, to the destruction of mankind,
Nourished two locks which graceful hung behind   20
In equal curls, and well conspired to deck
With shining ringlets the smooth ivory neck.
Love in these labyrinths his slaves detains,
And mighty hearts are held in slender chains.
With hairy springes[8] we the birds betray,   25
Slight lines of hair surprise the finny prey,
Fair tresses man's imperial race ensnare,
And beauty draws us with a single hair.
The adventurous Baron the bright locks admired,

6. It has been suggested that Pope intended here not "Bibles," but "bibelots," (trinkets), but this intepretation has not gained wide acceptance.

7. Belinda's maid, the "inferior priestess" mentioned in line 127.

8. Snares; pronounced *sprin-jez*.

He saw, he wished, and to the prize aspired.   30
Resolved to win, he meditates the way,
By force to ravish, or by fraud betray;
For when success a lover's toil attends,
Few ask if fraud or force attained his ends.

    For this, ere Phoebus rose, he had implored   35
Propitious Heaven, and every power adored,
But chiefly Love—to Love an altar built,
Of twelve vast French romances, neatly gilt.
There lay three garters, half a pair of gloves,
And all the trophies of his former loves.   40
With tender billet-doux he lights the pyre,
And breathes three amorous sighs to raise the fire.
Then prostrate falls, and begs with ardent eyes
Soon to obtain, and long possess the prize:
The powers gave ear, and granted half his prayer,   45
The rest the winds dispersed in empty air.

    But now secure the painted vessel glides,
The sunbeams trembling on the floating tides,
While melting music steals upon the sky,
And softened sounds along the waters die.   50
Smooth flow the waves, the zephyrs gently play,
Belinda smiled, and all the world was gay.
All but the Sylph—with careful thoughts oppressed,
The impending woe sat heavy on his breast.
He summons straight his denizens of air;   55
The lucid squadrons round the sails repair:
Soft o'er the shrouds aërial whispers breathe
That seemed but zephyrs to the train beneath.
Some to the sun their insect-wings unfold,
Waft on the breeze, or sink in clouds of gold.   60
Transparent forms too fine for mortal sight,
Their fluid bodies half dissolved in light,
Loose to the wind their airy garments flew,
Thin glittering textures of the filmy dew,
Dipped in the richest tincture of the skies,   65
Where light disports in ever-mingling dyes,
While every beam new transient colors flings,
Colors that change whene'er they wave their wings.
Amid the circle, on the gilded mast,
Superior by the head was Ariel placed;   70
His purple[9] pinions opening to the sun,
He raised his azure wand, and thus begun:
    "Ye Sylphs and Sylphids, to your chief give ear!
Fays, Fairies, Genii, Elves, and Daemons, hear!
Ye know the spheres and various tasks assigned   75
By laws eternal to the aërial kind.
Some in the fields of purest ether play,

---

9. In 18th-century poetic diction the word might mean "blood-red," "purple," or simply (as is likely here) "brightly colored." The word derives from Virgil, *Eclogue.* IX, 40, *purpureous.* An example of the Latinate nature of some poetic diction of the period.

And bask and whiten in the blaze of day.
Some guide the course of wandering orbs on high,
Or roll the planets through the boundless sky.   80
Some less refined, beneath the moon's pale light
Pursue the stars that shoot athwart the night,
Or suck the mists in grosser air below,
Or dip their pinions in the painted bow,
Or brew fierce tempests on the wintry main,   85
Or o'er the glebe[1] distill the kindly rain.
Others on earth o'er human race preside,
Watch all their ways, and all their actions guide:
Of these the chief the care of nations own,
And guard with arms divine the British Throne.   90
  "Our humbler province is to tend the Fair,
Not a less pleasing, though less glorious care:
To save the powder from too rude a gale,
Nor let the imprisoned essences exhale;
To draw fresh colors from the vernal flowers;   95
To steal from rainbows e'er they drop in showers
A brighter wash;[2] to curl their waving hairs,
Assist their blushes, and inspire their airs;
Nay oft, in dreams invention we bestow,
To change a flounce, or add a furbelow.   100
  "This day black omens threat the brightest fair,
That e'er deserved a watchful spirit's care;
Some dire disaster, or by force or slight,
But what, or where, the Fates have wrapped in night:
Whether the nymph shall break Diana's law,[3]   105
Or some frail china jar receive a flaw,
Or stain her honor or her new brocade,
Forget her prayers, or miss a masquerade,
Or lose her heart, or necklace, at a ball;
Or whether Heaven has doomed that Shock must fall.   110
Haste, then, ye spirits! to your charge repair:
The fluttering fan be Zephyretta's care;
The drops[4] to thee, Brillante, we consign;
And, Momentilla, let the watch be thine;
Do thou, Crispissa,[5] tend her favorite Lock;   115
Ariel himself shall be the guard of Shock.
  "To fifty chosen Sylphs, of special note,
We trust the important charge, the petticoat;
Oft have we known that sevenfold fence to fail,
Though stiff with hoops, and armed with ribs of whale.   120
Form a strong line about the silver bound,
And guard the wide circumference around.
  "Whatever spirit, careless of his charge,
His post neglects, or leaves the fair at large,
Shall feel sharp vengeance soon o'ertake his sins,   125

1. Cultiviated field.
2. Cosmetic lotion.
3. Diana was the goddess of chastity.
4. Diamond earrings. Observe the ap-
propriateness of the names of the Sylphs
to their assigned functions.
5. From Latin *crispere*, to curl.

Be stopped in vials, or transfixed with pins,
Or plunged in lakes of bitter washes lie,
Or wedged whole ages in a bodkin's eye;[6]
Gums and pomatums shall his flight restrain,
While clogged he beats his silken wings in vain,   130
Or alum styptics with contracting power
Shrink his thin essence like a riveled[7] flower:
Or, as Ixion[8] fixed, the wretch shall feel
The giddy motion of the whirling mill,
In fumes of burning chocolate shall glow,   135
And tremble at the sea that froths below!"
    He spoke; the spirits from the sails descend;
Some, orb in orb, around the nymph extend;
Some thread the mazy ringlets of her hair;
Some hang upon the pendants of her ear: 140
With beating hearts the dire event they wait,
Anxious, and trembling for the birth of Fate.

Canto III

    Close by those meads, forever crowned with flowers,
Where Thames with pride surveys his rising towers,
There stands a structure of majestic frame,
Which from the neighboring Hampton takes its name.[9]
Here Britain's statesmen oft the fall foredoom   5
Of foreign tyrants and of nymphs at home;
Here thou, great Anna! whom three realms obey,
Dost sometimes counsel take—and sometimes tea.
    Hither the heroes and the nymphs resort,
To taste awhile the pleasures of a court;   10
In various talk the instructive hours they passed,
Who gave the ball, or paid the visit last;
One speaks the glory of the British Queen,
And one describes a charming Indian screen;
A third interprets motions, looks, and eyes;   15
At every word a reputation dies.
Snuff, or the fan, supply each pause of chat,
With singing, laughing, ogling, and all that.
    Meanwhile, declining from the noon of day,
The sun obliquely shoots his burning ray;   20
The hungry judges soon the sentence sign,
And wretches hang that jurymen may dine;
The merchant from the Exchange returns in peace,
And the long labors of the toilet cease.
Belinda now, whom thirst of fame invites,   25
Burns to encounter two adventurous knights,

6. A "bodkin" is a blunt needle with a large eye, used for drawing ribbon through eyelets in the edging of women's garments.
7. To "rivel" is to "contract into wrinkles and corrugations" (Johnson's *Dictionary*).

8. In the Greek myth Ixion was punished in the underworld by being bound on an everturning wheel.
9. Hampton Court, the royal palace, about fifteen miles up the Thames from London.

At ombre[1] singly to decide their doom,
And swells her breast with conquests yet to come.
Straight the three bands prepare in arms to join,
Each band the number of the sacred nine.   30
Soon as she spreads her hand, the aërial guard
Descend, and sit on each important card:
First Ariel perched upon a Matadore,
Then each according to the rank they bore;
For Sylphs, yet mindful of their ancient race,   35
Are, as when women, wondrous fond of place.

 Behold, four Kings in majesty revered,
With hoary whiskers and a forky beard;
And four fair Queens whose hands sustain a flower,
The expressive emblem of their softer power;   40
Four Knaves in garbs succinct,[2] a trusty band,
Caps on their heads, and halberts in their hand;
And parti-colored troops, a shining train,
Draw forth to combat on the velvet plain.

 The skillful nymph reviews her force with·care;   45
"Let Spades be trumps!" she said, and trumps they were.

 Now move to war her sable Matadores,
In show like leaders of the swarthy Moors.
Spadillio first, unconquerable lord!
Led off two captive trumps, and swept the board.   50
As many more Manillio forced to yield,
And marched a victor from the verdant field.
Him Basto followed, but his fate more hard
Gained but one trump and one plebeian card.
With his broad saber next, a chief in years,   55
The hoary Majesty of Spades appears,
Puts forth one manly leg, to sight revealed,
The rest his many-colored robe concealed.
The rebel Knave, who dares his prince engage,
Proves the just victim of his royal rage.   60
Even mighty Pam,[3] that kings and queens o'erthrew
And mowed down armies in the fights of loo,
Sad chance of war! now destitute of aid,
Falls undistinguished by the victor Spade.

 Thus far both armies to Belinda yield;   65
Now to the Baron fate inclines the field.
His warlike amazon her host invades,

1. The game of ombre which Belinda plays against the Baron and another young man is too complicated for complete explication here. Pope has carefully arranged the cards so that Belinda wins. The Baron's hand is strong enough to be a threat, but the third player's is of little account. The hand is played exactly according to the rules of ombre, and Pope's description of the cards is equally accurate. Each player holds nine cards (line 30). The "Matadores" (line 33), when spades are trumps, are "Spadillio" (line 49), the ace of spades; "Manillio" (line 51), the two of spades; "Basto" (line 53), the ace of clubs; Belinda holds all three of these. (For a more complete description of ombre, see Appendix C, *The Rape of the Lock and Other Poems*, ed. Geoffrey Tillotson, in the Twickenham Edition of Pope's poems, Vol. II.)
2. Girded up.
3. The knave of clubs, the highest trump in the game of loo.

The imperial consort of the crown of Spades.
The Club's black tyrant first her victim died,
Spite of his haughty mien and barbarous pride.   70
What boots the regal circle on his head,
His giant limbs, in state unwieldy spread?
That long behind he trails his pompous robe,
And of all monarchs only grasps the globe?
　　The Baron now his Diamonds pours apace;   75
The embroidered King who shows but half his face,
And his refulgent Queen, with powers combined
Of broken troops an easy conquest find.
Clubs, Diamonds, Hearts, in wild disorder seen,
With throngs promiscuous strew the level green.   80
Thus when dispersed a routed army runs,
Of Asia's troops, and Afric's sable sons,
With like confusion different nations fly,
Of various habit, and of various dye,
The pierced battalions disunited fall   85
In heaps on heaps; one fate o'erwhelms them all.
　　The Knave of Diamonds tries his wily arts,
And wins (oh, shameful chance!) the Queen of Hearts.
At this, the blood the virgin's cheek forsook,
A livid paleness spreads o'er all her look;   90
She sees, and trembles at the approaching ill,
Just in the jaws of ruin, and Codille,[4]
And now (as oft in some distempered state)
On one nice trick depends the general fate.
An Ace of Hearts steps forth: the King unseen   95
Lurked in her hand, and mourned his captive Queen.
He springs to vengeance with an eager pace,
And falls like thunder on the prostrate Ace.
The nymph exulting fills with shouts the sky,
The walls, the woods, and long canals reply.   100
　　O thoughtless mortals! ever blind to fate,
Too soon dejected, and too soon elate:
Sudden these honors shall be snatched away,
And cursed forever this victorious day.
　　For lo! the board with cups and spoons is crowned,   105
The berries crackle, and the mill turns round;[5]
On shining altars of Japan[6] they raise
The silver lamp; the fiery spirits blaze:
From silver spouts the grateful liquors glide,
While China's earth receives the smoking tide.   110
At once they gratify their scent and taste,
And frequent cups prolong the rich repast.
Straight hover round the fair her airy band;
Some, as she sipped, the fuming liquor fanned,

---

4. The term applied to losing a hand
at cards.
5. I.e., coffee is roasted and ground.
6. I.e., small, lacquered tables. The word

"altars" suggests the ritualistic character of coffee-drinking in Belinda's
world.

Some o'er her lap their careful plumes displayed,   115
Trembling, and conscious of the rich brocade.
Coffee (which makes the politician wise,
And see through all things with his half-shut eyes)
Sent up in vapors to the Baron's brain
New stratagems, the radiant Lock to gain.   120
Ah, cease, rash youth! desist ere 'tis too late,
Fear the just Gods, and think of Scylla's fate![7]
Changed to a bird, and sent to flit in air,
She dearly pays for Nisus' injured hair!
    But when to mischief mortals bend their will,   125
How soon they find fit instruments of ill!
Just then, Clarissa drew with tempting grace
A two-edged weapon from her shining case:
So ladies in romance assist their knight,
Present the spear, and arm him for the fight.   130
He takes the gift with reverence, and extends
The little engine on his fingers' ends;
This just behind Belinda's neck he spread,
As o'er the fragrant steams she bends her head.
Swift to the Lock a thousand sprites repair,   135
A thousand wings, by turns, blow back the hair,
And thrice they twitched the diamond in her ear,
Thrice she looked back, and thrice the foe drew near.
Just in that instant, anxious Ariel sought
The close recesses of the virgin's thought;   140
As on the nosegay in her breast reclined,
He watched the ideas rising in her mind,
Sudden he viewed, in spite of all her art,
An earthly lover lurking at her heart.
Amazed, confused, he found his power expired,   145
Resigned to fate, and with a sigh retired.
    The Peer now spreads the glittering forfex[8] wide,
To enclose the Lock; now joins it, to divide.
Even then, before the fatal engine closed,
A wretched Sylph too fondly interposed;   150
Fate urged the shears, and cut the Sylph in twain
(But airy substance soon unites again):
The meeting points the sacred hair dissever
From the fair head, forever, and forever!
    Then flashed the living lightning from her eyes,   155
And screams of horror rend the affrighted skies.
Not louder shrieks to pitying heaven are cast,
When husbands, or when lapdogs breathe their last;
Or when rich china vessels fallen from high,
In glittering dust and painted fragments lie!   160

7. Scylla, daughter of Nisus, was turned into a sea bird because, for the sake of her love for Minos of Crete, who was besieging her father's city of Megara, she cut from her father's head the pur- ple lock on which his safety depended. She is not the Scylla of "Scylla and Charybdis."
8. Scissors.

"Let wreaths of triumph now my temples twine,"
The victor cried, "the glorious prize is mine!
While fish in streams, or birds delight in air,
Or in a coach and six the British Fair,
As long as *Atalantis*[9] shall be read,   165
Or the small pillow grace a lady's bed,
While visits shall be paid on solemn days,
When numerous wax-lights in bright order blaze,
While nymphs take treats, or assignations give,
So long my honor, name, and praise shall live!   170
What Time would spare, from Steel receives its date,
And monuments, like men, submit to fate!
Steel could the labor of the Gods destroy,
And strike to dust the imperial towers of Troy;
Steel could the works of mortal pride confound,   175
And hew triumphal arches to the ground.
What wonder then, fair nymph! thy hairs should feel,
The conquering force of unresisted Steel?"

Canto IV

But anxious cares the pensive nymph oppressed,
And secret passions labored in her breast.
Not youthful kings in battle seized alive,
Not scornful virgins who their charms survive,
Not ardent lovers robbed of all their bliss,   5
Not ancient ladies when refused a kiss,
Not tyrants fierce that unrepenting die,
Not Cynthia when her manteau's[1] pinned awry,
E'er felt such rage, resentment, and despair,
As thou, sad virgin! for thy ravished hair.   10
      For, that sad moment, when the Sylphs withdrew
And Ariel weeping from Belinda flew,
Umbriel,[2] a dusky, melancholy sprite
As ever sullied the fair face of light,
Down to the central earth, his proper scene,   15
Repaired to search the gloomy Cave of Spleen.[3]
      Swift on his sooty pinions flits the Gnome,
And in a vapor reached the dismal dome.
No cheerful breeze this sullen region knows,
The dreaded east is all the wind that blows.   20
Here in a grotto, sheltered close from air,
And screened in shades from day's detested glare,
She sighs forever on her pensive bed,
Pain at her side, and Megrim[4] at her head.
      Two handmaids wait the throne: alike in place,   25
But differing far in figure and in face.
Here stood Ill-Nature like an ancient maid,

---

9. Mrs. Manley's *New Atalantis* (1709)
was notorious for its thinly concealed
allusions to contemporary scandals.
1. Negligee or loose robe.

2. The name suggests shade and darkness.
3. Ill humor.
4. Headache.

Her wrinkled form in black and white arrayed;
With store of prayers for mornings, nights, and noons,
Her hand is filled; her bosom with lampoons.   30
 There Affectation, with a sickly mien,
Shows in her cheek the roses of eighteen,
Practiced to lisp, and hang the head aside,
Faints into airs, and languishes with pride,
On the rich quilt sinks with becoming woe,   35
Wrapped in a gown, for sickness and for show.
The fair ones feel such maladies as these,
When each new nightdress gives a new disease.
 A constant vapor[5] o'er the palace flies,
Strange phantoms rising as the mists arise;   40
Dreadful as hermit's dreams in haunted shades,
Or bright as visions of expiring maids.
Now glaring fiends, and snakes on rolling spires,[6]
Pale specters, gaping tombs, and purple fires;
Now lakes of liquid gold, Elysian scenes,   45
And crystal domes, and angels in machines.[7]
 Unnumbered throngs on every side are seen
Of bodies changed to various forms by Spleen.
Here living teapots stand, one arm held out,
One bent; the handle this, and that the spout: 50
A pipkin[8] there, like Homer's tripod, walks;
Here sighs a jar, and there a goose pie talks;
Men prove with child, as powerful fancy works,
And maids, turned bottles, call aloud for corks.
 Safe passed the Gnome through this fantastic band,   55
A branch of healing spleenwort[9] in his hand.
Then thus addressed the Power: "Hail, wayward Queen!
Who rule the sex to fifty from fifteen:
Parent of vapors and of female wit,
Who give the hysteric or poetic fit,   60
On various tempers act by various ways,
Make some take physic, others scribble plays;
Who cause the proud their visits to delay,
And send the godly in a pet to pray.
A nymph there is that all your power disdains,   65
And thousands more in equal mirth maintains.
But oh! if e'er thy Gnome could spoil a grace,
Or raise a pimple on a beauteous face,
Like citron-waters[1] matrons' cheeks inflame,
Or change complexions at a losing game;   70

---

5. Emblematic of "the vapors," i.e., hypochondria, melancholy, peevishness, often affected by fashionable women.
6. Coils.
7. Mechanical devices used in the theaters for spectacular effects. The fantasies of neurotic women here merge with the sensational stage effects popular with contemporary audiences.
8. An earthen pot. In *Iliad* XVIII.373–

77, Vulcan furnishes the gods with self-propelling "tripods" (three-legged stools).
9. An herb, efficacious against the spleen. Pope alludes to the golden bough that Aeneas and the Cumaean sybil carry with them for protection into the underworld in *Aeneid* VI.
1. Brandy flavored with orange or lemon peel.

If e'er with airy horns[2] I planted heads,
Or rumpled petticoats, or tumbled beds,
Or caused suspicion when no soul was rude,
Or discomposed the headdress of a prude,
O e'er to costive lapdog gave disease,   75
Which not the tears of brightest eyes could ease,
Hear me, and touch Belinda with chagrin:[3]
That single act gives half the world the spleen."
    The Goddess with a discontented air
Seems to reject him though she grants his prayer.   80
A wondrous bag with both her hands she binds,
Like that where once Ulysses held the winds;[4]
There she collects the force of female lungs,
Sighs, sobs, and passions, and the war of tongues.
A vial next she fills with fainting fears,   85
Soft sorrows, melting griefs, and flowing tears.
The Gnome rejoicing bears her gifts away,
Spreads his black wings, and slowly mounts to day.
    Sunk in Thalestris'[5] arms the nymph he found,
Her eyes dejected and her hair unbound.   90
Full o'er their heads the swelling bag he rent,
And all the Furies issued at the vent.
Belinda burns with more than mortal ire,
And fierce Thalestris fans the rising fire.
"O wretched maid!" she spread her hands, and cried   95
(While Hampton's echoes, "Wretched maid!" replied),
"Was it for this you took such constant care
The bodkin, comb, and essence to prepare?
For this your locks in paper durance bound,
For this with torturing irons wreathed around?   100
For this with fillets strained your tender head,
And bravely bore the double loads of lead?[6]
Gods! shall the ravisher display your hair,
While the fops envy, and the ladies stare!
Honor forbid! at whose unrivaled shrine   105
Ease, pleasure, virtue, all, our sex resign.
Methinks already I your tears survey,
Already hear the horrid things they say,
Already see you a degraded toast,
And all your honor in a whisper lost!   110
How shall I, then, your helpless fame defend?
'Twill then be infamy to seem your friend!

2. Horns, the symbol of the cuckold, the man whose wife has been unfaithful to him; here "airy," because they exist only in the jealous suspicions of the husband, the victim of the mischievous Umbriel.
3. Ill humor.
4. Aeolus (later conceived of as god of the winds) gave Ulysses a bag containing all the winds adverse to his voyage home. When his ship was in sight of Ithaca, his companions opened the bag and the storms that ensued drove Ulysses far away (*Odyssey* X.19 ff.).
5. The name is borrowed from a queen of the Amazons, hence a fierce and warlike woman. Thalestris, according to legend, traveled 30 days in order to have a child by Alexander the Great. Plutarch denies the story.
6. The frame on which the elaborate coiffures of the day were arranged.

And shall this prize, the inestimable prize,
Exposed through crystal to the gazing eyes,
And heightened by the diamond's circling rays,   115
On that rapacious hand forever blaze?
Sooner shall grass in Hyde Park Circus grow,
And wits take lodgings in the sound of Bow;[7]
Sooner let earth, air, sea, to chaos fall,
Men, monkeys, lapdogs, parrots, perish all!"   120
    She said; then raging to Sir Plume repairs,
And bids her beau demand the precious hairs
(Sir Plume of amber snuffbox justly vain,
And the nice conduct of a clouded cane).
With earnest eyes, and round unthinking face,   125
He first the snuffbox opened, then the case,
And thus broke out—"My Lord, why, what the devil!
Z——ds! damn the lock! 'fore Gad, you must be civil!
Plague on't! 'tis past a jest—nay prithee, pox!
Give her the hair"—he spoke, and rapped his box.   130
    "It grieves me much," replied the Peer again,
"Who speaks so well should ever speak in vain.
But by this Lock, this sacred Lock I swear
(Which never more shall join its parted hair;
Which never more its honors shall renew,   135
Clipped from the lovely head where late it grew),
That while my nostrils draw the vital air,
This hand, which won it, shall forever wear."
He spoke, and speaking, in proud triumph spread
The long-contended honors[8] of her head.   140
    But Umbriel, hateful Gnome, forbears not so;
He breaks the vial whence the sorrows flow.
Then see! the nymph in beauteous grief appears,
Her eyes half languishing, half drowned in tears;
On her heaved bosom hung her drooping head,   145
Which with a sigh she raised, and thus she said:
    "Forever cursed be this detested day,
Which snatched my best, my favorite curl away!
Happy! ah, ten times happy had I been,
If Hampton Court these eyes had never seen!   150
Yet am not I the first mistaken maid,
By love of courts to numerous ills betrayed.
Oh, had I rather unadmired remained
In some lone isle, or distant northern land;
Where the gilt chariot never marks the way,   155
Where none learn ombre, none e'er taste bohea![9]
There kept my charms concealed from mortal eye,
Like roses that in deserts bloom and die.
What moved my mind with youthful lords to roam?
Oh, had I stayed, and said my prayers at home!   160

7. A person born within sound of the bells of St. Mary-le-Bow in Cheapside is said to be a cockney. No fashionable wit would have so vulgar an address.
8. Ornaments, hence locks; a Latinism.
9. A costly sort of tea.

'Twas this the morning omens seemed to tell,
Thrice from my trembling hand the patch box[1] fell;
The tottering china shook without a wind,
Nay, Poll sat mute, and Shock was most unkind!
A Sylph too warned me of the threats of fate,   165
In mystic visions, now believed too late!
See the poor remnants of these slighted hairs!
My hands shall rend what e'en thy rapine spares.
These in two sable ringlets taught to break,
Once gave new beauties to the snowy neck;   170
The sister lock now sits uncouth, alone,
And in its fellow's fate foresees its own;
Uncurled it hangs, the fatal shears demands,
And tempts once more thy sacrilegious hands.
Oh, hadst thou, cruel! been content to seize   175
Hairs less in sight, or any hairs but these!"

Canto V

She said: the pitying audience melt in tears.
But Fate and Jove had stopped the Baron's ears.
In vain Thalestris with reproach assails,
For who can move when fair Belinda fails?
Not half so fixed the Trojan[2] could remain,   5
While Anna begged and Dido raged in vain.
Then grave Clarissa graceful waved her fan;
Silence ensued, and thus the nymph began:
    "Say why are beauties praised and honored most,
The wise man's passion, and the vain man's toast?   10
Why decked with all that land and sea afford,
Why angels called, and angel-like adored?
Why round our coaches crowd the white-gloved beaux,
Why bows the side box from its inmost rows?
How vain are all these glories, all our pains,   15
Unless good sense preserve what beauty gains;
That men may say when we the front box grace,
'Behold the first in virtue as in face!'
Oh! if to dance all night, and dress all day,
Charmed the smallpox, or chased old age away,   20
Who would not scorn what housewife's cares produce,
Or who would learn one earthly thing of use?
To patch, nay ogle, might become a saint,
Nor could it sure be such a sin to paint.
But since, alas! frail beauty must decay,   25
Curled or uncurled, since locks will turn to gray;
Since painted, or not painted, all shall fade,
And she who scorns a man must die a maid;

1. A box to hold the ornamental patches
of court plaster worn on the face by
both sexes. Cf. *Spectator* 81.
2. Aeneas, who forsook Dido at the
bidding of the gods, despite her reproaches and the supplications of her
sister Anna. Virgil compares him to a
steadfast oak that withstands a storm
(*Aeneid* IV.437–43).

What then remains but well our power to use,
And keep good humor still whate'er we lose?   30
And trust me, dear, good humor can prevail
When airs, and flights, and screams, and scolding fail.
Beauties in vain their pretty eyes may roll;
Charms strike the sight, but merit wins the soul."[3]
   So spoke the dame, but no applause ensued;   35
Belinda frowned, Thalestris called her prude.
"To arms, to arms!" the fierce virago cries,
And swift as lightning to the combat flies.
All side in parties, and begin the attack;
Fans clap, silks rustle, and tough whalebones crack;   40
Heroes' and heroines' shouts confusedly rise,
And bass and treble voices strike the skies.
No common weapons in their hands are found,
Like Gods they fight, nor dread a mortal wound.
   So when bold Homer makes the Gods engage,   45
And heavenly breasts with human passions rage;
'Gainst Pallas, Mars; Latona, Hermes arms;
And all Olympus rings with loud alarms:
Jove's thunder roars, heaven trembles all around,
Blue Neptune storms, the bellowing deeps resound: 50
Earth shakes her nodding towers, the ground gives way,
And the pale ghosts start at the flash of day!
   Triumphant Umbriel on a sconce's height
Clapped his glad wings, and sat to view the fight:
Propped on the bodkin spears, the sprites survey   55
The growing combat, or assist the fray.
   While through the press enraged Thalestris flies,
And scatters death around from both her eyes,
A beau and witling perished in the throng,
One died in metaphor, and one in song.   60
"O cruel nymph! a living death I bear,"
Cried Dapperwit, and sunk beside his chair.
A mournful glance Sir Fopling upwards cast,
"Those eyes are made so killing"—was his last.
Thus on Maeander's flowery margin lies   65
The expiring swan, and as he sings he dies.
   When bold Sir Plume had drawn Clarissa down,
Chloe stepped in, and killed him with a frown:
She smiled to see the doughty hero slain,
But, at her smile, the beau revived again.   70
   Now Jove suspends his golden scales in air,
Weighs the men's wits against the lady's hair;
The doubtful beam long nods from side to side;
At length the wits mount up, the hairs subside.
   See, fierce Belinda on the Baron flies,   75

---

3. The speech is a close parody of Pope's own translation of the speech of Sarpedon to Glaucus, first published in 1709 and slightly revised in his version of the *Iliad* (XII.371–96).

With more than usual lightning in her eyes;
Nor feared the chief the unequal fight to try,
Who sought no more than on his foe to die.
　But this bold lord with manly strength endued,
She with one finger and a thumb subdued: 　　　　　　80
Just where the breath of life his nostrils drew,
A charge of snuff the wily virgin threw;
The Gnomes direct, to every atom just,
The pungent grains of titillating dust.
Sudden, with starting tears each eye o'erflows, 　　85
And the high dome re-echoes to his nose.
　"Now meet thy fate," incensed Belinda cried,
And drew a deadly bodkin[4] from her side.
(The same, his ancient personage to deck,
Her great-great-grandsire wore about his neck, 　　90
In three seal rings; which after, melted down,
Formed a vast buckle for his widow's gown:
Her infant grandame's whistle next it grew,
The bells she jingled, and the whistle blew;
Then in a bodkin graced her mother's hairs, 　　　95
Which long she wore, and now Belinda wears.)
　"Boast not my fall," he cried, "insulting foe!
Thou by some other shalt be laid as low.
Nor think to die dejects my lofty mind:
All that I dread is leaving you behind! 　　　　　　100
Rather than so, ah, let me still survive,
And burn in Cupid's flames—but burn alive."
　"Restore the Lock!" she cries; and all around
"Restore the Lock!" the vaulted roofs rebound.
Not fierce Othello in so loud a strain 　　　　　　105
Roared for the handkerchief that caused his pain.[5]
But see how oft ambitious aims are crossed,
And chiefs contend till all the prize is lost!
The lock, obtained with guilt, and kept with pain,
In every place is sought, but sought in vain: 　　　110
With such a prize no mortal must be blessed,
So Heaven decrees! with Heaven who can contest?
　Some thought it mounted to the lunar sphere,
Since all things lost on earth are treasured there.
There heroes' wits are kept in ponderous vases, 　115
And beaux' in snuffboxes and tweezer cases.
There broken vows and deathbed alms are found,
And lovers' hearts with ends of riband bound,
The courtier's promises, and sick man's prayers,
The smiles of harlots, and the tears of heirs, 　　120
Cages for gnats, and chains to yoke a flea,
Dried butterflies, and tomes of casuistry.
　But trust the Muse—she saw it upward rise,

4. An ornamental pin shaped like a 　5. *Othello* III.iv.
dagger, to be worn in the hair.

Though marked by none but quick, poetic eyes
(So Rome's great founder to the heavens withdrew,[6]   125
To Proculus alone confessed in view);
A sudden star, it shot through liquid air,
And drew behind a radiant trail of hair.
Not Berenice's locks first rose so bright,[7]
The heavens bespangling with disheveled light.   130
The Sylphs behold it kindling as it flies,
And pleased pursue its progress through the skies.

    This the beau monde shall from the Mall[8] survey,
And hail with music its propitious ray.
This the blest lover shall for Venus take,   135
And send up vows from Rosamonda's Lake.[9]
This Partridge[1] soon shall view in cloudless skies,
When next he looks through Galileo's eyes;
And hence the egregious wizard shall foredoom
The fate of Louis, and the fall of Rome.   140

    Then cease, bright nymph! to mourn thy ravished hair,
Which adds new glory to the shining sphere!
Not all the tresses that fair head can boast,
Shall draw such envy as the Lock you lost.
For, after all the murders of your eye,   145
When, after millions slain, yourself shall die:
When those fair suns shall set, as set they must,
And all those tresses shall be laid in dust,
This Lock the Muse shall consecrate to fame,
And 'midst the stars inscribe Belinda's name.   150

1712   1714

Ode on Solitude[2]

Happy the man whose wish and care
    A few paternal acres bound,
Content to breathe his native air,
        In his own ground.

Whose herds with milk, whose fields with bread,   5
    Whose flocks supply him with attire,
Whose trees in summer yield him shade,
        In winter fire.

6. Romulus, the "founder" and first king of Rome, was snatched to heaven in a storm cloud while reviewing his army in the Campus Martius (Livy I. xvi).

7. Berenice, the wife of Ptolemy III, dedicated a lock of her hair to the gods to ensure her husband's safe return from war. It was turned into a constellation.

8. A walk laid out by Charles II in St. James's Park, a resort for strollers of all sorts.

9. In St. James's Park; associated with unhappy lovers.

1. John Partridge, the astrologer whose annually published predictions had been amusingly satirized by Swift and other wits in 1708. "Galileo's eyes": i.e., a telescope.

2. The hint for this poem was taken from Horace's well-known *Epode II*, which praises the simplicity and innocence of country life, a favorite literary theme in Pope's time.

Blest, who can unconcernedly find
   Hours, days, and years slide soft away,   10
In health of body, peace of mind,
          Quiet by day,

Sound sleep by night; study and ease,
   Together mixed; sweet recreation;
And innocence, which most does please   15
          With meditation.

Thus let me live, unseen, unknown;
   Thus unlamented let me die;
Steal from the world, and not a stone
          Tell where I lie.   20

ca. 1700–1709   1717, 1736

Epistle to Miss Blount[1]

ON HER LEAVING THE TOWN, AFTER THE CORONATION

As some fond virgin, whom her mother's care
Drags from the town to wholesome country air,
Just when she learns to roll a melting eye,
And hear a spark,[2] yet think no danger nigh;
From the dear man unwilling she must sever,   5
Yet takes one kiss before she parts forever:
Thus from the world fair Zephalinda[3] flew,
Saw others happy, and with sighs withdrew;
Not that their pleasures caused her discontent;
She sighed not that they stayed, but that she went.   10
   She went to plain-work,[4] and to purling brooks,
Old-fashioned halls, dull aunts, and croaking rooks:
She went from opera, park, assembly, play,
To morning walks, and prayers three hours a day;
To part her time 'twixt reading and bohea,[5]   15
To muse, and spill her solitary tea,
Or o'er cold coffee trifle with the spoon,
Count the slow clock, and dine exact at noon;[6]
Divert her eyes with pictures in the fire,
Hum half a tune, tell stories to the squire;   20
Up to her godly garret after seven,
There starve and pray, for that's the way to heaven.
   Some squire, perhaps, you take delight to rack,
Whose game is whist, whose treat a toast in sack;
Who visits with a gun, presents you birds,   25

1. Teresa Blount, sister of Pope's life-long friend Martha Blount. The "coronation" was that of George I (1714).
2. A fop, a beau.
3. A fanciful name adopted by Miss Blount.
4. "Needlework, as distinguished from embroidery" (Johnson's *Dictionary*).
5. A costly sort of tea.
6. The fashionable hour for dining in London was three or four o'clock. A noon dinner is a sign of old-fashioned rusticity.

Then gives a smacking buss, and cries—"No words!"
Or with his hounds comes hollowing from the stable,
Makes love with nods and knees beneath a table;
Whose laughs are hearty, though his jests are coarse,
And loves you best of all things—but his horse.   30
    In some fair evening, on your elbow laid,
You dream of triumphs in the rural shade;
In pensive thought recall the fancied scene,
See coronations rise on every green:
Before you pass the imaginary sights   35
Of lords and earls and dukes and gartered knights,
While the spread fan o'ershades your closing eyes;
Then gives one flirt,[7] and all the vision flies.
Thus vanish scepters, coronets, and balls,
And leave you in lone woods, or empty walls!   40
    So when your slave,[8] at some dear idle time
(Not plagued with headaches or the want of rhyme)
Stands in the streets, abstracted from the crew,
And while he seems to study, thinks of you;
Just when his fancy points [9] your sprightly eyes,   45
Or sees the blush of soft Parthenia [1] rise,
Gay [2] pats my shoulder, and you vanish quite;
Streets, chairs, and coxcombs rush upon my sight;
Vexed to be still in town, I knit my brow,
Look sour, and hum a tune—as you may now.   50

1717

Elegy to the Memory of an Unfortunate Lady[3]

    What beckoning ghost, along the moonlight shade
Invites my steps, and points to yonder glade?
'Tis she!—but why that bleeding bosom gored,
Why dimly gleams the visionary sword?
O ever beauteous, every friendly! tell,   5
Is it, in Heaven, a crime to love too well?
To bear too tender, or too firm a heart,
To act a lover's or a Roman's part? [4]
Is there no bright reversion [5] in the sky,
For those who greatly think, or bravely die?   10

7. I.e., opens and closes her fan with a jerk.
8. I.e., Pope.
9. Notices.
1. Martha Blount.
2. John Gay, the poet.
3. The subject of the poem is fanciful, although Pope had been interested in the misfortunes of two ladies, neither of whom much resembled the subject of this poem. Geoffrey Tillotson has plausibly suggested that lines 79–80 are addressed to the beautiful, witty Lady Mary Wortley Montagu, to whom Pope was romantically attached at this period. Later the two quarreled bitterly, for reasons no longer ascertainable, and Pope often attacked her in his satires under the pseudonym Sappho.
4. I.e., commit suicide, as the Roman Stoics taught that a man might do if he faced irremediable misery and misfortune.
5. "Succession (to an estate)" (Johnson's *Dictionary*).

Why bade ye else, ye Powers! her soul aspire
Above the vulgar flight of low desire?
Ambition first sprung from your blest abodes;
The glorious fault of angels and of gods: [5]
Thence to their images on earth it flows,   15
And in the breasts of kings and heroes glows.
Most souls, 'tis true, but peep out once an age,
Dull sullen prisoners in the body's cage:
Dim lights of life, that burn a length of years
Useless, unseen, as lamps in sepulchers;   20
Like Eastern kings a lazy state they keep,
And close confined to their own palace, sleep.
    From these perhaps (ere Nature bade her die)
Fate snatched her early to the pitying sky.
As into air the purer spirits flow,   25
And separate from their kindred dregs below;
So flew the soul to its congenial place.
Nor left one virtue to redeem her race. [6]
    But thou, false guardian of a charge too good,
Thou, mean deserter of thy brother's blood!   30
See on these ruby lips the trembling breath,
These cheeks, now fading at the blast of death;
Cold is that breast which warmed the world before,
And those love-darting eyes must roll no more.
Thus, if Eternal Justice rules the ball,   35
Thus shall your wives, and thus your children fall:
On all the line a sudden vengeance waits,
And frequent hearses shall besiege your gates.
There passengers shall stand, and pointing say
(While the long funerals blacken all the way),   40
Lo these were they, whose souls the Furies steeled,
And cursed with hearts unknowing how to yield.
Thus unlamented pass the proud away,
The gaze of fools, and pageant of a day!
So perish all, whose breast ne'er learned to glow   45
For others' good, or melt at others' woe.
    What can atone (oh, ever-injured shade!)
Thy fate unpitied, and thy rites unpaid?
No friend's complaint, no kind domestic tear
Pleased thy pale ghost, or graced thy mournful bier.   50
By foreign hands thy dying eyes were closed,
By foreign hands thy decent limbs composed,
By foreign hands thy humble grave adorned,
By strangers honored, and by strangers mourned!
What though no friends in sable weeds appear,   55
Grieve for an hour, perhaps, then mourn a year,
And bear about the mockery of woe
To midnight dances, and the public show?

5. Shakespeare's *Henry VIII* III.ii.   p. 70) has remarked on the "meta-
441–42.   physical" manner of lines 17–28.
6. Family. F. R. Leavis (*Revaluation*,

What though no weeping Loves thy ashes grace,
Nor polished marble emulate thy face?   60
What though no sacred earth allow thee room,
Nor hallowed dirge be muttered o'er thy tomb?[7]
Yet shall thy grave with rising flowers be dressed,
And the green turf lie lightly on thy breast:
There shall the morn her earliest tears bestow,   65
There the first roses of the year shall blow;
While angels with their silver wings o'ershade
The ground, now sacred by thy reliques made.
   So peaceful rests, without a stone, a name,
What once had beauty, titles, wealth, and fame.   70
How loved, how honored once, avails thee not,
To whom related, or by whom begot;
A heap of dust alone remains of thee,
'Tis all thou art, and all the proud shall be!
   Poets themselves must fall, like those they sung,   75
Deaf the praised ear, and mute the tuneful tongue.
Even he, whose soul now melts in mournful lays,
Shall shortly want the generous tear he pays;
Then from his closing eyes thy form shall part,
And the last pang shall tear thee from his heart,   80
Life's idle business at one gasp be o'er,
The Muse forgot, and thou beloved no more!

1717

Epistle to Robert, Earl of Oxford and Mortimer[1]

   Such were the notes thy once-loved Poet[2] sung,
Till Death untimely stopped his tuneful tongue.
Oh, just beheld and lost! admired and mourned!
With softest manners, gentlest arts, adorned!
Blessed in each science! blessed in every strain!   5
Dear to the Muse! to Harley dear—in vain!
   For him thou oft hast bid the world attend,
Fond to forget the statesman in the friend;
For Swift and him despised the farce of state,
The sober follies of the wise and great,   10
Dexterous the craving, fawning crowd to quit,
And pleased to 'scape from flattery to wit.[3]
   Absent or dead, still let a friend be dear
(A sigh the absent claims, the dead a tear);

7. In Roman Catholic countries suicides are not given Christian burial.
1. Robert Harley, Lord Treasurer in the Tory ministry that governed England from 1710 to Queen Anne's death in 1714, became the Earl of Oxford and Mortimer, after which he signed himself "Oxford." Oxford joined Swift, Pope, the queen's physician Dr. John Arbuthnot, John Gay, and Thomas Parnell in forming the Martinus Scriblerus Club in 1713.
2. Thomas Parnell (1679–1718), whose poems Pope edited in 1722, dedicating them to Oxford in this Epistle.
3. In the meetings of the Scriblerus Club.

Recall those nights that closed thy toilsome days,   15
Still hear thy Parnell in his living lays;
Who, careless now of interest, fame, or fate,
Perhaps forgets that Oxford e'er was great;
Or deeming meanest what we greatest call,
Beholds thee glorious only in thy fall.   20
 And sure if aught below the seats divine
Can touch immortals, 'tis a soul like thine;
A soul supreme, in each hard instance tried,
Above all pain, all passion, and all pride,
The rage of power, the blast of public breath,   25
The lust of lucre, and the dread of death.[4]
 In vain to deserts[5] thy retreat is made;
The Muse attends thee to thy silent shade;
'Tis hers the brave man's latest steps to trace,
Rejudge his acts, and dignify disgrace.   30
When Interest calls off all her sneaking train,
And all the obliged desert, and all the vain,
She waits, or to the scaffold or the cell,
When the last lingering friend has bid farewell.
Even now she shades thy evening walk with bays   35
(No hireling she, no prostitute to praise);
Even now, observant of the parting ray,
Eyes the calm sunset of thy various day,
Through fortune's cloud one truly great can see,
Nor fears to tell that Mortimer is he.   40

1722

4. In 1715 Oxford had been impeached on a charge of high treason and imprisoned in the Tower, where he remained until his acquittal in 1717.

5. The word implied not aridity but wildness. Actually Oxford retired to his family estate in Herefordshire.

An Essay on Man

Pope's philosophical poem, *An Essay on Man*, is a fragment of an ambitious but never completed scheme for what the poet referred to as his "ethic work," which was to have been a large survey of man and of the society which he has created. The work is dedicated to Henry St. John (pronounced *Sín-jun*), Viscount Bolingbroke (1678–1751), the brilliant, though erratic, Secretary of State in the Tory ministry of 1710–14, whom Pope had come to know through Swift. After the accession of George I he fled to France, attainted of treason, but was pardoned and allowed to return in 1723. He settled near Pope at Dawley Farm and a close friendship developed between the two men. In their conversations Bolingbroke, who fancied himself a philosopher, helped Pope to formulate the optimistic system that is expounded in this poem, though the notion that Pope merely versified ideas that Bolingbroke furnished him in prose is no longer considered valid.

 It is clear that the poem would have been pretty much what it is had the two men never met, for it expresses doctrines widely circulated and generally accepted at the time by enlightened minds throughout Europe.

The *Essay* gives memorable expression to ideas about the nature of the universe and man's place in it, ideas upon which 18th-century optimism rested. The evolutionary theories of the 19th century and the history of the first half of the 20th century have made such optimism untenable today; but this does not mean that the *Essay* is either trivial or cheap.

Pope's purpose is to "vindicate the ways of God to man," a phrase that consciously echoes *Paradise Lost* I.26. Like Milton, Pope faces the problem of the existence of evil in a world presumed to be the creation of a good God (a philosophical work that deals with this problem is called a "theodicy"). *Paradise Lost* is Biblical in content, Christian in doctrine; the *Essay on Man* avoids all specifically Christian doctrines, not because Pope disbelieved them, but because "man," the subject of the poem, includes millions who never heard of Christianity, and Pope is concerned with the universal. Milton tells a mythological story. Pope writes in abstract terms.

The *Essay* is divided into four Epistles. In the first Pope asserts the essential order and goodness of the universe and the rightness of man's place in it. The other Epistles deal with how man may emulate in his nature and in society the cosmic harmony revealed in the first Epistle. The second seeks to show how he may attain a psychological harmony which can become the basis of a virtuous life through the co-operation of self-love and the passions (both necessary to our complete humanity) with reason, the controller and director. The third is concerned with man in society, which, it teaches, was created through the co-operation of self-love (the egoistic drives that motivate us) and social love (our dependence on others, our inborn benevolence). The fourth is concerned with happiness, which lies within the reach of all, for it is dependent upon virtue, which becomes possible when—though only when—self-love is transmuted into love of man and love of God. Such, in brief summary, are Pope's main ideas in the poem. He has given them expression in splendid language, unforgettable phrases (many have detached themselves from the poem and have become a part of our daily speech), and astonishing metrical virtuosity; and though the poem is didactic, it is richly musical and is distinguished by subtly beautiful visual imagery.

From An Essay on Man

TO HENRY ST. JOHN, LORD BOLINGBROKE

Epistle I. Of the Nature and State of Man, With Respect to the Universe

Awake, my St. John! leave all meaner things
To low ambition, and the pride of kings.
Let us (since life can little more supply
Than just to look about us and to die)
Expatiate free[1] o'er all this scene of man;   5

1. Range freely.

A mighty maze! but not without a plan;
A wild, where weeds and flowers promiscuous shoot,
Or garden, tempting with forbidden fruit.
Together let us beat this ample field,
Try what the open, what the covert yield;   10
The latent tracts, the giddy heights, explore
Of all who blindly creep, or sightless soar;
Eye Nature's walks, shoot folly as it flies,
And catch the manners living as they rise;
Laugh where we must, be candid[2] where we can;   15
But vindicate the ways of God to man.[3]

    1. Say first, of God above, or man below,
What can we reason, but from what we know?
Of man, what see we but his station here,
From which to reason, or to which refer?   20
Through worlds unnumbered though the God be known,
'Tis ours to trace him only in our own.
He, who through vast immensity can pierce,
See worlds on worlds compose one universe,
Observe how system into system runs,   25
What other planets circle other suns,
What varied Being peoples every star,
May tell why Heaven has made us as we are.
But of this frame the bearings, and the ties,
The strong connections, nice dependencies,   30
Gradations just, has thy pervading soul
Looked through? or can a part contain the whole?
    Is the great chain, that draws all to agree,
And drawn supports, upheld by God, or thee?

    2. Presumptuous man! the reason wouldst thou find,   35
Why formed so weak, so little, and so blind?
First, if thou canst, the harder reason guess,
Why formed no weaker, blinder, and no less!
Ask of thy mother earth, why oaks are made
Taller or stronger than the weeds they shade?   40
Or ask of yonder argent fields above,
Why Jove's satellites[4] are less than Jove?
    Of systems possible, if 'tis confessed
That Wisdom Infinite must form the best,
Where all must full or not coherent be,   45
And all that rises, rise in due degree;
Then, in the scale of reasoning life, 'tis plain,
There must be, somewhere, such a rank as man:
And all the question (wrangle e'er so long)
Is only this, if God has placed him wrong?   50
    Respecting man, whatever wrong we call,
May, must be right, as relative to all.

2. Kindly.
3. Pope deliberately echoes *Paradise Lost* I.26.
4. In his *Dictionary* Johnson notes and condemns Pope's giving his word four syllables, as in Latin.

In human works, though labored on with pain,
A thousand movements scarce one purpose gain;
In God's, one single can its end produce;   55
Yet serves to second too some other use.
So man, who here seems principal alone,
Perhaps acts second to some sphere unknown,
Touches some wheel, or verges to some goal;
'Tis but a part we see, and not a whole.   60
    When the proud steed shall know why man restrains
His fiery course, or drives him o'er the plains;
When the dull ox, why now he breaks the clod,
Is now a victim, and now Egypt's god:
Then shall man's pride and dullness comprehend   65
His actions', passions', being's use and end;
Why doing, suffering, checked, impelled; and why
This hour a slave, the next a deity.
    Then say not man's imperfect, Heaven in fault;
Say rather, man's as perfect as he ought: 70
His knowledge measured to his state and place,
His time a moment, and a point his space.
If to be perfect in a certain sphere,[5]
What matter, soon or late, or here or there?
The blest today is as completely so,   75
As who began a thousand years ago.

    3. Heaven from all creatures hides the book of Fate,
All but the page prescribed, their present state:
From brutes what men, from men what spirits know:
Or who could suffer Being here below?   80
The lamb thy riot dooms to bleed today,
Had he thy reason, would he skip and play?
Pleased to the last, he crops the flowery food,
And licks the hand just raised to shed his blood.
O blindness to the future! kindly given,   85
That each may fill the circle marked by Heaven:
Who sees with equal eye, as God of all,
A hero perish, or a sparrow fall,
Atoms or systems[6] into ruin hurled,
And now a bubble burst, and now a world.   90
    Hope humbly then; with trembling pinions soar;
Wait the great teacher Death, and God adore!
What future bliss, he gives not thee to know,
But gives that hope to be thy blessing now.
Hope springs eternal in the human breast: 95
Man never is, but always to be blest:
The soul, uneasy and confined from home,
Rests and expatiates in a life to come.
    Lo! the poor Indian, whose untutored mind
Sees God in clouds, or hears him in the wind;   100
His soul proud Science never taught to stray

---

5. I.e., in one's "state and place."   6. Solar systems.

Far as the solar walk, or milky way;
Yet simple Nature to his hope has given,
Behind the cloud-topped hill, an humbler heaven;
Some safer world in depth of woods embraced,   105
Some happier island in the watery waste,
Where slaves once more their native land behold,
No fiends torment, no Christians thirst for gold!
To be, contents his natural desire,
He asks no angel's wing, no seraph's fire;   110
But thinks, admitted to that equal sky,
His faithful dog shall bear him company.

    4. Go, wiser thou! and, in thy scale of sense,
Weigh thy opinion against Providence;
Call imperfection what thou fancy'st such,   115
Say, here he gives too little, there too much;
Destroy all creatures for thy sport or gust,[7]
Yet cry, if man's unhappy, God's unjust;
If man alone engross not Heaven's high care,
Alone made perfect here, immortal there: 120
Snatch from his hand the balance and the rod,
Rejudge his justice, be the God of God!
In pride, in reasoning pride, our error lies;
All quit their sphere, and rush into the skies.
Pride still is aiming at the blest abodes,   125
Men would be angels, angels would be gods.
Aspiring to be gods, if angels fell,
Aspiring to be angels, men rebel:
And who but wishes to invert the laws
Of order, sins against the Eternal Cause.   130

    5. Ask for what end the heavenly bodies shine,
Earth for whose use? Pride answers, " 'Tis for mine:
For me kind Nature wakes her genial power,
Suckles each herb, and spreads out every flower;
Annual for me, the grape, the rose renew   135
The juice nectareous, and the balmy dew;
For me, the mine a thousand treasures brings;
For me, health gushes from a thousand springs;
Seas roll to waft me, suns to light me rise;
My footstool earth, my canopy the skies."   140
    But errs not Nature from this gracious end,
From burning suns when livid deaths descend,
When earthquakes swallow, or when tempests sweep
Towns to one grave, whole nations to the deep?
"No," 'tis replied, "the first Almighty Cause   145
Acts not by partial, but by general laws;
The exceptions few; some change since all began,
And what created perfect?"—Why then man?
If the great end be human happiness,

---

7. "Sense of tasting" (Johnson's *Dictionary*).

Then Nature deviates; and can man do less? 150
As much that end a constant course requires
Of showers and sunshine, as of man's desires;
As much eternal springs and cloudless skies,
As men forever temperate, calm, and wise.
If plagues or earthquakes break not Heaven's design, 155
Why then a Borgia, or a Catiline?[8]
Who knows but he whose hand the lightning forms,
Who heaves old ocean, and who wings the storms,
Pours fierce ambition in a Caesar's mind,
Or turns young Ammon[9] loose to scourge mankind? 160
From pride, from pride, our very reasoning springs;
Account for moral, as for natural things:
Why charge we Heaven in those, in these acquit?
In both, to reason right is to submit.

Better for us, perhaps, it might appear, 165
Were there all harmony, all virtue here; .
That never air or ocean felt the wind;
That never passion discomposed the mind: ·
But ALL subsists by elemental strife;
And passions are the elements of life. 170
The general ORDER, since the whole began,
Is kept in Nature, and is kept in man.

6. What would this man? Now upward will he soar,
And little less than angel, would be more;
Now looking downwards, just as grieved appears 175
To want the strength of bulls, the fur of bears.
Made for his use all creatures if he call,
Say what their use, had he the powers of all?
Nature to these, without profusion, kind,
The proper organs, proper powers assigned; 180
Each seeming want compénsated of course,
Here with degrees of swiftness, there of force;
All in exact proportion to the state;
Nothing to add, and nothing to abate.
Each beast, each insect, happy in its own; 185
Is Heaven unkind to man, and man alone?
Shall he alone, whom rational we call,
Be pleased with nothing, if not blessed with all?
The bliss of man (could pride that blessing find)
Is not to act or think beyond mankind; 190
No powers of body or of soul to share,
But what his nature and his state can bear.
Why has not man a microscopic eye?

---

8. The Renaissance Italian family of the Borgias were notorious for their crimes: ruthless lust for power, cruelty, rapaciousness, treachery, and murder (especially by poisoning); Cesare Borgia (1476–1507), son of Pope Alexander VI, is here referred to. Lucius Sergius Catiline (ca. 108–62 B.C.), an ambitious, greedy, and cruel conspirator against the Roman state, was denounced in Cicero's famous orations before the senate and in the Forum.
9. Alexander the Great.

For this plain reason, man is not a fly.
Say what the use, were finer optics given,   195
To inspect a mite, not comprehend the heaven?
Or touch, if tremblingly alive all o'er,
To smart and agonize at every pore?
Or quick effluvia[1] darting through the brain,
Die of a rose in aromatic pain?   200
If nature thundered in his opening ears,
And stunned him with the music of the spheres,
How would he wish that Heaven had left him still
The whispering zephyr, and the purling rill?
Who finds not Providence all good and wise,   205
Alike in what it gives, and what it denies?

    7. Far as creation's ample range extends,
The scale of sensual,[2] mental powers ascends:
Mark how it mounts, to man's imperial race,
From the green myriads in the peopled grass: 210
What modes of sight betwixt each wide extreme,
The mole's dim curtain, and the lynx's beam:[3]
Of smell, the headlong lioness between,
And hound sagacious[4] on the tainted green:
Of hearing, from the life that fills the flood,   215
To that which warbles through the vernal wood:
The spider's touch, how exquisitely fine!
Feels at each thread, and lives along the line:
In the nice[5] bee, what sense so subtly true
From poisonous herbs extracts the healing dew: 220
How instinct varies in the groveling swine,
Compared, half-reasoning elephant, with thine!
'Twixt that, and reason, what a nice barrier;[6]
Forever separate, yet forever near!
Remembrance and reflection how allied;   225
What thin partitions sense from thought divide:
And middle natures, how they long to join,
Yet never pass the insuperable line!
Without this just gradation, could they be
Subjected, these to those, or all to thee?   230
The powers of all subdued by thee alone,
Is not thy reason all these powers in one?

    8. See, through this air, this ocean, and this earth,
All matter quick, and bursting into birth.
Above, how high progressive life may go!   235
Around, how wide! how deep extend below!

1. According to the philosophy of Epicurus (adopted by Robert Boyle, the chemist, and other 17th-century scientists), the senses are stirred to perception by being bombarded through the pores by steady streams of "effluvia," incredibly thin and tiny—but material—images of the objects which surround us.
2. Sensory.
3. One of several early theories of vision held that the eye casts a beam of light which makes objects visible.
4. Quick of scent.
5. Exact, accurate.
6. Pronounced *ba-réer.*

Vast Chain of Being! which from God began,
Natures ethereal, human, angel, man,
Beast, bird, fish, insect, what no eye can see,
No glass can reach! from Infinite to thee,   240
From thee to nothing.—On superior powers
Were we to press, inferior might on ours:
Or in the full creation leave a void,
Where, one step broken, the great scale's destroyed:
From Nature's chain whatever link you strike,   245
Tenth or ten thousandth, breaks the chain alike.
      And, if each system in gradation roll
Alike essential to the amazing Whole,
The least confusion but in one, not all
That system only, but the Whole must fall.   250
Let earth unbalanced from her orbit fly,
Planets and suns run lawless through the sky,
Let ruling angels from their spheres be hurled,
Being on being wrecked, and world on world,
Heaven's whole foundations to their center nod,   255
And Nature tremble to the throne of God:
All this dread ORDER break—for whom? for thee?
Vile worm!—oh, madness, pride, impiety!

      9. What if the foot, ordained the dust to tread,
Or hand, to toil, aspired to be the head?   260
What if the head, the eye, or ear repined
To serve mere engines to the ruling Mind?[7]
Just as absurd for any part to claim
To be another, in this general frame:
Just as absurd, to mourn the tasks or pains,   265
The great directing MIND of ALL ordains.
      All are but parts of one stupendous whole,
Whose body Nature is, and God the soul;
That, changed through all, and yet in all the same,
Great in the earth, as in the ethereal frame,   270
Warms in the sun, refreshes in the breeze,
Glows in the stars, and blossoms in the trees,
Lives through all life, extends through all extent,
Spreads undivided, operates unspent,
Breathes in our soul, informs our mortal part,   275
As full, as perfect, in a hair as heart;
As full, as perfect, in vile man that mourns,
As the rapt seraph that adores and burns;
To him no high, no low, no great, no small;
He fills, he bounds, connects, and equals all.   280

      10. Cease then, nor ORDER imperfection name:
Our proper bliss depends on what we blame.
Know thy own point: this kind, this due degree
Of blindness, weakness, Heaven bestows on thee.

7. Cf. I Corinthians xii.14–26.

Submit—In this, or any other sphere,   285
Secure to be as blest as thou canst bear:
Safe in the hand of one disposing Power,
Or in the natal, or the mortal hour.
All Nature is but art, unknown to thee;
All chance, direction, which thou canst not see;   290
All discord, harmony not understood;
All partial evil, universal good:
And, spite of pride, in erring reason's spite,
One truth is clear: Whatever IS, is RIGHT.

From *Epistle II. Of the Nature and State of Man With Respect to Himself, as an Individual*

    1. Know then thyself, presume not God to scan;
The proper study of mankind is Man.
Placed on this isthmus of a middle state,
A being darkly wise, and rudely great:
With too much knowledge for the skeptic side,   5
With too much weakness for the Stoic's pride,
He hangs between; in doubt to act, or rest,
In doubt to deem himself a god, or beast;
In doubt his mind or body to prefer,
Born but to die, and reasoning but to err;   10
Alike in ignorance, his reason such,
Whether he thinks too little, or too much:
Chaos of thought and passion, all confused;
Still by himself abused, or disabused;
Created half to rise, and half to fall;   15
Great lord of all things, yet a prey to all;
Sole judge of truth, in endless error hurled:
The glory, jest, and riddle of the world!

* * *

1733

The Universal Prayer

Father of all! in every age,
    In every clime adored,
By saint, by savage, and by sage,
    Jehovah, Jove, or Lord!

Thou Great First Cause, least understood: 5
    Who all my sense confined
To know but this—that thou art good,
    And that myself am blind:

Yet gave me, in this dark estate,
    To see the good from ill;   10

And binding Nature fast in fate,
    Left free the human will.

What conscience dictates to be done,
    Or warns me not to do,
This, teach me more than Hell to shun,   15
    That, more than Heaven pursue.

What blessings thy free bounty gives,
    Let me not cast away;
For God is paid when man receives,
    To enjoy is to obey.   20

Yet not to earth's contracted span,
    Thy goodness let me bound,
Or think thee Lord alone of man,
    When thousand worlds are round:

Let not this weak, unknowing hand   25
    Presume thy bolts to throw,
And deal damnation round the land,
    On each I judge thy foe.

If I am right, thy grace impart,
    Still in the right to stay;   30
If I am wrong, oh teach my heart
    To find that better way.

Save me alike from foolish pride,
    Or impious discontent,
At aught thy wisdom has denied,   35
    Or aught thy goodness lent.

Teach me to feel another's woe,
    To hide the fault I see;
That mercy I to others show,
    That mercy show to me.   40

Mean though I am, not wholly so
    Since quickened by thy breath;
Oh lead me wheresoe'er I go,
    Through this day's life or death.

This day, be bread and peace my lot: 45
    All else beneath the sun,
Thou know'st if best bestowed or not,
    And let thy will be done.

To thee, whose temple is all space,
    Whose altar, earth, sea, skies!   50
One chorus let all being raise!
    All Nature's incense rise!

ca. 1715   1738

The First Satire of the Second Book of Horace Imitated[1]

TO MR. FORTESCUE[2]

P. There are (I scarce can think it, but am told),
There are, to whom my satire seems too bold:
Scarce to wise Peter[3] cómplaisant enough,
And something said of Chartres much too rough.
The lines are weak, another's pleased to say,   5
Lord Fanny[4] spins a thousand such a day.
Timorous by nature, of the rich in awe,
I come to counsel learned in the law:
You'll give me, like a friend, both sage and free,[4a]
Advice; and (as you use) without a fee.   10
    F. I'd write no more.
    P.   Not write? but then I think,
And for my soul I cannot sleep a wink.
I nod in company, I wake at night,
Fools rush into my head, and so I write.
    F. You could not do a worse thing for your life.   15
Why, if the nights seem tedious, take a wife:
Or rather truly, if your point be rest,
Lettuce and cowslip wine;[5] *Probatum est.*
But talk with Celsus,[6] Celsus will advise
Hartshorn, or something that shall close your eyes.   20
Or, if you needs must write, write Caesar's[7] praise,

1. In his Preface to the translation of Ovid's *Epistles* (1680), Dryden distinguished three methods of translation: "metaphrase," translating as nearly as possible word for word and line for line; "paraphrase," retaining the sense but not the literal wording of the original (the method that he used in translating Virgil, and Pope in translating Homer); and "imitation," following the general structure of the original, modernizing its allusions to circumstances, manners, and men, and assuming, as he says, "the liberty not only to vary from the words and sense, but to forsake them both" as occasion demands. It is this mode that Pope used in some of his major satires of the 1730's, *Imitations of Horace.*
    Experience had taught him that if in his satires he named actual people, he was charged with cruelty or slander, and if he used fictitious names, they were often identified by gossip with people he had not intended at all. General satire seemed to miss the mark. Satire aimed at individuals aroused sympathy for the victim and antagonism toward the satirist. When Bolingbroke pointed out that his situation was much like that which Horace had treated with wry humor in *Satires* II.i, Pope immediately set about "imitating" it, converting it into a completely contemporary, even a personal poem. It is a vigorous defense of Pope the satirist, who is presented in the heroic role of the disinterested friend and defender of virtue and truth in an evil time.
2. William Fortescue, the eminent lawyer, who, though a Whig and a supporter of Walpole, was a friend of Pope.
3. Peter Walter, a notorious moneylender; Francis Chartres, a debauchee and gambler. Pope mentions them in other satires.
4. John, Lord Hervey. See *Epistle to Dr. Arbuthnot*, line 305 and note. Fannius was a poetaster mentioned contemptuously by Horace (*Satires* I.iv.21–22 and I.x.80).
4a. Frank.
5. Used as soporifics; "*Probatum est*" may be freely rendered "a proved remedy."
6. A Roman writer on medicine, here used as a fictitious name for a physician. "Hartshorn," or buckshorn, was an herb used in treating the eyes and in sleeping potions.
7. George II's.

You'll gain at least a knighthood, or the bays.[8]

    P. What? like Sir Richard,[9] rumbling, rough, and fierce,
With arms, and George, and Brunswick crowd the verse?
Rend with tremendous sound your ears asunder,   25
With gun, drum, trumpet, blunderbuss, and thunder?
Or nobly wild, with Budgell's fire and force,
Paint angels trembling round his falling horse?[1]

    F. Then all your Muse's softer art display,
Let Carolina[2] smooth the tuneful lay,   30
Lull with Amelia's liquid name the Nine,
And sweetly flow through all the royal line.

    P. Alas! few verses touch their nicer ear;
They scarce can bear their laureate twice a year;[3]
And justly Caesar scorns the poet's lays,   35
It is to history he trusts for praise.

    F. Better be Cibber, I'll maintain it still,
Than ridicule all taste, blaspheme Quadrille,[4]
Abuse the City's best good men in meter,
And laugh at peers that put their trust in Peter.   40
Even those you touch not, hate you.

    P.   What should ail 'em?

    F. A hundred smart in Timon[5] and in Balaam:
The fewer still you name, you wound the more;
Bond is but one, but Harpax is a score.[6]

    P. Each mortal has his pleasure: none deny   45
Scarsdale his bottle, Darty his ham pie;
Ridotta[7] sips and dances, till she see
The doubling lusters[8] dance as fast as she;
F——[9] loves the senate, Hockley Hole his brother,
Like in all else, as one egg to another.   50
I love to pour out all myself, as plain
As downright Shippen, or as old Montaigne:[1]

8. The poet-laureateship.

9. Sir Richard Blackmore (1654–1729), London physician, knighted by William III for his Whig principles and his epics. Pope and all the "wits" laughed at his poems, with good reason. Observe the noisy emptiness of lines 23–26, which are intended to suggest Blackmore's inflated style.

1. Eustace Budgell, Addison's cousin, had sung the praises of the king's horse, which had been shot out from under him at the battle of Oudenarde (1708). George yearned for military glory.

2. Queen Caroline and the Princess Amelia. Contrast with the bombast of lines 25–26 the mellifluous emptiness of lines 30–32.

3. Colley Cibber (1671–1757), the laureate, wrote execrable official odes for each New Year and for the king's birthday.

4. A popular card game.

5. When in his *Epistle to the Earl of Burlington* (1731) Pope had described a fictitious "Timon," owner of a vulgar, ostentatious estate, the town had identified him with the Duke of Chandos and charged Pope with ingratitude to a friend. "Balaam": a fictitious London merchant whose rise and fall Pope recounts in his *Epistle to Lord Bathurst* (1732).

6. Dennis Bond, a notorious embezzler, mentioned by name in Pope's *Epistle to Bathurst*, line 100; "Harpax" (Greek for "robber") is a type of the miser in the same poem (lines 91–92).

7. A type name for a pleasure-loving woman. *Ridotto* is Italian for a social assembly with music and dancing.

8. Cut-glass chandeliers.

9. Stephen Fox, a Whig politician; "his brother": Henry, later Lord Holland. "Hockley Hole" was a bear garden.

1. William Shippen, the plain-spoken leader of the Jacobites in Parliament. The essays of Michel de Montaigne (1533–92) abound in self-revelation.

In them, as certain to be loved as seen,
The soul stood forth, nor kept a thought within;
In me what spots (for spots I have) appear,   55
Will prove at least the medium must be clear.
In this impartial glass, my Muse intends
Fair to expose myself, my foes, my friends;
Publish the present age, but where my text
Is vice too high, reserve it for the next: 60
My foes shall wish my life a longer date,
And every friend the less lament my fate.
My head and heart thus flowing through my quill,
Verse-man or prose-man, term me which you will,
Papist or Protestant, or both between,   65
Like good Erasmus[2] in an honest mean,
In moderation placing all my glory,
While Tories call me Whig, and Whigs a Tory.
Satire's my weapon, but I'm too discreet
To run amuck, and tilt at all I meet;   70
I only wear it in a land of hectors;
Thieves, supercargoes, sharpers, and directors.[3]
Save but our army! and let Jove encrust
Swords, pikes, and guns, with everlasting rust!
Peace is my dear delight—not Fleury's[4] more: 75
But touch me, and no minister so sore.
Whoe'er offends, at some unlucky time
Slides into verse, and hitches in a rhyme,
Sacred to ridicule his whole life long,
And the sad burden of some merry song.   80
    Slander or poison dread from Delia's rage,[5]
Hard words or hanging, if your judge be Page.[6]
From furious Sappho[7] scarce a milder fate,
P—xed[8] by her love, or libeled by her hate.
Its proper power to hurt, each creature feels;   85
Bulls aim their horns, and asses lift their heels;
'Tis a bear's talent not to kick, but hug;
And no man wonders he's not stung by Pug.[9]
So drink with Walters, or with Chartres eat,
They'll never poison you, they'll only cheat.   90
    Then, learned sir! (to cut the matter short)
Whate'er my fate, or well or ill at court,

2. Pope admired greatly the Dutch humanist Erasmus (1466–1536).
3. "Hectors": bullies; "supercargoes": officers in charge of the cargoes of merchant ships; "directors": i.e., of the collapsed South Sea Company, whose corruption was revealed by a Parliamentary inquiry when the company failed in 1720. But Pope, whose sympathies lay with the Tories and the landed gentry, is probably thinking generally of trade and finance.
4. Cardinal Fleury, minister of Louis XV of France, whose foreign policy was based on preserving peace.
5. Usually assumed to be Mary Howard, Countess of Delorain, a mistress of George II, who according to gossip had tried, in a fit of jealousy, to poison a Maid of Honor.
6. Sir Francis Page, a judge known for his bullying manner on the bench. Fielding describes him in action in *Tom Jones* VIII.xi.
7. Pope's most violent attack on Lady Mary Wortley Montagu.
8. Poxed, i.e., infected with syphilis.
9. The name of a pet dog or monkey.

Whether old age, with faint but cheerful ray,
Attends to gild the evening of my day,
Or Death's black wing already be displayed,   95
To wrap me in the universal shade;
Whether the darkened room to muse invite,
Or whitened wall provoke the skewer to write,[1]
In durance, exile, Bedlam, or the Mint,[2]
Like Lee or Budgell, I will rhyme and print.   100
    F. Alas, young man! your days can ne'er be long,
In flower of age you perish for a song!
Plums and directors, Shylock and his wife,[3]
Will club their testers, now, to take your life!
    P. What? armed for Virtue when I point the pen,   105
Brand the bold front of shameless guilty men,
Dash the proud gamester in his gilded car;
Bare the mean heart that lurks beneath a star;[4]
Can there be wanting, to defend her cause,
Lights of the Church, or guardians of the laws?   110
Could pensioned Boileau[5] lash in honest strain
Flatterers and bigots even in Louis' reign?
Could laureate Dryden pimp and friar engage,[6]
Yet neither Charles nor James be in a rage?
And I not strip the gilding off a knave,   115
Unplaced,[7] unpensioned, no man's heir, or slave?
I will, or perish in the generous cause.
Hear this, and tremble! you who 'scape the laws.
Yes, while I live, no rich or noble knave
Shall walk the world, in credit, to his grave.   120
TO VIRTUE ONLY AND HER FRIENDS A FRIEND,[8]
The world beside may murmur, or commend.
Know, all the distant din that world can keep,
Rolls o'er my grotto,[9] and but soothes my sleep.
There, my retreat the best companions grace,   125
Chiefs out of war, and statesmen out of place.
There St. John mingles with my friendly bowl
The feast of reason and the flow of soul:
And he, whose lightning pierced the Iberian lines,[1]

1. I.e., whether I go mad and am, like other madmen, locked up in a darkened room, or whether I am in prison with a whitewashed wall for paper and a skewer for pen.
2. "Bedlam": Bethlehem Hospital for the insane; "the Mint": an area in Southwark, where debtors were free from arrest. Nathaniel Lee (ca. 1653–92), the tragic poet, was confined for a while in Bedlam. Eustace Budgell, minor poet and relative of Addison, was in financial straits before his suicide in 1737.
3. Pope had thus referred to Lady Mary Wortley Montagu and her husband in his *Epistle to Bathurst*, line 96. A "plum" is slang for a man who (usually

dishonestly) has made £100,000; "testers" are sixpences.
4. The star worn on the chest by Knights of the Garter.
5. Nicolas Boileau-Despréaux (1636–1711), critic and distinguished satirist.
6. In his "Protestant play," *The Spanish Friar* (1681).
7. Holding no public office.
8. A translation of line 70 of Horace's poem, which Pope took as the motto of the satires that he wrote in the 1730's.
9. The subterranean passage under the road that separated his house at Twickenham from his garden became, in Pope's hands, a romantic grotto ornamented with minerals and shells.
1. Charles Mordaunt, Earl of Peter-

Now forms my quincunx,[2] and now ranks my vines,　130
Or tames the genius of the stubborn plain,
Almost as quickly as he conquered Spain.

　　Envy must own, I live among the great,
No pimp of pleasure, and no spy of state,
With eyes that pry not, tongue that ne'er repeats,　135
Fond to spread friendships, but to cover heats;
To help who want, to forward who excel;
This, all who know me, know; who love me, tell;
And who unknown defame me, let them be
Scribblers or peers, alike are mob to me.　140
This is my plea, on this I rest my cause—
What saith my counsel, learned in the laws?

　　F. Your plea is good. But still I say, beware!
Laws are explained by men—so have a care.
It stands on record, that in Richard's times　145
A man was hanged for very honest rhymes.[3]
Consult the statute: *quart*. I think, it is,
Edwardi sext. or *prim. et quint. Eliz.*
See *Libels, Satires*—here you have it—read.

　　P. *Libels* and *satires*! lawless things indeed!　150
But grave *epistles*, bringing vice to light,
Such as a king might read, a bishop write,
Such as Sir Robert[4] would approve—

　　F.　　　　　　　　　　　　　Indeed?
The case is altered—you may then proceed;
In such a cause the plaintiff will be hissed,　155
My lords the judges laugh, and you're dismissed.

　　　　　　　　　　　　　　　　　　　　　　1733

Epistle II. To a Lady[1]

OF THE CHARACTERS OF WOMEN

Nothing so true as what you once let fall,
"Most women have no characters at all."

borough (1658–1736), won renown in Spain (hence the allusion to "Iberian lines") during the campaign of 1705.
2. Trees or shrubs planted in fives: one at each corner of a square, one in the center.
3. Two rhymers have been suggested by scholars: John Ball, executed under Richard II in 1381 for his role in the Peasants' Revolt, and one Collingbourne, executed under Richard III for treasonable rhymes.
4. Sir Robert Walpole, the Prime Minister.
1. This is one of four poems that Pope grouped together under the title *Epistles to Several Persons*, but that have usually been known by the less appropriate title *Moral Essays*. They were conceived as

parts of Pope's ambitious "ethic work," of which only the first part, the *Essay on Man*, was completed. *Epistle I* treats the characters of men, *Epistle II* the characters of women. The other two epistles are concerned with the use of riches, a subject that engaged Pope's attention during the 1730's, since he distrusted the influence on private morals and public life of the rapidly growing wealth of England under the first Hanoverians.

　　Epistle II contains a series of brilliantly executed portraits (the metaphor of portrait painting dominates the poem) which among them illustrate the thesis that women are consistent only in being inconsistent. As we move from portrait to portrait, we not only observe

Matter too soft a lasting mark to bear,
And best distinguished by black, brown, or fair.

How many pictures[2] of one nymph we view,   5
All how unlike each other, all how true!
Arcadia's countess, here, in ermined pride,
Is, there, Pastora by a fountain side.
Here Fannia, leering on her own good man,
And there, a naked Leda with a swan.[3]   10
Let then the fair one beautifully cry,
In Magdalen's loose hair and lifted eye,
Or dressed in smiles of sweet Cecilia shine,[4]
With simpering angels, palms, and harps divine;
Whether the charmer sinner it, or saint it,   15
If folly grow romantic,[5] I must paint it.

Come then, the colors and the ground[6] prepare!
Dip in the rainbow, trick her off in air;
Choose a firm cloud, before it fall, and in it
Catch, ere she change, the Cynthia[7] of this minute.   20

Rufa, whose eye quick-glancing o'er the park,
Attracts each light gay meteor of a spark,
Agrees as ill with Rufa studying Locke,[8]
As Sappho's diamonds with her dirty smock,
Or Sappho at her toilet's greasy task,[9]   25
With Sappho fragrant at an evening masque:
So morning insects that in muck begun,
Shine, buzz, and flyblow in the setting sun.

ladies who are changeable and fickle in their own nature, but we also meet a variety of female characters—the affected, the slatternly, the soft-natured, the silly, the lewd, for instance—who remind us that ladies are as variegated as tulips (line 41).

Are the portraits imaginary or do they represent women whom Pope knew and whom his readers could recognize? This question exercised the gossips of Pope's own time and after; and it has occupied the attention of Pope's editors and commentators ever since his death. Many of the portraits indubitably allude to actual women (Sappho); some doubtless are composite (Atossa); others are mere types. Questions of identity, however, pertain rather to Pope's biography and character than to his art. It should matter little if at all to the reader first approaching Pope's satire whether in fact Atossa is Sarah, Duchess of Marlborough, or, as is much more likely, Katherine, Duchess of Buckinghamshire, or, most likely of all, Katherine combined with a few traits of Sarah. Occasionally, perhaps, a lady's name might have hinted to some of Pope's contemporaries that a real person was intended. Today the reader who is not a specialist will do well to neglect particular applications of Pope's satire and to concern himself with the generally,

the permanently human, which is always the center of Pope's works.

The "lady" of the title is Martha Blount (1690–1763), Pope's best-loved female friend, to whom he left the bulk of his property.
2. Ladies of the 17th and 18th centuries liked to have themselves painted in the costumes and attitudes of fanciful, mythological, or historical characters.
3. Leda was seduced by Zeus, who approached her in the form of a swan.
4. St. Mary Magdalen was often painted during the 17th century in the attitude described in line 12. St. Cecilia, the reputed inventor of the organ, was traditionally painted in the manner which Pope satirically glances at here.
5. Extravagant.
6. The first coatings of paint on the canvas before the figures in the picture are sketched in.
7. One of the names of Diana, goddess of the moon, a notoriously changeable heavenly body.
8. John Locke, author of *An Essay Concerning Human Understanding* (1690).
9. Lady Mary Wortley Montagu, though beautiful as a young woman, became notorious for her slatternly appearance and personal uncleanliness. Both Sappho and Lady Mary were female poets.

How soft is Silia! fearful to offend,
The frail one's advocate, the weak one's friend: 30
To her, Calista proved her conduct nice,
And good Simplicius asks of her advice.
Sudden, she storms! she raves! You tip the wink,
But spare your censure; Silia does not drink.
All eyes may see from what the change arose,   35
All eyes may see—a pimple on her nose.
    Papillia,[1] wedded to her amorous spark,
Sighs for the shades—"How charming is a park!"
A park is purchased, but the fair he sees
All bathed in tears—"Oh, odious, odious trees!"   40
    Ladies, like variegated tulips, show;
'Tis to their changes half their charms we owe;
Fine by defect, and delicately weak,
Their happy spots the nice admirer take,
'Twas thus Calypso[2] once each heart alarmed,   45
Awed without virtue, without beauty charmed;
Her tongue bewitched as oddly as her eyes,
Less wit than mimic, more a wit than wise;
Strange graces still, and stranger flights she had,
Was just not ugly, and was just not mad;   50
Yet ne'er so sure our passion to create,
As when she touched the brink of all we hate.
    Narcissa's[3] nature, tolerably mild,
To make a wash,[4] would hardly stew a child;
Has even been proved to grant a lover's prayer,   55
And paid a tradesman once to make him stare,
Gave alms at Easter, in a Christian trim,
And made a widow happy, for a whim.
Why then declare good nature is her scorn,
When 'tis by that alone she can be borne?   60
Why pique all mortals, yet affect a name?
A fool to pleasure, yet a slave to fame:
Now deep in Taylor and the *Book of Martyrs*,[5]
Now drinking citron[6] with his Grace and Chartres.
Now conscience chills her, and now passion burns;   65
And atheism and religion take their turns;
A very heathen in the carnal part,

1. The name comes from Latin for "butterfly."
2. The name is borrowed from the fascinating goddess who detained Odysseus on her island for seven years after the fall of Troy, thus preventing his return to his kingdom, Ithaca.
3. Type of extreme self-love. Narcissus, a beautiful youth, fell in love with his own image when he saw it reflected in a fountain.
4. Cosmetic lotion.
5. Jeremy Taylor, 17th-century Anglican divine, whose *Holy Living and Holy Dying* was often reprinted in the 18th century. John Foxe's *Acts and Monu-*

ments (usually referred to as Foxe's *Book of Martyrs*), 1563, was a household book in most Protestant families in the 17th and 18th centuries; a record of the Protestants who perished for their faith under the persecution of Mary Tudor (1553–58), it was instrumental in keeping anti-Catholic sentiments alive.
6. I.e., citron-water, brandy flavored with lemon or orange peel. "His Grace" is usually said to be the Duke of Wharton, an old enemy of Swift's and a notorious libertine; Francis Chartres: a debauchee often mentioned by Pope.

Yet still a sad, good Christian at her heart.
　　See Sin in state, majestically drunk;
Proud as a peeress, prouder as a punk;　　　　　　70
Chaste to her husband, frank[6a] to all beside,
A teeming mistress, but a barren bride.
What then? let blood and body bear the fault,
Her head's untouched, that noble seat of thought:
Such this day's doctrine—in another fit　　　　　75
She sins with poets through pure love of wit.
What has not fired her bosom or her brain?
Caesar and Tallboy,[7] Charles and Charlemagne.
As Helluo,[8] late dictator of the feast,
The nose of hautgout,[9] and the tip of taste,　　80
Criticked your wine, and analyzed your meat,
Yet on plain pudding deigned at home to eat;
So Philomedé,[1] lecturing all mankind
On the soft passion, and the taste refined,
The address, the delicacy—stoops at once,　　　85
And makes her hearty meal upon a dunce.
　　Flavia's a wit, has too much sense to pray;
To toast our wants and wishes, is her way;
Nor asks of God, but of her stars, to give
The mighty blessing, "while we live, to live."　　90
Then all for death, that opiate of the soul!
Lucretia's dagger,[2] Rosamonda's bowl.
Say, what can cause such impotence of mind?
A spark too fickle, or a spouse too kind.
Wise wretch! with pleasures too refined to please,　95
With too much spirit to be e'er at ease,
With too much quickness ever to be taught,
With too much thinking to have common thought:
You purchase pain with all that joy can give,
And die of nothing but a rage to live.　　　　　100
　　Turn then from wits; and look on Simo's mate,
No ass so meek, no ass so obstinate.
Or her, that owns her faults, but never mends,
Because she's honest, and the best of friends:
Or her, whose life the Church and scandal share,　105
Forever in a passion, or a prayer:
Or her, who laughs at hell, but (like her Grace)
Cries, "Ah! how charming, if there's no such place!"
Or who in sweet vicissitude appears
Of mirth and opium, ratafie[3] and tears,　　　110

6a. "Liberal; generous" (Johnson's *Dictionary*).

7. A crude young man in Richard Brome's comedy *The Jovial Crew* (1641) or the opera adapted from the play (1731); "Charles," as F. W. Bateson points out, "was a generic name for a footman in the period."

8. Latin for "glutton."

9. "Anything with a strong relish or strong scent, as overkept venison" (Johnson's *Dictionary*).

1. The name is Pope's adaptation of a Greek epithet meaning "laughter-loving," frequently applied to Aphrodite, the goddess of love.

2. Lucretia, violated by Tarquin, committed suicide; according to tradition, the "fair Rosamonda," mistress of Henry II, was forced by Queen Eleanor to drink poison.

3. "A fine liquor, prepared from the

The daily anodyne, and nightly draught,
To kill those foes to fair ones, time and thought.
Woman and fool are two hard things to hit,
For true no-meaning puzzles more than wit.
    But what are these to great Atossa's mind?[4]   115
Scarce once herself, by turns all womankind!
Who, with herself, or others, from her birth
Finds all her life one warfare upon earth:
Shines in exposing knaves, and painting fools,
Yet is whate'er she hates and ridicules.   120
No thought advances, but her eddy brain
Whisks it about, and down it goes again.
Full sixty years the world has been her trade,
The wisest fool much time has ever made.
From loveless youth to unrespected age,   125
No passion gratified except her rage.
So much the fury still outran the wit,
The pleasure missed her, and the scandal hit.
Who breaks with her, provokes revenge from hell,
But he's a bolder man who dares be well:[5]   130
Her every turn with violence pursued,
Nor more a storm her hate than gratitude:
To that each passion turns, or soon or late;
Love, if it makes her yield, must make her hate:
Superiors? death! and equals? what a curse!   135
But an inferior not dependent? worse.
Offend her, and she knows not to forgive;
Oblige her, and she'll hate you while you live:
But die, and she'll adore you—Then the bust
And temple rise—then fall again to dust.   140
Last night, her lord was all that's good and great;
A knave this morning, and his will a cheat.
Strange! by the means defeated of the ends,
By spirit robbed of power, by warmth of friends,
By wealth of followers! without one distress   145
Sick of herself through very selfishness!
Atossa, cursed with every granted prayer,
Childless with all her children, wants an heir.
To heirs unknown descends the unguarded store,
Or wanders, Heaven-directed, to the poor.   150
    Pictures like these, dear Madam, to design,
Asks no firm hand, and no unerring line;
Some wandering touches, some reflected light,
Some flying stroke alone can hit 'em right:
For how should equal colors do the knack?[6]   155
Chameleons who can paint in white and black?

---

kernels of apricots and spirits" (Johnson's *Dictionary*).
4. Atossa, daughter of Cyrus, Emperor of Persia (d. 529 B.C.). If the Duchess of Buckinghamshire is alluded to, the name is appropriate, for she was the natural daughter of James II.
5. Be in her favor.
6. Do the trick.

"Yet Chloe sure was formed without a spot—"
Nature in her then erred not, but forgot.
"With every pleasing, every prudent part,
Say, what can Chloe want?"—She wants a heart.   160
She speaks, behaves, and acts just as she ought;
But never, never, reached one generous thought.
Virtue she finds too painful an endeavor,
Content to dwell in decencies forever.
So very reasonable, so unmoved,   165
As never yet to love, or to be loved.
She, while her lover pants upon her breast,
Can mark[6a] the figures on an Indian chest;
And when she sees her friend in deep despair,
Observes how much a chintz exceeds mohair.   170
Forbid it Heaven, a favor or a debt
She e'er should cancel—but she may forget.
Safe is your secret still in Chloe's ear;
But none of Chloe's shall you ever hear.
Of all her dears she never slandered one,   175
But cares not if a thousand are undone.
Would Chloe know if you're alive or dead?
She bids her footman put it in her head.
Chloe is prudent—Would you too be wise?
Then never break your heart when Chloe dies.   180
    One certain portrait may (I grant) be seen,
Which Heaven has varnished out, and made a *Queen:*[7]
The same forever! and described by all
With Truth and Goodness, as with crown and ball.
Poets heap virtues, painters gems at will,   185
And show their zeal, and hide their want of skill.
'Tis well—but, artists! who can paint or write,
To draw the naked is your true delight.
That robe of quality so struts and swells,
None see what parts of Nature it conceals: 190
The exactest traits of body or of mind,
We owe to models of an humble kind.
If Queensberry[8] to strip there's no compelling,
'Tis from a handmaid we must take a Helen.
From peer or bishop 'tis no easy thing   195
To draw the man who loves his God, or king:
Alas! I copy (or my draft would fail)
From honest Mah'met[9] or plain Parson Hale.
    But grant, in public men sometimes are shown,
A woman's seen in private life alone: 200
Our bolder talents in full light displayed;
Your virtues open fairest in the shade.

6a. Pay attention to.
7. Pope refers as usual to Queen Caroline with disapprobation.
8. The Duchess of Queensberry, whom Pope valued because of her kindness
to his friend John Gay, had been a famous beauty.
9. Mahomet, a Turkish servant of George I; Dr. Stephen Hales was an Anglican clergyman and friend of Pope.

Bred to disguise, in public 'tis you hide;
There, none distinguish 'twixt your shame or pride,
Weakness or delicacy; all so nice,   205
That each may seem a virtue, or a vice.
    In men, we various ruling passions find;
In women, two almost divide the kind;
Those, only fixed, they first or last obey,
The love of pleasure, and the love of sway.   210
    That, Nature gives; and where the lesson taught
Is but to please, can pleasure seem a fault?
Experience, this; by man's oppression cursed,
They seek the second not to lose the first.
    Men, some to business, some to pleasure take;   215
But every woman is at heart a rake;
Men, some to quiet, some to public strife;
But every lady would be queen for life,
    Yet mark the fate of a whole sex of queens!
Power all their end, but beauty all the means: 220
In youth they conquer, with so wild a rage,
As leaves them scarce a subject in their age:
For foreign glory, foreign joy, they roam;
No thought of peace or happiness at home.
But wisdom's triumph is well-timed retreat,   225
As hard a science to the fair as great!
Beauties, like tyrants, old and friendless grown,
Yet hate repose, and dread to be alone,
Worn out in public, weary every eye,
Nor leave one sigh behind them when they die.   230
    Pleasures the sex, as children birds, pursue,
Still out of reach, yet never out of view,
Sure, if they catch, to spoil the toy at most,
To covet flying, and regret when lost:
At last, to follies youth could scarce defend,   235
It grows their age's prudence to pretend;
Ashamed to own they gave delight before,
Reduced to feign it, when they give no more:
As hags hold sabbaths,[1] less for joy than spite,
So these their merry, miserable night;   240
Still round and round the ghosts of beauty glide,
And haunt the places where their honor died.
    See how the world its veterans rewards!
A youth of frolics, an old age of cards;
Fair to no purpose, artful to no end,   245
Young without lovers, old without a friend;
A fop their passion, but their prize a sot;
Alive, ridiculous, and dead, forgot!
    Ah friend! to dazzle let the vain design;
To raise the thought, and touch the heart be thine!   250

---

1. Obscene rites popularly supposed to be held by witches ("hags"); "night," in the next line, refers to evenings on which ladies entertained guests.

That charm shall grow; while what fatigues the Ring[2]
Flaunts and goes down, an unregarded thing:
So when the sun's broad beam has tired the sight,
All mild ascends the moon's more sober light,
Serene in virgin modesty she shines,   255
And unobserved the glaring orb declines.
   Oh! blest with temper, whose unclouded ray
Can make tomorrow cheerful as today;
She, who can love a sister's charms, or hear
Sighs for a daughter with unwounded ear;   260
She, who ne'er answers till a husband cools,
Or, if she rules him, never shows she rules;
Charms by accepting, by submitting sways,
Yet has her humor most, when she obeys;
Let fops or fortune fly which way they will;   265
Disdains all loss of tickets[3] or Codille;
Spleen, vapors, or smallpox, above them all,
And mistress of herself, though China[4] fall.
   And yet, believe me, good as well as ill,
Woman's at best a contradiction still.   270
Heaven, when it strives to polish all it can
Its last best work, but forms a softer man;
Picks from each sex, to make the favorite blest,
Your love of pleasure, our desire of rest:
Blends, in exception to all general rules,   275
Your taste of follies, with our scorn of fools:
Reserve with frankness, art with truth allied,
Courage with softness, modesty with pride;
Fixed principles, with fancy ever new;
Shakes all together, and produces—you.   280
   Be this a woman's fame: with this unblest,
Toasts live a scorn, and queens may die a jest.
This Poebus promised (I forget the year)
When those blue eyes first opened on the sphere;
Ascendant Phoebus watched that hour with care,   285
Averted half your parents' simple prayer;
And gave you beauty, but denied the pelf
That buys your sex a tyrant o'er itself.
The generous god, who wit and gold refines,
And ripens spirits as he ripens mines,[5]   290
Kept dross for duchesses, the world shall know it,
To you gave sense, good humor, and a poet.

1735, 1744

---

2. The fashionable drive in Hyde Park.
3. I.e., lottery tickets; "Codille": the loss of a hand at the card games of ombre or quadrille.
4. Pope refers punningly to the china-ware which fashionable women collected enthusiastically.
5. Phoebus Apollo, as god of poetry "ripens wit"; as god of the sun, he "ripens mines," for respectable scientific theory held that the sun's rays mature precious metals in the earth.

Epistle to Dr. Arbuthnot[1]

Advertisement

TO THE FIRST PUBLICATION OF THIS *Epistle*

This paper is a sort of bill of complaint, begun many years since, and drawn up by snatches, as the several occasions offered. I had no thoughts of publishing it, till it pleased some persons of rank and fortune (the authors of *Verses to the Imitator of Horace,* and of an *Epistle to a Doctor of Divinity from a Nobleman at Hampton Court*) to attack, in a very extraordinary manner, not only my writings (of which, being public, the public is judge) but my person, morals, and family, whereof, to those who know me not, a truer information may be requisite. Being divided between the necessity to say something of myself, and my own laziness to undertake so awkward a task, I thought it the shortest way to put the last hand to this epistle. If it have anything pleasing, it will be that by which I am most desirous to please, the truth and

1. Dr. John Arbuthnot (1667–1735), to whom Pope addressed his best-known verse epistle, was distinguished both as a physician and as a man of wit. He had been one of the liveliest members of the Martinus Scriblerus Club, helping his friends to create the character and shape the career of the learned pedant whose *Memoirs* the Club had undertaken to write.

Pope had long been meditating such a poem, which was to be both an attack on his detractors and a defense of his own character and career. In his usual way he had jotted down hints, lines, couplets, fragments over a period of two decades, but the poem might never have been completed had it not been for two events: Arbuthnot, from his deathbed, wrote to urge Pope to continue his abhorrence of vice and to express it in his writings; and, during 1733, Pope was the victim of two bitter attacks by "persons of rank and fortune," as the "Advertisement" has it. The *Verses Addressed to the Imitator of Horace* was the work of Lady Mary Wortley Montagu, helped by her friend Lord Hervey (pronounced "Harvey"), a close friend and confidant of Queen Caroline; *An Epistle to a Doctor of Divinity from a Nobleman at Hampton Court* was the work of Lord Hervey alone. Lady Mary, it must be admitted, had provocation enough, especially in Pope's recent reference to her in *The First Satire of the Second Book of Horace,* lines 83–84; but Hervey had little to complain of beyond occasional covert references to him as "Lord Fanny." At any rate, the two scurrilous attacks goaded Pope into action, and the poem was completed by the end of the summer of 1734.

The *Epistle* is a masterpiece of poetic rhetoric. The very fact that it is addressed to Dr. Arbuthnot, a man who had the general approbation of the world because of his kindliness and probity, in some degree seems to guarantee the integrity of the "I" of the poem and to diminish the moral stature of his enemies. This acquisition of virtue through association, an effective stroke, is supported by every device of persuasive rhetoric: reasonable argument and emotional appeals, subtly suggestive imagery, and superbly controlled shifts in tone and style which help to sway the reader's judgment to the side of the speaker. The poem opens in the flat language of commonplace prose discourse, tinged with a wry humor and a tone of exasperation: "Shut, shut the door, good John! (fatigued, I said)" and as it progresses it rises or falls in language and style according to the emotions which the speaker expresses— anger, contempt, amusement, sarcasm, mock self-pity, indignation, hatred, affection, gratitude, tenderness—to return at the end to the homely tone of the opening.

It is not clear that Pope intended the poem to be thought of as a dialogue, as it has usually been printed since Warburton's edition of 1751. The original edition, while suggesting interruptions in the flow of the monologue, kept entirely to the form of a letter. The introduction of the friend, who speaks from time to time, of course converts the original letter into a dramatic dialogue.

the sentiment; and if anything offensive, it will be only to those I am least sorry to offend, the vicious or the ungenerous.

Many will know their own pictures in it, there being not a circumstance but what is true; but I have, for the most part, spared their names, and they may escape being laughed at, if they please.

I would have some of them know, it was owing to the request of the learned and candid friend to whom it is inscribed, that I make not as free use of theirs as they have done of mine. However, I shall have this advantage, and honor, on my side, that whereas, by their proceeding, any abuse may be directed at any man, no injury can possibly be done by mine, since a nameless character can never be found out, but by its truth and likeness. P.

P. Shut, shut the door, good John![2] (fatigued, I said),
Tie up the knocker, say I'm sick, I'm dead.
The Dog Star[3] rages! nay 'tis past a doubt
All Bedlam,[4] or Parnassus, is let out:
Fire in each eye, and papers in each hand,   5
They rave, recite, and madden round the land.
    What walls can guard me, or what shades can hide?
They pierce my thickets, through my grot[5] they glide,
By land, by water, they renew the charge,
They stop the chariot, and they board the barge.   10
No place is sacred, not the church is free;
Even Sunday shines no Sabbath day to me:
Then from the Mint[6] walks forth the man of rhyme,
Happy to catch me just at dinner time.
    Is there a parson, much bemused in beer,   15
A maudlin poetess, a rhyming peer,
A clerk foredoomed his father's soul to cross,
Who pens a stanza when he should engross?[7]
Is there who,[7a] locked from ink and paper, scrawls
With desperate charcoal round his darkened walls?   20
All fly to Twit'nam,[8] and in humble strain
Apply to me to keep them mad or vain.
Arthur,[9] whose giddy son neglects the laws,
Imputes to me and my damned works the cause:
Poor Cornus[1] sees his frantic wife elope,   25
And curses wit, and poetry, and Pope.

2. John Serle, Pope's gardener.
3. Sirius, associated with the period of greatest heat (and hence of madness) because it sets with the sun in late summer. August, in ancient Rome, was the season for reciting poetry.
4. Bethlehem Hospital for the insane in London.
5. See *First Satire of the Second Book of Horace*, line 124 and note.
5. A place in Southwark where debtors were free from arrest (they could not be arrested anywhere on Sundays).
7. Write out legal documents.

7a. Is there some madman who, locked up without ink or paper* * * ?
8. I.e., Twickenham, Pope's villa on the bank of the Thames, a few miles above Hampton Court.
9. Arthur Moore, whose son, James Moore Smythe, dabbled in literature. Moore Smythe had earned Pope's enmity by using in one of his plays some unpublished lines from Pope's *Epistle to a Lady* in spite of Pope's objections.
1. Latin for "horn," the traditional emblem of the cuckold.

Friend to my life (which did not you prolong,
The world had wanted many an idle song)
What drop or nostrum[2] can this plague remove?
Or which must end me, a fool's wrath or love?   30
A dire dilemma! either way I'm sped,[2a]
If foes, they write, if friends, they read me dead.
Seized and tied down to judge, how wretched I!
Who can't be silent, and who will not lie.
To laugh were want of goodness and of grace,   35
And to be grave exceeds all power of face.
I sit with sad civility, I read
With honest anguish and an aching head,
And drop at last, but in unwilling ears,
This saving counsel, "Keep your piece nine years."[3]   40
    "Nine years!" cries he, who high in Drury Lane,[4]
Lulled by soft zephyrs through the broken pane,
Rhymes ere he wakes, and prints before term[5] ends,
Obliged by hunger and request of friends:
"The piece, you think, is incorrect? why, take it,   45
I'm all submission, what you'd have it, make it."
    Three things another's modest wishes bound,
My friendship, and a prologue, and ten pound.
    Pitholeon[6] sends to me: "You know his Grace,
I want a patron; ask him for a place."   50
Pitholeon libeled me—"but here's a letter
Informs you, sir, 'twas when he knew no better.
Dare you refuse him? Curll[7] invites to dine,
He'll write a *Journal*, or he'll turn divine."[8]
Bless me! a packet.—"'Tis a stranger sues,   55
A virgin tragedy, an orphan Muse."
If I dislike it, "Furies, death, and rage!"
If I approve, "Commend it to the stage."
There (thank my stars) my whole commission ends,
The players and I are, luckily, no friends.   60
Fired that the house reject him, "'Sdeath, I'll print it,
And shame the fools—Your interest, sir, with Lintot!"[9]
Lintot, dull rogue, will think your price too much.
"Not, sir, if you revise it, and retouch."
All my demurs but double his attacks;   65
At last he whispers, "Do; and we go snacks."[1]

2. Medicine.
2a. Destroyed; killed (Johnson's *Dictionary*).
3. The advice of Horace in *Ars Poetica* (line 388).
4. I.e., living in a garret in Drury Lane, site of one of the theaters and the haunt of the profligate.
5. One of the four annual periods in which the law courts are in session and with which the publishing season coincided.
6. "A foolish poet of Rhodes, who pretended much to Greek" [Pope's note]; he is Leonard Welsted, who translated

Longinus and had attacked and slandered Pope. See line 375.
7. Edmund Curll, shrewd and disreputable bookseller, published pirated works, works falsely ascribed to reputable writers, scandalous biographies, and other ephemera. Pope had often attacked him and had assigned to him a low role in the *Dunciad*.
8. I.e., he will attack Pope in the *London Journal* or write a treatise on theology, as Welsted in fact did.
9. Bernard Lintot, publisher of Pope's Homer and other early works.
1. Go shares.

Glad of a quarrel, straight I clap the door,
"Sir, let me see your works and you no more."
   'Tis sung, when Midas' ears began to spring
(Midas, a sacred person and a king),   70
His very minister who spied them first,
(Some say his queen) was forced to speak, or burst.[2]
And is not mine, my friend, a sorer case,
When every coxcomb perks them in my face?
   A. Good friend, forbear! you deal in dangerous things.   75
I'd never name queens, ministers, or kings;
Keep close to ears, and those let asses prick;
'Tis nothing—— P. Nothing? if they bite and kick?
Out with it, *Dunciad!* let the secret pass,
That secret to each fool, that he's an ass: 80
The truth once told (and wherefore should we lie?)
The queen of Midas slept, and so may I.
   You think this cruel? take it for a rule,
No creature smarts so little as a fool.
Let peals of laughter, Codrus! round thee break,   85
Thou unconcerned canst hear the mighty crack.
Pit, box, and gallery in convulsions hurled,
Thou stand'st unshook amidst a bursting world.
Who shames a scribbler? break one cobweb through,
He spins the slight, self-pleasing thread anew: 90
Destroy his fib or sophistry, in vain;
The creature's at his dirty work again,
Throned in the center of his thin designs,
Proud of a vast extent of flimsy lines.
Whom have I hurt? has poet yet or peer   95
Lost the arched eyebrow or Parnassian sneer?
And has not Colley[3] still his lord and whore?
His butchers Henley? his freemasons Moore?
Does not one table Bavius[4] still admit?
Still to one bishop Philips seem a wit?   100
Still Sappho[5]—— A. Hold! for God's sake—you'll offend.
No names—be calm—learn prudence of a friend:
I too could write, and I am twice as tall;
But foes like these!—— P. One flatterer's worse than all.
Of all mad creatures, if the learn'd are right,   105

2. Midas, king of ancient Lydia, had the bad taste to prefer the flute-playing of Pan to that of Apollo, whereupon the god endowed him with ass's ears. It was his barber (not his wife or his minister) who discovered the secret and whispered it into a hole in the earth. The reference to "queen" and "minister" makes it plain that Pope is alluding to George II, Queen Caroline, and Walpole.
3. Colley Cibber, the laureate (see *First Satire of the Second Book of Horace*, lines 34 ff. and note). John

Henley, known as "Orator" Henley, an independent preacher of marked eccentricity, was popular among the lower orders, especially for his elocution.
4. The bad poet alluded to in Virgil's *Eclogues* III. The "Bishop" is Hugh Boulter, Bishop of Armagh; he had employed as his secretary Ambrose Philips (1674–1749), whose insipid and babbling simplicity of manner in poetry earned him the nickname of "Namby-Pamby."
5. Lady Mary Wortley Montagu.

It is the slaver kills, and not the bite.
A fool quite angry is quite innocent:
Alas! 'tis ten times worse when they repent.

   One dedicates in high heroic prose,
And ridicules beyond a hundred foes;
One from all Grub Street[6] will my fame defend,
And, more abusive, calls himself my friend.
This prints my letters,[7] that expects a bribe,
And others roar aloud, "Subscribe, subscribe!"[8]

   There are, who to my person pay their court: 115
I cough like Horace, and, though lean, am short;
Ammon's great son[9] one shoulder had too high,
Such Ovid's nose, and, "Sir! you have an eye—"
Go on, obliging creatures, make me see
All that disgraced my betters met in me.   120
Say for my comfort, languishing in bed,
"Just so immortal Maro[1] held his head":
And when I die, be sure you let me know
Great Homer died three thousand years ago.

   Why did I write? what sin to me unknown   125
Dipped me in ink, my parents', or my own?
As yet a child, nor yet a fool to fame,
I lisped in numbers, for the numbers came.
I left no calling for this idle trade,
No duty broke, no father disobeyed.   130
The Muse but served to ease some friend, not wife,
To help me through this long disease, my life,
To second, Arbuthnot! thy art and care,
And teach the being you preserved, to bear.[2]

   A. But why then publish? P. Granville the polite,   135
And knowing Walsh, would tell me I could write;
Well-natured Garth inflamed with early praise,
And Congreve loved, and Swift endured my lays;
The courtly Talbot, Somers, Sheffield, read;
Even mitered Rochester would nod the head,   140
And St. John's self (great Dryden's friends before)
With open arms received one poet more.[3]

6. A term denoting the whole society of literary, political, and journalistic hack writers.
7. In 1726 Curll had surreptitiously acquired and published without permission some of Pope's letters to Henry Cromwell.
8. To ensure the financial success of a work, the public was often asked to "subscribe" to it by taking a certain number of copies before printing was undertaken. Pope's Homer was published thus.
9. Alexander the Great. "Ovid's nose": Ovid's family name Naso suggests the Latin word *nasus* ("nose"), hence the pun.

1. Virgil.
2. Endure.
3. The purpose of this list is to establish Pope as the successor of Dryden and thus to place him far above his Grub-Street persecutors. George Granville, Lord Lansdowne, poet and statesman; William Walsh, poet and critic; Sir Samuel Garth, physician and mock-epic poet; William Congreve, the playwright; the statesmen Charles Talbot, Duke of Shrewsbury; Lord Sommers; John Sheffield, Duke of Buckinghamshire; and Francis Atterbury, Bishop of Rochester, had all been associated with Dryden in his later years and had all encouraged the young Pope.

Happy my studies, when by these approved!
Happier their author, when by these beloved!
From these the world will judge of men and books,   145
Not from the Burnets, Oldmixons, and Cookes.[4]
    Soft were my numbers; who could take offense
While pure description held the place of sense?
Like gentle Fanny's[5] was my flowery theme,
A painted mistress, or a purling stream.   150
Yet then did Gildon[6] draw his venal quill;
I wished the man a dinner, and sat still.
Yet then did Dennis[7] rave in furious fret;
I never answered, I was not in debt.
If want provoked, or madness made them print,   155
I waged no war with Bedlam or the Mint.
    Did some more sober critic come abroad?
If wrong, I smiled; if right, I kissed the rod.
Pains, reading, study are their just pretense,
And all they want is spirit, taste, and sense.   160
Commas and points they set exactly right,
And 'twere a sin to rob them of their mite.
Yet ne'er one sprig of laurel graced these ribalds,
From slashing Bentley down to piddling Tibbalds.[8]
Each wight who reads not, and but scans and spells,   165
Each word-catcher that lives on syllables,
Even such small critics some regard may claim,
Preserved in Milton's or in Shakespeare's name.
Pretty! in amber to observe the forms
Of hairs, or straws, or dirt, or grubs, or worms!   170
The things, we know, are neither rich nor rare,
But wonder how the devil they got there.
    Were others angry? I excused them too;
Well might they rage; I gave them but their due.
A man's true merit 'tis not hard to find;   175
But each man's secret standard in his mind,
That casting weight[9] pride adds to emptiness,
This, who can gratify? for who can guess?
The bard[1] whom pilfered pastorals renown,

4. Thomas Burnet, John Oldmixon, and Thomas Cooke; Pope identifies them in a note as "authors of secret and scandalous history."
5. John, Lord Hervey, whom Pope satirizes in the character of Sporus, lines 305–33 below.
6. Charles Gildon, minor critic and scribbler, who, Pope believed, early attacked him at the instigation of Addison; hence "venal quill."
7. John Dennis (see *Essay on Criticism*, line 270 and its note).
8. Richard Bentley (1662–1742), the eminent classical scholar, seemed to both Pope and Swift the perfect type of the pedant; he is called "slashing" because, in his edition of *Paradise Lost*

(1732), he had set in square brackets all passages which he disliked on the grounds they had been slipped into the poem without the blind poet's knowledge. Lewis Theobald (1688–1744), whose minute learning in Elizabethan literature had enabled him to expose Pope's defects as an editor of Shakespeare in 1726. Pope made him King of the Dunces in the *Dunciad* (1728).
9. The weight that turns the scale; here, the "deciding factor."
1. Ambrose Philips, Pope's rival in pastoral poetry in 1709, when their pastorals were published in Tonson's sixth *Miscellany*. Philips had also translated some Persian tales. Cf. line 100.

Who turns a Persian tale for half a crown,   180
Just writes to make his barrenness appear,
And strains from hard-bound brains eight lines a year:
He, who still wanting, though he lives on theft,
Steals much, spends little, yet has nothing left;
And he who now to sense, now nonsense leaning,   185
Means not, but blunders round about a meaning:
And he whose fustian's so sublimely bad,
It is not poetry, but prose run mad:
All these, my modest satire bade translate,
And owned that nine such poets made a Tate.[2]   190
How did they fume, and stamp, and roar, and chafe!
And swear, not Addison himself was safe.

Peace to all such! but were there one whose fires
True Genius kindles, and fair Fame inspires;
Blessed with each talent and each art to please,   195
And born to write, converse, and live with ease:
Should such a man, too fond to rule alone,
Bear, like the Turk, no brother near the throne;
View him with scornful, yet with jealous eyes,
And hate for arts that caused himself to rise;   200
Damn with faint praise, assent with civil leer,
And without sneering, teach the rest to sneer;
Willing to wound, and yet afraid to strike,
Just hint a fault, and hesitate dislike;
Alike reserved to blame or to commend,   205
A timorous foe, and a suspicious friend;
Dreading even fools; by flatterers besieged,
And so obliging that he ne'er obliged;
Like Cato, give his little senate[3] laws,
And sit attentive to his own applause;   210
While wits and Templars[4] every sentence raise,
And wonder with a foolish face of praise—
Who but must laugh, if such a man there be?
Who would not weep, if Atticus[5] were he?

What though my name stood rubric[6] on the walls   215
Or plastered posts, with claps, in capitals?
Or smoking forth, a hundred hawkers' load,
On wings of winds came flying all abroad?
I sought no homage from the race that write;
I kept, like Asian monarchs, from their sight: 220

2. Nahum Tate (1652–1715), poet laureate (1692–1715). His popular rewriting of Shakespeare's *King Lear* provided a happy ending; he wrote most of Part II of *Absalom and Achitophel*. The line refers to the old adage that it takes nine tailors to make one man.
3. Addison's tragedy *Cato* had been a sensational success in 1713. Pope had written the prologue, in which occurs the line, "While Cato gives his little senate laws." The satirical reference here is to Addison in the role of arbiter of taste among his friends and admirers, mostly Whigs, at Button's Coffee House. It was these people who had worked against the success of Pope's Homer.
4. Law students.
5. Pope's satiric pseudonym for Addison; Atticus (109–32 B.C.) was a wealthy man of letters and a friend of Cicero, known as a wise and disinterested man.
6. In red letters. "Claps": posters.

Poems I heeded (now berhymed so long)
No more than thou, great George! a birthday song.
I ne'er with wits or witlings passed my days
To spread about the itch of verse and praise;
Nor like a puppy daggled through the town   225
To fetch and carry sing-song up and down;
Nor at rehearsals sweat, and mouthed, and cried,
With handkerchief and orange at my side;
But sick of fops, and poetry, and prate,
To Bufo[7] left the whole Castalian state.   230
   Proud as Apollo on his forkéd hill,[8]
Sat full-blown Bufo, puffed by every quill;
Fed with soft dedication all day long,
Horace and he went hand in hand in song.
His library (where busts of poets dead   235
And a true Pindar stood without a head)
Received of wits an undistinguished race,
Who first his judgment asked, and then a place:
Much they extolled his pictures, much his seat,[9]
And flattered every day, and some days eat: 240
Till grown more frugal in his riper days,
He paid some bards with port, and some with praise;
To some a dry rehearsal was assigned,
And others (harder still) he paid in kind.
Dryden alone (what wonder?) came not nigh;   245
Dryden alone escaped this judging eye:
But still the great have kindness in reserve;
He helped to bury whom he helped to starve.
   May some choice patron bless each gray goose quill!
May every Bavius have his Bufo still!   250
So when a statesman wants a day's defense,
Or Envy holds a whole week's war with Sense,
Or simple Pride for flattery makes demands,
May dunce by dunce be whistled off my hands!
Blessed be the great! for those they take away,   255
And those they left me—for they left me Gay;[1]
Left me to see neglected genius bloom,
Neglected die, and tell it on his tomb;
Of all thy blameless life the sole return
My verse, and Queensberry weeping o'er thy urn!   260
Oh, let me live my own, and die so too!
("To live and die is all I have to do")
Maintain a poet's dignity and ease,

---

7. A type of tasteless patron of the arts. The Castalian spring on Mt. Parnassus was sacred to Apollo and the Muses.
8. Mt. Parnassus had two peaks, one sacred to Apollo, one to Bacchus.
9. Pronounced *sate*, and rhymed in next line with "eat" (*ate*). *Seat* means "estate."
1. John Gay (1685–1732), author of the *Beggar's Opera* (1728) and other delightful works, dear friend of Swift and Pope. His failure to obtain patronage from the court intensified Pope's hostility to the Whig administration and the queen. Gay spent the last years of his life under the protection of the Duke and Duchess of Queensberry.

And see what friends, and read what books I please;
Above a patron, though I condescend   265
Sometimes to call a minister my friend.
I was not born for courts or great affairs;
I pay my debts, believe, and say my prayers,
Can sleep without a poem in my head,
Nor know if Dennis be alive or dead.   270
    Why am I asked what next shall see the light?
Heavens! was I born for nothing but to write?
Has life no joys for me? or (to be grave)
Have I no friend to serve, no soul to save?
"I found him close with Swift"—"Indeed? no doubt"   275
Cries prating Balbus, "something will come out."
'Tis all in vain, deny it as I will.
"No, such a genius never can lie still,"
And then for mine obligingly mistakes
The first lampoon Sir Will or Bubo makes.[2]   280
Poor guiltless I! and can I choose but smile,
When every coxcomb knows me by my style?
    Cursed be the verse, how well soe'er it flow,
That tends to make one worthy man my foe,
Give Virtue scandal, Innocence a fear,   285
Or from the soft-eyed virgin steal a tear!
But he who hurts a harmless neighbor's peace,
Insults fallen worth, or Beauty in distress,
Who loves a lie, lame Slander helps about,
Who writes a libel, or who copies out: 290
That fop whose pride affects a patron's name,
Yet absent, wounds an author's honest fame;
Who can your merit selfishly approve,
And show the sense of it without the love;
Who has the vanity to call you friend,   295
Yet wants the honor, injured, to defend;
Who tells whate'er you think, whate'er you say,
And, if he lie not, must at least betray:
Who to the dean and silver bell can swear,
And sees at Cannons what was never there:[3]   300
Who reads but with a lust to misapply,
Make satire a lampoon, and fiction, lie:
A lash like mine no honest man shall dread,
But all such babbling blockheads in his stead.
    Let Sporus[4] tremble—— A. What? that thing of silk,   305
Sporus, that mere white curd of ass's milk?[5]
Satire or sense, alas! can Sporus feel?

---

2. Sir William Yonge, Whig politician and poetaster; George Bubb ("Bubo") Dodington was a Whig patron of letters.

3. Pope's enemies had accused him of satirizing Cannons, the ostentatious estate of the Duke of Chandos, in his description of Timon's villa in the *Epistle to Burlington*. This Pope quite justly denied. The bell of Timon's chapel was of silver, and there preached a dean who "never mentions Hell to ears polite."

4. John, Lord Hervey, effeminate courtier and confidant of Queen Caroline; see title footnote. The original Sporus was a boy, whom the Emperor Nero publicly married (see Suetonius' life of Nero in *The Twelve Caesars*).

5. Ass's milk was drunk by invalids.

Who breaks a butterfly upon a wheel?
  P. Yet let me flap this bug with gilded wings,
This painted child of dirt, that stinks and stings;   310
Whose buzz the witty and the fair annoys,
Yet wit ne'er tastes, and beauty ne'er enjoys;
So well-bred spaniels civilly delight
In mumbling of the game they dare not bite.
Eternal smiles his emptiness betray,   315
As shallow streams run dimpling all the way.
Whether in florid impotence he speaks,
And, as the prompter breathes, the puppet squeaks;
Or at the ear of Eve,[6] familiar toad,
Half froth, half venom, spits himself abroad,   320
In puns, or politics, or tales, or lies,
Or spite, or smut, or rhymes, or blasphemies.
His wit all seesaw between *that* and *this*,   ⎫
Now high, now low, now master up, now miss, ⎬
And he himself one vile antithesis.   ⎭ 325
Amphibious thing! that acting either part,
The trifling head or the corrupted heart,
Fop at the toilet, flatterer at the board,
Now trips a lady, and now struts a lord.
Eve's tempter thus the rabbins[7] have expressed,   330
A cherub's face, a reptile all the rest;
Beauty that shocks you, parts that none will trust,
Wit that can creep, and pride that licks the dust.
    Not Fortune's worshiper, nor Fashion's fool,
Not Lucre's madman, nor Ambition's tool,   335
Not proud, nor servile, be one poet's praise,
That if he pleased, he pleased by manly ways:
That flattery, even to kings, he held a shame,
And thought a lie in verse or prose the same:
That not in fancy's maze he wandered long,   340
But stooped[8] to truth, and moralized his song:
That not for fame, but Virtue's better end,
He stood the furious foe, the timid friend,
The damning critic, half approving wit,
The coxcomb hit, or fearing to be hit;   345
Laughed at the loss of friends he never had,
The dull, the proud, the wicked, and the mad;
The distant threats of vengeance on his head,
The blow unfelt, the tear he never shed;
The tale revived, the lie so oft o'erthrown,   350
The imputed trash, and dullness not his own;
The morals blackened when the writings 'scape,
The libeled person, and the pictured shape;[9]

6. "Eve" is the queen. The allusion is to *Paradise Lost* IV.799–809.
7. Scholars of and authorities on Jewish law and doctrine.
8. The falcon is said to "stoop" to its prey when it swoops down and seizes it in flight.
9. Pope's deformity was frequently ridiculed and occasionally caricatured.

Abuse on all he loved, or loved him, spread,
A friend in exile, or a father dead;   355
The whisper, that to greatness still too near,
Perhaps yet vibrates on his Sovereign's ear—
Welcome for thee, fair Virtue! all the past!
For thee, fair Virtue! welcome even the last!
   A. But why insult the poor, affront the great?   360
P. A knave's a knave to me in every state:
Alike my scorn, if he succeed or fail,
Sporus at court, or Japhet[1] in a jail,
A hireling scribbler, or a hireling peer,
Knight of the post[2] corrupt, or of the shire,   365
If on a pillory, or near a throne,
He gain his prince's ear, or lose his own.
   Yet soft by nature, more a dupe than wit,
Sappho[3] can tell you how this man was bit:
This dreaded satirist Dennis will confess   370
Foe to his pride, but friend to his distress:[4]
So humble, he has knocked at Tibbald's door,
Has drunk with Cibber, nay, has rhymed for Moore.
Full ten years slandered, did he once reply?
Three thousand suns went down on Welsted's lie.   375
To please a mistress one aspersed his life;
He lashed him not, but let her be his wife.
Let Budgell charge low Grub Street on his quill,
And write whate'er he pleased, except his will;[5]
Let the two Curlls of town and court,[6] abuse   380
His father, mother, body, soul, and muse.
Yet why? that father held it for a rule,
It was a sin to call our neighbor fool;
That harmless mother thought no wife a whore:
Hear this, and spare his family, James Moore!   385
Unspotted names, and memorable long,
If there be force in virtue, or in song.
   Of gentle blood (part shed in honor's cause,
While yet in Britain honor had applause)
Each parent sprung—— A. What fortune, pray?—— P. Their own,
And better got than Bestia's[7] from the throne.   391
Born to no pride, inheriting no strife,
Nor marrying discord in a noble wife,
Stranger to civil and religious rage,
The good man walked innoxious through his age.   395
No courts he saw, no suits would ever try,

1. Japhet Crook, a notorious forger.
2. One who lives by selling false evidence.
3. Lady Mary Wortley Montagu. "Bit": taken in; deceived.
4. Pope wrote the prologue to Cibber's *Provoked Husband* when that play was performed for Dennis's benefit, shortly before the old critic died.
5. Eustace Budgell attacked the *Grub Street Journal* for publishing what he took to be a squib by Pope charging him with having forged the will of Dr. Matthew Tindal.
6. I.e., the publisher and Lord Hervey.
7. Probably the Duke of Marlborough, whose vast fortune was made through the favor of Queen Anne. The actual Bestia was a corrupt Roman consul.

Nor dared an oath,[8] nor hazarded a lie.
Unlearn'd, he knew no schoolman's subtle art,
No language but the language of the heart.
By nature honest, by experience wise,   400
Healthy by temperance, and by exercise;
His life, though long, to sickness passed unknown,
His death was instant, and without a groan.
Oh, grant me thus to live, and thus to die!
Who sprung from kings shall know less joy than I.   405
    O friend! may each domestic bliss be thine!
Be no unpleasing melancholy mine:
Me, let the tender office long engage,
To rock the cradle of reposing Age,
With lenient arts extend a mother's breath,   410
Make Languor smile, and smooth the bed of Death,
Explore the thought, explain the asking eye,
And keep a while one parent from the sky![9]
On cares like these if length of days attend,
May Heaven, to bless those days, preserve my friend,   415
Preserve him social, cheerful, and serene,
And just as rich as when he served a Queen![1]
A. Whether that blessing be denied or given,
Thus far was right—the rest belong to Heaven.

1735

8. As a Catholic, Pope's father refused
to take the Oaths of Allegiance and Supremacy, and the oath against the
Pope. He thus rendered himself vulnerable to the many repressive anti-Catholic laws then in force.
9. Pope was a tender and devoted son.
His mother had died in 1733, and the

earliest version of these lines dates
from 1731, when the poet was nursing
her through a serious illness.
1. Pope alludes to the fact that Arbuthnot, a man of strict probity, left
the queen's service no wealthier than
when he entered it.

SAMUEL JOHNSON
(1709–1784)

1737:   Settles in London.
1747–55:   At work on the *Dictionary*.
1762:   Pensioned by the Crown.
1765:   Edition of Shakespeare.
1779, 1781: *Lives of the Poets*.

Throughout the 19th century it was generally agreed that although John-son himself was interesting, especially as a conversationalist, most of his works were unreadable. His poems were condemned as prosaic, his essays as tritely moralistic, his criticism as wrongheaded and tasteless. The case is altered today: a few of the poems, it is agreed, belong with the best of the century; the grave *Rambler* essays, which in his own time established his reputation as a stylist and a moralist, prove not so forbidding as we have been told they are; and the criticism is ranked with that of Dryden and Samuel Taylor Coleridge as the best in English. Boswell's Johnson is chiefly a conversationalist whose talk came hot from a mind that was wise, humane, honest, truthful, and well stored with knowledge drawn from books and experience. The talk is that of a wit and a poet who was quick to seize and to use the unexpected but appropriate image to illumi-nate truth as it was apprehended by a deeply moral imagination. Any fair examination of Johnson's best writings will demonstrate that for all its studied formality, Johnson's prose possesses most of the virtues of his con-versation. The object of the talker and of the moral essayist or critic proves in general to be the same—the search for truth in the wide field of human experience; and the wit and wisdom and energy of Johnson's spontaneous talk are also present in his prose.

Two examples must suffice here. When Mrs. Anna Williams wondered why a man should make a beast of himself through drunkenness, John-son answered that "he who makes a beast of himself gets rid of the pain of being a man." In this reply Mrs. Williams' tired metaphor is so charged with an awareness of the dark aspects of human life that it comes almost unbearably alive. Such moments characterize Johnson's writings as well. For instance, in reviewing the book of a fatuous would-be philosopher who blandly explained away the pains of poverty by declaring that a kindly providence compensates the poor by making them more hopeful, more healthy, more capable of relishing small pleasures and less sensitive to small annoyances than the rich, Johnson, who had known extreme pov-erty, retorted: "The poor indeed are insensible of many little vexations which sometimes embitter the possessions and pollute the enjoyment of the rich. They are not pained by casual incivility, or mortified by the mutilation of a compliment; but this happiness is like that of the male-factor who ceases to feel the cords that bind him when the pincers are tearing his flesh."

Johnson had himself known the pains of poverty. During his boyhood and youth, his father's financial circumstances steadily worsened, so that he was forced to leave Oxford before he had taken a degree. An imprudent marriage drove him to open a school which was unsuccessful; and the failure of the school prompted him to attempt to make his way as a writer in London. The years between 1737, when he first arrived there with his pupil David Garrick (later to become the leading actor of his generation), and 1755, when the publication of the *Dictionary* established his reputation, were very difficult. He supported himself at first as best he could by doing hack work for the *Gentleman's Magazine*, but gradually his own original writings began to attract attention, though hardly to support his wife and himself.

In 1746 Johnson published the *Plan* of his *Dictionary*, and the next seven years were occupied in compiling it—although he had been sanguine enough to count on finishing it in three years. Boswell remarks that "the world contemplated with wonder" a work "achieved by one man, while other countries had thought such undertakings fit only for whole academies." When in 1748 Dr. Adams, a friend from Oxford days, questioned his ability to carry out such a work alone in so short a time, and reminded him that the *Dictionary* of the French Academy had been compiled by forty academicians working for forty years, Johnson replied with humorous jingoism: "Sir, thus it is. This is the proportion. Let me see; forty times forty is sixteen hundred. As three to sixteen hundred, so is the proportion of an Englishman to a Frenchman."

Johnson's achievement in compiling the *Dictionary* becomes even greater when it is realized that he was writing some of his best essays and poems during the same period, for although the booksellers who published the *Dictionary* paid him what was then the large sum of £1575, it was not enough to enable him to support his household, buy materials, and pay the wages of the six amanuenses whom he employed year by year until the task was accomplished. He therefore had to exert himself to earn more money by writing. Thus, in 1749, his early tragedy *Irene* (pronounced I-re-nĕ) was produced at long last by his old friend Garrick, by then not only a successful actor but also the manager of Drury Lane. The play, deservedly, was not a success, though Johnson made some profit from it. In the same year appeared his finest poem, *The Vanity of Human Wishes*. The *Rambler* (1750–52) and the later *Idler* (1758–60), Johnson's very un-Addisonian imitations of the *Spectator*, found admiring readers and spread his reputation as a moralist throughout the island.

Boswell said of the *Rambler* essays that "in no writings whatever can be found more bark and steel [i.e., quinine and iron] for the mind." Moral strength and health; the importance of applying reason to experience; the testing of a man by what he does, not by what he says or merely "feels"; faith in God: these are the centers to which Johnson's moral writings always return. As such critics as Walter Jackson Bate remind us, what Johnson uniquely offers us is the quality of his understanding of the human condition, based on wide reading but always ultimately referred to his own passionate and often anguished experience. Such understanding had to be fought for again and again, as our two selections from the *Prayers and Meditations* show.

Johnson is thought of as the great generalizer, but what gives his generalizations strength is that they are rooted in the particulars of his self-knowledge. He had constantly to fight against what he called "filling the mind" with illusions, in order to avoid the call of duty, his own black melancholy, and the realties of life. The portrait (largely a self-portrait) of

Sober in *Idler* 31 is revealing: he occupies his idle hours with crafts and hobbies, and has now taken up chemistry—he "sits and counts the drops as they come from his retort, and forgets that, whilst a drop is falling, a moment flies away." So clear a vision is some distance away from the secure ease of the Addisonian essay.

His theme of themes is expressed in the title of his poem, *The Vanity of Human Wishes*, by which Johnson means the dangerous but all-pervasive illusion of what we now call wishful thinking, the feverish intrusion of our desires and hopes which distorts reality and interferes with the possibility of sensibly relying on what we have reason to expect. Almost all of Johnson's major writings—verse satire, moral essay, or the prose fable *Rasselas* (1759)—bear this theme. In *Rasselas* it is called "the hunger of imagination, which preys upon life," the seeing of things as one would like them to be, rather than as they are. The travelers who are the fable's protagonists pursue supposed guarantees of happiness; they reflect our naïve hopefulness, against the accumulation of contrary experience, that such a guarantee exists.

During this time of great activity, in which he produced the bulk of his moral writings, Johnson developed his characteristic style: the rotund periods, proceeding through balanced or parallel words; phrases or clauses moving to carefully controlled rhythms, in language that is characteristically general, often Latinate, and frequently polysyllabic. It is a style which is at the opposite extreme from Swift's simplicity or Addison's neatness. In Johnson's writings this style never becomes obscure or turgid, for even a very complex sentence reveals—as it should—the structure of the thought, and the learned words are always precisely used. "Sesquipedalian" words are not so frequent in Johnson's writings as his reputation for using them would imply. He learned many of them when he was reading early scientists to collect words for the *Dictionary*—such words as *obtund, exuberate, fugacity, frigorific*, which most people have been willing to forget. But he used many of these strange words in conversation as well as in his writings, often with a peculiarly Johnsonian felicity, although everyone is familiar with the notoriously infelicitous definition of *network* in the *Dictionary*: "Anything reticulated or decussated, at equal distances, with interstices between the intersections."

After Johnson received his pension in 1762, he no longer had to write for a living, and since he held that "no man but a blockhead" ever wrote for any other reason, he produced as little as he decently could during the last twenty years of his life. His edition of Shakespeare, long delayed, was published in 1765, with its fine preface and its fascinating notes, both textual and explicatory. Johnson's praise of Shakespeare and his discussion and destruction of the doctrine of the three unities are printed below. His last important work is the *Lives of the Poets*, which came out in two parts in 1779 and 1781. These biographical and critical prefaces were written at the instigation of a group of booksellers who had joined together to publish a large collection of the English poets and who wished to give their venture the prestige that it would acquire if Johnson took part in it. The poets to be included (except for four insisted on by Johnson) were selected by the booksellers, and their choice was determined by the current fashions. We have, therefore, a collection that begins with Cowley and Milton and ends with Gray and the poetaster Lord Lyttleton, and that omits poets whom we regard as "standard," such as Chaucer, Spenser, Sidney, or the metaphysicals.

In the *Lives of the Poets* and in the earlier *Life of Richard Savage* (1744), Johnson did much to advance the art of biography in England. The public had long been familiar with biography as panegyric or as scandalous memoir, and therefore Johnson's insistence on truth, even about the subject's defects, and on concrete, often minute, details was a new departure, disliked by many readers, as Boswell was to find when he followed his master's principles both in the *Journal of a Tour to the Hebrides* and in the *Life* itself. "The biographical part of literature is what I love most," Johnson said, for he found every biography useful in revealing human nature and the way men live. His insistence on truth in biography (and knowing that Boswell intended to write his life, he insisted that he should write it truthfully) was due to his conviction that the more truthful such a work is the more useful it will be to all of us who are concerned with the business of living. The value of the lives of the poets varies, for Johnson wrote some more casually than he did others. He is at his best as a critic when he draws up a general character of a writer's genius and when he discusses individual works.

Johnson's taste was conservative, and he therefore liked little in contemporary literature. He valued Richardson for his knowledge of the human heart, but he considered Fielding "low" and immoral, and Sterne merely perversely odd and trivial. Though he loved Collins, he regretted his fanciful subjects and "harsh" diction, and he offended many by his strictures on what he considered Gray's affectations. He poked gentle fun at his friend Thomas Warton's revival of antique words and "Ode, and elegy, and sonnet." But if he was conservative, he was no worshiper of authority, and least of all was he prone to follow mere theory. As a critic Johnson is always the empiricist, testing theory, as he tested all notions, by experience. His attitude toward the rules is perfectly expressed in these words from *Rambler* 156: "It ought to be the first endeavor of a writer to distinguish nature from custom; or that which is established because it is right, from that which is right only because it is established; that he may neither violate essential principles by a desire of novelty, nor debar himself from the attainment of beauties within his view, by a needless fear of breaking rules which no literary dictator has authority to enact." And the perfect illustration of this attitude is his treatment of the long-revered principle of the three dramatic unities in the Preface to Shakespeare.

That there were "essential principles" which any writer must follow seemed to him self-evident. He must adhere to universal truth and experience, i.e., to "Nature"; he must please, but he must also instruct; he must not offend against religion or promote immorality; he must avoid cold and slavish imitation of others, and he must not cultivate "singularity," the eccentrically original. In the passages from the *Lives of the Poets* below, some of his principles are illustrated. The well-known and influential discussion of metaphysical poetry, with its brilliant definition of "wit" as "a kind of *discordia concors*," at once illustrates Johnson's genius for formulating broad philosophical principles and reveals clearly why he equated the general with the natural. The notorious attack on Milton's *Lycidas*, which damaged Johnson's reputation as a critic for over a century, puzzles us until we recall that Johnson himself had his critical singularities, which in this case stood between him and a liking for a very great poem: he was justly contemptuous of 18th-century pastoral poetry, which was always conventional, artificial, and bookish, and which could be produced by mere imitation; and he had a great dislike on religious grounds for the Renaissance habit of mingling pagan and Christian materials in a poem. The praise of Dryden, Pope, and Shakespeare, on the other hand, is admirable because those poets, as was not the case with Donne or Milton, nobly illustrated the literary standards that Johnson respected throughout his career.

The Vanity of Human Wishes[1]

IN IMITATION OF THE TENTH SATIRE OF JUVENAL

Let Observation, with extensive view,
Survey mankind, from China to Peru;
Remark each anxious toil, each eager strife,
And watch the busy scenes of crowded life;
Then say how hope and fear, desire and hate   5
O'erspread with snares the clouded maze of fate,
Where wavering man, betrayed by venturous pride
To tread the dreary paths without a guide,
As treacherous phantoms in the mist delude,
Shuns fancied ills, or chases airy good;   10
How rarely Reason guides the stubborn choice,
Rules the bold hand, or prompts the suppliant voice;
How nations sink, by darling schemes oppressed,
When Vengeance listens to the fool's request.
Fate wings with every wish the afflictive dart,   15
Each gift of nature, and each grace of art;
With fatal heat impetuous courage glows,
With fatal sweetness elocution flows,
Impeachment stops the speaker's powerful breath,
And restless fire precipitates on death.   20

---

1. *The Vanity of Human Wishes* is an imitation of Juvenal's *Satire X*. Although it closely follows the order and the ideas of the Latin poem, it remains a very personal work, for Johnson has used the Roman Stoic's satire as a means of expressing his own Christian stoicism and his sense of the tragic in human life. He has tried to reproduce in English verse the qualities he thought especially Juvenalian: stateliness, pointed sentences, declamatory grandeur. The poem is difficult because of the extreme compactness of the style: every verse is forced to convey the greatest possible amount of meaning, and as a result the syntax is occasionally obscure. At first the language may seem too general, the frequent personifications mere abstractions. But although Johnson's poetic theory demanded that the poet should deal in the general rather than the particular (cf. his phrase "the grandeur of generality") he certainly did not intend that the general should become the merely abstract: observe, for example, how he makes ab-stract nouns concrete, active, and dramatic by using them as subjects of active and dramatic verbs: "Hate *dogs* their flight, and Insult *mocks* their end" (line 78). And when the more usual 18th-century combination of general adjective modifying general noun is used, the adjectives are carefully chosen for foreseen effects, as in lines 113–16 (in the first three lines they are used to create a cumulative effect of regal splendor, and in the last line a witty and intellectual impression of Cardinal Wolsey's pride and power): "At once is lost the pride of *awful* state, / The *golden* canopy, the *glittering* plate, / The *regal* palace, the *luxurious* board, / The *liveried* army, and the *menial* lord." The personified abstractions of Collins and Gray, however, are essentially pictorial, grouped in expressive attitudes as they would be in an allegorical painting. A comparison of their method of personification with Johnson's can be readily made by studying Gray's *Eton* ode, stanzas 5–8, along with lines 135–164 of the *Vanity*.

But scarce observed, the knowing and the bold
Fall in the general massacre of gold;
Wide-wasting pest! that rages unconfined,
And crowds with crimes the records of mankind;
For gold his sword the hireling ruffian draws,   25
For gold the hireling judge distorts the laws;
Wealth heaped on wealth, nor truth nor safety buys,
The dangers gather as the treasures rise.

    Let History tell where rival kings command,
And dubious title shakes the madded land,   30
When statutes glean the refuse of the sword,
How much more safe the vassal than the lord,
Low skulks the hind beneath the rage of power,
And leaves the wealthy traitor[2] in the Tower,
Untouched his cottage, and his slumbers sound,   35
Though Confiscation's vultures hover round.

    The needy traveler, serene and gay,
Walks the wild heath, and sings his toil away.
Does envy seize thee? crush the upbraiding joy,
Increase his riches and his peace destroy;   40
New fears in dire vicissitude invade,
The rustling brake[3] alarms, and quivering shade,
Nor light nor darkness bring his pain relief,
One shows the plunder, and one hides the thief.

    Yet still one general cry the skies assails,   45
And gain and grandeur load the tainted gales;
Few know the toiling statesman's fear or care,
The insidious rival and the gaping heir.

    Once more, Democritus,[4] arise on earth,
With cheerful wisdom and instructive mirth,   50
See motley life in modern trappings dressed,
And feed with varied fools the eternal jest:
Thou who couldst laugh where Want enchained Caprice,
Toil crushed Conceit, and man was of a piece;
Where Wealth unloved without a mourner died;   55
And scarce a sycophant was fed by Pride;
Where ne'er was known the form of mock debate,
Or seen a new-made mayor's unwieldy state;
Where change of favorites made no change of laws,
And senates heard before they judged a cause;   60
How wouldst thou shake at Britain's modish tribe,
Dart the quick taunt, and edge the piercing gibe?
Attentive truth and nature to descry,
And pierce each scene with philosophic eye,
To thee were solemn toys or empty show   65
The robes of pleasures and the veils of woe:
All aid the farce, and all thy mirth maintain,
Whose joys are causeless, or whose griefs are vain.

2. Johnson first wrote "bonny traitor," recalling the Jacobite uprising of 1745 and the execution of four of its Scot leaders.
3. Thicket.

4. A Greek philosopher of the late 5th century B.C., remembered as the "laughing philosopher" because men's follies only moved him to mirth.

Such was the scorn that filled the sage's mind,
Renewed at every glance on human kind; 70
How just that scorn ere yet thy voice declare,
Search every state, and canvass every prayer.

Unnumbered suppliants crowd Preferment's gate,
Athirst for wealth, and burning to be great;
Delusive Fortune hears the incessant call, 75
They mount, they shine, evaporate, and fall.
On every stage the foes of peace attend,
Hate dogs their flight, and Insult mocks their end.
Love ends with hope, the sinking statesman's door
Pours in the morning worshiper no more;[5] 80
For growing names the weekly scribbler lies,
To growing wealth the dedicator flies;
From every room descends the painted face,
That hung the bright palladium[6] of the place;
And smoked in kitchens, or in auctions sold, 85
To better features yields the frame of gold;
For now no more we trace in every line
Heroic worth, benevolence divine:
The form distorted justifies the fall,
And Detestation rids the indignant wall. 90

But will not Britain hear the last appeal,
Sign her foes' doom, or guard her favorites' zeal?
Through Freedom's sons no more remonstrance rings,
Degrading nobles and controlling kings;
Our supple tribes repress their patriot throats, 95
And ask no questions but the price of votes,
With weekly libels and septennial ale.[7]
Their wish is full to riot and to rail.

In full-blown dignity, see Wolsey[8] stand,
Law in his voice, and fortune in his hand: 100
To him the church, the realm, their powers consign,
Through him the rays of regal bounty shine;
Turned by his nod the stream of honor flows,
His smile alone security bestows:
Still to new heights his restless wishes tower, 105
Claim leads to claim, and power advances power;
Till conquest unresisted ceased to please,
And rights submitted, left him none to seize.
At length his sovereign frowns—the train of state
Mark the keen glance, and watch the sign to hate. 110
Where'er he turns, he meets a stranger's eye,
His suppliants scorn him, and his followers fly;

---

5. Statesmen gave interviews and received friends and petitioners at levees, or morning receptions.
6. An image of Pallas Athena, which fell from heaven and was preserved at Troy. Not until it was stolen by Diomedes could the city fall to the Greeks.
7. Ministers and even the king freely bought support by bribing members of Parliament, who in turn won elections by buying votes. "Weekly libels": politically motivated lampoons published in the weekly newspapers; "septennial ale": the ale given away by candidates at parliamentary elections, held at least every seven years.
8. Thomas Cardinal Wolsey (ca. 1475–1530), Lord Chancellor and favorite of Henry VIII. Shakespeare dramatized his fall in *Henry VIII*.

At once is lost the pride of awful state,
The golden canopy, the glittering plate,
The regal palace, the luxurious board,   115
The liveried army, and the menial lord.
With age, with cares, with maladies oppressed,
He seeks the refuge of monastic rest.
Grief aids disease, remembered folly stings,
And his last sighs reproach the faith of kings.   120
    Speak thou, whose thoughts at humble peace repine,
Shall Wolsey's wealth, with Wolsey's end be thine?
Or liv'st thou now, with safer pride content,
The wisest justice on the banks of Trent?
For why did Wolsey, near the steeps of fate,   125
On weak foundations raise the enormous weight?
Why but to sink beneath misfortune's blow,
With louder ruin to the gulfs below?
    What gave great Villiers[9] to the assassin's knife,
And fixed disease on Harley's closing life?   130
What murdered Wentworth, and what exiled Hyde,
By kings protected and to kings allied?
What but their wish indulged in courts to shine,
And power too great to keep or to resign?
    When first the college rolls receive his name,   135
The young enthusiast quits his ease for fame;
Resistless burns the fever of renown
Caught from the strong contagion of the gown:
O'er Bodley's dome his future labors spread,
And Bacon's mansion trembles o'er his head.[1]   140
Are these thy views? proceed, illustrious youth,
And Virtue guard thee to the throne of Truth!
Yet should thy soul indulge the generous heat,
Till captive Science yields her last retreat;
Should Reason guide thee with her brightest ray,   145
And pour on misty Doubt resistless day;
Should no false kindness lure to loose delight,
Nor praise relax, nor difficulty fright;
Should tempting Novelty thy cell refrain,
And Sloth effuse her opiate fumes in vain;   150
Should Beauty blunt on fops her fatal dart,
Nor claim the triumph of a lettered heart;
Should no disease thy torpid veins invade,
Nor Melancholy's phantoms haunt thy shade;

9. George Villiers, 1st Duke of Buckingham, favorite of James I and Charles
I, was assassinated in 1628. Mentioned
in the following lines are: Robert Harley, Earl of Oxford, Chancellor of the
Exchequer and later Lord Treasurer
under Queen Anne (1710–14), impeached and imprisoned by the Whigs
in 1715; Thomas Wentworth, Earl of
Strafford, intimate and adviser of
Charles I, impeached by the Long
Parliament and executed 1641; Edward Hyde, Earl of Clarendon ("to
kings allied" because his daughter
married James, Duke of York), Lord
Chancellor under Charles II; impeached
in 1667, he fled to the Continent.
1. "Bodley's dome" is the Bodleian Library, Oxford. Roger Bacon (ca. 1214–
94), scientist and philosopher, taught
at Oxford, where his study, according to
tradition, would collapse when a man
greater than he should appear at Oxford.

Yet hope not life from grief or danger free,   155
Nor think the doom of man reversed for thee:
Deign on the passing world to turn thine eyes,
And pause a while from letters, to be wise;
There mark what ills the scholar's life assail,
Toil, envy, want, the patron,[2] and the jail.   160
See nations slowly wise, and meanly just,
To buried merit raise the tardy bust.
If dreams yet flatter, once again attend,
Hear Lydiat's life, and Galileo's end.[3]

Nor deem, when Learning her last prize bestows,   165
The glittering eminence exempt from foes;
See when the vulgar 'scapes, despised or awed,
Rebellion's vengeful talons seize on Laud.[4]
From meaner minds though smaller fines content,
The plundered palace, or sequestered rent;[5]   170
Marked out by dangerous parts he meets the shock,
And fatal Learning leads him to the block:
Around his tomb let Art and Genius weep,
But hear his death, ye blockheads, hear and sleep.

The festal blazes, the triumphal show,   175
The ravished standard, and the captive foe,
The senate's thanks, the gazette's pompous tale,
With force resistless o'er the brave prevail.
Such bribes the rapid Greek[6] o'er Asia whirled,
For such the steady Romans shook the world;   180
For such in distant lands the Britons shine,
And stain with blood the Danube or the Rhine;
This power has praise that virtue scarce can warm,
Till fame supplies the universal charm.

Yet Reason frowns on War's unequal game,   185
Where wasted nations raise a single name,
And mortgaged states their grandsires' wreaths regret
From age to age in everlasting debt;
Wreaths which at last the dear-bought right convey
To rust on medals, or on stones decay.   190

On what foundation stands the warrior's pride,
How just his hopes, let Swedish Charles[7] decide;
A frame of adamant, a soul of fire,
No dangers fright him, and no labors tire;
O'er love, o'er fear, extends his wide domain,   195
Unconquered lord of pleasure and of pain;

2. In the first edition, "garret." For
the reason of the change see Boswell's
Life of Johnson.
3. Thomas Lydiat (1572–1646), Oxford scholar, died impoverished because
of his Royalist sympathies. Galileo
(1564–1642), the famous astronomer,
was imprisoned as a heretic by the
Inquisition in 1633; he died blind.
4. Appointed Archbishop of Canterbury
by Charles I, William Laud followed
rigorously high-church policies and was
executed by order of the Long Parliament in 1645.
5. During the Commonwealth, the
estates of many Royalists were pillaged
and their incomes confiscated ("sequestered") by the state.
6. Alexander the Great.
7. Charles XII of Sweden (1682–1718).
Defeated by the Russians at Pultowa
(1709), he escaped to Turkey and tried
to form an alliance against Russia
with the sultan. Returning to Sweden,
he attacked Norway and was killed in
the attack on Fredrikshald.

No joys to him pacific scepters yield,
War sounds the trump, he rushes to the field;
Behold surrounding kings their powers combine,
And one capitulate, and one resign;[8]   200
Peace courts his hand, but spreads her charms in vain;
"Think nothing gained," he cries, "till naught remain,
On Moscow's walls till Gothic standards fly,
And all be mine beneath the polar sky."
The march begins in military state,   205
And nations on his eye suspended wait;
Stern Famine guards the solitary coast,
And Winter barricades the realms of Frost;
He comes, nor want nor cold his course delay—
Hide, blushing Glory, hide Pultowa's day: 210
The vanquished hero leaves his broken bands,
And shows his miseries in distant lands;
Condemned a needy supplicant to wait,
While ladies interpose, and slaves debate.
But did not Chance at length her error mend?   215
Did no subverted empire mark his end?
Did rival monarchs give the fatal wound?
Or hostile millions press him to the ground?
His fall was destined to a barren strand,
A petty fortress, and a dubious hand;   220
He left the name at which the world grew pale,
To point a moral, or adorn a tale.
   All times their scenes of pompous woes afford,
From Persia's tyrant to Bavaria's lord.[9]
In gay hostility, and barbarous pride,   225
With half mankind embattled at his side,
Great Xerxes comes to seize the certain prey,
And starves exhausted regions in his way;
Attendant Flattery counts his myriads o'er,
Till counted myriads soothe his pride no more;   230
Fresh praise is tried till madness fires his mind,
The waves he lashes, and enchains the wind;
New powers are claimed, new powers are still bestowed,
Till rude resistance lops the spreading god;
The daring Greeks deride the martial show,   235
And heap their valleys with the gaudy foe;
The insulted sea with humbler thought he gains,
A single skiff to speed his flight remains;
The encumbered oar scarce leaves the dreaded coast
Through purple billows and a floating host.   240
   The bold Bavarian, in a luckless hour,
Tries the dread summits of Caesarean power,

8. Frederick IV of Denmark capitulated to Charles in 1700; Augustus II of Poland resigned his throne to Charles in 1704.
9. Xerxes ("Persia's tyrant") invaded Greece and was totally defeated in the sea battle off Salamis, 480 B.C.; the Elector Charles Albert ("Bavaria's Lord") caused the War of the Austrian Succession (1740–48) when he contested the crown of the Empire with Maria Theresa ("Fair Austria" in line 245).

With unexpected legions bursts away,
And sees defenseless realms receive his sway;
Short sway! fair Austria spreads her mournful charms,   245
The queen, the beauty, sets the world in arms;
From hill to hill the beacon's rousing blaze
Spreads wide the hope of plunder and of praise;
The fierce Croatian, and the wild Hussar,[1]
With all the sons of ravage crowd the war;   250
The baffled prince, in honor's flattering bloom
Of hasty greatness finds the fatal doom;
His foes' derision, and his subjects' blame,
And steals to death from anguish and from shame.

    Enlarge my life with multitude of days!   255
In health, in sickness, thus the suppliant prays;
Hides from himself his state, and shuns to know,
That life protracted is protracted woe.
Time hovers o'er, impatient to destroy,
And shuts up all the passages of joy;   260
In vain their gifts the bounteous seasons pour,
The fruit autumnal, and the vernal flower;
With listless eyes the dotard views the store,
He views, and wonders that they please no more;
Now pall the tasteless meats, and joyless wines,   265
And Luxury with sighs her slave resigns.
Approach, ye minstrels, try the soothing strain,
Diffuse the tuneful lenitives[2] of pain:
No sounds, alas! would touch the impervious ear,
Though dancing mountains witnessed Orpheus[2a] near;   270
Nor lute nor lyre his feeble powers attend,
Nor sweeter music of a virtuous friend,
But everlasting dictates crowd his tongue,
Perversely grave, or positively wrong.
The still returning tale, and lingering jest,   275
Perplex the fawning niece and pampered guest,
While growing hopes scarce awe the gathering sneer,
And scarce a legacy can bribe to hear;
The watchful guests still hint the last offense;
The daughter's petulance, the son's expense,   280
Improve his heady rage with treacherous skill,
And mold his passions till they make his will.
    Unnumbered maladies his joints invade,
Lay siege to life and press the dire blockade;
But unextinguished avarice still remains,   285
And dreaded losses aggravate his pains;
He turns, with anxious heart and crippled hands,
His bonds of debt, and mortgages of lands;
Or views his coffers with suspicious eyes,
Unlocks his gold, and counts it till he dies.   290

---

1. Hungarian light cavalry.
2. Medicines that relieve pain.
2a. A legendary poet who played on the lyre so beautifully that wild beasts were spellbound.

But grant, the virtues of a temperate prime
Bless with an age exempt from scorn or crime;
An age that melts with unperceived decay,
And glides in modest innocence away;
Whose peaceful day Benevolence endears,   295
Whose night congratulating Conscience cheers;
The general favorite as the general friend:
Such age there is, and who shall wish its end?
    Yet even on this her load Misfortune flings,
To press the weary minutes' flagging wings;   300
New sorrow rises as the day returns,
A sister sickens, or a daughter mourns.
Now kindred Merit fills the sable bier,
Now lacerated Friendship claims a tear;
Year chases year, decay pursues decay,   305
Still drops some joy from withering life away;
New forms arise, and different views engage,
Superfluous lags the veteran[3] on the stage,
Till pitying Nature signs the last release,
And bids afflicted Worth retire to peace.   310
    But few there are whom hours like these await,
Who set unclouded in the gulfs of Fate.
From Lydia's monarch[4] should the search descend,
By Solon cautioned to regard his end,
In life's last scene what prodigies surprise,   315
Fears of the brave, and follies of the wise!
From Marlborough's eyes the streams of dotage flow,
And Swift expires a driveler and a show.[5]
    The teeming mother, anxious for her race,
Begs for each birth the fortune of a face: 320
Yet Vane could tell what ills from beauty spring;[6]
And Sedley cursed the form that pleased a king.
Ye nymphs of rosy lips and radiant eyes,
Whom Pleasure keeps too busy to be wise,
Whom Joys with soft varieties invite,   325
By day the frolic, and the dance by night;
Who frown with vanity, who smile with art,
And ask the latest fashion of the heart;
What care, what rules your heedless charms shall save,
Each nymph your rival, and each youth your slave?   330
Against your fame with Fondness Hate combines,
The rival batters, and the lover mines.
With distant voice neglected Virtue calls,
Less heard and less, the faint remonstrance falls;
Tired with contempt, she quits the slippery reign,   335

3. A veteran of life, not of war.
4. Croesus, the wealthy and fortunate king, was warned by Solon not to count himself happy till he ceased to live. He lost his crown to Cyrus the Great of Persia.
5. John Churchill, Duke of Marlborough, England's brilliant general during most of the War of the Spanish Succession (1702–13); Jonathan Swift, who passed the last four years of his life in utter senility.
6. Anne Vane, mistress of Frederick, Prince of Wales (son of George II). Catherine Sedley, mistress of James II.

And Pride and Prudence take her seat in vain.
In crowd at once, where none the pass defend,
The harmless freedom, and the private friend.
The guardians yield, by force superior plied:
To Interest, Prudence; and to Flattery, Pride.   340
Now Beauty falls betrayed, despised, distressed,
And hissing Infamy proclaims the rest.
    Where then shall Hope and Fear their objects find?
Must dull Suspense corrupt the stagnant mind?
Must helpless man, in ignorance sedate,   345
Roll darkling down the torrent of his fate?
Must no dislike alarm, no wishes rise,
No cries invoke the mercies of the skies?
Inquirer, cease; petitions yet remain,
Which Heaven may hear, nor deem religion vain.   350
Still raise for good the supplicating voice,
But leave to Heaven the measure and the choice.
Safe in His power, whose eyes discern afar
The secret ambush of a specious prayer.
Implore His aid, in His decisions rest,   355
Secure, whate'er He gives, He gives the best.
Yet when the sense of sacred presence fires,
And strong devotion to the skies aspires,
Pour forth thy fervors for a healthful mind,
Obedient passions, and a will resigned;   360
For love, which scarce collective man can fill;
For patience sovereign o'er transmuted ill;
For faith, that panting for a happier seat,
Counts death kind Nature's signal of retreat:
These goods for man the laws of Heaven ordain,   365
These goods He grants, who grants the power to gain;
With these celestial Wisdom calms the mind,
And makes the happiness she does not find.

                                                    1749

To Miss ———[1]

ON HER PLAYING UPON THE HARPSICHORD IN A ROOM HUNG
WITH SOME FLOWER-PIECES OF HER OWN PAINTING

    When Stella strikes the tuneful string
    In scenes of imitated spring,
    Where Beauty lavishes her powers
    On beds of never-fading flowers,
    And pleasure propagates around   5
    Each charm of modulated sound,

1. Presumably Alicia Maria Carpenter, daughter of Lord Carpenter and later Countess of Egremont. Smith and McAdam, the editors of Johnson's poems, suggest that Johnson wrote this poem for his friend Henry Harvey to send as his own to Miss Carpenter.

Ah! think not, in the dangerous hour,
The nymph fictitious, as the flower;
But shun, rash youth, the gay alcove,
Nor tempt the snares of wily love.   10
      When charms thus press on every sense,
What thought of flight, or of defense?
Deceitful Hope, and vain Desire,
Forever flutter o'er her lyre,
Delighting, as the youth draws nigh,   15
To point the glances of her eye,
And forming, with unerring art,
New chains to hold the captive heart.
      But on these regions of delight,
Might Truth intrude with daring flight,   20
Could Stella, sprightly, fair and young,
One moment hear the moral song,
Instruction with her flowers might spring,
And Wisdom warble from her string.
      Mark, when from thousand mingled dyes   25
Thou see'st one pleasing form arise,
How active light, and thoughtful shade,
In greater scenes each other aid;
Mark, when the different notes agree
In friendly contrariety,   30
How passion's well-accorded strife
Gives all the harmony of life;
Thy pictures shall thy conduct frame,
Consistent still, though not the same,
Thy music teach the nobler art   35
To tune the regulated heart.

                                                          1746

Prologue Spoken by Mr. Garrick[1]

AT THE OPENING OF THE THEATRE ROYAL, DRURY LANE, 1747

      When Learning's triumph o'er her barbarous foes
First reared the stage, immortal Shakespeare rose;
Each change of many-colored life he drew,
Exhausted worlds, and then imagined new:
Existence saw him spurn her bounded reign,   5
And panting Time toiled after him in vain.
His powerful strokes presiding Truth impressed,
And unresisted Passion stormed the breast.
      Then Jonson came, instructed from the school
To please in method and invent by rule;   10
His studious patience and laborious art

1. David Garrick, the famous actor, had become joint patentee and manager of Drury Lane Theatre. Boswell says that this Prologue is unrivaled "for just and manly dramatic criticism."

By regular approach essayed the heart;
Cold Approbation gave the lingering bays,
For those who durst not censure, scarce could praise.[2]
A mortal born, he met the general doom,   15
But left, like Egypt's kings, a lasting tomb.
    The wits of Charles[3] found easier ways to fame,
Nor wished for Jonson's art, or Shakespeare's flame;
Themselves they studied; as they felt, they writ;
Intrigue was plot, obscenity was wit.   20
Vice always found a sympathetic friend;
They pleased their age, and did not aim to mend.
Yet bards like these aspired to lasting praise,
And proudly hoped to pimp in future days.
Their cause was general, their supports were strong,   25
Their slaves were willing, and their reign was long:
Till Shame regained the post that Sense betrayed,
And Virtue called Oblivion to her aid.
    Then, crushed by rules,[4] and weakened as refined,
For years the power of Tragedy declined;   30
From bard to bard the frigid caution crept,
Till Declamation roared while Passion slept;
Yet still did Virtue deign the stage to tread;
Philosophy remained though Nature fled;
But forced at length her ancient reign to quit,   35
She saw great Faustus[5] lay the ghost of Wit;
Exulting Folly hailed the joyous day,
And Pantomime and Song confirmed her sway.
    But who the coming changes can presage,
And mark the future periods of the stage?   40
Perhaps if skill could distant times explore,
New Behns,[6] new Durfeys, yet remain in store;
Perhaps where Lear has raved, and Hamlet died,
On flying cars new sorcerers may ride;[7]
Perhaps (for who can guess the effects of chance?)   45
Here Hunt may box, or Mahomet may dance.[8]
    Hard is his lot that, here by fortune placed,
Must watch the wild vicissitudes of taste;
With every meteor of caprice must play,
And chase the new-blown bubbles of the day.   50
Ah! let not censure term our fate our choice,
The stage but echoes back the public voice;
The drama's laws, the drama's patrons give,

2. Cf. Dryden's contrast of Shakespeare and Ben Jonson in his *Essay of Dramatic Poesy.*
3. The comic poets of the Restoration period.
4. Cf. Johnson's remarks on the dramatic unities in his preface to Shakespeare.
5. Dr. Faustus at that time was a popular subject for both farce and pantomime.

6. Aphra Behn (1640–89), adventuress, novelist, playwright; Thomas Durfey (1653–1723), satirist and writer of songs and plays.
7. It was a common complaint that the use of increasingly elaborate stage machinery was subordinating drama to mere spectacle.
8. Edward Hunt, a popular pugilist; Mahomet, a tightrope dancer.

For we that live to please, must please to live.
Then prompt no more the follies you decry,   55
As tyrants doom their tools of guilt to die;
'Tis yours this night to bid the reign commence
Of rescued Nature and reviving Sense;
To chase the charms of Sound, the pomp of Show,
For useful Mirth and salutary Woe;   60
Bid scenic Virtue form the rising age,
And Truth diffuse her radiance from the stage.

1747

On the Death of Dr. Robert Levet[1]

Condemned to Hope's delusive mine,
    As on we toil from day to day,
By sudden blasts, or slow decline,
    Our social comforts drop away.

Well tried through many a varying year,   5
    See Levet to the grave descend;
Officious,[2] innocent, sincere,
    Of every friendless name the friend.

Yet still he fills Affection's eye,
    Obscurely wise, and coarsely kind;   10
Nor, lettered Arrogance, deny
    Thy praise to merit unrefined.

When fainting Nature called for aid,
    And hovering Death prepared the blow,
His vigorous remedy displayed   15
    The power of art without the show.

In Misery's darkest cavern known,
    His useful care was ever nigh,
Where hopeless Anguish poured his groan,
    And lonely Want retired to die.   20

No summons mocked by chill delay,
    No petty gain disdained by pride,
The modest wants of every day
    The toil of every day supplied.

His virtues walked their narrow round,   25
    Nor made a pause, nor left a void;

1. An unlicensed physician, who lived in Johnson's house for many years and who died in 1782. His practice was among the very poor. Boswell wrote: "He was of a strange grotesque appearance, stiff and formal in his manner, and seldom said a word while any company was present."
2. "Kind, doing good offices" (Johnson's *Dictionary*).

And sure the Eternal Master found
    The single talent well employed.

The busy day, the peaceful night,
    Unfelt, uncounted, glided by;   30
His frame was firm, his powers were bright,
    Though now his eightieth year was nigh.

Then with no throbbing fiery pain,
    No cold gradations of decay,
Death broke at once the vital chain,   35
    And freed his soul the nearest way.

1783

A Short Song of Congratulation

Long-expected one and twenty
    Lingering year at last is flown,
Pomp and Pleasure, Pride and Plenty,
    Great Sir John,[1] are all your own.

Loosened from the minor's tether,   5
    Free to mortgage or to sell,
Wild as wind, and light as feather
    Bid the slaves of thrift farewell.

Call the Bettys, Kates, and Jennys
    Every name that laughs at Care,   10
Lavish of your grandsire's guineas,
    Show the spirit of an heir.

All that prey on vice and folly
    Joy to see their quarry fly,
Here the gamester light and jolly   15
    There the lender grave and sly.

Wealth, Sir John, was made to wander,
    Let it wander as it will;
See the jockey, see the pander,
    Bid them come, and take their fill.   20

When the bonny blade carouses,
    Pockets full, and spirits high,
What are acres? What are houses?
    Only dirt, or wet or dry.

If the guardian or the mother   25
    Tell the woes of willful waste,
Scorn their counsel and their pother,
    You can hang or drown at last.

1780

1794

1. Sir John Lade, nephew of Johnson's friend Henry Thrale. He came into his property in 1780, and, as Johnson fore- told, he had squandered it all by his death.

Rambler No. 5[1]

[On Spring]

TUESDAY, April 3, 1750

Et nunc omnis ager, nunc omnis parturit arbos,
Nunc frondent silvae, nunc formosissimus annus.
VIRGIL, *Eclogues* III. v. 56

Now ev'ry field, now ev'rv tree is green;
Now genial nature's fairest face is seen.
ELPHINSTON

Every man is sufficiently discontented with some circumstances of his present state, to suffer his imagination to range more or less in quest of future happiness, and to fix upon some point of time, in which, by the removal of the inconvenience which now perplexes him, or acquisition of the advantage which he at present wants, he shall find the condition of his life very much improved.

When this time, which is too often expected with great impatience, at last arrives, it generally comes without the blessing for which it was desired; but we solace ourselves with some new prospect, and press forward again with equal eagerness.

It is lucky for a man, in whom this temper prevails, when he turns his hopes upon things wholly out of his own power; since he forbears then to precipitate[2] his affairs, for the sake of the great event that is to complete his felicity, and waits for the blissful hour, with less neglect of the measures necessary to be taken in the mean time.

I have long known a person of this temper, who indulged his dream of happiness with less hurt to himself than such chimerical wishes commonly produce, and adjusted his scheme with such address, that his hopes were in full bloom three parts of the year, and in the other part never wholly blasted. Many, perhaps, would be desirous of learning by what means he procured to himself such a cheap and lasting satisfaction. It was gained by a constant practice of referring the removal of all his uneasiness to the coming of the next spring; if his health was impaired, the spring would restore it; if what he wanted was at a high price, it would fall in value in the spring.

The spring, indeed, did often come without any of these effects, but he was always certain that the next would be more propitious; nor was ever convinced that the present spring would fail him

1. The *Rambler*, almost wholly written by Johnson himself, appeared every Tuesday and Saturday from March 20, 1750, to March 14, 1752—years in which Johnson was writing the *Dictionary*. It is a successor of the *Tatler* and the *Spectator*, but it is much more serious in tone than the earlier periodicals. Johnson's reputation as a moralist and a stylist was established by these essays; because of them Boswell first conceived the ambition to seek Johnson's acquaintance.
2. "To hurry blindly or rashly" (Johnson's *Dictionary*).

before the middle of summer; for he always talked of the spring as coming till it was past, and when it was once past, everyone agreed with him that it was coming.

By long converse with this man, I am, perhaps, brought to feel immoderate pleasure in the contemplation of this delightful season; but I have the satisfaction of finding many, whom it can be no shame to resemble, infected with the same enthusiasm; for there is, I believe, scarce any poet of eminence, who has not left some testimony of his fondness for the flowers, the zephyrs, and the warblers of the spring. Nor has the most luxuriant imagination been able to describe the serenity and happiness of the golden age, otherwise than by giving a perpetual spring, as the highest reward of uncorrupted innocence.

There is, indeed, something inexpressibly pleasing, in the annual renovation of the world, and the new display of the treasures of nature. The cold and darkness of winter, with the naked deformity of every object on which we turn our eyes, make us rejoice at the succeeding season, as well for what we have escaped, as for what we may enjoy; and every budding flower, which a warm situation brings early to our view, is considered by us as a messenger to notify the approach of more joyous days.

The spring affords to a mind, so free from the disturbance of cares or passions as to be vacant[3] to calm amusements, almost every thing that our present state makes us capable of enjoying. The variegated verdure of the fields and woods, the succession of grateful odors, the voice of pleasure pouring out its notes on every side, with the gladness apparently conceived by every animal, from the growth of his food, and the clemency of the weather, throw over the whole earth an air of gaiety, significantly expressed by the smile of nature.

Yet there are men to whom these scenes are able to give no delight, and who hurry away from all the varieties of rural beauty, to lose their hours, and divert their thoughts by cards, or assemblies, a tavern dinner, or the prattle of the day.

It may be laid down as a position which will seldom deceive, that when a man cannot bear his own company there is something wrong. He must fly from himself, either because he feels a tediousness in life from the equipoise of an empty mind, which, having no tendency to one motion more than another but as it is impelled by some external power, must always have recourse to foreign objects; or he must be afraid of the intrusion of some unpleasing ideas, and, perhaps, is struggling to escape from the remembrance of a loss, the fear of a calamity, or some other thought of greater horror.

Those whom sorrow incapacitates to enjoy the pleasures of contemplation, may properly apply to such diversions, provided

3. "At leisure" (Johnson's *Dictionary*).

they are innocent, as lay strong hold on the attention; and those, whom fear of any future affliction chains down to misery, must endeavor to obviate the danger.

My considerations shall, on this occasion, be turned on such as are burthensome to themselves merely because they want subjects for reflection, and to whom the volume of nature is thrown open, without affording them pleasure or instruction, because they never learned to read the characters.

A French author has advanced this seeming paradox, that *very few men know how to take a walk*; and, indeed, it is true, that few know how to take a walk with a prospect of any other pleasure, than the same company would have afforded them at home.

There are animals that borrow their color from the neighboring body, and, consequently, vary their hue as they happen to change their place. In like manner it ought to be the endeavor of every man to derive his reflections from the objects about him; for it is to no purpose that he alters his position, if his attention continues fixed to the same point. The mind should be kept open to the access of every new idea, and so far disengaged from the predominance of particular thoughts, as easily to accommodate itself to occasional entertainment.

A man that has formed this habit of turning every new object to his entertainment, finds in the productions of nature an inexhaustible stock of materials upon which he can employ himself, without any temptations to envy or malevolence; faults, perhaps, seldom totally avoided by those, whose judgment is much exercised upon the works of art. He has always a certain prospect of discovering new reasons for adoring the sovereign author of the universe, and probable hopes of making some discovery of benefit to others, or of profit to himself. There is no doubt but many vegetables and animals have qualities that might be of great use, to the knowledge of which there is not required much force of penetration, or fatigue of study, but only frequent experiments, and close attention. What is said by the chemists of their darling mercury, is, perhaps, true of everybody through the whole creation, that if a thousand lives should be spent upon it, all its properties would not be found out.

Mankind must necessarily be diversified by various tastes, since life affords and requires such multiplicity of employments, and a nation of naturalists is neither to be hoped, or desired; but it is surely not improper to point out a fresh amusement to those who languish in health, and repine in plenty, for want of some source of diversion that may be less easily exhausted, and to inform the multitudes of both sexes, who are burthened with every new day, that there are many shows which they have not seen.

He that enlarges his curiosity after the works of nature, demonstrably multiplies the inlets to happiness; and, therefore, the younger part of my readers, to whom I dedicate this vernal speculation, must excuse me for calling upon them, to make use at once of the spring of the year, and the spring of life; to acquire, while their minds may be yet impressed with new images, a love of innocent pleasures, and an ardor for useful knowledge; and to remember, that a blighted spring makes a barren year, and that the vernal flowers, however beautiful and gay, are only intended by nature as preparatives to autumnal fruits.

1750

Idler No. 31[1]

[On Idleness]

SATURDAY, November 18, 1758

Many moralists have remarked, that Pride has of all human vices the widest dominion, appears in the greatest multiplicity of forms, and lies hid under the greatest variety of disguises; of disguises, which, like the moon's *veil of brightness*, are both *its luster and its shade*, and betray it to others, though they hide it from ourselves.

It is not my intention to degrade Pride from this pre-eminence of mischief, yet I know not whether Idleness may not maintain a very doubtful and obstinate competition.

There are some that profess Idleness in its full dignity, who call themselves the Idle, as Busiris in the play "calls himself the Proud";[2] who boast that they do nothing, and thank their stars that they have nothing to do; who sleep every night till they can sleep no longer, and rise only that exercise may enable them to sleep again; who prolong the reign of darkness by double curtains, and never see the sun but to "tell him how they hate his beams";[3] whose whole labor is to vary the postures of indulgence, and whose day differs from their night but as a couch or chair differs from a bed.

These are the true and open votaries of Idleness, for whom she weaves the garlands of poppies, and into whose cup she pours the waters of oblivion; who exist in a state of unruffled stupidity, forgetting and forgotten; who have long ceased to live, and at whose death the survivors can only say, that they have ceased to breathe.

But Idleness predominates in many lives where it is not suspected; for being a vice which terminates in itself, it may be enjoyed without injury to others; and is therefore not watched like Fraud, which endangers property, or like Pride, which naturally seeks its gratifications in another's inferiority. Idleness is a silent and peaceful quality, that neither raises envy by ostentation, nor hatred by opposition; and therefore nobody is busy to censure or detect it.

As Pride sometimes is hid under humility, Idleness is often covered by turbulence and hurry. He that neglects his known duty

---

1. Johnson wrote and published the *Idler*, a periodical similar to the *Rambler*, from 1758 until 1760.

2. Edward Young, *Busiris* (1719), I.13.
3. *Paradise Lost* IV.37.

and real employment, naturally endeavors to crowd his mind with something that may bar out the remembrance of his own folly, and does any thing but what he ought to do with eager diligence, that he may keep himself in his own favor.

Some are always in a state of preparation, occupied in previous measures, forming plans, accumulating materials, and providing for the main affair. These are certainly under the secret power of Idleness. Nothing is to be expected from the workman whose tools are forever to be sought. I was once told by a great master, that no man ever excelled in painting, who was eminently curious about pencils and colors.

There are others to whom Idleness dictates another expedient, by which life may be passed unprofitably away without the tediousness of many vacant hours. The art is, to fill the day with petty business, to have always something in hand which may raise curiosity, but not solicitude, and keep the mind in a state of action, but not of labor.

This art has for many years been practiced by my old friend Sober, with wonderful success. Sober is a man of strong desires and quick imagination, so exactly balanced by the love of ease, that they can seldom stimulate him to any difficult undertaking; they have, however, so much power, that they will not suffer him to lie quite at rest, and though they do not make him sufficiently useful to others, they make him at least weary of himself.

Mr. Sober's chief pleasure is conversation; there is no end of his talk or his attention; to speak or to hear is equally pleasing; for he still fancies that he is teaching or learning something, and is free for the time from his own reproaches.

But there is one time at night when he must go home, that his friends may sleep; and another time in the morning, when all the world agrees to shut out interruption. These are the moments of which poor Sober trembles at the thought. But the misery of these tiresome intervals, he has many means of alleviating. He has persuaded himself that the manual arts are undeservedly overlooked; he has observed in many trades the effects of close thought, and just ratiocination. From speculation he proceeded to practice, and supplied himself with the tools of a carpenter, with which he mended his coalbox very successfully, and which he still continues to employ, as he finds occasion.

He has attempted at other times the crafts of the shoemaker, tinman, plumber, and potter; in all these arts he has failed, and resolves to qualify himself for them by better information. But his daily amusement is chemistry. He has a small furnace, which he employs in distillation, and which has long been the solace of his life. He draws oils and waters, and essences and spirits, which he knows to be of no use; sits and counts the drops as they come from his retort, and forgets that, whilst a drop is falling, a moment flies away.

Poor Sober![4] I have often teased him with reproof, and he has often promised reformation; for no man is so much open to conviction as the Idler, but there is none on whom it operates so little. What will be the effect of this paper I know not; perhaps he will read it and laugh, and light the fire in his furnace; but my hope is that he will quit his trifles, and betake himself to rational and useful diligence.

From The History of Rasselas, Prince of Abyssinia[1]

Chapter I. *Description of a Palace in a Valley*

Ye who listen with credulity to the whispers of fancy, and pursue with eagerness the phantoms of hope; who expect that age will perform the promises of youth, and that the deficiencies of the present day will be supplied by the morrow—attend to the history of Rasselas, prince of Abyssinia.

Rasselas was the fourth son of the mighty emperor in whose dominions the Father of Waters[2] begins his course; whose bounty

4. Sober represents aspects of Johnson's own character. He was much given to indolence, and he performed chemical experiments in a small laboratory in his garret.

1. Johnson wrote *Rasselas* in January, 1759, during the evenings of one week, a remarkable instance of his ability to write rapidly and brilliantly under the pressure of necessity. His mother lay dying in Lichfield. Her son, famous for his *Dictionary*, was nonetheless oppressed by poverty and in great need of ready money with which to make her last days comfortable, pay her funeral expenses, and settle her small debts. He was paid £100 for the first edition of *Rasselas*, but not in time to attend her deathbed or her funeral. Because of these circumstances, the tale has often been read as an expression of the gloom of the moment; but acquaintance with Johnson's other writings and his conversation makes it plain that the book expresses his settled view of life and what human beings may reasonably expect from it.

Rasselas is a philosophical fable cast in the popular form of an Oriental tale, a type of fiction that owed its popularity to the vogue of the *Arabian Nights*, first translated into English in the early 18th century. Since the work is a fable, we should not approach it as a novel: psychologically credible characters and a series of intricately involved actions that lead to a necessary resolution and conclusion are not to be found in *Rasselas*. The action, the characters, the majestic prose rhythms, and the melancholy resonance of much of the language serve to articulate the theme, which is very similar to that of *The Vanity of Human Wishes*. Johnson formulated it in a magnificent phrase: the "hunger of imagination which preys incessantly upon life" (Chapter XXXII) and which lures us to "listen with credulity to the whispers of fancy and pursue with eagerness the phantoms of hope" (Chapter I). The tale is a gentle satire on one of the perennial topics of satirists, the folly of all of us who stubbornly cling to our illusions despite the evidence of experience. *Rasselas* is not all darkness and gloom, for Johnson's theme invites comic as well as tragic treatment, and some of the episodes evoke that laughter of the mind which is the effect of high comedy. In its main theme, however—the folly of cherishing the dream of ever attaining unalloyed happiness in a world which can never wholly satisfy our desires, however disinterested—and in many of the sayings of its characters, especially of the sage Imlac, *Rasselas* expresses some of Johnson's own deepest convictions.

2. The Nile.

pours down the streams of plenty, and scatters over half the world the harvests of Egypt.

According to the custom which has descended from age to age among the monarchs of the torrid zone, Rasselas was confined in a private palace, with the other sons and daughters of Abyssinian royalty, till the order of succession should call him to the throne.

The place which the wisdom or policy of antiquity had destined for the residence of the Abyssinian princes was a spacious valley[3] in the kingdom of Amhara, surrounded on every side by mountains, of which the summits overhang the middle part. The only passage by which it could be entered was a cavern that passed under a rock, of which it has long been disputed whether it was the work of nature or of human industry. The outlet of the cavern was concealed by a thick wood, and the mouth which opened into the valley was closed with gates of iron, forged by the artificers of ancient days, so massy that no man could, without the help of engines, open or shut them.

From the mountains on every side rivulets descended that filled all the valley with verdure and fertility, and formed a lake in the middle, inhabited by fish of every species, and frequented by every fowl whom nature has taught to dip the wing in water. This lake discharged its superfluities by a stream, which entered a dark cleft of the mountain on the northern side, and fell with dreadful noise from precipice to precipice till it was heard no more.

The sides of the mountains were covered with trees, the banks of the brooks were diversified with flowers; every blast shook spices from the rocks, and every month dropped fruits upon the ground. All animals that bite the grass, or browse the shrub, whether wild or tame, wandered in this extensive circuit, secured from beasts of prey by the mountains which confined them. On one part were flocks and herds feeding in the pastures, on another all the beasts of chase frisking in the lawns; the sprightly kid was bounding on the rocks, the subtle monkey frolicking in the trees, and the solemn elephant reposing in the shade. All the diversities of the world were brought together, the blessings of nature were collected, and its evils extracted and excluded.

The valley, wide and fruitful, supplied its inhabitants with the necessaries of life, and all delights and superfluities were added at the annual visit which the emperor paid his children, when the iron gate was opened to the sound of music, and during eight days everyone that resided in the valley was required to propose whatever might contribute to make seclusion pleasant, to fill up the

3. Johnson had read of the Happy Valley in the Portuguese Jesuit Father Lobo's book on Abyssinia, which he translated in 1735. The description in this and the immediately following paragraphs illustrates well enough Johnson's preference for the "general" over the "particular" (see Chapter X, below). It owes something to the description of the Garden in *Paradise Lost* IV, and Coleridge's *Kubla Khan* owes something to it.

vacancies of attention, and lessen the tediousness of time. Every desire was immediately granted. All the artificers of pleasure were called to gladden the festivity; the musicians exerted the power of harmony, and the dancers showed their activity before the princes, in hope that they should pass their lives in this blissful captivity, to which those only were admitted whose performance was thought able to add novelty to luxury. Such was the appearance of security and delight which this retirement afforded, that they to whom it was new always desired that it might be perpetual; and as those on whom the iron gate had once closed were never suffered to return, the effect of longer experience could not be known. Thus every year produced new schemes of delight and new competitors for imprisonment.

The palace stood on an eminence, raised about thirty paces above the surface of the lake. It was divided into many squares or courts, built with greater or less magnificence according to the rank of those for whom they were designed. The roofs were turned into arches of massy stone, joined with a cement that grew harder by time, and the building stood from century to century, deriding the solstitial rains and equinoctial hurricanes, without need of reparation.

This house, which was so large as to be fully known to none but some ancient officers, who successively inherited the secrets of the place, was built as if suspicion herself had dictated the plan. To every room there was an open and secret passage; every square had a communication with the rest, either from the upper stories by private galleries, or by subterranean passages from the lower apartments. Many of the columns had unsuspected cavities, in which a long race of monarchs had reposited their treasures. They then closed up the opening with marble, which was never to be removed but in the utmost exigencies of the kingdom, and recorded their accumulations in a book, which was itself concealed in a tower, not entered but by the emperor, attended by the prince who stood next in succession.

Chapter II. The Discontent of Rasselas in the Happy Valley

Here the sons and daughters of Abyssinia lived only to know the soft vicissitudes of pleasure and repose, attended by all that were skillful to delight, and gratified with whatever the senses can enjoy. They wandered in gardens of fragrance, and slept in the fortresses of security. Every art was practiced to make them pleased with their own condition. The sages who instructed them told them of nothing but the miseries of public life, and described all beyond the mountains as regions of calamity, where discord was always raging, and where man preyed upon man.

To heighten their opinion of their own felicity, they were daily entertained with songs, the subject of which was the *happy valley*.

Their appetites were excited by frequent enumerations of different enjoyments, and revelry and merriment was the business of every hour, from the dawn of morning to the close of even.

These methods were generally successful; few of the princes had ever wished to enlarge their bounds, but passed their lives in full conviction that they had all within their reach that art or nature could bestow, and pitied those whom fate had excluded from this seat of tranquility, as the sport of chance and the slaves of misery.

Thus they rose in the morning and lay down at night, pleased with each other and with themselves; all but Rasselas, who, in the twenty-sixth year of his age, began to withdraw himself from their pastimes and assemblies, and to delight in solitary walks and silent meditation. He often sat before tables covered with luxury, and forgot to taste the dainties that were placed before him; he rose abruptly in the midst of the song, and hastily retired beyond the sound of music. His attendants observed the change, and endeavored to renew his love of pleasure. He neglected their officiousness, repulsed their invitations, and spent day after day on the banks of rivulets sheltered with trees, where he sometimes listened to the birds in the branches, sometimes observed the fish playing in the stream, and anon cast his eyes upon the pastures and mountains filled with animals, of which some were biting the herbage, and some sleeping among the bushes.

This singularity of his humor made him much observed. One of the sages, in whose conversation he had formerly delighted, followed him secretly, in hope of discovering the cause of his disquiet. Rasselas, who knew not that anyone was near him, having for some time fixed his eyes upon the goats that were browsing among the rocks, began to compare their condition with his own.

"What," said he, "makes the difference between man and all the rest of the animal creation? Every beast that strays beside me has the same corporal necessities with myself; he is hungry, and crops the grass, he is thirsty, and drinks the stream, his thirst and hunger are appeased, he is satisfied, and sleeps; he rises again, and he is hungry, he is again fed, and is at rest. I am hungry and thirsty like him, but when thirst and hunger cease, I am not at rest; I am, like him, pained with want, but am not, like him, satisfied with fullness. The intermediate hours are tedious and gloomy; I long again to be hungry that I may again quicken my attention. The birds peck the berries or the corn, and fly away to the groves, where they sit in seeming happiness on the branches, and waste their lives in tuning one unvaried series of sounds. I likewise can call the lutanist and the singer, but the sounds that pleased me yesterday weary me today, and will grow yet more wearisome tomorrow. I can discover within me no power of perception which is not glutted with its proper pleasure, yet I do not feel myself delighted. Man has surely some latent sense for which this place affords no gratification, or he has some desires distinct from sense, which must be satisfied before he can be happy."

After this he lifted up his head, and seeing the moon rising, walked towards the palace. As he passed through the fields, and saw the animals around him, "Ye," said he, "are happy, and need not envy me that walk thus among you, burthened with myself; nor do I, ye gentle beings, envy your felicity, for it is not the felicity of man. I have many distresses from which ye are free; I fear pain when I do not feel it; I sometimes shrink at evils recollected, and sometimes start at evils anticipated. Surely the equity of Providence has balanced peculiar sufferings with peculiar enjoyments."

With observations like these the prince amused himself as he returned, uttering them with a plaintive voice, yet with a look that discovered him to feel some complacence in his own perspicacity, and to receive some solace of the miseries of life from consciousness of the delicacy with which he felt, and the eloquence with which he bewailed them. He mingled cheerfully in the diversions of the evening, and all rejoiced to find that his heart was lightened.

Chapter III. *The Wants of Him That Wants Nothing*

On the next day his old instructor, imagining that he had now made himself acquainted with his disease of mind, was in the hope of curing it by counsel, and officiously sought an opportunity of conference, which the prince, having long considered him as one whose intellects were exhausted, was not very willing to afford. "Why," said he, "does this man thus intrude upon me; shall I be never suffered to forget those lectures which pleased only while they were new, and to become new again must be forgotten?" He then walked into the wood, and composed himself to his usual meditations; when, before his thoughts had taken any settled form, he perceived his pursuer at his side, and was at first prompted by his impatience to go hastily away; but, being unwilling to offend a man whom he had once reverenced and still loved, he invited him to sit down with him on the bank.

The old man, thus encouraged, began to lament the change which had been lately observed in the prince, and to inquire why he so often retired from the pleasures of the palace, to loneliness and silence. "I fly from pleasure," said the prince, "because pleasure has ceased to please; I am lonely because I am miserable, and am unwilling to cloud with my presence the happiness of others." "You, sir," said the sage, "are the first who has complained of misery in the *happy valley*. I hope to convince you that your complaints have no real cause. You are here in full possession of all that the emperor of Abyssinia can bestow; here is neither labor to be endured nor danger to be dreaded, yet here is all that labor or danger can procure or purchase. Look round and tell me which of your wants is without supply; if you want nothing, how are you unhappy?"

"That I want nothing," said the prince, "or that I know not what I want, is the cause of my complaint; if I had any known want, I should have a certain wish; that wish would excite endeavor, and I should not then repine to see the sun move so slowly towards the western mountain, or lament when the day breaks, and sleep will no longer hide me from myself. When I see the kids and the lambs chasing one another, I fancy that I should be happy if I had something to pursue. But, possessing all that I can want, I find one day and one hour exactly like another, except that the latter is still more tedious than the former. Let your experience inform me how the day may now seem as short as in my childhood, while nature was yet fresh and every moment showed me what I never had observed before. I have already enjoyed too much; give me something to desire."

The old man was surprised at this new species of affliction and knew not what to reply, yet was unwilling to be silent. "Sir," said he, "if you had seen the miseries of the world you would know how to value your present state." "Now," said the prince, "you have given me something to desire. I shall long to see the miseries of the world, since the sight of them is necessary to happiness."[4]

Chapter X. Imlac's History Continued. A Dissertation upon Poetry

"Wherever I went, I found that poetry was considered as the highest learning, and regarded with a veneration somewhat approaching to that which man would pay to the angelic nature. And yet it fills me with wonder that, in almost all countries, the most ancient poets are considered as the best: whether it be that every other kind of knowledge is an acquisition gradually attained, and poetry is a gift conferred at once; or that the first poetry of every nation surprised them as a novelty, and retained the credit by consent which it received by accident at first; or whether, as the province of poetry is to describe nature and passion, which are always the same, the first writers took possession of the most striking objects for description and the most probable occurrences for fiction, and left nothing to those that followed them, but transcription of the same events, and new combinations of the same images—whatever be the reason, it is commonly observed that the early writers are in possession of nature, and their followers of art; that the first excel in strength and invention, and the latter in elegance and refinement.

4. In the chapters here omitted Rasselas, meditating escape, comes to know Imlac, a poet and "man of learning" who has experienced life in all its phases, and who, finally despairing of happiness, has willingly retired to the Happy Valley. Imlac's account of his experiences whets the prince's desire to see the world and make a "choice of life."

"I was desirous to add my name to this illustrious fraternity. I read all the poets of Persia and Arabia, and was able to repeat by memory the volumes that are suspended in the mosque of Mecca. But I soon found that no man was ever great by imitation. My desire of excellence impelled me to transfer my attention to nature and to life. Nature was to be my subject, and men to be my auditors: I could never describe what I had not seen; I could not hope to move those with delight or terror, whose interests and opinions I did not understand.

"Being now resolved to be a poet, I saw everything with a new purpose; my sphere of attention was suddenly magnified; no kind of knowledge was to be overlooked. I ranged mountains and deserts for images and resemblances, and pictured upon my mind every tree of the forest and flower of the valley. I observed with equal care the crags of the rock and the pinnacles of the palace. Sometimes I wandered along the mazes of the rivulet, and sometimes watched the changes of the summer clouds. To a poet nothing can be useless. Whatever is beautiful, and whatever is dreadful, must be familiar to his imagination; he must be conversant with all that is awfully vast or elegantly little. The plants of the garden, the animals of the wood, the minerals of the earth, and meteors of the sky, must all concur to store his mind with inexhaustible variety: for every idea[5] is useful for the enforcement or decoration of moral or religious truth; and he who knows most will have most power of diversifying his scenes, and of gratifying his reader with remote allusions and unexpected instruction.

"All the appearances of nature I was therefore careful to study, and every country which I have surveyed has contributed something to my poetical powers."

"In so wide a survey," said the prince, "you must surely have left much unobserved. I have lived till now within the circuit of these mountains, and yet cannot walk abroad without the sight of something which I have never beheld before, or never heeded."

"The business of a poet," said Imlac, "is to examine, not the individual, but the species; to remark general properties and large appearances; he does not number the streaks of the tulip, or describe the different shades in the verdure of the forest. He is to exhibit in his portraits of nature such prominent and striking features as recall the original to every mind, and must neglect the minuter discriminations, which one may have remarked and another have neglected, for those characteristics which are alike obvious to vigilance and carelessness.

"But the knowledge of nature is only half the task of a poet; he must be acquainted likewise with all the modes of life. His character requires that he estimate the happiness and misery of every condition; observe the power of all the passions in all their com-

5. Mental image.

binations, and trace the changes of the human mind, as they are modified by various institutions and accidental influences of climate or custom, from the sprightliness of infancy to the despondence of decrepitude. He must divest himself of the prejudices of his age or country; he must consider right and wrong in their abstracted and invariable state; he must disregard present laws and opinions, and rise to general and transcendental[6] truths, which will always be the same. He must, therefore, content himself with the slow progress of his name, contemn the applause of his own time, and commit his claims to the justice of posterity. He must write as the interpreter of nature and the legislator of mankind, and consider himself as presiding over the thoughts and manner of future generations, as a being superior to time and place.

"His labor is not yet at an end; he must know many languages and many sciences; and, that his style may be worthy of his thoughts, must by incessant practice familiarize to himself every delicacy of speech and grace of harmony."

Chapter XI. Imlac's Narrative Continued. A Hint on Pilgrimage

Imlac now felt the enthusiastic fit, and was proceeding to aggrandize his own profession, when the prince cried out: "Enough! thou hast convinced me that no human being can ever be a poet. Proceed with thy narration."

"To be a poet," said Imlac, "is indeed very difficult." "So difficult," returned the prince, "that I will at present hear no more of his labors. Tell me whither you went when you had seen Persia."

"From Persia," said the poet, "I traveled through Syria, and for three years resided in Palestine, where I conversed with great numbers of the northern and western nations of Europe, the nations which are now in possession of all power and all knowledge, whose armies are irresistible, and whose fleets command the remotest parts of the globe. When I compared these men with the natives of our own kingdom, and those that surround us, they appeared almost another order of beings. In their countries it is difficult to wish for anything that may not be obtained; a thousand arts, of which we never heard, are continually laboring for their convenience and pleasure; and whatever their own climate has denied them is supplied by their commerce."

"By what means," said the prince, "are the Europeans thus powerful, or why, since they can so easily visit Asia and Africa for trade or conquest, cannot the Asiatics and Africans invade their coasts, plant colonies in their ports, and give laws to their natural princes? The same wind that carries them back would bring us thither."

"They are more powerful, sir, than we," answered Imlac, "be-

6. "General; pervading many particulars" (Johnson's *Dictionary*).

cause they are wiser; knowledge will always predominate over ignorance, as man governs the other animals. But why their knowledge is more than ours, I know not what reason can be given, but the unsearchable will of the Supreme Being."

"When," said the prince with a sigh, "shall I be able to visit Palestine, and mingle with this mighty confluence of nations? Till that happy moment shall arrive, let me fill up the time with such representations as thou canst give me. I am not ignorant of the motive that assembles such numbers in that place, and cannot but consider it as the center of wisdom and piety, to which the best and wisest men of every land must be continually resorting."

"There are some nations," said Imlac, "that send few visitants to Palestine; for many numerous and learned sects in Europe concur to censure pilgrimage as superstitious, or deride it as ridiculous."

"You know," said the prince, "how little my life has made me acquainted with diversity of opinions. It will be too long to hear the arguments on both sides; you, that have considered them, tell me the result."

"Pilgrimage," said Imlac, "like many other acts of piety, may be reasonable or superstitious, according to the principles upon which it is performed. Long journeys in search of truth are not commanded. Truth, such as is necessary to the regulation of life, is always found where it is honestly sought. Change of place is no natural cause of the increase of piety, for it inevitably produces dissipation of mind. Yet, since men go every day to view the fields where great actions have been performed, and return with stronger impressions of the event, curiosity of the same kind may naturally dispose us to view that country whence our religion had its beginning; and I believe no man surveys those awful scenes without some confirmation of holy resolutions. That the Supreme Being may be more easily propitiated in one place than in another is the dream of idle superstition, but that some places may operate upon our own minds in an uncommon manner is an opinion which hourly experience will justify. He who supposes that his vices may be more successfully combated in Palestine, will, perhaps, find himself mistaken, yet he may go thither without folly; he who thinks they will be more freely pardoned, dishonors at once his reason and religion."

"These," said the prince, "are European distinctions. I will consider them another time. What have you found to be the effect of knowledge? Are those nations happier than we?"

"There is so much infelicity," said the poet, "in the world that scarce any man has leisure from his own distresses to estimate the comparative happiness of others. Knowledge is certainly one of the means of pleasure, as is confessed by the natural desire which every mind feels of increasing its ideas. Ignorance is mere privation, by which nothing can be produced; it is a vacuity in which the soul sits motionless and torpid for want of attraction; and, without knowing why, we always rejoice when we learn, and grieve when we forget. I am therefore inclined to conclude that if nothing counteracts the natural consequence of learning, we grow more happy as our minds take a wider range.

"In enumerating the particular comforts of life, we shall find many advantages on the side of the Europeans. They cure wounds and diseases with which we languish and perish. We suffer inclemencies of weather which they can obviate. They have engines for the despatch of many laborious works, which we must perform by manual industry. There is such communication between distant places that one friend can hardly be said to be absent from another. Their policy removes all public inconveniences; they have roads cut through their mountains, and bridges laid upon their rivers. And, if we descend to the privacies of life, their habitations are more commodious, and their possessions are more secure."

"They are surely happy," said the prince, "who have all these conveniencies, of which I envy none so much as the facility with which separated friends interchange their thoughts."

"The Europeans," answered Imlac, "are less unhappy than we, but they are not happy. Human life is everywhere a state in which much is to be endured, and little to be enjoyed."[7]

Chapter XVI. They Enter Cairo, and Find Every Man Happy

As they approached the city, which filled the strangers with astonishment, "This," said Imlac to the prince, "is the place where travelers and merchants assemble from all the corners of the earth. You will here find men of every character and every occupation. Commerce is here honorable. I will act as a merchant, and you shall live as strangers, who have no other end of travel than curiosity. It will soon be observed that we are rich; our reputation will procure us access to all whom we shall desire to know; you will see all the conditions of humanity, and enable yourself at leisure to make your *choice of life*."

They now entered the town, stunned by the noise, and offended by the crowds. Instruction had not yet so prevailed over habit, but that they wondered to see themselves pass undistinguished along the street, and met by the lowest of the people without reverence or notice. The princess could not at first bear the thought of being leveled with the vulgar, and for some days continued in her chamber, where she was served by her favorite, Pekuah, as in the palace of the valley.

7. In the omitted chapters Rasselas and Imlac tunnel through the mountain, starting from a cavern earlier discovered by Rasselas. Laden with wealth and guided by Imlac, Rasselas, his sister Nekayah, and her maid Pekuah escape from the Happy Valley and make their way to Cairo.

Imlac, who understood traffic,[8] sold part of the jewels the next day, and hired a house, which he adorned with such magnificence that he was immediately considered as a merchant of great wealth. His politeness attracted many acquaintance, and his generosity made him courted by many dependents. His table was crowded by men of every nation, who all admired his knowledge, and solicited his favor. His companions, not being able to mix in the conversation, could make no discovery of their ignorance or surprise, and were gradually initiated in the world as they gained knowledge of the language.

The prince had, by frequent lectures, been taught the use and nature of money; but the ladies could not for a long time comprehend what the merchants did with small pieces of gold and silver, or why things of so little use should be received as equivalent to the necessaries of life.

They studied the language two years, while Imlac was preparing to set before them the various ranks and conditions of mankind. He grew acquainted with all who had anything uncommon in their fortune or conduct. He frequented the voluptuous and the frugal, the idle and the busy, the merchants and the men of learning.

The prince being now able to converse with fluency, and having learned the caution necessary to be observed in his intercourse with strangers, began to accompany Imlac to places of resort, and to enter into all assemblies, that he might make his *choice of life.*

For some time he thought choice needless, because all appeared to him equally happy. Wherever he went he met gaiety and kindness, and heard the song of joy or the laugh of carelessness. He began to believe that the world overflowed with universal plenty, and that nothing was withheld either from want or merit; that every hand showered liberality, and every heart melted with benevolence: "And who then," says he, "will be suffered to be wretched?"

Imlac permitted the pleasing delusion, and was unwilling to crush the hope of inexperience, till one day, having sat awhile silent, "I know not," said the prince, "what can be the reason that I am more unhappy than any of our friends. I see them perpetually and unalterably cheerful, but feel my own mind restless and uneasy. I am unsatisfied with those pleasures which I seem most to court; I live in the crowds of jollity, not so much to enjoy company as to shun myself, and am only loud and merry to conceal my sadness."

"Every man," said Imlac, "may, by examining his own mind, guess what passes in the minds of others; when you feel that your own gaiety is counterfeit, it may justly lead you to suspect that of your companions not to be sincere. Envy is commonly reciprocal. We are long before we are convinced that happiness is never to be found, and each believes it possessed by others, to keep alive the

8. Commerce.

hope of obtaining it for himself. In the assembly where you passed the last night, there appeared such sprightliness of air, and volatility of fancy, as might have suited beings of an higher order, formed to inhabit serener regions, inaccessible to care or sorrow; yet, believe me, prince, there was not one who did not dread the moment when solitude should deliver him to the tyranny of reflection."

"This," said the prince, "may be true of others, since it is true of me; yet, whatever be the general infelicity of man, one condition is more happy than another, and wisdom surely directs us to take the least evil in the *choice of life*."

"The causes of good and evil," answered Imlac, "are so various and uncertain, so often entangled with each other, so diversified by various relations, and so much subject to accidents which cannot be foreseen, that he who would fix his condition upon incontestable reasons of preference must live and die inquiring and deliberating."

"But, surely," said Rasselas, "the wise men, to whom we listen with reverence and wonder, chose that mode of life for themselves which they thought most likely to make them happy."

"Very few," said the poet, "live by choice. Every man is placed in his present condition by causes which acted without his foresight, and with which he did not always willingly co-operate; and therefore you will rarely meet one who does not think the lot of his neighbor better than his own."

"I am pleased to think," said the prince, "that my birth has given me at least one advantage over others, by enabling me to determine for myself. I have here the world before me. I will review it at leisure; surely happiness is somewhere to be found."[9]

Chapter XVIII. The Prince Finds a Wise and Happy Man

As he was one day walking in the street, he saw a spacious building which all were, by the open doors, invited to enter: he followed the stream of people, and found it a hall or school of declamation, in which professors read lectures to their auditory. He fixed his eye upon a sage raised above the rest, who discoursed with great energy on the government of the passions. His look was venerable, his action graceful, his pronunciation clear, and his diction elegant. He showed with great strength of sentiment and variety of illustration that human nature is degraded and debased, when the lower faculties predominate over the higher; that when fancy, the parent of passion, usurps the dominion of the mind, nothing ensues but the natural effect of unlawful government, perturbation, and confusion; that she betrays the fortresses of the intellect to rebels, and excites her children to sedition against reason, their lawful sovereign. He compared reason to the sun, of which the light is constant, uniform and lasting; and fancy to a meteor, of bright but transitory luster,

9. In Chapter XVII, here omitted, Rasselas fails to find happiness among the gay and dissipated young men of Cairo.

irregular in its motion, and delusive in its direction.

He then communicated the various precepts given from time to time for the conquest of passion, and displayed the happiness of those who had obtained the important victory, after which man is no longer the slave of fear, nor the fool of hope; is no more emaciated by envy, inflamed by anger, emasculated by tenderness, or depressed by grief; but walks on calmly through the tumults or the privacies of life, as the sun pursues alike his course through the calm or the stormy sky.

He enumerated many examples of heroes immovable by pain or pleasure, who looked with indifference on those modes or accidents to which the vulgar give the names of good and evil. He exhorted his hearers to lay aside their prejudices, and arm themselves against the shafts of malice or misfortune, by invulnerable patience; concluding that this state only was happiness, and that his happiness was in everyone's power.

Rasselas listened to him with the veneration due to the instructions of a superior being, and, waiting for him at the door, humbly implored the liberty of visiting so great a master of true wisdom. The lecturer hesitated a moment, when Rasselas put a purse of gold into his hand, which he received with a mixture of joy and wonder.

"I have found," said the prince at his return to Imlac, "a man who can teach all that is necessary to be known; who, from the unshaken throne of rational fortitude, looks down on the scenes of life changing beneath him. He speaks, and attention watches his lips. He reasons, and conviction closes his periods. This man shall be my future guide; I will learn his doctrines, and imitate his life."

"Be not too hasty," said Imlac, "to trust or to admire the teachers of morality: they discourse like angels, but they live like men."

Rasselas, who could not conceive how any man could reason so forcibly without feeling the cogency of his own arguments, paid his visit in a few days, and was denied admission. He had now learned the power of money, and made his way by a piece of gold to the inner apartment, where he found the philosopher in a room half darkened, with his eyes misty and his face pale. "Sir," said he, "you are come at a time when all human friendship is useless; what I suffer cannot be remedied, what I have lost cannot be supplied. My daughter, my only daughter, from whose tenderness I expected all the comforts of my age, died last night of a fever. My views, my purposes, my hopes are at an end; I am now a lonely being, disunited from society."

"Sir," said the prince, "mortality is an event by which a wise man can never be surprised; we know that death is always near, and it should therefore always be expected." "Young man," answered the philosopher, "you speak like one that has never felt the pangs of separation." "Have you then forgot the precepts," said Rasselas, "which you so powerfully enforced? Has wisdom no strength to arm the heart against calamity? Consider that external things are naturally variable, but truth and reason are always the same." "What comfort," said the mourner, "can truth and reason afford me? Of what effect are they now, but to tell me that my daughter will not be restored?"

The prince, whose humanity would not suffer him to insult misery with reproof, went away, convinced of the emptiness of rhetorical sound, and the inefficacy of polished periods and studied sentences.

Chapter XIX. A Glimpse of Pastoral Life

He was still eager upon the same inquiry; and having heard of a hermit that lived near the lowest cataract of the Nile, and filled the whole country with the fame of his sanctity, resolved to visit his retreat, and inquire whether that felicity which public life could not afford was to be found in solitude; and whether a man whose age and virtue made him venerable could teach any peculiar art of shunning evils, or enduring them.

Imlac and the princess agreed to accompany him, and, after the necessary preparations, they began their journey. Their way lay through fields, where shepherds tended their flocks and the lambs were playing upon the pasture. "This," said the poet, "is the life which has been often celebrated for its innocence and quiet; let us pass the heat of the day among the shepherds' tents, and know whether all our searches are not to terminate in pastoral simplicity."

The proposal pleased them, and they induced the shepherds, by small presents and familiar questions, to tell their opinion of their own state. They were so rude and ignorant, so little able to compare the good with the evil of the occupation, and so indistinct in their narratives and descriptions, that very little could be learned from them. But it was evident that their hearts were cankered with discontent; that they considered themselves as condemned to labor for the luxury of the rich, and looked up with stupid malevolence toward those that were placed above them.

The princess pronounced with vehemence that she would never suffer these envious savages to be her companions, and that she should not soon be desirous of seeing any more specimens of rustic happiness; but could not believe that all the accounts of primeval pleasures were fabulous, and was yet in doubt whether life had anything that could be justly preferred to the placid gratifications of fields and woods. She hoped that the time would come, when, with a few virtuous and elegant companions, she could gather flowers planted by her own hand, fondle the lambs of her own ewe, and listen without care, among brooks and breezes, to one of her maidens reading in the shade.[1]

Chapter XXII. The Happiness of a Life Led According to Nature

Rasselas went often to an assembly of learned men, who met at stated times to unbend their minds and compare their opinions. Their manners were somewhat coarse, but their conversation was instructive, and their disputations acute, though sometimes too violent, and often continued till neither controvertist remembered upon what question they began. Some faults were almost general among them; everyone was desirous to dictate to the rest, and everyone was pleased to hear the genius or knowledge of another depreciated.

In this assembly Rasselas was relating his interview with the hermit, and the wonder with which he heard him censure a course of life which he had so deliberately chosen, and so laudably followed. The sentiments of the hearers were various. Some were of opinion that the folly of his choice had been justly punished by condemnation to perpetual perseverance. One of the youngest among them, with great vehemence, pronounced him an hypocrite. Some talked of the right of society to the labor of individuals, and considered retirement as a desertion of duty. Others readily allowed that there was a time when the claims of the public were satisfied, and when a man might properly sequester himself, to review his life and purify his heart.

One, who appeared more affected with the narrative than the rest, thought it likely that the hermit would in a few years go back to his retreat, and perhaps, if shame did not restrain, or death intercept him, return once more from his retreat into the world. "For the hope of happiness," said he, "is so strongly impressed that the longest experience is not able to efface it. Of the present state, whatever it be, we feel and are forced to confess the misery; yet when the same state is again at a distance, imagination paints it as desirable. But the time will surely come when desire will be no longer our torment, and no man shall be wretched but by his own fault."

"This," said a philosopher who had heard him with tokens of great impatience, "is the present condition of a wise man. The time is already come when none are wretched but by their own fault. Nothing is more idle than to inquire after happiness, which nature has kindly placed within our reach. The way to be happy is to live according to nature, in obedience to that universal and

1. In the omitted chapters the travelers discover the unease and danger of being wealthy, and then find the hermit, who, far from being piously content, is on the point of abandoning his hermitage and returning to society.

unalterable law with which every heart is originally impressed; which is not written on it by precept, but engraven by destiny, not instilled by education, but infused at our nativity. He that lives according to nature will suffer nothing from the delusions of hope, or importunities of desire; he will receive and reject with equability of temper, and act or suffer as the reason of things shall alternately prescribe. Other men may amuse themselves with subtle definitions, or intricate ratiocination. Let them learn to be wise by easier means; let them observe the hind of the forest, and the linnet of the grove; let them consider the life of animals, whose motions are regulated by instinct; they obey their guide, and are happy. Let us therefore, at length, cease to dispute, and learn to live; throw away the encumbrance of precepts, which they who utter them with so much pride and pomp do not understand, and carry with us this simple and intelligible maxim, that deviation from nature is deviation from happiness."

When he had spoken, he looked round him with a placid air, and enjoyed the consciousness of his own beneficence. "Sir," said the prince with great modesty, "as I, like all the rest of mankind, am desirous of felicity, my closest attention has been fixed upon your discourse. I doubt not the truth of a position which a man so learned has so confidently advanced. Let me only know what it is to live according to nature."

"When I find young men so humble and so docile," said the philosopher, "I can deny them no information which my studies have enabled me to afford. To live according to nature, is to act always with due regard to the fitness arising from the relations and qualities of causes and effects; to concur with the great and un-changeable scheme of universal felicity; to co-operate with the general disposition and tendency of the present system of things."

The prince soon found that this was one of the sages whom he should understand less as he heard him longer. He therefore bowed and was silent; and the philosopher, supposing him satisfied, and the rest vanquished, rose up and departed with the air of a man that had co-operated with the present system.[2]

From *Chapter XXVI. The Princess Continues Her Remarks upon Private Life*

Nekayah, perceiving her brother's attention fixed, proceeded in her narrative.

"In families where there is or is not poverty, there is commonly discord. If a kingdom be, as Imlac tells us, a great family, a family likewise is a little kingdom, torn with factions and exposed to revolutions. An unpracticed observer expects the love of parents and

2. In the omitted chapters Rasselas resolves to observe the happiness of men of high position, leaving the study of domestic life to his sister; they report their findings to each other.

children to be constant and equal; but this kindness seldom continues beyond the years of infancy: in a short time the children become rivals to their parents. Benefits are allayed[3] by reproaches, and gratitude debased by envy.

"Parents and children seldom act in concert; each child endeavors to appropriate the esteem or fondness of the parents, and the parents, with yet less temptation, betray each other to their children. Thus, some place their confidence in the father, and some in the mother, and by degrees the house is filled with artifices and feuds.

"The opinions of children and parents, of the young and the old, are naturally opposite, by the contrary effects of hope and despondence, of expectation and experience, without crime or folly on either side. The colors of life in youth and age appear different, as the face of nature in spring and winter. And how can children credit the assertions of parents, which their own eyes show them to be false?

"Few parents act in such a manner as much to enforce their maxims by the credit of their lives. The old man trusts wholly to slow contrivance and gradual progression; the youth expects to force his way by genius, vigor, and precipitance. The old man pays regard to riches, and the youth reverences virtue. The old man deifies prudence; the youth commits himself to magnanimity and chance. The young man, who intends no ill, believes that none is intended, and therefore acts with openness and candor; but his father, having suffered the injuries of fraud, is impelled to suspect, and too often allured to practice it. Age looks with anger on the temerity of youth, and youth with contempt on the scrupulosity[4] of age. Thus parents and children, for the greatest part, live on to love less and less; and, if those whom nature has thus closely united are the torments of each other, where shall we look for tenderness and consolation?"

"Surely," said the prince, "you must have been unfortunate in your choice of acquaintance: I am unwilling to believe that the most tender of all relations is thus impeded in its effects by natural necessity."

"Domestice discord," answered she, "is not inevitably and fatally necessary, but yet is not easily avoided. We seldom see that a whole family is virtuous; the good and evil cannot well agree, and the evil can yet less agree with one another. Even the virtuous fall sometimes to variance, when their virtues are of different kinds, and tending to extremes. In general, those parents have most reverence who most deserve it; for he that lives well cannot be despised.

"Many other evils infest private life. Some are the slaves of servants whom they have trusted with their affairs. Some are kept in continual anxiety to the caprice of rich relations, whom they cannot

3. To allay is "to join anything to another, so as to abate its predominant qualities" (Johnson's *Dictionary*).

4. "Fear of acting in any manner" (Johnson's *Dictionary*).

please, and dare not offend. Some husbands are imperious, and some wives perverse; and, as it is always more easy to do evil than good, though the wisdom or virtue of one can very rarely make many happy, the folly or vice of one may often make many miserable."

"If such be the general effect of marriage," said the prince, "I shall for the future think it dangerous to connect my interest with that of another, lest I should be unhappy by my partner's fault."

"I have met," said the princess, "with many who live single for that reason; but I never found that their prudence ought to raise envy. They dream away their time without friendship, without fondness, and are driven to rid themselves of the day, for which they have no use, by childish amusements, or vicious delights. They act as beings under the constant sense of some known inferiority that fills their minds with rancor, and their tongues with censure. They are peevish at home, and malevolent abroad; and, as the outlaws of human nature, make it their business and their pleasure to disturb that society which debars them from its privileges. To live without feeling or exciting sympathy, to be fortunate without adding to the felicity of others, or afflicted without tasting the balm of pity, is a state more gloomy than solitude; it is not retreat but exclusion from mankind. Marriage has many pains, but celibacy has no pleasures."[5] * * *

Chapter XXIX. *The Debate on Marriage Continued*

"The good of the whole," says Rasselas, "is the same with the good of all its parts. If marriage be best for mankind it must be evidently best for individuals, or a permanent and necessary duty must be the cause of evil, and some must be inevitably sacrificed to the convenience of others. In the estimate which you have made of the two states, it appears that the incommodities of a single life are, in a great measure, necessary and certain, but those of the conjugal state accidental and avoidable.

"I cannot forbear to flatter myself that prudence and benevolence will make marriage happy. The general folly of mankind is the cause of general complaint. What can be expected but disappointment and repentance from a choice made in the immaturity of youth, in the ardor of desire, without judgment, without foresight, without inquiry after conformity of opinions, similarity of manners, rectitude of judgment, or purity of sentiment.

"Such is the common process of marriage. A youth and maiden meeting by chance, or brought together by artifice, exchange glances, reciprocate civilities, go home, and dream of one another. Having little to divert attention, or diversify thought, they find

---

5. In the omitted chapters Rasselas reports that even the highest stations afford no happiness, and the conversation continues.

themselves uneasy when they are apart, and therefore conclude that they shall be happy together. They marry, and discover what nothing but voluntary blindness had before concealed; they wear out life in altercations, and charge nature with cruelty.

"From those early marriages proceeds likewise the rivalry of parents and children: the son is eager to enjoy the world before the father is willing to forsake it, and there is hardly room at once for two generations. The daughter begins to bloom before the mother can be content to fade, and neither can forbear to wish for the absence of the other.

"Surely all these evils may be avoided by that deliberation and delay which prudence prescribes to irrevocable choice. In the variety and jollity of youthful pleasures life may be well enough supported without the help of a partner. Longer time will increase experience, and wider views will allow better opportunities of inquiry and selection: one advantage, as least, will be certain; the parents will be visibly older than their children."

"What reason cannot collect," said Nekayah, "and what experiment has not yet taught, can be known only from the report of others. I have been told that late marriages are not eminently happy. This is a question too important to be neglected, and I have often proposed it to those, whose accuracy of remark, and comprehensiveness of knowledge, made their suffrages worthy of regard. They have generally determined that it is dangerous for a man and woman to suspend their fate upon each other, at a time when opinions are fixed, and habits are established; when friendships have been contracted on both sides, when life has been planned into method, and the mind has long enjoyed the contemplation of its own prospects.

"It is scarcely possible that two traveling through the world under the conduct of chance should have been both directed to the same path, and it will not often happen that either will quit the track which custom has made pleasing. When the desultory levity of youth has settled into regularity, it is soon succeeded by pride ashamed to yield, or obstinacy delighting to contend. And even though mutual esteem produces mutual desire to please, time itself, as it modifies unchangeably the external mien, determines likewise the direction of the passions, and gives an inflexible rigidity to the manners. Long customs are not easily broken: he that attempts to change the course of his own life very often labors in vain; and how shall we do that for others which we are seldom able to do for ourselves?"

"But surely," interposed the prince, "you suppose the chief motive of choice forgotten or neglected. Whenever I shall seek a wife, it shall be my first question, whether she be willing to be led by reason?"

"Thus it is," said Nekayah, "that philosophers are deceived. There are a thousand familiar disputes which reason never can decide; questions that elude investigation, and make logic ridiculous; cases where something must be done, and where little can be said. Consider the state of mankind, and inquire how few can be supposed to act upon any occasions, whether small or great, with all the reasons of action present to their minds. Wretched would be the pair above all names of wretchedness, who should be doomed to adjust by reason every morning all the minute detail of a domestic day.

"Those who marry at an advanced age will probably escape the encroachments of their children; but, in diminution of this advantage, they will be likely to leave them, ignorant and helpless, to a guardian's mercy: or, if that should not happen, they must at least go out of the world before they see those whom they love best either wise or great.

"From their children, if they have less to fear, they have less also to hope, and they lose, without equivalent, the joys of early love, and the convenience of uniting with manners pliant and minds susceptible of new impressions, which might wear away their dissimilitudes by long cohabitation, as soft bodies, by continual attrition, conform their surfaces to each other.

"I believe it will be found that those who marry late are best pleased with their children, and those who marry early with their partners."

"The union of these two affections," said Rasselas, "would produce all that could be wished. Perhaps there is a time when marriage might unite them, a time neither too early for the father, nor too late for the husband."

"Every hour," answered the princess, "confirms my prejudice in favor of the position so often uttered by the mouth of Imlac, 'That nature sets her gifts on the right hand and on the left.' Those conditions, which flatter hope and attract desire, are so constituted that, as we approach one, we recede from another. There are goods so opposed that we cannot seize both, but, by too much prudence, may pass between them at too great a distance to reach either. This is often the fate of long consideration; he does nothing who endeavors to do more than is allowed to humanity. Flatter not yourself with contrarieties of pleasure. Of the blessings set before you make your choice, and be content. No man can taste the fruits of autumn, while he is delighting his scent with the flowers of the spring: no man can, at the same time, fill his cup from the source and from the mouth of the Nile."[6]

6. In Chapter XXX, here omitted, Imlac proposes a visit to the Pyramids.

Chapter XXXI. They Visit the Pyramids

The resolution being thus taken, they set out the next day. They laid tents upon their camels, being resolved to stay among the pyramids till their curiosity was fully satisfied. They traveled gently, turned aside to everything remarkable, stopped from time to time and conversed with the inhabitants, and observed the various appearances of towns ruined and inhabited, of wild and cultivated nature.

When they came to the great pyramid, they were astonished at the extent of the base, and the height of the top. Imlac explained to them the principles upon which the pyramidal form was chosen for a fabric intended to coextend its duration with that of the world; he showed that its gradual diminution gave it such stability as defeated all the common attacks of the elements, and could scarcely be overthrown by earthquakes themselves, the least resistible of natural violence. A concussion that should shatter the pyramid would threaten the dissolution of the continent.

They measured all its dimensions, and pitched their tents at its foot. Next day they prepared to enter its interior apartments, and having hired the common guides, climbed up to the first passage, when the favorite of the princess, looking into the cavity, stepped back and trembled. "Pekuah," said the princess, "of what art thou afraid?" "Of the narrow entrance," answered the lady, "and of the dreadful gloom. I dare not inter a place which must surely be inhabited by unquiet souls. The original possessors of these dreadful vaults will start up before us, and perhaps shut us in forever." She spoke, and threw her arms round the neck of her mistress.

"If all your fear be of apparitions," said the prince, "I will promise you safety. There is no danger from the dead; he that is once buried will be seen no more."

"That the dead are seen no more," said Imlac, "I will not undertake to maintain, against the concurrent and unvaried testimony of all ages, and of all nations. There is no people, rude or learned, among whom apparitions of the dead are not related and believed. This opinion, which perhaps prevails as far as human nature is diffused, could become universal only by its truth; those that never heard of one another would not have agreed in a tale which nothing but experience can make credible. That it is doubted by single cavilers can very little weaken the general evidence; and some who deny it with their tongues confess it by their fears.

"Yet I do not mean to add new terrors to those which have already seized upon Pekuah. There can be no reason why specters should haunt the pyramid more than other places, or why they should have power or will to hurt innocence and purity. Our entrance is no violation of their privileges; we can take nothing from them, how then can we offend them?"

"My dear Pekuah," said the princess, "I will always go before you, and Imlac shall follow you. Remember that you are the companion of the princess of Abyssinia."

"If the princess is pleased that her servant should die," returned the lady, "let her command some death less dreadful than enclosure in this horrid cavern. You know I dare not disobey you; I must go if you command me, but if I once enter, I never shall come back."

The princess saw that her fear was too strong for expostulation or reproof, and, embracing her, told her that she should stay in the tent till their return. Pekuah was yet not satisfied, but entreated the princess not to pursue so dreadful a purpose as that of entering the recesses of the pyramid. "Though I cannot teach courage," said Nekayah, "I must not learn cowardice, nor leave at last undone what I came hither only to do."

Chapter XXXII. They Enter the Pyramid

Pekuah descended to the tents, and the rest entered the pyramid. They passed through the galleries, surveyed the vaults of marble, and examined the chest in which the body of the founder is supposed to have been reposited. They then sat down in one of the most spacious chambers to rest a while before they attempted to return.

"We have now," said Imlac, "gratified our minds with an exact view of the greatest work of man, except the wall of China.

"Of the wall it is very easy to assign the motive. It secured a wealthy and timorous nation from the incursions of barbarians, whose unskillfulness in arts made it easier for them to supply their wants by rapine than by industry, and who from time to time poured in upon the habitations of peaceful commerce, as vultures descend upon domestic fowl. Their celerity and fierceness made the wall necessary, and their ignorance made it efficacious.

"But for the pyramids, no reason has ever been given adequate to the cost and labor of the work. The narrowness of the chambers proves that it could afford no retreat from enemies, and treasures might have been reposited at far less expense with equal security. It seems to have been erected only in compliance with that hunger of imagination which preys incessantly upon life, and must be always appeased by some employment. Those who have already all that they can enjoy must enlarge their desires. He that has built for use till use is supplied, must begin to build for vanity, and extend his plan to the utmost power of human performance, that he may not be soon reduced to form another wish.

"I consider this mighty structure as a monument of the insufficiency of human enjoyments. A king, whose power is unlimited, and whose treasures surmount all real and imaginary wants, is compelled to solace, by the erection of a pyramid, the satiety of dominion and tastelessness of pleasures, and to amuse the tediousness of declining life by seeing thousands laboring without end, and one stone, for no purpose, laid upon another. Whoever thou art, that, not content with a moderate condition, imaginest happiness in royal magnificence, and dreamest that command or riches can feed the appetite of novelty with perpetual gratifications, survey the pyramids, and confess thy folly!"[7]

Chapter XLIV. The Dangerous Prevalence[8] of Imagination

"Disorders of intellect," answered Imlac, "happen much more often than superficial observers will easily believe. Perhaps, if we speak with rigorous exactness, no human mind is in its right state. There is no man whose imagination does not sometimes predominate over his reason, who can regulate his attention wholly by his will, and whose ideas will come and go at his command. No man will be found in whose mind airy notions do not sometimes tyrannize, and force him to hope or fear beyond the limits of sober probability. All power of fancy over reason is a degree of insanity; but while this power is such as we can control and repress, it is not visible to others, nor considered as any depravation of the mental faculties; it is not pronounced madness but when it comes ungovernable, and apparently influences speech or action.

"To indulge the power of fiction, and send imagination out upon the wing, is often the sport of those who delight too much in silent speculation. When we are alone we are not always busy; the labor of excogitation is too violent to last long; the ardor of inquiry will sometimes give way to idleness or satiety. He who has nothing external that can divert him must find pleasure in his own thoughts, and must conceive himself what he is not; for who is pleased with what he is? He then expatiates in boundless futurity, and culls from all imaginable conditions that which for the present moment he should most desire, amuses his desires with impossible enjoyments, and confers upon his pride unattainable dominion. The mind dances from scene to scene, unites all pleasures in all combinations, and riots in delights which nature and fortune, with all their bounty, cannot bestow.

"In time, some particular train of ideas fixes the attention; all other intellectual gratifications are rejected; the mind, in weariness

7. Chapters XXXIII-XLIII are here omitted. While the travelers are in the Pyramid, Pekuah is abducted by an Arab chieftain, from whom she is eventually ransomed. The travelers return to Cairo, and Imlac makes the acquaintance of an astronomer, who proves to be mad, having yielded to the delusion that he has learned to control the weather. Chapter XLIII concludes: "Rasselas * * * inquired of Imlac whether he thought such maladies of the mind frequent, and how they were contracted."
8. Predominance.

or leisure, recurs constantly to the favorite conception, and feasts on the luscious falsehood, whenever she is offended with the bitterness of truth. By degrees the reign of fancy is confirmed; she grows first imperious, and in time despotic. Then fictions begin to operate as realities, false opinions fasten upon the mind, and life passes in dreams of rapture or of anguish.

"This, sir, is one of the dangers of solitude, which the hermit has confessed not always to promote goodness, and the astronomer's misery has proved to be not always propitious to wisdom."

"I will no more," said the favorite, "imagine myself the queen of Abyssinia. I have often spent the hours which the princess gave to my own disposal, in adjusting ceremonies and regulating the court; I have repressed the pride of the powerful, and granted the petitions of the poor; I have built new palaces in more happy situations, planted groves upon the tops of mountains, and have exulted in the beneficence of royalty, till, when the princess entered, I had almost forgotten to bow down before her."

"And I," said the princess, "will not allow myself any more to play the shepherdess in my waking dreams. I have often soothed my thoughts with the quiet and innocence of pastoral employments, till I have in my chamber heard the winds whistle, and the sheep bleat; sometimes freed the lamb entangled in the thicket, and sometimes with my crook encountered the wolf. I have a dress like that of the village maids, which I put on to help my imagination, and a pipe on which I play softly, and suppose myself followed by my flocks."

"I will confess," said the prince, "an indulgence of fantastic delight more dangerous than yours. I have frequently endeavored to image the possibility of a perfect government, by which all wrong should be restrained, all vice reformed, and all the subjects preserved in tranquility and innocence. This thought produced innumerable schemes of reformation, and dictated many useful regulations and salutary edicts. This has been the sport, and sometimes the labor, of my solitude; and I start, when I think with how little anguish I once supposed the death of my father and my brothers."

"Such," says Imlac, "are the effects of visionary schemes; when we first form them, we know them to be absurd, but familiarize them by degrees, and in time lose sight of their folly."

Chapter XLV. They Discourse with an Old Man

The evening was now far past, and they rose to return home. As they walked along the bank of the Nile, delighted with the beams of the moon quivering on the water, they saw at a small distance an old man, whom the prince had often heard in the assembly of the sages. "Yonder," said he, "is one whose years have calmed his passions, but not clouded his reason. Let us close the disquisitions of the night by inquiring what are his sentiments of his own state, that we may know whether youth alone is to struggle with vexation, and whether any better hope remains for the latter part of life."

Here the sage approached and saluted them. They invited him to join their walk, and prattled a while, as acquaintance that had unexpectedly met one another. The old man was cheerful and talkative, and the way seemed short in his company. He was pleased to find himself not disregarded, accompanied them to their house, and, at the prince's request, entered with them. They placed him in the seat of honor, and set wine and conserves before him.

"Sir," said the princess, "an evening walk must give to a man of learning like you pleasures which ignorance and youth can hardly conceive. You know the qualities and the causes of all that you behold, the laws by which the river flows, the periods in which the planets perform their revolutions. Everything must supply you with contemplation, and renew the consciousness of your own dignity."

"Lady," answered he, "let the gay and the vigorous expect pleasure in their excursions; it is enough that age can obtain ease. To me the world has lost its novelty; I look round, and see what I remember to have seen in happier days. I rest against a tree, and consider that in the same shade I once disputed upon the annual overflow of the Nile with a friend who is now silent in the grave. I cast my eyes upward, fix them on the changing moon, and think with pain on the vicissitudes of life. I have ceased to take much delight in physical truth; for what have I to do with those things which I am soon to leave?"

"You may at least recreate yourself," said Imlac, "with the recollection of an honorable and useful life, and enjoy the praise which all agree to give you."

"Praise," said the sage with a sigh, "is to an old man an empty sound. I have neither mother to be delighted with the reputation of her son, nor wife to partake the honors of her husband. I have outlived my friends and my rivals. Nothing is now of much importance; for I cannot extend my interest beyond myself. Youth is delighted with applause, because it is considered as the earnest of some future good, and because the prospect of life is far extended; but to me, who am now declining to decrepitude, there is little to be feared from the malevolence of men, and yet less to be hoped from their affection or esteem. Something they may yet take away, but they can give me nothing. Riches would now be useless, and high employment would be pain. My retrospect of life recalls to my view many opportunities of good neglected, much time squandered upon trifles, and more lost in idleness and vacancy. I leave many great designs unattempted, and many great attempts unfinished. My mind is burthened with no heavy crime, and therefore I compose myself to tranquility; endeavor to abstract my thoughts from hopes and cares which, though reason knows them to be vain, still try to keep their old possession of the heart; expect,[9] with serene humility, that hour which nature cannot long delay; and hope to possess, in a better state, that happiness which here I could not find, and that virtue which here I have not attained."

He arose and went away, leaving his audience not much elated with the hope of long life. The prince consoled himself with remarking that it was not reasonable to be disappointed by this account; for age had never been considered as the season of felicity, and if it was possible to be easy in decline and weakness, it was likely that the days of vigor and alacrity might be happy; that the noon of life might be bright, if the evening could be calm.

The princess suspected that age was querulous and malignant, and delighted to repress the expectations of those who had newly entered the world. She had seen the possessors of estates look with envy on their heirs, and known many who enjoy pleasure no longer than they can confine it to themselves.

Pekuah conjectured that the man was older than he appeared, and was willing to impute his complaints to delirious dejection; or else supposed that he had been unfortunate, and was therefore discontented. "For nothing," said she, "is more common than to call our own condition the condition of life."

Imlac, who had no desire to see them depressed, smiled at the comforts which they could so readily procure to themselves, and remembered that, at the same age, he was equally confident of unmingled prosperity, and equally fertile of consolatory expedients. He forebore to force upon them unwelcome knowledge, which time itself would too soon impress. The princess and her lady retired; the madness of the astronomer hung upon their minds, and they desired Imlac to enter upon his office, and delay next morning the rising of the sun.[1]

Chapter XLIX. The Conclusion, in Which Nothing Is Concluded

It was now the time of the inundation of the Nile: a few days after their visit to the catacombs, the river began to rise.

They were confined to their house. The whole region being under water gave them no invitation to any excursions, and being well supplied with materials for talk, they diverted themselves with comparisons of the different forms of life which they had observed, and with various schemes of happiness which each of them had formed.

9. Await.
1. Chapters XLVI-XLVIII are here omitted. The travelers converse with the astronomer and learn that he too regrets his choice of life. A discourse on the nature of the soul (in the penultimate chapter) raises the hope of happiness in a future state.

Pekuah was never so much charmed with any place as the convent of St. Anthony, where the Arab restored her to the princess, and wished only to fill it with pious maidens, and to be made prioress of the order; she was weary of expectation and disgust,[2] and would gladly be fixed in some unvariable state.

The princess thought that, of all sublunary things, knowledge was the best: she desired first to learn all sciences, and then purposed to found a college of learned women, in which she would preside, that, by conversing with the old and educating the young, she might divide her time between the acquisition and communication of wisdom, and raise up for the next age models of prudence, and patterns of piety.

The prince desired a little kingdom, in which he might administer justice in his own person, and see all the parts of government with his own eyes; but he could never fix the limits of his dominion, and was always adding to the number of his subjects.

Imlac and the astronomer were contented to be driven along the stream of life, without directing their course to any particular port.

Of these wishes that they had formed, they well knew that none could be obtained. They deliberated a while what was to be done, and resolved, when the inundation should cease, to return to Abyssinia.[3]

1759

From Prayers and Meditations[1]

Easter Eve, 1761

Since the communion of last Easter, I have led a life so dissipated and useless, and my terrors and perplexities have so much increased, that I am under great depression and discouragement; yet I purpose to present myself before God tomorrow, with humble hope that he will not break the bruised reed.

Come unto me all ye that travail.[2]

I have resolved, I hope not presumptuously, till I am afraid to resolve again. Yet hoping in God, I steadfastly purpose to lead a new life. O God, enable me, for Jesus Christ's sake.

2. Aversion.
3. Probably not, as is often suggested, to the Happy Valley (in Chapter I we were told that none who leave the valley can ever return). Presumably the travelers return, with whatever wisdom they have gained, but also with their cherished illusions, to share the common destiny of mankind. But Johnson, hurrying to his conclusion, may have left the place to which they returned vague.

1. During much of his life Johnson observed with prayer and meditation certain seasons: his own birthday, the anniversary of the death of his wife, Good Friday, and Easter. He was accustomed to writing down his prayers and thoughts. This document gives a moving insight into his spiritual struggles and his sense of sin.
2. Matthew xi.28.

Good Friday, 1779, 11 P.M.

I am now to review the last year, and find little but dismal vacuity, neither business nor pleasure; much intended, and little done. My health is much broken; my nights afford me little rest. I have tried opium, but its help is counterbalanced with great disturbance; it prevents the spasms, but it hinders sleep. O God, have mercy on me.

Last week I published the *Lives of the Poets*, written, I hope, in such a manner as may tend to the promotion of piety.

In this last year I have made little acquisition; I have scarcely read anything. I maintain Mrs. [Desmoulins] and her daughter. Other good of myself I know not where to find, except a little charity.

But I am now in my seventieth year; what can be done, ought not to be delayed.

Rambler No. 4

[On Fiction]

Saturday, March 31, 1750

Simul et jucunda et idonea dicere vitae.
—HORACE, *Art of Poetry*, 334
And join both profit and delight in one.
—CREECH

The works of fiction with which the present generation seems more particularly delighted are such as exhibit life in its true state, diversified only by accidents that daily happen in the world, and influenced by passions and qualities which are really to be found in conversing with mankind.

This kind of writing may be termed, not improperly, the comedy of romance, and is to be conducted nearly by the rules of comic poetry. Its province is to bring about natural events by easy means, and to keep up curiosity without the help of wonder: it is therefore precluded from the machines[1] and expedients of the heroic romance, and can neither employ giants to snatch away a lady from the nuptial rites, nor knights to bring her back from captivity; it can neither bewilder its personages in deserts, nor lodge them in imaginary castles.

I remember a remark made by Scaliger upon Pontanus,[2] that all his writings are filled with the same images; and that if you take from him his lilies and his roses, his satyrs and his dryads, he will have nothing left that can be called poetry. In like manner, almost

1. The technical term in neoclassical critical theory for the supernatural agents who intervene in human affairs in epic and tragedy.

2. Julius Caesar Scaliger (1484–1558) criticized the Latin poems of the Italian poet Jovianus Pontanus (1426–1503).

all the fictions of the last age will vanish if you deprive them of a hermit and a wood, a battle and a shipwreck.

Why this wild strain of imagination found reception so long in polite and learned ages, it is not easy to conceive; but we cannot wonder that while readers could be procured, the authors were willing to continue it; for when a man had by practice gained some fluency of language, he had no further care than to retire to his closet, let loose his invention, and heat his mind with incredibilities; a book was thus produced without fear of criticism, without the toil of study, without knowledge of nature, or acquaintance with life.

The task of our present writers is very different; it requires, together with that learning which is to be gained from books, that experience which can never be attained by solitary diligence, but must arise from general converse and accurate observation of the living world. Their performances have, as Horace expresses it, *plus oneris quanto veniae minus*,[3] little indulgence, and therefore more difficulty. They are engaged in portraits of which everyone knows the original, and can detect any deviation from exactness of resemblance. Other writings are safe, except from the malice of learning, but these are in danger from every common reader; as the slipper ill executed was censured by a shoemaker who happened to stop in his way at the Venus of Appeles.[4]

But the fear of not being approved as just copiers of human manners is not the most important concern that an author of this sort ought to have before him. These books are written chiefly to the young, the ignorant, and the idle, to whom they serve as lectures of conduct, and introductions into life. They are the entertainment of minds unfurnished with ideas, and therefore easily susceptible of impressions; not fixed by principles, and therefore easily following the current of fancy; not informed by experience, and consequently open to every false suggestion and partial account.

That the highest degree of reverence should be paid to youth, and that nothing indecent should be suffered to approach their eyes or ears, are precepts extorted by sense and virtue from an ancient writer by no means eminent for chastity of thought. The same kind, though not the same degree, of caution, is required in everything which is laid before them, to secure them from unjust prejudices, perverse opinions, and incongruous combinations of images.

In the romances formerly written, every transaction and sentiment was so remote from all that passes among men that the reader was in very little danger of making any applications to himself; the virtues and crimes were equally beyond his sphere of activity; and

3. *Epistles* II.i.170.
4. According to Pliny the Younger (*Naturalis Historia* XXXV.85), the Greek painter Apelles of Kos (4th century B.C.) corrected the drawing of a sandal after hearing a shoemaker criticize it as faulty, but when the flattered artisan dared to find fault with the drawing of a leg, the artist bade him "stick to his last."

he amused himself with heroes and with traitors, deliverers and persecutors, as with beings of another species, whose actions were regulated upon motives of their own, and who had neither faults nor excellencies in common with himself.

But when an adventurer is leveled with the rest of the world, and acts in such scenes of the universal drama as may be the lot of any other man, young spectators fix their eyes upon him with closer attention, and hope, by observing his behavior and success, to regulate their own practices when they shall be engaged in the like part.

For this reason these familiar histories may perhaps be made of greater use than the solemnities of professed morality, and convey the knowledge of vice and virtue with more efficacy than axioms and definitions. But if the power of example is so great as to take possession of the memory by a kind of violence, and produce effects almost without the intervention of the will, care ought to be taken that when the choice is unrestrained, the best examples only should be exhibited; and that which is likely to operate so strongly should not be mischievous or uncertain in its effects.

The chief advantage which these fictions have over real life is that their authors are at liberty, though not to invent, yet to select objects, and to cull from the mass of mankind those individuals upon which the attention ought most to be employed; as a diamond, though it cannot be made, may be polished by art, and placed in such situation as to display that luster which before was buried among common stones.

It is justly considered as the greatest excellency of art to imitate nature; but it is necessary to distinguish those parts of nature which are most proper for imitation: greater care is still required in representing life, which is so often discolored by passion or deformed by wickedness. If the world be promiscuously described, I cannot see of what use it can be to read the account; or why it may not be as safe to turn the eye immediately upon mankind as upon a mirror which shows all that presents itself without discrimination.

It is therefore not a sufficient vindication of a character that it is drawn as it appears; for many characters ought never to be drawn: nor of a narrative that the train of events is agreeable to observation and experience; for that observation which is called knowledge of the world will be found much more frequently to make men cunning than good. The purpose of these writings is surely not only to show mankind, but to provide that they may be seen hereafter with less hazard; to teach the means of avoiding the snares which are laid by Treachery for Innocence, without infusing any wish for that superiority with which the betrayer flatters his vanity; to give the power of counteracting fraud without the temptation to practice it; to initiate youth by mock encounters in the art of necessary defense, and to increase prudence without impairing virtue.

Many writers, for the sake of following nature, so mingle good and bad qualities in their principal personages that they are both equally conspicuous; and as we accompany them through their adventures with delight, and are led by degrees to interest ourselves in their favor, we lose the abhorrence of their faults because they do not hinder our pleasure, or perhaps regard them with some kindness for being united with so much merit.

There have been men indeed splendidly wicked, whose endowments threw a brightness on their crimes, and whom scarce any villainy made perfectly detestable because they never could be wholly divested of their excellencies; but such have been in all ages the great corrupters of the world, and their resemblance ought no more to be preserved than the art of murdering without pain.

Some have advanced, without due attention to the consequence of this notion, that certain virtues have their correspondent faults, and therefore that to exhibit either apart is to deviate from probability. Thus men are observed by Swift to be "grateful in the same degree as they are resentful." This principle, with others of the same kind, supposes man to act from a brute impulse, and pursue a certain degree of inclination without any choice of the object; for, otherwise, though it should be allowed that gratitude and resentment arise from the same constitution of the passions, it follows not that they will be equally indulged when reason is consulted; yet, unless that consequence be admitted, this sagacious maxim becomes an empty sound, without any relation to practice or to life.

Nor is it evident that even the first motions to these effects are always in the same proportion. For pride, which produces quickness of resentment, will obstruct gratitude by unwillingness to admit that inferiority which obligation implies; and it is very unlikely that he who cannot think he receives a favor will acknowledge or repay it.

It is of the utmost importance to mankind that positions of this tendency should be laid open and confuted; for while men consider good and evil as springing from the same root, they will spare the one for the sake of the other, and in judging, if not of others at least of themselves, will be apt to estimate their virtues by their vices. To this fatal error all those will contribute who confound the colors of right and wrong, and, instead of helping to settle their boundaries, mix them with so much art that no common mind is able to disunite them.

In narratives where historical veracity has no place, I cannot discover why there should not be exhibited the most perfect idea of virtue; of virtue not angelical, nor above probability (for what we cannot credit, we shall never imitate), but the highest and purest that humanity can reach, which, exercised in such trials as the various revolutions of things shall bring upon it, may, by conquering some calamities and enduring others, teach us what we may hope, and what we can perform. Vice (for vice is necessary to be shown) should always disgust; nor should the graces of gaiety, nor the dignity of courage, be so united with it as to reconcile it to the mind. Wherever it appears, it should raise hatred by the malignity of its practices, and contempt by the meanness of its stratagems: for while it is supported by either parts or spirit, it will be seldom heartily abhorred. The Roman tyrant was content to be hated if he was but feared; [5] and there are thousands of the readers of romances willing to be thought wicked if they may be allowed to be wits. It is therefore to be steadily inculcated that virtue is the highest proof of understanding, and the only solid basis of greatness; and that vice is the natural consequence of narrow thoughts; that it begins in mistake, and ends in ignominy.

From The Preface to Shakespeare [1]
[*Shakespeare and General Nature*]

The poet of whose works I have undertaken the revision may now begin to assume the dignity of an ancient and claim the privilege of established fame and prescriptive veneration. He has long outlived his century, the term commonly fixed as the test of literary merit.[1a] Whatever advantages he might once derive from personal allusions, local customs, or temporary opinions, have for many years been lost; and every topic of merriment or motive of sorrow which the modes of artificial life afforded him now only obscure the scenes which they once illuminated. The effects of favor and competition are at an end; the tradition of his friendships and his enmities has perished; his works support no opinion with arguments nor

5. The Emperor Tiberius. See Suetonius' *Lives of the Caesars.*

1. This, the finest piece of Shakespeare criticism in the 18th century, is the culmination of a critical tradition that began with Nicholas Rowe's edition of the plays in 1709 (indeed with Dryden's critical remarks on Shakespeare) and that was continued by subsequent editors, notably Pope, Lewis Theobald, and William Warburton. Johnson's topics are in the main the conventional ones of 18th-century Shakespeare criticism: Shakespeare as the poet of nature, not of learning; as the creator of memorable characters; as a poet who supremely expresses and evokes the passions. Johnson follows his tradition in weighing Shakespeare's poetic virtues against his faults and finding that the virtues out-

weigh the faults. No one has praised Shakespeare more nobly and generously. The *Preface* is most original when Johnson attacks and dismisses the long-standing reverence in critical theory for the unities of time and place. By appealing to the experience of the play-goer, he demonstrates that, thanks to the imagination of the spectator, the playwright need not contain his action within a period of twenty-four hours or restrict it to one place throughout the drama.

Johnson's edition of Shakespeare also contained footnotes and brief introductions to each of the plays. We reprint here the introductory headnote to the two Henry IV plays.

1a. Horace, *Epistles* II.1.39.

supply any faction with invectives; they can neither indulge vanity nor gratify malignity; but are read without any other reason than the desire of pleasure, and are therefore praised only as pleasure is obtained; yet, thus unassisted by interest or passion, they have passed through variations of taste and changes of manners, and, as they devolved from one generation to another, have received new honors at every transmission.

But because human judgment, though it be gradually gaining upon certainty, never becomes infallible, and approbation, though long continued, may yet be only the approbation of prejudice or fashion, it is proper to inquire by what peculiarities of excellence Shakespeare has gained and kept the favor of his countrymen.

Nothing can please many, and please long, but just representations of general nature. Particular manners can be known to few, and therefore few only can judge how nearly they are copied. The irregular combinations of fanciful invention may delight awhile by that novelty of which the common satiety of life sends us all in quest; but the pleasures of sudden wonder are soon exhausted, and the mind can only repose on the stability of truth.

Shakespeare is, above all writers, at least above all modern writers, the poet of nature, the poet that holds up to his readers a faithful mirror of manners and of life. His characters are not modified by the customs of particular places, unpracticed by the rest of the world; by the peculiarities of studies or professions, which can operate but upon small numbers; or by the accidents of transient fashions or temporary opinions: they are the genuine progeny of common humanity, such as the world will always supply and observation will always find. His persons act and speak by the influence of those general passions and principles by which all minds are agitated and the whole system of life is continued in motion. In the writings of other poets a character is too often an individual: in those of Shakespeare it is commonly a species.

It is from this wide extension of design that so much instruction is derived. It is this which fills the plays of Shakespeare with practical axioms and domestic wisdom. It was said of Euripides[2] that every verse was a precept; and it may be said of Shakespeare that from his works may be collected a system of civil and economical prudence. Yet his real power is not shown in the splendor of particular passages, but by the progress of his fable and the tenor of his dialogue; and he that tries to recommend him by select quotations will succeed like the pedant in Hierocles[3] who, when he offered his house to sale, carried a brick in his pocket as a specimen.

It will not easily be imagined how much Shakespeare excels in accommodating his sentiments to real life but by comparing him

---

2. The Greek tragic poet (ca. 480–406 B.C.). The observation is Cicero's.

3. Hierocles of Alexandria, a Greek philosopher of the 5th century A.D.

with other authors. It was observed of the ancient schools of declamation that the more diligently they were frequented, the more was the student disqualified for the world, because he found nothing there which he should ever meet in any other place. The same remark may be applied to every stage but that of Shakespeare. The theater, when it is under any other direction, is peopled by such characters as were never seen, conversing in a language which was never heard, upon topics which will never arise in the commerce of mankind. But the dialogue of this author is often so evidently determined by the incident which produces it, and is pursued with so much ease and simplicity, that it seems scarcely to claim the merit of fiction, but to have been gleaned by diligent selection out of common conversation and common occurrences.

Upon every other stage the universal agent is love, by whose power all good and evil is distributed and every action quickened or retarded. To bring a lover, a lady, and a rival into the fable; to entangle them in contradictory obligations, perplex them with oppositions of interest, and harass them with violence of desires inconsistent with each other; to make them meet in rapture, and part in agony; to fill their mouths with hyperbolical joy and outrageous sorrow; to distress them as nothing human ever was distressed; to deliver them as nothing human ever was delivered, is the business of a modern dramatist. For this, probability is violated, life is misrepresented, and language is depraved. But love is only one of many passions; and as it has no great influence upon the sum of life, it has little operation in the dramas of a poet who caught his ideas from the living world and exhibited only what he saw before him. He knew that any other passion, as it was regular or exorbitant, was a cause of happiness or calamity.

Characters thus ample and general were not easily discriminated and preserved; yet perhaps no poet ever kept his personages more distinct from each other. I will not say with Pope that every speech may be assigned to the proper speaker,[4] because many speeches there are which have nothing characteristical; but perhaps though some may be equally adapted to every person, it will be difficult to find that any can be properly transferred from the present possessor to another claimant. The choice is right when there is reason for choice.

Other dramatists can only gain attention by hyperbolical or aggravated characters, by fabulous and unexampled excellence or depravity, as the writers of barbarous romances invigorated the reader by a giant and a dwarf; and he that should form his expectations of human affairs from the play or from the tale would be equally deceived. Shakespeare has no heroes; his scenes are occupied only by men, who act and speak as the reader thinks that he should himself

4. In the preface to his edition of Shakespeare's plays (1725).

have spoken or acted on the same occasion; even where the agency is supernatural, the dialogue is level with life. Other writers disguise the most natural passions and most frequent incidents so that he who contemplates them in the book will not know them in the world: Shakespeare approximates[5] the remote, and familiarizes the wonderful; the event which he represents will not happen, but, if it were possible, its effects would probably be such as he has assigned; and it may be said that he has not only shown human nature as it acts in real exigencies, but as it would be found in trials to which it cannot be exposed.

This therefore is the praise of Shakespeare, that his drama is the mirror of life; that he who has mazed his imagination in following the phantoms which other writers raise up before him, may here be cured of his delirious ecstasies by reading human sentiments in human language, by scenes from which a hermit may estimate the transactions of the world, and a confessor predict the progress of the passions.

[Shakespeare's Faults. The Three Dramatic Unities]

Shakespeare with his excellencies has likewise faults, and faults sufficient to obscure and overwhelm any other merit. I shall show them in the proportion in which they appear to me, without envious malignity or superstitious veneration. No question can be more innocently discussed than a dead poet's pretensions to renown; and little regard is due to that bigotry which sets candor[6] higher than truth.

His first defect is that to which may be imputed most of the evil in books or in men. He sacrifices virtue to convenience, and is so much more careful to please than to instruct that he seems to write without any moral purpose. From his writings indeed a system of social duty may be selected, for he that thinks reasonably must think morally, but his precepts and axioms drop casually from him; he makes no just distribution of good or evil, nor is always careful to show in the virtuous a disapprobation of the wicked; he carries his persons indifferently through right and wrong, and at the close dismisses them without further care, and leaves their examples to operate by chance. This fault the barbarity of his age cannot extenuate; for it is always a writer's duty to make the world better, and justice is a virtue independent on time or place.

The plots are often so loosely formed that a very slight consideration may improve them, and so carelessly pursued that he seems not always fully to comprehend his own design. He omits opportunities of instructing or delighting which the train of his story seems to force upon him, and apparently rejects those exhibitions

5. Brings near. 6. Kindness.

which would be more affecting for the sake of those which are more easy.

It may be observed that in many of his plays the latter part is evidently neglected. When he found himself near the end of his work, and in view of his reward, he shortened the labor to snatch the profit. He therefore remits his efforts where he should most vigorously exert them, and his catastrophe is improbably produced or imperfectly represented.

He had no regard to distinction of time or place, but gives to one age or nation, without scruple, the customs, institutions, and opinions of another, at the expense not only of likelihood but of possibility. These faults Pope has endeavored, with more zeal than judgment, to transfer to his imagined interpolators. We need not wonder to find Hector quoting Aristotle, when we see the loves of Theseus and Hippolyta combined with the Gothic mythology of fairies.[7] Shakespeare, indeed, was not the only violator of chronology, for in the same age Sidney, who wanted not the advantages of learning, has, in his *Arcadia*, confounded the pastoral with the feudal times, the days of innocence, quiet, and security with those of turbulence, violence, and adventure.

In his comic scenes he is seldom very successful when he engages his characters in reciprocations of smartness and contests of sarcasm; their jests are commonly gross, and their pleasantry licentious; neither his gentlemen nor his ladies have much delicacy, nor are sufficiently distinguished from his clowns by any appearance of refined manners. Whether he represented the real conversation of his time is not easy to determine: the reign of Elizabeth is commonly supposed to have been a time of stateliness, formality, and reserve; yet perhaps the relaxations of that severity were not very elegant. There must, however, have been always some modes of gaiety preferable to others, and a writer ought to choose the best.

In tragedy his performance seems constantly to be worse as his labor is more. The effusions of passion, which exigence forces out, are for the most part striking and energetic; but whenever he solicits his invention, or strains his faculties, the offspring of his throes is tumor,[8] meanness, tediousness, and obscurity.

In narration he affects a disproportionate pomp of diction and a wearisome train of circumlocution, and tells the incident imperfectly in many words which might have been more plainly delivered in few. Narration in dramatic poetry is naturally tedious, as it is unanimated and inactive, and obstructs the progress of the action; it should therefore always be rapid and enlivened by frequent interruption. Shakespeare found it an encumbrance, and instead of

7. In *Troilus and Cressida*, II.2.166, and in *Midsummer Night's Dream*, re- spectively.

8. Inflated grandeur, false magnificence.

lightening it by brevity, endeavored to recommend it by dignity and splendor.

His declamations or set speeches are commonly cold and weak, for his power was the power of nature; when he endeavored, like other tragic writers, to catch opportunities of amplification and, instead of inquiring what the occasion demanded, to show how much his stores of knowledge could supply, he seldom escapes without the pity or resentment of his reader.

It is incident to him to be now and then entangled with an unwieldy sentiment which he cannot well express, and will not reject; he struggles with it awhile, and, if it continues stubborn, comprises it in words such as occur, and leaves it to be disentangled and evolved by those who have more leisure to bestow upon it.

Not that always where the language is intricate the thought is subtle, or the image always great where the line is bulky; the equality of words to things is very often neglected, and trivial sentiments and vulgar[9] ideas disappoint the attention, to which they are recommended by sonorous epithets and swelling figures.

But the admirers of this great poet have most reason to complain when he approaches nearest to his highest excellence, and seems fully resolved to sink them in dejection and mollify them with tender emotions by the fall of greatness, the danger of innocence, or the crosses of love. What he does best, he soon ceases to do. He is not long soft and pathetic without some idle conceit or contemptible equivocation. He no sooner begins to move than he counteracts himself; and terror and pity, as they are rising in the mind, are checked and blasted by sudden frigidity.

A quibble[1] is to Shakespeare what luminous vapors are to the traveler: he follows it at all adventures; it is sure to lead him out of his way, and sure to engulf him in the mire. It has some malignant power over his mind, and its fascinations are irresistible. Whatever be the dignity or profundity of his disquisitions, whether he be enlarging knowledge or exalting affection, whether he be amusing[2] attention with incidents, or enchaining it in suspense, let but a quibble spring up before him, and he leaves his work unfinished. A quibble is the golden apple for which he will always turn aside from his career[3] or stoop from his elevation. A quibble, poor and barren as it is, gave him such delight that he was content to purchase it by the sacrifice of reason, propriety, and truth. A

9. "Mean; low; being of the common rate" (Johnson's *Dictionary*).
1. Pun.
2. "To entertain with tranquility; to fill with thoughts that engage the mind, without distracting it" (Johnson's *Dictionary*).

3. In Greek legend Atalanta refused to marry any man who could not defeat her in a foot race. Hippomenes won her by dropping, as he ran, three of the golden apples of the Hesperides, which she paused to pick up.

quibble was to him the fatal Cleopatra for which he lost the world, and was content to lose it.

It will be thought strange that in enumerating the defects of this writer, I have not yet mentioned his neglect of the unities; his violation of those laws which have been instituted and established by the joint authority of poets and critics.

For his other deviations from the art of writing, I resign him to critical justice without making any other demand in his favor than that which must be indulged to all human excellence: that his virtues be rated with his failings. But from the censure which this irregularity may bring upon him I shall, with due reverence to that learning which I must oppose, adventure to try how I can defend him.

His histories, being neither tragedies nor comedies, are not subject to any of their laws; nothing more is necessary to all the praise which they expect than that the changes of action be so prepared as to be understood; that the incidents be various and affecting, and the characters consistent, natural, and distinct. No other unity is intended, and therefore none is to be sought.

In his other works he has well enough preserved the unity of action. He has not, indeed, an intrigue regularly perplexed and regularly unraveled: he does not endeavor to hide his design only to discover it, for this is seldom the order of real events, and Shakespeare is the poet of nature: but his plan has commonly what Aristotle requires,[4] a beginning, a middle, and an end; one event is concatenated with another, and the conclusion follows by easy consequence. There are, perhaps, some incidents that might be spared, as in other poets there is much talk that only fills up time upon the stage; but the general system makes gradual advances, and the end of the play is the end of expectation.

To the unities of time and place he has shown no regard; and perhaps a nearer view of the principles on which they stand will diminish their value and withdraw from them the veneration which, from the time of Corneille,[5] they have very generally received, by discovering that they have given more trouble to the poet than pleasure to the auditor.

The necessity of observing the unities of time and place arises from the supposed necessity of making the drama credible. The critics hold it impossible that an action of months or years can be possibly believed to pass in three hours; or that the spectator can suppose himself to sit in the theater while ambassadors go and return between distant kings, while armies are levied and towns besieged, while an exile wanders and returns, or till he whom they saw court-

4. *Poetics* VII.
5. Pierre Corneille (1606–84), the French playwright, discussed the unities in his *Discours des trois unités* (1660).

ing his mistress shall lament the untimely fall of his son. The mind
revolts from evident falsehood, and fiction loses its force when it
departs from the resemblance of reality.

From the narrow limitation of time necessarily arises the contraction of place. The spectator who knows that he saw the first act
at Alexandria cannot suppose that he sees the next at Rome, at a
distance to which not the dragons of Medea could, in so short a
time, have transported him; he knows with certainty that he has
not changed his place; and he knows that place cannot change
itself, that what was a house cannot become a plain, that what was
Thebes can never be Persepolis.

Such is the triumphant language with which a critic exults over
the misery of an irregular poet, and exults commonly without resistance or reply. It is time, therefore, to tell him by the authority
of Shakespeare that he assumes, as an unquestionable principle, a
position which, while his breath is forming it into words, his understanding pronounces to be false. It is false that any representation
is mistaken for reality; that any dramatic fable in its materiality
was ever credible or, for a single moment, was ever credited.

The objection arising from the impossibility of passing the first
hour at Alexandria and the next at Rome supposes that when the
play opens the spectator really imagines himself at Alexandria, and
believes that his walk to the theater has been a voyage to Egypt,
and that he lives in the days of Antony and Cleopatra. Surely he
that imagines this may imagine more. He that can take the stage
at one time for the palace of the Ptolemies may take it in half an
hour for the promontory of Actium. Delusion, if delusion be admitted, has no certain limitation; if the spectator can be once persuaded that his old acquaintances are Alexander and Caesar, that
a room illuminated with candles is the plain of Pharsalia or the
bank of Granicus, he is in a state of elevation above the reach of
reason or of truth, and from the heights of empyrean poetry may
despise the circumscriptions of terrestrial nature. There is no reason
why a mind thus wandering in ecstasy should count the clock, or
why an hour should not be a century in that calenture[6] of the brain
that can make the stage a field.

The truth is that the spectators are always in their senses, and
know, from the first act to the last, that the stage is only a stage,
and that the players are only players. They came to hear a certain
number of lines recited with just gesture and elegant modulation.
The lines relate to some action, and an action must be in some
place; but the different actions that complete a story may be in
places very remote from each other; and where is the absurdity of

6. A delirium produced by tropical
heat, which causes sailors to leap into
the sea under the delusion that it is a
green field.

allowing that space to represent first Athens, and then Sicily, which was always known to be neither Sicily nor Athens but a modern theater?

By supposition, as place is introduced, time may be extended; the time required by the fable elapses, for the most part, between the acts; for, of so much of the action as is represented, the real and poetical duration is the same. If, in the first act, preparations for war against Mithridates are represented to be made in Rome, the event of the war may, without absurdity, be represented, in the catastrophe, as happening in Pontus; we know that there is neither war nor preparation for war; we know that we are neither in Rome nor Pontus, that neither Mithridates nor Lucullus are before us. The drama exhibits successive imitations of successive actions; and why may not the second imitation represent an action that happened years after the first, if it be so connected with it that nothing but time can be supposed to intervene? Time is, of all modes of existence, most obsequious[7] to the imagination; a lapse of years is as easily conceived as a passage of hours. In contemplation we easily contract the time of real actions, and therefore willingly permit it to be contracted when we only see their imitation.

It will be asked how the drama moves if it is not credited. It is credited with all the credit due to a drama. It is credited, whenever it moves, as a just picture of a real original; as representing to the auditor what he would himself feel if he were to do or suffer what is there feigned to be suffered or to be done. The reflection that strikes the heart is not that the evils before us are real evils, but that they are evils to which we ourselves may be exposed. If there be any fallacy, it is not that we fancy the players, but that we fancy ourselves, unhappy for a moment; but we rather lament the possibility than suppose the presence of misery, as a mother weeps over her babe when she remembers that death may take it from her. The delight of tragedy proceeds from our consciousness of fiction; if we thought murders and treasons real, they would please no more.

Imitations produce pain or pleasure, not because they are mistaken for realities, but because they bring realities to mind. When the imagination is recreated by a painted landscape, the trees are not supposed capable to give us shade or the fountains coolness; but we consider how we should be pleased with such fountains playing beside us and such woods waving over us. We are agitated in reading the history of *Henry the Fifth*; yet no man takes his book for the field of Agincourt. A dramatic exhibition is a book recited with concomitants that increase or diminish its effect. Familiar comedy is often more powerful on the theater than in the page; imperial tragedy is always less. The humor of Petruchio may be heightened by grimace; but what voice or what gesture can hope to

7. "Obedient; compliant" (Johnson's *Dictionary*).

add dignity or force to the soliloquy of Cato?[8]

A play read affects the mind like a play acted. It is therefore evident that the action is not supposed to be real; and it follows that between the acts a longer or shorter time may be allowed to pass, and that no more account of space or duration is to be taken by the auditor of a drama than by the reader of a narrative, before whom may pass in an hour the life of a hero or the revolutions of an empire.

Whether Shakespeare knew the unities and rejected them by design or deviated from them by happy ignorance, it is, I think, impossible to decide and useless to inquire. We may reasonably suppose that, when he rose to notice, he did not want[9] the counsels and admonitions of scholars and critics, and that he at last deliberately persisted in a practice which he might have begun by chance. As nothing is essential to the fable but unity of action, and as the unities of time and place arise evidently from false assumptions, and, by circumscribing the extent of the drama, lessen its variety, I cannot think it much to be lamented that they were not known by him, or not observed: nor, if such another poet could arise, should I very vehemently reproach him that his first act passed at Venice and his next in Cyprus.[1] Such violations of rules merely positive become the comprehensive genius of Shakespeare, and such censures are suitable to the minute and slender criticism of Voltaire.

> *Non usque adeo permiscuit imis*
> *Longus summa dies, ut non, si voce Metelli*
> *Serventur leges, malint a Caesare tolli.*[2]

Yet when I speak thus slightly of dramatic rules, I cannot but recollect how much wit and learning may be produced against me; before such authorities I am afraid to stand: not that I think the present question one of those that are to be decided by mere authority, but because it is to be suspected that these precepts have not been so easily received but for better reasons than I have yet been able to find. The result of my inquiries, in which it would be ludicrous to boast of impartiality, is that the unities of time and place are not essential to a just drama, that though they may sometimes conduce to pleasure, they are always to be sacrificed to the nobler beauties of variety and instruction; and that a play written with nice observation of critical rules is to be contemplated as an elaborate curiosity, as the product of superfluous and ostentatious art, by which is shown rather what is possible than what is necessary.

8. Petruchio is the hero of Shakespeare's comedy *The Taming of the Shrew*. In Addison's tragedy *Cato* (V.i), the hero soliloquizes on immortality shortly before committing suicide.
9. Lack.

1. As is the case in *Othello*.
2. Lucan, *Pharsalia* III.138–40: "The course of time has not wrought such confusion that the laws would not rather be trampled on by Caesar than saved by Metellus."

He that without diminution of any other excellence shall preserve all the unities unbroken deserves the like applause with the architect who shall display all the orders of architecture in a citadel without any deduction for its strength; but the principal beauty of a citadel is to exclude the enemy, and the greatest graces of a play are to copy nature and instruct life. * * *

[Henry IV]

None of Shakespeare's plays are more read than the first and second parts of *Henry the fourth*. Perhaps no author has ever in two plays afforded so much delight. The great events are interesting, for the fate of kingdoms depends upon them; the slighter occurrences are diverting, and, except one or two, sufficiently probable; the incidents are multiplied with wonderful fertility of invention, and the characters diversified with the utmost nicety of discernment, and the profoundest skill in the nature of man.

The prince, who is the hero both of the comic and tragic part, is a young man of great abilities and violent passions, whose sentiments are right, though his actions are wrong; whose virtues are obscured by negligence, and whose understanding is dissipated by levity. In his idle hours he is rather loose than wicked, and when the occasion forces out his latent qualities, he is great without effort, and brave without tumult. The trifler is roused into a hero, and the hero again reposes in the trifler. This character is great, original, and just.[3]

Percy is a rugged soldier, choleric, and quarrelsome, and has only the soldier's virtues, generosity and courage.

But Falstaff, unimitated, unimitable Falstaff, how shall I describe thee? Thou compound of sense and vice; of sense which may be admired but not esteemed, of vice which may be despised, but hardly detested. Falstaff is a character loaded with faults, and with those faults which naturally produce contempt. He is a thief, and a glutton, a coward, and a boaster, always ready to cheat the weak, and prey upon the poor; to terrify the timorous and insult the defenseless. At once obsequious and malignant, he satirizes in their absence those whom he lives by flattering. He is familiar with the prince only as an agent of vice, but of this familiarity he is so proud as not only to be supercilious and haughty with common men, but to think his interest of importance to the duke of Lancaster. Yet the man thus corrupt, thus despicable, makes himself necessary to the prince that despises him, by the most pleasing of all qualities, perpetual gaiety, by an unfailing power of exciting laughter, which is the more freely indulged, as his wit is not of the splendid or ambitious kind, but consists in easy escapes and sallies of levity, which make sport but raise no envy. It must be

3. **Exact.**

observed that he is stained with no enormous or sanguinary crimes, so that his licentiousness is not so offensive but that it may be borne for his mirth.

The moral to be drawn from this representation is that no man is more dangerous than he that with a will to corrupt, hath the power to please; and that neither wit nor honesty ought to think themselves safe with such a companion when they see Henry seduced by Falstaff.

1765

From LIVES OF THE POETS
From Cowley[1]
[*Metaphysical Wit*]

Wit, like all other things subject by their nature to the choice of man, has its changes and fashions, and at different times takes different forms. About the beginning of the seventeenth century appeared a race of writers that may be termed the metaphysical poets,[2] of whom in a criticism on the works of Cowley it is not improper to give some account.

The metaphysical poets were men of learning, and to show their learning was their whole endeavor; but, unluckily resolving to show it in rhyme, instead of writing poetry they only wrote verses, and very often such verses as stood the trial of the finger better than of the ear; for the modulation was so imperfect that they were only found to be verses by counting the syllables.

If the father of criticism[3] has rightly denominated poetry $\tau\epsilon\chi\nu\eta$ $\mu\iota\mu\eta\tau\iota\kappa\dot{\eta}$, *an imitative art*, these writers will without great wrong lose their right to the name of poets, for they cannot be said to have imitated anything: they neither copied nature nor life; neither painted the forms of matter nor represented the operations of intellect.

Those however who deny them to be poets allow them to be wits. Dryden confesses of himself and his contemporaries that they fall below Donne in it, but maintains that they surpass him in poetry.[4]

If wit be well described by Pope as being "that which has been often thought, but was never before so well expressed,"[5] they cer-

1. Abraham Cowley (1618–67) was much admired during the middle of the 17th century. His reputation began to decline before 1700, but he was remembered as a writer of false wit, especially in his love poems *The Mistress*.
2. Presumably Johnson took this now common designation from a hint in Dryden's *Discourse Concerning the Original and Progress of Satire*, 1693. Dryden condemned Donne because "he

affects the metaphysics * * * and perplexes the minds of the fair sex with nice speculations of philosophy, when he should engage their hearts, and entertain them with the softnesses of love" (*Essays*, ed. W. P. Ker, II.19).
3. Aristotle in his *Poetics*.
4. *Discourse * * * of Satire* (Ker II.102).
5. *Essay on Criticism*, lines 297–98.

tainly never attained nor ever sought it, for they endeavored to be singular in their thoughts, and were careless of their diction. But Pope's account of wit is undoubtedly erroneous; he depresses it below its natural dignity, and reduces it from strength of thought to happiness of language.

If by a more noble and more adequate conception that be considered as wit which is at once natural and new, that which though not obvious is, upon its first production, acknowledged to be just; if it be that which he that never found it, wonders how he missed; to wit of this kind the metaphysical poets have seldom risen. Their thoughts are often new, but seldom natural; they are not obvious, but neither are they just;[6] and the reader, far from wondering that he missed them, wonders more frequently by what perverseness of industry they were ever found.

But wit, abstracted from its effects upon the hearer, may be more rigorously and philosophically considered as a kind of *discordia concors*;[7] a combination of dissimilar images, or discovery of occult resemblances in things apparently unlike. Of wit, thus defined, they have more than enough. The most heterogeneous ideas are yoked by violence together; nature and art are ransacked for illustrations, comparisons, and allusions; their learning instructs, and their subtlety surprises; but the reader commonly thinks his improvement dearly bought, and, though he sometimes admires, is seldom pleased.

From this account of their compositions it will be readily inferred that they were not successful in representing or moving the affections. As they were wholly employed on something unexpected and surprising, they had no regard to that uniformity of sentiment which enables us to conceive and to excite the pains and the pleasure of other minds: they never inquired what on any occasion they should have said or done, but wrote rather as beholders than partakers of human nature; as beings looking upon good and evil, impassive and at leisure; as Epicurean deities making remarks on the actions of men and the vicissitudes of life, without interest and without emotion. Their courtship was void of fondness and their lamentation of sorrow. Their wish was only to say what they hoped had been never said before.

Nor was the sublime more within their reach than the pathetic; for they never attempted that comprehension and expanse of thought which at once fills the whole mind, and of which the first effect is sudden astonishment, and the second rational admiration. Sublimity is produced by aggregation, and littleness by dispersion. Great thoughts are always general, and consist in positions not

6. Exact, proper.
7. Literally, "a harmonious discord." Johnson is himself being witty in using this phrase, a familiar philosophical concept denoting the general harmony of God's creation despite its manifold and often contradictory particulars.

limited by exceptions, and in descriptions not descending to minuteness. It is with great propriety that subtlety, which in its original import means exility[8] of particles, is taken in its metaphorical meaning for nicety of distinction. Those writers who lay on the watch for novelty could have little hope of greatness; for great things cannot have escaped former observation. Their attempts were always analytic: they broke every image into fragments, and could no more represent by their slender conceits and labored particularities the prospects of nature or the scenes of life, than he who dissects a sunbeam with a prism can exhibit the wide effulgence of a summer noon.

What they wanted however of the sublime they endeavored to supply by hyperbole;[9] their amplification had no limits: they left not only reason but fancy behind them, and produced combinations of confused magnificence that not only could not be credited, but could not be imagined.

Yet great labor directed by great abilities is never wholly lost: if they frequently threw away their wit upon false conceits, they likewise sometimes struck out unexpected truth: if their conceits were farfetched, they were often worth the carriage.[10] To write on their plan it was at least necessary to read and think. No man could be born a metaphysical poet, nor assume the dignity of a writer by descriptions copied from descriptions, by imitations borrowed from imitations, by traditional imagery and hereditary similes, by readiness of rhyme and volubility of syllables.

1779

From Milton[1]
[Lycidas]

One of the poems on which much praise has been bestowed is *Lycidas;* of which the diction is harsh,[2] the rhymes uncertain, and the numbers unpleasing. What beauty there is, we must therefore seek in the sentiments and images. It is not to be considered as

8. Thinness.
9. An image heightened beyond reality (see Johnson's *Dictionary*).
10. In the *Life of Addison,* Johnson wrote: "A simile may be compared to lines converging at a point, and is more excellent as the lines approach from greater distance * * * "
1. Johnson's treatment of Milton as man and poet gave great offense to many ardent Miltonians in his own day and damaged his reputation as a critic in the following century. He did not ad-

mire Milton's character, and he detested his politics and religion. But no one has praised *Paradise Lost* more handsomely. Especially offensive in the 19th century was his attack on *Lycidas.* Johnson disliked modern pastorals, recognizing that the tradition had been worn threadbare. His views on the genre may be read in *Ramblers* 36 and 37.
2. This notorious word does not mean "unmelodious," but "strained, forced, affected, or labored."

the effusion of real passion; for passion runs not after remote allusions and obscure opinions. Passion plucks no berries from the myrtle and ivy, nor calls upon Arethuse and Mincius, nor tells of "rough satyrs and fauns with cloven heel." Where there is leisure for fiction there is little grief.

In this poem there is no nature, for there is no truth; there is no art, for there is nothing new. Its form is that of a pastoral, easy, vulgar, and therefore disgusting:[3] whatever images it can supply are long ago exhausted; and its inherent improbability always forces dissatisfaction on the mind. When Cowley tells of Hervey that they studied together, it is easy to suppose how much he must miss the companion of his labors and the partner of his discoveries;[4] but what image of tenderness can be excited by these lines!

> We drove afield, and both together heard
> What time the grayfly winds her sultry horn,
> Battening our flocks with the fresh dews of night.

We know that they never drove afield, and that they had no flocks to batten; and though it be allowed that the representation may be allegorical, the true meaning is so uncertain and remote that it is never sought because it cannot be known when it is found.

Among the flocks and copses and flowers appear the heathen deities, Jove and Phoebus, Neptune and Aeolus, with a long train of mythological imagery, such as a college easily supplies. Nothing can less display knowledge or less exercise invention than to tell how a shepherd has lost his companion and must now feed his flocks alone, without any judge of his skill in piping; and how one god asks another god what is become of Lycidas, and how neither god can tell. He who thus grieves will excite no sympathy; he who thus praises will confer no honor.

This poem has yet a grosser fault. With these trifling fictions are mingled the most awful and sacred truths, such as ought never to be polluted with such irreverent combinations. The shepherd likewise is now a feeder of sheep, and afterwards an ecclesiastical pastor, a superintendent of a Christian flock. Such equivocations are always unskillful; but here they are indecent,[5] and at least approach to impiety, of which, however, I believe the writer not to have been conscious.

Such is the power of reputation justly acquired that its blaze drives away the eye from nice examination. Surely no man could have fancied that he read *Lycidas* with pleasure had he not known its author.

---

3. I.e., displeasing ("disgusting") because its stale conventionality made it "vulgar" by putting it within the reach of the many.

4. Cowley's *On the Death of Mr. William Hervey* (1656).

5. Unbecoming, lacking in decorum.

[*L'Allegro. Il Penseroso*]

Of the two pieces, *L'Allegro* and *Il Penseroso*, I believe opinion is uniform; every man that reads them, reads them with pleasure. The author's design is not, what Theobald [1] has remarked, merely to show how objects derived their colors from the mind, by representing the operation of the same things upon the gay and the melancholy temper, or upon the same man as he is differently disposed; but rather how, among the successive variety of appearances, every disposition of mind takes hold on those by which it may be gratified.

The *cheerful* man hears the lark in the morning; the *pensive* man hears the nightingale in the evening. The *cheerful* man sees the cock strut, and hears the horn and hounds echo in the wood; then walks "not unseen" to observe the glory of the rising sun or listen to the singing milkmaid, and view the labors of the plowman and the mower; then casts his eyes about him over scenes of smiling plenty, and looks up to the distant tower, the residence of some fair inhabitant: thus he pursues rural gaiety through a day of labor or of play, and delights himself at night with the fanciful narratives of superstitious ignorance.

The *pensive* man at one time walks "unseen" to muse at midnight, and at another hears the sullen curfew. If the weather drives him home he sits in a room lighted only by "glowing embers"; or by a lonely lamp outwatches the North Star to discover the habitation of separate souls, and varies the shades of meditation by contemplating the magnificent or pathetic scenes of tragic and epic poetry. When the morning comes, a morning gloomy with rain and wind, he walks into the dark trackless woods, falls asleep by some murmuring water, and with melancholy enthusiasm expects some dream of prognostication or some music played by aerial performers.

Both Mirth and Melancholy are solitary, silent inhabitants of the breast that neither receive nor transmit communication: no mention is therefore made of a philosophical friend or a pleasant companion. The seriousness does not arise from any participation of calamity, nor the gaiety from the pleasures of the bottle.

The man of *cheerfulness* having exhausted the country tries what "towered cities" will afford, and mingles with scenes of splendor, gay assemblies, and nuptial festivities; but he mingles a mere spectator as, when the learned comedies of Jonson or the wild dramas of Shakespeare are exhibited, he attends the theater.

The *pensive* man never loses himself in crowds, but walks the cloister or frequents the cathedral. Milton probably had not yet forsaken the Church.

Both his characters delight in music; but he seems to think that

1. Lewis Theobald (1688–1744), the editor of Shakespeare and the enemy of Pope.

cheerful notes would have obtained from Pluto a complete dismission of Eurydice, of whom solemn sounds only procured a conditional release.

For the old age of Cheerfulness he makes no provision; but Melancholy he conducts with great dignity to the close of life. His Cheerfulness is without levity, and his Pensiveness without asperity.

Through these two poems the images are properly selected and nicely distinguished, but the colors of the diction seem not sufficiently discriminated. I know not whether the characters are kept sufficiently apart. No mirth can, indeed, be found in his melancholy; but I am afraid that I always meet some melancholy in his mirth. They are two noble efforts of imagination.

[Paradise Lost]

Those little pieces may be dispatched without much anxiety; a greater work calls for greater care. I am now to examine *Paradise Lost*, a poem which, considered with respect to design, may claim the first place, and with respect to performance the second, among the productions of the human mind.

By the general consent of critics the first praise of genius is due to the writer of an epic poem, as it requires an assemblage of all the powers which are singly sufficient for other compositions. Poetry is the art of uniting pleasure with truth, by calling imagination to the help of reason. Epic poetry undertakes to teach the most important truths by the most pleasing precepts, and therefore relates some great event in the most affecting manner. History must supply the writer with the rudiments of narration, which he must improve and exalt by a nobler art, must animate by dramatic energy, and diversify by retrospection and anticipation; morality must teach him the exact bounds and different shades of vice and virtue; from policy and the practice of life he has to learn the discriminations of character and the tendency of the passions, either single or combined; and physiology must supply him with illustrations and images. To put these materials to poetical use is required an imagination capable of painting nature and realizing fiction. Nor is he yet a poet till he has attained the whole extension of his language, distinguished all the delicacies of phrase, and all the colors of words, and learned to adjust their different sounds to all the varieties of metrical modulation.

Bossu is of opinion that the poet's first work is to find a *moral*, which his fable is afterwards to illustrate and establish.[1] This seems to have been the process only of Milton: the moral of other poems is incidental and consequent; in Milton's only it is essential and intrinsic. His purpose was the most useful and the most arduous: "to vindicate the ways of God to man"; to show the reasonableness

---

1. Père le Bossu wrote a treatise on the epic poem, *Traité du Poëme Épique*, 1675, much admired during the late 17th and early 18th centuries.

of religion, and the necessity of obedience to the Divine Law.

To convey this moral there must be a *fable*, a narration artfully constructed, so as to excite curiosity and surprise expectation. In this part of his work Milton must be confessed to have equaled every other poet. He has involved in his account of the Fall of Man the events which preceded, and those that were to follow it: he has interwoven the whole system of theology with such propriety that every part appears to be necessary, and scarcely any recital is wished shorter for the sake of quickening the progress of the main action.

The subject of an epic poem is naturally an event of great importance. That of Milton is not the destruction of a city, the conduct of a colony, or the foundation of an empire. His subject is the fate of worlds, the revolutions of heaven and of earth; rebellion against the Supreme King raised by the highest order of created beings; the overthrow of their host and the punishment of their crime; the creation of a new race of reasonable creatures; their original happiness and innocence, their forfeiture of immortality, and their restoration to hope and peace.

Great events can be hastened or retarded only by persons of elevated dignity. Before the greatness displayed in Milton's poem all other greatness shrinks away. The weakest of his agents are the highest and noblest of human beings, the original parents of mankind; with whose actions the elements consented; on whose rectitude or deviation of will depended the state of terrestrial nature and the condition of all the future inhabitants of the globe.

Of the other agents in the poem, the chief are such as it is irreverence to name on slight occasions. The rest were lower powers;

> of which the least could wield
> Those elements, and arm him with the force
> Of all their regions; [2]

powers which only the control of Omnipotence restrains from laying creation waste, and filling the vast expanse of space with ruin and confusion. To display the motives and actions of beings thus superior, so far as human reason can examine them or human imagination represent them, is the task which this mighty poet has undertaken and performed.

In the examination of epic poems much speculation is commonly employed upon the *characters*. The characters in the *Paradise Lost* which admit of examination are those of angels and of man; of angels good and evil, of man in his innocent and sinful state.

Among the angels the virtue of Raphael is mild and placid, of easy condescension and free communication; that of Michael is regal and lofty, and, as may seem, attentive to the dignity of his own nature. Abdiel and Gabriel appear occasionally, and act as every

2. *Paradise Lost* VI.221.

incident requires; the solitary fidelity of Abdiel is very amiably painted.[3]

Of the evil angels the characters are more diversified. To Satan, as Addison observes, such sentiments are given as suit "the most exalted and most depraved being." [4] Milton has been censured by Clarke for the impiety which sometimes breaks from Satan's mouth. For there are thoughts, as he justly remarks, which no observation of character can justify, because no good man would willingly permit them to pass, however transiently, through his own mind.[5] To make Satan speak as a rebel, without any such expressions as might taint the reader's imagination, was indeed one of the great difficulties in Milton's undertaking, and I cannot but think that he has extricated himself with great happiness. There is in Satan's speeches little that can give pain to a pious ear. The language of rebellion cannot be the same with that of obedience. The malignity of Satan foams in haughtiness and obstinacy; but his expressions are commonly general, and no otherwise offensive than as they are wicked.

The other chiefs of the celestial rebellion are very judiciously discriminated in the first and second books; and the ferocious character of Moloch appears, both in the battle and the council, with exact consistency.

To Adam and to Eve are given during their innocence such sentiments as innocence can generate and utter. Their love is pure benevolence and mutual veneration; their repasts are without luxury and their diligence without toil. Their addresses to their Maker have little more than the voice of admiration and gratitude. Fruition left them nothing to ask, and Innocence left them nothing to fear.

But with guilt enter distrust and discord, mutual accusation, and stubborn self-defense; they regard each other with alienated minds, and dread their Creator as the avenger of their transgression. At last they seek shelter in his mercy, soften to repentance, and melt in supplication. Both before and after the Fall the superiority of Adam is diligently sustained.

Of the *probable* and the *marvelous*,[6] two parts of a vulgar epic poem which immerge the critic in deep consideration, the *Paradise Lost* requires little to be said. It contains the history of a miracle, of Creation and Redemption; it displays the power and the mercy of the Supreme Being: the probable therefore is marvelous, and the marvelous is probable. The substance of the narrative is truth; and as truth allows no choice, it is, like necessity, superior to rule. To the accidental or adventitious parts, as to every thing human, some slight exceptions may be made. But the main fabric is immovably supported.

3. *Paradise Lost* V.803 ff.
4. *Spectator* 303.
5. John Clarke, *Essay upon Study*, 1731.

6. Actions in an epic poem which are wonderful because they exceed the probable.

It is justly remarked by Addison [7] that this poem has, by the nature of its subject, the advantage above all others, that it is universally and perpetually interesting. All mankind will, through all ages, bear the same relation to Adam and to Eve, and must partake of that good and evil which extend to themselves.

Of the *machinery*, so called from θεὸς ἀπὸ μηχανῆς [8] by which is meant the occasional interposition of supernatural power, another fertile topic of critical remarks, here is no room to speak, because every thing is done under the immediate and visible direction of Heaven; but the rule is so far observed that no part of the action could have been accomplished by any other means.

Of *episodes* [9] I think there are only two, contained in Raphael's relation of the war in heaven and Michael's prophetic account of the changes to happen in this world. Both are closely connected with the great action; one was necessary to Adam as a warning, the other as a consolation.

To the completeness or *integrity* of the design nothing can be objected; it has distinctly and clearly what Aristotle requires, a beginning, a middle, and an end. There is perhaps no poem of the same length from which so little can be taken without apparent mutilation. Here are no funeral games, nor is there any long description of a shield. The short digressions at the beginning of the third, seventh, and ninth books might doubtless be spared; but superfluities so beautiful who would take away? or who does not wish that the author of the *Iliad* had gratified succeeding ages with a little knowledge of himself? Perhaps no passages are more frequently or more attentively read than those extrinsic paragraphs; and since the end of poetry is pleasure, that cannot be unpoetical with which all are pleased.

The questions, whether the action of the poem be strictly *one*,[1] whether the poem can be properly termed *heroic*, and who is the hero, are raised by such readers as draw their principles of judgment rather from books than from reason. Milton, though he entitled *Paradise Lost* only a "poem," yet calls it himself "heroic song." [2] Dryden, petulantly and indecently, denies the heroism of Adam because he was overcome; but there is no reason why the hero should not be unfortunate except established practice, since success and virtue do not go necessarily together. Cato is the hero of Lucan, but Lucan's authority will not be suffered by Quintilian to decide. However, if success be necessary, Adam's deceiver was at last crushed; Adam was restored to his Maker's favor, and therefore may securely resume his human rank.

After the scheme and fabric of the poem must be considered its

7. *Spectator* 273.
8. Aristotle, *Poetics* XV.10. "Deus ex machina," the intervention of supernatural powers into the affairs of men.
9. Incidental but related narratives

within an epic poem. Johnson is citing *Paradise Lost* V.577 ff. and XI.334 ff.
1. I.e., a single action dealing with a single character.
2. *Paradise Lost* IX.25.

component parts, the sentiments, and the diction.

The *sentiments*, as expressive of manners or appropriated to characters, are for the greater part unexceptionably just. Splendid passages containing lessons of morality or precepts of prudence occur seldom. Such is the original formation of this poem that as it admits no human manners till the Fall, it can give little assistance to human conduct. Its end is to raise the thoughts above sublunary cares or pleasures. Yet the praise of that fortitude, with which Abdiel maintained his singularity of virtue against the scorn of multitudes, may be accommodated to all times; and Raphael's reproof of Adam's curiosity after the planetary motions, with the answer returned by Adam, may be confidently opposed to any rule of life which any poet has delivered.[3]

The thoughts which are occasionally called forth in the progress are such as could only be produced by an imagination in the highest degree fervid and active, to which materials were supplied by incessant study and unlimited curiosity. The heat of Milton's mind might be said to sublimate his learning, to throw off into his work the spirit of science, unmingled with its grosser parts.

He had considered creation in its whole extent, and his descriptions are therefore learned. He had accustomed his imagination to unrestrained indulgence, and his conceptions therefore were extensive. The characteristic quality of his poem is sublimity. He sometimes descends to the elegant, but his element is the great. He can occasionally invest himself with grace; but his natural port is gigantic loftiness. He can please when pleasure is required; but it is his peculiar power to astonish.

He seems to have been well acquainted with his own genius, and to know what it was that Nature had bestowed upon him more bountifully than upon others; the power of displaying the vast, illuminating the splendid, enforcing the awful, darkening the gloomy, and aggravating the dreadful: he therefore chose a subject on which too much could not be said, on which he might tire his fancy without the censure of extravagance.

* * *

The defects and faults of *Paradise Lost*, for faults and defects every work of man must have, it is the business of impartial criticism to discover. As in displaying the excellence of Milton I have not made long quotations, because of selecting beauties there had been no end, I shall in the same general manner mention that which seems to deserve censure; for what Englishman can take delight in transcribing passages, which, if they lessen the reputation of Milton, diminish in some degree the honor of our country?

* * *

The plan of *Paradise Lost* has this inconvenience, that it comprises neither human actions nor human manners. The man and

3. *Paradise Lost* VIII.65 ff.

woman who act and suffer are in a state which no other man or woman can ever know. The reader finds no transaction in which he can be engaged, beholds no condition in which he can by any effort of imagination place himself; he has, therefore, little natural curiosity or sympathy.

We all, indeed, feel the effects of Adam's disobedience; we all sin like Adam, and like him must all bewail our offenses; we have restless and insidious enemies in the fallen angels, and in the blessed spirits we have guardians and friends; in the Redemption of mankind we hope to be included: in the description of heaven and hell we are surely interested, as we are all to reside hereafter either in the regions of horror or of bliss.

But these truths are too important to be new: they have been taught to our infancy; they have mingled with our solitary thoughts and familiar conversation, and are habitually interwoven with the whole texture of life. Being therefore not new they raise no unaccustomed emotion in the mind: what we knew before, we cannot learn; what is not unexpected, cannot surprise.

Of the ideas suggested by these awful scenes, from some we recede with reverence, except when stated hours require their association; and from others we shrink with horror, or admit them only as salutary inflictions, as counterpoises to our interests and passions. Such images rather obstruct the career of fancy than incite it.

Pleasure and terror are indeed the genuine sources of poetry; but poetical pleasure must be such as human imagination can at least conceive, and poetical terror such as human strength and fortitude may combat. The good and evil of Eternity are too ponderous for the wings of wit; the mind sinks under them in passive helplessness, content with calm belief and humble adoration.

Known truths however may take a different appearance, and be conveyed to the mind by a new train of intermediate images. This Milton has undertaken, and performed with pregnancy and vigor of mind peculiar to himself. Whoever considers the few radical positions which the Scriptures afforded him will wonder by what energetic operation he expanded them to such extent and ramified them to so much variety, restrained as he was by religious reverence from licentiousness of fiction.

Here is a full display of the united force of study and genius; of a great accumulation of materials, with judgment to digest and fancy to combine them: Milton was able to select from nature or from story, from ancient fable or from modern science, whatever could illustrate or adorn his thoughts. An accumulation of knowledge impregnated his mind, fermented by study and exalted by imagination.

* * *

But original deficience cannot be supplied. The want of human interest is always felt. *Paradise Lost* is one of the books which the reader admires and lays down, and forgets to take up again. None ever wished it longer than it is. Its perusal is a duty rather than a pleasure. We read Milton for instruction, retire harassed and overburdened, and look elsewhere for recreation; we desert our master, and seek for companions.

* * *

Dryden remarks that Milton has some flats among his elevations.[4] This is only to say that all the parts are not equal. In every work one part must be for the sake of others; a palace must have passages, a poem must have transitions. It is no more to be required that wit should always be blazing than that the sun should always stand at noon. In a great work there is a vicissitude [5] of luminous and opaque parts, as there is in the world a succession of day and night. Milton, when he has expatiated in the sky, may be allowed sometimes to revisit earth; for what other author ever soared so high or sustained his flight so long?

* * *

The highest praise of genius is original invention. Milton cannot be said to have contrived the structure of an epic poem, and therefore owes reverence to that vigor and amplitude of mind to which all generations must be indebted for the art of poetical narration, for the texture of the fable, the variation of incidents, the interposition of dialogue, and all the stratagems that surprise and enchain attention. But of all the borrowers from Homer Milton is perhaps the least indebted. He was naturally a thinker for himself, confident of his own abilities and disdainful of help or hindrance; he did not refuse admission to the thoughts or images of his predecessors, but he did not seek them. From his contemporaries he neither courted nor received support; there is in his writings nothing by which the pride of other authors might be gratified or favor gained, no exchange of praise or solicitation of support. His great works were performed under discountenance and in blindness, but difficulties vanished at his touch; he was born for whatever is arduous; and his work is not the greatest of heroic poems, only because it is not the first.

1779

From Pope

[*Pope's Intellectual Character. Pope and Dryden Compared*]

Of his intellectual character, the constituent and fundamental principle was good sense, a prompt and intuitive perception of consonance and propriety. He saw immediately, of his own conceptions, what was to be chosen, and what was to be rejected; and, in

4. Preface to *Sylvae;* see Essays (ed. W. P. Ker), I.268.
5. Change.

the works of others, what was to be shunned, and what was to be copied.

But good sense alone is a sedate and quiescent quality, which manages its possessions well, but does not increase them; it collects few materials for its own operations, and preserves safety, but never gains supremacy. Pope had likewise genius; a mind active, ambitious, and adventurous, always investigating, always aspiring; in its widest searches still longing to go forward, in its highest flights still wishing to be higher; always imagining something greater than it knows, always endeavoring more than it can do.

To assist these powers, he is said to have had great strength and exactness of memory. That which he had heard or read was not easily lost; and he had before him not only what his own meditation suggested, but what he had found in other writers that might be accommodated to his present purpose.

These benefits of nature he improved by incessant and unwearied diligence; he had recourse to every source of intelligence, and lost no opportunity of information; he consulted the living as well as the dead; he read his compositions to his friends, and was never content with mediocrity when excellence could be attained. He considered poetry as the business of his life, and however he might seem to lament his occupation, he followed it with constancy: to make verses was his first labor, and to mend them was his last.

From his attention to poetry he was never diverted. If conversation offered anything that could be improved, he committed it to paper; if a thought, or perhaps an expression more happy than was common, rose to his mind, he was careful to write it; an independent distich was preserved for an opportunity of insertion, and some little fragments have been found containing lines, or parts of lines, to be wrought upon at some other time.

He was one of those few whose labor is their pleasure; he was never elevated to negligence, nor wearied to impatience; he never passed a fault unamended by indifference, nor quitted it by despair. He labored his works first to gain reputation, and afterwards to keep it.

Of composition there are different methods. Some employ at once memory and invention, and, with little intermediate use of the pen, form and polish large masses by continued meditation, and write their productions only when, in their own opinion, they have completed them. It is related of Virgil[1] that his custom was to pour out a great number of verses in the morning, and pass the day in retrenching exuberances and correcting inaccuracies. The method of Pope, as may be collected from his translation, was to write his first thoughts in his first words, and gradually to amplify, decorate, rectify, and refine them.

1. By Suetonius in his brief life of the poet.

With such faculties and such dispositions, he excelled every other writer in *poetical prudence;* he wrote in such a manner as might expose him to few hazards. He used almost always the same fabric of verse; and, indeed, by those few essays which he made of any other, he did not enlarge his reputation. Of this uniformity the certain consequence was readiness and dexterity. By perpetual practice, language had in his mind a systematical arrangement; having always the same use for words, he had words so selected and combined as to be ready at his call. This increase of facility he confessed himself to have perceived in the progress of his translation.

But what was yet of more importance, his effusions were always voluntary, and his subjects chosen by himself. His independence secured him from drudging at a task, and laboring upon a barren topic: he never exchanged praise for money, nor opened a shop of condolence or congratulation. His poems, therefore, were scarce ever temporary. He suffered coronations and royal marriages to pass without a song, and derived no opportunities from recent events, nor any popularity from the accidental disposition of his readers. He was never reduced to the necessity of soliciting the sun to shine upon a birthday, of calling the Graces and Virtues to a wedding, or of saying what multitudes have said before him. When he could produce nothing new, he was at liberty to be silent.

His publications were for the same reason never hasty. He is said to have sent nothing to the press till it had lain two years under his inspection: it is at least certain that he ventured nothing without nice examination. He suffered the tumult of imagination to subside, and the novelties of invention to grow familiar. He knew that the mind is always enamored of its own productions, and did not trust his first fondness. He consulted his friends, and listened with great willingness to criticism; and, what was of more importance, he consulted himself, and let nothing pass against his own judgment.

He professed to have learned his poetry from Dryden, whom, whenever an opportunity was presented, he praised through his whole life with unvaried liberality; and perhaps his character may receive some illustration, if he be compared with his master.

Integrity of understanding and nicety of discernment were not allotted in a less proportion to Dryden than to Pope. The rectitude of Dryden's mind was sufficiently shown by the dismission of his poetical prejudices, and the rejection of unnatural thoughts and rugged numbers. But Dryden never desired to apply all the judgment that he had. He wrote, and professed to write, merely for the people; and when he pleased others, he contented himself. He spent no time in struggles to rouse latent powers; he never attempted to make that better which was already good, nor often to mend what he must have known to be faulty. He wrote, as he tells us, with very little consideration; when occasion or necessity called upon him, he poured out what the present moment happened to supply, and, when once it had passed the press, ejected it from his mind; for when he had no pecuniary interest, he had no further solicitude.

Pope was not content to satisfy; he desired to excel, and therefore always endeavored to do his best: he did not court the candor, but dared the judgment of his reader, and, expecting no indulgence from others, he showed none to himself. He examined lines and words with minute and punctilious observation, and retouched every part with indefatigable diligence, till he had left nothing to be forgiven.

For this reason he kept his pieces very long in his hands, while he considered and reconsidered them. The only poems which can be supposed to have been written with such regard to the times as might hasten their publication were the two satires of *Thirty-Eight;* of which Dodsley[2] told me that they were brought to him by the author, that they might be fairly copied. "Almost every line," he said, "was then written twice over; I gave him a clean transcript, which he sent some time afterwards to me for the press, with almost every line written twice over a second time."

His declaration, that his care for his works ceased at their publication, was not strictly true. His parental attention never abandoned them; what he found amiss in the first edition, he silently corrected in those that followed. He appears to have revised the *Iliad,* and freed it from some of its imperfections; and the *Essay on Criticism* received many improvements after its first appearance. It will seldom be found that he altered without adding clearness, elegance, or vigor. Pope had perhaps the judgment of Dryden; but Dryden certainly wanted the diligence of Pope.

In acquired knowledge, the superiority must be allowed to Dryden, whose education was more scholastic, and who before he became an author had been allowed more time for study, with better means of information. His mind has a larger range, and he collects his images and illustrations from a more extensive circumference of science. Dryden knew more of man in his general nature, and Pope in his local manners. The notions of Dryden were formed by comprehensive speculation, and those of Pope by minute attention. There is more dignity in the knowledge of Dryden, and more certainty in that of Pope.

Poetry was not the sole praise of either; for both excelled likewise in prose; but Pope did not borrow his prose from his predecessor. The style of Dryden is capricious and varied, that of Pope is cautious and uniform; Dryden obeys the motions of his own mind,

2. Robert Dodsley, the publisher.

Pope constrains his mind to his own rules of composition. Dryden is sometimes vehement and rapid; Pope is always smooth, uniform, and gentle. Dryden's page is a natural field, rising into inequalities, and diversified by the varied exuberance of abundant vegetation; Pope's is a velvet lawn, shaven by the scythe, and leveled by the roller.

Of genius, that power which constitutes a poet; that quality without which judgment is cold and knowledge is inert; that energy which collects, combines, amplifies, and animates; the superiority must, with some hesitation, be allowed to Dryden. It is not to be inferred that of this poetical vigor Pope had only a little, because Dryden had more; for every other writer since Milton must give place to Pope; and even of Dryden it must be said that if he has brighter paragraphs, he has not better poems. Dryden's performances were always hasty, either excited by some external occasion, or extorted by domestic necessity; he composed without consideration, and published without correction. What his mind could supply at call, or gather in one excursion, was all that he sought, and all that he gave. The dilatory caution of Pope enabled him to condense his sentiments, to multiply his images, and to accumulate all that study might produce, or chance might supply. If the flights of Dryden therefore are higher, Pope continues longer on the wing. If of Dryden's fire the blaze is brighter, of Pope's the heat is more regular and constant. Dryden often surpasses expectation, and Pope never falls below it. Dryden is read with frequent astonishment, and Pope with perpetual delight.

This parallel will, I hope, when it is well considered, be found just; and if the reader should suspect me, as I suspect myself, of some partial fondness for the memory of Dryden, let him not too hastily condemn me; for meditation and inquiry may, perhaps, show him the reasonableness of my determination.

1781

JAMES BOSWELL
(1740–1795)

1763: Meets Samuel Johnson.
1768: Account of Corsica.
1773: Tour of the Highlands and the Hebrides with Johnson.
1791: *Life of Samuel Johnson.*

The discovery within the last three or four decades of a vast number of James Boswell's personal papers (formerly believed to have been destroyed by his literary executors) has made it possible to know the author of the *Life of Samuel Johnson* better, perhaps, than we can know any other person, dead or living. His published letters and journals (only a portion of those that exist) have made modern readers aware of the serious and absurd, the charming and repellent sides of his character. The journals are the work of a complicated man of genius, who perfected his art as a biographer through his almost lifelong habit of observing himself and recording with unique honesty and completeness his responses to widely varied experience. By the time he met Johnson, when he was only 23, he had already trained himself to listen, to observe, and to remember until he found time to set it all down in writing. Only very rarely, it seems, did he ever take notes of conversations while they were in progress, an action which would quickly have put an end to social discourse. His unusual memory, his instinctive sense of the characteristic, and his disciplined art enabled him in privacy to re-create and vividly preserve the many "scenes" which distinguish his journals as they do the *Life*.

Boswell was the elder son of Alexander Boswell of Auchinleck (pronounced *Aff-léck*) in Ayreshire, a judge who, by virtue of his high office, bore the courtesy title of Lord Auchinleck. As a member of an ancient family and heir to its large estate, Boswell was in the technical sense of the term a gentleman, with entrée into the best circles of Edinburgh and London—not, as he is sometimes represented, a climber who had to toady to his betters. By temperament he was unstable, prone to melancholy, given to romantic excesses of feeling, and thoroughly sensual. The combination of instability and sensuality led him early into the habitual dissipation that ultimately affected his health and shortened his life. After attending the Universities of Edinburgh and Glasgow, and studying law in Utrecht in Holland, he made the grand tour of Germany, Italy, and France, passing through Switzerland where he met and succeeded in captivating the two foremost French men of letters, Rousseau and Voltaire. He visited the beleaguered hero of Corsica, General Pasquale de Paoli, who was leading his people in their revolt against Genoa, and who seemed to European liberals to embody all the civic and military virtues of Republican Rome. Upon returning to England he wrote his first important work, *An Account of Corsica* (1768), which included the journal of his visit to Paoli. It was promptly translated into Dutch, German, French, and Italian, and its young author found himself with a modest European reputation.

By 1769, Boswell was established in what was to prove a successful law practice in Edinburgh and had married his cousin, Margaret Montgomerie. Whenever possible he made a jaunt to London in the spring, where he mingled dissipation with the soberer pleasures of intellectual life, especially in Johnson's circle. In 1773 Johnson, then 64, joined Boswell in a tour of the Highlands and the Hebrides. Boswell delighted in placing his elderly friend in situations which would bring out his essential character, and he was therefore very much pleased to bring Dr. Johnson to Scotland and into the primitive Highlands and the Hebrides, and to watch and record his responses to incidents and people along the way. Almost every aspect of the adventure should have made it impossible, or a least unpleasant. Johnson, far from young and after years of sedentary city living, found himself astride a horse in wild country or in open boats in autumn weather. As a devout Anglican, he was an outspoken enemy of the Presbyterian Church, the national church of Scotland. As a lover of London, he cared little or nothing for scenery and rural life, and even less for such primitive people as the Highlanders were at that time. Moreover, for

many years he had half-jestingly, half-seriously, made the Scots as a nation the butt of his satiric wit. But such were Boswell's social tact and
Johnson's vigor and curiosity that the tour was a great success. "There
have been many people," wrote Boswell of himself, "who built castles in
the air, but I believe I am the first that ever attempted to move into
them." The trip to the Hebrides is a fine example of this eminently Boswellian trait. Johnson's sober and unflattering account of the trip in his
Journey to the Western Isles of Scotland (1775) gave some offense to
Scottish national pride. Boswell's *Journal of a Tour to the Hebrides*
(1785), a preliminary study for the *Life*, is a lively and entertaining diary,
kept throughout the journey and approved, at least in part, by Johnson
himself.

In 1788, four years after Johnson's death, Boswell abandoned his Scotch
practice, removed with his family to London, was admitted to the English
bar (but never actually practiced), and, amidst domestic difficulties not
made less perplexing by his own frailties, began the *Life*. Fortunately he
had the help and encouragement of the distinguished literary scholar
Edmond Malone, without whose guidance he might never have finished his
task.

The *Life* is the work of an impressive literary artist who was dominated
by a Johnsonian regard for accuracy and truth. A lesser craftsman might
have been overwhelmed by the very abundance of material that Boswell
had to deal with: his own journals, all of Johnson's letters that he could
find, his voluminous writings, and every scrap of information that his
friends would furnish—all of which had to be collected, verified, and
somehow reduced to unity. The *Life* is a record not of Johnson alone
but of literary England during the last half of the century. Its pages are
populated by men as eminent in their way as was Johnson, most of whom
Boswell knew, all of whom are interesting to the reader. But Boswell
wrote with his eye on the object, and that object was Samuel Johnson,
to whom every detail in the book is relevant, toward whom such eminent
persons as Sir Joshua Reynolds, Edmund Burke, Oliver Goldsmith, Lord
Chesterfield—even the king himself—always face. Boswell's sense of unity
and of proportion is perfect. Although his book is dense with details, they
never impede the flow of the narrative. The movement is always forward,
individual episodes are designed to reveal the great protagonist in a variety
of aspects, and the world that Boswell created and populated is sustained
both by the animation of his own imagination and by the vitality of his
hero.

Boswell's gift is not only narrative: it is also dramatic. He himself was
a good deal of an actor and a superb mimic, with a flair for detecting the
characteristic gesture, word, tone, or trait. In reading the journals and
the *Life* one often feels that their author is a gifted theatrical improviser,
creating dramatic "scenes" (the word is a favorite of his) with living people, and playing simultaneously and with incredible sureness the several
roles of contriver of the dialogue, director of the plot, actor in the scene,
and applauding audience—for Boswell never failed to watch and applaud
or condemn his own curious conduct. The quintessence of Boswell as both
a social genius and a literary artist (the two complemented each other)
is to be found in his description of his visit to Voltaire: "I placed myself
by him. I touched the keys in unison with his imagination. I wish you had

heard the music." Boswell's art, as an interviewer, a conversationalist, and a biographer is, like all great art, the product of a deep and humane interpretative imagination. The scene with Voltaire, like all the famous scenes in the *Life*, is contrived with such apparent ease and by seemingly such simple means, that the genius responsible for them may go undetected by the casual reader.

Although the Johnson who has become a part of our heritage is largely Boswell's Johnson, there was much in his life about which Boswell had no first-hand knowledge, and there were aspects of his nature which he did not have much opportunity to observe. When Boswell met him, Johnson was 54, a widower, already established as "Dictionary" Johnson and the author of the *Rambler*, pensioned by the Crown and consequently no longer compelled to earn his living. Boswell knew nothing at first hand of Johnson's boyhood and youth in Lichfield, of his brief stay at Oxford, of his marriage, and of the long, difficult, and heroic years (more than a quarter of a century), during which Johnson made his way up from obscurity to eminence through difficulties that it is painful to imagine. Boswell knew him as the sage, the moralist, the scholar, the critic, and as a man moving in a largely male society in tavern, coffeehouse, and club. The chief glory of the *Life* is the conversation, always dominated by Johnson but not at all a monologue. It is the talk of a man, or rather of men, who have experienced broadly, read widely, observed and reflected on their observations, whose ideas are constantly brought to the test of experience, and whose experience is habitually transmuted into ideas. The book is as large as life and as human as its central character.

From Boswell on the Grand Tour
[*Boswell Interviews Voltaire*[1]]

And whence do I now write to you, my friend?[2] From the château of Monsieur de Voltaire. I had a letter for him from a Swiss colonel at The Hague. I came hither Monday and was presented to him. He received me with dignity and that air of a man who has been much in the world which a Frenchman acquires in perfection. I saw him for about half an hour before dinner. He was not in spirits. Yet he gave me some brilliant sallies. He did not dine with us, and I was obliged to post away immediately after dinner, because the gates of Geneva shut before five and Ferney is a good hour from town. I was by no means satisfied to have been so little time with the monarch of French literature. A happy scheme sprung up in my adventurous mind. Madame Denis, the niece of Monsieur de

1. Voltaire was the name assumed by François Marie Arouet (1694–1778), the most famous French writer of his generation. Playwright, poet, satirist, philosopher, enemy of the church, and irrepressible ironist, after a stormy career he was living in splendor at his chateau at Ferney near the border of Switzerland and France, just outside Geneva. His housekeeper and mistress was his niece Marie-Louise Denis. He and Jean-Jacques Rousseau, whom Boswell had just visited and whose avowed disciple he had become, were deadly enemies.
2. This passage is taken from a letter, dated 28 December, 1764, written to Boswell's closest friend, a young clergyman named William Temple.

Voltaire, had been extremely good to me. She is fond of our language. I wrote her a letter in English begging her interest to obtain for me the privilege of lodging a night under the roof of Monsieur de Voltaire, who, in opposition to our sun, rises in the evening. I was in the finest humor and my letter was full of wit. I told her, "I am a hardy and a vigorous Scot. You may mount me to the highest and coldest garret. I shall not even refuse to sleep upon two chairs in the bedchamber of your maid. I saw her pass through the room where we sat before dinner." I sent my letter on Tuesday by an express. It was shown to Monsieur de Voltaire, who with his own hand wrote this answer in the character of Madame Denis: "You will do us much honor and pleasure. We have few beds. But you will (*shall*) not sleep on two chairs. My uncle, though very sick, hath guessed at your merit. I know it better; for I have seen you longer." * * *

I returned yesterday to this enchanted castle. The magician appeared a very little before dinner. But in the evening he came into the drawing room in great spirits. I placed myself by him. I touched the keys in unison with his imagination. I wish you had heard the music. He was all brilliance. He gave me continued flashes of wit. I got him to speak English, which he does in a degree that made me now and then start up and cry, "Upon my soul this is astonishing!" When he talked our language he was animated with the soul of a Briton. He had bold flights. He had humor. He had an extravagance; he had a forcible oddity of style that the most comical of our *dramatis personae* could not have exceeded. He swore bloodily, as was the fashion when he was in England.[3] He hummed a ballad; he repeated nonsense. Then he talked of our Constitution with a noble enthusiasm. I was proud to hear this from the mouth of an illustrious Frenchman. At last we came upon religion. Then did he rage. The company went to supper. Monsieur de Voltaire and I remained in the drawing room with a great Bible before us; and if ever two mortal men disputed with vehemence, we did. Yes, upon that occasion he was one individual and I another. For a certain portion of time there was a fair opposition between Voltaire and Boswell. The daring bursts of his ridicule confounded my understanding. He stood like an orator of ancient Rome. Tully[4] was never more agitated than he was. He went too far. His aged frame trembled beneath him. He cried, "Oh, I am very sick; my head turns round," and he let himself gently fall upon an easy chair. He recovered. I resumed our conversation, but changed the tone. I talked to him serious and earnest. I demanded of him an honest confession of

3. In 1726, in order to avoid imprisonment because of a quarrel with a nobleman, Voltaire had gone into exile in England, where he remained for three years, meeting many distinguished English writers and statesmen and learning to admire the British Constitution and the English principle of religious toleration. His *Lettres philosophiques sur les Anglais* (1734) expressed his admiration of English institutions and is an indirect criticism of France.
4. Marcus Tullius Cicero.

his real sentiments. He gave it me with candor and with a mild eloquence which touched my heart. I did not believe him capable of thinking in the manner that he declared to me was "from the bottom of his heart." He expressed his veneration—his love—of the Supreme Being, and his entire resignation to the will of Him who is All-wise. He expressed his desire to resemble the Author of Goodness by being good himself. His sentiments go no farther. He does not inflame his mind with grand hopes of the immortality of the soul. He says it may be, but he knows nothing of it. And his mind is in perfect tranquility. I was moved; I was sorry. I doubted his sincerity. I called to him with emotion, "Are you sincere? are you really sincere?" He answered "Before God, I am." Then with the fire of him whose tragedies have so often shone on the theater of Paris, he said, "I suffer much. But I suffer with patience and resignation; not as a Christian—but as a man."

Temple, was not this an interesting scene? Would a journey from Scotland to Ferney have been too much to obtain such a remarkable interview? * * *

1764   1928

From The Life of Samuel Johnson, LL.D.

[*Plan of the* Life]

* * * Had Dr. Johnson written his own life, in conformity with the opinion which he has given, that every man's life may be best written by himself;[1] had he employed in the preservation of his own history, that clearness of narration and elegance of language in which he has embalmed so many eminent persons, the world would probably have had the most perfect example of biography that was ever exhibited. But although he at different times, in a desultory manner, committed to writing many particulars of the progress of his mind and fortunes, he never had persevering diligence enough to form them into a regular composition. Of these memorials a few have been preserved; but the greater part was consigned by him to the flames, a few days before his death.

As I had the honor and happiness of enjoying his friendship for upwards of twenty years; as I had the scheme of writing his life constantly in view; as he was well apprised of this circumstance, and from time to time obligingly satisfied my inquiries, by communicating to me the incidents of his early years; as I acquired a facility in recollecting, and was very assiduous in recording, his conversation, of which the extraordinary vigor and vivacity constituted one of the first features of his character; and as I have spared no pains in obtaining materials concerning him, from every quarter where I could discover that they were to be found, and have been favored

1. *Idler* 84.

with the most liberal communications by his friends; I flatter myself that few biographers have entered upon such a work as this with more advantages; independent of literary abilities, in which I am not vain enough to compare myself with some great names who have gone before me in this kind of writing. * * *

Instead of melting down my materials into one mass, and constantly speaking in my own person, by which I might have appeared to have more merit in the execution of the work, I have resolved to adopt and enlarge upon the excellent plan of Mr. Mason, in his *Memoirs of Gray*.[2] Wherever narrative is necessary to explain, connect, and supply, I furnish it to the best of my abilities; but in the chronological series of Johnson's life, which I trace as distinctly as I can, year by year, I produce, wherever it is in my power, his own minutes, letters, or conversation, being convinced that this mode is more lively, and will make my readers better acquainted with him than even most of those were who actually knew him, but could know him only partially; whereas there is here an accumulation of intelligence from various points, by which his character is more fully understood and illustrated.

Indeed I cannot conceive a more perfect mode of writing any man's life than not only relating all the most important events of it in their order, but interweaving what he privately wrote, and said, and thought; by which mankind are enabled as it were to see him live, and to "live o'er each scene"[3] with him, as he actually advanced through the several stages of his life. Had his other friends been as diligent and ardent as I was, he might have been almost entirely preserved. As it is, I will venture to say that he will be seen in this work more completely than any man who has ever yet lived.

And he will be seen as he really was; for I profess to write, not his panegyric, which must be all praise, but his Life; which, great and good as he was, must not be supposed to be entirely perfect. To be as he was, is indeed subject of panegyric enough to any man in this state of being; but in every picture there should be shade as well as light, and when I delineate him without reserve, I do what he himself recommended, both by his precept and his example. * * *

I am fully aware of the objections which may be made to the minuteness on some occasions of my detail of Johnson's conversation, and how happily it is adapted for the petty exercise of ridicule, by men of superficial understanding and ludicrous fancy; but I remain firm and confident in my opinion, that minute particulars are frequently characteristic, and always amusing, when they relate to a distinguished man. I am therefore exceedingly unwilling that

2. William Mason, poet and dramatist, published his life of Thomas Gray in 1774.   3. Pope's Prologue to Addison's *Cato*, line 4.

anything, however slight, which my illustrious friend thought it worth his while to express, with any degree of point, should perish. * * *

Of one thing I am certain, that considering how highly the small portion which we have of the table-talk and other anecdotes of our celebrated writers is valued, and how earnestly it is regretted that we have not more, I am justified in preserving rather too many of Johnson's sayings, than too few; especially as from the diversity of dispositions it cannot be known with certainty beforehand, whether what may seem trifling to some, and perhaps to the collector himself, may not be most agreeable to many; and the greater number that an author can please in any degree, the more pleasure does there arise to a benevolent mind. * * *

[Johnson's Early Years. Marriage and London]

[1709] Samuel Johnson was born at Lichfield, in Staffordshire, on the 18th of September, N.S.,[4] 1709; and his initiation into the Christian Church was not delayed; for his baptism is recorded, in the register of St. Mary's parish in that city, to have been performed on the day of his birth. His father is there styled *Gentleman*, a circumstance of which an ignorant panegyrist has praised him for not being proud; when the truth is, that the appellation of Gentleman, though now lost in the indiscriminate assumption of *Esquire*, was commonly taken by those who could not boast of gentility. His father was Michael Johnson, a native of Derbyshire, of obscure extraction, who settled in Lichfield as a bookseller and stationer. His mother was Sarah Ford, descended of an ancient race of substantial yeomanry in Warwickshire. They were well advanced in years when they married, and never had more than two children, both sons; Samuel, their first-born, who lived to be the illustrious character whose various excellence I am to endeavor to record, and Nathanael, who died in his twenty-fifth year.

Mr. Michael Johnson was a man of a large and robust body, and of a strong and active mind; yet, as in the most solid rocks veins of unsound substance are often discovered, there was in him a mixture of that disease, the nature of which eludes the most minute inquiry, though the effects are well known to be a weariness of life, an unconcern about those things which agitate the greater part of mankind, and a general sensation of gloomy wretchedness. From him then his son inherited, with some other qualities, "a vile melancholy," which in his too strong expression of any disturbance of the mind, "made him mad all his life, at least not sober." Michael

4. New Style. In 1752 Great Britain adopted the Gregorian Calendar, introduced in 1582 by Pope Gregory XIII, to correct the accumulated inaccuracies of Julius Caesar's calendar, which had been in use since 46 B.C. By 1752 the error amounted to eleven days. Dates before September 2, 1752, must therefore be corrected by adding eleven days or by using the Julian date, followed by "O.S." (Old Style).

was, however, forced by the narrowness of his circumstances to be very diligent in business, not only in his shop, but by occasionally resorting to several towns in the neighborhood, some of which were at a considerable distance from Lichfield. At that time booksellers' shops in the provincial towns of England were very rare, so that there was not one even in Birmingham, in which town old Mr. Johnson used to open a shop every market day. He was a pretty good Latin scholar, and a citizen so creditable as to be made one of the magistrates of Lichfield; and, being a man of good sense, and skill in his trade, he acquired a reasonable share of wealth, of which however he afterwards lost the greatest part, by engaging unsuccessfully in a manufacture of parchment. He was a zealous high-church man and royalist, and retained his attachment to the unfortunate house of Stuart, though he reconciled himself, by casuistical arguments of expediency and necessity, to take the oaths imposed by the prevailing power. * * *

Johnson's mother was a woman of distinguished understanding. I asked his old schoolfellow, Mr. Hector,[5] surgeon of Birmingham, if she was not vain of her son. He said, "She had too much good sense to be vain, but she knew her son's value." Her piety was not inferior to her understanding; and to her must be ascribed those early impressions of religion upon the mind of her son, from which the world afterwards derived so much benefit. He told me that he remembered distinctly having had the first notice of Heaven, "a place to which good people went," and hell, "a place to which bad people went," communicated to him by her, when a little child in bed with her; and that it might be the better fixed in his memory, she sent him to repeat it to Thomas Jackson, their manservant; he not being in the way, this was not done; but there was no occasion for any artificial aid for its preservation. * * *

[1728] That a man in Mr. Michael Johnson's circumstances should think of sending his son to the expensive University of Oxford, at his own charge, seems very improbable. The subject was too delicate to question Johnson upon. But I have been assured by Dr. Taylor[6] that the scheme never would have taken place had not a gentleman of Shropshire, one of his schoolfellows, spontaneously undertaken to support him at Oxford, in the character of his companion; though, in fact, he never received any assistance whatever from that gentleman.

He, however, went to Oxford, and was entered a Commoner of Pembroke College on the 31st of October, 1728, being then in his nineteenth year.

The Reverend Dr. Adams,[7] who afterwards presided over Pembroke College with universal esteem, told me he was present, and

5. Edmund Hector, a lifelong friend of Johnson's.
6. A well-to-do clergyman, who had been Johnson's school fellow in Lichfield.
7. The Rev William Adams, D.D., elected Master of Pembroke in 1775.

gave me some account of what passed on the night of Johnson's arrival at Oxford. On that evening, his father, who had anxiously accompanied him, found means to have him introduced to Mr. Jorden, who was to be his tutor. * * *

His father seemed very full of the merits of his son, and told the company he was a good scholar, and a poet, and wrote Latin verses. His figure and manner appeared strange to them; but he behaved modestly and sat silent, till upon something which occurred in the course of conversation, he suddenly struck in and quoted Macrobius; and thus he gave the first impression of that more extensive reading in which he had indulged himself.

His tutor, Mr. Jorden, fellow of Pembroke, was not, it seems, a man of such abilities as we should conceive requisite for the instructor of Samuel Johnson, who gave me the following account of him. "He was a very worthy man, but a heavy man, and I did not profit much by his instructions. Indeed, I did not attend him much. The first day after I came to college I waited upon him, and then stayed away four. On the sixth, Mr. Jorden asked me why I had not attended. I answered I had been sliding in Christ Church meadow. And this I said with as much *nonchalance* as I am now talking to you. I had no notion that I was wrong or irreverent to my tutor." BOSWELL: "That, Sir, was great fortitude of mind." JOHNSON: "No, Sir; stark insensibility." * * *

[1729] The "morbid melancholy," which was lurking in his constitution, and to which we may ascribe those particularities and that aversion to regular life, which, at a very early period, marked his character, gathered such strength in his twentieth year as to afflict him in a dreadful manner. While he was at Lichfield, in the college vacation of the year 1729, he felt himself overwhelmed with an horrible hypochondria, with perpetual irritation, fretfulness, and impatience; and with a dejection, gloom, and despair, which made existence misery. From this dismal malady he never afterwards was perfectly relieved; and all his labors, and all his enjoyments, were but temporary interruptions of its baleful influence. He told Mr. Paradise[8] that he was sometimes so languid and inefficient that he could not distinguish the hour upon the town-clock. * * *

To Johnson, whose supreme enjoyment was the exercise of his reason, the disturbance or obscuration of that faculty was the evil most to be dreaded. Insanity, therefore, was the object of his most dismal apprehension; and he fancied himself seized by it, or approaching to it, at the very time when he was giving proofs of a more than ordinary soundness and vigor of judgment. That his own diseased imagination should have so far deceived him, is strange; but it is stranger still that some of his friends should have given credit to his groundless opinion, when they had such undoubted

8. John Paradise, a member of the Essex Head Club, which Johnson founded in 1783.

proofs that it was totally fallacious; though it is by no means surprising that those who wish to depreciate him should, since his death, have laid hold of this circumstance, and insisted upon it with very unfair aggravation. * * *

Dr. Adams told me that Johnson, while he was at Pembroke College, "was caressed and loved by all about him, was a gay and frolicsome fellow, and passed there the happiest part of his life." But this is a striking proof of the fallacy of appearances, and how little any of us know of the real internal state even of those whom we see most frequently; for the truth is, that he was then depressed by poverty, and irritated by disease. When I mentioned to him this account as given me by Dr. Adams, he said, "Ah, Sir, I was mad and violent. It was bitterness which they mistook for frolic. I was miserably poor, and I thought to fight my way by my literature and my wit; so I disregarded all power and all authority." * * *

[1734] In a man whom religious education has secured from licentious indulgences, the passion of love, when once it has seized him, is exceedingly strong; being unimpaired by dissipation, and totally concentrated in one object. This was experienced by Johnson, when he became the fervent admirer of Mrs. Porter, after her first husband's death. Miss Porter told me that when he was first introduced to her mother, his appearance was very forbidding: he was then lean and lank, so that his immense structure of bones was hideously striking to the eye, and the scars of the scrofula were deeply visible. He also wore his hair,[9] which was straight and stiff, and separated behind: and he often had, seemingly, convulsive starts and odd gesticulations, which tended to excite at once surprise and ridicule. Mrs. Porter was so much engaged by his conversation that she overlooked all these external disadvantages, and said to her daughter, "This is the most sensible man that I ever saw in my life."

[1735] Though Mrs. Porter was double the age of Johnson, and her person and manner, as described to me by the late Mr. Garrick,[1] were by no means pleasing to others, she must have had a superiority of understanding and talents, as she certainly inspired him with a more than ordinary passion; and she having signified her willingness to accept of his hand, he went to Lichfield to ask his mother's consent to the marriage, which he could not but be conscious was a very imprudent scheme, both on account of their disparity of years and her want of fortune. But Mrs. Johnson knew too well the ardor of her son's temper, and was too tender a parent to oppose his inclinations.

I know not for what reason the marriage ceremony was not performed at Birmingham; but a resolution was taken that it should be at Derby, for which place the bride and bridegroom set out on horseback, I suppose in very good humor. But though Mr. Topham

9. I.e., he wore no wig.
1. David Garrick (1717–79), the most famous actor of his day. In 1736 he was one of Johnson's three pupils in an unsuccessful school at Edial.

Beauclerk[2] used archly to mention Johnson's having told him, with much gravity, "Sir, it was a love marriage on both sides," I have had from my illustrious friend the following curious account of their journey to church upon the nuptial morn:

9th July: "Sir, she had read the old romances, and had got into her head the fantastical notion that a woman of spirit should use her lover like a dog. So, Sir, at first she told me that I rode too fast, and she could not keep up with me; and, when I rode a little slower, she passed me, and complained that I lagged behind. I was not to be made the slave of caprice; and I resolved to begin as I meant to end. I therefore pushed on briskly, till I was fairly out of her sight. The road lay between two hedges, so I was sure she could not miss it; and I contrived that she should soon come up with me. When she did, I observed her to be in tears." * * *

[1737] Johnson now thought of trying his fortune in London, the great field of genius and exertion, where talents of every kind have the fullest scope and the highest encouragement. It is a memorable circumstance that his pupil David Garrick went thither at the same time, with intention to complete his education, and follow the profession of the law, from which he was soon diverted by his decided preference for the stage.[3] * * *

[1744] * * * He produced one work this year, fully sufficient to maintain the high reputation which he had acquired. This was *The Life of Richard Savage;*[4] a man of whom it is difficult to speak impartially without wondering that he was for some time the intimate companion of Johnson; for his character was marked by profligacy, insolence, and ingratitude: yet, as he undoubtedly had a warm and vigorous, though unregulated mind, had seen life in all its varieties, and been much in the company of the statesmen and wits of his time, he could communicate to Johnson an abundant supply of such materials as his philosophical curiosity most eagerly desired; and as Savage's misfortunes and misconduct had reduced him to the lowest state of wretchedness as a writer for bread, his visits to St. John's Gate[5] naturally brought Johnson and him together.

It is melancholy to reflect that Johnson and Savage were some-

2. Topham Beauclerk, a descendant of Charles II and the actress Nell Gwynn. He was brilliant and dissolute.

3. Johnson had hoped to complete his tragedy *Irene* and to get it produced, but ths was not accomplished until Garrick staged it in 1749. Meanwhile Johnson struggled against poverty, at first as a writer and translator for Edward Cave's *Gentleman's Magazine*. He gradually won recognition, but was never financially secure until he was pensioned in 1762. Garrick succeeded in the theater much more rapidly than did Johnson in literature.

4. Richard Savage, poet, courted and gained notoriety by claiming to be the illegitimate son of Earl Rivers and the Countess of Macclesfield, whose husband had divorced her because of her unfaithfulness with Rivers. Savage publicized his claim and persecuted his alleged mother. Johnson and many others believed Savage's story and resented what they considered the lady's inhumanity. Savage was a gifted man, but he lived in poverty as a hack writer, though he was long assisted by Pope and others. He died in a debtor's prison in Bristol in 1743.

5. Where Cave published the *Gentleman's Magazine*.

times in such extreme indigence that they could not pay for a lodging; so that they have wandered together whole nights in the streets. Yet in these almost incredible scenes of distress, we may suppose that Savage mentioned many of the anecdotes with which Johnson afterwards enriched the life of his unhappy companion, and those of other poets.

He told Sir Joshua Reynolds that one night in particular, when Savage and he walked round St. James's Square for want of a lodging, they were not at all depressed by their situation; but in high spirits and brimful of patriotism, traversed the square for several hours, inveighed against the minister, and "resolved they would *stand by their country*." * * *

[1752] That there should be a suspension of his literary labors during a part of the year 1752[6] will not seem strange when it is considered that soon after closing his *Rambler*, he suffered a loss which, there can be no doubt, affected him with the deepest distress. For on the 17th of March, O.S., his wife died. * * *

The following very solemn and affecting prayer was found, after Dr. Johnson's decease, by his servant, Mr. Francis Barber, who delivered it to my worthy friend the Reverend Mr. Strahan, Vicar of Islington, who at my earnest request has obligingly favored me with a copy of it, which he and I compared with the original:

"April 26, 1752, being after 12 at night of the 25th.

"O Lord! Governor of heaven and earth, in whose hands are embodied and departed spirits, if thou hast ordained the souls of the dead to minister to the living, and appointed my departed wife to have care of me, grant that I may enjoy the good effects of her attention and ministration, whether exercised by appearance, impulses, dreams or in any other manner agreeable to thy government. Forgive my presumption, enlighten my ignorance, and however meaner agents are employed, grant me the blessed influences of thy holy Spirit, through Jesus Christ our Lord. Amen." * * *

One night when Beauclerk and Langton[7] had supped at a tavern in London, and sat till about three in the morning, it came into their heads to go and knock up Johnson, and see if they could prevail on him to join them in a ramble. They rapped violently at the door of his chambers in the Temple,[8] till at last he appeared in his shirt, with his little black wig on the top of his head, instead of a nightcap, and a poker in his hand, imagining, probably, that some ruffians were coming to attack him. When he discovered who they were, and was told their errand, he smiled, and with great good

---

6. Johnson's important works written before the publication of the *Dictionary* are the poems *London* (1738) and *The Vanity of Human Wishes* (1749), the *Life of Savage* (1744), and the essays which made up his periodical *The Rambler* (1750–52).

7. Bennet Langton. As a boy he so much admired the *Rambler* that he

sought Johnson's acquaintance. They became lifelong friends.

8. Since Johnson lived in Inner Temple Lane between 1760 and 1765, the "frisk" could not have taken place in the year of his wife's death, where Boswell, for his own convenience, placed it.

humor agreed to their proposal: "What, is it you, you dogs! I'll have a frisk with you." He was soon dressed, and they sallied forth together into Covent Garden, where the greengrocers and fruiterers were beginning to arrange their hampers, just come in from the country. Johnson made some attempts to help them; but the honest gardeners stared so at his figure and manner and odd interference, that he soon saw his services were not relished. They then repaired to one of the neighboring taverns, and made a bowl of that liquor called *Bishop*,[9] which Johnson had always liked; while in joyous contempt of sleep, from which he had been roused, he repeated the festive lines,

> Short, O short then be thy reign,
> And give us to the world again![1]

They did not stay long, but walked down to the Thames, took a boat, and rowed to Billingsgate. Beauclerk and Johnson were so well pleased with their amusement that they resolved to persevere in dissipation for the rest of the day: but Langton deserted them, being engaged to breakfast with some young ladies. Johnson scolded him for "leaving his social friends, to go and sit with a set of wretched *un-idea'd* girls." Garrick being told of this ramble, said to him smartly, "I heard of your frolic t'other night. You'll be in the *Chronicle*." Upon which Johnson afterwards observed, "*He* durst not do such a thing. His *wife* would not *let* him!" * * *

[The Letter to Chesterfield]

[1754] Lord Chesterfield,[2] to whom Johnson had paid the high compliment of addressing to his Lordship the *Plan* of his *Dictionary*, had behaved to him in such a manner as to excite his contempt and indignation. The world has been for many years amused with a story confidently told, and as confidently repeated with additional circumstances, that a sudden disgust was taken by Johnson upon occasion of his having been one day kept long in waiting in his Lordship's antechamber, for which the reason assigned was that he had company with him; and that at last, when the door opened, out walked Colley Cibber;[3] and that Johnson was so violently provoked when he found for whom he had been so long excluded, that he went away in a passion, and never would return. I remember having mentioned this story to George Lord Lyttelton, who told me he was very intimate with Lord Chesterfield; and holding it as a well-known truth, defended Lord Chesterfield, by saying, that Cibber, who had been introduced familiarly by the back stairs, had

9. A drink made of wine, sugar, and either lemon or orange.
1. Misquoted from Lansdowne's *Drinking Song to Sleep*.
2. Philip Dormer Stanhope, Earl of Chesterfield (1694–1773), statesman, wit, man of fashion. His *Letters*, written for the guidance of his natural son, are famous for their worldly good sense and for their expression of the ideal of an 18th-century gentleman.
3. Colley Cibber (1671–1757), playwright, comic actor, and (after 1730) poet laureate. A fine actor but a very bad poet, Cibber was a constant object of ridicule by the wits of the town. Pope made him King of the Dunces in the *Dunciad* of 1743.

probably not been there above ten minutes. It may seem strange even to entertain a doubt concerning a story so long and so widely current, and thus implicitly adopted, if not sanctioned, by the authority which I have mentioned; but Johnson himself assured me that there was not the least foundation for it. He told me that there never was any particular incident which produced a quarrel between Lord Chesterfield and him; but that his Lordship's continued neglect was the reason why he resolved to have no connection with him. When the *Dictionary* was upon the eve of publication, Lord Chesterfield, who, it is said, had flattered himself with expectations that Johnson would dedicate the work to him, attempted, in a courtly manner, to soothe, and insinuate himself with the sage, conscious, as it should seem, of the cold indifference with which he had treated its learned author; and further attempted to conciliate him, by writing two papers in *The World*, in recommendation of the work; and it must be confessed that they contain some studied compliments, so finely turned, that if there had been no previous offense, it is probable that Johnson would have been highly delighted. Praise, in general, was pleasing to him; but by praise from a man of rank and elegant accomplishments, he was peculiarly gratified. * * *

This courtly device failed of its effect. Johnson, who thought that "all was false and hollow,"[4] despised the honeyed words, and was even indignant that Lord Chesterfield should, for a moment, imagine that he could be dupe of such an artifice. His expression to me concerning Lord Chesterfield, upon this occasion, was, "Sir, after making great professions, he had, for many years, taken no notice of me; but when my *Dictionary* was coming out, he fell a-scribbling in *The World* about it. Upon which, I wrote him a letter expressed in civil terms, but such as might show him that I did not mind what he said or wrote, and that I had done with him."

This is that celebrated letter of which so much has been said, and about which curiosity has been so long excited, without being gratified. I for many years solicited Johnson to favor me with a copy of it, that so excellent a composition might not be lost to posterity. He delayed from time to time to give it me; till at last in 1781, when we were on a visit at Mr. Dilly's,[5] at Southill in Bedfordshire, he was pleased to dictate it to me from memory. He afterwards found among his papers a copy of it, which he had dictated to Mr. Baretti,[6] with its title and corrections, in his own handwriting. This he gave to Mr. Langton; adding that if it were to come into print, he wished it to be from that copy. By Mr. Langton's kindness, I am enabled to enrich my work with a perfect transcript of what the world has so eagerly desired to see.

4. *Paradise Lost* II.112.
5. Southill was the country home of Charles and Edward Dilly, publishers. The firm published all of Boswell's serious works and shared in the publica- tion of Johnson's *Lives of the Poets* (1779–81).
6. Giuseppe Baretti, an Italian writer and lexicographer whom Johnson introduced into his circle.

To the Right Honorable the Earl of Chesterfield

February 7, 1755.

My Lord,

I have been lately informed, by the proprietor of *The World*, that two papers, in which my Dictionary is recommended to the public, were written by your Lordship. To be so distinguished, is an honor, which, being very little accustomed to favors from the great, I know not well how to receive, or in what terms to acknowledge.

When, upon some slight encouragement, I first visited your Lordship, I was overpowered, like the rest of mankind, by the enchantment of your address; and could not forbear to wish that I might boast myself *Le vainqueur du vainqueur de la terre*[7]—that I might obtain that regard for which I saw the world contending; but I found my attendance so little encouraged that neither pride nor modesty would suffer me to continue it. When I had once addressed your Lordship in public, I had exhausted all the art of pleasing which a retired and uncourtly scholar can possess. I had done all that I could; and no man is well pleased to have his all neglected, be it ever so little.

Seven years, my Lord, have now passed since I waited in your outward rooms, or was repulsed from your door; during which time I have been pushing on my work through difficulties of which it is useless to complain, and have brought it, at last, to the verge of publication, without one act of assistance, one word of encouragement, or one smile of favor. Such treatment I did not expect, for I never had a patron before.

The shepherd in Virgil grew at last acquainted with Love, and found him a native of the rocks.[8]

Is not a patron, my Lord, one who looks with unconcern on a man struggling for life in the water, and, when he has reached ground, encumbers him with help? The notice which you have been pleased to take of my labors, had it been early, had been kind; but it has been delayed till I am indifferent, and cannot enjoy it; till I am solitary, and cannot impart it; till I am known, and do not want it. I hope it is no very cynical asperity not to confess obligations where no benefit has been received, or to be unwilling that the public should consider me as owing that to a patron which Providence has enabled me to do for myself.

Having carried on my work thus far with so little obligation to any favorer of learning, I shall not be disappointed though I should conclude it, if less be possible, with less; for I have been long wakened from that dream of hope in which I once boasted myself with so much exultation, my Lord, your Lordship's most humble, most obedient servant,

Sam. Johnson.

"While this was the talk of the town," says Dr. Adams, in a letter to me, "I happened to visit Dr. Warburton,[9] who finding that

7. "The conqueror of the conqueror of the earth." From the first line of Scudéry's epic *Alaric* (1654).
8. *Eclogues* VIII.44.

9. William Warburton, Bishop of Gloucester, friend and literary executor of Pope, editor of Pope and Shakespeare, theological controversialist.

I was acquainted with Johnson, desired me earnestly to carry his compliments to him, and to tell him that he honored him for his manly behavior in rejecting these condescensions of Lord Chesterfield, and for resenting the treatment he had received from him, with a proper spirit. Johnson was visibly pleased with this compliment, for he had always a high opinion of Warburton. Indeed, the force of mind which appeared in this letter was congenial with that which Warburton himself amply possessed."

There is a curious minute circumstance which struck me, in comparing the various editions of Johnson's imitations of Juvenal. In the tenth satire, one of the couplets upon the vanity of wishes even for literary distinction stood thus:

> Yet think what ills the scholar's life assail,
> Pride, envy, want, the *garret*, and the jail.

But after experiencing the uneasiness which Lord Chesterfield's fallacious patronage made him feel, he dismissed the word *garret* from the sad group, and in all the subsequent editions the line stands

> Pride, envy, want, the *patron*, and the jail.

[1762] The accession of George the Third to the throne of these kingdoms[1] opened a new and brighter prospect to men of literary merit, who had been honored with no mark of royal favor in the preceding reign. His present Majesty's education in this country, as well as his taste and beneficence, prompted him to be the patron of science and the arts; and early this year Johnson, having been represented to him as a very learned and good man, without any certain provision, his Majesty was pleased to grant him a pension of three hundred pounds a year. The Earl of Bute,[2] who was then Prime Minister, had the honor to announce this instance of his Sovereign's bounty, concerning which many and various stories, all equally erroneous, have been propagated: maliciously representing it as a political bribe to Johnson, to desert his avowed principles, and become the tool of a government which he held to be founded in usurpation. I have taken care to have it in my power to refute them from the most authentic information. Lord Bute told me that Mr. Wedderburne, now Lord Loughborough, was the person who first mentioned this subject to him. Lord Loughborough told me that the pension was granted to Johnson solely as the reward of his literary merit, without any stipulation whatever, or even tacit understanding that he should write for administration. His Lordship added that he was confident the political tracts which Johnson afterwards did write, as they were entirely consonant with his

1. In 1760.
2. An intimate friend of George III's mother, he early gained an ascendancy over the young prince and was largely responsible for the king's autocratic views. He was hated in England both as a favorite and as a Scot.

own opinions, would have been written by him though no pension had been granted to him.[3] * * *

[A *Memorable Year: Boswell Meets Johnson*]

[1763] This is to me a memorable year; for in it I had the happiness to obtain the acquaintance of that extraordinary man whose memoirs I am now writing; an acquaintance which I shall ever esteem as one of the most fortunate circumstances in my life. * * *

Mr. Thomas Davies the actor, who then kept a bookseller's shop in Russel Street, Covent Garden, told me that Johnson was very much his friend, and came frequently to his house, where he more than once invited me to meet him; but by some unlucky accident or other he was prevented from coming to us. * * *

At last, on Monday the 16th of May, when I was sitting in Mr. Davies's back parlor, after having drunk tea with him and Mrs. Davies, Johnson unexpectedly came into the shop; and Mr. Davies having perceived him through the glass door in the room in which we were sitting, advancing towards us—he announced his awful approach to me, somewhat in the manner of an actor in the part of Horatio, when he addresses Hamlet on the appearance of his father's ghost, "Look, my Lord, it comes." I found that I had a very perfect idea of Johnson's figure, from the portrait of him painted by Sir Joshua Reynolds soon after he had published his *Dictionary*, in the attitude of sitting in his easy chair in deep meditation, which was the first picture his friend did for him, which Sir Joshua very kindly presented to me, and from which an engraving has been made for this work. Mr. Davies mentioned my name, and respectfully introduced me to him. I was much agitated; and recollecting his prejudice against the Scotch, of which I had heard much, I said to Davies, "Don't tell where I come from."—"From Scotland," cried Davies roguishly. "Mr. Johnson," said I, "I do indeed come from Scotland, but I cannot help it." I am willing to flatter myself that I meant this as light pleasantry to soothe and conciliate him, and not as an humiliating abasement at the expense of my country. But however that might be, this speech was somewhat unlucky; for with that quickness of wit for which he was so remarkable, he seized the expression "come from Scotland," which I used in the sense of being of that country; and, as if I had said that I had come away from it, or left it, retorted, "That, Sir, I find, is what a very great many of your countrymen cannot help." This stroke stunned me a good deal; and when we had sat down, I felt myself not a little embarrassed, and apprehensive of what might come next. He then addressed himself to Davies: "What do

3. Johnson's few political pamphlets in the 1770's invariably supported the policies of the Crown. The best-known is his answer to the American colonies, *Taxation No Tyranny* (1775). His dislike of the Americans was in large part due to the fact they owned slaves.

you think of Garrick? He has refused me an order for the play for Miss Williams,[4] because he knows the house will be full, and that an order would be worth three shillings." Eager to take any opening to get into conversation with him, I ventured to say, "O Sir, I cannot think Mr. Garrick would grudge such a trifle to you." "Sir," said he, with a stern look, "I have known David Garrick longer than you have done: and I know no right you have to talk to me on the subject." Perhaps I deserved this check; for it was rather presumptuous in me, an entire stranger, to express any doubt of the justice of his animadversion upon his old acquaintance and pupil. I now felt myself much mortified, and began to think that the hope which I had long indulged of obtaining his acquaintance was blasted. And, in truth, had not my ardor been uncommonly strong, and my resolution uncommonly persevering, so rough a reception might have deterred me forever from making any further attempts. Fortunately, however, I remained upon the field not wholly discomfited. * * *

I was highly pleased with the extraordinary vigor of his conversation, and regretted that I was drawn away from it by an engagement at another place. I had, for a part of the evening, been left alone with him, and had ventured to make an observation now and then, which he received very civilly; so that I was satisfied that though there was a roughness in his manner, there was no ill nature in his disposition. Davies followed me to the door, and when I complained to him a little of the hard blows which the great man had given me, he kindly took upon him to console me by saying, "Don't be uneasy. I can see he likes you very well."

A few days afterwards I called on Davies, and asked him if he thought I might take the liberty of waiting on Mr. Johnson at his chambers in the Temple. He said I certainly might, and that Mr. Johnson would take it as a compliment. So upon Tuesday the 24th of May, after having been enlivened by the witty sallies of Messieurs Thornton, Wilkes, Churchill, and Lloyd,[5] with whom I had passed the morning, I boldly repaired to Johnson. His chambers were on the first floor of No. 1, Inner Temple Lane, and I entered them with an impression given me by the Reverend Dr. Blair,[6] of Edinburgh, who had been introduced to him not long before, and described his having "found the giant in his den"; an expression, which, when I came to be pretty well acquainted with Johnson, I repeated to him, and he was diverted at this picturesque account

4. Mrs. Anna Williams (1706–83), a blind poet and friend of Mrs. Johnson. She continued to live in Johnson's house after his wife's death, and habitually sat up to make tea for him whenever he came home.
5. Bonnell Thornton, journalist; Charles Churchill, satirist; Robert Lloyd, poet and essayist. For Wilkes see a later episode. The four were bound together by a common love of wit and dissipation. Boswell enjoyed their company in 1763.
6. The Rev. Hugh Blair (1718–1800), Scottish divine and Professor of Rhetoric and Belles Lettres at the University of Edinburgh.

of himself. Dr. Blair had been presented to him by Dr. James Fordyce.[7] At this time the controversy concerning the pieces published by Mr. James Macpherson, as translations of *Ossian*, was at its height.[8] Johnson had all along denied their authenticity; and, what was still more provoking to their admirers, maintained that they had no merit. The subject having been introduced by Dr. Fordyce, Dr. Blair, relying on the internal evidence of their antiquity, asked Dr. Johnson whether he thought any man of a modern age could have written such poems? Johnson replied, "Yes, Sir, many men, many women, and many children." Johnson, at this time, did not know that Dr. Blair had just published a dissertation, not only defending their authenticity, but seriously ranking them with the poems of Homer and Virgil; and when he was afterwards informed of this circumstance, he expressed some displeasure at Dr. Fordyce's having suggested the topic, and said, "I am not sorry that they got thus much for their pains. Sir, it was like leading one to talk of a book when the author is concealed behind the door."

He received me very courteously; but, it must be confessed that his apartment, and furniture, and morning dress, were sufficiently uncouth. His brown suit of clothes looked very rusty; he had on a little old shriveled unpowdered wig, which was too small for his head; his shirt neck and knees of his breeches were loose; his black worsted stockings ill drawn up; and he had a pair of unbuckled shoes by way of slippers. But all these slovenly particularities were forgotten the moment that he began to talk. Some gentlemen, whom I do not recollect, were sitting with him; and when they went away, I also rose; but he said to me, "Nay, don't go." "Sir," said I, "I am afraid that I intrude upon you. It is benevolent to allow me to sit and hear you." He seemed pleased with this compliment, which I sincerely paid him, and answered, "Sir, I am obliged to any man who visits me." I have preserved the following short minute of what passed this day:

"Madness frequently discovers itself merely by unnecessary deviation from the usual modes of the world. My poor friend Smart showed the disturbance of his mind by falling upon his knees, and saying his prayers in the street, or in any other unusual place. Now although, rationally speaking, it is greater madness not to pray at all than to pray as Smart did, I am afraid there are so many who do not pray, that their understanding is not called in question."

Concerning this unfortunate poet, Christopher Smart, who was confined in a madhouse, he had, at another time, the following

7. A Scottish preacher.
8. Macpherson had imposed on most of his contemporaries, Scottish and English, by convincing them of the genuineness of prose poems which he had concocted but which he claimed to have translated from the original Gaelic of Ossian, a blind epic poet of the 3rd century. The vogue of the poems both in Europe and in America was enormous.

conversation with Dr. Burney:[9] BURNEY. "How does poor Smart do, Sir; is he likely to recover?" JOHNSON. "It seems as if his mind had ceased to struggle with the disease; for he grows fat upon it." BURNEY. "Perhaps, Sir, that may be from want of exercise." JOHNSON. "No, Sir; he has partly as much exercise as he used to have, for he digs in the garden. Indeed, before his confinement, he used for exercise to walk to the ale house; but he was *carried* back again. I did not think he ought to be shut up. His infirmities were not noxious to society. He insisted on people praying with him; and I'd as lief pray with Kit Smart as anyone else. Another charge was that he did not love clean linen; and I have no passion for it." —Johnson continued. "Mankind have a great aversion to intellectual labor; but even supposing knowledge to be easily attainable, more people would be content to be ignorant than would take even a little trouble to acquire it."

Talking of Garrick, he said, "He is the first man in the world for sprightly conversation."

When I rose a second time he again pressed me to stay, which I did. * * *

[Goldsmith. Sundry Opinions. Johnson Meets His King]

As Dr. Oliver Goldsmith will frequently appear in this narrative, I shall endeavor to make my readers in some degree acquainted with his singular character. He was a native of Ireland, and a contemporary with Mr. Burke[1] at Trinity College, Dublin, but did not then give much promise of future celebrity. He, however, observed to Mr. Malone,[2] that "though he made no great figure in mathematics, which was a study in much repute there, he could turn an ode of Horace into English better than any of them." He afterwards studied physic at Edinburgh, and upon the Continent; and I have been informed, was enabled to pursue his travels on foot, partly by demanding at universities to enter the lists as a disputant; by which, according to the custom of many of them, he was entitled to the premium of a crown, when luckily for him his challenge was not accepted; so that, as I once observed to Dr. Johnson, he *disputed* his passage through Europe. He then came to England, and was employed successively in the capacities of an usher[3] to an academy, a corrector of the press, a reviewer, and a writer for a newspaper. He had sagacity enough to cultivate assiduously the acquaintance of Johnson, and his faculties were gradually enlarged by the contemplation of such a model. To me and many others it

---

9. Dr. Charles Burney (1726–1814), historian of music and father of the novelist and diarist Fanny Burney, whom Johnson knew and loved in his old age.
1. Edmund Burke (1729–97), statesman, orator, and political philosopher.

2. Edmond Malone (1741–1812), distinguished editor and literary scholar. He helped Boswell in the writing and publication of the *Life*.
3. An assistant teacher; then a disagreeable and ill-paid job.

appeared that he studiously copied the manner of Johnson, though, indeed, upon a smaller scale.

At this time I think he had published nothing with his name, though it was pretty generally known that one Dr. *Goldsmith* was the author of *An Enquiry into the Present State of Polite Learning in Europe*, and of *The Citizen of the World*, a series of letters supposed to be written from London by a Chinese. No man had the art of displaying, with more advantage as a writer, whatever literary acquisitions he made. "*Nihil quod tetigit non ornavit.*"[4] His mind resembled a fertile, but thin soil. There was a quick, but not a strong vegetation, of whatever chanced to be thrown upon it. No deep root could be struck. The oak of the forest did not grow there; but the elegant shrubbery and the fragrant parterre[5] appeared in gay succession. It has been generally circulated and believed that he was a mere fool in conversation; but, in truth, this has been greatly exaggerated. He had, no doubt, a more than common share of that hurry of ideas which we often find in his countrymen, and which sometimes produces a laughable confusion in expressing them. He was very much what the French call *un étourdi*,[6] and from vanity and an eager desire of being conspicuous wherever he was, he frequently talked carelessly without knowledge of the subject, or even without thought. His person was short, his countenance coarse and vulgar, his deportment that of a scholar awkwardly affecting the easy gentleman. Those who were in any way distinguished, excited envy in him to so ridiculous an excess that the instances of it are hardly credible. When accompanying two beautiful young ladies with their mother on a tour in France, he was seriously angry that more attention was paid to them than to him; and once at the exhibition of the *Fantoccini* in London, when those who sat next him observed with what dexterity a puppet was made to toss a pike, he could not bear that it should have such praise, and exclaimed with some warmth, "Pshaw! I can do it better myself."[7] * * *

I had as my guests this evening at the Mitre Tavern, Dr. Johnson, Dr. Goldsmith, Mr. Thomas Davies, Mr. Eccles, an Irish gentleman, for whose agreeable company I was obliged to Mr. Davies, and the Reverend Mr. John Ogilvie,[8] who was desirous of being in company with my illustrious friend, while I, in my turn, was proud to have the honor of showing one of my countrymen upon what easy terms Johnson permitted me to live with him. * * *

Mr. Ogilvie was unlucky enough to choose for the topic of his

4. "He touched nothing that he did not adorn." From Johnson's epitaph for Goldsmith's monument in Westminster Abbey.
5. A flower garden with beds laid out in patterns.
6. One who acts without thought.

7. It is difficult to believe that Boswell did not recognize that Goldsmith was joking. Indeed, his entire characterization of Goldsmith is not without malice and distortion.
8. An eminent Scottish divine.

conversation the praises of his native country. He began with saying that there was very rich land round Edinburgh. Goldsmith, who had studied physic there, contradicted this, very untruly, with a sneering laugh. Disconcerted a little by this, Mr. Ogilvie then took new ground, where, I suppose, he thought himself perfectly safe; for he observed that Scotland had a great many noble wild prospects. JOHNSON. "I believe, Sir, you have a great many. Norway, too, has noble wild prospects; and Lapland is remarkable for prodigious noble wild prospects. But, Sir, let me tell you, the noblest prospect which a Scotchman ever sees, is the highroad that leads him to England!" This unexpected and pointed sally produced a roar of applause. After all, however, those who admire the rude grandeur of nature cannot deny it to Caledonia. * * *

At night Mr. Johnson and I supped in a private room at the Turk's Head Coffeehouse, in the Strand. "I encourage this house," said he, "for the mistress of it is a good civil woman, and has not much business.

"Sir, I love the acquaintance of young people; because, in the first place, I don't like to think myself growing old. In the next place, young acquaintances must last longest, if they do last; and then, Sir, young men have more virtue than old men: they have more generous sentiments in every respect. I love the young dogs of this age: they have more wit and humor and knowledge of life than we had; but then the dogs are not so good scholars. Sir, in my early years I read very hard. It is a sad reflection, but a true one, that I knew almost as much at eighteen as I do now. My judgment, to be sure, was not so good; but I had all the facts. I remember very well, when I was at Oxford, an old gentleman said to me, 'Young man, ply your book diligently now, and acquire a stock of knowledge; for when years come upon you, you will find that poring upon books will be but an irksome task.'" * * *

He again insisted on the duty of maintaining subordination of rank. "Sir, I would no more deprive a nobleman of his respect than of his money. I consider myself as acting a part in the great system of society, and I do to others as I would have them to do to me. I would behave to a nobleman as I should expect he would behave to me, were I a nobleman and he Sam. Johnson. Sir, there is one Mrs. Macaulay[9] in this town, a great republican. One day when I was at her house, I put on a very grave countenance, and said to her, 'Madam, I am now become a convert to your way of thinking. I am convinced that all mankind are upon an equal footing; and to give you an unquestionable proof, Madam, that I am in earnest, here is a very sensible, civil, well-behaved fellow citizen, your footman; I desire that he may be allowed to sit down and dine with us.' I thus, Sir, showed her the absurdity of the leveling doctrine.

9. Mrs. Catharine Macaulay, at this time much in the public eye as a female historian and a propounder of libertarian and egalitarian ideas.

She has never liked me since. Sir, your levelers wish to level *down* as far as themselves; but they cannot bear leveling *up* to themselves. They would all have some people under them; why not then have some people above them?" * * *

At supper this night he talked of good eating with uncommon satisfaction. "Some people," said he, "have a foolish way of not minding, or pretending not to mind, what they eat. For my part, I mind my belly very studiously, and very carefully; for I look upon it that he who does not mind his belly will hardly mind anything else." He now appeared to me *Jean Bull philosophe*,[1] and he was, for the moment, not only serious but vehement. Yet I have heard him, upon other occasions, talk with great contempt of people who were anxious to gratify their palates; and the 206th number of his *Rambler* is a masterly essay against gulosity.[2] His practice, indeed, I must acknowledge, may be considered as casting the balance of his different opinions upon this subject; for I never knew any man who relished good eating more than he did. When at table, he was totally absorbed in the business of the moment; his looks seemed riveted to his plate; nor would he, unless when in very high company, say one word, or even pay the least attention to what was said by others, till he had satisfied his appetite, which was so fierce, and indulged with such intenseness, that while in the act of eating, the veins of his forehead swelled, and generally a strong perspiration was visible. To those whose sensations were delicate, this could not but be disgusting; and it was doubtless not very suitable to the character of a philosopher, who should be distinguished by self-command. But it must be owned that Johnson, though he could be rigidly *abstemious*, was not a *temperate* man either in eating or drinking. He could refrain, but he could not use moderately. He told me that he had fasted two days without inconvenience, and that he had never been hungry but once. They who beheld with wonder how much he eat upon all occasions when his dinner was to his taste, could not easily conceive what he must have meant by hunger; and not only was he remarkable for the extraordinary quantity which he eat, but he was, or affected to be, a man of very nice discernment in the science of cookery. * * *

[1767] In February, 1767, there happened one of the most remarkable incidents of Johnson's life, which gratified his monarchical enthusiasm, and which he loved to relate with all its circumstances, when requested by his friends. This was his being honored by a private conversation with his Majesty, in the library at the Queen's house. He had frequently visited those splendid rooms and noble collection of books, which he used to say was more numerous and curious than he supposed any person could have made in the time which the King had employed. Mr. Barnard,

1. I.e., John Bull (the typical hard-headed Englishman) in the role of philosopher.
2. Greediness.

the librarian, took care that he should have every accommodation that could contribute to his ease and convenience, while indulging his literary taste in that place; so that he had here a very agreeable resource at leisure hours.

His Majesty having been informed of his occasional visits, was pleased to signify a desire that he should be told when Dr. Johnson came next to the library. Accordingly, the next time that Johnson did come, as soon as he was fairly engaged with a book, on which, while he sat by the fire, he seemed quite intent, Mr Barnard stole round to the apartment where the King was, and, in obedience to his Majesty's commands, mentioned that Dr. Johnson was then in the library. His Majesty said he was at leisure, and would go to him; upon which Mr. Barnard took one of the candles that stood on the King's table, and lighted his Majesty through a suite of rooms, till they came to a private door into the library, of which his Majesty had the key. Being entered, Mr. Barnard stepped forward hastily to Dr. Johnson, who was still in a profound study, and whispered him, "Sir, here is the King." Johnson started up, and stood still. His Majesty approached him, and at once was courteously easy.

His Majesty began by observing that he understood he came sometimes to the library; and then mentioning his having heard that the Doctor had been lately at Oxford, asked him if he was not fond of going thither. To which Johnson answered that he was indeed fond of going to Oxford sometimes, but was likewise glad to come back again. The King then asked him what they were doing at Oxford. Johnson answered, he could not much commend their diligence, but that in some respects they were mended, for they had put their press under better regulations, and were at that time printing Polybius. He was then asked whether there were better libraries at Oxford or Cambridge. He answered, he believed the Bodleian was larger than any they had at Cambridge; at the same time adding, "I hope, whether we have more books or not than they have at Cambridge, we shall make as good use of them as they do." Being asked whether All Souls or Christ Church library was the largest, he answered, "All Souls library is the largest we have, except the Bodleian." "Aye," said the King, "that is the public library."

His Majesty inquired if he was then writing anything. He answered, he was not, for he had pretty well told the world what he knew, and must now read to acquire more knowledge. The King, as it should seem with a view to urge him to rely on his own stores as an original writer, and to continue his labors, then said "I do not think you borrow much from anybody." Johnson said he thought he had already done his part as a writer. "I should have thought so too," said the King, "if you had not written so well."—

Johnson observed to me, upon this, that "No man could have paid a handsomer compliment; and it was fit for a king to pay. It was decisive." When asked by another friend, at Sir Joshua Reynolds's, whether he made any reply to this high compliment, he answered, "No, Sir. When the King had said it, it was to be so. It was not for me to bandy civilities with my sovereign." Perhaps no man who had spent his whole life in courts could have shown a more nice and dignified sense of true politeness than Johnson did in this instance. * * *

[Fear of Death]

[1769] When we were alone, I introduced the subject of death, and endeavored to maintain that the fear of it might be got over. I told him that David Hume said to me, he was no more uneasy to think he should *not be* after this life, than that he *had not been* before he began to exist. JOHNSON. "Sir, if he really thinks so, his perceptions are disturbed; he is mad: if he does not think so, he lies. He may tell you, he holds his finger in the flame of a candle, without feeling pain; would you believe him? When he dies, he at least gives up all he has." BOSWELL. "Foote,[3] Sir, told me, that when he was very ill he was not afraid to die." JOHNSON. "It is not true, Sir. Hold a pistol to Foote's breast, or to Hume's breast, and threaten to kill them, and you'll see how they behave." BOSWELL. "But may we not fortify our minds for the approach of death?" Here I am sensible I was in the wrong, to bring before his view what he ever looked upon with horror; for although when in a celestial frame, in his *Vanity of Human Wishes*, he has supposed death to be "kind Nature's signal for retreat," from this state of being to "a happier seat," his thoughts upon this awful change were in general full of dismal apprehensions. His mind resembled the vast amphitheater, the Colosseum at Rome. In the center stood his judgment, which, like a mighty gladiator, combated those apprehensions that, like the wild beasts of the arena, were all around in cells, ready to be let out upon him. After a conflict, he drives them back into their dens; but not killing them, they were still assailing him. To my question, whether we might not fortify our minds for the approach of death, he answered, in a passion, "No, Sir, let it alone. It matters not how a man dies, but how he lives. The act of dying is not of importance, it lasts so short a time." He added (with an earnest look), "A man knows it must be so, and submits. It will do him no good to whine."

I attempted to continue the conversation. He was so provoked that he said, "Give us no more of this"; and was thrown into such a state of agitation that he expressed himself in a way that alarmed

3. Samuel Foote, actor and dramatist, famous for his wit and his skill in mimicry.

and distressed me; showed an impatience that I should leave him, and when I was going away, called to me sternly, "Don't let us meet tomorrow." * * *

[*Ossian. "Talking for Victory"*]

MR. BOSWELL TO DR. JOHNSON

Edinburgh, Feb. 2, 1775.

* * * As to Macpherson, I am anxious to have from yourself a full and pointed account of what has passed between you and him. It is confidently told here that before your book[4] came out he sent to you, to let you know that he understood you meant to deny the authenticity of Ossian's poems; that the originals were in his possession; that you might have inspection of them, and might take the evidence of people skilled in the Erse language; and that he hoped, after this fair offer, you would not be so uncandid as to assert that he had refused reasonable proof. That you paid no regard to his message, but published your strong attack upon him; and then he wrote a letter to you, in such terms as he thought suited to one who had not acted as a man of veracity. * * *

What words were used by Mr. Macpherson in his letter to the venerable sage, I have never heard; but they are generally said to have been of a nature very different from the language of literary contest. Dr. Johnson's answer appeared in the newspapers of the day, and has since been frequently republished; but not with perfect accuracy. I give it as dictated to me by himself, written down in his presence, and authenticated by a note in his own handwriting, "*This, I think, is a true copy.*"

MR. JAMES MACPHERSON,

I received your foolish and impudent letter. Any violence offered me I shall do my best to repel; and what I cannot do for myself, the law shall do for me. I hope I shall never be deterred from detecting what I think a cheat, by the menaces of a ruffian.

What would you have me retract? I thought your book an imposture; I think it an imposture still. For this opinion I have given my reasons to the public, which I here dare you to refute. Your rage I defy. Your abilities, since your Homer, are not so formidable; and what I hear of your morals inclines me to pay regard not to what you shall say, but to what you shall prove. You may print this if you will.

SAM. JOHNSON.

Mr. Macpherson little knew the character of Dr. Johnson if he supposed that he could be easily intimidated; for no man was ever more remarkable for personal courage. He had, indeed, an awful dread of death, or rather, "of something after death"; and what rational man, who seriously thinks of quitting all that he has ever

---

4. Johnson's *Journey to the Western Islands* (1775), in which he had pub-licly expressed his views on the Ossianic poems.

known, and going into a new and unknown state of being, can be without that dread? But his fear was from reflection; his courage natural. His fear, in that one instance, was the result of philosophical and religious consideration. He feared death, but he feared nothing else, not even what might occasion death. Many instances of his resolution may be mentioned. One day, at Mr. Beauclerk's house in the country, when two large dogs were fighting, he went up to them, and beat them till they separated; and at another time, when told of the danger there was that a gun might burst if charged with many balls, he put in six or seven, and fired it off against a wall. Mr. Langton told me that when they were swimming together near Oxford, he cautioned Dr. Johnson against a pool which was reckoned particularly dangerous; upon which Johnson directly swam into it. He told me himself that one night he was attacked in the street by four men, to whom he would not yield, but kept them all at bay, till the watch came up, and carried both him and them to the roundhouse. In the playhouse at Lichfield, as Mr. Garrick informed me, Johnson having for a moment quitted a chair which was placed for him between the side-scenes, a gentleman took possession of it, and when Johnson on his return civilly demanded his seat, rudely refused to give it up; upon which Johnson laid hold of it, and tossed him and the chair into the pit. Foote, who so successfully revived the old comedy, by exhibiting living characters, had resolved to imitate Johnson on the stage, expecting great profits from his ridicule of so celebrated a man. Johnson being informed of his intention, and being at dinner at Mr. Thomas Davies's the bookseller, from whom I had the story, he asked Mr. Davies what was the common price of an oak stick; and being answered sixpence, "Why then, Sir," said he, "give me leave to send your servant to purchase me a shilling one. I'll have a double quantity; for I am told Foote means to *take me off*, as he calls it, and I am determined the fellow shall not do it with impunity." Davies took care to acquaint Foote of this, which effectually checked the wantonness of the mimic. Mr. Macpherson's menaces made Johnson provide himself with the same implement of defense; and had he been attacked, I have no doubt that, old as he was, he would have made his corporal prowess be felt as much as his intellectual. * * *

[1776] I mentioned a new gaming club, of which Mr. Beauclerk had given me an account, where the members played to a desperate extent. JOHNSON. "Depend upon it, Sir, this is mere talk. Who is ruined by gaming? You will not find six instances in an age. There is a strange rout made about deep play: whereas you have many more people ruined by adventurous trade, and yet we do not hear such an outcry against it." THRALE.[5] "There may be few people

5. Johnson met Henry Thrale, the
wealthy brewer, and his charming wife
Hester in 1765. Thereafter he was do-
mesticated as much as he wished to be

absolutely ruined by deep play; but very many are much hurt in their circumstances by it." JOHNSON. "Yes, Sir, and so are very many by other kinds of expense." I had heard him talk once before in the same manner; and at Oxford he said, he wished he had learnt to play at cards. The truth, however, is that he loved to display his ingenuity in argument; and therefore would sometimes in conversation maintain opinions which he was sensible were wrong, but in supporting which, his reasoning and wit would be most conspicuous. He would begin thus: "Why, Sir, as to the good or evil of card playing——" "Now, said Garrick, "he is thinking which side he shall take." He appeared to have a pleasure in contradiction, especially when any opinion whatever was delivered with an air of confidence; so that there was hardly any topic, if not one of the great truths of religion and morality, that he might not have been incited to argue, either for or against. Lord Elibank[6] had the highest admiration of his powers. He once observed to me, "Whatever opinion Johnson maintains, I will not say that he convinces me; but he never fails to show me that he has good reasons for it." I have heard Johnson pay his Lordship this high compliment: "I never was in Lord Elibank's company without learning something." * * *

[Dinner with Wilkes]

My worthy booksellers and friends, Messieurs Dilly in the Poultry, at whose hospitable and well-covered table I have seen a greater number of literary men than at any other, except that of Sir Joshua Reynolds, had invited me to meet Mr. Wilkes[7] and some more gentlemen on Wednesday, May 15. "Pray," said I, "let us have Dr. Johnson."—"What, with Mr. Wilkes? not for the world," said Mr. Edward Dilly, "Dr. Johnson would never forgive me."—"Come," said I, "if you'll let me negotiate for you, I will be answerable that all shall go well." DILLY. "Nay, if you will take it upon you, I am sure I shall be very happy to see them both here."

Notwithstanding the high veneration which I entertained for Dr. Johnson, I was sensible that he was sometimes a little actuated by the spirit of contradiction, and by means of that I hoped I

at their house at Streatham near London. There he enjoyed the good things of life, as well as the companionship of Mrs. Thrale and her children. Thrale died in 1781. His widow's marriage to Gabriel Piozzi, an Italian musician, in 1784, caused Johnson to quarrel with her and darkened the last months of his life.

6. Prominent in Scottish literary circles. Johnson, who admired him, had visited him on his tour of Scotland with Boswell in 1773.

7. John Wilkes (1727–97) was obnoxious to the Christian and Tory Johnson in every way. He was profane and

dissolute, and his personal life was a public scandal; for over a decade he had been notorious as a courageous, resourceful, and finally victorious opponent of the arbitrary and tyrannical policies of the king and his ministers, and had been the envenomed critic of Lord Bute, to whom Johnson owed his pension. When Johnson met him he had totally defeated his enemies, had served as Lord Mayor, and was again a Member of Parliament, a post from which he had been expelled and driven into exile as an outlaw in 1764. Boswell had found Wilkes a gay and congenial companion in Italy in 1764.

should gain my point. I was persuaded that if I had come upon him with a direct proposal, "Sir, will you dine in company with Jack Wilkes?" he would have flown into a passion, and would probably have answered, "Dine with Jack Wilkes, Sir! I'd as soon dine with Jack Ketch."[8] I therefore, while we were sitting quietly by ourselves at his house in an evening, took occasion to open my plan thus: "Mr. Dilly, Sir, sends his respectful compliments to you, and would be happy if you would do him the honor to dine with him on Wednesday next along with me, as I must soon go to Scotland." JOHNSON. "Sir, I am obliged to Mr. Dilly. I will wait upon him—" BOSWELL. "Provided, Sir, I suppose, that the company which he is to have, is agreeable to you." JOHNSON. "What do you mean, Sir? What do you take me for? Do you think I am so ignorant of the world as to imagine that I am to prescribe to a gentleman what company he is to have at his table?" BOSWELL. "I beg your pardon, Sir, for wishing to prevent you from meeting people whom you might not like. Perhaps he may have some of what he calls his patriotic[9] friends with him." JOHNSON. "Well, Sir, and what then? What care *I* for his *patriotic friends?* Poh!" BOSWELL. "I should not be surprised to find Jack Wilkes there." JOHNSON. "And if Jack Wilkes *should* be there, what is that to *me*, Sir? My dear friend, let us have no more of this. I am sorry to be angry with you; but really it is treating me strangely to talk to me as if I could not meet any company whatever, occasionally." BOSWELL. "Pray forgive me, Sir: I meant well. But you shall meet whoever comes, for me." Thus I secured him, and told Dilly that he would find him very well pleased to be one of his guests on the day appointed.

Upon the much-expected Wednesday, I called on him about half an hour before dinner, as I often did when we were to dine out together, to see that he was ready in time, and to accompany him. I found him buffeting his books, as upon a former occasion, covered with dust, and making no preparation for going abroad. "How is this, Sir?" said I. "Don't you recollect that you are to dine at Mr. Dilly's?" JOHNSON. "Sir, I did not think of going to Dilly's: it went out of my head. I have ordered dinner at home with Mrs. Williams." BOSWELL. "But, my dear Sir, you know you were engaged to Mr. Dilly, and I told him so. He will expect you, and will be much disappointed if you don't come." JOHNSON. "You must talk to Mrs. Williams about this."

Here was a sad dilemma. I feared that what I was so confident I had secured would yet be frustrated. He had accustomed himself

---

8. After the public hangman, Jack Ketch, died in 1686, his name became the common designation of all those who filled that office.
9. In Tory circles the word had come to be used ironically of those who op- posed the government. The "patriots" considered themselves the defenders of the ancient liberties of the English. They included the partisans of both Wilkes and of the American colonists.

to show Mrs. Williams such a degree of humane attention as frequently imposed some restraint upon him; and I knew that if she should be obstinate, he would not stir. I hastened downstairs to the blind lady's room, and told her I was in great uneasiness, for Dr. Johnson had engaged to me to dine this day at Mr. Dilly's, but that he had told me he had forgotten his engagement, and had ordered dinner at home. "Yes, Sir," said she, pretty peevishly, "Dr. Johnson is to dine at home."—"Madam," said I, "his respect for you is such that I know he will not leave you unless you absolutely desire it. But as you have so much of his company, I hope you will be good enough to forego it for a day; as Mr. Dilly is a very worthy man, has frequently had agreeable parties at his house for Dr. Johnson, and will be vexed if the Doctor neglects him today. And then, Madam, be pleased to consider my situation; I carried the message, and I assured Mr. Dilly that Dr. Johnson was to come, and no doubt he has made a dinner, and invited a company, and boasted of the honor he expected to have. I shall be quite disgraced if the Doctor is not there." She gradually softened to my solicitations, which were certainly as earnest as most entreaties to ladies upon any occasion, and was graciously pleased to empower me to tell Dr. Johnson that all things considered, she thought he should certainly go. I flew back to him, still in dust, and careless of what should be the event, "indifferent in his choice to go or stay";[1] but as soon as I had announced to him Mrs. Williams' consent, he roared, "Frank, a clean shirt," and was very soon dressed. When I had him fairly seated in a hackney coach with me, I exulted as much as a fortune hunter who has got an heiress into a post chaise with him to set out for Gretna Green.[2]

When we entered Mr. Dilly's drawing room, he found himself in the midst of a company he did not know. I kept myself snug and silent, watching how he would conduct himself. I observed him whispering to Mr. Dilly, "Who is that gentleman, Sir?"—"Mr. Arthur Lee."—JOHNSON. "Too, too, too" (under his breath), which was one of his habitual mutterings. Mr. Arthur Lee could not but be very obnoxious to Johnson, for he was not only a *patriot* but an *American*.[3] He was afterwards minister from the United States at the court of Madrid. "And who is the gentleman in lace?" —"Mr. Wilkes, Sir." This information confounded him still more; he had some difficulty to restrain himself, and taking up a book, sat down upon a window seat and read, or at least kept his eye upon it intently for some time, till he composed himself. His feel-

1. Addison's *Cato* V.i.40. Boswell cleverly adapts to his own purpose Cato's words, "Indifferent in his choice to sleep or die."
2. A village just across the Scottish border where runaway couples were married by the local innkeeper or the blacksmith.

3. Johnson was extremely hostile to the rebelling American colonists. On one occasion he said: "I am willing to love all mankind, except an American." Lee had been educated in England and Scotland, and had recently been admitted to the English bar. He had been a loyal supporter of Wilkes.

ings, I dare say, were awkward enough. But he no doubt recollected his having rated me for supposing that he could be at all disconcerted by any company, and he, therefore, resolutely set himself to behave quite as an easy man of the world, who could adapt himself at once to the disposition and manners of those whom he might chance to meet.

The cheering sound of "Dinner is upon the table," dissolved his reverie, and we *all* sat down without any symptom of ill humor. There were present, beside Mr. Wilkes, and Mr. Arthur Lee, who was an old companion of mine when he studied physic at Edinburgh, Mr. (now Sir John) Miller, Dr. Lettsom, and Mr. Slater the druggist. Mr. Wilkes placed himself next to Dr. Johnson, and behaved to him with so much attention and politeness that he gained upon him insensibly. No man eat more heartily than Johnson, or loved better what was nice and delicate. Mr. Wilkes was very assiduous in helping him to some fine veal. "Pray give me leave, Sir—It is better here—A little of the brown—Some fat, Sir—A little of the stuffing—Some gravy—Let me have the pleasure of giving you some butter—Allow me to recommend a squeeze of this orange—or the lemon, perhaps, may have more zest."— "Sir, Sir, I am obliged to you, Sir," cried Johnson, bowing, and turning his head to him with a look for some time of "surly virtue," but, in a short while, of complacency.

Foote being mentioned, Johnson said, "He is not a good mimic." One of the company added, "A merry Andrew, a buffoon." JOHNSON. "But he has wit too, and is not deficient in ideas, or in fertility and variety of imagery, and not empty of reading; he has knowledge enough to fill up his part. One species of wit he has in an eminent degree, that of escape. You drive him into a corner with both hands; but he's gone, Sir, when you think you have got him —like an animal that jumps over your head. Then he has a great range for wit; he never lets truth stand between him and a jest, and he is sometimes mighty coarse. Garrick is under many restraints from which Foote is free." WILKES. "Garrick's wit is more like Lord Chesterfield's." JOHNSON. "The first time I was in company with Foote was at Fitzherbert's. Having no good opinion of the fellow, I was resolved not to be pleased; and it is very difficult to please a man against his will. I went on eating my dinner pretty sullenly, affecting not to mind him. But the dog was so very comical, that I was obliged to lay down my knife and fork, throw myself back upon my chair, and fairly laugh it out. No, Sir, he was irresistible. He upon one occasion experienced, in an extraordinary degree, the efficacy of his powers of entertaining. Amongst the many and various modes which he tried of getting money, he became a partner with a small-beer[4] brewer, and he was to have a share of

---

4. Weak beer, served in the servants' hall.

the profits for procuring customers amongst his numerous acquaintance. Fitzherbert was one who took his small beer; but it was so bad that the servants resolved not to drink it. They were at some loss how to notify their resolution, being afraid of offending their master, who they knew liked Foote much as a companion. At last they fixed upon a little black boy, who was rather a favorite, to be their deputy, and deliver their remonstrance; and having invested him with the whole authority of the kitchen, he was to inform Mr. Fitzherbert, in all their names, upon a certain day, that they would drink Foote's small beer no longer. On that day Foote happened to dine at Fitzherbert's, and this boy served at table; he was so delighted with Foote's stories, and merriment, and grimace, that when he went downstairs, he told them, 'This is the finest man I have ever seen. I will not deliver your message. I will drink his small beer.' "

Somebody observed that Garrick could not have done this. WILKES. "Garrick would have made the small beer still smaller. He is now leaving the stage; but he will play *Scrub*[5] all his life." I knew that Johnson would let nobody attack Garrick but himself, as Garrick once said to me, and I had heard him praise his liberality; so to bring out his commendation of his celebrated pupil, I said, loudly, "I have heard Garrick is liberal." JOHNSON. "Yes, Sir, I know that Garrick has given away more money than any man in England that I am acquainted with, and that not from ostentatious views. Garrick was very poor when he began life; so when he came to have money, he probably was very unskillful in giving away, and saved when he should not. But Garrick began to be liberal as soon as he could; and I am of opinion, the reputation of avarice which he has had, has been very lucky for him, and prevented his having many enemies. You despise a man for avarice, but do not hate him. Garrick might have been much better attacked for living with more splendor than is suitable to a player: if they had had the wit to have assaulted him in that quarter, they might have galled him more. But they have kept clamoring about his avarice, which has rescued him from much obloquy and envy."

Talking of the great difficulty of obtaining authentic information for biography, Johnson told us, "When I was a young fellow I wanted to write the *Life of Dryden*, and in order to get materials, I applied to the only two persons then alive who had seen him; these were old Swinney,[6] and old Cibber. Swinney's information was no more than this, that at Will's Coffeehouse Dryden had a particular chair for himself, which was set by the fire in winter, and was then called his winter chair; and that it was carried out for him to the balcony in summer, and was then called his summer

---

5. The servant of Squire Sullen in George Farquhar's *Beaux' Stratagem:* a favorite role of Garrick's.
6. Owen Mac Swinney, a playwright.

chair. Cibber could tell no more but that he remembered him a decent old man, arbiter of critical disputes at Will's. You are to consider that Cibber was then at a great distance from Dryden, had perhaps one leg only in the room, and durst not draw in the other." BOSWELL. "Yet Cibber was a man of observation?" JOHNSON. "I think not." BOSWELL. "You will allow his *Apology* to be well done." JOHNSON. "Very well done, to be sure, Sir. That book is a striking proof of the justice of Pope's remark:

> Each might his several province well command,
> Would all but stoop to what they understand."[7]

BOSWELL. "And his plays are good." JOHNSON. "Yes; but that was his trade; *l'esprit du corps*: he had been all his life among players and play writers. I wondered that he had so little to say in conversation, for he had kept the best company, and learnt all that can be got by the ear. He abused Pindar to me, and then showed me an ode of his own, with an absurd couplet, making a linnet soar on an eagle's wing. I told him that when the ancients made a simile, they always made it like something real."

Mr. Wilkes remarked that "among all the bold flights of Shakespeare's imagination, the boldest was making Birnam Wood march to Dunsinane;[8] creating a wood where there never was a shrub; a wood in Scotland! ha! ha! ha!" And he also observed, that "the clannish slavery of the Highlands of Scotland was the single exception to Milton's remark of 'The mountain nymph, sweet Liberty,'[9] being worshiped in all hilly countries."—"When I was at Inverary," said he, "on a visit to my old friend, Archibald, Duke of Argyle, his dependents congratulated me on being such a favorite of his Grace. I said, 'It is then, gentlemen, truly lucky for me; for if I had displeased the Duke, and he had wished it, there is not a Campbell among you but would have been ready to bring John Wilkes's head to him in a charger. It would have been only

Off with his head! So much for Aylesbury.'[1]

I was then member for Aylesbury." * * *

Mr. Arthur Lee mentioned some Scotch who had taken possession of a barren part of America, and wondered why they should choose it. JOHNSON. "Why, Sir, all barrenness is comparative. The *Scotch* would not know it to be barren." BOSWELL. "Come, come, he is flattering the English. You have now been in Scotland, Sir, and say if you did not see meat and drink enough there." JOHNSON. "Why yes, Sir; meat and drink enough to give the inhabitants sufficient strength to run away from home." All these quick and lively sallies were said sportively, quite in jest, and with a smile, which

---

7. *Essay on Criticism* I.66–67.
8. *Macbeth* V.v.30–52.
9. *L'Allegro*, line 36.

1. "Off with his head! So much for Buckingham." A line in Cibber's version of Shakespeare's *Richard III*.

showed that he meant only wit. Upon this topic he and Mr. Wilkes could perfectly assimilate; here was a bond of union between them, and I was conscious that as both of them had visited Caledonia, both were fully satisfied of the strange narrow ignorance of those who imagine that it is a land of famine. But they amused themselves with persevering in the old jokes. When I claimed a superiority for Scotland over England in one respect, that no man can be arrested there for a debt merely because another swears it against him; but there must first be the judgment of a court of law ascertaining its justice; and that a seizure of the person, before judgment is obtained, can take place only if his creditor should swear that he is about to fly from the country, or, as it is technically expressed, is *in meditatione fugae:* WILKES. "That, I should think, may be safely sworn of all the Scotch nation." JOHNSON (to Mr. Wilkes). "You must know, Sir, I lately took my friend Boswell and showed him genuine civilized life in an English provincial town. I turned him loose at Lichfield, my native city, that he might see for once real civility: for you know he lives among savages in Scotland, and among rakes in London." WILKES. "Except when he is with grave, sober, decent people like you and me." JOHNSON (smiling). "And we ashamed of him."

They were quite frank and easy. Johnson told the story of his asking Mrs. Macaulay to allow her footman to sit down with them, to prove the ridiculousness of the argument for the equality of mankind; and he said to me afterwards, with a nod of satisfaction, "You saw Mr. Wilkes acquiesced." * * *

This record, though by no means so perfect as I could wish, will serve to give a notion of a very curious interview, which was not only pleasing at the time, but had the agreeable and benignant effect of reconciling any animosity and sweetening any acidity, which in the various bustle of political contest, had been produced in the minds of two men, who, though widely different, had so many things in common—classical learning, modern literature, wit, and humor, and ready repartee—that it would have been much to be regretted if they had been forever at a distance from each other.

Mr. Burke gave me much credit for this successful "negotiation"; and pleasantly said that there was nothing to equal it in the whole history of the *Corps Diplomatique.* * * *

[Dread of Solitude]

[1777] I talked to him of misery being "the doom of man" in this life, as displayed in his *Vanity of Human Wishes.* Yet I observed that things were done upon the supposition of happiness; grand houses were built, fine gardens were made, splendid places of public amusement were contrived, and crowded with company. JOHNSON. "Alas, Sir, these are all only struggles for happiness. When

I first entered Ranelagh,[2] it gave an expansion and gay sensation to my mind, such as I never experienced anywhere else. But, as Xerxes wept when he viewed his immense army, and considered that not one of that great multitude would be alive a hundred years afterwards, so it went to my heart to consider that there was not one in all that brilliant circle that was not afraid to go home and think; but that the thoughts of each individual there, would be distressing when alone." * * *

[*"A Bottom of Good Sense." Bet Flint.*
"Clear Your Mind of Cant"]

[1781] Talking of a very respectable author, he told us a curious circumstance in his life, which was that he had married a printer's devil.[3] REYNOLDS. "A printer's devil, Sir! Why, I thought a printer's devil was a creature with a black face and in rags." JOHNSON. "Yes, Sir. But I suppose, he had her face washed, and put clean clothes on her." Then looking very serious, and very earnest: "And she did not disgrace him; the woman had a bottom of good sense." The word *bottom* thus introduced was so ludicrous when contrasted with his gravity, that most of us could not forbear tittering and laughing; though I recollect that the Bishop of Killaloe kept his countenance with perfect steadiness, while Miss Hannah More[4] slyly hid her face behind a lady's back who sat on the same settee with her. His pride could not bear that any expression of his should excite ridicule, when he did not intend it; he therefore resolved to assume and exercise despotic power, glanced sternly around, and called out in a strong tone, "Where's the merriment?" Then collecting himself, and looking awful, to make us feel how he could impose restraint, and as it were searching his mind for a still more ludicrous word, he slowly pronounced, "I say the *woman* was *fundamentally* sensible"; as if he had said, "hear this now, and laugh if you dare." We all sat composed as at a funeral. * * *

He gave us an entertaining account of Bet Flint, a woman of the town, who, with some eccentric talents and much effrontery, forced herself upon his acquaintance. "Bet," said he, "wrote her own Life in verse, which she brought to me, wishing that I would furnish her with a Preface to it" (laughing). "I used to say of her that she was generally slut and drunkard; occasionally, whore and thief. She had, however, genteel lodgings, a spinnet on which she played, and a boy that walked before her chair. Poor Bet was taken up on a charge of stealing a counterpane, and tried at the Old Bailey. Chief Justice ———, who loved a wench, summed up favorably, and she was acquitted. After which Bet said, with a gay and

2. Pleasure gardens in Chelsea, where concerts were held; fireworks displayed, food and drink sold.
3. Apprentice in a print shop.

4. Hannah More (1745–1833), bluestocking and religious writer, one of the promoters of the Sunday School movement.

satisfied air, 'Now that the counterpane is *my own,* I shall make a petticoat of it.'" * * *

[1783] I have no minute of any interview with Johnson till Thursday, May 15, when I find what follows: BOSWELL. "I wish much to be in Parliament, Sir." JOHNSON. "Why, Sir, unless you come resolved to support any administration, you would be the worse for being in Parliament, because you would be obliged to live more expensively." BOSWELL. "Perhaps, Sir, I should be the less happy for being in Parliament. I never would sell my vote, and I should be vexed if things went wrong." JOHNSON. "That's cant,[5] Sir. It would not vex you more in the house than in the gallery: public affairs vex no man." BOSWELL. "Have not they vexed yourself a little, Sir? Have not you been vexed by all the turbulence of this reign, and by that absurd vote of the House of Commons, 'That the influence of the Crown has increased, is increasing, and ought to be diminished?'" JOHNSON. "Sir, I have never slept an hour less, nor eat an ounce less meat. I would have knocked the factious dogs on the head, to be sure; but I was not *vexed.*" BOSWELL. "I declare, Sir, upon my honor, I did imagine I was vexed, and took a pride in it; but it *was,* perhaps, cant; for I own I neither ate less, nor slept less." JOHNSON. "My dear friend, clear your *mind* of cant. You may *talk* as other people do: you may say to a man, 'Sir, I am your most humble servant.' You are *not* his most humble servant. You may say, 'These are bad times; it is a melancholy thing to be reserved to such times.' You don't mind the times. You tell a man, 'I am sorry you had such bad weather the last day of your journey, and were so much wet.' You don't care sixpence whether he is wet or dry. You may *talk* in this manner; it is a mode of talking in society: but don't *think* foolishly." * * *

[Johnson Prepares for Death]

My anxious apprehensions at parting with him this year proved to be but too well founded; for not long afterwards he had a dreadful stroke of the palsy, of which there are very full and accurate accounts in letters written by himself, to show with what composure of mind, and resignation to the Divine Will, his steady piety enabled him to behave. * * *

Two days after he wrote thus to Mrs. Thrale:

"On Monday, the 16th, I sat for my picture, and walked a considerable way with little inconvenience. In the afternoon and evening I felt myself light and easy, and began to plan schemes of life. Thus I went to bed, and in a short time waked and sat up, as has been long my custom, when I felt a confusion and indistinctness in my head, which lasted, I suppose, about half a minute. I was alarmed,

---

5. "A whining pretension to goodness in formal and affected terms" (Johnson's *Dictionary*).

and prayed God that however he might afflict my body, he would spare my understanding. This prayer, that I might try the integrity of my faculties, I made in Latin verse. The lines were not very good, but I knew them not to be very good: I made them easily, and concluded myself to be unimpaired in my faculties.

"Soon after I perceived that I had suffered a paralytic stroke, and that my speech was taken from me. I had no pain, and so little dejection in this dreadful state, that I wondered at my own apathy, and considered that perhaps death itself, when it should come, would excite less horror than seems now to attend it.

"In order to rouse the vocal organs, I took two drams. Wine has been celebrated for the production of eloquence. I put myself into violent motion, and I think repeated it; but all was vain. I then went to bed and strange as it may seem, I think slept. When I saw light, it was time to contrive what I should do. Though God stopped my speech, he left me my hand; I enjoyed a mercy which was not granted to my dear friend Lawrence,[6] who now perhaps overlooks me as I am writing, and rejoices that I have what he wanted. My first note was necessarily to my servant, who came in talking, and could not immediately comprehend why he should read what I put into his hands.

"I then wrote a card to Mr. Allen,[7] that I might have a discreet friend at hand, to act as occasion should require. In penning this note, I had some difficulty; my hand, I knew not how nor why, made wrong letters. I then wrote to Dr. Taylor to come to me, and bring Dr. Heberden; and I sent to Dr. Brocklesby, who is my neighbor.[8] My physicians are very friendly, and give me great hopes; but you may imagine my situation. I have so far recovered my vocal powers as to repeat the Lord's Prayer with no very imperfect articulation. My memory, I hope, yet remains as it was; but such an attack produces solicitude for the safety of every faculty." * * *

[1784] To Mr. Henry White, a young clergyman, with whom he now formed an intimacy, so as to talk to him with great freedom, he mentioned that he could not in general accuse himself of having been an undutiful son. "Once, indeed," said he, "I was disobedient; I refused to attend my father to Uttoxeter market. Pride was the source of that refusal, and the remembrance of it was painful. A few years ago, I desired to atone for this fault; I went to Uttoxeter in very bad weather, and stood for a considerable time bareheaded in the rain, on the spot where my father's stall used to stand. In contrition I stood, and I hope the penance was expiatory."

"I told him," says Miss Seward,[9] "in one of my latest visits to him, of a wonderful learned pig, which I had seen at Nottingham; and which did all that we have observed exhibited by dogs

6. Dr. Thomas Lawrence, president of the Royal College of Physicians and Johnson's own doctor, had died paralyzed shortly before this was written.
7. Edmund Allen, a printer, Johnson's landlord and neighbor.
8. These two physicians attended Johnson on his deathbed.
9. Anna Seward, "the Swan of Lichfield," a poet.

and horses. The subject amused him. 'Then,' said he, 'the pigs are a race unjustly calumniated. *Pig* has, it seems, not been wanting to *man*, but *man* to *pig*. We do not allow *time* for his education, we kill him at a year old.' Mr. Henry White, who was present, observed that if this instance had happened in or before Pope's time, he would not have been justified in instancing the swine as the lowest degree of groveling instinct.[1] Dr. Johnson seemed pleased with the observation, while the person who made it proceeded to remark that great torture must have been employed, ere the indocility of the animal could have been subdued. 'Certainly,' said the Doctor; 'but,' turning to me, 'how old is your pig?' I told him, three years old. 'Then,' said he, 'the pig has no cause to complain; he would have been killed the first year if he had not been *educated*, and protracted existence is a good recompense for very considerable degrees of torture.' "

[Johnson Faces Death]

As Johnson had now very faint hopes of recovery, and as Mrs. Thrale was no longer devoted to him, it might have been supposed that he would naturally have chosen to remain in the comfortable house of his beloved wife's daughter,[2] and end his life where he began it. But there was in him an animated and lofty spirit, and however complicated diseases might depress ordinary mortals, all who saw him, beheld and acknowledged the *invictum animum Catonis*.[3] Such was his intellectual ardor even at this time that he said to one friend, "Sir, I look upon every day to be lost, in which I do not make a new acquaintance"; and to another, when talking of his illness, "I will be conquered; I will not capitulate." And such was his love of London, so high a relish had he of its magnificent extent, and variety of intellectual entertainment, that he languished when absent from it, his mind having become quite luxurious from the long habit of enjoying the metropolis; and, therefore, although at Lichfield, surrounded with friends, who loved and revered him, and for whom he had a very sincere affection, he still found that such conversation as London affords, could be found nowhere else. These feelings, joined, probably, to some flattering hopes of aid from the eminent physicians and surgeons in London, who kindly and generously attended him without accepting fees, made him resolve to return to the capital. * * * Death had always been to him an object of terror; so that, though by no means happy, he still clung to life with an eagerness at which many have wondered. At any time when he was ill, he was very much pleased to be told that he looked better. An ingenious mem-

---

1. *Essay on Man* I.221.
2. Lucy Porter.
3. "The unconquered soul of Cato."

An adaptation of a phrase in Horace's *Odes* II.i.24.

ber of the Eumelian Club[4] informs me that upon one occasion when he said to him that he saw health returning to his cheek, Johnson seized him by the hand and exclaimed, "Sir, you are one of the kindest friends I ever had." * * *

Dr. Heberden, Dr. Brocklesby, Dr. Warren, and Dr. Butter, physicians, generously attended him, without accepting any fees, as did Mr. Cruikshank, surgeon; and all that could be done from professional skill and ability was tried, to prolong a life so truly valuable. He himself, indeed, having, on account of his very bad constitution, been perpetually applying himself to medical inquiries, united his own efforts with those of the gentlemen who attended him; and imagining that the dropsical collection of water which oppressed him might be drawn off by making incisions in his body, he, with his usual resolute defiance of pain, cut deep, when he thought that his surgeon had done it too tenderly.

About eight or ten days before his death, when Dr. Brocklesby paid him his morning visit, he seemed very low and desponding, and said, "I have been as a dying man all night." He then emphatically broke out in the words of Shakespeare:

> "Canst thou not minister to a mind diseased;
> Pluck from the memory a rooted sorrow,
> Raze out the written troubles of the brain,
> And with some sweet oblivious antidote
> Cleanse the stuffed bosom of that perilous stuff
> Which weighs upon the heart?"

To which Dr. Brocklesby readily answered, from the same great poet:

> "Therein the patient
> Must minister to himself."[5]

Johnson expressed himself much satisfied with the application. * * *

Amidst the melancholy clouds which hung over the dying Johnson, his characteristical manner showed itself on different occasions.

When Dr. Warren, in the usual style, hoped that he was better; his answer was, "No, Sir; you cannot conceive with what acceleration I advance towards death."

A man whom he had never seen before was employed one night to sit up with him. Being asked next morning how he liked his attendant, his answer was, "Not at all, Sir: the fellow's an idiot; he is as awkward as a turnspit[6] when first put into the wheel, and as sleepy as a dormouse."

Mr. Windham[7] having placed a pillow conveniently to support

---

4. A club to which Boswell and Reynolds belonged.
5. *Macbeth* V.iii.40–46.
6. A dog kept to turn the roasting-spit by running within a tread-wheel con-

nected to it (*NED*).
7. William Windham, one of Johnson's younger friends, later a Member of Parliament.

him, he thanked him for his kindness, and said, "That will do—all that a pillow can do." * * *

Johnson, with that native fortitude, which, amidst all his bodily distress and mental sufferings, never forsook him, asked Dr. Brocklesby, as a man in whom he had confidence, to tell him plainly whether he could recover. "Give me," said he, "a direct answer." The Doctor having first asked him if he could bear the whole truth, which way soever it might lead, and being answered that he could, declared that, in his opinion, he could not recover without a miracle. "Then," said Johnson, "I will take no more physic, not even my opiates; for I have prayed that I may render up my soul to God unclouded." In this resolution he persevered, and, at the same time, used only the weakest kinds of sustenance. Being pressed by Mr. Windham to take somewhat more generous nourishment, lest too low a diet should have the very effect which he dreaded, by debilitating his mind, he said, "I will take anything but inebriating sustenance."

The Reverend Mr. Strahan,[8] who was the son of his friend, and had been always one of his great favorites, had, during his last illness, the satisfaction of contributing to soothe and comfort him. That gentleman's house, at Islington, of which he is Vicar, afforded Johnson, occasionally and easily, an agreeable change of place and fresh air; and he attended also upon him in town in the discharge of the sacred offices of his profession.

Mr. Strahan has given me the agreeable assurance that, after being in much agitation, Johnson became quite composed, and continued so till his death.

Dr. Brocklesby, who will not be suspected of fanaticism, obliged me with the following account:

"For some time before his death, all his fears were calmed and absorbed by the prevalence of his faith, and his trust in the merits and *propitiation* of Jesus Christ." * * *

Johnson having thus in his mind the true Christian scheme, at once rational and consolatory, uniting justice and mercy in the Divinity, with the improvement of human nature, previous to his receiving the Holy Sacrament in his apartment, composed and fervently uttered this prayer:

"Almighty and most merciful Father, I am now as to human eyes, it seems, about to commemorate, for the last time, the death of thy Son Jesus Christ, our Saviour and Redeemer. Grant, O Lord, that my whole hope and confidence may be in his merits, and thy mercy; enforce and accept my imperfect repentance; make this commemoration available to the confirmation of my faith, the establishment

8. The Rev. George Strahan (pronounced *Strawn*), who later published Johnson's *Prayers and Meditations*.

of my hope, and the enlargement of my charity; and make the death of thy Son Jesus Christ effectual to my redemption. Have mercy upon me, and pardon the multitude of my offenses. Bless my friends; have mercy upon all men. Support me, by thy Holy Spirit, in the days of weakness, and at the hour of death; and receive me, at my death, to everlasting happiness, for the sake of Jesus Christ. Amen."

Having * * * made his will on the 8th and 9th of December, and settled all his worldly affairs, he languished till Monday, the 13th of that month, when he expired, about seven o'clock in the evening, with so little apparent pain that his attendants hardly perceived when his dissolution took place. * * *

1791

The Romantic Period

(1798-1832)

1789–1815: Revolutionary and Napoleonic period in France. 1789: The Revolution begins with the assembly of the States-General in May and the storming of the Bastille on July 14.—1793: King Louis XVI executed; England joins the alliance against France.—1793–94: The Reign of Terror under Robespierre.—1804: Napoleon crowned emperor. 1815: Napoleon defeated at Waterloo.

1798: *Lyrical Ballads* published anonymously by William Wordsworth and Samuel Taylor Coleridge.

1811–20: The Regency—George, Prince of Wales, acts as regent for George III, who was declared incurably insane.

1820: Accession of George IV.

1832: The Reform Bill carried in Parliament.

THE POLITICAL BACKGROUND: REVOLUTION AND REACTION

Following the common usage of historians of English literature, we will denote by the "Romantic period" the span between the year 1798, in which Wordsworth and Coleridge published their *Lyrical Ballads*, and 1832, when Sir Walter Scott died, when other major writers of the earlier century were either dead or no longer productive, and when the passage of the first Reform Bill, after more than three decades of political stagnation and repression, inaugurated the Victorian era of cautious readjustment of political power to conform to the economic and social realities of a new industrial age. This was a turbulent period in political and economic history, during which England was experiencing the ordeal of the change from its former status as a primarily agricultural society, where wealth and power had been largely concentrated in the landholding aristocracy, to a recognizably modern industrial nation, in which the balance of economic power was shifted to large-scale employers, who found themselves ranged against an immensely enlarging and increasingly restive working class. And this change occurred in a context first of the American and then of the much more radical French Revolution, of wars, of economic cycles of inflation and depression, and of the constant threat to the social structure from imported revolutionary ideologies to which the ruling classes responded by heresy-hunts and the repression of traditional liberties.

The early period of the French Revolution, marked by the Declaration of the Rights of Man and the storming of the Bastille to release the imprisoned political offenders, evoked enthusiastic support from English liberals and radicals alike. Two influential books indicate the radical social thinking stimulated by the Revolution. Tom Paine's *Rights of Man* (1791–92) justified the French Revolution against Edmund Burke's attack in his *Reflections on the Revolution in France* (1790), and advocated for England a democratic republic which was to be achieved, if lesser pressures failed, by popular revolution. More important for its influence on Wordsworth, Shelley, and other poets was William Godwin's *Inquiry Concerning Political Justice* (1793), which foretold an inevitable but peaceful evolution of society to a final stage in which all property would be equally distributed and all government would wither away. Later, however, English sympathizers dropped off as the Revolution followed its increasingly grim and violent course: the accession to power by the Jacobin extremists; the "September Massacres" of the imprisoned and helpless nobility in 1792, followed by the execution of the royal family; the invasion by the French Republic of the Rhineland and Netherlands, and its offer of armed assistance to all countries desiring to overthrow their governments, which brought England into the war against France; the guillotining of thousands in the Reign of Terror under Robespierre; and after the execution in their turn of the men who had directed the Terror, the emergence of Napoleon first as dictator and then as emperor of France. As Wordsworth wrote in *The Prelude* (XI.206–9),

> become oppressors in their turn,
> Frenchmen had changed a war of self-defense
> For one of conquest, losing sight of all
> Which they had struggled for * * *

For Wordsworth and all the English of liberal inclinations, these events posed a dilemma which has become familiar since the 1920's, in our parallel era of wars, revolutions, and the struggle by competing social ideologies—liberals had no clear choice, and no side they could wholeheartedly espouse. Napoleon, the child and champion of the French Revolution, had become an arch-aggressor, a despot, and the founder of a new dynasty; yet almost all those who opposed him did so for the wrong reasons, so that his final defeat at Waterloo in 1815 proved to be the triumph, not of progress and reform, but of reactionary despotisms throughout continental Europe.

In England this period of the wars against France and of the terrifying threat of the revolutionary spirit at home was one of harsh repressive measures. Public meetings were prohibited, habeas corpus suspended for the first time in over a hundred years, and advocates of even moderate measures of political change were persecuted as Jacobins, exponents of regicide and political terror, and were charged with high treason in time of war. In effect the Napoleonic wars put an end to reform, and to almost all genuine political life in England, for more than three decades. Although George III's attempt to revive the personal power of the Crown had been defeated by what G. M. Trevelyan calls "the new Tory oligarchy" under William Pitt the younger (1759–1806), the ruling classes—Whig and Tory—were still constituted much as they had been throughout the earlier part of the 18th century: aristocratic landholders and the higher Anglican clergy, with a popular leavening. And the Tories of this period saw themselves protecting the English constitution against the dangerous inroads of the democratic spirit of the French Revolution, much as the Whigs of 1689 had seen themselves as protectors of the same constitution against the Jacobites.

Yet this was the very time when profound economic and social changes were creating a desperate need for corresponding changes in political arrangements and politics, and new classes—manufacturing, rather than agricultural—were beginning to demand a power in government proportionate to their wealth. The "Industrial Revolution"—the shift in methods of manufacturing which resulted from the invention of power-driven machinery to replace hand labor—had begun in the mid-18th century with improvements in machines for processing textiles, and was given immense impetus when James Watt perfected the steam engine in 1765. In the succeeding decades steam replaced wind and water as the primary source of power in one after another type of manufacturing; and at once, after centuries of almost imperceptibly slow change, there began that constantly accelerating and still continuing alteration in economic and social conditions which shows no signs of slowing down in the foreseeable future. The application of steam power to manufacturing led to the massing of a new laboring population in the sprawling mill towns which burgeoned in central and northern England. In rural communities the destruction of home industry was accompanied by a rapid acceleration of the process—lamented by Oliver Goldsmith in *The Deserted Village* as early as 1770—of enclosing the old open-field and communally worked farms into privately owned agricultural holdings. This process was necessary for the more efficient methods of agriculture and animal breeding required to supply a growing population (although some of the land thus acquired was turned into vast private parks); in any case, it was achieved at the cost of creating a new landless class which either migrated to the industrial towns or remained as farm laborers, barely subsisting on starvation wages eked out by an inadequate dole. The landscape of England began to take on its modern appearance: the hitherto open rural areas subdivided into a checkerboard of fields enclosed by hedges and stone walls, and the factories of the mushrooming industrial and trading cities casting a pall of smoke over vast new areas of monotonous jerry-built houses and slum tenements. Meanwhile, the population was becoming increasingly polarized into what Disraeli later called the "Two Nations"—the two classes of capital and labor, the large owner or trader and the possessionless wageworker, the rich and the poor.

No attempt was made to regulate this movement from the old economic world to the new, not only because of the inertia of tradition and the power of vested interests, but because even the liberal reformers were dominated by the social philosophy of laissez faire. This theory of "let alone" holds that the general welfare can be ensured only by the free operation of economic laws; the government must maintain a policy of strict noninterference and leave each man to pursue his own private interests. For the great majority of the laboring class the results of this policy were inadequate wages, long hours of work under harsh discipline in sordid conditions, and the large-scale employment of women and children for tasks which destroyed both the body and the spirit. Reports by investigating committees on conditions in the coal mines, with male and female children of ten or even five years of age harnessed by the waist to heavy coal-sledges which they dragged by crawling on their hands and knees, read like lurid scenes from Dante's *Inferno*. The protracted French war, like other wars, was accompanied by high taxes, inflated prices, and shortages of food. In 1815 the conclusion of this war, when the enlargement of the working force by demobilized troops coincided with the fall in the wartime demand for goods, brought on the first modern industrial depression. Since the workers had no vote and were prevented by law from combining into labor unions, their sole recourse was to petitions, protest meetings, agitation, and hunger riots, which only frightened the ruling class into more repressive measures. In addition the introduction of new machines caused technological unemployment, and this provoked sporadic attempts by dispossessed workers to destroy the machines. After one such outbreak the House of Lords—despite Lord Byron's eloquent protest—passed a bill (1821) substituting death for transportation as the penalty for destroying the frames used for weaving in the stocking industry. In 1819 meetings of workers were organized to demand Parliamentary reform. In August of that year, a huge but orderly assembly at St. Peter's Fields, Manchester, was wantonly charged by troops, who killed nine and severely injured hundreds more; this was the notorious "Peterloo Massacre," so named as a parody on the Battle of Waterloo. The quick approval of this military action by the government evoked Percy Bysshe Shelley's scalding satire *The Masque of Anarchy* and inspired his poems for the working class, *England in 1819* and *Song to the Men of England*.

Suffering was largely confined to the poor, however, for all the while the landed classes, the industrialists, and many of the merchants prospered. In London the Regency period was for the leisure class a time of lavish display and moral laxity. In the provinces, the gentry in their great country houses carried on their familial and social concerns—so fully reflected in the novels of Jane Austen—almost untouched by great national and international events.

But the pressures for reform, while they might be repressed, could not be eliminated, especially since political disabilities were not limited to the working class. The right to vote was held by very few of the newly well-to-do; the shifts of population had increased the number of "rotten boroughs" (localities which, although now depopulated, kept their seats in the House of Commons, usually at the disposal of a single wealthy nobleman); while great new industrial cities such as Manchester had no representation at all. Gradually the working-class reformers acquired the support of the middle classes and the liberal Whigs. Finally, at a time of acute economic distress, and after a period of unprecedented agitation and disorders that threatened to break out into revolution, the first Reform Bill was carried in 1832, amid widespread rejoicing. It eliminated the rotten boroughs, redistributed parliamentary representation, and extended the vote. Although about half the middle class and almost all the working class remained still without a franchise, the principle of peaceful adjustment of conflicting interests by Parliamentary majority had been firmly established; and reform was to go on until, by stages, England acquired universal adult suffrage.

"THE SPIRIT OF THE AGE"

"Romanticism" has often been used by literary historians as though it were the name for a single essence or quality shared, in varying proportions, by all the principal writers of the Romantic period. But all attempts at a single definition of Romanticism fall far short of matching the variegated facts of a time which exceeds almost all ages of English literature in the range and diversity of its achievements. No writer in Wordsworth's lifetime thought of himself as a "Romantic," or as sharing an essential literary quality with all his important contemporaries; the word "Romantic" was not applied until half a century later, by English historians. Critics and reviewers contemporary with these writers treated them as independent individuals, or else grouped them (often invidiously, but with some basis in literary fact) into a number of separate schools: "the Lake School" of Wordsworth, Coleridge, and Robert Southey; "the Cockney School" of Leigh Hunt, Hazlitt, and associated writers, including John Keats; and "the Satanic School" of Byron, Shelley, and their followers.

Many of the major writers, however, did feel that there was something distinctive about their time—not a shared doctrine or literary quality, but a pervasive intellectual climate, which some of them called "the spirit of the age." They had the sense that (as Keats said in one of his sonnets) "Great spirits now on earth are sojourning," and that there was evidence all about of that release of energy, experimental boldness, and creative power which marks a literary renaissance. In his *Defense of Poetry* Shelley claimed that the literature of the age "has arisen as it were from a new birth. * * * It is impossible to read the compositions of the most celebrated writers of the present day without being startled with the electric life which burns within their words," and this is "less their spirit than the spirit of the age." Shelley explained this literary spirit as the inescapable accompaniment of political and social revolution; and other writers agreed. Francis Jeffrey, foremost conservative reviewer of the day, connected "the revolution in our literature" with "the agitations of the French Revolution, and the discussions as well as the hopes and terrors to which it gave occasion." William Hazlitt, who published a book of essays called *The Spirit of the Age*, described how, in his early youth, the French Revolution seemed "the dawn of a new era, a new impulse had been given to men's minds," so that "philosophy took a higher, poetry could afford a deeper range." The new poetry of the school of Wordsworth, he maintained, "had its origin in the French Revolution. * * * There was a mighty ferment in the heads of statesmen and poets, kings and people. * * * It was a time of promise, a renewal of the world—and of letters."

The imagination of Romantic writers was, indeed, preoccupied with the fact and idea of revolution. First the American and later, and to a much greater degree, the French Revolution seemed to promise that, by breaking free from outmoded concepts and institutions, man might also escape the oppression and sufferings which had hitherto seemed the inescapable condition of his existence, and establish a new and joyous world of liberty, equality, and fraternity. In the early period of the Revolution all the leading English writers except Edmund Burke were in sympathy with it, and Robert Burns, William Blake, Wordsworth, Coleridge, and Southey were among its most fervent adherents. Later, even after the first boundless expectations had been disappointed by the events in France, the younger writers, including Hazlitt, Hunt, Shelley, and Byron, felt that its example, when purged of its errors, still comprised man's best hope. The Revolution generated a feeling that this was a great age of new beginnings, when, by discarding inherited procedures and outworn customs, everything was possible; and not only in political and social arrangements, but in intellectual and literary enterprises as well. In his *Prelude* Wordsworth wrote the classic description of the intoxicating spirit of the early 1790's, with "France standing on the top of golden hours, / And human nature seeming born again," so that "not favored spots alone, but the whole Earth, / The beauty wore of promise." Something of this sense of suddenly expanding horizons and of limitless possibilities through new beginnings survived the shock of first disappointment at events in France and carried over to the year 1797, when Wordsworth and Coleridge, in excited daily communion, set out to revolutionize the theory and practice of poetry. The product of these discussions was the *Lyrical Ballads* of 1798.

POETIC THEORY AND POETIC PRACTICE

Wordsworth undertook to justify the new poetry by a critical manifesto or statement of poetic principles, in the form of an extended Preface to the second edition of *Lyrical Ballads* in 1800. In it he set himself in opposition to the literary *ancien régime*, those writers of the preceding century who, to his view, had imposed on poetry artificial conventions which distorted its free and natural development. Wordsworth's later critical writings were largely attempts to clarify, buttress, or qualify points made in his first declaration. Coleridge declared that the Preface was "half a child of my own brain"; and although he soon developed doubts about certain of Wordsworth's unguarded statements, and undertook to correct them in *Biographia Literaria* (1817), he did not question the necessity of Wordsworth's attempt to overturn the reigning tradition. In the fashion of innovators, Wordsworth was more concerned with justifying his program against what he regarded as the poetic Establishment than with doing strict historical justice to his predecessors. In the course of the 18th century there had been increasing opposition to the neoclassic tradition of Dryden, Pope, and Dr. Johnson and to the dominance of satire, verse essay, and the poetry of wit; and especially in the 1740's and later, there had emerged many of the critical concepts, as well as a number of the poetic subjects and forms, which were later exploited by Wordsworth and his contemporaries. Wordsworth's Preface nevertheless deserves its reputation as marking a turning point in English literature, for Wordsworth gathered up largely isolated ideas, organized them into a coherent theory based on explicit critical principles, and made them the rationale for his own massive achievements as a poet. We can conveniently use some of the concepts in this extremely influential essay as points of departure for a survey of distinctive elements in the theory and poetry of the Romantic period.

1. *The Concept of Poetry.*

In neoclassic theory, poetry had been regarded as primarily an imitation of human life—in a favorite figure, "a mirror held up to nature"—in a form designed to instruct and give artistic pleasure to the reader. Wordsworth, in a reiterated statement, defined all good poetry as "the spontaneous overflow of powerful feelings." In a reversal of earlier aesthetic theory, he thus located the source of poetry not in the outer world, but in the individual poet, and identified as its essential material not men and their actions, but the fluid feelings of the writer himself. Other Romantic theories, however various, concurred in this crucial point by referring to the mind and feelings of the individual writer, instead of to the outer world, for the source and substance of a poem. Many writers identified poetry (in metaphors parallel to Wordsworth's "overflow") as the "expression" or "utterance" or "exhibition" of emotion. Blake and Shelley described a poem as the poet's private imaginative vision, which they opposed to the ordinary world of public experience. Coleridge regarded poetry as the product of the poet's imagination which—by a process that Coleridge called "a dim analogue" of God's own creative activity—assimilates the materials of sense into an organic entity that does not imitate the created world, but constitutes an equivalent creation of its own.

In accordance with the view that poetry expresses the poet's own mind and feelings, Romantic poems to an extraordinary extent take as their subject matter, not the actions of other men, but the personal experiences, thoughts, and feelings of the poets who wrote them. The lyric poem written in the first person, which had earlier been regarded as a minor poetic kind, became a major Romantic form and was usually described as the most essentially poetic of all the genres. And in the Romantic lyric the "I" is often not a mere *dramatis persona*, a typical lyric speaker such as the Petrarchan lover or Cavalier gallant of Elizabethan and 17th-century love poems, but is recognizably the poet in his private person. In the poems of Coleridge and Keats, for example, the experiences and states of mind expressed by the lyric speaker often accord closely with the personal confessions in the poets' letters and journals. Even in his ostensibly fictional writings, narrative and dramatic, Byron usually invites his readers to identify the hero with the author, whether the hero is presented romantically (as in *Childe Harold*, *Manfred*, or the Oriental tales) or in an ironic perspective (as in *Don Juan*). An extreme example of this subjective tendency is Wordsworth's *Prelude*, which is a poem of epic length and epic seriousness about the growth of the poet's own mind, while Wordsworth's projected but incompleted poem *The Recluse* was to have been a huge trilogy concerning "the sensations and opinions of a poet living in retirement," the first and third parts to consist "chiefly of meditations in the Author's own person." In contemporary prose, the equivalent development was the vogue of the personal essays of Charles Lamb, Hazlitt, and Leigh Hunt, and the currency of the intellectual or spiritual autobiography, whether fictionalized (Thomas Carlyle's *Sartor Resartus*) or presented as unaltered fact (Coleridge's *Biographia Literaria*, Thomas De Quincey's *Confessions of an English Opium Eater* and *Autobiographic Sketches*).

Naturally enough, in the applied criticism of an age which viewed poetry as an expressive activity, there emerged for the first time the peculiarly modern tendency to read the great poetry of the past—including the poetry of Milton, Shakespeare, Dante, and even Homer—as a revelation, more or less disguised, of the deep inner personality of the poet. By 1827 Carlyle could say, with considerable truth, that the great question usually raised by "the best of our own critics at present is a question mainly of a psychological sort, to be answered by discovering and delineating the peculiar nature of the poet from his poetry."

2. *Poetic Spontaneity and Freedom.*

It will be noted that Wordsworth defined good poetry not merely as the overflow but as "the *spontaneous* overflow" of feelings. In traditional aesthetic theory, poetry had been regarded as supremely an art; an art perfected by painstaking endeavor, which in modern times could be practiced successfully only by a craftsman who had assimilated classical precedents, was aware of the "rules" governing the kind of poem he was writing, and (except for the felicities which, as Pope said, are "beyond the reach of art") deliberately employed tested means to achieve foreknown effects upon his audience. But to Wordsworth, although the writing of a poem may be preceded by reflection and followed by second thoughts and revisions, the immediate act of composition must be spontaneous— that is, unforced, arising from impulse, and free from all rules and the artful manipulation of means to foreseen ends—if the product is to be a genuine poem and not an artificial sham. Other important Romantic critics also voiced declarations of artistic independence. Keats listed as an "axiom" that "if poetry comes not as naturally as the leaves to a tree it had better not come at all." Blake insisted that he wrote from "Inspiration and Vision," and that his long "prophetic" poem, *Milton*, was given to him by an agency not himself, and "produced without Labor or Study." Shelley also maintained that it is "an error to assert that the finest passages of poetry are produced by labor and study," and suggested instead that they are the products of an unconscious creativity: "A great statue or picture grows under the power of the artist as a child in the mother's womb." "The definition of genius," Hazlitt remarked, "is that it acts unconsciously." Despite their theoretical insistence on the total autonomy and spontaneity of poetic activity, however, the surviving work-sheets of the Romantic poets, as well as the testimony of observers, show that they worked and reworked their texts no less arduously—if perhaps more immediately and intensely under the impetus of first conception—than the craftsmen of earlier ages. Coleridge, who believed that truth lies in a union of opposites, came closer to the facts of Romantic practice when he claimed that the act of composing poetry involves the psychological contraries "of passion and of will, of *spontaneous* impulse and of *voluntary* purpose."

The emphasis in this period on the free activity of the imagination is related to a characteristic insistence that the products of the precise and systematic intellect fall far short of matching the complexity, nuances, and ambiguities of concrete human experience. It is also in accord with the contemporary insistence on the essential role of instinct, intuition, and the feelings of "the heart" to supplement the judgments of the purely logical faculty, "the head," whether in the province of artistic beauty, philosophical and religious truth, or moral goodness. "Deep thinking," Coleridge wrote, "is attainable only by a man of deep feeling, and all truth is a species of revelation"; hence, "a metaphysical solution that does not tell you something in the heart is grievously to be suspected as apocryphal."

3. *Romantic "Nature Poetry."*

In his Preface Wordsworth wrote that "I have at all times endeavored to look steadily at my subject"; and in a supplementary Essay later attached to *Lyrical Ballads*, although he paid handsome tribute to James Thomson's descriptive poem *The Seasons*, he complained that, from Dryden through Pope, there is scarcely an image from external nature "from which it can be inferred that the eye of the poet had been steadily fixed on his object." A glance at the table of contents of any collection of Romantic poems will indicate the astonishing degree to which the natural scene and its flora and fauna have become a primary poetic subject; while Wordsworth, Shelley, and even more Coleridge and Keats, described natural phenomena with an accuracy of observation which, although it profited from the many descriptive poems that had followed upon *The Seasons*, exceeded 18th-century precedent in its ability to capture the sensuous nuance.

As a consequence of the prominence of landscape in this period, "Romantic poetry" has to the popular mind become almost synonymous with "nature poetry." Neither Romantic theory nor Romantic practice, however, justifies the opinion that the aim of this poetry was description for its own sake. Wordsworth in fact insisted that the ability to observe and describe objects accurately, "though indispensable to a Poet, is one which he employs only in submission to necessity, and never for a continuance of time: as its exercise supposes all the higher qualities of the mind to be passive, and in a state of subjection to external objects." And while most of the great Romantic lyrics—Wordsworth's *Tintern Abbey* and *Ode: Intimations of Immortality*, Coleridge's *Frost at Midnight* and *Dejection*, Shelley's *Ode to the West Wind*, Keats's *Nightingale*—begin with an aspect or change of aspect in the natural scene, this serves only as stimulus to the most characteristic human activity, that of thinking. Romantic "nature poems" are in fact descriptive-meditative poems, in which the presented scene usually serves to raise an emotional problem whose development and resolution constitute the organizing principle of the poem. As Wordsworth said, not nature, but "the Mind of Man" is "my haunt, and the main region of my song."

In addition, Romantic poems habitually imbue the landscape with human life, passion, and expressiveness. In part such descriptions represent the poetic equivalent of the current metaphysical concept of nature, which had developed in deliberate revolt against the world views of Descartes and other scientific philosophers of the 17th and 18th centuries, who had posited as the ultimate reality a mechanical world consisting of physical particles in motion. What is needed in philosophy, Coleridge wrote, is "the substitution of life and intelligence * * * for the philosophy of mechanism, which, in everything that is most worthy of the human intellect, strikes *Death*. * * * " But for many Romantic poets it was clearly also a matter of immediate, unthinking experience to respond to the outer universe as to a living entity which shares the feelings of the observer. James Thomson and other descriptive poets had described the physical universe as giving direct access to God, and even as itself possessing the attributes of divinity; in *Tintern Abbey* and other poems Wordsworth exhibits toward the landscape attitudes and sentiments which men had earlier felt not only for God, but also for a father, a mother, or a beloved woman. Elsewhere, as in the great passage on crossing Simplon Pass (see *The Prelude* VI.624 ff.), Wordsworth also revives the ancient theological concept that God's creation constitutes a symbol system, in a huge book of physical revelation parallel to the Revelation in the Scriptures—

> Characters of the great Apocalypse,
> The types and symbols of Eternity,
> Of first, and last, and midst, and without end.

This view of natural objects as symbols possessing a natural correspondence to the spiritual world (which had persisted in many esoteric philosophies as well as in Christian theology), served also as the theoretical understructure for a Romantic tendency, exhibited in its extreme form by Blake and Shelley, to write a symbolist poetry in which a rose, a sunflower, a mountain, a cave, or a cloud are presented as objects instinct with a significance beyond themselves. "I always seek in what I see," Shelley said, "the likeness of something beyond the present and tangible object."

4. The Glorification of the Commonplace.

In two lectures on Wordsworth, one in a series on *The English Poets* (1815) and another in *The Spirit of the Age* (1825), Hazlitt declared that the school of poetry founded by Wordsworth was the literary equivalent of the French Revolution, translating political changes into poetical experiments. The parallel between the political and poetical revolution was especially evident in the leveling tendency of Wordsworth's subject matter: "Kings and queens were dethroned from their rank and station in legitimate tragedy or epic poetry, as they were decapitated elsewhere. * * * The paradox [these poets] set out with was that all things are by nature equally fit subjects for poetry; or that if there is any preference to be given, those that are the meanest and most unpromising are the best. * * * They claimed kindred only with the commonest of the people. * * * "

What Hazlitt had in mind was Wordsworth's statement that the aim of *Lyrical Ballads* was "to choose incidents and situations from common life," and to use a "selection of language really spoken by men"; the special source of this subject matter and the principal model for this language, Wordsworth went on to say, is "humble and rustic life." As Hazlitt shrewdly saw, this was more a social than a distinctively literary definition of the proper materials and language for poetry. What Hazlitt failed to observe, however, was that Wordsworth represented not so much an abrupt break with tradition as the culmination of a tendency through the preceding century to dissolve the traditional hierarchy of the genres and the traditional theory of poetic decorum, according to which an appropriate level of style—high, middle, or low—had to be matched to the status of the poetic kinds, ranging from epic and tragedy at the top down to the pastoral and short lyric forms at the base. Versifiers of the later decades of the 18th century had experimented in the simple treatment of simple subjects, and Robert Burns—like Wordsworth, a sympathizer with the French Revolution—had achieved great poetic success in the serious representation of humble life in a language really spoken by rustics. But Wordsworth buttressed his poetic practice by a theory which inverted the old hierarchy by elevating humble and rustic life and the plain style, earlier appropriate to the lowly pastoral, into the principal subject and medium for poetry in general. And in his own practice, as Hazlitt also noted, Wordsworth went even further, and turned for the subjects of his serious poems not only to humble people but to the ignominious, the outcast, the delinquent—to "convicts, female vagrants, gypsies * * * idiot boys and mad mothers," as well as to "peasants, peddlers, and village barbers." Hence the outrage of Lord Byron, who alone among his great Romantic contemporaries insisted that Dryden and Pope had laid out the proper road for poetry, and who—in spite of his liberalism in politics— maintained allegiance both to aristocratic proprieties and traditional poetic decorum:

> "Peddlers," and "Boats," and "Wagons"! Oh! ye shades
> Of Pope and Dryden, are we come to this?

But in his democratization of poetry, Hazlitt insisted, Wordsworth was "the most original poet now living, and the one whose writings could the least be spared." And certainly it was Wordsworth, far more than any 18th-century predecessor, who effected an immense enlargement of our imaginative sympathies and brought into the province of serious literature a range of materials and interests which are still being diligently explored by major writers of the present day.

It should be noted, however, that Wordsworth's aim in *Lyrical Ballads* was not a mere reproductive realism, but as he announced in his Preface, to throw over "situations from common life * * * a certain coloring of imagination, whereby ordinary things should be presented to the mind in an unusual aspect." Or as Coleridge expanded this statement in *Biographia Literaria*, Chapter XIV, Wordsworth's object was "to give the charm of novelty to things of every day, and to excite a feeling analogous to the supernatural, by awakening the mind's attention from the lethargy of custom, and directing it to the loveliness and wonders of the world before us." As these passages indicate, Wordsworth's concern in his poetry was not only with "common life" but with "ordinary *things*"; no one can read *The Prelude*, for example, without noticing the extraordinary reverence which he attaches to such words as "common," "ordinary," "everyday," "humble," whether applied to people, to events, or to the visible scene. His aim throughout is to shake us out of the lethargy of custom so as to refresh our sense of wonder in the everyday, the trivial, and the familiar.

Dr. Johnson had said that "wonder is a pause of reason," and that "all wonder is the effect of novelty upon ignorance." But for many Romantic critics, to arouse in the sophisticated mind that sense of wonder felt by the ignorant and the naïve was a primary power of imagination and a major function of poetry. Commenting on the special imaginative quality of Wordsworth's early poetry (*Biographia*, Chapter VI), Coleridge commented: "To carry on the feelings of childhood into the powers of manhood; to combine the child's sense of wonder and novelty with the appearances, which every day for perhaps forty years had rendered familiar * * * this is the character and privilege of genius," and its effect on the reader is to awaken "freshness of sensation" in the representation of "familiar objects." Poetry, said Shelley in his *Defense of Poetry*, "reproduces the common universe" but "purges from our inward sight the film of familiarity which obscures from us the wonder of our being," and "creates anew the universe, after it has been blunted by reiteration." And in Carlyle's *Sartor Resartus* (1833–34), the chief—indeed the only— effect of the conversion of the protagonist from despairing unbelief is that he is able to sustain a sense of the "Natural Supernaturalism" in ordinary experience and so overcome the "custom" which "blinds us to the miraculousness of daily-recurring miracles."

Carlyle's terminology suggests that the Romantic attempt to apotheosize the lowly and the commonplace had a religious origin; it is a secular or nontheologial form of a central Christian doctrine: "the last shall be first." Wordsworth constantly endeavors to present a seemingly trivial person or thing or moment and show it suddenly transfigured, rendered luminous by an enduring and quasireligious significance. When he fails, as in the poem *We Are Seven*, the result verges on bathos. But often he wonderfully succeeds, as in his descriptions of such ordinary events as ice-skating, borrowing a rowboat without permission, and meeting an old blind beggar or a solitary leech-gatherer. In one of the events Wordsworth called "a spot of time," when he entered London for the first time, he describes how the "vulgar men about me, trivial forms * * * mean shapes" suddenly assumed a "weight and power" that lasted only a moment, "yet with Time it dwells, / And grateful memory, as a thing divine" (*The Prelude* VIII.543–59).

5. The Supernatural and "Strangeness in Beauty."

In most of his poems Coleridge, like Wordsworth, dealt with the everyday things of this world, and in *Frost at Midnight*, written in February of 1798, he showed how well he too could manage a natural supernaturalism and achieve the effect of wonder in the familiar. But according to the agreed division of labor between Wordsworth and Coleridge in writing *Lyrical Ballads*, Coleridge's special function, he tells us, was to achieve wonder by a frank violation of natural laws and the ordinary course of events, in poems of which "the incidents and agents were to be, in part at least, supernatural." And in *The Ancient Mariner, Christabel*, and *Kubla Khan*, Coleridge opened up to English poetry the realm of mystery and magic, in which ancient folklore, superstition, and demonology are used to startle and enthrall sophisticated readers by impressing them with the sense of occult powers and unknown modes of being. Such poems are usually set in the distant past or in faraway places, or both; the milieu of *Kubla Khan*, for example, exploits the exoticism both of the Middle Ages and of the Orient. Next to Coleridge, the greatest master of this Romantic mode was John Keats. In *La Belle Dame sans Merci* and *The Eve of St. Agnes* he adapted the old forms of ballad and romance to modern sophisticated use and, like Coleridge, exploited the charm of "the far away and long ago" by establishing a medieval setting for the events of magic and mystery. Hence the term "the medieval revival," frequently attached to the Romantic period, which comprehends also the ballad imitations and some of the verse tales and historical novels of Sir Walter Scott.

Another side of the tendency which Walter Pater later called "the addition of strangeness to beauty" was the Romantic interest in unusual modes of experience, of a kind which earlier writers had largely ignored as either too trivial or too aberrant for serious literary concern. Blake, Wordsworth, and Coleridge in their poetry explored aspects of those visionary states of consciousness which are common among children but which violate the standard categories of adult judgment. Coleridge was interested in mesmerism (what we now call hypnotism), shared with De Quincey a concern with dreams, nightmares, and the distortion of perception caused by drugs, and like Blake and Shelley, steeped himself in occult and esoteric doctrines—in "all the strange phantasms," as he called them, "that ever possessed your philosophy dreamers from Thoth the Egyptian to [Thomas] Taylor, the English Pagan." Byron exploited the fascination of the forbidden and the appeal of the terrifying Satanic hero. And Keats was extraordinarily sensitive to the ambivalence of human experience—to the mingling, at their highest intensity, of pleasure and pain, to the destructiveness of love, and to the erotic quality of the longing for death. Most of these phenomena had already been crudely explored by 18th-century writers of terror tales and Gothic fiction, and later in the 19th century all of them, sometimes exaggerated to the point of blatant abnormality, became the special literary province of Charles Baudelaire, Algernon Charles Swinburne, and other writers of the European Decadence.

INDIVIDUALISM, NONCONFORMITY, AND APOCALYPTIC EXPECTATION

Through the greater part of the 18th century, man had for the most part been viewed as a limited being in a strictly ordered and essentially unchanging world. A variety of philosophical and religious systems in this century coincided in a distrust of radical innovation, an emphasis on tradition and respect for the precedents established through the ages by the common sense of mankind, and the recommendation to man to set accessible goals and avoid extremes, whether in matters of politics, intellect, morality, or art. Many of the great literary works of the period, whatever their philosophical or religious differences, joined in attacking "pride," or man's persistent aspiration beyond the limits natural to his species. "The bliss of man," Pope wrote in *An Essay on Man*, "(could pride that blessing find) / Is not to act or think beyond mankind."

> This kind, this due degree
> Of blindness, weakness, Heaven bestows on thee.
> Submit.

The Romantic period, the age of burgeoning free enterprise and revolutionary hope, was also an age of radical individualism, in which both the philosophers and poets put an immensely higher estimate on man's potentialities and on his proper aims. In German post-Kantian philosophy, which generated many of the characteristic ideas of European Romanticism, the mind of man—what was called the "Subject" or "Ego"—took over various functions which had hitherto been the sole prerogative of Divinity. Most prominent was the rejection of a central 18th-century concept of the mind as a mirrorlike recipient of a universe already created and its replacement by the new concept of the mind as itself the creator of the universe it perceives. In the extreme version of the German idealist J. G. Fichte, all existence is a creation of the Ego, which sets up an external world merely to serve as a limit to itself, which it can then strive ceaselessly to overcome. The English founders of the new poetry also described the mind as creating its own experience, although they usually held that it performs this function in collaboration with the divine Creator, or with something given to it from without. Mind, wrote Coleridge in 1801, is "not passive" but "made in God's Image, and that too in the sublimest sense—the Image of the *Creator*." And Wordsworth declared in *The Prelude* (II.257–60) that the individual mind

> Doth, like an agent of the one great Mind
> Create, creator and receiver both,
> Working but in alliance with the works
> Which it beholds. * * *

Many Romantic writers also agreed that man's mind has an access beyond sense to the infinite, through a special faculty they called either Reason or Imagination. In *The Prelude* (VI.592 ff.) Wordsworth describes a flash of imagination "that has revealed / The invisible world," and affirms:

> Our destiny, our being's heart and home,
> Is with infinitude, and only there;
> With hope it is, hope that can never die,
> Effort, and expectation, and desire,
> And something evermore about to be.

The aspect of man which, to the moralists of the preceding age, had been his essential sin, or his tragic error, now becomes his glory and his triumph: he refuses to submit to his limitations and, though finite, persists in setting infinite, hence inaccessible goals. Wordsworth characteristically goes on to declare that "under such banners militant, the soul / Seeks for no trophies, struggles for no spoils"; for him, the militant striving is entirely spiritual, and ends in physical quietism and moral fortitude. But for other writers, especially in Germany, man's proper destiny is ceaseless activity—

a *"Streben nach dem Unendlichen,"* a striving for the infinite. This view is epitomized by Goethe's *Faust*, who in his quest for the unattainable violates ordinary moral limits, yet wins salvation by his very insatiability, which never stoops to contentment with any possibilities offered by this finite world. Man's infinite longing—in Shelley's phrase, "the desire of the moth for a star"—was a common theme also in the English literature of the day. "Less than everything," Blake announced, "cannot satisfy man." Shelley's *Alastor* and Keats's *Endymion* both represent the quest for an indefinable and inaccessible goal, and Byron's *Manfred* has for its hero a man whose "powers and will" reach beyond the limits of that human clay "which clogs the ethereal essence," so that "his aspirations / Have been beyond the dwellers of the earth."

In the contemporary theory of art, we find critics rejecting the neo-classic ideal of a limited intention, perfectly accomplished, in favor of "the glory of the imperfect," in which the artist's very failure attests the largeness of his aim. In a classic author like Sophocles, Coleridge said, "there is a completeness, a satisfying, an excellence, on which the mind can rest," but in Shakespeare there is "a dissatisfying, or falling short of perfection, yet so promising of our progression that we would not ex-change it for that repose of mind * * * " And in their own work, Ro-mantic writers often set themselves ambitious goals and experimented boldly in poetic language, versification, and design. They continued to cultivate a number of forms current in the later 18th century, including the sonnet, the extended lyric combining regional description and medita-tion, verse narratives of domestic and rural life, and songs written on the traditional themes of love, drink, and war. But especially in their longer poems, they struck out in new directions, and in the space of a few decades produced an astonishing variety of forms constructed on novel principles of organization and style. Blake's symbolic lyrics and visionary "prophetic" poems; Coleridge's strange ballad-narrative of sin and retribution, *The Ancient Mariner*; Wordsworth's epiclike spiritual autobiography, *The Prelude*; Shelley's cosmic symbolic drama, *Prometheus Unbound*; Keats's great sequence of *Odes* on the irreconcilable conflict in basic human de-sires; Byron's ironic survey of all European civilization, *Don Juan*—these depart sufficiently from their closest literary antecedents so that one might say of each of them, as Shelley said of *Don Juan*, that it was "something wholly new and relative to the age."

The great neoclassic writers had typically dealt with men as members of an organized, and usually an urban, society; of this society the author regarded himself as an integral part, its highest standards were those he spoke for, and to it as his audience he addressed himself. Some Romantic writers, on the other hand, deliberately isolated themselves from society. Wordsworth's projected masterwork he entitled *The Recluse*, and he de-scribed himself as "musing in solitude" on its subject, "the individual Mind that keeps her own / Inviolate retirement." And in almost all Words-worth's poems, long or short, the words "single," "solitary," "by oneself," "alone" constitute a leitmotif; again and again his imagination is re-leased by the sudden apparition of a single figure or object, standing out starkly against an undifferentiated background. Coleridge also, and still more strikingly, Byron and Shelley, liked to deal with a solitary protagonist who is separated from society because he has rejected it, or because it has rejected him; these poets thus introduced what developed into a persistent theme in many Victorian and modern writers, from Matthew Arnold through Thomas Mann, T. S. Eliot, and James Joyce—the theme of exile, of the disinherited mind which cannot find a spiritual home in its native land and society or in the whole modern world. The solitary Romantic nonconformist was sometimes also a great sinner. Writers of that time were fascinated by the outlaws of myth, legend, or history—Cain, Satan, Faust, the Wandering Jew or the great, flawed figure of Napoleon—about whom they wrote and on whom they modeled a number of their villains or their heroes. In Coleridge's *Ancient Mariner* (as in Wordsworth's *Guilt and Sorrow* and *Peter Bell*) the guilty outcast—"alone, alone, all, all alone"—is made to realize and expiate his sin against the community of living things, so that he may reassume his place in the social order. But in Byron the violator of conventional laws and limits remains proudly unrepentant. His hero Manfred, a compound of guilt and superhuman greatness, cannot be defeated by death, and wins the admiration even of the holy abbot by successfully defying the demons who, in the tradition of Marlowe's *Dr. Faustus,* have come to drag his soul to hell: I "was my own destroyer, and will be / My own hereafter * * * / Back, ye baffled fiends!" A more reputable Romantic hero, who turns up frequently in Byron and other writers and is made the protagonist of Shelley's greatest poem, is the Prometheus of Greek mythology. He shares with Satan the status of superlative nonconformity, since he sets himself in opposition to deity itself; unlike Satan, however, he is an unflawed nonconformist, because he acts as the champion rather than the enemy of the human race.

Nowhere is the Romantic combination of boundless aspiration and the reliance on the power of the individual mind better exhibited than in their literary treatment of the ultimate hope of mankind. The French Revolution had aroused in many sympathizers the millennial expectations which are deeply rooted in Hebrew and Christian tradition. "Few persons but those who have lived in it," Robert Southey reminisced in 1824, "can conceive or comprehend what the memory of the French Revolution was, nor what a visionary world seemed to open upon those who were just entering it. Old things seemed passing away, and nothing was dreamt of but the regeneration of the human race." Southey's language—like that of Wordsworth in *The Prelude* and Hazlitt in his autobiographical essays, when these writers described their early Revolutionary fervor—is Biblical; and it reflects the extent to which, in England, the Revolution was championed especially by members of radical Protestant sects, who envisioned it more or less explicitly on the model of Biblical prophecy. For the Biblical canon, which begins with the Creation, the felicity of Eden, and the abrupt Fall of Man, ends with the Apocalypse (literally, "Revelation" —the vision of the last things) of an equally abrupt return to felicity at Christ's Second Coming, first in an interim millennium (literally "one thousand years") of an earthly kingdom, and then, after the destruction of the original creation, in the eternity of "a new heaven and a new earth." The Biblical Book of Revelation symbolizes this ultimate event as a marriage between the holy city of New Jerusalem and Christ the Lamb. In 1794 Joseph Priestley, chemist, political radical, and leader of the Unitarian sect, published a sermon in which he interpreted the French Revolution as the stage preceding the millennium prophesied in Revelation. Coleridge in his *Religious Musings* (1794–96) followed Priestley in seeing the Revolution as the violent preliminary to the thousand years of earthly happiness, to be "followed by the passing away of this earth" in a new earth and heaven. And Blake's poems, *The French Revolution* (1791) and *America, a Prophecy* (1793), represent both these events, in apocalyptic terms, as portents of the last days of the fallen world.

The later course of the French Revolution, as we have seen, dashed the faith of most writers in violent political revolution as a way to the millennium. But a number of English poets did not abandon their apocalyptic hope; they salvaged it by giving it a new interpretation. They transferred the agency of apocalypse from mass action to the individual mind—from a political to a spiritual revolution—and proposed that "the new earth and new heaven" of Revelation is available here, now, to each man, if only he can make his visionary imagination triumph over his senses and logic-chopping understanding. Hence the extraordinary Romantic emphasis on a new way of *seeing* (which is the restoration of a lost earlier way of seeing) as man's chief aim in life. Blake's "Prophetic Books," for example, all deal with some aspect of the Fall and Redemption, and represent apocalypse as the recovery of the imaginative vision of things as they really are, seen "through and not with the eye." "The Last Judgment," he wrote, "is not Fable or Allegory, but Vision. * * * Vision or Imagination is a Representation of what Eternally Exists, Really and Unchangeably." "The Nature of my Work is Visionary or Imaginative; it is an Endeavor to Restore what the Ancients called the Golden Age." In some writers, this concept of the imaginative recreation of the old earth into a new earth is still expressed in the original Biblical metaphor of a marriage—although now it is not a marriage of the New Jerusalem with the Lamb, but a reintegration of man's inner faculties into spiritual unity, or else a marriage between man's mind and the external world. Coleridge put this latter version most succinctly, in *Dejection: An Ode*; it is the inner condition of "Joy," at life's highest moments, "Which, wedding nature to us, gives in dower / A new earth and new heaven." Wordsworth announced as the "high argument" for *The Recluse* (the same theme serves as underpattern for *The Prelude*) that "Paradise, and groves Elysian" are not "a history only of departed things"—

> For the discerning intellect of Man
> When wedded to this goodly universe
> In love and holy passion, shall find these
> A simple produce of the common day.

In Shelley's *Prometheus Unbound*, Prometheus represents archetypal man, whose total change of heart frees his imaginative capacity to envision a regenerate world; the fourth act symbolizes this event in the mode of a prodigious marriage celebration in which the whole cosmos participates. Carlyle's *Sartor Resartus*, to mention one more example, is the history of an individual's savage spiritual crisis and conversion, which turns out to be in fact the achievement of an individual apocalypse: "And I awoke to a new Heaven and a new Earth." But, as Carlyle goes on to indicate, this new earth is the same old earth, merely seen by his protagonist as though miraculously recreated, because he has learned to substitute the

"Imaginative" faculty for what Carlyle represents as the chief faculty of the 18th-century Enlightenment, the "Logical, Mensurative faculty," or "Understanding." Writing in 1830–31, at the close of the period historians have labeled "Romantic," Carlyle thus summed up the tendency of a generation of writers to retain the ancient faith in apocalypse, but to interpret it not as a change in the world, but as a change in man's world view.

WILLIAM BLAKE

(1757–1827)

1783:   *Poetical Sketches,* his first book of poems.
1794:   *Songs of Innocence and of Experience.*
1804–20: The two last and greatest "prophetic" poems, *Milton* and *Jerusalem.*

What Blake called his "Spiritual Life" was as varied, free, and dramatic as his "Corporeal Life" was simple, limited, and unadventurous. His father was a London haberdasher. His only formal education was in art: at the age of 10 he entered a drawing school and later studied for a time at the school of the Royal Academy of Arts. At 14 he was apprenticed for seven years to a well-known engraver, James Basire, read widely in his free time, and began to try his hand at poetry. At 24 he married Catherine Boucher, daughter of a market gardener. She was then illiterate, but Blake taught her to read and to help him in his engraving and printing. In the early and somewhat sentimentalized biographies, Catherine is represented as an ideal wife for an unorthodox and impecunious genius—gentle, forbearing, and resourceful, with an unswerving faith in her husband's visions and God-given powers. Blake, however, must have been a trying domestic partner, and his vehement attacks on the oppression and torment caused by a possessive, jealous female will, which reached a climax in 1793 and remained prominent in his writings for another decade, may well reflect a troubled period at home. The couple were childless.

The Blakes for a time enjoyed a moderate prosperity while Blake gave drawing lessons, illustrated books, and engraved designs made by other artists. When the demand for his work slackened, Blake in 1800 moved to a cottage at Felpham, on the Sussex seacoast, under the patronage of the wealthy poetaster, biographer, and amateur of the arts, William Hayley, who with the best of narrow intentions tried to transform Blake into a conventional artist and breadwinner. But the caged eagle soon rebelled. Hayley, Blake wrote, "is the Enemy of my Spiritual Life while he pretends to be the Friend of my Corporeal."

At Felpham in 1803 occurred an event that left a permanent mark on Blake's mind and art. He had an altercation with one John Scholfield, a private in the Royal Dragoons. Blake ordered the soldier out of his garden and, when the soldier replied with threats and curses against Blake and his wife, pushed him the fifty yards to the inn where he was quartered. Scholfield brought charges that Blake had uttered seditious statements about King and country. Despite Blake's insistence that Scholfield had perjured himself, he was indicted and brought to trial. Since England was at war with France, sedition was a hanging offense. Blake was acquitted; an event, according to a newspaper account, "which so gratified the auditory that the court was * * * thrown into an uproar by their noisy exultations." Nevertheless Scholfield, his fellow-soldier Cock, and other participants in the trial haunted Blake's imagination and were enlarged to demonic characters who play a sinister role in *Jerusalem*. The event exacerbated Blake's sense that ominous forces were at work in the contemporary world and led him to complicate the symbolic obliquities by which he veiled the unorthodoxy of his political, religious, and moral opinions, and the radicalism of the many allusions to contemporary affairs that he worked into his poems.

After three years at Felpham Blake moved back to London, determined to follow his "Divine Vision" though it meant a life of isolation, misunderstanding, and poverty. When his one great bid for public recognition, a one-man show put on in 1809, proved a total failure, Blake passed into almost complete obscurity. Only when he was in his 60's did he finally attract a small but devoted group of young painters who served as an audience for his work and his talk. Blake's old age was serene, self-confident, and joyous, largely free from the bursts of irascibility with which he had earlier responded to the shallowness and blindness of the English public. He died in his seventieth year.

Blake's first book of poems, *Poetical Sketches*, which he had printed when he was 26 years old, demonstrated his dissatisfaction with the reigning poetic tradition and his restless quest for new forms and techniques. For lyric models he turned back to the Elizabethan and early 17th-century poets, to the Ossianic poems, Collins, Thomas Chatterton, and other 18th-century writers outside the tradition of Pope; he also experimented with partial rhymes and novel rhythms and employed bold figures of speech that at times approximate the status of symbols. In *Songs of Innocence* (1789) Blake inaugurated the method of publication he used for all his later original works, a procedure he had partly invented. He drew text and illustrations as a total pictorial design with an acid-proof substance directly on the copper plate, then applied acid so that the design was left in relief. With this plate he printed a page, which he later colored with water colors by hand and bound with the other pages to make up a volume. The procedure of making the plates was laborious and time-consuming, and Blake struck off very few copies of his works; for example, of *Songs of Innocence and Experience* 27 copies (both complete and incomplete) are known to exist; of *The Book of Thel*, 15; of *The Marriage of Heaven and Hell*, 9; of *Milton*, 4; and of *Jerusalem*, 5. The existing works are a unique fusion of text, picture, and decoration; it must be remembered that to read Blake's poem in a printed text is to see only an abstraction from what, in its original version, was an integral and mutually illuminating combination of words and design.

In the *Songs of Innocence* Blake assumes the stance that he is writing "happy songs / Every child may joy to hear." They show the fallen world, however, as it appears to the limited view of a naïve and acquiescent innocence; and some of the songs, such as "The Chimney Sweeper" and "Holy Thursday," are deeply equivocal, hinting the possibility of a different evaluation of the events they represent. This "contrary" vision is expressed in *Songs of Experience* (1794), which reveal an ugly and terrifying world of poverty, disease, prostitution, war, exploitation, and social, institutional, and sexual repression. In the best of these Songs, such as *The Tyger* and *London*, Blake achieved his mature lyric technique of compressed metaphor and symbol which explode into a multiplicity of reference.

Gradually Blake's symbolic thinking about human history and his personal experience of life and suffering articulated themselves in the "Giant Forms" and their actions, which constitute a complete mythology. As Los said, speaking for all imaginative artists, "I must Create a System or be enslaved by another Man's." This coherent but constantly altering and enlarging system composed the subject matter, first of Blake's "minor prophecies," completed by 1795, and then of the major prophetic books on which he continued working until about 1820: *The Four Zoas, Milton,* and *Jerusalem.*

In his 60's Blake gave up poetry to devote himself to pictorial art. In the course of his life he produced hundreds of paintings and engravings, many of them illustrations for the work of other poets, including a representation of Chaucer's Canterbury pilgrims, a superb set of designs for the Book of Job, and a series of illustrations of Dante, on which he was still hard at work when he died. At the time of his death Blake was little known as an artist and almost entirely unknown as a poet. In the mid-19th century he acquired a group of admirers among the Pre-Raphaelites, who regarded him as a precursor, and since then his reputation and influence have been growing steadily both in England and abroad. Since the mid 1920's, Blake has finally come into his own, both in poetry and painting, as one of the most dedicated, intellectually challenging, and astonishingly original of artists.

The explication of Blake's large, cryptic, and complex prophetic books has been the preoccupation of many scholars. Blake wrote them in the persona, or "voice," of "the Bard / Who Present, Past, & Future sees"— that is, as a British poet who follows Spenser, and especially Milton, in a lineage going back to the poet-prophets of the Bible. "The Nature of my Work," he said, "is Visionary or Imaginative." What Blake meant by the key terms "vision" and "imagination," however, is often misrepresented by taking literally what he, speaking the traditional language of his great predecessors, intended in a figurative sense. "That which can be made Explicit to the Idiot," Blake declared, "is not worth my care." Blake was a born ironist who enjoyed mystifying his well-meaning but literal-minded friends and who took a defiant pleasure in shocking the dull and complacent "angels" of his day by being deliberately outrageous in representing his work and opinions.

Blake declared "warmly" that "all he knew was in the Bible," and that "The Old & New Testaments are the Great Code of Art." This is an exaggeration of the truth that all his prophetic writings deal, in various formulations, with some aspects of the over-all Biblical plot of the creation and fall of man, the history of the generations of man in the fallen world, redemption, and the promise of a recovery of Eden and of a New Jerusalem. These events, however, Blake interprets in his own way—a way for which he had considerable precedent, not so much in the Neoplatonic and occult thinkers with which some modern commentators align him as in the "spiritual" interpreters of the Bible among the radical Protestant sects in 17th- and 18th-century England. In *The French Revolution, America: A Proph-*

ecy, Europe: A Prophecy, and the trenchant prophetic satire, *A Marriage of Heaven and Hell*—all of which Blake wrote in the early 1790's while he was an ardent supporter of the French Revolution—he, like Wordsworth, Coleridge, Southey, and a number of radical English theologians, represented the contemporary Revolution as the purifying violence that, according to Biblical prophecy, was the portent of the imminent redemption of man and the world. In Blake's later writings, however, Orc, the fiery spirit of revolution, gives way as central personage to Los, the type of the visionary imagination in the fallen world—an index of Blake's shift of emphasis from apocalypse by revolution to apocalypse by imagination.

BLAKE'S MATURE MYTH

Blake's first attempt to articulate his full myth of mankind's present, past, and future was *The Four Zoas,* begun in 1796 or 1797—later than any of the works represented here. A passage from the opening statement of its theme will exemplify the long verse line (what Blake called "the march of long resounding strong heroic verse") in which he wrote all his Prophetic Books and will serve also to indicate in broad outline the myth, or visualizable imaginative form, in which Blake's thought embodied itself:

> Four Mighty Ones are in every Man: a Perfect Unity
> Cannot Exist, but from the Universal Brotherhood of Eden,
> The Universal Man. To Whom be Glory Evermore, Amen. * * *
> Los was the fourth immortal starry one, & in the Earth
> Of a bright Universe Empery attended day & night
> Days & nights of revolving joy, Urthona was his name
> In Eden; in the Auricular Nerves of Human life
> Which is the Earth of Eden, he his Emanations propagated. * * *
> Daughter of Beulah, Sing
> His fall into Division & his Resurrection to Unity.

Blake's mythical premise, or starting point, is not a transcendent God but "The Universal Man" who is himself God and who incorporates the cosmos as well. (Blake elsewhere describes this founding image as "the Human Form Divine" and names him "Albion.") The fall, in this myth, is not the fall of man away from God but a falling apart of primal man, a "fall into Division." In this event the original sin is what Blake calls "selfhood," the attempt of an isolated part to be self-sufficient. The break-up of the all-inclusive Universal Man in Eden into exiled parts, it is evident, identifies the fall of man with the creation—both of man and of nature, as we ordinarily know them. Universal Man divides first into the "Four Mighty Ones" who are the Zoas, or chief faculties of man, and these in turn divide sexually into male Spectres and female Emanations. (Thus in the quoted passage the Zoa known in the unfallen state as Urthona, the imaginative power, separates into the form of Los in the fallen world.) In addition to Eden there are three successively lower "states" of being in the fallen world, which Blake calls Beulah (a pastoral condition of easy and relaxed innocence, without clash of "contraries"), Generation (the realm of common human experience, suffering, and conflicting contraries), and Ulro (Blake's hell, the lowest state, or limit, of bleak rationality, tyranny, static negation, and isolated selfhood). The fallen world moves through the cycles of its history, successively approaching and falling away from redemption, until, by the agency of the Redeemer (who is equated with the human imagination and is most potently operative in the poet), it will culminate in an apocalypse. In terms of his controlling image of the Universal Man, Blake describes this apocalypse as a return to the original, undivided condition, "his Resurrection to Unity."

Blake, although he did not know it, shared with a number of contemporary German philosophers the point of view—it has in our own time become the prevailing point of view—that man's fall, and the malaise of modern culture, is essentially a mode of psychic disintegration, and that man's hope of recovery lies in a process of reintegration. As an imaginative poet, however, Blake does not present this view in abstract conceptual terms, but embodies it in picturable agents acting out an epic plot. What is confusing to many readers is that Blake uses different ways of representing the same vision of man in the world. For example, Blake alternates with his image of the division of Primal Man, the representation of the fall as a catastrophic alteration of vision in individual human beings. The result of this alteration was that the cosmos, which in the original mode of unified perception had been beheld as human and one, came to be seen as a multitude of isolated individuals in a de-humanized and alien nature. Conversely, the apocalypse toward which Blake—the imaginative artist who as an individual represents the mythical type-figure Los—is always working, is to enable all men to break through to a restored unity of vision. To such a vision all beings, together with the world they inhabit, will again be perceived as sharing the one life and the one humanity of that "Universal Brotherhood," the Human Form Divine, who is imaged as creating such a universe by the very act of so envisioning it. Although Blake decries, as the mythical being "Vala," what we ordinarily mean by "nature," it is a mistake to equate his views with any form of ascetic otherworldliness; he does not look forward to a consummation that will wipe out the fleshly and the natural world and replace it by a transcendental substitute. Blake maintained, on the contrary, that we achieve redemption by liberating and intensifying the bodily senses—as he said, by "an improvement of sensual enjoyment"—and by attaining and sustaining that mode of vision that does not cancel the fallen world, but transfigures it, by revealing the lineaments of its eternal imaginative form. That is what Blake means when, in A *Vision of the Last Judgment* (included below), he says that "The Nature of my Work is Visionary or Imaginative; it is an Endeavour to Restore what the Ancients called the Golden Age"; that "All Things are comprehended in their Eternal Forms in the Divine body of the Saviour . . . The Human Imagination"; and that in the moment of apocalyptic redemption "Error or Creation will be Burnt Up & then & not till then Truth or Eternity will appear. It is Burnt up the Moment Men cease to behold it." Accordingly, in the apocalypse that concludes *Jerusalem*, the reunion of Albion the Universal Man with Jerusalem, his emanation, is accompanied by a freeing of man's senses and the annihilation of his selfhood and results in the recovery of a lost mode of vision that sees all men in brotherhood, dwelling in a nature which, because it is humanized, is a place where individual men, united as One Man, can feel at home: "& they walked / To & fro in Eternity as One Man reflecting each in each & clearly seen / And seeing," in a setting which consists of "Human Forms identified, even Tree Metal Earth & Stone."

The text for all of Blake's writings is that of *The Poetry and Prose of*

William Blake, edited by David V. Erdman and Harold Bloom (New York, 1965). Blake's often erratic spelling and punctuation have been altered when the original form might mislead the modern reader.

From POETICAL SKETCHES[1]

Song

How sweet I roam'd from field to field,
    And tasted all the summer's pride,
'Till I the prince of love beheld,
    Who in the sunny beams did glide!

He shew'd me lilies for my hair,   5
    And blushing roses for my brow;
He led me through his gardens fair,
    Where all his golden pleasures grow.

With sweet May dews my wings were wet,
    And Phoebus fir'd my vocal rage;[2]   10
He caught me in his silken net,
    And shut me in his golden cage.

He loves to sit and hear me sing,
    Then, laughing, sports and plays with me;
Then stretches out my golden wing,   15
    And mocks my loss of liberty.

                          1783

To the Evening Star

Thou fair-hair'd angel of the evening,
Now, while the sun rests on the mountains, light
Thy bright torch of love; thy radiant crown
Put on, and smile upon our evening bed!
Smile on our loves; and, while thou drawest the   5
Blue curtains of the sky, scatter thy silver dew
On every flower that shuts its sweet eyes
In timely sleep. Let thy west wind sleep on

1. *Poetical Sketches,* Blake's only volume of poems to be set in type, went to press in 1783, but was never put on sale. A preface written by an anonymous friend apologized for the poems on the ground that they had been composed between the ages of 12 and 20. Although, like the work of other youthful poets, they echo earlier writers, many of them show remarkable originality. Some are radical experiments in meter and rhyme; *To the Evening Star* shows Blake's boldness in metaphor (lines 8–10); while in this same sonnet (lines 11–14) and in the *Song* ("How sweet I roam'd"), the images begin to assume the added reach of meaning that characterizes Blake's mature symbolism.
2. Fervor.

The lake; speak silence with thy glimmering eyes,
And wash the dusk with silver. Soon, full soon,   10
Dost thou withdraw; then the wolf rages wide,
And the lion glares thro' the dun forest:
The fleeces of our flocks are cover'd with
Thy sacred dew: protect them with thine influence.[3]

1783

Song[4]

Memory, hither come,
    And tune your merry notes;
And, while upon the wind,
    Your music floats,
I'll pore upon the stream,   5
Where sighing lovers dream,
And fish for fancies as they pass
Within the watery glass.

I'll drink of the clear stream,
    And hear the linnet's song;   10
And there I'll lie and dream
    The day along:
And, when night comes, I'll go
    To places fit for woe;
Walking along the darken'd valley,   15
    With silent Melancholy.

1783

Mad Song[5]

The wild winds weep,
    And the night is a-cold;
Come hither, Sleep,
    And my griefs infold:
But lo! the morning peeps   5
    Over the eastern steeps,
And the rustling birds of dawn
    The earth do scorn.

3. In astrology, the technical term for the occult power of stars over men.
4. Cf. *Under the Greenwood Tree* in *As You Like It* II.v.
5. Cf. the songs of the Fool in Shakespeare's great scene of madness and incipient madness in *King Lear*, Act. III. In a marginal comment on Spurzheim's *Observations on Insanity* (1817), Blake wrote: "Cowper came to me & said, 'O that I were insane always; I will never rest. * * * You retain health & yet are as mad as any of us all—over us all—mad as a refuge from unbelief—from Bacon Newton & Locke.' " (Cowper, like the other 18th-century poets, Christopher Smart and William Collins, went genuinely insane.)

Lo! to the vault
   Of pavéd heaven,   10
With sorrow fraught
   My notes are driven:
They strike the ear of night,
   Make weep the eyes of day;
They make mad the roaring winds,   15
   And the tempests play.

Like a fiend in a cloud
   With howling woe,
After night I do croud,
   And with night will go;   20
I turn my back to the east,
From whence comforts have increas'd;
For light doth seize my brain
With frantic pain.

                       1783

To the Muses

Whether on Ida's [6] shady brow,
   Or in the chambers of the East,
The chambers of the sun, that now
   From antient melody have ceas'd;

Whether in Heav'n ye wander fair,   5
   Or the green corners of the earth,
Or the blue regions of the air,
   Where the melodious winds have birth;

Whether on chrystal rocks ye rove,
   Beneath the bosom of the sea   10
Wand'ring in many a coral grove,
   Fair Nine, [7] forsaking Poetry!

How have you left the antient love
   That bards of old enjoy'd in you! [8]
The languid strings do scarcely move!   15
   The sound is forc'd, the notes are few!

                       1783

---

6. Ida is a mountain in southern Phrygia, celebrated in classical mythology.
7. The nine Muses.

8. The poem is Blake's lament, in the diction of latter 18th-century poetry, over the failure of the inspiration of the "bards," the older British poet-prophets.

From Songs of Innocence and of Experience

SHEWING THE TWO CONTRARY STATES OF THE HUMAN SOUL

From Songs of Innocence[1]

1789

The Author & Printer   W Blake

Introduction

Piping down the valleys wild
Piping songs of pleasant glee
On a cloud I saw a child,
And he laughing said to me,

"Pipe a song about a Lamb";   5
So I piped with merry chear;
"Piper pipe that song again"—
So I piped, he wept to hear.

"Drop thy pipe thy happy pipe
Sing thy songs of happy chear";   10
So I sung the same again
While he wept with joy to hear.

"Piper sit thee down and write
In a book that all may read"—
So he vanish'd from my sight.   15
And I pluck'd a hollow reed,

And I made a rural pen,
And I stain'd the water clear,
And I wrote my happy songs
Every child may joy to hear.   20

1789

1. *Songs of Innocence* was etched in 1789 and in 1794 was combined with other poems under the title above. Innocence is the state of the soul which, in these poems, is represented by the naïve outlook of the child who believes what he is told by his elders, and takes appearance for the reality and the best aspect of things for the whole truth. A number of the Songs represent this state in the mode of a pastoral or protected world. In other Songs, however, such as *The Chimney Sweeper* and *Holy Thursday*, a contrary possibility intrudes its ironic perspective, to reveal how precarious is the ignorantly innocent outlook upon the world.

But children need to grow up, and the state of innocence needs to yield to that of experience, which sees as real the world of materialism, poverty, oppression, prostitution, disease, and war, epitomized in the ghastly city of modern London. Some of the individual songs of innocence have a matched counterpart, or "contrary," in a terrifying song of experience; thus the meek lamb is replaced by the flaming, wrathful tiger. In Blake's later writings the "contrary states" become a dialectic of contraries, according to which naïve innocence must necessarily pass through and assimilate the opposing state of experience if it is to move on, by an act of imagination, to the third state, comprehending but transcending both the others, which he called "organized innocence."

The Lamb

Little Lamb, who made thee?
　Dost thou know who made thee?
Gave thee life & bid thee feed,
By the stream & o'er the mead;
Gave thee clothing of delight,　　　　5
Softest clothing wooly bright;
Gave thee such a tender voice,
Making all the vales rejoice!
　Little Lamb who made thee?
　Dost thou know who made thee?　　10

　Little Lamb I'll tell thee,
　Little Lamb I'll tell thee!
He is calléd by thy name,
For he calls himself a Lamb:
He is meek & he is mild,　　　　15
He became a little child:
I a child & thou a lamb,
We are calléd by his name.
　Little Lamb God bless thee.
　Little Lamb God bless thee.　　20

1789

The Divine Image

To Mercy, Pity, Peace, and Love,
All pray in their distress:
And to these virtues of delight
Return their thankfulness.

For Mercy, Pity, Peace, and Love,　　5
Is God, our father dear:
And Mercy, Pity, Peace, and Love,
Is Man, his child and care.

For Mercy has a human heart,
Pity, a human face:　　　　10
And Love, the human form divine,
And Peace, the human dress.

Then every man of every clime,
That prays in his distress,
Prays to the human form divine,　　15
Love, Mercy, Pity, Peace.

And all must love the human form,
In heathen, Turk, or Jew.
Where Mercy, Love, & Pity dwell,
There God is dwelling too.　　20

1789

The Chimney Sweeper

When my mother died I was very young,
And my father sold me while yet my tongue
Could scarcely cry " 'weep! 'weep! 'weep! 'weep!" [2]
So your chimneys I sweep & in soot I sleep.

There's little Tom Dacre, who cried when his head   5
That curl'd like a lambs back, was shav'd, so I said,
"Hush, Tom! never mind it, for when your head's bare,
You know that the soot cannot spoil your white hair."

And so he was quiet, & that very night,
As Tom was a-sleeping he had such a sight!   10
That thousands of sweepers, Dick, Joe, Ned, & Jack,
Were all of them lock'd up in coffins of black;

And by came an Angel who had a bright key,
And he open'd the coffins & set them all free;
Then down a green plain, leaping, laughing they run,   15
And wash in a river and shine in the Sun;

Then naked & white, all their bags left behind,
They rise upon clouds, and sport in the wind.
And the Angel told Tom, if he'd be a good boy,
He'd have God for his father & never want joy.   20

And so Tom awoke; and we rose in the dark
And got with our bags & our brushes to work.
Tho' the morning was cold, Tom was happy & warm;
So if all do their duty, they need not fear harm.

                                 1789

Nurse's Song

When the voices of children are heard on the green
And laughing is heard on the hill,
My heart is at rest within my breast
And everything else is still.

"Then come home my children, the sun is gone down   5
And the dews of night arise;
Come, come, leave off play, and let us away
Till the morning appears in the skies."

---

2. The child's lisping attempt at the chimney sweeper's street cry, "Sweep! Sweep!"

"No, no, let us play, for it is yet day
And we cannot go to sleep;   10
Besides, in the sky, the little birds fly
And the hills are all coverd with sheep."

"Well, well, go & play till the light fades away
And then go home to bed."
The little ones leapéd & shouted & laugh'd   15
And all the hills ecchoéd.

ca. 1784   1789

Holy Thursday[3]

'Twas on a Holy Thursday, their innocent faces clean,
The children walking two & two, in red & blue & green,
Grey headed beadles [4] walkd before with wands as white as snow,
Till into the high dome of Paul's they like Thames' waters flow.

O what a multitude they seemd, these flowers of London town!   5
Seated in companies they sit with radiance all their own.
The hum of multitudes was there, but multitudes of lambs,
Thousands of little boys & girls raising their innocent hands.

Now like a mighty wind they raise to heaven the voice of song,
Or like harmonious thunderings the seats of heaven among.   10
Beneath them sit the aged men, wise guardians of the poor;
Then cherish pity, lest you drive an angel from your door.[5]

ca. 1784   1789

The Little Black Boy

My mother bore me in the southern wild,
And I am black, but O! my soul is white;
White as an angel is the English child:
But I am black as if bereav'd of light.

My mother taught me underneath a tree,   5
And sitting down before the heat of day,
She took me on her lap and kisséd me,
And pointing to the east, began to say:

"Look on the rising sun: there God does live,
And gives his light, and gives his heat away;   10

---

3. In the English church, the Thursday celebrating the ascension of Jesus (forty days after Easter). It was the custom on this day to march the children from the charity schools of London to a service at St. Paul's Cathedral.

4. Lower church officers, one of whose duties is to keep order.

5. Hebrews xiii.2:"Be not forgetful to entertain strangers: for thereby some have entertained angels unawares."

And flowers and trees and beasts and men receive
Comfort in morning, joy in the noon day.

"And we are put on earth a little space,
That we may learn to bear the beams of love,
And these black bodies and this sun-burnt face   15
Is but a cloud, and like a shady grove.

"For when our souls have learn'd the heat to bear,
The cloud will vanish; we shall hear his voice,
Saying: 'Come out from the grove, my love & care,
And round my golden tent like lambs rejoice.' "   20

Thus did my mother say, and kisséd me;
And thus I say to little English boy:
When I from black and he from white cloud free,
And round the tent of God like lambs we joy,

I'll shade him from the heat till he can bear   25
To lean in joy upon our father's knee;
And then I'll stand and stroke his silver hair,
And be like him, and he will then love me.

1789

From Songs of Experience

1794

The Author & Printer   W Blake

Introduction

Hear the voice of the Bard!
Who Present, Past, & Future sees;
Whose ears have heard
The Holy Word
That walk'd among the ancient trees;[6]   5

Calling the lapséd Soul
And weeping in the evening dew;
That might controll
The starry pole,
And fallen, fallen light renew!   10

6. Genesis iii.8: "And [Adam and Eve] heard the voice of the Lord God walking in the garden in the cool of the day." The Bard, whose imagination is not bound by time, has heard the voice of the Lord in Eden and calls to the fallen ("lapsed") soul and to the fallen Earth to turn full to the light and stop its endless cycle of alternating light and darkness. In Blake's symbolism the starry sky ("floor") and the margin of the sea ("watery shore")—see the final stanza—are symbols of the rigid rational order and the temporal and spatial bondage imposed on the free imagination by the material world known through the "corporeal eye."

"O Earth, O Earth, return!
Arise from out the dewy grass;
Night is worn,
And the morn
Rises from the slumberous mass.   15

"Turn away no more;
Why wilt thou turn away?
The starry floor
The watry shore
Is giv'n thee till the break of day."   20

1794

Earth's Answer

Earth rais'd up her head,
From the darkness dread & drear.
Her light fled:
Stony dread!
And her locks cover'd with grey despair.   5

"Prison'd on watry shore
Starry Jealousy does keep my den,
Cold and hoar
Weeping o'er
I hear the Father of the ancient men.[7]   10

"Selfish father of men,
Cruel, jealous, selfish fear!
Can delight
Chain'd in night
The virgins of youth and morning bear?   15

"Does spring hide its joy
When buds and blossoms grow?
Does the sower
Sow by night,
Or the plowman in darkness plow?   20

"Break this heavy chain
That does freeze my bones around;
Selfish! vain!
Eternal bane!
That free Love with bondage bound."   25

1790–92   1794

7. The character Blake called "Urizen" in his later prophetic works. He represents perceptual, rational, and moral tyranny that binds the mind to the sensible order of time and space and imposes upon sexual desire (as upon all forms of creative human energy) the stultifying and distorting bondage of selfishness, fear, secrecy, shame, and jealousy.

The Clod & the Pebble

"Love seeketh not Itself to please,
Nor for itself hath any care;
But for another gives its ease,
And builds a Heaven in Hell's despair."

So sang a little Clod of Clay,   5
Trodden with the cattle's feet;
But a Pebble of the brook,
Warbled out these metres meet:

"Love seeketh only Self to please,
To bind another to its delight;   10
Joys in another's loss of ease,
And builds a Hell in Heaven's despite."

1790–92   1794

Holy Thursday

Is this a holy thing to see,
In a rich and fruitful land,
Babes reducd to misery,
Fed with cold and usurous hand?

Is that trembling cry a song?   5
Can it be a song of joy?
And so many children poor?
It is a land of poverty!

And their sun does never shine,
And their fields are bleak & bare,   10
And their ways are fill'd with thorns;
It is eternal winter there.

For where-e'er the sun does shine,
And where-e'er the rain does fall,
Babe can never hunger there,   15
Nor poverty the mind appall.

1790–92   1794

The Chimney Sweeper

A little black thing among the snow
Crying "'weep, 'weep," in notes of woe!
"Where are thy father & mother? say?"
"They are both gone up to the church to pray.

"Because I was happy upon the heath,   5
And smil'd among the winter's snow;
They clothéd me in the clothes of death,
And taught me to sing the notes of woe.

"And because I am happy, & dance & sing,
They think they have done me no injury,   10
And are gone to praise God & his Priest & King,
Who make up a heaven of our misery."

1790–92   1794

Nurse's Song

When the voices of children, are heard on the green
And whisprings are in the dale,
The days of my youth rise fresh in my mind,
My face turns green and pale.

Then come home my children, the sun is gone down   5
And the dews of night arise;
Your spring & your day are wasted in play,
And your winter and night in disguise.

1790–92   1794

The Sick Rose

O Rose, thou art sick.
The invisible worm
That flies in the night
In the howling storm

Has found out thy bed   5
Of crimson joy,
And his dark secret love
Does thy life destroy.

1790–92   1794

The Tyger

Tyger! Tyger! burning bright
In the forests of the night,
What immortal hand or eye
Could frame thy fearful symmetry?

In what distant deeps or skies   5
Burnt the fire of thine eyes?
On what wings dare he aspire?
What the hand, dare seize the fire?

And what shoulder, & what art,
Could twist the sinews of thy heart?   10

And when thy heart began to beat,
What dread hand? & what dread feet?

What the hammer? what the chain?
In what furnace was thy brain?
What the anvil? what dread grasp   15
Dare its deadly terrors clasp?

When the stars threw down their spears,
And water'd heaven with their tears,
Did he smile his work to see?
Did he who made the Lamb make thee?   20

Tyger! Tyger! burning bright
In the forests of the night,
What immortal hand or eye
Dare frame thy fearful symmetry?

1790–92   1794

Ah Sun-Flower

Ah Sun-flower! weary of time,
Who countest the steps of the Sun,
Seeking after that sweet golden clime
Where the traveller's journey is done;

Where the Youth pined away with desire,   5
And the pale Virgin shrouded in snow,
Arise from their graves and aspire,
Where my Sun-flower wishes to go.

1794

The Garden of Love

I went to the Garden of Love,
And saw what I never had seen:
A Chapel was built in the midst,
Where I used to play on the green.

And the gates of this Chapel were shut,   5
And "Thou shalt not" writ over the door;
So I turn'd to the Garden of Love,
That so many sweet flowers bore,

And I saw it was filled with graves,
And tomb-stones where flowers should be: 10
And Priests in black gowns were walking their rounds,
And binding with briars my joys & desires.

1790–92   1794

London

I wander thro' each charter'd [1] street,
Near where the charter'd Thames does flow,
And mark in every face I meet
Marks of weakness, marks of woe.

In every cry of every Man,   5
In every Infant's cry of fear,
In every voice, in every ban,[2]
The mind-forg'd manacles I hear.

How the Chimney-sweeper's cry
Every blackning Church appalls;   10
And the hapless Soldier's sigh
Runs in blood down Palace walls.

But most thro' midnight streets I hear
How the youthful Harlot's curse
Blasts the new-born Infant's tear,[3]   15
And blights with plagues the Marriage hearse.[4]

1790–92   1794

The Human Abstract[5]

Pity would be no more,
If we did not make somebody Poor;
And Mercy no more could be,
If all were as happy as we;

And mutual fear brings peace,   5
Till the selfish loves increase;
Then Cruelty knits a snare,
And spreads his baits with care.

He sits down with holy fears,
And waters the ground with tears;   10
Then Humility takes its root
Underneath his foot.

1. "Given liberty," but also, ironically, "pre-empted as private property, and rented out."
2. The various meanings of "ban" are relevant (political and legal prohibition, curse, public condemnation) as well as "banns" (marriage proclamation).
3. Implying prenatal blindness, resulting from a parent's venereal disease (the "plagues" of line 16) by earlier infection from the harlot.
4. In the older sense of "hearse": converts the marriage bed into a bier. Or possibly, since the current sense of the word had also come into use in Blake's day, "converts the marriage coach into a funeral hearse."
5. The matched contrary to *The Divine Image* in *Songs of Innocence*. The virtues of the earlier poem, "Mercy, Pity, Peace, and Love," are now seen as exploitation, cruelty, conflict, and hypocritical humility—the seed in the human brain of the Tree of Mystery, which darkens the natural world.

Soon spreads the dismal shade
Of Mystery over his head;
And the Catterpiller and Fly   15
Feed on the Mystery.

And it bears the fruit of Deceit,
Ruddy and sweet to eat;
And the Raven his nest has made
In its thickest shade.   20

The Gods of the earth and sea,
Sought thro' Nature to find this Tree,
But their search was all in vain:
There grows one in the Human Brain.

1790–92   1794

Infant Sorrow

My mother groand! my father wept.
Into the dangerous world I leapt:
Helpless, naked, piping loud;
Like a fiend hid in a cloud.

Struggling in my father's hands,   5
Striving against my swadling bands,
Bound and weary I thought best
To sulk upon my mother's breast.

1790–92   1794

A Poison Tree

I was angry with my friend:
I told my wrath, my wrath did end.
I was angry with my foe:
I told it not, my wrath did grow.

And I waterd it in fears,   5
Night & morning with my tears;
And I sunnéd it with smiles,
And with soft deceitful wiles.

And it grew both day and night,
Till it bore an apple bright.   10
And my foe beheld it shine,
And he knew that it was mine,

And into my garden stole,
When the night had veild the pole;
In the morning glad I see   15
My foe outstretchd beneath the tree.

1790–92   1794

To Tirzah[6]

Whate'er is Born of Mortal Birth
Must be consuméd with the Earth
To rise from Generation free;
Then what have I to do with thee?

The Sexes sprung from Shame & Pride,   5
Blow'd[7] in the morn: in evening died;
But Mercy changd Death into Sleep;
The Sexes rose to work & weep.

Thou, Mother of my Mortal part,
With cruelty didst mould my Heart,   10
And with false self-deceiving tears
Didst bind my Nostrils, Eyes, & Ears.

Didst close my Tongue in senseless clay
And me to Mortal Life betray.
The Death of Jesus set me free,   15
Then what have I to do with thee?

ca. 1805

A Divine Image[8]

Cruelty has a Human Heart
And Jealousy a Human Face,
Terror, the Human Form Divine,
And Secrecy, the Human Dress.

The Human Dress is forgéd Iron,   5
The Human Form, a fiery Forge,
The Human Face, a Furnace seal'd,
The Human Heart, its hungry Gorge.[9]

1790–91

6. Tirzah was the capital of the Northern Kingdom of Israel and is conceived by Blake in opposition to Jerusalem, capital of the Southern Kingdom of Judah, whose tribes had been redeemed from captivity. In this poem, which was added to late versions of *Songs of Experience*, Tirzah represents that necessity inherent in nature, the realm of "generation," from which the "mortal part" of man derives, and which enslaves his heart and senses. Blake antici-pates his emancipation from this bondage to the cycle of generation by the triumph of the imaginative over the natural body.
7. Blossomed.
8. After etching this poem Blake omitted it from *Songs of Experience*, probably because *The Human Abstract* served as a more comprehensive and subtle contrary to *The Divine Image*, in *Songs of Innocence*.
9. Throat.

The Book of Thel [1]

The Author & Printer Willm Blake, 1789

PLATE i [2]

THEL'S MOTTO

Does the Eagle know what is in the pit?
Or wilt thou go ask the Mole?
Can Wisdom be put in a silver rod?
Or Love in a golden bowl? [3]

PLATE 1

I

The daughters of Mne [4] Seraphim led round their sunny flocks,
All but the youngest; she in paleness sought the secret air,

1. Although Blake dated the engraved poem 1789, its composition probably extended to 1791, so that he was working on it at the time he was writing the *Songs of Innocence* and some of the *Songs of Experience*. *The Book of Thel* treats the same two "states" and implies the need to pass from primitive innocence through experience in order to achieve a higher, organized innocence; now, however, Blake employs the narrative instead of the lyrical mode and embodies aspects of the developing myth which was fully enacted in his later prophetic books. And like the major prophecies, this poem is written in the fourteener, a long line of seven stresses and (for the most part) fourteen syllables.

Thel—her name probably derives from a Greek word for "wish" or "will" and suggests the timid failure of a desire to fulfil itself—is a virgin dwelling in the Vales of Har, which is equivalent to the sheltered condition of pastoral peace and naïve innocence in Blake's *Songs of Innocence* and will develop into the "Beulah" of his prophetic books. In the fragile beauty of this realm of unrealized potentiality, Thel lives a two-dimensional mirror image of existence (line 9), a diaphanous, fading half-life. The Lily of the Valley and the Cloud—elements of the milieu in this mild realm without opposition or conflict—try to comfort her by describing their content with their roles in the cycle of innocent existence. Thel, however, since she is a human potentiality, finds such comfort inapplicable to her condition of unfulfillment and uselessness, as a virgin without a male contrary and as a shepherdess whose sheep run no risks and need no care. The Clod of Clay then speaks for her child, the voiceless

Worm, an emblem of phallic generation and a devourer of the mortal body in the fallen world; but the maternal Clay sees the role of the Worm, as well as her own, only from the perspective of primal innocence, hence of essential ignorance: "But how this is, sweet maid, I know not, and I cannot know." In her capacity, however, as the substance from which is formed the mortal body of man, the Clay invites Thel to try the experiment of dying into embodied life. With an abrupt and brutal shift in language and tone, Part IV expresses the shock of the revelation to Thel of the world of Generation and Experience—a revelation from which she flees in terror back to her sheltered, if inadequate, paradise.

The reader does not need to be an adept in Blakean mythology to recognize the symbolic reach of this poem over a large area of ordinary human experience—the elemental failure of nerve to meet the challenge of life as it is, the timid incapacity to risk the conflict, suffering, loss, and defeat without which there is no possibility either of growth or of any kind of creativity.

2. The plate numbers identify the page, each with its own pictorial design, as originally printed by Blake. They are reproduced here because they are frequently used for reference to Blake's writings.

3. Ecclesiastes xii.5–6 describes a time when "fears shall be in the way * * * and desire shall fail: because man goeth to his long home, and the mourners go about the streets: Or ever the silver cord be loosed, or the golden bowl be broken." Blake presumably changed the silver cord to a rod in order to make it, with the golden bowl, a sexual symbol.

To fade away like morning beauty from her mortal day;
Down by the river of Adona [5] her soft voice is heard,
And thus her gentle lamentation falls like morning dew: 5

"O life of this our spring! why fades the lotus of the water?
Why fade these children of the spring? born but to smile & fall.
Ah! Thel is like a watry bow, and like a parting cloud,
Like a reflection in a glass, like shadows in the water,
Like dreams of infants, like a smile upon an infant's face,   10
Like the dove's voice, like transient day, like music in the air.
Ah! gentle may I lay me down, and gentle rest my head,
And gentle sleep the sleep of death and gentle hear the voice
Of him that walketh in the garden in the evening time."[6]

The Lilly of the valley, breathing in the humble grass,   15
Answer'd the lovely maid and said: "I am a watry weed,
And I am very small, and love to dwell in lowly vales;
So weak, the gilded butterfly scarce perches on my head;
Yet I am visited from heaven, and he that smiles on all
Walks in the valley and each morn over me spreads his hand,   20
Saying: 'Rejoice, thou humble grass, thou new-born lilly flower,
Thou gentle maid of silent valleys and of modest brooks;
For thou shalt be clothed in light, and fed with morning manna,
Till summer's heat melts thee beside the fountains and the springs
To flourish in eternal vales.' Then why should Thel complain?   25

PLATE 2

Why should the mistress of the vales of Har utter a sigh?"

She ceasd & smild in tears, then sat down in her silver shrine.

Thel answerd: "O thou little virgin of the peaceful valley,
Giving to those that cannot crave, the voiceless, the o'ertired;
Thy breath doth nourish the innocent lamb, he smells thy milky
          garments,   5
He crops thy flowers, while thou sittest smiling in his face,
Wiping his mild and meekin [7] mouth from all contagious taints.
Thy wine doth purify the golden honey; thy perfume,
Which thou dost scatter on every little blade of grass that springs,
Revives the milkéd cow, & tames the fire-breathing steed.   10
But Thel is like a faint cloud kindled at the rising sun:
I vanish from my pearly throne, and who shall find my place?"

---

4. If not simply a misprint for "the,"
this may be, as Geoffrey Keynes says, a
variation upon "the mystical name, Bne
Seraphim." In the Bible, Seraphim are
the highest order of angels.
5. Possibly suggesting an equation of

the Vales of Har to Spenser's Garden of
Adonis in *The Faerie Queene* III.vi, as
well as to the paradisal garden in
Genesis (in line 14).
6. Genesis iii.8.
7. Humble.

"Queen of the vales," the Lilly answered, "ask the tender cloud,
And it shall tell thee why it glitters in the morning sky,
And why it scatters its bright beauty thro' the humid air.   15
Descend, O little cloud, & hover before the eyes of Thel."

The Cloud descended, and the Lilly bowd her modest head,
And went to mind her numerous charge among the verdant grass.

PLATE 3

II

"O little Cloud," the virgin said, "I charge thee tell to me,
Why thou complainest not when in one hour thou fade away:
Then we shall seek thee but not find; ah, Thel is like to Thee.
I pass away, yet I complain, and no one hears my voice."

The Cloud then shew'd his golden head & his bright form emerg'd,   5
Hovering and glittering on the air before the face of Thel.

"O virgin, know'st thou not our steeds drink of the golden springs
Where Luvah[8] doth renew his horses? Look'st thou on my youth,
And fearest thou, because I vanish and am seen no more,
Nothing remains? O maid, I tell thee, when I pass away,   10
It is to tenfold life, to love, to peace, and raptures holy:
Unseen descending, weigh my light wings upon balmy flowers,
And court the fair eyed dew, to take me to her shining tent;
The weeping virgin trembling kneels before the risen sun,
Till we arise link'd in a golden band, and never part,   15
But walk united, bearing food to all our tender flowers."

"Dost thou O little Cloud? I fear that I am not like thee;
For I walk through the vales of Har and smell the sweetest flowers,
But I feed not the little flowers; I hear the warbling birds,
But I feed not the warbling birds; they fly and seek their food; 20
But Thel delights in these no more, because I fade away,
And all shall say, 'Without a use this shining woman liv'd,
Or did she only live to be at death the food of worms?' "

The Cloud reclind upon his airy throne and answer'd thus:

"Then if thou art the food of worms, O virgin of the skies,   25
How great thy use, how great thy blessing! Every thing that lives
Lives not alone, nor for itself; fear not, and I will call
The weak worm from its lowly bed, and thou shalt hear its voice.
Come forth, worm of the silent valley, to thy pensive queen."

The helpless worm arose, and sat upon the Lilly's leaf,   30
And the bright Cloud saild on, to find his partner in the vale.

---

8. The earliest mention in Blake's work   passional and sexual aspect of man, re-
of one of his "Giant Forms," the Zoas.   pairs to the Vales of Har simply in
Luvah, the mythical embodiment of the   order to rest and water his horses.

PLATE 4

III

Then Thel astonish'd view'd the Worm upon its dewy bed.

"Art thou a Worm? Image of weakness, art thou but a Worm?
I see thee like an infant wrapped in the Lilly's leaf;
Ah, weep not, little voice, thou can'st not speak, but thou can'st weep.
Is this a Worm? I see thee lay helpless & naked, weeping,   5
And none to answer, none to cherish thee with mother's smiles."

The Clod of Clay heard the Worm's voice, & raisd her pitying head;
She bow'd over the weeping infant, and her life exhal'd
In milky fondness; then on Thel she fix'd her humble eyes.

"O beauty of the vales of Har! we live not for ourselves;   10
Thou seest me the meanest thing, and so I am indeed.
My bosom of itself is cold, and of itself is dark;

PLATE 5

But he that loves the lowly, pours his oil upon my head,
And kisses me, and binds his nuptial bands around my breast,
And says: 'Thou mother of my children, I have lovéd thee,
And I have given thee a crown that none can take away.'
But how this is, sweet maid, I know not, and I cannot know;   5
I ponder, and I cannot ponder; yet I live and love."

The daughter of beauty wip'd her pitying tears with her white veil,
And said: "Alas! I knew not this, and therefore did I weep.
That God would love a Worm, I knew, and punish the evil foot
That, wilful, bruis'd its helpless form; but that he cherish'd it   10
With milk and oil I never knew; and therefore did I weep,
And I complaind in the mild air, because I fade away,
And lay me down in thy cold bed, and leave my shining lot."

"Queen of the vales," the matron Clay answerd, "I heard thy sighs,
And all thy moans flew o'er my roof, but I have call'd them down. 15
Wilt thou, O Queen, enter my house? 'Tis given thee to enter
And to return; fear nothing, enter with thy virgin feet."

PLATE 6

IV

The eternal gates' terrific porter lifted the northern bar: 9
Thel enter'd in & saw the secrets of the land unknown.
She saw the couches of the dead, & where the fibrous roots

9. Homer, in *Odyssey* XIII, described the Cave of the Naiades, of which the northern gate is for men and the southern gate for gods. The Neoplatonist Porphyro had allegorized it as an account of the descent of the soul into matter. Blake has Thel use the northern gate to pass from the state before birth into incarnate life.

Of every heart on earth infixes deep its restless twists:
A land of sorrows & of tears where never smile was seen.   5

She wanderd in the land of clouds thro' valleys dark, listning
Dolours & lamentations; waiting oft beside a dewy grave,
She stood in silence, listning to the voices of the ground,
Till to her own grave plot she came, & there she sat down,
And heard this voice of sorrow breathéd from the hollow pit: 10

"Why cannot the Ear be closed to its own destruction?
Or the glistning Eye to the poison of a smile?
Why are Eyelids stord with arrows ready drawn,
Where a thousand fighting men in ambush lie?
Or an Eye of gifts & graces, show'ring fruits & coinéd gold?   15
Why a Tongue impress'd with honey from every wind?
Why an Ear, a whirlpool fierce to draw creations in?
Why a Nostril wide inhaling terror, trembling, & affright?
Why a tender curb upon the youthful burning boy?
Why a little curtain of flesh on the bed of our desire?" [1]   20

The Virgin started from her seat, & with a shriek
Fled back unhinderd till she came into the vales of Har.

THE END

1789–91

1. From Thel's grave issues, apparently, the voice of Thel herself, expressing how experience would seem to her timid and shrinking temperament, should she elect to live out her life in the human world. The catalogue of experience runs through the various senses to end with touch, the primary sexual sense.

The Marriage of Heaven and Hell

This, the most immediately accessible of Blake's longer works, is a vigorous, deliberately outrageous, and at times comic, onslaught against the timidly conventional and self-righteous members of society, as well as against many of the stock opinions of orthodox Christian piety and morality. The seeming simplicity of Blake's satiric attitude, however, is deceptive.

Initially, Blake accepts the terminology of middle-class Christian morality ("what the religious call Good & Evil") but reverses its values. In this conventional use Evil, which is manifested by the class of beings called Devils and which consigns a man to the orthodox Hell, is everything associated with the body and its desires and consists essentially of energy, abundance, act, freedom. And conventional Good, which is manifested by Angels and guarantees its adherents a place in the orthodox Heaven, is associated with the Soul (regarded as entirely separate from the body) and consists of the contrary qualities of reason, restraint, passivity, and prohibition. Blandly adopting this current nomenclature, Blake elects to assume the diabolic persona—what he calls "the voice of the Devil"—and to utter "Proverbs of Hell." This ironic stance produces a vein of satire which is in the great 18th-century tradition of sustained ironic reversal, represented by works such as Jonathan Swift's Modest Proposal.

But the transvaluation of standard criteria is only a first stage in Blake's complex irony, designed to startle the reader into recognizing the inadequacy of standard moral categories and stock responses. As he also says in the opening summary of his total argument, "Without Contraries is no progression," and "Reason and Energy" are both "necessary to Human existence." It turns out that Blake subordinates his satiric reversal of conventional values under a more inclusive point of view, according to which the real Good, as distinguished from the merely ironic Good, is not simply freedom from restraint, but a "marriage" of the contrary extremes of desire and restraint, energy and reason, the promptings of Hell and the limitations of Heaven—or as Blake calls these contraries, in the comprehensive terms he introduces in Plate 16, "the Prolific" and "the Devouring." These two classes, he adds, "should be enemies," and "whoever tries to reconcile them seeks to destroy existence." When Blake speaks not as moral satirist but as serious moralist, the good life is that abundant and strenuous life he describes as the sustained conflict, without victory or suppression, of simultaneous opposites.

Blake was stimulated to write this unique work in response to the books of the visionary Swedish theologian, Emanuel Swedenborg, whom he had at first admired but then had come to recognize as a conventional Angel in the disguise of a radical Devil. In Plate 3, the writings of Swedenborg are described as the winding clothes Blake discards as he is resurrected from the tomb of his past self, as a poet-prophet who heralds the apocalyptic promise of his age. For Blake wrote *The Marriage of Heaven and Hell* during the bright early years of the French Revolution, when he shared the expectations of a number of radical Englishmen, including the young poets Wordsworth, Coleridge, and Southey, that the Revolution was the universal violence which had been predicted by the Biblical prophets as a stage immediately preceding the millennium. The double role of *The Marriage* as both satire and revolutionary prophecy is made explicit in *A Song of Liberty*, which Blake engraved in 1792 and added as a coda.

The Marriage of Heaven and Hell

PLATE 2

The Argument

Rintrah [1] roars & shakes his fires in the burdend air;
Hungry clouds swag on the deep.

Once meek, and in a perilous path,
The just man kept his course along
The vale of death.   5

1. Rintrah plays the role of the angry Old Testament prophet Elijah as well as of John the Baptist, the voice "crying in the wilderness" (Matthew iii), preparing the way for Christ the Messiah. The "Argument" is a summary of the subject matter of the poem. The villain, who hypocritically assumes a "mild humility," represents the class of Angels in the *Marriage;* the just man is represented by Blake himself, a raging po[?] prophet in the guise of a "Devi[?] announces the apocalyptic p[?] imaginative redemption

Roses are planted where thorns grow,
And on the barren heath
Sing the honey bees.

Then the perilous path was planted,
And a river, and a spring,   10
On every cliff and tomb;
And on the bleached bones
Red clay [2] brought forth;

Till the villain left the paths of ease,
To walk in perilous paths, and drive   15
The just man into barren climes.

Now the sneaking serpent walks
In mild humility,
And the just man rages in the wilds
Where lions roam.   20

Rintrah roars & shakes his fires in the burdend air;
Hungry clouds swag [3] on the deep.

PLATE 3

As a new heaven is begun, and it is now thirty-three years since
its advent, the Eternal Hell revives.[4] And lo! Swedenborg is the
Angel sitting at the tomb; his writings are the linen clothes folded
up. Now is the dominion of Edom, & the return of Adam into
Paradise; see Isaiah xxxiv & XXXV Chap.[5]

Without Contraries is no progression. Attraction and Repulsion,
Reason and Energy, Love and Hate, are necessary to Human existence.

2. In Hebrew, the literal meaning of "Adam," or created man. There is also a probable reference to the Redeemer, the new Adam.
3. Sag or sway (or both).
4. The Swedish scientist and religious philosopher, Emanuel Swedenborg (1688–1772) had predicted, on the basis of his visions, that the Last Judgment and the coming of the Kingdom of Heaven would occur in 1757. This was precisely the year of Blake's birth. Now, in 1790, Blake is thirty-three, the age at which Christ had been resurrected from the tomb; appropriately, Blake rises from the tomb of his past life in his new role as imaginative artist who will redeem his age. But, Blake ironically comments, the works he will engrave in his resurrection will constitute the Eternal Hell, the contrary inevitably brought into simultaneous being by Swedenborg's limited New Heaven.
5. Isaiah xxxiv prophesies "the day of the Lord's vengeance," a time of violent destruction and bloodshed; Isaiah xxxv prophesies the redemption to follow, in which "the desert shall * * * blossom as the rose," "in the wilderness shall waters break out, and streams in the desert," and "no lion shall be there," but "an highway shall be there * * * and it shall be called the way of holiness." (Cf. "The Argument," lines 3–11, 20.) Blake combines with these chapters Isaiah lxiii, in which "Edom" is the place from which comes the man whose garments are red with the blood he has spilled; for as he says, "the day of vengeance is in mine heart, and the year of my redeemed is come." Blake interprets this last phrase as predicting the time when Adam would regain his lost Paradise.
With reference to affairs in 1790, Edom represents France, and the red man coming from Edom (to England) is the spirit of the French Revolution, which Blake represents as a portent of apocalyptic redemption and of the recovery of Paradise.

From these contraries spring what the religious call Good & Evil. Good is the passive that obeys Reason. Evil is the active springing from Energy.

Good is Heaven. Evil is Hell.

PLATE 4

The voice of the Devil

All Bibles or sacred codes have been the causes of the following Errors:

1. That Man has two real existing principles; Viz: a Body & a Soul.

2. That Energy, calld Evil, is alone from the Body, & that Reason, calld Good, is alone from the Soul.

3. That God will torment Man in Eternity for following his Energies. But the following Contraries to these are True:

1. Man has no Body distinct from his Soul; for that calld Body is a portion of Soul discernd by the five Senses, the chief inlets of Soul in this age.

2. Energy is the only life, and is from the Body; and Reason is the bound or outward circumference of Energy.

3. Energy is Eternal Delight

PLATE 5

Those who restrain desire, do so because theirs is weak enough to be restrained; and the restrainer or reason usurps its place & governs the unwilling.

And being restraind, it by degrees becomes passive, till it is only the shadow of desire.

The history of this is written in *Paradise Lost*,[6] & the Governor or Reason is call'd Messiah.

And the original Archangel, or possessor of the command of the heavenly host, is calld the Devil or Satan, and his children are call'd Sin & Death.[7]

But in the Book of Job, Milton's Messiah is call'd Satan.[8]

For this history has been adopted by both parties.

It indeed appear'd to Reason as if Desire was cast out; but the Devil's account is, that the Messi[PL 6]ah fell, & formed a heaven of what he stole from the Abyss.

This is shewn in the Gospel, where he prays to the Father to send the comforter or Desire that Reason may have Ideas to build

---

6. What follows, to the end of this section, is Blake's "diabolical" reading of Milton's *Paradise Lost*.
7. Satan's giving birth to Sin and then incestuously begetting Death upon her is described in II.745 ff.; the war in heaven, referred to three lines below, in which the Messiah defeated Satan and drove him out of heaven, is described in VI.824 ff.
8. Satan plays the role of the moral accuser and physical tormentor of Job.

on; [9] the Jehovah of the Bible being no other than he who dwells in flaming fire. Know that after Christ's death, he became Jehovah.

But in Milton, the Father is Destiny, the Son, a Ratio of the five senses,[1] & the Holy-ghost, Vacuum!

Note. The reason Milton wrote in fetters when he wrote of Angels & God, and at liberty when of Devils & Hell, is because he was a true Poet and of the Devil's party without knowing it.

A Memorable Fancy [2]

As I was walking among the fires of hell, delighted with the enjoyments of Genius, which to Angels look like torment and insanity, I collected some of their Proverbs; thinking that as the sayings used in a nation mark its character, so the Proverbs of Hell shew the nature of Infernal wisdom better than any description of buildings or garments.

When I came home, on the abyss of the five senses, where a flat sided steep frowns over the present world, I saw a mighty Devil folded in black clouds, hovering on the sides of the rock; with cor-[PL 7]roding fires he wrote the following sentence [3] now perceived by the minds of men, & read by them on earth:

> How do you know but ev'ry Bird that cuts the airy way,
> Is an immense world of delight, clos'd by your senses five?

Proverbs of Hell [4]

In seed time learn, in harvest teach, in winter enjoy.
Drive your cart and your plow over the bones of the dead.
The road of excess leads to the palace of wisdom.
Prudence is a rich ugly old maid courted by Incapacity.
He who desires but acts not, breeds pestilence.
The cut worm forgives the plow.
Dip him in the river who loves water.
A fool sees not the same tree that a wise man sees.
He whose face gives no light, shall never become a star.
Eternity is in love with the productions of time.
The busy bee has no time for sorrow.
The hours of folly are measur'd by the clock; but of wisdom, no

9. Possibly John xiv.16–17, where Christ says he "will pray the Father, and he shall give you another Comforter * * * even the Spirit of truth."
1. The Latin *ratio* means both "reason" and "sum." Blake applies the term to the 18th-century view, following the empirical philosophy of John Locke, that the content of the mind is limited to the sum of the experience acquired by the five senses.

2. A parody of what Swedenborg called "memorable relations" of his literal-minded visions of the eternal world.
3. The "mighty Devil" is Blake, as he sees himself reflected in the shiny plate on which he is etching this very passage with "corroding fires"—i.e., acid. See also the third from last sentence in Plate 14.
4. A "diabolic" version of the Book of Proverbs in the Old Testament.

clock can measure.

All wholsom food is caught without a net or a trap.

Bring out number, weight, & measure in a year of dearth.

No bird soars too high, if he soars with his own wings.

A dead body revenges not injuries.

The most sublime act is to set another before you.

If the fool would persist in his folly he would become wise.

Folly is the cloke of knavery.

Shame is Pride's cloke.

PLATE 8

Prisons are built with stones of Law, Brothels with bricks of Religion.

The pride of the peacock is the glory of God.

The lust of the goat is the bounty of God.

The wrath of the lion is the wisdom of God.

The nakedness of woman is the work of God.

Excess of sorrow laughs. Excess of joy weeps.

The roaring of lions, the howling of wolves, the raging of the stormy sea, and the destructive sword, are portions of eternity too great for the eye of man.

The fox condemns the trap, not himself.

Joys impregnate. Sorrows bring forth.

Let man wear the fell of the lion, woman the fleece of the sheep.

The bird a nest, the spider a web, man friendship.

The selfish, smiling fool & the sullen, frowning fool shall be both thought wise, that they may be a rod.

What is now proved was once only imagin'd.

The rat, the mouse, the fox, the rabbit watch the roots; the lion, the tyger, the horse, the elephant, watch the fruits.

The cistern contains: the fountain overflows.

One thought fills immensity.

Always be ready to speak your mind, and a base man will avoid you.

Every thing possible to be believ'd is an image of truth.

The eagle never lost so much time as when he submitted to learn of the crow.

PLATE 9

The fox provides for himself, but God provides for the lion.

Think in the morning, Act in the noon, Eat in the evening, Sleep in the night.

He who has sufferd you to impose on him knows you.

As the plow follows words, so God rewards prayers.

The tygers of wrath are wiser than the horses of instruction.

Expect poison from the standing water.

You never know what is enough unless you know what is more than enough.

Listen to the fools reproach! it is a kingly title!

The eyes of fire, the nostrils of air, the mouth of water, the beard of earth.

The weak in courage is strong in cunning.

The apple tree never asks the beech how he shall grow, nor the lion the horse, how he shall take his prey.

The thankful reciever bears a plentiful harvest.

If others had not been foolish, we should be so.

The soul of sweet delight can never be defil'd.

When thou seest an Eagle, thou seest a portion of Genius; lift up thy head!

As the catterpiller chooses the fairest leaves to lay her eggs on, so the priest lays his curse on the fairest joys.

To create a little flower is the labour of ages.

Damn braces: Bless relaxes.

The best wine is the oldest, the best water the newest.

Prayers plow not! Praises reap not!

Joys laugh not! Sorrows weep not!

PLATE 10

The head Sublime, the heart Pathos, the genitals Beauty, the hands & feet Proportion.

As the air to a bird or the sea to a fish, so is contempt to the contemptible.

The crow wish'd every thing was black, the owl that every thing was white.

Exuberance is Beauty.

If the lion was advised by the fox, he would be cunning.

Improvement makes strait roads, but the crooked roads without Improvement are roads of Genius.

Sooner murder an infant in its cradle than nurse unacted desires.

Where man is not, nature is barren.

Truth can never be told so as to be understood, and not be believ'd.

Enough! or Too much.

PLATE 11

The ancient Poets animated all sensible objects with Gods or Geniuses, calling them by the names and adorning them with the properties of woods, rivers, mountains, lakes, cities, nations, and whatever their enlarged & numerous senses could percieve.

And particularly they studied the genius of each city & country, placing it under its mental deity.

Till a system was formed, which some took advantage of & enslav'd the vulgar by attempting to realize or abstract the mental deities from their objects; thus began Priesthood,

Choosing forms of worship from poetic tales.

And at length they pronounced that the Gods had ordered such things.

Thus men forgot that All deities reside in the human breast.

PLATE 12

A Memorable Fancy

The Prophets Isaiah and Ezekiel dined with me, and I asked them how they dared so roundly to assert that God spake to them; and whether they did not think at the time that they would be misunderstood, & so be the cause of imposition.

Isaiah answer'd: "I saw no God, nor heard any, in a finite organical perception; but my senses discover'd the infinite in every thing, and as I was then perswaded, & remain confirm'd, that the voice of honest indignation is the voice of God, I cared not for consequences, but wrote."

Then I asked: "Does a firm perswasion that a thing is so, make it so?"

He replied: "All poets believe that it does, & in ages of imagination this firm perswasion removed mountains; but many are not capable of a firm perswasion of any thing."

Then Ezekiel said: "The philosophy of the East taught the first principles of human perception. Some nations held one principle for the origin & some another; we of Israel taught that the Poetic Genius (as you now call it) was the first principle and all the others merely derivative, which was the cause of our despising the Priests & Philosophers of other countries, and prophecying that all Gods [PL 13] would at last be proved to originate in ours & to be the tributaries of the Poetic Genius; it was this that our great poet, King David, desired so fervently & invokes so patheticly, saying by this he conquers enemies & governs kingdoms; and we so loved our God, that we cursed in his name all the deities of surrounding nations, and asserted that they had rebelled; from these opinions the vulgar came to think that all nations would at last be subject to the Jews."

"This," said he, "like all firm perswasions, is come to pass, for all nations believe the Jews' code and worship the Jews' god, and what greater subjection can be?"

I heard this with some wonder, & must confess my own conviction. After dinner I ask'd Isaiah to favour the world with his lost works; he said none of equal value was lost. Ezekiel said the same of his.

I also asked Isaiah what made him go naked and barefoot three years? He answerd, "the same that made our friend Diogenes, the Grecian." [5]

I then asked Ezekiel why he eat dung, & lay so long on his right & left side? [6] He answered, "the desire of raising other men into a

---

5. In Isaiah xx.2–3, the Lord commanded Isaiah to go "naked and barefoot" for three years. Diogenes was the 4th-century Greek Cynic, whose extreme repudiation of civilized customs gave rise to anecdotes that he had renounced clothing.

6. The Lord gave these instructions to the prophet Ezekiel, iv.4–6.

perception of the infinite; this the North American tribes practise, & is he honest who resists his genius or conscience only for the sake of present ease or gratification?"

PLATE 14

The ancient tradition that the world will be consumed in fire at the end of six thousand years is true, as I have heard from Hell.

For the cherub with his flaming sword is hereby commanded to leave his guard at tree of life; [7] and when he does, the whole creation will be consumed, and appear infinite and holy, whereas it now appears finite & corrupt.

This will come to pass by an improvement of sensual enjoyment.

But first the notion that man has a body distinct from his soul is to be expunged; this I shall do, by printing in the infernal method, by corrosives, which in Hell are salutary and medicinal, melting apparent surfaces away, and displaying the infinite which was hid.[8]

If the doors of perception were cleansed every thing would appear to man as it is, infinite.

For man has closed himself up, till he sees all things thro' narrow chinks of his cavern.

PLATE 15

A Memorable Fancy

I was in a Printing house in Hell & saw the method in which knowledge is transmitted from generation to generation.

In the first chamber was a Dragon-Man, clearing away the rubbish from a cave's mouth; within, a number of Dragons were hollowing the cave.

In the second chamber was a Viper folding round the rock & the cave, and others adorning it with gold, silver, and precious stones.

In the third chamber was an Eagle with wings and feathers of air; he caused the inside of the cave to be infinite; around were numbers of Eagle-like men, who built palaces in the immense cliffs.

In the fourth chamber were Lions of flaming fire, raging around & melting the metals into living fluids.

In the fifth chamber were Unnam'd forms, which cast the metals into the expanse.

There they were receiv'd by Men who occupied the sixth chamber, and took the forms of books & were arranged in libraries.[9]

---

7. In Genesis iii.24, when the Lord drove Adam and Eve from the Garden of Eden, he had placed Cherubims and a flaming sword at the eastern end "to keep the way of the tree of life."

8. See the preceding "Memorable Fancy," and footnote.
9. This Memorable Fancy is Blake's allegorical rendering of the creation and printing of works of imagination.

PLATE 16

The Giants who formed this world into its sensual existence, and now seem to live in it in chains, are in truth the causes of its life & the sources of all activity; but the chains are the cunning of weak and tame minds which have power to resist energy; according to the proverb, the weak in courage is strong in cunning.

Thus one portion of being is the Prolific, the other, the Devouring: to the Devourer it seems as if the producer was in his chains; but it is not so, he only takes portions of existence and fancies that the whole. ,

But the Prolific would cease to be Prolific unless the Devourer as a sea received the excess of his delights.[1]

Some will say, "Is not God alone the Prolific?" I answer, "God only Acts & Is, in existing beings or Men."

These two classes of men are always upon earth, & they should be enemies; whoever tries [PL 17] to reconcile them seeks to destroy existence.

Religion is an endeavour to reconcile the two.

Note. Jesus Christ did not wish to unite but to separate them, as in the Parable of sheep and goats! & he says, "I came not to send Peace but a Sword." [2]

Messiah or Satan or Tempter was formerly thought to be one of the Antediluvians [3] who are our Energies.

A Memorable Fancy

An Angel came to me and said: "O pitiable foolish young man! O horrible! O dreadful state! consider the hot burning dungeon thou art preparing for thyself to all eternity, to which thou art going in such career."

I said: "Perhaps you will be willing to shew me my eternal lot, & we will contemplate together upon it and see whether your lot or mine is most desirable."

So he took me thro' a stable & thro' a church & down into the church vault at the end of which was a mill; thro' the mill we went, and came to a cave; down the winding cavern we groped our tedious way till a void boundless as a nether sky appeard beneath us, & we held by the roots of trees and hung over this immensity, but I said: "If you please, we will commit ourselves to this void, and see whether Providence is here also, if you will not I will." But he answerd: "Do not presume, O young man, but as we here remain, behold thy lot which will soon appear when the darkness passes

---

1. The "Giants" in this section are man's creative energies, called "the Prolific," which are necessarily limited by their contrary, "the Devourer."

2. The parable of the sheep and the goats is in Matthew xxv.32–33; the saying of Christ, in Matthew x.34.
3. Men who lived before Noah's flood.

away." [4]

So I remaind with him sitting in the twisted [PL 18] root of an oak; he was suspended in a fungus which hung with the head downward into the deep.

By degrees we beheld the infinite Abyss, fiery as the smoke of a burning city; beneath us at an immense distance was the sun, black but shining; round it were fiery tracks on which revolv'd vast spiders, crawling after their prey, which flew, or rather swum in the infinite deep, in the most terrific shapes of animals sprung from corruption; & the air was full of them, & seemd composed of them; these are Devils, and are called Powers of the air. I now asked my companion which was my eternal lot? he said, "Between the black & white spiders."

But now, from between the black & white spiders a cloud and fire burst and rolled thro the deep, blackning all beneath, so that the nether deep grew black as a sea & rolled with a terrible noise; beneath us was nothing now to be seen but a black tempest, till looking east between the clouds & the waves, we saw a cataract of blood mixed with fire, and not many stones throw from us appeard and sunk again the scaly fold of a monstrous serpent. At last to the east, distant about three degrees, appeard a fiery crest above the waves. Slowly it reared like a ridge of golden rocks till we discovered two globes of crimson fire, from which the sea fled away in clouds of smoke; and now we saw it was the head of Leviathan; his forehead was divided into streaks of green & purple like those on a tyger's forehead: soon we saw his mouth & red gills hang just above the raging foam, tinging the black deep with beams of blood, advancing toward [PL 19] us with all the fury of a spiritual existence.

My friend the Angel climb'd up from his station into the mill; I remain'd alone, & then this appearance was no more, but I found myself sitting on a pleasant bank beside a river by moon light, hearing a harper who sung to the harp, & his theme was: "The man who never alters his opinion is like standing water, & breeds reptiles of the mind."

But I arose, and sought for the mill, & there I found my Angel, who surprised asked me how I escaped?

I answerd: "All that we saw was owing to your metaphysics: for when you ran away, I found myself on a bank by moonlight hearing

---

4. The "stable" is that where Jesus was born, which, allegorically, leads to the "church" founded in his name and to the "vault" where this institution effectually buried him. The "mill" in Blake is a symbol of mechanical and analytic philosophy; through this the pilgrims pass into the twisting cave of rationalistic theology and descend to an underworld which is an empty abyss. The point of this Blakean equivalent of a carnival fun house is that only after you have thoroughly confused yourself by this tortuous approach, and only if you then (as in the next two paragraphs) stare at this topsy-turvy emptiness long enough, will the void gradually assume the semblance of the comic horrors of the fantasied hell of angelic orthodoxy.

a harper. But now we have seen my eternal lot, shall I shew you yours? He laughd at my proposal; but I by force suddenly caught him in my arms, & flew westerly thro' the night, till we were elevated above the earth's shadow; then I flung myself with him directly into the body of the sun; here I clothed myself in white, & taking in my hand Swedenborg's volumes, sunk from the glorious clime, and passed all the planets till we came to Saturn; here I staid to rest & then leap'd into the void between Saturn & the fixed stars.

"Here," said I, "is your lot, in this space, if space it may be calld." Soon we saw the stable and the church, & I took him to the altar and open'd the Bible, and lo! it was a deep pit, into which I descended, driving the Angel before me; soon we saw seven houses of brick;[5] one we enterd; in it were a [PL 20] number of monkeys, baboons, & all of that species, chaind by the middle, grinning and snatching at one another, but withheld by the shortness of their chains: however, I saw that they sometimes grew numerous, and then the weak were caught by the strong, and with a grinning aspect, first coupled with & then devourd, by plucking off first one limb and then another till the body was left a helpless trunk. This, after grinning & kissing it with seeming fondness, they devourd too; and here & there I saw one savourily picking the flesh off of his own tail; as the stench terribly annoyd us both, we went into the mill, & I in my hand brought the skeleton of a body, which in the mill was Aristotle's Analytics.[6]

So the Angel said: "Thy phantasy has imposed upon me, & thou oughtest to be ashamed."

I answerd: "We impose on one another, & it is but lost time to converse with you whose works are only Analytics."

Opposition is true Friendship.

PLATE 21

I have always found that Angels have the vanity to speak of themselves as the only wise; this they do with a confident insolence sprouting from systematic reasoning.

Thus Swedenborg boasts that what he writes is new; tho' it is only the Contents or Index of already publish'd books.

A man carried a monkey about for a shew, & because he was a little wiser than the monkey, grew vain, and conciev'd himself as much wiser than seven men. It is so with Swedenborg; he shews the folly of churches & exposes hypocrites, till he imagines that all are religious, & himself the single [PL 22] one on earth that ever broke

---

5. The "seven churches which are in Asia," to which John addresses the Book of Revelation i.4. Blake now forces upon the angel his own diabolic view of angelic Biblical exegesis, theological speculation and disputation, and Hell—a view, Harold Bloom has remarked, which "makes monkeys out of the theologians."

6. Aristotle's treatises on logic.

a net.

Now hear a plain fact: Swedenborg has not written one new truth. Now hear another: he has written all the old falshoods.

And now hear the reason: He conversed with Angels who are all religious, & conversed not with Devils, who all hate religion, for he was incapable thro' his conceited notions.

Thus Swedenborg's writings are a recapitulation of all superficial opinions, and an analysis of the more sublime, but no further.

Have now another plain fact: Any man of mechanical talents may from the writings of Paracelsus or Jacob Behmen [7] produce ten thousand volumes of equal value with Swedenborg's, and from those of Dante or Shakespear, an infinite number.

But when he has done this, let him not say that he knows better than his master, for he only holds a candle in sunshine.

A Memorable Fancy

Once I saw a Devil in a flame of fire, who arose before an Angel that sat on a cloud, and the Devil utterd these words:

"The worship of God is, Honouring his gifts in other men, each according to his genius, and loving the [PL 23] greatest men best; those who envy or calumniate great men hate God, for there is no other God."

The Angel hearing this became almost blue; but mastering himself, he grew yellow, & at last white, pink, & smiling, and then replied:

"Thou Idolater, is not God One? & is not he visible in Jesus Christ? and has not Jesus Christ given his sanction to the law of ten commandments, and are not all other men fools, sinners, & nothings?"

The Devil answer'd; "Bray [8] a fool in a mortar with wheat, yet shall not his folly be beaten out of him; if Jesus Christ is the greatest man, you ought to love him in the greatest degree; now hear how he has given his sanction to the law of ten commandments: did he not mock at the sabbath, and so mock the sabbath's God? murder those who were murderd because of him? turn away the law from the woman taken in adultery? steal the labor of others to support him? bear false witness when he omitted making a defence before Pilate? covet when he pray'd for his disciples, and when he bid them shake off the dust of their feet against such as refused to lodge them? I tell you, no virtue can exist without breaking these ten commandments. Jesus was all virtue, and acted from im[PL

7. Paracelsus (1493–1541), a Swiss physician and a pioneer in empirical medicine, was also a prominent theorist of the occult. Behmen is Jakob Boehme (1575–1624), a German shoemaker who developed a theosophical system which has had great and persisting influence both on theological and metaphysical speculation.
8. Pound into small pieces.

24]pulse, not from rules."

When he had so spoken, I beheld the Angel, who stretched out his arms, embracing the flame of fire, & he was consumed and arose as Elijah.[9]

Note. This Angel, who is now become a Devil, is my particular friend; we often read the Bible together in its infernal or diabolical sense, which the world shall have if they behave well.

I have also The Bible of Hell,[1] which the world shall have whether they will or no.

One Law for the Lion & Ox is Oppression.

1790–93   1790–93

PLATE 25

A Song of Liberty [2]

1. The Eternal Female groand! it was heard over all the Earth.

2. Albion's[3] coast is sick, silent; the American meadows faint!

3. Shadows of Prophecy shiver along by the lakes and the rivers and mutter across the ocean: France, rend down thy dungeon!

4. Golden Spain, burst the barriers of old Rome!

5. Cast thy keys, O Rome, into the deep down falling, even to eternity down falling,

6. And weep.

7. In her trembling hands she took the new born terror, howling.

8. On those infinite mountains of light now barr'd out by the Atlantic sea,[4] the new born fire stood before the starry king!

9. Flag'd with grey brow'd snows and thunderous visages, the jealous wings wav'd over the deep.

10. The speary hand burned aloft, unbuckled was the shield, forth went the hand of jealousy among the flaming hair, and [PL 26] hurl'd the new born wonder thro' the starry night.

11. The fire, the fire, is falling!

12. Look up! look up! O citizen of London, enlarge thy countenance! O Jew, leave counting gold! return to thy oil and wine. O African! black African! (Go, wingéd thought, widen his forehead.)

---

9. The angry Old Testament prophet; see the opening "Argument," footnote.
1. I.e., the poems and designs that Blake is working on.
2. Blake etched this poem in 1792 and sometimes bound it as an appendix to *The Marriage of Heaven and Hell*. It recounts the birth, manifested in the contemporary events in France, of the flaming Spirit of Revolution (whom Blake later called Orc), and describes his conflict with the tyrannical sky-god

(whom Blake later called Urizen). The poem ends with the portent of the Spirit of Revolution shattering the ten commandments, or prohibitions against political, religious, and moral liberty, and bringing in a free and joyous new world.
3. England's.
4. The legendary continent of Atlantis, sunk beneath the sea; Blake uses it to represent the condition before the fall.

13. The fiery limbs, the flaming hair, shot like the sinking sun into the western sea.

14. Wak'd from his eternal sleep, the hoary element roaring fled away:

15. Down rushd, beating his wings in vain, the jealous king; his grey brow'd councellors, thunderous warriors, curl'd veterans, among helms, and shields, and chariots, horses, elephants; banners, castles, slings and rocks,

16. Falling, rushing, ruining! buried in the ruins, on Urthona's [5] dens;

17. All night beneath the ruins; then, their sullen flames, faded, emerge round the gloomy king,

18. With thunder and fire, leading his starry hosts thro' the waste wilderness [PL 27] he promulgates his ten commands, glancing his beamy eyelids over the deep in dark dismay,

19. Where the son of fire in his eastern cloud, while the morning plumes her golden breast,

20. Spurning the clouds written with curses, stamps the stony law to dust, loosing the eternal horses from the dens of night, crying:

Empire is no more! and now the lion & wolf shall cease.[6]

CHORUS

Let the Priests of the Raven of dawn, no longer in deadly black, with hoarse note curse the sons of joy. Nor his accepted brethren, whom, tyrant, he calls free, lay the bound or build the roof. Nor pale religious letchery call that virginity, that wishes but acts not!

For every thing that lives is Holy.

1792   1792

For the Sexes: The Gates of Paradise[1]

[*Prologue*]
Mutual Forgiveness of each Vice,
Such are the Gates of Paradise.
Against the Accuser's chief desire
Who walkd among the Stones of Fire
Jehovah's Finger Wrote the Law,   5
Then Wept! then rose in Zeal & Awe
And the Dead Corpse from Sinai's heat
Buried beneath his Mercy Seat.

---

5. In the later Prophetic Books, Urthona is the unfallen form of Los, who in the fallen world represents the poetic imagination, the agent working for the regeneration of humanity.

6. Cf. Isaiah's prophecy, lxv.17–25, of "new heavens and a new earth," when "the wolf and the lamb shall feed together, and the lion shall eat straw like the bullock."

1. The two poems reprinted here introduce and conclude a series of emblems (drawings with explanatory captions) that Blake issued first under the title *For Children: The Gates of Paradise* and later amplified and reissued under the present title.

O Christians, Christians! tell me Why
You rear it on your Altars high.   10

[*Epilogue*]
To The Accuser who is
The God of This World

Truly My Satan thou art but a Dunce,
And dost not know the Garment from the Man;
Every Harlot was a Virgin once,
Nor canst thou ever change Kate into Nan.

Tho thou art Worshipd by the Names Divine   5
Of Jesus & Jehovah: thou art still
The Son of Morn in weary Night's decline,
The lost Traveller's Dream under the Hill.

1793–ca. 1818   1793–ca. 1818

Poems from BLAKE'S NOTEBOOK[1]

Never Pain to Tell Thy Love

Never pain to tell thy love
Love that never told can be,
For the gentle wind does move
Silently, invisibly.

I told my love, I told my love,   5
I told her all my heart,
Trembling, cold, in ghastly fears—
Ah, she doth depart.

Soon as she was gone from me
A traveller came by   10
Silently, invisibly—
O, was no deny.

I Askéd a Thief

I askéd a thief to steal me a peach,
He turned up his eyes;
I ask'd a lithe lady to lie her down,
Holy & meek she cries.

1. A commonplace book in which Blake drew sketches and jotted down verses and memoranda between the late 1780's and 1810. It is known as the "Rossetti Notebook" because it later came into the possession of the poet and painter Dante Gabriel Rossetti. The manuscript was published by Geoffrey Keynes in 1935.

As soon as I went   5
An angel came.
He wink'd at the thief
And smild at the dame—

And without one word said
Had a peach from the tree   10
And still as a maid
Enjoy'd the lady.

1796

Mock on, Mock on, Voltaire, Rousseau

Mock on, Mock on, Voltaire, Rousseau;
Mock on, Mock on, 'tis all in vain.
You throw the sand against the wind,
And the wind blows it back again.

And every sand becomes a Gem   5
Reflected in the beams divine;
Blown back, they blind the mocking Eye,
But still in Israel's paths they shine.

The Atoms of Democritus
And Newton's Particles of light   10
Are sands upon the Red sea shore,
Where Israel's tents do shine so bright.

Morning

To find the Western path
Right thro the Gates of Wrath
I urge my way;
Sweet Mercy leads me on,
With soft repentant moan   5
I see the break of day.

The war of swords & spears
Melted by dewy tears
Exhales on high;
The Sun is freed from fears   10
And with soft grateful tears
Ascends the sky.

And Did Those Feet[1]

And did those feet in ancient time
Walk upon England's mountains green?

1. These quatrains occur in the Pref-   There is an ancient belief, still current
ace to Blake's prophetic poem *Milton*.   in parts of England, that Jesus came

And was the holy Lamb of God
On England's pleasant pastures seen?

And did the Countenance Divine   5
Shine forth upon our clouded hills?
And was Jerusalem builded here,
Among these dark Satanic Mills? 2

Bring me my Bow of burning gold:
Bring me my Arrows of desire:
Bring me my Spear: O clouds unfold!   10
Bring me my Chariot of fire!

I will not cease from Mental Fight,
Nor shall my Sword sleep in my hand,
Till we have built Jerusalem   15
In England's green & pleasant Land.

ca. 1804–10   ca. 1804–10

A Vision of The Last Judgment[1]

For the Year 1810
Additions to Blake's Catalogue of Pictures &c

The Last Judgment [will be] when all those are Cast away who trouble Religion with Questions concerning Good & Evil or Eating of the Tree of those Knowledges or Reasonings which hinder the Vision of God turning all into a Consuming fire. When Imaginative Art & Science & all Intellectual Gifts, all the Gifts of the Holy Ghost, are lookd upon as of no use & only Contention remains to Man then the Last Judgment begins & its Vision is seen by the Imaginative Eye of Every one according to the situation he holds.

[PAGE 68] The Last Judgment is not Fable or Allegory but Vision. Fable or Allegory are a totally distinct & inferior kind of

to England with Joseph of Arimathea. Blake adapts the legend to his own conception of a spiritual Israel, in which the significance of Biblical events are as relevant to England as to Palestine. By a particularly Blakean irony, this poem of mental war in the service of apocalyptic desire is widely used as a hymn by those of us whom Blake called "angels."

2. There may be an allusion here to industrial England; but the mill is primarily Blake's symbol for a mechanistic and utilitarian world view, according to which, as he said elsewhere, "the same dull round, even of a universe" becomes "a mill with complicated wheels."

1. In this essay Blake describes and comments on his painting of the Last Judgment, now lost, which is said to have measured seven by five feet and

to have included a thousand figures. The text has been transcribed and re-arranged, as the sequence of the pages indicate, from the scattered fragments in Blake's Notebook. The opening and closing parts are reprinted here as Blake's fullest, although cryptic, statements of what he means by vision. These sections deal with the relations of imaginative vision to allegory, Greek fable, and the Biblical story; to uncurbed human passion and intellectual power; to conventional and coercive virtue; to what is seen by the "corporeal" eye; to the arts; and to the Last Judgment and the apocalyptic redemption of man and the created world —an apocalypse which is to be achieved by the triumph over the bodily eye of human imagination, as manifested in the creative artist.

Poetry. Vision or Imagination is a Representation of what Eternally Exists, Really & Unchangeably. Fable or Allegory is Formd by the daughters of Memory. Imagination is Surrounded by the daughters of Inspiration who in the aggregate are calld Jerusalem. [P 69] Fable is Allegory but what Critics call The Fable is Vision itself. [P 68] The Hebrew Bible & the Gospel of Jesus are not Allegory but Eternal Vision or Imagination of All that Exists. Note here that Fable or Allegory is Seldom without some Vision. Pilgrim's Progress is full of it, the Greek Poets the same; but Allegory & Vision ought to be known as Two Distinct Things & so calld for the Sake of Eternal Life. Plato has made Socrates say that Poets & Prophets do not know or Understand what they write or Utter; this is a most Pernicious Falshood. If they do not, pray is an inferior Kind to be calld Knowing? Plato confutes himself.

The Last Judgment is one of these Stupendous Visions. I have represented it as I saw it. To different People it appears differently as [P 69] every thing else does for tho on Earth things seem Permanent they are less permanent than a Shadow as we all know too well.

The Nature of Visionary Fancy or Imagination is very little Known & the Eternal nature & permanence of its ever Existent Images is considered as less permanent than the things of Vegetative & Generative Nature; yet the Oak dies as well as the Lettuce, but Its Eternal Image & Individuality never dies, but renews by its seed. Just so the Imaginative Image returns by the seed of Contemplative Thought. The Writings of the Prophets illustrate these conceptions of the Visionary Fancy by their various sublime & Divine Images as seen in the Worlds of Vision. * * *

Let it here be Noted that the Greek Fables originated in Spiritual Mystery [P 72] and Real Visions Which are lost & clouded in Fable & Allegory while the Hebrew Bible & the Greek Gospel are Genuine, Preservd by the Saviour's Mercy. The Nature of my Work is Visionary or Imaginative. It is an Endeavour to Restore what the Ancients calld the Golden Age.

[PAGE 69] This world of Imagination is the World of Eternity; it is the Divine bosom into which we shall all go after the death of the Vegetated body. This World of Imagination is Infinite & Eternal whereas the world of Generation or Vegetation is Finite & for a small moment Temporal. There Exist in that Eternal World the Permanent Realities of Every Thing which we see reflected in this Vegetable Glass of Nature.

All Things are comprehended in their Eternal Forms in the Divine [P 70] body of the Saviour, the True Vine of Eternity, The Human Imagination, who appeard to Me as Coming to Judgment among his Saints & throwing off the Temporal that the Eternal

might be Establishd. Around him were seen the Images of Existences according to a certain order suited to my Imaginative Eye.
* * *

[PAGE 87] Men are admitted into Heaven not because they have
curbed & governd their Passions or have No Passions but because
they have Cultivated their Understandings. The Treasures of
Heaven are not Negations of Passion but Realities of Intellect from
which All the Passions Emanate Uncurbed in their Eternal Glory.
The Fool shall not enter into Heaven let him be ever so Holy.
Holiness is not The Price of Enterance into Heaven. Those who are
cast out Are All Those who, having no Passions of their own because No Intellect, Have spent their lives in Curbing & Governing
other People's by the Various arts of Poverty & Cruelty of all kinds.
Wo Wo Wo to you Hypocrites. Even Murder the Courts of Justice,
more merciful than the Church, are compelld to allow is not done
in Passion but in Cool Blooded Design & Intention.

The Modern Church Crucifies Christ with the Head Downwards.

[PAGE 92] Many Persons such as Paine & Voltaire with some of
the Ancient Greeks say we will not converse concerning Good &
Evil we will live in Paradise & Liberty. You may do so in Spirit but
not in the Mortal Body as you pretend, till after the Last Judgment;
for in Paradise they have no Corporeal & Mortal Body; that originated with the Fall & was calld Death & cannot be removed but by
a Last Judgment; while we are in the world of Mortality we Must
Suffer. The Whole Creation Groans to be deliverd; there will always be as many Hypocrites born as Honest Men & they will always
have superior Power in Mortal Things. You cannot have Liberty in
this World without what you call Moral Virtue & you cannot have
Moral Virtue without the Slavery of that half of the Human Race
who hate what you call Moral Virtue.

The Nature of Hatred & Envy & of All the Mischiefs in the World
are here depicted. No one Envies or Hates one of his Own Party;
even the devils love one another in their Way; they torment one
another for other reasons than Hate or Envy; these are only em-
ploya against the Just. Neither can Seth Envy Noah, or Elijah Envy
Abraham, but they may both of them Envy the Success [P 93] of
Satan or of Og or Molech. The Horse never Envies the Peacock nor
the Sheep the Goat but they Envy a Rival in Life & Existence whose
ways & means exceed their own, let him be of what Class of
Animals he will; a Dog will envy a Cat who is pamperd at the
expense of his comfort, as I have often seen. The Bible never tells
us that Devils torment one another thro Envy; it is thro this that
they torment the Just; but for what do they torment one another?
I answer, For the Coercive Laws of Hell, Moral Hypocrisy. They
torment a Hypocrite when he is discovered; they Punish a Failure

in the tormentor who has suffered the Subject of his torture to
Escape. In Hell all is Self Righteousness; there is no such thing
there as Forgiveness of Sin; he who does Forgive Sin is Crucified as
an Abettor of Criminals, & he who performs Works of Mercy in
Any shape whatever is punishd & if possible destroyd, not thro
Envy or Hatred or Malice but thro Self Righteousness that thinks
it does God service, which God is Satan. They do not Envy one
another; they contemn & despise one another.

Forgiveness of Sin is only at the Judgment Seat of Jesus the
Saviour, where the Accuser is cast out, not because he Sins but
because he torments the Just & makes them do what he condemns
as Sin & what he knows is opposite to their own Identity.

It is not because Angels are Holier than Men or Devils that
makes them Angels but because they do not Expect Holiness from
one another but from God only.

The Player is a liar when he Says Angels are happier than [P 94]
Men because they are better. Angels are happier than Men &
Devils because they are not always Prying after Good & Evil in one
Another & eating the Tree of Knowledge for Satan's Gratification.

Thinking as I do that the Creator of this World is a very Cruel
Being, & being a Worshipper of Christ, I cannot help saying: "the
Son O how unlike the Father!" First God Almighty comes with a
Thump on the Head. Then Jesus Christ comes with a balm to heal
it.

The Last Judgment is an Overwhelming of Bad Art & Science.
Mental Things are alone Real; what is Calld Corporeal Nobody
Knows of its dwelling Place; it is in Fallacy & its Existence an Imposture. Where is the Existence Out of Mind or Thought? Where
is it but in the Mind of a Fool? Some People flatter themselves that
there will be No Last Judgment & [P 95] that Bad Art will be
adopted & mixed with Good Art, That Error or Experiment will
make a Part of Truth, & they Boast that it is its Foundation. These
People flatter themselves; I will not Flatter them. Error is Created.
Truth is Eternal. Error or Creation will be Burned Up, & then & not
till then Truth or Eternity will appear. It is Burnt up the Moment
Men cease to behold it. I assert for My self that I do not behold
the Outward Creation & that to me it is hindrance & not Action;
it is as the Dirt upon my feet, No part of Me. "What," it will be
Questiond, "When the Sun rises do you not see a round Disk of fire
somewhat like a Guinea?" O no no, I see an Innumerable company
of the Heavenly host crying "Holy Holy Holy is the Lord God Almighty." I question not my Corporeal or Vegetative Eye any more
than I would Question a Window concerning a Sight. I look thro
it & not with it.

1810   1810

WILLIAM WORDSWORTH
(1770–1850)

1791–92: In France during the early period of the Revolution.
1797:   With his sister Dorothy at Alfoxden, Somersetshire, near Coleridge at Nether Stowey.
1798:   First edition of *Lyrical Ballads*.
1799:   William and Dorothy settle at Grasmere, in the Lake District.
1800:   Second edition of *Lyrical Ballads* in two volumes, with the famous Preface.
1807:   *Poems in Two Volumes;* end of the great decade.

Wordsworth was born in Cockermouth in West Cumberland, just on the northern fringe of the English Lake District; when his mother died, the 8-year-old boy was sent to school at Hawkshead, near Esthwaite Lake, in the heart of that thinly settled region which he and Coleridge were to transform into the poetic center of England. William and his three brothers boarded in the cottage of Ann Tyson, who gave the boys simple comfort, ample affection, and freedom to roam the countryside at will. A vigorous, willful, and sometimes moody boy, William spent his free days and sometimes "half the night" in the sports and rambles described in the first two books of *The Prelude*, "drinking in" (to use one of his favorite metaphors) the natural sights and sounds, and getting to know the cottagers, shepherds, and solitary wanderers who moved through his imagination and dreams into his later poetry. He also found time to read voraciously in the books owned by his young headmaster, William Taylor, who encouraged him in his inclination to poetry.

John Wordsworth, the poet's father, died suddenly when William was 13, leaving to his five children mainly the substantial sum owed him by Lord Lonsdale, whom he had served as attorney and as steward of the huge Lonsdale estate. That harsh and litigious nobleman managed to keep from paying the debt until he died in 1802. Wordsworth was nevertheless able to go up to St. John's College, Cambridge, in 1787, where he found very little in the limited curriculum of that time to appeal to him; he took his A.B. degree in 1791 without distinction.

During the summer vacation of his third year at Cambridge (1790), Wordsworth and his closest college friend, the Welshman Robert Jones, made a walking tour through France and the Alps (described in *The Prelude* VI) at the time when Frenchmen were joyously celebrating the first anniversary of the fall of the Bastille. Upon completing his course at Cambridge, Wordsworth spent four months in London, set off on another walking tour with Robert Jones through Wales (the time of the memorable ascent of Mount Snowdon in *The Prelude* XIV), and then went back alone to France in order to master the language and qualify as a traveling tutor.

In that year (between November, 1791, and December, 1792) Words-worth became a fervent "democrat" and proselyte of the French Revolution —which seemed to him, as to many other generous spirits, to promise a "glorious renovation"—and he had a passionate love affair with Annette Vallon, the impetuous and warm-hearted daughter of a French surgeon at Blois. It seems clear that Wordsworth and Annette planned to marry, despite their difference in religion and political inclinations (Annette be-longed to an old Catholic family whose sympathies were Royalist). But almost immediately after a daughter, Caroline, was born, lack of funds forced Wordsworth back to England. The outbreak of war between Eng-land and France made it impossible for him to rejoin Annette until they had drifted so far apart in sympathies that a permanent union no longer seemed practicable. Wordsworth's agonies of guilt, his divided loyalties be-tween England and France, his gradual disillusion with the course of the Revolution in France—as he describes them in *The Prelude* X and XI —brought him to the verge of an emotional breakdown, when "sick, wearied out with contrarieties," he "yielded up moral questions in despair." His suffering, his near-collapse, and the successful effort, after his sharp break with his own past, to re-establish "a saving intercourse with my true self" are the experiences which underlie many of Wordsworth's greatest poems.

At this critical point a young friend, Raisley Calvert, died and left Wordsworth a sum of money just sufficient to enable him to live solely by his poetry. He settled in a rent-free cottage at Racedown, Dorsetshire, with his beloved sister Dorothy, who now began her long career as con-fidante, inspirer, and secretary. At that same time Wordsworth met Samuel Taylor Coleridge; two years later he moved to Alfoxden to be near Coleridge, who lived four miles away at Nether Stowey. Here, his re-covery complete, he entered at the age of 27 upon the delayed spring-time of his poetic career.

Even while he had been an undergraduate at Cambridge, Coleridge had detected signs of genius in Wordsworth's rather conventional poem about his tour in the Alps, *Descriptive Sketches*, published in 1793. Now he hailed Wordsworth unreservedly as "the best poet of the age." The two men met almost daily, talked for hours about poetry, and composed prolifically. So close was their association that they lost almost all sense of individual proprietorship in a composition. We find the same phrases occurring in poems of Wordsworth and Coleridge, as well as in the de-lightful journals that Dorothy kept at the time; the two poets collaborated in some writings and freely traded thoughts and passages for others; and Coleridge even undertook to complete a few poems that Wordsworth had left unfinished

The result of their joint efforts was a small volume, published anony-mously in 1798, *Lyrical Ballads, With a Few Other Poems*. It opened with Coleridge's *Ancient Mariner*, included three other poems by Coleridge, a number of Wordsworth's verse anecdotes and psychological studies of humble people, some lyrics in which Wordsworth celebrated impulses from a vernal wood, and closed with Wordsworth's great descriptive and meditative poem in blank verse (not a "lyrical ballad," but one of the "other poems" of the title), *Tintern Abbey*. No other book of poems in

English so plainly announces a new literary departure. William Hazlitt wrote that when he heard Coleridge read some of these newly written poems aloud, "the sense of a new style and a new spirit in poetry came over me," with something of the effect "that arises from the turning up of the fresh soil, or of the first welcome breath of spring." The professional reviewers were less enthusiastic. Nevertheless *Lyrical Ballads* sold out in two years, and Wordsworth published over his own name a new edition, dated 1800, to which he added a second volume of poems, many of them written in homesickness during a long, cold, and friendless winter he and Dorothy had spent in Goslar, Germany, 1798–99. In his famous Preface to this edition, planned, like so many of the poems, in close consultation with Coleridge, Wordsworth enunciated the principles of the new criticism which served as rationale for the new poetry. Notable among the other works written in this prolific period is the austere and powerful tragic poem *The Ruined Cottage.*

Late in 1799 Wordsworth and Dorothy moved back permanently to their native lakes, settling at Grasmere in the little house later named thirteen-three. Coleridge, following them, rented Greta Hall at Keswick, ... 1802 Wordsworth finally came into his father's inheritance and, after an amicable settlement with Annette Vallon, married Mary Hutchinson, a Lake Country girl whom he had known since childhood. The course of his existence after that time was broken by various disasters: the drowning in 1805 of his favorite brother John, a sea captain whose ship was wrecked in a storm; the death of two of his five children in 1812; a gradual estrangement from Coleridge, culminating in an open quarrel (1810) from which they were not completely reconciled for almost two decades; and, from the 1830's on, the physical and mental decline of his sister Dorothy. The life of his middle age, however, was one of steadily increasing prosperity and reputation, as well as of political and religious conservatism. In 1813 an appointment as Stamp Distributor (that is, revenue collector) for Westmoreland was concrete evidence of his recognition as a national poet. Gradually Wordsworth's residences, as he moved into more and more commodious quarters, became standard places of resort for tourists; he was awarded honorary degrees and, in 1843, appointed poet laureate. He died in 1850 at the age of 80; only then did his executors publish his masterpiece, *The Prelude*, the autobiographical poem which he had begun in 1798 and completed, in its first version, in 1805, but which he had continued to revise and re-revise up to the last decade of his life.

Most of Wordsworth's greatest poetry had been written by 1807, when he published *Poems in Two Volumes*; and after *The Excursion* (1814) and the first collected edition of his poems (1815), although he continued to write voluminously, there is a conspicuous decline in his powers as a poet. The causes of what is often called "Wordsworth's anti-climax" have been much debated; the principal cause seems to be inherent in the very nature of his most characteristic writing. Wordsworth is above all the poet of the remembrance of things past, or as he himself put it, of "emotion recollected in tranquility." Some object or event in the present triggers a sudden renewal of feelings he had experienced in youth; the result is a poem exhibiting the sharp discrepancy between what Wordsworth called "two consciousnesses": himself as he is now and as he once was. But one's early emotional experience is not an inexhaustible resource for poetry. As Basil Willey has said, Wordsworth as a poet "was living upon capital"; and he knew it. As he says in *The Prelude* XII, while describing the recurrence of "spots of time" from his memories of childhood:

> The days gone by
> Return upon me almost from the dawn
> Of life: the hiding places of man's power
> Open; I would approach them, but they close.
> I see by glimpses now; when age comes on,
> May scarcely see at all. * * *

The past which Wordsworth recollected was one of emotional turmoil which is ordered, in the calmer present, into a hard-won equilibrium. The result was a poetry of excitation in calm; genius, as Wordsworth said, is "born to thrive by interchange / Of peace and excitation" (*Prelude* XIII.1–10). As time went on, however, the precarious equilibrium of his great creative period became a habit, and Wordsworth finally gained which in the *Ode to Duty* (composed in 1804), he l——ever is the same"—but at the expense of the agony and excitation which, under the calm surface ...powers his best and most characteristic poems.

Occasionally, in his middle and later life a jolting experience would revive the intensity of Wordsworth's remembered emotion, and also his earlier poetic strength. The moving sonnet *Surprised by Joy*, for example, was written in his forties at the abrupt realization that time was beginning to diminish his grief at the death some years earlier of his little daughter Catharine. And when Wordsworth was 65 years old, the sudden report of the death of James Hogg called up the memory of other and greater poets whom Wordsworth had loved and outlived; the result was an "Extempore Effusion," written in a return to the simple quatrains of the early *Lyrical Ballads* and with a recovery of the great elegiac voice which had uttered the dirges to Lucy, 35 years before.

From LYRICAL BALLADS
We Are Seven[1]

—A simple Child,
That lightly draws its breath,
And feels its life in every limb,
What should it know of death?

I met a little cottage Girl: 5
She was eight years old, she said;
Her hair was thick with many a curl
That clustered round her head.

---

1. "Written at Alfoxden in the spring of 1798. * * * The little girl who is the heroine I met within the area of Goodrich Castle in the year 1793" (Wordsworth). Wordsworth also tells us that he composed the last line of the last stanza first, and that Coleridge contributed the initial stanza.

She had a rustic, woodland air,
And she was wildly clad:
Her eyes were fair, and very fair;
—Her beauty made me glad.   10

"Sisters and brothers, little Maid,
How many may you be?"
"How many? Seven in all," she said,
And wondering looked at me.   15

"And where are they? I pray you tell."
She answered, "Seven are we;
And two of us at Conway dwell,
And two are gone to sea.   20

"Two of us in the churchyard lie,
My sister and my brother;
And, in the churchyard cottage, I
Dwell near them with my mother."

"You say that two at Conway dwell,   25
And two are gone to sea,
Yet ye are seven! I pray you tell,
Sweet Maid, how this may be."

Then did the little Maid reply,
"Seven boys and girls are we;   30
Two of us in the churchyard lie,
Beneath the churchyard tree."

"You run about, my little Maid,
Your limbs they are alive;
If two are in the churchyard laid,   35
Then ye are only five."

"Their graves are green, they may be seen,"
The little Maid replied,
"Twelve steps or more from my mother's door,
And they are side by side.   40

"My stockings there I often knit,
My kerchief there I hem;
And there upon the ground I sit,
And sing a song to them.

"And often after sunset, sir,   45
When it is light and fair,
I take my little porringer,[2]
And eat my supper there.

"The first that died was sister Jane;
In bed she moaning lay,   50
Till God released her of her pain;
And then she went away.

2. Bowl for porridge.

"So in the churchyard she was laid;
And, when the grass was dry,
Together round her grave we played,
My brother John and I.   55

"And when the ground was white with snow,
And I could run and slide,
My brother John was forced to go,
And he lies by her side."   60

"How many are you, then," said I,
"If they two are in heaven?"
Quick was the little Maid's reply,
"O master! we are seven."

"But they are dead; those two are dead!   65
Their spirits are in heaven!"
'Twas throwing words away; for still
The little Maid would have her will,
And said, "Nay, we are seven!"

1798   1798

Lines Written in Early Spring

I heard a thousand blended notes,
While in a grove I sate reclined,
In that sweet mood when pleasant thoughts
Bring sad thoughts to the mind.

To her fair works did Nature link   5
The human soul that through me ran;
And much it grieved my heart to think
What man has made of man.

Through primrose tufts, in that green bower,
The periwinkle[3] trailed its wreaths;   10
And 'tis my faith that every flower
Enjoys the air it breathes.

The birds around me hopped and played,
Their thoughts I cannot measure—
But the least motion which they made,   15
It seemed a thrill of pleasure.

The budding twigs spread out their fan,
To catch the breezy air;
And I must think, do all I can,
That there was pleasure there.   20

If this belief from heaven be sent,
If such be Nature's holy plan,[4]

3. A trailing evergreen plant with small blue flowers (U.S. myrtle).
4. The version of these lines printed in the *Lyrical Ballads* of 1798 mentioned neither heaven nor holiness: "If I these thoughts may not prevent, / If such be of my creed the plan."

Have I not reason to lament
What man has made of man?

1798   1798

Expostulation and Reply[1]

"Why, William, on that old gray stone,
Thus for the length of half a day,
Why, William, sit you thus alone,
And dream your time away?

"Where are your books?—that light bequeathed   5
To beings else forlorn and blind!
Up! up! and drink the spirit breathed
From dead men to their kind.

"You look round on your Mother Earth,
As if she for no purpose bore you;   10
As if you were her first-born birth,
And none had lived before you!"

One morning thus, by Esthwaite lake,
When life was sweet, I knew not why,
To me my good friend Matthew[2] spake,   15
And thus I made reply:

"The eye—it cannot choose but see;
We cannot bid the ear be still;
Our bodies feel, where'er they be,
Against or with our will.   20

"Nor less I deem that there are Powers
Which of themselves our minds impress;
That we can feed this mind of ours
In a wise passiveness.

"Think you, 'mid all this mighty sum   25
Of things forever speaking,
That nothing of itself will come,
But we must still be seeking?

"—Then ask not wherefore, here, alone,
Conversing[3] as I may,   30
I sit upon this old gray stone,
And dream my time away."

1798   1798

1. This and the following companion-poem have often been attacked—and defended—as Wordsworth's solemn deliverance on the comparative merits of nature and of books. But they are a dialogue between two friends who are intimate enough to rally one another by the usual device of overstating parts of a whole truth. Wordsworth said that the pieces originated in a conversation "with a friend who was somewhat unreasonably attached to modern books of moral philosophy," and also that the lore of "a wise passiveness" made the poem a favorite among Quakers.
2. A fictitious schoolmaster who plays a role in others of Wordsworth's early poems.
3. In the old sense of "communing" (with the "things forever speaking").

The Tables Turned

AN EVENING SCENE ON THE SAME SUBJECT

Up! up! my friend, and quit your books,
Or surely you'll grow double;
Up! up! my friend, and clear your looks;
Why all this toil and trouble?

The sun, above the mountain's head,   5
A freshening luster mellow
Through all the long green fields has spread,
His first sweet evening yellow.

Books! 'tis a dull and endless strife;
Come, hear the woodland linnet,[1]   10
How sweet his music! on my life,
There's more of wisdom in it.

And hark! how blithe the throstle[2] sings!
He, too, is no mean preacher;
Come forth into the light of things,   15
Let Nature be your teacher.

She has a world of ready wealth,
Our minds and hearts to bless—
Spontaneous wisdom breathed by health,
Truth breathed by cheerfulness.   20

One impulse from a vernal wood
May teach you more of man,
Of moral evil and of good,
Than all the sages can.

Sweet is the lore which Nature brings;   25
Our meddling intellect
Misshapes the beauteous forms of things—
We murder to dissect.

Enough of Science and of Art;
Close up those barren leaves;   30
Come forth, and bring with you a heart
That watches and receives.

1798   1798

To My Sister[1]

It is the first mild day of March:
Each minute sweeter than before,

---

1. A small finch, common in Europe.
2. The song thrush.
1. "Composed in front of Alfoxden House. * * * The larch mentioned in the first stanza was standing when I revisited the place in May, 1841, more than forty years after" (Wordsworth). The "Sister" is, of course, Dorothy, and "Edward" (named in line 13) is the boy Basil Montagu, then living with the Wordsworths.

The redbreast sings from the tall larch
That stands beside our door.

There is a blessing in the air,   5
Which seems a sense of joy to yield
To the bare trees, and mountains bare,
And grass in the green field.

My Sister! ('tis a wish of mine)
Now that our morning meal is done,   10
Make haste, your morning task resign;
Come forth and feel the sun.

Edward will come with you—and, pray,
Put on with speed your woodland dress,
And bring no book; for this one day   15
We'll give to idleness.

No joyless forms shall regulate
Our living calendar;
We from today, my Friend, will date
The opening of the year.   20

Love, now a universal birth,
From heart to heart is stealing;
From earth to man, from man to earth:
—It is the hour of feeling.

One moment now may give us more   25
Than years of toiling reason;
Our minds shall drink at every pore
The spirit of the season.

Some silent laws our hearts will make,
Which they shall long obey;   30
We for the year to come may take
Our temper from today.

And from the blessed power that rolls
About, below, above,
We'll frame the measure of our souls: 35
They shall be tuned to love.

Then come, my Sister! come, I pray,
With speed put on your woodland dress;
And bring no book: for this one day
We'll give to idleness.   40

1798   1798

Lines[1]

Composed a Few Miles Above Tintern Abbey
On Revisiting the Banks of the Wye
During a Tour. July 13, 1798

Five years have passed; five summers, with the length
Of five long winters! and again I hear
These waters, rolling from their mountain-springs
With a soft inland murmur. Once again
Do I behold these steep and lofty cliffs,   5
That on a wild secluded scene impress
Thoughts of more deep seclusion; and connect
The landscape with the quiet of the sky.
The day is come when I again repose
Here, under this dark sycamore, and view   10
These plots of cottage ground, these orchard tufts,
Which at this season, with their unripe fruits,
Are clad in one green hue, and lose themselves
'Mid groves and copses. Once again I see
These hedgerows, hardly hedgerows, little lines   15
Of sportive wood run wild; these pastoral farms,
Green to the very door; and wreaths of smoke
Sent up, in silence, from among the trees!
With some uncertain notice, as might seem
Of vagrant dwellers in the houseless woods,   20
Or of some Hermit's cave, where by his fire
The Hermit sits alone.

              These beauteous forms,
Through a long absence, have not been to me
As is a landscape to a blind man's eye;
But oft, in lonely rooms, and 'mid the din   25
Of towns and cities, I have owed to them,
In hours of weariness, sensations sweet,
Felt in the blood, and felt along the heart;
And passing even into my purer mind,
With tranquil restoration—feelings too   30
Of unremembered pleasure; such, perhaps,
As have no slight or trivial influence
On that best portion of a good man's life,

1. "No poem of mine was composed under circumstances more pleasant for me to remember than this. I began it upon leaving Tintern, after crossing the Wye, and concluded it just as I was entering Bristol in the evening, after a ramble of 4 or 5 days, with my sister. Not a line of it was altered, and not any part of it written down till I reached Bristol" (Wordsworth). The poem was printed as the last item in *Lyrical Ballads*.

Wordsworth had first visited the Wye valley and the ruins of Tintern Abbey, in Monmouthshire, while on a solitary walking tour in August of 1793, when he was 23 years old. The puzzling difference between the present landscape and the remembered "picture of the mind" (line 61) gives rise to an intricately organized meditation, in which the poet reviews his past, evaluates the present, and (through his sister as intermediary) anticipates the future, until he ends by rounding back quietly upon the scene which had been his point of departure.

His little, nameless, unremembered, acts
Of kindness and of love. Nor less, I trust, 35
To them I may have owed another gift,
Of aspect more sublime; that blessed mood,
In which the burthen of the mystery,
In which the heavy and the weary weight
Of all this unintelligible world, 40
Is lightened—that serene and blessed mood,
In which the affections gently lead us on—
Until, the breath of this corporeal frame
And even the motion of our human blood
Almost suspended, we are laid asleep 45
In body, and become a living soul;
While with an eye made quiet by the power
Of harmony, and the deep power of joy,
We see into the life of things.

                If this
Be but a vain belief, yet, oh! how oft— 50
In darkness and amid the many shapes
Of joyless daylight; when the fretful stir
Unprofitable, and the fever of the world,
Have hung upon the beatings of my heart—
How oft, in spirit, have I turned to thee, 55
O sylvan Wye! thou wanderer through the woods,
How often has my spirit turned to thee!

   And now, with gleams of half-extinguished thought
With many recognitions dim and faint,
And somewhat of a sad perplexity, 60
The picture of the mind revives again;
While here I stand, not only with the sense
Of present pleasure, but with pleasing thoughts
That in this moment there is life and food
For future years. And so I dare to hope, 65
Though changed, no doubt, from what I was when first
I came among these hills; when like a roe
I bounded o'er the mountains, by the sides
Of the deep rivers, and the lonely streams,
Wherever nature led—more like a man 70
Flying from something that he dreads than one
Who sought the thing he loved. For nature then
(The coarser pleasures of my boyish days,
And their glad animal movements all gone by)
To me was all in all.—I cannot paint 75
What then I was. The sounding cataract
Haunted me like a passion; the tall rock,
The mountain, and the deep and gloomy wood,
Their colors and their forms, were then to me
An appetite; a feeling and a love, 80

That had no need of a remoter charm,
By thought supplied, nor any interest
Unborrowed from the eye.—That time is past,
And all its aching joys are now no more,
And all its dizzy raptures.[2] Not for this   85
Faint[3] I, nor mourn nor murmur; other gifts
Have followed; for such loss, I would believe,
Abundant recompense. For I have learned
To look on nature, not as in the hour
Of thoughtless youth; but hearing oftentimes   90
The still, sad music of humanity,
Nor harsh nor grating, though of ample power
To chasten and subdue. And I have felt
A presence that disturbs me with the joy
Of elevated thoughts; a sense sublime   95
Of something far more deeply interfused,
Whose dwelling is the light of setting suns,
And the round ocean and the living air,
And the blue sky, and in the mind of man:
A motion and a spirit, that impels   100
All thinking things, all objects of all thought,
And rolls through all things. Therefore am I still
A lover of the meadows and the woods,
And mountains; and of all that we behold
From this green earth; of all the mighty world   105
Of eye, and ear—both what they half create,[4]
And what perceive; well pleased to recognize
In nature and the language of the sense
The anchor of my purest thoughts, the nurse,
The guide, the guardian of my heart, and soul   110
Of all my moral being.

           Nor perchance,
If I were not thus taught, should I the more
Suffer my genial spirits[5] to decay:
For thou art with me here upon the banks
Of this fair river; thou my dearest Friend,[6]   115

---

2. Lines 76 ff. contain Wordsworth's famous description of the three stages of his growing up, defined in terms of his evolving relations to the natural scene: the young boy's purely physical responsiveness (lines 73–74); the post-adolescent's aching, dizzy, and equivocal passions—a love which is more like dread (lines 67–72, 75–85: this was his state of mind on the occasion of his first visit); his present state (lines 85 ff.), in which for the first time he adds thought to sense. All his knowledge of human suffering, so painfully acquired in the interim, chastens him while it enriches the visible scene like a chord of music, and he has gained also awareness of an immanent "pres-ence" which links his mind and all the elements of the external world.
3. Lose heart.
4. The fact that apparent changes in the sensible world have turned out to be projected by the changing mind of the observer gives evidence that the faculties "half create" the world; the part that is "perceived" (line 107) is what has remained unchanged between the two visits. This view that the "creative sensibility" contributes to its own perceptions is often reiterated in the early books of *The Prelude*.
5. "Genial" is here the adjectival form of the noun "genius" ("native powers").
6. His sister Dorothy.

My dear, dear Friend; and in thy voice I catch
The language of my former heart, and read
My former pleasures in the shooting lights
Of thy wild eyes. Oh! yet a little while
May I behold in thee what I was once,   120
My dear, dear Sister! and this prayer I make,
Knowing that Nature never did betray
The heart that loved her; 'tis her privilege,
Through all the years of this our life, to lead
From joy to joy: for she can so inform   125
The mind that is within us, so impress
With quietness and beauty, and so feed
With lofty thoughts, that neither evil tongues,
Rash judgments, nor the sneers of selfish men,
Nor greetings where no kindness is, nor all   130
The dreary intercourse of daily life,
Shall e'er prevail against us, or disturb
Our cheerful faith, that all which we behold
Is full of blessings. Therefore let the moon
Shine on thee in thy solitary walk;   135
And let the misty mountain winds be free
To blow against thee: and, in after years,
When these wild ecstasies shall be matured
Into a sober pleasure; when thy mind
Shall be a mansion for all lovely forms,   140
Thy memory be as a dwelling place
For all sweet sounds and harmonies; oh! then,
If solitude, or fear, or pain, or grief
Should be thy portion, with what healing thoughts
Of tender joy wilt thou remember me,   145
And these my exhortations! Nor, perchance—
If I should be where I no more can hear
Thy voice, nor catch from thy wild eyes these gleams
Of past existence[7]—wilt thou then forget
That on the banks of this delightful stream   150
We stood together; and that I, so long
A worshiper of Nature, hither came
Unwearied in that service; rather say
With warmer love—oh! with far deeper zeal
Of holier love. Nor wilt thou then forget,   155
That after many wanderings, many years
Of absence, these steep woods and lofty cliffs,
And this green pastoral landscape, were to me
More dear, both for themselves and for thy sake!

1798

7. I.e., his own "past experience" five years before; see lines 116–19.

From Preface to the Second Edition

OF SEVERAL OF THE FOREGOING POEMS, PUBLISHED, WITH AN ADDITIONAL VOLUME, UNDER THE TITLE OF "LYRICAL BALLADS"[1]

The first volume of these poems has already been submitted to general perusal. It was published as an experiment, which I hoped might be of some use to ascertain how far, by fitting to metrical arrangement a selection of the real language of men in a state of vivid sensation, that sort of pleasure and that quantity of pleasure may be imparted, which a poet may rationally endeavor to impart.

I had formed no very inaccurate estimate of the probable effect of those poems: I flattered myself that they who should be pleased with them would read them with more than common pleasure; and, on the other hand, I was well aware that by those who should dislike them they would be read with more than common dislike. The result has differed from my expectation in this only, that a greater number have been pleased than I ventured to hope I should please.

Several of my friends are anxious for the success of these poems, from a belief that, if the views with which they were composed were indeed realized, a class of poetry would be produced, well adapted to interest mankind permanently, and not unimportant in the

1. The "Advertisement" prefixed to the first edition of *Lyrical Ballads* in 1798 said that the majority of the poems were "to be considered as experiments" to determine "how far the language of conversation in the middle and lower classes of society is adapted to the purposes of poetic pleasure." In the second edition of 1800 Wordsworth, relying in part on discussions with Coleridge, expanded this Advertisement into a justification of the new poetry on the basis of what he considered to be the principles of all good poetry. This Preface was enlarged in 1802, and altered later; the extract printed here includes these revisions.

Though the Preface has been one of the most discussed and influential of all critical essays, commentators still do not agree about precisely what were Wordsworth's major claims, or about the structure of his argument. It is clear, however, that Wordsworth tried to overthrow the basic theory, as well as the practice, of neoclassic poetry. When Wordsworth said that his principal object was "to choose incidents and situations from common life," he attacked the strict neoclassic view that the highest and most serious poetic kinds, such as epic and tragedy, were limited to the actions of kings, nobles, and heroes, and that only the lower poetic kinds, such as comedy and satire, might concern themselves with the lower social classes. Wordsworth thus translated his democratic sympathies into critical terms, overturning the precepts of traditional poetic "decorum" in order to justify the serious poetic treatment of peasants, children, criminals, and idiot boys. In addition Wordsworth undertook to write in "a selection of language really used by men," on the grounds that there can be no *"essential* difference between the language of prose and metrical composition." Here he opposed the basic neoclassic principle that in order to give its proper pleasure, the language of a poem must be artfully elevated over standard prose, by a special diction and figures of speech, in order to match itself to the height and dignity of its particular poetic kind. Wordsworth's own view of poetic diction is based on the new critical premise, at the heart of his theory, that "all good poetry is the spontaneous overflow of powerful feeling." The equivalence, therefore, between the language proper to a poet and the prose language "really spoken by men" is not one of vocabulary or grammar, but an equivalence in psychological origin—both, according to Wordsworth, ought to originate instinctively, as the words and figures of speech naturally prompted by the feelings of the speaker.

quality and in the multiplicity of its moral relations; and on this account they have advised me to prefix a systematic defense of the theory upon which the poems were written. But I was unwilling to undertake the task, knowing that on this occasion the reader would look coldly upon my arguments, since I might be suspected of having been principally influenced by the selfish and foolish hope of *reasoning* him into an approbation of these particular poems; and I was still more unwilling to undertake the task, because adequately to display the opinions, and fully to enforce the arguments, would require a space wholly disproportionate to a preface. For to treat the subject with the clearness and coherence of which it is susceptible, it would be necessary to give a full account of the present state of the public taste in this country, and to determine how far this taste is healthy or depraved; which, again, could not be determined, without pointing out in what manner language and the human mind act and react on each other, and without retracing the revolutions, not of literature alone, but likewise of society itself. I have therefore altogether declined to enter regularly upon this defense; yet I am sensible that that there would be something like impropriety in abruptly obtruding upon the public, without a few words of introduction, poems so materially different from those upon which general approbation is at present bestowed.

It is supposed that by the act of writing in verse an author makes a formal engagement that he will gratify certain known habits of association; that he not only thus apprises the reader that certain classes of ideas and expressions will be found in his book, but that others will be carefully excluded. This exponent or symbol held forth by metrical language must in different eras of literature have excited very different expectations: for example, in the age of Catullus, Terence, and Lucretius, and that of Statius or Claudian;[2] and in our own country, in the age of Shakespeare and Beaumont and Fletcher, and that of Donne and Cowley, or Dryden, or Pope. I will not take upon me to determine the exact import of the promise which, by the act of writing in verse, an author in the present day makes to his reader; but it will undoubtedly appear to many persons that I have not fulfilled the terms of an engagement thus voluntarily contracted. They who have been accustomed to the gaudiness and inane phraseology of many modern writers, if they persist in reading this book to its conclusion, will, no doubt, frequently have to struggle with feelings of strangeness and awkwardness; they will look round for poetry, and will be induced to inquire by what species of courtesy these attempts can be permitted to assume that title. I hope, therefore, the reader will not censure

2. Wordsworth has in mind the difference between the naturalness and simplicity of the first three Roman poets (who wrote in the last two centuries B.C.) and the elaborate artifice of the last two Roman poets (Statius wrote in the 1st and Claudian in the 4th century A.D.).

me for attempting to state what I have proposed to myself to perform; and also (as far as the limits of a preface will permit) to explain some of the chief reasons which have determined me in the choice of my purpose: that at least he may be spared any unpleasant feeling of disappointment, and that I myself may be protected from one of the most dishonorable accusations which can be brought against an author; namely, that of an indolence which prevents him from endeavoring to ascertain what is his duty, or, when his duty is ascertained, prevents him from performing it.

The principal object, then, proposed in these poems was to choose incidents and situations from common life, and to relate or describe them, throughout, as far as was possible, in a selection of language really used by men, and, at the same time, to throw over them a certain coloring of imagination, whereby ordinary things should be presented to the mind in an unusual aspect;[3] and further, and above all, to make these incidents and situations interesting by tracing in them, truly though not ostentatiously, the primary laws of our nature: chiefly, as far as regards the manner in which we associate ideas in a state of excitement. Humble and rustic life was generally chosen, because in that condition the essential passions of the heart find a better soil in which they can attain their maturity, are less under restraint, and speak a plainer and more emphatic language; because in that condition of life our elementary feelings co-exist in a state of greater simplicity, and consequently may be more accurately contemplated and more forcibly communicated; because the manners of rural life germinate from those elementary feelings, and, from the necessary character of rural occupations, are more easily comprehended, and are more durable; and, lastly, because in that condition the passions of men are incorporated with the beautiful and permanent forms of nature. The language, too, of these men has been adopted (purified indeed from what appear to be its real defects, from all lasting and rational causes of dislike or disgust) because such men hourly communicate with the best objects from which the best part of language is originally derived; and because, from their rank in society and the sameness and narrow circle of their intercourse, being less under the influence of social vanity, they convey their feelings and notions in simple and unelaborated expressions. Accordingly, such a language, arising out of repeated experience and regular feelings, is a more permanent and a far more philosophical language than that which is frequently substituted for it by poets, who think that they are conferring honor upon themselves and their art, in proportion as they separate themselves from the sympathies of men, and indulge in arbitrary and capricious habits of expression, in

---

3. Cf. Coleridge's account of their plan in *Biographia Literaria*, Chapter XIV.

order to furnish food for fickle tastes, and fickle appetites, of their own creation.[4]

I cannot, however, be insensible to the present outcry against the triviality and meanness, both of thought and language, which some of my contemporaries have occasionally introduced into their metrical compositions; and I acknowledge that this defect, where it exists, is more dishonorable to the writer's own character than false refinement or arbitrary innovation, though I should contend at the same time that it is far less pernicious in the sum of its consequences. From such verses the poems in these volumes will be found distinguished at least by one mark of difference, that each of them has a worthy *purpose*. Not that I always began to write with a distinct purpose formally conceived; but habits of meditation have, I trust, so prompted and regulated my feelings that my descriptions of such objects as strongly excite those feelings will be found to carry along with them a *purpose*. If this opinion be erroneous, I can have little right to the name of a poet. For all good poetry is the spontaneous overflow of powerful feelings; and though this be true, poems to which any value can be attached were never produced on any variety of subjects but by a man who, being possessed of more than usual organic sensibility, had also thought long and deeply. For our continued influxes of feeling are modified and directed by our thoughts, which are indeed the representatives of all our past feelings; and, as by contemplating the relation of these general representatives to each other, we discover what is really important to men, so, by the repetition and continuance of this act, our feelings will be connected with important subjects, till at length, if we be originally possessed of much sensibility, such habits of mind will be produced that, by obeying blindly and mechanically the impulses of those habits, we shall describe objects, and utter sentiments, of such a nature, and in such connection with each other, that the understanding of the reader must necessarily be in some degree enlightened, and his affections strengthened and purified.

It has been said that each of these poems has a purpose. Another circumstance must be mentioned which distinguishes these poems from the popular poetry of the day; it is this, that the feeling therein developed gives importance to the action and situation, and not the action and situation to the feeling.

A sense of false modesty shall not prevent me from asserting that the reader's attention is pointed to this mark of distinction, far less for the sake of these particular poems than from the general importance of the subject. The subject is indeed important! For

---

4. "It is worth while here to observe that the affecting parts of Chaucer are almost always expressed in language pure and universally intelligible even to this day" [Wordsworth's note].

the human mind is capable of being excited without the application of gross and violent stimulants; and he must have a very faint perception of its beauty and dignity who does not know this, and who does not further know that one being is elevated above another in proportion as he possesses this capability. It has therefore appeared to me that to endeavor to produce or enlarge this capability is one of the best services in which, at any period, a writer can be engaged; but this service, excellent at all times, is especially so at the present day. For a multitude of causes, unknown to former times, are now acting with a combined force to blunt the discriminating powers of the mind, and, unfitting it for all voluntary exertion, to reduce it to a state of almost savage torpor. The most effective of these causes are the great national events which are daily taking place, and the increasing accumulation of men in cities, where the uniformity of their occupations produces a craving for extraordinary incident, which the rapid communication of intelligence hourly gratifies.[5] To this tendency of life and manners the literature and theatrical exhibitions of the country have conformed themselves. The invaluable works of our elder writers, I had almost said the works of Shakespeare and Milton, are driven into neglect by frantic novels, sickly and stupid German tragedies,[6] and deluges of idle and extravagant stories in verse. When I think upon this degrading thirst after outrageous stimulation, I am almost ashamed to have spoken of the feeble endeavor made in these volumes to counteract it; and, reflecting upon the magnitude of the general evil, I should be oppressed with no dishonorable melancholy, had I not a deep impression of certain inherent and indestructible qualities of the human mind, and likewise of certain powers in the great and permanent objects that act upon it, which are equally inherent and indestructible; and were there not added to this impression a belief that the time is approaching when the evil will be systematically opposed by men of greater powers, and with far more distinguished success.

Having dwelt thus long on the subjects and aim of these poems, I shall request the reader's permission to apprise him of a few circumstances relating to their *style*, in order, among other reasons, that he may not censure me for not having performed what I never attempted. The reader will find the personifications of abstract ideas rarely occur in these volumes, and are utterly rejected, as an ordinary device to elevate the style, and raise it above prose. My purpose was to imitate, and, as far as possible, to adopt the very language of men; and assuredly such personifications do not make any

5. This was the period of the French Revolution, of the Industrial Revolution, and of the Napoleonic Wars.
6. Wordsworth probably had in mind the "Gothic" terror novels by writers such as Ann Radcliffe and M. G. Lewis, and the sentimental melodramas, then exceedingly popular in England, of August von Kotzebue and his German contemporaries.

natural or regular part of that language. They are, indeed, a figure of speech occasionally prompted by passion, and I have made use of them as such; but have endeavored utterly to reject them as a mechanical device of style, or as a family language which writers in meter seem to lay claim to by prescription. I have wished to keep the reader in the company of flesh and blood, persuaded that by so doing I shall interest him. Others who pursue a different track will interest him likewise; I do not interfere with their claim, but wish to prefer a claim of my own. There will also be found in these volumes little of what is usually called poetic diction; as much pains has been taken to avoid it as is ordinarily taken to produce it; this has been done for the reason already alleged, to bring my language near to the language of men; and further, because the pleasure which I have proposed to myself to impart is of a kind very different from that which is supposed by many persons to be the proper object of poetry. Without being culpably particular, I do not know how to give my reader a more exact notion of the style in which it was my wish and intention to write than by informing him that I have at all times endeavored to look steadily at my subject; consequently there is, I hope, in these poems little falsehood of description, and my ideas are expressed in language fitted to their respective importance. Something must have been gained by this practice, as it is friendly to one property of all good poetry, namely, good sense; but it has necessarily cut me off from a large portion of phrases and figures of speech which from father to son have long been regarded as the common inheritance of poets. I have also thought it expedient to restrict myself still further, having abstained from the use of many expressions, in themselves proper and beautiful, but which have been foolishly repeated by bad poets, till such feelings of disgust are connected with them as it is scarcely possible by any art of association to overpower.

If in a poem there should be found a series of lines, or even a single line, in which the language, though naturally arranged, and according to the strict laws of meter, does not differ from that of prose, there is a numerous class of critics, who, when they stumble upon these prosaisms, as they call them, imagine that they have made a notable discovery, and exult over the poet as over a man ignorant of his own profession. Now these men would establish a canon of criticism which the reader will conclude he must utterly reject, if he wishes to be pleased with these volumes. And it would be a most easy task to prove to him that not only the language of a large portion of every good poem, even of the most elevated character, must necessarily, except with reference to the meter, in no respect differ from that of good prose, but likewise that some of the most interesting parts of the best poems will be found to be strictly the language of prose when prose is well written. The truth of this assertion might be demonstrated by innumerable passages from almost all the poetical writings, even of Milton himself. To illustrate the subject in a general manner, I will here adduce a short composition of Gray, who was at the head of those who, by their reasonings, have attempted to widen the space of separation betwixt prose and metrical composition, and was more than any other man curiously elaborate in the structure of his own poetic diction.[7]

> In vain to me the smiling mornings shine,
> And reddening Phoebus lifts his golden fire:
> The birds in vain their amorous descant join,
> Or cheerful fields resume their green attire.
> These ears, alas! for other notes repine;
> *A different object do these eyes require;*
> *My lonely anguish melts no heart but mine;*
> *And in my breast the imperfect joys expire;*
> Yet morning smiles the busy race to cheer,
> And newborn pleasure brings to happier men;
> The fields to all their wonted tribute bear;
> To warm their little loves the birds complain.
> *I fruitless mourn to him that cannot hear,*
> *And weep the more because I weep in vain.*

It will easily be perceived that the only part of this sonnet which is of any value is the lines printed in italics; it is equally obvious that, except in the rhyme, and in the use of the single word "fruitless" for fruitlessly, which is so far a defect, the language of these lines does in no respect differ from that of prose.

By the foregoing quotation it has been shown that the language of prose may yet be well adapted to poetry; and it was previously asserted that a large portion of the language of every good poem can in no respect differ from that of good prose. We will go further. It may be safely affirmed that there neither is, nor can be, any *essential* difference between the language of prose and metrical composition. We are fond of tracing the resemblance between poetry and painting, and, accordingly, we call them sisters; but where shall we find bonds of connection sufficiently strict to typify the affinity betwixt metrical and prose composition? They both speak by and to the same organs; the bodies in which both of them are clothed may be said to be of the same substance, their affections are kindred, and almost identical, not necessarily differing even in degree; poetry[8] sheds no tears "such as angels weep," but natural

---

7. Thomas Gray had written that "the language of the age is never the language of poetry." The poem Wordsworth reproduces here is Gray's *Sonnet on the Death of Richard West*.
8. "I here use the word 'poetry' (though against my own judgment) as opposed to the word 'prose,' and synonymous with metrical composition. But much confusion has been introduced into criticism by this contradistinction of poetry and prose, instead of

and human tears; she can boast of no celestial ichor[9] that distinguishes her vital juices from those of prose; the same human blood circulates through the veins of them both. * * *

Taking up the subject, then, upon general grounds, let me ask what is meant by the word Poet? What is a poet? To whom does he address himself? And what language is to be expected from him? —He is a man speaking to men: a man, it is true, endowed with more lively sensibility, more enthusiasm and tenderness, who has a greater knowledge of human nature, and a more comprehensive soul, than are supposed to be common among mankind; a man pleased with his own passions and volitions, and who rejoices more than other men in the spirit of life that is in him; delighting to contemplate similar volitions and passions as manifested in the goings on of the universe, and habitually impelled to create them where he does not find them. To these qualities he has added a disposition to be affected more than other men by absent things as if they were present; an ability of conjuring up in himself passions which are indeed far from being the same as those produced by real events, yet (especially in those parts of the general sympathy which are pleasing and delightful) do more nearly resemble the passions produced by real events than anything which, from the motions of their own minds merely, other men are accustomed to feel in themselves—whence, and from practice, he has acquired a greater readiness and power in expressing what he thinks and feels, and especially those thoughts and feelings which, by his own choice, or from the structure of his own mind, arise in him without immediate external excitement.

But whatever portion of this faculty we may suppose even the greatest poet to possess, there cannot be a doubt that the language which it will suggest to him must often, in liveliness and truth, fall short of that which is uttered by men in real life under the actual pressure of those passions, certain shadows of which the poet thus produces, or feels to be produced, in himself.

However exalted a notion we would wish to cherish of the character of a poet, it is obvious that while he describes and imitates passions, his employment is in some degree mechanical, compared with the freedom and power of real and substantial action and suffering. So that it will be the wish of the poet to bring his feelings near to those of the persons whose feelings he describes; nay, for short spaces of time, perhaps, to let himself slip into an entire delusion, and even confound and identify his own feelings with theirs;

the more philosophical one of poetry and matter of fact, or science. The only strict antithesis to prose is meter; nor is this, in truth, a *strict* antithesis, because lines and passages of meter so naturally occur in writing prose that it would be scarcely possible to avoid them, even if it were desirable" [Wordsworth's note]. The quotation in the text is from *Paradise Lost* I.620.

9. In Greek mythology, the fluid in the veins of the gods.

modifying only the language which is thus suggested to him by a consideration that he describes for a particular purpose, that of giving pleasure. Here, then, he will apply the principle of selection which has been already insisted upon. He will depend upon this for removing what would otherwise be painful or disgusting in the passion; he will feel that there is no necessity to trick out or to elevate nature; and the more industriously he applies this principle the deeper will be his faith that no words which *his* fancy or imagination can suggest will be to be compared with those which are the emanations of reality and truth. * * *

The knowledge both of the poet and the man of science is pleasure; but the knowledge of the one cleaves to us as a necessary part of our existence, our natural and unalienable inheritance; the other is a personal and individual acquisition, slow to come to us, and by no habitual and direct sympathy connecting us with our fellow beings. The man of science seeks truth as a remote and unknown benefactor; he cherishes and loves it in his solitude; the poet, singing a song in which all human beings join with him, rejoices in the presence of truth as our visible friend and hourly companion. Poetry is the breath and finer spirit of all knowledge; it is the impassioned expression which is in the countenance of all science. Emphatically may it be said of the poet, as Shakespeare hath said of man, that "he looks before and after."[1] He is the rock of defense for human nature; an upholder and preserver, carrying everywhere with him relationship and love. In spite of difference of soil and climate, of language and manners, of laws and customs, in spite of things silently gone out of mind, and things violently destroyed, the poet binds together by passion and knowledge the vast empire of human society, as it is spread over the whole earth and over all time. The objects of the poet's thoughts are everywhere; though the eyes and senses of man are, it is true, his favorite guides, yet he will follow wheresoever he can find an atmosphere of sensation in which to move his wings. Poetry is the first and last of all knowledge—it is as immortal as the heart of man. If the labors of men of science should ever create any material revolution, direct or indirect, in our condition, and in the impressions which we habitually receive, the poet will sleep then no more than at present; he will be ready to follow the steps of the man of science, not only in those general indirect effects, but he will be at his side, carrying sensation into the midst of the objects of the science itself.[2] The remotest discoveries of the chemist, the botanist, or mineralogist will be as proper objects of the poet's art as any upon which it can be employed, if the time should ever come when these things shall be

---

1. *Hamlet* IV.iv.37.
2. Wordsworth heralds here, among other things, the modern poetry of the machine; he himself wrote an early example in the sonnet *Steamboats, Viaducts, and Railways.*

familiar to us, and the relations under which they are contemplated by the followers of these respective sciences shall be manifestly and palpably material to us as enjoying and suffering beings. If the time should ever come when what is now called science, thus familiarized to men, shall be ready to put on, as it were, a form of flesh and blood, the poet will lend his divine spirit to aid the transfiguration, and will welcome the being thus produced, as a dear and genuine inmate of the household of man.—It is not, then, to be supposed that anyone who holds that sublime notion of poetry which I have attempted to convey will break in upon the sanctity and truth of his pictures by transitory and accidental ornaments, and endeavor to excite admiration of himself by arts the necessity of which must manifestly depend upon the assumed meanness of his subject.

What has been thus far said applies to poetry in general, but especially to those parts of composition where the poet speaks through the mouths of his characters; and upon this point it appears to authorize the conclusion that there are few persons of good sense who would not allow that the dramatic parts of composition are defective, in proportion as they deviate from the real language of nature, and are colored by a diction of the poet's own, either peculiar to him as an individual poet or belonging simply to poets in general; to a body of men who, from the circumstance of their compositions being in meter, it is expected will employ a particular language.

It is not, then, in the dramatic parts of composition that we look for this distinction of language; but still it may be proper and necessary where the poet speaks to us in his own person and character. To this I answer by referring the reader to the description before given of a poet. Among the qualities there enumerated as principally conducing to form a poet, is implied nothing differing in kind from other men, but only in degree. The sum of what was said is that the poet is chiefly distinguished from other men by a greater promptness to think and feel without immediate external excitement, and a greater power in expressing such thoughts and feelings as are produced in him in that manner. But these passions and thoughts and feelings are the general passions and thoughts and feelings of men. And with what are they connected? Undoubtedly with our moral sentiments and animal[3] sensations, and with the causes which excite these; with the operations of the elements, and the appearances of the visible universe; with storm and sunshine, with the revolutions of the seasons, with cold and heat, with loss of friends and kindred, with injuries and resentments, gratitude and hope, with fear and sorrow. These, and the like, are the sensations and objects which the poet describes, as they are the sensations of

3. In the old sense: that which pertains to man's senses, as distinguished from his intellectual and moral aspects.

other men, and the objects which interest them. The poet thinks and feels in the spirit of human passions. How, then, can his language differ in any material degree from that of all other men who feel vividly and see clearly? It might be *proved* that it is impossible. But supposing that this were not the case, the poet might then be allowed to use a peculiar language when expressing his feelings for his own gratification, or that of men like himself. But poets do not write for poets alone, but for men. Unless, therefore, we are advocates for that admiration which subsists upon ignorance, and that pleasure which arises from hearing what we do not understand, the poet must descend from this supposed height; and, in order to excite rational sympathy, he must express himself as other men express themselves. To this it may be added that while he is only selecting from the real language of men, or, which amounts to the same thing, composing accurately in the spirit of such selection, he is treading upon safe ground, and we know what we are to expect from him. Our feelings are the same with respect to meter; for, as it may be proper to remind the reader, the distinction of meter is regular and uniform, and not, like that which is produced by what is usually called POETIC DICTION, arbitrary, and subject to infinite caprices upon which no calculation whatever can be made. In the one case, the reader is utterly at the mercy of the poet, respecting what imagery or diction he may choose to connect with the passion; whereas in the other, the meter obeys certain laws, to which the poet and reader both willingly submit because they are certain, and because no interference is made by them with the passion but such as the concurring testimony of ages has shown to heighten and improve the pleasure which coexists with it. * * *

I have said that poetry is the spontaneous overflow of powerful feelings: it takes its origin from emotion recollected in tranquillity: the emotion is contemplated till, by a species of reaction, the tranquillity gradually disappears, and an emotion, kindred to that which was before the subject of contemplation, is gradually produced, and does itself actually exist in the mind. In this mood successful composition generally begins, and in a mood similar to this it is carried on; but the emotion, of whatever kind, and in whatever degree, from various causes, is qualified by various pleasures, so that in describing any passions whatsoever, which are voluntarily described, the mind will, upon the whole, be in a state of enjoyment. If Nature be thus cautious to preserve in a state of enjoyment a being so employed, the poet ought to profit by the lesson held forth to him, and ought especially to take care that, whatever passions he communicates to his reader, those passions, if his reader's mind be sound and vigorous, should always be accompanied with an overbalance of pleasure. Now the music of harmonious metrical language, the sense of difficulty overcome, and the blind association of pleasure which has been previously received from works of rhyme or meter of the same or similar construction, an indistinct perception perpetually renewed of language closely resembling that of real life, and yet, in the circumstance of meter, differing from it so widely—all these imperceptibly make up a complex feeling of delight, which is of the most important use in tempering the painful feeling always found intermingled with powerful descriptions of the deeper passions. This effect is always produced in pathetic and impassioned poetry; while in lighter compositions the ease and gracefulness with which the poet manages his numbers are themselves confessedly a principal source of the gratification of the reader. All that it is *necessary* to say, however, upon this subject, may be effected by affirming, what few persons will deny, that of two descriptions, either of passions, manners, or characters each of them equally well executed, the one in prose and the other in verse, the verse will be read a hundred times where the prose is read once. * * *

If an author, by any single composition, has impressed us with respect for his talents, it is useful to consider this as affording a presumption that on other occasions, where we have been displeased, he nevertheless may not have written ill or absurdly; and further, to give him so much credit for this one composition as may induce us to review what has displeased us with more care than we should otherwise have bestowed upon it. This is not only an act of justice, but, in our decisions upon poetry especially, may conduce in a high degree to the improvement of our own taste; for an *accurate* taste in poetry and in all the other arts, as Sir Joshua Reynolds[4] has observed, is an *acquired* talent, which can only be produced by thought and a long-continued intercourse with the best models of composition. This is mentioned, not with so ridiculous a purpose as to prevent the most inexperienced reader from judging for himself (I have already said that I wish him to judge for himself), but merely to temper the rashness of decision, and to suggest that, if poetry be a subject on which much time has not been bestowed, the judgment may be erroneous; and that, in many cases, it necessarily will be so.

Nothing would, I know, have so effectually contributed to further the end which I have in view, as to have shown of what kind the pleasure is, and how that pleasure is produced, which is confessedly produced by metrical composition essentially different from that which I have here endeavored to recommend: for the reader will say that he has been pleased by such composition; and what more can be done for him? The power of any art is limited; and he will suspect that, if it be proposed to furnish him with new

4. Leading English portrait painter of the 18th century and author of *Discourses on Art* ((1769–1790).

friends, that can be only upon condition of his abandoning his old friends. Besides, as I have said, the reader is himself conscious of the pleasure which he has received from such composition, composition to which he has peculiarly attached the endearing name of poetry; and all men feel an habitual gratitude, and something of an honorable bigotry, for the objects which have long continued to please them: we not only wish to be pleased, but to be pleased in that particular way in which we have been accustomed to be pleased. There is in these feelings enough to resist a host of arguments; and I should be the less able to combat them successfully, as I am willing to allow that, in order entirely to enjoy the poetry which I am recommending, it would be necessary to give up much of what is ordinarily enjoyed. But, would my limits have permitted me to point out how this pleasure is produced, many obstacles might have been removed, and the reader assisted in perceiving that the powers of language are not so limited as he may suppose; and that it is possible for poetry to give other enjoyments, of a purer, more lasting, and more exquisite nature. This part of the subject has not been altogether neglected, but it has not been so much my present aim to prove that the interest excited by some other kinds of poetry is less vivid, and less worthy of the nobler powers of the mind, as to offer reasons for presuming that, if my purpose were fulfilled, a species of poetry would be produced which is genuine poetry, in its nature well adapted to interest mankind permanently, and likewise important in the multiplicity and quality of its moral relations.

From what has been said, and from a perusal of the poems, the reader will be able clearly to perceive the object which I had in view; he will determine how far it has been attained, and, what is a much more important question, whether it be worth attaining; and upon the decision of these two questions will rest my claim to the approbation of the public.

1800, 1802

Strange Fits of Passion Have I Known[1]

Strange fits of passion have I known:
And I will dare to tell,
But in the Lover's ear alone,
What once to me befell.

1. This and the four following pieces are often known as the "Lucy poems." All but the last were written in 1799, while Wordsworth and Dorothy were in Germany, and homesick. There has been diligent speculation about the identity of Lucy, but it remains speculation; the one certainty is that she is not the girl of Wordsworth's *Lucy Gray*, below. "Fits of passion": in an archaic sense, "sudden moods of intense grief."

When she I loved looked every day   5
Fresh as a rose in June,
I to her cottage bent my way,
Beneath an evening moon.

Upon the moon I fixed my eye,
All over the wide lea;   10
With quickening pace my horse drew nigh
Those paths so dear to me.

And now we reached the orchard plot;
And, as we climbed the hill,
The sinking moon to Lucy's cot   15
Came near, and nearer still.

In one of those sweet dreams I slept,
Kind Nature's gentlest boon!
And all the while my eyes I kept
On the descending moon.   20

My horse moved on; hoof after hoof
He raised, and never stopped:
When down behind the cottage roof,
At once, the bright moon dropped.

What fond and wayward thoughts will slide   25
Into a Lover's head!
"O mercy!" to myself I cried,
"If Lucy should be dead!"[2]

1799   1800

She Dwelt Among the Untrodden Ways

She dwelt among the untrodden ways
    Beside the springs of Dove.[3]
A Maid whom there were none to praise
    And very few to love;

A violet by a mossy stone   5
    Half hidden from the eye!
—Fair as a star, when only one
    Is shining in the sky.

She lived unknown, and few could know
    When Lucy ceased to be;   10
But she is in her grave, and, oh,
    The difference to me!

1799   1800

2. An additional stanza in an earlier
MS. version demonstrates how a poem
may profit by omitting a passage which
is, in itself, excellent poetry: "I told
her this: her laughter light / Is ringing
in my ears; / And when I think upon
that night / My eyes are dim with
tears."
3. There are several rivers by this
name in England, including one in the
Lake Country.

Three Years She Grew

Three years she grew in sun and shower,
Then Nature said, "A lovelier flower
On earth was never sown;
This Child I to myself will take;
She shall be mine, and I will make   5
A Lady of my own.

"Myself will to my darling be
Both law and impulse:[4] and with me
The Girl, in rock and plain,
In earth and heaven, in glade and bower,   10
Shall feel an overseeing power
To kindle or restrain.

"She shall be sportive as the fawn
That wild with glee across the lawn
Or up the mountain springs;
And hers shall be the breathing balm,   15
And hers the silence and the calm
Of mute insensate things.

"The floating clouds their state shall lend
To her; for her the willow bend;   20
Nor shall she fail to see
Even in the motions of the Storm
Grace that shall mold the Maiden's form
By silent sympathy.

"The stars of midnight shall be dear   25
To her; and she shall lean her ear
In many a secret place
Where rivulets dance their wayward round,
And beauty born of murmuring sound
Shall pass into her face.   30

"And vital feelings of delight
Shall rear her form to stately height,
Her virgin bosom swell;
Such thoughts to Lucy I will give
While she and I together live   35
Here in this happy dell."

Thus Nature spake—the work was done—
How soon my Lucy's race was run!
She died, and left to me
This health, this calm, and quiet scene;   40

4. Wordsworth recognizes in the moral
tutelage of nature a double influence,
"to kindle or restrain." Cf. *The Prel-*
ude I.301–2, where Wordsworth grows
up "fostered alike by beauty and by
fear."

The memory of what has been,
And never more will be.

1799 1800

A Slumber Did My Spirit Seal

A slumber did my spirit seal;
  I had no human fears:
She seemed a thing that could not feel
  The touch of earthly years.

No motion has she now, no force;   5
  She neither hears nor sees;
Rolled round in earth's diurnal[2] course,
  With rocks, and stones, and trees.

1799 1800

I Traveled Among Unknown Men

I traveled among unknown men,
  In lands beyond the sea;
Nor, England! did I know till then
  What love I bore to thee.

'Tis past, that melancholy dream!   5
  Nor will I quit thy shore
A second time; for still I seem
  To love thee more and more.

Among thy mountains did I feel
  The joy of my desire;   10
And she I cherished turned her wheel
  Beside an English fire.

Thy mornings showed, thy nights concealed,
  The bowers where Lucy played;
And thine too is the last green field   15
  That Lucy's eyes surveyed.

ca. 1801 1807

Lucy Gray[1]

OR SOLITUDE

Oft I had heard of Lucy Gray:
  And, when I crossed the wild,

---

2. Daily.
1. Written in 1799 while Wordsworth
was in Germany, and founded on a true
account of a young girl who drowned
when she lost her way in a snowstorm.
"The body however was found in the
canal. The way in which the incident
was treated and the spiritualizing of

I chanced to see at break of day
The solitary child.

No mate, no comrade Lucy knew;   5
She dwelt on a wide moor,
—The sweetest thing that ever grew
Beside a human door!

You yet may spy the fawn at play,
The hare upon the green;   10
But the sweet face of Lucy Gray
Will never more be seen.

"Tonight will be a stormy night—
You to the town must go;
And take a lantern, Child, to light   15
Your mother through the snow."

"That, Father! will I gladly do:
'Tis scarcely afternoon—
The minster[2] clock has just struck two,
And yonder is the moon!"   20

At this the Father raised his hook,
And snapped a faggot band;[3]
He plied his work—and Lucy took
The lantern in her hand.

Not blither is the mountain roe;   25
With many a wanton stroke
Her feet disperse the powdery snow,
That rises up like smoke.

The storm came on before its time;
She wandered up and down;   30
And many a hill did Lucy climb,
But never reached the town.

The wretched parents all that night
Went shouting far and wide;
But there was neither sound nor sight   35
To serve them for a guide.

At daybreak on a hill they stood
That overlooked the moor,
And thence they saw the bridge of wood,
A furlong[4] from their door.   40

They wept—and, turning homeward, cried,

the character might furnish hints for
contrasting the imaginative influences
which I have endeavored to throw over
common life with Crabbe's matter-of-
fact style of treating subjects of the
same kind" (Wordsworth). Compare
Wordsworth's statement (in the Preface to *Lyrical Ballads*) of his undertaking to throw over ordinary things
"a certain coloring of imagination."
2. Church.
3. Cord binding a bundle of sticks to
be used for fuel.
4. One eighth of a mile.

"In heaven we all shall meet";
—When in the snow the mother spied
The print of Lucy's feet.

Then downwards from the steep hill's edge   45
They tracked the footmarks small;
And through the broken hawthorn hedge,
And by the long stone wall;

And then an open field they crossed:
The marks were still the same;   50
They tracked them on, nor ever lost;
And to the bridge they came.

They followed from the snowy bank
Those footmarks, one by one,
Into the middle of the plank;   55
And further there were none!

—Yet some maintain that to this day
She is a living child;
That you may see sweet Lucy Gray
Upon the lonesome wild.   60

O'er rough and smooth she trips along,
And never looks behind;
And sings a solitary song
That whistles in the wind.

1799   1800

The Ruined Cottage   Wordsworth wrote *The Ruined Cottage* in
1797–98, but revised it several times before he finally published an expanded rendering of the story as Book I of *The Excursion,* in 1814. Not
until 1949 was *The Ruined Cottage,* as an independent poem, made available in the fifth volume of *The Poetical Works of William Wordsworth,*
edited by Ernest de Selincourt and Helen Darbishire, who printed a version
known as "MS. B." The version reprinted here is, however, from "MS. D,"
dating 1799 or 1800, as transcribed by Jonathan Wordsworth in *The Music of
Humanity: A Critical Study of Wordsworth's "Ruined Cottage"* (1968).

This is a shorter and better poem than the one reprinted in *The Poetical
Works.* The latter lacks the great concluding passage, lines 493–538, and
includes in Part I more than 250 lines describing the youthful development
of the peddler that are extraneous to the narrative proper and soften the
hard naturalism of the story by introducing into it, at considerable length,
the peddler's faith that nature teaches "deeply the lesson deep of love."
The version in the first book of *The Excursion* is longer still, is attenuated
in style, and attempts to mitigate the impact of Margaret's sufferings even
more by attributing to her a Christian piety which is conventional rather
than deeply realized. In the version reprinted here, however, we confront the

blank facts of "a tale of silent suffering"—suffering which is undeserved, unrationalized, and irremissive. Like the narrating poet, we attend in "the impotence of grief" as Margaret's anguish at the loss of her husband slowly bends and then breaks her spirit, before destroying her life. Her deterioration under this relentless pressure is a moral one, measured by the bleak details of the correlative deterioration of her untended garden and cottage. The event is "a common tale," and it poses the implicit question, What are we to make of human life, in which such things happen?

The peddler's recovery of heart turns, unexpectedly, on his recognition that this human tragedy takes place within the unceasing and neutral operation—as the narrator says, "the calm oblivious tendencies"—of nature. This nature, unmindful of man, his aims and suffering and work, quietly goes about the process of assimilating the human artifacts which have been wrought from it back into its own independent and continuing life. In a reversal as extreme as Wordsworth could make it, the peddler declares: "I turned away,/And walked along my road in happiness." By his artistry Wordsworth carries us along in imagination so that we too, whatever our own beliefs, feel what it is to be able to look upon and master the fact of human suffering, unsupported by any consoling creed of a beneficent power, whether in or out of nature.

Beyond any of Wordsworth's writings, even *Michael, The Ruined Cottage* demonstrates the distinctive quality of Wordsworth at his best— the quality Walter Raleigh identified more than a half century ago as his "calm and almost terrible strength."

The Ruined Cottage

First Part

'Twas Summer and the sun was mounted high.
Along the south the uplands feebly glared
Through a pale steam, and all the northern downs,
In clearer air ascending, shewed far off
Their surfaces with shadows dappled o'er   5
Of deep embattled clouds. Far as the sight
Could reach those many shadows lay in spots
Determined and unmoved, with steady beams
Of clear and pleasant sunshine interposed—
Pleasant to him who on the soft cool grass   10
Extends his careless limbs beside the root
Of some huge oak whose aged branches make
A twilight of their own, a dewy shade
Where the wren warbles while the dreaming man,
Half conscious of that soothing melody,   15
With sidelong eye looks out upon the scene,
By those impending branches made more soft,
More soft and distant.

Other lot was mine.
Across a bare wide Common I had toiled
With languid feet which by the slipp'ry ground   20
Were baffled still, and when I stretched myself
On the brown earth my limbs from very heat
Could find no rest, nor my weak arm disperse
The insect host which gathered round my face
And joined their murmurs to the tedious noise   25
Of seeds of bursting gorse that crackled round.
I rose and turned towards a group of trees
Which midway in that level stood alone;
And thither come at length, beneath a shade
Of clustering elms that sprang from the same root   30
I found a ruined house, four naked walls
That stared upon each other. I looked round
And near the door I saw an aged Man,
Alone and stretched upon the cottage bench,
An iron-pointed staff lay at his side.   35
With instantaneous joy I recognized
That pride of nature and of lowly life,
The venerable Armytage, a friend
As dear to me as is the setting sun.

                        Two days before   40
We had been fellow travelers. I knew
That he was in this neighborhood, and now
Delighted found him here in the cool shade.
He lay, his pack of rustic merchandise
Pillowing his head. I guess he had no thought   45
Of his way-wandering life. His eyes were shut,
The shadows of the breezy elms above
Dappled his face. With thirsty heat oppressed
At length I hailed him, glad to see his hat
Bedewed with waterdrops, as if the brim   50
Had newly scooped a running stream. He rose
And pointing to a sunflower, bade me climb
The [   ] wall where that same gaudy flower
Looked out upon the road.

                    It was a plot
Of garden ground now wild, its matted weeds   55
Marked with the steps of those whom as they passed,
The gooseberry trees that shot in long lank slips,
Or currants hanging from their leafless stems
In scanty strings, had tempted to o'erleap
The broken wall. Within that cheerless spot,   60
Where two tall hedgerows of thick alder boughs
Joined in a damp cold nook, I found a well
Half covered up with willow flowers and grass.
I slaked my thirst and to the shady bench
Returned, and while I stood unbonneted   65

To catch the motion of the cooler air,
The old Man said, "I see around me here
Things which you cannot see. We die, my Friend,
Nor we alone, but that which each man loved
And prized in his peculiar nook of earth   70
Dies with him, or is changed, and very soon
Even of the good is no memorial left.
The Poets, in their elegies and songs
Lamenting the departed, call the groves,
They call upon the hills and streams to mourn,   75
And senseless rocks—nor idly, for they speak
In these their invocations with a voice
Obedient to the strong creative power
Of human passion. Sympathies there are
More tranquil, yet perhaps of kindred birth,   80
That steal upon the meditative mind
And grow with thought. Beside yon spring I stood,
And eyed its waters till we seemed to feel
One sadness, they and I. For them a bond
Of brotherhood is broken; time has been   85
When every day the touch of human hand
Disturbed their stillness, and they ministered
To human comfort. When I stooped to drink
A spider's web hung to the water's edge,
And on the wet and slimy footstone lay   90
The useless fragment of a wooden bowl.
It moved my very heart.

                              The day has been
When I could never pass this road but she
Who lived within these walls, when I appeared,
A daughter's welcome gave me, and I loved her   95
As my own child. Oh Sir, the good die first,
And they whose hearts are dry as summer dust
Burn to the socket. Many a passenger
Has blessed poor Margaret for her gentle looks
When she upheld the cool refreshment drawn   100
From that forsaken spring, and no one came
But he was welcome, no one went away
But that it seemed she loved him. She is dead,
The worm is on her cheek, and this poor hut,
Stripped of its outward garb of household flowers, 105
Of rose and sweetbriar, offers to the wind
A cold bare wall whose earthy top is tricked
With weeds and the rank spear grass. She is dead,
And nettles rot and adders sun themselves
Where we have sate together while she nursed   110
Her infant at her breast. The unshod colt,
The wandring heifer and the Potter's ass,
Find shelter now within the chimney wall
Where I have seen her evening hearthstone blaze

And through the window spread upon the road 115
Its cheerful light. You will forgive me, sir,
But often on this cottage do I muse
As on a picture, till my wiser mind
Sinks, yielding to the foolishness of grief.

She had a husband, an industrious man, 120
Sober and steady. I have heard her say
That he was up and busy at his loom
In summer ere the mower's scythe had swept
The dewy grass, and in the early spring
Ere the last star had vanished. They who passed 125
At evening, from behind the garden fence
Might hear his busy spade, which he would ply
After his daily work till the daylight
Was gone, and every leaf and flower were lost
In the dark hedges. So they passed their days 130
In peace and comfort, and two pretty babes
Were their best hope next to the God in Heaven.

You may remember, now some ten years gone,
Two blighting seasons when the fields were left
With half a harvest. It pleased heaven to add 135
A worse affliction in the plague of war,
A happy land was stricken to the heart,
'Twas a sad time of sorrow and distress.
A wanderer among the cottages,
I with my pack of winter raiment saw 140
The hardships of that season. Many rich
Sunk down as in a dream among the poor,
And of the poor did many cease to be,
And their place knew them not. Meanwhile, abridged
Of daily comforts, gladly reconciled 145
To numerous self-denials, Margaret
Went struggling on through those calamitous years
With cheerful hope. But ere the second autumn
A fever seized her husband. In disease
He lingered long, and when his strength returned 150
He found the little he had stored to meet
The hour of accident, or crippling age,
Was all consumed. As I have said, 'twas now
A time of trouble: shoals of artisans
Were from their daily labor turned away 155
To hang for bread on parish charity,
They and their wives and children, happier far
Could they have lived as do the little birds
That peck along the hedges, or the kite
That makes her dwelling in the mountain rocks. 160

Ill fared it now with Robert, he who dwelt
In this poor cottage. At his door he stood
And whistled many a snatch of merry tunes

That had no mirth in them, or with his knife
Carved uncouth figures on the heads of sticks, 165
Then idly sought about through every nook
Of house or garden any casual task
Of use or ornament, and with a strange
Amusing but uneasy novelty
He blended where he might the various tasks 170
Of summer, autumn, winter, and of spring.
But this endured not, his good humor soon
Became a weight in which no pleasure was,
And poverty brought on a petted mood
And a sore temper. Day by day he drooped, 175
And he would leave his home, and to the town
Without an errand would he turn his steps,
Or wander here and there among the fields.
One while he would speak lightly of his babes
And with a cruel tongue, at other times 180
He played with them wild freaks of merriment,
And 'twas a piteous thing to see the looks
Of the poor innocent children. 'Every smile,'
Said Margaret to me here beneath these trees,
'Made my heart bleed.' " 185

            At this the old Man paused,
And looking up to those enormous elms
He said, " 'Tis now the hour of deepest noon.
At this still season of repose and peace,
This hour when all things which are not at rest
Are cheerful, while this multitude of flies 190
Fills all the air with happy melody,
Why should a tear be in an old man's eye?
Why should we thus with an untoward mind,
And in the weakness of humanity,
From natural wisdom turn our hearts away, 195
To natural comfort shut our eyes and ears,
And, feeding on disquiet, thus disturb
The calm of Nature with our restless thoughts?"

END OF THE FIRST PART

Second Part

He spake with somewhat of a solemn tone,
But when he ended there was in his face 200
Such easy cheerfulness, a look so mild,
That for a little time it stole away
All recollection, and that simple tale
Passed from my mind like a forgotten sound.
A while on trivial things we held discourse, 205
To me soon tasteless. In my own despite
I thought of that poor woman as of one

Whom I had known and loved. He had rehearsed
Her homely tale with such familiar power,
With such an active countenance, an eye   210
So busy, that the things of which he spake
Seemed present, and, attention now relaxed,
There was a heartfelt chillness in my veins.
I rose, and turning from that breezy shade
Went out into the open air, and stood   215
To drink the comfort of the warmer sun.
Long time I had not stayed ere, looking round
Upon that tranquil ruin, I returned
And begged of the old man that for my sake
He would resume his story.   220

                        He replied,
"It were a wantonness, and would demand
Severe reproof, if we were men whose hearts
Could hold vain dalliance with the misery
Even of the dead, contented thence to draw
A momentary pleasure, never marked   225
By reason, barren of all future good.
But we have known that there is often found
In mournful thoughts, and always might be found,
A power to virtue friendly; were't not so
I am a dreamer among men, indeed   230
An idle dreamer. 'Tis a common tale
By moving accidents uncharactered,
A tale of silent suffering, hardly clothed
In bodily form, and to the grosser sense
But ill adapted, scarcely palpable   235
To him who does not think. But at your bidding
I will proceed.

                  While thus it fared with them
To whom this cottage till that hapless year
Had been a blessed home, it was my chance
To travel in a country far remote;   240
And glad I was when, halting by yon gate
That leads from the green lane, again I saw
These lofty elm trees. Long I did not rest:
With many pleasant thoughts I cheered my way
O'er the flat common. At the door arrived,   245
I knocked, and when I entered, with the hope
Of usual greeting, Margaret looked at me
A little while, then turned her head away
Speechless, and sitting down upon a chair
Wept bitterly. I wist not what to do,   250
Or how to speak to her. Poor wretch, at last
She rose from off her seat, and then, oh Sir,

I cannot tell how she pronounced my name.
With fervent love, and with a face of grief
Unutterably helpless, and a look   255
That seemed to cling upon me, she enquired
If I had seen her husband. As she spake
A strange surprise and fear came to my heart,
Nor had I power to answer ere she told
That he had disappeared—just two months gone.   260
He left his house: two wretched days had passed,
And on the third by the first break of light,
Within her casement full in view she saw
A purse of gold.[1] 'I trembled at the sight,'
Said Margaret, 'for I knew it was his hand   265
That placed it there. And on that very day
By one, a stranger, from my husband sent,
The tidings came that he had joined a troop
Of soldiers going to a distant land.
He left me thus. Poor Man, he had not heart   270
To take farewell of me, and he feared
That I should follow with my babes, and sink
Beneath the misery of a soldier's life.'

This tale did Margaret tell with many tears,
And when she ended I had little power   275
To give her comfort, and was glad to take
Such words of hope from her own mouth as served
To cheer us both. But long we had not talked
Ere we built up a pile of better thoughts,
And with a brighter eye she looked around,   280
As if she had been shedding tears of joy.
We parted. It was then the early spring:
I left her busy with her garden tools,
And well remember, o'er that fence she looked,
And, while I paced along the footway path,   285
Called out and sent a blessing after me,
With tender cheerfulness, and with a voice
That seemed the very sound of happy thoughts.

    I roved o'er many a hill and many a dale
With this my weary load, in heat and cold,   290
Through many a wood and many an open ground,
In sunshine or in shade, in wet or fair,
Now blithe, now drooping, as it might befall;
My best companions now the driving winds
And now the 'trotting brooks' and whispering trees,   295
And now the music of my own sad steps,
With many a short-lived thought that passed between
And disappeared.

---

1. The "bounty" that her husband had
been paid for enlisting in the militia.
The shortage of volunteers and England's
sharply rising military needs had in some
counties forced the bounty up from
about £1 in 1757 to more than £16 in
1796 (J. R. Western, *English Militia
in the Eighteenth Century*, 1965, p.
276).

I came this way again
Towards the wane of summer, when the wheat
Was yellow, and the soft and bladed grass   300
Sprang up afresh and o'er the hay field spread
Its tender green. When I had reached the door
I found that she was absent. In the shade,
Where we now sit, I waited her return.
Her cottage in its outward look appeared   305
As cheerful as before, in any shew
Of neatness little changed, but that I thought
The honeysuckle crowded round the door,
And from the wall hung down in heavier tufts,
And knots of worthless stonecrop started out   310
Along the window's edge, and grew like weeds
Against the lower panes. I turned aside
And strolled into her garden. It was changed.
The unprofitable bindweed spread his bells
From side to side, and with unwieldy wreaths   315
Had dragged the rose from its sustaining wall
And bent it down to earth. The border tufts,
Daisy, and thrift, and lowly camomile,
And thyme, had straggled out into the paths
Which they were used to deck.   320

     Ere this an hour
Was wasted. Back I turned my restless steps,
And as I walked before the door it chanced
A stranger passed, and guessing whom I sought,
He said that she was used to ramble far.
The sun was sinking in the west, and now   325
I sate with sad impatience. From within
Her solitary infant cried aloud.
The spot though fair seemed very desolate,
The longer I remained more desolate;
And looking round I saw the cornerstones,   330
Till then unmarked, on either side the door
With dull red stains discolored, and stuck o'er
With tufts and hairs of wool, as if the sheep
That feed upon the commons thither came
Familiarly, and found a couching place   335
Even at her threshold.

    The house clock struck eight:
I turned and saw her distant a few steps.
Her face was pale and thin, her figure too
Was changed. As she unlocked the door she said,
'It grieves me you have waited here so long,   340
But in good truth I've wandered much of late,
And sometimes, to my shame I speak, have need
Of my best prayers to bring me back again.'
While on the board she spread our evening meal,

She told me she had lost her elder child,   345
That he for months had been a serving boy,
Apprenticed by the parish. 'I perceive
You look at me, and you have cause. Today
I have been traveling far, and many days
About the fields I wander, knowing this   350
Only, that what I seek I cannot find.
And so I waste my time: for I am changed,
And to myself,' she said, 'have done much wrong,
And to this helpless infant. I have slept
Weeping, and weeping I have waked. My tears   355
Have flowed as if my body were not such
As others are, and I could never die.
But I am now in mind and in my heart
More easy, and I hope,' she said, 'that heaven
Will give me patience to endure the things   360
Which I behold at home.'

                           It would have grieved
Your very soul to see her. Sir, I feel
The story linger in my heart. I fear
'Tis long and tedious, but my spirit clings
To that poor woman. So familiarly   365
Do I perceive her manner and her look
And presence, and so deeply do I feel
Her goodness, that not seldom in my walks
A momentary trance comes over me,
And to myself I seem to muse on one   370
By sorrow laid asleep or borne away,
A human being destined to awake
To human life, or something very near
To human life, when he shall come again
For whom she suffered. Sir, it would have grieved   375
Your very soul to see her: evermore
Her eyelids drooped, her eyes were downward cast,
And when she at her table gave me food
She did not look at me. Her voice was low,
Her body was subdued. In every act   380
Pertaining to her house affairs appeared
The careless stillness which a thinking mind
Gives to an idle matter. Still she sighed,
But yet no motion of the breast was seen,
No heaving of the heart. While by the fire   385
We sate together, sighs came on my ear,
I knew not how, and hardly whence they came.
I took my staff, and when I kissed her babe
The tears stood in her eyes. I left her then
With the best hope and comfort I could give: 390
She thanked me for my will, but for my hope
It seemed she did not thank me.

                                        I returned
And took my rounds along this road again
Ere on its sunny bank the primrose flower
Had chronicled the earliest day of spring.   395
I found her sad and drooping. She had learned
No tidings of her husband; if he lived,
She knew not that he lived; if he were dead,
She knew not he was dead. She seemed the same
In person or appearance, but her house   400
Bespoke a sleepy hand of negligence.
The floor was neither dry nor neat, the hearth
Was comfortless,
The windows too were dim, and her few books,
Which one upon the other heretofore   405
Had been piled up against the corner panes
In seemly order, now with straggling leaves
Lay scattered here and there, open or shut,
As they had chanced to fall. Her infant babe
Had from its mother caught the trick of grief,   410
And sighed among its playthings. Once again
I turned towards the garden gate, and saw
More plainly still that poverty and grief
Were now come nearer to her. The earth was hard,
With weeds defaced and knots of withered grass;   415
No ridges there appeared of clear black mould,
No winter greenness. Of her herbs and flowers
It seemed the better part were gnawed away
Or trampled on the earth. A chain of straw,
Which had been twisted round the tender stem   420
Of a young apple tree, lay at its root;
The bark was nibbled round by truant sheep.
Margaret stood near, her infant in her arms,
And, seeing that my eye was on the tree,
She said, 'I fear it will be dead and gone   425
Ere Robert come again.'

                                    Towards the house
Together we returned, and she inquired
If I had any hope. But for her Babe,
And for her little friendless Boy, she said,
She had no wish to live—that she must die   430
Of sorrow. Yet I saw the idle loom
Still in its place. His Sunday garments hung
Upon the selfsame nail, his very staff
Stood undisturbed behind the door. And when
I passed this way beaten by Autumn winds,   435
She told me that her little babe was dead,
And she was left alone. That very time,
I yet remember, through the miry lane
She walked with me a mile, when the bare trees

Trickled with foggy damps, and in such sort   440
That any heart had ached to hear her, begged
That wheresoe'r I went I still would ask
For him whom she had lost. We parted then,
Our final parting; for from that time forth
Did many seasons pass ere I returned   445
Into this tract again.

              Five tedious years
She lingered in unquiet widowhood,
A wife and widow. Needs must it have been
A sore heart-wasting. I have heard, my friend,
That in that broken arbor she would sit   450
The idle length of half a sabbath day;
There, where you see the toadstool's lazy head;
And when a dog passed by she still would quit
The shade and look abroad. On this old Bench
For hours she sate, and evermore her eye   455
Was busy in the distance, shaping things
Which made her heart beat quick. Seest thou that path?—
The green sward now has broken its gray line—
There to and fro she paced through many a day
Of the warm summer, from a belt of flax   460
That girt her waist, spinning the long-drawn thread
With backward steps. Yet ever as there passed
A man whose garments shewed the Soldier's red,
Or crippled Mendicant in Sailor's garb,
The little child who sate to turn the wheel   465
Ceased from his toil, and she, with faltering voice,
Expecting still to hear her husband's fate,
Made many a fond inquiry; and when they
Whose presence gave no comfort, were gone by,
Her heart was still more sad. And by yon gate,   470
Which bars the traveler's road, she often stood,
And when a stranger horseman came, the latch
Would lift, and in his face look wistfully,
Most happy if from aught discovered there
Of tender feeling she might dare repeat   475
The same sad question.

              Meanwhile her poor hut
Sunk to decay; for he was gone, whose hand
At the first nippings of October frost
Closed up each chink, and with fresh bands of straw
Chequered the green-grown thatch. And so she lived   480
Through the long winter, reckless and alone,
Till this reft house, by frost, and thaw, and rain,
Was sapped; and when she slept, the nightly damps
Did chill her breast, and in the stormy day
Her tattered clothes were ruffled by the wind   485
Even at the side of her own fire. Yet still

She loved this wretched spot, nor would for worlds
Have parted hence; and still that length of road,
And this rude bench, one torturing hope endeared,
Fast rooted at her heart. And here, my friend,   490
In sickness she remained; and here she died,
Last human tenant of these ruined walls."

The old Man ceased: he saw that I was moved.
From that low bench rising instinctively,
I turned aside in weakness, nor had power   495
To thank him for the tale which he had told.
I stood, and leaning o'er the garden gate
Reviewed that Woman's sufferings; and it seemed
To comfort me while with a brother's love
I blessed her in the impotence of grief.   500
At length towards the cottage I returned
Fondly, and traced with milder interest,
That secret spirit of humanity
Which, 'mid the calm oblivious tendencies
Of nature, 'mid her plants, her weeds and flowers,   505
And silent overgrowings, still survived.
The old man seeing this resumed, and said,
"My friend, enough to sorrow have you given,
The purposes of Wisdom ask no more:
Be wise and cheerful, and no longer read   510
The forms of things with an unworthy eye.
She sleeps in the calm earth, and peace is here.
I well remember that those very plumes,
Those weeds, and the high spear grass on that wall,
By mist and silent raindrops silvered o'er,   515
As once I passed, did to my mind convey
So still an image of tranquillity,
So calm and still, and looked so beautiful
Amid the uneasy thoughts which filled my mind,
That what we feel of sorrow and despair   520
From ruin and from change, and all the grief
The passing shews of being leave behind,
Appeared an idle dream that could not live
Where meditation was. I turned away,
And walked along my road in happiness."   525

    He ceased. By this the sun declining shot
A slant and mellow radiance, which began
To fall upon us where beneath the trees
We sate on that low bench. And now we felt,
Admonished thus, the sweet hour coming on: 530
A linnet warbled from those lofty elms,
A thrush sang loud, and other melodies
At distance heard, peopled the milder air.
The old man rose and hoisted up his load.
Together casting then a farewell look   535

Upon those silent walls, we left the shade;
And, ere the stars were visible, attained
A rustic inn, our evening resting place.

THE END

1797–ca. 1799   1968

Michael[1]

A PASTORAL POEM

If from the public way you turn your steps
Up the tumultuous brook of Greenhead Ghyll,[2]
You will suppose that with an upright path
Your feet must struggle; in such bold ascent
The pastoral mountains front you, face to face.   5
But, courage! for around that boisterous brook
The mountains have all opened out themselves,
And made a hidden valley of their own.
No habitation can be seen; but they
Who journey thither find themselves alone   10
With a few sheep, with rocks and stones, and kites[3]
That overhead are sailing in the sky.
It is in truth an utter solitude;
Nor should I have made mention of this dell
But for one object which you might pass by,   15
Might see and notice not. Beside the brook
Appears a straggling heap of unhewn stones!
And to that simple object appertains
A story—unenriched with strange events,
Yet not unfit, I deem, for the fireside,   20
Or for the summer shade. It was the first
Of those domestic tales that spake to me
Of Shepherds, dwellers in the valleys, men
Whom I already loved—not verily
For their own sakes, but for the fields and hills   25
Where was their occupation and abode.
And hence this Tale, while I was yet a Boy
Careless of books, yet having felt the power
Of Nature, by the gentle agency
Of natural objects, led me on to feel   30

1. This poem is founded on the actual misfortunes of a family at Grasmere. "The sheepfold," Wordsworth said, "on which so much of the poem turns, remains, or rather the ruins of it." He wrote to Thomas Poole, on April 9, 1801, that he had attempted to picture a man "agitated by two of the most powerful affections of the human heart; the parental affection, and the love of property, *landed* property, including the feelings of inheritance, home, and personal and family independence." The subtitle shows Wordsworth's shift of the term "pastoral" from aristocratic make-believe to the tragic suffering of people in what he called "humble and rustic life."
2. Greenhead Ghyll (a ghyll is a ravine forming the bed of a stream) is not far from Wordsworth's cottage at Grasmere. The other places named in the poem are also in that vicinity.
3. Hawks.

For passions that were not my own, and think
(At random and imperfectly indeed)
On man, the heart of man, and human life.
Therefore, although it be a history
Homely and rude, I will relate the same   35
For the delight of a few natural hearts;
And, with yet fonder feeling, for the sake
Of youthful Poets, who among these hills
Will be my second self when I am gone.

    Upon the forest side in Grasmere Vale   40
There dwelt a Shepherd, Michael was his name;
An old man, stout of heart, and strong of limb.
His bodily frame had been from youth to age
Of an unusual strength: his mind was keen,
Intense, and frugal, apt for all affairs,   45
And in his shepherd's calling he was prompt
And watchful more than ordinary men.
Hence had he learned the meaning of all winds,
Of blasts of every tone; and oftentimes,
When others heeded not, he heard the South   50
Make subterraneous music, like the noise
Of bagpipers on distant Highland hills.
The Shepherd, at such warning, of his flock
Bethought him, and he to himself would say,
"The winds are now devising work for me!"   55
And, truly, at all times, the storm, that drives
The traveler to a shelter, summoned him
Up to the mountains: he had been alone
Amid the heart of many thousand mists,
That came to him, and left him, on the heights.   60
So lived he till his eightieth year was past.
And grossly that man errs, who should suppose
That the green valleys, and the streams and rocks,
Were things indifferent to the Shepherd's thoughts.
Fields, where with cheerful spirits he had breathed   65
The common air; hills, which with vigorous step
He had so often climbed; which had impressed
So many incidents upon his mind
Of hardship, skill or courage, joy or fear;
Which, like a book, preserved the memory   70
Of the dumb animals, whom he had saved,
Had fed or sheltered, linking to such acts
The certainty of honorable gain;
Those fields, those hills—what could they less? had laid
Strong hold on his affections, were to him   75
A pleasurable feeling of blind love,
The pleasure which there is in life itself.

His days had not been passed in singleness.
His Helpmate was a comely matron, old—
Though younger than himself full twenty years.   80
She was a woman of a stirring life,
Whose heart was in her house; two wheels she had
Of antique form: this large, for spinning wool;
That small, for flax; and, if one wheel had rest,
It was because the other was at work.   85
The Pair had but one inmate in their house,
An only Child, who had been born to them
When Michael, telling o'er his years, began
To deem that he was old—in shepherd's phrase,
With one foot in the grave. This only Son,   90
With two brave sheep dogs tried in many a storm,
The one of an inestimable worth,
Made all their household. I may truly say,
That they were as a proverb in the vale
For endless industry. When day was gone,   95
And from their occupations out of doors
The Son and Father were come home, even then,
Their labor did not cease; unless when all
Turned to the cleanly supper board, and there,
Each with a mess of pottage and skimmed milk,   100
Sat round the basket piled with oaten cakes,
And their plain homemade cheese. Yet when the meal
Was ended, Luke (for so the Son was named)
And his old Father both betook themselves
To such convenient work as might employ   105
Their hands by the fireside; perhaps to card
Wool for the Housewife's spindle, or repair
Some injury done to sickle, flail, or scythe,
Or other implement of house or field.

Down from the ceiling, by the chimney's edge,   110
That in our ancient uncouth country style
With huge and black projection overbrowed
Large space beneath, as duly as the light
Of day grew dim the Housewife hung a lamp;
An aged utensil, which had performed   115
Service beyond all others of its kind.
Early at evening did it burn—and late,
Surviving comrade of uncounted hours,
Which, going by from year to year, had found,
And left, the couple neither gay perhaps   120
Nor cheerful, yet with objects and with hopes,
Living a life of eager industry.
And now, when Luke had reached his eighteenth year,
There by the light of this old lamp they sate,
Father and Son, while far into the night   125

The Housewife plied her own peculiar work,
Making the cottage through the silent hours
Murmur as with the sound of summer flies.
This light was famous in its neighborhood,
And was a public symbol of the life   130
That thrifty Pair had lived. For, as it chanced,
Their cottage on a plot of rising ground
Stood single, with large prospect, north and south,
High into Easedale, up to Dunmail Raise,
And westward to the village near the lake;   135
And from this constant light, so regular,
And so far seen, the House itself, by all
Who dwelt within the limits of the vale,
Both old and young, was named The Evening Star.

Thus living on through such a length of years   140
The Shepherd, if he loved himself, must needs
Have loved his Helpmate; but to Michael's heart
This son of his old age was yet more dear—
Less from instinctive tenderness, the same
Fond spirit that blindly works in the blood of all—   145
Than that a child, more than all other gifts
That earth can offer to declining man,
Brings hope with it, and forward-looking thoughts,
And stirrings of inquietude, when they
By tendency of nature needs must fail.   150
Exceeding was the love he bare to him,
His heart and his heart's joy! For oftentimes
Old Michael, while he was a babe in arms,
Had done him female service, not alone
For pastime and delight, as is the use   155
Of fathers, but with patient mind enforced
To acts of tenderness; and he had rocked
His cradle, as with a woman's gentle hand.

And in a later time, ere yet the Boy
Had put on boy's attire, did Michael love,   160
Albeit of a stern unbending mind,
To have the Young-one in his sight, when he
Wrought in the field, or on his shepherd's stool
Sate with a fettered sheep before him stretched
Under the large old oak, that near his door   165
Stood single, and, from matchless depth of shade,
Chosen for the Shearer's covert from the sun,
Thence in our rustic dialect was called
The Clipping Tree, a name which yet it bears.
There, while they two were sitting in the shade,   170
With others round them, earnest all and blithe,
Would Michael exercise his heart with looks

Of fond correction and reproof bestowed
Upon the Child, if he disturbed the sheep
By catching at their legs, or with his shouts   175
Scared them, while they lay still beneath the shears.

    And when by Heaven's good grace the boy grew up
A healthy Lad, and carried in his cheek
Two steady roses that were five years old;
Then Michael from a winter coppice⁴ cut   180
With his own hand a sapling, which he hooped
With iron, making it throughout in all
Due requisites a perfect shepherd's staff,
And gave it to the Boy; wherewith equipped
He as a watchman oftentimes was placed   185
At gate or gap, to stem or turn the flock;
And, to his office prematurely called,
There stood the urchin, as you will divine,
Something between a hindrance and a help;
And for this cause not always, I believe,   190
Receiving from his Father hire of praise;
Though nought was left undone which staff, or voice,
Or looks, or threatening gestures, could perform.

    But soon as Luke, full ten years old, could stand
Against the mountain blasts, and to the heights,   195
Not fearing toil, nor length of weary ways,
He with his Father daily went, and they
Were as companions, why should I relate
That objects which the Shepherd loved before
Were dearer now? that from the Boy there came   200
Feelings and emanations—things which were
Light to the sun and music to the wind;
And that the old Man's heart seemed born again?

    Thus in his Father's sight the Boy grew up:
And now, when he had reached his eighteenth year,   205
He was his comfort and his daily hope.

    While in this sort the simple household lived
From day to day, to Michael's ear there came
Distressful tidings. Long before the time
Of which I speak, the Shepherd had been bound   210
In surety for his brother's son, a man
Of an industrious life, and ample means;
But unforeseen misfortunes suddenly
Had pressed upon him; and old Michael now
Was summoned to discharge the forfeiture,   215
A grievous penalty, but little less
Than half his substance. This unlooked-for claim,
At the first hearing, for a moment took

4. Grove of small trees.

More hope out of his life than he supposed
That any old man ever could have lost.   220
As soon as he had armed himself with strength
To look his trouble in the face, it seemed
The Shepherd's sole resource to sell at once
A portion of his patrimonial fields.
Such was his first resolve; he thought again,   225
And his heart failed him. "Isabel," said he,
Two evenings after he had heard the news,
"I have been toiling more than seventy years,
And in the open sunshine of God's love
Have we all lived; yet, if these fields of ours   230
Should pass into a stranger's hand, I think
That I could not lie quiet in my grave.
Our lot is a hard lot; the sun himself
Has scarcely been more diligent than I;
And I have lived to be a fool at last   235
To my own family. An evil man
That was, and made an evil choice, if he
Were false to us; and, if he were not false,
There are ten thousand to whom loss like this
Had been no sorrow. I forgive him—but   240
'Twere better to be dumb than to talk thus.

        "When I began, my purpose was to speak
Of remedies and of a cheerful hope.
Our Luke shall leave us, Isabel; the land
Shall not go from us, and it shall be free;   245
He shall possess it, free as is the wind
That passes over it. We have, thou know'st,
Another kinsman—he will be our friend
In this distress. He is a prosperous man,
Thriving in trade—and Luke to him shall go,   250
And with his kinsman's help and his own thrift
He quickly will repair this loss, and then
He may return to us. If here he stay,
What can be done? Where everyone is poor,
What can be gained?"
                        At this the old Man paused,   255
And Isabel sat silent, for her mind
Was busy, looking back into past times.
There's Richard Bateman,[5] thought she to herself,
He was a parish boy—at the church door
They made a gathering for him, shillings, pence,   260
And halfpennies, wherewith the neighbors bought
A basket, which they filled with peddler's wares;

5. "The story alluded to here is well known in the country. The chapel is called Ings Chapel and is on the road leading from Kendal to Ambleside" [Wordsworth's note].

And, with this basket on his arm, the lad
Went up to London, found a master there,
Who, out of many, chose the trusty boy   265
To go and overlook his merchandise
Beyond the seas; where he grew wondrous rich,
And left estates and monies to the poor,
And, at his birthplace, built a chapel floored
With marble, which he sent from foreign lands.   270
These thoughts, and many others of like sort,
Passed quickly through the mind of Isabel,
And her face brightened. The old Man was glad,
And thus resumed: "Well, Isabel! this scheme
These two days has been meat and drink to me.   275
Far more than we have lost is left us yet.
We have enough—I wish indeed that I
Were younger—but this hope is a good hope.
Make ready Luke's best garments, of the best
Buy for him more, and let us send him forth   280
Tomorrow, or the next day, or tonight:
If he *could* go, the Boy should go tonight."

　　Here Michael ceased, and to the fields went forth
With a light heart. The Housewife for five days
Was restless morn and night, and all day long   285
Wrought on with her best fingers to prepare
Things needful for the journey of her son.
But Isabel was glad when Sunday came
To stop her in her work; for, when she lay
By Michael's side, she through the last two nights   290
Heard him, how he was troubled in his sleep;
And when they rose at morning she could see
That all his hopes were gone. That day at noon
She said to Luke, while they two by themselves
Were sitting at the door, "Thou must not go;   295
We have no other Child but thee to lose,
None to remember—do not go away,
For if thou leave thy Father he will die."
The Youth made answer with a jocund voice;
And Isabel, when she had told her fears,   300
Recovered heart. That evening her best fare
Did she bring forth, and all together sat
Like happy people round a Christmas fire.

　　With daylight Isabel resumed her work;
And all the ensuing week the house appeared   305
As cheerful as a grove in spring; at length
The expected letter from their kinsman came,
With kind assurances that he would do
His utmost for the welfare of the Boy;

To which requests were added that forthwith 310
He might be sent to him. Ten times or more
The letter was read over; Isabel
Went forth to show it to the neighbors round;
Nor was there at that time on English land
A prouder heart than Luke's. When Isabel 315
Had to her house returned, the old Man said,
"He shall depart tomorrow." To this word
The Housewife answered, talking much of things
Which, if at such short notice he should go,
Would surely be forgotten. But at length 320
She gave consent, and Michael was at ease.

Near the tumultuous brook of Greenhead Ghyll,
In that deep valley, Michael had designed
To build a Sheepfold;[6] and, before he heard
The tidings of his melancholy loss, 325
For this same purpose he had gathered up
A heap of stones, which by the streamlet's edge
Lay thrown together, ready for the work.
With Luke that evening thitherward he walked;
And soon as they had reached the place he stopped, 330
And thus the old Man spake to him: "My son,
Tomorrow thou wilt leave me: with full heart
I look upon thee, for thou art the same
That wert a promise to me ere thy birth,
And all thy life hast been my daily joy. 335
I will relate to thee some little part
Of our two histories; 'twill do thee good
When thou art from me, even if I should touch
On things thou canst not know of. After thou
First cam'st into the world—as oft befalls 340
To newborn infants—thou didst sleep away
Two days, and blessings from thy Father's tongue
Then fell upon thee. Day by day passed on,
And still I loved thee with increasing love.
Never to living ear came sweeter sounds 345
Than when I heard thee by our own fireside
First uttering, without words, a natural tune;
While thou, a feeding babe, didst in thy joy
Sing at thy Mother's breast. Month followed month,
And in the open fields my life was passed 350
And on the mountains; else I think that thou
Hadst been brought up upon thy Father's knees.
But we were playmates, Luke; among these hills,
As well thou knowest, in us the old and young
Have played together, nor with me didst thou 355
Lack any pleasure which a boy can know."

6. Pen for sheep. "A sheepfold in these mountains is an unroofed building of stone walls, with different divisions" [Wordsworth's note].

Luke had a manly heart; but at these words
He sobbed aloud. The old Man grasped his hand,
And said, "Nay, do not take it so—I see
That these are things of which I need not speak.   360
Even to the utmost I have been to thee
A kind and a good Father: and herein
I but repay a gift which I myself
Received at others' hands; for, though now old
Beyond the common life of man, I still   365
Remember them who loved me in my youth.
Both of them sleep together; here they lived,
As all their Forefathers had done; and, when
At length their time was come, they were not loath
To give their bodies to the family mold.   370
I wished that thou shouldst live the life they lived,
But 'tis a long time to look back, my Son,
And see so little gain from threescore years.
These fields were burthened[7] when they came to me;
Till I was forty years of age, not more   375
Than half of my inheritance was mine.
I toiled and toiled; God blessed me in my work,
And till these three weeks past the land was free.
It looks as if it never could endure
Another master. Heaven forgive me, Luke,   380
If I judge ill for thee, but it seems good
That thou shouldst go."
                              At this the old Man paused;
Then, pointing to the stones near which they stood,
Thus, after a short silence, he resumed:
"This was a work for us; and now, my Son,   385
It is a work for me. But, lay one stone—
Here, lay it for me, Luke, with thine own hands.
Nay, Boy, be of good hope—we both may live
To see a better day. At eighty-four
I still am strong and hale; do thou thy part;   390
I will do mine. I will begin again
With many tasks that were resigned to thee:
Up to the heights, and in among the storms,
Will I without thee go again, and do
All works which I was wont to do alone,   395
Before I knew thy face. Heaven bless thee, Boy!
Thy heart these two weeks has been beating fast
With many hopes; it should be so—yes—yes—
I knew that thou couldst never have a wish
To leave me, Luke; thou hast been bound to me   400
Only by links of love; when thou art gone,
What will be left to us!—But I forget
My purposes. Lay now the cornerstone,
As I requested; and hereafter, Luke,

7. I.e., mortgaged

When thou art gone away, should evil men   405
Be thy companions, think of me, my Son,
And of this moment; hither turn thy thoughts,
And God will strengthen thee; amid all fear
And all temptation, Luke, I pray that thou
May'st bear in mind the life thy Fathers lived,   410
Who, being innocent, did for that cause
Bestir them in good deeds. Now, fare thee well—
When thou return'st, thou in this place wilt see
A work which is not here: a covenant
'Twill be between us; but, whatever fate   415
Befall thee, I shall love thee to the last,
And bear thy memory with me to the grave."

The Shepherd ended here; and Luke stooped down,
And, as his Father had requested, laid
The first stone of the Sheepfold. At the sight   420
The old Man's grief broke from him; to his heart
He pressed his Son, he kisséd him and wept;
And to the house together they returned.
Hushed was that House in peace, or seeming peace
Ere the night fell; with morrow's dawn the Boy   425
Began his journey, and, when he had reached
The public way, he put on a bold face;
And all the neighbors, as he passed their doors,
Came forth with wishes and with farewell prayers,
That followed him till he was out of sight.   430

A good report did from their kinsman come,
Of Luke and his well-doing; and the Boy
Wrote loving letters, full of wondrous news,
Which, as the Housewife phrased it, were throughout
"The prettiest letters that were ever seen."   435
Both parents read them with rejoicing hearts.
So, many months passed on; and once again
The Shepherd went about his daily work
With confident and cheerful thoughts; and now
Sometimes when he could find a leisure hour   440
He to that valley took his way, and there
Wrought at the Sheepfold. Meantime Luke began
To slacken in his duty; and, at length,
He in the dissolute city gave himself
To evil courses; ignominy and shame   445
Fell on him, so that he was driven at last
To seek a hiding place beyond the seas.

There is a comfort in the strength of love;
'Twill make a thing endurable, which else
Would overset the brain, or break the heart;   450
I have conversed with more than one who well
Remember the old Man, and what he was

Years after he had heard this heavy news.
His bodily frame had been from youth to age
Of an unusual strength. Among the rocks   455
He went, and still looked up to sun and cloud,
And listened to the wind; and, as before,
Performed all kinds of labor for his sheep,
And for the land, his small inheritance.
And to that hollow dell from time to time   460
Did he repair, to build the Fold of which
His flock had need. 'Tis not forgotten yet
The pity which was then in every heart
For the old Man—and 'tis believed by all
That many and many a day he thither went,   465
And never lifted up a single stone.

There, by the Sheepfold, sometimes was he seen
Sitting alone, or with his faithful Dog,
Then old, beside him, lying at his feet.
The length of full seven years, from time to time,   470
He at the building of this Sheepfold wrought,
And left the work unfinished when he died.
Three years, or little more, did Isabel
Survive her Husband: at her death the estate
Was sold, and went into a stranger's hand.   475
The Cottage which was named The Evening Star
Is gone—the plowshare has been through the ground
On which it stood; great changes have been wrought
In all the neighborhood; yet the oak is left
That grew beside their door; and the remains   480
Of the unfinished Sheepfold may be seen
Beside the boisterous brook of Greenhead Ghyll.
Oct. 11–Dec. 9, 1800   1800

Written in March[2]

WHILE RESTING ON THE BRIDGE AT THE FOOT
OF BROTHER'S WATER

The cock is crowing,
The stream is flowing,
The small birds twitter,
The lake doth glitter,
The green field sleeps in the sun;   5
The oldest and youngest
Are at work with the strongest;
The cattle are grazing,
Their heads never raising;
There are forty feeding like one!   10

2. From Dorothy Wordsworth's *Jour-*
nals for April 16, 1802: "When we
came to Brother's Water I left William
sitting on the bridge. * * * When I
returned I found William writing a
poem descriptive of the sights and

Like an army defeated
The snow hath retreated,
And now doth fare ill
On the top of the bare hill;
The plowboy is whooping—anon—anon: 15
There's joy in the mountains;
There's life in the fountains;
Small clouds are sailing,
Blue sky prevailing;
The rain is over and gone!   20

1802   1807

Resolution and Independence[1]

1

There was a roaring in the wind all night;
The rain came heavily and fell in floods;
But now the sun is rising calm and bright;
The birds are singing in the distant woods;
Over his own sweet voice the stock dove broods;   5
The jay makes answer as the magpie chatters;
And all the air is filled with pleasant noise of waters.

2

All things that love the sun are out of doors;
The sky rejoices in the morning's birth;
The grass is bright with raindrops; on the moors   10
The hare is running races in her mirth;
And with her feet she from the plashy earth
Raises a mist; that, glittering in the sun,
Runs with her all the way, wherever she doth run.

3

I was a Traveler then upon the moor;   15
I saw the hare that raced about with joy;
I heard the woods and distant waters roar;
Or heard them not, as happy as a boy:
The pleasant season did my heart employ:

sounds we saw and heard. There was the gentle flowing of the stream, the glittering, lively lake * * * behind us, a flat pasture with forty-two cattle feeding. * * * William finished the poem before we got to the foot of Kirkstone."
1. "This old man I met a few hundred yards from my cottage at Town End, Grasmere [October 3, 1800]; and the account of him is taken from his own mouth. I was in the state of feeling described in the beginning of the poem, while crossing over Barton Fell from Mr. Clarkson's, at the foot of Ullswater, towards Askam. The image of the hare I then observed on the ridge of the Fell" (Wordsworth). Two years later the trivial events, recollected in tranquillity, were transformed into this splendid example of Wordsworth's spontaneous mythmaking. In stanzas 8 ff., under Wordsworth's visionary stare, the still old man, sent as "by peculiar grace," is metamorphosed into a sequence of figures both more and less than human, until in the end he modulates into the archetypal figure of the eternal and haunted wanderer, of whom Coleridge's Ancient Mariner had been the most recent embodiment. Unlike Coleridge's, however, Wordsworth's is a natural supernaturalism, for the old leech-gatherer remains stubbornly matter-of-fact, and the event realistic.

My old remembrances went from me wholly;   20
And all the ways of men, so vain and melancholy.

4

But, as it sometimes chanceth, from the might
Of joy in minds that can no further go,
As high as we have mounted in delight
In our dejection do we sink as low;   25
To me that morning did it happen so;
And fears and fancies thick upon me came;
Dim sadness—and blind thoughts, I knew not, nor could name.

5

I heard the skylark warbling in the sky;
And I bethought me of the playful hare: 30
Even such a happy Child of earth am I;
Even as these blissful creatures do I fare;
Far from the world I walk, and from all care;
But there may come another day to me—
Solitude, pain of heart, distress, and poverty.   35

6

My whole life I have lived in pleasant thought,
As if life's business were a summer mood;
As if all needful things would come unsought
To genial faith, still rich in genial good;
But how can he expect that others should   40
Build for him, sow for him, and at his call
Love him, who for himself will take no heed at all?

7

I thought of Chatterton,[2] the marvelous Boy,
The sleepless Soul that perished in his pride;
Of him who walked in glory and in joy   45
Following his plow, along the mountainside;[3]
By our own spirits are we deified:
We Poets in our youth begin in gladness,
But thereof come in the end despondency and madness.

8

Now, whether it were by peculiar grace,   50
A leading from above, a something given,
Yet it befell that, in this lonely place,
When I with these untoward thoughts had striven,
Beside a pool bare to the eye of heaven
I saw a Man before me unawares: 55
The oldest man he seemed that ever wore gray hairs.

9

As a huge stone is sometimes seen to lie
Couched on the bald top of an eminence;
Wonder to all who do the same espy,

---

2. Thomas Chatterton (1752–70), a
poet of great talent who, in his loneliness and dire poverty, poisoned himself at the age of 17 and so became the
prime Romantic symbol of neglected

young genius.
3. Robert Burns, also considered at
that time as a natural poet who died
young and poor, without adequate recognition.

By what means it could thither come, and whence; 60
So that it seems a thing endued with sense:
Like a sea beast crawled forth, that on a shelf
Of rock or sand reposeth, there to sun itself;

10

Such seemed this Man,⁴ not all alive nor dead,
Nor all asleep—in his extreme old age; 65
His body was bent double, feet and head
Coming together in life's pilgrimage;
As if some dire constraint of pain, or rage
Of sickness felt by him in times long past,
A more than human weight upon his frame had cast. 70

11

Himself he propped, limbs, body, and pale face,
Upon a long gray staff of shaven wood;
And, still as I drew near with gentle pace,
Upon the margin of that moorish flood
Motionless as a cloud that old Man stood, 75
That heareth not the loud winds when they call,
And moveth all together, if it move at all.

12

At length, himself unsettling, he the pond
Stirred with his staff, and fixedly did look
Upon the muddy water, which he conned, 80
As if he had been reading in a book;
And now a stranger's privilege I took,
And, drawing to his side, to him did say,
"This morning gives us promise of a glorious day."

13

A gentle answer did the old Man make, 85
In courteous speech which forth he slowly drew;
And him with further words I thus bespake,
"What occupation do you there pursue?
This is a lonesome place for one like you."
Ere he replied, a flash of mild surprise 90
Broke from the sable orbs of his yet-vivid eyes.

14

His words came feebly, from a feeble chest,
But each in solemn order followed each,
With something of a lofty utterance dressed—
Choice word and measured phrase, above the reach 95
Of ordinary men; a stately speech;
Such as grave livers⁵ do in Scotland use,
Religious men, who give to God and man their dues.

4. In Wordsworth's own analysis of this passage, he says that the stone is endowed with something of life, the sea beast is stripped of some of its life to assimilate it to the stone, and the old man divested of enough life and motion to make "the two objects unite and coalesce in just comparison"; he used the passage to demonstrate his theory of how the "conferring, the abstracting, and the modifying powers of the Imagination * * * are all brought into conjunction" (Preface to the *Poems* of 1815). Compare Coleridge's analysis of the imagination in *Biographia Literaria*, Chapter XIII.
5. Those who live gravely.

15

He told, that to these waters he had come
To gather leeches,[6] being old and poor:
Employment hazardous and wearisome!
And he had many hardships to endure:
From pond to pond he roamed, from moor to moor;
Housing, with God's good help, by choice or chance;
And in this way he gained an honest maintenance.   105

16

The old Man still stood talking by my side;
But now his voice to me was like a stream
Scarce heard; nor word from word could I divide;
And the whole body of the Man did seem
Like one whom I had met with in a dream;   110
Or like a man from some far region sent,
To give me human strength, by apt admonishment.

17

My former thoughts returned: the fear that kills;
And hope that is unwilling to be fed;
Cold, pain, and labor, and all fleshly ills;   115
And mighty Poets in their misery dead.
—Perplexed, and longing to be comforted,
My question eagerly did I renew,
"How is it that you live, and what is it you do?"

18

He with a smile did then his words repeat;   120
And said that, gathering leeches, far and wide
He traveled, stirring thus about his feet
The waters of the pools where they abide.
"Once I could meet with them on every side,
But they have dwindled long by slow decay;   125
Yet still I persevere, and find them where I may."

19

While he was talking thus, the lonely place,
The old Man's shape, and speech—all troubled me:
In my mind's eye I seemed to see him pace
About the weary moors continually,   130
Wandering about alone and silently.
While I these thoughts within myself pursued,
He, having made a pause, the same discourse renewed.

20

And soon with this he other matter blended,   135
Cheerfully uttered, with demeanor kind,
But stately in the main; and, when he ended,
I could have laughed myself to scorn to find
In that decrepit Man so firm a mind.
"God," said I, "be my help and stay[7] secure;   140
I'll think of the Leech Gatherer on the lonely moor!"

May 3–July 4, 1802   1807

6. Leeches were used to draw blood for curative purposes. A leech-gatherer, barelegged in shallow water, stirred the water to rouse them, and then picked them off his skin.
7. Support (a noun).

The Green Linnet[1]

Beneath these fruit-tree boughs that shed
Their snow-white blossoms on my head,
With brightest sunshine round me spread
    Of spring's unclouded weather,
In this sequestered nook how sweet   5
To sit upon my orchard seat!
And birds and flowers once more to greet,
    My last year's friends together.

One have I marked, the happiest guest
In all this covert of the blest: 10
Hail to thee, far above the rest
    In joy of voice and pinion!
Thou, Linnet! in thy green array,
Presiding Spirit here today,
Dost lead the revels of the May;   15
    And this is thy dominion.

While birds, and butterflies, and flowers,
Make all one band of paramours,
Thou, ranging up and down the bowers,
    Art sole in thy employment: 20
A Life, a Presence like the Air,
Scattering thy gladness without care,
Too blest with any one to pair;
    Thyself thy own enjoyment.

Amid yon tuft of hazel trees,   25
That twinkle to the gusty breeze,
Behold him perched in ecstasies,
    Yet seeming still to hover;
There! where the flutter of his wings
Upon his back and body flings   30
Shadows and sunny glimmerings,
    That cover him all over.

My dazzled sight he oft deceives,
A brother of the dancing leaves;
Then flits, and from the cottage eaves   35
    Pours forth his song in gushes;
As if by that exulting strain
He mocked and treated with disdain
The voiceless Form he chose to feign,
    While fluttering in the bushes.   40

1803   1807

1. Coleridge used the last two stanzas to demonstrate Wordsworth's "perfect truth of nature in his images and descriptions." The extent and particularity of this description, however, are rare in Wordsworth, despite his reputation as a "nature poet."

Yew Trees[1]

There is a Yew Tree, pride of Lorton Vale,
Which to this day stands single, in the midst
Of its own darkness, as it stood of yore:
Not loath to furnish weapons for the bands
Of Umfraville or Percy ere they marched   5
To Scotland's heaths; or those that crossed the sea
And drew their sounding bows at Azincour,
Perhaps at earlier Crecy, or Poictiers.
Of vast circumference and gloom profound
This solitary Tree! a living thing   10
Produced too slowly ever to decay;
Of form and aspect too magnificent
To be destroyed. But worthier still of note
Are those fraternal Four of Borrowdale,
Joined in one solemn and capacious grove;   15
Huge trunks! and each particular trunk a growth
Of intertwisted fibers serpentine
Up-coiling, and inveterately convolved;
Nor uninformed with Phantasy, and looks
That threaten the profane—a pillared shade,   20
Upon whose grassless floor of red-brown hue,
By sheddings from the pining umbrage[2] tinged
Perennially—beneath whose sable roof
Of boughs, as if for festal purpose decked
With unrejoicing berries—ghostly Shapes   25
May meet at noontide; Fear and trembling Hope,
Silence and Foresight; Death the Skeleton
And Time the Shadow—there to celebrate,
As in a natural temple scattered o'er
With altars undisturbed of mossy stone,   30
United worship; or in mute repose
To lie, and listen to the mountain flood
Murmuring from Glaramara's[3] inmost caves.

ca. 1803   1815

I Wandered Lonely As a Cloud[4]

I wandered lonely as a cloud
That floats on high o'er vales and hills,

---

1. An evergreen tree; its wood was used for the bows which won the English victories mentioned in the poem, in the late medieval wars against Scotland and France. In the *Biographia Literaria*, Chapter XXII, Coleridge cited lines 13 ff. as a prime example of the faculty of imagination, in which Wordsworth "stands nearest of all modern writers to Shakespeare and Milton; and yet in a kind perfectly unborrowed and his own."
2. Foliage that casts a shade.
3. Mountain rising from Borrowdale valley, in the Lake Country.
4. The last stanza describes the kind of recollection in tranquillity from which this poem arose, two years after

When all at once I saw a crowd,
A host, of golden daffodils;
Beside the lake, beneath the trees,   5
Fluttering and dancing in the breeze.

Continuous as the stars that shine
And twinkle on the milky way,
They stretched in never-ending line
Along the margin of a bay: 10
Ten thousand saw I at a glance,
Tossing their heads in sprightly dance.

The waves beside them danced; but they
Outdid the sparkling waves in glee;
A poet could not but be gay,   15
In such a jocund company;
I gazed—and gazed—but little thought
What wealth the show to me had brought:

For oft, when on my couch I lie
In vacant or in pensive mood,   20
They flash upon that inward eye
Which is the bliss of solitude;
And then my heart with pleasure fills,
And dances with the daffodils.

1804   1807

My Heart Leaps Up

My heart leaps up when I behold
    A rainbow in the sky:
So was it when my life began;
So is it now I am a man;
So be it when I shall grow old,   5
    Or let me die!
The Child is father of the Man;
And I could wish my days to be
Bound each to each by natural piety.[1]

March 26, 1802   1807

the original experience. This event
Dorothy Wordsworth described in her
Journals for April 15, 1802; the occasion was a walk past the shore of
Ullswater: "I never saw daffodils so
beautiful. They grew among the mossy
stones about and about them; some
rested their heads upon these stones, as
on a pillow, for weariness; and the
rest tossed and reeled and danced, and

seemed as if they verily laughed with
the wind, that blew upon them over
the lake; they looked so gay, ever
glancing, ever changing."
1. As distinguished from piety based
on the Scriptures; a continuing responsiveness to the miracle of ordinary
things is the religious sentiment that
binds Wordsworth's maturity to his
childhood.

Ode: Intimations of Immortality   "This was composed dur-
ing my residence at Town End, Grasmere; two years at least passed be-

tween the writing of the four first stanzas and the remaining part. To the attentive and competent reader the whole sufficiently explains itself; but there may be no harm in adverting here to particular feelings or *experiences* of my own mind on which the structure of the poem partly rests. Nothing was more difficult for me in childhood than to admit the notion of death as a state applicable to my own being. I have said elsewhere

> —A simple child,
> That lightly draws its breath,
> And feels its life in every limb,
> What should it know of death!—

But it was not so much from [feelings] of animal vivacity that *my* difficulty came as from a sense of the indomitableness of the spirit within me. I used to brood over the stories of Enoch and Elijah, and almost to persuade myself that, whatever might become of others, I should be translated, in something of the same way, to heaven. With a feeling congenial to this, I was often unable to think of external things as having external existence, and I communed with all that I saw as something not apart from, but inherent in, my own immaterial nature. Many times while going to school have I grasped at a wall or tree to recall myself from this abyss of idealism to the reality. At that time I was afraid of such processes. In later periods of life I have deplored, as we have all reason to do, a subjugation of an opposite character, and have rejoiced over the remembrances, as is expressed in the lines—

> Obstinate questionings
> Of sense and outward things,
> Fallings from us, vanishings; etc.

To that dreamlike vividness and splendor which invest objects of sight in childhood, everyone, I believe, if he would look back, could bear testimony, and I need not dwell upon it here: but having in the Poem regarded it as presumptive evidence of a prior state of existence, I think it right to protest against a conclusion, which has given pain to some good and pious persons, that I meant to inculcate such a belief. It is far too shadowy a notion to be recommended to faith, as more than an element in our instincts of immortality. But let us bear in mind that, though the idea is not advanced in revelation, there is nothing there to contradict it, and the fall of Man presents an analogy in its favor. Accordingly, a pre-existent state has entered into the popular creeds of many nations; and, among all persons acquainted with classic literature, is known as an ingredient in Platonic philosophy. Archimedes said that he could move the world if he had a point whereon to rest his machine. Who has not felt the same aspirations as regards the world of his own mind? Having to wield some of its elements when I was impelled to write this Poem on the 'Immortality of the Soul,' I took hold of the notion of pre-existence as having sufficient foundation in humanity for authorizing me to make for my purpose the best use of it I could as a Poet" (Wordsworth).

As Wordsworth says, Plato held the doctrine that the soul is immortal and exists separately from the body both before birth and after death. But while the *Ode* proposes that the soul only gradually loses "the vision splendid" after birth, Plato maintained the contrary: that the knowledge of the eternal Ideas, which the soul had acquired by direct acquaintance, is totally lost at the instant of birth, and must be gradually "recollected" by philosophical discipline in the course of this life (*Phaedo* 73–77). Wordsworth's concept resembles more closely the view of some Neo-Platonists that the glory of the unborn soul is gradually quenched by its descent into the darkness of matter.

Wordsworth was troubled by objections to the Christian heterodoxy of this apparent claim for the pre-existence, in addition to the orthodox belief in the survival, of the soul. He insisted that he did not intend to assert this as doctrine, but only to use it as a premise, a poetic postulate, not necessarily to be credited outside the poem, enabling him to deal "as a poet" with an experience to which everyone, as he says, "if he would look back, could bear testimony." The basic problem is a universal human one: that the loss of youth involves the loss of a freshness and radiance investing all experience. Coleridge's *Dejection: An Ode,* which he wrote after he had heard the first four stanzas of Wordsworth's poem, employs a similar figurative technique for a comparable, though more devastating, experience of loss. As with all poems so large and rich as this one, there are divergent interpretations of its purport, emphases, and organization; but almost all commentators agree that this poem is the equal of the best in the difficult and elevated form of the irregular Pindaric ode. The Catholic poet G. M. Hopkins remarked: "For my part I should think St. George and St. Thomas of Canterbury wore roses in heaven for England's sake on the day that *Ode,* not without their intercession, was penned."

The original version of this poem had as its title only "Ode," and then as epigraph *"Paulo maiora canamus"* ("Let us sing of somewhat higher things") from Virgil's *Eclogue IV.*

Ode

INTIMATIONS OF IMMORTALITY FROM RECOLLECTIONS OF EARLY CHILDHOOD

The Child is father of the Man;
And I could wish my days to be
Bound each to each by natural piety.[1]

1

There was a time when meadow, grove, and stream,
The earth, and every common sight,
        To me did seem
        Apparelled in celestial light,
The glory and the freshness of a dream.
It is not now as it hath been of yore—
        Turn whereso'er I may,
        By night or day,
The things which I have seen I now can see no more.   5

1. The concluding lines of Wordsworth's *My Heart Leaps Up.*

2

The Rainbow comes and goes, 10
And lovely is the Rose,
The Moon doth with delight
Look round her when the heavens are bare,
Waters on a starry night
Are beautiful and fair; 15
The sunshine is a glorious birth;
But yet I know, where'er I go,
That there hath passed away a glory from the earth.

3

Now, while the birds thus sing a joyous song,
And while the young lambs bound 20
As to the tabor's sound,[2]
To me alone there came a thought of grief:
A timely utterance[3] gave that thought relief,
And I again am strong:
The cataracts blow their trumpets from the steep; 25
No more shall grief of mine the season wrong;
I hear the Echoes through the mountains throng,
The Winds come to me from the fields of sleep,[4]
And all the earth is gay;
Land and sea 30
Give themselves up to jollity,
And with the heart of May
Doth every Beast keep holiday—
Thou Child of Joy,
Shout round me, let me hear thy shouts, thou happy 35
Shepherd-boy!

4

Ye blessed Creatures, I have heard the call
Ye to each other make; I see
The heavens laugh with you in your jubilee;
My heart is at your festival, 40
My head hath its coronal,[5]
The fullness of your bliss, I feel—I feel it all.
Oh, evil day! if I were sullen
While Earth herself is adorning,
This sweet May morning, 45
And the Children are culling
On every side,

2. A tabor is a small drum often used to beat time for dancing.
3. Perhaps *My Heart Leaps Up*, perhaps *Resolution and Independence*, perhaps not a poem at all.
4. Of the many suggested interpretations, the simplest is "from the fields where they were sleeping." Wordsworth often associated a rising wind with the revival of spirit and poetic inspiration; see, e.g., the opening passage of *The Prelude*.
5. Circlet of wild flowers, with which the shepherd boys trimmed their hats in May.

In a thousand valleys far and wide,
    Fresh flowers; while the sun shines warm,
And the Babe leaps up on his Mother's arm—   50
    I hear, I hear, with joy I hear!
    —But there's a Tree, of many, one,
A single Field which I have looked upon,
Both of them speak of something that is gone:
        The Pansy at my feet   55
        Doth the same tale repeat:
Whither is fled the visionary gleam?
Where is it now, the glory and the dream?

         5

Our birth is but a sleep and a forgetting:
The Soul that rises with us, our life's Star,[6]   60
       Hath had elsewhere its setting,
         And cometh from afar:
       Not in entire forgetfulness,
       And not in utter nakedness,
But trailing clouds of glory do we come   65
       From God, who is our home:
Heaven lies about us in our infancy!
Shades of the prison-house begin to close
        Upon the growing Boy
        But he   70
Beholds the light, and whence it flows,
        He sees it in his joy;
The Youth, who daily farther from the east
        Must travel, still is Nature's Priest,
        And by the vision splendid   75
        Is on his way attended;
At length the Man perceives it die away,
And fade into the light of common day.

         6

Earth fills her lap with pleasures of her own;
Yearnings she hath in her own natural kind,   80
And, even with something of a Mother's mind,
       And no unworthy aim,
       The homely[7] Nurse doth all she can
To make her foster child, her Inmate Man,
       Forget the glories he hath known,   85
And that imperial palace whence he came.

         7

Behold the Child among his newborn blisses,
A six-years' Darling of a pygmy size!
See, where 'mid work of his own hand he lies,
Fretted[8] by sallies of his mother's kisses,   90
With light upon him from his father's eyes!

---

6. **The sun, as metaphor for the soul.**   friendly."
7. In the old sense, "simple and   8. Checkered over.

See, at his feet, some little plan or chart,
Some fragment from his dream of human life,
Shaped by himself with newly-learned art;
  A wedding or a festival,   95
  A mourning or a funeral;
   And this hath now his heart,
   And unto this he frames his song;
    Then will he fit his tongue
To dialogues of business, love, or strife;   100
   But it will not be long
   Ere this be thrown aside,
   And with new joy and pride
The little Actor cons another part;
Filling from time to time his "humorous stage"[9]   105
With all the Persons, down to palsied Age,
That Life brings with her in her equipage;
   As if his whole vocation
   Were endless imitation.

8

Thou, whose exterior semblance doth belie   110
   Thy Soul's immensity;
Thou best Philosopher, who yet dost keep
Thy heritage, thou Eye among the blind,
That, deaf and silent, read'st the eternal deep,
Haunted forever by the eternal mind—   115
   Mighty Prophet! Seer blest!
   On whom those truths do rest,
Which we are toiling all our lives to find,
In darkness lost, the darkness of the grave;
Thou, over whom thy Immortality   120
Broods like the Day, a Master o'er a Slave,
A Presence which is not to be put by;
Thou little Child, yet glorious in the might
Of heaven-born freedom on thy being's height,
Why with such earnest pains dost thou provoke   125
The years to bring the inevitable yoke,
Thus blindly with thy blessedness at strife?
Full soon thy Soul shall have her earthly freight,
And custom lie upon thee with a weight,
Heavy as frost, and deep almost as life!   130

9

   O joy! that in our embers
   Is something that doth live,
   That nature yet remembers
   What was so fugitive!
The thought of our past years in me doth breed   135
Perpetual benediction: not indeed
For that which is most worthy to be blest;
Delight and liberty, the simple creed

9. From a sonnet by Samuel Daniel, Elizabethan poet. In Daniel's age, "humerous" meant "capricious," and also referred to the various characters and temperaments ("humors") represented in drama.

Of Childhood, whether busy or at rest,
With new-fledged hope still fluttering in his breast— 140
     Not for these I raise
     The song of thanks and praise;
But for those obstinate questionings
Of sense and outward things,
Fallings from us, vanishings; 145
Blank misgivings of a Creature
Moving about in worlds not realized,[1]
High instincts before which our mortal **Nature**
Did tremble like a guilty Thing surprised;
     But for those first affections, 150
     Those shadowy recollections,
     Which, be they what they may,
Are yet the fountain light of all our day,
Are yet a master light of all our seeing;
     Uphold us, cherish, and have power to **make** 155
Our noisy years seem moments in the being
Of the eternal Silence: truths that wake,
     To perish never;
Which neither listlessness, nor mad endeavor,
     Nor Man nor Boy, 160
Nor all that is at enmity with joy,
Can utterly abolish or destroy!
     Hence in a season of calm weather
     Though inland far we be,
Our Souls have sight of that immortal sea 165
     Which brought us hither,
     Can in a moment travel thither,
And see the Children sport upon the shore,
And hear the mighty waters rolling evermore.

10

Then sing, ye Birds, sing, sing a joyous song! 170
     And let the young Lambs bound
     As to the tabor's sound!
We in thought will join your throng,
     Ye that pipe and ye that play,
     Ye that through your hearts today 175
     Feel the gladness of the May!
What though the radiance which was once so bright
Be now forever taken from my sight,
     Though nothing can bring back the hour
Of splendor in the grass, of glory in the flower; 180
     We will grieve not, rather find
     Strength in what remains behind;
     In the primal sympathy
     Which having been must ever be;
     In the soothing thoughts that spring 185
     Out of human suffering;

1. Not seeming real; see Wordsworth's comment in the headnote to the *Ode*.

In the faith that looks through death,
In years that bring the philosophic mind.

11

And O, ye Fountains, Meadows, Hills, and Groves,
Forebode not any severing of our loves! 190
Yet in my heart of hearts I feel your might;
I only have relinquished one delight
To live beneath your more habitual sway.
I love the Brooks which down their channels fret,
Even more than when I tripped lightly as they; 195
The innocent brightness of a newborn Day
      Is lovely yet;
The clouds that gather round the setting sun
Do take a sober coloring from an eye
That hath kept watch o'er man's mortality; 200
Another race hath been, and other palms are won[2].
Thanks to the human heart by which we live,
Thanks to its tenderness, its joys, and fears,
To me the meanest flower that blows can give
Thoughts that do often lie too deep for tears. 205

1802–4   1807

Ode to Duty[1]

Jam non consilio bonus, sed more eo perductus, ut non tantum recte facere possim, sed nisi recte facere non possim.

Stern Daughter of the Voice of God![2]
O Duty! if that name thou love

2. In Greece, foot races were often run for the prize of a branch or wreath of palm.

1. "This Ode * * * is on the model of Gray's *Ode to Adversity* which is copied from Horace's *Ode to Fortune.* Many and many a time have I been twitted by my wife and sister for having forgotten this dedication of myself to the stern lawgiver" (Wordsworth).

This poem merits its reputation as a departure from Wordsworth's earlier poems and ideas. In it he abandons the descriptive-meditative pattern of his *Tintern Abbey* and *Ode: Intimations of Immortality* and reverts to the standard 18th-century form of an ode addressed to a personified abstraction. The moral idea of this poem also represents Wordsworth's reversion from his youthful reliance on natural impulse to a more orthodox ethical tradition. The poem makes no reference to that "Nature" which earlier had constituted for Wordsworth "both law and impulse," and, in *Tintern Abbey*, had been called "The guide, the guardian of my heart, and soul / Of all my moral being." The Duty, "Stern

Daughter of the Voice of God," to which Wordsworth now commends himself, is the same concept as Milton's "right reason," God's representative in man, which Christian humanists had developed by combining the stern morality of the pagan Stoics with the concept of the inner voice of the Christian "conscience." (In one MS. variant Wordsworth described Duty as "sent from God" to keep us to the road "which conscience hath pronounced the best.")

The epigraph is translated, "Now I am not good by taking thought, but have been brought by habit to such a point that it is not so much that I am able to act rightly, but that I am unable to act except rightly." Added in 1837, it is an adaptation from *Moral Epistles* CXX.10 by Seneca (4 B.C.–A.D. 65), Stoic philosopher and writer of tragedies.

2. Cf. *Paradise Lost* IX.652–54: "God so commanded, and left that Command / Sole Daughter of his voice; the rest, we live / Law to ourselves, our Reason is our Law."

Who are a light to guide, a rod
To check the erring, and reprove;
Thou, who art victory and law
When empty terrors overawe;
From vain temptations dost set free;
And calm'st the weary strife of frail humanity!

There are who ask not if thine eye
Be on them; who, in love and truth,
Where no misgiving is, rely
Upon the genial sense[3] of youth:
Glad Hearts! without reproach or blot;
Who do thy work, and know it not:
Oh! if through confidence misplaced
They fail, thy saving arms, dread Power! around them cast.

Serene will be our days and bright,
And happy will our nature be,
When love is an unerring light,
And joy its own security.
And they a blissful course may hold
Even now, who, not unwisely bold,
Live in the spirit of this creed;
Yet seek thy firm support, according to their need.

I, loving freedom, and untried,
No sport of every random gust,
Yet being to myself a guide,
Too blindly have reposed my trust;
And oft, when in my heart was heard
Thy timely mandate, I deferred
The task, in smoother walks to stray;
But thee I now would serve more strictly, if I may.

Through no disturbance of my soul,
Or strong compunction[4] in me wrought,
I supplicate for thy control;
But in the quietness of thought:
Me this unchartered freedom tires;
I feel the weight of chance desires:
My hopes no more must change their name,
I long for a repose that ever is the same.

Stern Lawgiver! yet thou dost wear
The Godhead's most benignant grace;
Nor know we anything so fair
As is the smile upon thy face:
Flowers laugh before thee on their beds
And fragrance in thy footing treads;

5

10

15

20

25

30

35

40

45

3. Innate good nature.
4. In the older sense, "sting of con-   science," "remorse."

Thou dost preserve the stars from wrong;[5]
And the most ancient heavens, through thee, are fresh and strong.

To humbler functions, awful Power!
I call thee: I myself commend
Unto thy guidance from this hour;   50
Oh, let my weakness have an end!
Give unto me, made lowly wise,[6]
The spirit of self-sacrifice;
The confidence of reason give;   55
And in the light of truth thy Bondman let me live!
ca. 1804   1807

The Solitary Reaper[1]

Behold her, single in the field,
Yon solitary Highland Lass!
Reaping and singing by herself;
Stop here, or gently pass!
Alone she cuts and binds the grain,   5
And sings a melancholy strain;
O listen! for the Vale profound
Is overflowing with the sound.

No Nightingale did ever chaunt
More welcome notes to weary bands   10
Of travelers in some shady haunt,
Among Arabian sands;
A voice so thrilling ne'er was heard
In springtime from the Cuckoo bird,
Breaking the silence of the seas   15
Among the farthest Hebrides.

Will no one tell me what she sings?[2]—
Perhaps the plaintive numbers flow
For old, unhappy, far-off things,
And battles long ago;   20
Or is it some more humble lay,

5. Wordsworth's parallel between the moral law and the laws governing the motion of the stars is illuminated by Kant's famous statement: "Two things fill the mind with ever new and increasing admiration and awe * * * the starry heavens above and the moral law within."
6. Another echo from Milton, whose Christian-humanist ethic pervades this ode. The angel Raphael had advised Adam (*Paradise Lost* VIII.173–74), "Be lowly wise: / Think only what concerns thee and thy being."
1. One of the rare poems not based on Wordsworth's own experience. Wordsworth tells us that it was suggested by a passage in Thomas Wilkinson's *Tour of Scotland* (1824), which he had seen in MS.: "Passed by a female who was reaping alone, she sung in Erse [the Gaelic language of Scotland] as she bended over her sickle, the sweetest human voice I ever heard. Her strains were tenderly melancholy, and felt delicious long after they were heard no more."
2. Wordsworth did not understand Erse, the language in which she sings.

Familiar matter of today?
Some natural sorrow, loss, or pain,
That has been, and may be again?

Whate'er the theme, the Maiden sang   25
As if her song could have no ending;
I saw her singing at her work,
And o'er the sickle bending—
I listened, motionless and still;
And, as I mounted up the hill,   30
The music in my heart I bore,
Long after it was heard no more.

November 5, 1805   1807

Elegiac Stanzas

SUGGESTED BY A PICTURE OF PEELE CASTLE, IN A STORM, PAINTED BY SIR GEORGE BEAUMONT[1]

I was thy neighbor once, thou rugged Pile!
Four summer weeks I dwelt in sight of thee:
I saw thee every day; and all the while
Thy Form was sleeping on a glassy sea.

So pure the sky, so quiet was the air!   5
So like, so very like, was day to day!
Whene'er I looked, thy Image still was there;
It trembled, but it never passed away.

How perfect was the calm! it seemed no sleep;
No mood, which season takes away, or brings: 10
I could have fancied that the mighty Deep
Was even the gentlest of all gentle Things.

Ah! then, if mine had been the Painter's hand,
To express what then I saw; and add the gleam,
The light that never was, on sea or land,   15
The consecration, and the Poet's dream;

I would have planted thee, thou hoary Pile
Amid a world how different from this!
Beside a sea that could not cease to smile;
On tranquil land, beneath a sky of bliss.   20

Thou shouldst have seemed a treasure house divine
Of peaceful years; a chronicle of heaven—
Of all the sunbeams that did ever shine
The very sweetest had to thee been given.

1. Sir George Beaumont, a wealthy landscape painter, was Wordsworth's patron and close friend. Peele Castle is on a promontory opposite Rampside, Lancashire, where Wordsworth had spent a month in 1794, eleven years before he saw Beaumont's painting.

A Picture had it been of lasting ease,   25
Elysium[2] quiet, without toil or strife;
No motion but the moving tide, a breeze,
Or merely silent Nature's breathing life.

Such, in the fond illusion of my heart,
Such Picture would I at that time have made,   30
And seen the soul of truth in every part,
A steadfast peace that might not be betrayed

So once it would have been—'tis so no more;
I have submitted to a new control:
A power is gone, which nothing can restore;   35
A deep distress hath humanized my Soul.[3]

Not for a moment could I now behold
A smiling sea, and be what I have been:
The feeling of my loss will ne'er be old;
This, which I know, I speak with mind serene.   40

Then, Beaumont, Friend! who would have been the Friend,
If he had lived, of him whom I deplore,
This work of thine I blame not, but commend;
This sea in anger, and that dismal shore.

O 'tis a passionate Work!—yet wise and well,   45
Well chosen is the spirit that is here;
That Hulk which labors in the deadly swell,
This rueful sky, this pageantry of fear!

And this huge Castle, standing here sublime,
I love to see the look with which it braves,   50
Cased in the unfeeling armor of old time,
The lightning, the fierce wind, and trampling waves.

Farewell, farewell the heart that lives alone,
Housed in a dream, at distance from the Kind![4]
Such happiness, wherever it be known,   55
Is to be pitied; for 'tis surely blind.

But welcome fortitude, and patient cheer,
And frequent sights of what is to be borne!
Such sights, or worse, as are before me here.—
Not without hope we suffer and we mourn.   60
1805   1807

2. Elysium, in classical mythology, was the peaceful place where those favored by the gods dwelled after death.
3. Captain John Wordsworth, Wil-

liam's brother, had been drowned in a shipwreck on February 5, 1805. He is referred to in lines 41–42.
4. Mankind.

Sonnets

Composed upon Westminster Bridge, September 3, 1802[1]

Earth has not anything to show more fair:
Dull would he be of soul who could pass by
A sight so touching in its majesty;
This City now doth, like a garment, wear
The beauty of the morning; silent, bare,⁣   5
Ships, towers, domes, theaters, and temples lie
Open unto the fields, and to the sky;
All bright and glittering in the smokeless air.
Never did sun more beautifully steep
In his first splendor, valley, rock, or hill;⁣   10
Ne'er saw I, never felt, a calm so deep!
The river glideth at his own sweet will:
Dear God! the very houses seem asleep;
And all that mighty heart is lying still!

1802   1807

It Is a Beauteous Evening[2]

It is a beauteous evening, calm and free,
The holy time is quiet as a Nun
Breathless with adoration; the broad sun
Is sinking down in its tranquility;
The gentleness of heaven broods o'er the Sea:⁣   5
Listen! the mighty Being is awake,
And doth with his eternal motion make
A sound like thunder—everlastingly.
Dear Child! dear Girl! that walkest with me here,
If thou appear untouched by solemn thought,⁣   10
Thy nature is not therefore less divine:
Thou liest in Abraham's bosom[3] all the year,
And worship'st at the Temple's inner shrine,
God being with thee when we know it not.

1802   1807

1. "Composed on the roof of a coach, on my way to France" (Wordsworth). The date of this trip, however, was not September 3, but July 31, 1802. The conflict of feelings attending Wordsworth's brief return to France, where he had once been a revolutionist and the lover of Annette Vallon, evoked a number of personal and political sonnets, among them the three which follow.

2. "This was composed on the beach near Calais in the autumn of 1802" (Wordsworth). The girl walking with Wordsworth is Caroline, his natural daughter by Annette Vallon.
3. Where the souls destined for heaven rest after death. Luke xvi.22: "And it came to pass, that the beggar died, and was carried by the angels into Abraham's bosom."

Composed in the Valley Near Dover, On the Day of Landing

Here, on our native soil, we breathe once more.
The cock that crows, the smoke that curls, that sound
Of bells—those boys who in yon meadow ground
In white-sleeved shirts are playing; and the roar
Of the waves breaking on the chalky shore—   5
All, all are English. Oft have I looked round
With joy in Kent's green vales; but never found
Myself so satisfied in heart before.
Europe is yet in bonds; but let that pass,
Thought for another moment. Thou art free   10
My Country! and 'tis joy enough and pride
For one hour's perfect bliss, to tread the grass
Of England once again, and hear and see,
With such a dear Companion[4] at my side.

August 30, 1802   1807

London, 1802[5]

Milton! thou shouldst be living at this hour:
England hath need of thee: she is a fen
Of stagnant waters: altar, sword, and pen,
Fireside, the heroic wealth of hall and bower,
Have forefeited their ancient English dower   5
Of inward happiness. We are selfish men;
Oh! raise us up, return to us again;
And give us manners, virtue, freedom, power.
Thy soul was like a Star, and dwelt apart;
Thou hadst a voice whose sound was like the sea: 10
Pure as the naked heavens, majestic, free,
So didst thou travel on life's common way,
In cheerful godliness; and yet thy heart
The lowliest duties on herself did lay.

September, 1802   1807

The World Is Too Much with Us

The world is too much with us; late and soon,
Getting and spending, we lay waste our powers;

---

4. Dorothy Wordsworth.
5. One of a series "written immediately after my return from France to London, when I could not but be struck, as here described, with the vanity and parade of our own country * * * as contrasted with the quiet, and I may say the desolation, that the revolution had produced in France" (Wordsworth).

Little we see in Nature that is ours;
We have given our hearts away, a sordid boon![6]
This Sea that bares her bosom to the moon,   5
The winds that will be howling at all hours,
And are up-gathered now like sleeping flowers,
For this, for everything, we are out of tune;
It moves us not.—Great God! I'd rather be
A Pagan suckled in a creed outworn;   10
So might I, standing on this pleasant lea,
Have glimpses that would make me less forlorn;
Have sight of Proteus rising from the sea;
Or hear old Triton blow his wreathéd horn.[7]

1807

Surprised by Joy[8]

Surprised by joy—impatient as the Wind
I turned to share the transport—Oh! with whom
But thee, deep buried in the silent tomb,
That spot which no vicissitude can find?
Love, faithful love, recalled thee to my mind—   5
But how could I forget thee? Through what power,
Even for the least division of an hour,
Have I been so beguiled as to be blind
To my most grievous loss!—That thought's return
Was the worst pang that sorrow ever bore,   10
Save one, one only, when I stood forlorn,
Knowing my heart's best treasure was no more;
That neither present time, nor years unborn
Could to my sight that heavenly face restore.

1815

Composed by the Side of Grasmere Lake

Clouds, lingering yet, extend in solid bars
Through the gray west; and lo! these waters, steeled
By breezeless air to smoothest polish, yield
A vivid repetition of the stars;
Jove, Venus, and the ruddy crest of Mars[9]   5
Amid his fellows beauteously revealed
At happy distance from earth's groaning field,
Where ruthless mortals wage incessant wars.
Is it a mirror?—or the nether Sphere[1]

6. Gift; it is the act of giving the heart away that is sordid.
7. Proteus: an old man of the sea who (in the *Odyssey*) can assume a variety of shapes. Triton: a sea deity, usually represented as blowing on a conch shell.
8. "This was in fact suggested by my daughter Catharine, long after her death" (Wordsworth). Catharine Wordsworth died June 4, 1812, at the age of 4.
9. Roman god of war.
1. The earth, region below the sphere of the moon.

Opening to view the abyss in which she feeds
Her own calm fires?—But list! a voice is near;
Great Pan himself low-whispering through the reeds,
"Be thankful, thou; for, if unholy deeds
Ravage the world, tranquillity is here!"

1807   1819

Afterthought[2]

I thought of thee,[3] my partner and my guide,
As being passed away.—Vain sympathies!
For, backward, Duddon! as I cast my eyes,
I see what was, and is, and will abide;
Still glides the Stream, and shall forever glide;   5
The Form remains, the Function never dies;
While we, the brave, the mighty, and the wise,
We Men, who in our morn of youth defied
The elements, must vanish—be it so!
Enough, if something from our hands have power   10
To live, and act, and serve the future hour;
And if, as toward the silent tomb we go,
Through love, through hope, and faith's transcendant dower,[4]
We feel that we are greater than we know.

1820

Mutability[5]

From low to high doth dissolution climb,
And sink from high to low, along a scale
Of awful notes, whose concord shall not fail;
A musical but melancholy chime,
Which they can hear who meddle not with crime,   5
Nor avarice, nor over-anxious care.
Truth fails not; but her outward forms that bear
The longest date do melt like frosty rime,
That in the morning whitened hill and plain
And is no more; drop like the tower sublime   10

2. The last in the sonnet sequence *The River Duddon*, which traces the course of the river from its source in the Lake Country to its terminus in the Irish Sea. The description of the course of a river, combined with the incidental meditations which the changing scene evokes, had been a common poetic formula in the "local poems" of the 18th century, but Wordsworth employs it here for a memorable state- ment of one of his reiterated topics: the flow of water as an emblem of permanence in change.
3. I.e., the river.
4. Endowment, gift.
5. This great sonnet interrupts a rather pedestrian sequence, *Ecclesiastical Sonnets*, dealing with the history and ceremonies of the church in England.

Of yesterday, which royally did wear
His crown of weeds, but could not even sustain
Some casual shout that broke the silent air,
Or the unimaginable touch of Time.

1821   1822

Steamboats, Viaducts, and Railways[6]

Motions and Means, on land and sea at war
With old poetic feeling, not for this,
Shall ye, by Poets even, be judged amiss!
Nor shall your presence, howsoe'er it mar
The loveliness of Nature, prove a bar   5
To the Mind's gaining that prophetic sense
Of future change, that point of vision, whence
May be discovered what in soul ye are.
In spite of all that beauty may disown
In your harsh features, Nature doth embrace   10
Her lawful offspring in Man's art; and Time,
Pleased with your triumphs o'er his brother Space,
Accepts from your bold hands the proffered crown
Of hope, and smiles on you with cheer sublime.

1833   1835

Extempore Effusion upon the Death of James Hogg[1]

When first, descending from the moorlands,
I saw the Stream of Yarrow[2] glide
Along a bare and open valley,
The Ettrick Shepherd[3] was my guide.

When last along its banks I wandered,   5
Through groves that had begun to shed

6. In late middle age Wordsworth demonstrates, as he had predicted in the Preface to *Lyrical Ballads*, that the poet will assimilate to his subject' matter the "material revolution" produced by science. Unlike most poets, furthermore, he boldly accepts as evidences of man's progress even the unlovely encroachments of technology upon his beloved natural scene.
1. Wordsworth's niece relates how Wordsworth was deeply moved by finding unexpectedly in a newspaper the account of the death of the poet James Hogg. "Half an hour afterwards he came into the room where the ladies were sitting and asked Miss Hutchinson [his sister-in-law] to write down some lines which he had just composed." All the poets named here, several of Wordsworth's closest friends among them, had died between 1832 and 1835.
2. A river in the southeast of Scotland.
3. James Hogg, the "Ettrick Shepherd" (he was born in Ettrick Forest, and was for a time a shepherd), was discovered as a writer by Sir Walter Scott, and became well known as a poet, essayist, and editor.

Their golden leaves upon the pathways,
My steps the Border-minstrel[4] led.

The mighty Minstrel breathes no longer,
'Mid moldering ruins low he lies;   10
And death upon the braes[5] of Yarrow,
Has closed the Shepherd-poet's eyes:

Nor has the rolling year twice measured,
From sign to sign, its steadfast course,
Since every mortal power of Coleridge   15
Was frozen at its marvelous source;

The rapt One, of the godlike forehead,
The heaven-eyed creature sleeps in earth:
And Lamb, the frolic and the gentle,
Has vanished from his lonely hearth.   20

Like clouds that rake the mountain summits,
Or waves that own no curbing hand,
How fast has brother followed brother,
From sunshine to the sunless land!

Yet I, whose lids from infant slumber   25
Were earlier raised, remain to hear
A timid voice, that asks in whispers,
"Who next will drop and disappear?"

Our haughty life is crowned with darkness,
Like London with its own black wreath,   30
On which with thee, O Crabbe![6] forth-looking,
I gazed from Hampstead's breezy heath.

As if but yesterday departed,
Thou too art gone before; but why,
O'er ripe fruit, seasonably gathered,   35
Should frail survivors heave a sigh?

Mourn rather for that holy Spirit,
Sweet as the spring, as ocean deep;
For her[7] who, ere her summer faded,
Has sunk into a breathless sleep.   40

No more of old romantic sorrows,
For slaughtered Youth or lovelorn Maid!
With sharper grief is Yarrow smitten,
And Ettrick mourns with her their Poet dead.

November 21, 1835   1835

4. Sir Walter Scott.
5. The sloping banks of a stream.
6. George Crabbe, the poet of rural
and village life.
7. Felicia Hemans, a minor but prolific
poetess, who died when only 42. She is
best known in America for *The Landing of the Pilgrim Fathers* and *The
Boy Stood on the Burning Deck.*

From The Recluse[1]

["*Prospectus*"]

On Man, on Nature, and on Human Life,
Musing in solitude, I oft perceive
Fair trains of imagery before me rise,
Accompanied by feelings of delight
Pure, or with no unpleasing sadness mixed;   5
And I am conscious of affecting thoughts
And dear remembrances, whose presence soothes
Or elevates the Mind, intent to weigh
The good and evil of our mortal state.
—To these emotions, whencesoe'er they come,   10
Whether from breath of outward circumstance,
Or from the Soul—an impulse to herself—
I would give utterance in numerous verse.[2]
Of Truth, of Grandeur, Beauty, Love, and Hope,
And melancholy Fear subdued by Faith;   15
Of blessed consolations in distress;
Of moral strength, and intellectual Power;
Of joy in widest commonalty spread;
Of the individual Mind that keeps her own
Inviolate retirement, subject there   20
To Conscience only, and the law supreme
Of that Intelligence which governs all,
I sing—"fit audience let me find though few!"[3]

1. Through most of his poetic life Wordsworth labored intermittently at a long philosophic poem called *The Recluse*, which he intended to be his masterwork. It was to consist of an autobiographical introduction (the poem now called *The Prelude*) and three long parts; of these three he completed only Book I of Part I ("Home at Grasmere") and the whole of Part II, called *The Excursion*. In the Preface to *The Excursion*, published separately in 1814, Wordsworth printed this long extract (the concluding section of "Home at Grasmere") to serve "as a kind of *Prospectus* of the design and scope of the whole Poem"—i.e., of the entire *Recluse*.

The first version of this "Prospectus" was probably drafted as early as 1798. In language thronged with echoes from *Paradise Lost*, Wordsworth announces an undertaking which he conceives to be no less inspired and sublime than Milton's. In it he will move higher than heaven and deeper than hell, past scenes evoking greater fear than Erebus and greater awe than

Jehovah; but without ever leaving "the Mind of Man— / My haunt, and the main region of my song" (lines 40–41). And his "high argument" is that Paradise need not remain Paradise lost, for it can be regained; not, however, as in Revelation xxi, by the marriage between the New Jerusalem and Christ the Lamb, but by a marriage between the "intellect of Man" and "this goodly universe," and the resulting new "creation * * * which they with blended might / Accomplish" (lines 47–71). In no other passage does Wordsworth reveal so clearly the extent to which he assimilates to his poetry the Biblical scheme of Milton's epic—assigning, however, the active role, from creation to redemption, to the human faculties, in their vital interaction with the external universe.

2. Harmonious verse; an echo of *Paradise Lost* V.150. The inspiring "breath of outward circumstance" parallels the "correspondent breeze" in the opening passage of *The Prelude*, just below.

3. *Paradise Lost* VII.31.

So prayed, more gaining than he asked, the Bard—
In holiest mood. Urania,[4] I shall need   25
Thy guidance, or a greater Muse, if such
Descend to earth or dwell in highest heaven!
For I must tread on shadowy ground, must sink
Deep—and, aloft ascending, breathe in worlds
To which the heaven of heavens [4a] is but a veil.   30
All strength—all terror, single or in bands,
That ever was put forth in personal form—
Jehovah—with his thunder, and the choir
Of shouting Angels, and the empyreal thrones[5]—
I pass them unalarmed. Not Chaos, not   35
The darkest pit of lowest Erebus,[6]
Nor aught of blinder vacancy, scooped out
By help of dreams—can breed such fear and awe
As fall upon us often when we look
Into our Minds, into the Mind of Man—   40
My haunt, and the main region of my song.
—Beauty—a living Presence of the earth,
Surpassing the most fair ideal Forms
Which craft of delicate Spirits hath composed
From earth's materials—waits upon my steps;   45
Pitches her tents before me as I move,
An hourly neighbor. Paradise, and groves
Elysian,[7] Fortunate Fields—like those of old
Sought in the Atlantic Main—why should they be
A history only of departed things,   50
Or a mere fiction of what never was?
For the discerning intellect of Man,
When wedded to this goodly universe
In love and holy passion, shall find these
A simple produce of the common day.   55
—I, long before the blissful hour arrives,
Would chant, in lonely peace, the spousal[8] verse
Of this great consummation—and, by words
Which speak of nothing more than what we are,
Would I arouse the sensual from their sleep   60
Of Death, and win the vacant and the vain
To noble raptures; while my voice proclaims
How exquisitely the individual Mind
(And the progressive powers perhaps no less
Of the whole species) to the external World   65
Is fitted—and how exquisitely, too—

---

4. The Muse whom Milton had invoked in *Paradise Lost*. In pagan
myth, Urania had been the Muse of
astronomy.
4a. In *Paradise Lost* the dwelling place,
beyond the visible heaven, of God and
his angels.
5. *Paradise Lost* II.430.
6. In classical myth, a dark region of
the underworld; often used as a name
for hell by Christian writers.

7. Elysium, in Greek myth, was the
place where men favored by the gods
live a happy life after death. It was
sometimes identified with the "Islands
of the Blessed," reputed to be located
far out in the western sea—hence
"sought in the Atlantic Main." See
Horace, *Epodes* XVI.
8. Marital; hence a "spousal verse" is
an epithalamion.

Theme this but little heard of among men—
The external World is fitted to the Mind;
And the creation (by no lower name
Can it be called) which they with blended might   70
Accomplish—this is our high argument.[9]
—Such grateful haunts foregoing, if I oft
Must turn elsewhere—to travel near the tribes
And fellowships of men, and see ill sights
Of madding passions mutually inflamed;   75
Must hear Humanity in fields and groves
Pipe solitary anguish; or must hang
Brooding above the fierce confederate storm
Of sorrow, barricadoed[1] evermore
Within the walls of cities—may these sounds   80
Have their authentic comment; that even these
Hearing, I be not downcast or forlorn!—
Descend, prophetic Spirit! that inspir'st
The human Soul of universal earth,
Dreaming on things to come;[2] and dost possess   85
A metropolitan[3] temple in the hearts
Of mighty Poets: upon me bestow
A gift of genuine insight; that my Song
With starlike virtue in its place may shine,
Shedding benignant influence, and secure,   90
Itself, from all malevolent effect
Of those mutations that extend their sway
Throughout the nether sphere![4]—And if with this
I mix more lowly matter; with the thing
Contemplated, describe the Mind and Man   95
Contemplating; and who, and what he was—
The transitory Being that beheld
The Vision; when and where, and how he lived—
Be not this labor useless. If such theme
May sort with highest objects, then—dread Power!   100
Whose gracious favor is the primal source
Of all illumination—may my Life
Express the image of a better time,
More wise desires, and simpler manners—nurse
My Heart in genuine freedom—all pure thoughts   105
Be with me—so shall thy unfailing love
Guide, and support, and cheer me to the end!

ca. 1798–1814   1814

---

9. Theme, as in *Paradise Lost* I.24: "the height of this great Argument."
1. Barricaded, as in *Paradise Lost* VIII.241.
2. Cf. "the prophetic soul / Of the wide world dreaming on things to come" (Shakespeare, *Sonnet* CVII).
3. Designating the principal seat of a

religion.
4. In the Ptolemaic world picture, the spheres of the heavenly bodies were immutable, and only the earth (the "nether sphere," or region below the sphere of the moon) was subject to change. Compare *Paradise Lost* VII.375 and X.656–64.

The Prelude   Wordsworth originally planned, in 1798, to incorporate an account of his own poetic development within his projected philosophical poem, *The Recluse*, but decided in the following year to make these materials into an independent poem, addressed to S. T. Coleridge, which would serve as a prefatory work to *The Recluse*. "The preparatory poem is biographical," Wordsworth wrote in his Preface to *The Excursion* (1814), "and conducts the history of the Author's mind to the point when he was emboldened to hope that his faculties were sufficiently matured for entering upon the arduous labor which he had proposed to himself." Most of Books I and II were written in 1798–99; and by May, 1805, Wordsworth had completed the first version of the entire poem. For the next 35 years, however, he kept tinkering with the text, and it was not published until 1850, three months after Wordsworth's death. The author himself referred to the manuscript only as a poem "on my own earlier life," or "on the growth of my own mind." The apt title, *The Prelude*, was bestowed on it by Mrs. Wordsworth.

Wordsworth was well aware that "it was a thing unprecedented in literary history that a man should talk so much about himself." But it should be recognized that Wordsworth deals with himself only, in Coleridge's term, as the "I-representative." The events of his life are presented, not as they had seemed to him at the time they occurred, but reinterpreted in tranquility and shaped into an artistic pattern; and the protagonist of the poem is not really Wordsworth the private person, but the poet's mind, or more specifically, the poetic imagination. "This faculty," Wordsworth wrote in the last book (XIV.193–94), "hath been the feeding source / Of our long labor"; and the account of its emergence, development, impairment, and restoration, he goes on to say, constitutes the plot, or narrative principle, of the whole of *The Prelude*.

When he had finished *The Prelude* Wordsworth felt, in disappointment, that it was "far below what I had seemed capable of executing"; and at the close of the poem he described it as only preliminary to his "building up a Work that shall endure" (XIV.311). This later work was never finished. But in the sustained treatment of his remembrance of things past, Wordsworth had in fact found his great and original poetic subject; and though he did not realize it, in writing the prelude to his masterpiece he had written the masterpiece itself.

From The Prelude[1]
or
Growth of a Poet's Mind
AN AUTOBIOGRAPHICAL POEM

From *Book I. Introduction—Childhood and Schooltime*

Oh there is blessing in this gentle breeze,[2]
A visitant that while it fans my cheek
Doth seem half-conscious of the joy it brings
From the green fields, and from yon azure sky.
Whate'er its mission, the soft breeze can come   5
To none more grateful than to me; escaped
From the vast city,[3] where I long had pined
A discontented sojourner: now free,
Free as a bird to settle where I will.
What dwelling shall receive me? in what vale   10
Shall be my harbor? underneath what grove
Shall I take up my home? and what clear stream
Shall with its murmur lull me into rest?
The earth is all before me.[4] With a heart
Joyous, nor scared at its own liberty,   15
I look about; and should the chosen guide
Be nothing better than a wandering cloud,
I cannot miss my way. I breathe again!
Trances of thought and mountings of the mind
Come fast upon me: it is shaken off,   20
That burthen of my own unnatural self,
The heavy weight of many a weary day
Not mine, and such as were not made for me.
Long months of peace (if such bold word accord
With any promises of human life),   25

1. The first version of *The Prelude*, completed in 1805, together with variant passages from Wordsworth's later MSS., was published by Ernest de Selincourt in 1926. The text reproduced here is Wordsworth's final version of 1850.
2. Wordsworth says, lines 46–50, that the preceding lines were uttered in the circumstances they describe. Until recently it was the standard opinion that the occasion was September of 1795 when Wordsworth, released from financial worries by a legacy, was on his way to find a home in Racedown, Dorset. It is much more likely, however, that the lines refer primarily to his walk to what was to be his home at Grasmere, late in 1797, deliberately fused with details from an earlier trip to Racedown. In 1804 this passage was adopted as the preamble for *The Prelude*, where it replaces the epic device (as in *Paradise Lost*) of the opening prayer to the Muse for inspiration. To be "inspired" is, in its literal sense, to be blown into by a divinity: Wordsworth begins his poem with a literal wind, the "breath of heaven," which (lines 33–42) becomes the stimulus for a correspondent inner breeze, marking both a spring-like revival of the spirit after a wintry season and a burst of poetic power which Wordsworth equates with the inspiration of the Biblical prophets when touched by the Holy Spirit (lines 50–54). The revivifying breeze, material and spiritual, recurs as a kind of leitmotif in *The Prelude*, and also became the radical metaphor of Coleridge's *Dejection: An Ode* and Shelley's *Ode to the West Wind*.
3. London, where Wordsworth had lived February to August, 1795.
4. The first of many echoes of *Paradise Lost*: "The world was all before them" (XII.646).

Long months of ease and undisturbed delight
Are mine in prospect; whither shall I turn,
By road or pathway, or through trackless field,
Uphill or down, or shall some floating thing
Upon the river point me out my course?   30

Dear Liberty! Yet what would it avail
But for a gift that consecrates the joy?
For I, methought, while the sweet breath of heaven
Was blowing on my body, felt within
A correspondent breeze, that gently moved   35
With quickening virtue,[5] but is now become
A tempest, a redundant energy,
Vexing its own creation. Thanks to both,
And their congenial[6] powers, that, while they join
In breaking up a long-continued frost,   40
Bring with them vernal promises, the hope
Of active days urged on by flying hours—
Days of sweet leisure, taxed with patient thought
Abstruse, nor wanting punctual service high,
Matins and vespers of harmonious verse!   45

Thus far, O Friend![7] did I, not used to make
A present joy the matter of a song,[8]
Pour forth that day my soul in measured strains
That would not be forgotten, and are here
Recorded: to the open fields I told   50
A prophecy: poetic numbers came
Spontaneously to clothe in priestly robe
A renovated spirit singled out,
Such hope was mine, for holy services.
My own voice cheered me, and, far more, the mind's   55
Internal echo of the imperfect sound;
To both I listened, drawing from them both
A cheerful confidence in things to come.

* * *

Fair seedtime had my soul, and I grew up
Fostered alike by beauty and by fear:[9]
Much favored in my birthplace, and no less
In that belovéd Vale[1] to which erelong
We were transplanted—there were we let loose   305
For sports of wider range. Ere I had told

---

5. Reviving power.
6. Kindred.
7. Here begins *The Prelude* proper, composed 1798–1805. The "Friend" is Samuel Taylor Coleridge, to whom the entire poem is addressed as a kind of immense verse letter. For Coleridge's reply, see *To William Wordsworth.*
8. His poetry, as Wordsworth said in the Preface to *Lyrical Ballads,* usually originates as "emotion recollected in

tranquility," not, as in the preamble just preceding, during the actual experience it describes.
9. Wordsworth refers repeatedly to the double impulse of nature, "both law and impulse * * * / To kindle or restrain," as he said in *Three Years She Grew* (lines 8–12).
1. The valley of Esthwaite, the location of Hawkshead, where Wordsworth attended school.

Ten birthdays, when among the mountain slopes
Frost, and the breath of frosty wind, had snapped
The last autumnal crocus, 'twas my joy
With store of springes[2] o'er my shoulder hung   310
To range the open heights where woodcocks run
Along the smooth green turf. Through half the night,
Scudding away from snare to snare, I plied
That anxious visitation—moon and stars
Were shining o'er my head. I was alone,   315
And seemed to be a trouble to the peace
That dwelt among them. Sometimes it befell
In these night wanderings, that a strong desire
O'erpowered my better reason, and the bird
Which was the captive of another's toil   320
Became my prey; and when the deed was done
I heard among the solitary hills
Low breathings coming after me, and sounds
Of undistinguishable motion, steps
Almost as silent as the turf they trod.   325

　　Nor less, when spring had warmed the cultured Vale,
Moved we as plunderers where the mother bird
Had in high places built her lodge; though mean
Our object and inglorious, yet the end
Was not ignoble. Oh! when I have hung   330
Above the raven's nest, by knots of grass
And half-inch fissures in the slippery rock
But ill sustained, and almost (so it seemed)
Suspended by the blast that blew amain,
Shouldering the naked crag, oh, at that time   335
While on the perilous ridge I hung alone,
With what strange utterance did the loud dry wind
Blow through my ear! the sky seemed not a sky
Of earth—and with what motion moved the clouds!

　　Dust as we are, the immortal spirit grows   340
Like harmony in music; there is a dark
Inscrutable workmanship that reconciles
Discordant elements, makes them cling together
In one society. How strange that all
The terrors, pains, and early miseries,   345
Regrets, vexations, lassitudes interfused
Within my mind, should e'er have borne a part,
And that a needful part, in making up
The calm existence that is mine when I
Am worthy of myself! Praise to the end!   350
Thanks to the means which Nature deigned to employ;
Whether her fearless visitings, or those
That came with soft alarm, like hurtless light
Opening the peaceful clouds; or she may use

2. Bird snares.

Severer interventions, ministry   355
More palpable, as best might suit her aim.[3]

One summer evening (led by her) I found
A little boat tied to a willow tree
Within a rocky cave, its usual home.
Straight I unloosed her chain, and stepping in   360
Pushed from the shore. It was an act of stealth
And troubled pleasure, nor without the voice
Of mountain echoes did my boat move on;
Leaving behind her still, on either side,
Small circles glittering idly in the moon,   365
Until they melted all into one track
Of sparkling light. But now, like one who rows,
Proud of his skill, to reach a chosen point
With an unswerving line, I fixed my view
Upon the summit of a craggy ridge,   370
The horizon's utmost boundary; for above
Was nothing but the stars and the gray sky.
She was an elfin pinnace;[4] lustily
I dipped my oars into the silent lake,
And, as I rose upon the stroke, my boat   375
Went heaving through the water like a swan;
When, from behind that craggy steep till then
The horizon's bound, a huge peak, black and huge,
As if with voluntary power instinct,
Upreared its head.[5] I struck and struck again,   380
And growing still in stature the grim shape
Towered up between me and the stars, and still,
For so it seemed, with purpose of its own
And measured motion like a living thing,
Strode after me. With trembling oars I turned,   385
And through the silent water stole my way
Back to the covert of the willow tree;
There in her mooring place I left my bark,
And through the meadows homeward went, in grave
And serious mood; but after I had seen   390
That spectacle, for many days, my brain
Worked with a dim and undetermined sense
Of unknown modes of being; o'er my thoughts
There hung a darkness, call it solitude
Or blank desertion. No familiar shapes   395
Remained, no pleasant images of trees,
Of sea or sky, no colors of green fields;
But huge and mighty forms, that do not live

3. A restatement of the double ministry of nature described in line 302;
what follows is a second example of
discipline by fear.
4. Small boat.
5. In order to direct his boat in a
straight line, the rower has fixed his
eye on a point in the ridge of the
nearby shore, which blocks out the
landscape behind. As he moves farther
out, the black peak suddenly rears into
his altering angle of vision and seems
to stride closer with each stroke of the
oars.

Like living men, moved slowly through the mind
By day, and were a trouble to my dreams.   400

    Wisdom and Spirit of the universe!
Thou Soul that art the eternity of thought,
That givest to forms and images a breath
And everlasting motion, not in vain
By day or starlight thus from my first dawn   405
Of childhood didst thou intertwine for me
The passions that build up our human soul;
Not with the mean and vulgar works of man,
But with high objects, with enduring things—
With life and nature—purifying thus   410
The elements of feeling and of thought,
And sanctifying, by such discipline,
Both pain and fear, until we recognize
A grandeur in the beatings of the heart.
Nor was this fellowship vouchsafed to me   415
With stinted kindness. In November days,
When vapors rolling down the valley made
A lonely scene more lonesome, among woods,
At noon and 'mid the calm of summer nights,
When, by the margin of the trembling lake,   420
Beneath the gloomy hills homeward I went
In solitude, such intercourse was mine;
Mine was it in the fields both day and night,
And by the waters, all the summer long.

    And in the frosty season, when the sun   425
Was set, and visible for many a mile
The cottage windows blazed through twilight gloom,
I heeded not their summons: happy time
It was indeed for all of us—for me
It was a time of rapture! Clear and loud   430
The village clock tolled six—I wheeled about,
Proud and exulting like an untired horse
That cares not for his home. All shod with steel,
We hissed along the polished ice in games
Confederate, imitative of the chase   435
And woodland pleasures—the resounding horn,
The pack loud chiming, and the hunted hare.
So through the darkness and the cold we flew,
And not a voice was idle; with the din
Smitten, the precipices rang aloud;   440
The leafless trees and every icy crag
Tinkled like iron; while far distant hills
Into the tumult sent an alien sound
Of melancholy not unnoticed, while the stars
Eastward were sparkling clear, and in the west   445
The orange sky of evening died away.
Not seldom from the uproar I retired

Into a silent bay, or sportively
Glanced sideway, leaving the tumultuous throng,
To cut across the reflex[6] of a star   450
That fled, and, flying still before me, gleamed
Upon the glassy plain; and oftentimes,
When we had given our bodies to the wind,
And all the shadowy banks on either side
Came sweeping through the darkness, spinning still   455
The rapid line of motion, then at once
Have I, reclining back upon my heels,
Stopped short; yet still the solitary cliffs
Wheeled by me—even as if the earth had rolled
With visible motion her diurnal round!   460
Behind me did they stretch in solemn train,
Feebler and feebler, and I stood and watched
Till all was tranquil as a dreamless sleep.

 Ye Presences of Nature in the sky
And on the earth! Ye Visions of the hills!   465
And Souls of lonely places![7] can I think
A vulgar hope was yours when ye employed
Such ministry, when ye, through many a year
Haunting me thus among my boyish sports,
On caves and trees, upon the woods and hills,   470
Impressed upon all forms the characters
Of danger or desire; and thus did make
The surface of the universal earth
With triumph and delight, with hope and fear,
Work like a sea? * * *   475

 Nor, sedulous as I have been to trace
How Nature by extrinsic passion first   545
Peopled the mind with forms sublime or fair,[8]
And made me love them, may I here omit
How other pleasures have been mine, and joys
Of subtler origin; how I have felt,
Not seldom even in that tempestuous time,   550
Those hallowed and pure motions of the sense
Which seem, in their simplicity, to own
An intellectual[9] charm; that calm delight
Which, if I err not, surely must belong
To those first-born affinities that fit   555
Our new existence to existing things,
And, in our dawn of being, constitute
The bond of union between life and joy.

6. Reflection.
7. In this period Wordsworth referred both to a single "Spirit" or "Soul" of the universe as a whole (e.g., lines 401–2, above) and to plural "Presences" and "Souls" inanimating the various parts of the universe.
8. The passion at first was "extrinsic" because felt not for nature itself, but for nature as associated with the outdoor activities he loved. He now goes on to distinguish other "subtler" pleasures, felt in the very process of sensing the natural objects themselves.
9. As though they were abstract concepts rather than sensations.

Yes, I remember when the changeful earth,
And twice five summers on my mind had stamped   560
The faces of the moving year, even then
I held unconscious intercourse with beauty
Old as creation, drinking in a pure
Organic pleasure from the silver wreaths
Of curling mist, or from the level plain   565
Of waters colored by impending[1] clouds.

The sands of Westmoreland, the creeks and bays
Of Cumbria's[2] rocky limits, they can tell
How, when the Sea threw off his evening shade,
And to the shepherd's hut on distant hills   570
Sent welcome notice of the rising moon,
How I have stood, to fancies such as these
A stranger, linking with the spectacle
No conscious memory of a kindred sight,
And bringing with me no peculiar sense   575
Of quietness or peace; yet have I stood,
Even while mine eye hath moved o'er many a league
Of shining water, gathering as it seemed,
Through every hairbreadth in that field of light,
New pleasure like a bee among the flowers.   580

Thus oft amid those fits of vulgar[3] joy
Which, through all seasons, on a child's pursuits
Are prompt attendants, 'mid that giddy bliss
Which, like a tempest, works along the blood
And is forgotten; even then I felt   585
Gleams like the flashing of a shield—the earth
And common face of Nature spake to me
Rememberable things; sometimes, 'tis true,
By chance collisions and quaint accidents
(Like those ill-sorted unions, work supposed   590
Of evil-minded fairies), yet not vain
Nor profitless, if haply they impressed
Collateral[4] objects and appearances,
Albeit lifeless then, and doomed to sleep
Until maturer seasons called them forth   595
To impregnate and to elevate the mind.
—And if the vulgar joy by its own weight
Wearied itself out of the memory,
The scenes which were a witness of that joy
Remained in their substantial lineaments   600
Depicted on the brain, and to the eye
Were visible, a daily sight; and thus
By the impressive discipline of fear,
By pleasure and repeated happiness,
So frequently repeated, and by force   605

1. Overhanging.
2. Cumberland's.

3. Commonplace.
4. Accompanying but subordinate.

Of obscure feelings representative
Of things forgotten, these same scenes so bright,
So beautiful, so majestic in themselves,
Though yet the day was distant, did become
Habitually dear, and all their forms   610
And changeful colors by invisible links
Were fastened to the affections. * * *

From *Book II. Schooltime* (*continued*)

Blest the infant Babe
(For with my best conjecture I would trace
Our Being's earthly progress),[1] blest the Babe,
Nursed in his Mother's arms, who sinks to sleep   235
Rocked on his Mother's breast; who with his soul
Drinks in the feelings of his Mother's eye!
For him, in one dear Presence, there exists
A virtue which irradiates and exalts
Objects through widest intercourse of sense.   240
No outcast he, bewildered and depressed:
Along his infant veins are interfused
The gravitation and the filial bond
Of nature that connect him with the world.
Is there a flower, to which he points with hand   245
Too weak to gather it, already love
Drawn from love's purest earthly fount for him
Hath beautified that flower; already shades
Of pity cast from inward tenderness
Do fall around him upon aught that bears   250
Unsightly marks of violence or harm.
Emphatically such a Being lives,
Frail creature as he is, helpless as frail,
An inmate of this active universe.
For feeling has to him imparted power   255
That through the growing faculties of sense
Doth like an agent of the one great Mind
Create, creator and receiver both,[2]
Working but in alliance with the works
Which it beholds.—Such, verily, is the first   260
Poetic spirit of our human life,
By uniform control of after years,
In most, abated or suppressed; in some,
Through every change of growth and of decay,
Pre-eminent till death. * * *   265

1. Like the modern psychologist, Wordsworth recognized the importance of earliest infancy in the development of the individual mind and temperament, although he had then to invent the terms with which to analyze infant psychology.
2. Like Coleridge (see *Biographia Lite-* *raria*, Chapter XIII), Wordsworth describes the mind in perception as partially creating the world it seems passively to receive. In the succeeding passage (lines 360–74) Wordsworth repeats this concept in various metaphors signifying the give-and-take of outer world and inner mind and emotion.

'Twere long to tell
What spring and autumn, what the winter snows,
And what the summer shade, what day and night,
Evening and morning, sleep and waking, thought   355
From sources inexhaustible, poured forth
To feed the spirit of religious love
In which I walked with Nature. But let this
Be not forgotten, that I still retained
My first creative sensibility;   360
That by the regular action of the world
My soul was unsubdued. A plastic power
Abode with me; a forming hand, at times
Rebellious, acting in a devious mood;
A local spirit of his own, at war   365
With general tendency, but, for the most,
Subservient strictly to external things
With which it communed. An auxiliar light
Came from my mind, which on the setting sun
Bestowed new splendor; the melodious birds,   370
The fluttering breezes, fountains that run on
Murmuring so sweetly in themselves, obeyed
A like dominion, and the midnight storm
Grew darker in the presence of my eye:
Hence my obeisance, my devotion hence,   375
And hence my transport.
                        Nor should this, perchance,
Pass unrecorded, that I still had loved
The exercise and produce of a toil,
Than analytic industry to me
More pleasing, and whose character I deem   380
Is more poetic as resembling more
Creative agency. The song would speak
Of that interminable building reared
By observation of affinities
In objects where no brotherhood exists   385
To passive minds. My seventeenth year was come;
And, whether from this habit rooted now
So deeply in my mind, or from excess
In the great social principle of life
Coercing all things into sympathy,   390
To unorganic natures were transferred
My own enjoyments; or the power of truth
Coming in revelation, did converse
With things that really are;[3] I, at this time,
Saw blessings spread around me like a sea.   395
Thus while the days flew by, and years passed on,

---

3. Wordsworth is careful to indicate that there are two possible explanations for his sense that life pervades the inorganic as well as organic world: it may be the illusory result of a projection of his own inner life, or it may be the perception of an objective truth.

From Nature and her overflowing soul,
I had received so much, that all my thoughts
Were steeped in feeling; I was only then
Contented, when with bliss ineffable   400
I felt the sentiment of Being spread
O'er all that moves and all that seemeth still;
O'er all that, lost beyond the reach of thought
And human knowledge, to the human eye
Invisible, yet liveth to the heart;   405
O'er all that leaps and runs, and shouts and sings,
Or beats the gladsome air; o'er all that glides
Beneath the wave, yea, in the wave itself,
And mighty depth of waters. Wonder not
'f high the transport, great the joy I felt,   410
Communing in this sort through earth and heaven
With every form of creature, as it looked
Towards the Uncreated with a countenance
Of adoration, with an eye of love.[4]
One song they sang, and it was audible,   415
Most audible, then, when the fleshly ear,
O'ercome by humblest prelude of that strain,
Forgot her functions, and slept undisturbed.[5]

* * *

From *Book III. Residence at Cambridge*

The Evangelist St. John my patron was:[1]
Three Gothic courts are his, and in the first
Was my abiding place, a nook obscure;
Right underneath, the College kitchens made
A humming sound, less tunable than bees,   50
But hardly less industrious; with shrill notes
Of sharp command and scolding intermixed.
Near me hung Trinity's[2] loquacious clock,
Who never let the quarters, night or day,
Slip by him unproclaimed, and told the hours   55
Twice over with a male and female voice.
Her pealing organ was my neighbor too;
And from my pillow, looking forth by light
Of moon or favoring stars, I could behold
The antechapel where the statue stood   60
Of Newton with his prism and silent face,
The marble index of a mind forever
Voyaging through strange seas of Thought, alone.

---

4. Wordsworth did not add lines 412–
14, giving a Christian frame to his experience of the "one life," until very
late, in 1839.
5. Cf. this description of the trance
state, like that of religious mystics,
with *Tintern Abbey*, lines 41–49.
1. Wordsworth was a student at St.

John's College, Cambridge University,
from 1787 to 1791.
2. Trinity College adjoins St. John's.
Roubiliac's statue of Newton, holding
the prism with which he had conducted
the experiments described in his *Optics*,
stands in the west end of Trinity chapel.

Of College labors, of the Lecturer's room
All studded round, as thick as chairs could stand,   65
With loyal students faithful to their books,
Half-and-half idlers, hardy recusants,
And honest dunces—of important days,
Examinations, when the man was weighed
As in a balance! of excessive hopes,   70
Tremblings withal and commendable fears,
Small jealousies, and triumphs good or bad,
Let others that know more speak as they know.
Such glory was but little sought by me,
And little won. Yet from the first crude days   75
Of settling time in this untried abode,
I was disturbed at times by prudent thoughts,
Wishing to hope without a hope, some fears
About my future worldly maintenance,
And, more than all, a strangeness in the mind,   80
A feeling that I was not for that hour,
Nor for that place. * * *

It hath been told that when the first delight
That flashed upon me from this novel show
Had failed, the mind returned into herself;
Yet true it is that I had made a change
In climate, and my nature's outward coat   205
Changed also slowly and insensibly.
Full oft the quiet and exalted thoughts
Of loneliness gave way to empty noise
And superficial pastimes; now and then
Forced labor, and more frequently forced hopes;   210
And, worst of all, a treasonable growth
Of indecisive judgments, that impaired
And shook the mind's simplicity.—And yet
This was a gladsome time. Could I behold—
Who, less insensible than sodden clay   215
In a sea river's bed at ebb of tide,
Could have beheld—with undelighted heart,
So many happy youths, so wide and fair
A congregation in its budding time
Of health, and hope, and beauty, all at once   220
So many divers samples from the growth
Of life's sweet season—could have seen unmoved
That miscellaneous garland of wild flowers
Decking the matron temples of a place
So famous through the world? To me, at least,   225
It was a goodly prospect: for, in sooth,
Though I had learnt betimes to stand unpropped,
And independent musings pleased me so
That spells seemed on me when I was alone,
Yet could I only cleave to solitude   230

In lonely places; if a throng was near
That way I leaned by nature; for my heart
Was social, and loved idleness and joy.

* * *

Companionships,
Friendships, acquaintances, were welcome all.
We sauntered, played, or rioted;[3] we talked
Unprofitable talk at morning hours;
Drifted about along the streets and walks,   250
Read lazily in trivial books, went forth
To gallop through the country in blind zeal
Of senseless horsemanship, or on the breast
Of Cam[4] sailed boisterously, and let the stars
Come forth, perhaps without one quiet thought.   255

* * *

Thus in submissive idleness, my Friend!
The laboring time of autumn, winter, spring,
Eight months! rolled pleasingly away; the ninth   630
Came and returned me to my native hills.

From *Book IV. Summer Vacation*[1]

Yes, that heartless chase
Of trivial pleasures was a poor exchange
For books and nature at that early age.
'Tis true some casual knowledge might be gained   300
Of character or life; but at that time,
Of manners put to school I took small note,
And all my deeper passions lay elsewhere.
Far better had it been to exalt the mind
By solitary study, to uphold   305
Intense desire through meditative peace;
And yet, for chastisement of these regrets,
The memory of one particular hour
Doth here rise up against me. 'Mid a throng
Of maids and youths, old men, and matrons staid,   310
A medley of all tempers, I had passed
The night in dancing, gaiety, and mirth,
With din of instruments and shuffling feet,
And glancing forms, and tapers glittering,
And unaimed prattle flying up and down;   315
Spirits upon the stretch, and here and there
Slight shocks of young love-liking interspersed,
Whose transient pleasure mounted to the head,

3. This was a period of low ebb in the
intellectual vigor and discipline of
Cambridge, so that Wordsworth was
able to indulge generously in the fringe
activities of university life.
4. The river Cam, which flows through
Cambridge.

1. Wordsworth spent his first summer
vacation from the university at Hawkshead. In this passage he describes an
experience during the walk home after
an all-night dance.

And tingled through the veins. Ere we retired,
The cock had crowed, and now the eastern sky   320
Was kindling, not unseen, from humble copse
And open field, through which the pathway wound,
And homeward led my steps. Magnificent
The morning rose, in memorable pomp,
Glorious as e'er I had beheld—in front,   325
The sea lay laughing at a distance; near,
The solid mountains shone, bright as the clouds,
Grain-tinctured,[2] drenched in empyrean light;
And in the meadows and the lower grounds
Was all the sweetness of a common dawn—   330
Dews, vapors, and the melody of birds,
And laborers going forth to till the fields.
Ah! need I say, dear Friend! that to the brim
My heart was full; I made no vows, but vows
Were then made for me; bond unknown to me   335
Was given, that I should be, else sinning greatly,
A dedicated Spirit. On I walked
In thankful blessedness, which yet survives.

* * *

From *Book* V. *Books*

　　　　　　Oh! why hath not the Mind   45
Some element to stamp her image on
In nature somewhat nearer to her own?
Why, gifted with such powers to send abroad
Her spirit, must it lodge in shrines so frail?[1]

　　One day, when from my lips a like complaint   50
Had fallen in presence of a studious friend,
He with a smile made answer, that in truth
'Twas going far to seek disquietude;
But on the front of his reproof confessed
That he himself had oftentimes given way   55
To kindred hauntings. Whereupon I told,
That once in the stillness of a summer's noon,
While I was seated in a rocky cave
By the seaside, perusing, so it chanced,
The famous history of the errant knight   60
Recorded by Cervantes,[2] these same thoughts
Beset me, and to height unusual rose,
While listlessly I sate, and, having closed
The book, had turned my eyes toward the wide sea.

2. Crimson. The "empyrean" was, in ancient thought, the outer sphere of the universe, composed of pure fire.
1. Wordsworth is describing his recurrent fear that some holocaust might wipe out all books, the frail and perishable repositories of all man's wisdom and poetry.
2. I.e., Don Quixote. Wordsworth's nightmare involves all the elements of the poet's last waking experience. Mathematics had flourished among the Arabs—hence the Arabian rider (lines 75 ff.).

On poetry and geometric truth, 65
And their high privilege of lasting life,
From all internal injury exempt,
I mused upon these chiefly; and at length,
My senses yielding to the sultry air,
Sleep seized me, and I passed into a dream. 70
I saw before me stretched a boundless plain
Of sandy wilderness, all black and void,
And as I looked around, distress and fear
Came creeping over me, when at my side,
Close at my side, an uncouth shape appeared 75
Upon a dromedary, mounted high.
He seemed an Arab of the Bedouin tribes:
A lance he bore, and underneath one arm
A stone, and in the opposite hand a shell
Of a surpassing brightness. At the sight 80
Much I rejoiced, not doubting but a guide
Was present, one who with unerring skill
Would through the desert lead me; and while yet
I looked and looked, self-questioned what this freight
Which the newcomer carried through the waste 85
Could mean, the Arab told me that the stone
(To give it in the language of the dream)
Was "Euclid's Elements";[3] and "This," said he,
"Is something of more worth"; and at the word
Stretched forth the shell, so beautiful in shape, 90
In color so resplendent, with command
That I should hold it to my ear. I did so,
And heard that instant in an unknown tongue,
Which yet I understood, articulate sounds,
A loud prophetic blast of harmony; 95
An Ode, in passion uttered, which foretold
Destruction to the children of the earth
By deluge, now at hand. No sooner ceased
The song, than the Arab with calm look declared
That all would come to pass of which the voice 100
Had given forewarning, and that he himself
Was going then to bury those two books:
The one that held acquaintance with the stars,
And wedded soul to soul in purest bond
Of reason, undisturbed by space or time; 105
The other that was a god, yea, many gods,
Had voices more than all the winds, with power
To exhilarate the spirit, and to soothe,
Through every clime, the heart of human kind.
While this was uttering, strange as it may seem, 110
I wondered not, although I plainly saw
The one to be a stone, the other a shell;

3. Euclid was a Greek mathematician; be used as a textbook into the 19th cen-
his celebrated book on plane geometry tury.
and the theory of numbers continued to

Nor doubted once but that they both were books,
Having a perfect faith in all that passed.
Far stronger, now, grew the desire I felt   115
To cleave unto this man; but when I prayed
To share his enterprise, he hurried on
Reckless[4] of me: I followed, not unseen,
For oftentimes he cast a backward look,
Grasping his twofold treasure.—Lance in rest,   120
He rode, I keeping pace with him; and now
He, to my fancy, had become the knight
Whose tale Cervantes tells; yet not the knight,
But was an Arab of the desert too;
Of these was neither, and was both at once.   125
His countenance, meanwhile, grew more disturbed;
And, looking backwards when he looked, mine eyes
Saw, over half the wilderness diffused,
A bed of glittering light: I asked the cause:
"It is," said he, "the waters of the deep   130
Gathering upon us"; quickening then the pace
Of the unwieldy creature he bestrode,
He left me: I called after him aloud;
He heeded not; but, with his twofold charge
Still in his grasp, before me, full in view,   135
Went hurrying o'er the illimitable waste,
With the fleet waters of a drowning world
In chase of him; whereat I waked in terror,
And saw the sea before me, and the book,
In which I had been reading, at my side.   140

* * *

There was a Boy: ye knew him well, ye cliffs
And islands of Winander!—many a time   365
At evening, when the earliest stars began
To move along the edges of the hills,
Rising or setting, would he stand alone
Beneath the trees or by the glimmering lake,
And there, with fingers interwoven, both hands   370
Pressed closely palm to palm, and to his mouth
Uplifted, he, as through an instrument,
Blew mimic hootings to the silent owls,
That they might answer him; and they would shout
Across the watery vale, and shout again,   375
Responsive to his call, with quivering peals,
And long halloos and screams, and echoes loud,
Redoubled and redoubled, concourse wild
Of jocund din; and, when a lengthened pause
Of silence came and baffled his best skill,   380
Then sometimes, in that silence while he hung
Listening, a gentle shock of mild surprise

4. Neglectful.

Has carried far into his heart the voice
Of mountain torrents; or the visible scene
Would enter unawares into his mind,   385
With all its solemn imagery, its rocks,
Its woods, and that uncertain heaven, received
Into the bosom of the steady lake.[5]

* * *

Here must we pause: this only let me add,
From heart experience, and in humblest sense   585
Of modesty, that he, who in his youth
A daily wanderer among woods and fields
With living Nature hath been intimate,
Not only in that raw unpracticed time
Is stirred to ecstasy, as others are,   590
By glittering verse; but further, doth receive,
In measure only dealt out to himself,
Knowledge and increase of enduring joy
From the great Nature that exists in works
Of mighty Poets.[6] Visionary power   595
Attends the motions of the viewless winds,
Embodied in the mystery of words:
There, darkness makes abode, and all the host
Of shadowy things work endless changes—there,
As in a mansion like their proper home,   600
Even forms and substances are circumfused
By that transparent veil with light divine,
And, through the turnings intricate of verse,
Present themselves as objects recognized,
In flashes, and with glory not their own.   605

From Book VI. *Cambridge and the Alps*

When the third summer freed us from restraint,[1]
A youthful friend, he too a mountaineer,
Not slow to share my wishes, took his staff,
And sallying forth, we journeyed side by side,   325
Bound to the distant Alps. A hardy slight
Did this unprecedented course imply
Of college studies and their set rewards;[2]

5. Coleridge wrote of the last line and a half ("that uncertain heaven * * * lake"): "Had I met these lines running wild in the deserts of Arabia, I should instantly have screamed out, 'Wordsworth.' "
6. Having found a set of symbols in nature, Wordsworth now finds nature in the symbol systems of "mighty poets," in one of his characteristically sonorous passages of splendid obscurity.
1. After reviewing briefly his second and third years at Cambridge, Wordsworth here describes his trip through France and Switzerland with a college friend, Robert Jones, in the succeeding summer vacation, 1790. France was then in the "golden hours" of the early period of the Revolution; the fall of the Bastille had occurred on July 14 of the preceding year.
2. English universities allow much longer vacations than those in America, on the optimistic assumption that they will be used primarily for intensive study. Wordsworth is facing his final examinations in the next college year.

Nor had, in truth, the scheme been formed by me
Without uneasy forethought of the pain,   330
The censures, and ill-omening, of those
To whom my worldly interests were dear.
But Nature then was sovereign in my mind,
And mighty forms, seizing a youthful fancy,
Had given a charter to irregular hopes.   335
In any age of uneventful calm
Among the nations, surely would my heart
Have been possessed by similar desire;
But Europe at that time was thrilled with joy,
France standing on the top of golden hours,   340
And human nature seeming born again.

                        * * *

When from the Vallais we had turned, and clomb
Along the Simplon's steep and rugged road,[3]
Following a band of muleteers, we reached
A halting place, where all together took   565
Their noontide meal. Hastily rose our guide,
Leaving us at the board; awhile we lingered,
Then paced the beaten downward way that led
Right to a rough stream's edge, and there broke off;
The only track now visible was one   570
That from the torrent's further brink held forth
Conspicuous invitation to ascend
A lofty mountain. After brief delay
Crossing the unbridged stream, that road we took,
And clomb with eagerness, till anxious fears   575
Intruded, for we failed to overtake
Our comrades gone before. By fortunate chance,
While every moment added doubt to doubt,
A peasant met us, from whose mouth we learned
That to the spot which had perplexed us first   580
We must descend, and there should find the road,
Which in the stony channel of the stream
Lay a few steps, and then along its banks;
And, that our future course, all plain to sight,
Was downwards, with the current of that stream.   585
Loath to believe what we so grieved to hear,
For still we had hopes that pointed to the clouds,
We questioned him again, and yet again;
But every word that from the peasant's lips
Came in reply, translated by our feelings,   590
Ended in this—*that we had crossed the Alps.*[4]

3. The Simplon Pass through the Alps.
4. As Dorothy Wordsworth baldly put
it later on, "The ambition of youth
was disappointed at these tidings." The
visionary experience that follows occurred not in the Alps but at the time
of writing the passage, as the 1805 text
explicitly says: "Imagination! lifting
up itself / Before the eye and progress
of my Song." Wordsworth goes on to
interpret it as a revelation that man's
glory consists in the infinite striving of
his insatiable spirit.

Imagination—here the Power so called
Through sad incompetence of human speech,
That awful Power rose from the mind's abyss
Like an unfathered vapor[5] that enwraps,   595
At once, some lonely traveler. I was lost;
Halted without an effort to break through;
But to my conscious soul I now can say—
"I recognize thy glory": in such strength
Of usurpation, when the light of sense   600
Goes out, but with a flash that has revealed
The invisible world, doth greatness make abode,
There harbors; whether we be young or old,
Our destiny, our being's heart and home,
Is with infinitude, and only there;   605
With hope it is, hope that can never die,
Effort, and expectation, and desire,
And something evermore about to be.
Under such banners militant, the soul
Seeks for no trophies, struggles for no spoils   610
That may attest her prowess, blest in thoughts
That are their own perfection and reward,
Strong in herself and in beatitude[6]
That hides her, like the mighty flood of Nile
Poured from his fount of Abyssinian clouds   615
To fertilize the whole Egyptian plain.

The melancholy slackening that ensued
Upon those tidings by the peasant given
Was soon dislodged. Downwards we hurried fast,
And, with the half-shaped road which we had missed,   620
Entered a narrow chasm. The brook and road
Were fellow travelers in this gloomy strait,
And with them did we journey several hours
At a slow pace. The immeasurable height
Of woods decaying, never to be decayed,   625
The stationary blasts of waterfalls,
And in the narrow rent at every turn
Winds thwarting winds, bewildered and forlorn,
The torrents shooting from the clear blue sky,
The rocks that muttered close upon our ears,   630
Black drizzling crags that spake by the wayside
As if a voice were in them, the sick sight
And giddy prospect of the raving stream,
The unfettered clouds and region of the Heavens,
Tumult and peace, the darkness and the light—   635
Were all like workings of one mind, the features
Of the same face, blossoms upon one tree;
Characters of the great Apocalypse,[7]

---

5. Sudden vapor from no apparent source.

6. The ultimate blessedness or happiness.

7. The objects in this natural scene, exhibiting a coincidence of all oppo-

The types and symbols of Eternity,
Of first, and last, and midst, and without end.[8]   640

* * *

From *Book VII. Residence in London*

Rise up, thou monstrous anthill on the plain
Of a too busy world![1] Before me flow,   150
Thou endless stream of men and moving things!
Thy everyday appearance, as it strikes—
With wonder heightened, or sublimed by awe—
On strangers, of all ages; the quick dance
Of colors, lights, and forms; the deafening din;   155
The comers and the goers face to face,
Face after face; the string of dazzling wares,
Shop after shop, with symbols, blazoned names,[2]
And all the tradesman's honors overhead:
Here, fronts of houses, like a title page,   160
With letters huge inscribed from top to toe,
Stationed above the door, like guardian saints;
There, allegoric shapes, female or male,
Or physiognomies of real men,
Land warriors, kings, or admirals of the sea,   165
Boyle,[3] Shakespeare, Newton, or the attractive head
Of some quack doctor, famous in his day.

* * *

From these sights   675
Take one—that ancient festival, the Fair,
Holden where martyrs suffered in past time,
And named of St. Bartholomew;[4] there, see
A work completed to our hands, that lays,
If any spectacle on earth can do,   680
The whole creative powers of man asleep!—
For once, the Muse's help will we implore,
And she shall lodge us, wafted on her wings,
Above the press and danger of the crowd,
Upon some showman's platform. What a shock   685

sites, are like the written words of the
Apocalypse—i.e., of the Book of Revelation, the last book of the New Testament.
8. In *Paradise Lost* V.153–165 Milton
says that the things created declare
their Creator, and calls on all to extol
"him first, him last, him midst, and
without end."
1. This is how London struck the
young man from the country in the
three and a half months he spent there
in 1791.
2. The names ostentatiously inscribed
on the shop signs.
3. Robert Boyle, the great 17th-cen-
tury physicist and chemist. "Attrac-

tive": i.e., drawing people to him.
4. This huge fair was long held in
Smithfield, the place where, on St.
Bartholomew's Day, August 24, Protestants had been executed in Queen
Mary's reign. The scene, which for
Wordsworth laid "the whole creative
powers of man asleep" (line 681), is
exactly the kind that most stimulates
those writers (including Chaucer,
Shakespeare, and Dickens) who take
inspiration from the vigor and bustle
of variegated humanity. But "before
it could touch [Wordsworth] near," as
Walter Raleigh said, "an experience
had to be simple and isolated."

For eyes and ears! what anarchy and din,
Barbarian and infernal—a phantasma,[5]
Monstrous in color, motion, shape, sight, sound!
Below, the open space, through every nook
Of the wide area, twinkles, is alive   690
With heads; the midway region, and above,
Is thronged with staring pictures and huge scrolls,
Dumb proclamations of the Prodigies;
With chattering monkeys dangling from their poles,
And children whirling in their roundabouts;[6]   695
With those that stretch the neck and strain the eyes,
And crack the voice in rivalship, the crowd
Inviting; with buffoons against buffoons
Grimacing, writhing, screaming—him who grinds
The hurdy-gurdy, at the fiddle weaves,   700
Rattles the salt box, thumps the kettledrum,
And him who at the trumpet puffs his cheeks,
The silver-collared Negro with his timbrel,
Equestrians, tumblers, women, girls, and boys,
Blue-breeched, pink-vested, with high-towering plumes.   705
All movables of wonder, from all parts,
Are here—Albinos, painted Indians, Dwarfs,
The Horse of knowledge,[7] and the learned Pig,
The Stone-eater, the man that swallows fire,
Giants, Ventriloquists, the Invisible Girl,   710
The Bust that speaks and moves its goggling eyes,
The Waxwork, Clockwork, all the marvelous craft
Of modern Merlins,[8] Wild Beasts, Puppet-shows,
All out-o'-the-way, farfetched, perverted things,
All freaks of nature, all Promethean[9] thoughts   715
Of man, his dullness, madness, and their feats
All jumbled up together, to compose
A Parliament of Monsters. Tents and Booths
Meanwhile, as if the whole were one vast mill,
Are vomiting, receiving on all sides,   720
Men, Women, three-years' Children, Babes in arms.

    Oh, blank confusion! true epitome
Of what the mighty City is herself
To thousands upon thousands of her sons,
Living amid the same perpetual whirl   725
Of trivial objects, melted and reduced
To one identity, by differences
That have no law, no meaning, and no end—
Oppression, under which even highest minds
Must labor, whence the strongest are not free.   730
But though the picture weary out the eye,

5. Fantasy of a disordered mind.
6. Merry-go-rounds.
7. A horse trained to tap out answers
to numerical questions, etc.
8. Magicians. Merlin was the magician

in the Arthurian romances.
9. Creative, or highly inventive. Prometheus, in Greek mythology, made
man out of clay and taught him the
arts.

By nature an unmanageable sight,
It is not wholly so to him who looks
In steadiness, who hath among least things
An under-sense of greatest; sees the parts   735
As parts, but with a feeling of the whole.

* * *

From *Book VIII. Retrospect—Love of Nature* Leading to Love of Man[1]

For me, when my affections first were led
From kindred, friends, and playmates, to partake
Love for the human creature's absolute self,
That noticeable kindliness of heart
Sprang out of fountains, there abounding most,   125
Where sovereign Nature dictated the tasks
And occupations which her beauty adorned,
And Shepherds were the men that pleased me first.

* * *

A rambling schoolboy, thus
I felt his presence in his own domain,
As of a lord and master, or a power,
Or genius, under Nature, under God,
Presiding; and severest solitude   260
Had more commanding looks when he was there.
When up the lonely brooks on rainy days
Angling I went, or trod the trackless hills
By mists bewildered, suddenly mine eyes
Have glanced upon him distant a few steps,   265
In size a giant, stalking through thick fog,
His sheep like Greenland bears; [1a] or, as he stepped
Beyond the boundary line of some hill-shadow,
His form hath flashed upon me, glorified
By the deep radiance of the setting sun;[2]   270
Or him have I descried in distant sky,
A solitary object and sublime,
Above all height! like an aerial cross
Stationed alone upon a spiry rock
Of the Chartreuse, for worship.[3] Thus was man   275

1. In this book Wordsworth reviews the first 21 years of his life in order to trace the transfer of his earlier feelings for nature to shepherds and other humble people who carry on their lonely duties almost as though they were moving parts of the landscape (cf. *Michael*, lines 1–39). Wordsworth's central concern is to describe the early development in his relatively inexperienced mind of an Image, or conceptual model, of the largeness, worth, and almost sacred dignity of generic Man (lines 256–81); an Image which proved invulnerable to the acid bath of his later experience of the vulgarity, meanness, and evil of which individual men are capable (lines 317–22).
1a. Polar bears.
2. A "glory" is a mountain phenomenon in which the enlarged figure of a man is seen projected by the sun upon the mist, with a radiance about its head. Cf. Coleridge's *Dejection*, line 54.
3. In his tour of the Alps Wordsworth had been deeply impressed by the Chartreuse, a Carthusian monastery in

Ennobled outwardly before my sight,
And thus my heart was early introduced
To an unconscious love and reverence
Of human nature; hence the human form
To me became an index of delight, 280
Of grace and honor, power and worthiness.
Meanwhile this creature—spiritual almost
As those of books, but more exalted far;
Far more of an imaginative form
Than the gay Corin[4] of the groves, who lives 285
For his own fancies, or to dance by the hour,
In coronal, with Phyllis in the midst—
Was, for the purposes of kind,[5] a man
With the most common; husband, father; learned,
Could teach, admonish; suffered with the rest 290
From vice and folly, wretchedness and fear;
Of this I little saw, cared less for it,
But something must have felt.
                 Call ye these appearances—
Which I beheld of shepherds in my youth,
This sanctity of Nature given to man— 295
A shadow, a delusion, ye who pore
On the dead letter, miss the spirit of things;
Whose truth is not a motion or a shape
Instinct with vital functions, but a block
Or waxen image which yourselves have made, 300
And ye adore! But blessed be the God
Of Nature and of Man that this was so;
That men before my inexperienced eyes
Did first present themselves thus purified,
Removed, and to a distance that was fit: 305
And so we all of us in some degree
Are led to knowledge, whencesoever led,
And howsoever; were it otherwise,
And we found evil fast as we find good
In our first years, or think that it is found, 310
How could the innocent heart bear up and live!
But doubly fortunate my lot; not here
Alone, that something of a better life
Perhaps was round me than it is the privilege
Of most to move in, but that first I looked 315
At Man through objects that were great or fair;
First communed with him by their help. And thus
Was founded a sure safeguard and defense
Against the weight of meanness, selfish cares,

the French Alps, with its soaring cross
visible against the sky. There is an
overtone here of the Christlike divinity
investing the "common" man (line
289).
4. "Corin" and "Phyllis," dancing in

their "coronals," or wreaths of flowers,
were stock characters in earlier pastoral literature.
5. I.e., in carrying out the tasks of
humankind.

Coarse manners, vulgar passions, that beat in   320
On all sides from the ordinary world
In which we traffic. * * *

    Yet deem not, Friend! that human kind with me   340
Thus early took a place pre-eminent;
Nature herself was, at this unripe time,
But secondary to my own pursuits
And animals activities, and all
Their trivial pleasures;[6] and when these had drooped   345
And gradually expired, and Nature, prized
For her own sake, became my joy, even then—
And upwards through late youth, until not less
Than two-and-twenty summers had been told—
Was Man in my affections and regards   350
Subordinate to her, her visible forms
And viewless agencies: a passion, she,
A rapture often, and immediate love
Ever at hand; he, only a delight
Occasional, an accidental grace,   355
His hour being not yet come. * * *

From *Book IX. Residence in France*[1]

France lured me forth; the realm that I had crossed
So lately, journeying toward the snow-clad Alps.
But now, relinquishing the scrip and staff,[2]   35
And all enjoyment which the summer sun
Sheds round the steps of those who meet the day
With motion constant as his own, I went
Prepared to sojourn in a pleasant town,
Washed by the current of the stately Loire.[3]   40

    Through Paris lay my readiest course, and there
Sojourning a few days, I visited,
In haste, each spot of old or recent fame,
The latter chiefly; from the field of Mars   45
Down to the suburbs of St. Antony,
And from Mont Martyr southward to the Dome
Of Geneviève.[4] In both her clamorous Halls,

6. Cf. Wordsworth's account of the stages of his development in *Tintern Abbey*, lines 65–92 and note.
1. Wordsworth's second visit to France, while he was 21 and 22 years of age (1791–92), came during a crucial period of the French Revolution. This book deals with Wordsworth's stay at Paris, Orléans, and Blois, when he developed his passionate partisanship for the French people and the revolutionary cause.
2. The "scrip" (the bag or knapsack) and the "staff" are the traditional emblems of the foot pilgrim.

3. Orléans, on the Loire river, where Wordsworth stayed from late November, 1791, until he moved to Blois early the next year.
4. The "field of Mars" (the Champ de Mars), where Louis XVI swore fidelity to the new constitution. "The suburbs of St. Anthony": Faubourg St. Antoine, near the Bastille, a working-class quarter and center of revolutionary violence. "Mont Martyr": Montmartre, a hill on which revolutionary meetings were held. The "dome of Geneviève" became the Panthéon, a burial place for notable Frenchmen.

The National Synod[5] and the Jacobins,
I saw the Revolutionary Power   50
Toss like a ship at anchor, rocked by storms;
The Arcades I traversed, in the Palace huge
Of Orléans;[6] coasted round and round the line
Of Tavern, Brothel, Gaming-house, and Shop,
Great rendezvous of worst and best, the walk   55
Of all who had a purpose, or had not;
I stared and listened, with a stranger's ears.
To Hawkers and Haranguers, hubbub wild!
And hissing Factionists with ardent eyes,
In knots, or pairs, or single. Not a look   60
Hope takes, or Doubt or Fear is forced to wear,
But seemed there present; and I scanned them all,
Watched every gesture uncontrollable,
Of anger, and vexation, and despite,
All side by side, and struggling face to face,   65
With gaiety and dissolute idleness.

　　Where silent zephyrs sported with the dust
Of the Bastille, I sate in the open sun,
And from the rubbish gathered up a stone,
And pocketed the relic, in the guise   70
Of an enthusiast: yet, in honest truth,
I looked for something that I could not find,
Affecting more emotion than I felt;
For 'tis most certain that these various sights,
However potent their first shock, with me   75
Appeared to recompense the traveler's pains
Less than the painted Magdalene of Le Brun,[7]
A beauty exquisitely wrought, with hair
Disheveled, gleaming eyes, and rueful cheek
Pale and bedropped with overflowing tears.   80

　　　　　　* * *

　　　　　　　For myself, I fear   110
Now in connection with so great a theme
To speak (as I must be compelled to do)
Of one so unimportant; night by night
Did I frequent the formal haunts of men,
Whom, in the city, privilege of birth   115
Sequestered from the rest, societies
Polished in arts, and in punctilio[8] versed;
Whence, and from deeper causes, all discourse
Of good and evil of the time was shunned

5. The newly formed National Assembly. "Jacobins": the club of radical democratic revolutionists, named for the ancient convent of St. Jacques, their meeting place.
6. The arcades in the courtyard of the Palais Royal, a shopping center and Parisian rendezvous.
7. A theatrical painting of the weeping Mary Magdalene by Charles Le Brun (1619–90), then regarded as a religious masterpiece.
8. The niceties of social manners.

With scrupulous care; but these restrictions soon   120
Proved tedious, and I gradually withdrew
Into a noisier world, and thus ere long
Became a patriot;[9] and my heart was all
Given to the people, and my love was theirs.

* * *

    Among that band of Officers was one,
Already hinted at, of other mold—
A patriot, thence rejected by the rest,   290
And with an oriental loathing spurned,
As of a different caste.[1] A meeker man
Than this lived never, nor a more benign,
Meek though enthusiastic. Injuries
Made *him* more gracious, and his nature then   295
Did breathe its sweetness out most sensibly,
As aromatic flowers on Alpine turf,
When foot hath crushed them. He through the events
Of that great change wandered in perfect faith,
As through a book, an old romance, or tale   300
Of Fairy, or some dream of actions wrought
Behind the summer clouds. By birth he ranked
With the most noble, but unto the poor
Among mankind he was in service bound,
As by some tie invisible, oaths professed   305
To a religious order. Man he loved
As man; and, to the mean and the obscure,
And all the homely[2] in their homely works,
Transferred a courtesy which had no air
Of condescension; but did rather seem   310
A passion and a gallantry, like that
Which he, a soldier, in his idler day
Had paid to woman: somewhat vain he was,
Or seemed so, yet it was not vanity,
But fondness, and a kind of radiant joy   315
Diffused around him, while he was intent
On works of love or freedom, or revolved
Complacently[3] the progress of a cause,
Whereof he was a part: yet this was meek
And placid, and took nothing from the man   320
That was delightful. Oft in solitude
With him did I discourse about the end
Of civil government, and its wisest forms;
Of ancient loyalty, and chartered rights,
Custom and habit, novelty and change;   325
Of self-respect, and virtue in the few

9. A republican in politics.
1. This memorable character sketch is
of Michel Beaupuy, fifteen years older
than Wordsworth, and one of the rare
republicans among the officer corps of
the regular army. By doctrine and
force of character he did much to shape
Wordsworth's radical sympathies.
2. Lowly.
3. With quiet satisfaction.

For patrimonial honor set apart,
And ignorance in the laboring multitude.
For he, to all intolerance indisposed,
Balanced these contemplations in his mind;   330
And I, who at that time was scarcely dipped
Into the turmoil, bore a sounder judgment
Than later days allowed; carried about me,
With less alloy to its integrity,
The experience of past ages, as, through help   335
Of books and common life, it makes sure way
To youthful minds, by objects over near
Not pressed upon, nor dazzled or misled
By struggling with the crowd for present ends.

* * *

                    Yet not the less,
Hatred of absolute rule, where will of one
Is law for all, and of that barren pride
In them who, by immunities unjust,
Between the sovereign and the people stand,   505
His helper and not theirs, laid stronger hold
Daily upon me, mixed with pity too
And love; for where hope is, there love will be
For the abject multitude. And when we chanced
One day to meet a hunger-bitten girl,   510
Who crept along fitting her languid gait
Unto a heifer's motion, by a cord
Tied to her arm, and picking thus from the lane
Its sustenance, while the girl with pallid hands
Was busy knitting in a heartless mood   515
Of solitude, and at the sight my friend
In agitation said, " 'Tis against *that*
That we are fighting," I with him believed
That a benignant spirit was abroad
Which might not be withstood, that poverty   520
Abject as this would in a little time
Be found no more, that we should see the earth
Unthwarted in her wish to recompense
The meek, the lowly, patient child of toil,
All institutes forever blotted out   525
That legalized exclusion, empty pomp
Abolished, sensual state and cruel power
Whether by edict of the one or few;
And finally, as sum and crown of all,
Should see the people having a strong hand   530
In framing their own laws; whence better days
To all mankind.[4] * * *

4. The following political aims constituted the radicalism of Wordsworth
and Beaupuy: elimination of the extreme of poverty; the rewards of tillage to go to the tiller of the land; all
careers opened to talents; abolition of
absolute power, whether by a monarch
or an oligarchy; and a greatly extended franchise.

From *Book X. Residence in France (continued)*[1]

Cheered with this hope,[2] to Paris I returned,
And ranged, with ardor heretofore unfelt,
The spacious city, and in progress passed   50
The prison[3] where the unhappy Monarch lay,
Associate with his children and his wife
In bondage; and the palace, lately stormed
With roar of cannon by a furious host.
I crossed the square (an empty area then!)   55
Of the Carrousel, where so late had lain
The dead, upon the dying heaped, and gazed
On this and other spots, as doth a man
Upon a volume whose contents he knows
Are memorable, but from him locked up,   60
Being written in a tongue he cannot read,
So that he questions the mute leaves with pain,
And half upbraids their silence. But that night
I felt most deeply in what world I was,
What ground I trod on, and what air I breathed.   65
High was my room and lonely, near the roof
Of a large mansion or hotel, a lodge
That would have pleased me in more quiet times;
Nor was it wholly without pleasure then.
With unextinguished taper I kept watch,   70
Reading at intervals; the fear gone by
Pressed on me almost like a fear to come.
I thought of those September massacres,
Divided from me by one little month,
Saw them and touched:[4] the rest was conjured up   75
From tragic fictions or true history,
Remembrances and dim admonishments.
The horse is taught his manage,[5] and no star
Of wildest course but treads back his own steps;
For the spent hurricane the air provides   80
As fierce a successor; the tide retreats
But to return out of its hiding place
In the great deep; all things have second birth;
The earthquake is not satisfied at once;
And in this way I wrought upon myself,   85
Until I seemed to hear a voice that cried,

1. At this period, October, 1792–August, 1794, Wordsworth's revolutionary enthusiasm was at its height.
2. The Parisian mob had stormed the Tuileries; the king had been deposed and imprisoned; and the Commune had organized the "September Massacres," in which 3,000 Royalist suspects were murdered. Wordsworth's "hope" was that the moderates were now taking over and would eliminate further violence.

3. I.e., the "Temple," where Louis XVI was held prisoner. "The palace" is the Tuileries; in front of this is the great square of "the Carrousel," where a number of the mob storming the palace had been killed.
4. I.e., his imagination of the September Massacres was so vivid as to be palpable.
5. The French *manège*, the prescribed action and paces of a trained horse.

To the whole city, "Sleep no more." The trance
Fled with the voice to which it had given birth;
But vainly comments of a calmer mind
Promised soft peace and sweet forgetfulness.   90
The place, all hushed and silent as it was,
Appeared unfit for the repose of night,
Defenseless as a wood where tigers roam.

* * *

                    In this frame of mind,
Dragged by a chain of harsh necessity,
So seemed it—now I thankfully acknowledge,
Forced by the gracious providence of Heaven—
To England I returned,[6] else (though assured   225
That I both was and must be of small weight,
No better than a landsman on the deck
Of a ship struggling with a hideous storm)
Doubtless, I should have then made common cause
With some who perished; haply perished too,   230
A poor mistaken and bewildered offering—
Should to the breast of Nature have gone back,
With all my resolutions, all my hopes,
A Poet only to myself, to men
Useless, and even, belovéd Friend! a soul   235
To thee unknown![7] * * *

What, then, were my emotions, when in arms
Britain put forth her freeborn strength in league,
Oh, pity and shame! with those confederate Powers![8]   265
Not in my single self alone I found,
But in the minds of all ingenuous youth,
Change and subversion from that hour. No shock
Given to my moral nature had I known
Down to that very moment; neither lapse   270
Nor turn of sentiment that might be named
A revolution, save at this one time;
All else was progress on the selfsame path
On which, with a diversity of pace,
I had been traveling: this a stride at once   275
Into another region. As a light
And pliant harebell, swinging in the breeze
On some gray rock—its birthplace—so had I

6. Forced by the "harsh necessity" of a lack of money, Wordsworth returned to England late in 1792.
7. Wordsworth did not meet Coleridge, the belovéd "Friend," until 1795.
8. England joined the war against France in February, 1793. The great moral crisis which almost wrecked Wordsworth's life began with this sudden split between his profound attachments to the English land (the development of which he had described in the early books of *The Prelude*) and his later but heartfelt identification with the cause of the French Revolution. What had seemed a single and coherent development suddenly became split into conflicting parts. The moral turmoil he goes on to describe is remarkably parallel to that of many young radicals of the 1930's and later, who had staked their hopes for mankind on the Russian Revolution.

Wantoned, fast rooted on the ancient tower
Of my belovéd country, wishing not   280
A happier fortune than to wither there:
Now was I from that pleasant station torn
And tossed about in whirlwind. I rejoiced,
Yea, afterwards—truth most painful to record!—
Exulted, in the triumph of my soul,   285
When Englishmen by thousands were o'erthrown,
Left without glory on the field, or driven,
Brave hearts! to shameful flight.[9] It was a grief—
Grief call it not, 'twas anything but that—
A conflict of sensations without name,   290
Of which *he* only, who may love the sight
Of a village steeple, as I do, can judge,
When, in the congregation bending all
To their great Father, prayers were offered up,
Or praises for our country's victories;   295
And, 'mid the simple worshipers, perchance
I only, like an uninvited guest
Whom no one owned, sate silent, shall I add,
Fed on the day of vengeance yet to come.

* * *

Most melancholy at that time, O Friend!
Were my day thoughts—my nights were miserable;[10]
Through months, through years, long after the last beat
Of those atrocities, the hour of sleep   400
To me came rarely charged with natural gifts,
Such ghastly visions had I of despair
And tyranny, and implements of death;
And innocent victims sinking under fear,
And momentary hope, and worn-out prayer,   405
Each in his separate cell, or penned in crowds
For sacrifice, and struggling with fond mirth
And levity in dungeons, where the dust
Was laid with tears. Then suddenly the scene
Changed, and the unbroken dream entangled me   410
In long orations, which I strove to plead
Before unjust tribunals—with a voice
Laboring, a brain confounded, and a sense,
Deathlike, of treacherous desertion, felt
In the last place of refuge—my own soul.   415

* * *

From *Book XI. France* (concluded)[1]

O pleasant exercise of hope and joy!   105
For mighty were the auxiliars which then stood

9. The French defeated the English in the battle of Hondschoote, September 6, 1793.
10. The Reign of Terror, under Robes-
pierre, had begun with the execution of the moderate Girondist leaders in October and November, 1793.
1. Book XI deals with the year from

Upon our side, us who were strong in love!
Bliss was it in that dawn to be alive,
But to be young was very Heaven! O times,
In which the meager, stale, forbidding ways   110
Of custom, law, and statute, took at once
The attraction of a country in romance!
When Reason seemed the most to assert her rights
When most intent on making of herself
A prime enchantress—to assist the work,   115
Which then was going forward in her name!
Not favored spots alone, but the whole Earth,
The beauty wore of promise—that which sets
(As at some moments might not be unfelt
Among the bowers of Paradise itself)   120
The budding rose above the rose full blown.[2]
What temper at the prospect did not wake
To happiness unthought of? The inert
Were roused, and lively natures rapt away!
They who had fed their childhood upon dreams,   125
The playfellows of fancy, who had made
All powers of swiftness, subtlety, and strength
Their ministers—who in lordly wise had stirred
Among the grandest objects of the sense,
And dealt with whatsoever they found there   130
As if they had within some lurking right
To wield it—they, too, who of gentle mood
Had watched all gentle motions, and to these
Had fitted their own thoughts, schemers more mild,
And in the region of their peaceful selves—   135
Now was it that *both* found, the meek and lofty
Did both find helpers to their hearts' desire,
And stuff at hand, plastic as they could wish—
Were called upon to exercise their skill,
Not in Utopia, subterranean fields,   140
Or some secreted island, Heaven knows where!
But in the very world, which is the world
Of all of us—the place where, in the end,
We find our happiness, or not at all!

    Why should I not confess that Earth was then   145
To me, what an inheritance, new-fallen,
Seems, when the first time visited, to one
Who thither comes to find in it his home?
He walks about and looks upon the spot

August, 1794, through September, 1795: Wordsworth's growing disillusionment with the French Revolution, his recourse to abstract theories of man and politics, his despair and nervous breakdown, and the beginning of his recovery when he moved from London to Racedown.

2. A statement of the Romantic theme of the glory of the imperfect, which sets a higher value on promise than on achievement.

With cordial transport, molds it and remolds,   150
And is half-pleased with things that are amiss,
'Twill be such joy to see them disappear.

* * *

But now, become oppressors in their turn,
Frenchmen had changed a war of self-defense
For one of conquest,[3] losing sight of all
Which they had struggled for: now mounted up,
Openly in the eye of earth and heaven,   210
The scale of liberty.[4] I read her doom.
With anger vexed, with disappointment sore,
But not dismayed, nor taking to the shame
Of a false prophet. While resentment rose,
Striving to hide, what nought could heal, the wounds   215
Of mortified presumption, I adhered
More firmly to old tenets, and, to prove
Their temper, strained them more; and thus, in heat
Of contest, did opinions every day
Grow into consequence, till round my mind   220
They clung, as if they were its life, nay more,
The very being of the immortal soul.

* * *

I summoned my best skill, and toiled, intent
To anatomize the frame of social life,   280
Yea, the whole body of society
Searched to its heart.[5] Share with me, Friend! the wish
That some dramatic tale, endued with shapes
Livelier, and flinging out less guarded words
Than suit the work we fashion, might set forth   285
What then I learned, or think I learned, of truth,
And the errors into which I fell, betrayed
By present objects, and by reasonings false
From their beginnings, inasmuch as drawn
Out of a heart that had been turned aside   290
From Nature's way by outward accidents,
And which was thus confounded, more and more
Misguided, and misguiding. So I fared,
Dragging all precepts, judgments, maxims, creeds,
Like culprits to the bar; calling the mind,   295
Suspiciously, to establish in plain day
Her titles and her honors; now believing,
Now disbelieving; endlessly perplexed

3. In late 1794 and early 1795 French troops had successes in Spain, Italy, Holland, and Germany.
4. I.e., the desire for power now outweighed the love of liberty.
5. Disappointed in the course of the actual Revolution, Wordsworth turned to the theories of William Godwin and other philosophers of the Enlighten-

ment. These theorists attempted to deduce the laws of ethics and government from rational premises; they fatally omitted, as Wordsworth later maintained, to take account of the moral promptings and loyalties of man's "heart"—i.e., of his instinctual and feelingful nature (see lines 353–56).

With impulse, motive, right and wrong, the ground
Of obligation, what the rule and whence   300
The sanction; till, demanding formal *proof*,
And seeking it in everything, I lost
All feeling of conviction, and, in fine,[6]
Sick, wearied out with contrarieties,
Yielded up moral questions in despair.   305

    This was the crisis of that strong disease,
This the soul's last and lowest ebb; I drooped,
Deeming our blessed reason of least use
Where wanted most * * *

            Then it was—
Thanks to the bounteous Giver of all good!—
That the belovéd Sister[7] in whose sight   335
Those days were passed, now speaking in a voice
Of sudden admonition—like a brook
That did but *cross* a lonely road, and now
Is seen, heard, felt, and caught at every turn,
Companion never lost through many a league—   340
Maintained for me a saving intercourse
With my true self;[8] for, though bedimmed and changed
Much, as it seemed, I was no further changed
Than as a clouded and a waning moon;
She whispered still that brightness would return;   345
She, in the midst of all, preserved me still
A Poet, made me seek beneath that name,
And that alone, my office upon earth;
And, lastly, as hereafter will be shown,
If willing audience fail not, Nature's self,   350
By all varieties of human love
Assisted, led me back through opening day
To those sweet counsels between head and heart
Whence grew that genuine knowledge, fraught with peace,
Which, through the later sinkings of this cause,   355
Hath still upheld me, and upholds me now
In the catastrophe (for so they dream,
And nothing less), when, finally to close
And seal up all the gains of France, a Pope
Is summoned in, to crown an Emperor[9] * * *   360

6. At last.
7. After a long separation, from 1791 to 1794, Dorothy Wordsworth came to live with her brother at Racedown in 1795, and continued a member of his household until her death.
8. Dorothy and the renewed influence of nature (line 350) healed the inner fracture between his earlier and later self, which Wordsworth had described in Book X, lines 268 ff.
9. The ultimate blow to liberal hopes for France when, on December 2, 1804, Napoleon summoned Pope Pius VII to officiate at the ceremony elevating him to Emperor. At the last moment, Napoleon took the crown and donned it himself.

From *Book XII. Imagination and Taste,*
How Impaired and Restored[1]

There are in our existence spots of time,
That with distinct pre-eminence retain
A renovating virtue, whence—depressed   210
By false opinion and contentious thought,
Or aught of heavier or more deadly weight,
In trivial occupations, and the round
Of ordinary intercourse—our minds
Are nourished and invisibly repaired;   215
A virtue, by which pleasure is enhanced,
That penetrates, enables us to mount,
When high, more high, and lifts us up when fallen.
This efficacious spirit chiefly lurks
Among those passages of life that give   220
Profoundest knowledge to what point, and how,
The mind is lord and master—outward sense
The obedient servant of her will. Such moments
Are scattered everywhere, taking their date
From our first childhood. I remember well,   225
That once, while yet my inexperienced hand
Could scarcely hold a bridle, with proud hopes
I mounted, and we journeyed towards the hills:
An ancient servant of my father's house
Was with me, my encourager and guide;   230
We had not traveled long, ere some mischance
Disjoined me from my comrade; and, through fear
Dismounting, down the rough and stony moor
I led my horse, and, stumbling on, at length
Came to a bottom, where in former times   235
A murderer had been hung in iron chains.
The gibbet-mast had moldered down, the bones
And iron case were gone; but on the turf,
Hard by, soon after that fell deed was wrought,
Some unknown hand had carved the murderer's name.   240
The monumental letters were inscribed
In times long past; but still, from year to year
By superstition of the neighborhood,
The grass is cleared away, and to this hour
The characters are fresh and visible: 245

1. Book XII reviews the "impairment" and gradual recovery of Wordsworth's creative sensibility in response to the natural world; its climax is the famed description of the "spots of time." These are moments of experience of what is in itself ordinary (line 254), but becomes luminous with a profound significance that, since it is bestowed by the perceiver, evidences the imaginative power of the perceiving mind (lines 220–23, 275–77). The recollection of these indelible scenes nourishes and repairs the mind in those periods of depression or distraction when the imagination flags (lines 210–215). Wordsworth also recognizes (lines 277–86) that the recollection of such spots of time from his own early experience is the source of his greatest poetry, and that this source is not inexhaustible.

A casual glance had shown them, and I fled,
Faltering and faint, and ignorant of the road;
Then, reascending the bare common, saw
A naked pool that lay beneath the hills,
The beacon on the summit, and more near,   250
A girl, who bore a pitcher on her head,
And seemed with difficult steps to force her way
Against the blowing wind. It was, in truth,
An ordinary sight; but I should need
Colors and words that are unknown to man,   255
To paint the visionary dreariness
Which, while I looked all round for my lost guide,
Invested moorland waste and naked pool,
The beacon crowning the lone eminence,
The female and her garments vexed and tossed   260
By the strong wind. When, in the blessed hours
Of early love, the loved one at my side,
I roamed, in daily presence of this scene,
Upon the naked pool and dreary crags,
And on the melancholy beacon, fell   265
A spirit of pleasure and youth's golden gleam;
And think ye not with radiance more sublime
For these remembrances, and for the power
They had left behind? So feeling comes in aid
Of feeling, and diversity of strength   270
Attends us, if but once we have been strong.
Oh! mystery of man, from what a depth
Proceed thy honors. I am lost, but see
In simple childhood something of the base
On which thy greatness stands; but this I feel,   275
That from thyself it comes, that thou must give,
Else never canst receive. The days gone by
Return upon me almost from the dawn
Of life: the hiding places of man's power
Open; I would approach them, but they close.   280
I see by glimpses now; when age comes on,
May scarcely see at all; and I would give,
While yet we may, as far as words can give,
Substance and life to what I feel, enshrining,
Such is my hope, the spirit of the Past   285
For future restoration.—Yet another
Of these memorials:
                           One Christmas time,
On the glad eve of its dear holidays,
Feverish, and tired, and restless, I went forth
Into the fields, impatient for the sight   290
Of those led palfreys² that should bear us home;
My brothers and myself. There rose a crag,
That, from the meeting point of two highways

2. Small saddle horses.

Ascending, overlooked them both, far stretched;
Thither, uncertain on which road to fix   295
My expectation, thither I repaired,
Scoutlike, and gained the summit; 'twas a day
Tempestuous, dark, and wild, and on the grass
I sate half-sheltered by a naked wall;
Upon my right hand couched a single sheep,   300
Upon my left a blasted hawthorn stood;
With those companions at my side, I watched,
Straining my eyes intensely, as the mist
Gave intermitting prospect of the copse
And plain beneath. Ere we to school returned—   305
That dreary time—ere we had been ten days
Sojourners in my father's house, he died;
And I and my three brothers, orphans then,
Followed his body to the grave. The event,
With all the sorrow that it brought, appeared   310
A chastisement; and when I called to mind
That day so lately passed, when from the crag
I looked in such anxiety of hope,
With trite reflections of morality,
Yet in the deepest passion, I bowed low   315
To God, who thus corrected my desires;
And, afterwards, the wind and sleety rain,
And all the business of the elements,
The single sheep, and the one blasted tree,
And the bleak music from that old stone wall,   320
The noise of wood and water, and the mist
That on the line of each of those two roads
Advanced in such indisputable shapes;[3]
All these were kindred spectacles and sounds
To which I oft repaired, and thence would drink,   325
As at a fountain; and on winter nights,
Down to this very time, when storm and rain
Beat on my roof, or, haply, at noonday,
While in a grove I walk, whose lofty trees,
Laden with summer's thickest foliage, rock   330
In a strong wind, some working of the spirit,
Some inward agitations thence are brought,
Whate'er their office, whether to beguile
Thoughts over busy in the course they took,
Or animate an hour of vacant ease.   335

From *Book XIII. Imagination and Taste,*
How Impaired and Restored (concluded)

Here, calling up to mind what then I saw,[1]
A youthful traveler, and see daily now

3. I.e., shapes one didn't dare dispute
with.
1. Wordsworth has described, as part
of his imaginative recovery, his learning to look again with sympathy upon
"the unassuming things that hold / A

In the familiar circuit of my home,
Here might I pause, and bend in reverence
To Nature, and the power of human minds,   225
To men as they are men within themselves.
How oft high service is performed within,
When all the external man is rude in show—
Not like a temple rich with pomp and gold,
But a mere mountain chapel, that protects   230
Its simple worshipers from sun and shower.
Of these, said I, shall be my song; of these,
If future years mature me for the task,
Will I record the praises, making verse
Deal boldly with substantial things; in truth   235
And sanctity of passion, speak of these,
That justice may be done, obeisance paid
Where it is due: thus haply shall I teach,
Inspire; through unadulterated ears
Pour rapture, tenderness, and hope—my theme   240
No other than the very heart of man,
As found among the best of those who live,
Not unexalted by religious faith,
Nor uninformed by books, good books, though few,
In Nature's presence; thence may I select   245
Sorrow, that is not sorrow, but delight;
And miserable love, that is not pain
To hear of, for the glory that redounds
Therefrom to human kind, and what we are.
Be mine to follow with no timid step   250
Where knowledge leads me: it shall be my pride
That I have dared to tread this holy ground,
Speaking no dream, but things oracular;
Matter not lightly to be heard by those
Who to the letter of the outward promise   255
Do read the invisible soul;[2] by men adroit
In speech, and for communion with the world
Accomplished; minds whose faculties are then
Most active when they are most eloquent,
And elevated most when most admired.   260
Men may be found of other mold than these,
Who are their own upholders, to themselves
Encouragement, and energy, and will,
Expressing liveliest thoughts in lively words
As native passion dictates. * * *   265

silent station in this beauteous world,"
and his finding again "in Man an object of delight." Now he shows how, in
reaction against his concern with great
actions detached from moral purpose
which constituted the French Revolution, he came to embrace the poetic
doctrines of the Preface to *Lyrical Ballads*. He will write of simple, lowly
men, whose patient endurance of suffering redounds to the glory of human
kind, and who speak a language which
is the spontaneous overflow of powerful
feeling (lines 263–64).
2. I.e., this doctrine will not be lightly
accepted by those who judge a man's
inner worth by his exterior seeming.

From Book XIV. *Conclusion*

In one of those excursions (may they ne'er
Fade from remembrance!) through the northern tracts
Of Cambria ranging with a youthful friend,[1]
I left Bethgelert's huts at couching time,
And westward took my way, to see the sun   5
Rise, from the top of Snowdon. To the door
Of a rude cottage at the mountain's base
We came, and roused the shepherd who attends
The adventurous stranger's steps, a trusty guide;
Then, cheered by short refreshment, sallied forth.   10

It was a close, warm, breezeless summer night,
Wan, dull, and glaring, with a dripping fog
Low-hung and thick that covered all the sky;
But, undiscouraged, we began to climb
The mountainside. The mist soon girt us round,   15
And, after ordinary travelers' talk
With our conductor, pensively we sank
Each into commerce with his private thoughts;
Thus did we breast the ascent, and by myself
Was nothing either seen or heard that checked   20
Those musings or diverted, save that once
The shepherd's lurcher,[2] who, among the crags,
Had to his joy unearthed a hedgehog, teased
His coiled-up prey with barkings turbulent.
This small adventure, for even such it seemed   25
In that wild place and at the dead of night,
Being over and forgotten, on we wound
In silence as before. With forehead bent
Earthward, as if in opposition set
Against an enemy, I panted up   30
With eager pace, and no less eager thoughts.
Thus might we wear a midnight hour away,
Ascending at loose distance each from each,
And I, as chanced, the foremost of the band;
When at my feet the ground appeared to brighten,   35
And with a step or two seemed brighter still;
Nor was time given to ask or learn the cause,
For instantly a light upon the turf
Fell like a flash, and lo! as I looked up,
The Moon hung naked in a firmament   40

1. Wordsworth climbed Mt. Snowdon, the highest peak in Wales ("Cambria"), with Robert Jones, the friend with whom he had also tramped through the Alps (Book VI). The climb started from the village of Bethgelert at "couching time," the time of night when the sheep lie down to sleep. This event had taken place in 1791 (or possibly 1793); Wordsworth presents it out of its chronological order to introduce at this point a great natural "type" or "emblem" (lines 66, 70) for the mind, and especially for the activity of the imagination, whose "restoration" he has described in the two preceding books.
2. A crossbred dog, used to hunt hares.

Of azure without cloud, and at my feet
Rested a silent sea of hoary mist.
A hundred hills their dusky backs upheaved
All over this still ocean; and beyond,
Far, far beyond, the solid vapors stretched,   45
In headlands, tongues, and promontory shapes,
Into the main Atlantic, that appeared
To dwindle, and give up his majesty,
Usurped upon far as the sight could reach.
Not so the ethereal vault; encroachment none   50
Was there, nor loss;[3] only the inferior stars
Had disappeared, or shed a fainter light
In the clear presence of the full-orbed Moon,
Who, from her sovereign elevation, gazed
Upon the billowy ocean, as it lay   55
All meek and silent, save that through a rift—
Not distant from the shore whereon we stood,
A fixed, abysmal, gloomy, breathing-place—
Mounted the roar of waters, torrents, streams
Innumerable, roaring with one voice!   60
Heard over earth and sea, and, in that hour,
For so it seemed, felt by the starry heavens.

When into air had partially dissolved
That vision, given to spirits of the night
And three chance human wanderers, in calm thought   65
Reflected, it appeared to me the type
Of a majestic intellect, its acts
And its possessions, what it has and craves,
What in itself it is, and would become.
There I beheld the emblem of a mind   70
That feeds upon infinity, that broods
Over the dark abyss, intent to hear
Its voices issuing forth to silent light
In one continuous stream; a mind sustained
By recognitions of transcendent power,   75
In sense conducting to ideal form,
In soul of more than mortal privilege.[4]
One function, above all, of such a mind
Had Nature shadowed there, by putting forth,
'Mid circumstances awful and sublime,   80
That mutual domination which she loves
To exert upon the face of outward things,
So molded, joined, abstracted, so endowed
With interchangeable supremacy,
That men, least sensitive, see, hear, perceive,   85

3. The mist projected in various shapes over the Atlantic Ocean, but did not "encroach" upon the heavens overhead.
4. The sense of lines 74–77 may be that the mind recognizes its transcendent power to idealize objects in the realm of sense and to exceed the limits of mortality in the realm of soul.

And cannot choose but feel. The power, which all
Acknowledge when thus moved, which Nature thus
To bodily sense exhibits, is the express
Resemblance of that glorious faculty
That higher minds bear with them as their own.[5]   90
This is the very spirit in which they deal
With the whole compass of the universe:
They from their native selves can send abroad
Kindred mutations; for themselves create
A like existence; and, whene'er it dawns   95
Created for them, catch it, or are caught
By its inevitable mastery,
Like angels stopped upon the wing by sound
Of harmony from Heaven's remotest spheres.
Them the enduring and the transient both   100
Serve to exalt; they build up greatest things
From least suggestions; ever on the watch,
Willing to work and to be wrought upon,
They need not extraordinary calls
To rouse them; in a world of life they live,   105
By sensible impressions not enthralled,
But by their quickening impulse made more prompt
To hold fit converse with the spiritual world,
And with the generations of mankind
Spread over time, past, present, and to come,   110
Age after age, till Time shall be no more.
Such minds are truly from the Deity,
For they are Powers; and hence the highest bliss
That flesh can know is theirs—the consciousness
Of Whom they are, habitually infused   115
Through every image and through every thought,
And all affections by communion raised
From earth to heaven, from human to divine;
Hence endless occupation for the Soul,
Whether discursive or intuitive;[6]   120
Hence cheerfulness for acts of daily life,
Emotions which best foresight need not fear,
Most worthy then of trust when most intense.
Hence, amid ills that vex and wrongs that crush
Our hearts—if here the words of Holy Writ   125
May with fit reverence be applied—that peace
Which passeth understanding,[7] that repose

5. The "glorious faculty" is the imagination, which in its exhibition of mastery over sense—through its power to alter and re-create what is given to it in perception (lines 93–106)—is analogous to that aspect of the outer scene, in which the ordinary landscape is transfigured by the moonlit mist. Compare the mind as "lord and master" of outward sense in Book XII, lines 221–23.

6. An echo of *Paradise Lost* V.488. The "discursive" reason undertakes to reach truths through a logical sequence of premises, observations, and conclusions; the "intuitive" reason comprehends truths immediately.

7. Philippians iv.7: "the peace of God, which passeth all understanding." This passage of Christian piety was added by Wordsworth in a late revision.

In moral judgments which from this pure source
Must come, or will by man be sought in vain.

* * *

Never did I, in quest of right and wrong,
Tamper with conscience from a private aim;
Nor was in any public hope the dupe
Of selfish passions; nor did ever yield
Willfully to mean cares or low pursuits,
But shrunk with apprehensive jealousy   155
From every combination which might aid
The tendency, too potent in itself,
Of use and custom to bow down the soul
Under a growing weight of vulgar sense,
And substitute a universe of death   160
For that which moves with light and life informed,
Actual, divine, and true. To fear and love,
To love as prime and chief, for there fear ends,
Be this ascribed;[8] to early intercourse,
In presence of sublime or beautiful forms,   165
With the adverse principles of pain and joy—
Evil as one is rashly named by men
Who know not what they speak. By love subsists
All lasting grandeur, by pervading love;
That gone, we are as dust. * * *   170

    This spiritual Love acts not nor can exist
Without Imagination,[9] which, in truth,
Is but another name for absolute power   190
And clearest insight, amplitude of mind,
And Reason in her most exalted mood.
This faculty hath been the feeding source
Of our long labor: we have traced the stream
From the blind cavern whence is faintly heard   195
Its natal murmur; followed it to light
And open day; accompanied its course
Among the ways of Nature, for a time
Lost sight of it bewildered and engulfed;
Then given it greeting as it rose once more   200
In strength, reflecting from its placid breast
The works of man and face of human life;
And lastly, from its progress have we drawn
Faith in life endless, the sustaining thought
Of human Being, Eternity, and God.[1]   205

8. Wordsworth's mind, he had said early in *The Prelude*, had been "fostered alike by beauty and by fear" (I.302); that is, by the opposing but equally necessary principles of the beautiful and terrifying aspects of nature. Now, in his conclusion, the principles of fear and pain are said to be ultimately transcended by their "adverse principles" of love and joy.
9. Cf. Shelley's *Defense of Poetry:* "The great secret of morals is love; or a going out of our own nature. * * * The great instrument of moral good is the imagination."
1. In the 1805 version, this read: "The feeling of life endless, the great thought / By which we live, Infinity and God."

Imagination having been our theme,
So also hath that intellectual Love,
For they are each in each, and cannot stand
Dividually.[2] * * *

And now, O Friend![3] this history is brought
To its appointed close: the discipline
And consummation of a Poet's mind,
In everything that stood most prominent,   305
Have faithfully been pictured; we have reached
The time (our guiding object from the first)
When we may, not presumptuously, I hope,
Suppose my powers so far confirmed, and such
My knowledge, as to make me capable   310
Of building up a work that shall endure.

* * *

Oh! yet a few short years of useful life,   430
And all will be complete, thy race be run,
Thy monument of glory will be raised;
Then, though (too weak to tread the ways of truth)
This age fall back to old idolatry,
Though men return to servitude as fast   435
As the tide ebbs, to ignominy and shame,
By nations sink together,[4] we shall still
Find solace—knowing what we have learnt to know,
Rich in true happiness if allowed to be
Faithful alike in forwarding a day   440
Of firmer trust, joint laborers in the work
(Should Providence such grace to us vouchsafe)
Of their deliverance, surely yet to come.
Prophets of Nature, we to them will speak
A lasting inspiration, sanctified   445
By reason, blest by faith: what we have loved,
Others will love, and we will teach them how;
Instruct them how the mind of man becomes
A thousand times more beautiful than the earth
On which he dwells, above this frame of things   450
(Which, 'mid all revolution in the hopes
And fears of men, doth still remain unchanged)
In beauty exalted, as it is itself
Of quality and fabric more divine.[5]

1799–1805   1850

2. Separately.
3. Coleridge, to whom the "thy" in lines 431–32 also refers.
4. I.e., though men—whole nations of them together—sink to ignominy and shame.
5. Cf. Wordsworth's statement about "the Mind of Man * * * the main region of my song," in *The Recluse*, lines 40–41.

SAMUEL TAYLOR COLERIDGE
(1772–1834)

1797: At Nether Stowey, Somersetshire; the Wordsworths settle nearby, at Alfoxden.

1798: *Lyrical Ballads*, which included *The Ancient Mariner* and several other poems by Coleridge.

1800: Moves to Greta Hall, Keswick, thirteen miles from the Wordsworths at Grasmere.

1816: Final residence at Highgate, near London, under the care of Dr. James Gillman.

1817: *Biographia Literaria*.

In *The Prelude* Wordsworth, recording his gratitude to the mountains, lakes, and winds "that dwell among the hills where I was born," commiserates with Coleridge because "thou, my Friend! wert reared / In the great city, 'mid far other scenes." Coleridge had in fact been born in the small town of Ottery St. Mary, in rural Devonshire; but upon the death of his father he had been sent to school at Christ's Hospital, in London. He was a dreamy, enthusiastic, and extraordinarily precocious schoolboy; Charles Lamb, his schoolmate and lifelong friend, in his essay on Christ's Hospital has given us a vivid sketch of Coleridge's loneliness, his learning, and his eloquence. When in 1791 Coleridge went up to Jesus College, Cambridge, he was an accomplished scholar; but he found little intellectual stimulation at the university, fell into idleness, dissoluteness, and debt, and in despair fled to London and enlisted in the Light Dragoons under the alias of Silas Tomkyn Comberbacke—probably the most inept cavalryman in the long history of the British army. Although rescued by his brothers and sent back to Cambridge, he left in 1794 without a degree.

In June, 1794, Coleridge met Robert Southey, then a student at Oxford who, like himself, had poetic aspirations, was a radical in religion and politics, and sympathized with the republican experiment in France. Together the two young men planned to establish an ideal democratic community in America for which Coleridge coined the name "Pantisocracy," signifying an equal rule by all. A plausible American real-estate agent persuaded them that the ideal location would be on the banks of the Susquehanna, in Pennsylvania. Twelve men undertook to go; and since perpetuation of the scheme required offspring, hence wives, Coleridge dutifully became engaged to Sara Fricker, conveniently at hand as the sister of Southey's fiancée. The Pantisocracy scheme collapsed, but at Southey's insistence Coleridge went through with the marriage, "resolved," as he said, "but wretched." Later Coleridge's radicalism waned, and he became a conservative—a highly philosophical one—in politics, and a staunch Anglican in religion.

Despite this inauspicious beginning, Coleridge was at first happy in his marriage. When Wordsworth (whom Coleridge met in 1795, and almost immediately judged "the best poet of the age") brought his sister Dorothy to settle at Alfoxden, only three miles from the Coleridges at Nether Stowey, the period of intimate communication and poetic collaboration began which was the golden time of Coleridge's life. An annuity of £150, granted to Coleridge by Thomas and Josiah Wedgwood, sons of the founder of the famous pottery firm, came just in time to deflect him from assuming a post as a Unitarian minister. After their momentous joint publication of *Lyrical Ballads* in 1798, Coleridge and the Wordsworths spent a winter in Germany, where Coleridge attended the University of Göttingen and began the lifelong study of Kant and the post-Kantian German philosophers and critics which helped to alter profoundly his thinking about philosophy, religion, and aesthetics.

Back in England, Coleridge in 1800 followed the Wordsworths to the Lake District, settling at Greta Hall, Keswick. He had become gradually disaffected from his wife, and in 1799 he fell helplessly and hopelessly in love with Sara Hutchinson, whose sister, Mary, Wordsworth married three years later. All his life Coleridge had suffered from numerous painful physical ailments; Wordsworth has described how sometimes, in a sudden spasm of agony, Coleridge would "throw himself down and writhe like a worm upon the ground." According to the standard medical prescription of the time, Coleridge had long been taking laudanum (opium dissolved in alcohol). In 1800–1801 heavy dosages taken for attacks of rheumatism made opium a necessity to him, and Coleridge soon recognized that the drug was a worse evil than the diseases it did not cure. *Dejection: An Ode*, published in 1802, was Coleridge's despairing farewell to health, happiness, and poetic creativity. A two-year sojourn on the Mediterranean island of Malta, intended to restore his health, instead completed his decline. When he returned to England in the late summer of 1806 he was a broken man, an inveterate drug addict, estranged from his wife, suffering from agonies of remorse, and subject to terrifying nightmares of guilt and despair from which his own shrieks awakened him. A bitter quarrel with Wordsworth in 1810 marked the nadir of his life and expectations.

Under these conditions Coleridge's literary efforts, however sporadic and fragmentary, were little short of heroic. In 1808 he gave his first course of public lectures in London, and in the next eleven years followed these with other series on both literary and philosophical topics. He wrote for newspapers and singlehandedly undertook to write, publish, and distribute a periodical, *The Friend*, which lasted for some fourteen months after January, 1809. A tragedy, *Remorse*, had in 1813 a very successful run of twenty performances at the Drury Lane Theatre. In 1816 he took up residence at Highgate, a northern suburb of London, under the supervision of the excellent and endlessly patient physician James Gillman, who managed to control, although not to eliminate, Coleridge's consumption of opium. The next three years were Coleridge's most sustained period of literary activity: while continuing to lecture and to write for the newspapers on a variety of subjects, he published the *Biographia Literaria*, *Zapolya* (a drama), a book consisting of the essays in *The Friend* (revised and greatly enlarged), two collections of poems, and several important treatises on philosophical and religious subjects; in these he undertook to establish a metaphysical basis for the Trinitarian theology to which he had turned after his youthful period of Unitarianism.

The remaining years of his life, which he spent with Dr. and Mrs. Gillman, were quieter and happier than any he had known since the turn of the century. He came to a peaceful understanding with his wife and was reconciled to Wordsworth, with whom he toured the Rhineland in 1828. His rooms at Highgate became a center for friends, for the London literati, and for a steady stream of pilgrims from England and America. They came to hear one of the wonders of the age, the Sage of Highgate's conversation—or monologue—for even in his decline, Coleridge's talk never entirely lost the almost incantatory power which Hazlitt has immortalized in *My First Acquaintance with Poets*. When he died, Coleridge left his friends with the sense that an imcomparable intellect had vanished from the world. "The most *wonderful* man that I have ever known," Wordsworth declared, his voice breaking; and Charles Lamb: "His great and dear spirit haunts me. * * * Never saw I his likeness, nor probably the world can see again."

Coleridge's friends, however, abetted by Coleridge's own merciless self-judgments, set current the opinion, still common, that Coleridge was great in promise but not in performance. Even in his buoyant youth, before opium had drained his strength and weakened his will, Coleridge described his own character as "indolence capable of energies"; and it is true that while his mind was incessantly active and fertile, he always lacked application and staying power. After *The Ancient Mariner*, most of the poems he completed were written, like the first version of *Dejection: An Ode*, at a single sitting, in a burst of inspiration or spasm of intense effort. Writings which required sustained planning and application were either left unfinished or, like the *Biographia Literaria*, made up of brilliant sections patched together and eked out with filler, in a desperate effort to meet a deadline. Many of his best speculations Coleridge merely confided to his notebooks and the ears of his friends, incorporated in letters, and poured out upon the margins of his own and other people's books.

Even so, it is only when measured against his own immense potentialities that Coleridge's achievements appear minor. In opposition to the prevailing British philosophy of empiricism and associationism, Coleridge for most of his mature life expounded his views of the mind as creative in perception, intuitive in its discovery of the first premises of metaphysics and religion, and capable of a poetic re-creation of the world of sense by the fusing and shaping power of the "secondary imagination." Within the decade after Coleridge died, John Stuart Mill, the most acute student of contemporary thought, announced that Coleridge was one of "the two great seminal minds of England," the most important instigator and representative of the conservative intellectual movement of the day. Time has proved Mill's estimate of Coleridge to be just, for his influence is strongly evident in 19th-century English and American traditions of philosophical idealism, enlightened political conservatism, and liberal interpretations of Trinitarian theology. By present consensus, Coleridge is also one of the greatest and most influential of literary theorists; his ideas have become central points of reference even in many of the new critics who depreciate the Romantic poetry for which Coleridge, in his criticism, attempted to provide a rationale. And Coleridge's writings in verse, though small in bulk, are the work of a major and notably original poet.

Here, too, we tend to underestimate Coleridge's versatility—this time because of our preoccupation with his three poems of mystery and magic, *The Ancient Mariner, Christabel,* and *Kubla Khan.* These are indeed great and unprecedented achievements, but Coleridge wrote them all within a few years, and then dropped the mode. No less impressive in their own way are the blank-verse poems of the lonely and meditative mind which, by an extension of his term for one of them, are called "Conversation Poems"; in the best of these, *Frost at Midnight,* Coleridge perfected that characteristic pattern of integrally related description and meditation which Wordsworth immediately adopted in *Tintern Abbey.* Coleridge himself adapted this pattern to the larger requirements of *Dejection,* a high achievement in a genre in which very few poets have been successful, the irregular Pindaric ode. The verse epistle *To William Wordsworth* is at once a movingly personal poem, the most revealing comment ever made about *The Prelude,* and a noble tribute to a friend whom Coleridge thought the greatest poet since Milton. And even when he had mainly given up poetry, after 1805, Coleridge continued to write occasional short lyrics (represented below) which are remarkable equally for their quality, their diversity, and the extent to which they have been neglected by anthologists.

The Eolian Harp[1]

COMPOSED AT CLEVEDON, SOMERSETSHIRE

My pensive Sara! thy soft cheek reclined
Thus on mine arm, most soothing sweet it is
To sit beside our Cot, our Cot o'ergrown

---

1. Named for Aeolus, god of the winds, the harp has strings stretched over a rectangular sounding box. The strings are tuned in unison. When placed in an opened window, the harp (also called "Eolian lute," "Eolian lyre," "wind harp") responds to the altering wind by sequences of musical chords. This instrument, which seems to voice nature's own music, was a favorite household furnishing in the period, and was repeatedly alluded to in Romantic poetry; see Geoffrey Grigson, *The Harp of Aeolus and Other Essays* (1947). It served also as one of the recurrent Romantic images for the mind—either the mind in poetic inspiration, as in the last stanza of Shelley's *Ode to the West Wind,* or else the mind in perception, responding to an intellectual breeze by trembling into consciousness, as in this poem.

Coleridge, however, no sooner puts forward this concept than he retracts it, for it comes too close to the heresy of pantheism, which identifies God with the nature that, in the orthodox view, is His creation.

Coleridge wrote this poem to Sara Fricker, whom he married on October 4, 1795, and took to a cottage at Clevedon, overlooking the Bristol Channel. He later made changes in the original version; the famous lines 26–33, for example, were not incorporated until 1817. It was Coleridge's first achievement in the important Romantic form of the sustained blank-verse lyric of description and meditation, in the mode of conversation addressed to a silent auditor, which he perfected in *Frost at Midnight,* and which Wordsworth adopted for *Tintern Abbey.*

With white-flowered Jasmin, and the broad-leaved Myrtle,
(Meet emblems they of Innocence and Love!)   5
And watch the clouds, that late were rich with light,
Slow saddening round, and mark the star of eve
Serenely brilliant (such should Wisdom be)
Shine opposite! How exquisite the scents
Snatched from yon bean-field! and the world so hushed!   10
The stilly murmur of the distant Sea
Tells us of silence.
                         And that simplest Lute,
Placed length-ways in the clasping casement, hark!
How by the desultory breeze caressed,
Like some coy maid half yielding to her lover,   15
It pours such sweet upbraiding, as must needs
Tempt to repeat the wrong! And now, its strings
Boldlier swept, the long sequacious[2] notes
Over delicious surges sink and rise,
Such a soft floating witchery of sound   20
As twilight Elfins make, when they at eve
Voyage on gentle gales from Fairy-Land,
Where Melodies round honey-dropping flowers,
Footless and wild, like birds of Paradise,[3]
Nor pause, nor perch, hovering on untamed wing!   25
O! the one Life within us and abroad,
Which meets all motion and becomes its soul,
A light in sound, a sound-like power in light,
Rhythm in all thought, and joyance everywhere—
Methinks, it should have been impossible   30
Not to love all things in a world so filled;
Where the breeze warbles, and the mute still air
Is Music slumbering on her instrument.

    And thus, my Love! as on the midway slope
Of yonder hill I stretch my limbs at noon,   35
Whilst through my half-closed eyelids I behold
The sunbeams dance, like diamonds, on the main,
And tranquil muse upon tranquillity:
Full many a thought uncalled and undetained,
And many idle flitting phantasies,   40
Traverse my indolent and passive brain,
As wild and various as the random gales
That swell and flutter on this subject Lute!

    And what if all of animated nature
Be but organic Harps diversely framed,   45
That tremble into thought, as o'er them sweeps
Plastic and vast, one intellectual breeze,
At once the Soul of each, and God of all?

2. Successive.
3. Brilliantly colored birds, found in New Guinea and adjacent islands. The native practice of removing the legs when preparing the skin led Europeans to believe that the birds were footless and spent their lives hovering in the air and feeding on nectar.

But thy more serious eye a mild reproof
Darts, O belovéd Woman! nor such thoughts   50
Dim and unhallowed dost thou not reject,
And biddest me walk humbly with my God.
Meek Daughter in the family of Christ!
Well hast thou said and holily dispraised
These shapings of the unregenerate mind;   55
Bubbles that glitter as they rise and break
On vain Philosophy's aye-babbling spring.
For never guiltless may I speak of him,
The Incomprehensible! save when with awe
I praise him, and with Faith that inly *feels*;   60
Who with his saving mercies healéd me,
A sinful and most miserable man,
Wildered and dark, and gave me to possess
Peace, and this Cot, and thee, heart-honored Maid!

1795   1796

The Rime of the Ancient Mariner[1]

IN SEVEN PARTS

Facile credo, plures esse Naturas invisibiles quam visibiles in rerum universitate. Sed horum [sic] *omnium familiam quis nobis enarrabit? et gradus et cognationes et discrimina et singulorum munera? Quid agunt? quae loca habitant? Harum rerum notitiam semper ambivit ingenium humanum, nunquam attigit. Juvat, interea, non diffiteor, quandoque in animo, tanquam in tabulâ, majoris et melioris mundi imaginem contemplari: ne mens assuefacta hodiernae vitae minutiis se contrahat nimis, et tota subsidat in pusillas cogitationes. Sed veritati interea invigilandum est, modusque servandus, ut certa ab incertis, diem a nocte, distinguamus.*

T. BURNET, *Archaeol. Phil.* p. 68.[2]

Argument

How a Ship, having first sailed to the Equator, was driven by storms to the cold Country towards the South Pole; how the Ancient Mari-

1. Coleridge describes the origin of this poem in the opening section of Chapter XIV of *Biographia Literaria*. In a note on his *We Are Seven*, dictated to Isabella Fenwick in 1843, Wordsworth added some details. The poem, based on a dream of Coleridge's friend Cruikshank, was originally planned as a collaboration between the two friends, to pay the expense of a walking tour they took with Dorothy Wordsworth in November of 1797. Before he dropped out of the enterprise, Wordsworth suggested the shooting of the albatross and the navigation of the ship by the dead men; he also contributed lines 13–16 and 226–27.

The version of *The Ancient Mariner* printed in *Lyrical Ballads* (1798) contained many archaic words and spellings. In later editions Coleridge greatly improved the poem by pruning the archaisms, and by other revisions; he also added the Latin epigraph and the marginal glosses.

2. Latin epigraph: "I readily believe that there are more invisible than visible Natures in the universe. But who will explain for us the family of all these beings, and the ranks and relations and distinguishing features and functions of each? What do they do? What places do they inhabit? The human mind has always sought the knowl-

ner cruelly and in contempt of the laws of hospitality killed a Sea-
bird and how he was followed by many and strange Judgments: and
in what manner he came back to his own Country.

Part I

An ancient Mar-
iner meeteth
three Gallants
bidden to a wed-
ding feast, and
detaineth one.

It is an ancient Mariner
And he stoppeth one of three.
—"By thy long gray beard and glittering eye,
Now wherefore stopp'st thou me?

The Bridegroom's doors are opened wide,   5
And I am next of kin;
The guests are met, the feast is set:
May'st hear the merry din."

He holds him with his skinny hand,
"There was a ship," quoth he.   10
"Hold off! unhand me, graybeard loon!"
Eftsoons[3] his hand dropped he.

The Wedding
Guest is spell-
bound by the eye
of the old seafar-
ing man, and
constrained to
hear his tale.

He holds him with his glittering eye—
The Wedding Guest stood still,
And listens like a three years' child: 15
The Mariner hath his will.

The Wedding Guest sat on a stone:
He cannot choose but hear;
And thus spake on that ancient man,
The bright-eyed Mariner.   20

"The ship was cheered, the harbor cleared,
Merrily did we drop
Below the kirk,[4] below the hill,

The Mariner
tells how the
ship sailed south-
ward with a good
wind and fair
weather, till it
reached the Line.

Below the lighthouse top.

The Sun came up upon the left,   25
Out of the sea came he!
And he shone bright, and on the right
Went down into the sea.

Higher and higher every day,
Till over the mast at noon[5]—"   30
The Wedding Guest here beat his breast,
For he heard the loud bassoon.

edge of these things, but never attained
it. Meanwhile I do not deny that it is
helpful sometimes to contemplate in
the mind, as on a tablet, the image
of a greater and better world, lest the
intellect, habituated to the petty things
of daily life, narrow itself and sink
wholly into trivial thoughts. But at the
same time we must be watchful for the
truth and keep a sense of proportion,
so that we may distinguish the certain
from the uncertain, day from night."
Adapted by Coleridge from Thomas
Burnet, *Archaeologiae philosophicae*
(1692).
3. At once.
4. Church.
5. I.e., the ship had reached the equator (the "Line").

The Wedding
Guest heareth
the bridal music;
but the Mariner
continueth his
tale.

The bride hath paced into the hall,
Red as a rose is she;
Nodding their heads before her goes   35
The merry minstrelsy.

The Wedding Guest he beat his breast,
Yet he cannot choose but hear;
And thus spake on that ancient man,
The bright-eyed Mariner.   40

The ship driven
by a storm to-
ward the South
Pole.

"And now the STORM-BLAST came, and he
Was tyrannous and strong;
He struck with his o'ertaking wings,
And chased us south along.

With sloping masts and dipping prow,   45
As who pursued with yell and blow
Still treads the shadow of his foe,
And forward bends his head,
The ship drove fast, loud roared the blast,
And southward aye we fled.   50

And now there came both mist and snow,
And it grew wondrous cold:
And ice, mast-high, came floating by,
As green as emerald.

The land of ice,
and of fearful
sounds where no
living thing was
to be seen.

And through the drifts the snowy clifts[6]   55
Did send a dismal sheen:
Nor shapes of men nor beasts we ken—
The ice was all between.

The ice was here, the ice was there,
The ice was all around: 60
It cracked and growled, and roared and howled,
Like noises in a swound![7]

Till a great sea
bird, called the
Albatross, came
through the
snow-fog, and
was received
with great joy
and hospitality.

At length did cross an Albatross,
Thorough the fog it came;
As if it had been a Christian soul,   65
We hailed it in God's name.

It ate the food it ne'er had eat,
And round and round it flew.
The ice did split with a thunder-fit;
The helmsman steered us through!   70

And lo! the Al-
batross proveth
a bird of good
omen, and fol-
loweth the ship
as it returned
northward
through fog and
floating ice.

And a good south wind sprung up behind;
The Albatross did follow,
And every day, for food or play,
Came to the mariners' hollo!

In mist or cloud, on mast or shroud,[8]   75
It perched for vespers nine;

6. Cliffs.   8. Rope supporting the mast.
7. Swoon.

Whiles all the night, through fog-smoke white,
Glimmered the white Moon-shine."

"God save thee, ancient Mariner!
From the fiends, that plague thee thus!—
Why look'st thou so?"—With my crossbow
I shot the ALBATROSS.

Part II

The Sun now rose upon the right:[9]
Out of the sea came he,
Still hid in mist, and on the left
Went down into the sea.

And the good south wind still blew behind,
But no sweet bird did follow,
Nor any day for food or play
Came to the mariners' hollo!

And I had done a hellish thing,
And it would work 'em woe:
For all averred, I had killed the bird
That made the breeze to blow.
Ah wretch! said they, the bird to slay,
That made the breeze to blow!

Nor dim nor red, like God's own head,
The glorious Sun uprist:
Then all averred, I had killed the bird
That brought the fog and mist.
'Twas right, said they, such birds to slay,
That bring the fog and mist.

The fair breeze blew, the white foam flew,
The furrow followed free;
We were the first that ever burst
Into that silent sea.

Down dropped the breeze, the sails dropped down,
'Twas sad as sad could be;
And we did speak only to break
The silence of the sea!

All in a hot and copper sky,
The bloody Sun, at noon,
Right up above the mast did stand,
No bigger than the Moon.

Day after day, day after day,
We stuck, nor breath nor motion;
As idle as a painted ship
Upon a painted ocean.

9. I.e., having rounded Cape Horn, the ship heads north into the Pacific.

And the Alba-
tross begins to
be avenged.

Water, water, everywhere,
And all the boards did shrink;   120
Water, water, everywhere,
Nor any drop to drink.

The very deep did rot: O Christ!
That ever this should be!
Yea, slimy things did crawl with legs   125
Upon the slimy sea.

About, about, in reel and rout
The death-fires[1] danced at night;
The water, like a witch's oils,
Burnt green, and blue and white.   130

And some in dreams assuréd were
Of the Spirit that plagued us so;

A Spirit had
followed them;
one of the invis-
ible inhabitants
of this planet,

Nine fathom deep he had followed us
From the land of mist and snow.

neither departed souls nor angels; concerning whom the learned Jew, Josephus, and
the Platonic Constantinopolitan, Michael Psellus, may be consulted. They are very
numerous, and there is no climate or element without one or more.

And every tongue, through utter drought,   135
Was withered at the root;
We could not speak, no more than if
We had been choked with soot.

Ah! well-a-day! what evil looks

The shipmates,
in their sore dis-
tress, would fain
throw the whole
guilt on the an-
cient Mariner: in

Had I from old and young!   140
Instead of the cross, the Albatross
About my neck was hung.

sign whereof they hang the dead sea bird round his neck.

Part III

There passed a weary time. Each throat
Was parched, and glazed each eye.
A weary time! a weary time!   145
How glazed each weary eye,

The ancient Mar-
iner beholdeth a
sign in the ele-
ment afar off.

When looking westward, I beheld
A something in the sky.

At first it seemed a little speck,
And then it seemed a mist;   150
It moved and moved, and took at last
A certain shape, I wist.[2]

A speck, a mist, a shape, I wist!
And still it neared and neared:

1. The corposant, or St. Elmo's fire, an atmospheric electricity on a ship's mast or rigging, believed by the super-stitious sailor to portend disaster.
2. Knew.

As if it dodged a water sprite,   155
It plunged and tacked and veered.

At its nearer ap-
proach, it seem-
eth him to be a
ship; and at a
dear ransom he
freeth his speech
from the bonds
of thirst.

With throats unslaked, with black lips baked,
We could nor laugh nor wail;
Through utter drought all dumb we stood!
I bit my arm, I sucked the blood,   160
And cried, A sail! a sail!

With throats unslaked, with black lips baked,
Agape they heard me call:

A flash of joy;

Gramercy![3] they for joy did grin,
And all at once their breath drew in,   165
As they were drinking all.

And horror fol-
lows. For can it
be a ship that
comes onward
without wind or
tide?

See! see! (I cried) she tacks no more!
Hither to work us weal;[4]
Without a breeze, without a tide,
She steadies with upright keel!   170

The western wave was all aflame.
The day was well nigh done!
Almost upon the western wave
Rested the broad bright Sun;
When that strange shape drove suddenly   175
Betwixt us and the Sun.

It seemeth him
but the skeleton
of a ship.

And straight the Sun was flecked with bars,
(Heaven's Mother send us grace!)
As if through a dungeon grate he peered
With broad and burning face.   180

And its ribs are
seen as bars on
the face of the
setting Sun.

Alas! (thought I, and my heart beat loud)
How fast she nears and nears!
Are those *her* sails that glance in the Sun,
Like restless gossameres?[5]

The Specter-
Woman and her
Deathmate, and
no other on
board the skele-
ton ship.

Are those *her* ribs through which the Sun   185
Did peer, as through a grate?
And is that Woman all her crew?
Is that a DEATH? and are there two?
Is DEATH that woman's mate?

Like vessel, like
crew!

Her lips were red, *her* looks were free,   190
Her locks were yellow as gold:
Her skin was as white as leprosy,
The Nightmare LIFE-IN-DEATH was she,
Who thicks man's blood with cold.

Death and Life-
in-Death have
diced for the
ship's crew, and
she (the latter)
winneth the an-
cient Mariner.

The naked hulk alongside came,   195
And the twain were casting dice;
"The game is done! I've won! I've won!"
Quoth she, and whistles thrice.

---

3. From the French *grand-merci*, "great
thanks."

4. Benefit.
5. Filmy cobwebs floating in the air.

No twilight
within the courts
of the Sun.
The Sun's rim dips; the stars rush out:
At one stride comes the dark;   200
With far-heard whisper, o'er the sea,
Off shot the specter bark.

At the rising of
the Moon,
We listened and looked sideways up!
Fear at my heart, as at a cup,
My lifeblood seemed to sip!   205
The stars were dim, and thick the night,
The steersman's face by his lamp gleamed white;
From the sails the dew did drip—
Till clomb above the eastern bar
The hornéd Moon, with one bright star   210
Within the nether tip.[5a]

One after an-
other,
One after one, by the star-dogged Moon,
Too quick for groan or sigh,
Each turned his face with ghastly pang,
And cursed me with his eye.   215

His shipmates
drop down dead.
Four times fifty living men,
(And I heard nor sigh nor groan)
With heavy thump, a lifeless lump,
They dropped down one by one.

But Life-in-
Death begins her
work on the an-
cient Mariner.
The souls did from their bodies fly—   220
They fled to bliss or woe!
And every soul, it passed me by,
Like the whizz of my crossbow!

Part IV

The Wedding
Guest feareth
that a Spirit is
talking to him;
"I fear thee, ancient Mariner!
I fear thy skinny hand!   225
And thou art long, and lank, and brown,
As is the ribbed sea-sand.

I fear thee and thy glittering eye,
And thy skinny hand, so brown."—
But the ancient
Mariner assureth
him of his bodily
life, and pro-
ceedeth to relate
his horrible pen-
ance.
Fear not, fear not, thou Wedding Guest!   230
This body dropped not down.

Alone, alone, all, all alone,
Alone on a wide wide sea!
And never a saint took pity on
My soul in agony.   235

He despiseth the
creatures of the
calm,
The many men, so beautiful!
And they all dead did lie:
And a thousand thousand slimy things
Lived on; and so did I.

5a. An omen of impending evil.

And envieth that they should live, and so many lie dead.

I looked upon the rotting sea,   240
And drew my eyes away;
I looked upon the rotting deck,
And there the dead men lay.

I looked to heaven, and tried to pray;
But or ever a prayer had gushed,   245
A wicked whisper came, and made
My heart as dry as dust.

I closed my lids, and kept them close,
And the balls like pulses beat;
For the sky and the sea, and the sea and the sky   250
Lay like a load on my weary eye,
And the dead were at my feet.

But the curse liveth for him in the eye of the dead men.

The cold sweat melted from their limbs,
Nor rot nor reek did they:
The look with which they looked on me   255
Had never passed away.

An orphan's curse would drag to hell
A spirit from on high;
But oh! more horrible than that
Is the curse in a dead man's eye!   260
Seven days, seven nights, I saw that curse,
And yet I could not die.

In his loneliness and fixedness he yearneth towards the journeying Moon, and the stars that still sojourn, yet still move onward; and everywhere the blue sky belongs to them, and is their appointed rest, and their native country and their own natural homes, which they enter unannounced, as lords that are certainly expected and yet there is a silent joy at their arrival.

The moving Moon went up the sky,
And nowhere did abide:
Softly she was going up,   265
And a star or two beside—

Her beams bemocked the sultry main,
Like April hoar-frost spread;
But where the ship's huge shadow lay,
The charmèd water burnt alway   270
A still and awful red.

By the light of the Moon he beholdeth God's creatures of the great calm.

Beyond the shadow of the ship,
I watched the water snakes:
They moved in tracks of shining white,
And when they reared, the elfish light   275
Fell off in hoary flakes.

Within the shadow of the ship
I watched their rich attire:
Blue, glossy green, and velvet black,
They coiled and swam; and every track   280
Was a flash of golden fire.

Their beauty and their happiness.

O happy living things! no tongue
Their beauty might declare:

A spring of love gushed from my heart,

And I blessed them unaware:
Sure my kind saint took pity on me,
And I blessed them unaware. 285

The selfsame moment I could pray;
And from my neck so free
The Albatross fell off, and sank
Like lead into the sea. 290

Part V

Oh sleep! it is a gentle thing,
Beloved from pole to pole!
To Mary Queen the praise be given!
She sent the gentle sleep from Heaven,
That slid into my soul. 295

The silly[6] buckets on the deck,
That had so long remained,
I dreamt that they were filled with dew;
And when I awoke, it rained. 300

My lips were wet, my throat was cold,
My garments all were dank;
Sure I had drunken in my dreams,
And still my body drank.

I moved, and could not feel my limbs: 305
I was so light—almost
I thought that I had died in sleep,
And was a blessed ghost.

And soon I heard a roaring wind:
It did not come anear; 310
But with its sound it shook the sails,
That were so thin and sere.

The upper air burst into life!
And a hundred fire-flags sheen,[7]
To and fro they were hurried about! 315
And to and fro, and in and out,
The wan stars danced between.

And the coming wind did roar more loud,
And the sails did sigh like sedge;[8]
And the rain poured down from one black cloud; 320
The Moon was at its edge.

The thick black cloud was cleft, and still
The Moon was at its side:
Like waters shot from some high crag,
The lightning fell with never a jag, 325
A river steep and wide.

6. In the archaic sense: blessed, happy.   tralis, or Southern Lights.
7. Shone. These are the Aurora Aus-   8. A rushlike plant growing in wet soil.

The bodies of
the ship's crew
are inspirited,
and the ship
moves on;

The loud wind never reached the ship,
Yet now the ship moved on!
Beneath the lightning and the Moon
The dead men gave a groan.   330

They groaned, they stirred, they all uprose,
Nor spake, nor moved their eyes;
It had been strange, even in a dream,
To have seen those dead men rise.

The helmsman steered, the ship moved on;   335
Yet never a breeze up-blew;
The mariners all 'gan work the ropes,
Where they were wont to do;
They raised their limbs like lifeless tools—
We were a ghastly crew.   340

The body of my brother's son
Stood by me, knee to knee:
The body and I pulled at one rope,
But he said nought to me.

But not by the
souls of the men,
nor by demons
of earth or mid-
dle air, but by a
blessed troop of
angelic spirits,
sent down by
the invocation of
the guardian
saint.

"I fear thee, ancient Mariner!"   345
Be calm, thou Wedding Guest!
'Twas not those souls that fled in pain,
Which to their corses⁹ came again,
But a troop of spirits blest:

For when it dawned—they dropped their arms,   350
And clustered round the mast;
Sweet sounds rose slowly through their mouths,
And from their bodies passed.

Around, around, flew each sweet sound,
Then darted to the Sun;
Slowly the sounds came back again,   355
Now mixed, now one by one.

Sometimes a-dropping from the sky
I heard the skylark sing;
Sometimes all little birds that are,   360
How they seemed to fill the sea and air
With their sweet jargoning!¹

And now 'twas like all instruments,
Now like a lonely flute;
And now it is an angel's song,   365
That makes the heavens be mute.

It ceased; yet still the sails made on
A pleasant noise till noon,
A noise like of a hidden brook

9. Corpses.   1. In Middle English, "warbling."

In the leafy month of June,
That to the sleeping woods all night
Singeth a quiet tune. 370

Till noon we quietly sailed on,
Yet never a breeze did breathe:
Slowly and smoothly went the ship, 375
Moved onward from beneath.

The lonesome Spirit from the South Pole carries on the ship as far as the Line, in obedience to the angelic troop, but still requireth vengeance.

Under the keel nine fathom deep,
From the land of mist and snow,
The spirit slid: and it was he
That made the ship to go. 380
The sails at noon left off their tune,
And the ship stood still also.

The Sun, right up above the mast,
Had fixed her to the ocean:
But in a minute she 'gan stir, 385
With a short uneasy motion—
Backwards and forwards half her length
With a short uneasy motion.

Then like a pawing horse let go,
She made a sudden bound: 390
It flung the blood into my head,
And I fell down in a swound.

The Polar Spirit's fellow demons, the invisible inhabitants of the element, take part in his wrong; and two of them relate, one to the other, that penance long and heavy for the ancient Mariner hath been accorded to the Polar Spirit, who returneth southward.

How long in that same fit I lay,
I have not[2] to declare;
But ere my living life returned, 395
I heard and in my soul discerned
Two voices in the air.

"Is it he?" quoth one, "Is this the man?
By him who died on cross,
With his cruel bow he laid full low 400
The harmless Albatross.

The spirit who bideth by himself
In the land of mist and snow,
He loved the bird that loved the man
Who shot him with his bow." 405

The other was a softer voice,
As soft as honeydew:
Quoth he, "The man hath penance done,
And penance more will do."

Part VI

FIRST VOICE

"But tell me, tell me! speak again,
Thy soft response renewing— 410

2. I.e., have not the knowledge.

What makes that ship drive on so fast?
What is the ocean doing?"

SECOND VOICE

"Still as a slave before his lord,
The ocean hath no blast;
His great bright eye most silently   415
Up to the Moon is cast—

If he may know which way to go;
For she guides him smooth or grim.
See, brother, see! how graciously   420
She looketh down on him."

FIRST VOICE

The Mariner hath been cast into a trance; for the angelic power causeth the vessel to drive northward faster than human life could endure.

"But why drives on that ship so fast,
Without or wave or wind?"

SECOND VOICE

"The air is cut away before,
And closes from behind.   425

Fly, brother, fly! more high, more high!
Or we shall be belated:
For slow and slow that ship will go,
When the Mariner's trance is abated."

The supernatural motion is retarded; the Mariner awakes, and his penance begins anew.

I woke, and we were sailing on   430
As in a gentle weather:
'Twas night, calm night, the moon was high;
The dead men stood together.

All stood together on the deck,
For a charnel-dungeon fitter:
All fixed on me their stony eyes,   435
That in the Moon did glitter.

The pang, the curse, with which they died,
Had never passed away:
I could not draw my eyes from theirs,   440
Nor turn them up to pray.

The curse is finally expiated.

And now this spell was snapped: once more
I viewed the ocean green,
And looked far forth, yet little saw
Of what had else been seen—   445

Like one, that on a lonesome road
Doth walk in fear and dread,
And having once turned round walks on,
And turns no more his head;
Because he knows, a frightful fiend   450
Doth close behind him tread.

But soon there breathed a wind on me,
Nor sound nor motion made:
Its path was not upon the sea,
In ripple or in shade.   455

It raised my hair, it fanned my cheek
Like a meadow-gale of spring—
It mingled strangely with my fears,
Yet it felt like a welcoming.

Swiftly, swiftly flew the ship,   460
Yet she sailed softly too:
Sweetly, sweetly blew the breeze—
On me alone it blew.

*And the ancient
Mariner behold-
eth his native
country.*

Oh! dream of joy! is this indeed
The lighthouse top I see?   465
Is this the hill? is this the kirk?
Is this mine own countree?

We drifted o'er the harbor bar,
And I with sobs did pray—
O let me be awake, my God!   470
Or let me sleep alway.

The harbor bay was clear as glass,
So smoothly it was strewn!
And on the bay the moonlight lay,
And the shadow of the Moon.   475

The rock shone bright, the kirk no less,
That stands above the rock:
The moonlight steeped in silentness
The steady weathercock.

And the bay was white with silent light,   480
Till rising from the same,

*The angelic
spirits leave the
dead bodies,*

Full many shapes, that shadows were,
In crimson colors came.

*And appear in
their own forms
of light.*

A little distance from the prow
Those crimson shadows were: 485
I turned my eyes upon the deck—
Oh, Christ! what saw I there!

Each corse lay flat, lifeless and flat,
And, by the holy rood!³
A man all light, a seraph man,   490
On every corse there stood.

This seraph band, each waved his hand:
It was a heavenly sight!

3. Cross. "Seraph": a shining celestial being, highest in the ranks of the angels.

They stood as signals to the land,
Each one a lovely light;   495

This seraph band, each waved his hand,
No voice did they impart—
No voice; but oh! the silence sank
Like music on my heart.

But soon I heard the dash of oars,   500
I heard the Pilot's cheer;
My head was turned perforce away
And I saw a boat appear.

The Pilot and the Pilot's boy,
I heard them coming fast: 505
Dear Lord in Heaven! it was a joy
The dead men could not blast.

I saw a third—I heard his voice:
It is the Hermit good!
He singeth loud his godly hymns   510
That he makes in the wood.
He'll shrieve my soul, he'll wash away
The Albatross's blood.

Part VII

The Hermit of the Wood

This Hermit good lives in that wood
Which slopes down to the sea.   515
How loudly his sweet voice he rears!
He loves to talk with marineres
That come from a far countree.

He kneels at morn, and noon, and eve—
He hath a cushion plump: 520
It is the moss that wholly hides
The rotted old oak stump.

The skiff boat neared: I heard them talk,
"Why, this is strange, I trow!
Where are those lights so many and fair,   525
That signal made but now?"

Approacheth the ship with wonder.

"Strange, by my faith!" the Hermit said—
"And they answered not our cheer!
The planks looked warped! and see those sails,
How thin they are and sere!   530
I never saw aught like to them,
Unless perchance it were

Brown skeletons of leaves that lag
My forest-brook along;
When the ivy tod[4] is heavy with snow,   535

4. Clump of ivy.

And the owlet whoops to the wolf below,
That eats the she-wolf's young."

"Dear Lord! it hath a fiendish look,"
The Pilot made reply,
"I am a-feared"—"Push on, push on!"   540
Said the Hermit cheerily.

The boat came closer to the ship,
But I nor spake nor stirred;
The boat came close beneath the ship,
And straight a sound was heard.   545

The ship sud-
denly sinketh.
Under the water it rumbled on,
Still louder and more dread:
It reached the ship, it split the bay;
The ship went down like lead.

The ancient
Mariner is saved
in the Pilot's
boat.
Stunned by that loud and dreadful sound,   550
Which sky and ocean smote,
Like one that hath been seven days drowned
My body lay afloat;
But swift as dreams, myself I found
Within the Pilot's boat.   555

Upon the whirl, where sank the ship,
The boat spun round and round;
And all was still, save that the hill
Was telling of the sound.

I moved my lips—the Pilot shrieked   560
And fell down in a fit;
The holy Hermit raised his eyes,
And prayed where he did sit.

I took the oars: the Pilot's boy,
Who now doth crazy go,   565
Laughed loud and long, and all the while
His eyes went to and fro.
"Ha! ha!" quoth he, "full plain I see,
The Devil knows how to row."

And now, all in my own countree,   570
I stood on the firm land!
The Hermit stepped forth from the boat,
And scarcely he could stand.

The ancient
Mariner ear-
nestly entreateth
the Hermit to
shrieve him; and
the penance of
life falls on him.
"O shrieve me, shrieve me, holy man!"
The Hermit crossed his brow.[5]   575
"Say quick," quoth he, "I bid thee say—
What manner of man art thou?"

5. Made the sign of the cross on his forehead.

Forthwith this frame of mine was wrenched
With a woeful agony,
Which forced me to begin my tale;   580
And then it left me free.

*And ever and
anon throughout
his future life an
agony constrain-
eth him to travel
from land to
land;*

Since then, at an uncertain hour,
That agony returns:
And till my ghastly tale is told,
This heart within me burns.   585

I pass, like night, from land to land;
I have strange power of speech;
That moment that his face I see,
I know the man that must hear me:
To him my tale I teach.   590

What loud uproar bursts from that door!
The wedding guests are there:
But in the garden-bower the bride
And bridemaids singing are:
And hark the little vesper bell,   595
Which biddeth me to prayer!

O Wedding Guest! this soul hath been
Alone on a wide wide sea:
So lonely 'twas, that God himself
Scarce seeméd there to be.   600

O sweeter than the marriage feast,
'Tis sweeter far to me,
To walk together to the kirk
With a goodly company!—

To walk together to the kirk,   605
And all together pray,
While each to his great Father bends,
Old men, and babes, and loving friends
And youths and maidens gay!

*And to teach, by
his own exam-
ple, love and rev-
erence to all
things that God
made and loveth.*

Farewell, farewell! but this I tell   610
To thee, thou Wedding Guest!
He prayeth well, who loveth well
Both man and bird and beast.

He prayeth best, who loveth best
All things both great and small;   615
For the dear God who loveth us,
He made and loveth all.

The Mariner, whose eye is bright,
Whose beard with age is hoar,
Is gone: and now the Wedding Guest   620
Turned from the bridegroom's door.

He went like one that hath been stunned,
And is of sense forlorn:[6]
A sadder and a wiser man,
He rose the morrow morn.   625

1797–98   1798

Kubla Khan

OR A VISION IN A DREAM. A FRAGMENT

The following fragment is here published at the request of a poet of great and deserved celebrity,[1] and, as far as the author's own opinions are concerned, rather as a psychological curiosity, than on the ground of any supposed *poetic* merits.

In the summer of the year 1797, the author, then in ill health, had retired to a lonely farmhouse between Porlock and Linton, on the Exmoor confines of Somerset and Devonshire. In consequence of a slight indisposition, an anodyne had been prescribed, from the effects of which he fell asleep in his chair at the moment that he was reading the following sentence, or words of the same substance, in *Purchas's Pilgrimage:* "Here the Khan Kubla commanded a palace to be built, and a stately garden thereunto. And thus ten miles of fertile ground were inclosed with a wall."[2] The author continued for about three hours in a profound sleep, at least of the external senses,[3] during which time he has the most vivid confidence that he could not have composed less than from two to three hundred lines; if that indeed can be called composition in which all the images rose up before him as *things*, with a parallel production of the correspondent expressions, without any sensation or consciousness of effort. On awaking he appeared to himself to have a distinct recollection of the whole, and taking his pen, ink, and paper, instantly and eagerly wrote down the lines that are here preserved. At this moment he was unfortunately called out by a person on business from Porlock, and detained by him above an hour, and on his return to his room, found, to his no small surprise and mortification, that though he still retained some vague and dim

6. Forsaken.
1. Lord Byron.
2. "In Xamdu did Cublai Can build a stately Palace, encompassing sixteene miles of plaine ground with a wall, wherein are fertile Meddowes, pleasant springs, delightfull Streames, and all sorts of beasts of chase and game, and in the middest thereof a sumptuous house of pleasure, which may be removed from place to place." From Samuel Purchas, *Purchas his Pilgrimage* (1613). The historical Kublai

Khan founded the Mongol dynasty in China in the 13th century.
3. In a note on a manuscript copy of *Kubla Khan,* Coleridge gave a more precise account of the nature of this "sleep": "This fragment with a good deal more, not recoverable, composed, in a sort of reverie brought on by two grains of opium, taken to check a dysentery, at a farmhouse between Porlock and Linton, a quarter of a mile from Culbone Church, in the fall of the year, 1797."

recollection of the general purport of the vision, yet, with the exception of some eight or ten scattered lines and images, all the rest had passed away like the images on the surface of a stream into which a stone has been cast, but, alas! without the after restoration of the latter!

> Then all the charm
> Is broken—all that phantom world so fair
> Vanishes, and a thousand circlets spread,
> And each misshape[s] the other. Stay awhile,
> Poor youth! who scarcely dar'st lift up thine eyes—
> The stream will soon renew its smoothness, soon
> The visions will return! And lo, he stays,
> And soon the fragments dim of lovely forms
> Come trembling back, unite, and now once more
> The pool becomes a mirror.
>
> [From Coleridge's *The Picture; or, the Lover's Resolution*,
> lines 91–100]

Yet from the still surviving recollections in his mind, the author has frequently purposed to finish for himself what had been originally, as it were, given to him. Σαμερον αδιον ασω:[4] but the tomorrow is yet to come.

> In Xanadu did Kubla Khan
> A stately pleasure dome decree:
> Where Alph, the sacred river, ran
> Through caverns measureless to man
>   Down to a sunless sea. 5
> So twice five miles of fertile ground
> With walls and towers were girdled round:
> And there were gardens bright with sinuous rills,
> Where blossomed many an incense-bearing tree;
> And here were forests ancient as the hills, 10
> Enfolding sunny spots of greenery.
>
> But oh! that deep romantic chasm which slanted
> Down the green hill athwart a cedarn cover!
> A savage place! as holy and enchanted
> As e'er beneath a waning moon was haunted 15
> By woman wailing for her demon lover!
> And from this chasm, with ceaseless turmoil seething,
> As if this earth in fast thick pants were breathing,
> A mighty fountain momently was forced:
> Amid whose swift half-intermitted burst 20
> Huge fragments vaulted like rebounding hail,
> Or chaffy grain beneath the thresher's flail:

---

4. "I shall sing a sweeter song today." In the edition of 1834, Σαμερον ("today") was changed to αυριον ("tomorrow"). Coleridge had in mind Theocritus, *Idyls* I.145: ἐς ὕστερον ἄδιον ᾁσῶ ("I shall sing a sweeter song on a later day").

And 'mid these dancing rocks at once and ever
It flung up momently the sacred river.
Five miles meandering with a mazy motion   25
Through wood and dale the sacred river ran,
Then reached the caverns measureless to man,
And sank in tumult to a lifeless ocean:
And 'mid this tumult Kubla heard from far
Ancestral voices prophesying war!   30
   The shadow of the dome of pleasure
   Floated midway on the waves;
   Where was heard the mingled measure
   From the fountain and the caves.
It was a miracle of rare device,   35
A sunny pleasure dome with caves of ice!

A damsel with a dulcimer
In a vision once I saw:
It was an Abyssinian maid,
And on her dulcimer she played,   40
Singing of Mount Abora.
Could I revive within me
Her symphony and song,
To such a deep delight 'twould win me,
That with music loud and long,   45
I would build that dome in air,
That sunny dome! those caves of ice!
And all who heard should see them there,
And all should cry, Beware! Beware!
His flashing eyes, his floating hair!   50
Weave a circle round him thrice,[5]
And close your eyes with holy dread,
For he on honeydew hath fed,
And drunk the milk of Paradise.

ca. 1797–98   1816

Christabel[1]

Preface

The first part of the following poem was written in the year
1797, at Stowey, in the county of Somerset. The second part, after
my return from Germany, in the year 1800, at Keswick, Cumber-

5. A magic ritual, to protect the inspired poet from intrusion.
1. Coleridge had planned to publish *Christabel* in the second edition of *Lyrical Ballads* (1800), but had not been able to complete the poem. When *Christabel* was finally published in 1816 in its present fragmentary state, Coleridge still had hopes of finishing

it, for the Preface contained this sentence (deleted in the edition of 1834): "But as, in my very first conception of the tale, I had the whole present to my mind, with the wholeness, no less than the liveliness of a vision, I trust that I shall be able to embody in verse the three parts yet to come, in the course of the present year."

land. It is probable that if the poem had been finished at either
of the former periods, or if even the first and second part had been
published in the year 1800, the impression of its originality would
have been much greater than I dare at present expect. But for this
I have only my own indolence to blame. The dates are mentioned
for the exclusive purpose of precluding charges of plagiarism or
servile imitation from myself. For there is amongst us a set of
critics, who seem to hold that every possible thought and image
is traditional; who have no notion that there are such things as
fountains in the world, small as well as great; and who would therefore charitably derive every rill they behold flowing from a perfora-
tion made in some other man's tank. I am confident, however, that
as far as the present poem is concerned, the celebrated poets[2] whose
writings I might be suspected of having imitated, either in particular passages, or in the tone and the spirit of the whole, would be
among the first to vindicate me from the charge, and who, on any
striking coincidence, would permit me to address them in this doggerel version of two monkish Latin hexameters.

> 'Tis mine and it is likewise yours;
> But an if this will not do;
> Let it be mine, good friend! for I
> Am the poorer of the two.

I have only to add that the meter of Christabel is not, properly
speaking, irregular, though it may seem so from its being founded
on a new principle: namely, that of counting in each line the accents, not the syllables.[3] Though the latter may vary from seven
to twelve, yet in each line the accents will be found to be only four.
Nevertheless, this occasional variation in number of syllables is not
introduced wantonly, or for the mere ends of convenience, but in
correspondence with some transition in the nature of the imagery
or passion.

Part I

'Tis the middle of night by the castle clock,
And the owls have awakened the crowing cock;
Tu—whit!——Tu—whoo!
And hark, again! the crowing cock,
How drowsily it crew.   5

---

2. Sir Walter Scott and Lord Byron,
who had read and admired *Christabel*
while it circulated in manuscript. Coleridge has in mind Scott's *Lay of the
Last Minstrel* (1805) and Byron's
Siege of Corinth (1816), which showed
the influence of *Christabel*, especially
in their meter.
3. Much of the older English versification had, in practice, been based on the
stress, or "accent," and some of it
shows as much freedom in varying the
number of syllables as does *Christabel*.
Coleridge is, however, departing from
the 18th-century theory of versification,
which maintained that English meter
is based on a recurrent number of syllables in each line, and not on a recurrent number of stresses.

Sir Leoline, the Baron rich,
Hath a toothless mastiff bitch;
From her kennel beneath the rock
She maketh answer to the clock,
Four for the quarters, and twelve for the hour;   10
Ever and aye, by shine and shower,
Sixteen short howls, not over loud;
Some say she sees my lady's shroud.

Is the night chilly and dark?
The night is chilly, but not dark.   15
The thin gray cloud is spread on high,
It covers but not hides the sky.
The moon is behind, and at the full;
And yet she looks both small and dull.
The night is chill, the cloud is gray: 20
'Tis a month before the month of May,
And the spring comes slowly up this way.

The lovely lady, Christabel,
Whom her father loves so well,
What makes her in the wood so late,   25
A furlong from the castle gate?
She had dreams all yesternight
Of her own betrothéd knight;
And she in the midnight wood will pray
For the weal[4] of her lover that's far away.   30

She stole along, she nothing spoke,
The sighs she heaved were soft and low,
And naught was green upon the oak
But moss and rarest mistletoe:
She kneels beneath the huge oak tree,   35
And in silence prayeth she.

The lady sprang up suddenly,
The lovely lady, Christabel!
It moaned as near, as near can be,
But what it is she cannot tell.—   40
On the other side it seems to be,
Of the huge, broad-breasted, old oak tree.

The night is chill; the forest bare;
Is it the wind that moaneth bleak?
There is not wind enough in the air   45
To move away the ringlet curl
From the lovely lady's cheek—
There is not wind enough to twirl
The one red leaf, the last of its clan,
That dances as often as dance it can,   50

---

4. Well-being.

Hanging so light, and hanging so high,
On the topmost twig that looks up at the sky.

Hush, beating heart of Christabel!
Jesu, Maria, shield her well!
She folded her arms beneath her cloak,   55
And stole to the other side of the oak.
　　　What sees she there?

There she sees a damsel bright,
Dressed in a silken robe of white,
That shadowy in the moonlight shone: 60
The neck that made that white robe wan,
Her stately neck, and arms were bare;
Her blue-veined feet unsandaled were,
And wildly glittered here and there
The gems entangled in her hair.   65
I guess, 'twas frightful there to see
A lady so richly clad as she—
Beautiful exceedingly!

Mary mother, save me now!
(Said Christabel), And who art thou?   70

The lady strange made answer meet,[5]
And her voice was faint and sweet—
Have pity on my sore distress,
I scarce can speak for weariness:
Stretch forth thy hand, and have no fear!   75
Said Christabel, How camest thou here?
And the lady, whose voice was faint and sweet,
Did thus pursue her answer meet—

My sire is of a noble line,
And my name is Geraldine: 80
Five warriors seized me yestermorn,
Me, even me, a maid forlorn:
They choked my cries with force and fright,
And tied me on a palfrey white.
The palfrey was as fleet as wind,   85
And they rode furiously behind.
They spurred amain,[6] their steeds were white:
And once we crossed the shade of night.
As sure as Heaven shall rescue me,
I have no thought what men they be;   90
Nor do I know how long it is
(For I have lain entranced, I wis[7])
Since one, the tallest of the five,
Took me from the palfrey's back,
A weary woman, scarce alive.   95

5. Appropriate.
6. At top speed.
7. I believe; Coleridge's minsinterpre-

tation of the Middle English adverb
"ywis," meaning "certainly."

Some muttered words his comrades spoke:
He placed me underneath this oak;
He swore they would return with haste;
Whither they went I cannot tell—
I thought I heard, some minutes past,   100
Sounds as of a castle bell.
Stretch forth thy hand (thus ended she),
And help a wretched maid to flee.

Then Christabel stretched forth her hand,
And comforted fair Geraldine: 105
O well, bright dame! may you command
The service of Sir Leoline;
And gladly our stout chivalry
Will he send forth and friends withal
To guide and guard you safe and free   110
Home to your noble father's hall.

She rose: and forth with steps they passed
That strove to be, and were not, fast.
Her gracious stars the lady blessed,
And thus spake on sweet Christabel: 115
All our household are at rest,
The hall as silent as the cell;
Sir Leoline is weak in health,
And may not well awakened be,
But we will move as if in stealth,   120
And I beseech your courtesy,
This night, to share your couch with me.

They crossed the moat, and Christabel
Took the key that fitted well;
A little door she opened straight,   125
All in the middle of the gate;
The gate that was ironed within and without,
Where an army in battle array had marched out.
The lady sank, belike through pain,
And Christabel with might and main   130
Lifted her up, a weary weight,
Over the threshold of the gate:[8]
Then the lady rose again,
And moved, as she were not in pain.

So free from danger, free from fear,   135
They crossed the court: right glad they were.
And Christabel devoutly cried
To the lady by her side,
Praise we the Virgin all divine
Who hath rescued thee from thy distress!   140

8. She cannot cross the threshold by her own power because it has been blessed against evil spirits; this is the first of several indications that Geraldine is a malign being.

Alas, alas! said Geraldine,
I cannot speak for weariness.
So free from danger, free from fear,
They crossed the court: right glad they were.

Outside her kennel, the mastiff old   145
Lay fast asleep, in moonshine cold.
The mastiff old did not awake,
Yet she an angry moan did make!
And what can ail the mastiff bitch?
Never till now she uttered yell   150
Beneath the eye of Christabel.
Perhaps it is the owlet's scritch:
For what can ail the mastiff bitch?

They passed the hall, that echoes still,
Pass as lightly as you will!   155
The brands were flat, the brands were dying,
Amid their own white ashes lying;
But when the lady passed, there came
A tongue of light, a fit of flame;
And Christabel saw the lady's eye,   160
And nothing else saw she thereby,
Save the boss of the shield of Sir Leoline tall,
Which hung in a murky old niche in the wall.
O softly tread, said Christabel,
My father seldom sleepeth well.   165

Sweet Christabel her feet doth bare,
And jealous of the listening air
They steal their way from stair to stair,
Now in glimmer, and now in gloom,
And now they pass the Baron's room,   170
As still as death, with stifled breath!
And now have reached her chamber door;
And now doth Geraldine press down
The rushes of the chamber floor.

The moon shines dim in the open air,   175
And not a moonbeam enters here.
But they without its light can see
The chamber carved so curiously,
Carved with figures strange and sweet,
All made out of the carver's brain,   180
For a lady's chamber meet:
The lamp with twofold silver chain
Is fastened to an angel's feet.

The silver lamp burns dead and dim;
But Christabel the lamp will trim.   185
She trimmed the lamp, and made it bright,
And left it swinging to and fro,

While Geraldine, in wretched plight,
Sank down upon the floor below.

O weary lady, Geraldine,   190
I pray you, drink this cordial wine!
It is a wine of virtuous powers;
My mother made it of wild flowers.

And will your mother pity me,
Who am a maiden most forlorn?   195
Christabel answered—Woe is me!
She died the hour that I was born.
I have heard the gray-haired friar tell
How on her deathbed she did say,
That she should hear the castle bell   200
Strike twelve upon my wedding day.
O mother dear! that thou wert here!
I would, said Geraldine, she were!
But soon with altered voice, said she—
"Off, wandering mother! Peak and pine!   205
I have power to bid thee flee."
Alas! what ails poor Geraldine?
Why stares she with unsettled eye?
Can she the bodiless dead espy?
And why with hollow voice cries she,   210
"Off, woman, off! this hour is mine—
Though thou her guardian spirit be,
Off, woman, off! 'tis given to me."

Then Christabel knelt by the lady's side,
And raised to heaven her eyes so blue—   215
Alas! said she, this ghastly ride—
Dear lady! it hath 'wildered you!
The lady wiped her moist cold brow,
And faintly said, " 'tis over now!"

Again the wild-flower wine she drank: 220
Her fair large eyes 'gan glitter bright,
And from the floor whereon she sank,
The lofty lady stood upright:
She was most beautiful to see,
Like a lady of a far countree.   225

And thus the lofty lady spake—
"All they who live in the upper sky,
Do love you, holy Christabel!
And you love them, and for their sake
And for the good which me befell,   230
Even I in my degree will try,
Fair maiden, to requite you well.
But now unrobe yourself; for I
Must pray, ere yet in bed I lie."

Quoth Christabel, So let it be!   235
And as the lady bade, did she.
Her gentle limbs did she undress,
And lay down in her loveliness.

But through her brain of weal and woe
So many thoughts moved to and fro,   240
That vain it were her lids to close;
So halfway from the bed she rose,
And on her elbow did recline
To look at the lady Geraldine.

Beneath the lamp the lady bowed,   245
And slowly rolled her eyes around;
Then drawing in her breath aloud,
Like one that shuddered, she unbound
The cincture[9] from beneath her breast:
Her silken robe, and inner vest,   250
Dropped to her feet, and full in view,
Behold! her bosom and half her side——
A sight to dream of, not to tell!
O shield her! shield sweet Christabel!

Yet Geraldine nor speaks nor stirs;   255
Ah! what a stricken look was hers!
Deep from within she seems halfway
To lift some weight with sick assay,
And eyes the maid and seeks delay;
Then suddenly, as one defied,   260
Collects herself in scorn and pride,
And lay down by the maiden's side!—
And in her arms the maid she took,
            Ah well-a-day!
And with low voice and doleful look   265
These words did say:
"In the touch of this bosom there worketh a spell,
Which is lord of thy utterance, Christabel!
Thou knowest tonight, and wilt know tomorrow,
This mark of my shame, this seal of my sorrow;   270
      But vainly thou warrest,
         For this is alone in
      Thy power to declare,
         That in the dim forest
      Thou heard'st a low moaning,   275
And found'st a bright lady, surpassingly fair;
And didst bring her home with thee in love and in charity,
To shield her and shelter her from the damp air."

The Conclusion to Part I

It was a lovely sight to see
The lady Christabel, when she   280

9. Belt.

Was praying at the old oak tree.
    Amid the jagged shadows
    Of mossy leafless boughs,
    Kneeling in the moonlight,
    To make her gentle vows;   285
Her slender palms together pressed,
Heaving sometimes on her breast;
Her face resigned to bliss or bale[1]—
Her face, oh call it fair not pale,
And both blue eyes more bright than clear,   290
Each about to have a tear.

With open eyes (ah woe is me!)
Asleep, and dreaming fearfully,
Fearfully dreaming, yet I wis,
Dreaming that alone, which is—   295
O sorrow and shame! Can this be she,
The lady, who knelt at the old oak tree?
And lo! the worker of these harms,
That holds the maiden in her arms,
Seems to slumber still and mild,   300
As a mother with her child.

A star hath set, a star hath risen,
O Geraldine! since arms of thine
Have been the lovely lady's prison.
O Geraldine! one hour was thine—   305
Thou'st had thy will! By tairn[2] and rill,
The night birds all that hour were still.
But now they are jubilant anew,
From cliff and tower, tu—whoo! tu—whoo!
Tu—whoo! tu—whoo! from wood and fell![3]   310

And see! the lady Christabel
Gathers herself from out her trance;
Her limbs relax, her countenance
Grows sad and soft; the smooth thin lids
Close o'er her eyes; and tears she sheds—   315
Large tears that leave the lashes bright!
And oft the while she seems to smile
As infants at a sudden light!

Yea, she doth smile, and she doth weep,
Like a youthful hermitess,
Beauteous in a wilderness,   320
Who, praying always, prays in sleep.
And, if she move unquietly,
Perchance, 'tis but the blood so free
Comes back and tingles in her feet.   325
No doubt, she hath a vision sweet.

1. Evil, sorrow.
2. Tarn, a mountain pool.
3. Elevated moor, or hill.

What if her guardian spirit 'twere,
What if she knew her mother near?
But this she knows, in joys and woes,
That saints will aid if men will call: 330
For the blue sky bends over all!

Part II

Each matin bell, the Baron saith,
Knells us back to a world of death.
These words Sir Leoline first said,
When he rose and found his lady dead: 335
These words Sir Leoline will say
Many a morn to his dying day!

And hence the custom and law began
That still at dawn the sacristan,
Who duly pulls the heavy bell,
Five and forty beads must tell[4]   340
Between each stroke—a warning knell,
Which not a soul can choose but hear
From Bratha Head to Wyndermere.[5]

Saith Bracy the bard, So let it knell!   345
And let the drowsy sacristan
Still count as slowly as he can!
There is no lack of such, I ween,
As well fill up the space between.
In Langdale Pike[6] and Witch's Lair,   350
And Dungeon Ghyll[7] so foully rent,
With ropes of rock and bells of air
Three sinful sextons' ghosts are pent,
Who all give back, one after t'other,
The death note to their living brother;   355
And oft too, by the knell offended,
Just as their one! two! three! is ended,
The devil mocks the doleful tale
With a merry peal from Borodale.

The air is still! through mist and cloud   360
That merry peal comes ringing loud;
And Geraldine shakes off her dread,
And rises lightly from the bed;
Puts on her silken vestments white,
And tricks her hair in lovely plight,[8]   365
And nothing doubting of her spell
Awakens the lady Christabel.

---

4. Pray while "telling" (keeping count on) the beads of a rosary. "Sacristan": sexton.
5. These and the following names are of localities in the English Lake Country.
6. Peak.
7. Ravine forming the bed of a stream.
8. Plait.

"Sleep you, sweet lady Christabel?
I trust that you have rested well."

And Christabel awoke and spied   370
The same who lay down by her side—
O rather say, the same whom she
Raised up beneath the old oak tree!
Nay, fairer yet! and yet more fair!
For she belike hath drunken deep   375
Of all the blessedness of sleep!
And while she spake, her looks, her air
Such gentle thankfulness declare,
That (so it seemed) her girded vests
Grew tight beneath her heaving breasts. 380
"Sure I have sinned!" said Christabel,
"Now heaven be praised if all be well!"
And in low faltering tones, yet sweet,
Did she the lofty lady greet
With such perplexity of mind   385
As dreams too lively leave behind.

So quickly she rose, and quickly arrayed
Her maiden limbs, and having prayed
That He, who on the cross did groan,
Might wash away her sins unknown,   390
She forthwith led fair Geraldine
To meet her sire, Sir Leoline.

The lovely maid and the lady tall
Are pacing both into the hall,
And pacing on through page and groom,   395
Enter the Baron's presence-room.

The Baron rose, and while he pressed
His gentle daughter to his breast,
With cheerful wonder in his eyes
The lady Geraldine espies,   400
And gave such welcome to the same,
As might beseem so bright a dame!

But when he heard the lady's tale,
And when she told her father's name,
Why waxed Sir Leoline so pale,   405
Murmuring o'er the name again,
Lord Roland de Vaux of Tryermaine?

Alas! they had been friends in youth;
But whispering tongues can poison truth;
And constancy lives in realms above;   410
And life is thorny; and youth is vain;
And to be wroth with one we love
Doth work like madness in the brain.
And thus it chanced, as I divine,

With Roland and Sir Leoline. 415
Each spake words of high disdain
And insult to his heart's best brother:
They parted—ne'er to meet again!
But never either found another
To free the hollow heart from paining— 420
They stood aloof, the scars remaining,
Like cliffs which had been rent asunder;
A dreary sea now flows between—
But neither heat, nor frost, nor thunder,
Shall wholly do away, I ween, 425
The marks of that which once hath been.

Sir Leoline, a moment's space,
Stood gazing on the damsel's face:
And the youthful Lord of Tryermaine
Came back upon his heart again. 430

O then the Baron forgot his age,
His noble heart swelled high with rage;
He swore by the wounds in Jesu's side
He would proclaim it far and wide,
With trump and solemn heraldry, 435
That they, who thus had wronged the dame,
Were base as spotted infamy!
"And if they dare deny the same,
My herald shall appoint a week,
And let the recreant traitors seek 440
My tourney court—that there and then
I may dislodge their reptile souls
From the bodies and forms of men!"
He spake: his eye in lightning rolls!
For the lady was ruthlessly seized; and he kenned 445
In the beautiful lady the child of his friend!

And now the tears were on his face,
And fondly in his arms he took
Fair Geraldine, who met the embrace,
Prolonging it with joyous look. 450
Which when she viewed, a vision fell
Upon the soul of Christabel,
The vision of fear, the touch and pain!
She shrunk and shuddered, and saw again—
(Ah, woe is me! Was it for thee, 455
Thou gentle maid! such sights to see?)

Again she saw that bosom old,
Again she felt that bosom cold,
And drew in her breath with a hissing sound:
Whereat the Knight turned wildly round, 460
And nothing saw, but his own sweet maid
With eyes upraised, as one that prayed.

The touch, the sight, had passed away,
And in its stead that vision blest,
Which comforted her after-rest 465
While in the lady's arms she lay,
Had put a rapture in her breast,
And on her lips and o'er her eyes
Spread smiles like light!
            With new surprise,
"What ails then my belovéd child?" 470
The Baron said—His daughter mild
Made answer, "All will yet be well!"
I ween, she had no power to tell
Aught else: so mighty was the spell.

Yet he, who saw this Geraldine, 475
Had deemed her sure a thing divine:
Such sorrow with such grace she blended,
As if she feared she had offended
Sweet Christabel, that gentle maid!
And with such lowly tones she prayed 480
She might be sent without delay
Home to her father's mansion.
               "Nay!
Nay, by my soul!" said Leoline.
"Ho! Bracy the bard, the charge be thine!
Go thou, with music sweet and loud,
And take two steeds with trappings proud, 485
And take the youth whom thou lov'st best
To bear thy harp, and learn thy song,
And clothe you both in solemn vest,
And over the mountains haste along,
Lest wandering folk, that are abroad, 490
Detain you on the valley road.

"And when he has crossed the Irthing flood,
My merry bard! he hastes, he hastes
Up Knorren Moor, through Halegarth Wood,
And reaches soon that castle good 495
Which stands and threatens Scotland's wastes.

"Bard Bracy! bard Bracy! your horses are fleet,
Ye must ride up the hall, your music so sweet,
More loud than your horses' echoing feet!
And loud and loud to Lord Roland call, 500
Thy daughter is safe in Langdale hall!
Thy beautiful daughter is safe and free—
Sir Leoline greets thee thus through me!
He bids thee come without delay
With all thy numerous array 505
And take thy lovely daughter home:
And he will meet thee on the way

With all his numerous array
White with their panting palfreys' foam: 510
And, by mine honor! I will say,
That I repent me of the day
When I spake words of fierce disdain
To Roland de Vaux of Tryermaine!—
For since that evil hour hath flown,   515
Many a summer's sun hath shone;
Yet ne'er found I a friend again
Like Roland de Vaux of Tryermaine."

The lady fell, and clasped his knees,
Her face upraised, her eyes o'erflowing;   520
And Bracy replied, with faltering voice,
His gracious Hail on all bestowing!—
"Thy words, thou sire of Christabel,
Are sweeter than my harp can tell;
Yet might I gain a boon of thee,   525
This day my journey should not be,
So strange a dream hath come to me,
That I had vowed with music loud
To clear yon wood from thing unblest,
Warned by a vision in my rest!   530
For in my sleep I saw that dove,
That gentle bird, whom thou dost love,
And call'st by thy own daughter's name—
Sir Leoline! I saw the same
Fluttering, and uttering fearful moan,   535
Among the green herbs in the forest alone.
Which when I saw and when I heard,
I wondered what might ail the bird;
For nothing near it could I see,
Save the grass and green herbs underneath the old tree. 540

"And in my dream methought I went
To search out what might there be found;
And what the sweet bird's trouble meant,
That thus lay fluttering on the ground.
I went and peered, and could descry   545
No cause for her distressful cry;
But yet for her dear lady's sake
I stooped, methought, the dove to take,
When lo! I saw a bright green snake
Coiled around its wings and neck.   550
Green as the herbs on which it couched,
Close by the dove's its head it crouched;
And with the dove it heaves and stirs,
Swelling its neck as she swelled hers!
I woke; it was the midnight hour,   555
The clock was echoing in the tower;
But though my slumber was gone by,

This dream it would not pass away—
It seems to live upon my eye!
And thence I vowed this selfsame day 560
With music strong and saintly song
To wander through the forest bare,
Lest aught unholy loiter there."

Thus Bracy said: the Baron, the while,
Half-listening heard him with a smile; 565
Then turned to Lady Geraldine,
His eyes made up of wonder and love;
And said in courtly accents fine,
"Sweet maid, Lord Roland's beauteous dove,
With arms more strong than harp or song, 570
Thy sire and I will crush the snake!"
He kissed her forehead as he spake,
And Geraldine in maiden wise
Casting down her large bright eyes,
With blushing cheek and courtesy fine 575
She turned her from Sir Leoline;
Softly gathering up her train,
That o'er her right arm fell again;
And folded her arms across her chest,
And couched her head upon her breast, 580
And looked askance at Christabel——
Jesu, Maria, shield her well!

A snake's small eye blinks dull and shy;
And the lady's eyes they shrunk in her head,
Each shrunk up to a serpent's eye, 585
And with somewhat of malice, and more of dread,
At Christabel she looked askance!—
One moment—and the sight was fled!
But Christabel in dizzy trance
Stumbling on the unsteady ground 590
Shuddered aloud, with a hissing sound;
And Geraldine again turned round,
And like a thing, that sought relief,
Full of wonder and full of grief,
She rolled her large bright eyes divine 595
Wildly on Sir Leoline.

The maid, alas! her thoughts are gone,
She nothing sees—no sight but one!
The maid, devoid of guile and sin,
I know not how, in fearful wise, 600
So deeply had she drunken in
That look, those shrunken serpent eyes,
That all her features were resigned
To this sole image in her mind:
And passively did imitate 605

That look of dull and treacherous hate!
And thus she stood, in dizzy trance,
Still picturing that look askance
With forced unconscious sympathy
Full before her father's view—   610
As far as such a look could be
In eyes so innocent and blue!

And whence the trance was o'er, the maid
Paused awhile, and inly prayed:
Then falling at the Baron's feet,   615
"By my mother's soul do I entreat
That thou this woman send away!"
She said: and more she could not say:
For what she knew she could not tell,
O'ermastered by the mighty spell.   620

Why is thy cheek so wan and wild,
Sir Leoline? Thy only child
Lies at thy feet, thy joy, thy pride,
So fair, so innocent, so mild;
The same, for whom thy lady died!   625
O by the pangs of her dear mother
Think thou no evil of thy child!
For her, and thee, and for no other,
She prayed the moment ere she died:
Prayed that the babe for whom she died,   630
Might prove her dear lord's joy and pride!
        That prayer her deadly pangs beguiled,
                Sir Leoline!
        And wouldst thou wrong thy only child,
                Her child and thine?   635

Within the Baron's heart and brain
If thoughts, like these, had any share,
They only swelled his rage and pain,
And did but work confusion there.
His heart was cleft with pain and rage,   640
His cheeks they quivered, his eyes were wild,
Dishonored thus in his old age;
Dishonored by his only child,
And all his hospitality
To the wronged daughter of his friend   645
By more than woman's jealousy
Brought thus to a disgraceful end—
He rolled his eye with stern regard
Upon the gentle minstrel bard,
And said in tones abrupt, austere—   650
"Why, Bracy! dost thou loiter here?
I bade thee hence!" The bard obeyed;
And turning from his own sweet maid,

The aged knight, Sir Leoline,
Led forth the lady Geraldine!   655

The Conclusion to Part II

A little child, a limber elf,
Singing, dancing to itself,
A fairy thing with red round cheeks,
That always finds, and never seeks,
Makes such a vision to the sight   660
As fills a father's eyes with light;
And pleasures flow in so thick and fast
Upon his heart, that he at last
Must needs express his love's excess
With words of unmeant bitterness.   665
Perhaps 'tis pretty to force together
Thoughts so all unlike each other;
To mutter and mock a broken charm,
To dally with wrong that does no harm.
Perhaps 'tis tender too and pretty   670
At each wild word to feel within
A sweet recoil of love and pity.
And what, if in a world of sin
(O sorrow and shame should this be true!)
Such giddiness of heart and brain   675
Comes seldom save from rage and pain,
So talks as it's most used to do.

ca. 1797–1801   1816

Frost at Midnight[1]

The Frost performs its secret ministry,
Unhelped by any wind. The owlet's cry
Came loud—and hark, again! loud as before.
The inmates of my cottage, all at rest,
Have left me to that solitude, which suits   5
Abstruser musings: save that at my side
My cradled infant slumbers peacefully.
'Tis calm indeed! so calm, that it disturbs
And vexes meditation with its strange
And extreme silentness. Sea, hill, and wood,   10
This populous village! Sea, and hill, and wood,
With all the numberless goings-on of life,
Inaudible as dreams! the thin blue flame
Lies on my low-burnt fire, and quivers not;
Only that film,[2] which fluttered on the grate,   15

---

1. The scene is Coleridge's cottage at Nether Stowey; the infant in line 7 is his son Hartley.

2. "In all parts of the kingdom these films are called *strangers* and supposed to portend the arrival of some absent

Still flutters there, the sole unquiet thing.
Methinks its motion in this hush of nature
Gives it dim sympathies with me who live,
Making it a companionable form,
Whose puny flaps and freaks the idling Spirit   20
By its own moods interprets, everywhere
Echo or mirror seeking of itself,
And makes a toy of Thought.

      But O! how oft,
How oft, at school, with most believing mind,
Presageful, have I gazed upon the bars,   25
To watch that fluttering *stranger!* and as oft
With unclosed lids, already had I dreamt
Of my sweet birthplace,[3] and the old church tower,
Whose bells, the poor man's only music, rang
From morn to evening, all the hot fair-day,   30
So sweetly, that they stirred and haunted me
With a wild pleasure, falling on mine ear
Most like articulate sounds of things to come!
So gazed I, till the soothing things, I dreamt,
Lulled me to sleep, and sleep prolonged my dreams!   35
And so I brooded all the following morn,
Awed by the stern preceptor's face,[4] mine eye
Fixed with mock study on my swimming book:
Save if the door half opened, and I snatched
A hasty glance, and still my heart leaped up,   40
For still I hoped to see the *stranger's* face,
Townsman, or aunt, or sister more beloved,
My playmate when we both were clothed alike![5]

  Dear Babe, that sleepest cradled by my side,
Whose gentle breathings, heard in this deep calm,   45
Fill up the interspersèd vacancies
And momentary pauses of the thought!
My babe so beautiful! it thrills my heart
With tender gladness, thus to look at thee,
And think that thou shalt learn far other lore,   50
And in far other scenes! For I was reared
In the great city, pent 'mid cloisters dim,
And saw nought lovely but the sky and stars.
But *thou*, my babe! shalt wander like a breeze
By lakes and sandy shores, beneath the crags   55
Of ancient mountain, and beneath the clouds,
Which image in their bulk both lakes and shores

friend" [Coleridge's note]. The "film"
is a piece of soot fluttering on the bar
of the grate; it was one of various
signs which, according to popular English belief of the time, foretold an unexpected visitor. See also lines 26 and
41.
3. Coleridge was born at Ottery St.

Mary, Devonshire, but went to school
in London, beginning at the age of 9.
4. The "stern preceptor" at Coleridge's
school, Christ's Hospital, was the Rev.
James Boyer, whom Coleridge describes
in *Biographia Literaria*, Chapter I.
5. I.e., when both Coleridge and his
sister Ann still wore infant clothes.

And mountain crags: so shalt thou see and hear
The lovely shapes and sounds intelligible
Of that eternal language, which thy God   60
Utters, who from eternity doth teach
Himself in all, and all things in himself.
Great universal Teacher! he shall mold
Thy spirit, and by giving make it ask.

Therefore all seasons shall be sweet to thee,   65
Whether the summer clothe the general earth
With greenness, or the redbreast sit and sing
Betwixt the tufts of snow on the bare branch
Of mossy apple tree, while the nigh thatch
Smokes in the sun-thaw; whether the eave-drops fall   70
Heard only in the trances of the blast,
Or if the secret ministry of frost
Shall hang them up in silent icicles,
Quietly shining to the quiet Moon.

February, 1798   1798

Dejection: An Ode[1]

> Late, late yestreen I saw the new Moon,
> With the old Moon in her arms;
> And I fear, I fear, my master dear!
> We shall have a deadly storm.
> *Ballad of Sir Patrick Spence*

1

Well! If the bard was weather-wise, who made
The grand old ballad of Sir Patrick Spence,
This night, so tranquil now, will not go hence
Unroused by winds, that ply a busier trade
Than those which mold yon cloud in lazy flakes,   5
Or the dull sobbing draft, that moans and rakes
Upon the strings of this Aeolian lute,[2]

---

1. This poem originated in a verse letter of 340 lines, called *A Letter to ———*, which Coleridge wrote on the night of April 4, 1802, after hearing the opening stanzas of *Ode: Intimations of Immortality,* which Wordsworth had just composed. The *Letter* was addressed to Sara Hutchinson (whom Coleridge sometimes called "Asra"), the sister of Wordsworth's fiancée Mary. It picked up the theme of a loss in the quality of perceptual experience which Wordsworth had presented at the beginning of his *Ode.* In his original poem, Coleridge lamented at length his unhappy marriage and the hopelessness of his love for Sara Hutchinson. In the next six months Coleridge deleted more than half the original lines, revised and reordered the remaining passages, and so transformed a long verse confession into the compact and dignified *Dejection: An Ode.* He published the *Ode,* in substantially its present form, on October 4, 1802, Wordsworth's wedding day—and also the seventh anniversary of Coleridge's own disastrous marriage to Sara Fricker. Coleridge's implicit concern with the marital relation emerges in the marriage metaphors of lines 49 and 67–70.

2. A stringed instrument played upon by the wind; see Coleridge's *The Eolian Harp,* note 1.

Which better far were mute.
For lo! the New-moon winter-bright!
And overspread with phantom light,   10
(With swimming phantom light o'erspread
But rimmed and circled by a silver thread)
I see the old Moon in her lap, foretelling
    The coming-on of rain and squally blast.
And oh! that even now the gust were swelling,   15
    And the slant night shower driving loud and fast!
Those sounds which oft have raised me, whilst they awed,
    And sent my soul abroad,
Might now perhaps their wonted³ impulse give,
Might startle this dull pain, and make it move and live!   20

2

A grief without a pang, void, dark, and drear,
    A stifled, drowsy, unimpassioned grief,
    Which finds no natural outlet, no relief,
        In word, or sigh, or tear—
O Lady!⁴ in this wan and heartless mood,   25
To other thoughts by yonder throstle wooed,
    All this long eve, so balmy and serene,
Have I been gazing on the western sky,
    And its peculiar tint of yellow green:
And still I gaze—and with how blank an eye!   30
And those thin clouds above, in flakes and bars,
That give away their motion to the stars;
Those stars, that glide behind them or between,
Now sparkling, now bedimmed, but always seen:
Yon crescent Moon, as fixed as if it grew   35
In its own cloudless, starless lake of blue;
I see them all so excellently fair,
I see, not feel, how beautiful they are!

3

        My genial⁵ spirits fail;
        And what can these avail   40
To lift the smothering weight from off my breast?
        It were a vain endeavor,
        Though I should gaze forever
On that green light that lingers in the west:
I may not hope from outward forms to win   45
The passion and the life, whose fountains are within.

4

O Lady! we receive but what we give,
And in our life alone does Nature live:

---

3. Customary.
4. In the original version "Sara"—i.e.,
Sara Hutchinson, with whom Coleridge
was hopelessly in love. After intervening versions, in which the poem was
addressed first to "William" (Words-

worth) and then to "Edmund," Coleridge introduced the noncommittal
"Lady" in 1817.
5. In its old use as the adjective form
of "genius": "My innate powers fail."

Ours is her wedding garment, ours her shroud![6]
And would we aught behold, of higher worth,   50
Than that inanimate cold world allowed
To the poor loveless ever-anxious crowd,
    Ah! from the soul itself must issue forth
A light, a glory,[7] a fair luminous cloud
        Enveloping the Earth—   55
And from the soul itself must there be sent
    A sweet and potent voice, of its own birth,
Of all sweet sounds the life and element!

5

O pure of heart! thou need'st not ask of me
What this strong music in the soul may be!   60
    What, and wherein it doth exist,
    This light, this glory, this fair luminous mist,
    This beautiful and beauty-making power.
    Joy,[8] virtuous Lady! Joy that ne'er was given,
Save to the pure, and in their purest hour,   65
Life, and Life's effluence, cloud at once and shower,
Joy, Lady! is the spirit and the power,
Which wedding Nature to us gives in dower
    A new Earth and new Heaven,[9]
Undreamt of by the sensual and the proud—   70
Joy is the sweet voice, Joy the luminous cloud—
        We in ourselves rejoice!
And thence flows all that charms or ear or sight,
    All melodies the echoes of that voice,
All colors a suffusion from that light.   75

6

There was a time when, though my path was rough,
    This joy within me dallied with distress,
And all misfortunes were but as the stuff
    Whence Fancy made me dreams of happiness:
For hope grew round me, like the twining vine,   80
And fruits, and foliage, not my own, seemed mine.
But now afflictions bow me down to earth:
Nor care I that they rob me of my mirth;
    But oh! each visitation
Suspends what nature gave me at my birth,   85
    My shaping spirit of Imagination.

6. I.e., whether nature is experienced as "inanimate" (line 51) or in living interchange with the observer depends on the apathy or joyous vitality of the observer's own spirit.

7. Coleridge commonly used "glory" not in the sense of a halo, merely, but as a term for a mountain phenomenon in which a walker sees his own figure projected by the sun in the mist, enlarged, and with a circle of light around its head. See Coleridge's *Constancy to an Ideal Object,* line 30.

8. Coleridge often uses "Joy" for a sense of abounding vitality and of harmony between one's inner life and the life of nature. He sometimes calls the contrary "exsiccation," or spiritual dryness.

9. The sense of this passage becomes clearer if line 68 is punctuated, as in one of Coleridge's quotations from his own poem in an essay: "Which, wedding Nature to us, gives in dower"; i.e., "Joy" is the condition which (overcoming the alienation between man's mind and its milieu) marries us to "Nature," and gives by way of wedding portion ("dower") the experience of a renovated outer world.

For not to think of what I needs must feel,
    But to be still and patient, all I can;
And happly by abstruse research to steal
    From my own nature all the natural man—   90
This was my sole resource, my only plan:
Till that which suits a part infects the whole,
And now is almost grown the habit of my soul.

7

Hence, viper thoughts, that coil around my mind,
    Reality's dark dream!   95
I turn from you, and listen to the wind,
    Which long has raved unnoticed. What a scream
Of agony by torture lengthened out
That lute sent forth! Thou Wind, that rav'st without,
    Bare crag, or mountain tairn,[1] or blasted tree,   100
Or pine grove whither woodman never clomb,
Or lonely house, long held the witches' home,
    Methinks were fitter instruments for thee,
Mad lutanist! who in this month of showers,
Of dark-brown gardens, and of peeping flowers,   105
Mak'st devils' yule,[2] with worse than wintry song,
The blossoms, buds, and timorous leaves among.
    Thou actor, perfect in all tragic sounds!
Thou mighty poet, e'en to frenzy bold!
        What tell'st thou now about?   110
        'Tis of the rushing of an host in rout,
    With groans, of trampled men, with smarting wounds—
At once they groan with pain, and shudder with the cold!
But hush! there is a pause of deepest silence!
    And all that noise, as of a rushing crowd,   115
With groans, and tremulous shudderings—all is over—
    It tells another tale, with sounds less deep and loud!
        A tale of less affright,
        And tempered with delight,
As Otway's[3] self had framed the tender lay—   120
        'Tis of a little child
        Upon a lonesome wild,
Not far from home, but she hath lost her way:
And now moans low in bitter grief and fear,
And now screams loud, and hopes to make her mother hear.   125

8

'Tis midnight, but small thoughts have I of sleep:
Full seldom may my friend such vigils keep!
Visit her, gentle Sleep! with wings of healing,
    And may this storm be but a mountain birth,[4]
    May all the stars hang bright above her dwelling,   130

1. Tarn, or mountain pool.
2. Christmas, in the perverted form in which it is celebrated by devils.
3. Thomas Otway (1652–85), a dramatist noted for the pathos of his tragic passages. The poet originally named was "William," and the allusion was probably to Wordsworth's *Lucy Gray*.
4. Probably, "May this be a typical mountain storm, short though violent," although it is possible that Coleridge intended an allusion to Horace's phrase, "the mountain labored and brought forth a mouse."

Silent as though they watched the sleeping Earth!
With light heart may she rise,
Gay fancy, cheerful eyes,
Joy lift her spirit, joy attune her voice;
To her may all things live, from pole to pole,   135
Their life the eddying of her living soul!
O simple spirit, guided from above,
Dear Lady! friend devoutest of my choice,
Thus mayest thou ever, evermore rejoice.

April 4, 1802   1802, 1817

What Is Life?[5]

Resembles life what once was deemed of light,
Too ample in itself for human sight?
An absolute self—an element ungrounded—
All that we see, all colors of all shade
    By encroach of darkness made?—   5
Is very life by consciousness unbounded?
And all the thoughts, pains, joys of mortal breath,
A war-embrace of wrestling life and death?

1804   1829

Phantom[6]

All look and likeness caught from earth
All accident of kin and birth,
Had passed away. There was no trace
Of aught on that illumined face,
Upraised beneath the rifted stone   5
But of one spirit all her own—
She, she herself, and only she,
Shone through her body visibly.

1804   1834

To William Wordsworth

COMPOSED ON THE NIGHT AFTER HIS RECITATION OF A POEM
ON THE GROWTH OF AN INDIVIDUAL MIND[1]

Friend of the wise! and teacher of the good!
Into my heart have I received that lay

5. Written by Coleridge in a notebook
kept at Malta in 1804, in order, he
said, "to try a meter." It expresses a
conception of life as a sustained opposition between the life principle and
the death principle, in which the latter
is the inevitable victor.
6. A notebook Coleridge kept at Malta
in 1804 makes it clear that the poem
describes the appearance of Sara Hutchinson in a dream.

1. This was the poem (later called *The
Prelude*) addressed to Coleridge, which
Wordsworth had completed in 1805.
After Coleridge returned from Malta,
very low in health and spirits, Wordsworth read the poem aloud to him on
the evenings of almost two weeks.
Coleridge wrote most of his poem immediately the reading was completed,
on January 7, 1807.

More than historic, that prophetic lay
Wherein (high theme by thee first sung aright)
Of the foundations and the building up   5
Of a Human Spirit thou hast dared to tell
What may be told, to the understanding mind
Revealable; and what within the mind
By vital breathings secret as the soul
Of vernal growth, oft quickens in the heart   10
Thoughts all too deep for words!²—

                      Theme hard as high!
Of smiles spontaneous, and mysterious fears
(The first-born they of Reason and twin birth),
Of tides obedient to external force,
And currents self-determined, as might seem,   15
Or by some inner Power; of moments awful,
Now in thy inner life, and now abroad,
When power streamed from thee, and thy soul received
The light reflected, as a light bestowed—
Of fancies fair, and milder hours of youth,   20
Hyblean³ murmurs of poetic thought
Industrious in its joy, in vales and glens
Native or outland, lakes and famous hills!
Or on the lonely highroad, when the stars
Were rising; or by secret mountain streams,   25
The guides and the companions of thy way!

Of more than Fancy, of the Social Sense
Distending wide, and man beloved as man,
Where France in all her towns lay vibrating
Like some becalméd bark beneath the burst   30
Of Heaven's immediate thunder, when no cloud
Is visible, or shadow on the main.
For thou wert there, thine own brows garlanded,
Amid the tremor of a realm aglow,
Amid a mighty nation jubilant,   35
When from the general heart of human kind
Hope sprang forth like a full-born deity!
——Of that dear Hope afflicted and struck down,
So summoned homeward, thenceforth calm and sure
From the dread watchtower of man's absolute self,   40
With light unwaning on her eyes, to look
Far on—herself a glory to behold,
The Angel of the vision! Then (last strain)
Of Duty, chosen Laws controlling choice,
Action and joy!—An Orphic song⁴ indeed,   45

2. Wordsworth had described the effect on his mind of the animating breeze ("vital breathings") in *The Prelude,* I.1-44 "Thoughts * * * words" echoes the last line of his *Intimations* ode. Coleridge then summarizes the major themes and events of *The Prelude.*

3. Sweet.
4. As enchanting and oracular as the song of the legendary Orpheus. The allusion is probably also to the Orphic mysteries, involving spiritual death and rebirth; see lines 61-66.

A song divine of high and passionate thoughts
To their own music chaunted!

           O great bard!
Ere that last strain dying awed the air,
With steadfast eye I viewed thee in the choir
Of ever-enduring men. The truly great   50
Have all one age, and from one visible space
Shed influence! They, both in power and act,
Are permanent, and Time is not with them,
Save as it worketh for them, they in it.
Nor less a sacred roll, than those of old,   55
And to be placed, as they, with gradual fame
Among the archives of mankind, thy work
Makes audible a linkéd lay of Truth,
Of Truth profound a sweet continuous lay,
Not learnt, but native, her own natural notes!   60
Ah! as I listened with a heart forlorn,
The pulses of my being beat anew:
And even as Life returns upon the drowned,[5]
Life's joy rekindling roused a throng of pains—
Keen pangs of Love, awakening as a babe   65
Turbulent, with an outcry in the heart;
And fears self-willed, that shunned the eye of Hope;
And Hope that scarce would know itself from Fear;
Sense of past Youth, and Manhood come in vain,
And Genius given, and Knowledge won in vain;   70
And all which I had culled in wood-walks wild,
And all which patient toil had reared, and all,
Commune with thee had opened out—but flowers
Strewed on my corse, and borne upon my bier
In the same coffin, for the selfsame grave!   75

    That way no more! and ill beseems it me,
Who came a welcomer in herald's guise,
Singing of Glory, and Futurity,
To wander back on such unhealthful road,
Plucking the poisons of self-harm! And ill   80
Such intertwine beseems triumphal wreaths
Strewed before thy advancing!

              Nor do thou,
Sage bard! impair the memory of that hour
Of thy communion with my nobler mind[6]
By pity or grief, already felt too long!   85
Nor let my words import more blame than needs.
The tumult rose and ceased: for Peace is nigh
Where Wisdom's voice has found a listening heart.
Amid the howl of more than wintry storms,
The Halcyon[7] hears the voice of vernal hours   90

5. A death-in-life is also described in,
e.g., *Dejection* and *Epitaph*.
6. I.e., during the early association between the two poets (1797-98).
7. A fabled bird, able to calm the sea,
where it nested in winter.

Already on the wing.

Eve following eve,[8]
Dear tranquil time, when the sweet sense of Home
Is sweetest! moments for their own sake hailed
And more desired, more precious, for thy song,
In silence listening, like a devout child,   95
My soul lay passive, by thy various strain
Driven as in surges now beneath the stars,
With momentary stars of my own birth,
Fair constellated foam, still darting off
Into the darkness; now a tranquil sea,   100
Outspread and bright, yet swelling to the moon.

And when—O friend! my comforter and guide!
Strong in thyself, and powerful to give strength!—
Thy long sustainéd song finally closed,
And thy deep voice had ceased—yet thou thyself   105
Wert still before my eyes, and round us both
That happy vision of belovéd faces—
Scarce conscious, and yet conscious of its close
I sate, my being blended in one thought
(Thought was it? or aspiration? or resolve?)   110
Absorbed, yet hanging still upon the sound—
And when I rose, I found myself in prayer.

January 7, 1807   1817

Recollections of Love

1

How warm this woodland wild recess!
　　Love surely hath been breathing here;
　　And this sweet bed of heath, my dear!
Swells up, then sinks with faint caress,
　　As if to have you yet more near.   5

2

Eight springs have flown since last I lay
　　On seaward Quantock's heathy hills,
　　Where quiet sounds from hidden rills
Float here and there, like things astray,
　　And high o'erhead the skylark shrills.   10

3

No voice as yet had made the air
　　Be music with your name; yet why
　　That asking look? that yearning sigh?
That sense of promise every where?
　　Belovéd! flew your spirit by?   15

4

As when a mother doth explore

8. The evenings during which Wordsworth read his poem aloud.

The rose mark on her long-lost child,
I met, I loved you, maiden mild!
As whom I long had loved before—
So deeply had I been beguiled.   20

5

You stood before me like a thought,
A dream remembered in a dream.
But when those meek eyes first did seem
To tell me, Love within you wrought—
O Greta,[1] dear domestic stream!   25

6

Has not, since then, Love's prompture deep,
Has not Love's whisper evermore
Been ceaseless, as thy gentle roar?
Sole voice, when other voices sleep,
Dear under-song in clamor's hour.   30

ca. 1807   1817

On Donne's Poetry[2]

With Donne, whose muse on dromedary trots,
Wreathe iron pokers into truelove knots;
Rhyme's sturdy cripple, fancy's maze and clue,
Wit's forge and fire-blast, meaning's press and screw.

ca. 1818   1836

Work Without Hope

LINES COMPOSED 21ST FEBRUARY 1825

All Nature seems at work. Slugs leave their lair—
The bees are stirring—birds are on the wing—
And Winter slumbering in the open air
Wears on his smiling face a dream of Spring!
And I the while, the sole unbusy thing,   5
Nor honey make, nor pair, nor build, nor sing.

Yet well I ken the banks where amaranths[3] blow,
Have traced the fount whence streams of nectar flow.
Bloom, O ye amaranths! bloom for whom ye may,
For me ye bloom not! Glide, rich streams, away!   10
With lips unbrightened, wreathless brow, I stroll:
And would you learn the spells that drowse my soul?
Work without Hope draws nectar in a sieve,
And Hope without an object cannot live.

1825   1828

1. The river Greta, which flowed past Coleridge's home in Keswick, in the Lake Country.
2. Donne as a poet had been in eclipse for most of the 18th century. This terse and penetrating comment shows the Romantic poet's great, though qualified, respect for the master of the metaphysical style.
3. Mythical flowers that bloom perpetually.

Constancy to an Ideal Object

Since all that beat about in Nature's range
Or veer or vanish, why should'st thou remain
The only constant in a world of change,
O yearning Thought! that liv'st but in the brain?
Call to the Hours, that in the distance play,   5
The faery people of the future day——
Fond[1] Thought! not one of all that shining swarm
Will breathe on thee with life-enkindling breath,
Till when, like strangers shelt'ring from a storm,
Hope and Despair meet in the porch of Death!   10
Yet still thou haunt'st me; and though well I see,
She[1a] is not thou, and only thou art she,
Still, still as though some dear embodied Good,
Some living Love before my eyes there stood
With answering look a ready ear to lend,   15
I mourn to thee and say—"Ah! loveliest friend!
That this the meed[2] of all my toils might be,
To have a home, an English home, and thee!"
Vain repetition! Home and thou are one.
The peaceful'st cot the moon shall shine upon,   20
Lulled by the thrush and wakened by the lark,
Without thee were but a becalméd bark,
Whose Helmsman on an ocean waste and wide
Sits mute and pale his moldering helm beside.

And art thou nothing? Such thou art, as when   25
The woodman winding westward up the glen
At wintry dawn, where o'er the sheep-track's maze
The viewless snow-mist weaves a glist'ning haze,
Sees full before him, gliding without tread,
An image with a glory round its head;[3]   30
The enamored rustic worships its fair hues,
Nor knows he makes the shadow he pursues!

1828

Phantom or Fact

A DIALOGUE IN VERSE

AUTHOR

A lovely form there sate beside my bed,
And such a feeding calm its presence shed,
A tender love so pure from earthly leaven,
That I unnethe[1] the fancy might control,
'Twas my own spirit newly come from heaven,   5
Wooing its gentle way into my soul!
But ah! the change—It had not stirred, and yet—

---

1. Foolish.
1a. Sara Hutchinson.
2. Reward.
3. A projected image of oneself in the
mist. See Coleridge's *Dejection: An Ode*, line 54.
1. With difficulty.

Alas! that change how fain would I forget!
That shrinking back, like one that had mistook!
That weary, wandering, disavowing look!   10
'Twas all another, feature, look, and frame,
And still, methought, I knew, it was the same!

FRIEND

This riddling tale, to what does it belong?
Is't history? vision? or an idle song?
Or rather say at once, within what space   15
Of time this wild disastrous change took place?

AUTHOR

Call it a moment's work (and such it seems)
This tale's a fragment from the life of dreams;
But say that years matured the silent strife,
And 'tis a record from the dream of life.   20

ca. 1830   1834

Epitaph[1]

Stop, Christian passer-by!—Stop, child of God,
And read with gentle breast. Beneath this sod
A poet lies, or that which once seemed he.
O lift one thought in prayer for S. T. C.;
That he who many a year with toil of breath
Found death in life, may here find life in death!
Mercy for praise—to be forgiven for[2] fame
He asked, and hoped, through Christ. Do thou the same!

1833   1834

From Biographia Literaria[1]
From *Chapter I*

The discipline of his taste at school—Bowles's sonnets—Compari-
son between the poets before and since Mr. Pope.

* * * At school I enjoyed the inestimable advantage of a very

---

1. Written by Coleridge the year before he died. One version that he sent in a letter had as title: "Epitaph on a Poet little known, yet better known by the Initials of his name than by the Name Itself."
2. " 'For' in the sense of 'instead of' " [Coleridge's note].
1. In March, 1815, Coleridge was preparing a collected edition of his poems, and planned to include "a general preface * * * on the principles of philosophic and genial criticism." Characteristically, the materials developed as

Coleridge worked on them, until, on July 29, he declared that the preface had been extended into a complete work, "an Autobiographia Literaria"; it was to consist of two main parts, "my literary life and opinions, as far as poetry and *poetical* criticism [are] concerned," and a critique of Wordsworth's theory of poetic diction. This work was ready by 17 September 1815, but the *Biographia Literaria*, in two volumes, was not published until July, 1817. The delay was caused by a series of miscalculations by his printer, which

sensible, though at the same time a very severe master. He[2] early molded my taste to the preference of Demosthenes to Cicero, of Homer and Theocritus to Virgil, and again of Virgil to Ovid. He habituated me to compare Lucretius (in such extracts as I then read), Terence, and, above all, the chaster poems of Catullus not only with the Roman poets of the so-called silver and brazen ages but with even those of the Augustan era; and, on grounds of plain sense and universal logic, to see and assert the superiority of the former in the truth and nativeness both of their thoughts and diction. At the same time that we were studying the Greek tragic poets, he made us read Shakespeare and Milton as lessons; and they were the lessons, too, which required most time and trouble to *bring up*, so as to escape his censure. I learnt from him that poetry, even that of the loftiest and, seemingly, that of the wildest odes, had a logic of its own as severe as that of science; and more difficult, because more subtle, more complex, and dependent on more, and more fugitive, causes. In the truly great poets, he would say, there is a reason assignable, not only for every word, but for the position of every word; and I well remember that, availing himself of the synonyms to the Homer of Didymus,[3] he made us attempt to show, with regard to each, *why* it would not have answered the same purpose, and *wherein* consisted the peculiar fitness of the word in the original text.

In our own English compositions (at least for the last three years of our school education) he showed no mercy to phrase, metaphor, or image unsupported by a sound sense, or where the same sense might have been conveyed with equal force and dignity in plainer words. Lute, harp, and lyre, muse, muses, and inspirations, Pegasus, Parnassus, and Hippocrene were all an abomina-

---

forced Coleridge to add miscellaneous materials needed to eke out the length of his original manuscript.

The critique of Wordsworth's theory of diction, which Coleridge had been planning ever since 1802, when he had detected "a radical difference in our theoretical opinions respecting poetry," is long, detailed, and subtly reasoned. In the selection from Chapter XVII, below, Coleridge agrees with Wordsworth's general aim of reforming the artifices of modern poetic diction, but he sharply denies Wordsworth's claim that there is no essential difference between the language of poetry and the language really spoken by men. The other selections printed here are devoted mainly to the central principle of Coleridge's own critical theory, the distinction between the mechanical "fancy" and the organic "imagination." Thus the biographical section of the *Biographia* (Chapters I and IV), dealing with the development of his poetic

taste and theory, describes his gradual realization, climaxed by his first exposure to Wordsworth's poetry, "that fancy and imagination were two distinct and widely different faculties." The conclusion to Chapter XIII tersely summarizes this distinction, and the definition of poetry, at the end of Chapter XIV, develops at somewhat greater length the nature of the process and products of the "synthetic and magical power * * * of imagination." These cryptic paragraphs have proved to be the most widely discussed and influential passages ever written by an English critic.

2. "The Rev. James Boyer, many years Head Master of the Grammar School, Christ's Hospital" [Coleridge's note]. See also Charles Lamb's essay, *Christ's Hospital Five-and-Thirty Years Ago*.
3. Didymus of Alexandria (ca. 65 B.C.– A.D. 10) was the author of a commentary on the text of Homer.

tion to him. In fancy I can almost hear him now, exclaiming, "Harp? Harp? Lyre? Pen and ink, boy, you mean! Muse, boy, muse? Your nurse's daughter, you mean! Pierian spring? Oh, aye! the cloister pump, I suppose!" Nay, certain introductions, similes, and examples were placed by name on a list of interdiction. Among the similes there was, I remember, that of the manchineel fruit,[4] as suiting equally well with too many subjects, in which, however, it yielded the palm at once to the example of Alexander and Clytus,[5] which was equally good and apt whatever might be the theme. Was it ambition? Alexander and Clytus! Flattery? Alexander and Clytus! Anger? Drunkenness? Pride? Friendship? Ingratitude? Late repentance? Still, still Alexander and Clytus! At length the praises of agriculture having been exemplified in the sagacious observation that, had Alexander been holding the plow, he would not have run his friend Clytus through with a spear, this tried and serviceable old friend was banished by public edict *in secula seculorum*.[6] I have sometimes ventured to think that a list of this kind or an *index expurgatorius* of certain well-known and ever returning phrases, both introductory and transitional, including the large assortment of modest egotisms and flattering illeisms,[7] etc., etc., might be hung up in our law courts and both Houses of Parliament with great advantage to the public as an important saving of national time, an incalculable relief to his Majesty's ministers; but, above all, as insuring the thanks of country attorneys and their clients, who have private bills to carry through the House.

Be this as it may, there was one custom of our master's which I cannot pass over in silence, because I think it imitable and worthy of imitation. He would often permit our theme exercises, under some pretext of want of time, to accumulate till each lad had four or five to be looked over. Then placing the whole number *abreast* on his desk, he would ask the writer why this or that sentence might not have found as appropriate a place under this or that other thesis; and if no satisfying answer could be returned and two faults of the same kind were found in one exercise, the irrevocable verdict followed, the exercise was torn up, and another on the same subject to be produced, in addition to the tasks of the day. The reader will, I trust, excuse this tribute of recollection to a man whose severities, even now, not seldom furnish the dreams by which the blind fancy would fain interpret to the mind the painful sensations of distempered sleep; but neither lessen nor dim the deep sense of my moral and intellectual obligations. He sent us to the university excellent Latin and Greek scholars and tolerable

4. Poisonous, though attractive in appearance.
5. Plutarch's *Life* of Alexander the Great relates that the king killed his friend Clytus in a drunken quarrel.

6. Forever ("for centuries of centuries").
7. Excessive use of the pronoun "he" (in Latin, *ille*).

Hebraists. Yet our classical knowledge was the least of the good gifts which we derived from his zealous and conscientious tutorage. He is now gone to his final reward, full of years and full of honors, even of those honors which were dearest to his heart as gratefully bestowed by that school, and still binding him to the interests of that school in which he had been himself educated and to which during his whole life he was a dedicated thing. * * *

I had just entered on my seventeenth year when the sonnets of Mr. Bowles,[8] twenty in number, and just then published in a quarto pamphlet, were first made known and presented to me by a schoolfellow who had quitted us for the university and who, during the whole time that he was in our first form (or in our school language, a Grecian), had been my patron and protector. I refer to Dr. Middleton, the truly learned and every way excellent Bishop of Calcutta * * *

It was a double pleasure to me, and still remains a tender recollection, that I should have received from a friend so revered the first knowledge of a poet by whose works, year after year, I was so enthusiastically delighted and inspired. My earliest acquaintances will not have forgotten the undisciplined eagerness and impetuous zeal with which I laboured to make proselytes, not only of my companions, but of all with whom I conversed, of whatever rank and in whatever place. As my school finances did not permit me to purchase copies I made, within less than a year and a half, more than forty transcriptions, as the best presents I could offer to those who had in any way won my regard. And with almost equal delight did I receive the three or four following publications of the same author.

Though I have seen and known enough of mankind to be well aware that I shall perhaps stand alone in my creed, and that it will be well if I subject myself to no worse charge than that of singularity, I am not therefore deterred from avowing that I regard and ever have regarded the obligations of intellect among the most sacred of the claims of gratitude. A valuable thought, or a particular train of thoughts, gives me additional pleasure when I can safely refer and attribute it to the conversation or correspondence of another. My obligations to Mr. Bowles were indeed important and for radical good. At a very premature age, even before my fifteenth year, I had bewildered myself in metaphysics and in theological controversy. Nothing else pleased me. History and particular facts lost all interest in my mind. Poetry (though for a

8. William Lisle Bowles (1762–1850) published in 1789 two editions of a collection of sonnets setting forth, in simple and fluent language, the pensive meditations evoked from a traveler by the varying scene. Coleridge's immense admiration for Bowles (which was shared to a lesser degree by Wordsworth) has puzzled literary historians; but Bowles did point the way to the long lyric of description and meditation, in heightened colloquial language, which became a major Romantic genre.

schoolboy of that age I was above par in English versification and had already produced two or three compositions which, I may venture to say without reference to my age, were somewhat above mediocrity, and which had gained me more credit than the sound good sense of my old master was at all pleased with), poetry itself, yea novels and romances, became insipid to me. In my friendless wanderings on our leave-days (for I was an orphan, and had scarce any connections in London), highly was I delighted if any passenger, especially if he were dressed in black,[9] would enter into conversation with me. For I soon found the means of directing it to my favorite subjects

> Of providence, foreknowledge, will, and fate,
> Fixed fate, free will, foreknowledge absolute,
> And found no end, in wandering mazes lost.[1]

This preposterous pursuit was, beyond doubt, injurious both to my natural powers and to the progress of my education. It would perhaps have been destructive had it been continued; but from this I was auspiciously withdrawn, partly indeed by an accidental introduction to an amiable family,[2] chiefly however by the genial influence of a style of poetry so tender and yet so manly, so natural and real, and yet so dignified and harmonious, as the sonnets, etc., of Mr. Bowles! Well were it for me, perhaps, had I never relapsed into the same mental disease; if I had continued to pluck the flower and reap the harvest from the cultivated surface, instead of delving in the unwholesome quicksilver mines of metaphysic depths. But if in after time I have sought a refuge from bodily pain and mismanaged sensibility in abstruse researches, which exercised the strength and subtlety of the understanding without awakening the feelings of the heart; still there was a long and blessed interval, during which my natural faculties were allowed to expand and my original tendencies to develop themselves; my fancy, and the love of nature, and the sense of beauty in forms and sounds.

The second advantage which I owe to my early perusal and admiration of these poems (to which let me add, though known to me at a somewhat later period, the *Lewesdon Hill* of Mr. Crow)[3] bears more immediately on my present subject. Among those with whom I conversed there were, of course, very many who had formed their taste and their notions of poetry from the writings of Mr. Pope and his followers: or to speak more generally, in that school of French poetry condensed and invigorated by English understanding which had predominated from the last century. I was not blind

9. I.e., if he were a clergyman.
1. *Paradise Lost* II.559–61.
2. The family of Mary Evans, with whom Coleridge fell deeply in love in 1788.
3. William Crow(e) (1745–1829) published in 1788 *Lewesdon Hill*, a long poem in blank verse which, like Bowles's sonnets, combined descriptions of the natural scene with associated moral and personal reflections.

to the merits of this school, yet as from inexperience of the world and consequent want of sympathy with the general subjects of these poems they gave me little pleasure, I doubtless undervalued the *kind*, and with the presumption of youth withheld from its masters the legitimate name of poets. I saw that the excellence of this kind consisted in just and acute observations on men and manners in an artificial state of society as its matter and substance, and in the logic of wit conveyed in smooth and strong epigrammatic couplets as its *form*. Even when the subject was addressed to the fancy or the intellect, as in the *Rape of the Lock* or the *Essay on Man*; nay, when it was a consecutive narration, as in that astonishing product of matchless talent and ingenuity, Pope's translation of the *Iliad*; still a *point* was looked for at the end of each second line, and the whole was as it were a sorites or, if I may exchange a logical for a grammatical metaphor, a *conjunction disjunctive*,[4] of epigrams. Meantime the matter and diction seemed to me characterized not so much by poetic thoughts as by thoughts *translated* into the language of poetry. On this last point I had occasion to render my own thoughts gradually more and more plain to myself by frequent amicable disputes concerning Darwin's *Botanic Garden*,[5] which for some years was greatly extolled, not only by the *reading* public in general, but even by those whose genius and natural robustness of understanding enabled them afterwards to act foremost in dissipating these "painted mists" that occasionally rise from the marshes at the foot of Parnassus. During my first Cambridge vacation I assisted a friend in a contribution for a literary society in Devonshire, and in this I remember to have compared Darwin's work to the Russian palace of ice, glittering, cold, and transitory. In the same essay too I assigned sundry reasons, chiefly drawn from a comparison of passages in the Latin poets with the original Greek from which they were borrowed, for the preference of Collins's odes to those of Gray, and of the simile in Shakespeare:

> How like a younker or a prodigal
> The scarfed bark puts from her native bay,
> Hugged and embraced by the strumpet wind!
> How like the prodigal doth she return,
> With over-weathered ribs and ragged sails,
> Lean, rent and beggared by the strumpet wind![6]

to the imitation in the *Bard*:

> Fair laughs the morn, and soft the zephyr blows
> While proudly riding o'er the azure realm

---

4. "Sorites": a procession of logical propositions; "*conjunction disjunctive*": a word which connects the parts of a sentence but expresses an alternative or opposition: "or," "but," "lest," etc.

5. Published in 1789–91 by Erasmus Darwin (1731–1802); a long poem in closed couplets, presenting the science of botany in elaborate allegories.
6. *Merchant of Venice* II.vi.14–19.

In gallant trim the gilded vessel goes;
YOUTH on the prow, and PLEASURE at the helm;
Regardless of the sweeping whirlwind's sway,
That, hushed in grim repose, expects its evening prey.[7]

(In which, by the bye, the words "realm" and "sway" are rhymes dearly purchased.) I preferred the original, on the ground that in the imitation it depended wholly in the compositor's putting, or not putting, a small capital both in this and in many other passages of the same poet whether the words should be personifications or mere abstracts. I mention this because, in referring various lines in Gray to their original in Shakespeare and Milton, and in the clear perception how completely all the propriety was lost in the transfer, I was at that early period led to a conjecture which, many years afterwards, was recalled to me from the same thought having been started in conversation, but far more ably, and developed more fully, by Mr. Wordsworth; namely, that this style of poetry which I have characterized above as translations of prose thoughts into poetic language had been kept up by, if it did not wholly arise from, the custom of writing Latin verses and the great importance attached to these exercises in our public schools. Whatever might have been the case in the fifteenth century, when the use of the Latin tongue was so general among learned men that Erasmus is said to have forgotten his native language; yet in the present day it is not to be supposed that a youth can think in Latin, or that he can have any other reliance on the force or fitness of his phrases but the authority of the author from whence he had adopted them. Consequently he must first prepare his thoughts and then pick out from Virgil, Horace, Ovid, or perhaps more compendiously, from his *Gradus*,[8] halves and quarters of lines in which to embody them.

I never object to a certain degree of disputatiousness in a young man from the age of seventeen to that of four or five and twenty, provided I find him always arguing on one side of the question. The controversies occasioned by my unfeigned zeal for the honor of a favorite contemporary, then known to me only by his works, were of great advantage in the formation and establishment of my taste and critical opinions. In my defense of the lines running into each other instead of closing at each couplet, and of natural language, neither bookish nor vulgar, neither redolent of the lamp nor of the kennel, such as *I will remember thee*; instead of the same thought tricked up in the rag-fair finery of

——Thy image on her wing
Before my Fancy's eye shall Memory bring,

7. Thomas Gray, *The Bard* (1757).
8. *Gradus ad Parnassum* ("Stairway to Parnassus"), a dictionary of Latin words, synonyms, and descriptive epithets, illustrated from the Latin poets. It was long used as a school text in Latin composition.

I had continually to adduce the meter and diction of the Greek poets from Homer to Theocritus inclusive; and still more of our elder English poets from Chaucer to Milton. Nor was this all. But as it was my constant reply to authorities brought against me from later poets of great name that no authority could avail in opposition to Truth, Nature, Logic, and the Laws of Universal Grammar; actuated too by my former passion for metaphysical investigations, I labored at a solid foundation on which permanently to ground my opinions in the component faculties of the human mind itself and their comparative dignity and importance. According to the faculty or source from which the pleasure given by any poem or passage was derived I estimated the merit of such poem or passage. As the result of all my reading and meditation, I abstracted two critical aphorisms, deeming them to comprise the conditions and criteria of poetic style: first, that not the poem which we have *read*, but that to which we *return* with the greatest pleasure, possesses the genuine power and claims the name of *essential* poetry. Second, that whatever lines can be translated into other words of the same language without diminution of their significance, either in sense of association or in any worthy feeling, are so far vicious in their diction. Be it however observed that I excluded from the list of worthy feelings the pleasure derived from mere novelty in the reader, and the desire of exciting wonderment at his powers in the author. Oftentimes since then, in perusing French tragedies, I have fancied two marks of admiration at the end of each line, as hieroglyphics of the author's own admiration at his own cleverness. Our genuine admiration of a great poet is a continuous undercurrent of feeling; it is everywhere present, but seldom anywhere as a separate excitement. I was wont boldly to affirm that it would be scarcely more difficult to push a stone out from the pyramids with the bare hand than to alter a word, or the position of a word, in Milton or Shakespeare (in their most important works at least), without making the auther say something else, or something worse, than he does say. One great distinction I appeared to myself to see plainly, between even the characteristic faults of our elder poets and the false beauties of the moderns. In the former, from Donne to Cowley, we find the most fantastic out-of-the-way thoughts, but in the most pure and genuine mother English; in the latter, the most obvious thoughts, in language the most fantastic and arbitrary. Our faulty elder poets sacrificed the passion and passionate flow of poetry to the subtleties of intellect and to the starts of wit; the moderns to the glare and glitter of a perpetual yet broken and heterogeneous imagery, or rather to an amphibious something, made up half of image and half of abstract[9] meaning. The one

9. "I remember a ludicrous instance in the poem of a young tradesman: 'No more will I endure Love's pleasing pain, / Or round my *heart's leg* tie his galling chain' " [Coleridge's note].

sacrificed the heart to the head, the other both heart and head to point and drapery. * * *

From *Chapter IV*

Mr. Wordsworth's earlier poems—On fancy and imagination— The investigation of the distinction important to the fine arts.

* * * During the last year of my residence at Cambridge I became acquainted with Mr. Wordsworth's first publication, entitled *Descriptive Sketches;*[1] and seldom, if ever, was the emergence of an original poetic genius above the literary horizon more evidently announced. In the form, style, and manner of the whole poem, and in the structure of the particular lines and periods, there is a harshness and acerbity connected and combined with words and images all aglow which might recall those products of the vegetable world, where gorgeous blossoms rise out of the hard and thorny rind and shell within which the rich fruit was elaborating. The language was not only peculiar and strong, but at times knotty and contorted, as by its own impatient strength; while the novelty and struggling crowd of images acting in conjunction with the difficulties of the style demanded always a greater closeness of attention than poetry (at all events than descriptive poetry) has a right to claim. It not seldom therefore justified the complaint of obscurity. In the following extract I have sometimes fancied that I saw an emblem of the poem itself and of the author's genius as it was then displayed:

> 'Tis storm; and hid in mist from hour to hour,
> All day the floods a deepening murmur pour,
> The sky is veiled, and every cheerful sight;
> Dark is the region as with coming night;
> And yet what frequent bursts of overpowering light!
> Triumphant on the bosom of the storm,
> Glances the fire-clad eagle's wheeling form;
> Eastward, in long perspective glittering, shine
> The wood-crowned cliffs that o'er the lake recline;
> Wide o'er the Alps a hundred streams unfold,
> At once to pillars turned that flame with gold;
> Behind his sail the peasant strives to shun
> The West, that burns like one dilated sun,
> Where in a mighty crucible expire
> The mountains, glowing hot, like coals of fire.[2]

The poetic Psyche, in its process to full development, undergoes as many changes as its Greek namesake, the butterfly.[3] And it is

1. Published 1793, the year before Coleridge left Cambridge; a long descriptive-meditative poem in closed couplets.
2. *Descriptive Sketches* (1815 version), lines 332 ff.
3. "In Greek, Psyche is the common name for the soul and the butterfly" [Coleridge's note].

remarkable how soon genius clears and purifies itself from the faults and errors of its earliest products; faults which, in its earliest compositions, are the more obtrusive and confluent because, as heterogeneous elements which had only a temporary use, they constitute the very *ferment* by which themselves are carried off. Or we may compare them to some diseases, which must work on the humors and be thrown out on the surface in order to secure the patient from their future recurrence. I was in my twenty-fourth year when I had the happiness of knowing Mr. Wordsworth personally;[4] and, while memory lasts, I shall hardly forget the sudden effect produced on my mind by his recitation of a manuscript poem which still remains unpublished, but of which the stanza and tone of style were the same as those of *The Female Vagrant* as originally printed in the first volume of the *Lyrical Ballads*.[5] There was here no mark of strained thought or forced diction, no crowd or turbulence of imagery, and, as the poet hath himself well described in his lines on revisiting the Wye, manly reflection and human associations had given both variety and an additional interest to natural objects which in the passion and appetite of the first love they had seemed to him neither to need or permit.[6] The occasional obscurities which had risen from an imperfect control over the resources of his native language had almost wholly disappeared, together with that worse defect of arbitrary and illogical phrases, at once hackneyed and fantastic, which hold so distinguished a place in the *technique* of ordinary poetry and will, more or less, alloy the earlier poems of the truest genius, unless the attention has been specifically directed to their worthlessness and incongruity. I did not perceive anything particular in the mere style of the poem alluded to during its recitation, except indeed such difference as was not separable from the thought and manner; and the Spenserian stanza which always, more or less, recalls to the reader's mind Spenser's own style, would doubtless have authorized in my then opinion a more frequent descent to the phrases of ordinary life than could, without an ill effect, have been hazarded in the heroic couplet. It was not however the freedom from false taste, whether as to common defects or to those more properly his own, which made so unusual an impression on my feelings immediately, and subsequently on my judgment. It was the union of deep feeling with profound thought; the fine balance of truth in observing with the imaginative faculty in modifying the objects observed; and above all the original gift of spreading the tone, the *atmosphere*, and with it the depth and height of the ideal world, around forms,

---

4. The meeting occurred in September, 1795.
5. *Guilt and Sorrow*, composed between 1791 and 1794; a revised portion of this poem was published as *The Female Vagrant* in *Lyrical Ballads* (1798).
6. Wordsworth's *Tintern Abbey*, lines 76 ff.

incidents, and situations of which, for the common view, custom had bedimmed all the luster, had dried up the sparkle and the dew-drops. "To find no contradiction in the union of old and new, to contemplate the Ancient of Days and all his works with feelings as fresh as if all had then sprang forth at the first creative fiat, characterizes the mind that feels the riddle of the world and may help to unravel it. To carry on the feelings of childhood into the powers of manhood; to combine the child's sense of wonder and novelty with the appearances which every day for perhaps forty years had rendered familiar:

> With sun and moon and stars throughout the year
> And man and woman;[7]

this is the character and privilege of genius, and one of the marks which distinguish genius from talents. And therefore it is the prime merit of genius, and its most unequivocal mode of manifestation, so to represent familiar objects as to awaken in the minds of others a kindred feeling concerning them, and that freshness of sensation which is the constant accompaniment of mental no less than of bodily convalescence. Who has not a thousand times seen snow fall on water? Who has not watched it with a new feeling from the time that he has read Burns' comparison of sensual pleasure:

> To snow that falls upon a river
> A moment white—then gone forever![8]

In poems, equally as in philosophic disquisitions, genius produces the strongest impressions of novelty while it rescues the most ad-mitted truths from the impotence caused by the very circumstance of their universal admission. Truths of all others the most awful and mysterious, yet being at the same time of universal interest, are too often considered as *so* true, that they lose all the life and efficiency of truth and lie bedridden in the dormitory of the soul side by side with the most despised and exploded errors." *The Friend*, p. 76, No. 5.[9]

This excellence, which in all Mr. Wordsworth's writings is more or less predominant and which constitutes the character of his mind, I no sooner felt than I sought to understand. Repeated medi-tations led me first to suspect (and a more intimate analysis of the human faculties, their appropriate marks, functions, and effects, matured my conjecture into full conviction) that fancy and imagi-nation were two distinct and widely different faculties, instead of being, according to the general belief, either two names with one meaning, or at furthest the lower and higher degree of one and the same power. It is not, I own, easy to conceive a more apposite

7. Altered from Milton's sonnet *To Mr. Cyriack Skinner upon his Blindness.*
8. Altered from Burns, *Tam o' Shanter,* lines 61–62.
9. *The Friend* was a periodical pub-lished by Coleridge (1809–10).

translation of the Greek *phantasia* than the Latin *imaginatio;* but it is equally true that in all societies there exists an instinct of growth, a certain collective unconscious good sense working progressively to desynonymize those words originally of the same meaning which the conflux of dialects had supplied to the more homogeneous languages, as the Greek and German, and which the same cause, joined with accidents of translation from original works of different countries, occasion in mixed languages like our own. The first and most important point to be proved is that two conceptions perfectly distinct are confused under one and the same word, and (this done) to appropriate that word exclusively to one meaning, and the synonym (should there be one) to the other. But if (as will be often the case in the arts and sciences) no synonym exists, we must either invent or borrow a word. In the present instance the appropriation had already begun and been legitimated in the derivative adjective: Milton had a highily *imaginative*, Cowley a very *fanciful*, mind. If therefore I should succeed in establishing the actual existence of two faculties generally different, the nomenclature would be at once determined. To the faculty by which I had characterized Milton we should confine the term *imagination;* while the other would be contra-distinguished as *fancy.* Now were it once fully ascertained that this division is no less grounded in nature than that of delirium from mania, or Otway's

Lutes, lobsters, seas of milk, and ships of amber,[1]

from Shakespeare's

What! have his daughters brought him to this pass?[2]

or from the preceding apostrophe to the elements, the theory of the fine arts and of poetry in particular could not, I thought, but derive some additional and important light. It would in its immediate effects furnish a torch of guidance to the philosophical critic, and ultimately to the poet himself. In energetic minds truth soon changes by domestication into power; and from directing in the discrimination and appraisal of the product becomes influencive in the production. To admire on principle is the only way to imitate without loss of originality. * * *

From *Chapter XIII*

On the imagination, or esemplastic[3] power.

* * * The IMAGINATION, then, I consider either as primary, or secondary. The primary IMAGINATION I hold to be the living power and prime agent of all human perception, and as a repetition in

---

1. Thomas Otway, in *Venice Preserved* (1682), wrote "laurels" in place of "lobsters" (V.ii.151).
2. *King Lear* III.iv.63.
3. Coleridge coined this word and used it to mean "molding into unity."

the finite mind of the eternal act of creation in the infinite I AM. The secondary I consider as an echo of the former, coexisting with the conscious will, yet still as identical with the primary in the *kind* of its agency, and differing only in *degree*, and in the *mode* of its operation. It dissolves, diffuses, dissipates, in order to recreate; or where this process is rendered impossible, yet still, at all events, it struggles to idealize and to unify. It is essentially *vital*, even as all objects (*as* objects) are essentially fixed and dead.

FANCY, on the contrary, has no other counters to play with but fixities and definites. The fancy is indeed no other than a mode of memory emancipated from the order of time and space; and blended with, and modified by that empirical phenomenon of the will which we express by the word CHOICE. But equally with the ordinary memory it must receive all its materials ready made from the law of association.[4] * * *

Chapter XIV

Occasion of the Lyrical Ballads, *and the objects originally proposed—Preface to the second edition—The ensuing controversy, its causes and acrimony—Philosophic definitions of a poem and poetry with scholia.*[5]

During the first year that Mr. Wordsworth and I were neighbors[6] our conversations turned frequently on the two cardinal points of poetry, the power of exciting the sympathy of the reader by a faithful adherence to the truth of nature, and the power of giving the interest of novelty by the modifying colors of imagination.[7] The sudden charm which accidents of light and shade, which moonlight or sunset diffused over a known and familiar landscape, appeared to represent the practicability of combining both. These are the poetry of nature. The thought suggested itself (to which of us I do not recollect) that a series of poems might be composed of two sorts. In the one, the incidents and agents were to be, in part at least, supernatural; and the excellence aimed at was to consist in the interesting of the affections by the dramatic truth of such emotions as would naturally accompany such situations, supposing them real. And real in *this* sense they have been to every human being who, from whatever source of delusion, has at any

4. Coleridge conceives God's creation to be a continuous process, which has an analogy in the creative perception ("primary imagination") of all human minds. The creative process is repeated, or "echoed," on still a third level, by the "secondary imagination" of the poet, which dissolves the products of primary perception in order to shape them into a new and unified creation—the imaginative passage or poem. The "fancy," on the other hand, can only manipulate "fixities and definites" which, linked by association, come to it ready-made from perception. Its products, therefore, are not re-creations (echoes of God's original creative process), but mosaic-like reassemblies of existing bits and pieces.
5. Additional remarks, after a philosophic demonstration.
6. At Nether Stowey and Alfoxden, Somerset, in 1797.
7. Cf. Wordsworth's account in his Preface to *Lyrical Ballads*.

time believed himself under supernatural agency. For the second class, subjects were to be chosen from ordinary life; the characters and incidents were to be such as will be found in every village and its vicinity where there is a meditative and feeling mind to seek after them, or to notice them when they present themselves.

In this idea originated the plan of the *Lyrical Ballads*; in which it was agreed that my endeavors should be directed to persons and characters supernatural, or at least romantic; yet so as to transfer from our inward nature a human interest and a semblance of truth sufficient to procure for these shadows of imagination that willing suspension of disbelief for the moment, which constitutes poetic faith. Mr. Wordsworth, on the other hand, was to propose to himself as his object to give the charm of novelty to things of every day, and to excite a feeling analogous to the supernatural, by awakening the mind's attention from the lethargy of custom and directing it to the loveliness and the wonders of the world before us; an inexhaustible treasure, but for which, in consequence of the film of familiarity and selfish solicitude, we have eyes yet see not, ears that hear not, and hearts that neither feel nor understand.[8]

With this view I wrote the *Ancient Mariner*, and was preparing, among other poems, the *Dark Ladie*, and the *Christabel*, in which I should have more nearly realized my ideal than I had done in my first attempt. But Mr. Wordsworth's industry had proved so much more successful and the number of his poems so much greater, that my compositions, instead of forming a balance, appeared rather an interpolation of heterogeneous matter.[9] Mr. Wordsworth added two or three poems written in his own character, in the impassioned, lofty, and sustained diction which is characteristic of his genius. In this form the *Lyrical Ballads* were published; and were presented by him, as an *experiment*,[1] whether subjects which from their nature rejected the usual ornaments and extra-colloquial style of poems in general might not be so managed in the language of ordinary life as to produce the pleasurable interest which it is the peculiar business of poetry to impart. To the second edition[2] he added a preface of considerable length; in which, notwithstanding some passages of apparently a contrary import, he was understood to contend for the extension of this style to poetry of all kinds, and to reject as vicious and indefensible all phrases and forms of style that were not included in what he (unfortunately, I think, adopting an equivocal expression) called the language of *real* life. From this preface, prefixed to poems in which it was impossible to deny the presence of original genius, however mistaken its direction might

8. Cf. Isaiah vi.9–10.
9. The first edition of *Lyrical Ballads*, published anonymously in 1798, contained nineteen poems by Wordsworth, four by Coleridge.

1. "Experiments" was also the word used by Wordsworth in his "Advertisement" to the first edition.
2. Of 1800.

be deemed, arose the whole long continued controversy.[3] For from the conjunction of perceived power with supposed heresy I explain the inveteracy and in some instances, I grieve to say, the acrimonious passions with which the controversy has been conducted by the assailants.

Had Mr. Wordsworth's poems been the silly, the childish things which they were for a long time described as being; had they been really distinguished from the compositions of other poets merely by meanness of language and inanity of thought; had they indeed contained nothing more than what is found in the parodies and pretended imitations of them; they must have sunk at once, a dead weight, into the slough of oblivion, and have dragged the preface along with them. But year after year increased the number of Mr. Wordsworth's admirers. They were found too not in the lower classes of the reading public, but chiefly among young men of strong sensibility and meditative minds; and their admiration (inflamed perhaps in some degree by opposition) was distinguished by its intensity, I might almost say, by its *religious* fervor. These facts, and the intellectual energy of the author, which was more or less consciously felt where it was outwardly and even boisterously denied, meeting with sentiments of aversion to his opinions and of alarm at their consequences, produced an eddy of criticism which would of itself have borne up the poems by the violence with which it whirled them round and round. With many parts of this preface, in the sense attributed to them and which the words undoubtedly seem to authorize, I never concurred; but, on the contrary objected to them as erroneous in principle, and as contradictory (in appearance at least) both to other parts of the same preface and to the author's own practice in the greater number of the poems themselves. Mr. Wordsworth in his recent collection[4] has, I find, degraded this prefatory disquisition to the end of his second volume, to be read or not at the reader's choice. But he has not, as far as I can discover, announced any change in his poetic creed. At all events, considering it as the source of a controversy in which I have been honored more than I deserve by the frequent conjunction of my name with his, I think it expedient to declare once for all in what points I coincide with his opinions, and in what points I altogether differ. But in order to render myself intelligible I must previously, in as few words as possible, explain my ideas, first, of a POEM; and secondly, of POETRY itself, in *kind* and in *essence*.

The office of philosophical *disquisition* consists in just *distinction;* while it is the privilege of the philosopher to preserve himself constantly aware that distinction is not division. In order to ob-

3. The controversy over Wordsworth's theory and poetical practice in the literary journals of the day.

4. Wordsworth's *Poems,* two volumes, 1815.

tain adequate notions of any truth, we must intellectually separate its distinguishable parts; and this is the technical *process* of philosophy. But having so done, we must then restore them in our conceptions to the unity in which they actually coexist; and this is the *result* of philosophy. A poem contains the same elements as a prose composition; the difference therefore must consist in a different combination of them, in consequence of a different object proposed. According to the difference of the object will be the difference of the combination. It is possible that the object may be merely to facilitate the recollection of any given facts or observations by artificial arrangement; and the composition will be a poem, merely because it is distinguished from prose by meter, or by rhyme, or by both conjointly. In this, the lowest sense, a man might attribute the name of a poem to the well-known enumeration of the days in the several months:

> Thirty days hath September
> April, June, and November, etc.

and others of the same class and purpose. And as a particular pleasure is found in anticipating the recurrence of sounds and quantities, all compositions that have this charm superadded, whatever be their contents, *may* be entitled poems.

So much for the superficial *form.* A difference of object and contents supplies an additional ground of distinction. The immediate purpose may be the communication of truths; either of truth absolute and demonstrable, as in works of science; or of facts experienced and recorded, as in history. Pleasure, and that of the highest and most permanent kind, may *result* from the *atttainment* of the end; but it is not itself the immediate end. In other works the communication of pleasure may be the immediate purpose; and though truth, either moral or intellectual, ought to be the *ultimate* end, yet this will distinguish the character of the author, not the class to which the work belongs. Blessed indeed is that state of society in which the immediate purpose would be baffled by the perversion of the proper ultimate end; in which no charm of diction or imagery could exempt the Bathyllus even of an Anacreon, or the Alexis of Virgil,[5] from disgust and aversion!

But the communication of pleasure may be the immediate object of a work not metrically composed; and that object may have been in a high degree attained, as in novels and romances. Would then the mere superaddition of meter, with or without rhyme, entitle *these* to the name of poems? The answer is that nothing can permanently please which does not contain in itself the reason why it is so, and not otherwise. If meter be superadded, all other

5. The reference is to poems of homosexual love. "Bathyllus" was a beautiful boy praised by Anacreon, a Greek lyric poet (ca. 560–475 B.C.); "Alexis" was a young man loved by the shepherd Corydon in Virgil's *Eclogues* II.

parts must be made consonant with it. They must be such as to justify the perpetual and distinct attention to each part which an exact correspondent recurrence of accent and sound are calculated to excite. The final definition then, so deduced, may be thus worded. A poem is that species of composition which is opposed to works of science by proposing for its *immediate* object pleasure, not truth; and from all other species (having *this* object in common with it) it is discriminated by proposing to itself such delight from the *whole* as is compatible with a distinct gratification from each component *part*.

Controversy is not seldom excited in consequence of the disputants attaching each a different meaning to the same word; and in few instances has this been more striking than in disputes concerning the present subject. If a man chooses to call every composi-⁺ion a poem which is rhyme, or measure, or both, I must leave his opinion uncontroverted. The distinction is at least competent to characterize the writer's intention. If it were subjoined that the whole is likewise entertaining or affecting as a tale or as a series of interesting reflections, I of course admit this as another fit ingredient of a poem and an additional merit. But if the definition sought for be that of a *legitimate* poem, I answer it must be one the parts of which mutually support and explain each other; all in their proportion harmonizing with, and supporting the purpose and known influences of metrical arrangement. The philosophic critics of all ages coincide with the ultimate judgment of all countries in equally denying the praises of a just poem on the one hand to a series of striking lines or distichs,[6] each of which absorbing the whole attention of the reader to itself disjoins it from its context and makes it a separate whole, instead of a harmonizing part; and on the other hand, to an unsustained composition, from which the reader collects rapidly the general result unattracted by the component parts. The reader should be carried forward, not merely or chiefly by the mechanical impulse of curiosity, or by a restless desire to arrive at the final solution; but by the pleasurable activity of mind excited by the attractions of the journey itself. Like the motion of a serpent, which the Egyptians made the emblem of intellectual power; or like the path of sound through the air; at every step he pauses and half recedes, and from the retrogressive movement collects the force which again carries him onward. *"Praecipitandus est liber spiritus,"* says Petronius Arbiter most happily.[7] The epithet *liber* here balances the preceding verb; and it is not easy to conceive more meaning condensed in fewer words.

But if this should be admitted as a satisfactory character of a poem, we have still to seek for a definition of poetry. The writings

6. Pairs of lines.
7. "The free spirit [of the poet] must be hurled onward." From the *Satyricon,* by the lively Roman satirist, Petronius Arbiter (1st century A.D.).

of Plato, and Bishop Taylor, and the *Theoria Sacra* of Burnet,[8] furnish undeniable proofs that poetry of the highest kind may exist without meter, and even without the contradistinguishing objects of a poem. The first chapter of Isaiah (indeed a very large proportion of the whole book) is poetry in the most emphatic sense; yet it would be not less irrational than strange to assert that pleasure, and not truth, was the immediate object of the prophet. In short, whatever *specific* import we attach to the word poetry, there will be found involved in it, as a necessary consequence, that a poem of any length neither can be, nor ought to be, all poetry.[9] Yet if a harmonious whole is to be produced, the remaining parts must be preserved *in keeping* with the poetry; and this can be no otherwise effected than by such a studied selection and artificial arrangement as will partake of *one*, though not a *peculiar*, property of poetry. And this again can be no other than the property of exciting a more continuous and equal attention than the language of prose aims at, whether colloquial or written.

My own conclusions on the nature of poetry, in the strictest use of the word, have been in part anticipated in the preceding disquisition on the fancy and imagination. What is poetry? is so nearly the same question with, what is a poet? that the answer to the one is involved in the solution of the other. For it is a distinction resulting from the poetic genius itself, which sustains and modifies the images, thoughts, and emotions of the poet's own mind. The poet, described in *ideal* perfection, brings the whole soul of man into activity, with the subordination of its faculties to each other, according to their relative worth and dignity. He diffuses a tone and spirit of unity that blends and (as it were) *fuses*, each into each, by that synthetic and magical power to which we have exclusively appropriated the name of imagination. This power, first put in action by the will and understanding and retained under their irremissive, though gentle and unnoticed, control (*laxis effertur habenis*[1]) reveals itself in the balance or reconciliation of opposite or discordant qualities:[2] of sameness, with difference; of the general, with the concrete; the idea, with the image; the individual, with the representative; the sense of novelty and freshness, with old and familiar objects; a more than usual state of emotion,

---

8. Bishop Jeremy Taylor (1613–67), author of *Holy Living* and *Holy Dying;* Thomas Burnet, author of *The Sacred Theory of the Earth* (1681–89). Coleridge greatly admired the elaborate and sonorous prose of both these writers; he took from a work by Burnet the Latin motto for *The Ancient Mariner.*
9. Coleridge does not use the word "poetry" in the usual way, as a term for the class of all metrical compositions, but to designate those passages, whether in verse or prose, produced by the mind of genius in its supreme mo-

ments of imaginative activity.
1. I.e., driven with loosened reins.
2. Here Coleridge introduces into English criticism the concept that the highest poetry incorporates and reconciles opposite or discordant elements; under the names of "irony" and "paradox," this concept has become a primary criterion of the "new criticism" of our day. Although admittedly derived from Coleridge, the concept, by a further irony, has usually been employed to derogate Romantic poetry.

with more than usual order; judgment ever awake and steady self-possession, with enthusiasm and feeling profound or vehement; and while it blends and harmonizes the natural and the artificial, still subordinates art to nature; the manner to the matter; and our admiration of the poet to our sympathy with the poetry. "Doubtless," as Sir John Davies observes of the soul (and his words may with slight alteration be applied, and even more appropriately, to the poetic IMAGINATION):

> Doubtless this could not be, but that she turns
> Bodies to spirit by sublimation strange,
> As fire converts to fire the things it burns,
> As we our food into our nature change.
>
> From their gross matter she abstracts their forms,
> And draws a kind of quintessence from things;
> Which to her proper nature she transforms
> To bear them light on her celestial wings.
>
> Thus does she, when from individual states
> She doth abstract the universal kinds;
> Which then reclothed in divers names and fates
> Steal access through our senses to our minds.[3]

Finally, GOOD SENSE is the BODY of poetic genius, FANCY its DRAPERY, MOTION its LIFE, and IMAGINATION the SOUL that is everywhere, and in each; and forms all into one graceful and intelligent whole.

From *Chapter XVII*

Examination of the tenets peculiar to Mr. Wordsworth—Rustic life (above all, low and rustic life) especially unfavorable to the formation of a human diction—The best parts of language the products of philosophers, not clowns or shepherds—Poetry essentially ideal and generic—The language of Milton as much the language of real life, yea, incomparably more so than that of the cottager.

As far then as Mr. Wordsworth in his preface contended, and most ably contended, for a reformation in our poetic diction, as far as he has evinced the truth of passion, and the *dramatic* propriety of those figures and metaphors in the original poets which, stripped of their justifying reasons and converted into mere artifices of connection or ornament, constitute the characteristic falsity in the poetic style of the moderns; and as far as he has, with equal acuteness and clearness, pointed out the process by which this change was effected and the resemblances between that state into which the reader's mind is thrown by the pleasurable confusion of

3. Adapted from John Davies' *Nosce Teipsum* ("Know Thyself"), a philosophical poem (1599).

thought from an unaccustomed train of words and images and that state which is induced by the natural language of impassioned feeling, he undertook a useful task and deserves all praise, both for the attempt and for the execution. The provocations to this remonstrance in behalf of truth and nature were still of perpetual recurrence before and after the publication of this preface. I cannot likewise but add that the comparison of such poems of merit as have been given to the public within the last ten or twelve years with the majority of those produced previously to the appearance of that preface leave no doubt on my mind that Mr. Wordsworth is fully justified in believing his efforts to have been by no means ineffectual. Not only in the verses of those who have professed their admiration of his genius, but even of those who have distinguished themselves by hostility to his theory and depreciation of his writings, are the impressions of his principles plainly visible. It is possible that with these principles others may have been blended, which are not equally evident, and some which are unsteady and subvertible from the narrowness or imperfection of their basis. But it is more than possible that these errors of defect or exaggeration, by kindling and feeding the controversy, may have conduced not only to the wider propagation of the accompanying truths, but that, by their frequent presentation to the mind in an excited state they may have won for them a more permanent and practical result. A man will borrow a part from his opponent the more easily, if he feels himself justified in continuing to reject a part. While there remain important points in which he can still feel himself in the right, in which he still finds firm footing for continued resistance, he will gradually adopt those opinions which were the least remote from his own convictions as not less congruous with his own theory than with that which he reprobates. In like manner, with a kind of instinctive prudence, he will abandon by little and little his weakest posts, till at length he seems to forget that they had ever belonged to him, or affects to consider them at most as accidental and "petty annexments," the removal of which leaves the citadel unhurt and unendangered.

My own differences from certain supposed parts of Mr. Wordsworth's theory ground themselves on the assumption that his words had been rightly interpreted, as purporting that the proper diction for poetry in general consists altogether in a language taken, with due exceptions, from the mouths of men in real life, a language which actually constitutes the natural conversation of men under the influence of natural feelings.[4] My objection is, first, that in *any* sense this rule is applicable only to *certain* classes of poetry; secondly, that even to these classes it is not applicable, except in

4. Wordsworth, Preface to *Lyrical Ballads* (1800): "a selection of the real language of men in a state of vivid sensation. * * * " The language of men of "humble and rustic life" has been adopted.

such a sense as hath never by anyone (as far as I know or have read) been denied or doubted; and, lastly, that as far as, and in that degree in which it is *practicable*, yet as a *rule* it is useless, if not injurious, and therefore either need not or ought not to be practiced. * * *

Here let me be permitted to remind the reader that the positions which I controvert are contained in the sentences—"a selection of the REAL language of men"; "the language of these men (i.e., men in low and rustic life) I propose to myself to imitate, and as far as possible to adopt the very language of men." "Between the language of prose and that of metrical composition there neither is, nor can be any essential difference." It is against these exclusively that my opposition is directed.

I object, in the very first instance, to an equivocation in the use of the word "real." Every man's language varies according to the extent of his knowledge, the activity of his faculties and the depth or quickness of his feelings. Every man's language has, first, its *individualities*; secondly, the common properties of the *class* to which he belongs; and thirdly, words and phrases of *universal* use. The language of Hooker, Bacon, Bishop Taylor, and Burke differs from the common language of the learned class only by the superior number and novelty of the thoughts and relations which they had to convey. The language of Algernon Sidney[5] differs not at all from that which every well-educated gentleman would wish to write, and (with due allowances for the undeliberateness and less connected train of thinking natural and proper to conversation) such as he would wish to talk. Neither one or the other differ half as much from the general language of cultivated society as the language of Mr. Wordsworth's homeliest composition differs from that of a common peasant. For "real" therefore we must substitute *ordinary*, or *lingua communis*. And this, we have proved, is no more to be found in the phraseology of low and rustic life than in that of any other class. Omit the peculiarities of each, and the result of course must be common to all. And assuredly the omissions and changes to be made in the language of rustics before it could be transferred to any species of poem, except the drama or other professed imitation, are at least as numerous and weighty as would be required in adapting to the same purpose the ordinary language of tradesmen and manufacturers. Not to mention that the language so highly extolled by Mr. Wordsworth varies in every county, nay, in every village, according to the accidental character of the clergyman, the existence or nonexistence of schools; or even, perhaps, as the exciseman, publican, or barber happen to be, or not to be, zealous politicians and readers of the weekly newspaper *pro*

---

5. Algernon Sidney (1622–83), republican soldier and statesman, author of *Discourses Concerning Government*.

bono publico.[6] Anterior to cultivation the *lingua communis* of every country, as Dante has well observed, exists everywhere in parts and nowhere as a whole.[7]

Neither is the case rendered at all more tenable by the addition of the words "in a state of excitement."[8] For the nature of a man's words, when he is strongly affected by joy, grief, or anger, must necessarily depend on the number and quality of the general truths, conceptions, and images, and of the words expressing them, with which his mind had been previously stored. For the property of passion is not to *create*, but to set in increased activity. At least, whatever new connections of thoughts or images, or (which is equally, if not more than equally, the appropriate effect of strong excitement) whatever generalizations of truth or experience the heat of passion may produce, yet the terms of their conveyance must have pre-existed in his former conversations, and are only collected and crowded together by the unusual stimulation. It is indeed very possible to adopt in a poem the unmeaning repetitions, habitual phrases, and other blank counters which an unfurnished or confused understanding interposes at short intervals in order to keep hold of his subject which is still slipping from him, and to give him time for recollection; or in mere aid of vacancy, as in the scanty companies of a country stage the same player pops backwards and forwards, in order to prevent the appearance of empty spaces, in the procession of *Macbeth* or *Henry VIIIth*. But what assistance to the poet or ornament to the poem these can supply, I am at a loss to conjecture. Nothing assuredly can differ either in origin or in mode more widely from the apparent tautologies of intense and turbulent feeling in which the passion is greater and of longer endurance than to be exhausted or satisfied by a single representation of the image or incident exciting it. Such repetitions I admit to be a beauty of the highest kind; as illustrated by Mr. Wordsworth himself from the song of Deborah. "At her feet he bowed, he fell, he lay down: at her feet he bowed, he fell: where he bowed, there he fell down dead."[9]

1815   1817

From Lectures on Shakespeare[1]
[Fancy and Imagination in Shakespeare's Poetry]

In the preceding lecture we have examined with what armor clothed and with what titles authorized Shakespeare came forward

6. "For the public welfare."
7. In *De vulgari eloquentia* ("On the Vulgar Tongue") Dante discusses—and affirms—the fitness for poetry of the unlocalized Italian vernacular.
8. Wordsworth: "the manner in which we associate ideas in a state of excite-

ment."
9. Judges v.27. Cited by Wordsworth in a note to *The Thorn* as an example of the natural tautology of "impassioned feelings."
1. Although Coleridge's series of public lectures on Shakespeare and other

as a poet to demand the throne of fame as the dramatic poet of England; we have now to observe and retrace the excellencies which compelled even his contemporaries to seat him on that throne, although there were giants in those days contending for the same honor. Hereafter we shall endeavor to make out the title of the English drama, as created by and existing in Shakespeare, and its right to the supremacy of dramatic excellence in general. I have endeavored to prove that he had shown himself a *poet*, previously to his appearance [as] a dramatic poet—and that had no *Lear*, no *Othello*, no *Henry the Fourth*, no *Twelfth Night* appeared, we must have admitted that Shakespeare possessed the chief if not all the requisites of a poet—namely, deep feeling and exquisite sense of beauty, both as exhibited to the eye in combinations of form, and to the ear in sweet and appropriate melody (with the exception of Spenser he is [the sweetest of English poets]); that these feelings were under the command of *his own will*—that in his very first productions he projected his mind out of his own particular being, and felt and made others feel, on subjects [in] no way connected with himself, except by force of contemplation, and that sublime faculty, by which a great mind becomes that which it meditates on. To this we are to add the affectionate love of nature and natural objects, without which no man could have observed so steadily, or painted so truly and passionately the very minutest beauties of the external world. Next, we have shown that he possessed fancy, considered as the faculty of bringing together images dissimilar in the main by some one point or more of likeness distinguished.[2]

> Full gently now she takes him by the hand,
> A lily prisoned in a jail of snow,
> Or ivory in an alabaster band—
> So white a friend engirts so white a foe.

Still mounting, we find undoubted proof in his mind of imagination, or the power by which one image or feeling is made to modify many others and by a sort of *fusion to force many into one*—that which after showed itself in such might and energy in *Lear*, where the deep anguish of a father spreads the feeling of ingratitude and cruelty over the very elements of heaven. Various are the workings

poets contained much of his best criticism, he published none of this material, leaving only fragmentary remains of his lectures in notebooks, scraps of manuscript, and notes written in the margins of books. The following selections, which develop some of the basic ideas presented in *Biographia Literaria*, are taken from T. M. Raysor's edition, based on Coleridge's manuscripts and on contemporary reports, of *Coleridge's Shakespearean Criticism* (1930).

2. Coleridge here applies the distinction between fancy and imagination presented in *Biographia Literaria*, Chapter XIII. This passage from the narrative poem *Venus and Adonis* (lines 361–64) is an instance of fancy because the elements brought together remain an assemblage of recognizable and independent "fixities and definites," despite the isolated points of likeness which form the grounds of the comparison.

of this greatest faculty of the human mind—both passionate and tranquil. In its tranquil and purely pleasurable operation, it acts chiefly by producing out of many things, as they would have appeared in the description of an ordinary mind, described slowly and in unimpassioned succession, a oneness, even as nature, the greatest of poets, acts upon us when we open our eyes upon an extended prospect. Thus the flight of Adonis from the enamored goddess in the dusk of evening—

> Look how a bright star shooteth from the sky—
> So glides he in the night from Venus' eye.[3]

How many images and feelings are here brought together without effort and without discord—the beauty of Adonis—the rapidity of his flight—the yearning yet hopelessness of the enamored gazer—and a shadowy ideal character thrown over the whole.[4]—Or it acts by impressing the stamp of humanity, of human feeling, over inanimate objects * * *

> Lo, here the gentle lark, weary of rest,
> From his moist cabinet mounts up on high
> And wakes the morning, from whose silver breast
> The sun ariseth in his majesty;
> Who doth the world so gloriously behold
> That cedar tops and hills seem burnished gold.

And lastly, which belongs only to a great poet, the power of so carrying on the eye of the reader as to make him almost lose the consciousness of words—to make him *see* everything—and this without exciting any painful or laborious attention, without any *anatomy* of description (a fault not uncommon in descriptive poetry) but with the sweetness and easy movement of nature.

Lastly, he previously to his dramas, gave proof of a most profound, energetic, and philosophical mind, without which he might have been a very delightful poet, but not the great dramatic poet * * * But chance and his powerful instinct combined to lead him to his proper province—in the conquest of which we are to consider both the difficulties that opposed him, and the advantages. ca. 1808

[Mechanic vs. Organic Form][5]

The subject of the present lecture is no less than a question submitted to your understandings, emancipated from national prej-

3. *Venus and Adonis*, lines 815–16.
4. An instance of imagination, Coleridge claims, because the component parts—the shooting star and the flight of Adonis, together with the feelings with which both are perceived—dissolve into a new and seamless unity, different in character from the sum of its parts. In the following instance (lines 853–58), the imagination is said to fuse the neutral and inanimate objects with the human nature and feelings of the observer.
5. Coleridge is opposing the earlier view that, because he violates the critical "rules" based on classical drama,

udice: Are the plays of Shakespeare works of rude uncultivated genius, in which the splendor of the parts compensates, if aught can compensate, for the barbarous shapelessness and irregularity of the whole? To which not only the French critics, but even his own English admirers, say [yes]. Or is the form equally admirable with the matter, the judgment of the great poet not less deserving of our wonder than his genius? Or to repeat the question in other words, is Shakespeare a great dramatic poet on account only of these beauties and excellencies which he possesses in common with the ancients, but with diminished claims to our love and honor to the full extent of his difference from them? Or are these very differences additional proofs of poetic wisdom, at once results and symbols of living power as contrasted with lifeless mechanism, of free and rival originality as contradistinguished from servile imitation, or more accurately, [from] a blind copying of effects instead of a true imitation of the essential principles? Imagine not I am about to oppose genius to rules. No! the comparative value of these rules is the very cause to be tried. The spirit of poetry, like all other living powers, must of necessity circumscribe itself by rules, were it only to unite power with beauty. It must embody in order to reveal itself; but a living body is of necessity an organized one— and what is organization but the connection of parts to a whole, so that each part is at once end and means! This is no discovery of criticism; it is a necessity of the human mind—and all nations have felt and obeyed it, in the invention of meter and measured sounds as the vehicle and involucrum[6] of poetry, itself a fellow growth from the same life, even as the bark is to the tree.

No work of true genius dare want its appropriate form; neither indeed is there any danger of this. As it must not, so neither can it, be lawless! For it is even this that constitutes its genius—the power of acting creatively under laws of its own origination. How then comes it that not only single Zoili,[7] but whole nations have combined in unhesitating condemnation of our great dramatist, as a sort of African nature, fertile in beautiful monsters, as a wild heath where islands of fertility look greener from the surrounding waste, where the loveliest plants now shine out among unsightly weeds and now are choked by their parasitic growth, so intertwined

Shakespeare is a highly irregular dramatist whose occasional successes are the result of innate and untutored genius, operating without artistry or judgment. Coleridge's refutation is based on his distinction between the "mechanical form" conceived by neoclassical criticism, and "organic form." Mechanical form results from imposing a pattern of pre-existing rules on the literary material. Shakespeare's organic form, on the other hand, evolves like a plant by an inner principle, according not to rules but to the laws of its own growth, until it achieves an organic unity—a living interdependence of parts and whole in which, as Coleridge says, "each part is at once end and means." The concept of "organic form," in one or another interpretation, has become a cardinal principle in much modern criticism.

6. Outer covering of part of a plant.
7. Plural of "Zoilus," who in classical times was the standard example of a bad critic.

that we cannot disentangle the weed without snapping the flower. In this statement I have had no reference to the vulgar abuse of Voltaire,[8] save as far as his charges are coincident with the decisions of his commentators and (so they tell you) his almost idolatrous admirers. The true ground of the mistake, as has been well remarked by a continental critic,[9] lies in the confounding mechanical regularity with organic form. The form is mechanic when on any given material we impress a predetermined form, not necessarily arising out of the properties of the material, as when to a mass of wet clay we give whatever shape we wish it to retain when hardened. The organic form, on the other hand, is innate; it shapes as it develops itself from within, and the fulness of its development is one and the same with the perfection of its outward form. Such is the life, such the form. Nature, the prime genial artist, inexhaustible in diverse powers, is equally inexhaustible in forms. Each exterior is the physiognomy of the being within, its true image reflected and thrown out from the concave mirror. And even such is the appropriate excellence of her chosen poet, of our own Shakespeare, himself a nature humanized, a genial understanding directing self-consciously a power and an implicit wisdom deeper than consciousness.[1]   1930

8. Voltaire (1694–1778) wrote critiques treating Shakespeare as a barbarous, irregular, and sometimes indecent natural genius.
9. August Wilhelm Schlegel, German critic and literary historian, whose *Lec-*

tures on Dramatic Art and Literature (1808–9) present many of the ideas Coleridge develops in this lecture.
1. I.e., the organic process of the imagination is in part unconscious.

GEORGE GORDON, LORD BYRON
(1788–1824)

1812:   *Childe Harold*, Cantos I and II.
1813–14: The Oriental tales, including *The Giaour, The Corsair, Lara.*
1816:   Separation from Lady Byron; leaves England, never to return.
1818:   Begins *Don Juan.*
1823:   Joins the Greek war for liberation from the Turks.

In his *History of English Literature*, written in the late 1850's, the French critic Hippolyte Taine gave only a few condescending pages to Wordsworth, Coleridge, Shelley, and Keats, and then devoted a long enthusiastic chapter to Lord Byron, "the greatest and most English of these artists; he is so great and so English that from him alone we shall learn more truths of his country and of his age than from all the rest together." Byron had achieved an immense European reputation during his own lifetime, while his great English contemporaries were admired only by small coteries in England and America, and through much of the 19th century he continued to be rated as one of the greatest of English poets and the very prototype of literary Romanticism. His influence was felt everywhere, not only among minor writers—in the two or three decades after his death, most European poets struck Byronic attitudes—but among the greatest poets and novelists (including Goethe in Germany, Balzac and Stendhal in France, Pushkin and Dostoevsky in Russia, and Melville in America), painters (especially Delacroix), and composers (especially Beethoven and Berlioz).

These facts may startle the contemporary student, who has been brought up in the modern estimate of Byron as the least important and the least Romantic of the five great English poets of his day. Neither Byron's critical theories nor his literary achievements fit easily into the standard categories ascribed to the "Romantic movement" in England, and his poems have little in common with the characteristic innovations of Wordsworth, Coleridge, Keats, or Shelley. Only Shelley, among these writers, thought highly of either Byron or his work; while Byron spoke slightingly of all of them except Shelley, and in fact insisted that, measured against the poetic practice of Pope, he and his contemporaries were "all in the wrong, one as much as another * * * we are upon a wrong revolutionary poetical system, or systems, not worth a damn in itself." Byron's masterpiece, *Don Juan,* is an instance of that favorite neoclassic type, a satire against modern civilization, which has much more in common with the methods and aims of Pope, Swift, Voltaire, or Sterne than with those of his own contemporaries. Even Byron's lyrics are old-fashioned: many are in the 18th-century gentlemanly mode of witty extemporization and epigram (*Written after Swimming from Sestos to Abydos*) or continue the Cavalier tradition of poetic gallantry and the elaborate deployment of a compliment to a lady (*She Walks in Beauty* or *There Be None of Beauty's Daughters*).

Byron's chief claim to be called an arch-Romantic is that he provided his age with what Taine called its "ruling personage; that is, the model that contemporaries invest with their admiration and sympathy." This personage is the "Byronic hero." He occurs in many guises in Byron's romances and dramas, but his central and recurrent attribute is that of a saturnine, passionate, moody, and remorse-torn but unrepentant sinner, who, in proud moral isolation, relies on his absolute self against all institutional and moral trammels on the display of individuality. This figure, infusing the archrebel in a nonpolitical form with a strong erotic interest, gathered together and embodied the implicit yearnings of Byron's time, was imitated in life as well as in art, and helped shape the intellectual as well as the cultural history of the later 19th century. Bertrand Russell, in his *History of Western Philosophy*, gives a chapter to Byron—not because he was a systematic thinker, but because "Byronism," the attitude of "Titanic cosmic self-assertion," established an outlook and way of feeling that entered 19th-century philosophy and eventually helped to form Nietzsche's concept of the Superman, the great hero who stands outside the jurisdiction of the ordinary criteria of good and evil.

Byron's contemporaries insisted on identifying the author with his fictional characters. But Byron's letters and the testimony of his friends show that, except for recurrent moods of black depression, his own temperament was in many respects the antithesis to that of his heroes. He was passionate and willful, but when in good humor he could be very much a man of the world in the 18th-century style—gregarious, lively, tolerant, and a witty conversationalist capable of taking an ironic attitude toward his own foibles as well as those of other men. The aloof hauteur he exhibited in public was largely a mask to hide his painful diffidence when in a strange company; he possessed devoted friends, both men and women, and among them he was usually unassuming, companionable, sometimes even exuberant, and tactful; to his household dependents he was unfailingly generous and tenaciously loyal. But if Byronism was largely a fiction, produced by a collaboration between Byron's imagination and that of his public, then the fiction was historically more important than the poet in his actual person.

Byron was descended from two aristocratic families, both of them colorful, violent, and dissolute. His grandfather was an admiral known as "Foulweather Jack"; his great-uncle was the fifth Baron Byron, known to his rural neighbors as the "Wicked Lord," who was tried by his peers for killing his kinsman, William Chaworth, in a drunken duel; his father, Captain John Byron, was a rake and fortune-hunter who rapidly dissipated the patrimony of two wealthy wives. Byron's mother was a Scotswoman, Catherine Gordon of Gight, the last descendant of a line of lawless Scottish lairds. After her husband died (Byron was then 3), she brought up her son in near poverty in Aberdeen, where he was indoctrinated with the Calvinistic morality of Scottish Presbyterianism. Mrs. Byron was an ill-educated and almost pathologically irascible woman, who nevertheless had an abiding love for her son; they fought violently when together, but corresponded affectionately enough when apart, until her death in 1811.

When Byron was 10, the death of his great-uncle, preceded by that of more immediate heirs to the title, made him the sixth Lord Byron. In a fashion suitable to his new eminence he was sent to Harrow School, then to Trinity College, Cambridge. Byron had been born with a clubfoot, which was made worse by inept medical treatment, and this defect all his life caused him physical suffering and agonized embarrassment. His lameness increased his avidity for athletic prowess, and he played cricket and made himself an expert boxer, fencer, and horseman, and a powerful swimmer. He was also sexually precocious; when only 7, he fell in love with a little cousin, Mary Duff, and so violently that ten years later news of her marriage threw him into convulsions. Both at Cambridge and at his ancestral estate of Newstead, he engaged with more than ordinary vigor in the expensive pursuits and fashionable dissipations of a young Regency lord— at college he had richly furnished rooms, a carriage and retinue, a tame bear, and a mistress whom he liked to disguise as a boy. As a result, despite a sizeable and increasing income, Byron got into financial difficulties from which he did not entirely extricate himself until late in his life. In the course of his schooling he formed many close friendships, the most important with John Cam Hobhouse, a sturdy political liberal and common-sense moralist who exerted a steadying influence throughout Byron's turbulent life.

Despite his distractions at the university, Byron found time to try his hand at lyric verse, which was published in 1807 in a slim and conventional volume entitled *Hours of Idleness*. This was treated with unmerited harshness by the pontifical *Edinburgh Review*, and Byron was provoked to write in reply his first important poem, *English Bards and Scotch Reviewers*, a vigorous satire in the couplet style of the late 18th-century followers of Pope, in which he incorporated skillful but tactless ridicule of all his major poetic contemporaries, including Scott, Wordsworth, and Coleridge.

After attaining his M.A. degree and his majority, Byron set out with Hobhouse in 1809 on a tour through Portugal and Spain to Malta, and then to little-known Albania, Greece, and Asia Minor. In this adventurous two-year excursion, Byron accumulated materials which he wove into most of his important poems, including his last work, *Don Juan*. The first literary product was *Childe Harold*; he wrote the opening two cantos while on the tour which the poem describes, published them in 1812 soon after his return to England, and, in his own oft-quoted phrase, "awoke one morning and found myself famous." He became the literary and social celebrity of fashionable London, enjoying an unprecedented success, which he at once increased by his series of highly readable Near-Eastern verse tales; in these the Byronic hero, in various embodiments, flaunts his misanthropy and undergoes a variety of violent and romantic adventures which current gossip attributed to the author himself. In his chronic shortage of money, Byron could well have used the huge income from these publications, but instead maintained his status as an aristocratic amateur by giving the royalties away. Occupying his inherited seat in the House of Lords, Byron also became briefly active on the extreme liberal side of the Whig party and spoke courageously in defense of the Nottingham weavers who, made desperate by technological unemployment, had resorted to destroying the new textile machines; he also supported other liberal measures, including that of Catholic Emancipation.

In the meantime Byron found himself besieged by women. He was extraordinarily handsome—"so beautiful a countenance," Coleridge wrote, "I scarcely ever saw. * * * his eyes the open portals of the sun—things of light, and for light"; because of a constitutional tendency to obesity, however, Byron was able to maintain his beauty only by recurring again and again to a starvation diet of biscuits, soda water, and strong cathartics. Often as a result of female initiative rather than his own, Byron incurred a sequence of liaisons with ladies of fashion. One of these, the flamboyant, eccentric, and hysterical young Lady Caroline Lamb, caused him so much distress by her frenzied pursuit and public tantrums that Byron turned for relief to marriage with Annabella Milbanke, who was in every way Lady Caroline's opposite, for she was naïve, unworldly, intellectual (with a special passion for mathematics), and not a little priggish; she persuaded herself that she could make Byron over in her own image. This ill-starred marriage produced a daughter (Augusta Ada) and many scenes in which Byron, goaded by financial difficulties, behaved so frantically that his wife suspected his sanity; after only one year, the union ended in a legal separation. The final blow came when Lady Byron discovered her husband's incestuous relations with his half sister, Augusta Leigh. The two had been raised apart, so that they were almost strangers when they met as adults; also, Byron seems to have had one attribute in common with the Byronic hero—a compulsion to try forbidden experience (including, as we now know, homosexual love affairs), joined with a tendency to court his own destruction. The facts of the case have long been violently disputed, but now there remains no room for doubt concerning the validity of the charge. Byron's affection for his sister, however guilty, was deep and genuine, and endured all through his life. This affair proved a delicious morsel even to the jaded palate of the dissolute Regency society; Byron was ostracized by all but a few friends, and finally forced to leave England forever on April 25, 1816.

Byron now resumed the travels incorporated in the third and fourth cantos of *Childe Harold*. At Geneva he lived for several months in close and intellectually fruitful relation to Shelley, who was accompanied by his wife, Mary Godwin, and by his wife's stepsister, Claire Clairmont—a misguided girl of 17 who had forced herself upon Byron while he was still in England and who in January, 1817, bore him a daughter, Allegra. In the fall of 1817 Byron established himself in Venice, where he inaugurated various affairs that culminated in a period of frenzied debauchery which, Byron estimated, involved more than 200 women, mainly of the lower classes. This period was nevertheless one of great literary creativity: often working through the later hours of the night, he finished his tragedy *Manfred*, wrote the fourth canto of *Childe Harold*, and after turning out *Beppo*, a short rehearsal in the narrative style and stanza of *Don Juan*, began the composition of *Don Juan* itself. In the colloquial ottava rima, Byron finally learned to write poetry as well as he had written prose.

Exhausted and bored by promiscuity, Byron in 1819 settled into a placid and relatively faithful relationship with Teresa Guiccioli, the young wife of the elderly Count Alessandro Guiccioli; according to the Italian upper-class mores of the times, having contracted a marriage of convenience, she could now with propriety attach Byron to herself as a *cavalier servente*. Through Teresa's nationalistic family, the Gambas, Byron became involved in the Carbonari plot against Austrian control over northern Italy. When the Gambas were forced by the authorities to move to Pisa, Byron followed them there, and for the second time joined Shelley. There grew up about the two friends the "Pisan Circle," which in addition to the Gambas included Shelley's friends Thomas Medwin and Edward and Jane Williams, as well as the Greek nationalist leader Prince Mavrocordatos, the picturesque Irish Count Taaffe, and the flamboyant and mendacious adventurer Edward Trelawny, who seems to have stepped out of one of Byron's romances. They were later joined by Leigh Hunt and his family, whom Shelley enlisted in a short-lived scheme to publish a new radical political journal, the *Liberal*. The circle was gradually broken up, first by Shelley's anger over Byron's treatment of his daughter Allegra (Byron, refusing any association with the mother, Claire Clairmont, had sent the child to be brought up as a Catholic in an Italian convent, where she died of a fever in 1822); then by the expulsion of the Gambas, whom Byron followed to Genoa; and finally by the drowning of Shelley and Williams in July, 1822.

Byron meanwhile had been steadily at work on a series of closet tragedies (including *Cain*, *Sardanapalus*, and *Marino Faliero*) and on *The*

Vision of Judgment, a superb satire directed against a sycophantic poem, *A Vision of Judgment*, in which the poet laureate, Robert Southey, had memorialized the death of King George III. He also continued writing his great series of incomparably vivid, informative, and witty letters to his friends in England. But increasingly Byron devoted himself to the continuation of *Don Juan*. He had always been diffident in his self-judgments and easily swayed by literary advice. But now, confident that he had at last found his métier and was accomplishing a masterpiece, Byron kept on, in spite of persistent objections against the supposed immorality of the poem by the English public, by his publisher, John Murray, by his friends and well-wishers, and by his extremely decorous mistress, the Countess Guiccioli—by almost everyone, in fact, except the idealist, Shelley, who thought *Juan* incomparably better than anything he himself could write, and insisted "that every word of it is pregnant with immortality."

Byron finally broke off literature for action: he organized an expedition to assist in the Greek war for independence from the Turks. He knew too well the conditions in Greece, and had too skeptical an estimate of human nature, to entertain great hope of success; but he was bored with love, with the domesticity of his relations to Teresa, and in some moods, with life itself. He had, in addition, by his own writings helped to kindle European enthusiasm for the Greek cause, and now felt honor-bound to try what could be done. In the dismal, marshy town of Missolonghi he lived a Spartan existence, undertaking to train troops whom he had himself subsidized and exhibiting great practical grasp and power of leadership amid an incredible confusion of factionalism, intrigue, and military ineptitude until, worn out, he succumbed to a series of feverish attacks and died just after he had reached his 36th birthday. Harold Nicolson, the historian of these events in *Byron: The Last Journey*, wrote: "Lord Byron accomplished nothing at Missolonghi except his own suicide; but by that single act of heroism he secured the liberation of Greece." To this day Byron is revered by the Greek people as a national hero.

Students of Byron still feel, as his friends had felt, the magnetic attraction of his paradoxical and variable temperament. As Mary Shelley wrote six years after his death, when she read Thomas Moore's edition of his *Letters and Journals:* "The Lord Byron I find there is our Lord Byron—the fascinating—faulty—childish—philosophical being—daring the world—docile to a private circle—impetuous and indolent—gloomy and yet more gay than any other. * * * [I become] reconciled (as I used to in his lifetime) to those waywardnesses which annoyed me when he was away, through the delightful and buoyant tone of his conversation and manners." Of his inner discordances, Byron himself was well aware; he told his friend Lady Blessington: "I am so changeable, being everything by turns and nothing long—I am such a strange *mélange* of good and evil, that it would be difficult to describe me." Yet he remained faithful to his own code: a determination always to tell the truth as he saw it about the world and about himself—his refusal, unlike most of us, to suppress or conceal any of his moods is in fact what made him seem so contradictory—and a passionate dedication to the freedom of nations and individuals. As he went on to say to Lady Blessington: "There are but two sentiments to which I am constant—a strong love of liberty, and a detestation of cant."

Written After Swimming from Sestos to Abydos[1]

1

If, in the month of dark December,
Leander, who was nightly wont
(What maid will not the tale remember?)
To cross thy stream, broad Hellespont!

2

If, when the wintry tempest roared,   5
He sped to Hero, nothing loath,
And thus of old thy current poured,
Fair Venus! how I pity both!

3

For *me*, degenerate modern wretch,
Though in the genial month of May,   10
My dripping limbs I faintly stretch,
And think I've done a feat today.

4

But since he crossed the rapid tide,
According to the doubtful story,
To woo—and—Lord knows what beside,   15
And swam for Love, as I for Glory;

5

'Twere hard to say who fared the best:
Sad mortals! thus the gods still plague you!
He lost his labor, I my jest;
For he was drowned, and I've the ague.   20

1810   1812

When We Two Parted

When we two parted
In silence and tears,
Half broken-hearted
To sever for years,

1. The Hellespont (now called the Dardanelles) is the narrow strait between Europe and Asia. In the ancient story, retold in Christopher Marlowe's *Hero and Leander*, young Leander of Abydos, on the Asian side, swam nightly to visit Hero, a priestess of the goddess Venus at Sestos, until he was drowned when he made the attempt in a storm. Byron and a young Lt. Ekenhead swam the Hellespont in the reverse direction on May 3, 1810. Byron alternated between complacency and humor in his many references to the event. In a note to the poem, Byron mentions that the distance was "upwards of four English miles, though the actual breadth is barely one. The rapidity of the current is such that no boat can row directly across. * * * The water was extremely cold, from the melting of the mountain snows."

Pale grew thy cheek and cold,   5
    Colder thy kiss;
Truly that hour foretold
    Sorrow to this.

The dew of the morning
    Sunk chill on my brow—   10
It felt like the warning
    Of what I feel now.
Thy vows are all broken,
    And light is thy fame;
I hear thy name spoken,   15
    And share in its shame.

They name thee before me,
    A knell to mine ear;
A shudder comes o'er me—
    Why wert thou so dear?   20
They know not I knew thee,
    Who knew thee too well—
Long, long shall I rue thee,
    Too deeply to tell.

In secret we met—   25
    In silence I grieve,
That thy heart could forget,
    Thy spirit deceive.
If I should meet thee
    After long years,   30
How should I greet thee?—
    With silence and tears.

1813   1816

She Walks in Beauty[1]

1

She walks in beauty, like the night
    Of cloudless climes and starry skies;
And all that's best of dark and bright
    Meet in her aspect and her eyes:
Thus mellowed to that tender light   5
    Which heaven to gaudy day denies.

2

One shade the more, one ray the less,
    Had half impaired the nameless grace

1. One of the lyrics in *Hebrew Melodies* (1815), written to be set to adaptations of traditional Jewish tunes by the young musician Isaac Nathan. Byron wrote the lines the morning after he had met his beautiful young cousin by marriage, Mrs. Robert John Wilmot, who wore a black mourning gown brightened with spangles.

Which waves in every raven tress,
    Or softly lightens o'er her face;
Where thoughts serenely sweet express   10
    How pure, how dear their dwelling place.

3

And on that cheek, and o'er that brow,
    So soft, so calm, yet eloquent,
The smiles that win, the tints that glow,   15
    But tell of days in goodness spent,
A mind at peace with all below,
    A heart whose love is innocent!

June 12, 1814   1815

Stanzas for Music

There Be None of Beauty's Daughters

1

There be none of Beauty's daughters
    With a magic like thee;
And like music on the waters
    Is thy sweet voice to me:
When, as if its sound were causing   5
    The charméd ocean's pausing,
The waves lie still and gleaming,
And the lulled winds seem dreaming;

2

And the midnight moon is weaving
    Her bright chain o'er the deep;   10
Whose breast is gently heaving,
    As an infant's asleep:
So the spirit bows before thee,
To listen and adore thee;
With a full but soft emotion,   15
Like the swell of summer's ocean.

1816   1816

They Say That Hope Is Happiness

1

They say that Hope is happiness;
    But genuine Love must prize the past,
And Memory wakes the thoughts that bless:
    They rose the first—they set the last;

2

And all that Memory loves the most   5
    Was once our only Hope to be,
And all that Hope adored and lost
    Hath melted into Memory.

3

Alas! it is delusion all;
  The future cheats us from afar,   10
Nor can we be what we recall,
  Nor dare we think on what we are.

1816   1829

Darkness[1]

I had a dream, which was not all a dream.
The bright sun was extinguished, and the stars
Did wander darkling[2] in the eternal space,
Rayless, and pathless, and the icy earth
Swung blind and blackening in the moonless air;   5
Morn came and went—and came, and brought no day,
And men forgot their passions in the dread
Of this their desolation; and all hearts
Were chilled into a selfish prayer for light:
And they did live by watchfires—and the thrones,   10
The palaces of crownéd kings—the huts,
The habitations of all things which dwell,
Were burnt for beacons; cities were consumed,
And men were gathered round their blazing homes
To look once more into each other's face;   15
Happy were those who dwelt within the eye
Of the volcanoes, and their mountain torch:
A fearful hope was all the world contained;
Forests were set on fire—but hour by hour
They fell and faded—and the crackling trunks   20
Extinguished with a crash—and all was black.
The brows of men by the despairing light
Wore an unearthly aspect, as by fits
The flashes fell upon them; some lay down
And hid their eyes and wept; and some did rest   25
Their chins upon their clenchéd hands, and smiled;
And others hurried to and fro, and fed
Their funeral piles with fuel, and looked up
With mad disquietude on the dull sky,
The pall of a past world; and then again   30
With curses cast them down upon the dust,
And gnashed their teeth and howled: the wild birds shrieked
And, terrified, did flutter on the ground,
And flap their useless wings; the wildest brutes
Came tame and tremulous; and vipers crawled   35
And twined themselves among the multitude,

1. A powerfully imagined blank-verse
description of the end of life on earth—
a speculation hardly less common in
Byron's time than in ours.
2. In the dark.

Hissing, but stingless—they were slain for food;
And War, which for a moment was no more,
Did glut himself again—a meal was bought
With blood, and each sate sullenly apart   40
Gorging himself in gloom: no love was left;
All earth was but one thought—and that was death
Immediate and inglorious; and the pang
Of famine fed upon all entrails—men
Died, and their bones were tombless as their flesh;   45
The meager by the meager were devoured,
Even dogs assailed their masters, all save one,
And he was faithful to a corse, and kept
The birds and beasts and famished men at bay,
Till hunger clung them, or the dropping dead   50
Lured their lank jaws; himself sought out no food,
But with a piteous and perpetual moan,
And a quick desolate cry, licking the hand
Which answered not with a caress—he died.
The crowd was famished by degrees; but two   55
Of an enormous city did survive,
And they were enemies: they met beside
The dying embers of an altar place,
Where had been heaped a mass of holy things
For an unholy usage; they raked up,   60
And shivering scraped with their cold skeleton hands
The feeble ashes, and their feeble breath
Blew for a little life, and made a flame
Which was a mockery; then they lifted up
Their eyes as it grew lighter, and beheld   65
Each other's aspects—saw, and shrieked, and died—
Even of their mutual hideousness they died,
Unknowing who he was upon whose brow
Famine had written Fiend. The world was void,
The populous and the powerful was a lump   70
Seasonless, herbless, treeless, manless, lifeless—
A lump of death—a chaos of hard clay.
The rivers, lakes, and ocean all stood still,
And nothing stirred within their silent depths;
Ships sailorless lay rotting on the sea,   75
And their masts fell down piecemeal: as they dropped
They slept on the abyss without a surge—
The waves were dead; the tides were in their grave,
The Moon, their mistress, had expired before;
The winds were withered in the stagnant air,   80
And the clouds perished; Darkness had no need
Of aid from them—She was the Universe.

1816   1816

From Childe Harold's Pilgrimage[1]

A ROMAUNT[2]

From *Canto I*

1

Oh, thou! in Hellas deemed of heavenly birth,
Muse! formed or fabled at the minstrel's will!
Since shamed full oft by later lyres on earth,
Mine dares not call thee from thy sacred hill:
Yet there I've wandered by thy vaunted rill;   5
Yes! sighed o'er Delphi's long-deserted shrine,
Where, save that feeble fountain, all is still;
Nor mote my shell awake the weary Nine[3]
To grace so plain a tale—this lowly lay of mine.

2

Whilome[4] in Albion's isle there dwelt a youth,   10
Who ne in virtue's ways did take delight;
But spent his days in riot most uncouth,
And vexed with mirth the drowsy ear of Night.
Ah, me! in sooth he was a shameless wight,

1. *Childe Harold* is a travelogue, narrated by a melancholy, passionate, well-read, and very eloquent tourist. Byron wrote most of the first two cantos while on the tour through Spain, Portugal, Albania, and Greece which these cantos describe; when he published them, in 1812, they made him at one stroke the best known and most talked about living English poet. Byron took up *Childe Harold* again in 1816, during the European tour he made after the breakup of his marriage. Canto III, published in 1816, moves through Belgium, up the Rhine, and then to Switzerland and the Alps. Canto IV, published in 1818, describes the great cities and monuments of Italy.

Byron chose for his poem the Spenserian stanza, and like James Thomson (in the *Castle of Indolence*) and other 18th-century predecessors, he attempted in the first canto to imitate, in a serio-comic fashion, the archaic language of his Elizabethan model. (The word "Childe" itself is the ancient term for a young noble awaiting knighthood.) But Byron soon dropped the archaisms; and in the last two cantos, he adapts Spenser's mellifluous stanza to his own assured and brassy magniloquence.

In the Preface to his first two cantos, Byron had insisted that the narrator, Childe Harold, was "a fictitious character," merely "the child of imagination." But in the manuscript version of

these cantos, he had himself called his hero "Childe Burun," the early form of his own family name; the world insisted on identifying the character as well as the travels of the protagonist with those of the author; and in the fourth canto Byron, abandoning the third-person *dramatis persona*, spoke out frankly in the first person.

In its shock tactics of apostrophes, imperatives, exclamations, hyperbole, and abrupt changes in subject, pace, and mood, the style of *Childe Harold* is without close parallel in English; to it Goethe applied the terms *Keckheit, Kühnheit, und Grandiosität:* "daring, dash, and grandiosity." It is no small feat in the author to have converted a meticulously accurate tourist's record of scenes, memorials, and museums into a dramatic and passionate experience. The result is like seeing Europe by flashes of lightning, for everything is presented, not as it is in itself, but as it affects the violent sensibility of that new cultural phenomenon, the Romantic Man of Feeling.

2. A romance, or narrative of adventure.

3. The "shell" is a lyre (Hermes is fabled to have invented the lyre by stretching strings over the hollow of a tortoise shell); the "Nine" are the Muses, whose "vaunted rill" (line 5) was the Castalian spring. "Mote": may.

4. Once upon a time.

Sore given to revel and ungodly glee;   15
Few earthly things found favor in his sight
Save concubines and carnal companie,
And flaunting wassailers[5] of high and low degree.

3

Childe Harold was he hight—but whence his name
And lineage long, it suits me not to say;   20
Suffice it that perchance they were of fame,
And had been glorious in another day:
But one sad losel[6] soils a name for aye,
However mighty in the olden time;
Nor all that heralds rake from coffined clay,   25
Nor florid prose, nor honeyed lies of rhyme,
Can blazon evil deeds, or consecrate a crime.

4

Childe Harold basked him in the noontide sun,
Disporting there like any other fly;
Nor deemed before his little day was done   30
One blast might chill him into misery.
But long ere scarce a third of his passed by,
Worse than adversity the Childe befell;
He felt the fullness of satiety:
Then loathed he in his native land to dwell,   35
Which seemed to him more lone than eremite's[7] sad cell.

5

For he through Sin's long labyrinth had run,
Nor made atonement when he did amiss;
Had sighed to many though he loved but one,
And that loved one, alas! could ne'er be his.   40
Ah, happy she! to 'scape from him whose kiss
Had been pollution unto aught so chaste;
Who soon had left her charms for vulgar bliss,
And spoiled her goodly lands to gild his waste,
Nor calm domestic peace had ever deigned to taste.   45

6

And now Childe Harold was sore sick at heart,
And from his fellow bacchanals would flee;
'Tis said, at times the sullen tear would start,
But Pride congealed the drop within his ee:[8]
Apart he stalked in joyless reverie,   50
And from his native land resolved to go,
And visit scorching climes beyond the sea;
With pleasure drugged, he almost longed for woe,
And e'en for change of scene would seek the shades below.

* * *

5. Brazen topers.
6. Rascal. Byron's great-uncle, the 5th
Lord Byron, had killed a kinsman in a
drunken duel.
7. A religious hermit.
8. Eye.

From *Canto III*

1

Is thy face like thy mother's, my fair child!
Ada![1] sole daughter of my house and heart?
When last I saw thy young blue eyes they smiled,
And then we parted—not as now we part,
But with a hope.—
          Awaking with a start,   5
The waters heave around me; and on high
The winds lift up their voices: I depart,
Whither I know not; but the hour's gone by,
When Albion's[2] lessening shores could grieve or glad mine eye.

2

Once more upon the waters! yet once more!   10
And the waves bound beneath me as a steed
That knows his rider. Welcome to their roar!
Swift be their guidance, wheresoe'er it lead!
Though the strained mast should quiver as a reed,
And the rent canvas fluttering strew the gale,   15
Still must I on; for I am as a weed,
Flung from the rock on Ocean's foam, to sail
Where'er the surge may sweep, the tempest's breath prevail.

3

In my youth's summer[3] I did sing of One,
The wandering outlaw of his own dark mind;   20
Again I seize the theme, then but begun,
And bear it with me, as the rushing wind
Bears the cloud onwards: in that tale I find
The furrows of long thought, and dried-up tears,
Which, ebbing, leave a sterile track behind,   25
O'er which all heavily the journeying years
Plod the last sands of life—where not a flower appears.

4

Since my young days of passion—joy, or pain—
Perchance my heart and harp have lost a string,
And both may jar:[4] it may be that in vain   30
I would essay as I have sung to sing.
Yet, though a dreary strain, to this I cling,
So that it wean me from the weary dream
Of selfish grief or gladness—so it fling
Forgetfulness around me—it shall seem   35
To me, though to none else, a not ungrateful theme.

5

He, who grown aged in this world of woe,
In deeds, not years, piercing the depths of life,

1. Byron's daughter, Augusta Ada, born December, 1816, a month before her parents separated. Byron's "hope" (line 5) had been for a reconciliation, but he was never to see Ada again.

2. England's.

3. Byron wrote Canto I at 21; he is now 28.

4. Sound discordant.

So that no wonder waits him—nor below
Can love, or sorrow, fame, ambition, strife, 40
Cut to his heart again with the keen knife
Of silent, sharp endurance—he can tell
Why thought seeks refuge in lone caves, yet rife
With airy images, and shapes which dwell
Still unimpaired, though old, in the soul's haunted cell. 45

6

'Tis to create, and in creating live
A being more intense, that we endow
With form our fancy, gaining as we give
The life we image, even as I do now.
What am I? Nothing: but not so art thou, 50
Soul of my thought!⁵ with whom I traverse earth,
Invisible but gazing, as I glow
Mixed with thy spirit, blended with thy birth,
And feeling still with thee in my crushed feelings' dearth.

7

Yet must I think less wildly—I *have* thought 55
Too long and darkly, till my brain became,
In its own eddy boiling and o'erwrought,
A whirling gulf of phantasy and flame:
And thus, untaught in youth my heart to tame,
My springs of life were poisoned. 'Tis too late! 60
Yet am I changed; though still enough the same
In strength to bear what time can not abate,
And feed on bitter fruits without accusing Fate.

8

Something too much of this—but now 'tis past,
And the spell closes with its silent seal.⁶ 65
Long absent HAROLD reappears at last;
He of the breast which fain no more would feel,
Wrung with the wounds which kill not but ne'er heal;
Yet Time, who changes all, had altered him
In soul and aspect as in age: years steal 70
Fire from the mind as vigor from the limb,
And life's enchanted cup but sparkles near the brim.

9

His had been quaffed too quickly, and he found
The dregs were wormwood; but he filled again,
And from a purer fount, on holier ground, 75
And deemed its spring perpetual; but in vain!
Still round him clung invisibly a chain
Which galled forever, fettering though unseen,
And heavy though it clanked not; worn with pain,
Which pined although it spoke not, and grew keen, 80
Entering with every step he took through many a scene.

5. I.e., Childe Harold, his literary creation.

6. I.e., he sets the seal of silence on his
personal tale ("spell").

10

Secure in guarded coldness, he had mixed
Again in fancied safety with his kind,
And deemed his spirit now so firmly fixed
And sheathed with an invulnerable mind,   85
That, if no joy, no sorrow lurked behind;
And he, as one, might 'midst the many stand
Unheeded, searching through the crowd to find
Fit speculation—such as in strange land
He found in wonderworks of God and Nature's hand.   90

11

But who can view the ripened rose, nor seek
To wear it? who can curiously behold
The smoothness and the sheen of beauty's cheek,
Nor feel the heart can never all grow old?
Who can contemplate Fame through clouds unfold   95
The star which rises o'er her steep, nor climb?
Harold, once more within the vortex, rolled
On with the giddy circle, chasing Time,
Yet with a nobler aim than in his youth's fond[7] prime.

12

But soon he knew himself the most unfit   100
Of men to herd with Man, with whom he held
Little in common; untaught to submit
His thoughts to others, though his soul was quelled
In youth by his own thoughts; still uncompelled,
He would not yield dominion of his mind   105
To spirits against whom his own rebelled,
Proud though in desolation; which could find
A life within itself, to breathe without mankind.

13

Where rose the mountains, there to him were friends;
Where rolled the ocean, thereon was his home;   110
Where a blue sky, and glowing clime, extends,
He had the passion and the power to roam;
The desert, forest, cavern, breaker's foam,
Were unto him companionship; they spake
A mutual language, clearer than the tome   115
Of his land's tongue, which he would oft forsake
For Nature's pages glassed[8] by sunbeams on the lake.

14

Like the Chaldean,[9] he could watch the stars,
Till he had peopled them with beings bright
As their own beams; and earth, and earth-born jars,   120
And human frailties, were forgotten quite:
Could he have kept his spirit to that flight
He had been happy; but this clay will sink
Its spark immortal, envying it the light

7. Foolish.
8. Made glassy.
9. A people of ancient Babylonia, expert in astronomy.

To which it mounts, as if to break the link   125
That keeps us from yon heaven which woos us to its brink.

15

But in Man's dwellings he became a thing
Restless and worn, and stern and wearisome,
Drooped as a wild-born falcon with clipped wing,
To whom the boundless air alone were home: 130
Then came his fit again, which to o'ercome,
As eagerly the barred-up bird will beat
His breast and beak against his wiry dome
Till the blood tinge his plumage, so the heat
Of his impeded soul would through his bosom eat.   135

16

Self-exiled Harold wanders forth again,
With nought of hope left—but with less of gloom;
The very knowledge that he lived in vain,
That all was over on this side the tomb,
Had made Despair a smilingness assume,   140
Which, though 'twere wild—as on the plundered wreck
When mariners would madly meet their doom
With draughts intemperate on the sinking deck—
Did yet inspire a cheer which he forebore to check.

17

Stop!—for thy tread is on an Empire's dust!   145
An Earthquake's spoil is sepulchered below!
Is the spot marked with no colossal bust,
Nor column trophied for triumphal show?
None;[1] but the moral's truth tells simpler so,
As the ground was before, thus let it be—   150
How that red rain hath made the harvest grow!
And is this all the world has gained by thee,
Thou first and last of fields, king-making Victory?

18

And Harold stands upon this place of skulls,
The grave of France, the deadly Waterloo!   155
How in an hour the power which gave annuls
Its gifts, transferring fame as fleeting too!
In "pride of place" here last the eagle flew,[2]
Then tore with bloody talon the rent plain,
Pierced by the shaft of banded nations through;   160
Ambition's life and labors all were vain;
He wears the shattered links of the world's broken chain.[3]

19

Fit retribution! Gaul[4] may champ the bit
And foam in fetters—but is Earth more free?

1. Napoleon's defeat at Waterloo, near
Brussels, had occurred only the year
before, on June 18, 1815.
2. The eagle was the standard of Napoleon. "Pride of place" is a term from
falconry, meaning the highest point of
flight (cf. *Macbeth* II.iv.12).

3. Napoleon was then a prisoner at St.
Helena.
4. France. Byron, like Shelley and other
liberals, saw the defeat of the Napoleonic tyranny as at the same time a victory for tyrannous kings and the forces
of extreme reaction throughout Europe.

Did nations combat to make *One* submit; 165
Or league to teach all kings true sovereignty?
What! shall reviving Thralldom again be
The patched-up idol of enlightened days?
Shall we, who struck the Lion down, shall we
Pay the Wolf homage? proffering lowly gaze 170
And servile knees to thrones? No; *prove*[5] before ye praise!

20

If not, o'er one fallen despot boast no more!
In vain fair cheeks were furrowed with hot tears
For Europe's flowers long rooted up before
The trampler of her vineyards; in vain years 175
Of death, depopulation, bondage, fears,
Have all been borne, and broken by the accord
Of roused-up millions: all that most endears
Glory is when the myrtle wreathes a sword
Such as Harmodius drew on Athens' tyrant lord.[6] 180

21

There was a sound of revelry by night,
And Belgium's capital had gathered then
Her Beauty and her Chivalry, and bright
The lamps shone o'er fair women and brave men;[7]
A thousand hearts beat happily; and when 185
Music arose with its voluptuous swell,
Soft eyes looked love to eyes which spake again,
And all went merry as a marriage bell—
But hush! hark! a deep sound strikes like a rising knell!

22

Did ye not hear it?—No; 'twas but the wind, 190
Or the car rattling o'er the stony street;
On with the dance! let joy be unconfined;
No sleep till morn, when Youth and Pleasure meet
To chase the glowing Hours with flying feet—
But hark!—that heavy sound breaks in once more, 195
As if the clouds its echo would repeat;
And nearer, clearer, deadlier than before!
Arm! Arm! it is—it is—the cannon's opening roar!

23

Within a windowed niche of that high hall
Sate Brunswick's fated chieftain;[8] he did hear 200
That sound the first amidst the festival,
And caught its tone with Death's prophetic ear;
And when they smiled because he deemed it near,

5. Await the test (proof) of experience.
6. In 514 B.C. Harmodius and Aristogei-
ton, hiding their daggers in myrtle
(symbol of love), killed Hipparchus,
tyrant of Athens.
7. This famous ball, given by the
Duchess of Richmond on the eve of the
battle of Quatre Bras, which opened the
conflict at Waterloo, is also described

in Thackeray's *Vanity Fair*, Chapters
29–30.
8. The Duke of Brunswick, nephew of
George III of England, was killed in the
battle of Quatre Bras, just as his
father, commanding the Prussian army
against Napoleon, had been killed at
Auerstedt in 1806 (line 205).

His heart more truly knew that peal too well
Which stretched his father on a bloody bier,   205
And roused the vengeance blood alone could quell:
He rushed into the field, and, foremost fighting, fell.

24

Ah! then and there was hurrying to and fro,
And gathering tears, and tremblings of distress,
And cheeks all pale, which but an hour ago   210
Blushed at the praise of their own loveliness;
And there were sudden partings, such as press
The life from out young hearts, and choking sighs
Which ne'er might be repeated; who could guess
If ever more should meet those mutual eyes,   215
Since upon night so sweet such awful morn could rise!

25

And there was mounting in hot haste: the steed,
The mustering squadron, and the clattering car,
Went pouring forward with impetuous speed,
And swiftly forming in the ranks of war;   220
And the deep thunder peal on peal afar;
And near, the beat of the alarming drum
Roused up the soldier ere the morning star;
While thronged the citizens with terror dumb,
Or whispering, with white lips—"The foe! They come! they come!"

26

And wild and high the "Cameron's gathering"⁹ rose!   226
The war-note of Lochiel, which Albyn's hills
Have heard, and heard, too, have her Saxon foes—
How in the noon of night that pibroch¹ thrills,
Savage and shrill! But with the breath which fills   230
Their mountain pipe, so fill the mountaineers
With the fierce native daring which instills
The stirring memory of a thousand years,
And Evan's, Donald's fame² rings in each clansman's ears!

27

And Ardennes³ waves above them her green leaves,   235
Dewy with nature's teardrops, as they pass,
Grieving, if aught inanimate e'er grieves,
Over the unreturning brave—alas!
Ere evening to be trodden like the grass
Which now beneath them, but above shall grow   240
In its next verdure, when this fiery mass
Of living valor, rolling on the foe
And burning with high hope, shall molder cold and low.

---

9. The clan song of the Camerons, whose chief was called "Lochiel," after his estate. "Albyn's": Scotland's.
1. Bagpipe music, usually warlike in character.
2. Sir Evan and Donald Cameron, famous warriors in the Stuart cause in the 17th and 18th centuries.
3. A forested region covering parts of Belgium, France, and Luxembourg, which became a battlefield again in both World Wars.

28

Last noon beheld them full of lusty life,
Last eve in Beauty's circle proudly gay,   245
The midnight brought the signal-sound of strife,
The morn the marshaling in arms—the day
Battle's magnificently-stern array!
The thunderclouds close o'er it, which when rent
The earth is covered thick with other clay,   250
Which her own clay shall cover, heaped and pent,
Rider and horse—friend, foe—in one red burial blent!

* * *

36

There sunk the greatest, nor the worst of men,[4]
Whose spirit antithetically mixed
One moment of the mightiest, and again
On little objects with like firmness fixed,
Extreme in all things! hadst thou been betwixt,   320
Thy throne had still been thine, or never been;
For daring made thy rise as fall: thou seek'st
Even now to reassume the imperial mien,
And shake again the world, the Thunderer of the scene!

37

Conqueror and captive of the earth art thou!   325
She trembles at thee still, and thy wild name
Was ne'er more bruited in men's minds than now
That thou are nothing, save the jest of Fame,
Who wooed thee once, thy vassal, and became
The flatterer of thy fierceness, till thou wert   330
A god unto thyself; nor less the same
To the astounded kingdoms all inert,
Who deemed thee for a time whate'er thou didst assert.

38

Oh, more or less than man—in high or low,
Battling with nations, flying from the field;   335
Now making monarchs' necks thy footstool, now
More than thy meanest soldier taught to yield;
An empire thou couldst crush, command, rebuild,
But govern not thy pettiest passion, nor,
However deeply in men's spirits skilled,   340
Look through thine own, nor curb the lust of war,
Nor learn that tempted Fate will leave the loftiest star.

39

Yet well thy soul hath brooked the turning tide
With that untaught innate philosophy,
Which, be it wisdom, coldness, or deep pride,   345
Is gall and wormwood to an enemy.
When the whole host of hatred stood hard by,
To watch and mock thee shrinking, thou hast smiled

4. I.e., Napoleon.

With a sedate and all-enduring eye—
When Fortune fled her spoiled and favorite child,   350
He stood unbowed beneath the ills upon him piled.

40

Sager than in thy fortunes; for in them
Ambition steeled thee on too far to show
That just habitual scorn, which could contemn
Men and their thoughts; 'twas wise to feel, not so   355
To wear it ever on thy lip and brow,
And spurn the instruments thou wert to use
Till they were turned unto thine overthrow:
'Tis but a worthless world to win or lose;
So hath it proved to thee and all such lot[5] who choose.   360

41

If, like a tower upon a headlong rock,
Thou hadst been made to stand or fall alone,
Such scorn of man had helped to brave the shock;
But men's thoughts were the steps which paved thy throne,
Their admiration thy best weapon shone;   365
The part of Philip's son[6] was thine, not then
(Unless aside thy purple had been thrown)
Like stern Diogenes[7] to mock at men;
For sceptered cynics earth were far too wide a den.

42

But quiet to quick bosoms is a hell,   370
And *there* hath been thy bane; there is a fire
And motion of the soul which will not dwell
In its own narrow being, but aspire
Beyond the fitting medium of desire;
And, but once kindled, quenchless evermore,   375
Preys upon high adventure, nor can tire
Of aught but rest; a fever at the core,
Fatal to him who bears, to all who ever bore.

43

This makes the madmen who have made men mad
By their contagion; Conquerors and Kings,   380
Founders of sects and systems, to whom add
Sophists, Bards, Statesmen, all unquiet things
Which stir too strongly the soul's secret springs,
And are themselves the fools to those they fool;
Envied, yet how unenviable! what stings   385
Are theirs! One breast laid open were a school
Which would unteach mankind the lust to shine or rule.

44

Their breath is agitation, and their life
A storm whereon they ride, to sink at last;

5. Hazard.
6. Alexander the Great, son of Philip of Macedon.
7. The Greek philosopher of Cynicism, contemporary of Alexander. It is related

that Alexander was so struck by his independence of mind that he said, "If I were not Alexander, I should wish to be Diogenes"; hence the allusion in line 369.

And yet so nursed and bigoted to strife,   390
That should their days, surviving perils past,
Melt to calm twilight, they feel overcast
With sorrow and supineness, and so die;
Even as a flame unfed which runs to waste
With its own flickering, or a sword laid by,   395
Which eats into itself and rusts ingloriously.

45

He who ascends to mountain tops, shall find
The loftiest peaks most wrapped in clouds and snow;
He who surpasses or subdues mankind,
Must look down on the hate of those below.   400
Though high *above* the sun of glory glow,
And far *beneath* the earth and ocean spread,
Round him are icy rocks, and loudly blow
Contending tempests on his naked head,
And thus reward the toils which to those summits led.[8] 405

* * *

52

Thus Harold inly said, and passed along,   460
Yet not insensibly to all which here
Awoke the jocund birds to early song
In glens which might have made even exile dear:
Though on his brow were graven lines austere,
And tranquil sternness which had ta'en the place   465
Of feelings fierier far but less severe,
Joy was not always absent from his face,
But o'er it in such scenes would steal with transient trace.

53

Nor was all love shut from him, though his days
Of passion had consumed themselves to dust.   470
It is in vain that we would coldly gaze
On such as smile upon us; the heart must
Leap kindly back to kindness, though disgust
Hath weaned it from all wordlings: thus he felt,
For there was soft remembrance, and sweet trust   475
In one fond breast,[3] to which his own would melt,
And in its tenderer hour on that his bosom dwelt.

54

And he had learned to love—I know not why,
For this in such as him seems strange of mood—
The helpless looks of blooming infancy,   480
Even in its earliest nurture; what subdued,
To change like this, a mind so far imbued
With scorn of man, it little boots to know;
But thus it was; and though in solitude

8. In the stanzas here omitted, Harold is abruptly sent sailing up the Rhine, meditating on the "thousand battles" that "have assailed thy banks."

3. Commentators agree that the reference is to Byron's half sister, Augusta Leigh.

Small power the nipped affections have to grow,   485
In him this glowed when all beside had ceased to glow.

55

And there was one soft breast, as hath been said,
Which unto his was bound by stronger ties
Than the church links withal; and, though unwed,
That love was pure, and, far above disguise,   490
Had stood the test of mortal enmities
Still undivided, and cemented more
By peril, dreaded most in female eyes;
But this was firm, and from a foreign shore
Well to that heart might his these absent greetings pour!   495

* * *

68

Lake Leman[4] woos me with its crystal face,
The mirror where the stars and mountains view
The stillness of their aspect in each trace   645
Its clear depth yields of their far height and hue:
There is too much of man here, to look through
With a fit mind the might which I behold;
But soon in me shall Loneliness renew   650
Thoughts hid, but not less cherished than of old,
Ere mingling with the herd had penned me in their fold.

69

To fly from, need not be to hate, mankind:
All are not fit with them to stir and toil,
Nor is it discontent to keep the mind   655
Deep in its fountain, lest it overboil
In the hot throng, where we become the spoil
Of our infection, till too late and long
We may deplore and struggle with the coil,[5]
In wretched interchange of wrong for wrong   660
Midst a contentious world, striving where none are strong.

70

There, in a moment, we may plunge our years
In fatal penitence, and in the blight
Of our own soul turn all our blood to tears,
And color things to come with hues of night;   665
The race of life becomes a hopeless flight
To those that walk in darkness: on the sea,
The boldest steer but where their ports invite,
But there are wanderers o'er Eternity
Whose bark drives on and on, and anchored ne'er shall be.   670

71

Is it not better, then, to be alone,
And love earth only for its earthly sake?
By the blue rushing of the arrowy Rhone,
Or the pure bosom of its nursing lake,
Which feeds it as a mother who doth make   675

---

4. The Lake of Geneva, Switzerland.   5. Tumult.

A fair but froward infant her own care,
Kissing its cries away as these awake—
Is it not better thus our lives to wear,
Than join the crushing crowd, doomed to inflict or bear?

72

I live not in myself, but I become   680
Portion of that around me; and to me
High mountains are a feeling, but the hum
Of human cities torture: I can see
Nothing to loathe in nature, save to be
A link reluctant in a fleshly chain,   685
Classed among creatures, when the soul can flee,
And with the sky, the peak, the heaving plain
Of ocean, or the stars, mingle, and not in vain.[6]

73

And thus I am absorbed, and this is life:
I look upon the peopled desert past,   690
As on a place of agony and strife,
Where, for some sin, to sorrow I was cast,
To act and suffer, but remount at last
With a fresh pinion; which I feel to spring,
Though young, yet waxing vigorous, as the blast   695
Which it would cope with, on delighted wing,
Spurning the clay-cold bonds which round our being cling.

74

And when, at length, the mind shall be all free
From what it hates in this degraded form,
Reft of its carnal life, save what shall be   700
Existent happier in the fly and worm—
When elements to elements conform,
And dust is as it should be, shall I not
Feel all I see, less dazzling, but more warm?
The bodiless thought? the Spirit of each spot?   705
Of which, even now, I share at times the immortal lot?

75

Are not the mountains, waves, and skies a part
Of me and of my soul, as I of them?
Is not the love of these deep in my heart
With a pure passion? should I not contemn   710
All objects, if compared with these? and stem
A tide of suffering, rather than forego
Such feelings for the hard and worldly phlegm
Of those whose eyes are only turned below,
Gazing upon the ground, with thoughts which dare not glow?   715

* * *

6. Byron had lived in close contact with
Shelley at Geneva and had toured the
lake with him. At the time, he was
introduced to concepts of nature held
by Shelley and Wordsworth, whom
Shelley had pressed on Byron's attention; these ideas are reflected in Canto
III, but the voice is Byron's. Byron said
of this canto: "I was half mad during
the time of its composition, between
metaphysics, mountains, lakes, love unextinguishable, thoughts unutterable,
and the nightmare of my own delin-
quencies."

85

Clear, placid Leman! thy contrasted lake,
With the wild world I dwelt in, is a thing
Which warns me with its stillness to forsake
Earth's troubled waters for a purer spring.   800
This quiet sail is as a noiseless wing
To waft me from distraction; once I loved
Torn ocean's roar, but thy soft murmuring
Sounds sweet as if a sister's voice reproved,
That I with stern delights should e'er have been so moved.   805

86

It is the hush of night, and all between
Thy margin and the mountains, dusk, yet clear,
Mellowed and mingling, yet distinctly seen,
Save darkened Jura,[7] whose capped heights appear
Precipitously steep; and drawing near,   810
There breathes a living fragrance from the shore,
Of flowers yet fresh with childhood; on the ear
Drops the light drip of the suspended oar,
Or chirps the grasshopper one good-night carol more.

87

He is an evening reveler, who makes   815
His life an infancy, and sings his fill;
At intervals, some bird from out the brakes[8]
Starts into voice a moment, then is still.
There seems a floating whisper on the hill,
But that is fancy, for the starlight dews   820
All silently their tears of love instill,
Weeping themselves away, till they infuse
Deep into Nature's breast the spirit of her hues.

88

Ye stars! which are the poetry of heaven!
If in your bright leaves we would read the fate   825
Of men and empires—'tis to be forgiven,
That in our aspirations to be great,
Our destinies o'erleap their mortal state,
And claim a kindred with you; for ye are
A beauty and a mystery, and create   830
In us such love and reverence from afar
That fortune—fame—power—life have named themselves a Star.

89

All heaven and earth are still—though not in sleep,
But breathless, as we grow when feeling most;
And silent, as we stand in thoughts too deep—   835
All heaven and earth are still. From the high host
Of stars to the lulled lake and mountain coast,
All is concentered in a life intense,
Where not a beam, nor air, nor leaf is lost,

7. The mountain range between Swit-   Lake of Geneva.
zerland and France, visible from the   8. Thickets.

But hath a part of being, and a sense   840
Of that which is of all Creator and defense.

90

Then stirs the feeling infinite, so felt
In solitude, where we are *least* alone;
A truth, which through our being then doth melt
And purifies from self: it is a tone,   845
The soul and source of music, which makes known
Eternal harmony, and sheds a charm,
Like to the fabled Cytherea's zone,[9]
Binding all things with beauty—'twould disarm
The specter Death, had he substantial power to harm.   850

91

Not vainly did the early Persian make
His altar the high places and the peak
Of earth-o'ergazing mountains, and thus take
A fit and unwalled temple, there to seek
The Spirit, in whose honor shrines are weak   855
Upreared of human hands. Come, and compare
Columns and idol-dwellings, Goth or Greek,
With Nature's realms of worship, earth and air,
Nor fix on fond abodes to circumscribe thy prayer!

92

The sky is changed!—and such a change! Oh night,   860
And storm, and darkness, ye are wondrous strong,
Yet lovely in your strength, as is the light
Of a dark eye in woman! Far along,
From peak to peak, the rattling crags among,
Leaps the live thunder! Not from one lone cloud,   865
But every mountain now hath found a tongue,
And Jura answers, through her misty shroud,
Back to the joyous Alps, who call to her aloud!

93

And this is in the night—Most glorious night!
Thou wert not sent for slumber! let me be   870
A sharer in thy fierce and far delight—
A portion of the tempest and of thee!
How the lit lake shines, a phosphoric sea,
And the big rain comes dancing to the earth!
And now again 'tis black—and now, the glee   875
Of the loud hills shakes with its mountain mirth,
As if they did rejoice o'er a young earthquake's birth.

94

Now, where the swift Rhone cleaves his way between
Heights which appear as lovers who have parted
In hate, whose mining depths so intervene   880
That they can meet no more, though brokenhearted!
Though in their souls, which thus each other thwarted,
Love was the very root of the fond rage

9. The sash of Venus, which conferred the power to attract love.

Which blighted their life's bloom, and then departed—
Itself expired, but leaving them an age   885
Of years all winters—war within themselves to wage:

95

Now, where the quick Rhone thus hath cleft his way,
The mightiest of the storms hath ta'en his stand:
For here, not one, but many, make their play,
And fling their thunderbolts from hand to hand,   890
Flashing and cast around: of all the band,
The brightest through these parted hills hath forked
His lightnings—as if he did understand,
That in such gaps as desolation worked,
There the hot shaft should blast whatever therein lurked.   895

96

Sky—mountains—river—winds—lake—lightnings! ye,
With night, and clouds, and thunder, and a soul
To make these felt and feeling, well may be
Things that have made me watchful; the far roll
Of your departing voices, is the knoll[1]   900
Of what in me is sleepless—if I rest.
But where of ye, oh tempests! is the goal?
Are ye like those within the human breast?
Or do ye find at length, like eagles, some high nest?

97

Could I embody and unbosom now   905
That which is most within me—could I wreak
My thoughts upon expression, and thus throw
Soul, heart, mind, passions, feelings, strong or weak,
All that I would have sought, and all I seek,
Bear, know, feel—and yet breathe—into *one* word,   910
And that one word were lightning, I would speak;
But as it is, I live and die unheard,
With a most voiceless thought, sheathing it as a sword.

98

The morn is up again, the dewy morn,
With breath all incense and with cheek all bloom,   915
Laughing the clouds away with playful scorn,
And living as if earth contained no tomb—
And glowing into day; we may resume
The march of our existence; and thus I,
Still on thy shores, fair Leman! may find room   920
And food for meditation, nor pass by
Much, that may give us pause, if pondered fittingly.

* * *

113

I have not loved the world, nor the world me;
I have not flattered its rank breath, nor bowed   1050
To its idolatries a patient knee—
Nor coined my cheek to smiles—nor cried aloud

1. Knell (old form).

In worship of an echo; in the crowd
They could not deem me one of such; I stood
Among them, but not of them; in a shroud   1055
Of thoughts which were not their thoughts, and still could,
Had I not filed[2] my mind, which thus itself subdued.

114

I have not loved the world, nor the world me—
But let us part fair foes; I do believe,
Though I have found them not, that there may be   1060
Words which are things, hopes which will not deceive,
And virtues which are merciful nor weave
Snares for the failing: I would also deem
O'er others' griefs that some sincerely grieve;
That two, or one, are almost what they seem—   1065
That goodness is no name, and happiness no dream.

115

My daughter! with thy name this song begun—
My daughter! with thy name thus much shall end!—
I see thee not—I hear thee not—but none
Can be so wrapped in thee; thou art the friend   1070
To whom the shadows of far years extend:
Albeit my brow thou never shouldst behold,
My voice shall with thy future visions blend,
And reach into thy heart—when mine is cold—
A token and a tone even from thy father's mold.   1075

116

To aid thy mind's development—to watch
Thy dawn of little joys—to sit and see
Almost thy very growth—to view thee catch
Knowledge of objects—wonders yet to thee!
To hold thee lightly on a gentle knee,   1080
And print on thy soft cheek a parent's kiss—
This, it should seem, was not reserved for me;
Yet this was in my nature—as it is,
I know not what is there, yet something like to this.

117

Yet, though dull Hate as duty should be taught,   1085
I know that thou wilt love me; though my name
Should be shut from thee, as a spell still fraught
With desolation, and a broken claim;
Though the grave closed between us—'twere the same;
I know that thou wilt love me; though to drain   1090
My blood from out thy being were an aim
And an attainment—all would be in vain—
Still thou wouldst love me, still that more than life retain.

118

The child of love—though born in bitterness
And nurtured in convulsion! Of thy sire   1095

---

2. Defiled. In a note Byron refers to *Macbeth* III.i.65 ("For Banquo's issue have
I filed my mind").

These were the elements, and thine no less.
As yet such are around thee, but thy fire
Shall be more tempered and thy hope far higher.
Sweet be thy cradled slumbers! O'er the sea,
And from the mountains where I now respire,   1100
Fain would I waft such blessing upon thee,
As, with a sigh, I deem thou mightst have been to me!

From *Canto IV*

1

I stood in Venice, on the Bridge of Sighs,[1]
A palace and a prison on each hand:
I saw from out the wave her structures rise
As from the stroke of the enchanter's wand:
A thousand years their cloudy wings expand   5
Around me, and a dying Glory smiles
O'er the far times, when many a subject land
Looked to the wingéd Lion's[2] marble piles,
Where Venice sate in state, throned on her hundred isles!

2

She looks a sea Cybele,[3] fresh from ocean,   10
Rising with her tiara of proud towers
At airy distance, with majestic motion,
A ruler of the waters and their powers:
And such she was—her daughters had their dowers
From spoils of nations, and the exhaustless East   15
Poured in her lap all gems in sparkling showers:
In purple was she robed, and of her feast
Monarchs partook, and deemed their dignity increased.

3

In Venice Tasso's echoes are no more,
And silent rows the songless gondolier;[4]   20
Her palaces are crumbling to the shore,
And music meets not always now the ear:
Those days are gone—but Beauty still is here;
States fall, arts fade—but Nature doth not die,
Nor yet forget how Venice once was dear,   25
The pleasant place of all festivity,
The revel of the earth, the masque of Italy![5]

4

But unto us she hath a spell beyond
Her name in story, and her long array
Of mighty shadows, whose dim forms despond   30

1. A covered bridge between the Doge's Palace and the prison of San Marco.
2. The emblem of St. Mark, patron saint of Venice.
3. A nature goddess, sometimes represented wearing a crown ("tiara") of towers.
4. The gondoliers once had the custom of chanting stanzas of Tasso's *Jerusalem Delivered*.
5. "Masques" were lavish dramatic entertainments popular in the courts of the Renaissance, involving songs, dances, and elaborate costumes and staging.

Above the dogeless city's[6] vanished sway:
Ours is a trophy which will not decay
With the Rialto;[7] Shylock and the Moor
And Pierre cannot be swept or worn away—
The keystones of the arch! though all were o'er,   35
For us repeopled were[8] the solitary shore.

* * *

178

There is a pleasure in the pathless woods,
There is a rapture on the lonely shore,   1595
There is society where none intrudes,
By the deep sea, and music in its roar:
I love not Man the less, but Nature more,
From these our interviews, in which I steal
From all I may be, or have been before,   1600
To mingle with the Universe, and feel
What I can ne'er express, yet can not all conceal.

179

Roll on, thou deep and dark blue Ocean—roll!
Ten thousand fleets sweep over thee in vain;
Man marks the earth with ruin—his control   1605
Stops with the shore; upon the watery plain
The wrecks are all thy deed, nor doth remain
A shadow of man's ravage, save his own,
When, for a moment, like a drop of rain,
He sinks into thy depths with bubbling groan,   1610
Without a grave, unknelled, uncoffined, and unknown.

180

His steps are not upon thy paths—thy fields
Are not a spoil for him—thou dost arise
And shake him from thee; the vile strength he wields
For earth's destruction thou dost all despise,   1615
Spurning him from thy bosom to the skies,
And send'st him, shivering in thy playful spray
And howling, to his Gods, where haply lies
His petty hope in some near port or bay,
And dashest him again to earth—there let him lay.[9]   1620

181

The armaments which thunderstrike the walls
Of rock-built cities, bidding nations quake
And monarchs tremble in their capitals,
The oak leviathans,[1] whose huge ribs make
Their clay creator the vain title take   1625
Of lord of thee, and arbiter of war—

6. The last duke ("doge") of Venice was deposed by Napoleon in 1797.
7. The business district in Venice, a setting in *The Merchant of Venice* and *Othello* ("the Moor"), and also in Thomas Otway's tragedy, *Venice Preserved* (1682), in which Pierre (line 34) is a leading character.

8. Would be.
9. For "lie." Denounced by many critics, this has been called the most notorious solecism in English poetry. But Byron, like other English aristocrats of the time, deliberately affected a cavalier indifference to commonplace grammar.
1. Warships.

These are thy toys, and, as the snowy flake,
They melt into thy yeast of waves, which mar
Alike the Armada's pride or spoils of Trafalgar.[2]

182

Thy shores are empires, changed in all save thee—   1630
Assyria, Greece, Rome, Carthage, what are they?
Thy waters washed them power while they were free,
And many a tyrant since; their shores obey
The stranger, slave, or savage; their decay
Has dried up realms to deserts—not so thou,   1635
Unchangeable save to thy wild waves' play;
Time writes no wrinkle on thine azure brow—
Such as creation's dawn beheld, thou rollest now.

183

Thou glorious mirror, where the Almighty's form
Glasses[3] itself in tempests; in all time,   1640
Calm or convulsed—in breeze, or gale, or storm,
Icing the pole, or in the torrid clime
Dark-heaving—boundless, endless, and sublime—
The image of Eternity—the throne
Of the Invisible; even from out thy slime   1645
The monsters of the deep are made; each zone
Obeys thee; thou goest forth, dread, fathomless, alone.

184

And I have loved thee, Ocean! and my joy
Of youthful sports was on thy breast to be
Borne, like thy bubbles, onward: from a boy   1650
I wantoned with thy breakers—they to me
Were a delight; and if the freshening sea
Made them a terror—'twas a pleasing fear,
For I was as it were a child of thee,
And trusted to thy billows far and near,   1655
And laid my hand upon thy mane—as I do here.

185

My task is done—my song hath ceased—my theme
Has died into an echo; it is fit
The spell should break of this protracted dream.
The torch shall be extinguished which hath lit   1660
My midnight lamp—and what is writ, is writ—
Would it were worthier! but I am not now
That which I have been—and my visions flit
Less palpably before me—and the glow
Which in my spirit dwelt is fluttering, faint, and low.   1665

186

Farewell! a word that must be, and hath been—
A sound which makes us linger—yet—farewell!
Ye! who have traced the Pilgrim to the scene

2. The Spanish Armada, defeated by
the English in 1588, lost many ships in
a storm; another storm was responsible
for the loss of a number of French ships
that Nelson had captured at Trafalgar
(1805).
3. Mirrors.

Which is his last, if in your memories dwell
A thought which once was his, if on ye swell   1670
A single recollection, not in vain
He wore his sandal shoon and scallop shell;[4]
Farewell! with *him* alone may rest the pain,
If such there were—with *you*, the moral of his strain!

1812, 1816, 1818

So We'll Go No More A-Roving[1]

1

So we'll go no more a-roving
   So late into the night,
Though the heart be still as loving,
   And the moon be still as bright.

2

For the sword outwears its sheath,   5
   And the soul wears out the breast,
And the heart must pause to breathe,
   And Love itself have rest.

3

Though the night was made for loving,
   And the day returns too soon,   10
Yet we'll go no more a-roving
   By the light of the moon.

1817   1836

4. Sandals and a scallop shell (worn on the hat) were traditional emblems of pilgrims to holy shrines. of travel by land and travel by sea.
1. Included in a letter to Thomas Moore, February 28, 1817, and written in the Lenten aftermath of a spell of feverish dissipation in the Carnival season at Venice. Byron wrote, "I find 'the sword wearing out the scabbard,' though I have but just turned the corner of twenty-nine." The poem is based on the refrain of a Scottish song, *The Jolly Beggar:* "And we'll gang nae mair a roving / Sae late into the nicht * * * "

Don Juan   Byron began his masterpiece (pronounced in the English fashion, *Don Joó-un*) in July of 1818, published it in installments, beginning with Cantos I and II in 1819, and continued working on it almost until his death. He extemporized the poem from episode to episode; "I *have* no plan," he said, "I *had* no plan; but I had or have materials." The work was composed with remarkable speed (the 888 lines of Canto XIII, for example, were accomplished within a week), and it seeks to give the effect of improvisation and comprehensiveness rather than of compression; it ought to be read rapidly, at a conversational pace.

The poem breaks off in the sixteenth canto, but even in its unfinished state *Don Juan* is the longest satire, and one of the longest of all poems, written in English. Its hero, the Spanish libertine, had in the original legend been superhuman in his sexual energy and wickedness. Throughout

Byron's version the unspoken but persistent joke is that this violent and archetypal *homme fatal* of European legend is in fact more acted upon than active—never the seducer, always the seduced. Unfailingly amiable and well-intentioned, he is guilty largely of youth, charm, and a courteous and compliant spirit. The ladies do all the rest.

The chief models for the poem were the Italian seriocomic versions of medieval chivalric romances; the genre had been introduced by Pulci in the 15th century and achieved its greatest success in Ariosto's *Orlando Furioso* (1516). From these writers Byron caught the mixed moods and violent oscillations between the sublime and the ridiculous, as well as the easy, colloquial management of the complex ottava rima—an eight-line stanza in which the initial interlaced rhymes (*ababab*) build up to the comic turn in the final pat couplet (*cc*). Byron was influenced in·the English use of this Italian form by a mildly amusing poem published in 1817, under the pseudonym of "Whistlecraft," by his friend John Hookham Frere. Other recognizable antecedents of *Don Juan* are Swift's *Gulliver's Travels* and Johnson's *Rasselas*, which also employed the naïve traveler as a satiric device, and Laurence Sterne's novel, *Tristram Shandy*, with its comic exploitation of a narrative medium blatantly subject to the whimsy of the author. But even the most original literary works play variations upon inherited conventions. Shelley at once recognized his friend's poem for what it was, "something wholly new and relative to the age."

Byron's most trusted literary advisers thought the poem disgracefully immoral, and John Murray took the precaution of printing the first two installments without identifying either Byron as the author or himself as the publisher. In our own day, however, the most common complaint is not that *Don Juan* is immoral, but that it is morally nihilistic—that the poem is destructive without limit, since it proposes no positive values as a base for the satire, but sees life, in the words of one critic, as "a strange meaningless pageant." Yet Byron insisted that *Don Juan* is "a satire on *abuses* of the present state of society," and "the most moral of poems." Though the final phrase exaggerates, it has a foundation of truth. What the poem most frequently attacks, in love, religion, and social relations, are very considerable vices—sham, hypocrisy, complacency, oppression, greed, and lust. Furthermore, the satire constantly, though silently, assumes as moral positives the qualities of courage, loyalty, generosity, and, above all, total candor; it merely implies that these virtues are excessively rare, and that the modern world is not constituted to reward, to encourage, or even to recognize them when they make their appearance. And far from being intimidatingly nihilistic, *Don Juan* is always and zestfully on the side of life, in its abundant variety. "As to *Don Juan*," Byron wrote elatedly to a friend, "confess—confess, you dog and be candid. * * * It may be profligate, but is it not *life*, is it not *the thing*?"

Another critical complaint is that the slender plot of the poem is buried under an excess of authorial digression. It is a mistake, however, to read *Don Juan* primarily for the story. The controlling element is not the narrative but the narrator: his play of mind and volatility of mood constitute the center of interest, and his temperament gives the work its unity. The poem is really an incessant monologue, in the course of which a story manages to be told. It opens with the first-person pronoun and immediately lets us into the story-teller's predicament: "I want a hero * * * " The voice then goes on, for almost two thousand stanzas, with effortless volubility and bewildering shifts of mood and perspective, using the occasion of Juan's misadventures to confide to us the speaker's thoughts and judgments upon all the major institutions, activities, and values of Western society.

What Byron discovered in *Don Juan* was how to give literary expression to that aspect of his temperament which, in real life, his self-consciousness and reserve permitted him to display only in the security of a circle of intimate friends or in his wonderfully vivacious letters to people he trusted. The poet who in his brilliantly successful youth created the gloomy and misanthropic Byronic hero, in his later and sadder life created a character (not the hero, but the narrator of *Don Juan*) who is one of the great comic inventions in literature.

From Don Juan
Fragment[1]

I would to heaven that I were so much clay,
    As I am blood, bone, marrow, passion, feeling—
Because at least the past were passed away—
    And for the future—(but I write this reeling,
Having got drunk exceedingly today,   5
    So that I seem to stand upon the ceiling)
I say—the future is a serious matter—
And so—for God's sake—hock[2] and soda water!

From *Canto I*

1

I want a hero: an uncommon want,
    When every year and month sends forth a new one,
Till, after cloying the gazettes with cant,
    The age discovers he is not the true one;
Of such as these I should not care to vaunt,   5
    I'll therefore take our ancient friend Don Juan—
We all have seen him, in the pantomime,[1]
Sent to the devil somewhat ere his time.

* * *

5

Brave men were living before Agamemnon[2]
    And since, exceeding valorous and sage,
A good deal like him too, though quite the same none;   35

---

1. This stanza was written on the back of part of the MS. of Canto I.
2. A white Rhine wine, from the German *Hochheimer*.
1. The Juan legend was a popular subject in English pantomime.
2. In Homer's *Iliad*, the king commanding the Greeks in the siege of Troy. This line is translated from an ode by Horace.

But then they shone not on the poet's page,
And so have been forgotten—I condemn none,
  But can't find any in the present age
Fit for my poem (that is, for my new one);
So, as I said, I'll take my friend Don Juan.   40

6

Most epic poets plunge *"in medias res"*[3]
  (Horace makes this the heroic turnpike road),
And then your hero tells, whene'er you please,
  What went before—by way of episode,
While seated after dinner at his ease,   45
  Beside his mistress in some soft abode,
Palace, or garden, paradise, or cavern,
Which serves the happy couple for a tavern.

7

That is the usual method, but not mine—
  My way is to begin with the beginning;   50
The regularity of my design
  Forbids all wandering as the worst of sinning,
And therefore I shall open with a line
  (Although it cost me half an hour in spinning)
Narrating somewhat of Don Juan's father,   55
And also of his mother, if you'd rather.

8

In Seville was he born, a pleasant city,
  Famous for oranges and women—he
Who has not seen it will be much to pity,
  So says the proverb—and I quite agree;   60
Of all the Spanish towns is none more pretty,
  Cadiz perhaps—but that you soon may see—
Don Juan's parents lived beside the river,
A noble stream, and called the Guadalquivir.

9

His father's name was Jóse[4]—*Don*, of course,   65
  A true Hidalgo, free from every stain
Of Moor or Hebrew blood, he traced his source
  Through the most Gothic gentlemen of Spain;
A better cavalier ne'er mounted horse,
  Or, being mounted, e'er got down again,   70
Than Jóse, who begot our hero, who
Begot—but that's to come—Well, to renew:

10

His mother was a learned lady, famed
  For every branch of every science known—
In every Christian language ever named,
  With virtues equaled by her wit alone: 75
She made the cleverest people quite ashamed,
  And even the good with inward envy groan,

---

3. "Into the middle of things" (Horace, *Ars Poetica* 148).

4. Normally "José," of course; Byron transferred the accent for his meter.

Finding themselves so very much exceeded
In their own way by all the things that she did.   80

11

Her memory was a mine: she knew by heart
    All Calderon and greater part of Lopé,[5]
So that if any actor missed his part
    She could have served him for the prompter's copy;
For her Feinagle's[6] were an useless art,   85
    And he himself obliged to shut up shop—he
Could never make a memory so fine as
That which adorned the brain of Donna Inez.

12

Her favorite science was the mathematical,
    Her noblest virtue was her magnanimity,   90
Her wit (she sometimes tried at wit) was Attic[7] all,
    Her serious sayings darkened to sublimity;
In short, in all things she was fairly what I call
    A prodigy—her morning dress was dimity,
Her evening silk, or, in the summer, muslin,   95
And other stuffs, with which I won't stay puzzling.

13

She knew the Latin—that is, "the Lord's prayer,"
    And Greek—the alphabet—I'm nearly sure;
She read some French romances here and there,
    Although her mode of speaking was not pure;   100
For native Spanish she had no great care,
    At least her conversation was obscure;
Her thoughts were theorems, her words a problem,
As if she deemed that mystery would ennoble 'em.

* * *

22

'Tis pity learned virgins ever wed
    With persons of no sort of education,
Or gentlemen, who, though well born and bred,   170
    Grow tired of scientific conversation:
I don't choose to say much upon this head,
    I'm a plain man, and in a single station,
But—Oh! ye lords of ladies intellectual.   175
Inform us truly, have they not henpecked you all?

23

Don Jóse and his lady quarrelled—*why*,
    Not any of the many could divine,
Though several thousand people chose to try,
    'Twas surely no concern of theirs nor mine;
I loathe that low vice, curiosity;   180
    But if there's anything in which I shine,

5. Lope de Vega and Calderón de la Barca, the great Spanish dramatists of the early 17th century.
6. Gregor von Feinagle, a German expert on mnemonics, who had lectured in England in 1811.
7. Athenian. The common phrase "Attic salt" signifies the famed wit of the Athenians.

'Tis in arranging all my friends' affairs,
Not having, of my own, domestic cares.

24

And so I interfered, and with the best   185
   Intentions, but their treatment was not kind;
I think the foolish people were possessed,
   For neither of them could I ever find,
Although their porter afterwards confessed—
   But that's no matter, and the worst's behind,   190
For little Juan o'er me threw, downstairs,
A pail of housemaid's water unawares.

25

A little curly-headed, good-for-nothing,
   And mischief-making monkey from his birth;
His parents ne'er agreed except in doting   195
   Upon the most unquiet imp on earth;
Instead of quarreling, had they been but both in
   Their senses, they'd have sent young master forth
To school, or had him soundly whipped at home,
To teach him manners for the time to come.   200

26

Don Jóse and the Donna Inez led
   For some time an unhappy sort of life,
Wishing each other, not divorced, but dead;
   They lived respectably as man and wife,
Their conduct was exceedingly well-bred,   205
   And gave no outward signs of inward strife,
Until at length the smothered fire broke out,
And put the business past all kind of doubt.

27

For Inez called some druggists and physicians,
   And tried to prove her loving lord was *mad*,[8]   210
But as he had some lucid intermissions,
   She next decided he was only *bad*;
Yet when they asked her for her depositions,
   No sort of explanation could be had,
Save that her duty both to man and God   215
Required this conduct—which seemed very odd.

28

She kept a journal, where his faults were noted,
   And opened certain trunks of books and letters,
All which might, if occasion served, be quoted;
   And then she had all Seville for abettors,   220
Besides her good old grandmother (who doted);
   The hearers of her case became repeaters,
Then advocates, inquisitors, and judges,
Some for amusement, others for old grudges.

8. Lady Byron had thought her husband might be insane, and sought medical advice on the matter. This and other passages obviously allude to his wife, although Byron insisted that Donna Inez was not intended to be a caricature of Lady Byron.

29

And then this best and meekest woman bore   225
    With such serenity her husband's woes,
Just as the Spartan ladies did of yore,
    Who saw their spouses killed, and nobly chose
Never to say a word about them more—
    Calmly she heard each calumny that rose,   230
And saw *his* agonies with such sublimity,
That all the world exclaimed, "What magnanimity!"

* * *

32

Their friends had tried at reconciliation,
    Then their relations, who made matters worse   250
('Twere hard to tell upon a like occasion
    To whom it may be best to have recourse—
I can't say much for friend or yet relation);
    The lawyers did their utmost for divorce,
But scarce a fee was paid on either side   255
Before, unluckily, Don Jóse died.

33

He died: and most unluckily, because
    According to all hints I could collect
From counsel learned in those kinds of laws
    (Although their talk's obscure and circumspect),   260
His death contrived to spoil a charming cause;
    A thousand pities also with respect
To public feeling, which on this occasion
Was manifested in a great sensation.

* * *

37

Dying intestate, Juan was sole heir
    To a chancery suit,[9] and messuages, and lands,   290
Which, with a long minority and care,
    Promised to turn out well in proper hands:
Inez became sole guardian, which was fair,
    And answered but to nature's just demands;
An only son left with an only mother   295
Is brought up much more wisely than another.

38

Sagest of women, even of widows, she
    Resolved that Juan should be quite a paragon,
And worthy of the noblest pedigree
    (His sire was of Castile, his dam from Aragon).   300
Then for accomplishments of chivalry,
    In case our lord the king should go to war again,
He learned the arts of riding, fencing, gunnery,
And how to scale a fortress—or a nunnery.

9. A suit in what was then the highest   "Messuages": houses and the adjoining
English court, notorious for its delays.   lands.

39

But that which Donna Inez most desired,
    And saw into herself each day before all
The learned tutors whom for him she hired,
    Was that his breeding should be strictly moral:
Much into all his studies she inquired,
    And so they were submitted first to her, all,   310
Arts, sciences, no branch was made a mystery
To Juan's eyes, excepting natural history.[1]

40

The languages, especially the dead,
    The sciences, and most of all the abstruse,
The arts, at least all such as could be said   315
    To be the most remote from common use,
In all these he was much and deeply read;
    But not a page of anything that's loose,
Or hints continuation of the species,
Was ever suffered, lest he should grow vicious.   320

41

His classic studies made a little puzzle,
    Because of filthy loves of gods and goddesses,
Who in the earlier ages raised a bustle,
    But never put on pantaloons or bodices;
His reverend tutors had at times a tussle,   325
    And for their *Aeneids*, *Iliads*, and *Odysseys*,
Were forced to make an odd sort of apology,
For Donna Inez dreaded the mythology.

42

Ovid's a rake, as half his verses show him,
    Anacreon's morals are a still worse sample,   330
Catullus scarcely has a decent poem,
    I don't think Sappho's *Ode* a good example,
Although Longinus tells us there is no hymn
    Where the sublime soars forth on wings more ample;[2]
But Virgil's songs are pure, except that horrid one   335
Beginning with "*Formosum Pastor Corydon*."[3]

43

Lucretius' irreligion[4] is too strong
    For early stomachs, to prove wholesome food;
I can't help thinking Juvenal[5] was wrong,
    Although no doubt his real intent was good,   340
For speaking out so plainly in his song,
    So much indeed as to be downright rude;

305

1. Which includes biology and physiology.
2. The Greek rhetorician Longinus praises a passage from Sappho in *On the Sublime* X.
3. Virgil's *Eclogue II* begins: "The shepherd, Corydon, burned with love for the handsome Alexis."
4. In *De rerum natura* ("On the Nature of Things") Lucretius sets out to show that the universe can be explained without reference to any god.
5. The Latin satires of Juvenal attacked the corruption of Roman society in the first century A.D.

And then what proper person can be partial
To all those nauseous epigrams of Martial?

44

Juan was taught from out the best edition,   345
    Expurgated by learned men, who place,
Judiciously, from out the schoolboy's vision,
    The grosser parts; but fearful to deface
Too much their modest bard by this omission,
    And pitying sore his mutilated case,   350
They only add them all in an appendix,[6]
Which saves, in fact, the trouble of an index.

* * *

52

For my part I say nothing—nothing—but
    This I will say—my reasons are my own—   410
That if I had an only son to put
    To school (as God be praised that I have none)
'Tis not with Donna Inez I would shut
    Him up to learn his catechism alone,
No—no—I'd send him out betimes to college,   415
For there it was I picked up my own knowledge.

53

For there one learns—'tis not for me to boast,
    Though I acquired—but I pass over *that*,
As well as all the Greek I since have lost:
    I say that there's the place—but *"Verbum sat,"*[7]   420
I think I picked up too, as well as most,
    Knowledge of matters—but no matter *what*—
I never married—but, I think, I know
That sons should not be educated so.

54

Young Juan now was sixteen years of age,   425
    Tall, handsome, slender, but well knit: he seemed
Active, though not so sprightly, as a page;
    And everybody but his mother deemed
Him almost man; but she flew in a rage
    And bit her lips (for else she might have screamed)   430
If any said so, for to be precocious
Was in her eyes a thing the most atrocious.

55

Amongst her numerous acquaintance, all
    Selected for discretion and devotion,
There was the Donna Julia, whom to call   435
    Pretty were but to give a feeble notion
Of many charms in her as natural
    As sweetness to the flower, or salt to ocean,
Her zone[8] to Venus, or his bow to Cupid
(But this last simile is trite and stupid).   440

6. "Fact! There is, or was, such an edition, with all the obnoxious epigrams
of Martial placed by themselves at the
end" [Byron's note].
7. A word [to the wise] is sufficient.
8. Girdle.

56

The darkness of her Oriental eye
   Accorded with her Moorish origin
(Her blood was not all Spanish, by the by;
   In Spain, you know, this is a sort of sin).
When proud Granada fell, and, forced to fly,   445
   Boabdil wept,[9] of Donna Julia's kin
Some went to Africa, some stayed in Spain,
Her great-great-grandmamma chose to remain.

57

She married (I forget the pedigree)
   With an hidalgo,[1] who transmitted down   450
His blood less noble than such blood should be;
   At such alliances his sires would frown,
In that point so precise in each degree
   That they bred *in and in*, as might be shown,
Marrying their cousins—nay, their aunts, and nieces,   455
Which always spoils the breed, if it increases.

58

This heathenish cross restored the breed again,
   Ruined its blood, but much improved its flesh;
For from a root the ugliest in old Spain
   Sprung up a branch as beautiful as fresh;   460
The sons no more were short, the daughters plain:
   But there's a rumor which I fain would hush,
'Tis said that Donna Julia's grandmamma
Produced her Don more heirs at love than law.

59

However this might be, the race went on   465
   Improving still through every generation,
Until it centered in an only son,
   Who left an only daughter; my narration
May have suggested that this single one
   Could be but Julia (whom on this occasion   470
I shall have much to speak about), and she
Was married, charming, chaste, and twenty-three.

60

Her eye (I'm very fond of handsome eyes)
   Was large and dark, suppressing half its fire
Until she spoke, then through its soft disguise   475
   Flashed an expression more of pride than ire,
And love than either; and there would arise
   A something in them which was not desire,
But would have been, perhaps, but for the soul
Which struggled through and chastened down the whole.   480

61

Her glossy hair was clustered o'er a brow
   Bright with intelligence, and fair, and smooth;

9. The last Moorish king of Granada
(then a province in Spain) wept when
his capital fell to the Spaniards (1492).

1. A Spanish nobleman of the lower
class.

Her eyebrow's shape was like the aërial bow,
  Her cheek all purple with the beam of youth,
Mounting, at times, to a transparent glow,   485
  As if her veins ran lightning; she, in sooth,
Possessed an air and grace by no means common:
  Her stature tall—I hate a dumpy woman.

62

Wedded she was some years, and to a man
  Of fifty, and such husbands are in plenty;   490
And yet, I think, instead of such a ONE
  'Twere better to have TWO of five-and-twenty,
Especially in countries near the sun:
  And now I think on't, "*mi vien in mente*,"[2]
Ladies even of the most uneasy virtue   495
  Prefer a spouse whose age is short of thirty.

63

'Tis a sad thing, I cannot choose but say,
  And all the fault of that indecent sun,
Who cannot leave alone our helpless clay,
  But will keep baking, broiling, burning on,   500
That howsoever people fast and pray,
  The flesh is frail, and so the soul undone:
What men call gallantry, and gods adultery,
Is much more common where the climate's sultry.

64

Happy the nations of the moral North!   505
  Where all is virtue, and the winter season
Sends sin, without a rag on, shivering forth
  ('Twas snow that brought St. Anthony to reason);[3]
Where juries cast up what a wife is worth
  By laying whate'er sum, in mulct,[4] they please on 510
The lover, who must pay a handsome price,
Because it is a marketable vice.

65

Alfonso was the name of Julia's lord,
  A man well looking for his years, and who
Was neither much beloved nor yet abhorred: 515
  They lived together as most people do,
Suffering each other's foibles by accord,
  And not exactly either *one* or *two*;
Yet he was jealous, though he did not show it,
For jealousy dislikes the world to know it.

* * *

69

Juan she saw, and, as a pretty child,   545
  Caressed him often—such a thing might be
Quite innocently done, and harmless styled,

2. "It comes to my mind."
3. "For the particulars of St. Anthony's recipe for hot blood in cold weather, see Mr. Alban Butler's *Lives of the Saints*" [Byron's note].
4. By way of a fine or legal penalty.

When she had twenty years, and thirteen he;
But I am not so sure I should have smiled
　　When he was sixteen, Julia twenty-three;　　　　550
These few short years make wondrous alterations,
Particularly amongst sunburnt nations.

70

Whate'er the cause might be, they had become
　　Changed; for the dame grew distant, the youth shy,
Their looks cast down, their greetings almost dumb,　　555
　　And much embarrassment in either eye;
There surely will be little doubt with some
　　That Donna Julia knew the reason why,
But as for Juan, he had no more notion
Than he who never saw the sea, of ocean.　　　　560

71

Yet Julia's very coldness still was kind,
　　And tremulously gentle her small hand
Withdrew itself from his, but left behind
　　A little pressure, thrilling, and so bland
And slight, so very slight, that to the mind　　　　565
　　'Twas but a doubt; but ne'er magician's wand
Wrought change with all Armida's[5] fairy art
Like what this light touch left on Juan's heart.

72

And if she met him, though she smiled no more,
　　She looked a sadness sweeter than her smile,　　570
As if her heart had deeper thoughts in store
　　She must not own, but cherished more the while,
For that compression in its burning core;
　　Even innocence itself has many a wile,
And will not dare to trust itself with truth,　　　　575
And love is taught hypocrisy from youth.

* * *

76

She vowed she never would see Juan more,
　　And next day paid a visit to his mother,
And looked extremely at the opening door,
　　Which, by the Virgin's grace, let in another;
Grateful she was, and yet a little sore—　　　　605
　　Again it opens, it can be no other,
'Tis surely Juan now—No! I'm afraid
That night the Virgin was no further prayed.

77

She now determined that a virtuous woman
　　Should rather face and overcome temptation,
That flight was base and dastardly, and no man　　610
　　Should ever give her heart the least sensation;
That is to say, a thought beyond the common

5. The sorceress who seduces Rinaldo in Tasso's *Jerusalem Delivered.*

Preference, that we must feel upon occasion,
For people who are pleasanter than others,   615
But then they only seem so many brothers.

78

And even if by chance—and who can tell?
   The devil's so very sly—she should discover
That all within was not so very well,
   And, if still free, that such or such a lover   620
Might please perhaps, a virtuous wife can quell
   Such thoughts, and be the better when they're over;
And if the man should ask, 'tis but denial:
I recommend young ladies to make trial.

79

And then there are such things as love divine,   625
   Bright and immaculate, unmixed and pure,
Such as the angels think so very fine,
   And matrons, who would be no less secure,
Platonic, perfect, "just such love as mine":
   Thus Julia said—and thought so, to be sure,   630
And so I'd have her think, were I the man
On whom her reveries celestial ran.

* * *

86

So much for Julia. Now we'll turn to Juan.
   Poor little fellow! he had no idea
Of his own case, and never hit the true one;
   In feelings quick as Ovid's Miss Medea,[6]
He puzzled over what he found a new one,   685
   But not as yet imagined it could be a
Thing quite in course, and not at all alarming,
Which, with a little patience, might grow charming.

* * *

90

Young Juan wandered by the glassy brooks,
   Thinking unutterable things; he threw
Himself at length within the leafy nooks   715
   Where the wild branch of the cork forest grew;
There poets find materials for their books,
   And every now and then we read them through,
So that their plan and prosody are eligible,
Unless, like Wordsworth, they prove unintelligible. 720

91

He, Juan (and not Wordsworth), so pursued
   His self-communion with his own high soul,
Until his mighty heart, in its great mood,
   Had mitigated part, though not the whole
Of its disease; he did the best he could   725

---

6. In *Metamorphoses* VII, Ovid tells the story of Medea's mad infatuation for Jason.

With things not very subject to control,
And turned, without perceiving his condition,
Like Coleridge, into a metaphysician.

92

He thought about himself, and the whole earth,
    Of man the wonderful, and of the stars,   730
And how the deuce they ever could have birth;
    And then he thought of earthquakes, and of wars,
How many miles the moon might have in girth,
    Of air-balloons, and of the many bars
To perfect knowledge of the boundless skies—   735
And then he thought of Donna Julia's eyes.

93

In thoughts like these true wisdom may discern
    Longings sublime, and aspirations high,
Which some are born with, but the most part learn
    To plague themselves withal, they know not why: 740
'Twas strange that one so young should thus concern
    His brain about the action of the sky;
If *you* think 'twas philosophy that this did,
I can't help thinking puberty assisted.

94

He pored upon the leaves, and on the flowers,   745
    And heard a voice in all the winds; and then
He thought of wood nymphs and immortal bowers,
    And how the goddesses came down to men:
He missed the pathway, he forgot the hours,
    And when he looked upon his watch again,   750
He found how much old Time had been a winner—
He also found that he had lost his dinner.

             * * *

103

'Twas on a summer's day—the sixth of June—
    I like to be particular in dates,
Not only of the age, and year, but moon;
    They are a sort of post house, where the Fates   820
Change horses, making history change its tune,
    Then spur away o'er empires and o'er states,
Leaving at last not much besides chronology,
Excepting the post-obits[7] of theology.

104

'Twas on the sixth of June, about the hour   825
    Of half-past six—perhaps still nearer seven—
When Julia sate within as pretty a bower
    As e'er held houri in that heathenish heaven
Described by Mahomet, and Anacreon Moore,[8]

7. I.e., post-obit bonds (*post obitum*, "after death"): loans to an heir which fall due after the death of the person whose estate he is to inherit. Byron's meaning is probably that only theology purports to tell us what rewards are due in heaven.

8. Byron's friend, the poet Thomas Moore, who had translated the *Odes* of Anacreon; Byron is alluding to the

To whom the lyre and laurels have been given,   830
With all the trophies of triumphant song—
He won them well, and may he wear them long!

105

She sate, but not alone; I know not well
  How this same interview had taken place,
And even if I knew, I should not tell—   835
  People should hold their tongues in any case;
No matter how or why the thing befell,
  But there she and Juan, face to face—
When two such faces are so, 'twould be wise,
But very difficult, to shut their eyes.   840

106

How beautiful she looked! her conscious[9] heart
  Glowed in her cheek, and yet she felt no wrong.
Oh Love! how perfect is thy mystic art,
  Strengthening the weak, and trampling on the strong,
How self-deceitful is the sagest part   845
  Of mortals whom thy lure hath led along—
The precipice she stood on was immense,
So was her creed[1] in her own innocence.

107

She thought of her own strength, and Juan's youth,
  And of the folly of all prudish fears,
Victorious virtue, and domestic truth,   850
  And then of Don Alfonso's fifty years:
I wish these last had not occurred, in sooth,
  Because that number rarely much endears,
And through all climes, the snowy and the sunny,
Sounds ill in love, whate'er it may in money.   855

* * *

113

The sun set, and up rose the yellow moon:
  The devil's in the moon for mischief; they
Who called her CHASTE, methinks, began too soon
  Their nomenclature; there is not a day,
The longest, not the twenty-first of June,   900
  Sees half the business in a wicked way
On which three single hours of moonshine smile—
And then she looks so modest all the while.

114

There is a dangerous silence in that hour,   905
  A stillness, which leaves room for the full soul
To open all itself, without the power
  Of calling wholly back its self-control;
The silver light which, hallowing tree and tower,
  Sheds beauty and deep softness o'er the whole,   910

tale of *Paradise and the Peri* in   9. Feelingful.
Moore's Oriental poem *Lalla Rookh*.   1. Belief.

Breathes also to the heart, and o'er it throws
A loving languor, which is not repose.

115

And Julia sate with Juan, half embraced
    And half retiring from the glowing arm,
Which trembled like the bosom where 'twas placed;   915
    Yet still she must have thought there was no harm,
Or else 'twere easy to withdraw her waist;
    But then the situation had its charm,
And then——God knows what next——I can't go on;
I'm almost sorry that I e'er begun.   920

116

Oh Plato! Plato! you have paved the way,
    With your confounded fantasies, to more
Immoral conduct by the fancied sway
    Your system feigns o'er the controlless core
Of human hearts, than all the long array   925
    Of poets and romancers: You're a bore,
A charlatan, a coxcomb—and have been,
At best, no better than a go-between.

117

And Julia's voice was lost, except in sighs,
    Until too late for useful conversation;   930
The tears were gushing from her gentle eyes,
    I wish, indeed, they had not had occasion,
But who, alas! can love, and then be wise?
    Not that remorse did not oppose temptation;
A little still she strove, and much repented,   935
And whispering "I will ne'er consent"—consented.

* * *

126

'Tis sweet to win, no matter how, one's laurels
    By blood or ink; 'tis sweet to put an end
To strife; 'tis sometimes sweet to have our quarrels,
    Particularly with a tiresome friend:
Sweet is old wine in bottles, ale in barrels;   1005
    Dear is the helpless creature we defend
Against the world; and dear the schoolboy spot
We ne'er forget, though there we are forgot.

127

But sweeter still than this, than these, than all,
    Is first and passionate love—it stands alone,   1010
Like Adam's recollection of his fall;
    The tree of knowledge has been plucked—all's known—
And life yields nothing further to recall
    Worthy of this ambrosial sin, so shown,
No doubt in fable, as the unforgiven   1015
Fire which Prometheus[2] filched for us from heaven.

* * *

2. The Titan Prometheus incurred the wrath of Jupiter by stealing fire for mankind from heaven.

133

Man's a phenomenon, one knows not what,
　And wonderful beyond all wondrous measure;
'Tis pity though, in this sublime world, that
　Pleasure's a sin, and sometimes sin's a pleasure;　　1060
Few mortals know what end they would be at,
　But whether glory, power, or love, or treasure,
The path is through perplexing ways, and when
The goal is gained, we die, you know—and then——

134

What then?—I do not know, no more do you——　　1065
　And so good night.—Return we to our story:
'Twas in November, when fine days are few,
　And the far mountains wax a little hoary,
And clap a white cape on their mantles blue;
　And the sea dashes round the promontory,　　1070
And the loud breaker boils against the rock,
And sober suns must set at five o'clock.

135

'Twas, as the watchmen say, a cloudy night;
　No moon, no stars, the wind was low or loud
By gusts, and many a sparkling hearth was bright　　1075
　With the piled wood, round which the family crowd;
There's something cheerful in that sort of light,
　Even as a summer sky's without a cloud:
I'm fond of fire, and crickets, and all that,
A lobster salad, and champagne, and chat.　　1080

136

'Twas midnight—Donna Julia was in bed,
　Sleeping, most probably—when at her door
Arose a clatter might awake the dead,
　If they had never been awoke before,
And that they have been so we all have read,　　1085
　And are to be so, at the least, once more;
The door was fastened, but with voice and fist
First knocks were heard, then "Madam—Madam—hist!

137

"For God's sake, Madam—Madam—here's my master,
　With more than half the city at his back——　　1090
Was ever heard of such a cursed disaster!
　'Tis not my fault—I kept good watch—Alack!
Do, pray, undo the bolt a little faster——
　They're on the stair just now, and in a crack
Will all be here; perhaps he yet may fly——　　1095
Surely the window's not so *very* high!"

138

By this time Don Alfonso was arrived,
　With torches, friends, and servants in great number;
The major part of them had long been wived,
　And therefore paused not to disturb the slumber　　1100
Of any wicked woman, who contrived

By stealth her husband's temples to encumber:[3]
Examples of this kind are so contagious,
Were *one* not punished, *all* would be outrageous.

139

I can't tell how, or why, or what suspicion   1105
   Could enter into Don Alfonso's head;
But for a cavalier of his condition[4]
   It surely was exceedingly ill-bred,
Without a word of previous admonition,
   To hold a levee[5] round his lady's bed,   1110
And summon lackeys, armed with fire and sword,
To prove himself the thing he most abhorred.

140

Poor Donna Julia! starting as from sleep
   (Mind that I do not say she had not slept),
Began at once to scream, and yawn, and weep;   1115
   Her maid, Antonia, who was an adept,
Contrived to fling the bedclothes in a heap,
   As if she had just now from out them crept:
I can't tell why she should take all this trouble
To prove her mistress had been sleeping double.   1120

141

But Julia mistress, and Antonia maid,
   Appeared like two poor harmless women, who
Of goblins, but still more of men, afraid,
   Had thought one man might be deterred by two,
And therefore side by side were gently laid,   1125
   Until the hours of absence should run through,
And truant husband should return, and say,
"My dear, I was the first who came away."

142

Now Julia found at length a voice, and cried,
   "In heaven's name, Don Alfonso, what d'ye mean?   1130
Has madness seized you? would that I had died
   Ere such a monster's victim I had been!
What may this midnight violence betide,
   A sudden fit of drunkenness or spleen?
Dare you suspect me, whom the thought would kill?   1135
Search, then, the room!"—Alfonso said, "I will."

143

He searched, *they* searched, and rummaged everywhere,
   Closet and clothes-press, chest and window seat,
And found much linen, lace, and several pair
   Of stockings, slippers, brushes, combs, complete,   1140
With other articles of ladies fair,
   To keep them beautiful, or leave them neat:
Arras they pricked and curtains with their swords,
And wounded several shutters, and some boards.

3. Horns growing on the forehead were   4. Rank.
the traditional emblem of the cuckolded   5. Morning reception.
husband.

144

Under the bed they searched, and there they found—⠀⠀⠀1145
⠀⠀No matter what—it was not that they sought;
They opened windows, gazing if the ground
⠀⠀Had signs or footmarks, but the earth said nought;
And then they stared each other's faces round:
⠀⠀'Tis odd, not one of all these seekers thought,⠀⠀⠀1150
And seems to me almost a sort of blunder,
Of looking *in* the bed as well as under.

145

During this inquisition Julia's tongue
⠀⠀Was not asleep—"Yes, search and search," she cried,
"Insult on insult heap, and wrong on wrong!⠀⠀⠀1155
⠀⠀It was for this that I became a bride!
For this in silence I have suffered long
⠀⠀A husband like Alfonso at my side;
But now I'll bear no more, nor here remain,
If there be law or lawyers in all Spain.⠀⠀⠀1160

146

"Yes, Don Alfonso! husband now no more,
⠀⠀If ever you indeed deserved the name,
Is't worthy of your years?—you have threescore—
⠀⠀Fifty, or sixty, it is all the same—
Is't wise or fitting, causeless to explore⠀⠀⠀1165
⠀⠀For facts against a virtuous woman's fame?
Ungrateful, perjured, barbarous Don Alfonso,
How dare you think your lady would go on so?"

* * *

159

The Senhor Don Alfonso stood confused;⠀⠀⠀1265
⠀⠀Antonia bustled round the ransacked room,
And, turning up her nose, with looks abused
⠀⠀Her master, and his myrmidons, of whom
Not one, except the attorney, was amused;
⠀⠀He, like Achates,[6] faithful to the tomb,⠀⠀⠀1270
So there were quarrels, cared not for the cause,
Knowing they must be settled by the laws.

160

With prying snub nose, and small eyes, he stood,
⠀⠀Following Antonia's motions here and there,
With much suspicion in his attitude;⠀⠀⠀1275
⠀⠀For reputations he had little care;
So that a suit or action were made good,
⠀⠀Small pity had he for the young and fair,
And ne'er believed in negatives, till these
Were proved by competent false witnesses.⠀⠀⠀1280

6. The *fidus Achates* ("faithful Achates") of Virgil's *Aeneid*, whose loyalty to Aeneas has become proverbial.

161

But Don Alfonso stood with downcast looks,
   And, truth to say, he made a foolish figure;
When, after searching in five hundred nooks,
   And treating a young wife with so much rigor,
He gained no point, except some self-rebukes,   1285
   Added to those his lady with such vigor
Had poured upon him for the last half hour,
Quick, thick, and heavy—as a thundershower.

162

At first he tried to hammer an excuse,
   To which the sole reply was tears, and sobs,   1290
And indications of hysterics, whose
   Prologue is always certain throes, and throbs,
Gasps, and whatever else the owners choose—
   Alfonso saw his wife, and thought of Job's;[7]
He saw too, in perspective, her relations,   1295
And then he tried to muster all his patience.

163

He stood in act to speak, or rather stammer,
   But sage Antonia cut him short before
The anvil of his speech received the hammer,
   With "Pray, sir, leave the room, and say no more,   1300
Or madam dies."—Alfonso muttered, "D—n her."
   But nothing else, the time of words was o'er;
He cast a rueful look or two, and did,
He knew not wherefore, that which he was bid.

164

With him retired his "*posse comitatus*,"[8]   1305
   The attorney last, who lingered near the door
Reluctantly, still tarrying there as late as
   Antonia let him—not a little sore
At this most strange and unexplained "*hiatus*"
   In Don Alfonso's facts, which just now wore   1310
An awkward look; as he revolved the case,
The door was fastened in his legal face.

165

No sooner was it bolted, than—Oh shame!
   Oh sin! Oh sorrow! and Oh womankind!
How can you do such things and keep your fame,
   Unless this world, and t'other too, be blind?   1315
Nothing so dear as an unfilched good name!
   But to proceed—for there is more behind:
With much heartfelt reluctance be it said,
Young Juan slipped, half-smothered, from the bed.   1320

7. Job's wife had advised her afflicted husband to "curse God, and die" (Job ii.9).
8. The complete form of the modern word "posse" (*posse comitatus* means literally "power of the county," i.e., the body of citizens summoned by a sheriff to preserve order in the county).

166

He had been hid—I don't pretend to say
  How, nor can I indeed describe the where—
Young, slender, and packed easily, he lay,
  No doubt, in little compass, round or square;
But pity him I neither must nor may   1325
  His suffocation by that pretty pair;
'Twere better, sure, to die so, than be shut
With maudlin Clarence in his malmsey butt.[9]

* * *

169

What's to be done? Alfonso will be back   1345
  The moment he has sent his fools away.
Antonia's skill was put upon the rack,
  But no device could be brought into play—
And how to parry the renewed attack?
  Besides, it wanted but few hours of day: 1350
Antonia puzzled; Julia did not speak,
But pressed her bloodless lip to Juan's cheek.

170

He turned his lip to hers, and with his hand
  Called back the tangles of her wandering hair;
Even then their love they could not all command,   1355
  And half forgot their danger and despair:
Antonia's patience now was at a stand—
  "Come, come, 'tis no time now for fooling there,"
She whispered, in great wrath—"I must deposit
This pretty gentleman within the closet."   1360

* * *

173

Now, Don Alfonso entering, but alone,
  Closed the oration of the trusty maid:
She loitered, and he told her to be gone,
  An order somewhat sullenly obeyed;   1380
However, present remedy was none,
  And no great good seemed answered if she stayed:
Regarding both with slow and sidelong view,
She snuffed the candle, curtsied, and withdrew.

174

Alfonso paused a minute—then begun   1385
  Some strange excuses for his late proceeding;
He would not justify what he had done,
  To say the best, it was extreme ill-breeding;
But there were ample reasons for it, none
  Of which he specified in this his pleading: 1390

9. The Duke of Clarence, brother of Richard III, was reputed to have been assassinated by being drowned in a cask ("butt") of malmsey, a sweet and aromatic wine.

His speech was a fine sample, on the whole,
Of rhetoric, which the learned call *"rigmarole."*[1]

* * *

180

Alfonso closed his speech, and begged her pardon,
   Which Julia half withheld, and then half granted,
And laid conditions, he thought very hard on,   1435
   Denying several little things he wanted:
He stood like Adam lingering near his garden,
   With useless penitence perplexed and haunted,
Beseeching she no further would refuse,
When, lo! he stumbled o'er a pair of shoes.   1440

181

A pair of shoes!—what then? not much, if they
   Are such as fit with ladies' feet, but these
(No one can tell how much I grieve to say)
   Were masculine; to see them, and to seize,
Was but a moment's act.—Ah! well-a-day!   1445
   My teeth begin to chatter, my veins freeze—
Alfonso first examined well their fashion,
And then flew out into another passion.

182

He left the room for his relinquished sword,
   And Julia instant to the closet flew.
"Fly, Juan, fly! for heaven's sake—not a word—   1450
   The door is open—you may yet slip through
The passage you so often have explored—
   Here is the garden key—Fly—fly—Adieu!
Haste—haste! I hear Alfonso's hurrying feet—   1455
Day has not broke—there's no one in the street."

183

None can say that this was not good advice,
   The only mischief was, it came too late;
Of all experience 'tis the usual price,
   A sort of income tax laid on by fate: 1460
Juan had reached the room door in a trice,
   And might have done so by the garden gate,
But met Alfonso in his dressing gown,
Who threatened death—so Juan knocked him down.

184

Dire was the scuffle, and out went the light;   1465
   Antonia cried out "Rape!" and Julia "Fire!"
But not a servant stirred to aid the fight.
   Alfonso, pommeled to his heart's desire,
Swore lustily he'd be revenged this night;
   And Juan, too, blasphemed an octave higher;   1470
His blood was up: though young, he was a Tartar,[2]
And not at all disposed to prove a martyr.

---

1. Illogical sequence of vague statements.

2. "To catch a Tartar" is to tackle someone too strong for his assailant.

185

Alfonso's sword had dropped ere he could draw it,
 And they continued battling hand to hand,
For Juan very luckily ne'er saw it;   1475
 His temper not being under great command,
If at that moment he had chanced to claw it,
 Alfonso's days had not been in the land
Much longer.—Think of husbands', lover's lives!
And how ye may be doubly widows—wives!   1480

186

Alfonso grappled to detain the foe,
 And Juan throttled him to get away,
And blood ('twas from the nose) began to flow;
 At last, as they more faintly wrestling lay,
Juan contrived to give an awkward blow,   1485
 And then his only garment quite gave way;
He fled, like Joseph,[3] leaving it; but there,
I doubt, all likeness ends between the pair.

187

Lights came at length, and men, and maids, who found
 An awkward spectacle their eyes before;
Antonia in hysterics, Julia swooned,   1490
 Alfonso leaning, breathless, by the door;
Some half-torn drapery scattered on the ground,
 Some blood, and several footsteps, but no more:
Juan the gate gained, turned the key about,   1495
And liking not the inside, locked the out.

188

Here ends this canto.—Need I sing, or say,
 How Juan, naked, favored by the night,
Who favors what she should not, found his way,
 And reached his home in an unseemly plight?   1500
The pleasant scandal which arose next day,
 The nine days' wonder which was brought to light,
And how Alfonso sued for a divorce,
Were in the English newspapers, of course.

189

If you would like to see the whole proceedings,   1505
 The depositions, and the cause at full,
The names of all the witnesses, the pleadings
 Of counsel to nonsuit,[4] or to annul,
There's more than one edition, and the readings
 Are various, but they none of them are dull;   1510
The best is that in shorthand ta'en by Gurney,[5]
Who to Madrid on purpose made a journey.

---

3. In Genesis xxxix.7 ff. the chaste
Joseph flees from the advances of Poti-
phar's wife, leaving "his garment in
her hand."
4. Judgment against the plaintiff for
failure to establish his case.
5. William B. Gurney, official shorthand
writer for the Houses of Parliament and
a famous court reporter.

190

But Donna Inez, to divert the train
    Of one of the most circulating scandals
That had for centuries been known in Spain,   1515
    At least since the retirement of the Vandals,[6]
First vowed (and never had she vowed in vain)
    To Virgin Mary several pounds of candles;
And then, by the advice of some old ladies,
She sent her son to be shipped off from Cadiz.   1520

191

She had resolved that he should travel through
    All European climes, by land or sea,
To mend his former morals, and get new,
    Especially in France and Italy
(At least this is the thing most people do).   1525
    Julia was sent into a convent; she
Grieved, but, perhaps, her feelings may be better
Shown in the following copy of her letter:

192

"They tell me 'tis decided; you depart:
    'Tis wise—'tis well, but not the less a pain;   1530
I have no further claim on your young heart,
    Mine is the victim, and would be again;
To love too much has been the only art
    I used—I write in haste, and if a stain
Be on this sheet, 'tis not what it appears;   1535
My eyeballs burn and throb, but have no tears.

193

"I loved, I love you, for this love have lost
    State, station, heaven, mankind's, my own esteem,
And yet cannot regret what it hath cost,
    So dear is still the memory of that dream;   1540
Yet, if I name my guilt, 'tis not to boast,
    None can deem harshlier of me than I deem:
I trace this scrawl because I cannot rest—
I've nothing to reproach, or to request.

194

"Man's love is of man's life a thing apart,   1545
    'Tis woman's whole existence; man may range
The court, camp, church, the vessel, and the mart;
    Sword, gown, gain, glory, offer in exchange
Pride, fame, ambition, to fill up his heart,
    And few there are whom these cannot estrange;   1550
Men have all these resources, we but one,
To love again, and be again undone."

* * *

6. The Germanic tribe which overran Spain and other parts of southern Europe in the 4th and 5th centuries; notorious for rape and violence.

198

This note was written upon gilt-edged paper
　With a neat little crow-quill, slight and new;
Her small white hand could hardly reach the taper,[7]
　It trembled as magnetic needles do,　　　　　　　　1580
And yet she did not let one tear escape her;
　The seal a sunflower; *"Elle vous suit partout,"*[8]
The motto, cut upon a white cornelian;
　The wax was superfine, its hue vermilion.

199

This was Don Juan's earliest scrape; but whether　　　1585
　I shall proceed with his adventures is
Dependent on the public altogether;
　We'll see, however, what they say to this,
Their favor in an author's cap's a feather,
　And no great mischief's done by their caprice;　　1590
And if their approbation we experience,
Perhaps they'll have some more about a year hence.

200

My poem's epic, and is meant to be
　Divided in twelve books; each book containing,
With love, and war, a heavy gale at sea,　　　　　　1595
　A list of ships, and captains, and kings reigning,
New characters; the episodes are three;
　A panoramic view of hell's in training,
After the style of Virgil and of Homer,
So that my name of Epic's no misnomer.　　　　　　　1600

201

All these things will be specified in time,
　With strict regard to Aristotle's rules,
The *Vade Mecum*[9] of the true sublime,
　Which makes so many poets, and some fools:
Prose poets like blank verse, I'm fond of rhyme,　　1605
　Good workmen never quarrel with their tools;
I've got new mythological machinery,
And very handsome supernatural scenery.

202

There's only one slight difference between
　Me and my epic brethren gone before,　　　　　　　1610
And here the advantage is my own, I ween
　(Not that I have not several merits more,
But this will more peculiarly be seen):
　They so embellish that 'tis quite a bore
Their labyrinth of fables to thread through,　　　　1615
Whereas this story's actually true.

---

7. The candle (in order to melt wax to seal the letter).
8. "She follows you everywhere."
9. Handbook (Latin, "go with me");

Byron is deriding the interpretation of Aristotle's *Poetics* ("rules") as a guide for writing epic and tragedy.

203

If any person doubt it, I appeal
    To history, tradition, and to facts,
To newspapers, whose truth all know and feel,
    To plays in five, and operas in three acts;   1620
All these confirm my statement a good deal,
    But that which more completely faith exacts
Is that myself, and several now in Seville,
Saw Juan's last elopement with the devil.[1]

204

If ever I should condescend to prose,   1625
    I'll write poetical commandments, which
Shall supersede beyond all doubt all those
    That went before; in these I shall enrich
My text with many things that no one knows,
    And carry precept to the highest pitch: 1630
I'll call the work "Longinus o'er a Bottle,
Or Every Poet his *own* Aristotle."

205

Thou shalt believe in Milton, Dryden, Pope;[2]
    Thou shalt not set up Wordsworth, Coleridge, Southey;
Because the first is crazed beyond all hope,   1635
    The second drunk, the third so quaint and mouthy:
With Crabbe it may be difficult to cope,
    And Campbell's Hippocrene[3] is somewhat drouthy:
Thou shalt not steal from Samuel Rogers, nor
Commit—flirtation with the muse of Moore.[4]   1640

206

Thou shalt not covet Mr. Sotheby's Muse,[5]
    His Pegasus, nor anything that's his;
Thou shalt not bear false witness like "the Blues"[6]
    (There's one, at least, is very fond of this);
Thou shalt not write, in short, but what I choose: 1645
    This is true criticism, and you may kiss—
Exactly as you please, or not,—the rod;
But if you don't, I'll lay it on, by G—d!

207

If any person should presume to assert
    This story is not moral, first I pray   1650
That they will not cry out before they're hurt,
    Then that they'll read it o'er again, and say

1. The usual plays on the Juan legend ended with Juan in hell; a recent version is George Bernard Shaw's *Man and Superman*.
2. This is one of many passages, in prose and verse, in which Byron vigorously defended Dryden and Pope against his Romantic contemporaries.
3. Fountain on Mt. Helicon whose waters supposedly gave inspiration.
4. George Crabbe, whom Byron admired, was the author of *The Village* (1783) and other realistic poems of

rural life. Thomas Campbell, Samuel Rogers, and Thomas Moore were minor poets of the Romantic period; the last two were close friends of Byron's (cf. line 829 and note).
5. William Sotheby, contemporary poet and translator, was a wealthy man (see line 1642). Pegasus was the winged horse, symbolizing poetic inspiration.
6. I.e., "bluestockings," a contemporary term for pedantic lady intellectuals, among whom Byron numbered his wife (line 1644).

(But, doubtless, nobody will be so pert)
    That this is not a moral tale, though gay;
Besides, in Canto Twelfth, I mean to show   1655
The very place where wicked people go.

* * *

213

But now at thirty years my hair is gray
    (I wonder what it will be like at forty?
I thought of a peruke[7] the other day)—
    My heart is not much greener; and, in short, I   1700
Have squandered my whole summer while 'twas May,
    And feel no more the spirit to retort; I
Have spent my life, both interest and principal,
And deem not, what I deemed, my soul invincible.

214

No more—no more—Oh! never more on me   1705
    The freshness of the heart can fall like dew,
Which out of all the lovely things we see
    Extracts emotions beautiful and new,
Hived in our bosoms like the bag o' the bee:
    Think'st thou the honey with those objects grew?   1710
Alas! 'twas not in them, but in thy power
To double even the sweetness of a flower.

215

No more—no more—Oh! never more, my heart,
    Canst thou be my sole world, my universe!
Once all in all, but now a thing apart,   1715
    Thou canst not be my blessing or my curse:
The illusion's gone forever, and thou art
    Insensible, I trust, but none the worse,
And in thy stead I've got a deal of judgment,
Though heaven knows how it ever found a lodgment.   1720

216

My days of love are over; me no more
    The charms of maid, wife, and still less of widow
Can make the fool of which they made before—
    In short, I must not lead the life I did do;
The credulous hope of mutual minds is o'er,   1725
    The copious use of claret is forbid too,
So for a good old-gentlemanly vice,
I think I must take up with avarice.

* * *

219

What are the hopes of man? Old Egypt's King   1745
    Cheops erected the first pyramid
And largest, thinking it was just the thing
    To keep his memory whole, and mummy hid:
But somebody or other rummaging

7. Wig.

Burglariously broke his coffin's lid: 1750
Let not a monument give you or me hopes,
Since not a pinch of dust remains of Cheops.

220

But I, being fond of true philosophy,
    Say very often to myself, "Alas!
All things that have been born were born to die,   1755
    And flesh (which Death mows down to hay) is grass;
You've passed your youth not so unpleasantly,
    And if you had it o'er again—'twould pass—
So thank your stars that matters are no worse,
And read your Bible, sir, and mind your purse."   1760

221

But for the present, gentle reader! and
    Still gentler purchaser! the bard—that's I—
Must, with permission, shake you by the hand,
    And so your humble servant, and good-by!
We meet again, if we should understand   1765
    Each other; and if not, I shall not try
Your patience further than by this short sample—
'Twere well if others followed my example.

222

"Go, little book, from this my solitude!
    I cast thee on the waters—go thy ways!   1770
And if, as I believe, thy vein be good,
    The world will find thee after many days."
When Southey's read, and Wordsworth understood,
    I can't help putting in my claim to praise—
The four first rhymes are Southey's, every line:[8]   1775
For God's sake, reader! take them not for mine!

From *Canto II*

8

But to our tale: the Donna Inez sent
    Her son to Cadiz only to embark;
To stay there had not answered her intent,
    But why?—we leave the reader in the dark—   60
'Twas for a voyage the young man was meant,
    As if a Spanish ship were Noah's ark,
To wean him from the wickedness of earth,
And send him like a dove of promise forth.

9

Don Juan bade his valet pack his things   65
    According to direction, then received
A lecture and some money: for four springs
    He was to travel; and though Inez grieved
(As every kind of parting has its stings),
    She hoped he would improve—perhaps believed: 70

8. The lines occur in the last stanza of Southey's *Epilogue to the Lay of the Laureate.*

A letter, too, she gave (he never read it)
Of good advice—and two or three of credit.

* * *

11

Juan embarked—the ship got under way,
    The wind was fair, the water passing rough;
A devil of a sea rolls in that bay,
    As I, who've crossed it oft, know well enough;
And, standing upon deck, the dashing spray   85
    Flies in one's face, and makes it weather-tough:
And there he stood to take, and take again,
His first—perhaps his last—farewell of Spain.

12

I can't but say it is an awkward sight
    To see one's native land receding through   90
The growing waters; it unmans one quite,
    Especially when life is rather new:
I recollect Great Britain's coast looks white,
    But almost every other country's blue,
When gazing on them, mystified by distance,   95
We enter on our nautical existence.

* * *

17

And Juan wept, and much he sighed and thought,
    While his salt tears dropped into the salt sea,   130
"Sweets to the sweet" (I like so much to quote;
    You must excuse this extract—'tis where she,
The Queen of Denmark, for Ophelia brought
    Flowers to the grave);[1] and, sobbing often, he
Reflected on his present situation,   135
And seriously resolved on reformation.

18

"Farewell, my Spain! a long farewell!" he cried,
    "Perhaps I may revisit thee no more,
But die, as many an exiled heart hath died,
    Of its own thirst to see again thy shore: 140
Farewell, where Guadalquiver's waters glide!
    Farewell, my mother! and, since all is o'er,
Farewell, too, dearest Julia!—(here he drew
Her letter out again, and read it through).

19

"And oh! if e'er I should forget, I swear—   145
    But that's impossible, and cannot be—
Sooner shall this blue ocean melt to air,
    Sooner shall earth resolve itself to sea,
Than I resign thine image, oh, my fair!
    Or think of anything, excepting thee;   150

1. Hamlet V.i.266.

A mind diseased no remedy can physic—
(Here the ship gave a lurch, and he grew seasick.)

20

"Sooner shall heaven kiss earth—(here he fell sicker)
  Oh, Julia! what is every other woe?—
(For God's sake let me have a glass of liquor;   155
  Pedro, Battista, help me down below.)
Julia, my love—(you rascal, Pedro, quicker)—
  Oh, Julia!—(this cursed vessel pitches so)—
Beloved Julia, hear me still beseeching!"
(Here he grew inarticulate with retching.)   160

21

He felt that chilling heaviness of heart,
  Or rather stomach, which, alas! attends,
Beyond the best apothecary's art,
  The loss of love, the treachery of friends,
Or death of those we dote on, when a part   165
  Of us dies with them as each fond hope ends:
No doubt he would have been much more pathetic,
But the sea acted as a strong emetic.[2]

* * *

49

'Twas twilight, and the sunless day went down   385
  Over the waste of waters; like a veil,
Which, if withdrawn, would but disclose the frown
  Of one whose hate is masked but to assail.
Thus to their hopeless eyes the night was shown,
  And grimly darkled o'er the faces pale,   390
And the dim desolate deep: twelve days had Fear
Been their familiar, and now Death was here.

50

Some trial had been making at a raft,
  With little hope in such a rolling sea,
A sort of thing at which one would have laughed,   395
  If any laughter at such times could be,
Unless with people who too much have quaffed,
  And have a kind of wild and horrid glee,
Half epileptical, and half hysterical—
Their preservation would have been a miracle.   400

51

At half-past eight o'clock, booms, hencoops, spars,
  And all things, for a chance, had been cast loose
That still could keep afloat the struggling tars,
  For yet they strove, although of no great use:
There was no light in heaven but a few stars,   405
  The boats put off o'ercrowded with their crews;
She gave a heel, and then a lurch to port,
And, going down head foremost—sunk, in short.

2. In stanzas 22–48 (here omitted) the   violent storm, which leaves her a help-
ship, bound for Leghorn, runs into a   less, sinking wreck.

52

Then rose from sea to sky the wild farewell—
  Then shrieked the timid, and stood still the brave—   410
Then some leaped overboard with dreadful yell,
  As eager to anticipate their grave;
And the sea yawned around her like a hell,
  And down she sucked with her the whirling wave,
Like one who grapples with his enemy,   415
And strives to strangle him before he die.

53

And first one universal shriek there rushed,
  Louder than the loud ocean, like a crash
Of echoing thunder; and then all was hushed,
  Save the wild wind and the remorseless dash   420
Of billows; but at intervals there gushed,
  Accompanied with a convulsive splash,
A solitary shriek, the bubbling cry
Of some strong swimmer in his agony.

* * *

56

Juan got into the longboat, and there
  Contrived to help Pedrillo[3] to a place;
It seemed as if they had exchanged their care,
  For Juan wore the magisterial face
Which courage gives, while poor Pedrillo's pair   445
  Of eyes were crying for their owner's ease:
Battista, though (a name called shortly Tita),
Was lost by getting at some aqua-vita.[4]

57

Pedro, his valet, too, he tried to save,
  But the same cause, conducive to his loss,
Left him so drunk, he jumped into the wave   450
  As o'er the cutter's edge he tried to cross,
And so he found a wine-and-watery grave;
  They could not rescue him although so close,
Because the sea ran higher every minute,   455
And for the boat—the crew kept crowding in it.

* * *

103

As they drew nigh the land, which now was seen
  Unequal in its aspect here and there,
They felt the freshness of its growing green,
  That waved in forest tops, and smoothed the air,   820
And fell upon their glazed eyes like a screen
  From glistening waves, and skies so hot and bare—
Lovely seemed any object that should sweep
Away the vast, salt, dread, eternal deep.

---

3. Juan's tutor.   4. Brandy.

104

The shore looked wild, without a trace of man,   825
    And girt by formidable waves; but they
Were mad for land, and thus their course they ran,
    Though right ahead the roaring breakers lay:
A reef between them also now began
    To show its boiling surf and bounding spray,   830
But finding no place for their landing better,
They ran the boat for shore—and overset her.

105

But in his native stream, the Guadalquiver,
    Juan to lave his youthful limbs was wont;
And having learnt to swim in that sweet river,   835
    Had often turned the art to some account:
A better swimmer you could scarce see ever,
    He could, perhaps, have passed the Hellespont,
As once (a feat on which ourselves we prided)
Leander, Mr. Ekenhead, and I did.[5]   840

106

So, here, though faint, emaciated, and stark,
    He buoyed his boyish limbs, and strove to ply
With the quick wave, and gain, ere it was dark,
    The beach which lay before him, high and dry:
The greatest danger here was from a shark,   845
    That carried off his neighbor by the thigh;
As for the other two, they could not swim,
So nobody arrived on shore but him.

107

Nor yet had he arrived but for the oar,
    Which, providentially for him, was washed   850
Just as his feeble arms could strike no more,
    And the hard wave o'erwhelmed him as 'twas dashed
Within his grasp; he clung to it, and sore
    The waters beat while he thereto was lashed:
At last, with swimming, wading, scrambling, he   855
Rolled on the beach, half senseless, from the sea:

108

There, breathless, with his digging nails he clung
    Fast to the sand, lest the returning wave,
From whose reluctant roar his life he wrung,
    Should suck him back to her insatiate grave: 860
And there he lay, full length, where he was flung,
    Before the entrance of a cliff-worn cave,
With just enough of life to feel its pain,
And deem that it was saved, perhaps, in vain.

109

With slow and staggering effort he arose,   865
    But sunk again upon his bleeding knee

5. Like Leander in the myth, Byron and Lt. Ekenhead had swum the Helles- pont on May 3, 1810. See *Written After Swimming from Sestos to Abydos.*

And quivering hand; and then he looked for those
  Who long had been his mates upon the sea;
But none of them appeared to share his woes,
  Save one, a corpse, from out the famished three,   870
Who died two days before, and now had found
An unknown barren beach for burial ground.

110

And as he gazed, his dizzy brain spun fast,
  And down he sunk; and as he sunk, the sand
Swam round and round, and all his senses passed: 875
  He fell upon his side, and his stretched hand
Drooped dripping on the oar (their jurymast),
  And, like a withered lily, on the land
His slender frame and pallid aspect lay,
As fair a thing as e'er was formed of clay.   880

111

How long in his damp trance young Juan lay
  He knew not, for the earth was gone for him,
And time had nothing more of night nor day
  For his congealing blood, and senses dim;
And how this heavy faintness passed away   885
  He knew not, till each painful pulse and limb,
And tingling vein seemed throbbing back to life,
For Death, though vanquished, still retired with strife.

112

His eyes he opened, shut, again unclosed,
  For all was doubt and dizziness; he thought   890
He still was in the boat, and had but dozed,
  And felt again with his despair o'erwrought,
And wished it death in which he had reposed,
  And then once more his feelings back were brought,
And slowly by his swimming eyes was seen   895
A lovely female face of seventeen.

113

'Twas bending close o'er his, and the small mouth
  Seemed almost prying into his for breath;
And chafing him, the soft warm hand of youth
  Recalled his answering spirits back from death;   900
And, bathing his chill temples, tried to soothe
  Each pulse to animation, till beneath
Its gentle touch and trembling care, a sigh
To these kind efforts made a low reply.

114

Then was the cordial poured, and mantle flung   905
  Around his scarce-clad limbs; and the fair arm
Raised higher the faint head which o'er it hung;
  And her transparent cheek, all pure and warm,
Pillowed his deathlike forehead; then she wrung
  His dewy curls, long drenched by every storm;   910

And watched with eagerness each throb that drew
A sigh from his heaved bosom—and hers, too.

115

And lifting him with care into the cave,
   The gentle girl, and her attendant—one
Young, yet her elder, and of brow less grave,   915
   And more robust of figure—then begun
To kindle fire, and as the new flames gave
   Light to the rocks that roofed them, which the sun
Had never seen, the maid, or whatsoe'er
She was, appeared distinct, and tall, and fair.   920

116

Her brow was overhung with coins of gold,
   That sparkled o'er the auburn of her hair,
Her clustering hair, whose longer locks were rolled
   In braids behind; and though her stature were
Even of the highest for a female mold,   925
   They nearly reached her heel; and in her air
There was a something which bespoke command,
As one who was a lady in the land.

117

Her hair, I said, was auburn; but her eyes
   Were black as death, their lashes the same hue,   930
Of downcast length, in whose silk shadow lies
   Deepest attraction; for when to the view
Forth from its raven fringe the full glance flies,
   Ne'er with such force the swiftest arrow flew;
'Tis as the snake late coiled, who pours his length,   935
And hurls at once his venom and his strength.

                      *   *   *

123

And these two tended him, and cheered him both
   With food and raiment, and those soft attentions,
Which are (as I must own) of female growth,
   And have ten thousand delicate inventions: 980
They made a most superior mess of broth,
   A thing which poesy but seldom mentions,
But the best dish that e'er was cooked since Homer's
Achilles ordered dinner for newcomers.[6]

124

I'll tell you who they were, this female pair,
   Lest they should seem princesses in disguise;
Besides, I hate all mystery, and that air
   Of claptrap, which your recent poets prize;
And so, in short, the girls they really were
   They shall appear before your curious eyes,   990
Mistress and maid; the first was only daughter
Of an old man, who lived upon the water.

6. A reference to the lavish feast with which Achilles entertained Ajax, Phoenix,
and Ulysses (*Iliad* IX.193 ff.).

125

A fisherman he had been in his youth,
  And still a sort of fisherman was he;
But other speculations were, in sooth,
  Added to his connection with the sea,   995
Perhaps not so respectable, in truth:
  A little smuggling, and some piracy,
Left him, at last, the sole of many masters
Of an ill-gotten million of piasters.[7]   1000

126

A fisher, therefore, was he—though of men,
  Like Peter the Apostle[8]—and he fished
For wandering merchant vessels, now and then,
  And sometimes caught as many as he wished;
The cargoes he confiscated, and gain   1005
  He sought in the slave market too, and dished
Full many a morsel for that Turkish trade,
By which, no doubt, a good deal may be made.

127

He was a Greek, and on his isle had built
  (One of the wild and smaller Cyclades[9])   1010
A very handsome house from out his guilt,
  And there he lived exceedingly at ease;
Heaven knows what cash he got or blood he spilt,
  A sad[1] old fellow was he, if you please;
But this I know, it was a spacious building,   1015
Full of barbaric carving, paint, and gilding.

128

He had an only daughter, called Haidée,
  The greatest heiress of the Eastern Isles;
Besides, so very beautiful was she,
  Her dowry was as nothing to her smiles: 1020
Still in her teens, and like a lovely tree
  She grew to womanhood, and between whiles
Rejected several suitors, just to learn
How to accept a better in his turn.

129

And walking out upon the beach, below   1025
  The cliff, towards sunset, on that day she found,
Insensible—not dead, but nearly so—
  Don Juan, almost famished, and half drowned;
But being naked, she was shocked, you know,
  Yet deemed herself in common pity bound,   1030
As far as in her lay, "to take him in,
A stranger"[2] dying, with so white a skin.

7. Near Eastern coins.
8. Christ's words to Peter and Andrew, both fishermen: "Follow me, and I will make you fishers of men" (Matthew iv.19).
9. A group of islands in the Aegean Sea.
1. In the playful sense: "wicked."
2. Cf. Matthew xxv.35: "I was a stranger, and ye took me in."

130

But taking him into her father's house
    Was not exactly the best way to save,
But like conveying to the cat the mouse,   1035
    Or people in a trance into their grave;
Because the good old man had so much *"νοῦς,"*[3]
    Unlike the honest Arab thieves so brave,
He would have hospitably cured the stranger
And sold him instantly when out of danger.   1040

131

And therefore, with her maid, she thought it best
    (A virgin always on her maid relies)
To place him in the cave for present rest:
    And when, at last, he opened his black eyes,
Their charity increased about their guest;   1045
    And their compassion grew to such a size,
It opened half the turnpike gates to heaven
(St. Paul says 'tis the toll which must be given).[4]

* * *

141

And Haidée met the morning face to face;
    Her own was freshest, though a feverish flush
Had dyed it with the headlong blood, whose race
    From heart to cheek is curbed into a blush,
Like to a torrent which a mountain's base,   1125
    That overpowers some Alpine river's rush,
Checks to a lake, whose waves in circles spread;
Or the Red Sea—but the sea is not red.

142

And down the cliff the island virgin came,
    And near the cave her quick light footsteps drew,   1130
While the sun smiled on her with his first flame,
    And young Aurora[5] kissed her lips with dew,
Taking her for a sister; just the same
    Mistake you would have made on seeing the two,
Although the mortal, quite as fresh and fair,   1135
Had all the advantage, too, of not being air.

143

And when into the cavern Haidée stepped
    All timidly, yet rapidly, she saw
That like an infant Juan sweetly slept;
    And then she stopped, and stood as if in awe   1140
(For sleep is awful), and on tiptoe crept
    And wrapped him closer, lest the air, too raw,
Should reach his blood, then o'er him still as death
Bent, with hushed lips, that drank his scarce-drawn breath.

* * *

3. Nous, "intelligence"; in England,   4. I Corinthians xiii.13.
pronounced so as to rhyme with "mouse."   5. The dawn.

148

And she bent o'er him, and he lay beneath,
   Hushed as the babe upon its mother's breast,
Drooped as the willow when no winds can breathe,
   Lulled like the depth of ocean when at rest,   1180
Fair as the crowning rose of the whole wreath,
   Soft as the callow cygnet[6] in its nest;
In short, he was a very pretty fellow,
Although his woes had turned him rather yellow.

149

He woke and gazed, and would have slept again,   1185
   But the fair face which met his eyes forbade
Those eyes to close, though weariness and pain
   Had further sleep a further pleasure made;
For woman's face was never formed in vain
   For Juan, so that even when he prayed   1190
He turned from grisly saints, and martyrs hairy,
To the sweet portraits of the Virgin Mary.

150

And thus upon his elbow he arose,
   And looked upon the lady, in whose cheek
The pale contended with the purple rose,   1195
   As with an effort she began to speak;
Her eyes were eloquent, her words would pose,
   Although she told him, in good modern Greek,
With an Ionian accent, low and sweet,
That he was faint, and must not talk, but eat.   1200

* * *

168

And every day by daybreak—rather early
   For Juan, who was somewhat fond of rest—
She came into the cave, but it was merely
   To see her bird reposing in his nest;   1340
And she would softly stir his locks so curly,
   Without disturbing her yet slumbering guest,
Breathing all gently o'er his cheek and mouth,
As o'er a bed of roses the sweet South.[7]

169

And every morn his color freshlier came,   1345
   And every day helped on his convalescence;
'Twas well, because health in the human frame
   Is pleasant, besides being true love's essence,
For health and idleness to passion's flame
   Are oil and gunpowder; and some good lessons   1350
Are also learnt from Ceres[8] and from Bacchus,
Without whom Venus will not long attack us.

6. Young swan.   8. Goddess of the grain.
7. The south wind.

170

While Venus fills the heart (without heart really
  Love, though good always, is not quite so good),
Ceres presents a plate of vermicelli—   1355
  For love must be sustained like flesh and blood—
While Bacchus pours out wine, or hands a jelly:
  Eggs, oysters, too, are amatory food;
But who is their purveyor from above
Heaven knows—it may be Neptune, Pan, or Jove.   1360

171

When Juan woke he found some good things ready,
  A bath, a breakfast, and the finest eyes
That ever made a youthful heart less steady,
  Besides her maid's, as pretty for their size;
But I have spoken of all this already—   1365
  And repetition's tiresome and unwise—
Well—Juan, after bathing in the sea,
Came always back to coffee and Haidée.

172

Both were so young, and one so innocent,
  That bathing passed for nothing; Juan seemed   1370
To her, as 'twere, the kind of being sent,
  Of whom these two years she had nightly dreamed,
A something to be loved, a creature meant
  To be her happiness, and whom she deemed
To render happy; all who joy would win   1375
Must share it—Happiness was born a twin.

173

It was such pleasure to behold him, such
  Enlargement of existence to partake
Nature with him, to thrill beneath his touch,
  To watch him slumbering, and to see him wake: 1380
To live with him forever were too much;
  But then the thought of parting made her quake:
He was her own, her ocean-treasure, cast
Like a rich wreck—her first love, and her last.

174

And thus a moon rolled on, and fair Haidée   1385
  Paid daily visits to her boy, and took
Such plentiful precautions, that still he
  Remained unknown within his craggy nook;
At last her father's prows put out to sea,
  For certain merchantmen upon the look,   1390
Not as of yore to carry off an Io,[9]
But three Ragusan vessels, bound for Scio.[1]

175

Then came her freedom, for she had no mother,
  So that, her father being at sea, she was

9. Io, a mistress of Zeus persecuted by his jealous wife Hera, was kidnaped by Phoenician merchants.

1. Ragusa (or Dubrovnik), is an Adriatic port; Scio is the Italian name for Chios, an island near Turkey.

Free as a married woman, or such other   1395
    Female, as where she likes may freely pass,
Without even the encumbrance of a brother,
    The freest she that ever gazed on glass:
I speak of Christian lands in this comparison,
Where wives, at least, are seldom kept in garrison.   1400

176

Now she prolonged her visits and her talk
    (For they must talk), and he had learnt to say
So much as to propose to take a walk—
    For little had he wandered since the day
On which, like a young flower snapped from the stalk,   1405
    Drooping and dewy on the beach he lay—
And thus they walked out in the afternoon,
And saw the sun set opposite the moon.

177

It was a wild and breaker-beaten coast,
    With cliffs above, and a broad sandy shore,
Guarded by shoals and rocks as by an host,   1410
    With here and there a creek, whose aspect wore
A better welcome to the tempest-tossed;
    And rarely ceased the haughty billow's roar,
Save on the dead long summer days, which make   1415
The outstretched ocean glitter like a lake.

178

And the small ripple split upon the beach
    Scarcely o'erpass'd the cream of your champagne,
When o'er the brim the sparkling bumpers reach,
    That spring dew of the spirit! the heart's rain!   1420
Few things surpass old wine; and they may preach
    Who please—the more because they preach in vain—
Let us have wine and woman, mirth and laughter,
Sermons and soda water the day after.

179

Man, being reasonable, must get drunk;   1425
    The best of life is but intoxication:
Glory, the grape, love, gold, in these are sunk
    The hopes of all men, and of every nation;
Without their sap, how branchless were the trunk
    Of life's strange tree, so fruitful on occasion:
But to return—Get very drunk; and when   1430
You wake with headache, you shall see what then.

180

Ring for your valet—bid him quickly bring
    Some hock and soda water, then you'll know
A pleasure worthy Xerxes the great king:[2]
    For not the blest sherbet, sublimed with snow,   1435
Nor the first sparkle of the desert spring,

2. Xerxes, 5th-century Persian king, was said to have offered a reward to anyone who could discover a new kind of pleasure.

Nor Burgundy in all its sunset glow,
After long travel, ennui, love, or slaughter,
Vie with that draught of hock and soda water.   1440

181

The coast—I think it was the coast that I
    Was just describing—Yes, it *was* the coast—
Lay at this period quiet as the sky,
    The sands untumbled, the blue waves untossed,
And all was stillness, save the sea bird's cry,   1445
    And dolphin's leap, and little billow crossed
By some low rock or shelve, that made it fret
Against the boundary it scarcely wet.

182

And forth they wandered, her sire being gone,
    As I have said, upon an expedition;   1450
And mother, brother, guardian, she had none,
    Save Zoë, who, although with due precision
She waited on her lady with the sun,
    Thought daily service was her only mission,
Bringing warm water, wreathing her long tresses,   1455
And asking now and then for cast-off dresses.

183

It was the cooling hour, just when the rounded
    Red sun sinks down behind the azure hill,
Which then seems as if the whole earth it bounded,
    Circling all nature, hushed, and dim, and still,   1460
With the far mountain crescent half surrounded
    On one side, and the deep sea calm and chill
Upon the other, and the rosy sky,
With one star sparkling through it like an eye.

184

And thus they wandered forth, and hand in hand,   1465
    Over the shining pebbles and the shells,
Glided along the smooth and hardened sand,
    And in the worn and wild receptacles
Worked by the storms, yet worked as it were planned,
    In hollow halls, with sparry roofs and cells,   1470
They turned to rest; and, each clasped by an arm,
Yielded to the deep twilight's purple charm.

185

They looked up to the sky, whose floating glow
    Spread like a rosy ocean, vast and bright;
They gazed upon the glittering sea below,   1475
    Whence the broad moon rose circling into sight;
They heard the waves splash, and the wind so low,
    And saw each other's dark eyes darting light
Into each other—and, beholding this,
Their lips drew near, and clung into a kiss;   1480

186

A long, long kiss, a kiss of youth, and love,
  And beauty, all concéntrating like rays
Into one focus, kindled from above;
  Such kisses as belong to early days,
Where heart, and soul, and sense, in concert move,   1485
  And the blood's lava, and the pulse a blaze,
Each kiss a heart-quake—for a kiss's strength,
I think, it must be reckoned by its length.

187

By length I mean duration; theirs endured
  Heaven knows how long—no doubt they never reckoned;   1490
And if they had, they could not have secured
  The sum of their sensations to a second:
They had not spoken; but they felt allured,
  As if their souls and lips each other beckoned,
Which, being joined, like swarming bees they clung—   1495
Their hearts the flowers from whence the honey sprung.

188

They were alone, but not alone as they
  Who shut in chambers think it loneliness;
The silent ocean, and the starlight bay,
  The twilight glow, which momently grew less,   1500
The voiceless sands, and dropping caves, that lay
  Around them, made them to each other press,
As if there were no life beneath the sky
Save theirs, and that their life could never die.

189

They feared no eyes nor ears on that lone beach,   1505
  They felt no terrors from the night, they were
All in all to each other: though their speech
  Was broken words, they *thought* a language there—
And all the burning tongues the passions teach
  Found in one sigh the best interpreter   1510
Of nature's oracle—first love—that all
Which Eve has left her daughters since her fall.

190

Haidée spoke not of scruples, asked no vows,
  Nor offered any; she had never heard
Of plight and promises to be a spouse,   1515
  Or perils by a loving maid incurred;
She was all which pure ignorance allows,
  And flew to her young mate like a young bird;
And never having dreamt of falsehood, she
Had not one word to say of constancy.[3]   1520

191

She loved, and was belovéd—she adored,
  And she was worshiped; after nature's fashion,

3. Byron said, with reference to Haidée:
"I was, and am, penetrated with the
conviction that women only know evil
from men, whereas men have no criterion to judge of purity or goodness but
woman."

Their intense souls, into each other poured,
    If souls could die, had perished in that passion—
But by degrees their senses were restored,   1525
    Again to be o'ercome, again to dash on;
And, beating 'gainst *his* bosom, Haidée's heart
Felt as if never more to beat apart.

192

Alas! they were so young, so beautiful,
    So lonely, loving, helpless, and the hour   1530
Was that in which the heart is always full,
    And, having o'er itself no further power,
Prompts deeds eternity cannot annul,
    But pays off moments in an endless shower
Of hell-fire—all prepared for people giving   1535
Pleasure or pain to one another living.

193

Alas! for Juan and Haidée! they were
    So loving and so lovely—till then never,
Excepting our first parents, such a pair
    Had run the risk of being damned forever;   1540
And Haidée, being devout as well as fair,
    Had, doubtless, heard about the Stygian river,[4]
And hell and purgatory—but forgot
Just in the very crisis she should not.

194

They look upon each other, and their eyes   1545
    Gleam in the moonlight; and her white arm clasps
Round Juan's head, and his around hers lies
    Half buried in the tresses which it grasps;
She sits upon his knee, and drinks his sighs,
    He hers, until they end in broken gasps;   1550
And thus they form a group that's quite antique,
Half naked, loving, natural, and Greek.

195

And when those deep and burning moments passed,
    And Juan sunk to sleep within her arms,
She slept not, but all tenderly, though fast,   1555
    Sustained his head upon her bosom's charms;
And now and then her eye to heaven is cast,
    And then on the pale cheek her breast now warms,
Pillowed on her o'erflowing heart, which pants
With all it granted, and with all it grants.   1560

196

An infant when it gazes on a light,
    A child the moment when it drains the breast,
A devotee when soars the Host[5] in sight,
    An Arab with a stranger for a guest,
A sailor when the prize has struck[6] in fight,   1565

4. The Styx, which flows through
Hades.
5. The Eucharistic wafer.

6. Has lowered its flag in token of
surrender.

A miser filling his most hoarded chest,
Feel rapture; but not such true joy are reaping
As they who watch o'er what they love while sleeping.

197

For there it lies so tranquil, so beloved,
   All that it hath of life with us is living;   1570
So gentle, stirless, helpless, and unmoved,
   And all unconscious of the joy 'tis giving;
All it hath felt, inflicted, passed, and proved,
   Hushed into depths beyond the watcher's diving;
There lies the thing we love with all its errors   1575
And all its charms, like death without its terrors.

198

The lady watched her lover—and that hour
   Of Love's, and Night's, and Ocean's solitude,
O'erflowed her soul with their united power;
   Amidst the barren sand and rocks so rude   1580
She and her wave-worn love had made their bower,
   Where nought upon their passion could intrude,
And all the stars that crowded the blue space
Saw nothing happier than her glowing face.

199

Alas! the love of women! it is known   1585
   To be a lovely and a fearful thing;
For all of theirs upon that die is thrown,
   And if 'tis lost, life hath no more to bring
To them but mockeries of the past alone,
   And their revenge is as the tiger's spring,   1590
Deadly, and quick, and crushing; yet, as real
Torture is theirs, what they inflict they feel.

200

They are right; for man, to man so oft unjust,
   Is always so to women; one sole bond
Awaits them, treachery is all their trust;   1595
   Taught to conceal, their bursting hearts despond
Over their idol, till some wealthier lust
   Buys them in marriage—and what rests beyond?
A thankless husband, next a faithless lover,
Then dressing, nursing, praying, and all's over.   1600

201

Some take a lover, some take drams or prayers,
   Some mind their household, others dissipation,
Some run away, and but exchange their cares,
   Losing the advantage of a virtuous station;
Few changes e'er can better their affairs,   1605
   Theirs being an unnatural situation,
From the dull palace to the dirty hovel:
Some play the devil, and then write a novel.[7]

7. The impetuous and hysterical Lady Caroline Lamb, having thrown herself at Byron and been after a time rejected, incorporated incidents from the affair in her novel, *Glenarvon* (1816).

202

Haidée was Nature's bride, and knew not this;
 Haidée was Passion's child, born where the sun   1610
Showers triple light, and scorches even the kiss
 Of his gazelle-eyed daughters; she was one
Made but to love, to feel that she was his
 Who was her chosen: what was said or done
Elsewhere was nothing. She had nought to fear,   1615
Hope, care, nor love beyond, her heart beat *here*.

203

And oh! that quickening of the heart, that beat!
 How much it costs us! yet each rising throb
Is in its cause as its effect so sweet,
 That Wisdom, ever on the watch to rob   1620
Joy of its alchemy, and to repeat
 Fine truths; even Conscience, too, has a tough job
To make us understand each good old maxim,
So good—I wonder Castlereagh[8] don't tax 'em.

204

And now 'twas done—on the lone shore were plighted   1625
 Their hearts; the stars, their nuptial torches, shed
Beauty upon the beautiful they lighted:
 Ocean their witness, and the cave their bed,
By their own feelings hallowed and united,
 Their priest was Solitude, and they were wed: 1630
And they were happy, for to their young eyes
Each was an angel, and earth paradise.

* * *

208

But Juan! had he quite forgotten Julia?
 And should he have forgotten her so soon?
I can't but say it seems to me mostly truly a
 Perplexing question; but, no doubt, the moon   1660
Does these things for us, and whenever newly a
 Strong palpitation rises, 'tis her boon,
Else how the devil is it that fresh features
Have such a charm for us poor human creatures?

209

I hate inconstancy—I loathe, detest,   1665
 Abhor, condemn, abjure the mortal made
Of such quicksilver clay that in his breast
 No permanent foundation can be laid;
Love, constant love, has been my constant guest—
 And yet last night, being at a masquerade,   1670
I saw the prettiest creature, fresh from Milan,
Which gave me some sensations like a villain.

8. Robert Stewart, Viscount Castlereagh, British Foreign Secretary from 1812 to 1822.

210

But soon Philosophy came to my aid,
 And whispered, "Think of every sacred tie!"
"I will, my dear Philosophy!" I said,   1675
 "But then her teeth, and then, oh, Heaven! her eye!
I'll just inquire if she be wife or maid,
 Or neither—out of curiosity."
"Stop!" cried Philosophy, with air so Grecian
(Though she was masked then as a fair Venetian);   1680

211

"Stop!" so I stopped.—But to return: that which
 Men call inconstancy is nothing more
Than admiration due where nature's rich
 Profusion with young beauty covers o'er
Some favored object; and as in the niche   1685
 A lovely statue we almost adore,
This sort of adoration of the real
Is but a heightening of the "beau ideal."[9]

212

'Tis the perception of the beautiful,
 A fine extension of the faculties,   1690
Platonic, universal, wonderful,
 Drawn from the stars, and filtered through the skies,
Without which life would be extremely dull;
 In short, it is the use of our own eyes,
With one or two small senses added, just   1695
To hint that flesh is formed of fiery dust.

213

Yet 'tis a painful feeling, and unwilling,
 For surely if we always could perceive
In the same object graces quite as killing
 As when she rose upon us like an Eve,   1700
'Twould save us many a heartache, many a shilling
 (For we must get them anyhow, or grieve),
Whereas, if one sole lady pleased forever,
How pleasant for the heart, as well as liver!

* * *

216

In the meantime, without proceeding more
 In this anatomy, I've finished now
Two hundred and odd stanzas as before,
 That being about the number I'll allow
Each canto of the twelve, or twenty-four;   1725
 And, laying down my pen, I make my bow,
Leaving Don Juan and Haidée to plead
For them and theirs with all who deign to read.

9. Ideal beauty.

From *Canto III*

1

Hail, Muse! et cetera.—We left Juan sleeping,
Pillowed upon a fair and happy breast,
And watched by eyes that never yet knew weeping,
And loved by a young heart, too deeply blest
To feel the poison through her spirit creeping,   5
Or know who rested there, a foe to rest,
Had soiled the current of her sinless years,
And turned her pure heart's purest blood to tears!

2

Oh, Love! what is it in this world of ours
Which makes it fatal to be loved? Ah why   10
With cypress branches[1] hast thou wreathed thy bowers,
And made thy best interpreter a sigh?
As those who dote on odors pluck the flowers,
And place them on their breast—but place to die—
Thus the frail beings we would fondly cherish   15
Are laid within our bosoms but to perish.

3

In her first passion woman loves her lover,
In all the others all she loves is love,
Which grows a habit she can ne'er get over,
And fits her loosely—like an easy glove,   20
As you may find, whene'er you like to prove her:
One man alone at first her heart can move;
She then prefers him in the plural number,
Not finding that the additions much encumber.

4

I know not if the fault be men's or theirs;   25
But one thing's pretty sure; a woman planted[2]
(Unless at once she plunge for life in prayers)
After a decent time must be gallanted;
Although, no doubt, her first of love affairs
Is that to which her heart is wholly granted;   30
Yet there are some, they say, who have had *none,*
But those who have ne'er end with only *one.*

5

'Tis melancholy, and a fearful sign
Of human frailty, folly, also crime,
That love and marriage rarely can combine,   35
Although they both are born in the same clime;
Marriage from love, like vinegar from wine—
A sad, sour, sober beverage—by time
Is sharpened from its high celestial flavor,
Down to a very homely household savor.   40

---

1. Signifying sorrow.   2. Abandoned (from the French *planter là,* to leave in the lurch).

6

There's something of antipathy, as 'twere,
   Between their present and their future state;
A kind of flattery that's hardly fair
   Is used until the truth arrives too late—
Yet what can people do, except despair?   45
   The same things change their names at such a rate;
For instance—passion in a lover's glorious,
But in a husband is pronounced uxorious.

7

Men grow ashamed of being so very fond;
   They sometimes also get a little tired   50
(But that, of course, is rare), and then despond:
   The same things cannot always be admired,
Yet 'tis "so nominated in the bond,"[3]
   That both are tied till one shall have expired.
Sad thought! to lose the spouse that was adorning   55
Our days, and put one's servants into mourning.

8

There's doubtless something in domestic doings
   Which forms, in fact, true love's antithesis;
Romances paint at full length people's wooings,
   But only give a bust of marriages;   60
For no one cares for matrimonial cooings,
   There's nothing wrong in a connubial kiss:
Think you, if Laura had been Petrarch's wife,
He would have written sonnets all his life?

9

All tragedies are finished by a death,   65
   All comedies are ended by a marriage;
The future states of both are left to faith,
   For authors fear description might disparage
The worlds to come of both, or fall beneath,
   And then both worlds would punish their miscarriage;   70
So leaving each their priest and prayer book ready,
They say no more of Death or of the Lady.[4]

10

The only two that in my recollection
   Have sung of heaven and hell, or marriage, are
Dante and Milton, and of both the affection   75
   Was hapless in their nuptials, for some bar
Of fault or temper ruined the connection
   (Such things, in fact, it don't ask much to mar);
But Dante's Beatrice and Milton's Eve
Were not drawn from their spouses, you conceive.   80

11

Some persons say that Dante meant theology
   By Beatrice, and not a mistress—I,

3. Shylock: "Is it so nominated in the bond?" *The Merchant of Venice* IV.i.254.

4. Alluding to a popular ballad, *Death and the Lady.*

Although my opinion may require apology,
  Deem this a commentator's phantasy,
Unless indeed it was from his own knowledge he   85
  Decided thus, and showed good reason why;
I think that Dante's more abstruse ecstatics
Meant to personify the mathematics.

12

Haidée and Juan were not married, but
  The fault was theirs, not mine: it is not fair,   90
Chaste reader, then, in any way to put
  The blame on me, unless you wish they were;
Then if you'd have them wedded, please to shut
  The book which treats of this erroneous pair,
Before the consequences grow too awful;   95
'Tis dangerous to read of loves unlawful.

13

Yet they were happy—happy in the illicit
  Indulgence of their innocent desires;
But more imprudent grown with every visit,
  Haidée forgot the island was her sire's;   100
When we have what we like, 'tis hard to miss it,
  At least in the beginning, ere one tires;
Thus she came often, not a moment losing,
Whilst her piratical papa was cruising.

14

Let not his mode of raising cash seem strange,   105
  Although he fleeced the flags of every nation,
For into a prime minister but change
  His title, and 'tis nothing but taxation;
But he, more modest, took an humbler range
  Of life, and in an honester vocation   110
Pursued o'er the high seas his watery journey,
And merely practiced as a sea attorney.

15

The good old gentleman had been detained
  By winds and waves, and some important captures;
And, in the hope of more, at sea remained,   115
  Although a squall or two had damped his raptures,
By swamping one of the prizes; he had chained
  His prisoners, dividing them like chapters
In numbered lots; they all had cuffs and collars,
And averaged each from ten to a hundred dollars.   120

* * *

19

Then having settled his marine affairs,   145
  Despatching single cruisers here and there,
His vessel having need of some repairs,
  He shaped his course to where his daughter fair
Continued still her hospitable cares;
  But that part of the coast being shoal and bare,   150

And rough with reefs which ran out many a mile,
His port lay on the other side o' the isle.

20

And there he went ashore without delay,
　Having no customhouse nor quarantine
To ask him awkward questions on the way
　About the time and place where he had been:
He left his ship to be hove down next day,
　With orders to the people to careen;[5]
So that all hands were busy beyond measure,
In getting out goods, ballast, guns, and treasure.

* * *

27

He saw his white walls shining in the sun,
　His garden trees all shadowy and green;
He heard his rivulet's light bubbling run,
　The distant dog-bark; and perceived between
The umbrage of the wood so cool and dun,
　The moving figures, and the sparkling sheen
Of arms (in the East all arm)—and various dyes
Of colored garbs, as bright as butterflies.

28

And as the spot where they appear he nears,
　Surprised at these unwonted signs of idling,
He hears—alas! no music of the spheres,
　But an unhallowed, earthly sound of fiddling!
A melody which made him doubt his ears,
　The cause being past his guessing or unriddling;
A pipe, too, and a drum, and shortly after,
A most unoriental roar of laughter.

* * *

38

He did not know (alas! how men will lie)
　That a report (especially the Greeks)
Avouched his death (such people never die),
　And put his house in mourning several weeks—
But now their eyes and also lips were dry;
　The bloom, too, had returned to Haidée's cheeks.
Her tears, too, being returned into their fount,
She now kept house upon her own account.

39

Hence all this rice, meat, dancing, wine, and fiddling,
　Which turned the isle into a place of pleasure;
The servants all were getting drunk or idling,
　A life which made them happy beyond measure.
Her father's hospitality seemed middling,
　Compared with what Haidée did with his treasure;
'Twas wonderful how things went on improving,
While she had not one hour to spare from loving.

5. To tip a vessel on its side in order to clean and repair its hull.

40

Perhaps you think in stumbling on this feast,
   He flew into a passion, and in fact
There was no mighty reason to be pleased;   315
   Perhaps you prophesy some sudden act,
The whip, the rack, or dungeon at the least,
   To teach his people to be more exact,
And that, proceeding at a very high rate,
He showed the royal penchants of a pirate.   320

41

You're wrong.—He was the mildest mannered man
   That ever scuttled ship or cut a throat;
With such true breeding of a gentleman,
   You never could divine his real thought,
No courtier could, and scarcely woman can   325
   Gird more deceit within a petticoat;
Pity he loved adventurous life's variety,
He was so great a loss to good society.

* * *

48

Not that he was not sometimes rash or so,
   But never in his real and serious mood;
Then calm, concéntrated, and still, and slow,
   He lay coiled like the boa in the wood;   380
With him it never was a word and blow,
   His angry word once o'er, he shed no blood,
But in his silence there was much to rue,
And his *one* blow left little work for *two*.

49

He asked no further questions, and proceeded   385
   On to the house, but by a private way,
So that the few who met him hardly heeded,
   So little they expected him that day;
If love paternal in his bosom pleaded
   For Haidée's sake is more than I can say,   390
But certainly to one deemed dead returning,
This revel seemed a curious mode of mourning.

50

If all the dead could now return to life
   (Which God forbid!), or some, or a great many,
For instance, if a husband or his wife   395
   (Nuptial examples are as good as any),
No doubt whate'er might be their former strife,
   The present weather would be much more rainy—
Tears shed into the grave of the connection
Would share most probably its resurrection.   400

51

He entered in the house no more his home,
   A thing to human feelings the most trying,

And harder for the heart to overcome,
   Perhaps, than even the mental pangs of dying;
To find our hearthstone turned into a tomb,
   And round its once warm precincts palely lying   405
The ashes of our hopes, is a deep grief,
Beyond a single gentleman's belief.

52

He entered in the house—his home no more,
   For without hearts there is no home—and felt   410
The solitude of passing his own door
   Without a welcome: *there* he long had dwelt,
There his few peaceful days Time had swept o'er,
   There his warm bosom and keen eye would melt
Over the innocence of that sweet child,   415
His only shrine of feelings undefiled.

53

He was a man of a strange temperament,
   Of mild demeanor though of savage mood,
Moderate in all his habits, and content
   With temperance in pleasure, as in food,   420
Quick to perceive, and strong to bear, and meant
   For something better, if not wholly good;
His country's wrongs and his despair to save her
Had stung him from a slave to an enslaver.

* * *

96

But let me to my story: I must own,
   If I have any fault, it is digression—
Leaving my people to proceed alone,
   While I soliloquize beyond expression;
But these are my addresses from the throne,   860
   Which put off business to the ensuing session:
Forgetting each omission is a loss to
The world, not quite so great as Ariosto.[6]

* * *

101

T' our tale.—The feast was over, the slaves gone,
   The dwarfs and dancing girls had all retired;
The Arab lore and poet's song were done,
   And every sound of revelry expired;
The lady and her lover, left alone,   900
   The rosy flood of twilight's sky admired—
Ave Maria![7] o'er the earth and sea,
That heavenliest hour of Heaven is worthiest thee!

6. Byron warmly admired this poet, author of *Orlando Furioso* (1532), the greatest of the Italian chivalric romances.
7. "Hail, Mary": these words open a Roman Catholic prayer. *Ave Maria* is sometimes used to refer to evening (or morning), since the prayer is part of the service at these times.

102

Ave Maria! blessed be the hour!   905
   The time, the clime, the spot, where I so oft
Have felt that moment in its fullest power
   Sink o'er the earth so beautiful and soft,
While swung the deep bell in the distant tower,
   Or the faint dying day-hymn stole aloft,   910
And not a breath crept through the rosy air,
And yet the forest leaves seemed stirred with prayer.

103

Ave Maria! 'tis the hour of prayer!
   Ave Maria! 'tis the hour of love!
Ave Maria! may our spirits dare   915
   Look up to thine and to thy Son's above!
Ave Maria! oh that face so fair!
   Those downcast eyes beneath the Almighty dove—
What though 'tis but a pictured image strike—
That painting is no idol—'tis too like.   920

104

Some kinder casuists are pleased to say,
   In nameless print—that I have no devotion;
But set those persons down with me to pray,
   And you shall see who has the properest notion
Of getting into heaven the shortest way;   925
   My altars are the mountains and the ocean,
Earth, air, stars—all that springs from the great **Whole**,
Who hath produced, and will receive the soul.

* * *

From *Canto IV*

3

As boy, I thought myself a clever fellow,
   And wished that others held the same opinion;
They took it up when my days grew more mellow,
   And other minds acknowledged my dominion: 20
Now my sere fancy "falls into the yellow
   Leaf,"[1] and Imagination droops her pinion,
And the sad truth which hovers o'er my desk
Turns what was once romantic to burlesque.

4

And if I laugh at any mortal thing,   25
   'Tis that I may not weep; and if I weep,
'Tis that our nature **cannot** always bring
   Itself to apathy, for we must steep
Our hearts first in the depths of Lethe's spring,
   Ere what we least wish to behold will sleep: 30
Thetis baptized her mortal son in Styx;[2]
A mortal mother would on Lethe fix.

1. Cf. *Macbeth* V.iii.22–23: "My way   yellow leaf."
of life / Is fallen into the sere, the   2. The river in Hades into which the

5

Some have accused me of a strange design
   Against the creed and morals of the land,
And trace it in this poem every line: 35
   I don't pretend that I quite understand
My own meaning when I would be *very* fine;
   But the fact is that I have nothing planned,
Unless it were to be a moment merry,
A novel word in my vocabulary.   40

6

To the kind reader of our sober clime
   This way of writing will appear exotic;
Pulci[3] was sire of the half-serious rhyme,
   Who sang when chivalry was more Quixotic,
And reveled in the fancies of the time,   45
   True knights, chaste dames, huge giants, kings despotic;
But all these, save the last, being obsolete,
I chose a modern subject as more meet.

7

How I have treated it, I do not know;
   Perhaps no better than they have treated me   50
Who have imputed such designs as show
   Not what they saw, but what they wished to see:
But if it gives them pleasure, be it so;
   This is a liberal age, and thoughts are free:
Meantime Apollo plucks me by the ear,   55
And tells me to resume my story here.

* * *

26

Juan and Haidée gazed upon each other
   With swimming looks of speechless tenderness,
Which mixed all feelings, friend, child, lover, brother,
   All that the best can mingle and express
When two pure hearts are poured in one another,   205
   And love too much, and yet cannot love less;
But almost sanctify the sweet excess
By the immortal wish and power to bless.

27

Mixed in each other's arms, and heart in heart,
   Why did they not then die?—they had lived too long   210
Should an hour come to bid them breathe apart;
   Years could but bring them cruel things or wrong;
The world was not for them, nor the world's art
   For beings passionate as Sappho's song;
Love was born *with* them, *in* them, so intense,   215
It was their very spirit—not a sense.

nymph Thetis dipped Achilles, to make
him invulnerable. Lethe, another river
in Hades, brings oblivion of life.
3. Author of the *Morgante Maggiore*,

prototype of the Italian seriocomic romance from which Byron derived the
stanza and manner of *Don Iuan*. See the
introduction to *Don Juan*.

28

They should have lived together deep in woods,
    Unseen as sings the nightingale; they were
Unfit to mix in these thick solitudes
    Called social, haunts of Hate, and Vice, and Care: 220
How lonely every freeborn creature broods!
    The sweetest songbirds nestle in a pair;
The eagle soars alone; the gull and crow
Flock o'er their carrion, just like men below.

29

Now pillowed cheek to cheek, in loving sleep,   225
    Haidée and Juan their siesta took,
A gentle slumber, but it was not deep,
    Forever and anon a something shook
Juan, and shuddering o'er his frame would creep;
    And Haidée's sweet lips murmured like a brook   230
A wordless music, and her face so fair
Stirred with her dream, as rose-leaves with the air;

30

Or as the stirring of a deep clear stream
    Within an Alpine hollow, when the wind
Walks o'er it, was she shaken by the dream,   235
    The mystical usurper of the mind—
O'erpowering us to be whate'er may seem
    Good to the soul which we no more can bind;
Strange state of being! (for 'tis still to be)
Senseless to feel, and with sealed eyes to see.   240

31

She dreamed of being alone on the seashore,
    Chained to a rock; she knew not how, but stir
She could not from the spot, and the loud roar
    Grew, and each wave rose roughly, threatening her;
And o'er her upper lip they seemed to pour,   245
    Until she sobbed for breath, and soon they were
Foaming o'er her lone head, so fierce and high—
Each broke to drown her, yet she could not die.

32

Anon—she was released, and then she strayed
    O'er the sharp shingles[4] with her bleeding feet,   250
And stumbled almost every step she made;
    And something rolled before her in a sheet,
Which she must still pursue howe'er afraid;
    'Twas white and indistinct, nor stopped to meet
Her glance nor grasp, for still she gazed and grasped,   255
And ran, but it escaped her as she clasped.

33

The dream changed—in a cave she stood, its walls
    Were hung with marble icicles; the work
Of ages on its water-fretted halls,

4. Loose pebbles.

Where waves might wash, and seals might breed and lurk;
Her hair was dripping, and the very balls   261
    Of her black eyes seemed turned to tears, and murk
The sharp rocks looked below each drop they caught,
Which froze to marble as it fell, she thought.

34

And wet, and cold, and lifeless at her feet,   265
    Pale as the foam that frothed on his dead brow,
Which she essayed in vain to clear (how sweet
    Were once her cares, how idle seemed they now!),
Lay Juan, nor could aught renew the beat
    Of his quenched heart; and the sea dirges low   270
Rang in her sad ears like a mermaid's song,
And that brief dream appeared a life too long.

35

And gazing on the dead, she thought his face
    Faded, or altered into something new—
Like to her father's features, till each trace   275
    More like and like to Lambro's aspect grew—
With all his keen worn look and Grecian grace;
    And starting, she awoke, and what to view?
Oh! Powers of Heaven! what dark eye meets she there?
'Tis—'tis her father's—fixed upon the pair!   280

36

Then shrieking, she arose, and shrieking fell,
    With joy and sorrow, hope and fear, to see
Him whom she deemed a habitant where dwell
    The ocean-buried, risen from death, to be
Perchance the death of one she loved too well: 285
    Dear as her father had been to Haidée,
It was a moment of that awful kind—
I have seen such—but must not call to mind.

37

Up Juan sprung to Haidée's bitter shriek,
    And caught her falling, and from off the wall   290
Snatched down his saber, in hot haste to wreak
    Vengeance on him who was the cause of all:
Then Lambro, who till now forebore to speak,
    Smiled scornfully, and said, "Within my call,
A thousand scimitars await the word;   295
Put up, young man, put up your silly sword."

38

And Haidée clung around him; "Juan, 'tis—
    'Tis Lambro—'tis my father! Kneel with me—
He will forgive us—yes—it must be—yes.
    Oh! dearest father, in this agony   300
Of pleasure and of pain—even while I kiss
    Thy garment's hem with transport, can it be
That doubt should mingle with my filial joy?
Deal with me as thou wilt, but spare this boy."

39

High and inscrutable the old man stood,   305
  Calm in his voice, and calm within his eye—
Not always signs with him of calmest mood:
  He looked upon her, but gave no reply;
Then turned to Juan, in whose cheek the blood
  Oft came and went, as there resolved to die;   310
In arms, at least, he stood, in act to spring
On the first foe whom Lambro's call might bring.

40

"Young man, your sword"; so Lambro once more said:
  Juan replied, "Not while this arm is free."
The old man's cheek grew pale, but not with dread,   315
  And drawing from his belt a pistol, he
Replied, "Your blood be then on your own head."
  Then looked close at the flint, as if to see
'Twas fresh—for he had lately used the lock[5]—
And next proceeded quietly to cock.   320

41

It has a strange quick jar upon the ear,
  That cocking of a pistol, when you know
A moment more will bring the sight to bear
  Upon your person, twelve yards off, or so;
A gentlemanly distance,[6] not too near,   325
  If you have got a former friend for foe;
But after being fired at once or twice,
The ear becomes more Irish, and less nice.[7]

42

Lambro presented, and one instant more
  Had stopped this Canto, and Don Juan's breath,   330
When Haidée threw herself her boy before;
  Stern as her sire: "On me," she cried, "let death
Descend—the fault is mine; this fatal shore
  He found—but sought not. I have pledged my faith;
I love him—I will die with him: I knew   335
Your nature's firmness—know your daughter's too."

43

A minute past, and she had been all tears,
  And tenderness, and infancy; but now
She stood as one who championed human fears—
  Pale, statue-like, and stern, she wooed the blow; 340
And tall beyond her sex, and their compeers,[8]
  She drew up to her height, as if to show
A fairer mark; and with a fixed eye scanned
Her father's face—but never stopped his hand.

5. That part of the gun which explodes   pensity of hotheaded young Irishmen
the charge.   to fight duels.
6. I.e., dueling distance.   8. I.e., she was the match in height of
7. Finicky. Byron alludes to the pro-   Lambro and Juan.

44

He gazed on her, and she on him; 'twas strange   345
   How like they looked! the expression was the same;
Serenely savage, with a little change
   In the large dark eye's mutual-darted flame;
For she, too, was as one who could avenge,
   If cause should be—a lioness, though tame;   350
Her father's blood before her father's face
Boiled up, and proved her truly of his race.

45

I said they were alike, their features and
   Their stature differing but in sex and years;
Even to the delicacy of their hand   355
   There was resemblance, such as true blood wears;
And now to see them, thus divided, stand
   In fixed ferocity, when joyous tears,
And sweet sensations, should have welcomed both,
Show what the passions are in their full growth.   360

46

The father paused a moment, then withdrew
   His weapon, and replaced it; but stood still,
And looking on her, as to look her through,
   "Not I," he said, "have sought this stranger's ill;
Not I have made this desolation: few   365
   Would bear such outrage, and forbear to kill;
But I must do my duty—how thou hast
Done thine, the present vouches for the past.

47

"Let him disarm; or, by my father's head,
   His own shall roll before you like a ball!"   370
He raised his whistle as the word he said,
   And blew; another answered to the call,
And rushing in disorderly, though led,
   And armed from boot to turban, one and all,
Some twenty of his train came, rank on rank;   375
He gave the word, "Arrest or slay the Frank."[9]

48

Then, with a sudden movement, he withdrew
   His daughter; while compressed within his clasp,
'Twixt her and Juan interposed the crew;
   In vain she struggled in her father's grasp—   380
His arms were like a serpent's coil: then flew
   Upon their prey, as darts an angry asp,
The file of pirates; save the foremost, who
Had fallen, with his right shoulder half cut through.

49

The second had his cheek laid open; but   385
   The third, a wary, cool old sworder, took
The blows upon his cutlass, and then put

9. Term used in the Near East to designate a western European.

His own well in; so well, ere you could look,
His man was floored, and helpless at his foot,
 With the blood running like a little brook   390
From two smart saber gashes, deep and red—
One on the arm, the other on the head.

50

And then they bound him where he fell, and bore
 Juan from the apartment: with a sign
Old Lambro bade them take him to the shore,   395
 Where lay some ships which were to sail at nine.
They laid him in a boat, and plied the oar
 Until they reached some galliots,[1] placed in line;
On board of one of these, and under hatches,
They stowed him, with strict orders to the watches.   400

51

The world is full of strange vicissitudes,
 And here was one exceedingly unpleasant:
A gentleman so rich in the world's goods,
 Handsome and young, enjoying all the present,
Just at the very time when he least broods   405
 On such a thing is suddenly to sea sent,
Wounded and chained, so that he cannot move,
And all because a lady fell in love.

* * *

56

Afric is all the sun's, and as her earth
 Her human clay is kindled; full of power
For good or evil, burning from its birth,
 The Moorish blood partakes the planet's hour,
And like the soil beneath it will bring forth: 445
 Beauty and love were Haidée's mother's dower;
But her large dark eye showed deep Passion's force,
Though sleeping like a lion near a source.

57

Her daughter, tempered with a milder ray,
 Like summer clouds all silvery, smooth, and fair,
Till slowly charged with thunder they display   450
 Terror to earth, and tempest to the air,
Had held till now her soft and milky way;
 But overwrought with passion and despair,
The fire burst forth from her Numidian[2] veins,   455
Even as the simoom[3] sweeps the blasted plains.

58

The last sight which she saw was Juan's gore,
 And he himself o'ermastered and cut down;
His blood was running on the very floor
 Where late he trod, her beautiful, her own;   460

1. A small, fast galley, propelled both   3. A violent, hot, dust-laden desert
by oars and sails.   wind.
2. North African.

Thus much she viewed an instant and no more—
   Her struggles ceased with one convulsive groan;
On her sire's arm, which until now scarce held
Her writhing, fell she like a cedar felled.

59

A vein had burst, and her sweet lips' pure dyes   465
   Were dabbled with the deep blood which ran o'er;
And her head drooped, as when the lily lies
   O'ercharged with rain: her summoned handmaids bore
Their lady to her couch with gushing eyes;
   Of herbs and cordials they produced their store,   470
But she defied all means they could employ,
Like one life could not hold, nor death destroy.

60

Days lay she in that state unchanged, though chill—
   With nothing livid,[4] still her lips were red;
She had no pulse, but death seemed absent still;   475
   No hideous sign proclaimed her surely dead;
Corruption came not in each mind to kill
   All hope; to look upon her sweet face bred
New thoughts of life, for it seemed full of soul—
She had so much, earth could not claim the whole.   480

* * *

69

Twelve days and nights she withered thus; at last,   545
   Without a groan, or sigh, or glance, to show
A parting pang, the spirit from her passed:
   And they who watched her nearest could not know
The very instant, till the change that cast
   Her sweet face into shadow, dull and slow,   550
Glazed o'er her eyes—the beautiful, the black—
Oh! to possess such luster—and then lack!

70

She died, but not alone; she held within
   A second principle of life, which might
Have dawned a fair and sinless child of sin;   555
   But closed its little being without light,
And went down to the grave unborn, wherein
   Blossom and bough lie withered with one blight;
In vain the dews of Heaven descend above
The bleeding flower and blasted fruit of love.   560

71

Thus lived—thus died she; never more on her
   Shall sorrow light, or shame. She was not made
Through years or moons the inner weight to bear,
   Which colder hearts endure till they are laid
By age in earth; her days and pleasures were   565
   Brief, but delightful—such as had not stayed

4. I.e., she was ashen pale.

Long with her destiny; but she sleeps well
By the seashore, whereon she loved to dwell.

72

That isle is now all desolate and bare,
　　Its dwellings down, its tenants passed away;　　　570
None but her own and father's grave is there,
　　And nothing outward tells of human clay;
Ye could not know where lies a thing so fair,
　　No stone is there to show, no tongue to say
What was; no dirge, except the hollow sea's,　　　575
In some shape; let none think to fly the danger,
Mourns o'er the beauty of the Cyclades.

73

But many a Greek maid in a loving song
　　Sighs o'er her name; and many an islander
With her sire's story makes the night less long;
　　Valor was his, and beauty dwelt with her:　　　580
If she loved rashly, her life paid for wrong—
　　A heavy price must all pay who thus err,
In some shape; let none think to fly the danger,
For soon or late Love is his own avenger.[5]

* * *

1818–23　　　　　　　　　　　　　　　　　　　　1819–24

The Vision of Judgment[1]

By Quevedo Redivivus[2]

SUGGESTED BY THE COMPOSITION SO ENTITLED BY THE AUTHOR OF
Wat Tyler

"A Daniel come to judgment! yea, a Daniel!
I thank thee, Jew, for teaching me that word."[3]

5. Juan's adventures continue: he is sold as a slave in Constantinople, has an episode in the harem of the sultana, engages in the Russian siege of Ismail, becomes "man-mistress" to Catherine the Great of Russia, and, in Canto X, is sent on a diplomatic mission to England. He is a guest at a great English country house, a subject of interest to several very beautiful women, when the poem breaks off in the sixteenth canto.

1. Although originally an ardent supporter of the French Revolution, Robert Southey soon turned a Tory and in 1813 was appointed poet laureate. Four years after the appointment he was dismayed by the unauthorized publication of his radical poetical drama *Wat Tyler*, which he had written in 1794 but had prudently left in manuscript. Byron reminds him of it in the subtitle. When King George III died in 1820—Shelley in his *Sonnet: England in 1819* had called him, accurately enough, "an old, mad, blind, despised, and dying king"— Southey did his official duty by writing

A Vision of Judgment (1821). In this fulsome eulogy George III goes to heaven, confounds such detractors as John Wilkes and Junius, and obtains a testimonial of noble character from his old enemy, George Washington. The vision ends with the King, beatified, ceremoniously admitted to heaven.

Byron, responding to reports that Southey was vilifying him, had ridiculed the poet in his "Dedication" to Canto I of *Don Juan*. In the Preface to his *Vision of Judgment*, Southey then exhibited his bad judgment by denouncing Byron as head of the "Satanic School" of poetry, combining "lascivious" passages with "a satanic spirit of pride and audacious impiety." Byron immediately responded with *The Vision of Judgment*, in which he purports to tell the true story of how, with the unwitting help of Southey, King George had really managed to get into heaven. The poem is in the genre of the satiric attack on literary "dunces" by Dryden and Pope, but is written in the ottava

1

Saint Peter sat by the celestial gate:
  His keys were rusty, and the lock was dull,
So little trouble had been given of late;
  Not that the place by any means was full,
But since the Gallic era "eighty-eight"[4]   5
  The devils had ta'en a longer, stronger pull,
And "a pull altogether," as they say
At sea—which drew most souls another way.

2

The angels all were singing out of tune,
  And hoarse with having little else to do,   10
Excepting to wind up the sun and moon,
  Or curb a runaway young star or two,
Or wild colt of a comet, which too soon
  Broke out of bounds o'er th' ethereal blue,
Splitting some planet with its playful tail,   15
As boats are sometimes by a wanton whale.

3

The guardian seraphs had retired on high,
  Finding their charges past all care below;
Terrestrial business filled nought in the sky
  Save the recording angel's black bureau;   20
Who found, indeed, the facts to multiply
  With such rapidity of vice and woe,
That he had stripped off both his wings in quills,
And yet was in arrear of human ills.

4

His business so augmented of late years,   25
  That he was forced, against his will no doubt
(Just like those cherubs, earthly ministers),
  For some resource to turn himself about,
And claim the help of his celestial peers,
  To aid him ere he should be quite worn out   30
By the increased demand for his remarks;
Six angels and twelve saints were named his clerks.

5

This was a handsome board—at least for heaven;
  And yet they had even then enough to do,
So many conquerors' cars were daily driven,   35
  So many kingdoms fitted up anew;
Each day too slew its thousands six or seven,
  Till at the crowning carnage, Waterloo,
They threw their pens down in divine disgust—
The page was so besmeared with blood and dust.   40

rima stanza and the easy colloquial manner of Byron's *Don Juan*. In its quick, sure characterization, the pace and economy of its narrative, its inventiveness in detail, above all in the high spirits and unfailing good humor with which the author demolishes his opponent, this poem represents Byron at his masterful best.

2. "Quevedo Revived." Quevedo was a 17th-century Spanish author of *Sueños,* "Visions," written in prose and predominantly satirical in tone.
3. Quoted, not quite accurately, from *The Merchant of Venice,* IV.i.340–41.
4. The last year of the old régime in France, before the outbreak of the Revolution in 1789.

6

This by the way; 'tis not mine to record
  What angels shrink from: even the very devil
On this occasion his own work abhorred,
  So surfeited with the infernal revel:
Though he himself had sharpened every sword,   45
  It almost quenched his innate thirst of evil.
(Here Satan's sole good work deserves insertion—
'Tis, that he has both generals in reversion.[5])

7

Let's skip a few short years of hollow peace,
  Which peopled earth no better, hell as wont,   50
And heaven none—they form the tyrant's lease,
  With nothing but new names subscribed upon 't;
'Twill one day finish: meantime they increase,
  "With seven heads and ten horns," and all in front,
Like Saint John's foretold beast;[6] but ours are born   55
Less formidable in the head than horn.

8

In the first year of freedom's second dawn[7]
  Died George the Third; although no tyrant, one
Who shielded tyrants, till each sense withdrawn
  Left him nor mental nor external sun: 60
A better farmer ne'er brushed dew from lawn,
  A worse king never left a realm undone!
He died—but left his subjects still behind,
One half as mad—and t'other no less blind.

9

He died! his death made no great stir on earth;   65
  His burial made some pomp; there was profusion
Of velvet, gilding, brass, and no great dearth
  Of aught but tears—save those shed by collusion.
For these things may be bought at their true worth;
  Of elegy there was the due infusion—   70
Bought also; and the torches, cloaks, and banners,
Heralds, and relics of old Gothic manners,

10

Formed a sepulchral melodrame. Of all
  The fools who flocked to swell or see the show,
Who cared about the corpse? The funeral   75
  Made the attraction, and the black the woe.
There throbbed not there a thought which pierced the pall;
  And when the gorgeous coffin was laid low,
It seemed the mockery of hell to fold
The rottenness of eighty years in gold.   80

5. Satan has the legal right to the future possession of both Napoleon and Wellington, the commanding officers at the Battle of Waterloo.
6. The Book of Revelation describes such a beast, xiii.1.
7. 1820 was a year of new revolutionary movements in Italy and other countries of southern Europe.

11

So mix his body with the dust! It might
    Return to what it *must* far sooner, were
The natural compound left alone to fight
    Its way back into earth, and fire, and air;
But the unnatural balsams[8] merely blight   85
    What nature made him at his birth, as bare
As the mere million's base unmummied clay—
Yet all his spices but prolong decay.

12

He's dead—and upper earth with him has done;
    He's buried; save the undertaker's bill,   90
Or lapidary scrawl,[9] the world is gone
    For him, unless he left a German will;
But where's the proctor who will ask his son?[1]
    In whom his qualities are reigning still,
Except that household virtue, most uncommon,   95
Of constancy to a bad, ugly woman.

13

"God save the king!" It is a large economy
    In God to save the like; but if he will
Be saving, all the better; for not one am I
    Of those who think damnation better still: 100
I hardly know too if not quite alone am I
    In this small hope of bettering future ill
By circumscribing, with some slight restriction,
The eternity of hell's hot jurisdiction.

14

I know this is unpopular; I know   105
    'Tis blasphemous; I know one may be damned
For hoping no one else may e'er be so;
    I know my catechism; I know we're crammed
With the best doctrines till we quite o'erflow;
    I know that all save England's church have shammed,   110
And that the other twice two hundred churches
And synagogues have made a *damned* bad purchase.

15

God help us all! God help me too! I am,
    God knows, as helpless as the devil can wish,
And not a whit more difficult to damn,   115
    Than is to bring to land a late-hooked fish,
Or to the butcher to purvey the lamb;
    Not that I'm fit for such a noble dish,
As one day will be that immortal fry
Of almost everybody born to die.   120

16

Saint Peter sat by the celestial gate,
    And nodded o'er his keys; when, lo! there came

---

8. I.e., embalming fluids.
9. Inscription cut into a stone monument.
1. A King's Proctor is an official who intervenes in the probate of a will, when chicanery is suspected. Byron alludes

to the scandal that the will of George I, of the German House of Hanover, had been hidden by his son, George II, who was the grandfather of the late George III.

A wondrous noise he had not heard of late—
    A rushing sound of wind, and stream, and flame;
In short, a roar of things extremely great,   125
    Which would have made aught save a saint exclaim;
But he, with first a start and then a wink,
Said, "There's another star gone out, I think!"

17

But ere he could return to his repose,
    A cherub flapped his right wing o'er his eyes—   130
At which St. Peter yawned, and rubbed his nose:
    "Saint porter," said the angel, "prithee rise!"
Waving a goodly wing, which glowed, as glows
    An earthly peacock's tail, with heavenly dyes:
To which the saint replied, "Well, what's the matter?   135
"Is Lucifer come back with all this clatter?"

18

"No," quoth the cherub; "George the Third is dead."
    "And who *is* George the Third?" replied the apostle:
"*What George? what Third?*" "The king of England," said
    The angel. "Well! he won't find kings to jostle   140
Him on his way; but does he wear his head;
    Because the last we saw here had a tustle,
And ne'er would have got into heaven's good graces,
Had he not flung his head in all our faces.[2]

19

"He was, if I remember, king of France;   145
    That head of his, which could not keep a crown
On earth, yet ventured in my face to advance
    A claim to those of martyrs—like my own:
If I had had my sword, as I had once
    When I cut ears off, I had cut him down;[3]   150
But having but my *keys,* and not my brand,
I only knocked his head from out his hand.

20

"And then he set up such a headless howl,
    That all the saints came out and took him in;
And there he sits by St. Paul, cheek by jowl;   155
    That fellow Paul—the parvenu! The skin
Of St. Bartholomew,[4] which makes his cowl
    In heaven, and upon earth redeemed his sin
So as to make a martyr, never sped
Better than did this weak and wooden head.   160

21

"But had it come up here upon its shoulders,
    There would have been a different tale to tell:
The fellow-feeling in the saint's beholders
    Seems to have acted on them like a spell;

2. Louis XVI, who had been guillotined in January, 1793.
3. When the officers came to take Jesus, "Simon Peter having a sword drew it, and smote the high priest's servant, and cut off his right ear" (John xviii.10). "Brand," line 151, is archaic for "sword."
4. According to tradition, the martyred St. Bartholomew was flayed alive.

And so this very foolish head heaven solders   165
   Back on its trunk: it may be very well,
And seems the custom here to overthrow
Whatever has been wisely done below."

22

The angel answered, "Peter! do not pout:
   The king who comes has head and all entire,   170
And never knew much what it was about—
   He did as doth the puppet—by its wire,
And will be judged like all the rest, no doubt:
   My business and your own is not to inquire
Into such matters, but to mind our cue—   175
Which is to act as we are bid to do."

23

While thus they spake, the angelic caravan,
   Arriving like a rush of mighty wind,
Cleaving the fields of space, as doth the swan
   Some silver stream (say Ganges, Nile, or Inde,   180
Or Thames, or Tweed), and 'midst them an old man
   With an old soul, and both extremely blind,
Halted before the gate, and in his shroud
Seated their fellow traveler on a cloud.

24

But bringing up the rear of this bright host   185
   A Spirit of a different aspect waved
His wings, like thunder clouds above some coast
   Whose barren beach with frequent wrecks is paved;
His brow was like the deep when tempest-tossed;
   Fierce and unfathomable thoughts engraved   190
Eternal wrath on his immortal face,
And *where* he gazed a gloom pervaded space.

25

As he drew near, he gazed upon the gate
   Ne'er to be entered more by him or Sin,
With such a glance of supernatural hate,   195
   As made Saint Peter wish himself within;
He pattered with his keys at a great rate,
   And sweated through his apostolic skin:
Of course his perspiration was but ichor,[5]
Or some such other spiritual liquor.   200

26

The very cherubs huddled all together,
   Like birds when soars the falcon; and they felt
A tingling to the tip of every feather,
   And formed a circle like Orion's belt
Around their poor old charge; who scarce knew whither   205
   His guards had led him, though they gently dealt
With royal manes[6] (for by many stories,
And true, we learn the angels all are Tories).

---

5. The fluid in the veins of the gods.
6. In Roman religion, spirits of the dead (pronounced *mā'nēz*).

27

As things were in this posture, the gate flew
    Asunder, and the flashing of its hinges   210
Flung over space an universal hue
    Of many-colored flame, until its tinges
Reached even our speck of earth, and made a new
    Aurora borealis spread its fringes
O'er the North Pole; the same seen, when ice-bound,   215
By Captain Parry's[7] crew, in "Melville's Sound."

28

And from the gate thrown open issued beaming
    A beautiful and mighty Thing of Light,
Radiant with glory, like a banner streaming
    Victorious from some world-o'erthrowing fight: 220
My poor comparisons must needs be teeming
    With earthly likenesses, for here the night
Of clay obscures our best conceptions, saving
Johanna Southcote,[8] or Bob Southey raving.

29

'Twas the archangel Michael: all men know   225
    The make of angels and archangels, since
There's scarce a scribbler has not one to show,
    From the fiends' leader to the angels' prince.
There also are some altarpieces, though
    I really can't say that they much evince   230
One's inner notions of immortal spirits;
But let the connoisseurs explain *their* merits.

30

Michael flew forth in glory and in good;
    A goodly work of him from whom all glory
And good arise; the portal past—he stood;   235
    Before him the young cherubs and saints hoary—
(I say *young*, begging to be understood
    By looks, not years; and should be very sorry
To state, they were not older than St. Peter,
But merely that they seemed a little sweeter).   240

31

The cherubs and the saints bowed down before
    That arch-angelic hierarch, the first
Of essences angelical, who wore
    The aspect of a god; but this ne'er nursed
Pride in his heavenly bosom, in whose core   245
    No thought, save for his Master's service, durst
Intrude, however glorified and high;
He knew him but the viceroy of the sky.

7. Captain William Edward Parry, in his account of his *Voyage in 1819–20*, in search of a northwest passage.
8. Joanna Southcott (1750–1814) was a servant girl who, claiming direct communications from the Almighty, became head of a religious sect. In 1813 she proclaimed that she was about to give birth to a son, Shiloh, who would redeem the world. The pregnancy turned out to be a tumor, of which she died the following year.

32

He and the somber silent Spirit met—
    They knew each other both for good and ill;   250
Such was their power, that neither could forget
    His former friend and future foe; but still
There was a high, immortal, proud regret
    In either's eye, as if 'twere less their will
Than destiny to make the eternal years   255
Their date of war, and their "champ clos"[9] the spheres.

33

But here they were in neutral space: we know
    From Job, that Satan hath the power to pay
A heavenly visit thrice a year or so;
    And that the "sons of God," like those of clay,   260
Must keep him company;[1] and we might show
    From the same book, in how polite a way
The dialogue is held between the Powers
Of Good and Evil—but 'twould take up hours.

34

And this is not a theologic tract,   265
    To prove with Hebrew and with Arabic
If Job be allegory or a fact,
    But a true narrative; and thus I pick
From out the whole but such and such an act
    As sets aside the slightest thought of trick.   270
'Tis every tittle true, beyond suspicion,
And accurate as any other vision.

35

The spirits were in neutral space, before
    The gate of heaven; like eastern thresholds is
The place where Death's grand cause is argued o'er,[2]   275
    And souls despatched to that world or to this;
And therefore Michael and the other wore
    A civil aspect: though they did not kiss,
Yet still between his Darkness and his Brightness
There passed a mutual glance of great politeness.   280

36

The Archangel bowed, not like a modern beau,
    But with a graceful oriental bend,
Pressing one radiant arm just where below
    The heart in good men is supposed to tend.
He turned as to an equal, not too low,   285
    But kindly; Satan met his ancient friend
With more hauteur, as might an old Castilian
Poor noble meet a mushroom rich civilian.[3]

---

9. "Enclosed field," the arena for knightly tournaments.
1. Job i.6. "There was a day when the sons of God came to present themselves before the Lord, and Satan came also among them."
2. The gateways of walled cities in the Middle East were sometimes used for public debates and to administer justice.
3. Byron contrasts ancient Spanish noblemen with *nouveaux riches* who spring up as rapidly as mushrooms.

37

He merely bent his diabolic brow
    An instant; and then raising it, he stood   290
In act to assert his right or wrong, and show
    Cause why King George by no means could or should
Make out a case to be exempt from woe
    Eternal, more than other kings, endued
With better sense and hearts, whom history mentions,   295
Who long have "paved hell with their good intentions."[4]

38

Michael began: "What wouldst thou with this man,
    Now dead, and brought before the Lord? What ill
Hath he wrought since his mortal race began,
    That thou canst claim him? Speak! and do thy will,   300
If it be just: if in this earthly span
    He hath been greatly failing to fulfil
His duties as a king and mortal, say,
And he is thine; if not, let him have way."

39

"Michael!" replied the Prince of Air, "even here,   305
    Before the Gate of him thou servest, must
I claim my subject: and will make appear
    That as he was my worshiper in dust,
So shall he be in spirit, although dear
    To thee and thine, because nor wine nor lust   310
Were of his weaknesses; yet on the throne
He reigned o'er millions to serve me alone.

40

"Look to *our* earth, or rather *mine*; it was,
    Once, more thy master's: but I triumph not
In this poor planet's conquest; nor, alas!   315
    Need he thou servest envy me my lot:
With all the myriads of bright worlds which pass
    In worship round him, he may have forgot
Yon weak creation of such paltry things:
I think few worth damnation save their kings—   320

41

"And these but as a kind of quitrent,[5] to
    Assert my right as lord: and even had
I such an inclination, 'twere (as you
    Well know) superfluous; they are grown so bad,
That hell has nothing better left to do   325
    Than leave them to themselves: so much more mad
And evil by their own internal curse,
Heaven cannot make them better, nor I worse.

42

"Look to the earth, I said, and say again:
    When this old, blind, mad, helpless, weak, poor worm   330
Began in youth's first bloom and flush to reign,

4. An old English proverb.
5. A fixed rent, paid in place of services to a feudal lord.

The world and he both wore a different form,
And much of earth and all the watery plain
    Of ocean called him king: through many a storm
His isles had floated on the abyss of time;
    For the rough virtues chose them for their clime.   335

43

"He came to his scepter young; he leaves it old:
    Look to the state in which he found his realm,
And left it; and his annals too behold,
    How to a minion first he gave the helm,[6]   340
How grew upon his heart a thirst for gold,
    The beggar's vice, which can but overwhelm
The meanest hearts; and for the rest, but glance
Thine eye along America and France.

44

" 'Tis true, he was a tool from first to last   345
    (I have the workmen safe); but as a tool
So let him be consumed. From out the past
    Of ages, since mankind have known the rule
Of monarchs—from the bloody rolls amassed
    Of sin and slaughter—from the Caesar's school,   350
Take the worst pupil; and produce a reign
More drenched with gore, more cumbered with the slain.

45

"He ever warred with freedom and the free:
    Nations as men, home subjects, foreign foes,
So that[7] they uttered the word 'Liberty!'   355
    Found George the Third their first opponent. Whose
History was ever stained as his will be
    With national and individual woes?
I grant his household abstinence; I grant
His neutral virtues, which most monarchs want;   360

46

"I know he was a constant consort; own
    He was a decent sire, and middling lord.
All this is much, and most upon a throne;
    As temperance, if at Apicius' board,[8]
Is more than at an anchorite's[9] supper shown.   365
    I grant him all the kindest can accord;
And this was well for him, but not for those
Millions who found him what oppression chose.

47

"The New World shook him off; the Old yet groans
    Beneath what he and his prepared, if not
Completed: he leaves heirs on many thrones   370
    To all his vices, without what begot
Compassion for him—his tame virtues; drones

---

6. The unpopular Earl of Bute, whom
George III made Prime Minister in
1802.
7. "Provided that."

8. I.e., At the table of Apicius (a famed
Roman gourmet in the time of Augustus).
9. A religious hermit's.

Who sleep, or despots who have now forgot
A lesson which shall be re-taught them, wake   375
Upon the thrones of earth; but let them quake!
                    48
"Five millions of the primitive,[1] who hold
    The faith which makes ye great on earth, implored
A *part* of that vast *all* they held of old—
    Freedom to worship—not alone your Lord,   380
Michael, but you, and you, Saint Peter! Cold
    Must be your souls, if you have not abhorred
The foe to Catholic participation
In all the license of a Christian nation.
                    49
"True! he allowed them to pray God; but as   385
    A consequence of prayer, refused the law
Which would have placed them upon the same base
    With those who did not hold the saints in awe."
But here Saint Peter started from his place,
    And cried, "You may the prisoner withdraw: 390
Ere heaven shall ope her portals to this Guelph,[2]
While I am guard, may I be damned myself!
                    50
"Sooner will I with Cerberus[3] exchange
    My office (and *his* is no sinecure)
Than see this royal Bedlam bigot range   395
    The azure fields of heaven, of that be sure!"
"Saint!" replied Satan, "you do well to avenge
    The wrongs he made your satellites endure;
And if to this exchange you should be given,
I'll try to coax *our* Cerberus up to heaven."   400
                    51
Here Michael interposed: "Good saint! and devil!
    Pray, not so fast; you both outrun discretion.
Saint Peter! you were wont to be more civil!
    Satan! excuse this warmth of his expression,
And condescension to the vulgar's level: 405
    Even saints sometimes forget themselves in session.
Have you got more to say?"—"No."—"If you please,
I'll trouble you to call your witnesses."
                    52
Then Satan turned and waved his swarthy hand,
    Which stirred with its electric qualities   410
Clouds farther off than we can understand,
    Although we find him sometimes in our skies;
Infernal thunder shook both sea and land
    In all the planets, and hell's batteries

1. The Irish Catholics. In 1795 George
had opposed the Catholic Emancipation
Bill, which gave Roman Catholics the
right to hold public offices (line 383).

2. The House of Hanover was descended from the German Guelphs.
3. The three-headed dog guarding the
entrance to Hades.

Let off the artillery, which Milton mentions
  As one of Satan's most sublime inventions.[4]

53
This was a signal unto such damned souls
  As have the privilege of their damnation
Extended far beyond the mere controls
  Of worlds past, present, or to come; no station
Is theirs particularly in the rolls
  Of hell assigned; but where their inclination
Or business carries them in search of game,
They may range freely—being damned the same.

54
They're proud of this—as very well they may,
  It being a sort of knighthood, or gilt key
Stuck in their loins;[5] or like an "entré"
  Up the back stairs, or such freemasonry.
I borrow my comparisons from clay,
  Being clay myself. Let not those spirits be
Offended with such base low likenesses;
We know their posts are nobler far than these.

55
When the great signal ran from heaven to hell—
  About ten million times the distance reckoned
From our sun to its earth, as we can tell
  How much time it takes up, even to a second,
For every ray that travels to dispel
  The fogs of London, through which, dimly beaconed,
The weathercocks are gilt some thrice a year,
If that the *summer* is not too severe—

56
I say that I can tell—'twas half a minute:
  I know the solar beams take up more time
Ere, packed up for their journey, they begin it;
  But then their telegraph[6] is less sublime,
And if they ran a race, they would not win it
  'Gainst Satan's couriers bound for their own clime.
The sun takes up some years for every ray
To reach its goal—the devil not half a day.

57
Upon the verge of space, about the size
  Of half-a-crown, a little speck appeared
(I've seen a something like it in the skies
  In the Aegean, ere a squall); it neared,
And, growing bigger, took another guise;
  Like an aërial ship it tacked, and steered,

415

420

425

430

435

440

445

450

4. In *Paradise Lost* VI. 469 ff., Satan
announced his invention of the cannon
for use in the war in heaven.
5. A gold key hung from the belt be-

tokens certain official positions at the
English court.
6. In its original sense, any apparatus
for transmitting signals at a distance.

Or *was* steered (I am doubtful of the grammar 455
Of the last phrase, which makes the stanza stammer—

58

But take your choice); and then it grew a cloud;
And so it was—a cloud of witnesses.
But such a cloud! No land e'er saw a crowd
    Of locusts numerous as the heavens saw these; 460
They shadowed with their myriads space; their loud
    And varied cries were like those of wild geese
(If nations may be likened to a goose),
And realized the phrase of "hell broke loose."[7]

59

Here crashed a sturdy oath of stout John Bull, 465
    Who damned away his eyes as heretofore:
There Paddy brogued "By Jasus!"—"What's your wull?"
    The temperate Scot exclaimed: the French ghost swore
In certain terms I shan't translate in full,
    As the first coachman will; and 'midst the war, 470
The voice of Jonathan was heard to express,
"*Our* president is going to war, I guess."[8]

60

Besides there were the Spaniard, Dutch, and Dane;
    In short, an universal shoal of shades,
From Otaheite's isle[9] to Salisbury Plain, 475
    Of all climes and professions, years and trades,
Ready to swear against the good king's reign,
    Bitter as clubs in cards are against spades;
All summoned by this grand "subpoena," to
Try if kings mayn't be damned like me or you. 480

61

When Michael saw this host, he first grew pale,
    As angels can; next, like Italian twilight,
He turned all colors—as a peacock's tail,
    Or sunset streaming through a Gothic skylight
In some old abbey, or a trout not stale, 485
    Or distant lightning on the horizon *by* night,
Or a fresh rainbow, or a grand review
Of thirty regiments in red, green, and blue.

62

Then he addressed himself to Satan: "Why—
    My good old friend, for such I deem you, though 490
Our different parties make us fight so shy,
    I ne'er mistake you for a *personal* foe;
Our difference is *political*, and I
    Trust that, whatever may occur below,
You know my great respect for you: and this 495
Makes me regret whate'er you do amiss—

---

7. *Paradise Lost* IV. 918.
8. "Brother Jonathan" was the name applied to America and Americans, now replaced by "Uncle Sam"; the "I guess" was used by Byron as an obvious Ameri- canism. This was written during the troubled Anglo-American relations after the War of 1812.
9. The old name for Tahiti.

63

"Why, my dear Lucifer, would you abuse
  My call for witnesses? I did not mean
That you should half of earth and hell produce;
  'Tis even superfluous, since two honest, clean,   500
True testimonies are enough: we lose
  Our time, nay, our eternity, between
The accusation and defense: if we
Hear both, 'twill stretch our immortality."

64

Satan replied, "To me the matter is   505
  Indifferent, in a personal point of view:
I can have fifty better souls than this
  With far less trouble than we have gone through
Already; and I merely argued his
  Late majesty of Britain's case with you   510
Upon a point of form: you may dispose
Of him; I've kings enough below, God knows!"

65

Thus spoke the Demon (late called "multifaced"
  By multo-scribbling Southey[1]). "Then we'll call
One or two persons of the myriads placed   515
  Around our congress, and dispense with all
The rest," quoth Michael: "Who may be so graced
  As to speak first? there's choice enough—who shall
It be?" Then Satan answered, "There are many;
But you may choose Jack Wilkes[2] as well as any."   520

66

A merry, cock-eyed, curious-looking sprite
  Upon the instant started from the throng,
Dressed in a fashion now forgotten quite;
  For all the fashions of the flesh stick long
By people in the next world; where unite   525
  All the costumes since Adam's, right or wrong,
From Eve's fig leaf down to the petticoat,
Almost as scanty, of days less remote.

67

The spirit looked around upon the crowds
  Assembled, and exclaimed, "My friends of all   530
The spheres, we shall catch cold amongst these clouds;
  So let's to business: why this general call?
If those are freeholders I see in shrouds,
  And 'tis for an election that they bawl,
Behold a candidate with unturned coat!   535
Saint Peter, may I count upon your vote?"

1. In *A Vision of Judgment* V. 70.
2. John Wilkes (1727–97), notorious
libertine, wit, and courageous political
radical, who in 1764 was expelled from
the House of Commons and driven into
exile for his libelous attack on George
III in his weekly periodical, *The North*
Briton. He later came back to England,
became Lord Mayor of London, and was
triumphantly returned to Parliament.
For a supreme example of the wit and
aplomb for which Byron admired Wilkes,
see Boswell's account of Dr. Johnson's
dinner with him in Volume 1.

68

"Sir," replied Michael, "you mistake; these things
   Are of a former life, and what we do
Above is more august; to judge of kings
   Is the tribunal met: so now you know."   540
"Then I presume those gentlemen with wings,"
   Said Wilkes, "are cherubs; and that soul below
Looks much like George the Third, but to my mind
A good deal older—Bless me! is he blind?"

69

"He is what you behold him, and his doom   545
   Depends upon his deeds," the Angel said.
"If you have aught to arraign in him, the tomb
   Gives license to the humblest beggar's head
To lift itself against the loftiest."—"Some,"
   Said Wilkes, "don't wait to see them laid in lead,   550
For such a liberty—and I, for one,
Have told them what I thought beneath the sun."

70

"*Above* the sun repeat, then, what thou hast
   To urge against him," said the Archangel. "Why,"
Replied the spirit, "since old scores are past,   555
   Must I turn evidence? In faith, not I.
Besides, I beat him hollow at the last,
   With all his Lords and Commons:[3] in the sky
I don't like ripping up old stories, since
His conduct was but natural in a prince.   560

71

"Foolish, no doubt, and wicked, to oppress
   A poor unlucky devil without a shilling;
But then I blame the man himself much less
   Than Bute and Grafton,[4] and shall be unwilling
To see him punished here for their excess,   565
   Since they were both damned long ago, and still in
Their place below: for me, I have forgiven,
And vote his 'habeas corpus' into heaven."

72

"Wilkes," said the Devil, "I understand all this;
   You turned to half a courtier ere you died,[5]   570
And seem to think it would not be amiss
   To grow a whole one on the other side
Of Charon's ferry;[6] you forget that *his*
   Reign is concluded; whatsoe'er betide,
He won't be sovereign more: you've lost your labor   575
For at the best he will but be your neighbor.

---

3. In 1782 Wilkes succeeded in getting
the House of Commons to expunge
the record of his expulsion.
4. The Duke of Grafton, like the Earl
of Bute, was a minister subservient to
George III.

5. Wilkes in his latter years softened his
opposition and moved in higher social
circles.
6. In Greek mythology, Charon ferried
the dead to the underworld across the
river Styx.

73

"However, I knew what to think of it,
　　When I beheld you in your jesting way
Flitting and whispering round about the spit
　　Where Belial, upon duty for the day,　　　　　　580
With Fox's lard was basting William Pitt,[7]
　　His pupil; I knew what to think, I say:
That fellow even in hell breeds farther ills;
I'll have him *gagged*—'twas one of his own bills.[8]

74

"Call Junius!"[9] From the crowd a shadow stalked,　585
　　And at the name there was a general squeeze,
So that the very ghosts no longer walked
　　In comfort, at their own aërial ease,
But were all rammed, and jammed (but to be balked,
　　As we shall see), and jostled hands and knees,　590
Like wind compressed and pent within a bladder,
Or like a human colic, which is sadder.

75

The shadow came—a tall, thin, gray-haired figure,
　　That looked as it had been a shade on earth;
Quick in its motions, with an air of vigor,　　　　595
　　But nought to mark its breeding or its birth:
Now it waxed little, then again grew bigger,
　　With now an air of gloom, or savage mirth;
But as you gazed upon its features, they
Changed every instant—to *what*, none could say.　600

76

The more intently the ghosts gazed, the less
　　Could they distinguish whose the features were;
The Devil himself seemed puzzled even to guess;
　　They varied like a dream—now here, now there;
And several people swore from out the press,　　605
　　They knew him perfectly; and one could swear
He was his father: upon which another
Was sure he was his mother's cousin's brother:

77

Another, that he was a duke, or knight,
　　An orator, a lawyer, or a priest,
A nabob,[1] a man-midwife; but the wight　　　　610
　　Mysterious changed his countenance at least
As oft as they their minds: though in full sight
　　He stood, the puzzle only was increased;

---

7. Charles James Fox, statesman and political opponent of William Pitt, prime minister under George III, was notably corpulent.
8. The Alien and Sedition Bills of 1795 severely restricted freedom of speech and of the press.
9. Pseudonym of the writer of a brilliant series of letters (1769–71), attacking supporters of George III and the King himself. His identity is an unsolved political mystery; among more than

fifty possibilities proposed are Edmund Burke, John Horne Tooke, and Sir Philip Francis, mentioned in lines 631–32. When the letters were published as a book, the title-page read: *Letters of Junius, Stat Nominis Umbra* ("he stands, the shadow of a name"); hence the allusions, lines 593 ff., 667. The Latin phrase is from Lucan's *Pharsalia* I.135.
1. A man of great wealth, especially one who has returned to England with a fortune acquired in India.

The man was a phantasmagoria in   615
    Himself—he was so volatile and thin.

78

The moment that you had pronounced him *one*,
    Presto! his face changed, and he was another;
And when that change was hardly well put on,
    It varied, till I don't think his own mother   620
(If that he had a mother) would her son
    Have known, he shifted so from one to t'other;
Till guessing from a pleasure grew a task,
At this epistolary "Iron Mask."[2]

79

For sometimes he like Cerberus would seem—   625
    "Three gentlemen at once" (as sagely says
Good Mrs. Malaprop[3]); then you might deem
    That he was not even *one*; now many rays
Were flashing round him; and now a thick steam
    Hid him from sight—like fogs on London days: 630
Now Burke, now Tooke, he grew to people's fancies,
And certes often like Sir Philip Francis.

80

I've an hypothesis—'tis quite my own;
    I never let it out till now, for fear
Of doing people harm about the throne,   635
    And injuring some minister or peer,
On whom the stigma might perhaps be blown;
    It is—my gentle public, lend thine ear!
'Tis, that what Junius we are wont to call
Was *really, truly*, nobody at all.   640

81

I don't see wherefore letters should not be
    Written without hands, since we daily view
Them written without heads; and books, we see,
    Are filled as well without the latter too:
And really till we fix on somebody   645
    For certain sure to claim them as his due,
Their author, like the Niger's mouth,[4] will bother
The world to say if *there* be mouth or author.

82

"And who and what art thou?" the Archangel said.
    "For *that* you may consult my title page,"   650
Replied this mighty shadow of a shade:
    "If I have kept my secret half an age,
I scarce shall tell it now."—"Canst thou upbraid,"
    Continued Michael, "George Rex, or allege

---

2. "The Man in the Iron Mask" was
a state prisoner in the reign of Louis
XIV, whose identity was thus concealed.
3. A character in R. B. Sheridan's
The Rivals, who comically misused

words; the word "malapropism" derives from her name.
4. Several recent British expeditions to
explore the course of the river Niger,
in western Africa, had ended in failure.

Aught further?" Junius answered, "You had better   655
First ask him for *his* answer to my letter:

83

"My charges upon record will outlast
    The brass of both his epitaph and tomb."
"Repent'st thou not," said Michael, "of some past
    Exaggeration? something which may doom   660
Thyself if false, as him if true? Thou wast
    Too bitter—is it not so?—in thy gloom
Of passion?"—"Passion!" cried the phantom dim,
"I loved my country, and I hated him.

84

"What I have written, I have written:[5] let   665
    The rest be on his head or mine!" So spoke
Old "Nominis Umbra"; and while speaking yet,
    Away he melted in celestial smoke.
Then Satan said to Michael, "Don't forget
    To call George Washington, and John Horne Tooke,[6]   670
And Franklin"—but at this time there was heard
A cry for room, though not a phantom stirred.

85

At length with jostling, elbowing, and the aid
    Of cherubim appointed to that post,
The devil Asmodeus[7] to the circle made   675
    His way, and looked as if his journey cost
Some trouble. When his burden down he laid,
    "What's this?" cried Michael; "why, 'tis not a ghost?"
"I know it," quoth the incubus; "but he
Shall be one, if you leave the affair to me.   680

86

"Confound the renegado! I have sprained
    My left wing, he's so heavy; one would think
Some of his works about his neck were chained.
    But to the point; while hovering o'er the brink
Of Skiddaw (where as usual it still rained),[8]   685
    I saw a taper, far below me, wink,
And stooping, caught this fellow at a libel—
No less on history than the Holy Bible.

87

"The former is the devil's scripture, and
    The latter yours, good Michael: so the affair   690
Belongs to all of us, you understand.
    I snatched him up just as you see him there,
And brought him off for sentence out of hand:
    I've scarcely been ten minutes in the air—
At least a quarter it can hardly be: 695
I dare say that his wife is still at tea."

5. Said by Pilate, John xix.22.
6. A prominent English opponent of the
war against the American colonies; see
note to line 585.
7. The devil in Le Sage's *Le Diable*

Boiteux ("The Lame Devil"), published
1707, who carries Don Cleofas to the
summit of San Salvador.
8. Mount Skiddaw, near Southey's home
in the Lake Country.

88

Here Satan said, "I know this man of old,
    And have expected him for some time here;
A sillier fellow you will scarce behold,
    Or more conceited in his petty sphere: 700
But surely it was not worth while to fold
    Such trash below your wing, Asmodeus dear:
We had the poor wretch safe (without being bored
With carriage) coming of his own accord.

89

"But since he's here, let's see what he has done."   705
    "Done!" cried Asmodeus, "he anticipates
The very business you are now upon,
    And scribbles as if head clerk to the Fates.
Who knows to what his ribaldry may run,
    When such an ass as this, like Balaam's,[9] prates?"   710
"Let's hear," quoth Michael, "what he has to say:
You know we're bound to that in every way."

90

Now the bard, glad to get an audience, which
    By no means often was his case below,
Began to cough, and hawk, and hem, and pitch   715
    His voice into that awful note of woe
To all unhappy hearers within reach
    Of poets when the tide of rhyme's in flow;
But stuck fast with his first hexameter,
Not one of all whose gouty feet would stir.   720

91

But ere the spavined dactyls[1] could be spurred
    Into recitative, in great dismay
Both cherubim and seraphim were heard
    To murmur loudly through their long array;
And Michael rose ere he could get a word   725
    Of all his foundered verses under way,
And cried, "For God's sake stop, my friend! 'twere best—
Non Di, non homines[2]—you know the rest."

92

A general bustle spread throughout the throng,
    Which seemed to hold all verse in detestation;   730
The angels had of course enough of song
    When upon service; and the generation
Of ghosts had heard too much in life, not long
    Before, to profit by a new occasion:

9. Balaam's ass was granted speech in
Numbers xxii.28 ff.
1. Southey's *A Vision of Judgment* was
written in dactylic hexameters, a very
awkward measure in English. A "spavined" horse is a lame one.

2. Horace, *Art of Poetry*, 372–73: "me-
diocribus esse poetis / Non homines,
non di, non concessere columnae" ("mediocrity in poets has never been tolerated
by either men, or gods, or booksellers").

The monarch, mute till then, exclaimed, "What! what!   735
Pye³ come again? No more—no more of that!"

93

The tumult grew; an universal cough
     Convulsed the skies, as during a debate,
When Castlereagh⁴ has been up long enough
     (Before he was first minister of state,
I mean—the *slaves hear now*); some cried "Off, off!"   740
     As at a farce; till, grown quite desperate,
The bard Saint Peter prayed to interpose
(Himself an author)⁵ only for his prose.

94

The varlet was not an ill-favored knave;   745
     A good deal like a vulture in the face,
With a hook nose and a hawk's eye, which gave
     A smart and sharper-looking sort of grace
To his whole aspect, which, though rather grave,
     Was by no means so ugly as his case;   750
But that, indeed, was hopeless as can be,
Quite a poetic felony "*de se.*"⁶

95

Then Michael blew his trump, and stilled the noise
     With one still greater, as is yet the mode
On earth besides; except some grumbling voice,   755
     Which now and then will make a slight inroad
Upon decorous silence, few will twice
     Lift up their lungs when fairly overcrowed;
And now the bard could plead his own bad cause,
With all the attitudes of self-applause.   760

96

He said—(I only give the heads)—he said,
     He meant no harm in scribbling; 'twas his way
Upon all topics; 'twas, besides, his bread,
     Of which he buttered both sides; 'twould delay
Too long the assembly (he was pleased to dread),   765
     And take up rather more time than a day,
To name his works—he would but cite a few—
"Wat Tyler"—"Rhymes on Blenheim"—"Waterloo."

97

He had written praises of a regicide;⁷
     He had written praises of all kings what ever;
He had written for republics far and wide,   770
     And then against them bitterer than ever:

---

3. Henry James Pye, a bad and much ridiculed poet, Southey's predecessor as poet laureate.
4. Viscount Castlereagh was foreign secretary when Byron wrote his poem. "The slaves hear now": i.e., now that he is Prime Minister members of the House of Commons listen obsequiously.

5. The reference is to the first and second epistles of Peter, very short books in the New Testament.
6. A felony "upon himself"; that is, suicide.
7. In an early poem on Henry Martin, one of the judges who had condemned Charles I to be beheaded.

For pantisocracy[8] he once had cried
    Aloud, a scheme less moral than 'twas clever;
Then grew a hearty anti-jacobin—   775
Had turned his coat—and would have turned his skin.

98

He had sung against all battles, and again
    In their high praise and glory; he had called
Reviewing "the ungentle craft,"[9] and then
    Become as base a critic as e'er crawled—   780
Fed, paid, and pampered by the very men
    By whom his muse and morals had been mauled:
He had written much blank verse, and blanker prose,
And more of both than anybody knows.

99

He had written Wesley's life—here turning round   785
    To Satan, "Sir, I'm ready to write yours,
In two octavo volumes, nicely bound,
    With notes and preface, all that most allures
The pious purchaser; and there's no ground
    For fear, for I can choose my own reviewers: 790
So let me have the proper documents,
That I may add you to my other saints."

100

Satan bowed, and was silent. "Well, if you,
    With amiable modesty, decline
My offer, what says Michael? There are few   795
    Whose memoirs could be rendered more divine.
Mine is a pen of all work; not so new
    As it was once, but I would make you shine
Like your own trumpet. By the way, my own
Has more of brass in it, and is as well blown.   800

101

"But talking about trumpets, here's my Vision!
    Now you shall judge, all people; yes, you shall
Judge with my judgment, and by my decision
    Be guided who shall enter heaven or fall.
I settle all these things by intuition,   805
    Times present, past, to come, heaven, hell, and all,
Like King Alfonso.[1] When I thus see double,
I save the Deity some worlds of trouble."

102

He ceased, and drew forth an MS.; and no
    Persuasion on the part of devils, saints,   810
Or angels, now could stop the torrent; so

---

8. An ideal community that Southey and Coleridge, in 1794–95, had planned to set up in America on the banks of the Susquehanna. The scheme was utopian, but in no way immoral.
9. In Southey's *The Remains of Henry Kirke White*, Vol. I (1808).

1. "King Alphonso [of Castile, in the 13th century] speaking of the Ptolemean system, said that had he been consulted at the creation of the world, he would have spared the Maker some absurdities" [Byron's note].

He read the first three lines of the contents;
  But at the fourth, the whole spiritual show
    Had vanished, with variety of scents,
Ambrosial and sulphureous, as they sprang,   815
  Like lightning, off from his "melodious twang."[2]

103

Those grand heroics acted as a spell:
  The angels stopped their ears and plied their pinions;
The devils ran howling, deafened, down to hell;
  The ghosts fled, gibbering, for their own dominions—   820
    (For 'tis not yet decided where they dwell,
And I leave every man to his opinions);
  Michael took refuge in his trump—but, lo!
His teeth were set on edge, he could not blow!

104

Saint Peter, who has hitherto been known   825
  For an impetuous saint, upraised his keys,
And at the fifth line knocked the poet down;
  Who fell like Phaëton,[3] but more at ease,
Into his lake, for there he did not drown;
  A different web being by the Destinies   830
Woven for the Laureate's final wreath, whene'er
Reform shall happen either here or there.

105

He first sank to the bottom—like his works,
  But soon rose to the surface—like himself;
For all corrupted things are buoyed like corks,
  By their own rottenness, light as an elf,   835
Or wisp that flits o'er a morass: he lurks,
  It may be, still, like dull books on a shelf,
In his own den, to scrawl some "Life" or "Vision,"
As Welborn says—"the devil turned precisian."[4]   840

106

As for the rest, to come to the conclusion
  Of this true dream, the telescope is gone
Which kept my optics free from all delusion,
  And showed me what I in my turn have shown;
All I saw farther, in the last confusion,   845
  Was, that King George slipped into heaven for one;
And when the tumult dwindled to a calm,
I left him practising the hundredth psalm.[5]

1821   1822

---

2. John Aubrey in his *Miscellanies upon Various Subjects* (1696) had described a ghost that vanished "with a curious perfume, and most melodious twang."
3. Phaethon, son of Apollo, tried to drive his father's chariot, the sun. He could not control the horses and was struck down into the sea by a thunderbolt of Zeus. The satiric point is that Apollo is the god of poetry as well as of the sun.
4. A "precisian" is a Puritan. Spoken by Welborn in Massinger's play, *A New Way to Pay Old Debts* (1626), I.i.6.
5. Which contains the relevant line, "Enter into his gates with thanksgiving."

Stanzas to the Po[1]

River, that rollest by the ancient walls,
　　Where dwells the Lady of my love, when she
Walks by thy brink, and there perchance recalls
　　A faint and fleeting memory of me;

What if thy deep and ample stream should be　　　　5
　　A mirror of my heart, where she may read
The thousand thoughts I now betray to thee,
　　Wild as thy wave, and headlong as thy speed!

What do I say—a mirror of my heart?
　　Are not thy waters sweeping, dark, and strong?　　10
Such as my feelings were and are, thou art;
　　And such as thou art were my passions long.

Time may have somewhat tamed them—not forever;
　　Thou overflow'st thy banks, and not for aye
Thy bosom overboils, congenial river!　　　　　　　15
　　Thy floods subside, and mine have sunk away—

But left long wrecks behind: and now again,
　　Borne in our old unchanged career, we move:
Thou tendest wildly onwards to the main.
　　And I—to loving *one* I should not love.　　　　20

The current I behold will sweep beneath
　　Her native walls, and murmur at her feet;
Her eyes will look on thee, when she shall breathe
　　The twilight air, unharmed by summer's heat.

She will look on thee—I have looked on thee,　　　25
　　Full of that thought; and, from that moment, ne'er
Thy waters could I dream of, name, or see,
　　Without the inseparable sigh for her!

Her bright eyes will be imaged in thy stream—
　　Yes! they will meet the wave I gaze on now:　　30
Mine cannot witness, even in a dream,
　　That happy wave repass me in its flow!

The wave that bears my tears returns no more:
　　Will she return by whom that wave shall sweep?
Both tread thy banks, both wander on thy shore,　　35
　　I by thy source, she by the dark-blue deep.

1. This powerful lyric was written a
month or two after Byron had fallen in
love with the 19-year-old Italian Teresa
Guiccioli. The Po is a river in northern
Italy that flows into the Adriatic.

But that which keepeth us apart is not
    Distance, nor depth of wave, nor space of earth,
But the distraction of a various lot,
    As various as the climates of our birth.   40

A stranger loves the Lady of the land,
    Born far beyond the mountains, but his blood
Is all meridian,[2] as if never fanned
    By the black wind that chills the polar flood.

My blood is all meridian; were it not,   45
    I had not left my clime, nor should I be,
In spite of tortures, ne'er to be forgot,
    A slave again of love—at least of thee.

'Tis vain to struggle—let me perish young—
    Live as I lived, and love as I have loved;   50
To dust if I return, from dust I sprung,
    And then, at least, my heart can ne'er be moved.

1819   1824

When a Man Hath No Freedom to Fight for at Home[1]

When a man hath no freedom to fight for at home,
    Let him combat for that of his neighbors;
Let him think of the glories of Greece and of Rome,
    And get knocked on his head for his labors.

To do good to mankind is the chivalrous plan,   5
    And is always as nobly requited;
Then battle for freedom wherever you can,
    And, if not shot or hanged, you'll get knighted.

November 5, 1820   1824

Stanzas Written on the Road Between Florence and Pisa

Oh, talk not to me of a name great in story—
The days of our youth are the days of our glory;

2. Southern.
1. The ironist's attitude toward gratuitous enlistment in a foreign war for national freedom—a cause to which Byron gave his own life less than four years later.

And the myrtle and ivy of sweet two-and-twenty
Are worth all your laurels,[1] though ever so plenty.

What are garlands and crowns to the brow that is wrinkled? 5
'Tis but as a dead-flower with May-dew besprinkled:
Then away with all such from the head that is hoary!
What care I for the wreaths that can *only* give glory?

Oh FAME!—if I e'er took delight in thy praises,
'Twas less for the sake of thy high-sounding phrases, 10
Than to see the bright eyes of the dear one discover
She thought that I was not unworthy to love her.

There chiefly I sought thee, *there* only I found thee;
Her glance was the best of the rays that surround thee;
When it sparkled o'er aught that was bright in my story, 15
I knew it was love, and I felt it was glory.

November, 1821   1830

1. Myrtle was sacred to Venus, goddess of love, and ivy to Bacchus, god of wine and revelry; a laurel crown was awarded by the Greeks as a mark of high honor.

PERCY BYSSHE SHELLEY
(1792–1822)

1811: Is expelled from Oxford and elopes with Harriet West-
        brook.
1818: Leaves England for Italy, never to return.
1819: The great year: *Prometheus Unbound, The Cenci, Ode
        to the West Wind,* and some of his best lyrics.
1820: Settles in Pisa and its vicinity; the "Pisan Circle."

Although he was an extreme heretic and nonconformist in all his life and thought, Shelley emerged from a solidly conservative background. His ancestors had been Sussex aristocrats since early in the 17th century; his grandfather, Sir Bysshe Shelley, made himself the richest man in Horsham, Sussex; his father, Timothy Shelley, was a hardheaded and conventional member of Parliament; Percy Shelley himself was in line for a baronetcy, and as befitted his station, was sent to be educated at Eton and at Oxford. He was slight of build, eccentric in manner, and unskilled in sports or fighting, and as a consequence, was mercilessly baited by older and stronger boys. Even then he saw the petty tyranny of schoolmasters and schoolmates as representative of man's general inhumanity to man, and dedicated his life to a war against all injustice and oppression. He describes the experience in the Dedication to *The Revolt of Islam:*

> So without shame, I spoke: "I will be wise,
> And just, and free, and mild, if in me lies
> Such power, for I grow weary to behold
> The selfish and the strong still tyrannize
> Without reproach or check." I then controlled
> My tears, my heart grew calm, and I was meek and bold.

At Oxford in the autumn of 1810 Shelley's closest friend was Thomas Jefferson Hogg, a self-centered and self-confident young man who shared Shelley's love of philosophy and scorn of orthodoxy. The two collaborated on a pamphlet, *The Necessity of Atheism*, which claimed that God's existence cannot be proved on empirical grounds. Shelley refused to repudiate the document before the authorities and, to his great shock and grief, was peremptorily expelled, terminating a university career that had lasted only six months. This event opened a breach between Shelley and his father that widened over the years.

Shelley went to London where, eager for a test of his zeal for social justice, he took up the cause of Harriet Westbrook, the pretty and warm-hearted daughter of a well-to-do tavern keeper, whose father, Shelley wrote to Hogg, "has persecuted her in a most horrible way by endeavoring to compel her to go to school." Harriet threw herself on Shelley's protection, and "gratitude and admiration," he wrote, "all demand that I shall love her *forever*." He eloped with Harriet to Edinburgh and married her, though against his firm conviction that marriage was a tyrannical and degrading social institution. He was then 18 years of age, and his bride 16. The young couple moved restlessly from place to place, living on a small allowance granted reluctantly by their families. In February of 1812, accompanied by Harriet's sister Eliza, they traveled to Dublin to distribute Shelley's *Address to the Irish People* and otherwise take part in the movement for Catholic emancipation and for the amelioration of the oppressed and poverty-stricken people.

Back in London, Shelley became a disciple of the radical social philosopher William Godwin, author of the *Inquiry Concerning Political Justice*. In 1813 he printed privately his first important work, *Queen Mab*, a long prophetic poem set in the fantastic frame of the journey of a disembodied soul through space, to whom the fairy Mab reveals in visions the woeful past, the dreadful present, and the utopian future. Announcing that "there is no God!" Mab decries institutional religion and codified morality as the causes of social evil. She predicts, by the action of the all-ruling goddess Necessity, the withering away of all institutions, and the return of man to his natural state of goodness and felicity.

In the following spring Shelley, who had drifted apart from Harriet, fell in love with the beautiful Mary Wollstonecraft Godwin. Acting according to his conviction that cohabitation without love is immoral, he abandoned Harriet, fled to France with Mary (taking along her half sister, Claire Clairmont), and—still acting in accordance with his belief in nonexclusive love—invited Harriet to come live with them in the relationship of a sister. Shelley's elopement with Mary outraged even her father, though his theoretical views of marriage had been no less liberal than Shelley's, and despite the fact that Shelley, himself in financial difficulties, had earlier taken over Godwin's very substantial debts. When he returned to London, Shelley found that the general public, his family, and most of his friends regarded him not only as an atheist and revolutionary, but also as a gross immoralist. When, two years later, Harriet drowned herself in a fit of despair, the courts denied Shelley the custody of their two children. Shelley married Mary Godwin and, in 1818, moved to Italy; thereafter he saw himself in the role of an alien and outcast, scorned and rejected by the mankind to whose welfare he had dedicated his powers and his life.

In Italy he resumed his restless existence, moving from town to town and house to house. His health was usually bad. Although the death of his grandfather in 1815 had provided a substantial income, he dissipated so much of it by his warmhearted but improvident support of William Godwin, Leigh Hunt, and other indigent pensioners that he was constantly short of money and harried by creditors. Within nine months, in 1818–19, Clara and William, the beloved children of Percy and Mary Shelley, both died. This tragedy threw Mary into a state of apathy and self-absorption which destroyed the earlier harmony of her relationship with her husband, and from which even the birth of another son, Percy Florence, could not entirely rescue her.

In these desperate circumstances, in a state sometimes verging on despair, and knowing that he almost entirely lacked a literary audience, Shelley wrote his greatest works. In 1819 he completed his masterpiece, *Prometheus Unbound*, and wrote a fine tragedy, *The Cenci*, as well as a number of lyric poems, two satires (*The Mask of Anarchy* and *Peter Bell the Third*), and a penetrating political essay, *A Philosophical View of Reform*. His works of the next two years include *A Defense of Poetry*; *Epipsychidion*, a rhapsodic vision of love as a union, beyond earthly limits, with what the title identifies as "the soul out of my soul"; *Adonais*, his noble elegy on the death of Keats; and *Hellas*, a lyrical drama evoked by the Greek war for liberation from the Turks in which he again projected his vision of a new golden age. These writings, unlike the early *Queen Mab*, are the products of a mind enlarged and chastened by tragic experience, deepened by incessant philosophical speculation, and richly stored with the harvest of his reading—which Shelley carried on, as his friend Hogg said, "in season and out of season, at table, in bed, and especially during a walk," until he became one of the most erudite of poets. His delight in scientific discoveries and speculations continued, but his earlier zest for Gothic terrors and the social theories of the radical 18th-century optimists had given way to an absorption in Greek tragedy, Milton's *Paradise Lost*, and the Bible. While he did not give up his hopes for a millennial future (he wore a ring with the motto *Il buon tempo verrà*—"the good time will come"), he now attributed the evils of present society to man's own moral failures, and grounded the possibility of radical social reform upon a prior reform of man's moral nature through the redeeming power of love. Though often thought of as a simple-minded doctrinaire, Shelley in fact possessed a complex and energetically inquisitive intelligence which never halted at a fixed mental position; all his writings represent, not final solutions, but stages in a ceaseless exploration.

The poems of Shelley's maturity also exhibit the effect of his intensive study of Plato and the Neo-Platonists. From his early childhood, Shelley had lived in two worlds. One was the world of his everyday experience, the world of suffering, oppression, and cruelty, which he found intolerable; the other was an imagined world of absolute justice, goodness, and love. To such a mind Platonism was congenial, for it sees the cosmos as divided between the passing and shadowy domain of sense experience and the criterion world of Forms, perfect, eternal, out of time and space, the locus of all Reality, Beauty, and Goodness, of which the world of sense is only a distant and illusory reflection. The earlier interpretations of Shelley as an outright (if somewhat confused) Platonic idealist have been drastically modified by recent investigations of Shelley's reading, and of his philosophical essays, as well as his poetry. He was a close student of the English empirical tradition, which limits knowledge to valid reasoning upon what is given in sense-experience, and felt a special affinity, within this tradition, to the radical scepticism of David Hume. Very early in his career he wrote, in a note to *Queen Mab*, "All that we have a right to infer from our ignorance of any event is that we do not know it"; and later: we quickly reach "the verge where words abandon us, and what wonder if we grow dizzy to look down the dark abyss of how little we know." Shelley was indeed an idealist, but as C. E. Pulos has shown in *The Deep Truth: A Study of Shelley's Scepticism*, his was "a qualified idealism," holding provisionally to the ideas envisioned by an imagination which transcends experience, but refusing to assert of these ideas specific attributes outside the limits of experience. On this ground he steadfastly refused, for example, to affirm the survival of conscious life and personal identity beyond the grave; what we know is that this life ends in death, and what happens thereafter, as he said in *Prometheus Unbound*, however we may imagine it, "is known / But to the uncommunicating dead." The *Hymn to Intellectual Beauty* is often represented as the central instance of Shelley's Platonism; in fact, the poem expressly rejects positive assertions about the nature, controlling causes, and ends of this "unseen Power," which have been proposed either by doctrinaire philosophy or dogmatic religion. Shelley also puts forward the concept of another Power, the ultimate principle that governs all process, the way things actually happen—the Power "in the likeness of the Arve" in *Mont Blanc*, the "mighty darkness" and shapeless form that is Demogorgon in *Prometheus Unbound*; but this principle is represented as inaccessible to the knowing mind and totally indifferent to human ends, so that, although capable of being turned to great good, it is equally capable of bringing destruction to all that we most value. To the mature Shelley the hope that good will triumph in a millennial condition on earth is not an intellectual certainty, but only an essential virtue, a moral *sine qua non*. The indefeasible hope in the ultimate redemption of life by love and the imagination does not guarantee its achievement, but it keeps open the possibility of such achievement, and releases man's imaginative and creative potentialities which are its only available means. We must cling to hope, for its contrary, despair, does guarantee its own validity, by ensuring the permanence of the desperate conditions before which the mind has surrendered its aspirations.

When in 1820 the Shelleys settled finally at Pisa, he came closer to finding contentment than at any time in his adult life. A group of friends, Shelley's "Pisan Circle," gathered around them, including for a while Lord Byron and the swashbuckling young Cornishman, Edward Trelawney. Chief in Shelley's affections, however, were Edward Williams, a retired lieutenant of the army of the East India Company, and his charming common-law wife, Jane, with whom Shelley carried on a flirtation and to whom he addressed some of his best lyrics and verse letters. The end came suddenly, and in a fashion pre-visioned in the ecstatic last stanza of *Adonais*, where Shelley had described his spirit as a ship driven by a violent storm out into the dark unknown to join the disembodied soul of Adonais. On July 8, 1822, Shelley and Edward Williams were sailing their open boat, the *Don Juan*, from Leghorn to their summer house near Lerici, on the Gulf of Spezzia. A violent squall blew up and swamped the boat. When several days later the bodies were washed ashore they were cremated, and Shelley's ashes were buried in the Protestant Cemetery at Rome, near the graves of John Keats and of William Shelley, the poet's young son. He left unfinished *The Triumph of Life* which, in its sustained narrative power, boldness of design, and stylistic concentration was a new departure for Shelley and, in the estimation of many readers, promised to be his greatest poem.

Byron, who did not pay moral compliments lightly, wrote to John Murray at the time of Shelley's death: "You were all brutally mistaken about Shelley, who was, without exception, the *best* and least selfish man I ever knew. I never knew one who was not a beast in comparison." The tragedy of Shelley's short life was that, in attempting to live in this world according to his ideas of what ought to be, he brought disaster and suffering upon himself and those he loved; as he himself recognized when he wrote to Mary the year before he died: "Good, far more than evil impulses, love, far more than hatred, has been to me * * * the source of all sorts of mischief."

To many of the new critics in the decades after 1920 (and despite the reverence toward him of W. B. Yeats, an admitted master of the poetry they most admire), Shelley has served as the very model of what poetry should not be, a favorite resort for supposed examples of intellectual and emotional immaturity, shoddy workmanship, unvisualizable descriptions, and incoherent imagery. But the attack has elicited a number of able defenders, whose close reading of Shelley's poems have increasingly verified Wordsworth's perception that "Shelley is one of the best *artists* of us all: I mean in workmanship of style." Shelley's expansion of the metrical and sonantal resources of verse is without recent parallel in the history of English literature. Furthermore, his successful poems show an astonishing range of voice, from the sovereign order in rage of *Ode to the West Wind*, through the calm and heroic dignity of the utterances of Prometheus, and the near approximation to the inexpressible in the representation of the transfiguration of Asia and in the visionary conclusion of *Adonais*, to—and most surprising, in a poet who almost entirely lacked an audience—the assured urbanity, the effortless command of the tone and the language of a cultivated man of the world, which is exemplified in passages that Shelley wrote all through his mature career, but most sustainedly in the great lyrics and verse letters that he composed during the last year of his life.

Mutability

We are as clouds that veil the midnight moon;
　How restlessly they speed, and gleam, and quiver,
Streaking the darkness radiantly!—yet soon
　Night closes round, and they are lost forever:

Or like forgotten lyres, whose dissonant strings 　　　　5
　Give various response to each varying blast,
To whose frail frame no second motion brings
　One mood or modulation like the last.

We rest.—A dream has power to poison sleep;
　We rise.—One wandering thought pollutes the day; 　10
We feel, conceive or reason, laugh or weep;
　Embrace fond woe, or cast our cares away:

It is the same!—For, be it joy or sorrow,
　The path of its departure still is free:
Man's yesterday may ne'er be like his morrow; 　　　　15
　Nought may endure but Mutability.

　　　　　　　　　　　　　　　　　　　　1816

Mont Blanc[1]

LINES WRITTEN IN THE VALE OF CHAMOUNI

1

The everlasting universe of things
Flows through the mind, and rolls its rapid waves,

1. Shelley wrote of this poem: "It was composed under the immediate impression of the deep and powerful feelings excited by the objects which it attempts to describe; and, as an indisciplined overflowing of the soul, rests its claim to approbation on an attempt to imitate the untamable wildness and inaccessible solemnity from which those feelings sprang."

Shelley's comment points to two important attributes of *Mont Blanc*. First, he attempts, as in other poems (supremely in *Ode to the West Wind*), to make the poem iconic, or directly imitative—in the over-all impetus, but interpolated *ritardandi*, of its blank verse, syntax, and imagery—of the alternating "wildness" and "solemnity" of the scene and the consonant thought and feelings it evokes. Second, this work belongs to the genre of the "local" poem, a descriptive-meditative presentation of a precisely identified landscape. In this respect it resembles Wordsworth's *Tintern Abbey*, the major influence on *Mont Blanc*. Shelley's poem, like Wordsworth's, emphasizes the interchange between mind and nature in perception and goes on to

pose the question of the significance of nature to man; it proposes, however, a very different answer to that question.

The poem raises the central problem about the nature and human significance of "Power," the ultimate principle behind all natural and mental process. The symbol of this Power is the river Arve (lines 16–17), which has its "secret throne" at the summit of Mont Blanc, the highest peak in Europe, and beyond human access. The process of the Arve begins with the ceaseless but unseen fall of snow and the unheard play of winds at the far height of the mountain, becomes the Mer de Glace glacier, moves inexorably down the mountain, and melts into the river, which runs through its ravine into the valley of Chamonix in southeastern France. Shelley's answers to all questions about this Power are austerely skeptical. He postulates only that "the power is there," at the inaccessible peak of Mont Blanc (lines 127 ff.), but it is "remote, serene, and inaccessible" (lines 96–97): Shelly refuses to invest it with anthropomorphic intentions or values.

What we do know is that this Power,

Now dark—now glittering—now reflecting gloom—
Now lending splendor, where from secret springs
The source of human thought its tribute brings   5
Of waters—with a sound but half its own,
Such as a feeble brook will oft assume
In the wild woods, among the mountains lone,
Where waterfalls around it leap forever,
Where woods and winds contend, and a vast river   10
Over its rocks ceaselessly bursts and raves.

2

Thus thou, Ravine of Arve—dark, deep Ravine—
Thou many-colored, many-voicéd vale,
Over whose pines, and crags, and caverns sail
Fast cloud-shadows and sunbeams: awful scene,   15
Where Power in likeness of the Arve comes down
From the ice-gulfs that gird his secret throne,
Bursting through these dark mountains like the flame
Of lightning through the tempest; thou dost lie,
Thy giant brood of pines around thee clinging,   20
Children of elder time, in whose devotion
The chainless winds still come and ever came
To drink their odors, and their mighty swinging
To hear—an old and solemn harmony;
Thine earthly rainbows stretched across the sweep   25
Of the aethereal waterfall, whose veil
Robes some unsculptured image; the strange sleep
Which when the voices of the desert fail
Wraps all in its own deep eternity;
Thy caverns echoing to the Arve's commotion,   30
A loud, lone sound no other sound can tame;
Thou art pervaded with that ceaseless motion,
Thou art the path of that unresting sound—
Dizzy Ravine! and when I gaze on thee
I seem as in a trance sublime and strange   35
To muse on my own separate fantasy,
My own, my human mind, which passively
Now renders and receives fast influencings,
Holding an unremitting interchange
With the clear universe of things around;[2]   40

as, in its embodiment as a glacier, it descends from its secret throne into the human ken, remorselessly destroys all things, animal and human (lines 100–20); yet in its simultaneous form as a river (lines 120–26), it with equal moral indifference is the "breath and blood of distant lands," and the source of life-giving rain. It is the enlightened human will alone which can convert this purposeless destroyer and preserver to moral purposefulness, by harnessing process as means to its own human ends, even to the revolutionary end of total reform by the repeal of "Large codes of

fraud and woe" (lines 80–83). The poem ends like *Ode to the West Wind*, with a rhetorical question, of which the implication is that phenomenal nature is in itself but a universal blank, except as it is invested with human significance by the imagination of observing man. Shelley comes close here to the central theme of the modern American poet, Wallace Stevens, for whom the human imagination confronts an alien and neutral nature and creates the order and meaning it does not find.

2. This passage is remarkably parallel

One legion of wild thoughts, whose wandering wings
Now float above thy darkness, and now rest
Where that or thou art no unbidden guest,
In the still cave of the witch Poesy,
Seeking among the shadows that pass by   45
Ghosts of all things that are, some shade of thee,
Some phantom, some faint image; till the breast
From which they fled recalls them, thou art there!

3

Some say that gleams of a remoter world
Visit the soul in sleep, that death is slumber,   50
And that its shapes the busy thoughts outnumber
Of those who wake and live. I look on high;
Has some unknown omnipotence unfurled
The veil of life and death? or do I lie
In dream, and does the mightier world of sleep   55
Spread far around and inaccessibly
Its circles? For the very spirit fails,
Driven like a homeless cloud from steep to steep
That vanishes among the viewless[3] gales!
Far, far above, piercing the infinite sky,   60
Mont Blanc appears—still, snowy, and serene—
Its subject mountains their unearthly forms
Pile around it, ice and rock; broad vales between
Of frozen floods, unfathomable deeps,
Blue as the overhanging heaven, that spread   65
And wind among the accumulated steeps;
A desert peopled by the storms alone,
Save when the eagle brings some hunter's bone,
And the wolf tracks her there—how hideously
Its shapes are heaped around! rude, bare, and high,   70
Ghastly, and scarred, and riven. Is this the scene
Where the old Earthquake-daemon taught her young
Ruin? Were these their toys? or did a sea
Of fire envelop once this silent snow?[4]
None can reply—all seems eternal now.   75
The wilderness has a mysterious tongue
Which teaches awful doubt, or faith so mild,
So solemn, so serene, that man may be,
But for such faith,[5] with nature reconciled;
Thou hast a voice, great Mountain, to repeal   80
Large codes of fraud and woe; not understood

---

to a passage in Wordsworth's *Prelude* which (since the poem was not published until 1850) Shelley could not have read. See above, in *The Prelude,* XIV, 63 ff., where in the landscape viewed from Mount Snowdon, Wordsworth discovers the "type" or "emblem" of the human mind.

3. Invisible.

4. An allusion to theories current in Shelley's day that the earth was origi-nally a smooth globe, and that moun-tains were formed by catastrophic earthquakes, by floods, or by a bursting forth of fire from the earth's interior.

5. "Simply by holding such a faith"— such as Wordsworth's "cheerful faith" (lines 133–34) in *Tintern Abbey* "that all which we behold / Is full of bless-ings." In Shelley's balance of possibil-ities, the landscape is equally capable of teaching this faith and "awful doubt."

By all, but which the wise, and great, and good
Interpret, or make felt, or deeply feel.

4

The fields, the lakes, the forests, and the streams,
Ocean, and all the living things that dwell   85
Within the daedal[6] earth; lightning, and rain,
Earthquake, and fiery flood, and hurricane,
The torpor of the year when feeble dreams
Visit the hidden buds, or dreamless sleep
Holds every future leaf and flower; the bound   90
With which from that detested trance they leap;
The works and ways of man, their death and birth,
And that of him and all that his may be;
All things that move and breathe with toil and sound
Are born and die; revolve, subside, and swell.   95
Power dwells apart in its tranquillity,
Remote, serene, and inaccessible:
And *this*, the naked countenance of earth,
On which I gaze, even these primaeval mountains
Teach the adverting mind. The glaciers creep   100
Like snakes that watch their prey, from their far fountains,
Slow rolling on; there, many a precipice,
Frost and the Sun in scorn of mortal power
Have piled: dome, pyramid, and pinnacle,
A city of death, distinct with many a tower   105
And wall impregnable of beaming ice.
Yet not a city, but a flood of ruin
Is there, that from the boundaries of the sky
Rolls its perpetual stream; vast pines are strewing
Its destined path, or in the mangled soil   110
Branchless and shattered stand; the rocks, drawn down
From yon remotest waste, have overthrown
The limits of the dead and living world,
Never to be reclaimed. The dwelling place
Of insects, beasts, and birds, becomes its spoil   115
Their food and their retreat for ever gone,
So much of life and joy is lost. The race
Of man flies far in dread; his work and dwelling
Vanish, like smoke before the tempest's stream,
And their place is not known. Below, vast caves   120
Shine in the rushing torrents' restless gleam,
Which from those secret chasms in tumult welling[7]
Meet in the vale, and one majestic River,
The breath and blood of distant lands, forever
Rolls its loud waters to the ocean waves,   125
Breathes its swift vapors to the circling air.

---

6. Intricately formed; derived from
Daedalus, builder of the labyrinth in
Crete.
7. Like lines 9–11, an echo of Coleridge's description of the chasm and
sacred river in *Kubla Khan*, lines 11–24.
In writing *Mont Blanc* Shelley probably
remembered also Coleridge's *Hymn before Sun-Rise, in the Vale of Chamouni.*

5

Mont Blanc yet gleams on high—the power is there,
The still and solemn power of many sights,
And many sounds, and much of life and death.
In the calm darkness of the moonless nights,   130
In the lone glare of day, the snows descend
Upon that Mountain; none beholds them there,
Nor when the flakes burn in the sinking sun,
Or the star-beams dart through them—Winds contend
Silently there, and heap the snow with breath   135
Rapid and strong, but silently! Its home
The voiceless lightning in these solitudes
Keeps innocently, and like vapor broods
Over the snow. The secret Strength of things
Which governs thought, and to the infinite dome   140
Of Heaven is as a law, inhabits thee!
And what were thou,[8] and earth, and stars, and sea,
If to the human mind's imaginings
Silence and solitude were vacancy?
July 23, 1816   1817

Hymn to Intellectual Beauty[1]

1

The awful shadow of some unseen Power
    Floats though unseen among us—visiting
    This various world with as inconstant wing
As summer winds that creep from flower to flower—
Like moonbeams that behind some piny mountain shower,   5
        It visits with inconstant glance
        Each human heart and countenance;
Like hues and harmonies of evening—
    Like clouds in starlight widely spread—
    Like memory of music fled—   10
        Like aught that for its grace may be
Dear, and yet dearer for its mystery.

8. Mont Blanc.
1. "Intellectual" here signifies non-material. Intellectual Beauty is an "unseen Power" because it is beyond access by sense experience. It is an entity postulated to account for occasional states of awareness which lend splendor, grace, and truth to both the natural world and to man's moral consciousness. The attempts of philosophy, superstition, and religion (stanza 3) to identify and control the mystery, which is outside the limits of human knowledge, are equally vain. Yet to this mystery (stanzas 5–7), at its first unexpected visitation in his youth, Shelley had dedicated his powers, and to it he now prays as he passes the noon of life.

2

Spirit of BEAUTY, that dost consecrate
  With thine own hues all thou dost shine upon
  Of human thought or form—where art thou gone?   15
Why dost thou pass away and leave our state,
This dim vast vale of tears, vacant and desolate?
    Ask why the sunlight not forever·
    Weaves rainbows o'er yon mountain river,
Why aught should fail and fade that once is shown,   20
    Why fear and dream and death and birth
    Cast on the daylight of this earth
    Such gloom—why man has such a scope
For love and hate, despondency and hope?

3

No voice from some sublimer world hath ever   25
  To sage or poet these responses given—
  Therefore the names of Demon, Ghost, and Heaven,
Remain the records of their vain endeavor,
Frail spells—whose uttered charm might not avail to sever,
    From all we hear and all we see,   30
    Doubt, chance, and mutability.
Thy light alone—like mist o'er mountains driven,
    Or music by the night wind sent·
    Through strings of some still instrument,
    Or moonlight on a midnight stream,   35
Gives grace and truth to life's unquiet dream.

4

Love, Hope, and Self-esteem, like clouds depart
  And come, for some uncertain moments lent.
  Man were immortal, and omnipotent,
Didst thou, unknown and awful as thou art,   40
Keep with thy glorious train firm state within his heart.
    Thou messenger of sympathies,
    That wax and wane in lovers' eyes—
Thou—that to human thought art nourishment,
    Like darkness to a dying flame!   45
    Depart not as thy shadow came,
    Depart not—lest the grave should be,
Like life and fear, a dark reality.

5

While yet a boy I sought for ghosts, and sped
  Through many a listening chamber, cave and ruin,   50
  And starlight wood, with fearful steps pursuing
Hopes of high talk with the departed dead.[2]
I called on poisonous names with which our youth is fed;
    I was not heard—I saw them not—
    When musing deeply on the lot   55

2. A reference to Shelley's youthful attempts to evoke ghosts and to practice magic. The "poisonous names" in the following line are probably elements of the religious rituals he had been taught as a boy.

Of life, at that sweet time when winds are wooing
    All vital things that wake to bring
    News of birds and blossoming—
    Sudden, thy shadow fell on me;
I shrieked, and clasped my hands in ecstasy!   60

6

I vowed that I would dedicate my powers
    To thee and thine—have I not kept the vow?
    With beating heart and streaming eyes, even now
I call the phantoms of a thousand hours
Each from his voiceless grave: they have in visioned bowers   65
    Of studious zeal or love's delight
    Outwatched with me the envious night[3]—
They know that never joy illumed my brow
    Unlinked with hope that thou wouldst free
    This world from its dark slavery,   70
    That thou—O awful LOVELINESS,
Wouldst give whate'er these words cannot express.

7

The day becomes more solemn and serene
    When noon is past—there is a harmony
    In autumn, and a luster in its sky,   75
Which through the summer is not heard or seen,
As if it could not be, as if it had not been!
    Thus let thy power, which like the truth
    Of nature on my passive youth
Descended, to my onward life supply   80
    Its calm—to one who worships thee,
    And every form containing thee,
    Whom, SPIRIT fair, thy spells did bind
To fear himself, and love all human kind.

1816   1817

Ozymandias[1]

I met a traveler from an antique land
Who said: Two vast and trunkless legs of stone
Stand in the desert . . . Near them, on the sand,
Half sunk, a shattered visage lies, whose frown,
And wrinkled lip, and sneer of cold command,   5
Tell that its sculptor well those passions read

---

3. I.e., watched until the night, envious of their delight, had reluctantly departed.

1. According to a passage in Diodorus Siculus, the Greek historian of the 1st century B.C., the largest statue in Egypt had the inscription: "I am Ozymandias, king of kings; if anyone wishes to know what I am and where I lie, let him surpass me in some of my exploits." Ozymandias was Ramses II of Egypt, 13th century B.C.

Which yet survive, stamped on these lifeless things,
The hand that mocked them, and the heart that fed:[2]
And on the pedestal these words appear:
"My name is Ozymandias, king of kings: 10
Look on my works, ye Mighty, and despair!"
Nothing beside remains. Round the decay
Of that colossal wreck, boundless and bare
The lone and level sands stretch far away.

1817   1818

Sonnet

Lift not the painted veil which those who live
Call Life: though unreal shapes be pictured there,
And it but mimic all we would believe
With colors idly spread—behind, lurk Fear
And Hope, twin Destinies; who ever weave   5
Their shadows, o'er the chasm, sightless and drear.
I knew one who had lifted it—he sought,
For his lost heart was tender, things to love,
But found them not, alas! nor was there aught
The world contains, the which he could approve.   10
Through the unheeding many he did move,
A splendor among shadows, a bright blot
Upon this gloomy scene, a Spirit that strove
For truth, and like the Preacher[3] found it not.

1818   1824

Stanzas Written in Dejection, Near Naples[1]

1

The sun is warm, the sky is clear,
    The waves are dancing fast and bright,
Blue isles and snowy mountains wear
    The purple noon's transparent might,
    The breath of the moist earth is light,   5
        Around its unexpanded buds;

---

2. The sculptured passions survive the
hand of the sculptor who had "mocked"
(i.e., both represented and derided)
them, as well as the heart of the king
which had been their source.
3. Author of the skeptical and pessimistic Book of Ecclesiastes in the Old
Testament.

1. Shelley's first wife, Harriet, had
drowned herself; Clara, his baby
daughter by Mary Shelley, had just
died; and Shelley himself was plagued
by ill health, pain, financial worries,
and the sense that he had failed as a
poet.

Like many a voice of one delight,
The winds, the birds, the ocean floods,
The City's voice itself is soft like Solitude's.

2

I see the Deep's untrampled floor 10
With green and purple seaweeds strown;
I see the waves upon the shore,
Like light dissolved in star-showers, thrown:
I sit upon the sands alone—
The lightning of the noontide ocean 15
Is flashing round me, and a tone
Arises from its measured motion;
How sweet! did any heart now share in my emotion.

3

Alas! I have nor hope nor health,
Nor peace within nor calm around, 20
Nor that content surpassing wealth
The sage in meditation found,
And walked with inward glory crowned—
Nor fame, nor power, nor love, nor leisure.
Others I see whom these surround— 25
Smiling they live, and call life pleasure;
To me that cup has been dealt in another measure.

4

Yet now despair itself is mild,
Even as the winds and waters are;
I could lie down like a tired child, 30
And weep away the life of care
Which I have borne and yet must bear,
Till death like sleep might steal on me,
And I might feel in the warm air
My cheek grow cold, and hear the sea 35
Breathe o'er my dying brain its last monotony.

5

Some might lament that I were cold,
As I, when this sweet day is gone,
Which my lost heart, too soon grown old,
Insults with this untimely moan; 40
They might lament—for I am one
Whom men love not—and yet regret,
Unlike this day, which, when the sun
Shall on its stainless glory set,
Will linger, though enjoyed, like joy in memory yet.[2] 45

December, 1818   1824

2. I.e., the few men who may lament
his passing will find the remembrance
flawed by his failings, but this stainless
day, even after the enjoyment of it is
past, will leave a memory of flawless
joy.

Song to the Men of England[1]

1

Men of England, wherefore plow
For the lords who lay ye low?
Wherefore weave with toil and care
The rich robes your tyrants wear?

2

Wherefore feed, and clothe, and save,   5
From the cradle to the grave,
Those ungrateful drones who would
Drain your sweat—nay, drink your blood?

3

Wherefore, Bees of England, forge
Many a weapon, chain, and scourge,   10
That these stingless drones may spoil
The forced produce of your toil?

4

Have ye leisure, comfort, calm,
Shelter, food, love's gentle balm?
Or what is it ye buy so dear   15
With your pain and with your fear?

5

The seed ye sow, another reaps;
The wealth ye find, another keeps;
The robes ye weave, another wears;
The arms ye forge, another bears.   20

6

Sow seed—but let no tyrant reap;
Find wealth—let no impostor heap;
Weave robes—let not the idle wear;
Forge arms—in your defense to bear.

7

Shrink to your cellars, holes, and cells;   25
In halls ye deck another dwells.
Why shake the chains ye wrought? Ye see
The steel ye tempered glance on ye.

8

With plow and spade, and hoe and loom,
Trace your grave, and build your tomb,   30
And weave your winding sheet, till fair
England be your sepulcher.

1819   1839

1. This and the following poem were written at a time of turbulent unrest among English workers, after the return of many thousands of soldiers from the Napoleonic Wars had led to the first great depression of the new industrial age. The poems express Shelley's hope for a proletarian revolution. This song was originally planned as one of a series of poems for workingmen, but Shelley gave up the project. It has become, as Shelley hoped, a hymn of the British labor movement.

England in 1819

An old, mad, blind, despised, and dying king[1]—
Princes, the dregs of their dull race, who flow
Through public scorn—mud from a muddy spring;
Rulers who neither see, nor feel, nor know,
But leechlike to their fainting country cling,   5
Till they drop, blind in blood, without a blow;
A people starved and stabbed in the untilled field—
An army, which liberticide and prey
Makes as a two-edged sword to all who wield;
Golden and sanguine laws[2] which tempt and slay;   10
Religion Christless, Godless—a book sealed;
A Senate—Time's worst statute unrepealed[3]—
Are graves, from which a glorious Phantom[4] may
Burst, to illumine our tempestuous day.

1819   1839

The Indian Serenade[1]

1

I arise from dreams of thee
In the first sweet sleep of night.
When the winds are breathing low,
And the stars are shining bright:
I arise from dreams of thee,   5
And a spirit in my feet
Hath led me—who knows how?
To thy chamber window, Sweet!

2

The wandering airs they faint
On the dark, the silent stream—   10
The Champak[2] odors fail
Like sweet thoughts in a dream;
The nightingale's complaint,
It dies upon her heart—
As I must on thine,   15
Oh, beloved as thou art!

3

Oh lift me from the grass!
I die! I faint! I fail!
Let thy love in kisses rain
On my lips and eyelids pale.   20
My cheek is cold and white, alas!

1. George III, who died in the next year, 1820.
2. Laws bought with gold, and leading to bloodshed.
3. The law imposing disabilities upon Roman Catholics.
4. I.e., the revolution.

1. It is a mistake to read this as an utterance by Shelley himself. The poem is explicitly a dramatic lyric, sung by an imagined East-Indian lover in an exotic landscape, and exhibits the conventional extravagance of a serenade.
2. An Indian species of magnolia.

My heart beats loud and fast—
Oh! press it to thine own again,
Where it will break at last.

1819   1822

Ode to the West Wind[1]

1

O wild West Wind, thou breath of Autumn's being,
Thou, from whose unseen presence the leaves dead
Are driven, like ghosts from an enchanter fleeing,

Yellow, and black, and pale, and hectic red,
Pestilence-stricken multitudes: O thou,   5
Who chariotest to their dark wintry bed

The wingéd seeds, where they lie cold and low,
Each like a corpse within its grave, until
Thine azure sister of the Spring[2] shall blow

Her clarion[3] o'er the dreaming earth, and fill   10
(Driving sweet buds like flocks to feed in air)
With living hues and odors plain and hill:

Wild Spirit, which art moving everywhere;
Destroyer and preserver; hear, oh, hear!

2

Thou on whose stream, mid the steep sky's commotion,   15
Loose clouds like earth's decaying leaves are shed,
Shook from the tangled boughs of Heaven and Ocean,[4]

Angels of rain and lightning: there are spread
On the blue surface of thine aëry surge,
Like the bright hair uplifted from the head   20

1. "This poem was conceived and chiefly written in a wood that skirts the Arno, near Florence, and on a day when that tempestuous wind, whose temperature is at once mild and animating, was collecting the vapors which pour down the autumnal rains" [Shelley's note]. As in other major Romantic poems— see, for example, the opening of Wordsworth's *Prelude*, Coleridge's *Dejection*, and the conclusion to Shelley's *Adonais* —the rising wind, linked with the cycle of the seasons, is presented as the outer correspondent to an inner change from apathy and a deathlike torpor to renewed spiritual vitality, and from imaginative sterility to a burst of creative power which is paralleled to the inspiration of the Biblical prophets. In Hebrew, Greek, and many other languages, the words for wind, breath, soul, and inspiration are all identical or related. Thus Shelley's west wind is a "spirit" (the Latin *spiritus:* wind,

breath, soul, and the root word in "inspiration"), the "breath of Autumn's being," which on earth, sky, and sea destroys in the autumn in order to revive in the spring. Around this central image the poem weaves various cycles of death and regeneration—vegetational, human, and divine.

The remarkable stanza used in this ode was developed by Shelley from the interlaced tercets (three-line units) of the Italian *terza rima: aba bcb cdc,* etc. Shelley's stanza consists of a set of four such tercets, closed by a couplet rhyming with the middle line of the preceding tercet: *aba bcb cdc ded ee.*
2. The reviving wind that will blow in the spring.
3. A high, shrill trumpet; compare "the trumpet of a prophecy" in line 69.
4. I.e., the fragmentary clouds ("leaves") are torn by the wind from the larger clouds formed by a union of the air with the water vapor (the

Of some fierce Maenad,[5] even from the dim verge
Of the horizon to the zenith's height,
The locks of the approaching storm. Thou dirge

Of the dying year, to which this closing night
Will be the dome of a vast sepulcher,   25
Vaulted with all thy congregated might

Of vapours, from whose solid atmosphere
Black rain, and fire, and hail will burst: oh, hear!

3

Thou who didst waken from his summer dreams
The blue Mediterranean, where he lay,   30
Lulled by the coil of his crystálline streams,[6]

Beside a pumice[7] isle in Baiae's bay,
And saw in sleep old palaces and towers
Quivering within the wave's intenser day,[8]

All overgrown with azure moss and flowers   35
So sweet, the sense faints picturing them! Thou
For whose path the Atlantic's level powers

Cleave themselves into chasms, while far below
The sea-blooms and the oozy woods which wear
The sapless foliage of the ocean, know   40

Thy voice, and suddenly grow gray with fear,
And tremble and despoil themselves:[9] oh, hear!

4

If I were a dead leaf thou mightest bear;
If I were a swift cloud to fly with thee;
A wave to pant beneath thy power, and share   45

The impulse of thy strength, only less free
Than thou, O uncontrollable! If even
I were as in my boyhood, and could be

The comrade of thy wanderings over Heaven,
As then, when to outstrip thy skyey speed   50
Scarce seemed a vision; I would ne'er have striven

As thus with thee in prayer in my sore need.
Oh, lift me as a wave, a leaf, a cloud!
I fall upon the thorns of life! I bleed!

"tangled boughs of Heaven and Ocean"). "Angels" suggests the old sense: messengers, harbingers.

5. A female votary who danced frenziedly in the worship of Dionysus (or Bacchus), the Greek god of wine and vegetation. As vegetation god, he was fabled to die in the fall and to be resurrected in the spring; hence, there is a glancing allusion here to a mythic cycle of death and rebirth.
6. The currents that flow in the Mediterranean Sea, sometimes with a visible difference in color.

7. Formed of a porous volcanic stone. "Baiae's bay," west of Naples, was the locale of imposing villas erected by Roman emperors.
8. Shelley once observed that, when seen reflected in water, colors are "more vivid yet blended with more harmony." 9. "The phenomenon * * * is well known to naturalists. The vegetation at the bottom of the sea * * * sympathizes with that of the land in the change of seasons" [Shelley's note].

A heavy weight of hours has chained and bowed   55
One too like thee: tameless, and swift, and proud.

5

Make me thy lyre,[1] even as the forest is:
What if my leaves are falling like its own!
The tumult of thy mighty harmonies

Will take from both a deep, autumnal tone,   60
Sweet though in sadness. Be thou, Spirit fierce,
My spirit! Be thou me, impetuous one!

Drive my dead thoughts over the universe
Like withered leaves to quicken a new birth!
And, by the incantation of this verse,   65

Scatter, as from an unextinguished hearth
Ashes and sparks, my words among mankind!
Be through my lips to unawakened earth

The trumpet of a prophecy! O Wind,
If Winter comes, can Spring be far behind?   70

1819   1820

1. The Aeolian lyre, or wind harp,   for the response of the human mind to
which responds to the wind with a   the wind in Wordsworth's *Prelude* and
musical chord. This image is also used   Coleridge's *Eolian Harp* and *Dejection*.

Prometheus Unbound

Shelley composed this work in Italy between the autumn of 1818 and the close of 1819 and published it the following summer. Upon its completion he wrote in a letter, "It is a drama, with characters and mechanism of a kind yet unattempted; and I think the execution is better than any of my former attempts." It is based upon the *Prometheus Bound* of Aeschylus, which dramatizes the sufferings of Prometheus, unrepentant champion of mankind, who, because he had stolen fire from heaven, was condemned by Zeus to be chained to Mt. Caucasus and to be tortured by a vulture feeding upon his liver. Shelley continued Aeschylus' story, but transformed it into a symbolic drama about the origin of evil and its elimination. In such earlier writings as *Queen Mab* Shelley had expressed his belief that injustice and suffering can be eliminated by an external revolution which will wipe out or radically reform existing social, political, and religious institutions. Implicit in *Prometheus Unbound*, on the other hand, is the view that both the origin of evil and the possibility of reform are the moral responsibility of man himself. Social chaos and wars are a gigantic projection of man's moral disorder and inner division and conflict: tyrants are the outer representatives of the tyranny of man's baser over his better elements; hatred for others is an expression of self-contempt; and successful political reform is impossible unless man has first reformed his own nature at its deep roots, by substituting selfless love for divisive hate. Shelley thus incorporates into his secular myth of universal regeneration by an apocalypse of man's moral imagination, the ethical teaching of Christ on the Mount, as well as the highest classical morality represented in the *Prometheus* of Aeschylus. And Shelley warns (IV.562 ff.) that even should such a victory take place—the reintegration of splintered man, and the consequent restoration of an order which is at once moral and political, and which releases all man's creative powers in art and science—the price of its continuation is an unremitting vigilance lest the serpent deep in human nature should break loose and start the cycle of fall into division and conflict all over again.

Shelley wrote in his Preface that Prometheus is, "as it were, the type of the highest perfection of moral and intellectual nature." But he also warned that it is a mistake to suppose that the poem contains "a reasoned system on the theory of human life. Didactic poetry is my abhorrence." *Prometheus Unbound* is not a dramatized philosophical essay, nor a moral allegory, but a large and very intricate imaginative construction which involves premises about the nature of man and the springs of morality and creativity. The non-Christian poet, Yeats, called it one of "the sacred books of the world," and the Christian critic, C. S. Lewis, found in it many of the powers of Dante. Many readers argue, at any rate, that, with *The Triumph of Life* and some of the longer lyrics, *Prometheus Unbound* constitutes a weighty claim to rank Shelley as among the major poets.

From Prometheus Unbound

A LYRICAL DRAMA

Dramatis Personae

PROMETHEUS	HERCULES
DEMOGORGON	THE PHANTASM OF JUPITER
JUPITER	THE SPIRIT OF THE EARTH
THE EARTH	THE SPIRIT OF THE MOON
OCEAN	SPIRITS OF THE HOURS
APOLLO	SPIRITS
MERCURY	ECHOES
ASIA ⎫	FAUNS
PANTHEA ⎬ *Oceanides*	FURIES
IONE ⎭	

From *Act I*

SCENE—*A Ravine of Icy Rocks in the Indian Caucasus.* PROMETHEUS *is discovered bound to the Precipice.* PANTHEA *and* IONE *are seated at his feet. Time, night. During the Scene, morning slowly breaks.*

PROMETHEUS. Monarch of Gods and Daemons,[1] and all Spirits
   But One, who throng those bright and rolling worlds
   Which Thou and I alone of living things
   Behold with sleepless eyes! regard this Earth
   Made multitudinous with thy slaves, whom thou
   Requitest for knee-worship, prayer, and praise,   5
   And toil, and hecatombs[2] of broken hearts,
   With fear and self-contempt and barren hope.

1. Prometheus is addressing Jupiter.
2. In Greek, "a hundred oxen" (slaugh-   tered as a sacrifice to the gods).

Whilst me, who am thy foe, eyeless in hate,[3]
Hast thou made reign and triumph, to thy scorn,   10
O'er mine own misery and thy vain revenge.
Three thousand years of sleep-unsheltered hours,
And moments aye divided by keen pangs
Till they seemed years, torture and solitude,
Scorn and despair—these are mine empire—   15
More glorious far than that which thou surveyest
From thine unenvied throne, O Mighty God!
Almighty, had I deigned[4] to share the shame
Of thine ill tyranny, and hung not here
Nailed to this wall of eagle-baffling mountain,   20
Black, wintry, dead, unmeasured; without herb,
Insect, or beast, or shape or sound of life.
Ah me! alas, pain, pain ever, forever!

No change, no pause, no hope! Yet I endure.
I ask the Earth, have not the mountains felt?   25
I ask yon Heaven, the all-beholding Sun,
Has it not seen? The Sea, in storm or calm,
Heaven's ever-changing Shadow, spread below,
Have its deaf waves not heard my agony?
Ah me! alas, pain, pain ever, forever!   30

The crawling glaciers pierce me with the spears
Of their moon-freezing crystals, the bright chains
Eat with their burning cold into my bones.
Heaven's wingéd hound,[5] polluting from thy lips
His beak in poison not his own, tears up   35
My heart; and shapeless sights come wandering by,
The ghastly people of the realm of dream,
Mocking me: and the Earthquake-fiends are charged
To wrench the rivets from my quivering wounds
When the rocks split and close again behind: 40
While from their loud abysses howling throng
The genii of the storm, urging the rage
Of whirlwind, and afflict me with keen hail.
And yet to me welcome is day and night,
Whether one breaks the hoar frost of the morn,   45
Or starry, dim, and slow, the other climbs
The leaden-colored east; for then they lead
The wingless, crawling hours, one among whom
—As some dark Priest hales the reluctant victim
Shall drag thee, cruel King, to kiss the blood   50
From these pale feet,[6] which then might trample thee
If they disdained not such a prostrate slave.
Disdain! Ah no! I pity thee.[7] What ruin

3. Blinded by hate.
4. I.e., you would have been all-power-ful, if I had deigned.
5. The vulture, tearing daily at Prometheus' heart, was kissed by Jupiter by way of reward.
6. One of a number of implied paral-

lels between the agony of Prometheus and the passion of Christ.
7. At this early point occurs the technical crisis of the play: the beginning of Prometheus' change of heart from hate to compassion, which is consummated in

Will hunt thee undefended through wide Heaven!
How will thy soul, cloven to its depth with terror,   55
Gape like a hell within! I speak in grief,
Not exultation, for I hate no more,
As then ere misery made me wise. The curse
Once breathed on thee I would recall. Ye Mountains,
Whose many-voicéd Echoes, through the mist   60
Of cataracts, flung the thunder of that spell!
Ye icy Springs, stagnant with wrinkling frost,
Which vibrated to hear me, and then crept
Shuddering through India! Thou serenest Air,
Through which the Sun walks burning without beams!   65
And ye swift Whirlwinds, who on poiséd wings
Hung mute and moveless o'er yon hushed abyss,
As thunder, louder than your own, made rock
The orbéd world! If then my words had power,
Though I am changed so that aught evil wish   70
Is dead within; although no memory be
Of what is hate, let them not lose it now!⁸
What was that curse? for ye all heard me speak.⁹

* * *

PHANTASM

Fiend, I defy thee! with a calm, fixed mind,
      All that thou canst inflict I bid thee do;
Foul Tyrant both of Gods and Humankind,
      One only being shalt thou not subdue.   265
Rain then thy plagues upon me here,
Ghastly disease, and frenzying fear;
And let alternate frost and fire
Eat into me, and be thine ire
Lightning, and cutting hail, and legioned forms   270
Of furies, driving by upon the wounding storms.

Aye, do thy worst. Thou art omnipotent.
      O'er all things but thyself I gave thee power,
And my own will. Be thy swift mischiefs sent
      To blast mankind, from yon ethereal tower.   275
Let thy malignant spirit move
In darkness over those I love:
On me and mine I imprecate
The utmost torture of thy hate;
And thus devote to sleepless agony,   280
This undeclining head while thou must reign on high.

lines 303–5. The rest of the symbolic drama gradually unfolds the consequences of this moral triumph—of which Prometheus himself (like Coleridge's Ancient Mariner when he blessed the water snakes) is at this time entirely unaware.
8. I.e., let my words not lose their power now.
9. In the passage here omitted, none dares to repeat the curse Prometheus had proclaimed against Jupiter for fear of that god's vengeance. Prometheus is finally. forced to call up the Phantasm of Jupiter himself who, in the next excerpt, repeats the curse.

But thou, who art the God and Lord: O, thou,
　　Who fillest with thy soul this world of woe,
To whom all things of Earth and Heaven do bow
　　In fear and worship: all-prevailing foe!　　　285
I curse thee! let a sufferer's curse
Clasp thee, his torturer, like remorse;
Till thine Infinity shall be
A robe of envenomed agony;
And thine Omnipotence a crown of pain,　　　290
To cling like burning gold round thy dissolving brain.

Heap on thy soul, by virtue of this Curse,
　　Ill deeds, then be thou damned, beholding good;
Both infinite as is the universe,
　　And thou, and thy self-torturing solitude.　　　295
An awful image of calm power
Though now thou sittest, let the hour
Come, when thou must appear to be
That which thou art internally;
And after many a false and fruitless crime　　　300
Scorn track thy lagging fall through boundless space and time.

PROMETHEUS. Were these my words, O Parent?
THE EARTH.　　　　　　　　　　　　They were thine.
PROMETHEUS. It doth repent me: words are quick and vain;
　　Grief for awhile is blind, and so was mine.
　　I wish no living thing to suffer pain.　　　305

THE EARTH

　　　Misery, Oh misery to me,
　　That Jove at length should vanquish thee.[1]
　　Wail, howl aloud, Land and Sea,
　　The Earth's rent heart shall answer ye.
Howl, Spirits of the living and the dead,　　　310
Your refuge, your defense lies fallen and vanquishéd.

FIRST ECHO
Lies fallen and vanquishéd!

SECOND ECHO
Fallen and vanquishéd!

IONE[2]
Fear not: 'tis but some passing spasm,
The Titan is unvanquished still.　　　315

* * *

---

1. In this extreme instance of dramatic irony, Earth mistakes mercy for submission, and therefore interprets Prometheus' victory as his defeat.

2. Ione, Panthea, and Asia (in the following scene) are sisters and Oceanids —i.e., daughters of Oceanus.

From Act II[1]

SCENE IV—*The Cave of* DEMOGORGON. ASIA *and* PANTHEA.

PANTHEA. What veiléd form sits on that ebon throne?
ASIA. The veil has fallen.
PANTHEA.   I see a mighty darkness
   Filling the seat of power, and rays of gloom
   Dart round, as light from the meridian sun.
   —Ungazed upon and shapeless; neither limb,   5
   Nor form, nor outline; yet we feel it is
   A living Spirit.
DEMOGORGON.   Ask what thou wouldst know.
ASIA. What canst thou tell?
DEMOGORGON.   All things thou dar'st demand.
ASIA. Who made the living world?
DEMOGORGON.   God.
ASIA.   Who made all
   That it contains? thought, passion, reason, will,   10
   Imagination?
DEMOGORGON. God: Almighty God.
ASIA. Who made that sense[2] which, when the winds of Spring
   In rarest visitation, or the voice
   Of one beloved heard in youth alone,
   Fills the faint eyes with falling tears which dim   15
   The radiant looks of unbewailing flowers,
   And leaves this peopled earth a solitude
   When it returns no more?
DEMOGORGON.   Merciful God.
ASIA. And who made terror, madness, crime, remorse,
   Which from the links of the great chain of things,   20
   To every thought within the mind of man
   Sway and drag heavily, and each one reels
   Under the load towards the pit of death;
   Abandoned hope, and love that turns to hate;
   And self-contempt, bitterer to drink than blood;   25

1. Act II has opened with Asia, the feminine principle and embodiment of love, who was separated from Prometheus at the moment of his fall into divisive hate, in a lovely Indian valley at the first hour of the first dawn of the spring season of redemption. Asia and her sister Panthea have been led, by a sweet and irresistible compulsion, first to the portal and then down into the depths of the cave of Demogorgon—the central enigma of Shelley's poem.
   Commentators have usually equated Demogorgon with *necessity*, but the interpretation, though pertinent, is too neat and confining. More flexibly, he can be thought of as *process*, the inexorable way in which things evolve. But the ultimate mover of that process —the ultimate reason for things—must remain, Shelley skeptically insists, a mystery beyond the limits of accessible knowledge. Demogorgon, like the inaccessible Power represented by the Arve in *Mont Blanc* (above), is implacable, neutral, and the more terrifying because he himself is ignorant of the principle that controls him. He serves merely to stimulate Asia to ask once more the ultimate and persistent questions about the "why" of creation, good, and evil. But "the deep truth is imageless" (line 116). Demogorgon can give merely riddling answers, which in fact tell Asia only what she herself has thought already (lines 121–23). The one question he can answer unequivocally is not "why," but "when": the hour in the process when Prometheus shall arise. That hour (line 128) is now.
2. Presumably the sense by which one is aware of the "unseen Power" which Shelley calls "Intellectual Beauty"; see *Hymn to Intellectual Beauty,* stanza 2.

Pain, whose unheeded and familiar speech
Is howling, and keen shrieks, day after day;
And Hell, or the sharp fear of Hell?[3]

DEMOGORGON.   He reigns.

ASIA. Utter his name: a world pining in pain
  Asks but his name: curses shall drag him down.   30

DEMOGORGON. He reigns.

ASIA.   I feel, I know it: who?

DEMOGORGON.   He reigns.

ASIA. Who reigns? There was the Heaven and Earth at first,
  And Light and Love; then Saturn,[4] from whose throne
  Time fell, an envious shadow: such the state
  Of the earth's primal spirits beneath his sway,   35
  As the calm joy of flowers and living leaves
  Before the wind or sun has withered them
  And semivital worms; but he refused
  The birthright of their being, knowledge, power,
  The skill which wields the elements, the thought   40
  Which pierces this dim universe like light,
  Self-empire, and the majesty of love;
  For thirst of which they fainted. Then Prometheus
  Gave wisdom, which is strength, to Jupiter,
  And with this law alone, "Let man be free,"   45
  Clothed him with the dominion of wide Heaven.
  To know nor faith, nor love, nor law; to be
  Omnipotent but friendless is to reign;
  And Jove now reigned; for on the race of man
  First famine, and then toil, and then disease,   50
  Strife, wounds, and ghastly death unseen before,
  Fell; and the unseasonable seasons drove
  With alternating shafts of frost and fire,
  Their shelterless, pale tribes to mountain caves:
  And in their desert hearts fierce wants he sent,   55
  And mad disquietudes, and shadows idle
  Of unreal good, which levied mutual war,
  So ruining the lair wherein they raged.
  Prometheus saw, and waked the legioned hopes
  Which sleep within folded Elysian flowers,   60
  Nepenthe, Moly, Amaranth,[5] fadeless blooms,
  That they might hide with thin and rainbow wings
  The shape of Death; and Love he sent to bind
  The disunited tendrils of that vine
  Which bears the wine of life, the human heart;   65
  And he tamed fire which, like some beast of prey,
  Most terrible, but lovely, played beneath
  The frown of man; and tortured to his will

3. The nouns "hope," "love," etc. (lines
24–28), are all objects of the verb
"made" (line 19).
4. In Greek myth, Saturn's reign was
the golden age. In Asia's version, it
was for men the age of happy but totally ignorant innocence.
5. These are medicinal flowers in Greek
myth. Asia (lines 59–97) is describing
the various sciences and arts given to
man by Prometheus, the culture-bringer.

Iron and gold, the slaves and signs of power,
And gems and poisons, and all subtlest forms   70
Hidden beneath the mountains and the waves.
He gave man speech, and speech created thought,
Which is the measure of the universe;
And Science struck the thrones of earth and heaven,
Which shook, but fell not; and the harmonious mind   75
Poured itself forth in all-prophetic song;
And music lifted up the listening spirit
Until it walked, exempt from mortal care,
Godlike, o'er the clear billows of sweet sound;
And human hands first mimicked and then mocked,[6]   80
With molded limbs more lovely than its own,
The human form, till marble grew divine;
And mothers, gazing, drank the love men see
Reflected in their race, behold, and perish.[7]
He told the hidden power of herbs and springs,   85
And Disease drank and slept. Death grew like sleep.
He taught the implicated orbits woven
Of the wide-wandering stars; and how the sun
Changes his lair, and by what secret spell
The pale moon is transformed, when her broad eye   90
Gazes not on the interlunar[8] sea:
He taught to rule, as life directs the limbs,
The tempest-wingéd chariots of the Ocean,
And the Celt knew the Indian.[9] Cities then
Were built, and through their snowlike columns flowed 95
The warm winds, and the azure ether shone,
And the blue sea and shadowy hills were seen.
Such, the alleviations of his state,
Prometheus gave to man, for which he hangs
Withering in destined pain: but who rains down   100
Evil, the immedicable plague,[1] which, while
Man looks on his creation like a God
And sees that it is glorious, drives him on,
The wreck of his own will, the scorn of earth,
The outcast, the abandoned, the alone?   105
Not Jove: while yet his frown shook Heaven, aye, when
His adversary from adamantine chains
Cursed him, he trembled like a slave. Declare
Who is his master? Is he too a slave?
DEMOGORGON. All spirits are enslaved which serve things evil: 110
Thou knowest if Jupiter be such or no.
ASIA. Whom calledst thou God?

6. I.e., sculptors first merely reproduced, but later improved upon
("mocked"), the beauty of the human
form. Cf. *Ozymandias*, line 8.
7. Expectant mothers looked at the
beautiful statues so that their children
might, by prenatal influence, be born
with that beauty which makes beholders
die of love.
8. The phase between old and new
moon, when the moon is invisible.
9. The reference is to the ships in
which the Celtic (here, British) races of
Europe were able to sail to India.
1. The disease not curable by medicine.

DEMOGORGON.   I spoke but as ye speak;
For Jove is the supreme of living things.
ASIA. Who is the master of the slave?
DEMOGORGON.   If the abysm
Could vomit forth its secrets.—But a voice   115
Is wanting, the deep truth is imageless;[2]
For what would it avail to bid thee gaze
On the revolving world? What to bid speak
Fate, Time, Occasion, Chance, and Change? To these
All things are subject but eternal Love.   120
ASIA. So much I asked before, and my heart gave
The response thou hast given; and of such truths
Each to itself must be the oracle.
One more demand; and do thou answer me
As mine own soul would answer, did it know   125
That which I ask. Prometheus shall arise
Henceforth the sun of this rejoicing world:
When shall the destined hour arrive?
DEMOGORGON.   Behold![3]
ASIA. The rocks are cloven, and through the purple night
I see cars drawn by rainbow-wingéd steeds   130
Which trample the dim winds: in each there stands
A wild-eyed charioteer urging their flight.
Some look behind, as fiends pursued them there,
And yet I see no shapes but the keen stars:
Others, with burning eyes, lean forth, and drink   135
With eager lips the wind of their own speed, .
As if the thing they loved fled on before,
And now, even now, they clasped it. Their bright locks
Stream like a comet's flashing hair: they all
Sweep onward.
DEMOGORGON.   These are the immortal Hours,   140
Of whom thou didst demand. One waits for thee.
ASIA. A spirit with a dreadful countenance
Checks its dark chariot by the craggy gulf.
Unlike thy brethren, ghastly charioteer,
Who art thou? Whither wouldst thou bear me? Speak!   145
SPIRIT. I am the shadow of a destiny
More dread than is my aspect: ere yon planet
Has set, the darkness[4] which ascends with me
Shall wrap in lasting night heaven's kingless throne.
ASIA. What meanest thou?
PANTHEA.   That terrible shadow floats   150
Up from its throne, as may the lurid smoke
Of earthquake-ruined cities o'er the sea.

---

2. Three years earlier Shelley had written (*On Life*): "How vain is it to think that words can penetrate the mystery of our being!" And in a note on *Hellas* he was to say, three years later, that "the Gordian knot of the origin of evil" cannot be disentangled by assertions.

3. Demogorgon's answer is a gesture: he points to the approaching chariots ("cars").

4. I.e., Demogorgon, who is ascending (lines 150–55) to effect the dethronement of Jupiter.

Lo! it ascends the car; the coursers fly
Terrified: watch its path among the stars
Blackening the night!
ASIA.   Thus I am answered: strange!   155
PANTHEA. See, near the verge, another chariot stays;
An ivory shell inlaid with crimson fire,
Which comes and goes within its sculptured rim
Of delicate strange tracery; the young spirit
That guides it has the dovelike eyes of hope;   160
How its soft smiles attract the soul! as light
Lures wingéd insects through the lampless air.[5]

SPIRIT

My coursers are fed with the lightning,
    They drink of the whirlwind's stream,
And when the red morning is bright'ning   165
    They bathe in the fresh sunbeam;
They have strength for their swiftness I deem,
Then ascend with me, daughter of Ocean.

I desire: and their speed makes night kindle;
    I fear: they outstrip the Typhoon;   170
Ere the cloud piled on Atlas can dwindle
    We encircle the earth and the moon:
We shall rest from long labors at noon:
Then ascend with me, daughter of Ocean.

SCENE V—*The Car pauses within a Cloud on the top of a snowy
Mountain. ASIA, PANTHEA, and the SPIRIT OF THE HOUR.*

SPIRIT

On the brink of the night and the morning
    My coursers are wont to respire;
But the Earth has just whispered a warning
    That their flight must be swifter than fire:
They shall drink the hot speed of desire!   5

ASIA. Thou breathest on their nostrils, but my breath
    Would give them swifter speed.
SPIRIT.   Alas! it could not.
PANTHEA. Oh Spirit! pause, and tell whence is the light
    Which fills this cloud? the sun is yet unrisen.
SPIRIT. The sun will rise not until noon.[6] Apollo   10
    Is held in heaven by wonder; and the light
    Which fills this vapor, as the aërial hue
    Of fountain-gazing roses fills the water,
    Flows from thy mighty sister.
PANTHEA.   Yes, I feel—
ASIA. What is it with thee, sister? Thou art pale.   15
PANTHEA. How thou art changed! I dare not look on thee;

---

5. The ancient image of the soul,
"psyche," was a moth. The chariot described here by Panthea will carry Asia
to a reunion with Prometheus.
6. Noon will be the time of the reunion between Prometheus and Asia.

I feel but see thee not. I scarce endure
The radiance of thy beauty.[7] Some good change
Is working in the elements, which suffer
Thy presence thus unveiled. The Nereids tell   20
That on the day when the clear hyaline
Was cloven at thine uprise, and thou didst stand
Within a veinéd shell,[8] which floated on
Over the calm floor of the crystal sea,
Among the Aegean isles, and by the shores   25
Which bear thy name, love, like the atmosphere
Of the sun's fire filling the living world,
Burst from thee, and illumined earth and heaven
And the deep ocean and the sunless caves
And all that dwells within them, till grief cast   30
Eclipse upon the soul from which it came:[9]
Such art thou now; nor is it I alone,
Thy sister, thy companion, thine own chosen one,
But the whole world which seeks thy sympathy.
Hearest thou not sound i' the air which speak the love   35
Of all articulate beings? Feelest thou not
The inanimate winds enamored of thee? List!   [*Music.*]

ASIA. Thy words are sweeter than aught else but his
Whose echoes they are: yet all love is sweet,
Given or returned. Common as light is love,   40
And its familiar voice wearies not ever.
Like the wide heaven, the all-sustaining air,
It makes the reptile equal to the God:
They who inspire it most are fortunate,
As I am now; but those who feel it most   45
Are happier still, after long sufferings,
As I shall soon become.

PANTHEA.   List! Spirits speak.

VOICE IN THE AIR[1] [*singing*]

Life of Life! thy lips enkindle
    With their love the breath between them;
And thy smiles before they dwindle   50
    Make the cold air fire; then screen them
In those looks, where whoso gazes
Faints, entangled in their mazes.

Child of Light! thy limbs are burning
    Through the vest which seems to hide them;   55
As the radiant lines of morning

7. In an earlier scene, Panthea had envisioned in a dream the radiant and eternal inner form of Prometheus emerging through his "wound-worn limbs." The corresponding transfiguration of Asia, prepared for by her descent to the underworld, now takes place.
8. The story told by the Nereids (sea nymphs) serves to associate Asia with Aphrodite, goddess of love, emerging (as in Botticelli's painting) from the Mediterranean on a seashell. "Hyaline": the glassy sea.
9. The inner radiance, now revived, had been obliterated at the time of Asia's separation from Prometheus.
1. The voice describes, in a dizzying whirl of optical paradoxes, what it feels like to look upon the naked essence of love and beauty.

Through the clouds ere they divide them;
And this atmosphere divinest
Shrouds thee wheresoe'er thou shinest.

Fair are others; none beholds thee,   60
  But thy voice sounds low and tender
Like the fairest, for it folds thee
  From the sight, that liquid splendor,
And all feel, yet see thee never,
As I feel now, lost forever!   65

Lamp of Earth! where'er thou movest
  Its dim shapes are clad with brightness,
And the souls of whom thou lovest
  Walk upon the winds with lightness,
Till they fail, as I am failing,   70
Dizzy, lost, yet unbewailing!

ASIA

My soul is an enchanted boat,
  Which, like a sleeping swan, doth float
Upon the silver waves of thy sweet singing;
  And thine doth like an angel sit   75
  Beside a helm conducting it,
Whilst all the winds with melody are ringing.
  It seems to float ever, forever,
  Upon that many-winding river,
  Between mountains, woods, abysses,   80
  A paradise of wildernesses!
Till, like one in slumber bound,
Borne to the ocean, I float down, around,
Into a sea profound, of ever-spreading sound:

  Meanwhile thy spirit lifts its pinions   85
  In music's most serene dominions;
Catching the winds that fan that happy heaven.
  And we sail on, away, afar,
  Without a course, without a star,
But, by the instinct of sweet music driven;   90
  Till through Elysian garden islets
  By thee, most beautiful of pilots,
  Where never mortal pinnace glided,
  The boat of my desire is guided:
Realms where the air we breathe is love,   95
Which in the winds and on the waves doth move,
Harmonizing this earth with what we feel above.

  We have passed Age's icy caves,
  And Manhood's dark and tossing waves,
And Youth's smooth ocean, smiling to betray: 100
  Beyond the glassy gulfs we flee
  Of shadow-peopled Infancy,

Through Death and Birth, to a diviner day;[2]
  A paradise of vaulted bowers,
  Lit by downward-gazing flowers, 105
And watery paths that wind between
  Wildernesses calm and green,
Peopled by shapes too bright to see,
And rest, having beheld; somewhat like thee;
Which walk upon the sea, and chant melodiously! 110

From *Act III*

SCENE I—*Heaven.* JUPITER *on his Throne;* THETIS *and the other Deities assembled.*

JUPITER. Ye congregated powers of heaven, who share
  The glory and the strength of him ye serve,
  Rejoice! henceforth I am omnipotent.
  All else had been subdued to me; alone
  The soul of man, like unextinguished fire, 5
  Yet burns towards heaven with fierce reproach, and doubt,
  And lamentation, and reluctant prayer,
  Hurling up insurrection, which might make
  Our antique empire insecure, though built
  On eldest faith, and hell's coeval, fear; 10
  And though my curses through the pendulous air,
  Like snow on herbless peaks, fall flake by flake,
  And cling to it;[1] though under my wrath's night
  It climbs the crags of life, step after step,
  Which wound it, as ice wounds unsandaled feet, 15
  It yet remains supreme o'er misery,
  Aspiring, unrepressed, yet soon to fall:
  Even now have I begotten a strange wonder,
  That fatal child,[2] the terror of the earth,
  Who waits but till the destined hour arrive, 20
  Bearing from Demogorgon's vacant throne
  The dreadful might of ever-living limbs
  Which clothed that awful spirit unbeheld,
  To redescend, and trample out the spark.[3]
  Pour forth heaven's wine, Idaean Ganymede,[4] 25
  And let it fill the Daedal cups like fire,
  And from the flower-inwoven soil divine
  Ye all-triumphant harmonies arise,
  As dew from earth under the twilight stars:
  Drink! be the nectar circling through your veins 30

2. Asia is describing what it feels like to be transfigured—in the image of moving backward down the stream of time, through youth and infancy and birth itself, in order to die to this life and be born again to a "diviner" existence.
1. I.e., "the soul of man," line 5 (as also in lines 14 and 16).
2. The son of Jupiter and Thetis; Jupiter believes that the "fatal child" will

assume the bodily form of the conquered Demogorgon and then return to announce his victory and to trample out the resistance of Prometheus.
3. The "spark" of Prometheus' defiance.
4. Ganymede had been seized on Mt. Ida by an eagle and carried to heaven to be Jupiter's cupbearer. "Daedal": skillfully wrought (from the name of the Greek craftsman, Daedalus).

The soul of joy, ye ever-living Gods,
Till exultation burst in one wide voice
Like music from Elysian winds.
                         And thou
Ascend beside me, veiléd in the light
Of the desire which makes thee one with me,   35
Thetis, bright image of eternity!
When thou didst cry, "Insufferable might!⁵
God! Spare me! I sustain not the quick flames,
The penetrating presence; all my being,
Like him whom the Numidian seps⁶ did thaw   40
Into a dew with poison, is dissolved,
Sinking through its foundations": even then
Two mighty spirits, mingling, made a third
Mightier than either, which, unbodied now,
Between us floats, felt, although unbeheld,   45
Waiting the incarnation, which ascends,
(Hear ye the thunder of the fiery wheels
Griding⁷ the winds?) from Demogorgon's throne.
Victory! victory! Feel'st thou not, O world,
The earthquake of his chariot thundering up   50
Olympus?

    [*The Car of the* HOUR *arrives.* DEMOGORGON *descends, and moves towards the Throne of* JUPITER.]
              Awful shape, what art thou? Speak!
DEMOGORGON. Eternity. Demand no direr name.
Descend, and follow me down the abyss.
I am thy child,⁸ as thou wert Saturn's child;
Mightier than thee: and we must dwell together   55
Henceforth in darkness. Lift thy lightnings not.
The tyranny of heaven none may retain,
Or reassume, or hold, succeeding thee:
Yet if thou wilt, as 'tis the destiny
Of trodden worms to writhe till they are dead,   60
Put forth thy might.
JUPITER.   Detested prodigy!
Even thus beneath the deep Titanian prisons
I trample thee! thou lingerest?
                  Mercy! mercy!
No pity, no release, no respite! Oh,
That thou wouldst make mine enemy my judge,   65
Even where he hangs, seared by my long revenge,
On Caucasus! he would not doom me thus.
Gentle, and just, and dreadless, is he not
The monarch of the world?⁹ What then art thou?

---

5. This description of the union of Jupiter and Thetis is a grotesque parody of the reunion of Prometheus and Asia.
6. A serpent of Numidia (North Africa) whose bite was thought to cause putrefaction.
7. Cutting with a rasping sound.

8. Ironically, and in a figurative sense: Demogorgon's function follows from Jupiter's actions.
9. The ultimate irony: Jupiter appeals to those very qualities of Prometheus for which he has hitherto persecuted him, begging for a mercy which Prome-

No refuge! no appeal!
      Sink with me then,   70
We two will sink on the wide waves of ruin,
Even as a vulture and a snake outspent
Drop, twisted in inextricable fight,
Into a shoreless sea. Let hell unlock
Its mounded oceans of tempestuous fire,   75
And whelm on them into the bottomless void
This desolated world, and thee, and me,
The conqueror and the conquered, and the wreck
Of that for which they combated.
         Ai! Ai!
The elements obey me not. I sink   80
Dizzily down, ever, forever, down.
And, like a cloud, mine enemy above
Darkens my fall with victory! Ai, Ai!

From SCENE IV—*A Forest. In the Background a Cave.* PROME-
THEUS, ASIA, PANTHEA, IONE, *and the* SPIRIT OF THE EARTH.[1]

* * *

[*The* SPIRIT OF THE HOUR *enters.*]
PROMETHEUS. We feel what thou hast heard and seen: yet speak.
SPIRIT OF THE HOUR. Soon as the sound had ceased whose thunder
  filled
The abysses of the sky and the wide earth,
There was a change: the impalpable thin air   100
And the all-circling sunlight were transformed,
As if the sense of love dissolved in them
Had folded itself round the sphered world.
My vision then grew clear, and I could see
Into the mysteries of the universe: 105
Dizzy as with delight I floated down,
Winnowing the lightsome air with languid plumes,
My coursers sought their birthplace in the sun,
Where they henceforth will live exempt from toil,
Pasturing flowers of vegetable fire;   110
And where my moonlike car will stand within
A temple, gazed upon by Phidian forms[2]
Of thee, and Asia, and the Earth, and me,
And you fair nymphs looking the love we feel—
In memory of the tidings it has borne—   115
Beneath a dome fretted with graven flowers,

theus has already granted him; but
Prometheus' change from vengefulness
to mercy is in fact the cause of Jupiter's
present downfall.
1. After Jupiter's annihilation (described in Scene ii), Hercules unbinds
Prometheus, who is reunited with Asia
and retires to a cave "where we will
sit and talk of time and change /
* * * ourselves unchanged." In the
speech which concludes the act (re-

printed here) the Spirit of the Hour describes what happened when he sounded
the trumpet of human and social regeneration.
2. The crescent-shaped ("moonlike")
chariot, its apocalyptic mission accomplished, will be frozen to the immobility of stone, and will be surrounded
by the sculptured forms of other agents
in the drama. Phidias (5th century
B.C.) was the noblest of Greek sculptors.

Poised on twelve columns of resplendent stone,
And open to the bright and liquid sky.
Yoked to it by an amphisbaenic snake[3]
The likeness of those wingéd steeds will mock[4]   120
The flight from which they find repose. Alas,
Whither has wandered now my partial[5] tongue
When all remains untold which ye would hear?
As I have said, I floated to the earth:
It was, as it is still, the pain of bliss   125
To move, to breathe, to be; I wandering went
Among the haunts and dwellings of mankind,
And first was disappointed not to see
Such mighty change as I had felt within
Expressed in outward things; but soon I looked,   130
And behold, thrones were kingless, and men walked
One with the other even as spirits do,
None fawned, none trampled; hate, disdain, or fear,
Self-love or self-contempt, on human brows
No more inscribed, as o'er the gate of hell,   135
"All hope abandon ye who enter here";[6]
None frowned, none trembled, none with eager fear
Gazed on another's eye of cold command,
Until the subject of a tyrant's will
Became, worse fate, the abject of his own,[7]   140
Which spurred him, like an outspent horse, to death.
None wrought his lips in truth-entangling lines
Which smiled the lie his tongue disdained to speak;
None, with firm sneer, trod out in his own heart
The sparks of love and hope till there remained   145
Those bitter ashes, a soul self-consumed,
And the wretch crept a vampire among men,
Infecting all with his own hideous ill;
None talked that common, false, cold, hollow talk
Which makes the heart deny the *yes* it breathes,   150
Yet question that unmeant hypocrisy
With such a self-mistrust as has no name.
And women, too, frank, beautiful, and kind
As the free heaven which rains fresh light and dew
On the wide earth, past; gentle radiant forms,   155
From custom's evil taint exempt and pure;
Speaking the wisdom once they could not think,
Looking emotions once they feared to feel,
And changed to all which once they dared not be,
Yet being now, made earth like heaven; nor pride,   160
Nor jealousy, nor envy, nor ill shame,

---

3. A mythical snake with a head at either end; it serves here as a symbolic warning that a reversal of the process of redemption is always possible. Cf. IV.561–69.
4. "Imitate" and also, in their statu-esque immobility, "mock at" the flight that they represent.
5. Biased, self-concerned.
6. Dante, *Inferno* III.9.
7. I.e., abjectly subject to his own will.

The bitterest of those drops of treasured gall,
Spoilt the sweet taste of the nepenthe,[8] love.

Thrones, altars, judgment-seats, and prisons; wherein,
And beside which, by wretched men were borne   165
Scepters, tiaras, swords, and chains, and tomes
Of reasoned wrong, glozed on[9] by ignorance,
Were like those monstrous and barbaric shapes,
The ghosts of a no-more-remembered fame,
Which, from their unworn obelisks, look forth   170
In triumph o'er the palaces and tombs
Of those who were their conquerors: moldering round,
These imaged to the pride of kings and priests
A dark yet mighty faith, a power as wide
As is the world it wasted, and are now   175
But an astonishment; even so the tools
And emblems of its last captivity,
Amid the dwellings of the peopled earth,
Stand, not o'erthrown, but unregarded now.
And those foul shapes,[1] abhorred by god and man—   180
Which, under many a name and many a form
Strange, savage, ghastly, dark, and execrable,
Were Jupiter, the tyrant of the world;
And which the nations, panic-stricken, served
With blood, and hearts broken by long hope, and love   185
Dragged to his altars soiled and garlandless,
And slain amid men's unreclaiming tears,
Flattering the thing they feared, which fear was hate—
Frown, moldering fast, o'er their abandoned shrines:
The painted veil, by those who were, called life,[2]   190
Which mimicked, as with colors idly spread,
All men believed or hoped, is torn aside;
The loathsome mask has fallen, the man remains—
Scepterless, free, uncircumscribed—but man:
Equal, unclassed, tribeless, and nationless,   195
Exempt from awe, worship, degree, the king
Over himself; just, gentle, wise: but man
Passionless?—no, yet free from guilt or pain,
Which were, for his will made or suffered them,
Nor yet exempt, though ruling them like slaves,   200
From chance, and death, and mutability,
The clogs of that which else might oversoar
The loftiest star of unascended heaven,
Pinnacled dim in the intense inane.[3]

8. A fabled drug bringing forgetfulness of pain and sorrow.
9. Annotated.
1. The variously named gods which claimed human sacrifice—all really manifestations of Jupiter (line 183).
2. I.e., which was thought to be life (reality) by men as they were before their regeneration.
3. I.e., a dim point in the extreme of empty space. If regenerate man were to be entirely released from the material conditions of chance, death, and change (line 201), he would cease to be man at all, becoming, what even the stars are not, a pure ideal.

From Act IV[1]

SCENE—*A Part of the Forest near the Cave of Prometheus.*

* * *

THE EARTH

The joy, the triumph, the delight, the madness!
The boundless, overflowing, bursting gladness,   320
The vaporous exultation not to be confined![2]
Ha! ha! the animation of delight
Which wraps me, like an atmosphere of light,
And bears me as a cloud is borne by its own wind.

THE MOON

Brother mine, calm wanderer,   325
Happy globe of land and air,
Some Spirit[3] is darted like a beam from thee,
Which penetrates my frozen frame,
And passes with the warmth of flame,
With love, and odor, and deep melody   330
Through me, through me!

THE EARTH

Ha! ha! the caverns of my hollow mountains,
My cloven fire-crags, sound-exulting fountains
Laugh with a vast and inextinguishable laughter.
The oceans, and the deserts, and the abysses,   335
And the deep air's unmeasured wildernesses,
Answer from all their clouds and billows, echoing after.

They cry aloud as I do. Sceptered curse,[4]
Who all our green and azure universe
Threatenedst to muffle round with black destruction, sending   340
A solid cloud to rain hot thunderstones,
And splinter and knead down my children's bones,
All I bring forth, to one void mass battering and blending—

Until each craglike tower, and storied column,
Palace, and obelisk, and temple solemn,   345

---

1. The original drama, completed in the spring of 1819, contained only three acts. Later that year Shelley, feeling the need for a more impressive climax, added the fourth act by way of a great choral conclusion. The rejuvenation of man is reflected throughout the universe, and the apocalyptic vision of a new heaven and earth is presented, as in Revelation xxi, in the symbol of a marriage: "And I saw a new heaven and a new earth: for the first heaven and the first earth were passed away; and there was no more sea. And I John saw the holy city, new Jerusalem, coming down from God out of heaven, prepared as a bride adorned for her husband." Shelley extends this marital figure to the cosmos (including, in the excerpt here, the earth and moon), in a total renewal of love and relationship that reflects the central reunion of Prometheus and Asia and represents the reintegration of a split and conflicting humanity. In the coda, Demogorgon sums up the meaning of the whole.

2. Literally, the earth's gases are bursting out through its volcanoes.

3. Represented physically by gravitational force, exerted by the moving earth upon its circling satellite.

4. Jupiter.

My imperial mountains crowned with cloud, and snow, and fire;
  My sealike forests, every blade and blossom
  Which finds a grave or cradle in my bosom,
Were stamped by thy strong hate into a lifeless mire:

    How art thou sunk, withdrawn, covered, drunk up   350
    By thirsty nothing, as the brackish cup
Drained by a desert troop, a little drop for all;
    And from beneath, around, within, above,
    Filling thy void annihilation, love
Burst in like light on caves cloven by the thunder ball.   355

THE MOON

    The snow upon my lifeless mountains
    Is loosened into living fountains,
My solid oceans flow, and sing, and shine:
    A spirit from my heart bursts forth,
    It clothes with unexpected birth   360
My cold bare bosom: Oh! it must be thine
      On mine, on mine!

    Gazing on thee I feel, I know
    Green stalks burst forth, and bright flowers grow,
And living shapes upon my bosom move: 365
    Music is in the sea and air,
    Wingéd clouds soar here and there,
Dark with the rain new buds are dreaming of:
    'Tis love, all love!

THE EARTH

It interpenetrates my granite mass,   370
Through tangled roots and trodden clay doth pass
Into the utmost leaves and delicatest flowers;
    Upon the winds, among the clouds 'tis spread,
    It wakes a life in the forgotten dead,
They breathe a spirit up from their obscurest bowers.   375

    And like a storm bursting its cloudy prison
    With thunder, and with whirlwind, has arisen
Out of the lampless caves of unimagined being:
    With earthquake shock and swiftness making shiver
    Thought's stagnant chaos, unremoved forever,[5]   380
Till hate, and fear, and pain, light-vanquished shadows, fleeing,

    Leave Man, who was a many-sided mirror,
    Which could distort to many a shape of error,
This true fair world of things, a sea reflecting love;
    Which over all his kind, as the sun's heaven   385
    Gliding o'er ocean, smooth, serene, and even,
Darting from starry depths radiance and life, doth move:

    Leave Man, even as a leprous child is left,
    Who follows a sick beast to some warm cleft

5. I.e., never to be removed.

Of rocks, through which the might of healing springs is poured; 390
  Then when it wanders home with rosy smile,
  Unconscious, and its mother fears awhile
It is a spirit, then, weeps on her child restored.

  Man, oh, not men![6] a chain of linkèd thought,
  Of love and might to be divided not, 395
Compelling the elements with adamantine stress;
  As the sun rules,[7] even with a tyrant's gaze,
  The unquiet republic of the maze
Of planets, struggling fierce towards heaven's free wilderness.

  Man, one harmonious soul of many a soul, 400
  Whose nature is its own divine control,
Where all things flow to all, as rivers to the sea;
  Familiar acts are beautiful through love;
  Labor, and pain, and grief, in life's green grove
Sport like tame beasts, none knew how gentle they could be! 405

  His will, with all mean passions, bad delights,
  And selfish cares, its trembling satellites,
A spirit ill to guide, but mighty to obey,
  Is as a tempest-wingèd ship, whose helm
  Love rules, through waves which dare not overwhelm, 410
Forcing life's wildest shores to own its sovereign sway.

  All things confess his strength. Through the cold mass
  Of marble and of color his dreams pass;
Bright threads whence mothers weave the robes their children wear;
  Language is a perpetual Orphic song,[8] 415
  Which rules with Daedal harmony a throng
Of thoughts and forms, which else senseless and shapeless were.

  The lightning is his slave;[9] heaven's utmost deep
  Gives up her stars, and like a flock of sheep
They pass before his eye, are numbered, and roll on! 420
  The tempest is his steed, he strides the air;
  And the abyss shouts from her depth laid bare,
Heaven, hast thou secrets? Man unveils me; I have none.

THE MOON

  The shadow of white death has passed
  From my path in heaven at last, 425
A clinging shroud of solid frost and sleep;
  And through my newly-woven bowers,
  Wander happy paramours,
Less mighty, but as mild as those who keep
  Thy vales more deep. 430

6. Human society, once splintered into isolated individuals by hate and conflict, is now described as bound by love and commonalty of thought into a single macrocosmic Man.
7. By its gravitational attraction.
8. Like the music of Orpheus, which attracted and controlled beasts, rocks, and trees. "Daedal" (next line): skillful, intricate.
9. The Earth describes the scientific and technological triumphs of regenerate man.

THE EARTH

As the dissolving warmth of dawn may fold
A half unfrozen dew-globe, green, and gold,
And crystalline, till it becomes a wingéd mist,
And wanders up the vault of the blue day,
Outlives the noon, and on the sun's last ray   435
Hangs o'er the sea, a fleece of fire and amethyst.

THE MOON

Thou art folded, thou art lying
In the light which is undying
Of thine own joy, and heaven's smile divine;
All suns and constellations shower   440
On thee a light, a life, a power
Which doth array thy sphere; thou pourest thine
    On mine, on mine!

THE EARTH

I spin beneath my pyramid of night,[1]
Which points into the heavens dreaming delight,   445
Murmuring victorious joy in my enchanted sleep;
As a youth lulled in love-dreams faintly sighing,
Under the shadow of his beauty lying,
Which round his rest a watch of light and warmth doth keep.

THE MOON

As in the soft and sweet eclipse,   450
When soul meets soul on lovers' lips,
High hearts are calm, and brightest eyes are dull;
So when thy shadow falls on me,[1a]
Then am I mute and still, by thee
Covered; of thy love, Orb most beautiful,   455
    Full, oh, too full!

Thou art speeding round the sun
Brightest world of many a one;
Green and azure sphere which shinest
With a light which is divinest   460
Among all the lamps of Heaven
To whom life and light is given;
I, thy crystal paramour
Borne beside thee by a power
Like the polar Paradise,   465
Magnet-like of lovers' eyes;[2]
I, a most enamored maiden
Whose weak brain is overladen
With the pleasure of her love,
Maniac-like around thee move   470
Gazing, an insatiate bride,
On thy form from every side

1. The conic shadow cast by the earth as it intercepts the sun's light.
1a. In the eclipse of the moon; cf. line 450.

2. Circling the earth, the moon keeps her face constantly toward it.

Like a Maenad,[3] round the cup
Which Agave lifted up
In the weird Cadmaean forest. 475
Brother, wheresoe'er thou soarest
I must hurry, whirl, and follow
Through the heavens wide and hollow,
Sheltered by the warm embrace
Of thy soul from hungry space, 480
Drinking from thy sense and sight
Beauty, majesty, and might,
As a lover or a chameleon
Grows like what it looks upon,
As a violet's gentle eye 485
Gazes on the azure sky
Until its hue grows like what it beholds,
As a gray and watery mist
Glows like solid amethyst
Athwart the western mountain it enfolds, 490
When the sunset sleeps
Upon its snow—

THE EARTH

And the weak day weeps[4]
That it should be so.
Oh, gentle Moon, the voice of thy delight 495
Falls on me like thy clear and tender light
Soothing the seaman, borne the summer night,
Through isles forever calm;
Oh, gentle Moon, thy crystal accents pierce
The caverns of my pride's deep universe, 500
Charming the tiger joy, whose tramplings fierce
Made wounds which need thy balm.

* * *

DEMOGORGON

Man, who wert once a despot and a slave;
A dupe and a deceiver; a decay;
A traveler from the cradle to the grave 550
Through the dim night of this immortal day:

ALL

Speak: thy strong words may never pass away.

DEMOGORGON

This is the day which down the void abysm
At the Earth-born's[5] spell yawns for Heaven's despotism,
And Conquest is dragged captive through the deep:[6] 555

3. The Maenads were female participants in the ecstatic worship of Dionysus, or Bacchus. Agave, daughter of
King Cadmus (lines 474–75), in a
blind frenzy tore her own son Pentheus
to bits when he was caught spying on
the Dionysiac rites.
4. I.e., the dew at nightfall.
5. Prometheus'.
6. Ephesians iv.8: "When [Christ]
ascended up on high, he led captivity
captive."

Love, from its awful throne of patient power
In the wise heart, from the last giddy hour
  Of dread endurance, from the slippery, steep,
And narrow verge of craglike agony, springs   560
And folds over the world its healing wings.

Gentleness, Virtue, Wisdom, and Endurance,
These are the seals of that most firm assurance
  Which bars the pit over Destruction's strength;
And if, with infirm hand, Eternity,   565
Mother of many acts and hours, should free
  The serpent that would clasp her with his length;[7]
These are the spells by which to reassume
An empire o'er the disentangled doom:[8]

To suffer woes which Hope thinks infinite;   570
To forgive wrongs darker than death or night;
  To defy Power, which seems omnipotent;
To love, and bear; to hope till Hope creates
From its own wreck the thing it contemplates;
  Neither to change, nor falter, nor repent;   575
This, like thy glory, Titan, is to be
Good, great and joyous, beautiful and free;
This is alone Life, Joy, Empire, and Victory.
1818–19   1820

The Cloud

I bring fresh showers for the thirsting flowers,
  From the seas and the streams;
I bear light shade for the leaves when laid
  In their noonday dreams.
From my wings are shaken the dews that waken   5
  The sweet buds every one,
When rocked to rest on their mother's breast,
  As she dances about the sun.
I wield the flail of the lashing hail,
  And whiten the green plains under,   10
And then again I dissolve it in rain,
  And laugh as I pass in thunder.

I sift the snow on the mountains below,
  And their great pines groan aghast;
And all the night 'tis my pillow white,   15
  While I sleep in the arms of the blast.

7. A final reminder that the serpent incessantly struggles to break loose and start the cycle of evil all over again. Felicity must continue to be earned.
8. Shelley's four cardinal virtues (line 562), which seal the serpent in the pit, also constitute the magic formulas ("spells") by which to remaster him, should he again break loose. These virtues are expanded upon in the concluding lines (570–75).

Sublime on the towers of my skyey bowers,
    Lightning my pilot[1] sits;
In a cavern under is fettered the thunder,
    It struggles and howls at fits;[2]   20
Over earth and ocean, with gentle motion,
    This pilot is guiding me,
Lured by the love of the genii that move
    In the depths of the purple sea;
Over the rills, and the crags, and the hills,   25
    Over the lakes and the plains,
Wherever he dream, under mountain or stream,
    The Spirit he loves remains;
And I all the while bask in Heaven's blue smile,[3]
    Whilst he is dissolving in rains.   30

The sanguine Sunrise, with his meteor eyes,
    And his burning plumes outspread,
Leaps on the back of my sailing rack,[4]
    When the morning star shines dead;
As on the jag of a mountain crag,   35
    Which an earthquake rocks and swings,
An eagle alit one moment may sit
    In the light of its golden wings.
And when Sunset may breathe, from the lit sea beneath,
    Its ardors of rest and of love,   40
And the crimson pall of eve may fall
    From the depth of Heaven above,
With wings folded I rest, on mine aëry nest,
    As still as a brooding dove.

That orbéd maiden with white fire laden,   45
    Whom mortals call the Moon,
Glides glimmering o'er my fleecelike floor,
    By the midnight breezes strewn;
And wherever the beat of her unseen feet,
    Which only the angels hear,   50
May have broken the woof[5] of my tent's thin roof,
    The stars peep behind her and peer;
And I laugh to see them whirl and flee,
    Like a swarm of golden bees,
When I widen the rent in my wind-built tent,   55
    Till the calm rivers, lakes, and seas,
Like strips of the sky fallen through me on high,
    Are each paved with the moon and these.[6]

I bind the Sun's throne with a burning zone,[7]
    And the Moon's with a girdle of pearl;   60

1. The atmospheric electricity which guides the movements of the cloud; it is "lured" (line 23) by the attraction of an opposite charge.
2. Fitfully.
3. The upper part of the cloud re- mains exposed to the sun.
4. High, broken clouds, driven by the wind.
5. Texture.
6. I.e., the stars.
7. Girdle, belt.

The volcanoes are dim, and the stars reel and swim,
    When the whirlwinds my banner unfurl.
From cape to cape, with a bridgelike shape,
    Over a torrent sea,
Sunbeam-proof, I hang like a roof—   65
    The mountains its columns be.
The triumphal arch through which I march
    With hurricane, fire, and snow,
When the Powers of the air are chained to my chair,
    Is the million-colored bow;   70
The sphere-fire[8] above its soft colors wove,
    While the moist Earth was laughing below.

I am the daughter of Earth and Water,
    And the nursling of the Sky;
I pass through the pores of the ocean and shores;   75
    I change, but I cannot die.
For after the rain when with never a stain
    The pavilion of Heaven is bare,
And the winds and sunbeams with their convex gleams
    Build up the blue dome of air,[9]   80
I silently laugh at my own cenotaph,[1]
    And out of the caverns of rain,
Like a child from the womb, like a ghost[2] from the tomb,
    I arise and unbuild it again.

                                                            1820

To a Skylark[1]

Hail to thee, blithe Spirit!
    Bird thou never wert,
That from Heaven, or near it,
    Pourest thy full heart
In profuse strains of unpremeditated art.   5

Higher still and higher
    From the earth thou springest
Like a cloud of fire;
    The blue deep thou wingest,
And singing still dost soar, and soaring ever singest.   10

In the golden lightning
    Of the sunken sun,
O'er which clouds are bright'ning,

8. The sunlight.
9. The blue color of the sky; the
phenomenon results from the way "sunbeams" are filtered through the atmosphere.
1. The memorial monument ("cenotaph") of the dead cloud is the cloudless blue dome.

2. Soul, spirit.
1. The bird, freed from the bonds of
earth and soaring beyond the reach of
all the physical senses except hearing,
is made the emblem of a nonmaterial
spirit of pure joy, beyond access by
human sense; see lines 15, 61.

Thou dost float and run;
Like an unbodied joy whose race is just begun. 15

The pale purple even
Melts around thy flight
Like a star of Heaven,
In the broad daylight
Thou art unseen, but yet I hear thy shrill delight, 20

Keen as are the arrows
Of that silver sphere,[2]
Whose intense lamp narrows
In the white dawn clear
Until we hardly see—we feel that it is there. 25

All the earth and air
With thy voice is loud,
As, when night is bare,
From one lonely cloud
The moon rains out her beams, and Heaven is overflowed. 30

What thou art we know not;
What is most like thee?
From rainbow clouds there flow not
Drops so bright to see
As from thy presence showers a rain of melody. 35

Like a Poet hidden
In the light of thought,
Singing hymns unbidden,
Till the world is wrought
To sympathy with hopes and fears it heeded not: 40

Like a high-born maiden
In a palace tower
Soothing her love-laden
Soul in secret hour
With music sweet as love, which overflows her bower: 45

Like a glowworm golden
In a dell of dew,
Scattering unbeholden
Its aërial hue
Among the flowers and grass, which screen it from the view! 50

Like a rose embowered
In its own green leaves,
By warm winds deflowered,[3]
Till the scent it gives
Makes faint with too much sweet those heavy-wingèd thieves:[4] 55

---

2. The morning star.
3. In the double sense: fertilized, and
stripped of its petals.
4. The "warm winds," line 53.

Sound of vernal showers
    On the twinkling grass,
Rain-awakened flowers,
    All that ever was
Joyous, and clear, and fresh, thy music doth surpass: 60

Teach us, Sprite[5] or Bird,
    What sweet thoughts are thine:
I have never heard
    Praise of love or wine
That panted forth a flood of rapture so divine.   65

Chorus Hymeneal,[6]
    Or triumphal chant,
Matched with thine would be all
    But an empty vaunt,
A thing wherein we feel there is some hidden want.   70

What objects are the fountains
    Of thy happy strain?
What fields, or waves, or mountains?
    What shapes of sky or plain?
What love of thine own kind? what ignorance of pain?   75

With thy clear keen joyance
    Languor cannot be:
Shadow of annoyance
    Never came near thee:
Thou lovest—but ne'er knew love's sad satiety.   80

Waking or asleep,
    Thou of death must deem
Things more true and deep
    Than we mortals dream,
Or how could thy notes flow in such a crystal stream?   85

We look before and after,
    And pine for what is not:
Our sincerest laughter
    With some pain is fraught;
Our sweetest songs are those that tell of saddest thought.   90

Yet if we could scorn
    Hate, and pride, and fear;
If we were things born
    Not to shed a tear,
I know not how thy joy we ever should come near.   95

Better than all measures
    Of delightful sound,
Better than all treasures

5. Spirit.
6. Celebrating a marriage (from Hymen, Greek god of marriage).

That in books are found,
Thy skill to poet were, thou scorner of the ground!   100

Teach me half the gladness
  That thy brain must know,
Such harmonious madness
  From my lips would flow
The world should listen then—as I am listening now.   105

1820   1820

Hymn of Apollo[1]

1

The sleepless Hours who watch me as I lie,
  Curtained with star-inwoven tapestries
From the broad moonlight of the sky,
  Fanning the busy dreams from my dim eyes—
Waken me when their Mother, the gray Dawn,   5
Tells them that dreams and that the moon is gone.

2

Then I arise, and climbing Heaven's blue dome,
  I walk over the mountains and the waves,
Leaving my robe upon the ocean foam;
  My footsteps pave the clouds with fire; the caves   10
Are filled with my bright presence, and the air
Leaves the green Earth to my embraces bare.

3

The sunbeams are my shafts, with which I kill
  Deceit, that loves the night and fears the day;
All men who do or even imagine ill   15
  Fly me, and from the glory of my ray
Good minds and open actions take new might,
Until diminished by the reign of Night.

4

I feed the clouds, the rainbows and the flowers
  With their aethereal colors; the moon's globe   20
And the pure stars in their eternal bowers
  Are cinctured[2] with my power as with a robe;
Whatever lamps on Earth or Heaven may shine
Are portions of one power, which is mine.

5

I stand at noon upon the peak of Heaven,   25
  Then with unwilling steps I wander down
Into the clouds of the Atlantic even;

1. Written, with the companion piece that follows, for the opening scene in Mary Shelley's verse drama *Midas*. Apollo, god of the sun, of healing, and of poetry and the other arts, sings this serenely Olympian hymn in a contest with Pan, the goatlike deity of flocks, forests, and wild life. In the play, old Tmolus, a mountain god who judges the contest, awards the prize to Apollo; when Midas, a mortal, objects, preferring Pan's song of natural desire, passions, and suffering, Apollo affixes on him asses' ears.
2. Girdled.

For grief that I depart they weep and frown:
What look is more delightful than the smile
With which I soothe them from the western isle?   30

6

I am the eye with which the Universe
   Beholds itself and knows itself divine;
All harmony of instrument or verse,
   All prophecy, all medicine is mine,
All light of art or nature; to my song   35
Victory and praise in its own right belong.

1820   1824

Hymn of Pan[1]

1

From the forests and highlands
   We come, we come;
From the river-girt islands,
   Where loud waves are dumb
     Listening to my sweet pipings.   5
The wind in the reeds and the rushes,
   The bees on the bells of thyme,
The birds on the myrtle bushes,
   The cicale[2] above in the lime,
And the lizards below in the grass,   10
Were as silent as ever old Tmolus was,
     Listening to my sweet pipings.

2

Liquid Peneus[3] was flowing,
   And all dark Tempe lay
In Pelion's shadow, outgrowing
   The light of the dying day,   15
     Speeded by my sweet pipings.
The Sileni, and Sylvans, and Fauns,[4]
   And the Nymphs of the woods and the waves,
To the edge of the moist river lawns,   20
   And the brink of the dewy caves,
And all that did then attend and follow,
Were silent with love, as you now, Apollo,
     With envy of my sweet pipings.

3

I sang of the dancing stars,   25
   I sang of the daedal[5] Earth,

1. Pan's reply to Apollo in his singing
contest; see *Hymn of Apollo*, note 1.
2. Locust.
3. The river Peneus flows through the
lovely valley of Tempe, not far from
Mt. Pelion; the locale is Thessaly, in
northeastern Greece.
4. The male sileni, sylvans, and fauns,
and the female nymphs, are all minor
rural or woodland deities.
5. Ingeniously formed.

And of Heaven—and the giant wars,[6]
  And Love, and Death, and Birth—
  And then I changed my pipings—
Singing how down the vale of Maenalus   30
  I pursued a maiden and clasped a reed.[7]
Gods and men, we are all deluded thus!
  It breaks in our bosom and then we bleed:
All wept, as I think both ye now would,
If envy or age had not frozen your blood,   35
  At the sorrow of my sweet pipings.

1820   1824

The Two Spirits: An Allegory[1]

FIRST SPIRIT

O thou, who plumed with strong desire
  Wouldst float above the earth, beware!
A Shadow tracks thy flight of fire—
      Night is coming!
Bright are the regions of the air,   5
And among the winds and beams
  It were delight to wander there—
      Night is coming!

SECOND SPIRIT

The deathless stars are bright above;
  If I would cross the shade of night,[2]   10
Within my heart is the lamp of love,
      And that is day!
And the moon will smile with gentle light
On my golden plumes where'er they move;
  The meteors will linger round my flight,   15
      And make night day.

FIRST SPIRIT

But if the whirlwinds of darkness waken
  Hail, and lightning, and stormy rain;
See, the bounds of the air are shaken—

---

6. I.e., the ancient wars of the giants, sons of Earth, against the gods of Olympus.
7. Pan pursued the nymph, Syrinx, but as he caught her, she turned into a reed. From it was made Pan's pipe, the "syrinx."
1. The Second Spirit speaks for the poet's unquenchable desire, accepting the risk involved in the attempt to soar above the limits of earth and its cycle of night into the light of the sun; the First Spirit speaks for the timidity that

would bind the poet, safe but somnolent, to darkness and the "dull earth." The last two stanzas pose, without resolving, alternate possibilities: that the aspiring spirit ends up in an eddy, trapped amid the frozen mountain heights of the earth, or else that, in the course of an overflight which is successful, his inner light makes night day for other weary but undefeated travelers.
2. The shadow cast by the earth in the light of the sun; cf. *Prometheus Unbound* IV.444–45.

Night is coming! 20
The red swift clouds of the hurricane
Yon declining sun have overtaken,
The clash of the hail sweeps over the plain—
Night is coming!

SECOND SPIRIT

I see the light, and I hear the sound; 25
I'll sail on the flood of the tempest dark,
With the calm within and the light around
Which makes night day:
And thou, when the gloom is deep and stark,
Look from thy dull earth, slumber-bound, 30
My moonlike flight thou then mayst mark
On high, far away.

———————

Some say there is a precipice
Where one vast pine is frozen to ruin
O'er piles of snow and chasms of ice 35
Mid Alpine mountains;
And that the languid storm pursuing
That wingéd shape, forever flies
Round those hoar branches, aye renewing
Its aëry fountains. 40

Some say when nights are dry and clear,
And the death-dews sleep on the morass,
Sweet whispers are heard by the traveler,
Which make night day:
And a silver shape like his early love doth pass 45
Upborne by her wild and glittering hair,
And when he awakes on the fragrant grass,
He finds night day.

1820   1824

The Tower of Famine[1]

Amid the desolation of a city,
Which was the cradle, and is now the grave
Of an extinguished people—so that Pity

Weeps o'er the shipwrecks of Oblivion's wave,
There stands the Tower of Famine. It is built 5
Upon some prison-homes, whose dwellers rave

1. At Pisa there still exists the prison of Ugolino, which goes by the name of "La Torre della Fame"; in the adjoining building the galley slaves are confined. It is situated on the Ponte al Marc on the Arno [note either by Shelley or Mary Shelley]. The story of Ugolino is told in Dante's *Inferno*, XXXIII. He was a Guelf of the late 13th century who having made himself master of Pisa by treachery was overthrown and, together with two sons and two grandsons, locked up in the tower and left to starve to death.

For bread, and gold, and blood: Pain, linked to Guilt,
Agitates the light flame of their hours,
Until its vital oil is spent or spilt.

There stands the pile, a tower amid the towers   10
And sacred domes; each marble-ribbéd roof,
The brazen-gated temples, and the bowers

Of solitary wealth—the tempest-proof
Pavilions of the dark Italian air—
Are by its presence dimmed—they stand aloof,   15

And are withdrawn—so that the world is bare;
As if a specter wrapped in shapeless terror
Amid a company of ladies fair

Should glide and glow, till it became a mirror
Of all their beauty, and their hair and hue,   20
The life of their sweet eyes, with all its error,
Should be absorbed, till they to marble grew.

1820   1829

To Night[1]

1

Swiftly walk o'er the western wave,
    Spirit of Night!
Out of the misty eastern cave,
Where, all the long and lone daylight,
Thou wovest dreams of joy and fear,   5
Which make thee terrible and dear—
    Swift be thy flight!

2

Wrap thy form in a mantle gray,
    Star-inwrought!
Blind with thine hair the eyes of Day;   10
Kiss her until she be wearied out,
Then wander o'er city, and sea, and land,
Touching all with thine opiate wand—
    Come, long-sought!

3

When I arose and saw the dawn,   15
    I sighed for thee;
When light rode high, and the dew was gone,
And noon lay heavy on flower and tree,
And the weary Day turned to his rest,
Lingering like an unloved guest,   20
    I sighed for thee.

1. In a number of Shelley's poems night and darkness, as opposed to the clarity of the day, are emblems of the myste-rious and primordial powers of the poetic imagination. See, e.g., the opening of *The Triumph of Life*, below.

4

Thy brother Death came, and cried,
    "Wouldst thou me?"
Thy sweet child Sleep, the filmy-eyed,
Murmured like a noontide bee,   25
"Shall I nestle near thy side?
Wouldst thou me?"—And I replied,
    "No, not thee!"

5

Death will come when thou art dead,
    Soon, too soon—   30
Sleep will come when thou art fled;
Of neither would I ask the boon
I ask of thee, belovéd Night—
Swift be thine approaching flight,
    Come soon, soon!   35

1821   1824

To ———

Music, when soft voices die,
Vibrates in the memory—
Odors, when sweet violets sicken,
Live within the sense they quicken.
Rose leaves, when the rose is dead,   5
Are heaped for the belovéd's bed;[1]
And so thy thoughts,[2] when thou art gone,
Love itself shall slumber on.

1821   1824

A Lament

1

O world! O life! O time!
On whose last steps I climb,
    Trembling at that where I had stood before;
When will return the glory of your prime?
    No more—Oh, never more!   5

2

Out of the day and night
A joy has taken flight;
    Fresh spring, and summer, and winter hoar,
Move my faint heart with grief, but with delight
    No more—Oh, never more!   10

1821   1824

1. The fallen petals form a bed for
the dead rose.   2. I.e., my thoughts of thee.

When Passion's Trance Is Overpast

1

When passion's trance is overpast,
If tenderness and truth could last,
Or live, whilst all wild feelings keep
Some mortal slumber, dark and deep,
I should not weep, I should not weep!   5

2

It were enough to feel, to see,
Thy soft eyes gazing tenderly,
And dream the rest—and burn and be
The secret food of fires unseen,
Couldst thou but be as thou hast been.   10

3

After the slumber of the year
The woodland violets reappear;
All things revive in field or grove,
And sky and sea, but two, which move
And form all others, life and love.   15

1821   1824

Choruses from Hellas[1]

Worlds on Worlds

Worlds on worlds are rolling ever
     From creation to decay,
Like the bubbles on a river
     Sparkling, bursting, borne away.
But they[2] are still immortal   5
Who, through birth's orient[3] portal
And death's dark chasm hurrying to and fro,
     Clothe their unceasing flight
     In the brief dust and light

1. *Hellas*, a closet drama written in the autumn of 1821 and published the next year, was inspired by the Greek war for independence against the Turks. In his Preface Shelley declared that he regarded this revolution as only part of a larger pattern in this "age of the war of the oppressed against the oppressors"; he believed that it contained the promise of the final overthrow of all tyranny. The choruses below are sung by Greek captive women. The first chorus describes the emergence of Christ into the revolving cycle of history; the second chorus concludes the drama. Shelley wrote in a note that this final chorus prophesies "darkly a period of regeneration and happiness"— in other words, a return to the golden age, and a final stop to the rolling of the historical cycle. Shelley said that the coming of this millennium is far from certain, but based his hope on the precedent of Isaiah's messianic prophecy and on the prediction of a return to the golden time of Saturn in Virgil's *Eclogues* IV.
2. The immortal "beings which inhabit the planets and * * * clothe themselves in matter" [Shelley's note]. Shelley adopts the ancient notion that each of the planets possesses a supervising spirit.
3. Eastern.

Gathered around their chariots as they go;   10
    New shapes they still may weave,
    New gods, new laws receive,
Bright or dim are they as the robes they last
    On Death's bare ribs had cast.

A power from the unknown God,   15
    A Promethean conqueror,[4] came;
Like a triumphal path he trod
    The thorns of death and shame.
    A mortal shape to him
    Was like the vapor dim   20
Which the orient planet animates with light;
    Hell, Sin, and Slavery came,
    Like bloodhounds mild and tame,
Nor preyed, until their Lord had taken flight;
    The moon of Mahomet[5]   25
    Arose, and it shall set:
While blazoned as on Heaven's immortal noon
    The cross leads generations on.

Swift as the radiant shapes of sleep
    From one whose dreams are Paradise   30
Fly, when the fond wretch wakes to weep,
    And Day peers forth with her blank eyes;
    So fleet, so fain, so fair,
    The Powers of earth and air
Fled from the folding-star[6] of Bethlehem: 35
    Apollo, Pan, and Love,
    And even Olympian Jove
Grew weak, for killing Truth had glared on them;
    Our hills and seas and streams,
    Dispeopled of their dreams,   40
Their waters turned to blood, their dew to tears,
    Wailed for the golden years.

The World's Great Age

The world's great age begins anew,
    The golden years return,[7]
The earth doth like a snake renew
    Her winter weeds[8] outworn:
Heaven smiles, and faiths and empires gleam,   5
    Like wrecks of a dissolving dream.

---

4. Christ, whom Shelley compares to
Prometheus, who brought fire and the
arts of civilization to mankind.
5. The crescent, emblem of Moham-
medanism, which was founded six centuries after the birth of Christ.
6. The star of evening, the time when
sheep are driven into the sheepfold;
hence, "folding." Shelley goes on to de-

scribe the pagan gods of earth and
Olympus fleeing before the star of
Bethlehem.
7. According to Greek myth, the first
period of mankind was the golden age.
8. Clothes, especially mourning garments; "weeds" also suggest the dead
vegetation of winter.

A brighter Hellas rears its mountains
    From waves serener far;
A new Peneus[9] rolls his fountains
    Against the morning star.   10
Where fairer Tempes bloom, there sleep
Young Cyclads[1] on a sunnier deep.

A loftier Argo[2] cleaves the main,
    Fraught with a later prize;
Another Orpheus[3] sings again,   15
    And loves, and weeps, and dies.
A new Ulysses leaves once more
Calypso[4] for his native shore.

Oh, write no more the tale of Troy,
    If earth Death's scroll must be!   20
Nor mix with Laian rage[5] the joy
    Which dawns upon the free:
Although a subtler Sphinx renew
Riddles of death Thebes never knew.

Another Athens shall arise,   25
    And to remoter time
Bequeath, like sunset to the skies,
    The splendor of its prime;
And leave, if nought so bright may live,
All earth can take or Heaven can give.   30

Saturn and Love their long repose
    Shall burst, more bright and good
Than all who fell, than One who rose,
    Than many unsubdued:[6]
Not gold, not blood, their altar dowers,   35
But votive tears and symbol flowers.

Oh, cease! must hate and death return?
    Cease! must men kill and die?
Cease! drain not to its dregs the urn
    Of bitter prophecy.   40
The world is weary of the past,
Oh, might it die or rest at last!

1822

9. The river that flows through the beautiful vale of Tempe (line 11).
1. The Cyclades, Greek islands in the Aegean Sea.
2. On which Jason sailed in his quest for the Golden Fleece.
3. The legendary player on the lyre who was torn to pieces by the frenzied Thracian women while he was mourning the death of his wife, Eurydice.
4. The nymph deserted by Ulysses on his voyage back from the Trojan War to his native Ithaca.
5. King Laius of Thebes was killed in an angry quarrel by his son Oedipus, who did not recognize his father. Shortly thereafter, Oedipus delivered Thebes from the ravages of the Sphinx by answering its riddle (lines 23–24).
6. "Saturn and Love were among the deities of a real or imaginary state of innocence and happiness. 'All' those 'who fell' [are] the Gods of Greece, Asia, and Egypt; the 'One who rose' [is] Jesus Christ * * * and the 'many unsubdued' [are] the monstrous objects of the idolatry of China, India, the Antarctic islands, and the native tribes of America" [Shelley's note].

Adonais[1]

AN ELEGY ON THE DEATH OF JOHN KEATS, AUTHOR OF ENDYMION, HYPERION, ETC.

[Thou wert the morning star among the living,
  Ere thy fair light had fled—
Now, having died, thou art as Hesperus, giving
  New splendor to the dead.][2]

1

I weep for Adonais—he is dead!
O, weep for Adonais! though our tears
Thaw not the frost which binds so dear a head!
And thou, sad Hour, selected from all years
To mourn our loss, rouse thy obscure compeers,   5
And teach them thine own sorrow, say: "With me
Died Adonais; till the Future dares
Forget the Past, his fate and fame shall be
An echo and a light unto eternity!"

---

1. John Keats died in Rome February 23, 1821, and was buried there in the Protestant Cemetery. Shelley had met Keats, had invited him to be his guest at Pisa, and had gradually come to recognize him as "among the writers of the highest genius who have adorned our age" (Preface to *Adonais*). The name "Adonais" is derived from Adonis, the handsome youth who had been loved by the goddess Venus and slain by a wild boar; the function of the beast in this poem is attributed to the anonymous author of a vituperative review of Keats's *Endymion* in the *Quarterly Review*, April, 1818 (now known to be John Wilson Croker), whom Shelley mistakenly believed to be responsible for Keats's illness and death. The alteration of "Adonis" to "Adonais" has evoked a good deal of discussion. Recently Earl Wasserman has argued persuasively that it is a fusion of "Adonis" (who had been worshiped as a vegetation deity) with "Adonai," one of the Old Testament names of God; in this procedure Shelley would be following the speculative mythographers of his day, a number of whom identified Adonis with Adonai as god of the sun and of fertility.

Shelley described *Adonais* in a letter as a "highly wrought piece of art." Its artistry consists in part in the care with which it follows the conventions of the pastoral elegy, established more than two thousand years earlier by the Greek Sicilian poets Theocritus, Bion, and Moschus—Shelley had himself translated into English Bion's *Lament for Adonis* and Moschus' *Lament for Bion*. We recognize the centuries-old poetic ritual in many verbal echoes, and in such devices as the mournful and accusing invocation to a muse (stanzas 2–4), the sympathetic participation of nature in the death of the poet (stanzas 14–17), the procession of appropriate mourners (stanzas 30–35), the denunciation of unworthy practitioners of the pastoral or literary art (stanzas 17, 27–29, 36–37); and above all in the shift from despair at the finality of human death (lines 64, 190: "*He* will awake no more, oh, never more!") to consolation in the sudden and contradictory discovery that the grave is a gate to a higher existence (line 343: "Peace, peace! he is not dead, he doth not sleep"). These familiar elements Shelley reinterprets with astonishing inventiveness and transforms into a densely symbolic poetic construction; *Adonais* ranks with Milton's *Lycidas* among the supreme examples of the exacting form of the pastoral elegy.

2. This is Shelley's own translation of a Greek epigram, attributed to Plato, which he had prefixed to *Adonais* as a motto. (See also *The Triumph of Life*, below, line 256.) The reference is to the planet Venus, which appears both as the morning star, Lucifer, and the evening star, Hesperus or Vesper. Shelley makes of this phenomenon—the hidden identity of a single star under various aspects, and its persistence even when invisible in daylight—a key element in his symbolism for Adonais' triumph over death. See stanzas 44–46.

2

Where wert thou, mighty Mother,[3] when he lay,   10
When thy Son lay, pierced by the shaft which flies
In darkness? where was lorn Urania
When Adonais died? With veiléd eyes,
'Mid listening Echoes, in her Paradise
She sate, while one,[4] with soft enamored breath,   15
Rekindled all the fading melodies,
With which, like flowers that mock the corse[5] beneath,
He had adorned and hid the coming bulk of Death.

3

Oh, weep for Adonais—he is dead!
Wake, melancholy Mother, wake and weep!   20
Yet wherefore? Quench within their burning bed
Thy fiery tears, and let thy loud heart keep
Like his, a mute and uncomplaining sleep;
For he is gone, where all things wise and fair
Descend—oh, dream not that the amorous Deep   25
Will yet restore him to the vital air;
Death feeds on his mute voice, and laughs at our despair.

4

Most musical of mourners, weep again!
Lament anew, Urania!—He[6] died,
Who was the Sire of an immortal strain,   30
Blind, old, and lonely, when his country's pride,
The priest, the slave, and the liberticide,
Trampled and mocked with many a loathéd rite
Of lust and blood; he went, unterrified,
Into the gulf of death; but his clear Sprite[7]   35
Yet reigns o'er earth; the third[8] among the sons of light.

5

Must musical of mourners, weep anew!
Not all to that bright station dared to climb;
And happier they their happiness who knew,
Whose tapers yet burn through that night of time   40
In which suns perished; others more sublime,
Struck by the envious wrath of man or god,
Have sunk, extinct in their refulgent prime;
And some yet live, treading the thorny road,
Which leads, through toil and hate, to Fame's serene abode.   45

6

But now, thy youngest, dearest one, has perished—
The nursling of thy widowhood, who grew,
Like a pale flower by some sad maiden cherished,

3. Urania, originally the Muse of astronomy. But the name was also an epithet for Aphrodite or Venus, and Shelley converts the Venus who, in Greek myth, had been the lover of Adonis into the mother of Adonais and, like the *Venus Genetrix* of Lucretius' *On the Nature of Things,* the "mighty Mother" of all earthly life.
4. I.e., the echo of Keats's own poems.
5. Corpse.
6. Milton, who had already adopted Urania as the muse of *Paradise Lost.*
7. Spirit.
8. The latest of the great epic poets, after Homer and Dante.

And fed with truelove tears, instead of dew;[9]
Most musical of mourners, weep anew!   50
Thy extreme[1] hope, the loveliest and the last,
The bloom, whose petals nipped before they blew
Died on the promise of the fruit, is waste;
The broken lily lies—the storm is overpast.

7

To that high Capital,[2] where kingly Death   55
Keeps his pale court in beauty and decay,
He came; and bought, with price of purest breath,
A grave among the eternal.—Come away!
Haste, while the vault of blue Italian day
Is yet his fitting charnel-roof! while still   60
He lies, as if in dewy sleep he lay;
Awake him not! surely he takes his fill
Of deep and liquid rest, forgetful of all ill.

8

He will awake no more, oh, never more!—
Within the twilight chamber spreads apace   65
The shadow of white Death, and at the door
Invisible Corruption waits to trace
His extreme way to her dim dwelling place;
The eternal Hunger sits, but pity and awe
Soothe her pale rage, nor dares she to deface   70
So fair a prey, till darkness, and the law
Of change, shall o'er his sleep the mortal curtain draw.

9

Oh, weep for Adonais!—The quick Dreams,[3]
The passion-wingéd Ministers of thought,
Who were his flocks, whom near the living streams   75
Of his young spirit he fed, and whom he taught
The love which was its music, wander not—
Wander no more, from kindling brain to brain,
But droop there, whence they sprung; and mourn their lot
Round the cold heart, where, after their sweet pain,   80
They ne'er will gather strength, or find a home again.

10

And one with trembling hands clasps his cold head,
And fans him with her moonlight wings, and cries:
"Our love, our hope, our sorrow, is not dead;
See, on the silken fringe of his faint eyes,   85
Like dew upon a sleeping flower, there lies
A tear some Dream has loosened from his brain."
Lost Angel of a ruined Paradise![4]
She knew not 'twas her own; as with no stain
She faded, like a cloud which had outwept its rain.   90

9. An allusion to an incident in Keats's *Isabella*.
1. Last.
2. Rome.
3. The products of his poetic imagination.
4. Lost messenger ("angel") from a destroyed creative imagination.

11

One from a lucid urn of starry dew
Washed his light limbs as if embalming them;
Another clipped her profuse locks, and threw
The wreath upon him, like an anadem,[5]
Which frozen tears instead of pearls begem;   95
Another in her willful grief would break
Her bow and wingéd reeds, as if to stem
A greater loss with one which was more weak,
And dull the barbéd fire against his frozen cheek.

12

Another Splendor on his mouth alit,   100
That mouth, whence it was wont to draw the breath
Which gave it strength to pierce the guarded wit,[6]
And pass into the panting heart beneath
With lightning and with music: the damp death
Quenched its caress upon his icy lips;   105
And, as a dying meteor stains a wreath
Of moonlight vapor, which the cold night clips,[7]
It flushed through his pale limbs, and passed to its eclipse.

13

And others came . . . Desires and Adorations,
Wingéd Persuasions and veiled Destinies,   110
Splendors, and Glooms, and glimmering Incarnations
Of hopes and fears, and twilight Phantasies;
And Sorrow, with her family of Sighs,
And Pleasure, blind with tears, led by the gleam
Of her own dying smile instead of eyes,   115
Came in slow pomp—the moving pomp might seem
Like pageantry of mist on an autumnal stream.

14

All he had loved, and molded into thought,
From shape, and hue, and odor, and sweet sound,
Lamented Adonais. Morning sought   120
Her eastern watch-tower, and her hair unbound,
Wet with the tears which should adorn the ground,
Dimmed the aërial eyes that kindle day;
Afar the melancholy thunder moaned,
Pale Ocean in unquiet slumber lay,   125
And the wild Winds flew round, sobbing in their dismay.

15

Lost Echo sits amid the voiceless mountains,
And feeds her grief with his remembered lay,
And will no more reply to winds or fountains,
Or amorous birds perched on the young green spray,   130
Or herdsman's horn, or bell at closing day;
Since she can mimic not his lips, more dear
Than those for whose disdain she pined away

---

5. A rich garland.
6. The cautious intellect of the listener.
7. "Cuts off," or else, in the older sense, "embraces."

Into a shadow of all sounds[8]—a drear
Murmur, between their songs, is all the woodmen hear.   135

16

Grief made the young Spring wild, and she threw down
Her kindling buds, as if she Autumn were,
Or they dead leaves; since her delight is flown,
For whom should she have waked the sullen year?
To Phoebus was not Hyacinth so dear[9]   140
Nor to himself Narcissus, as to both
Thou, Adonais: wan they stand and sere
Amid the fain companions of their youth,
With dew all turned to tears; odor, to sighing ruth.[1]

17

Thy spirit's sister, the lorn nightingale   145
Mourns not her mate with such melodious pain;
Not so the eagle, who like thee could scale
Heaven, and could nourish in the sun's domain
Her mighty youth with morning,[2] doth complain,
Soaring and screaming round her empty nest,   150
As Albion[3] wails for thee: the curse of Cain
Light on his[4] head who pierced thy innocent breast,
And scared the angel soul that was its earthly guest!

18

Ah, woe is me! Winter is come and gone,
But grief returns with the revolving year;   155
The airs and streams renew their joyous tone;
The ants, the bees, the swallows reappear;
Fresh leaves and flowers deck the dead Seasons' bier;
The amorous birds now pair in every brake,[5]
And build their mossy homes in field and brere;   160
And the green lizard, and the golden snake,
Like unimprisoned flames, out of their trance awake.

19

Through wood and stream and field and hill and Ocean
A quickening life from the Earth's heart has burst
As it has ever done, with change and motion,   165
From the great morning of the world when first
God dawned on Chaos; in its stream immersed,
The lamps of Heaven flash with a softer light;
All baser things pant with life's sacred thirst,
Diffuse themselves, and spend in love's delight,   170
The beauty and the joy of their renewéd might.

---

8. Because of her unrequited love for
Narcissus, who was enamored of his
own reflection (line 141), the nymph
Echo pined away until she was only a
voice.
9. Young Hyacinthus was loved by
Phoebus Apollo, who accidentally killed
him in a game of quoits. Apollo made
the hyacinth flower spring from his
blood.

1. Pity.
2. In legend, the aged eagle, to renew
his youth, flies toward the sun until his
old plumage is burned off and the film
cleared away from his eyes.
3. England.
4. I.e., the reviewer of Keats's *Endymion* (see title footnote above).
5. Thicket. "Brere": briar.

20

The leprous corpse, touched by this spirit tender,
Exhales itself in flowers of gentle breath;
Like incarnations of the stars, when splendor
Is changed to fragrance, they illumine death   175
And mock the merry worm that wakes beneath;
Nought we know, dies. Shall that alone which knows
Be as a sword consumed before the sheath
By sightless lightning?[6]—the intense atom glows
A moment, then is quenched in a most cold repose.   180

21

Alas! that all we loved of him should be,
But for our grief, as if it had not been,
And grief itself be mortal! Woe is me!
Whence are we, and why are we? of what scene
The actors or spectators? Great and mean   185
Meet massed in death, who lends what life must borrow.[7]
As long as skies are blue, and fields are green,
Evening must usher night, night urge the morrow,
Month follow month with woe, and year wake year to sorrow.

22

He will awake no more, oh, never more!   190
"Wake thou," cried Misery, "childless Mother, rise
Out of thy sleep, and slake, in thy heart's core,
A wound more fierce than his, with tears and sighs."
And all the Dreams that watched Urania's eyes,
And all the Echoes whom their sister's song   195
Had held in holy silence, cried: "Arise!"
Swift as a Thought by the snake Memory stung,
From her ambrosial rest the fading Splendor[8] sprung.

23

She rose like an autumnal Night, that springs
Out of the East, and follows wild and drear   200
The golden Day, which, on eternal wings,
Even as a ghost abandoning a bier,
Had left the Earth a corpse. Sorrow and fear
So struck, so roused, so rapt Urania;
So saddened round her like an atmosphere   205
Of stormy mist; so swept her on her way
Even to the mournful place where Adonais lay.

24

Out of her secret Paradise she sped,
Through camps and cities rough with stone, and steel,
And human hearts, which to her aery tread   210
Yielding not, wounded the invisible
Palms of her tender feet where'er they fell:

6. I.e., the material world, which the mind knows, survives. Shall only the knowing mind be destroyed, like a sword melted by invisible ("sightless") lightning, while the sheath (the body, or material vehicle of the mind) survives?
7. I.e., life is a short-term loan from death.
8. Urania.

And barbéd tongues, and thoughts more sharp than they,
Rent the soft Form they never could repel,
Whose sacred blood, like the young tears of May,   215
Paved with eternal flowers that undeserving way.

25

In the death chamber for a moment Death,
Shamed by the presence of that living Might,
Blushed to annihilation, and the breath
Revisited those lips, and Life's pale light   220
Flashed through those limbs, so late her dear delight.
"Leave me not wild and drear and comfortless,
As silent lightning leaves the starless night!
Leave me not!" cried Urania: her distress
Roused Death: Death rose and smiled, and met her vain caress.

26

"Stay yet awhile! speak to me once again;   226
Kiss me, so long but as a kiss may live;
And in my heartless breast[9] and burning brain
That word, that kiss, shall all thoughts else survive,
With food of saddest memory kept alive,   230
Now thou art dead, as if it were a part
Of thee, my Adonais! I would give
All that I am to be as thou now art!
But I am chained to Time, and cannot thence depart!

27

"O gentle child, beautiful as thou wert,   235
Why didst thou leave the trodden paths of men
Too soon, and with weak hands though mighty heart
Dare the unpastured dragon in his den?
Defenseless as thou wert, oh, where was then
Wisdom the mirrored shield, or scorn the spear?[1]   240
Or hadst thou waited the full cycle, when
Thy spirit should have filled its crescent sphere,
The monsters of life's waste had fled from thee like deer.

28

"The herded wolves, bold only to pursue;
The obscene ravens, clamorous o'er the dead;   245
The vultures to the conqueror's banner true
Who feed where Desolation first has fed,
And whose wings rain contagion—how they fled,
When, like Apollo, from his golden bow
The Pythian of the age[2] one arrow sped   250
And smiled!—The spoilers tempt no second blow,
They fawn on the proud feet that spurn them lying low.

9. Because her heart has been given to Adonais.
1. Young defenseless Keats confronting the literary reviewers is paralleled with Perseus in the myth, who attacked Medusa (the "dragon") with his spear, avoiding her direct gaze (which turned men into stone) by looking only at her reflection in his shield.
2. Apollo was called "the Pythian" because he had slain the dragon Python; the allusion here is to Byron, who "slew" the critics in *English Bards and Scotch Reviewers* (1809).

29

"The sun comes forth, and many reptiles spawn;
He sets, and each ephemeral insect then
Is gathered into death without a dawn,   255
And the immortal stars awake again;
So is it in the world of living men:
A godlike mind soars forth, in its delight
Making earth bare and veiling heaven,[3] and when
It sinks, the swarms that dimmed or shared its light   260
Leave to its kindred lamps[4] the spirit's awful night."

30

Thus ceased she: and the mountain shepherds came,
Their garlands sere, their magic mantles rent;
The Pilgrim of Eternity,[5] whose fame
Over his living head like Heaven is bent,   265
An early but enduring monument,
Came, veiling all the lightnings of his song
In sorrow; from her wilds Ierne sent
The sweetest lyrist[6] of her saddest wrong,
And Love taught Grief to fall like music from his tongue.   270

31

Midst others of less note, came one frail Form,[7]
A phantom among men; companionless
As the last cloud of an expiring storm
Whose thunder is its knell; he, as I guess,
Had gazed on Nature's naked loveliness,   275
Actaeon-like,[8] and now he fled astray
With feeble steps o'er the world's wilderness,
And his own thoughts, along that rugged way,
Pursued, like raging hounds, their father and their prey.

32

A pardlike[9] Spirit beautiful and swift—   280
A Love in desolation masked—a Power
Girt round with weakness—it can scarce uplift
The weight of the superincumbent hour;
It is a dying lamp, a falling shower,
A breaking billow—even whilst we speak   285
Is it not broken? On the withering flower
The killing sun smiles brightly: on a cheek
The life can burn in blood, even while the heart may break.

33

His head was bound with pansies overblown,
And faded violets, white, and pied, and blue;   290
And a light spear topped with a cypress cone,

3. As the sun reveals the earth but veils the other stars.
4. The other stars, or divine minds.
5. Byron, who had referred to Childe Harold as one of the "wanderers o'er eternity" (III.669).
6. Thomas Moore (1779–1852) the poet from Ireland ("Ierne").
7. Shelley himself.
8. Actaeon while hunting came upon Diana bathing, and in punishment was turned into a stag and torn to pieces by his own hounds.
9. Leopardlike.

Round whose rude shaft dark ivy tresses grew[1]
Yet dripping with the forest's noonday dew,
Vibrated, as the ever-beating heart
Shook the weak hand that grasped it; of that crew   295
He came the last, neglected and apart;
A herd-abandoned deer struck by the hunter's dart.

34
All stood aloof, and at his partial[2] moan
Smiled through their tears; well knew that gentle band
Who in another's fate now wept his own,   300
As in the accents of an unknown land
He sung new sorrow; sad Urania scanned
The Stranger's mien, and murmured: "Who art thou?"
He answered not, but with a sudden hand
Made bare his branded and ensanguined brow,   305
Which was like Cain's or Christ's[3]—oh! that it should be so!

35
What softer voice is hushed over the dead?
Athwart what brow is that dark mantle thrown?
What form leans sadly o'er the white deathbed,
In mockery[4] of monumental stone,   310
The heavy heart heaving without a moan?
If it be he,[5] who, gentlest of the wise,
Taught, soothed, loved, honored the departed one,
Let me not vex, with inharmonious sighs,
The silence of that heart's accepted sacrifice.   315

36
Our Adonais has drunk poison—oh!
What deaf and viperous murderer could crown
Life's early cup with such a draught of woe?
The nameless worm[6] would now itself disown:
It felt, yet could escape, the magic tone   320
Whose prelude held[7] all envy, hate, and wrong,
But what was howling in one breast alone,
Silent with expectation of the song,
Whose master's hand is cold, whose silver lyre unstrung.

37
Live thou, whose infamy is not thy fame!   325
Live! fear no heavier chastisement from me,
Thou noteless blot on a remembered name!
But be thyself, and know thyself to be!
And ever at thy season be thou free
To spill the venom when thy fangs o'erflow;   330

---

1. Like the thyrsus, the leaf-entwined staff carried by Dionysus, deity of vegetation.
2. I.e., with reference to himself.
3. His bloody ("ensanguined") brow bore a mark like that with which God had branded Cain for murdering Abel —or like that left by Christ's crown of thorns.
4. Imitation.
5. Leigh Hunt, close friend both of Keats and Shelley.
6. Serpent. In accordance with the journalistic custom of that time, the reviewer of *Endymion* had remained "nameless."
7. Held back, checked.

Remorse and Self-contempt shall cling to thee;
Hot Shame shall burn upon thy secret brow,
And like a beaten hound tremble thou shalt—as now.

38

Nor let us weep that our delight is fled
Far from these carrion kites that scream below; 335
He wakes or sleeps with the enduring dead;
Thou canst not soar where he is sitting now.—
Dust to the dust! but the pure spirit shall flow
Back to the burning fountain whence it came,
A portion of the Eternal,[8] which must glow 340
Through time and change, unquenchably the same,
Whilst thy cold embers[9] choke the sordid hearth of shame.

39

Peace, peace! he is not dead, he doth not sleep—
He hath awakened from the dream of life—
'Tis we, who lost in stormy visions, keep 345
With phantoms an unprofitable strife,
And in mad trance, strike with our spirit's knife
Invulnerable nothings.—*We* decay
Like corpses in a charnel; fear and grief
Convulse us and consume us day by day, 350
And cold hopes swarm like worms within our living clay.

40

He has outsoared the shadow of our night;[1]
Envy and calumny and hate and pain,
And that unrest which men miscall delight,
Can touch him not and torture not again; 355
From the contagion of the world's slow stain
He is secure, and now can never mourn
A heart grown cold, a head grown gray in vain;
Nor, when the spirit's self has ceased to burn,
With sparkless ashes load an unlamented urn. 360

41

He lives, he wakes—'tis Death is dead, not he;
Mourn not for Adonais.—Thou young Dawn,
Turn all thy dew to splendor, for from thee
The spirit thou lamentest is not gone;
Ye caverns and ye forests, cease to moan! 365
Cease, ye faint flowers and fountains, and thou Air,
Which like a mourning veil thy scarf hadst thrown
O'er the abandoned Earth, now leave it bare
Even to the joyous stars which smile on its despair![2]

8. According to a Neo-Platonic world view, all mortal life is an overflow from the Absolute, imaged as the eternal fountain, and also as the radiant light-source, of life, which emanates down through the dross of matter (stanza 43) and recirculates continuously to its source. The recognition of this fact is the turning point of the poem: it leads to the **discovery** that our existence in the material world is but "the dream of life"—that it is, in fact, the real death.
9. I.e., the reviewer's ashes.
1. Keats has soared beyond night, which Shelley (it is one of his favorite figures) accurately describes as the shadow cast by the earth as it intercepts the radiance of the sun.
2. Again the science is accurate: it is the envelope of air around the earth

42

He is made one with Nature: there is heard   370
His voice in all her music, from the moan
Of thunder, to the song of night's sweet bird;
He is a presence to be felt and known
In darkness and in light, from herb and stone,
Spreading itself where'er that Power may move   375
Which has withdrawn his being to its own;
Which wields the world with never-wearied love,
Sustains it from beneath, and kindles it above.

43

He is a portion of the loveliness
Which once he made more lovely: he doth bear   380
His part, while the one Spirit's plastic[3] stress
Sweeps through the dull dense world, compelling there
All new successions to the forms they wear;
Torturing th' unwilling dross that checks its flight
To its own likeness, as each mass may bear;[4]   385
And bursting in its beauty and its might
From trees and beasts and men into the Heaven's light.

44

The splendors of the firmament of time
May be eclipsed, but are extinguished not;
Like stars to their appointed height they climb,   390
And death is a low mist which cannot blot
The brightness it may veil.[5] When lofty thought
Lifts a young heart above its mortal lair,
And love and life contend in it, for what
Shall be its earthly doom, the dead live there[6]   395
And move like winds of light on dark and stormy air.

45

The inheritors of unfulfilled renown[7]
Rose from their thrones, built beyond mortal thought,
Far in the Unapparent. Chatterton
Rose pale—his solemn agony had not   400
Yet faded from him; Sidney, as he fought
And as he fell and as he lived and loved

(lines 366–67) which, by diffusing and reflecting the sunlight, renders the stars invisible in the daytime.

3. Molding, shaping.

4. I.e. to the degree that a particular substance will permit. The concept is an ancient one, that different kinds of matter offer variable resistance to the attempt of Spirit to realize itself on earth. The stars ("the Heaven's light," line 387) are of such a refined matter that they can approximate to the pure radiance of the "one Spirit" itself.

5. The spirits of great poets ("splendors of the firmament of time"), like stars in daylight, continue to exist even when invisible to earthly eyes because "eclipsed" or "veiled" by death. In Shelley's image, the viewpoint is transferred from earth to airless interstellar space: from this station we see that the radiance of a star persists, even if it is temporarily "eclipsed" from the earth by the intervention of another heavenly body, or "veiled" by the "low mist" of the atmosphere.

6. I.e., in that "young heart" (line 393).

7. Poets who died young, before achieving their full measure of renown. Thomas Chatterton (1752–70) committed suicide at 17, Sir Philip Sidney (1554–86) died in battle at 32, and Lucan killed himself at 26 to escape Nero's sentence of death.

Sublimely mild, a Spirit without spot,
  Arose; and Lucan, by his death approved:[8]
Oblivion as they rose shrank like a thing reproved.   405

46

And many more, whose names on Earth are dark,
  But whose transmitted effluence cannot die
So long as fire outlives the parent spark,
  Rose, robed in dazzling immortality.
    "Thou art become as one of us," they cry,   410
"It was for thee yon kingless sphere has long
Swung blind in unascended majesty,
    Silent alone amid an Heaven of Song.
Assume thy wingéd throne, thou Vesper of our throng!"[9]

47

Who mourns for Adonais? Oh, come forth,   415
  Fond wretch! and know thyself and him aright.
Clasp with thy panting soul the pendulous[1] Earth;
  As from a center, dart thy spirit's light
Beyond all worlds, until its spacious might
  Satiate the void circumference: then shrink   420
    Even to a point within our day and night;[2]
And keep thy heart light lest it make thee sink
When hope has kindled hope, and lured thee to the brink.

48

Or go to Rome, which is the sepulcher,
  Oh, not of him, but of our joy: 'tis nought   425
That ages, empires, and religions there
  Lie buried in the ravage they have wrought;
For such as he can lend—they borrow not
  Glory from those who made the world their prey;
    And he is gathered to the kings of thought   430
Who waged contention with their time's decay,
And of the past are all that cannot pass away.

49

Go thou to Rome—at once the Paradise,
  The grave, the city, and the wilderness;
And where its wrecks like shattered mountains rise,   435
  And flowering weeds, and fragrant copses dress
The bones of Desolation's nakedness
  Pass, till the spirit of the spot shall lead
Thy footsteps to a slope of green access[3]
    Where, like an infant's smile, over the dead   440
A light of laughing flowers along the grass is spread;

8. Justified, proved worthy.
9. Adonais assumes his rightful place in the unoccupied sphere of Vesper, the evening star. See the epigraph and cf. lines 35–36. Shelley also adopts here the ancient view of the music of the spheres ("an Heaven of Song").
1. Suspended.
2. Shelley asks the wretch so foolish ("fond") as to mourn Adonais to stretch his imagination to encompass the poet's present cosmic viewpoint (see stanza 55 and note 5) and then contract ("shrink") back to his ordinary tiny station on earth where, unlike Adonais, we have an alternation of day and night (life and death).
3. The Protestant Cemetery, Keats's burial place.

50

And gray walls molder round, on which dull Time
Feeds, like slow fire upon a hoary brand;
And one keen pyramid with wedge sublime,[4]
Pavilioning the dust of him who planned   445
This refuge for his memory, doth stand
Like flame transformed to marble; and beneath,
A field is spread, on which a newer band[5]
Have pitched in Heaven's smile their camp of death,
Welcoming him we lose with scarce extinguished breath.   450

51

Here pause: these graves are all too young as yet
To have outgrown the sorrow which consigned
Its charge to each; and if the seal is set,
Here, on one fountain of a mourning mind,
Break it not thou! too surely shalt thou find   455
Thine own well full, if thou returnest home,
Of tears and gall. From the world's bitter wind
Seek shelter in the shadow of the tomb.
What Adonais is, why fear we to become?

52

The One[6] remains, the many change and pass;   460
Heaven's light forever shines, Earth's shadows fly;
Life, like a dome of many-colored glass,
Stains the white radiance of Eternity,
Until Death tramples it to fragments.—Die,
If thou wouldst be with that which thou dost seek!   465
Follow where all is fled!—Rome's azure sky,
Flowers, ruins, statues, music, words, are weak
The glory they transfuse with fitting truth to speak.

53

Why linger, why turn back, why shrink, my Heart?
Thy hopes are gone before: from all things here   470
They have departed; thou shouldst now depart!
A light is passed from the revolving year,
And man, and woman; and what still is dear
Attracts to crush, repels to make thee wither.
The soft sky smiles—the low wind whispers near: 475
'Tis Adonais calls! oh, hasten thither,
No more let Life divide what Death can join together.

54

That Light whose smile kindles the Universe,
That Beauty in which all things work and move,
That Benediction which the eclipsing Curse   480
Of birth can quench not, that sustaining Love
Which through the web of being blindly wove

---

4. The tomb of Gaius Cestius, a Roman
statesman.
5. The recently buried dead (the cemetery
had been established not long before), including Shelley's 3-year-old

son, William, referred to in lines
453–55.
6. The Absolute, the one fountain of
all light, of lines 339–40.

By man and beast and earth and air and sea,
Burns bright or dim, as each are mirrors of [6a]
The fire for which all thirst,[7] now beams on me,   485
Consuming the last clouds of cold mortality.

55

The breath whose might I have invoked in song[8]
Descends on me; my spirit's bark is driven,
Far from the shore, far from the trembling throng
Whose sails were never to the tempest given;   490
The massy earth and spheréd skies are riven!
I am borne darkly, fearfully, afar;
Whilst, burning through the inmost veil of Heaven,
The soul of Adonais, like a star,
Beacons from the abode where the Eternal are.   495
June, 1821   1821

Lines: When the Lamp Is Shattered

1

When the lamp is shattered
The light in the dust lies dead—
When the cloud is scattered
The rainbow's glory is shed.
When the lute is broken,   5
Sweet tones are remembered not;
When the lips have spoken,
Loved accents are soon forgot.

2

As music and splendor
Survive not the lamp and the lute,   10
The heart's echoes render
No song when the spirit is mute—
No song but sad dirges,
Like the wind through a ruined cell,
Or the mournful surges   15
That ring the dead seaman's knell.

3

When hearts have once mingled
Love first leaves the well-built nest;[1]
The weak one is singled
To endure what it once possessed.   20
O Love! who bewailest
The frailty of all things here,

6a. According to the degree that each
mirrors.
7. The inordinate "thirst" of the human spirit to return to its source in
the "burning fountain" of eternal light,
beauty, and love (lines 339–40).
8. The reference is to the "breath of
Autumn's being," which Shelley had

"invoked," or prayed for, two years
before, in the last two stanzas of *Ode
to the West Wind*. Lines 488–90 describe what it feels like to be "inspired"—literally, breathed or blown
into.
1. I.e., Love first flies away from the
stronger heart.

Why choose you the frailest[2]
For your cradle, your home, and your bier?

4

Its passions will rock thee   25
As the storms rock the ravens on high;
  Bright reason will mock thee,
Like the sun from a wintry sky.
    From thy nest every rafter
Will rot, and thine eagle home[3]   30
    Leave thee naked to laughter,
When leaves fall and cold winds come.

1822   1824

A Dirge

Rough wind, that moanest loud
    Grief too sad for song;
Wild wind, when sullen cloud
    Knells all the night long;
Sad storm, whose tears are vain,   5
Bare woods, whose branches strain,
Deep caves and dreary main—
    Wail, for the world's wrong!

1822   1824

To Jane: The Invitation[1]

Best and brightest, come away!
Fairer far than this fair Day,
Which, like thee to those in sorrow,
Comes to bid a sweet good-morrow
To the rough Year just awake   5
In its cradle on the brake.
The brightest hour of unborn Spring,
Through the winter wandering,
Found, it seems, the halcyon Morn
To hoar February born.   10
Bending from Heaven, in azure mirth,
It kissed the forehead of the Earth,
And smiled upon the silent sea,
And bade the frozen streams be free,

2. The heart.
3. The nest of Love (the heart), like
that of the eagle, is exposed to the winter sun and vulnerable to the winter
weather.
1. "Jane" is Jane Williams, common-

law wife of Edward Williams, Shelley's
close friend. This invitation to an outdoor excursion exemplifies Shelley's grace
and urbanity, writing in the ancient tradition of the verse letter.

And waked to music all their fountains,   15
And breathed upon the frozen mountains,
And like a prophetess of May
Strewed flowers upon the barren way,
Making the wintry world appear
Like one on whom thou smilest, dear.   20
Away, away, from men and towns,
To the wild wood and the downs—
To the silent wilderness
Where the soul need not repress
Its music lest it should not find   25
An echo in another's mind,
While the touch of Nature's art
Harmonizes heart to heart.
I leave this notice on my door
For each accustomed visitor: 30
"I am gone into the fields
To take what this sweet hour yields;
Reflection, you may come tomorrow,
Sit by the fireside with Sorrow.—
You with the unpaid bill, Despair—   35
You, tiresome verse-reciter, Care—
I will pay you in the grave—
Death will listen to your stave.
Expectation too, be off!
Today is for itself enough;   40
Hope, in pity mock not Woe
With smiles, nor follow where I go;
Long having lived on thy sweet food,
At length I find one moment's good
After long pain—with all your love,   45
This you never told me of."

Radiant Sister of the Day,
Awake! arise! and come away!
To the wild woods and the plains,
And the pools where winter rains   50
Image all their roof of leaves,
Where the pine its garland weaves
Of sapless green and ivy dun
Round stems that never kiss the sun;
Where the lawns and pastures be,   55
And the sandhills of the sea;
Where the melting hoarfrost wets
The daisy-star that never sets,
And windflowers, and violets,
Which yet join not scent to hue,   60
Crown the pale year weak and new;
When the night is left behind
In the deep east, dun and blind,

And the blue noon is over us,
And the multitudinous   65
Billows murmur at our feet,
Where the earth and ocean meet,
And all things seem only one
In the universal sun.

1822   1824

To Jane: The Keen Stars Were Twinkling

1

The keen stars were twinkling,
And the fair moon was rising among them,
     Dear Jane!
The guitar was tinkling,
But the notes were not sweet till you sung them   5
     Again.

2

As the moon's soft splendor
O'er the faint cold starlight of Heaven
     Is thrown,
So your voice most tender   10
To the strings without soul had then given
     Its own.

3

The stars will awaken,
Though the moon sleep a full hour later,
     Tonight;   15
No leaf will be shaken
Whilst the dews of your melody scatter
     Delight.

4

Though the sound overpowers,
Sing again, with your dear voice revealing   20
     A tone
Of some world far from ours,
Where music and moonlight and feeling
     Are one.

1822   1832

Lines Written in the Bay of Lerici[1]

She left me at the silent time
When the moon had ceased to climb
The azure path of Heaven's steep,
And like an albatross asleep,

---

1. Another of Shelley's last lyrics, inspired by Jane Williams.

Balanced on her wings of light,   5
Hovered in the purple night,
Ere she sought her ocean nest
In the chambers of the West.
She left me, and I stayed alone
Thinking over every tone   10
Which, though silent to the ear,
The enchanted heart could hear,
Like notes which die when born, but still
Haunt the echoes of the hill;
And feeling ever—oh, too much!—   15
The soft vibration of her touch,
As if her gentle hand, even now,
Lightly trembled on my brow;
And thus, although she absent were,
Memory gave me all of her   20
That even Fancy dares to claim:
Her presence had made weak and tame
All passions, and I lived alone
In the time which is our own;
The past and future were forgot,   25
As they had been, and would be, not.
But soon, the guardian angel gone,
The daemon[2] reassumed his throne
In my faint heart. I dare not speak
My thoughts, but thus disturbed and weak   30
I sat and saw the vessels glide
Over the ocean bright and wide,
Like spirit-wingéd chariots sent
O'er some serenest element
For ministrations strange and far;   35
As if to some Elysian star
They sailed for drink to medicine
Such sweet and bitter pain as mine.
And the wind that winged their flight
From the land came fresh and light,   40
And the scent of sleeping flowers,
And the coolness of the hours
Of dew, and sweet warmth left by day,
Were scattered o'er the twinkling bay.
And the fisher with his lamp   45
And spear about the low rocks damp
Crept, and struck the fish which came
To worship the delusive flame.
Too happy they, whose pleasure sought
Extinguishes all sense and thought   50
Of the regret that pleasure leaves,
Destroying life alone, not peace!

1822   1862

2. I.e., the passions, with compulsion to look before and after.

The Triumph of Life Shelley left this poem in process when he died in early July, 1822. He took its central event from Petrarch's six *Trionfi*, "triumph" having the meaning of the Latin *triumphus*, the ceremonial entrance of a victorious general into ancient Rome in a procession which included his prisoners of war. The poem is strongly influenced by Dante's *Divine Comedy*, not only in its *terza rima* (the verse form also of Petrarch's *Trionfi*) but also in over-all conception, in a number of narrative details, and in style. It is notable that Shelley, like Keats in *The Fall of Hyperion*, left unfinished at his death a long poem in the form of a Dantean dream-vision, in which the poet faces up to the discovery that human history has been a continuous process of human suffering and defeat —and, in Shelley's version, an almost unrelieved narrative of human weakness and evil-doing.

We ought to be cautious, however, of a current tendency to dramatize Shelley's career by imposing on it the form of a tragic plot, moving inexorably to the dead end of *The Triumph of Life*, from which there was no exit except the poet's own death. The vision in the poem of the frantic, quiescent, or despairing captives in the procession of Life—including all who have in the least degree compromised in spirit or aspiration with the passions, temptations, or values of the fleshly life and the material world— is a desolate one, but its darkness is not unrelieved. There are the "sacred few" among humanity who have not compromised at all. The band of "mighty captives" chained to Life's car represent a full spectrum of relative worth, from mighty villains to mighty heroes. And although we lack Shelley's answer to the question posed at the end of the fragment—"then, what is Life?"—there is no definitive evidence that he planned to depart from the precedent of all his other long poems, in which he allowed some scope of possibility for redeeming life by the cardinal Shelleyan virtues; and above all by that love which, as he says near the close of *The Triumph of Life* (lines 472–76), led Dante safely "from the lowest depths of Hell" through Purgatory to Heaven and back to earth.

But any statement of how Shelley would have ended this fragment is speculative. What is certain is the vitality, the tone, and the timbre of the poetic voice in the portion before us. No other narrative poem quite matches in its opening the puissance, impetus, and assurance of Shelley's forty-line induction, as the sun springs forth like a bridegroom coming out of his chamber, to be greeted with the quiet ceremonies of natural worship by the revolving world, to whom it brings light, heat, and joyous reawakening—to all except the poet who, having waked while the world slept in darkness, now composes himself to sleep as the world awakes, to undergo, in the transparent darkness of a trance, the crisis of his vision. And the promise of this extraordinary opening is fulfilled in the unflagging narrative drive, and in the ease, clarity, and precision of language, of the rest of the poem, which expresses an *élan* even in its grimmest passages.

The Triumph of Life does not sound like the voice of a defeated poet at the end of his tether, but of a poet who, just attaining the height of his powers, was making a masterful new beginning, when fate slit the thin spun life.

The Triumph of Life[1]

Swift as a spirit hastening to his task
    Of glory & of good, the Sun sprang forth
Rejoicing in his splendour, & the mask

Of darkness fell from the awakened Earth.
    The smokeless altars of the mountain snows   5
    Flamed above crimson clouds, & at the birth

Of light, the Ocean's orison[2] arose
    To which the birds tempered their matin lay.
All flowers in field or forest which unclose

    Their trembling eyelids to the kiss of day,   10
Swinging their censers in the element,
    With orient[3] incense lit by the new ray

Burned slow & inconsumably, & sent
    Their odorous sighs up to the smiling air,
And in succession due, did Continent,   15

    Isle, Ocean, & all things that in them wear
The form & character of mortal mould
    Rise as the Sun their father rose, to bear

Their portion of the toil which he of old
    Took as his own & then imposed on them;   20
But I, whom thoughts which must remain untold

Had kept as wakeful as the stars that gem
    The cone of night,[4] now they were laid asleep,
    Stretched my faint limbs beneath the hoary stem

Which an old chestnut flung athwart the steep   25
    Of a green Apennine:[5] before me fled
The night; behind me rose the day; the Deep

    Was at my feet, & Heaven above my head
When a strange trance over my fancy grew
    Which was not slumber, for the shade it spread   30

1. The text is that newly edited from Shelley's manuscript by Donald H. Reiman, in *Shelley's "The Triumph of Life": A Critical Study* (Urbana, Illinois, 1965). Shelley left a difficult and uncompleted manuscript draft; as Reiman says, "had Shelley lived, he would have revised and corrected [it] extensively." In the best tradition of modern textual scholarship, the editor has worked out Shelley's final intentions "both from the physical evidence of the manuscript and from the prosodic laws of *terza rima*." We reprint Reiman's text unaltered (without his careful textual notes) as much closer than the earlier published versions to what Shelley actually wrote. Blank spaces in the text reproduce blanks in the manuscript; some marks of punctuation (e.g., quotation marks) are Reiman's.
2. Prayer; to which (in the next line) the birds tuned their chanted morning prayer.
3. Morning.
4. The conical shadow cast by the earth as it intercepts the sunlight.
5. One of the Apennines, the chain of mountains extending down the Italian peninsula.

Was so transparent that the scene came through
    As clear as when a veil of light is drawn
O'er evening hills they glimmer;[6] and I knew

    That I had felt the freshness of that dawn,
Bathed in the same cold dew my brow & hair 35
    And sate as thus upon that slope of lawn

Under the self same bough, & heard as there
    The birds, the fountains & the Ocean hold
Sweet talk in music through the enamoured air.
    And then a Vision on my brain was rolled . . 40

As in that trance of wondrous thought I lay
    This was the tenour of my waking dream.
Methought I sate beside a public way

    Thick strewn with summer dust, & a great stream
Of people there was hurrying to & fro 45
    Numerous as gnats upon the evening gleam,

All hastening onward, yet none seemed to know
    Whither he went, or whence he came, or why
He made one of the multitude, yet so

    Was borne amid the crowd as through the sky 50
One of the million leaves of summer's bier.—
    Old age & youth, manhood & infancy,

Mixed in one mighty torrent did appear,
    Some flying from the thing they feared & some
Seeking the object of another's fear, 55

    And others as with steps towards the tomb
Pored on the trodden worms that crawled beneath,
    And others mournfully within the gloom

Of their own shadow walked, and called it death . . .
    And some fled from it[7] as it were a ghost, 60
Half fainting in the affliction of vain breath.

    But more with motions which each other crost
Pursued or shunned the shadows the clouds threw
    Or birds within the noonday ether lost,

Upon that path where flowers never grew; 65
    And weary with vain toil & faint for thirst
Heard not the fountains whose melodious dew

    Out of their mossy cells forever burst
Nor felt the breeze which from the forest told
    Of grassy paths, & wood lawns interspersed 70

---

6. "They" refers to "hills," in the same line.   7. I.e., from their own shadow (line 59).

With overarching elms & caverns cold,
    And violet banks where sweet dreams brood, but they
Pursued their serious folly as of old . . . .

    And as I gazed methought that in the way
The throng grew wilder, as the woods of June   75
    When the South wind shakes the extinguished day.—

And a cold glare, intenser than the noon
    But icy cold, obscured with   light
The Sun as he the stars. Like the young moon

    When on the sunlit limits of the night   80
Her white shell trembles amid crimson air
    And whilst the sleeping tempest gathers might

Doth, as a herald of its coming, bear
    The ghost of her dead Mother, whose dim form
Bends in dark ether from her infant's chair,[8]   85

    So came a chariot on the silent storm
Of its own rushing splendour, and a Shape
    So sate within as one whom years deform

Beneath a dusky hood & double cape
    Crouching within the shadow of a tomb,   90
And o'er what seemed the head, a cloud like crape,

    Was bent a dun & faint etherial gloom
Tempering the light; upon the chariot's beam
    A Janus-visaged[9] Shadow did assume

The guidance of that wonder-wingéd team.   95
    The Shapes which drew it in thick lightnings
Were lost: I heard alone on the air's soft stream

    The music of their ever moving wings.
All the four faces of that charioteer
    Had their eyes banded . . . little profit brings   100

Speed in the van & blindness in the rear,
    Nor then avail the beams that quench the Sun
Or that his banded eyes could pierce the sphere

    Of all that is, has been, or will be done.—
So ill was the car guided, but it past   105
    With solemn speed majestically on . . .

8. The crescent new moon bearing the faint outline of the full moon in its arms—the omen of a coming storm, as in Coleridge's *Dejection: An Ode*, epigraph and lines 9–14. The parallel is to the crescent-formed chariot bearing the dark Shape of Life.
9. The Roman god Janus was represented with two faces, looking before and after. The shadowy charioteer guiding his team (which is invisible in the glare), however, has four faces, all of them blindfolded ("banded," line 100). Harold Bloom points out that this description of the chariot of Life is a parodic version of Ezekiel's vision of a divine chariot in the likeness of four living creatures, each having four faces, and in their progress forming rings which "were full of eyes" (Ezekiel i.4–28); echoed in *Paradise Lost* VI. 749–72.

The crowd gave way, & I arose aghast,
 Or seemed to rise, so mighty was the trance,
And saw like clouds upon the thunder blast

  The million with fierce song and maniac dance   110
Raging around; such seemed the jubilee
  As when to greet some conqueror's advance

Imperial Rome poured forth her living sea
 From senatehouse & prison & theatre
When Freedom left those who upon the free   115

  Had bound a yoke which soon they stooped to bear.[1]

Nor wanted here the true similitude
 Of a triumphal pageant, for where'er

The chariot rolled a captive multitude
  Was driven; althose who had grown old in power 120
Or misery,—all who have their age subdued,

  By action or by suffering, and whose hour
Was drained to its last sand in weal or woe,
  So that the trunk survived both fruit & flower;

All those whose fame or infamy must grow   125
 Till the great winter lay the form & name
Of their own earth with them forever low,[2]

  All but the sacred few who could not tame
Their spirits to the Conqueror, but as soon
  As they had touched the world with living flame 130

Fled back like eagles to their native noon,
 Or those who put aside the diadem
Of earthly thrones or gems, till the last one

  Were there;—for they of Athens & Jerusalem[3]
Were neither mid the mighty captives seen   135
  Nor mid the ribald crowd that followed them

Or fled before . . Now swift, fierce & obscene
 The wild dance maddens in the van, & those
Who lead it, fleet as shadows on the green,

  Outspeed the chariot & without repose   140
Mix with each other in tempestuous measure
  To savage music . . . . Wilder as it grows,

---

1. I.e., free men who are enslaved become subservient in spirit.
2. Until the world shall end in ice.
3. The "captive multitude" (line 119) following the chariot include all the men whose exceptional power or talent had made them famous or infamous (line 125), except the "sacred few." The latter are divided into two classes: those who having touched the world with their purifying flame had died young, and those who having lived into older age had resisted the corrupting influence of "earthly thrones and gems" (line 133). These few included, doubtless, Socrates and Jesus ("of Athens and Jerusalem," line 134), but how many others the text does not specify.

They, tortured by the agonizing pleasure,
  Convulsed & on the rapid whirlwinds spun
Of that fierce spirit, whose unholy leisure   145

  Was soothed by mischief since the world begun,
Throw back their heads & loose their streaming hair,
  And in their dance round her who dims the Sun

Maidens & youths fling their wild arms in air
  As their feet twinkle; they recede, and now   150
Bending within each other's atmosphere

  Kindle invisibly; and as they glow
Like moths by light attracted & repelled,
  Oft to new bright destruction come & go.

Till like two clouds into one vale impelled   155
  That shake the mountains when their lightnings mingle
And die in rain,—the fiery band which held

  Their natures, snaps . . . ere the shock cease to tingle
One falls and then another in the path
  Senseless, nor is the desolation single,   160

Yet ere I can say *where* the chariot hath
  Past over them; nor other trace I find
But as of foam after the Ocean's wrath

  Is spent upon the desert shore.—Behind,
Old men, and women foully disarrayed   165
  Shake their grey hair in the insulting wind,

Limp in the dance & strain with limbs decayed
  To reach the car of light which leaves them still
Farther behind & deeper in the shade.

  But not the less with impotence of will   170
They wheel, though ghastly shadows interpose
  Round them & round each other, and fulfill

Their work and to the dust whence they arose
  Sink & corruption veils them as they lie
And frost in these performs what fire in those.[4]   175

  Struck to the heart by this sad pageantry,
Half to myself I said, "And what is this?
  Whose shape is that within the car? & why"—

4. The narrator sees three separate companies of captives: (1) the "maidens and youths" who in a Dionysian intoxication, dance in an erotic frenzy, meet, couple, and fall senseless, to be crushed by the onrushing chariot (lines 137–64); (2) the foul and ribald "old men and women" at the rear of the total procession, attempting impotently to perform the same dance as the young (lines 136, 164–75); (3) the "mighty captives," men with high capacities for good who have to various degrees been corrupted by Life, who are chained to the chariot in the middle of the procession (lines 119–27, 135). (In the Roman triumphs, the captive chieftains were bound to the conqueror's chariot, to heighten their dishonor.)

I would have added—"is all here amiss?"
    But a voice answered . . "Life" . . . I turned & knew   180
(O Heaven have mercy on such wretchedness!)

    That what I thought was an old root which grew
To strange distortion out of the hill side
    Was indeed one of that deluded crew,

And that the grass which methought hung so wide   185
    And white, was but his thin discoloured hair,
And that the holes it vainly sought to hide

    Were or had been eyes.—"If thou canst forbear
To join the dance, which I had well forborne,"[5]

    Said the grim Feature, of my thought aware,   190

"I will now tell that which to this deep scorn
    Led me & my companions, and relate
The progress of the pageant since the morn;

    "If thirst of knowledge doth not thus abate,
Follow it even to the night, but I   195
    Am weary" . . . Then like one who with the weight

Of his own words is staggered, wearily
    He paused, and ere he could resume, I cried,
"First who art thou?" . . . "Before thy memory

    "I feared, loved, hated, suffered, did, & died,[6]   200
And if the spark with which Heaven lit my spirit
    Earth had with purer nutriment supplied

"Corruption would not now thus much inherit
    Of what was once Rousseau—nor this disguise
Stained that within which still disdains to wear it.—   205

    "If I have been extinguished, yet there rise
A thousand beacons from the spark I bore."—[7]
    "And who are those chained to the car?" "The Wise,

"The great, the unforgotten: they who wore
    Mitres & helms & crowns, or wreathes of light,[8]   210
Signs of thought's empire over thought; their lore

    "Taught them not this—to know themselves; their might
Could not repress the mutiny within,
    And for the morn of truth they feigned, deep night

---

5. I.e., which I would have done well to avoid. "Feature": in the old sense, "form," "shape."
6. I.e., Rousseau had lived and died before Shelley was born.
7. The sparks of Rousseau's writings had lighted a thousand signal fires—including that of the French Revolution, of which one child was Napoleon, de-

scribed in lines 215–27.
8. I.e., mitered churchmen, helmeted soldiers, crowned kings, and philosophers adorned with wreaths composed of light. With line 208 Rousseau takes up the description in detail of the captives chained to the chariot (see footnote for line 175).

"Caught them ere evening." "Who is he with chin
    Upon his breast and hands crost on his chain?"
"The Child of a fierce hour; he sought to win   215

    "The world, and lost all it did contain
Of greatness, in its hope destroyed; & more
    Of fame & peace than Virtue's self can gain   220

"Without the opportunity which bore
    Him on its eagle's pinion to the peak
From which a thousand climbers have before

    "Fall'n as Napoleon fell."—I felt my cheek
Alter to see the great form pass away   225
    Whose grasp had left the giant world so weak

That every pigmy kicked it as it lay—
    And much I grieved to think how power & will
In opposition rule our mortal day—

    And why God made irreconcilable   230
Good & the means of good;[9] and for despair
    I half disdained mine eye's desire to fill

With the spent vision of the times that were
    And scarce have ceased to be . . . "Dost thou behold,"
Said then my guide, "those spoilers spoiled, Voltaire,   235

    "Frederic, & Kant, Catherine, & Leopold,[1]
Chained hoary anarchs,[2] demagogue & sage
    Whose name the fresh world thinks already old—

"For in the battle Life & they did wage
    She remained conqueror—I was overcome   240
By my own heart alone,[3] which neither age

    "Nor tears nor infamy nor now the tomb
Could temper to its object."—"Let them pass"—
    I cried—"the world & its mysterious doom

"Is not so much more glorious than it was   245
    That I desire to worship those who drew
New figures on its false & fragile glass

    "As the old faded."—"Figures ever new
Rise on the bubble, paint them how you may;
    We have but thrown, as those before us threw,   250

---

9. I.e., the possession of the will to do good is opposed to the possession of power, the means to accomplish good.
1. Presumably Voltaire (the immensely influential thinker and man of letters of the French Enlightenment) is the "demagogue"; Frederick the Great of Prussia, Catherine the Great of Russia, and Leopold II of the Holy Roman Empire, all influenced by Voltaire's ideas, are the "anarchs"; and Immanuel Kant (the great German philosopher writing at the end of the Enlightenment) is the "sage."
2. Leaders who bring about anarchy.
3. While these others were conquered by Life, Rousseau was self-conquered by his own heart's limitless desires, which no experience could moderate ("temper") to contentment with an achievable object or satisfaction.

"Our shadows on it as it past away.
    But mark, how chained to the triumphal chair
The mighty phantoms of an elder day—

"All that is mortal of great Plato there
Expiates the joy & woe his master knew not;[4]   255
    That star that ruled his doom was far too fair—

"And Life, where long that flower of Heaven grew not,
    Conquered the heart by love which gold or pain
Or age or sloth or slavery could subdue not—

"And near   walk the   twain,   260
The tutor & his pupil,[5] whom Dominion
    Followed as tame as vulture in a chain.—

"The world was darkened beneath either pinion
Of him whom from the flock of conquerors
Fame singled as her thunderbearing minion;   265

"The other long outlived both woes & wars,
Throned in new thoughts of men, and still had kept
    The jealous keys of truth's eternal doors

"If Bacon's spirit   had not leapt
Like lightning out of darkness; he compelled   270
The Proteus shape of Nature's as it slept

"To wake & to unbar the caves that held
The treasure of the secrets of its reign—
    See the great bards of old who inly quelled

"The passions which they sung, as by their strain   275
    May well be known:[6] their living melody
Tempers its own contagion to the vein

"Of those who are infected with it—I
Have suffered what I wrote, or viler pain!—

"And so my words were seeds of misery—   280
Even as the deeds of others."—Not as theirs," [6a]
    I said—he pointed to a company

In which I recognized amid the heirs
  Of Caesar's crime from him to Constantine,[7]
The Anarchs old whose force & murderous snares   285

  Had founded many a sceptre bearing line
And spread the plague of blood & gold abroad,
  And Gregory & John[8] and men divine

Who rose like shadows between Man & god
  Till that eclipse, still hanging under Heaven,   290
Was worshipped by the world o'er which they strode

  For the true Sun it quenched.—"Their power was given
But to destroy," replied the leader—"I
  Am one of those who have created, even

"If it be but a world of agony."—   295
  "Whence camest thou & whither goest thou?
How did thy course begin," I said, "& why?

  "Mine eyes are sick of this perpetual flow
Of people, & my heart of one sad thought.—
  Speak." [9] "Whence I came, partly I seem to know,   300

"And how & by what paths I have been brought
  To this dread pass, methinks even thou mayst guess;
Why this should be my mind can compass not;

  "Whither the conqueror hurries me still less.
But follow thou, & from spectator turn   305
  Actor or victim in this wretchedness,

"And what thou wouldst be taught I then may learn
  From thee.—Now listen . . . In the April prime
When all the forest tops began to burn

  "With kindling green, touched by the azure clime   310
Of the young year, I found myself asleep
  Under a mountain which from unknown time

"Had yawned into a cavern high & deep,
  And from it came a gentle rivulet
Whose water like clear air in its calm sweep   315

  "Bent the soft grass & kept for ever wet
The stems of the sweet flowers, and filled the grove
  With sound which all who hear must needs forget

7. The crime of destroying the Roman Republic by becoming dictator and so opening the line of Roman emperors extending to Constantine, who inaugurated the Christian rule of Rome early in the 4th century. The "Anarchs" are the founders of later European dynasties in the Christian period.
8. Pope Gregory the Great established the independent political power of the papacy; "John," presumably, simply be-cause it has been a name frequently assumed by Popes.
9. The rest of the fragment consists of Rousseau's allegorical account of his own life, in response to the only two of the narrator's questions (lines 296–97) which, he says, the limitations of his knowledge permit him partially to answer. "April prime": Spring, the first season of the year.

"All pleasure & all pain, all hate & love,
    Which they had known before that hour of rest: 320
A sleeping mother then would dream not of

    "The only child who died upon her breast
At eventide, a king would mourn no more
    The crown of which his brow was dispossest

"When the sun lingered o'er the Ocean floor   325
    To gild his rival's new prosperity.—
Thou wouldst forget thus vainly to deplore

    "Ills, which if ills, can find no cure from thee,
The thought of which no other sleep will quell
    Nor other music blot from memory—   330

"So sweet & deep is the oblivious[1] spell.—
    Whether my life had been before that sleep
The Heaven which I imagine, or a Hell

    "Like this harsh world in which I wake to weep,
I know not. I arose & for a space   335
    The scene of woods & waters seemed to keep,

"Though it was now broad day, a gentle trace
    Of light diviner than the common Sun
Sheds on the common Earth, but all the place

    "Was filled with many sounds woven into one   340
Oblivious melody, confusing sense
    Amid the gliding waves & shadows dun;

"And as I looked the bright omnipresence
    Of morning through the orient[2] cavern flowed,
And the Sun's image radiantly intense   345

    "Burned on the waters of the well that glowed
Like gold, and threaded all the forest maze
    With winding paths of emerald fire—there stood

"Amid the sun, as he amid the blaze
    Of his own glory, on the vibrating   350
Floor of the fountain, paved with flashing rays,

    "A shape all light, which with one hand did fling
Dew on the earth, as if she were the Dawn[3]
    Whose invisible rain forever seemed to sing

1. Causing forgetfulness. Shelley models Rousseau's account of his life in part on Rousseau's own writings and in part on Wordsworth's metaphoric description, in *Intimations Ode*, of the westward course of man's life, substituting his own skepticism for Wordsworth's certainties.

2. Lit from the east. The cavern runs from east to west through the mountain, and as Rousseau grows older he follows the course of its stream westward.

3. "The shape all light," of which the meaning has been much disputed, probably signifies the false Rousseauistic (and in Shelley's view, Wordsworthian) ideal of the state of nature and of trust in the natural human instincts. The attractive feminine shape is formed by a reflection of the sun's light from the earthly medium of water and leads Rousseau on only to betray him (lines 382 ff., 405 ff.).

"A silver music on the mossy lawn,   355
  And still before her on the dusky grass
Iris⁴ her many coloured scarf had drawn.—

 "In her right hand she bore a crystal glass
Mantling with bright Nepenthe;⁵—the fierce splendour
  Fell from her as she moved under the mass   360

"Of the deep cavern, & with palms so tender
  Their tread broke not the mirror of its billow,
Glided along the river, and did bend her

 "Head under the dark boughs, till like a willow
Her fair hair swept the bosom of the stream   365
  That whispered with delight to be their pillow.—

"As one enamoured is upborne in dream
  O'er lily-paven lakes mid silver mist
To wondrous music, so this shape might seem

 "Partly to tread the waves with feet which kist   370
The dancing foam, partly to glide along
  The airs that roughened the moist amethyst,

"Or the slant morning beams that fell among
  The trees, or the soft shadows of the trees;
And her feet ever to the ceaseless song   375

 "Of leaves & winds & waves & birds & bees
And falling drops moved in a measure new
  Yet sweet, as on the summer evening breeze

"Up from the lake a shape of golden dew
  Between two rocks, athwart the rising moon,   380
Moves up the east, where eagle never flew.—

 "And still her feet, no less than the sweet tune
To which they moved, seemed as they moved, to blot
  The thoughts of him who gazed on them, & soon

"All that was seemed as if it had been not,   385
  As if the gazer's mind was strewn beneath
Her feet like embers, & she, thought by thought,

 "Trampled its fires into the dust of death,
As Day upon the threshold of the east
  Treads out the lamps of night, until the breath   390

---

4. The rainbow; here it signifies the prismatic colors of the refracted light of the sun.
5. A drug causing total forgetfulness. The sinister suggestion subtly introduced in the description of the shape ("the fierce splendor," line 359) is heightened by echoes from Milton's *Comus*, lines 671 ff., in which the enchanter Comus (born of Circe, "daughter of the Sun") tries to seduce the Lady by a beverage which Milton compared to Nepenthe.

"Of darkness reillumines even the least
　　Of heaven's living eyes[6]—like day she came,
Making the night a dream; and ere she ceased

"To move, as one between desire and shame
Suspended, I said—'If, as it doth seem,　　　　　　　　395
　　Thou comest from the realm without a name,

" 'Into this valley of perpetual dream,
　　Shew whence I came, and where I am, and why—
Pass not away upon the passing stream.'

" 'Arise and quench thy thirst,' was her reply.　　　400
And as a shut lily, stricken by the wand
　　Of dewy morning's vital alchemy,

"I rose; and, bending at her sweet command,
　　Touched with faint lips the cup she raised,
And suddenly my brain became as sand　　　　　　　　405

"Where the first wave had more than half erased
The track of deer on desert Labrador,
　　Whilst the fierce wolf from which they fled amazed

"Leaves his stamp visibly upon the shore
　　Until the second bursts—so on my sight　　　　　　410
Burst a new Vision never seen before.—

"And the fair shape waned in the coming light
As veil by veil the silent splendour drops
　　From Lucifer, amid the chrysolite[7]

"Of sunrise ere it strike the mountain tops—　　　　415
　　And as the presence of that fairest planet
Although unseen is felt by one who hopes

"That his day's path may end as he began it
In that star's smile, whose light is like the scent
　　Of a jonquil when evening breezes fan it,　　　　　420

"Or the soft note in which his dear lament
　　The Brescian shepherd[8] breathes, or the caress
That turned his weary slumber to content.—

"So knew I in that light's severe excess
The presence of that shape which on the stream　　　425
　　Moved, as I moved along the wilderness,

"More dimly than a day appearing dream,
　　The ghost of a forgotten form of sleep,
A light from Heaven whose half extinguished beam

---

6. I.e., the stars.
7. A greenish gem.
8. The favorite song, *Stanco di pascolar le pecorelle,* is a Brescian national air

[Mary Shelley's note]. The title translates, "I am tired of pasturing the sheep." Brescia: a region in northern Italy.

"Through the sick day in which we wake to weep   430
Glimmers, forever sought, forever lost.—
    So did that shape its obscure tenour keep

"Beside my path, as silent as a ghost;[9]
    But the new Vision, and its cold bright car,
With savage music, stunning music, crost   435

"The forest, and as if from some dread war
Triumphantly returning, the loud million
    Fiercely extolled the fortune of her star.—

"A moving arch of victory the vermilion
    And green & azure plumes of Iris had   440
Built high over her wind-winged pavilion,

"And underneath aetherial glory clad
The wilderness, and far before her flew
    The tempest of the splendour which forbade

"Shadow to fall from leaf or stone;—the crew   445
    Seemed in that light like atomies[1] that dance
Within a sunbeam.—Some upon the new

"Embroidery of flowers that did enhance
The grassy vesture of the desart, played,
    Forgetful of the chariot's swift advance;   450

"Others stood gazing till within the shade
    Of the great mountain its light left them dim.—
Others outspeeded it, and others made

"Circles around it like the clouds that swim
Round the high moon in a bright sea of air,   455
    And more did follow, with exulting hymn,

"The chariot & the captives fettered there,
    But all like bubbles on an eddying flood
Fell into the same track at last & were

"Borne onward.—I among the multitude   460
Was swept; me sweetest flowers delayed not long,
    Me not the shadow nor the solitude,

"Me not the falling stream's Lethean song,
    Me, not the phantom of that early form
Which moved upon its motion,—but among   465

"The thickest billows of the living storm
I plunged, and bared my bosom to the clime
    Of that cold light, whose airs too soon deform.—

9. In lines 410–33 the brilliance of the chariot of Life makes the fair shape fade until, like the morning (and evening) star, Lucifer (line 414) in the daytime, its presence is felt, although no longer seen. (Cf. *To a Skylark*, above, lines 21–25.)
1. Particles of dust.

"Before the chariot had begun to climb
 The opposing steep of that mysterious dell,
Behold a wonder worthy of the rhyme   470

"Of him[2] whom from the lowest depths of Hell
Through every Paradise & through all glory
 Love led serene, & who returned to tell

"In words of hate & awe the wondrous story   475
 How all things are transfigured, except Love;
For deaf as is a sea which wrath makes hoary

"The world can hear not the sweet notes that move
The sphere[3] whose light is melody to lovers—
 A wonder worthy of his rhyme—the grove   480

"Grew dense with shadows to its inmost covers,
 The earth was grey with phantoms, & the air
Was peopled with dim forms, as when there hovers

"A flock of vampire-bats before the glare
Of the tropic sun, bringing ere evening   485
 Strange night upon some Indian isle,—thus were

"Phantoms diffused around, & some did fling
 Shadows of shadows, yet unlike themselves,
Behind them, some like eaglets on the wing

"Were lost in the white blaze, others like elves 490
Danced in a thousand unimagined shapes
 Upon the sunny streams & grassy shelves;

"And others sate chattering like restless apes
 On vulgar paws and voluble like fire.
Some made a cradle of the ermined capes   495

"Of kingly mantles, some upon the tiar[4]
Of pontiffs sate like vultures, others played
 Within the crown which girt with empire

"A baby's or an idiot's brow, & made
 Their nests in it; the old anatomies[5]   500
Sate hatching their bare brood under the shade

"Of demon wings, and laughed from their dead eyes
To reassume the delegated power
 Arrayed in which these worms did monarchize

---

2. Dante, who in *The Divine Comedy* was kept safe by Love in his pilgrimage.
3. The third sphere of the planet Venus (Love), in Dante's Ptolemaic universe.
4. The tiara, or triple crown of the popes.

5. Skeletonlike monsters.
6. The monarchs who had made the earth one great cemetery ("charnel") were like grave-worms, for they fed upon the corpses they had slaughtered.

"Who make this earth their charnel.[6]—Others more   505
  Humble, like falcons sate upon the fist
Of common men, and round their heads did soar,

  "Or like small gnats & flies, as thick as mist
On evening marshes, thronged about the brow
  Of lawyer, statesman, priest & theorist,   510

"And others like discoloured flakes of snow
  On fairest bosoms & the sunniest hair
Fell, and were melted by the youthful glow

  "Which they extinguished; for like tears, they were
A veil to those from whose faint lids they rained   515
  In drops of sorrow.—I became aware

"Of whence those forms proceeded which thus stained
  The track in which we moved; after brief space
From every form the beauty slowly waned,

  "From every firmest limb & fairest face   520
The strength & freshness fell like dust, & left
  The action & the shape without the grace

"Of life;[7] the marble brow of youth was cleft
  With care, and in the eyes where once hope shone
Desire like a lioness bereft   525

  "Of its last cub, glared ere it died; each one
Of that great crowd sent forth incessantly
  These shadows, numerous as the dead leaves blown

"In Autumn evening from a poplar tree—
  Each, like himself & like each other were,   530
At first, but soon distorted, seemed to be

  "Obscure clouds moulded by the casual air;
And of this stuff the car's creative ray
  Wrought all the busy phantoms that were there

"As the sun shapes the clouds—thus, on the way   535
  Mask after mask fell from the countenance
And form of all, and long before the day

  "Was old, the joy which waked like Heaven's glance
The sleepers in the oblivious valley, died,
  And some grew weary of the ghastly dance   540

"And fell, as I have fallen by the way side,
  Those soonest from whose forms most shadows past
And least of strength & beauty did abide."—

7. In lines 481–523, the shadows and phantoms originate (lines 516–37) in the qualities of beauty, strength, and freshness, which fall like masks away from the men and women in the procession, as their hope degenerates into mere desire. These shadows of lost physical qualities are soon distorted by the currents of the air and miscreated into phantoms by the light from the car of Life.

"Then, what is Life?" I said . . . the cripple cast
His eye upon the car which now had rolled 545
  Onward, as if that look must be the last,

And answered . . . . "Happy those for whom the fold
  Of
1822   1824

From A Defense of Poetry[1]
Part I

According to one mode of regarding those two classes of mental
action, which are called reason and imagination, the former may
be considered as mind contemplating the relations borne by one
thought to another, however produced; and the latter, as mind
acting upon those thoughts so as to color them with its own light,
and composing from them, as from elements, other thoughts, each
containing within itself the principle of its own integrity. The one[2]
is the τὸ ποιεῖν,[3] or the principle of synthesis, and has for its objects

---

1. In 1820 Shelley's good friend Thomas Love Peacock published an ironic essay, *The Four Ages of Poetry*, in which he took the position that poetry is a primitive use of language which once had a function in a barbarous society, but has become a useless anachronism in this age of science and technology. Peacock was himself a poet, as well as the best contemporary prose satirist, and Shelley saw the joke; but he also recognized that the position which Peacock had ironically assumed was very close to that actually held in his day by Utilitarian philosophers and material-minded laymen who either attacked or contemptuously ignored the imaginative faculty and its achievements. He therefore undertook, as he good-humoredly wrote to Peacock, "to break a lance with you * * * in honor of my mistress Urania," even though he was only "the knight of the shield of shadow and the lance of gossamere." The result was *The Defense of Poetry*, planned to consist of three parts. The last two parts were never written, and even the existing section, written in 1821, remained unpublished until 1840, eighteen years after Shelley's death.

For many decades Shelley's *Defense* was regarded as one of the very few classic essays in literary criticism. Its reputation, however, has diminished in the recent era of the new criticism. The chief interest since the 1920's has been in applied commentary and the kind of critical theory that is oriented toward providing useful distinctions for the close analysis of particular literary texts. But

Shelley's main enterprise, although different, is no less valid and a rarer achievement in the history of critical writings. His emphasis is on the universal and permanent forms, qualities, and values that all great poems, as products of imagination, possess in common; on those aspects, as he puts it, in which time, person, and place "are convertible with respect to the highest poetry without injuring it as poetry." More than this: Shelley extends the term "poet" to comprehend all the creative minds that break out of the limitations of their age and place to approximate the enduring and general forms of value—including not only writers in verse and prose, but artists, legislators, and prophets, as well as the founders of a new organization of society, morality, or religion. The very range of the *Defense* gives it unequaled importance as a ringing claim for the validity and indispensability of the visionary and creative imagination in all the great human concerns. Nor has any later writer exceeded the cogency of the attack, which Shelley includes, on our acquisitive society and its narrowly material concept of utility and progress, which has permitted man to make enormous progress in science and in his material well-being without a proportionate development of his "poetical faculty," the moral imagination; with the grotesque result, as Shelley says, that "man, having enslaved the elements, remains himself a slave."

2. I.e., the imagination.
3. "Making." The Greek word from which "poet" derives means "maker."

those forms which are common to universal nature and existence itself; the other is the τὸ λογίζειν,[4] or principle of analysis, and its action regards the relations of things simply as relations; considering thoughts, not in their integral unity, but as the algebraical representations which conduct to certain general results. Reason is the enumeration of quantities already known; imagination is the perception of the value of those quantities, both separately and as a whole. Reason respects the differences, and imagination the similitudes of things. Reason is to the imagination as the instrument to the agent, as the body to the spirit, as the shadow to the substance.[5] * * *

In the youth of the world, men dance and sing and imitate natural objects, observing in these actions, as in all others, a certain rhythm or order. And, although all men observe a similar, they observe not the same order, in the motions of the dance, in the melody of the song, in the combinations of language, in the series of their imitations of natural objects. For there is a certain order or rhythm belonging to each of these classes of mimetic representation, from which the hearer and the spectator receive an intenser and purer pleasure than from any other: the sense of an approximation to this order has been called taste by modern writers. Every man in the infancy of art observes an order which approximates more or less closely to that from which this highest delight results; but the diversity is not sufficiently marked, as that its gradations should be sensible, except in those instances where the predominance of this faculty of approximation to the beautiful (for so we may be permitted to name the relation between this highest pleasure and its cause) is very great. Those in whom it exists in excess are poets, in the most universal sense of the word; and the pleasure resulting from the manner in which they express the influence of society or nature upon their own minds communicates itself to others, and gathers a sort of reduplication from that community. Their language is vitally metaphorical; that is, it marks the before unapprehended relations of things and perpetuates their apprehension, until the words which represent them become, through time, signs for portions or classes of thoughts[6] instead of pictures of integral thoughts; and then if no new poets should arise to create afresh the associations which have been thus disorganized, language will be dead to all the nobler purposes of human intercourse. These similitudes or relations are finely said by Lord Bacon to be "the same footsteps of nature impressed upon the various subjects of

and the term "maker" had been adopted by Renaissance defenders of poetry. Sir Philip Sidney, in his *Apology for Poetry* (1595), which Shelley had carefully studied, said: "The Greeks named him poet. * * * It cometh of this word *poiein*, which is *to make;* wherein * * * we Englishmen have met with the Greeks in calling him a maker. * * * "

4. "Calculating," "reasoning."

5. In the paragraph here omitted, Shelley defines poetry as "the expression of the imagination"; it is "connate with the origin of man."

6. I.e., abstract concepts.

the world,"[7] and he considers the faculty which perceives them as
the storehouse of axioms common to all knowledge. In the infancy
of society every author is necessarily a poet, because language itself
is poetry; and to be a poet is to apprehend the true and the beautiful, in a word, the good which exists in the relation, subsisting first,
between existence and perception, and secondly, between perception and expression. Every original language near to its source is
in itself the chaos of a cyclic poem; the copiousness of lexicography
and the distinctions of grammar are the works of a later age, and
are merely the catalogue and the form of the creations of poetry.

But poets, or those who imagine and express this indestructible
order, are not only the authors of language and of music, of the
dance, and architecture, and statuary, and painting; they are the
institutors of laws, and the founders of civil society, and the inventors of the arts of life, and the teachers, who draw into a certain propinquity with the beautiful and the true that partial apprehension of the agencies of the invisible world which is called religion.[8] Hence all original religions are allegorical, or susceptible of
allegory, and, like Janus,[9] have a double face of false and true.
Poets, according to the circumstances of the age and nation in
which they appeared, were called, in the earlier epochs of the world,
legislators, or prophets;[1] a poet essentially comprises and unites
both these characters. For he not only beholds intensely the present
as it is, and discovers those laws according to which present things
ought to be ordered, but he beholds the future in the present, and
his thoughts are the germs of the flower and the fruit of latest time.
Not that I assert poets to be prophets in the gross sense of the word,
or that they can foretell the form as surely as they foreknow the
spirit of events: such is the pretense of superstition, which would
make poetry an attribute of prophecy, rather than prophecy an attribute of poetry. A poet participates in the eternal, the infinite,
and the one; as far as relates to his conceptions, time and place
and number are not. The grammatical forms which express the
moods of time, and the difference of persons, and the distinction
of place are convertible with respect to the highest poetry without
injuring it as poetry; and the choruses of Aeschylus, and the Book
of Job, and Dante's *Paradiso*, would afford, more than any other
writings, examples of this fact, if the limits of this essay did not
forbid citation. The creations of sculpture, painting, and music, are
illustrations still more decisive. * * *

A poem is the very image of life expressed in its eternal truth.
There is this difference between a story and a poem, that a story

---

7. *"De augmentis scientiarum* I.iii"
[Shelley's note].
8. Shelley thus deliberately enlarges the
discussion to include all creative insights or imaginative break-throughs of
mankind in whatever area they may oc-

cur.
9. Roman god of doorways, with two
heads which face in opposite directions.
1. The term *vates* ("prophet") was
sometimes applied to poets by the Romans.

is a catalogue of detached facts, which have no other bond of connection than time, place, circumstance, cause, and effect; the other is the creation of actions according to the unchangeable forms of human nature as existing in the mind of the Creator, which is itself the image of all other minds. The one is partial, and applies only to a definite period of time and a certain combination of events which can never again recur; the other is universal, and contains within itself the germ of a relation to whatever motives or actions have place in the possible varieties of human nature. Time, which destroys the beauty and the use of the story of particular facts, stripped of the poetry which should invest them, augments that of poetry, and forever develops new and wonderful applications of the eternal truth which it contains. Hence epitomes have been called the moths of just history; they eat out the poetry of it.[2] A story of particular facts is a mirror which obscures and distorts that which should be beautiful; poetry is a mirror which makes beautiful that which is distorted.

The parts of a composition may be poetical, without the composition as a whole being a poem. A single sentence may be considered as a whole, though it may be found in the midst of a series of unassimilated portions; a single word even may be a spark of inextinguishable thought. And thus all the great historians, Herodotus, Plutarch, Livy, were poets; and although the plan of these writers, especially that of Livy, restrained them from developing this faculty in its highest degree, they make copious and ample amends for their subjection, by filling all the interstices of their subjects with living images.

Having determined what is poetry, and who are poets, let us proceed to estimate its effects upon society.

Poetry is ever accompanied with pleasure: all spirits on which it falls open themselves to receive the wisdom which is mingled with its delight. In the infancy of the world neither poets themselves nor their auditors are fully aware of the excellence of poetry, for it acts in a divine and unapprehended manner, beyond and above consciousness; and it is reserved for future generations to contemplate and measure the mighty cause and effect in all the strength and splendor of their union. Even in modern times, no living poet ever arrived at the fullness of his fame; the jury which sits in judgment upon a poet, belonging as he does to all time, must be composed of his peers: it must be impaneled by time from the selectest of the wise of many generations. A poet is a nightingale, who sits in darkness and sings to cheer its own solitude with sweet sounds; his auditors are as men entranced by the melody of an unseen musician, who feel that they are moved and softened, yet know not whence or why. The poems of Homer and his contemporaries

2. Cf. Bacon's *Advancement of Learning* II.ii.4; "epitomes" are abstracts or   condensations.

were the delight of infant Greece; they were the elements of that social system which is the column upon which all succeeding civilization has reposed. Homer embodied the ideal perfection of his age in human character; nor can we doubt that those who read his verses were awakened to an ambition of becoming like to Achilles, Hector, and Ulysses; the truth and beauty of friendship, patriotism, and persevering devotion to an object were unveiled to their depths in these immortal creations; the sentiments of the auditors must have been refined and enlarged by a sympathy with such great and lovely impersonations, until from admiring they imitated, and from imitation they identified themselves with the objects of their admiration. Nor let it be objected that these characters are remote from moral perfection and that they can by no means be considered as edifying patterns for general imitation. Every epoch, under names more or less specious, has deified its peculiar errors; revenge is the naked idol of the worship of a semi-barbarous age, and self-deceit is the veiled image of unknown evil, before which luxury and satiety lie prostrate. But a poet considers the vices of his contemporaries as a temporary dress in which his creations must be arrayed and which cover without concealing the eternal proportions of their beauty. An epic or dramatic personage is understood to wear them around his soul, as he may the ancient armor or the modern uniform around his body; whilst it is easy to conceive a dress more graceful than either. The beauty of the internal nature cannot be so far concealed by its accidental vesture, but that the spirit of its form shall communicate itself to the very disguise, and indicate the shape it hides from the manner in which it is worn. A majestic form and graceful motions will express themselves through the most barbarous and tasteless costume. Few poets of the highest class have chosen to exhibit the beauty of their conceptions in its naked truth and splendor; and it is doubtful whether the alloy of costume, habit, etc., be not necessary to temper this planetary music[3] for mortal ears.

The whole objection, however, of the immorality of poetry[4] rests upon a misconception of the manner in which poetry acts to produce the moral improvement of man. Ethical science[5] arranges the elements which poetry has created, and propounds schemes and proposes examples of civil and domestic life; nor is it for want of admirable doctrines that men hate, and despise, and censure, and deceive, and subjugate one another. But poetry acts in another and diviner manner. It awakens and enlarges the mind itself by rendering it the receptacle of a thousand unapprehended combinations of thought. Poetry lifts the veil from the hidden beauty of the world,

3. The music of the revolving crystalline spheres of the planets, inaudible to human ears.

4. In the preceding paragraph Shelley has been implicitly dealing with the charge, voiced by Plato, that poetry is immoral because it presents evil characters acting evilly.

5. Moral philosophy.

and makes familiar objects be as if they were not familiar; it reproduces all that it represents, and the impersonations clothed in its Elysian light stand thenceforward in the minds of those who have once contemplated them, as memorials of that gentle and exalted content[6] which extends itself over all thoughts and actions with which it coexists. The great secret of morals is love, or a going out of our own nature, and an identification of ourselves with the beautiful which exists in thought, action, or person not our own. A man, to be greatly good, must imagine intensely and comprehensively; he must put himself in the place of another and of many others; the pains and pleasures of his species must become his own. The great instrument of moral good is the imagination;[7] and poetry administers to the effect by acting upon the cause. Poetry enlarges the circumference of the imagination by replenishing it with thoughts of ever new delight, which have the power of attracting and assimilating to their own nature all other thoughts and which form new intervals and interstices whose void forever craves fresh food. Poetry strengthens that faculty which is the organ of the moral nature of man, in the same manner as exercise strengthens a limb. A poet therefore would do ill to embody his own conceptions of right and wrong, which are usually those of his place and time, in his poetical creations, which participate in neither. By this assumption of the inferior office of interpreting the effect, in which perhaps after all he might acquit himself but imperfectly, he would resign a glory in a participation in the cause.[8] There was little danger that Homer, or any of the eternal poets, should have so far misunderstood themselves as to have abdicated this throne of their widest dominion. Those in whom the poetical faculty, though great, is less intense, as Euripides, Lucan, Tasso, Spenser, have frequently affected[9] a moral aim, and the effect of their poetry is diminished in exact proportion to the degree in which they compel us to advert to this purpose.[1] * * *

It is difficult to define pleasure in its highest sense; the definition involving a number of apparent paradoxes. For, from an inexplicable defect of harmony in the constitution of human nature, the pain of the inferior is frequently connected with the pleasures of the

6. Contentment, total satisfaction.
7. Central to Shelley's theory is the concept of the sympathetic imagination—the faculty by which an individual is enabled to overleap the limits of his own nervous system and identify himself with the thoughts and feelings of other men. Shelley claims that the faculty which in poetry enables us to share the joys and sufferings of invented characters is also the basis of all morality, for it compels us to feel for others as we feel for ourselves.
8. The "effect," or the particular moral

standards set up by the imagination, is contrasted to the "cause" of all morality, the imagination itself.
9. Assumed, adopted.
1. In the omitted passage Shelley reviews the history of drama and poetry in relation to civilization and morality and proceeds to refute the charge that poets are less useful than "reasoners and merchants." He begins by defining utility in terms of pleasure, and then distinguishes between the lower (physical and material) and the higher (imaginative) pleasures.

superior portions of our being. Sorrow, terror, anguish, despair itself, are often the chosen expressions of an approximation to the highest good. Our sympathy in tragic fiction depends on this principle; tragedy delights by affording a shadow of the pleasure which exists in pain. This is the source also of the melancholy which is inseparable from the sweetest melody. The pleasure that is in sorrow is sweeter than the pleasure of pleasure itself. And hence the saying, "It is better to go to the house of mourning, than to the house of mirth"[2]—not that this highest species of pleasure is necessarily linked with pain. The delight of love and friendship, the ecstasy of the admiration of nature, the joy of the perception and still more of the creation of poetry, is often wholly unalloyed.

The production and assurance of pleasure in this highest sense is true utility. Those who produce and preserve this pleasure are poets or poetical philosophers.

The exertions of Locke, Hume, Gibbon, Voltaire, Rousseau,[3] and their disciples in favor of oppressed and deluded humanity are entitled to the gratitude of mankind. Yet it is easy to calculate the degree of moral and intellectual improvement which the world would have exhibited, had they never lived. A little more nonsense would have been talked for a century or two; and perhaps a few more men, women, and children burnt as heretics. We might not at this moment have been congratulating each other on the abolition of the Inquisition in Spain.[4] But it exceeds all imagination to conceive what would have been the moral condition of the world if neither Dante, Petrarch, Boccaccio, Chaucer, Shakespeare, Calderon, Lord Bacon, nor Milton had ever existed; if Raphael and Michael Angelo had never been born; if the Hebrew poetry had never been translated; if a revival of the study of Greek literature had never taken place; if no monuments of ancient sculpture had been handed down to us; and if the poetry of the religion of the ancient world had been extinguished together with its belief. The human mind could never, except by the intervention of these excitements, have been awakened to the invention of the grosser sciences, and that application of analytical reasoning to the aberrations of society, which it is now attempted to exalt over the direct expression of the inventive and creative faculty itself.

We have more moral, political, and historical wisdom than we know how to reduce into practice; we have more scientific and economical knowledge than can be accommodated to the just distribution of the produce which it multiplies. The poetry in these systems of thought is concealed by the accumulation of facts and calculating processes. There is no want of knowledge respecting

2. Ecclesiastes vii.2.
3. "Although Rousseau has been thus classed, he was essentially a poet. The others, even Voltaire, were mere reasoners" [Shelley's note].
4. In 1820.

what is wisest and best in morals, government, and political economy, or at least, what is wiser and better than what men now practise and endure. But we let "*I dare not* wait upon *I would,* like the
poor cat in the adage."[5] We want the creative faculty to imagine
that which we know; we want the generous impulse to act that
which we imagine; we want the poetry of life; our calculations have
outrun our conception; we have eaten more than we can digest.
The cultivation of those sciences which have enlarged the limits
of the empire of man over the external world has, for want of the
poetical faculty, proportionally circumscribed those of the internal
world; and man, having enslaved the elements, remains himself a
slave. To what but a cultivation of the mechanical arts in a degree
disproportioned to the presence of the creative faculty, which is
the basis of all knowledge, is to be attributed the abuse of all invention for abridging and combining labor, to the exasperation of
the inequality of mankind? From what other cause has it arisen
that the discoveries which should have lightened have added a
weight to the curse imposed on Adam? Thus poetry and the principle of Self, of which money is the visible incarnation, are the God
and Mammon of the world.

The functions of the poetical faculty are twofold: by one it creates new materials of knowledge and power and pleasure; by the
other it engenders in the mind a desire to reproduce and arrange
them according to a certain rhythm and order which may be called
the beautiful and the good. The cultivation of poetry is never more
to be desired than at periods when, from an excess of the selfish
and calculating principle, the accumulation of the materials of
external life exceed the quantity of the power of assimilating them
to the internal laws of human nature. The body has then become
too unwieldy for that which animates it.

Poetry is indeed something divine. It is at once the center and
circumference of knowledge; it is that which comprehends all science, and that to which all science must be referred. It is at the
same time the root and blossom of all other systems of thought;
it is that from which all spring, and that which adorns all; and
that which, if blighted, denies the fruit and the seed, and withholds
from the barren world the nourishment and the succession of the
scions of the tree of life. It is the perfect and consummate surface
and bloom of all things; it is as the odor and the color of the rose
to the texture of the elements which compose it, as the form and
the splendor of unfaded beauty to the secrets of anatomy and corruption. What were virtue, love, patriotism, friendship; what were
the scenery of this beautiful universe which we inhabit; what were
our consolations on this side of the grave—and what were our aspirations beyond it, if poetry did not ascend to bring light and fire

5. *Macbeth* I.vii.44–45.

from those eternal regions where the owl-winged faculty of calculation dare not ever soar? Poetry is not like reasoning, a power to be
exerted according to the determination of the will. A man cannot
say, "I will compose poetry." The greatest poet even cannot say
it; for the mind in creation is as a fading coal, which some invisible
influence, like an inconstant wind, awakens to transitory brightness;
this power arises from within, like the color of a flower which fades
and changes as it is developed, and the conscious portions of our
natures are unprophetic either of its approach or its departure.[6]
Could this influence be durable in its original purity and force, it
is impossible to predict the greatness of the results; but when composition begins, inspiration is already on the decline, and the most
glorious poetry that has ever been communicated to the world is
probably a feeble shadow of the original conceptions of the poet.
I appeal to the greatest poets of the present day, whether it be not
an error to assert that the finest passages of poetry are produced by
labor and study. The toil and the delay recommended by critics can
be justly interpreted to mean no more than a careful observation
of the inspired moments, and an artificial connection of the spaces
between their suggestions by the intertexture of conventional expressions—a necessity only imposed by the limitedness of the poetical faculty itself; for Milton conceived the *Paradise Lost* as a
whole before he executed it in portions. We have his own authority
also for the muse having "dictated" to him the "unpremeditated
song."[7] And let this be an answer to those who would allege the
fifty-six various readings of the first line of the *Orlando Furioso*.[8]
Compositions so produced are to poetry what mosaic is to painting.
This instinct and intuition of the poetical faculty is still more observable in the plastic and pictorial arts: a great statue or picture
grows under the power of the artist as a child in the mother's
womb; and the very mind which directs the hands in formation
is incapable of accounting to itself for the origin, the gradations,
or the media of the process.

Poetry is the record of the best and happiest[9] moments of
the happiest and best minds. We are aware of evanescent
visitations of thought and feeling sometimes associated with
place or person, sometimes regarding our own mind alone, and
always arising unforeseen and departing unbidden, but elevating
and delightful beyond all expression: so that even in the desire and
regret they leave, there cannot but be pleasure, participating as it
does in the nature of its object. It is as it were the interpenetration

6. This passage reiterates the ancient
belief that the highest poetry is "inspired," and therefore occurs independently of the intention, effort, or consciousness of the poet. Unlike earlier
critics, however, Shelley attributes such
poetry not to a god or muse outside
the poet, but to the unconscious depths
within the poet's own mind.
7. *Paradise Lost* IX.21–24.
8. The epic romance by the 16th-cen-
tury Italian poet Ariosto.
9. In the double sense of "most joyous" and "most apt or felicitous in invention."

of a diviner nature through our own; but its footsteps are like those of a wind over the sea, which the coming calm erases, and whose traces remain only, as on the wrinkled sand which paves it. These and corresponding conditions of being are experienced principally by those of the most delicate sensibility and the most enlarged imagination; and the state of mind produced by them is at war with every base desire. The enthusiasm of virtue, love, patriotism, and friendship is essentially linked with such emotions; and whilst they last, self appears as what it is, an atom to a universe. Poets are not only subject to these experiences as spirits of the most refined organization, but they can color all that they combine with the evanescent hues of this ethereal world; a word or a trait in the representation of a scene or a passion will touch the enchanted chord, and reanimate, in those who have ever experienced these emotions, the sleeping, the cold, the buried image of the past. Poetry thus makes immortal all that is best and most beautiful in the world; it arrests the vanishing apparitions which haunt the interlunations[1] of life, and, veiling them or in language or in form, sends them forth among mankind, bearing sweet news of kindred joy to those with whom their sisters abide—abide, because there is no portal of expression from the caverns of the spirit which they inhabit into the universe of things. Poetry redeems from decay the visitations of the divinity in man.

Poetry turns all things to loveliness; it exalts the beauty of that which is most beautiful, and it adds beauty to that which is most deformed; it marries exultation and horror, grief and pleasure, eternity and change; it subdues to union, under its light yoke, all irreconcilable things. It transmutes all that it touches, and every form moving within the radiance of its presence is changed by wondrous sympathy to an incarnation of the spirit which it breathes: its secret alchemy turns to potable gold the poisonous waters which flow from death through life; it strips the veil of familiarity from the world, and lays bare the naked and sleeping beauty, which is the spirit of its forms.

All things exist as they are perceived—at least in relation to the percipient. "The mind is its own place, and of itself can make a heaven of hell, a hell of heaven."[2] But poetry defeats the curse which binds us to be subjected to the accident of surrounding impressions. And whether it spreads its own figured curtain, or withdraws life's dark veil from before the scene of things, it equally creates for us a being within our being. It makes us the inhabitants of a world to which the familiar world is a chaos. It reproduces the common universe of which we are portions and percipients, and it purges from our inward sight the film of familiarity which obscures from us the wonder of our being. It compels us to feel that

1. The dark intervals between the old and new moon.   2. Satan's speech, *Paradise Lost* I.254–55.

which we perceive, and to imagine that which we know. It creates anew the universe,[3] after it has been annihilated in our minds by the recurrence of impressions blunted by reiteration. It justifies the bold and true words of Tasso: *Non merita nome di creatore, se non Iddio ed il Poeta.*[4]

A poet, as he is the author to others of the highest wisdom, pleasure, virtue, and glory, so he ought personally to be the happiest, the best, the wisest, and the most illustrious of men. As to his glory, let time be challenged to declare whether the fame of any other institutor of human life be comparable to that of a poet. That he is the wisest, the happiest, and the best, inasmuch as he is a poet, is equally incontrovertible: the greatest poets have been men of the most spotless virtue, of the most consummate prudence, and, if we would look into the interior of their lives, the most fortunate of men; and the exceptions, as they regard those who possessed the poetic faculty in a high yet inferior degree, will be found on consideration to confine rather than destroy the rule. Let us for a moment stoop to the arbitration of popular breath, and usurping and uniting in our own persons the incompatible characters of accuser, witness, judge, and executioner, let us decide without trial, testimony, or form, that certain motives of those who are "there sitting where we dare not soar,"[5] are reprehensible. Let us assume that Homer was a drunkard, that Virgil was a flatterer, that Horace was a coward, that Tasso was a madman, that Lord Bacon was a peculator, that Raphael was a libertine, that Spenser was a poet laureate. It is inconsistent with this division of our subject to cite living poets, but posterity has done ample justice to the great names now referred to. Their errors have been weighed and found to have been dust in the balance; if their sins "were as scarlet, they are now white as snow":[6] they have been washed in the blood of the mediator and redeemer, time. Observe in what a ludicrous chaos the imputations of real or fictitious crime have been confused in the contemporary calumnies against poetry and poets;[7] consider how little is, as it appears—or appears, as it is; look to your own motives, and judge not, lest ye be judged.

Poetry, as has been said, differs in this respect from logic, that it is not subject to the control of the active powers of the mind, and that its birth and recurrence have no necessary connection with

3. Shelley's version of a widespread Romantic doctrine: the poetic imagination is, like God, creative, because it re-creates or makes new the old universe. One way in which it does so is by revealing the wonder in the familiar; cf. Coleridge, *Biographia Literaria*, Chapter IV, above, on "freshness of sensation," or "the child's sense of wonder and novelty" combined with the oldest and most familiar appearances.

4. "No one merits the name of Creator except God and the Poet." The sense, though not the exact wording, is to be found in Tasso, the 16th-century Italian poet.

5. *Paradise Lost* IV.829.
6. Isaiah i.18.
7. Shelley's defense of Lord Byron and himself against the charges of immorality frequently voiced by contemporary reviewers.

the consciousness or will. It is presumptuous to determine that these[8] are the necessary conditions of all mental causation, when mental effects are experienced unsusceptible of being referred to them. The frequent recurrence of the poetical power, it is obvious to suppose, may produce in the mind a habit of order and harmony correlative with its own nature and with its effects upon other minds. But in the intervals of inspiration, and they may be frequent without being durable, a poet becomes a man, and is abandoned to the sudden reflux of the influences under which others habitually live. But as he is more delicately organized than other men, and sensible to pain and pleasure, both his own and that of others, in a degree unknown to them, he will avoid the one and pursue the other with an ardor proportioned to this difference. And he renders himself obnoxious to calumny when he neglects to observe the circumstances under which these objects of universal pursuit and flight have disguised themselves in one another's garments.

But there is nothing necessarily evil in this error, and thus cruelty, envy, revenge, avarice, and the passions purely evil have never formed any portion of the popular imputations on the lives of poets.

I have thought it most favorable to the cause of truth to set down these remarks according to the order in which they were suggested to my mind, by a consideration of the subject itself, instead of observing the formality of a polemical reply;[9] but if the view which they contain be just, they will be found to involve a refutation of the arguers against poetry, so far at least as regards the first division of the subject. I can readily conjecture what should have moved the gall of some learned and intelligent writers who quarrel with certain versifiers; I confess myself, like them, unwilling to be stunned by the Theseids[1] of the hoarse Codri of the day. Bavius and Maevius undoubtedly are, as they ever were, insufferable persons. But it belongs to a philosophical critic to distinguish rather than confound.

The first part of these remarks has related to poetry in its elements and principles; and it has been shown, as well as the narrow limits assigned them would permit, that what is called poetry, in a restricted sense, has a common source with all other forms of order and of beauty, according to which the materials of human life are susceptible of being arranged, and which is poetry in a universal sense.

The second part[2] will have for its object an application of these

---

8. I.e., consciousness and will. The concept that some mental processes are "unconscious" (outside our awareness or control) was developed in the late 18th and early 19th centuries.
9. I.e., to Peacock's *Four Ages of Poetry*.
1. Epic poems about Theseus. Codrus

(plural "Codri") was the author of a long, dull *Theseid*, attacked by Juvenal in *Satires* I; "Bavius and Maevius" were would-be poets satirized by Virgil in *Eclogues* III.
2. Shelley completed only the first part of his *Defense*.

principles of the present state of the cultivation of poetry, and a defense of the attempt to idealize the modern forms of manners and opinions, and compel them into a subordination to the imaginative and creative faculty. For the literature of England, an energetic development of which has ever preceded or accompanied a great and free development of the national will, has arisen as it were from a new birth. In spite of the low-thoughted envy which would undervalue contemporary merit, our own will be a memorable age in intellectual achievements, and we live among such philosophers and poets as surpass beyond comparison any who have appeared since the last national struggle for civil and religious liberty.[3] The most unfailing herald, companion, and follower of the awakening of a great people to work a beneficial change in opinion or institution is poetry. At such periods there is an accumulation of the power of communicating and receiving intense and impassioned conceptions respecting man and nature. The persons in whom this power resides may often, as far as regards many portions of their nature, have little apparent correspondence with that spirit of good of which they are the ministers. But even whilst they deny and abjure, they are yet compelled to serve the power which is seated on the throne of their own soul. It is impossible to read the compositions of the most celebrated writers of the present day without being startled with the electric life which burns within their words. They measure the circumference and sound the depths of human nature with a comprehensive and all-penetrating spirit, and they are themselves perhaps the most sincerely astonished at its manifestations; for it is less their spirit than the spirit of the age.[4] Poets are the hierophants[5] of an unapprehended inspiration; the mirrors of the gigantic shadows which futurity casts upon the present; the words which express what they understand not; the trumpets which sing to battle and feel not what they inspire; the influence which is moved not, but moves.[6] Poets are the unacknowledged legislators of the world.

1821   1840

---

3. The age of Milton and the English Civil War.
4. More than any contemporary Shelley recognized the existence and greatness of what we now call "the Romantic movement" in poetry and thought, as well as its relation to the ferment of ideas and aspirations produced by the French Revolution.
5. Priests, the expositors of sacred mysteries.
6. Aristotle had said that God is the "Unmoved Mover" of the universe.

JOHN KEATS
(1795–1821)

1817: *Poems*, Keats's first book.
1818: *Endymion*.
1819: Keats's *annus mirabilis*, in which he writes almost all
his greatest poems.
1820: Publishes the volume *Lamia, Isabella, The Eve of St.
Agnes, and Other Poems*.

No major poet has had a less propitious origin. Keats's father was head
ostler at a London livery stable; he married his employer's daughter and
inherited the business. Mrs. Keats, by all reports, was a strongly sensuous
woman, and a rather casual but affectionate mother to her four children
—John (the first-born), his two brothers, and a sister. Keats was sent to
the Reverend John Clarke's private school at Enfield, where he was a
noisy, high-spirited boy; despite his small physique (when full-grown, he
was barely over five feet in height), he distinguished himself in skylarking
and fist-fights. Here Keats had the good fortune to have as a teacher
Charles Cowden Clarke, son of the headmaster, who later became himself
a man of letters; he encouraged Keats's passion for reading and, both at
school and in the course of their later friendship, introduced him to
Spenser and other poets, to music, and to the theater.

When Keats was 8 his father was killed by a fall from a horse, and
when he was 14, his mother died of tuberculosis. Although the livery
stable had prospered, and £8,000 had been left in trust to the children
by Keats's grandmother, the estate remained tied up in a Chancery suit
for all of Keats's lifetime. The children's guardian, Richard Abbey, was
an unimaginative and practical-minded businessman; he took Keats out
of school at the age of 15 and bound him apprentice to Thomas Hammond, a surgeon and apothecary at Edmonton. In 1815 Keats carried on
his medical studies at Guy's Hospital, London, and the next year qualified
to practice as an apothecary—but almost immediately, over his guardian's
protests, he abandoned medicine for poetry.

This decision was influenced by Keats's friendship with Leigh Hunt,
then editor of the *Examiner* and a leading political radical, a minor poet,
and a prolific writer of criticism and periodical essays. Hunt, the first
successful author of Keats's acquaintance, added his enthusiastic encouragement of Keat's poetic efforts to that of Clarke. More important, Hunt
introduced him to writers greater than himself, Hazlitt, Lamb, and Shelley, as well as to Benjamin Robert Haydon, painter of grandiose historical
and religious canvases. Through Hunt Keats also met John Hamilton
Reynolds, and then Charles Wentworth Dilke and Charles Brown, men
who became his intimate friends and provided him with an essential cir-

cumstance for a fledgling poet, a sympathetic and appreciative audience.

The rapidity and sureness of Keats's development has no match. He did not even undertake poetry until his 18th year, and for the next few years produced album verse which was at best merely competent and at times exhibited a labored vulgarity of sentiment and phrasing. Suddenly, in 1816, he spoke out loud and bold in *On First Looking into Chapman's Homer*, a major sonnet in the grand style. Later that same year he wrote *Sleep and Poetry*, in which he laid out for himself a poetic program deliberately modeled on the careers of the greatest poets, asking only

> for ten years, that I may overwhelm
> Myself in poesy; so I may do the deed
> That my own soul has to itself decreed.

For even while his health was good, Keats felt a foreboding of early death, and applied himself to his art with a desperate urgency. In 1817 Keats went on to compose *Endymion*, an ambitious undertaking of more than 4,000 lines. It is a profuse and often obscure allegory of the poet's search for the ideal of beauty and happiness, but in a number of single passages, it already exhibits the sure movement and phrasing of his mature poetic style. But Keats's critical judgment and aspiration exceeded his achievement: long before he completed it, he declared impatiently that he carried on with the "slipshod" *Endymion* only as a poetic exercise and "trial of invention" and began to block out the more ambitious *Hyperion*, conceived on the model of Milton's *Paradise Lost* in that most demanding of forms, the epic poem. The extent of his success in achieving the Miltonic manner is what made Keats leave off before *Hyperion* was finished, for he recognized that he was uncommonly susceptible to poetic influences, and regarded this as a threat to his poetic individuality. "I will write independently," he insisted. "The Genius of Poetry must work out its own salvation in a man." He had refused the chance of intimacy with Shelley "that I might have my own unfettered scope"; he had broken away from Leigh Hunt's influence lest he get "the reputation of Hunt's *élève*"; now he shied away from domination by Milton's idiosyncratic and powerfully infectious style.

With the year 1818 began a series of disappointments and disasters which culminated in Keats's mortal illness. Sentimental legend used to fix the blame upon two anonymous articles: a scurrilous attack on Keats as a member of the "Cockney School" (that is, Leigh Hunt's radical literary circle) which appeared in the heavily Tory *Blackwood's Magazine*, and a savage mauling of *Endymion* in the *Quarterly Review*. Shelley gave impetus to this myth by his description of Keats as "a pale flower" in *Adonais*, and Byron, who knew even less about Keats, asserted that he was "snuffed out by an article." But in fact, Keats had the good sense to recognize that the attacks were motivated by Tory bias and class snobbery, and he had already passed his own severe judgment on *Endymion*: "My own domestic criticism," he said, "has given me pain without comparison beyond what *Blackwood* or the *Quarterly* could possibly inflict." More important was the financial distress of his brother George and his young bride, who had just emigrated to Kentucky and lost their money in an ill-advised investment; Keats, himself always short of funds, had now to turn to literary journey-work to eke out the family income. His younger brother Tom contracted tuberculosis, and the poet, in constant attendance upon him through the later months of 1818, helplessly watched him waste away until his death that December. In the spring and summer of that year Keats had taken a strenuous walking tour in the English Lake Country, Scotland, and Ireland; it was a glorious adventure, but a totally exhausting one in wet, cold weather, and Keats returned in August with a chronically ulcerated throat made increasingly ominous by the shadow of the tuberculosis which had killed his mother and brother. And in the late fall of 1818 Keats fell desperately, unwillingly, helplessly in love with Fanny Brawne. This pretty, vivacious, and mildly flirtatious girl of 18 had little interest in poetry, but she possessed an alert and sensible mind and loved Keats sincerely, and might well have made him an excellent wife. They became engaged, but Keats's dedication to poetry, his poverty, and his growing illness made marriage impossible and love a torment.

In this period of acute distress and emotional turmoil, within five years of his first trying his hand at poetry, Keats achieved the culmination of his brief poetic career. Between January and September of 1819, masterpiece followed masterpiece in astonishing succession: *The Eve of St. Agnes*, *La Belle Dame sans Merci*, all six of the great *Odes*, *Lamia*, and a sufficient number of fine sonnets to make him, with Wordsworth, the major Romantic craftsman in that form. All of these poems possess the distinctive qualities of the work of Keats's maturity: a slow-paced, gracious movement; a concreteness of description in which all the senses—tactile, gustatory, kinetic, organic, as well as visual and auditory—combine to give the total apprehension of an experience; an intense delight at the sheer existence of things outside himself, the poet seeming to lose his own identity in the fullness of identification with the object he contemplates; and a concentrated felicity of phrasing which reminded Keats's friends, as it has so many critics since, of the language of Shakespeare. And under the rich sensuous surface we find Keats's characteristic presentation of all experience as a tangle of inseparable but irreconcilable opposites. He finds melancholy in delight, and pleasure in pain; he feels the highest intensity of love as an approximation to death; he inclines equally toward a life of indolence and "sensation" and toward a life of thought; he is aware both of the attraction of an imaginative dream world without "disagreeables" and the remorseless pressure of the actual; he aspires at the same time for aesthetic detachment (what in his letters he called "negative capability") and for social responsibility.

His letters, no less remarkable than his poetry, show that Keats felt on his pulses the conflicts he dramatized in his major poems. Above all, they reveal him wrestling with the problem of evil and suffering in the world— what to make of our lives in the discovery that "the world is full of misery and heartbreak, pain, sickness and oppression." To the end of his life Keats, with stubborn courage, refused to seek comfort by substituting for the complexity and contradictions of experience, and of a life which must find its justification in this world, either the simplicity of inherited philosophical doctrines or the absolutes of a religious creed. At the close of his poetic career, in the latter part of 1819, Keats began to rework the epic *Hyperion* into the form of a dream vision which he called *The*

Fall of Hyperion. In the introductory section of this fragment the poet is told by the prophetess Moneta that he has hitherto been merely a dreamer; he must know that

> The poet and the dreamer are distinct,
> Diverse, sheer opposite, antipodes,

and that the height of poetry can only be reached by

> those to whom the miseries of the world
> Are misery, and will not let them rest.

Keats was seemingly planning to undertake a new direction and subject matter, when death intervened.

On the night of February 3, 1820, he coughed up some blood. He refused to evade the truth: "I cannot be deceived in that color; that drop of blood is my death warrant. I must die." That spring and summer a series of hemorrhages rapidly weakened him. In the autumn he allowed himself to be persuaded to seek a milder climate in Italy in the company of Joseph Severn, a young painter; but these last months were only what he called "a posthumous existence." He died in Rome on February 23, 1821, and was buried in the Protestant Cemetery. At times the agony of his disease, the apparent frustration of his hopes for great poetic achievement, and the despair of his passion for Fanny Brawne combined to compel even Keats's brave spirit to bitterness, resentment, and jealousy, but he always recovered his gallantry. His last letter, written to Charles Brown, concludes: "I can scarcely bid you good-bye, even in a letter. I always made an awkward bow. God bless you! John Keats."

No one can read Keats's poems and letters without an undersense of the immense waste of so extraordinary an intellect and genius cut off so early. What he might have accomplished is beyond conjecture; what we do know is that his achievement, when he stopped writing at the age of 24, greatly exceeds that at the corresponding age of Chaucer, Shakespeare, or Milton.

On First Looking into Chapman's Homer[1]

> Much have I traveled in the realms of gold,
>   And many goodly states and kingdoms seen;
>   Round many western islands have I been
> Which bards in fealty to Apollo hold.
> Oft of one wide expanse had I been told   5
>   That deep-browed Homer ruled as his demesne;[2]
>   Yet did I never breathe its pure serene[3]

1. Keats's former schoolteacher, Charles Cowden Clarke, introduced him to Homer in the vigorous translation of the Elizabethan poet George Chapman. They read through the night, and Keats walked home at dawn; this sonnet, his first great poem, reached Clarke by the ten o'clock mail that same morning. That it was Balboa, not Cortez, who caught his first sight of the Pacific from the heights of Darien, in Panama, matters to history but not to poetry.
2. Realm, feudal possession.
3. Clear expanse of air.

Till I heard Chapman speak out loud and bold:
Then felt I like some watcher of the skies
    When a new planet swims into his ken;   10
Or like stout Cortez when with eagle eyes
    He stared at the Pacific—and all his men
Looked at each other with a wild surmise—
    Silent, upon a peak in Darien.

October, 1816   1816

From Sleep and Poetry[1]

* * *

O for ten years, that I may overwhelm
Myself in poesy; so I may do the deed
That my own soul has to itself decreed.
Then will I pass the countries that I see
In long perspective, and continually   100
Taste their pure fountains. First the realm I'll pass
Of Flora, and old Pan:[2] sleep in the grass,
Feed upon apples red, and strawberries,
And choose each pleasure that my fancy sees;
Catch the white-handed nymphs in shady places,   105
To woo sweet kisses from averted faces—
Play with their fingers, touch their shoulders white
Into a pretty shrinking with a bite
As hard as lips can make it: till agreed,
A lovely tale of human life we'll read.   110
And one will teach a tame dove how it best
May fan the cool air gently o'er my rest;
Another, bending o'er her nimble tread,
Will set a green robe floating round her head,
And still will dance with ever varied ease,   115
Smiling upon the flowers and the trees:
Another will entice me on, and on
Through almond blossoms and rich cinnamon;
Till in the bosom of a leafy world

1. At the early age of 21, Keats set himself a rigorous regimen of poetic training modeled on the course followed by the greatest poets. Virgil had established the pattern of beginning with pastoral writing and proceeding gradually to the point at which he was ready to undertake the epic, and this pattern had been deliberately followed by Spenser and Milton. Keats's version of this program, as he describes it here, is to begin with the realm of "Flora, and old Pan" (line 102) and, within ten years, to climb up to the level of poetry dealing with "the agonies, the strife / Of human hearts" (lines 124–25). The latter achievement Keats found best represented among his contemporaries by Wordsworth and, less successfully, by Shelley—Keats's vision of the chariot of poesy (lines 125–154) echoes Shelley's allegorical visions. The program Keats set himself is illuminated by his analysis of Wordsworth's progress in his letter to J. H. Reynolds of May 3, 1818.
2. I.e., the carefree pastoral world. Flora was the Roman goddess of flowers, and Pan the Greek god of pastures, woods, and animal life.

We rest in silence, like two gems upcurled   120
In the recesses of a pearly shell.

And can I ever bid these joys farewell?
Yes, I must pass them for a nobler life,
Where I may find the agonies, the strife
Of human hearts: for lo! I see afar   125
O'ersailing the blue cragginess, a car[3]
And steeds with streamy manes—the charioteer
Looks out upon the winds with glorious fear:
And now the numerous tramplings quiver lightly
Along a huge cloud's ridge; and now with sprightly   130
Wheel downward come they into fresher skies,
Tipped round with silver from the sun's bright eyes.
Still downward with capacious whirl they glide;
And now I see them on the green-hill's side
In breezy rest among the nodding stalks.   135
The charioteer with wond'rous gesture talks
To the trees and mountains; and there soon appear
Shapes of delight, of mystery, and fear,
Passing along before a dusky space
Made by some mighty oaks: as they would chase   140
Some ever-fleeting music on they sweep.
Lo! how they murmur, laugh, and smile, and weep:
Some with upholden hand and mouth severe;
Some with their faces muffled to the ear
Between their arms; some, clear in youthful bloom,   145
Go glad and smilingly athwart the gloom;
Some looking back, and some with upward gaze;
Yes, thousands in a thousand different ways
Flit onward—now a lovely wreath of girls
Dancing their sleek hair into tangled curls;   150
And now broad wings. Most awfully intent
The driver of those steeds is forward bent,
And seems to listen: O that I might know
All that he writes with such a hurrying glow.

The visions all are fled—the car is fled   155
Into the light of heaven, and in their stead
A sense of real things comes doubly strong,
And, like a muddy stream, would bear along
My soul to nothingness: but I will strive
Against all doubtings, and will keep alive   160
The thought of that same chariot, and the strange
Journey it went * * *

Nov.–Dec., 1816   1817

3. This chariot, with its "charioteer" (line 127), represents the higher poetic imagination, which bodies forth (line 138), the matters "of delight, of mystery, and fear" that characterize the grander poetic forms.

On Seeing the Elgin Marbles for the First Time[4]

My spirit is too weak; mortality
  Weighs heavily on me like unwilling sleep,
  And each imagined pinnacle and steep
Of godlike hardship tells me I must die
Like a sick eagle looking at the sky.   5
  Yet 'tis a gentle luxury to weep,
  That I have not the cloudy winds to keep
Fresh for the opening of the morning's eye.
Such dim-conceivéd glories of the brain
  Bring round the heart an indescribable feud;   10
So do these wonders a most dizzy pain,
  That mingles Grecian grandeur with the rude
Wasting of old Time—with a billowy main,
  A sun, a shadow of a magnitude.

                                1817

On the Sea

It keeps eternal whisperings around
  Desolate shores, and with its mighty swell
  Gluts twice ten thousand Caverns, till the spell
Of Hecate leaves them their old shadowy sound.
Often 'tis in such gentle temper found,   5
  That scarcely will the very smallest shell
  Be moved for days from where it sometime fell,
When last the winds of Heaven were unbound.
Oh ye! who have your eyeballs vexed and tired,
  Feast them upon the wideness of the Sea;   10
    Oh ye! whose ears are dinned with uproar rude,
  Or fed too much with cloying melody—
    Sit ye near some old Cavern's Mouth and brood,
Until ye start, as if the sea nymphs quired!

1817   1817

From Endymion[1]

A POETIC ROMANCE

Preface

  Knowing within myself the manner in which this Poem has been produced, it is not without a feeling of regret that I make it

4. Lord Elgin had brought to England in 1806 the marble statues and friezes which adorned the Parthenon at Athens; in 1816 they were purchased by the government for the British Museum. Keats's response to his first sight of these time-worn memorials of Grecian artistry is characteristically intense, mixed, and subtly analyzed.

1. This poem of more than 4,000 lines (based on the classical myth of a mortal beloved by the goddess of the moon)

public.

What manner I mean, will be quite clear to the reader, who must soon perceive great inexperience, immaturity, and every error denoting a feverish attempt, rather than a deed accomplished. The two first books, and indeed the two last, I feel sensible are not of such completion as to warrant their passing the press; nor should they if I thought a year's castigation would do them any good—it will not: the foundations are too sandy. It is just that this young ster should die away: a sad thought for me, if I had not some hope that while it is dwindling I may be plotting, and fitting myself for verses fit to live.

This may be speaking too presumptuously, and may deserve a punishment: but no feeling man will be forward.to inflict it: he will leave me alone, with the conviction that there is not a fiercer hell than the failure in a great object. This is not written with the least atom of purpose to forestall criticisms of course, but from the desire I have to conciliate men who are competent to look, and who do look with a zealous eye, to the honor of English literature.

The imagination of a boy is healthy, and the mature imagination of a man is healthy; but there is a space of life between, in which the soul is in a ferment, the character undecided, the way of life uncertain, the ambition thick-sighted: thence proceeds mawkishness, and all the thousand bitters which those men I speak of must necessarily taste in going over the following pages.

I hope I have not in too late a day touched the beautiful mythology of Greece, and dulled its brightness: for I wish to try once more,[2] before I bid it farewell.

TEIGNMOUTH, April 10, 1818.

From *Book I*
[A THING OF BEAUTY]

A thing of beauty is a joy forever:
Its loveliness increases; it will never
Pass into nothingness; but still will keep
A bower quiet for us, and a sleep

tells of Endymion's long and agonized search for an immortal goddess whom he had seen in several visions. In the course of his wanderings he comes upon an Indian maid who had been abandoned by the followers of Bacchus, and to his utter despair succumbs to a sensual passion for her, in apparent betrayal of his love for his heavenly ideal. In the resolution, the Indian maid reveals that she is herself Cynthia (Diana), goddess of the moon, and also the celestial goddess of his earlier visions.

Keats set himself to writing a long poem before he was entirely ready in range of knowledge, clarity of thought,

or stylistic assurance; the poem reaches a high level only in single passages. The interpretation which seems best to fit the text is that ideal love and imaginative beauty are to be found only by way of instinctual impulses and earthly passion, which the ideal repeats, in one of Keats's phrases, "in a finer tone." The poem's constitution is so cloudy, however, that its purport is disputed. But Keats has disarmed all external criticism by his self-criticism in the candid and insightful Preface, which has become a classic statement of the characteristics of unripe genius.

2. In *Hyperion*, which Keats was already planning.

Full of sweet dreams, and health, and quiet breathing. 5
Therefore, on every morrow, are we wreathing
A flowery band to bind us to the earth,
Spite of despondence, of the inhuman dearth
Of noble natures, of the gloomy days,
Of all the unhealthy and o'er-darkened ways 10
Made for our searching: yes, in spite of all,
Some shape of beauty moves away the pall
From our dark spirits. Such the sun, the moon,
Trees old, and young, sprouting a shady boon
For simple sheep; and such are daffodils 15
With the green world they live in; and clear rills
That for themselves a cooling covert make
'Gainst the hot season; the mid-forest brake,[3]
Rich with a sprinkling of fair musk-rose blooms:
And such too is the grandeur of the dooms[4] 20
We have imagined for the mighty dead;
All lovely tales that we have heard or read:
An endless fountain of immortal drink,
Pouring unto us from the heaven's brink.[5]

Nor do we merely feel these essences 25
For one short hour; no, even as the trees
That whisper round a temple become soon
Dear as the temple's self, so does the moon,
The passion poesy, glories infinite,
Haunt us till they become a cheering light 30
Unto our souls, and bound to us so fast,
That, whether there be shine, or gloom o'ercast,
They always must be with us, or we die.

Therefore, 'tis with full happiness that I
Will trace the story of Endymion. 35
The very music of the name has gone
Into my being, and each pleasant scene
Is growing fresh before me as the green
Of our own valleys * * *

[THE "PLEASURE THERMOMETER"]

"Peona![6] ever have I longed to slake
My thirst for the world's praises: nothing base, 770
No merely slumberous phantasm, could unlace
The stubborn canvas for my voyage prepared—
Though now 'tis tattered; leaving my bark bared
And sullenly drifting: yet my higher hope

3. Thicket.
4. Judgments.
5. The poet sets up, and searches to resolve, the basic opposition between the inevitably "mortal" pleasures in this life and the conceived possibility of "immortal" delight. Thus "essences" (line 25) seem to be the things of
beauty in this world, purged of the alloy of sadness and mutability that spoils ordinary experience. The central passage dealing with this theme is below, Book I, lines 777 ff.
6. The sister to whom Endymion confides his troubles.

Is of too wide, too rainbow-large a scope,   775
To fret at myriads of earthly wrecks.
Wherein lies happiness?[7] In that which becks
Our ready minds to fellowship divine,
A fellowship with essence; till we shine,
Full alchemized,[8] and free of space. Behold   780
The clear religion of heaven! Fold
A rose leaf round thy finger's taperness,
And soothe thy lips: hist, when the airy stress
Of music's kiss impregnates the free winds,
And with a sympathetic touch unbinds   785
Aeolian[9] magic from their lucid wombs:
Then old songs waken from enclouded tombs;
Old ditties sigh above their father's grave;
Ghosts of melodious prophesyings rave
Round every spot where trod Apollo's foot;   790
Bronze clarions awake, and faintly bruit,[1]
Where long ago a giant battle was;
And, from the turf, a lullaby doth pass
In every place where infant Orpheus slept.
Feel we these things?—that moment have we stepped   795
Into a sort of oneness, and our state
Is like a floating spirit's. But there are
Richer entanglements, enthrallments far
More self-destroying, leading, by degrees,
To the chief intensity: the crown of these   800
Is made of love and friendship, and sits high
Upon the forehead of humanity.
All its more ponderous and bulky worth
Is friendship, whence there ever issues forth
A steady splendor; but at the tiptop,   805
There hangs by unseen film, an orbèd drop
Of light, and that is love: its influence,
Thrown in our eyes, genders a novel sense,
At which we start and fret; till in the end,
Melting into its radiance, we blend,   810
Mingle, and so become a part of it—

7. Of lines 777–857, Keats wrote to his publisher, John Taylor: "When I wrote it, it was the regular stepping of the Imagination towards a Truth. My having written that Argument will perhaps be of the greatest Service to me of anything I ever did—It set before me at once the gradations of Happiness even like a kind of Pleasure Thermometer, and is my first step towards the chief attempt in the Drama—the playing of different Natures with Joy and Sorrow." The gradations on this "Pleasure Thermometer" mark the stages on the way to what Keats calls "happiness" (line 777)—his secular version of the religious concept of "felicity" which, in the orthodox view, is to be achieved by a surrender of oneself to God. For Keats the way to happiness lies through a fusion of ourselves, first sensuously, with the lovely objects of nature and art (lines 781–97), then on a higher level, with other human beings through "love and friendship" (line 801) but in the final degree, only through sexual love. By this "self-destroying," or total loss of personal identity through our imaginative identification with a beloved person outside ourselves, we escape from the material and spatial limits, and from the self-centered condition, of ordinary experience, to achieve a "fellowship with essence," which is a kind of immortality within our mortal existence (line 844).
8. Transformed by alchemy from a base to a precious metal.
9. From Aeolus, god of winds.
1. Make a sound.

Nor with aught else can our souls interknit
So wingedly: when we combine therewith,
Life's self is nourished by its proper pith,[2]
And we are nurtured like a pelican brood.[3]   815
Aye, so delicious is the unsating food,
That men, who might have towered in the van
Of all the congregated world, to fan
And winnow from the coming step of time
All chaff of custom, wipe away all slime   820
Left by men-slugs and human serpentry,
Have been content to let occasion die,
Whilst they did sleep in love's elysium.
And, truly, I would rather be struck dumb,
Than speak against this ardent listlessness: 825
For I have ever thought that it might bless
The world with benefits unknowingly;
As does the nightingale, upperchéd high,
And cloistered among cool and bunchéd leaves—
She sings but to her love, nor e'er conceives   830
How tiptoe Night holds back her dark gray hood.[4]
Just so may love, although 'tis understood
The mere commingling of passionate breath,
Produce more than our searching witnesseth:
What I know not: but who, of men, can tell   835
That flowers would bloom, or that green fruit would swell
To melting pulp, that fish would have bright mail,
The earth its dower of river, wood, and vale,
The meadows runnels, runnels pebble-stones,
The seed its harvest, or the lute its tones,   840
Tones ravishment, or ravishment its sweet
If human souls did never kiss and greet?

"Now, if this earthly love has power to make
Men's being mortal, immortal; to shake
Ambition from their memories, and brim   845
Their measure of content: what merest whim,
Seems all this poor endeavor after fame,
To one, who keeps within his steadfast aim
A love immortal, an immortal too.
Look not so 'wildered; for these things are true,   850
And never can be born of atomies[5]
That buzz about our slumbers, like brain-flies,
Leaving us fancy-sick. No, no, I'm sure,
My restless spirit never could endure
To brood so long upon one luxury,   855
Unless it did, though fearfully, espy
A hope beyond the shadow of a dream."

---

2. Its own elemental substance.
3. Young pelicans were once thought to feed on their mother's flesh; so our life be nourished by their mother's blood; so our life is nourished by another's life, with which it fuses in love.
4. I.e., in order better to hear.
5. Mites, tiny flying insects.

From *Book IV*

[THE CAVE OF QUIETUDE[1]]

There lies a den,
Beyond the seeming confines of the space
Made for the soul to wander in and trace
Its own existence, of remotest glooms.   515
Dark regions are around it, where the tombs
Of buried griefs the spirit sees, but scarce
One hour doth linger weeping, for the pierce
Of new-born woe it feels more inly smart:
And in these regions many a venomed dart   520
At random flies; they are the proper home
Of every ill: the man is yet to come
Who hath not journeyed in this native hell.
But few have ever felt how calm and well
Sleep may be had in that deep den of all.   525
There anguish does not sting; nor pleasure pall:
Woe-hurricanes beat ever at the gate,
Yet all is still within and desolate.
Beset with painful gusts, within ye hear
No sound so loud as when on curtained bier   530
The death-watch tick[2] is stifled. Enter none
Who strive therefore: on the sudden it is won.
Just when the sufferer begins to burn,
Then it is free to him; and from an urn,
Still fed by melting ice, he takes a draught—   535
Young Semele[3] such richness never quaffed
In her maternal longing! Happy gloom!
Dark Paradise! where pale becomes the bloom
Of health by due; where silence dreariest
Is most articulate; where hopes infest;   540
Where those eyes are the brightest far that keep
Their lids shut longest in a dreamless sleep.
O happy spirit-home! O wondrous soul!
Pregnant with such a den to save the whole

1. Endymion, although divided between his heavenly and earthly loves, has surrendered to his passion for the human Indian maiden. A pair of winged horses have carried the couple aloft, but as Endymion turns to his bride, she dissolves in the cold moonlight, leaving him alone. He plunges into the "Cave of Quietude"—a mental state (a "native hell," line 523) of total desolation, a "Dark Paradise" of pain and despair so extreme that they become indistinguishable from their own opposites of pleasure and happiness. Compare this description to the lesson of the nature of "high tragedy"—the aesthetic contemplation of human suffering which has passed beyond the bounds of both pain and pleasure—which the poet reads in the "wan" but "bright-blanched" face of Moneta; below, *The Fall of Hyperion*, I.256–82.
2. The death-watch beetle makes a sound like the ticking of a watch, supposed to portend death.
3. Semele presumptuously prayed that Jove unite with her not as man but as a god. When he did so, she was consumed by flames, but conceived Bacchus who was rescued by Jove from the maternal ashes.

In thine own depth.[4] Hail, gentle Carian![5]   545
For, never since thy griefs and woes began,
Hast thou felt so content: a grievous feud
Hath led thee to this Cave of Quietude.
Aye, his lulled soul was there, although upborne
With dangerous speed: and so he did not mourn   550
Because he knew not whither he was going.
So happy was he, not the aërial blowing
Of trumpets at clear parley[6] from the east
Could rouse from that fine relish, that high feast.
They stung the feathered horse:[7] with fierce alarm   555
He flapped towards the sound. Alas, no charm
Could lift Endymion's head, or he had viewed
A skyey masque,[8] a pinioned multitude—
And silvery was its passing: voices sweet
Warbling the while as if to lull and greet   560
The wanderer in his path. Thus warbled they,
While past the vision went in bright array.[9]

Apr.–Nov., 1817   1818

In Drear-Nighted December

1

In drear-nighted December,
    Too happy, happy tree,
Thy branches ne'er remember
    Their green felicity:
    The north cannot undo them   5
    With a sleety whistle through them;
Nor frozen thawings glue them
    From budding at the prime.[1]

2

In drear-nighted December,
    Too happy, happy brook,   10
Thy bubblings ne'er remember
    Apollo's[2] summer look;
    But with a sweet forgetting,
    They stay their crystal fretting,
Never, never petting[3]   15
    About the frozen time.

---

4. The apparent meaning is that the soul, in the utter depth of its suffering, can produce a cave ("den") of quietude in which to heal itself.
5. Endymion was a native of Caria, in Asia Minor.
6. A trumpet call to assembly.
7. The winged horse on whose back Endymion lay.
8. A dramatic entertainment, involving dialogue, song, and dance by masked actors. "Pinioned": winged.
9. The flying chorus in this masque go on to sing a celebration of Diana's coming marriage—to Endymion himself, although he, listening, does not know it.
1. The earliest period; hence, spring.
2. I.e., the sun's.
3. Fretting.

3

Ah! would 'twere so with many
  A gentle girl and boy!
But were there ever any
      Writhed not of passéd joy?   20
  The feel of *not* to feel it,[4]
When there is none to heal it
Nor numbéd sense to steel it,
  Was never said in rhyme.

December, 1817   1829

On Sitting Down to Read *King Lear* Once Again[1]

O golden-tongued Romance with serene lute!
  Fair pluméd Siren! Queen of far away!
  Leave melodizing on this wintry day,
Shut up thine olden pages, and be mute:
Adieu! for once again the fierce dispute   5
  Betwixt damnation and impassioned clay
  Must I burn through; once more humbly essay
The bitter-sweet of this Shakespearean fruit.
Chief Poet! and ye clouds of Albion,[2]
  Begetters of our deep eternal theme,   10
When through the old oak forest I am gone,
  Let me not wander in a barren dream,
But when I am consuméd in the fire,
Give me new Phoenix[3] wings to fly at my desire.

January, 1818   1838, 1848

When I Have Fears[4]

When I have fears that I may cease to be
  Before my pen has gleaned my teeming brain,
Before high-piléd books, in charact'ry,[5]
  Hold like rich garners the full-ripened grain;
When I behold, upon the night's starred face,   5
  Huge cloudy symbols of a high romance,

---

4. This version of line 21, from a recently discovered autograph copy, is adopted in preference to the earlier version in the printed form of the poem: "To know the change and feel it."
1. Keats pauses in revising *Endymion: A Poetic Romance* to read again Shakespeare's great tragedy. The word "Siren" (line 2) indicates Keats's feeling that Romance was enticing him from the poet's prime duty, to deal with "the agonies, the strife / Of human hearts" (*Sleep and Poetry*, lines 124–125).

2. Albion is the old Celtic name for England; *King Lear* is set in Celtic Britain. The "oak forest" of line 11 refers either to *King Lear* or (more likely) to the romance, *Endymion*.
3. The fabulous bird which periodically burns itself to death in order to rise anew from the ashes.
4. The first, and one of the most successful, of Keats's attempts at the sonnet in the Shakespearean rhyme scheme.
5. Characters; written or printed letters of the alphabet.

And think that I may never live to trace
  Their shadows, with the magic hand of chance;
And when I feel, fair creature of an hour,
  That I shall never look upon thee more,   10
Never have relish in the faery power
  Of unreflecting love!—then on the shore
Of the wide world I stand alone, and think
Till Love and Fame to nothingness do sink.

January, 1818   1848

To Homer

Standing aloof in giant ignorance,
  Of thee I hear and of the Cyclades,[6]
As one who sits ashore and longs perchance
  To visit dolphin-coral in deep seas.
So thou wast blind!—but then the veil was rent;   5
  For Jove uncurtained Heaven to let thee live,
And Neptune made for thee a spumy tent,
  And Pan made sing for thee his forest-hive;
Aye, on the shores of darkness there is light,
  And precipices show untrodden green;   10
There is a budding morrow in midnight,
  There is a triple sight in blindness keen;
Such seeing hadst thou, as it once befell
To Dian, Queen of Earth, and Heaven, and Hell.[7]

1818   1848

The Eve of St. Agnes[1]

1

St. Agnes' Eve—Ah, bitter chill it was!
  The owl, for all his feathers, was a-cold;
The hare limped trembling through the frozen grass,

6. A group of islands in the Aegean Sea, off Greece; Keats's allusion is to his ignorance of the Greek language.

7. In later cults Diana was worshiped as a three-figured goddess, the deity of nature and of the moon, as well as queen of hell. The "triple sight" which blind Homer paradoxically commands is of these three regions, and also of heaven, sea, and earth (the realms of Jove, Neptune, and Pan, lines 6–8).

1. St. Agnes, martyred ca. 303 at the age of 13, is the patron saint of virgins. Legend has it that if a virtuous young girl performs the proper ritual, she will dream of her future husband on the evening before St. Agnes' Day, which falls on January 21. Keats combined this superstition with the Romeo and Juliet theme of young love thwarted by feuding families and told the story in a sequence of sensuously evolving Spenserian stanzas. The luxurious product has been called "a colored dream," but it is a complexly meaningful dream, in which the strong contrasts of heat and cold, crimson and silver, youth and age, revelry and austere penance, sensuality and chastity, life and death, hell and heaven, assume symbolic values, and are used to show forth the extremes of spirituality and grossness which are mediated by a candid physicality, the difference between the dream and the reality of passion, and the ambivalences at the center of human love. The poem is Keats's first complete success in sustained narrative.

And silent was the flock in woolly fold:
Numb were the Beadsman's[2] fingers, while he told   5
His rosary, and while his frosted breath,
Like pious incense from a censer old,
Seemed taking flight for heaven, without a death,
Past the sweet Virgin's picture, while his prayer he saith.

2

His prayer he saith, this patient, holy man;   10
Then takes his lamp, and riseth from his knees,
And back returneth, meager, barefoot, wan,
Along the chapel aisle by slow degrees:
The sculptured dead, on each side, seem to freeze,
Imprisoned in black, purgatorial rails: 15
Knights, ladies, praying in dumb orat'ries,[3]
He passeth by; and his weak spirit fails
To think[4] how they may ache in icy hoods and mails.

3

Northward he turneth through a little door,
And scarce three steps, ere Music's golden tongue   20
Flattered[5] to tears this aged man and poor;
But no—already had his deathbell rung:
The joys of all his life were said and sung:
His was harsh penance on St. Agnes' Eve:
Another way he went, and soon among   25
Rough ashes sat he for his soul's reprieve,
And all night kept awake, for sinner's sake to grieve.

4

That ancient Beadsman heard the prelude soft;
And so it chanced, for many a door was wide,
From hurry to and fro. Soon, up aloft,   30
The silver, snarling trumpets 'gan to chide:
The level chambers, ready with their pride,[6]
Were glowing to receive a thousand guests:
The carvéd angels, ever eager-eyed,
Stared, where upon their heads the cornice rests,   35
With hair blown back, and wings put cross-wise on their breasts.

5

At length burst in the argent revelry,[7]
With plume, tiara, and all rich array,
Numerous as shadows haunting fairily
The brain, new stuffed, in youth, with triumphs gay   40
Of old romance. These let us wish away,
And turn, sole-thoughted, to one Lady there,
Whose heart had brooded, all that wintry day,
On love, and winged St. Agnes' saintly care,
As she had heard old dames full many times declare.   45

---

2. A "beadsman" is paid to pray for
his benefactor. He "tells" (counts) the
beads of his rosary, to keep track of
his prayers.
3. Silent chapels.

4. I.e., when he thinks.
5. Beguiled, charmed.
6. Ostentation.
7. Silver-clad revelers.

6

They told her how, upon St. Agnes' Eve,
Young virgins might have visions of delight,
And soft adorings from their loves receive
Upon the honeyed middle of the night,
If ceremonies due they did aright;   50
As, supperless to bed they must retire,
And couch supine their beauties, lily white;
Nor look behind, nor sideways, but require
Of Heaven with upward eyes for all that they desire.

7

Full of this whim was thoughtful Madeline: 55
The music, yearning like a God in pain,
She scarcely heard: her maiden eyes divine,
Fixed on the floor, saw many a sweeping train
Pass by—she heeded not at all: in vain
Came many a tiptoe, amorous cavalier,   60
And back retired; not cooled by high disdain;
But she saw not: her heart was otherwhere:
She sighed for Agnes' dreams, the sweetest of the year.

8

She danced along with vague, regardless eyes,
Anxious her lips, her breathing quick and short: 65
The hallowed hour was near at hand: she sighs
Amid the timbrels,[8] and the thronged resort
Of whisperers in anger, or in sport;
'Mid looks of love, defiance, hate, and scorn,
Hoodwinked with faery fancy;[9] all amort,   70
Save to St. Agnes and her lambs unshorn,[1]
And all the bliss to be before tomorrow morn.

9

So, purposing each moment to retire,
She lingered still. Meantime, across the moors,
Had come young Porphyro, with heart on fire   75
For Madeline. Beside the portal doors,
Buttressed from moonlight,[2] stands he, and implores
All saints to give him sight of Madeline,
But for one moment in the tedious hours,
That he might gaze and worship all unseen;   80
Perchance speak, kneel, touch, kiss—in sooth such things have been.

10

He ventures in: let no buzzed whisper tell:
All eyes be muffled, or a hundred swords
Will storm his heart, Love's fev'rous citadel:
For him, those chambers held barbarian hordes,   85
Hyena foemen, and hot-blooded lords,

8. Small drums.
9. She was blinded ("hoodwinked"—as though the eyes were covered by a hood) by her charmed imagination; "all amort": as though dead.
1. On St. Agnes' Day it was the custom to offer lambs' wool at the altar, to be made into cloth by nuns.
2. Sheltered from the moonlight by the buttresses (the supports projecting from the wall).

Whose very dogs would execrations howl
Against his lineage: not one breast affords
Him any mercy, in that mansion foul,
Save one old beldame,[3] weak in body and in soul.   90

11

Ah, happy chance! the aged creature came,
Shuffling along with ivory-headed wand,[4]
To where he stood, hid from the torch's flame,
Behind a broad hall-pillar, far beyond
The sound of merriment and chorus bland:[5]   95
He startled her; but soon she knew his face,
And grasped his fingers in her palsied hand,
Saying, "Mercy, Porphyro! hie thee from this place;
They are all here tonight, the whole bloodthirsty race!

12

"Get hence! get hence! there's dwarfish Hildebrand;   100
He had a fever late, and in the fit
He curséd thee and thine, both house and land:
Then there's that old Lord Maurice, not a whit
More tame for his gray hairs—Alas me! flit!
Flit like a ghost away."—"Ah, Gossip[6] dear,   105
We're safe enough; here in this armchair sit,
And tell me how"—"Good Saints! not here, not here;
Follow me, child, or else these stones will be thy bier."

13

He followed through a lowly archéd way,
Brushing the cobwebs with his lofty plume,   110
And as she muttered "Well-a—well-a-day!"
He found him in a little moonlight room,
Pale, latticed, chill, and silent as a tomb.
"Now tell me where is Madeline," said he,
"O tell me, Angela, by the holy loom   115
Which none but secret sisterhood may see,
When they St. Agnes' wool are weaving piously."

14

"St. Agnes! Ah! it is St. Agnes' Eve—
Yet men will murder upon holy days:
Thou must hold water in a witch's sieve,[7]   120
And be liege lord of all the Elves and Fays,
To venture so: it fills me with amaze
To see thee, Porphyro!—St. Agnes' Eve!
God's help! my lady fair the conjuror plays[8]
This very night: good angels her deceive!   125
But let me laugh awhile, I've mickle[9] time to grieve."

15

Feebly she laugheth in the languid moon,

---

3. Old (and usually, homely) woman; an ironic development in English from the French meaning, "lovely lady."
4. Staff.
5. Soft.
6. In the old sense: godmother, or old friend.
7. A sieve made to hold water by witchcraft.
8. I.e., in her attempt to evoke the vision of her lover.
9. Much.

While Porphyro upon her face doth look,
Like puzzled urchin on an aged crone
Who keepeth closed a wondrous riddle-book,   130
As spectacled she sits in chimney nook.
But soon his eyes grew brilliant, when she told
His lady's purpose; and he scarce could brook[1]
Tears, at the thought of those enchantments cold,
And Madeline asleep in lap of legends old.   135

16

Sudden a thought came like a full-blown rose,
Flushing his brow, and in his painéd heart
Made purple riot: then doth he propose
A stratagem, that makes the beldame start:
"A cruel man and impious thou art: 140
Sweet lady, let her pray, and sleep, and dream
Alone with her good angels, far apart
From wicked men like thee. Go, go!—I deem
Thou canst not surely be the same that thou didst seem."

17

"I will not harm her, by all saints I swear,"   145
Quoth Porphyro: "O may I ne'er find grace
When my weak voice shall whisper its last prayer,
If one of her soft ringlets I displace,
Or look with ruffian passion in her face:
Good Angela, believe me by these tears;   150
Or I will, even in a moment's space,
Awake, with horrid shout, my foemen's ears,
And beard them, though they be more fanged than wolves and
    bears."

18

"Ah! why wilt thou affright a feeble soul?
A poor, weak, palsy-stricken, churchyard thing,   155
Whose passing bell[2] may ere the midnight toll;
Whose prayers for thee, each morn and evening,
Were never missed."—Thus plaining,[3] doth she bring
A gentler speech from burning Porphyro;
So woeful, and of such deep sorrowing,   160
That Angela gives promise she will do
Whatever he shall wish, betide her weal or woe.

19

Which was, to lead him, in close secrecy,
Even to Madeline's chamber, and there hide
Him in a closet, of such privacy   165
That he might see her beauty unespied,
And win perhaps that night a peerless bride,
While legioned faeries paced the coverlet,
And pale enchantment held her sleepy-eyed.

1. "Brook" ordinarily means "endure,"   2. Death knell.
although Keats apparently uses it for   3. Complaining.
"restrain."

Never on such a night have lovers met,   170
Since Merlin paid his Demon all the monstrous debt.[4]

20

"It shall be as thou wishest," said the Dame:
"All cates[5] and dainties shall be storéd there
Quickly on this feast night: by the tambour frame[6]
Her own lute thou wilt see: no time to spare,   175
For I am slow and feeble, and scarce dare
On such a catering trust my dizzy head.
Wait here, my child, with patience; kneel in prayer
The while: Ah! thou must needs the lady wed,
Or may I never leave my grave among the dead."   180

21

So saying, she hobbled off with busy fear.
The lover's endless minutes slowly passed:
The dame returned, and whispered in his ear
To follow her; with aged eyes aghast
From fright of dim espial. Safe at last,   185
Through many a dusky gallery, they gain
The maiden's chamber, silken, hushed, and chaste;
Where Porphyro took covert, pleased amain.[7]
His poor guide hurried back with agues in her brain.

22

Her falt'ring hand upon the balustrade,   190
Old Angela was feeling for the stair,
When Madeline, St. Agnes' charméd maid,
Rose, like a missioned spirit,[8] unaware:
With silver taper's light, and pious care,
She turned, and down the aged gossip led   195
To a safe level matting. Now prepare,
Young Porphyro, for gazing on that bed;
She comes, she comes again, like ringdove frayed[9] and fled.

23

Out went the taper as she hurried in;
Its little smoke, in pallid moonshine, died: 200
She closed the door, she panted, all akin
To spirits of the air, and visions wide:
No uttered syllable, or, woe betide!
But to her heart, her heart was voluble,
Paining with eloquence her balmy side;   205
As though a tongueless nightingale should swell
Her throat in vain, and die, heart-stifled, in her dell.

24

A casement high and triple-arched there was,
All garlanded with carven imag'ries
Of fruits, and flowers, and bunches of knot-grass,   210

4. It is not clear what episode in the Arthurian legends this refers to—possibly the one in which Merlin, the magician, paid for his magic with his life when the wily lady Vivien turned one of his own spells against him.

5. Delicacies.
6. A drum-shaped embroidery frame.
7. Mightily.
8. Like an angel sent on a mission.
9. Frightened.

And diamonded with panes of quaint device,
Innumerable of stains and splendid dyes,
As are the tiger moth's deep-damasked wings;
And in the midst, 'mong thousand heraldries,
And twilight saints, and dim emblazonings, 215
A shielded scutcheon blushed with blood of queens and kings.[1]

25

Full on this casement shone the wintry moon,
And threw warm gules[2] on Madeline's fair breast,
As down she knelt for heaven's grace and boon;[3]
Rose-bloom fell on her hands, together pressed, 220
And on her silver cross soft amethyst,
And on her hair a glory, like a saint:
She seemed a splendid angel, newly dressed,
Save wings, for heaven—Porphyro grew faint:
She knelt, so pure a thing, so free from mortal taint. 225

26

Anon his heart revives: her vespers done,
Of all its wreathéd pearls her hair she frees;
Unclasps her warméd jewels one by one;
Loosens her fragrant bodice; by degrees
Her rich attire creeps rustling to her knees: 230
Half-hidden, like a mermaid in sea-weed,
Pensive awhile she dreams awake, and sees,
In fancy, fair St. Agnes in her bed,
But dares not look behind, or all the charm is fled.

27

Soon, trembling in her soft and chilly nest, 235
In sort of wakeful swoon, perplexed[4] she lay,
Until the poppied warmth of sleep oppressed
Her soothéd limbs, and soul fatigued away;
Flown, like a thought, until the morrow-day;
Blissfully havened both from joy and pain; 240
Clasped like a missal where swart Paynims pray;[5]
Blinded alike from sunshine and from rain,
As though a rose should shut, and be a bud again.

28

Stol'n to this paradise, and so entranced,
Porphyro gazed upon her empty dress, 245
And listened to her breathing, if it chanced
To wake into a slumberous tenderness;
Which when he heard, that minute did he bless,
And breathed himself: then from the closet crept,
Noiseless as fear in a wide wilderness, 250

---

1. In the stained glass are represented many genealogical symbols ("heraldries") and other dim-colored devices ("emblazonings"); among these, a shield-shaped escutcheon signified by its colored symbols that the family was of royal lineage (of the "blood of queens and kings").
2. In heraldry, the color red.

3. Gift, blessing.
4. In a confused state between waking and sleeping.
5. Variously interpreted; perhaps: held tightly, cherished, like a Christian prayer book ("missal") in a land where the religion is that of dark-skinned pagans ("swart Paynims").

And over the hushed carpet, silent, stepped,
And 'tween the curtains peeped, where, lo!—how fast she slept.

29

Then by the bedside, where the faded moon
Made a dim, silver twilight, soft he set
A table, and, half anguished, threw thereon   255
A cloth of woven crimson, gold, and jet—
O for some drowsy Morphean amulet![6]
The boisterous, midnight, festive clarion,[7]
The kettledrum, and far-heard clarinet,
Affray his ears, though but in dying tone—   260
The hall door shuts again, and all the noise is gone.

30

And still she slept an azure-lidded sleep,
In blanchéd linen, smooth, and lavendered,
While he from forth the closet brought a heap
Of candied apple, quince, and plum, and gourd;[8]   265
With jellies soother than the creamy curd,
And lucent syrups, tinct with cinnamon;
Manna and dates, in argosy transferred
From Fez;[9] and spicéd dainties, every one,
From silken Samarcand to cedared Lebanon.   270

31

These delicates he heaped with glowing hand
On golden dishes and in baskets bright
Of wreathéd silver: sumptuous they stand
In the retired quiet of the night,
Filling the chilly room with perfume light.—   275
"And now, my love, my seraph[1] fair, awake!
Thou art my heaven, and I thine eremite:[2]
Open thine eyes, for meek St. Agnes' sake,
Or I shall drowse beside thee, so my soul doth ache."

32

Thus whispering, his warm, unnervéd arm   280
Sank in her pillow. Shaded was her dream
By the dusk curtains: 'twas a midnight charm
Impossible to melt as icéd stream:
The lustrous salvers in the moonlight gleam;
Broad golden fringe upon the carpet lies: 285
It seemed he never, never could redeem
From such a steadfast spell his lady's eyes;
So mused awhile, entoiled in wooféd fantasies.[3]

33

Awakening up, he took her hollow lute—
Tumultuous—and, in chords that tenderest be,   290

6. Sleep-producing charm.
7. High-pitched trumpet.
8. Melon. According to the legend, the dream lover would bring the virgin a feast of delicacies.
9. I.e., jellies softer ("soother") than the curds of cream, clear ("lucent") syrups tinged with cinnamon, and sweet gums ("manna") and dates transported in a great merchant ship ("argosy") from Fez.
1. One of the highest order of angels.
2. A religious hermit.
3. Entangled in a weave of fantasies.

He played an ancient ditty, long since mute,
In Provence called "*La belle dame sans merci*":[4]
Close to her ear touching the melody;
Wherewith disturbed, she uttered a soft moan:
He ceased—she panted quick—and suddenly   295
Her blue affrayéd eyes wide open shone:
Upon his knees he sank, pale as smooth-sculptured stone.

34

Her eyes were open, but she still beheld,
Now wide awake, the vision of her sleep:
There was a painful change, that nigh expelled   300
The blisses of her dream so pure and deep,
At which fair Madeline began to weep,
And moan forth witless words with many a sigh;
While still her gaze on Porphyro would keep,
Who knelt, with joinéd hands and piteous eye,   305
Fearing to move or speak, she looked so dreamingly.

35

"Ah, Porphyro!" said she, "but even now
Thy voice was at sweet tremble in mine ear,
Made tunable with every sweetest vow;
And those sad eyes were spiritual and clear: 310
How changed thou art! how pallid, chill, and drear!
Give me that voice again, my Porphyro,
Those looks immortal, those complainings dear!
Oh leave me not in this eternal woe,
For if thou diest, my Love, I know not where to go."   315

36

Beyond a mortal man impassioned far
At these voluptuous accents, he arose,
Ethereal, flushed, and like a throbbing star
Seen mid the sapphire heaven's deep repose;
Into her dream he melted, as the rose   320
Blendeth its odor with the violet—
Solution sweet: meantime the frost-wind blows
Like Love's alarum pattering the sharp sleet
Against the windowpanes; St. Agnes' moon hath set.

37

'Tis dark: quick pattereth the flaw-blown[5] sleet: 325
"This is no dream, my bride, my Madeline!"
'Tis dark: the icéd gusts still rave and beat:
"No dream, alas! alas! and woe is mine!
Porphyro will leave me here to fade and pine.—
Cruel! what traitor could thee hither bring?   330
I curse not, for my heart is lost in thine,
Though thou forsakest a deceivéd thing—
A dove forlorn and lost with sick unprunéd wing."

---

4. "The Lovely Lady Without Pity,"
by the medieval poet, Alain Chartier.
Keats later used the title for his own
    ballad.
    5. Gust-blown.

38

"My Madeline! sweet dreamer! lovely bride!
Say, may I be for aye thy vassal blest? 335
Thy beauty's shield, heart-shaped and vermeil[6] dyed?
Ah, silver shrine, here will I take my rest
After so many hours of toil and quest,
A famished pilgrim—saved by miracle.
Though I have found, I will not rob thy nest 340
Saving of thy sweet self; if thou think'st well
To trust, fair Madeline, to no rude infidel.

39

"Hark! 'tis an elfin-storm from faery land,
Of haggard[7] seeming, but a boon indeed:
Arise—arise! the morning is at hand— 345
The bloated wassaillers[8] will never heed—
Let us away, my love, with happy speed;
There are no ears to hear, or eyes to see—
Drowned all in Rhenish and the sleepy mead:[9]
Awake! arise! my love, and fearless be, 350
For o'er the southern moors I have a home for thee."

40

She hurried at his words, beset with fears,
For there were sleeping dragons all around,
At glaring watch, perhaps, with ready spears—
Down the wide stairs a darkling[1] way they found.— 355
In all the house was heard no human sound.
A chain-drooped lamp was flickering by each door;
The arras, rich with horseman, hawk, and hound,
Fluttered in the besieging wind's uproar;
And the long carpets rose along the gusty floor. 360

41

They glide, like phantoms, into the wide hall;
Like phantoms, to the iron porch, they glide;
Where lay the Porter, in uneasy sprawl,
With a huge empty flagon by his side:
The wakeful bloodhound rose, and shook his hide, 365
But his sagacious eye an inmate owns:[2]
By one, and one, the bolts full easy slide:
The chains lie silent on the footworn stones;
The key turns, and the door upon its hinges groans.

42

And they are gone: aye, ages long ago 370
These lovers fled away into the storm.
That night the Baron dreamt of many a woe,
And all his warrior-guests, with shade and form
Of witch, and demon, and large coffin-worm,
Were long be-nightmared. Angela the old 375

---

6. Vermilion.
7. Wild, untamed (originally, a wild hawk).
8. Drunken carousers.
9. Rhine wine and the sleep-producing
mead (a heavy fermented drink made with honey).
1. In the dark.
2. Acknowledges a member of the household.

Died palsy-twitched, with meager face deform;
  The Beadsman, after thousand aves[3] told,
For aye unsought for slept among his ashes cold.
Jan.–Feb., 1819   1820

Bright Star[4]

Bright star, would I were steadfast as thou art—
  Not in lone splendor hung aloft the night
And watching, with eternal lids apart,
  Like nature's patient, sleepless Eremite,[5]
The moving waters at their priestlike task   5
  Of pure ablution[6] round earth's human shores,
Or gazing on the new soft fallen mask
  Of snow upon the mountains and the moors—
No—yet still steadfast, still unchangeable,
  Pillowed upon my fair love's ripening breast,   10
To feel forever its soft fall and swell,
  Awake forever in a sweet unrest,
Still, still to hear her tender-taken breath,
And so live ever—or else swoon to death.[7]

1819   1838

Why Did I Laugh Tonight?[8]

Why did I laugh tonight? No voice will tell:
  No God, no Demon of severe response,
Deigns to reply from Heaven or from Hell.
  Then to my human heart I turn at once.
Heart! Thou and I are here sad and alone;   5
  I say, why did I laugh? O mortal pain!
O Darkness! Darkness! ever must I moan,
  To question Heaven and Hell and Heart in vain.
Why did I laugh? I know this Being's lease,
  My fancy to its utmost blisses spreads;   10
Yet would I on this very midnight cease,
  And the world's gaudy ensigns[9] see in shreds;

---

3. The prayers beginning *Ave Maria*
("Hail Mary").
4. While on a tour of the Lake Country in 1818, Keats had said that the
austere scenes "refine one's sensual vision into a sort of north star which
can never cease to be open lidded and
steadfast over the wonders of the great
Power"; the thought developed into
this sonnet. This used to be called
Keats's last sonnet, since it was believed that Keats composed it on his
way to death in Italy in September,
1820, at which time he copied it into
his volume of Shakespeare. But a MS.
draft dated 1819 has since been found.

5. Hermit, religious solitary.
6. Washing, as part of a religious rite.
7. In the earlier version: "Half passionless, and so swoon on to death."
8. In the letter to his brother and sister-
in-law, George and Georgiana Keats,
into which he copied this sonnet, March
19, 1819, Keats wrote: "Though the
first steps to it were through my human
passions, they went away, and I wrote
with my Mind—and perhaps I must
confess a little bit of my heart. * * * I
went to bed, and enjoyed an uninterrupted sleep. Sane I went to bed and
sane I arose."
9. Banners.

Verse, Fame, and Beauty are intense indeed,
But Death intenser—Death is Life's high meed.

March, 1819   1848

La Belle Dame sans Merci[1]

O what can ail thee, Knight at arms,
　　Alone and palely loitering?
The sedge has withered from the Lake
　　And no birds sing!

O what can ail thee, Knight at arms,   5
　　So haggard, and so woebegone?
The squirrel's granary is full
　　And the harvest's done.

I see a lily on thy brow
　　With anguish moist and fever dew,   10
And on thy cheeks a fading rose
　　Fast withereth too.

I met a Lady in the Meads,
　　Full beautiful, a faery's child,
Her hair was long, her foot was light   15
　　And her eyes were wild.

I made a Garland for her head,
　　And bracelets too, and fragrant Zone;[2]
She looked at me as she did love
　　And made sweet moan.   20

I set her on my pacing steed
　　And nothing else saw all day long,
For sidelong would she bend and sing
　　A faery's song.

She found me roots of relish sweet,   25
　　And honey wild, and manna dew,
And sure in language strange she said
　　"I love thee true."

She took me to her elfin grot
　　And there she wept and sighed full sore,   30
And there I shut her wild wild eyes
　　With kisses four.

1. The title, though not the subject matter, was taken from a medieval poem by Alain Chartier and means "The Lovely Lady Without Pity." The story of a mortal destroyed by his love for a supernatural *femme fatale* has been told repeatedly in myth, fairy tale, and ballad, but never so hauntingly. The metrical key to its effect is the poignant and richly suggestive suspension achieved by shortening to two stresses the final line of each stanza.

We print here Keats's first version, written in a letter to his brother and sister-in-law. The version published in 1820, "Ah, what can ail thee, wretched wight," is a rare instance in which Keats weakened a poem by revision.

Keats imitates a frequent procedure of folk ballads by casting the poem into the dialogue form. The first three stanzas are addressed to the Knight, and the rest of the poem is his reply.

2. Girdle.

And there she lulléd me asleep,
  And there I dreamed, Ah Woe betide!
The latest[3] dream I ever dreamt   35
  On the cold hill side.

I saw pale Kings, and Princes too,
  Pale warriors, death-pale were they all;
They cried, "La belle dame sans merci
  Thee hath in thrall!"   40

I saw their starved lips in the gloam
  With horrid warning gapéd wide,
And I awoke, and found me here
  On the cold hill's side.

And this is why I sojourn here,   45
  Alone and palely loitering;
Though the sedge is withered from the Lake
  And no birds sing.

April, 1819   1820

On the Sonnet[1]

If by dull rhymes our English must be chained,
  And, like Andromeda,[2] the Sonnet sweet
Fettered, in spite of painéd loveliness;
Let us find out, if we must be constrained,
  Sandals more interwoven and complete   5
To fit the naked foot of poesy;
Let us inspect the lyre, and weigh the stress
Of every chord,[3] and see what may be gained
  By ear industrious, and attention meet;
Misers of sound and syllable, no less   10
Than Midas[4] of his coinage, let us be
  Jealous of dead leaves in the bay-wreath crown;
So, if we may not let the Muse be free,
  She will be bound with garlands of her own.

April, 1819   1848

To Sleep

O soft embalmer of the still midnight,
  Shutting, with careful fingers and benign,

3. Last.
1. In a letter including this sonnet, Keats wrote that "I have been endeavoring to discover a better sonnet stanza than we have," objecting especially to the "pouncing rhymes" of the Petrarchan form and the inevitable tick of the closing couplet in the Shakespearean stanza. This and the two following poems exemplify Keats's experiments with variations upon these conventional sonnet patterns.
2. Andromeda was chained to a rock in order to placate a sea monster, but was rescued by Perseus.
3. Lyre-string.
4. King Midas was granted his wish that all he touched should turn to gold.

Our gloom-pleased eyes, embowered from the light,
    Enshaded in forgetfulness divine;
O soothest[1] Sleep! if so it please thee, close   5
    In midst of this thine hymn my willing eyes,
Or wait the amen, ere thy poppy[2] throws
    Around my bed its lulling charities;
Then save me, or the passéd day will shine
    Upon my pillow, breeding many woes;   10
      Save me from curious[3] conscience, that still lords
Its strength for darkness, burrowing like a mole;
    Turn the key deftly in the oiléd wards,[4]
And seal the hushéd casket of my soul.

April, 1819   1838, 1848

On Fame

"You cannot eat your cake and have it too."
                            —*Proverb*

How fevered is the man, who cannot look
    Upon his mortal days with temperate blood,
Who vexes all the leaves of his life's book,
    And robs his fair name of its maidenhood;
It is as if the rose should pluck herself,   5
    Or the ripe plum finger its misty bloom,
As if a Naiad,[5] like a meddling elf,
    Should darken her pure grot with muddy gloom;
But the rose leaves herself upon the briar,
    For winds to kiss and grateful bees to feed,   10
And the ripe plum still wears its dim attire;
      The undisturbéd lake has crystal space;
      Why then should man, teasing the world for grace,
Spoil his salvation for a fierce miscreed?[6]

April, 1819   1848

Ode to Psyche[1]

O Goddess! hear these tuneless numbers, wrung
    By sweet enforcement and remembrance dear,

1. Softest.
2. Opium is made from the dried juice of the opium poppy.
3. Scrupulous. "Lords": marshals, sets in order.
4. The ridges in a lock which determine the pattern of the key.
5. Water nymph.
6. I.e., the falsé doctrine ("miscreed") that the award of salvation ("grace") can be won by achieving fame in this world. Cf. Milton's *Lycidas*, lines 78 ff.: "Fame is no plant that grows on mortal soil. * * * "
1. This poem initiated the sequence of five great odes that Keats wrote in late April and in May, 1819. Since it is copied into the same journal-letter which included *On the Sonnet*, it is likely that Keats's experiments with sonnet schemes led to the development of the intricate and varied stanzas of his odes, and also that Keats abandoned the sonnet upon discovering the richer possibilities of the more spacious form. In a letter of April 30, 1819, Keats said that of all his poems up to that time, *Psyche* "is the first and the only one with which I have taken even moderate pains. I have for the most part dashed off my

And pardon that thy secrets should be sung
    Even into thine own soft-conchéd[2] ear:
Surely I dreamt today, or did I see   5
    The wingéd Psyche with awakened eyes?[2a]
I wandered in a forest thoughtlessly,
    And, on the sudden, fainting with surprise,
Saw two fair creatures, couchéd side by side
    In deepest grass, beneath the whisp'ring roof   10
Of leaves and trembled blossoms, where there ran
        A brooklet, scarce espied:

'Mid hushed, cool-rooted flowers, fragrant-eyed,
    Blue, silver-white, and budded Tyrian,[3]
They lay calm-breathing on the bedded grass;   15
    Their arms embracéd, and their pinions[4] too;
Their lips touched not, but had not bade adieu,
    As if disjoinéd by soft-handed slumber,
And ready still past kisses to outnumber
    At tender eye-dawn of aurorean love:[5]   20
        The wingéd boy I knew;
But who wast thou, O happy, happy dove?
        His Psyche true!

O latest born and loveliest vision far
    Of all Olympus' faded hierarchy![6]   25
Fairer than Phoebe's sapphire-regioned star,[7]
    Or Vesper, amorous glowworm of the sky;
Fairer than these, though temple thou hast none,
    Nor altar heaped with flowers;
Nor virgin choir to make delicious moan   30
    Upon the midnight hours;
No voice, no lute, no pipe, no incense sweet
    From chain-swung censer teeming;

lines in a hurry. This I have done leisurely—I think it reads the more richly for it and will I hope encourage me to write other things in even a more peaceable and healthy spirit." In the story told by the Roman author Apuleius in the 2nd century A.D., Psyche was a lovely mortal beloved by Cupid, "the winged boy," son of Venus. After various tribulations, imposed by Venus because she was jealous of Psyche's beauty, Psyche was wedded to Cupid and translated to heaven as an immortal.

The tendency in recent criticism of Keats is to read the *Ode* as a quasi-allegory, in which Psyche (in Greek: soul, or mind) represents "the human-soul-in-love" (Harold Bloom) or else the modern inward-oriented poetry of the mind (W. J. Bate). To this latter-day goddess, Keats in the last two stanzas promises to establish a place of worship within "some untrodden region" of his own mind, with himself as poet-priest and prophet.

2. Soft and shaped like a seashell.
2a. Another of Keats's inquiries into the relation of dreams to poetic vision; see, e.g., *Sleep and Poetry*, the concluding line of *Ode to a Nightingale*, the opening section of *The Fall of Hyperion: A Dream*.
3. The purple dye anciently made in Tyre.
4. Wings.
5. Aurora was the goddess of the dawn.
6. The ranks of the classic gods of Mt. Olympus. "You must recollect that Psyche was not embodied as a goddess before the time of Apuleius the Platonist who lived after the Augustan age, and consequently the goddess was never worshiped or sacrificed to with any of the ancient fervor—and perhaps never thought of in the old religion" (Keats, letter of April 30, 1819).
7. The moon, supervised by the goddess Phoebe (Diana). "Vesper": the evening star.

No shrine, no grove, no oracle, no heat
    Of pale-mouthed prophet dreaming.   35

O brightest! though too late for antique vows,
    Too, too late for the fond believing lyre,
When holy were the haunted forest boughs,
    Holy the air, the water, and the fire;
Yet even in these days so far retired   40
    From happy pieties, thy lucent fans,[8]
      Fluttering among the faint Olympians,
I see, and sing, by my own eyes inspired.
So let me be thy choir, and make a moan
      Upon the midnight hours;   45
Thy voice, thy lute, thy pipe, thy incense sweet
    From swingéd censer teeming;
Thy shrine, thy grove, thy oracle, thy heat
    Of pale-mouthed prophet dreaming.
Yes, I will be thy priest, and build a fane[9]   50
    In some untrodden region of my mind,
Where branchéd thoughts, new grown with pleasant pain,
    Instead of pines shall murmur in the wind:
Far, far around shall those dark-clustered trees
    Fledge[1] the wild-ridged mountains steep by steep;   55
And there by zephyrs, streams, and birds, and bees,
    The moss-lain Dryads[2] shall be lulled to sleep;
And in the midst of this wide quietness
A rosy sanctuary will I dress
With the wreathed trellis of a working brain,   60
    With buds, and bells, and stars without a name,
With all the gardener Fancy e'er could feign,
    Who breeding flowers, will never breed the same:
And there shall be for thee all soft delight
    That shadowy thought can win,   65
A bright torch, and a casement ope at night,
    To let the warm Love[3] in!

April, 1819   1820

Ode on a Grecian Urn[1]

1

Thou still unravished bride of quietness,
    Thou foster child of silence and slow time,

---

8. Shining wings.
9. Temple.
1. I.e., the trees shall stand, rank against rank, like layers of feathers.
2. Wood nymphs.
3. I.e., Cupid, god of love.
1. This urn, with its sculptured reliefs of Dionysian ecstasies, panting young lovers in flight and pursuit, a pastoral piper under spring foliage, and the quiet celebration of communal pieties, resembles parts of various vases, sculptures, and paintings; but it existed in all its particulars only in Keats's imagination. In the urn—which captures moments of intense experience in attitudes of grace and freezes them into marble immobility—Keats found the perfect correlative for his persistent concern with the longing for permanence in a world of change. The interpretation of the details with which Keats devel-

Sylvan[2] historian, who canst thus express
 A flowery tale more sweetly than our rhyme:
What leaf-fringed legend haunts about thy shape   5
  Of deities or mortals, or of both,
   In Tempe or the dales of Arcady?[3]
  What men or gods are these? What maidens loath?
What mad pursuit? What struggle to escape?
  What pipes and timbrels? What wild ecstasy? 10

2

Heard melodies are sweet, but those unheard
 Are sweeter; therefore, ye soft pipes, play on;
Not to the sensual ear,[4] but, more endeared,
 Pipe to the spirit ditties of no tone:
Fair youth, beneath the trees, thou canst not leave 15
 Thy song, nor ever can those trees be bare;
  Bold Lover, never, never canst thou kiss,
Though winning near the goal—yet, do not grieve;
 She cannot fade, though thou hast not thy bliss,
 Forever wilt thou love, and she be fair! 20

3

Ah, happy, happy boughs! that cannot shed
 Your leaves, nor ever bid the Spring adieu;
And, happy melodist, unwearièd,
 Forever piping songs forever new;
More happy love! more happy, happy love! 25
 Forever warm and still to be enjoyed,
  Forever panting, and forever young;
All breathing human passion far above,
 That leaves a heart high-sorrowful and cloyed,
 A burning forehead, and a parching tongue. 30

4

Who are these coming to the sacrifice?
 To what green altar, O mysterious priest,
Lead'st thou that heifer lowing at the skies,
 And all her silken flanks with garlands dressed?
What little town by river or sea shore, 35
 Or mountain-built with peaceful citadel,
  Is emptied of this folk, this pious morn?
And, little town, thy streets forevermore
 Will silent be; and not a soul to tell
 Why thou art desolate, can e'er return. 40

5

O Attic[5] shape! Fair attitude! with brede
    Of marble men and maidens overwrought,[6]
With forest branches and the trodden weed;
    Thou, silent form, dost tease us out of thought
As doth eternity: Cold Pastoral!   45
    When old age shall this generation waste,
      Thou shalt remain, in midst of other woe
    Than ours, a friend to man, to whom thou say'st,
    "Beauty is truth, truth beauty,"[7]—that is all
      Ye know on earth, and all ye need to know.   50
May, 1819   1820

Ode to a Nightingale[1]

1

My heart aches, and a drowsy numbness pains
    My sense, as though of hemlock[2] I had drunk,
Or emptied some dull opiate to the drains
    One minute past, and Lethe-wards[3] had sunk:
'Tis not through envy of thy happy lot,   5
    But being too happy in thine happiness—
      That thou, light-wingéd Dryad of the trees,
        In some melodious plot
    Of beechen green, and shadows numberless,
      Singest of summer in full-throated ease.   10

2

O, for a draught of vintage! that hath been
    Cooled a long age in the deep-delvéd earth,
Tasting of Flora[4] and the country green,
    Dance, and Provençal song,[5] and sunburnt mirth!

5. Greek. Attica was the region of Greece in which Athens was located.

6. Ornamented all over ("overwrought") with an interwoven pattern ("brede").

7. The quotation marks around this phrase are found in the volume of poems Keats published in 1820; but there are no quotation marks in the version printed in *Annals of the Fine Arts* that same year, or in the four transcripts of the poem made by Keats's friends. This discrepancy has encouraged the diversity of critical interpretations of the last two lines. Leading critics disagree whether the whole of these lines is said by the urn, or "Beauty is truth, truth beauty" by the urn and the rest by Keats or else by an invented lyric speaker; whether the "ye" in the last line is addressed to the lyric speaker, to the readers, to the urn, or to the figures on the urn; whether "all ye know" is that beauty is truth, or this plus the statement in lines 46–48; and whether "beauty is truth" is a universal and profound metaphysical proposition, or an overstatement uttered in the course of a dramatic dialogue, or simply nonsense. (The various commentaries are collected in *Keats's Well-Read Urn,* ed. H. T. Lyon, 1958).

1. Charles Brown, with whom Keats was then living in Hampstead, wrote: "In the spring of 1819 a nightingale had built her nest near my house. Keats felt a tranquil and continual joy in her song; and one morning he took his chair from the breakfast table to the grass plot under a plum tree, where he sat for two or three hours. When he came into the house, I perceived he had some scraps of paper in his hand, and these he was quietly thrusting behind the books. On inquiry, I found those scraps, four or five in number, contained his poetic feeling on the song of our nightingale."

2. A poisonous herb, not the North American evergreen tree.

3. Toward Lethe, the river in Hades whose waters cause forgetfulness.

4. Roman goddess of flowers, or the flowers themselves.

5. Provence, in southern France, was in

O for a beaker full of the warm South,   15
   Full of the true, the blushful Hippocrene,[6]
      With beaded bubbles winking at the brim,
         And purple-stainéd mouth;
   That I might drink, and leave the world unseen,
      And with thee fade away into the forest dim: 20

3

Fade far away, dissolve, and quite forget
   What thou among the leaves hast never known,
The weariness, the fever, and the fret
   Here, where men sit and hear each other groan;
Where palsy shakes a few, sad, last gray hairs,   25
   Where youth grows pale, and specter-thin, and dies;[7]
      Where but to think is to be full of sorrow
         And leaden-eyed despairs,
   Where Beauty cannot keep her lustrous eyes,
      Or new Love pine at them beyond tomorrow.   30

4

Away! away! for I will fly to thee,
   Not charioted by Bacchus and his pards,
But on the viewless wings of Poesy,[8]
   Though the dull brain perplexes and retards:
Already with thee! tender is the night,   35
   And haply the Queen-Moon is on her throne,
      Clustered around by all her starry Fays;[9]
         But here there is no light,
   Save what from heaven is with the breezes blown
      Through verdurous[1] glooms and winding mossy ways.   40

5

I cannot see what flowers are at my feet,
   Nor what soft incense hangs upon the boughs,
But, in embalméd[2] darkness, guess each sweet
   Wherewith the seasonable month endows
The grass, the thicket, and the fruit tree wild;   45
   White hawthorn, and the pastoral eglantine;[3]
      Fast fading violets covered up in leaves;
         And mid-May's eldest child,
   The coming musk-rose, full of dewy wine,
      The murmurous haunt of flies on summer eves.   50

6

Darkling[4] I listen; and for many a time
   I have been half in love with easeful Death,

---

the late Middle Ages renowned for its troubadours, the writers and singers of love songs.
6. Pronounced *Hip'-ocreen:* fountain of the Muses on Mt. Helicon; hence, the waters of inspiration, here applied metaphorically to a beaker of wine.
7. Keats's brother, Tom, wasted by tuberculosis, had died the previous winter.
8. I.e., not by getting drunk on wine (the "vintage" of stanza two), but on the invisible ("viewless") wings of the poetic fancy. (Bacchus, god of wine, was sometimes represented in a chariot drawn by "pards"—leopards.)
9. Fairies.
1. Green-foliaged.
2. Perfumed.
3. Sweetbrier, or honeysuckle.
4. In the dark.

Called him soft names in many a muséd[5] rhyme,
   To take into the air my quiet breath;
Now more than ever seems it rich to die,   55
   To cease upon the midnight with no pain,
     While thou art pouring forth thy soul abroad
        In such an ecstasy!
Still wouldst thou sing, and I have ears in vain—
   To thy high requiem become a sod.   60

       7
Thou wast not born for death, immortal Bird!
   No hungry generations tread thee down;
The voice I hear this passing night was heard
   In ancient days by emperor and clown:
Perhaps the selfsame song that found a path   65
   Through the sad heart of Ruth,[7] when, sick for home,
     She stood in tears amid the alien corn;[8]
        The same that ofttimes hath
   Charmed magic casements, opening on the foam
   Of perilous seas, in faery lands forlorn.   70

       8
Forlorn![9] the very word is like a bell
   To toll me back from thee to my sole self!
Adieu! the fancy[10] cannot cheat so well
   As she is famed to do, deceiving elf.
Adieu! adieu! thy plaintive anthem[11] fades   75
   Past the near meadows, over the still stream,
     Up the hill side; and now 'tis buried deep
        In the next valley-glades:
     Was it a vision, or a waking dream?
     Fled is that music:—Do I wake or sleep?[1]   80
May, 1819   1819, 1820

5. Meditated. Two earlier poems ("rhymes") by Keats which called on "easeful Death" are the sonnets *Why Did I Laugh?* and *Bright Star.*
7. The young widow in the Biblical Book of Ruth.
8. I.e., wheat.
9. One critic has said that "forlorn"—which means "long past" as well as "sorrowful"—"has its feet in two worlds," the faeryland of imagination and the woe of reality to which the word reawakens the lyric speaker.
10. I.e., "the viewless wings of Poesy" of line 33.
11. Hymn. As the lyric speaker's own mood changes, the interpreted quality of the bird song alters from the flawless happiness of stanza 1, to the "high requiem" of line 60, to the sadness of the broken vision at the end.
1. See *Ode to Psyche,* above, note to line 6.

Ode on Melancholy

This is Keats's best-known statement of his recurrent theme of the inextricable contrarieties of life. The remarkable last stanza, in which Melancholy becomes a veiled goddess in a mystery religion, implies that it is the tragic human destiny that beauty, joy, and life itself take their quality and value from the very fact that they are transitory, and turn into their opposites.

   The poem originally had the following opening stanza, which Keats canceled in MS:

Though you should build a bark of dead men's bones,
  And rear a phantom gibbet for a mast,
Stitch creeds together for a sail, with groans
  To fill it out, blood-stainéd and aghast;
Although your rudder be a dragon's tail
  Long severed, yet still hard with agony,
    Your cordage large uprootings from the skull
Of bald Medusa, certes you would fail
  To find the Melancholy—whether she
    Dreameth in any isle of Lethe dull.

Ode on Melancholy

1

No, no, go not to Lethe,[2] neither twist
  Wolfsbane, tight-rooted, for its poisonous wine;
Nor suffer thy pale forehead to be kissed
  By nightshade,[3] ruby grape of Proserpine;
Make not your rosary of yew-berries,[4]   5
  Nor let the beetle, nor the death-moth be
    Your mournful Psyche,[5] nor the downy owl
A partner in your sorrow's mysteries;[6]
  For shade to shade will come too drowsily,
    And drown the wakeful anguish of the soul.[7]   10

2

But when the melancholy fit shall fall
  Sudden from heaven like a weeping cloud,
That fosters the droop-headed flowers all,
  And hides the green hill in an April shroud;
Then glut thy sorrow on a morning rose,   15
  Or on the rainbow of the salt sand-wave,
    Or on the wealth of globéd peonies;
Or if thy mistress some rich anger shows,
  Imprison her soft hand, and let her rave,
    And feed deep, deep upon her peerless eyes.   20

3

She[8] dwells with Beauty—Beauty that must die;
  And Joy, whose hand is ever at his lips
Bidding adieu; and aching Pleasure nigh,
  Turning to Poison while the bee-mouth sips:
Aye, in the very temple of Delight   25
  Veiled Melancholy has her sov'reign shrine,

2. The waters of forgetfulness in Hades.
3. "Nightshade" and "wolfsbane" (line 2) are poisonous plants. Proserpine is the wife of Pluto and queen of the infernal regions.
4. A symbol of death.
5. In ancient times Psyche (the soul) was sometimes represented as a butterfly or moth, fluttering out of the mouth of a dying man. The allusion may also be to the death's-head moth, which has skull-like markings on its back. The "beetle" of line 6 refers to replicas of the large black beetle, the scarab, which were often placed by Egyptians in their tombs as a symbol of resurrection.
6. Secret religious rites.
7. I.e., the intensity of sorrow is merely dulled when it is put next to other sorrows; it needs contrast to heighten it.
8. I.e., Melancholy, personified as a goddess whose chief place of worship ("shrine," line 26) is located "in the very temple of Delight" (line 25).

Though seen of none save him whose strenuous tongue
Can burst Joy's grape against his palate fine;⁹
His soul shall taste the sadness of her might,
    And be among her cloudy trophies hung.¹   30
May, 1819   1820

9. Sensitive, subtly discriminative.   practice of hanging trophies in the
1. A reference to the Greek and Roman   temples of the gods.

Lamia   Keats himself cited, as the source of his plot, a story in Robert
Burton's *Anatomy of Melancholy* (1621): "One Menippus Lycius, a young
man twenty-five years of age, that going betwixt Cenchreas and Corinth,
met such a phantasm in the habit of a fair gentlewoman, which, taking
him by the hand, carried him home to her house, in the suburbs of Corinth. * * * The young man, a philosopher, otherwise staid and discreet,
able to moderate his passions, though not this of love, tarried with her a
while to his great content, and at last married her, to whose wedding,
amongst other guests, came Apollonius; who, by some probable conjectures,
found her out to be a serpent, a lamia; and that all her furniture was, like
Tantalus' gold, described by Homer, no substance but mere illusions. When
she saw herself descried, she wept, and desired Apollonius to be silent, but
he would not be moved, and thereupon she, plate, house, and all that was
in it, vanished in an instant: many thousands took notice of this fact, for
it was done in the midst of Greece."

In ancient demonology, a "lamia"—pronounced *lā'-mĭ-a*—was a monster
in woman's form who preyed on human beings. There are various clues
(see especially Part II, 229–38) that Keats invested the ancient legend with
allegorical significance. Its interpretation, however, and even the inclination
of Keats's own sympathies in the contest between Lamia and Apollonius,
have been disputed. It is possible that Keats failed to make up his mind, or
wavered in the course of composition. What seems to be Keats's indecision,
however, may in fact indicate that he intended to present an inevitably
fatal situation, in which no one is entirely blameless or blameworthy, and
no character is meant to monopolize either our sympathy or antipathy.
Lamia is an enchantress, a liar, and a calculating expert in *amour;* but she
apparently intends no harm, is genuinely in love, and is very beautiful. And
both male protagonists exhibit culpable extremes which alienate our sympathy. Lycius, though an attractive young lover, is gullible, a slave to his
passions, and capable of gratuitous cruelty; while Apollonius, though realistically clear-sighted, is rigid, puritanical, and inhumane.

The poem, written between late June and early September, 1819, is a
return, after the Spenserian stanzas of *The Eve of St. Agnes,* to the pentameter couplets Keats had used in *Endymion* and other early narrative
poems. But Keats had in the meantime been studying Dryden's closed and
strong-paced couplets. The initial lines of Dryden's version of Boccaccio's
story *Cymon and Iphigenia* will show the kind of narrative model which
helped Keats make the technical transition from the fluent but sprawling
gracefulness of the opening of *Endymion* to the vigor and economy of the
opening of *Lamia:*

In that sweet isle where Venus keeps her court,
And every grace, and all the loves, resort;
Where either sex is formed of softer earth,
And takes the bent of pleasure from their birth;
There lived a Cyprian lord, above the rest
Wise, wealthy, with a numerous issue blest;

* * *

Lamia

Part I

Upon a time, before the faery broods
Drove Nymph and Satyr from the prosperous woods,[1]
Before King Oberon's bright diadem,
Scepter, and mantle, clasped with dewy gem,
Frighted away the Dryads and the Fauns
From rushes green, and brakes,[2] and cowslipped lawns,   5
The ever-smitten Hermes empty left
His golden throne, bent warm on amorous theft:[3]
From high Olympus had he stolen light,
On this side of Jove's clouds, to escape the sight   10
Of his great summoner, and made retreat
Into a forest on the shores of Crete.
For somewhere in that sacred island dwelt
A nymph, to whom all hooféd Satyrs knelt;
At whose white feet the languid Tritons[4] poured   15
Pearls, while on land they withered and adored.
Fast by the springs where she to bathe was wont,
And in those meads where sometimes she might haunt,
Were strewn rich gifts, unknown to any Muse,
Though Fancy's casket were unlocked to choose.   20
Ah, what a world of love was at her feet!
So Hermes thought, and a celestial heat
Burnt from his wingéd heels to either ear,
That from a whiteness, as the lily clear,
Blushed into roses 'mid his golden hair,   25
Fallen in jealous curls about his shoulders bare.[5]
From vale to vale, from wood to wood, he flew,
Breathing upon the flowers his passion new,
And wound with many a river to its head,
To find where this sweet nymph prepared her secret bed: 30
In vain; the sweet nymph might nowhere be found,
And so he rested, on the lonely ground,

1. Nymphs and satyrs—like the dryads and fauns in line 5—were all minor classical deities of the woods and fields, said here to have been driven off by Oberon, king of the fairies, who were supernatural beings of the postclassical era.
2. Thickets.
3. Hermes (or Mercury), wing-footed messenger at the summons of Jove (line 11), was notoriously amorous.
4. Minor sea gods.
5. The curls clung jealously to his bare shoulders. This line is the first of a number of Alexandrines, a device for introducing variety of movement that Keats learned from Dryden. Another such device is the triplet in lines 61–63.

Of the Wood-Gods, and even the very trees.
There as he stood, he heard a mournful voice,   35
Such as once heard, in gentle heart, destroys
All pain but pity: thus the lone voice spake:
"When from this wreathed tomb shall I awake!
When move in a sweet body fit for life,
And love, and pleasure, and the ruddy strife   40
Of hearts and lips! Ah, miserable me!"
The God, dove-footed,[6] glided silently
Round bush and tree, soft-brushing, in his speed,
The taller grasses and full-flowering weed,
Until he found a palpitating snake,   45
Bright, and cirque-couchant[7] in a dusky brake.

She was a gordian[8] shape of dazzling hue,
Vermilion-spotted, golden, green, and blue;
Striped like a zebra, freckled like a pard,
Eyed like a peacock,[9] and all crimson barred;   50
And full of silver moons, that, as she breathed,
Dissolved, or brighter shone, or interwreathed
Their lusters with the gloomier tapestries—
So rainbow-sided, touched with miseries,
She seemed, at once, some penanced lady elf,   55
Some demon's mistress, or the demon's self.
Upon her crest she wore a wannish[1] fire
Sprinkled with stars, like Ariadne's tiar:[2]
Her head was serpent, but ah, bitter-sweet!
She had a woman's mouth with all its pearls[3] complete: 60
And for her eyes: what could such eyes do there
But weep, and weep, that they were born so fair?
As Proserpine still weeps for her Sicilian air.[4]
Her throat was serpent, but the words she spake
Came, as through bubbling honey, for Love's sake,   65
And thus; while Hermes on his pinions lay,
Like a stooped falcon[5] ere he takes his prey.

"Fair Hermes, crowned with feathers, fluttering light,
I had a splendid dream of thee last night:
I saw thee sitting, on a throne of gold,   70
Among the Gods, upon Olympus old,
The only sad one; for thou didst not hear
The soft, lute-fingered Muses chaunting clear,
Nor even Apollo when he sang alone,
Deaf to his throbbing throat's long, long melodious moan. 75
I dreamt I saw thee, robed in purple flakes,
Break amorous through the clouds, as morning breaks,

6. Quietly as a dove.
7. Lying in a circular coil.
8. Intricately twisted, like the knot tied by King Gordius, which no one could undo.
9. Having multicolored spots, like the "eyes" in a peacock's tail. "Pard": leopard.
1. Rather dark.
2. Ariadne, who was transformed into a constellation, had been represented in a painting by Titian wearing a symbolic crown, or tiara ("tiar"), of stars.
3. "Pearls" had become almost a synonym for teeth in Elizabethan poetry.
4. Proserpine had been carried off to Hades by Pluto from the field of Enna, in Sicily.
5. "Stoop" is the term for the plunge of a falcon upon his prey.

And, swiftly as bright Phoebean dart,[6]
Strike for the Cretan isle; and here thou art!
Too gentle Hermes, hast thou found the maid?"   80
Whereat the star of Lethe[7] not delayed
His rosy eloquence and thus inquired:
"Thou smooth-lipped serpent, surely high inspired!
Thou beauteous wreath, with melancholy eyes,
Possess whatever bliss thou canst devise,   85
Telling me only where my nymph is fled—
Where she doth breathe!" "Bright planet, thou hast said,"
Returned the snake, "but seal with oaths, fair God!"
"I swear," said Hermes, "by my serpent rod,
And by thine eyes, and by thy starry crown!"   90
Light flew his earnest words, among the blossoms blown.
Then thus again the brilliance feminine:
"Too frail of heart! for this lost nymph of thine,
Free as the air, invisibly, she strays
About these thornless wilds; her pleasant days   95
She tastes unseen; unseen her nimble feet
Leave traces in the grass and flowers sweet;
From weary tendrils, and bowed branches green,
She plucks the fruit unseen, she bathes unseen:
And by my power is her beauty veiled   100
To keep it unaffronted, unassailed
By the love-glances of unlovely eyes,
Of Satyrs, Fauns, and bleared Silenus'[8] sighs.
Pale grew her immortality, for woe
Of all these lovers, and she grievéd so   105
I took compassion on her, bade her steep
Her hair in weïrd[9] syrups, that would keep
Her loveliness invisible, yet free
To wander as she loves, in liberty.
Thou shalt behold her, Hermes, thou alone,   110
If thou wilt, as thou swearest, grant my boon!"
Then, once again, the charméd God began
An oath, and through the serpent's ears it ran
Warm, tremulous, devout, psalterian.[1]
Ravished, she lifted her Circean[2] head,   115
Blushed a live damask, and swift-lisping said,
"I was a woman, let me have once more
A woman's shape, and charming as before.
I love a youth of Corinth—O the bliss!
Give me my woman's form, and place me where he is.   120
Stoop, Hermes, let me breathe upon thy brow,
And thou shalt see thy sweet nymph even now."
The God on half-shut feathers sank serene,

6. A ray of Phoebus Apollo, god of the sun.
7. Hermes, when he appeared like a star on the banks of Lethe, in the darkness of Hades. (One of Hermes' offices was to guide the souls of the dead to the lower regions.)
8. Silenus was a satyr, tutor of Bacchus, and always drunk.
9. Magical; Keats makes the word a dissyllable.
1. Either "like a psalm" or "like the sound of the psaltery" (an ancient stringed instrument).
2. Like that of Circe, the enchantress in the *Odyssey*. "Live damask": a living damask rose (large and fragrant pink rose).

She breathed upon his eyes, and swift was seen
Of both the guarded nymph near-smiling on the green.   125
It was no dream; or say a dream it was,
Real are the dreams of Gods, and smoothly pass
Their pleasures in a long immortal dream.
One warm, flushed moment, hovering, it might seem
Dashed by the wood-nymph's beauty, so he burned;   130
Then, lighting on the printless verdure, turned
To the swooned serpent, and with languid arm,
Delicate, put to proof the lithe Caducean charm.[3]
So done, upon the nymph his eyes he bent
Full of adoring tears and blandishment,   135
And towards her stepped: she, like a moon in wane,
Faded before him, cowered, nor could restrain
Her fearful sobs, self-folding like a flower
That faints into itself at evening hour:
But the God fostering her chilléd hand,   140
She felt the warmth, her eyelids opened bland,[4]
And, like new flowers at morning song of bees,
Bloomed, and gave up her honey to the lees.[5]
Into the green-recesséd woods they flew;
Nor grew they pale, as mortal lovers do.   145

    Left to herself, the serpent now began
To change; her elfin blood in madness ran,
Her mouth foamed, and the grass, therewith besprent,[6]
Withered at dew so sweet and virulent;
Her eyes in torture fixed, and anguish drear,   150
Hot, glazed, and wide, with lid-lashes all sear,
Flashed phosphor and sharp sparks, without one cooling tear.
The colors all inflamed throughout her train,
She writhed about, convulsed with scarlet pain:
A deep volcanian[7] yellow took the place   155
Of all her milder-moonéd body's grace;
And, as the lava ravishes the mead,
Spoilt all her silver mail, and golden brede;[8]
Made gloom of all her frecklings, streaks and bars,
Eclipsed her crescents, and licked up her stars: 160
So that, in moments few, she was undressed
Of all her sapphires, greens, and amethyst,
And rubious-argent:[9] of all these bereft,
Nothing but pain and ugliness were left.
Still shone her crown; that vanished, also she   165
Melted and disappeared as suddenly;
And in the air, her new voice luting soft,
Cried, "Lycius! gentle Lycius!"—Borne aloft
With the bright mists about the mountains hoar
These words dissolved: Crete's forests heard no more.   170

3. I.e., put to the test the magic of the flexible Caduceus (Hermes' official staff).
4. Softly.
5. Dregs.
6. Sprinkled.
7. The color of sulphur (thrown up by a volcano), in contrast to her former silvery moon color.
8. "Mail": interlinked rings, as in a coat of armor; "brede": embroidery, interwoven pattern.
9. Silvery red.

Whither fled Lamia, now a lady bright,
A full-born beauty new and exquisite?
She fled into that valley they pass o'er
Who go to Corinth from Cenchreas' shore;[1]
And rested at the foot of those wild hills,   175
The rugged founts of the Peraean rills,
And of that other ridge whose barren back
Stretches, with all its mist and cloudy rack,
Southwestward to Cleone. There she stood
About a young bird's flutter from a wood,   180
Fair, on a sloping green of mossy tread,
By a clear pool, wherein she passionéd[2]
To see herself escaped from so sore ills,
While her robes flaunted with the daffodils.

Ah, happy Lycius!—for she was a maid   185
More beautiful than ever twisted braid,
Or sighed, or blushed, or on spring-flowered lea[3]
Spread a green kirtle to the minstrelsy:
A virgin purest lipped, yet in the lore
Of love deep learnéd to the red heart's core: 190
Not one hour old, yet of sciential brain
To unperplex bliss from its neighbor pain;[4]
Define their pettish limits, and estrange
Their points of contact, and swift counterchange;
Intrigue with the specious chaos,[5] and dispart   195
Its most ambiguous atoms with sure art;
As though in Cupid's college she had spent
Sweet days a lovely graduate, still unshent,[6]
And kept his rosy terms in idle languishment.

Why this fair creature chose so faerily   200
By the wayside to linger, we shall see;
But first 'tis fit to tell how she could muse
And dream, when in the serpent prison-house,
Of all she list[7] strange or magnificent:
How, ever, where she willed, her spirit went;   205
Whether to faint Elysium, or where
Down through tress-lifting waves the Nereids[8] fair
Wind into Thetis' bower by many a pearly stair;
Or where God Bacchus drains his cups divine,
Stretched out, at ease, beneath a glutinous pine;   210
Or where in Pluto's gardens palatine
Mulciber's columns gleam in far piazzian line.[9]

1. Cenchrea (Keats's "Cenchreas")
was a harbor of Corinth, in southern
Greece.
2. Felt intense excitement.
3. Meadow; "kirtle": gown.
4. I.e., of knowledgeable ("sciential")
brain to disentangle ("unperplex") bliss
from its closely-related pain, to define
their quarreled-over ("pettish") limits,
and to separate out ("estrange") their
points of contact and the swift changes
of each condition into its opposite. Cf.
Keats's *Ode on Melancholy*, lines 25–26.
5. I.e., turn to her own artful purpose
the seeming ("specious") chaos.
6. Unspoiled. "Rosy terms": the terms
spent studying in "Cupid's college."
7. Wished.
8. Sea nymphs, of whom Thetis (the
mother of Achilles) was one.
9. I.e., columns made by Mulciber

And sometimes into cities she would send
Her dream, with feast and rioting to blend;
And once, while among mortals dreaming thus,   215
She saw the young Corinthian Lycius
Charioting foremost in the envious race,
Like a young Jove with calm uneager face,
And fell into a swooning love of him.
Now on the moth-time of that evening dim   220
He would return that way, as well she knew,
To Corinth from the shore; for freshly blew
The eastern soft wind, and his galley now
Grated the quaystones with her brazen prow
In port Cenchreas, from Egina isle   225
Fresh anchored; whither he had been awhile
To sacrifice to Jove, whose temple there
Waits with high marble doors for blood and incense rare.
Jove heard his vows, and bettered his desire;
For by some freakful chance he made retire   230
From his companions, and set forth to walk,
Perhaps grown wearied of their Corinth talk:
Over the solitary hills he fared,
Thoughtless at first, but ere eve's star appeared
His phantasy was lost, where reason fades,   235
In the calmed twilight of Platonic shades.[1]
Lamia beheld him coming, near, more near—
Close to her passing, in indifference drear,
His silent sandals swept the mossy green;
So neighbored to him, and yet so unseen   240
She stood: he passed, shut up in mysteries,
His mind wrapped like his mantle, while her eyes
Followed his steps, and her neck regal white
Turned—syllabling thus, "Ah, Lycius bright
And will you leave me on the hills alone?   245
Lycius, look back! and be some pity shown."
He did; not with cold wonder fearingly,
But Orpheus-like at an Eurydice;[2]
For so delicious were the words she sung,
It seemed he had loved them a whole summer long: 250
And soon his eyes had drunk her beauty up,
Leaving no drop in the bewildering cup,
And still the cup was full—while he, afraid
Lest she should vanish ere his lip had paid
Due adoration, thus began to adore;   255
Her soft look growing coy, she saw his chain so sure:
"Leave thee alone! Look back! Ah, Goddess, see
Whether my eyes can ever turn from thee!
For pity do not this sad heart belie[3]—

(Vulcan, god of fire and metalworking)
gleam in long lines around open courts
(piazzas). "Palatine": palatial.
1. I.e., he was absorbed in musing
about the obscurities of Plato's philosophy.
2. As Orpheus looked at Eurydice in

Hades. Orpheus was allowed by Pluto
to lead Eurydice back to earth on condition that he not look back at her, but
he could not resist doing so, and lost
her once more.
3. Be false to.

Even as thou vanishest so shall I die.   260
Stay! though a Naiad of the rivers, stay!
To thy far wishes will thy streams obey:
Stay! though the greenest woods be thy domain,
Alone they can drink up the morning rain:
Though a descended Pleiad,[4] will not one   265
Of thine harmonious sisters keep in tune
Thy spheres, and as thy silver proxy shine?
So sweetly to these ravished ears of mine
Came thy sweet greeting, that if thou shouldst fade
Thy memory will waste me to a shade—   270
For pity do not melt!"—"If I should stay,"
Said Lamia, "here, upon this floor of clay,
And pain my steps upon these flowers too rough,
What canst thou say or do of charm enough
To dull the nice[5] remembrance of my home?   275
Thou canst not ask me with thee here to roam
Over these hills and vales, where no joy is—
Empty of immortality and bliss!
Thou art a scholar, Lycius, and must know
That finer spirits cannot breathe below   280
In human climes, and live: Alas! poor youth,
What taste of purer air hast thou to soothe
My essence? What serener palaces,
Where I may all my many senses please,
And by mysterious sleights a hundred thirsts appease?   285
It cannot be—Adieu!" So said, she rose
Tiptoe with white arms spread. He, sick to lose
The amorous promise of her lone complain,
Swooned, murmuring of love, and pale with pain.
The cruel lady, without any show   290
Of sorrow for her tender favorite's woe,
But rather, if her eyes could brighter be,
With brighter eyes and slow amenity,
Put her new lips to his, and gave afresh
The life she had so tangled in her mesh: 295
And as he from one trance was wakening
Into another, she began to sing,
Happy in beauty, life, and love, and everything,
A song of love, too sweet for earthly lyres,
While, like held breath, the stars drew in their panting fires. 300
And then she whispered in such trembling tone,
As those who, safe together met alone
For the first time through many anguished days,
Use other speech than looks; bidding him raise
His drooping head, and clear his soul of doubt,   305
For that she was a woman, and without
Any more subtle fluid in her veins
Than throbbing blood, and that the selfsame pains
Inhabited her frail-strung heart as his.

4. One of the seven sisters composing   5. Detailed, minutely accurate.
the constellation Pleiades.

And next she wondered how his eyes could miss   310
Her face so long in Corinth, where, she said,
She dwelt but half retired, and there had led
Days happy as the gold coin could invent
Without the aid of love; yet in content
Till she saw him, as once she passed him by,   315
Where 'gainst a column he leant thoughtfully
At Venus' temple porch, 'mid baskets heaped
Of amorous herbs and flowers, newly reaped
Late on that eve, as 'twas the night before
The Adonian feast;[6] whereof she saw no more,   320
But wept alone those days, for why should she adore?
Lycius from death awoke into amaze,
To see her still, and singing so sweet lays;
Then from amaze into delight he fell
To hear her whisper woman's lore so well;   325
And every word she spake enticed him on
To unperplexed delight[7] and pleasure known.
Let the mad poets say whate'er they please
Of the sweets of Faeries, Peris,[8] Goddesses,
There is not such a treat among them all,   330
Haunters of cavern, lake, and waterfall,
As a real woman, lineal indeed
From Pyrrha's pebbles[9] or old Adam's seed.
Thus gentle Lamia judged, and judged aright,
That Lycius could not love in half a fright,   335
So threw the goddess off, and won his heart
More pleasantly by playing woman's part,
With no more awe than what her beauty gave,
That, while it smote, still guaranteed to save.
Lycius to all made eloquent reply,   340
Marrying to every word a twinborn sigh;
And last, pointing to Corinth, asked her sweet,
If 'twas too far that night for her soft feet.
The way was short, for Lamia's eagerness
Made, by a spell, the triple league decrease   345
To a few paces; not at all surmised
By blinded Lycius, so in her comprised.[1]
They passed the city gates, he knew not how,
So noiseless, and he never thought to know.

As men talk in a dream, so Corinth all,   350
Throughout her palaces imperial,
And all her populous streets and temples lewd,[2]
Muttered, like tempest in the distance brewed,
To the wide-spreaded night above her towers.
Men, women, rich and poor, in the cool hours,   355

6. The feast of Adonis, beloved by Venus.
7. I.e., delight not mixed with its neighbor, pain; see line 192.
8. Fairylike creatures in Persian mythology.
9. Descended from the pebbles with which, in Greek myth, Pyrrha and Deucalion repeopled the earth after the flood.
1. Bound up.
2. Temples of Venus, whose worship sometimes involved ritual prostitution.

Shuffled their sandals o'er the pavement white,
Companioned or alone; while many a light
Flared, here and there, from wealthy festivals
And threw their moving shadows on the walls,
Or found them clustered in the corniced shade   360
Of some arched temple door, or dusky colonnade.

Muffling his face, of greeting friends in fear,
Her fingers he pressed hard, as one came near
With curled gray beard, sharp eyes, and smooth bald crown,
Slow-stepped, and robed in philosophic gown: 365
Lycius shrank closer, as they met and passed,
Into his mantle, adding wings to haste,
While hurried Lamia trembled: "Ah," said he,
"Why do you shudder, love, so ruefully?
Why does your tender palm dissolve in dew?"—   370
"I'm wearied," said fair Lamia: "tell me who
Is that old man? I cannot bring to mind
His features—Lycius! wherefore did you blind
Yourself from his quick eyes?" Lycius replied,
" 'Tis Apollonius sage, my trusty guide   375
And good instructor; but tonight he seems
The ghost of folly haunting my sweet dreams."

While yet he spake they had arrived before
A pillared porch, with lofty portal door,
Where hung a silver lamp, whose phosphor glow   380
Reflected in the slabbéd steps below,
Mild as a star in water; for so new,
And so unsullied was the marble hue,
So through the crystal polish, liquid fine,
Ran the dark veins, that none but feet divine   385
Could e'er have touched there. Sounds Aeolian[3]
Breathed from the hinges, as the ample span
Of the wide doors disclosed a place unknown
Some time to any, but those two alone,
And a few Persian mutes, who that same year   390
Were seen about the markets: none knew where
They could inhabit; the most curious
Were foiled, who watched to trace them to their house:
And but the flitter-wingéd verse must tell,
For truth's sake, what woe afterwards befell,   395
'Twould humor many a heart to leave them thus,
Shut from the busy world of more incredulous.

Part II

Love in a hut, with water and a crust,
Is—Love, forgive us!—cinders, ashes, dust;
Love in a palace is perhaps at last
More grievous torment than a hermit's fast:

3. Like sounds from the wind harp (Aeolus is god of winds), which responds
musically to a current of air.

That is a doubtful tale from faery land,   5
Hard for the non-elect to understand.
Had Lycius lived to hand his story down,
He might have given the moral a fresh frown,
Or clenched it quite: but too short was their bliss
To breed distrust and hate, that make the soft voice hiss.   10
Beside, there, nightly, with terrific glare,
Love, jealous grown of so complete a pair,
Hovered and buzzed his wings, with fearful roar,
Above the lintel of their chamber door,
And down the passage cast a glow upon the floor.   15

For all this came a ruin: side by side
They were enthronéd, in the eventide,
Upon a couch, near to a curtaining
Whose airy texture, from a golden string,
Floated into the room, and let appear   20
Unveiled the summer heaven, blue and clear,
Betwixt two marble shafts: there they reposed,
Where use had made it sweet, with eyelids closed,
Saving a tithe which love still open kept,
That they might see each other while they almost slept;   25
When from the slope side of a suburb hill,
Deafening the swallow's twitter, came a thrill
Of trumpets—Lycius started—the sounds fled,
But left a thought, a buzzing in his head.
For the first time, since first he harbored in   30
That purple-linéd palace of sweet sin,
His spirit passed beyond its golden bourn
Into the noisy world almost forsworn.
The lady, ever watchful, penetrant,
Saw this with pain, so arguing a want   35
Of something more, more than her empery[4]
Of joys; and she began to moan and sigh
Because he mused beyond her, knowing well
That but a moment's thought is passion's passing bell.[5]
"Why do you sigh, fair creature?" whispered he: 40
"Why do you think?" returned she tenderly:
"You have deserted me—where am I now?
Not in your heart while care weighs on your brow:
No, no, you have dismissed me; and I go
From your breast houseless: aye, it must be so."   45
He answered, bending to her open eyes,
Where he was mirrored small in paradise,
"My silver planet, both of eve and morn![6]
Why will you plead yourself so sad forlorn,
While I am striving how to fill my heart   50
With deeper crimson, and a double smart?
How to entangle, trammel up, and snare
Your soul in mine, and labyrinth you there

4. Empire.
5. Death knell.
6. The planet Venus, which is both the morning and the evening star.

Like the hid scent in an unbudded rose?
Aye, a sweet kiss—you see your mighty woes.[7]
My thoughts! shall I unveil them? Listen then!   55
What mortal hath a prize, that other men
May be confounded and abashed withal,
But lets it sometimes pace abroad majestical,
And triumph, as in thee I should rejoice   60
Amid the hoarse alarm of Corinth's voice.
Let my foes choke, and my friends shout afar,
While through the thronged streets your bridal car
Wheels round its dazzling spokes."—The lady's cheek
Trembled; she nothing said, but, pale and meek,   65
Arose and knelt before him, wept a rain
Of sorrows at his words; at last with pain
Beseeching him, the while his hand she wrung,
To change his purpose. He thereat was stung,
Perverse, with stronger fancy to reclaim   70
Her wild and timid nature to his aim:
Besides, for all his love, in self-despite,
Against his better self, he took delight
Luxurious in her sorrows, soft and new.
His passion, cruel grown, took on a hue   75
Fierce and sanguineous as 'twas possible
In one whose brow had no dark veins to swell.
Fine was the mitigated fury, like
Apollo's presence when in act to strike
The serpent—Ha, the serpent! certes, she   80
Was none. She burnt, she loved the tyranny,
And, all subdued, consented to the hour
When to the bridal he should lead his paramour.
Whispering in midnight silence, said the youth,
"Sure some sweet name thou hast, though, by my truth,   85
I have not asked it, ever thinking thee
Not mortal, but of heavenly progeny,
As still I do. Hast any mortal name,
Fit appellation for this dazzling frame?
Or friends or kinsfolk on the cited earth,   90
To share our marriage feast and nuptial mirth?"
"I have no friends," said Lamia, "no, not one;
My presence in wide Corinth hardly known:
My parents' bones are in their dusty urns
Sepulchered, where no kindled incense burns,   95
Seeing all their luckless race are dead, save me,
And I neglect the holy rite for thee.
Even as you list invite your many guests;
But if, as now it seems, your vision rests
With any pleasure on me, do not bid   100
Old Apollonius—from him keep me hid."
Lycius, perplexed at words so blind and blank,

7. Playfully: "You see how great your troubles were!"

Made close inquiry; from whose touch she shrank,
Feigning a sleep; and he to the dull shade
Of deep sleep in a moment was betrayed.   105

It was the custom then to bring away
The bride from home at blushing shut of day,
Veiled, in a chariot, heralded along
By strewn flowers, torches, and a marriage song,
With other pageants: but this fair unknown   110
Had not a friend. So being left alone
(Lycius was gone to summon all his kin),
And knowing surely she could never win
His foolish heart from its mad pompousness,
She set herself, high-thoughted, how to dress   115
The misery in fit magnificence.
She did so, but 'tis doubtful how and whence
Came, and who were her subtle servitors.
About the halls, and to and from the doors,
There was a noise of wings, till in short space   120
The glowing banquet room shone with wide-archéd grace.
A haunting music, sole perhaps and lone
Supportress of the faery roof, made moan
Throughout, as fearful the whole charm might fade.
Fresh carvéd cedar, mimicking a glade   125
Of palm and plantain, met from either side,
High in the midst, in honor of the bride:
Two palms and then two plaintains, and so on,
From either side their stems branched one to one
All down the aisléd place; and beneath all   130
There ran a stream of lamps straight on from wall to wall.
So canopied, lay an untasted feast
Teeming with odors. Lamia, regal dressed,
Silently paced about, and as she went,
In pale contented sort of discontent,   135
Missioned her viewless servants to enrich
The fretted[8] splendor of each nook and niche.
Between the tree stems, marbled plain at first,
Came jasper panels; then, anon, there burst
Forth creeping imagery of slighter trees,   140
And with the larger wove in small intricacies.
Approving all, she faded at self-will,
And shut the chamber up, close, hushed and still,
Complete and ready for the revels rude,
When dreadful[9] guests would come to spoil her solitude.   145

The day appeared, and all the gossip rout.
O senseless Lycius! Madman! wherefore flout
The silent-blessing fate, warm cloistered hours,
And show to common eyes these secret bowers?

8. Adorned with fretwork (interlaced   9. Terrifying.
patterns).

The herd approached; each guest, with busy brain,   150
Arriving at the portal, gazed amain,[1]
And entered marveling: for they knew the street,
Remembered it from childhood all complete
Without a gap, yet ne'er before had seen
That royal porch, that high-built fair demesne;[2]   155
So in they hurried all, 'mazed, curious and keen:
Save one, who looked thereon with eye severe,
And with calm-planted steps walked in austere;
'Twas Apollonius: something too he laughed,
As though some knotty problem, that had daft[3]   160
His patient thought, had now begun to thaw,
And solve and melt—'twas just as he foresaw.

He met within the murmurous vestibule
His young disciple. " 'Tis no common rule,
Lycius," said he, "for uninvited guest   165
To force himself upon you, and infest
With an unbidden presence the bright throng
Of younger friends; yet must I do this wrong,
And you forgive me." Lycius blushed, and led
The old man through the inner doors broad-spread;   170
With reconciling words and courteous mien
Turning into sweet milk the sophist's spleen.

Of wealthy luster was the banquet room,
Filled with pervading brilliance and perfume:
Before each lucid panel fuming stood   175
A censer fed with myrrh and spicéd wood,
Each by a sacred tripod held aloft,
Whose slender feet wide-swerved upon the soft
Wool-wooféd[4] carpets: fifty wreaths of smoke
From fifty censers their light voyage took   180
To the high roof, still mimicked as they rose
Along the mirrored walls by twin-clouds odorous.
Twelve spheréd tables, by silk seats ensphered,
High as the level of a man's breast reared
On libbard's[5] paws, upheld the heavy gold   185
Of cups and goblets, and the store thrice told
Of Ceres' horn[6] and, in huge vessels, wine
Come from the gloomy tun with merry shine.
Thus loaded with a feast the tables stood,
Each shrining in the midst the image of a God.   190

When in an antechamber every guest
Had felt the cold full sponge to pleasure pressed,
By minist'ring slaves, upon his hands and feet,
And fragrant oils with ceremony meet

1. Intently.
2. Estate.
3. Baffled, bewildered.
4. Woven.

5. Leopard's.
6. The horn of plenty, overflowing with the products of Ceres, goddess of vegetation.

Poured on his hair, they all moved to the feast   195
In white robes, and themselves in order placed
Around the silken couches, wondering
Whence all this mighty cost and blaze of wealth could spring.

Soft went the music the soft air along,
While fluent Greek a voweled undersong   200
Kept up among the guests, discoursing low
At first, for scarcely was the wine at flow;
But when the happy vintage touched their brains,
Louder they talk, and louder come the strains
Of powerful instruments—the gorgeous dyes,   205
The space, the splendor of the draperies,
The roof of awful richness, nectarous cheer,
Beautiful slaves, and Lamia's self, appear,
Now, when the wine has done its rosy deed,
And every soul from human trammels freed,   210
No more so strange; for merry wine, sweet wine,
Will make Elysian shades not too fair, too divine.
Soon was God Bacchus at meridian height;
Flushed were their cheeks, and bright eyes double bright:
Garlands of every green, and every scent   215
From vales deflowered, or forest trees branch-rent,
In baskets of bright osiered[7] gold were brought
High as the handles heaped, to suit the thought
Of every guest; that each, as he did please,
Might fancy-fit his brows, silk-pillowed at his ease.   220

What wreath for Lamia? What for Lycius?
What for the sage, old Apollonius?
Upon her aching forehead be there hung
The leaves of willow and of adder's tongue;[8]
And for the youth, quick, let us strip for him   225
The thyrsus,[9] that his watching eyes may swim
Into forgetfulness; and, for the sage,
Let spear-grass and the spiteful thistle wage
War on his temples. Do not all charms fly
At the mere touch of cold philosophy?[1]   230
There was an awful[2] rainbow once in heaven:
We know her woof, her texture; she is given
In the dull catalogue of common things.
Philosophy will clip an Angel's wings,
Conquer all mysteries by rule and line,   235
Empty the haunted air, and gnoméd mine[3]—

---

7. Plaited. An "osier" is a willow rod used in weaving baskets.
8. A fern whose spikes resemble a serpent's tongue.
9. The vine-covered staff of Bacchus, used to signify drunkenness.
1. "Philosophy" in the sense of "natural philosophy," or science. Benjamin Haydon tells in his *Autobiography* how,
at a hard-drinking and high-spirited dinner party, Keats had agreed with Charles Lamb (to what extent jokingly, is not clear) that Newton's *Optics* "had destroyed all the poetry of the rainbow by reducing it to the prismatic colors."
2. Awe-inspiring.
3. Gnomes were guardians of mines.

Unweave a rainbow, as it erewhile made
The tender-personed Lamia melt into a shade.

By her glad Lycius sitting, in chief place,
Scarce saw in all the room another face,   240
Till, checking his love trance, a cup he took
Full brimmed, and opposite sent forth a look
'Cross the broad table, to beseech a glance
From his old teacher's wrinkled countenance,
And pledge him.[4] The bald-head philosopher   245
Had fixed his eye, without a twinkle or stir
Full on the alarmèd beauty of the bride,
Brow-beating her fair form, and troubling her sweet pride.
Lycius then pressed her hand, with devout touch,
As pale it lay upon the rosy couch: 250
'Twas icy, and the cold ran through his veins;
Then sudden it grew hot, and all the pains
Of an unnatural heat shot to his heart.
"Lamia, what means this? Wherefore dost thou start?
Know'st thou that man?" Poor Lamia answered not.   255
He gazed into her eyes, and not a jot
Owned[5] they the lovelorn piteous appeal:
More, more he gazed: his human senses reel:
Some hungry spell that loveliness absorbs;
There was no recognition in those orbs.   260
"Lamia!" he cried—and no soft-toned reply.
The many heard, and the loud revelry
Grew hush; the stately music no more breathes;
The myrtle[5a] sickened in a thousand wreaths.
By faint degrees, voice, lute, and pleasure ceased;   265
A deadly silence step by step increased,
Until it seemed a horrid presence there,
And not a man but felt the terror in his hair.
"Lamia!" he shrieked; and nothing but the shriek
With its sad echo did the silence break.   270
"Begone, foul dream!" he cried, gazing again
In the bride's face, where now no azure vein
Wandered on fair-spaced temples; no soft bloom
Misted the cheek; no passion to illume
The deep-recessèd vision—all was blight;   275
Lamia, no longer fair, there sat a deadly white.
"Shut, shut those juggling[6] eyes, thou ruthless man!
Turn them aside, wretch! or the righteous ban
Of all the Gods, whose dreadful images
Here represent their shadowy presences,   280
May pierce them on the sudden with the thorn
Of painful blindness; leaving thee forlorn,
In trembling dotage to the feeblest fright
Of conscience, for their long offended might,

4. Drink a toast to him.   of love.
5. Acknowledged.   6. Deceiving, full of trickery.
5a. Sacred to Venus, hence an emblem

For all thine impious proud-heart sophistries,   285
Unlawful magic, and enticing lies.
Corinthians! look upon that gray-beard wretch!
Mark how, possessed, his lashless eyelids stretch
Around his demon eyes! Corinthians, see!
My sweet bride withers at their potency."   290
"Fool!" said the sophist, in an undertone
Gruff with contempt; which a death-nighing moan
From Lycius answered, as heart-struck and lost,
He sank supine beside the aching ghost.
"Fool! Fool!" repeated he, while his eyes still   295
Relented not, nor moved; "from every ill
Of life have I preserved thee to this day,
And shall I see thee made a serpent's prey?"
Then Lamia breathed death breath; the sophist's eye,
Like a sharp spear, went through her utterly,   300
Keen, cruel, perceant,[7] stinging: she, as well
As her weak hand could any meaning tell,
Motioned him to be silent; vainly so,
He looked and looked again a level—No!
"A serpent!" echoed he; no sooner said,   305
Than with a frightful scream she vanishéd:
And Lycius' arms were empty of delight,
As were his limbs of life, from that same night.
On the high couch he lay!—his friends came round—
Supported him—no pulse, or breath they found,   310
And, in its marriage robe, the heavy body wound.

July–Aug., 1819   1820

7. Piercing.

The Fall of Hyperion

In September of 1818, at the close of his twenty-third year and while he was serving as nurse to his dying brother Tom, Keats undertook an epic poem, modeled on *Paradise Lost*, which he called *Hyperion*. Its subject, the displacement of Saturn and his fellow Titans by Zeus and the other Olympians, was taken from Greek mythology, but the primary epic question, like that in *Paradise Lost*, was *unde malum?*—whence and why evil? Keats set out to represent an answer, not in terms of the Christian or any other religious creed, but in humanistic terms, delimited to man and his natural milieu. The Titans had been equable and benign gods, ruling in the Saturnian, or golden, age of general felicity. Yet at the beginning of the poem all the Titans except Hyperion, god of the sun, have been dethroned; and the uncomprehending Saturn again and again raises the question, Who? Why? How? Is there blank unreason and injustice at the heart of the universe? Oceanus, god of the sea, offers a valid but incomplete solution: the gods, though themselves blameless, have fallen in the natural progression of things, according to which each stage of development is fated to give place to a higher excellence, "for 'tis the eternal law / That first in beauty should be first in might." And it is the part of wisdom and virtue among the Titans to accept this truth uncomplainingly,

>   for to bear all naked truths,
>   And to envisage circumstance, all calm,
>   That is the top of sovereignty.

In Book III of the original *Hyperion* this is supplemented by the experience of Apollo, still a youth on earth but destined to displace Hyperion
among the heavenly powers. He lives in "aching ignorance" of the universe
and its processes, but he is aware of his ignorance and avid for knowledge.
To him appears Mnemosyne, herself a Titan, but one who has deserted
her fellow gods "For prophecies of thee, and for the sake / Of loveliness
new born." Suddenly Apollo reads in the face of Mnemosyne—goddess of
memory, who will be mother of the muses, and so of all the arts—the
silent record of the defeat of the Titans and at once soars to the knowledge
that he seeks: the deep understanding, at once intoxicating and agonizing,
that life involves process, and process entails change and suffering, and that
there can be no creative progress except by the defeat and destruction of
the preceding stage. Apollo cries out:

>   Knowledge enormous makes a god of me.
>   Names, deeds, gray legends, dire events, rebellions,
>   Majesties, sovran voices, agonies,
>   Creations and destroyings, all at once
>   Pour into the wide hollows of my brain
>   And deify me, as if of some blithe wine
>   Or elixir peerless I had drunk,
>   And so become immortal.

This is an enlargement of Apollo's awareness to encompass the sense of the
tragic nature of life which it has been the Titans' deficiency to lack. As
the fragment breaks off Apollo is transfigured, like one who should "with
fierce convulse / Die into life," not only into the god of the sun, who has
earned the right to displace Hyperion, but also into the god of the highest
poetry.

This extraordinary fragment Keats wrote mainly in the two months
between late September and December, 1818, and he abandoned it entirely
by April of 1819. Late that summer, however, he took up the theme again,
under the title *The Fall of Hyperion: A Dream*. This time his primary
model is Dante, especially the *Purgatorio*, which he had been carefully
studying in Cary's translation. In *The Divine Comedy* all the narrated
events had been represented as a vision granted to Dante at the beginning
of the poem. In similar fashion Keats begins his new poem with a long
induction in which the poet, in a dream, earns the right to a vision finally
granted him by Moneta (her Latin name suggests "the Admonisher"), who
replaces Mnemosyne; this vision incorporates the epic events narrated in the
first *Hyperion*. The induction, in effect, shifts the center of poetic concern
from the epic action to the evolving consciousness of the narrative poet
himself, as he seeks his identity and status; it serves also to displace the
earlier ordeal through which Apollo had become god of poetry by the
ordeal of this particular poet.

As early as *Sleep and Poetry* (1816), Keats had begun to explore the
baffling relation of dreams to insight, of wishful fantasies and illusions to
imaginative truth, of the life of actuality and of humane action to the
contemplative vision of the poet; and he had worked these matters into
his poetic program to move from the realm of "Flora, and old Pan" to
the "nobler life" of "the agonies, the strife / Of human hearts." He con-

tinued to widen these speculations in *Endymion* and a number of his shorter poems; and his letters show his ceaseless effort to assimilate his ever-enlarging experience, his sharpening sense of suffering humanity, and his awareness of the need for some equivalent of the "salvation" offered by a religious creed he could not accept, into his theory and program of poetry. (See especially the letters, included here, on "The Chambers of Human Life" and on "The Vale of Soul-Making.") Into the induction to the long "Dream" which constitutes *The Fall of Hyperion*, Keats works the results of his sustained attempts to differentiate escapist dreams, as well as the creeds of the religious "fanatic," from the imaginative vision of the poet; he presents these results as progressive discoveries which he had made at the various stages of his own development as a poet. The induction, therefore, is Keats's equivalent of a poem he never saw, Wordsworth's *Prelude*, the account of "the Growth of a Poet's Mind." But whereas Wordsworth had represented his evolution of mind, up to and through the crisis in which he discovered his poetic identity, in the mode of literal autobiography, Keats instead employs the pattern of a ritual initiation. In the course of this agonizing rite of passage the poet progresses, in quantum leaps of expanding awareness of what it is to be human, and a poet of humanity, to the stage at which, having passed through and beyond the sufferings of ordinary experience to achieve aesthetic insight and distance—the power (line 304) "To see as a god sees"— he has defined the kind of poet he is and earned the right to essay his epic poem of tragic suffering.

A number of reasons impelled Keats to abandon *The Fall of Hyperion* at the sixty-first line of the second Canto. Keats wrote to Reynolds on September 21, 1819:

I have given up Hyperion . . . Miltonic verse cannot be written but in an artful or rather artist's humour. I wish to give myself up to other sensations. English ought to be kept up. It may be interesting to you to pick out some lines from Hyperion and put a mark X to the false beauty proceeding from art, and one ‖ to the true voice of feeling.

The two *Hyperions* are astonishing achievements; but they are achievements, as Keats, with his matchless acumen in self-criticism recognized, which have the air of artistic *tours de force*, written in an age in which the high artifice of the epic matter and style had ceased to be the natural voice of the poet. In the same letter Keats mentions having composed two days earlier the ode *To Autumn*; in this, his last and most flawless major poem, the poet had envisaged the circumstance of the cycle of life and death, all calm, and had uttered his experience in the true voice of feeling.

The Fall of Hyperion

A DREAM

Canto I

Fanatics have their dreams, wherewith they weave
A paradise for a sect; the savage too
From forth the loftiest fashion of his sleep

Guesses at Heaven; pity these have not
Traced upon vellum or wild Indian leaf   5
The shadows of melodious utterance.
But bare of laurel they live, dream, and die;
For Poesy alone can tell her dreams,
With the fine spell of words alone can save
Imagination from the sable chain   10
And dumb enchantment. Who alive can say,
"Thou art no Poet—may'st not tell thy dreams"?
Since every man whose soul is not a clod
Hath visions, and would speak, if he had loved,
And been well nurtured in his mother tongue.   15
Whether the dream now purposed to rehearse
Be poet's or fanatic's will be known
When this warm scribe, my hand, is in the grave.

Methought I stood where trees of every clime,
Palm, myrtle, oak, and sycamore, and beech,   20
With plantain, and spice-blossoms, made a screen;
In neighborhood of fountains (by the noise
Soft-showering in my ears), and (by the touch
Of scent) not far from roses. Turning round
I saw an arbor with a drooping roof   25
Of trellis vines, and bells, and larger blooms,
Like floral censers, swinging light in air;
Before its wreathéd doorway, on a mound
Of moss, was spread a feast of summer fruits,
Which, nearer seen, seemed refuse of a meal   30
By angel tasted or our Mother Eve;[1]
For empty shells were scattered on the grass,
And grape-stalks but half bare, and remnants more,
Sweet smelling, whose pure kinds I could not know.
Still was more plenty than the fabled horn[2]   35
Thrice emptied could pour forth, at banqueting
For Proserpine returned to her own fields,[3]
Where the white heifers low. And appetite
More yearning than on Earth I ever felt
Growing within, I ate deliciously;   40
And, after not long, thirsted, for thereby
Stood a cool vessel of transparent juice,
Sipped by the wandered bee, the which I took,
And, pledging all the mortals of the world,
And all the dead whose names are in our lips,   45
Drank. That full draught is parent of my theme.[4]
No Asian poppy nor elixir fine

1. In *Paradise Lost* V.321 ff., Eve serves
the visiting angel, Raphael, with a meal
of fruits and fruit juices. Keats thus
adapts Milton's Eden to represent the
early stage of his own experience and
poetry.
2. The cornucopia, or horn of plenty.

3. When Proserpine each year is released
by her husband, Pluto, god of the underworld, for a sojourn on earth, it is the
beginning of spring.
4. The drink puts the poet to sleep and
effects the dream within a dream which
constitutes the rest of his poem.

Of the soon-fading jealous Caliphat;[5]
No poison gendered in close monkish cell,
To thin the scarlet conclave of old men,[6]   50
Could so have rapt unwilling life away.
Among the fragrant husks and berries crushed,
Upon the grass I struggled hard against
The domineering potion; but in vain:
The cloudy swoon came on, and down I sunk,   55
Like a Silenus[7] on an antique vase.
How long I slumbered 'tis a chance to guess.
When sense of life returned, I started up
As if with wings; but the fair trees were gone,
The mossy mound and arbor were no more: 60
I looked around upon the carvéd sides
Of an old sanctuary with roof august,
Builded so high, it seemed that filméd clouds
Might spread beneath, as o'er the stars of heaven;
So old the place was, I remembered none   65
The like upon the Earth: what I had seen
Of gray cathedrals, buttressed walls, rent towers,
The superannuations of sunk realms,
Or Nature's rocks toiled hard in waves and winds,
Seemed but the faulture of decrepit things   70
To that eternal doméd Monument.—
Upon the marble at my feet there lay
Store of strange vessels and large draperies,
Which needs had been of dyed asbestos wove,
Or in that place the moth could not corrupt,[8]   75
So white the linen, so, in some, distinct
Ran imageries from a somber loom.
All in a mingled heap confused there lay
Robes, golden tongs, censer and chafing dish,
Girdles, and chains, and holy jewelries.[9]   80

    Turning from these with awe, once more I raised
My eyes to fathom the space every way;
The embosséd roof, the silent massy range
Of columns north and south, ending in mist
Of nothing; then to eastward, where black gates   85
Were shut against the sunrise evermore.[1]
Then to the west I looked, and saw far off
An image, huge of feature as a cloud,
At level of whose feet an altar slept,
To be approached on either side by steps,   90

5. A council of Caliphs, Mohammedan
rulers, who plot to kill each other with
a poisonous draft ("elixir").
6. The Cardinals of the Catholic Church.
7. An elderly satyr, usually represented
as dead drunk.
8. Matthew vi.20. "Lay up for yourselves treasures in heaven, where neither
moth nor rust doth corrupt."

9. Offerings to the gods were spread on
the floor of Greek temples.
1. The poet cannot turn back to his
origin in the east, and the ways north
and south lead nowhere; he must travel
the way of mortal life toward the sunset. Cf. the westering course of the sun
in Wordsworth's *Ode: Intimations of
Immortality.*

And marble balustrade, and patient travail
To count with toil the innumerable degrees.
Towards the altar sober-paced I went,
Repressing haste, as too unholy there;
And, coming nearer, saw beside the shrine   95
One minist'ring;[2] and there arose a flame.
When in mid-May the sickening East wind
Shifts sudden to the south, the small warm rain
Melts out the frozen incense from all flowers,
And fills the air with so much pleasant health   100
That even the dying man forgets his shroud;
Even so that lofty sacrificial fire,
Sending forth Maian[3] incense, spread around
Forgetfulness of everything but bliss,
And clouded all the altar with soft smoke;   105
From whose white fragrant curtains thus I heard
Language pronounced: "If thou canst not ascend
These steps,[4] die on that marble where thou art.
Thy flesh, near cousin to the common dust,
Will parch for lack of nutriment—thy bones   110
Will wither in few years, and vanish so
That not the quickest eye could find a grain
Of what thou now art on that pavement cold.
The sands of thy short life are spent this hour,
And no hand in the universe can turn   115
Thy hourglass, if these gummed leaves be burnt
Ere thou canst mount up these immortal steps."
I heard, I looked: two senses both at once,
So fine, so subtle, felt the tyranny
Of that fierce threat and the hard task proposed.   120
Prodigious seemed the toil; the leaves were yet
Burning—when suddenly a palsied chill
Struck from the paved level up my limbs,
And was ascending quick to put cold grasp
Upon those streams that pulse beside the throat: 125
I shrieked, and the sharp anguish of my shriek
Stung my own ears—I strove hard to escape
The numbness; strove to gain the lowest step.
Slow, heavy, deadly was my pace: the cold
Grew stifling, suffocating, at the heart;   130
And when I clasped my hands I felt them not.
One minute before death, my iced foot touched
The lowest stair; and as it touched, life seemed
To pour in at the toes: I mounted up,
As once fair angels on a ladder flew   135
From the green turf to Heaven.[5] "Holy Power,"

2. Who identifies herself, line 226, as
Moneta.
3. Maia was one of the Pleiades, a
daughter of Atlas and (by Zeus) the
mother of Hermes.
4. These steps which the poet must ascend to knowledge were probably suggested by the stairs going up the steep
side of the Purgatorial Mount, in Dante's
Purgatorio.
5. The ladder by which, in a dream,
Jacob saw angels passing between heaven
and earth; Genesis xxviii.12 and *Para-*
dise Lost III.510–15.

Cried I, approaching near the hornéd shrine,[6]
"What am I that should so be saved from death?
What am I that another death come not
To choke my utterance sacrilegious, here?"   140
Then said the veiléd shadow: "Thou hast felt
What 'tis to die and live again before
Thy fated hour, that thou hadst power to do so
Is thy own safety; thou hast dated on
Thy doom."[7] "High Prophetess," said I, "purge off,   145
Benign, if so it please thee, my mind's film."
"None can usurp this height," returned that shade,
"But those to whom the miseries of the world
Are misery, and will not let them rest.
All else who find a haven in the world,   150
Where they may thoughtless sleep away their days,
If by a chance into this fane[8] they come,
Rot on the pavement where thou rottedst half."[9]
"Are there not thousands in the world," said I,
Encouraged by the sooth voice of the shade,   155
"Who love their fellows even to the death,
Who feel the giant agony of the world,
And more, like slaves to poor humanity,
Labor for mortal good? I sure should see
Other men here; but I am here alone."   160
"Those whom thou spak'st of are no vision'ries,"
Rejoined that voice. "They are no dreamers weak,
They seek no wonder but the human face;
No music but a happy-noted voice—
They come not here, they have no thought to come—   165
And thou art here, for thou art less than they.
What benefit canst thou, or all thy tribe,
To the great world? Thou art a dreaming thing,
A fever of thyself—think of the earth;
What bliss even in hope is there for thee?   170
What haven? every creature hath its home;
Every sole man hath days of joy and pain,
Whether his labors be sublime or low—
The pain alone, the joy alone, distinct.
Only the dreamer venoms all his days,   175
Bearing more woe than all his sins deserve.
Therefore, that happiness be somewhat shared,
Such things as thou art are admitted oft
Into like gardens thou didst pass erewhile,
And suffered in these temples: for that cause   180
Thou standest safe beneath this statue's knees."
"That I am favored for unworthiness,

---

6. As e.g., in Exodus xxvii.2, "And thou shalt make the horns of [the altar] upon the four corners thereof." In his description of the temple and its accoutrements, Keats deliberately mingles Hebrew, Christian, and pagan elements, to represent the poet's passage through the stage represented by all religions, which are "dreams" made into the creed for "a sect" (lines 1–18).
7. I.e., you have postponed the time when you will be judged.
8. Temple.
9. I.e., "where you halfway rotted."

By such propitious parley medicined
In sickness not ignoble, I rejoice,
Aye, and could weep for love of such award."   185
So answered I, continuing, "If it please,
[1][Majestic shadow, tell me: sure not all
Those melodies sung into the World's ear
Are useless: sure a poet is a sage;
A humanist, physician to all men.   190
That I am none I feel, as vultures feel
They are no birds when eagles are abroad.
What am I then: Thou spakest of my tribe:
What tribe?" The tall shade veiled in drooping white
Then spake, so much more earnest, that the breath   195
Moved the thin linen folds that drooping hung
About a golden censer from the hand
Pendent—"Art thou not of the dreamer tribe?
The poet and the dreamer are distinct,
Diverse, sheer opposite, antipodes.   200
The one pours out a balm upon the World,
The other vexes it." Then shouted I
Spite of myself, and with a Pythia's spleen,[2]
"Apollo! faded! O far flown Apollo!
Where is thy misty pestilence[3] to creep   205
Into the dwellings, through the door crannies
Of all mock lyrists, large self worshipers
And careless Hectorers in proud bad verse?[4]
Though I breathe death with them it will be life
To see them sprawl before me into graves.][5]   210

1. Keats's friend, Richard Woodhouse, crossed out lines 187–210 in a manuscript of the poem, with the marginal comment at the first line, "Keats seems to have intended to erase this and the next twenty-one lines"; perhaps his ground for this opinion is the repetition between lines 187 and 211, and between lines 194–98 and 216–20. Since there is no good evidence, however, that Keats planned to do more than merely revise this crucial passage, it is usually reprinted (as here) in brackets.
2. With the anger ("spleen") of the Pythia, the priestess who served at Delphi as the oracle of Apollo, the god of poetry.
3. Probably the foul vapors which were said to issue from the earth and intoxicate the Delphic oracle.
4. This has been conjectured as referring to Byron, or else to several contemporaries, including Shelley and Wordsworth. But the poetic types, not individuals, are all that matter to Keats's argument.
5. In lines 147–210, we find a series of progressive distinctions: (1) between humanitarians who feel for "the miseries of the world" and those men who are "thoughtless" sleepers (lines 147–53);

(2) within the class of humanitarians, between those who actively "benefit * * * the great world" and the poets who are "visionaries" and "dreamers" (lines 161–69); (3) and within the class of poets, between those who are merely dreamers and those who are sages and healers (lines 187–202). As in the colloquy between Asia and Demogorgon (see above, Shelley's *Prometheus Unbound*, II.1–128), the interchange here represents, in dramatized form, a process of inner analysis and self-discovery on the part of the questing poet. Moneta's charges should not be read as final judgments but as tests to determine the "tribe" to which he belongs—tests he passes by the nature of the responses he makes. The fact that Moneta continuously alters the categories by which she judges him signifies that, in the very course of his self-investigation, he changes and grows into what he is at the end of the process. At this point, the fact that the narrator himself proceeds to bring charges against self-indulgent and irresponsible poets distinguishes him from the class of poets he denounces and thus shows that he is ready for the final stage of his ordeal, his initiation into the realm of the highest poetry,

Majestic shadow, tell me where I am,
Whose altar this; for whom this incense curls;
What image this whose face I cannot see,
For the broad marble knees; and who thou art,
Of accent feminine so courteous?"   215

Then the tall shade, in drooping linens veiled,
Spoke out, so much more earnest, that her breath
Stirred the thin folds of gauze that drooping hung
About a golden censer from her hand
Pendent; and by her voice I knew she shed   220
Long-treasured tears. "This temple, sad and lone,
Is all spared from the thunder of a war
Foughten long since by giant hierarchy
Against rebellion: this old image here,
Whose carvéd features wrinkled as he fell,   225
Is Saturn's; I Moneta, left supreme,
Sole Priestess of his desolation."
I had no words to answer, for my tongue,
Useless, could find about its rooféd home
No syllable of a fit majesty   230
To make rejoinder to Moneta's mourn.
There was a silence, while the altar's blaze
Was fainting for sweet food. I looked thereon,
And on the pavéd floor, where nigh were piled
Faggots of cinnamon, and many heaps   235
Of other crispéd spice-wood; then again
I looked upon the altar, and its horns
Whitened with ashes, and its lang'rous flame,
And then upon the offerings again;
And so by turns—till sad Moneta cried,   240
"The sacrifice is done, but not the less
Will I be kind to thee for thy good will.
My power, which to me is still a curse,
Shall be to thee a wonder; for the scenes
Still swooning vivid through my globéd brain,   245
With an electral changing misery,
Thou shalt with those dull mortal eyes behold,
Free from all pain, if wonder pain thee not."
As near as an immortal's spheréd words
Could to a mother's soften, were these last: 250
And yet I had a terror of her robes,
And chiefly of the veils, that from her brow
Hung pale, and curtained her in mysteries,
That made my heart too small to hold its blood.
This saw that Goddess, and with sacred hand   255
Parted the veils. Then saw I a wan face,
Not pined by human sorrows, but bright-blanched

through the revelation of the "high tragedy" (line 277) of what it means to be human. This ultimate enlightenment, which begins with line 291 and which was intended to constitute the remainder of the poem, is a vision in a dream within a dream (see line 46 and footnote).

By an immortal sickness which kills not;
It works a constant change, which happy death
Can put no end to; deathwards progressing   260
To no death was that visage; it had passed
The lily and the snow; and beyond these
I must not think now, though I saw that face—
But for her eyes I should have fled away.
They held me back, with a benignant light,   265
Soft mitigated by divinest lids
Half-closed, and visionless entire they seemed
Of all external things; they saw me not,
But in blank splendor, beamed like the mild moon,
Who comforts those she sees not, who knows not   270
What eyes are upward cast. As I had found
A grain of gold upon a mountain's side,
And twinged with avarice strained out my eyes
To search its sullen entrails rich with ore,
So at the view of sad Moneta's brow,   275
I ached to see what things the hollow brain
Behind enwombéd: what high tragedy
In the dark secret chambers of her skull
Was acting, that could give so dread a stress
To her cold lips, and fill with such a light   280
Her planetary eyes; and touch her voice
With such a sorrow. "Shade of Memory!"
Cried I, with act adorant at her feet,
"By all the gloom hung round thy fallen house,
By this last temple, by the golden age,   285
By great Apollo, thy dear Foster Child,
And by thyself, forlorn divinity,
The pale Omega⁶ of a withered race,
Let me behold, according as thou saidst,
What in thy brain so ferments to and fro!"   290
No sooner had this conjuration passed
My devout lips, than side by side we stood
(Like a stunt bramble by a solemn pine)
Deep in the shady sadness of a vale,⁷
Far sunken from the healthy breath of morn,   295
Far from the fiery noon and eve's one star.
Onward I looked beneath the gloomy boughs,
And saw, what first I thought an image huge,
Like to the image pedestaled so high
In Saturn's temple. Then Moneta's voice   300
Came brief upon mine ear: "So Saturn sat
When he had lost his Realms—" whereon there grew
A power within me of enormous ken
To see as a god sees, and take the depth

---

6. The long *O*, final letter of the Greek alphabet; hence, "last member."
7. This was the opening line of the original *Hyperion*. The rest of the poem is a revised version of part of that first text, with the poet now represented as allowed to envision the course of events which Moneta remembers (lines 282, 289–90).

Of things as nimbly as the outward eye   305
Can size and shape pervade. The lofty theme
At those few words hung vast before my mind,
With half-unraveled web. I set myself
Upon an eagle's watch, that I might see,
And seeing ne'er forget. No stir of life   310
Was in this shrouded vale, not so much air
As in the zoning[8] of a summer's day
Robs not one light seed from the feathered grass,
But where the dead leaf fell there did it rest:
A stream went voiceless by, still deadened more   315
By reason of the fallen Divinity
Spreading more shade; the Naiad[9] 'mid her reeds
Pressed her cold finger closer to her lips.
    Along the margin-sand large footmarks went
No farther than to where old Saturn's feet   320
Had rested, and there slept, how long a sleep!
Degraded, cold, upon the sodden ground
His old right hand lay nerveless, listless, dead,
Unsceptred; and his realmless eyes[1] were closed,
While his bowed head seemed listening to the Earth,   325
His ancient mother,[2] for some comfort yet.

    It seemed no force could wake him from his place;
But there came one who, with a kindred hand
Touched his wide shoulders after bending low
With reverence, though to one who knew it not.   330
Then came the grievèd voice of Mnemosyne,[3]
And grieved I hearkened. "That divinity
Whom thou saw'st step from yon forlornest wood,
And with slow pace approach our fallen King,
Is Thea,[4] softest-natured of our Brood."   335
I marked the Goddess in fair statuary
Surpassing wan Moneta by the head,[5]
And in her sorrow nearer woman's tears.
There was a listening fear in her regard,
As if calamity had but begun;   340
As if the vanward clouds[6] of evil days
Had spent their malice, and the sullen rear
Was with its stored thunder laboring up.
One hand she pressed upon that aching spot
Where beats the human heart, as if just there,   345
Though an immortal, she felt cruel pain;
The other upon Saturn's bended neck
She laid, and to the level of his hollow ear
Leaning with parted lips, some words she spoke

8. Course.
9. Water nymph.
1. Saturn's eyes, when open, express the fact that he has lost his realm.
2. Saturn and the other Titans were the children of Heaven and Earth.
3. A slip; Moneta was Mnemosyne in the first *Hyperion*.
4. Sister and wife of Hyperion.
5. I.e., Thea was a head taller than Moneta.
6. The front line of clouds.

In solemn tenor and deep organ tune;   350
Some mourning words, which in our feeble tongue
Would come in this-like accenting; how frail
To that large utterance of the early Gods!

   "Saturn! look up—and for what, poor lost King?[7]
I have no comfort for thee; no, not one;   355
I cannot cry, 'Wherefore thus sleepest thou?'
For Heaven is parted from thee, and the Earth
Knows thee not, so afflicted, for a God;
And Ocean too, with all its solemn noise,
Has from thy scepter passed, and all the air   360
Is emptied of thine hoary majesty:
Thy thunder, captious at the new command,
Rumbles reluctant o'er our fallen house;
And thy sharp lightning, in unpracticed hands,
Scorches and burns our once serene domain.   365
With such remorseless speed still come new woes,
That unbelief has not a space to breathe.[8]
Saturn! sleep on—me thoughtless,[1] why should I
Thus violate thy slumbrous solitude?
Why should I ope thy melancholy eyes?   370
Saturn! sleep on, while at thy feet I weep."

   As when upon a trancéd summer-night
Forests, branch-charméd by the earnest stars,[2]
Dream, and so dream all night without a noise,
Save from one gradual solitary gust,   375
Swelling upon the silence; dying off;
As if the ebbing air had but one wave;
So came these words, and went; the while in tears
She pressed her fair large forehead to the earth,
Just where her fallen hair might spread in curls,   380
A soft and silken mat for Saturn's feet.
Long, long those two were postured motionless,
Like sculpture builded up upon the grave
Of their own power. A long awful time
I looked upon them: still they were the same;   385
The frozen God still bending to the earth,
And the sad Goddess weeping at his feet,
Moneta silent. Without stay or prop,
But my own weak mortality, I bore
The load of this eternal quietude,   390
The unchanging gloom, and the three fixéd shapes
Ponderous upon my senses, a whole moon.
For by my burning brain I measured sure

7. Keats several times recalls *King Lear*,
in representing the condition of Saturn.
8. I.e., that disbelief has not an instant
to catch its breath.
1. I.e., how thoughtless I am!
2. Keats here sacrifices to epic severity
a notable figure in the first *Hyperion*
I, 72 ff., "As when, upon a trancéd
summer-night / Those green-robed senators of mighty woods, / Tall oaks,
branch-charméd by the earnest stars, /
Dream * * *.

Her silver seasons shedded on the night,
And ever day by day methought I grew 395
More gaunt and ghostly. Oftentimes I prayed
Intense, that Death would take me from the Vale
And all its burdens—gasping with despair
Of change, hour after hour I cursed myself;
Until old Saturn raised his faded eyes, 400
And looked around and saw his kingdom gone,
And all the gloom and sorrow of the place,
And that fair kneeling Goddess at his feet.
As the moist scent of flowers, and grass, and leaves,
Fills forest dells with a pervading air, 405
Known to the woodland nostril, so the words
Of Saturn filled the mossy glooms around,
Even to the hollows of time-eaten oaks,
And to the windings of the foxes' holes,
With sad low tones, while thus he spake, and sent 410
Strange musings to the solitary Pan.
"Moan, brethren, moan; for we are swallowed up
And buried from all godlike exercise
Of influence benign on planets pale,
And peaceful sway above man's harvesting, 415
And all those acts which Deity supreme
Doth ease its heart of love in. Moan and wail,
Moan, brethren, moan; for lo, the rebel spheres
Spin round, the stars their ancient courses keep,
Clouds still with shadowy moisture haunt the earth, 420
Still suck their fill of light from sun and moon;
Still buds the tree, and still the sea-shores murmur;
There is no death in all the Universe,
No smell of death—there shall be death[3]—moan, moan;
Moan, Cybele,[4] moan; for thy pernicious Babes 425
Have changed a god into a shaking palsy.
Moan, brethren, moan, for I have no strength left;
Weak as the reed—weak—feeble as my voice—
Oh, oh, the pain, the pain of feebleness.
Moan, moan, for still I thaw—or give me help; 430
Throw down those Imps,[5] and give me victory.
Let me hear other groans, and trumpets blown
Of triumph calm, and hymns of festival,
From the gold peaks of heaven's high-piléd clouds;
Voices of soft proclaim,[6] and silver stir 435
Of strings in hollow shells; and let there be
Beautiful things made new for the surprise
Of the sky-children." So he feebly ceased,
With such a poor and sickly sounding pause,
Methought I heard some old man of the earth 440

---

3. The passing of the Saturnian golden age (paralleled by Keats with the fable of the loss of Eden) has introduced suffering, and will also introduce death.
4. Pronounced Sĭb′elē; the wife of Saturn and mother of the Olympian gods, who have overthrown their parents.
5. I.e., his rebellious children.
6. Used as a noun, "proclamation."

Bewailing earthly loss; nor could my eyes
And ears act with that pleasant unison of sense
Which marries sweet sound with the grace of form,
And dolorous accent from a tragic harp
With large-limbed visions.[7]—More I scrutinized: 445
Still fixed he sat beneath the sable trees,
Whose arms spread straggling in wild serpent forms,
With leaves all hushed; his awful presence there
(Now all was silent) gave a deadly lie
To what I erewhile heard—only his lips   450
Trembled amid the white curls of his beard.
They told the truth, though, round, the snowy locks
Hung nobly, as upon the face of heaven
A mid-day fleece of clouds. Thea arose,
And stretched her white arm through the hollow dark,   455
Pointing some whither: whereat he too rose
Like a vast giant, seen by men at sea
To grow pale from the waves at dull midnight.[8]
They melted from my sight into the woods;
Ere I could turn, Moneta cried, "These twain   460
Are speeding to the families of grief,
Where roofed in by black rocks they waste, in pain
And darkness, for no hope."—And she spake on,
As ye may read who can unwearied pass
Onward from the Antechamber of this dream,   465
Where even at the open doors awhile
I must delay, and glean my memory
Of her high phrase—perhaps no further dare.

Canto II

"Mortal, that thou may'st understand aright,
I humanize my sayings to thine ear,
Making comparisons of earthly things;
Or thou might'st better listen to the wind,
Whose language is to thee a barren noise,   5
Though it blows legend-laden through the trees.—
In melancholy realms big tears are shed,
More sorrow like to this, and suchlike woe,
Too huge for mortal tongue, or pen of scribe.
The Titans fierce, self hid or prison bound,   10
Groan for the old allegiance[9] once more,
Listening in their doom for Saturn's voice.
But one of our whole eagle-brood still keeps
His sov'reignty, and rule, and majesty;
Blazing Hyperion on his orbéd fire   15
Still sits, still snuffs the incense teeming up
From Man to the Sun's God—yet unsecure,
For as upon the earth dire prodigies[1]

7. I.e., he could not attach this speech, like that of a feebly complaining old mortal, to the visible form of the large-limbed god who uttered it.
8. I.e., like a giant who is seen by men at sea to emerge, pale, from the waves.
9. The meter requires four syllables: al-lé-gĭ-ánce.
1. Terrifying omens.

Fright and perplex, so also shudders he;
Nor at dog's howl or gloom-bird's even screech,   20
Or the familiar visitings of one
Upon the first toll of his passing bell:[2]
But horrors, portioned to a giant nerve,
Make great Hyperion ache. His palace bright,
Bastioned with pyramids of glowing gold,   25
And touched with shade of bronzéd obelisks,
Glares a blood-red through all the thousand courts,
Arches, and domes, and fiery galleries;
And all its curtains of Aurorian clouds
Flush angerly; when he would taste the wreaths   30
Of incense breathed aloft from sacred hills,
Instead of sweets, his ample palate takes
Savor of poisonous brass and metals sick.
Wherefore when harbored in the sleepy West,
After the full completion of fair day,   35
For rest divine upon exalted couch
And slumber in the arms of melody,
He paces through the pleasant hours of ease
With strides colossal, on from hall to hall,
While far within each aisle and deep recess   40
His wingéd minions in close clusters stand
Amazed, and full of fear; like anxious men,
Who on a wide plain gather in sad troops,
When earthquakes jar their battlements and towers.
Even now, while Saturn, roused from icy trance,   45
Goes, step for step, with Thea from yon woods,
Hyperion, leaving twilight in the rear,
Is sloping to the threshold of the West.—
Thither we tend."—Now in clear light I stood,
Relieved from the dusk vale. Mnemosyne[3]   50
Was sitting on a square-edged polished stone,
That in its lucid depth reflected pure
Her priestess-garments. My quick eyes ran on
From stately nave to nave, from vault to vault,
Through bow'rs of fragrant and enwreathéd light   55
And diamond-pavéd lustrous long arcades.
Anon rushed by the bright Hyperion;
His flaming robes streamed out beyond his heels,
And gave a roar, as if of earthly fire,
That scared away the meek ethereal hours,   60
And made their dove-wings tremble. On he flared.

1819   1856

2. Lines 20–22 might be paraphrased: "Not, however, at such portents as a dog's howl or the evening screech of the owl, nor with the well-known feelings ["visitings"] of someone when he hears the first stroke of his own death knell * * *" It had been the English custom to ring the church bell when a person was close to death, to invite hearers to pray for his departing soul. See, e.g., Shakespeare, *Venus and Adonis*, lines 701–2; and for "visitings," *Macbeth* I.v. 46.

3. As in I, 331, a slip for "Moneta."

To Autumn[1]

1

Season of mists and mellow fruitfulness,
　　Close bosom-friend of the maturing sun;
Conspiring with him how to load and bless
　　With fruit the vines that round the thatch-eaves run;
To bend with apples the mossed cottage-trees,　　　　　5
　　And fill all fruit with ripeness to the core;
　　　　To swell the gourd, and plump the hazel shells
　　With a sweet kernel; to set budding more,
And still more, later flowers for the bees,
Until they think warm days will never cease,　　　　10
　　　　For Summer has o'er-brimmed their clammy cells.

2

Who hath not seen thee oft amid thy store?
　　Sometimes whoever seeks abroad may find
Thee sitting careless on a granary floor,
　　Thy hair soft-lifted by the winnowing[2] wind;　　　15
Or on a half-reaped furrow sound asleep,
　　Drowsed with the fume of poppies, while thy hook[3]
　　　　Spares the next swath and all its twinéd flowers:
And sometimes like a gleaner thou dost keep
　　Steady thy laden head across a brook;　　　　　20
　　Or by a cider-press, with patient look,
　　　　Thou watchest the last oozings hours by hours.

3

Where are the songs of Spring? Aye, where are they?
　　Think not of them, thou hast thy music too—
While barred clouds bloom the soft-dying day,　　　25
　　And touch the stubble-plains with rosy hue;
Then in a wailful choir the small gnats mourn
　　Among the river sallows,[4] borne aloft
　　　　Or sinking as the light wind lives or dies;
And full-grown lambs loud bleat from hilly bourn;[4a]　　30
　　Hedge crickets sing; and now with treble soft
　　The redbreast whistles from a garden croft;[5]
　　　　And gathering swallows twitter in the skies.

September 19, 1819　　　　　　　　　　　　　　　1820

---

1. Two days after this serene and gracious ode was composed, Keats wrote to J. H. Reynolds: "I never liked stubble fields so much as now—Aye, better than the chilly green of the spring. Somehow a stubble plain looks warm—in the same way that some pictures look warm—this struck me so much in my Sunday's walk that I composed upon it."
2. To "winnow" is to fan the chaff from the grain.
3. Scythe.
4. Willows.
4a. Region.
5. A "croft" is an enclosed plot of farm land.

This Living Hand[1]

This living hand, now warm and capable
Of earnest grasping, would, if it were cold
And in the icy silence of the tomb,
So haunt thy days and chill thy dreaming nights
That thou wouldst wish thine own heart dry of blood   5
So in my veins red life might stream again,
And thou be conscience-calmed—see here it is—
I hold it towards you.

Late 1819?   1898

1. Found written in the margin of a page of Keats's unfinished satire, *The Cap and Bells*, and commonly assumed to have been addressed to Fanny Brawne.

Letters   Keats's letters constitute a running commentary on his life, reading, thinking, and writing. They demonstrate an extraordinary intelligence, whose very lack of academic or technical training gives its expression a freedom from jargon and standard categories that is equally challenging and rewarding to the reader. Keats's early reputation as a poet of pure luxury, sensation, and art for art's sake has been revolutionized since, early this century, critics began to pay close attention to his letters. For Keats thought hard and persistently about life and art, and any seed of an ethical or critical idea that he picked up from his intellectual contemporaries (Hazlitt, Coleridge, Wordsworth) instantly germinated and flourished in the rich soil of his imagination. What T. S. Eliot said about the metaphysical poets applies equally to Keats in his letters: his "mode of feeling was directly and freshly altered by [his] reading and thought." And like Donne, he looked not only into the heart, but literally, "into the cerebral cortex, the nervous system, and the digestive tract." A number of Keats's casual comments on the poet and on poetry included below—especially those dealing with what we now call empathy, and with "negative capability"— have become standard points of reference in aesthetic theory. But nothing that Keats said did he himself regard as ultimate; each statement constituted only a stage in his continuing exploration into what he called "the mystery."

The text below is that of the edition of the *Letters* by Hyder E. Rollins (1958), which reproduces the original MSS. precisely, so that the reader may follow Keats's pen as, throwing spelling and grammar to the winds, it strains to keep up with the rush of his thoughts.

To Benjamin Bailey[1]
[*The Authenticity of the Imagination*]

[November 22, 1817]

My dear Bailey,
    * * * O I wish I was as certain of the end of all your troubles as

1. Bailey was one of Keats's closest friends. Keats had stayed with him the month before at Oxford, where Bailey was an undergraduate.

that of your momentary start about the authenticity of the Imagination. I am certain of nothing but of the holiness of the Heart's affections and the truth of Imagination—What the imagination seizes as Beauty must be truth[2]—whether it existed before or not— for I have the same Idea of all our Passions as of Love they are all in their sublime, creative of essential Beauty—In a Word, you may know my favorite Speculation by my first Book and the little song I sent in my last[3]—which is a representation from the fancy of the probable mode of operating in these Matters—The Imagination may be compared to Adam's dream[4]—he awoke and found it truth. I am the more zealous in this affair, because I have never yet been able to perceive how any thing can be known for truth by consequitive reasoning[5]—and yet it must be—Can it be that even the greatest Philosopher ever ~~when~~ arrived at his goal without putting aside numerous objections—However it may be, O for a Life of Sensations[6] rather than of Thoughts! It is "a Vision in the form of Youth" a Shadow of reality to come—and this consideration has further conv[i]nced me for it has come as auxiliary to another favorite Speculation of mine, that we shall enjoy ourselves here after by having what we called happiness on Earth repeated in a finer tone and so repeated[7]—And yet such a fate can only befall those who delight in sensation rather than hunger as you do after Truth— Adam's dream will do here and seems to be a conviction that Imagination and its empyreal reflection is the same as human Life and its spiritual repetition. But as I was saying—the simple imaginative Mind may have its rewards in the repeti[ti]on of its own silent Working coming continually on the spirit with a fine suddenness— to compare great things with small—have you never by being surprised with an old Melody—in a delicious place—by a delicious voice, fe[l]t over again your very speculations and surmises at the time it first operated on your soul—do you not remember forming to yourself the singer's face more beautiful that[8] it was possible and yet with the elevation of the Moment you did not think so—even then you were mounted on the Wings of Imagination so high—that the Prototype must be here after—that delicious face you will see— What a time! I am continually running away from the subject— sure this cannot be exactly the case with a complex Mind—one that is imaginative and at the same time careful of its fruits—who would exist partly on sensation partly on thought—to whom it is necessary that years should bring the philosophic Mind[9]—such an one I con-

2. The phrase occurs in a poetic context at the close of *Ode on a Grecian Urn.* Try substituting "real," or "reality," where Keats uses the word "truth."
3. The song was "O Sorrow," from *Endymion.*
4. In *Paradise Lost* VIII.452–90, Adam dreams that Eve has been created, and awakes to find her real.
5. Consecutive reasoning—reasoning which moves by logical steps.
6. Not only sense experiences, but also the intuitive perceptions of truths, as opposed to truth achieved by consecutive reasoning.
7. Cf. the "Pleasure Thermometer" in *Endymion,* Book I, lines 777 ff.
8. For "than."
9. An echo of Wordsworth, *Ode: Intimations of Immortality,* line 187.

sider your's and therefore it is necessary to your eternal Happiness that you not only ~~have~~ drink this old Wine of Heaven which I shall call the redigestion of our most ethereal Musings on Earth; but also increase in knowledge and know all things. I am glad to hear you are in a fair Way for Easter—you will soon get through your unpleasant reading and then!—but the world is full of troubles and I have not much reason to think myself pesterd with many—I think Jane or Marianne has a better opinion of me than I deserve—for really and truly I do not think my Brothers illness connected with mine—you know more of the real Cause than they do—nor have I any chance of being rack'd as you have been[1]—you perhaps at one time thought there was such a thing as Worldly Happiness to be arrived at, at certain periods of time marked out—you have of necessity from your disposition been thus led away—I scarcely remember counting upon any Happiness—I look not for it if it be not in the present hour—nothing startles me beyond the Moment. The setting sun will always set me to rights—or if a Sparrow come before my Window I take part in its existence and pick about the Gravel. The first thing that strikes me on hea[r]ing a Misfortune having befalled another is this. Well it cannot be helped.—he will have the pleasure of trying the resourses of his spirit, and I beg now my dear Bailey that hereafter should you observe any thing cold in me not to but[2] it to the account of heartlessness but abstraction—for I assure you I sometimes feel not the influence of a Passion or Affection during a whole week—and so long this sometimes continues I begin to suspect myself and the genuiness of my feelings at other times—thinking them a few barren Tragedy-tears * * *

> Your affectionate friend
> John Keats—

To George and Thomas Keats
[Negative Capability]

[December 21, 27 (?), 1817]

My dear Brothers

I must crave your pardon for not having written ere this * * * I spent Friday evening with Wells[1] & went the next morning to see *Death on the Pale horse*. It is a wonderful picture, when West's age is considered;[2] But there is nothing to be intense upon; no women one feels mad to kiss; no face swelling into reality. the excellence of every Art is its intensity, capable of making all disagreeables evapo-

1. Keats's friends Jane and Marianne Reynolds feared that Keats's ill health at this time threatened tuberculosis, from which his brother Tom was suffering. Bailey had recently suffered pain (been "racked") because of an unsuccessful love affair.
2. For "put."
1. Charles Wells, a former schoolmate of Tom Keats and, for a time, a friend of John Keats.
2. Benjamin West (1738–1820), painter of historical pictures, was an American who moved to England and became president of the Royal Academy. The "Christ Rejected" mentioned a few sentences farther on is also by West.

rate, from their being in close relationship with Beauty & Truth[3]—
Examine King Lear & you will find this examplified throughout; but
in this picture we have unpleasantness without any momentous
depth of speculation excited, in which to bury its repulsiveness—
The picture is larger than Christ rejected—I dined with Haydon[4]
the sunday after you left, & had a very pleasant day, I dined too
(for I have been out too much lately) with Horace Smith & met his
two Brothers with Hill & Kingston & one Du Bois,[5] they only served
to convince me, how superior humour is to wit in respect to enjoyment—These men say things which make one start, without making
one feel, they are all alike; their manners are alike; they all know
fashionables; they have a mannerism in their very eating & drinking,
in their mere handling a Decanter—They talked of Kean[6] & his
low company—Would I were with that company instead of yours
said I to myself! I know such like acquaintance will never do for
me & yet I am going to Reynolds, on wednesday—Brown & Dilke[7]
walked with me & back from the Christmas pantomime.[8] I had not
a dispute but a disquisition with Dilke, on various subjects; several
things dovetailed in my mind, & at once it struck me, what quality
went to form a Man of Achievement especially in Literature &
which Shakespeare posessed so enormously—I mean *Negative Capability*,[9] that is when man is capable of being in uncertainties, Mysteries, doubts, without any irritable reaching after fact & reason—
Coleridge, for instance, would let go by a fine isolated verisimilitude
caught from the Penetralium[1] of mystery, from being incapable of
remaining content with half knowledge. This pursued through Volumes would perhaps take us no further than this, that with a great
poet the sense of Beauty overcomes every other consideration, or
rather obliterates all consideration.

3. Keats's solution to a problem at
least as old as Aristotle: why do we
enjoy the aesthetic representation of a
subject which in real life would be ugly
or painful?
4. Keats's close friend, Benjamin Haydon, painter of grandiose historical and
religious pictures.
5. Horace Smith was one of the best
known literary wits of the day; the
others mentioned were men of letters
or of literary interests.
6. Edmund Kean, the noted Shakespearean actor of the early 19th century.
7. John Hamilton Reynolds, 'Charles
Armitage Brown, and Charles Wentworth Dilke were all writers and friends
of Keats.
8. Christmas pantomimes were performed each year at Drury Lane and
Covent Garden.
9. This famous and elusive phrase has
accumulated a heavy body of commentary. Two points may here suffice: (1)
Keats is concerned with a central aesthetic question of his day: to distinguish between what was called the "objective" poet, who simply and imper-
sonally presents his material, and the
"subjective" or "sentimental" poet, who
presents his material as it appears when
viewed through his personal interests,
beliefs, and feelings. The poet of "negative capability" is the objective poet.
(See the letter to Reynolds, Feb. 3,
1818, below.) (2) Keats goes on to
propose that, within a poem, the presentation of matter in an artistic form
that appeals to our "sense of Beauty"
is enough, independently of its truth or
falsity when considered outside the
poem according to nonartistic logical
criteria. T. S. Eliot illuminated an
important aspect of Keats's meaning
when he observed that a theory "which
has entered into poetry is established,
for its truth or falsity in one sense
ceases to matter, and its truth in another sense is proved" (*The Metaphysical Poets*).
1. The Latin *penetralia* signified the
innermost and most secret parts of a
temple.

Shelley's poem[2] is out & there are words about its being objected too, as much as Queen Mab was. Poor Shelley I think he has his Quota of good qualities, in sooth la!! Write soon to your most sincere friend & affectionate Brother

John

To John Hamilton Reynolds[1]
[*Wordsworth's Poetry*]

[February 3, 1818]

My dear Reynolds,

* * * It may be said that we ought to read our Contemporaries. that Wordsworth &c should have their due from us. but for the sake of a few fine imaginative or domestic passages, are we to be bullied into a certain Philosophy engendered in the whims of an Egotist[2]— Every man has his speculations, but every man does not brood and peacock over them till he makes a false coinage and deceives himself—Many a man can travel to the very bourne[2a] of Heaven, and yet want confidence to put down his halfseeing. Sancho[3] will invent a Journey heavenward as well as any body. We hate poetry that has a palpable design upon us—and if we do not agree, seems to put its hand in its breeches pocket. Poetry should be great & unobtrusive, a thing which enters into one's soul, and does not startle it or amaze it with itself but with its subject.—How beautiful are the retired flowers! how would they lose their beauty were they to throng into the highway crying out, admire me I am a violet! dote upon me I am a primrose! Modern poets differ from the Elizabethans in this. Each of the moderns like an Elector of Hanover governs his petty state, & knows how many straws are swept daily from the Causeways in all his dominions & has a continual itching that all the Housewives should have their coppers well scoured: the antients were ~~Emperors of large~~ Emperors of vast Provinces, they had only heard of the remote ones and scarcely cared to visit them.—I will cut all this—I will have no more of Wordsworth or Hunt[4] in particular—Why should we be of the tribe of Manasseh, when we can wander with Esau?[5] why should we kick against the Pricks, when we

2. *Laon and Cythna* (1817), which dealt with incest, and had to be recalled by the author; it was revised and republished as *The Revolt of Islam* (1818). *Queen Mab* (1813) was a youthful poem in which Shelley presented his radical program for the achievement of the millennium by the elimination of "kings, priests, and statesmen," and the reform of human institutions.
1. Reynolds, a close friend, was at this time an insurance clerk and also an able, though minor, poet and man of letters.
2. Keats immensely admired Wordsworth, as succeeding letters will show,

and learned more from him than from any poetic contemporary. He had reservations, however, about the subjective and didactic qualities of Wordsworth's poetry (see the letter to George and Thomas Keats, above)—reservations which, in some moods, he stated in unflattering terms.
2a. Boundary.
3. Sancho Panza, the earthy squire in *Don Quixote*.
4. Leigh Hunt, a poet who earlier had strongly influenced Keats's style.
5. I.e., why should we remain in a conventional way of life (as did the tribe of Manasseh, which followed the

can walk on Roses?"Why should we be owls, when we can be Eagles? Why be teased with "nice Eyed wagtails," when we have in sight "the Cherub Contemplation"?[6]—Why with Wordsworths "Matthew with a bough of wilding in his hand" when we can have Jacques "under an oak &c"[7]—The secret of the Bough of Wilding will run through your head faster than I can write it—Old Matthew spoke to him some years ago on some nothing, & because he happens in an Evening Walk to imagine the figure of the old man—he must stamp it down in black & white, and it is henceforth sacred—I don't mean to deny Wordsworth's grandeur & Hunt's merit, but I mean to say we need not be teazed with grandeur & merit—when we can have them uncontaminated & unobtrusive. Let us have the old Poets, & robin Hood[8] Your letter and its sonnets gave me more pleasure than will the 4th Book of Childe Harold[9] & the whole of any body's life & opinions. * * *

Y[r] sincere friend and Coscribbler
John Keats.

To John Taylor[1]
[Keats's Axioms in Poetry]

[February 27, 1818]

My dear Taylor,
Your alteration strikes me as being a great improvement—the page looks much better. * * * It is a sorry thing for me that any one should have to overcome Prejudices in reading my Verses— that affects me more than any hypercriticism on any particular Passage. In *Endymion* I have most likely but moved into the Go-cart from the leading strings. In Poetry I have a few Axioms, and you will see how far I am from their Centre. 1st I think Poetry should surprise by a fine excess and not by Singularity—it should strike the Reader as a wording of his own highest thoughts, and appear almost a Remembrance—2nd Its touches of Beauty should never be half way therby making the reader breathless instead of content: the rise, the progress, the setting of imagery should like the Sun come natural natural too him—shine over him and set soberly although in magnificence leaving him in the Luxury of twilight—but it is easier to think what Poetry should be than to write it—and this leads me on to another axiom. That if Poetry comes not as naturally

conventional paths of Old Testament history) when we can become adventurers (like Esau, who sold his birthright in Genesis xxv.29–34 and became a domestic outlaw).
6. The first phrase is from Hunt's *Nymphs*, the second from Milton's *Il Penseroso* (line 54).
7. The Wordsworth phrase is from his poem *The Two April Mornings* (a "wilding" is an uncultivated tree or plant, especially the wild apple tree).

Jacques is in *As You Like It* (see II.i.31).
8. A reference to two sonnets on Robin Hood by Reynolds which he had sent to Keats.
9. Canto IV of Byron's *Childe Harold* was being eagerly awaited by English readers.
1. Member of the publishing firm of Taylor and Hessey, to whom Keats wrote this letter while *Endymion* was being put through the press.

as the Leaves to a tree it had better not come at all. However it may
be with me I cannot help looking into new countries with "O for a
Muse of fire to ascend!"[2]—If Endymion serves me as a Pioneer perhaps I ought to be content. I have great reason to be content, for
thank God I can read and perhaps understand Shakspeare to his
depths, and I have I am sure many friends, who, if I fail, will
attribute any change in my Life and Temper to Humbleness rather
than to Pride—to a cowering under the Wings of great Poets rather
than to a Bitterness that I am not appreciated. I am anxious to get
Endymion printed that I may forget it and proceed. * * *

Your sincere and oblig⁴ friend
John Keats—

P.S. You shall have a sho[r]t *Preface* in good time—

To John Hamilton Reynolds
[*Milton, Wordsworth, and the Chambers of Human Life*]

[May 3, 1818]

My dear Reynolds.

     * * * Were I to study physic or rather Medicine again,—I feel
it would not make the least difference in my Poetry; when the Mind
is in its infancy a Bias ~~in~~ is in reality a Bias, but when we have acquired more strength, a Bias becomes no Bias. Every department of
knowledge we see excellent and calculated towards a great whole.
I am so convinced of this, that I am glad at not having given away
my medical Books, which I shall again look over to keep alive the
little I know thitherwards; and moreover intend through you and
Rice to become a sort of Pip-civilian.[1] An extensive knowledge is
needful to thinking people—it takes away the heat and fever; and
helps, by widening speculation, to ease the Burden of the Mystery:[2]
a thing I begin to understand a little, and which weighed upon you
in the most gloomy and true sentence in your Letter. The difference
of high Sensations with and without knowledge appears to me this
—in the latter case we are falling continually ten thousand fathoms
deep and being blown up again without wings and with all [the]
horror of a ~~Case~~ bare shoulderd Creature—in the former case, our
shoulders are fledged,[3] and we go thro' the same ~~Fir~~ air and space
without fear. * * *

     You say "I fear there is little chance of any thing else in this
life." You seem by that to have been going through with a more
painful and acute ~~test~~ zest the same labyrinth that I have—I have

---

2. Altered from Shakespeare's *Henry V*, Prologue, line 1.
1. Apparently, "a small-scale lay-man." James Rice, a lawyer, was one of Keats's favorite friends.
2. *Tintern Abbey*, line 38. Here begins

Keats's wonderfully insightful expansion of the significance of this and
other phrases and passages in Wordsworth.
3. Grow wings.

come to the same conclusion thus far. My Branchings out therefrom have been numerous: one of them is the consideration of Wordsworth's genius and as a help, in the manner of gold being the meridian Line of worldly wealth,—how he differs from Milton.[4]—And here I have nothing but surmises, from an uncertainty whether Miltons apparently less anxiety for Humanity proceeds from his seeing further or no than Wordsworth: And whether Wordsworth has in truth epic passion, and martyrs himself to the human heart, the main region of his song[5]—In regard to his genius alone—we find what he says true as far as we have experienced and we can judge no further but by larger experience—for axioms in philosophy are not axioms until they are proved upon our pulses: We read fine—— things but never feel them to thee[6] full until we have gone the same steps as the Author.—I know this is not plain; you will know exactly my meaning when I say, that now I shall relish Hamlet more than I ever have done—Or, better—You are sensible no man can set down Venery[7] as a bestial or joyless thing until he is sick of it and therefore all philosophizing on it would be mere wording. Until we are sick, we understand not;—in fine, as Byron says, "Knowledge is Sorrow";[8] and I go on to say that "Sorrow is Wisdom"—and further for aught we can know for certainty! "Wisdom is folly" * * *

I will return to Wordsworth—whether or no he has an extended vision or a circumscribed grandeur—whether he is an eagle in his nest, or on the wing—And to be more explicit and to show you how tall I stand by the giant, I will put down a simile of human life as far as I now perceive it; that is, to the point to which I say we both have arrived at—Well—I compare human life to a large Mansion of Many Apartments, two of which I can only describe, the doors of the rest being as yet shut upon me—The first we step into we call the infant or thoughtless Chamber, in which we remain as long as we do not think—We remain there a long while, and notwithstanding the doors of the second Chamber remain wide open, showing a bright appearance, we care not to hasten to it; but are at length imperceptibly impelled by the awakening of the thinking principle —within us—we no sooner get into the second Chamber, which I shall call the Chamber of Maiden-Thought,[9] than we become intoxicated with the light and the atmosphere, we see nothing but pleasant wonders, and think of delaying there for ever in delight: However among the effects this breathing is father of is that tremendous one of sharpening one's vision into the ~~head~~ heart and nature of Man—of convincing ones nerves that the World is full

---

4. I.e., as gold is the standard of material wealth (in the way that the meridian line of Greenwich Observatory, England, is the reference for measuring degrees of longitude), so Milton is the standard of poetic value, by which we may measure Wordsworth.

5. Cf. "Prospectus" to *The Recluse*, line 41.
6. For "the."
7. Sexual indulgence.
8. *Manfred* I.i.10: "Sorrow is knowledge."
9. I.e., innocent thought.

of Misery and Heartbreak, Pain, Sickness and oppression—whereby This Chamber of Maiden Thought becomes gradually darken'd and at the same time on all sides of it many doors are set open—but all dark—all leading to dark passages—We see not the ballance of good and evil. We are in a Mist—*We* are now in that state—We feel the "burden of the Mystery," To this point was Wordsworth come, as far as I can conceive when he wrote "Tintern Abbey" and it seems to me that his Genius is explorative of those dark Passages. Now if we live, and go on thinking, we too shall explore them. he is a Genius and superior [to] us, in so far as he can, more than we, make discoveries, and shed a light in them—Here I must think Wordsworth is deeper than Milton—though I think it has depended more upon the general and gregarious advance of intellect, than individual greatness of Mind—From the Paradise Lost and the other Works of Milton, I hope it is not too presuming, even between ourselves to say, his Philosophy, human and divine, may be tolerably understood by one not much advanced in years, In his time englishmen were just emancipated from a great superstition—and Men had got hold of certain points and resting places in reasoning which were too newly born to be doubted, and too much ~~oppressed~~ opposed by the Mass of Europe not to be thought etherial and authentically divine—who could gainsay his ideas on virtue, vice, and Chastity in Comus, just at the time of the dismissal of Cod-pieces[1] and a hundred other disgraces? who would not rest satisfied with his hintings at good and evil in the Paradise Lost, when just free from the inquisition and burning in Smithfield?[2] The Reformation produced such immediate and great benefits, that Protestantism was considered under the immediate eye of heaven, and its own remaining Dogmas and superstitions, then, as it were, regenerated, constituted those resting places and seeming sure points of Reasoning—from that I have mentioned, Milton, whatever he may have thought in the sequel,[3] appears to have been content with these by his writings—He did not think into the human heart, as Wordsworth has done—Yet Milton as a Philosop[h]er, had sure as great powers as Wordsworth—What is then to be inferr'd? O many things—It proves there is really a grand march of intellect—, It proves that a mighty providence subdues the mightiest Minds to the service of the time being, whether it be in human Knowledge or Religion— * * *

Your affectionate friend
John Keats.

1. In the 15th and 16th centuries the codpiece was a flap, often ornamental, which covered an opening in the front of men's breeches.

2. An open place northwest of the walls of the City of London where, in the 16th century, heretics were burned.
3. I.e., later on.

To Richard Woodhouse[1]

[*A Poet Has No Identity*]

[October 27, 1818]

My dear Woodhouse,

Your Letter gave me a great satisfaction; more on account of its friendliness, than any relish of that matter in it which is accounted so acceptable in the "genus irritabile"[2] The best answer I can give you is in a clerklike manner to make some observations on two principle points, which seem to point like indices into the midst of the whole pro and con, about genius, and views and atchievements and ambition and cœtera. 1st As to the poetical Character itself, (I mean that sort of which, if I am any thing, I am a Member; that sort distinguished from the wordsworthian or egotistical sublime; which is a thing per se and stands alone) it is not itself—it has no self—it is every thing and nothing—It has no character—it enjoys light and shade; it lives in gusto, be it foul or fair, high or low, rich or poor, mean or elevated—It has as much delight in conceiving an Iago as an Imogen.[3] What shocks the virtuous philosop[h]er, delights the camelion[4] Poet. It does no harm from its relish of the dark side of things any more than from its taste for the bright one; because they both end in speculation.[5] A Poet is the most unpoetical of any thing in existence; because he has no Identity—he is continually in for[6]—and filling some other Body—The Sun, the Moon, the Sea and Men and Women who are creatures of impulse are poetical and have about them an unchangeable attribute—the poet has none; no identity—he is certainly the most unpoetical of all God's Creatures. If then he has no self, and if I am a Poet, where is the Wonder that I should say I would ~~right~~ write no more? Might I not at that very instant [have] been cogitating on the Characters of saturn and Ops?[7] It is a wretched thing to confess; but is a very fact that not one word I ever utter can be taken for granted as an opinion growing out of my identical nature—how can it, when I have no nature? When I am in a room with People if I ever am free from speculating on creations of my own brain, then not myself goes home to myself: but the identity of every one in the room

1. Woodhouse was a young lawyer with literary interests who recognized Keats's talents and prepared, or preserved, manuscript copies of many of his poems and letters.
2. "The irritable race," a phrase Horace had applied to poets.
3. Iago is the villain in Shakespeare's *Othello* and Imogen the virtuous heroine of his *Cymbeline*.
4. The chameleon is a lizard which camouflages itself by matching its color to its surroundings.

5. "In speculation" here means "in contemplation"—i.e., without affecting our practical judgment or actions.
6. Instead of "in for," Keats may have intended to write "informing."
6a. Woodhouse had written Keats a letter, expressing concern at a remark by Keats that, since former writers had preempted the best poetic materials and styles, there was nothing new left for the modern poet.
7. Characters in Keats's *Hyperion*.

begins to to press upon me[8] that, I am in a very little time an[ni]-
hilated—not only among Men; it would be the same in a Nursery
of children: I know not whether I make myself wholly understood:
I hope enough so to let you see that no dependence is to be placed
on what I said that day.

In the second place I will speak of my views, and of the life I
purpose to myself—I am ambitious of doing the world some good:
if I should be spared that may be the work of maturer years—in the
interval I will assay to reach to as high a summit in Poetry as the
nerve[9] bestowed upon me will suffer. The faint conceptions I have
of Poems to come brings the blood frequently into my forehead—
All I hope is that I may not lose all interest in human affairs—that
the solitary indifference I feel for applause even from the finest
Spirits, will not blunt any acuteness of vision I may have. I do not
think it will—I feel assured I should write from the mere yearning
and fondness I have for the Beautiful even if my night's labours
should be burnt every morning and no eye ever shine upon them.
But even now I am perhaps not speaking from myself; but from
some character in whose soul I now live. I am sure however that
this next sentence is from myself. I feel your anxiety, good opinion
and friendliness in the highest degree, and am

> Your's most sincerely
> John Keats

To George and Georgiana Keats[1]
["*The Vale of Soul-Making*"]

[February 14–May 3, 1819]

My Dear Brother & Sister——

* * * I have this moment received a note from Haslam[2] in
which he expects the death of his Father who has been for some
time in a state of insensibility—his mother bears up he says very
well—I shall go to twon[3] tommorrow to see him. This is the world
—thus we cannot expect to give way many hours to pleasure—Circumstances are like Clouds continually gathering and bursting—
While we are laughing the seed of some trouble is put into ~~he~~ the
wide arable land of events—while we are laughing it sprouts is[4]
grows and suddenly bears a poison fruit which we must pluck—
Even so we have leisure to reason on the misfortunes of our friends;
our own touch us too nearly for words. Very few men have ever

---

8. Perhaps "*so* to press upon me."
9. Sinew.
1. Keats's younger brother and his
wife, who had emigrated to Louisville,
Kentucky, in 1818. This is part of a
long letter, which Keats wrote over a

period of several months.
2. William Haslam, a young businessman and intimate friend.
3. For "town."
4. For "it."

arrived at a complete disinterestedness of Mind: very few have been influenced by a pure desire of the benefit of others—in the greater part of the Benefactors ~of~ & to Humanity some meretricious motive has sullied their greatness—some melodramatic scenery has facinated them—From the manner in which I feel Haslam's misfortune I perceive how far I am from any humble standard of disinterestedness—Yet this feeling ought to be carried to its highest pitch, as there is no fear of its ever injuring society—which it would do I fear pushed to an extremity—For in wild nature the Hawk would loose his Breakfast of Robins and the Robin his of Worms The Lion must starve as well as the swallow—The greater part of Men make their way with the same instinctiveness, the same unwandering eye from their purposes, the same animal eagerness as the Hawk—The Hawk wants a Mate, so does the Man—look at them both they set about it and procure on[e] in the same manner —They want both a nest and they both set about one in the same manner—they get their food in the same manner—The noble animal Man for his amusement smokes his pipe—the Hawk balances about the Clouds—that is the only difference of their leisures. This it is that makes the Amusement of Life—to a speculative Mind. I go among the Feilds and catch a glimpse of a stoat[5] or a fieldmouse peeping out of the withered grass—the creature hath a purpose and its eyes are bright with it—I go amongst the buildings of a city and I see a Man hurrying along—to what? The Creature has a purpose and his eyes are bright with it. But then as Wordsworth says, "we have all one human heart"[6]—there is an ellectric fire in human nature tending to purify—so that among these human creature[s] there is continully some birth of new heroism—The pity is that we must wonder at it: as we should at finding a pearl in rubbish—I have no doubt that thousands of people never heard of have had hearts comp[l]etely disinterested: I can remember but two—Socrates and Jesus—their Histories evince it—What I heard a little time ago, Taylor observe with respect to Socrates, may be said of Jesus— That he was so great a~s~ man that though he transmitted no writing of his own to posterity, we have his Mind and his sayings and his greatness handed to us by others. It is to be lamented that the history of the latter was written and revised by Men interested in the pious frauds of Religion. Yet through all this I see his splendour. Even here though I myself am pursueing the same instinctive course as the veriest human animal you can think of—I am however young writing at random—straining at particles of light in the midst of a great darkness—without knowing the bearing of any one assertion of any one opinion. Yet may I not in this be free from sin?[7] May

5. A weasel.
6. *The Old Cumberland Beggar*, line 153.

7. Keats speculates that though his instinctive course is not, any more than an animal's, "disinterested" (free from

there not be superior beings amused with any graceful, though instinctive attitude my mind my[8] fall into, as I am entertained with the alertness of a Stoat or the anxiety of a Deer? Though a quarrel in the streets is a thing to be hated, the energies displayed in it are fine; the commonest Man shows a grace in his quarrel—By a superior being our reasoning[s] may take the same tone—though erroneous they may be fine—This is the very thing in which consists poetry; and if so it is not so fine a thing as philosophy—For the same reason that an eagle is not so fine a thing as a truth—Give me this credit—Do you not think I strive—to know myself? Give me this credit—and you will not think that on my own accou[n]t I repeat Milton's lines

> "How charming is divine Philosophy
> Not harsh and crabbed as dull fools suppose
> But musical as is Apollo's lute"—[9]

No—no for myself—feeling grateful as I do to have got into a state of mind to relish them properly—Nothing ever becomes real till it is experienced—Even a Proverb is no proverb to you till your Life has illustrated it— * * *

The common cognomen of this world among the misguided and superstitious is "a vale of tears" from which we are to be redeemed by a certain arbitary interposition of God and taken to Heaven—What a little circumscribe[d] straightened notion! Call the world if you Please "The vale of Soul-making" Then you will find out the use of the world (I am speaking now in the highest terms for human nature admitting it to be immortal which I will here take for granted for the purpose of showing a thought which has struck me concerning it) I say "*Soul making*" Soul as distinguished from an Intelligence—There may be intelligences or sparks of the divinity in millions—but they are not Souls ~~the~~ till they acquire identities, till each one is personally itself. I[n]telligences are atoms of perception —they know and they see and they are pure, in short they are God —how then are Souls to be made? How then are these sparks which are God to have identity given them—so as ever to possess a bliss peculiar to each ones individual existence? How, but by the medium of a world like this? This point I sincerely wish to consider because I think it a grander system of salvation than the chrystean religion —or rather it is a system of Spirit-creation[1]—This is effected by

selfish interests), it may still be, like an animal's, natural, hence innocent and possessed of an innate grace and beauty. He further supposes that this may be the nature of poetry, also, as distinguished from the deliberate and self-conscious process of philosophical reasoning. Compare the letter on "Negative Capability," Dec. 21, 1817, above.
8. For "may."
9. *Comus*, lines 475–77.

1. Keats is struggling magnificently for an analogy which will embody his solution to the ancient riddle of evil, as an alternative to what he understands to be the Christian view: evil exists as a test of man's merit of salvation in heaven, and this world is only a proving ground for a later and better life. Keats proposes that the function of the human experience of sorrow and

three grand materials acting the one upon the other for a series of years—These three Materials are the *Intelligence*—the *human heart* (as distinguished from intelligence or Mind) and the *World* or *Elemental space* suited for the proper action of *Mind and Heart* on each other for the purpose of forming the *Soul* or *Intelligence destined to possess the sense of Identity*. I can scarcely express what I but dimly perceive—and yet I think I perceive it—that you may judge the more clearly I will put it in the most homely form possible— I will call the *world* a School instituted for the purpose of teaching little children to read—I will call the *human heart* the *horn Book*[2] used in that School—and I will call the *Child able to read, the Soul* made from that *school* and its *hornbook*. Do you not see how necessary a World of Pains and troubles is to school an Intelligence and make it a soul? A Place where the heart must feel and suffer in a thousand diverse ways! Not merely is the Heart a Hornbook, It is the Minds Bible, it is the Minds experience, it is the teat from which the Mind or intelligence sucks its identity—As various as the Lives of Men are—so various become their souls, and thus does God make individual beings, Souls, Identical Souls of the sparks of his own essence—This appears to me a faint sketch of a system of Salvation which does not affront our reason and humanity—I am convinced that many difficulties which christians labour under would vanish before it—There is one wh[i]ch even now Strikes me—the Salvation of Children—In them the Spark or intelligence returns to God, without any identity—it having had no time to learn of, and be altered by, the heart—or seat of the human Passions—It is pretty generally suspected that the chr[i]stian scheme has been coppied from the ancient persian and greek Philosophers. Why may they not have made this simple thing even more simple for common apprehension by introducing Mediators and Personages in the same manner as in the hethen mythology abstractions are personified— Seriously I think it probable that this System of Soul-making—may have been the Parent of all the more palpable and personal Schemes of Redemption, among the Zoroastrians the Christians and the Hindoos. For as one part of the human species must have their carved Jupiter; so another part must have the palpable and named Mediatior and saviour, their Christ their Oromanes and their Vishnu[2a]—

---

pain is to feed and discipline the formless and unstocked "intelligence" that a man possesses at birth, and thus to shape it into a rich and coherent "identity," or "soul." This result provides a justification ("salvation") for our suffering life on its own terms; that is, experience is its own reward, and not in heaven, but on earth. The passage is Keats's version of what Wordsworth says in the last two stanzas of his

Ode: Intimations of Immortality.
2. A child's primer, which used to consist of a sheet of paper mounted on thin wood, protected by a sheet of transparent horn.
2a. Oromanes (Ahriman) was the principle of evil, locked in a persisting struggle with Ormazd, the principle of good, in the Zoroastrian religion. Vishnu was the deity who creates and preserves the world, in Hindu belief.

If what I have said should not be plain enough, as I fear it may not be, I will but[3] you in the place where I began in this series of thoughts—I mean, I began by seeing how man was formed by circumstances—and what are circumstances?—but touchstones of his heart—? and what are touch stones?—but proovings of his hearrt? —and what are proovings of his heart but fortifiers or alterers of his nature? and what is his altered nature but his soul?—and what was his soul before it came into the world and had These provings and alterations and perfectionings?—An intelligences—without Identity —and how is this Identity to be made? Through the medium of the Heart? And how is the heart to become this Medium but in a world of Circumstances?—There now I think what with Poetry and Theology you may thank your Stars that my pen is not very long winded— * * *

This is the 3ᵈ of May & every thing is in delightful forwardness; the violets are not withered, before the peeping of the first rose; You must let me know every thing, how parcels go & come, what papers you have, & what Newspapers you want, & other things— God bless you my dear Brother & Sister

Your ever Affectionate Brother
John Keats—

To Percy Bysshe Shelley[1]

["*Load Every Rift with Ore*"]

[August 16, 1820]

My dear Shelley,

I am very much gratified that you, in a foreign country, and with a mind almost over occupied, should write to me in the strain of the Letter beside me. If I do not take advantage of your invitation it will be prevented by a circumstance I have very much at heart to prophesy[2]—There is no doubt that an english winter would put an end to me, and do so in a lingering hateful manner, therefore I must either voyage or journey to Italy as a soldier marches up to a battery. My nerves at present are the worst part of me, yet they feel soothed when I think that come what extreme may, I shall not be destined to remain in one spot long enough to take a hatred of any four particular bed-posts. I am glad you take any pleasure in my poor Poem;[3]—which I would willingly take the trouble to unwrite, if possible, did I care so much as I have done about Reputation. I received a copy of the Cenci,[4] as from yourself from Hunt. There

3. For "put."
1. Written in reply to a letter urging Keats (who was ill) to spend the winter with the Shelleys in Pisa.
2. His own death.
3. Keats's *Endymion*, Shelley had written, contains treasures, "though treas-

ures poured forth with indistinct profusion." Keats here responds with advice in kind.
4. Shelley's blank-verse tragedy, *The Cenci*, had been published in the spring of 1820.

is only one part of it I am judge of; the Poetry, and dramatic effect, which by many spirits now a days is considered the mammon. A modern work it is said must have a purpose, which may be the God —*an artist* must serve Mammon[5]—he must have "self concentration" selfishness perhaps. You I am sure will forgive me for sincerely remarking that you might curb your magnanimity and be more of an artist, and "load every rift"[6] of your subject with ore. The thought of such discipline must fall like cold chains upon you, who perhaps never sat with your wings furl'd for six Months together. And is not this extraordina[r]y talk for the writer of Endymion? whose mind was like a pack of scattered cards—I am pick'd up and sorted to a pip.[7] My Imagination is a Monastry and I am its Monk—you must explain my metap⁽ᵉˢ⁾[8] to yourself. I am in expectation of Prometheus[9] every day. Could I have my own wish for its interest effected you would have it still in manuscript—or be but now putting an end to the second act. I remember you advising me not to publish my first-blights, on Hampstead heath—I am returning advice upon your hands. Most of the Poems in the volume I send you[1] have been written above two years, and would never have been publish'd but from a hope of gain; so you see I am inclined enough to take your advice now. I must exp[r]ess once more my deep sense of your kindness, adding my sincere thanks and respects for Mrs Shelley. In the hope of soon seeing you I remain

most sincerely yours,
John Keats—

5. Matthew vi.24, and Luke xvi.13: "Ye cannot serve God and mammon."
6. Spenser, *Faerie Queene* II.vii.28: "With rich metall loaded every rifte."
7. Perfectly ordered; all the suits in the deck matched up ("pips" are the conventional spots on playing cards).

8. I.e., "metaphysics."
9. *Prometheus Unbound,* of which Shelley had promised Keats a copy.
1. Keats's volume of 1820, including *Lamia, The Eve of St. Agnes,* and the *Odes.* When Shelley drowned, he had this small book open in his pocket.

The Victorian Age

(1832-1901)

1832: The First Reform Bill.
1837: Victoria becomes queen.
1846: The Corn Laws repealed.
1851: The Great Exhibition in London.
1859: Charles Darwin's *Origin of Species* published.
1870–71: Franco-Prussian War.
1901: Death of Victoria.

AN AGE OF EXPANSION

During the long reign of Queen Victoria England reached her highest point of development as a world power. In the 18th century the pivotal city of Western civilization had been Paris; by the second half of the 19th century this center of influence had shifted to London, a city which expanded from about 2 million inhabitants when Victoria came to the throne to 6.5 million at the time of her death. The rapid growth of London is one of the many indications of the most important development of the age: the shift from a way of life based on the ownership of land to a modern urban economy based on trade and manufacturing. "We have been living, as it were, the life of three hundred years in thirty." This was the impression formed by Dr. Thomas Arnold during the early stages of England's industrialization. By the end of the century—after the resources of steam power had been more fully exploited for fast railways and iron ships, for looms, printing presses, and farmers' combines, and after the introduction of the telegraph, intercontinental cable, anesthetics, and universal compulsory education—an observer might have felt that three thousand years rather than three hundred had been crammed into his lifetime.

Because England was the first country to become industrialized, her transformation was an especially painful one, but being first had a compensation: it was profitable. An early start enabled England to capture markets all over the globe. Her cotton and other manufactured products were exported in English ships, a merchant fleet whose size was without parallel in other countries. The profits gained from her trade led also to extensive capital investments in all continents (especially in the underdeveloped sections of her own Empire) so that after England had become the world's workshop, London became, from 1870 on, the world's banker.

The effect of these developments on Victorian character has been described by the historian David Thomson. The period, he says in *England and the Nineteenth Century,* "is one of strenuous activity and dynamic change, of ferment of ideas and recurrent social unrest, of great inventiveness and expansion." And he adds:

The whole meaning of Victorian England is lost if it is thought of as a country of stuffy complacency and black top-hatted moral priggery. Its frowsty crinolines and dingy hansom cabs, its gas-lit houses and over-ornate draperies, concealed a people engaged in a tremendously exciting adventure—the daring experiment of fitting industrial man into a democratic society. Their failures, faults, and ludicrous shortcomings are all too apparent: but the days when Mr. Lytton Strachey could afford to laugh at the foibles of the "Eminent Victorians" have passed, and we must ask ourselves the question of whether we *can* laugh at our great-grandfathers' attempts to solve problems to which we have so far failed to find an answer. At least the Victorians found greatness, stability, and peace: and the whole world, marveling, envied them for it.

The reactions of Victorian writers to the fast-paced expansion of England were various. A few, such as Thomas Babington Macaulay (1800–59), relished the spectacle as wholly delightful. During the prosperous 1850's Macaulay's essays and histories, with their recitations of the statistics of industrial growth, constituted a Hymn to Progress as well as a celebration of the superior qualities of the English people—"the greatest and most highly civilized people that ever the world saw," Macaulay wrote. And later in the century there were lesser jingoists whose writings confidently pointed out the reasons for further national self-congratulation. More representative, perhaps, was Tennyson. Such poems as *Locksley Hall* may remind us of Macaulay's confidence in the blessings of progress, yet Tennyson's capacity to relish industrial change was only sporadic. Much of the time he felt instead like those writers in the camp opposite to Macaulay, nostalgic writers who perceived that leadership in commerce and industry was being paid for at a terrible price in human happiness. In their experience a so-called "progress" had been gained only by abandoning the traditional rhythms of life and traditional patterns of human relationships which had sustained mankind for centuries. In the melancholy poetry of Matthew Arnold this note is often struck:

> For what wears out the life of mortal men?
> 'Tis that from change to change their being rolls;
> 'Tis that repeated shocks, again, again,
> Exhaust the energy of strongest souls.

An occasional ride on a roller coaster may be exhilarating, but to be chained aboard for a lifetime is a nightmare.

Despite the industrial and political pre-eminence of England during the period, it is evident that most perceptive Victorians suffered from an anxious sense of something lost, a sense too of being displaced persons in a world made alien by technological changes which had been exploited too quickly for the adaptive powers of the human psyche. In this respect, as in many others, the Victorians may remind us of their English-speaking counterparts in America during the second half of the 20th century who have taken over a leading position in the Western world with similar mixed feelings of satisfaction and anxiety.

CRITICAL REACTIONS AGAINST VICTORIANS IN THE TWENTIETH CENTURY

To suggest a similarity between the Victorians and ourselves (a similarity, not an identity) seems a necessary preliminary for a reading of their writings. Literary history requires of us a double perspective. We should be able to see our predecessors as like ourselves; otherwise they will appear to us as mere monsters. We should also be able to see them as unlike ourselves; otherwise they are stripped of their distinctive coloration in time. In the earlier decades of the 20th century, most literary critics were incapable of exercising this double perspective. In their eyes the Victorian writers were monsters, grotesque and remote as the dinosaurs and yet, paradoxically, still threatening. Having been brought up as children to believe that Tennyson and Thackeray were great writers, they had to assert their independence by demonstrating that Tennyson and Thackeray were sometimes absurd and therefore of no consequence. Lytton Strachey's skillful puncturing of over-inflated Victorian balloons is characteristic of the Edwardian (1901–10) and Georgian (1911–36) attitudes. One encounters these attitudes, in subtler form, in the Georgian novelist Virginia Woolf. Her book *Orlando* is a delightful fictionalized survey of English literature from Elizabethan times to 1928, in which the Victorians are presented in terms of dampness, rain, and proliferating vegetation:

Ivy grew in unparalleled profusion. Houses that had been of bare stone were smothered in greenery. * * * And just as the ivy and the evergreen rioted in the damp earth outside, so did the same fertility show itself within. The life of the average woman was a succession of childbirths. * * * Giant cauliflowers towered deck above deck till they rivaled * * * the elm trees themselves. Hens laid incessantly eggs of no special tint. * * * The whole sky itself as it spread wide above the British Isles was nothing but a vast feather bed.

Two comments can be made about this witty description. One is that it accurately identifies a distinguishing quality of Victorian life and literature: creative energy. A second is that the author of the passage did not admire such creative energy. In fact she felt terrified by it as if it might smother her. Mrs. Woolf was the daughter of Sir Leslie Stephen (1832–1904), himself an eminent Victorian. Growing up under such towering shadows, she and her generation had to fight back. And her father himself provided the kind of ammunition needed to attack him. Had he not stated fatuously that Hardy's *Return of the Native*, a novel now discussed in our high schools, was "too passionate" for publication? Yet the demolishing of these Victorian predecessors was achieved by a narrowing of sympathies. As Mrs. Woolf herself says of her heroine, Orlando: "The spirit of the nineteenth century was antipathetic to her in the extreme, and thus it took her and broke her, and she was aware of her defeat at its hands."

The Georgian reaction against the Victorians is perhaps now only a matter of the history of taste, but it needs airing here because its aftereffects have lingered. Most readers today enjoy the writings of Dickens and Browning, Arnold and Newman, George Eliot and Emily Brontë. Yet sometimes these same readers, with curious inconsistency, employ the term "Victorian" in an exclusively pejorative sense. Most of us would rather be called a thief than a prude, and if the connotation of "Victorian" is narrowed down to suggest "prude" and nothing else, we remain seriously hampered in enjoying to the full what the Victorian writers accomplished. Sympathy may not be essential, but condescension is fatal to understanding.

At the opposite extreme is the more recent tendency to sentimentalize minor aspects of the age. The kind of antiquarian zeal that today fosters enthusiasm for Victorian stuffed birds or quaint gables is of little help in approaching Victorian literature. What is required is that we be wary of outmoded suppositions about the nature of the Victorian age and that we see these writers not as smothering monsters but as artists who "lived, felt dawn, saw sunset glow, loved and were loved"—as a poet said of a later generation that perished between 1914 and 1918 on the battlefields of Flanders. In some of the more recent studies of Victorian literature we have admirable instances of how it can best be read, studies in which Browning and T. S. Eliot, instead of being merely pitted against each other, are regarded as adjacent and complementary links in the continuous chain of which English literature is made up.

Before seeking further to characterize the age and its literature, we should consider a second difficulty about the term "Victorian." For a period almost seventy years in length we can hardly expect our generalizations to be uniformly applicable. It may be legitimate to categorize as "Victorian" both the writings of Thomas Carlyle at the beginning of the period and of Oscar Wilde at the end, but we should do so with our eyes open to the gap that stretches between the worlds of these two writers. As a preliminary corrective it is helpful to subdivide the age into three phases: Early Victorian (1832–48); Mid-Victorian (1848–70); and Late Victorian (1870–1901).

THE EARLY PERIOD (1832–48): A TIME OF TROUBLES

The early phase has been sometimes characterized as the Time of Troubles. In 1832 the passing of a Reform Bill had seemed to satisfy many of the demands of the middle classes, who were gradually taking over control of England's economy. The bill extended the right to vote to all men owning property worth ten pounds or more in annual rent. In effect the voting public hereafter included the lower middle classes but not the working classes (the latter had to wait their turn until 1867 when a second Reform Bill was passed). Even more important than the extension of the franchise was the abolition in 1832 of an archaic electoral system whereby some of the new industrial cities were unrepresented in Parliament while "rotten boroughs" (communities which had become depopulated) elected the nominees of the local squire. Because it broke up the monopoly of power that the conservative landowners had so long enjoyed (the Tory party had been in office almost continuously from 1783 until 1830), the Reform Bill represents the beginning of a new age. Yet this celebrated piece of legislation could hardly be expected to solve all of the economic, social, and political problems that had been building up while England was developing into a modern democratic and industrialized state. In the early 1840's a severe depression, with widespread unemployment, led to rioting. Even without the provocation of unemployment, conditions in the new industrial and coal-mining areas were sufficiently inflammatory to create fears of revolution. Workers and their families in the slums of such cities as Manchester lived like packs of rats in a sewer, and the conditions under which women and children toiled in mines and factories were unimaginably brutal. Elizabeth Barrett's poem *The Cry of the Children* (1843) may strike us as hysterical exaggeration, but it was based upon reliable evidence concerning children of five years of age who dragged heavy tubs of coal through low-ceilinged mine-passages for sixteen hours a day. Life in early Victorian mines and factories was much like Thomas Hobbes's "state of nature"—"poor, nasty, brutish, and short."

The owners of mines and factories are invariably blamed for such conditions, yet these owners regarded themselves as innocent, and with some justification, for they were wedded to an economic theory of laissez faire which assumed that unregulated working conditions would ultimately benefit everyone. A sense of the seemingly hopeless complexity of the situation during the Hungry 1840's is provided by an entry for 1842 in the diary of the statesman Charles Greville, an entry written at the same time that Carlyle was making his contribution to the "Condition of England Question," *Past and Present*. Conditions in the north of England, Greville reports, were "appalling."

There is an immense and continually increasing population, no adequate demand for labor, * * * no confidence, but a universal alarm, disquietude, and discontent. Nobody can sell anything. * * * Certainly I have never seen * * * so serious a state of things as that which now stares us in the face; and this after thirty years of uninterrupted peace, and the most ample scope afforded for the development of all our resources. * * * One remarkable feature in the present condition of affairs is that nobody can account for it, and nobody pretends to be able to point out any remedy.

In reality many remedies were being pointed out. One of the most striking was put forward by the Chartists, a large organization of workingmen. In 1838 the organization drew up a "People's Charter" advocating the extension of the right to vote, the use of secret balloting, and other legislative reforms. For ten years the Chartist leaders engaged in agitation to have their program adopted by Parliament. Their fiery speeches, addressed to large mobs of discontented men, alarmed those who were not themselves suffering from hunger. In *Locksley Hall*, Tennyson seems to have had the Chartist mobs in mind when he pictured the threat posed by this time of troubles: "Slowly comes a hungry people, as a lion, creeping nigher, / Glares at one that nods and winks behind a slowly-dying fire." Although in the eyes of posterity the Chartist program seems an eminently reasonable one, it was premature in the 1840's. More immediately feasible was the agitation to abolish the high tariffs on imported grains, tariffs known as the Corn Laws (the word "corn" in England refers to wheat and other grains). These high tariffs had been established to protect English farm products from having to compete with low-priced products imported from abroad. Landowners and farmers fought to keep these tariffs in force so that high prices for their wheat would be assured, but the rest of the population suffered severely from the exorbitant price of bread or, in years of bad crops, from scarcity of food. In 1845 serious crop failures in England and the outbreak of potato blight in Ireland convinced Sir Robert Peel, the Tory Prime Minister, that traditional protectionism must be abandoned. In 1846 the Corn Laws were repealed by Parliament, and the way was paved for the introduction of a system of Free Trade whereby goods could be imported with the payment of only minimal tariff duties. Although Free Trade did not eradicate the slums of Manchester, it worked well for many years and helped to relieve the major crisis of the Victorian economy. In 1848, when armed revolutions were exploding violently in every country of Europe, England was relatively unaffected. A monster Chartist demonstration fizzled out harmlessly in London, and Englishmen settled down to enjoy two decades of prosperity.

This Time of Troubles left its mark on some early Victorian literature. "Insurrection is a most sad necessity," Carlyle writes in his *Past and Present,* "and governors who wait for that to instruct them are surely getting into the fatalest courses." A similar refrain runs through Carlyle's history *The French Revolution* (1837), with its warning that an irresponsible English government might suffer the same fate as the irresponsible government of Louis XVI had suffered. The warning is a reminder that if the Victorians were not so obsessed as we are with the possibilities of the outbreak of an international war, they did feel they were living under the shadow of a possible civil war. Memories of the French Reign of Terror lasted longer than memories of Trafalgar and Waterloo, memories freshened by later outbreaks of civil strife, "the red fool-fury of the Seine" as Tennyson described one of the violent overturnings of government in France. It is the novelists of the 1840's and early 1850's, however, who show the most marked response to the industrial and political scene. Vivid records of these conditions are to be found in the fiction of Charles Kingsley (1819–75), Mrs. Gaskell (1810–65), and Benjamin Disraeli (1804–81), a novelist who became Prime Minister. For his novel *Sybil* (1845) Disraeli chose an appropriate subtitle, *The Two Nations*—a phrase that pointed up the line dividing the England of the rich from the other nation, the England of the poor. The novels of Charles Dickens (1812–70) can also be related to these developments. *Pickwick Papers,* his first novel, appearing in the same year as Victoria's accession, was predominantly a gay-spirited comedy, but each of his later books shows a more somber dissatisfaction with the shortcomings of the Victorian social scene. The indignant social criticism in such late novels as *Our Mutual Friend* indicates how Dickens continued to represent in the 1860's a frame of mind more appropriate for the 1840's.

THE MID-VICTORIAN PERIOD (1848–70): ECONOMIC PROSPERITY
AND RELIGIOUS CONTROVERSY

Dickens' mood of indignation was unrepresentative but not unique after 1848. It was shared, for example, by John Ruskin, who abandoned the criticism of art during this period in order to expose the faults of Victorian industry and commerce, as in his prophetic history of architecture, *The Stones of Venice* (1853) or in his attacks upon laissez-faire economics in *Unto This Last* (1862). Generally speaking, however, the comfortable and commonsensical novels of Anthony Trollope (1815–82) are a more characteristic reflection of the mid-Victorian attitude towards the social and political scene. This second phase of the Victorian age had many harassing problems, but it was a time of prosperity. On the whole its institutions worked well. Even the badly-bungled war against Russia in the Crimea (1854–56) did not seriously affect the growing sense of satisfaction that the challenging difficulties of the 1840's had been solved or would be solved by English wisdom and energy. The monarchy was proving its worth in a modern setting. The queen and her husband, Prince Albert, had more than merely adapted themselves to a state in which the middle class had become dominant; they were themselves models of middle-class domesticity and devotion to duty. The aristocracy was discovering that Free Trade was enriching rather than impoverishing their estates; agriculture flourished together with trade and industry. And through a succession of Factory Acts in Parliament, which restricted child labor and limited hours of employment, the condition of the working classes was also being gradually improved. When we speak of Victorian complacency or stability or optimism, we are usually referring to this mid-Victorian phase—"The Age of Improvement," as the historian Asa Briggs has called it. "Of all the decades in our history," writes G. M. Young, "a wise man would choose the eighteen-fifties to be young in."

In 1851 Prince Albert opened the Great Exhibition in Hyde Park where a gigantic glass greenhouse, the Crystal Palace, had been erected to display the exhibits of modern industry and science. Although the Crystal Palace has been later cited as an example of Victorian bad taste in the arts, it was one of the first buildings constructed according to modern architectural principles in which materials such as glass and iron are employed for purely functional ends (much late Victorian furniture, on the other hand, with its fantastic and irrelevant ornamentation, was constructed according to the opposite principle). The building itself, as well as the exhibits, symbolized the triumphant feats of Victorian technology. As Benjamin Disraeli (later to become Prime Minister) wrote to a friend in 1862: "It is a privilege to live in this age of rapid and brilliant events. What an error to consider it a utilitarian age. It is one of infinite romance."

In the strenuous assertiveness of some of Robert Browning's poetry one might detect parallels to the confident mood inspired by the Great Exhibition. Generally, however, most mid-Victorian poetry and critical prose was less preoccupied with technology, economics, and politics than with the conflict between religion and science. This conflict was not, of course, altogether a new one. Tennyson's *In Memoriam* (1850), like much mid-Victorian literature, carries on the religious debates of earlier decades, debates concerning the role of the church and the authority of the Bible, and the claims of scientific reasoning to be the most reliable method of discovering truth. These debates, in their earlier form, had been generally between the Utilitarians, the followers of Jeremy Bentham (1772–1832) and the philosophical conservatives, the followers of S. T. Coleridge. As John Stuart Mill demonstrates in his excellent essays on Bentham and Coleridge, these two writers divided between them the allegiance of all thoughtful men in England. Bentham and his disciples, such as James Mill (the father of John Stuart Mill), were reformers of a distinctive cast of mind. Their aim was to test all institutions, government or church or the law, in the light of human reason and common sense in order to determine whether such institutions were useful—that is, whether they contributed to the greatest happiness of the greatest numbers of men. This "Utilitarian" test was an extremely effective method of correcting inefficiencies in government administration: the drastic remodeling of the Civil

Service in Victorian England was a tribute to Benthamite thinking. The fact that some procedures in government or law had been established for hundreds of years did not daunt Bentham in the least. Man's traditional customs, the very past itself, were of little interest to his logical mind; everything had to be tested afresh in terms of the Utilitarian formula. Such a test, if applied to a long-established institution like the Church of England, or to religious belief in general, could have, and did have, disruptive effects. Was religious belief useful for the needs of a reasonable man? To the Benthamites the answer was evident: religious belief was merely an outmoded superstition.

Opponents of Utilitarianism, including Coleridge, argued that Bentham's view of human nature was unrealistically narrow, that man had always needed a faith as profoundly as he had needed food, and that if reason seemed to demonstrate the irrelevance of religion then reason must be an inadequate mode of arriving at truth. These anti-Utilitarians were of two types. The first were those such as Carlyle, who abandoned institutional Christianity yet sought to retain some sort of substitute religious belief— a quest that is vividly described in Carlyle's spiritual autobiography, *Sartor Resartus*. Others, led by John Henry Newman, argued that only a power-ful, dogmatic, and traditional religious institution could withstand the at-tacks of irreverent thinkers of the Benthamite stamp. In the 1830's and 1840's (before he was converted to Roman Catholicism), Newman became the leader of an impressive crusade to strengthen the Church of England. The movement he headed is known under various names including "The Oxford Movement," because it originated at Oxford University, or as "Tractarianism," because Newman and his conservative followers developed their arguments in defense of a High Church in a series of pamphlets or tracts, or as "Puseyism," because Edward Pusey, an Oxford clergyman, shared with Newman the leadership in these developments. Whatever name it went by, Newman's campaign produced a lively controversy. When Arthur Hugh Clough and Matthew Arnold were at Oxford in the early 1840's, the university was seething with religious debates, debates that were to have a marked effect on the poetry written by both men in the 1850's.

In mid-Victorian England these controversies continued, but with an added intensification. Leadership in the anticlerical position passed grad-ually from the Utilitarians to some of the leaders of science, in particular to Thomas Henry Huxley, the lieutenant of Charles Darwin. Although many English scientists were themselves men of strong religious convic-tions, the impact of their scientific discoveries seemed consistently damag-ing to established faiths. Complaining about the "flimsiness" of his own religious faith in 1851, Ruskin exclaimed: "If only the Geologists would let me alone, I could do very well, but those dreadful hammers! I hear the clink of them at the end of every cadence of the Bible verses."

The damage lamented by Ruskin was effected in two ways. First was the application of a scientific attitude of mind towards a study of the Bible itself. This kind of investigation, developed especially in Germany, was known as the "Higher Criticism." Instead of treating the Bible as a sacredly infallible document, scientifically-minded scholars examined it as a mere text of history and presented evidence about its composition that believers, especially in Protestant countries, found disconcerting, to say the least. The second kind of damage was effected by the view of man implicit in the discoveries of Geology and Astronomy, the new and "Terrible Muses" of literature, as Tennyson called them in a late poem. Geology, by extending the history of the earth backwards millions of years, reduced the stature of man in time. The revolution effected by geology during the Victorian age was described by John Tyndall, an eminent physicist, in an address at Belfast in 1874. In the 18th century, Tyndall notes, men had an "unwavering trust" in the "chronology of the Old Testament," but in Victorian times men have had to become accustomed to "the idea that not for six thousand, nor for sixty thousand, nor for six thousand thousand, but for aeons embracing untold millions of years, this earth has been the theater of life and death. The riddle of the rocks has been read by the geologist and paleontologist, from sub-Cambrian depths to the deposits thickening over the sea bottoms of today. And upon the leaves of that stone book are * * * stamped the characters, plainer and surer than those formed by the ink of history, which carry the mind back into abysses of past time." And if geology reduced the stature of man in time, astronomy, by extending a knowledge of stellar distances to dizzying expanses, reduced the stature of man in space. To Tennyson's speaker in *Maud* (1855) the stars are "innumerable" tyrants of "iron skies." They are "Cold fires, yet with power to burn and brand / His nothingness into man."

In the mid-Victorian period a further reduction into "nothingness" was effected by Biology. Darwin's great treatise, *The Origin of Species* (1859), was interpreted by the nonscientific public in a variety of ways. Some chose to assume that evolution was synonymous with progress, but most readers recognized that Darwin's theory of natural selection conflicted not only with the concept of creation derived from the Bible but also with long-established assumptions of the values attached to man's special role in the world. Darwin's later treatise, *The Descent of Man* (1871), raised more explicitly the spectral question of man's identification with the animal kingdom. If the principle of survival of the fittest was accepted as the key to conduct, there remained the inquiry: fittest for what?

Disputes about evolutionary science, like the disputes about the Oxford Movement, are a reminder that beneath the placidly prosperous surface of the mid-Victorian age there were serious conflicts and anxieties. In the same year as the Great Exhibition, with its celebration of the triumphs of trade and industry, Charles Kingsley described the painful estrangements in Victorian households that had been brought about by religious differences. "The young men and women of our day are fast parting from their parents and each other; the more thoughtful are wandering either towards Rome, towards sheer materialism, or towards an unchristian and unphilosophic spiritualism."

THE LATE PERIOD (1870–1901): DECAY OF VICTORIAN VALUES

The third phase of the Victorian age is more difficult to categorize. At first glance its point of view seems merely an extension of mid-Victorianism whose golden glow lingered on through the Jubilee years of 1887 and 1897 (years celebrating the fiftieth and sixtieth anniversaries of the queen's accession) down to 1914. For many Victorians, this final phase of the century was a time of serenity and security, the age of house parties and long weekends in the country. In the amber of Henry James's prose is immortalized a sense of the comfortable pace of these pleasant, well-fed gatherings. Life in London, too, was for many an exhilarating heyday. In *My Life and Loves*, the Irish-American Frank Harris, often a severe critic of the English scene, records his recollections of the gaiety of London in the 1880's: "London: who would give even an idea of its varied delights: London, the center of civilization, the queen city of the world without a peer in the multitude of its attractions, as superior to Paris as Paris is to New York." Yet as the leading social critic of the 1860's, Matthew Arnold, had tried to show, there were anomalies in the seemingly smooth-working institutions of mid-Victorian England, and after 1870 flaws became evident. The sudden emergence of Bismarck's Germany after the defeat of France in 1871 was progressively to confront England with powerful threats to her naval and military position and also to her exclusive pre-eminence in trade and industry. The recovery of the United States after the Civil War likewise provided serious competition from a new quarter. In 1873 and 1874 economic depressions occurred of so severe a nature that the rate of emigration rose to an alarming degree. Also threatening to the domestic balance of power was the growth of labor as a political and economic force. In 1867, under Disraeli's guidance, a second Reform Bill had been passed which extended the right to vote to sections of the working classes, and this, together with the subsequent development of trade unions, made labor a political force to be reckoned with. Although Gilbert and Sullivan's comic opera *Iolanthe* had said that "every boy and every gal that's born into the world alive / Is either a little Liberal, or else a little Conserva-tive," it would not be long before this lyric of the year 1882 would require a corrective footnote. A third party, the Labour Party, was about to be added, a party dedicated to a very different conception of the role of the state than that held by the earlier generations of Whigs and Tories. The new party represented a wide variety of shades of social-ism. Some labor leaders were disciples of the Tory-Socialism of John Ruskin and shared his idealistic conviction that the middle-class economic and political system, with its distrust of state interference, was irresponsible and immoral. Other labor leaders had been infected instead by the revolutionary theories of Karl Marx and Friedrich Engels as expounded in their *Communist Manifesto* of 1847 and in Marx's *Capital* (1867, 1885, 1895). Perhaps the first English author of note to be connected with Marxism was the poet and painter William Morris. Morris, himself a man of some independent means, was too much of an individualist to follow consistently an orthodox Marxist line, but he did share with Marx a conviction that utopia could be achieved only after the working classes had, by revolution, taken control of government and industry.

In much of the literature of this final phase of Victorianism we can sense an over-all change of attitudes. Some of the late Victorian writers expressed the change openly by simply attacking the major mid-Victorian idols. Samuel Butler (1835–1902), for example, set about demolishing Darwin, Tennyson, and Prime Minister Gladstone, figures whose aura of authority reminded him of his own father. For the more worldly and casual-mannered Prime Minister Disraeli, on the other hand, Butler could express considerable admiration, as can be seen in the following characteristically witty evaluation he made of "Dizzy" in 1881: "Earnestness was his greatest danger, but if he did not quite overcome it (as who indeed can? it is the last enemy that shall be subdued), he managed to veil it with a fair amount of success." In his novel, *The Way of All Flesh*, much of which was written in the 1870's, Butler satirized family life. In particular he made fun of the tyrannical self-righteousness of a Victorian father, his own father (a clergyman) serving as his model. Butler's open revolt was perhaps premature. More typical were Walter Pater and his followers, writers who concluded that the striving of their predecessors was ultimately pointless, that the answers to man's problems are not to be found, and that our role is to enjoy the fleeting moments of beauty in "this short day of frost and sun." It is symptomatic of this shift in point of view that Edward FitzGerald's beautiful translation of the *Rubáiyát of Omar Khayyám* (1859), with its melancholy theme that life's problems are insoluble, went virtually unnoticed in the 1860's but became a popular favorite in subsequent decades. The most dramatic illustration of the shift is provided by the life and works of Pater's disciple, Oscar Wilde. In Dickens' *David Copperfield*, the hero affirms: "I have always been thoroughly in earnest." Forty-four years later, in Wilde's comedy, *The Importance of Being Earnest* (1895), we see what happened to this typical mid-Victorian word, "earnest." In Wilde's deft dialogue the word is reduced to a pun, a key joke in this comic spectacle of earlier Victorian values being turned upside down.

EARNESTNESS, RESPECTABILITY, AND THE EVANGELICALS

Wilde's decades, the 1880's and 1890's, when being earnest was apparently not important, can be legitimately overlooked if we are trying to categorize the Victorian age as a whole instead of distinguishing the stages of its development. Why has the term "earnest" been so often applied to the typical Victorian writers? It should be noted that the quality of earnestness (or as some historians call it, more appropriately, "eagerness") was not strained. It did not exclude high spirits and humor. An age which relished the comic genius of Dickens and Thackeray, the grotesque humor of Browning and Carlyle, the nonsensical whimsy of Edward Lear and Lewis Carroll, was not exclusively dedicated to mere solemnity. Nevertheless the general Victorian preference was for the mood of *Il Penseroso* rather than *L'Allegro*. This earnestness of spirit can best be accounted for by distinguishing it not from what came after but from what went before it.

The connections between literature in the Romantic and Victorian ages are close. Victorian poets as different as Browning and Swinburne both derive from Shelley. Tennyson is a follower of Keats, Arnold is a follower of Wordsworth, and many other instances of such continuity and influence may be cited. If we are looking for a dividing point, however, we may find one in Carlyle's well-known advice to his contemporaries in 1834: "Close thy Byron; open thy *Goethe*." Carlyle's advice could be interpreted in two ways. The first is with reference to literary forms. By ceasing to use Byron as a model, a Victorian writer might avoid the wild excesses, the lack of controlled form of much Romantic writing. Byron himself foresaw that such a reformation was necessary. "We are all on a wrong tack ('Lakers and all)," he wrote. "Our successors will have to go back to the riding school * * * and learn to ride the great horse." Some of Byron's Victorian successors ignored his prediction; they too rode Pegasus bareback as casually as he had done. The novels of the Brontë sisters, for example, are Byronic; *Wuthering Heights* and *Jane Eyre* (both published in 1847) have affinities with the Gothic novels popular in Byron's day. The prose of Carlyle himself is Byronic. Yet several Victorian poets, Tennyson in particular, do fulfill Byron's prediction. The energy of Romantic literature persists, but it is channeled into a stricter concern for disciplined forms, "Nature still," as Alexander Pope recommended, "but Nature methodized." Tennyson's Virgilian sense of vowel sounds and Dante Gabriel Rossetti's polished polysyllables are symptomatic of the change. Matthew Arnold, too, at least in his literary criticism, is evidently a classical riding master. It is significant that the Romantic poet most influential in the Victorian age was Keats, the most form-conscious of the Romantics, rather than Byron.

As for Carlyle himself, when he advised his contemporaries to close their volumes of Byron he was not primarily concerned with a chastening of literary forms. He was saying, in effect: "Stop moping. There is work to be done, work that requires the earnest efforts of all of us." Byronism, in this context, meant the easy-going aristocratic code that had been dominant during the Regency, with its preference for a happy-go-lucky enjoyment of the physical pleasures of life, for hunting and hard drinking and lounging. Lord Melbourne, Victoria's first Prime Minister, embodied such a view of life and found himself out of place under the new dispensation—an "autumn rose" as Strachey called him. Carlyle's gospel, on the other hand, was soon to be extremely timely for the new generation. From 1830 on there developed what the historian Arnold Toynbee calls a "challenge." The earnest strivings of the Victorians provided the needed "response." The strenuous transformation of English political, social, economic, and literary life is evidence that the volumes of Byron (as thus interpreted) had been closed.

A further indication of the timeliness of Carlyle's call to action in *Sartor Resartus* is its Evangelical tone. "Evangelical," a term commonly used in all discussions of 19th-century literature, requires some explanation. In its strictest sense "Evangelical" refers to part of a branch of the Church of England called the Low Church. In the 18th century many Anglicans had been profoundly affected by the teachings of John Wesley. Without setting up a separate church, they had sought to instill some of Wesley's ideals and religious enthusiasm into the phlegmatic and easy-going Established Church of which they were members. Zealously dedicated to good causes (they were responsible for the emancipation of all the slaves in the British Empire as early as 1833), advocates of a strict puritan code of morality, and righteously censorious of worldliness in others, the Evangelicals became a powerful and active minority in the early part of the 19th century. Much of their power depended on the fact that their view of life and religion was virtually identical with that of a much larger group, the Nonconformists—that is, the Baptists, Methodists, Congregationalists, and other Protestant sects outside the Church of England. When united for action with this large group of sects, whose membership included a generous proportion of successful businessmen, the Evangelicals were a formidable force. For this reason, the term "Evangelical" is often stretched to refer to the puritan code and spiritual zeal shared by this combination of the Protestant sects and the Evangelical wing of the church.

Finally, the term "Evangelical" has been loosely applied to cover any kind of enthusiastic concern for reform. It is thus used to describe anyone infected with the *spirit* of the Evangelical movement even though he does not subscribe to its ethical code or its beliefs. This loose use of the term may be a mere sleight-of-hand trick, but it enables the historian to equate Evangelicalism with early Victorianism. Seen in this light, even secular reformers such as Jeremy Bentham and his Utilitarian followers could be classified as Evangelical in spirit. Bentham was no churchman; as his earnest-minded disciple J. S. Mill described him, he was "the great questioner of things established." Yet because the sober effort of the Utilitarians was responsible for many of the major reforms of government and administration in the Victorian age, it could be said that the Utilitarians showed signs of having been lastingly infected by a religious spirit which they had outwardly rejected. Less incongruously, the spirit of Evangelicalism can be detected among the school of thinkers opposed to Bentham, the conservative school of Coleridge. The revival of conservatism was most dramatically manifested not in politics but in the Oxford Movement in religion. Although Newman and his Tractarian followers of the 1830's and 1840's were of course opposed to the theological position of the true Evangelicals, the fervor with which they set about reforming the Anglican Church by instilling fresh energy into its doctrines and rituals is similar to the fervor of Evangelical theologians such as Thomas Scott, whose teachings left a permanent mark on Newman himself.

Victorian earnestness may therefore be explained partly as a response to a challenging situation and partly as rooted in an active religious movement that left its stamp on agnostics as well as on believers. Arnold's friend Arthur Clough, who became a skeptic, attributed his own persistent obsession with problems of conscience to the Evangelical revival. The movement "beginning with Wesleyanism, and culminating at last in Puseyism" was responsible, he said, for an "over-excitation of the religious sense, resulting in this irrational, almost animal irritability of conscience." George Eliot (pseudonym of Mary Ann Evans; 1819–80) is another example of this Evangelical legacy. After having abandoned Christianity and having flouted convention by living for years with a married man, she devoted her novels to painstaking analyses of problems of conscience and moral choice. It would be difficult to name a Victorian writer of any consequence who remained an Evangelical in the true sense of the term; it would be equally difficult to name one who was not affected by what Evangelicalism had stood for.

If we also consider the puritan code of morality advocated by the Nonconformists and Evangelicals rather than their earnestness of spirit, it is once more apparent why Carlyle's recommendation to close the volumes of Byron was appropriate. During Byron's lifetime those advocating the puritan code had been a minority. After 1832 they gradually came to represent if not a numerical majority at least the most potent voice in Victorian England. And they were not reluctant to make that voice heard.

The code of puritanism and respectability, which the middle classes imposed on England, is symbolized by the joyless Victorian Sunday. In 1837, a new Sunday Observance Bill was introduced into Parliament, a bill that provoked Dickens into protesting against its strict prohibition of harmless entertainments on the Sabbath. Although the Bill did not quite pass, the Sober Sunday ritual became established by custom if not by law. To later generations, even more noteworthy was the puritans' standard of sexual behavior, with its intense concern for female innocence—or, as its opponents contended, for female ignorance. The history of Victorian asceticism is nevertheless much more complex than common supposition allows, as may be suggested by the fact that in 1850 8,000 prostitutes were known by the police to be operating in London. In the city of Leeds, a few years earlier, statistics indicate that there were two churches and 39 chapels or meeting houses to compete with 451 taverns and 98 brothels. For a striking corrective to the commonly accepted suppositions about Victorian asceticism, Steven Marcus' study of the sexual habits of different classes of mid-19th-century English society, *The Other Victorians* (1966), may be consulted.

The middle-class puritan code was largely derived from the Old Testament, but it also reflected commercial experience in which sobriety, hard work, and a joyless abstention from worldly pleasures paid off, paradoxically enough, in worldly success. Intermixed with this ascetic code was an insistence upon respectability—an insistence reflecting the insecurity of a newly powerful class in a fluid society, a class anxious to have a fixed set of manners by which to live and to measure themselves and the families of others. Hence developed the phenomenon of "Mrs. Grundyism": conformity in its worst sense—that is, external conformity.

It is against this background that John Stuart Mill's essay *On Liberty* should be read. The status of liberty in Victorian England was actually one of the most outstanding achievements of the age. For continental agitators of Left, Right, or Center in politics, Victorian England was the land of freedom, an asylum where the policeman was a friendly protector instead of an instrument of tyranny. To this asylum flocked General Torrijos (whose plot against the Spanish monarchy involved Tennyson); Mazzini, the Italian nationalist; Louis Napoleon of France; Kossuth, the Hungarian patriot; Prince Metternich of Austria; and Karl Marx himself, whose major work, *Capital*, was conceived in the Reading Room of the British Museum. The Victorian achievement in religious as well as political freedom is also impressive. Atheist orators such as Charles Bradlaugh enjoyed the privilege of addressing large audiences. As Amy Cruse affirms, "no age has done more towards giving religious freedom in thought and speech and practice."

Under such circumstances, we may wonder why Mill considered liberty a problem worth writing a treatise about in 1859. Mill was inspired by his experience that individuality is threatened not merely by political tyrannies or entrenched religions. It is threatened also by the less tangible pressures exerted by society itself, in particular by the middle-class conventions which weighed upon the nonconformist in society rather than upon the Nonconformist in religion. In Hardy's late-Victorian novel, *Jude the Obscure*, a novel which contributed to the breakdown of the puritan code in literature, it is revealing that when the heroine resolves to leave her husband she justifies her action by citing a passage from Mill's *On Liberty*.

THE DIVERSITY OF VICTORIAN LITERATURE

The weight of the puritan code on the literature of early and mid-Victorian England was, as we might expect, considerable. It was most evident in the novels, for novels were commonly read aloud in family gatherings, and the need to avoid topics which might cause embarrassment to young girls established taboos that the novelist could not dare ignore, although he might sometimes skillfully circumvent them. Thackeray and others offered protests, but it was not until near the end of the century or later that the novelists broke clear of the restrictions imposed on them by the demands of their middle-class public. The poets, and also the writers of that important Victorian form, the extended essay, fared better. When Browning was writing *The Ring and the Book* he was obviously unconcerned about whether his poem might raise blushes on prudish cheeks, and Swinburne's *Poems and Ballads* flouts the taboos in the manner of the French poets whom he admired. Both volumes appeared in the 1860's at the same time as the essays of Matthew Arnold with their attacks on the narrowness of the puritan middle-class mind.

Too much can be made of the importance of these quaint taboos as literary conventions in the Victorian age. A much more significant kind of pressure from the Victorian audience on its writers was one that they were themselves inclined to comply with rather than to repudiate or circumvent. This was the desire on the part of readers to be guided and edified. The desire stems from a combination of the various strands of Victorian character we have been here considering: the earnest preoccupation with problems of a new age, the sense of anxious uncertainty as an established order gives way, and the strain of puritanism which may dismiss entertainment as mere entertainment. The newly expanding reading public, despite its air of solid confidence, wanted help from its authors, and its authors were understandably flattered by the request. Only a few, such as D. G. Rossetti, ignored it; the others all exhibit, in varying degrees, an air of prophecy and mission. Carlyle in his lectures *On Heroes* identifies the writer or "Poet" such as Shakespeare with the great prophets such as Mahomet, and in his own writings it is evident that he sought to make his mark as a seer rather than as a mere man of letters. The very high status that even Matthew Arnold claimed for literature is evident in his statement that "most of what now passes with us for religion and philosophy will be replaced by poetry." Perhaps the most extreme example of a Victorian writer with a sense of mission is, however, John Ruskin, a writer who had opinions on everything from Botticelli to how to build sheepfolds. Tennyson, here as in most instances, is more representative. To provide firm guidance in problems of science and religion, the destiny of nations and daily life, was a task that sometimes appealed to Tennyson and sometimes appalled him. As we might expect, several of his poems are concerned with the dilemma of a writer's divided duty towards his public and his art—a dilemma that has become even more acute in the 20th century as the reading public has further expanded.

The existence of this dilemma may help to explain another characteristic of Victorian literature: its variety both in style and in subject matter. Variety is in part a symptom of the Victorian writer's bold independence and his zest for literary experiment for its own sake, but it is also a symptom of an absence of any final general agreement concerning the function of literature and art in a democratic society. The writer and his audience might usually agree that instruction was a desirable attribute of a work of literature, but what was to constitute the instruction and what was the appropriate mode in which to convey it? Tennyson's poem *The Lotos-Eaters* (1842) and Browning's poem *The Bishop Orders his Tomb* (1845) were published within the space of three years. The one is in the grand manner of English poetry, the culmination of a poetic tradition emphasizing beautiful cadences and vowel sounds: "To watch the crisping ripples on the beach, / And tender curving lines of creamy spray." The colloquial speech of Browning's bishop, as he hisses his hatred of a rival, seems to belong to a different century: "Shrewd was that snatch from out the corner south / He graced his carrion with, God curse the same!" And if we ignore the stylistic differences here and concentrate upon a possible similarity—that both poems, like many Victorian writings, evoke the past of myth and history—what is to be done to align these works with other works of the same period? What resemblance is there to Dickens' *Oliver Twist* (1838) for example, with its realistic scenes of a sordid workhouse, or to Carlyle's *Past and Present* (1843) with its idiosyncratic manner of exposing the sufferings of the Victorian poor, or to John Ruskin's *Modern Painters* (1843) with its rhapsodic celebrations of alpine scenery and romantic sunsets? In one of his early letters Matthew Arnold complained to a friend of the "multitudinousness" of the age, and as a literary critic Arnold sought to provide for himself as a poet, and for his contemporaries in general, a set of classical critical principles which would correct this anarchical diversity and would reimpose some kind of order. Arnold's achievement as a critic and poet is indeed impressive, yet it can hardly be said that he succeeded in persuading his contemporaries to accept him as a Victorian Aristotle. The "multitudinousness" was too overpowering, even for him. As a result, most candid literary historians admit that while we may confidently identify the distinguishing characteristics of individual Victorian writers, of a Browning, a Dickens, or a Newman, it is extremely difficult to devise satisfactory statements about Victorian literature that are generally applicable to most or all of these writers. This admission is distressing to tidy minds, but in itself it tells us something distinctive about Victorian literature as a whole. Variety may frustrate the pleasure of ready classification, but it provides interesting challenges of its own.

THOMAS CARLYLE
(1795–1881)

1833: *Sartor Resartus* published in *Fraser's Magazine*.
1834: Moves to London from Craigenputtock in Scotland.
1837: *The French Revolution* published.
1843: *Past and Present* published.
1866: Death of Jane Carlyle.

W. B. Yeats once asked William Morris what writers had inspired the socialist movement of the 1880's, and Morris replied: "Oh, Ruskin and Carlyle, but somebody should have been beside Carlyle and punched his head every five minutes." Morris's mixed feelings of admiration and exasperation are typical of the response Carlyle evokes in many readers. Anyone approaching his prose for the first time should expect to be sometimes bewildered. Like George Bernard Shaw, Carlyle discovered, early in life, that exaggeration can be a highly effective way of gaining the attention of an audience. But it can also be a way of distracting an audience unfamiliar with the idiosyncrasies of his rhetoric and unprepared for the distinctive enjoyments his writings can provide.

One of the idiosyncrasies of his prose is that it is meant to be read aloud. As a talker Carlyle was as famous in his day as Dr. Johnson in his. Charles Darwin testified that he was "the best worth listening to of any man I know." No Boswell has adequately recorded this talk, but no Boswell was needed, for Carlyle has contrived to get the sound of his own spoken voice into his writings. It is a noisy and emphatic voice, startling upon first acquaintance. To become familiar with its unusual sounds and rhythms, one can best begin by reading aloud from some of Carlyle's portraits of his contemporaries which are included in the following selections. Many of these colorful portraits are from his letters, and it becomes evident that the mannerisms of the author were simply the mannerisms of the man and were congenial and appropriate for the author's purposes.

Carlyle was 41 years old when Victoria became queen of England. He had been born in the same year as Keats, yet he is rarely grouped with his contemporaries among the Romantic writers. Instead his name is linked with younger men such as Dickens, Browning, and Ruskin, the early generation of Victorian writers. The classification is fitting, for it was Carlyle's role to foresee the problems that were to preoccupy the Victorians and early to report upon his experiences in confronting these problems. After 1837 his loud voice began to attract an audience, and he soon became one of the most influential figures of the age, affecting the attitudes of scientists, statesmen, and especially of men of letters. His wife once complained that Ralph Waldo Emerson had no ideas (except mad ones) that he had not derived from Carlyle. "But pray, Mrs. Carlyle," replied a friend, *"who has?"* "

Before attaining such prestige among the Victorians, however, Carlyle had a long wait. His early career is the dramatic story of struggles against narrowness of background, poverty, ill-health, and religious uncertainties.

Carlyle was born in Ecclefechan, a village in Scotland, the eldest child of a large family. His mother, at the time of her marriage, had been illiterate. His father, James Carlyle, a stonemason and later a farmer, was proudly characterized by his son as a peasant. The key to the character of James Carlyle was the Scottish Calvinism which he instilled into the members of his household. Frugality, hard work, a tender but undemonstrative family loyalty, and a peculiar blend of self-denial and self-righteousness were characteristic features of Carlyle's childhood home. The stamp of its discipline, imprinted upon him for life, can be detected even in Carlyle's sense of humor, which was highly developed yet limited. The trivial banter of London's bohemia did not merely bore him; it drove him to furious repudiations. His incapacity to enjoy the fun of Charles Lamb is comparable to his father's stern rejection of workmen who wasted time.

With his father's aid the young Carlyle was educated at Annan Academy and at Edinburgh University, the subject of his special interest being mathematics; he left without taking a degree. It was his parents' hope that their son would become a clergyman, but in this respect Thomas made a severe break with his ancestry. He was a prodigious reader, and his exposure to such skeptical writers as Hume, Voltaire, and Gibbon had undermined his faith. Gibbon's *Decline and Fall of the Roman Empire*, he told Emerson, was "the splendid bridge from the old world to the new." By the time he was 23, Carlyle had crossed the bridge and had abandoned his Christian faith and his proposed career as a clergyman. During the period in which he was thinking through his religious position, he supported himself by teaching school in Scotland, and later by tutoring private pupils, but from 1824 to the end of his life he relied exclusively upon his writings for his livelihood. His early writings consisted of translations, biographies, and critical studies of Goethe and other German authors, to whose view of life he was deeply attracted. The German Romantics (loosely grouped by Carlyle under the label "Mystics") were the second most important influence on his life and character, exceeded only by his early family experiences. Aided by the writings of these German poets and philosophers, he arrived finally at a faith in life that served as a substitute for the Christian faith he had lost.

His most significant early essay, *Characteristics*, appeared in *The Edinburgh Review* in 1831. A year earlier he had begun writing his full-length autobiographical novel, *Sartor Resartus*, a work which he had great difficulty in persuading anyone to publish. In book form *Sartor* first appeared in America in 1836, where Carlyle's follower, Emerson, had prepared an enthusiastic audience for this unusual work. His American following (which was later to become a vast one) did little at first, however, to relieve the poverty in which he still found himself after fifteen years of writing. In 1837 the tide at last turned when he published *The French Revolution*. "O it has been a great success, dear," his wife assured him, but her husband, embittered by the long struggle, was incredulous that the sought-for recognition had at last come to him.

It was in character for his wife, Jane Welsh Carlyle, to be less surprised by his success than he was. That Thomas Carlyle was a genius had been an article of faith to her from her first meeting with him in 1821. A clever girl, the daughter of a doctor of good family, Jane Welsh had many suitors. When in 1826 she finally accepted Carlyle, her family and friends were shocked. This peasant's son, of no fixed employment, seemed a fantastic choice. Subsequent events seemed to confirm her family's verdict. Not long after marriage, Carlyle insisted upon their retiring to a remote farm at Craigenputtock where for six years (1828–34) this sociable woman was obliged to live in isolation and loneliness. After they moved to London in 1834 and settled in a house on Cheyne Walk in Chelsea, Jane Carlyle was considerably happier and enjoyed her role as hostess. Her husband, however, remained a difficult man to live with. His stomach ailments, irascible nerves, and preoccupation with his writings, as well as the lionizing to which he was subjected, left him with little inclination for domestic amenities.

This marriage of the Carlyles has aroused almost as much interest as that of the Brownings. Their friend the Reverend W. H. Brookfield (whose marriage was an unhappy one) once said cynically that marrying is "dipping into a pitcher of snakes for the chance of an eel," and partisan biographers have argued that Jane Welsh drew a snake instead of an eel. Even without such partisanship, it is easy to be sorry for the wife. Yet if we study her letters, before and after her marriage, it is evident that she got what she asked for. She wanted a man of genius who would change the world. She paid for what she wanted by years of comparative poverty, ill health, and loneliness. Just before her death in 1866, she had the satisfaction of enjoying to the full a high point of her husband's triumph when the peasant's son she had chosen returned to Scotland to deliver his inaugural address as Lord Rector of Edinburgh University.

During the first thirty years of Carlyle's residence in London he wrote extensive historical works and many pamphlets concerning contemporary issues. After *The French Revolution* he edited, in 1845, the *Letters and Speeches of Oliver Cromwell*, a Puritan leader of heroic dimensions in Carlyle's eyes, and later wrote a full-length biography, *The History of Friedrich II of Prussia, Called Frederick the Great* (1858–65). Carlyle's pamphleteering is seen at its best in *Past and Present* (1843) and in its most violent phase in his *Latter-Day Pamphlets* (1850). Following the death of his wife, he wrote very little. For the remaining fifteen years of his life he confined himself to reading, or to talking to the stream of visitors who called at Cheyne Walk to listen to the "Sage of Chelsea," as he came to be called. In 1874 he accepted the Prussian Order of Merit from Bismarck but declined an English baronetcy offered by Disraeli. In 1881 he died and was buried near his family in Ecclefechan churchyard.

To understand Carlyle's role as historian, biographer, and social critic, it is essential to understand his attitude towards religion. The qualities of his prose style as well as his mature evaluation of past and present are ultimately attributable to religious experiences undergone in his earlier years. By the time he was 23, he had been shorn of his faith in Christianity. At this stage, as Carlyle observed with dismay, many men seemed content simply to stop. A Utilitarian such as James Mill or some of his common-sensical professors at the University of Edinburgh regarded society and the universe itself as machines. To such men the machines might sometimes seem complex, but they were not mysterious, for machines are subject to man's control and understanding through reason and observation. To Carlyle, and to many others, life without a sense of the divine was a mean-ingless nightmare. In the first part of "The Everlasting No," a chapter of *Sartor Resartus*, he gives a memorable picture of the horrors of such a soulless world that drove him in 1822 to thoughts of suicide. The 18th-century Enlightenment had left him not in light but in darkness. As William Barrett says of modern man, in his study of 20th-century Ex-istentialism: "The individual is thrust out of the sheltered nest that society has provided. He can no longer hide his nakedness by the old disguises."

Barrett's choice of terms here is identical with Carlyle's metaphor of the "Clothes Philosophy." The naked man seeks clothing for protection. One solution, represented by Coleridge and his followers, was to repudiate the skepticism of Voltaire and Hume and to return to the protective be-liefs and rituals of the Christian church. To Carlyle such a return was pointless. The traditional Christian coverings were worn out—"Hebrew Old Clothes" he called them. His own solution, described in "The Ever-lasting Yea," was to tailor a new suit of beliefs from German philosophy, shreds of Scottish Calvinism, and his own observations. The following sum-marizes his basic religious attitude: "Gods die with the men who have con-ceived them. But the god-stuff roars eternally, like the sea. * * * Even the gods must be born again. We must be born again." Although this passage is from *The Plumed Serpent*, by D. H. Lawrence (a writer who resembles Carlyle at almost every point), it might have come from any one of Car-lyle's own books—most especially from *Sartor Resartus*, in which he de-scribes his being born again—his "Fire-baptism"—into a new secular faith.

On what evidence was the new faith based? Carlyle and Lawrence might contend that the word "evidence" is irrelevant here. Or Carlyle might cite the religious experience itself, the moment of insight when he saw the realities behind the appearances. He might also cite his realization that all the sciences he had studied had failed to answer the important ques-tions confronting man, which remain what he called "mysteries." From this latter realization there derives what seems an anti-intellectual strain in Carlyle. He speaks often of the limitations of the conscious analytic intellect and praises instead the instinctive responses of the unconsciously healthy soul, responses which include a sense of religious awe.

The most appropriate term to describe Carlyle's central position is *vi-talism*. The presence of energy in the world was, in itself, for him, a sign of the godhead. Carlyle therefore judges everything in terms of the pres-ence or absence of some vital spark. The minds of men, books, societies, churches, or even landscapes, are rated as alive or dead, dynamic or merely mechanical. The government of Louis XVI, for example, was obviously moribund, doomed to be swept away by the dynamic forces of the French Revolution. The government of Victorian England seemed likewise to be doomed unless infused with vital energies of leadership and an awareness of the real needs of mankind. When an editor complained that his essay *Characteristics* was "inscrutable," Carlyle remarked: "My own fear was that it might be too *scrutable*; for it indicates decisively enough that Society (in my view) is utterly condemned to destruction, and even now beginning its long travail-throes of Newbirth."

This preoccupation with revolution and the destruction of the old orders suggests that Carlyle's politics were radical, but his position is bewilderingly difficult to classify. During the Hungry 1840's, he was one of the most outspoken critics of middle-class bunglings and of the economic theory of laissez faire which, in his opinion, was ultimately responsible for these bunglings. On behalf of the millions of people suffering from the miseries attendant upon a major breakdown of industry and agriculture he did strenuous work. At other times, because of his insistence upon strong and heroic leadership, Carlyle appears to be a violent conservative, or, as some have argued, virtually a fascist. That some aspects of his political position are similar to fascism is beyond dispute. The theory of democracy seemed to him to be based on an unrealistic premise about the basic needs of mankind, and he had no confidence that democratic institutions could work efficiently. A few men in every age are, in his view, leaders; the rest are followers and are happy only as followers. Society should be organized so that these gifted leaders can have scope to govern effectively. Such leaders are, for Carlyle, heroes. George Bernard Shaw, who learned much from Carlyle, would call them supermen. Liberals and democrats, however, might call them dictators. Although Carlyle was aware that the Western world was committed to a faith in a system of balloting and of legislative debate, he was confident that the system would eventually break down. The democratic assumption that all voters are equally capable of choice and the assumption that men value liberty more than they value order seemed to him nonsense. To all of us nurtured in presuppositions about the virtues of the democratic system of politics, it is instructive to confront this potent Victorian critic of democracy. But it is also instructive to observe how his political authoritarianism became intensified as he grew older. In his earlier writings Carlyle was arguing, in effect, that in politics, as well as in religion, men need the guiding hand of some kind of father. In his later writings, on the other hand, he seems to be arguing for the need of some kind of ruthless commander. His opinions about how governors should treat Negro workers on the Jamaica plantations make painful reading. As he himself said, these fierce *Latter-Day Pamphlets* had "divided me altogether from the mob of 'Progress-of-the-Species' and other vulgar." One distinction should, however, be noted. Concerning the English and Irish laborers thrown out of work by economic circumstances Carlyle writes with affectionate compassion. But toward anyone who does not *want* to work (as he had been informed was the case in Jamaica), he writes with the savage contempt of the hard-working northerner. Once more the test remains for Carlyle the presence or absence of energy.

The effect of vitalism on Carlyle's prose style will also be evident. At the time he began to write, the essayists of the 18th century, Samuel Johnson in particular, were the models of good prose. Carlyle recognized that their style, however admirable an instrument for reasoning, analysis, and generalized exposition, did not suit his purposes. Like a poet, he wanted to convey the sense of experience itself. Like a preacher or prophet, he wanted to exhort or inspire his readers rather than to develop a chain of logical argument. Like a psychoanalyst, he wanted to explore the unconscious and irrational levels of human life, the hidden nine tenths of the iceberg rather than the conscious and rational fraction above the surface. To this end he developed his highly individual manner of writing, with its vivid imagery of fire and barnyard and zoo, its mixture of Biblical rhythms and explosive talk, and its inverted and unorthodox syntax. Classicists may complain, as Landor did, that the result is not English. Carlyle would reply that it is not 18th-century English, but that his style was appropriate for a Victorian who reports of revolutions in society and in thought. In reply to a friend who had protested about his stylistic experiments Carlyle exclaimed: "Do you reckon this really a time for Purism of Style? I do not: with whole ragged battalions of Scott's Novel Scotch, with Irish, German, French, and even Newspaper Cockney * * * storming in on us, and the whole structure of our Johnsonian English breaking up from its foundations—revolution *there* as visible as anywhere else!" Carlyle's defense of his style can be tested by his history, *The French Revolution*. One may agree or disagree with the historian's explanations of how the fire started or how it was extinguished. But the fire itself is unquestionably there before us, roaring, palpable, giving off a heat of its own.

In 1847 Emerson made his second visit to Carlyle in England and recorded his impressions of his writings and talk: "In Carlyle, as in Byron, one is more struck with the rhetoric than with the matter. He has manly superiority rather than intellectuality, and so makes good hard hits all the time. There is more character than intellect in every sentence, herein strongly resembling Samuel Johnson." We should misunderstand Emerson if we took this verdict to be unkind. What he says has the virtue of putting Carlyle into the appropriate company of Byron and Dr. Johnson instead of Immanuel Kant and St. Thomas Aquinas. There are readers in the 20th century, of whom D. H. Lawrence was one, who find Carlyle's religious position, even his political position, worthy of imitation. But for most readers he survives rather as a man of letters, the inventor of a distinctive and extremely effective prose medium which can bring to life for us the very texture of events in scenes such as when a king confronts a guillotine, a young agnostic confronts the devil, or a talker such as Coleridge stupefies an audience of admiring disciples.

[Carlyle's Portraits of His Contemporaries][1]

[KING WILLIAM IV AT 69]

The old King came driving to the ground, near where I was standing: he was in regimentals [2] with a most copious plume of feathers, so that while he sat all shrunk together in the open carriage, you saw little else but a lock of feathers, and might have taken our Defender of the Faith for some singular species of *Clocker* [3] coming thither. On dismounting, he showed an innocent respectable old face; straddled out his legs greatly (which seemed weak), rested on his heels, *stiddering* [4] himself, and looked round with much simplicity what they wanted next with him. The Review itself was a wheeling and marching of foot and horse, several thousands; a flaring and a blaring from trumpet and drum, with artillery-vollies, sham-charges, and then a continued explosion of musketry and cannon from the whole posse of them, like a long explosion of Mount Ætna: all very grand.

[From a letter to his mother, July 19, 1835]

[QUEEN VICTORIA AT 18]

Yesterday, going through one of the Parks, I saw the poor little Queen. She was in an open carriage, preceded by three or four swift red-coated troopers; all off for Windsor just as I happened to pass. Another carriage or carriages followed with maids-of-honour, etc.: the whole drove very fast. It seemed to me the poor little Queen was a bit modest, nice sonsy [5] little lassie; blue eyes, light hair, fine white skin; of extremely small stature: she looked timid, anxious, almost frightened; for the people looked at her in perfect silence; one old liveryman alone touched his hat to her: I was heartily sorry for the poor bairn,—tho' perhaps she might have said as Parson Swan did, "*Greet* [6] not for me brethren; for verily, yea verily, I

---

1. Carlyle once said that "human Portraits, faithfully drawn, are of all pictures the welcomest on human walls." With his pen, rather than with brush, he himself has created a strikingly colorful gallery of his contemporaries.

A few of the following selections (all of them excerpted by the present editor) were written for publication, in particular the elaborate portrait of Coleridge; the majority of them, however, are from his letters. They are thus sketches rather than portraits—sometimes, in fact, caricatures. As Charles Sanders, a biographer, has shown, Carlyle has earned the title of the Victorian Rembrandt. But with his sharp eye for absurdities he is often the Victorian Daumier or Rowlandson. This element of caricature can be partly explained in terms of difference of age. It will be noted that most of the celebrities described were men older than Carlyle, and he had the customary determination of youth to make fun of the pretensions of an older and established generation. In Carlyle's case there was the additional urge to be irreverent in that he was a provincial in a great metropolis with the provincial's need to assert his independence of judgment.

The portraits are not presented chronologically. The first two are sketches of royalty; the others are of English writers. Titles for each portrait have been assigned by the editor.

2. I.e., in military uniform.
3. Clucking hen (Scottish).
4. Steadying (Scottish).
5. Sweet (Scottish).
6. Weep.

greet not for mysel'." It is a strange thing to look at the fashion of this world!

[From a letter to his mother, April 12, 1838]

[CHARLES LAMB AT 56]

Charles Lamb I sincerely believe to be in some considerable degree *insane*. A more pitiful, ricketty, gasping, staggering, stammering Tom fool I do not know. He is witty by denying truisms, and abjuring good manners. His speech wriggles hither and thither with an incessant painful fluctuation; not an opinion in it or a fact or even a phrase that you can thank him for: more like a convulsion fit than natural systole and diastole.—Besides he is now a confirmed shameless drunkard: *asks* vehemently for gin-and-water in strangers' houses; tipples until he is utterly mad, and is only not thrown out of doors because he is too much despised for taking such trouble with him. Poor Lamb! Poor England where such a despicable abortion is named genius!—He said: There are just two things I regret in English History; first that Guy Faux's plot did not take effect (there would have been so glorious an *explosion*); second that the Royalists did not hang Milton (then we might have laughed at them); etc., etc.

[From *Notebooks*, November 2, 1831]

[SAMUEL TAYLOR COLERIDGE AT 53] [7]

Coleridge sat on the brow of Highgate Hill, in those years, looking down on London and its smoke-tumult, like a sage escaped from the inanity of life's battle; attracting towards him the thoughts of innumerable brave souls still engaged there. His express contributions to poetry, philosophy, or any specific province of human literature or enlightenment, had been small and sadly intermittent; but he had, especially among young inquiring men, a higher than literary, a kind of prophetic or magician character. He was thought to hold, he alone in England, the key of German and other Transcendentalisms; knew the sublime secret of believing by "the reason" what "the understanding" had been obliged to fling out as incredible; and could still, after Hume and Voltaire had done their best and worst with him, profess himself an orthodox Christian, and say and print to the Church of England, with its singular old rubrics and surplices at Allhallowtide,[8] *Esto perpetua*. A sublime man; who, alone in those dark days, had saved his crown of spiritual

7. In 1816 Coleridge moved to a London suburb as a permanent guest in the home of James Gillman. Here he received visits from admirers of his philosophy such as Carlyle's friend, John Sterling, from whose biography, by Carlyle, this selection has been taken. Carlyle's visits were made during his first residence in London in 1824–25.

8. November 1, a festival in honor of all the saints, celebrated by the Roman Catholic and Angelican Churches. The Latin means, "Be thou everlasting"— the last words of Paolo Sarpi (1552–1623), theologian and historian, addressed to the city of Venice.

manhood; escaping from the black materialisms, and revolutionary deluges, with "God, Freedom, Immortality" still his: a king of men. The practical intellects of the world did not much heed him, or carelessly reckoned him a metaphysical dreamer: but to the rising spirits of the young generation he had this dusky sublime character; and sat there as a kind of *Magus*,[9] girt in mystery and enigma; his Dodona [1] oak-grove (Mr. Gillman's house at Highgate) whispering strange things, uncertain whether oracles or jargon.

The Gillmans did not encourage much company, or excitation of any sort, round their sage; nevertheless access to him, if a youth did reverently wish it, was not difficult. He would stroll about the pleasant garden with you, sit in the pleasant rooms of the place,—perhaps take you to his own peculiar room, high up, with a rearward view, which was the chief view of all. A really charming outlook, in fine weather. Close at hand, wide sweep of flowery leafy gardens, their few houses mostly hidden, the very chimney-pots veiled under blossomy umbrage, flowed gloriously down hill, gloriously issuing in wide-tufted undulating plain-country, rich in all charms of field and town. Waving blooming country of the brightest green; dotted all over with handsome villas, handsome groves; crossed by roads and human traffic, here inaudible or heard only as a musical hum: and behind all swam, under olive-tinted haze, the illimitable limitary ocean of London, with its domes and steeples definite in the sun, big Paul's and the many memories attached to it hanging high over all. Nowhere, of its kind, could you see a grander prospect on a bright summer day, with the set of the air going southward,—southward, and so draping with the city-smoke not *you* but the city. Here for hours would Coleridge talk, concerning all conceivable or inconceivable things; and liked nothing better than to have an intelligent, or failing that, even a silent and patient human listener. He distinguished himself to all that ever heard him as at least the most surprising talker extant in this world,—and to some small minority, by no means to all, as the most excellent.

The good man, he was now getting old, towards sixty perhaps; and gave you the idea of a life that had been full of sufferings; a life heavy-laden, half-vanquished, still swimming painfully in seas of manifold physical and other bewilderment. Brow and head were round, and of massive weight, but the face was flabby and irresolute. The deep eyes, of a light hazel, were as full of sorrow as of inspiration; confused pain looked mildly from them, as in a kind of mild astonishment. The whole figure and air, good and amiable otherwise, might be called flabby and irresolute; expressive of weakness

9. An oriental magician or sorcerer.
1. An oracle in Greece. Prophecies were voiced by priests who interpreted the rustling sounds made by oak leaves stirred by the wind.

under possibility of strength. He hung loosely on his limbs, with knees bent, and stooping attitude; in walking, he rather shuffled than decisively stept; and a lady once remarked, he never could fix which side of the garden walk would suit him best, but continually shifted, in corkscrew fashion, and kept trying both. A heavy-laden, high-aspiring and surely much-suffering man. His voice, naturally soft and good, had contracted itself into a plaintive snuffle and singsong; he spoke as if preaching,—you would have said, preaching earnestly and also hopelessly the weightiest things. I still recollect his "object" and "subject," terms of continual recurrence in the Kantean province; and how he sang and snuffled them into "om-m-mject" and "sum-m-mject," with a kind of solemn shake or quaver, as he rolled along. No talk, in his century or in any other, could be more surprising. * * *

Nothing could be more copious than his talk; and furthermore it was always, virtually or literally, of the nature of a monologue; suffering no interruption, however reverent; hastily putting aside all foreign additions, annotations, or most ingenuous desires for elucidation, as well-meant superfluities which would never do. Besides, it was talk not flowing anywhither like a river, but spreading everywhither in inextricable currents and regurgitations like a lake or sea; terribly deficient in definite goal or aim, nay often in logical intelligibility; *what* you were to believe or do, on any earthly or heavenly thing, obstinately refusing to appear from it. So that, most times, you felt logically lost; swamped near to drowning in this tide of ingenious vocables, spreading out boundless as if to submerge the world.

To sit as a passive bucket and be pumped into, whether you consent or not, can in the long-run be exhilarating to no creature; how eloquent soever the flood of utterance that is descending. But if it be withal a confused unintelligible flood of utterance, threatening to submerge all known landmarks of thought, and drown the world and you!—I have heard Coleridge talk, with eager musical energy, two stricken hours, his face radiant and moist, and communicate no meaning whatsoever to any individual of his hearers,—certain of whom, I for one, still kept eagerly listening in hope; the most had long before given up, and formed (if the room were large enough) secondary humming groups of their own. He began anywhere: you put some question to him, made some suggestive observation: instead of answering this, or decidedly setting out towards answer of it, he would accumulate formidable apparatus, logical swim-bladders, transcendental life-preservers and other precautionary and vehiculatory gear, for setting out; perhaps did at last get under way, —but was swiftly solicited, turned aside by the glance of some radiant new game on this hand or that, into new courses; and ever into new; and before long into all the Universe, where it was uncertain what game you would catch, or whether any.

His talk, alas, was distinguished, like himself, by irresolution: it disliked to be troubled with conditions, abstinences, definite fulfilments;—loved to wander at its own sweet will, and make its auditor and his claims and humble wishes a mere passive bucket for itself! He had knowledge about many things and topics, much curious reading; but generally all topics led him, after a pass or two, into the high seas of theosophic philosophy, the hazy infinitude of Kantean transcendentalism, with its "sum-m-mjects" and "om-m-mjects." Sad enough; for with such indolent impatience of the claims and ignorances of others, he had not the least talent for explaining this or anything unknown to them; and you swam and fluttered in the mistiest wide unintelligible deluge of things, for most part in a rather profitless uncomfortable manner.

Glorious islets, too, I have seen rise out of the haze; but they were few, and soon swallowed in the general element again. Balmy sunny islets, islets of the blest and the intelligible:—on which occasions those secondary humming groups would all cease humming, and hang breathless upon the eloquent words; till once your islet got wrapt in the mist again, and they could recommence humming. * * * Coleridge was not without what talkers call wit, and there were touches of prickly sarcasm in him, contemptuous enough of the world and its idols and popular dignitaries; he had traits even of poetic humour: but in general he seemed deficient in laughter; or indeed in sympathy for concrete human things either on the sunny or on the stormy side. One right peal of concrete laughter at some convicted flesh-and-blood absurdity, one burst of noble indignation at some injustice or depravity, rubbing elbows with us on this solid Earth, how strange would it have been in that Kantean haze-world, and how infinitely cheering amid its vacant air-castles and dim-melting ghosts and shadows! None such ever came. His life had been an abstract thinking and dreaming, idealistic, passed amid the ghosts of defunct bodies and of unborn ones. The moaning singsong of that theosophico-metaphysical monotony left on you, at last, a very dreary feeling. * * *

But indeed, to the young ardent mind, instinct with pious nobleness, yet driven to the grim deserts of Radicalism for a faith, his speculations had a charm much more than literary, a charm almost religious and prophetic. The constant gist of his discourse was lamentation over the sunk condition of the world; which he recognised to be given-up to Atheism and Materialism, full of mere sordid misbeliefs, mispursuits and misresults. All Science had become mechanical; the science not of men, but of a kind of human beavers. Churches themselves had died away into a godless mechanical condition; and stood there as mere Cases of Articles, mere Forms of Churches; like the dried carcasses of once-swift camels, which you find left withering in the thirst of the universal desert, —ghastly portents for the present, beneficent ships of the desert no more. Men's souls were blinded, hebetated,[2] and sunk under the influence of Atheism and Materialism, and Hume and Voltaire: the world for the present was as an extinct world, deserted of God, and incapable of welldoing till it changed its heart and spirit. This, expressed I think with less of indignation and with more of long-drawn querulousness, was always recognisable as the ground-tone: —in which truly a pious young heart, driven into Radicalism and the opposition party, could not but recognise a too sorrowful truth; and ask of the Oracle, with all earnestness, What remedy, then?

The remedy, though Coleridge himself professed to see it as in sunbeams, could not, except by processes unspeakably difficult, be described to you at all. On the whole, those dead Churches, this dead English Church especially, must be brought to life again. Why not? It was not dead; the soul of it, in this parched-up body, was tragically asleep only. Atheistic Philosophy was true on its side, and Hume and Voltaire could on their own ground speak irrefrag-ably for themselves against any Church: but lift the Church and them into a higher sphere of argument, *they* died into inanition, the Church revivified itself into pristine florid vigour,—became once more a living ship of the desert, and invincibly bore you over stock and stone. But how, but how! By attending to the "reason" of man, said Coleridge, and duly chaining-up the "understanding" of man: the *Vernunft* (Reason) and *Verstand* (Understanding) of the Ger-mans, it all turned upon these, if you could well understand them, —which you couldn't. For the rest, Mr. Coleridge had on the anvil various Books, especially was about to write one grand Book *On the Logos*, which would help to bridge the chasm for us. So much appeared, however: Churches, though proved false (as you had im-agined), were still true (as you were to imagine): here was an Artist who could burn you up an old Church, root and branch; and then as the Alchymists professed to do with organic substances in gen-eral, distil you an "Astral Spirit" from the ashes, which was the very image of the old burnt article, its airdrawn counterpart,— this you still had, or might get, and draw uses from, if you could. Wait till the Book on the Logos were done;—alas, till your own terrene eyes, blind with conceit and the dust of logic, were purged, subtilised and spiritualised into the sharpness of vision requisite for discerning such an "om-m-mject."—The ingenuous young Eng-lish head, of those days, stood strangely puzzled by such revelations; uncertain whether it were getting inspired, or getting infatuated

2. Dulled.

into flat imbecility; and strange effulgence, of new day or else of deeper meteoric night, coloured the horizon of the future for it.

[From *Life of John Sterling*, 1851]

[WILLIAM WORDSWORTH IN HIS SEVENTIES]

On a summer morning (let us call it 1840 then) I was apprised by Taylor[3] that Wordsworth had come to town, and would meet a small party of us at a certain tavern in St. James's Street, at breakfast, to which I was invited for the given day and hour. We had a pretty little room, quiet though looking street-ward (tavern's name is quite lost to me); the morning sun was pleasantly tinting the opposite houses, a balmy, calm and sunlight morning. Wordsworth, I think, arrived just along with me; we had still five minutes of sauntering and miscellaneous talking before the whole were assembled. I do not positively remember any of them, except that James Spedding[1] was there, and that the others, not above five or six in whole, were polite intelligent quiet persons, and, except Taylor and Wordsworth, not of any special distinction in the world. Breakfast was pleasant, fairly beyond the common of such things. Wordsworth seemed in good tone, and, much to Taylor's satisfaction, talked a great deal; about "poetic" correspondents of his own (i.e. correspondents for the sake of his poetry; especially one such who had sent him, from Canton, an excellent chest of tea; correspondent grinningly applauded by us all); then about ruralities and miscellanies. * * * These were the first topics. Then finally about literature, literary laws, practices, observances, at considerable length, and turning wholly on the mechanical part, including even a good deal of shallow enough etymology, from me and others, which was well received. On all this Wordsworth enlarged with evident satisfaction, and was joyfully reverent of the "wells of English undefiled";[2] though stone dumb as to the deeper rules and wells of Eternal Truth and Harmony, which you were to try and set forth by said undefiled wells of English or what other speech you had! To me a little disappointing, but not much; though it would have given me pleasure had the robust veteran man emerged a little out of vocables into things, now and then, as he never once chanced to do. For the rest, he talked well in his way; with veracity, easy brevity and force, as a wise tradesman would of his tools and workshop,—and as no unwise one could. His voice was good, frank and sonorous, though practically clear distinct and forcible rather than melodious; the tone of him businesslike, sedately confident; no discourtesy, yet no anxiety about being courteous. A fine whole-

3. Henry Taylor, contemporary play-wright.
1. Editor of the works of Francis Ba-con.
2. Spenser, *Faerie Queene* IV.ii.32—referring to Chaucer.

some rusticity, fresh as his mountain breezes, sat well on the stalwart veteran, and on all he said and did. You would have said he was a usually taciturn man; glad to unlock himself to audience sympathetic and intelligent, when such offered itself. His face bore marks of much, not always peaceful, meditation; the look of it not bland or benevolent so much as close impregnable and hard: a man *multa tacere loquive paratus*,[3] in a world where he had experienced no lack of contradictions as he strode along! The eyes were not very brilliant, but they had a quiet clearness; there was enough of brow and well shaped; rather too much of cheek ("horse face" I have heard satirists say); face of squarish shape and decidedly longish, as I think the head itself was (its "length" going horizontal); he was large-boned, lean, but still firm-knit tall and strong-looking when he stood, a right good old steel-grey figure, with rustic simplicity and dignity about him, and a vivacious strength looking through him which might have suited one of those old steel-grey markgrafs[4] whom Henry the Fowler set up to ward the "marches" and do battle with the intrusive heathen in a stalwart and judicious manner.

On this and other occasional visits of his, I saw Wordsworth a number of times, at dinner, in evening parties; and we grew a little more familiar, but without much increase of real intimacy or affection springing up between us. He was willing to talk with me in a corner, in noisy extensive circles, having weak eyes, and little loving the general babble current in such places. One evening, probably about this time, I got him upon the subject of great poets, who I thought might be admirable equally to us both; but was rather mistaken, as I gradually found. Pope's partial failure I was prepared for; less for the narrowish limits visible in Milton and others. I tried him with Burns, of whom he had sung tender recognition; but Burns also turned out to be a limited inferior creature, any genius he had a theme for one's pathos rather; even Shakespeare himself had his blind sides, his limitations; gradually it became apparent to me that of transcendent unlimited there was, to this critic, probably but one specimen known, Wordsworth himself! He by no means said so, or hinted so, in words; but on the whole it was all I gathered from him in this considerable *tête-à-tête* of ours; and it was not an agreeable conquest. New notion as to poetry or poet I had not in the smallest degree got; but my insight into the depths of Wordsworth's pride in himself had considerably augmented; and it did not increase my love of him; though I did not in the least hate it either, so quiet was it, so fixed, unappealing, like a dim old lichened crag on the wayside, the private meaning of which, in con-

3. "Prepared to speak out or to pass over much in silence."
4. Governors appointed by Henry I of Germany, "the Fowler" (876–936), to guard the borders ("marches") of his kingdom.

trast with any public meaning it had, you recognised with a kind of not wholly melancholy grin. * * *

During the last seven or ten years of his life, Wordsworth felt himself to be a recognised lion, in certain considerable London circles, and was in the habit of coming up to town with his wife for a month or two every season, to enjoy his quiet triumph and collect his bits of tribute *tales quales*.[5] * * * Wordsworth took his bit of lionism very quietly, with a smile sardonic rather than triumphant, and certainly got no harm by it, if he got or expected little good. His wife, a small, withered, puckered, winking lady, who never spoke, seemed to be more in earnest about the affair, and was visibly and sometimes ridiculously assiduous to secure her proper place of precedence at table. * * * The light was always afflictive to his eyes; he carried in his pocket something like a skeleton brass candlestick, in which, setting it on the dinner-table, between him and the most afflictive or nearest of the chief lights, he touched a little spring, and there flirted out, at the top of his brass implement, a small vertical green circle which prettily enough threw his eyes into shade, and screened him from that sorrow. In proof of his equanimity as lion I remember, in connection with this green shade, one little glimpse. * * * Dinner was large, luminous, sumptuous; I sat a long way from Wordsworth; dessert I think had come in, and certainly there reigned in all quarters a cackle as of Babel (only politer perhaps), which far up in Wordsworth's quarter (who was leftward on my side of the table) seemed to have taken a sententious, rather louder, logical and quasi-scientific turn, heartily unimportant to gods and men, so far as I could judge of it and of the other babble reigning. I looked upwards, leftwards, the coast being luckily for a moment clear; there, far off, beautifully screened in the shadow of his vertical green circle, which was on the farther side of him, sate Wordsworth, silent, slowly but steadily gnawing some portion of what I judged to be raisins, with his eye and attention placidly fixed on these and these alone. The sight of whom, and of his rock-like indifference to the babble, quasi-scientific and other, with attention turned on the small practical alone, was comfortable and amusing to me, who felt like him but could not eat raisins. This little glimpse I could still paint, so clear and bright is it, and this shall be symbolical of all.

In a few years, I forget in how many and when, these Wordsworth appearances in London ceased; we heard, not of ill-health perhaps, but of increasing love of rest; at length of the long sleep's coming; and never saw Wordsworth more. One felt his death as the extinction of a public light, but not otherwise.

[From *Reminiscences*, 1867, 1881]

5. Of such a sort.

[ALFRED TENNYSON AT 34]

Alfred is one of the few British or Foreign Figures (a not increasing number I think!) who are and remain beautiful to me;—a true human soul, or some authentic approximation thereto, to whom your own soul can say, Brother!—However, I doubt he will not come; he often skips me, in these brief visits to Town; skips everybody indeed; being a man solitary and sad, as certain men are, dwelling in an element of gloom,—carrying a bit of Chaos about him, in short, which he is manufacturing into Cosmos!

Alfred is the son of a Lincolnshire Gentleman Farmer, I think; indeed, you see in his verses that he is a native of "moated granges," and green, fat pastures, not of mountains and their torrents and storms. He had his breeding at Cambridge, as if for the Law or Church; being master of a small annuity on his Father's decease, he preferred clubbing with his Mother and some Sisters, to live unpromoted and write Poems. In this way he lives still, now here, now there; the family always within reach of London, never in it; he himself making rare and brief visits, lodging in some old comrade's rooms. I think he must be under forty, not much under it. One of the finest-looking men in the world. A great shock of rough dusty-dark hair; bright-laughing hazel eyes; massive aquiline face, most massive yet most delicate; of sallow-brown complexion, almost Indian-looking; clothes cynically loose, free-and-easy;—smokes infinite tobacco. His voice is musical metallic,—fit for loud laughter and piercing wail, and all that may lie between; speech and speculation free and plenteous: I do not meet, in these late decades, such company over a pipe!—We shall see what he will grow to. He is often unwell; very chaotic,—his way is through Chaos and the Bottomless and Pathless; not handy for making out many miles upon.

[From a letter to Emerson, August 5, 1844]

[WILLIAM MAKEPEACE THACKERAY AT 42]

Thackeray has very rarely come athwart me since his return: he is a big fellow, soul and body; of many gifts and qualities (particularly in the Hogarth[6] line, with a dash of Sterne[7] superadded), of enormous *appetite* withal, and very uncertain and chaotic in all points except his *outer breeding*, which is fixed enough, and *perfect* according to the modern English style. I rather dread explosions in his history. A *big*, fierce, weeping, hungry man; not a strong one.

[From a letter to Emerson, September 9, 1853]

---

6. William Hogarth (1697–1764), a realistic and satirical painter of English life.

7. Laurence Sterne (1713–68), whose novels are often sentimental.

From Characteristics[1]

The healthy know not of their health, but only the sick: this is the Physician's Aphorism; and applicable in a far wider sense than he gives it. We may say, it holds no less in moral, intellectual, political, poetical, than in merely corporeal therapeutics; that wherever, or in what shape soever, powers of the sort which can be named *vital* are at work, herein lies the test of their working right or working wrong.

In the Body, for example, as all doctors are agreed, the first condition of complete health is, that each organ perform its function unconsciously, unheeded; let but any organ announce its separate existence, were it even boastfully, and for pleasure, not for pain, then already has one of those unfortunate "false centres of sensibility" established itself, already is derangement there. The perfection of bodily well-being is, that the collective bodily activities seem one; and be manifested, moreover, not in themselves, but in the action they accomplish. * * *

However, without venturing into the abstruse, or too eagerly asking Why and How, in things where our answer must needs prove, in great part, an echo of the question, let us be content to remark farther, in the merely historical way, how that Aphorism of the bodily Physician holds good in quite other departments. Of the Soul, with her activities, we shall find it no less true than of the Body: nay, cry the Spiritualists, is not that very division of the unity, Man, into a dualism of Soul and Body, itself the symptom of disease; as, perhaps, your frightful theory of Materialism, of his being but a Body, and therefore, at least, once more a unity, may be the paroxysm which was critical, and the beginning of cure! But omitting this, we observe, with confidence enough, that the truly strong mind, view it as Intellect, as Morality, or under any other aspect, is nowise the mind acquainted with its strength; that here

1. First published in the *Edinburgh Review*, ostensibly as a review of two books of philosophy which had appeared in 1830 and 1831: *An Essay on the Origin and Prospects of Man* by Thomas Hope, and *Philosophical Lectures* by Friedrich von Schlegel. Hope was a Utilitarian writer, and his analytical treatise may have inspired the first half of the essay, in which Carlyle exposes what seems to him the most characteristic symptom of modern man's diseased state of mind and spirit: self-consciousness. Schlegel's book, an example of the German transcendental philosophy which Carlyle admired, may have inspired the second half of his essay, in which he points out the encouraging prospects for the future if mankind can find a new religious faith. Yet it is only near the end of *Characteristics* that Carlyle finally refers directly to these two books as such, for his real object, as his title suggests, is not to write a mere book review but to describe the state of mind and society characteristic of the age. This early essay, even in the necessarily abridged form adopted here, contains in embryo all the basic religious and political ideas that Carlyle was to develop in his later writings.

as before the sign of health is Unconsciousness. In our inward, as
in our outward world, what is mechanical lies open to us; not what
is dynamical and has vitality. Of our Thinking, we might say, it is
but the mere upper surface that we shape into articulate Thoughts;
—underneath the region of argument and conscious discourse, lies
the region of meditation; here, in its quiet mysterious depths, dwells
what vital force is in us; here, if aught is to be created, and not
merely manufactured and communicated, must the work go on.
Manufacture is intelligible, but trivial; Creation is great, and cannot be understood. Thus if the Debater and Demonstrator, whom
we may rank as the lowest of true thinkers, knows what he has done,
and how he did it, the Artist, whom we rank as the highest, knows
not; must speak of Inspiration, and in one or the other dialect, call
his work the gift of a divinity.

But on the whole "genius is ever a secret to itself";[2] of this old
truth we have, on all sides, daily evidence. The Shakespeare takes
no airs for writing *Hamlet* and the *Tempest*, understands not that
it is anything surprising: Milton, again, is more conscious of his
faculty, which accordingly is an inferior one. On the other hand,
what cackling and strutting must we not often hear and see, when,
in some shape of academical prolusion, maiden speech, review article, this or the other well-fledged goose has produced its goose-egg,
of quite measurable value, were it the pink of its whole kind; and
wonders why all mortals do not wonder!

Foolish enough, too, was the College Tutor's surprise at Walter
Shandy:[3] how, though unread in Aristotle, he could nevertheless
argue; and not knowing the name of any dialectic tool, handled
them all to perfection. Is it the skilfulest anatomist that cuts the
best figure[4] at Sadler's Wells? or does the boxer hit better for
knowing that he has a *flexor longus* and a *flexor brevis?*[5] But indeed, as in the higher case of the Poet, so here in that of the
Speaker and Inquirer, the true force is an unconscious one. The
healthy Understanding, we should say, is not the Logical, argumentative, but the Intuitive; for the end of Understanding is not
to prove and find reasons, but to know and believe. Of logic, and
its limits, and uses and abuses, there were much to be said and examined; one fact, however, which chiefly concerns us here, has long
been familiar: that the man of logic and the man of insight; the
Reasoner and the Discoverer, or even Knower, are quite separable,
—indeed, for most part, quite separate characters. In practical matters, for example, has it not become almost proverbial that the man
of logic cannot prosper? This is he whom business-people call Sys-

---

2. From an essay by the German poet
J. C. F. von Schiller (1759–1805).
3. Laurence Sterne, *Tristram Shandy*
I.xix.

4. Makes the most striking appearance.
"Sadler's Wells" refers to a London
theater.
5. Technical terms for bodily muscles.

tematic and Theoriser and Word-monger; his *vital* intellectual force lies dormant or extinct, his whole force is mechanical, conscious: of such a one it is foreseen that, when once confronted with the infinite complexities of the real world, his little compact theorem of the world will be found wanting; that unless he can throw it overboard and become a new creature, he will necessarily founder. * * * Never since the beginning of Time was there, that we hear or read of, so intensely self-conscious a Society. Our whole relations to the Universe and to our fellow-man have become an Inquiry, a Doubt; nothing will go on of its own accord, and do its function quietly; but all things must be probed into, the whole working of man's world be anatomically studied. Alas, anatomically studied, that it may be medically aided! Till at length indeed, we have come to such a pass, that except in this same *medicine,* with its artifices and appliances, few can so much as imagine any strength or hope to remain for us. The whole Life of Society must now be carried on by drugs: doctor after doctor appears with his nostrum, of Co-operative Societies, Universal Suffrage, Cottage-and-Cow systems, Repression of Population, Vote by Ballot. To such height has the dyspepsia of Society reached; as indeed the constant grinding internal pain, or from time to time the mad spasmodic throes, of all Society do otherwise too mournfully indicate.

Far be it from us to attribute, as some unwise persons do, the disease itself to this unhappy sensation that there is a disease! The Encyclopedists[6] did not produce the troubles of France; but the troubles of France produced the Encyclopedists, and much else. The Self-consciousness is the symptom merely; nay, it is also the attempt towards cure. We record the fact, without special censure; not wondering that Society should feel itself, and in all ways complain of aches and twinges, for it has suffered enough. * * *

But leaving this, let us rather look within, into the Spiritual condition of Society, and see what aspects and prospects offer themselves there. * * * To begin with our highest Spiritual function, with Religion, we might ask, Whither has Religion now fled? Of Churches and their establishments we here say nothing; nor of the unhappy domains of Unbelief, and how innumerable men, blinded in their minds, have grown to "live without God in the world";[7] but, taking the fairest side of the matter, we ask, What is the nature of that same Religion, which still lingers in the hearts of the few who are called, and call themselves, specially the Religious? Is it a healthy religion, vital, unconscious of itself; that shines forth spontaneously in doing of the Work, or even in preaching of the Word? Unhappily, no. Instead of heroic martyr Conduct, and in-

---

6. Diderot, Voltaire, and other critics of the established order in France who were contributors to the *Encyclopédie*

(1751–52, 1776–80).
7. Cf. Ephesians ii.12.

spired and soul-inspiring Eloquence, whereby Religion itself were brought home to our living bosoms, to live and reign there, we have "Discourses on the Evidences,"[8] endeavouring, with smallest result, to make it probable that such a thing as Religion exists. The most enthusiastic Evangelicals do not preach a Gospel, but keep describing how it should and might be preached: to awaken the sacred fire of faith, as by a sacred contagion, is not their endeavour; but, at most, to describe how Faith shows and acts, and scientifically distinguish true Faith from false. Religion, like all else, is conscious of itself, listens to itself; it becomes less and less creative, vital; more and more mechanical. Considered as a whole, the Christian Religion of late ages has been continually dissipating itself into Metaphysics; and threatens now to disappear, as some rivers do, in deserts of barren sand.

Of Literature, and its deep-seated, wide-spread maladies, why speak? Literature is but a branch of Religion, and always participates in its character: however, in our time, it is the only branch that still shows any greenness; and, as some think, must one day become the main stem. * * * Nay, is not the diseased self-conscious state of Literature disclosed in this one fact, which lies so near us here, the prevalence of Reviewing! Sterne's wish for a reader "that would give-up the reins of his imagination into his author's hands, and be pleased he knew not why, and cared not wherefore,"[9] might lead him a long journey now. Indeed, for our best class of readers, the chief pleasure, a very stinted one, is this same knowing of the Why; which many a Kames and Bossu[1] has been, ineffectually enough, endeavouring to teach us: till at last these also have laid down their trade; and now your Reviewer is a mere *taster*; who tastes, and says, by the evidence of such palate, such tongue, as he has got, It is good, It is bad. Was it thus that the French carried out certain inferior creatures on their Algerine Expedition, to taste the wells for them, and try whether they were poisoned? Far be it from us to disparage our own craft, whereby we have our living! Only we must note these things: that Reviewing spreads with strange vigour; that such a man as Byron reckons the Reviewer and the Poet equal; that at the last Leipzig Fair, there was advertised a Review of Reviews. By and by it will be found that all Literature has become one boundless self-devouring Review; and, as in London routs,[2] we have to *do* nothing, but only to *see* others do nothing.—Thus does Literature also, like a sick thing, superabundantly "listen to itself."

No less is this unhealthy symptom manifest, if we cast a glance

8. *Evidences of Christianity* (1794) by William Paley, a Utilitarian theologian.
9. Sterne's *Tristram Shandy* (III.xii).
1. Henry Home, Lord Kames (1696–

1782), author of *Elements of Criticism;* René le Bossu (1631–89), French literary critic.
2. Fashionable **gatherings.**

on our Philosophy, on the character of our speculative Thinking.
Nay already, as above hinted, the mere existence and necessity of a
Philosophy is an evil. Man is sent hither not to question, but to
work: "the end of man," it was long ago written, "is an Action,
not a Thought."[3] In the perfect state, all Thought were but the
picture and inspiring symbol of Action; Philosophy, except as Poetry
and Religion, would have no being. And yet how, in this imperfect
state, can it be avoided, can it be dispensed with? Man stands as
in the centre of Nature; his fraction of Time encircled by Eternity,
his handbreadth of Space encircled by Infinitude: how shall he forbear asking himself, What am I; and Whence; and Whither? How
too, except in slight partial hints, in kind asseverations and assurances, such as a mother quiets her fretfully inquisitive child with,
shall he get answer to such inquiries?

The disease of Metaphysics, accordingly, is a perennial one. In
all ages, those questions of Death and Immortality, Origin of Evil,
Freedom and Necessity, must, under new forms, anew make their
appearance; ever, from time to time, must the attempt to shape
for ourselves some Theorem of the Universe be repeated. And ever
unsuccessfully: for what Theorem of the Infinite can the Finite
render complete? We, the whole species of Mankind, and our whole
existence and history, are but a floating speck in the illimitable
ocean of the All; yet *in* that ocean; indissoluble portion thereof;
partaking of its infinite tendencies: borne this way and that by its
deep-swelling tides, and grand ocean currents;—of which what
faintest chance is there that we should ever exhaust the significance,
ascertain the goings and comings? A region of Doubt, therefore,
hovers forever in the background; in Action alone can we have certainty. Nay properly Doubt is the indispensable inexhaustible material whereon Action works, which Action has to fashion into Certainty and Reality; only on a canvas of Darkness, such is man's way
of being, could the many-coloured picture of our Life paint itself
and shine. * * *

Now this is specially the misery which has fallen on man in our
Era. Belief, Faith has well-nigh vanished from the world. The
youth on awakening in this wondrous Universe no longer finds a
competent theory of its wonders. Time was, when if he asked himself, What is man, What are the duties of man? the answer stood
ready written for him. But now the ancient "ground-plan of the
All" belies itself when brought into contact with reality; Mother
Church has, to the most, become a superannuated Step-mother,
whose lessons go disregarded; or are spurned at, and scornfully gainsaid. For young Valour and thirst of Action no ideal Chivalry invites to heroism, prescribes what is heroic: the old ideal of Man-

---

3. Aristotle, *Ethics* I.iii.

hood has grown obsolete, and the new is still invisible to us, and we grope after it in darkness, one clutching this phantom, another that; Werterism,[4] Byronism, even Brummelism, each has its day. For Contemplation and love of Wisdom, no Cloister now opens its religious shades; the Thinker must, in all senses, wander homeless, too often aimless, looking up to a Heaven which is dead for him, round to an Earth which is deaf. Action, in those old days, was easy, was voluntary, for the divine worth of human things lay acknowledged; Speculation was wholesome, for it ranged itself as the handmaid of Action; what could not so range itself died out by its natural death, by neglect. Loyalty still hallowed obedience, and made rule noble; there was still something to be loyal to: the Godlike stood embodied under many a symbol in men's interests and business; the Finite shadowed forth the Infinite; Eternity looked through Time. The Life of man was encompassed and overcanopied by a glory of Heaven, even as his dwelling-place by the azure vault.

How changed in these new days! Truly may it be said, the Divinity has withdrawn from the Earth; or veils himself in that widewasting Whirlwind of a departing Era, wherein the fewest can discern his goings. Not Godhead, but an iron, ignoble circle of Necessity embraces all things; binds the youth of these times into a sluggish thrall, or else exasperates him into a rebel. Heroic Action is paralysed; for what worth now remains unquestionable with him? At the fervid period when his whole nature cries aloud for Action, there is nothing sacred under whose banner he can act; the course and kind and conditions of free Action are all but undiscoverable. Doubt storms-in on him through every avenue; inquiries of the deepest, painfulest sort must be engaged with; and the invincible energy of young years waste itself in sceptical, suicidal cavillings; in passionate "questionings of Destiny," whereto no answer will be returned.

For men, in whom the old perennial principle of Hunger (be it Hunger of the poor Day-drudge who stills it with eighteenpence a-day, or of the ambitious Place-hunter who can nowise still it with so little) suffices to fill-up existence, the case is bad; but not the worst. These men have an aim, such as it is; and can steer towards it, with chagrin enough truly; yet, as their hands are kept full, without desperation. Unhappier are they to whom a higher instinct has been given; who struggle to be persons, not machines; to whom the Universe is not a warehouse, or at best a fancy-bazaar, but a mystic temple and hall of doom. For such men there lie properly two courses open. The lower, yet still an estimable class, take up with worn-out Symbols of the Godlike; keep trimming and trucking be-

4. The cultivation of melancholy based on the model of Goethe's novel, *The Sorrows of Young Werther*. "Brummelism": a fad for wearing elegant clothes in the manner of Beau Brummel, a dandy of George IV's time.

tween these and Hypocrisy, purblindly enough, miserably enough. A numerous intermediate class end in Denial; and form a theory that there is no theory; that nothing is certain in the world, except this fact of Pleasure being pleasant; so they try to realise what trifling modicum of Pleasure they can come at, and to live contented therewith, winking hard. Of these we speak not here; but only of the second nobler class, who also have dared to say No and cannot yet say Yea; but feel that in the No they dwell as in a Golgotha, where life enters not, where peace is not appointed them.

Hard, for most part, is the fate of such men; the harder the nobler they are. In dim forecastings, wrestles within them the "Divine Idea of the World" yet will nowhere visibly reveal itself. They have to realise a Worship for themselves, or live unworshipping. The Godlike has vanished from the world; and they, by the strong cry of their soul's agony, like true wonder-workers, must again evoke its presence. This miracle is their appointed task; which they must accomplish, or die wretchedly: this miracle has been accomplished by such; but not in our land; our land yet knows not of it. Behold a Byron, in melodious tones, "cursing his day": he mistakes earthborn passionate Desire for heaven-inspired Freewill; without heavenly load-star, rushes madly into the dance of meteoric lights that hover on the mad Mahlstrom; and goes down among its eddies. Hear a Shelley filling the earth with inarticulate wail; like the infinite, inarticulate grief and weeping of forsaken infants. A noble Friedrich Schlegel,[5] stupefied in that fearful loneliness, as of a silenced battle-field, flies back to Catholicism; as a child might to its slain mother's bosom, and cling there. In lower regions, how many a poor Hazlitt must wander on God's verdant earth, like the Unblest on burning deserts; passionately dig wells, and draw up only the dry quicksand; believe that he is seeking Truth, yet only wrestle among endless Sophisms, doing desperate battle as with spectre-hosts; and die and make no sign!

To the better order of such minds any mad joy of Denial has long since ceased: the problem is not now to deny, but to ascertain and perform. Once in destroying the False, there was a certain inspiration; but now the genius of Destruction has done its work, there is now nothing more to destroy. The doom of the Old has long been pronounced, and irrevocable; the Old has passed away: but, alas, the New appears not in its stead; the Time is still in pangs of travail with the New. Man has walked by the light of conflagrations, and amid the sound of falling cities; and now there is darkness, and long watching till it be morning. The voice even of the faithful can but exclaim: "As yet struggles the twelfth hour of the Night: birds of darkness are on the wing, spectres uproar,

5. German literary critic and leader of the Romantic school (1772–1829). In 1808 he joined the Roman Catholic Church.

the dead walk, the living dream.—Thou, Eternal Providence, wilt cause the day to dawn!"[6]

Such being the condition, temporal and spiritual, of the world at our Epoch, can we wonder that the world "listens to itself," and struggles and writhes, everywhere externally and internally, like a thing in pain? Nay, is not even this unhealthy action of the world's Organisation, if the symptom of universal disease, yet also the symptom and sole means of restoration and cure? The effort of Nature, exerting her medicative force to cast-out foreign impediments, and once more become One, become whole? In Practice, still more in Opinion, which is the precursor and prototype of Practice, there must needs be collision, convulsion; much has to be ground away. Thought must needs be Doubt and Inquiry before it can again be Affirmation and Sacred Precept. Innumerable "Philosophies of Man," contending in boundless hubbub, must annihilate each other, before an inspired Poesy and Faith for Man can fashion itself together. * * *

For ourselves, the loud discord which jars in these two Works,[7] in innumerable works of the like import, and generally in all the Thought and Action of this period, does not any longer utterly confuse us. Unhappy who, in such a time, felt not, at all conjunctures, ineradicably in his heart the knowledge that a God made this Universe, and a Demon not! And shall Evil always prosper, then? Out of all Evil comes Good; and no Good that is possible but shall one day be real. Deep and sad as is our feeling that we stand yet in the bodeful Night; equally deep, indestructible is our assurance that the Morning also will not fail. Nay already, as we look round, streaks of a dayspring are in the east; it is dawning; when the time shall be fulfilled, it will be day. The progress of man towards higher and nobler developments of whatever is highest and noblest in him, lies not only prophesied to Faith, but now written to the eye of Observation, so that he who runs may read.

One great step of progress, for example, we should say, in actual circumstances, was this same; the clear ascertainment that we are in progress. About the grand Course of Providence, and his final Purposes with us, we can know nothing, or almost nothing: man begins in darkness, ends in darkness; mystery is everywhere around us and in us, under our feet, among our hands. Nevertheless so much has become evident to every one, that this wondrous Mankind is advancing somewhither; that at least all human things are, have been and forever will be, in Movement and Change;—as, indeed, for beings that exist in Time, by virtue of Time, and are made

6. "Jean Paul's *Hesperus*" [Carlyle's note]. Jean Paul Richter (1763–1825) was a German humorist.

7. Books by Hope and Schlegel. See the title note.

of Time, might have been long since understood. In some provinces, it is true, as in Experimental Science, this discovery is an old one; but in most others it belongs wholly to these latter days. How often, in former ages, by eternal Creeds, eternal Forms of Government and the like, has it been attempted, fiercely enough, and with destructive violence, to chain the Future under the Past; and say to the Providence, whose ways with man are mysterious, and through the great deep: Hitherto shalt thou come, but no farther! A wholly insane attempt; and for man himself, could it prosper, the frightfulest of all enchantments, a very Life-in-Death. Man's task here below, the destiny of every individual man, is to be in turns Apprentice and Workman; or say rather, Scholar, Teacher, Discoverer: by nature he has a strength for learning, for imitating; but also a strength for acting, for knowing on his own account. Are we not in a world seen to be Infinite; the relations lying closest together modified by those latest discovered and lying farthest asunder? Could you ever spell-bind man into a Scholar merely, so that he had nothing to discover, to correct; could you ever establish a Theory of the Universe that were entire, unimprovable, and which needed only to be got by heart; man then were spiritually defunct, the Species we now name Man had ceased to exist. But the gods, kinder to us than we are to ourselves, have forbidden such suicidal acts. As Phlogiston[8] is displaced by Oxygen, and the Epicycles of Ptolemy by the Ellipses of Kepler,[9] so does Paganism give place to Catholicism, Tyranny to Monarchy, and Feudalism to Representative Government,—where also the process does not stop. Perfection of Practice, like completeness of Opinion, is always approaching, never arrived; Truth, in the words of Schiller, *immer wird, nie ist*; never *is*, always *is a-being*.

Sad, truly, were our condition did we know but this, that Change is universal and inevitable. Launched into a dark shoreless sea of Pyrrhonism, what would remain for us but to sail aimless, hopeless; or make madly merry, while the devouring Death had not yet ingulfed us? As indeed, we have seen many, and still see many do. Nevertheless so stands it not. The venerator of the Past (and to what pure heart is the Past, in that "moonlight of memory," other than sad and holy?) sorrows not over its departure, as one utterly bereaved. The true Past departs not, nothing that was worthy in the Past departs; no Truth or Goodness realised by man ever dies, or can die; but is all still here, and, recognised or not, lives and works through endless changes. If all things, to speak in the German dialect, are discerned by us, and exist for us, in an element of

Time, and therefore of Mortality and Mutability; yet Time itself reposes on Eternity: the truly Great and Transcendental has its basis and substance in Eternity; stands revealed to us as Eternity in a vesture of Time. Thus in all Poetry, Worship, Art, Society, as one form passes into another, nothing is lost: it is but the superficial, as it were the *body* only, that grows obsolete and dies; under the mortal body lies a *soul* which is immortal; which anew incarnates itself in fairer revelation; and the Present is the living sumtotal of the whole Past.

In Change, therefore, there is nothing terrible, nothing supernatural: on the contrary, it lies in the very essence of our lot and life in this world. To-day is not yesterday: we ourselves change; how can our Works and Thoughts, if they are always to be the fittest, continue always the same? Change, indeed, is painful; yet ever needful; and if Memory have its force and worth, so also has Hope. Nay, if we look well to it, what is all Derangement, and necessity of great Change, in itself such an evil, but the product simply of *increased resources* which the old *methods* can no longer administer; of new wealth which the old coffers will no longer contain? What is it, for example, that in our own day bursts asunder the bonds of ancient Political Systems, and perplexes all Europe with the fear of Change, but even this: the increase of social resources, which the old social methods will no longer sufficiently administer? The new omnipotence of the Steam-engine is hewing asunder quite other mountains than the physical. Have not our economical distresses, those barnyard Conflagrations[1] themselves, the frightfulest madness of our mad epoch, their rise also in what is a real increase: increase of Men; of human Force; properly, in such a Planet as ours, the most precious of all increases? It is true again, the ancient methods of administration will no longer suffice. Must the indomitable millions, full of old Saxon energy and fire, lie cooped-up in this Western Nook, choking one another, as in a Blackhole of Calcutta,[2] while a whole fertile untenanted Earth, desolate for want of the ploughshare, cries: Come and till me, come and reap me?[3] If the ancient Captains can no longer yield guidance, new must be sought after: for the difficulty lies not in nature, but in artifice; the European Calcutta-Blackhole has no walls but air ones and paper ones. —So too, Scepticism itself, with its innumerable mischiefs, what is it but the sour fruit of a most blessed increase, that of Knowledge; a fruit too that will not always continue *sour*?

In fact, much as we have said and mourned about the unproduc-

---

1. Rick-burning in the 1820's and 1830's by disgruntled farm laborers in England.

2. A small room in which 146 European men and women were imprisoned by the Indians in 1756. After one night, only 23 remained alive.

3. Carlyle often urged emigration to America as a solution to the over-crowding of Europe. One of his brothers did emigrate, and became a farmer in Ontario, Canada.

tive prevalence of Metaphysics, it was not without some insight into the use that lies in them. Metaphysical Speculation, if a necessary evil, is the forerunner of much good. The fever of Scepticism must needs burn itself out, and burn out thereby the Impurities that caused it; then again will there be clearness, health. The principle of life, which now struggles painfully, in the outer, thin and barren domain of the Conscious or Mechanical, may then withdraw into its inner sanctuaries, its abysses of mystery and miracle; withdraw deeper than ever into that domain of the Unconscious, by nature infinite and inexhaustible; and creatively work there. From that mystic region, and from that alone, all wonders, all Poesies, and Religions, and Social Systems have proceeded: the like wonders, and greater and higher, lie slumbering there; and, brooded on by the spirit of the waters, will evolve themselves, and rise like exhalations from the Deep. * * *

Remarkable it is, truly, how everywhere the eternal fact begins again to be recognised, that there is a Godlike in human affairs; that God not only made us and beholds us, but is in us and around us; that the Age of Miracles, as it ever was, now is. Such recognition we discern on all hands and in all countries: in each country after its own fashion. In France, among the younger nobler minds, strangely enough; where, in their loud contention with the Actual and Conscious, the Ideal or Unconscious is, for the time, without exponent; where Religion means not the parent of Polity, as of all that is highest, but Polity itself; and this and the other earnest man has not been wanting, who could audibly whisper to himself: "Go to, I will make religion." In England still more strangely; as in all things, worthy England will have its way: by the shrieking of hysterical women,[4] casting out of devils, and other "gifts of the Holy Ghost." Well might Jean Paul say, in this his twelfth hour of the Night, "the living dream"; well might he say, "the dead walk."[5] Meanwhile let us rejoice rather that so much has been seen into, were it through never so diffracting media, and never so madly distorted; that in all dialects, though but half-articulately, this high Gospel begins to be preached: Man is still Man. The genius of Mechanism, as was once before predicted, will not always sit like a choking incubus on our soul; but at length, when by a new magic Word the old spell is broken, become our slave, and as familiar-spirit do all our bidding. "We are near awakening when we dream that we dream."[6]

He that has an eye and a heart can even now say: Why should I falter? Light has come into the world; to such as love Light, so

---

4. An allusion to followers of Carlyle's friend, the preacher Edward Irving. Women in Irving's congregation asserted that they had acquired the gift of tongues.

5. See note 6 above, Jean Paul's *Hesperus.*
6. Quoted from a work by the German poet Novalis (1772–1801).

as Light must be loved, with a boundless all-doing, all-enduring love. For the rest, let that vain struggle to read the mystery of the Infinite cease to harass us. It is a mystery which, through all ages, we shall only read here a line of, there another line of. Do we not already know that the name of the Infinite is GOOD, is GOD? Here on Earth we are as Soldiers, fighting in a foreign land; that understand not the plan of the campaign, and have no need to understand it; seeing well what is at our hand to be done. Let us do it like Soldiers; with submission, with courage, with a heroic joy. "Whatsoever thy hand findeth to do, do it with all thy might."[7] Behind us, behind each one of us, lie Six Thousand Years of human effort, human conquest: before us is the boundless Time, with its as yet uncreated and unconquered Continents and Eldorados, which we, even we, have to conquer, to create; and from the bosom of Eternity there shine for us celestial guiding stars.

> "My inheritance how wide and fair!
> Time is my fair seed-field, of Time I'm heir."[8]

1831   1831

From Sartor Resartus[1]
Chapter VII. *The Everlasting No*

Under the strange nebulous envelopment, wherein our Professor has now shrouded himself, no doubt but his spiritual nature is nevertheless progressive, and growing: for how can the "Son of

7. Ecclesiastes ix.10.
8. From Goethe's romance, *Wilhelm Meisters Wanderjahre* (1821).
1. *Sartor Resartus* is a combination of novel, autobiography, and essay. To present some of his own experiences, Carlyle invented a hero, Professor Diogenes Teufelsdröckh of Germany, whose name itself (meaning "God-Begotten Devil's Dung") suggests the grotesque and fantastic humor which Carlyle used to expound a serious treatise. Teufelsdröckh tells the story of his unhappiness in love and of his difficulties in religion. He also airs his opinions on a variety of subjects. Interspersed between the Professor's words (which are in quotation marks) are the remarks of an editor, also imaginary, who has the task of putting together the story from assorted documents written by Teufelsdröckh. The title, meaning "The Tailor Re-Tailored," refers to the editor's role of patching the story together. The title also refers to Carlyle's so-called "Clothes Philosophy," which is expounded by the hero in many chapters of *Sartor*. In effect this Clothes Philosophy is an attempt to demon-strate the difference between the appearances of things and their reality. The appearance of a man depends upon the costume he wears; the reality of a man is the body underneath the costume. By analogy, Carlyle suggests that institutions, such as churches or governments, are like clothes. They may be useful "visible emblems" of the spiritual forces which they cover, but they wear out and have to be replaced by new clothes. The Christian church, for example, which once expressed man's permanent religious desires, is, in Carlyle's terms, worn out and must be discarded. But the underlying religious spirit must be recognized and kept alive at all costs. In this respect, the Clothes Philosophy has much in common with the theory of archetypal experiences developed in the 20th century by the psychiatrist Carl Jung. Carlyle extends his analogy, however, into many other areas. Clothes hide the body just as the world of nature cloaks the reality of God and as the body itself cloaks the reality of man's soul. The discovery of these realities behind the appearances is, for Carlyle and for his

Time," in any case, stand still? We behold him, through those dim years, in a state of crisis, of transition: his mad Pilgrimings, and general solution into aimless Discontinuity, what is all this but a mad Fermentation; wherefrom, the fiercer it is, the clearer product will one day evolve itself?

Such transitions are ever full of pain: thus the Eagle when he moults is sickly; and, to attain his new beak, must harshly dash-off the old one upon rocks. What Stoicism soever our Wanderer, in his individual acts and motions, may affect, it is clear that there is a hot fever of anarchy and misery raging within; coruscations of which flash out: as, indeed, how could there be other? Have we not seen him disappointed, bemocked of Destiny, through long years? All that the young heart might desire and pray for has been denied; nay, as in the last worst instance, offered and then snatched away. Ever an "excellent Passivity"; but of useful, reasonable Activity, essential to the former as Food to Hunger, nothing granted: till at length, in this wild Pilgrimage, he must forcibly seize for himself an Activity, though useless, unreasonable. Alas, his cup of bitterness, which had been filling drop by drop, ever since that first "ruddy morning" in the Hinterschlag Gymnasium,[2] was at the very lip; and then with that poison-drop, of the Towgood-and-Blumine business,[3] it runs over, and even hisses over in a deluge of foam.

He himself says once, with more justice than originality: "Man is, properly speaking, based upon Hope, he has no other possession but Hope; this world of his is emphatically the Place of Hope." What, then, was our Professor's possession? We see him, for the present, quite shut-out from Hope; looking not into the golden orient, but vaguely all round into a dim copper firmament, pregnant with earthquake and tornado.

Alas, shut-out from Hope, in a deeper sense than we yet dream of! For, as he wanders wearisomely through this world, he has now lost all tidings of another and higher. Full of religion, or at least of religiosity, as our Friend has since exhibited himself, he hides not that, in those days, he was wholly irreligious: "Doubt had darkened into Unbelief," says he; "shade after shade goes grimly over your soul, till you have the fixed, starless, Tartarean black." To such readers as have reflected, what can be called reflecting, on man's life, and happily discovered, in contradiction to much Profit-

---

hero, the initial stage of a solution to the dilemmas of life.

Teufelsdröckh's religious development, as described in the following chapters, may be contrasted with J. S. Mill's account of his own crisis of spirit in his *Autobiography*.

2. "Smite-Behind Grammar School";

Teufelsdröckh's unhappiness had begun with his loneliness at this school.

3. Blumine, a girl loved by Teufelsdröckh, had married his friend Towgood. His distress is pictured in the preceding chapter, entitled "Sorrows of Teufelsdröckh."

and-loss Philosophy,[4] speculative and practical, that Soul is *not* synonymous with Stomach; who understand, therefore, in our Friend's words, "that, for man's well-being, Faith is properly the one thing needful; how, with it, Martyrs, otherwise weak, can cheerfully endure the shame and the cross; and without it, Worldlings puke-up their sick existence, by suicide, in the midst of luxury": to such it will be clear that, for a pure moral nature, the loss of his religious Belief was the loss of everything. Unhappy young man! All wounds, the crush of long-continued Destitution, the stab of false Friendship and of false Love, all wounds in thy so genial heart, would have healed again, had not its life-warmth been withdrawn. Well might he exclaim, in his wild way: "Is there no God, then; but at best an absentee God, sitting idle, ever since the first Sabbath, at the outside of his Universe, and *seeing* it go? Has the word Duty no meaning; is what we call Duty no divine Messenger and Guide, but a false earthly Fantasm, made-up of Desire and Fear, of emanations from the Gallows and from Dr. Graham's Celestial-Bed?[5] Happiness of an approving Conscience! Did not Paul of Tarsus, whom admiring men have since named Saint, feel that *he* was 'the chief of sinners';[6] and Nero of Rome, jocund in spirit (*wohlgemuth*), spend much of his time in fiddling? Foolish Word-monger and Motive-grinder, who in thy Logic-mill hast an earthly mechanism for the Godlike itself, and wouldst fain grind me out Virtue from the husks of Pleasure,—I tell thee, Nay! To the unregenerate Prometheus Vinctus[7] of a man, it is ever the bitterest aggravation of his wretchedness that he is conscious of Virtue, that he feels himself the victim not of suffering only, but of injustice. What then? Is the heroic inspiration we name Virtue but some Passion; some bubble of the blood, bubbling in the direction others *profit* by? I know not: only this I know, If what thou namest Happiness be our true aim, then are we all astray. With Stupidity and sound Digestion man may front much. But what, in these dull unimaginative days, are the terrors of Conscience to the diseases of the Liver! Not on Morality, but on Cookery, let us build our stronghold: there brandishing our frying-pan, as censer, let us offer sweet incense to the Devil, and live at ease on the fat things *he* has provided for his Elect!"

Thus has the bewildered Wanderer to stand, as so many have done,

4. Utilitarian theory of ethics that our actions should be based on calculating the sum of pleasures and pains which would result from such actions. This "hedonistic calculus" horrified Carlyle because it left out of account man's religious instincts.
5. James Graham (1745–94), a quack doctor, had invented an elaborate bed which was supposed to cure sterility in couples using it. In this passage the bed is apparently a symbol of sexual desires.
6. See I Timothy i.15.
7. I.e., Prometheus Bound; this is also the title of a play by Aeschylus depicting the sufferings of a hero who defied Zeus.

shouting question after question into the Sibyl-cave of Destiny,[8] and receive no Answer but an Echo. It is all a grim Desert, this once-fair world of his; wherein is heard only the howling of wild-beasts, or the shrieks of despairing, hate-filled men; and no Pillar of Cloud by day, and no Pillar of Fire by night,[9] any longer guides the Pilgrim. To such length has the spirit of Inquiry carried him. "But what boots it (*was thut's*)?" cries he: "it is but the common lot in this era. Not having come to spiritual majority prior to the *Siècle de Louis Quinze*,[1] and not being born purely a Loghead (*Dummkopf*), thou hast no other outlook. The whole world is, like thee, sold to Unbelief; their old Temples of the Godhead, which for long have not been rainproof, crumble down; and men ask now: Where is the Godhead; our eyes never saw him?"

Pitiful enough were it, for all these wild utterances, to call our Diogenes wicked. Unprofitable servants as we all are, perhaps at no era of his life was he more decisively the Servant of Goodness, the Servant of God, than even now when doubting God's existence. "One circumstance I note," says he: "after all the nameless woe that Inquiry, which for me, what it is not always, was genuine Love of Truth, had wrought me, I nevertheless still loved Truth, and would bate no jot of my allegiance to her. 'Truth'! I cried, 'though the Heavens crush me for following her: no Falsehood! though a whole celestial Lubberland[2] were the price of Apostasy.' In conduct it was the same. Had a divine Messenger from the clouds, or miraculous Handwriting on the wall, convincingly proclaimed to me *This thou shalt do*, with what passionate readiness, as I often thought, would I have done it, had it been leaping into the infernal Fire. Thus, in spite of all Motive-grinders, and Mechanical Profit-and-Loss Philosophies, with the sick ophthalmia and hallucination they had brought on, was the Infinite nature of Duty still dimly present to me: living without God in the world, of God's light I was not utterly bereft; if my as yet sealed eyes, with their unspeakable longing, could nowhere see Him, nevertheless in my heart He was present, and His heaven-written Law still stood legible and sacred there."

Meanwhile, under all these tribulations, and temporal and spiritual destitutions, what must the Wanderer, in his silent soul, have endured! "The painfullest feeling," writes he, "is that of your own Feebleness (*Unkraft*); ever, as the English Milton says, to be weak is the true misery.[3] And yet of your Strength there is and can be no clear feeling, save by what you have prospered in, by what you have done. Between vague wavering Capability and fixed indubitable Performance, what a difference! A certain inarticulate Self-conscious-

---

8. An allusion to Virgil's *Aeneid* VI. 36 ff., where Aeneas questions the Cumaean sibyl.
9. Exodus xiii.21.
1. "The Century of Louis XV," an allusion to Voltaire's history of the skeptical and enquiring spirit of 18th-

century France during the reign of Louis XV (1710–74): *Précis du Siècle de Louis XV*.
2. Land of Plenty.
3. *Paradise Lost* I.157: "Fallen cherub, to be weak is miserable."

ness dwells dimly in us; which only our Works can render articulate and decisively discernible. Our Works are the mirror wherein the spirit first sees its natural lineaments. Hence, too, the folly of that impossible Precept, *Know thyself;*[4] till it be translated into this partially possible one, *Know what thou canst work-at.*

"But for me, so strangely unprosperous had I been, the net-result of my Workings amounted as yet simply to—Nothing. How then could I believe in my Strength, when there was as yet no mirror to see it in? Ever did this agitating, yet, as I now perceive, quite frivolous question, remain to me insoluble: Hast thou a certain Faculty, a certain Worth, such even as the most have not; or art thou the completest Dullard of these modern times? Alas! the fearful Unbelief is unbelief in yourself; and how could I believe? Had not my first, last Faith in myself, when even to me the Heavens seemed laid open, and I dared to love, been all-too cruelly belied? The speculative Mystery of Life grew ever more mysterious to me: neither in the practical Mystery[5] had I made the slightest progress, but been everywhere buffeted, foiled, and contemptuously cast-out. A feeble unit in the middle of a threatening Infinitude, I seemed to have nothing given me but eyes, whereby to discern my own wretchedness. Invisible yet impenetrable walls, as of Enchantment, divided me from all living: was there, in the wide world, any true bosom I could press trustfully to mine? O Heaven, No, there was none! I kept a lock upon my lips: why should I speak much with that shifting variety of so-called Friends, in whose withered, vain and too-hungry souls Friendship was but an incredible tradition? In such cases, your resource is to talk little, and that little mostly from the Newspapers. Now when I look back, it was a strange isolation I then lived in. The men and women around me, even speaking with me, were but Figures; I had, practically, forgotten that they were alive, that they were not merely automatic. In midst of their crowded streets and assemblages, I walked solitary; and (except as it was my own heart, not another's, that I kept devouring) savage also, as the tiger in his jungle. Some comfort it would have been, could I, like a Faust,[6] have fancied myself tempted and tormented of the Devil; for a Hell, as I imagine, without Life, though only diabolic Life, were more frightful: but in our age of Down-pulling and Disbelief, the very Devil has been pulled down, you cannot so much as believe in a Devil. To me the Universe was all void of Life, of Purpose, of Volition, even of Hostility: it was one huge, dead, immeasurable Steam-engine, rolling on, in its dead indifference, to grind me limb from limb. O, the vast, gloomy, solitary Golgotha,[7] and Mill of

---

4. This maxim was inscribed in gold letters over the portico of the temple at Delphi.
5. A profession or practical occupation.

6. Faust, the hero of a drama by Goethe, was tempted by the Devil.
7. Calvary, the place where Christ was crucified.

Death! Why was the Living banished thither companionless, conscious? Why, if there is no Devil; nay, unless the Devil is your God?"

A prey incessantly to such corrosions, might not, moreover, as the worst aggravation to them, the iron constitution even of a Teufelsdröckh threaten to fail? We conjecture that he has known sickness; and, in spite of his locomotive habits, perhaps sickness of the chronic sort. Hear this, for example: "How beautiful to die of broken-heart, on Paper! Quite another thing in practice; every window of your Feeling, even of your Intellect, as it were, begrimed and mud-bespattered, so that no pure ray can enter; a whole Drugshop in your inwards; the fordone soul drowning slowly in quagmires of Disgust!"

Putting all which external and internal miseries together, may we not find in the following sentences, quite in our Professor's still vein, significance enough? "From Suicide a certain aftershine (*Nachschein*) of Christianity withheld me: perhaps also a certain indolence of character; for, was not that a remedy I had at any time within reach? Often, however, was there a question present to me: Should some one now, at the turning of that corner, blow thee suddenly out of Space, into the other World, or other No-World, by pistol-shot,—how were it? On which ground, too, I have often, in sea-storms and sieged cities and other death-scenes, exhibited an imperturbability, which passed, falsely enough, for courage.

"So had it lasted," concludes the Wanderer, "so had it lasted, as in bitter protracted Death-agony, through long years. The heart within me, unvisited by any heavenly dewdrop, was smouldering in sulphurous, slow-consuming fire. Almost since earliest memory I had shed no tear; or once only when I, murmuring half-audibly, recited Faust's Deathsong, that wild *Selig der den er im Siegesglanze findet* (Happy whom *he* finds in Battle's splendour),[8] and thought that of this last Friend[9] even I was not forsaken, that Destiny itself could not doom me not to die. Having no hope, neither had I any definite fear, were it of Man or of Devil: nay, I often felt as if it might be solacing, could the Arch-Devil himself, though in Tartarean terrors, but rise to me, that I might tell him a little of my mind. And yet, strangly enough, I lived in a continual, indefinite, pining fear; tremulous, pusillanimous, apprehensive of I knew not what: it seemed as if all things in the Heavens above and the Earth beneath would hurt me; as if the Heavens and the Earth were but boundless jaws of a devouring monster, wherein I, palpitating, waited to be devoured.

"Full of such humour, and perhaps the miserablest man in the whole French Capital or Suburbs, was I, one sultry Dogday,[1] after much perambulation, toiling along the dirty little *Rue Saint-Thomas de l'Enfer*,[2] among civic rubbish enough, in a close atmosphere, and over pavements hot as Nebuchadnezzar's Furnace; whereby doubtless my spirits were little cheered; when, all at once, there rose a Thought in me, and I asked myself: 'What *art* thou afraid of? Wherefore, like a coward, dost thou forever pip and whimper, and go cowering and trembling? Despicable biped! what is the sumtotal of the worst that lies before thee? Death? Well, Death; and say the pangs of Tophet[3] too, and all that the Devil and Man may, will or can do against thee! Hast thou not a heart; canst thou not suffer whatsoever it be; and, as a Child of Freedom, though outcast, trample Tophet itself under thy feet, while it consumes thee? Let it come, then; I will meet it and defy it!' And as I so thought, there rushed like a stream of fire over my whole soul; and I shook base Fear away from me forever. I was strong, of unknown strength; a spirit, almost a god. Ever from that time, the temper of my misery was changed: not Fear or whining Sorrow was it, but Indignation and grim fire-eyed Defiance.

"Thus had the EVERLASTING NO[4] (*das ewige Nein*) pealed authoritatively through all the recesses of my Being, of my ME; and then was it that my whole ME stood up, in native God-created majesty, and with emphasis recorded its Protest. Such a Protest, the most important transaction in Life, may that same Indignation and Defiance, in a psychological point of view, be fitly called. The Everlasting No had said: 'Behold, thou art fatherless, outcast, and the Universe is mine (the Devil's)'; to which my whole Me now made answer: '*I am not thine, but Free, and forever hate thee!*'

"It is from this hour that I incline to date my Spiritual Newbirth, or Baphometic Fire-baptism;[5] perhaps I directly thereupon began to be a Man."

Chapter VIII. Centre of Indifference

Though, after this "Baphometic Fire-baptism" of his, our Wanderer signifies that his Unrest was but increased; as indeed, "Indignation and Defiance," especially against things in general, are not the most peaceable inmates; yet can the Psychologist surmise that it was no longer a quite hopeless Unrest; that henceforth it had at least a

1. A hot and unwholesome summer period, coinciding with the prominence of Sirius, the Dog Star, is called the season of the dog days.
2. "St. Thomas-of-Hell Street." In later life Carlyle admitted that this incident was based upon his own experience during a walk in Edinburgh (rather than in Paris) when he was 26 or 27 years of age. For a period of three weeks, he said, he had been suffering from "total sleeplessness."

3. Hell.
4. This phrase does not signify the hero's protest. It represents the sum of all the forces that had denied meaning to life. These negative forces, which had hitherto held the hero in bondage, are repudiated by his saying, "No!" to the "Everlasting No."
5. A transformation by a flash of spiritual illumination. The term may derive from Baphomet, an idol that inspired such spiritual experiences.

fixed centre to revolve round. For the fire-baptised soul, long so scathed and thunder-riven, here feels its own Freedom, which feeling is its Baphometic Baptism: the citadel of its whole kingdom it has thus gained by assault, and will keep inexpugnable; outwards from which the remaining dominions, not indeed without hard battling, will doubtless by degrees be conquered and pacificated. Under another figure, we might say, if in that great moment, in the *Rue Saint-Thomas de l'Enfer*, the old inward Satanic School[1] was not yet thrown out of doors, it received peremptory judicial notice to quit; —whereby, for the rest, its howl-chantings, Ernulphus-cursings,[2] and rebellious gnashings of teeth, might, in the meanwhile, become only the more tumultuous, and difficult to keep secret.

Accordingly, if we scrutinise these Pilgrimings well, there is perhaps discernible henceforth a certain incipient method in their madness. Not wholly as a Spectre does Teufelsdröckh now storm through the world; at worst as a spectre-fighting Man, nay who will one day be a Spectre-queller. If pilgriming restlessly to so many "Saints' Wells," [3] and ever without quenching of his thirst, he nevertheless finds little secular wells, whereby from time to time some alleviation is ministered. In a word, he is now, if not ceasing, yet intermitting to "eat his own heart"; and clutches round him outwardly on the NOT-ME for wholesomer food. Does not the following glimpse exhibit him in a much more natural state?

"Towns also and Cities, especially the ancient, I failed not to look upon with interest. How beautiful to see thereby, as through a long vista, into the remote Time; to have as it were, an actual section of almost the earliest Past brought safe into the Present, and set before your eyes! There, in that old City, was a live ember of Culinary Fire put down, say only two-thousand years ago; and there, burning more or less triumphantly, with such fuel as the region yielded, it has burnt, and still burns, and thou thyself seest the very smoke thereof. Ah! and the far more mysterious live ember of Vital Fire was then also put down there; and still miraculously burns and spreads; and the smoke and ashes thereof (in these Judgment-Halls and Church-yards), and its bellows-engines (in these Churches), thou still seest; and its flame, looking out from every kind countenance, and every hateful one, still warms thee or scorches thee.

"Of Man's Activity and Attainment the chief results are aeriform, mystic, and preserved in Tradition only: such are his Forms of Government, with the Authority they rest on; his Customs, or Fashions both of Cloth-habits and of Soul-habits; much more his collec-

1. A term coined by Robert Southey to characterize the self-assertive and rebellious temper of the poetry of Byron and Shelley.
2. A curse devised by Ernulf (1040–1124), Bishop of Rochester, when sentencing persons to excommunication. See

Sterne's *Tristram Shandy* III.xi.
3. Holy fountains or wells whose waters were reputed to restore health. Here a figurative allusion to Teufelsdröckh's unsuccessful search, at this time, for a religious solution to his problems.

tive stock of Handicrafts, the whole Faculty he has acquired of manipulating Nature: all these things, as indispensable and priceless as they are, cannot in any way be fixed under lock and key, but must flit, spirit-like, on impalpable vehicles, from Father to Son; if you demand sight of them, they are nowhere to be met with. Visible Plowmen and Hammermen there have been, ever from Cain and Tubalcain downwards: [4] but where does your accumulated Agricultural, Metallurgic, and other Manufacturing SKILL lie warehoused? It transmits itself on the atmospheric air, on the sun's rays (by Hearing and by Vision); it is a thing aeriform, impalpable, of quite spiritual sort. In like manner, ask me not. Where are the LAWS where is the GOVERNMENT? In vain wilt thou go to Schönbrunn, to Downing Street, to the Palais Bourbon: [5] thou findest nothing there but brick or stone houses, and some bundles of Papers tied with tape. Where, then, is that same cunningly-devised almighty Government of theirs to be laid hands on? Everywhere, yet nowhere: seen only in its works, this too is a thing aeriform, invisible; or if you will, mystic and miraculous. So spiritual (*geistig*) is our whole daily Life: all that we do springs out of Mystery, Spirit, invisible Force; only like a little Cloud-image, or Armida's Palace,[6] air-built, does the Actual body itself forth from the great mystic Deep.

"Visible and tangible products of the Past, again, I reckon-up to the extent of three. Cities, with their Cabinets and Arsenals; then tilled Fields, to either or to both of which divisions Roads with their Bridges, may belong; and thirdly—Books. In which third truly, the last invented, lies a worth far surpassing that of the two others. Wondrous indeed is the virtue of a true Book. Not like a dead city of stones, yearly crumbling, yearly needing repair; more like a tilled field, but then a spiritual field: like a spiritual tree, let me rather say, it stands from year to year, and from age to age (we have Books that already number some hundred-and-fifty human ages); and yearly comes its new produce of leaves (Commentaries, Deductions, Philosophical, Political Systems; or were it only Sermons, Pamphlets, Journalistic Essays), every one of which is talismanic and thaumaturgic,[7] for it can persuade men. O thou who art able to write a Book, which once in the two centuries or oftener there is a man gifted to do, envy not him whom they name City-builder, and inexpressibly pity him whom they name Conqueror or City-burner! Thou too art a Conqueror and Victor; but of the true sort, namely over the Devil: thou too hast built what will outlast all marble and metal, and be a wonder-bringing City of the Mind, a Temple and Seminary and Prophetic Mount, whereto all kindreds of the Earth will pilgrim. —Fool! why journeyest thou wearisomely, in thy antiquarian fervour, to gaze on the stone pyramids of Geeza, or the clay ones of

---

4. See Genesis, iv.1–22.
5. Headquarters of government in Vienna, London, and Paris, respectively.
6. The magic palace of a beautiful enchantress in Tasso's *Jerusalem Delivered*.
7. Miracle-working.

Sacchara?[8] These stand there, as I can tell thee, idle and inert, looking over the Desert, foolishly enough, for the last three-thousand years: but canst thou not open thy Hebrew BIBLE, then, or even Luther's Version thereof?"

No less satisfactory is his sudden appearance not in Battle, yet on some Battle-field; which, we soon gather, must be that of Wagram;[9] so that here, for once, is a certain approximation to distinctiveness of date. Omitting much, let us impart what follows:

"Horrible enough! A whole Marchfeld[1] strewed with shell-splinters, cannon-shot, ruined tumbrils, and dead men and horses; stragglers still remaining not so much as buried. And those red mould heaps: ay, there lie the Shells of Men, out of which all the Life and Virtue has been blown; and now are they swept together, and crammed-down out of sight, like blown Egg-shells!—Did Nature, when she bade the Donau bring down his mould-cargoes from the Carinthian and Carpathian Heights, and spread them out here into the softest, richest level,—intend thee, O Marchfeld, for a corn-bearing Nursery, whereon her children might be nursed; or for a Cockpit, wherein they might the more commodiously be throttled and tattered? Were thy three broad Highways, meeting here from the ends of Europe, made for Ammunition-wagons, then? Were thy Wagrams and Stillfrieds[2] but so many ready-built Casemates,[3] wherein the house of Hapsburg might batter with artillery, and with artillery be battered? König Ottokar, amid yonder hillocks, dies under Rodolf's truncheon; here Kaiser Franz falls a-swoon under Napoleon's: within which five centuries, to omit the others, how has thy breast, fair Plain, been defaced and defiled! The greensward is torn-up and trampled-down; man's fond care of it, his fruit-trees, hedge-rows, and pleasant dwellings, blown away with gunpowder; and the kind seedfield lies a desolate, hideous Place of Sculls.— Nevertheless, Nature is at work; neither shall these Powder-Devilkins with their utmost devilry gainsay her: but all that gore and carnage will be shrouded-in, absorbed into manure; and next year the Marchfeld will be green, nay greener. Thrifty unwearied Nature, ever out of our great waste educing some little profit of thy own,— how dost thou, from the very carcass of the Killer, bring Life for the Living![4]

"What, speaking in quite unofficial language, is the net-purport and upshot of war? To my own knowledge, for example, there dwell

8. Pyramids at Ghizeh and Sakkara near Cairo.
9. A village in Austria; site of Napoleon's victory over the Austrians, July, 1809.
1. A fertile plain in Austria whose soil (according to Teufelsdröckh) was brought down from the Carpathian mountains by the Danube (Donau) River.
2. Stillfried was the site of a battle in which Ottokar, King ("könig") of Bohemia, was killed by the forces of Rudolph of Hapsburg in 1278. In 1809 the Hapsburg armies, under Emperor Francis ("Franz") I, were in turn defeated by Napoleon at nearby Wagram.
3. Fortified chambers.
4. Cf. Byron's reflections on the battlefield at Waterloo: "How that red rain hath made the harvest grow!"—*Childe Harold's Pilgrimage,* III.xvii.150.

and toil, in the British village of Dumdrudge, usually some five-hundred souls. From these, by certain 'Natural Enemies' [5] of the French, there are successively selected, during the French war, say thirty able-bodied men: Dumdrudge, at her own expense, has suckled and nursed them: she has, not without difficulty and sorrow, fed them up to manhood, and even trained them to crafts, so that one can weave, another build, another hammer, and the weakest can stand under thirty stone avoirdupois. Nevertheless, amid much weeping and swearing, they are selected; all dressed in red; and shipped away, at the public charges, some two-thousand miles, or say only to the south of Spain;[6] and fed there till wanted. And now to that same spot, in the south of Spain, are thirty similar French artisans, from a French Dumdrudge, in like manner wending: till at length, after infinite effort, the two parties come into actual juxtaposition; and Thirty stands fronting Thirty, each with a gun in his hand. Straightway the word 'Fire!' is given: and they blow the souls out of one another; and in place of sixty brisk useful craftsmen, the world has sixty dead carcasses, which it must bury, and anew shed tears for. Had these men any quarrel? Busy as the Devil is, not the smallest! They lived far enough apart; were the entirest strangers; nay, in so wide a Universe, there was even, unconsciously, by Commerce, some mutual helpfulness between them. How then? Simpleton! their Governors had fallen-out; and, instead of shooting one another, had the cunning to make these poor blockheads shoot.— Alas, so is it in Deutschland, and hitherto in all other lands; still as of old, 'what devilry soever Kings do, the Greeks must pay the piper!'[7]—In that fiction of the English Smollet,[8] it is true, the final Cessation of War is perhaps prophetically shadowed forth; where the two Natural Enemies, in person, take each a Tobacco-pipe, filled with Brimstone; light the same, and smoke in one another's faces, till the weaker gives in: but from such predicted Peace-Era, what blood-filled trenches, and contentious centuries, may still divide us!'

Thus can the Professor, at least in lucid intervals, look away from his own sorrows, over the many-coloured world, and pertinently enough note what is passing there. We may remark, indeed, that for the matter of spiritual culture, if for nothing else, perhaps few periods of his life were richer than this. Internally, there is the most momentous instructive Course of Practical Philosophy, with Experiments, going on; towards the right comprehension of which his Peripatetic[9] habits, favourable to Meditation, might help him rather than hinder. Externally, again, as he wanders to and fro, there are, if for the longing heart little substance, yet for the seeing eye

5. Term often used in English newspapers to account for the frequency of wars between the English and French.
6. Where British armies fought against Napoleon, 1808–14.
7. Cf. Horace, *Epistles*, I.ii.14.

8. See Chapter XLI of *The Adventures of Ferdinand Count Fathom* by Tobias Smollett (1721–71).
9. Walking about, after the manner of Aristotle who delivered his lectures while walking in the Lyceum.

sights enough: in these so boundless Travels of his, granting that
the Satanic School was even partially kept down, what an incredible
knowledge of our Planet, and its Inhabitants and their Works, that
is to say, of all knowable things, might not Teufelsdröckh acquire!

"I have read in most Public Libraries," says he, "including those
of Constantinople and Samarcand: in most Colleges, except the
Chinese Mandarin ones, I have studied, or seen that there was no
studying. Unknown Languages have I oftenest gathered from their
natural repertory, the Air, by my organ of Hearing; Statistics, Geo-
graphics, Topographics came, through the Eye, almost of their own
accord. The ways of Man, how he seeks food, and warmth, and protection for himself, in most regions, are ocularly known to me. Like
the great Hadrian,[1] I meted-out much of the terraqueous Globe with
a pair of Compasses[2] that belonged to myself only.

"Of great Scenes why speak? Three summer days, I lingered reflecting, and even composing (*dichtete*), by the Pine-chasms of
Vaucluse; and in that clear Lakelet[3] moistened my bread. I have sat
under the Palm-trees of Tadmor;[4] smoked a pipe among the ruins
of Babylon. The great Wall of China I have seen; and can testify
that it is of gray brick, coped and covered with granite, and shows
only second-rate masonry.—Great Events, also, have not I witnessed? Kings sweated-down (*ausgemergelt*) into Berlin-and-Milan
Customhouse-Officers;[5] the World well won, and the World well
lost;[6] oftener than once a hundred-thousand individuals shot (by
each other) in one day. All kindreds and peoples and nations dashed
together, and shifted and shovelled into heaps, that they might ferment there, and in time unite. The birth-pangs of Democracy,[7]
wherewith convulsed Europe was groaning in cries that reached
Heaven, could not escape me.

"For great Men I have ever had the warmest predilection; and can
perhaps boast that few such in this era have wholly escaped me.
Great Men are the inspired (speaking and acting) Texts of that
divine BOOK OF REVELATION, whereof a Chapter is completed from
epoch to epoch, and by some named HISTORY; to which inspired
Texts your numerous talented men, and your innumerable untalented men, are the better or worse exegetic Commentaries, and
wagonload of too-stupid, heretical or orthodox, weekly Sermons. For
my study, the inspired Texts themselves! Thus did not I, in very
early days, having disguised me as tavern-waiter, stand behind

---

1. Roman emperor (76–138) who traveled extensively throughout his empire.
2. I.e., legs.
3. A pool at the base of a mountain in
Vaucluse in southern France. The adjacent "Pine-chasms" were one of Petrarch's favorite haunts. For Teufelsdröckh the area served as one of the
"secular wells" that helped to restore
him to spiritual health.

4. Palmyra in Syria.
5. Napoleon reduced some of Europe's
kings to the status of mere tax collectors
for his regime.
6. Cf. the title of Dryden's play *All
for Love, or the World Well Lost.*
7. As manifested in the revolutionary
outbreaks in France (1789 and 1830)
and in the agitations in England preceding the Reform Bill of 1832.

the field-chairs, under that shady Tree at Treisnitz by the Jena High-way; [8] waiting upon the great Schiller and greater Goethe; and hear-ing what I have not forgotten. For—"

—But at this point the Editor recalls his principle of caution, some time ago laid down, and must suppress much. Let not the sacredness of Laurelled, still more, of Crowned Heads, be tampered with. Should we, at a future day, find circumstances altered, and the time come for Publication, then may these glimpses into the privacy of the Illustrious be conceded; which for the present were little better than treacherous, perhaps traitorous Eavesdroppings. Of Lord Byron, therefore, of Pope Pius, Emperor Tarakwang, and the "White Water-roses" [9] (Chinese Carbonari) with their mysteries, no notice here! Of Napoleon himself we shall only, glancing from afar, remark that Teufelsdröckh's relation to him seems to have been of very varied character. At first we find our poor Professor on the point of being shot as a spy; then taken into private conversation, even pinched on the ear, yet presented with no money; at last indignantly dismissed, almost thrown out of doors, as an "Ideologist." "He him-self," says the Professor, "was among the completest Ideologists, at least Ideopraxists: [1] in the Idea (*in der Idee*) he lived, moved and fought. The man was a Divine Missionary, though unconscious of it; and preached, through the cannon's throat, that great doctrine, *La carrière ouverte aux talens* (The Tools to him that can handle them), which is our ultimate Political Evangel, wherein alone can liberty lie. Madly enough he preached, it is true, as Enthusiasts [2] and first Missionaries are wont, with imperfect utterance, amid much frothy rant; yet as articulately perhaps as the case admitted. Or call him, of you will, an American Backwoodsman, who had to fell un-penetrated forests, and battle with innumerable wolves, and did not entirely forbear strong liquor, rioting, and even theft; whom, notwithstanding, the peaceful Sower will follow, and, as he cuts the boundless harvest, bless."

More legitimate and decisively authentic is Teufelsdröckh's ap-pearance and emergence (we know not well whence) in the solitude of the North Cape, on that June Midnight. He has a "light-blue Spanish cloak" hanging round him, as his "most commodious, principal, indeed sole upper-garment"; and stands there, on the World-promontory, looking over the infinite Brine, like a little blue Belfry (as we figure), now motionless indeed, yet ready, if stirred, to ring quaintest changes.

"Silence as of death," writes he; "for Midnight, even in the Arctic latitudes, has its character: nothing but the granite cliffs ruddy-tinged, the peaceable gurgle of that slow-heaving Polar Ocean, over

8. Where Goethe and Schiller met dur-ing the 1790's when they were collabo-rating on their writings.
9. Like the Carbonari in Italy, a secret revolutionary society in China during the regime of Emperor "Tarakwang" (Tao Kuang, 1821–50).
1. Those who put ideas into practice.
2. Religious fanatics.

which in the utmost North the great Sun hangs low and lazy, as if
he too were slumbering. Yet is his cloud-couch wrought of crimson
and cloth-of-gold; yet does his light stream over the mirror of
waters, like a tremulous fire-pillar, shooting downwards to the abyss,
and hide itself under my feet. In such moments, Solitude also is invaluable; for who would speak, or be looked on, when behind him
lies all Europe and Africa, fast asleep, except the watchmen; and
before him the silent Immensity, and Palace of the Eternal, whereof
our Sun is but a porch-lamp?

"Nevertheless, in this solemn moment comes a man, or monster,
scrambling from among the rock-hollows; and, shaggy, huge as the
Hyperborean [3] Bear, hails me in Russian speech: most probably,
therefore, a Russian Smuggler. With courteous brevity, I signify my
indifference to contraband trade, my humane intentions, yet strong
wish to be private. In vain: the monster, counting doubtless on his
superior stature, and minded to make sport for himself, or perhaps
profit, were it with murder, continues to advance; ever assailing me
with his importunate train-oil[4] breath; and now has advanced, till
we stand both on the verge of the rock, the deep Sea rippling
greedily down below. What argument will avail? On the thick
Hyperborean, cherubic reasoning, seraphic eloquence were lost. Prepared for such extremity, I, deftly enough, whisk aside one step;
draw out, from my interior reservoirs, a sufficient Birmingham
Horse-pistol, and say, 'Be so obliging as retire, Friend (*Er ziehe sich
zurück, Freund*), and with promptitude!' This logic even the Hyperborean understands: fast enough, with apologetic, petitionary
growl, he sidles off; and, except for suicidal as well as homicidal
purposes, need not return.

"Such I hold to be the genuine use of Gunpowder: that it makes
all men alike tall. Nay, if thou be cooler, cleverer than I, if thou have
more *Mind*, though all but no *Body* whatever, then canst thou kill
me first, and are the taller. Hereby, at last, is the Goliath powerless,
and the David resistless; savage Animalism is nothing, inventive
Spiritualism is all.

"With respect to Duels, indeed, I have my own ideas. Few things,
in this so surprising world, strike me with more surprise. Two little
visual Spectra of men, hovering with insecure enough cohesion in
the midst of the UNFATHOMABLE, and to dissolve therein, at any
rate, very soon,—make pause at the distance of twelve paces asunder;
whirl round; and, simultaneously by the cunningest mechanism, explode one another into Dissolution; and off-hand become Air, and
Nonextant! Deuce on it (*verdammt*), the little spitfires!—Nay, I
think with old Hugo von Trimberg:[5] 'God must needs laugh outright, could such a thing be, to see his wondrous Manikins here
below.' "

3. From the far North.   5. Medieval poet (1260–1309).
4. Whale oil.

But amid these specialties, let us not forget the great generality, which is our Chief guest here: How prospered the inner man of Teufelsdröckh under so much outward shifting? Does Legion [6] still lurk in him, though repressed; or has he exorcised that Devil's Brood? We can answer that the symptoms continue promising. Experience is the grand spiritual Doctor; and with him Teufelsdröckh has been long a patient, swallowing many a bitter bolus.[7] Unless our poor Friend belong to the numerous class of Incurables, which seems not likely, some cure will doubtless be effected. We should rather say that Legion, or the Satanic School, was now pretty well extirpated and cast out, but next to nothing introduced in its room; whereby the heart remains, for the while, in a quiet but no comfortable state.

"At length, after so much roasting," thus writes our Autobiographer, "I was what you might name calcined. Pray only that it be not rather, as is the more frequent issue, reduced to a *caput-mortuum!*[8] But in any case, by mere dint of practice, I had grown familiar with many things. Wretchedness was still wretched; but I could now partly see through it, and despise it. Which highest mortal, in this inane Existence, had I not found a Shadow-hunter, or Shadow-hunted; and, when I looked through his brave garnitures, miserable enough? Thy wishes have all been sniffed aside, thought I: but what, had they ever been all granted! Did not the Boy Alexander weep because he had not two Planets to conquer; or a whole Solar System; or after that, a whole Universe? *Ach Gott*, when I gazed into these Stars, have they not looked-down on me as if with pity, from their serene spaces; like Eyes glistening with heavenly tears over the little lot of man! Thousands of human generations, all as noisy as our own, have been swallowed-up of Time, and there remains no wreck of them any more; and Arcturus and Orion and Sirius and the Pleiades are still shining in their courses, clear and young, as when the Shepherd first noted them in the plain of Shinar.[9] Pshaw! what is this paltry little Dog-cage[1] of an Earth; what art thou that sittest whining there? Thou art still Nothing, Nobody: true; but who, then, is Something, Somebody? For thee the Family of Man has no use; it rejects thee; thou art wholly as a dissevered limb: so be it; perhaps it is better so!"

Too-heavy-laden Teufelsdröckh! Yet surely his bands are loosening; one day he will hurl the burden far from him, and bound forth free and with a second youth.

6. Unclean spirits as described in Mark v.9.
7. Large pill.
8. Death's head.
9. The shepherd is probably Abraham, who was commanded by the Lord to "tell the stars, if thou be able to number them" (Genesis xv.5). Shinar was a plain in the Sumerian region (in mod-ern times, Iraq). Abraham migrated from the Sumerian city of Ur (Genesis x.10; xi.31).
1. A drum-shaped cage that turns when a dog runs inside the cylinder. This dog-powered device, attached to a kitchen spit, was used for turning joints of meat during roasting.

Chapter IX. The Everlasting Yea

"Temptations in the Wilderness!"[2] exclaims Teufelsdröckh: "Have we not all to be tried with such? Not so easily can the old Adam, lodged in us by birth, be dispossessed. Our Life is compassed round with Necessity; yet is the meaning of Life itself no other than Freedom, than Voluntary Force: thus have we a warfare; in the beginning, especially, a hard-fought battle. For the God-given mandate, *Work thou in Welldoing*, lies mysteriously written, in Promethean[3] Prophetic Characters, in our hearts; and leaves us no rest, night or day, till it be deciphered and obeyed; till it burn forth, in our conduct, a visible, acted Gospel of Freedom. And as the clay-given mandate, *Eat thou and be filled*, at the same time persuasively proclaims itself through every nerve,—must not there be a confusion, a contest, before the better Influence can become the upper?

"To me nothing seems more natural than that the Son of Man, when such God-given mandate first prophetically stirs within him, and the Clay must now be vanquished, or vanquish,—should be carried of the spirit into grim Solitudes, and there fronting the Tempter do grimmest battle with him; defiantly setting him at naught, till he yield and fly. Name it as we choose: with or without visible Devil, whether in the natural Desert of rocks and sands, or in the populous moral Desert of selfishness and baseness,—to such Temptation are we all called. Unhappy if we are not! Unhappy if we are but Half-men, in whom that divine handwriting has never blazed forth, all-subduing, in true sun-splendour; but quivers dubiously amid meaner lights: or smoulders, in dull pain, in darkness, under earthly vapours!—Our Wilderness is the wide World in an Atheistic Century; our Forty Days are long years of suffering and fasting: nevertheless, to these also comes an end. Yes, to me also was given, if not Victory, yet the consciousness of Battle, and the resolve to persevere therein while life or faculty is left. To me also, entangled in the enchanted forests, demon-peopled, doleful of sight and of sound, it was given, after weariest wanderings, to work out my way into the higher sunlit slopes—of that Mountain which has no summit, or whose summit is in Heaven only!"

He says elsewhere, under a less ambitious figure; as figures are, once for all, natural to him: "Has not thy Life been that of most sufficient men (*tüchtigen Männer*) thou hast known in this generation? An outflush of foolish young Enthusiasm, like the first

2. Matthew iv.1.
3. Fiery or fiery-spirited, an allusion to Prometheus, the defiant Titan who brought the secret of fire-making to man.

fallow-crop, wherein are as many weeds as valuable herbs: this all parched away, under the Droughts of practical and spiritual Unbelief, as Disappointment, in thought and act, often-repeated gave rise to Doubt, and Doubt gradually settled into Denial! If I have had a second-crop, and now see the perennial greensward, and sit under umbrageous[4] cedars, which defy all Drought (and Doubt); herein too, be the Heavens praised, I am not without examples, and even exemplars."

So that, for Teufelsdröckh also, there has been a "glorious revolution":[5] these mad shadow-hunting and shadow-hunted Pilgrimings of his were but some purifying "Temptation in the Wilderness," before his Apostolic work (such as it was) could begin; which Temptation is now happily over, and the Devil once more worsted! Was "that high moment in the *Rue de l'Enfer*," then, properly the turning-point of the battle; when the Fiend said, *Worship me or be torn in shreds*; and was answered valiantly with an *Apage Satana?*[6] —Singular Teufelsdröckh, would thou hadst told thy singular story in plain words! But it is fruitless to look there, in those Paper-bags,[7] for such. Nothing but innuendoes, figurative crotchets: a typical Shadow, fitfully wavering, prophetico-satiric; no clear logical Picture. "How paint to the sensual eye," asks he once, "what passes in the Holy-of-Holies of Man's Soul; in what words, known to these profane times, speak even afar-off of the unspeakable?" We ask in turn: Why perplex these times, profane as they are, with needless obscurity, by omission and by commission? Not mystical only is our Professor, but whimsical; and involves himself, now more than ever, in eye-bewildering *chiaroscuro*.[8] Successive glimpses, here faithfully imparted, our more gifted readers must endeavour to combine for their own behoof.

He says: "The hot Harmattan wind[9] had raged itself out; its howl went silent within me; and the long-deafened soul could now hear. I paused in my wild wanderings; and sat me down to wait, and consider; for it was as if the hour of change drew nigh. I seemed to surrender, to renounce utterly, and say: Fly, then, false shadows of Hope; I will chase you no more, I will believe you no more. And ye too, haggard spectres of Fear, I care not for you; ye too are all shadows and a lie. Let me rest here: for I am way-weary and life-weary; I will rest here, were it but to die: to die or to live is alike to me; alike insignificant."—And again: "Here, then, as I lay in that CENTRE OF INDIFFERENCE; cast, doubtless by benignant upper Influence, into a healing sleep, the heavy dreams rolled gradually away, and I awoke to a new Heaven and a new Earth.[1] The first

4. Shady.
5. The overthrow of James II of England in 1688.
6. "Get thee hence, Satan!" (Matthew iv.8–10).
7. Bags containing documents and writings by Teufelsdröckh.
8. Light and shade.
9. A hot dry wind in Africa.
1. Revelation xxi.1.

preliminary moral Act, Annihilation of Self (*Selbsttödtung*), had been happily accomplished; and my mind's eyes were now unsealed, and its hands ungyved."[2]

Might we not also conjecture that the following passage refers to his Locality, during this same "healing sleep"; that his Pilgrim-staff lies cast aside here, on "the high table-land"; and indeed that the repose is already taking wholesome effect on him? If it were not that the tone, in some parts, has more of riancy,[3] even of levity, than we could have expected! However, in Teufelsdröckh, there is always the strangest Dualism: light dancing, with guitar-music, will be going on in the fore-court, while by fits from within comes the faint whimpering of woe and wail. We transcribe the piece entire:

"Beautiful it was to sit there, as in my skyey Tent, musing and meditating; on the high table-land, in front of the Mountains; over me, as roof, the azure Dome, and around me, for walls, four azure-flowing curtains,—namely, of the Four azure winds, on whose bottom-fringes also I have seen gilding. And then to fancy the fair Castles that stood sheltered in these Mountain hollows; with their green flower-lawns, and white dames and damosels, lovely enough: or better still, the straw-roofed Cottages, wherein stood many a Mother baking bread, with her children round her:—all hidden and protectingly folded-up in the valley-folds; yet there and alive, as sure as if I beheld them. Or to see, as well as fancy, the nine Towns and Villages, that lay round my mountain-seat, which, in still weather, were wont to speak to me (by their steeple-bells) with metal tongue; and, in almost all weather, proclaimed their vitality by repeated Smoke-clouds; whereon, as on a culinary horologe,[4] I might read the hour of the day. For it was the smoke of cookery, as kind housewives at morning, midday, eventide, were boiling their husbands' kettles; and ever a blue pillar rose up into the air, successively or simultaneously, from each of the nine, saying, as plainly as smoke could say: Such and such a meal is getting ready here. Not uninteresting! For you have the whole Borough, with all its love-makings and scandal-mongeries, contentions and content-ments, as in miniature, and could cover it all with your hat.—If, in my wide Wayfarings, I had learned to look into the business of the World in its details, here perhaps was the place for combining it into general propositions, and deducing inferences therefrom.

"Often also could I see the black Tempest marching in anger through the Distance: round some Schreckhorn,[5] as yet grim-blue, would the eddying vapour gather, and there tumultuously eddy, and flow down like a mad witch's hair; till, after a space, it vanished, and, in the clear sunbeam, your Schreckhorn stood smiling grim-

2. Unfettered.
3. Gaiety.
4. Clock.

5. "Peak of Terror." A mountain in Switzerland.

white, for the vapour had held snow. How thou fermentest and elaboratest, in thy great fermenting-vat and laboratory of an Atmosphere, of a World, O Nature!—Or what is Nature? Ha! why do I not name thee GOD? Art not thou the 'Living Garment of God'? O Heavens, is it, in very deed, HE, then, that ever speaks through thee; that lives and loves in thee, that lives and loves in me?

"Fore-shadows, call them rather fore-splendours, of that Truth, and Beginning of Truths, fell mysteriously over my soul. Sweeter than Dayspring to the Shipwrecked in Nova Zembla;[6] ah, like the mother's voice to her little child that strays bewildered, weeping, in unknown tumults; like soft streamings of celestial music to my too-exasperated heart, came that Evangel. The Universe is not dead and demoniacal, a charnel-house with spectres; but godlike, and my Father's!

"With other eyes, too, could I now look upon my fellow man; with an infinite Love, an infinite Pity. Poor, wandering, wayward man! Art thou not tired, and beaten with stripes, even as I am? Ever, whether thou bear the royal mantle or the beggar's gabardine, art thou not so weary, so heavy-laden; and thy Bed of Rest is but a Grave. O my Brother, my Brother, why cannot I shelter thee in my bosom, and wipe away all tears from thy eyes! Truly, the din of many-voiced Life, which, in this solitude, with the mind's organ, I could hear, was no longer a maddening discord, but a melting one; like inarticulate cries, and sobbings of a dumb creature, which in the ear of Heaven are prayers. The poor Earth, with her poor joys, was now my needy Mother, not my cruel Stepdame; man, with his so mad Wants and so mean Endeavours, had become the dearer to me; and even for his sufferings and his sins, I now first named him Brother. Thus I was standing in the porch of that '*Sanctuary of Sorrow*';[7] by strange, steep ways had I too been guided thither; and ere long its sacred gates would open, and the '*Divine Depth of Sorrow*' lie disclosed to me."

The Professor says, he here first got eye on the Knot that had been strangling him, and straightway could unfasten it, and was free. "A vain interminable controversy," writes he, "touching what is at present called Origin of Evil, or some such thing, arises in every soul, since the beginning of the world; and in every soul, that would pass from idle Suffering into actual Endeavouring, must first be put an end to. The most, in our time, have to go content with a simple, incomplete enough Suppression of this controversy; to a few some Solution of it is indispensable. In every new era, too, such Solution comes-out in different terms; and ever the Solution

6. A Dutch sea captain, whose ship was wrecked off the island of Nova Zembla in the Arctic in 1596, recorded in his journal his thankfulness at the coming of daylight.
7. Adapted from Goethe's *Wilhelm Meister*.

of the last era has become obsolete, and is found unserviceable. For it is man's nature to change his Dialect from century to century; he cannot help it though he would. The authentic *Church-Catechism* of our present century has not yet fallen into my hands: meanwhile, for my own private behoof, I attempt to elucidate the matter so. Man's Unhappiness, as I construe, comes of his Greatness; it is because there is an Infinite in him, which with all his cunning he cannot quite bury under the Finite. Will the whole Finance Ministers and Upholsterers and Confectioners of modern Europe undertake, in joint-stock company, to make one Shoeblack HAPPY? They cannot accomplish it, above an hour or two; for the Shoeblack also has a Soul quite other than his Stomach; and would require, if you consider it, for his permanent satisfaction and saturation, simply this allotment, no more, and no less: *God's infinite Universe altogether to himself*, therein to enjoy infinitely, and fill every wish as fast as it rose. Oceans of Hochheimer,[8] a Throat like that of Ophiuchus:[9] speak not of them; to the infinite Shoeblack they are as nothing. No sooner is your ocean filled, than he grumbles that it might have been of better vintage. Try him with half of a Universe, of an Omnipotence, he sets to quarrelling with the proprietor of the other half, and declares himself the most maltreated of men.—Always there is a black spot in our sunshine: it is even as I said, the *Shadow of Ourselves*.

"But the whim we have of Happiness is somewhat thus. By certain valuations, and averages, of our own striking, we come upon some sort of average terrestrial lot; this we fancy belongs to us by nature, and of indefeasible right. It is simple payment of our wages, of our deserts; requires neither thanks nor complaint; only such *overplus* as there may be do we account Happiness; any *deficit* again is Misery. Now consider that we have the valuation of our own deserts ourselves, and what a fund of Self-conceit there is in each of us,—do you wonder that the balance should so often dip the wrong way, and many a Blockhead cry: See there, what a payment; was ever worthy gentleman so used!—I tell thee, Blockhead, it all comes of thy Vanity; of what thou *fanciest* those same deserts of thine to be. Fancy that thou deservest to be hanged (as is most likely), thou wilt feel it happiness to be only shot: fancy that thou deservest to be hanged in a hair-halter, it will be a luxury to die in hemp.

"So true is it, what I then say, that *the Fraction of Life can be increased in value not so much by increasing your Numerator as by lessening your Denominator*. Nay, unless my Algebra deceive me, *Unity* itself divided by *Zero* will give *Infinity*. Make thy claim of wages a zero, then; thou hast the world under thy feet. Well did

8. Rhine wine or hock from Hochheim.   9. The serpent in the constellation Serpentarius.

the Wisest of our time write: 'It is only with Renunciation (*Ent-sagen*) that Life, properly speaking, can be said to begin.'[1]

"I asked myself: What is this that, ever since earliest years, thou hast been fretting and fuming, and lamenting and self-tormenting, on account of? Say it in a word: is it not because thou art not HAPPY? Because the THOU (sweet gentleman) is not sufficiently honoured, nourished, soft-bedded, and lovingly cared for? Foolish soul! What Act of Legislature was there that *thou* shouldst be Happy? A little while ago thou hadst no right to *be* at all. What if thou wert born and predestined not to be Happy, but to be Un-happy! Art thou nothing other than a Vulture, then, that fliest through the Universe seeking after somewhat to *eat*; and shrieking dolefully because carrion enough is not given thee? Close thy *Byron*; open thy *Goethe*."

"*Es leuchtet mir ein*,[2] I see a glimpse of it!" cries he elsewhere: "there is in man a HIGHER than Love of Happiness: he can do without Happiness, and instead thereof find Blessedness! Was it not to preach-forth this same HIGHER that sages and martyrs, the Poet and the Priest, in all times, have spoken and suffered; bearing testimony, through life and through death, of the Godlike that is in Man, and how in the Godlike only has he Strength and Free-dom? Which God-inspired Doctrine art thou also honoured to be taught; O Heavens! and broken with manifold merciful Afflictions, even till thou become contrite, and learn it! O, thank thy Destiny for these; thankfully bear what yet remain: thou hadst need of them; the Self in thee needed to be annihilated. By benignant fever-paroxysms is Life rooting out the deep-seated chronic Diseases, and triumphs over Death. On the roaring billows of Time, thou art not engulfed, but borne aloft into the azure of Eternity. Love not Pleasure; love God.[3] This is the EVERLASTING YEA, wherein all contradiction is solved: wherein whoso walks and works, it is well with him."

And again: "Small is it that thou canst trample the Earth with its injuries under thy feet, as old Greek Zeno[4] trained thee: thou canst love the Earth while it injures thee, and even because it in-jures thee; for this a Greater than Zeno was needed, and he too was sent. Knowest thou that '*Worship of Sorrow*'?[5] The Temple thereof, founded some eighteen centuries ago, now lies in ruins, overgrown with jungle, the habitation of doleful creatures: never-theless, venture forward; in a low crypt, arched out of falling frag-ments, thou findest the Altar still there, and its sacred Lamp peren-nially burning."

1. Adapted from *Wilhelm Meister;* "the wisest of our time" is Goethe.
2. An exclamation of Wilhelm Meister's.
3. II Timothy iii.4.
4. Greek Stoic philosopher of the 3rd century B.C. After being injured in a fall Zeno is reputed to have struck the earth with his hand as if the earth were responsible for his injury. After-wards he committed suicide. Hence he is said to "trample the Earth."
5. Christianity.

Without pretending to comment on which strange utterances, the Editor will only remark, that there lies beside them much of a still more questionable character; unsuited to the general apprehension; nay wherein he himself does not see his way. Nebulous disquisitions on Religion, yet not without bursts of splendour; on the "perennial continuance of Inspiration"; on Prophecy; that there are "true Priests, as well as Baal-Priests,[6] in our own day": with more of the like sort. We select some fractions, by way of finish to this farrago.

"Cease, my much-respected Herr von Voltaire," thus apostrophises the Professor: "shut thy sweet voice; for the task appointed thee seems finished. Sufficiently hast thou demonstrated this proposition, considerable or otherwise: That the Mythus of the Christian Religion looks not in the eighteenth century as it did in the eighth. Alas, were thy six-and-thirty quartos, and the six-and-thirty thousand other quartos and folios, and flying sheets or reams, printed before and since on the same subject, all needed to convince us of so little! But what next? Wilt thou help us to embody the divine Spirit of that Religion in a new Mythus, in a new vehicle and vesture, that our Souls, otherwise too like perishing, may live? What! thou hast no faculty in that kind? Only a torch for burning, no hammer for building? Take our thanks, then, and ——— thyself away.

"Meanwhile what are antiquated Mythuses to me? Or is the God present, felt in my own heart, a thing which Herr von Voltaire will dispute out of me; or dispute into me? To the 'Worship of Sorrow' ascribe what origin and genesis thou pleasest, *has* not that Worship originated, and been generated; is it not *here*? Feel it in thy heart, and then say whether it is of God! This is Belief; all else is Opinion, —for which latter whoso will let him worry and be worried."

"Neither," observes he elsewhere, "shall ye tear-out one another's eyes, struggling over 'Plenary Inspiration,'[7] and suchlike: try rather to get a little even Partial Inspiration, each of you for himself. One BIBLE I know, of whose Plenary Inspiration doubt is not so much as possible; nay with my own eyes I saw the God's-Hand writing it: thereof all other Bibles are but leaves,—say, in Picture-Writing to assist the weaker faculty."

Or, to give the wearied reader relief, and bring it to an end, let him take the following perhaps more intelligible passage:

"To me, in this our life," says the Professor, "which is an internecine warfare with the Time-spirit, other warfare seems questionable. Hast thou in any way a Contention with thy brother, I advise thee, think well what the meaning thereof is. If thou gauge

---

6. False priests. See I Kings xviii.17–40.
7. Doctrine: that all statements in the Bible are supernaturally inspired and authoritative. Voltaire had sought to demonstrate that this doctrine was absurd.

it to the bottom, it is simply this: 'Fellow, see! thou art taking more than thy share of Happiness in the world, something from *my* share: which, by the Heavens, thou shalt not; nay I will fight thee rather.'—Alas, and the whole lot to be divided is such a beggarly matter, truly a 'feast of shells,'[8] for the substance has been spilled out: not enough to quench one Appetite; and the collective human species clutching at them!—Can we not, in all such cases, rather say: 'Take it, thou too-ravenous individual; take that pitiful additional fraction of a share, which I reckoned mine, but which thou so wantest; take it with a blessing: would to Heaven I had enough for thee!'—If Fichte's *Wissenschaftslehre*[9] be, 'to a certain extent, Applied Christianity,' surely to a still greater extent, so is this. We have here not a Whole Duty of Man,[1] yet a Half Duty, namely the Passive half: could we but do it, as we can demonstrate it!

"But indeed Conviction, were it never so excellent, is worthless till it convert itself into Conduct. Nay properly Conviction is not possible till then; inasmuch as all Speculation is by nature endless, formless, a vortex amid vortices: only by a felt indubitable certainty of Experience does it find any centre to revolve round, and so fashion itself into a system. Most true is it, as a wise man teaches us, that 'Doubt of any sort cannot be removed except by Action.'[2] On which ground, too, let him who gropes painfully in darkness or uncertain light, and prays vehemently that the dawn may ripen into day, lay this other precept well to heart, which to me was of invaluable service: '*Do the Duty which lies nearest thee*,' which thou knowest to be a Duty! Thy second Duty will already have become clearer.

"May we not say, however, that the hour of Spiritual Enfranchisement is even this: When your Ideal World, wherein the whole man has been dimly struggling and inexpressibly languishing to work, becomes revealed, and thrown open; and you discover, with amazement enough, like the Lothario in *Wilhelm Meister*, that your 'America is here or nowhere'? The Situation that has not its Duty, its Ideal, was never yet occupied by man. Yes here, in this poor, miserable, hampered, despicable Actual, wherein thou even now standest, here or nowhere is thy Ideal: work it out therefrom; and working, believe, live, be free. Fool! the Ideal is in thyself, the impediment too is in thyself: thy Condition is but the stuff thou art to shape that same Ideal out of: what matters whether such stuff be of this sort or that, so the Form thou give it be heroic, be poetic? O thou that pinest in the imprisonment of the Actual, and criest bitterly to the gods for a kingdom wherein to rule and create, know

8. Empty eggshells.
9. "The Doctrine of Knowledge"; by the German philosopher Johann Gottlieb Fichte (1762–1814).
1. Title of an anonymous book of religious instruction first published in 1659.
2. This and the following quotation are from Goethe's *Wilhelm Meister*.

this of a truth: the thing thou seekest is already with thee, 'here or nowhere,' couldst thou only see!

"But it is with man's Soul as it was with Nature: the beginning of Creation is—Light.[3] Till the eye have vision, the whole members are in bonds.[4] Divine moment, when over the tempest-tost Soul, as once over the wild-weltering Chaos, it is spoken: Let there be Light! Ever to the greatest that has felt such moment, is it not miraculous and God-announcing; even as, under simpler figures, to the simplest and least. The mad primeval Discord is hushed; the rudely-jumbled conflicting elements bind themselves into separate Firmaments: deep silent rock-foundations are built beneath; and the skyey vault with its everlasting Luminaries above: instead of a dark wasteful Chaos, we have a blooming, fertile, heaven-encompassed World.

"I too could now say to myself: Be no longer a Chaos, but a World, or even Worldkin. Produce! Produce! Were it but the pitifullest infinitesimal fraction of a Product, produce it, in God's name! 'Tis the utmost thou hast in thee: out with it, then. Up, up! Whatsoever thy hand findeth to do, do it with thy whole might. Work while it is called Today; for the Night cometh, wherein no man can work."[5]

1830–31   1833–34

From The French Revolution[1]

September in Paris[2]

The tocsin is pealing its loudest, the clocks inaudibly striking *Three,* when poor Abbé Sicard,[3] with some thirty other Nonjurant

3. Cf. Genesis i.3.
4. Cf. Matthew vi.22–23.
5. Adapted from Ecclesiastes ix.10 and John ix.4.
1. To tell the story of the French Revolution, Carlyle uses an imaginary reporter as his narrator. This reporter voices the feelings of the revolutionary party. At times he expresses pity towards the victims of the revolution, but for the most part he is at one with the force he calls "Patriotism," praising those leaders who are ardently dedicated to overthrowing the corrupt feudal order. He thus speaks appropriately in the first person plural: "Give *us* arms." This method of day-to-day eyewitnessing of events contributes to the effect of immediacy that Carlyle sought in what he himself called his "wild savage Book, itself a kind of French Revolution."
A second feature of his method is the device of weaving into the narrative a number of direct quotations from the sources he had consulted during the three years devoted to writing the his-

tory. Although later historians have been able to point out inaccuracies in *The French Revolution,* Carlyle did base his account on extensive researches. G. M. Trevelyan has said of him that he was not only a great writer but also "in his own strange way, a great historian." Perhaps the most satisfactory comment on *The French Revolution* is J. S. Mill's statement in his review of 1837: "This is not so much a history as an epic poem, and notwithstanding * * * the truest of histories."
2. Part III, Book 1, Chapter iv. In September, 1792, the revolutionary party under Georges Jacques Danton and Jean Paul Marat urged desperate measures to defend Paris from the invading armies of Austria and Prussia. Hysterical fears of a counterrevolutionary "fifth column" in Paris led to the so-called September Massacres, in which 1,400 political prisoners were slaughtered in four days.
3. The head of a school for the deaf and dumb in Paris; he died in 1822.

Priests,[4] in six carriages, fare along the streets, from their preliminary House of Detention at the Townhall, westward towards the
Prison of the Abbaye. Carriages enough stand deserted on the
streets; these six move on,—through angry multitudes, cursing as
they move. Accursed Aristocrat Tartuffes,[5] this is the pass ye have
brought us to! And now ye will break the Prisons, and set Capet
Veto[6] on horseback to ride over us? Out upon you, Priests of
Beelzebub and Moloch; of Tartuffery, Mammon and the Prussian
Gallows,—which ye name Mother-Church and God!—Such reproaches have the poor Nonjurants to endure, and worse; spoken
in on them by frantic Patriots, who mount even on the carriage-
steps; the very Guards hardly refraining. Pull up your carriage-
blinds?—No! answers Patriotism, clapping its horny paw on the car-
riage-blind, and crushing it down again. Patience in oppression has
limits: we are close on the Abbaye, it has lasted long: a poor Nonjurant, of quicker temper, smites the horny paw with his cane; nay,
finding solacement in it, smites the unkempt head, sharply and
again more sharply, twice over,—seen clearly of us and of the
world. It is the last that we see clearly. Alas, next moment, the
carriages are locked and blocked in endless raging tumults; in yells
deaf to the cry for mercy, which answer the cry for mercy with
sabre-thrusts through the heart. The thirty Priests are torn out, are
massacred about the Prison-Gate, one after one,—only the poor
Abbé Sicard, whom one Moton a watchmaker, knowing him, heroically tried to save and secrete in the Prison, escapes to tell;—and
it is Night and Orcus,[7] and Murder's snaky-sparkling head *has* risen
in the murk!—

From Sunday afternoon (exclusive of intervals and pauses not
final) till Thursday evening, there follow consecutively a Hundred
Hours. Which hundred hours are to be reckoned with the hours
of the Bartholomew Butchery, of the Armagnac Massacres, Sicilian
Vespers, or whatsoever is savagest in the annals of this world. Horrible the hour when man's soul, in its paroxysm, spurns asunder the
barriers and rules; and shows what dens and depths are in it! For
Night and Orcus, as we say, as was long prophesied, have burst
forth, here in this Paris, from their subterranean imprisonment:
hideous, dim-confused; which it is painful to look on; and yet
which cannot, and indeed which should not, be forgotten.

The Reader, who looks earnestly through this dim Phantasmagory
of the Pit, will discern few fixed certain objects; and yet still a few.

4. Priests who had refused to swear
allegiance to the new church constitution established by the National Assembly in 1791.
5. Hypocrites (from the title of
Molière's play).
6. I.e., the king (Louis XVI). The
"Nonjurant Priests" were accused of
favoring the restoration to the king of
his power to veto legislation, a power
he had lost after August 10, 1792. At
the same time he had been stripped of
his royal titles and was thereafter referred to simply as Louis Capet, the
family name of an early dynasty of
French kings (Louis XVI was a Bourbon).
7. Hades, the underworld of the dead.

He will observe, in this Abbaye Prison, the sudden massacre of the Priests being once over, a strange Court of Justice, or call it Court of Revenge and Wild-Justice, swiftly fashion itself, and take seat round a table, with the Prison-Registers spread before it;—Stanislas Maillard, Bastille-hero, famed Leader of the Menads,[8] presiding. O Stanislas, one hoped to meet thee elsewhere than here; thou shifty Riding-Usher, with an inkling of Law! This work also thou hadst to do; and then—to depart for ever from our eyes. At *La Force*, at the *Châtelet*, the *Conciergerie*, the like Court forms itself, with the like accompaniments: the thing that one man does, other men can do. There are some Seven Prisons in Paris, full of Aristocrats with conspiracies;—nay not even *Bicêtre* and *Salpêtrière* shall escape, with their Forgers of Assignats:[9] and there are seventy times seven hundred Patriot hearts in a state of frenzy. Scoundrel hearts also there are; as perfect, say, as the Earth holds,—if such are needed. To whom, in this mood, law is as no-law; and killing, by what name soever called, is but work to be done.

So sit these sudden Courts of Wild-Justice, with the Prison-Registers before them; unwonted wild tumult howling all round; the Prisoners in dread expectancy within. Swift: a name is called; bolts jingle, a Prisoner is there. A few questions are put; swiftly this sudden Jury decides: Royalist Plotter or not? Clearly not; in that case, Let the Prisoner be enlarged with *Vive la Nation*. Probably yea; then still, Let the Prisoner be enlarged, but without *Vive la Nation*; or else it may run. Let the Prisoner be conducted to La Force. At La Force again their formula is, Let the Prisoner be conducted to the Abbaye.—"To La Force then!" Volunteer bailiffs seize the doomed man; he is at the outer gate; "enlarged," or "conducted," not into La Force, but into a howling sea; forth, under an arch of wild sabres, axes and pikes; and sinks, hewn asunder. And another sinks, and another; and there forms itself a piled heap of corpses, and the kennels begin to run red. Fancy the yells of these men, their faces of sweat and blood; the crueller shrieks of these women, for there are women too; and a fellow-mortal hurled naked into it all! Jourgniac de Saint-Méard has seen battle, has seen an effervescent Regiment du Roi in mutiny; but the bravest heart may quail at this. The Swiss Prisoners, remnants of the Tenth of August,[1] "clasped each other spasmodically, and hung back; grey veterans crying: 'Mercy, Messieurs; ah, mercy!' But there was no mercy. Suddenly, however, one of these men steps forward. He had on a blue frock coat; he seemed about thirty, his stature was above common, his look noble and martial. 'I go first,' said he,

8. Frenzied women of Greece, followers of Dionysus. Maillard had led a mob of women in the march to Versailles in October, 1789.
9. Paper money issued by the French revolutionary government. Royalists accused of forging such currency had been imprisoned.
1. Remnants of the Swiss Guards, most of whom had been massacred on August 10, 1792, when defending the king's palace from a mob.

'since it must be so: adieu!' Then dashing his hat sharply behind
him: 'Which way?' cried he to the Brigands: 'Show it me, then.'
They open the folding gate; he is announced to the multitude. He
stands a moment motionless; then plunges forth among the pikes,
and dies of a thousand wounds."

Man after man is cut down; the sabres need sharpening, the killers refresh themselves from wine-jugs. Onward and onward goes
the butchery; the loud yells wearying down into bass growls. A
sombre-faced shifting multitude looks on; in dull approval, or dull
disapproval; in dull recognition that it is Necessity. "An *Anglais*
in drab greatcoat" was seen, or seemed to be seen, serving liquor
from his own drambottle;—for what purpose, "if not set on by
Pitt," Satan and himself know best! Witty Dr. Moore grew sick
on approaching, and turned into another street.—Quick enough
goes this Jury-Court; and rigorous. The brave are not spared, nor
the beautiful, nor the weak. Old M. de Montmorin, the Minister's
Brother, was acquitted by the Tribunal of the Seventeenth; and
conducted back, elbowed by howling galleries; but is not acquitted
here. Princess de Lamballe[2] has lain down on bed: "Madame, you
are to be removed to the Abbaye." "I do not wish to remove; I
am well enough here." There is a need-be for removing. She will
arrange her dress a little, then; rude voices answer, "You have not
far to go." She too is led to the hell-gate; a manifest Queen's-Friend.
She shivers back, at the sight of bloody sabres; but there is no return: Onwards! That fair hind head is cleft with the axe; the neck
is severed. That fair body is cut in fragments; with indignities, and
obscene horrors of moustachio *grands-lèvres*,[3] which human nature
would fain find incredible,—which shall be read in the original
language only. She was beautiful, she was good, she had known
no happiness. Young hearts, generation after generation, will think
with themselves: O worthy of worship, thou king-descended, god-
descended, and poor sister-woman! why was not I there; and some
Sword Balmung[4] or Thor's Hammer in my hand? Her head is fixed
on a pike; paraded under the windows of the Temple; that a still
more hated, a Marie Antoinette, may see. One Municipal, in the
Temple with the Royal Prisoners at the moment, said, "Look out."
Another eagerly whispered, "Do not look." The circuit of the Temple is guarded, in these hours, by a long stretched tricolor riband:
terror enters, and the clangour of infinite tumult; hitherto not
regicide, though that too may come.

But it is more edifying to note what thrillings of affection, what
fragments of wild virtues turn up in this shaking asunder of man's

2. Great-granddaughter of the King
of Sardinia; she had married a Bourbon, was early widowed, and later became a close friend of Queen Marie
Antoinette, with whom she had been
imprisoned.
3. "Thick lips"—a figure of speech to
characterize the mob.
4. The sharp sword of Siegfried, hero
of the *Nibelungenlied*.

existence; for of these too there is a proportion. Note old Marquis Cazotte: he is doomed to die; but his young Daughter clasps him in her arms, with an inspiration of eloquence, with a love which is stronger than very death: the heart of the killers themselves is touched by it; the old man is spared. Yet he was guilty, if plotting for his King is guilt: in ten days more, a Court of Law condemned him, and he had to die elsewhere; bequeathing his Daughter a lock of his old grey hair. Or note old M. de Sombreuil, who also had a Daughter:—My Father is not an Aristocrat: O good gentlemen, I will swear it, and testify it, and in all ways prove it; we are not; we hate Aristocrats! "Wilt thou drink Aristocrats' blood?" The man lifts blood (if universal Rumour can be credited); the poor maiden does drink. "This Sombreuil is innocent then!" Yes, indeed,—and now note, most of all, how the bloody pikes, at this news, do rattle to the ground; and the tiger-yells become bursts of jubilee over a brother saved; and the old man and his daughter are clasped to bloody bosoms, with hot tears; and borne home in triumph of V*ive la Nation*, the killers refusing even money! Does it seem strange, this temper of theirs? It seems very certain, well proved by Royalist testimony in other instances; and very significant.

Place de la Révolution[1]

To this conclusion, then, hast thou come, O hapless Louis! The Son of Sixty Kings is to die on the Scaffold by form of Law. Under Sixty Kings this same form of Law, form of Society, has been fashioning itself together, these thousand years; and has become, one way and other, a most strange Machine. Surely, if needful, it is also frightful, this Machine; dead, blind; not what it should be; which, with swift stroke, or by cold slow torture, has wasted the lives and souls of innumerable men. And behold now a King himself, or say rather Kinghood in his person, is to expire here in cruel tortures;—like a Phalaris[2] shut in the belly of his own red-heated Brazen Bull! It is ever so; and thou shouldst know it, O haughty tyrannous man: injustice breeds injustice; curses and falsehoods do verily return "always *home*," wide as they may wander. Innocent Louis bears the sins of many generations: he too experiences that man's tribunal is not in this Earth; that if he had no Higher one, it were not well with him.

A King dying by such violence appeals impressively to the imagination; as the like must do, and ought to do. And yet at bottom it is not the King dying, but the man! Kingship is a coat: the grand loss is of the skin. The man from whom you take his Life, to him

1. Part III, Book 2, Chapter viii. On January 20, 1793, by a small majority, the Convention of Delegates in Paris had voted for the death of the king.

2. A Sicilian tyrant whose victims were roasted alive by being confined inside the brass figure of a bull under which a fire was lit.

can the whole combined world do *more?* Lally[3] went on his hurdle; his mouth filled with a gag. Miserablest mortals, doomed for picking pockets, have a whole five-act Tragedy in them, in that dumb pain, as they go to the gallows, unregarded; they consume the cup of trembling down to the lees. For Kings and for Beggars, for the justly doomed and the unjustly, it is a hard thing to die. Pity them all: thy utmost pity, with all aids and appliances and throne-and-scaffold contrasts, how far short is it of the thing pitied!

A Confessor has come; Abbé Edgeworth, of Irish extraction, whom the King knew by good report, has come promptly on this solemn mission. Leave the Earth alone, then, thou hapless King; it with its malice will go its way, thou also canst go thine. A hard scene yet remains: the parting with our loved ones. Kind hearts, environed in the same grim peril with us; to be left *here!* Let the Reader look with the eyes of Valet Cléry,[4] through these glass-doors, where also the Municipality watches; and see the cruellest of scenes:

"At half-past eight, the door of the ante-room opened: the Queen appeared first, leading her Son by the hand; then Madame Royale[5] and Madame Elizabeth: they all flung themselves into the arms of the King. Silence reigned for some minutes; interrupted only by sobs. The Queen made a movement to lead his Majesty towards the inner room, where M. Edgeworth was waiting unknown to them: 'No,' said the King, 'let us go into the dining-room, it is there only that I can see you.' They entered there; I shut the door of it, which was of glass. The King sat down, the Queen on his left hand, Madame Elizabeth on his right, Madame Royale almost in front; the young Prince remained standing between his Father's legs. They all leaned towards him, and often held him embraced. This scene of woe lasted an hour and three quarters; during which we could hear nothing; we could see only that always when the King spoke, the sobbings of the Princesses redoubled, continued for some minutes; and that then the King began again to speak." —And so our meetings and our partings do now end! The sorrows we gave each other; the poor joys we faithfully shared, and all our lovings and our sufferings, and confused toilings under the earthly Sun, are over. Thou good soul, I shall never, never through all ages of Time, see thee any more!—NEVER! O Reader, knowest thou that hard word?

For nearly two hours this agony lasts; then they tear themselves asunder. "Promise that you will see us on the morrow." He promises:—Ah yes, yes; yet once; and go now, ye loved ones; cry to God

3. A French general who was accused unjustly of treachery and executed in 1766. The gag in his mouth was presumably to prevent his protesting his innocence.
4. The valet who attended the king dur-

ing his imprisonment and who later published a journal.
5. The king's daughter, the Duchesse d'Angoulême (1778–1851); Madame Elizabeth was the king's sister, guillotined a year later.

for yourselves and me!—It was a hard scene, but it is over. He will not see them on the morrow. The Queen, in passing through the ante-room, glanced at the Cerberus Municipals;[6] and, with woman's vehemence, said through her tears, "*Vous êtes tous des scélérats.*"[7]

King Louis slept sound, till five in the morning, when Cléry, as he had been ordered, awoke him. Cléry dressed his hair: while this went forward, Louis took a ring from his watch, and kept trying it on his finger; it was his wedding-ring, which he is now to return to the Queen as a mute farewell. At half-past six, he took the Sacrament; and continued in devotion, and conference with Abbé Edgeworth. He will not see his Family: it were too hard to bear.

At eight, the Municipals enter: the King gives them his Will, and messages and effects; which they, at first, brutally refuse to take charge of: he gives them a roll of gold pieces, a hundred and twenty-five louis; these are to be returned to Malesherbes,[8] who had lent them. At nine, Santerre[9] says the hour is come. The King begs yet to retire for three minutes. At the end of three minutes, Santerre again says the hour is come. "Stamping on the ground with his right foot, Louis answers: '*Partons*, Let us go.' "—How the rolling of those drums comes in, through the Temple bastions and bulwarks, on the heart of a queenly wife; soon to be a widow! He is gone, then, and has not seen us? A Queen weeps bitterly; a King's Sister and Children. Over all these Four does Death also hover: all shall perish miserably save one; she, as Duchesse d'Angoulême, will live,—not happily.

At the Temple Gate were some faint cries, perhaps from voices of Pitiful women: "*Grâce!*[1] *Grâce!*" Through the rest of the streets there is silence as of the grave. No man not armed is allowed to be there: the armed, did any even pity, dare not express it, each man overawed by all his neighbours. All windows are down, none seen looking through them. All shops are shut. No wheel-carriage rolls, this morning, in these streets but one only. Eighty-thousand armed men stand ranked, like armed statues of men; cannons bristle, cannoneers with match burning, but no word or movement: it is as a city enchanted into silence and stone: one carriage with its escort, slowly rumbling, is the only sound. Louis reads, in his Book of Devotion, the Prayers of the Dying: clatter of this death-march falls sharp on the ear, in the great silence; but the thought would fain struggle heavenward, and forget the Earth.

As the clocks strike ten, behold the Place de la Révolution, once Place de Louis Quinze: the Guillotine, mounted near the old

---

6. Municipal officers, likened to Cerberus, the three-headed dog that guarded the entrance to Hades.
7. "You are all scoundrels."
8. A delegate who had defended the king. He was guillotined a year later.
9. A Jacobin leader who commanded the troops in Paris.
1. "Mercy!"

Pedestal where once stood the Statue of that Louis! Far round, all bristles with cannons and armed men: spectators crowding in the rear; D'Orléans Égalité[2] there in cabriolet. Swift messengers, *hoquetons*, speed to the Townhall, every three minutes: near by is the Convention sitting,—vengeful for Lepelletier.[3] Heedless of all, Louis reads his Prayers of the Dying; not till five minutes yet has he finished; then the Carriage opens. What temper he is in? Ten different witnesses will give ten different accounts of it. He is in the collision of all tempers; arrived now at the black Mahlstrom and descent of Death: in sorrow, in indignation, in resignation struggling to be resigned. "Take care of M. Edgeworth," he straitly charges the Lieutenant who is sitting with them: then they two descend.

The drums are beating: "*Taisez-vous*, Silence!" he cries "in a terrible voice, *d'une voix terrible*." He mounts the scaffold, not without delay; he is in puce[4] coat, breeches of grey, white stockings. He strips off the coat; stands disclosed in a sleeve-waistcoat of white flannel. The Executioners approach to bind him: he spurns, resists; Abbé Edgeworth has to remind him how the Saviour, in whom men trust, submitted to be bound. His hands are tied, his head bare; the fatal moment is come. He advances to the edge of the Scaffold, "his face very red," and says: "Frenchmen, I die innocent: it is from the Scaffold and near appearing before God that I tell you so. I pardon my enemies; I desire that France——" A General on horseback, Santerre or another, prances out, with uplifted hand: "*Tambours!*" The drums drown the voice. "Executioners, do your duty!" The Executioners, desperate lest themselves be murdered (for Santerre and his Armed Ranks will strike, if they do not), seize the hapless Louis: six of them desperate, him singly desperate, struggling there; and bind him to their plank. Abbé Edgeworth, stooping, bespeaks him: "Son of Saint Louis,[5] ascend to Heaven." The Axe clanks down; a King's Life is shorn away. It is Monday the 21st of January 1793. He was aged Thirty-eight years four months and twenty-eight days.

Executioner Samson shows the Head: fierce shout of *Vive la République* rises, and swells; caps raised on bayonets, hats waving: students of the College of Four Nations take it up, on the far Quais; fling it over Paris. D'Orléans drives off in his cabriolet: the Townhall Councillors rub their hands, saying, "It is done, It is done." There is dipping of handkerchiefs, of pike-points in the blood. Headsman Samson, though he afterwards denied it, sells locks of the hair: fractions of the puce coat are long after worn in

2. The Duc d'Orléans, a Royalist who had become a revolutionary leader, was called Égalité (Equality). Despite his having voted for the king's death, he was himself executed in 1793.
3. A delegate who had voted for the king's death and was killed by a Royalist sympathizer.
4. Dull red.
5. Louis IX, king of France (reigned 1226–70).

rings.—And so, in some half-hour it is done; and the multitude has all departed. Pastry-cooks, coffee-sellers, milkmen sing out their trivial quotidian cries: the world wags on, as if this were a common day. In the coffee-houses that evening, says Prudhomme, Patriot shook hands with Patriot in a more cordial manner than usual. Not till some days after, according to Mercier, did public men see what a grave thing it was.

From *Cause and Effect*[1]

* * * Yes, Reader, here is the miracle. Out of that putrescent rubbish of Scepticism, Sensualism, Sentimentalism, hollow Machiavelism, such a Faith has verily risen; flaming in the heart of a People. A whole People, awakening as it were to consciousness in deep misery, believes that it is within reach of a Fraternal Heaven-on-Earth. With longing arms, it struggles to embrace the Unspeakable; cannot embrace it, owing to certain causes.—Seldom do we find that a whole People can be said to have any Faith at all; except in things which it can eat and handle. Whensoever it gets any Faith, its history becomes spirit-stirring, noteworthy. But since the time when steel Europe shook itself simultaneously at the word of Hermit Peter,[2] and rushed towards the Sepulchre where God had lain, there was no universal impulse of Faith that one could note. Since Protestantism went silent, no Luther's voice, no Zisca's[3] drum any longer proclaiming that God's truth was *not* the Devil's Lie; and the Last of the Cameronians[4] (Renwick was the name of him; honour to the name of the brave!) sank, shot, on the Castle-hill of Edinburgh, there was no partial impulse of Faith among Nations. Till now, behold, once more, this French Nation believes! Herein, we say, in that astonishing Faith of theirs, lies the miracle. It is a Faith undoubtedly of the more prodigious sort, even among Faiths; and will embody itself in prodigies. It is the soul of that world-prodigy named French Revolution; whereat the world still gazes and shudders.

But, for the rest, let no man ask History to explain by cause and effect how the business proceeded henceforth. This battle of Mountain and Gironde,[5] and what follows, is the battle of Fanaticisms

---

1. Part III, Book 3, Chapter i. Between the execution of the king and the advent of Napoleon, the revolutionary movement in France suffered from dissension and counterrevolutionary outbreaks which led to the Reign of Terror (1793–94). During this period most of the political leaders and thousands of their followers lost their lives. Before recommencing his narrative, Carlyle pauses, in this chapter, to consider some of the forces underlying these developments.
2. Leader of the First Crusade to Palestine in the late 11th century.
3. Ca. 1360–1424; successful general and leader of the Hussites, a religious sect in Bohemia.
4. A 17th-century Scottish sect. See Sir Walter Scott's novel, *The Heart of Midlothian.*
5. The Girondists were a party of moderate revolutionaries, often of middle-class backgrounds. They were liquidated (as the Marxists say) by their opponents, the Jacobins, who were more adept in controlling the populace. Because the Jacobin delegates in the Na-

and Miracles; unsuitable for cause and effect. The sound of it, to the mind, is as a hubbub of voices in distraction; little of articulate is to be gathered by long listening and studying; only battle-tumult, shouts of triumph, shrieks of despair. The Mountain has left no Memoirs; the Girondins have left Memoirs, which are too often little other than long-drawn Interjections, of *Woe is me,* and *Cursed be ye*. So soon as History can philosophically delineate the conflagration of a kindled Fireship,[6] she may try this other task. Here lay the bitumen-stratum, there the brimstone one; so ran the vein of gunpowder, of nitre, terebinth[7] and foul grease: this, were she inquisitive enough, History might partly know. But how they acted and reacted below decks, one fire-stratum playing into the other, by its nature and the art of man, now when all hands ran raging, and the flames lashed high over shrouds and topmast: this let not History attempt.

The Fireship is old France, the old French Form of Life; her crew a Generation of men. Wild are their cries and their ragings there, like spirits tormented in that flame. But, on the whole, are they not *gone,* O Reader? Their Fireship and they, frightening the world, have sailed away; its flames and its thunders quite away, into the Deep of Time. One thing therefore History will do: pity them all; for it went hard with them all. Not even the seagreen Incorruptible[8] but shall have some pity, some human love, though it takes an effort. And now, so much once thoroughly attained, the rest will become easier. To the eye of equal brotherly pity, innumerable perversions dissipate themselves; exaggerations and execrations fall off, of their own accord. Standing wistfully on the safe shore, we will look, and see, what is of interest to us, what is adapted to us.

1834–37   1837

---

tional Assembly sat in the most elevated place, the party was sometimes called the "Mountain."
6. A ship filled with combustibles (such as gunpowder and brimstone) which is set adrift among enemy ship-

ping to create havoc.
7. Turpentine.
8. Maximilien Robespierre, "the Incorruptible"; chief of the Jacobin party and principal instigator of the Reign of Terror.

From Past and Present[1]

From *Democracy*

If the Serene Highnesses and Majesties do not take note of that,[2] then, as I perceive, *that* will take note of itself! The time for levity, insincerity, and idle babble and play-acting, in all kinds, is gone by; it is a serious, grave time. Old long-vexed questions, not yet solved in logical words or parliamentary laws, are fast solving themselves in facts, somewhat unblessed to behold! This largest of questions, this question of Work and Wages, which ought, had we heeded Heaven's voice, to have begun two generations ago or more, cannot be delayed longer without hearing Earth's voice. "Labour" will verily need to be somewhat "organized," as they say,—God knows with what difficulty. Man will actually need to have his debts and earnings a little better paid by man; which, let Parliaments speak of them, or be silent of them, are eternally his due from man, and cannot, without penalty and at length not without death-penalty,[3] be withheld. How much ought to cease among us straightway; how much ought to begin straightway, while the hours yet are!

Truly they are strange results to which this of leaving all to "Cash"; of quietly shutting up the God's Temple, and gradually opening wide-open the Mammon's Temple, with "Laissez-faire, and Every man for himself,"—have led us in these days! We have Upper, speaking Classes, who indeed do "speak" as never man spake before; the withered flimsiness, godless baseness and barrenness of whose Speech might of itself indicate what kind of Doing and practical Governing went on under it! For Speech is the gaseous element out of which most kinds of Practice and Performance,

1. In 1842 there were reputedly 1.5 million unemployed in England (out of a population of 18 million). The closing of factories and the reduction of wages led to severe rioting in the manufacturing districts. Bread-hungry mobs (as well as the Chartist mobs who demanded political reforms) caused many observers to dread that a large-scale revolution was imminent. Carlyle was himself so appalled by the plight of the industrial workers that he postponed his researches into the life and times of Cromwell in order to air his views on the contemporary crisis. *Past and Present*, a book written in seven weeks, was a call for heroic leadership. Cromwell and other historic leaders are cited, but the principal example from the past is Abbot Samson, a medieval monk who established order in the monasteries under his charge. Carlyle hoped that the "Captains of Industry"

might provide a comparable leadership in 1843. He was aware that the spread of democracy was inevitable, but he had little confidence in it as a method of producing leaders. Nor did he have any confidence, at this time, in the landed aristocracy who seemed to him preoccupied with fox-hunting, preserving their game, and upholding the tariffs on grain (the Corn Laws). In place of a "Do nothing Aristocracy" there was need for a "Working Aristocracy." The first selection here printed is from Book III, Chapter 13.

2. The previous chapter, "Reward," had urged that English manufacturers needed the help of everyone, and that Parliament should remove the tariffs (Corn Laws) restricting the growth of trade and industry.

3. I.e., by the outbreak of a revolution, as in France.

especially all kinds of moral Performance, condense themselves, and take shape; as the one is, so will the other be. Descending, accordingly, into the Dumb Class in its Stockport Cellars[4] and Poor-Law Bastilles,[5] have we not to announce that they are hitherto unexampled in the History of Adam's Posterity?

Life was never a May-game for men: in all times the lot of the dumb millions born to toil was defaced with manifold sufferings, injustices, heavy burdens, avoidable and unavoidable; not play at all, but hard work that made the sinews sore and the heart sore. As bond-slaves, *villani, bordarii, sochemanni,* nay indeed as dukes, earls and kings, men were oftentimes made weary of their life; and had to say, in the sweat of their brow and of their soul, Behold, it is not sport, it is grim earnest, and our back can bear no more! Who knows not what massacrings and harryings there have been; grinding, long-continuing, unbearable injustices,—till the heart had to rise in madness, and some *"Eu Sachsen, nimith euer sachses,* You Saxons, out with your gully-knives, then!" You Saxons, some "arrestment," partial "arrestment of the Knaves and Dastards" has become indispensable!—The page of Dryasdust[6] is heavy with such details.

And yet I will venture to believe that in no time, since the beginnings of Society, was the lot of those same dumb millions of toilers so entirely unbearable as it is even in the days now passing over us. It is not to die, or even to die of hunger, that makes a man wretched; many men have died; all men must die,—the last exit of us all is in a Fire-Chariot of Pain.[7] But it is to live miserable we know not why; to work sore and yet gain nothing; to be heartworn, weary, yet isolated, unrelated, girt-in with a cold universal Laissez-faire: it is to die slowly all our life long, imprisoned in a deaf, dead, Infinite Injustice, as in the accursed iron belly of a Phalaris' Bull![8] This is and remains for ever intolerable to all men whom God has made. Do we wonder at French Revolutions, Chartisms, Revolts of Three Days? The times, if we will consider them, are really unexampled.

Never before did I hear of an Irish Widow reduced to "prove her sisterhood by dying of typhus-fever and infecting seventeen persons,"—saying in such undeniable way, "You *see,* I was your sister!"[9] Sisterhood, brotherhood, was often forgotten; but not till the rise of these ultimate Mammon and Shotbelt Gospels[1] did I ever

4. In a cellar in the slum district of Stockport, an industrial town near Manchester, three children were poisoned by their starving parents in order to collect insurance benefits from a burial society.
5. I.e. workhouse for the unemployed.
6. An imaginary author of dull histories.
7. Cf. II Kings ii.11–12.
8. Phalaris was a Sicilian tyrant whose victims were roasted alive by being confined inside the brass figure of a bull under which a fire was lit.
9. An incident referred to several times in *Past and Present.* Dickens in *Bleak House* also showed how indifference to the lack of sanitation in London slums led to the spread of disease to other parts of the city.
1. "Mammon Gospel" signifies the pursuit of wealth according to the eco-

see it so expressly denied. If no pious Lord or *Law-ward* would re-member it, always some pious Lady (*"Hlaf dig,"* Benefactress, *"Loaf-giveress,"* they say she is,—blessings on her beautiful heart!) was there, with mild mother-voice and hand, to remember it; some pious thoughtful *Elder,* what we now call "Prester," *Presbyter* or "Priest," was there to put all men in mind of it, in the name of the God who had made all.

Not even in Black Dahomey[2] was it ever, I think, forgotten to the typhus-fever length. Mungo Park,[3] resourceless, had sunk down to die under the Negro Village-Tree, a horrible White object in the eyes of all. But in the poor Black Woman, and her daughter who stood aghast at him, whose earthly wealth and funded capital consisted of one small calabash of rice, there lived a heart richer than *"Laissez-faire"*: they, with a royal munificence, boiled their rice for him; they sang all night to him, spinning assiduous on their cotton distaffs, as he lay to sleep: "Let us pity the poor white man; no mother has he to fetch him milk, no sister to grind him corn!" Thou poor black Noble One,—thou *Lady* too: did not a God make thee too; was there not in thee too something of a God!—

Gurth,[4] born thrall of Cedric the Saxon, has been greatly pitied by Dryasdust and others. Gurth, with the brass collar round his neck, tending Cedric's pigs in the glades of the wood, is not what I call an exemplar of human felicity: but Gurth, with the sky above him, with the free air and tinted boscage and umbrage round him, and in him at least the certainty of supper and social lodging when he came home; Gurth to me seems happy, in comparison with many a Lancashire and Buckinghamshire man, of these days, not born thrall of anybody! Gurth's brass collar did not gall him: Cedric *deserved* to be his Master. The pigs were Cedric's, but Gurth too would get his parings of them. Gurth had the inexpressible satisfaction of feeling himself related indissolubly, though in a rude brass-collar way, to his fellow-mortals in this Earth. He had superiors, inferiors, equals.—Gurth is now "emancipated" long since; has what we call "Liberty." Liberty, I am told, is a Divine thing. Liberty when it becomes the "Liberty to die by starvation" is not so divine!

Liberty? The true liberty of a man, you would say, consisted in his finding out, or being forced to find out, the right path, and to walk thereon. To learn, or to be taught, what work he actually was able for; and then by permission, persuasion, and even compulsion, to set about doing of the same! That is his true blessed-

nomic code of laissez faire, whereby no one took the responsibility of caring for the starving widow. The meaning of "Shotbelt" has not been identified.

2. A state in west Africa where savage customs, such as human sacrifice and

cannibalism, persisted.

3. Explorer and author of *Travels in the Interior of Africa* (1799). In 1806 he was killed by African natives.

4. A swineherd described in Scott's *Ivanhoe.*

ness, honour, "liberty" and maximum of wellbeing: if liberty be not that, I for one have small care about liberty. You do not allow a palpable madman to leap over precipices; you violate his liberty, you that are wise; and keep him, were it in strait-waistcoats, away from the precipices! Every stupid, every cowardly and foolish man is but a less palpable madman: his true liberty were that a wiser man, that any and every wiser man, could, by brass collars, or in whatever milder or sharper way, lay hold of him when he was going wrong, and order and compel him to go a little righter. O, if thou really art my *Senior*, Seigneur, my *Elder*, Presbyter or Priest, —if thou art in very deed my *Wiser*, may a beneficent instinct lead and impel thee to "conquer" me, to command me! If thou do know better than I what is good and right, I conjure thee in the name of God, force me to do it; were it by never such brass collars, whips and handcuffs, leave me not to walk over precipices! That I have been called, by all the Newspapers, a "free man" will avail me little, if my pilgrimage have ended in death and wreck. O that the Newspapers had called me slave, coward, fool, or what it pleased their sweet voices to name me, and I had attained not death, but life!—Liberty requires new definitions.

A conscious abhorrence and intolerance of Folly, of Baseness, Stupidity, Poltroonery and all that brood of things, dwells deep in some men: still deeper in others an *un*conscious abhorrence and intolerance, clothed moreover by the beneficent Supreme Powers in what stout appetites, energies, egoisms so-called, are suitable to it;—these latter are your Conquerors, Romans, Normans, Russians, Indo-English; Founders of what we call Aristocracies. Which indeed have they not the most "divine right" to found;—being themselves very truly Ἄριστοι, BRAVEST, BEST; and conquering generally a confused rabble of WORST, or at lowest, clearly enough, of WORSE? I think their divine right, tried, with affirmatory verdict, in the greatest Law-Court known to me, was good! A class of men who are dreadfully exclaimed against by Dryasdust; of whom nevertheless beneficent Nature has oftentimes had need; and may, alas, again have need.

When, across the hundredfold poor scepticisms, trivialisms, and constitutional cobwebberies of Dryasdust, you catch any glimpse of a William the Conqueror,[5] a Tancred of Hauteville[6] or such like,—do you not discern veritably some rude outline of a true God-made King; whom not the Champion of England[7] cased in

---

5. King William I of England (reigned 1066–87), surnamed the Conqueror after the Battle of Hastings in 1066. Being an illegitimate son, he also bore the surname of William the Bastard. Although some historians condemn William as a ruthless ruler, he is ranked . by Carlyle as a hero because of his strong and efficient government. Wil-

liam fulfilled the requirements of the kingly hero described by Carlyle in his lectures *On Heroes:* a man fittest "to *command* over us * * * to tell us what we are to *do.*"
6. Norman hero of the First Crusade.
7. An official who goes through a formality, at coronation ceremonies, of demanding whether anyone challenges

tin, but all Nature and the Universe were calling to the throne?
It is absolutely necessary that he get thither. Nature does not mean
her poor Saxon children to perish, of obesity, stupor or other malady, as yet: a stern Ruler and Line of Rulers therefore is called in,
—a stern but most beneficent *perpetual House-Surgeon* is by Nature herself called in, and even the appropriate *fees* are provided
for him! Dryasdust talks lamentably about Hereward[8] and the Fen
Counties; fate of Earl Waltheof;[9] Yorkshire and the North reduced
to ashes; all of which is undoubtedly lamentable. But even Dryasdust apprises me of one fact: "A child, in this William's reign,
might have carried a purse of gold from end to end of England."
My erudite friend, it is a fact which outweighs a thousand! Sweep
away thy constitutional, sentimental, and other cobwebberies; look
eye to eye, if thou still have any eye, in the face of this big burly
William Bastard: thou wilt see a fellow of most flashing discernment, of most strong lion-heart;—in whom, as it were, within a
frame of oak and iron, the gods have planted the soul of "a man
of genius"! Dost thou call that nothing? I call it an immense thing!
—Rage enough was in this Willelmus Conquaestor, rage enough
for his occasions;—and yet the essential element of him, as of all
such men, is not scorching *fire*, but shining illuminative *light*. Fire
and light are strangely interchangeable; nay, at bottom, I have
found them different forms of the same most godlike "elementary
substance" in our world: a thing worth stating in these days. The
essential element of this Conquaestor is, first of all, the most sun-
eyed perception of what *is* really what on this God's-Earth;—which,
thou wilt find, does mean at bottom "Justice," and "Virtues" not
a few: *Conformity* to what the Maker has seen good to make; that,
I suppose, will mean Justice and a Virtue or two?—

Dost thou think Willelmus Conquaestor would have tolerated
ten years' jargon, one hour's jargon, on the propriety of killing
Cotton-manufactures by partridge Corn-Laws?[1] I fancy, this was
not the man to knock out of his night's-rest with nothing but a
noisy bedlamism in your mouth! "Assist us still better to bush the
partridges; strangle Plugson who spins the shirts?"[2]—*"Par la Splendeur de Dieu!"*[3]—Dost thou think Willelmus Conquaestor, in this
new time, with Steam-engine Captains of Industry on one hand

the right of the monarch to ascend the
throne. He wears full armor ("cased in
tin"). A symbol for Carlyle of outworn feudal customs.
8. Hereward the Wake, an outlaw
whose exploits against William the
Conqueror made him seem a romantic
figure like Robin Hood.
9. His execution in 1075, on a supposedly trumped-up charge, is cited as
a blot on William's record as king.
1. See the title note.

2. This speech sums up the pleas of
the High Tariff lobby in Parliament.
"Keep the Corn Laws intact so that
the aristocratic landlords may continue
to enjoy shooting partridges on their
estates; subdue the manufacturing leaders by preventing trade." ("Plugson
of Undershot" was Carlyle's term to
describe the new class of industrial
leaders.)
3. "By the splendor of God!"—one of
William's oaths.

of him, and Joe-Manton Captains of Idleness[4] on the other, would have doubted which *was* really the BEST; which did deserve strangling, and which not?

I have a certain indestructible regard for Willelmus Conquaestor. A resident House-Surgeon, provided by Nature for her beloved English People, and even furnished with the requisite fees, as I said; for he by no means felt himself doing Nature's work, this Willelmus, but his own work exclusively! And his own work withal it was; informed *"par la Splendeur de Dieu."*—I say, it is necessary to get the work out of such a man, however harsh that be! When a world, not yet doomed for death, is rushing down to ever-deeper Baseness and Confusion, it is a dire necessity of Nature's to bring in her ARISTOCRACIES, her BEST, even by forcible methods. When their descendants or representatives cease entirely to *be* the Best, Nature's poor world will very soon rush down again to Baseness; and it becomes a dire necessity of Nature's to cast them out. Hence French Revolutions, Five-point Charters, Democracies, and a mournful list of *Etceteras*, in these our afflicted times. * * *

Democracy, the chase of Liberty in that direction, shall go its full course; unrestrained by him of Pferdefuss-Quacksalber, or any of *his* household. The Toiling Millions of Mankind, in most vital need and passionate instinctive desire of Guidance, shall cast away False-Guidance; and hope, for an hour, that No-Guidance will suffice them: but it can be for an hour only. The smallest item of human Slavery is the oppression of man by his Mock-Superiors; the palpablest, but I say at bottom the smallest. Let him shake off such oppression, trample it indignantly under his feet; I blame him not, I pity and commend him. But oppression by your Mock-Superiors well shaken off, the grand problem yet remains to solve: That of finding government by your Real-Superiors! Alas, how shall we ever learn the solution of that, benighted, bewildered, sniffing, sneering, godforgetting unfortunates as we are? It is a work for centuries; to be taught us by tribulations, confusions, insurrections, obstructions; who knows if not by conflagration and despair! It is a lesson inclusive of all other lessons; the hardest of all lessons to learn. * * *

Captains of Industry[1]

If I believed that Mammonism with its adjuncts was to continue henceforth the one serious principle of our existence, I should reckon it idle to solicit remedial measures from any Government, the disease being insusceptible of remedy. Government can do much, but it can in no wise do all. Government, as the most conspicuous object in Society, is called upon to give signal of what

4. The idle aristocracy who wasted time shooting partridges with guns made by Joseph Manton, a London gunsmith.

1. From Book IV, Chapter 4.

shall be done; and, in many ways, to preside over, further, and command the doing of it. But the Government cannot do, by all its signalling and commanding, what the Society is radically indisposed to do. In the long-run every Government is the exact symbol of its People, with their wisdom and unwisdom; we have to say, Like People like Government.—The main substance of this immense Problem of Organizing Labour, and first of all of Managing the Working Classes, will, it is very clear, have to be solved by those who stand practically in the middle of it; by those who themselves work and preside over work. Of all that can be enacted by any Parliament in regard to it, the germs must already lie potentially extant in those two Classes, who are to obey such enactment. A Human Chaos *in* which there is no light, you vainly attempt to irradiate by light shed *on* it: order never can arise there.

But it is my firm conviction that the "Hell of England" will *cease* to be that of "not making money"; that we shall get a nobler Hell and a nobler Heaven! I anticipate light *in* the Human Chaos, glimmering, shining more and more; under manifold true signals from without That light shall shine. Our deity no longer being Mammon,—O Heavens, each man will then say to himself: "Why such deadly haste to make money? I shall not go to Hell, even if I do not make money! There is another Hell, I am told!" Competition, at railway-speed, in all branches of commerce and work will then abate:—good felt-hats for the head, in every sense, instead of seven-feet lath-and-plaster hats on wheels,[2] will then be discoverable! Bubble-periods,[3] with their panics and commercial crises, will again become infrequent; steady modest industry will take the place of gambling speculation. To be a noble Master, among noble Workers, will again be the first ambition with some few; to be a rich Master only the second. How the Inventive Genius of England, with the whirr of its bobbins and billy-rollers[4] shoved somewhat into the backgrounds of the brain, will contrive and devise, not cheaper produce exclusively, but fairer distribution of the produce at its present cheapness! By degrees, we shall again have a Society with something of Heroism in it, something of Heaven's Blessing on it; we shall again have, as my German friend[5] asserts, "instead of Mammon-Feudalism with unsold cotton-shirts and Preservation of the Game, noble just Industrialism and Government by the Wisest!"

It is with the hope of awakening here and there a British man to know himself for a man and divine soul, that a few words of parting admonition, to all persons to whom the Heavenly Powers

---

2. A London hatter's mode of advertising. Carlyle considered most advertisements to be wasteful.
3. Periods of violent fluctuation in the stock market caused by unsound speculating.
4. Machines used to prepare cotton or wool for spinning.
5. Teufelsdröckh, the hero of *Sartor Resartus*.

have lent power of any kind in this land, may now be addressed. And first to those same Master-Workers, Leaders of Industry; who stand nearest, and in fact powerfullest, though not most prominent, being as yet in too many senses a Virtuality rather than an Actuality.

The Leaders of Industry, if Industry is ever to be led, are virtually the Captains of the World; if there be no nobleness in them, there will never be an Aristocracy more. But let the Captains of Industry consider: once again, are they born of other clay than the old Captains of Slaughter; doomed for ever to be not Chivalry, but a mere gold-plated *Doggery*,—what the French well name *Canaille*, "Doggery" with more or less gold carrion at its disposal? Captains of Industry are the true Fighters, henceforth recognizable as the only true ones: Fighters against Chaos, Necessity and the Devils and Jötuns;[6] and lead on Mankind in that great, and alone true, and universal warfare; the stars in their courses fighting for them, and all Heaven and all Earth saying audibly, Well done! Let the Captains of Industry retire into their own hearts, and ask solemnly, If there is nothing but vulturous hunger for fine wines, valet reputation and gilt carriages, discoverable there? Of hearts made by the Almighty God I will not believe such a thing. Deep-hidden under wretchedest god-forgetting Cants, Epicurisms, Dead-Sea Apisms;[7] forgotten as under foullest fat Lethe mud and weeds, there is yet, in all hearts born into this God's-World, a spark of the Godlike slumbering. Awake, O nightmare sleepers; awake, arise, or be for ever fallen! This is not playhouse poetry; it is sober fact. Our England, our world cannot live as it is. It will connect itself with a God again, or go down with nameless throes and fire-consummation to the Devils. Thou who feelest aught of such a Godlike stirring in thee, any faintest intimation of it as through heavy-laden dreams, follow *it*, I conjure thee. Arise, save thyself, be one of those that save thy country.

Bucaniers,[8] Chactaw Indians, whose supreme aim in fighting is that they may get the scalps, the money, that they may amass scalps and money; out of such came no Chivalry, and never will! Out of such came only gore and wreck, infernal rage and misery; desperation quenched in annihilation. Behold it, I bid thee, behold there, and consider! What is it that thou have a hundred thousand-pound bills laid up in thy strong-room, a hundred scalps hung up in thy wigwam? I value not them or thee. Thy scalps and thy thousand-pound bills are as yet nothing, if no nobleness from

6. Giants of Scandinavian mythology.
7. A tribe of men living near the Dead Sea were transformed into apes because they had ignored the prophecies of Moses. This story, of Mohammedan origin, is used by Carlyle to represent the possible fate of nations which are indifferent to their social problems.
8. Buccaneers.

within irradiate them; if no Chivalry, in action, or in embryo ever struggling towards birth and action, be there.

Love of men cannot be bought by cash-payment; and without love, men cannot endure to be together. You cannot lead a Fighting World without having it regimented, chivalried: the thing, in a day, becomes impossible; all men in it, the highest at first, the very lowest at last, discern consciously, or by a noble instinct, this necessity. And can you any more continue to lead a Working World unregimented, anarchic? I answer, and the Heavens and Earth are now answering, No! The thing becomes not "in a day" impossible; but in some two generations it does. Yes, when fathers and mothers, in Stockport hunger-cellars, begin to eat their children, and Irish widows have to prove their relationship by dying of typhus-fever; and amid Governing "Corporations of the Best and Bravest," busy to preserve their game by "bushing," dark millions of God's human creatures start up in mad Chartisms, impracticable Sacred-Months, and Manchester Insurrections;[9]—and there is a virtual Industrial Aristocracy as yet only half-alive, spell-bound amid money-bags and ledgers; and an actual Idle Aristocracy seemingly near dead in somnolent delusions, in trespasses and double-barrels;[1] "sliding," as on inclined-planes, which every new year they *soap* with new Hansard's-jargon[2] under God's sky, and so are "sliding" ever faster, towards a "scale" and balance-scale whereon is written *Thou art found Wanting:*—in such days, after a generation or two, I say, it does become, even to the low and simple, very palpably impossible! No Working World, any more than a Fighting World, can be led on without a noble Chivalry of Work, and laws and fixed rules which follow out of that,—far nobler than any Chivalry of Fighting was. As an anarchic multitude on mere Supply-and-demand, it is becoming inevitable that we dwindle in horrid suicidal convulsion, and self-abrasion, frightful to the imagination, into *Chactaw* Workers. With wigwams and scalps,—with palaces and thousand-pound bills; with savagery, depopulation, chaotic desolation! Good Heavens, will not one French Revolution and Reign of Terror suffice us, but must there be two? There will be two if needed; there will be twenty if needed; there will be precisely as many as are needed. The Laws of Nature will have themselves fulfilled. That is a thing certain to me.

Your gallant battle-hosts and work-hosts, as the others did, will need to be made loyally yours; they must and will be regulated, methodically secured in their just share of conquest under you;—

9. In 1819 a large open-air labor meeting in Manchester was broken up by charging cavalry. Thirteen men and women were massacred, and many others were wounded.
1. Carlyle is suggesting that the only concern of the landed aristocrats is to keep trespassers off their game preserves and reserve shooting rights to themselves.
2. Parliamentary oratory, as in Hansard's printed record of debates in the House of Commons.

joined with you in veritable brotherhood, sonhood, by quite other and deeper ties than those of temporary day's wages! How would mere redcoated regiments, to say nothing of chivalries, fight for you, if you could discharge them on the evening of the battle, on payment of the stipulated shillings,—and they discharge you on the morning of it! Chelsea Hospitals,[3] pensions, promotions, rigorous lasting covenant on the one side and on the other, are indispensable even for a hired fighter. The Feudal Baron, much more, —how could he subsist with mere temporary mercenaries round him, at sixpence a day; ready to go over to the other side, if sevenpence were offered? He could not have subsisted;—and his noble instinct saved him from the necessity of even trying! The Feudal Baron had a Man's Soul in him; to which anarchy, mutiny, and the other fruits of temporary mercenaries, were intolerable: he had never been a Baron otherwise, but had continued a Chactaw and Bucanier. He felt it precious, and at last it became habitual, and his fruitful enlarged existence included it as a necessity, to have men round him who in heart loved him; whose life he watched over with rigour yet with love; who were prepared to give their life for him, if need came. It was beautiful; it was human! Man lives not otherwise, nor can live contented, anywhere or anywhen. Isolation is the sum-total of wretchedness to man. To be cut off, to be left solitary: to have a world alien, not your world; all a hostile camp for you; not a home at all, of hearts and faces who are yours, whose you are! It is the frightfullest enchantment; too truly a work of the Evil One. To have neither superior, nor inferior, nor equal, united manlike to you. Without father, without child, without brother. Man knows no sadder destiny. "How is each of us," exclaims Jean Paul,[4] "so lonely in the wide bosom of the All!" Encased each as in his transparent "ice-palace"; our brother visible in his, making signals and gesticulations to us;—visible, but for ever unattainable: on his bosom we shall never rest, nor he on ours. It was not a God that did this; no!

Awake, ye noble Workers, warriors in the one true war: all this must be remedied. It is you who are already half-alive, whom I will welcome into life; whom I will conjure in God's name to shake off your enchanted sleep, and live wholly! Cease to count scalps, gold-purses; not in these lies your or our salvation. Even these, if you count only these, will not be left. Let bucaniering be put far from you; alter, speedily abrogate all laws of the bucaniers, if you would gain any victory that shall endure. Let God's justice, let pity, nobleness and manly valour, with more gold-purses or with fewer, testify themselves in this your brief Life-transit to all the Eternities, the Gods and Silences. It is to you I call; for ye are not dead, ye

---

3. Home for disabled veterans.   4. Jean Paul Richter (1763–1825), German humorist.

are already half-alive: there is in you a sleepless dauntless energy, the prime-matter of all nobleness in man. Honour to you in your kind. It is to you I call: ye know at least this, That the mandate of God to His creature man is: Work! The future Epic of the World rests not with those that are near dead, but with those that are alive, and those that are coming into life.

Look around you. Your world-hosts are all in mutiny, in confusion, destitution; on the eve of fiery wreck and madness! They will not march farther for you, on the sixpence a day and supply-and-demand principle: they will not; nor ought they, nor can they. Ye shall reduce them to order, begin reducing them. To order, to just subordination; noble loyalty in return for noble guidance. Their souls are driven nigh mad; let yours be sane and ever saner. Not as a bewildered bewildering mob; but as a firm regimented mass, with real captains over them, will these men march any more. All human interests, combined human endeavours, and social growths in this world, have, at a certain stage of their development, required organizing: and Work, the grandest of human interests, does now require it.

God knows, the task will be hard: but no noble task was ever easy. This task will wear away your lives, and the lives of your sons and grandsons: but for what purpose, if not for tasks like this, were lives given to men? Ye shall cease to count your thousand-pound scalps, the noble of you shall cease! Nay, the very scalps, as I say, will not long be left if you count on these. Ye shall cease wholly to be barbarous vulturous Chactaws, and become noble European Nineteenth-Century Men. Ye shall know that Mammon, in never such gigs[5] and flunkey "respectabilities," is not the alone God; that of himself he is but a Devil, and even a Brute-god.

Difficult? Yes, it will be difficult. The short-fibre cotton; that too was difficult. The waste cotton-shrub, long useless, disobedient, as the thistle by the wayside,—have ye not conquered it; made it into beautiful bandana webs; white woven shirts for men; bright-tinted air-garments wherein flit goddesses? Ye have shivered mountains asunder, made the hard iron pliant to you as soft putty: the Forest-giants, Marsh-jötuns bear sheaves of golden grain; Aegir the Sea-demon[6] himself stretches his back for a sleek highway to you, and on Firehorses and Windhorses ye career. Ye are most strong. Thor red-bearded, with his blue sun-eyes, with his cheery heart and strong thunder-hammer, he and you have prevailed. Ye are most strong, ye Sons of the icy North, of the far East,—far marching from your rugged Eastern Wildernesses, hitherward from the grey Dawn of Time! Ye are Sons of the *Jötun*-land; the land of Diffi-

5. To own a gig (a light carriage) was a sign of respectable status comparable to owning certain kinds of automobiles today. Carlyle ridiculed the passion for respectability as "gigmanity."

6. From Scandinavian mythology.

culties Conquered. Difficult? You must try this thing. Once try it
with the understanding that it will and shall have to be done. Try
it as ye try the paltrier thing, making of money! I will bet on you
once more, against all Jötuns, Tailor-gods,[7] Double-barrelled Law-
wards, and Denizens of Chaos whatsoever!

1843   1843

7. False gods.

ALFRED, LORD TENNYSON
(1809–1892)

1830: *Poems Chiefly Lyrical.*
1833: Death of Arthur Hallam.
1842: *Poems.*
1850: *In Memoriam.* Tennyson appointed poet laureate.
1859: *Idylls of the King* (first four books).

In the earlier years of the 20th century, an easy way to arouse laughter
at a gathering of intelligent people was to recite aloud some poem by
Tennyson such as *Flower in the Crannied Wall.* A high falsetto voice
might add to the effect but was not essential, for the company would
laugh not because this was a bad poem but simply because it was a poem
by Tennyson. Samuel Butler, who anticipated early 20th-century tastes,
has a characteristic entry in his *Notebooks:* "Talking it over, we agreed that
Blake was no good because he learnt Italian at 60 in order to study Dante,
and we knew Dante was no good because he was so fond of Virgil, and
Virgil was no good because Tennyson ran him, and as for Tennyson—well,
Tennyson goes without saying." It was inevitable that the almost hysterical
repudiation of their Victorian predecessors by the Edwardians and Georgians would be directed most damagingly against Tennyson, the so-called
spokesman of the Victorian age, the poet whose works were on the book-
shelves of almost every family of readers in England and the United States
from 1850 onwards. As Thomas Hardy noted sadly in *An Ancient to Ancients,*

> The bower we shrined to Tennyson,
>   Gentlemen,
> Is roof-wrecked; damps there drip upon
> Sagged seats, the creeper-nails are rust,
> The spider is sole denizen.

Hardy's obituary was premature. Tennyson's "bower" has to a considerable extent been rebuilt. The scale of the vast building has been wisely
reduced, but the best of his poems are now established upon foundations of
more solid critical appreciation. And when we enjoy such poems as *Ulysses*
or *Tears, Idle Tears* we may wonder what perversity of taste led earlier
critics to write off the delight to be found in this "lord of language"—as

Tennyson himself addresses his favorite predecessor, Virgil. The Edwardians might reply, however, that they had read other poems by Tennyson than *Ulysses*. They had been brought up to admire such sentimental pieces as *The May Queen*, his popular idyls of rural life, and his newspaper verses. And the Edwardians had here a point, for in such poems, Tennyson was certainly vulnerable. *Enoch Arden* gained him the title that Walt Whitman longed for, "The Poet of the People," but his more enduring reputation, as J. Churton Collins predicted in 1891, was to be as "the poet of the cultured." A year later, Tennyson himself made an accurate prophecy of his status in his lines on *Poets and Critics*:

> What is true at last will tell:
> Few at first will place thee well;
> Some too low would have thee shine,
> Some too high—no fault of thine—
> Hold thine own, and work thy will!

Like his poetry, Tennyson's life and character have been reassessed in the 20th century. To many of his contemporaries he seemed a remote wizard, secure in his laureate's robes, a man whose life had been sheltered, marred only by the loss of his best friend in youth. During much of his career Tennyson may have been isolated, but his was not a sheltered life in the real sense of the word. Although he grew up in a parsonage, it was not the kind of parsonage one encounters in the novels of Jane Austen. His family could have supplied materials instead for one of William Faulkner's novels about the American South. It was a household dominated by frictions and loyalties and broodings over ancestral inheritances, in which the children showed marked strains of instability and eccentricity.

Alfred was the fourth son in a family of twelve children. One of his brothers had to be confined to an insane asylum for life; another was long a victim of the opium habit; another had violent quarrels with his father, who had become a drunkard. This father, the Reverend Dr. George Tennyson, was the eldest son of a wealthy landowner. He had been obliged to become a clergyman, a profession he disliked, because he had been disinherited in favor of his younger brother. George Tennyson therefore settled in a small rectory at Somersby in Lincolnshire where he tutored his sons in classical and modern languages to prepare them for entering the university.

Before leaving this strange household for Cambridge, Alfred had already demonstrated a flair for writing verse—precocious exercises in the manner of Milton or Byron or the Elizabethan dramatists. He had even published a volume in 1827, in collaboration with his brother Charles, *Poems by Two Brothers*. This feat drew him to the attention of a group of gifted undergraduates at Cambridge, the "Apostles," who encouraged him to devote his life to poetry. Up until this time, the young man had known scarcely anyone outside the circle of his own family. Despite his massive frame and powerful physique, he was painfully shy, and the friendships he found at Cambridge, as well as the intellectual and political discussions in which he participated, served to give him confidence and to widen his horizons as a poet. The most important of these friendships was with Arthur Hallam, a leader of the Apostles, who later became engaged to Tennyson's sister. Hallam's sudden death, in 1833, seemed an overwhelming calamity to his friend. Not only the long elegy *In Memoriam* but many of Tennyson's other poems are tributes to this early friendship.

Alfred's career at Cambridge was interrupted and finally broken off in 1831 by family dissensions and financial need, and he returned home to study and practice the craft of poetry. His early volumes (1830 and 1832) were attacked as "obscure" or "affected" by some of the reviewers. Tennyson suffered acutely under hostile criticism, but he also profited from it. His volume of 1842 demonstrated a remarkable advance in taste and technical excellence, and in 1850 he at last attained fame and full critical recognition with *In Memoriam*. In the same year he became poet laureate in succession to Wordsworth. The struggle during the previous twenty years had been made especially painful by the long postponement of his marriage to Emily Sellwood, with whom he had fallen in love in 1836 but could not marry, because of poverty, until 1850.

His life thereafter was a comfortable one. He was as popular as Byron had been, and his fame lasted for much longer. The earnings from his poetry (sometimes exceeding £10,000 a year) enabled him to purchase a house in the country and to enjoy the kind of seclusion he liked. His notoriety was enhanced, like that of G. B. Shaw and Walt Whitman, by his colorful appearance. Huge and shaggy, in cloak and broadbrimmed hat, gruff in manner as a farmer, he impressed everyone as what is called a "character." He also had a booming voice, when reading his poetry, that electrified listeners much as Dylan Thomas electrified audiences in the 20th century: "mouthing out his hollow o's and a's, / Deep-chested music." Moreover, for many Victorian readers, he seemed not only a great poetical phrasemaker and a striking individual but also a wise man whose occasional pronouncements on politics or world affairs represented the national voice itself. In 1884 he accepted a peerage. In 1892 he died and was buried in Westminster Abbey.

It is often said that success was bad for Tennyson, and that after *In Memoriam* his poetic power seriously declined. That in his last 42 years certain of his mannerisms became accentuated is true. One of the difficulties of his dignified blank verse was, as he said himself, that it is hard to describe commonplace objects and "at the same time to retain poetical elevation." The ornateness of his later style sometimes betrayed him into such blunders as describing a basketful of fish as "Enoch's ocean spoil / In ocean-smelling osier." In others of his later poems, those dealing with national affairs, there is also an increased shrillness of tone—a mannerism accentuated by Tennyson's realizing that like Dickens he had a vast public behind him to back up his pronouncements.

It is foolish, however, to try to shelve all of Tennyson's later productions. In 1855 he published his experimental monologue *Maud*, perhaps his finest long poem. In 1859 he published four books of his *Idylls of the King*, a large-scale epic which occupied most of his energies in the second half of his career. About this late poem, completed in twelve books, in 1888, there is less agreement. Some readers consider it to be complacent— mere "lollipops," as Carlyle called it. Yet *Idylls of the King* is not simply a hymn to progress. It records, instead, a cycle of change from a society that has emerged from a wasteland into civilization but which may revert to a wasteland once more. In any event, even if this ambitious epic does not show Tennyson in his best vein, there is no sign of decline in his late lyrics. The 80-year-old poet who wrote *Crossing the Bar* had certainly not lost his touch.

The problem of Tennyson's development is really of more significance for the period before 1850 rather than afterwards. W. H. Auden has stated that Tennyson had "the finest ear, perhaps, of any English poet." The interesting point is that Tennyson did not have such an ear: he developed it. Studies of the original versions of his poems in the 1830 and 1832 volumes demonstrate that not only was his taste uncertain at the outset of his career but that his sense of meter was originally unreliable. The harmonics he was to achieve from 1842 onwards had to be learned just as a pianist with a weak left hand has to overcome his weakness by constant exercise. Like Chaucer or Keats or Pope, Tennyson studied his predecessors assiduously to perfect his technique. Anyone wanting to learn the traditional craft of English verse can study with profit the various stages of revision that such poems as *The Lotos-Eaters* were subjected to by this painstaking and artful poet.

If the early Tennyson was uncertain of meter, he had other skills that were immediately in evidence. One of these was a capacity for linking scenery to states of mind. As early as 1835, J. S. Mill identified the special kind of scene-painting to be found in early poems such as *Mariana:* " * * * not the power of producing that rather vapid species of composition usually termed descriptive poetry * * * but the power of *creating* scenery, in keeping with some state of human feeling so fitted to it as to be the embodied symbol of it, and to summon up the state of feeling itself, with a force not to be surpassed by anything but reality."

A second aspect of Tennyson's early development was his increased preoccupation with problems of his day. If J. S. Mill praised his capacity to render landscape, he also urged, in his review, Tennyson's further responsibilities—to "cultivate, and with no half devotion, philosophy as well as poetry." Advice of this kind Tennyson was already predisposed to heed. The death of Hallam, the religious uncertainties which he had himself experienced, together with his own extensive study of writings by geologists, astronomers, and biologists, led him to confront many of the religious issues that bewildered his generation and later generations. The result was *In Memoriam* (1850), a long elegy written over a period of seventeen years, embodying the poet's reflections on man's relation to God and to nature.

Was Tennyson intellectually equipped to deal with the great questions raised in *In Memoriam?* The answer may depend on a reader's religious and philosophical presuppositions. Some, such as T. H. Huxley, considered Tennyson an intellectual giant, a thinker who had mastered the scientific thought of his century and fully confronted the issues it raised. Others dismissed Tennyson, in this phase, as a lightweight. Auden went so far as to call him the "stupidest" of English poets. We might say more accurately that his mind was slow, ponderous, brooding, and we should add that for the composition of *In Memoriam* such qualities of mind were assets, not liabilities. In these terms we can understand when Tennyson's poetry really fails to measure up: it is when he writes of events of the moment over which his thoughts and feelings have had no time to brood. Several of his poems are essentially newspaper pieces. They are Letters to the Editor, in effect, with the ephemeral heat and simplicity we expect of such productions. *The Charge of the Light Brigade,* inspired by a report in *The Times* of a cavalry charge at Balaclava during the Crimean War, is one of the best of his productions in this category. His *Dedication* of *Idylls of the King* to Prince Albert is also related to this kind of occasional verse and is included in the following selections as a representative example of a Victorian period piece.

Tennyson's poems of contemporary events were inevitably popular in his own day. So too were those poems where, as in *Locksley Hall,* he dipped into the future. The technological changes wrought by Victorian inventors and engineers fascinated him. Sometimes they gave him an assurance of human progress as swaggeringly exultant as that of Macaulay. At other times the horrors of industrialism's by-products in the slums, the bloodshed of war, the greed of the newly rich, destroyed his hopes that man was evolving upwards. Such a late poem as *The Dawn* embodies an attitude which he found in Virgil: "Thou majestic in thy sadness at the doubtful doom of human kind."

For despite Tennyson's fascination with technological developments, he was essentially a poet of the countryside, a man whose whole being was conditioned by the recurring rhythms of rural rather than urban life. He had the countryman's awareness of traditional roots and his sense of the past. It is appropriate that most of his best poems are about the past, not about the present or future. The past is his great theme: his own past (as in *All Along the Valley*), his country's past (as in *The Revenge*), the past of mankind, the past of the world itself:

> There rolls the deep where grew the tree.
> O earth, what changes hast thou seen!
> There where the long street roars hath been
> The stillness of the central sea.

Tennyson is the first major writer to express this awareness of the vast extent of geological time that has haunted human consciousness since Victorian scientists exposed the history of the earth's crust. In his more usual vein, however, it is the recorded past of mankind that inspires him, the classical past in particular. Classical themes, as Douglas Bush has noted, "generally banished from his mind what was timid, parochial, sentimental * * * and evoked his special gifts and most authentic emotions, his rich and wistful sense of the past, his love of nature, and his power of style."

One returns, finally then, to the question of language. At the time of his death, a critic complained that Tennyson was merely "a discoverer of words rather than of ideas." The same complaint has been made by George Bernard Shaw and others—not about Tennyson but about Shakespeare.

The Kraken[1]

Below the thunders of the upper deep,
Far, far beneath in the abysmal sea,

1. A mythical sea beast of gigantic size.

His ancient, dreamless, uninvaded sleep
The Kraken sleepeth: faintest sunlights flee
About his shadowy sides; above him swell   5
Huge sponges of millennial growth and height;
And far away into the sickly light,
From many a wondrous grot and secret cell
Unnumbered and enormous polypi[2]
Winnow with giant arms the slumbering green.   10
There hath he lain for ages, and will lie
Battening upon huge sea worms in his sleep,
Until the latter fire[3] shall heat the deep;
Then once by man and angels to be seen,
In roaring he shall rise and on the surface die.   15

1830

Mariana[1]

"Mariana in the moated grange."
Measure for Measure

With blackest moss the flower plots
    Were thickly crusted, one and all;
The rusted nails fell from the knots
    That held the pear to the gable wall.
The broken sheds looked sad and strange: 5
    Unlifted was the clinking latch;
    Weeded and worn the ancient thatch
Upon the lonely moated grange.
        She only said, "My life is dreary,
            He cometh not," she said;   10
        She said, "I am aweary, aweary,
            I would that I were dead!"

Her tears fell with the dews at even;
    Her tears fell ere the dews were dried;
She could not look on the sweet heaven,   15
    Either at morn or eventide.
After the flitting of the bats,
    When thickest dark did trance the sky,
    She drew her casement curtain by,
And glanced athwart the glooming flats.   20
        She only said, "The night is dreary,
            He cometh not," she said;
        She said, "I am aweary, aweary,
            I would that I were dead!"

2. Octopuses.
3. Fire which would finally consume the world. See Revelation xvi.3–9.
1. Mariana, in Shakespeare's *Measure for Measure* (III.i.277), waits in a grange (an outlying farmhouse) for her lover who has deserted her.

Upon the middle of the night,   25
   Waking she heard the nightfowl crow;
The cock sung out an hour ere light;
   From the dark fen the oxen's low
Came to her; without hope of change,
   In sleep she seemed to walk forlorn,   30
   Till cold winds woke the gray-eyed morn
About the lonely moated grange.
     She only said, "The day is dreary,
      He cometh not," she said;
     She said, "I am aweary, aweary,   35
      I would that I were dead!"

About a stonecast from the wall
   A sluice with blackened waters slept,
And o'er it many, round and small,
   The clustered marish[2] mosses crept.   40
Hard by a poplar shook alway,
   All silver-green with gnarlèd bark:
   For leagues no other tree did mark
The level waste, the rounding gray.
     She only said, "My life is dreary,   45
      He cometh not," she said;
     She said, "I am aweary, aweary,
      I would that I were dead!"

And ever when the moon was low,
   And the shrill winds were up and away,   50
In the white curtain, to and fro,
   She saw the gusty shadow sway.
But when the moon was very low,
   And wild winds bound within their cell,
   The shadow of the poplar fell   55
Upon her bed, across her brow.
     She only said, "The night is dreary,
      He cometh not," she said;
     She said, "I am aweary, aweary,
      I would that I were dead!"   60

All day within the dreamy house,
   The doors upon their hinges creaked;
The blue fly sung in the pane; the mouse
   Behind the moldering wainscot shrieked,
Or from the crevice peered about.   65
   Old faces glimmered through the doors,
   Old footsteps trod the upper floors,
Old voices called her from without.
     She only said, "My life is dreary,
      He cometh not," she said;   70
     She said, "I am aweary, aweary,
      I would that I were dead!"

2. Marsh.

The sparrow's chirrup on the roof,
   The slow clock ticking, and the sound
Which to the wooing wind aloof   75
   The poplar made, did all confound
Her sense; but most she loathed the hour
   When the thick-moted sunbeam lay
Athwart the chambers, and the day
Was sloping toward his western bower.   80
   Then, said she, "I am very dreary,
     He will not come," she said;
   She wept, "I am aweary, aweary,
     Oh God, that I were dead!"

                            1830

Sonnet

She took the dappled partridge flecked with blood,
   And in her hand the drooping pheasant bare,
   And by his feet she held the woolly hare,
And like a master painting where she stood,
Looked some new goddess of an English wood.   5
   Nor could I find an imperfection there,
   Nor blame the wanton act that showed so fair—
To me whatever freak[3] she plays is good.
Hers is the fairest Life that breathes with breath,
   And *their* still plumes and azure eyelids closed   10
     Made quiet Death so beautiful to see
That Death lent grace to Life and Life to Death
   And in one image Life and Death reposed,
     To make my love an Immortality.

ca. 1830   1931

The Lady of Shalott
Part I

On either side the river lie
Long fields of barley and of rye,
That clothe the wold[1] and meet the sky;
And through the field the road runs by
   To many-towered Camelot;[2]   5
And up and down the people go,
Gazing where the lilies blow[3]
Round an island there below,
   The island of Shalott.

3. Prank.
1. Rolling plains.
2. Legendary city in which King

Arthur's palace was located.
3. Bloom.

Willows whiten, aspens quiver,   10
Little breezes dusk and shiver
Through the wave that runs forever
By the island in the river
   Flowing down to Camelot.
Four gray walls, and four gray towers,   15
Overlook a space of flowers,
And the silent isle imbowers
   The Lady of Shalott.

By the margin, willow-veiled,
Slide the heavy barges trailed   20
By slow horses; and unhailed
The shallop⁴ flitteth silken-sailed
   Skimming down to Camelot:
But who hath seen her wave her hand?
Or at the casement seen her stand?   25
Or is she known in all the land,
   The Lady of Shalott?

Only reapers, reaping early
In among the bearded barley,
Hear a song that echoes cheerly   30
From the river winding clearly,
   Down to towered Camelot;
And by the moon the reaper weary,
Piling sheaves in uplands airy,
Listening, whispers " 'Tis the fairy   35
   Lady of Shalott."

Part II

There she weaves by night and day
A magic web with colors gay.
She has heard a whisper say,
A curse is on her if she stay   40
   To look down to Camelot.
She knows not what the curse may be,
And so she weaveth steadily,
And little other care hath she,
   The Lady of Shalott.   45

And moving through a mirror clear
That hangs before her all the year,
Shadows of the world appear.
There she sees the highway near
   Winding down to Camelot;   50
There the river eddy whirls,
And there the surly village churls,
And the red cloaks of market girls,
   Pass onward from Shalott.

4. A light open boat.

Sometimes a troop of damsels glad,   55
An abbot on an ambling pad,[5]
Sometimes a curly shepherd lad,
Or long-haired page in crimson clad,
    Goes by to towered Camelot;
And sometimes through the mirror blue   60
The knights come riding two and two:
She hath no loyal knight and true,
    The Lady of Shalott.

But in her web she still delights
To weave the mirror's magic sights,   65
For often through the silent nights
A funeral, with plumes and lights
    And music, went to Camelot;
Or when the moon was overhead,
Came two young lovers lately wed: 70
"I am half sick of shadows," said
    The Lady of Shalott.

Part III

A bowshot from her bower eaves,
He rode between the barley sheaves,
The sun came dazzling through the leaves,   75
And flamed upon the brazen greaves[6]
    Of bold Sir Lancelot.
A red-cross knight[7] forever kneeled
To a lady in his shield,
That sparkled on the yellow field,   80
    Beside remote Shalott.

The gemmy bridle glittered free,
Like to some branch of stars we see
Hung in the golden Galaxy.
The bridle bells rang merrily   85
    As he rode down to Camelot;
And from his blazoned baldric[8] slung
A mighty silver bugle hung,
And as he rode his armor rung,
    Beside remote Shalott.   90

All in the blue unclouded weather
Thick-jeweled shone the saddle leather,
The helmet and the helmet-feather
Burned like one burning flame together,
    As he rode down to Camelot;   95
As often through the purple night,
Below the starry clusters bright,

5. Easy-paced horse.
6. Armor protecting the leg below the knee.
7. Cf. Spenser's *Faerie Queene* I.
8. A richly decorated sash worn diagonally across the breast.

Some bearded meteor, trailing light,
    Moves over still Shalott.

His broad clear brow in sunlight glowed;   100
On burnished hooves his war horse trode;
From underneath his helmet flowed
His coal-black curls as on he rode,
    As he rode down to Camelot.
From the bank and from the river   105
He flashed into the crystal mirror,
"Tirra lirra," by the river
    Sang Sir Lancelot.

She left the web, she left the loom,
She made three paces through the room,   110
She saw the water lily bloom,
She saw the helmet and the plume,
    She looked down to Camelot.
Out flew the web and floated wide;
The mirror cracked from side to side;   115
"The curse is come upon me," cried
    The Lady of Shalott.

Part IV

In the stormy east wind straining,
The pale yellow woods were waning,
The broad stream in his banks complaining,   120
Heavily the low sky raining
    Over towered Camelot;
Down she came and found a boat
Beneath a willow left afloat,
And round about the prow she wrote   125
    The Lady of Shalott.

And down the river's dim expanse
Like some bold seër in a trance,
Seeing all his own mischance—
With a glassy countenance   130
    Did she look to Camelot.
And at the closing of the day
She loosed the chain, and down she lay;
The broad stream bore her far away,
    The Lady of Shalott.   135

Lying, robed in snowy white
That loosely flew to left and right—
The leaves upon her falling light—
Through the noises of the night
    She floated down to Camelot;   140
And as the boat-head wound along
The willowy hills and fields among,

They heard her singing her last song,
    The Lady of Shalott.

Heard a carol, mournful, holy,   145
Chanted loudly, chanted lowly,
Till her blood was frozen slowly,
And her eyes were darkened wholly,
    Turned to towered Camelot.
For ere she reached upon the tide   150
The first house by the waterside,
Singing in her song she died,
    The Lady of Shalott.

Under tower and balcony,
By garden wall and gallery,   155
A gleaming shape she floated by,
Dead-pale between the houses high,
    Silent into Camelot.
Out upon the wharfs they came,
Knight and burgher, lord and dame,   160
And round the prow they read her name,
    The Lady of Shalott.

Who is this? and what is here?
And in the lighted palace near
Died the sound of royal cheer;   165
And they crossed themselves for fear,
    All the knights at Camelot:
But Lancelot mused a little space;
He said, "She has a lovely face;
God in his mercy lend her grace,   170
    The Lady of Shalott."

1832, 1842

The Lotos-Eaters[1]

"Courage!" he[2] said, and pointed toward the land,
"This mounting wave will roll us shoreward soon."
In the afternoon they came unto a land[3]

1. Based on a short episode from the *Odyssey* (IX.82–97) in which the weary Greek veterans of the Trojan War are tempted by a desire to abandon their long voyage homeward. As Odysseus later reported: "On the tenth day we set foot on the land of the lotos-eaters who eat a flowering food. * * * I sent forth certain of my company [who] * * * mixed with the men of the lotos-eaters who * * * gave them of the lotos to taste. Now whosoever of them did eat the honey-sweet fruit of the lotos had no more wish to bring tidings nor to come back, but there he chose to abide * * * forgetful of his homeward way."

Tennyson expands Homer's brief account into an elaborate picture of weariness and the desire for rest and death. The descriptions in the first stanzas are similar to Spenser's *Faerie Queene* (II.vi). The final section derives, in part, from Lucretius' conception of the gods in *De rerum natura*.
2. Odysseus (or Ulysses).
3. The repetition of "land" from line 1 was deliberate; Tennyson said that

In which it seeméd always afternoon.
All round the coast the languid air did swoon, 5
Breathing like one that hath a weary dream.
Full-faced above the valley stood the moon;
And, like a downward smoke, the slender stream
Along the cliff to fall and pause and fall did seem.

A land of streams! some, like a downward smoke, 10
Slow-dropping veils of thinnest lawn,[4] did go;
And some through wavering lights and shadows broke,
Rolling a slumbrous sheet of foam below.
They saw the gleaming river seaward flow
From the inner land; far off, three mountaintops 15
Three silent pinnacles of aged snow,
Stood sunset-flushed; and, dewed with showery drops,
Up-clomb the shadowy pine above the woven copse.

The charméd sunset lingered low adown
In the red West; through mountain clefts the dale 20
Was seen far inland, and the yellow down[5]
Bordered with palm, and many a winding vale
And meadow, set with slender galingale;[6]
A land where all things always seemed the same!
And round about the keel with faces pale, 25
Dark faces pale against that rosy flame,
The mild-eyed melancholy Lotos-eaters came.

Branches they bore of that enchanted stem,
Laden with flower and fruit, whereof they gave
To each, but whoso did receive of them 30
And taste, to him the gushing of the wave
Far far away did seem to mourn and rave
On alien shores; and if his fellow spake,
His voice was thin, as voices from the grave;
And deep-asleep he seemed, yet all awake, 35
And music in his ears his beating heart did make.

They sat them down upon the yellow sand,
Between the sun and moon upon the shore;
And sweet it was to dream of Fatherland,
Of child, and wife, and slave; but evermore 40
Most weary seemed the sea, weary the oar,
Weary the wandering fields of barren foam.
Then some one said, "We will return no more";
And all at once they sang, "Our island home[7]
Is far beyond the wave; we will no longer roam." 45

this "no rhyme" was "lazier" in its
effect. Compare "afternoon" (lines 3–4)
and the rhyming of "adown" and
"down" (lines 19, 21).

4. A fine, thin linen.
5. An open plain on high ground.
6. A plant resembling tall coarse grass.
7. Ithaca.

Choric Song[8]

1

There is sweet music here that softer falls
Than petals from blown roses on the grass,
Or night-dews on still waters between walls
Of shadowy granite, in a gleaming pass;
Music that gentlier on the spirit lies,   50
Than tired eyelids upon tired eyes;
Music that brings sweet sleep down from the blissful skies.
Here are cool mosses deep,
And through the moss the ivies creep,
And in the stream the long-leaved flowers weep,   55
And from the craggy ledge the poppy hangs in sleep.

2

Why are we weighed upon with heaviness,
And utterly consumed with sharp distress,
While all things else have rest from weariness?
All things have rest: why should we toil alone,   60
We only toil, who are the first of things,
And make perpetual moan,
Still from one sorrow to another thrown;
Nor ever fold our wings,
And cease from wanderings,   65
Nor steep our brows in slumber's holy balm;
Nor harken what the inner spirit sings,
"There is no joy but calm!"—
Why should we only toil, the roof and crown of things?

3

Lo! in the middle of the wood,   70
The folded leaf is wooed from out the bud
With winds upon the branch, and there
Grows green and broad, and takes no care,
Sun-steeped at noon, and in the moon
Nightly dew-fed; and turning yellow   75
Falls, and floats adown the air.
Lo! sweetened with the summer light,
The full-juiced apple, waxing over-mellow,
Drops in a silent autumn night.
All its allotted length of days   80
The flower ripens in its place,
Ripens and fades, and falls, and hath no toil,
Fast-rooted in the fruitful soil.

4

Hateful is the dark blue sky,
Vaulted o'er the dark blue sea.   85
Death is the end of life; ah, why

8. Sung by the mariners.

Should life all labor be?
Let us alone. Time driveth onward fast,
And in a little while our lips are dumb.
Let us alone. What is it that will last?   90
All things are taken from us, and become
Portions and parcels of the dreadful past.
Let us alone. What pleasure can we have
To war with evil? Is there any peace
In ever climbing up the climbing wave?   95
All things have rest, and ripen toward the grave
In silence—ripen, fall, and cease:
Give us long rest or death, dark death, or dreamful ease.

5

How sweet it were, hearing the downward stream,
With half-shut eyes ever to seem   100
Falling asleep in a half-dream!
To dream and dream, like yonder amber light,
Which will not leave the myrrh-bush on the height;
To hear each other's whispered speech;
Eating the Lotos day by day,   105
To watch the crisping⁹ ripples on the beach,
And tender curving lines of creamy spray;
To lend our hearts and spirits wholly
To the influence of mild-minded melancholy;
To muse and brood and live again in memory,   110
With those old faces of our infancy
Heaped over with a mound of grass,
Two handfuls of white dust, shut in an urn of brass!

6

Dear is the memory of our wedded lives,
And dear the last embraces of our wives   115
And their warm tears; but all hath suffered change;
For surely now our household hearths are cold,
Our sons inherit us, our looks are strange,
And we should come like ghosts to trouble joy.
Or else the island princes¹ overbold   120
Have eat our substance, and the minstrel sings
Before them of the ten years' war in Troy,
And our great deeds, as half-forgotten things.
Is there confusion in the little isle?
Let what is broken so remain.   125
The Gods are hard to reconcile;
'Tis hard to settle order once again.
There *is* confusion worse than death,
Trouble on trouble, pain on pain,
Long labor unto aged breath,   130
Sore tasks to hearts worn out by many wars
And eyes grown dim with gazing on the pilot-stars.

9. Curling.   1. Penelope's suitors.

7

But, propped on beds of amaranth[2] and moly,
How sweet—while warm airs lull us, blowing lowly—
With half-dropped eyelid still,   135
Beneath a heaven dark and holy,
To watch the long bright river drawing slowly
His waters from the purple hill—
To hear the dewy echoes calling
From cave to cave through the thick-twined vine—   140
To watch the emerald-colored water falling
Through many a woven acanthus wreath divine!
Only to hear and see the far-off sparkling brine,
Only to hear were sweet, stretched out beneath the pine.

8

The Lotos blooms below the barren peak,   145
The Lotos blows by every winding creek;
All day the wind breathes low with mellower tone;
Through every hollow cave and alley lone
Round and round the spicy downs the yellow Lotos dust is blown.
We have had enough of action, and of motion we,   150
Rolled to starboard, rolled to larboard, when the surge was seething
    free,
Where the wallowing monster spouted his foam-fountains in the sea.
Let us swear an oath, and keep it with an equal mind,
In the hollow Lotos land to live and lie reclined
On the hills like Gods together, careless of mankind.   155
For they lie beside their nectar, and the bolts[3] are hurled
Far below them in the valleys, and the clouds are lightly curled
Round their golden houses, girdled with the gleaming world;
Where they smile in secret, looking over wasted lands,
Blight and famine, plague and earthquake, roaring deeps and fiery
    sands,   160
Clanging fights, and flaming towns, and sinking ships, and praying
    hands.
But they smile, they find a music centered in a doleful song
Steaming up, a lamentation and an ancient tale of wrong,
Like a tale of little meaning though the words are strong;
Chanted from an ill-used race of men that cleave the soil,   165
Sow the seed, and reap the harvest with enduring toil,
Storing yearly little dues of wheat, and wine and oil;
Till they perish and they suffer—some, 'tis whispered—down in hell
Suffer endless anguish, others in Elysian valleys dwell,
Resting weary limbs at last on beds of asphodel.[4]   170
Surely, surely, slumber is more sweet than toil, the shore
Than labor in the deep mid-ocean, wind and wave and oar;
O, rest ye, brother mariners, we will not wander more.

1832, 1842

2. A legendary unfading flower;   3. Thunderbolts.
"moly": a flower with magical prop- 4. A yellow lilylike flower supposed to
erties, mentioned by Homer.   grow in the Elysian valleys.

You Ask Me, Why, Though Ill at Ease[5]

You ask me, why, though ill at ease,
   Within this region I subsist,
   Whose spirits falter in the mist,
And languish for the purple seas.

It is the land that freemen till,   5
   That sober-suited Freedom chose,
   The land, where girt with friends or foes
A man may speak the thing he will;

A land of settled government,
   A land of just and old renown,   10
   Where Freedom slowly broadens down
From precedent to precedent;

Where faction seldom gathers head,
   But, by degrees to fullness wrought,
   The strength of some diffusive thought   15
Hath time and space to work and spread.

Should banded unions[6] persecute
   Opinion, and induce a time
   When single thought is civil crime,
And individual freedom mute,   20

Though power should make from land to land
   The name of Britain trebly great—
   Though every channel of the State
Should fill and choke with golden sand—

Yet waft me from the harbor-mouth,   25
   Wild wind! I seek a warmer sky,
   And I will see before I die
The palms and temples of the South.

1833   1842

Morte d'Arthur[1]
The Epic

At Francis Allen's on the Christmas eve—
The game of forfeits done—the girls all kissed

---

5. Written at the time of the disturbances during and after the passing of the Reform Bill of 1832.
6. Any organized political groups, not necessarily trade unions.

1. At the age of 24, Tennyson proposed to write a long epic poem in twelve books on the subject of King Arthur and the knights of the Round Table, but harsh reviews discouraged

Beneath the sacred bush[2] and passed away—
The parson Holmes, the poet Everard Hall,
The host, and I sat round the wassail-bowl, 5
Then halfway ebbed; and there we held a talk,
How all the old honor had from Christmas gone,
Or gone or dwindled down to some odd games
In some odd nooks like this; till I, tired out
With cutting eights that day upon the pond, 10
Where, three times slipping from the outer edge,
I bumped the ice into three several stars,
Fell in a doze; and half-awake I heard
The parson taking wide and wider sweeps,
Now harping on the church-commissioners,[3] 15
Now hawking at geology and schism;
Until I woke, and found him settled down
Upon the general decay of faith
Right through the world: "at home was little left,
And none abroad; there was no anchor, none, 20
To hold by." Francis, laughing, clapped his hand
On Everard's shoulder, with "I hold by him."
"And I," quoth Everard, "by the wassail-bowl."
"Why yes," I said, "we knew your gift that way
At college; but another which you had— 25
I mean of verse (for so we held it then),
What came of that?" "You know," said Frank, "he burnt
His epic, his King Arthur, some twelve books"—
And then to me demanding why: "O, sir,
He thought that nothing new was said, or else 30
Something so said 'twas nothing—that a truth
Looks freshest in the fashion of the day;
God knows; he has a mint of reasons; ask.
It pleased *me* well enough." "Nay, nay," said Hall,
"Why take the style of those heroic times? 35
For nature brings not back the mastodon,
Nor we those times; and why should any man
Remodel models? these twelve books of mine
Were faint Homeric echoes, nothing-worth,
Mere chaff and draff, much better burnt." "But I," 40

him for many years from completing his plan. By 1838 he had completed one book of the twelve, the story of King Arthur's death, which was published in 1842 under the title *Morte d'Arthur*. In this earlier version, the story is framed by a short introductory section called *The Epic* (lines 1–51) and an epilogue (lines 324–54) describing a party on Christmas Eve in modern times, at which a poet reads *Morte d'Arthur* to a group of friends. The facetious and easy conversational style of this introductory section is in marked contrast to the heroic manner of the main story.

Later, in 1869, Tennyson incorporated *Morte d'Arthur* into his long narrative poem, *Idylls of the King*. Under a new title, *The Passing of Arthur*, it appears there as the twelfth book of the *Idylls*. At this time Tennyson discarded *The Epic* framework and added some lines to the main story, but in effect *Morte d'Arthur* may be read as an example of *Idylls of the King*.
2. Mistletoe.
3. Commissioners appointed by the government in 1835 to regulate finances of the Anglican Church.

Said Francis, "picked the eleventh from this hearth,
And have it; keep a thing, its use will come.
I hoard it as a sugarplum for Holmes."
He laughed, and I, though sleepy, like a horse
That hears the corn-bin open, pricked my ears;   45
For I remembered Everard's college fame
When we were Freshmen. Then at my request
He brought it; and the poet, little urged,
But with some prelude of disparagement,
Read, mouthing out his hollow o's and a's,   50
Deep-chested music, and to this result.

Morte d'Arthur

So all day long the noise of battle rolled
Among the mountains by the winter sea,
Until King Arthur's table, man by man,
Had fallen in Lyonnesse[4] about their lord,   55
King Arthur; then, because his wound was deep,
The bold Sir Bedivere uplifted him,
Sir Bedivere, the last of all his knights,
And bore him to a chapel nigh the field,
A broken chancel with a broken cross,   60
That stood on a dark strait of barren land.
On one side lay the ocean, and on one
Lay a great water, and the moon was full.
Then spake King Arthur to Sir Bedivere:
"The sequel of today unsolders all   65
The goodliest fellowship of famous knights
Whereof this world holds record. Such a sleep
They sleep—the men I loved. I think that we
Shall never more, at any future time,
Delight our souls with talk of knightly deeds,   70
Walking about the gardens and the halls
Of Camelot, as in the days that were.
I perish by this people which I made—
Though Merlin sware that I should come again
To rule once more—but let what will be be,   75
I am so deeply smitten through the helm
That without help I cannot last till morn.
Thou therefore take my brand[5] Excalibur,
Which was my pride; for thou rememberest how
In those old days, one summer noon, an arm   80
Rose up from out the bosom of the lake,
Clothed in white samite,[6] mystic, wonderful,
Holding the sword—and how I rowed across
And took it, and have worn it, like a king;
And, wheresoever I am sung or told   85
In aftertime, this also shall be known.

4. Legendary country off the coast of   5. Sword.
Cornwall.   6. A rich, heavy silk.

But now delay not; take Excalibur,
And fling him far into the middle mere;[7]
Watch what thou seest, and lightly[8] bring me word."
    To him replied the bold Sir Bedivere: 90
"It is not meet, Sir King, to leave thee thus,
Aidless, alone, and smitten through the helm.
A little thing may harm a wounded man.
Yet I thy hest will all perform at full,
Watch what I see, and lightly bring thee word."   95
    So saying, from the ruined shrine he stepped
And in the moon athwart the place of tombs,
Where lay the mighty bones of ancient men,
Old knights, and over them the sea wind sang
Shrill, chill, with flakes of foam. He, stepping down   100
By zigzag paths and juts of pointed rock,
Came on the shining levels of the lake.
    There drew he forth the brand Excalibur,
And o'er him, drawing it, the winter moon,
Brightening the skirts of a long cloud, ran forth   105
And sparkled keen with frost against the hilt;
For all the haft twinkled with diamond sparks,
Myriads of topaz-lights, and jacinth-work[9]
Of subtlest jewelry. He gazed so long
That both his eyes were dazzled, as he stood,   110
This way and that dividing the swift mind,
In act to throw; but at the last it seemed
Better to leave Excalibur concealed
There in the many-knotted water-flags,
That whistled stiff and dry about the marge.   115
So strode he back slow to the wounded king.
    Then spake King Arthur to Sir Bedivere:
"Hast thou performed my mission which I gave?
What is it thou hast seen, or what hast heard?"
    And answer made the bold Sir Bedivere: 120
"I heard the ripple washing in the reeds,
And the wild water lapping on the crag."
    To whom replied King Arthur, faint and pale:
"Thou hast betrayed thy nature and thy name,
Not rendering true answer, as beseemed   125
Thy fealty, nor like a noble knight;
For surer sign had followed, either hand,
Or voice, or else a motion of the mere.
This is a shameful thing for men to lie.
Yet now, I charge thee, quickly go again   130
As thou art lief[1] and dear, and do the thing
I bade thee, watch, and lightly bring me word."
    Then went Sir Bedivere the second time
Across the ridge, and paced beside the mere,

---

7. Middle of the lake.   9. A "jacinth" is a red-colored gem.
8. Quickly.   1. Beloved.

Counting the dewy pebbles, fixed in thought;   135
But when he saw the wonder of the hilt,
How curiously[2] and strangely chased, he smote
His palms together, and he cried aloud:
    "And if indeed I cast the brand away,
Surely a precious thing, one worthy note,   140
Should thus be lost forever from the earth,
Which might have pleased the eyes of many men.
What good should follow this, if this were done?
What harm, undone? deep harm to disobey,
Seeing obedience is the bond of rule.   145
Were it well to obey then, if a king demand
An act unprofitable, against himself?
The king is sick, and knows not what he does.
What record, or what relic of my lord
Should be to aftertime, but empty breath   150
And rumors of a doubt? but were this kept,
Stored in some treasure-house of mighty kings,
Some one might show it at a joust of arms,
Saying, 'King Arthur's sword, Excalibur,
Wrought by the lonely maiden of the lake;   155
Nine years she wrought it, sitting in the deeps
Upon the hidden bases of the hills.'
So might some old man speak in the aftertime
To all the people, winning reverence;
But now much honor and much fame were lost."   160
    So spake he, clouded with his own conceit,[3]
And hid Excalibur the second time,
And so strode back slow to the wounded king.
    Then spoke King Arthur, breathing heavily:
"What is it thou hast seen, or what hast heard?"   165
    And answer made the bold Sir Bedivere:
"I heard the water lapping on the crag,
And the long ripple washing in the reeds."
    To whom replied King Arthur, much in wrath:
"Ah, miserable and unkind, untrue,   170
Unknightly, traitor-hearted! Woe is me!
Authority forgets a dying king,
Laid widowed of the power in his eye
That bowed the will. I see thee what thou art,
For thou, the latest-left of all my knights,   175
In whom should meet the offices of all,
Thou wouldst betray me for the precious hilt;
Either from lust of gold, or like a girl
Valuing the giddy pleasure of the eyes.
Yet, for a man may fail in duty twice,   180
And the third time may prosper, get thee hence;
But, if thou spare to fling Excalibur,
I will arise and slay thee with my hands."

2. Skillfully; "chased": adorned.   3. Vain and foolish fancies.

Then quickly rose Sir Bedivere, and ran,
And, leaping down the ridges lightly, plunged   185
Among the bulrush-beds, and clutched the sword,
And strongly wheeled and threw it. The great brand
Made lightnings in the splendor of the moon,
And flashing round and round, and whirled in an arch,
Shot like a streamer of the northern morn,[4]   190
Seen where the moving isles of winter shock[5]
By night, with noises of the northern sea.
So flashed and fell the brand Excalibur;
But ere he dipped the surface, rose an arm
Clothed in white samite, mystic, wonderful,   195
And caught him by the hilt, and brandished him
Three times, and drew him under in the mere.
And lightly went the other to the king.
    Then spoke King Arthur, drawing thicker breath:
"Now see I by thine eyes that this is done.   200
Speak out; what is it thou hast heard, or seen?"
    And answer made the bold Sir Bedivere:
"Sir King, I closed mine eyelids, lest the gems
Should blind my purpose, for I never saw,
Nor shall see, here or elsewhere, till I die,   205
Not though I live three lives of mortal men,
So great a miracle as yonder hilt.
Then with both hands I flung him, wheeling him;
But when I looked again, behold an arm,
Clothed in white samite, mystic, wonderful,   210
That caught him by the hilt, and brandished him
Three times, and drew him under in the mere."
    And answer made King Arthur, breathing hard:
"My end draws nigh; 'tis time that I were gone.
Make broad thy shoulders to receive my weight,   215
And bear me to the margin; yet I fear
My wound hath taken cold, and I shall die."
    So saying, from the pavement he half rose,
Slowly, with pain, reclining on his arm,
And looking wistfully with wide blue eyes   220
As in a picture. Him Sir Bedivere
Remorsefully regarded through his tears,
And would have spoken, but he found not words,
Then took with care, and kneeling on one knee,
O'er both his shoulders drew the languid hands,   225
And rising bore him through the place of tombs.
    But, as he walked, King Arthur panted hard,
Like one that feels a nightmare on his bed
When all the house is mute. So sighed the king,
Muttering and murmuring at his ear, "Quick, quick!   230
I fear it is too late, and I shall die."
    But the other swiftly strode from ridge to ridge,

4. The northern lights.   5. I.e., where the icebergs collide.

Clothed with his breath, and looking, as he walked,
Larger than human on the frozen hills.
He heard the deep behind him, and a cry   235
Before. His own thought drove him like a goad.
Dry clashed his harness in the icy caves
And barren chasms, and all to left and right
The bare black cliff clanged round him, as he based
His feet on juts of slippery crag that rang   240
Sharp-smitten with the dint of arméd heels—
And on a sudden, lo! the level lake,
And the long glories of the winter moon.
    Then saw they how there hove a dusky barge,
Dark as a funeral scarf from stem to stern,   245
Beneath them; and descending they were ware
That all the decks were dense with stately forms
Black-stoled, black-hooded, like a dream—by these
Three queens with crowns of gold—and from them rose
A cry that shivered to the tingling stars,   250
And, as it were one voice, an agony
Of lamentation, like a wind that shrills
All night in a waste land, where no one comes,
Or hath come, since the making of the world.
    Then murmured Arthur, "Place me in the barge,"   255
And to the barge they came. There those three queens
Put forth their hands, and took the king, and wept.
But she that rose the tallest of them all
And fairest laid his head upon her lap,
And loosed the shattered casque,[6] and chafed his hands, 260
And called him by his name, complaining loud,
And dropping bitter tears against his brow
Striped with dark blood; for all his face was white
And colorless, and like the withered moon
Smote by the fresh beam of the springing east;   265
And all his greaves and cuisses dashed with drops
Of onset;[7] and the light and lustrous curls—
That made his forehead like a rising sun
High from the dais-throne—were parched with dust;
Or, clotted into points and hanging loose,   270
Mixed with the knightly growth that fringed his lips.
So like a shattered column lay the king;
Not like that Arthur who, with lance in rest,
From spur to plume a star of tournament,
Shot through the lists at Camelot, and charged   275
Before the eyes of ladies and of kings.
    Then loudly cried the bold Sir Bedivere:
"Ah! my Lord Arthur, whither shall I go?
Where shall I hide my forehead and my eyes?

6. Helmet.
7. "Greaves": armor to protect the leg below the knee, "cuisses": armor to protect the front of the thighs, "onset": blood from the battle.

For now I see the true old times are dead,   280
When every morning brought a noble chance,
And every chance brought out a noble knight.
Such times have been not since the light that led
The holy Elders with the gift of myrrh.[8]
But now the whole ROUND TABLE is dissolved   285
Which was an image of the mighty world;
And I, the last, go forth companionless,
And the days darken round me, and the years,
Among new men, strange faces, other minds."
   And slowly answered Arthur from the barge: 290
"The old order changeth, yielding place to new,
And God fulfills himself in many ways,
Lest one good custom should corrupt the world.
Comfort thyself: what comfort is in me?
I have lived my life, and that which I have done   295
May He within himself make pure! but thou,
If thou shouldst never see my face again,
Pray for my soul. More things are wrought by prayer
Than this world dreams of. Wherefore, let thy voice
Rise like a fountain for me night and day.   300
For what are men better than sheep or goats
That nourish a blind life within the brain,
If, knowing God, they lift not hands of prayer
Both for themselves and those who call them friend?
For so the whole round earth is every way   305
Bound by gold chains about the feet of God.
But now farewell. I am going a long way
With these thou seest—if indeed I go—
For all my mind is clouded with a doubt—
To the island-valley of Avilion;[9]   310
Where falls not hail, or rain, or any snow,
Nor ever wind blows loudly, but it lies
Deep-meadowed, happy, fair with orchard lawns
And bowery hollows crowned with summer sea,
Where I will heal me of my grievous wound."   315
   So said he, and the barge with oar and sail
Moved from the brink, like some full-breasted swan
That, fluting a wild carol ere her death,
Ruffles her pure cold plume, and takes the flood
With swarthy webs. Long stood Sir Bedivere   320
Revolving many memories, till the hull
Looked one black dot against the verge of dawn,
And on the mere the wailing died away.

    Here ended Hall, and our last light, that long
Had winked and threatened darkness, flared and fell;   325

8. I.e., the star that guided the three kings ("Elders") to the Christ Child at Bethlehem.
9. Avalon, in Celtic mythology and medieval romance, the Vale of the Blessed where heroes enjoyed life after death.

At which the parson, sent to sleep with sound,
And waked with silence, grunted "Good!" but we
Sat rapt: it was the tone with which he read—
Perhaps some modern touches here and there
Redeemed it from the charge of nothingness—   330
Or else we loved the man, and prized his work;
I know not; but we sitting, as I said,
The cock crew loud, as at that time of year
The lusty bird takes every hour for dawn.
Then Francis, muttering, like a man ill-used,   335
"There now—that's nothing!" drew a little back,
And drove his heel into the smoldered log,
That sent a blast of sparkles up the flue.
And so to bed, where yet in sleep I seemed
To sail with Arthur under looming shores,   340
Point after point; till on to dawn, when dreams
Begin to feel the truth and stir of day,
To me, methought, who waited with the crowd,
There came a bark that, blowing forward, bore
King Arthur, like a modern gentleman   345
Of stateliest port; and all the people cried,
"Arthur is come again: he cannot die."
Then those that stood upon the hills behind
Repeated—"Come again, and thrice as fair";
And, further inland, voices echoed—"Come   350
With all good things, and war shall be no more."
At this a hundred bells began to peal,
That with the sound I woke, and heard indeed
The clear church bells ring in the Christmas morn.

1833–38   1842

Ulysses[1]

It little profits that an idle king,
By this still hearth, among these barren crags,
Matched with an aged wife, I mete and dole
Unequal laws[2] unto a savage race,
That hoard, and sleep, and feed, and know not me.   5

1. According to Dante, after Ulysses had returned home to Ithaca and had settled down to rule his island kingdom, he became restless and desired to set out on another voyage of exploration to the west. In old age he persuaded a band of his followers to accompany him on such a voyage. "Consider your origin," he addressed them, "ye were not formed to live like brutes, but to follow virtue and knowledge" (*Inferno* XXVI).
The contrast between the conscien-tious administrator, Telemachus, and the energetic quester, his father, has been variously interpreted. A few readers argue that Ulysses is not repre-sented in the monologue as a great hero but as irresponsible. Tennyson himself stated that the poem expressed his own "need of going forward and braving the struggle of life" after the death of Hallam.
2. Measure out rewards and punish-ments.

I cannot rest from travel; I will drink
Life to the lees. All times I have enjoyed
Greatly, have suffered greatly, both with those
That loved me, and alone; on shore, and when
Through scudding drifts[3] the rainy Hyades   10
Vexed the dim sea. I am become a name;
For always roaming with a hungry heart
Much have I seen and known—cities of men
And manners, climates, councils, governments,
Myself not least, but honored of them all—   15
And drunk delight of battle with my peers,
Far on the ringing plains of windy Troy.
I am a part of all that I have met;
Yet all experience is an arch wherethrough
Gleams that untraveled world whose margin fades   20
Forever and forever when I move.
How dull it is to pause, to make an end,
To rust unburnished, not to shine in use!
As though to breathe were life! Life piled on life
Were all too little, and of one to me   25
Little remains; but every hour is saved
From that eternal silence, something more,
A bringer of new things; and vile it were
For some three suns to store and hoard myself,
And this gray spirit yearning in desire   30
To follow knowledge like a sinking star,
Beyond the utmost bound of human thought.

    This is my son, mine own Telemachus,
To whom I leave the scepter and the isle—
Well-loved of me, discerning to fulfill   35
This labor, by slow prudence to make mild
A rugged people, and through soft degrees
Subdue them to the useful and the good.
Most blameless is he, centered in the sphere
Of common duties, decent not to fail   40
In offices of tenderness, and pay
Meet adoration to my household gods,
When I am gone. He works his work, I mine.

    There lies the port; the vessel puffs her sail;
There gloom the dark, broad seas. My mariners,   45
Souls that have toiled, and wrought, and thought with me—
That ever with a frolic welcome took
The thunder and the sunshine, and opposed
Free hearts, free foreheads—you and I are old;
Old age hath yet his honor and his toil.   50
Death closes all; but something ere the end,
Some work of noble note, may yet be done,

3. Driving showers of spray and rain;   whose rising was assumed to be fol-
the "Hyades" are a group of stars   lowed by rain.

Not unbecoming men that strove with Gods.
The lights begin to twinkle from the rocks;
The long day wanes; the slow moon climbs; the deep   55
Moans round with many voices. Come, my friends,
'Tis not too late to seek a newer world.
Push off, and sitting well in order smite
The sounding furrows; for my purpose holds
To sail beyond the sunset, and the baths   60
Of all the western stars,[4] until I die.
It may be that the gulfs will wash us down;
It may be we shall touch the Happy Isles,[5]
And see the great Achilles, whom we knew.
Though much is taken, much abides; and though   65
We are not now that strength which in old days
Moved earth and heaven, that which we are, we are—
One equal temper of heroic hearts,
Made weak by time and fate, but strong in will
To strive, to seek, to find, and not to yield.   70

1833   1842

Tithonus[1]

The woods decay, the woods decay and fall,
The vapors weep their burthen to the ground,
Man comes and tills the field and lies beneath,
And after many a summer dies the swan.[2]
Me only cruel immortality   5
Consumes; I wither slowly in thine arms,[3]
Here at the quiet limit of the world,
A white-haired shadow roaming like a dream
The ever-silent spaces of the East,
Far-folded mists, and gleaming halls of morn.   10
    Alas! for this gray shadow, once a man—
So glorious in his beauty and thy choice,
Who madest him thy chosen, that he seemed
To his great heart none other than a God!
I asked thee, "Give me immortality."   15
Then didst thou grant mine asking with a smile,
Like wealthy men who care not how they give.
But thy strong Hours indignant worked their wills,

4. The outer ocean or river which, in Greek cosmology, surrounded the flat circle of the earth, and into which the stars descended.
5. Elysium, or the Islands of the Blessed, where heroes such as Achilles were supposed to enjoy life after death. These islands were thought to be in the far-western ocean.
1. Tithonus, a Trojan prince, was loved by the goddess of the dawn, Eos or Aurora, who obtained for him the gift of living forever but neglected to obtain for him the gift of everlasting youth. In the monologue, Tithonus appears as an aged man, dwelling still in the palace of the goddess, and cut off by his frustrating predicament from the normal cycle of human life which culminates in death. To him immortality, not death, is "cruel."
2. Some species of swans live for at least fifty years.
3. I.e., the arms of Eos.

And beat me down and marred and wasted me,
And though they could not end me, left me maimed   20
To dwell in presence of immortal youth,
Immortal age beside immortal youth,
And all I was in ashes. Can thy love,
Thy beauty, make amends, though even now,
Close over us, the silver star,[4] thy guide,   25
Shines in those tremulous eyes that fill with tears
To hear me? Let me go; take back thy gift.
Why should a man desire in any way
To vary from the kindly race of men,
Or pass beyond the goal of ordinance[5]   30
Where all should pause, as is most meet for all?
    A soft air fans the cloud apart; there comes
A glimpse of that dark world where I was born.
Once more the old mysterious glimmer steals
From thy pure brows, and from thy shoulders pure,   35
And bosom beating with a heart renewed.
Thy cheek begins to redden through the gloom,
Thy sweet eyes brighten slowly close to mine,
Ere yet they blind the stars, and the wild team[6]
Which love thee, yearning for thy yoke, arise,   40
And shake the darkness from their loosened manes,
And beat the twilight into flakes of fire.
    Lo! ever thus thou growest beautiful
In silence, then before thine answer given
Departest, and thy tears are on my cheek.   45
    Why wilt thou ever scare me with thy tears,
And make me tremble lest a saying learnt,
In days far-off, on that dark earth, be true?
"The Gods themselves cannot recall their gifts."
    Ay me! ay me! with what another heart   50
In days far-off, and with what other eyes
I used to watch—if I be he that watched—
The lucid outline forming round thee; saw
The dim curls kindle into sunny rings;
Changed with thy mystic change, and felt my blood   55
Glow with the glow that slowly crimsoned all
Thy presence and thy portals, while I lay,
Mouth, forehead, eyelids, growing dewy-warm
With kisses balmier than half-opening buds
Of April, and could hear the lips that kissed   60
Whispering I knew not what of wild and sweet,
Like that strange song I heard Apollo sing,
While Ilion like a mist rose into towers.[7]
    Yet hold me not forever in thine East;

4. The morning star that precedes the dawn.
5. What is decreed or ordained as human destiny.
6. The horses that draw Eos' chariot into the sky at daybreak.
7. The walls of Troy (Ilion) were supposed to have been built to the strains of Apollo's music.

How can my nature longer mix with thine?   65
Coldly thy rosy shadows bathe me, cold
Are all thy lights, and cold my wrinkled feet
Upon thy glimmering thresholds, when the steam
Floats up from those dim fields about the homes
Of happy men that have the power to die,   70
And grassy barrows of the happier dead.
Release me, and restore me to the ground.
Thou seest all things, thou wilt see my grave;
Thou wilt renew thy beauty morn by morn,
I earth in earth forget these empty courts,   75
And thee returning on thy silver wheels.

1833, 1859   1860

Break, Break, Break

Break, break, break,
    On thy cold gray stones, O Sea!
And I would that my tongue could utter
    The thoughts that arise in me.

O, well for the fisherman's boy,   5
    That he shouts with his sister at play!
O, well for the sailor lad,
    That he sings in his boat on the bay!

And the stately ships go on
    To their haven under the hill;   10
But O for the touch of a vanished hand,
    And the sound of a voice that is still!

Break, break, break,
    At the foot of thy crags, O Sea!
But the tender grace of a day that is dead   15
    Will never come back to me.

1834   1842

Locksley Hall[1]

Comrades, leave me here a little, while as yet 'tis early morn;
Leave me here, and when you want me, sound upon the bugle horn.

1. The situation in this poem—of a young man's being jilted by a girl who chose to marry a wealthy landowner—may have been suggested to Tennyson by the experience of his brother. Frederick Tennyson, a hot-tempered man, had fallen in love with his cousin, Julia Tennyson, and was similarly unsuccessful. It may also have been inspired by Tennyson's own frustrated courtship of Rosa Baring who rejected the young poet in favor of a wealthy suitor. Concerning the ranting tone of the speaker (a tone accentuated by the heavily marked trochaic meter), Tennyson himself said: "The whole poem represents young life, its good side, its deficiencies, and its yearnings."

'Tis the place, and all around it, as of old, the curlews call,
Dreary gleams[2] about the moorland flying over Locksley Hall;

Locksley Hall, that in the distance overlooks the sandy tracts,   5
And the hollow ocean-ridges roaring into cataracts.

Many a night from yonder ivied casement, ere I went to rest,
Did I look on great Orion sloping slowly to the west.

Many a night I saw the Pleiads,[3] rising through the mellow shade,
Glitter like a swarm of fireflies tangled in a silver braid.   10

Here about the beach I wandered, nourishing a youth sublime
With the fairy tales of science, and the long result of time;

When the centuries behind me like a fruitful land reposed;
When I clung to all the present for the promise that it closed;[4]

When I dipped into the future far as human eye could see,   15
Saw the vision of the world and all the wonder that would be.—

In the spring a fuller crimson comes upon the robin's breast;
In the spring the wanton lapwing gets himself another crest;

In the spring a livelier iris changes on the burnished dove;
In the spring a young man's fancy lightly turns to thoughts of love.   20

Then her cheek was pale and thinner than should be for one so young,
And her eyes on all my motions with a mute observance hung.

And I said, "My cousin Amy, speak, and speak the truth to me,
Trust me, cousin, all the current of my being sets to thee."

On her pallid cheek and forehead came a color and a light,   25
As I have seen the rosy red flushing in the northern night.

And she turned—her bosom shaken with a sudden storm of sighs—
All the spirit deeply dawning in the dark of hazel eyes—

Saying, "I have hid my feelings, fearing they should do me wrong";
Saying, "Dost thou love me, cousin?" weeping, "I have loved thee
    long."   30

Love took up the glass of Time, and turned it in his glowing hands;
Every moment, lightly shaken, ran itself in golden sands.

Love took up the harp of Life, and smote on all the chords with
    might;
Smote the chord of Self, that, trembling, passed in music out of
    sight.

Many a morning on the moorland did we hear the copses ring,   35
And her whisper thronged my pulses with the fullness of the spring.

---

2. Tennyson stated that "gleams" does
not refer to "curlews" flying but to
streaks of light.

3. The Pleiades, a seven-starred constellation.

4. Enclosed.

Many an evening by the waters did we watch the stately ships,
And our spirits rushed together at the touching of the lips.

O my cousin, shallow-hearted! O my Amy, mine no more!
O the dreary, dreary moorland! O the barren, barren shore! 40

Falser than all fancy fathoms, falser than all songs have sung,
Puppet to a father's threat, and servile to a shrewish tongue!

Is it well to wish thee happy?—having known me—to decline
On a range of lower feelings and a narrower heart than mine!

Yet it shall be; thou shalt lower to his level day by day, 45
What is fine within thee growing coarse to sympathize with clay.

As the husband is, the wife is; thou art mated with a clown,[5]
And the grossness of his nature will have weight to drag thee down.

He will hold thee, when his passion shall have spent its novel force,
Something better than his dog, a little dearer than his horse. 50

What is this? his eyes are heavy; think not they are glazed with wine.
Go to him, it is thy duty; kiss him, take his hand in thine.

It may be my lord is weary, that his brain is overwrought;
Soothe him with thy finer fancies, touch him with thy lighter
    thought.

He will answer to the purpose, easy things to understand— 55
Better thou wert dead before me, though I slew thee with my hand!

Better thou and I were lying, hidden from the heart's disgrace,
Rolled in one another's arms, and silent in a last embrace.

Cursed be the social wants that sin against the strength of youth!
Cursed be the social lies that warp us from the living truth! 60

Cursed be the sickly forms that err from honest Nature's rule!
Cursed be the gold that gilds the straitened[6] forehead of the fool!

Well—'tis well that I should bluster!—Hadst thou less unworthy
    proved—
Would to God—for I had loved thee more than ever wife was loved.

Am I mad, that I should cherish that which bears but bitter fruit? 65
I will pluck it from my bosom, though my heart be at the root.

Never, though my mortal summers to such length of years should
    come
As the many-wintered crow[7] that leads the clanging rookery home.

Where is comfort? in division of the records of the mind?
Can I part her from herself, and love her, as I knew her, kind? 70

I remember one that perished; sweetly did she speak and move;
Such a one do I remember, whom to look at was to love.

5. Boor.   7. A rook, a long-lived bird.
6. Narrowed.

Can I think of her as dead, and love her for the love she bore?
No—she never loved me truly; love is love for evermore.

Comfort? comfort scorned of devils! this is truth the poet[8] sings,   75
That a sorrow's crown of sorrow is remembering happier things.

Drug thy memories, lest thou learn it, lest thy heart be put to proof,
In the dead unhappy night, and when the rain is on the roof.

Like a dog, he hunts in dreams, and thou art staring at the wall,
Where the dying night-lamp flickers, and the shadows rise and
    fall.
         80

Then a hand shall pass before thee, pointing to his drunken sleep,
To thy widowed[9] marriage-pillows, to the tears that thou wilt weep.

Thou shalt hear the "Never, never," whispered by the phantom years.
And a song from out the distance in the ringing of thine ears;

And an eye shall vex thee, looking ancient kindness on thy pain.   85
Turn thee, turn thee on thy pillow; get thee to thy rest again.

Nay, but Nature brings thee solace; for a tender voice will cry.
'Tis a purer life than thine, a lip to drain thy trouble dry.

Baby lips will laugh me down; my latest rival brings thee rest.
Baby fingers, waxen touches, press me from the mother's breast.   90

O, the child too clothes the father with a dearness not his due.
Half is thine and half is his; it will be worthy of the two.

O, I see thee old and formal, fitted to thy petty part,
With a little hoard of maxims preaching down a daughter's heart.

"They were dangerous guides the feelings—she herself was not ex-
    empt—
         95
Truly, she herself had suffered"—Perish in thy self-contempt!

Overlive it—lower yet—be happy! wherefore should I care?
I myself must mix with action, lest I wither by despair.

What is that which I should turn to, lighting upon days like these?
Every door is barred with gold, and opens but to golden keys.   100

Every gate is thronged with suitors, all the markets overflow.
I have but an angry fancy; what is that which I should do?

I had been content to perish, falling on the foeman's ground,
When the ranks are rolled in vapor, and the winds are laid with
    sound.[1]

But the jingling of the guinea helps the hurt that Honor feels,   105
And the nations do but murmur, snarling at each other's heels.

---

8. Dante (*Inferno* V.121–23).
9. Presumably figurative. Her marriage
having become a mockery, she is widowed.
1. It was once believed that the firing
of artillery stilled the winds.

Can I but relive in sadness? I will turn that earlier page.
Hide me from my deep emotion, O thou wondrous Mother-Age![2]

Make me feel the wild pulsation that I felt before the strife,
When I heard my days before me, and the tumult of my life;   110

Yearning for the large excitement that the coming years would yield,
Eager-hearted as a boy when first he leaves his father's field,

And at night along the dusky highway near and nearer drawn,
Sees in heaven the light of London flaring like a dreary dawn;

And his spirit leaps within him to be gone before him then,   115
Underneath the light he looks at, in among the throngs of men;

Men, my brothers, men the workers, ever reaping something new;
That which they have done but earnest[3] of the things that they shall
do.

For I dipped into the future, far as human eye could see,
Saw the Vision of the world, and all the wonder that would be;   120

Saw the heavens fill with commerce, argosies of magic sails,[4]
Pilots of the purple twilight, dropping down with costly bales;

Heard the heavens fill with shouting, and there rained a ghastly dew
From the nations' airy navies grappling in the central blue;

Far along the world-wide whisper of the south wind rushing
warm,   125
With the standards of the peoples plunging through the thunderstorm;

Till the war drum throbbed no longer, and the battle flags were
furled
In the Parliament of man, the Federation of the world.

There the common sense of most shall hold a fretful realm in awe,
And the kindly earth shall slumber, lapped in universal law.   130

So I triumphed ere my passion sweeping through me left me dry,
Left me with the palsied heart, and left me with the jaundiced eye;

Eye, to which all order festers, all things here are out of joint.
Science moves, but slowly, slowly, creeping on from point to point;

Slowly comes a hungry people, as a lion, creeping nigher,   135
Glares at one that nods and winks behind a slowly-dying fire.

Yet I doubt not through the ages one increasing purpose runs,
And the thoughts of men are widened with the process of the suns.

What is that to him that reaps not harvest of his youthful joys,
Though the deep heart of existence beat forever like a boy's?   140

2. Perhaps signifying the consolations of a future age of progress. See also line 185.

3. A pledge.

4. Probably airships, such as balloons.

Knowledge comes, but wisdom lingers, and I linger on the shore,
And the individual withers, and the world is more and more.

Knowledge comes, but wisdom lingers, and he bears a laden breast,
Full of sad experience, moving toward the stillness of his rest.

Hark, my merry comrades call me, sounding on the bugle horn,   145
They to whom my foolish passion were a target for their scorn.

Shall it not be scorn to me to harp on such a moldered string?
I am shamed through all my nature to have loved so slight a thing.

Weakness to be wroth with weakness! woman's pleasure, woman's
        pain—
Nature made them blinder motions bounded in a shallower brain.   150

Woman is the lesser man, and all thy passions, matched with mine,
Are as moonlight unto sunlight, and as water unto wine—

Here at least, where nature sickens, nothing. Ah, for some retreat
Deep in yonder shining Orient, where my life began to beat,

Where in wild Mahratta-battle[5] fell my father evil-starred—   155
I was left a trampled orphan, and a selfish uncle's ward.

Or to burst all links of habit—there to wander far away,
On from island unto island at the gateways of the day.

Larger constellations burning, mellow moons and happy skies,
Breadths of tropic shade and palms in cluster, knots of Paradise.   160

Never comes the trader, never floats an European flag,
Slides the bird o'er lustrous woodland, swings the trailer[6] from the
        crag;

Droops the heavy-blossomed bower, hangs the heavy-fruited tree—
Summer isles of Eden lying in dark purple spheres of sea.

There methinks would be enjoyment more than in this march of
        mind,   165
In the steamship, in the railway, in the thoughts that shake man-
        kind.

There the passions cramped no longer shall have scope and breath-
        ing space;
I will take some savage woman, she shall rear my dusky race.

Iron-jointed, supple-sinewed, they shall dive, and they shall run,
Catch the wild goat by the hair, and hurl their lances in the sun;   170

Whistle back the parrot's call, and leap the rainbows of the brooks,
Not with blinded eyesight poring over miserable books—

Fool, again the dream, the fancy! but I *know* my words are wild,
But I count the gray barbarian lower than the Christian child.

5. A reference to wars waged by a   in India (1803 and 1817).
Hindu people against the British forces   6. A vine.

I, to herd with narrow foreheads, vacant of our glorious gains.   175
Like a beast with lower pleasures, like a beast with lower pains!

Mated with a squalid savage—what to me were sun or clime?
I the heir of all the ages, in the foremost files of time—

I that rather held it better men should perish one by one,
Than that earth should stand at gaze like Joshua's moon in
   Ajalon![7]   180

Not in vain the distance beacons. Forward, forward let us range,
Let the great world spin forever down the ringing grooves[8] of change.

Through the shadow of the globe we sweep into the younger day;
Better fifty years of Europe than a cycle of Cathay.[9]

Mother-Age—for mine I knew not—help me as when life begun;   185
Rift the hills, and roll the waters, flash the lightnings, weigh the sun.

O, I see the crescent promise of my spirit hath not set.
Ancient founts of inspiration well through all my fancy yet.

Howsoever these things be, a long farewell to Locksley Hall!
Now for me the woods may wither, now for me the roof-tree fall.   190

Comes a vapor from the margin, blackening over heath and holt,
Cramming all the blast before it, in its breast a thunderbolt.

Let it fall on Locksley Hall, with rain or hail, or fire or snow;
For the mighty wind arises, roaring seaward, and I go.

                                                    1842

Move Eastward, Happy Earth

Move eastward, happy earth, and leave
   Yon orange sunset waning slow;
From fringes of the faded eve,
   O happy planet, eastward go,
Till over thy dark shoulder glow   5
   Thy silver sister-world,[1] and rise
   To glass herself in dewy eyes
That watch me from the glen below.

Ah, bear me with thee, smoothly borne,
   Dip forward under starry light,   10

---

7. At the command of Joshua, the sun and moon stood still while the Israelites completed the slaughter of their enemies in the valley of Ajalon (Joshua x.12–13).
8. Railroad tracks. Tennyson at one time had the impression that train wheels ran in grooved rails.
9. China, regarded in the 19th century as a static, unprogressive country.
1. The planet Venus, or perhaps the moon, which will be reflected in the eyes of the speaker's beloved.

And move me to my marriage morn,
And round again to happy night.

ca. 1836   1842

Lines

Here[2] often, when a child I lay reclined,
  I took delight in this locality.
Here stood the infant Ilion of the mind,
  And here the Grecian ships did seem to be.
And here again I come, and only find   5
  The drain-cut levels of the marshy lea—
Gray sea banks and pale sunsets—dreary wind,
  Dim shores, dense rains, and heavy-clouded sea!

1837   1850

The Eagle: A Fragment

He clasps the crag with crooked hands;
Close to the sun in lonely lands,
Ringed with the azure world, he stands.

The wrinkled sea beneath him crawls;
He watches from his mountain walls,
And like a thunderbolt he falls.   5

1851

Songs from THE PRINCESS[1]
Sweet and Low

Sweet and low, sweet and low,
  Wind of the western sea,
Low, low, breathe and blow,
  Wind of the western sea!
Over the rolling waters go,   5
Come from the dying moon, and blow,
  Blow him again to me;
While my little one, while my pretty one, sleeps.

---

2. At Mablethorpe, on the Lincolnshire coast.
1. *The Princess* is a story of the role of women in modern society. As a long narrative love poem, *The Princess* has not been highly regarded, and parodies such as Gilbert and Sullivan's *Princess* *Ida* have exposed the flaws in the story. What saves the poem is its use of interludes in which occasional songs were sung. These songs rank among the finest of Tennyson's lyrics, and various 19th- and 20th-century composers have set them to music.

Sleep and rest, sleep and rest,
    Father will come to thee soon;   10
Rest, rest, on mother's breast,
    Father will come to thee soon;
Father will come to his babe in the nest,
Silver sails all out of the west
    Under the silver moon;   15
Sleep, my little one, sleep, my pretty one, sleep.

                    1850

The Splendor Falls

The splendor falls on castle walls
    And snowy summits old in story;
The long light shakes across the lakes,
    And the wild cataract leaps in glory.
Blow, bugle, blow, set the wild echoes flying,   5
Blow, bugle; answer, echoes, dying, dying, dying.

O, hark, O, hear! how thin and clear,
    And thinner, clearer, farther going!
O, sweet and far from cliff and scar[2]
    The horns of Elfland faintly blowing!   10
Blow, let us hear the purple glens replying,
Blow, bugle; answer, echoes, dying, dying, dying.

O love, they die in yon rich sky,
    They faint on hill or field or river;
Our echoes roll from soul to soul,   15
    And grow forever and forever.
Blow, bugle, blow, set the wild echoes flying,
And answer, echoes, answer, dying, dying, dying.

                    1850

Tears, Idle Tears

Tears, idle tears, I know not what they mean,
Tears from the depth of some divine despair
Rise in the heart, and gather to the eyes,
In looking on the happy autumn-fields,
And thinking of the days that are no more.   5

Fresh as the first beam glittering on a sail,
That brings our friends up from the underworld,
Sad as the last which reddens over one

---

2. Mountainside.

That sinks with all we love below the verge;
So sad, so fresh, the days that are no more.   10

   Ah, sad and strange as in dark summer dawns
The earliest pipe of half-awakened birds
To dying ears, when unto dying eyes
The casement slowly grows a glimmering square;
So sad, so strange, the days that are no more.   15

   Dear as remembered kisses after death,
And sweet as those by hopeless fancy feigned
On lips that are for others; deep as love,
Deep as first love, and wild with all regret;
O Death in Life, the days that are no more!   20

1847

Ask Me No More

Ask me no more: the moon may draw the sea;
   The cloud may stoop from heaven and take the shape,
   With fold to fold, of mountain or of cape;
But O too fond, when have I answered thee?
         Ask me no more.   5

Ask me no more: what answer should I give?
   I love not hollow cheek or faded eye:
   Yet, O my friend, I will not have thee die!
Ask me no more, lest I should bid thee live;
         Ask me no more.   10

Ask me no more: thy fate and mine are sealed;
   I strove against the stream and all in vain;
   Let the great river take me to the main.
No more, dear love, for at a touch I yield;
         Ask me no more.   15

1850

Now Sleeps the Crimson Petal

Now sleeps the crimson petal, now the white:
Nor waves the cypress in the palace walk;
Nor winks the gold fin in the porphyry font.
The firefly wakens; waken thou with me.

Now droops the milk-white peacock like a ghost,   5
And like a ghost she glimmers on to me.

Now lies the Earth all Danaë[3] to the stars,
And all thy heart lies open unto me.

Now slides the silent meteor on, and leaves
A shining furrow, as thy thoughts in me.   10

Now folds the lily all her sweetness up,
And slips into the bosom of the lake.
So fold thyself, my dearest, thou, and slip
Into my bosom and be lost in me.

                                                        1847

Come Down, O Maid

Come down, O maid, from yonder mountain height.
What pleasure lives in height (the shepherd sang),
In height and cold, the splendor of the hills?
But cease to move so near the heavens, and cease
To glide a sunbeam by the blasted pine,   5
To sit a star upon the sparkling spire;
And come, for Love is of the valley, come,
For Love is of the valley, come thou down
And find him; by the happy threshold, he,
Or hand in hand with Plenty in the maize,   10
Or red with spirted purple of the vats,
Or foxlike in the vine;[4] nor cares to walk
With Death and Morning on the Silver Horns,[5]
Nor wilt thou snare him in the white ravine,
Nor find him dropped upon the firths of ice,[6]   15
That huddling slant in furrow-cloven falls
To roll the torrent out of dusky doors.[7]
But follow; let the torrent dance thee down
To find him in the valley; let the wild
Lean-headed eagles yelp alone, and leave   20
The monstrous ledges there to slope, and spill
Their thousand wreaths of dangling water-smoke,
That like a broken purpose waste in air.
So waste not thou, but come; for all the vales
Await thee; azure pillars of the hearth[8]   25
Arise to thee; the children call, and I
Thy shepherd pipe, and sweet is every sound,
Sweeter thy voice, but every sound is sweet;

3. Danaë, a Greek princess, was confined in a metal tower by her father
to prevent suitors from coming near
her. Zeus, however, succeeded in visiting her in the form of a shower of
gold. Their offspring was the hero,
Perseus.
4. This image comes from the Song
of Solomon ii.15.

5. Mountain peaks.
6. Glaciers.
7. Heaps of rock and refuse at the
base of a glacier through which the
mountain torrent forces its way down
to the valley below.
8. Columns of smoke from the houses
in the valley.

Myriads of rivulets hurrying through the lawn,
The moan of doves in immemorial elms,   30
And murmuring of innumerable bees.

1847

In Memoriam A. H. H.   Like most of Tennyson's writings, *In Memoriam* shows his debt to earlier poetry, yet its structure is strikingly different from such traditional elegies as Milton's *Lycidas* or Shelley's *Adonais*. Resembling a song cycle more than a symphony, it is made up of individual lyric units, seemingly self-sustaining, that may be enjoyed by themselves even though the full pleasure to be derived from each component depends upon its relationship to the poem as a whole. The circumstances of the poem's composition help to explain how this new kind of elegy was evolved. The sudden death of Arthur Hallam at the age of 22 had a profound effect on Tennyson. The young poet had cherished Hallam not only as his closest friend and the fiancé of his sister but as an all-wise counselor upon whose judgment he depended for guidance. This fatherly prop having been pulled away, Tennyson was overwhelmed with doubts about the meaning of life and man's role in the universe, doubts reinforced by his own study of geology and other sciences. As a kind of poetic diary recording the variety of his feelings and reflections he began to compose a series of lyrics. These "short swallow-flights of song," as he calls them, written at intervals over a period of seventeen years, were later grouped into one long elegy in which a progressive development from despair to some sort of hope, as in section 95, is recorded.

Some of the early sections of the poem resemble traditional pastoral elegies, including those portraying the voyage during which Hallam's body was brought to England for burial (sections 9–11, 13–15, 19). Other early sections portraying the speaker's loneliness, in which even Christmas festivities seem joyless (section 28), are more distinctive. With the passage of time, indicated by anniversaries and by recurring changes of the seasons, the speaker comes to accept the loss and to assert his belief in life and in an afterlife. In particular the recurring Christmases (sections 28, 78, 104) indicate the stages of his development, yet the pattern of progress in the poem is not a simple unimpeded movement upwards. Dramatic conflicts recur throughout. Thus the most intense expression of doubt occurs not at the beginning of *In Memoriam* but as late as sections 54, 55, and 56.

The quatrain form in which the whole poem is written is usually called the "*In Memoriam* stanza," although it had been occasionally used by earlier poets. So rigid a form taxed Tennyson's ingenuity in achieveing variety, but it is one of several means by which the diverse parts of the poem are knitted together.

The introductory section, consisting of eleven stanzas, is commonly referred to as the "Prologue," although Tennyson did not assign a title to it. It was written in 1849 after the rest of the poem was complete.

From In Memoriam A. H. H.

OBIIT MDCCCXXXIII

Strong Son of God, immortal Love,
　Whom we, that have not seen thy face,
　By faith, and faith alone, embrace,
Believing where we cannot prove;[1]

Thine are these orbs[2] of light and shade;　　　　5
　Thou madest Life in man and brute;
　Thou madest Death; and lo, thy foot
Is on the skull which thou hast made.

Thou wilt not leave us in the dust:
　Thou madest man, he knows not why,　　　　10
　He thinks he was not made to die;
And thou hast made him: thou art just.

Thou seemest human and divine,
　The highest, holiest manhood, thou.
　Our wills are ours, we know not how;　　　　15
Our wills are ours, to make them thine.

Our little systems[3] have their day;
　They have their day and cease to be;
　They are but broken lights of thee,
And thou, O Lord, art more than they.　　　　20

We have but faith: we cannot know,
　For knowledge is of things we see;
　And yet we trust it comes from thee,
A beam in darkness: let it grow.

Let knowledge grow from more to more,　　　　25
　But more of reverence in us dwell;
　That mind and soul, according well,
May make one music as before,[4]

But vaster. We are fools and slight;
　We mock thee when we do not fear:　　　　30
　But help thy foolish ones to bear;
Help thy vain worlds to bear thy light.

Forgive what seemed my sin in me,
　What seemed my worth since I began;
　For merit lives from man to man,　　　　35
And not from man, O Lord, to thee.

1. See John xx.24–29, in which Jesus rebukes Thomas for his doubts concerning the Resurrection: "Blessed are they that have not seen, and yet have believed."
2. Planets.
3. Systems of religion and philosophy.
4. As in the days of fixed religious faith.

Forgive my grief for one removed,
　　Thy creature, whom I found so fair.
　　I trust he lives in thee, and there
I find him worthier to be loved.　　　　　　　　40

Forgive these wild and wandering cries,
　　Confusions of a wasted [5] youth;
　　Forgive them where they fail in truth,
And in thy wisdom make me wise.

1849

1

I held it truth, with him who sings
　　To one clear harp in divers tones,[6]
　　That men may rise on stepping stones
Of their dead selves to higher things.

But who shall so forecast the years　　　　　　5
　　And find in loss a gain to match?
　　Or reach a hand through time to catch
The far-off interest of tears?

Let Love clasp Grief lest both be drowned,
　　Let darkness keep her raven gloss.　　　　　10
　　Ah, sweeter to be drunk with loss,
To dance with Death, to beat the ground,

Than that the victor Hours should scorn
　　The long result of love, and boast,
　　"Behold the man that loved and lost,　　　　15
But all he was is overworn."

2

Old yew, which graspest at the stones
　　That name the underlying dead,
　　Thy fibers net the dreamless head,
Thy roots are wrapped about the bones.

The seasons bring the flower again,　　　　　　5
　　And bring the firstling to the flock;
　　And in the dusk of thee the clock
Beats out the little lives of men.

O, not for thee the glow, the bloom,
　　Who changest not in any gale,　　　　　　　10
　　Nor branding summer suns avail
To touch thy thousand years of gloom; [7]

And gazing on thee, sullen tree,
　　Sick for [8] thy stubborn hardihood,

---

5. Desolated.
6. Identified by Tennyson as Goethe.
7. The ancient yew tree, growing in
the grounds near the clock tower and
church where Hallam was to be buried,
seems neither to blossom in spring nor
change from its dark mournful color
in summer.
8. Envying or longing to share.

I seem to fail from out my blood   15
And grow incorporate into thee.

3

O Sorrow, cruel fellowship,
    O Priestess in the vaults of Death,
    O sweet and bitter in a breath,
What whispers from thy lying lip?

"The stars," she whispers, "blindly run;   5
    A web is woven across the sky;
    From out waste places comes a cry,
And murmurs from the dying sun;

"And all the phantom, Nature, stands—
    With all the music in her tone,   10
    A hollow echo of my own—
A hollow form with empty hands."

And shall I take a thing so blind,
    Embrace her [9] as my natural good;
    Or crush her, like a vice of blood,   15
Upon the threshold of the mind?

4

To Sleep I give my powers away;
    My will is bondsman to the dark;
    I sit within a helmless bark,
And with my heart I muse and say:

O heart, how fares it with thee now,   5
    That thou should fail from thy desire,
    Who scarcely darest to inquire,
"What is it makes me beat so low?"

Something it is which thou hast lost,
    Some pleasure from thine early years.   10
    Break thou deep vase of chilling tears,
That grief hath shaken into frost!

Such clouds of nameless trouble cross
    All night below the darkened eyes;
    With morning wakes the will, and cries,   15
"Thou shalt not be the fool of loss."

5

I sometimes hold it half a sin
    To put in words the grief I feel;
    For words, like Nature, half reveal
And half conceal the Soul within.

But, for the unquiet heart and brain,   5
    A use in measured language lies;
    The sad mechanic exercise,
Like dull narcotics, numbing pain.

9. I.e., sorrow.

In words, like weeds,[1] I'll wrap me o'er,
  Like coarsest clothes against the cold;
  But that large grief which these enfold
Is given in outline and no more.

* * *

7

Dark house,[2] by which once more I stand
  Here in the long unlovely street,
  Doors, where my heart was used to beat
So quickly, waiting for a hand,

A hand that can be clasped no more—
  Behold me, for I cannot sleep,
  And like a guilty thing I creep
At earliest morning to the door.

He is not here; but far away
  The noise of life begins again,
  And ghastly through the drizzling rain
On the bald street breaks the blank day.

* * *

9

Fair ship, that from the Italian shore
  Sailest the placid ocean-plains
  With my lost Arthur's loved remains,
Spread thy full wings, and waft him o'er.

So draw him home to those that mourn
  In vain; a favorable speed
  Ruffle thy mirrored mast, and lead
Through prosperous floods his holy urn.

All night no ruder air perplex
  Thy sliding keel, till Phosphor,[3] bright
  As our pure love, through early light
Shall glimmer on the dewey decks.

Sphere all your lights around, above;
  Sleep, gentle heavens, before the prow;
  Sleep, gentle winds, as he sleeps now,
My friend, the brother of my love;

My Arthur, whom I shall not see
  Till all my widowed race be run;
  Dear as the mother to the son,
More than my brothers are to me.

10

I hear the noise about thy keel;
  I hear the bell struck in the night;
  I see the cabin window bright;
  I see the sailor at the wheel.

1. Garments.
2. House on Wimpole Street, in London, where Hallam had lived.
3. The morning star.

Thou bring'st the sailor to his wife,   5
   And traveled men from foreign lands;
   And letters unto trembling hands;
And, thy dark freight, a vanished life.

So bring him; we have idle dreams;
   This look of quiet flatters thus   10
   Our home-bred fancies. O, to us,
The fools of habit, sweeter seems

To rest beneath the clover sod,
   That takes the sunshine and the rains,
   Or where the kneeling hamlet drains   15
The chalice of the grapes of God; [4]

Than if with thee the roaring wells
   Should gulf him fathom-deep in brine,
   And hands so often clasped in mine,
Should toss with tangle [5] and with shells.   20

11

Calm is the morn without a sound,
   Calm as to suit a calmer grief,
   And only through the faded leaf
The chestnut pattering to the ground;

Calm and deep peace on this high wold, [6]   5
   And on these dews that drench the furze,
   And all the silvery gossamers
That twinkle into green and gold;

Calm and still light on yon great plain
   That sweeps with all its autumn bowers,   10
   And crowded farms and lessenings towers,
To mingle with the bounding main;

Calm and deep peace in this wide air,
   These leaves that redden to the fall,
   And in my heart, if calm at all,   15
If any calm, a calm despair;

Calm on the seas, and silver sleep,
   And waves that sway themselves in rest,
   And dead calm in that noble breast
Which heaves but with the heaving deep. [7]   20

* * *

13

Tears of the widower, when he sees
   A late-lost form that sleep reveals,

---

4. Referring to a burial inside a church building rather than in the churchyard.
5. Seaweed.
6. High and open countryside.
7. It is now the autumn of 1833, and the poet imagines that Hallam's body was already being brought back by ship to England. The date of the actual voyage seems to have been later in the year.

And moves his doubtful arms, and feels
Her place is empty, fall like these;

Which weep a loss forever new,   5
  A void where heart on heart reposed;
  And, where warm hands have pressed and closed,
Silence, till I be silent too;

Which weep the comrade of my choice,
  An awful thought, a life removed,   10
  The human-hearted man I loved,
A Spirit, not a breathing voice.

Come, Time, and teach me, many years,
  I do not suffer in a dream;
  For now so strange do these things seem,   15
Mine eyes have leisure for their tears,

My fancies time to rise on wing,
  And glance about the approaching sails,
  As though they brought but merchants' bales,
And not the burthen that they bring.[8]   20

14

If one should bring me this report,
  That thou[9] hadst touched the land today,
  And I went down unto the quay,
And found thee lying in the port;

And standing, muffled round with woe,   5
  Should see thy passengers in rank
  Come stepping lightly down the plank
And beckoning unto those they know;

And if along with these should come
  The man I held as half divine,   10
  Should strike a sudden hand in mine,
And ask a thousand things of home;

And I should tell him all my pain,
  And how my life had drooped of late,
  And he should sorrow o'er my state   15
And marvel what possessed my brain;

And I perceived no touch of change,
  No hint of death in all his frame,
  But found him all in all the same,
I should not feel it to be strange.   20

15

Tonight the winds begin to rise
  And roar from yonder dropping day;

---

8. The speaker asks Time to teach him to confront the awesome fact of what has happened (line 10) so that he will not delude himself by fancying the ship is bearing only merchandise and not the body of his friend.
9. I.e., the ship.

The last red leaf is whirled away,
The rooks are blown about the skies;

The forest cracked, the waters curled,   5
   The cattle huddled on the lea;
   And wildly dashed on tower and tree
The sunbeam strikes along the world:

And but for fancies, which aver
   That all thy [1] motions gently pass   10
   Athwart a plane of molten glass,
I scarce could brook the strain and stir

That makes the barren branches loud;
   And but for fear it is not so,
   The wild unrest that lives in woe   15
Would dote and pore on yonder cloud

That rises upward always higher,
   And onward drags a laboring breast,
   And topples round the dreary west,
A looming bastion fringed with fire.   20

* * *
19

The Danube to the Severn [2] gave
   The darkened heart that beat no more;
   They laid him by the pleasant shore,
And in the hearing of the wave.

There twice a day the Severn fills;   5
   The salt sea water passes by,
   And hushes half the babbling Wye, [3]
And makes a silence in the hills.

The Wye is hushed nor moved along,
   And hushed my deepest grief of all,   10
   When filled with tears that cannot fall,
I brim with sorrow drowning song.

The tide flows down, the wave again
   Is vocal in its wooded walls;
   My deeper anguish also falls,   15
And I can speak a little then.

* * *
21

I sing to him that rests below,
   And, since the grasses round me wave,

---

1. I.e., the ship's.
2. Hallam died at Vienna on the Danube. His burial place is on the banks of the Severn, a tidal river in the southwest of England.
3. The water of the Wye River, a tributary of the Severn, is dammed up as the tide flows in, and its sound is silenced until, with the turn of the tide, its "wave" once more becomes "vocal" (lines 13–14); these stanzas were written at Tintern Abbey in the Wye River country.

I take the grasses of the grave,[4]
And make them pipes whereon to blow.

The traveler hears me now and then,   5
  And sometimes harshly will he speak:
  "This fellow would make weakness weak,
And melt the waxen hearts of men."

Another answers: "Let him be,
  He loves to make parade of pain,   10
  That with his piping he may gain
The praise that comes to constancy."

A third is wroth: "Is this an hour
  For private sorrow's barren song,
  When more and more the people throng   15
The chairs and thrones of civil power?

"A time to sicken and to swoon,
  When Science reaches forth her arms [5]
  To feel from world to world, and charms
Her secret from the latest moon?" [6]   20

Behold, ye speak an idle thing;
  Ye never knew the sacred dust.
  I do but sing because I must,
And pipe but as the linnets sing;

And one is glad; her note is gay,   25
  For now her little ones have ranged;
  And one is sad; her note is changed,
Because her brood is stolen away.

22

The path by which we twain did go,
  Which led by tracts that pleased us well,
  Through four sweet years arose and fell,
From flower to flower, from snow to snow;

And we with singing cheered the way,   5
  And, crowned with all the season lent,
  From April on to April went,
And glad at heart from May to May.

But where the path we walked began
  To slant the fifth autumnal slope,[7]   10
  As we descended following Hope,
There sat the Shadow feared of man;

4. The speaker assumes that the burial
was in the churchyard; in fact, Hallam's body was interred in a vault inside St. Andrews church at Clevedon,
Somersetshire, on January 3, 1834. See
section 10, lines 11–16.
5. Astronomical instruments such as telescopes.
6. Probably alluding to the discovery,
in 1846, of the planet Neptune and its
moon.
7. Hallam died in early autumn (September 15, 1833) in the fifth year of
the friendship.

Who broke our fair companionship,
 And spread his mantle dark and cold,
 And wrapped thee formless in the fold,   15
And dulled the murmur on thy lip,

And bore thee where I could not see
 Nor follow, though I walk in haste,
 And think that somewhere in the waste
The Shadow sits and waits for me.   20

23

Now, sometimes in my sorrow shut,
 Or breaking into song by fits,
 Alone, alone, to where he sits,
The Shadow cloaked from head to foot,

Who keeps the keys of all the creeds,   5
 I wander, often falling lame,
 And looking back to whence I came,
Or on to where the pathway leads;

And crying, How changed from where it ran
 Through lands where not a leaf was dumb, 10
 But all the lavish hills would hum
The murmur of a happy Pan;

When each by turns was guide to each,
 And Fancy light from Fancy caught,
 And Thought leapt out to wed with Thought 15
Ere Thought could wed itself with Speech;

And all we met was fair and good,
 And all was good that Time could bring,
 And all the secret of the Spring
Moved in the chambers of the blood;   20

And many an old philosophy
 On Argive heights divinely sang,[8]
 And round us all the thicket rang
To many a flute of Arcady.[9]

24

And was the day of my delight
 As pure and perfect as I say?
 The very source and fount of day
Is dashed with wandering isles of night.[1]

If all was good and fair we met,   5
 This earth had been the Paradise
 It never looked to human eyes
Since our first sun arose and set.

And is it that the haze of grief
 Makes former gladness loom so great? 10

---

8. In classical times the Greek city of Argos was renowned for its music.
9. Sheep-raising region in Greece associated with pastoral poetry.
1. Moving spots on the sun.

The lowness of the present state,
That sets the past in this relief?

Or that the past will always win
A glory from its being far,
And orb into the perfect star   15
We saw not when we moved therein? [2]

25

I know that this was Life—the track
Whereon with equal feet we fared;
And then, as now, the day prepared
The daily burden for the back.

But this it was that made me move   5
As light as carrier birds in air;
I loved the weight I had to bear,
Because it needed help of Love;

Nor could I weary, heart or limb,
When mighty Love would cleave in twain   10
The lading of a single pain,
And part it, giving half to him.

26

Still onward winds the dreary way;
I with it, for I long to prove
No lapse of moons can canker Love,
Whatever fickle tongues may say.

And if that eye which watches guilt   5
And goodness, and hath power to see
Within the green the mouldered tree,
And towers fallen as soon as built—

O, if indeed that eye foresee
Or see—in Him is no before—   10
In more of life true life no more
And Love the indifference to be,

Then might I find, ere yet the morn
Breaks hither over Indian seas,
That Shadow waiting with the keys,   15
To shroud me from my proper scorn.[3]

27

I envy not in any moods
The captive void of noble rage,
The linnet born within the cage,
That never knew the summer woods;

2. The speaker speculates whether past experiences seem so much more "pure and perfect" (line 2) than present ones because they are far distant from us in time just as our planet Earth would have the deceptive appearance of being a perfect orb if we viewed it from a great distance in space, as from another planet. See *Locksley Hall Sixty Years After*, lines 187–92.

3. The Deity, being outside time, sees (rather than foresees) whether or not the rest of life ("more of life," line 11) will be pointless. If pointless then the way for the speaker to deal with his self-scorn ("proper scorn") might be to seek death.

I envy not the beast that takes·   5
  His license in the field of time,
  Unfettered by the sense of crime,
To whom a conscience never wakes;

Nor, what may count itself as blest,
  The heart that never plighted troth   10
  But stagnates in the weeds of sloth;
Nor any want-begotten rest.[4]

I hold it true, whate'er befall;
  I feel it, when I sorrow most;
  'Tis better to have loved and lost   15
Than never to have loved at all.

28

The time draws near the birth of Christ.[5]
  The moon is hid, the night is still;
  The Christmas bells from hill to hill
Answer each other in the mist.

Four voices of four hamlets round,   5
  From far and near, on mead and moor,
  Swell out and fail, as if a door
Were shut between me and the sound;

Each voice four changes [6] on the wind,
  That now dilate, and now decrease,   10
  Peace and goodwill, goodwill and peace,
Peace and goodwill, to all mankind.

This year I slept and woke with pain,
  I almost wished no more to wake,
  And that my hold on life would break   15
Before I heard those bells again;

But they my troubled spirit rule,
  For they controlled me when a boy;
  They bring me sorrow touched with joy,
The merry, merry bells of Yule.   20

* * *

30

With trembling fingers did we weave
  The holly round the Christmas hearth;
  A rainy cloud possessed the earth,
And sadly fell our Christmas eve.

At our old pastimes in the hall   5
  We gamboled, making vain pretense
  Of gladness, with an awful sense
Of one mute Shadow watching all.

---

4. Complacency resulting from some deficiency or "want."
5. The first Christmas after Hallam's death (1833); the setting is Tennyson's family home in Lincolnshire.
6. Different sequences in which church bells are pealed.

We paused: the winds were in the beech;
   We heard them sweep the winter land;
   And in a circle hand-in-hand
Sat silent, looking each at each.   10

Then echo-like our voices rang;
   We sung, though every eye was dim,
   A merry song we sang with him   15
Last year; impetuously we sang.

We ceased; a gentler feeling crept
   Upon us: surely rest is meet.[7]
   "They rest," we said, "their sleep is sweet,"
And silence followed, and we wept.   20

Our voices took a higher range;
   Once more we sang: "They do not die
   Nor lose their mortal sympathy,
Nor change to us, although they change;

"Rapt [8] from the fickle and the frail   25
   With gathered power, yet the same,
   Pierces the keen seraphic flame
From orb to orb,[9] from veil to veil."

Rise, happy morn, rise, holy morn,
   Draw forth the cheerful day from night: 30
   O Father, touch the east, and light
The light that shone when Hope was born.

* * *

34

My own dim life should teach me this,
   That life shall live forevermore,
   Else earth is darkness at the core,
And dust and ashes all that is;

This round of green, this orb of flame,   5
   Fantastic beauty; such as lurks
   In some wild poet, when he works
Without a conscience or an aim.[1]

What then were God to such as I?
   'Twere hardly worth my while to choose   10
   Of things all mortal, or to use
A little patience ere I die;

'Twere best at once to sink to peace,
   Like birds the charming serpent draws,[2]

7. Proper or appropriate.
8. Carried away from.
9. The angelic spirit ("flame") of the dead moves from star to star.
1. Perhaps Thomas Lovell Beddoes, a brilliantly promising but erratic poet, admired by Tennyson, who committed suicide in 1849.
2. Some snakes are reputed to capture their prey by casting a charm.

To drop head-foremost in the jaws   15
Of vacant darkness and to cease.

35

Yet if some voice that man could trust
    Should murmur from the narrow house,
    "The cheeks drop in, the body bows;
Man dies, nor is there hope in dust";

Might I not say? "Yet even here,   5
    But for one hour, O Love, I strive
    To keep so sweet a thing alive."
But I should turn mine ears and hear

The moanings of the homeless sea,
    The sound of streams that swift or slow   10
    Draw down Aeonian hills,[3] and sow
The dust of continents to be;

And Love would answer with a sigh,
    "The sound of that forgetful shore
    Will change my sweetness more and more,   15
Half-dead to know that I shall die."

O me, what profits it to put
    An idle case? If Death were seen
    At first as Death, Love had not been,
Or been in narrowest working shut,   20

Mere fellowship of sluggish moods,
    Or in his coarsest Satyr-shape
    Had bruised the herb and crushed the grape,
And basked and battened in the woods.[4]

* * *

39

Old warder of these buried bones,
    And answering now my random stroke
    With fruitful cloud and living smoke,
Dark yew, that graspest at the stones

And dippest toward the dreamless head,   5
    To thee too comes the golden hour
    When flower is feeling after flower; [5]
But Sorrow—fixed upon the dead,

And darkening the dark graves of men—
    What whispered from her lying lips?   10

3. Hills that are aeons old, seemingly everlasting.
4. Lines 18 ff. may be paraphrased: if we knew death to be final and that no afterlife were possible, love could not exist except on a primitive or bestial level.

5. The ancient yew tree in the graveyard was described in section 2 as never changing. Now the speaker discovers that in the flowering season, if the tree is struck ("my random stroke," line 2), it gives off a cloud of golden pollen.

Thy gloom is kindled at the tips,[6]
And passes into gloom again.

* * *

44

How fares it with the happy dead?
    For here the man is more and more;
    But he forgets the days before
God closed the doorways of his head.[7]

The days have vanished, tone and tint,   5
    And yet perhaps the hoarding sense [8]
    Gives out at times (he knows not whence)
A little flash, a mystic hint;

And in the long harmonious years
    (If Death so taste Lethean springs [9])   10
    May some dim touch of earthly things
Surprise thee ranging with thy peers.

If such a dreamy touch should fall,
    O turn thee round, resolve the doubt;
    My guardian angel will speak out   15
In that high place, and tell thee all.

* * *

47

That each, who seems a separate whole,
    Should move his rounds,[1] and fusing all
    The skirts [2] of self again, should fall
Remerging in the general Soul,

Is faith as vague as all unsweet.   5
    Eternal form shall still divide
    The eternal soul from all beside;
And I shall know him when we meet;

And we shall sit at endless feast,
    Enjoying each the other's good.   10
    What vaster dream can hit the mood
Of Love on earth? He seeks at least

Upon the last and sharpest height,
    Before the spirits fade away,
    Some landing place, to clasp and say,   15
"Farewell! We lose ourselves in light."

6. Only the tips of the yew-branches are in flower.
7. This difficult stanza has been variously interpreted. If "man" (line 2) refers to the dead, the passage means that in our living world the dead man is more and more remembered, but that he, in the afterworld, is shut off through death from remembering past experiences on earth. Alternatively if "man" refers to living mankind rather than to the "happy dead," the passage means that as man grows up (line 2) he forgets his earliest infancy, especially the two-year period before the sutures of his skull are closed.
8. Memory.
9. I.e., springs of forgetfulness.
1. I.e., go through the customary circuit of life.
2. Outer edges or fringes.

48

If these brief lays, of Sorrow born,
　　Were taken to be such as closed
　　Grave doubts and answers here proposed,
Then these were such as men might scorn.

Her [3] care is not to part and prove;　　　　5
　　She takes, when harsher moods remit,
　　What slender shade of doubt may flit,
And makes it vassal unto love;

And hence, indeed, she sports with words,
　　But better serves a wholesome law,　　　10
　　And holds it sin and shame to draw
The deepest measure from the chords;

Nor dare she trust a larger lay,
　　But rather loosens from the lip
　　Short swallow-flights of song, that dip　　15
Their wings in tears, and skim away.

* * *

50

Be near me when my light is low,
　　When the blood creeps, and the nerves prick
　　And tingle; and the heart is sick,
And all the wheels of being slow.

Be near me when the sensuous frame　　　5
　　Is racked with pangs that conquer trust;
　　And Time, a maniac scattering dust,
And Life, a Fury slinging flame.

Be near me when my faith is dry,
　　And men the flies of latter spring,　　　10
　　That lay their eggs, and sting and sing
And weave their petty cells and die.

Be near me when I fade away,
　　To point the term of human strife,
　　And on the low dark verge of life　　　15
The twilight of eternal day.

* * *

54

O, yet we trust that somehow good
　　Will be the final goal of ill,
　　To pangs of nature, sins of will,
Defects of doubt, and taints of blood;

That nothing walks with aimless feet;　　　5
　　That not one life shall be destroyed,

3. I.e., sorrow's.

Or cast as rubbish to the void,
When God hath made the pile complete;

That not a worm is cloven in vain;
   That not a moth with vain desire   10
   Is shriveled in a fruitless fire,
Or but subserves another's gain.

Behold, we know not anything;
   I can but trust that good shall fall
   At last—far off—at last, to all,   15
And every winter change to spring.

So runs my dream; but what am I?
   An infant crying in the night;
   An infant crying for the light,
And with no language but a cry.   20

55

The wish, that of the living whole
   No life may fail beyond the grave,
   Derives it not from what we have
The likest God within the soul?

Are God and Nature then at strife,   5
   That Nature lends such evil dreams?
   So careful of the type [4] she seems,
So careless of the single life,

That I, considering everywhere
   Her secret meaning in her deeds,   10
   And finding that of fifty seeds
She often brings but one to bear,

I falter where I firmly trod,
   And falling with my weight of cares
   Upon the great world's altar-stairs   15
That slope through darkness up to God,

I stretch lame hands of faith, and grope,
   And gather dust and chaff, and call
   To what I feel is Lord of all,
And faintly trust the larger hope.[5]   20

56

"So careful of the type?" but no.
   From scarpéd [6] cliff and quarried stone
   She [7] cries, "A thousand types are gone;
I care for nothing, all shall go.

"Thou makest thine appeal to me: 5
   I bring to life, I bring to death;
   The spirit does but mean the breath:
I know no more." And he, shall he,

---

4. Species.
5. As expressed in lines 1–2 of this section.

6. Cut away so that the strata are exposed.
7. Nature.

Man, her last work, who seemed so fair,
  Such splendid purpose in his eyes,
  Who rolled the psalm to wintry skies,   10
Who built him fanes [8] of fruitless prayer,

Who trusted God was love indeed
  And love Creation's final law—
  Though Nature, red in tooth and claw   15
With ravine, shrieked against his creed—

Who loved, who suffered countless ills,
  Who battled for the True, the Just,
  Be blown about the desert dust,
Or sealed within the iron hills? [9]   20

No more? A monster then, a dream,
  A discord. Dragons of the prime,
  That tare [1] each other in their slime,
Were mellow music matched with [2] him.

O life as futile, then, as frail!   25
  O for thy voice to soothe and bless!
  What hope of answer, or redress?
Behind the veil, behind the veil.

57

Peace; come away: [3] the song of woe
  Is after all an earthly song.
  Peace; come away: we do him wrong
To sing so wildly: let us go.

Come; let us go: your cheeks are pale;   5
  But half my life I leave behind.
  Methinks my friend is richly shrined;
But I shall pass, my work will fail.

Yet in these ears, till hearing dies,
  One set slow bell will seem to toll   10
  The passing of the sweetest soul
That ever looked with human eyes.

I hear it now, and o'er and o'er,
  Eternal greetings to the dead;
  And "Ave, [4] Ave, Ave," said,   15
"Adieu, adieu," forevermore.

58

In those sad words I took farewell.
  Like echoes in sepulchral halls,
  As drop by drop the water falls
In vaults and catacombs, they fell;

8. Temples.
9. Preserved like fossils in rock.
1. Tore (archaic).
2. In comparison with.

3. Perhaps addressed to Emily Tennyson, the poet's sister and Hallam's fiancée.
4. Hail.

And, falling, idly broke the peace   5
 Of hearts that beat from day to day,
 Half-conscious of their dying clay,
And those cold crypts where they shall cease.

The high Muse answered: "Wherefore grieve
 Thy brethren with a fruitless tear?   10
 Abide a little longer here,
And thou shalt take a nobler leave."

59

O Sorrow, wilt thou live with me
 No casual mistress, but a wife,
 My bosom friend and half of life;
As I confess it needs must be?

O Sorrow, wilt thou rule my blood,   5
 Be sometimes lovely like a bride,
 And put thy harsher moods aside,
If thou wilt have me wise and good?

My centered passion cannot move,
 Nor will it lessen from today;   10
 But I'll have leave at times to play
As with the creature of my love;

And set thee forth, for thou art mine,
 With so much hope for years to come,
 That, howsoe'er I know thee, some   15
Could hardly tell what name were thine.

* * *

64

Dost thou [5] look back on what hath been,
 As some divinely gifted man,
 Whose life in low estate began
And on a simple village green;

Who breaks his birth's invidious bar,   5
 And grasps the skirts of happy chance,
 And breasts the blows of circumstance,
And grapples with his evil star;

Who makes by force his merit known
 And lives to clutch the golden keys,[6]   10
 To mold a mighty state's decrees,
And shape the whisper of the throne;

And moving up from high to higher,
 Becomes on Fortune's crowning slope
 The pillar of a people's hope,   15
The center of a world's desire;

---

5. I.e., Hallam.   6. Badges of high public office.

Yet feels, as in a pensive dream,
   When all his active powers are still,
   A distant dearness in the hill,
A secret sweetness in the stream,   20

The limit of his narrower fate,
   While yet beside its vocal springs
   He played at counselors and kings,
With one that was his earliest mate;

Who plows with pain his native lea   25
   And reaps the labor of his hands,
   Or in the furrow musing stands:
"Does my old friend remember me?"

* * *
67
When on my bed the moonlight falls,
   I know that in thy place of rest
   By that broad water of the west [7]
There comes a glory on the walls:

Thy marble bright in dark appears,   5
   As slowly steals a silver flame
   Along the letters of thy name,
And o'er the number of thy years.

The mystic glory swims away,
   From off my bed the moonlight dies;   10
   And closing eaves of wearied eyes
I sleep till dusk is dipped in gray;

And then I know the mist is drawn
   A lucid veil from coast to coast,
   And in the dark church like a ghost   15
Thy tablet glimmers to the dawn.

* * *
70
I cannot see the features right,
   When on the gloom I strive to paint
   The face I know; the hues are faint
And mix with hollow masks of night;

Cloud-towers by ghostly masons wrought,   5
   A gulf that ever shuts and gapes,
   A hand that points, and palléd [8] shapes
In shadowy thoroughfares of thought;

And crowds that stream from yawning doors,
   And shoals of puckered faces drive;   10

---

7. The Severn River.   8. Dim or pale.

Dark bulks that tumble half alive,
And lazy lengths on boundless shores;

Till all at once beyond the will
    I hear a wizard music roll,
    And through a lattice on the soul   15
Looks thy fair face and makes it still.

71

Sleep, kinsman thou to death and trance
    And madness, thou [9] has forged at last
    A night-long present of the past
In which we went through summer France.[1]

Hadst thou such credit with the soul?   5
    Then bring an opiate trebly strong,
    Drug down the blindfold sense of wrong,
That so my pleasure may be whole;

While now we talk as once we talked
    Of men and minds, the dust of change,   10
    The days that grow to something strange,
In walking as of old we walked

Beside the river's wooded reach,
    The fortress, and the mountain ridge,
    The cataract flashing from the bridge,   15
The breaker breaking on the beach.

72

Risest thou thus, dim dawn, again,[2]
    And how lest, issuing out of night,
    With blasts that blow the poplar white,
And lash with storm the streaming pane?

Day, when my crowned estate [3] begun   5
    To pine in that reverse of doom,[4]
    Which sickened every living bloom,
And blurred the splendor of the sun;

Who usherest in the dolorous hour
    With thy quick tears that make the rose   10
    Pull sideways, and the daisy close
Her crimson fringes to the shower;

Who mightst have heaved a windless flame
    Up the deep East, or, whispering, played
    A checker-work of beam and shade   15
Along the hills, yet looked the same,

---

9. I.e., sleep.
1. In the summer of 1830, Hallam and Tennyson went through southern France en route to Spain.
2. September 15, 1834, the first anniversary of Hallam's death.
3. State of happiness.
4. The reversal of disaster which doom brought upon him when Hallam died.

As wan, as chill, as wild as now;
    Day, marked as with some hideous crime,
    When the dark hand struck down through time,
And canceled nature's best: but thou,   20

Lift as thou mayst thy burthened brows
    Through clouds that drench the morning star,
    And whirl the ungarnered sheaf afar,
And sow the sky with flying boughs,

And up thy vault with roaring sound   25
    Climb thy thick noon, disastrous day;
    Touch thy dull goal of joyless gray,
And hide thy shame beneath the ground.

* * *
75
I leave thy praises unexpressed
    In verse that brings myself relief,
    And by the measure of my grief
I leave thy greatness to be guessed.

What practice howsoe'er expert   5
    In fitting aptest words to things,
    Or voice the richest-toned that sings,
Hath power to give thee as thou wert?

I care not in these fading days
    To raise a cry that lasts not long,   10
    And round thee with the breeze of song
To stir a little dust of praise.

Thy leaf has perished in the green,
    And, while we breathe beneath the sun,
    The world which credits what is done   15
Is cold to all that might have been.

So here shall silence guard thy fame;
    But somewhere, out of human view,
    Whate'er thy hands are set to do
Is wrought with tumult of acclaim.   20

* * *
78
Again at Christmas [5] did we weave
    The holly round the Christmas hearth;
    The silent snow possessed the earth,
And calmly fell our Christmas eve.

The yule clog [6] sparkled keen with frost,   5
    No wing of wind the region swept,

5. The second Christmas (1834) after Hallam's death.
6. Log.

But over all things brooding slept
The quiet sense of something lost.

As in the winters left behind,
 Again our ancient games had place,   10
 The mimic picture's [7] breathing grace,
And dance and song and hoodman-blind.

Who showed a token of distress?
 No single tear, no mark of pain—
 O sorrow, then can sorrow wane?   15
O grief, can grief be changed to less?

O last regret, regret can die!
 No—mixed with all this mystic frame,
 Her [8] deep relations are the same,
But with long use her tears are dry.   20

* * *
82

I wage not any feud with Death
 For changes wrought on form and face;
 No lower life that earth's embrace
May breed with him can fright my faith.

Eternal process moving on,   5
 From state to state the spirit walks;
 And these are but the shattered stalks,
Or ruined chrysalis of one.

Nor blame I Death, because he bare
 The use of virtue out of earth;
 I know transplanted human worth   10
Will bloom to profit, otherwhere.

For this alone on Death I wreak
 The wrath that garners in my heart:
 He put our lives so far apart   15
We cannot hear each other speak.
83

Dip down upon the northern shore,
 O sweet new-year [9] delaying long;
 Thou doest expectant Nature wrong;
Delaying long, delay no more.

What stays thee from the clouded noons,   5
 Thy sweetness from its proper place?
 Can trouble live with April days,
Or sadness in the summer moons?

7. A game in which the participants
pose in the manner of some famous
statue or painting and the spectators
try to guess what work of art is being
mimicked.
8. I.e., sorrow's.
9. Spring of 1835.

Bring orchis, bring the foxglove spire,
  The little speedwell's [1] darling blue,
  Deep tulips dashed with fiery dew,   10
Laburnums, dropping-wells of fire.

O thou, new-year, delaying long,
  Delayest the sorrow in my blood,
  That longs to burst a frozen bud   15
And flood a fresher throat with song.

84

When I contemplate all alone
  The life that had been thine below,
  And fix my thoughts on all the glow
To which thy crescent would have grown,

I see thee sitting crowned with good,   5
  A central warmth diffusing bliss
  In glance and smile, and clasp and kiss,
On all the branches of thy blood;

Thy blood, my friend, and partly mine;
  For now the day was drawing on,   10
  When thou shouldst link thy life with one
Of mine own house, and boys of thine

Had babbled "Uncle" on my knee;
  But that remorseless iron hour
  Made cypress of her orange flower,[2]   15
Despair of hope, and earth of thee.

I seem to meet their least desire,
  To clap their cheeks, to call them mine.
  I see their unborn faces shine
Beside the never-lighted fire.   20

I see myself an honored guest,
  Thy partner in the flowery walk
  Of letters, genial table talk,
Or deep dispute, and graceful jest;

While now thy prosperous labor fills   25
  The lips of men with honest praise,
  And sun by sun the happy days
Descend below the golden hills

With promise of a morn as fair;
  And all the train of bounteous hours   30
  Conduct, by paths of growing powers,
To reverence and the silver hair;

1. A blue spring flower.
2. Orange blossoms are associated with brides—here the poet's sister, Emily Tennyson, to whom Hallam had been engaged.

Till slowly worn her earthly robe,
   Her lavish mission richly wrought,
   Leaving great legacies of thought,   35
Thy spirit should fail from off the globe;

What time mine own might also flee,
   As linked with thine in love and fate,
   And, hovering o'er the dolorous strait
To the other shore, involved in thee,   40

Arrive at last the blessed goal,
   And He that died in Holy Land
   Would reach us out the shining hand,
And take us as a single soul.

What reed was that on which I leant?   45
   Ah, backward fancy, wherefore wake
   The old bitterness again, and break
The low beginnings of content?

* * *

86

Sweet after showers, ambrosial air,
   That rollest from the gorgeous gloom
   Of evening over brake and bloom
And meadow, slowly breathing bare

The round of space,[3] and rapt below   5
   Through all the dewy-tasseled wood,
   And shadowing down the hornéd flood [4]
In ripples, fan my brows and blow

The fever from my cheek, and sigh
   The full new life that feeds they breath   10
   Throughout my frame, till Doubt and Death,
Ill brethren, let the fancy fly

From belt to belt of crimson seas
   On leagues of odor streaming far,
   To where in yonder orient star   15
A hundred spirits whisper "Peace."

87

I passed beside the reverend walls [5]
   In which of old I wore the gown;
   I roved at random through the town,
And saw the tumult of the halls;

And heard once more in college fanes   5
   The storm their high-built organs make,

3. Air that is slowly clearing the clouds
from the sky.
4. Crescent-shaped body of water.

5. Of Trinity College, Cambridge University.

And thunder-music, rolling, shake
The prophet blazoned on the panes;

And caught once more the distant shout,
The measured pulse of racing oars   10
Among the willows; paced the shores
And many a bridge, and all about

The same gray flats again, and felt
The same, but not the same; and last
Up that long walk of limes I passed   15
To see the rooms in which he dwelt.

Another name was on the door.
I lingered; all within was noise
Of songs, and clapping hands, and boys
That crashed the glass and beat the floor; 20

Where once we held debate, a band
Of youthful friends,[6] on mind and art,
And labor, and the changing mart,
And all the framework of the land;

When one would aim an arrow fair,   25
But send it slackly from the string;
And one would pierce an outer ring,
And one an inner, here and there;

And last the master bowman, he,
Would cleave the mark. A willing ear   30
We lent him. Who but hung to hear
The rapt oration flowing free

From point to point, with power and grace
And music in the bounds of law,[7]
To those conclusions when we saw   35
The God within him light his face,

And seem to lift the form, and glow
In azure orbits heavenly-wise;
And over those ethereal eyes
The bar of Michael Angelo?[8]   40

88

Wild bird, whose warble, liquid sweet,
Rings Eden through the budded quicks,[9]

6. The "Apostles," an undergraduate club to which Tennyson and Hallam had belonged.
7. An essay presented by Hallam at Cambridge in 1831 provides an example of his skill in theological argument (see *The Writings of Arthur Hallam*, edited by T. H. V. Motter, 1943, pp. 198–213). This essay, much admired by Tennyson, may have influenced the main argument of *In Memoriam*. In his essay Hallam develops an idea he had stated in a letter to Tennyson's sister: "It is by the heart, not by the head, that we must all be convinced of the two great fundamental truths, the reality of Love, and the reality of Evil." See also *In Memoriam*, section 109, lines 1–8 below.
8. Hallam, like Michelangelo, had a prominent ridge of bone above his eyes.
9. Hawthorn hedges. The "wild bird" is presumably a nightingale.

O tell me where the senses mix,
O tell me where the passions meet,

Whence radiate: fierce extremes employ   45
   Thy spirits in the darkening leaf,[1]
   And in the midmost heart of grief
Thy passion clasps a secret joy;

And I—my harp would prelude woe—
   I cannot all command the strings;   50
   The glory of the sum of things
Will flash along the chords and go.

89

Witch elms that counterchange the floor
Of this flat lawn with dusk and bright;[2]
   And thou, with all thy breadth and height
Of foliage, towering sycamore;

How often, hither wandering down,   5
   My Arthur found your shadows fair,
   And shook to all the liberal air
The dust and din and steam of town!

He brought an eye for all he saw;
   He mixed in all our simple sports;   10
   They pleased him, fresh from brawling courts
And dusty purlieus of the law.[3]

O joy to him in this retreat,
   Immantled in ambrosial dark,
   To drink the cooler air, and mark   15
The landscape winking through the heat!

O sound to rout the brood of cares,
   The sweep of scythe in morning dew,
   The gust that round the garden flew,
And tumbled half the mellowing pears!   20

O bliss, when all in circle drawn
   About him, heart and ear were fed
   To hear him, as he lay and read
The Tuscan poets[4] on the lawn!

Or in the all-golden afternoon   25
   A guest, or happy sister, sung,
   Or here she brought the harp and flung
A ballad to the brightening moon.

Nor less it pleased in livelier moods,
   Beyond the bounding hill to stray,   30

1. Cf. Keats' *Ode to a Nightingale* (lines 10 and 60) and his sonnet on *King Lear*, line 5.
2. Shadows of the elm tree checker the lawn at Somersby, the Tennysons' country home.
3. Hallam became a law student in London after leaving Cambridge.
4. Petrarch and Dante.

And break the livelong summer day
With banquet in the distant woods;

Whereat we glanced from theme to theme,
Discussed the books to love or hate,
Or touched the changes of the state,   35
Or threaded some Socratic dream;[5]

But if I praised the busy town,
He loved to rail against it still,
For "ground in yonder social mill
We rub each other's angles down,   40

"And merge," he said, "in form and gloss
The picturesque of man and man."
We talked: the stream beneath us ran,
The wine-flask lying couched in moss,

Or cooled within the glooming wave;   45
And last, returning from afar,
Before the crimson-circled star [6]
Had fallen into her father's grave,

And brushing ankle-deep in flowers,
We heard behind the woodbine veil
The milk that bubbled in [7] the pail,   50
And buzzings of the honeyed hours.

* * *

91

When rosy plumelets tuft the larch,
And rarely [8] pipes the mounted thrush,
Or underneath the barren bush
Flits by the sea-blue bird [9] of March;

Come, wear the form by which I know   5
Thy spirit in time among thy peers;
The hope of unaccomplished years
Be large and lucid round thy brow.

When summer's hourly-mellowing change
May breathe, with many roses sweet,   10
Upon the thousand waves of wheat
That ripple round the lowly grange,

Come; not in watches of the night,
But where the sunbeam broodeth warm,
Come, beauteous in thine after form,   15
And like a finer light in light.

* * *

---

5. I.e., worked our way through some discourse of Socrates (as recorded by Plato).
6. Venus, which will sink into the west as the sun has done. According to the nebular hypothesis, planets were flung from the sun into the outer spaces of our solar system; in this sense the sun is the "father" of planets.
7. Into.
8. Exquisitely.
9. Kingfisher.

93

I shall not see thee. Dare I say
   No spirit ever brake the band
   That stays him from the native land
Where first he walked when clasped in clay? [1]

No visual shade of someone lost,   5
   But he, the Spirit himself, may come
   Where all the nerve of sense is numb,
Spirit to Spirit, Ghost to Ghost.

Oh, therefore from thy sightless [2] range
   With gods in unconjectured bliss,   10
   Oh, from the distance of the abyss
Of tenfold-complicated change,

Descend, and touch, and enter; hear
   The wish too strong for words to name,
   That in this blindness of the frame [3]   15
My Ghost may feel that thine is near.

94

How pure at heart and sound in head,
   With what divine affections bold
   Should be the man whose thought would hold
An hour's communion with the dead.

In vain shalt thou, or any, call   5
   The spirits from their golden day,
   Except, like them, thou too canst say,
My spirit is at peace with all.

They haunt the silence of the breast,
   Imaginations calm and fair,   10
   The memory like a cloudless air,
The conscience as a sea at rest;

But when the heart is full of din,
   And doubt beside the portal waits,
   They can but listen at the gates,   15
And hear the household jar within.

95

By night we lingered on the lawn,
   For underfoot the herb was dry;
   And genial warmth; and o'er the sky
The silvery haze of summer drawn;

And calm that let the tapers burn   5
   Unwavering: not a cricket chirred;
   The brook alone far off was heard,
And on the board the fluttering urn. [4]

---

1. I.e., when he was alive and clothed   3. The living body.
in flesh.   4. Urn to boil water for tea or coffee.
2. Invisible.

And bats went round in fragrant skies,
   And wheeled or lit the filmy shapes [5]   10
   That haunt the dusk, with ermine capes
And woolly breasts and beaded eyes;

While now we sang old songs that pealed
   From knoll to knoll, where, couched at ease,
   The white kine glimmered, and the trees   15
Laid their dark arms [6] about the field.

But when those others, one by one,
   Withdrew themselves from me and night,
   And in the house light after light
Went out, and I was all alone,   20

A hunger seized my heart; I read
   Of that glad year which once had been,
   In those fallen leaves which kept their green,
The noble letters of the dead.

And strangely on the silence broke   25
   The silent-speaking words, and strange
   Was love's dumb cry defying change
To test his worth; and strangely spoke

The faith, the vigor, bold to dwell
   On doubts that drive the coward back,   30
   And keen through wordy snares to track
Suggestion to her inmost cell.

So word by word, and line by line,
   The dead man touched me from the past,
   And all at once it seemed at last   35
The [7] living soul was flashed on mine,

And mine in this [8] was wound, and whirled
   About empyreal heights of thought,
   And came on that which is, and caught
The deep pulsations of the world,   40

Aeonian music measuring out
   The steps of Time—the shocks of Chance—
   The blows of Death. At length my trance
Was canceled, stricken through with doubt.[9]

5. The white-winged night moths called ermine moths.
6. Cast the shadows of their branches.
7. Printed "His" in the first edition; and line 37 read, in the first edition, "And mine in his was wound."
8. The music of the universe which has pulsated for aeons of time.
9. In a letter of 1874 replying to an enquiry about his experience of mystical trances, Tennyson wrote: "A kind of waking trance I have frequently had, quite up from boyhood, when I have been all alone. This has generally come upon me through repeating my own name two or three times to myself silently, till all at once, as it were out of the intensity of the consciousness of individuality, the individuality itself seemed to dissolve and fade away into boundless being, and this not a confused state, but the clearest of the clearest, the surest of the surest, the weirdest of the weirdest, utterly beyond words,

Vague words! but ah, how hard to frame   45
  In matter-molded forms of speech,
  Or even for intellect to reach
Through memory that which I became.

Till now the doubtful dusk revealed
  The knolls once more where, couched at ease,   50
  The white kine glimmered, and the trees
Laid their dark arms about the field;

And sucked from out the distant gloom
  A breeze began to tremble o'er
  The large leaves of the sycamore,   55
And fluctuate all the still perfume,

And gathering freshlier overhead,
  Rocked the full-foliaged elms, and swung
  The heavy-folded rose, and flung
The lilies to and fro, and said,   60

"The dawn, the dawn," and died away;
  And East and West, without a breath,
  Mixed their dim lights, like life and death,
To broaden into boundless day.

96

You say, but with no touch of scorn,
  Sweet-hearted, you,[1] whose light blue eyes
  Are tender over drowning flies,
You tell me, doubt is Devil-born.

I know not: one [2] indeed I knew   5
  In many a subtle question versed,
  Who touched a jarring lyre at first,
But ever strove to make it true;

Perplexed in faith, but pure in deeds,
  At last he beat his music out.   10
  There lives more faith in honest doubt,
Believe me, than in half the creeds.

He fought his doubts and gathered strength,
  He would not make his judgment blind,
  He faced the specters of the mind   15
And laid them; thus he came at length

To find a stronger faith his own,
  And Power was with him in the night,

where death was an almost laughable impossibility, the loss of personality (if so it were) seeming no extinction but the only true life. * * * This might * * * be the state which St. Paul describes, 'Whether in the body I cannot tell, or whether out of the body I cannot tell.' * * * I am ashamed of my feeble description. Have I not said the state is utterly beyond words? But in a moment, when I come back to my normal state of 'sanity,' I am ready to fight for *mein liebes Ich* [my dear self], and hold that it will last for aeons of aeons."—*Alfred Lord Tennyson, A Memoir*, 1897, I, 320.

1. A woman of simple faith.
2. Hallam.

Which makes the darkness and the light,
And dwells not in the light alone,   20

But in the darkness and the cloud,[3]
  As over Sinaï's peaks of old,
  While Israel made their gods of gold,
Although the trumpet blew so loud.

* * *
99
Risest thou thus, dim dawn, again,[4]
  So loud with voices of the birds,
  So thick with lowings of the herds,
Day, when I lost the flower of men;

Who tremblest through thy darkling red   5
  On yon swollen brook that bubbles fast [5]
  By meadows breathing of the past,
And woodlands holy to the dead;

Who murmurest in the foliage eaves
  A song that slights the coming care,[6]   10
  And Autumn laying here and there
A fiery finger on the leaves;

Who wakenest with thy balmy breath
  To myriads on the genial earth,
  Memories of bridal, or of birth,[7]   15
And unto myriads more, of death.

Oh, wheresoever those [8] may be,
  Betwixt the slumber of the poles,
  Today they count as kindred souls;
They know me not, but mourn with me.   20

* * *
103
On that last night before we went
  From out the doors where I was bred,[9]
  I dreamed a vision of the dead,
Which left my after-morn content.

Methought I dwelt within a hall,   5
  And maidens with me; distant hills
  From hidden summits fed with rills
A river sliding by the wall.

---

3. See Exodus xix.16–25. After veiling
Mount Sinai in a "cloud" of smoke,
God addressed Moses from the darkness.
4. September 15, 1835, the second anniversary of Hallam's death.
5. Reflections of the clouded red light
of dawn quiver on the surface of the
fast-moving water.
6. I.e., disregards future events such as
death or the coming of autumn. Cf.
Shelley's *Ode to the West Wind.*

7. Cf. *Epilogue,* below, lines 117–28.
8. I.e., the "myriads" who remember
death.
9. In 1837 Tennyson and his family
moved away from their home in Lincolnshire, which had been closely associated
with his friendship with Hallam. In section 104 the move seems to occur in
1835, the year of the third Christmas
after Hallam's death.

> The hall with harp and carol rang.
> > They sang of what is wise and good   10
> > And graceful. In the center stood
> A statue veiled, to which they sang;
>
> And which, though veiled, was known to me,
> > The shape of him I loved, and love
> > Forever. Then flew in a dove   15
> And brought a summons from the sea; [1]
>
> And when they learnt that I must go,
> > They wept and wailed, but led the way
> > To where the little shallop [2] lay
> At anchor in the flood below;   20
>
> And on by many a level mead,
> > And shadowing bluff that made the banks,
> > We glided winding under ranks
> Of iris and the golden reed;
>
> And still as vaster grew the shore   25
> > And rolled the floods in grander space,
> > The maidens gathered strength and grace
> And presence, lordlier than before;
>
> And I myself, who sat apart
> > And watched them, waxed in every limb;   30
> > I felt the thews of Anakim, [3]
> The pulses of a Titan's heart;
>
> As one would sing the death of war,
> > And one would chant the history
> > Of that great race which is to be, [4]   35
> And one the shaping of a star;
>
> Until the forward-creeping tides
> > Began to foam, and we to draw
> > From deep to deep, to where we saw
> A great ship lift her shining sides. [5]   40
>
> The man we loved was there on deck,
> > But thrice as large as man he bent
> > To greet us. Up the side I went,
> And fell in silence on his neck;
>
> Whereat those maidens with one mind   45
> > Bewailed their lot; I did them wrong:

1. Cf. *Crossing the Bar:* "And one clear call for me."
2. A light open boat.
3. Plural of *Anak;* i.e., a reference to the giant sons of Anak. See Numbers xiii.33. The Titans (line 32) were giants of Greek mythology.
4. See the account of the "crowning race" in *Epilogue,* below, lines 128–44.
5. Cf. *Morte d'Arthur,* lines 255–322, in which Bedivere is left behind as Arthur's barge, the ship of death, sails away. In the present dream vision, not only is the speaker taken aboard but also his companions, who represent the creative arts of this world—"all the human powers and talents that do not pass with life but go along with it," as Tennyson said of this passage.

"We served thee here," they said, "so long,
And wilt thou leave us now behind?"

So rapt [6] I was, they could not win
    An answer from my lips, but he
    Replying, "Enter likewise ye
And go with us:" they entered in.   50

And while the wind began to sweep
    A music out of sheet and shroud,
    We steered her toward a crimson cloud   55
That landlike slept along the deep.

104

The time draws near the birth of Christ; [7]
    The moon is hid, the night is still;
    A single church below the hill
Is pealing, folded in the mist.

A single peal of bells below,   5
    That wakens at this hour of rest
    A single murmur in the breast,
That these are not the bells I know.

Like strangers' voices here they sound,
    In lands where not a memory strays,   10
    Nor landmark breathes of other days,
But all is new unhallowed ground.

* * *

106

Ring out, wild bells, to the wild sky,
    The flying cloud, the frosty light:
    The year is dying in the night;
Ring out, wild bells, and let him die.

Ring out the old, ring in the new,   5
    Ring, happy bells, across the snow:
    The year is going, let him go;
Ring out the false, ring in the true.

Ring out the grief that saps the mind,
    For those that here we see no more;   10
    Ring out the feud of rich and poor,
Ring in redress to all mankind.

Ring out a slowly dying cause,
    And ancient forms of party strife;
    Ring in the nobler modes of life,   15
With sweeter manners, purer laws.

Ring out the want, the care, the sin,
    The faithless coldness of the times;

---

6. Entranced.   7. See note 9 to section 103.

Ring out, ring out my mournful rhymes,
But ring the fuller minstrel in.   20

Ring out false pride in place and blood,
   The civic slander and the spite;
   Ring in the love of truth and right,
Ring in the common love of good.

Ring out old shapes of foul disease;   25
   Ring out the narrowing lust of gold;
   Ring out the thousand wars of old,
Ring in the thousand years of peace.

Ring in the valiant man and free,
   The larger heart, the kindlier hand;   30
   Ring out the darkness of the land,
Ring in the Christ that is to be.[8]

107

It is the day when he was born,[9]
   A bitter day that early sank
   Behind a purple-frosty bank
Of vapor, leaving night forlorn.

The time admits not flowers or leaves   5
   To deck the banquet. Fiercely flies
   The blast of North and East, and ice
Makes daggers at the sharpened eaves,

And bristles all the brakes and thorns
   To yon hard crescent, as she hangs   10
   Above the wood which grides [1] and clangs
Its leafless ribs and iron horns

Together, in the drifts [2] that pass
   To darken on the rolling brine
   That breaks the coast. But fetch the wine,   15
Arrange the board and brim the glass;

Bring in great logs and let them lie,
   To make a solid core of heat;
   Be cheerful-minded, talk and treat
Of all things even as he were by;   20

We keep the day. With festal cheer,
   With books and music, surely we
   Will drink to him, whate'er he be,
And sing the songs he loved to hear.

* * *

8. These allusions to the second coming of Christ and to the millennium are derived from Revelation xx, but Tennyson has interpreted the Biblical account in his own way. He once told his son of his conviction that "the forms of Christian religion would alter; but that the spirit of Christ would still grow from more to more."
9. February 1.
1. Clashes with a strident noise.
2. Either cloud-drifts or clouds of snow.

109

Heart-affluence in discursive talk
  From household fountains never dry;
  The critic clearness of an eye
That saw through all the Muses' walk; [3]

Seraphic intellect and force   5
  To seize and throw the doubts of man;
  Impassioned logic, which outran
The hearer in its fiery course;

High nature amorous of the good,
  But touched with no ascetic gloom;   10
  And passion pure in snowy bloom
Through all the years of April blood;

A love of freedom rarely felt,
  Of freedom in her regal seat
  Of England; not the schoolboy heat,   15
The blind hysterics of the Celt; [4]

And manhood fused with female grace
  In such a sort, the child would twine
  A trustful hand, unasked, in thine,
And find his comfort in thy face;   20

All these have been, and thee mine eyes
  Have looked on: if they looked in vain,
  My shame is greater who remain,
Nor let thy wisdom make me wise.

* * *

115

Now fades the last long streak of snow,
  Now burgeons every maze of quick [5]
  About the flowering squares, [6] and thick
By ashen roots the violets blow.

Now rings the woodland loud and long,   5
  The distance takes a lovelier hue,
  And drowned in yonder living blue
The lark becomes a sightless song.

Now dance the lights on lawn and lea,
  The flocks are whiter down the vale,   10
  And milkier every milky sail
On winding stream or distant sea;

Where now the seamew pipes, or dives
  In yonder greening gleam, and fly
  The happy birds, that change their sky   15
To build and brood, that live their lives

3. The realm of art and literature.   section 127, lines 7–8.
4. In particular the French at the time   5. In hawthorn hedges.
of the Revolution of 1789. See also   6. Fields.

From land to land; and in my breast
   Spring wakens too, and my regret
   Becomes an April violet,
And buds and blossoms like the rest.   20

* * *

118

Contémplate all this work of Time,
   The giant laboring in his youth;
   Nor dream of human love and truth,
As dying Nature's earth and lime;

But trust that those we call the dead   5
   Are breathers of an ampler day
   For ever nobler ends. They [7] say,
The solid earth whereon we tread

In tracts of fluent heat began,
   And grew to seeming-random forms,   10
   The seeming prey of cyclic storms,
Till at the last arose the man;

Who throve and branched from clime to clime,
   The herald of a higher race,
   And of himself in higher place,   15
If so he type [8] this work of time

Within himself, from more to more;
   Or, crowned with attributes of woe
   Like glories, move his course, and show
That life is not as idle ore,   20

But iron dug from central gloom,
   And heated hot with burning fears,
   And dipped in baths of hissing tears,
And battered with the shocks of doom

To shape and use. Arise and fly   25
   The reeling Faun, the sensual feast;
   Move upward, working out the beast,
And let the ape and tiger die.

119

Doors, where my heart was used to beat
   So quickly, not as one that weeps
   I come once more; the city sleeps;
I smell the meadow in the street;

I hear a chirp of birds; I see   5
   Betwixt the black fronts long-withdrawn
   A light blue lane of early dawn,
And think of early days and thee,

---

7. Geologists and astronomers.   8. Emulate, prefigure as a type.

And bless thee, for thy lips are bland,
   And bright the friendship of thine eye;   10
   And in my thoughts with scarce a sigh
I take the pressure of thine hand.

* * *
120
I trust I have not wasted breath:
   I think we are not wholly brain,
   Magnetic mockeries; [9] not in vain,
Like Paul [1] with beasts, I fought with Death;

Not only cunning casts in clay: 5
   Let Science prove we are, and then
   What matters Science unto men,
At least to me? I would not stay.

Let him, the wiser man [2] who springs
   Hereafter, up from childhood shape   10
   His action like the greater ape,
But I was *born* to other things.
121
Sad Hesper [3] o'er the buried sun
   And ready, thou, to die with him,
   Thou watchest all things ever dim
And dimmer, and a glory done.

The team is loosened from the wain,[4]   5
   The boat is drawn upon the shore;
   Thou listenest to the closing door,
And life is darkened in the brain.

Bright Phosphor,[5] fresher for the night,
   By thee the world's great work is heard   10
   Beginning, and the wakeful bird;
Behind thee comes the greater light.

The market boat is on the stream,
   And voices hail it from the brink;
   Thou hear'st the village hammer clink,   15
And see'st the moving of the team.

Sweet Hesper-Phosphor, double name [6]
   For what is one, the first, the last,
   Thou, like my present and my past,
Thy place is changed; thou art the same.   20

* * *

9. Mechanisms operated by responses to electrical forces.
1. I Corinthians xv.32.
2. Spoken ironically.
3. Evening star.
4. Hay wagon.
5. Morning star.
6. The same planet, Venus, is both evening star and morning star.

123

There rolls the deep where grew the tree.
   O earth, what changes hast thou seen!
   There where the long street roars hath been
The stillness of the central sea.[7]

The hills are shadows, and they flow   5
   From form to form, and nothing stands;
   They melt like mist, the solid lands,
Like clouds they shape themselves and go.

But in my spirit will I dwell,
   And dream my dream, and hold it true;   10
   For though my lips may breathe adieu,
I cannot think the thing farewell.

124

That which we dare invoke to bless;
   Our dearest faith; our ghastliest doubt;
   He, They, One, All; within, without;
The Power in darkness whom we guess—

I found Him not in world or sun,   5
   Or eagle's wing, or insect's eye,[8]
   Nor through the questions men may try,
The petty cobwebs we have spun.

If e'er when faith had fallen asleep,
   I heard a voice, "believe no more,"   10
   And heard an ever-breaking shore
That tumbled in the Godless deep,

A warmth within the breast would melt
   The freezing reason's colder part,
   And like a man in wrath the heart   15
Stood up and answered, "I have felt."

No, like a child in doubt and fear:
   But that blind clamor made me wise;
   Then was I as a child that cries,
But, crying, knows his father near;   20

And what I am beheld again
   What is, and no man understands;

---

7. Cf. a passage from Sir Charles Lyell's *The Principles of Geology* (1832), a book well-known to Tennyson. In discussing the "interchange of sea and land" that has occurred "on the surface of our globe" Lyell remarks: "In the Mediterranean alone, many flourishing inland towns and a still greater number of ports now stand where the sea rolled its waves since the era when civilized nations first grew in Europe."

8. He does not discover satisfactory proof of God's existence in the 18th-century argument that because objects in nature are designed there must exist a designer.

And out of darkness came the hands
That reach through nature, molding men.

* * *

126

Love is and was my lord and king,
   And in his presence I attend
   To hear the tidings of my friend,
Which every hour his couriers bring.

Love is and was my king and lord,
   And will be, though as yet I keep 5
   Within the court on earth, and sleep
Encompassed by his faithful guard,

And hear at times a sentinel
   Who moves about from place to place,
   And whispers to the worlds of space, 10
In the deep night, that all is well.

127

And all is well, though faith and form [9]
   Be sundered in the night of fear;
   Well roars the storm to those that hear
A deeper voice across the storm,

Proclaiming social truth shall spread, 5
   And justice, even though thrice again
   The red fool-fury of the Seine
Should pile her barricades with dead.[1]

But ill for him that wears a crown,
   And him, the lazar,[2] in his rags!
   They tremble, the sustaining crags; 10
The spires of ice are toppled down,

And molten up, and roar in flood;
   The fortress crashes from on high,
   The brute earth lightens [3] to the sky,
And the great Aeon [4] sinks in blood, 15

And compassed by the fires of hell,
   While thou, dear spirit, happy star,
   O'erlook'st the tumult from afar,
And smilest, knowing all is well. 20

* * *

9. Traditional institutions through which faith was formerly expressed, such as the Church. See Carlyle's essay, *Characteristics*, above.
1. Revolutionary uprisings in France, in each of which a king lost his throne (line 9): in 1789 against Louis XVI, in 1830 against Charles X, and in 1848 against Louis Philippe. The third (line 6) would have been a prophesy if, as Tennyson recollected, section 126 was finished at a date earlier than 1848.
2. Pauper suffering from disease.
3. Is lit up by fire.
4. A vast tract of time, here perhaps modern western civilization.

129

Dear friend, faroff, my lost desire,
  So far, so near in woe and weal,
  O loved the most, when most I feel
There is a lower and a higher;

Known and unknown, human, divine;   5
  Sweet human hand and lips and eye;
  Dear heavenly friend that canst not die,
Mine, mine, forever, ever mine;

Strange friend, past, present, and to be;
  Loved deeplier, darklier understood;   10
  Behold, I dream a dream of good,
And mingle all the world with thee.

130

Thy voice is on the rolling air;
  I hear thee where the waters run;
  Thou standest in the rising sun,
And in the setting thou art fair.

What art thou then? I cannot guess;   5
  But though I seem in star and flower
  To feel thee some diffusive power,
I do not therefore love thee less.

My love involves the love before;
  My love is vaster passion now;   10
  Tho' mix'd with God and Nature thou,
I seem to love thee more and more.

Far off thou art, but ever nigh;
  I have thee still, and I rejoice;
  I prosper, circled with thy voice;   15
I shall not lose thee tho' I die.

131

O living will [5] that shalt endure
  When all that seems shall suffer shock,
  Rise in the spiritual rock,[6]
Flow through our deeds and make them pure,

That we may lift from out of dust   5
  A voice as unto him that hears,
  A cry above the conquered years
To one that with us works, and trust,

With faith that comes of self-control,
  The truths that never can be proved   10
  Until we close with all we loved,
And all we flow from, soul in soul.

---

5. Tennyson later commented that he
meant here the moral will of mankind.

6. Christ (see I Corinthians x.4).

From *Epilogue* [7]

* * *

And rise, O moon, from yonder down,
   Till over down and over dale
   All night the shining vapor sail
And pass the silent-lighted town,

The white-faced halls, the glancing rills,   5
   And catch at every mountain head,
   And o'er the friths [8] that branch and spread
Their sleeping silver through the hills;

And touch with shade the bridal doors,
   With tender gloom the roof, the wall;   10
   And breaking let the splendor fall
To spangle all the happy shores

By which they rest, and ocean sounds,
   And, star and system rolling past,
   A soul shall draw from out the vast   15
And strike his being into bounds,

And, moved through life of lower phase,
   Result in man,[9] be born and think,
   And act and love, a closer link
Betwixt us and the crowning race   20

Of those that, eye to eye, shall look
   On knowledge; under whose command
   Is Earth and Earth's, and in their hand
Is Nature like an open book;

No longer half-akin to brute,   25
   For all we thought and loved and did,
   And hoped, and suffered, is but seed
Of what in them is flower and fruit;

Whereof the man that with me trod
   This planet was a noble type   30
   Appearing ere the times were ripe,
That friend of mine who lives in God,

That God, which ever lives and loves,
   One God, one law, one element,
   And one far-off divine event,   35
To which the whole creation moves.

1833–50   1850

7. The *Epilogue* describes the wedding day of Tennyson's sister Cecilia to Edmund Lushington. At the conclusion (reprinted here) the speaker reflects upon their moonlit wedding night and the kind of offspring which will result from their union.

8. Inlets of the sea.
9. A child will be conceived and will develop in embryo through various stages. This development is similar to the evolution of man from the animal to the human level and perhaps to a future higher stage of development.

The Charge of the Light Brigade[1]

1

Half a league, half a league,
Half a league onward,
All in the valley of Death
   Rode the six hundred.
"Forward, the Light Brigade!   5
Charge for the guns!" he said.
Into the valley of Death
   Rode the six hundred.

2

"Forward, the Light Brigade!"
Was there a man dismayed?   10
Not though the soldier knew
   Someone had blundered.
Theirs not to make reply,
Theirs not to reason why,
Theirs but to do and die.   15
Into the valley of Death
   Rode the six hundred.

3

Cannon to right of them,
Cannon to left of them,
Cannon in front of them   20
   Volleyed and thundered;
Stormed at with shot and shell,
Boldly they rode and well,
Into the jaws of Death,
Into the mouth of hell   25
   Rode the six hundred.

4

Flashed all their sabers bare,
Flashed as they turned in air
Sab'ring the gunners there,
Charging an army, while   30
   All the world wondered.
Plunged in the battery smoke
Right through the line they broke;
Cossack and Russian
Reeled from the saber stroke   35
   Shattered and sundered.

1. During the Crimean War, owing to confusion of orders, a brigade of British cavalry charged some entrenched batteries of Russian artillery. This blunder cost the lives of three fourths of the 600 horsemen engaged (see Cecil Woodham-Smith, *The Reason Why*, 1954). Tennyson rapidly composed his "ballad" (as he called the poem) after reading an account of the battle in a newspaper.

Then they rode back, but not,
    Not the six hundred.

        5
Cannon to right of them,
Cannon to left of them,
Cannon behind them   40
    Volleyed and thundered;
Stormed at with shot and shell,
While horse and hero fell,
They that had fought so well   45
Came through the jaws of Death,
Back from the mouth of hell,
All that was left of them,
    Left of six hundred.

        6
When can their glory fade?
O the wild charge they made!   50
    All the world wondered.
Honor the charge they made!
Honor the Light Brigade,
    Noble six hundred!   55

1854   1854

From Maud[1]

VIII

She came to the village church,
And sat by a pillar alone;
An angel watching an urn
Wept over her, carved in stone;
And once, but once, she lifted her eyes,   305
And suddenly, sweetly, strangely blushed
To find they were met by my own;
And suddenly, sweetly, my heart beat stronger
And thicker, until I heard no longer
The snowy-banded, dilettante,   310
Delicate-handed priest intone;
And thought, is it pride? and mused and sighed,
"No surely, now it cannot be pride."

* * *

1. The speaker is a young man, living alone in the country, whose disillusionment after his father's suicide has left him full of a bitterness that borders on madness. He is restored to sanity and intense happiness when he discovers that Maud, the beautiful daughter of a local landowner, accepts his love for him. The following selections tell of his proposal to her and her acceptance of him. Later in the poem he loses Maud after killing her brother in a duel.

    Maud was a poem that Tennyson especially enjoyed reading aloud. He called it "a little *Hamlet*," but it is closer to *Romeo and Juliet* in its picture of love in the midst of family feuds.

XVI

Catch not my breath, O clamorous heart,
Let not my tongue be a thrall to my eye,
For I must tell her before we part,
I must tell her, or die.

* * *

XVIII

1

I have led her home, my love, my only friend.
There is none like her, none.   600
And never yet so warmly ran my blood
And sweetly, on and on
Calming itself to the long-wished-for end,
Full to the banks, close on the promised good.

2

None like her, none.   605
Just now the dry-tongued laurels' pattering talk
Seemed her light foot along the garden walk,
And shook my heart to think she comes once more.
But even then I heard her close the door;
The gates of heaven are closed, and she is gone.   610

3

There is none like her, none,
Nor will be when our summers have deceased.
O, art thou[2] sighing for Lebanon
In the long breeze that streams to thy delicious East,
Sighing for Lebanon,   615
Dark cedar, though thy limbs have here increased,
Upon a pastoral slope as fair,
And looking to the South and fed
With honeyed rain and delicate air,
And haunted by the starry head   620
Of her whose gentle will has changed my fate,
And made my life a perfumed altar-flame;
And over whom thy darkness must have spread
With such delight as theirs of old, thy great
Forefathers of the thornless garden, there   625
Shadowing the snow-limbed Eve from whom she came?

4

Here will I lie, while these long branches sway,
And you fair stars that crown a happy day
Go in and out as if at merry play,
Who am no more so all forlorn   630
As when it seemed far better to be born
To labor and the mattock-hardened hand
Than nursed at ease and brought to understand
A sad astrology,[3] the boundless plan

2. The cedar-of-Lebanon tree in Maud's   3. Astronomy.
garden.

That makes you tyrants in your iron skies, 635
Innumerable, pitiless, passionless eyes,
Cold fires, yet with power to burn and brand
His nothingness into man.

5

But now shine on, and what care I,
Who in this stormy gulf have found a pearl 640
The countercharm of space and hollow sky,[4]
And do accept my madness, and would die
To save from some slight shame one simple girl?—

6

Would die, for sullen-seeming Death may give
More life to Love than is or ever was 645
In our low world, where yet 'tis sweet to live.
Let no one ask me how it came to pass;
It seems that I am happy, that to me
A livelier emerald twinkles in the grass,
A purer sapphire melts into the sea. 650

7

Not die, but live a life of truest breath,
And teach true life to fight with mortal wrongs.
O, why should Love, like men in drinking songs,
Spice his fair banquet with the dust of death?
Make answer, Maud my bliss, 655
Maud made my Maud by that long loving kiss,
Life of my life, wilt thou not answer this?
"The dusky strand of Death inwoven here
With dear Love's tie, makes Love himself more dear."

8

Is that enchanted moan only the swell 660
Of the long waves that roll in yonder bay?
And hark the clock within, the silver knell
Of twelve sweet hours that passed in bridal white,
And died to live, long as my pulses play;
But now by this my love has closed her sight 665
And given false death[5] her hand, and stolen away
To dreamful wastes where footless fancies dwell
Among the fragments of the golden day.
May nothing there her maiden grace affright!
Dear heart, I feel with thee the drowsy spell. 670
My bride to be, my evermore delight,
My own heart's heart, my ownest own, farewell;
It is but for a little space I go.
And ye[6] meanwhile far over moor and fell
Beat to the noiseless music of the night! 675
Has our whole earth gone nearer to the glow
Of your soft splendors that you look so bright?
I have climbed nearer out of lonely hell.

4. Something that offsets his former 5. I.e., sleep.
fears of the vastness of space revealed 6. The stars.
by modern astronomy.

Beat, happy stars, timing with things below,
Beat with my heart more blest than heart can tell,　　680
Blest, but for some dark undercurrent woe
That seems to draw—but it shall not be so;
Let all be well, be well.

* * *

1855

In the Valley of Cauteretz[7]

All along the valley, stream that flashest white,
Deepening thy voice with the deepening of the night,
All along the valley, where thy waters flow,
I walked with one I loved two and thirty years ago.
All along the valley, while I walked today,　　5
The two and thirty years were a mist that rolls away;
For all along the valley, down thy rocky bed,
Thy living voice to me was as the voice of the dead,
And all along the valley, by rock and cave and tree,
The voice of the dead was a living voice to me.　　10

1861　　　　　　　　　　　　　　　　　　　　　　　　1864

From Idylls of the King
Dedication[1]

These to His Memory—since he held them dear,
Perchance as finding there unconsciously
Some image of himself—I dedicate,
I dedicate, I consecrate with tears—
These Idylls.

　　　　　And indeed he seems to me　　5
Scarce other than my king's ideal knight,
"Who reverenced his conscience as his king;
Whose glory was, redressing human wrong;
Who spake no slander, no, nor listened to it;
Who loved one only and who clave to her—"[2]　　10

---

7. A valley in the French Pyrenees visited by Tennyson and Hallam in 1830 and revisited by Tennyson in 1861.
1. Tennyson's dedication of his *Idylls* to Prince Albert, Queen Victoria's husband, who had died in 1861, could be dismissed as a mere formality on the part of the poet laureate, but it was more. Because of his earnest dedication to duty, his statesmanship, his work for peace, Albert seemed to Tennyson to have been almost a modern reincarnation of King Arthur.

Concerning the *Idylls* as a poem, see the Tennyson introduction. *Morte d'Arthur*, included above, may be read as a representative *Idyll*; in a slightly revised form, it became the final book of the twelve-book cycle.
2. A paraphrase of King Arthur's words (*Idylls* XI.472) summarizing the ideals of the knights of the Round Table.

Her—over all whose realms to their last isle,
Commingled with the gloom of imminent war,
The shadow of his loss drew like eclipse,
Darkening the world. We have lost him; he is gone.
We know him now; all narrow jealousies   15
Are silent, and we see him as he moved,
How modest, kindly, all-accomplished, wise,
With what sublime repression of himself,
And in what limits, and how tenderly;
Not swaying to this faction or to that;   20
Not making his high place the lawless perch
Of winged ambitions, nor a vantage-ground
For pleasure; but through all this tract of years
Wearing the white flower of a blameless life,
Before a thousand peering littlenesses,   25
In that fierce light which beats upon a throne,
And blackens every blot: for where is he,
Who dares foreshadow for an only son
A lovelier life, a more unstained, than his?
Or how should England dreaming of *his* sons   30
Hope more for these than some inheritance
Of such a life, a heart, a mind as thine,
Thou noble Father of her Kings to be,
Laborious for her people and her poor—
Voice in the rich dawn of an ampler day—   35
Far-sighted summoner of War and Waste
To fruitful strifes and rivalries of peace—
Sweet nature gilded by the gracious gleam
Of letters, dear to Science, dear to Art,
Dear to thy land[3] and ours, a Prince indeed,   40
Beyond all titles, and a household name,
Hereafter, through all times, Albert the Good.

Break not, O woman's-heart, but still endure;
Break not, for thou art Royal, but endure,
Remembering all the beauty of that star   45
Which shone so close beside Thee that ye made
One light together, but has passed and leaves
The Crown a lonely splendor.

                  May all love,
His love, unseen but felt, o'ershadow thee,
The love of all thy sons encompass thee,
The love of all thy daughters cherish thee,   50
The love of all thy people comfort thee,
Till God's love set thee at his side again!

                                       1862

3. Albert was a native of Saxe-Coburg in Germany.

In Love, If Love Be Love[4]

In love, if love be Love, if love be ours,
Faith and unfaith can ne'er be equal powers:
Unfaith in aught is want of faith in all.

It is the little rift[5] within the lute,
That by and by will make the music mute,　　　　　5
And ever widening slowly silence all.

The little rift within the lover's lute
Or little pitted speck in garnered fruit,
That rotting inward slowly molders all.

It is not worth the keeping: let it go:　　　　　10
But shall it? answer, darling, answer, no.
And trust me not at all or all in all.

Northern Farmer[1]

NEW STYLE

1

Dosn't thou 'ear my 'erse's[2] legs, as they canters awaäy?
Proputty,[3] proputty, proputty—that's what I 'ears 'em saäy.
Proputty, proputty, proputty—Sam, thou's an ass for thy paäins;
Theer's moor sense i' one o' 'is legs, nor in all thy braäins.

2

Woä—theer's a craw[4] to pluck wi' tha, Sam: yon's Parson's 'ouse—
Dosn't thou knaw that a man mun be eäther a man or a mouse?　　6
Time to think on it then; for thou'll be twenty to weeäk.[5]
Proputty, proputty—woä then, woä—let ma 'ear mysén[6] speäk.

3

Me an' thy muther, Sammy, 'as beän a-talkin' o' thee;
Thou's beän talkin' to muther, an' she beän a-tellin' it me.　　10
Thou'll not marry for munny—thou's sweet upo' Parson's lass—
Noä—thou'll marry for luvv—an' we boäth on us thinks tha an ass.

4

Seeäed her todaäy goä by—Saäint's-daäy—they was ringing the bells.
She's a beauty, thou thinks—an' soä is scoors o' gells,[7]

4. Sung by Vivien in her successful attempt to seduce Merlin, the magician (*Idylls* VI.385 ff.).
5. Crack.
1. This monologue exemplifies the diversity of Tennyson's talents. A passionate attachment to land and property, which was portrayed sympathetically by Wordsworth in *Michael*, is here represented humorously. The harsh common sense of the farmer's attitude towards love and marriage is reinforced by his jaw-breaking north-English dialect.

This is the second of a pair of monologues in dialect. In the first, *Northern Farmer: Old Style*, the speaker is a bailiff who has spent his life supervising the farmlands of a wealthy squire. In the second, the "new style" farmer is himself an independent landowner.
2. Horse's.
3. Property.
4. Crow.
5. This week.
6. Myself.
7. Scores of girls.

Them as 'as munny an' all—wot's a beauty?—the flower as blaws. 15
But proputty, proputty sticks, an' proputty, proputty graws.

5

Do'ant be stunt;[8] taäke time. I knaws what maäkes tha sa mad.
Warn't I craäzed fur the lasses mysén when I wur a lad?
But I knawed a Quaäker feller as often 'as towd[9] ma this:
"Doänt thou marry for munny, but goä wheer munny is!" 20

6

An' I went wheer munny war; an' thy muther coom to 'and,
Wi' lots o' munny laaïd by, an' a nicetish bit o' land.
Maäybe she warn't a beauty—I niver giv it a thowt—
But warn't she as good to cuddle an' kıss as a lass as 'ant nowt?[1]

7

Parson's lass 'ant nowt, an' she weänt 'a nowt[2] when 'e's deäd, 25
Mun be a guvness, lad, or summut, and addle[3] her breäd.
Why? fur 'e's nobbut[4] a curate, an' weänt niver get hissén clear,
An' 'e maäde the bed as 'e ligs[5] on afoor 'e coomed to the shere.

8

An' thin 'e coomed to the parish wi' lots o' Varsity debt,
Stook to his taaïl they did, an' 'e 'ant got shut on 'em[6] yet. 30
An' 'e ligs on 'is back i' the grip,[7] wi' noän to lend 'im a shuvv,
Woorse nor a far-weltered yowe;[8] fur, Sammy, 'e married fur luvv.

9

Luvv? what's luvv? thou can luvv thy lass an' 'er munny too,
Maäkin' 'em goä togither, as they've good right to do.
Couldn' I luvv thy muther by cause o' 'er munny laaïd by? 35
Naäy—fur I luvved 'er a vast sight moor fur it; reäson why.

10

Aye, an' thy muther says thou wants to marry the lass,
Cooms of a gentleman burn;[9] an' we boäth on us thinks tha an ass.
Woä then, proputty, wiltha?—an ass as near as mays nowt[1]—
Woä then, wiltha? dangtha!—the bees is as fell as owt.[2] 40

11

Breäk me a bit o' the esh[3] for his 'eäd, lad, out o' the fence!
Gentleman burn! what's gentleman burn? is it shillins an' pence?
Proputty, proputty's ivrything 'ere, an', Sammy, I'm blest
If it isn't the saäme oop yonder, fur them as 'as it's the best.

12

Tis'n them as 'as munny as breäks into 'ouses an' steäls, 45
Them as 'as coäts to their backs an' taäkes their regular meäls.
Noä, but it's them as niver knaws wheer a meäl's to be 'ad.
Taäke my word for it, Sammy, the poor in a loomp is bad.

8. Stubborn.
9. Told.
1. Has nothing.
2. Won't have anything.
3. Earn.
4. Only.
5. Lies; "shere": shire.
6. Rid of them.

7. Ditch.
8. Ewe lying on her back.
9. Born.
1. Makes nothing.
2. The flies are as mean as anything.
3. A branch of ash leaves (to keep the flies off the horse's head).

13

Them or thir feythers, tha sees, mun 'a beän a laäzy lot,
Fur work mun 'a gone to the gittin' whiniver munny was got.   50
Feyther 'ad ammost nowt; leästways 'is munny was 'id.
But 'e tued an' moiled[4] issén deäd, an' 'e died a good un, 'e did.

14

Looök thou theer wheer Wrigglesby beck[5] cooms out by the 'ill!
Feyther run oop[6] to the farm, an' I runs oop to the mill;
An' I'll run oop to the brig,[7] an' that thou'll live to see;   55
And if thou marries a good un I'll leäve the land to thee.

15

Thim's my noätions, Sammy, wheerby I meäns to stick;
But if thou marries a bad un, I'll leäve the land to Dick.—
Coom oop, proputty, proputty—that's what I 'ears 'im saäy—
Proputty, proputty, proputty—canter an' canter awaäy.   60

1869

Flower in the Crannied Wall

Flower in the crannied wall,
I pluck you out of the crannies,
I hold you here, root and all, in my hand,
Little flower—but *if* I could understand
What you are, root and all, and all in all,   5
I should know what God and man is.

1869

The Revenge[1]

A BALLAD OF THE FLEET

1

At Flores in the Azores Sir Richard Grenville lay,
And a pinnace, like a fluttered bird, came flying from far away:
"Spanish ships of war at sea! we have sighted fifty-three!"
Then sware Lord Thomas Howard: " 'Fore God I am no coward;
But I cannot meet them here, for my ships are out of gear,   5
And the half my men are sick. I must fly, but follow quick.
We are six ships of the line; can we fight with fifty-three?"

2

Then spake Sir Richard Grenville: "I know you are no coward;
You fly them for a moment to fight with them again.
But I've ninety men and more that are lying sick ashore.   10

4. Toiled and drudged.
5. Brook.
6. I.e., father's property ran up.
7. Bridge.
1. Based on Sir Walter Ralegh's ac-

count of an engagement in 1591 off
the coast of Flores, one of the islands
of the Azores, in which five Spanish
ships were sunk by the *Revenge* during
a fifteen-hour battle.

I should count myself the coward if I left them, my Lord Howard,
To these Inquisition dogs and the devildoms of Spain."

3

So Lord Howard passed away with five ships of war that day,
Till he melted like a cloud in the silent summer heaven;
But Sir Richard bore in hand all his sick men from the land   15
Very carefully and slow,
Men of Bideford in Devon,
And we laid them on the ballast down below;
For we brought them all aboard,
And they blessed him in their pain, that they were not left to
    Spain,   20
To the thumbscrew and the stake, for the glory of the Lord.

4

He had only a hundred seamen to work the ship and to fight,
And he sailed away from Flores till the Spaniard came in sight,
With his huge sea-castles heaving upon the weather bow.
"Shall we fight or shall we fly?   25
Good Sir Richard, tell us now,
For to fight is but to die!
There'll be little of us left by the time this sun be set."
And Sir Richard said again: "We be all good English men.
Let us bang these dogs of Seville, the children of the devil,   30
For I never turned my back upon Don or devil yet."

5

Sir Richard spoke and he laughed, and we roared a hurrah, and so
The little Revenge ran on sheer into the heart of the foe,
With her hundred fighters on deck, and her ninety sick below;
For half of their fleet to the right and half to the left were seen,   35
And the little Revenge ran on through the long sea lane between.

6

Thousands of their soldiers looked down from their decks and
    laughed,
Thousands of their seamen made mock at the mad little craft
Running on and on, till delayed
By their mountain-like San Philip that, of fifteen hundred tons,   40
And up-shadowing high above us with her yawning tiers of guns,
Took the breath from our sails, and we stayed.

7

And while now the great San Philip hung above us like a cloud
Whence the thunderbolt will fall
Long and loud,   45
Four galleons drew away
From the Spanish fleet that day,
And two upon the larboard and two the starboard lay,
And the battle thunder broke from them all.

8

But anon the great San Philip, she bethought herself and went,   50
Having that within her womb that had left her ill content;
And the rest they came aboard us, and they fought us hand to hand,

For a dozen times they came with their pikes and musqueteers,
And a dozen times we shook 'em off as a dog that shakes his ears
When he leaps from the water to the land.   55

9

And the sun went down, and the stars came out far over the summer
    sea,
But never a moment ceased the fight of the one and the fifty-three.
Ship after ship, the whole night long, their high-built galleons came,
Ship after ship, the whole night long, with her battle thunder and
    flame;
Ship after ship, the whole night long, drew back with her dead and
    her shame.   60
For some were sunk and many were shattered, and so could fight us
    no more—
God of battles, was ever a battle like this in the world before?

10

For he said, "Fight on! fight on!"
Though his vessel was all but a wreck;
And it chanced that, when half of the short summer night was
    gone,   65
With a grisly wound to be dressed he had left the deck,
But a bullet struck him that was dressing it suddenly dead,
And himself he was wounded again in the side and the head,
And he said, "Fight on! fight on!"

11

And the night went down, and the sun smiled out far over the
    summer sea,   70
And the Spanish fleet with broken sides lay round us all in a ring;
But they dared not touch us again, for they feared that we still could
    sting,
So they watched what the end would be.
And we had not fought them in vain,
But in perilous plight were we,   75
Seeing forty of our poor hundred were slain,
And half of the rest of us maimed for life
In the crash of the cannonades and the desperate strife;
And the sick men down in the hold were most of them stark and
    cold,
And the pikes were all broken or bent, and the powder was all of
    it spent;   80
And the masts and the rigging were lying over the side;
But Sir Richard cried in his English pride:
"We have fought such a fight for a day and a night
As may never be fought again!
We have won great glory, my men!   85
And a day less or more
At sea or ashore,
We die—does it matter when?
Sink me the ship, Master Gunner—sink her, split her in twain!
Fall into the hands of God, not into the hands of Spain!"   90

12

And the gunner said, "Aye, aye," but the seamen made reply:
"We have children, we have wives,
And the Lord hath spared our lives.
We will make the Spaniard promise, if we yield, to let us go;
We shall live to fight again and to strike another blow."
And the lion there lay dying, and they yielded to the foe. 95

13

And the stately Spanish men to their flagship bore him then,
Where they laid him by the mast, old Sir Richard caught at last,
And they praised him to his face with their courtly foreign grace;
But he rose upon their decks, and he cried:
"I have fought for Queen and Faith like a valiant man and true; 100
I have only done my duty as a man is bound to do.
With a joyful spirit I Sir Richard Grenville die!"
And he fell upon their decks, and he died.

14

And they stared at the dead that had been so valiant and true, 105
And had holden the power and glory of Spain so cheap
That he dared her with one little ship and his English few;
Was he devil or man? He was devil for aught they knew,
But they sank his body with honor down into the deep,
And they manned the Revenge with a swarthier alien crew, 110
And away she sailed with her loss and longed for her own;
When a wind from the lands they had ruined awoke from sleep,
And the water began to heave and the weather to moan,
And or ever that evening ended a great gale blew,
And a wave like the wave that is raised by an earthquake grew, 115
Till it smote on their hulls and their sails and their masts and their
flags,
And the whole sea plunged and fell on the shot-shattered navy of
Spain,
And the little Revenge herself went down by the island crags
To be lost evermore in the main.

1878

To Virgil

WRITTEN AT THE REQUEST OF THE MANTUANS[1] FOR THE NINETEENTH CENTENARY OF VIRGIL'S DEATH

1

Roman Virgil, thou that singest
    Ilion's lofty temples robed in fire,
Ilion falling, Rome arising,
    wars, and filial faith, and Dido's pyre;[2]

---

1. Inhabitants of Mantua, the city near which Virgil was born.
2. The allusions in this stanza are to incidents in Virgil's *Aeneid*, especially the fall of Troy (Ilion).

2

Landscape-lover, lord of language
  more than he that sang the "Works and Days,"[3]
All the chosen coin of fancy
  flashing out from many a golden phrase;

3

Thou that singest wheat and woodland,
  tilth and vineyard, hive and horse and herd;
All the charm of all the Muses
  often flowering in a lonely word;   5

4

Poet of the happy Tityrus[4]
  piping underneath his beechen bowers;
Poet of the poet-satyr[5]
  whom the laughing shepherd bound with flowers;

5

Chanter of the Pollio,[6] glorying
  in the blissful years again to be,
Summers of the snakeless meadow,
  unlaborious earth and oarless sea;   10

6

Thou that seest Universal
  Nature moved by Universal Mind;
Thou majestic in thy sadness
  at the doubtful doom of human kind;

7

Light among the vanished ages;
  star that gildest yet this phantom shore;
Golden branch[7] amid the shadows,
  kings and realms that pass to rise no more;

8

Now thy Forum roars no longer,
  fallen every purple Caesar's dome—   15
Though thine ocean-roll of rhythm
  sound forever of Imperial Rome—

9

Now the Rome of slaves hath perished,
  and the Rome of freemen[8] holds her place,
I, from out the Northern Island
  sundered once from all the human race,

10

I salute thee, Mantovano,[9]
  I that loved thee since my day began,
Wielder of the stateliest measure
  ever molded by the lips of man.   20

1882   1882

3. Hesiod, a Greek poet, whose *Works and Days* anticipated Virgil's *Georgics* in its pictures of farm life.
4. A shepherd in Virgil's *Eclogue* I.
5. Silenus, in *Eclogue* VI.
6. A friend of Virgil's who is celebrated in *Eclogue* IV.

7. A golden bough enabled Aeneas to enter the world of the shades. See *Aeneid* VI.208 ff.
8. Italy had only recently been liberated and unified.
9. Mantuan.

"Frater Ave atque Vale"[1]

Row us out from Desenzano,[2] to your Sirmione row!
So they rowed, and there we landed—"O venusta Sirmio!"
There to me through all the groves of olive in the summer glow,
There beneath the Roman ruin where the purple flowers grow,
Came that "Ave atque Vale" of the Poet's hopeless woe,   5
Tenderest of Roman poets nineteen hundred years ago,
"Frater Ave atque Vale"—as we wandered to and fro
Gazing at the Lydian[3] laughter of the Garda Lake below
Sweet Catullus's all-but-island, olive-silvery Sirmio!

1880   1883

To E. FitzGerald[1]

Old Fitz, who from your suburb grange,
    Where once I tarried for a while,
Glance at the wheeling orb of change,
    And greet it with a kindly smile;
Whom yet I see as there you sit   5
    Beneath your sheltering garden-tree,
And watch your doves about you flit,
    And plant on shoulder, hand, and knee,
Or on your head their rosy feet,
    As if they knew your diet spares   10
Whatever moved in that full sheet
    Let down to Peter at his prayers;[2]
Who live on milk and meal and grass;
    And once for ten long weeks I tried
Your table of Pythagoras,[3]   15
    And seemed at first "a thing enskied,"
As Shakespeare has it,[4] airy-light
    To float above the ways of men,
Then fell from that half-spiritual height

1. "Brother, hail and farewell," a line from an elegy by the Roman poet Catullus on the death of his brother (CI.10). Tennyson himself had recently lost his brother Charles.

2. A town on Lake Garda in Italy, which Tennyson visited in 1880. Sirmione is a beautiful peninsula jutting into the lake, on which Catullus had his summer home. Catullus' poem in honor of the locality includes the phrase "O venusta Sirmio!" ("O lovely Sirmio!").

3. The Etruscans, who settled near Lake Garda, were thought to be descended from the Lydians of Asia Minor.

1. Edward FitzGerald, translator of the *Rubáiyát of Omar Khayyám* (the "golden Eastern lay"), was an early admirer of Tennyson's poetry and a friend of long standing. This dedication in the form of a verse letter was to introduce an early poem by Tennyson entitled *Tiresias*. Before the letter and poem reached him in 1883 FitzGerald died.

2. I.e., meat, fish, or fowl. See Acts x.11–12.

3. Greek philosopher and vegetarian. FitzGerald made several unsuccessful attempts to regulate Tennyson's eating habits as well as to diminish his daily consumption of a pint of port wine and vast quantities of pipe tobacco.

4. *Measure for Measure* I.iv.34.

Chilled, till I tasted flesh again   20
   One night when earth was winter-black,
      And all the heavens flashed in frost;
   And on me, half-asleep, came back
      That wholesome heat the blood had lost,
And set me climbing icy capes   25
   And glaciers, over which there rolled
To meet me long-armed vines with grapes
   Of Eshcol hugeness;[5] for the cold
Without, and warmth within me, wrought
   To mold the dream; but none can say   30
That Lenten fare makes Lenten thought
   Who reads your golden Eastern lay,
Than which I know no version done
   In English more divinely well;
A planet equal to the sun   35
   Which cast it, that large infidel
Your Omar; and your Omar drew
   Full-handed plaudits from our best
In modern letters, and from two,
   Old friends outvaluing all the rest,   40
Two voices heard on earth no more;
   But we old friends are still alive,
And I am nearing seventy-four,
   While you have touched at seventy-five,
And so I send a birthday line   45
   Of greeting; and my son, who dipped
In some forgotten book of mine
   With sallow scraps of manuscript,
And dating many a year ago,
   Has hit on this, which you will take,   50
My Fitz, and welcome, as I know,
   Less for its own than for the sake
Of one recalling gracious times,
   When, in our younger London days,
You found some merit in my rhymes,   55
   And I more pleasure in your praise.

1883   1885

Locksley Hall Sixty Years After [1]

Late, my grandson! half the morning have I paced these sandy tracts,
Watched again the hollow ridges roaring into cataracts,

Wandered back to living boyhood while I heard the curlews call,
I myself so close on death, and death itself in Locksley Hall.

---

5. See Numbers xiii.23.
1. Tennyson insisted that this poem
was a "dramatic impersonation," not
an autobiography. The ranting tone is

therefore as appropriate to the lonely
80-year-old speaker of 1886 as it was
for the jilted young man in the original
Locksley Hall (published in 1842 but

So—your happy suit was blasted—she the faultless, the divine;   5
And you liken—boyish babble—this boy-love of yours with mine.

I myself have often babbled doubtless of a foolish past;
Babble, babble; our old England may go down in babble at last.

"Curse him!" curse your fellow-victim? call him dotard in your rage?
Eyes that lured a doting boyhood well might fool a dotard's age.   10

Jilted for a wealthier! wealthier? yet perhaps she was not wise;
I remember how you kissed the miniature with those sweet eyes.

In the hall there hangs a painting—Amy's arms about my neck—
Happy children in a sunbeam sitting on the ribs of wreck.

In my life there was a picture, she that clasped my neck had flown;   15
I was left within the shadow sitting on the wreck alone.

Yours has been a slighter ailment, will you sicken for her sake?
You, not you! your modern amorist is of easier, earthlier make.

Amy loved me, Amy failed me, Amy was a timid child;
But your Judith—but your worldling—*she* had never driven me wild.   20

She that holds the diamond necklace dearer than the golden ring,
She that finds a winter sunset² fairer than a morn of spring.

She that in her heart is brooding on his briefer lease of life,
While she vows "till death shall part us," she the would-be-widow
    wife.

She the worldling born of worldlings—father, mother—be content,   25
Even the homely farm can teach us there is something in descent.

Yonder in that chapel, slowly sinking now into the ground,
Lies the warrior, my forefather, with his feet upon the hound.

Crossed! ³ for once he sailed the sea to crush the Moslem in his
    pride;
Dead the warrior, dead his glory, dead the cause in which he died.   30

Yet how often I and Amy in the moldering aisle have stood,
Gazing for one pensive moment on that founder of our blood.

There again I stood today, and where of old we knelt in prayer,
Close beneath the casement crimson with the shield of Locksley—
    there,

presumably set in 1826). Although the speaker's tone has remained the same during the 60 years that have passed, his attitudes towards progress, immortality, and democracy have changed considerably. Also changed is his view of the Squire of Locksley Hall, who has just died—the feudal past as represented by his former rival for the hand of his cousin Amy.

Tennyson told his son that later gener-

ations of readers might find that the two poems were his "most historically interesting" productions, in their descriptions of his century at two different points in its development.
2. The elderly man whom Judith chose to marry.
3. The crossed feet of the statue on top of the tomb indicate that the speaker's ancestor had served in the Crusades.

All in white Italian marble, looking still as if she smiled,   35
Lies my Amy dead in childbirth, dead the mother, dead the child.

Dead—and sixty years ago, and dead her aged husband now—
I, this old white-headed dreamer, stoopt and kissed her marble brow.

Gone the fires of youth, the follies, furies, curses, passionate tears,
Gone like fires and floods and earthquakes of the planet's dawning
    years.   40

Fires that shook me once, but now to silent ashes fallen away.
Cold upon the dead volcano sleeps the gleam of dying day.

Gone the tyrant of my youth,[4] and mute below the chancel stones,
All his virtues—I forgive them—black in white above his bones.[5]

Gone the comrades of my bivouac, some in fight against the foe,   45
Some through age and slow diseases, gone as all on earth will go.

Gone with whom for forty years my life in golden sequence ran,
She with all the charm of woman, she with all the breadth of man,

Strong in will and rich in wisdom, Edith, yet so lowly-sweet,
Woman to her inmost heart, and woman to her tender feet,   50

Very woman of very woman, nurse of ailing body and mind,
She that linked again the broken chain that bound me to my kind.

Here today was Amy with me, while I wandered down the coast,
Near us Edith's holy shadow, smiling at the slighter ghost.

Gone our sailor son thy father, Leonard early lost at sea;   55
Thou alone, my boy, of Amy's kin and mine are left to me.

Gone thy tender-natured mother, wearying to be left alone,
Pining for the stronger heart that once had beat beside her own.

Truth, for truth is truth, he worshiped, being true as he was brave;
Good, for good is good, he followed, yet he looked beyond the
    grave.[6]   60

Wiser there than you, that crowning barren Death as lord of all,
Deem this over-tragic drama's closing curtain is the pall!

Beautiful was death in him, who saw the death, but kept the deck,
Saving women and their babes, and sinking with the sinking wreck,

Gone forever! Ever? no—for since our dying race began,   65
Ever, ever, and forever was the leading light of man.

---

4. A "selfish uncle" who became his
guardian after the death of his father.
See *Locksley Hall,* line 156.
5. I.e., black-lettered inscription carved
on a slab of white marble set into the
floor of the church.

6. These lines were written in April,
1886, after Tennyson received news of
the death of his 32 year old son, Lionel,
who had been returning from India to
England.

Those that in barbarian burials killed the slave, and slew the wife
Felt within themselves the sacred passion of the second life.

Indian warriors dream of ampler hunting grounds beyond the night;
Even the black Australian dying hopes he shall return, a white.   70

Truth for truth, and good for good! The good, the true, the pure,
    the just—
Take the charm "Forever" from them, and they crumble into dust.

Gone the cry of "Forward, Forward," lost within a growing gloom;
Lost, or only heard in silence from the silence of a tomb.

Half the marvels of my morning, triumphs over time and space,   75
Staled by frequence, shrunk by usage into commonest common-
    place!

"Forward" rang the voices then, and of the many mine was one.
Let us hush this cry of "Forward" till ten thousand years have gone.

Far among the vanished races, old Assyrian kings would flay
Captives whom they caught in battle—iron-hearted victors they.   80

Ages after, while in Asia, he that led the wile Moguls
Timur built his ghastly tower of eighty thousand human skulls,[7]

Then, and here in Edward's time, an age of noblest English names,
Christian conquerors took and flung the conquered Christian into
    flames.[8]

Love your enemy, bless your haters, said the Greatest of the great;   85
Christian love among the Churches looked the twin of heathen hate.

From the golden alms of Blessing man had coined himself a curse:
Rome of Caesar, Rome of Peter, which was crueler? which was
    worse?

France had shown a light to all men, preached a Gospel, all men's
    good;
Celtic Demos[9] rose a Demon, shrieked and slaked the light with
    blood.   90

Hope was ever on her mountain, watching till the day begun—
Crowned with sunlight—over darkness—from the still unrisen sun.

Have we grown at last beyond the passions of the primal clan?
"Kill your enemy, for you hate him," still, "your enemy" was a man.

Have we sunk below them? peasants maim the helpless horse, and
    drive   95
Innocent cattle under thatch, and burn the kindlier brutes alive.[1]

7. Timur or Tamerlane (1336–1405), Mogul ruler whose conquests included the Persian City, Isfahan, where the skulls of thousands of the slaughtered inhabitants were piled up.
8. In the reign of Edward VI (1547–53), Catholics were persecuted; in the reign of Mary (1553–58), Protestants were persecuted.
9. I.e., the common people; here, the reference is to the mass executions and slaughterings during the French Revolution.
1. In the 1880's, peasants agitating against landlords in Ireland destroyed cattle and farm buildings.

Brutes, the brutes are not your wrongers—burnt at midnight, found
  at morn,
Twisted hard in mortal agony with their offspring, born-unborn,

Clinging to the silent mother! Are we devils? are we men?
Sweet Saint Francis of Assisi, would that he were here again,[2]   100

He that in his Catholic wholeness used to call the very flowers
Sisters, brothers—and the beasts—whose pains are hardly less than
  ours!

Chaos, Cosmos! Cosmos, Chaos! who can tell how all will end?
Read the wide world's annals, you, and take their wisdom for your
  friend.

Hope the best, but hold the Present fatal daughter of the Past,   105
Shape your heart to front the hour, but dream not that the hour will
  last.

Aye, if dynamite and revolver[3] leave you courage to be wise—
When was age so crammed with menace? madness? written, spoken
  lies?

Envy wears the mask of Love, and, laughing sober fact to scorn,
Cries to weakest as to strongest, "Ye are equals, equal-born."   110

Equal-born? O, yes, if yonder hill be level with the flat.
Charm us, orator, till the lion look no larger than the cat,

Till the cat through that mirage of overheated language loom
Larger than the lion—Demos end in working its own doom.

Russia bursts our Indian barrier,[4] shall we fight her? shall we yield? 115
Pause! before you sound the trumpet, hear the voices from the field.

Those three hundred millions under one Imperial scepter now,
Shall we hold them? shall we loose them? take the suffrage of the
  plow.[5]

Nay, but these[6] would feel and follow Truth if only you and you,
Rivals of realm-ruining party, when you speak were wholly true.   120

Plowmen, shepherds, have I found, and more than once, and still
  could find,
Sons of God, and kings of men in utter nobleness of mind,

2. St. Francis (1182–1226), whose
fondness for animals and birds was noteworthy.
3. Bombings and shootings, as in the
Anarchist Riot in Haymarket Square,
Chicago, May 4, 1886.
4. The British regarded Afghanistan as
a buffer between Russia and India; in
1885 a Russian attack against an Afghan
border force (an incident known as the
Panjdeh scare) brought Britain and Russia to the brink of war.
5. I.e., let the farm laborers' vote decide
whether Britain should try to hold India
as part of Queen Victoria's Empire
(which it had become in 1877) or to
withdraw and let the 300 million people
of India confront the threat of Russian
invasion on their own.
6. Farm laborers, to whom Parliament
granted the right to vote in 1884. As a
member of the House of Lords Tennyson himself had voted for this measure
but with considerable reluctance because
it seemed to him premature.

Truthful, trustful, looking upward to the practiced hustings-liar; [7]
So the higher wields the lower, while the lower is the higher.

Here and there a cotter's babe is royal-born by right divine;   125
Here and there my lord is lower than his oxen or his swine.

Chaos, Cosmos! Cosmos, Chaos! once again the sickening game;
Freedom, free to slay herself, and dying while they shout her name.

Step by step we gained a freedom known to Europe, known to all;
Step by step we rose to greatness—through the tonguesters we may
    fall.   130

You that woo the Voices [8]—tell them "old experience is a fool,"
Teach your flattered kings that only those who cannot read can rule.

Pluck the mighty from their seat, but set no meek ones in their
    place;
Pillory Wisdom in your markets, pelt your offal at her face.

Tumble Nature heel o'er head, and, yelling with the yelling street, 135
Set the feet above the brain and swear the brain is in the feet.

Bring the old dark ages back without the faith, without the hope,
Break the State, the Church, the Throne, and roll their ruins down
    the slope.

Authors—essayist, atheist, novelist, realist, rhymester, play your part,
Paint the mortal shame of nature with the living hues of art.   140

Rip your brothers' vices open, strip your own foul passions bare;
Down with Reticence, down with Reverence—forward—naked—let
    them stare.

Feed the budding rose of boyhood with the drainage of your sewer;
Send the drain into the fountain, lest the stream should issue pure.

Set the maiden fancies wallowing in the troughs of Zolaism [9]—   145
Forward, forward, aye, and backward, downward too into the abysm!

Do your best to charm the worst, to lower the rising race of men;
Have we risen from out the beast, then back into the beast again?

Only "dust to dust" for me that sicken at your lawless din,
Dust in wholesome old-world dust before the newer world begin.   150

Heated am I? you—you wonder—well, it scarce becomes mine age—
Patience! let the dying actor mouth his last upon the stage.

7. I.e., a lying politician making a campaign speech on a platform.
8. Votes.
9. When translations of the novels of
Emile Zola (1840–1902) began appearing in England in 1884 his publisher
was prosecuted and a violent controversy
ensued. Zola's emphasis on the animal
nature of his characters and his frank
treatment of their sexual lives (especially those of the working classes) appealed to the younger generation of
English writers but seemed shockingly
distasteful to some of Tennyson's contemporaries.

Cries of unprogressive dotage ere the dotard fall asleep?
Noises of a current narrowing, not the music of a deep?

Aye, for doubtless I am old, and think gray thoughts, for I am gray; 155
After all the stormy changes shall we find a changeless May?

After madness, after massacre, Jacobinism and Jacquerie,[1]
Some diviner force to guide us through the days I shall not see?

When the schemes and all the systems, kingdoms and republics fall,
Something kindlier, higher, holier—all for each and each for all? 160

All the full-brain, half-brain races, led by Justice, Love, and Truth;
All the millions one at length, with all the visions of my youth?

All diseases quenched by Science, no man halt, or deaf or blind;
Stronger ever born of weaker, lustier body, larger mind?

Earth at last a warless world, a single race, a single tongue— 165
I have seen her far away—for is not Earth as yet so young?—

Every tiger madness muzzled, every serpent passion killed,
Every grim ravine a garden, every blazing desert tilled,

Robed in universal harvest up to either pole she smiles,
Universal ocean softly washing all her warless isles. 170

Warless? when her tens are thousands, and her thousands millions,
then—
All her harvest all too narrow—who can fancy warless men?

Warless? war will die out late then. Will it ever? late or soon?
Can it, till this outworn earth be dead as yon dead world the moon?

Dead the new astronomy calls her.—On this day and at this hour, 175
In this gap between the sandhills, whence you see the Locksley
tower,

Here we met, our latest meeting—Amy—sixty years ago—
She and I—the moon was falling greenish through a rosy glow,

Just above the gateway tower, and even where you see her now—
Here we stood and clasped each other, swore the seeming-deathless
vow.— 180

Dead, but how her living glory lights the hall, the dune, the grass!
Yet the moonlight is the sunlight, and the sun himself will pass.

Venus near her! smiling downward at this earthlier earth of ours,
Closer on the sun, perhaps a world of never fading flowers.[2]

1. The Jacobins were an extremist Rev-olutionary party in France; a "Jac-querie" is an uprising of peasants against landholders, the name being derived from a peasants' revolt against the no-bles of Northern France in 1358.
2. The evening star, being closer to the sun, may be a more perfect planet than ours, but as the speaker also speculates (line 184), its beautiful appearance may be deceptive and life there be troubled by war and other evils as is life on earth.

Hesper, whom the poet called the Bringer home of all good things [3]— 185
All good things may move in Hesper, perfect peoples, perfect kings.

Hesper—Venus—were we native to that splendor or in Mars,
We should see the globe we groan in, fairest of their evening stars.

Could we dream of wars and carnage, craft and madness, lust and
   spite,
Roaring London, raving Paris, in that point of peaceful light? 190

Might we not in glancing heavenward on a star so silver-fair,
Yearn, and clasp the hands and murmur, "Would to God that we
   were there"?

Forward, backward, backward, forward, in the immeasurable sea,
Swayed by vaster ebbs and flows than can be known to you or me.

All the suns—are these but symbols of innumerable man, 195
Man or Mind that sees a shadow of the planner or the plan?

Is there evil but on earth? or pain in every peopled sphere?
Well, be grateful for the sounding watchword "Evolution" here,

Evolution ever climbing after some ideal good,
And Reversion ever dragging Evolution in the mud. 200

What are men that He should heed us? cried the king of sacred
   song; [4]
Insects of an hour, that hourly work their brother insect wrong,

While the silent heavens roll, and suns along their fiery way,
All their planets whirling round them, flash a million miles a day.

Many an aeon moulded earth before her highest, man, was born, 205
Many an aeon too may pass when earth is manless and forlorn,

Earth so huge, and yet so bounded—pools of salt, and plots of
   land—
Shallow skin of green and azure—chains of mountain, grains of
   sand!

Only That which made us meant us to be mightier by and by,
Set the sphere of all the boundless heavens within the human eye, 210

Sent the shadow of Himself, the boundless, through the human
   soul;
Boundless inward in the atom, boundless outward in the Whole.

•   •   •   •   •   •   •

Here is Locksley Hall, my grandson, here the lion-guarded gate.
Not tonight in Locksley Hall—tomorrow—you, you come so late.

---

3. Hesper or Venus, was addressed by   *Wasteland*, line 221-222 and see also
the Greek poet Sappho "Oh, Hesperus!   *In Memoriam*, sec. 121.
Thou bringest all things home." Cf. *The*   4. King David. See Psalm viii.4.

Wrecked—your train—or all but wrecked? a shattered wheel? a
    vicious boy!   215
Good, this forward,[5] you that preach it, is it well to wish you joy?

Is it well that while we range with Science, glorying in the Time,
City children soak and blacken soul and sense in city slime?

There among the glooming alleys Progress halts on palsied feet,
Crime and hunger cast our maidens by the thousand on the street. 220

There the master scrimps his haggard sempstress of her daily bread,
There a single sordid attic holds the living and the dead.

There the smoldering fire of fever creeps across the rotted floor,
And the crowded couch of incest in the warrens of the poor.

Nay, your pardon, cry your "Forward," yours are hope and youth,
    but I—   225
Eighty winters leave the dog too lame to follow with the cry,

Lame and old, and past his time, and passing now into the night;
Yet I would the rising race were half as eager for the light.

Light the fading gleam of even? light the glimmer of the dawn?
Aged eyes may take the growing glimmer for the gleam withdrawn. 230

Far away beyond her myriad coming changes earth will be
Something other than the wildest modern guess of you and me.

Earth may reach her earthly-worst, of if she gain her earthly-best,
Would she find her human offspring this ideal man at rest?

Forward then, but still remember how the course of Time will
    swerve,   235
Crook and turn upon itself in many a backward streaming curve.

Not the Hall tonight, my grandson! Death and Silence hold their
    own.
Leave the master [6] in the first dark hour of his last sleep alone.

Worthier soul was he than I am, sound and honest, rustic Squire,
Kindly landlord, boon companion—youthful jealousy is a liar. 240

Cast the poison from your bosom, oust the madness from your
    brain.
Let the trampled serpent show you that you have not lived in vain.

Youthful! youth and age are scholars yet but in the lower school,
Nor is he the wisest man who never proved himself a fool.

5. Cf. *Locksley Hall*, line 181. "Forward" had been the young man's watchword for progress into the future, a
progress associated with railway journeys. Now his grandson's railway journey
has been disrupted by the vandalism of
"a vicious boy" (line 215), an embodiment of the underprivileged classes of
modern industrial society who may wreck
the progress that Science seemed to
promise.
6. Amy's husband, the feudal-style master and squire of Locksley Hall, as contrasted with the master as capitalist
employer of line 221.

Yonder lies our young sea village—Art and Grace are less and less: 245
Science grows and Beauty dwindles—roofs of slated hideousness!

There is one old hostel left us where they swing the Locksley shield,
Till the peasant cow shall butt the "lion passant" from his field.[7]

Poor old Heraldry, poor old History, poor old Poetry, passing hence,
In the common deluge drowning old political common sense! 250

Poor old voice of eighty crying after voices that have fled!
All I loved are vanished voices, all my steps are on the dead.

All the world is ghost to me, and as the phantom disappears,
Forward far and far from here is all the hope of eighty years.

.   .   .   .

In this hostel—I remember—I repent it o'er his grave— 255
Like a clown—by chance he met me—I refused the hand he gave.

From that casement where the trailer mantles all the moldering
     bricks—
I was then in early boyhood, Edith but a child of six—

While I sheltered in this archway from a day of driving showers—
Peeped the winsome face of Edith like a flower among the flowers. 260

Here tonight! the Hall tomorrow, when they toll the chapel bell!
Shall I hear in one dark room a wailing, "I have loved thee well"?

Then a peal that shakes the portal—one has come to claim his bride,
Her that shrank, and put me from her, shrieked, and started from
     my side—

Silent echoes! You, my Leonard, use and not abuse your day, 265
Move among your people, know them, follow him [8] who led the way,

Strove for sixty widowed years to help his homelier brother men,
Served the poor, and built the cottage, raised the school, and drained
     the fen.

Hears he now the voice that wronged him? who shall swear it cannot
     be?
Earth would never touch her worst, were one in fifty such as he. 270

Ere she gain her heavenly-best, a God must mingle with game.
Nay, there may be those about us whom we neither see nor name,

Felt within us as ourselves, the Powers of Good, the Powers of Ill,
Strowing balm, or shedding poison in the fountains of the will.

Follow you the star that lights a desert pathway, yours or mine. 275
Forward, till you see the Highest Human Nature is divine.

---

7. In heraldry "field" refers to the entire surface of the shield on which the coat-of-arms was painted. The Locksley shield, featuring a running lion ("lion passant"), appears on the signboard outside the old inn. On the "peasant cow" see lines 95–99 and 118.
8. Amy's husband.

Follow Light, and do the Right—for man can half-control his
  doom—
Till you find the deathless Angel seated in the vacant tomb.[9]

Forward, let the stormy moment fly and mingle with the past.
I that loathed have come to love him. Love will conquer at the last.   280

Gone at eighty, mine own age, and I and you will bear the pall;
Then I leave thee lord and master, latest lord of Locksley Hall.
1886   1886

By an Evolutionist

The Lord let the house of a brute to the soul of a man,
  And the man said, "Am I your debtor?"
And the Lord—"Not yet: but make it as clean as you can,
  And then I will let you a better."

1

If my body come from brutes, my soul uncertain, or a fable,   5
  Why not bask amid the senses while the sun of morning shines,
I, the finer brute rejoicing in my hounds, and in my stable,
  Youth and health, and birth and wealth, and choice of women
    and of wines?

2

What has thou done for me, grim Old Age, save breaking my bones
    on the rack?
  Would I had passed in the morning that looks so bright from
    afar!   10

OLD AGE

Done for thee? starved the wild beast that was linked with thee
    eighty years back.
  Less weight now for the ladder-of-heaven that hangs on a star.

1

If my body come from brutes, though somewhat finer than their
    own,
  I am heir, and this my kingdom. Shall the royal voice be mute?
No, but if the rebel subject seek to drag me from the throne,   15
  Hold the scepter, Human Soul, and rule thy province of the brute.

2

I have climbed to the snows of Age, and I gaze at a field in the
    Past,
  Where I sank with the body at times in the sloughs of a low
    desire,

---

9. The angel who rolled back the stone from the tomb of Christ. See Matthew,
28—1–7.

But I hear no yelp of the beast, and the Man is quiet at last
   As he stands on the heights of his life with a glimpse of a height
     that is higher.   20

      1889

June Bracken and Heather

TO ———[1]

There on the top of the down,
The wild heather round me and over me June's high blue,
When I looked at the bracken so bright and the heather so brown,
I thought to myself I would offer this book to you,
This, and my love together,   5
To you that are seventy-seven,
With a faith as clear as the heights of the June-blue heaven,
And a fancy as summer-new
As the green of the bracken amid the gloom of the heather.

      1892

The Dawn

"You are but children."
—EGYPTIAN PRIEST TO SOLON

     Red of the Dawn!
Screams of a babe in the red-hot palms of a Moloch [2] of Tyre,
   Man with his brotherless dinner on man in the tropical wood,
   Priests in the name of the Lord passing souls through fire to the
     fire,
Head-hunters and boats of Dahomey [3] that float upon human blood!

     Red of the Dawn!   6
Godless fury of peoples, and Christless frolic of kings,
   And the bolt of war dashing down upon cities and blazing farms,
   For Babylon was a child newborn, and Rome was a babe in arms,
And London and Paris and all the rest are as yet but in leading
     strings.   10

     Dawn not Day,
While scandal is mouthing a bloodless name at *her* cannibal feast,
   And rake-ruined bodies and souls go down in a common wreck,
   And the Press of a thousand cities is prized for it smells of the
     beast,
Or easily violates virgin Truth for a coin or a check.   15

     Dawn not Day!
Is it Shame, so few should have climbed from the dens in the level

---

1. Addressed to Tennyson's wife as a dedication to a volume of poems.
2. A god to whom children were sacrificed as burnt offerings.

3. West African country in which the custom of human sacrifice persisted in the 19th century. In 1892, after a war, Dahomey became a French colony.

below,
Men, with a heart and a soul, no slaves of a four-footed will?
But if twenty million of summers are stored in the sunlight still,
We are far from the noon of man, there is time for the race to grow.

Red of the Dawn!   21
Is it turning a fainter red? So be it, but when shall we lay
   The Ghost of the Brute that is walking and haunting us yet, and
      be free?
   In a hundred, a thousand winters? Ah, what will *our* children be?
The men of a hundred thousand, a million summers away?   25
                                                    1892

The Silent Voices

When the dumb Hour, clothed in black,
Brings the Dreams about my bed,
Call me not so often back,
Silent Voices of the dead,
Toward the lowland ways behind me,   5
And the sunlight that is gone!
Call me rather, silent voices,
Forward to the starry track
Glimmering up the heights beyond me
On, and always on!   10
                                                    1892

Crossing the Bar[1]

Sunset and evening star,
   And one clear call for me!
And may there be no moaning of the bar,[2]
   When I put out to sea,

But such a tide as moving seems asleep,   5
   Too full for sound and foam,
When that which drew from out the boundless deep
   Turns again home.

Twilight and evening bell,
   And after that the dark!   10
And may there be no sadness of farewell,
   When I embark;

For though from out our bourne[3] of Time and Place
   The flood may bear me far,
I hope to see my Pilot face to face   15
   When I have crossed the bar.

1889   1889

1. Although not the last poem written
by Tennyson, *Crossing the Bar* appears,
at his request, as the final poem in all
collections of his work.

2. Mournful sound of the ocean beating
on a sand bar at the mouth of a harbor.
3. Boundary.

ROBERT BROWNING
(1812–1889)

1846:   Marriage to Elizabeth Barrett and residence in Italy.
1855:   *Men and Women* published.
1861:   Death of Elizabeth Barrett Browning.
1868–69: *The Ring and the Book* published.

During the years of his marriage Robert Browning was sometimes referred to as "Mrs. Browning's husband." Elizabeth Barrett, who seems to us now a minor figure, was at that time a famous poet while her husband was a relatively unknown experimenter whose poems were greeted with misunderstanding or indifference. Not until the 1860's did he at last gain a public and become recognized as the rival or equal of Tennyson. In the 20th century his reputation has persisted, but in an unusual way: his poetry is admired by two groups of readers widely different in tastes. To one group his work is a moral tonic. Such readers appreciate him as a man who lived bravely and as a writer who showed life to be a joyful battle, the imperfections of this world being remedied, under the dispensations of an all-loving God, by the perfections of the next. Typical of this group are the Browning Societies which have flourished in England and America. Members of these societies usually regard their poet as a wise philosopher and religious teacher who resolved the doubts which had troubled Arnold and Tennyson and which have continued to trouble later generations of less confident writers.

A second group of readers enjoy Browning less for his attempt to solve problems of religious doubt than for his attempt to solve the problems of how poetry should be written. Such poets as Ezra Pound and Robert Lowell value him as a major artist. These readers recognize that more than any other 19th-century poet (even including Hopkins), it was Browning who energetically hacked through a trail that has subsequently become the main road of 20th-century poetry. In *Poetry and the Age* Randall Jarrell, speaking of present-day poetry, remarks how "the dramatic monologue, which once had depended for its effect upon being a departure from the norm of poetry, now became in one form or another the norm." Browning did not invent the dramatic monologue, but he established it as a norm.

The dramatic monologue, as Browning uses it, enables the reader, speaker, and poet to be located at an appropriate distance from each other, aligned in such a way that the reader must work *through* the words of the speaker toward the meaning of the poet himself. For example, in the well-known early monologue *My Last Duchess*, we listen to the Duke as he speaks of his dead wife, and it is almost as if we were overhearing a man talking into the telephone of a booth adjacent to ours. From his one-sided conversation we piece together the situation, both past and present, and we infer what sort of woman the Duchess really was, and what sort of man is the Duke. Ultimately we may also infer what the poet himself thinks of the speaker he has created. In this instance, from evidence outside the poem we know that Browning had a special aversion for domestic tyrants. His own father-in-law was to provide him with a striking example of the breed, and it is revealing that in his longest poem, *The Ring and the Book*, he once more explored the story of another domestic tyrant who, like the Duke, was irritated by his wife's virtues. Yet from *My Last Duchess* itself, if we exclude external evidence, it is interesting to note how persuasive is the Duke's own side of the story:

> She had
> A heart—how shall I say?—too soon made glad,
> Too easily impressed; she liked whate'er
> She looked on, and her looks went everywhere.

Although Browning contrives that our verdict as jurymen will be a just one, he does allow us a considerable amount of latitude. And in some of his later monologues we are really obliged to grope toward a choice. In reading *A Grammarian's Funeral*, for example, can we be sure that the central character is a hero? Or is he merely a fool? Browning has not made the answer easy for us.

In addition to his experiments with the dramatic monologue Browning also made experiments with language and syntax. The grotesque rhymes and jaw-breaking diction which he often employs have been repugnant to some critics; George Santayana, for instance, dismissed him as a clumsy barbarian. But to those who understand Browning's aims, the incongruities of language are not literally incongruous but functional, a humorous and appropriate counterpart to an imperfect world. Ezra Pound's tribute to "Old Hippety-Hop o' the accents," as he addresses Browning, is both affectionate and memorable:

> Heart that was big as the bowels of Vesuvius
> Words that were winged as her sparks in eruption,
> Eagled and thundered as Jupiter Pluvius
> Sound in your wind past all signs o' corruption.

This capacity to attract the admiration of such a diversity of readers, sophisticated and unsophisticated, is one of several ways in which Browning's writings can be likened to those of Dickens and Shakespeare.

The personal life of Robert Browning falls into three phases: his years as a child and young bachelor, as a husband, and as a widower. Each of these phases is most appropriately considered in relation to his development as a poet.

He was born in Camberwell, a London suburb, within a few months of the births of Dickens and Thackeray. His father, a bank clerk, was a learned man with an extensive library. His mother was a kindly, religious-minded woman, interested in music, whose love for her brilliant son was warmly reciprocated. Until the time of his marriage at the age of 34 Browning was rarely absent from his parents' home. He attended a boarding school near Camberwell, traveled a little, and was a student at the University of London for a short period, but he preferred to pursue his education at home where he was tutored in foreign languages, music, boxing, and horsemanship, and where he read omnivorously. From this unusual education he acquired a store of knowledge upon which to draw for the background of his poems.

The "obscurity" of which his contemporaries complained in his earlier poetry may be partly accounted for by the circumstances of Browning's education. He was inclined to assume that his out-of-the-ordinary learning was generally shared by educated readers. Often it was not. But the obscurity of such poems as *Sordello* is attributable not only to the nature of Browning's learning but to the poet's anxious desire to avoid exposing himself too explicitly before his readers. His first poem, *Pauline*, published when he was 21, had been modeled on the example of Shelley, the most personal of poets. When a review by John Stuart Mill pointed out that the young author was parading a "morbid state" of self-worship, Browning was overwhelmed with embarrassment. He resolved to avoid confessional writings thereafter.

One way of reducing the personal element in his poetry was to write plays instead of soul-searching narratives or lyrics. In 1836, encouraged by the actor W. C. Macready, Browning began work on his first play, *Strafford*, a historical tragedy that lasted only four nights when it was produced at a London theater in 1837. For ten years the young writer struggled to produce other plays that would better hold the attention of an audience, but as stage productions they all remained failures. Browning nevertheless profited from this otherwise disheartening experience. Writing dialogue for actors led him to explore another form more congenial to his genius, the dramatic monologue, a form that enabled him through imaginary speakers to avoid explicit autobiography and yet did not demand that these speakers act out their story with the speed or the simplifications that stage production demands.

Browning's resolution to avoid the subjective manner of Shelley did not preclude his being influenced by the earlier poet in other ways. At 14, when he first discovered Shelley's works, he became an atheist and liberal. Although he outgrew the atheism, after a struggle, and also the extreme phases of his liberalism, he retained from Shelley's influence something permanent and more difficult to define: an ardent dedication to ideals (often undefined ideals) and an energetic striving toward goals (often undefined goals). This quality of aspiration is much more mixed with earthiness—even worldliness—in Browning's character than in Shelley's. To soar upwards on a skylark's wing was not to Browning's taste. He is more like Robert Frost's swinger of birches who climbs a tree toward heaven but is anxious to swing down to earth again before getting too far away.

Yet the element of worldliness should not obscure from us Browning's ardent romanticism. His love affair with Elizabeth Barrett was romantic in several of the senses of that hard-worked adjective. It is easy to see why the well-known story of their courtship has been retold by novelists, dramatists, and movie-producers, for the situation had the dramatic ingredients of Browning's own favorite story of St. George rescuing the maiden from the dragon. Almost everything seemed unpropitious when Browning met Elizabeth Barrett in 1845. She was six years older than he was, a semi-invalid, jealously guarded by her possessively tyrannical father. But love, as the poet was to say later, is best, and love swept aside all obstacles. After their elopement to Italy, the former semi-invalid was soon enjoying good health and a full life. The husband likewise seemed to thrive during the years of this remarkable marriage. Like many English poets he was especially at ease in the warm lands of the Mediterranean. His most memorable volume of poems, *Men and Women* (1855), reflects his enjoyment of Italy: its picturesque landscapes and lively street scenes as well as its monuments from the past—its Renaissance past in particular, a period of expanding energies which was congenial to his own expansive temperament.

The happy fifteen-year sojourn in Italy ended in 1861 with Elizabeth's death. The widower returned to London with his son. During the 28 years remaining to him, the quantity of verse he produced did not diminish. Nor, during the first decade, did it decrease in quality. His greatest single work, *The Ring and the Book*, a poem on the vast scale of a long novel, was published in 1868. His later writings, however, suffer from a certain mechanical repetition of mannerism and an excess of argumentation—faults into which he may have been lead by the unqualified enthusiasm of his admirers, for it was during this period that he gained his great following. When he died, in 1889, he was buried in Westminster Abbey.

During these London years Browning became abundantly fond of social life. He dined at the homes of friends and at clubs, where he enjoyed port wine and conversation. He would talk loudly and emphatically about many topics—except his own poetry, about which he was usually reticent. His reticence bothered many of his admirers. American women visiting in London, after having looked forward to meeting the author whose poems had inspired them to higher things, were disappointed—almost appalled—when they met the man at a dinner party. He did not "look like a poet." His late poem *House* may show why he gave such an impression. Behind the façade of the hearty diner-out, Browning could live and think as he pleased, just as he had discovered in writing his monologues the advantage, for him, of indirect speaking. Each speaker of monologue provides a mask for the poet.

Despite his bursts of outspokenness, Browning's character is thus not so clearly known to us as that of Tennyson or Arnold or Carlyle. Hardy once said that Browning's character seemed to him "*the* literary puzzle of the 19th century." To solve the puzzle one biographer, Mrs. Betty Miller, has tried to show that Browning was not such a happy and confident person as he is usually represented to have been, an impression that can be reinforced by the note of desperation in such poems as *Childe Roland*. This eccentric interpretation has at least the merit of suggesting that like Yeats (a poet preoccupied with masks) Browning was a more complex man than some of his admirers have been willing to recognize.

Just as Browning's character is harder to identify than that of Tennyson, so also are his poems more difficult to relate to the age in which they were written than are the sometimes topical poems of Tennyson. Our first impression may be that there is no connection whatever. Bishops and painters of the Renaissance, physicians of the Roman Empire, musicians of 18th-century Germany—as we explore this gallery of talking portraits we seem to be in a world of time long past, remote from the world of steam engines and disputes about man's descent from the ape.

Yet our first impression is misleading. Many of these portraits explore problems that confronted Browning's contemporaries, especially problems of faith and doubt, good and evil, and problems of the function of the artist in modern life. *Caliban upon Setebos*, for example, is a highly topical critique of Darwinism and of natural (as opposed to supernatural) religions. Browning's own attitude towards these topics is partially concealed because of his use of speakers and of settings from earlier ages, yet we do encounter certain recurrent religious assumptions that we can safely assign to the poet himself. The most recurrent is that God has created an imperfect world as a kind of testing-ground, a "vale of soul-making," as Keats had said. It followed, for Browning's purposes, that man's soul must be immortal and that heaven itself be perfect. As Abt Vogler affirms: "On the earth the broken arcs; in the heaven, a perfect round." Armed with such a faith, Browning gives the impression that he was himself untroubled by the doubts that gnawed at the hearts of Arnold and Clough and Tennyson. The "evidence" presented by historical criticism of the Bible he could dismiss as simply irrelevant, just as D. H. Lawrence, a later romantic, disposed of evolution by contending that he did not feel the evidence for it in his solar plexus.

This kind of religious conviction attracts many readers who expect poetry to provide uplift and reassurances. Other readers find it an insurmountable obstacle, as fatuous as Macaulay's faith in progress. To what extent our capacity to enjoy the writings of an author is hindered if his religious position seems repellent to us is one of the most important problems in modern criticism. The problem is much too vast to explore here, but there is at least room to insert a qualifying clause to modify the indictment that Browning's critics too hastily draw up against his cheerful religious position. A blind optimist might be simply unreadable, but Browning's optimism was not blind. Few writers, in fact, seem to have been more aware of the existence of evil. His gallery of villains—murderers, sadistic husbands, mean and petty manipulators—is an extraordinary one. Nothing is more essential to a fair-minded study of his poetry than our recognition that his apparent optimism is consistently being tested by his bringing to light the evils of man's nature. Readers who prefer to dispose of his writings by pinning them down in a formulated phrase, instead of reading them with attention, invariably cite the following lines as summing up all of Browning:

> God's in his heaven—
> All's right with the world!

But if we turn to the poem in which these lines appear, we have to modify our formulation. *Pippa Passes* is a collection of sordid tales such as one encounters on the front page of the most lurid style of newspaper. The heroine, who works in a sweatshop 364 days a year, is about to be sent to Rome as a prostitute; a man and woman living in adultery have just murdered the woman's husband; a waspish set of Bohemians have tricked a youth into marriage. Because Pippa's innocence seems to counteract the sordidness of the other scenes, we may say afterwards that God is in his heaven. But that all's right with the world is merely affirmed by the girl; the poem does not show it.

A second aspect of Browning's poetry that separates it from the Victorian age is its style. The most representative Victorian poets such as Tennyson or Dante Gabriel Rossetti write in the manner of Keats, Milton, Spenser, and of classical poets such as Virgil. Theirs is the central stylistic tradition in English poetry, one which favors smoothly polished texture and pleasing liquidity of sound. Browning draws from a different tradition, more colloquial and discordant, a tradition which includes the poetry of John Donne, the soliloquies of Shakespeare, the comic verse of the early 19th-century poet Thomas Hood, and certain features of the narrative style of Chaucer. Of most significance are Browning's affinities with Donne. Both poets sacrifice, on occasion, the pleasures of harmony and of a consistent elevation of tone by using a harshly discordant style and unexpected juxtapositions that startle us into an awareness of a world of everyday realities and trivialities. Browning's late poem, *The Householder*, is an excellent example of this Donne-like vein. Readers who dislike this kind of poetry in Browning or in Donne argue that it suffers from prosiness. Oscar Wilde once described the novelist George Meredith as "a prose Browning." And so, he added, was Browning. Wilde's joke may help us to relate Browning to his contemporaries. For if Browning seems out of step with his fellow Victorian poets, he is by no means out of step with his contemporaries in prose. The grotesque, which plays such a prominent role in the style and subject matter of Carlyle and Dickens, and in the aesthetic theories of John Ruskin, is equally prominent in Browning's verse:

> Fee, faw, fum! bubble and squeak!
> Blessedest Thursday's the fat of the week.
> Rumble and tumble, sleek and rough,
> Stinking and savory, smug and gruff.

These opening lines of *Holy-Cross Day* display a similar kind of noisy jocularity in presenting a situation of grave seriousness as that used by Carlyle in his *French Revolution*.

The link between Browning and the Victorian prose writers is not limited to style. With the later generation of Victorian novelists, George Eliot, George Meredith, and Henry James, Browning shares a central preoccupation. Like Eliot in particular, he was interested in exposing the devious ways in which our minds work and the complexity of our motives. "My stress lay on incidents in the development of a human soul," he wrote; "little else is worth study." His psychological insights can be illustrated in such poems as *The Bishop Orders His Tomb* or *Fra Lippo Lippi*. Although these are spoken monologues, not inner monologues in the manner of James Joyce, yet the insight into the workings of the minds of men is similarly acute. As in reading Joyce, we must be on our guard to follow the rapid shifts of the speaker's mental processes as jumps are made from one cluster of associations to another.

But Browning's role as a forerunner of 20th-century literature should not blind us to his essential Victorianism. Energy is the most characteristic aspect of his writing, and energy is perhaps the most characteristic aspect of Victorian literature in general. Often, of course, such energy was misdirected. Gerard Manley Hopkins identified this failing precisely when he complained of Browning's "Broad Church" way of talking, like "a man bouncing up from table with his mouth full of bread and cheese and saying that he meant to stand no blasted nonsense." At its best, however, such buoyancy is a virtue imparting a creative vitality to all of Browning's writings.

Porphyria's Lover[1]

The rain set early in tonight,
    The sullen wind was soon awake,
It tore the elm-tops down for spite,
    And did its worst to vex the lake:
    I listened with heart fit to break.   5
When glided in Porphyria; straight
    She shut the cold out and the storm,
And kneeled and made the cheerless grate
    Blaze up, and all the cottage warm;
    Which done, she rose, and from her form   10
Withdrew the dripping cloak and shawl,
    And laid her soiled gloves by, untied
Her hat and let the damp hair fall,
    And, last, she sat down by my side
    And called me. When no voice replied,   15
She put my arm about her waist,
    And made her smooth white shoulder bare,
And all her yellow hair displaced,
    And, stooping, made my cheek lie there,
    And spread, o'er all, her yellow hair,   20
Murmuring how she loved me—she
    Too weak, for all her heart's endeavor,
To set its struggling passion free
    From pride, and vainer ties dissever,
    And give herself to me forever.   25
But passion sometimes would prevail,
    Nor could tonight's gay feast restrain
A sudden thought of one so pale
    For love of her, and all in vain:
    So, she was come through wind and rain.   30
Be sure I looked up at her eyes
    Happy and proud; at last I knew
Porphyria worshiped me: surprise
    Made my heart swell, and still it grew
    While I debated what to do.   35
That moment she was mine, mine, fair,
    Perfectly pure and good: I found
A thing to do, and all her hair
    In one long yellow string I wound
    Three times her little throat around,   40
And strangled her. No pain felt she;
    I am quite sure she felt no pain.
As a shut bud that holds a bee,

1. One of a pair of monologues originally published under the title *Mad-*
house Cells, a title that emphasized the
abnormal state of mind of the speaker.

I warily oped her lids: again
Laughed the blue eyes without a stain.   45
And I untightened next the tress
About her neck; her cheek once more
Blushed bright beneath my burning kiss:
I propped her head up as before,
Only, this time my shoulder bore   50
Her head, which droops upon it still:
The smiling rosy little head,
So glad it has its utmost will,
That all it scorned at once is fled,
And I, its love, am gained instead!   55
Porphyria's love: she guessed not how
Her darling one wish would be heard.
And thus we sit together now,
And all night long we have not stirred,
And yet God has not said a word!   60

1834   1836, 1842

Soliloquy of the Spanish Cloister[1]

1

Gr-r-r—there go, my heart's abhorrence!
Water your damned flowerpots, do!
If hate killed men, Brother Lawrence,
God's blood, would not mine kill you!
What? your myrtle bush wants trimming?   5
Oh, that rose has prior claims—
Needs its leaden vase filled brimming?
Hell dry you up with its flames!

2

At the meal we sit together:
Salve tibi![2] I must hear   10
Wise talk of the kind of weather,
Sort of season, time of year:
Not a plenteous cork crop: scarcely
Dare we hope oak-galls,[3] *I doubt:*
What's the Latin name for "parsley"?   15
What's the Greek name for Swine's Snout?

3

Whew! We'll have our platter burnished,
Laid with care on our own shelf!
With a fire-new spoon we're furnished,
And a goblet for ourself,   20

1. No period of history is specified in this poem. The monastery setting is timeless and serves to intensify the pressure of meanness and hatred that is boiling up in the speaker.

2. "Hail to thee!" This and other speeches in italics are supposed to be the words of Brother Lawrence.
3. Abnormal outgrowths on oak trees, used for tanning.

Rinsed like something sacrificial
    Ere 'tis fit to touch our chaps[4]—
Marked with L. for our initial!
    (He-he! There his lily snaps!)

4

Saint, forsooth! While brown Dolores   25
    Squats outside the Convent bank
With Sanchicha, telling stories,
    Steeping tresses in the tank,
Blue-black, lustrous, thick like horsehairs,
    —Can't I see his dead eye glow,   30
Bright as 'twere a Barbary corsair's?[5]
    (That is, if he'd let it show!)

5

When he finishes refection,[6]
    Knife and fork he never lays
Cross-wise, to my recollection,   35
    As do I, in Jesu's praise.
I the Trinity illustrate,
    Drinking watered orange pulp—
In three sips the Arian[7] frustrate;
    While he drains his at one gulp.   40

6

Oh, those melons? If he's able
    We're to have a feast! so nice!
One goes to the Abbot's table,
    All of us get each a slice.
How go on your flowers? None double?   45
    Not one fruit-sort can you spy?
Strange!—And I, too, at such trouble,
    Keep them close-nipped on the sly!

7

There's a great text in Galatians,[8]
    Once you trip on it, entails   50
Twenty-nine distinct damnations,
    One sure, if another fails:
If I trip him just a-dying,
    Sure of heaven as sure can be,
Spin him round and send him flying
    Off to hell, a Manichee?[9]   55

8

Or, my scrofulous French novel
    On gray paper with blunt type!

4. Jaws.
5. Pirate of the Barbary Coast of northern Africa, renowned for fierceness and lechery.
6. Dinner.
7. Heretical followers of Arius (256–336), who denied the doctrine of the Trinity.
8. The speaker hopes to obtain Lawrence's damnation by luring him into a heresy, this to be accomplished by exposing him to the difficult task of interpreting "Galatians" in an unswervingly orthodox way. In Galatians v.15–23, St. Paul specifies an assortment of "works of the flesh" that lead to damnation, which could make up a total of "twenty-nine."
9. A heretic, a follower of the Persian prophet of the 3rd century, Mani.

Simply glance at it, you grovel
    Hand and foot in Belial's gripe: 60
If I double down its pages
    At the woeful sixteenth print,
When he gathers his greengages,
    Ope a sieve and slip it in't?

9

Or, there's Satan!—one might venture   65
    Pledge one's soul to him,[1] yet leave
Such a flaw in the indenture
    As he'd miss till, past retrieve,
Blasted lay that rose-acacia
    We're so proud of! *Hy, Zy, Hine . . .*[2]   70
'St, there's Vespers! *Plena gratiá*
    Ave, Virgo![3] Gr-r-r—you swine!

ca. 1839   1842

My Last Duchess[1]

FERRARA

That's my last Duchess painted on the wall,
Looking as if she were alive. I call
That piece a wonder, now: Frà Pandolf's[2] hands
Worked busily a day, and there she stands.
Will't please you sit and look at her? I said   5
"Frà Pandolf" by design, for never read
Strangers like you that pictured countenance,
The depth and passion of its earnest glance,
But to myself they turned (since none puts by
The curtain I have drawn for you, but I)   10
And seemed as they would ask me, if they durst,
How such a glance came there; so, not the first
Are you to turn and ask thus Sir, 'twas not
Her husband's presence only, called that spot
Of joy into the Duchess' cheek: perhaps   15
Frà Pandolf chanced to say "Her mantle laps
Over my lady's wrist too much," or "Paint
Must never hope to reproduce the faint
Half-flush that dies along her throat": such stuff
Was courtesy, she thought, and cause enough   20

---

1. The speaker would pledge his own soul to Satan in return for blasting Lawrence and his "rose-acacia," but the pledge would be so cleverly worded that the speaker would not have to pay, himself, his debt to Satan. There would be an escape-clause, a "flaw in the indenture," for himself.
2. Perhaps the opening of a mysterious curse against Lawrence.
3. "Full of grace, Hail, Virgin!" The speaker's twisted state of mind may be reflected in his mixed-up version of the prayer to Mary: "Ave, Maria, gratia plena."

1. The poem is based on incidents in the life of Alfonso II, Duke of Ferrara in Italy, whose first wife, Lucrezia, a young girl, died in 1561 after three years of marriage. Following her death, the Duke negotiated through an agent to marry a niece of the Count of Tyrol. Browning represents the Duke as addressing this agent.
2. Brother Pandolf, an imaginary painter.

For calling up that spot of joy. She had
A heart—how shall I say?—too soon made glad,
Too easily impressed; she liked whate'er
She looked on, and her looks went everywhere.
Sir, 'twas all one! My favor at her breast,   25
The dropping of the daylight in the West,
The bough of cherries some officious fool
Broke in the orchard for her, the white mule
She rode with round the terrace—all and each
Would draw from her alike the approving speech,   30
Or blush, at least. She thanked men—good! but thanked
Somehow—I know not how—as if she ranked
My gift of a nine-hundred-years-old name
With anybody's gift. Who'd stoop to blame
This sort of trifling? Even had you skill   35
In speech—(which I have not)—to make your will
Quite clear to such an one, and say, "Just this
Or that in you disgusts me; here you miss,
Or there exceed the mark"—and if she let
Herself be lessoned so, nor plainly set   40
Her wits to yours, forsooth, and made excuse
—E'en then would be some stooping; and I choose
Never to stoop. Oh sir, she smiled, no doubt,
Whene'er I passed her; but who passed without
Much the same smile? This grew; I gave commands;   45
Then all smiles stopped together. There she stands
As if alive. Will't please you rise? We'll meet
The company below, then. I repeat,
The Count your master's known munificence
Is ample warrant that no just pretense   50
Of mine for dowry will be disallowed;
Though his fair daughter's self, as I avowed
At starting, is my object. Nay, we'll go
Together down, sir. Notice Neptune, though,
Taming a sea horse, thought a rarity,   55
Which Claus of Innsbruck[3] cast in bronze for me!

1842   1842

The Laboratory
Ancien Régime

1

Now that I, tying thy glass mask tightly,
May gaze thro' these faint smokes curling whitely,
As thou pliest thy trade in this devil's-smithy—
Which is the poison to poison her, prithee?

2

He is with her, and they know that I know   5
Where they are, what they do: they believe my tears flow
While they laugh, laugh at me, at me fled to the drear
Empty church, to pray God in, for them!—I am here.

3. An unidentified or imaginary sculptor. The Count of Tyrol had his capital at Innsbruck.

3

Grind away, moisten and mash up thy paste,
Pound at thy powder—I am not in haste!   10
Better sit thus, and observe thy strange things,
Than go where men wait me and dance at the King's.

4

That in the mortar—you call it a gum?
Ah, the brave tree whence such gold oozings come!
And yonder soft phial, the exquisite blue,   15
Sure to taste sweetly, is that poison too?

5

Had I but all of them, thee and thy treasures,
What a wild crowd of invisible pleasures!
To carry pure death in an earring, a casket,
A signet, a fan-mount, a filigree basket!   20

6

Soon, at the King's,[1] a mere lozenge to give,
And Pauline should have just thirty minutes to live!
But to light a pastile, and Elise, with her head
And her breast and her arms and her hands, should drop dead!

7

Quick—is it finished? The color's too grim!   25
Why not soft like the phial's, enticing and dim?
Let it brighten her drink, let her turn it and stir,
And try it and taste, ere she fix and prefer!

8

What a drop! She's not little, no minion [2] like me!
That's why she ensnared him: this never will free   30
The soul from those masculine eyes—say, "no!"
To that pulse's magnificent come-and-go.

9

For only last night, as they whispered, I brought
My own eyes to bear on her so, that I thought
Could I keep them one half minute fixed, she would fall   35
Shriveled; she fell not; yet this does it all!

10

Not that I bid you spare her the pain;
Let death be felt and the proof remain:
Brand, burn up, bite into its grace—
He is sure to remember her dying face!   40

11

Is it done? Take my mask off! Nay, be not morose;
It kills her, and this prevents seeing it close:
The delicate droplet, my whole fortune's fee!
If it hurts her, beside, can it ever hurt me?

1. Probably King Louis XIV of France (1643–1715). In the 1670's a police investigation disclosed that an extraordinary number of women and men attached to the King's court had been disposing of rivals and enemies by poisonings. Some 36 of the accused courtiers and the dealers from whom they had purchased poisons were punished by torture and burnt to death.
2. A dainty and delicate person.

12

Now, take all my jewels, gorge gold to your fill,   45
You may kiss me, old man, on my mouth if you will!
But brush this dust off me, lest horror it brings
Ere I know it—next moment I dance at the King's!
ca. 1844   1844

The Lost Leader[1]

1

Just for a handful of silver he left us,
   Just for a riband to stick in his coat—
Found the one gift of which fortune bereft us,
   Lost all the others she lets us devote;
They, with the gold to give, doled him out silver,   5
   So much was theirs who so little allowed:
How all our copper had gone for his service!
   Rags—were they purple, his heart had been proud!
We that had loved him so, followed him, honored him,
   Lived in his mild and magnificent eye,   10
Learned his great language, caught his clear accents,
   Made him our pattern to live and to die!
Shakespeare was of us, Milton was for us,
   Burns, Shelley, were with us—they watch from their graves!
He alone breaks from the van[2] and the freemen   15
   —He alone sinks to the rear and the slaves!

2

We shall march prospering—not through his presence;
   Songs may inspirit us—not from his lyre;
Deeds will be done—while he boasts his quiescence,
   Still bidding crouch whom the rest bade aspire: 20
Blot out his name, then, record one lost soul more,
   One task more declined, one more footpath untrod,
One more devils'-triumph and sorrow for angels,
   One wrong more to man, one more insult to God!
Life's night begins: let him never come back to us!   25
   There would be doubt, hesitation and pain,
Forced praise on our part—the glimmer of twilight,
   Never glad confident morning again!
Best fight on well, for we taught him—strike gallantly,
   Menace our heart ere we master his own;   30
Then let him receive the new knowledge and wait us,
   Pardoned in heaven, the first by the throne!
1843   1845

1. William Wordsworth, who had been an ardent liberal in his youth, had become a political conservative in later years. In old age, when he accepted a grant of money from the government ("a handful of silver") and also the office of poet laureate ("a riband to stick in his coat"), he alienated some of his young admirers such as Browning, whose liberalism was then as ardent as Wordsworth's had once been.
   Cf. J. G. Whittier's poem *Ichabod*, which embodies a similar sense of sorrowful indignation over the apostasy of Daniel Webster, a great leader formerly admired by the poet.
2. Vanguard of the army of liberalism.

How They Brought the Good News
from Ghent to Aix[1]

(16—)

1

I sprang to the stirrup, and Joris, and he;
I galloped, Dirck galloped, we galloped all three;
"Good speed!" cried the watch, as the gate-bolts undrew;
"Speed!" echoed the wall to us galloping through;
Behind shut the postern, the lights sank to rest,   5
And into the midnight we galloped abreast.

2

Not a word to each other; we kept the great pace
Neck by neck, stride by stride, never changing our place;
I turned in my saddle and made its girths tight,
Then shortened each stirrup, and set the pique[2] right,   10
Rebuckled the cheek-strap, chained slacker the bit,
Nor galloped less steadily Roland a whit.

3

'Twas moonset at starting; but while we drew near
Lokeren, the cocks crew and twilight dawned clear;
At Boom, a great yellow star came out to see;   15
At Düffeld, 'twas morning as plain as could be;
And from Mecheln church-steeple we heard the half-chime,
So, Joris broke silence with, "Yet there is time!"

4

At Aershot, up leaped of a sudden the sun,
And against him the cattle stood black every one,   20
To stare through the mist at us galloping past,
And I saw my stout galloper Roland at last,
With resolute shoulders, each butting away
The haze, as some bluff river headland its spray:

5

And his low head and crest, just one sharp ear bent back   25
For my voice, and the other pricked out on his track;
And one eye's black intelligence—ever that glance
O'er its white edge at me, his own master, askance!
And the thick heavy spume-flakes which ay and anon
His fierce lips shook upwards in galloping on.   30

6

By Hasselt, Dirck groaned; and cried Joris, "Stay spur!
Your Roos galloped bravely, the fault's not in her,
We'll remember at Aix"—for one heard the quick wheeze
Of her chest, saw the stretched neck and staggering knees,
And sunk tail, and horrible heave of the flank,   35
As down on her haunches she shuddered and sank.

1. The distance between Ghent, in Flanders, and Aix-la-Chapelle is about one hundred miles. Browning said that the incident, occurring during the wars between Flanders and Spain, was an imaginary one.
2. Spur or pommel.

7

So, we were left galloping, Joris and I,
Past Looz and past Tongres, no cloud in the sky;
The broad sun above laughed a pitiless laugh,
'Neath our feet broke the brittle bright stubble like chaff;   40
Till over by Dalhem a dome-spire sprang white,
And "Gallop," gasped Joris, "for Aix is in sight!"

8

"How they'll greet us!"—and all in a moment his roan
Rolled neck and croup over, lay dead as a stone;
And there was my Roland to bear the whole weight   45
Of the news which alone could save Aix from her fate,
With his nostrils like pits full of blood to the brim,
And with circles of red for his eye-sockets' rim.

9

Then I cast loose my buffcoat, each holster let fall,
Shook off both my jack boots, let go belt and all,   50
Stood up in the stirrup, leaned, patted his ear,
Called my Roland his pet name, my horse without peer;
Clapped my hands, laughed and sang, any noise, bad or good,
Till at length into Aix Roland galloped and stood.

10

And all I remember is—friends flocking round   55
As I sat with his head 'twixt my knees on the ground;
And no voice but was praising this Roland of mine,
As I poured down his throat our last measure of wine,
Which (the burgesses voted by common consent)
Was no more than his due who brought good news from Ghent.   60
ca. 1844   1845

Home-Thoughts, from Abroad

1

Oh, to be in England
Now that April's there,
And whoever wakes in England
Sees, some morning, unaware,
That the lowest boughs and the brushwood sheaf   5
Round the elm-tree bole are in tiny leaf,
While the chaffinch sings on the orchard bough
In England—now!

2

And after April, when May follows,
And the whitethroat builds, and all the swallows!   10
Hark, where my blossomed peartree in the hedge
Leans to the field and scatters on the clover
Blossoms and dewdrops—at the bent spray's edge—
That's the wise thrush; he sings each song twice over,

Lest you should think he never could recapture   15
The first fine careless rapture!
And though the fields look rough with hoary dew,
All will be gay when noontide wakes anew
The buttercups, the little children's dower
—Far brighter than this gaudy melon-flower!   20

ca. 1845   1845

Home-Thoughts, from the Sea

Nobly, nobly Cape Saint Vincent[1] to the northwest died away;
Sunset ran, one glorious blood-red, reeking into Cadiz Bay;
Bluish 'mid the burning water, full in face Trafalgar[2] lay;
In the dimmest northeast distance dawned Gibraltar grand and gray;
"Here and here did England help me: how can I help England?"—
     say,   5
Whoso turns as I, this evening, turn to God to praise and pray,
While Jove's planet[3] rises yonder, silent over Africa.

1844   1845

The Bishop Orders His Tomb at
Saint Praxed's Church[1]

ROME, 15—

Vanity, saith the preacher, vanity![2]
Draw round my bed: is Anselm keeping back?
Nephews—sons mine . . . ah God, I know not! Well—
She, men would have to be your mother once,
Old Gandolf envied me, so fair she was!   5
What's done is done, and she is dead beside,
Dead long ago, and I am Bishop since,
And as she died so must we die ourselves,
And thence ye may perceive the world's a dream.
Life, how and what is it? As here I lie   10

1. Off the coast of Portugal, scene of British naval victory under Admiral Nelson (1797).
2. A cape in Spain, where Nelson won his great victory over Napoleon's fleets (1805).
3. Jupiter.

1. In *Fra Lippo Lippi* Browning represents the dawn of the Renaissance in Italy, with its fresh zest for "the beauty and the wonder and the power" of man's experiences in this world. In the present monologue he portrays a later stage of the Renaissance when such worldliness, full-blown, had infected even some of the leading churchmen of Italy. Browning's portrait of the dying bishop is, however, not primarily a satire against corruption in the church. It is a brilliant exposition of the workings of a mind, a mind that has been conditioned by special historical circumstances. The Victorian historian of art, John Ruskin, said of this poem: "I know of no other piece of modern English, prose or poetry, in which there is so much told, as in these lines, of the Renaissance spirit—its worldliness, inconsistency, pride, hypocrisy, ignorance of itself, love of art, of luxury, and of good Latin. It is nearly all that I have said of the central Renaissance in thirty pages of the *Stones of Venice*, put into as many lines, Browning's also being the antecedent work."

St. Praxed's Church was named in honor of St. Praxedes, a Roman virgin of the 2nd century who gave her riches to poor Christians. Both the bishop and his predecessor, Gandolf, are imaginary persons.
2. Cf. Ecclesiastes i.2.

In this state chamber, dying by degrees,
Hours and long hours in the dead night, I ask
"Do I live, am I dead?" Peace, peace seems all.
Saint Praxed's ever was the church for peace;
And so, about this tomb of mine. I fought   15
With tooth and nail to save my niche, ye know:
—Old Gandolf cozened[3] me, despite my care;
Shrewd was that snatch from out the corner south
He graced his carrion with, God curse the same!
Yet still my niche is not so cramped but thence   20
One sees the pulpit o' the epistle side,[4]
And somewhat of the choir, those silent seats,
And up into the aery dome where live
The angels, and a sunbeam's sure to lurk:
And I shall fill my slab of basalt[5] there,   25
And 'neath my tabernacle[6] take my rest,
With those nine columns round me, two and two,
The odd one at my feet where Anselm stands:
Peach-blossom marble all, the rare, the ripe
As fresh-poured red wine of a mighty pulse.[7]   30
—Old Gandolf with his paltry onion-stone,[8]
Put me where I may look at him! True peach,
Rosy and flawless: how I earned the prize!
Draw close: that conflagration of my church
—What then? So much was saved if aught were missed!   35
My sons, ye would not be my death? Go dig
The white-grape vineyard where the oil-press stood,
Drop water gently till the surface sink,
And if ye find . . . Ah God, I know not, I! . . .
Bedded in store of rotten fig leaves soft,   40
And corded up in a tight olive-frail,[9]
Some lump, ah God, of *lapis lazuli*,[1]
Big as a Jew's head cut off at the nape,
Blue as a vein o'er the Madonna's breast . . .
Sons, all have I bequeathed you, villas, all,   45
That brave Frascati[2] villa with its bath,
So, let the blue lump poise between my knees,
Like God the Father's globe on both his hands
Ye worship in the Jesu Church[3] so gay,
For Gandolf shall not choose but see and burst!   50
Swift as a weaver's shuttle fleet our years:[4]
Man goeth to the grave, and where is he?

3. Cheated.
4. The Epistles of the New Testament are read from the right-hand side of the altar (as one faces it).
5. Dark-colored igneous rock.
6. Stone canopy or tentlike roof, presumably supported by the "nine columns" under which the sculptured effigy of the Bishop would lie on the slab of basalt.
7. Browning uses "pulse" in the special sense of a pulpy mash of fermented grapes from which a strong wine might be poured off. In a later poem, the *Epilogue* to *Pacchiarotto*, he likens such wine to "viscous blood" that has been "squeezed gold" from the "pulp" of the grapes.
8. An inferior marble that peels in layers.
9. Basket for holding olives.
1. Valuable bright blue stone.
2. Suburb of Rome, used as a resort by wealthy Italians.
3. Il Gesù, a Jesuit church in Rome.
4. Cf. Job vii.6.

Did I say basalt for my slab, sons? Black[5]—
'Twas ever antique-black I meant! How else
Shall ye contrast my frieze[6] to come beneath?   55
The bas-relief in bronze ye promised me,
Those Pans and Nymphs ye wot of, and perchance
Some tripod, thyrsus, with a vase or so,
The Saviour at his sermon on the mount,
Saint Praxed in a glory, and one Pan   60
Ready to twitch the Nymph's last garment off,
And Moses with the tables[7] . . . but I know
Ye mark me not! What do they whisper thee,
Child of my bowels, Anselm? Ah, ye hope
To revel down my villas while I gasp   65
Bricked o'er with beggar's moldy travertine[8]
Which Gandolf from his tomb-top chuckles at!
Nay, boys, ye love me—all of jasper, then!
'Tis jasper ye stand pledged to, lest I grieve
My bath must needs be left behind, alas!   70
One block, pure green as a pistachio nut,
There's plenty jasper somewhere in the world—
And have I not Saint Praxed's ear to pray
Horses for ye, and brown Greek manuscripts,
And mistresses with great smooth marbly limbs?   75
—That's if ye carve my epitaph aright,
Choice Latin, picked phrase, Tully's[9] every word,
No gaudy ware like Gandolf's second line—
Tully, my masters? Ulpian[1] serves his need!
And then how I shall lie through centuries,   80
And hear the blessed mutter of the mass,
And see God made and eaten all day long,[2]
And feel the steady candle flame, and taste
Good strong thick stupefying incense-smoke!
For as I lie here, hours of the dead night,   85
Dying in state and by such slow degrees,
I fold my arms as if they clasped a crook,[3]
And stretch my feet forth straight as stone can point,
And let the bedclothes, for a mortcloth,[4] drop
Into great laps and folds of sculptor's-work: 90
And as yon tapers dwindle, and strange thoughts
Grow, with a certain humming in my ears,

5. Black marble.
6. Continuous band of sculpture.
7. The "bas-relief" (or sculpture in which the figures do not project far from the background surface) would consist of a mixture of pagan and religious scenes (lines 57–62). Among the former would be a "tripod," on which priestesses at the oracle of Delphi sat to make their prophecies, and a "thyrsus," a long staff carried in processions in honor of Bacchus, the god of wine. The religious scenes would include St. Praxed with her halo ("a glory") and Moses with the stone tablets ("tables") on which the Ten Com-

mandments were written. Such intermingling of classical and Christian traditions is characteristic of the Renaissance.
8. Italian limestone.
9. A familiar name for Marcus Tullius Cicero, whose writing was the model, during the Renaissance, of classical Latin prose.
1. Late Latin prose-writer, not considered a model of good style.
2. Reference to the doctrine of transubstantiation.
3. Bishop's staff or crozier.
4. Rich cloth spread over a dead body or coffin.

About the life before I lived this life,
And this life too, popes, cardinals, and priests,
Saint Praxed at his sermon on the mount,[5]   95
Your tall pale mother with her talking eyes,
And new-found agate urns as fresh as day,
And marble's language, Latin pure, discreet
—Aha, ELUCESCEBAT[6] quoth our friend?
No Tully, said I, Ulpian at the best!   100
Evil and brief hath been my pilgrimage.
All *lapis*, all, sons! Else I give the Pope
My villas! Will ye ever eat my heart?
Ever your eyes were as a lizard's quick,
They glitter like your mother's for my soul,   105
Or ye would heighten my impoverished frieze,
Piece out its starved design, and fill my vase
With grapes, and add a vizor and a Term,[7]
And to the tripod ye would tie a lynx
That in his struggle throws the thyrsus down,   110
To comfort me on my entablature[8]
Whereon I am to lie till I must ask
"Do I live, am I dead?" There, leave me, there!
For ye have stabbed me with ingratitude
To death—ye wish it—God, ye wish it! Stone—   115
Gritstone,[9] a-crumble! Clammy squares which sweat
As if the corpse they keep were oozing through—
And no more *lapis* to delight the world!
Well go! I bless ye. Fewer tapers there,
But in a row: and, going, turn your backs   120
—Aye, like departing altar-ministrants,
And leave me in my church, the church for peace,
That I may watch at leisure if he leers—
Old Gandolf, at me, from his onion-stone,
As still he envied me, so fair she was!   125

1844   1845

Meeting at Night[1]

1

The gray sea and the long black land;
And the yellow half-moon large and low;
And the startled little waves that leap

---

5. The bishop is confusing St. Praxed (a woman) with Christ—an indication that his mind is wandering.
6. Word from Gandolf's epitaph meaning "he was illustrious." The bishop considers the form of the verb to be in "gaudy" bad taste. If the epitaph had been copied from Cicero instead of from Ulpian, the word would have been *elucebat*.
7. "Vizor": part of a helmet, often represented in sculpture. "Term": statue of Terminus, the Roman god of boundaries, usually represented without arms.
8. Horizontal platform supporting a statue or effigy.
9. Coarse sandstone such as that used for grindstones.
1. This poem and the one which follows it appeared originally under the single title *Night and Morning*. The speaker in both is a man.

In fiery ringlets from their sleep,
As I gain the cove with pushing prow,   5
And quench its speed i' the slushy sand.

2

Then a mile of warm sea-scented beach;
Three fields to cross till a farm appears;
A tap at the pane, the quick sharp scratch
And blue spurt of a lighted match,   10
And a voice less loud, through its joys and fears,
Than the two hearts beating each to each!

1845

Parting at Morning

Round the cape of a sudden came the sea,
And the sun looked over the mountain's rim:
And straight was a path of gold for him,[2]
And the need of a world of men for me.

1845

A Toccata of Galuppi's[1]

1

Oh, Galuppi, Baldassaro, this is very sad to find!
I can hardly misconceive you; it would prove me deaf and blind;
But although I take your meaning, 'tis with such a heavy mind!

2

Here you come with your old music, and here's all the good it brings.
What, they lived once thus at Venice where the merchants were
    the kings,   5
Where Saint Mark's is, where the Doges used to wed the sea with
    rings?[2]

2. The sun.
1. There are three speakers in this short poem. The first is a 19th-century scientist in England who is listening to a musical composition by Baldassaro Galuppi (1706–85), a Venetian. The music evokes for this scientist the voice of the dead composer (the third speaker) who comments upon the pointless and butterfly-like frivolity of his 18th-century contemporaries. The second group of voices is made up of comments by members of Galuppi's audience as they respond to the different moods of his clavichord-playing during a party which the scientist imagines to have taken place in Venice.
    A "toccata" is defined in Grove's *Dictionary of Music* as a "touch-piece,

or a composition intended to exhibit the touch and execution of the performer." The same authority states that "no particular composition was taken as the basis of the poem," but Browning is known to have himself played on the organ some unpublished compositions by Galuppi, and one of these, not yet identified, may have occasioned the poem. Browning's interest in music was keen, and his knowledge of the art was more extensive than that of most English poets.
2. An annual ceremony in which the Doge, the Venetian chief magistrate, threw a ring into the water to symbolize the bond between his city, with its maritime empire, and the sea.

3

Aye, because the sea's the street there; and 'tis arched by . . . what
  you call
. . . Shylock's bridge[3] with houses on it, where they kept the carnival:
I was never out of England—it's as if I saw it all.

4

Did young people take their pleasure when the sea was warm in
  May?   10
Balls and masks[4] begun at midnight, burning ever to midday,
When they made up fresh adventures for the morrow, do you say?

5

Was a lady such a lady, cheeks so round and lips so red—
On her neck the small face buoyant, like a bellflower on its bed,
O'er the breast's superb abundance where a man might base his
  head?   15

6

Well, and it was graceful of them—they'd break talk off and afford
—She, to bite her mask's black velvet—he, to finger on his sword,
While you sat and played toccatas, stately at the clavichord?[5]

7

What? Those lesser thirds so plaintive, sixths diminished, sigh on
  sigh,
Told them something? Those suspensions, those solutions—"Must
  we die?"   20
Those commiserating sevenths[6]—"Life might last! we can but
  try!"

8

"Were you happy?"—"Yes."—"And are you still as happy?"—
  "Yes. And you?"
—"Then, more kisses!"—"Did *I* stop them, when a million seemed
  so few?"
Hark, the dominant's persistence till it must be answered to!

9

So, an octave struck the answer. Oh, they praised you, I dare say! 25
"Brave Galuppi! that was music; good alike at grave and gay!
I can always leave off talking when I hear a master play!"

10

Then they left you for their pleasure: till in due time, one by one,
Some with lives that came to nothing, some with deeds as well un-
  done,   29
Death stepped tacitly and took them where they never see the sun.

3. The Rialto, a bridge over the Grand
Canal.
4. Masquerades.
5. A keyboard instrument in which the
strings are struck by metal hammers.
As a mechanism it resembles a piano,
but the sound is more like that of a
harpsichord.
6. This term and others in these lines
all refer to the technical devices used
by Galuppi to produce alternating moods
in his music, conflict in each instance
being resolved into harmony. Thus the
"dominant" (the fifth note of the
scale), after being persistently sounded,
is answered by a resolving chord (lines
24–25).

11

But when I sit down to reason, think to take my stand nor swerve,
While I triumph o'er a secret wrung from nature's close reserve,
In you come with your cold music till I creep through every nerve.

12

Yes, you, like a ghostly cricket, creaking where a house was burned:
"Dust and ashes, dead and done with, Venice spent what Venice
earned.   35
The soul, doubtless, is immortal—where a soul can be discerned.

13

"Yours for instance: you know physics, something of geology,
Mathematics are your pastime; souls shall rise in their degree;
Butterflies may dread extinction—you'll not die, it cannot be!

14

"As for Venice and her people, merely born to bloom and drop, 40
Here on earth they bore their fruitage, mirth and folly were the
crop:
What of soul was left, I wonder, when the kissing had to stop?

15

"Dust and ashes!" So you creak it, and I want the heart to scold.
Dear dead women, with such hair, too—what's become of all the
gold   44
Used to hang and brush their bosoms? I feel chilly and grown old.
ca. 1847   1855

Memorabilia[1]

1

Ah, did you once see Shelley plain,
    And did he stop and speak to you
And did you speak to him again?
    How strange it seems and new!

2

But you were living before that,   5
    And also you are living after;
And the memory I started at—
    My starting moves your laughter.

3

I crossed a moor, with a name of its own
    And a certain use in the world no doubt,   10
Yet a hand's-breadth of it shines alone
    'Mid the blank miles round about:

1. The title means "things worth remembering." Browning reports that he
once met a stranger in a bookstore who
mentioned having talked with Shelley.
"Suddenly the stranger paused, and
burst into laughter as he observed me
staring at him with blanched face.
* * * I still vividly remember how
strangely the presence of a man who
had seen and spoken with Shelley affected me."

4

For there I picked up on the heather
    And there I put inside my breast
A molted feather, an eagle feather!   15
    Well, I forget the rest.

ca. 1851   1855

Love Among the Ruins[1]

1

Where the quiet-colored end of evening smiles,
    Miles and miles
On the solitary pastures where our sheep
    Half-asleep
Tinkle homeward through the twilight, stray or stop   5
    As they crop—
Was the site once of a city great and gay
    (So they say),
Of our country's very capital, its prince
    Ages since   10
Held his court in, gathered councils, wielding far
    Peace or war.

2

Now—the country does not even boast a tree,
    As you see,
To distinguish slopes of verdure, certain rills   15
    From the hills
Intersect and give a name to (else they run
    Into one),
Where the domed and daring palace shot its spires
    Up like fires   20
O'er the hundred-gated circuit of a wall
    Bounding all,
Made of marble, men might march on nor be pressed,
    Twelve abreast.

3

And such plenty and perfection, see, of grass   25
    Never was!
Such a carpet as, this summertime, o'erspreads
    And embeds
Every vestige of the city, guessed alone,
    Stock or stone—   30
Where a multitude of men breathed joy and woe
    Long ago;
Lust of glory pricked their hearts up, dread of shame
    Struck them tame;

1. The ruins may be those of such cities as Babylon or Nineveh or one of the Etruscan cities of Italy.
  The unusual stanza used in this poem was invented by Browning. The contrast between past and present, which is the core of the poem, is reinforced by devoting one half of each stanza to the past and the other half to the present.

And that glory and that shame alike, the gold 35
    Bought and sold.

4

Now—the single little turret that remains
    On the plains,
By the caper overrooted, by the gourd
    Overscored, 40
While the patching houseleek's[2] head of blossom winks
    Through the chinks—
Marks the basement whence a tower in ancient time
    Sprang sublime,
And a burning ring, all round, the chariots traced 45
    As they raced,
And the monarch and his minions and his dames
    Viewed the games.

5

And I know, while thus the quiet-colored eve
    Smiles to leave
To their folding, all our many-tinkling fleece 50
    In such peace,
And the slopes and rills in undistinguished gray
    Melt away—
That a girl with eager eyes and yellow hair 55
    Waits me there
In the turret whence the charioteers caught soul
    For the goal,
When the king looked, where she looks now, breathless, dumb
    Till I come. 60

6

But he looked upon the city, every side,
    Far and wide,
All the mountains topped with temples, all the glades'
    Colonnades,
All the causeys,[3] bridges, aqueducts—and then, 65
    All the men!
When I do come, she will speak not, she will stand,
    Either hand
On my shoulder, give her eyes the first embrace
    Of my face, 70
Ere we rush, ere we extinguish sight and speech
    Each on each.

7

In one year they sent a million fighters forth
    South and north,
And they built their gods a brazen pillar high 75
    As the sky,
Yet reserved a thousand chariots in full force—
    Gold, of course,

---

2. Common European plant, with petals clustered in the shape of rosettes.

3. Causeways or roads raised above low ground.

Oh heart! oh blood that freezes, blood that burns!
  Earth's returns   80
For whole centuries of folly, noise, and sin!
  Shut them in,
With their triumphs and their glories and the rest!
  Love is best.

1852   1855

Women and Roses[1]

1

I dream of a red-rose tree.
And which of its roses three
Is the dearest rose to me?

2

Round and round, like a dance of snow
In a dazzling drift, as its guardians, go   5
Floating the women faded for ages,
Sculptured in stone, on the poet's pages.
Then follow women fresh and gay,
Living and loving and loved today.
Last, in the rear, flee the multitude of maidens,   10
Beauties yet unborn. And all, to one cadence,
They circle their rose on my rose tree.

3

Dear rose, thy term is reached,
Thy leaf hangs loose and bleached:
Bees pass it unimpeached.[2]   15

4

Stay then, stoop, since I cannot climb,
You, great shapes of the antique time!
How shall I fix you, fire you, freeze you,
Break my heart at your feet to please you?
Oh, to possess and be possessed!   20
Hearts that beat 'neath each pallid breast!
Once but of love, the poesy, the passion,
Drink but once and die!—In vain, the same fashion,
They circle their rose on my rose tree.

5

Dear rose, thy joy's undimmed,   25
Thy cup is ruby-rimmed,
Thy cup's heart nectar-brimmed.

6

Deep, as drops from a statue's plinth[3]
The bee sucked in by the hyacinth,

1. Like Chaucer in the *Romaunt of the Rose* and also like Tennyson in *Maud*, the speaker in the following dream lyric associates roses with fair women and a garden of roses with the garden of love. The beautiful women of the past are first evoked (stanzas 3, 4); then those of the present (stanzas 5, 6); and finally those of the future (stanzas 7, 8). All, however, elude him.
2. Unhindered.
3. Base.

So will I bury me while burning,   30
Quench like him at a plunge my yearning,
Eyes in your eyes, lips on your lips!
Fold me fast where the cincture⁴ slips,
Prison all my soul in eternities of pleasure,
Girdle me for once! But no—the old measure,   35
They circle their rose on my rose tree.

7

Dear rose without a thorn,
Thy bud's the babe unborn:
First streak of a new morn.

8

Wings, lend wings for the cold, the clear!   40
What is far conquers what is near.
Roses will bloom nor want beholders,
Sprung from the dust where our flesh molders.
What shall arrive with the cycle's change?
A novel grace and a beauty strange.   45
I will make an Eve, be the artist that began her,
Shaped her to his mind!—Alas! in like manner
They circle their rose on my rose tree.

1852   1855

"Childe Roland to the Dark Tower Came"¹

(SEE EDGAR'S SONG IN "LEAR")

1

My first thought was, he lied in every word,
That hoary cripple, with malicious eye
Askance² to watch the working of his lie
On mine, and mouth scarce able to afford

4. Ornamental belt worn by women, usually across the hips.
1. Browning stated that this poem "came upon me as a kind of dream," and that it was written in one day. Although the poem was among those of his own writings that pleased him most, he was reluctant to explain what the dream (or nightmare) signified. He once agreed with a friend's suggestion that the meaning might be expressed in the statement: "He that endureth to the end shall be saved." Most readers have responded to the poem in this way, finding in the story of Roland's quest an inspiring expression of defiance and courage. Other readers find the poem to be more expressive of despair than of enduring hope, and it is at least true that the landscape is as grim and nightmarelike as in such 20th-century writings as T. S. Eliot's *Hollow Men*

or Franz Kafka's *Penal Colony*. It has been said of *Childe Roland* that every reader can be his own allegorist, and such a poem thus poses a further large question of whether or not total comprehension of a work is always essential for appreciation of literature.

The lines from Shakespeare's *King Lear* (III.iv.187–90), from which the title is taken, are spoken when Lear is about to enter a hovel on the heath, and Edgar, feigning madness, chants the fragment of a song reminiscent of quests and challenges in fairly tales: "Child Rowland to the dark tower came; / His word was still / 'Fie, foh, and fum! / I smell the blood of a British man.' " A "childe" is a youth of gentle birth, usually a candidate for knighthood.

2. Squinting sidewise.

Suppression of the glee, that pursed and scored   5
    Its edge, at one more victim gained thereby.

2

What else should he be set for, with his staff?
    What, save to waylay with his lies, ensnare
    All travelers who might find him posted there,
And ask the road? I guessed what skull-like laugh   10
Would break, what crutch 'gin write my epitaph
    For pastime in the dusty thoroughfare,

3

If at his counsel I should turn aside
    Into that ominous tract which, all agree,
    Hides the Dark Tower. Yet acquiescingly   15
I did turn as he pointed: neither pride
Nor hope rekindling at the end descried,
    So much as gladness that some end might be.

4

For, what with my whole world-wide wandering,
    What with my search drawn out through years, my hope 20
    Dwindled into a ghost not fit to cope
With that obstreperous joy success would bring,
I hardly tried now to rebuke the spring
    My heart made, finding failure in its scope.

5

As when a sick man very near to death[3]   25
    Seems dead indeed, and feels begin and end
    The tears and takes the farewell of each friend,
And hears one bid the other go, draw breath
Freelier outside ("since all is o'er," he saith,
    "And the blow fallen no grieving can amend"),   30

6

While some discuss if near the other graves
    Be room enough for this, and when a day
    Suits best for carrying the corpse away,
With care about the banners, scarves and staves:
And still the man hears all, and only craves   35
    He may not shame such tender love and stay.

7

Thus, I had so long suffered in this quest,
    Heard failure prophesied so oft, been writ
    So many times among "The Band"—to wit,
The knights who to the Dark Tower's search addressed   40
Their steps—that just to fail as they, seemed best,
    And all the doubt was now—should I be fit?

8

So, quiet as despair, I turned from him,
    That hateful cripple, out of his highway
    Into the path he pointed. All the day   45

---

3. Cf. *A Valediction: Forbidding Mourning*, lines 1–4, by John Donne, a poet much admired by Browning.

Had been a dreary one at best, and dim
Was settling to its close, yet shot one grim
    Red leer to see the plain catch its estray.[4]

9

For mark! no sooner was I fairly found
    Pledged to the plain, after a pace or two,   50
    Than, pausing to throw backward a last view
O'er the safe road, 'twas gone; gray plain all round:
Nothing but plain to the horizon's bound.
    I might go on; naught else remained to do.

10

So, on I went. I think I never saw   55
    Such starved ignoble nature; nothing throve:
    For flowers—as well expect a cedar grove!
But cockle,[5] spurge, according to their law
Might propagate their kind, with none to awe,
    You'd think; a burr had been a treasure trove.   60

11

No! penury, inertness and grimace,
    In some strange sort, were the land's portion. "See
    Or shut your eyes," said Nature peevishly,
"It nothing skills: I cannot help my case;
'Tis the Last Judgment's fire must cure this place,   65
    Calcine[6] its clods and set my prisoners free."

12

If there pushed any ragged thistle stalk
    Above its mates, the head was chopped; the bents[7]
    Were jealous else. What made those holes and rents
In the dock's[8] harsh swarth leaves, bruised as to balk   70
All hope of greenness? 'tis a brute must walk
    Pashing their life out, with a brute's intents.

13

As for the grass, it grew as scant as hair
    In leprosy; thin dry blades pricked the mud
    Which underneath looked kneaded up with blood.   75
One stiff blind horse, his every bone a-stare,
Stood stupefied, however he came there:
    Thrust out past service from the devil's stud!

14

Alive? he might be dead for aught I know,
    With that red gaunt and colloped[9] neck a-strain,   80
    And shut eyes underneath the rusty mane;
Seldom went such grotesqueness with such woe;
I never saw a brute I hated so;
    He must be wicked to deserve such pain.

---

4. Literally, a domestic animal that has strayed away from its home.
5. A weed that bears burrs. "Spurge" is a bitter-juiced weed.
6. Turn to powder by heat.
7. Coarse, stiff grasses.
8. Coarse plant.
9. Ridged.

15

I shut my eyes and turned them on my heart.   85
    As a man calls for wine before he fights,
    I asked one draught of earlier, happier sights,
Ere fitly I could hope to play my part.
Think first, fight afterwards—the soldier's art:
    One taste of the old time sets all to rights.   90

16

Not it! I fancied Cuthbert's reddening face
    Beneath its garniture of curly gold,
    Dear fellow, till I almost felt him fold
An arm in mine to fix me to the place,
That way he used. Alas, one night's disgrace!   95
    Out went my heart's new fire and left it cold.

17

Giles then, the soul of honor—there he stands
    Frank as ten years ago when knighted first.
    What honest man should dare (he said) he durst.
Good—but the scene shifts—faugh! what hangman hands   100
Pin to his breast a parchment? His own bands
    Read it. Poor traitor, spit upon and cursed!

18

Better this present than a past like that;
    Back therefore to my darkening path again!
    No sound, no sight as far as eye could strain.   105
Will the night send a howlet[1] or a bat?
I asked: when something on the dismal flat
    Came to arrest my thoughts and change their train.

19

A sudden little river crossed my path
    As unexpected as a serpent comes.   110
    No sluggish tide congenial to the glooms;
This, as it frothed by, might have been a bath
For the fiend's glowing hoof—to see the wrath
    Of its black eddy bespate[2] with flakes and spumes.

20

So petty yet so spiteful! All along,   115
    Low scrubby alders kneeled down over it;
    Drenched willows flung them headlong in a fit
Of mute despair, a suicidal throng:
The river which had done them all the wrong,
    Whate'er that was, rolled by, deterred no whit.   120

21

Which, while I forded—good saints, how I feared
    To set my foot upon a dead man's cheek,
    Each step, or feel the spear I thrust to seek
For hollows, tangled in his hair or beard!
—It may have been a water rat I speared,   125
    But, ugh! it sounded like a baby's shriek.

1. Owl.   2. Bespattered.

22

Glad was I when I reached the other bank.
    Now for a better country. Vain presage!
    Who were the strugglers, what war did they wage,
Whose savage trample thus could pad the dank   130
Soil to a plash? Toads in a poisoned tank,
    Or wild cats in a red-hot iron cage—

23

The fight must so have seemed in that fell cirque.[3]
    What penned them there, with all the plain to choose?
    No footprint leading to that horrid mews,[4]   135
None out of it. Mad brewage set to work
Their brains, no doubt, like galley slaves the Turk
    Pits for his pastime, Christians against Jews.

24

And more than that—a furlong on—why, there!
    What bad use was that engine for, that wheel,   140
    Or brake,[5] not wheel—that harrow fit to reel
Men's bodies out like silk? with all the air
Of Tophet's[6] tool, on earth left unaware,
    Or brought to sharpen its rusty teeth of steel.

25

Then came a bit of stubbed ground, once a wood,   145
    Next a marsh, it would seem, and now mere earth
    Desperate and done with; (so a fool finds mirth,
Makes a thing and then mars it, till his mood
Changes and off he goes!) within a rood[7]—
    Bog, clay and rubble, sand and stark black dearth.   150

26

Now blotches rankling, colored gay and grim,
    Now patches where some leanness of the soil's
    Broke into moss or substances like boils;
Then came some palsied oak, a cleft in him
Like a distorted mouth that splits its rim   155
    Gaping at death, and dies while it recoils.

27

And just as far as ever from the end!
    Naught in the distance but the evening, naught
    To point my footstep further! At the thought,
A great black bird, Apollyon's[8] bosom friend,   160
Sailed past, nor beat his wide wing dragon-penned[9]
    That brushed my cap—perchance the guide I sought.

28

For, looking up, aware I somehow grew,
    'Spite of the dusk, the plain had given place
    All round to mountains—with such name to grace   165

3. Dreadful arena.
4. Enclosed stable yard.
5. A toothed machine used for separating the fibers of flax or hemp. Here an instrument of torture.
6. Hell's.
7. A distance of sixteen feet.
8. The devil's.
9. With wings or pinions like those of a dragon.

Mere ugly heights and heaps now stolen in view.
How thus they had surprised me—solve it, you!
How to get from them was no clearer case.

29

Yet half I seemed to recognize some trick
Of mischief happened to me, God knows when—   170
In a bad dream perhaps. Here ended, then,
Progress this way. When, in the very nick
Of giving up, one time more, came a click
As when a trap shuts—you're inside the den!

30

Burningly it came on me all at once,   175
This was the place! those two hills on the right,
Crouched like two bulls locked horn in horn in fight;
While to the left, a tall scalped mountain . . . Dunce,
Dotard, a-dozing at the very nonce,[1]
After a life spent training for the sight!   180

31

What in the midst lay but the Tower itself?
The round squat turret, blind as the fool's heart,
Built of brown stone, without a counterpart
In the whole world. The tempest's mocking elf
Points to the shipman thus the unseen shelf   185
He strikes on, only when the timbers start.

32

Not see? because of night perhaps?—why, day
Came back again for that! before it left,
The dying sunset kindled through a cleft:
The hills, like giants at a hunting, lay,   190
Chin upon hand, to see the game at bay—
"Now stab and end the creature—to the heft!"[2]

33

Not hear? when noise was everywhere! it tolled
Increasing like a bell. Names in my ears
Of all the lost adventurers my peers—   195
How such a one was strong, and such was bold,
And such was fortunate, yet each of old
Lost, lost! one moment knelled the woe of years.

34

There they stood, ranged along the hillsides, met
To view the last of me, a living frame   200
For one more picture! in a sheet of flame
I saw them and I knew them all. And yet
Dauntless the slug-horn[3] to my lips I set,
And blew. *"Childe Roland to the Dark Tower came."*

1852   1855

---

1. Moment.
2. Handle of dagger or sword.
3. A trumpet, probably made from the horn of an ox.

Up at a Villa—Down in the City

(AS DISTINGUISHED BY AN ITALIAN PERSON OF QUALITY)

1
Had I but plenty of money, money enough and to spare,
The house for me, no doubt, were a house in the city square;
Ah, such a life, such a life, as one leads at the window there!

2
Something to see, by Bacchus, something to hear, at least!
There, the whole day long, one's life is a perfect feast;
While up at a villa one lives, I maintain it, no more than a beast. 5

3
Well now, look at our villa! stuck like the horn of a bull
Just on a mountain edge as bare as the creature's skull,
Save a mere shag of a bush with hardly a leaf to pull!
—I scratch my own,[1] sometimes, to see if the hair's turned wool. 10

4
But the city, oh the city—the square with the houses! Why?
They are stone-faced, white as a curd, there's something to take the
    eye!
Houses in four straight lines, not a single front awry;
You watch who crosses and gossips, who saunters, who hurries by;
Green blinds, as a matter of course, to draw when the sun gets
    high;
And the shops with fanciful signs which are painted properly. 15

5
What of a villa? Though winter be over in March by rights,
'Tis May perhaps ere the snow shall have withered well off the
    heights:
You've the brown plowed land before, where the oxen steam and
    wheeze,
And the hills over-smoked behind by the faint gray olive trees. 20

6
Is it better in May, I ask you? You've summer all at once;
In a day he leaps complete with a few strong April suns.
'Mid the sharp short emerald wheat, scarce risen three fingers well,
The wild tulip, at end of its tube, blows out its great red bell
Like a thin clear bubble of blood, for the children to pick and
    sell. 25

7
Is it ever hot in the square? There's a fountain to spout and splash!
In the shade it sings and springs; in the shine such foam-bows flash
On the horses with curling fish-tails, that prance and paddle and
    pash

1. I.e., my own skull.

Round the lady atop in her conch—fifty gazers do not abash,
Though all that she wears is some weeds round her waist in a sort
   of sash.   30

8

All the year long at the villa, nothing to see though you linger,
Except yon cypress that points like death's lean lifted forefinger.
Some think fireflies pretty, when they mix i' the corn and mingle,
Or thrid[2] the stinking hemp till the stalks of it seem a-tingle.
Late August or early September, the stunning cicala is shrill,   35
And the bees keep their tiresome whine round the resinous firs on
   the hill.
Enough of the seasons—I spare you the months of the fever and
   chill.

9

Ere you open your eyes in the city, the blessed church bells begin:
No sooner the bells leave off than the diligence[3] rattles in:
You get the pick of the news, and it costs you never a pin.   40
By-and-by there's the traveling doctor gives pills, lets blood, draws
   teeth;
Or the Pulcinello-trumpet[4] breaks up the market beneath.
At the post office such a scene-picture[5]—the new play, piping hot!
And a notice how, only this morning, three liberal thieves[6] were
   shot.
Above it, behold the Archbishop's most fatherly of rebukes,   45
And beneath, with his crown and his lion, some little new law of
   the Duke's!
Or a sonnet with flowery marge, to the Reverend Don So-and-so
Who is Dante, Boccaccio, Petrarca, Saint Jerome, and Cicero,
"And moreover," (the sonnet goes rhyming) "the skirts of Saint
   Paul has reached,
Having preached us those six Lent-lectures more unctuous than
   ever he preached."   50
Noon strikes—here sweeps the procession; our Lady borne smiling
   and smart
With a pink gauze gown all spangles, and seven swords[7] stuck in
   her heart!
Bang-whang-whang goes the drum, tootle-te-tootle the fife;
No keeping one's haunches still: it's the greatest pleasure in life.

10

But bless you, it's dear—it's dear! fowls, wine, at double the rate. 55
They have clapped a new tax upon salt, and what oil pays passing
   the gate[8]
It's a horror to think of. And so, the villa for me, not the city!

---

2. Thread their way through.
3. Stagecoach.
4. Trumpet announcing the puppet show, in which Pulcinello is the clown.
5. Picture advertising a coming play.
6. The men were republicans, opposed to Austrian rule, but "thieves" in the eyes of the speaker.
7. The swords symbolize the seven sorrows of Our Lady, the Virgin Mary.
8. Inside the gates of the city, produce was subject to special taxes.

Beggars can scarcely be choosers: but still—ah, the pity, the pity!
Look, two and two go the priests, then the monks with cowls and
    sandals,   60
And the penitents dressed in white shirts, a-holding the yellow
    candles;
One, he carries a flag up straight, and another a cross with handles,
And the Duke's guard brings up the rear, for the better prevention
    of scandals:
Bang-whang-whang goes the drum, *tootle-te-tootle* the fife.
Oh, a day in the city square, there is no such pleasure in life!   65

                                        1855

Respectability

1

Dear, had the world in its caprice
    Deigned to proclaim "I know you both,
    Have recognized your plighted troth,
Am sponsor for you: live in peace!"—
How many precious months and years   5
    Of youth had passed, that speed so fast,
    Before we found it out at last,
The world, and what it fears?

2

How much of priceless life were spent
    With men that every virtue decks,   10
    And women models of their sex,
Society's true ornament—
Ere we dared wander, nights like this,
    Through wind and rain, and watch the Seine,
    And feel the Boulevard break again   15
To warmth and light and bliss?

3

I know! the world proscribes not love;
    Allows my fingers to caress
    Your lips' contour and downiness,
Provided it supply a glove.
The world's good word!—the Institute![1]   20
    Guizot receives Montalembert!
    Eh? Down the court three lampions[2] flare:
Put forward your best foot!

ca. 1852   1855

---

1. A building in Paris, which the lovers are approaching in their walk. The speaker is reminded that at a meeting of the French Academy, held in the Institute, occurred a glaring instance of the hypocrisy which he thinks is characteristic of all social relations.

In 1852, François Guizot had delivered a flowery speech of welcome in honor of Charles Montalembert, an author whom Guizot at heart despised.
2. Ornamental lamps illuminating the courtyard of the Institute.

Fra Lippo Lippi[1]

I am poor brother Lippo, by your leave!
You need not clap your torches to my face.
Zooks,[2] what's to blame? you think you see a monk!
What, 'tis past midnight, and you go the rounds,
And here you catch me at an alley's end   5
Where sportive ladies leave their doors ajar?
The Carmine's[3] my cloister: hunt it up,
Do—harry out, if you must show your zeal,
Whatever rat, there, haps on his wrong hole,
And nip each softling of a wee white mouse,   10
Weke, weke, that's crept to keep him company!
Aha, you know your betters! Then, you'll take
Your hand away that's fiddling on my throat,
And please to know me likewise. Who am I?
Why, one, sir, who is lodging with a friend   15
Three streets off—he's a certain . . . how d'ye call?
Master—a . . . Cosimo of the Medici,[4]
I' the house that caps the corner. Boh! you were best!
Remember and tell me, the day you're hanged,
How you affected such a gullet's gripe![5]   20
But you,[6] sir, it concerns you that your knaves
Pick up a manner nor discredit you:
Zooks, are we pilchards,[7] that they sweep the streets
And count fair prize what comes into their net?
He's Judas to a tittle, that man is![8]   25
Just such a face! Why, sir, you make amends.
Lord, I'm not angry! Bid your hangdogs go
Drink out this quarter-florin to the health
Of the munificent House that harbors me
(And many more beside, lads! more beside!)   30
And all's come square again. I'd like his face—
His, elbowing on his comrade in the door

1. This monologue portrays the dawn
of the Renaissance in Italy at a point
when the medieval attitude towards life
and art was about to be displaced by
a fresh appreciation of earthly pleasures. It was from Giorgio Vasari's *Lives
of the Painters* that Browning derived
most of his information about the life
of the Florentine painter and friar,
Lippo Lippi (1406–69), but the theory
of art propounded by Lippi in the poem
was developed by the poet himself.
Browning's own partiality for this poem
may be attributed, in part, to his having
identified himself with his hero, an artist whose aesthetic principles made him
a misfit among his more pharisaical
contemporaries.

2. A shortened version of "Gadzooks,"
a mild oath now obscure in meaning
but perhaps resembling a phrase still
in use: "God's truth."
3. Italian for "Carmelite," an order of
mendicant friars to which Lippi belongs.
4. Lippi's patron, banker and virtual
ruler of Florence.
5. I.e., how you had the arrogance to
choke the gullet of someone with my
connections.
6. The officer in charge of the patrol
of policemen or watchmen.
7. Small fish.
8. I.e., one of the watchmen has a
face that would serve as a model for
a painting of Judas.

With the pike and lantern—for the slave that holds
John Baptist's head a-dangle by the hair
With one hand ("Look you, now," as who should say)   35
And his weapon in the other, yet unwiped!
It's not your chance to have a bit of chalk,
A wood-coal or the like? or you should see!
Yes, I'm the painter, since you style me so.
What, brother Lippo's doings, up and down,   40
You know them and they take you? like enough!
I saw the proper twinkle in your eye—
'Tell you, I liked your looks at very first.
Let's sit and set things straight now, hip to haunch.
Here's spring come, and the nights one makes up bands   45
To roam the town and sing out carnival,⁹
And I've been three weeks shut within my mew,¹
A-painting for the great man, saints and saints
And saints again. I could not paint all night—
Ouf! I leaned out of window for fresh air.   50
There came a hurry of feet and little feet,
A sweep of lute-strings, laughs, and whifts of song—
Flower o' the broom,
Take away love, and our earth is a tomb!
Flower o' the quince,   55
*I let Lisa go, and what good in life since?*²
Flower o' the thyme—and so on. Round they went.
Scarce had they turned the corner when a titter
Like the skipping of rabbits by moonlight—three slim shapes,
And a face that looked up . . . zooks, sir, flesh and blood, 60
That's all I'm made of! Into shreds it went,
Curtain and counterpane and coverlet,
All the bed-furniture—a dozen knots,
There was a ladder! Down I let myself,
Hands and feet, scrambling somehow, and so dropped,   65
And after them. I came up with the fun
Hard by Saint Laurence,³ hail fellow, well met—
Flower o' the rose,
If I've been merry, what matter who knows?
And so as I was stealing back again   70
To get to bed and have a bit of sleep
Ere I rise up tomorrow and go work
On Jerome knocking at his poor old breast
With his great round stone to subdue the flesh,⁴
You snap me of the sudden. Ah, I see!   75
Though your eye twinkles still, you shake your head—
Mine's shaved—a monk, you say—the sting's in that!
If Master Cosimo announced himself,

---

9. Season of revelry before the commencement of Lent.
1. Private den.
2. This and other interspersed flower-
songs are called *stornelli* in Italy.

3. San Lorenzo, a church in Florence.
4. A picture of St. Jerome (ca. 340–
420), whose ascetic observances were
hardly a congenial subject for such a
painter as Lippi.

Mum's the word naturally; but a monk!
Come, what am I a beast for? tell us, now!   80
I was a baby when my mother died
And father died and left me in the street.
I starved there, God knows how, a year or two
On fig skins, melon parings, rinds and shucks,
Refuse and rubbish. One fine frosty day,   85
My stomach being empty as your hat,
The wind doubled me up and down I went.
Old Aunt Lapaccia trussed me with one hand
(Its fellow was a stinger as I knew),
And so along the wall, over the bridge,   90
By the straight cut to the convent. Six words there,
While I stood munching my first bread that month:
"So, boy, you're minded," quoth the good fat father
Wiping his own mouth, 'twas refection time[5]—
"To quit this very miserable world?   95
Will you renounce" . . . . "the mouthful of bread?" thought I;
By no means! Brief, they made a monk of me;
I did renounce the world, its pride and greed,
Palace, farm, villa, shop, and banking house,
Trash, such as these poor devils of Medici   100
Have given their hearts to—all at eight years old.
Well, sir, I found in time, you may be sure,
'Twas not for nothing—the good bellyful,
The warm serge and the rope that goes all round,
And day-long blessed idleness beside!   105
"Let's see what the urchin's fit for"—that came next.
Not overmuch their way, I must confess.
Such a to-do! They tried me with their books:
Lord, they'd have taught me Latin in pure waste!
Flower o' the clove,   110
All the Latin I construe is "amo," I love!
But, mind you, when a boy starves in the streets
Eight years together, as my fortune was,
Watching folk's faces to know who will fling
The bit of half-stripped grape bunch he desires,   115
And who will curse or kick him for his pains—
Which gentleman processional and fine,
Holding a candle to the Sacrament,
Will wink and let him lift a plate and catch
The droppings of the wax to sell again,   120
Or holla for the Eight[6] and have him whipped—
How say I?—nay, which dog bites, which lets drop
His bone from the heap of offal in the street—
Why, soul and sense of him grow sharp alike,
He learns the look of things, and none the less   125
For admonition from the hunger-pinch.
I had a store of such remarks, be sure,

5. Mealtime.   6. Florentine magistrates.

Which, after I found leisure, turned to use.
I drew men's faces on my copybooks,
Scrawled them within the antiphonary's marge,[7]   130
Joined legs and arms to the long music-notes,
Found eyes and nose and chin for A's and B's,
And made a string of pictures of the world
Betwixt the ins and outs of verb and noun,
On the wall, the bench, the door. The monks looked black.   135
"Nay," quoth the Prior,[8] "turn him out, d' ye say?
In no wise. Lose a crow and catch a lark.
What if at last we get our man of parts,
We Carmelites, like those Camaldolese
And Preaching Friars,[9] to do our church up fine   140
And put the front on it that ought to be!"
And hereupon he bade me daub away.
Thank you! my head being crammed, the walls a blank,
Never was such prompt disemburdening.
First, every sort of monk, the black and white,   145
I drew them, fat and lean: then, folk at church,
From good old gossips waiting to confess
Their cribs of barrel droppings, candle ends—
To the breathless fellow at the altar-foot,
Fresh from his murder, safe and sitting there   150
With the little children round him in a row
Of admiration, half for his beard and half
For that white anger of his victim's son
Shaking a fist at him with one fierce arm,
Signing himself with the other because of Christ   155
(Whose sad face on the cross sees only this
After the passion[1] of a thousand years)
Till some poor girl, her apron o'er her head
(Which the intense eyes looked through), came at eve
On tiptoe, said a word, dropped in a loaf,   160
Her pair of earrings and a bunch of flowers
(The brute took growling), prayed, and so was gone.
I painted all, then cried " 'Tis ask and have;
Choose, for more's ready!"—laid the ladder flat,
And showed my covered bit of cloister wall.   165
The monks closed in a circle and praised loud
Till checked, taught what to see and not to see,
Being simple bodies—"That's the very man!
Look at the boy who stoops to pat the dog!
That woman's like the Prior's niece who comes   170
To care about his asthma: it's the life!"
But there my triumph's straw-fire flared and funked;[2]
Their betters took their turn to see and say:
The Prior and the learned pulled a face

7. Margin of music book used for   gious orders, respectively.
choral singing.   1. Sufferings.
8. Head of a Carmelite convent.   2. Went up in smoke.
9. Benedictine and Dominican reli-

And stopped all that in no time. "How? what's here?   175
Quite from the mark of painting, bless us all!
Faces, arms, legs and bodies like the true
As much as pea and pea! it's devil's game!
Your business is not to catch men with show,
With homage to the perishable clay,   180
But lift them over it, ignore it all,
Make them forget there's such a thing as flesh.
Your business is to paint the souls of men—
Man's soul, and it's a fire, smoke . . . no, it's not . . .
It's vapor done up like a newborn babe—   185
(In that shape when you die it leaves your mouth)
It's . . . well, what matters talking, it's the soul!
Give us no more of body than shows soul!
Here's Giotto,[3] with his Saint a-praising God,
That sets us praising—why not stop with him?   190
Why put all thoughts of praise out of our head
With wonder at lines, colors, and what not?
Paint the soul, never mind the legs and arms!
Rub all out, try at it a second time.
Oh, that white smallish female with the breasts,   195
She's just my niece . . . Herodias,[4] I would say—
Who went and danced and got men's heads cut off!
Have it all out!" Now, is this sense, I ask?
A fine way to paint soul, by painting body
So ill, the eye can't stop there, must go further   200
And can't fare worse! Thus, yellow does for white
When what you put for yellow's simply black,
And any sort of meaning looks intense
When all beside itself means and looks naught.
Why can't a painter lift each foot in turn,   205
Left foot and right foot, go a double step,
Make his flesh liker and his soul more like,
Both in their order? Take the prettiest face,
The Prior's niece . . . patron-saint—is it so pretty
You can't discover if it means hope, fear,   210
Sorrow or joy? won't beauty go with these?
Suppose I've made her eyes all right and blue,
Can't I take breath and try to add life's flash,
And then add soul and heighten them threefold?
Or say there's beauty with no soul at all—   215
(I never saw it—put the case the same—)
If you get simple beauty and naught else,
You get about the best thing God invents:
That's somewhat: and you'll find the soul you have missed,
Within yourself, when you return him thanks.   220

3. Great Florentine painter (1276–
1337), whose stylized pictures of religious subjects were admired as models
of pre-Renaissance art.
4. See Matthew, xiv.1–12, for an ac-

count of John the Baptist's execution
after he had aroused the displeasure of
Herodias, sister-in-law of King Herod.
It was her daughter, Salome, who performed the dance.

"Rub all out!" Well, well, there's my life, in short,
And so the thing has gone on ever since.
I'm grown a man no doubt, I've broken bounds:
You should not take a fellow eight years old
And make him swear to never kiss the girls.   225
I'm my own master, paint now as I please—
Having a friend, you see, in the Corner-house!5
Lord, it's fast holding by the rings in front—
Those great rings serve more purposes than just
To plant a flag in, or tie up a horse!   230
And yet the old schooling sticks, the old grave eyes
Are peeping o'er my shoulder as I work,
The heads shake still—"It's art's decline, my son!
You're not of the true painters, great and old;
Brother Angelico's the man, you'll find;   235
Brother Lorenzo stands his single peer:6
Fag on at flesh, you'll never make the third!"
Flower o' the pine,
You keep your mistr . . . . manners, and I'll stick to mine!
I'm not the third, then: bless us, they must know!   240
Don't you think they're the likeliest to know,
They with their Latin? So, I swallow my rage,
Clench my teeth, suck my lips in tight, and paint
To please them—sometimes do and sometimes don't;
For, doing most, there's pretty sure to come   245
A turn, some warm eve finds me at my saints—
A laugh, a cry, the business of the world—
(*Flower o' the peach,*
Death for us all, and his own life for each!)
And my whole soul revolves, the cup runs over,   250
The world and life's too big to pass for a dream,
And I do these wild things in sheer despite,
And play the fooleries you catch me at,
In pure rage! The old mill-horse, out at grass
After hard years, throws up his stiff heels so,   255
Although the miller does not preach to him
The only good of grass is to make chaff.7
What would men have? Do they like grass or no—
May they or mayn't they? all I want's the thing
Settled forever one way. As it is,   260
You tell too many lies and hurt yourself:
You don't like what you only like too much,
You do like what, if given you at your word,
You find abundantly detestable.
For me, I think I speak as I was taught;   265
I always see the garden and God there
A-making man's wife: and, my lesson learned,

5. The Medici palace.
6. Fra Angelico (1387–1455) and Lorenzo Monaco (1370–1425), whose

paintings were in the approved traditional manner.
7. Straw.

The value and significance of flesh,
I can't unlearn ten minutes afterwards.

    You understand me: I'm a beast, I know.   270
But see, now—why, I see as certainly
As that the morning star's about to shine,
What will hap some day. We've a youngster here
Comes to our convent, studies what I do,
Slouches and stares and lets no atom drop: 275
His name is Guidi[8]—he'll not mind the monks—
They call him Hulking Tom, he lets them talk—
He picks my practice up—he'll paint apace,
I hope so—though I never live so long,
I know what's sure to follow. You be judge!   280
You speak no Latin more than I, belike;
However, you're my man, you've seen the world
—The beauty and the wonder and the power,
The shapes of things, their colors, lights and shades,
Changes, surprises—and God made it all!   285
—For what? Do you feel thankful, aye or no,
For this fair town's face, yonder river's line,
The mountain round it and the sky above,
Much more the figures of man, woman, child,
These are the frame to? What's it all about?   290
To be passed over, despised? or dwelt upon,
Wondered at? oh, this last of course!—you say.
But why not do as well as say—paint these
Just as they are, careless what comes of it?
God's works—paint any one, and count it crime   295
To let a truth slip. Don't object, "His works
Are here already; nature is complete:
Suppose you reproduce her—(which you can't)
There's no advantage! You must beat her, then."
For, don't you mark? we're made so that we love   300
First when we see them painted, things we have passed
Perhaps a hundred times nor cared to see;
And so they are better, painted—better to us,
Which is the same thing. Art was given for that;
God uses us to help each other so,   305
Lending our minds out. Have you noticed, now,
Your cullion's[9] hanging face? A bit of chalk,
And trust me but you should, though! How much more,
If I drew higher things with the same truth!
That were to take the Prior's pulpit-place,   310
Interpret God to all of you! Oh, oh,
It makes me mad to see what men shall do
And we in our graves! This world's no blot for us,
Nor blank; it means intensely, and means good:

---

8. Guidi or Masaccio (1401–28), a painter who may have been Lippi's master rather than his pupil. Like Lippi he was in revolt against the medieval theory of art.
9. Rascal's.

To find its meaning is my meat and drink.   315
"Aye, but you don't so instigate to prayer!"
Strikes in the Prior: "when your meaning's plain
It does not say to folk—remember matins,
Or, mind you fast next Friday!" Why, for this
What need of art at all? A skull and bones,   320
Two bits of stick nailed crosswise, or, what's best,
A bell to chime the hour with, does as well.
I painted a Saint Laurence[1] six months since
At Prato, splashed the fresco in fine style:
"How looks my painting, now the scaffold's down?"   325
I ask a brother: "Hugely," he returns—
"Already not one phiz of your three slaves
Who turn the Deacon off his toasted side,
But's scratched and prodded to our heart's content,
The pious people have so eased their own   330
With coming to say prayers there in a rage:
We get on fast to see the bricks beneath.
Expect another job this time next year,
For pity and religion grow i' the crowd—
Your painting serves its purpose!" Hang the fools!   335

        —That is—you'll not mistake an idle word
Spoke in a huff by a poor monk, God wot,
Tasting the air this spicy night which turns
The unaccustomed head like Chianti wine!
Oh, the church knows! don't misreport me, now!   340
It's natural a poor monk out of bounds
Should have his apt word to excuse himself:
And hearken how I plot to make amends.
I have bethought me: I shall paint a piece
. . . There's for you! Give me six months, then go, see   345
Something in Sant' Ambrogio's![2] Bless the nuns!
They want a cast o' my office.[3] I shall paint
God in the midst, Madonna and her babe,
Ringed by a bowery flowery angel brood,
Lilies and vestments and white faces, sweet   350
As puff on puff of grated orris-root
When ladies crowd to Church at midsummer.
And then i' the front, of course a saint or two—
Saint John, because he saves the Florentines,
Saint Ambrose, who puts down in black and white   355
The convent's friends and gives them a long day,
And Job, I must have him there past mistake,
The man of Uz (and Us without the z,
Painters who need his patience). Well, all these
Secured at their devotion, up shall come   360

1. A scene representing the fiery martyr- 2. A convent church in Florence.
dom of Saint Laurence; a "fresco" is   3. Sample of my work. The completed
painted quickly on fresh plaster over   painting, which Browning saw in Flor-
a surface of bricks. Prato is a town   ence, is Lippi's "Coronation of the
near Florence.   Virgin."

Out of a corner when you least expect,
As one by a dark stair into a great light,
Music and talking, who but Lippo! I!—
Mazed, motionless and moonstruck—I'm the man!
Back I shrink—what is this I see and hear?   365
I, caught up with my monk's things by mistake,
My old serge gown and rope that goes all round,
I, in this presence, this pure company!
Where's a hole, where's a corner for escape?
Then steps a sweet angelic slip of a thing   370
Forward, puts out a soft palm—"Not so fast!"
—Addresses the celestial presence, "nay—
He made you and devised you, after all,
Though he's none of you! Could Saint John there draw—
His camel-hair⁴ make up a painting-brush?   375
We come to brother Lippo for all that,
Iste perfecit opus!"⁵ So, all smile—
I shuffle sideways with my blushing face
Under the cover of a hundred wings
Thrown like a spread of kirtles⁶ when you're gay   380
And play hot cockles,⁷ all the doors being shut,
Till, wholly unexpected, in there pops
The hothead husband! Thus I scuttle off
To some safe bench behind, not letting go
The palm of her, the little lily thing   385
That spoke the good word for me in the nick,
Like the Prior's niece . . . Saint Lucy, I would say.
And so all's saved for me, and for the church
A pretty picture gained. Go, six months hence!
Your hand, sir, and good-by: no lights, no lights!   390
The street's hushed, and I know my own way back,
Don't fear me! There's the gray beginning. Zooks!
ca. 1853   1855

In a Year

1

Never any more,
    While I live,
Need I hope to see his face
    As before.
Once his love grown chill,   5
    Mine may strive:
Bitterly we re-embrace,
    Single still.

4. "And John was clothed with camel's
hair" (Mark i.6).
5. "This man made the work." In this
painting, as later completed, these
words appear beside a figure which
Browning took to be Lippi's self-portrait.
6. Skirts.
7. A game in which a player wears a
blindfold.

2

Was it something said,
    Something done,
Vexed him? was it touch of hand,
    Turn of head?
Strange! that very way
    Love begun:
I as little understand
    Love's decay.

3

When I sewed or drew,
    I recall
How he looked as if I sung
    —Sweetly too.
If I spoke a word,
    First of all
Up his cheek the color sprung,
    Then he heard.

4

Sitting by my side,
    At my feet,
So he breathed but air I breathed,
    Satisfied!
I, too, at love's brim
    Touched the sweet:
I would die if death bequeathed
    Sweet to him.

5

"Speak, I love thee best!"
    He exclaimed:
"Let thy love my own foretell!"
    I confessed:
"Clasp my heart on thine
    Now unblamed,
Since upon thy soul as well
    Hangeth mine!"

6

Was it wrong to own,
    Being truth?
Why should all the giving prove
    His alone?
I had wealth and ease,
    Beauty, youth:
Since my lover gave me love,
    I gave these.

7

That was all I meant
    —To be just,
And the passion I had raised,
    To content.

Since he chose to change
    Gold for dust,
If I gave him what he praised   55
    Was it strange?

8

Would he loved me yet,
    On and on,
While I found some way undreamed
    —Paid my debt!   60
Gave more life and more,
    Till, all gone,
He should smile, "She never seemed
    Mine before.

9

"What, she felt the while,   65
    Must I think?
Love's so different with us men!"
    He should smile:
"Dying for my sake—
    White and pink!   70
Can't we touch these bubbles then
    But they break?"

10

Dear, the pang is brief,
    Do thy part,
Have thy pleasure! How perplexed   75
    Grows belief!
Well, this cold clay clod
    Was man's heart:
Crumble it, and what comes next?
    Is it God?   80

          1855

The Last Ride Together

1

I said—Then, dearest, since 'tis so,
Since now at length my fate I know,
Since nothing all my love avails,
Since all, my life seemed meant for, fails,
    Since this was written and needs must be—   5
My whole heart rises up to bless
Your name in pride and thankfulness!
Take back the hope you gave—I claim
Only a memory of the same,
—And this beside, if you will not blame,   10
    Your leave for one more last ride with me.

2

My mistress bent that brow of hers;
Those deep dark eyes where pride demurs
When pity would be softening through,
Fixed me a breathing-while or two   15
     With life or death in the balance: right!
The blood replenished me again;
My last thought was at least not vain:
I and my mistress, side by side
Shall be together, breathe and ride,   20
So, one day more am I deified.
     Who knows but the world may end tonight?

3

Hush! if you saw some western cloud
All billowy-bosomed, over-bowed
By many benedictions—sun's   25
And moon's and evening star's at once—
     And so, you, looking and loving best,
Conscious grew, your passion drew
Cloud, sunset, moonrise, star-shine too,
Down on you, near and yet more near,   30
Till flesh must fade for heaven was here!—
Thus leant she and lingered[1]—joy and fear!
     Thus lay she a moment on my breast.

4

Then we began to ride. My soul
Smoothed itself out, a long-cramped scroll   35
Freshening and fluttering in the wind.
Past hopes already lay behind.
     What need to strive with a life awry?
Had I said that, had I done this,
So might I gain, so might I miss.   40
Might she have loved me? just as well
She might have hated, who can tell!
Where had I been now if the worst befell?
     And here we are riding, she and I.

5

Fail I alone, in words and deeds?   45
Why, all men strive and who succeeds?
We rode; it seemed my spirit flew,
Saw other regions, cities new,
     As the world rushed by on either side.
I thought—All labor, yet no less   50
Bear up beneath their unsuccess.
Look at the end of work, contrast
The petty done, the undone vast,
This present of theirs with the hopeful past!
     I hoped she would love me; here we ride.   55

---

1. Before she mounts her horse.

6

What hand and brain went ever paired?
What heart alike conceived and dared?
What act proved all its thought had been?
What will but felt the fleshly screen?
    We ride and I see her bosom heave.   60
There's many a crown for who can reach.
Ten lines, a statesman's life in each![2]
The flag stuck on a heap of bones,
A soldier's doing! what atones?
They scratch his name on the Abbey stones.   65
    My riding is better, by their leave.

7

What does it all mean, poet? Well,
Your brains beat into rhythm, you tell
What we felt only; you expressed
You hold things beautiful the best,   70
    And pace them in rhyme so, side by side.
'Tis something, nay 'tis much: but then,
Have you yourself what's best for men?
Are you—poor, sick, old ere your time—
Nearer one whit your own sublime   75
Than we who never have turned a rhyme?
    Sing, riding's a joy! For me, I ride.

8

And you, great sculptor—so, you gave
A score of years to Art, her slave,
And that's your Venus, whence we turn   80
To yonder girl that fords the burn![3]
    You acquiesce, and shall I repine?
What, man of music, you grown gray
With notes and nothing else to say,
Is this your sole praise from a friend,   85
"Greatly his opera's strains intend,
But in music we know how fashions end!"
    I gave my youth; but we ride, in fine.[4]

9

Who knows what's fit for us? Had fate
Proposed bliss here should sublimate   90
My being—had I signed the bond—
Still one must lead some life beyond,
    Have a bliss to die with, dim-descried.
This foot once planted on the goal,
This glory-garland round my soul,   95
Could I descry such? Try and test!
I sink back shuddering from the quest.

2. If a man tries hard enough, he may be crowned with what seems to be success. He might become, for example, an eminent "statesman." Yet his only memorial would be a short sketch of his career ("ten lines") in some history or biographical dictionary.
3. Crosses the brook.
4. In short.

Earth being so good, would Heaven seem best?[5]
Now, Heaven and she are beyond this ride.

10

And yet—she has not spoke so long!   100
What if heaven be that, fair and strong
At life's best, with our eyes upturned
Whither life's flower is first discerned,
We, fixed so, ever should so abide?
What if we still ride on, we two   105
With life forever old yet new,
Changed not in kind but in degree,
The instant made eternity—
And heaven just prove that I and she
Ride, ride together, forever ride?   110

1855

Andrea del Sarto[1]

(CALLED "THE FAULTLESS PAINTER")

But do not let us quarrel any more,
No, my Lucrezia; bear with me for once:
Sit down and all shall happen as you wish.
You turn your face, but does it bring your heart?
I'll work then for your friend's friend, never fear,   5
Treat his own subject after his own way,
Fix his own time, accept too his own price,
And shut the money into this small hand
When next it takes mine. Will it? tenderly?
Oh, I'll content him—but tomorrow, Love!   10
I often am much wearier than you think,

5. If fate had decreed that he could possess his mistress fully, life on earth would have been so blissful that heaven could offer nothing for him to look forward to after death. Hence (he argues) to preserve "a bliss to die with" (line 93), it is better that she never really became his on earth.
1. This portrait of Andrea del Sarto (1486–1531) was derived from a biography written by his pupil, Giorgio Vasari, author of *The Lives of the Painters*. Vasari's account seeks to explain why this Florentine master, one of the most skillful painters of the Renaissance, never altogether fulfilled the promise he had shown early in his career and why he had never arrived (in Vasari's opinion) at the level of such artists as Raphael. Vasari noted that Andrea suffered from "a certain timidity of mind * * * which rendered it impossible that those evidences of ardor and animation, which are proper to the more exalted character, should

ever appear in him."
Browning also follows Vasari's account of Andrea's marriage to a beautiful widow, Lucrezia, "an artful woman who made him do as she pleased in all things." Vasari reports that Andrea's "immoderate love for her soon caused him to neglect the studies demanded by his art," and that this infatuation had "more influence over him than the glory and honor towards which he had begun to make such hopeful advances."
Browning's poem has often been praised for its exposition of a paradoxical theory of success and failure, but it has other qualities as well. Its slow-paced, enervated blank-verse line, its setting of a quiet evening in autumn, its comparative lack of the movement and noise that we expect in Browning's energetic verse create a unity of impression that is unobtrusive yet effective.

This evening more than usual, and it seems
As if—forgive now—should you let me sit
Here by the window with your hand in mine
And look a half-hour forth on Fiesole,[2]   15
Both of one mind, as married people use,
Quietly, quietly the evening through,
I might get up tomorrow to my work
Cheerful and fresh as ever. Let us try.
Tomorrow, how you shall be glad for this!   20
Your soft hand is a woman of itself,
And mine the man's bared breast she curls inside.
Don't count the time lost, neither; you must serve
For each of the five pictures we require:
It saves a model. So! keep looking so—   25
My serpentining beauty, rounds on rounds![3]
—How could you ever prick those perfect ears,
Even to put the pearl there! oh, so sweet—
My face, my moon, my everybody's moon,
Which everybody looks on and calls his,   30
And, I suppose, is looked on by in turn,
While she looks—no one's: very dear, no less.[4]
You smile? why, there's my picture ready made,
There's what we painters call our harmony!
A common grayness silvers everything[5]—   35
All in a twilight, you and I alike
—You, at the point of your first pride in me
(That's gone you know)—but I, at every point;
My youth, my hope, my art, being all toned down
To yonder sober pleasant Fiesole.   40
There's the bell clinking from the chapel top;
That length of convent wall across the way
Holds the trees safer, huddled more inside;
The last monk leaves the garden; days decrease,
And autumn grows, autumn in everything.   45
Eh? the whole seems to fall into a shape
As if I saw alike my work and self
And all that I was born to be and do,
A twilight-piece. Love, we are in God's hand.
How strange now, looks the life he makes us lead;   50
So free we seem, so fettered fast we are!
I feel he laid the fetter: let it lie!
This chamber for example—turn your head—
All that's behind us! You don't understand
Nor care to understand about my art,   55
But you can hear at least when people speak:
And that cartoon,[6] the second from the door

2. A suburb on the hills overlooking Florence.
3. Coils of hair like the coils of a serpent.
4. Her affections are centered upon no one person, not even upon her husband.
yet she is nevertheless dear to him. Cf. *My Last Duchess*, lines 23–24.
5. The predominant color in many of Andrea's paintings is silver gray.
6. Drawing.

—It is the thing, Love! so such things should be—
Behold Madonna!—I am bold to say.
I can do with my pencil what I know,   60
What I see, what at bottom of my heart
I wish for, if I ever wish so deep—
Do easily, too—when I say, perfectly,
I do not boast, perhaps: yourself are judge,
Who listened to the Legate's[7] talk last week,   65
And just as much they used to say in France.
At any rate 'tis easy, all of it!
No sketches first, no studies, that's long past:
I do what many dream of, all their lives,
—Dream? strive to do, and agonize to do,   70
And fail in doing. I could count twenty such
On twice your fingers, and not leave this town,
Who strive—you don't know how the others strive
To paint a little thing like that you smeared
Carelessly passing with your robes afloat—   75
Yet do much less, so much less, Someone[8] says
(I know his name, no matter)—so much less!
Well, less is more, Lucrezia: I am judged.
There burns a truer light of God in them,
In their vexed beating stuffed and stopped-up brain,   80
Heart, or whate'er else, than goes on to prompt
This low-pulsed forthright craftsman's hand of mine.
Their works drop groundward, but themselves, I know,
Reach many a time a heaven that's shut to me,
Enter and take their place there sure enough,   85
Though they come back and cannot tell the world.
My works are nearer heaven, but I sit here.
The sudden blood of these men! at a word—
Praise them, it boils, or blame them, it boils too.
I, painting from myself and to myself,   90
Know what I do, am unmoved by men's blame
Or their praise either. Somebody remarks
Morello's[9] outline there is wrongly traced,
His hue mistaken; what of that? or else,
Rightly traced and well ordered; what of that?   95
Speak as they please, what does the mountain care?
Ah, but a man's reach should exceed his grasp,
Or what's a heaven for? All is silver-gray
Placid and perfect with my art: the worse!
I know both what I want and what might gain,   100
And yet how profitless to know, to sigh
"Had I been two, another and myself,
Our head would have o'erlooked the world!"[1] No doubt.
Yonder's a work now, of that famous youth

7. A deputy of the Pope.
8. Probably Michelangelo (1475–1564).
9. A mountain peak outside Florence.
1. I.e., if I had been both an aspiring,

dedicated, and soul-conscious artist as well as a faultless craftsman, the combination would have been unsurpassable. See also line 140 ("we half-men").

The Urbinate[2] who died five years ago.   105
('Tis copied, George Vasari sent it me.)[3]
Well, I can fancy how he did it all,
Pouring his soul, with kings and popes to see,
Reaching, that heaven might so replenish him,
Above and through his art—for it gives way;   110
That arm is wrongly put—and there again—
A fault to pardon in the drawing's lines,
Its body, so to speak: its soul is right,
He means right—that, a child may understand.
Still, what an arm! and I could alter it: 115
But all the play, the insight and the stretch—
Out of me, out of me! And wherefore out?
Had you enjoined them on me, given me soul,
We might have risen to Rafael, I and you!
Nay, Love, you did give all I asked, I think—   120
More than I merit, yes, by many times.
But had you—oh, with the same perfect brow,
And perfect eyes, and more than perfect mouth,
And the low voice my soul hears, as a bird
The fowler's pipe,[4] and follows to the snare—   125
Had you, with these the same, but brought a mind!
Some women do so. Had the mouth there urged
"God and the glory! never care for gain.
The present by the future, what is that?
Live for fame, side by side with Agnolo![5]   130
Rafael is waiting: up to God, all three!"
I might have done it for you. So it seems:
Perhaps not. All is as God overrules.
Beside, incentives come from the soul's self;
The rest avail not. Why do I need you?   135
What wife had Rafael, or has Agnolo?
In this world, who can do a thing, will not;
And who would do it, cannot, I perceive:
Yet the will's somewhat—somewhat, too, the power—
And thus we half-men struggle. At the end,   140
God, I conclude, compensates, punishes.
'Tis safer for me, if the award be strict,
That I am something underrated here.
Poor this long while, despised, to speak the truth.
I dared not, do you know, leave home all day,   145
For fear of chancing on the Paris lords.
The best is when they pass and look aside;
But they speak sometimes; I must bear it all.
Well may they speak! That Francis,[6] that first time,

2. Raphael (1483–1520), born at Ur-
bino.
3. In saying that the painting is a
copy, Andrea may perhaps be concerned
to prevent Lucrezia from selling it.
4. Whistle or call used by hunters to
lure wildfowl into range.

5. Michelangelo.
6. King Francis I of France had invited Andrea to his court at Fontainebleau and warmly encouraged him in
his painting. On returning to Florence,
however, Andrea is reputed to have
stolen some funds entrusted to him by

And that long festal year at Fontainebleau! 150
I surely then could sometimes leave the ground,
Put on the glory, Rafael's daily wear,
In that humane great monarch's golden look—
One finger in his beard or twisted curl
Over his mouth's good mark that made the smile, 155
One arm about my shoulder, round my neck,
The jingle of his gold chain in my ear,
I painting proudly with his breath on me,
All his court round him, seeing with his eyes,
Such frank French eyes, and such a fire of souls 160
Profuse, my hand kept plying by those hearts—
And, best of all, this, this, this face beyond,
This in the background, waiting on my work,
To crown the issue with a last reward!
A good time, was it not, my kingly days? 165
And had you not grown restless . . . but I know—
'Tis done and past; 'twas right, my instinct said;
Too live the life grew, golden and not gray,
And I'm the weak-eyed bat no sun should tempt
Out of the grange whose four walls make his world.[7] 170
How could it end in any other way?
You called me, and I came home to your heart.
The triumph was—to reach and stay there; since
I reached it ere the triumph, what is lost?
Let my hands frame your face in your hair's gold, 175
You beautiful Lucrezia that are mine!
"Rafael did this, Andrea painted that;
The Roman's is the better when you pray,
But still the other's Virgin was his wife—"
Men will excuse me. I am glad to judge 180
Both pictures in your presence; clearer grows
My better fortune, I resolve to think.
For, do you know, Lucrezia, as God lives,
Said one day Agnolo, his very self,
To Rafael . . . I have known it all these years . . . 185
(When the young man was flaming out his thoughts
Upon a palace wall for Rome to see,
Too lifted up in heart because of it)
"Friend, there's a certain sorry little scrub
Goes up and down our Florence, none cares how, 190
Who, were he set to plan and execute
As you are, pricked on by your popes and kings,
Would bring the sweat into that brow of yours!"
To Rafael's—And indeed the arm is wrong.
I hardly dare . . . yet, only you to see, 195

Francis, and to please Lucrezia he built
a house with the money. Now he is
afraid of being insulted by "Paris lords"
on the streets.
7. The bat, a creature of evening,
thrives best in the confines of the
"four walls" of a farm building
("grange"). See also line 261 in which
Andrea thinks of heaven as a place of
four walls.

Give the chalk here—quick, thus the line should go!
Aye, but the soul! he's Rafael! rub it out!
Still, all I care for, if he spoke the truth,
(What he? why, who but Michel Agnolo?
Do you forget already words like those?)   200
If really there was such a chance, so lost—
Is, whether you're—not grateful—but more pleased.
Well, let me think so. And you smile indeed!
This hour has been an hour! Another smile?
If you would sit thus by me every night   205
I should work better, do you comprehend?
I mean that I should earn more, give you more.
See, it is settled dusk now; there's a star;
Morello's gone, the watch-lights show the wall,
The cue-owls[8] speak the name we call them by.   210
Come from the window, love—come in, at last,
Inside the melancholy little house
We built to be so gay with. God is just.
King Francis may forgive me: oft at nights
When I look up from painting, eyes tired out,   215
The walls become illumined, brick from brick
Distinct, instead of mortar, fierce bright gold,
That gold of his I did cement them with!
Let us but love each other. Must you go?
That Cousin here again? he waits outside?   220
Must see you—you, and not with me? Those loans?
More gaming debts to pay?[9] you smiled for that?
Well, let smiles buy me! have you more to spend?
While hand and eye and something of a heart
Are left me, work's my ware, and what's it worth? 225
I'll pay my fancy. Only let me sit
The gray remainder of the evening out,
Idle, you call it, and muse perfectly
How I could paint, were I but back in France,
One picture, just one more—the Virgin's face,   230
Not yours this time! I want you at my side
To hear them—that is, Michel Agnolo—
Judge all I do and tell you of its worth.
Will you? Tomorrow, satisfy your friend.
I take the subjects for his corridor,   235
Finish the portrait out of hand—there, there,
And throw him in another thing or two
If he demurs; the whole should prove enough
To pay for this same Cousin's freak. Beside,
What's better and what's all I care about,   240
Get you the thirteen scudi[1] for the ruff!

8. An owl whose cry sounds like the Italian word *ciù*.
9. Lucrezia's "Cousin" (or lover or "friend") owes gambling debts to a creditor. Andrea has already contracted (lines 5–10) to pay off these debts by painting some pictures according to the creditor's specifications. Now he agrees to pay off further debts.
1. Italian coins.

Love, does that please you? Ah, but what does he,
The Cousin! What does he to please you more?

I am grown peaceful as old age tonight.
I regret little, I would change still less.   245
Since there my past life lies, why alter it?
The very wrong to Francis!—it is true
I took his coin, was tempted and complied,
And built this house and sinned, and all is said.
My father and my mother died of want.[2]   250
Well, had I riches of my own? you see
How one gets rich! Let each one bear his lot.
They were born poor, lived poor, and poor they died:
And I have labored somewhat in my time
And not been paid profusely. Some good son   255
Paint my two hundred pictures—let him try!
No doubt, there's something strikes a balance. Yes,
You loved me quite enough, it seems tonight.
This must suffice me here. What would one have?
In heaven, perhaps, new chances, one more chance—   260
Four great walls in the New Jerusalem,
Meted on each side by the angel's reed,[3]
For Leonard,[4] Rafael, Agnolo and me
To cover—the three first without a wife,
While I have mine! So—still they overcome   265
Because there's still Lucrezia—as I choose.

Again the Cousin's whistle! Go, my Love.
ca. 1853   1855

Two in the Campagna[1]

1

I wonder do you feel today
        As I have felt since, hand in hand,
We sat down on the grass, to stray
        In spirit better through the land,
This morn of Rome and May?   5

2

For me, I touched a thought, I know,
        Has tantalized me many times,
(Like turns of thread the spiders throw
        Mocking across our path) for rhymes
To catch at and let go.   10

2. According to Vasari, Andrea's infatuation for Lucrezia prompted him
to stop supporting his poverty-stricken
parents.
3. Measuring rod. For "New Jerusalem," see Revelation xxi.10–21.

4. Leonardo da Vinci (1452–1519).
1. The Campagna is the name for the
level plains and pasture lands near
Rome where the ruins of ancient cities
are overrun with wild flowers.

3
Help me to hold it! First it left
    The yellowing fennel,[2] run to seed
There, branching from the brickwork's cleft,
    Some old tomb's ruin: yonder weed
Took up the floating weft,[3]   15

4
Where one small orange cup amassed
    Five beetles—blind and green they grope
Among the honey-meal: and last,
    Everywhere on the grassy slope
I traced it. Hold it fast!   20

5
The champaign[4] with its endless fleece
    Of feathery grasses everywhere!
Silence and passion, joy and peace,
    An everlasting wash of air—
Rome's ghost since her decease.   25

6
Such life here, through such lengths of hours,
    Such miracles performed in play,
Such primal naked forms of flowers,
    Such letting nature have her way
While heaven looks from its towers!   30

7
How say you? Let us, O my dove,
    Let us be unashamed of soul,
As earth lies bare to heaven above!
    How is it under our control
To love or not to love?   35

8
I would that you were all to me,
    You that are just so much, no more.
Nor yours nor mine, nor slave nor free!
    Where does the fault lie? What the core
O' the wound, since wound must be?   40

9
I would I could adopt your will,
    See with your eyes, and set my heart
Beating by yours, and drink my fill
    At your soul's springs—your part my part
In life, for good and ill.   45

10
No. I yearn upward, touch you close,
    Then stand away. I kiss your cheek,
Catch your soul's warmth—I pluck the rose
    And love it more than tongue can speak—
Then the good minute goes.   50

2. A yellow-flowered plant from which
a pungent spice is derived.
3. Threads crossing from side to side
of a web.
4. Here, the Campagna.

11

Already how am I so far
    Out of that minute? Must I go
Still like the thistle-ball, no bar,
    Onward, whenever light winds blow,
Fixed by no friendly star?   55

12

Just when I seemed about to learn!
    Where is the thread now? Off again!
The old trick! Only I discern—
    Infinite passion, and the pain
Of finite hearts that yearn.   60

1854   1855

A Grammarian's Funeral[1]

SHORTLY AFTER THE REVIVAL OF LEARNING IN EUROPE

Let us begin and carry up this corpse,
    Singing together.
Leave we the common crofts, the vulgar thorpes[2]
    Each in its tether[3]
Sleeping safe on the bosom of the plain,   5
    Cared for till cock-crow:
Look out if yonder be not day again
    Rimming the rock-row!
That's the appropriate country; there, man's thought,
    Rarer, intenser,   10
Self-gathered for an outbreak, as it ought,
    Chafes in the censer.
Leave we the unlettered plain its herd and crop;[4]
    Seek we sepulture
On a tall mountain, citied to the top,   15
    Crowded with culture!
All the peaks soar, but one the rest excels;
    Clouds overcome it;
No! yonder sparkle is the citadel's
    Circling its summit.   20

1. The speaker is one of the students who are bearing the body of their scholarly master to the mountaintop for burial. The student's defense of the dead grammarian's idealistic dedication to knowledge and faith in a future life is expressed in some of the harshest-sounding and most laborious verse ever written by Browning. It is this grotesque combination of opposites (soaring idealism in conjunction with harsh or petty realities) that gives *A Grammarian's Funeral* its distinctive tone.
  No model for the grammarian has been specifically identified. Browning seems to have had in mind the kind of early Renaissance scholar whose devotion to the Greek language made it possible for others to enjoy the more recognizably significant aspects of the revival of learning.
2. "Crofts" are small tracts of land farmed by peasants; "thorpes" are villages.
3. Restricted to a narrow sphere like an animal tied to a stake.
4. Flatlands at the base of the mountain which are populated by illiterate shepherds and peasants. "Sepulture": burial place.

Thither our path lies; wind we up the heights:
    Wait ye the warning?
Our low life was the level's and the night's;
    He's for the morning.
Step to a tune, square chests, erect each head,   25
    'Ware[5] the beholders!
This is our master, famous, calm, and dead,
    Borne on our shoulders.

Sleep, crop and herd! sleep, darkling thorpe and croft,
    Safe from the weather!   30
He, whom we convoy to his grave aloft,
    Singing together,
He was a man born with thy face and throat,
    Lyric Apollo![6]
Long he lived nameless: how should spring take note   35
    Winter would follow?
Till lo, the little touch, and youth was gone!
    Cramped and diminished,
Moaned he, "New measures, other feet anon!
    My dance is finished?"   40
No, that's the world's way: (keep the mountain-side,
    Make for the city!)
He knew the signal, and stepped on with pride
    Over men's pity;
Left play for work, and grappled with the world   45
    Bent on escaping:
"What's in the scroll," quoth he, "thou keepest furled?
    Show me their shaping,
Theirs who most studied man, the bard and sage—
    Give!"—So, he gowned him,[7]   50
Straight got by heart that book to its last page:
    Learned, we found him.
Yea, but we found him bald too, eyes like lead,
    Accents uncertain:
"Time to taste life," another would have said,   55
    "Up with the curtain!"
This man said rather, "Actual life comes next?
    Patience a moment!
Grant I have mastered learning's crabbed text,
    Still there's the comment.[8]   60
Let me know all! Prate not of most or least,
    Painful or easy!
Even to the crumbs I'd fain eat up the feast,
    Aye, nor feel queasy."
Oh, such a life as he resolved to live,   65
    When he had learned it,

5. Look out for!
6. God of music and embodiment of male beauty.
7. Dressed in academic gown; became a scholar.
8. Commentaries or annotations upon a text.

When he had gathered all books had to give!
    Sooner, he spurned it.
Image the whole, then execute the parts—
    Fancy the fabric   70
Quite, ere you build, ere steel strike fire from quartz,
    Ere mortar dab brick!

(Here's the town gate reached: there's the market place
    Gaping before us.)
Yea, this in him was the peculiar grace   75
    (Hearten our chorus!)
That before living he'd learn how to live—
    No end to learning:
Earn the means first—God surely will contrive
    Use for our earning.   80
Others mistrust and say, "But time escapes:
    Live now or never!"
He said, "What's time? Leave Now for dogs and apes!
    Man has Forever."
Back to his book then: deeper drooped his head: 85
    Calculus[9] racked him:
Leaden before, his eyes grew dross of lead:
    Tussis[1] attacked him.
"Now, master, take a little rest!"—not he!
    (Caution redoubled,   90
Step two abreast, the way winds narrowly!)
    Not a whit troubled
Back to his studies, fresher than at first,
    Fierce as a dragon
He (soul-hydroptic[2] with a sacred thirst)   95
    Sucked at the flagon.
Oh, if we draw a circle premature,
    Heedless of far gain,
Greedy for quick returns of profit, sure
    Bad is our bargain!   100
Was it not great? did not he throw on God
    (He loves the burthen)—
God's task to make the heavenly period
    Perfect the earthen?
Did not he magnify the mind, show clear   105
    Just what it all meant?
He would not discount life, as fools do here,
    Paid by installment.
He ventured neck or nothing—heaven's success
    Found, or earth's failure: 110
"Wilt thou trust death or not?" He answered "Yes:
    Hence with life's pale lure!"
That low man seeks a little thing to do,
    Sees it and does it:

9. A stone such as a gallstone.   2. Insatiably soul-thirsty.
1. A cough.

This high man, with a great thing to pursue,   115
    Dies ere he knows it.
That low man goes on adding one to one,
    His hundred's soon hit:
This high man, aiming at a million,
    Misses an unit.[3]   120
That, has the world here—should he need the next,
    Let the world mind him!
This, throws himself on God, and unperplexed
    Seeking shall find him.
So, with the throttling hands of death at strife,   125
    Ground he at grammar;
Still, through the rattle, parts of speech were rife:
    While he could stammer
He settled *Hoti's* business—let it be!—
    Properly based *Oun*—   130
Gave us the doctrine of the enclitic *De*,[4]
    Dead from the waist down.
Well, here's the platform, here's the proper place:
    Hail to your purlieus,
All ye highfliers of the feathered race,   135
    Swallows and curlews!
Here's the top peak; the multitude below
    Live, for they can, there:
This man decided not to Live but Know—
    Bury this man there?   140
Here—here's his place, where meteors shoot, clouds form,
    Lightnings are loosened,
Stars come and go! Let joy break with the storm,
    Peace let the dew send!
Lofty designs must close in like effects: 145
    Loftily lying,
Leave him—still loftier than the world suspects,
    Living and dying.

ca. 1854   1855

Confessions

1

What is he buzzing in my ears?
    "Now that I come to die,
Do I view the world as a vale of tears?"
    Ah, reverend sir, not I!

2

What I viewed there once, what I view again   5
    Where the physic bottles stand

3. A small item such as some trifling worldly pleasure.
4. *"Hoti," "Oun,"* and *"De"* are Greek particles meaning "that," "then," and "towards." An unaccented word such as *de* is "enclitic" when it affects the accentuation of a word adjacent to it.

On the table's edge—is a suburb lane,
    With a wall to my bedside hand.

3

That lane sloped, much as the bottles do,
    From a house you could descry   10
O'er the garden wall: is the curtain blue
    Or green to a healthy eye?

4

To mine, it serves for the old June weather
    Blue above lane and wall;
And that farthest bottle labeled "Ether"   15
    Is the house o'ertopping all.

5

At a terrace, somewhere near the stopper,
    There watched for me, one June,
A girl: I know, sir, it's improper,
    My poor mind's out of tune.   20

6

Only, there was a way . . . you crept
    Close by the side to dodge
Eyes in the house, two eyes except:
    They styled their house "The Lodge."

7

What right had a lounger up their lane?   25
    But, by creeping very close,
With the good wall's help—their eyes might strain
    And stretch themselves to O's,

8

Yet never catch her and me together,
    As she left the attic, there,
By the rim of the bottle labeled "Ether,"   30
    And stole from stair to stair,

9

And stood by the rose-wreathed gate. Alas,
    We loved, sir—used to meet:
How sad and bad and mad it was—   35
    But then, how it was sweet!

ca. 1859   1864

Youth and Art

1

It once might have been, once only:
    We lodged in a street together,
You, a sparrow on the housetop lonely,
    I, a lone she-bird of his feather.

2

Your trade was with sticks and clay,
    You thumbed, thrust, patted, and polished,   5
Then laughed, "They will see some day
    Smith made, and Gibson[1] demolished."

3

My business was song, song, song;
    I chirped, cheeped, trilled, and twittered,   10
"Kate Brown's on the boards ere long,
    And Grisi's[2] existence embittered!"

4

I earned no more by a warble
    Than you by a sketch in plaster;
You wanted a piece of marble,   15
    I needed a music master.

5

We studied hard in our styles,
    Chipped each at a crust like Hindoos,
For air looked out on the tiles,
    For fun watched each other's windows.   20

6

You lounged, like a boy of the South,
    Cap and blouse—nay, a bit of beard, too;
Or you got it, rubbing your mouth
    With fingers the clay adhered to.

7

And I—soon managed to find   25
    Weak points in the flower-fence facing,
Was forced to put up a blind
    And be safe in my corset lacing.

8

No harm! It was not my fault
    If you never turned your eye's tail up,   30
As I shook upon E *in alt*,[3]
    Or ran the chromatic scale up:

9

For spring bade the sparrows pair,
    And the boys and girls gave guesses,
And stalls in our street looked rare   35
    With bulrush and watercresses.

10

Why did not you pinch a flower
    In a pellet of clay and fling it?
Why did not I put a power
    Of thanks in a look, or sing it?   40

11

I did look, sharp as a lynx,
    (And yet the memory rankles)

1. John Gibson (1790–1866), English
sculptor.
2. Giulia Grisi (1811–69), a famous
Italian soprano.
3. High E.

When models arrived, some minx
    Tripped upstairs, she and her ankles.

12

But I think I gave you as good!   45
    "That foreign fellow—who can know
How she pays, in a playful mood,
    For his tuning her that piano?"

13

Could you say so, and never say
    "Suppose we join hands and fortunes,   50
And I fetch her from over the way,
    Her, piano, and long tunes and short tunes"?

14

No, no: you would not be rash,
    Nor I rasher and something over:
You've to settle yet Gibson's hash,   55
    And Grisi yet lives in clover.

15

But you meet the Prince[4] at the Board,
    I'm queen myself at *bals-paré*,[5]
I've married a rich old lord,
    And you're dubbed knight and an **R. A.**   60

16

Each life unfulfilled, you see;
    It hangs still, patchy and scrappy:
We have not sighed deep, laughed free,
    Starved, feasted, despaired—been happy.

17

And nobody calls you a dunce,   65
    And people suppose me clever:
This could but have happened once,
    And we missed it, lost it forever.

ca. 1860   1864

4. Perhaps Prince Albert, a patron of the arts. Now that the sculptor has acquired a title and is an "R. A." (a member of the respectable Royal Academy of Arts), he serves on committees or boards with the prince.
5. Fancy-dress balls.

Caliban upon Setebos

Two closely related controversies of the Victorian period led Browning to write this poem (whose title means "Caliban's thoughts about Setebos"). The first, stimulated by Darwin, was concerned with man's origins and his relation to other animals. Caliban, the half-man and half-monster of Shakespeare's *Tempest*, provided the poet with a model of how the mind of a primitive creature may operate. The second controversy concerned the nature of God and God's responsibility for the existence of suffering in the world. Like many men, Caliban thinks of God's nature as similar to his own. His anthropomorphic conception of the deity, whom he calls Setebos, is confined to what he has observed of life on his island and to what he has observed of himself. From the former derives his "natural theology," that is, his identifying the character of God from evidences provided by nature rather than from the evidence of supernatural revelation. From the latter, his observation of his own character, derives Caliban's conception of God's willful power. Caliban himself admires power and thinks of God in Calvinistic terms as a being who selects at random some creatures who are to be saved and others who are to be condemned to suffer.

An obstacle for the reader is Caliban's use of the third person pronoun. He says that he "never speaks his mind save housed as now"— that is, he thinks if he is adequately hidden under the slush in his cave, the deity will not catch him thinking; he may remind us of the hero of George Orwell's 1984 trying to evade the Thought Police. But to make especially sure of not being caught, Caliban refers to himself in the third person. Thus " 'Will sprawl" means "Caliban will sprawl" (an apostrophe before the verb usually indicates that Caliban himself is the implied subject). Only occasionally does he slip into the first person (e.g., line 56 or 68), when he feels sure that Setebos will not hear him. The deity is also referred to in the third person but with an initial capital letter ("He").

Caliban upon Setebos

OR NATURAL THEOLOGY IN THE ISLAND

"Thou thoughtest that I was altogether such a one as thyself."[1]

['Will sprawl, now that the heat of day is best,
Flat on his belly in the pit's much mire,
With elbows wide, fists clenched to prop his chin.
And, while he kicks both feet in the cool slush,
And feels about his spine small eft-things[2] course,   5
Run in and out each arm, and make him laugh:
And while above his head a pompion plant,[3]
Coating the cave-top as a brow its eye,
Creeps down to touch and tickle hair and beard,
And now a flower drops with a bee inside,   10
And now a fruit to snap at, catch and crunch—
He looks out o'er yon sea which sunbeams cross
And recross till they weave a spider web
(Meshes of fire, some great fish breaks at times)
And talks to his own self, howe'er he please,   15
Touching that other, whom his dam[4] called God.
Because to talk about Him, vexes—ha,
Could He but know! and time to vex is now,
When talk is safer than in wintertime.
Moreover Prosper[5] and Miranda sleep   20

1. Psalm 1.21. The speaker is God.
2. Water lizards.
3. Pumpkin plant.
4. Caliban's mother, Sycorax.

5. Prospero the magician, who is Caliban's master in *The Tempest*. Miranda is Prospero's daughter.

In confidence he drudges at their task,
And it is good to cheat the pair, and gibe,
Letting the rank tongue blossom into speech.]

Setebos, Setebos, and Setebos!
'Thinketh, He dwelleth i' the cold o' the moon.   25

'Thinketh He made it, with the sun to match,
But not the stars; the stars came otherwise;
Only made clouds, winds, meteors, such as that:
Also this isle, what lives and grows thereon,
And snaky sea which rounds and ends the same.   30

'Thinketh, it came of being ill at ease:
He hated that He cannot change His cold,
Nor cure its ache. 'Hath spied an icy fish
That longed to 'scape the rock-stream where she lived,
And thaw herself within the lukewarm brine   35
O' the lazy sea her stream thrusts far amid,
A crystal spike 'twixt two warm walls of wave;[6]
Only, she ever sickened, found repulse
At the other kind of water, not her life,
(Green-dense and dim-delicious, bred o' the sun)   40
Flounced back from bliss she was not born to breathe,
And in her old bounds buried her despair,
Hating and loving warmth alike: so He.

'Thinketh, He made thereat the sun, this isle,
Trees and the fowls here, beast and creeping thing.   45
Yon otter, sleek-wet, black, lithe as a leech;
Yon auk,[7] one fire-eye in a ball of foam,
That floats and feeds; a certain badger brown
He hath watched hunt with that slant white-wedge eye
By moonlight; and the pie[8] with the long tongue   50
That pricks deep into oakwarts for a worm,
And says a plain word when she finds her prize,
But will not eat the ants; the ants themselves
That build a wall of seeds and settled stalks
About their hole—He made all these and more,   55
Made all we see, and us, in spite: how else?
He could not, Himself, make a second self
To be His mate; as well have made Himself:
He would not make what he mislikes or slights,
An eyesore to Him, or not worth His pains: 60
But did, in envy, listlessness, or sport,
Make what Himself would fain, in a manner, be—
Weaker in most points, stronger in a few,
Worthy, and yet mere playthings all the while,
Things He admires and mocks too—that is it.   65

6. I.e., the thin stream of cold water   7. Sea bird.
which is driven into the warm ocean   8. Magpie.
like a spike between walls.

Because, so brave, so better though they be,
It nothing skills if He begin to plague.[9]
Look now, I melt a gourd-fruit into mash,
Add honeycomb and pods, I have perceived,
Which bite like finches when they bill and kiss—   70
Then, when froth rises bladdery,[1] drink up all,
Quick, quick, till maggots scamper through my brain;
Last, throw me on my back i' the seeded thyme,
And wanton, wishing I were born a bird.
Put case, unable to be what I wish,   75
I yet could make a live bird out of clay:
Would not I take clay, pinch my Caliban
Able to fly?—for, there, see, he hath wings,
And great comb like the hoopoe's[2] to admire,
And there, a sting to do his foes offense,   80
There, and I will that he begin to live,
Fly to yon rock-top, nip me off the horns
Of grigs[3] high up that make the merry din,
Saucy through their veined wings, and mind me not.
In which feat, if his leg snapped, brittle clay,   85
And he lay stupid-like—why, I should laugh;
And if he, spying me, should fall to weep,
Beseech me to be good, repair his wrong,
Bid his poor leg smart less or grow again—
Well, as the chance were, this might take or else   90
Not take my fancy: I might hear his cry,
And give the mankin three sound legs for one,
Or pluck the other off, leave him like an egg,
And lessoned he was mine and merely clay.
Were this no pleasure, lying in the thyme,   95
Drinking the mash, with brain become alive,
Making and marring clay at will? So He.

'Thinketh, such shows nor right nor wrong in Him,
Nor kind, nor cruel: He is strong and Lord.
'Am strong myself compared to yonder crabs   100
That march now from the mountain to the sea;
'Let twenty pass, and stone the twenty-first,
Loving not, hating not, just choosing so.
'Say, the first straggler that boasts purple spots
Shall join the file, one pincer twisted off;   105
'Say, this bruised fellow shall receive a worm,
And two worms he whose nippers end in red;
As it likes me each time, I do: so He.

Well then, 'supposeth He is good i' the main,
Placable if His mind and ways were guessed,   110
But rougher than His handiwork, be sure!

9. I.e., our superior virtues are of no   1. Bubbly.
help to us if God elects to inflict plagues 2. Bird with bright plumage.
upon us.   3. Grasshoppers.

Oh, He hath made things worthier than Himself,
And envieth that, so helped, such things do more
Than He who made them! What consoles but this?
That they, unless through Him, do naught at all,   115
And must submit: what other use in things?
'Hath cut a pipe of pithless elder-joint
That, blown through, gives exact the scream o' the jay
When from her wing you twitch the feathers blue:
Sound this, and little birds that hate the jay   120
Flock within stone's throw, glad their foe is hurt:
Put case such pipe could prattle and boast forsooth,
"I catch the birds, I am the crafty thing,
I make the cry my maker cannot make
With his great round mouth; he must blow through mine!"   125
Would not I smash it with my foot? So He.

But wherefore rough, why cold and ill at ease?
Aha, that is a question! Ask, for that,
What knows—the something over Setebos
That made Him, or He, may be, found and fought,   130
Worsted, drove off and did to nothing,[4] perchance.
There may be something quiet o'er His head,
Out of His reach, that feels nor joy nor grief,
Since both derive from weakness in some way.
I joy because the quails come; would not joy   135
Could I bring quails here when I have a mind:
This Quiet, all it hath a mind to, doth.
'Esteemeth stars the outposts of its couch,
But never spends much thought nor care that way.
It may look up, work up—the worse for those   140
It works on! 'Careth but for Setebos[5]
The many-handed as a cuttlefish,
Who, making Himself feared through what He does,
Looks up, first, and perceives he cannot soar
To what is quiet and hath happy life;   145
Next looks down here, and out of very spite
Makes this a bauble-world to ape yon real,
These good things to match those as hips[6] do grapes.
'Tis solace making baubles, aye, and sport.
Himself peeped late, eyed Prosper at his books   150
Careless and lofty, lord now of the isle:
Vexed, 'stitched a book of broad leaves, arrow-shaped,
Wrote thereon, he knows what, prodigious words;
Has peeled a wand and called it by a name;
Weareth at whiles for an enchanter's robe   155
The eyed skin of a supple oncelot;[7]

4. Completely overcame.
5. Caliban is concerned to appease only Setebos, not the other deity—the Quiet.
6. Hard fruits produced by wild roses.

7. Browning may have invented this term from the Spanish *oncela* or from the French *ocelot*. Both words signify a leopard or spotted wildcat.

And hath an ounce[8] sleeker than youngling mole,
A four-legged serpent he makes cower and couch,
Now snarl, now hold its breath and mind his eye,
And saith she is Miranda and my wife: 160
'Keeps for his Ariel[9] a tall pouch-bill crane
He bids go wade for fish and straight disgorge;
Also a sea beast, lumpish, which he snared,
Blinded the eyes of, and brought somewhat tame,
And split its toe-webs, and now pens the drudge   165
In a hole o' the rock and calls him Caliban;
A bitter heart that bides its time and bites.
'Plays thus at being Prosper in a way,
Taketh his mirth with make-believes: so He.

His dam held that the Quiet made all things   170
Which Setebos vexed only: 'holds not so.
Who made them weak, meant weakness He might vex.
Had He meant other, while His hand was in,
Why not make horny eyes no thorn could prick,
Or plate my scalp with bone against the snow,   175
Or overscale my flesh 'neath joint and joint,
Like an orc's[1] armor? Aye—so spoil His sport!
He is the One now: only He doth all.

'Saith, He may like, perchance, what profits Him.
Aye, himself loves what does him good; but why?   180
'Gets good no otherwise. This blinded beast
Loves whoso places flesh-meat on his nose,
But, had he eyes, would want no help, but hate
Or love, just as it liked him: He hath eyes.
Also it pleaseth Setebos to work,   185
Use all His hands, and exercise much craft,
By no means for the love of what is worked.
'Tasteth, himself, no finer good i' the world
When all goes right, in this safe summertime,
And he wants little, hungers, aches not much,   190
Than trying what to do with wit and strength.
'Falls to make something: 'piled yon pile of turfs,
And squared and stuck there squares of soft white chalk,
And, with a fish-tooth, scratched a moon on each,
And set up endwise certain spikes of tree,   195
And crowned the whole with a sloth's skull a-top,
Found dead i' the woods, too hard for one to kill.
No use at all i' the work, for work's sole sake;
'Shall some day knock it down again: so He.

'Saith He is terrible: watch His feats in proof!   200
One hurricane will spoil six good months' hope.
He hath a spite against me, that I know,

8. A large, ferocious leopard, six or   Prospero.
seven feet in length.   1. Killer whale's.
9. In *The Tempest*, a spirit who serves

Just as He favors Prosper, who knows why?
So it is, all the same, as well I find.
'Wove wattles half the winter, fenced them firm   205
With stone and stake to stop she-tortoises
Crawling to lay their eggs here: well, one wave,
Feeling the foot of Him upon its neck,
Gaped as a snake does, lolled out its large tongue,
And licked the whole labor flat; so much for spite.   210
'Saw a ball[2] flame down late (yonder it lies)
Where, half an hour before, I slept i' the shade:
Often they scatter sparkles: there is force!
'Dug up a newt He may have envied once
And turned to stone, shut up inside a stone.   215
Please Him and hinder this?—What Prosper does?[3]
Aha, if He would tell me how! Not He!
There is the sport: discover how or die!
All need not die, for of the things o' the isle
Some flee afar, some dive, some run up trees;   220
Those at His mercy—why, they please Him most
When . . . when . . . well, never try the same way twice!
Repeat what act has pleased, He may grow wroth.
You must not know His ways, and play Him off,
Sure of the issue. 'Doth the like himself: 225
'Spareth a squirrel that it nothing fears
But steals the nut from underneath my thumb,
And when I threat, bites stoutly in defense:
'Spareth an urchin[4] that contrariwise
Curls up into a ball, pretending death   230
For fright at my approach: the two ways please.
But what would move my choler more than this,
That either creature counted on its life
Tomorrow and next day and all days to come,
Saying, forsooth, in the inmost of its heart,   235
"Because he did so yesterday with me,
And otherwise with such another brute,
So must he do henceforth and always."—Aye?
Would teach the reasoning couple what "must" means!
'Doth as he likes, or wherefore Lord? So He.   240

'Conceiveth all things will continue thus,
And we shall have to live in fear of Him
So long as He lives, keeps His strength: no change,
If He have done His best, make no new world
To please Him more, so leave off watching this—   245
If He surprise not even the Quiet's self
Some strange day—or, suppose, grow into it
As grubs grow butterflies: else, here are we,
And there is He, and nowhere help at all.

2. Meteorite.
3. I.e., shall I please Setebos, as
Prospero does, and thus prevent my

being punished as the newt was punished?
4. Hedgehog.

'Believeth with the life, the pain shall stop.   250
His dam held different, that after death
He both plagued enemies and feasted friends:
Idly![5] He doth His worst in this our life,
Giving just respite lest we die through pain,
Saving last pain for worst—with which, an end.   255
Meanwhile, the best way to escape His ire
Is, not to seem too happy. 'Sees, himself,
Yonder two flies, with purple films and pink,
Bask on the pompion-bell above: kills both.
'Sees two black painful beetles roll their ball   260
On head and tail as if to save their lives:
Moves them the stick away they strive to clear.

Even so, 'would have Him misconceive, suppose
This Caliban strives hard and ails no less,
And always, above all else, envies Him;   265
Wherefore he mainly dances on dark nights,
Moans in the sun, gets under holes to laugh,
And never speaks his mind save housed as now:
Outside, 'groans, curses. If He caught me here,
O'erheard this speech, and asked "What chucklest at?"   270
'Would, to appease Him, cut a finger off,
Or of my three kid yearlings burn the best,
Or let the toothsome apples rot on tree,
Or push my tame beast for the orc to taste:
While myself lit a fire, and made a song   275
And sung it, "*What I hate, be consecrate
To celebrate Thee and Thy state, no mate
For Thee; what see for envy in poor me?*"
Hoping the while, since evils sometimes mend,
Warts rub away and sores are cured with slime,   280
That some strange day, will either the Quiet catch
And conquer Setebos, or likelier He
Decrepit may doze, doze, as good as die.

————————

[What, what? A curtain o'er the world at once!
Crickets stop hissing; not a bird—or, yes,   285
There scuds His raven that has told Him all!
It was fool's play this prattling! Ha! The wind
Shoulders the pillared dust, death's house o' the move,
And fast invading fires begin! White blaze—
A tree's head snaps—and there, there, there, there, there,   290
His thunder follows! Fool to gibe at Him!
Lo! 'Lieth flat and loveth Setebos!
'Maketh his teeth meet through his upper lip,

5. I.e., Caliban thinks his mother's opinion was wrong or idle. God's sport with man is confined to this world; there is no afterlife.

Will let those quails fly, will not eat this month
    One little mess of whelks,[6] so he may 'scape!]

ca. 1860   295

                                                    1864

Prospice[7]

Fear death?—to feel the fog in my throat,
    The mist in my face,
When the snows begin, and the blasts denote
    I am nearing the place,
The power of the night, the press of the storm,   5
    The post of the foe;
Where he stands, the Arch Fear in a visible form,
    Yet the strong man must go:
For the journey is done and the summit attained,
    And the barriers fall,   10
Though a battle's to fight ere the guerdon be gained,
    The reward of it all.
I was ever a fighter, so—one fight more,
    The best and the last!
I would hate that death bandaged my eyes, and forbore,   15
    And bade me creep past.
No! let me taste the whole of it, fare like my peers
    The heroes of old,
Bear the brunt, in a minute pay glad life's arrears
    Of pain, darkness, and cold.   20
For sudden the worst turns the best to the brave,
    The black minute's at end,
And the elements' rage, the fiend-voices that rave,
    Shall dwindle, shall blend,
Shall change, shall become first a peace out of pain,   25
    Then a light, then thy breast,
O thou soul of my soul![8] I shall clasp thee again,
    And with God be the rest!

ca. 1861   1864

Abt Vogler[1]

(AFTER HE HAS BEEN EXTEMPORIZING UPON THE MUSICAL INSTRUMENT OF HIS INVENTION)

1

Would that the structure brave, the manifold music I build,
    Bidding my organ obey, calling its keys to their work,

6. Shellfish.
7. The title means "Look forward."
8. Browning's wife.
1. Georg Joseph Vogler (1749–1814),

a German priest and musician, held
the honorary title of *Abbé* or *Abt*. As
a composer, teacher, and designer of
musical instruments he was well known

Claiming each slave of the sound, at a touch, as when Solomon
willed
    Armies of angels that soar, legions of demons that lurk,
Man, brute, reptile, fly—alien of end and of aim,
    Adverse, each from the other heaven-high, hell-deep removed— 5
Should rush into sight at once as he named the ineffable Name,[2]
    And pile him a palace straight, to pleasure the princess he
loved!

2

Would it might tarry like his, the beautiful building of mine,
    This which my keys in a crowd pressed and importuned to
raise! 10
Ah, one and all, how they helped, would dispart now and now com-
bine,
    Zealous to hasten the work, heighten their master his praise!
And one would bury his brow with a blind plunge down to hell,
    Burrow awhile and build, broad on the roots of things,
Then up again swim into sight, having based me my palace well, 15
    Founded it, fearless of flame, flat on the nether springs.

3

And another would mount and march, like the excellent minion he
was,
    Aye, another and yet another, one crowd but with many a crest,
Raising my rampired walls of gold as transparent as glass,
    Eager to do and die, yield each his place to the rest: 20
For higher still and higher (as a runner tips with fire,
    When a great illumination surprises a festal night—
Outlining round and round Rome's dome from space to spire)[3]
    Up, the pinnacled glory reached, and the pride of my soul was
in sight.

4

In sight? Not half! for it seemed, it was certain, to match man's
birth,
    Nature in turn conceived, obeying an impulse as I; 25
And the emulous heaven yearned down, made effort to reach the
earth,
    As the earth had done her best, in my passion, to scale the sky:

in his own day, but he was most famous as an extemporizer at the organ. Browning's soliloquy represents Vogler at the organ joyfully improvising a piece of music and then reflecting upon the ephemeral existence of such a unique work of art and of its possible relation to God's purposes in heaven and on earth. In this connection, a suggestive comparison can be made between Browning's conception of a palace of music inhabited by the "wonderful Dead" and W. B. Yeats's conception of a heaven of art in his Byzantium poems.

A characteristic feature of *Abt Vogler* is the use of exceptionally long sentences, densely packed with details,

which may evoke for us the effects of rolling organ music. The resulting movement is markedly different from the brisk staccato rhythms of *A Toccata of Galuppi's*.

The "musical instrument of his invention" is a compact organ called the Orchestrion.
2. According to Jewish legend, King Solomon (because he possessed a seal inscribed with the "ineffable Name" of God) had the power of compelling the demons of earth and air to perform his bidding.
3. On festival nights the dome of St. Peter's in Rome is illuminated by a series of lights ignited by a torchbearer.

Novel splendors burst forth, grew familiar and dwelt with mine,
 Not a point nor peak but found and fixed its wandering star; 30
Meteor-moons, balls of blaze: and they did not pale nor pine,
 For earth had attained to heaven, there was no more near nor
  far.

5

Nay more; for there wanted not who walked in the glare and glow,
 Presences plain in the place; or, fresh from the Protoplast,[4]
Furnished for ages to come, when a kindlier wind should blow, 35
 Lured now to begin and live, in a house to their liking at last;
Or else the wonderful Dead who have passed through the body and
  gone,
 But were back once more to breathe in an old world worth
  their new:
What never had been, was now; what was, as it shall be anon;
 And what is—shall I say, matched both? for I was made per-
  fect too. 40

6

All through my keys that gave their sounds to a wish of my soul,
 All through my soul that praised as its wish flowed visibly forth,
All through music and me! For think, had I painted the whole,
 Why, there it had stood, to see, nor the process so wonder-
  worth:
Had I written the same, made verse—still, effect proceeds from
  cause, 45
 Ye know why the forms are fair, ye hear how the tale is told;
It is all triumphant art, but art in obedience to laws,
 Painter and poet are proud in the artist-list enrolled—

7

But here is the finger of God, a flash of the will that can,
 Existent behind all laws, that made them and, lo, they are! 50
And I know not if, save in this, such gift be allowed to man,
 That out of three sounds he frame, not a fourth sound, but a
  star.[5]
Consider it well: each tone of our scale in itself is naught;
 It is everywhere in the world—loud, soft, and all is said:
Give it to me to use! I mix it with two in my thought: 55
 And, there! Ye have heard and seen: consider and bow the
  head!

8

Well, it is gone at last, the palace of music I reared;
 Gone! and the good tears start, the praises that come too slow;
For one is assured at first, one scarce can say that he feared,
 That he even gave it a thought, the gone thing was to go. 60
Never to be again! But many more of the kind
 As good, nay, better perchance: is this your comfort to me?

---

4. The original or archetypal form of a species. The "presences" from this source are beings of the future, not yet existing, who are "lured" into life by the music. Cf. *Women and Roses*, stanzas 7 and 8.

5. I.e., the musician's combining of three notes into a new harmonic unit is a creative act as miraculous as the creation of a star.

To me, who must be saved because I cling with my mind
    To the same, same self, same love, same God: aye, what was,
      shall be.

9

Therefore to whom turn I but to thee, the ineffable Name?   65
    Builder and maker, thou, of houses not made with hands![6]
What, have fear of change from thee who art ever the same?
    Doubt that thy power can fill the heart that thy power expands?
There shall never be one lost good! What was, shall live as before;
    The evil is null, is naught, is silence implying sound;   70
What was good shall be good, with, for evil, so much good more;
    On the earth the broken arcs; in the heaven, a perfect round.

10

All we have willed or hoped or dreamed of good shall exist;
    Not its semblance, but itself; no beauty, nor good, nor power
Whose voice has gone forth, but each survives for the melodist   75
    When eternity affirms the conception of an hour.
The high that proved too high, the heroic for earth too hard,
    The passion that left the ground to lose itself in the sky,
Are music sent up to God by the lover and the bard;
    Enough that he heard it once: we shall hear it by-and-by.   80

11

And what is our failure here but a triumph's evidence
    For the fullness of the days? Have we withered or agonized?
Why else was the pause prolonged but that singing might issue
      thence?
    Why rushed the discords in but that harmony should be
      prized?
Sorrow is hard to bear, and doubt is slow to clear,   85
    Each sufferer says his say, his scheme of the weal and woe:
But God has a few of us whom he whispers in the ear;
    The rest may reason and welcome: 'tis we musicians know.

12

Well, it is earth with me; silence resumes her reign:
    I will be patient and proud, and soberly acquiesce.   90
Give me the keys. I feel for the common chord again,
    Sliding by semitones, till I sink to the minor—yes,
And I blunt it into a ninth, and I stand on alien ground,
    Surveying awhile the heights I rolled from into the deep;
Which, hark, I have dared and done, for my resting place is
      found,   95
    The C Major of this life:[7] so, now I will try to sleep.

1864

6. See II Corinthians v.1, in which St. Paul speaks of "a building of God, an house not made with hands, eternal in the heavens."

7. Vogler's last moments of playing express first his sadness that he cannot remain forever among the "heights" of the music he has temporarily created, and afterwards his acceptance of this return to man's ordinary existence. Thus he plays in a "minor" key, pauses for a short space on the "alien ground" of a "ninth" (a discord which requires a resolution), and finally concludes in "C Major," a key without sharps or flats and representing the plane of ordinary life.

Rabbi Ben Ezra[1]

1

Grow old along with me!
   The best is yet to be,
The last of life, for which the first was made:
   Our times are in His hand
   Who saith, "A whole I planned,
Youth shows but half; trust God: see all nor be afraid!"

2

Not that, amassing flowers,
   Youth sighed, "Which rose make ours,
Which lily leave and then as best recall?"
   Not that, admiring stars,
   It yearned, "Nor Jove, nor Mars;
Mine be some figured flame which blends, transcends them all!"

3

Not for such hopes and fears
   Annulling youth's brief years,
Do I remonstrate: folly wide the mark!
   Rather I prize the doubt
   Low kinds exist without,
Finished and finite clods, untroubled by a spark.

4

Poor vaunt of life indeed,
   Were man but formed to feed
On joy, to solely seek and find and feast:
   Such feasting ended, then
   As sure an end to men;
Irks care the crop-full bird? Frets doubt the maw-crammed beast?[2]

5

Rejoice we are allied
   To That which doth provide
And not partake, effect and not receive!
   A spark disturbs our clod;
   Nearer we hold of God
Who gives, than of His tribes that take, I must believe.

6

Then, welcome each rebuff
   That turns earth's smoothness rough,
Each sting that bids nor sit nor stand but go!
   Be our joys three parts pain!

1. The speaker, Abraham Ibn Ezra (ca. 1092–1167), was an eminent Biblical scholar of Spain, but Browning makes little attempt to present him as a distinct individual or to relate him to the age in which he lived. Unlike the more characteristic monologues, *Rabbi Ben Ezra* is not dramatic but declamatory.
2. I.e., does care disturb a bird whose gullet ("crop") is full of food? does doubt trouble an animal whose stomach ("maw") is full?

Strive, and hold cheap the strain;
Learn, nor account the pang; dare, never grudge the throe![3]   35

7

For thence—a paradox
  Which comforts while it mocks—
Shall life succeed in that it seems to fail:
  What I aspired to be,
  And was not, comforts me: 40
A brute I might have been, but would not sink i' the scale.

8

What is he but a brute
  Whose flesh has soul to suit,
Whose spirit works lest arms and legs want play?
  To man, propose this test—   45
  Thy body at its best,
How far can that project thy soul on its lone way?

9

Yet gifts should prove their use:
  I own the Past profuse
Of power each side, perfection every turn: 50
  Eyes, ears took in their dole,
  Brain treasured up the whole;
Should not the heart beat once, "How good to live and learn"?

10

Not once beat, "Praise be Thine!
  I see the whole design,   55
I, who saw power, see now love perfect too:
  Perfect I call Thy plan:
  Thanks that I was a man!
Maker, remake, complete—I trust what Thou shalt do!"   60

11

For pleasant is this flesh;
  Our soul, in its rose-mesh[4]
Pulled ever to the earth, still yearns for rest;
  Would we some prize might hold
  To match those manifold   65
Possessions of the brute—gain most, as we did best!

12

Let us not always say,
  "Spite of this flesh today
I strove, made head, gained ground upon the whole!"
  As the bird wings and sings,   70
  Let us cry, "All good things
Are ours, nor soul helps flesh more, now, than flesh helps soul!"

13

Therefore I summon age
  To grant youth's heritage,
Life's struggle having so far reached its term: 75

3. Anguish.

4. The body which holds the soul in its net.

Thence shall I pass, approved
A man, for aye removed
From the developed brute; a god though in the germ.

14

And I shall thereupon
Take rest, ere I be gone   80
Once more on my adventure brave and new:[5]
Fearless and unperplexed,
When I wage battle next,
What weapons to select, what armor to indue.[6]

15

Youth ended, I shall try   85
My gain or loss thereby;
Leave the fire ashes,[7] what survives is gold:
And I shall weigh the same,
Give life its praise or blame:
Young, all lay in dispute; I shall know, being old.   90

16

For note, when evening shuts,
A certain moment cuts
The deed off, calls the glory from the gray:
A whisper from the west
Shoots—"Add this to the rest,   95
Take it and try its worth: here dies another day."

17

So, still within this life,
Though lifted o'er its strife,
Let me discern, compare, pronounce at last,
"This rage was right i' the main,   100
That acquiescence vain:
The Future I may face now I have proved the Past."

18

For more is not reserved
To man, with soul just nerved
To act tomorrow what he learns today: 105
Here, work enough to watch
The Master work, and catch
Hints of the proper craft, tricks of the tool's true play.

19

As it was better, youth
Should strive, through acts uncouth,   110
Toward making, than repose on aught found made:
So, better, age, exempt
From strife, should know, than tempt[8]
Further. Thou waitedst age: wait death nor be afraid!

20

Enough now, if the Right   115
And Good and Infinite

---

5. In the next life.   7. If the fire leaves ashes.
6. Put on.   8. Attempt.

Be named here, as thou callest thy hand thine own,
  With knowledge absolute,
  Subject to no dispute
From fools that crowded youth, nor let thee feel alone.[9] 120

21

  Be there, for once and all,
  Severed great minds from small,
Announced to each his station in the Past!
  Was I, the world arraigned,[1]
  Were they, my soul disdained, 125
Right? Let age speak the truth and give us peace at last!

22

  Now, who shall arbitrate?
  Ten men love what I hate,
Shun what I follow, slight what I receive;
  Ten, who in ears and eyes 130
  Match me: we all surmise,
They this thing, and I that: whom shall my soul believe?

23

  Not on the vulgar mass
  Called "work," must sentence pass,
Things done, that took the eye and had the price; 135
  O'er which, from level stand,
  The low world laid its hand,
Found straightway to its mind, could value in a trice:

24

  But all, the world's coarse thumb
  And finger failed to plumb, 140
So passed in making up the main account;
  All instincts immature,
  All purposes unsure,
That weighed not as his work, yet swelled the man's amount:

25

  Thoughts hardly to be packed 145
  Into a narrow act,
Fancies that broke through language and escaped;
  All I could never be,
  All, men ignored in me,
This, I was worth to God, whose wheel[2] the pitcher shaped. 150

26

  Aye, note that Potter's wheel,
  That metaphor! and feel
Why time spins fast, why passive lies our clay—
  Thou, to whom fools propound,[3]

9. Stanzas 20 and 21 affirm that in age we can more readily think independently than in youth. Maturity enables us to ignore the pressure of having to conform to the thinking of the crowd of small-minded people.
1. Was I, whom the world arraigned.
2. The potting-wheel on which the speaker's highest qualities of soul were shaped into an enduring "pitcher" by God. See Isaiah lxiv.8.
3. Perhaps addressed to Omar Khayyám, whose poem, *The Rubáiyát*, urged men to eat, drink, and be merry. Edward FitzGerald's translation of Omar's poem had appeared in 1859.

When the wine makes its round,   155
"Since life fleets, all is change; the Past gone, seize today!"

27

Fool! All that is, at all,
Lasts ever, past recall;
Earth changes, but thy soul and God stand sure:
What entered into thee,   160
That was, is, and shall be:
Time's wheel runs back or stops: Potter and clay endure.

28

He fixed thee 'mid this dance
Of plastic circumstance,
This Present, thou, forsooth, wouldst fain arrest:[4]   165
Machinery just meant
To give thy soul its bent,
Try thee and turn thee forth, sufficiently impressed.

29

What though the earlier grooves
Which ran the laughing loves   170
Around thy base,[5] no longer pause and press?
What though, about thy rim,
Skull-things in order grim
Grow out, in graver mood, obey the sterner stress?

30

Look not thou down but up!   175
To uses of a cup,
The festal board, lamp's flash, and trumpet's peal,
The new wine's foaming flow,
The Master's lips a-glow!
Thou, heaven's consummate cup, what need'st thou with earth's
    wheel?   180

31

But I need, now as then,
Thee, God, who moldest men;
And since, not even while the whirl was worst,
Did I—to the wheel of life
With shapes and colors rife,   185
Bound dizzily—mistake my end, to slake Thy thirst:

32

So, take and use Thy work:
Amend what flaws may lurk,
What strain o' the stuff, what warpings past the aim!
My times be in Thy hand!   190
Perfect the cup as planned!
Let age approve of youth, and death complete the same!
ca. 1862   1864

4. I.e., you would be glad to stop   of your life.
("arrest") time at this present point   5. Base of the clay pitcher.

Apparent Failure

"We shall soon lose a celebrated building."
PARIS NEWSPAPER

1

No, for I'll save it! Seven years since,
    I passed through Paris, stopped a day
To see the baptism of your Prince;[1]
    Saw, made my bow, and went my way:
Walking the heat and headache off,   5
    I took the Seine-side, you surmise,
Thought of the Congress, Gortschakoff,
    Cavour's appeal and Buol's replies,[2]
So sauntered till—what met my eyes?

2

Only the Doric little Morgue!   10
    The dead-house where you show your drowned:
Petrarch's Vaucluse makes proud the Sorgue,[3]
    Your Morgue has made the Seine renowned.
One pays one's debt in such a case;
    I plucked up heart and entered—stalked,   15
Keeping a tolerable face
    Compared with some whose cheeks were chalked:
Let them! No Briton's to be balked!

3

First came the silent gazers; next,
    A screen of glass, we're thankful for;   20
Last, the sight's self, the sermon's text,
    The three men who did most abhor
Their life in Paris yesterday,
    So killed themselves: and now, enthroned
Each on his copper couch, they lay   25
    Fronting me, waiting to be owned.
I thought, and think, their sin's atoned.

4

Poor men, God made, and all for that!
    The reverence struck me; o'er each head
Religiously was hung its hat,   30
    Each coat dripped by the owner's bed,
Sacred from touch: each had his berth,
    His bounds, his proper place of rest,
Who last night tenanted on earth

1. Prince Louis, son of Napoleon III, was baptized in June, 1856. Browning had witnessed the event.
2. The Congress of Paris which met in 1856 to establish peace terms after the Crimean War. Russia was represented by Prince Alexander Gortscha-koff, Piedmont by Count Cavour, and Austria by Count von Buol-Schauen-stein.
3. The Sorgue River is renowned because the poet Petrarch lived in Vaucluse, a village on its banks.

Some arch, where twelve such slept abreast— 35
Unless the plain asphalt seemed best.

5

How did it happen, my poor boy?
You wanted to be Buonaparte
And have the Tuileries[4] for toy,
    And could not, so it broke your heart? 40
You, old one by his side, I judge,
    Were, red as blood, a socialist,
A leveler! Does the Empire grudge
    You've gained what no Republic missed?
Be quiet, and unclench your fist! 45

6

And this—why, he was red in vain,
    Or black[5]—poor fellow that is blue!
What fancy was it turned your brain?
    Oh, women were the prize for you!
Money gets women, cards and dice 50
    Get money, and ill luck gets just
The copper couch and one clear nice
    Cool squirt of water o'er your bust,
The right thing to extinguish lust!

7

It's wiser being good than bad; 55
    It's safer being meek than fierce:
It's fitter being sane than mad.
    My own hope is, a sun will pierce
The thickest cloud earth ever stretched;
    That, after Last, returns the First, 60
Though a wide compass round be fetched;
    That what began best, can't end worst,
Nor what God blessed once, prove accursed.

1863   1864

O Lyric Love[1]

O lyric Love, half angel and half bird
And all a wonder and a wild desire—
Boldest of hearts that ever braved the sun,
Took sanctuary within the holier blue,
And sang a kindred soul out to his face— 5
Yet human at the red-ripe of the heart—

4. The palace in Paris where the kings of France had resided.
5. Reference to a gambling game, *rouge-et-noir*, in which red or black may win the stakes.
1. These lines, which conclude Book I of *The Ring and the Book*, are addressed to the poet's wife, who had died in 1861. Ten out of the twelve books of this long poem are dramatic monologues, each speaker commenting upon the murder of Pompilia Franceschini by her husband, Guido. In Books I and XII, however, Browning usually speaks, as in this dedicatory passage, in his own person.

When the first summons from the darkling earth
Reached thee amid thy chambers, blanched their blue,
And bared them of the glory—to drop down,
To toil for man, to suffer or to die—   10
This is the same voice: can thy soul know change?
Hail then, and hearken from the realms of help!
Never may I commence my song, my due
To God who best taught song by gift of thee,
Except with bent head and beseeching hand—   15
That still, despite the distance and the dark,
What was, again may be; some interchange
Of grace, some splendor once thy very thought,
Some benediction anciently thy smile:
—Never conclude, but raising hand and head   20
Thither where eyes, that cannot reach, yet yearn
For all hope, all sustainment, all reward,
Their utmost up and on—so blessing back
In those thy realms of help, that heaven thy home,
Some whiteness which, I judge, thy face makes proud,   25
Some wanness where, I think, thy foot may fall!

                                                1868

The Householder

[*Epilogue to* Fifine at the Fair]

1

Savage I was sitting in my house, late, lone:
   Dreary, weary with the long day's work:
Head of me, heart of me, stupid as a stone:
   Tongue-tied now, now blaspheming like a Turk;
When, in a moment, just a knock, call, cry,   5
   Half a pang and all a rapture, there again were we!—
"What, and is it really you again?" quoth I:
   "I again, what else did you expect?" quoth She.

2

"Never mind, hie away from this old house—
   Every crumbling brick embrowned with sin and shame!   10
Quick, in its corners ere certain shapes arouse!
   Let them—every devil of the night—lay claim,
Make and mend, or rap and rend, for me! Good-by!
   God be their guard from disturbance at their glee,
Till, crash, comes down the carcass in a heap!" quoth I: 15
   "Nay, but there's a decency required!" quoth She.

3

"Ah, but if you knew how time has dragged, days, nights!
   All the neighbor-talk with man and maid—such men!
All the fuss and trouble of street sounds, window sights:
   All the worry of flapping door and echoing roof; and then,   20

All the fancies . . . Who were they had leave, dared try
  Darker arts that almost struck despair in me?
If you knew but how I dwelt down here!" quoth I:
  "And was I so better off up there?" quoth She.

4

"Help and get it over! *Reunited to his wife*   25
  (How draw up the paper lets the parish-people know?)
Lies M., or N., departed from this life,
  Day the this or that, month and year the so and so.
What i' the way of final flourish? Prose, verse? Try!
  Affliction sore long time he bore, or, what is it to be?   30
Till God did please to grant him ease. Do end!" quoth I:
  "I end with—Love is all and Death is naught!" quoth She.

1872   1872

House

1

Shall I sonnet-sing you about myself?
  Do I live in a house you would like to see?
Is it scant of gear, has it store of pelf?
  "Unlock my heart with a sonnet-key?"

2

Invite the world, as my betters have done?   5
  "Take notice: this building remains on view,
Its suites of reception every one,
  Its private apartment and bedroom too;

3

"For a ticket, apply to the Publisher."
  No: thanking the public, I must decline.   10
A peep through my window, if folk prefer;
  But, please you, not foot over threshold of mine!

4

I have mixed with a crowd and heard free talk
  In a foreign land where an earthquake chanced:
And a house stood gaping, naught to balk   15
  Man's eye wherever he gazed or glanced.

5

The whole of the frontage shaven sheer,
  The inside gaped: exposed to day,
Right and wrong and common and queer,
  Bare, as the palm of your hand, it lay.   20

6

The owner? Oh, he had been crushed, no doubt!
  "Odd tables and chairs for a man of wealth!
What a parcel of musty old books about!
  He smoked—no wonder he lost his health!

7

"I doubt if he bathed before he dressed.   25
  A brazier?—the pagan, he burned perfumes!

You see it is proved, what the neighbors guessed:
  His wife and himself had separate rooms."
               8

Friends, the goodman of the house at least
  Kept house to himself till an earthquake came:
'Tis the fall of its frontage permits you feast   30
  On the inside arrangement you praise or blame.

               9
Outside should suffice for evidence:
  And whoso desires to penetrate
Deeper, must dive by the spirit-sense—
  No optics like yours, at any rate!   35

             10
."Hoity toity! A street to explore,
  Your house the exception! *'With this same key
Shakespeare unlocked his heart,'* once more!" [2]
  Did Shakespeare? If so, the less Shakespeare he!   40
                        1876

To Edward FitzGerald[1]

I chanced upon a new book yesterday;
I opened it, and, where my finger lay
'Twixt page and uncut page, these words I read—
Some six or seven at most—and learned thereby
That you, FitzGerald, whom by ear and eye
  She never knew, "thanked God my wife was dead."   5
Aye, dead! and were yourself alive, good Fitz,
How to return you thanks would task my wits.
  Kicking you seems the common lot of curs—
While more appropriate greeting lends you grace,
Surely to spit there glorifies your face—   10
  Spitting from lips once sanctified by hers.

1889   1889

2. The quotation is from Wordsworth's *Scorn Not the Sonnet,* which praises the sonnet form as the one in which Shakespeare had revealed his true self. In theory, if not in practice, Browning strongly disapproved of a poet who "unlocked his heart" in public. A striking example of this failing was *The House of Life,* a sonnet sequence by D. G. Rossetti, published in 1870. It has been conjectured that the glimpses into the intimacies of domestic life and love relations, featured in Rossetti's sonnets, probably prompted Browning to present his case on behalf of an artist's right to privacy and need for reticence.

1. In 1861 FitzGerald wrote to a friend: "Mrs. Browning's death is rather a relief to me, I must say: no more *Aurora Leighs* [title of a popular poem by Mrs. Browning], thank God! * * * She and her sex had better mind the kitchen and the children." Browning discovered the passage among FitzGerald's posthumously published letters and in white heat wrote this rejoinder which was published in the *Athenaeum.* In defense of his poem, Browning wrote a long and eloquent letter to the Tennysons (who had been close friends of FitzGerald), which has been published in the *Times Literary Supplement* (June 3, 1965), 464.

Epilogue to *Asolando*[2]

At the midnight in the silence of the sleep-time,
    When you[3] set your fancies free,
Will they pass to where—by death, fools think, imprisoned—
Low he lies who once so loved you, whom you loved so,
        —Pity me?   5
Oh to love so, be so loved, yet so mistaken!
    What had I on earth to do
With the slothful, with the mawkish, the unmanly?
Like the aimless, helpless, hopeless, did I drivel
        —Being—who?   10

One who never turned his back but marched breast forward,
    Never doubted clouds would break,
Never dreamed, though right were worsted, wrong would triumph,
Held we fall to rise, are baffled to fight better,
        Sleep to wake.   15

No, at noonday in the bustle of man's work-time
    Greet the unseen[4] with a cheer!
Bid him forward, breast and back as either should be,
"Strive and thrive!" cry, "Speed—fight on, fare ever
        There as here!"   20
1889   1890

2. The final poem in *Asolando,* a volume published on the day of Browning's death. Browning is said to have recognized that because the third stanza sounded "like bragging" he ought to consider canceling it. "But it's the simple truth," he added, "and as it's true, it shall stand."
3. Any loved person who survives the speaker.
4. The speaker, after he is dead.

MATTHEW ARNOLD
(1822–1888)

1853: *Poems* (with Preface) published.
1857: Elected Professor of Poetry at Oxford.
1869: *Culture and Anarchy* published.

How is a full and enjoyable life to be lived in a modern industrial society? This was the recurrent topic in the poetry and prose of Matthew Arnold. In his poetry the question itself is raised; in his prose some answers are attempted. Arnold's mode of posing such questions may not always satisfy us, and his answers may sometimes be simply wrong. What is less excusable, as he himself said of Ruskin, is that he could be not only wrong but dogmatic when he was wrong. On the whole, however, his writings have fared well with posterity. "The misapprehensiveness of his age is exactly what a poet is sent to remedy," wrote Browning. Oddly enough it is to Arnold's work rather than to Browning's that the statement seems more appropriate. And its applicability to Arnold has persisted from Victorian times to ours, in part because the "misapprehensiveness" has also persisted. Of all the major Victorian writers, as F. R. Leavis has said, it is Arnold who, "because of the peculiar quality of his intelligence and the peculiar nature of his relation to his time, will repay special study in a way no others will."

Matthew Arnold was born in Laleham, a village in the valley of the Thames. That his childhood was spent in the vicinity of a river seems appropriate, for clear-flowing streams were later to appear in his poems as symbols of serenity. At 6, Arnold was moved to Rugby School where his father, Dr. Thomas Arnold, had become headmaster. As a clergyman Dr. Arnold was a leader of the liberal or Broad Church and hence one of the principal opponents of John Henry Newman. As a headmaster he became famous as an educational reformer, a teacher who instilled into his pupils an earnest preoccupation with moral and social issues and also an awareness of the connection between liberal studies and modern life. At Rugby his eldest son, Matthew, was directly exposed to the powerful force of the father's mind and character. The son's attitude towards this force was a mixture of attraction and repulsion. That he was permanently influenced by his father is evident in his poems and in his writings on religion and politics, but like many sons of clergymen, he made a determined effort in his youth to be different. At Oxford he behaved like a character from one of Evelyn Waugh's early novels. Elegantly and colorfully dressed, alternately languid or merry in manner, he attracted attention as a dandy whose irreverent jokes irritated his more solemn undergraduate friends and acquaintances. With Rugby standards he appeared to have no connection. Even his studies did not seem to occupy him seriously. By a session of cramming, he managed to earn second-class honors in his final examinations, a near disaster that was redeemed by his election to a fellowship at Oriel College.

Arnold's biographers usually dismiss his youthful frivolity of spirit as a temporary pose or mask, but it was more. It remained to color his prose style, brightening his most serious criticism with geniality and wit. For most readers the jauntiness of his prose is a virtue, although for others it is offensive. Anyone suspicious of urbanity and irony would applaud Whitman's sour comment that Arnold is "one of the dudes of literature." A more appropriate estimate of his manner is provided by Arnold's own description of Sainte-Beuve as a critic: "a critic of measure, not exuberant; of the center, not provincial * * * with gay and amiable temper, his manner as good as his matter—the '*critique souriant*' [smiling critic]."

Unlike Tennyson or Carlyle, Arnold had to confine his writing and reading to his spare time. In 1847 he took the post of private secretary to Lord Lansdowne, and in 1851, the year of his marriage, he became an inspector of schools, a position which he held for 35 years. Although his work as an inspector may have reduced his output as a writer, it had several advantages. His extensive traveling in England took him to the homes of the more ardently Protestant middle classes, and when he criticized the dullness of middle-class life (as he often did), Arnold knew his subject intimately. His position also led to travel on the Continent to study the schools of Europe. As a critic of English education he was thus able to make helpful comparisons and to draw on a stock of fresh ideas in the same way as in his literary criticism he used his knowledge of French, German, Italian, and classical literatures to measure the achievements of English writers. Despite the monotony of much of his work as an inspector, Arnold became convinced of its importance. It was work that contributed to what he regarded as the most important need of his century: the development of a satisfactory system of education for the middle classes.

In 1849 Arnold published *The Strayed Reveler*, the first of his volumes of poetry. Eight years later, as a tribute to his poetic achievement, he was elected to the Professorship of Poetry at Oxford, a part-time position which he held for ten years. Later, like Dickens and Thackeray before him, Arnold toured America in order to make money by lecturing. For his two visits (1883 and 1886) there was the further inducement of seeing his daughter Lucy, who had married an American. Two years after his second visit to the United States, Arnold died of a sudden heart attack.

Arnold's career as a writer can be divided roughly into four periods. In the 1850's appeared most of his poems; in the 1860's, his literary criticism and social criticism; in the 1870's, his religious and educational writings, and in the 1880's, his second set of essays in literary criticism.

About his career as a poet, two questions are repeatedly asked. The first is whether his poetry is as effective or better than his prose; the second is why he virtually stopped writing poetry after 1860. The first has, of course, been variously answered. Many would endorse Tennyson's request in a letter: "Tell Mat not to write any more of those prose things like *Literature and Dogma*, but to give us something like his *Thyrsis, Scholar Gypsy*, or *Forsaken Merman*." At the opposite extreme is a recent critic, J. D. Jump, who has a high regard for Arnold's prose but considers only one of the poems to have merit: *Dover Beach*. Such readers complain, and with good cause, of Arnold's bad habits as a poet: for example, his excessive reliance upon italics instead of upon meter as a method of emphasizing the meaning of a line. Or they cite the prosy flatness with which he opens his fine sonnet *To a Friend*: "Who prop, thou ask'st, in these bad days, my mind?" Contrariwise, when Arnold leaves the flat plane of versified reflections and attempts to scale the heights of what he called "the grand style," there is a different kind of uncertainty which becomes evident, as in *Sohrab and Rustum*, in the over-elaborated similes. Yet the success of such lovely poems as *Thyrsis* is more than enough to overcome the indictments of the critics. Often, as in *Thyrsis*, he is at his best as a poet of nature. Settings of seashore or river or mountaintop provide something more than picturesque backdrops for these poems; they function to draw the meaning together. A concern for rendering outdoor nature may seem a curious accomplishment for so sophisticated a writer, but as his contemporaries noted, Arnold is in this respect, as in several others, similar to Thomas Gray.

Arnold's own verdict on the qualities of his poetry is a reasonable one. In a letter to his mother, in 1869, he writes: "My poems represent, on the whole, the main movement of mind of the last quarter of a century, and thus they will probably have their day as people become conscious to themselves of what that movement of mind is, and interested in the literary productions which reflect it. It might be fairly urged that I have less poetical sentiment than Tennyson, and less intellectual vigor and abundance than Browning; yet, because I have perhaps more of a fusion of the two than either of them, and have more regularly applied that fusion to the main line of modern development, I am likely enough to have my turn, as they have had theirs."

The emphasis in the letter upon "movement of mind" suggests that Arnold's poetry and prose should be studied together. Such an approach can be fruitful provided that it does not obscure the important difference between Arnold the poet and Arnold the critic. T. S. Eliot once said of his own writings that "in one's prose reflections one may be legitimately occupied with ideals, whereas in the writing of verse, one can deal only with actuality." Arnold's writings provide a nice verification of Eliot's seeming paradox. As a poet he usually records his own experiences, his own feelings of loneliness and isolation as a lover, his longing for a serenity that he cannot find, his melancholy sense of the passing of youth (more than for many men, Arnold's thirtieth birthday was an awesome landmark after which he felt, he said, "three parts iced over"). Above all he records his despair in a universe in which man's role seemed as incongruous as it was later to seem to Thomas Hardy. In a memorable passage of his *Stanzas from the Grande Chartreuse* he describes himself as "wandering between two worlds, one dead, / The other powerless to be born." And addressing the representatives of a faith which seems to him dead, he cries: "Take me, cowled forms, and fence me round, / Till I possess my soul again."

As a poet, then, like T. S. Eliot and W. H. Auden, Arnold provides a record of a sick individual in a sick society. This was "actuality" as he experienced it. As a prose-writer, a formulator of "ideals," he seeks a different role. It is the role of what Auden calls the "healer" of a sick society, or as he himself called Goethe, the "Physician of the iron age." And in this difference we have a clue to the question previously raised: why did Arnold virtually abandon the writing of poetry and shift into criticism? Among other reasons he abandoned it because he was dissatisfied with the kind of poetry he himself was writing.

In one of his excellent letters to his friend Arthur Hugh Clough in the 1850's (letters which provide the best insight we have into Arnold's mind and tastes) this note of dissatisfaction is struck: "I am glad you like the *Gypsy Scholar*—but what does it *do* for you? Homer *animates*—Shakespeare *animates*—in its poor way I think *Sohrab and Rustum animates*—the *Gypsy Scholar* at best awakens a pleasing melancholy. But this is not what we want." It is evident that early in his career Arnold had evolved a theory of what poetry should do for its readers, a theory based, in part, on his impression of what classical poetry had achieved. To help make life bearable, poetry, in Arnold's view, must bring joy. As he says in the Preface to his *Poems* in 1853, it must "inspirit and rejoice the reader"; it must "convey a charm, and infuse delight." Such a demand does not exclude tragic poetry but does exclude works "in which suffering finds no vent in action; in which a continual state of mental distress is prolonged." Of Charlotte Brontë's novel *Villette* he says witheringly: "The writer's mind contains nothing but hunger, rebellion, and rage. * * * No fine writing can hide this thoroughly, and it will be fatal to her in the long run." Judged by such a standard, most 19th-century poems, including *Empedocles on Etna* and others by Arnold, were unsatisfactory. And when Arnold tried himself to write poems which would meet his own requirements—*Sohrab* *and Rustum* or *Balder Dead*—he was not at his best. By the late 1850's he thus found himself at a dead end. By turning aside to literary criticism he was able partially to escape the dilemma. In his prose his melancholy and "morbid" personality was subordinated to the resolutely cheerful and purposeful character he had created for himself by an effort of will.

Arnold's two volumes of *Essays in Criticism* (1865 and 1888) repeatedly shows how authors as different as Marcus Aurelius, Tolstoy, Homer, and Wordsworth provide the virtues he sought in his reading. Among these virtues was plainness of style. Although he could on occasion recommend the richness of language of such poets as Keats or Tennyson—their "natural magic" as he himself called it—Arnold's usual preference was for literature that was unadorned. And beyond stylistic excellences the principal virtue he admired as a critic was what he called the quality of "high seriousness." Given a world in which formal religion appeared to be of subordinate importance, it became increasingly important to Arnold that the poet must be a serious thinker who could offer guidance for his readers. Arnold's attitude towards religion helps to account for his finally asking perhaps too much from literature. Excessive expectations underlie his most glaring blunder as a critic: his solemnly inadequate discussion of Chaucer's lack of high seriousness in *The Study of Poetry*.

In *The Function of Criticism* it is apparent that Arnold regarded good literary criticism, as he regarded literature itself, as a potent force in producing a civilized society. From a close study of this basic essay one could forecast the third stage of his career: his excursion into the criticism of society which was to culminate in *Culture and Anarchy* (1869) and *Friendship's Garland* (1871).

Arnold's starting point as a critic of society is different from that of Carlyle and John Ruskin. The older prophets attacked the Victorian middle classes on the grounds of their materialism, their selfish indifference to the sufferings of the poor—their immorality, in effect. Arnold argued instead that the "Philistines," as he called them, were not so much wicked as ignorant, narrow-minded, and suffering from the dullness of their private lives. This novel analysis was reinforced by Arnold's conviction that the world of the future would be a middle-class world, a world dominated therefore by a class inadequately equipped for leadership and inadequately equipped to enjoy civilized living.

To establish this point, Arnold employed cajolery, satire, and even quotations from the newspapers with considerable effect. He also employed catchwords (such as "sweetness and light") which have remained useful slogans even though they are an obstacle to understanding the complexities of his position. His view of civilization, for example, was pared down to a four-point formula of the four "powers": conduct, intellect and knowledge, beauty, social life and manners. The formula was simple and workable. Applying it to French or American civilizations, he had a scale by which to show up the virtues of different countries as well as their inadequacies. Applying the formula to his own country, Arnold usually awarded the Victorian middle classes an "A" in the first category (of conduct) but a failing grade in the other three categories.

Arnold's relentless exposure of middle-class narrow-mindedness eventually led him into the arena of religious controversy. As a critic of religious institutions he was arguing, in effect, that just as the middle classes did not know how to lead full lives, so also did they not know how to read the Bible intelligently or attend church intelligently. His three full-length studies of the Bible, including *Literature and Dogma* (1873), are best considered in this way as a postscript to his social criticism. The Bible, to Arnold, was a great work of literature like the *Odyssey*, and the Church of England was a great national institution like Parliament. Both Bible and church must be preserved not because historical Christianity was credible but because both, when properly understood, were agents of what he called "culture"—they contributed to making mankind more civilized.

The term *culture* is perhaps Arnold's most familiar catchword, although what he meant by it has sometimes been misunderstood. For him the term connotes the qualities of an open-minded intelligence (as described in *The Function of Criticism*)—a refusal to take things on authority. In this respect, Arnold appears close to T. H. Huxley and J. S. Mill. But the word also connotes a full awareness of man's past and a capacity to enjoy the best works of art, literature, history, and philosophy that have come down to us from that past. As a way of viewing life in all its aspects, including the social, political, and religious, culture represents for Arnold the most effective way of curing the ills of a sick society. It is his principal prescription.

To attempt to define culture brings one to a final aspect of Arnold's career as a critic: his writings on education, in which he sought to make cultural values, as he said, "prevail." Most obviously these writings comprise his reply to Huxley in his admirably reasoned essay, *Literature and Science*, as well as his volumes of official reports written as an inspector of schools. Less obviously they comprise all of his prose. At the core of these writings is his belief that good education is the crucial need for modern man. Arnold was essentially a great teacher raised to the nth degree. He has the faults of a teacher: a tendency to repeat himself, to lean too hard on formulated phrases, and he displays something of the lectern manner at times. He also has the great teacher's virtues, in particular the virtue of skillfully conveying to us the conviction on which all his arguments are based. This conviction is that the humanist tradition of which he is the expositor can enable the individual man or woman to live life more fully as well as to change the course of society. For these values Arnold fought. He boxed with the gloves on—kid gloves, his opponents used to say—and he provided a lively exhibition of footwork that is a pleasure in itself for us to witness. Yet the gracefulness of the display should not obscure the fact that he is landing hard blows squarely on what Carlyle called the vast blockheadism.

Although his lifelong attacks against the inadequacies of puritanism make Arnold one of the most anti-Victorian figures of the Victorian age, there is an assumption behind his attacks that is itself characteristically Victorian. This assumption is that the puritan middle classes *can* be changed, that they are, as we would more clumsily say, educable. In 1852, writing to Clough on the subject of equality (a political objective in which he believed by conviction if not by instinct), he observed: "I am more and more convinced that the world tends to become more comfortable for the mass, and more uncomfortable for those of any natural gift or distinction—and it is as well perhaps that it should be so—for hitherto the gifted have astonished and delighted the world, but not trained or inspired or in any real way changed it." Arnold's gifts as a poet and critic enabled him to do both: to delight the world and also to change it.

Shakespeare

Others abide our question. Thou art free.
We ask and ask—Thou smilest and art still,
Out-topping knowledge. For the loftiest hill,
Who to the stars uncrowns his majesty,

Planting his steadfast footsteps in the sea,[1]   5
Making the heaven of heavens his dwelling place,
Spares but the cloudy border of his base
To the foiled searching of mortality;
And thou, who didst the stars and sunbeams know,
Self-schooled, self-scanned, self-honored, self-secure,   10
Didst tread on earth unguessed at.—Better so!

All pains the immortal spirit must endure,
All weakness which impairs, all griefs which bow,
Find their sole speech in that victorious brow.

1844   1849

In Harmony with Nature[2]

TO A PREACHER

"In harmony with Nature?" Restless fool,
Who with such heat dost preach what were to thee,
When true, the last impossibility—
To be like Nature strong, like Nature cool!

Know, man hath all which Nature hath, but more,   5
And in that *more* lie all his hopes of good.
Nature is cruel, man is sick of blood;
Nature is stubborn, man would fain adore;

Nature is fickle, man hath need of rest;
Nature forgives no debt, and fears no grave;   10
Man would be mild, and with safe conscience blest.

Man must begin, know this, where Nature ends;
Nature and man can never be fast friends.
Fool, if thou canst not pass her, rest her slave!

1844(?)   1849

1. Cf. William Cowper's Olney Hymn 35: "God moves in a mysterious way / His wonders to perform; / He plants his footsteps in the sea, / And rides upon the storm."
2. Originally entitled: "To an Independent Preacher, who preached that we should be 'In Harmony with Nature.'"

To a Friend

Who prop, thou ask'st, in these bad days, my mind?—
He much, the old man,[3] who, clearest-souled of men,
Saw The Wide Prospect, and the Asian Fen,
And Tmolus hill, and Smyrna bay, though blind.

Much he, whose friendship I not long since won,   5
That halting slave, who in Nicopolis [4]
Taught Arrian, when Vespasian's brutal son [5]
Cleared Rome of what most shamed him. But be his

My special thanks, whose even-balanced soul,
From first youth tested up to extreme old age,   10
Business could not make dull, nor passion wild;

Who saw life steadily, and saw it whole;
The mellow glory of the Attic stage,
Singer of sweet Colonus,[4] and its child.

          1849

The Forsaken Merman[1]

Come, dear children, let us away;
Down and away below!
Now my brothers call from the bay,
Now the great winds shoreward blow,
Now the salt tides seaward flow;   5
Now the wild white horses play,
Champ and chafe and toss in the spray.
Children dear, let us away!
This way, this way!

Call her once before you go—   10
Call once yet!
In a voice that she will know:
"Margaret! Margaret!"
Children's voices should be dear
(Call once more) to a mother's ear;   15

3. Homer, who was reputed to have been born in Smyrna, a seaport of what is now Turkey. From Smyrna he saw across the sea to Europe ("The Wide Prospect") as well as to the nearby marshes ("Fen") and mountain ranges ("Tmolus hill") of Asia Minor.

4. Epictetus, a lame philosopher who was exiled to Nicopolis where he taught Stoicism to Arrian, a Greek historian.

5. I.e., the Emperor Domitian (81–96). Because the philosophers had "shamed" him, he had ordered their expulsion from Rome.

4. Sophocles (496–406 B.C.), a native of Colonus, sang of his town in his *Oedipus at Colonus*.

1. For a comparison of Arnold's skillful telling of this story with the Danish version from which he derived it, see C. B. Tinker and H. F. Lowry: *The Poetry of Arnold: A Commentary* (1940), pp. 129–132.

Children's voices, wild with pain—
Surely she will come again!
Call her once and come away;
This way, this way!
"Mother dear, we cannot stay!   20
The wild white horses foam and fret."
Margaret! Margaret!

Come, dear children, come away down;
Call no more!
One last look at the white-walled town,   25
And the little gray church on the windy shore,
Then come down!
She will not come though you call all day;
Come away, come away!

Children dear, was it yesterday   30
We heard the sweet bells over the bay?
In the caverns where we lay,
Through the surf and through the swell,
The far-off sound of a silver bell?
Sand-strewn caverns, cool and deep,   35
Where the winds are all asleep;
Where the spent lights quiver and gleam,
Where the salt weed sways in the stream,
Where the sea beasts, ranged all round,
Feed in the ooze of their pasture ground;   40
Where the sea snakes coil and twine,
Dry their mail and bask in the brine;
Where great whales come sailing by,
Sail and sail, with unshut eye,
Round the world for ever and aye?   45
When did music come this way?
Children dear, was it yesterday?

Children dear, was it yesterday
(Call yet once) that she went away?
Once she sate with you and me,   50
On a red gold throne in the heart of the sea,
And the youngest sate on her knee.
She combed its bright hair, and she tended it well,
When down swung the sound of a far-off bell.
She sighed, she looked up through the clear green sea;   55
She said: "I must go, for my kinsfolk pray
In the little gray church on the shore today.
'Twill be Easter time in the world—ah me!
And I lose my poor soul, Merman! here with thee."
I said: "Go up, dear heart, through the waves;   60
Say thy prayer, and come back to the kind sea caves!"
She smiled, she went up through the surf in the bay.
Children dear, was it yesterday?

Children dear, were we long alone?
"The sea grows stormy, the little ones moan; 65
Long prayers," I said, "in the world they say;
Come!" I said; and we rose through the surf in the bay.
We went up the beach, by the sandy down
Where the sea stocks bloom, to the white-walled town;
Through the narrow paved streets, where all was still, 70
To the little gray church on the windy hill.
From the church came a murmur of folk at their prayers,
But we stood without in the cold blowing airs.
We climbed on the graves, on the stones worn with rains,
And we gazed up the aisle through the small leaded panes. 75
She sate by the pillar; we saw her clear:
"Margaret, hist! come quick, we are here!
Dear heart," I said, "we are long alone;
The sea grows stormy, the little ones moan."
But, ah, she gave me never a look, 80
For her eyes were sealed to the holy book!
Loud prays the priest; shut stands the door.
Come away, children, call no more!
Come away, come down, call no more!

Down, down, down! 85
Down to the depths of the sea!
She sits at her wheel in the humming town,
Singing most joyfully.
Hark what she sings: "O joy, O joy,
For the humming street, and the child with its toy! 90
For the priest, and the bell, and the holy well;
For the wheel where I spun,
And the blessed light of the sun!"
And so she sings her fill,
Singing most joyfully, 95
Till the spindle drops from her hand,
And the whizzing wheel stands still.
She steals to the window, and looks at the sand,
And over the sand at the sea;
And her eyes are set in a stare; 100
And anon there breaks a sigh,
And anon there drops a tear,
From a sorrow-clouded eye,
And a heart sorrow-laden,
A long, long sigh; 105
For the cold strange eyes of a little Mermaiden
And the gleam of her golden hair.

Come away, away children;
Come children, come down!
The hoarse wind blows coldly;
Lights shine in the town. 110
She will start from her slumber

When gusts shake the door;
She will hear the winds howling,
Will hear the waves roar.   115
We shall see, while above us
The waves roar and whirl,
A ceiling of amber,
A pavement of pearl.
Singing: "Here came a mortal,   120
But faithless was she!
And alone dwell forever
The kings of the sea."

But, children, at midnight,
When soft the winds blow,   125
When clear falls the moonlight,
When spring tides are low;
When sweet airs come seaward
From heaths starred with broom,
And high rocks throw mildly   130
On the blanched sands a gloom;
Up the still, glistening beaches,
Up the creeks we will hie,
Over banks of bright seaweed
The ebb tide leaves dry.   135
We will gaze, from the sand hills,
At the white, sleeping town;
At the church on the hillside—
And then come back down.
Singing: "There dwells a loved one,   140
But cruel is she!
She left lonely forever
The kings of the sea."

                                            1849

Isolation. To Marguerite[1]

We were apart; yet, day by day,
I bade my heart more constant be.
I bade it keep the world away,
And grow a home for only thee;
Nor feared but thy love likewise grew,   5
Like mine, each day, more tried, more true.

The fault was grave! I might have known,
What far too soon, alas! I learned—
The heart can bind itself alone,
And faith may oft be unreturned.   10

1. Addressed to a girl Arnold is reputed to have met in Switzerland in the late 1840's.

Self-swayed our feelings ebb and swell—
Thou lov'st no more—Farewell! Farewell!

Farewell!—and thou, thou lonely heart,[2]
Which never yet without remorse
Even for a moment didst depart 15
From thy remote and sphéréd course
To haunt the place where passions reign—
Back to thy solitude again!

Back! with the conscious thrill of shame
Which Luna[3] felt, that summer night, 20
Flash through her pure immortal frame,
When she forsook the starry height
To hang over Endymion's sleep
Upon the pine-grown Latmian steep.

Yet she, chaste queen, had never proved 25
How vain a thing is mortal love,
Wandering in Heaven, far removed.
But thou hast long had place to prove
This truth—to prove, and make thine own:
"Thou hast been, shalt be, art, alone." 30

Or, if not quite alone, yet they
Which touch thee are unmating things—
Ocean and clouds and night and day;
Lorn autumns and triumphant springs;
And life, and others' joy and pain, 35
And love, if love, of happier men.

Of happier men—for they, at least,
Have *dreamed* two human hearts might blend
In one, and were through faith released
From isolation without end 40
Prolonged; nor knew, although not less
Alone than thou, their loneliness.

1857

To Marguerite—Continued

Yes! in the sea of life enisled,
With echoing straits between us thrown,
Dotting the shoreless watery wild,
We mortal millions live *alone*.
The islands feel the enclasping flow, 5
And then their endless bounds they know.

2. Presumably the speaker's heart, not
Marguerite's.
3. Luna (or Diana), the goddess of
chastity and of the moon, fell in love
with Endymion, a handsome shepherd,
whom she discovered asleep on Mt.
Latmos.

But when the moon their hollows lights,
And they are swept by balms of spring,
And in their glens, on starry nights,
The nightingales divinely sing;   10
And lovely notes, from shore to shore,
Across the sounds and channels pour—

Oh! then a longing like despair
Is to their farthest caverns sent;
For surely once, they feel, we were   15
Parts of a single continent!
Now round us spreads the watery plain—
Oh might our marges meet again!

Who ordered that their longing's fire
Should be, as soon as kindled, cooled?   20
Who renders vain their deep desire?—
A God, a God their severance ruled!
And bade betwixt their shores to be
The unplumbed, salt, estranging sea.

ca. 1849   1852

The Buried Life

Light flows our war of mocking words, and yet,
Behold, with tears mine eyes are wet!
I feel a nameless sadness o'er me roll.
Yes, yes, we know that we can jest,
We know, we know that we can smile!   5
But there's a something in this breast,
To which thy light words bring no rest,
And thy gay smiles no anodyne.
Give me thy hand, and hush awhile,
And turn those limpid eyes on mine,   10
And let me read there, love! thy inmost soul.

Alas! is even love too weak
To unlock the heart, and let it speak?
Are even lovers powerless to reveal
To one another what indeed they feel?   15
I knew the mass of men concealed
Their thoughts, for fear that if revealed
They would by other men be met
With blank indifference, or with blame reproved;
I knew they lived and moved   20
Tricked in disguises, alien to the rest
Of men, and alien to themselves—and yet
The same heart beats in every human breast!

But we, my love!—doth a like spell benumb
Our hearts, our voices?—must we too be dumb?   25

Ah! well for us, if even we,
Even for a moment, can get free
Our heart, and have our lips unchained;
For that which seals them hath been deep-ordained!

Fate, which foresaw   30
How frivolous a baby man would be—
By what distractions he would be possessed,
How he would pour himself in every strife,
And well-nigh change his own identity—
That it might keep from his capricious play   35
His genuine self, and force him to obey
Even in his own despite his being's law,
Bade through the deep recesses of our breast
The unregarded river of our life
Pursue with indiscernible flow its way;   40
And that we should not see
The buried stream, and seem to be
Eddying at large in blind uncertainty,
Though driving on with it eternally.

But often, in the world's most crowded streets,[1]
But often, in the din of strife,   45
There rises an unspeakable desire
After the knowledge of our buried life;
A thirst to spend our fire and restless force
In tracking out our true, original course;   50
A longing to inquire
Into the mystery of this heart which beats
So wild, so deep in us—to know
Whence our lives come and where they go.
And many a man in his own breast then delves,   55
But deep enough, alas! none ever mines.
And we have been on many thousand lines,
And we have shown, on each, spirit and power;
But hardly have we, for one little hour,
Been on our own line, have we been ourselves—   60
Hardly had skill to utter one of all
The nameless feelings that course through our breast,
But they course on forever unexpressed.
And long we try in vain to speak and act
Our hidden self, and what we say and do   65
Is eloquent, is well—but 'tis not true!
And then we will no more be racked
With inward striving, and demand

1. This passage, like many others in Arnold's poetry, illustrates the impact on his writings of Wordsworth. In this instance cf. Wordsworth's *Tintern Abbey*, lines 25-27: "But oft, in lonely rooms, and 'mid the din / Of towns and cities, I have owed to them, / In hours of weariness, sensations sweet."

Of all the thousand nothings of the hour
Their stupefying power;   70
Ah yes, and they benumb us at our call!
Yet still, from time to time, vague and forlorn,
From the soul's subterranean depth upborne
As from an infinitely distant land,
Come airs, and floating echoes, and convey   75
A melancholy into all our day.[2]

Only—but this is rare—
When a beloved hand is laid in ours,
When, jaded with the rush and glare
Of the interminable hours,   80
Our eyes can in another's eyes read clear,
When our world-deafened ear
Is by the tones of a loved voice caressed—
A bolt is shot back somewhere in our breast,
And a lost pulse of feeling stirs again.   85
The eye sinks inward, and the heart lies plain,
And what we mean, we say, and what we would, we know.
A man becomes aware of his life's flow,
And hears its winding murmur; and he sees
The meadows where it glides, the sun, the breeze.   90

And there arrives a lull in the hot race
Wherein he doth forever chase
That flying and elusive shadow, rest.
An air of coolness plays upon his face,
And an unwonted calm pervades his breast.   95
And then he thinks he knows
The hills where his life rose,
And the sea where it goes.

                                                                    1852

Stanzas in Memory of the Author of *Obermann*[3]

NOVEMBER, 1849

In front the awful Alpine track
Crawls up its rocky stair;

2. Cf. Wordsworth's *Ode: Intimations of Immortality,* lines 151–53: "Those shadowy recollections, / Which, be they what they may, / Are yet the fountain light of all our day."

3. The author of *Obermann* (1804), an epistolary novel, was a French essayist, E. P. de Senancour (1770–1846). The hero is a recluse living in a mountain chalet in the Lake Geneva district of Switzerland. The book's melancholy reflections and its celebration of Alpine scenery combined to establish its vogue among a select group of readers. When Arnold discovered the book in 1847 it made "an extraordinary impression" on him. In 1869 he published an essay on Senancour, and his poems refer often to *Obermann* as representative of qualities Arnold sometimes admired in writers of the Romantic Movement. In a note of 1868 he wrote: "The influence of Rousseau, and certain affinities with more famous and fortunate authors of his own day—Chateaubriand and Madame de Staël—are everywhere visible in Senancour. * * * The stir of all the main forces, by which modern life is and has been impelled, lives in the letters of *Obermann;* the dissolving agencies of the

The autumn storm-winds drive the rack,[4]
Close o'er it, in the air.

Behind are the abandoned baths [5]
Mute in their meadows lone;
The leaves are on the valley paths,
The mists are on the Rhone—

The white mists rolling like a sea!
I hear the torrents roar.
—Yes, Obermann, all speaks of thee;
I feel thee near once more!

I turn thy leaves! I feel their breath
Once more upon me roll;
That air of languor, cold, and death,
Which brooded o'er thy soul.

Fly hence, poor wretch, whoe'er thou art,
Condemned to cast about,
All shipwreck in thy own weak heart,
For comfort from without!

A fever in these pages burns
Beneath the calm they feign;
A wounded human spirit turns,
Here, on its bed of pain.

Yes, though the virgin mountain air
Fresh through these pages blows;
Though to these leaves the glaciers spare
The soul of their white snows;

Though here a mountain murmur swells
Of many a dark-boughed pine;
Though, as you read, you hear the bells
Of the high-pasturing kine—

Yet, through the hum of torrent lone,
And brooding mountain bee,
There sobs I know not what ground tone
Of human agony.

Is it for this, because the sound
Is fraught too deep with pain,
That, Obermann! the world around
So little loves thy strain?

eighteenth century, the fiery storm of the French Revolution, the first faint promise and dawn of that new world which our own time is but now more fully bringing to light—all these are to be felt * * * there. To me, indeed, it will always seem that the impressiveness of this production can hardly be rated too high." Arnold composed his elegy during a visit to Switzerland in the autumn of 1849.

Eighteen years later he stated in a letter that the poem records "my separation of myself, finally, from him [Senancour] and his influence."
4. Mass of clouds.
5. The Baths of Leuk. This poem was conceived, and partly composed, in the valley going down from the foot of the Gemmi Pass towards the Rhone [Arnold's note].

Some secrets may the poet tell,
For the world loves new ways;
To tell too deep ones is not well—
It knows not what he says.

Yet of the spirits who have reigned   45
In this our troubled day,
I know but two, who have attained,
Save thee, to see their way.

By England's lakes, in gray old age,
His quiet home one keeps;   50
And one, the strong much toiling sage,
In German Weimar sleeps.

But Wordsworth's eyes avert their ken
From half of human fate;
And Goethe's course few sons of men   55
May think to emulate.

For he pursued a lonely road,
His eyes on Nature's plan;
Neither made man too much a God,
Nor God too much a man.   60

Strong was he, with a spirit free
From mists, and sane, and clear;
Clearer, how much! than ours—yet we
Have a worse course to steer.

For though his manhood bore the blast   65
Of a tremendous time,
Yet in a tranquil world was passed
His tender youthful prime.[6]

But we, brought forth and reared in hours
Of change, alarm, surprise—   70
What shelter to grow ripe is ours?
What leisure to grow wise?

Like children bathing on the shore,
Buried a wave beneath,
The second wave succeeds, before   75
We have had time to breathe.

Too fast we live, too much are tried,
Too harassed, to attain
Wordsworth's sweet calm, or Goethe's wide
And luminous view to gain.   80

And then we turn, thou sadder sage,
To thee! we feel thy spell!

6. Goethe (1749–1832) lived 40 years before the outbreak of the French Revolution.

—The hopeless tangle of our age,
Thou too hast scanned it well!

Immovable thou sittest, still   85
As death, composed to bear!
Thy head is clear, thy feeling chill,
And icy thy despair.

Yes, as the son of Thetis [7] said,
I hear thee saying now: 90
Greater by far than thou are dead;
Strive not! die also thou!

Ah! two desires toss about
The poet's feverish blood.
One drives him to the world without,   95
And one to solitude.

The glow, he cries, *the thrill of life,*
Where, where do these abound?—
Not in the world, not in the strife
Of men, shall they be found.   100

He who hath watched, not shared, the strife,
Knows how the day hath gone.
He only lives with the world's life,
Who hath renounced his own.

To thee we come, then! Clouds are rolled   105
Where thou, O seer! art set;
Thy realm of thought is drear and cold—
The world is colder yet!

And thou hast pleasures, too, to share
With those who come to thee—   110
Balms floating on thy mountain air,
And healing sights to see.

How often, where the slopes are green
On Jaman,[8] hast thou sate
By some high chalet door, and seen   115
The summer day grow late;

And darkness steal o'er the wet grass
With the pale crocus starred,
And reach that glimmering sheet of glass
Beneath the piny sward,   120

Lake Leman's waters, far below!
And watched the rosy light
Fade from the distant peaks of snow;
And on the air of night

---

7. Achilles. See *Iliad* XXI. 106–13.   8. A mountain on the shores of Lake
Geneva.

Heard accents of the eternal tongue 125
Through the pine branches play—
Listened, and felt thyself grow young!
Listened and wept—Away!

Away the dreams that but deceive
And thou, sad guide, adieu! 130
I go, fate drives me; but I leave
Half of my life with you.

We, in some unknown Power's employ,
Move on a rigorous line;
Can neither, when we will, enjoy, 135
Nor, when we will, resign.

I in the world must live; but thou,
Thou melancholy shade!
Wilt not, if thou canst see me now,
Condemn me, nor upbraid. 140

For thou art gone away from earth,
And place with those dost claim,
The Children of the Second Birth,[9]
Whom the world could not tame;

And with that small, transfigured band, 145
Whom many a different way
Conducted to their common land,
Thou learn'st to think as they.

Christian and pagan, king and slave,
Soldier and anchorite, 150
Distinctions we esteen so grave,
Are nothing in their sight.

They do not ask, who pined unseen,
Who was on action hurled,
Whose one bond is, that all have been 155
Unspotted by the world.

There without anger thou wilt see
Him who obeys thy spell
No more, so he but rest, like thee,
Unsoiled!—and so, farewell. 160

Farewell!—Whether thou now liest near
That much-loved inland sea,
The ripples of whose blue waves cheer
Vevey and Meillerie:[1]

And in that gracious region bland, 165
Where with clear rustling wave

9. "Except a man be born again, he cannot see the kingdom of God" (John iii.3).
1. Towns in the Lake Geneva region.

Senancour, as Arnold learned later, had been buried in a suburb of Paris, "The Capital of Pleasure" (line 179).

The scented pines of Switzerland
Stand dark round thy green grave,

Between the dusty vineyard walls
Issuing on that green place   170
The early peasant still recalls
The pensive stranger's face,

And stoops to clear thy moss-grown date
Ere he plods on again—
Or whether, by maligner fate,   175
Among the swarms of men,

Where between granite terraces
The blue Seine rolls her wave,
The Capital of Pleasure sees
The hardly-heard-of grave—   180

Farewell! Under the sky we part,
In this stern Alpine dell.
O unstrung will! O broken heart!
A last, a last farewell!

1849   1852

Memorial Verses[1]

APRIL, 1850

Goethe in Weimar sleeps, and Greece,
Long since, saw Byron's struggle cease.
But one such death remained to come;
The last poetic voice is dumb—
We stand today by Wordsworth's tomb.   5

When Byron's eyes were shut in death,
We bowed our head and held our breath.
He taught us little; but our soul
Had *felt* him like the thunder's roll.
With shivering heart the strife we saw   10
Of passion with eternal law;
And yet with reverential awe
We watched the fount of fiery life
Which served for that Titanic strife.

When Goethe's death was told, we said: 15
Sunk, then, is Europe's sagest head.
Physician of the iron age,

1. This elegy was written shortly after Wordsworth had died in April, 1850, at the age of 80. Arnold had known the poet as a man and deeply admired his writings—as is evident not only in this poem but in his late essay, *Wordsworth*. Byron, who died in Greece in 1824, had affected Arnold profoundly in his youth, but later that strenuous "Titanic" poetry seemed to him less satisfactory, its value limited by its lack of serenity. His final verdict on Byron can be encountered in his essay in *Essays in Criticism: Second Series*. Goethe, who died in 1832, was regarded by Arnold as a great philosophical poet and the most significant man of letters of the early 19th century.

Goethe has done his pilgrimage.
He took the suffering human race,
He read each wound, each weakness clear;   20
And struck his finger on the place,
And said: *Thou ailest here, and here!*
He looked on Europe's dying hour
Of fitful dream and feverish power;
His eye plunged down the weltering strife,   25
The turmoil of expiring life—
He said: *The end is everywhere,*
Art still has truth, take refuge there!
And he was happy, if to know
Causes of things, and far below   30
His feet to see the lurid flow
Of terror, and insane distress,
And headlong fate, be happiness.

    And Wordsworth!—Ah, pale ghosts, rejoice!
For never has such soothing voice   35
Been to your shadowy world conveyed,
Since erst, a morn, some wandering shade
Heard the clear song of Orpheus[2] come
Through Hades, and the mournful gloom.
Wordsworth has gone from us—and ye,   40
Ah, may ye feel his voice as we!
He too upon a wintry clime
Had fallen—on this iron time
Of doubts, disputes, distractions, fears.
He found us when the age had bound   45
Our souls in its benumbing round;
He spoke, and loosed our heart in tears.
He laid us as we lay at birth
On the cool flowery lap of earth,
Smiles broke from us and we had ease;   50
The hills were round us, and the breeze
Went o'er the sunlit fields again;
Our foreheads felt the wind and rain.
Our youth returned; for there was shed
On spirits that had long been dead,   55
Spirits dried up and closely furled,
The freshness of the early world.

    Ah! since dark days still bring to light
Man's prudence and man's fiery might,
Time may restore us in his course   60
Goethe's sage mind and Byron's force;
But where will Europe's latter hour
Again find Wordsworth's healing power?
Others will teach us how to dare,
And against fear our breast to steel;   65

2. By means of his beautiful music,   in his search for the shade of his dead
Orpheus won his way through Hades   wife, Eurydice.

Others will strengthen us to bear—
But who, ah! who, will make us feel?
The cloud of mortal destiny,
Others will front it fearlessly—
But who, like him, will put it by?   70

    Keep fresh the grass upon his grave
O Rotha,[3] with thy living wave!
Sing him thy best! for few or none
Hears thy voice right, now he is gone.

1850   1850

Longing

Come to me in my dreams, and then
By day I shall be well again!
For then the night will more than pay
The hopeless longing of the day.

Come, as thou cam'st a thousand times,   5
A messenger from radiant climes,
And smile on thy new world, and be
As kind to others as to me!

Or, as thou never cam'st in sooth,
Come now, and let me dream it truth;   10
And part my hair, and kiss my brow,
And say: *My love! why sufferest thou?*

Come to me in my dreams, and then
By day I shall be well again!
For then the night will more than pay   15
The hopeless longing of the day.

1852

Lines Written in Kensington Gardens[4]

In this lone, open glade I lie,
Screened by deep boughs on either hand;
And at its end, to stay the eye,
Those black-crowned, red-boled pine trees stand!

Birds here make song, each bird has his,   5
Across the girdling city's hum.
How green under the boughs it is!
How thick the tremulous sheep-cries come![5]

---

3. A river near Wordsworth's burial place.
4. A park in the heart of London.
5. Sheep are sometimes grazed in London parks.

Sometimes a child will cross the glade
To take his nurse his broken toy;   10
Sometimes a thrush flit overhead
Deep in her unknown day's employ.

Here at my feet what wonders pass,
What endless, active life is here!
What blowing daisies, fragrant grass!   15
An air-stirred forest, fresh and clear.

Scarce fresher is the mountain sod
Where the tired angler lies, stretched out,
And, eased of basket and of rod,
Counts his day's spoil, the spotted trout.   20

In the huge world, which roars hard by,
Be others happy if they can!
But in my helpless cradle I
Was breathed on by the rural Pan.

I, on men's impious uproar hurled,   25
Think often, as I hear them rave,
That peace has left the upper world
And now keeps only in the grave.

Yet here is peace forever new!
When I who watch them am away,   30
Still all things in this glade go through
The changes of their quiet day.

Then to their happy rest they pass!
The flowers upclose, the birds are fed,
The night comes down upon the grass,   35
The child sleeps warmly in his bed.

Calm soul of all things! make it mine
To feel, amid the city's jar,
That there abides a piece of thine,
Man did not make, and cannot mar.   40

The will to neither strive nor cry,
The power to feel with others give!
Calm, calm me more! nor let me die
Before I have begun to live.

       1852

Philomela[1]

> Hark! ah, the nightingale—
> The tawny-throated!

1. The Greek tale of violence evoked by the song of the nightingale concerned two sisters, Philomela and Procne. In Arnold's version, Philomela was married to a king of Thrace. After learning that her husband had raped

Hark, from that moonlit cedar what a burst!
What triumph! hark!—what pain!

O wanderer from a Grecian shore,   5
Still, after many years, in distant lands,
Still nourishing in thy bewildered brain
That wild, unquenched, deep-sunken, old-world pain—
Say, will it never heal?
And can this fragrant lawn   10
With its cool trees, and night,
And the sweet, tranquil Thames,
And moonshine, and the dew,
To thy racked heart and brain
Afford no balm?   15

Dost thou tonight behold,
Here, through the moonlight on this English grass,
The unfriendly palace in the Thracian wild?
Dost thou again peruse
With hot cheeks and seared eyes   20
The too clear web,[2] and thy dumb sister's shame?
Dost thou once more assay
Thy flight, and feel come over thee,
Poor fugitive, the feathery change
Once more, and once more seem to make resound   25
With love and hate, triumph and agony,
Lone Daulis, and the high Cephissian vale?[3]
Listen, Eugenia[4]—
How thick the bursts come crowding through the leaves!
Again—thou hearest?   30
Eternal passion!
Eternal pain!

1848   1853

Requiescat[5]

Strew on her roses, roses,
    And never a spray of yew!
In quiet she reposes;
    Ah, would that I did too!

Her mirth the world required;   5
    She bathed it in smiles of glee.

Procne and cut out her tongue to prevent the outrage being discovered, Philomela was transformed into a nightingale.
2. A picture in needlework made by
Procne to tell what had happened to
her.

3. Daulis, a city in Phocis, where
Philomela's transformation took place;
the "Cephissian vale" was a river valley in Phocis.
4. Unidentified listener.
5. "May she rest."

But her heart was tired, tired,
    And now they let her be.

Her life was turning, turning,
    In mazes of heat and sound.   10
But for peace her soul was yearning,
    And now peace laps her round.

Her cabined, ample spirit,
    It fluttered and failed for breath.
Tonight it doth inherit   15
    The vasty hall of death.

                                       1853

The Scholar Gypsy

The story of a 17th-century student who left Oxford and joined a band of gypsies had made a strong impression on Arnold. In the poem he wistfully imagines that the spirit of this scholar is still to be encountered in the Cumner countryside near Oxford, having achieved immortality by a serene pursuit of the secret of human existence. Like Keats's nightingale, the scholar has escaped "the weariness, the fever, and the fret" of modern life.

At the outset, the poet addresses a shepherd who has been helping him in his search for traces of the scholar. The shepherd is addressed as "you." After line 61, with the shift to "thou" and "thy," the person addressed is the scholar himself, and the poet thereafter sometimes uses the pronoun "we" to indicate he is speaking for all mankind of later generations.

About the setting Arnold wrote to his brother Tom on May 15, 1857: "You alone of my brothers are associated with that life at Oxford, the *freest* and most delightful part, perhaps, of my life, when with you and Clough and Walrond I shook off all the bonds and formalities of the place, and enjoyed the spring of life and that unforgotten Oxfordshire and Berkshire country. Do you remember a poem of mine called 'The Scholar Gipsy'? It was meant to fix the remembrance of those delightful wanderings of ours in the Cumner Hills."

The passage from Joseph Glanvill's *Vanity of Dogmatizing* (1661) which inspired the poem was included by Arnold as a note:

There was very lately a lad in the University of Oxford, who was by his poverty forced to leave his studies there; and at last to join himself to a company of vagabond gypsies. Among these extravagant people, by the insinuating subtilty of his carriage, he quickly got so much of their love and esteem as that they discovered to him their mystery. After he had been a pretty while exercised in the trade, there chanced to ride by a couple of scholars, who had formerly been of his acquaintance. They quickly spied out their old friend among the gypsies; and he gave them an account of the necessity which drove him to that kind of life, and told them that the people he went with were not such imposters as they were taken for, but that they had a traditional kind of learning among them, and could do wonders by the power of imagination, their fancy binding that of others: that himself had learned much of their art, and when he had compassed the whole secret, he intended, he said, to leave their company, and give the world an account of what he had learned.

The Scholar Gypsy

Go, for they call you, shepherd, from the hill;
  Go, shepherd, and untie the wattled cotes![1]
    No longer leave thy wistful flock unfed,
    Nor let thy bawling fellows rack their throats,
      Nor the cropped herbage shoot another head.   5
      But when the fields are still,
    And the tired men and dogs all gone to rest,
      And only the white sheep are sometimes seen
      Cross and recross the strips of moon-blanched green,
Come, shepherd, and again begin the quest!   10

Here, where the reaper was at work of late—
  In this high field's dark corner, where he leaves
    His coat, his basket, and his earthen cruse,[2]
    And in the sun all morning binds the sheaves,
      Then here, at noon, comes back his stores to use—   15
      Here will I sit and wait,
    While to my ear from uplands far away
      The bleating of the folded[3] flocks is borne,
      With distant cries of reapers in the corn[4]—
All the live murmur of a summer's day.   20

Screened is this nook o'er the high, half-reaped field,
  And here till sundown, shepherd! will I be.
    Through the thick corn the scarlet poppies peep,
    And round green roots and yellowing stalks I see
      Pale pink convolvulus in tendrils creep;   25
      And air-swept lindens yield
    Their scent, and rustle down their perfumed showers
      Of bloom on the bent grass[5] where I am laid,
      And bower me from the August sun with shade;
And the eye travels down to Oxford's towers.   30

And near me on the grass lies Glanvill's book—
  Come, let me read the oft-read tale again!
    The story of the Oxford scholar poor,
    Of pregnant parts[6] and quick inventive brain,
      Who, tired of knocking at preferment's door,   35
      One summer morn forsook
    His friends, and went to learn the gypsy lore,
      And roamed the world with that wild brotherhood,
      And came, as most men deemed, to little good,
But came to Oxford and his friends no more.   40

But once, years after, in the country lanes,
  Two scholars, whom at college erst he knew,

---

1. Sheepfolds woven from sticks.
2. Pot or jug for carrying his drink.
3. Penned up.

4. Grain or wheat.
5. A stiff kind of grass.
6. Teeming with ideas.

Met him, and of his way of life inquired;
Whereat he answered, that the gypsy crew,
   His mates, had arts to rule as they desired   45
      The workings of men's brains,
And they can bind them to what thoughts they will.
   "And I," he said, "the secret of their art,
   When fully learned, will to the world impart;
But it needs heaven-sent moments for this skill."   50

This said, he left them, and returned no more.—
   But rumors hung about the countryside,
   That the lost Scholar long was seen to stray,
   Seen by rare glimpses, pensive and tongue-tied,
      In hat of antique shape, and cloak of gray,   55
      The same the gypsies wore.
Shepherds had met him on the Hurst[8] in spring;
   At some lone alehouse in the Berkshire moors,
   On the warm ingle-bench,[9] the smock-frocked boors
Had found him seated at their entering,   60

But, 'mid their drink and clatter, he would fly.
   And I myself seem half to know thy looks,
      And put the shepherds, wanderer! on thy trace;
And boys who in lone wheatfields scare the rooks[9]
      I ask if thou hast passed their quiet place;   65
      Or in my boat I lie
Moored to the cool bank in the summer heats,
   'Mid wide grass meadows which the sunshine fills,
   And watch the warm, green-muffled Cumner hills,
And wonder if thou haunt'st their shy retreats.   70

For most, I know, thou lov'st retired ground!
   Thee at the ferry Oxford riders blithe,
      Returning home on summer nights, have met
Crossing the stripling Thames[1] at Bab-lock-hithe,
      Trailing in the cool stream thy fingers wet,   75
      As the punt's rope chops round;[2]
And leaning backward in a pensive dream,
   And fostering in thy lap a heap of flowers
   Plucked in shy fields and distant Wychwood bowers,
And thine eyes resting on the moonlit stream.   80

And then they land, and thou art seen no more!—

---

7. A hill near Oxford. All the place names in the poem (except those in the final two stanzas) refer to the countryside near Oxford.
8. Fireside bench. "Boors," here, are rustics.
9. Boys hired to frighten crows away from eating wheat grains. See Hardy's novel *Jude the Obscure*, I.ii.
1. I.e., the narrow upper reaches of the river before it broadens out to its full width.
2. The scholar's flat-bottomed boat ("punt") is tied up by a rope at the river bank near the ferry-crossing like the speaker's boat (in the previous stanza), which was "moored to the cool bank." The motion of the boat as it is stirred by the current of the river causes the chopping sound of the rope in the water.

Maidens, who from the distant hamlets come
　To dance around the Fyfield elm in May,
Oft through the darkening fields have seen thee roam,
　Or cross a stile into the public way.　　　　　　85
　　Oft thou hast given them store
Of flowers—the frail-leafed, white anemone,
　Dark bluebells drenched with dews of summer eves,
　And purple orchises with spotted leaves—
But none hath words she can report of thee.　　90

And, above Godstow Bridge, when hay time's here
　In June, and many a scythe in sunshine flames,
　Men who through those wide fields of breezy grass
Where black-winged swallows haunt the glittering Thames,
　To bathe in the abandoned lasher pass,[3]　　95
　　Have often passed thee near
Sitting upon the river bank o'ergrown;
　Marked thine outlandish garb, thy figure spare,
　Thy dark vague eyes, and soft abstracted air—
But, when they came from bathing, thou wast gone!　　100

At some lone homestead in the Cumner hills,
　Where at her open door the housewife darns,
　Thou hast been seen, or hanging on a gate
To watch the threshers in the mossy barns.
　Children, who early range these slopes and late　　105
　　For cresses from the rills,
Have known thee eying, all an April day,
　The springing pastures and the feeding kine;
　And marked thee, when the stars come out and shine,
Through the long dewy grass move slow away.　　110

In autumn, on the skirts of Bagley Wood—
　Where most the gypsies by the turf-edged way
　Pitch their smoked tents, and every bush you see
With scarlet patches tagged and shreds of gray,
　Above the forest ground called Thessaly—　　115
　　The blackbird, picking food,
Sees thee, nor stops his meal, nor fears at all;
　So often has he known thee past him stray,
　Rapt, twirling in thy hand a withered spray,
And waiting for the spark from heaven to fall.　　120

And once, in winter, on the causeway chill
　Where home through flooded fields foot-travelers go,
　Have I not passed thee on the wooden bridge,
Wrapped in thy cloak and battling with the snow,
　Thy face tow'rd Hinksey and its wintry ridge?　　125
　　And thou hast climbed the hill,
And gained the white brow of the Cumner range;

---

3. Water that spills over a dam or weir.　　　4. The dining hall of an Oxford college.

Turned once to watch, while thick the snowflakes fall,
  The line of festal light in Christ Church hall[4]—
    Then sought thy straw in some sequestered grange.   130

But what—I dream! Two hundred years are flown
  Since first thy story ran through Oxford halls,
    And the grave Glanvill did the tale inscribe
  That thou wert wandered from the studious walls
    To learn strange arts, and join a gypsy tribe;   135
      And thou from earth art gone
  Long since, and in some quiet churchyard laid—
    Some country nook, where o'er thy unknown grave
    Tall grasses and white flowering nettles wave,
  Under a dark, red-fruited yew tree's shade.   140

—No, no, thou hast not felt the lapse of hours!
  For what wears out the life of mortal men?
    'Tis that from change to change their being rolls;
    'Tis that repeated shocks, again, again,
      Exhaust the energy of strongest souls   145
        And numb the elastic powers.
  Till having used our nerves with bliss and teen,[5]
    And tired upon a thousand schemes our wit,
    To the just-pausing Genius[6] we remit
  Our worn-out life, and are—what we have been.   150

Thou hast not lived, why should'st thou perish, so?
  Thou hadst *one* aim, *one* business, *one* desire;
    Else wert thou long since numbered with the dead!
  Else hadst thou spent, like other men, thy fire!
    The generations of thy peers are fled,   155
      And we ourselves shall go;
  But thou possessest an immortal lot,
    And we imagine thee exempt from age
    And living as thou liv'st on Glanvill's page,
  Because thou hadst—what we, alas! have not.   160

For early didst thou leave the world, with powers
  Fresh, undiverted to the world without,
    Firm to their mark, not spent on other things;
  Free from the sick fatigue, the languid doubt,
    Which much to have tried, in much been baffled, brings.   165
      O life unlike to ours!
  Who fluctuate idly without term or scope,
    Of whom each strives, nor knows for what he strives,
    And each half[7] lives a hundred different lives;
  Who wait like thee, but not, like thee, in hope.   170

Thou waitest for the spark from heaven! and we,
  Light half-believers of our casual creeds,
    Who never deeply felt, nor clearly willed,

---

4. The dining hall of an Oxford college.
5. Vexation.
6. Perhaps the spirit of the universe, which pauses briefly to receive back the life given to us.
7. An adverb modifying "lives."

Whose insight never has borne fruit in deeds,
  Whose vague resolves never have been fulfilled;   175
    For whom each year we see
Breeds new beginnings, disappointments new;
  Who hesitate and falter life away,
  And lose tomorrow the ground won today—
Ah! do not we, wanderer! await it too?   180
Yes, we await it!—but it still delays,
  And then we suffer! and amongst us one,[8]
    Who most has suffered, takes dejectedly
His seat upon the intellectual throne;
  And all his store of sad experience he   185
    Lays bare of wretched days;
Tells us his misery's birth and growth and signs,
  And how the dying spark of hope was fed,
  And how the breast was soothed, and how the head,
And all his hourly varied anodynes.   190

This for our wisest! and we others pine,
  And wish the long unhappy dream would end,
    And waive all claim to bliss, and try to bear;
With close-lipped patience for our only friend,
  Sad patience, too near neighbor to despair—   195
    But none has hope like thine!
Thou through the fields and through the woods dost stray,
  Roaming the countryside, a truant boy,
  Nursing thy project in unclouded joy,
And every doubt long blown by time away.   200

O born in days when wits were fresh and clear,
  And life ran gaily as the sparkling Thames;
    Before this strange disease of modern life,
With its sick hurry, its divided aims,
  Its heads o'ertaxed, its palsied hearts, was rife— 205
    Fly hence, our contact fear!
Still fly, plunge deeper in the bowering wood!
  Averse, as Dido[9] did with gesture stern
  From her false friend's approach in Hades turn,
Wave us away, and keep thy solitude!   210

Still nursing the unconquerable hope,
  Still clutching the inviolable shade,
    With a free, onward impulse brushing through,
By night, the silvered branches of the glade—
  Far on the forest skirts, where none pursue.   215
    On some mild pastoral slope
Emerge, and resting on the moonlit pales
  Freshen thy flowers as in former years
  With dew, or listen with enchanted ears,

8. Probably Tennyson, whose *In Memoriam* had appeared in 1850, or perhaps Goethe.
9. Dido committed suicide after her lover, Aeneas, deserted her. When he later encountered her in Hades, she turned sternly away from him.

From the dark dingles,[10] to the nightingales!   220

But fly our paths, our feverish contact fly!
   For strong the infection of our mental strife,
      Which, though it gives no bliss, yet spoils for rest;
   And we should win thee from thy own fair life,
      Like us distracted, and like us unblest.   225
         Soon, soon thy cheer would die,
   Thy hopes grow timorous, and unfixed thy powers,
   And thy clear aims be cross and shifting made;
   And then thy glad perennial youth would fade,
   Fade, and grow old at last, and die like ours.   230

Then fly our greetings, fly our speech and smiles!
   —As some grave Tyrian trader, from the sea,
      Descried at sunrise an emerging prow
   Lifting the cool-haired creepers stealthily,
      The fringes of a southward-facing brow   235
         Among the Aegean isles;
   And saw the merry Grecian coaster come,
      Freighted with amber grapes, and Chian wine,
      Green, bursting figs, and tunnies[1] steeped in brine—
   And knew the intruders on his ancient home,   240

The young lighthearted masters of the waves—
   And snatched his rudder, and shook out more sail;
      And day and night held on indignantly
   O'er the blue Midland waters with the gale,
      Betwixt the Syrtes[2] and soft Sicily,   245
         To where the Atlantic raves
   Outside the western straits; and unbent sails
      There, where down cloudy cliffs, through sheets of foam,
      Shy traffickers, the dark Iberians[3] come;
   And on the beach undid his corded bales.[4]   250

                                            1853

10. Small deep valleys.
1. Tuna fish.
2. Shoals off the coast of North Africa.
3. Dark inhabitants of Spain and Portugal—perhaps associated with gypsies.
4. The elaborate simile of the final two stanzas has been variously interpreted and misinterpreted. The trader from Tyre is disconcerted when, peering out through the foliage ("fringes") that screens his hiding place, he sees noisy intruders entering his harbor. Like the Scholar Gypsy, when similarly intruded upon by hearty extroverts, he resolves to flee and seek a new home. The reference (line 249) to the Iberians as "*shy* traffickers" (traders) is explained by Kenneth Allott as having been derived from Herodotus' *History* (IV.196). Herodotus describes a distinctive method of selling goods established by Carthaginian merchants who used to sail through the straits of Gibraltar to trade with the inhabitants of the coast of West Africa. The Carthaginians would leave bales of their merchandise on display along the beaches and, without having seen their prospective customers, would return to their ships. The shy natives would then come down from their inland hiding places and set gold beside the bales they wished to buy. When the natives withdrew in their turn, the Carthaginians would return to the beach and decide whether payments were adequate, a process repeated until agreement was reached. On the Atlantic coasts this method of bargaining persisted into the 19th century. As William Beloe, a translator of Herodotus, noted in 1844: "In this manner they transact their exchange without seeing one another, or without the least instance of dishonesty * * * on either side." For the solitary Tyrian trader such a procedure, with its avoidance of *contact* (line 221), would have been especially appropriate.

Dover Beach

The sea is calm tonight.
The tide is full, the moon lies fair
Upon the straits—on the French coast the light
Gleams and is gone; the cliffs of England stand,
Glimmering and vast, out in the tranquil bay.   5
Come to the window, sweet is the night air!
Only, from the long line of spray
Where the sea meets the moon-blanched land,
Listen! you hear the grating roar[1]
Of pebbles which the waves draw back, and fling,   10
At their return, up the high strand,
Begin, and cease, and then again begin,
With tremulous cadence slow, and bring
The eternal note of sadness in.

Sophocles long ago   15
Heard it on the Aegean, and it brought
Into his mind the turbid ebb and flow
Of human misery;[2] we
Find also in the sound a thought,
Hearing it by this distant northern sea.   20

The Sea of Faith
Was once, too, at the full, and round earth's shore
Lay like the folds of a bright girdle furled.[3]
But now I only hear
Its melancholy, long, withdrawing roar,   25
Retreating, to the breath
Of the night wind, down the vast edges drear
And naked shingles[4] of the world.

Ah, love, let us be true
To one another! for the world, which seems   30
To lie before us like a land of dreams,
So various, so beautiful, so new,
Hath really neither joy, nor love, nor light,
Nor certitude, nor peace, nor help for pain;
And we are here as on a darkling plain   35

---

1. Cf. Wordsworth's *It Is a Beauteous Evening*: "Listen! the mighty Being is awake, / And doth with his eternal motion make / A sound like thunder—everlastingly."
2. See Sophocles' *Antigone*, lines 583 ff.
3. This difficult line means, in general, that at high tide the sea envelops the land closely. Its forces are "gathered" up (to use Wordsworth's term for it) like the "folds" of bright clothing ("girdle") which have been compressed ("furled"). At ebb tide, as the sea retreats, it is unfurled and spread out. It still surrounds the shoreline but not as an "enclasping flow" (as Arnold speaks of the sea in *To Marguerite, Continued*). See also *2 Henry IV*, III.i.49–51: "to see / The beachy girdle of the ocean / Too wide for Neptune's hips."
4. Beaches covered with pebbles.

Swept with confused alarms of struggle and flight,
Where ignorant armies [5] clash by night.
ca. 1851   1867

Stanzas from the Grande Chartreuse[1]

Through Alpine meadows soft-suffused
With rain, where thick the crocus blows,
Past the dark forges long disused,
The mule track from Saint Laurent goes.
The bridge is crossed, and slow we ride,   5
Through forest, up the mountainside.

The autumnal evening darkens round,
The wind is up, and drives the rain;
While, hark! far down, with strangled sound
Doth the Dead Guier's[2] stream complain,   10
Where that wet smoke, among the woods,
Over his boiling cauldron broods.

Swift rush the spectral vapors white
Past limestone scars [3] with ragged pines,
Showing—then blotting from our sight!—   15
Halt—through the cloud-drift something shines!
High in the valley, wet and drear,
The huts of Courrerie appear.

Strike leftward! cries our guide; and higher
Mounts up the stony forest way.   20
At last the encircling trees retire;
Look! through the showery twilight gray
What pointed roofs are these advance?—
A palace of the Kings of France?

Approach, for what we seek is here!   25
Alight, and sparely sup, and wait
For rest in this outbuilding near;
Then cross the sward and reach that gate.
Knock; pass the wicket! Thou art come
To the Carthusians' world-famed home.   30

5. Perhaps the revolutions of 1848 or
a reference to the siege of Rome by the
French in 1849. The date of composition
of the poem is unknown, although generally assumed to be 1851.
1. A monastery situated high in the
French Alps. It was established in 1084
by St. Bruno, founder of the Carthusians
(line 30), whose austere regimen of
solitary contemplation, fasting, and religious exercises (lines 37–44) had remained virtually unchanged for centuries.

Arnold visited the site September 7,
1851, accompanied by his bride. His account may be compared with that by
Wordsworth (*Prelude* VI. 416–88) who
had made a similar visit in 1790.
2. The Guiers Mort river flows down
from the monastery and joins the Guiers
Vif in the valley below. Wordsworth
speaks of the two rivers as "the sister
streams of Life and Death."
3. Precipices.

The silent courts, where night and day
Into their stone-carved basins cold
The splashing icy fountains play—
The humid corridors behold!
Where, ghostlike in the deepening night,   35
Cowled forms brush by in gleaming white.

The chapel, where no organ's peal
Invests the stern and naked prayer—
With penitential cries they kneel
And wrestle; rising then, with bare   40
And white uplifted faces stand,
Passing the Host from hand to hand;[4]

Each takes, and then his visage wan
Is buried in his cowl once more.
The cells!—the suffering Son of Man   45
Upon the wall—the knee-worn floor—
And where they sleep, that wooden bed,
Which shall their coffin be, when dead![5]

The library, where tract and tome
Not to feed priestly pride are there,   50
To hymn the conquering march of Rome,
Nor yet to amuse, as ours are!
They paint of souls the inner strife,
Their drops of blood, their death in life.

The garden, overgrown—yet mild,   55
See, fragrant herbs[6] are flowering there!
Strong children of the Alpine wild
Whose culture is the brethren's care;
Of human tasks their only one,
And cheerful works beneath the sun.   60

Those halls, too, destined to contain
Each its own pilgrim-host of old,
From England, Germany, or Spain—
All are before me! I behold
The House, the Brotherhood austere!   65
—And what am I, that I am here?

For rigorous teachers seized my youth,
And purged its faith, and trimmed its fire,
Showed me the high, white star of Truth,

4. Arnold, during his short visit, may not actually have witnessed the service of the Mass in the monastery. The consecrated wafer (the Host) is not passed from the hand of the officiating priest to the hands of the communicant (as is the practice in Arnold's own Anglican church) but placed, instead, on the tongue of the communicant (who kneels rather than stands). See Tinker and Lowry, *The Poetry of Matthew Arnold: A Commentary*, pp. 249–51.
5. A Carthusian is buried on a wooden plank but does not sleep in a coffin.
6. From which the liqueur, Chartreuse, is manufactured. Sales of this liqueur provide the principal revenues for upkeep of the monastery.

There bade me gaze, and there aspire.   70
Even now their whispers pierce the gloom:
W*hat dost thou in this living tomb?*

Forgive me, masters of the mind![7]
At whose behest I long ago
So much unlearnt, so much resigned—   75
I come not here to be your foe!
I seek these anchorites, not in ruth,[8]
To curse and to deny your truth;

Not as their friend, or child, I speak!
But as, on some far northern strand,   80
Thinking of his own Gods, a Greek
In pity and mournful awe might stand
Before some fallen Runic stone—[9]
For both were faiths, and both are gone.

Wandering between two worlds, one dead,   85
The other powerless to be born,
With nowhere yet to rest my head,
Like these, on earth I wait forlorn.
Their faith, my tears, the world deride—
I come to shed them at their side.   90

Oh, hide me in your gloom profound,
Ye solemn seats of holy pain!
Take me, cowled forms, and fence me round,
Till I possess my soul again;
Till free my thoughts before me roll,   95
Not chafed by hourly false control!

For the world cries your faith is now
But a dead time's exploded dream;
My melancholy, sciolists[1] say,
Is a passed mode, an outworn theme—   100
As if the world had ever had
A faith, or sciolists been sad!

Ah, if it *be* passed, take away,
At least, the restlessness, the pain;
Be man henceforth no more a prey   105
To these out-dated stings again!
The nobleness of grief is gone—
Ah, leave us not the fret alone!

7. Writers whose insistence upon testing
religious beliefs in the light of fact and
reason persuaded Arnold that faith in
Christianity (especially in the Roman
Catholic or Anglo Catholic forms) was
no longer tenable in the modern world.
8. Remorse for having adopted the ra-
tionalist view of Christianity.
9. A monument inscribed in Teutonic
letters (runes), emblematic of a Nordic
religion that has become extinct. The
relic reminds the Greek that his own religion is likewise dying and will soon be
extinct. See Arnold's *Preface* of 1853,
second paragraph.
1. Superficial-minded persons who pretend to know the answers to all questions.

But—if you[2] cannot give us ease—
Last of the race of them who grieve   110
Here leave us to die out with these
Last of the people who believe!
Silent, while years engrave the brow;
Silent—the best are silent now.

Achilles[3] ponders in his tent,   115
The kings of modern thought[4] are dumb;
Silent they are, though not content,
And wait to see the future come.
They have the grief men had of yore,
But they contend and cry no more.   120

Our fathers[5] watered with their tears
This sea of time whereon we sail,
Their voices were in all men's ears
Who passed within their puissant hail.
Still the same ocean round us raves,   125
But we stand mute, and watch the waves.

For what availed it, all the noise
And outcry of the former men?—
Say, have their sons achieved more joys,
Say, is life lighter now than then?   130
The sufferers died, they left their pain—
The pangs which tortured them remain.

What helps it now, that Byron bore,
With haughty scorn which mocked the smart,
Through Europe to the Aetolian shore[6]   135
The pageant of his bleeding heart?
That thousands counted every groan,
And Europe made his woe her own?

What boots it, Shelley! that the breeze
Carried thy lovely wail away,   140
Musical through Italian trees
Which fringe thy soft blue Spezzian bay?[7]
Inheritors of thy distress
Have restless hearts one throb the less?

2. It is not clear whether the speaker has resumed addressing his "rigorous teachers" (line 67) or (as would seem more likely) a combination of the sciolists, who scorn the speaker's melancholy and the worldly, who scorn the faith of the monks. See his address to the "sons of the world" (lines 160–68).
3. Achilles, after the death of Patroclus, refused to participate in the Trojan war; hence similar to modern intellectual leaders who refuse to speak out about their frustrated sense of alienation.
4. Variously but never satisfactorily identified as Newman or Carlyle (the latter was said to have preached the gospel of silence in 40 volumes). Another advocate of stoical silence was the French poet, Alfred de Vigny (1797–1863).
5. Predecessors among the Romantic writers such as Byron.
6. Region in Greece where Byron died.
7. The Gulf of Spezzia in Italy where Shelley was drowned.

Or are we easier, to have read, 145
O Obermann![8] the sad, stern page,
Which tells us how thou hidd'st thy head
From the fierce tempest of thine age
In the lone brakes of Fontainebleau,
Or chalets near the Alpine snow? 150

Ye slumber in your silent grave!—
The world, which for an idle day
Grace to your mood of sadness gave,
Long since hath flung her weeds[9] away.
The eternal trifler[1] breaks your spell; 155
But we—we learnt your lore too well!

Years hence, perhaps, may dawn an age,
More fortunate, alas! than we,
Which without hardness will be sage,
And gay without frivolity. 160
Sons of the world, oh, speed those years;
But, while we wait, allow our tears!

Allow them! We admire with awe
The exulting thunder of your race;
You give the universe your law, 165
You triumph over time and space!
Your pride of life, your tireless powers,
We laud them, but they are not ours.

We are like children reared in shade
Beneath some old-world abbey wall, 170
Forgotten in a forest glade,
And secret from the eyes of all.
Deep, deep the greenwood round them waves,
Their abbey, and its close[2] of graves!

But, where the road runs near the stream, 175
Oft through the trees they catch a glance
Of passing troops in the sun's beam—
Pennon, and plume, and flashing lance!
Forth to the world those soldiers fare,
To life, to cities, and to war! 180

And through the wood, another way,
Faint bugle notes from far are borne,
Where hunters gather, staghounds bay,[3]
Round some fair forest-lodge at morn.
Gay dames are there, in sylvan green; 185
Laughter and cries—those notes between!

---

8. Melancholy hero of *Obermann* (1804),
a novel by Senancour.
9. Mourning clothes.
1. The sciolist, as in line 99.

2. Enclosure.
3. Cf. the contrast between recluses **and**
hunters in *The Scholar Gypsy*, lines 71–
81.

The banners flashing through the trees
Make their blood dance and chain their eyes;
That bugle music on the breeze
Arrests them with a charmed surprise.   190
Banner by turns and bugle woo:
Ye shy recluses, follow too!

O children, what do ye reply?—
"Action and pleasure, will ye roam
Through these secluded dells to cry   195
And call us?—but too late ye come!
Too late for us your call ye blow,
Whose bent was taken long ago.

"Long since we pace this shadowed nave;
We watch those yellow tapers shine,   200
Emblems of hope over the grave,
In the high altar's depth divine;
The organ carries to our ear
Its accents of another sphere.

"Fenced early in this cloistral round   205
Of reverie, of shade, of prayer,
How should we grow in other ground?
How can we flower in foreign air?
—Pass, banners, pass, and bugles, cease;
And leave our desert to its peace!"   210

1852(?)   1855

Thyrsis[1]

A MONODY, TO COMMEMORATE THE AUTHOR'S FRIEND,
ARTHUR HUGH CLOUGH, WHO DIED AT FLORENCE, 1861

How changed is here each spot man makes or fills!
In the two Hinkseys[2] nothing keeps the same;

1. In the 1840's, at Oxford, Clough had been one of Arnold's closest friends. After the death of this fellow poet, twenty years later, Arnold revisited the Thames-valley countryside which they had explored together. The familiar scenes prompted him to review the changes wrought by time on the ideals shared in his Oxford days with Clough, ideals symbolized, in part, by a distant elm and by the story of the Scholar Gypsy. The survival of these ideals in the face of the difficulties of modern life is the subject of this elegy. Unlike Tennyson in such elegies as *In Memoriam*, Arnold rarely touches here upon other kinds of immortality.

As a framework for his elegy, Arnold draws on the same Greek and Latin pastoral tradition from which Milton's *Lycidas* and Shelley's *Adonais* were derived. Hence Clough is referred to by one of the traditional names for a shepherd-poet, Thyrsis, and Arnold himself as Corydon. The sense of distancing which results from this traditional elegiac mode is reduced considerably by the realism of the setting with its bleak wintry landscape at twilight, a landscape which is brightened, in turn, by evocations of the return of hopeful springtime.

2. The villages of North Hinksey and South Hinksey.

The village street its haunted mansion lacks,
And from the sign is gone Sibylla's name,[3]
   And from the roofs the twisted chimney stacks—   5
     Are ye too changed, ye hills?
See, 'tis no foot of unfamiliar men
   Tonight from Oxford up your pathway strays!
   Here came I often, often, in old days—
Thyrsis and I; we still had Thyrsis then.   10

Runs it not here, the track by Childsworth Farm,
   Past the high wood, to where the elm tree crowns
     The hill behind whose ridge the sunset flames?
The signal-elm, that looks on Ilsley Downs,
     The Vale, the three lone weirs, the youthful Thames?—   15
      This winter eve is warm,
   Humid the air! leafless, yet soft as spring,
     The tender purple spray on copse and briers!
   And that sweet city with her dreaming spires,
   She needs not June for beauty's heightening,   20

Lovely all times she lies, lovely tonight!—
   Only, methinks, some loss of habit's power
     Befalls me wandering through this upland dim.
Once passed I blindfold here, at any hour;
     Now seldom come I, since I came with him.   25
      That single elm tree bright
   Against the west—I miss it! is it gone?
     We prized it dearly; while it stood, we said,
   Our friend, the Gypsy Scholar, was not dead;
   While the tree lived, he in these fields lived on.   30

Too rare, too rare, grow now my visits here,
   But once I knew each field, each flower, each stick;
     And with the countryfolk acquaintance made
By barn in threshing time, by new-built rick.
     Here, too, our shepherd pipes we first assayed.   35
      Ah me! this many a year
   My pipe is lost, my shepherd's holiday!
     Needs must I lose them, needs with heavy heart
   Into the world and wave of men depart;
   But Thyrsis of his own will went away.[4]   40

It irked him to be here, he could not rest.
   He loved each simple joy the country yields,
     He loved his mates; but yet he could not keep,[5]
For that a shadow loured on the fields,
     Here with the shepherds and the silly[6] sheep.   45
      Some life of men unblest

He knew, which made him droop, and filled his head.
  He went; his piping took a troubled sound
  Of storms[7] that rage outside our happy ground;
He could not wait their passing, he is dead.   50

So, some tempestuous morn in early June,
  When the year's primal burst of bloom is o'er,
  Before the roses and the longest day—
When garden walks and all the grassy floor
  With blossoms red and white of fallen May   55
  And chestnut flowers are strewn—
So have I heard the cuckoo's parting cry,
  From the wet field, through the vexed garden trees,
  Come with the volleying rain and tossing breeze:
The bloom is gone, and with the bloom go I!   60

Too quick despairer, wherefore wilt thou go?
  Soon will the high Midsummer pomps come on,
  Soon will the musk carnations break and swell,
Soon shall we have gold-dusted snapdragon,
  Sweet-william with his homely cottage smell,   65
  And stocks in fragrant blow;
Roses that down the alleys shine afar,
  And open, jasmine-muffled lattices,
  And groups under the dreaming garden trees,
And the full moon, and the white evening star.   70

He hearkens not! light comer, he is flown!
  What matters it? next year he will return,
  And we shall have him in the sweet spring days,
With whitening hedges, and uncrumpling fern,
  And bluebells trembling by the forest ways,   75
  And scent of hay new-mown.
But Thyrsis never more we swains shall see;
  See him come back, and cut a smoother reed,
  And blow a strain the world at last shall heed—
For Time, not Corydon, hath conquered thee!   80

Alack, for Corydon no rival now!—
  But when Sicilian shepherds lost a mate,
  Some good survivor with his flute would go,
Piping a ditty sad for Bion's fate;[8]
  And cross the unpermitted ferry's flow,[9]   85
  And relax Pluto's brow,
And make leap up with joy the beauteous head
  Of Proserpine, among whose crownéd hair
  Are flowers first opened on Sicilian air,
And flute his friend, like Orpheus, from the dead.[1]   90

7. Religious and political controversies.
8. Moschus, a Greek poet, composed a pastoral elegy upon the death of the poet Bion in Sicily.
9. The river Styx across which the dead were ferried to the underworld where Pluto ruled with his queen, Proserpine.
In spring, Proserpine's returning above ground in Sicily would cause the flowers to blossom.
1. Orpheus' music enabled him to enter the "unpermitted" realms of the dead and to bring his wife, Eurydice, back with him to the land of the living.

O easy access to the hearer's grace
 When Dorian shepherds[2] sang to Proserpine!
  For she herself had trod Sicilian fields,
 She knew the Dorian water's gush divine,
  She knew each lily white which Enna yields,[3] 95
   Each rose with blushing face;
 She loved the Dorian pipe, the Dorian strain.
  But ah, of our poor Thames she never heard!
  Her foot the Cummer cowslips never stirred;
 And we should tease her with our plaint in vain! 100

Well! wind-dispersed and vain the words will be,
 Yet, Thyrsis, let me give my grief its hour
  In the old haunt, and find our tree-topped hill!
 Who, if not I, for questing here hath power?
  I know the wood which hides the daffodil, 105
   I know the Fyfield tree,
 I know what white, what purple fritillaries[4]
  The grassy harvest of the river fields,
  Above by Ensham, down by Sandford, yields,
 And what sedged brooks are Thames's tributaries; 110

I know these slopes; who knows them if not I?—
 But many a dingle[5] on the loved hillside,
  With thorns once studded, old, white-blossomed trees,
 Where thick the cowslips grew, and far descried
  High towered the spikes of purple orchises, 115
   Hath since our day put by
 The coronals of that forgotten time;
  Down each green bank hath gone the plowboy's team,
  And only in the hidden brookside gleam
 Primroses, orphans of the flowery prime. 120

Where is the girl, who by the boatman's door,
 Above the locks, above the boating throng,
  Unmoored our skiff when through the Wytham flats,
 Red loosestrife[6] and blond meadowsweet among
  And darting swallows and light water-gnats, 125
   We tracked the shy Thames shore?
 Where are the mowers, who, as the tiny swell
  Of our boat passing heaved the river grass,
  Stood with suspended scythe to see us pass?—
 They all are gone, and thou art gone as well! 130

Yes, thou art gone! and round me too the night
 In ever-nearing circle weaves her shade.
  I see her veil draw soft across the day,

2. The Dorian Greeks had colonized Sicily, the home of pastoral poetry.
3. From a meadow near Enna, a Sicilian town, Proserpine had been carried off to the underworld by Pluto (or Dis). Cf. the touchstone lines admired by Arnold in *Paradise Lost* (IV.268–71): "that fair field / Of Enna, where Proserpine gathering flowers, / Herself a fairer flower, by gloomy Dis / Was gathered * * * "
4. Flowers commonly found in moist meadows.
5. Small deep valley.
6. Flowers which grow on banks of streams.

I feel her slowly chilling breath invade
    The cheek grown thin, the brown hair sprent[7] with gray;   135
      I feel her finger light
Laid pausefully upon life's headlong train;
    The foot less prompt to meet the morning dew,
    The heart less bounding at emotion new,
And hope, once crushed, less quick to spring again.   140

And long the way appears, which seemed so short
    To the less practiced eye of sanguine youth;
    And high the mountaintops, in cloudy air,
The mountaintops where is the throne of Truth,[8]
    Tops in life's morning sun so bright and bare!   145
      Unbreachable the fort
Of the long-battered world uplifts its wall;
    And strange and vain the earthly turmoil grows,
    And near and real the charm of thy repose,
And night as welcome as a friend would fall.   150

But hush! the upland hath a sudden loss
    Of quiet!—Look, adown the dusk hillside,
    A troop of Oxford hunters going home,
As in old days, jovial and talking, ride!
    From hunting with the Berkshire hounds they come.   155
      Quick! let me fly, and cross
Into yon farther field!—'Tis done; and see,
    Backed by the sunset, which doth glorify
    The orange and pale violet evening sky,
Bare on its lonely ridge, the Tree! the Tree!   160

I take the omen! Eve lets down her veil,
    The white fog creeps from bush to bush about,
    The west unflushes, the high stars grow bright,
And in the scattered farms the lights come out.
    I cannot reach the signal-tree tonight,   165
      Yet, happy omen, hail!
Hear it from thy broad lucent Arno vale[9]
    (For there thine earth-forgetting eyelids keep
    The morningless and unawakening sleep
Under the flowery oleanders pale),   170

Hear it, O Thyrsis, still our tree is there!—
    Ah, vain! These English fields, this upland dim,
    These brambles pale with mist engarlanded,
That lone, sky-pointing tree, are not for him;
    To a boon southern country he is fled,   175
      And now in happier air,
Wandering with the great Mother's[1] train divine

7. Sprinkled.
8. Cf. Pope's *Essay on Criticism*, ll.220–32.
9. Clough was buried in Florence, which is situated in the valley of the Arno River.

1. Demeter (whose name may mean Earth Mother) was worshiped as the goddess of agriculture. The "immortal chants" (line 181) would be sung in her honor by her followers, members of the "train divine" (line 176).

(And purer or more subtle soul than thee,
I trow, the mighty Mother doth not see)
Within a folding of the Apennine,[2]   180

Thou hearest the immortal chants of old!—
Putting his sickle to the perilous grain
In the hot cornfield of the Phrygian king,[3]
For thee the Lityerses song again
Young Daphnis with his silver voice doth sing;   185
Sings his Sicilian fold,
His sheep, his hapless love, his blinded eyes—
And how a call celestial round him rang,
And heavenward from the fountain brink he sprang,
And all the marvel of the golden skies.   190

There thou art gone, and me thou leavest here
Sole in these fields! yet will I not despair.
Despair I will not, while I yet descry
'Neath the mild canopy of English air
That lonely tree against the western sky.   195
Still, still these slopes, 'tis clear,
Our Gypsy Scholar haunts, outliving thee!
Fields where soft sheep from cages pull the hay,
Woods with anemones in flower till May,
Know him a wanderer still; then why not me?   200

A fugitive and gracious light he seeks,
Shy to illumine; and I seek it too.
This does not come with houses or with gold,
With place, with honor, and a flattering crew;
'Tis not in the world's market bought and sold—   205
But the smooth-slipping weeks
Drop by, and leave its seeker still untired;
Out of the heed of mortals he is gone,
He wends unfollowed, he must house alone;
Yet on he fares, by his own heart inspired.   210

Thou too, O Thyrsis, on like quest wast bound;
Thou wanderedst with me for a little hour!
Men gave thee nothing; but this happy quest,
If men esteemed thee feeble, gave thee power,

2. Mountains near Florence.
3. Arnold includes a note from Servius' commentary on Virgil's *Eclogues:* "Daphnis, the ideal Sicilian shepherd of Greek pastoral poetry, was said to have followed into Phrygia his mistress Piplea, who had been carried off by robbers, and to have found her in the power of the king of Phrygia, Lityerses. Lityerses used to make strangers try a contest with him in reaping corn, and to put them to death if he overcame them. Hercules arrived in time to save Daphnis, took upon himself the reaping contest with Lityerses, overcame him, and slew him. The Lityerses song connected with this tradition was, like the Linus song, one of the early plaintive strains of Greek popular poetry, and used to be sung by corn reapers. Other traditions represented Daphnis as beloved by a nymph who exacted from him an oath to love no one else. He fell in love with a princess, and was struck blind by the jealous nymph. Mercury, who was his father, raised him to heaven, and made a fountain spring up in the place from which he ascended. At this fountain the Sicilians offered yearly sacrifices."

If men procured thee trouble, gave thee rest.   215
    And this rude Cumner ground,
Its fir-topped Hurst, its farms, its quiet fields,
    Here cam'st thou in thy jocund youthful time,
    Here was thine height of strength, thy golden prime!
And still the haunt beloved a virtue yields.   220

What though the music of thy rustic flute
    Kept not for long its happy, country tone;
      Lost it soo soon, and learnt a stormy note[4]
Of men contention-tossed, of men who groan,
      Which tasked thy pipe too sore, and tired thy throat—   225
        It failed, and thou wast mute!
Yet hadst thou alway visions of our light,
    And long with men of care thou couldst not stay,
    And soon thy foot resumed its wandering way,
Left human haunt, and on alone till night.   230

Too rare, too rare, grow now my visits here!
    'Mid city noise, not, as with thee of yore,
      Thyrsis! in reach of sheep-bells is my home.
—Then through the great town's harsh, heart-wearying roar,
    Let in thy voice a whisper often come,   235
      To chase fatigue and fear:
Why faintest thou? I wandered till I died.
Roam on! The light we sought is shining still.
Dost thou ask proof? Our tree yet crowns the hill,
Our Scholar travels yet the loved hillside.   240

1866

Palladium

Set where the upper streams of Simois[5] flow
Was the Palladium,[6] high 'mid rock and wood;
And Hector was in Ilium, far below,
And fought, and saw it not—but there it stood!

It stood, and sun and moonshine rained their light   5
On the pure columns of its glen-built hall.
Backward and forward rolled the waves of fight
Round Troy—but while this stood, Troy could not fall.

So, in its lovely moonlight, lives the soul.
Mountains surround it, and sweet virgin air;   10
Cold plashing, past it, crystal waters roll;
We visit it by moments, ah, too rare!

4. Clough's poetry often dealt with contemporary religious problems.
5. A river near Troy.
6. An ancient statue of the goddess
Pallas Athena. The safety of Troy
(Ilium) was thought to depend upon the
statue's being retained in the city.

We shall renew the battle in the plain
Tomorrow—red with blood will Xanthus[7] be;
Hector and Ajax will be there again,   15
Helen will come upon the wall to see.

Then we shall rust in shade, or shine in strife,
And fluctuate 'twixt blind hopes and blind despairs,
And fancy that we put forth all our life,
And never know how with the soul it fares.   20

Still doth the soul, from its lone fastness high,
Upon our life a ruling effluence send.
And when it fails, fight as we will, we die;
And while it lasts, we cannot wholly end.

                                                             1867

The Better Part

Long fed on boundless hopes, O race of man,
How angrily thou spurn'st all simpler fare!
"Christ," someone says, "was human as we are;
No judge eyes us from Heaven, our sin to scan;

"We live no more, when we have done our span."—   5
"Well, then, for Christ," thou answerest, "who can care?
From sin, which Heaven records not, why forbear?
Live we like brutes our life without a plan!"

So answerest thou; but why not rather say:
"Hath man no second life?—*Pitch this one high!*   10
Sits there no judge in Heaven, our sin to see?—

"*More strictly, then, the inward judge obey!*
Was Christ a man like us? Ah! let us try
If we, then, too, can be such men as he!"

                                                             1867

Growing Old[1]

What is it to grow old?
Is it to lose the glory of the form,
The luster of the eye?
Is it for beauty to forego her wreath?
—Yes, but not this alone.   5

7. A river near Troy.
1. Arnold's poem may have been
prompted as a rejoinder to Browning's
enthusiastic picture of old age in
Rabbi Ben Ezra (1864).

Is it to feel our strength—
Not our bloom only, but our strength—decay?
Is it to feel each limb
Grow stiffer, every function less exact,
Each nerve more loosely strung?   10

Yes, this, and more; but not
Ah, 'tis not what in youth we dreamed 'twould be!
'Tis not to have our life
Mellowed and softened as with sunset glow,
A golden day's decline.   15

'Tis not to see the world
As from a height, with rapt prophetic eyes,
And heart profoundly stirred;
And weep, and feel the fullness of the past,[2]
The years that are no more.   20

It is to spend long days
And not once feel that we were ever young;
It is to add, immured
In the hot prison of the present, month
To month with weary pain.   25

It is to suffer this,
And feel but half, and feebly, what we feel.
Deep in our hidden heart
Festers the dull remembrance of a change,
But no emotion—none.   30

It is—last stage of all—
When we are frozen up within, and quite
The phantom of ourselves,
To hear the world applaud the hollow ghost
Which blamed the living man.   35

1867

The Last Word

Creep into thy narrow bed,
Creep, and let no more be said!
Vain thy onset! all stands fast.
Thou thyself must break at last.

Let the long contention cease!   5
Geese are swans, and swans are geese.
Let them have it how they will!
Thou art tired; best be still.

2. Cf. Tennyson's *Tears, Idle Tears.*

They out-talked thee, hissed thee, tore thee?
Better men fared thus before thee;   10
Fired their ringing shot and passed,
Hotly charged—and sank at last.

Charge once more, then, and be dumb!
Let the victors, when they come,
When the forts of folly fall,
Find thy body by the wall!

1867

Preface to *Poems* (1853)

In two small volumes of poems, published anonymously, one in
1849, the other in 1852, many of the poems which compose the
present volume have already appeared. The rest are now published
for the first time.

I have, in the present collection, omitted the poem from which
the volume published in 1852 took its title.[1] I have done so, not
because the subject of it was a Sicilian Greek born between two and
three thousand years ago, although many persons would think this a
sufficient reason. Neither have I done so because I had, in my own
opinion, failed in the delineation which I intended to effect. I intended to delineate the feelings of one of the last of the Greek religious philosophers, one of the family of Orpheus and Musaeus,[2]
having survived his fellows, living on into a time when the habits of
Greek thought and feeling had begun fast to change, character to
dwindle, the influence of the Sophists[3] to prevail. Into the feelings of
a man so situated there entered much that we are accustomed
to consider as exclusively modern; how much, the fragments[4] of
Empedocles himself which remain to us are sufficient at least to
indicate. What those who are familiar only with the great monuments of early Greek genius suppose to be its exclusive character-

1. *Empedocles on Etna,* the long poem
that supplied the title for Arnold's second collection of poems, portrays the
disillusioned reflections of the Greek
philosopher and scientist Empedocles and
culminates in the speaker's suicide on
Mount Etna in Sicily, in the 5th century
B.C. Because of his dissatisfaction with
what he calls the "morbid" tone of
Empedocles on Etna Arnold continued to
exclude it from his volumes of poetry
until 1867 when he reprinted it at the
request, he said, "of a man of genius,
whom it had the honor and good fortune
to interest—Mr. Robert Browning." It
should be noted that in the arguments
developed in the *Preface* against his own
poem (and against 19th-century poetry
in general) Arnold is exclusively concerned with narrative and dramatic po-

etry. The *Preface,* as he himself remarked
in 1854, "leaves * * * untouched the
question, how far, and in what manner,
the opinions there expressed respecting
the choice of subjects apply to lyric poetry; that region of the poetical field
which is chiefly cultivated at present."
2. Pupil of the poet and musician Orpheus. The latter was the legendary
founder of the Orphic religion that flourished in 6th-century Greece and later declined.
3. Greek rhetoricians, often criticized because of their reputed concern for niceties
of expression over substance of knowledge.
4. Empedocles' writings (medical and
scientific treatises in verse) have survived only in fragments.

istics, have disappeared; the calm, the cheerfulness, the disinterested objectivity have disappeared; the dialogue of the mind with itself has commenced; modern problems have presented themselves, we hear already the doubts, we witness the discouragement, of Hamlet and of Faust.

The representation of such a man's feelings must be interesting, if consistently drawn. We all naturally take pleasure, says Aristotle, in any imitation or representation whatever;[5] this is the basis of our love of poetry; and we take pleasure in them, he adds, because all knowledge is naturally agreeable to us; not to the philosopher only, but to mankind at large. Every representation therefore which is consistently drawn may be supposed to be interesting, inasmuch as it gratifies this natural interest in knowledge of all kinds. What is *not* interesting is that which does not add to our knowledge of any kind; that which is vaguely conceived and loosely drawn; a representation which is general, indeterminate, and faint, instead of being particular, precise, and firm.

Any accurate representation may therefore be expected to be interesting; but, if the representation be a poetical one, more than this is demanded. It is demanded, not only that it shall interest, but also that it shall inspirit and rejoice the reader; that it shall convey a charm, and infuse delight. For the Muses, as Hesiod says, were born that they might be "a forgetfulness of evils, and a truce from cares":[6] and it is not enough that the poet should add to the knowledge of men, it is required of him also that he should add to their happiness. "All art," says Schiller, "is dedicated to Joy, and there is no higher and no more serious problem, than how to make men happy. The right art is that alone, which creates the highest enjoyment."[7]

A poetical work, therefore, is not yet justified when it has been shown to be an accurate, and therefore interesting representation; it has to be shown also that it is a representation from which men can derive enjoyment. In presence of the most tragic circumstances, represented in a work of Art, the feeling of enjoyment, as is well known, may still subsist; the representation of the most utter calamity, of the liveliest anguish, is not sufficient to destroy it; the more tragic the situation, the deeper becomes the enjoyment; and the situation is more tragic in proportion as it becomes more terrible.

What then are the situations, from the representation of which, though accurate, no poetical enjoyment can be derived? They are those in which the suffering finds no vent in action; in which a continuous state of mental distress is prolonged, unrelieved by

5. See Aristotle, *Poetics*, especially 1, 2, 4, 7, 14.
6. From *Theogony* 52–56, by the early Greek poet Hesiod.
7. J. C. F. von Schiller, *On the Use of* the Chorus in Tragedy, prefatory essay to *The Bride of Messina* (1803). See *Friedrich Schiller's Works* (1903), VIII, 224.

incident, hope, or resistance; in which there is everything to be endured, nothing to be done. In such situations there is inevitably something morbid, in the description of them something monotonous. When they occur in actual life, they are painful, not tragic; the representation of them in poetry is painful also.

To this class of situations, poetically faulty as it appears to me, that of Empedocles, as I have endeavored to represent him, belongs; and I have therefore excluded the poem from the present collection.

And why, it may be asked, have I entered into this explanation respecting a matter so unimportant as the admission or exclusion of the poem in question? I have done so, because I was anxious to avow that the sole reason for its exclusion was that which has been stated above; and that it has not been excluded in deference to the opinion which many critics of the present day appear to entertain against subjects chosen from distant times and countries: against the choice, in short, of any subjects but modern ones.

"The poet," it is said, and by an intelligent critic, "the poet who would really fix the public attention must leave the exhausted past, and draw his subjects from matters of present import, and *therefore* both of interest and novelty."[8]

Now this view I believe to be completely false. It is worth examining, inasmuch as it is a fair sample of a class of critical dicta everywhere current at the present day, having a philosophical form and air, but no real basis in fact; and which are calculated to vitiate the judgment of readers of poetry, while they exert, so far as they are adopted, a misleading influence on the practice of those who write it.

What are the eternal objects of poetry, among all nations and at all times? They are actions; human actions; possessing an inherent interest in themselves, and which are to be communicated in an interesting manner by the art of the poet.[9] Vainly will the latter imagine that he has everything in his own power; that he can make an intrinsically inferior action equally delightful with a more excellent one by his treatment of it; he may indeed compel us to admire his skill, but his work will possess, within itself, an incurable defect.

The poet, then, has in the first place to select an excellent action; and what actions are the most excellent? Those, certainly, which most powerfully appeal to the great primary human affections: to those elementary feelings which subsist permanently in the race, and which are independent of time. These feelings are permanent and the same; that which interests them is permanent and the same also. The modernness or antiquity of an action, therefore, has nothing to do with its fitness for poetical representation; this de-

8. In the *Spectator* of April 2nd, 1853. The words quoted were not used with reference to poems of mine [Arnold's note]. According to Arnold the "intelligent critic" was R. S. Rintoul, editor of the *Spectator*.
9. Cf. Aristotle, *Poetics* 6.

pends upon its inherent qualities. To the elementary part of our nature, to our passions, that which is great and passionate is eternally interesting; and interesting solely in proportion to its greatness and to its passion. A great human action of a thousand years ago is more interesting to it than a smaller human action of today, even though upon the representation of this last the most consummate skill may have been expended, and though it has the advantage of appealing by its modern language, familiar manners, and contemporary allusions, to all our transient feelings and interests. These, however, have no right to demand of a poetical work that it shall satisfy them; their claims are to be directed elsewhere. Poetical works belong to the domain of our permanent passions; let them interest these, and the voice of all subordinate claims upon them is at once silenced.

Achilles, Prometheus, Clytemnestra, Dido—what modern poem presents personages as interesting, even to us moderns, as these personages of an "exhausted past"? We have the domestic epic dealing with the details of modern life which pass daily under our eyes;[1] we have poems representing modern personages in contact with the problems of modern life, morel, intellectual, and social; these works have been produced by poets the most distinguished of their nation and time; yet I fearlessly assert that *Hermann and Dorothea, Childe Harold, Jocelyn, The Excursion,*[2] leave the reader cold in comparison with the effect produced upon him by the latter books of the *Iliad,* by the *Oresteia,*[3] or by the episode of Dido.[4] And why is this? Simply because in the three last-named cases the action is greater, the personages nobler, the situations more intense: and this is the true basis of the interest in a poetical work, and this alone.

It may be urged, however, that past actions may be interesting in themselves, but that they are not to be adopted by the modern poet, because it is impossible for him to have them clearly present to his own mind, and he cannot therefore feel them deeply, nor represent them forcibly. But this is not necessarily the case. The externals of a past action, indeed, he cannot know with the precision of a contemporary; but his business is with its essentials. The outward man of Oedipus or of Macbeth, the houses in which they lived, the ceremonies of their courts, he cannot accurately figure to himself; but neither do they essentially concern him. His business is with their inward man; with their feelings and behavior in certain tragic situations, which engage their passions as men; these have in them nothing local and casual; they are as accessible to the modern poet as to a contemporary.

---

1. Perhaps alluding to such poems as Tennyson's *The Princess* (1847) and Alexander Smith's *Life Drama* (1853).
2. Long poems by Goethe (1797), Byron (1818), Lamartine (1836), and Words-worth (1814), respectively.
3. A trilogy of plays by Aeschylus concerned with the stories of Agamemnon, Clytemnestra, and their son, Orestes.
4. See Virgil's *Aeneid* IV.

The date of an action, then, signifies nothing: the action itself, its selection and construction, this is what is all-important. This the Greeks understood far more clearly than we do. The radical difference between their poetical theory and ours consists, as it appears to me, in this: that, with them, the poetical character of the action in itself, and the conduct of it, was the first consideration; with us, attention is fixed mainly on the value of the separate thoughts and images which occur in the treatment of an action. They regarded the whole; we regard the parts. With them, the action predominated over the expression of it; with us, the expression predominates over the action. Not that they failed in expression, or were inattentive to it; on the contrary, they are the highest models of expression, the unapproached masters of the *grand style:* but their expression is so excellent because it is so admirably kept in its right degree of prominence; because it is so simple and so well subordinated; because it draws its force directly from the pregnancy of the matter which it conveys. For what reason was the Greek tragic poet confined to so limited a range of subjects? Because there are so few actions which unite in themselves, in the highest degree, the conditions of excellence: and it was not thought that on any but an excellent subject could an excellent poem be constructed. A few actions, therefore, eminently adapted for tragedy, maintained almost exclusive possession of the Greek tragic stage; their significance appeared inexhaustible; they were as permanent problems, perpetually offered to the genius of every fresh poet. This too is the reason of what appears to us moderns a certain baldness of expression in Greek tragedy; of the triviality with which we often reproach the remarks of the chorus, where it takes part in the dialogue: that the action itself, the situation of Orestes, or Merope, or Alcmaeon,[5] was to stand the central point of interest, unforgotten, absorbing, principal; that no accessories were for a moment to distract the spectator's attention from this; that the tone of the parts was to be perpetually kept down, in order not to impair the grandiose effect of the whole. The terrible old mythic story on which the drama was founded stood, before he entered the theater, traced in its bare outlines upon the spectator's mind; it stood in his memory, as a group of statuary, faintly seen, at the end of a long and dark vista: then came the poet, embodying outlines, developing situations, not a word wasted, not a sentiment capriciously thrown in: stroke upon stroke, the drama proceeded: the light deepened upon the group; more and more it revealed itself to the riveted gaze of the spectator: until at last, when the final words were spoken, it stood before him in broad sunlight, a model of immortal beauty.

5. Merope, queen of Messene in Greece, appears in plays by Euripides and in Arnold's own play *Merope* (1858). Alcmaeon was the son of a legendary Greek hero, who like Orestes, avenged his father's death by killing his mother. He was the subject of several Greek plays now lost.

This was what a Greek critic demanded; this was what a Greek poet endeavored to effect. It signified nothing to what time an action belonged; we do not find that the *Persae* occupied a particularly high rank among the dramas of Aeschylus, because it represented a matter of contemporary interest:[6] this was not what a cultivated Athenian required; he required that the permanent elements of his nature should be moved; and dramas of which the action, though taken from a long-distant mythic time, yet was calculated to accomplish this in a higher degree than that of the *Persae*, stood higher in his estimation accordingly. The Greeks felt, no doubt, with their exquisite sagacity of taste, that an action of present times was too near them, too much mixed up with what was accidental and passing, to form a sufficiently grand, detached, and self-subsistent object for a tragic poem: such objects belonged to the domain of the comic poet, and of the lighter kinds of poetry. For the more serious kinds, for *pragmatic* poetry, to use an excellent expression of Polybius,[7] they were more difficult and severe in the range of subjects which they permitted. Their theory and practice alike, the admirable treatise of Aristotle, and the unrivaled works of their poets, exclaim with a thousand tongues—"All depends upon the subject; choose a fitting action, penetrate yourself with the feeling of its situations; this done, everything else will follow."

But for all kinds of poetry alike there was one point on which they were rigidly exacting; the adaptability of the subject to the kind of poetry selected, and the careful construction of the poem.

How different a way of thinking from this is ours! We can hardly at the present day understand what Menander[8] meant when he told a man who inquired as to the progress of his comedy that he had finished it, not having yet written a single line, because he had constructed the action of it in his mind. A modern critic would have assured him that the merit of his piece depended on the brilliant things which arose under his pen as he went along. We have poems which seem to exist merely for the sake of single lines and passages; not for the sake of producing any total impression. We have critics who seem to direct their attention merely to detached expressions, to the language about the action, not to the action itself. I verily think that the majority of them do not in their hearts believe that there is such a thing as a total impression to be derived from a poem at all, or to be demanded from a poet; they think the term a commonplace of metaphysical criticism. They will permit the poet to select any action he pleases, and to suffer that action to go as it will, provided he gratifies them with occasional bursts of fine writing, and with a shower of isolated

6. Aeschylus' *Persians* (472 B.C.) portrays the Greek victory over the Persian invaders, which had occurred only a few years before the play was produced.

7. Greek historian (202–120 B.C.).
8. Greek writer of comedies (342–292 B.C.).

thoughts and images. That is, they permit him to leave their poetical sense ungratified, provided that he gratifies their rhetorical sense and their curiosity. Of his neglecting to gratify these, there is little danger. He needs rather to be warned against the danger of attempting to gratify these alone; he needs rather to be perpetually reminded to prefer his action to everything else; so to treat this, as to permit its inherent excellences to develop themselves, without interruption from the intrusion of his personal peculiarities; most fortunate, when he most entirely succeeds in effecting himself, and in enabling a noble action to subsist as it did in nature.

But the modern critic not only permits a false practice; he absolutely prescribes false aims.—"A true allegory of the state of one's own mind in a representative history," the poet is told, "is perhaps the highest thing that one can attempt in the way of poetry." [9] And accordingly he attempts it. An allegory of the state of one's own mind, the highest problem of an art which imitates actions! No assuredly, it is not, it never can be so: no great poetical work has ever been produced with such an aim. *Faust* itself, in which something of the kind is attempted, wonderful passages as it contains, and in spite of the unsurpassed beauty of the scenes which relate to Margaret, *Faust* itself, judged as a whole, and judged strictly as a poetical work, is defective: its illustrious author, the greatest poet of modern times, the greatest critic of all times, would have been the first to acknowledge it; he only defended his work, indeed, by asserting it to be "something incommensurable."[1]

The confusion of the present times is great, the multitude of voices counseling different things bewildering, the number of existing works capable of attracting a young writer's attention and of becoming his models, immense. What he wants is a hand to guide him through the confusion, a voice to prescribe to him the aim which he should keep in view, and to explain to him that the value of the literary works which offer themselves to his attention is relative to their power of helping him forward on his road towards this aim. Such a guide the English writer at the present day will nowhere find. Failing this, all that can be looked for, all indeed that can be desired is, that his attention should be fixed on excellent models; that he may reproduce, at any rate, something of their excellence, by penetrating himself with their works and by catching their spirit, if he cannot be taught to produce what is excellent independently.

Foremost among these models for the English writer stands Shakespeare: a name the greatest perhaps of all poetical names;

9. *North British Review*, **XIX** (August, 1853), 180 (U.S. edition). Arnold seems not to have noticed that Goethe (a critic he revered) had been cited earlier in the article as the authority for this critical generalization.

1. J. Eckermann, *Conversations with Goethe*, Jan. 3, 1830.

a name never to be mentioned without reverence. I will venture, however, to express a doubt, whether the influence of his works, excellent and fruitful for the readers of poetry, for the great majority, has been of unmixed advantage to the writers of it. Shakespeare indeed chose excellent subjects; the world could afford no better than Macbeth, or Romeo and Juliet, or Othello: he had no theory respecting the necessity of choosing subjects of present import, or the paramount interest attaching to allegories of the state of one's own mind; like all great poets, he knew well what constituted a poetical action; like them, wherever he found such an action, he took it; like them, too, he found his best in past times. But to these general characteristics of all great poets he added a special one of his own; a gift, namely, of happy, abundant, and ingenious expression, eminent and unrivaled: so eminent as irresistibly to strike the attention first in him, and even to throw into comparative shade his other excellences as a poet. Here has been the mischief. These other excellences were his fundamental excellences *as a poet*; what distinguishes the artist from the mere amateur, says Goethe, is *Architectonicè* in the highest sense;[2] that power of execution, which creates, forms, and constitutes: not the profoundness of single thoughts, not the richness of imagery, not the abundance of illustration. But these attractive accessories of a poetical work being more easily seized than the spirit of the whole, and these accessories being possessed by Shakespeare in an unequaled degree, a young writer having recourse to Shakespeare as his model runs great risk of being vanquished and absorbed by them, and, in consequence, of reproducing, according to the measure of his power, these, and these alone.[3] Of this preponderating quality of Shakespeare's genius, accordingly almost the whole of modern English poetry has, it appears to me, felt the influence. To the exclusive attention on the part of his imitators to this it is in a great degree owing, that of the majority of modern poetical works the details alone are valuable, the composition worthless. In reading them one is perpetually reminded of that terrible sentence on a modern French poet: *Il dit tout ce qu'il veut, mais malheureusement il n'a rien à dire.*[4]

Let me give an instance of what I mean. I will take it from the works of the very chief among those who seem to have been formed in the school of Shakespeare: of one whose exquisite

2. In Goethe's essay *Concerning the So-called Dilettantism* (1799) in his *Werke,* 1851, XXV, 322.
3. Cf. Arnold's letter to Clough (Oct. 28, 1852): "More and more I feel that the difference between a mature and a youthful age of the world compels the poetry of the former to use great plainness of speech * * * and that Keats and Shelley were on a false track when they set themselves to reproduce the exuberance of expression, the charm, the richness of images, and the felicity, of the Elizabethan poets."
4. "He says everything he wishes to, but unfortunately he has nothing to say"— a comment on Théophile Gautier (1811–72) whose emphasis on style was severely criticized by Arnold in his late essay *Wordsworth* (see below).

genius and pathetic death render him forever interesting. I will take the poem of *Isabella, or the Pot of Basil*, by Keats. I choose this rather than the *Endymion*, because the latter work (which a modern critic has classed with the *Fairy Queen!*[5]) although undoubtedly there blows through it the breath of genius, is yet as a whole so utterly incoherent, as not strictly to merit the name of a poem at all. The poem of *Isabella*, then, is a perfect treasurehouse of graceful and felicitous words and images: almost in every stanza there occurs one of those vivid and picturesque turns of expression, by which the object is made to flash upon the eye of the mind, and which thrill the reader with a sudden delight. This one short poem contains, perhaps, a greater number of happy single expressions which one could quote than all the extant tragedies of Sophocles. But the action, the story? The action in itself is an excellent one; but so feebly is it conceived by the poet, so loosely constructed, that the effect produced by it, in and for itself, is absolutely null. Let the reader, after he has finished the poem of Keats, turn to the same story in the *Decameron*:[6] he will then feel how pregnant and interesting the same action has become in the hands of a great artist, who above all things delineates his object; who subordinates expression to that which it is designed to express.

I have said that the imitators of Shakespeare, fixing their attention on his wonderful gift of expression, have directed their imitation to this, neglecting his other excellences. These excellences, the fundamental excellences of poetical art, Shakespeare no doubt possessed them—possessed many of them in a splendid degree; but it may perhaps be doubted whether even he himself did not sometimes give scope to his faculty of expression to the prejudice of a higher poetical duty. For we must never forget that Shakespeare is the great poet he is from his skill in discerning and firmly conceiving an excellent action, from his power of intensely feeling a situation, of intimately associating himself with a character; not from his gift of expression, which rather even leads him astray, degenerating sometimes into a fondness for curiosity of expression, into an irritability of fancy, which seems to make it impossible for him to say a thing plainly, even when the press of the action demands the very directest language, or its level character the very simplest. Mr. Hallam, than whom it is impossible to find a saner and more judicious critic, has had the courage (for at the present day it needs courage) to remark, how extremely and faultily difficult Shakespeare's language often is.[7] It is so: you may find main scenes in some of his greatest tragedies, *King Lear* for instance, where the language is so artificial, so curiously tortured,

5. In the *North British Review*, XIX (Aug., 1853), 172, 74, Keats' *Endymion* is twice linked with Spenser's *Faerie Queene* as "leisurely compositions of the sweet sensuous order."

6. Boccaccio's *Decameron*, 4th day, 5th novel.
7. Henry Hallam, historian (1779–1859), *Introduction to the Literature of Europe* (1838–39), Ch. 23.

and so difficult, that every speech has to be read two or three times before its meaning can be comprehended. This over-curiousness of expression is indeed but the excessive employment of a wonderful gift—of the power of saying a thing in a happier way than any other man; nevertheless, it is carried so far that one understands what M. Guizot meant, when he said that Shakespeare appears in his language to have tried all styles except that of simplicity.[8] He has not the severe and scrupulous self-restraint of the ancients, partly no doubt, because he had a far less cultivated and exacting audience. He has indeed a far wider range than they had, a far richer fertility of thought; in this respect he rises above them. In his strong conception of his subject, in the genuine way in which he is penetrated with it, he resembles them, and is unlike the moderns. But in the accurate limitation of it, the conscientious rejection of superfluities, the simple and rigorous development of it from the first line of his work to the last, he falls below them, and comes nearer to the moderns. In his chief works, besides what he has of his own, he has the elementary soundness of the ancients; he has their important action and their large and broad manner; but he has not their purity of method. He is therefore a less safe model; for what he has of his own is personal, and inseparable from his own rich nature; it may be imitated and exaggerated, it cannot be learned or applied as an art. He is above all suggestive; more valuable, therefore, to young writers as men than as artists. But clearness of arrangement, rigor of development, simplicity of style—these may to a certain extent be learned; and these may, I am convinced, be learned best from the ancients, who although infinitely less suggestive than Shakespeare, are thus, to the artist, more instructive.

What, then, it will be asked, are the ancients to be our sole models? the ancients with their comparatively narrow range of experience, and their widely different circumstances? Not, certainly, that which is narrow in the ancients, nor that in which we can no longer sympathize. An action like the action of the *Antigone* of Sophocles, which turns upon the conflict between the heroine's duty to her brother's corpse and that to the laws of her country, is no longer one in which it is possible that we should feel a deep interest. I am speaking too, it will be remembered, not of the best sources of intellectual stimulus for the general reader, but of the best models of instruction for the individual writer. This last may certainly learn of the ancients, better than anywhere else, three things which it is vitally important for him to know: the all-importance of the choice of a subject; the necessity of accurate construction; and the subordinate character of expression. He will learn from them how unspeakably superior

8. F. P. G. Guizot, French historian (1787–1874), discussing Shakespeare's sonnets in his *Shakespeare et son Temps* (1852), p. 114.

is the effect of the one moral impression left by a great action treated as a whole, to the effect produced by the most striking single thought or by the happiest image. As he penetrates into the spirit of the great classical works, as he becomes gradually aware of their intense significance, their noble simplicity, and their calm pathos, he will be convinced that it is this effect, unity and profoundness of moral impression, at which the ancient poets aimed; that it is this which constitutes the grandeur of their works, and which makes them immortal. He will desire to direct his own efforts towards producing the same effect. Above all, he will deliver himself from the jargon of modern criticism, and escape the danger of producing poetical works conceived in the spirit of the passing time, and which partake of its transitoriness.

The present age makes great claims upon us; we owe it service, it will not be satisfied without our admiration. I know not how it is, but their commerce with the ancients appears to me to produce, in those who constantly practice it, a steadying and composing effect upon their judgment, not of literary works only, but of men and events in general. They are like persons who have had a very weighty and impressive experience; they are more truly than others under the empire of facts, and more independent of the language current among those with whom they live. They wish neither to applaud nor to revile their age; they wish to know what it is, what it can give them, and whether this is what they want. What they want, they know very well; they want to educe and cultivate what is best and noblest in themselves; they know, too, that this is no easy task—χαλεπὸν, as Pittacus said, χαλεπὸν ἐσθλὸν ἔμμεναι[9]—and they ask themselves sincerely whether their age and its literature can assist them in the attempt. If they are endeavoring to practice any art, they remember the plain and simple proceedings of the old artists, who attained their grand results by penetrating themselves with some noble and significant action, not by inflating themselves with a belief in the pre-eminent importance and greatness of their own times. They do not talk of their mission, nor of interpreting their age, nor of the coming poet; all this, they know, is the mere delirium of vanity; their business is not to praise their age, but to afford to the men who live in it the highest pleasure which they are capable of feeling. If asked to afford this by means of subjects drawn from the age itself, they ask what special fitness the present age has for supplying them. They are told that it is an era of progress, an age commissioned to carry out the great ideas of industrial development and social amelioration. They reply that with all this they can do nothing; that the elements they need for the exercise of their art are great actions, calculated powerfully and delightfully to affect what is permanent in the human soul;

9. "It is hard to be good." An aphorism of Pittacus, a Greek sage, 7th century B.C.

that so far as the present age can supply such actions, they will gladly make use of them; but that an age wanting in moral grandeur can with difficulty supply such, and an age of spiritual discomfort with difficulty be powerfully and delightfully affected by them.

A host of voices will indignantly rejoin that the present age is inferior to the past neither in moral grandeur nor in spiritual health. He who possesses the discipline I speak of will content himself with remembering the judgments passed upon the present age, in this respect, by the two men, the one of strongest head, the other of widest culture, whom it has produced; by Goethe and by Niebuhr.[1] It will be sufficient for him that he knows the opinions held by these two great men respecting the present age and its literature; and that he feels assured in his own mind that their aims and demands upon life were such as he would wish, at any rate, his own to be; and their judgment as to what is impeding and disabling such as he may safely follow. He will not, however, maintain a hostile attitude towards the false pretensions of his age: he will content himself with not being overwhelmed by them. He will esteem himself fortunate if he can succeed in banishing from his mind all feelings of contradiction, and irritation, and impatience; in order to delight himself with the contemplation of some noble action of a heroic time, and to enable others, through his representation of it, to delight in it also.

I am far indeed from making any claim, for myself, that I possess this discipline; or for the following poems, that they breathe its spirit. But I say, that in the sincere endeavor to learn and practice, amid the bewildering confusion of our times, what is sound and true in poetical art, I seemed to myself to find the only sure guidance, the only solid footing, among the ancients. They, at any rate, knew what they wanted in art, and we do not. It is this uncertainty which is disheartening, and not hostile criticism. How often have I felt this when reading words of disparagement or of cavil: that it is the uncertainty as to what is really to be aimed at which makes our difficulty, not the dissatisfaction of the critic, who himself suffers from the same uncertainty. *Non me tua fervida terrent Dicta;* . . . *Dii me terrent, et Jupiter hostis.*[2]

Two kinds of *dilettanti,* says Goethe, there are in poetry: he who neglects the indispensable mechanical part, and thinks he has done enough if he shows spirituality and feeling; and he who seeks to arrive at poetry merely by mechanism, in which he can acquire an artisan's readiness, and is without soul and matter.[3] And he adds, that the first does most harm to art, and the last to

1. B. G. Niebuhr (1776–1831), German historian.
2. Virgil, *Aeneid* XII. 894–95: "Your fiery speeches do not frighten me; it is the gods and the enmity of Jupiter that

frighten me" (Turnus, a warrior abandoned by the gods, is replying to Aeneas who has taunted him with being afraid).
3. See note 2, Goethe's essay, above.

himself. If we must be *dilettanti*; if it is impossible for us, under the circumstances amidst which we live, to think clearly, to feel nobly, and to delineate firmly; if we cannot attain to the mastery of the great artists; let us, at least, have so much respect for our art as to prefer it to ourselves. Let us not bewilder our successors; let us transmit to them the practice of poetry, with its boundaries and wholesome regulative laws, under which excellent works may again, perhaps, at some future time, be produced, not yet fallen into oblivion through our neglect, not yet condemned and canceled by the influence of their eternal enemy, caprice.

From The Function of Criticism at the Present Time[1]

Many objections have been made to a proposition which, in some remarks of mine on translating Homer,[2] I ventured to put forth; a proposition about criticism, and its importance at the present day. I said: "Of the literature of France and Germany, as of the intellect of Europe in general, the main effort, for now many years, has been a critical effort; the endeavor, in all branches of knowledge, theology, philosophy, history, art, science, to see the object as in itself it really is." I added, that owing to the operation in English literature of certain causes, "almost the last thing for which one would come to English literature is just that very thing which now Europe most desires—criticism"; and that the power and value of English literature was thereby impaired. More than one rejoinder declared that the importance I here assigned to criticism was excessive, and asserted the inherent superiority of the creative effort of the human spirit over its critical effort. And the other day, having been led by a Mr. Shairp's excellent notice of Wordsworth[3] to turn again to his biography, I found, in the words of this great man, whom I, for one, must always listen to with the profoundest respect,

---

1. This essay served as an introduction to Arnold's volume of *Essays in Criticism* (1865). As a declaration of intentions, it can serve as a standard for measuring his total accomplishment in criticism. The essay makes us aware that criticism, for Arnold, meant a great deal more than casual book-reviewing or mere censoriousness. He was not a Utilitarian, yet his object in this essay is to show that good criticism is useful. Creative writers, he argues, can profit in a special way from good criticism, but all of us can also derive from it benefits of the greatest value. In particular, we may develop a civilized attitude of mind in which to examine the social, political, aesthetic, and religious problems which confront us.
2. *On Translating Homer* (1861).
3. J. C. Shairp's essay *Wordsworth:*

The Man and the Poet was published in 1864. Arnold comments in a footnote: "I cannot help thinking that a practice, common in England during the last century, and still followed in France, of printing a notice of this kind—a notice by a competent critic—to serve as an introduction to an eminent author's works, might be revived among us with advantage. To introduce all succeeding editions of Wordsworth, Mr. Shairp's notice might, it seems to me, excellently serve; it is written from the point of view of an admirer, nay, of a disciple, and that is right; but then the disciple must be also, as in this case he is, a critic, a man of letters, not, as too often happens, some relation or friend with no qualification for his task except affection for his author."

a sentence passed on the critic's business, which seems to justify every possible disparagement of it. Wordsworth says in one of his letters:

"The writers in these publications (the Reviews), while they prosecute their inglorious employment, cannot be supposed to be in a state of mind very favorable for being affected by the finer influences of a thing so pure as genuine poetry."

And a trustworthy reporter of his conversation quotes a more elaborate judgment to the same effect:

"Wordsworth holds the critical power very low, infinitely lower than the inventive; and he said today that if the quantity of time consumed in writing critiques on the works of others were given to original composition, of whatever kind it might be, it would be much better employed; it would make a man find out sooner his own level, and it would do infinitely less mischief. A false or malicious criticism may do much injury to the minds of others; a stupid invention, either in prose or verse, is quite harmless."

It is almost too much to expect of poor human nature, that a man capable of producing some effect in one line of literature, should, for the greater good of society, voluntarily doom himself to impotence and obscurity in another. Still less is this to be expected from men addicted to the composition of the "false or malicious criticism" of which Wordsworth speaks. However, everybody would admit that a false or malicious criticism had better never have been written. Everybody, too, would be willing to admit, as a general proposition, that the critical faculty is lower than the inventive. But is it true that criticism is really, in itself, a baneful and injurious employment; is it true that all time given to writing critiques on the works of others would be much better employed if it were given to original composition, of whatever kind this may be? Is it true that Johnson had better have gone on producing more *Irenes*[4] instead of writing his *Lives of the Poets*; nay, is it certain that Wordsworth himself was better employed in making his Ecclesiastical Sonnets[5] than when he made his celebrated Preface so full of criticism, and criticism of the works of others? Wordsworth was himself a great critic, and it is to be sincerely regretted that he has not left us more criticism; Goethe was one of the greatest of critics, and we may sincerely congratulate ourselves that he has left us so much criticism. Without wasting time over the exaggeration which Wordsworth's judgment on criticism clearly contains, or over an attempt to trace the causes—not difficult, I think, to be traced—which may have led Wordsworth to this exaggeration, a critic may

4. *Irene* is the name of a clumsy play by Samuel Johnson.
5. A sonnet sequence by Wordsworth, usually regarded as minor verse. The Preface is to his *Lyrical Ballads* of 1800.

with advantage seize an occasion for trying his own conscience, and for asking himself of what real service, at any given moment, the practice of criticism either is or may be made to his own mind and spirit, and to the minds and spirits of others.

The critical power is of lower rank than the creative. True; but in assenting to this proposition, one or two things are to be kept in mind. It is undeniable that the exercise of a creative power, that a free creative activity, is the highest function of man; it is proved to be so by man's finding in it his true happiness. But it is undeniable, also, that men may have the sense of exercising this free creative activity in other ways than in producing great works of literature or art; if it were not so, all but a very few men would be shut out from the true happiness of all men. They may have it in well-doing, they may have it in learning, they may have it even in criticizing. This is one thing to be kept in mind. Another is, that the exercise of the creative power in the production of great works of literature or art, however high this exercise of it may rank, is not at all epochs and under all conditions possible; and that therefore labor may be vainly spent in attempting it, which might with more fruit be used in preparing for it, in rendering it possible. This creative power works with elements, with materials; what if it has not those materials, those elements, ready for its use? In that case it must surely wait till they are ready. Now, in literature—I will limit myself to literature, for it is about literature that the question arises—the elements with which the creative power works are ideas; the best ideas on every matter which literature touches, current at the time. At any rate we may lay it down as certain that in modern literature no manifestation of the creative power not working with these can be very important or fruitful. And I say *current* at the time, not merely accessible at the time; for creative literary genius does not principally show itself in discovering new ideas, that is rather the business of the philosopher. The grand work of literary genius is a work of synthesis and exposition, not of analysis and discovery; its gift lies in the faculty of being happily inspired by a certain intellectual and spiritual atmosphere, by a certain order of ideas, when it finds itself in them; of dealing divinely with these ideas, presenting them in the most effective and attractive combinations—making beautiful works with them, in short. But it must have the atmosphere, it must find itself amidst the order of ideas, in order to work freely; and these it is not so easy to command. This is why great creative epochs in literature are so rare, this is why there is so much that is unsatisfactory in the productions of many men of real genius; because, for the creation of a masterwork of literature two powers must concur, the power of the man and the power of the moment, and the man is not enough without the moment; the creative power has, for its happy exercise, appointed elements, and those elements are not in its own control.

Nay, they are more within the control of the critical power. It is the business of the critical power, as I said in the words already quoted, "in all branches of knowledge, theology, philosophy, history, art, science, to see the object as in itself it really is." Thus it tends, at last, to make an intellectual situation of which the creative power can profitably avail itself. It tends to establish an order of ideas, if not absolutely true, yet true by comparison with that which it displaces; to make the best ideas prevail. Presently these new ideas reach society, the touch of truth is the touch of life, and there is a stir and growth everywhere; out of this stir and growth come the creative epochs of literature.

Or, to narrow our range, and quit these considerations of the general march of genius and of society—considerations which are apt to become too abstract and impalpable—everyone can see that a poet, for instance, ought to know life and the world before dealing with them in poetry; and life and the world being in modern times very complex things, the creation of a modern poet, to be worth much, implies a great critical effort behind it; else it must be a comparatively poor, barren, and short-lived affair. This is why Byron's poetry had so little endurance in it, and Goethe's so much; both Byron and Goethe had a great productive power, but Goethe's was nourished by a great critical effort providing the true materials for it, and Byron's was not; Goethe knew life and the world, the poet's necessary subjects, much more comprehensively and thoroughly than Byron. He knew a great deal more of them, and he knew them much more as they really are.

It has long seemed to me that the burst of creative activity in our literature, through the first quarter of this century, had about it in fact something premature; and that from this cause its productions are doomed, most of them, in spite of the sanguine hopes which accompanied and do still accompany them, to prove hardly more lasting than the productions of far less splendid epochs. And this prematureness comes from its having proceeded without having its proper data, without sufficient materials to work with. In other words, the English poetry of the first quarter of this century, with plenty of energy, plenty of creative force, did not know enough. This makes Byron so empty of matter, Shelley so incoherent, Wordsworth even, profound as he is, yet so wanting in completeness and variety. Wordsworth cared little for books, and disparaged Goethe. I admire Wordsworth, as he is, so much that I cannot wish him different; and it is vain, no doubt, to imagine such a man different from what he is, to suppose that he *could* have been different. But surely the one thing wanting to make Wordsworth an even greater poet than he is—his thought richer, and his influence of wider application—was that he should have read more books, among them, no doubt, those of that Goethe whom he disparaged without reading him.

But to speak of books and reading may easily lead to a misunderstanding here. It was not really books and reading that lacked to our poetry at this epoch: Shelley had plenty of reading, Coleridge had immense reading. Pindar and Sophocles—as we all say so glibly, and often with so little discernment of the real import of what we are saying—had not many books; Shakespeare was no deep reader. True; but in the Greece of Pindar and Sophocles, in the England of Shakespeare, the poet lived in a current of ideas in the highest degree animating and nourishing to the creative power; society was, in the fullest measure, permeated by fresh thought, intelligent and alive. And this state of things is the true basis for the creative power's exercise, in this it finds its data, its materials, truly ready for its hand; all the books and reading in the world are only valuable as they are helps to this. Even when this does not actually exist, books and reading may enable a man to construct a kind of semblance of it in his own mind, a world of knowledge and intelligence in which he may live and work. This is by no means an equivalent to the artist for the nationally diffused life and thought of the epochs of Sophocles or Shakespeare; but, besides that it may be a means of preparation for such epochs, it does really constitute, if many share in it, a quickening and sustaining atmosphere of great value. Such an atmosphere the many-sided learning and the long and widely combined critical effort of Germany formed for Goethe, when he lived and worked. There was no national glow of life and thought there as in the Athens of Pericles[6] or the England of Elizabeth. That was the poet's weakness. But there was a sort of equivalent for it in the complete culture and unfettered thinking of a large body of Germans. That was his strength. In the England of the first quarter of this century there was neither a national glow of life and thought, such as we had in the age of Elizabeth, nor yet a culture and a force of learning and criticism such as were to be found in Germany. Therefore the creative power of poetry wanted, for success in the highest sense, materials and a basis; a thorough interpretation of the world was necessarily denied to it.

At first sight it seems strange that out of the immense stir of the French Revolution and its age should not have come a crop of works of genius equal to that which came out of the stir of the great productive time of Greece, or out of that of the Renascence, with its powerful episode the Reformation. But the truth is that the stir of the French Revolution took a character which essentially distinguished it from such movements as these. These were, in the main, disinterestedly intellectual and spiritual movements; movements in which the human spirit looked for its satisfaction in itself

6. Pericles (d. 429 B.C.), the leading statesman of Athens during a period of the city's most outstanding achievements in art, literature, and politics.

and in the increased play of its own activity. The French Revolution took a political, practical character. The movement, which went on in France under the old *régime*, from 1700 to 1789, was far more really akin than that of the Revolution itself to the movement of the Renascence; the France of Voltaire and Rousseau told far more powerfully upon the mind of Europe than the France of the Revolution. Goethe reproached this last expressly with having "thrown quiet culture back." Nay, and the true key to how much in our Byron, even in our Wordsworth, is this!—that they had their source in a great movement of feeling, not in a great movement of mind. The French Revolution, however—that object of so much blind love and so much blind hatred—found undoubtedly its motive power in the intelligence of men, and not in their practical sense; this is what distinguishes it from the English Revolution of Charles the First's time. This is what makes it a more spiritual event than our Revolution, an event of much more powerful and world-wide interest, though practically less successful; it appeals to an order of ideas which are universal, certain, permanent. 1789 asked of a thing, Is it rational? 1642 asked of a thing, Is it legal? or, when it went furthest, Is it according to conscience? This is the English fashion, a fashion to be treated, within its own sphere, with the highest respect; for its success, within its own sphere, has been prodigious. But what is law in one place is not law in another; what is law here today is not law even here tomorrow; and as for conscience, what is binding on one man's conscience is not binding on another's. The old woman who threw her stool at the head of the surpliced minister in St. Giles's Church at Edinburgh[7] obeyed an impulse to which millions of the human race may be permitted to remain strangers. But the prescriptions of reason are absolute, unchanging, of universal validity; *to count by tens is the easiest way of counting*—that is a proposition of which everyone, from here to the Antipodes, feels the force; at least I should say so if we did not live in a country where it is not impossible that any morning we may find a letter in the *Times* declaring that a decimal coinage is an absurdity.[7a] That a whole nation should have been penetrated with an enthusiasm for pure reason, and with an ardent zeal for making its prescriptions triumph, is a very remarkable thing, when we consider how little of mind, or anything so worthy and quickening as mind, comes into the motives which alone, in general, impel great masses of men. In spite of the extravagant direction given to this enthusiasm, in spite of the crimes and follies in which it lost itself, the French Revolution derives from the force, truth, and universality of the ideas which it took for its law, and from the passion

7. In 1637 rioting broke out in Scotland against a new kind of church service prescribed by Charles I. The riot was started by an old woman hurling a stool at a clergyman.
7a. In 1863 a proposal in Parliament to introduce the French decimal system for weights and measures had provoked articles in the *Times* defending the English system (of ounces and pounds or inches and feet) as more practical.

with which it could inspire a multitude for these ideas, a unique and still living power; it is—it will probably long remain—the greatest, the most animating event in history. And as no sincere passion for the things of the mind, even though it turn out in many respects an unfortunate passion, is ever quite thrown away and quite barren of good, France has reaped from hers one fruit—the natural and legitimate fruit though not precisely the grand fruit she expected: she is the country in Europe where *the people* is most alive.

But the mania for giving an immediate political and practical application to all these fine ideas of the reason was fatal. Here an Englishman is in his element: on this theme we can all go on for hours. And all we are in the habit of saying on it has undoubtedly a great deal of truth. Ideas cannot be too much prized in and for themselves, cannot be too much lived with; but to transport them abruptly into the world of politics and practice, violently to revolutionize this world to their bidding—that is quite another thing. There is the world of ideas and there is the world of practice; the French are often for suppressing the one and the English the other; but neither is to be suppressed. A member of the House of Commons said to me the other day: "That a thing is an anomaly, I consider to be no objection to it whatever." I venture to think he was wrong; that a thing is an anomaly *is* an objection to it, but absolutely and in the sphere of ideas: it is not necessarily, under such and such circumstances, or at such and such a moment, an objection to it in the sphere of politics and practice. Joubert[8] has said beautifully: "*C'est la force et le droit qui règlent toutes choses dans le monde; la force en attendant le droit.*"—"Force and right are the governors of this world; force till right is ready." *Force till right is ready*; and till right is ready, force, the existing order of things, is justified, is the legitimate ruler. But right is something moral, and implies inward recognition, free assent of the will; we are not ready for right—*right, so far as we are concerned, is not ready*—until we have attained this sense of seeing it and willing it. The way in which for us it may change and transform force, the existing order of things, and become, in its turn, the legitimate ruler of the world, should depend on the way in which, when our time comes, we see it and will it. Therefore for other people enamored of their own newly discerned right, to attempt to impose it upon us as ours, and violently to substitute their right for our force, is an act of tyranny, and to be resisted. It sets at nought the second great half of our maxim, *force till right is ready*. This was the grand error of the French Revolution; and its movement of ideas, by quitting the intellectual sphere and rushing furiously into the political sphere, ran, indeed, a prodigious and memorable course, but produced no such intellectual fruit as the movement of ideas of the Renascence,

8. Joseph Joubert (1754–1824), French moralist about whom Arnold wrote one of his *Essays in Criticism.*

and created, in opposition to itself, what I may call an *epoch of concentration*. The great force of that epoch of concentration was England; and the great voice of that epoch of concentration was Burke.[9] It is the fashion to treat Burke's writings on the French Revolution as superannuated and conquered by the event; as the eloquent but unphilosophical tirades of bigotry and prejudice. I will not deny that they are often disfigured by the violence and passion of the moment, and that in some directions Burke's view was bounded, and his observation therefore at fault. But on the whole, and for those who can make the needful corrections, what distinguishes these writings is their profound, permanent, fruitful, philosophical truth. They contain the true philosophy of an epoch of concentration, dissipate the heavy atmosphere which its own nature is apt to engender round it, and make its resistance rational instead of mechanical.

But Burke is so great because, almost alone in England, he brings thought to bear upon politics, he saturates politics with thought. It is his accident that his ideas were at the service of an epoch of concentration, not of an epoch of expansion; it is his characteristic that he so lived by ideas, and had such a source of them welling up within him, that he could float even an epoch of concentration and English Tory politics with them. It does not hurt him that Dr. Price[1] and the Liberals were enraged with him; it does not even hurt him that George the Third and the Tories were enchanted with him. His greatness is that he lived in a world which neither English Liberalism nor English Toryism is apt to enter—the world of ideas, not the world of catchwords and party habits. So far is it from being really true of him that he "to party gave up what was meant for mankind,"[2] that at the very end of his fierce struggle with the French Revolution, after all his invectives against its false pretensions, hollowness, and madness, with his sincere convictions of its michievousness, he can close a memorandum on the best means of combating it, some of the last pages [2a] he ever wrote—the *Thoughts on French Affairs*, in December 1791—with these striking words:

"The evil is stated, in my opinion, as it exists. The remedy must be where power, wisdom, and information, I hope, are more united with good intentions than they can be with me. I have done with this subject, I believe, forever. It has given me many anxious moments for the last two years. *If a great change is to be made in human affairs, the minds of men will be fitted to it; the general opinions and feelings will draw that way. Every fear, every hope will*

---

9. Edmund Burke (1729–97), prominent statesman and author of *Reflections on the French Revolution* (1790), which expressed the conservative opposition to revolutionary theories.
1. Richard Price (1723–91), a pro-revolutionary clergyman who was an opponent of Burke's.

2. See Oliver Goldsmith's poem, *Retaliation* (1774).
2a. Arnold was mistaken; Burke continued to write for another six years after 1791. According to Arnold's editor, R. H. Super, the mistake was caused by misunderstanding a passage in one of Burke's letters.

forward it; and then they who persist in opposing this mighty current in human affairs, will appear rather to resist the decrees of Providence itself, than the mere designs of men. They will not be resolute and firm, but perverse and obstinate."

That return of Burke upon himself has always seemed to me one of the finest things in English literature, or indeed in any literature. That is what I call living by ideas: when one side of a question has long had your earnest support, when all your feelings are engaged, when you hear all round you no language but one, when your party talks this language like a steam engine and can imagine no other— still to be able to think, still to be irresistibly carried, if so it be, by the current of thought to the opposite side of the question, and, like Balaam,[3] to be unable to speak anything *but what the Lord has put in your mouth.* I know nothing more striking, and I must add that I know nothing more un-English.

For the Englishman in general is like my friend the Member of Parliament, and believes, point-blank, that for a thing to be an anomaly is absolutely no objection to it whatever. He is like the Lord Auckland of Burke's day, who, in a memorandum on the French Revolution, talks of certain "miscreants, assuming the name of philosophers, who have presumed themselves capable of establishing a new system of society." The Englishman has been called a political animal, and he values what is political and practical so much that ideas easily become objects of dislike in his eyes, and thinkers, "miscreants," because ideas and thinkers have rashly meddled with politics and practice. This would be all very well if the dislike and neglect confined themselves to ideas transported out of their own sphere, and meddling rashly with practice; but they are inevitably extended to ideas as such, and to the whole life of intelligence; practice is everything, a free play of the mind is nothing. The notion of the free play of the mind upon all subjects being a pleasure in itself, being an object of desire, being an essential provider of elements without which a nation's spirit, whatever compensations it may have for them, must, in the long run, die of inanition, hardly enters into an Englishman's thoughts. It is noticeable that the word *curiosity*, which in other languages is used in a good sense, to mean, as a high and fine quality of man's nature, just this disinterested love of a free play of the mind on all subjects, for its own sake—it is noticeable, I say, that this word has in our language no sense of the kind, no sense but a rather bad and disparaging one. But criticism, real criticism, is essentially the exercise of this very quality. It obeys an instinct prompting it to try to know the best that is known and thought in the world, irrespectively of practice, politics, and everything of the kind; and to value knowledge and thought as they approach this best, without the intrusion

3. Cf. Numbers xxii.38.

of any other considerations whatever. This is an instinct for which there is, I think, little original sympathy in the practical English nature, and what there was of it has undergone a long benumbing period of blight and suppression in the epoch of concentration which followed the French Revolution.

But epochs of concentration cannot well endure forever; epochs of expansion, in the due course of things, follow them. Such an epoch of expansion seems to be opening in this country. In the first place all danger of a hostile forcible pressure of foreign ideas upon our practice has long disappeared; like the traveler in the fable, therefore, we begin to wear our cloak a little more loosely.[4] Then, with a long peace, the ideas of Europe steal gradually and amicably in, and mingle, though in infinitesimally small quantities at a time, with our own notions. Then, too, in spite of all that is said about the absorbing and brutalizing influence of our passionate material progress, it seems to me indisputable that this progress is likely, though not certain, to lead in the end to an apparition of intellectual life; and that man, after he has made himself perfectly comfortable and has now to determine what to do with himself next, may begin to remember that he has a mind, and that the mind may be made the source of great pleasure. I grant it is mainly the privilege of faith, at present, to discern this end to our railways, our business, and our fortune-making; but we shall see if, here as elsewhere, faith is not in the end the true prophet. Our ease, our traveling, and our unbounded liberty to hold just as hard and securely as we please to the practice to which our notions have given birth, all tend to beget an inclination to deal a little more freely with these notions themselves, to canvass them a little, to penetrate a little into their real nature. Flutterings of curiosity, in the foreign sense of the word, appear amongst us, and it is in these that criticism must look to find its account. Criticism first; a time of true creative activity, perhaps—which, as I have said, must inevitably be preceded amongst us by a time of criticism—hereafter, when criticism has done its work.

It is of the last importance that English criticism should clearly discern what rule for its course, in order to avail itself of the field now opening to it, and to produce fruit for the future, it ought to take. The rule may be summed up in one word—*disinterestedness*.[5] And how is criticism to show disinterestedness? By keeping aloof from what is called "the practical view of things"; by resolutely following the law of its own nature, which is to be a free play of the mind on all subjects which it touches. By steadily refusing to lend itself to any of those ulterior, political, practical considerations about ideas, which plenty of people will be sure to attach to them,

4. See Aesop's fable of the wind and the sun.
5. This key word in Arnold's argument connotes independence and objectivity of mind. It should not be confused, as it often is, with mere lack of interest.

which perhaps ought often to be attached to them, which in this country at any rate are certain to be attached to them quite sufficiently, but which criticism has really nothing to do with. Its business is, as I have said, simply to know the best that is known and thought in the world, and by in its turn making this known, to create a current of true and fresh ideas. Its business is to do this with inflexible honesty, with due ability; but its business is to do no more, and to leave alone all questions of practical consequences and applications, questions which will never fail to have due prominence given to them. Else criticism, besides being really false to its own nature, merely continues in the old rut which it has hitherto followed in this country, and will certainly miss the chance now given to it. For what is at present the bane of criticism in this country? It is that practical considerations cling to it and stifle it. It subserves interests not its own. Our organs of criticism are organs of men and parties having practical ends to serve, and with them those practical ends are the first thing and the play of mind the second; so much play of mind as is compatible with the prosecution of those practical ends is all that is wanted. An organ like the *Revue des Deux Mondes*,[6] having for its main function to understand and utter the best that is known and thought in the world, existing, it may be said, as just an organ for a free play of the mind, we have not. But we have the *Edinburgh Review*, existing as an organ of the old Whigs, and for as much play of mind as may suit its being that; we have the *Quarterly Review*, existing as an organ of the Tories, and for as much play of mind as may suit its being that; we have the *British Quarterly Review*, existing as an organ of the political Dissenters, and for as much play of mind as may suit its being that; we have the *Times*, existing as an organ of the common, satisfied, well-to-do Englishman, and for as much play of mind as may suit its being that. And so on through all the various fractions, political and religious, of our society; every fraction has, as such, its organ of criticism, but the notion of combining all fractions in the common pleasure of a free disinterested play of mind meets with no favor. Directly this play of mind wants to have more scope, and to forget the pressure of practical considerations a little, it is checked, it is made to feel the chain. We saw this the other day in the extinction, so much to be regretted, of the *Home and Foreign Review*.[6a] Perhaps in no organ of criticism in this country was there so much knowledge, so much play of mind; but these could not save it. The *Dublin Review* subordinates play of mind to the practical business of English and Irish Catholicism, and lives. It must needs be that men should act in sects and parties, that each of these sects and parties should have its organ, and should make

6. An international magazine of exceptionally high quality, founded in Paris in 1829.

6a. A liberal Catholic periodical, founded in 1862, which ceased publication in 1864.

this organ subserve the interests of its action; but it would be well, too, that there should be a criticism, not the minister of these interests, not their enemy, but absolutely and entirely independent of them. No other criticism will ever attain any real authority or make any real way towards its end—the creating a current of true and fresh ideas.

It is because criticism has so little kept in the pure intellectual sphere, has so little detached itself from practice, has been so directly polemical and controversial, that it has so ill accomplished, in this country, its best spiritual work; which is to keep man from a self-satisfaction which is retarding and vulgarizing, to lead him towards perfection, by making his mind dwell upon what is excellent in itself, and the absolute beauty and fitness of things. A polemical practical criticism makes men blind even to the ideal imperfection of their practice, makes them willingly assert its ideal perfection, in order the better to secure it against attack; and clearly this is narrowing and baneful for them. If they were reassured on the practical side, speculative considerations of ideal perfection they might be brought to entertain, and their spiritual horizon would thus gradually widen. Sir Charles Adderley[7] says to the Warwickshire farmers:

"Talk of the improvement of breed! Why, the race we ourselves represent, the men and women, the old Anglo-Saxon race, are the best breed in the whole world. . . . The absence of a too enervating climate, too unclouded skies, and a too luxurious nature, has produced so vigorous a race of people, and has rendered us so superior to all the world."

Mr. Roebuck[8] says to the Sheffield cutlers:

"I look around me and ask what is the state of England? Is not property safe? Is not every man able to say what he likes? Can you not walk from one end of England to the other in perfect security? I ask you whether, the world over or in past history, there is anything like it? Nothing. I pray that our unrivaled happiness may last."

Now obviously there is a peril for poor human nature in words and thoughts of such exuberant self-satisfaction, until we find ourselves safe in the streets of the Celestial City.

> *Das wenige verschwindet leicht dem Blicke*
> *Der vorwärts sieht, wie viel noch übrig bleibt—*[9]

says Goethe; "the little that is done seems nothing when we look forward and see how much we have yet to do." Clearly this is a

7. 1814–1905; conservative politician and wealthy landowner.
8. John Arthur Roebuck (1801–79), radical politician and representative in

Parliament for the industrial city of Sheffield.
9. Goethe's *Iphigenie auf Tauris* I.ii.91–92.

better line of reflection for weak humanity, so long as it remains on this earthly field of labor and trial.

But neither Sir Charles Adderley nor Mr. Roebuck is by nature inaccessible to considerations of this sort. They only lose sight of them owing to the controversial life we all lead, and the practical form which all speculation takes with us. They have in view opponents whose aim is not ideal, but practical; and in their zeal to uphold their own practice against these innovators, they go so far as even to attribute to this practice an ideal perfection. Somebody has been wanting to introduce a six-pound franchise,[1] or to abolish church-rates, or to collect agricultural statistics by force, or to diminish local self-government. How natural, in reply to such proposals, very likely improper or ill-timed, to go a little beyond the mark and to say stoutly, "Such a race of people as we stand, so superior to all the world! The old Anglo-Saxon race, the best breed in the whole world! I pray that our unrivaled happiness may last! I ask you whether, the world over or in past history, there is anything like it?" And so long as criticism answers this dithyramb by insisting that the old Anglo-Saxon race would be still more superior to all others if it had no church-rates, or that our unrivaled happiness would last yet longer with a six-pound franchise, so long will the strain, "The best breed in the whole world!" swell louder and louder, everything ideal and refining will be lost out of sight, and both the assailed and their critics will remain in a sphere, to say the truth, perfectly unvital, a sphere in which spiritual progression is impossible. But let criticism leave church-rates and the franchise alone, and in the most candid spirit, without a single lurking thought of practical innovation, confront with our dithyramb this paragraph on which I stumbled in a newspaper immediately after reading Mr. Roebuck:

"A shocking child murder has just been committed at Nottingham. A girl named Wragg left the workhouse there on Saturday morning with her young illegitimate child. The child was soon afterwards found dead on Mapperly Hills, having been strangled. Wragg is in custody."

Nothing but that; but, in juxtaposition with the absolute eulogies of Sir Charles Adderley and Mr. Roebuck, how eloquent, how suggestive are those few lines! "Our old Anglo-Saxon breed, the best in the whole world!"—how much that is harsh and ill-favored there is in this best! Wragg! If we are to talk of ideal perfection, of "the best in the whole world," has anyone reflected what a touch of grossness in our race, what an original shortcoming in the more delicate spiritual perceptions, is shown by the natural growth amongst us of such hideous names—Higginbottom, Stiggins, Bugg!

1. A radical proposal to extend the right to vote to anyone owning land worth £6 annual rent. "Church-rates": taxes supporting the Church of England.

In Ionia and Attica they were luckier in this respect than "the best race in the world"; by the Ilissus[2] there was no Wragg, poor thing! And "our unrivaled happiness"—what an element of grimness, bareness, and hideousness mixes with it and blurs it; the workhouse, the dismal Mapperly Hills[2a]—how dismal those who have seen them will remember—the gloom, the smoke, the cold, the strangled illegitimate child! "I ask you whether, the world over or in past history, there is anything like it?" Perhaps not, one is inclined to answer; but at any rate, in that case, the world is very much to be pitied. And the final touch—short, bleak and inhuman: *Wragg is in custody.* The sex lost in the confusion of our unrivaled happiness; or (shall I say?) the superfluous Christian name lopped off by the straightforward vigor of our old Anglo-Saxon breed! There is profit for the spirit in such contrasts as this; criticism serves the cause of perfection by establishing them. By eluding sterile conflict, by refusing to remain in the sphere where alone narrow and relative conceptions have any worth and validity, criticism may diminish its momentary importance, but only in this way has it a chance of gaining admittance for those wider and more perfect conceptions to which all its duty is really owed. Mr. Roebuck will have a poor opinion of an adversary who replies to his defiant songs of triumph only by murmuring under his breath, *Wragg is in custody*; but in no other way will these songs of triumph be induced gradually to moderate themselves, to get rid of what in them is excessive and offensive, and to fall into a softer and truer key.

It will be said that it is a very subtle and indirect action which I am thus prescribing for criticism, and that, by embracing in this manner the Indian virtue of detachment and abandoning the sphere of practical life, it condemns itself to a slow and obscure work. Slow and obscure it may be, but it is the only proper work of criticism. The mass of mankind will never have any ardent zeal for seeing things as they are; very inadequate ideas will always satisfy them. On these inadequate ideas reposes, and must repose, the general practice of the world. That is as much as saying that whoever sets himself to see things as they are will find himself one of a very small circle; but it is only by this small circle resolutely doing its own work that adequate ideas will ever get current at all. The rush and roar of practical life will always have a dizzying and attracting effect upon the most collected spectator, and tend to draw him into its vortex; most of all will this be the case where that life is so powerful as it is in England. But it is only by remaining collected, and refusing to lend himself to the point of view of the practical man, that the critic can do the practical man any service; and it is only by the greatest sincerity in pursuing his own course, and by at last convincing even the practical man of his sin-

2. A stream in Attica, Greece.
2a. Adjacent to the coal-mining and industrial area of Nottingham (later associated with the writings of D. H. Lawrence).

cerity, that he can escape misunderstandings which perpetually threaten him.

For the practical man is not apt for fine distinctions, and yet in these distinctions truth and the highest culture greatly find their account. But it is not easy to lead a practical man—unless you reassure him as to your practical intentions, you have no chance of leading him—to see that a thing which he has always been used to look at from one side only, which he greatly values, and which, looked at from that side, quite deserves, perhaps, all the prizing and admiring which he bestows upon it—that this thing, looked at from another side, may appear much less beneficent and beautiful, and yet retain all its claims to our practical allegiance. Where shall we find language innocent enough, how shall we make the spotless purity of our intentions evident enough, to enable us to say to the political Englishman that the British Constitution itself, which, seen from the practical side, looks such a magnificent organ of progress and virtue, seen from the speculative side—with its compromises, its love of facts, its horror of theory, its studied avoidance of clear thoughts—that, seen from this side, our august Constitution sometimes looks—forgive me, shade of Lord Somers![3]—a colossal machine for the manufacture of Philistines?[4] How is Cobbett[5] to say this and not be misunderstood, blackened as he is with the smoke of a lifelong conflict in the field of political practice? how is Mr. Carlyle to say it and not be misunderstood, after his furious raid into this field with his *Latter-day Pamphlets?* how is Mr. Ruskin, after his pugnacious political economy?[6] I say, the critic must keep out of the region of immediate practice in the political, social, humanitarian sphere if he wants to make a beginning for that more free speculative treatment of things, which may perhaps one day make its benefits felt even in this sphere, but in a natural and thence irresistible manner.

Do what he will, however, the critic will still remain exposed to frequent misunderstandings, and nowhere so much as in this country. For here people are particularly indisposed even to comprehend that without this free disinterested treatment of things, truth and the highest culture are out of the question. So immersed are they in practical life, so accustomed to take all their notions from this life and its processes, that they are apt to think that truth and culture themselves can be reached by the processes of this life, and that it is an impertinent singularity to think of reaching them in

3. John Somers (1651–1716), statesman responsible for formulating the Declaration of Rights.
4. The unenlightened middle classes whose opposition to the men of culture is parallel to the Biblical tribe which fought against the people of Israel, "the children of light." Arnold's repeated use of this parallel has established the term in our language.
5. William Cobbett (1762–1835), vehement reformer whose political position anticipated that of Dickens.
6. Reference to *Unto this Last* (1862) in which Ruskin shifted from art criticism to an attack on traditional theories of economics.

any other. "We are all *terrae filii*,"[7] cries their eloquent advocate; "all Philistines together. Away with the notion of proceeding by any other course than the course dear to the Philistines; let us have a social movement, let us organize and combine a party to pursue truth and new thought, let us call it *the liberal party*, and let us all stick to each other, and back each other up. Let us have no nonsense about independent criticism, and intellectual delicacy, and the few and the many. Don't let us trouble ourselves about foreign thought; we shall invent the whole thing for ourselves as we go along. If one of us speaks well, applaud him; if one of us speaks ill, applaud him too; we are all in the same movement, we are all liberals, we are all in pursuit of truth." In this way the pursuit of truth becomes really a social, practical, pleasurable affair, almost requiring a chairman, a secretary, and advertisements; with the excitement of an occasional scandal, with a little resistance to give the happy sense of difficulty overcome; but, in general, plenty of bustle and very little thought. To act is so easy, as Goethe says; to think is so hard! It is true that the critic has many temptations to go with the stream, to make one of the party movement, one of these *terrae filii*; it seems ungracious to refuse to be a *terrae filius* when so many excellent people are; but the critic's duty is to refuse, or, if resistance is vain, at least to cry with Obermann: *Périssons en résistant*.[8] * * *

For criticism, these are elementary laws; but they never can be popular, and in this country they have been very little followed, and one meets with immense obstacles in following them. That is a reason for asserting them again and again. Criticism must maintain its independence of the practical spirit and its aims. Even with well-meant efforts of the practical spirit it must express dissatisfaction, if in the sphere of the ideal they seem impoverishing and limiting. It must not hurry on to the goal because of its practical importance. It must be patient, and know how to wait; and flexible, and know how to attach itself to things and how to withdraw from them. It must be apt to study and praise elements that for the fullness of spiritual perfection are wanted, even though they belong to a power which in the practical sphere may be maleficent. It must be apt to discern the spiritual shortcomings or illusions of powers that in the practical sphere may be beneficent. And this without any notion of favoring or injuring, in the practical sphere, one power or the other; without any notion of playing off, in this sphere, one power against the other. When one looks, for instance, at the English Divorce Court—an institution which perhaps has its practical conveniences, but which in the

7. "Sons of the earth."
8. "Let us die resisting." Three paragraphs are omitted here. They consist of a highly allusive account of a controversy concerning Biblical history. The discussion further illustrates the difficulties of a critic's remaining impartial.

ideal sphere is so hideous; an institution which neither makes divorce impossible nor makes it decent, which allows a man to get rid of his wife, or a wife of her husband, but makes them drag one another first, for the public edification, through a mire of unutterable infamy—when one looks at this charming institution, I say, with its crowded trials, its newspaper reports, and its money compensations, this institution in which the gross unregenerate British Philistine has indeed stamped an image of himself—one may be permitted to find the marriage theory of Catholicism refreshing and elevating. Or when Protestantism, in virtue of its supposed rational and intellectual origin, gives the law to criticism too magisterially, criticism may and must remind it that its pretensions, in this respect, are illusive and do it harm; that the Reformation was a moral rather than an intellectual event; that Luther's theory of grace no more exactly reflects the mind of the spirit than Bossuet's philosophy of history[9] reflects it; and that there is no more antecedent probability of the Bishop of Durham's[1] stock of ideas being agreeable to perfect reason than of Pope Pius the Ninth's. But criticism will not on that account forget the achievements of Protestantism in the practical and moral sphere; nor that, even in the intellectual sphere, Protestantism, though in a blind and stumbling manner, carried forward the Renascence, while Catholicism threw itself violently across its path.

I lately heard a man of thought and energy contrasting the want of ardor and movement which he now found amongst young men in this country with what he remembered in his own youth, twenty years ago. "What reformers we were then!" he exclaimed; "What a zeal we had! how we canvassed every institution in Church and State, and were prepared to remodel them all on first principles!" He was inclined to regret, as a spiritual flagging, the lull which he saw. I am disposed rather to regard it as a pause in which the turn to a new mode of spiritual progress is being accomplished. Everything was long seen, by the young and ardent amongst us, in inseparable connection with politics and practical life. We have pretty well exhausted the benefits of seeing things in this connection, we have got all that can be got by so seeing them. Let us try a more disinterested mode of seeing them; let us betake ourselves more to the serener life of the mind and spirit. This life, too, may have its excesses and dangers; but they are not for us at present. Let us think of quietly enlarging our stock of true and fresh ideas, and not, as soon as we get an idea or half an idea, be running out with it into the street, and trying to make it rule there. Our ideas will, in the end, shape the world all the better for matur-

9. Bishop Jacques Bossuet (1627–1704) whose theory of history is limited by its Roman Catholic bias (in Arnold's view), just as Martin Luther's exclusive view of grace reflects the bias of extreme Protestantism.
1. An Anglican bishop.

ing a little. Perhaps in fifty years' time it will in the English House of Commons be an objection to an institution that it is an anomaly, and my friend the Member of Parliament will shudder in his grave. But let us in the meanwhile rather endeavor that in twenty years' time it may, in English literature, be an objection to a proposition that it is absurd. That will be a change so vast, that the imagination almost fails to grasp it. *Ab integro saeclorum nascitur ordo.*[2]

If I have insisted so much on the course which criticism must take where politics and religion are concerned, it is because, where these burning matters are in question, it is most likely to go astray. I have wished, above all, to insist on the attitude which criticism should adopt towards things in general; on its right tone and temper of mind. But then comes another question as to the subject matter which literary criticism should most seek. Here, in general, its course is determined for it by the idea which is the law of its being; the idea of a disinterested endeavor to learn and propagate the best that is known and thought in the world, and thus to establish a current of fresh and true ideas. By the very nature of things, as England is not all the world, much of the best that is known and thought in the world cannot be of English growth, must be foreign; by the nature of things, again, it is just this that we are least likely to know, while English thought is streaming in upon us from all sides, and takes excellent care that we shall not be ignorant of its existence. The English critic of literature, therefore, must dwell much on foreign thought, and with particular heed on any part of it, which, while significant and fruitful in itself, is for any reason specially likely to escape him. Again, judging is often spoken of as the critic's one business, and so in some sense it is; but the judgment which almost insensibly forms itself in a fair and clear mind, along with fresh knowledge, is the valuable one; and thus knowledge, and ever fresh knowledge, must be the critic's great concern for himself. And it is by communicating fresh knowledge, and letting his own judgment pass along with it—but insensibly, and in the second place, not the first, as a sort of companion and clue, not as an abstract lawgiver—that the critic will generally do most good to his readers. Sometimes, no doubt, for the sake of establishing an author's place in literature, and his relation to a central standard (and if this is not done, how are we to get at our *best in the world?*) criticism may have to deal with a subject matter so familiar that fresh knowledge is out of the question, and then it must be all judgment; an enunciation and detailed application of principles. Here the great safeguard is never to let oneself become abstract, always to retain an intimate and lively consciousness of the truth of what one is saying, and, the moment this fails us, to be sure that something is wrong. Still under all circumstances,

2. "Order is born from the renewal of the ages" (Virgil, *Eclogues* IV.5).

this mere judgment and application of principles is, in itself, not the most satisfactory work to the critic; like mathematics, it is tautological, and cannot well give us, like fresh learning, the sense of creative activity.

But stop, some one will say; all this talk is of no practical use to us whatever; this criticism of yours is not what we have in our minds when we speak of criticism; when we speak of critics and criticism, we mean critics and criticism of the current English literature of the day; when you offer to tell criticism its function, it is to this criticism that we expect you to address yourself. I am sorry for it, for I am afraid I must disappoint these expectations. I am bound by my own definition of criticism: *a disinterested endeavor to learn and propagate the best that is known and thought in the world.* How much of current English literature comes into this "best that is known and thought in the world"? Not very much I fear; certainly less, at this moment, than of the current literature of France or Germany. Well, then, am I to alter my definition of criticism, in order to meet the requirements of a number of practicing English critics, who, after all, are free in their choice of a business? That would be making criticism lend itself just to one of those alien practical considerations, which, I have said, are so fatal to it. One may say, indeed, to those who have to deal with the mass—so much better disregarded—of current English literature, that they may at all events endeavor, in dealing with this, to try it, so far as they can, by the standard of the best that is known and thought in the world; one may say, that to get anywhere near this standard, every critic should try and possess one great literature, at least, besides his own; and the more unlike his own, the better. But, after all, the criticism I am really concerned with— the criticism which alone can much help us for the future, the criticism which, throughout Europe, is at the present day meant, when so much stress is laid on the importance of criticism and the critical spirit—is a criticism which regards Europe as being, for intellectual and spiritual purposes, one great confederation, bound to a joint action and working to a common result; and whose members have, for their proper outfit, a knowledge of Greek, Roman, and Eastern antiquity, and of one another. Special, local, and temporary advantages being put out of account, that modern nation will in the intellectual and spiritual sphere make most progress, which most thoroughly carries out this program. And what is that but saying that we too, all of us, as individuals, the more thoroughly we carry it out, shall make the more progress?

There is so much inviting us!—what are we to take? what will nourish us in growth towards perfection? That is the question which, with the immense field of life and of literature lying before him, the critic has to answer; for himself first, and afterwards for others. In this idea of the critic's business the essays brought together in the following pages have had their origin; in this idea, widely different as are their subjects, they have, perhaps, their unity.

I conclude with what I said at the beginning: to have the sense of creative activity is the great happiness and the great proof of being alive, and it is not denied to criticism to have it; but then criticism must be sincere, simple, flexible, ardent, ever widening its knowledge. Then it may have, in no contemptible measure, a joyful sense of creative activity; a sense which a man of insight and conscience will prefer to what he might derive from a poor, starved, fragmentary, inadequate creation. And at some epochs no other creation is possible.

Still, in full measure, the sense of creative activity belongs only to genuine creation; in literature we must never forget that. But what true man of letters ever can forget it? It is no such common matter for a gifted nature to come into possession of a current of true and living ideas, and to produce amidst the inspiration of them, that we are likely to underrate it. The epochs of Aeschylus and Shakespeare make us feel their pre-eminence. In an epoch like those is, no doubt, the true life of literature; there is the promised land, towards which criticism can only beckon. That promised land it will not be ours to enter, and we shall die in the wilderness: but to have desired to enter it, to have saluted it from afar, is already, perhaps, the best distinction among contemporaries; it will certainly be the best title to esteem with posterity.

1864, 1865

From Maurice de Guérin[1]
[A Definition of Poetry]

The grand power of poetry is its interpretative power; by which I mean, not a power of drawing out in black and white an explanation of the mystery of the universe, but the power of so dealing with things as to awaken in us a wonderfully full, new, and intimate sense of them, and of our relations with them. When this sense is awakened in us, as to objects without us, we feel ourselves to be in contact with the essential nature of those objects, to be no longer bewildered and oppressed by them, but to have their secret, and to be in harmony with them; and this feeling calms and satisfies us as no other can. Poetry, indeed, interprets in another way besides this; but one of its two ways of interpreting, of exercising its highest power, is by awakening this sense in us. I will not now inquire whether this sense is illusive, whether it can be proved not to be

1. 1810–39; a minor French poet. The essay was included in *Essays in Criticism: First Series.*

illusive, whether it does absolutely make us possess the real nature of things; all I say is, that poetry can awaken it in us, and that to awaken it is one of the highest powers of poetry. The interpretations of science do not give us this intimate sense of objects as the interpretations of poetry give it; they appeal to a limited faculty, and not to the whole man. * * *

I have said that poetry interprets in two ways; it interprets by expressing, with magical felicity, the physiognomy and movement of the outward world, and it interprets by expressing, with inspired conviction, the ideas and laws of the inward world of man's moral and spiritual nature. In other words, poetry in interpretative both by having *natural magic* in it, and by having *moral profundity*. In both ways it illuminates man; it gives him a satisfying sense of reality; it reconciles him with himself and the universe. Thus Aeschylus's "δράσαντι παθεῖν"[2] and his "ἀνήριθμον γέλασμα"[3] are alike interpretative. Shakespeare interprets both when he says,

> Full many a glorious morning have I seen,
> Flatter the mountaintops with sovereign eye;[4]

and when he says,

> There's a divinity that shapes our ends,
> Rough-hew them as we will.[5]

These great poets unite in themselves the faculty of both kinds of interpretation, the naturalistic and the moral. But it is observable that in the poets who unite both kinds, the latter (the moral) usually ends by making itself the master. In Shakespeare the two kinds seem wonderfully to balance one another; but even in him the balance leans; his expression tends to become too little sensuous and simple, too much intellectualized. The same thing may be yet more strongly affirmed of Lucretius and of Wordsworth. In Shelley there is not a balance of the two gifts, nor even a coexistence of them, but there is a passionate straining after them both, and this is what makes Shelley, as a man, so interesting; I will not now inquire how much Shelley achieves as a poet, but whatever he achieves, he in general fails to achieve natural magic in his expression; in Mr. Palgrave's charming *Treasury*[6] may be seen a gallery of his failures.[7] But in Keats and Guérin, in whom the faculty of

2. "The doer must suffer." From Aeschylus' *Choephori* (line 313).
3. "Countless laughter." From Aeschylus' *Prometheus Bound* (line 90).
4. Shakespeare, *Sonnets* XXXIII.1–2.
5. *Hamlet* V.ii.10–11.
6. Francis Palgrave's anthology of poems, *The Golden Treasury*, was first published in 1861.
7. "Compare, for example, his *Lines Written in the Euganean Hills*, with Keats's *Ode to Autumn* . . . The latter

piece *renders* Nature; the former *tries to render* her. I will not deny, however, that Shelley has natural magic in his rhythm; what I deny is, that he has it in his language. It always seems to me that the right sphere for Shelley's genius was the sphere of music, not of poetry; the medium of sounds he can master, but to master the more difficult medium of words he has neither intellectual force enough nor sanity enough" [Arnold's note].

naturalistic interpretation is overpoweringly predominant, the natural magic is perfect; when they speak of the world they speak like Adam naming by divine inspiration the creatures; their expression corresponds with the thing's essential reality.

1863, 1865

From Culture and Anarchy[1]
From *Chapter I. Sweetness and Light*

[PURITANISM AND CULTURE]

The impulse of the English race towards moral development and self-conquest has nowhere so powerfully manifested itself as in Puritanism. Nowhere has Puritanism found so adequate an expression as in the religious organization of the Independents.[2] The modern Independents have a newspaper, the *Nonconformist*, written with great sincerity and ability. The motto, the standard, the profession of faith which this organ of theirs carries aloft, is: "The Dissidence of Dissent and the Protestantism of the Protestant religion." There is sweetness and light, and an ideal of complete harmonious human perfection! One need not go to culture and poetry to find language to judge it. Religion, with its instinct for perfection, supplies language to judge it, language, too, which is in our mouths every day. "Finally, be of one mind, united in feeling," says St. Peter.[3] There is an ideal which judges the Puritan ideal: "The Dissidence of Dissent and the Protestantism of the Protestant religion!" And religious organizations like this are what people believe in, rest in, would give their lives for! Such, I say, is the wonderful virtue of even the beginnings of perfection, of having conquered even the plain faults of our animality, that the religious organization which has helped us to do it can seem to us some-

1. As a critic of social life, Arnold sought to test Victorian institutions according to whether they seemed to him civilized. A characteristic quality of the civilized state of mind is summed up, for his purposes, in his formula "sweetness and light," a phrase suggesting reasonableness of temper and intellectual insight. Arnold derived the phrase from a fable contrasting the spider with the bee in Swift's *Battle of the Books*. The spider (representing a narrow, self-centered, and uncultured mind) spins out of itself "nothing at all but flybane and cobweb." The bee (representing a cultured mind that has drawn nourishment from the humanist tradition) ranges far and wide and brings to its hive honey and also wax out of which candles may be made. Therefore the bee, Swift says, furnishes mankind "with the two noblest of things, which are sweetness and light."
The three following excerpts illustrate aspects of Arnold's indictment of the middle classes for their lack of sweetness and light. The first and third expose the narrowness and dullness of middle-class Puritan religious institutions in both the 17th and 19th centuries. The second, "Doing As One Likes," shows the limitations of the middle-class political bias and the irresponsibility of *laissez faire*. Here Arnold is most close to Carlyle and Ruskin. These three extracts indicate why it has been said that Matthew Arnold discovered the foibles of Main Street fifty years before Sinclair Lewis exposed them in his novels of American life.
2. A 17th-century Puritan group (of which Cromwell was an adherent), allied with the Congregationalists.
3. Cf. I Peter iii.8.

thing precious, salutary, and to be propagated, even when it wears such a brand of imperfection on its forehead as this. And men have got such a habit of giving to the language of religion a special application, of making it a mere jargon, that for the condemnation which religion itself passes on the shortcomings of their religious organizations they have no ear; they are sure to cheat themselves and to explain this condemnation away. They can only be reached by the criticism which culture, like poetry, speaking a language not to be sophisticated, and resolutely testing these organizations by the ideal of a human perfection complete on all sides, applies to them.

But men of culture and poetry, it will be said, are again and again failing, and failing conspicuously, in the necessary first stage to a harmonious perfection, in the subduing of the great obvious faults of our animality, which it is the glory of these religious organizations to have helped us to subdue. True, they do often so fail. They have often been without the virtues as well as the faults of the Puritan; it has been one of their dangers that they so felt the Puritan's faults that they too much neglected the practice of his virtues. I will not, however, exculpate them at the Puritan's expense. They have often failed in morality, and morality is indispensable. And they have been punished for their failure, as the Puritan has been rewarded for his performance. They have been punished wherein they erred; but their ideal of beauty, of sweetness and light, and a human nature complete on all its sides, remains the true ideal of perfection still; just as the Puritan's ideal of perfection remains narrow and inadequate, although for what he did well he has been richly rewarded. Notwithstanding the mighty results of the Pilgrim Fathers' voyage, they and their standard of perfection are rightly judged when we figure to ourselves Shakespeare or Virgil—souls in whom sweetness and light, and all that in human nature is most humane, were eminent—accompanying them on their voyage, and think what intolerable company Shakespeare and Virgil would have found them! In the same way let us judge the religious organizations which we see all around us. Do not let us deny the good and the happiness which they have accomplished; but do not let us fail to see clearly that their idea of human perfection is narrow and inadequate, and that the Dissidence of Dissent and the Protestantism of the Protestant religion will never bring humanity to its true goal. As I said with regard to wealth: Let us look at the life of those who live in and for it—so I say with regard to the religious organizations. Look at the life imaged in such a newspaper as the *Nonconformist*—a life of jealousy of the Establishment,[4] disputes, tea-meetings, openings of chapels, sermons; and then think of it as an ideal of a human life completing

4. The Church of England or the Established Church.

itself on all sides, and aspiring with all its organs after sweetness, light, and perfection!

1867, 1869

From *Chapter II. Doing As One Likes*

* * * When I began to speak of culture, I insisted on our bondage to machinery, on our proneness to value machinery as an end in itself, without looking beyond it to the end for which alone, in truth, it is valuable. Freedom, I said, was one of those things which we thus worshiped in itself, without enough regarding the ends for which freedom is to be desired. In our common notions and talk about freedom, we eminently show our idolatry of machinery. Our prevalent notion is—and I quoted a number of instances to prove it—that it is a most happy and important thing for a man merely to be able to do as he likes. On what he is to do when he is thus free to do as he likes, we do not lay so much stress. Our familiar praise of the British Constitution under which we live, is that it is a system of checks—a system which stops and paralyzes any power in interfering with the free action of individuals. To this effect Mr. Bright,[1] who loves to walk in the old ways of the Constitution, said forcibly in one of his great speeches, what many other people are every day saying less forcibly, that the central idea of English life and politics is *the assertion of personal liberty*. Evidently this is so; but evidently, also, as feudalism, which with its ideas, and habits of subordination was for many centuries silently behind the British Constitution, dies out, and we are left with nothing but our system of checks, and our notion of its being the great right and happiness of an Englishman to do as far as possible what he likes, we are in danger of drifting towards anarchy. We have not the notion, so familiar on the Continent and to antiquity, of *the State*—the nation in its collective and corporate character, entrusted with stringent powers for the general advantage, and controlling individual wills in the name of an interest wider than that of individuals. We say, what is very true, that this notion is often made instrumental to tyranny; we say that a State is in reality made up of the individuals who compose it, and that every individual is the best judge of his own interests. Our leading class is an aristocracy, and no aristocracy likes the notion of a State-authority greater than itself, with a stringent administrative machinery superseding the decorative inutilities of lord-lieutenancy, deputy-lieutenancy, and the *posse comitatus*,[2] which are all in its own hands. Our middle class, the great representative of trade and Dissent, with its maxims of every man for himself in business, every man for himself in religion, dreads

1. John Bright, 19th-century orator and reformer.
2. I.e., "power of the county"—a feudal method of enforcing law by local authorities instead of by agencies of the central government.

a powerful administration which might somehow interfere with it; and besides, it has its own decorative inutilities of vestrymanship and guardianship, which are to this class what lord-lieutenancy and the county magistracy are to the aristocratic class, and a stringent administration might either take these functions out of its hands, or prevent its exercising them in its own comfortable, independent manner, as at present.

Then as to our working class. This class, pressed constantly by the hard daily compulsion of material wants, is naturally the very center and stronghold of our national idea, that it is man's ideal right and felicity to do as he likes. I think I have somewhere related how M. Michelet[3] said to me of the people of France, that it was "a nation of barbarians civilized by the conscription." He meant that through their military service the idea of public duty and of discipline was brought to the mind of these masses, in other respects so raw and uncultivated. Our masses are quite as raw and uncultivated as the French; and so far from their having the idea of public duty and of discipline, superior to the individual's self-will, brought to their mind by a universal obligation of military service, such as that of the conscription—so far from their having this, the very idea of a conscription is so at variance with our English notion of the prime right and blessedness of doing as one likes, that I remember the manager of the Clay Cross works in Derbyshire told me during the Crimean war, when our want of soldiers was much felt and some people were talking of a conscription, that sooner than submit to a conscription the population of that district would flee to the mines, and lead a sort of Robin Hood life underground.

For a long time, as I have said, the strong feudal habits of subordination and deference continued to tell upon the working class. The modern spirit has now almost entirely dissolved those habits, and the anarchical tendency of our worship of freedom in and for itself, of our superstitious faith, as I say, in machinery, is becoming very manifest. More and more, because of this our blind faith in machinery, because of our want of light to enable us to look beyond machinery to the end for which machinery is valuable, this and that man, and this and that body of men, all over the country, are beginning to assert and put in practice an Englishman's right to do what he likes; his right to march where he likes, meet where he likes, enter where he likes, hoot as he likes, threaten as he likes, smash as he likes.[4] All this, I say, tends to anarchy; and though a number of excellent people, and particularly my friends of the Liberal or progressive party, as they call themselves, are kind enough to reassure us by saying that these are trifles, that a few

3. Jules Michelet (1798–1874), French historian.
4. Reference to the riots of 1866 in which a London mob demolished the iron railings enclosing Hyde Park.

transient outbreaks of rowdyism signify nothing, that our system of liberty is one which itself cures all the evils which it works, that the educated and intelligent classes stand in overwhelming strength and majestic repose, ready, like our military force in riots, to act at a moment's notice—yet one finds that one's Liberal friends generally say this because they have such faith in themselves and their nostrums, when they shall return, as the public welfare requires, to place and power. But this faith of theirs one cannot exactly share, when one has so long had them and their nostrums at work, and see that they have not prevented our coming to our present embarrassed condition. And one finds, also, that the outbreaks of rowdyism tend to become less and less of trifles, to become more frequent rather than less frequent; and that meanwhile our educated and intelligent classes remain in their majestic repose, and somehow or other, whatever happens, their overwhelming strength, like our military force in riots, never does act.

How, indeed, *should* their overwhelming strength act, when the man who gives an inflammatory lecture, or breaks down the park railings, or invades a Secretary of State's office, is only following an Englishman's impulse to do as he likes; and our own conscience tells us that we ourselves have always regarded this impulse as something primary and sacred? Mr. Murphy[5] lectures at Birmingham, and showers on the Catholic population of that town "words," says the Home Secretary, "only fit to be addressed to thieves or murderers." What then? Mr. Murphy has his own reasons of several kinds. He suspects the Roman Catholic Church of designs upon Mrs. Murphy; and he says if mayors and magistrates do not care for their wives and daughters, he does. But, above all, he is doing as he likes; or, in worthier language, asserting his personal liberty. "I will carry out my lectures if they walk over my body as a dead corpse, and I say to the Mayor of Birmingham that he is my servant while I am in Birmingham, and as my servant he must do his duty and protect me." Touching and beautiful words, which find a sympathetic chord in every British bosom! The moment it is plainly put before us that a man is asserting his personal liberty, we are half disarmed; because we are believers in freedom, and not in some dream of a right reason to which the assertion of our freedom is to be subordinated. Accordingly, the Secretary of State had to say that although the lecturer's language was "only fit to be addressed to thieves or murderers," yet, "I do not think he is to be deprived, I do not think that anything I have said could justify the inference that he is to be deprived, of the right of protection in a place built by him for the purpose of these lectures; because the language was not language which afforded grounds for a criminal

5. An orator whose inflammatory anti-Catholic public speech *The Errors of* *the Roman Church* led to rioting in Birmingham and other cities in 1867.

prosecution." No, nor to be silenced by Mayor, or Home Secretary, or any administrative authority on earth, simply on their notion of what is discreet and reasonable! This is in perfect consonance with our public opinion, and with our national love for the assertion of personal liberty. * * *

From *Chapter V. Porro Unum Est Necessarium* [1]

* * *Sweetness and light evidently have to do with the bent or side in humanity which we call Hellenic. Greek intelligence has obviously for its essence the instinct for what Plato calls the true, firm, intelligible law of things; the law of light, of seeing things as they are. Even in the natural sciences, where the Greeks had not time and means adequately to apply this instinct, and where we have gone a great deal further than they did, it is this instinct which is the root of the whole matter and the ground of all our success; and this instinct the world has mainly learnt of the Greeks, inasmuch as they are humanity's most signal manifestation of it. Greek art, again, Greek beauty, have their root in the same impulse to see things as they really are, inasmuch as Greek art and beauty rest on fidelity to nature—the *best* nature—and on a delicate discrimination of what this best nature is. To say we work for sweetness and light, then, is only another way of saying that we work for Hellenism. But, oh! cry many people, sweetness and light are not enough; you must put strength or energy along with them, and make a kind of trinity of strength, sweetness and light, and then, perhaps, you may do some good. That is to say, we are to join Hebraism, strictness of the moral conscience, and manful walking by the best light we have, together with Hellenism, inculcate both, and rehearse the praises of both.

Or, rather, we may praise both in conjunction, but we must be careful to praise Hebraism most. "Culture," says an acute, though somewhat rigid critic, Mr. Sidgwick,[2] "diffuses sweetness and light. I do not undervalue these blessings, but religion gives fire and strength, and the world wants fire and strength even more than sweetness and light." By religion, let me explain, Mr. Sidgwick here means particularly that Puritanism on the insufficiency of which I have been commenting and to which he says I am unfair. Now, no doubt, it is possible to be a fanatical partisan of light and the instincts which push us to it, a fanatical enemy of strict-

1. Luke x.42: "But one thing is needful." This chapter develops a contrast established in Ch. IV between *Hebraism* (Puritan morality and energetic devotion to work) and *Hellenism* (cultivation of the aesthetic and intellectual understanding of life). The Puritan middle classes, according to Arnold, think that the "one thing needful" is the Hebraic form of virtue.
2. Henry Sidgwick, philosopher (1838–1900), whose article on Arnold appeared in *Macmillan's Magazine*, Aug., 1867.

ness of moral conscience and the instincts which push us to it. A fanaticism of this sort deforms and vulgarizes the well-known work, in some respects so remarkable, of the late Mr. Buckle.[3] Such a fanaticism carries its own mark with it, in lacking sweetness; and its own penalty, in that, lacking sweetness, it comes in the end to lack light too. And the Greeks—the great exponents of humanity's bent for sweetness and light united, of its perception that the truth of things must be at the same time beauty—singularly escaped the fanaticism which we moderns, whether we Hellenize or whether we Hebraize, are so apt to show. They arrived—though failing, as has been said, to give adequate practical satisfaction to the claims of man's moral side—at the idea of a comprehensive adjustment of the claims of both the sides in man, the moral as well as the intellectual, of a full estimate of both, and of a reconciliation of both; an idea which is philosophically of the greatest value, and the best of lessons for us moderns. So we ought to have no difficulty in conceding to Mr. Sidgwick that manful walking by the best light one has—fire and strength as he calls it—has its high value as well as culture, the endeavor to see things in their truth and beauty, the pursuit of sweetness and light. But whether at this or that time, and to this or that set of persons, one ought to insist most on the praises of fire and strength, or on the praises of sweetness and light, must depend, one would think, on the circumstances and needs of that particular time and those particular persons. And all that we have been saying, and indeed any glance at the world around us, shows that with us, with the most respectable and strongest part of us, the ruling force is now, and long has been, a Puritan force—the care for fire and strength, strictness of conscience, Hebraism, rather than the care for sweetness and light, spontaneity of consciousness, Hellenism.

Well, then, what is the good of our now rehearsing the praises of fire and strength to ourselves, who dwell too exclusively on them already? When Mr. Sidgwick says so broadly, that the world wants fire and strength even more than sweetness and light, is he not carried away by a turn for broad generalization?; does he not forget that the world is not all of one piece, and every piece with the same needs at the same time? It may be true that the Roman world at the beginning of our era, or Leo the Tenth's Court at the time of the Reformation, or French society in the eighteenth century,[4] needed fire and strength even more than sweetness and light. But can it be said that the Barbarians who overran the empire needed fire and strength even more than sweetness and light; or

3. Henry Thomas Buckle (1821–62), author of *A History of Civilization*.
4. Societies representing an excess of sophisticated worldliness as at the courts of such a Roman emperor as Nero (A.D. 54–68), or Pope Leo X (1513–21), or Louis XV (1715–74).

that the Puritans needed them more; or that Mr. Murphy, the Birmingham lecturer, and the Rev. W. Cattle[5] and his friends, need them more?

The Puritan's great danger is that he imagines himself in possession of a rule telling him the *unum necessarium*, or one thing needful, and that he then remains satisfied with a very crude conception of what this rule really is and what it tells him, thinks he has now knowledge and henceforth needs only to act, and, in this dangerous state of assurance and self-satisfaction, proceeds to give full swing to a number of the instincts of his ordinary self. Some of the instincts of his ordinary self he has, by the help of his rule of life, conquered; but others which he has not conquered by this help he is so far from perceiving to need subjugation, and to be instincts of an inferior self, that he even fancies it to be his right and duty, in virtue of having conquered a limited part of himself, to give unchecked swing to the remainder. He is, I say, a victim of Hebraism, of the tendency to cultivate strictness of conscience rather than spontaneity of consciousness. And what he wants is a larger conception of human nature, showing him the number of other points at which his nature must come to its best, besides the points which he himself knows and thinks of. There is no *unum necessarium*, or one thing needful, which can free human nature from the obligation of trying to come to its best at all these points. The real *unum necessarium* for us is to come to our best at all points. Instead of our "one thing needful," justifying in us vulgarity, hideousness, ignorance, violence— our vulgarity, hideousness, ignorance, violence, are really so many touchstones which try our one thing needful, and which prove that in the state, at any rate, in which we ourselves have it, it is not all we want. And as the force which encourages us to stand staunch and fast by the rule and ground we have is Hebraism, so the force which encourages us to go back upon this rule, and to try the very ground on which we appear to stand, is Hellenism —a turn for giving our consciousness free play and enlarging its range. And what I say is, not that Hellenism is always for everybody more wanted than Hebraism, but that for the Rev. W. Cattle at this particular moment, and for the great majority of us his fellow countrymen, it is more wanted.

* * *

The newspapers a short time ago contained an account of the suicide of a Mr. Smith, secretary to some insurance company, who, it was said, "labored under the apprehension that he would come

5. A Nonconformist clergyman who was chairman of the anti-Catholic meeting addressed by Murphy in 1867. See "Doing As One Likes," above.

to poverty, and that he was eternally lost." And when I read these words, it occurred to me that the poor man who came to such a mournful end was, in truth, a kind of type—by the selection of his two grand objects of concern, by their isolation from everything else, and their juxtaposition to one another—of all the strongest, most respectable, and most representative part of our nation. "He labored under the apprehension that he would come to poverty, and that he was eternally lost." The whole middle class have a conception of things—a conception which makes us call them Philistines—just like that of this poor man; though we are seldom, of course, shocked by seeing it take the distressing, violently morbid, and fatal turn, which it took with him. But how generally, with how many of us, are the main concerns of life limited to these two: the concern for making money, and the concern for saving our souls! And how entirely does the narrow and mechanical conception of our secular business proceed from a narrow and mechanical conception of our religious business! What havoc do the united conceptions make of our lives! It is because the second-named of these two master-concerns presents to us the one thing needful in so fixed, narrow, and mechanical a way, that so ignoble a fellow master-concern to it as the first-named becomes possible; and, having been once admitted, takes the same rigid and absolute character as the other.

Poor Mr. Smith had sincerely the nobler master-concern as well as the meaner—the concern for saving his soul (according to the narrow and mechanical conception which Puritanism has of what the salvation of the soul is), as well as the concern for making money. But let us remark how many people there are, especially outside the limits of the serious and conscientious middle class to which Mr. Smith belonged, who take up with a meaner master-concern—whether it be pleasure, or field sports, or bodily exercises, or business, or popular agitation—who take up with one of these exclusively, and neglect Mr. Smith's nobler master-concern, because of the mechanical form which Hebraism has given to this noble master-concern. Hebraism makes it stand, as we have said, as something talismanic, isolated, and all-sufficient, justifying our giving our ordinary selves free play in bodily exercises, or business, or popular agitation, if we have made our account square with this master-concern; and, if we have not, rendering other things indifferent, and our ordinary self all we have to follow, and to follow with all the energy that is in us, till we do. Whereas the idea of perfection at all points, the encouraging in ourselves spontaneity of consciousness, the letting a free play of thought live and flow around all our activity, the indisposition to allow one side of our activity to stand as so all-important and all-sufficing that it makes other sides indifferent—this bent of mind in us may not only check us in following unreservedly a mean master-concern of any kind, but may even, also, bring new life and movement into that side of us with which alone Hebraism concerns itself, and awaken a healthier and less mechanical activity there. Hellenism may thus actually serve to further the designs of Hebraism.

* * *

1868, 1869

From Wordsworth[1]

* * * Wordsworth has been in his grave for some thirty years, and certainly his lovers and admirers cannot flatter themselves that this great and steady light of glory as yet shines over him. He is not fully recognized at home; he is not recognized at all abroad. Yet I firmly believe that the poetical performance of Wordsworth is, after that of Shakespeare and Milton, of which all the world now recognizes the worth, undoubtedly the most considerable in our language from the Elizabethan age to the present time. Chaucer is anterior; and on other grounds, too, he cannot well be brought into the comparison. But taking the roll of our chief poetical names, besides Shakespeare and Milton, from the age of Elizabeth downwards, and going through it—Spenser, Dryden, Pope, Gray, Goldsmith, Cowper, Burns, Coleridge, Scott, Campbell, Moore, Byron, Shelley, Keats (I mention those only who are dead)—I think it certain that Wordsworth's name deserves to stand, and will finally stand, above them all. Several of the poets named have gifts and excellences which Wordsworth has not. But taking the performance of each as a whole, I say that Wordsworth seems to me to have left a body of poetical work superior in power, in interest, in the qualities which give enduring freshness, to that which any one of the others has left.

But this is not enough to say. I think it certain, further, that if we take the chief poetical names of the Continent since the death of Molière, and, omitting Goethe, confront the remaining names with that of Wordsworth, the result is the same. Let us take Klopstock, Lessing, Schiller, Uhland, Rückert, and Heine for Germany; Filicaia, Alfieri, Manzoni, and Leopardi for Italy; Racine, Boileau, Voltaire, André Chénier, Béranger, Lamartine, Musset, M. Victor

1. In one of his letters to Clough, Arnold remarked that those who cannot read Greek literature "should read nothing but Milton and parts of Wordsworth: the state should see to it." The following essay, which served as the introduction to a volume of Wordsworth's poems selected by Arnold, demonstrates the reasons for this admiration. A further tribute to Wordsworth is expressed in Arnold's poem *Memorial Verses*. The opening paragraphs of the essay, which are omitted here, review the history of Wordsworth's reputation.

Hugo (he has been so long celebrated that although he still lives I may be permitted to name him) for France. Several of these, again, have evidently gifts and excellences to which Wordsworth can make no pretension. But in real poetical achievement it seems to me indubitable that to Wordsworth, here again, belongs the palm. It seems to me that Wordsworth has left behind him a body of poetical work which wears, and will wear, better on the whole than the performance of any one of these personages, so far more brilliant and celebrated, most of them, than the homely poet of Rydal.[2] Wordsworth's performance in poetry is on the whole, in power, in interest, in the qualities which give enduring freshness, superior to theirs.

This is a high claim to make for Wordsworth. But if it is a just claim, if Wordsworth's place among the poets who have appeared in the last two or three centuries is after Shakespeare, Molière, Milton, Goethe, indeed, but before all the rest, then in time Wordsworth will have his due. We shall recognize him in his place, as we recognize Shakespeare and Milton; and not only we ourselves shall recognize him, but he will be recognized by Europe also. Meanwhile, those who recognize him already may do well, perhaps, to ask themselves whether there are not in the case of Wordsworth certain special obstacles which hinder or delay his due recognition by others, and whether these obstacles are not in some measure removable.

The *Excursion* and the *Prelude*, his poems of greatest bulk, are by no means Wordsworth's best work. His best work is in his shorter pieces, and many indeed are there of these which are of first-rate excellence. But in his seven volumes the pieces of high merit are mingled with a mass of pieces very inferior to them; so inferior to them that it seems wonderful how the same poet should have produced both. Shakespeare frequently has lines and passages in a strain quite false, and which are entirely unworthy of him. But one can imagine him smiling if one could meet him in the Elysian Fields and tell him so; smiling and replying that he knew it perfectly well himself, and what did it matter? But with Wordsworth the case is different. Work altogether inferior, work quite uninspired, flat, and dull, is produced by him with evident unconsciousness of its defects, and he presents it to us with the same faith and seriousness as his best work. Now a drama or an epic fill the mind, and one does not look beyond them; but in a collection of short pieces the impression made by one piece requires to be continued and sustained by the piece following. In reading Wordsworth the impression made by one of his fine pieces is too often dulled and

2. Rydal Mount, Wordsworth's home in the Lake District.

spoiled by a very inferior piece coming after it.

Wordsworth composed verses during a space of some sixty years; and it is no exaggeration to say that within one single decade of those years, between 1798 and 1808, almost all his really first-rate work was produced. A mass of inferior work remains, work done before and after this golden prime, imbedding the first-rate work and clogging it, obstructing our approach to it, chilling, not unfrequently, the high-wrought mood with which we leave it. To be recognized far and wide as a great poet, to be possible and receivable as a classic, Wordsworth needs to be relieved of a great deal of the poetical baggage which now encumbers him. To administer this relief is indispensable, unless he is to continue to be a poet for the few only—a poet valued far below his real worth by the world.[3] * * *

Disengaged from the quantity of inferior work which now obscures them, the best poems of Wordsworth, I hear many people say, would indeed stand out in great beauty, but they would prove to be very few in number, scarcely more than a half a dozen. I maintain, on the other hand, that what strikes me with admiration, what establishes in my opinion Wordsworth's superiority, is the great and ample body of powerful work which remains to him, even after all his inferior work has been cleared away. He gives us so much to rest upon, so much which communicates his spirit and engages ours!

This is of very great importance. If it were a comparison of single pieces, or of three or four pieces, by each poet, I do not say that Wordsworth would stand decisively above Gray, or Burns, or Coleridge, or Keats, or Manzoni, or Heine. It is in his ampler body of powerful work that I find his superiority. His good work itself, his work which counts, is not all of it, of course, of equal value. Some kinds of poetry are in themselves lower kinds than others. The ballad kind is a lower kind: the didactic kind, still more, is a lower kind. Poetry of this latter sort counts, too, sometimes, by its biographical interest partly, not by its poetical interest pure and simple; but then this can only be when the poet producing it has the power and importance of Wordsworth, a power and importance which he assuredly did not establish by such didactic poetry alone. Altogether, it is, I say, by the great body of powerful and significant work which remains to him, after every reduction and deduction has been made, that Wordsworth's superiority is proved.

To exhibit this body of Wordsworth's best work, to clear away obstructions from around it, and to let it speak for itself, is what every lover of Wordsworth should desire. Until this has been done,

---

3. Two paragraphs, here omitted, criticize Wordsworth's system of classifying his poems.

Wordsworth, whom we, to whom he is dear, all of us know and feel to be so great a poet, has not had a fair chance before the world. When once it has been done, he will make his way best, not by our advocacy of him, but by his own worth and power. We may safely leave him to make his way thus, we who believe that a superior worth and power in poetry finds in mankind a sense responsive to it and disposed at last to recognize it. Yet at the outset, before he has been duly known and recognized, we may do Wordsworth a service, perhaps, by indicating in what his superior power and worth will be found to consist, and in what it will not.

Long ago, in speaking of Homer, I said that the noble and profound application of ideas to life is the most essential part of poetic greatness. I said that a great poet receives his distinctive character of superiority from his application, under the conditions immutably fixed by the laws of poetic beauty and poetic truth, from his application, I say, to his subject, whatever it may be, of the ideas

On man, on nature, and on human life,[4]

which he has acquired for himself. The line quoted is Wordsworth's own; and his superiority arises from his powerful use, in his best pieces, his powerful application to his subject, of ideas "on man, on nature, and on human life."

Voltaire, with his signal acuteness, most truly remarked that "no nation has treated in poetry moral ideas with more energy and depth than the English nation." And he adds: "There, it seems to me, is the great merit of the English poets." Voltaire does not mean, by "treating in poetry moral ideas," the composing moral and didactic poems—that brings us but a very little way in poetry. He means just the same thing as was meant when I spoke above "of the noble and profound application of ideas to life"; and he means the application of these ideas under the conditions fixed for us by the laws of poetic beauty and poetic truth. If it is said that to call these ideas *moral* ideas is to introduce a strong and injurious limitation, I answer that it is to do nothing of the kind, because moral ideas are really so main a part of human life. The question, *how to live*, is itself a moral idea; and it is the question which most interests every man, and with which, in some way or other, he is perpetually occupied. A large sense is of course to be given to the term *moral*. Whatever bears upon the question, "how to live," comes under it.

> Nor love thy life, nor hate; but, what thou liv'st,
> Live well; how long or short, permit to heaven.[5]

---

4. *The Recluse,* line 754.   5. *Paradise Lost* XI.553–54.

In those fine lines Milton utters, as everyone at once perceives, a moral idea. Yes, but so too, when Keats consoles the forward-bending lover on the Grecian Urn, the lover arrested and presented in immortal relief by the sculptor's hand before he can kiss, with the line,

> Forever wilt thou love, and she be fair,[6]

he utters a moral idea. When Shakespeare says that

> We are such stuff
> As dreams are made on, and our little life
> Is rounded with a sleep,[7]

he utters a moral idea.

Voltaire was right in thinking that the energetic and profound treatment of moral ideas, in this large sense, is what distinguishes the English poetry. He sincerely meant praise, not dispraise or hint of limitation; and they err who suppose that poetic limitation is a necessary consequence of the fact, the fact being granted as Voltaire states it. If what distinguishes the greatest poets is their powerful and profound application of ideas to life, which surely no good critic will deny, then to prefix to the term ideas here the term moral makes hardly any difference, because human life itself is in so preponderating a degree moral.

It is important, therefore, to hold fast to this: that poetry is at bottom a criticism of life; that the greatness of a poet lies in his powerful and beautiful application of ideas to life—to the question: How to live. Morals are often treated in a narrow and false fashion; they are bound up with systems of thought and belief which have had their day; they are fallen into the hands of pedants and professional dealers; they grow tiresome to some of us. We find attraction, at times, even in a poetry of revolt against them; in a poetry which might take for its motto Omar Khayyám's words: "Let us make up in the tavern for the time which we have wasted in the mosque." Or we find attractions in a poetry indifferent to them: in a poetry where the contents may be what they will, but where the form is studied and exquisite. We delude ourselves in either case; and the best cure for our delusion is to let our minds rest upon that great and inexhaustible word *life*, until we learn to enter into its meaning. A poetry of revolt against moral ideas is a poetry of revolt against life; a poetry of indifference towards moral ideas is a poetry of indifference towards *life*.

Epictetus had a happy figure for things like the play of the senses, or literary form and finish, or argumentative ingenuity, in compari-

---

6. *Ode on a Grecian Urn,* line 20.   7. *The Tempest* IV.i.156–58.

son with "the best and master thing" for us, as he called it, the concern, how to live. Some people were afraid of them, he said, or they disliked and undervalued them. Such people were wrong; they were unthankful or cowardly. But the things might also be over-prized, and treated as final when they are not. They bear to life the relation which inns bear to home. "As if a man, journeying home, and finding a nice inn on the road, and liking it, were to stay forever at the inn! Man, thou hast forgotten thine object; thy journey was not *to* this, but *through* this. 'But this inn is taking.' And how many other inns, too, are taking, and how many fields and meadows! but as places of passage merely. You have an object, which is this: to get home, to do your duty to your family, friends, and fellow-countrymen, to attain inward freedom, serenity, happiness, contentment. Style takes your fancy, arguing takes your fancy, and you forget your home and want to make your abode with them and to stay with them, on the plea that they are taking. Who denies that they are taking? but as places of passage, as inns. And when I say this, you suppose me to be attacking the care for style, the care for argument. I am not; I attack the resting in them, the not looking to the end which is beyond them."

Now, when we come across a poet like Theophile Gautier[8] we have a poet who has taken up his abode at an inn, and never got farther. There may be inducements to this or that one of us, at this or that moment, to find delight in him, to cleave to him; but after all, we do not change the truth about him—we only stay ourselves in his inn along with him. And when we come across a poet like Wordsworth, who sings

> Of truth, of grandeur, beauty, love, and hope,
> And melancholy fear subdued by faith,
> Of blessed consolations in distress,
> Of moral strength and intellectual power,
> Of joy in widest commonalty spread—[9]

then we have a poet intent on "the best and master thing," and who prosecutes his journey home. We say, for brevity's sake, that he deals with *life*, because he deals with that in which life really consists. This is what Voltaire means to praise in the English poets— this dealing with what is really life. But always it is the mark of the greatest poets that they deal with it; and to say that the English

8. Théophile Gautier (1811–72), a poet whose preoccupation with "literary form and finish" and indifference towards edification in literature made him an important exponent of art for art's sake in France, like D. G. Rossetti in England. Arnold often deplored his fellow Victorians' fondness for the stunning phrasemaking of such poets as Tennyson, Keats, and Rossetti.
9. *The Recluse.* lines 767–71.

poets are remarkable for dealing with it, is only another way of saying, what is true, that in poetry the English genius has especially shown its power.

Wordsworth deals with it, and his greatness lies in his dealing with it so powerfully. I have named a number of celebrated poets above all of whom he, in my opinion, deserves to be placed. He is to be placed above poets like Voltaire, Dryden, Pope, Lessing, Schiller, because these famous personages, with a thousand gifts and merits, never, or scarcely ever, attain the distinctive accent and utterance of the high and genuine poets—

Quique pii vates et Phoebo digna locuti,[1]

at all. Burns, Keats, Heine, not to speak of others in our list, have this accent—who can doubt it? And at the same time they have treasures of humor, felicity, passion, for which in Wordsworth we shall look in vain. Where, then, is Wordsworth's superiority? It is here; he deals with more of *life* than they do; he deals with *life*, as a whole, more powerfully.

No Wordsworthian will doubt this. Nay, the fervent Wordsworthian will add, as Mr. Leslie Stephen does, that Wordsworth's poetry is precious because his philosophy is sound; that his "ethical system is as distinctive and capable of exposition as Bishop Butler's"; that his poetry is informed by ideas which "fall spontaneously into a scientific system of thought."[2] But we must be on our guard against the Wordsworthians, if we want to secure for Wordsworth his due rank as a poet. The Wordsworthians are apt to praise him for the wrong things, and to lay far too much stress upon what they call his philosophy. His poetry is the reality, his philosophy—so far, at least, as it may put on the form and habit of "a scientific system of thought," and the more that it puts them on—is the illusion. Perhaps we shall one day learn to make this proposition general, and to say: Poetry is the reality, philosophy the illusion. But in Wordsworth's case, at any rate, we cannot do him justice until we dismiss his formal philosophy.

The *Excursion* abounds with philosophy and therefore the *Excursion* is to the Wordsworthian what it never can be to the disinterested lover of poetry—a satisfactory work. "Duty exists," says Wordsworth, in the *Excursion*; and then he proceeds thus—

> . . . Immutably survive,
> For our support, the measures and the forms,
> Which an abstract Intelligence supplies,

---

1. "Those devout bards who utter things worthy of Phoebus" (Virgil, *Aeneid* VI.662).

2. From an essay on "Wordsworth's Ethics" in *Hours in a Library* by Leslie Stephen (1832–1904).

Whose kingdom is, where time and space are not.[3]

And the Wordsworthian is delighted, and thinks that here is a sweet union of philosophy and poetry. But the disinterested lover of poetry will feel that the lines carry us really not a step farther than the proposition which they would interpret; that they are a tissue of elevated but abstract verbiage, alien to the very nature of poetry.

Or let us come direct to the center of Wordsworth's philosophy, as "an ethical system, as distinctive and capable of systematical exposition as Bishop Butler's"—

> . . . One adequate support
> For the calamities of mortal life
> Exists, one only—an assured belief
> That the procession of our fate, howe'er
> Sad or disturbed, is ordered by a Being
> Of infinite benevolence and power;
> Whose everlasting purposes embrace
> All accidents, converting them to good.[4]

That is doctrine such as we hear in church too, religious and philosophic doctrine; and the attached Wordsworthian loves passages of such doctrine, and brings them forward in proof of his poet's excellence. But however true the doctrine may be, it has, as here presented, none of the characters of *poetic* truth, the kind of truth which we require from a poet, and in which Wordsworth is really strong.

Even the "intimations" of the famous *Ode,* those cornerstones of the supposed philosophic system of Wordsworth—the idea of the high instincts and affections coming out in childhood, testifying of a divine home recently left, and fading away as our life proceeds—this idea, of undeniable beauty as a play of fancy, has itself not the character of poetic truth of the best kind; it has no real solidity. The instinct of delight in Nature and her beauty had no doubt extraordinary strength in Wordsworth himself as a child. But to say that universally this instinct is mighty in childhood, and tends to die away afterwards, is to say what is extremely doubtful. In many people, perhaps with the majority of educated persons, the love of nature is nearly imperceptible at ten years old, but strong and operative at thirty. In general we may say of these high instincts of early childhood, the base of the alleged systematic philosophy of Wordsworth, what Thucydides says of the early achievements of the Greek race: "It is impossible to speak with certainty of what is so remote; but from all that we can really investigate, I should say

---

3. *The Excursion* IV.73–76.   4. *The Excursion* IV.10–17.

that they were no very great things."

Finally, the "scientific system of thought" in Wordsworth gives us at least such poetry as this, which the devout Wordsworthian accepts—

> O for the coming of that glorious time
> When, prizing knowledge as her noblest wealth
> And best protection, this Imperial Realm,
> While she exacts allegiance, shall admit
> An obligation, on her part, to *teach*
> Them who are born to serve her and obey;
> Binding herself by statute to secure,
> For all the children whom her soil maintains,
> The rudiments of letters, and inform
> The mind with moral and religious truth.[5]

Wordsworth calls Voltaire dull, and surely the production of these un-Voltairian lines must have been imposed on him as a judgment! One can hear them being quoted at a Social Science Congress; one can call up the whole scene. A great room in one of our dismal provincial towns; dusty air and jaded afternoon daylight; benches full of men with bald heads and women in spectacles; an orator lifting up his face from a manuscript written within and without to declaim these lines of Wordsworth; and in the soul of any poor child of nature who may have wandered in thither, an unutterable sense of lamentation, and mourning, and woe!

"But turn we," as Wordsworth says, "from these bold, bad men,"[6] the haunters of Social Science Congresses. And let us be on our guard, too, against the exhibitors and extollers of a "scientific system of thought" in Wordsworth's poetry. The poetry will never be seen aright while they thus exhibit it. The cause of its greatness is simple, and may be told quite simply. Wordsworth's poetry is great because of the extraordinary power with which Wordsworth feels the joy offered to us in nature, the joy offered to us in the simple primary affections and duties; and because of the extraordinary power with which, in case after case, he shows us this joy, and renders it so as to make us share it.

The source of joy from which he thus draws is the truest and most unfailing source of joy accessible to man. It is also accessible universally. Wordsworth brings us word, therefore, according to his own strong and characteristic line, he brings us word

> Of joy in widest commonalty spread.[7]

Here is an immense advantage for a poet. Wordsworth tells of what all seek, and tells of it at its truest and best source, and yet a

5. *The Excursion* IX.293–302.　　　*Fleming.*
6. In Wordsworth's poem *To the Lady*　7. *The Recluse*, line 771.

source where all may go and draw for it.

Nevertheless, we are not to suppose that everything is precious which Wordsworth, standing even at this perennial and beautiful source, may give us. Wordsworthians are apt to talk as if it must be. They will speak with the same reverence of *The Sailor's Mother*, for example, as of *Lucy Gray*. They do their master harm by such lack of discrimination. *Lucy Gray* is a beautiful success; *The Sailor's Mother* is a failure. To give aright what he wishes to give, to interpret and render successfully, is not always within Wordsworth's own command. It is within no poet's command; here is the part of the Muse, the inspiration, the God, the "not ourselves." In Wordsworth's case, the accident, for so it may almost be called, of inspiration, is of peculiar importance. No poet, perhaps, is so evidently filled with a new and sacred energy when the inspiration is upon him; no poet, when it fails him, is so left "weak as is a breaking wave."[8] I remember hearing him say that "Goethe's poetry was not inevitable enough." The remark is striking and true; no line in Goethe, as Goethe said himself, but its maker knew well how it came there. Wordsworth is right, Goethe's poetry is not inevitable; not inevitable enough. But Wordsworth's poetry, when he is at his best, is inevitable, as inevitable as Nature herself. It might seem that Nature not only gave him the matter for his poem, but wrote his poem for him. He has no style. He was too conversant with Milton not to catch at times his master's manner, and he has fine Miltonic lines; but he has no assured poetic style of his own, like Milton. When he seeks to have a style he falls into ponderosity and pomposity. In the *Excursion* we have his style, as an artistic product of his own creation; and although Jeffrey[9] completely failed to recognize Wordsworth's real greatness, he was yet not wrong in saying of the *Excursion*, as a work of poetic style: "This will never do." And yet magical as is that power, which Wordsworth has not, of assured and possessed poetic style, he has something which is an equivalent for it.

Everyone who has any sense for these things feels the subtle turn, the heightening, which is given to a poet's verse by his genius for style. We can feel it in the

> After life's fitful fever he sleeps well[1]—

of Shakespeare; in the

> . . . though fall'n on evil days,
> On evil days though fall'n, and evil tongues[2]—

8. Wordsworth, *A Poet's Epitaph*, line 58.
9. Francis Jeffrey (1773–1850), contributor to the *Edinburgh Review*.
1. *Macbeth* III.ii.23.
2. *Paradise Lost* VII.25–26.

of Milton. It is the incomparable charm of Milton's power of poetic style which gives such worth to *Paradise Regained*, and makes a great poem of a work in which Milton's imagination does not soar high. Wordsworth has in constant possession, and at command, no style of this kind; but he had too poetic a nature, and had read the great poets too well, not to catch, as I have already remarked, something of it occasionally. We find it not only in his Miltonic lines; we find it in such a phrase as this, where the manner is his own, not Milton's—

> the fierce confederate storm
> Of sorrow barricadoed evermore
> Within the walls of cities;[3]

although even here, perhaps, the power of style which is undeniable, is more properly that of eloquent prose than the subtle heightening and change wrought by genuine poetic style. It is style, again, and the elevation given by style, which chiefly makes the effectiveness of *Laodameia*. Still the right sort of verse to choose from Wordsworth, if we are to seize his true and most characteristic form of expression, is a line like this from *Michael*—

> And never lifted up a single stone.

There is nothing subtle in it, no heightening, no study of poetic style, strictly so called, at all; yet it is expression of the highest and most truly expressive kind.

Wordsworth owed much to Burns, and a style of perfect plainness, relying for effect solely on the weight and force of that which with entire fidelity it utters, Burns could show him.

> The poor inhabitant below
> Was quick to learn and wise to know,
> And keenly felt the friendly glow
> And softer flame;
> But thoughtless follies laid him low
> And stained his name.[4]

Everyone will be conscious of a likeness here to Wordsworth; and if Wordsworth did great things with this nobly plain manner, we must remember, what indeed he himself would always have been forward to acknowledge, that Burns used it before him.

Still Wordsworth's use of it has something unique and unmatchable. Nature herself seems, I say, to take the pen out of his hand, and to write for him with her own bare, sheer, penetrating power. This arises from two causes: from the profound sincereness with which Wordsworth feels his subject, and also from the profoundly sincere and natural character of his subject itself. He can and will treat such a subject with nothing but the most plain, first-hand, al-

3. *The Recluse*, lines 831–33.   4. From Burns's *A Bard's Epitaph*.

most austere naturalness. His expression may often be called bald, as, for instance, in the poem of *Resolution and Independence;* but it is bald as the bare mountaintops are bald, with a baldness which is full of grandeur.

Wherever we meet with the successful balance, in Wordsworth, of profound truth of subject with profound truth of execution, he is unique. His best poems are those which most perfectly exhibit this balance. I have a warm admiration for *Laodameia* and for the great *Ode;* but if I am to tell the very truth, I find *Laodameia* not wholly free from something artificial, and the great *Ode* not wholly free from something declamatory. If I had to pick out poems of a kind most perfectly to show Wordsworth's unique power, I should rather choose poems such as *Michael, The Fountain, The Highland Reaper.*[5] And poems with the peculiar and unique beauty which distinguishes these, Wordsworth produced in considerable number; besides very many other poems of which the worth, although not so rare as the worth of these, is still exceedingly high.

On the whole, then, as I said at the beginning, not only is Wordsworth eminent by reason of the goodness of his best work, but he is eminent also by reason of the great body of good work which he has left to us. With the ancients I will not compare him. In many respects the ancients are far above us, and yet there is something that we demand which they can never give. Leaving the ancients, let us come to the poets and poetry of Christendom. Dante, Shakespeare, Molière, Milton, Goethe are altogether larger and more splendid luminaries in the poetical heaven than Wordsworth. But I know not where else, among the moderns, we are to find his superiors.

To disengage the poems which show his power, and to present them to the English-speaking public and to the world, is the object of this volume. I by no means say that it contains all which in Wordsworth's poems is interesting. Except in the case of *Margaret,* a story composed separately from the rest of the *Excursion,* and which belongs to a different part of England, I have not ventured on detaching portions of poems, or on giving any piece otherwise than as Wordsworth himself gave it. But under the conditions imposed by this reserve, the volume contains, I think, everything, or nearly everything, which may best serve him with the majority of lovers of poetry, nothing which may disserve him.

I have spoken lightly of Wordsworthians; and if we are to get Wordsworth recognized by the public and by the world, we must recommend him not in the spirit of a clique, but in the spirit of disinterested lovers of poetry. But I am a Wordsworthian myself. I can read with pleasure and edification *Peter Bell,* and the whole series of *Ecclesiastical Sonnets,* and the address to Mr. Wilkinson's

5. I.e., *The Solitary Reaper.*

spade, and even the *Thanksgiving Ode*—everything of Wordsworth, I think, except *Vaudracour and Julia*. It is not for nothing that one has been brought up in the veneration of a man so truly worthy of homage; that one has seen him and heard him, lived in his neighborhood, and been familiar with his country. No Wordsworthian has a tenderer affection for this pure and sage master than I, or is less really offended by his defects. But Wordsworth is something more than the pure and sage master of a small band of devoted followers, and we ought not to rest satisfied until he is seen to be what he is. He is one of the very chief glories of English Poetry; and by nothing is England so glorious as by her poetry. Let us lay aside every weight which hinders our getting him recognized as this, and let our one study be to bring to pass, as widely as possible and as truly as possible, his own word concerning his poems: "They will co-operate with the benign tendencies in human nature and society, and will, in their degree, be efficacious in making men wiser, better, and happier."[6]

1879

The Study of Poetry[1]

"The future of poetry is immense, because in poetry, where it is worthy of its high destinies, our race, as time goes on, will find an ever surer and surer stay. There is not a creed which is not shaken, not an accredited dogma which is not shown to be questionable, not a received tradition which does not threaten to dissolve. Our religion has materialized itself in the fact, in the supposed fact; it has attached its emotion to the fact, and now the fact is failing it. But for poetry the idea is everything; the rest is a world of illusion, of divine illusion. Poetry attaches its emotion to the idea; the idea *is* the fact. The strongest part of our religion today is its unconscious poetry."

Let me be permitted to quote these words of my own, as uttering the thought which should, in my opinion, go with us and govern

6. Wordsworth's letter to Lady Beaumont, May 21, 1807.

1. Aside from its vindication of the importance of literature, this essay is an interesting example of the variety of Arnold's own reading. To know literature in only one language seemed to him not to know literature. His personal *Notebooks* show that throughout his active life he continued to read books in French, German, Italian, Latin, and Greek. His favorite authors in these languages are used by him as a means of testing English poetry. The testing is sometimes a severe one. Readers may also protest that despite Arnold's own wit, his essay is limited by an incomplete recognition of the values of comic literature, a shortcoming abundantly evident in the discussion of Chaucer. Nevertheless, whether we agree or disagree with some of Arnold's verdicts, we can be attracted by the combination of traditionalism and impressionism on which these verdicts are based, and we can enjoy the memorable phrasemaking in which the verdicts are expressed. *The Study of Poetry* has been extraordinarily potent in shaping literary tastes in England and in America.

us in all our study of poetry. In the present work[2] it is the course of one great contributory stream to the world-river of poetry that we are invited to follow. We are here invited to trace the stream of English poetry. But whether we set ourselves, as here, to follow only one of the several streams that make the mighty river of poetry, or whether we seek to know them all, our governing thought should be the same. We should conceive of poetry worthily, and more highly than it has been the custom to conceive of it. We should conceive of it as capable of higher uses, and called to higher destinies, than those which in general men have assigned to it hitherto. More and more mankind will discover that we have to turn to poetry to interpret life for us, to console us, to sustain us. Without poetry, our science will appear incomplete; and most of what now passes with us for religion and philosophy will be replaced by poetry. Science, I say, will appear incomplete without it. For finely and truly does Wordsworth call poetry "the impassioned expression which is in the countenance of all science";[3] and what is a countenance without its expression? Again, Wordsworth finely and truly calls poetry "the breath and finer spirit of all knowledge": our religion, parading evidences such as those on which the popular mind relies now; our philosophy, pluming itself on its reasonings about causation and finite and infinite being; what are they but the shadows and dreams and false shows of knowledge? The day will come when we shall wonder at ourselves for having trusted to them, for having taken them seriously; and the more we perceive their hollowness, the more we shall prize "the breath and finer spirit of knowledge" offered to us by poetry.

But if we conceive thus highly of the destinies of poetry, we must also set our standard for poetry high, since poetry, to be capable of fulfilling such high destinies, must be poetry of a high order of excellence. We must accustom ourselves to a high standard and to a strict judgment. Sainte-Beuve[4] relates that Napoleon one day said, when somebody was spoken of in his presence as a charlatan: "Charlatan as much as you please; but where is there *not* charlatanism?"—"Yes," answers Sainte-Beuve, "in politics, in the art of governing mankind, that is perhaps true. But in the order of thought, in art, the glory, the eternal honor is that charlatanism shall find no entrance; herein lies the inviolableness of that noble portion of man's being." It is admirably said, and let us hold fast to it. In poetry, which is thought and art in one, it is the glory, the eternal honor, that charlatanism shall find no entrance; that this noble sphere be kept inviolate and inviolable. Charlatanism is for confusing or obliterating the distinctions between excellent and in-

2. An anthology of English poetry for which Arnold's essay served as the introduction.
3. See Wordsworth's Preface to *Lyrical*

Ballads.
4. Charles Augustin Sainte-Beuve (1804–69), French critic who influenced Arnold.

ferior, sound and unsound or only half-sound, true and untrue or only half-true. It is charlatanism, conscious or unconscious, whenever we confuse or obliterate these. And in poetry, more than anywhere else, it is unpermissible to confuse or obliterate them. For in poetry the distinction between excellent and inferior, sound and unsound or only half-sound, true and untrue or only half-true, is of paramount importance. It is of paramount importance because of the high destinies of poetry. In poetry, as a criticism of life under the conditions fixed for such a criticism by the laws of poetic truth and poetic beauty, the spirit of our race will find, we have said, as time goes on and as other helps fail, its consolation and stay. But the consolation and stay will be of power in proportion to the power of the criticism of life. And the criticism of life will be of power in proportion as the poetry conveying it is excellent rather than inferior, sound rather than unsound or half-sound, true rather than untrue or half-true.

The best poetry is what we want; the best poetry will be found to have a power of forming, sustaining, and delighting us, as nothing else can. A clearer, deeper sense of the best in poetry, and of the strength and joy to be drawn from it, is the most precious benefit which we can gather from a poetical collection such as the present. And yet in the very nature and conduct of such a collection there is inevitably something which tends to obscure in us the consciousness of what our benefit should be, and to distract us from the pursuit of it. We should therefore steadily set it before our minds at the outset, and should compel ourselves to revert constantly to the thought of it as we proceed.

Yes; constantly in reading poetry, a sense for the best, the really excellent, and of the strength and joy to be drawn from it, should be present in our minds and should govern our estimate of what we read. But this real estimate, the only true one, is liable to be superseded, if we are not watchful, by two other kinds of estimate, the historic estimate and the personal estimate, both of which are fallacious. A poet or a poem may count to us historically, they may count to us on grounds personal to ourselves, and they may count to us really. They may count to us historically. The course of development of a nation's language, thought, and poetry, is profoundly interesting; and by regarding a poet's work as a stage in this course of development we may easily bring ourselves to make it of more importance as poetry than in itself it really is, we may come to use a language of quite exaggerated praise in criticizing it; in short, to overrate it. So arises in our poetic judgments the fallacy caused by the estimate which we may call historic. Then, again, a poet or a poem may count to us on grounds personal to ourselves. Our personal affinities, likings, and circumstances, have great power to sway our estimate of this or that poet's work, and to make us attach more importance to it as poetry than in itself it really possesses, because to us it is, or has been, of high importance. Here also we overrate the object of our interest, and apply to it a language of praise which is quite exaggerated. And thus we get the source of a second fallacy in our poetic judgments—the fallacy caused by an estimate which we may call personal.

Both fallacies are natural. It is evident how naturally the study of the history and development of a poetry may incline a man to pause over reputations and works once conspicuous but now obscure, and to quarrel with a careless public for skipping, in obedience to mere tradition and habit, from one famous name or work in its national poetry to another, ignorant of what it misses, and of the reason for keeping what it keeps, and of the whole process of growth in its poetry. The French have become diligent students of their own early poetry, which they long neglected; the study makes many of them dissatisfied with their so-called classical poetry, the court-tragedy of the seventeenth century, a poetry which Pellisson[5] long ago reproached with its want of the true poetic stamp, with its *politesse stérile et rampante*,[6] but which nevertheless has reigned in France as absolutely as if it had been the perfection of classical poetry indeed. The dissatisfaction is natural; yet a lively and accomplished critic, M. Charles d'Héricault, the editor of Clément Marot,[7] goes too far when he says that "the cloud of glory playing round a classic is a mist as dangerous to the future of a literature as it is intolerable for the purposes of history." "It hinders," he goes on, "it hinders us from seeing more than one single point, the culminating and exceptional point; the summary, fictitious and arbitrary, of a thought and of a work. It substitutes a halo for a physiognomy, it puts a statue where there was once a man, and hiding from us all trace of the labor, the attempts, the weaknesses, the failures, it claims not study but veneration; it does not show us how the thing is done, it imposes upon us a model. Above all, for the historian this creation of classic personages is inadmissible; for it withdraws the poet from his time, from his proper life, it breaks historical relationships, it blinds criticism by conventional admiration, and renders the investigation of literary origins unacceptable. It gives us a human personage no longer, but a God seated immovable amidst His perfect work, like Jupiter on Olympus; and hardly will it be possible for the young student, to whom such work is exhibited at such a distance from him, to believe that it did not issue ready made from that divine head."

All this is brilliantly and tellingly said, but we must plead for a

5. Paul Pellison, 17th-century French critic.
6. "Conventionality that is barren and bombastic."
7. D'Héricault's edition of Marot was published in 1868. The graceful poetry of Clément Marot (ca. 1495–1544) was admired and imitated in late 19th-century England, sometimes at the expense of overlooking the excellences of the more severely classical 17th-century French poets such as Racine.

distinction. Everything depends on the reality of a poet's classic character. If he is a dubious classic, let us sift him; if he is a false classic, let us explode him. But if he is a real classic, if his work belongs to the class of the very best (for this is the true and right meaning of the word *classic, classical*), then the great thing for us is to feel and enjoy his work as deeply as ever we can, and to appreciate the wide difference between it and all work which has not the same high character. This is what is salutary, this is what is formative; this is the great benefit to be got from the study of poetry. Everything which interferes with it, which hinders it, is injurious. True, we must read our classic with open eyes, and not with eyes blinded with superstition; we must perceive when his work comes short, when it drops out of the class of the very best, and we must rate it, in such cases, at its proper value. But the use of this negative criticism is not in itself, it is entirely in its enabling us to have a clearer sense and a deeper enjoyment of what is truly excellent. To trace the labor, the attempts, the weaknesses, the failures of a genuine classic, to acquaint oneself with his time and his life and his historical relationships, is mere literary dilettantism unless it has that clear sense and deeper enjoyment for its end. It may be said that the more we know about a classic the better we shall enjoy him; and, if we lived as long as Methuselah and had all of us heads of perfect clearness and wills of perfect steadfastness, this might be true in fact as it is plausible in theory. But the case here is much the same as the case with the Greek and Latin studies of our schoolboys. The elaborate philological groundwork which we require them to lay is in theory an admirable preparation for appreciating the Greek and Latin authors worthily. The more thoroughly we lay the groundwork, the better we shall be able, it may be said, to enjoy the authors. True, if time were not so short, and schoolboys' wits not so soon tired and their power of attention exhausted; only, as it is, the elaborate philological preparation goes on, but the authors are little known and less enjoyed. So with the investigator of "historic origins" in poetry. He ought to enjoy the true classic all the better for his investigations; he often is distracted from the enjoyment of the best, and with the less good he overbusies himself, and is prone to overrate it in proportion to the trouble which it has cost him.

The idea of tracing historic origins and historical relationships cannot be absent from a compilation like the present. And naturally the poets to be exhibited in it will be assigned to those persons for exhibition who are known to prize them highly, rather than to those who have no special inclination towards them. Moreover the very occupation with an author, and the business of exhibiting him, disposes us to affirm and amplify his importance. In the present work, therefore, we are sure of frequent temptation to adopt the historic estimate, or the personal estimate, and to forget the real estimate; which latter, nevertheless, we must employ if we are to make poetry yield us its full benefit. So high is that benefit, the benefit of clearly feeling and of deeply enjoying the really excellent, the truly classic in poetry, that we do well, I say, to set it fixedly before our minds as our object in studying poets and poetry, and to make the desire of attaining it the one principle to which, as the *Imitation* says, whatever we may read or come to know, we always return. *Cum multa legeris et cognoveris, ad unum semper oportet redire principium.*[8]

The historic estimate is likely in especial to affect our judgment and our language when we are dealing with ancient poets; the personal estimate when we are dealing with poets our contemporaries, or at any rate modern. The exaggerations due to the historic estimate are not in themselves, perhaps, of very much gravity. Their report hardly enters the general ear; probably they do not always impose even on the literary men who adopt them. But they lead to a dangerous abuse of language. So we hear Cædmon,[9] amongst our own poets, compared to Milton. I have already noticed the enthusiasm of one accomplished French critic for "historic origins." Another eminent French critic, M. Vitet, comments upon that famous document of the early poetry of his nation, the *Chanson de Roland.*[1] It is indeed a most interesting document. The *joculator* or *jongleur*[2] Taillefer, who was with William the Conqueror's army at Hastings, marched before the Norman troops, so said the tradition, singing "of Charlemagne and of Roland and of Oliver, and of the vassals who died at Roncevaux"; and it is suggested that in the *Chanson de Roland* by one Turoldus or *Théroulde*, a poem preserved in a manuscript of the twelfth century in the Bodleian Library at Oxford, we have certainly the matter, perhaps even some of the words, of the chant which Taillefer sang. The poem has vigor and freshness; it is not without pathos. But M. Vitet is not satisfied with seeing in it a document of some poetic value, and of very high historic and linguistic value; he sees in it a grand and beautiful work, a monument of epic genius. In its general design he finds the grandiose conception, in its details he finds the constant union of simplicity with greatness, which are the marks, he truly says, of the genuine epic, and distinguish it from the artificial epic of literary ages. One thinks of Homer; this is the sort of praise which is given to Homer, and justly given. Higher praise there cannot well be, and it is the praise due to epic poetry of the highest order only, and to no other. Let us try, then, the *Chanson de Ro-*

---

8. "When you have read and learned many things, you ought always to return to the one principle" (*The Imitation of Christ* III.43, famous devotional work by Thomas à Kempis, 1380–1471).
9. 7th-century Old English poet.

1. 11th-century epic poem in Old French which tells of the wars of Charlemagne against the Moors in Spain, and of the bravery of the French leaders, Roland and Oliver.
2. I.e., minstrel.

land at its best. Roland, mortally wounded, lays himself down under a pine tree, with his face turned towards Spain and the enemy—

> De plusurs choses à remembrer li prist,
> De tantes teres cume li bers cunquist,
> De dulce France, des humes de sun lign,
> De Carlemagne sun seignor ki l'nurrit.[3]

That is primitive work, I repeat, with an undeniable poetic quality of its own. It deserves such praise, and such praise is sufficient for it. But now turn to Homer—

> Ὣς φάτο τοὺς δ' ἤδη κάτεχεν φυσίζοος αἶα
> ἐν Λακεδαίμονι αὖθι, φίλῃ ἐν πατρίδι γαίῃ.[4]

We are here in another world, another order of poetry altogether; here is rightly due such supreme praise as that which M. Vitet gives to the *Chanson de Roland*. If our words are to have any meaning, if our judgments are to have any solidity, we must not heap that supreme praise upon poetry of an order immeasurably inferior.

Indeed there can be no more useful help for discovering what poetry belongs to the class of the truly excellent, and can therefore do us most good, than to have always in one's mind lines and expressions of the great masters, and to apply them as a touchstone to other poetry. Of course we are not to require this other poetry to resemble them; it may be very dissimilar. But if we have any tact we shall find them, when we have lodged them well in our minds, an infallible touchstone for detecting the presence or absence of high poetic quality, and also the degree of this quality, in all other poetry which we may place beside them. Short passages, even single lines, will serve our turn quite sufficiently. Take the two lines which I have just quoted from Homer, the poet's comment on Helen's mention of her brothers—or take his

> Ἆ δειλώ, τί σφῶϊ δόμεν Πηλῆϊ ἄνακτι
> θνητῷ; ὑμεῖς δ' ἐστὸν ἀγήρω τ' ἀθανάτω τε.
> ἦ ἵνα δυστήνοισι μετ' ἀνδράσιν ἄλγε' ἔχητον;[5]

the address of Zeus to the horses of Peleus—or take finally his

> Καὶ σέ, γέρον, τὸ πρὶν μὲν ἀκούομεν ὄλβιον εἶναι·[6]

3. " 'Then began he to call many things to remembrance—all the lands which his valor conquered and pleasant France, and the men of his lineage, and Charlemagne his liege lord who nourished him.' *Chanson de Roland* III.939–42" [Arnold's note].
4. " 'So said she; they long since in Earth's soft arms were reposing, / There, in their own dear land, their fatherland, Lacedaemon.' *Iliad* III.243–

44 (translated by Dr. Hawtrey)" [Arnold's note].
5. " 'Ah, unhappy pair, why gave we you to King Peleus, to a mortal? but ye are without old age, and immortal. Was it that with men born to misery ye might have sorrow?' *Iliad* XVII.443–45" [Arnold's note].
6. " 'Nay, and thou too, old man, in former days wast, as we hear, happy.' *Iliad* XXIV.543" [Arnold's note].

the words of Achilles to Priam, a suppliant before him Take that incomparable line and a half of Dante, Ugolino's tremendous words—

> Io no piangeva; sì dentro impietrai.
> Piangevan elli . . .[7]

take the lovely words of Beatrice to Virgil—

> Io son fatta da Dio, sua mercè, tale,
> Che la vostra miseria non mi tange,
> Nè fiamma d'esto incendio non m'assale . . .[8]

take the simple, but perfect, single line—

> In la sua volontade è nostra pace.[9]

Take of Shakespeare a line or two of Henry the Fourth's expostulation with sleep—

> Wilt thou upon the high and giddy mast
> Seal up the shipboy's eyes, and rock his brains
> In cradle of the rude imperious surge . . .[1]

and take, as well, Hamlet's dying request to Horatio—

> If thou didst ever hold me in thy heart,
> Absent thee from felicity awhile,
> And in this harsh world draw thy breath in pain,
> To tell my story . . .[2]

Take of Milton that Miltonic passage—

> Darkened so, yet shone
> Above them all the archangel; but his face
> Deep scars of thunder had intrenched, and care
> Sat on his faded cheek . . .[3]

add two such lines as—

> And courage never to submit or yield
> And what is else not to be overcome . . .[4]

and finish with the exquisite close to the loss of Proserpine, the loss

> . . . which cost Ceres all that pain
> To seek her through the world.[5]

---

7. " 'I wailed not, so of stone I grew within; *they* wailed.' *Inferno* XXXIII. 49–50" [Arnold's note].
8. " 'Of such sort hath God, thanked be His mercy, made me, that your misery toucheth me not, neither doth the flame of this fire strike me.' *Inferno* II.91–93" [Arnold's note].

9. " 'In His will is our peace.' *Paradiso* III.85" [Arnold's note].
1. *2 Henry IV* III.i.18–20.
2. *Hamlet* V.ii.357–60.
3. *Paradise Lost* I.599–602.
4. *Ibid.* I.108–9.
5. *Ibid.* IV.271–72.

These few lines, if we have tact and can use them, are enough even
of themselves to keep clear and sound our judgments about poetry,
to save us from fallacious estimates of it, to conduct us to a real
estimate.

The specimens I have quoted differ widely from one another,
but they have in common this: the possession of the very highest
poetical quality. If we are thoroughly penetrated by their power,
we shall find that we have acquired a sense enabling us, whatever
poetry may be laid before us, to feel the degree in which a high
poetical quality is present or wanting there. Critics give themselves
great labor to draw out what in the abstract constitutes the characters of a high quality of poetry. It is much better simply to have
recourse to concrete examples—to take specimens of poetry of
the high, the very highest quality, and to say: The characters
of a high quality of poetry are what is expressed *there*. They
are far better recognized by being felt in the verse of the master, than by being perused in the prose of the critic. Nevertheless if we are urgently pressed to give some critical account of them,
we may safely, perhaps, venture on laying down, not indeed how
and why the characters arise, but where and in what they arise.
They are in the matter and substance of the poetry, and they are
in its manner and style. Both of these, the substance and matter
on the one hand, the style and manner on the other, have a mark,
an accent, of high beauty, worth, and power. But if we are asked
to define this mark and accent in the abstract, our answer must
be: No, for we should thereby be darkening the question, not clearing it. The mark and accent are as given by the substance and matter of that poetry, by the style and manner of that poetry, and of
all other poetry which is akin to it in quality.

Only one thing we may add as to the substance and matter of
poetry, guiding ourselves by Aristotle's profound observation that
the superiority of poetry over history consists in its possessing
a higher truth and a higher seriousness (φιλοσοφώτερον καὶ
σπουδαιότερον).[6] Let us add, therefore, to what we have said, this:
that the substance and matter of the best poetry acquire their special character from possessing, in an eminent degree, truth and
seriousness. We may add yet further, what is in itself evident, that
to the style and manner of the best poetry their special character,
their accent, is given by their diction, and, even yet more, by their
movement. And though we distinguish between the two characters,
the two accents, of superiority, yet they are nevertheless vitally
connected one with the other. The superior character of truth and
seriousness, in the matter and substance of the best poetry, is inseparable from the superiority of diction and movement marking
its style and manner. The two superiorities are closely related, and

6. Aristotle, *Poetics* IX.

are in steadfast proportion one to the other. So far as high poetic truth and seriousness are wanting to a poet's matter and substance, so far also, we may be sure, will a high poetic stamp of diction and movement be wanting to his style and manner. In proportion as this high stamp of diction and movement, again, is absent from a poet's style and manner, we shall find, also, that high poetic truth and seriousness are absent from his substance and matter.

So stated, these are but dry generalities; their whole force lies in their application. And I could wish every student of poetry to make the application of them for himself. Made by himself, the application would impress itself upon his mind far more deeply than made by me. Neither will my limits allow me to make any full application of the generalities above propounded; but in the hope of bringing out, at any rate, some significance in them, and of establishing an important principle more firmly by their means, I will, in the space which remains to me, follow rapidly from the commencement the course of our English poetry with them in my view.

Once more I return to the early poetry of France, with which our own poetry, in its origins, is indissolubly connected. In the twelfth and thirteenth centuries, that seed time of all modern language and literature, the poetry of France had a clear predominance in Europe. Of the two divisions of that poetry, its productions in the *langue d'oïl* and its productions in the *langue d'oc*,[7] the poetry of the *langue d'oc*, of southern France, of the troubadours, is of importance because of its effect on Italian literature—the first literature of modern Europe to strike the true and grand note, and to bring forth, as in Dante and Petrarch it brought forth, classics. But the predominance of French poetry in Europe, during the twelfth and thirteenth centuries, is due to its poetry of the *langue d'oïl*, the poetry of northern France and of the tongue which is now the French language. In the twelfth century the bloom of this romance poetry was earlier and stronger in England, at the court of our Anglo-Norman kings, than in France itself. But it was a bloom of French poetry; and as our native poetry formed itself, it formed itself out of this. The romance poems which took possession of the heart and imagination of Europe in the twelfth and thirteenth centuries are French; "they are," as Southey justly says, "the pride of French literature, nor have we anything which can be placed in competition with them." Themes were supplied from all quarters: but the romance setting which was common to them all, and which gained the ear of Europe, was French. This constituted for the French poetry, literature, and language, at the height of the Middle Age, an unchallenged predominance. The

7. Medieval dialects of France; in the northern dialect, from which modern French derives, the word *oui* ("yes") was pronounced *oïl;* in the southern dialect it was pronounced *oc*.

Italian Brunetto Latini, the master of Dante, wrote his *Treasure* in French because, he says, "*la parleure en est plus délitable et plus commune à toutes gens.*"[8] In the same century, the thirteenth, the French romance writer, Christian of Troyes, formulates the claims, in chivalry and letters, of France, his native country, as follows:

> *Or vous ert par ce livre apris,*
> *Que Gresse ot de chevalerie*
> *Le premier los et de clergie;*
> *Puis vint chevalerie à Rome,*
> *Et de la clergie la some,*
> *Qui ore est en France venue.*
> *Diex doinst qu'ele i soit retenue*
> *Et que li lius li abelisse*
> *Tant que de France n'isse*
> *L'onor qui s'i est arestée!*

"Now by this book you will learn that first Greece had the renown for chivalry and letters; then chivalry and the primacy in letters passed to Rome, and now it is come to France. God grant it may be kept there; and that the place may please it so well, that the honor which has come to make stay in France may never depart thence!"

Yet it is now all gone, this French romance poetry, of which the weight of substance and the power of style are not unfairly represented by this extract from Christian of Troyes. Only by means of the historic estimate can we persuade ourselves now to think that any of it is of poetical importance.

But in the fourteenth century there comes an Englishman nourished on this poetry; taught his trade by this poetry, getting words, rhyme, meter from this poetry; for even of that stanza which the Italians used, and which Chaucer derived immediately from the Italians, the basis and suggestion was probably given in France. Chaucer (I have already named him) fascinated his contemporaries, but so too did Christian of Troyes and Wolfram of Eschenbach.[9] Chaucer's power of fascination, however, is enduring; his poetical importance does not need the assistance of the historic estimate; it is real. He is a genuine source of joy and strength, which is flowing still for us and will flow always. He will be read, as time goes on, far more generally than he is read now. His language is a cause of difficulty for us; but so also, and I think in quite as great a degree, is the language of Burns. In Chaucer's case, as in that of Burns, it is a difficulty to be unhesitatingly accepted and overcome.

If we ask ourselves wherein consists the immense superiority of Chaucer's poetry over the romance poetry—why it is that in passing from this to Chaucer we suddenly feel ourselves to be in an-

8. "French speech is more delightful and more commonly known to all peo- ples."
9. 12th-century German poet.

other world, we shall find that his superiority is both in the substance of his poetry and in the style of his poetry. His superiority in substance is given by his large, free, simple, clear yet kindly view of human life—so unlike the total want, in the romance poets, of all intelligent command of it. Chaucer has not their helplessness; he has gained the power to survey the world from a central, a truly human point of view. We have only to call to mind the Prologue to *The Canterbury Tales*. The right comment upon it is Dryden's: "It is sufficient to say, according to the proverb, that *here is God's plenty*." And again: "He is a perpetual fountain of good sense."[1] It is by a large, free, sound representation of things, that poetry, this high criticism of life, has truth of substance; and Chaucer's poetry has truth of substance.

Of his style and manner, if we think first of the romance poetry and then of Chaucer's divine liquidness of diction, his divine fluidity of movement, it is difficult to speak temperately. They are irresistible, and justify all the rapture with which his successors speak of his "gold dewdrops of speech."[2] Johnson misses the point entirely when he finds fault with Dryden for ascribing to Chaucer the first refinement of our numbers, and says that Gower[3] also can show smooth numbers and easy rhymes. The refinement of our numbers means something far more than this. A nation may have versifiers with smooth numbers and easy rhymes, and yet may have no real poetry at all. Chaucer is the father of our splendid English poetry; he is our "well of English undefiled,"[4] because by the lovely charm of his diction, the lovely charm of his movement, he makes an epoch and founds a tradition. In Spenser, Shakespeare, Milton, Keats, we can follow the tradition of the liquid diction, the fluid movement, of Chaucer; at one time it is his liquid diction of which in these poets we feel the virtue, and at another time it is his fluid movement. And the virtue is irresistible.

Bounded as is my space, I must yet find room for an example of Chaucer's virtue, as I have given examples to show the virtue of the great classics. I feel disposed to say that a single line is enough to show the charm of Chaucer's verse; that merely one line like this—

O martyr souded[5] in virginitee!

has a virtue of manner and movement such as we shall not find in all the verse of romance poetry—but this is saying nothing. The

---

1. Both quotations are from Dryden's Preface to his *Fables* (1700).
2. *The Life of Our Lady*, a poem by John Lydgate (ca. 1370–ca. 1451).
3. John Gower (ca. 1325–1408), friend of Chaucer and author of the *Confessio Amantis*, a long poem in octosyllabic couplets.

4. Said of Chaucer by Spenser (*Faerie Queene* IV.ii.32).
5. "The French *soudé:* soldered, fixed fast" [Arnold's note]. The line is from the Prioress's Tale (line 127): Chaucer wrote "souded to" rather than "souded in."

virtue is such as we shall not find, perhaps, in all English poetry, outside the poets whom I have named as the special inheritors of Chaucer's tradition. A single line, however, is too little if we have not the strain of Chaucer's verse well in our memory; let us take a stanza. It is from *The Prioress's Tale*, the story of the Christian child murdered in a Jewry—

> My throte is cut unto my nekke-bone
> Saidè this child, and as by way of kinde
> I should have deyd, yea, longè time agone;
> But Jesu Christ, as ye in bookès finde,
> Will that his glory last and be in minde,
> And for the worship of his mother dere
> Yet may I sing O *Alma* loud and clere.

Wordsworth has modernized this Tale, and to feel how delicate and evanescent is the charm of verse, we have only to read Wordsworth's first three lines of this stanza after Chaucer's—

> My throat is cut unto the bone, I trow,
> Said this young child, and by the law of kind
> I should have died, yea, many hours ago.

The charm is departed. It is often said that the power of liquidness and fluidity in Chaucer's verse was dependent upon a free, a licentious dealing with language, such as is now impossible; upon a liberty, such as Burns too enjoyed, of making words like *neck, bird,* into a dissyllable by adding to them, and words like *cause, rhyme,* into a dissyllable by sounding the *e* mute. It is true that Chaucer's fluidity is conjoined with this liberty, and is admirably served by it; but we ought not to say that it was dependent upon it. It was dependent upon his talent. Other poets with a like liberty do not attain to the fluidity of Chaucer; Burns himself does not attain to it. Poets, again, who have a talent akin to Chaucer's, such as Shakespeare or Keats, have known how to attain to his fluidity without the like liberty.

And yet Chaucer is not one of the great classics. His poetry transcends and effaces, easily and without effort, all the romance poetry of Catholic Christendom; it transcends and effaces all the English poetry contemporary with it, it transcends and effaces all the English poetry subsequent to it down to the age of Elizabeth. Of such avail is poetic truth of substance, in its natural and necessary union with poetic truth of style. And yet, I say, Chaucer is not one of the great classics. He has not their accent. What is wanting to him is suggested by the mere mention of the name of the first great classic of Christendom, the immortal poet who died eighty years before Chaucer—Dante. The accent of such verse as

In la sua volontade è nostra pace . . .

is altogether beyond Chaucer's reach; we praise him, but we feel that this accent is out of the question for him. It may be said that it was necessarily out of the reach of any poet in the England of that stage of growth. Possibly; but we are to adopt a real, not a historic, estimate of poetry. However we may account for its absence, something is wanting, then, to the poetry of Chaucer, which poetry must have before it can be placed in the glorious class of the best. And there is no doubt what that something is. It is the σπουδαιότης, the high and excellent seriousness, which Aristotle assigns as one of the grand virtues of poetry. The substance of Chaucer's poetry, his view of things and his criticism of life, has largeness, freedom, shrewdness, benignity; but it has not this high seriousness. Homer's criticism of life has it, Dante's has it, Shakespeare's has it. It is this chiefly which gives to our spirits what they can rest upon; and with the increasing demands of our modern ages upon poetry, this virtue of giving us what we can rest upon will be more and more highly esteemed. A voice from the slums of Paris, fifty or sixty years after Chaucer, the voice of poor Villon[6] out of his life of riot and crime, has at its happy moments (as, for instance, in the last stanza of *La Belle Heaulmière*[7]) more of this important poetic virtue of seriousness than all the productions of Chaucer. But its apparition in Villon, and in men like Villon, is fitful; the greatness of the great poets, the power of their criticism of life, is that their virtue is sustained.

To our praise, therefore, of Chaucer as a poet there must be this limitation: he lacks the high seriousness of the great classics, and therewith an important part of their virtue. Still, the main fact for us to bear in mind about Chaucer is his sterling value according to that real estimate which we firmly adopt for all poets. He has poetic truth of substance, though he has not high poetic seriousness, and corresponding to his truth of substance he has an exquisite virtue of style and manner. With him is born our real poetry.

For my present purpose I need not dwell on our Elizabethan poetry, or on the continuation and close of this poetry in Milton. We all of us profess to be agreed in the estimate of this poetry; we all of us recognize it as great poetry, our greatest, and Shake-

---

6. François Villon (1431–84), French poet and vagabond.
7. "The name *Heaulmière* is said to be derived from a headdress (helm) worn as a mask by courtesans. In Villon's ballad, a poor old creature of this class laments her days of youth and beauty. The last stanza of the ballad runs thus —'*Ainsi le bon temps regretons / Entre nous, pauvres vieilles sottes, / Assises bas, à croppetons, / Tout en ung tas comme pelottes; / A petit feu de chenevottes / Tost allumées, tost estainctes, / Et jadis fusmes si mignottes! / Ainsi en prend à maintz et maintes.*' [It may be translated:] 'Thus amongst ourselves we regret the good time, poor silly old things, low-seated on our heels, all in a heap like so many balls; by a little fire of hemp stalks, soon lighted, soon spent. And once we were such darlings! So fares it with many and many a one'" [Arnold's note].

speare and Milton as our poetical classics. The real estimate, here, has universal currency. With the next age of our poetry divergency and difficulty begin. An historic estimate of that poetry has established itself; and the question is, whether it will be found to coincide with the real estimate.

The age of Dryden, together with our whole eighteenth century which followed it, sincerely believed itself to have produced poetical classics of its own, and even to have made advance, in poetry, beyond all its predecessors. Dryden regards as not seriously disputable the opinion "that the sweetness of English verse was never understood or practiced by our fathers."[8] Cowley could see nothing at all in Chaucer's poetry. Dryden heartily admired it, and, as we have seen, praised its matter admirably; but of its exquisite manner and movement all he can find to say is that "there is the rude sweetness of a Scotch tune in it, which is natural and pleasing, though not perfect."[9] Addison, wishing to praise Chaucer's numbers, compares them with Dryden's own. And all through the eighteenth century, and down even into our own times, the stereotyped phrase of approbation for good verse found in our early poetry has been, that it even approached the verse of Dryden, Addison, Pope, and Johnson.

Are Dryden and Pope poetical classics? Is the historic estimate, which represents them as such, and which has been so long established that it cannot easily give way, the real estimate? Wordsworth and Coleridge, as is well known, denied it; but the authority of Wordsworth and Coleridge does not weigh much with the young generation, and there are many signs to show that the eighteenth century and its judgments are coming into favor again. Are the favorite poets of the eighteenth century classics?

It is impossible within my present limits to discuss the question fully. And what man of letters would not shrink from seeming to dispose dictatorially of the claims of two men who are, at any rate, such masters in letters as Dryden and Pope; two men of such admirable talent, both of them, and one of them, Dryden, a man, on all sides, of such energetic and genial power? And yet, if we are to gain the full benefit from poetry, we must have the real estimate of it. I cast about for some mode of arriving, in the present case, at such an estimate without offense. And perhaps the best way is to begin, as it is easy to begin, with cordial praise.

When we find Chapman, the Elizabethan translator of Homer, expressing himself in his preface thus: "Though truth in her very nakedness sits in so deep a pit, that from Gades to Aurora and Ganges few eyes can sound her, I hope yet those few here will so

8. Dryden's *Essay on Dramatic Poesy.*
Cowley is the poet Abraham Cowley
(1618–67).
9. Dryden's Preface to his *Fables.*

discover and confirm that, the date being out of her darkness in this morning of our poet, he shall now gird his temples with the sun," we pronounce that such a prose is intolerable. When we find Milton writing: "And long it was not after, when I was confirmed in this opinion, that he, who would not be frustrate of his hope to write well hereafter in laudable things, ought himself to be a true poem"[1]—we pronounce that such a prose has its own grandeur, but that it is obsolete and inconvenient. But when we find Dryden telling us: "What Virgil wrote in the vigor of his age, in plenty and at ease, I have undertaken to translate in my declining years; struggling with wants, oppressed with sickness, curbed in my genius, liable to be misconstrued in all I write"[2]—then we exclaim that here at last we have the true English prose, a prose such as we would all gladly use if we only knew how. Yet Dryden was Milton's contemporary.

But after the Restoration the time had come when our nation felt the imperious need of a fit prose. So, too, the time had likewise come when our nation felt the imperious need of freeing itself from the absorbing preoccupation which religion in the Puritan age had exercised. It was impossible that this freedom should be brought about without some negative excess, without some neglect and impairment of the religious life of the soul; and the spiritual history of the eighteenth century shows us that the freedom was not achieved without them. Still, the freedom was achieved; the preoccupation, an undoubtedly baneful and retarding one if it had continued, was got rid of. And as with religion amongst us at that period, so it was also with letters. A fit prose was a necessity; but it was impossible that a fit prose should establish itself amongst us without some touch of frost to the imaginative life of the soul. The needful qualities for a fit prose are regularity, uniformity, precision, balance. The men of letters, whose destiny it may be to bring their nation to the attainment of a fit prose, must of necessity, whether they work in prose or in verse, give a predominating, an almost exclusive attention to the qualities of regularity, uniformity, precision, balance. But an almost exclusive attention to these qualities involves some repression and silencing of poetry.

We are to regard Dryden as the puissant and glorious founder, Pope as the splendid high priest, of our age of prose and reason, of our excellent and indispensable eighteenth century. For the purposes of their mission and destiny their poetry, like their prose, is admirable. Do you ask me whether Dryden's verse, take it almost where you will, is not good?

> A milk-white Hind, immortal and unchanged,
> Fed on the lawns and in the forest ranged.[3]

1. Milton's *Apology for Smectymnuus.*   in his translation of Virgil.
2. Dryden's *Postscript to the Reader*   3. *The Hind and the Panther* I.1–2.

I answer: Admirable for the purposes of the inaugurator of an age of prose and reason. Do you ask me whether Pope's verse, take it almost where you will, is not good?

> To Hounslow Heath I point, and Banstead Down;
> Thence comes your mutton, and these chicks my own.[4]

I answer: Admirable for the purposes of the high priest of an age of prose and reason. But do you ask me whether such verse proceeds from men with an adequate poetic criticism of life, from men whose criticism of life has a high seriousness, or even, without that high seriousness, has poetic largeness, freedom, insight, benignity? Do you ask me whether the application of ideas to life in the verse of these men, often a powerful application, no doubt, is a powerful *poetic* application? Do you ask me whether the poetry of these men has either the matter or the inseparable manner of such an adequate poetic criticism; whether it has the accent of

> Absent thee from felicity awhile . . .

or of

> And what is else not to be overcome . . .

or of

> O martyr souded in virginitee!

I answer: It has not and cannot have them; it is the poetry of the builders of an age of prose and reason. Though they may write in verse, though they may in a certain sense be masters of the art of versification, Dryden and Pope are not classics of our poetry, they are classics of our prose.

Gray is our poetical classic of that literature and age; the position of Gray is singular, and demands a word of notice here. He has not the volume or the power of poets who, coming in times more favorable, have attained to an independent criticism of life. But he lived with the great poets, he lived, above all, with the Greeks, through perpetually studying and enjoying them; and he caught their poetic point of view for regarding life, caught their poetic manner. The point of view and the manner are not self-sprung in him, he caught them of others; and he had not the free and abundant use of them. But whereas Addison and Pope never had the use of them, Gray had the use of them at times. He is the scantiest and frailest of classics in our poetry, but he is a classic.

And now, after Gray, we are met, as we draw towards the end of the eighteenth century, we are met by the great name of Burns. We enter now on times where the personal estimate of poets begins to be rife, and where the real estimate of them is not reached

4. *Imitations of Horace,* Satire II.ii.143–44.

without difficulty. But in spite of the disturbing pressures of personal partiality, of national partiality, let us try to reach a real estimate of the poetry of Burns.

By his English poetry Burns in general belongs to the eighteenth century, and has little importance for us.

> Mark ruffian Violence, distained with crimes,
> Rousing elate in these degenerate times;
> View unsuspecting Innocence a prey,
> As guileful Fraud points out the erring way;
> While subtle Litigation's pliant tongue
> The life-blood equal sucks of Right and Wrong![5]

Evidently this is not the real Burns, or his name and fame would have disappeared long ago. Nor is Clarinda's love-poet, Sylvander,[6] the real Burns either. But he tells us himself: "These English songs gravel me to death. I have not the command of the language that I have of my native tongue. In fact, I think that my ideas are more barren in English than in Scotch. I have been at *Duncan Gray* to dress it in English, but all I can do is desperately stupid."[7] We English turn naturally, in Burns, to the poems in our own language, because we can read them easily; but in those poems we have not the real Burns.

The real Burns is of course in his Scotch poems. Let us boldly say that of much of this poetry, a poetry dealing perpetually with Scotch drink, Scotch religion, and Scotch manners, a Scotchman's estimate is apt to be personal. A Scotchman is used to this world of Scotch drink, Scotch religion, and Scotch manners; he has a tenderness for it; he meets its poet half way. In this tender mood he reads pieces like the *Holy Fair* or *Halloween*. But this world of Scotch drink, Scotch religion, and Scotch manners is against a poet, not for him, when it is not a partial countryman who reads him; for in itself it is not a beautiful world, and no one can deny that it is of advantage to a poet to deal with a beautiful world. Burns's world of Scotch drink, Scotch religion, and Scotch manners, is often a harsh, a sordid, a repulsive world; even the world of his *Cotter's Saturday Night* is not a beautiful world. No doubt a poet's criticism of life may have such truth and power that it triumphs over its world and delights us. Burns may triumph over his world, often he does triumph over his world, but let us observe how and where. Burns is the first case we have had where the bias of the personal estimate tends to mislead; let us look at him closely, he can bear it.

Many of his admirers will tell us that we have Burns, convivial, genuine, delightful, here—

5. *On the Death of Lord President Dundas*, lines 25–30.
6. Burns, styling himself Sylvander, carried on an idyllic correspondence with a Mrs. Maclehose, addressing her as Clarinda.
7. Letter to George Thomson, October 19, 1794.

Leeze me on drink! it gies us mair
    Than either school or college;
It kindles wit, it waukens lair,
    It pangs us fou o' knowledge.
Be't whisky gill or penny wheep
    Or ony stronger potion,
It never fails, on drinking deep,
    To kittle up our notion
        By night or day.[8]

There is a great deal of that sort of thing in Burns, and it is unsatisfactory, not because it is bacchanalian poetry, but because it
has not that accent of sincerity which bacchanalian poetry, to do
it justice, very often has. There is something in it of bravado, something which makes us feel that we have not the man speaking to
us with his real voice; something, therefore, poetically unsound.

With still more confidence will his admirers tell us that we have
the genuine Burns, the great poet, when his strain asserts the independence, equality, dignity, of men, as in the famous song *For
A' That and A' That*—

A prince can mak' a belted knight,
    A marquis, duke, and a' that;
But an honest man's aboon his might,
    Guid faith he mauna fa' that!
For a' that, and a' that,
    Their dignities, and a' that,
The pith o' sense, and pride o' worth,
    Are higher rank than a' that.

Here they find his grand, genuine touches; and still more, when
this puissant genius, who so often set morality at defiance, falls
moralizing—

The sacred lowe o' weel-placed love
    Luxuriantly indulge it;
But never tempt th' illicit rove,
    Though naething should divulge it.
I waive the quantum o' the sin,
    The hazard o' concealing,
But och! it hardens a' within,
    And petrifies the feeling.[9]

Or in a higher strain—

Who made the heart, 'tis He alone
    Decidedly can try us;
He knows each chord, its various tone;
    Each spring, its various bias.
Then at the balance let's be mute,

8. *The Holy Fair*, lines 163–71.   9. *Epistle to a Young Friend*, lines 41–48.

We never can adjust it;
What's *done* we partly may compute,
But know not what's resisted.[1]

Or in a better strain yet, a strain, his admirers will say, unsurpassable—

To make a happy fireside clime
To weans and wife,
That's the true pathos and sublime
Of human life.[2]

There is criticism of life for you, the admirers of Burns will say to us; there is the application of ideas to life! There is, undoubtedly. The doctrine of the last-quoted lines coincides almost exactly with what was the aim and end, Xenophon tells us, of all the teaching of Socrates. And the application is a powerful one; made by a man of vigorous understanding, and (need I say?) a master of language.

But for supreme poetical success more is required than the powerful application of ideas to life; it must be an application under the conditions fixed by the laws of poetic truth and poetic beauty. Those laws fix as an essential condition, in the poet's treatment of such matters as are here in question, high seriousness—the high seriousness which comes from absolute sincerity. The accent of high seriousness, born of absolute sincerity, is what gives to such verse as

In la sua volontade è nostra pace . . .

to such criticism of life as Dante's, its power. Is this accent felt in the passages which I have been quoting from Burns? Surely not; surely, if our sense is quick, we must perceive that we have not in those passages a voice from the very inmost soul of the genuine Burns; he is not speaking to us from these depths, he is more or less preaching. And the compensation for admiring such passages less, for missing the perfect poetic accent in them, will be that we shall admire more the poetry where that accent is found.

No; Burns, like Chaucer, comes short of the high seriousness of the great classics, and the virtue of matter and manner which goes with that high seriousness is wanting to his work. At moments he touches it in a profound and passionate melancholy, as in those four immortal lines taken by Byron as a motto for *The Bride of Abydos*, but which have in them a depth of poetic quality such as resides in no verse of Byron's own—

Had we never loved sae kindly,
Had we never loved sae blindly,

1. *Address to the Unco Guid*, lines 57–64. 2. *Epistle to Dr. Blacklock*, lines 51–54.

> Never met, or never parted,
> We had ne'er been broken-hearted.[3]

But a whole poem of that quality Burns cannot make; the rest, in the *Farewell to Nancy*, is verbiage.

We arrive best at the real estimate of Burns, I think, by conceiving his work as having truth of matter and truth of manner, but not the accent or the poetic virtue of the highest masters. His genuine criticism of life, when the sheer poet in him speaks, is ironic; it is not—

> Thou Power Supreme, whose mighty scheme
> These woes of mine fulfill,
> Here firm I rest, they must be best
> Because they are Thy will![4]

It is far rather: "Whistle owre the lave o't!"[5] Yet we may say of him as of Chaucer, that of life and the world, as they come before him, his view is large, free, shrewd, benignant—truly poetic, therefore; and his manner of rendering what he sees is to match. But we must note, at the same time, his great difference from Chaucer. The freedom of Chaucer is heightened, in Burns, by a fiery, reckless energy; the benignity of Chaucer deepens, in Burns, into an overwhelming sense of the pathos of things—of the pathos of human nature, the pathos, also, of nonhuman nature. Instead of the fluidity of Chaucer's manner, the manner of Burns has spring, bounding swiftness. Burns is by far the greater force, though he has perhaps less charm. The world of Chaucer is fairer, richer, more significant than that of Burns; but when the largeness and freedom of Burns get full sweep, as in *Tam o' Shanter*, or still more in that puissant and splendid production, *The Jolly Beggars*, his world may be what it will, his poetic genius triumphs over it. In the world of *The Jolly Beggars* there is more than hideousness and squalor, there is bestiality; yet the piece is a superb poetic success. It has a breadth, truth, and power which make the famous scene in Auerbach's Cellar, of Goethe's *Faust*, seem artificial and tame beside it, and which are only matched by Shakespeare and Aristophanes.

Here, where his largeness and freedom serve him so admirably, and also in those poems and songs where to shrewdness he adds infinite archness and wit, and to benignity infinite pathos, where his manner is flawless, and a perfect poetic whole is the result— in things like the address to the mouse whose home he had ruined, in things like *Duncan Gray, Tam Glen, Whistle and I'll Come to You, My Lad, Auld Lang Syne* (this list might be made much longer)—here we have the genuine Burns, of whom the real esti-

---

3. *Ae Fond Kiss* (also called *A Farewell to Nancy*), lines 13–16.
4. *Winter: A Dirge*, lines 17–20.

5. "Whistle over what's left of it." The phrase is a refrain from one of Burns's poems.

mate must be high indeed. Not a classic, nor with the excellent
σπουδαιότης[6] of the great classics, nor with a verse rising to a criticism of life and a virtue like theirs; but a poet with thorough truth
of substance and an answering truth of style, giving us a poetry
sound to the core. We all of us have a leaning towards the pathetic,
and may be inclined perhaps to prize Burns most for his touches
of piercing, sometimes almost intolerable, pathos; for verse like—

> We twa hae paidl't i' the burn
> From mornin' sun till dine;
> But seas between us braid hae roared
> Sin auld lang syne . . .[7]

where he is as lovely as he is sound. But perhaps it is by the perfection of soundness of his lighter and archer masterpieces that
he is poetically most wholesome for us. For the votary misled by
a personal estimate of Shelley, as so many of us have been, are,
and will be—of that beautiful spirit building his many-colored haze
of words and images

> Pinnacled dim in the intense inane[8]—

no contact can be wholesomer than the contact with Burns at his
archest and soundest. Side by side with the

> On the brink of the night and the morning
> My coursers are wont to respire,
> But the Earth has just whispered a warning
> That their flight must be swifter than fire . . .[9]

of *Prometheus Unbound*, how salutary, how very salutary, to place
this from *Tam Glen*—

> My minnie does constantly deave me
> And bids me beware o' young men;
> They flatter, she says, to deceive me;
> But wha can think sae o' Tam Glen?

But we enter on burning ground as we approach the poetry of
times so near to us—poetry like that of Byron, Shelley, and Wordsworth—of which the estimates are so often not only personal, but
personal with passion. For my purpose, it is enough to have taken
the single case of Burns, the first poet we come to of whose work
the estimate formed is evidently apt to be personal, and to have
suggested how we may proceed, using the poetry of the great classics
as a sort of touchstone, to correct this estimate, as we had previously
corrected by the same means the historic estimate where we met
with it. A collection like the present, with its succession of cele-

---

6. "High seriousness." iv.204.
7. *Auld Lang Syne*, lines 17–20. 9. *Ibid*. II.v.1–4.
8. Shelley, *Prometheus Unbound* III.

brated names and celebrated poems, offers a good opportunity to
us for resolutely endeavoring to make our estimates of poetry real.
I have sought to point out a method which will help us in making
them so, and to exhibit it in use so far as to put anyone who likes
in a way of applying it for himself.

At any rate the end to which the method and the estimate are
designed to lead, and from leading to which, if they do lead to it,
they get their whole value—the benefit of being able clearly to feel
and deeply to enjoy the best, the truly classic, in poetry—is an end,
let me say it once more at parting, of supreme importance. We are
often told that an era is opening in which we are to see multitudes
of a common sort of readers, and masses of a common sort of literature; that such readers do not want and could not relish anything better than such literature, and that to provide it is becoming a vast and profitable industry. Even if good literature entirely
lost currency with the world, it would still be abundantly worth
while to continue to enjoy it by oneself. But it never will lose currency with the world, in spite of momentary appearances; it never
will lose supremacy. Currency and supremacy are insured to it, not
indeed by the world's deliberate and conscious choice, but by something far deeper—by the instinct of self-preservation in humanity.

1880

Literature and Science[1]

Practical people talk with a smile of Plato and of his absolute
ideas: and it is impossible to deny that Plato's ideas do often seem
unpractical and unpracticable, and especially when one views them
in connection with the life of a great work-a-day world like the
United States. The necessary staple of the life of such a world
Plato regards with disdain; handicraft and trade and the working
professions he regards with disdain; but what becomes of the life
of an industrial modern community if you take handicraft and
trade and the working professions out of it? The base mechanic
arts and handicrafts, says Plato, bring about a natural weakness
in the principle of excellence in a man, so that he cannot govern
the ignoble growths in him, but nurses them, and cannot understand fostering any other. Those who exercise such arts and trades,
as they have their bodies, he says, marred by their vulgar businesses,

1. Delivered as a lecture during Arnold's tour of the United States in
1883, and published in *Discourses in
America* (1885), this essay has become
a classic contribution to a subject endlessly debated. Its main argument was
summed up by Stuart P. Sherman: "If

Arnold had said outright that the study
of letters helps us to *bear* the grand
results of science, he would not have
been guilty of a superficial epigram; he
would have spoken from the depths of
his experience."

so they have their souls, too, bowed and broken by them. And if one of these uncomely people has a mind to seek self-culture and philosophy, Plato compares him to a bald little tinker, who has scraped together money, and has got his release from service, and has had a bath, and bought a new coat, and is rigged out like a bridegroom about to marry the daughter of his master who has fallen into poor and helpless estate.

Nor do the working professions fare any better than trade at the hands of Plato. He draws for us an inimitable picture of the working lawyer, and of his life of bondage; he shows how this bondage from his youth up has stunted and warped him, and made him small and crooked of soul, encompassing him with difficulties which he is not man enough to rely on justice and truth as means to encounter, but has recourse, for help out of them, to falsehood and wrong. And so, says Plato, this poor creature is bent and broken, and grows up from boy to man without a particle of soundness in him, although exceedingly smart and clever in his own esteem.

One cannot refuse to admire the artist who draws these pictures. But we say to ourselves that his ideas show the influence of a primitive and obsolete order of things, when the warrior caste and the priestly caste were alone in honor, and the humble work of the world was done by slaves. We have now changed all that; the modern majesty consists in work, as Emerson declares; and in work, we may add, principally of such plain and dusty kind as the work of cultivators of the ground, handicraftsmen, men of trade and business, men of the working professions. Above all is this true in a great industrious community such as that of the United States.

Now education, many people go on to say, is still mainly governed by the ideas of men like Plato, who lived when the warrior caste and the priestly or philosophical class were alone in honor, and the really useful part of the community were slaves. It is an education fitted for persons of leisure in such a community. This education passed from Greece and Rome to the feudal communities of Europe, where also the warrior caste and the priestly caste were alone held in honor, and where the really useful and working part of the community, though not nominally slaves as in the pagan world, were practically not much better off than slaves, and not more seriously regarded. And how absurd it is, people end by saying, to inflict this education upon an industrious modern community, where very few indeed are persons of leisure, and the mass to be considered has not leisure, but is bound, for its own great good, and for the great good of the world at large, to plain labor and to industrial pursuits, and the education in question tends necessarily to make men dissatisfied with these pursuits and unfitted for them!

That is what is said. So far I must defend Plato, as to plead that his view of education and studies is in the general, as it seems to me, sound enough, and fitted for all sorts and conditions of men, whatever their pursuits may be. "An intelligent man," says Plato, "will prize those studies which result in his soul getting soberness, righteousness, and wisdom, and will less value the others."[2] I cannot consider *that* a bad description of the aim of education, and of the motives which should govern us in the choice of studies, whether we are preparing ourselves for a hereditary seat in the English House of Lords or for the pork trade in Chicago.

Still I admit that Plato's world was not ours, that his scorn of trade and handicraft is fantastic, that he had no conception of a great industrial community such as that of the United States, and that such a community must and will shape its education to suit its own needs. If the usual education handed down to it from the past does not suit it, it will certainly before long drop this and try another. The usual education in the past has been mainly literary. The question is whether the studies which were long supposed to be the best for all of us are practically the best now; whether others are not better. The tyranny of the past, many think, weighs on us injuriously in the predominance given to letters in education. The question is raised whether, to meet the needs of our modern life, the predominance ought not now to pass from letters to science; and naturally the question is nowhere raised with more energy than here in the United States. The design of abasing what is called "mere literary instruction and education," and of exalting what is called "sound, extensive, and practical scientific knowledge," is, in this intensely modern world of the United States, even more perhaps than in Europe, a very popular design, and makes great and rapid progress.

I am going to ask whether the present movement for ousting letters from their old predominance in education, and for transferring the predominance in education to the natural sciences, whether this brisk and flourishing movement ought to prevail, and whether it is likely that in the end it really will prevail. An objection may be raised which I will anticipate. My own studies have been almost wholly in letters, and my visits to the field of the natural sciences have been very slight and inadequate, although those sciences have always strongly moved my curiosity. A man of letters, it will perhaps be said, is not competent to discuss the comparative merits of letters and natural science as means of education. To this objection I reply, first of all, that his incompetence, if he attempts the discussion but is really incompetent for it, will be abundantly visible; nobody will be taken in; he will have plenty of sharp observers and critics to save mankind from that danger. But the line I am going to follow is, as you will soon discover, so extremely

2. Plato, *Republic* IX.591.

simple, that perhaps it may be followed without failure even by one who for a more ambitious line of discussion would be quite incompetent.

Some of you may possibly remember a phrase of mine which has been the object of a good deal of comment; an observation to the effect that in our culture, the aim being *to know ourselves and the world*, we have, as the means to this end, *to know the best which has been thought and said in the world*.[3] A man of science, who is also an excellent writer and the very prince of debaters, Professor Huxley, in a discourse at the opening of Sir Josiah Mason's college at Birmingham,[4] laying hold of this phrase, expanded it by quoting some more words of mine, which are these: "The civilized world is to be regarded as now being, for intellectual and spiritual purposes, one great confederation, bound to a joint action and working to a common result; and whose members have for their proper outfit a knowledge of Greek, Roman, and Eastern antiquity, and of one another. Special local and temporary advantages being put out of account, that modern nation will in the intellectual and spiritual sphere make most progress, which most thoroughly carries out this program."

Now on my phrase, thus enlarged, Professor Huxley remarks that when I speak of the above-mentioned knowledge as enabling us to know ourselves and the world, I assert *literature* to contain the materials which suffice for thus making us know ourselves and the world. But it is not by any means clear, says he, that after having learnt all which ancient and modern literatures have to tell us, we have laid a sufficiently broad and deep foundation for that criticism of life, that knowledge of ourselves and the world, which constitutes culture. On the contrary, Professor Huxley declares that he finds himself "wholly unable to admit that either nations or individuals will really advance, if their oufit draws nothing from the stores of physical science. An army without weapons of precision, and with no particular base of operations, might more hopefully enter upon a campaign on the Rhine, than a man, devoid of a knowledge of what physical science has done in the last century, upon a criticism of life."

This shows how needful it is for those who are to discuss any matter together, to have a common understanding as to the sense of the terms they employ—how needful, and how difficult. What Professor Huxley says, implies just the reproach which is so often brought against the study of belles-lettres, as they are called: that the study is an elegant one, but slight and ineffectual; a smattering of Greek and Latin and other ornamental things, of little use for anyone whose object is to get at truth, and to be a practical man.

3. See *The Function of Criticism at the Present Time.*   4. See T. H. Huxley's lecture *Science and Culture.*

So, too, M. Renan[5] talks of the "superficial humanism" of a school course which treats us as if we were all going to be poets, writers, preachers, orators, and he opposes this humanism to positive science, or the critical search after truth. And there is always a tendency in those who are remonstrating against the predominance of letters in education, to understand by letters belles-lettres, and by belles-lettres a superficial humanism, the opposite of science or true knowledge.

But when we talk of knowing Greek and Roman antiquity, for instance, which is the knowledge people have called the humanities, I for my part mean a knowledge which is something more than a superficial humanism, mainly decorative. "I call all teaching *scientific*," says Wolf,[6] the critic of Homer, "which is systematically laid out and followed up to its original sources. For example: a knowledge of classical antiquity is scientific when the remains of classical antiquity are correctly studied in the original languages." There can be no doubt that Wolf is perfectly right; that all learning is scientific which is systematically laid out and followed up to its original sources, and that a genuine humanism is scientific.

When I speak of knowing Greek and Roman antiquity, therefore, as a help to knowing ourselves and the world, I mean more than a knowledge of so much vocabulary, so much grammar, so many portions of authors in the Greek and Latin languages, I mean knowing the Greeks and Romans, and their life and genius, and what they were and did in the world; what we get from them, and what is its value. That, at least, is the ideal; and when we talk of endeavoring to know Greek and Roman antiquity, as a help to knowing ourselves and the world, we mean endeavoring so to know them as to satisfy this ideal, however much we may still fall short of it.

The same also as to knowing our own and other modern nations, with the like aim of getting to understand ourselves and the world. To know the best that has been thought and said by the modern nations, is to know, says Professor Huxley, "only what modern *literatures* have to tell us; it is the criticism of life contained in modern literature." And yet "the distinctive character of our times," he urges, "lies in the vast and constantly increasing part which is played by natural knowledge." And how, therefore, can a man, devoid of knowledge of what physical science has done in the last century, enter hopefully upon a criticism of modern life?

Let us, I say, be agreed about the meaning of the terms we are using. I talk of knowing the best which has been thought and uttered in the world; Professor Huxley says this means knowing *literature*. Literature is a large word; it may mean everything writ-

5. Ernest Renan (1823–92), French religious philosopher and author of *The Life of Jesus*. 6. Friedrich August Wolf (1759–1824), German scholar.

ten with letters or printed in a book. Euclid's *Elements* and New-ton's *Principia* are thus literature. All knowledge that reaches us through books is literature. But by literature Professor Huxley means belles-lettres. He means to make me say, that knowing the best which has been thought and said by the modern nations is knowing their belles-lettres and no more. And this is no sufficient equipment, he argues, for a criticism of modern life. But as I do not mean, by knowing ancient Rome, knowing merely more or less of Latin belles-lettres, and taking no account of Rome's mili-tary, and political, and legal, and administrative work in the world; and as, by knowing ancient Greece, I understand knowing her as the giver of Greek art, and the guide to a free and right use of reason and to scientific method, and the founder of our mathe-matics and physics and astronomy and biology—I understand know-ing her as all this, and not merely knowing certain Greek poems, and histories, and treatises, and speeches—so as to the knowledge of modern nations also. By knowing modern nations, I mean not merely knowing their belles-lettres, but knowing also what has been done by such men as Copernicus, Galileo, Newton, Darwin. "Our ancestors learned," says Professor Huxley, "that the earth is the center of the visible universe, and that man is the cynosure of things terrestrial; and more especially was it inculcated that the course of nature had no fixed order, but that it could be, and constantly was, altered." "But for us now," continues Professor Huxley, "the no-tions of the beginning and the end of the world entertained by our forefathers are no longer credible. It is very certain that the earth is not the chief body in the material universe, and that the world is not subordinated to man's use. It is even more certain that nature is the expression of a definite order, with which nothing interferes." "And yet," he cries, "the purely classical education advocated by the representatives of the humanists in our day gives no inkling of all this."

In due place and time I will just touch upon that vexed question of classical education; but at present the question is as to what is meant by knowing the best which modern nations have thought and said. It is not knowing their belles-lettres merely which is meant. To know Italian belles-lettres is not to know Italy, and to know English belles-lettres is not to know England. Into knowing Italy and England there comes a great deal more, Galileo and New-ton amongst it. The reproach of being a superficial humanism, a tincture of belles-lettres, may attach rightly enough to some other disciplines; but to the particular discipline recommended when I proposed knowing the best that has been thought and said in the world, it does not apply. In that best I certainly include what in modern times has been thought and said by the great observers and knowers of nature.

There is, therefore, really no question between Professor Huxley and me as to whether knowing the great results of the modern scientific study of nature is not required as a part of our culture, as well as knowing the products of literature and art. But to follow the processes by which those results are reached, ought, say the friends of physical science, to be made the staple of education for the bulk of mankind. And here there does arise a question between those whom Professor Huxley calls with playful sarcasm "the Levites of culture," and those whom the poor humanist is sometimes apt to regard as its Nebuchadnezzars.[7]

The great results of the scientific investigation of nature we are agreed upon knowing, but how much of our study are we bound to give to the processes by which those results are reached? The results have their visible bearing on human life. But all the processes, too, all the items of fact, by which those results are reached and established, are interesting. All knowledge is interesting to a wise man, and the knowledge of nature is interesting to all men. It is very interesting to know, that, from the albuminous white of the egg, the chick in the egg gets the materials for its flesh, bones, blood, and feathers; while, from the fatty yolk of the egg, it gets the heat and energy which enable it at length to break its shell and begin the world. It is less interesting, perhaps, but still it is interesting, to know that when a taper burns, the wax is converted into carbonic acid and water. Moreover, it is quite true that the habit of dealing with facts, which is given by the study of nature, is, as the friends of physical science praise it for being, an excellent discipline. The appeal, in the study of nature, is constantly to observation and experiment; not only is it said that the thing is so, but we can be made to see that it is so. Not only does a man tell us that when a taper burns the wax is converted into carbonic acid and water, as a man may tell us, if he likes, that Charon[8] is punting his ferry boat on the river Styx, or that Victor Hugo is a sublime poet, or Mr. Gladstone the most admirable of statesmen; but we are made to see that the conversion into carbonic acid and water does actually happen. This reality of natural knowledge it is, which makes the friends of physical science contrast it, as a knowledge of things, with the humanist's knowledge, which is, say they, a knowledge of words. And hence Professor Huxley is moved to lay it down that, "for the purpose of attaining real culture, an exclusively scientific education is at least as effectual as an exclusively literary education." And a certain President of the Section for Mechanical Science in the British Association is, in Scripture phrase, "very bold," and de-

---

7. Huxley implied that the humanists are hidebound conservatives like the Levites, priests who were preoccupied with traditional ritual observances. Arnold implies that the scientists may be like Nebuchadnezzar, a Babylonian king who destroyed the temple of Jerusalem.
8. Boatman in Greek mythology who conducted the souls of the dead across the river Styx.

clares that if a man, in his mental training, "has substituted literature and history for natural science, he has chosen the less useful
alternative." But whether we go these lengths or not, we must all
admit that in natural science the habit gained of dealing with facts
is a most valuable discipline, and that everyone should have some
experience of it.

More than this, however, is demanded by the reformers. It is
proposed to make the training in natural science the main part of
education, for the great majority of mankind at any rate. And here,
I confess, I part company with the friends of physical science, with
whom up to this point I have been agreeing. In differing from
them, however, I wish to proceed with the utmost caution and diffidence. The smallness of my own acquaintance with the disciplines
of natural science is ever before my mind, and I am fearful of doing
these disciplines an injustice. The ability and pugnacity of the
partisans of natural science make them formidable persons to contradict. The tone of tentative inquiry, which befits a being of dim
faculties and bounded knowledge, is the tone I would wish to take
and not to depart from. At present it seems to me, that those who
are for giving to natural knowledge, as they call it, the chief place
in the education of the majority of mankind, leave one important
thing out of their account: the constitution of human nature. But
I put this forward on the strength of some facts not at all recondite,
very far from it; facts capable of being stated in the simplest possible fashion, and to which, if I so state them, the man of science
will, I am sure, be willing to allow their due weight.

Deny the facts altogether, I think, he hardly can. He can hardly
deny, that when we set ourselves to enumerate the powers which
go to the building up of human life, and say that they are the
power of conduct, the power of intellect and knowledge, the power
of beauty, and the power of social life and manners—he can hardly
deny that this scheme, though drawn in rough and plain lines
enough, and not pretending to scientific exactness, does yet give a
fairly true representation of the matter. Human nature is built up
by these powers; we have the need for them all. When we have
rightly met and adjusted the claims of them all, we shall then be in
a fair way for getting soberness and righteousness, with wisdom.
This is evident enough, and the friends of physical science would
admit it.

But perhaps they may not have sufficiently observed another
thing: namely, that the several powers just mentioned are not isolated, but there is, in the generality of mankind, a perpetual tendency to relate them one to another in divers ways. With one such
way of relating them I am particularly concerned now. Following
our instinct for intellect and knowledge, we acquire pieces of knowledge; and presently, in the generality of men, there arises the desire

to relate these pieces of knowledge to our sense for conduct, to our sense for beauty—and there is weariness and dissatisfaction if the desire is balked. Now in this desire lies, I think, the strength of that hold which letters have upon us.

All knowledge is, as I said just now, interesting; and even items of knowledge which from the nature of the case cannot well be related, but must stand isolated in our thoughts, have their interest. Even lists of exceptions have their interest. If we are studying Greek accents, it is interesting to know that *pais* and *pas*, and some other monosyllables of the same form of declension, do not take the circumflex upon the last syllable of the genitive plural, but vary, in this respect, from the common rule. If we are studying physiology, it is interesting to know that the pulmonary artery carries dark blood and the pulmonary vein carries bright blood, departing in this respect from the common rule for the division of labor between the veins and the arteries. But everyone knows how we seek naturally to combine the pieces of our knowledge together, to bring them under general rules, to relate them to principles; and how unsatisfactory and tiresome it would be to go on forever learning lists of exceptions, or accumulating items of fact which must stand isolated.

Well, that same need of relating our knowledge, which operates here within the sphere of our knowledge itself, we shall find operating, also, outside that sphere. We experience, as we go on learning and knowing—the vast majority of us experience—the need of relating what we have learnt and known to the sense which we have in us for conduct, to the sense which we have in us for beauty.

A certain Greek prophetess of Mantineia in Arcadia, Diotima by name, once explained to the philosopher Socrates that love, and impulse, and bent of all kinds, is, in fact, nothing else but the desire in men that good should forever be present to them. This desire for good, Diotima assured Socrates, is our fundamental desire, of which fundamental desire every impulse in us is only some one particular form.[9] And therefore this fundamental desire it is, I suppose—this desire in men that good should be forever present to them—which acts in us when we feel the impulse for relating our knowledge to our sense for conduct and to our sense for beauty. At any rate, with men in general the instinct exists. Such is human nature. And the instinct, it will be admitted, is innocent, and human nature is preserved by our following the lead of its innocent instincts. Therefore, in seeking to gratify this instinct in question, we are following the instinct of self-preservation in humanity.

But, no doubt, some kinds of knowledge cannot be made to directly serve the instinct in question, cannot be directly related to the sense for beauty, to the sense for conduct. These are instrument

9. Plato, *Symposium* 201–7.

knowledges; they lead on to other knowledges, which can. A man who passes his life in instrument knowledges is a specialist. They may be invaluable as instruments to something beyond, for those who have the gift thus to employ them; and they may be disciplines in themselves wherein it is useful for everyone to have some schooling. But it is inconceivable that the generality of men should pass all their mental life with Greek accents or with formal logic. My friend Professor Sylvester,[1] who is one of the first mathematicians in the world, holds transcendental doctrines as to the virtue of mathematics, but those doctrines are not for common men. In the very Senate House and heart of our English Cambridge[2] I once ventured, though not without an apology for my profaneness, to hazard the opinion that for the majority of mankind a little of mathematics, even, goes a long way. Of course this is quite consistent with their being of immense importance as an instrument to something else; but it is the few who have the aptitude for thus using them, not the bulk of mankind.

The natural sciences do not, however, stand on the same footing with these instrument knowledges. Experience shows us that the generality of men will find more interest in learning that, when a taper burns, the wax is converted into carbonic acid and water, or in learning the explanation of the phenomenon of dew, or in learning how the circulation of the blood is carried on, than they find in learning that the genitive plural of *pais* and *pas* does not take the circumflex on the termination. And one piece of natural knowledge is added to another, and others are added to that, and at last we come to propositions so interesting as Mr. Darwin's famous proposition that "our ancestor was a hairy quadruped furnished with a tail and pointed ears, probably arboreal in his habits." Or we come to propositions of such reach and magnitude as those which Professor Huxley delivers, when he says that the notions of our forefathers about the beginning and the end of the world were all wrong, and that nature is the expression of a definite order with which nothing interferes.

Interesting, indeed, these results of science are, important they are, and we should all of us be acquainted with them. But what I now wish you to mark is, that we are still, when they are propounded to us and we receive them, we are still in the sphere of intellect and knowledge. And for the generality of men there will be found, I say, to arise, when they have duly taken in the proposition that their ancestor was "a hairy quadruped furnished with a tail and pointed ears, probably arboreal in his habits," there will be found to arise an invincible desire to relate this proposition to

1. James T. Sylvester, professor of mathematics at Johns Hopkins University.
2. At Cambridge University, mathematics have been traditionally emphasized. In its original form, *Literature and Science* had been delivered as a lecture at Cambridge.

the sense in us for conduct, and to the sense in us for beauty. But this the men of science will not do for us, and will hardly even profess to do. They will give us other pieces of knowledge, other facts, about other animals and their ancestors, or about plants, or about stones, or about stars; and they may finally bring us to those great "general conceptions of the universe, which are forced upon us all," says Professor Huxley, "by the progress of physical science." But still it will be *knowledge* only which they give us; knowledge not put for us into relation with our sense for conduct, our sense for beauty, and touched with emotion by being so put; not thus put for us, and therefore, to the majority of mankind, after a certain while, unsatisfying, wearying.

Not to the born naturalist, I admit. But what do we mean by a born naturalist? We mean a man in whom the zeal for observing nature is so uncommonly strong and eminent, that it marks him off from the bulk of mankind. Such a man will pass his life happily in collecting natural knowledge and reasoning upon it, and will ask for nothing, or hardly anything, more. I have heard it said that the sagacious and admirable naturalist whom we lost not very long ago, Mr. Darwin, once owned to a friend that for his part he did not experience the necessity for two things which most men find so necessary to them—religion and poetry; science and the domestic affections, he thought, were enough. To a born naturalist, I can well understand that this should seem so. So absorbing is his occupation with nature, so strong his love for his occupation, that he goes on acquiring natural knowledge and reasoning upon it, and has little time or inclination for thinking about getting it related to the desire in man for conduct, the desire in man for beauty. He relates it to them for himself as he goes along, so far as he feels the need; and he draws from the domestic affections all the additional solace necessary. But then Darwins are extremely rare. Another great and admirable master of natural knowledge, Faraday,[3] was a Sandemanian. That is to say, he related his knowledge to his instinct for conduct and to his instinct for beauty, by the aid of that respectable Scottish sectary,[4] Robert Sandeman. And so strong, in general, is the demand of religion and poetry to have their share in a man, to associate themselves with his knowing, and to relieve and rejoice it, that, probably, for one man amongst us with the disposition to do as Darwin did in this respect, there are at least fifty with the disposition to do as Faraday.

Education lays hold upon us, in fact, by satisfying this demand. Professor Huxley holds up to scorn medieval education, with its neglect of the knowledge of nature, its poverty even of literary studies, its formal logic devoted to "showing how and why that

---

3. Michael Faraday (1791–1867), famous chemist.
4. I.e., a zealous member of a sect.

Robert Sandeman (1718–71) was the founder of a Scottish sect bearing his name.

which the Church said was true must be true." But the great medieval Universities were not brought into being, we may be sure, by the zeal for giving a jejune and contemptible education. Kings have been their nursing fathers, and queens have been their nursing mothers, but not for this. The medieval Universities came into being, because the supposed knowledge, delivered by Scripture and the Church, so deeply engaged men's hearts, by so simply, easily, and powerfully relating itself to their desire for conduct, their desire for beauty. All other knowledge was dominated by this supposed knowledge and was subordinated to it, because of the surpassing strength of the hold which it gained upon the affections of men, by allying itself profoundly with their sense for conduct, their sense for beauty.

But now, says Professor Huxley, conceptions of the universe fatal to the notions held by our forefathers have been forced upon us by physical science. Grant to him that they are thus fatal, that the new conceptions must and will soon become current everywhere, and that everyone will finally perceive them to be fatal to the beliefs of our forefathers. The need of humane letters, as they are truly called, because they serve the paramount desire in men that good should be forever present to them—the need of humane letters, to establish a relation between the new conceptions, and our instinct for beauty, our instinct for conduct, is only the more visible. The Middle Age could do without humane letters, as it could do without the study of nature, because its supposed knowledge was made to engage its emotions so powerfully. Grant that the supposed knowledge disappears, its power of being made to engage the emotions will of course disappear along with it—but the emotions themselves, and their claim to be engaged and satisfied, will remain. Now if we find by experience that humane letters have an undeniable power of engaging the emotions, the importance of humane letters in a man's training becomes not less, but greater, in proportion to the success of modern science in extirpating what it calls "medieval thinking."

Have humane letters, then, have poetry and eloquence, the power here attributed to them of engaging the emotions, and do they exercise it? And if they have it and exercise it, *how* do they exercise it, so as to exert an influence upon man's sense for conduct, his sense for beauty? Finally, even if they both can and do exert an influence upon the senses in question, how are they to relate to them the results—the modern results—of natural science? All these questions may be asked. First, have poetry and eloquence the power of calling out the emotions? The appeal is to experience. Experience shows that for the vast majority of men, for mankind in general, they have the power. Next, do they exercise it? They do. But then, *how* do they exercise it so as to affect man's sense for

conduct, his sense for beauty? And this is perhaps a case for applying the Preacher's words: "Though a man labor to seek it out, yet
he shall not find it; yea, farther, though a wise man think to know
it, yet shall he not be able to find it."[5] Why should it be one thing,
in its effect upon the emotions, to say, "Patience is a virtue," and
quite another thing, in its effect upon the emotions, to say with
Homer,

$$\tau\lambda\eta\tau\grave{o}\nu\ \gamma\grave{a}\rho\ \text{Μοῖραι}\ \theta\upsilon\mu\grave{o}\nu\ \theta\acute{\epsilon}\sigma\alpha\nu\ \grave{a}\nu\theta\rho\acute{\omega}\pi\omega\iota\sigma\iota\nu^{6}—$$

"for an enduring heart have the destinies appointed to the children
of men"? Why should it be one thing, in its effect upon the emotions, to say with the philosopher Spinoza, *Felicitas in eo consistit
quod homo suum esse conservare potest*—"Man's happiness consists in his being able to preserve his own essence,"[7] and quite another thing, in its effect upon the emotions, to say with the Gospel,
"What is a man advantaged, if he gain the whole world, and lose
himself, forfeit himself?"[8] How does this difference of effect arise?
I cannot tell, and I am not much concerned to know; the important
thing is that it does arise, and that we can profit by it. But how,
finally, are poetry and eloquence to exercise the power of relating
the modern results of natural science to man's instinct for conduct,
his instinct for beauty? And here again I answer that I do not
know *how* they will exercise it, but that they can and will exercise
it I am sure. I do not mean that modern philosophical poets and
modern philosophical moralists are to come and relate for us, in
express terms, the results of modern scientific research to our instinct for conduct, our instinct for beauty. But I mean that we shall
find, as a matter of experience, if we know the best that has been
thought and uttered in the world, we shall find that the art and
poetry and eloquence of men who lived, perhaps, long ago, who
had the most limited natural knowledge, who had the most erroneous conceptions about many important matters, we shall find
that this art, and poetry, and eloquence, have in fact not only the
power of refreshing and delighting us, they have also the power—
such is the strength and worth, in essentials, of their authors' criticism of life—they have a fortifying, and elevating, and quickening,
and suggestive power, capable of wonderfully helping us to relate
the results of modern science to our need for conduct, our need
for beauty. Homer's conceptions of the physical universe were, I
imagine, grotesque; but really, under the shock of hearing from
modern science that "the world is not subordinated to man's use,
and that man is not the cynosure of things terrestrial," I could, for
my own part, desire no better comfort than Homer's line which I
quoted just now,

5. "Ecclesiastes viii.17" [Arnold's note].
6. *"Iliad* XXIV.49" [Arnold's note].
7. Spinoza, *Ethics* IV.xviii.
8. Cf. Luke ix.25.

τλητὸν γὰρ Μοῖραι θυμὸν θέσαν ἀνθρώποισιν—

"for an enduring heart have the destinies appointed to the children of men"!

And the more that men's minds are cleared, the more that the results of science are frankly accepted, the more that poetry and eloquence come to be received and studied as what in truth they really are—the criticism of life by gifted men, alive and active with extraordinary power at an unusual number of points—so much the more will the value of humane letters, and of art also, which is an utterance having a like kind of power with theirs, be felt and acknowledged, and their place in education be secured.

Let us therefore, all of us, avoid indeed as much as possible any invidious comparison between the merits of humane letters, as means of education, and the merits of the natural sciences. But when some President of a Section for Mechanical Science insists on making the comparison, and tells us that "he who in his training has substituted literature and history for natural science has chosen the less useful alternative," let us make answer to him that the student of humane letters only, will, at least, know also the great general conceptions brought in by modern physical science; for science, as Professor Huxley says, forces them upon us all. But the student of the natural sciences only, will, by our very hypothesis, know nothing of humane letters; not to mention that in setting himself to be perpetually accumulating natural knowledge, he sets himself to do what only specialists have in general the gift for doing genially. And so he will probably be unsatisfied, or at any rate incomplete, and even more incomplete than the student of humane letters only.

I once mentioned in a school report, how a young man in one of our English training colleges having to paraphrase the passage in *Macbeth* beginning,

Can'st thou not minister to a mind diseased?[9]

turned this line into, "Can you not wait upon the lunatic?" And I remarked what a curious state of things it would be, if every pupil of our national schools knew, let us say, that the moon is two thousand one hundred and sixty miles in diameter, and thought at the same time that a good paraphrase for

Can'st thou not minister to a mind diseased?

was, "Can you not wait upon the lunatic?" If one is driven to choose, I think I would rather have a young person ignorant about the moon's diameter, but aware that "Can you not wait upon the lunatic?" is bad, than a young person whose education had been

9. *Macbeth* V.iii.40.

such as to manage things the other way.

Or to go higher than the pupils of our national schools. I have in my mind's eye a member of our British Parliament who comes to travel here in America, who afterwards relates his travels, and who shows a really masterly knowledge of the geology of this great country and of its mining capabilities, but who ends by gravely suggesting that the United States should borrow a prince from our Royal Family, and should make him their king, and should create a House of Lords of great landed proprietors after the pattern of ours; and then America, he thinks, would have her future happily and perfectly secured. Surely, in this case, the President of the Section for Mechanical Science would himself hardly say that our member of Parliament, by concentrating himself upon geology and mineralogy, and so on, and not attending to literature and history, had "chosen the more useful alternative."

If then there is to be separation and option between humane letters on the one hand, and the natural sciences on the other, the great majority of mankind, all who have not exceptional and overpowering aptitudes for the study of nature, would do well, I cannot but think, to chose to be educated in humane letters rather than in the natural sciences. Letters will call out their being at more points, will make them live more.

I said that before I ended I would just touch on the question of classical education, and I will keep my word. Even if literature is to retain a large place in our education, yet Latin and Greek, say the friends of progress, will certainly have to go. Greek is the grand offender in the eyes of these gentlemen. The attackers of the established course of study think that against Greek, at any rate, they have irresistible arguments. Literature may perhaps be needed in education, they say; but why on earth should it be Greek literature? Why not French or German? Nay, "has not an Englishman models in his own literature of every kind of excellence?"[1] As before, it is not on any weak pleadings of my own that I rely for convincing the gainsayers; it is on the constitution of human nature itself, and on the instinct of self-preservation in humanity. The instinct for beauty is set in human nature, as surely as the instinct for knowledge is set there, or the instinct for conduct. If the instinct for beauty is served by Greek literature and art as it is served by no other literature and art, we may trust to the instinct of self-preservation in humanity for keeping Greek as part of our culture. We may trust to it for even making the study of Greek more prevalent than it is now. Greek will come, I hope, some day to be studied more rationally than at present; but it will be increasingly studied as men increasingly feel the need in them for beauty, and how powerfully Greek art and Greek literature can serve this need.

1. Quoted from Huxley's *Science and Culture*.

Women will again study Greek, as Lady Jane Grey[2] did; I believe that in that chain of forts, with which the fair host of the Amazons are now engirdling our English universities,[3] I find that here in America, in colleges like Smith College in Massachusetts, and Vassar College in the State of New York, and in the happy families of the mixed universities out West, they are studying it already.

Defuit una mihi symmetria prisca—"The antique symmetry was the one thing wanting to me," said Leonardo da Vinci; and he was an Italian. I will not presume to speak for the Americans, but I am sure that, in the Englishman, the want of this admirable symmetry of the Greeks is a thousand times more great and crying than in any Italian. The results of the want show themselves most glaringly, perhaps, in our architecture, but they show themselves, also, in all our art. *Fit details strictly combined, in view of a large general result nobly conceived;* that is just the beautiful *symmetria prisca* of the Greeks, and it is just where we English fail, where all our art fails. Striking ideas we have, and well-executed details we have; but that high symmetry which, with satisfying and delightful effect, combines them, we seldom or never have. The glorious beauty of the Acropolis at Athens did not come from single fine things stuck about on that hill, a statue here, a gateway there—no, it arose from all things being perfectly combined for a supreme total effect. What must not an Englishman feel about our deficiencies in this respect, as the sense for beauty, whereof this symmetry is an essential element, awakens and strengthens within him! what will not one day be his respect and desire for Greece and its *symmetria prisca*, when the scales drop from his eyes as he walks the London streets, and he sees such a lesson in meanness as the Strand, for instance, in its true deformity! But here we are coming to our friend Mr. Ruskin's province,[4] and I will not intrude upon it, for he is its very sufficient guardian.

And so we at last find, it seems, we find flowing in favor of the humanities the natural and necessary stream of things, which seemed against them when we started. The "hairy quadruped furnished with a tail and pointed ears, probably arboreal in his habits," this good fellow carried hidden in his nature, apparently, something destined to develop into a necessity for humane letters. Nay, more; we seem finally to be even led to the further conclusion that our hairy ancestor carried in his nature, also, a necessity for Greek.

And therefore, to say the truth, I cannot really think that humane letters are in much actual danger of being thrust out from their leading place in education, in spite of the array of authorities against

2. Lady Jane Grey (1537–54) was reputed to be a learned scholar in Greek. She was proclaimed Queen of England in 1553, but was forced to abdicate the throne nine days afterwards. Later she was executed by order of Queen Mary.

3. Colleges for women at Oxford and Cambridge.

4. In such books as *The Stones of Venice* John Ruskin (1819–1900) had criticized the "meanness" of Victorian architecture.

them at this moment. So long as human nature is what it is, their attractions will remain irresistible. As with Greek, so with letters generally: they will some day come, we may hope, to be studied more rationally, but they will not lose their place. What will happen will rather be that there will be crowded into education other matters besides, far too many; there will be, perhaps, a period of unsettlement and confusion and false tendency; but letters will not in the end lose their leading place. If they lose it for a time, they will get it back again. We shall be brought back to them by our wants and aspirations. And a poor humanist may possess his soul in patience, neither strive nor cry, admit the energy and brilliancy of the partisans of physical science, and their present favor with the public, to be far greater than his own, and still have a happy faith that the nature of things works silently on behalf of the studies which he loves, and that, while we shall all have to acquaint ourselves with the great results reached by modern science, and to give ourselves as much training in its disciplines as we can conveniently carry, yet the majority of men will always require humane letters; and so much the more, as they have the more and the greater results of science to relate to the need in man for conduct, and to the need in him for beauty.

1882, 1885

JOHN STUART MILL
(1806–1873)

In many American colleges the writings of J. S. Mill are studied in courses in government or in philosophy, and it may therefore be asked why they should also have a place in the study of literature. It is evident that Mill is the least literary of the important Victorian prose writers. His analytic mind, preoccupied with abstractions rather than with the concrete details that are the concern of the more typical man of letters, his self-effacing manner, and his relatively colorless style are the marks of a writer whose value lies in his generalizations from experience rather than in the rendering of particular experiences for their own sake. Yet a knowledge of Mill's writings is essential to our understanding of Victorian literature. He is one of the leading figures in the intellectual history of his century, a thinker whose honest grappling with the political and religious problems of his age was to have a profound influence on writers as diverse as Arnold, Swinburne, and Hardy.

Mill was educated at home in London under the direction of his father, James Mill, a leader of the Utilitarians. James Mill believed that ordinary schooling fails to develop our intellectual capacities early enough, and he demonstrated his point by the extraordinary results he achieved in training his son. As a child John Stuart Mill read Greek and Latin, and as a boy he could carry on intelligent discussions of problems in mathematics, philosophy, and economics. By the time he was 14, as he reports in his *Autobiography*, his intensive education enabled him to start his career "with an advantage of a quarter of a century" over his contemporaries.

Mill worked in the office of the East India Company for many years and also served a term in Parliament in the 1860's, but his principal energies were devoted to his writings on such subjects as logic and philosophy, political principles, and economics. He began as a disciple of the Utilitarian theories of his father and of Jeremy Bentham but became gradually dissatisfied with the narrowness of their conception of human motives. His honesty and open-mindedness enabled him to appreciate the values of such anti-Utilitarians as Coleridge and Carlyle, and, whenever possible, to incorporate some of these values into the Utilitarian system. His essay on Coleridge's enlightened conservatism in politics and religion is a striking example of Mill's capacity for sympathetic understanding. In part this sympathy was gained by the lesson he learned through experiencing a nervous breakdown during his early 20's. This painful event, described in the chapter of his *Autobiography* included below, taught him that the lack of concern for the affections and emotions of men, characteristic of the Utilitarian system of thought (and typified by his own education), was a fatal flaw in that system. His tribute to the therapeutic value of art (because of its effect on human emotions), both in his *Autobiography* and in his early essay *What Is Poetry*, would have astonished Mill's master, Bentham, who had equated poetry with pushpin, a trifling game.

Mill's emotional life was also broadened by his love for Harriet Taylor, a married woman who eventually became his wife. Under her influence he became an advocate for the cause of female emancipation, one of several unpopular causes to which he was dedicated. The subjection of women was, however, only one aspect of the tyranny against which he fought. His fundamental concern was to prevent the subjection of individuals in a democracy. His classic treatise *On Liberty* (1859) is not a traditional liberal attack against tyrannical kings or dictators; it is an attack against tyrannical majorities. Mill foresaw that in democracies such as America, the pressure toward conformity might crush all individualists (intellectual individualists in particular) to the level of what he called a "collective mediocrity." Throughout all of his writings, even in his discussions of the advantages of socialism, Mill is concerned with demonstrating that the individual is more important than institutions such as church or state. In *On Liberty* we find a characteristic example of the sequence of his reasoning, but here, where the theme of individualism is central, his logic is charged with eloquence.

What Is Poetry?

It has often been asked, What Is Poetry? And many and various are the answers which have been returned. The vulgarest of all— one with which no person possessed of the faculties to which poetry addresses itself can ever have been satisfied—is that which confounds poetry with metrical composition; yet to this wretched mockery of a definition many have been led back by the failure of all their attempts to find any other that would distinguish what they have been accustomed to call poetry from much which they have known only under other names.

That, however, the word "poetry" imports something quite peculiar in its nature; something which may exist in what is called prose as well as in verse; something which does not even require the instrument of words, but can speak through the other audible symbols called musical sounds, and even through the visible ones which are the language of sculpture, painting, and architecture— all this, we believe, is and must be felt, though perhaps indistinctly, by all upon whom poetry in any of its shapes produces any impression beyond that of tickling the ear. The distinction between poetry and what is not poetry, whether explained or not, is felt to be fundamental; and, where every one feels a difference, a difference there must be. All other appearances may be fallacious; but the appearance of a difference is a real difference. Appearances too, like other things, must have a cause; and that which can cause anything, even an illusion, must be a reality. And hence, while a half-philosophy disdains the classifications and distinctions indicated by popular language, philosophy carried to its highest point frames new ones, but rarely sets aside the old, content with correcting and regularizing them. It cuts fresh channels for thought, but does not fill up such as it finds ready-made: it traces, on the countrary, more deeply, broadly, and distinctly, those into which the current has spontaneously flowed.

Let us then attempt, in the way of modest inquiry, not to coerce and confine Nature within the bounds of an arbitrary definition, but rather to find the boundaries which she herself has set, and erect a barrier round them; not calling mankind to account for having misapplied the word "poetry," but attempting to clear up the conception which they already attach to it, and to bring forward as a distinct principle that which, as a vague feeling, has really guided them in their employment of the term.

The object of poetry is confessedly to act upon the emotions; and therein is poetry sufficiently distinguished from what Wordsworth affirms to be its logical opposite; namely, not prose, but matter of fact, or science.[1] The one addresses itself to the belief; the other, to the feelings. The one does its work by convincing or persuading; the other, by moving. The one acts by presenting a proposition to the understanding; the other, by offering interesting objects of contemplation to the sensibilities.

This, however, leaves us very far from a definition of poetry. This distinguishes it from one thing; but we are bound to distinguish it from everything. To bring thoughts or images before the mind, for the purpose of acting upon the emotions, does not belong to poetry alone. It is equally the province (for example) of the novelist: and yet the faculty of the poet and that of the novelist are as distinct as any other two faculties; as the faculties of the novelist and of the orator, or of the poet and the metaphysician. The two characters may be united, as characters most disparate may; but they have no natural connection.

Many of the greatest poems are in the form of fictitious narratives; and, in almost all good serious fictions, there is true poetry. But there is a radical distinction between the interest felt in a story as such, and the interest excited by poetry; for the one is derived from incident, the other from the representation of feeling. In one, the source of the emotion excited is the exhibition of a state or states of human sensibility; in the other, of a series of states of mere outward circumstances. Now, all minds are capable of being affected more or less by representations of the latter kind, and all, or almost all, by those of the former; yet the two sources of interest correspond to two distinct and (as respects their greatest development) mutually exclusive characters of mind.

At what age is the passion for a story, for almost any kind of story, merely as a story, the most intense? In childhood. But that also is the age at which poetry, even of the simplest description, is least relished and least understood; because the feelings with which it is especially conversant are yet undeveloped, and, not having been even in the slightest degree experienced, cannot be sympathized with. In what stage of the progress of society, again, is storytelling most valued, and the storyteller in greatest request and honor? In a rude state like that of the Tartars and Arabs at this day, and of almost all nations in the earliest ages. But, in this state of society, there is little poetry except ballads, which are mostly narrative—that is, essentially stories—and derive their principal interest from the incidents. Considered as poetry, they are of the lowest and most elementary kind: the feelings depicted, or rather indicated, are the simplest our nature has; such joys and griefs as the immediate pressure of some outward event excites in rude minds, which live wholly immersed in outward things, and have never, either from choice or a force they could not resist,

1. See above, Wordsworth's Preface to *Lyrical Ballads*.

turned themselves to the contemplation of the world within. Passing now from childhood, and from the childhood of society, to the grown-up men and women of this most grown-up and unchildlike age, the minds and hearts of greatest depth and elevation are commonly those which take greatest delight in poetry: the shallowest and emptiest, on the contrary, are, at all events, not those least addicted to novel-reading. This accords, too, with all analogous experience of human nature. The sort of persons whom not merely in books, but in their lives, we find perpetually engaged in hunting for excitement from without, are invariably those who do not possess, either in the vigor of their intellectual powers or in the depth of their sensibilities, that which would enable them to find ample excitement nearer home. The most idle and frivolous persons take a natural delight in fictitious narrative: the excitement it affords is of the kind which comes from without. Such persons are rarely lovers of poetry, though they may fancy themselves so because they relish novels in verse. But poetry, which is the delineation of the deeper and more secret workings of human emotion, is interesting only to those to whom it recalls what they have felt, or whose imagination it stirs up to conceive what they could feel, or what they might have been able to feel, had their outward circumstances been different.

Poetry, when it is really such, is truth; and fiction also, if it is good for anything, is truth: but they are different truths. The truth of poetry is to paint the human soul truly: the truth of fiction is to give a true picture of life. The two kinds of knowledge are different, and come by different ways, come mostly to different persons. Great poets are often proverbially ignorant of life. What they know has come by observation of themselves: they have found within them one highly delicate and sensitive specimen of human nature, on which the laws of emotion are written in large characters, such as can be read off without much study. Other knowledge of mankind, such as comes to men of the world by outward experience, is not indispensable to them as poets: but, to the novelist, such knowledge is all in all; he has to describe outward things, not the inward man; actions and events, not feelings; and it will not do for him to be numbered among those, who, as Madame Roland said of Brissot, know man, but not *men*.[2]

All this is no bar to the possibility of combining both elements, poetry and narrative or incident, in the same work, and calling it either a novel or a poem; but so may red and white combine on the same human features or on the same canvas. There is one order of composition which requires the union of poetry and incident, each in its highest kind—the dramatic. Even there, the two elements are perfectly distinguishable, and may exist of un-

<hr />

2. Jacques Pierre Brissot (1754–93), a leading reformer during the French Revolution, is characterized in the *Mém-* *oires* of Jeanne Manon Roland (1754–93).

equal quality and in the most various proportion. The incidents of a dramatic poem may be scanty and ineffective, though the delineation of passion and character may be of the highest order, as in Goethe's admirable "Torquato Tasso"; or, again, the story as a mere story may be well got up for effect, as is the case with some of the most trashy productions of the Minerva Press: [3] it may even be, what those are not, a coherent and probable series of events, though there be scarcely a feeling exhibited which is not represented falsely, or in a manner absolutely commonplace. The combination of the two excellences is what renders Shakespeare so generally acceptable, each sort of readers finding in him what is suitable to their faculties. To the many, he is great as a storyteller; to the few, as a poet.

In limiting poetry to the delineation of states of feeling, and denying the name where nothing is delineated but outward objects, we may be thought to have done what we promised to avoid— to have not found, but made, a definition in opposition to the usage of language, since it is established by common consent that there is a poetry called descriptive. We deny the charge. Description is not poetry because there is descriptive poetry, no more than science is poetry because there is such a thing as a didactic poem. But an object which admits of being described, or a truth which may fill a place in a scientific treatise, may also furnish an occasion for the generation of poetry, which we thereupon choose to call descriptive or didactic. The poetry is not in the object itself, nor in the scientific truth itself, but in the state of mind in which the one and the other may be contemplated. The mere delineation of the dimensions and colors of external objects is not poetry, no more than a geometrical ground-plan of St. Peter's or Westminster Abbey is painting. Descriptive poetry consists, no doubt, in description, but in description of things as they appear, not as they are; and it paints them, not in their bare and natural lineaments, but seen through the medium and arrayed in the colors of the imagination set in action by the feelings. If a poet describes a lion, he does not describe him as a naturalist would, nor even as a traveler would, who was intent upon stating the truth, the whole truth, and nothing but the truth. He describes him by imagery, that is, by suggesting the most striking likenesses and contrasts which might occur to a mind contemplating a lion, in the state of awe, wonder, or terror, which the spectacle naturally excites, or is, on the occasion, supposed to excite. Now, this is describing the lion professedly, but the state of excitement of the spectator really. The lion may be described falsely or with exaggeration and the poetry be all the better: but, if the human emotion be not painted with scrupulous truth, the poetry is bad poetry; i.e., is not poetry at all, but a failure.

Thus far, our progress towards a clear view of the essentials of

3. Early 19th-century publishing house that fostered the production of sentimental novels.

poetry has brought us very close to the last two attempts at a definition of poetry which we happen to have seen in print, both of them by poets, and men of genius. The one is by Ebenezer Elliott, the author of "Corn-law Rhymes," and other poems of still greater merit. "Poetry," says he, "is impassioned truth." [4] The other is by a writer in "Blackwood's Magazine," and comes, we think, still nearer the mark. He defines poetry, "man's thoughts tinged by his feelings." There is in either definition a near approximation to what we are in search of. Every truth which a human being can enunciate, every thought, even every outward impression, which can enter into his consciousness, may become poetry, when shown through any impassioned medium; when invested with the coloring of joy, or grief, or pity, or affection, or admiration, or reverence, or awe, or even hatred or terror; and, unless so colored, nothing, be it as interesting as it may, is poetry. But both these definitions fail to discriminate between poetry and eloquence. Eloquence, as well as poetry, is impassioned truth; eloquence, as well as poetry, is thoughts colored by the feelings. Yet common apprehension and philosophic criticism alike recognize a distinction between the two: there is much that everyone would call eloquence, which no one would think of classing as poetry. A question will sometimes arise, whether some particular author is a poet; and those who maintain the negative commonly allow, that, though not a poet, he is a highly eloquent writer. The distinction between poetry and eloquence appears to us to be equally fundamental with the distinction between poetry and narrative, or between poetry and description, while it is still farther from having been satisfactorily cleared up than either of the others.

Poetry and eloquence are both alike the expression or utterance of feeling: but, if we may be excused the antithesis, we should say that eloquence is *heard*; poetry is *over*heard. Eloquence supposes an audience. The peculiarity of poetry appears to us to lie in the poet's utter unconsciousness of a listener. Poetry is feeling confessing itself to itself in moments of solitude, and embodying itself in symbols which are the nearest possible representations of the feeling in the exact shape in which it exists in the poet's mind. Eloquence is feeling pouring itself out to other minds, courting their sympathy, or endeavoring to influence their belief, or move them to passion or to action.

All poetry is of the nature of soliloquy. It may be said that poetry which is printed on hot-pressed paper, and sold at a bookseller's shop, is a soliloquy in full dress and on the stage. It is so; but there is nothing absurd in the idea of such a mode of soliloquizing. What we have said to ourselves we may tell to others afterwards; what we have said or done in solitude we may voluntarily reproduce when we know that other eyes are upon us. But

4. Preface to *Corn-Law Rhymes* (1828) by Ebenezer Elliot (1781–1849).

no trace of consciousness that any eyes are upon us must be visible in the work itself. The actor knows that there is an audience present: but, if he act as though he knew it, he acts ill. A poet may write poetry, not only with the intention of printing it, but for the express purpose of being paid for it. That it should *be* poetry, being written under such influences, is less probable, not, however, impossible; but no otherwise possible than if he can succeed in excluding from his work every vestige of such lookings-forth into the outward and every-day world, and can express his emotions exactly as he has felt them in solitude, or as he is conscious that he should feel them, though they were to remain for ever unuttered, or (at the lowest) as he knows that others feel them in similar circumstances of solitude. But when he turns round, and addresses himself to another person; when the act of utterance is not itself the end, but a means to an end—viz., by the feelings he himself expresses, to work upon the feelings, or upon the belief or the will of another; when the expression of his emotions, or of his thoughts tinged by his emotions, is tinged also by that purpose, by that desire of making an impression upon another mind—then it ceases to be poetry, and becomes eloquence.

Poetry, accordingly, is the natural fruit of solitude and meditation; eloquence, of intercourse with the world. The persons who have most feeling of their own, if intellectual culture has given them a language in which to express it, have the highest faculty of poetry: those who best understand the feelings of others are the most eloquent. The persons and the nations who commonly excel in poetry as those whose character and tastes render them least dependent upon the applause or sympathy or concurrence of the world in general. Those to whom that applause, that sympathy, that concurrence, are most necessary, generally excel most in eloquence. And hence, perhaps, the French, who are the least poetical of all great and intellectual nations, are among the most eloquent; the French also being the most sociable, the vainest, and the least self-dependent.

If the above be, as we believe, the true theory of the distinction commonly admitted between eloquence and poetry, or even though it be not so, yet if, as we cannot doubt, the distinction above stated be a real bona fide distinction, it will be found to hold, not merely in the language of words, but in all other language, and to intersect the whole domain of art.

Take, for example, music. We shall find in that art, so peculiarly the expression of passion, two perfectly distinct styles—one of which may be called the poetry, the other the oratory, of music. This difference, being seized, would put an end to much musical sectarianism. There has been much contention whether the music of the modern Italian school, that of Rossini,[5] and his suc-

5. G. A. Rossini (1792–1868), composer of operas.

cessors, be impassioned or not. Without doubt, the passion it expresses is not the musing, meditative tenderness or pathos or grief of Mozart or Beethoven; yet it is passion, but garrulous passion, the passion which pours itself into other ears, and therein the better calculated for dramatic effect, having a natural adaptation for dialogue. Mozart also is great in musical oratory; but his most touching compositions are in the opposite style, that of soliloquy. Who can imagine "Dove sono" [6] *heard?* We imagine it *overheard.*

Purely pathetic music commonly partakes of soliloquy. The soul is absorbed in its distress and, though there may be bystanders, it is not thinking of them. When the mind is looking within, and not without, its state does not often or rapidly vary; and hence the even, uninterrupted flow, approaching almost to monotony, which a good reader or a good singer will give to words or music of a pensive or melancholy cast. But grief, taking the form of a prayer or of a complaint, becomes oratorical: no longer low and even and subdued, it assumes a more emphatic rhythm, a more rapidly returning accent; instead of a few slow, equal notes, following one after another at regular intervals, it crowds note upon note, and often assumes a hurry and bustle like joy. Those who are familiar with some of the best of Rossini's serious compositions, such as the air "Tu che i miseri conforti," [7] in the opera of "Tancredi," or the duet "Ebben per mia memoria," [8] in "La Gazza Ladra," will at once understand and feel our meaning. Both are highly tragic and passionate: the passion of both is that of oratory, not poetry. The like may be said of that most moving invocation in Beethoven's "Fidelio,"

> "Komm, Hoffnung, lass das letzte Stern
> Der Müde nicht erbleichen "—[9]

in which Madame Schröder Devrient exhibited such consummate powers of pathetic expression. How different from Winter's beautiful "Paga fui," [1] the very soul of melancholy exhaling itself in solitude! fuller of meaning, and therefore more profoundly poetical, than the words for which it was composed; for it seems to express, not simple melancholy, but the melancholy of remorse.

If from vocal music we now pass to instrumental, we may have a specimen of musical oratory in any fine military symphony or march; while the poetry of music seems to have attained its consummation in Beethoven's "Overture to Egmont," so wonderful in its mixed expression of grandeur and melancholy.

---

6. "Where are fled [the lovely moments?]"—soprano aria from Act III of Mozart's opera *The Marriage of Figaro.*
7. "You, who give comfort to the wretched," soprano aria from Rossini's *Tancredi* (1813).
8. "Indeed according to my memory," soprano aria from Rossini's *La Gazza Ladra* (1817).
9. "Come, Hope, let not the weary person's last star fade out." Aria from *Fidelio* (1805). Mill seems to be quoting from memory. The passage should read: "Komm, Hoffnung, lass den letzten Stern / Der Müden nicht erbleichen."
1. "I have been contented." Aria from the once-popular opera *Il Ratto di Proserpina* by Peter Winter (1775–1825), first performed in London in 1804.

In the arts which speak to the eye, the same distinctions will be found to hold, not only between poetry and oratory, but between poetry, oratory, narrative, and simple imitation or description.

Pure description is exemplified in a mere portrait or a mere landscape, productions of art, it is true, but of the mechanical rather than of the fine arts; being works of simple imitation, not creation. We say, a mere portrait or a mere landscape; because it is possible for a portrait or a landscape, without ceasing to be such, to be also a picture, like Turner's [2] landscapes, and the great portraits by Titian or Vandyke.

Whatever in painting or sculpture expresses human feeling— or character, which is only a certain state of feeling grown habitual —may be called, according to circumstances, the poetry or the eloquence of the painter's or the sculptor's art: the poetry, if the feeling declares itself by such signs as escape from us when we are unconscious of being seen; the oratory, if the signs are those we use for the purpose of voluntary communication.

The narrative style answers to what is called historical painting, which it is the fashion among connoisseurs to treat as the climax of the pictorial art. That it is the most difficult branch of the art, we do not doubt, because, in its perfection, it includes the perfection of all the other branches; as, in like manner, an epic poem, though, in so far as it is epic (i.e., narrative), it is not poetry at all, is yet esteemed the greatest effort of poetic genius, because there is no kind whatever of poetry which may not appropriately find a place in it. But an historical picture as such, that is, as the representation of an incident, must necessarily, as it seems to us, be poor and ineffective. The narrative powers of painting are extremely limited. Scarcely any picture, scarcely even any series of pictures, tells its own story without the aid of an interpreter. But it is the single figures, which, to us, are the great charm even of an historical picture. It is in these that the power of the art is really seen. In the attempt to narrate, visible and permanent signs are too far behind the fugitive audible ones, which follow so fast one after another; while the faces and figures in a narrative picture, even though they be Titian's, stand still. Who would not prefer one "Virgin and Child" of Raphael to all the pictures which Rubens, with his fat, frouzy Dutch Venuses, ever painted?—though Rubens, besides excelling almost everyone in his mastery over the mechanical parts of his art, often shows real genius in *grouping* his figures, the peculiar problem of historical painting. But then, who, except a mere student of drawing and coloring, ever cared to look twice at any of the figures themselves? The power of painting lies in poetry, of which Rubens had not the slightest tincture, not in narrative, wherein he might have excelled.

2. J. W. M. Turner (1775–1851), English landscape painter.

The single figures, however, in an historical picture, are rather the eloquence of painting than the poetry. They mostly (unless they are quite out of place in the picture) express the feelings of one person as modified by the presence of others. Accordingly, the minds whose bent leads them rather to eloquence than to poetry rush to historical painting. The French painters, for instance, seldom attempt, because they could make nothing of, single heads, like those glorious ones of the Italian masters with which they might feed themselves day after day in their own Louvre. They must all be historical; and they are, almost to a man, attitudinizers. If we wished to give any young artist the most impressive warning our imagination could devise against that kind of vice in the pictorial which corresponds to rant in the histrionic art, we would advise him to walk once up and once down the gallery of the Luxembourg.[3] Every figure in French painting or statuary seems to be showing itself off before spectators. They are not poetical, but in the worst style of corrupted eloquence.

1833, 1859

From Coleridge[1]

The name of Coleridge is one of the few English names of our time which are likely to be oftener pronounced, and to become symbolical of more important things, in proportion as the inward workings of the age manifest themselves more and more in outward facts. Bentham[2] excepted, no Englishman of recent date has left his impress so deeply in the opinions and mental tendencies of those among us who attempt to enlighten their practice by philosophical meditation. If it be true, as Lord Bacon affirms, that a knowledge of the speculative opinions of the men between twenty and thirty years of age is the great source of political prophecy, the existence of Coleridge will show itself by no slight or ambiguous traces in the coming history of our country; for no one has contributed more to shape the opinions of those among its younger men, who can be said to have opinions at all.

The influence of Coleridge, like that of Bentham, extends far beyond those who share in the peculiarities of his religious or philosophical creed. He has been the great awakener in this country of the spirit of philosophy, within the bounds of traditional opinions. He has been, almost as truly as Bentham, "the great questioner of things established"; for a questioner needs not necessarily

3. A palace in Paris, where paintings of scenes from French history were exhibited.
1. In his *Autobiography* Mill discusses Samuel Taylor Coleridge as a poet. In the present essay he discusses Coleridge as a political and religious philosopher whose conversation and writings had a profound influence on Mill's contemporaries in the 1820's and 1830's.
2. Jeremy Bentham (1748–1832), originator of Utilitarian theories of politics and ethics.

be an enemy. By Bentham, beyond all others, men have been led
to ask themselves, in regard to any ancient or received opinion, Is
it true? and by Coleridge, What is the meaning of it? The one
took his stand *outside* the received opinion, and surveyed it as an
entire stranger to it: the other looked at it from within, and endeavored to see it with the eyes of a believer in it; to discover by
what apparent facts it was at first suggested, and by what appearances it has ever since been rendered continually credible—
has seemed, to a succession of persons, to be a faithful interpretation
of their experience. Bentham judged a proposition true or false as
it accorded or not with the result of his own inquiries; and did not
search very curiously into what might be meant by the proposition,
when it obviously did not mean what he thought true. With Coleridge, on the contrary, the very fact that any doctrine had been
believed by thoughtful men, and received by whole nations or
generations of mankind, was part of the problem to be solved; was
one of the phenomena to be accounted for. And, as Bentham's
short and easy method of referring all to the selfish interests of
aristocracies or priests or lawyers, or some other species of imposters, could not satisfy a man who saw so much farther into the
complexities of the human intellect and feelings, he considered the
long or extensive prevalence of any opinion as a presumption that
it was not altogether a fallacy; that, to its first authors at least, it
was the result of a struggle to express in words something which had
a reality to them, though perhaps not to many of those who have
since received the doctrine by mere tradition. The long duration of
a belief, he thought, is at least proof of an adaptation in it to
some portion or other of the human mind: and if, on digging down
to the root, we do not find, as is generally the case, some truth, we
shall find some natural want or requirement of human nature which
the doctrine in question is fitted to satisfy; among which wants the
instincts of selfishness and of credulity have a place, but by no
means an exclusive one. From this difference in the points of view
of the two philosophers, and from the too rigid adherence of each
to his own, it was to be expected that Bentham should continually
miss the truth which is in the traditional opinions, and Coleridge
that which is out of them and at variance with them. But it was also
likely that each would find, or show the way to finding, much of
what the other missed.

It is hardly possible to speak of Coleridge, and his position
among his contemporaries, without reverting to Bentham: they are
connected by two of the closest bonds of association—resemblance and contrast. It would be difficult to find two persons of philosophic eminence more exactly the contrary of one another. Compare their modes of treatment of any subject, and you might fancy
them inhabitants of different worlds. They seem to have scarcely

a principle or a premise in common. Each of them sees scarcely any thing but what the other does not see. Bentham would have regarded Coleridge with a peculiar measure of the good-humored contempt with which he was accustomed to regard all modes of philosophizing different from his own. Coleridge would probably have made Bentham one of the exceptions to the enlarged and liberal appreciation which (to the credit of *his* mode of philosophizing) he extended to most thinkers of any eminence from whom he differed. But contraries, as logicians say, are but *quae in eodem genere maxime distant*—the things which are farthest from one another in the same kind. These two agreed in being the men, who, in their age and country, did most to enforce, by precept and example, the necessity of a philosophy. They agreed in making it their occupation to recall opinions to first principles; taking no proposition for granted without examining into the grounds of it, and ascertaining that it possessed the kind and degree of evidence suitable to its nature. They agreed in recognizing that sound theory is the only foundation for sound practice; and that whoever despises theory, let him give himself what airs of wisdom he may, is self-convicted of being a quack. If a book were to be compiled containing all the best things ever said on the rule-of-thumb school of political craftsmanship, and on the insufficiency for practical purposes of what the mere practical man calls experience, it is difficult to say whether the collection would be more indebted to the writings of Bentham or of Coleridge. They agreed, too, in perceiving that the groundwork of all other philosophy must be laid in the philosophy of the mind. To lay this foundation deeply and strongly, and to raise a superstructure in accordance with it, were the objects to which their lives were devoted. They employed, indeed, for the most part, different materials; but as the materials of both were real observations, the genuine product of experience, the results will, in the end, be found, not hostile, but supplementary, to one another. Of their methods of philosophizing, the same thing may be said: they were different, yet both were legitimate logical processes. In every respect, the two men are each other's "completing counterpart": the strong points of each correspond to the weak points of the other. Whoever could master the premises and combine the methods of both would possess the entire English philosophy of his age. Coleridge used to say that every one is born either a Platonist or an Aristotelian: it may be similarly affirmed that every Englishman of the present day is by implication either a Benthamite or a Coleridgian; holds views of human affairs which can only be proved true on the principles either of Bentham or of Coleridge. * * *

1840

From On Liberty

From *Chapter III. Of Individuality As One of the Elements of Well-Being*

* * * Few persons, out of Germany, even comprehend the meaning of the doctrine which Wilhelm von Humboldt, so eminent both as a savant and as a politician, made the text of a treatise— that "the end of man, or that which is prescribed by the eternal or immutable dictates of reason, and not suggested by vague and transient desires, is the highest and most harmonious development of his powers to a complete and consistent whole"; that, therefore, the object "towards which every human being must ceaselessly direct his efforts, and on which especially those who design to influence their fellow men must ever keep their eyes, is the individuality of power and development"; that for this there are two requisites, "freedom, and variety of situations"; and that from the union of these arise "individual vigor and manifold diversity," which combine themselves in "originality."[1]

Little, however, as people are accustomed to a doctrine like that of Von Humboldt, and surprising as it may be to them to find so high a value attached to individuality, the question, one must nevertheless think, can only be one of degree. No one's idea of excellence in conduct is that people should do absolutely nothing but copy one another. No one would assert that people ought not to put into their mode of life, and into the conduct of their concerns, any impress whatever of their own judgment, or of their own individual character. On the other hand, it would be absurd to pretend that people ought to live as if nothing whatever had been known in the world before they came into it; as if experience had as yet done nothing towards showing that one mode of existence, or conduct, is preferable to another. Nobody denies that people should be so taught and trained in youth, as to know and benefit by the ascertained results of human experience. But it is the privilege and proper condition of a human being, arrived at the maturity of his faculties, to use and interpret experience in his own way. It is for him to find out what part of recorded experience is properly applicable to his own circumstances and character. The traditions and customs of other people are, to a certain extent, evidence of what their experience has taught *them;* presumptive evidence, and as such, have a claim to his deference: but, in the first place, their experience may be too narrow; or they may not have interpreted it rightly. Secondly, their interpretation of experience may be

1. From *The Sphere and Duties of Government,* by Baron Wilhelm von Humboldt (1767–1835), Prussian statesman and man of letters. Orig- inally written in 1791, this treatise was first published in Germany in 1852 and was translated into English in 1854.

correct, but unsuitable to him. Customs are made for customary circumstances, and customary characters; and his circumstances or his character may be uncustomary. Thirdly, though the customs be both good as customs, and suitable to him, yet to conform to custom, merely *as* custom, does not educate or develop in him any of the qualities which are the distinctive endowment of a human being. The human faculties of perception, judgment, discriminative feeling, mental activity, and even moral preference are exercised only in making a choice. He who does anything because it is the custom makes no choice. He gains no practice either in discerning or in desiring what is best. The mental and moral, like the muscular powers, are improved only by being used. The faculties are called into no exercise by doing a thing merely because others do it, no more than by believing a thing only because others believe it. If the grounds of an opinion are not conclusive to the person's own reason, his reason cannot be strengthened, but is likely to be weakened, by his adopting it: and if the inducements to an act are not such as are consentaneous[2] to his own feelings and character (where affection, or the rights of others, are not concerned) it is so much done towards rendering his feelings and character inert and torpid, instead of active and energetic.

He who lets the world, or his own portion of it, choose his plan of life for him has no need of any other faculty than the apelike one of imitation. He who chooses his plan for himself employs all his faculties. He must use observation to see, reasoning and judgment to foresee, activity to gather materials for decision, discrimination to decide, and when he has decided, firmness and self-control to hold to his deliberate decision. And these qualities he requires and exercises exactly in proportion as the part of his conduct which he determines according to his own judgment and feelings is a large one. It is possible that he might be guided in some good path, and kept out of harm's way, without any of these things. But what will be his comparative worth as a human being? It really is of importance, not only what men do, but also what manner of men they are that do it. Among the works of man, which human life is rightly employed in perfecting and beautifying, the first in importance surely is man himself. Supposing it were possible to get houses built, corn grown, battles fought, causes tried, and even churches erected and prayers said, by machinery—by automatons in human form—it would be a considerable loss to exchange for these automatons even the men and women who at present inhabit the more civilized parts of the world, and who assuredly are but starved specimens of what nature can and will produce. Human nature is not a machine to be built after a model, and set to do exactly the work prescribed for it, but a tree, which requires to grow and develop itself on all sides, according to the tendency of the inward forces

2. Agreeable.

which make it a living thing.

It will probably be conceded that it is desirable people should exercise their understandings, and that an intelligent following of custom, or even occasionally an intelligent deviation from custom, is better than a blind and simply mechanical adhesion to it. To a certain extent it is admitted that our understanding should be our own: but there is not the same willingness to admit that our desires and impulses should be our own likewise; or that to possess impulses of our own, and of any strength, is anything but a peril and a snare. Yet desires and impulses are as much a part of a perfect human being, as beliefs and restraints: and strong impulses are only perilous when not properly balanced; when one set of aims and inclinations is developed into strength, while others, which ought to coexist with them, remain weak and inactive. It is not because men's desires are strong that they act ill; it is because their consciences are weak. There is no natural connection between strong impulses and a weak conscience. The natural connection is the other way. To say that one person's desires and feelings are stronger and more various than those of another is merely to say that he has more of the raw material of human nature, and is therefore capable, perhaps of more evil, but certainly of more good. Strong impulses are but another name for energy. Energy may be turned to bad uses; but more good may always be made of an energetic nature than of an indolent and impassive one. Those who have most natural feeling are always those whose cultivated feelings may be made the strongest. The same strong susceptibilities which make the personal impulses vivid and powerful are also the source from whence are generated the most passionate love of virture, and the sternest self-control. It is through the cultivation of these that society both does its duty and protects its interests: not by rejecting the stuff of which heroes are made, because it knows not how to make them. A person whose desires and impulses are his own—are the expression of his own nature, as it has been developed and modified by his own culture—is said to have a character. One whose desires and impulses are not his own, has no character, no more than a steam engine has a character. If, in addition to being his own, his impulses are strong, and are under the government of a strong will, he has an energetic character. Whoever thinks that individuality of desires and impulses should not be encouraged to unfold itself must maintain that society has no need of strong natures—is not the better for containing many persons who have much character—and that a high general average of energy is not desirable.

In some early states of society, these forces might be, and were, too much ahead of the power which society then possessed of disciplining and controlling them. There has been a time when the element of spontaneity and individuality was in excess, and the social principle had a hard struggle with it. The difficulty then was to induce men of strong bodies or minds to pay obedience to any rules which required them to control their impulses. To overcome this difficulty, law and discipline, like the Popes struggling against the Emperors, asserted a power over the whole man, claiming to control all his life in order to control his character—which society had not found any other sufficient means of binding. But society has now fairly got the better of individuality; and the danger which threatens human nature is not the excess, but the deficiency, of personal impulses and preferences. Things are vastly changed, since the passions of those who were strong by station or by personal endowment were in a state of habitual rebellion against laws and ordinances, and required to be rigorously chained up to enable the persons within their reach to enjoy any particle of security. In our times, from the highest class of society down to the lowest, everyone lives as under the eye of a hostile and dreaded censorship. Not only in what concerns others, but in what concerns only themselves, the individual or the family do not ask themselves—what do I prefer? or, what would suit my character and disposition? or, what would allow the best and highest in me to have fair play, and enable it to grow and thrive? They ask themselves, what is suitable to my position? what is usually done by persons of my station and pecuniary circumstances? or (worse still) what is usually done by persons of a station and circumstances superior to mine? I do not mean that they choose what is customary, in preference to what suits their own inclination. It does not occur to them to have any inclination, except for what is customary. Thus the mind itself is bowed to the yoke: even in what people do for pleasure, conformity is the first thing thought of; they like in crowds; they exercise choice only among things commonly done: peculiarity of taste, eccentricity of conduct, are shunned equally with crimes: until by dint of not following their own nature, they have no nature to follow: their human capacities are withered and starved: they become incapable of any strong wishes or native pleasures, and are generally without either opinions or feelings of home growth, or properly their own. Now is this, or is it not, the desirable condition of human nature?

It is so, on the Calvinistic theory. According to that, the one great offense of man is self-will. All the good of which humanity is capable is comprised in obedience. You have no choice; thus you must do, and no otherwise: "whatever is not a duty is a sin." Human nature being radically corrupt, there is no redemption for anyone until human nature is killed within him. To one holding this theory of life, crushing out any of the human faculties, capacities, and susceptibilities is no evil: man needs no capacity but that of surrendering himself to the will of God: and if he uses any of his faculties for any other purpose but to do that supposed will more effectually, he is better without them. This is the theory of Calvinism; and it is held, in a mitigated form, by many who do not consider themselves Calvinists; the mitigation consisting in giving a less ascetic interpretation to the alleged will of God; asserting it to be his will that mankind should gratify some of their inclinations; of course not in the manner they themselves prefer, but in the way of obedience, that is, in a way prescribed to them by authority; and, therefore, by the necessary conditions of the case, the same for all.

In some such insidious form there is at present a strong tendency to this narrow theory of life, and to the pinched and hidebound type of human character which it patronizes. Many persons, no doubt, sincerely think that human beings thus cramped and dwarfed are as their Maker designed them to be; just as many have thought that trees are a much finer thing when clipped into pollards,[3] or cut out into figures of animals, than as nature made them. But if it be any part of religion to believe that man was made by a good Being, it is more consistent with that faith to believe that this Being gave all human faculties that they might be cultivated and unfolded, not rooted out and consumed, and that he takes delight in every nearer approach made by his creatures to the ideal conception embodied in them, every increase in any of their capabilities of comprehension, of action, or of enjoyment. There is a different type of human excellence from the Calvinistic; a conception of humanity as having its nature bestowed on it for other purposes than merely to be abnegated. "Pagan self-assertion" is one of the elements of human worth, as well as "Christian self-denial."[4] There is a Greek ideal of self-development, which the Platonic and Christian ideal of self-government blends with, but does not supersede. It may be better to be a John Knox than an Alcibiades, but it is better to be a Pericles than either;[5] nor would a Pericles, if we had one in these days, be without anything good which belonged to John Knox.

It is not by wearing down into uniformity all that is individual in themselves, but by cultivating it and calling it forth, within the limits imposed by the rights and interests of others, that human beings become a noble and beautiful object of contemplation; and as the works partake the character of those who do them, by the same process human life also becomes rich, diversified, and animating, furnishing more abundant aliment to high thoughts and elevating feelings, and strengthening the tie which binds every individual to the race, by making the race infinitely better worth belonging to. In proportion to the development of his individuality, each person becomes more valuable to himself, and is therefore capable of being more valuable to others. There is a greater fullness

3. Trees that acquire an artificial shape by being cut back so as to produce a mass of dense foliage.
4. From the *Essays* (1848) of John Sterling, a minor writer and friend of Thomas Carlyle's.

5. John Knox (1505–72) was the stern Scottish Calvinist reformer; Alcibiades (450–404 B.C.) was a dissolute Athenian commander, and Pericles (500–429 B.C.) was a model statesman in Athens.

of life about his own existence, and when there is more life in the units there is more in the mass which is composed of them. As much compression as is necessary to prevent the stronger specimens of human nature from encroaching on the rights of others cannot be dispensed with; but for this there is ample compensation even in the point of view of human development. The means of development which the individual loses by being prevented from gratifying his inclinations to the injury of others are chiefly obtained at the expense of the development of other people. And even to himself there is a full equivalent in the better development of the social part of his nature, rendered possible by the restraint put upon the selfish part. To be held to rigid rules of justice for the sake of others develops the feelings and capacities which have the good of others for their object. But to be restrained in things not affecting their good, by their mere displeasure, develops nothing valuable, except such force of character as may unfold itself in resisting the restraint. If acquiesced in, it dulls and blunts the whole nature. To give any fair play to the nature of each, it is essential that different persons should be allowed to lead different lives. In proportion as this latitude has been exercised in any age, has that age been noteworthy to posterity. Even despotism does not produce its worst effects, so long as individuality exists under it; and whatever crushes individuality is despotism, by whatever name it may be called, and whether it professes to be enforcing the will of God or the injunctions of men.

Having said that Individuality is the same thing with development, and that it is only the cultivation of individuality which produces, or can produce, well-developed human beings, I might here close the argument: for what more or better can be said of any condition of human affairs than that it brings human beings themselves nearer to the best thing they can be? or what worse can be said of any obstruction to good than that it prevents this? Doubtless, however, these considerations will not suffice to convince those who most need convincing; and it is necessary further to show that these developed human beings are of some use to the undeveloped—to point out to those who do not desire liberty, and would not avail themselves of it, that they may be in some intelligible manner rewarded for allowing other people to make use of it without hindrance.

In the first place, then, I would suggest that they might possibly learn something from them. It will not be denied by anybody, that originality is a valuable element in human affairs. There is always need of persons not only to discover new truths, and point out when what were once truths are true no longer, but also to commence new practices, and set the example of more enlightened conduct, and better taste and sense in human life. This cannot well be gainsaid by anybody who does not believe that the world has already attained perfection in all its ways and practices. It is true that this benefit is not capable of being rendered by everybody alike: there are but few persons, in comparison with the whole of mankind, whose experiments, if adopted by others, would be likely to be any improvement on established practice. But these few are the salt of the earth; without them, human life would become a stagnant pool. Not only is it they who introduce good things which did not before exist; it is they who keep the life in those which already existed. If there were nothing new to be done, would human intellect cease to be necessary? Would it be a reason why those who do the old things should forget why they are done, and do them like cattle, not like human beings? There is only too great a tendency in the best beliefs and practices to degenerate into the mechanical; and unless there were a succession of persons whose ever-recurring originality prevents the grounds of those beliefs and practices from becoming merely traditional, such dead matter would not resist the smallest shock from anything really alive, and there would be no reason why civilization should not die out, as in the Byzantine Empire. Persons of genius, it is true, are, and are always likely to be, a small minority; but in order to have them, it is necessary to preserve the soil in which they grow. Genius can only breathe freely in an *atmosphere* of freedom. Persons of genius are, *ex vi termini*,[6] more individual than any other people—less capable, consequently, of fitting themselves, without hurtful compression, into any of the small number of molds which society provides in order to save its members the trouble of forming their own character. If from timidity they consent to be forced into one of these molds, and to let all that part of themselves which cannot expand under the pressure remain unexpanded, society will be little the better for their genius. If they are of a strong character, and break their fetters, they become a mark for the society which has not succeeded in reducing them to commonplace, to point at with solemn warning as "wild," "erratic," and the like; much as if one should complain of the Niagara River for not flowing smoothly between its banks like a Dutch canal.

I insist thus emphatically on the importance of genius, and the necessity of allowing it to unfold itself freely both in thought and in practice, being well aware that no one will deny the position in theory, but knowing also that almost everyone, in reality, is totally indifferent to it. People think genius a fine thing if it enables a man to write an exciting poem, or paint a picture. But in its true sense, that of originality in thought and action, though no one says that it is not a thing to be admired, nearly all, at heart, think that they can do very well without it. Unhappily this is too natural to be wondered at. Originality is the one thing which unoriginal minds cannot feel the use of. They cannot see what it is to do for

6. Latin for "by force of the term," i.e., by definition.

them: how should they? If they could see what it would do for them, it would not be originality. The first service which originality has to render them is that of opening their eyes: which being once fully done, they would have a chance of being themselves original. Meanwhile, recollecting that nothing was ever yet done which some-one was not the first to do, and that all good things which exist are the fruits of originality, let them be modest enough to believe that there is something still left for it to accomplish, and assure them-selves that they are more in need of originality, the less they are conscious of the want.

In sober truth, whatever homage may be professed, or even paid, to real or supposed mental superiority, the general tendency of things throughout the world is to render mediocrity the ascendant power among mankind. In ancient history, in the middle ages, and in a diminishing degree through the long transition from feudality to the present time, the individual was a power in himself; and if he had either great talents or a high social position, he was a con-siderable power. At present individuals are lost in the crowd. In politics it is almost a triviality to say that public opinion now rules the world. The only power deserving the name is that of masses, and of governments while they make themselves the organ of the tend-encies and instincts of masses. This is as true in the moral and social relations of private life as in public transactions. Those whose opinions go by the name of public opinion, are not always the same sort of public: in America they are the whole white population; in England, chiefly the middle class. But they are always a mass, that is to say, collective mediocrity. And what is a still greater novelty, the mass do not now take their opinions from dignitaries in Church or State, from ostensible leaders, or from books. Their thinking is done for them by men much like themselves, addressing them or speaking in their name, on the spur of the moment, through the newspapers. I am not complaining of all this. I do not assert that anything better is compatible, as a general rule, with the present low state of the human mind. But that does not hinder the govern-ment of mediocrity from being mediocre government. No govern-ment by a democracy or a numerous aristocracy, either in its political acts or in the opinions, qualities, and tone of mind which it fosters, ever did or could rise above mediocrity, except in so far as the sovereign Many have let themselves be guided (which in their best times they always have done) by the counsels and influence of a more highly gifted and instructed One or Few. The initiation of all wise or noble things, comes and must come from individuals; generally at first from some one individual. The honor and glory of the average man is that he is capable of following that initiative; that he can respond internally to wise and noble things, and be led to them with his eyes open. I am not countenancing the sort of "hero worship" which applauds the strong man of genius for forcibly seizing on the government of the world and making it do his bidding in spite of itself. All he can claim is freedom to point out the way. The power of compelling others into it is not only inconsistent with the freedom and development of all the rest, but corrupting to the strong man himself. It does seem, however, that when the opinions of masses of merely average men are everywhere become or becoming the dominant power, the counterpoise and corrective to that tendency would be the more and more pronounced individuality of those who stand on the higher eminences of thought. It is in these circumstances most especially that exceptional individuals, instead of being deterred, should be encouraged in acting differently from the mass. In other times there was no advantage in their doing so, unless they acted not only differently, but better. In this age, the mere example of nonconformity, the mere refusal to bend the knee to custom, is itself a service. Precisely because the tyranny of opinion is such as to make eccentricity a reproach, it is desirable, in order to break through that tyranny, that people should be eccentric. Eccentricity has always abounded when and where strength of character has abounded; and the amount of eccentricity in a society has generally been proportional to the amount of genius, mental vigor, and moral courage which it contained. That so few now dare to be eccentric marks the chief danger of the time. * * *

There is one characteristic of the present direction of public opinion, peculiarly calculated to make it intolerant of any marked demonstration of individuality. The general average of mankind are not only moderate in intellect, but also moderate in inclinations: they have no tastes or wishes strong enough to incline them to do anything unusual, and they consequently do not understand those who have, and class all such with the wild and intemperate whom they are accustomed to look down upon. Now, in addition to this fact which is general, we have only to suppose that a strong movement has set in towards the improvement of morals, and it is evident what we have to expect. In these days such a movement has set in; much has actually been effected in the way of increased regularity of conduct, and discouragement of excesses; and there is a philanthropic spirit abroad, for the exercise of which there is no more inviting field than the moral and prudential improvement of our fellow creatures. These tendencies of the times cause the public to be more disposed than at most former periods to prescribe general rules of conduct, and endeavor to make everyone conform to the approved standard. And that standard, express or tacit, is to desire nothing strongly. Its ideal of character is to be without any marked character; to maim by compression, like a Chinese lady's foot, every part of human nature which stands out prominently, and tends to make the person markedly dissimilar in outline to commonplace humanity.

As is usually the case with ideals which exclude one half of what is desirable, the present standard of approbation produces only an inferior imitation of the other half. Instead of great energies guided by vigorous reason, and strong feelings strongly controlled by a conscientious will, its result is weak feelings and weak energies, which therefore can be kept in outward conformity to rule without any strength either of will or reason. Already energetic characters on any large scale are becoming merely traditional. There is now scarcely any outlet for energy in this country except business. The energy expended in this may still be regarded as considerable. What little is left from that employment, is expended on some hobby; which may be a useful, even a philanthropic hobby, but is always some one thing, and generally a thing of small dimensions. The greatness of England is now all collective: individually small, we only appear capable of anything great by our habit of combining; and with this our moral and religious philanthropies are perfectly contented. But it was men of another stamp than this that made England what it has been; and men of another stamp will be needed to prevent its decline.

The despotism of custom is everywhere the standing hindrance to human advancement, being in unceasing antagonism to that disposition to aim at something better than customary, which is called, according to circumstances, the spirit of liberty, or that of progress or improvement. The spirit of improvement is not always a spirit of liberty, for it may aim at forcing improvements on an unwilling people; and the spirit of liberty, in so far as it resists such attempts, may ally itself locally and temporarily with the opponents of improvement; but the only unfailing and permanent source of improvement is liberty, since by it there are as many possible independent centers of improvement as there are individuals. The progressive principle, however, in either shape, whether as the love of liberty or of improvement, is antagonistic to the sway of Custom, involving at least emancipation from that yoke; and the contest between the two constitutes the chief interest of the history of mankind. The greater part of the world has, properly speaking, no history, because the depotism of Custom is complete. This is the case over the whole East. Custom is there, in all things, the final appeal; justice and right mean conformity to custom; the argument of custom no one, unless some tyrant intoxicated with power, thinks of resisting. And we see the result. Those nations must once have had originality; they did not start out of the ground populous, lettered, and versed in many of the arts of life; they made themselves all this, and were then the greatest and most powerful nations of the world. What are they now? The subjects or dependants of tribes whose forefathers wandered in the forests when theirs had magnificent palaces and gorgeous temples, but over whom custom exercised only a divided rule with liberty and progress. A people, it appears, may be progressive for a certain length of time, and then stop: when does it stop? When it ceases to possess individuality. If a similar change should befall the nations of Europe, it will not be in exactly the same shape: the despotism of custom with which these nations are threatened is not precisely stationariness. It proscribes singularity, but it does not preclude change, provided all change together. We have discarded the fixed costumes of our forefathers; everyone must still dress like other people, but the fashion may change once or twice a year. We thus take care that when there is change it shall be for change's sake, and not from any idea of beauty or convenience; for the same idea of beauty or convenience would not strike all the world at the same moment, and be simultaneously thrown aside by all at another moment. But we are progressive as well as changeable: we continually make new inventions in mechanical things, and keep them until they are again superseded by better; we are eager for improvement in politics, in education, even in morals, though in this last our idea of improvement chiefly consists in persuading or forcing other people to be as good as ourselves. It is not progress that we object to; on the contrary, we flatter ourselves that we are the most progressive people who ever lived. It is individuality that we war against: we should think we had done wonders if we had made ourselves all alike; forgetting that the unlikeness of one person to another is generally the first thing which draws the attention of either to the imperfection of his own type, and the superiority of another, or the possibility, by combining the advantages of both, of producing something better than either. We have a warning example in China—a nation of much talent, and, in some respects, even wisdom, owing to the rare good fortune of having been provided at an early period with a particularly good set of customs, the work, in some measure, of men to whom even the most enlightened European must accord, under certain limitations, the title of sages and philosophers. They are remarkable, too, in the excellence of their apparatus for impressing, as far as possible, the best wisdom they possess upon every mind in the community, and securing that those who have appropriated most of it shall occupy the posts of honor and power. Surely the people who did this have discovered the secret of human progressiveness, and must have kept themselves steadily at the head of the movement of the world. On the contrary, they have become stationary—have remained so for thousands of years; and if they are ever to be farther improved, it must be by foreigners. They have succeeded beyond all hope in what English philanthropists are so industriously working at—in making a people all alike, all governing their thoughts and conduct by the same maxims and rules; and these are the fruits. The modern regime of public opinion is, in an unorganized form, what the Chinese educational and political systems are in an organized; and unless individuality shall be able successfully to assert itself against this yoke, Europe, notwithstanding its noble antecedents and its professed Christianity, will tend to become another China. * * *

1859

From Autobiography
From *Chapter V. A Crisis in My Mental History.*
One Stage Onward

For some years after this time[1] I wrote very little, and nothing regularly, for publication: and great were the advantages which I derived from the intermission. It was of no common importance to me, at this period, to be able to digest and mature my thoughts for my own mind only, without any immediate call for giving them out in print. Had I gone on writing, it would have much disturbed the important transformation in my opinions and character, which took place during those years. The origin of this transformation, or at least the process by which I was prepared for it, can only be explained by turning some distance back.

From the winter of 1821, when I first read Bentham, and especially from the commencement of the *Westminster Review*, I had what might truly be called an object in life; to be a reformer of the world. My conception of my own happiness was entirely identified with this object. The personal sympathies I wished for were those of fellow laborers in this enterprise. I endeavored to pick up as many flowers as I could by the way; but as a serious and permanent personal satisfaction to rest upon, my whole reliance was placed on this; and I was accustomed to felicitate myself on the certainty of a happy life which I enjoyed, through placing my happiness in something durable and distant, in which some progress might be always making, while it could never be exhausted by complete attainment. This did very well for several years, during which the general improvement going on in the world and the idea of myself as engaged with others in struggling to promote it, seemed enough to fill up an interesting and animated existence. But the time came when I awakened from this as from a dream. It was in the autumn of 1826. I was in a dull state of nerves, such as everybody is occasionally liable to; unsusceptible to enjoyment or pleasurable excitement; one of those moods when what is pleasure at other times becomes insipid or indifferent; the state, I should think, in which converts to Methodism usually are, when smitten by their first "conviction of sin." In this frame of mind it occurred to me to put

1. 1828. Mill had been contributing articles to the *Westminster Review*.

the question directly to myself: "Suppose that all your objects in life were realized; that all the changes in institutions and opinions which you are looking forward to could be completely effected at this very instant: would this be a great joy and happiness to you?" And an irrepressible self-consciousness distinctly answered, "No!" At this my heart sank within me: the whole foundation on which my life was constructed fell down. All my happiness was to have been found in the continual pursuit of this end. The end had ceased to charm, and how could there ever again be any interest in the means? I seemed to have nothing left to live for.

At first I hoped that the cloud would pass away of itself; but it did not. A night's sleep, the sovereign remedy for the smaller vexations of life, had no effect on it. I awoke to a renewed consciousness of the woeful fact. I carried it with me into all companies, into all occupations. Hardly anything had power to cause me even a few minutes' oblivion of it. For some months the cloud seemed to grow thicker and thicker. The lines in Coleridge's *Dejection*—I was not then acquainted with them—exactly describe my case:

> A grief without a pang, void, dark and drear,
> A drowsy, stifled, unimpassioned grief,
> Which finds no natural outlet or relief
> In word, or sigh, or tear.[2]

In vain I sought relief from my favorite books; those memorials of past nobleness and greatness from which I had always hitherto drawn strength and animation. I read them now without feeling, or with the accustomed feeling minus all its charm; and I became persuaded that my love of mankind, and of excellence for its own sake, had worn itself out. I sought no comfort by speaking to others of what I felt. If I had loved anyone sufficiently to make confiding my griefs a necessity, I should not have been in the condition I was. I felt, too, that mine was not an interesting, or in any way respectable distress. There was nothing in it to attract sympathy. Advice, if I had known where to seek it, would have been most precious. The words of Macbeth to the physician[3] often occurred to my thoughts. But there was no one on whom I could build the faintest hope of such assistance. My father, to whom it would have been natural to me to have recourse in any practical difficulties, was the last person to whom, in such a case as this, I looked for help. Everything convinced me that he had no knowledge of any such mental state as I was suffering from, and that even if he could be made to understand it, he was not the physician who could heal it. My education, which was wholly his work, had been conducted without any regard to the possibility of its ending in this result; and I saw no use in giving him the pain of thinking

2. *Dejection: An Ode*, lines 21–24.
3. "Canst thou not minister to a mind diseas'd * * * ?" (*Macbeth* V.iii.40–44).

that his plans had failed, when the failure was probably irremediable, and, at all events, beyond the power of *his* remedies. Of other friends, I had at that time none to whom I had any hope of making my condition intelligible. It was however abundantly intelligible to myself; and the more I dwelt upon it, the more hopeless it appeared.

My course of study had led me to believe that all mental and moral feelings and qualities, whether of a good or of a bad kind, were the results of association; that we love one thing, and hate another, take pleasure in one sort of action or contemplation, and pain in another sort, through the clinging of pleasurable or painful ideas to those things, from the effect of education or of experience. As a corollary from this, I had always heard it maintained by my father, and was myself convinced, that the object of education should be to form the strongest possible associations of the salutary class; associations of pleasure with all things beneficial to the great whole, and of pain with all things hurtful to it. This doctrine appeared inexpugnable; but it now seemed to me, on retrospect, that my teachers had occupied themselves but superficially with the means of forming and keeping up these salutary associations. They seemed to have trusted altogether to the old familiar instruments, praise and blame, reward and punishment. Now, I did not doubt that by these means, begun early, and applied unremittingly, intense associations of pain and pleasure, especially of pain, might be created, and might produce desires and aversions capable of lasting undiminished to the end of life. But there must always be something artificial and casual in associations thus produced. The pains and pleasures thus forcibly associated with things are not connected with them by any natural tie; and it is therefore, I thought, essential to the durability of these associations that they should have beome so intense and inveterate as to be practically indissoluble, before the habitual exercise of the power of analysis had commenced. For I now saw, or thought I saw, what I had always before received with incredulity—that the habit of analysis has a tendency to wear away the feelings: as indeed it has, when no other mental habit is cultivated, and the analyzing spirit remains without its natural complements and correctives. The very excellence of analysis (I argued) is that it tends to weaken and undermine whatever is the result of prejudice; that it enables us mentally to separate ideas which have only casually clung together: and no associations whatever could ultimately resist this dissolving force, were it not that we owe to analysis our clearest knowledge of the permanent sequences in nature; the real connections between Things, not dependent on our will and feelings; natural laws, by virtue of which, in many cases, one thing is inseparable from another in fact; which laws, in proportion as they are clearly perceived and imaginatively realized, cause our ideas of things which are always joined together in Nature to cohere more and more closely in our thoughts. Analytic habits may thus even strengthen the associations between causes and effects, means and ends, but tend altogether to weaken those which are, to speak familiarly, a *mere* matter of feeling. They are therefore (I thought) favorable to prudence and clear-sightedness, but a perpetual worm at the root both of the passions and of the virtues; and, above all, fearfully undermine all desires, and all pleasures, which are the effects of association, that is, according to the theory I held, all except the purely physical and organic; of the entire insufficiency of which to make life desirable, no one had a stronger conviction than I had. These were the laws of human nature, by which, as it seemed to me, I had been brought to my present state. All those to whom I looked up were of opinion that the pleasure of sympathy with human beings, and the feelings which made the good of others, and especially of mankind on a large scale, the object of existence, were the greatest and surest sources of happiness. Of the truth of this I was convinced, but to know that a feeling would make me happy if I had it, did not give me the feeling. My education, I thought, had failed to create these feelings in sufficient strength to resist the dissolving influence of analysis, while the whole course of my intellectual cultivation had made precocious and premature analysis the inveterate habit of my mind. I was thus, as I said to myself, left stranded at the commencement of my voyage, with a well-equipped ship and a rudder, but no sail; without any real desire for the ends which I had been so carefully fitted out to work for: no delight in virtue, or the general good, but also just as little in anything else. The fountains of vanity and ambition seemed to have dried up within me, as completely as those of benevolence. I had had (as I reflected) some gratification of vanity at too early an age: I had obtained some distinction, and felt myself of some importance, before the desire of distinction and of importance had grown into a passion: and little as it was which I had attained, yet having been attained too early, like all pleasures enjoyed too soon, it had made me *blasé* and indifferent to the pursuit. Thus neither selfish nor unselfish pleasures were pleasures to me. And there seemed no power in nature sufficient to begin the formation of my character anew, and create in a mind now irretrievably analytic, fresh associations of pleasure with any of the objects of human desire.

These were the thoughts which mingled with the dry heavy dejection of the melancholy winter of 1826–7. During this time I was not incapable of my usual occupations. I went on with them mechanically, by the mere force of habit. I had been so drilled in a certain sort of mental exercise that I could still carry it on when all the spirit had gone out of it. I even composed and spoke several speeches at the debating society, how, or with what degree of success, I know not. Of four years continual speaking at that society, this is the only year of which I remember next to nothing. Two lines of Coleridge, in whom alone of all writers I have found a true description of what I felt, were often in my thoughts, not at this time (for I had never read them), but in a later period of the same mental malady:

> Work without hope draws nectar in a sieve,
> And hope without an object cannot live.[4]

In all probability my case was by no means so peculiar as I fancied it, and I doubt not that many others have passed through a similar state; but the idiosyncrasies of my education had given to the general phenomenon a special character, which made it seem the natural effect of causes that it was hardly possible for time to remove. I frequently asked myself if I could, or if I was bound to go on living, when life must be passed in this manner. I generally answered to myself, that I did not think I could possibly bear it beyond a year. When, however, not more than half that duration of time had elapsed, a small ray of light broke in upon my gloom. I was reading, accidentally, Marmontel's *Mémoires*,[5] and came to the passage which relates his father's death, the distressed position of the family, and the sudden inspiration by which he, then a mere boy, felt and made them feel that he would be everything to them—would supply the place of all that they had lost. A vivid conception of that scene and its feelings came over me, and I was moved to tears. From this moment my burden grew lighter. The oppression of the thought that all feeling was dead within me was gone. I was no longer hopeless: I was not a stock or a stone. I had still, it seemed, some of the material out of which all worth of character, and all capacity for happiness, are made. Relieved from my ever present sense of irremediable wretchedness, I gradually found that the ordinary incidents of life could again give me some pleasure; that I could again find enjoyment, not intense, but sufficient for cheerfulness, in sunshine and sky, in books, in conversation, in public affairs; and that there was, once more, excitement, though of a moderate kind, in exerting myself for my opinions, and for the public good. Thus the cloud gradually drew off, and I again enjoyed life: and though I had several relapses, some of which lasted many months, I never again was as miserable as I had been.

The experiences of this period had two very marked effects on my opinions and character. In the first place, they led me to adopt a theory of life, very unlike that on which I had before acted, and

---

4. From Coleridge's short poem *Work Without Hope*.   5. J. F. Marmontel (1723–99), whose *Mémoires* were published in 1804.

having much in common with what at that time I certainly had never heard of, the anti-self-consciousness theory of Carlyle.[6] I never, indeed, wavered in the conviction that happiness is the test of all rules of conduct, and the end of life. But I now thought that this end was only to be attained by not making it the direct end. Those only are happy (I thought) who have their minds fixed on some object other than their own happiness; on the happiness of others, on the improvement of mankind, even on some art or pursuit, followed not as a means, but as itself an ideal end. Aiming thus at something else, they find happiness by the way. The enjoyments of life (such was now my theory) are sufficient to make it a pleasant thing, when they are taken *en passant*, without being made a principal object. Once make them so, and they are immediately felt to be insufficient. They will not bear a scrutinizing examination. Ask yourself whether you are happy, and you cease to be so. The only chance is to treat, not happiness, but some end external to it, as the purpose of life. Let your self-consciousness, your scrutiny, your self-interrogation exhaust themselves on that; and if otherwise fortunately circumstanced you will inhale happiness with the air you breathe, without dwelling on it or thinking about it, without either forestalling it in imagination, or putting it to flight by fatal questioning. This theory now became the basis of my philosophy of life. And I still hold to it as the best theory for all those who have but a moderate degree of sensibility and of capacity for enjoyment, that is, for the great majority of mankind.

The other important change which my opinions at this time underwent was that I, for the first time, gave its proper place, among the prime necessities of human well-being, to the internal culture of the individual. I ceased to attach almost exclusive importance to the ordering of outward circumstances, and the training of the human being for speculation and for action.

I had now learnt by experience that the passive susceptibilities needed to be cultivated as well as the active capacities, and required to be nourished and enriched as well as guided. I did not, for an instant, lose sight of, or undervalue, that part of the truth which I had seen before; I never turned recreant to intellectual culture, or ceased to consider the power and practice of analysis as an essential condition both of individual and of social improvement. But I thought that it had consequences which required to be corrected, by joining other kinds of cultivation with it. The maintenance of a due balance among the faculties now seemed to me of primary importance. The cultivation of the feelings became one of the cardinal points in my ethical and philosophical creed. And my thoughts and inclinations turned in an increasing degree toward

6. See Carlyle's *Characteristics* and Chapter IX of *Sartor Resartus*, "The Everlasting Yea."

whatever seemed capable of being instrumental to that object.

I now began to find meaning in the things which I had read or heard about the importance of poetry and art as instruments of human culture. But it was some time longer before I began to know this by personal experience. The only one of the imaginative arts in which I had from childhood taken great pleasure was music; the best effect of which (and in this it surpasses perhaps every other art) consists in exciting enthusiasm; in winding up to a high pitch those feelings of an elevated kind which are already in the character, but to which this excitement gives a glow and a fervor, which, though transitory at its utmost height, is precious for sustaining them at other times. This effect of music I had often experienced; but like all my pleasurable susceptibilities it was suspended during the gloomy period. I had sought relief again and again from this quarter, but found none. After the tide had turned, and I was in process of recovery, I had been helped forward by music, but in a much less elevated manner. I at this time first became acquainted with Weber's *Oberon*,[7] and the extreme pleasure which I drew from its delicious melodies did me good, by showing me a source of pleasure to which I was as susceptible as ever. The good, however, was much impaired by the thought that the pleasure of music (as is quite true of such pleasure as this was, that of mere tune) fades with familiarity, and requires either to be revived by intermittence, or fed by continual novelty. And it is very characteristic both of my then state, and of the general tone of my mind at this period of my life, that I was seriously tormented by the thought of the exhaustibility of musical combinations. The octave consists only of five tones and two semitones, which can be put together in only a limited number of ways, of which but a small proportion are beautiful: most of these, it seemed to me, must have been already discovered, and there could not be room for a long succession of Mozarts and Webers, to strike out, as these had done, entirely new and surpassingly rich veins of musical beauty. This source of anxiety may, perhaps, be thought to resemble that of the philosophers of Laputa,[8] who feared lest the sun should be burnt out. It was, however, connected with the best feature in my character, and the only good point to be found in my very unromantic and in no way honorable distress. For though my dejection, honestly looked at, could not be called other than egotistical, produced by the ruin, as I thought, of my fabric of happiness, yet the destiny of mankind in general was ever in my thoughts, and could not be separated from my own. I felt that the flaw in my life must be a flaw in life itself; that the question was whether, if the reformers of society and government could succeed in their objects, and every person in the

---

7. A romantic opera composed by Carl Maria von Weber (1786–1826).   8. See *Gulliver's Travels*, Part III.

community were free and in a state of physical comfort, the pleasures of life, being no longer kept up by struggle and privation, would cease to be pleasures. And I felt that unless I could see my way to some better hope than this for human happiness in general, my dejection must continue; but that if I could see such an outlet, I should then look on the world with pleasure; content as far as I was myself concerned, with any fair share of the general lot.

This state of my thoughts and feelings made the fact of my reading Wordsworth for the first time (in the autumn of 1828), an important event in my life. I took up the collection of his poems from curiosity, with no expectation of mental relief from it, though I had before resorted to poetry with that hope. In the worst period of my depression, I had read through the whole of Byron (then new to me), to try whether a poet, whose peculiar department was supposed to be that of the intenser feelings, could rouse any feeling in me. As might be expected, I got no good from this reading, but the reverse. The poet's state of mind was too like my own. His was the lament of a man who had worn out all pleasures, and who seemed to think that life, to all who possess the good things of it, must necessarily be the vapid, uninteresting thing which I found it. His Harold and Manfred had the same burden on them which I had; and I was not in a frame of mind to desire any comfort from the vehement sensual passion of his Giaours, or the sullenness of his Laras.[9] But while Byron was exactly what did not suit my condition, Wordsworth was exactly what did. I had looked into *The Excursion*[1] two or three years before, and found little in it; and I should probably have found as little had I read it at this time. But the miscellaneous poems, in the two-volume edition of 1815 (to which little of value was added in the latter part of the author's life), proved to be the precise thing for my mental wants at that particular juncture.

In the first place, these poems addressed themselves powerfully to one of the strongest of my pleasurable susceptibilities, the love of rural objects and natural scenery; to which I had been indebted not only for much of the pleasure of my life, but quite recently for relief from one of my longest relapses into depression. In this power of rural beauty over me, there was a foundation laid for taking pleasure in Wordsworth's poetry; the more so, as his scenery lies mostly among mountains, which, owing to my early Pyrenean excursion,[2] were my ideal of natural beauty. But Wordsworth would never have had any great effect on me, if he had merely placed

9. The heroes of some of Byron's early poems were usually gloomy and self-preoccupied. Mill refers here to *Childe Harold's Pilgrimage* (1812–18), *Manfred* (1817), *The Giaour* (1813) and *Lara* (1814).
1. A long meditative poem by Words-

worth, published in 1814.
2. At 15 Mill had been deeply affected by the landscape of the Pyrenees in Spain, a mountainous region which also made a strong impression upon Tennyson.

before me beautiful pictures of natural scenery. Scott does this still better than Wordsworth, and a very second-rate landscape does it more effectually than any poet. What made Wordsworth's poems a medicine for my state of mind, was that they expressed, not mere outward beauty, but states of feeling, and of thought colored by feeling, under the excitement of beauty. They seemed to be the very culture of the feelings, which I was in quest of. In them I seemed to draw from a source of inward joy, of sympathetic and imaginative pleasure, which could be shared in by all human beings; which had no connection with struggle or imperfection, but would be made richer by every improvement in the physical or social condition of mankind. From them I seemed to learn what would be the perennial sources of happiness, when all the greater evils of life shall have been removed. And I felt myself at once better and happier as I came under their influence. There have certainly been, even in our own age, greater poets than Wordsworth; but poetry of deeper and loftier feeling could not have done for me at that time what his did. I needed to be made to feel that there was real, permanent happiness in tranquil contemplation. Wordsworth taught me this, not only without turning away from, but with a greatly increased interest in the common feelings and common destiny of human beings. And the delight which these poems gave me proved that with culture of this sort, there was nothing to dread from the most confirmed habit of analysis. At the conclusion of the Poems came the famous *Ode*, falsely called Platonic, *Intimations of Immortality:* in which, along with more than his usual sweetness of melody and rhythm, and along with the two passages of grand imagery but bad philosophy so often quoted, I found that he too had had similar experience to mine; that he also had felt that the first freshness of youthful enjoyment of life was not lasting; but that he had sought for compensation, and found it, in the way in which he was now teaching me to find it. The result was that I gradually, but completely, emerged from my habitual depression, and was never again subject to it. I long continued to value Wordsworth less according to his intrinsic merits than by the measure of what he had done for me. Compared with the greatest poets, he may be said to be the poet of unpoetical natures, possessed of quiet and contemplative tastes. But unpoetical natures are precisely those which require poetic cultivation. This cultivation Wordsworth is much more fitted to give than poets who are intrinsically far more poets than he. * * *

1873

The Twentieth Century

1914–18: World War I.
1918: Gerard Manley Hopkins' poetry published.
1922: T. S. Eliot's *The Waste Land*.
1922: James Joyce's *Ulysses*.
1928: W. B. Yeats's *The Tower*.
1930: Period of depression and unemployment begins.
1939–45: World War II.

THE END OF VICTORIANISM

Cultural movements do not proceed neatly by centuries, and this section, which for convenience we call "the twentieth century," begins really with the late 19th, when the sense of the passing of a major phase of English history was already in the air. Queen Victoria's Jubilee in 1887 and, even more, her Diamond Jubilee in 1897 were felt even by contemporaries to mark the end of an era. As the 19th century drew to a close there were many manifestations of a weakening of traditional stabilities. The aesthetic movement, with its insistence on "art for art's sake," assaulted the assumptions about the nature and function of art held by ordinary middle-class readers, deliberately, provocatively. It helped to widen the breach between artists and writers on the one hand and the "Philistine" public on the other —a breach whose earlier symptom was Matthew Arnold's war on the Philistines in *Culture and Anarchy* and which was later to result in the "alienation of the artist" that is now a commonplace of criticism. This was more than a purely English matter. From France came the tradition of the bohemian life that scorned the limits imposed by conventional ideas of respectability, together with other notions of the artist as rejecting and rejected by ordinary society, which in different ways fostered the view of the alienated artist. The life and work of the French Symbolist poets in France, the early novels of Thomas Mann in Germany (especially *Buddenbrooks*, 1901), and Joyce's *Portrait of the Artist as a Young Man* (1916) show some of the very different ways in which this attitude revealed itself in literature all over Europe. In England, the growth of popular education as a result of the Education Act of 1870, which finally made elementary education compulsory and universal, led to the rapid emergence of a large, unsophisticated literary public at whom new kinds of journalism, in particular the cheap "yellow press," were directed. A public that was literate but not in any real sense educated increased steadily throughout the 19th century, and one result of this was the splitting up of the audience for literature into "highbrows," "lowbrows," and "middlebrows." Although in earlier periods there had been different kinds of audience for different kinds of writing, the split now developed with unprecedented speed and to an unprecedented degree because of the mass production of "popular" literature for the semiliterate. The fragmentation of the reading public now merged with the artist's war on the Philistine (and indeed was one of the causes of that war in the first place) to widen the gap between popular art and art esteemed only by the sophisticated and the expert. This is part of the background of modern literature all over the Western world.

Another manifestation—or at least accompaniment—of the end of the Victorian age was the rise of various kinds of pessimism and stoicism. The novels and poetry of Thomas Hardy show one kind of pessimism (and it *was* pessimism, even if Hardy himself repudiated the term), and the poems of A. E. Housman show another variety, while a real or affected stoicism is to be found not only in these writers but also in many minor writers of the last decade of the 19th century and the first decade of the 20th. Examples of this stoicism—the determination to stand for human dignity by enduring bravely, with a "stiff upper lip," whatever fate may bring—range from Robert Louis Stevenson's essays and the rhetorically assertive poems of the editor and journalist W. E. Henley, to Rudyard Kipling's *Jungle Books* and many of his short stories, the last stanza of Housman's *The Chestnut Casts His Flambeaux* ("Bear them we can, and if we can we must") and Yeats's "They know that Hamlet and Lear are gay."

Although the high tide of anti-Victorianism was marked by the publication in 1918 of that classic of ironic debunking, *Eminent Victorians* by Lytton Strachey (1880–1932), the criticism of the normal attitudes and preconceptions of the Victorian middle classes first became really violent in the last two decades of the 19th century. No one could have been more savage in his attacks on the Victorian conceptions of the family, education, and religion than Samuel Butler, whose novel *The Way of All Flesh* (completed in 1884, posthumously published in 1903) is still the bitterest indictment in English literature of the Victorian way of life. The chorus of questioning of Victorian assumptions grew ever louder as the century drew to an end; sounding prominently in it was the voice of the young Bernard Shaw, one of Butler's greatest admirers. The position of women, too, was rapidly changing during this period. The Married Woman's Property Act of 1882, which allowed married women to own property in their own right; the admission of women to the universities at different times during the latter part of the century; the fight for women's suffrage, which was not won until 1918 (and not fully won until 1928)—these events marked a change in the attitude to women and in the part they played in the national life as well as in the relation between the sexes, which is reflected in a variety of ways in the literature of the period.

The Boer War (1899–1902), fought by the British to establish political and economic control over the Boer republics of South Africa, marked both the high point of and the reaction against British imperialism. It was a war against which many British intellectuals protested and one which the British in the end were slightly ashamed of having won. The development

of the British Empire into the British Commonwealth (i.e., into an association of self-governing countries) continued in fits and starts throughout
the first half of the 20th century, with imperialist and anti-imperialist
sentiment often meeting head on; writers as far apart as Kipling and E. M.
Forster occupied themselves with the problem. The Irish question also
caused a great deal of excitement from the beginning of the period until
well into the 1920's. A steadily rising Irish nationalism protested with increasing violence against the political subordination of Ireland to the
British Crown and government. In World War I some Irish nationalists
sought German help in rebelling against Britain, and this exacerbated feeling on both sides. No one can fully understand William Butler Yeats or
James Joyce without some awareness of the Irish struggle for independence,
the feelings of Anglo-Irish men of letters on this burning topic, and the
way in which the Irish Literary Revival of the late 19th and early 20th
centuries (with which Yeats was much concerned) reflected a determination
to achieve a vigorous national life culturally even if the road seemed
blocked politically.

THE IMPACT OF WORLD WAR I

Edwardian England (1901–10) was very conscious of being no longer
Victorian. Edward VII stamped his character on the decade in which
he reigned. It was a vulgar age of conspicuous enjoyment by those who
could afford it, and writers and artists kept well away from implication in
high society (though there were some conspicuous exceptions): in general,
there was no equivalent in this period of Queen Victoria's interest in Tennyson. The alienation of artists and intellectuals was proceeding apace. From
1910 (when George V came to the throne) until war broke out in August,
1914, Britain achieved a temporary equilibrium between Victorian earnestness and Edwardian flashiness; in retrospect that "Georgian" period seems
peculiarly golden, the last phase of assurance and stability before the old
order throughout Europe broke up in violence with results that are still
with us. Yet even then, under the surface, there was restlessness and experimentation. If this was the age of Rupert Brooke, it was also the age of
T. S. Eliot's first experiments in a disturbingly new kind of poetry.

"Edwardian" as a term applied to English cultural history suggests a
period in which the social and economic stabilities of the Victorian age—
country houses with numerous servants, a flourishing and confident middle
class, a strict hierarchy of social classes—remained unimpaired, though on
the level of ideas there was a sense of change and liberation. "Georgian"
refers largely to the lull before the storm of World War I.

The quiet traditionalism of much of the verse that appeared in the volumes of *Georgian Poetry* edited by Edward Marsh between 1911 and 1920
represented an attempt to wall in the garden of English poetry against the
disruptive forces of modern civilization. Cultured meditations on the
English countryside ("I love the mossy quietness / That grows upon the
great stone flags") alternated with self-conscious exercises in the exotic
("When I was but thirteen or so / I went into a golden land, / Chim-
borazo, Cotopaxi, / Took me by the hand"). Sometimes the magical note
was authentic, as in many of Walter de la Mare's poems, and sometimes
the meditative strain was original and impressive, as in the poetry of Edward Thomas. But as World War I went on, with more and more poets

killed and the survivors increasingly disillusioned, the whole world on which the Georgian imagination rested came to appear unreal. A patriotic poem such as Rupert Brooke's *The Soldier* became a ridiculous anachronism in the face of modern trench warfare, and the even more blatantly patriotic note sounded by other Georgian poets (as in John Freeman's *Happy Is England Now*, which claimed that "there's not a nobleness of heart, hand, brain / But shines the purer; happiest is England now / In those that fight") came to seem positively obscene. The savage ironies of Siegfried Sassoon's war poems and the combination of pity and irony in those of Wilfred Owen portrayed a world undreamed of in the golden years from 1910 to 1914. Over four years of tremendous slaughter under appalling conditions (the battle casualties were many times greater than those in World War II), the wiping out of virtually a whole generation of young men, the shattering of so many illusions and ideals made World War I a watershed in European civilization. No one had been prepared for what actually happened in that war—in contrast to World War II, so long anticipated and predicted by a generation brought up on the grim war books of World War I. The experience was traumatic. It left throughout all Europe a sense that the bases of civilization had been destroyed, that all traditional values had been wiped out, and we see this reflected in different ways in *The Waste Land* of Eliot and the early novels and stories of Aldous Huxley.

THE POETIC REVOLUTION

A technical revolution in poetry was going on side by side with shifts in attitude. The Imagist movement, influenced by T. E. Hulme's insistence on hard, clear, precise images and encouraged by Ezra Pound when he lived in London just before World War I, fought against romantic fuzziness and facile emotionalism in poetry. The movement developed simultaneously on both sides of the Atlantic, and its early members included Amy Lowell, Richard Aldington, Hilda Doolittle, John Gould Fletcher, and F. S. Flint. As Flint explained in an article in March, 1913, Imagists insisted on "direct treatment of the 'thing,' whether subjective or objective," on the avoidance of all words "that did not contribute to the presentation," and on a freer metrical movement than a strict adherence to "the sequence of a metronome" could allow. All this encouraged precision in imagery and freedom of rhythmic movement, but more was required for the production of poetry of any real scope and interest. Imagism went in for the short, sharply etched, descriptive lyric, but it had no technique for the production of longer and more complex poems. Other new ideas about poetry helped to provide this technique. Sir Herbert Grierson's great edition of the poems of John Donne in 1912 both reflected and helped to encourage a new enthusiasm for 17th-century metaphysical poetry. The revival of interest in metaphysical wit brought with it a desire on the part of some pioneering poets to introduce into their poetry a much higher degree of intellectual complexity than had been found among the Victorians or the Georgians. The full subtlety of French Symbolist poetry also now came to be appreciated; it had been admired in the 90's, but for its dreamy suggestiveness rather than for its imagistic precision and complexity. At the same time a need was felt to bring poetic language and rhythms closer to those of conversation, or at least to spice the formalities of poetic utterance with echoes of the colloquial and even the slangy. Irony, which made possible several levels of discourse simultaneously, and wit, with the use of puns (banished from serious poetry for over 200 years), helped to achieve that union of thought and passion which T. S. Eliot, in his review of Grierson's anthology of metaphysical poetry (1921), saw as characteristic of the metaphysicals and wished to bring back into modern poetry. A new critical and a new creative movement in poetry went hand in hand, with Eliot the high priest of both. It was Eliot who extended the scope of Imagism by bringing the English metaphysicals and the French Symbolists (as well as the English Jacobean dramatists) to the rescue, thus adding new criteria of complexity and allusiveness to the criteria of concreteness and precision stressed by the Imagists. It was Eliot, too, who introduced into modern English and American poetry the kind of irony achieved by shifting suddenly from the formal to the colloquial or by oblique allusions to objects or ideas that contrasted sharply with those carried by the surface meaning of the poem. Thus between, say, 1911 (the first year of the Georgian poets) and 1922 (the year of the publication of *The Waste Land*) a major revolution occurred in English—and for that matter American—poetic theory and practice—a revolution which determined the way in which most serious poets and critics now think about their art. If one compares the poems in Palgrave's *Golden Treasury*, a Victorian anthology which was still used as a basic school text in Britain in the 1930's, with those in a number of academic anthologies of the mid-20th century, the change in poetic taste will become startlingly apparent. In the critical discussion, if not always in the allotment of space, Donne rather than Spenser becomes the great poet of the 16th- and 17th-century period; Gerard Manley Hopkins replaces Tennyson as the great 19th-century poet; and in general what one might call the metaphysical-Symbolist tradition predominates over both the cultivated self-pity of the Romantic-Victorian tradition and the Platonic-meditative strain of both the Elizabethans and (in his own way) Wordsworth.

The posthumous publication by Robert Bridges in 1918 of the poetry of Gerard Manley Hopkins encouraged further experimentation in language and rhythms. Hopkins combined absolute precision of the individual image with a complex ordering of images and a new kind of metrical patterning. The young poets of the early 1930's—W. H. Auden, Stephen Spender, C. Day Lewis—were much influenced by Hopkins as well as by Eliot (now the presiding genius of modern English and American poetry) and by a variety of other poets from the 16th-century John Skelton to Wilfred Owen. And even when the almost flamboyant new tones of Dylan Thomas were first sounded in the late 1930's, the influence of Hopkins could still be heard. It is only since World War II that a new generation of young English poets (including Donald Davie, Elizabeth Jennings, and Philip Larkin), searching for what has been called "purity of diction," have turned away from both the 17th century and the poetry of Hopkins and Eliot to seek a poetry which avoids all kinds of verbal excess in its desire for quiet luminosity and unpretentious truth.

Meanwhile the remarkable career of W. B. Yeats, stretching across the whole modern period, showed how a truly great poet can at the same time reflect the varying developments of his age and maintain an unmistakably individual accent. Beginning among the aesthetes of the 90's, turning later to a more tough and spare ironic language without losing his characteristic verbal magic, working out his own notions of symbolism and bringing them in different ways into his poetry, developing in his full maturity a rich symbolic and metaphysical poetry with its own curiously haunting cadences and its imagery both shockingly realistic and movingly suggestive, Yeats's work is itself a history of English poetry between 1890 and 1939. Yet he is always Yeats, unique and inimitable—without doubt the greatest English-speaking poet of his age.

NEW METHODS IN FICTION

One can trace three major influences on the changes in attitude and technique in the modern novel. The first is the novelist's realization that the general background of belief which united him with his public in a common sense of what was significant in experience had disappeared. The public values of the Victorian novel, in which major crises of plot could be shown through changes in the social or financial or marital status of the chief characters, gave way to more personally conceived notions of value, dependent on the novelist's intuitions and sensibilities rather than on public agreement. "To believe that your impressions hold good for others," Virginia Woolf once wrote (discussing Jane Austen), "is to be released from the cramp and confinement of personality." The modern novelist could no longer believe this: he had to fall back on personality, drawing his criterion of significance in human affairs (and thus his principle of selection) from his own intuitions, so that he needed to find ways of convincing the reader that his own private sense of what was significant in experience was truly valid. A new technical burden was thus imposed on the novelist's prose, for it had now to build up a world of values instead of drawing on an existing world of values. Virginia Woolf tried to solve the problem by using some of the devices of poetry in order to suggest the novelist's own sense of value and vision of the world. Joyce, on the other hand, made no attempt to convey a single personal attitude, but reacted to the breakdown of public values by employing a kind of writing so multiple in its implications that it conveyed numerous points of view simultaneously, the author being totally objective and committed to none of them—a mode which required remarkable technical virtuosity.

The second influence on the changes in attitude and technique in the modern novel was a new view of time; time was not a series of chronological moments to be presented by the novelist in sequence with an occasional deliberate retrospect ("this reminded him of," "he recalled that"), but as a continuous flow in the consciousness of the individual, with the "already" continuously merging into the "not yet" and retrospect merging into anticipation. This influence is closely bound up with a third: the new notions of the nature of consciousness, which derived in a general way from Sigmund Freud and Carl Jung but were also part of the spirit of the age and discernible even in those novelists who had not read either psychologist. Consciousness is multiple; the past is always present in it at some level and is continually coloring one's present reaction. Marcel Proust in France, in his great novel sequence *Remembrance of Things*

Past (1913–28), had explored the ways in which the past impinges on the present and consciousness is determined by memory. The view that a man *is* his memories, that his present is the sum of his past, that if we dig into a man's consciousness we can tell the whole truth about him without waiting for a chronological sequence of time to take him through a series of testing circumstances, inevitably led to a technical revolution in the novel. For now, by exploring in depth into consciousness and memory rather than proceeding lengthwise along the dimension of time, a novelist could write a novel concerned ostensibly with only one day of the hero's life (Joyce's *Ulysses* and Virginia Woolf's *Mrs. Dalloway*). This view of multiple levels of consciousness existing simultaneously, coupled with the view of time as a constant flow rather than a series of separate moments, meant that a novelist preferred to plunge into the consciousness of his characters in order to tell his story rather than to provide an external framework of chronological narrative. The "stream-of-consciousness" technique, where the author tries to render directly the very fabric of his character's consciousness without reporting it in formal, quoted remarks, was developed in the 1920's as an important new technique of the English novel. It made for more difficult reading, at least for those accustomed only to the methods of the older English novel. No "porch" was constructed at the front of the novel to put the reader in possession of necessary preliminary information: such information emerged, as the novel progressed, from the consciousness of each character as it responded to the present with echoes of its past. No conventional signposts were put up to tell the reader where he was, for that was felt to interfere with the immediacy of the impression. But once the reader learns how to find his way in this unsignposted territory, he is rewarded by new delicacies of perception and new subtleties of presentation.

Concentration on the "stream of consciousness" and on the association of ideas within the individual consciousness led inevitably to stress on the essential loneliness of the individual. For all consciousnesses are unique and isolated, and if this unique, private world is the real world in which men live, if the public values to which they must pay lip service in the social world in which they move are not the real values which give meaning to their personality, then each man is condemned to live in the prison of his own incommunicable consciousness. How is true communication possible in such a world? The public gestures imposed upon us by society never correspond to our real inward needs. They are conventional in the bad sense, mechanical, imposing a crude standardization on the infinite subtlety of experience. If we do try to give out a sign from our real selves, that sign is bound to be misunderstood when read by some other self in the light of that self's quite other personality. The theme of such modern fiction is thus the possibility of love, the establishment of emotional communication, in a community of private consciousnesses. This, is, in different ways, the theme of Joyce, of Lawrence, of Virginia Woolf, and of Forster, and (on a rather different scale and not always so directly) of Conrad. The search for communion and the inevitable isolation of Leopold Bloom in *Ulysses* is symbolic of the human condition as seen by the modern novelist. Similar investigations of this basic condition are Forster's explorations of the conventions which seem to be helps to living but which in fact prevent true human contacts, and Virginia Woolf's delicate projections of the relation between the self's need for privacy and the self's need for genuine communication. The theme of all Lawrence's novels is human relationships, the ideal of which he restlessly explored with shifting emphasis throughout his career; such relationships can be all too easily distorted by the mechanical conventions of society, by notions of respectability or propriety, by all the shams and frauds of middle-class life, by the demands of power or money or success. One might almost say that the greatest modern novels are about the difficulty, and at the same time the inevitability, of being human. The dilemma of the human condition is never really solved in these novelists; but knowledge that the dilemma is shared—a knowledge so brilliantly conveyed in *Ulysses* and so wryly proffered by Forster—can both illuminate and comfort.

THE DRAMA

Modern drama begins in a sense with the witty drawing-room comedies of Oscar Wilde; yet Wilde founded no dramatic school. His wit was personal and irresponsible, unlike the wit of Restoration comedy, which reflected an attitude to the relation between the sexes which was part of a view of society held by a whole (if a small) social class. Bernard Shaw brought still another kind of wit into drama—not Wilde's exhibitionist sparkle nor yet the assured sophistication of the Restoration dramatists, but the provocative paradox that was meant to tease and disturb, to challenge the complacency of the audience. Shaw's discussion plays were given dramatic life through the mastery of theatrical techniques which he learned during his years as a dramatic critic. In his general attitudes Shaw represents the anti-Victorianism of the late Victorians; his long life should not obscure the fact that his first—and some of his best—plays belong to the 90's. Other attempts by 20th-century dramatists to debate social questions on the stage—by Galsworthy, for example—deserve respect for their humanity and intelligence and sometimes for their theatrical craftsmanship, but they lack Shaw's verbal and intellectual brilliance and his superb capacity to entertain. We must turn to Ireland to find another really impressive variety of dramatic activity. The Irish Literary Theatre was founded in 1899, with Yeats's early play *The Countess Cathleen* as its first production. The founders—Yeats, Lady Gregory, George Moore, and Edward Martyn—wanted to make a contribution to an Irish literary revival, but they were influenced also by the Independent Theatre in London, founded in 1891 by J. T. Grein in order to encourage new developments in the drama. In 1902 the Irish Literary Theatre was able to maintain a permanent all-Irish company and changed its name to the Irish National Theatre, which moved in 1904 to the Abbey Theatre, by which name it has since been known. Many of the plays produced at the Abbey Theatre were only of local and ephemeral interest, but J. M. Synge's use of the speech and imagination of Irish country people, Yeats's powerful symbolic use of themes from old Irish legend, and Sean O'Casey's use of the Irish civil war as a background for plays combining tragic melodrama, humor of character, and irony of circumstance, brought new kinds of vitality to the theater. T. S. Eliot attempted with considerable success to revive a ritual poetic drama in England with his *Murder in the Cathedral* (1935). His later attempts to combine religious symbolism with the box-office appeal of amusing society comedy (as in *The Cocktail Party*, 1950), though impressive technical achievements, were not wholly successful: the combination of contemporary social chatter with profound religious symbolism produces an unevenness of tone and disturbing shifts in levels of realism. Elsewhere in modern drama the conflict between realism and symbolism (first clearly seen in Ibsen) is acted out in a variety of ways.

BRITISH-AMERICAN LITERARY RELATIONS

The relationship between British and American literature has been closer in the present century than at any other time. It is true that American dependence on English literature in earlier periods resulted in a certain kind of closeness of relationship, but the really individual American writers—Walt Whitman, Herman Melville, Mark Twain, for example—turned deliberately away from the English literary scene in order to avoid this dependence. Henry James, who lived mainly in England from 1876 until his death in 1916, becoming a British citizen in 1915, was a pioneer in the development of what might be called an Anglo-American sensibility. The American poet Robert Frost lived in England from 1912 to 1915, published his first book of poems there, and had a close literary and personal association with the English poet Edward Thomas. A more revolutionary American poet, Ezra Pound, lived in England from 1908 to 1920, and it was from England that he launched the Imagist movement, which proved equally influential on both sides of the Atlantic. In the modern period most of the significant literary movements have been common to the two countries; indeed, the most significant movement of all—the revolution in poetic taste and practice associated with the work of T. S. Eliot—was an Anglo-American phenomenon. The American Eliot turned British subject and the English Auden turned American citizen are symbolic of the whole literary situation—as is I. A. Richards, who, after years in Cambridge, England, now teaches at Harvard in Cambridge, Massachusetts. In poetry and criticism, at least, the modern achievement has been in considerable degree Anglo-American (although the individuality and uniqueness of each poet is, of course, undeniable—Yeats on one side of the Atlantic and Wallace Stevens on the other, for example).

THOMAS HARDY
(1840–1928)

1872–96: Career as novelist, ending with *Jude the Obscure.*
1898:   *Wessex Poems*, first collection of poetry.

Thomas Hardy was born near Dorchester, in that area of southwest England that he was to make the "Wessex" of his novels. He attended local schools until the age of 15, when he was articled to a Dorchester architect with whom he worked for six years. In 1861 he went to London to continue his studies and to practice as an architect. Meanwhile he was completing his general education informally through his own erratic reading, and becoming more and more interested in both fiction and poetry. After some early attempts at writing both short stories and poems, he decided to concentrate on fiction. His first novel was rejected by the publishers in 1868 on the advice of George Meredith, who nevertheless advised Hardy to write another. The result was *Desperate Remedies*, published anonymously in 1871, followed the next year by his first real success (also published anonymously), *Under the Greenwood Tree*. Hardy's career as a novelist was now well launched; he gave up his architectural work and produced a series of novels that ended with *Jude the Obscure* in 1896. The hostile reception of this novel sent him back to poetry. His remarkable epic-drama of the Napoleonic Wars, *The Dynasts*, came out in three parts between 1903 and 1908; after this he wrote mostly lyric poetry.

Hardy's novels, set in a predominantly rural "Wessex," show the forces of nature outside and inside man combining to shape human destiny. Against a background of immemorial agricultural labor, with ancient monuments such as Stonehenge or an old Roman amphitheater reminding us of the human past, he presents characters at the mercy of their own passions or finding temporary salvation in the age-old rhythms of rural work or rural recreation. Men in Hardy's fiction are not masters of their fates; they are at the mercy of the indifferent forces which manipulate their behavior and their relations with others; but they can achieve dignity through endurance, and heroism through simple strength of character. The characteristic Victorian novelist—e.g., Dickens and Thackeray—was concerned with the behavior and problems of men in a given social milieu, which he described in detail; Hardy preferred to go directly for the elemental in human behavior with a minimum of contemporary social detail. Most of Hardy's novels are tragic, though *Under the Greenwood Tree* has an idyllic character possessed by no other of his novels. But even here the happy ending is achieved only by ending the story with the marriage of the hero and heroine and refusing to go further; the texture of the narrative, for all its moments of gaiety and charm, has already suggested the bitter ironies of which life is capable. His later work explores those ironies with sometimes an almost malevolent staging of coincidence in order to emphasize the disparity between human desire and ambition on the one hand and what fate has in store for the characters on the other. But fate is not a wholly external force. Men are driven by the demands of their own nature as much as by anything from outside them. *Tess of the D'Urbervilles* (1891) is the story of an intelligent and sensitive girl, daughter of a poor family, driven to murder and so to death by hanging, by a concatenation of events and circumstances so bitterly ironic that many readers find it the darkest of Hardy's novels, while others would award that distinction to *Jude the Obscure*, the disturbingly powerful account of an ambitious rustic trapped between his intellect and his sensuality and as a result delivered to destruction.

Hardy himself denied that he was a pessimist, calling himself a "meliorist," i.e., one who believes that the world may be made better by human effort. But there is little sign of "meliorism" in either his most important novels or his lyric poetry. In his poems—which alone are represented here because no extract could do justice to Hardy's power as a novelist—many of his characteristic attitudes and ideas and many of his favorite situations can be found. A number of his poems are verse anecdotes illustrating the perversity of fate, the disastrous or ironic coincidence. But his best poems go beyond this mood to present with quiet gravity and a carefully controlled elegiac feeling some aspect of human sorrow or loss or frustration or regret, always projected through a particular, fully realized situation. *Hap* shows Hardy in the characteristic mood of complaining about the irony of human destiny in a universe ruled by chance; but a poem such as *The Walk* (one of a group of poems written after the death of his first wife in 1912) gives, with remarkable power, concrete embodiment to a sense of loss. That power—we see it also in *A Broken Appointment* and *She Hears the Storm*—is achieved through a kind of verbal as well as an emotional integrity. Hardy's poetry, like his prose, often has a self-taught air about it; both can be odd or pretentious or awkward or clumsy. But at their best both his poetry and his prose have an air of persuasive authenticity. The association of a given emotion with particular visual memories in *Neutral Tones*, for example, is impressive because it carries such extraordinary conviction; and it carries that conviction because the rhythms and rhymes are handled so as to suggest the kind of utterance actually wrung from the poet (consider, e.g., the curious dead fall of "They had fallen from an ash, and were gray"). At the same time, Hardy will use an antique or a poetic word or phrase ("thereby," "a-wing") if it fits in with the movement of the poem and keeps him from having to stop and search for something more deft: the result is an effect not of artificiality but of spontaneity. Hardy's use of ballad rhythms often helps to give an elemental quality to his poetry, suggesting that this incident or situation, carefully particularized though it is, nevertheless stands for some profound and recurring themes in human experience.

Sometimes in Hardy's poetry the quiet lilt of the verse and the fall of the rhymes convey a deep but controlled emotion, as in *Drummer Hodge*, where the sense of a simple English soldier buried in a far distant land and mingling with an earth that will produce vegetation so different from anything known in England is poignantly expressed. *In Time of "The Breaking of Nations"* conveys with stark clarity the same awareness of the processes of nature continuing in spite of cataclysms caused by human folly in the novels. The sadness in Hardy—his inability to believe in the government of the world by a benevolent God, his sense of the waste and frustration involved in human life, his insistent irony when faced with moral or metaphysical questions—is part of the late Victorian mood. We can see something like it in A. E. Housman, and there is an earlier version of Victorian pessimism in Edward FitzGerald's *Rubáiyát of Omar Khayyám*, published when Hardy was 19. Yet Hardy's characteristic themes and attitudes cannot be related simply to the reaction to new scientific and philosophical ideas (Darwin's theory of evolution, for example) that we see in so many forms in late 19th-century literature. The favorite poetic mood of both Tennyson and Arnold was also an elegiac one (e.g., in Tennyson's *Break, Break, Break* and Arnold's *Dover Beach*), but this is not Hardy's mood. The sad-sweet cadences of Victorian self-pity are not to be found in Hardy's poetry, which is sterner, as though braced by a long look at the worst. It is this sternness—sometimes amounting to ruggedness—together with his verbal and emotional integrity, his refusal ever to surrender to mere poetic fashion, his quietly searching individual accent, that has helped to bring about the steady rise in Hardy's poetic reputation in recent years, so that today he is regarded not only as a distinguished novelist but also as a great English poet.

Hap[1]

If but some vengeful god would call to me
From up the sky, and laugh: "Thou suffering thing,
Know that thy sorrow is my ecstasy,
That thy love's loss is my hate's profiting!"

Then would I bear it, clench myself, and die,   5
Steeled by the sense of ire unmerited;
Half-eased in that a Powerfuller than I
Had willed and meted me the tears I shed.

But not so. How arrives it joy lies slain,
And why unblooms the best hope ever sown?   10
—Crass Casualty obstructs the sun and rain,
And dicing Time for gladness casts a moan. . . .
These purblind Doomsters[2] had as readily strown
Blisses about my pilgrimage as pain.

1866   1898

The Impercipient

(AT A CATHEDRAL SERVICE)

That with this bright believing band
        I have no claim to be,
That faiths by which my comrades stand
        Seem fantasies to me,

1. I.e., chance (as also "Casualty," line 11).
2. Half-blind judges.

And mirage-mists their Shining Land,
    Is a strange destiny.

Why thus my soul should be consigned
    To infelicity,
Why always I must feel as blind
    To sights my brethren see,
Why joys they've found I cannot find,
    Abides a mystery.

Since heart of mine knows not that ease
    Which they know; since it be
That He who breathes All's Well to these
    Breathes no All's-Well to me,
My lack might move their sympathies
    And Christian charity!

I am like a gazer who should mark
    An inland company
Standing upfingered, with, "Hark! hark!
    The glorious distant sea!"
And feel, "Alas, 'tis but yon dark
    And wind-swept pine to me!"

Yet I would bear my shortcomings
    With meet tranquillity,
But for the charge that blessed things
    I'd liefer not have be.
O, doth a bird deprived of wings
    Go earth-bound willfully!

  .   .   .   .   .

Enough. As yet disquiet clings
    About us. Rest shall we.

                                    1898

Neutral Tones

We stood by a pond that winter day,
And the sun was white, as though chidden of God,
And a few leaves lay on the starving sod;
        —They had fallen from an ash, and were gray.

Your eyes on me were as eyes that rove
Over tedious riddles of years ago;
And some words played between us to and fro
        On which lost the more by our love.

The smile on your mouth was the deadest thing
Alive enough to have strength to die;

And a grin of bitterness swept thereby
    Like an ominous bird a-wing. . . .
Since then, keen lessons that love deceives,
And wrings with wrong, have shaped to me
Your face, and the God-cursed sun, and a tree,   15
    And a pond edged with grayish leaves.

1867   1898

I Look into My Glass

I look into my glass,
And view my wasting skin,
And say, "Would God it came to pass
My heart had shrunk as thin!"

For then, I, undistressed   5
By hearts grown cold to me,
Could lonely wait my endless rest
With equanimity.

But Time, to make me grieve,
Part steals, lets part abide;   10
And shakes this fragile frame at eve
With throbbings of noontide.

                                        1898

A Broken Appointment

        You did not come,
And marching Time drew on, and wore me numb.—
Yet less for loss of your dear presence there
Than that I thus found lacking in your make
That high compassion which can overbear   5
Reluctance for pure loving-kindness' sake
Grieved I, when, as the hope-hour stroked its sum,
        You did not come.

        You love not me,
And love alone can lend you loyalty;   10
—I know and knew it. But, unto the store
Of human deeds divine in all but name,
Was it not worth a little hour or more
To add yet this: Once you, a woman, came
To soothe a time-torn man; even though it be   15
        You love not me?

                                        1902

Drummer Hodge

1

They throw in Drummer Hodge, to rest
    Uncoffined—just as found:
His landmark is a kopje-crest[1]
    That breaks the veldt around;
And foreign constellations west[2]   5
    Each night above his mound.

2

Young Hodge the Drummer never knew—
    Fresh from his Wessex home—
The meaning of the broad Karoo,[3]
    The Bush, the dusty loam,   10
And why uprose to nightly view
    Strange stars amid the gloam.

3

Yet portion of that unknown plain
    Will Hodge forever be;
His homely Northern breast and brain   15
    Grow to some Southern tree,
And strange-eyed constellations reign
    His stars eternally.

1902

Lausanne[4]

IN GIBBON'S OLD GARDEN: 11–12 P.M.

JUNE 27, 1897

(*The 110th anniversary of the completion of the* Decline *and* Fall *at the same hour and place*)

A spirit seems to pass,
Formal in pose, but grave withal and grand:
He contemplates a volume in his hand,
And far lamps fleck him through the thin acacias.

1. South African Dutch (Afrikaans) word for a small hill. "Veldt": Afrikaans for a plain or prairie. The poem is a lament for an English soldier killed in the Boer War (1899–1902).
2. Set. The "foreign constellations" are those visible only in the southern hemisphere.
3. A dry table-land region in South Africa (usually spelled "Karroo"). "The Bush": British Colonial word for an uncleared area of land.
4. Edward Gibbon finished his monumental *History of the Decline and Fall of the Roman Empire* (6 vols., 1776–88) in Lausanne, Switzerland, where he lived from 1783 until his death. Gibbon records in his *Memoirs of My Life and Writings* that "It was on the day, or rather night, of the 27th of June, 1787, that I wrote the last lines of the last page, in a summer-house in my garden," and goes on to describe his emotions on having completed his life's work. Gibbon, a skeptic, saw himself fighting for truth against prejudice and superstition.

           Anon the book is closed,   5
     With "It is finished!" And at the alley's end
     He turns, and when on me his glances bend
As from the Past comes speech—small, muted, yet composed.

           "How fares the Truth now?—Ill?
     —Do pens but slily further her advance?   10
     May one not speed her but in phrase askance?[5]
Do scribes aver the Comic to be Reverend still?[6]

           "Still rule those minds on earth
     At whom sage Milton's wormwood words were hurled:
     'Truth like a bastard comes into the world   15
Never without ill fame to him who gives her birth'?"[7]
1897   1902

The Darkling[1] Thrush

     I leant upon a coppice gate[2]
         When Frost was specter-gray,
     And Winter's dregs made desolate
         The weakening eye of day.
     The tangled bine-stems[3] scored the sky   5
         Like strings of broken lyres,
     And all mankind that haunted nigh
         Had sought their household fires.

     The land's sharp features seemed to be
         The Century's corpse[4] outleant,   10
     His crypt the cloudy canopy,
         The wind his death-lament.
     The ancient pulse of germ and birth
         Was shrunken hard and dry,
     And every spirit upon earth   15
         Seemed fervorless as I.

     At once a voice arose among
         The bleak twigs overhead
     In a fullhearted evensong
         Of joy illimited;   20
     An aged thrush, frail, gaunt, and small,
         In blast-beruffled plume,
     Had chosen thus to fling his soul
         Upon the growing gloom.

5. Oblique.
6. I.e., do theological writers still claim respect for what is ridiculous on the grounds that it is ancient and venerable?
7. From Milton's *Areopagitica* (1644), defending liberty of the press.

1. In the dark.
2. Gate leading to a small wood or thicket.
3. Twining stems of shrubs.
4. This poem was written on December 31, 1900. the last day of the 19th century.

So little cause for carolings   25
    Of such ecstatic sound
Was written on terrestrial things
    Afar or nigh around,
That I could think there trembled through
    His happy good-night air   30
Some blessed Hope, whereof he knew
    And I was unaware.

1900   1902

A Trampwoman's Tragedy

(182–)

1

From Wynyard's Gap [1] the livelong day,
    The livelong day,
We beat afoot the northward way
    We had traveled times before.
The sun-blaze burning on our backs,   5
Our shoulders sticking to our packs,
By fosseway,[2] fields, and turnpike tracks
    We skirted sad Sedge-Moor.

2

Full twenty miles we jaunted on,
    We jaunted on—   10
My fancy-man, and jeering John,
    And Mother Lee, and I.
And, as the sun drew down to west,
We climbed the toilsome Poldon [3] crest,
And saw, of landskip sights the best,   15
    The inn that beamed thereby.

3

For months we had padded side by side,
    Ay, side by side
Through the Great Forest, Blackmoor wide,
    And where the Parret ran.   20
We'd faced the gusts on Mendip ridge,
Had crossed the Yeo unhelped by bridge,
Been stung by every Marshwood midge,
    I and my fancy-man.

1. The places here named are in Somerset, in southwest England on the northern edge of the area which Hardy called "Wessex" and of which his native Dorset, the county south and southwest of Somerset, reaching to the English Channel, was the major part.
2. Path running along a ditch. See note 4 below.
3. Sad (line 8) because of the Battle of Sedgemoor (1685) when the rebellion of the Duke of Monmouth against James II was crushed with excessive cruelty. "This plain [Sedgemoor], intersected by ditches known as *rhines,* * * * is broken by isolated hills and lower ridges, of which the most conspicuous are Brent Knoll near Burnham, the Isle of Avalon, rising with Glastonbury Tor as its highest point, and the long low ridge of Polden ending to the west in a steep bluff." *Encyclopaedia Britannica,* 11th edition, 1911.

4

Lone inns we loved, my man and I,   25
  My man and I;
"King's Stag," "Windwhistle" [4] high and dry,
  "The Horse" on Hintock Green.
The cosy house at Wynyard's Gap,
"The Hut" renowned on Bredy Knap,   30
And many another wayside tap
  Where folk might sit unseen.

5

Now as we trudged—O deadly day,
  O deadly day!—
I teased my fancy-man in play   35
  And wanton idleness.
I walked alongside jeering John,
I laid his hand my waist upon;
I would not bend my glances on
  My lover's dark distress.   40

6

Thus Poldon top at last we won,
  At last we won,
And gained the inn at sink of sun
  Far-famed as "Marshal's Elm."[5]
Beneath us figured tor and lea,   45
From Mendip to the western sea—
I doubt if finer sight there be
  Within this royal realm.

7

Inside the settle all a-row—
  All four a-row   50
We sat, I next to John, to show
  That he had wooed and won.
And then he took me on his knee,
And swore it was his turn to be
My favored mate, and Mother Lee   55
  Passed to my former one.

8

Then in a voice I had never heard,
  I had never heard,
My only Love to me: "One word,
  My lady, if you please!   60
Whose is the child you are like to bear?—
His? After all my months o' care?"
God knows 'twas not! But, O despair!
  I nodded—still to tease.

4. "The highness and dryness of Windwhistle Inn was impressed upon the writer two or three years ago, when, after climbing on a hot afternoon to the beautiful spot near which it stands and entering the inn for tea, he was informed by the landlady that none could be had, unless he would fetch water from a valley half a mile off, the house containing not a drop, owing to its situation. However, a tantalizing row of full barrels behind her back testified to a wetness of a certain sort, which was not at that time desired" [Hardy's note].
5. " 'Marshal's Elm,' so picturesquely situated, is no longer an inn, though the house, or part of it, still remains. It used to exhibit a fine old swinging sign" [Hardy's note].

9

Then up he sprung, and with his knife—   65
    And with his knife
He let out jeering Johnny's life,
    Yes; there, at set of sun.
The slant ray through the window nigh
Gilded John's blood and glazing eye,   70
Ere scarcely Mother Lee and I
    Knew that the deed was done.

10

The taverns tell the gloomy tale,
    The gloomy tale,
How that at Ivel-chester jail   75
    My Love, my sweetheart swung;
Though stained till now by no misdeed
Save one horse ta'en in time o' need;
(Blue Jimmy stole right many a steed
    Ere his last fling he flung).[6]   80

11

Thereaft I walked the world alone,
    Alone, alone!
On his death-day I gave my groan
    And dropt his dead-born child.
'Twas nigh the jail, beneath a tree,   85
None tending me; for Mother Lee
Had died at Glaston, leaving me
    Unfriended on the wild.

12

And in the night as I lay weak,
    As I lay weak,   90
The leaves a-falling on my cheek,
    The red moon low declined—
The ghost of him I'd die to kiss
Rose up and said: "Ah, tell me this!
Was the child mine, or was it his?   95
    Speak, that I rest may find!"

13

O doubt not but I told him then,
    I told him then,
That I had kept me from all men
    Since we joined lips and swore.   100
Whereat he smiled, and thinned away
As the wind stirred to call up day . . .
    —'Tis past! And here alone I stray
    Haunting the Western Moor.

April, 1902   1909

6. " 'Blue Jimmy' was a notorious horse stealer of Wessex in those days, who appropriated more than a hundred horses before he was caught, among others one belonging to a neighbor of the writer's grandfather. He was hanged at the now demolished Ivel-chester or Ilchester jail above mentioned—that building formerly of so many sinister associations in the minds of the local peasantry, and the continual haunt of fever, which at last led to its condemnation. Its site is now an innocent-looking green meadow" [Hardy's note].

Let Me Enjoy

(MINOR KEY)

1

Let me enjoy the earth no less
Because the all-enacting Might
That fashioned forth its loveliness
Had other aims than my delight.

2

About my path there flits a Fair, 5
Who throws me not a word or sign;
I'll charm me with her ignoring air,
And laud the lips not meant for mine.

3

From manuscripts of moving song
Inspired by scenes and dreams unknown 10
I'll pour out raptures that belong
To others, as they were my own.

4

And some day hence, towards Paradise
And all its blest—if such should be—
I will lift glad, afar-off eyes, 15
Though it contain no place for me.

1909

The Rash Bride

AN EXPERIENCE OF THE MELLSTOCK QUIRE[1]

1

We Christmas-caroled down the Vale, and up the Vale, and
round the Vale,
We played and sang that night as we were yearly wont to do—
A carol in a minor key, a carol in the major D,
Then at each house: "Good wishes: many Christmas joys to you!"

2

Next, to the widow's John and I and all the rest drew on.
And I 5
Discerned that John could hardly hold the tongue of him for joy.
The widow was a sweet young thing whom John was bent on
marrying,
And quiring at her casement seemed romantic to the boy.

3

"She'll make reply, I trust," said he, "to our salute? She must!"
said he,
"And then I will accost her gently—much to her surprise!— 10
For knowing not I am with you here, when I speak up and call
her dear
A tenderness will fill her voice, a bashfulness her eyes."

4

So, by her window-square we stood; ay, with our lanterns there
we stood,

1. Choir.

And he along with us—not singing, waiting for a sign;
And when we'd quired her carols three a light was lit and out
    looked she,   15
A shawl about her bedgown, and her color red as wine.

5

And sweetly then she bowed her thanks, and smiled, and
    spoke aloud her thanks;
When lo, behind her back there, in the room, a man appeared.
I knew him—one from Woolcomb way—Giles Swetman—
    honest as the day,
But eager, hasty; and I felt that some strange trouble neared.   20

6

"How comes he there? . . . Suppose," said we, "she's wed of
    late! Who knows?" said we.
—"She married yestermorning—only mother yet has known
The secret o't!" shrilled one small boy. "But now I've told,
    let's wish 'em joy!"
A heavy fall aroused us: John had gone down like a stone.

7

We rushed to him and caught him round, and lifted him, and
    brought him round,   25
When, hearing something wrong had happened, oped the
    window she:
"Has one of you fallen ill?" she asked, "by these night
    labors overtasked?"
None answered. That she'd done poor John a cruel turn felt we.

8

Till up spoke Michael: "Fie, young dame! You've broke your
    promise, sly young dame,
By forming this new tie, young dame, and jilting John so true,   30
Who trudged tonight to sing to 'ee because he thought he'd
    bring to 'ee
Good wishes as your coming spouse. May ye such trifling rue!"

9

Her man had said no word at all; but being behind had heard
    it all,
And now cried: "Neighbors, on my soul I knew not 'twas
    like this!"
And then to her: "If I had known you'd had in tow not me
    alone,   35
No wife should you have been of mine. It is a dear bought bliss!"

10

She changed death-white, and heaved a cry: we'd never heard
    so grieved a cry
As came from her at this from him: heartbroken quite seemed
    she;
And suddenly, as we looked on, she turned, and rushed; and
    she was gone,
Whither, her husband, following after, knew not; nor knew we.   40

11

We searched till dawn about the house; within the house,
    without the house,

We searched among the laurel boughs that grew beneath the
  wall,
And then among the crocks and things, and stores for winter
  junketings,
In linhay,[2] loft, and dairy; but we found her not at all.

12

Then John rushed in: "O friends," he said, "hear this, this,
  this!" and bends his head: 45
"I've—searched round by the—*well*, and find the cover open
  wide!
I am fearful that—I can't say what . . . Bring lanterns, and
  some cords to knot."
We did so, and we went and stood the deep dark hole beside.

13

And then they, ropes in hand, and I—ay, John, and all the
  band, and I
Let down a lantern to the depths—some hundred feet and
  more;   50
It glimmered like a fog-dimmed star; and there, beside its light,
  afar,
White drapery floated, and we knew the meaning that it bore.

14

The rest is naught. . . . We buried her o' Sunday. Neighbors
  carried her;
And Swetman—he who'd married her—now miserablest
  of men,
Walked mourning first; and then walked John; just quivering,
  but composed anon;   55
And we the quire formed round the grave, as was the custom
  then.

15

Our old bass player, as I recall—his white hair blown—but why
  recall!—
His viol upstrapped, bent figure—doomed to follow her full
  soon—
Stood bowing, pale and tremulous; and next to him the rest
  of us. . . .
We sang the Ninetieth Psalm [3] to her—set to Saint Stephen's
  tune.   60

1909

One We Knew

(M. H.[4] 1772–1857)

She told how they used to form for the country dances—
  "The Triumph," "The New-rigged Ship"—
To the light of the guttering wax in the paneled manses
  And in cots to the blink of a dip.[5]

---

2. Shed.
3. A favorite psalm at funerals, contrasting God's eternity with the brevity
of human life.

4. Hardy's grandmother.
5. I.e., in cottages by the light of a
candle.

She spoke of the wild "poussetting" and "allemanding" [6]   5
   On carpet, on oak, and on sod;
And the two long rows of ladies and gentlemen standing,
   And the figures the couples trod.

She showed us the spot where the maypole was yearly planted,
   And where the bandsmen stood   10
While breeched and kerchiefed partners whirled, and panted
   To choose each other for good.

She told of that far-back day when they learnt astounded
   Of the death of the King of France:
Of the Terror; and then of Bonaparte's unbounded   15
   Ambition and arrogance.

Of how his threats woke warlike preparations
   Along the southern strand,
And how each night brought tremors and trepidations
   Lest morning should see him land.   20

She said she had often heard the gibbet creaking
   As it swayed in the lightning flash,
Had caught from the neighboring town a small child's shrieking
   At the cart tail under the lash. . . .

With cap-framed face and long gaze into the embers—   25
   We seated around her knees—
She would dwell on such dead themes, not as one who remembers,
   But rather as one who sees.

She seemed one left behind of a band gone distant
   So far that no tongue could hail: 30
Past things retold were to her as things existent,
   Things present but as a tale.
May 20, 1902   1909

She Hears the Storm

   There was a time in former years—
      While my rooftree was his—
   When I should have been distressed by fears
      At such a night as this!

   I should have murmured anxiously,   5
      "The pricking rain strikes cold;
   His road is bare of hedge or tree,
      And he is getting old."

   But now the fitful chimney-roar,
      The drone of Thorncombe trees,   10

6. To pousette is to dance round with hands joined; allemande is the name of a dance originating in Germany.

The Froom in flood upon the moor,
    The mud of Mellstock Leaze,[7]

The candle slanting sooty wicked,
    The thuds upon the thatch,
The eaves-drops on the window flicked,   15
    The clacking garden-hatch,[8]

And what they mean to wayfarers,
    I scarcely heed or mind;
He has won that storm-tight roof of hers
    Which Earth grants all her kind.   20

                    1909

Channel Firing[1]

That night your great guns, unawares,
Shook all our coffins as we lay,
And broke the chancel window-squares,
We thought it was the Judgment Day
And sat upright. While drearisome   5
Arose the howl of wakened hounds:
The mouse let fall the altar-crumb,
The worms drew back into the mounds,

The glebe cow[2] drooled. Till God called, "No;
It's gunnery practice out at sea   10
Just as before you went below;
The world is as it used to be:

"All nations striving strong to make
Red war yet redder. Mad as hatters
They do no more for Christés[3] sake   15
Than you who are helpless in such matters.

"That this is not the judgment hour
For some of them's a blessed thing,
For if it were they'd have to scour
Hell's floor for so much threatening. . . .   20

"Ha, ha. It will be warmer when
I blow the trumpet (if indeed
I ever do; for you are men,
And rest eternal sorely need)."

---

7. The place names in Hardy's fictional "Wessex" were often invented ("Thorncombe," "Mellstock Leaze"), but he also used the names of real locations, as in "A Trampwoman's Tragedy." The standard edition of Hardy's novels has a map of "Wessex" showing the locale of both the real and the invented names. "The Froom" is presumably the river Frome, flowing through Dorsetshire and Somerset.
8. Gate.

1. Written in April, 1914, when Anglo-German naval rivalry was growing steadily more acute; the title refers to gunnery practice in the English Channel. Four months later (August 4) World War I broke out.
2. I.e., cow on a small plot of land belonging to a cottage (a "glebe" is a small field).
3. The archaic spelling and pronunciation suggests a ballad note of doom.

So down we lay again. "I wonder,   25
Will the world ever saner be,"
Said one, "than when He sent us under
In our indifferent century!"

And many a skeleton shook his head.
"Instead of preaching forty year,"   30
My neighbor Parson Thirdly said,
"I wish I had stuck to pipes and beer."

Again the guns disturbed the hour,
Roaring their readiness to avenge,
As far inland as Stourton Tower,   35
And Camelot, and starlit Stonehenge.[4]

1914   1914

The Convergence of the Twain

(LINES ON THE LOSS OF THE "TITANIC")[1]

1

In a solitude of the sea
Deep from human vanity,
And the Pride of Life that planned her, stilly couches she.

2

Steel chambers, late the pyres
Of her salamandrine fires,[2]   5
Cold currents thrid, and turn to rhythmic tidal lyres.

3

Over the mirrors meant
To glass the opulent
The sea worm crawls—grotesque, slimed, dumb, indifferent.

4

Jewels in joy designed   10
To ravish the sensuous mind
Lie lightless, all their sparkles bleared and black and blind.

5

Dim moon-eyed fishes near
Gaze at the gilded gear
And query: "What does this vaingloriousness down here?" . . . 15

4. Again the "Wessex" place names
from various sources: Stonehenge is
the famous prehistoric stone circle on
Salisbury Plain; Camelot was the
legendary location of King Arthur's
court and the Round Table. There is
a real river Stour in Dorset, and a
town called Stour Head, which Hardy
calls "Stourton."
1. The *Titanic* was the largest and
most luxurious ocean liner of her day.
Considered unsinkable, she sank with
great loss of life on April 15, 1912,
on her maiden voyage from Southampton to America, after colliding with an
iceberg.
2. Probably "fires in which nothing
could survive" (although, since the
salamander is a lizardlike animal supposed to be able to live in fire, "salamandrine" usually means "able to resist or to live in fire"). In the next line,
"thrid" is the archaic past tense of
the verb "thread."

6

Well: while was fashioning
This creature of cleaving wing,
The Immanent Will[3] that stirs and urges everything

7

Prepared a sinister mate
For her—so gaily great—
A Shape of Ice, for the time far and dissociate.   20

8

And as the smart ship grew
In stature, grace, and hue,
In shadowy silent distance grew the Iceberg too.

9

Alien they seemed to be: 25
No mortal eye could see
The intimate welding of their later history,

10

Or sign that they were bent
By paths coincident
On being anon twin halves of one august event,   30

11

Till the Spinner of the Years
Said "Now!" And each one hears,
And consummation comes, and jars two hemispheres.

1912   1912, 1914

Ah, Are You Digging on My Grave?

"Ah, are you digging on my grave,
     My loved one?—planting rue?"[1]
—"No: yesterday he went to wed
One of the brightest wealth has bred.
'It cannot hurt her now,' he said,   5
     'That I should not be true.' "

"Then who is digging on my grave?
     My nearest dearest kin?"
—"Ah, no: they sit and think, 'What use!
What good will planting flowers produce?   10
No tendance of her mound can loose
     Her spirit from Death's gin.' "[2]

"But someone digs upon my grave?
     My enemy?—prodding sly?"
—"Nay: when she heard you had passed the Gate   15
That shuts on all flesh soon or late,
She thought you no more worth her hate,
     And cares not where you lie."

3. The force (blind, but slowly gaining consciousness throughout history)
which drives the world, according to
Hardy's philosophy.

1. A yellow-flowered herb, traditionally an emblem of sorrow ("rue" is
also an archaic word for "sorrow").
2. Trap.

"Then, who is digging on my grave?
  Say—since I have not guessed!"
—"O it is I, my mistress dear,   20
Your little dog, who still lives near,
And much I hope my movements here
  Have not disturbed your rest?"

"Ah yes! *You* dig upon my grave . . .
  Why flashed it not on me   25
That one true heart was left behind!
What feeling do we ever find
To equal among human kind
  A dog's fidelity!"   30

"Mistress, I dug upon your grave
  To bury a bone, in case
I should be hungry near this spot
When passing on my daily trot.
I am sorry, but I quite forgot   35
  It was your resting place."

             1914

Under the Waterfall

"Whenever I plunge my arm, like this,
In a basin of water, I never miss
The sweet sharp sense of a fugitive day
Fetched back from its thickening shroud of gray.
    Hence the only prime   5
    And real love-rhyme
    That I know by heart,
    And that leaves no smart,
Is the purl of a little valley fall
About three spans wide and two spans tall   10
Over a table of solid rock,
And into a scoop of the self-same block;
The purl of a runlet that never ceases
In stir of kingdoms, in wars, in peaces;
With a hollow boiling voice it speaks   15
And has spoken since hills were turfless peaks."

"And why gives this the only prime
Idea to you of a real love rhyme?
And why does plunging your arm in a bowl
Full of spring water, bring throbs to your soul?"   20

"Well, under the fall, in a crease of the stone,
Though where precisely none ever has known,
Jammed darkly, nothing to show how prized,
And by now with its smoothness opalized,

Is a drinking glass: 25
For, down that pass
My lover and I
Walked under a sky
Of blue with a leaf-wove awning of green,
In the burn of August, to paint the scene, 30
And we placed our basket of fruit and wine
By the runlet's rim, where we sat to dine;
And when we had drunk from the glass together,
Arched by the oak-copse from the weather,
I held the vessel to rinse in the fall, 35
Where it slipped, and sank, and was past recall,
Though we stooped and plumbed the little abyss
With long bared arms. There the glass still is.
And, as said, if I thrust my arm below
Cold water in basin or bowl, a throe 40
From the past awakens a sense of that time,
And the glass we used, and the cascade's rhyme.
The basin seems the pool, and its edge
The hard smooth face of the brookside ledge,
And the leafy pattern of chinaware 45
The hanging plants that were bathing there.

"By night, by day, when it shines or lours,
There lies intact that chalice of ours,
And its presence adds to the rhyme of love
Persistently sung by the fall above. 50
No lip has touched it since his and mine
In turns therefrom sipped lovers' wine."

1914

The Walk

You did not walk with me
Of late to the hilltop tree
By the gated ways,
As in earlier days;
You were weak and lame, 5
So you never came,
And I went alone, and I did not mind,
Not thinking of you as left behind.

I walked up there today
Just in the former way; 10
Surveyed around
The familiar ground
By myself again:
What difference, then?
Only that underlying sense 15
Of the look of a room on returning thence.

1914

During Wind and Rain

They sing their dearest songs—
He, she, all of them—yea,
Treble and tenor and bass,
    And one to play;
With the candles mooning each face. . . .   5
    Ah, no; the years O!
How the sick leaves reel down in throngs!

They clear the creeping moss—
Elders and juniors—aye,
Making the pathways neat   10
    And the garden gay;
And they build a shady seat. . . .
    Ah, no; the years, the years;
See, the white stormbirds wing across!

They are blithely breakfasting all—   15
Men and maidens—yea,
Under the summer tree,
    With a glimpse of the bay,
While pet fowl come to the knee. . . .
    Ah, no; the years O!   20
And the rotten rose is ripped from the wall.

They change to a high new house,
He, she, all of them—aye,
Clocks and carpets and chairs
    On the lawn all day,
And brightest things that are theirs. . . .   25
    Ah, no; the years, the years;
Down their carved names the raindrop plows.

                                                    1917

In Time of "The Breaking of Nations"[1]

1
Only a man harrowing clods
    In a slow silent walk
With an old horse that stumbles and nods
    Half asleep as they stalk.

2
Only thin smoke without flame   5
    From the heaps of couch-grass;
Yet this will go onward the same
    Though Dynasties pass.

3
Yonder a maid and her wight
    Come whispering by;   10
War's annals will cloud into night
    Ere their story die.

1915   1916

1. Cf. "Thou art my battle ax and weapons of war: for with thee will I break in pieces the nations" (Jeremiah li.20). The poem was written during World War I.

GERARD MANLEY HOPKINS
(1844–1889)

1866: Joins the Roman Catholic Church.
1877: Ordained.
1918: Posthumous publication of his poems by Bridges.

Gerard Manley Hopkins was educated at Highgate School, London, and at Balliol College, Oxford, where he studied classics and was influenced by the Oxford Movement, that revival of the ritualistic and dogmatic side of Christianity which began as a movement within the Church of England but which ended by taking many of its adherents, including the leading figure in the movement, John Henry Newman, to the Roman Catholic Church. After a period of spiritual turmoil Hopkins joined the Roman Catholic Church in 1866, sponsored by Newman, and two years later entered the Society of Jesus. He was ordained in 1877, and after serving as priest in a number of parishes, including one in a working-class area of Liverpool where the squalor disturbed him deeply, he was in 1884 appointed Professor of Classics at University College, Dublin.

A devoted Jesuit performing faithfully the duties assigned to him by his superiors, Hopkins was also a sensitive poet fascinated by language and rhythm and a passionately keen observer of the color and form and detail of the world of nature. The claims of religion and the duties of his religious profession were paramount, but his aesthetic interests (which included an interest in painting and music) asserted themselves with sometimes painful force, and it was not always easy for him to reconcile his religious vocation with his poetic genius. Before entering the Society of Jesus he burned his finished poems (though working copies survive) and did not write poetry again until late in 1875 or early in 1876. Hopkins went through periods of deep depression, of a listless sense of failure, and of that deep spiritual emptiness which mystics know as "the dark night of the soul" and see as one of the necessary stages on the road to spiritual fulfillment. This mood of spiritual desolation is expressed in the so-called "terrible sonnets," written between 1885 and 1889. But Hopkins also enjoyed moods of intense pleasure in the natural world, linked with a profound sense of natural beauty as a reflection of divine reality, and it is this combination of the most passionate and particularized apprehension of the sounds, shapes, and colors of the English countryside with the religious awareness of God as revealed through these sounds, shapes and colors, that is the theme of much of his poetry.

Hopkins' poems were never published in his lifetime. In spite of his eager interest in poetry and in technical problems of writing verse—an interest which is reflected in all its variety and intensity in the letters he wrote to his friends Robert Bridges (later poet laureate) and R. W. Dixon—Hopkins subordinated his poetry to his duties as a Jesuit and never sought any public fame as a poet. He resisted the suggestion made by Bridges and others in 1879 that he publish some of his poems, as he felt that his religious superiors would not approve. It is doubtful in any case whether his poetry would have been appreciated or even understood in the 19th century, for it flouted most of the contemporary expectations of what poetry should be. One of his aims was to rejuvenate the language of poetry, and he did so in a variety of ways. Sometimes he placed a familiar and much-used word in a new and startling context to bring out a lost aspect of its original meaning (e.g., addressing God as "sir" in *Thou Art Indeed Just, Lord*); sometimes he revived older words or used dialect words or phrases (such as "all road ever" in *Felix Randal*); sometimes he coined new words on the analogy of existing ones (e.g., "leafmeal" in *Spring and Fall*). He also employed devices found in other poetic modes, such as Anglo-Saxon and Welsh, to find new ways of giving exact and arresting expression to an impression or an idea or a combination of both; and he used unusual combinations of words and unusual word order to achieve the exact curve of the meaning. His study of the medieval philosopher Duns Scotus had encouraged this interest in "individuation" or "this-ness" (*haecceitas*) as a clue to the nature of reality. The essential inward pattern of the expression, what he called "inscape," was his primary concern. "No doubt," he wrote to Bridges, "my poetry errs on the side of oddness * * * but as air, melody, is what strikes me most of all in music and design in painting, so design, pattern, or what I am in the habit of calling 'inscape' is what I above all aim at in poetry. Now it is the virtue of design, pattern, or inscape to be distinctive and it is the vice of distinctiveness to become queer. This vice I cannot have escaped." Bridges, though recognizing his friend's genius, was often more aware of the oddness than of the distinctiveness; a later generation, reacting against the mellifluous poeticizings of an attenuated Romantic tradition, saw in the power and originality of Hopkins' expression not only something tremendously impressive in itself but also an invitation to experiment in new uses of language and new poetic rhythms.

Hopkins' interest in rhythms was as great as his interest in words. In his letters he developed a theory of "sprung rhythm" which broke away from the standard conception of poetic rhythms as consisting of a number of metrical feet, each having a fixed number of syllables, some stressed and some unstressed, with a limited number of possible variations and substitutions. Intead, he saw rhythm in poetry as much more flexible, much more like time and tempo in music, where the rhythmic effects are controlled by the number of beats in the measure (rather than the number of notes) and the general pattern of rising or falling movement. He also experimented with various ways of running lines into each other and of manipulating groups of "slack" or unaccented syllables within the line. He often used accent marks, which draw the reader's attention to the way the stresses fall in the line. All these devices help to produce his characteristic "sprung rhythm," which gives his poetry a different sound from that of other Victorian verse, a sound in many respects more like that of English and American poetry since Eliot.

The remarkable swinging movement of the opening of *The Windhover* is a characteristic triumph of Hopkins' rhythmic effects. He called the rhythm here "falling," meaning that the stress comes first in each foot. (The first word, "I," is conceived of as an introductory light beat outside the main movement of the line.) Hopkins himself scanned the first four lines in this way:

I caught this morning morning's minion, king-
  dom of daylight's dauphin, dapple-dawn-drawn Falcon, in his riding
Of the rolling level underneath him steady air, and striding
High there, how he rung upon the rein of a wimpling wing * * *

The stressed syllables are marked /, while the curved line underneath a
syllable marks what he called "hangers" or "outriders," which he defined
as "one, two, or three slack syllables added to a foot and not counted in
the nominal scanning." He remarked elsewhere that "the strong syllable
in an outriding foot has always a great stress and after the outrider follows
a short pause." Thus the first syllable in "dauphin" and in "Falcon" is
marked with a double stress-mark. The curious plunging effect which this
rhythm achieves—reproducing so effectively the movement of the bird
which is being described—is heightened by the sense of urgent forward
movement achieved by splitting "kingdom" between two lines and rhyming the first syllable ("king-") with the unstressed syllable "ing" of "riding" in the next line as well as, more obviously, with "wing" in line 4.
The hyphenating of groups of words, as in "dapple-dawn-drawn," is another common device of Hopkins: it can achieve a variety of effects, with
each word in the hyphenated group modifying and coloring the other to
achieve a simultaneous blend of meaning both more immediate and more
subtle in its impact on the reader than the same words could produce if
linked more conventionally by conjunctions. Hopkins always tried to
squeeze all water out of his language, to avoid all unnecessary words that
are required only as grammatical signs and so are liable to dissipate the
meaning. To concentrate meaning (so that when the poem is finally made
out its meaning "explodes," as he once put it) rather than to dissipate it
was always Hopkins' aim.

Other devices used by Hopkins include patterns of alliteration (e.g.,
God's Grandeur, line 3: "It gathers to a greatness, like the *ooze of oil*");
internal rhymes (line 6: "And all is *seared* with trade; *bleared*, *smeared*
with toil"); varieties of assonance (lines 11–14: "West," "went,"
"breast"); and different kinds of sound patterns which he adapted from
the traditions of Welsh poetry.

In its kind of imagery, too, and in the way in which the imagery works,
Hopkins' poetry differs sharply from that of, say, Tennyson or Rossetti.
In such a poem as *The Starlight Night* we are struck not only by the
arresting imperatives with which it opens and the echoes of Anglo-Saxon
poetic devices in "fire-folk" and "circle-citadel" but also by the remarkable way in which excitement at an aspect of the natural world moves
into a religious affirmation. This is achieved partly by a punning use of
language unknown in serious English poetry since the 17th century. In
line 13, for example, the harvested sheaves ("shocks") are to be safely
housed in the barn. But "shocks" also suggests the other and more familiar
sense of the word—"the thousand natural shocks that flesh is heir to"
(*Hamlet*). By buying the beauty of nature with prayer (lines 8 ff.), we
learn to see God in nature and to possess both nature and God. Thus by
"owning" nature we have a home for it—and for ourselves, protecting

both the "shocks" of corn and ourselves from the shocks of life. At the conclusion Christ and his saints are brought into this communion of the sheltered and protected: it becomes now the communion of saints and that, we now learn, is what "the fire-folk sitting in the air" really suggested. And what other 19th-century poet would have used the language of the auction room in talking of the beauty of nature and its relation to religious practices? ("Buy then! bid then!—What?—Prayer, patience, alms, vows.")

This combination of the startlingly colloquial and the strikingly unusual is an important feature of Hopkins' poetry. *The Lantern Out of Doors* begins with a simple, colloquial use of English ("And who goes there? / I think * * * "). The surface thought is also simple: we meet people in daily life who interest us momentarily, but our paths cross briefly and they disappear and we forget about them, because "out of sight is out of mind" (and notice the way Hopkins introduces a homely proverb here). Christ, on the other hand, never forgets people; He is always interested in them; He is their ransom, their rescue, and their eternal friend. There is, however, much more than this in the poem. The word "interests" in line 2 is not a normal poetic word; it arrests us by its very ordinariness. As the poem develops, it comes to suggest not only its obvious, primary meaning but its financial meaning (as in "to lend at interest"). The thought is: people whose character makes them valuable pass by but soon disappear when they are bought by death or distance. Although death or distance buys or consumes them, so that they are lost to sight, Christ continues to "mind" them—in the sense (still common in Scotland) of "remember" them as well as "look after" them, as a man minds his property. Christ's *interest* is their *ransom*: the implication is that Christ gives the interest on his property to ransom man—but of course the word "interest" is also used in its more obvious meaning. Or consider lines 5 and following. The sense is that men beautiful in "mould" (shape) disappear in the "mould" (the earth of the grave): their very beauty suggests their mortality. Or we could follow out the double meaning of "kind" in the phrase "foot follows kind." This combination of the colloquial and the formal, the building up of complex patterns of meaning through the multiple suggestiveness given to words in their poetic context, is what so excited 20th-century poets when they discovered Hopkins.

This discovery was made in 1918, long after Hopkins' death, when Bridges first brought out an edition of Hopkins' poems. By the time the second edition appeared, with an introduction by Charles Williams, in 1930, Hopkins' position was established; the younger poets, such as W. H. Auden and later Dylan Thomas, turned to him enthusiastically as one of their masters. Hopkins is thus in a sense a 20-century poet born out of his time who had to wait until the present century for posthumous appreciation and influence.

The text of the selections given here follows that of the third edition of Hopkins' poems (1948), edited by W. H. Gardner, which is now the standard text.

God's Grandeur

The world is charged with the grandeur of God.
　　It will flame out, like shining from shook foil;[1]
　　It gathers to a greatness, like the ooze of oil
Crushed.[2] Why do men then now not reck his rod?
Generations have trod, have trod, have trod;   5
　　And all is seared with trade; bleared, smeared with toil;
　　And wears man's smudge and shares man's smell: the soil
Is bare now, nor can foot feel, being shod.

And for all this, nature is never spent;
　　There lives the dearest freshness deep down things;   10
And though the last lights off the black West went
　　Oh, morning, at the brown brink eastward, springs—
Because the Holy Ghost over the bent
　　World broods with warm breast and with ah! bright wings.

1877   1918

The Starlight Night

Look at the stars! look, look up at the skies!
　　O look at all the fire-folk sitting in the air!
　　The bright boroughs, the circle-citadels there!
Down in dim woods the diamond delves! the elves'-eyes!
The grey lawns cold where gold,[3] where quickgold lies!
　　Wind-beat whitebeam! airy abeles [4] set on a flare!
　　Flake-doves sent floating forth at a farmyard scare!—
Ah well! it is all a purchase, all is a prize.

Buy then! bid then!—What?—Prayer, patience, alms, vows.
Look, look: a May-mess,[5] like on orchard boughs!
Look! March-bloom, like on mealed-with-yellow[6] sallows!
These are indeed the barn; withindoors house
The shocks.[7] This piece-bright paling[8] shuts the spouse
　　Christ home, Christ and his mother and all his hallows.[9]

1877   1918

1. "I mean foil in the sense of leaf or tinsel * * * Shaken goldfoil gives off broad glares like sheet lightning and also, and this is true of nothing else, owing to its zigzag dints and creasings and network of small many cornered facets, a sort of fork lightning too" (Hopkins, *Letters*).
2. From olives.
3. Dewdrops, referred to also as "quickgold" (a word coined by analogy with "quicksilver" and thus suggesting the gleaming and volatile nature of dewdrops).
4. White poplars.
5. A profusion of May—i.e., suggesting a mass of May blossoms, such as pear blossoms ("like on orchard boughs"). "May" is also another name for the white hawthorn. There may be religious overtones, with "May" suggesting "Mary" (the Virgin) and "mess" suggesting "Mass" (the Catholic rite).
6. Yellow-spotted. "Sallows" are a variety of willow tree.
7. Sheaves of corn: see discussion of this poem in the Hopkins introduction.
8. Fencing. It is "piece-bright," i.e., bright as a gold or silver coin. "Piece" in this sense suggests the thirty pieces of silver for which Judas betrayed Christ: but line 9 implies that we can buy both Christ and the beauty of nature with a very different kind of coin.
9. Saints.

Spring

Nothing is so beautiful as spring—
    When weeds, in wheels, shoot long and lovely and lush;
    Thrush's eggs look little low heavens, and thrush
Through the echoing timber does so rinse and wring
The ear, it strikes like lightnings to hear him sing;   5
    The glassy peartree leaves and blooms, they brush
    The descending blue; that blue is all in a rush
With richness; the racing lambs too have fair their fling.

What is all this juice and all this joy?
    A strain of the earth's sweet being in the beginning   10
In Eden garden.—Have, get, before it cloy,
    Before it cloud, Christ, lord, and sour with sinning,
Innocent mind and Mayday in girl and boy,
Most, O maid's[1] child, thy choice and worthy the winning. .

1877   1918

The Lantern Out of Doors

Sometimes a lantern moves along the night,
    That interests our eyes. And who goes there?
    I think; where from and bound, I wonder, where,
With, all down darkness wide, his wading light?

Men go by me whom either beauty bright   5
    In mould or mind or what not else makes rare:
    They rain against our much-thick and marsh air
Rich beams, till death or distance buys them quite.

Death or distance soon consumes them: wind
    What most I may eye after,[2] be in at the end   10
I cannot, and out of sight is out of mind.

Christ minds; Christ's interest, what to avow or amend
    There, éyes them, heart wánts, care haúnts, foot fóllows kínd,
    Their ránsom, théir rescue, ánd first, fást, last friénd.[3]

1877   1918

1. The Virgin Mary's. May is a popular form of the word "Mary," so "Mayday" in line 13 also suggests "Mary's day," day of innocence and purity. Cf. note 3 to *The Starlight Night.*
2. W. H. Gardner notes that the entire verb in this passage is "wind eye after." "I mean that the eye winds only in the sense that its focus or point of sight winds and that coin-cides with a point of the object and winds with that. For the object, a lantern passing further and further away and bearing now east now west of one right line, is truly and properly described as winding" (Hopkins, *Letters*).
3. For a discussion of the language in this poem, see the Hopkins introduction.

The Windhover[1]

TO CHRIST OUR LORD

I caught this morning morning's minion,[2] king-
   dom of daylight's dauphin,[3] dapple-dawn-drawn Falcon, in
     his riding
Of the rolling level underneath him steady air, and striding
High there, how he rung upon the rein[4] of a wimpling wing
In his ecstasy! then off, off forth on swing,
   As a skate's heel sweeps smooth on a bow-bend: the hurl
     and gliding   5
Rebuffed the big wind. My heart in hiding
Stirred for a bird,—the achieve of, the mastery of the thing!

Brute beauty and valour and act, oh, air, pride, plume, here
   Buckle![5] AND[6] the fire that breaks from thee then, a billion   10
Times told lovelier, more dangerous, O my chevalier!

   No wonder of it: shéer plód makes plough down sillion[7]
Shine, and blue-bleak embers, ah my dear,
   Fall, gall themselves, and gash gold-vermilion.

1877   1918

Pied Beauty

Glory be to God for dappled things—
   For skies of couple-colour as a brinded[1] cow;
     For rose-moles all in stipple[2] upon trout that swim;

1. Kestrel, called "windhover" because it hovers in the air, head to wind. This poem, which Hopkins considered "the best thing I ever wrote" (*Letters*), has been variously explicated. The main thought seems to be that the ecstatic flying of the bird stirs the poet's heart ("in hiding," for the poet is a priest, with his heart hidden away from earthly things in the service of God). In the combination of beauty, strength, and glory which the poet sees in the bird, he sees an emblem of the beauty, strength, and glory of Christ, whom he addresses as "my chevalier" (line 11). It is "dangerous" to see these qualities in Christ, for we look to Christ for lessons in humility and the enduring of suffering. But it is "no wonder" (lines 12–14) that Christ's humility and suffering are bound up with His glory and pride; many things include their opposites; "sheer plod" can make the ploughshare shine, as it cuts its furrow, and a black coal in a fire can fall over and break and reveal its red-hot interior, its "gold-vermilion" gashes suggesting *both* beauty and pride *and* Christ's wounds and suffering.
2. Darling.
3. Heir (literally, the title of the

eldest son of the king of France); the word carries overtones of chivalry and splendor.
4. There is an implied comparison to a horse circling around its trainer at the end of a long rein. "Wimpling": rippling.
5. The obvious sense here is "join," though some critics have understood it as "bend" or "break" and some have taken it as an imperative in that sense. But see note 1. Hopkins is celebrating the point at which animal beauty, strength, bearing, and fine display all join.
6. Hopkins emphasizes the "AND" to draw attention from the admiration of the bird to the sense of Christ behind it which that admiration brings. A movement from appreciation of the life of nature to a religious sense of the God reflected in nature is found in very many of Hopkins' poems.
7. The ridge between two furrows of a plowed field. Hopkins uses this archaic word perhaps to suggest an overtone from "silica" (the mineral which in the form of gleaming particles of quartz often makes dull rocks shine).
1. Brindled, streaked.
2. Dots or small spots.

Fresh-firecoal chestnut-falls;[3] finches' wings;
　　Landscape plotted and pieced[4]—fold, fallow, and plough;　5
　And áll trádes, their gear and tackle and trim.[5]

All things counter,[6] original, spare, strange;
　　Whatever is fickle, freckled (who knows how?)
　　With swift, slow; sweet, sour; adazzle, dim;
　He fathers-forth whose beauty is past change:　　　　　10
　　　　Praise him.

1877　　　　　　　　　　　　　　　　　　　　　1918

Hurrahing in Harvest

Summer ends now; now, barbarous in beauty, the stocks[7] arise
　Around; up above, what wind-walks! what lovely
　　　behaviour
　Of silk-sack clouds! has wilder, wilful-wavier

Meal-drift moulded ever and melted across skies?
I walk, I lift up, I lift up heart, eyes,
　Down all that glory in the heavens to glean our Saviour;　　5
　And, éyes, heárt, what looks, what lips yet gave you a
Rapturous love's greeting of realer, of rounder replies?

And the azurous hung hills are his world-wielding shoulder
　Majestic—as a stallion stalwart, very-violet-sweet!—　　10
These things, these things were here and but the beholder
　Wanting; which two when they once meet,
The heart rears wings bold and bolder
　And hurls for him, O half hurls earth for him off under
　　　his feet.

1877　　　　　　　　　　　　　　　　　　　　　1918

Binsey Poplars

FELLED 1879

My aspens dear, whose airy cages quelled,
　Quelled or quenched in leaves the leaping sun,
　All felled, felled, are all felled;
　　Of a fresh and following folded rank[1]
　　　　Not spared, not one　　　　　　　　5
　　　　That dandled a sandalled
　　　Shadow that swam or sank
On meadow and river and wind-wandering weed-winding bank.

3. Chestnuts stripped of their husks
after being roasted in "fresh-firecoal."
4. Divided into rectangles of different
colors, as the English landscape appears. "Fold": enclosure for animals;
"fallow": a field plowed but left un-
sown for a season.
5. Equipment.
6. Contrary, i.e., in contrasted patterns or colors. "Spare": rare.
7. Stooks (or shocks: see "The Starlight Night") are sheaves of corn placed
upright, supporting each other at an
angle, for drying.
1. Row of trees with alternate trees
set off at an angle, making the row
"folded."

O if we but knew what we do
    When we delve[2] or hew—   10
Hack and rack[3] the growing green!
    Since country is so tender
To touch, her being só slender,
That, like this sleek and seeing ball[4]
But a prick will make no eye at all,   15
Where we, even where we mean
    To mend her we end her,
    When we hew or delve:
After-comers cannot guess the beauty been.
Ten or twelve, only ten or twelve   20
    Strokes of havoc únselve[5]
    The sweet especial scene,
Rural scene, a rural scene,
Sweet especial rural scene.

1879   1918

Duns Scotus's Oxford[6]

Towery city and branchy between towers;
Cuckoo-echoing, bell-swarmèd, lark-charmèd, rook-racked, river-
    rounded;
The dapple-eared lily below thee; that country and town did
Once encounter in, here coped[7] and poisèd powers;

Thou hast a base and brickish skirt[8] there, sours   5
That neighbour-nature thy grey beauty is grounded
Best in; graceless growth, thou hast confounded
Rural rural keeping[9]—folk, flocks, and flowers.

Yet ah! this air I gather and I release
He lived on; these weeds and waters, these walls are what   10
He haunted who of all men most sways my spirits to peace;

Of realty[1] the rarest-veinèd unraveller; a not
Rivalled insight, be rival Italy or Greece;
Who fired France for Mary without spot.[2]

1879   1918

2. Dig.
3. Torture.
4. The eye.
5. Rob it of its "self" or individuality.
6. Duns Scotus, the 13th-century Scholastic philosopher, is supposed to have taught at Oxford ca. 1301. Hopkins admired him greatly; when he came upon two of Scotus's commentaries in 1872 he was "flush with a new stroke of enthusiasm. * * * When I took in any inscape of the sky or sea I thought of Scotus" (*Note-books*). In this poem he builds up an impression of medieval Oxford, then links this to Scotus

through himself ("this air I gather and I release / He lived on") to end with a tribute to him.
7. Set off one against the other.
8. Refers to the appearance of 19th-century brick houses in north Oxford. Note the characteristic omission of the relative pronoun before "sours."
9. I.e., you have spoiled the effect of a rural city presiding over its rural environment.
1. Reality.
2. Reference to Scotus's work in spreading the cult of the Virgin Mary in France.

Felix Randal

Felix Randal the farrier,[1] O he is dead then? my duty all ended,
Who have watched his mould of man, big-boned and hardy-hand-
    some
Pining, pining, till time when reason rambled in it and some
Fatal four disorders, fleshed there, all contended?

Sickness broke him. Impatient he cursed at first, but mended   5
Being anointed and all; though a heavenlier heart began some
Months earlier, since I had our sweet reprieve and ransom
Tendered to him.[2] Ah well, God rest him all road ever[3] he offended!

This seeing the sick endears them to us, us too it endears.
My tongue had taught thee comfort, touch had quenched thy
    tears,
Thy tears that touched my heart, child, Felix, poor Felix Randal;   10

How far from then forethought of, all thy more boisterous years,
When thou at the random[4] grim forge, powerful amidst peers,
Didst fettle[5] for the great grey drayhorse his bright and battering
    sandal!

1880   1918

Spring and Fall

TO A YOUNG CHILD

Márgarét, are you gríeving
Over Goldengrove unleaving?
Leáves, líke the things of man, you
With your fresh thoughts care for, can you?
Áh! ás the heart grows older   5
It will come to such sights colder
By and by, nor spare a sigh
Though worlds of wanwood leafmeal[6] lie;
And yet you wíll weep and know why.
Now no matter, child, the name: 10
Sórrow's spríngs áre the same.

1. Blacksmith.
2. Had heard his confession and given him absolution.
3. In whatever way.
4. Built with stones of irregular shapes and sizes.
5. Prepare.
6. "I take *wanwood* to be a noun (the meaning 'bloodless' being combined with the older meaning 'dark,' 'livid' —O.E. *wann*). *Leafmeal* I take for an adverb, made 'by substitution' from *piecemeal* on the analogy of Shakespeare's *inch-meal* and *limb-meal*: hence it suggests the leaves falling one by one, then rotting to form pale, mealy fragments" [W. H. Gardner's note].

Nor mouth had, no nor mind, expressed
What heart heard of, ghost guessed: [7]
It ís the blight man was born for,
It is Margaret you mourn for.

1880   15
                                                            1918

Inversnaid [8]

This darksome burn,[9] horseback brown,
His rollrock highroad roaring down,
In coop and in comb [1] the fleece of his foam
Flutes and low to the lake falls home.

A windpuff-bonnet óf fáwn-fróth   5
Turns and twindles [2] over the broth
Of a pool so pitchblack, féll-frówning,
It rounds and rounds Despair to drowning.

Degged [3] with dew, dappled with dew
Are the groins of the braes [4] that the brook treads through,   10
Wiry heathpacks, flitches [5] of fern,
And the beadbonny ash that sits over the burn.

What would the world be, once bereft
Of wet and of wildness? Let them be left,
O let them be left, wildness and wet;   15
Long live the weeds and the wilderness yet.
1881   1918

[Carrion Comfort] [6]

Not, I'll not, carrion comfort, Despair, not feast on thee;
Not untwist—slack they may be—these last strands of man
In me ór, most weary, cry *I can no more.* I can;
Can something, hope, wish day come, not choose not to be.
But ah, but O thou terrible, why wouldst thou rude on me   5
Thy wring-world right foot rock?[7] lay a lionlimb against me? scan

7. "*Ghost,* spirit (of the living), with a proleptic suggestion of 'phantom'—the living spirit foreknowing, through sensory experience, its own state after death. Lines 8 and 14 connect the Fall of the Leaf with the Fall of Man: 'and unto dust shalt thou return' (Genesis iii.18)" [W. H. Gardner's note].
8. On Loch Lomondside, Scotland, famous for its rushing stream and waterfall.
9. Stream.
1. "Coop": hollow; "comb": crest.

2. Apparently Hopkins' coinage: twists and dwindles.
3. Sprinkled.
4. Hills.
5. Tufts, clumps.
6. Title supplied by Bridges in the 1918 edition. This is one of the "terrible sonnets," as are the two poems that follow.
7. Why wouldst thou turn roughly against me thy right foot that wrings the world?

With darksome devouring eyes my bruisèd bones? and fan,
O in turns of tempest, me heaped there; me frantic to avoid thee
   and flee?

   Why? That my chaff might fly; my grain lie, sheer and clear.
Nay in all that toil, that coil,[8] since (seems) I kissed the rod,   10
Hand rather, my heart lo! lapped strength, stole joy, would laugh,
   chéer.
Cheer whom though? the hero whose heaven-handling flung me,
   fóot tród
Me? or me that fought him? O which one? is it each one? That
   night, that year
Of now done darkness I wretch lay wrestling with (my God!) my
   God.

1885   1918

———

[No Worst, There Is None][9]

No worst, there is none. Pitched past pitch of grief,
More pangs will, schooled at forepangs, wilder wring.
Comforter, where, where is your comforting?
Mary, mother of us, where is your relief?

My cries heave, herds-long,[1] huddle in a main, a chief   5
Woe, world-sorrow; on an age-old anvil wince and sing—
Then lull, then leave off. Fury had shrieked "No ling-
ering! Let me be fell:[2] force I must be brief."

   O the mind, mind has mountains; cliffs of fall
Frightful, sheer, no-man-fathomed. Hold them cheap   10
May who ne'er hung there. Nor does long our small
Durance[3] deal with that steep or deep. Here! creep,
Wretch, under a comfort serves in a whirlwind: all
Life death does end and each day dies with sleep.

1885   1918

[Thou Art Indeed Just, Lord]

*Justus quidem tu es, Domine, si disputem tecum: verumtamen
justa loquar ad te: Quare via impiorum prosperatur? etc.*[4]

---

8. Disturbance.
9. Untitled by Hopkins. Cf. the description of "desolation" in the *Spiritual Exercises* of St. Ignatius Loyola, founder of the Jesuit order: "a darkening of the soul, trouble of mind, movement to base and earthly things, restlessness of various agitations and temptations, moving to distrust, loss of hope, loss of love; when the soul feels herself thoroughly apathetic, sad, and as it were separated from her Creator and Lord."
1. Coming in large numbers and in a long series, like herds of cattle following each other. "Main" (like "chief") is an adjective, qualifying "woe."
2. Fierce: "Force" means here "perforce."
3. Endurance.
4. The Latin is the Vulgate version of Jeremiah xii.1, which reads in the King James version: "Righteous art thou, O Lord, when I plead with thee: yet let me talk with thee of thy judgments: Wherefore doth the way of the wicked prosper? * * * " This Latin quotation was Hopkins' title.

Thou art indeed just, Lord, if I contend
With thee; but, sir, so what I plead is just.
Why do sinners' ways prosper? and why must
Disappointment all I endeavour end?
    Wert thou my enemy, O thou my friend,   5
How wouldst thou worse, I wonder, than thou dost
Defeat, thwart me? Oh, the sots and thralls of lust
Do in spare hours more thrive than I that spend,
Sir, life upon thy cause. See, banks and brakes[5]
Now, leavèd how thick! lacèd they are again   10
With fretty[6] chervil, look, and fresh wind shakes
Them; birds build—but not I build; no, but strain,
Time's eunuch, and not breed one work that wakes.
Mine,[7] O thou lord of life, send my roots rain.

1889   1918

5. Clumps of fern.
6. Fretted, with interlacing pattern.
"Chervil" is a member of the parsley
family.
7. "Mine" may refer to "roots," emphasizing that the poet wants God to
send "*my* roots rain" since every other
creature is flourishing, or it may mean
"my God."

GEORGE BERNARD SHAW
(1856–1950)

1876: Settles in London.
1892: *Widowers' Houses* produced.
1898: Publication of *Plays Pleasant and Unpleasant*, including
      Arms and the Man.
1923: *Saint Joan.*

Bernard Shaw was born in Dublin of English stock, one of the galaxy of Anglo-Irishmen (they include Swift, Sheridan, Edmund Burke, and Yeats) who have contributed so brilliantly to English literature. He left school at the age of 14 and worked for five years (1871–76) in a land agent's office. He went to London in 1876, his mother having settled there in order to improve her prospects as a music teacher, and began his literary career as a writer of unsuccessful novels. He soon became interested in social reform: in 1884 he was one of the founders of the Fabian Society, an organization dedicated to the promotion of socialism by gradual stages. Although he was friendly with the most important socialist thinkers in England in the late 19th century, including Sidney and Beatrice Webb and William Morris, Shaw was never a conventional socialist. His social and political attitude was affected by his belief in an active and individually *willed* kind of evolution, urged on by what he called the Life Force, and by his admiration of vitality and power. He inherited from his gifted mother a love of music and learned from her to know and admire Mozartian opera; he also became a great champion of Richard Wagner, and in his regular music criticism, first for the London *Star* and then for the *World*, not only displayed his enthusiasms with lively wit but also introduced a new standard in judging both performers and composers, often mocking conventional taste and fashionable preferences. In 1895 he became dramatic critic for the *Saturday Review* (a London periodical): his deliberately provocative reviews stirred up contemporary English ideas about plays and acting and enlarged the intellectual horizons of his readers. He championed Henrik Ibsen as well as Wagner, and published in 1891 a study of Ibsen entitled *The Quintessence of Ibsenism* which presented the Norwegian dramatist as a realistic and reforming playwright who addressed himself to the problems of modern life and introduced genuine *discussion* in his dialogue. The more profound and symbolic Ibsen whom we admire today was not Shaw's Ibsen, and it is significant that for him the great plays were those which attacked middle-class conventionality and hypocrisy rather than those which probed more subtly and poetically into deeper aspects of experience.

His training in music and dramatic criticism, his interest in social reform, his admiration for Wagner and Ibsen, the influence of Samuel Butler (author of *Erewhon* and *The Way of All Flesh* and the great satirist of Victorian life and thought) helped to make Shaw a playwright who on the one hand knew all the conventional tricks of the theater and on the other was determined to use the drama as he conceived Ibsen to have used it—as a means of shaking theater audiences out of their complacencies, hypocrisies, and thoughtless acquiescence in all kinds of social evil.

Reviewing new plays over a period of years had given Shaw an expert knowledge of the structural devices employed by the authors of the "well-made play" (adroitly plotted theatrical entertainment) of the late 19th century; and when he came to write his own plays he was able to use conventional dramatic structure and even conventional themes for highly unconventional purposes. From the beginning his aim as a dramatist was to shock his audiences into taking a new view of their society and the moral problems that arose out of it. "I must warn my readers," he wrote, "that my attacks are directed against themselves, not against my stage figures." Not only did he delight in standing the popular view on its head, but he went further: beginning by persuading his audience by means of dramatic action and dialogue that the conventional hero was the villain and the conventional villain was the hero, he would swing everything around again to show that the conventional hero was the hero after all, but in a very different sense from that which the audience had originally thought. He followed this pattern in *Man and Superman*, *Major Barbara*, and *Arms and the Man*. He used paradox, both in the action and even more in the dialogue, to dazzle and even bewilder his audiences—only to demonstate that their absurd conventional views and unconscious hypocrisies were responsible for their bewilderment. Having thus destroyed the audience's self-confidence he would organize the dialogue (or sometimes a monologue) in order to allow one of his splendidly vital (but never conventionally heroic) heroes to put across the Shavian vision of society or politics or religion or whatever was the main theme of the play. And all the time he entertained and fascinated by his wit as well as by his sheer sense of fun. Sometimes this sense of fun led him to conclude a serious critical comedy in sheer farce—as in *You Never Can Tell* (1900)—but on the whole Shaw combined entertainment and intellectual provocation to bring a new kind of critical wit into English drama. The wit of Oscar Wilde's comedies had no specific critical implications; it drew on the conventions of society not in order to expose them but in order to get the maximum number of epigrams out of their delightful inconsistencies and absurdities. Shaw's wit was put at the service of a genuine passion for reform, and even if he sometimes assumed the posture of a licensed clown—a posture which members of the public were all too ready to accept as his natural one, for it enabled them to laugh off the disturbing paradoxes he thrust at them—he remained to the end a crusader as well as an entertainer.

Shaw's first play, *Widowers' Houses* (produced in 1892), dealt in a characteristically provocative manner with the problem of slum landlordism: even here, with a subject easily compartmentalized into moral blacks and whites, Shaw's techniques of reversal and inversion keep revealing new aspects of the problem, so that, instead of merely condemning the landlord, the audience is forced to comprehend the entire complex of social and economic conditions that produced the problem. *Mrs. Warren's Profession*, written in 1893, was for a long time banned from the public theater because of its concern with the tabooed subject of prostitution; it is not, however, simply about prostitution, but about well-meaning brothel-keepers and the laws of supply and demand, which it explores with boldness and wit, again substituting the revelation of causes and consequences for simple moral indignation. In 1898 Shaw published *Plays Pleasant and Unpleasant,* with long provocative prefaces attacking a great variety of things, including theatrical censorship; the plays included *Arms and the Man, Candida, The Man of Destiny,* and (among the "unpleasant") *Widowers' Houses* and *Mrs. Warren's Profession.* Among his later plays, *John Bull's Other Island* (1904) is a characteristic contribution to the discussion of Ireland's grievances against the English; *Man and Superman* (1904) is an ambitious attempt to project through comedy his views of how the Life Force works in ordinary life and contains some brilliant scenes, though the play as a whole is rather too long and too talkative; *The Doctor's Dilemma* (1906) exposes both doctors and artists while exploring some of the moral problems in which they can become involved; *Major Barbara* (1907) shows Shaw's characteristic admiration of success and energy and his contempt for those evangelists who attempt to promote religion by giving soup to the poor instead of trying to convert the strong and successful; *Pygmalion* (1912) is a brilliant exploration of the relation between social class and accent in England, which has since been made into the extraordinarily popular musical comedy, *My Fair Lady. Heartbreak House* (1917), subtitled "a fantasia in the Russian manner on English themes," suggests the Russian dramatist Chekhov in its depiction of the imminent collapse of a civilization, but it is essentially Shavian, and the finest example of what Eric Bentley has called the "disquisitory" Shavian play, based on the interplay of ideas in dialogue. *The Apple Cart* (1929) is a paradoxical treatment of the problems of monarchy and democracy done with a mischievous desire to shock equally both Left- and Right-wing thinkers and again shows that admiration of the strong man which is Shaw's personal heresy and goes oddly with his socialism.

Back to Methuselah (1921) was Shaw's most ambitious work, and the one which he considered his masterpiece. But it is in fact the dullest of his plays. Shaw's picture of the Life Force eventually enabling men to improve the human species to the point where they can live long enough to become little more than disembodied intellects reveals a curious coldness and abstraction at the heart of his thought. *Saint Joan* (1923), his one tragedy and often regarded as his finest play, is brilliant in its way, but it is really a comedy containing one tragic scene rather than a tragedy. Shaw had no historical imagination. He makes the past interesting by analogizing it to the present and gets his comic effects by interpreting historical characters as though they were the kind of characters who would be doing the same sort of thing today. The result is often very amusing, but it yields no real insight. Saint Joan as a girl with inspired common sense is a refreshing, funny, and, up to a point, a persuasive portrait—but this portrait is not compatible with the image of Joan as religious martyr, which Shaw does not know how to paint. Similarly, in that most entertaining play *Caesar and Cleopatra* (which is, incidentally, most brilliant theatrically) Shaw's wit takes the form of interpreting the main characters as though they lived in the 19th century. Caesar becomes a 19th-century liberal and his secretary Britannicus is a Victorian Philistine: this gives a kind of reality to the past, but at the cost of losing a dimension.

Shaw continued throughout his long and active career to tease and provoke the public with his plays and prefaces. He is at his best when he uses effective dramatic devices and brilliantly entertaining dialogue in order to expose contradictions, inconsistencies, gaps between the pretended and the real, in contemporary attitudes and behavior. In *Arms and the Man* he does this admirably. It is a deliberately antiromantic play, if by romanticism one means "fictitious morals and fictitious good conduct, shedding fictitious glory on overcrowding, disease, crime, drink, war, cruelty, infant mortality * * *" It exhibits what Shaw called "natural morality" as against the "romantic morality" of those who objected to it. We see in this play Shaw's characteristic device of continually transposing the parts of conventional hero and conventional villain. First we think Bluntschli, the soldier in danger of capture and death, is a military hero; then we see him as a coward who prefers chocolate to bullets; then we find that he is capable of a brave resignation to death; and in the end, after many further transformations, he emerges as a new sort of hero—the *efficient* man. And it is he who wins the heroine, who also keeps changing before our eyes until we finally see her—as we do so many of Shaw's heroines —as the girl led by the Life Force to seek out as her mate the most efficient and vital man available. Similar transformations occur in our view of Louka and Sergius. These teasing shifts in ways of presenting a character represent more than a successful dramatic trick: this is how Shaw makes his audiences look again and again at the particular situation he is presenting, until they have shed all illusions bred either by convention or by facile anticonventionality.

Shaw was an ardent believer in spelling reform, and, while awaiting a reformed alphabet and phonetic spelling, introduced some minor simplifications in his own spelling which he insisted on his publishers retaining. These simplifications (omission of the apostrophe in a number of contractions, for example) are retained in the text here printed.

From Preface to *Plays Pleasant*[1]
[*Arms and the Man*]

* * * There is no reason, however, why I should take this haughty attitude towards those representative critics whose complaint is that my plays, though not unentertaining, lack the elevation of sentiment and seriousness of purpose of Shakespear and Ibsen. They can find, under the surface brilliancy for which they give me credit, no coherent thought or sympathy, and accuse me, in various terms and degrees, of an inhuman and freakish wantonness; of preoccupation with "the seamy side of life"; of paradox, cynicism, and eccentricity, reducible, as some contend, to a trite formula of treating bad as good, and good as bad, important as trivial, and trivial as important, serious as laughable, and laughable as serious, and so forth. As to this formula I can only say that if any gentleman is simple enough to think that even a good comic opera can be produced by it, I invite him to try his hand, and see whether anything remotely resembling one of my plays will result.

I could explain the matter easily enough if I chose; but the result would be that the people who misunderstand the plays would misunderstand the explanation ten times more. The particular exceptions taken are seldom more than symptoms of the underlying fundamental disagreement between the romantic morality of the critics and the realistic morality of the plays. For example, I am quite aware that the much criticized Swiss officer in *Arms and the Man* is not a conventional stage soldier. He suffers from want of food and sleep; his nerves go to pieces after three days under fire, ending in the horrors of a rout and pursuit; he has found by experience that it is more important to have a few bits of chocolate to eat in the field than cartridges for his revolver. When many of my critics rejected these circumstances as fantastically improbable and cynically unnatural, it was not necessary to argue them into common sense: all I had to do was to brain them, so to speak, with the first half dozen military authorities at hand, beginning with the present Commander in Chief. But when it proved that such unromantic (but all the more dramatic) facts implied to them a denial of the existence of courage, patriotism, faith, hope, and charity, I saw that it was not really mere matter of fact that was at issue between us. One strongly Liberal critic, who had received my first play with the most generous encouragement, declared, when *Arms and the Man* was produced, that I had struck a wanton blow at the cause of liberty in the Balkan Peninsula by mentioning that it was

1. First printed in the second volume ("Containing the Four Pleasant Plays") of *Plays Pleasant and Unpleasant* (1898), this Preface later, with some changes, became the Preface to *Arms and the Man.* The earlier text is followed here.

not a matter of course for a Bulgarian in 1885 to wash his hands every day. My Liberal critic no doubt saw soon afterwards the squabble, reported all through Europe, between Stambouiloff[2] and an eminent lady of the Bulgarian court who took exception to his neglect of his fingernails. After that came the news of his ferocious assassination, and a description of the room prepared for the reception of visitors by his widow, who draped it with black, and decorated it with photographs of the mutilated body of her husband. Here was a sufficiently sensational confirmation of the accuracy of my sketch of the theatrical nature of the first apings of western civilization by spirited races just emerging from slavery. But it had no bearing on the real issue between my critic and myself, which was, whether the political and religious idealism which had inspired the rescue of these Balkan principalities from the despotism of the Turk, and converted miserably enslaved provinces into hopeful and gallant little states, will survive the general onslaught on idealism which is implicit, and indeed explicit, in *Arms and the Man* and the realistic plays of the modern school. For my part I hope not; for idealism, which is only a flattering name for romance in politics and morals, is as obnoxious to me as romance in ethics or religion. In spite of a Liberal Revolution or two, I can no longer be satisfied with fictitious morals and fictitious good conduct, shedding fictitious glory on overcrowding, disease, crime, drink, war, cruelty, infant mortality, and all the other commonplaces of civilization which drive men to the theatre to make foolish pretences that these things are progress, science, morals, religion, patriotism, imperial supremacy, national greatness and all the other names the newspapers call them. On the other hand, I see plenty of good in the world working itself out as fast as the idealist will allow it; and if they would only let it alone and learn to respect reality, which would include the beneficial exercise of respecting themselves, and incidentally respecting me, we should all get along much better and faster. At all events, I do not see moral chaos and anarchy as the alternative to romantic convention; and I am not going to pretend that I do to please the less clear-sighted people who are convinced that the world is only held together by the force of unanimous, strenuous, eloquent, trumpet-tongued lying. To me the tragedy and comedy of life lie in the consequences, sometimes terrible, sometimes ludicrous, of our persistent attempts to found our institutions on the ideals suggested to our imaginations by our half-satisfied passions, instead of on a genuinely scientific natural history. And with that hint as to what I am driving at, I withdraw and ring up the curtain.

2. Stefan Stambolov (Stambouiloff), was a Bulgarian politician, nationalist leader and premier from 1887 to 1894. He was fatally wounded by an assassin on July 15, 1895.

Arms and the Man[1]

Act I

Night: A lady's bedchamber in Bulgaria, in a small town near the Dragoman Pass, late in November in the year 1885. Through an open window with a little balcony a peak of the Balkans, wonderfully white and beautiful in the starlit snow, seems quite close at hand, though it is really miles away. The interior of the room is not like anything to be seen in the west of Europe. It is half rich Bulgarian, half cheap Viennese. Above the head of the bed, which stands against a little wall cutting off the left-hand corner of the room, is a painted wooden shrine, blue and gold, with an ivory image of Christ, and a light ha·ging before it in a pierced metal ball suspended by three chains. The principal seat, placed towards the other side of the room and opposite the window, is a Turkish ottoman. The counterpane and hangings of the bed, the window curtains, the little carpet, and all the ornamental textile fabrics in the room are oriental and gorgeous; the paper on the walls is occidental and paltry. The washstand, against the wall on the side nearest the ottoman and window, consists of an enamelled iron basin with a pail beneath it in a painted metal frame, and a single towel on the rail at the side. The dressing table, between the bed and the window, is a common pine table, covered with a cloth of many colours, with an expensive toilet mirror on it. The door is on the side nearest the bed; and there is a chest of drawers between. This chest of drawers is also covered by a variegated native cloth; and on it there is a pile of paper-backed novels, a box of chocolate creams, and a miniature easel with a large photograph of an extremely handsome officer, whose lofty bearing and magnetic glance can be felt even from the portrait. The room is lighted by a candle on the chest of drawers, and another on the dressing table with a box of matches beside it.

The window is hinged doorwise and stands wide open. Outside, a pair of wooden shutters, opening outwards, also stand open. On the balcony a young lady, intensely conscious of the romantic beauty of the night, and of the fact that her own youth and beauty

---

1. The title comes from the first line of Virgil's *Aeneid*, *Arma virumque cano*, "Arms and the man I sing." The play takes place in 1885 and 1886, during the last days of the Serbo-Bulgarian War (Act I) and the ensuing Treaty of Bucharest (Acts II and III). Less than twenty years before, Bulgaria had at last achieved a measure of proud independence after five centuries of oppressive Turkish rule, although Eastern Rumelia (formerly southern Bulgaria) remained subject to the sultan. In 1885 nationalist leaders in Eastern Rumelia revolted in an attempt to unite the two Bulgarias. The neighboring kingdom of Serbia, ostensibly fearing an upset of the balance of power in the Balkans, proclaimed war, but its army was brilliantly defeated by the largely untrained Bulgarian army in November of 1885—shortly before the beginning of Shaw's play. The Bulgarians were, however, prevented from pursuing their victory by the intervention of Austria and the Treaty of Bucharest (March 3, 1886). The interest of the larger powers in Balkan affairs explains the presence of or allusion to Russian and Austrian officers in the play.

Since later printings of the play contain some inaccuracies, our text has been collated with that of the Ayot St. Lawrence edition (1930–32).

are part of it, is gazing at the snowy Balkans. She is in her night-gown, well covered by a long mantle of furs, worth, on a moderate estimate, about three times the furniture of the room.

Her reverie is interrupted by her mother, Catherine Petkoff, a woman over forty, imperiously energetic, with magnificent black hair and eyes, who might be a very splendid specimen of the wife of a mountain farmer, but is determined to be a Viennese lady, and to that end wears a fashionable tea gown on all occasions.

CATHERINE. [*entering hastily, full of good news*] Raina! [*She pronounces it Rah-eena, with the stress on the ee.*] Raina! [*She goes to the bed, expecting to find Raina there.*] Why, where—? [*Raina looks into the room*]. Heavens, child! are you out in the night air instead of in your bed? Youll catch your death. Louka told me you were asleep.

RAINA. [*dreamily*] I sent her away. I wanted to be alone. The stars are so beautiful! What is the matter?

CATHERINE. Such news! There has been a battle.

RAINA. [*her eyes dilating*] Ah! [*She comes eagerly to Catherine.*]

CATHERINE. A great battle at Slivnitza! A victory! And it was won by Sergius.

RAINA. [*with a cry of delight*] Ah! [*They embrace rapturously*] Oh, mother! [*Then, with sudden anxiety*] Is father safe?

CATHERINE. Of course: he sends me the news. Sergius is the hero of the hour, the idol of the regiment.

RAINA. Tell me, tell me. How was it? [*Ecstatically*] Oh, mother! mother! mother! [*She pulls her mother down on the ottoman; and they kiss one another frantically.*]

CATHERINE. [*with surging enthusiasm*] You cant guess how splendid it is. A cavalry charge! think of that! He defied our Russian commanders—acted without orders—led a charge on his own responsibility—headed it himself—was the first man to sweep through their guns. Cant you see it, Raina: our gallant splendid Bulgarians with their swords and eyes flashing, thundering down like an avalanche and scattering the wretched Serbs and their dandified Austrian officers like chaff. And you! you kept Sergius waiting a year before you would be betrothed to him. Oh, if you have a drop of Bulgarian blood in your veins, you will worship him when he comes back.

RAINA. What will he care for my poor little worship after the acclamations of a whole army of heroes? But no matter: I am so happy! so proud! [*She rises and walks about excitedly.*] It proves that all our ideas were real after all.

CATHERINE. [*indignantly*] Our ideas real! What do you mean?

RAINA. Our ideas of what Sergius would do. Our patriotism. Our heroic ideals. I sometimes used to doubt whether they were anything but dreams. Oh, what faithless little creatures girls are! When I buckled on Sergius's sword he looked so noble: it was treason to think of disillusion or humiliation or failure. And yet —and yet—[*She sits down again suddenly*] Promise me youll never tell him.

CATHERINE. Dont ask me for promises until I know what I'm promising.

RAINA. Well, it came into my head just as he was holding me in his arms and looking into my eyes, that perhaps we only had our heroic ideas because we are so fond of reading Byron and Pushkin,[2] and because we were so delighted with the opera that season at Bucharest. Real life is so seldom like that! indeed never, as far as I knew it then. [*Remorsefully*] Only think, mother: I doubted him: I wondered whether all his heroic qualities and his soldier-ship might not prove mere imagination when he went into a real battle. I had an uneasy fear that he might cut a poor figure there beside all those clever officers from the Tsar's court.

CATHERINE. A poor figure! Shame on you! The Serbs have Austrian officers who are just as clever as the Russians; but we have beaten them in every battle for all that.

RAINA. [*laughing and snuggling against her mother*] Yes: I was only a prosaic little coward. Oh, to think that it was all true! that Sergius is just as splendid and noble as he looks! that the world is really a glorious world for women who can see its glory and men who can act its romance! What happiness! what unspeakable fulfilment!

They are interrupted by the entry of Louka, a handsome proud girl in a pretty Bulgarian peasant's dress with double apron, so defiant that her servility to Raina is almost insolent. She is afraid of Catherine, but even with her goes as far as she dares.

LOUKA. If you please, madam, all the windows are to be closed and the shutters made fast. They say there may be shooting in the streets. [*Raina and Catherine rise together, alarmed.*] The Serbs are being chased right back through the pass; and they say they may run into the town. Our cavalry will be after them; and our people will be ready for them, you may be sure, now theyre running away. [*She goes out on the balcony, and pulls the outside shutters to; then steps back into the room.*]

CATHERINE. [*businesslike, housekeeping instincts aroused*] I must see that everything is made safe downstairs.

RAINA. I wish our people were not so cruel. What glory is there in killing wretched fugitives?

CATHERINE. Cruel! Do you suppose they would hesitate to kill you —or worse?

RAINA. [*to Louka*] Leave the shutters so that I can just close them if I hear any noise.

CATHERINE. [*authoritatively, turning on her way to the door*] Oh no, dear: you must keep them fastened. You would be sure to drop off to sleep and leave them open. Make them fast, Louka.

LOUKA. Yes, madam. [*She fastens them.*]

RAINA. Dont be anxious about me. The moment I hear a shot, I shall blow out the candles and roll myself up in bed with my ears well covered.

2. Alexander Pushkin (1799–1837), generally recognized as the great Rus- sian Romantic poet; he was influenced by Byron.

CATHERINE. Quite the wisest thing you can do, my love. Goodnight.

RAINA. Goodnight. [*Her emotion comes back for a moment.*] Wish me joy [*They kiss.*] This is the happiest night of my life—if only there are no fugitives.

CATHERINE. Go to bed, dear; and dont think of them. [*She goes out.*]

LOUKA. [*secretly to Raina*] If you would like the shutters open, just give them a push like this [*she pushes them: they open: she pulls them to again*]. One of them ought to be bolted at the bottom; but the bolt's gone.

RAINA. [*with dignity, reproving her*] Thanks, Louka; but we must do what we are told. [*Louka makes a grimace.*] Goodnight.

LOUKA. [*carelessly*] Goodnight. [*She goes out, swaggering.*]

Raina, left alone, takes off her fur cloak and throws it on the ottoman. Then she goes to the chest of drawers, and adores the portrait there with feelings that are beyond all expression. She does not kiss it or press it to her breast, or shew it any mark of bodily affection; but she takes it in her hands and elevates it, like a priestess.

RAINA. [*looking up at the picture*] Oh, I shall never be unworthy of you any more, my soul's hero: never, never, never. [*She replaces it reverently. Then she selects a novel from the little pile of books. She turns over the leaves dreamily; finds her page; turns the book inside out at it; and, with a happy sigh, gets into bed and prepares to read herself to sleep. But before abandoning herself to fiction, she raises her eyes once more, thinking of the blessed reality, and murmurs*] My hero! my hero!

A distant shot breaks the quiet of the night. She starts, listening; and two more shots, much nearer, follow, startling her so that she scrambles out of bed, and hastily blows out the candle on the chest of drawers. Then, putting her fingers in her ears, she runs to the dressing table, blows out the light there, and hurries back to bed in the dark, nothing being visible but the glimmer of the light in the pierced ball before the image, and the starlight seen through the slits at the top of the shutters. The firing breaks out again: there is a startling fusillade quite close at hand. Whilst it is still echoing, the shutters disappear, pulled open from without; and for an instant the rectangle of snowy starlight flashes out with the figure of a man silhouetted in black upon it. The shutters close immediately; and the room is dark again. But the silence is now broken by the sound of panting. Then there is a scratch; and the flame of a match is seen in the middle of the room.

RAINA. [*crouching on the bed*] Who's there? [*The match is out instantly.*] Who's there? Who is that?

A MAN'S VOICE. [*in the darkness, subduedly, but threateningly*] Sh—sh! Dont call out; or youll be shot. Be good; and no harm will happen to you. [*She is heard leaving her bed, and making for the door.*] Take care: it's no use trying to run away.

RAINA. But who—

THE VOICE. [*warning*] Remember: if you raise your voice my revolver will go off. [*Commandingly*] Strike a light and let me see

2252 · *George Bernard Shaw*

you. Do you hear. [*Another moment of silence and darkness as she retreats to the chest of drawers. Then she lights a candle; and the mystery is at an end. He is a man of about 35, in a deplorable plight, bespattered with mud and blood and snow, his belt and the strap of his revolver case keeping together the torn ruins of the blue tunic of a Serbian artillery officer. All that the candle-light and his unwashed unkempt condition make it possible to discern is that he is of middling stature and undistinguished appearance, with strong neck and shoulders, roundish obstinate looking head covered with short crisp bronze curls, clear quick eyes and good brows and mouth, hopelessly prosaic nose like that of a strong minded baby, trim soldierlike carriage and energetic manner, and with all his wits about him in spite of his desperate predicament: even with a sense of the humor of it, without, however, the least intention of trifling with it or throwing away a chance. Reckoning up what he can guess about Raina: her age, her social position, her character, and the extent to which she is frightened, he continues, more politely but still most determinedly*] Excuse my disturbing you; but you recognize my uniform? Serb! If I'm caught I shall be killed. [*Menacingly*] Do you understand that?*

RAINA. Yes.

THE MAN. Well, I dont intend to get killed if I can help it. [*Still more formidably*] Do you understand that? [*He locks the door quickly but quietly.*]

RAINA. [*disdainfully*] I suppose not. [*She draws herself up superbly, and looks him straight in the face, adding, with cutting emphasis*] Some soldiers, I know, are afraid to die.

THE MAN. [*with grim goodhumor*] All of them, dear lady, all of them, believe me. It is our duty to live as long as we can. Now, if you raise an alarm—

RAINA. [*cutting him short*] You will shoot me. How do you know that I am afraid to die?

THE MAN. [*cunningly*] Ah; but suppose I dont shoot you, what will happen then? A lot of your cavalry will burst into this pretty room of yours and slaughter me here like a pig; for I'll fight like a demon: they shant get me into the street to amuse themselves with: I know what they are. Are you prepared to receive that sort of company in your present undress? [*Raina, suddenly conscious of her nightgown, instinctively shrinks and gathers it more closely about her neck. He watches her and adds pitilessly*] Hardly presentable, eh? [*She turns to the ottoman. He raises his pistol instantly, and cries*] Stop! [*She stops.*] Where are you going?

RAINA. [*with dignified patience*] Only to get my cloak.

THE MAN. [*passing swiftly to the ottoman and snatching the cloak*] A good idea! I'll keep the cloak; and youll take care that nobody comes in and sees you without it. This is a better weapon than the revolver: eh? [*He throws the pistol down on the ottoman.*]

RAINA. [*revolted*] It is not the weapon of a gentleman!

THE MAN. It's good enough for a man with only you to stand between him and death. [*As they look at one another for a moment, Raina hardly able to believe that even a Serbian officer can be so cynically and selfishly unchivalrous, they are startled by a sharp fusillade in the street. The chill of imminent death hushes the man's voice as he adds*] Do you hear? If you are going to bring those blackguards in on me you shall receive them as you are.

Clamor and disturbance. The pursuers in the street batter at the house door, shouting Open the door! Open the door! Wake up, will you! *A man servant's voice calls to them angrily from within* This is Major Petkoff's house: you cant come in here; *but a renewal of the clamor, and a torrent of blows on the door, end with his letting a chain down with a clank, followed by a rush of heavy footsteps and a din of triumphant yells, dominated at last by the voice of Catherine, indignantly addressing an officer with* What does this mean, sir? Do you know where you are? *The noise subsides suddenly.*

LOUKA. [*outside, knocking at the bedroom door*] My lady! my lady! get up quick and open the door. If you dont they will break it down.

The fugitive throws up his head with the gesture of a man who sees that it is all over with him, and drops the manner he has been assuming to intimidate Raina.

THE MAN. [*sincerely and kindly*] No use, dear: I'm done for. [*Flinging the cloak to her*] Quick! wrap yourself up: theyre coming.

RAINA. Oh, thank you. [*She wraps herself up with intense relief*].

THE MAN. [*between his teeth*] Dont mention it.

RAINA. [*anxiously*] What will you do?

THE MAN. [*grimly*] The first man in will find out. Keep out of the way; and dont look. It wont last long; but it will not be nice. [*He draws his sabre and faces the door, waiting.*]

RAINA. [*impulsively*] I'll help you. I'll save you.

THE MAN. You cant.

RAINA. I can. I'll hide you. [*She drags him towards the window*]. Here! behind the curtains.

THE MAN. [*yielding to her*] Theres just half a chance, if you keep your head.

RAINA. [*drawing the curtain before him*] S-sh! [*She makes for the ottoman.*]

THE MAN. [*putting out his head*] Remember—

RAINA. [*running back to him*] Yes?

THE MAN.—nine soldiers out of ten are born fools.

RAINA. Oh! [*She draws the curtain angrily before him.*]

THE MAN. [*looking out at the other side*] If they find me, I promise you a fight: a devil of a fight.

She stamps at him. He disappears hastily. She takes off her cloak, and throws it across the foot of the bed. Then, with a sleepy, disturbed air, she opens the door. Louka enters excitedly.

LOUKA. One of those beasts of Serbs has been seen climbing up the waterpipe to your balcony. Our men want to search for him; and they are so wild and drunk and furious. [*She makes for the other side of the room to get as far from the door as possible.*] My lady says you are to dress at once and to—[*She sees the revolver lying on the ottoman, and stops, petrified.*]

RAINA. [*as if annoyed at being disturbed*] They shall not search here. Why have they been let in?

CATHERINE. [*coming in hastily*] Raina, darling, are you safe? Have you seen anyone or heard anything?

RAINA. I heard the shooting. Surely the soldiers will not dare come in here?

CATHERINE. I have found a Russian officer, thank Heaven: he knows Sergius. [*Speaking through the door to someone outside*] Sir: will you come in now. My daughter will receive you.

A young Russian officer, in Bulgarian uniform, enters, sword in hand.

OFFICER. [*with soft feline politeness and stiff military carriage*] Good evening, gracious lady. I am sorry to intrude; but there is a Serb hiding on the balcony. Will you and the gracious lady your mother please to withdraw whilst we search?

RAINA. [*petulantly*] Nonsense, sir: you can see that there is no one on the balcony. [*She throws the shutters wide open and stands with her back to the curtain where the man is hidden, pointing to the moonlit balcony. A couple of shots are fired right under the window; and a bullet shatters the glass opposite Raina, who winks and gasps, but stands her ground; whilst Catherine screams, and the officer, with a cry of* Take care! *rushes to the balcony.*]

THE OFFICER. [*on the balcony, shouting savagely down to the street*] Cease firing there, you fools: do you hear? Cease firing, damn you! [*He glares down for a moment; then turns to Raina, trying to resume his polite manner.*] Could anyone have got in without your knowledge? Were you asleep?

RAINA. No: I have not been to bed.

THE OFFICER. [*impatiently, coming back into the room*] Your neighbors have their heads so full of runaway Serbs that they see them everywhere. [*Politely*] Gracious lady: a thousand pardons. Goodnight. [*Military bow, which Raina returns coldly. Another to Catherine, who follows him out.*]

Raina closes the shutters. She turns and sees Louka, who has been watching the scene curiously.

RAINA. Dont leave my mother, Louka, until the soldiers go away.

Louka glances at Raina, at the ottoman, at the curtain; then purses her lips secretively, laughs insolently, and goes out. Raina, highly offended by this demonstration, follows her to the door, and shuts it behind her with a slam, locking it violently. The man immediately steps out from behind the curtain, sheathing his sabre. Then, dismissing the danger from his mind in a businesslike way, he comes affably to Raina.

THE MAN. A narrow shave; but a miss is as good as a mile. Dear young lady: your servant to the death. I wish for your sake I had joined the Bulgarian army instead of the other one. I am not a native Serb.

RAINA. [*haughtily*] No: you are one of the Austrians who set the Serbs on to rob us of our national liberty, and who officer their army for them. We hate them!

THE MAN. Austrian! not I. Dont hate me, dear young lady. I am a Swiss, fighting merely as a professional soldier. I joined the Serbs because they came first on the road from Switzerland. Be generous: youve beaten us hollow.

RAINA. Have I not been generous?

THE MAN. Noble! Heroic! But I'm not saved yet. This particular rush will soon pass through; but the pursuit will go on all night by fits and starts. I must take my chance to get off in a quiet interval. [*Pleasantly*] You dont mind my waiting just a minute or two, do you?

RAINA. [*putting on her most genteel society manner*] Oh, not at all. Wont you sit down?

THE MAN. Thanks. [*He sits on the foot of the bed.*]

Raina walks with studied elegance to the ottoman and sits down. Unfortunately she sits on the pistol, and jumps up with a shriek. The man, all nerves, shies like a frightened horse to the other side of the room.

THE MAN. [*irritably*] Dont frighten me like that. What is it?

RAINA. Your revolver! It was staring that officer in the face all the time. What an escape!

THE MAN. [*vexed at being unnecessarily terrified*] Oh, is that all?

RAINA. [*staring at him rather superciliously as she conceives a poorer and poorer opinion of him, and feels proportionately more and more at her ease*] I am sorry I frightened you. [*She takes up the pistol and hands it to him.*] Pray take it to protect yourself against me.

THE MAN. [*grinning wearily at the sarcasm as he takes the pistol*] No use, dear young lady: theres nothing in it. It's not loaded. [*He makes a grimace at it, and drops it disparagingly into his revolver case.*]

RAINA. Load it by all means.

THE MAN. Ive no ammunition. What use are cartridges in battle? I always carry chocolate instead; and I finished the last cake of that hours ago.

RAINA. [*outraged in her most cherished ideals of manhood*] Chocolate! Do you stuff your pockets with sweets—like a schoolboy—even in the field?

THE MAN. [*grinning*] Yes: isnt it contemptible? [*Hungrily*] I wish I had some now.

RAINA. Allow me. [*She sails away scornfully to the chest of drawers, and returns with the box of confectionery in her hand.*] I am sorry I have eaten them all except these. [*She offers him the box.*]

THE MAN. [*ravenously*] Youre an angel! [*He gobbles the contents.*] Creams! Delicious! [*He looks anxiously to see whether there are any more. There are none: he can only scrape the box with his fingers and suck them. When that nourishment is exhausted he accepts the inevitable with pathetic goodhumor, and says, with grateful emotion*] Bless you, dear lady! You can always tell an old soldier by the inside of his holsters and cartridge boxes. The young ones carry pistols and cartridges: the old ones, grub. Thank you. [*He hands back the box. She snatches it contemptuously from him and throws it away. He shies again, as if she had meant to strike him.*] Ugh! Dont do things so suddenly, gracious lady. It's mean to revenge yourself because I frightened you just now.

RAINA. [*loftily*] Frighten me! Do you know, sir, that though I am only a woman, I think I am at heart as brave as you.

THE MAN. I should think so. You havnt been under fire for three days as I have. I can stand two days without shewing it much; but no man can stand three days: I'm as nervous as a mouse. [*He sits down on the ottoman, and takes his head in his hands.*] Would you like to see me cry?

RAINA. [*alarmed*] No.

THE MAN. If you would, all you have to do is to scold me just as if I were a little boy and you my nurse. If I were in camp now, theyd play all sorts of tricks on me.

RAINA. [*a little moved*] I'm sorry. I wont scold you. [*Touched by the sympathy in her tone, he raises his head and looks gratefully at her: she immediately draws back and says stiffly*] You must excuse me: our soldiers are not like that. [*She moves away from the ottoman.*]

THE MAN. Oh yes they are. There are only two sorts of soldiers: old ones and young ones. Ive served fourteen years: half of your fellows never smelt powder before. Why, how is it that youve just beaten us? Sheer ignorance of the art of war, nothing else. [*Indignantly*] I never saw anything so unprofessional.

RAINA. [*ironically*] Oh! was it unprofessional to beat you?

THE MAN. Well, come! is it professional to throw a regiment of cavalry on a battery of machine guns, with the dead certainty that if the guns go off not a horse or man will ever get within fifty yards of the fire? I couldnt believe my eyes when I saw it.

RAINA. [*eagerly turning to him, as all her enthusiasm and her dreams of glory rush back on her*] Did you see the great cavalry charge? Oh, tell me about it. Describe it to me.

THE MAN. You never saw a cavalry charge, did you?

RAINA. How could I?

THE MAN. Ah, perhaps not. No: of course not! Well, it's a funny sight. It's like slinging a handful of peas against a window pane: first one comes; then two or three close behind him; and then all the rest in a lump.

RAINA. [*her eyes dilating as she raises her clasped hands ecstatically*] Yes, first One! the bravest of the brave!

THE MAN. [*prosaically*] Hm! you should see the poor devil pulling at his horse.

RAINA. Why should he pull at his horse?

THE MAN. [*impatient of so stupid a question*] It's running away with him, of course: do you suppose the fellow wants to get there before the others and be killed? Then they all come. You can tell

the young ones by their wildness and their slashing. The old ones
come bunched up under the number one guard: they know that
theyre mere projectiles, and that it's no use trying to fight. The
wounds are mostly broken knees, from the horses cannoning together.

RAINA. Ugh! But I dont believe the first man is a coward. I know
he is a hero!

THE MAN. [*goodhumoredly*] Thats what youd have said if youd seen
the first man in the charge today.

RAINA. [*breathless, forgiving him everything*] Ah, I knew it! Tell
me. Tell me about him.

THE MAN. He did it like an operatic tenor. A regular handsome
fellow, with flashing eyes and lovely moustache, shouting his
war-cry and charging like Don Quixote at the windmills. We did
laugh.

RAINA. You dared to laugh!

THE MAN. Yes; but when the sergeant ran up as white as a sheet,
and told us theyd sent us the wrong ammunition, and that we
couldnt fire a round for the next ten minutes, we laughed at the
other side of our mouths. I never felt so sick in my life; though
Ive been in one or two very tight places. And I hadnt even a
revolver cartridge: only chocolate. We'd no bayonets: nothing.
Of course, they just cut us to bits. And there was Don Quixote
flourishing like a drum major, thinking he'd done the cleverest
thing ever known, whereas he ought to be courtmartialled for it.
Of all the fools ever let loose on a field of battle, that man must
be the very maddest. He and his regiment simply committed suicide; only the pistol missed fire: thats all.

RAINA. [*deeply wounded, but steadfastly loyal to her ideals*] Indeed!
Would you know him again if you saw him?

THE MAN. Shall I ever forget him!

*She again goes to the chest of drawers. He watches her with a
vague hope that she may have something more for him to eat. She
takes the portrait from its stand and brings it to him.*

RAINA. That is a photograph of the gentleman—the patriot and
hero—to whom I am betrothed.

THE MAN. [*recognizing it with a shock*] I'm really very sorry. [*Looking at her*] Was it fair to lead me on? [*He looks at the portrait
again*] Yes: thats Don Quixote: not a doubt of it. [*He stifles a
laugh.*]

RAINA. [*quickly*] Why do you laugh?

THE MAN. [*apologetic, but still greatly tickled*] I didnt laugh, I assure
you. At least I didnt mean to. But when I think of him charging
the windmills and imagining he was doing the finest thing—[*He
chokes with suppressed laughter.*]

RAINA. [*sternly*] Give me back the portrait, sir.

THE MAN. [*with sincere remorse*] Of course. Certainly. I'm really
very sorry. [*He hands her the picture. She deliberately kisses it
and looks him straight in the face before returning to the chest
of drawers to replace it. He follows her, apologizing.*] Perhaps

I'm quite wrong, you know: no doubt I am. Most likely he had got wind of the cartridge business somehow, and knew it was a safe job.

RAINA. That is to say, he was a pretender and a coward! You did not dare say that before.

THE MAN. [*with a comic gesture of despair*] It's no use, dear lady: I cant make you see it from the professional point of view. [*As he turns away to get back to the ottoman, a couple of distant shots threaten renewed trouble.*]

RAINA. [*sternly, as she sees him listening to the shots*] So much the better for you!

THE MAN. [*turning*] How?

RAINA. You are my enemy; and you are at my mercy. What would I do if I were a professional soldier?

THE MAN. Ah, true, dear young lady: youre always right. I know how good youve been to me: to my last hour I shall remember those three chocolate creams. It was unsoldierly; but it was angelic.

RAINA. [*coldly*] Thank you. And now I will do a soldierly thing. You cannot stay here after what you have just said about my future husband; but I will go out on the balcony and see whether it is safe for you to climb down into the street. [*She turns to the window.*]

THE MAN. [*changing countenance*] Down that waterpipe! Stop! Wait! I cant! I darent! The very thought of it makes me giddy. I came up it fast enough with death behind me. But to face it now in cold blood—! [*He sinks on the ottoman.*] It's no use: I give up: I'm beaten. Give the alarm. [*He drops his head on his hands in the deepest dejection.*]

RAINA. [*disarmed by pity*] Come: dont be disheartened. [*She stoops over him almost maternally: he shakes his head.*] Oh, you are a very poor soldier: a chocolate cream soldier! Come, cheer up! it takes less courage to climb down than to face capture: remember that.

THE MAN. [*dreamily, lulled by her voice*] No: capture only means death; and death is sleep: oh, sleep, sleep, sleep, undisturbed sleep! Climbing down the pipe means doing something—exerting myself—thinking! Death ten times over first.

RAINA. [*softly and wonderingly, catching the rhythm of his weariness*] Are you as sleepy as that?

THE MAN. Ive not had two hours undisturbed sleep since I joined. I havnt closed my eyes for forty-eight hours.

RAINA. [*at her wit's end*] But what am I to do with you?

THE MAN. [*staggering up, roused by her desperation*] Of course. I must do something. [*He shakes himself; pulls himself together; and speaks with rallied vigor and courage.*] You see, sleep or no sleep, hunger or no hunger, tired or not tired, you can always do a thing when you know it must be done. Well, that pipe must be got down: [*he hits himself on the chest*] do you hear that, you chocolate cream soldier? [*He turns to the window.*]

RAINA. [*anxiously*] But if you fall?

THE MAN. I shall sleep as if the stones were a feather bed. Goodbye. [*He makes boldly for the window; and his hand is on the shutter when there is a terrible burst of firing in the street beneath.*]

RAINA. [*rushing to him*] Stop! [*She seizes him recklessly, and pulls him quite round.*] Theyll kill you.

THE MAN. [*coolly, but attentively*] Never mind: this sort of thing is all in my day's work. I'm bound to take my chance. [*Decisively*] Now do what I tell you. Put out the candle; so that they shant see the light when I open the shutters. And keep away from the window, whatever you do. If they see me theyre sure to have a shot at me.

RAINA. [*clinging to him*] Theyre sure to see you: it's bright moonlight. I'll save you. Oh, how can you be so indifferent! You want me to save you, dont you?

THE MAN. I really dont want to be troublesome. [*She shakes him in her impatience.*] I am not indifferent, dear young lady, I assure you. But how is it to be done?

RAINA. Come away from the window. [*She takes him firmly back to the middle of the room. The moment she releases him he turns mechanically towards the window again. She seizes him and turns him back, exclaiming*] Please! [*He becomes motionless, like a hypnotized rabbit, his fatigue gaining fast on him. She releases him, and addresses him patronizingly.*] Now listen. You must trust to our hospitality. You do not yet know in whose house you are. I am a Petkoff.

THE MAN. A pet what?

RAINA. [*rather indignantly*] I mean that I belong to the family of the Petkoffs, the richest and best known in our country.

THE MAN. Oh yes, of course. I beg your pardon. The Petkoffs, to be sure. How stupid of me!

RAINA. You know you never heard of them until this moment. How can you stoop to pretend!

THE MAN. Forgive me: I'm too tired to think; and the change of subject was too much for me. Dont scold me.

RAINA. I forgot. It might make you cry. [*He nods, quite seriously. She pouts and then resumes her patronizing tone.*] I must tell you that my father holds the highest command of any Bulgarian in our army. He is [*proudly*] a Major.

THE MAN. [*pretending to be deeply impressed*] A Major! Bless me! Think of that!

RAINA. You shewed great ignorance in thinking that it was necessary to climb up to the balcony because ours is the only private house that has two rows of windows. There is a flight of stairs inside to get up and down by.

THE MAN. Stairs! How grand! You live in great luxury indeed, dear young lady.

RAINA. Do you know what a library is?

THE MAN. A library? A roomful of books?

RAINA. Yes. We have one, the only one in Bulgaria.

THE MAN. Actually a real library! I should like to see that.

RAINA. [*affectedly*] I tell you these things to shew you that you are not in the house of ignorant country folk who would kill you the moment they saw your Serbian uniform, but among civilized people. We go to Bucharest every year for the opera season; and I have spent a whole month in Vienna.

THE MAN. I saw that, dear young lady. I saw at once that you knew the world.

RAINA. Have you ever seen the opera of Ernani?[3]

THE MAN. Is that the one with the devil in it in red velvet, and a soldiers' chorus?

RAINA. [*contemptuously*] No!

THE MAN. [*stifling a heavy sigh of weariness*] Then I dont know it.

RAINA. I thought you might have remembered the great scene where Ernani, flying from his foes just as you are tonight, takes refuge in the castle of his bitterest enemy, an old Castilian noble. The noble refuses to give him up. His guest is sacred to him.

THE MAN. [*quickly, waking up a little*] Have your people got that notion?

RAINA. [*with dignity*] My mother and I can understand that notion, as you call it. And if instead of threatening me with your pistol as you did you had simply thrown yourself as a fugitive on our hospitality, you would have been as safe as in your father's house.

THE MAN. Quite sure?

RAINA. [*turning her back on him in disgust*] Oh, it is useless to try to make you understand.

THE MAN. Dont be angry: you see how awkward it would be for me if there was any mistake. My father is a very hospitable man: he keeps six hotels; but I couldnt trust him as far as that. What about your father?

RAINA. He is away at Slivnitza fighting for his country. I answer for your safety. There is my hand in pledge of it. Will that reassure you? [*She offers him her hand.*]

THE MAN. [*looking dubiously at his own hand*] Better not touch my hand, dear young lady. I must have a wash first.

RAINA. [*touched*] That is very nice of you. I see that you are a gentleman.

THE MAN. [*puzzled*] Eh?

RAINA. You must not think I am surprised. Bulgarians of really good standing—people in our position—wash their hands nearly every day. So you see I can appreciate your delicacy. You may take my hand. [*She offers it again.*]

THE MAN. [*kissing it with his hands behind his back*] Thanks, gracious young lady: I feel safe at last. And now would you mind breaking the news to your mother? I had better not stay here secretly longer than is necessary.

RAINA. If you will be so good as to keep perfectly still whilst I am away.

THE MAN. Certainly. [*He sits down on the ottoman.*]

Raina goes to the bed and wraps herself in the fur cloak. His eyes

3. Opera by Verdi, first produced in 1844, based on Victor Hugo's tragedy *Hernani*.

*close. She goes to the door. Turning for a last look at him, she sees
that he is dropping off to sleep.*

RAINA. [*at the door*] You are not going asleep, are you? [*He murmurs inarticulately: she runs to him and shakes him.*] Do you
hear? Wake up: you are falling asleep.

THE MAN. Eh? Falling aslee—? Oh no: not the least in the world:
I was only thinking. It's all right: I'm wide awake.

RAINA. [*severely*] Will you please stand up while I am away. [*He
rises reluctantly.*] All the time, mind.

THE MAN. [*standing unsteadily*] Certainly. Certainly: you may depend on me.

*Raina looks doubtfully at him. He smiles weakly. She goes reluctantly, turning again at the door, and almost catching him in the
act of yawning. She goes out.*

THE MAN. [*drowsily*] Sleep, sleep, sleep, sleep, slee—[*The words
trail off into a murmur. He wakes again with a shock on the
point of falling.*] Where am I? Thats what I want to know:
where am I? Must keep awake. Nothing keeps me awake except
danger: remember that: [*intently*] danger, danger, danger, dan—
[*trailing off again: another shock*] Wheres danger? Mus' find it.
[*He starts off vaguely round the room in search of it*] What am
I looking for? Sleep—danger—dont know. [*He stumbles against
the bed.*] Ah yes: now I know. All right now. I'm to go to bed,
but not to sleep. Be sure not to sleep, because of danger. Not to
lie down either, only sit down. [*He sits on the bed. A blissful expression comes into his face.*] Ah! [*With a happy sigh he sinks
back at full length; lifts his boots into the bed with a final effort;
and falls fast asleep instantly.*]

Catherine comes in, followed by Raina.

RAINA. [*looking at the ottoman*] He's gone! I left him here.

CATHERINE. Here! Then he must have climbed down from the—

RAINA. [*seeing him*] Oh! [*She points.*]

CATHERINE. [*scandalized*] Well! [*She strides to the bed, Raina following until she is opposite her on the other side.*] He's fast
asleep. The brute!

RAINA. [*anxiously*] Sh!

CATHERINE. [*shaking him*] Sir! [*Shaking him again, harder*] Sir!!
[*Vehemently, shaking very hard*] Sir!!!

RAINA. [*catching her arm*] Dont, mamma; the poor darling is worn
out. Let him sleep.

CATHERINE. [*letting him go, and turning amazed to Raina*] The poor
darling! Raina!!! [*She looks sternly at her daughter.*]

The man sleeps profoundly.

Act II

*The sixth of March, 1886. In the garden of Major Petkoff's
house. It is a fine spring morning: the garden looks fresh and pretty.
Beyond the paling the tops of a couple of minarets can be seen,
shewing that there is a valley there, with the little town in it. A
few miles further the Balkan mountains rise and shut in the land-*

scape. Looking towards them from within the garden, the side of the house is seen on the left, with a garden door reached by a little flight of steps. On the right the stable yard, with its gateway, encroaches on the garden. There are fruit bushes along the paling and house, covered with washing spread out to dry. A path runs by the house, and rises by two steps at the corner, where it turns out of sight. In the middle, a small table, with two bent wood chairs at it, is laid for breakfast with Turkish coffee pot, cups, rolls, etc.; but the cups have been used and the bread broken. There is a wooden garden seat against the wall on the right.

Louka, smoking a cigaret, is standing between the table and the house, turning her back with angry disdain on a man servant who is lecturing her. He is a middle-aged man of cool temperament and low but clear and keen intelligence, with the complacency of the servant who values himself on his rank in servitude, and the imperturbability of the accurate calculator who has no illusions. He wears a white Bulgarian costume: jacket with embroidered border, sash, wide knickerbockers, and decorated gaiters. His head is shaved up to the crown, giving him a high Japanese forehead. His name is Nicola.

NICOLA. Be warned in time, Louka: mend your manners. I know the mistress. She is so grand that she never dreams that any servant could dare be disrespectful to her; but if she once suspects that you are defying her, out you go.

LOUKA. I do defy her. I will defy her. What do I care for her?

NICOLA. If you quarrel with the family, I never can marry you. It's the same as if you quarrelled with me!

LOUKA. You take her part against me, do you?

NICOLA. [*sedately*] I shall always be dependent on the good will of the family. When I leave their service and start a shop in Sofia, their custom will be half my capital: their bad word would ruin me.

LOUKA. You have no spirit. I should like to catch them saying a word against me!

NICOLA. [*pityingly*] I should have expected more sense from you, Louka. But youre young: youre young!

LOUKA. Yes; and you like me the better for it, dont you? But I know some family secrets they wouldnt care to have told, young as I am. Let them quarrel with me if they dare!

NICOLA. [*with compassionate superiority*] Do you know what they would do if they heard you talk like that?

LOUKA. What could they do?

NICOLA. Discharge you for untruthfulness. Who would believe any stories you told after that? Who would give you another situation? Who in this house would dare be seen speaking to you ever again? How long would your father be left on his little farm? [*She impatiently throws away the end of her cigaret, and stamps on it.*] Child: you dont know the power such high people have over the like of you and me when we try to rise out of our poverty against them. [*He goes close to her and lowers his voice.*] Look at me, ten years in their service. Do you think I know no secrets? I know things about the mistress that she wouldnt have the master know for a thousand levas.[4] I know things about him that she wouldnt let him hear the last of for six months if I blabbed them to her. I know things about Raina that would break off her match with Sergius if—

LOUKA. [*turning on him quickly*] How do you know? I never told you!

NICOLA. [*opening his eyes cunningly*] So thats your little secret, is it? I thought it might be something like that. Well, you take my advice and be respectful; and make the mistress feel that no matter what you know or dont know, she can depend on you to hold your tongue and serve the family faithfully. Thats what they like; and thats how youll make most out of them.

LOUKA. [*with searching scorn*] You have the soul of a servant, Nicola.

NICOLA. [*complacently*] Yes: thats the secret of success in service.

A loud knocking with a whip handle on a wooden door is heard from the stable yard.

MALE VOICE OUTSIDE. Hollo! Hollo there! Nicola!

LOUKA. Master! back from the war!

NICOLA. [*quickly*] My word for it, Louka, the war's over. Off with you and get some fresh coffee. [*He runs out into the stable yard.*]

LOUKA. [*as she collects the coffee pot and cups on the tray, and carries it into the house*] Youll never put the soul of a servant into me.

Major Petkoff comes from the stable yard, followed by Nicola. He is a cheerful, excitable, insignificant, unpolished man of about 50, naturally unambitious except as to his income and his importance in local society, but just now greatly pleased with the military rank which the war has thrust on him as a man of consequence in his town. The fever of plucky patriotism which the Serbian attack roused in all the Bulgarians has pulled him through the war; but he is obviously glad to be home again.

PETKOFF. [*pointing to the table with his whip*] Breakfast out here, eh?

NICOLA. Yes, sir. The mistress and Miss Raina have just gone in.

PETKOFF. [*sitting down and taking a roll*] Go in and say Ive come; and get me some fresh coffee.

NICOLA. It's coming, sir. [*He goes to the house door. Louka, with fresh coffee, a clean cup, and a brandy bottle on her tray, meets him.*] Have you told the mistress?

LOUKA. Yes: she's coming.

Nicola goes into the house. Louka brings the coffee to the table.

PETKOFF. Well: the Serbs havnt run away with you, have they?

LOUKA. No, sir.

PETKOFF. Thats right. Have you brought me some cognac?

LOUKA. [*putting the bottle on the table*] Here, sir.

PETKOFF. Thats right. [*He pours some into his coffee.*]

4. The *lev* was the Bulgarian monetary unit, equal to about a cent (Shaw apparently thought the plural, *leva*, was the singular).

Catherine, who, having at this early hour made only a very per-functory toilet, wears a Bulgarian apron over a once brilliant but now half worn-out dressing gown, and a colored handkerchief tied over her thick black hair, comes from the house with Turkish slippers on her bare feet, looking astonishingly handsome and stately under all the circumstances. Louka goes into the house.

CATHERINE. My dear Paul: what a surprise for us! [*She stoops over the back of his chair to kiss him.*] Have they brought you fresh coffee?

PETKOFF. Yes: Louka's been looking after me. The war's over. The treaty was signed three days ago at Bucharest; and the decree for our army to demobilize was issued yesterday.

CATHERINE. [*springing erect, with flashing eyes*] Paul: have you let the Austrians force you to make peace?

PETKOFF. [*submissively*] My dear: they didnt consult me. What could I do? [*She sits down and turns away from him.*] But of course we saw to it that the treaty was an honorable one. It declares peace—

CATHERINE. [*outraged*] Peace!

PETKOFF. [*appeasing her*]—but not friendly relations: remember that. They wanted to put that in; but I insisted on its being struck out. What more could I do?

CATHERINE. You could have annexed Serbia and made Prince Alexander[5] Emperor of the Balkans. Thats what I would have done.

PETKOFF. I dont doubt it in the least, my dear. But I should have had to subdue the whole Austrian Empire first; and that would have kept me too long away from you. I missed you greatly.

CATHERINE. [*relenting*] Ah! [*She stretches her hand affectionately across the table to squeeze his.*]

PETKOFF. And how have you been, my dear?

CATHERINE. Oh, my usual sore throats: thats all.

PETKOFF. [*with conviction*] That comes from washing your neck every day. Ive often told you so.

CATHERINE. Nonsense, Paul!

PETKOFF. [*over his coffee and cigaret*] I dont believe in going too far with these modern customs. All this washing cant be good for the health: it's not natural. There was an Englishman at Philippopolis who used to wet himself all over with cold water every morning when he got up. Disgusting! It all comes from the English: their climate makes them so dirty that they have to be perpetually washing themselves. Look at my father! he never had a bath in his life; and he lived to be ninety-eight, the healthiest man in Bulgaria. I dont mind a good wash once a week to keep up my position; but once a day is carrying the thing to a ridiculous extreme.

CATHERINE. You are a barbarian at heart still, Paul. I hope you behaved yourself before all those Russian officers.

PETKOFF. I did my best. I took care to let them know that we have a library.

5. Prince Alexander of Battenberg, first elected ruler of Bulgaria (reigned 1879–86).

CATHERINE. Ah; but you didnt tell them that we have an electric bell in it? I have had one put up.

PETKOFF. Whats an electric bell?

CATHERINE. You touch a button; something tinkles in the kitchen; and then Nicola comes up.

PETKOFF. Why not shout for him?

CATHERINE. Civilized people never shout for their servants. Ive learnt that while you were away.

PETKOFF. Well, I'll tell you something Ive learnt too. Civilized people dont hang out their washing to dry where visitors can see it; so youd better have all that [*indicating the clothes on the bushes*] put somewhere else.

CATHERINE. Oh, thats absurd, Paul: I dont believe really refined people notice such things.

SERGIUS. [*knocking at the stable gates*] Gate, Nicola!

PETKOFF. Theres Sergius. [*Shouting*] Hollo, Nicola!

CATHERINE. Oh, dont shout, Paul: it really isnt nice.

PETKOFF. Bosh! [*He shouts louder than before*] Nicola!

NICOLA. [*appearing at the house door*] Yes, sir.

PETKOFF. Are you deaf? Dont you hear Major Saranoff knocking? Bring him round this way. [*He pronounces the name with the stress on the second syllable: Sarahnoff*].

NICOLA. Yes, major. [*He goes into the stable yard.*]

PETKOFF. You must talk to him, my dear, until Raina takes him off our hands. He bores my life out about our not promoting him. Over my head, if you please.

CATHERINE. He certainly ought to be promoted when he marries Raina. Besides, the country should insist on having at least one native general.

PETKOFF. Yes; so that he could throw away whole brigades instead of regiments. It's no use, my dear: he hasnt the slightest chance of promotion until we're quite sure that the peace will be a lasting one.

NICOLA. [*at the gate, announcing*] Major Sergius Saranoff! [*He goes into the house and returns presently with a third chair, which he places at the table. He then withdraws.*]

Major Sergius Saranoff, the original of the portrait in Raina's room, is a tall romantically handsome man, with the physical hardihood, the high spirit, and the susceptible imagination of an untamed mountaineer chieftain. But his remarkable personal distinction is of a characteristically civilized type. The ridges of his eyebrows, curving with an interrogative twist round the projections at the outer corners; his jealously observant eye; his nose, thin, keen, and apprehensive in spite of the pugnacious high bridge and large nostril; his assertive chin would not be out of place in a Parisian salon, shewing that the clever imaginative barbarian has an acute critical faculty which has been thrown into intense activity by the arrival of western civilization in the Balkans. The result is precisely what the advent of nineteenth century thought first produced in England: to wit, Byronism. By his brooding on the perpetual failure, not only of others, but of himself, to live up to his ideals; by his consequent cynical scorn for humanity; by his jejune credulity as to the absolute validity of his concepts and the unworthiness of the world in disregarding them; by his wincings and mockeries under the sting of the petty disillusions which every hour spent among men brings to his sensitive observation, he has acquired the half tragic, half ironic air, the mysterious moodiness, the suggestion of a strange and terrible history that has left nothing but undying re-morse, by which Childe Harold[6] fascinated the grandmothers of his English contemporaries. It is clear that here or nowhere is Raina's ideal hero. Catherine is hardly less enthusiastic about him than her daughter, and much less reserved in shewing her enthusiasm. As he enters from the stable gate, she rises effusively to greet him. Pet-koff is distinctly less disposed to make a fuss about him.

PETKOFF. Here already, Sergius! Glad to see you.

CATHERINE. My dear Sergius! [*She holds out both her hands.*]

SERGIUS. [*kissing them with scrupulous gallantry*] My dear mother, if I may call you so.

PETKOFF. [*drily*] Mother-in-law, Sergius: mother-in-law! Sit down; and have some coffee.

SERGIUS. Thank you: none for me. [*He gets away from the table with a certain distaste for Petkoff's enjoyment of it, and posts himself with conscious dignity against the rail of the steps leading to the house.*]

CATHERINE. You look superb. The campaign has improved you, Sergius. Everybody here is mad about you. We were all wild with enthusiasm about that magnificent cavalry charge.

SERGIUS. [*with grave irony*] Madam: it was the cradle and the grave of my military reputation.

CATHERINE. How so?

SERGIUS. I won the battle the wrong way when our worthy Russian generals were losing it the right way. In short, I upset their plans, and wounded their self-esteem. Two Cossack colonels had their regiments routed on the most correct principles of scientific war-fare. Two major-generals got killed strictly according to military etiquette. The two colonels are now major-generals; and I am still a simple major.

CATHERINE. You shall not remain so, Sergius. The women are on your side; and they will see that justice is done you.

SERGIUS. It is too late. I have only waited for the peace to send in my resignation.

PETKOFF. [*dropping his cup in his amazement*] Your resignation!

CATHERINE. Oh, you must withdraw it!

SERGIUS. [*with resolute measured emphasis, folding his arms*] I never withdraw.

PETKOFF. [*vexed*] Now who could have supposed you were going to do such a thing?

---

6. Hero of Byron's famous travel poem, *Childe Harold* (1812, 1816, 1818), an epitome of the Romantic Man of Feeling.

SERGIUS. [*with fire*] Everyone that knew me. But enough of myself and my affairs. How is Raina; and where is Raina?

RAINA. [*suddenly coming round the corner of the house and standing at the top of the steps in the path*] Raina is here.

She makes a charming picture as they turn to look at her. She wears an underdress of pale green silk, draped with an overdress of thin ecru canvas embroidered with gold. She is crowned with a dainty eastern cap of gold tinsel. Sergius goes impulsively to meet her. Posing regally, she presents her hand: he drops chivalrously on one knee and kisses it.

PETKOFF. [*aside to Catherine, beaming with parental pride*] Pretty, isnt it? She always appears at the right moment.

CATHERINE. [*impatiently*] Yes; she listens for it. It is an abominable habit.

Sergius leads Raina forward with splendid gallantry. When they arrive at the table, she turns to him with a bend of the head: he bows; and thus they separate, he coming to his place and she going behind her father's chair.

RAINA. [*stooping and kissing her father*] Dear father! Welcome home!

PETKOFF. [*patting her cheek*] My little pet girl. [*He kisses her. She goes to the chair left by Nicola for Sergius, and sits down.*]

CATHERINE. And so youre no longer a soldier, Sergius.

SERGIUS. I am no longer a soldier. Soldiering, my dear madam, is the coward's art of attacking mercilessly when you are strong, and keeping out of harm's way when you are weak. That is the whole secret of successful fighting. Get your enemy at a disadvantage; and never, on any account, fight him on equal terms.

PETKOFF. They wouldnt let us make a fair stand-up fight of it. However, I suppose soldiering has to be a trade like any other trade.

SERGIUS. Precisely. But I have no ambition to shine as a tradesman; so I have taken the advice of that bagman of a captain that settled the exchange of prisoners with us at Pirot, and given it up.

PETKOFF. What! that Swiss fellow? Sergius: Ive often thought of that exchange since. He over-reached us about those horses.

SERGIUS. Of course he over-reached us. His father was a hotel and livery stable keeper; and he owed his first step to his knowledge of horse-dealing. [*With mock enthusiasm*] Ah, he was a soldier: every inch a soldier! If only I had bought the horses for my regiment instead of foolishly leading it into danger, I should have been a field-marshal now!

CATHERINE. A Swiss? What was he doing in the Serbian army?

PETKOFF. A volunteer, of course: keen on picking up his profession. [*Chuckling*] We shouldnt have been able to begin fighting if these foreigners hadnt shewn us how to do it: we knew nothing about it; and neither did the Serbs. Egad, thered have been no war without them!

RAINA. Are there many Swiss officers in the Serbian Army?

PETKOFF. No. All Austrians, just as our officers were all Russians. This was the only Swiss I came across. I'll never trust a Swiss again. He humbugged us into giving him fifty ablebodied men for two hundred worn out chargers. They werent even eatable!

SERGIUS. We were two children in the hands of that consummate soldier, major: simply two innocent little children.

RAINA. What was he like?

CATHERINE. Oh, Raina, what a silly question!

SERGIUS. He was like a commercial traveller in uniform. Bourgeois to his boots!

PETKOFF. [*grinning*] Sergius: tell Catherine that queer story his friend told us about how he escaped after Slivnitza. You remember. About his being hid by two women.

SERGIUS. [*with bitter irony*] Oh yes: quite a romance! He was serving in the very battery I so unprofessionally charged. Being a thorough soldier, he ran away like the rest of them, with our cavalry at his heels. To escape their sabres he climbed a waterpipe and made his way into the bedroom of a young Bulgarian lady. The young lady was enchanted by his persuasive commercial traveller's manners. She very modestly entertained him for an hour or so, and then called in her mother lest her conduct should appear unmaidenly. The old lady was equally fascinated; and the fugitive was sent on his way in the morning, disguised in an old coat belonging to the master of the house, who was away at the war.

RAINA. [*rising with marked stateliness*] Your life in the camp has made you coarse, Sergius. I did not think you would have repeated such a story before me. [*She turns away coldy.*]

CATHERINE. [*also rising*] She is right, Sergius. If such women exist, we should be spared the knowledge of them.

PETKOFF. Pooh! nonsense! what does it matter?

SERGIUS. [*ashamed*] No, Petkoff: I was wrong. [*To Raina, with earnest humility*] I beg your pardon. I have behaved abominably. Forgive me, Raina. [*She bows reservedly.*] And you too, madam. [*Catherine bows graciously and sits down. He proceeds solemnly, again addressing Raina*] The glimpses I have had of the seamy side of life during the last few months have made me cynical; but I should not have brought my cynicism here: least of all into your presence, Raina. I— [*Here, turning to the others, he is evidently going to begin a long speech when the Major interrupts him.*]

PETKOFF. Stuff and nonsense, Sergius! Thats quite enough fuss about nothing: a soldier's daughter should be able to stand up without flinching to a little strong conversation. [*He rises.*] Come: it's time for us to get to business. We have to make up our minds how those three regiments are to get back to Philippopolis: theres no forage for them on the Sofia route. [*He goes towards the house.*] Come along. [*Sergius is about to follow him when Catherine rises and intervenes.*]

CATHERINE. Oh, Paul, cant you spare Sergius for a few moments? Raina has hardly seen him yet. Perhaps I can help you to settle about the regiments.

SERGIUS. [*protesting*] My dear madam, impossible: you—

CATHERINE. [*stopping him playfully*] You stay here, my dear Sergius: theres no hurry. I have a word or two to say to Paul. [*Sergius instantly bows and steps back.*] Now, dear [*taking Petkoff's arm*]: come and see the electric bell.

PETKOFF. Oh, very well, very well.

They go into the house together affectionately. Sergius, left alone with Raina, looks anxiously at her, fearing that she is still offended. She smiles, and stretches out her arms to him.

SERGIUS. [*hastening to her*] Am I forgiven?

RAINA. [*placing her hands on his shoulders as she looks up at him with admiration and worship*] My hero! My king!

SERGIUS. My queen! [*He kisses her on the forehead.*]

RAINA. How I have envied you, Sergius! You have been out in the world, on the field of battle, able to prove yourself there worthy of any woman in the world; whilst I have had to sit at home inactive—dreaming—useless—doing nothing that could give me the right to call myself worthy of any man.

SERGIUS. Dearest: all my deeds have been yours. You inspired me. I have gone through the war like a knight in a tournament with his lady looking down at him!

RAINA. And you have never been absent from my thoughts for a moment. [*Very solemnly*] Sergius: I think we two have found the higher love. When I think of you, I feel that I could never do a base deed, or think an ignoble thought.

SERGIUS. My lady and my saint! [*He clasps her reverently.*]

RAINA. [*returning his embrace*] My lord and my—

SERGIUS. Sh—sh! Let me be the worshipper, dear. You little know how unworthy even the best man is of a girl's pure passion!

RAINA. I trust you. I love you. You will never disappoint me, Sergius. [*Louka is heard singing within the house. They quickly release each other.*] I cant pretend to talk indifferently before her: my heart is too full. [*Louka comes from the house with her tray. She goes to the table, and begins to clear it, with her back turned to them.*] I will get my hat; and then we can go out until lunch time. Wouldnt you like that?

SERGIUS. Be quick. If you are away five minutes, it will seem five hours. [*Raina runs to the top of the steps, and turns there to exchange looks with him and wave him a kiss with both hands. He looks after her with emotion for a moment; then turns slowly away, his face radiant with the loftiest exaltation. The movement shifts his field of vision, into the corner of which there now comes the tail of Louka's double apron. His attention is arrested at once. He takes a stealthy look at her, and begins to twirl his moustache mischievously, with his left hand akimbo on his hip. Finally, striking the ground with his heels in something of a cavalry swagger, he strolls over to the other side of the table, opposite her, and says*] Louka: do you know what the higher love is?

LOUKA. [*astonished*] No, sir.

SERGIUS. Very fatiguing thing to keep up for any length of time,

Louka. One feels the need of some relief after it.

LOUKA. [*innocently*] Perhaps you would like some coffee, sir? [*She stretches her hand across the table for the coffee pot.*]

SERGIUS. [*taking her hand*] Thank you, Louka.

LOUKA. [*pretending to pull*] Oh, sir, you know I didnt mean that. I'm surprised at you!

SERGIUS. [*coming clear of the table and drawing her with him*] I am surprised at myself, Louka. What would Sergius, the hero of Slivnitza, say if he saw me now? What would Sergius, the apostle of the higher love, say if he saw me now? What would the half dozen Sergiuses who keep popping in and out of this handsome figure of mine say if they caught us here? [*Letting go her hand and slipping his arm dexterously round her waist*] Do you consider my figure handsome, Louka?

LOUKA. Let me go, sir. I shall be disgraced. [*She struggles: he holds her inexorably.*] Oh, will you let go?

SERGIUS. [*looking straight into her eyes*] No.

LOUKA. Then stand back where we cant be seen. Have you no common sense?

SERGIUS. Ah! thats reasonable. [*He takes her into the stableyard gateway, where they are hidden from the house.*]

LOUKA. [*plaintively*] I may have been seen from the windows: Miss Raina is sure to be spying about after you.

SERGIUS. [*stung: letting her go*] Take care, Louka. I may be worthless enough to betray the higher love; but do not you insult it.

LOUKA. [*demurely*] Not for the world, sir, I'm sure. May I go on with my work, please, now?

SERGIUS. [*again putting his arm round her*] You are a provoking little witch, Louka. If you were in love with me, would you spy out of windows on me?

LOUKA. Well, you see, sir, since you say you are half a dozen different gentlemen all at once, I should have a great deal to look after.

SERGIUS. [*charmed*] Witty as well as pretty. [*He tries to kiss her.*]

LOUKA. [*avoiding him*] No: I dont want your kisses. Gentlefolk are all alike: you making love to me behind Miss Raina's back; and she doing the same behind yours.

SERGIUS. [*recoiling a step*] Louka!

LOUKA. It shews how little you really care.

SERGIUS. [*dropping his familiarity, and speaking with freezing politeness*] If our conversation is to continue, Louka, you will please remember that a gentleman does not discuss the conduct of the lady he is engaged to with her maid.

LOUKA. It's so hard to know what a gentleman considers right. I thought from your trying to kiss me that you had given up being so particular.

SERGIUS. [*turning from her and striking his forehead as he comes back into the garden from the gateway*] Devil! devil!

LOUKA. Ha! ha! I expect one of the six of you is very like me, sir; though I am only Miss Raina's maid. [*She goes back to her work at the table, taking no further notice of him.*]

SERGIUS. [*speaking to himself*] Which of the six is the real man? thats the question that torments me. One of them is a hero, another a buffoon, another a humbug, another perhaps a bit of a blackguard. [*He pauses, and looks furtively at Louka as he adds, with deep bitterness*] And one, at least, is a coward: jealous, like all cowards. [*He goes to the table.*] Louka.

LOUKA. Yes?

SERGIUS. Who is my rival?

LOUKA. You shall never get that out of me, for love or money.

SERGIUS. Why?

LOUKA. Never mind why. Besides, you would tell that I told you; and I should lose my place.

SERGIUS. [*holding out his right hand in affirmation*] No! on the honor of a—[*He checks himself; and his hand drops, nerveless, as he concludes sardonically*]—of a man capable of behaving as I have been behaving for the last five minutes. Who is he?

LOUKA. I dont know. I never saw him. I only heard his voice through the door of her room.

SERGIUS. Damnation! How dare you?

LOUKA. [*retreating*] Oh, I mean no harm: youve no right to take up my words like that. The mistress knows all about it. And I tell you that if that gentleman ever comes here again, Miss Raina will marry him, whether he likes it or not. I know the difference between the sort of manner you and she put on before one another and the real manner.

Sergius shivers as if she had stabbed him. Then, setting his face like iron, he strides grimly to her, and grips her above the elbows with both hands.

SERGIUS. Now listen you to me.

LOUKA. [*wincing*] Not so tight: youre hurting me.

SERGIUS. That doesn't matter. You have stained my honor by making me a party to your eavesdropping. And you have betrayed your mistress.

LOUKA. [*writhing*] Please—

SERGIUS. That shews that you are an abominable little clod of common clay, with the soul of a servant. [*He lets her go as if she were an unclean thing, and turns away, dusting his hands of her, to the bench by the wall, where he sits down with averted head, meditating gloomily.*]

LOUKA. [*whimpering angrily with her hands up her sleeves, feeling her bruised arms*] You know how to hurt with your tongue as well as with your hands. But I dont care, now Ive found out that whatever clay I'm made of, youre made of the same. As for her, she's a liar; and her fine airs are a cheat; and I'm worth six of her. [*She shakes the pain off hardily; tosses her head; and sets to work to put the things on the tray.*]

He looks doubtfully at her. She finishes packing the tray, and laps the cloth over the edges, so as to carry all out together. As she stoops to lift it, he rises.

SERGIUS. Louka! [*She stops and looks defiantly at him.*] A gentleman has no right to hurt a woman under any circumstances. [*With profound humility, uncovering his head*] I beg your pardon.

LOUKA. That sort of apology may satisfy a lady. Of what use is it to a servant?

SERGIUS. [*rudely crossed in his chivalry, throws it off with a bitter laugh, and says slightingly*] Oh! you wish to be paid for the hurt! [*He puts on his shako, and takes some money from his pocket.*]

LOUKA. [*her eyes filling with tears in spite of herself*] No: I want my hurt made well.

SERGIUS. [*sobered by her tone*] How?

She rolls up her left sleeve; clasps her arm with the thumb and fingers of her right hand; and looks down at the bruise. Then she raises her head and looks straight at him. Finally, with a superb gesture, she presents her arm to be kissed. Amazed, he looks at her; at the arm; at her again; hesitates; and then, with shuddering intensity, exclaims Never! *and gets away as far as possible from her.*

Her arm drops. Without a word, and with unaffected dignity, she takes her tray, and is approaching the house when Raina returns, wearing a hat and jacket in the height of the Vienna fashion of the previous year, 1885. Louka makes way proudly for her, and then goes into the house.

RAINA. I'm ready. Whats the matter? [*Gaily*] Have you been flirting with Louka?

SERGIUS. [*hastily*] No, no. How can you think such a thing?

RAINA. [*ashamed of herself*] Forgive me, dear: it was only a jest. I am so happy today.

He goes quickly to her, and kisses her hand remorsefully. Catherine comes out and calls to them from the top of the steps.

CATHERINE. [*coming down to them*] I am sorry to disturb you, children; but Paul is distracted over those three regiments. He doesnt know how to send them to Philippopolis; and he objects to every suggestion of mine. You must go and help him, Sergius. He is in the library.

RAINA. [*disappointed*] But we are just going out for a walk.

SERGIUS. I shall not be long. Wait for me just five minutes. [*He runs up the steps to the door.*]

RAINA. [*following him to the foot of the steps and looking up at him with timid coquetry*] I shall go round and wait in full view of the library windows. Be sure you draw father's attention to me. If you are a moment longer than five minutes, I shall go in and fetch you, regiments or no regiments.

SERGIUS. [*laughing*] Very well. [*He goes in.*]

Raina watches him until he is out of her sight. Then, with a perceptible relaxation of manner, she begins to pace up and down the garden in a brown study.

CATHERINE. Imagine their meeting that Swiss and hearing the whole story! The very first thing your father asked for was the old coat we sent him off in. A nice mess you have got us into!

RAINA. [*gazing thoughtfully at the gravel as she walks*] The little beast!

CATHERINE. Little beast! What little beast?

RAINA. To go and tell! Oh, if I had him here, I'd cram him with chocolate creams til he couldnt ever speak again!

CATHERINE. Dont talk such stuff. Tell me the truth, Raina. How long was he in your room before you came to me?

RAINA. [*whisking round and recommencing her march in the opposite direction*] Oh, I forget.

CATHERINE. You cannot forget! Did he really climb up after the soldiers were gone; or was he there when that officer searched the room?

RAINA. No. Yes: I think he must have been there then.

CATHERINE. You think! Oh, Raina! Raina! Will anything ever make you straightforward? If Sergius finds out, it will be all over between you.

RAINA. [*with cool impertinence*] Oh, I know Sergius is your pet. I sometimes wish you could marry him instead of me. You would just suit him. You would pet him, and spoil him, and mother him to perfection.

CATHERINE. [*opening her eyes very widely indeed*] Well, upon my word!

RAINA. [*capriciously: half to herself*] I always feel a longing to do or say something dreadful to him—to shock his propriety—to scandalize the five senses out of him. [*To Catherine, perversely*] I dont care whether he finds out about the chocolate cream soldier or not. I half hope he may.[*She again turns and strolls flippantly away up the path to the corner of the house.*]

CATHERINE. And what should I be able to say to your father, pray?

RAINA. [*over her shoulder, from the top of the two steps*] Oh, poor father! As if he could help himself! [*She turns the corner and passes out of sight.*]

CATHERINE. [*looking after her, her fingers itching*] Oh, if you were only ten years younger! [*Louka comes from the house with a salver, which she carries hanging down by her side.*] Well?

LOUKA. Theres a gentleman just called, madam. A Serbian officer.

CATHERINE. [*flaming*] A Serb! And how dare he—[*checking herself bitterly*] Oh, I forgot. We are at peace now. I suppose we shall have them calling every day to pay their compliments. Well: if he is an officer why dont you tell your master? He is in the library with Major Saranoff. Why do you come to me?

LOUKA. But he asks for you, madam. And I dont think he knows who you are: he said the lady of the house. He gave me this little ticket for you. [*She takes a card out of her bosom; puts it on the salver; and offers it to Catherine.*]

CATHERINE. [*reading*] "Captain Bluntschli"? Thats a German name.

LOUKA. Swiss, madam, I think.

CATHERINE. [*with a bound that makes Louka jump back*] Swiss! What is he like?

LOUKA. [*timidly*] He has a big carpet bag, madam.

CATHERINE. Oh Heavens! he's come to return the coat. Send him away: say we're not at home: ask him to leave his address and I'll write to him. Oh stop: that will never do. Wait! [*She throws herself into a chair to think it out. Louka waits.*] The master and Major Saranoff are busy in the library, arnt they?

LOUKA. Yes, madam.

CATHERINE. [*decisively*] Bring the gentleman out here at once. [*Peremptorily*] And be very polite to him. Dont delay. Here [*impatiently snatching the salver from her*]: leave that here; and go straight back to him.

LOUKA. Yes, madam [*going*].

CATHERINE. Louka!

LOUKA. [*stopping*] Yes, madam.

CATHERINE. Is the library door shut?

LOUKA. I think so, madam.

CATHERINE. If not, shut it as you pass through.

LOUKA. Yes, madam [*going.*]

CATHERINE. Stop [*Louka stops*]. He will have to go that way [*indicating the gate of the stable yard*]. Tell Nicola to bring his bag here after him. Dont forget.

LOUKA. [*surprised*] His bag?

CATHERINE. Yes: here: as soon as possible. [*Vehemently*] Be quick! [*Louka runs into the house. Catherine snatches her apron off and throws it behind a bush. She then takes up the salver and uses it as a mirror, with the result that the handkerchief tied round her head follows the apron. A touch to her hair and a shake to her dressing gown make her presentable.*] Oh, how? how? how can a man be such a fool! Such a moment to select! [*Louka appears at the door of the house, announcing* Captain Bluntschli. *She stands aside at the top of the steps to let him pass before she goes in again. He is the man of the midnight adventure in Raina's room, clean, well brushed, smartly uniformed, and out of trouble, but still unmistakably the same man. The moment Louka's back is turned, Catherine swoops on him with impetuous, urgent, coaxing appeal.*] Captain Bluntschli: I am very glad to see you; but you must leave this house at once. [*He raises his eyebrows.*] My husband has just returned with my future son-in-law; and they know nothing. If they did, the consequences would be terrible. You are a foreigner: you do not feel our national animosities as we do. We still hate the Serbs: the effect of the peace on my husband has been to make him feel like a lion baulked of his prey. If he discovers our secret, he will never forgive me; and my daughter's life will hardly be safe. Will you, like the chivalrous gentleman and soldier you are, leave at once before he finds you here?

BLUNTSCHLI. [*disappointed, but philosophical*] At once, gracious lady. I only came to thank you and return the coat you lent me. If you will allow me to take it out of my bag and leave it with your servant as I pass out, I need detain you no further. [*He turns to go into the house.*]

CATHERINE. [*catching him by the sleeve*] Oh, you must not think of going back that way. [*Coaxing him across to the stable gates*] This is the shortest way out. Many thanks. So glad to have been of service to you. Good-bye.

BLUNTSCHLI. But my bag?

CATHERINE. It shall be sent on. You will leave me your address.

BLUNTSCHLI. True. Allow me. [*He takes out his cardcase, and stops to write his address, keeping Catherine in an agony of impatience. As he hands her the card, Petkoff, hatless, rushes from the house in a fluster of hospitality, followed by Sergius.*]

PETKOFF. [*as he hurries down the steps*] My dear Captain Bluntschli—

CATHERINE. Oh Heavens! [*She sinks on the seat against the wall.*]

PETKOFF. [*too preoccupied to notice her as he shakes Bluntschli's hand heartily*] Those stupid people of mine thought I was out here, instead of in the—haw!—library [*he cannot mention the library without betraying how proud he is of it*]. I saw you through the window. I was wondering why you didnt come in. Saranoff is with me: you remember him, dont you?

SERGIUS. [*saluting humorously, and then offering his hand with great charm of manner*] Welcome, our friend the enemy!

PETKOFF. No longer the enemy, happily. [*Rather anxiously*] I hope youve called as a friend, and not about horses or prisoners.

CATHERINE. Oh, quite as a friend, Paul. I was just asking Captain Bluntschli to stay to lunch; but he declares he must go at once.

SERGIUS. [*sardonically*] Impossible, Bluntschli. We want you here badly. We have to send on three cavalry regiments to Philippopolis; and we dont in the least know how to do it.

BLUNTSCHLI. [*suddenly attentive and businesslike*] Philippopolis? The forage is the trouble, I suppose.

PETKOFF. [*eagerly*] Yes: thats it. [*To Sergius*] He sees the whole thing at once.

BLUNTSCHLI. I think I can shew you how to manage that.

SERGIUS. Invaluable man! Come along! [*Towering over Bluntschli, he puts his hand on his shouder and takes him to the steps, Petkoff following.*]

Raina comes from the house as Bluntschli puts his foot on the first step.

RAINA. Oh! The chocolate cream soldier!

Bluntschli stands rigid. Sergius, amazed, looks at Raina, then at Petkoff, who looks back at him and then at his wife.

CATHERINE. [*with commanding presence of mind*] My dear Raina, dont you see that we have a guest here? Captain Bluntschli: one of our new Serbian friends.

Raina bows: Bluntschli bows.

RAINA. How silly of me! [*She comes down into the centre of the group, between Bluntschli and Petkoff.*] I made a beautiful ornament this morning for the ice pudding; and that stupid Nicola has just put down a pile of plates on it and spoilt it. [*To Bluntschli, winningly*] I hope you didn't think that you were the chocolate cream soldier, Captain Bluntschli.

BLUNTSCHLI. [*laughing*] I assure you I did. [*Stealing a whimsical glance at her*] Your explanation was a relief.

PETKOFF. [*suspiciously, to Raina*] And since when, pray, have you taken to cooking?

CATHERINE. Oh, whilst you were away. It is her latest fancy.

PETKOFF. [*testily*] And has Nicola taken to drinking? He used to be careful enough. First he shews Captain Bluntschli out here when he knew quite well I was in the library; and then he goes downstairs and breaks Raina's chocolate soldier. He must— [*Nicola appears at the top of the steps with the bag. He descends; places it respectfully before Bluntschli; and waits for further orders. General amazement. Nicola, unconscious of the effect he is producing, looks perfectly satisfied with himself. When Petkoff recovers his power of speech, he breaks out at him with*] Are you mad, Nicola?

NICOLA. [*taken aback*] Sir?

PETKOFF. What have you brought that for?

NICOLA. My lady's orders, major. Louka told me that—

CATHERINE. [*interrupting him*] My orders! Why should I order you to bring Captain Bluntschli's luggage out here? What are you thinking of, Nicola?

NICOLA. [*after a moment's bewilderment, picking up the bag as he addresses Bluntschli with the very perfection of servile discretion*] I beg your pardon, captain, I am sure. [*To Catherine*] My fault, madam: I hope youll overlook it. [*He bows, and is going to the steps with the bag, when Petkoff addresses him angrily.*]

PETKOFF. Youd better go and slam that bag, too, down on Miss Raina's ice pudding! [*This is too much for Nicola. The bag drops from his hand almost on his master's toes, eliciting a roar of*] Begone, you butter-fingered donkey.

NICOLA. [*snatching up the bag, and escaping into the house*] Yes, major.

CATHERINE. Oh, never mind. Paul: dont be angry.

PETKOFF. [*blustering*] Scoundrel! He's got out of hand while I was away. I'll teach him. Infernal blackguard! The sack next Saturday! I'll clear out the whole establishment—[*He is stifled by the caresses of his wife and daughter, who hang round his neck, petting him*].

CATHERINE.⎱ [*together*] ⎰Now, now, now, it mustnt be angry. He
RAINA. ⎰   ⎱Wow, wow, wow: not on your first day at
  ⎰meant no harm. Be good to please me, dear.
  ⎱home. I'll make another ice pudding. Tch-
  ⎰Sh-sh-sh-sh!
  ⎱ch-ch!

PETKOFF. [*yielding*] Oh well, never mind. Come, Bluntschli: lets have no more nonsense about going away. You know very well youre not going back to Switzerland yet. Until you do go back youll stay with us.

RAINA. Oh, do, Captain Bluntschli.

PETKOFF. [*to Catherine*] Now, Catherine: it's of you he's afraid. Press him: and he'll stay.

CATHERINE. Of course I shall be only too delighted if [*appealingly*] Captain Bluntschli really wishes to stay. He knows my wishes.

BLUNTSCHLI. [*in his driest military manner*] I am at madam's orders.

SERGIUS. [*cordially*] That settles it!

PETKOFF. [*heartily*] Of course!

RAINA. You see you must stay.

BLUNTSCHLI. [*smiling*] Well, if I must, I must.

Gesture of despair from Catherine.

Act III

In the library after lunch. It is not much of a library. Its literary equipment consists of a single fixed shelf stocked with old paper covered novels, broken backed, coffee stained, torn and thumbed; and a couple of little hanging shelves with a few gift books on them: the rest of the wall space being occupied by trophies of war and the chase. But it is a most comfortable sitting room. A row of three large windows shews a mountain panorama, just now seen in one of its friendliest aspects in the mellowing afternoon light. In the corner next the right-hand window a square earthenware stove, a perfect tower of glistening pottery, rises nearly to the ceiling and guarantees plenty of warmth. The ottoman is like that in Raina's room, and similarly placed; and the window seats are luxurious with decorated cushions. There is one object, however, hopelessly out of keeping with its surroundings. This is a small kitchen table, much the worse for wear, fitted as a writing table with an old canister full of pens, an eggcup filled with ink, and a deplorable scrap of heavily used pink blotting paper.

At the side of this table, which stands to the left of anyone facing the window, Bluntschli is hard at work with a couple of maps before him, writing orders. At the head of it sits Sergius, who is supposed to be also at work, but is actually gnawing the feather of a pen, and contemplating Bluntschli's quick, sure, businesslike progress with a mixture of envious irritation at his own incapacity and awestruck wonder at an ability which seems to him almost miraculous, though its prosaic character forbids him to esteem it. The Major is comfortably established on the ottoman, with a newspaper in his hand and the tube of his hookah within easy reach. Catherine sits at the stove, with her back to them, embroidering. Raina, reclining on the divan, is gazing in a daydream out at the Balkan landscape, with a neglected novel in her lap.

The door is on the same side as the stove, farther from the window. The button of the electric bell is at the opposite side, behind Bluntschli.

PETKOFF. [*looking up from his paper to watch how they are getting on at the table*] Are you sure I cant help in any way, Bluntschli?

BLUNTSCHLI. [*without interrupting his writing or looking up*] Quite sure, thank you. Saranoff and I will manage it.

SERGIUS. [*grimly*] Yes: we'll manage it. He finds out what to do; draws up the orders; and I sign em. Division of labor! [*Bluntschli passes him a paper.*] Another one? Thank you. [*He plants the paper squarely before him; sets his chair carefully parallel to it; and signs with his cheek on his elbow and his protruded tongue following the movements of his pen.*] This hand is more accustomed to the sword than to the pen.

PETKOFF. It's very good of you, Bluntschli: it is indeed, to let yourself be put upon in this way. Now are you quite sure I can do nothing?

CATHERINE. [*in a low warning tone*] You can stop interrupting, Paul.

PETKOFF. [*starting and looking round at her*] Eh? Oh! Quite right, my love: quite right. [*He takes his newspaper up again, but presently lets it drop.*] Ah, you havnt been campaigning, Catherine: you dont know how pleasant it is for us to sit here, after a good lunch, with nothing to do but enjoy ourselves. Theres only one thing I want to make me thoroughly comfortable.

CATHERINE. What is that?

PETKOFF. My old coat. I'm not at home in this one: I feel as if I were on parade.

CATHERINE. My dear Paul, how absurd you are about that old coat! It must be hanging in the blue closet where you left it.

PETKOFF. My dear Catherine, I tell you Ive looked there. Am I to believe my own eyes or not? [*Catherine rises and crosses the room to press the button of the electric bell.*] What are you shewing off that bell for? [*She looks at him majestically, and silently resumes her chair and her needlework.*] My dear: if you think the obstinacy of your sex can make a coat out of two old dressing gowns of Raina's, your waterproof, and my mackintosh, youre mistaken. Thats exactly what the blue closet contains at present. *Nicola presents himself.*

CATHERINE. Nicola: go to the blue closet and bring your master's old coat here: the braided one he wears in the house.

NICOLA. Yes, madame. [*He goes out.*]

PETKOFF. Catherine.

CATHERINE. Yes, Paul.

PETKOFF. I bet you any piece of jewellery you like to order from Sofia against a week's housekeeping money that the coat isnt there.

CATHERINE. Done, Paul!

PETKOFF. [*excited by the prospect of a gamble*] Come: heres an opportunity for some sport. Wholl bet on it? Bluntschli: I'll give you six to one.

BLUNTSCHLI. [*imperturbably*] It would be robbing you, major. Madame is sure to be right. [*Without looking up, he passes another batch of papers to Sergius.*]

SERGIUS. [*also excited*] Bravo, Switzerland! Major: I bet my best charger against an Arab mare for Raina that Nicola finds the coat in the blue closet.

PETKOFF. [*eagerly*] Your best char—

CATHERINE. [*hastily interrupting him*] Dont be foolish, Paul. An

Arabian mare will cost you 50,000 levas.

RAINA. [*suddenly coming out of her picturesque revery*] Really, mother, if you are going to take the jewellery, I dont see why you should grudge me my Arab.

Nicola comes back with the coat, and brings it to Petkoff, who can hardly believe his eyes.

CATHERINE. Where was it, Nicola?

NICOLA. Hanging in the blue closet, madame.

PETKOFF. Well, I am d—

CATHERINE. [*stopping him*] Paul!

PETKOFF. I could have sworn it wasnt there. Age is beginning to tell on me. I'm getting hallucinations. [*To Nicola*] Here: help me to change. Excuse me, Bluntschli. [*He begins changing coats, Nicola acting as valet.*] Remember: I didnt take that bet of yours, Sergius. Youd better give Raina that Arab steed yourself, since youve roused her expectations. Eh, Raina? [*He looks round at her; but she is again rapt in the landscape. With a little gush of parental affection and pride, he points her out to them, and says*] She's dreaming, as usual.

SERGIUS. Assuredly she shall not be the loser.

PETKOFF. So much the better for her. I shant come off so cheaply, I expect. [*The change is now complete. Nicola goes out with the discarded coat.*] Ah, now I feel at home at last. [*He sits down and takes his newspaper with a grunt of relief.*]

BLUNTSCHLI. [*to Sergius, handing a paper*] Thats the last order.

PETKOFF. [*jumping up*] What! Finished?

BLUNTSCHLI. Finished.

PETKOFF. [*with childlike envy*] Havnt you anything for me to sign?

BLUNTSCHLI. Not necessary. His signature will do.

PETKOFF. [*inflating his chest and thumping it*] Ah well, I think weve done a thundering good day's work. Can I do anything more?

BLUNTSCHLI. You had better both see the fellows that are to take these. [*Sergius rises*] Pack them off at once; and shew them that Ive marked on the orders the time they should hand them in by. Tell them that if they stop to drink or tell stories—if theyre five minutes late, theyll have the skin taken off their backs.

SERGIUS. [*stiffening indignantly*] I'll say so. [*He strides to the door.*] And if one of them is man enough to spit in my face for insulting him, I'll buy his discharge and give him a pension. [*He goes out.*]

BLUNTSCHLI. [*confidentially*] Just see that he talks to them properly, major, will you?

PETKOFF. [*officiously*] Quite right, Bluntschli, quite right. I'll see to it. [*He goes to the door importantly, but hesitates on the threshold.*] By the bye, Catherine, you may as well come too. Theyll be far more frightened of you than of me.

CATHERINE. [*putting down her embroidery*] I daresay I had better. You would only splutter at them. [*She goes out, Petkoff holding the door for her and following her.*]

BLUNTSCHLI. What an army! They make cannons out of cherry trees; and the officers send for their wives to keep discipline! [*He begins to fold and docket the papers.*]

Raina, who has risen from the divan, marches slowly down the room with her hands clasped behind her, and looks mischievously at him.

RAINA. You look ever so much nicer than when we last met. [*He looks up, surprised.*] What have you done to yourself?

BLUNTSCHLI. Washed; brushed; good night's sleep and breakfast. Thats all.

RAINA. Did you get back safely that morning?

BLUNTSCHLI. Quite, thanks.

RAINA. Were they angry with you for running away from Sergius's charge?

BLUNTSCHLI [*grinning*] No: they were glad; because theyd all just run away themselves.

RAINA. [*going to the table, and leaning over it towards him*] It must have made a lovely story for them: all that about me and my room.

BLUNTSCHLI. Capital story. But I only told it to one of them: a particular friend.

RAINA. On whose discretion you could absolutely rely?

BLUNTSCHLI. Absolutely.

RAINA. Hm! He told it all to my father and Sergius the day you exchanged the prisoners. [*She turns away and strolls carelessly across to the other side of the room.*]

BLUNTSCHLI. [*deeply concerned, and half incredulous*] No! You dont mean that, do you?

RAINA. [*turning, with sudden earnestness*] I do indeed. But they dont know that it was in this house you took refuge. If Sergius knew, he would challenge you and kill you in a duel.

BLUNTSCHLI. Bless me! then dont tell him.

RAINA. Please be serious, Captain Bluntschli. Can you not realize what it is to me to deceive him? I want to be quite perfect with Sergius: no meanness, no smallness, no deceit. My relation to him is the one really beautiful and noble part of my life. I hope you can understand that.

BLUNTSCHLI. [*sceptically*] You mean that you wouldnt like him to find out that the story about the ice pudding was a––a––a––You know.

RAINA. [*wincing*] Ah, dont talk of it in that flippant way. I lied: I know it. But I did it to save your life. He would have killed you. That was the second time I ever uttered a falsehood. [*Bluntschli rises quickly and looks doubtfully and somewhat severely at her.*] Do you remember the first time?

BLUNTSCHLI. I! No. Was I present?

RAINA. Yes; and I told the officer who was searching for you that you were not present.

BLUNTSCHLI. True. I should have remembered it.

RAINA. [*greatly encouraged*] Ah, it is natural that you should forget it first. It cost you nothing: it cost me a lie! A lie!

She sits down on the ottoman, looking straight before her with her hands clasped around her knee. Bluntschli, quite touched, goes to the ottoman with a particularly reassuring and considerate air, and sits down beside her.

BLUNTSCHLI. My dear young lady, dont let this worry you. Remember: I'm a soldier. Now what are the two things that happen to a soldier so often that he comes to think nothing of them? One is hearing people tell lies [*Raina recoils*]: the other is getting his life saved in all sorts of ways by all sorts of people.

RAINA. [*rising in indignant protest*] And so he becomes a creature incapable of faith and of gratitude.

BLUNTSCHLI. [*making a wry face*] Do you like gratitude? I dont. If pity is akin to love, gratitude is akin to the other thing.

RAINA. Gratitude! [*Turning on him*] If you are incapable of gratitude you are incapable of any noble sentiment. Even animals are grateful. Oh, I see now exactly what you think of me! You were not surprised to hear me lie. To you it was something I probably did every day! every hour! That is how men think of women. [*She paces the room tragically.*]

BLUNTSCHLI. [*dubiously*] Theres reason in everything. You said youd told only two lies in your whole life. Dear young lady: isnt that rather a short allowance? I'm quite a straightforward man myself; but it wouldnt last me a whole morning.

RAINA. [*staring haughtily at him*] Do you know, sir, that you are insulting me?

BLUNTSCHLI. I cant help it. When you strike that noble attitude and speak in that thrilling voice, I admire you; but I find it impossible to believe a single word you say.

RAINA. [*superbly*] Captain Bluntschli!

BLUNTSCHLI. [*unmoved*] Yes?

RAINA. [*standing over him, as if she could not believe her senses*] Do you mean what you said just now? Do you know what you said just now?

BLUNTSCHLI. I do.

RAINA. [*gasping*] I! I!!! [*She points to herself incredulously, meaning "I, Raina Petkoff, tell lies!" He meets her gaze unflinchingly. She suddenly sits down beside him, and adds, with a complete change of manner from the heroic to a babyish familiarity*] How did you find me out?

BLUNTSCHLI [*promptly*] Instinct, dear young lady. Instinct, and experience of the world.

RAINA. [*wonderingly*] Do you know, you are the first man I ever met who did not take me seriously?

BLUNTSCHLI. You mean, dont you, that I am the first man that has ever taken you quite seriously?

RAINA. Yes: I suppose I do mean that. [*Cosily, quite at her ease with him*] How strange it is to be talked to in such a way! You know, Ive always gone on like that.

BLUNTSCHLI. You mean the—?

RAINA. I mean the noble attitude and the thrilling voice. [*They laugh together.*] I did it when I was a tiny child to my nurse. She believed in it. I do it before my parents. They believe in it. I do it before Sergius. He believes in it.

BLUNTSCHLI. Yes: he's a little in that line himself, isnt he?

RAINA. [*startled*] Oh! Do you think so?

BLUNTSCHLI. You know him better than I do.

RAINA. I wonder—I wonder is he? If I thought that—! [*Discouraged*] Ah, well: what does it matter? I suppose, now youve found me out, you despise me.

BLUNTSCHLI. [*warmly, rising*] No, my dear young lady, no, no, no a thousand times. It's part of your youth: part of your charm. I'm like all the rest of them: the nurse, your parents, Sergius: I'm your infatuated admirer.

RAINA. [*pleased*] Really?

BLUNTSCHLI. [*slapping his breast smartly with his hand, German fashion*] Hand aufs Herz![7] Really and truly.

RAINA. [*very happy*] But what did you think of me for giving you my portrait?

BLUNTSCHLI. [*astonished*] Your portrait! You never gave me your portrait.

RAINA. [*quickly*] Do you mean to say you never got it?

BLUNTSCHLI. No. [*He sits down beside her, with renewed interest, and says, with some complacency*] When did you send it to me?

RAINA. [*indignantly*] I did not send it to you. [*She turns her head away, and adds, reluctantly*] It was in the pocket of that coat.

BLUNTSCHLI. [*pursing his lips and rounding his eyes*] Oh-o-oh! I never found it. It must be there still.

RAINA. [*springing up*] There still! for my father to find the first time he puts his hand in his pocket! Oh, how could you be so stupid?

BLUNTSCHLI. [*rising also*] It doesnt matter: I suppose it's only a photograph: how can he tell who it was intended for? Tell him he put it there himself.

RAINA. [*bitterly*] Yes: that is so clever! isnt it? [*Distractedly*] Oh! what shall I do?

BLUNTSCHLI. Ah, I see. You wrote something on it. That was rash.

RAINA. [*vexed almost to tears*] Oh, to have done such a thing for you, who care no more—except to laugh at me—oh! Are you sure nobody has touched it?

BLUNTSCHLI. Well, I cant be quite sure. You see, I couldnt carry it about with me all the time: one cant take much luggage on active service.

RAINA. What did you do with it?

BLUNTSCHLI. When I got through to Pirot I had to put it in safe keeping somehow. I thought of the railway cloak room; but thats the surest place to get looted in modern warfare. So I pawned it.

RAINA. Pawned it!!!

BLUNTSCHLI. I know it doesnt sound nice; but it was much the safest

7. "Hand on heart" (German).

plan. I redeemed it the day before yesterday. Heaven only knows whether the pawnbroker cleared out the pockets or not.

RAINA. [*furious: throwing the words right into his face*] You have a low shopkeeping mind. You think of things that would never come into a gentleman's head.

BLUNTSCHLI. [*phlegmatically*] Thats the Swiss national character, dear lady. [*He returns to the table.*]

RAINA. Oh, I wish I had never met you. [*She flounces away, and sits at the window fuming.*]

Louka comes in with a heap of letters and telegrams on her salver, and crosses, with her bold free gait, to the table. Her left sleeve is looped up to the shoulder with a brooch, shewing her naked arm, with a broad gilt bracelet covering the bruise.

LOUKA. [*to Bluntschli*] For you. [*She empties the salver with a fling on to the table.*] The messenger is waiting. [*She is determined not to be civil to an enemy, even if she must bring him his letters.*]

BLUNTSCHLI. [*to Raina*] Will you excuse me: the last postal delivery that reached me was three weeks ago. These are the subsequent accumulations. Four telegrams: a week old. [*He opens one.*] Oho! Bad news!

RAINA. [*rising and advancing a little remorsefully*] Bad news?

BLUNTSCHLI. My father's dead. [*He looks at the telegram with his lips pursed, musing on the unexpected change in his arrangements. Louka crosses herself hastily.*]

RAINA. Oh, how very sad!

BLUNTSCHLI. Yes: I shall have to start for home in an hour. He has left a lot of big hotels behind him to be looked after. [*He takes up a fat letter in a long blue envelope.*] Here's a whacking letter from the family solicitor. [*He puts out the enclosures and glances over them.*] Great Heavens! Seventy! Two hundred! [*In a crescendo of dismay*] Four hundred! Four thousand!! Nine thousand six hundred!!! What on earth am I to do with them all?

RAINA. [*timidly*] Nine thousand hotels?

BLUNTSCHLI. Hotels! nonsense. If you only knew! Oh, it's too ridiculous! Excuse me: I must give my fellow orders about starting. [*He leaves the room hastily, with the documents in his hand.*]

LOUKA. [*knowing instinctively that she can annoy Raina by disparaging Bluntschli*] He has not much heart, that Swiss. He has not a word of grief for his poor father.

RAINA. [*bitterly*] Grief! A man who has been doing nothing but killing people for years! What does he care? What does any soldier care? [*She goes to the door, restraining her tears with difficulty.*]

LOUKA. Major Saranoff has been fighting too; and he has plenty of heart left. [*Raina, at the door, draws herself up haughtily and goes out.*] Aha! I thought you wouldnt get much feeling out of your soldier. [*She is following Raina when Nicola enters with an armful of logs for the stove.*]

NICOLA. [*grinning amorously at her*] Ive been trying all the afternoon to get a minute alone with you, my girl. [*His countenance changes as he notices her arm.*] Why, what fashion is that of wearing your sleeve, child?

LOUKA. [*proudly*] My own fashion.

NICOLA. Indeed! If the mistress catches you, she'll talk to you. [*He puts the logs down, and seats himself comfortably on the ottoman.*]

LOUKA. Is that any reason why you should take it on yourself to talk to me?

NICOLA. Come! dont be so contrairy with me. Ive some good news for you. [*She sits down beside him. He takes out some paper money. Louka, with an eager gleam in her eyes, tries to snatch it; but he shifts it quickly to his left hand, out of her reach.*] See! a twenty leva bill! Sergius gave me that, out of pure swagger. A fool and his money are soon parted. Theres ten levas more. The Swiss gave me that for backing up the mistress's and Raina's lies about him. He's no fool, he isnt. You should have heard old Catherine downstairs as polite as you please to me, telling me not to mind the Major being a little impatient; for they knew what a good servant I was—after making a fool and a liar of me before them all! The twenty will go to our savings; and you shall have the ten to spend if youll only talk to me so as to remind me I'm a human being. I get tired of being a servant occasionally.

LOUKA. Yes: sell your manhood for 30 levas, and buy me for 10! [*Rising scornfully*] Keep your money. You were born to be a servant. I was not. When you set up your shop you will only be everybody's servant instead of somebody's servant. [*She goes moodily to the table and seats herself regally in Sergius's chair.*]

NICOLA. [*picking up his logs, and going to the stove*] Ah, wait til you see. We shall have our evenings to ourselves; and I shall be master in my own house, I promise you. [*He throws the logs down and kneels at the stove.*]

LOUKA. You shall never be master in mine.

NICOLA. [*turning, still on his knees, and squatting down rather forlornly on his calves, daunted by her implacable disdain*] You have a great ambition in you, Louka. Remember: if any luck comes to you, it was I that made a woman of you.

LOUKA. You!

NICOLA. [*scrambling up and going to her*] Yes, me. Who was it made you give up wearing a couple of pounds of false black hair on your head and reddening your lips and cheeks like any other Bulgarian girl! I did. Who taught you to trim your nails, and keep your hands clean, and be dainty about yourself, like a fine Russian lady! Me: do you hear that? me! [*She tosses her head defiantly; and he turns away, adding more coolly*] Ive often thought that if Raina were out of the way, and you just a little less of a fool and Sergius just a little more of one, you might come to be one of my grandest customers, instead of only being my wife and costing me money.

LOUKA. I believe you would rather be my servant than my husband. You would make more out of me. Oh, I know that soul of yours.

NICOLA. [*going closer to her for greater emphasis*] Never you mind my soul; but just listen to my advice. If you want to be a lady, your present behavior to me wont do at all, unless when we're alone. It's too sharp and impudent; and impudence is a sort of familiarity: it shews affection for me. And dont you try being high and mighty with me, either. Youre like all country girls: you think it's genteel to treat a servant the way I treat a stable-boy. Thats only your ignorance; and dont you forget it. And dont be so ready to defy everybody. Act as if you expected to have your own way, not as if you expected to be ordered about. The way to get on as a lady is the same as the way to get on as a servant: youve got to know your place: thats the secret of it. And you may depend on me to know my place if you get promoted. Think over it, my girl. I'll stand by you: one servant should always stand by another.

LOUKA. [*rising impatiently*] Oh, I must behave in my own way. You take all the courage out of me with your cold-blooded wisdom. Go and put those logs in the fire: thats the sort of thing you understand.

Before Nicola can retort, Sergius comes in. He checks himself a moment on seeing Louka; then goes to the stove.

SERGIUS. [*to Nicola*] I am not in the way of your work, I hope.

NICOLA. [*in a smooth, elderly manner*] Oh no, sir: thank you kindly. I was only speaking to this foolish girl about her habit of running up here to the library whenever she gets a chance, to look at the books. Thats the worst of her education, sir: it gives her habits above her station. [*To Louka*] Make that table tidy, Louka, for the Major. [*He goes out sedately.*]

Louka, without looking at Sergius, pretends to arrange the papers on the table. He crosses slowly to her, and studies the arrangement of her sleeve reflectively.

SERGIUS. Let me see: is there a mark there? [*He turns up the bracelet and sees the bruise made by his grasp. She stands motionless, not looking at him: fascinated, but on her guard*] Ffff! Does it hurt?

LOUKA. Yes.

SERGIUS. Shall I cure it?

LOUKA. [*instantly withdrawing herself proudly, but still not looking at him*] No. You cannot cure it now.

SERGIUS. [*masterfully*] Quite sure? [*He makes a movement as if to take her in his arms.*]

LOUKA. Dont trifle with me, please. An officer should not trifle with a servant.

SERGIUS. [*indicating the bruise with a merciless stroke of his forefinger*] That was no trifle, Louka.

LOUKA. [*flinching; then looking at him for the first time*] Are you sorry?

SERGIUS. [*with measured emphasis, folding his arms*] I am never sorry.

LOUKA. [*wistfully*] I wish I could believe a man could be as unlike a woman as that. I wonder are you really a brave man?

SERGIUS. [*unaffectedly, relaxing his attitude*] Yes: I am a brave man. My heart jumped like a woman's at the first shot; but in the charge I found that I was brave. Yes: that at least is real about me.

LOUKA. Did you find in the charge that the men whose fathers are poor like mine were any less brave than the men who are rich like you?

SERGIUS. [*with bitter levity*] Not a bit. They all slashed and cursed and yelled like heroes. Psha! the courage to rage and kill is cheap. I have an English bull terrier who has as much of that sort of courage as the whole Bulgarian nation, and the whole Russian nation at its back. But he lets my groom thrash him, all the same. Thats your soldier all over! No, Louka: your poor men can cut throats; but they are afraid of their officers; they put up with insults and blows; they stand by and see one another punished like children: aye, and help to do it when they are ordered. And the officers!!! Well [*with a short harsh laugh*] I am an officer. Oh, [*fervently*] give me the man who will defy to the death any power on earth or in heaven that sets itself up against his own will and conscience: he alone is the brave man.

LOUKA. How easy it is to talk! Men never seem to me to grow up: they all have schoolboy's ideas. You dont know what true courage is.

SERGIUS. [*ironically*] Indeed! I am willing to be instructed. [*He sits on the ottoman, sprawling magnificently.*]

LOUKA. Look at me! How much am I allowed to have my own will? I have to get your room ready for you: to sweep and dust, to fetch and carry. How could that degrade me if it did not degrade you to have it done for you? But [*with subdued passion*] if I were Empress of Russia, above everyone in the world, then!! Ah then, though according to you I could shew no courage at all, you should see, you should see.

SERGIUS. What would you do, most noble Empress?

LOUKA. I would marry the man I loved, which no other queen in Europe has the courage to do. If I loved you, though you would be as far beneath me as I am beneath you, I would dare to be the equal of my inferior. Would you dare as much if you loved me? No: if you felt the beginnings of love for me you would not let it grow. You would not dare: you would marry a rich man's daughter because you would be afraid of what other people would say of you.

SERGIUS. [*bounding up*] You lie: it is not so, by all the stars! If I loved you, and I were the Tsar himself, I would set you on the throne by my side. You know that I love another woman, a woman as high above you as heaven is above earth. And you are jealous of her.

LOUKA. I have no reason to be. She will never marry you now. The man I told you of has come back. She will marry the Swiss.

SERGIUS. [*recoiling*] The Swiss!

LOUKA. A man worth ten of you. Then you can come to me; and I will refuse you. You are not good enough for me. [*She turns to the door.*]

SERGIUS. [*springing after her and catching her fiercely in his arms*] I will kill the Swiss; and afterwards I will do as I please with you.

LOUKA. [*in his arms, passive and steadfast*] The Swiss will kill you, perhaps. He has beaten you in love. He may beat you in war.

SERGIUS. [*tormentedly*] Do you think I believe that she—she! whose worst thoughts are higher than your best ones, is capable of trifling with another man behind my back?

LOUKA. Do you think she would believe the Swiss if he told her now that I am in your arms?

SERGIUS. [*releasing her in despair*] Damnation! Oh, damnation! Mockery! mockery everywhere! everything I think is mocked by everything I do. [*He strikes himself frantically on the breast.*] Coward! liar! fool! Shall I kill myself like a man, or live and pretend to laugh at myself? [*She again turns to go.*] Louka! [*She stops near the door.*] Remember: you belong to me.

LOUKA. [*turning*] What does that mean? An insult?

SERGIUS. [*commandingly*] It means that you love me, and that I have had you here in my arms, and will perhaps have you there again. Whether that is an insult I neither know nor care: take it as you please. But [*vehemently*] I will not be a coward and a trifler. If I choose to love you, I dare marry you, in spite of all Bulgaria. If these hands ever touch you again, they shall touch my affianced bride.

LOUKA. We shall see whether you dare keep your word. And take care. I will not wait long.

SERGIUS. [*again folding his arms and standing motionless in the middle of the room*] Yes: we shall see. And you shall wait my pleasure.

Bluntschli, much preoccupied, with his papers still in his hand, enters, leaving the door open for Louka to go out. He goes across to the table, glancing at her as he passes. Sergius, without altering his resolute attitude, watches him steadily. Louka goes out, leaving the door open.

BLUNTSCHLI. [*absently, sitting at the table as before, and putting down his papers*] Thats a remarkable looking young woman.

SERGIUS. [*gravely, without moving*] Captain Bluntschli.

BLUNTSCHLI. Eh?

SERGIUS. You have deceived me. You are my rival. I brook no rivals. At six o'clock I shall be in the drilling-ground on the Klissoura road, alone, on horseback, with my sabre. Do you understand?

BLUNTSCHLI. [*staring, but sitting quite at his ease*] Oh, thank you: thats a cavalry man's proposal. I'm in the artillery; and I have the choice of weapons. If I go, I shall take a machine gun. And there shall be no mistake about the cartridges this time.

SERGIUS. [*flushing, but with deadly coldness*] Take care, sir. It is not our custom in Bulgaria to allow invitations of that kind to be trifled with.

BLUNTSCHLI. [*warmly*] Pooh! dont talk to me about Bulgaria. You dont know what fighting is. But have it your own way. Bring your sabre along. I'll meet you.

SERGIUS. [*fiercely delighted to find his opponent a man of spirit*] Well said, Switzer. Shall I lend you my best horse?

BLUNTSCHLI. No: damn your horse! thank you all the same, my dear fellow. [*Raina comes in, and hears the next sentence.*] I shall fight you on foot. Horseback's too dangerous; I dont want to kill you if I can help it.

RAINA. [*hurrying forward anxiously*] I have heard what Captain Bluntschli said, Sergius. You are going to fight. Why? [*Sergius turns away in silence, and goes to the stove, where he stands watching her as she continues, to Bluntschli*] What about?

BLUNTSCHLI. I dont know: he hasnt told me. Better not interfere, dear young lady. No harm will be done: Ive often acted as sword instructor. He wont be able to touch me; and I'll not hurt him. It will save explanations. In the morning I shall be off home; and youll never see me or hear of me again. You and he will **then** make it up and live happily ever after.

RAINA. [*turning away deeply hurt, almost with a sob in her voice*] I never said I wanted to see you again.

SERGIUS. [*striding forward*] Ha! That is a confession.

RAINA. [*haughtily*] What do you mean?

SERGIUS. You love that man!

RAINA. [*scandalized*] Sergius!

SERGIUS. You allow him to make love to you behind my back, just as you treat me as your affianced husband behind his. Bluntschli: you knew our relations; and you deceived me. It is for that that I call you to account, not for having received favors I never enjoyed.

BLUNTSCHLI. [*jumping up indignantly*] Stuff! Rubbish! I have received no favors. Why, the young lady doesnt even know whether I'm married or not.

RAINA. [*forgetting herself*] Oh! [*Collapsing on the ottoman*] Are you?

SERGIUS. You see the young lady's concern, Captain Bluntschli. Denial is useless. You have enjoyed the privilege of being received in her own room, late at night—

BLUNTSCHLI. [*interrupting him pepperily*] Yes, you blockhead! she received me with a pistol at her head. Your cavalry were at my heels. I'd have blown out her brains if she'd uttered a cry.

SERGIUS. [*taken aback*] Bluntschli! Raina: is this true?

RAINA. [*rising in wrathful majesty*] Oh, how dare you, how dare you?

BLUNTSCHLI. Apologize, man: apologize. [*He resumes his seat at the table.*]

SERGIUS [*with the old measured emphasis, folding his arms*] I never apologize!

RAINA. [*passionately*] This is the doing of that friend of yours, Captain Bluntschli. It is he who is spreading this horrible story about me. [*She walks about excitedly.*]

BLUNTSCHLI. No: he's dead. Burnt alive!

RAINA. [*stopping, shocked*] Burnt alive!

BLUNTSCHLI. Shot in the hip in a woodyard. Couldnt drag himself out. Your fellows' shells set the timber on fire and burnt him, with half a dozen other poor devils in the same predicament.

RAINA. How horrible!

SERGIUS. And how ridiculous! Oh, war! war! the dream of patriots and heroes! A fraud, Bluntschli. A hollow sham, like love.

RAINA. [*outraged*] Like love! You say that before me!

BLUNTSCHLI. Come, Saranoff: that matter is explained.

SERGIUS. A hollow sham, I say. Would you have come back here if nothing had passed between you except at the muzzle of your pistol? Raina is mistaken about your friend who was burnt. He was not my informant.

RAINA. Who then? [*Suddenly guessing the truth*] Ah, Louka! my maid! my servant! You were with her this morning all that time after—after—Oh, what sort of god is this I have been worshipping! [*He meets her gaze with sardonic enjoyment of her disenchantment. Angered all the more, she goes closer to him, and says, in a lower, intenser tone*] Do you know that I looked out of the window as I went upstairs, to have another sight of my hero; and I saw something I did not understand then. I know now that you were making love to her.

SERGIUS. [*with grim humor*] You saw that?

RAINA. Only too well. [*She turns away, and throws herself on the divan under the centre window, quite overcome.*]

SERGIUS. [*cynically*] Raina: our romance is shattered. Life's a farce.

BLUNTSCHLI. [*to Raina, whimsically*] You see: he's found himself out now.

SERGIUS. [*going to him*] Bluntschli: I have allowed you to call me a blockhead. You may now call me a coward as well. I refuse to fight you. Do you know why?

BLUNTSCHLI. No; but it doesnt matter. I didnt ask the reason when you cried on; and I dont ask the reason now that you cry off. I'm a professional soldier! I fight when I have to, and am very glad to get out of it when I havnt to. Youre only an amateur: you think fighting's an amusement.

SERGIUS. [*sitting down at the table, nose to nose with him*] You shall hear the reason all the same, my professional. The reason is that it takes two men—real men—men of heart, blood and honor—to make a genuine combat. I could no more fight with you than I could make love to an ugly woman. Youve no magnetism: youre not a man: youre a machine.

BLUNTSCHLI. [*apologetically*] Quite true, quite true. I always was that sort of chap. I'm very sorry.

SERGIUS. Psha!

BLUNTSCHLI. But now that youve found that life isnt a farce, but something quite sensible and serious, what further obstacle is there to your happiness?

RAINA. [*rising*] You are very solicitous about my happiness and his.

Do you forget his new love—Louka? It is not you that he must fight now, but his rival, Nicola.

SERGIUS. Rival!! [*bounding half across the room*]

RAINA. Dont you know that theyre engaged?

SERGIUS. Nicola! Are fresh abysses opening? Nicola!!

RAINA. [*sarcastically*] A shocking sacrifice, isnt it? Such beauty! such intellect! such modesty! wasted on a middle-aged servant man. Really, Sergius, you cannot stand by and allow such a thing. It would be unworthy of your chivalry.

SERGIUS. [*losing all self-control*] Viper! Viper! [*He rushes to and fro, raging.*]

BLUNTSCHLI. Look here, Saranoff: youre getting the worst of this.

RAINA. [*getting angrier*] Do you realize what he has done, Captain Bluntschli? He has set this girl as a spy on us; and her reward is that he makes love to her.

SERGIUS. False! Monstrous!

RAINA. Monstrous! [*Confronting him*] Do you deny that she told you about Captain Bluntschli being in my room?

SERGIUS. No; but—

RAINA. [*interrupting*] Do you deny that you were making love to her when she told you?

SERGIUS. No; but I tell you—

RAINA. [*cutting him short contemptuously*] It is unnecessary to tell us anything more. That is quite enough for us. [*She turns away from him and sweeps majestically back to the window.*]

BLUNTSCHLI. [*quietly, as Sergius, in an agony of mortification, sinks on the ottoman, clutching his averted head between his fists*] I told you you were getting the worst of it, Saranoff.

SERGIUS. Tiger cat!

RAINA. [*running excitedly to Bluntschli*] You hear this man calling me names, Captain Bluntschli?

BLUNTSCHLI. What else can he do, dear lady? He must defend himself somehow. Come [*very persuasively*]: dont quarrel. What good does it do?

Raina, with a gasp, sits down on the ottoman, and after a vain effort to look vexedly at Bluntschli, falls a victim to her sense of humor, and actually leans back babyishly against the writhing shoulder of Sergius.

SERGIUS. Engaged to Nicola! Ha! ha! Ah well, Bluntschli, you are right to take this huge imposture of a world coolly.

RAINA. [*quaintly to Bluntschli, with an intuitive guess at his state of mind*] I daresay you think us a couple of grown-up babies, dont you?

SERGIUS. [*grinning savagely*] He does: he does. Swiss civilization nursetending Bulgarian barbarism, eh?

BLUNTSCHLI. [*blushing*] Not at all, I assure you. I'm only very glad to get you two quieted. There! there! let's be pleasant and talk it over in a friendly way. Where is this other young lady?

RAINA. Listening at the door, probably.

SERGIUS. [*shivering as if a bullet had struck him, and speaking with quiet but deep indignation*] I will prove that that, at least, is a calumny. [*He goes with dignity to the door and opens it. A yell of fury bursts from him as he looks out. He darts into the passage, and returns dragging in Louka, whom he flings violently against the table, exclaiming*] Judge her, Bluntschli. You, the cool impartial man: judge the eavesdropper.

Louka stands her ground, proud and silent.

BLUNTSCHLI. [*shaking his head*] I mustnt judge her. I once listened myself outside a tent when there was a mutiny brewing. It's all a question of the degree of provocation. My life was at stake.

LOUKA. My love was at stake. I am not ashamed.

RAINA. [*contemptuously*] Your love! Your curiosity, you mean.

LOUKA. [*facing her and returning her contempt with interest*] My love, stronger than anything you can feel, even for your chocolate cream soldier.

SERGIUS. [*with quick suspicion, to Louka*] What does that mean?

LOUKA. [*fiercely*] I mean—

SERGIUS. [*interrupting her slightingly*] Oh, I remember: the ice pudding. A paltry taunt, girl!

Major Petkoff enters, in his shirtsleeves.

PETKOFF. Excuse my shirtsleeves, gentlemen. Raina: somebody has been wearing that coat of mine: I'll swear it. Somebody with a differently shaped back. It's all burst open at the sleeve. Your mother is mending it. I wish she'd make haste: I shall catch cold. [*He looks more attentively at them.*] Is anything the matter?

RAINA. No. [*She sits down at the stove, with a tranquil air.*]

SERGIUS. Oh no.[*He sits down at the end of the table, as at first.*]

BLUNTSCHLI. [*who is already seated*] Nothing. Nothing.

PETKOFF. [*sitting down on the ottoman in his old place*] Thats all right. [*He notices Louka.*] Anything the matter, Louka?

LOUKA. No, sir.

PETKOFF. [*genially*] Thats all right. [*He sneezes.*] Go and ask your mistress for my coat, like a good girl, will you?

Nicola enters with the coat. Louka makes a pretence of having business in the room by taking the little table with the hookah away to the wall near the windows.

RAINA. [*rising quickly as she sees the coat on Nicola's arm*] Here it is, papa. Give it to me, Nicola; and do you put some more wood on the fire. [*She takes the coat, and brings it to the Major, who stands up to put it on. Nicola attends to the fire.*]

PETKOFF. [*to Raina, teasing her affectionately*] Aha! Going to be very good to poor old papa just for one day after his return from the wars, eh?

RAINA. [*with solemn reproach*] Ah, how can you say that to me, father?

PETKOFF. Well, well, only a joke, little one. Come: give me a kiss. [*She kisses him.*] Now give me the coat.

RAINA. No: I am going to put it on for you. Turn your back. [*He turns his back and feels behind him with his arms for the sleeves. She dexterously takes the photograph from the pocket and throws it on the table before Bluntschli, who covers it with a sheet of paper under the very nose of Sergius, who looks on amazed, with his suspicions roused in the highest degree. She then helps Petkoff on with his coat.*] There, dear! Now are you comfortable?

PETKOFF. Quite, little love. Thanks. [*He sits down; and Raina returns to her seat near the stove.*] Oh, by the bye, Ive found something funny. Whats the meaning of this? [*He puts his hand into the picked pocket.*] Eh? Hallo! [*He tries the other pocket.*] Well, I could have sworn—! [*Much puzzled, he tries the breast pocket.*] I wonder—[*trying the original pocket*] Where can it—? [*He rises, exclaiming*] Your mother's taken it!

RAINA. [*very red*] Taken what?

PETKOFF. Your photograph, with the inscription: "Raina, to her Chocolate Cream Soldier: a Souvenir." Now you know theres something more in this than meets the eye; and I'm going to find it out. [*Shouting*] Nicola!

NICOLA. [*coming to him*] Sir!

PETKOFF. Did you spoil any pastry of Miss Raina's this morning?

NICOLA. You heard Miss Raina say that I did, sir.

PETKOFF. I know that, you idiot. Was it true?

NICOLA. I am sure Miss Raina is incapable of saying anything that is not true, sir.

PETKOFF. Are you? Then I'm not. [*Turning to the others*] Come: do you think I dont see it all? [*He goes to Sergius, and slaps him on the shoulder.*] Sergius: youre the chocolate cream soldier, arnt you?

SERGIUS. [*starting up*] I! A chocolate cream soldier! Certainly not.

PETKOFF. Not! [*He looks at them. They are all very serious and very conscious.*] Do you mean to tell me that Raina sends things like that to other men?

SERGIUS. [*enigmatically*] The world is not such an innocent place as we used to think, Petkoff.

BLUNTSCHLI. [*rising*] It's all right, major. I'm the chocolate cream soldier. [*Petkoff and Sergius are equally astonished.*] The gracious young lady saved my life by giving me chocolate creams when I was starving: shall I ever forget their flavour! My late friend Stolz told you the story at Pirot. I was the fugitive.

PETKOFF. You! [*He gasps.*] Sergius: do you remember how those two women went on this morning when we mentioned it? [*Sergius smiles cynically. Petkoff confronts Raina severely.*] Youre a nice young woman, arnt you?

RAINA. [*bitterly*] Major Saranoff has changed his mind. And when I wrote that on the photograph, I did not know that Captain Bluntschli was married.

BLUNTSCHLI. [*startled into vehement protest*] I'm not married.

RAINA. [*with deep reproach*] You said you were.

BLUNTSCHLI. I did not. I positively did not. I never was married in my life.

PETKOFF. [*exasperated*] Raina: will you kindly inform me, if I am not asking too much, which of these gentlemen you are engaged to?

RAINA. To neither of them. This young lady [*introducing Louka, who faces them all proudly*] is the object of Major Saranoff's affections at present.

PETKOFF. Louka! Are you mad, Sergius? Why, this girl's engaged to Nicola.

NICOLA. I beg your pardon, sir. There is a mistake. Louka is not engaged to me.

PETKOFF. Not engaged to you, you scoundrel! Why, you had twenty-five levas from me on the day of your betrothal; and she had that gilt bracelet from Miss Raina.

NICOLA. [*with cool unction*] We gave it out so, sir. But it was only to give Louka protection. She had a soul above her station; and I have been no more than her confidential servant. I intend, as you know, sir, to set up a shop later on in Sofia; and I look forward to her custom and recommendation should she marry into the nobility. [*He goes out with impressive discretion, leaving them all staring after him.*]

PETKOFF. [*breaking the silence*] Well, I am—hm!

SERGIUS. This is either the finest heroism or the most crawling baseness. Which is it, Bluntschli?

BLUNTSCHLI. Never mind whether it's heroism or baseness. Nicola's the ablest man Ive met in Bulgaria. I'll make him manager of a hotel if he can speak French and German.

LOUKA. [*suddenly breaking out at Sergius*] I have been insulted by everyone here. You set them the example. You owe me an apology.

Sergius, like a repeating clock of which the spring has been touched, immediately begins to fold his arms.

BLUNTSCHLI. [*before he can speak*] It's no use. He never apologizes.

LOUKA. Not to you, his equal and his enemy. To me, his poor servant, he will not refuse to apologize.

SERGIUS. [*approvingly*] You are right. [*He bends his knee in his grandest manner*] Forgive me.

LOUKA. I forgive you. [*She timidly gives him her hand, which he kisses.*] That touch makes me your affianced wife.

SERGIUS. [*springing up*] Ah! I forgot that.

LOUKA. [*coldly*] You can withdraw if you like.

SERGIUS. Withdraw! Never! You belong to me. [*He puts his arm about her.*]

Catherine comes in and finds Louka in Sergius's arms, with all the rest gazing at them in bewildered astonishment.

CATHERINE. What does this mean?

Sergius releases Louka.

PETKOFF. Well, my dear, it appears that Sergius is going to marry Louka instead of Raina. [*She is about to break out indignantly at him: he stops her by exclaiming testily*] Dont blame me: Ive nothing to do with it. [*He retreats to the stove.*]

CATHERINE. Marry Louka! Sergius: you are bound by your word to us!

SERGIUS. [*folding his arms*] Nothing binds me.

BLUNTSCHLI. [*much pleased by this piece of common sense*] Saranoff: your hand. My congratulations. These heroics of yours have their practical side after all. [*To Louka*] Gracious young lady: the best wishes of a good Republican! [*He kisses her hand, to Raina's great disgust, and returns to his seat.*]

CATHERINE. Louka: you have been telling stories.

LOUKA. I have done Raina no harm.

CATHERINE. [*haughtily*] Raina!

Raina, equally indignant, almost snorts at the liberty.

LOUKA. I have a right to call her Raina: she calls me Louka. I told Major Saranoff she would never marry him if the Swiss gentleman came back.

BLUNTSCHLI. [*rising, much surprised*] Hallo!

LOUKA. [*turning to Raina*] I thought you were fonder of him than of Sergius. You know best whether I was right.

BLUNTSCHLI. What nonsense! I assure you, my dear major, my dear madame, the gracious young lady simply saved my life, nothing else. She never cared two straws for me. Why, bless my heart and soul, look at the young lady and look at me. She, rich, young, beautiful, with her imagination full of fairy princes and noble natures and cavalry charges and goodness knows what! And I, a commonplace Swiss soldier who hardly knows what a decent life is after fifteen years of barracks and battles: a vagabond, a man who has spoiled all his chances in life through an incurably romantic disposition, a man—

SERGIUS. [*starting as if a needle had pricked him and interrupting Bluntschli in incredulous amazement*] Excuse me, Bluntschli: what did you say had spoiled your chances in life?

BLUNTSCHLI. [*promptly*] An incurably romantic disposition. I ran away from home twice when I was a boy. I went into the army instead of into my father's business. I climbed the balcony of this house when a man of sense would have dived into the nearest cellar. I came sneaking back here to have another look at the young lady when any other man of my age would have sent the coat back—

PETKOFF. My coat!

BLUNTSCHLI.—yes: thats the coat I mean—would have sent it back and gone quietly home. Do you suppose I am the sort of fellow a young girl falls in love with? Why, look at our ages! I'm thirty-four: I dont suppose the young lady is much over seventeen. [*This estimate produces a marked sensation, all the rest turning and staring at one another. He proceeds innocently*] All that adventure which was life or death to me, was only a schoolgirl's game to her—chocolate creams and hide and seek. Heres the proof! [*He takes the photograph from the table.*] Now, I ask you, would a woman who took the affair seriously have sent me this and written on it "Raina, to her Chocolate Cream Soldier: a Souvenir"? [*He exhibits the photograph triumphantly, as if it settled the matter beyond all possibility of refutation.*]

PETKOFF. Thats what I was looking for. How the deuce did it get there? [*He comes from the stove to look at it, and sits down on the ottoman.*]

BLUNTSCHLI. [*to Raina, complacently*] I have put everything right, I hope, gracious young lady.

RAINA. [*going to the table to face him*] I quite agree with your account of yourself. You are a romantic idiot. [*Bluntschli is unspeakably taken aback.*] Next time, I hope you will know the difference between a schoolgirl of seventeen and a woman of twenty-three.

BLUNTSCHLI. [*stupefied*] Twenty-three!

Raina snaps the photograph contemptuously from his hand; tears it up; throws the pieces in his face; and sweeps back to her former place.

SERGIUS. [*with grim enjoyment of his rival's discomfiture*] Bluntschli: my one last belief is gone. Your sagacity is a fraud, like everything else. You have less sense than even I!

BLUNTSCHLI. [*overwhelmed*] Twenty-three! Twenty-three!! [*He considers.*] Hm! [*swiftly making up his mind and coming to his host*] In that case, Major Petkoff, I beg to propose formally to become a suitor for your daughter's hand, in place of Major Saranoff retired.

RAINA. You dare!

BLUNTSCHLI. If you were twenty-three when you said those things to me this afternoon, I shall take them seriously.

CATHERINE. [*loftily polite*] I doubt, sir, whether you quite realize either my daughter's position or that of Major Sergius Saranoff, whose place you propose to take. The Petkoffs and the Saranoffs are known as the richest and most important families in the country. Our position is almost historical: we can go back for twenty years.

PETKOFF. Oh, never mind that, Catherine. [*To Bluntschli*] We should be most happy, Bluntschli, if it were only a question of your position; but hang it, you know, Raina is accustomed to a very comfortable establishment. Sergius keeps twenty horses.

BLUNTSCHLI. But who wants twenty horses? We're not going to keep a circus.

CATHERINE. [*severely*] My daughter, sir, is accustomed to a first-rate stable.

RAINA. Hush, mother: youre making me ridiculous.

BLUNTSCHLI. Oh well, if it comes to a question of an establishment, here goes! [*He darts impetuously to the table; seizes the papers in the blue envelope; and turns to Sergius.*] How many horses did you say?

SERGIUS. Twenty, noble Switzer.

BLUNTSCHLI. I have two hundred horses. [*They are amazed.*] How many carriages?

SERGIUS. Three.

BLUNTSCHLI. I have seventy. Twenty-four of them will hold twelve inside, besides two on the box, without counting the driver and conductor. How many tablecloths have you?

SERGIUS. How the deuce do I know?

BLUNTSCHLI. Have you four thousand?

SERGIUS. No.

BLUNTSCHLI. I have. I have nine thousand six hundred pairs of sheets and blankets, with two thousand four hundred eider-down quilts. I have ten thousand knives and forks, and the same quantity of dessert spoons. I have three hundred servants. I have six palatial establishments, besides two livery stables, a tea garden, and a private house. I have four medals for distinguished services; I have the rank of an officer and the standing of a gentleman; and I have three native languages. Shew me any man in Bulgaria that can offer as much!

PETKOFF. [*with childish awe*] Are you Emperor of Switzerland?

BLUNTSCHLI. My rank is the highest known in Switzerland: I am a free citizen.

CATHERINE. Then, Captain Bluntschli, since you are my daughter's choice—

RAINA. [*mutinously*] He's not.

CATHERINE. [*ignoring her*]—I shall not stand in the way of her happiness. [*Petkoff is about to speak*] That is Major Petkoff's feeling also.

PETKOFF. Oh, I shall be only too glad. Two hundred horses! Whew!

SERGIUS. What says the lady?

RAINA. [*pretending to sulk*] The lady says that he can keep his table-cloths and his omnibuses. I am not here to be sold to the highest bidder. [*She turns her back on him.*]

BLUNTSCHLI. I wont take that answer. I appealed to you as a fugitive, a beggar, and a starving man. You accepted me. You gave me your hand to kiss, your bed to sleep in, and your roof to shelter me.

RAINA. I did not give them to the Emperor of Switzerland.

BLUNTSCHLI. Thats just what I say. [*He catches her by the shoulders and turns her face-to-face with him.*] Now tell us whom you did give them to.

RAINA. [*succumbing with a shy smile*] To my chocolate cream soldier.

BLUNTSCHLI. [*with a boyish laugh of delight*] Thatll do. Thank you. [*He looks at his watch and suddenly becomes businesslike.*] Time's up, major. Youve managed those regiments so well that youre sure to be asked to get rid of some of the infantry of the Timok division. Send them home by way of Lom Palanka. Saranoff: dont get married until I come back: I shall be here punctually at five in the evening on Tuesday fortnight. Gracious ladies [*his heels click*] good evening. [*He makes them a military bow, and goes.*]

SERGIUS. What a man! Is he a man?

1894   1898

JOSEPH CONRAD
(1857–1924)

1875–94: Career as a seaman.
1895:   *Almayer's Folly.*
1904:   *Nostromo.*

Joseph Conrad was born Jozef Teodor Konrad Nalecz Korzeniowski in
Poland (then under Russian rule), son of a Polish patriot who suffered
exile in Russia for his Polish nationalist activities and died in 1869, leaving
Conrad to be brought up by a maternal uncle. At the age of 15 he amazed
everybody by announcing his passionate desire to go to sea; he was eventually allowed to go to Marseilles in 1874, and from there he made a number of voyages on French merchant ships to Martinique and the West
Indies. In 1878 he signed on an English ship which brought him to the
east coast English port of Lowestoft, where (still as an ordinary seaman)
he joined the crew of a small coasting vessel plying between Lowestoft
and Newcastle. In six voyages between these two ports he learned English.
Thus launched on a career in the British merchant service, Conrad sailed
on a variety of British ships to the Orient and elsewhere and eventually
gained his master's certificate in 1886, the year when he became a naturalized British subject. He received his first command in 1888, and in 1890
took a steamboat up the Congo River in nightmarish circumstances (described in *Heart of Darkness*) which produced severe illness and permanently haunted his imagination. In the early 1890's he was already thinking of turning some of his Malayan experiences into English fiction, and
in 1892–93, when serving as first mate on the *Torrens* sailing from London
to Adelaide, he revealed to a sympathetic passenger that he had begun a
novel (*Almayer's Folly*), while on the return journey he impressed John
Galsworthy, who was a passenger, with his conversation. Though possessed of a master's certificate, Conrad found it difficult to get the kind of
job as master that he wished, and occasionally he had to serve in lesser
capacities. His difficulty in obtaining a command, together with the interest aroused by *Almayer's Folly* when it was published in 1895, helped
to turn him away from the sea to a career as a writer. He settled in London and in 1896 married an English girl; this son of a Polish patriot
turned merchant seaman turned writer was henceforth an English novelist.

Conrad was for a long time regarded as a sea writer whose exotic descriptions of eastern landscapes and exploitation of the romantic atmosphere
of Malaya and other unfamiliar regions gave his work a special kind of
richness and splendor. But this is only one, and not in the last analysis
the most important, aspect of his work. More and more Conrad used the
sea and the circumstances of life on shipboard or in remote eastern settlements as means of exploring certain profound moral ambiguities in human
experience. In *The Nigger of the "Narcissus"* (1897) he shows how a dying
Negro seaman corrupts the morale of a ship's crew by the very fact that his
plight produces sympathy, thus symbolically presenting one of his commonest themes—the necessity and at the same time the dangers of human

contact. In *Lord Jim* (1900), using the device of an intermediate narrator, he probes the meaning of a gross failure of duty on the part of a romantic and idealistic young sailor, and by presenting the hero's history from a series of different points of view keeps the moral questioning continuing to the end. The use of intermediate narrators and multiple points of view is common in Conrad; it is his favorite way of suggesting the complexity of experience and the difficulty of judging human actions. In *Heart of Darkness* he draws on his Congo River experience to create an atmosphere of darkness and horror in the midst of which the hero recognizes a deep inner kinship with the corrupt villain, the Belgian trader who has lost all his earlier ideals to succumb to the worst elements in the native life he had hoped to improve.

This notion of the difficulty of true communion, coupled with the idea that communion can be unexpectedly forced on us—sometimes with someone who may be on the surface our moral opposite, so that we can at times be compelled into a mysterious recognition of our opposite as our true self—is found in many of Conrad's works; it provides one of the underlying themes of *The Secret Sharer* (1912). This story can be enjoyed for the clarity and power with which Conrad renders the atmosphere of the Gulf of Siam as felt by a young sea captain on taking on his first command, but it also uses situation and incident symbolically in order to suggest some of the paradoxes of identity and sympathy.

Other stories and novels explore the ways in which the codes we live by are tested in moments of crisis, revealing either their inadequacy or our own. Imagination can corrupt (as with Lord Jim), or save (as in *The Shadow Line*; 1917); and there are times when total lack of it can see a man through (Captain M'Whirr in *Typhoon*, 1902), though a similar lack in other circumstances can render a man comically ridiculous (Captain Mitchell in *Nostromo*, 1904).

Nostromo, a profound and subtle study of the corrupting effects of politics and "material interests" on personal relationships (set in an imaginary South American republic), is now generally regarded as Conrad's greatest work. His two other political novels—*The Secret Agent* (1906) and *Under Western Eyes* (1910)—have also recently come into their own. The latter is the story of a Russian student who becomes involuntarily associated with antigovernment violence in Czarist Russia and is irresistibly maneuvered by circumstances into a position where, although a government spy, he has to pretend to be a revolutionary among revolutionaries. This is the ultimate in human loneliness and incommunicability—when you must consistently pretend to be the opposite of what you are. It is a story of Dostoievskian power, and shows a very different Conrad from the picturesque sea-dreamer pictured by the earlier critics. Conrad was as much a pessimist as Hardy, but he projected his pessimism in subtler ways. He was also a great master of English prose, an astonishing fact when we realize that he was 21 before he learned any English, and that to the end of his life he spoke English with a thick foreign accent.

Preface to *The Nigger of the "Narcissus"* [1]

[The Task of the Artist]

A work that aspires, however humbly, to the condition of art should carry its justification in every line. And art itself may be defined as a single-minded attempt to render the highest kind of justice to the visible universe, by bringing to light the truth, manifold and one, underlying its every aspect. It is an attempt to find in its forms, in its colors, in its light, in its shadows, in the aspects of matter and in the facts of life, what of each is fundamental, what is enduring and essential—their one illuminating and convincing quality—the very truth of their existence. The artist, then, like the thinker or the scientist, seeks the truth and makes his appeal. Impressed by the aspect of the world the thinker plunges into ideas, the scientist into facts—whence, presently, emerging they make their appeal to those qualities of our being that fit us best for the hazardous enterprise of living. They speak authoritatively to our common-sense, to our intelligence, to our desire of peace or to our desire of unrest; not seldom to our prejudices, sometimes to our fears, often to our egoism—but always to our credulity. And their words are heard with reverence, for their concern is with weighty matters: with the cultivation of our minds and the proper care of our bodies, with the attainment of our ambitions, with the perfection of the means and the glorification of our precious aims.

It is otherwise with the artist.

Confronted by the same enigmatical spectacle the artist descends within himself, and in that lonely region of stress and strife, if he be deserving and fortunate, he finds the terms of his appeal. His appeal is made to our less obvious capacities: to that part of our nature which, because of the warlike conditions of existence, is necessarily kept out of sight within the more resisting and hard qualities—like the vulnerable body within a steel armor. His appeal is less loud, more profound, less distinct, more stirring—and sooner forgotten. Yet its effect endures forever. The changing wisdom of successive generations discards ideas, questions facts, demolishes theories. But the artist appeals to that part of our being which is not dependent on wisdom: to that in us which is a gift and not an acquisition—and, therefore, more permanently enduring. He

---

1. *The Nigger of the "Narcissus"* was written in 1896–97, shortly after his marriage, and published first in *The New Review*, August–December 1897, and then in book form in 1898. The novel, in the words of Jocelyn Baines, Conrad's biographer, "is the culmination of Conrad's apprenticeship as a novelist." Conrad took particular pleasure in writing the book, and later called it "the story by which, as a creative artist, I stand or fall." It was with the feeling that he was now wholly dedicated to writing and had finally (in his own words) "done with the sea" that, a few months after finishing the novel, he wrote the preface in which he defined his aims as an artist. The preface first appeared in the 1898 edition.

speaks to our capacity for delight and wonder, to the sense of mystery surrounding our lives; to our sense of pity, and beauty, and pain; to the latent feeling of fellowship with all creation—and to the subtle but invincible conviction of solidarity that knits together the loneliness of innumerable hearts, to the solidarity in dreams, in joy, in sorrow, in aspirations, in illusions, in hope, in fear, which binds men to each other, which binds together all humanity—the dead to the living and the living to the unborn.

It is only some such train of thought, or rather of feeling, that can in a measure explain the aim of the attempt, made in the tale which follows,[2] to present an unrestful episode in the obscure lives of a few individuals out of all the disregarded multitude of the bewildered, the simple and the voiceless. For, if any part of truth dwells in the belief confessed above, it becomes evident that there is not a place of splendor or a dark corner of the earth that does not deserve if only a passing glance of wonder and pity. The motive, then, may be held to justify the matter of the work; but this preface, which is simply an avowal of endeavor, cannot end here—for the avowal is not yet complete.

Fiction—if it at all aspires to be art—appeals to temperament. And in truth it must be, like painting, like music, like all art, the appeal of one temperament to all the other innumerable temperaments whose subtle and resistless power endows passing events with their true meaning, and creates the moral, the emotional atmosphere of the place and time. Such an appeal, to be effective, must be an impression conveyed through the senses; and, in fact, it cannot be made in any other way, because temperament, whether individual or collective, is not amenable to persuasion. All art, therefore, appeals primarily to the senses, and the artistic aim when expressing itself in written words must also make its appeal through the senses, if its high desire is to reach the secret spring of responsive emotions. It must strenuously aspire to the plasticity of sculpture, to the color of painting, and to the magic suggestiveness of music—which is the art of arts. And it is only through complete, unswerving devotion to the perfect blending of form and substance; it is only through an unremitting, never-discouraged care for the shape and ring of sentences that an approach can be made to plasticity, to color, and that the light of magic suggestiveness may be brought to play for an evanescent instant over the commonplace surface of words: of the old, old words, worn thin, defaced by ages of careless usage.

The sincere endeavor to accomplish that creative task, to go as far on that road as his strength will carry him, to go undeterred by faltering, weariness, or reproach, is the only valid justification for the worker in prose. And if his conscience is clear, his answer to

---

2. I.e., *The Nigger of the "Narcissus."*

those who in the fullness of a wisdom which looks for immediate profit, demand specifically to be edified, consoled, amused; who demand to be promptly improved, or encouraged, or frightened, or shocked, or charmed, must run thus:—My task which I am trying to achieve is, by the power of the written word, to make you hear, to make you feel—it is, before all, to make you *see*. That—and no more, and it is everything. If I succeed, you shall find there, according to your deserts, encouragement, consolation, fear, charm—all you demand—and, perhaps, also that glimpse of truth for which you have forgotten to ask.

To snatch, in a moment of courage, from the remorseless rush of time a passing phase of life, is only the beginning of the task. The task approached in tenderness and faith is to hold up unquestioningly, without choice and without fear, the rescued fragment before all eyes in the light of a sincere mood. It is to show its vibration, its color, its form; and through its movement, its form, and its color, reveal the substance of its truth—disclose its inspiring secret: the stress and passion within the core of each convincing moment. In a single-minded attempt of that kind, if one be deserving and fortunate, one may perchance attain to such clearness of sincerity that at last the presented vision of regret or pity, of terror or mirth, shall awaken in the hearts of the beholders that feeling of unavoidable solidarity; of the solidarity in mysterious origin, in toil, in joy, in hope, in uncertain fate, which binds men to each other and all mankind to the visible world.

It is evident that he who, rightly or wrongly, holds by the convictions expressed above cannot be faithful to any one of the temporary formulas of his craft. The enduring part of them—the truth which each only imperfectly veils—should abide with him as the most precious of his possessions, but they all—Realism, Romanticism, Naturalism, even the unofficial sentimentalism (which, like the poor,[3] is exceedingly difficult to get rid of)—all these gods must, after a short period of fellowship, abandon him—even on the very threshold of the temple—to the stammerings of his conscience and to the outspoken consciousness of the difficulties of his work. In that uneasy solitude the supreme cry of Art for Art, itself, loses the exciting ring of its apparent immorality. It sounds far off. It has ceased to be a cry, and is heard only as a whisper, often incomprehensible, but at times and faintly encouraging.

Sometimes, stretched at ease in the shade of a roadside tree, we watch the motions of a laborer in a distant field, and after a time, begin to wonder languidly as to what the fellow may be at. We watch the movements of his body, the waving of his arms; we see him bend down, stand up, hesitate, begin again. It may add to the charm of an idle hour to be told the purpose of his exertions. If we

3. "For the poor always ye have with you." John xii.8.

know he is trying to lift a stone, to dig a ditch, to uproot a stump, we look with a more real interest at his efforts; we are disposed to condone the jar of his agitation upon the restfulness of the landscape; and even, if in a brotherly frame of mind, we may bring ourselves to forgive his failure. We understand his object, and, after all, the fellow has tried, and perhaps he had not the strength—and perhaps he had not the knowledge. We forgive, go on our way— and forget.

And so it is with the workmen of art. Art is long and life is short,[4] and success is very far off. And thus, doubtful of strength to travel so far, we talk a little about the aim—the aim of art, which, like life itself, is inspiring, difficult—obscured by mists. It is not in the clear logic of a triumphant conclusion; it is not in the unveiling of one of those heartless secrets which are called the Laws of Nature. It is not less great, but only more difficult.

To arrest, for the space of a breath, the hands busy about the work of the earth, and compel men entranced by the sight of distant goals to glance for a moment at the surrounding vision of form and color, of sunshine and shadows; to make them pause for a look, for a sigh, for a smile—such is the aim, difficult and evanescent, and reserved only for a very few to achieve. But sometimes, by the deserving and the fortunate, even that task is accomplished. And when it is accomplished—behold!—all the truth of life is there: a moment of vision, a sigh, a smile—and the return to an eternal rest.
1897   1898

Youth[1]

This could have occurred nowhere but in England, where men and sea interpenetrate, so to speak—the sea entering into the life of most men, and the men knowing something or everything about the sea, in the way of amusement, of travel, or of bread-winning.

We were sitting round a mahogany table that reflected the bottle, the claret-glasses, and our faces as we leaned on our elbows. There was a director of companies, an accountant, a lawyer, Marlow, and myself. The director had been a *Conway*[2] boy, the accountant had served four years at sea, the lawyer—a fine crusted Tory, High Churchman, the best of old fellows, the soul of honor—had been

4. Cf. the Latin proverb (deriving from a dictum of the Greek physician Hippocrates) *ars longa, vita brevis,* "art is long and life is short." Chaucer rendered it, "The lyf so short, the craft so long to lerne" (*The Parlement of Foules*) and Longfellow, "Art is long, and Time is fleeting" (*A Psalm of Life*).
1. This story is derived from Conrad's own experience at sea. In an "author's note," written in 1917, Conrad remarked that " 'Youth' is a feat of memory. It is a record of experience; but that experience, in its facts, in its inwardness and in its outward coloring, begins and ends in myself." The real ship was called the *Palestine*, and Conrad changed the name to *Judea;* he did not alter the name of the captain, Beard, or that of the mate, Mahon.
2. The *Conway* was a training ship on which student officers for the British merchant marine gained sea experience.

chief officer in the P. & O.[3] service in the good old days when mail-boats were square-rigged at least on two masts, and used to come down the China Sea before a fair monsoon with stun'sails set alow and aloft. We all began life in the merchant service. Between the five of us there was the strong bond of the sea, and also the fellow-ship of the craft, which no amount of enthusiasm for yachting, cruising, and so on can give, since one is only the amusement of life and the other is life itself.

Marlow (at least I think that is how he spelt his name) told the story, or rather the chronicle, of a voyage:

"Yes, I have seen a little of the Eastern seas; but what I remem-ber best is my first voyage there. You fellows know there are those voyages that seem ordered for the illustration of life, that might stand for a symbol of existence. You fight, work, sweat, nearly kill yourself, sometimes do kill yourself, trying to accomplish some-thing—and you can't. Not from any fault of yours. You simply can do nothing, neither great nor little—not a thing in the world—not even marry an old maid, or get a wretched 600-ton cargo of coal to its port of destination.

"It was altogether a memorable affair. It was my first voyage to the East, and my first voyage as second mate; it was also my skip-per's first command. You'll admit it was time. He was sixty if a day; a little man, with a broad, not very straight back, with bowed shoulders and one leg more bandy than the other, he had that queer twisted-about appearance you see so often in men who work in the fields. He had a nutcracker face—chin and nose trying to come together over a sunken mouth—and it was framed in iron-gray fluffy hair, that looked like a chin-strap of cotton-wool sprinkled with coal-dust. And he had blue eyes in that old face of his, which were amazingly like a boy's, with that candid expression some quite common men preserve to the end of their days by a rare internal gift of simplicity of heart and rectitude of soul. What induced him to accept me was a wonder. I had come out of a crack Australian clipper, where I had been third officer, and he seemed to have a prejudice against crack clippers as aristocratic and high-toned. He said to me, 'You know, in this ship you will have to work.' I said I had to work in every ship I had ever been in. 'Ah, but this is dif-ferent, and you gentlemen out of them big ships; . . . but there! I dare say you will do. Join tomorrow.'

"I joined tomorrow. It was twenty-two years ago; and I was just twenty. How time passes! It was one of the happiest days of my life. Fancy! Second mate for the first time—a really responsible officer! I wouldn't have thrown up my new billet for a fortune. The mate looked me over carefully. He was also an old chap, but of another stamp. He had a Roman nose, a snow-white, long beard, and his

3. "Pacific and Oriental," a famous British line shipping to the Far East.

name was Mahon, but he insisted that it should be pronounced Mann. He was well connected; yet there was something wrong with his luck, and he had never got on.

"As to the captain, he had been for years in coasters, then in the Mediterranean, and last in the West Indian trade. He had never been round the Capes.[4] He could just write a kind of sketchy hand, and didn't care for writing at all. Both were thorough good seamen of course, and between those two old chaps I felt like a small boy between two grandfathers.

"The ship also was old. Her name was the *Judea*. Queer name, isn't it? She belonged to a man Wilmer, Wilcox—some name like that; but he has been bankrupt and dead these twenty years or more, and his name don't matter. She had been laid up in Shadwell basin for ever so long. You may imagine her state. She was all rust, dust, grime—soot aloft, dirt on deck. To me it was like coming out of a palace into a ruined cottage. She was about 400 tons, had a primitive windlass, wooden latches to the doors, not a bit of brass about her, and a big square stern. There was on it, below her name in big letters, a lot of scrollwork, with the gilt off, and some sort of a coat of arms, with the motto 'Do or Die' underneath. I remember it took my fancy immensely. There was a touch of romance in it, something that made me love the old thing—something that appealed to my youth!

"We left London in ballast—sand ballast—to load a cargo of coal in a northern port for Bangkok. Bangkok! I thrilled. I had been six years at sea, but had only seen Melbourne and Sydney, very good places, charming places in their way—but Bangkok!

"We worked out of the Thames under canvas, with a North Sea pilot on board. His name was Jermyn, and he dodged all day long about the galley drying his handkerchief before the stove. Apparently he never slept. He was a dismal man, with a perpetual tear sparkling at the end of his nose, who either had been in trouble, or was in trouble, or expected to be in trouble—couldn't be happy unless something went wrong. He mistrusted my youth, my common sense, and my seamanship, and made a point of showing it in a hundred little ways. I dare say he was right. It seems to me I knew very little then, and I know not much more now; but I cherish a hate for that Jermyn to this day.

"We were a week working up as far as Yarmouth Roads, and then we got into a gale—the famous October gale of twenty-two years ago. It was wind, lightning, sleet, snow, and a terrific sea. We were flying light, and you may imagine how bad it was when I tell you we had smashed bulwarks and a flooded deck. On the second night she shifted her ballast into the lee bow, and by that time we

4. The Cape of Good Hope, at the southwestern tip of the African continent, and Cape Horn, the southernmost point of South America.

had been blown off somewhere on the Dogger Bank. There was nothing for it but go below with shovels and try to right her, and there we were in that vast hold, gloomy like a cavern, the tallow dips stuck and flickering on the beams, the gale howling above, the ship tossing about like mad on her side; there we all were, Jermyn, the captain, everyone, hardly able to keep our feet, engaged on that gravedigger's work, and trying to toss shovelfuls of wet sand up to windward. At every tumble of the ship you could see vaguely in the dim light men falling down with a great flourish of shovels. One of the ship's boys (we had two), impressed by the weirdness of the scene, wept as if his heart would break. We could hear him blubbering somewhere in the shadows.

"On the third day the gale died out, and by and by a north-country tug picked us up. We took sixteen days in all to get from London to the Tyne![5] When we got into dock we had lost our turn for loading, and they hauled us off to a pier where we remained for a month. Mrs. Beard (the captain's name was Beard) came from Colchester to see the old man. She lived on board. The crew of runners had left, and there remained only the officers, one boy and the steward, a mulatto who answered to the name of Abraham. Mrs. Beard was an old woman, with a face all wrinkled and ruddy like a winter apple, and the figure of a young girl. She caught sight of me once, sewing on a button, and insisted on having my shirts to repair. This was something different from the captains' wives I had known on board crack clippers. When I brought her the shirts, she said: 'And the socks? They want mending, I am sure, and John's—Captain Beard's—things are all in order now. I would be glad of something to do.' Bless the old woman. She overhauled my outfit for me, and meantime I read for the first time *Sartor Resartus* and Burnaby's *Ride to Khiva*.[6] I didn't understand much of the first then; but I remember I preferred the soldier to the philosopher at the time; a preference which life has only confirmed. One was a man, the other was either more—or less. However, they are both dead and Mrs. Beard is dead, and youth, strength, genius, thoughts, achievements, simple hearts—all dies. . . . No matter.

"They loaded us at last. We shipped a crew. Eight able seamen and two boys. We hauled off one evening to the buoys at the dock-gates, ready to go out, and with a fair prospect of beginning the voyage next day. Mrs. Beard was to start for home by a late train.

5. A river in the northeast of England, on which the port of Newcastle-on-Tyne is situated. It flows into the North Sea at Tynemouth, nearly 300 miles north of London.
6. A once-popular travel book, published in 1876, by the English soldier and traveler Frederick Gustavus Barnaby (1842–85), describing his 300-mile winter journey on horseback across the Russian steppes. Khiva is now in the Uzbek Soviet Socialist Republic of the U.S.S.R.

When the ship was fast we went to tea. We sat rather silent through the meal—Mahon, the old couple, and I. I finished first, and slipped away for a smoke, my cabin being in a deckhouse just against the poop.[7] It was high water, blowing fresh with a drizzle; the double dock-gates were opened, and the steam colliers were going in and out in the darkness with their lights burning bright, a great plashing of propellers, rattling of winches, and a lot of hailing on the pierheads. I watched the procession of head-lights gliding high and of green lights gliding low in the night, when suddenly a red gleam flashed at me, vanished, came into view again, and remained. The fore-end of a steamer loomed up close. I shouted down the cabin, 'Come up, quick!' and then heard a startled voice saying afar in the dark, 'Stop her, sir.' A bell jingled. Another voice cried warningly, 'We are going right into that bark, sir.' The answer to this was a gruff 'All right,' and the next thing was a heavy crash as the steamer struck a glancing blow with the bluff of her bow about our fore-rigging. There was a moment of confusion, yelling, and running about. Steam roared. Then somebody was heard saying, 'All clear, sir.' . . . 'Are you all right?' asked the gruff voice. I had jumped forward to see the damage, and hailed back, 'I think so.' 'Easy astern,' said the gruff voice. A bell jingled. 'What steamer is that?' screamed Mahon. By that time she was no more to us than a bulky shadow maneuvering a little way off. They shouted at us some name—a woman's name, Miranda or Melissa—or some such thing. 'This means another month in this beastly hole,' said Mahon to me, as we peered with lamps about the splintered bulwarks and broken braces. 'But where's the captain?'

"We had not heard or seen anything of him all that time. We went aft to look. A doleful voice arose hailing somewhere in the middle of the dock, '*Judea* ahoy!' . . . How the devil did he get there? . . . 'Hallo!' we shouted. 'I am adrift in our boat without oars,' he cried. A belated water-man offered his services, and Mahon struck a bargain with him for a half crown to tow our skipper alongside; but it was Mrs. Beard that came up the ladder first. They had been floating about the dock in that mizzly cold rain for nearly an hour. I was never so surprised in my life.

"It appears that when he heard my shout 'Come up' he understood at once what was the matter, caught up his wife, ran on deck, and across, and down into our boat, which was fast to the ladder. Not bad for a sixty-year-old. Just imagine that old fellow saving heroically in his arms that old woman—the woman of his life. He set her down on a thwart, and was ready to climb back on board when the painter came adrift somehow, and away they went together. Of course in the confusion we did not hear him shouting.

7. Raised deck, often forming the roof of the cabin, at ship's stern.

He looked abashed. She said cheerfully, 'I suppose it does not matter my losing the train now?' 'No, Jenny—you go below and get warm,' he growled. Then to us: 'A sailor has no business with a wife—I say. There I was, out of the ship. Well, no harm done this time. Let's go and look at what that fool of a steamer smashed.'

"It wasn't much, but it delayed us three weeks. At the end of that time, the captain being engaged with his agents, I carried Mrs. Beard's bag to the railway station and put her all comfy into a third-class carriage. She lowered the window to say, 'You are a good young man. If you see John—Captain Beard—without his muffler at night, just remind him from me to keep his throat well wrapped up.' 'Certainly, Mrs. Beard,' I said. 'You are a good young man; I noticed how attentive you are to John—to Captain——' The train pulled out suddenly; I took my cap off to the old woman: I never saw her again. . . . Pass the bottle.

"We went to sea next day. When we made that start for Bangkok we had been already three months out of London. We had expected to be a fortnight or so—at the outside.

"It was January, and the weather was beautiful—the beautiful sunny winter weather that has more charm than in the summertime, because it is unexpected, and crisp, and you know it won't, it can't, last long. It's like a windfall, like a godsend, like an unexpected piece of luck.

"It lasted all down the North Sea, all down Channel; and it lasted till we were three hundred miles or so to the westward of the Lizards; [8] then the wind went round to the sou'west and began to pipe up. In two days it blew a gale. The *Judea*, hove to, wallowed on the Atlantic like an old candle-box. It blew day after day: it blew with spite, without interval, without mercy, without rest. The world was nothing but an immensity of great foaming waves rushing at us, under a sky low enough to touch with the hand and dirty like a smoked ceiling. In the stormy space surrounding us there was as much flying spray as air. Day after day and night after night there was nothing round the ship but the howl of the wind, the tumult of the sea, the noise of water pouring over her deck. There was no rest for her and no rest for us. She tossed, she pitched, she stood on her head, she sat on her tail, she rolled, she groaned, and we had to hold on while on deck and cling to our bunks when below, in a constant effort of body and worry of mind.

"One night Mahon spoke through the small window of my berth. It opened right into my very bed, and I was lying there sleepless, in my boots, feeling as though I had not slept for years, and could not if I tried. He said excitedly:

---

8. Lizard Head, peninsula in southwest England, on the coast of Cornwall, terminating in Lizard Point, the southern-most point in England.

" 'You got the sounding-rod in here, Marlow? I can't get the pumps to suck. By God! It's no child's play.'

"I gave him the sounding rod and lay down again, trying to think of various things—but I thought only of the pumps. When I came on deck they were still at it, and my watch relieved at the pumps. By the light of the lantern brought on deck to examine the sounding rod I caught a glimpse of their weary, serious faces. We pumped all the four hours. We pumped all night, all day, all the week—watch and watch. She was working herself loose, and leaked badly—not enough to drown us at once, but enough to kill us with the work at the pumps. And while we pumped the ship was going from us piecemeal: the bulwarks went, the stanchions were torn out, the ventilators smashed, the cabin door burst in. There was not a dry spot in the ship. She was being gutted bit by bit. The long-boat changed, as if by magic, into matchwood where she stood in her gripes. I had lashed her myself, and was rather proud of my handiwork, which had withstood so long the malice of the sea. And we pumped. And there was no break in the weather. The sea was white like a sheet of foam, like a caldron of boiling milk; there was not a break in the clouds, no—not the size of a man's hand—no, not for so much as ten seconds. There was for us no sky, there were for us no stars, no sun, no universe—nothing but angry clouds and an infuriated sea. We pumped watch and watch, for dear life; and it seemed to last for months, for years, for all eternity, as though we had been dead and gone to a hell for sailors. We forgot the day of the week, the name of the month, what year it was, and whether we had ever been ashore. The sails blew away, she lay broadside on under a weather-cloth, the ocean poured over her, and we did not care. We turned those handles, and had the eyes of idiots. As soon as we had crawled on deck I used to take a round turn with a rope about the men, the pumps, and the mainmast, and we turned, we turned incessantly, with the water to our waists, to our necks, over our heads. It was all one. We had forgotten how it felt to be dry.

"And there was somewhere in me the thought: By Jove! this is the deuce of an adventure—something you read about; and it is my first voyage as second mate—and I am only twenty—and here I am lasting it out as well as any of these men, and keeping my chaps up to the mark. I was pleased. I would not have given up the experience for worlds. I had moments of exultation. Whenever the old dismantled craft pitched heavily with her counter high in the air, she seemed to me to throw up, like an appeal, like a defiance, like a cry to the clouds without mercy, the words written on her stern: '*Judea*, London: Do or Die.'

"O youth! The strength of it, the faith of it, the imagination of it! To me she was not an old rattletrap carting about the world a lot of coal for a freight—to me she was the endeavor, the test, the trial of life. I think of her with pleasure, with affection, with regret —as you would think of someone dead you have loved. I shall never forget her. . . . Pass the bottle.

"One night when tied to the mast, as I explained, we were pumping on, deafened with the wind, and without spirit enough in us to wish ourselves dead, a heavy sea crashed aboard and swept clean over us. As soon as I got my breath I shouted, as in duty bound, 'Keep on, boys!' when suddenly I felt something hard floating on deck strike the calf of my leg. I made a grab at it and missed. It was so dark we could not see each other's faces within a foot—you understand.

"After that thump the ship kept quiet for a while, and the thing, whatever it was, struck my leg again. This time I caught it— and it was a saucepan. At first, being stupid with fatigue and thinking of nothing but the pumps, I did not understand what I had in my hand. Suddenly it dawned upon me, and I shouted, 'Boys, the house on deck is gone. Leave this, and let's look for the cook.'

"There was a deck-house forward, which contained the galley, the cook's berth, and the quarters of the crew. As we had expected for days to see it swept away, the hands had been ordered to sleep in the cabin—the only safe place in the ship. The steward, Abraham, however, persisted in clinging to his berth, stupidly, like a mule— from sheer fright I believe, like an animal that won't leave a stable falling in an earthquake. So we went to look for him. It was chancing death, since once out of our lashings we were as exposed as if on a raft. But we went. The house was shattered as if a shell had exploded inside. Most of it had gone overboard—stove, men's quarters, and their property, all was gone; but two posts, holding a portion of the bulkhead to which Abraham's bunk was attached, remained as if by a miracle. We groped in the ruins and came upon this, and there he was, sitting in his bunk, surrounded by foam and wreckage, jabbering cheerfully to himself. He was out of his mind; completely and forever mad, with this sudden shock coming upon the fag-end of his endurance. We snatched him up, lugged him aft, and pitched him headfirst down the cabin companion. You understand there was no time to carry him down with infinite precautions and wait to see how he got on. Those below would pick him up at the bottom of the stairs all right. We were in a hurry to go back to the pumps. That business could not wait. A bad leak is an inhuman thing.

"One would think that the sole purpose of that fiendish gale had been to make a lunatic of that poor devil of a mulatto. It eased before morning, and next day the sky cleared, and as the sea went down the leak took up. When it came to bending a fresh set of sails the crew demanded to put back—and really there was nothing else to do. Boats gone, decks swept clean, cabin gutted, men without a stitch but what they stood in, stores spoiled, ship strained. We put her head for home, and—would you believe it? The wind came east right in our teeth. It blew fresh, it blew continuously. We had to beat up every inch of the way, but she did not leak so badly, the water keeping comparatively smooth. Two hours' pumping in every four is no joke—but it kept her afloat as far as Falmouth.[9]

"The good people there live on casualties of the sea, and no doubt were glad to see us. A hungry crowd of shipwrights sharpened their chisels at the sight of that carcass of a ship. And, by Jove! they had pretty pickings off us before they were done. I fancy the owner was already in a tight place. There were delays. Then it was decided to take part of the cargo out and caulk her topsides. This was done, the repairs finished, cargo reshipped; a new crew came on board, and we went out—for Bangkok. At the end of a week we were back again. The crew said they weren't going to Bangkok—a hundred and fifty days' passage—in a something hooker that wanted pumping eight hours out of the twenty-four; and the nautical papers inserted again the little paragraph: '*Judea*. Bark. Tyne to Bangkok; coals; put back to Falmouth leaky and with crew refusing duty.'

"There were more delays—more tinkering. The owner came down for a day, and said she was as right as a little fiddle. Poor old Captain Beard looked like the ghost of a Geordie[1] skipper—through the worry and humiliation of it. Remember he was sixty, and it was his first command. Mahon said it was a foolish business, and would end badly. I loved the ship more than ever, and wanted awfully to get to Bangkok. To Bangkok! Magic name, blessed name. Mesopotamia wasn't a patch on it.[2] Remember I was twenty, and it was my first second-mate's billet, and the East was waiting for me.

"We went out and anchored in the outer roads with a fresh crew—the third. She leaked worse than ever. It was as if those confounded shipwrights had actually made a hole in her. This time we did not even go outside. The crew simply refused to man the windlass.

"They towed us back to the inner harbor, and we became a fixture, a feature, an institution of the place. People pointed us out to visitors as 'That 'ere barque that's going to Bangkok—has been here six months—put back three times.' On holidays the small

---

9. Port on southwest English coast, in Cornwall.
1. A "Geordie" is a native of Tyneside, in northeast England. (See note 5 above.)
2. David Garrick, the 18th-century Eng-lish actor, said that "that blessed word Mesopotamia" in the mouth of the famous preacher George Whitefield had the power of making people laugh or cry.

boys pulling about in boats would hail, '*Judea*, ahoy!' and if a head showed above the rail shouted, 'Where you bound to?—Bangkok?' and jeered. We were only three on board. The poor old skipper mooned in the cabin. Mahon undertook the cooking, and unexpectedly developed all a Frenchman's genius for preparing nice little messes. I looked languidly after the rigging. We became citizens of Falmouth. Every shopkeeper knew us. At the barber's or tobacconist's they asked familiarly, 'Do you think you will ever get to Bangkok?' Meantime the owner, the underwriters, and the charterers squabbled amongst themselves in London, and our pay went on. . . . Pass the bottle.

"It was horrid. Morally it was worse than pumping for life. It seemed as though we had been forgotten by the world, belonged to nobody, would get nowhere; it seemed that, as if bewitched, we would have to live for ever and ever in that inner harbor, a derision and a byword to generations of long-shore loafers and dishonest boatmen. I obtained three months' pay and a five days' leave, and made a rush for London. It took me a day to get there and pretty well another to come back—but three months' pay went all the same. I don't know what I did with it. I went to a music-hall, I believe, lunched, dined, and supped in a swell place in Regent Street, and was back on time, with nothing but a complete set of Byron's works and a new railway rug to show for three months' work. The boatman who pulled me off to the ship said: 'Hallo! I thought you had left the old thing. *She* will never get to Bangkok.' 'That's all *you* know about it,' I said, scornfully—but I didn't like that prophecy at all.

"Suddenly a man, some kind of agent to somebody, appeared with full powers. He had grog blossoms all over his face, an indomitable energy, and was a jolly soul. We leaped into life again. A hulk came alongside, took our cargo, and then we went into dry dock to get our copper stripped. No wonder she leaked. The poor thing, strained beyond endurance by the gale, had, as if in disgust, spat out all the oakum of her lower seams. She was recaulked, new-coppered, and made as tight as a bottle. We went back to the hulk and reshipped our cargo.

"Then, on a fine moonlight night, all the rats left the ship.

"We had been infested with them. They had destroyed our sails, consumed more stores than the crew, affably shared our beds and our dangers, and now, when the ship was made seaworthy, concluded to clear out. I called Mahon to enjoy the spectacle. Rat after rat appeared on our rail, took a last look over his shoulder, and leaped with a hollow thud into the empty hulk. We tried to count them, but soon lost the tale. Mahon said: 'Well, well! don't talk to me about the intelligence of rats. They ought to have left before, when we had that narrow squeak from foundering. There you have the proof how silly is the superstition about them. They leave a good ship for an old rotten hulk, where there is nothing to eat, too, the fools! . . . I don't believe they know what is safe or what is good for them, any more than you or I.'

"And after some more talk we agreed that the wisdom of rats had been grossly overrated, being in fact no greater than that of men.

"The story of the ship was known, by this, all up the Channel from Land's End to the Forelands, and we could get no crew on the south coast. They sent us one all complete from Liverpool, and we left once more—for Bangkok.

"We had fair breezes, smooth water right into the tropics, and the old *Judea* lumbered along in the sunshine. When she went eight knots everything cracked aloft, and we tied our caps to our heads; but mostly she strolled on at the rate of three miles an hour. What could you expect? She was tired—that old ship. Her youth was where mine is—where yours is—you fellows who listen to this yarn; and what friend would throw your years and your weariness in your face? We didn't grumble at her. To us aft, at least, it seemed as though we had been born in her, reared in her, had lived in her for ages, had never known any other ship. I would just as soon have abused the old village church at home for not being a cathedral.

"And for me there was also my youth to make me patient. There was all the East before me, and all life, and the thought that I had been tried in that ship and had come out pretty well. And I thought of men of old who, centuries ago, went that road in ships that sailed no better, to the land of palms, and spices, and yellow sands, and of brown nations ruled by kings more cruel than Nero the Roman, and more splendid than Solomon the Jew. The old barque lumbered on, heavy with her age and the burden of her cargo, while I lived the life of youth in ignorance and hope. She lumbered on through an interminable procession of days; and the fresh gilding flashed back at the setting sun, seemed to cry out over the darkening sea the words painted on her stern, '*Judea*, London. Do or Die.'

"Then we entered the Indian Ocean and steered northerly for Java Head. The winds were light. Weeks slipped by. She crawled on, do or die, and people at home began to think of posting us as overdue.

"One Saturday evening, I being off duty, the men asked me to give them an extra bucket of water or so—for washing clothes. As I did not wish to screw on the fresh-water pump so late, I went forward whistling, and with a key in my hand to unlock the forepeak scuttle, [3] intending to serve the water out of a spare tank we kept there.

"The smell down below was as unexpected as it was frightful. One would have thought hundreds of paraffin lamps had been flaring and smoking in that hole for days. I was glad to get out. The man with me coughed and said, 'Funny smell, sir.' I answered negligently, 'It's good for the health, they say,' and walked aft.

"The first thing I did was to put my head down the square of the midship ventilator. As I lifted the lid a visible breath, something like a thin fog, a puff of faint haze, rose from the opening. The ascending air was hot, and had a heavy, sooty, paraffiny smell. I gave one sniff, and put down the lid gently. It was no use choking myself. The cargo was on fire.

"Next day she began to smoke in earnest. You see it was to be expected, for though the coal was of a safe kind, that cargo had been so handled, so broken up with handling, that it looked more like smithy coal than anything else. Then it had been wetted—more than once. It rained all the time we were taking it back from the hulk, and now with this long passage it got heated, and there was another case of spontaneous combustion.

"The captain called us into the cabin. He had a chart spread on the table, and looked unhappy. He said, 'The coast of West Australia is near, but I mean to proceed to our destination. It is the hurricane month, too; but we will just keep her head for Bangkok, and fight the fire. No more putting back anywhere, if we all get roasted. We will try first to stifle this 'ere damned combustion by want of air.'

"We tried. We battened down everything, and still she smoked. The smoke kept coming out through imperceptible crevices; it forced itself through bulkheads and covers; it oozed here and there and everywhere in slender threads, in an invisible film, in an incomprehensible manner. It made its way into the cabin, into the forecastle; it poisoned the sheltered places on the deck; it could be sniffed as high as the mainyard. It was clear that if the smoke came out the air came in. This was disheartening. This combustion refused to be stifled.

"We resolved to try water, and took the hatches off. Enormous volumes of smoke, whitish, yellowish, thick, greasy, misty, choking, ascended as high as the trucks. All hands cleared out aft. Then the poisonous cloud blew away, and we went back to work in a smoke that was no thicker now than that of an ordinary factory chimney.

"We rigged the force pump, got the hose along, and by and by it burst. Well, it was as old as the ship—a prehistoric hose, and

3. A covered hatchway (small opening) in the deck of a ship.

past repair. Then we pumped with the feeble head pump, drew water with buckets, and in this way managed in time to pour lots of Indian Ocean into the main hatch. The bright stream flashed in sunshine, fell into a layer of white crawling smoke, and vanished on the black surface of coal. Steam ascended mingling with the smoke. We poured salt water as into a barrel without a bottom. It was our fate to pump in that ship, to pump out of her, to pump into her; and after keeping water out of her to save ourselves from being drowned, we frantically poured water into her to save ourselves from being burnt.

"And she crawled on, do or die, in the serene weather. The sky was a miracle of purity, a miracle of azure. The sea was polished, was blue, was pellucid, was sparkling like a precious stone, extending on all sides, all round to the horizon—as if the whole terrestrial globe had been one jewel, one colossal sapphire, a single gem fashioned into a planet. And on the luster of the great calm waters the *Judea* glided imperceptibly, enveloped in languid and unclean vapors, in a lazy cloud that drifted to leeward, light and slow; a pestiferous cloud defiling the splendor of sea and sky.

"All this time of course we saw no fire. The cargo smoldered at the bottom somewhere. Once Mahon, as we were working side by side, said to me with a queer smile: 'Now, if she would only spring a tidy leak—like that time when we first left the Channel— it would put a stopper on this fire. Wouldn't it?' I remarked irrelevantly, 'Do you remember the rats?'

"We fought the fire and sailed the ship too as carefully as though nothing had been the matter. The steward cooked and attended on us. Of the other twelve men, eight worked while four rested. Everyone took his turn, captain included. There was equality, and if not exactly fraternity, then a deal of good feeling. Sometimes a man, as he dashed a bucketful of water down the hatchway, would yell out, 'Hurrah for Bangkok!' and the rest laughed. But generally we were taciturn and serious—and thirsty. Oh! how thirsty! And we had to be careful with the water. Strict allowance. The ship smoked, the sun blazed. . . . Pass the bottle.

"We tried everything. We even made an attempt to dig down to the fire. No good, of course. No man could remain more than a minute below. Mahon, who went first, fainted there, and the man who went to fetch him out did likewise. We lugged them out on deck. Then I leaped down to show how easily it could be done. They had learned wisdom by that time, and contented themselves by fishing for me with a chainhook tied to a broom handle, I believe. I did not offer to go and fetch up my shovel, which was left down below.

"Things began to look bad. We put the longboat into the

water. The second boat was ready to swing out. We had also another, a fourteen-foot thing, on davits aft, where it was quite safe.

"Then, behold, the smoke suddenly decreased. We redoubled our efforts to flood the bottom of the ship. In two days there was no smoke at all. Everybody was on the broad grin. This was on a Friday. On Saturday no work, but sailing the ship of course, was done. The men washed their clothes and their faces for the first time in a fortnight, and had a special dinner given them. They spoke of spontaneous combustion with contempt, and implied *they* were the boys to put out combustions. Somehow we all felt as though we each had inherited a large fortune. But a beastly smell of burning hung about the ship. Captain Beard had hollow eyes and sunken cheeks. I had never noticed so much before how twisted and bowed he was. He and Mahon prowled soberly about hatches and ventilators, sniffing. It struck me suddenly poor Mahon was a very, very old chap. As to me, I was as pleased and proud as though I had helped to win a great naval battle. O! Youth!

"The night was fine. In the morning a homeward-bound ship passed us hull down—the first we had seen for months; but we were nearing the land at last, Java Head being about 190 miles off, and nearly due north.

"Next day it was my watch on deck from eight to twelve. At breakfast the captain observed, 'It's wonderful how that smell hangs about the cabin.' About ten, the mate being on the poop, I stepped down on the main deck for a moment. The carpenter's bench stood abaft the mainmast: I leaned against it sucking at my pipe, and the carpenter, a young chap, came to talk to me. He remarked, 'I think we have done very well, haven't we?' and then I perceived with annoyance the fool was trying to tilt the bench. I said curtly, 'Don't, Chips,' and immediately became aware of a queer sensation, of an absurd delusion—I seemed somehow to be in the air. I heard all round me like a pent-up breath released—as if a thousand giants simultaneously had said Phoo!—and felt a dull concussion which made my ribs ache suddenly. No doubt about it—I was in the air, and my body was describing a short parabola. But short as it was, I had the time to think several thoughts in, as far as I can remember, the following order: 'This can't be the carpenter—What is it?—Some accident—Submarine volcano?—Coals, gas!—By Jove! We are being blown up—Everybody's dead—I am falling into the after-hatch—I see fire in it.'

"The coaldust suspended in the air of the hold had glowed dull-red at the moment of the explosion. In the twinkling of an eye, in an infinitesimal fraction of a second since the first tilt of the bench, I was sprawling full length on the cargo. I picked myself up and scrambled out. It was quick like a rebound. The deck was a wilderness of smashed timber, lying crosswise like trees in a wood after a hurricane; an immense curtain of solid rags waved gently before me—it was the mainsail blown to strips. I thought: the masts will be toppling over directly; and to get out of the way bolted on all fours towards the poop ladder. The first person I saw was Mahon, with eyes like saucers, his mouth open, and the long white hair standing straight on end round his head like a silver halo. He was just about to go down when the sight of the main deck stirring, heaving up, and changing into splinters before his eyes, petrified him on the top step. I stared at him in unbelief, and he stared at me with a queer kind of shocked curiosity. I did not know that I had no hair, no eyebrows, no eye-lashes, that my young mustache was burnt off, that my face was black, one cheek laid open, my nose cut, and my chin bleeding. I had lost my cap, one of my slippers, and my shirt was torn to rags. Of all this I was not aware. I was amazed to see the ship still afloat, the poop deck whole—and, most of all, to see anybody alive. Also the peace of the sky and the serenity of the sea were distinctly surprising. I suppose I expected to see them convulsed with horror. . . . Pass the bottle.

"There was a voice hailing the ship from somewhere—in the air, in the sky—I couldn't tell. Presently I saw the captain—and he was mad. He asked me eagerly, 'Where's the cabin table?' and to hear such a question was a frightful shock. I had just been blown up, you understand, and vibrated with that experience—I wasn't quite sure whether I was alive. Mahon began to stamp with both feet and yelled at him, 'Good God! don't you see the deck's blown out of her?' I found my voice, and stammered out as if conscious of some gross neglect of duty, 'I don't know where the cabin table is.' It was like an absurd dream.

"Do you know what he wanted next? Well, he wanted to trim the yards. Very placidly, and as if lost in thought, he insisted on having the foreyard squared. 'I don't know if there's anybody alive,' said Mahon, almost tearfully. 'Surely,' he said gently, 'there will be enough left to square the foreyard.'

"The old chap, it seems, was in his own berth winding up the chronometers, when the shock sent him spinning. Immediately it occurred to him—as he said afterwards—that the ship had struck something, and ran out into the cabin. There, he saw, the cabin table had vanished somewhere. The deck being blown up, it had fallen down into the lazarette [4] of course. Where we had our break-fast that morning he saw only a great hole in the floor. This ap-peared to him so awfully mysterious, and impressed him so immensely, that what he saw and heard after he got on deck were

4. Space between decks.

mere trifles in comparison. And, mark, he noticed directly the wheel deserted and his bark off her course—and his only thought was to get that miserable, stripped, undecked, smoldering shell of a ship back again with her head pointing at her port of destination. Bangkok! That's what he was after. I tell you this quiet, bowed, bandy-legged, almost deformed little man was immense in the singleness of his idea and in his placid ignorance of our agitation. He motioned us forward with a commanding gesture, and went to take the wheel himself.

"Yes; that was the first thing we did—trim the yards of that wreck! No one was killed, or even disabled, but everyone was more or less hurt. You should have seen them! Some were in rags, with black faces, like coal heavers, like sweeps, and had bullet heads that seemed closely cropped, but were in fact singed to the skin. Others, of the watch below, awakened by being shot out from their collapsing bunks, shivered incessantly, and kept on groaning even as we went about our work. But they all worked. That crew of Liverpool hard cases had in them the right stuff. It's my experience they always have. It is the sea that gives it—the vastness, the loneliness surrounding their dark stolid souls. Ah! Well! We stumbled, we crept, we fell, we barked our shins on the wreckage, we hauled. The masts stood, but we did not know how much they might be charred down below. It was nearly calm, but a long swell ran from the west and made her roll. They might go at any moment. We looked at them with apprehension. One could not foresee which way they would fall.

"Then we retreated aft and looked about us. The deck was a tangle of planks on edge, of planks on end, of splinters, of ruined woodwork. The masts rose from that chaos like big trees above a matted undergrowth. The interstices of that mass of wreckage were full of something whitish, sluggish, stirring—of something that was like a greasy fog. The smoke of the invisible fire was coming up again, was trailing, like a poisonous thick mist in some valley choked with dead wood. Already lazy wisps were beginning to curl upwards amongst the mass of splinters. Here and there a piece of timber, stuck upright, resembled a post. Half of a fife-rail had been shot through the foresail, and the sky made a patch of glorious blue in the ignobly soiled canvas. A portion of several boards holding together had fallen across the rail, and one end protruded overboard, like a gangway leading upon nothing, like a gangway leading over the deep sea, leading to death—as if inviting us to walk the plank at once and be done with our ridiculous troubles. And still the air, the sky—a ghost, something invisible was hailing the ship.

"Someone had the sense to look over, and there was the

helmsman, who had impulsively jumped overboard, anxious to come back. He yelled and swam lustily like a merman, keeping up with the ship. We threw him a rope, and presently he stood amongst us streaming with water and very crestfallen. The captain had surrendered the wheel, and apart, elbow on rail and chin in hand, gazed at the sea wistfully. We asked ourselves, What next? I thought, Now, this is something like. This is great. I wonder what will happen. O youth!

"Suddenly Mahon sighted a steamer far astern. Captain Beard said, 'We may do something with her yet.' We hoisted two flags, which said in the international language of the sea, 'On fire. Want immediate assistance.' The steamer grew bigger rapidly, and by and by spoke with two flags on her foremast, 'I am coming to your assistance.'

"In half an hour she was abreast, to windward, within hail, and rolling slightly, with her engines stopped. We lost our composure, and yelled all together with excitement, 'We've been blown up.' A man in a white helmet, on the bridge, cried, 'Yes! All right! all right!' and he nodded his head, and smiled, and made soothing motions with his hand as though at a lot of frightened children. One of the boats dropped in the water, and walked towards us upon the sea with her long oars. Four Calashes pulled a swinging stroke. This was my first sight of Malay seamen. I've known them since, but what struck me then was their unconcern; they came alongside, and even the bowman standing up and holding to our main-chains with the boat-hook did not deign to lift his head for a glance. I thought people who had been blown up deserved more attention.

"A little man, dry like a chip and agile like a monkey, clambered up. It was the mate of the steamer. He gave one look, and cried, 'O boys—you had better quit!'

"We were silent. He talked apart with the captain for a time— seemed to argue with him. Then they went away together to the steamer.

"When our skipper came back we learned that the steamer was the *Somerville*, Captain Nash, from West Australia to Singapore via Batavia with mails, and that the agreement was she should tow us to Anjer or Batavia, if possible, where we could extinguish the fire by scuttling,[5] and then proceed on our voyage—to Bangkok! The old man seemed excited. 'We will do it yet,' he said to Mahon, fiercely. He shook his fist at the sky. Nobody else said a word.

"At noon the steamer began to tow. She went ahead slim and high, and what was left of the *Judea* followed at the end of seventy

5. I.e., sinking the boat by cutting a hole in the side or bottom.

fathom of tow-rope—followed her swiftly like a cloud of smoke
with mastheads protruding above. We went aloft to furl the sails.
We coughed on the yards, and were careful about the bunts.[6] Do
you see the lot of us there, putting a neat furl on the sails of that
ship doomed to arrive nowhere? There was not a man who didn't
think that at any moment the masts would topple over. From
aloft we could not see the ship for smoke, and they worked carefully, passing the gaskets with even turns. 'Harbor furl—aloft there!'
cried Mahon from below.

"You understand this? I don't think one of those chaps expected
to get down in the usual way. When we did I heard them saying
to each other, 'Well, I thought we would come down overboard,
in a lump—sticks and all—blame me if I didn't.' 'That's what I
was thinking to myself,' would answer wearily another battered
and bandaged scarecrow. And, mind, these were men without the
drilled-in habit of obedience. To an onlooker they would be a lot
of profane scallywags without a redeeming point. What made
them do it—what made them obey me when I, thinking consciously how fine it was, made them drop the bunt of the foresail
twice to try and do it better? What? They had no professional
reputation—no examples, no praise. It wasn't a sense of duty; they
all knew well enough how to shirk, and laze, and dodge—when they
had a mind to it—and mostly they had. Was it the two pounds
ten a month that sent them there? They didn't think their pay
half good enough. No; it was something in them, something inborn
and subtle and everlasting. I don't say positively that the crew
of a French or German merchantman wouldn't have done it, but
I doubt whether it would have been done in the same way. There
was a completeness in it, something solid like a principle, and
masterful like an instinct—a disclosure of something secret—of
that hidden something, that gift of good or evil that makes racial
difference, that shapes the fate of nations.

"It was that night at ten that, for the first time since we had
been fighting it, we saw the fire. The speed of the towing had
fanned the smoldering destruction. A blue gleam appeared forward, shining below the wreck of the deck. It wavered in patches,
it seemed to stir and creep like the light of a glowworm. I saw it
first, and told Mahon. 'Then the game's up,' he said. 'We had
better stop this towing, or she will burst out suddenly fore and
aft before we can clear out.' We set up a yell; rang bells to attract
their attention; they towed on. At last Mahon and I had to crawl
forward and cut the rope with an ax. There was no time to cast
off the lashings. Red tongues could be seen licking the wilderness of splinters under our feet as we made our way back to the
poop.

6. The middle part of a furled sail, gathered into a bunch.

"Of course they very soon found out in the steamer that the rope was gone. She gave a loud blast of her whistle, her lights were seen sweeping in a wide circle, she came up ranging close alongside, and stopped. We were all in a tight group on the poop looking at her. Every man had saved a little bundle or a bag. Suddenly a conical flame with a twisted top shot up forward and threw upon the black sea a circle of light, with the two vessels side by side and heaving gently in its center. Captain Beard had been sitting on the gratings still and mute for hours, but now he rose slowly and advanced in front of us, to the mizzen-shrouds. Captain Nash hailed: 'Come along! Look sharp. I have mailbags on board. I will take you and your boats to Singapore.'

" 'Thank you! No!' said our skipper. 'We must see the last of the ship.'

" 'I can't stand by any longer,' shouted the other. 'Mails—you know.'

" 'Ay! ay! We are all right.'

" 'Very well! I'll report you in Singapore. . . . Good-by!'

"He waved his hands. Our men dropped their bundles quietly. The steamer moved ahead, and passing out of the circle of light, vanished at once from our sight, dazzled by the fire which burned fiercely. And then I knew that I would see the East first as commander of a small boat. I thought it fine; and the fidelity to the old ship was fine. We should see the last of her. Oh, the glamor of youth! Oh, the fire of it, more dazzling than the flames of the burning ship, throwing a magic light on the wide earth, leaping audaciously to the sky, presently to be quenched by time, more cruel, more pitiless, more bitter than the sea—and like the flames of the burning ship surrounded by an impenetrable night.

"The old man warned us in his gentle and inflexible way that it was part of our duty to save for the underwriters as much as we could of the ship's gear. Accordingly we went to work aft, while she blazed forward to give us plenty of light. We lugged out a lot of rubbish. What didn't we save? An old barometer fixed with an absurd quantity of screws nearly cost me my life: a sudden rush of smoke came upon me, and I just got away in time. There were various stores, bolts of canvas, coils of rope; the poop looked like a marine bazaar, and the boats were lumbered to the gunwales. One would have thought the old man wanted to take as much as he could of his first command with him. He was very, very quiet, but off his balance evidently. Would you believe it? He wanted to take a length of old stream-cable and a kedge anchor with him in the longboat. We said, 'Ay, ay, sir,' deferentially, and on the quiet let the things slip overboard. The heavy medicine chest went that way, two bags of green coffee, tins of paint—fancy, paint!—a whole lot of things. Then I was ordered with two hands into the boats to make a stowage and get them ready against the time it would be proper for us to leave the ship.

"We put everything straight, stepped the long-boat's mast for our skipper, who was to take charge of her, and I was not sorry to sit down for a moment. My face felt raw, every limb ached as if broken, I was aware of all my ribs, and would have sworn to a twist in the backbone. The boats, fast astern, lay in a deep shadow, and all around I could see the circle of the sea lighted by the fire. A gigantic flame arose forward straight and clear. It flared fierce, with noises like the whirr of wings, with rumbles as of thunder. There were cracks, detonations, and from the cone of flame the sparks flew upwards, as man is born to trouble,[7] to leaky ships, and to ships that burn.

"What bothered me was that the ship, lying broadside to the swell and to such wind as there was—a mere breath—the boats would not keep astern where they were safe, but persisted, in a pig-headed way boats have, in getting under the counter and then swinging alongside. They were knocking about dangerously and coming near the flame, while the ship rolled on them, and, of course, there was always the danger of the masts going over the side at any moment. I and my two boat-keepers kept them off as best as we could, with oars and boat-hooks; but to be constantly at it became exasperating, since there was no reason why we should not leave at once. We could not see those on board, nor could we imagine what caused the delay. The boat-keepers were swearing feebly, and I had not only my share of the work but also had to keep at it two men who showed a constant inclination to lay themselves down and let things slide.

"At last I hailed, 'On deck there,' and someone looked over. 'We're ready here,' I said. The head disappeared, and very soon popped up again. 'The captain says, All right, sir, and to keep the boats well clear of the ship.'

"Half an hour passed. Suddenly there was a frightful racket, rattle, clanking of chain, hiss of water, and millions of sparks flew up into the shivering column of smoke that stood leaning slightly above the ship. The cat-heads had burned away, and the two red-hot anchors had gone to the bottom, tearing out after them two hundred fathom of red-hot chain. The ship trembled, the mass of flame swayed as if ready to collapse, and the fore-topgallant mast fell. It darted down like an arrow of fire, shot under, and instantly leaping up within an oar's-length of the

7. "Yet man is born unto trouble as the sparks fly upward." Job v.7.

boats, floated quietly, very black on the luminous sea. I hailed the deck again. After some time a man in an unexpectedly cheerful but also muffled tone, as though he had been trying to speak with his mouth shut, informed me, 'Coming directly, sir,' and vanished. For a long time I heard nothing but the whirr and roar of the fire. There were also whistling sounds. The boats jumped, tugged at the painters, ran at each other playfully, knocked their sides together, or, do what we would, swung in a bunch against the ship's side. I couldn't stand it any longer, and swarming up a rope, clambered aboard over the stern.

"It was as bright as day. Coming up like this, the sheet of fire facing me was a terrifying sight, and the heat seemed hardly bearable at first. On a settee cushion dragged out of the cabin Captain Beard, his legs drawn up and one arm under his head, slept with the light playing on him. Do you know what the rest were busy about? They were sitting on deck right aft, round an open case, eating bread and cheese and drinking bottled stout.

"On the background of flames twisting in fierce tongues above their heads they seemed at home like salamanders, and looked like a band of desperate pirates. The fire sparkled in the whites of their eyes, gleamed on patches of white skin seen through the torn shirts. Each had the marks as of a battle about him— bandaged heads, tied-up arms, a strip of dirty rags around a knee— and each man had a bottle between his legs and a chunk of cheese in his hand. Mahon got up. With his handsome and disreputable head, his hooked profile, his long white beard, and with an uncorked bottle in his hand, he resembled one of those reckless sea robbers of old making merry amidst violence and disaster. 'The last meal on board,' he explained solemnly. 'We had nothing to eat all day, and it was no use leaving all this.' He flourished the bottle and indicated the sleeping skipper. 'He said he couldn't swallow anything, so I got him to lie down,' he went on; and as I stared, 'I don't know whether you are aware, young fellow, the man had no sleep to speak of for days—and there will be dam' little sleep in the boats.' 'There will be no boats by and by if you fool about much longer,' I said, indignantly. I walked up to the skipper and shook him by the shoulder. At last he opened his eyes, but did not move. 'Time to leave her, sir,' I said quietly.

"He got up painfully, looked at the flames, at the sea sparkling round the ship, and black, black as ink farther away; he looked at the stars shining dim through a thin veil of smoke in a sky black, black as Erebus.[8]

" 'Youngest first,' he said.

"And the ordinary seaman, wiping his mouth with the back of

8. In Greek mythology, the entry to Hades, the underworld; hence, total darkness.

his hand, got up, clambered over the taffrail and vanished. Others followed. One, on the point of going over, stopped short to drain his bottle, and with a great swing of his arm flung it at the fire. 'Take this!' he cried.

"The skipper lingered disconsolately, and we left him to commune alone for a while with his first command. Then I went up again and brought him away at last. It was time. The ironwork on the poop was hot to the touch.

"Then the painter of the long-boat was cut, and the three boats, tied together, drifted clear of the ship. It was just sixteen hours after the explosion when we abandoned her. Mahon had charge of the second boat, and I had the smallest—the fourteen-foot thing. The long-boat would have taken the lot of us; but the skipper said we must save as much property as we could—for the underwriters—and so I got my first command. I had two men with me, a bag of biscuits, a few tins of meat, and a breaker of water. I was ordered to keep close to the long-boat, that in case of bad weather we might be taken into her.

"And do you know what I thought? I thought I would part company as soon as I could. I wanted to have my first command all to myself. I wasn't going to sail in a squadron if there were a chance for independent cruising. I would make land by myself. I would beat the other boats. Youth! All youth! The silly, charming, beautiful youth.

"But we did not make a start at once. We must see the last of the ship. And so the boats drifted about that night, heaving and setting on the swell. The men dozed, waked, sighed, groaned. I looked at the burning ship.

"Between the darkness of earth and heaven she was burning fiercely upon a disc of purple sea shot by the blood-red play of gleams; upon a disc of water glittering and sinister. A high, clear flame, an immense and lonely flame, ascended from the ocean, and from its summit the black smoke poured continuously at the sky. She burned furiously; mournful and imposing like a funeral pile kindled in the night, surrounded by the sea, watched over by the stars. A magnificent death had come like a grace, like a gift, like a reward to that old ship at the end of her laborious days. The surrender of her weary ghost to the keeping of stars and sea was stirring like the sight of a glorious triumph. The masts fell just before daybreak, and for a moment there was a burst and turmoil of sparks that seemed to fill with flying fire the night patient and watchful, the vast night lying silent upon the sea. At daylight she was only a charred shell, floating still under a cloud of smoke and bearing a glowing mass of coal within.

"Then the oars were got out, and the boats forming in a line

moved round her remains as if in procession—the long-boat leading. As we pulled across her stern a slim dart of fire shot out
viciously at us, and suddenly she went down, head first, in a great
hiss of steam. The unconsumed stern was the last to sink; but
the paint had gone, had cracked, had peeled off, and there were
no letters, there was no word, no stubborn device that was like
her soul, to flash at the rising sun her creed and her name.

"We made our way north. A breeze sprang up, and about noon
all the boats came together for the last time. I had no mast or
sail in mine, but I made a mast out of a spare oar and hoisted
a boat-awning for a sail, with a boathook for a yard. She was
certainly over-masted, but I had the satisfaction of knowing that
with the wind aft I could beat the other two. I had to wait for
them. Then we all had a look at the captain's chart, and, after a
sociable meal of hard bread and water, got our last instructions.
These were simple: steer north, and keep together as much as
possible. 'Be careful with that jury-rig,[9] Marlow,' said the captain;
and Mahon, as I sailed proudly past his boat, wrinkled his curved
nose and hailed, 'You will sail that ship of yours under water, if
you don't look out, young fellow.' He was a malicious old man—
and may the deep sea where he sleeps now rock him gently, rock
him tenderly to the end of time!

"Before sunset a thick rain-squall passed over the two boats,
which were far astern, and that was the last I saw of them for a
time. Next day I sat steering my cockle-shell—my first command—
with nothing but water and sky round me. I did sight in the
afternoon the upper sails of a ship far away, but said nothing, and
my men did not notice her. You see I was afraid she might be
homeward bound, and I had no mind to turn back from the
portals of the East. I was steering for Java—another blessed name—
like Bangkok, you know. I steered many days.

"I need not tell you what it is to be knocking about in an open
boat. I remember nights and days of calm, when we pulled, we
pulled, and the boat seemed to stand still, as if bewitched within
the circle of the sea horizon. I remember the heat, the deluge of
rain-squalls that kept us baling for dear life (but filled our water-
cask), and I remember sixteen hours on end with a mouth dry as a
cinder and a steering-oar over the stern to keep my first command
head on to a breaking sea. I did not know how good a man I was
till then. I remember the drawn faces, the dejected figures of my
two men, and I remember my youth and the feeling that will
never come back any more—the feeling that I could last forever,
outlast the sea, the earth, and all men; the deceitful feeling that
lures us on to joys, to perils, to love, to vain effort—to death;
the triumphant conviction of strength, the heat of life in the

9. Temporary rig.

handful of dust, the glow in the heart that with every year grows dim, grows cold, grows small, and expires—and expires, too soon, too soon—before life itself.

"And this is how I see the East. I have seen its secret places and have looked into its very soul; but now I see it always from a small boat, a high outline of mountains, blue and afar in the morning; like faint mist at noon; a jagged wall of purple at sunset. I have the feel of the oar in my hand, the vision of a scorching blue sea in my eyes. And I see a bay, a wide bay, smooth as glass and polished like ice, shimmering in the dark. A red light burns far off upon the gloom of the land, and the night is soft and warm. We drag at the oars with aching arms, and suddenly a puff of wind, a puff faint and tepid and laden with strange odors of blossoms, of aromatic wood, comes out of the still night—the first sigh of the East on my face. That I can never forget. It was impalpable and enslaving, like a charm, like a whispered promise of mysterious delight.

"We had been pulling this finishing spell for eleven hours. Two pulled, and he whose turn it was to rest sat at the tiller. We had made out the red light in that bay and steered for it, guessing it must mark some small coasting port. We passed two vessels, out-landish and high-sterned, sleeping at anchor, and, approaching the light, now very dim, ran the boat's nose against the end of a jutting wharf. We were blind with fatigue. My men dropped the oars and fell off the thwarts as if dead. I made fast to a pile. A current rippled softly. The scented obscurity of the shore was grouped into vast masses, a density of colossal clumps of vegetation, probably—mute and fantastic shapes. And at their foot the semi-circle of a beach gleamed faintly, like an illusion. There was not a light, not a stir, not a sound. The mysterious East faced me, perfumed like a flower, silent like death, dark like a grave.

"And I sat weary beyond expression, exulting like a conqueror, sleepless and entranced as if before a profound, a fateful enigma.

"A splashing of oars, a measured dip reverberating on the level of water, intensified by the silence of the shore into loud claps, made me jump up. A boat, a European boat, was coming in. I invoked the name of the dead; I hailed: '*Judea* ahoy!' A thin shout answered.

"It was the captain. I had beaten the flagship by three hours, and I was glad to hear the old man's voice again, tremulous and tired. 'Is it you, Marlow?' 'Mind the end of that jetty, sir,' I cried.

"He approached cautiously, and brought up with the deep-sea lead-line which we had saved—for the underwriters. I eased my painter and fell alongside. He sat, a broken figure at the stern, wet with dew, his hands clasped in his lap. His men were asleep already. 'I had a terrible time of it,' he murmured. 'Mahon is behind—not very far.' We conversed in whispers, in low whispers, as if afraid to wake up the land. Guns, thunder, earthquakes would not have awakened the men just then.

"Looking round as we talked, I saw away at sea a bright light traveling in the night. 'There's a steamer passing the bay,' I said. She was not passing, she was entering, and she even came close and anchored. 'I wish,' said the old man, 'you would find out whether she is English. Perhaps they could give us a passage somewhere.' He seemed nervously anxious. So by dint of punching and kicking I started one of my men into a state of somnambulism, and giving him an oar, took another and pulled towards the lights of the steamer.

"There was a murmur of voices in her, metallic hollow clangs of the engine-room, footsteps on the deck. Her ports shone, round like dilated eyes. Shapes moved about, and there was a shadowy man high up on the bridge. He heard my oars.

"And then, before I could open my lips, the East spoke to me, but it was in a Western voice. A torrent of words was poured into the engimatical, the fateful silence; outlandish, angry words, mixed with words and even whole sentences of good English, less strange but even more surprising. The voice swore and cursed violently; it riddled the solemn peace of the bay by a volley of abuse. It began by calling me Pig, and from that went crescendo into unmentionable adjectives—in English. The man up there raged aloud in two languages, and with a sincerity in his fury that almost convinced me I had, in some way, sinned against the harmony of the universe. I could hardly see him, but began to think he would work himself into a fit.

"Suddenly he ceased, and I could hear him snorting and blowing like a porpoise. I said:

" 'What steamer is this, pray?'

" 'Eh? What's this? And who are you?'

" 'Castaway crew of an English barque burnt at sea. We came here tonight. I am the second mate. The captain is in the long-boat, and wishes to know if you would give us a passage somewhere.'

" 'Oh, my goodness! I say. . . . This is the *Celestial* from Singapore on her return trip. I'll arrange with your captain in the morning, . . . and, . . . I say, . . . did you hear me just now?'

" 'I should think the whole bay heard you.'

" 'I thought you were a shore-boat. Now, look here—this infernal lazy scoundrel of a caretaker has gone to sleep again—curse him. The light is out, and I nearly ran foul of the end of this damned jetty. This is the third time he plays me this trick. Now, I ask you, can anybody stand this kind of thing? It's enough to drive a man out of his mind. I'll report him. . . . I'll get the Assistant Resident to give him the sack, by—! See—there's no light. It's out, isn't it? I take you to witness the light's out. There should be a light, you know. A red light on the—'

" 'There was a light,' I said mildly.

" 'But it's out, man! What's the use of talking like this? You can see for yourself it's out—don't you? If you had to take a valuable steamer along this God-forsaken coast you would want a light, too. I'll kick him from end to end of his miserable wharf. You'll see if I don't. I will—'

" 'So I may tell my captain you'll take us?' I broke in.

" 'Yes, I'll take you. Good night,' he said, brusquely.

"I pulled back, made fast again to the jetty, and then went to sleep at last. I had faced the silence of the East. I had heard some of its language. But when I opened my eyes again the silence was as complete as though it had never been broken. I was lying in a flood of light, and the sky had never looked so far, so high, before. I opened my eyes and lay without moving.

"And then I saw the men of the East—they were looking at me. The whole length of the jetty was full of people. I saw brown, bronze, yellow faces, the black eyes, the glitter, the color of an Eastern crowd. And all these beings stared without a murmur, without a sigh, without a movement. They stared down at the boats, at the sleeping men who at night had come to them from the sea. Nothing moved. The fronds of palms stood still against the sky. Not a branch stirred along the shore, and the brown roofs of hidden houses peeped through the green foliage, through the big leaves that hung shining and still like leaves forged of heavy metal. This was the East of the ancient navigators, so old, so mysterious, resplendent and somber, living and unchanged, full of danger and promise. And these were the men. I sat up suddenly. A wave of movement passed through the crowd from end to end, passed along the heads, swayed the bodies, ran along the jetty like a ripple on the water, like a breath of wind on a field—and all was still again. I see it now—the wide sweep of the bay, the glittering sands, the wealth of green infinite and varied, the sea blue like the sea of a dream, the crowd of attentive faces, the blaze of vivid color—the water reflecting it all, the curve of the shore, the jetty, the high-sterned outlandish craft floating still, and the three boats with the tired men from the West sleeping, unconscious of the land and the people and of the violence of sunshine. They slept thrown across the thwarts, curled on bottom-boards, in the careless attitudes of death. The head of the old skipper, leaning back in the stern of the long-boat, had fallen on his breast, and he looked as though he would never wake. Farther out old Mahon's face was upturned to the sky, with the long white beard spread out on his breast, as though he had been shot where he sat at the tiller; and a man, all in a heap in the bows of the boat, slept with both arms embracing the stem-head and with his cheek laid on the gunwale. The East looked at them without a sound.

"I have known its fascination since; I have seen the mysterious shores, the still water, the lands of brown nations, where a stealthy Nemesis lies in wait, pursues, overtakes so many of the conquering race, who are proud of their wisdom, of their knowledge, of their strength. But for me all the East is contained in that vision of my youth. It is all in that moment when I opened my young eyes on it. I came upon it from a tussle with the sea—and I was young—and I saw it looking at me. And this is all that is left of it! Only a moment; a moment of strength, of romance, glamor—of youth! . . . A flick of sunshine upon a strange shore, the time to remember, the time for a sigh, and—good-bye!—Night—Good-bye . . . !"

He drank.

"Ah! The good old time—the good old time. Youth and the sea. Glamor and the sea! The good, strong sea, the salt, bitter sea, that could whisper to you and roar at you and knock your breath out of you."

He drank again.

"By all that's wonderful it is the sea, I believe, the sea itself—or is it youth alone? Who can tell? But you here—you all had something out of life: money, love—whatever one gets on shore—and, tell me, wasn't that the best time, that time when we were young at sea; young and had nothing, on the sea that gives nothing, except hard knocks—and sometimes a chance to feel your strength —that only—that you all regret?"

And we all nodded at him: the man of finance, the man of accounts, the man of law, we all nodded at him over the polished table that like a still sheet of brown water reflected our faces, lined, wrinkled; our faces marked by toil, by deceptions, by success, by love; our weary eyes looking still, looking always, looking anxiously for something out of life, that while it is expected is already gone—has passed unseen, in a sigh, in a flash— together with the youth, with the strength, with the romance of illusions.

1898

1898, 1902

The Secret Sharer

I

On my right hand there were lines of fishing stakes resembling a mysterious system of half-submerged bamboo fences, incomprehensible in its division of the domain of tropical fishes, and crazy of aspect as if abandoned forever by some nomad tribe of fishermen now gone to the other end of the ocean; for there was no sign of human habitation as far as the eye could reach. To the left a group of barren islets, suggesting ruins of stone walls, towers, and blockhouses, had its foundations set in a blue sea that itself looked solid, so still and stable did it lie below my feet; even the track of light from the westering sun shone smoothly, without that animated glitter which tells of an imperceptible ripple. And when I turned my head to take a parting glance at the tug which had just left us anchored outside the bar, I saw the straight line of the flat shore joined to the stable sea, edge to edge, with a perfect and unmarked closeness, in one leveled floor half brown, half blue under the enormous dome of the sky. Corresponding in their insignificance to the islets of the sea, two small clumps of trees, one on each side of the only fault in the impeccable joint, marked the mouth of the river Meinam we had just left on the first preparatory stage of our homeward journey; and, far back on the inland level, a larger and loftier mass, the grove surrounding the great Paknam pagoda, was the only thing on which the eye could rest from the vain task of exploring the monotonous sweep of the horizon. Here and there gleams as of a few scattered pieces of silver marked the windings of the great river; and on the nearest of them, just within the bar, the tug steaming right into the land become lost to my sight, hull and funnel and masts, as though the impassive earth had swallowed her up without an effort, without a tremor. My eye followed the light cloud of her smoke, now here, now there, above the plain, according to the devious curves of the stream, but always fainter and farther away, till I lost it at last behind the miter-shaped hill of the great pagoda. And then I was left alone with my ship, anchored at the head of the Gulf of Siam.

She floated at the starting point of a long journey, very still in an immense stillness, the shadows of her spars flung far to the eastward by the setting sun. At that moment I was alone on her decks. There was not a sound in her—and around us nothing moved, nothing lived, not a canoe on the water, not a bird in the air, not a cloud in the sky. In this breathless pause at the threshold of a long passage we seemed to be measuring our fitness for a long and arduous enterprise, the appointed task of both our existences to be carried out, far from all human eyes, with only sky and sea for spectators and for judges.

There must have been some glare in the air to interfere with one's sight, because it was only just before the sun left us that my roaming eyes made out beyond the highest ridge of the principal islet of the group something which did away with the solemnity of perfect solitude. The tide of darkness flowed on swiftly; and with tropical suddenness a swarm of stars came out above the shadowy earth, while I lingered yet, my hand resting lightly on my ship's rail as if on the shoulder of a trusted friend. But, with all that multitude of celestial bodies staring down at one, the comfort of quiet communion with her was gone for good. And there were also disturbing sounds by this time—voices, footsteps forward; the steward flitted along the main deck, a busily ministering spirit; a hand bell tinkled urgently under the poop deck. . . .

I found my two officers waiting for me near the supper table, in the lighted cuddy.[1] We sat down at once, and as I helped the chief mate, I said:

"Are you aware that there is a ship anchored inside the islands? I saw her mastheads above the ridge as the sun went down."

He raised sharply his simple face, overcharged by a terrible growth of whisker, and emitted his usual ejaculations: "Bless my soul, sir! You don't say so!"

My second mate was a sound-cheeked, silent young man, grave beyond his years, I thought; but as our eyes happened to meet I detected a slight quiver on his lips. I looked down at once. It was not my part to encourage sneering on board my ship. It must be said, too, that I knew very little of my officers. In consequence of certain events of no particular significance, except to myself, I had been appointed to the command only a fortnight before. Neither did I know much of the hands forward. All these people had been together for eighteen months or so, and my position was that of the only stranger on board. I mention this because it has some bearing on what is to follow. But what I felt most was my being a stranger to the ship; and if all the truth must be told, I was somewhat of a stranger to myself. The youngest man on board (barring the second mate), and untried as yet by a position of the fullest responsibility, I was willing to take the adequacy of the others for granted. They had simply to be equal to their tasks: but I wondered how far I should turn out faithful to that ideal conception of one's own personality every man sets up for himself secretly.

Meantime the chief mate, with an almost visible effect of collaboration on the part of his round eyes and frightful whiskers, was

1. Cabin.

trying to evolve a theory of the anchored ship. His dominant trait was to take all things into earnest consideration. He was of a painstaking turn of mind. As he used to say, he "liked to account to himself" for practically everything that came in his way, down to a miserable scorpion he had found in his cabin a week before. The why and the wherefore of that scorpion—how it got on board and came to select his room rather than the pantry (which was a dark place and more what a scorpion would be partial to), and how on earth it managed to drown itself in the inkwell of his writing desk —had exercised him infinitely. The ship within the islands was much more easily accounted for; and just as we were about to rise from the table he made his pronouncement. She was, he doubted not, a ship from home lately arrived. Probably she drew too much water to cross the bar except at the top of spring tides. Therefore she went into that natural harbor to wait for a few days in preference to remaining in an open roadstead.

"That's so," confirmed the second mate, suddenly, in his slightly hoarse voice. "She draws over twenty feet. She's the Liverpool ship *Sephora* with a cargo of coal. Hundred and twenty-three days from Cardiff."

We looked at him in surprise.

"The tugboat skipper told me when he came on board for your letters, sir," explained the young man. "He expects to take her up the river the day after tomorrow."

After thus overwhelming us with the extent of his information he slipped out of the cabin. The mate observed regretfully that he "could not account for that young fellow's whims." What prevented him telling us all about it at once, he wanted to know.

I detained him as he was making a move. For the last two days the crew had had plenty of hard work, and the night before they had very little sleep. I felt painfully that I—a stranger—was doing something unusual when I directed him to let all hands turn in without setting an anchor watch.[2] I proposed to keep on deck myself till one o'clock or thereabouts. I would get the second mate to relieve me at that hour.

"He will turn out the cook and the steward at four," I concluded, "and then give you a call. Of course at the slightest sign of any sort of wind we'll have the hands up and make a start at once."

He concealed his astonishment. "Very well, sir." Outside the cuddy he put his head in the second mate's door to inform him of my unheard-of caprice to take a five hours' anchor watch on myself. I heard the other raise his voice incredulously: "What? The captain himself?" Then a few more murmurs, a door closed, then another. A few moments later I went on deck.

2. I.e., a part of the ship's crew kept on duty while the ship lies at anchor.

My strangeness, which had made me sleepless, had prompted that unconventional arrangement, as if I had expected in those solitary hours of the night to get on terms with the ship of which I knew nothing, manned by men of whom I knew very little more. Fast alongside a wharf, littered like any ship in port with a tangle of unrelated things, invaded by unrelated shore people, I had hardly seen her yet properly. Now, as she lay cleared for sea, the stretch of her main deck seemed to me very fine under the stars. Very fine, very roomy for her size, and very inviting. I descended the poop and paced the waist, my mind picturing to myself the coming passage through the Malay Archipelago, down the Indian Ocean, and up the Atlantic. All its phases were familiar enough to me, every characteristic, all the alternatives which were likely to face me on the high seas—everything! . . . except the novel responsibility of command. But I took heart from the reasonable thought that the ship was like other ships, the men like other men, and that the sea was not likely to keep any special surprises expressly for my discomfiture.

Arrived at that comforting conclusion, I bethought myself of a cigar and went below to get it. All was still down there. Everybody at the after end of the ship was sleeping profoundly. I came out again on the quarter-deck, agreebly at ease in my sleeping suit on that warm breathless night, barefooted, a glowing cigar in my teeth, and, going forward, I was met by the profound silence of the fore end of the ship. Only as I passed the door of the forecastle I heard a deep, quiet, trustful sigh of some sleeper inside. And suddenly I rejoiced in the great security of the sea as compared with the unrest of the land, in my choice of that untempted life presenting no disquieting problems, invested with an elementary moral beauty by the absolute straightforwardness of its appeal and by the singleness of its purpose.

The riding light in the fore-rigging burned with a clear, untroubled, as if symbolic, flame, confident and bright in the mysterious shades of the night. Passing on my way aft along the other side of the ship, I observed that the rope side ladder, put over, no doubt, for the master of the tug when he came to fetch away our letters, had not been hauled in as it should have been. I became annoyed at this, for exactitude in small matters is the very soul of discipline. Then I reflected that I had myself peremptorily dismissed my officers from duty, and by my own act had prevented the anchor watch being formally set and things properly attended to. I asked myself whether it was wise ever to interfere with the established routine of duties even from the kindest of motives. My action might have made me appear eccentric. Goodness only knew how that absurdly whiskered mate would "account" for my conduct, and what the whole ship thought of that informality of their new captain. I was vexed with myself.

Not from compunction certainly, but, as it were mechanically, I proceeded to get the ladder in myself. Now a side ladder of that sort is a light affair and comes in easily, yet my vigorous tug, which should have brought it flying on board, merely recoiled upon my body in a totally unexpected jerk. What the devil! . . . I was so astounded by the immovableness of that ladder that I remained stock-still, trying to account for it to myself like that imbecile mate of mine. In the end, of course, I put my head over the rail.

The side of the ship made an opaque belt of shadow on the darkling glassy shimmer of the sea. But I saw at once something elongated and pale floating very close to the ladder. Before I could form a guess a faint flash of phosphorescent light, which seemed to issue suddenly from the naked body of a man, flickered in the sleeping water with the elusive, silent play of summer lightning in a night sky. With a gasp I saw revealed to my stare a pair of feet, the long legs, a broad livid back immersed right up to the neck in a greenish cadaverous glow. One hand, awash, clutched the bottom rung of the ladder. He was complete but for the head. A headless corpse! The cigar dropped out of my gaping mouth with a tiny plop and a short hiss quite audible in the absolute stillness of all things under heaven. At that I suppose he raised up his face, a dimly pale oval in the shadow of the ship's side. But even then I could only barely make out down there the shape of his black-haired head. However, it was enough for the horrid, frost-bound sensation which had gripped me about the chest to pass off. The moment of vain exclamations was past, too. I only climbed on the spare spar and leaned over the rail as far as I could, to bring my eyes nearer to that mystery floating alongside.

As he hung by the ladder, like a resting swimmer, the sea lightning played about his limbs at every stir; and he appeared in it ghastly, silvery, fishlike. He remained as mute as a fish, too. He made no motion to get out of the water, either. It was inconceivable that he should not attempt to come on board, and strangely troubling to suspect that perhaps he did not want to. And my first words were prompted by just that troubled incertitude.

"What's the matter?" I asked in my ordinary tone, speaking down to the face upturned exactly under mine.

"Cramp," it answered, no louder. Then slightly anxious, "I say, no need to call anyone."

"I was not going to," I said.

"Are you alone on deck?"

"Yes."

I had somehow the impression that he was on the point of letting go the ladder to swim away beyond my ken—mysterious as he came. But, for the moment, this being appearing as if he had risen from the bottom of the sea (it was certainly the nearest land to the ship) wanted only to know the time. I told him. And he, down there, tentatively:

"I suppose your captain's turned in?"

"I am sure he isn't," I said.

He seemed to struggle with himself, for I heard something like the low, bitter murmur of doubt. "What's the good?" His next words came out with a hesitating effort.

"Look here, my man. Could you call him out quietly?"

I thought the time had come to declare myself.

"*I* am the captain."

I heard a "By Jove!" whispered at the level of the water. The phosphorescence flashed in the swirl of the water all about his limbs, his other hand seized the ladder.

"My name's Leggatt."

The voice was calm and resolute. A good voice. The self-possession of that man had somehow induced a corresponding state in myself. It was very quietly that I remarked:

"You must be a good swimmer."

"Yes. I've been in the water practically since nine o'clock. The question for me now is whether I am to let go this ladder and go on swimming till I sink from exhaustion, or—to come on board here."

I felt this was no mere formula of desperate speech, but a real alternative in the view of a strong soul. I should have gathered from this that he was young; indeed, it is only the young who are ever confronted by such clear issues. But at the time it was pure intuition on my part. A mysterious communication was established already between us two—in the face of that silent, darkened tropical sea. I was young, too; young enough to make no comment. The man in the water began suddenly to climb up the ladder, and I hastened away from the rail to fetch some clothes.

Before entering the cabin I stood still, listening in the lobby at the foot of the stairs. A faint snore came through the closed door of the chief mate's room. The second mate's door was on the hook, but the darkness in there was absolutely soundless. He, too, was young and could sleep like a stone. Remained the steward, but he was not likely to wake up before he was called. I got a sleeping suit out of my room and, coming back on deck, saw the naked man from the sea sitting on the main hatch, glimmering white in the darkness, his elbows on his knees and his head in his hands. In a moment he had concealed his damp body in a sleeping suit of the same gray-stripe pattern as the one I was wearing and followed me like my double on the poop. Together we moved right aft, bare-footed, silent.

"What is it?" I asked in a deadened voice, taking the lighted lamp out of the binnacle,[3] and raising it to his face.

"An ugly business."

He had rather regular features; a good mouth; light eyes under somewhat heavy, dark eyebrows; a smooth, square forehead; no growth on his cheeks; a small, brown mustache, and a well-shaped, round chin. His expression was concentrated, meditative, under the inspecting light of the lamp I held up to his face; such as a man thinking hard in solitude might wear. My sleeping suit was just right for his size. A well-knit young fellow of twenty-five at most. He caught his lower lip with the edge of white, even teeth.

"Yes," I said, replacing the lamp in the binnacle. The warm, heavy tropical night closed upon his head again.

"There's a ship over there," he murmured.

"Yes, I know. The *Sephora*. Did you know of us?"

"Hadn't the slightest idea. I am the mate of her——" He paused and corrected himself. "I should say I *was*."

"Aha! Something wrong?"

"Yes. Very wrong indeed. I've killed a man."

"What do you mean? Just now?"

"No, on the passage. Weeks ago. Thirty-nine south. When I say a man——"

"Fit of temper," I suggested, confidently.

The shadowy, dark head, like mine, seemed to nod imperceptibly above the ghostly gray of my sleeping suit. It was, in the night, as though I had been faced by my own reflection in the depths of a somber and immense mirror.

"A pretty thing to have to own up to for a Conway boy,"[4] mur-mured my double, distinctly.

"You're a Conway boy?"

"I am," he said, as if startled. Then, slowly . . . "Perhaps you too——"

It was so; but being a couple of years older I had left before he joined. After a quick interchange of dates a silence fell; and I thought suddenly of my absurd mate with his terrific whiskers and the "Bless my soul—you don't say so" type of intellect. My double gave me an inkling of his thoughts by saying:

"My father's a parson in Norfolk. Do you see me before a judge and jury on that charge? For myself I can't see the necessity. There are fellows that an angel from heaven—— And I am not that. He was one of those creatures that are just simmering all the time with

3. A stand on the deck, near the helm, on which the compass rests.   4. See footnote 2 to *Youth*, above.

a silly sort of wickedness. Miserable devils that have no business to live at all. He wouldn't do his duty and wouldn't let anybody else do theirs. But what's the good of talking! You know well enough the sort of ill-conditioned snarling cur—"

He appealed to me as if our experiences had been as identical as our clothes. And I knew well enough the pestiferous danger of such a character where there are no means of legal repression. And I knew well enough also that my double there was no homicidal ruffian. I did not think of asking him for details, and he told me the story roughly in brusque, disconnected sentences. I needed no more. I saw it all going on as though I were myself inside that other sleeping suit.

"It happened while we were setting a reefed foresail, at dusk. Reefed foresail! You understand the sort of weather. The only sail we had left to keep the ship running; so you may guess what it had been like for days. Anxious sort of job, that. He gave me some of his cursed insolence at the sheet. I tell you I was overdone with this terrific weather that seemed to have no end to it. Terrific, I tell you—and a deep ship. I believe the fellow himself was half crazed with funk. It was no time for gentlemanly reproof, so I turned round and felled him like an ox. He up and at me. We closed just as an awful sea made for the ship. All hands saw it coming and took to the rigging, but I had him by the throat, and went on shaking him like a rat, the men above us yelling, 'Look out! look out!' Then a crash as if the sky had fallen on my head. They say that for over ten minutes hardly anything was to be seen of the ship—just the three masts and a bit of the forecastle head and of the poop all awash driving along in a smother of foam. It was a miracle that they found us, jammed together behind the fore-bits. It's clear that I meant business, because I was holding him by the throat still when they picked us up. He was black in the face. It was too much for them. It seems they rushed us aft together, gripped as we were, screaming 'Murder!' like a lot of lunatics, and broke into the cuddy. And the ship running for her life, touch and go all the time, any minute her last in a sea fit to turn your hair gray only a-looking at it. I understand that the skipper, too, started raving like the rest of them. The man had been deprived of sleep for more than a week, and to have this sprung on him at the height of a furious gale nearly drove him out of his mind. I wonder they didn't fling me overboard after getting the carcass of their precious shipmate out of my fingers. They had rather a job to separate us, I've been told. A sufficiently fierce story to make an old judge and a respectable jury sit up a bit. The first thing I heard when I came to myself was the maddening howling of that endless gale, and on that the voice of the old man. He was hanging on to my bunk, staring into my face out of his sou'wester.

" 'Mr. Leggatt, you have killed a man. You can act no longer as chief mate of this ship.' "

His care to subdue his voice made it sound monotonous. He rested a hand on the end of the skylight to steady himself with, and all that time did not stir a limb, so far as I could see. "Nice little tale for a quiet tea party," he concluded in the same tone.

One of my hands, too, rested on the end of the skylight; neither did I stir a limb, so far as I knew. We stood less than a foot from each other. It occurred to me that if old "Bless my soul—you don't say so" were to put his head up the companion and catch sight of us, he would think he was seeing double, or imagine himself come upon a scene of weird witchcraft; the strange captain having a quiet confabulation by the wheel with his own gray ghost. I became very much concerned to prevent anything of the sort. I heard the other's soothing undertone.

"My father's a parson in Norfolk," it said. Evidently he had forgotten he had told me this important fact before. Truly a nice little tale.

"You had better slip down into my stateroom now," I said, moving off stealthily. My double followed my movements; our bare feet made no sound; I let him in, closed the door with care, and, after giving a call to the second mate, returned on deck for my relief.

"Not much sign of any wind yet," I remarked when he approached.

"No, sir. Not much," he assented, sleepily, in his hoarse voice, with just enough deference, no more, and barely suppressing a yawn.

"Well, that's all you have to look out for. You have got your orders."

"Yes, sir."

I paced a turn or two on the poop and saw him take up his position face forward with his elbow in the rat-lines of the mizzen-rigging before I went below. The mate's faint snoring was still going on peacefully. The cuddy lamp was burning over the table on which stood a vase with flowers, a polite attention from the ships' provision merchant—the last flowers we should see for the next three months at the very least. Two bunches of bananas hung from the beam symmetrically, one on each side of the rudder casing. Everything was as before in the ship—except that two of her captain's sleeping suits were simultaneously in use, one motionless in the cuddy, the other keeping very still in the captain's stateroom.

It must be explained here that my cabin had the form of the capital letter L, the door being within the angle and opening into the short part of the letter. A couch was to the left, the bed-place to the right; my writing desk and the chronometers' table faced the door. But anyone opening it, unless he stepped right inside, had no view of what I call the long (or vertical) part of the letter. It contained some lockers surmounted by a bookcase; and a few clothes, a thick jacket or two, caps, oilskin coat, and such like, hung on hooks. There was at the bottom of that part a door opening into my bathroom, which could be entered also directly from the saloon.[5] But that way was never used.

The mysterious arrival had discovered the advantage of this particular shape. Entering my room, lighted strongly by a big bulkhead lamp swung on gimbals[6] above my writing desk, I did not see him anywhere till he stepped out quietly from behind the coats hung in the recessed part.

"I heard somebody moving about, and went in there at once," he whispered.

I, too, spoke under my breath.

"Nobody is likely to come in here without knocking and getting permission."

He nodded. His face was thin and the sunburn faded, as though he had been ill. And no wonder. He had been, I heard presently, kept under arrest in his cabin for nearly seven weeks. But there was nothing sickly in his eyes or in his expression. He was not a bit like me, really; yet, as we stood leaning over my bed-place, whispering side by side, with our dark heads together and our backs to the door, anybody bold enough to open it stealthily would have been treated to the uncanny sight of a double captain busy talking in whispers with his other self.

"But all this doesn't tell me how you came to hang on to our side ladder," I inquired, in the hardly audible murmurs we used, after he had told me something more of the proceedings on board the *Sephora* once the bad weather was over.

"When we sighted Java Head I had had time to think all those matters out several times over. I had six weeks of doing nothing else, and with only an hour or so every evening for a tramp on the quarter-deck."

He whispered, his arms folded on the side of my bed-place, staring through the open port. And I could imagine perfectly the manner of this thinking out—a stubborn if not a steadfast operation; something of which I should have been perfectly incapable.

"I reckoned it would be dark before we closed with the land," he continued, so low that I had to strain my hearing, near as we were to each other, shoulder touching shoulder almost. "So I asked to speak to the old man. He always seemed very sick when he came to see me—as if he could not look me in the face. You know, that foresail saved the ship. She was too deep to have run long under bare poles. And it was I that managed to set it for him. Anyway,

5. I.e., the officers' dining room.
6. Device for suspending articles in
order to keep them in a horizontal
position whatever the ship's motion.

he came. When I had him in my cabin—he stood by the door looking at me as if I had the halter around my neck already—I asked
him right away to leave my cabin door unlocked at night while the
ship was going through Sunda Straits.[7] There would be the Java
coast within two or three miles, off Angier Point. I wanted nothing
more. I've had a prize for swimming my second year in the Conway."

"I can believe it," I breathed out.

"God only knows why they locked me in every night. To see
some of their faces you'd have thought they were afraid I'd go
about at night strangling people. Am I a murdering brute? Do I
look it? By Jove! if I had been he wouldn't have trusted himself like
that into my room. You'll say I might have chucked him aside and
bolted out, there and then—it was dark already. Well, no. And
for the same reason I wouldn't think of trying to smash the door.
There would have been a rush to stop me at the noise, and I did
not mean to get into a confounded scrimmage. Somebody else
might have got killed—for I would not have broken out only to
get chucked back, and I did not want any more of that work. He
refused, looking more sick than ever. He was afraid of the men, and
also of that old second mate of his who had been sailing with him
for years—a gray-headed old humbug; and his steward, too, had
been with him devil knows how long—seventeen years or more—a
dogmatic sort of loafer who hated me like poison, just because I was
the chief mate. No chief mate ever made more than one voyage in
the *Sephora*, you know. Those two old chaps ran the ship. Devil
only knows what the skipper wasn't afraid of (all his nerve went to
pieces altogether in that hellish spell of bad weather we had)—of
what the law would do to him—of his wife, perhaps. Oh, yes!
she's on board. Though I don't think she would have meddled.
She would have been only too glad to have me out of the ship in
any way. The 'brand of Cain'[8] business, don't you see. That's all
right. I was ready enough to go off wandering on the face of the
earth—and that was price enough to pay for an Abel of that sort.
Anyhow, he wouldn't listen to me. 'This thing must take its course.
I represent the law here.' He was shaking life a leaf. 'So you won't?'
'No!' 'Then I hope you will be able to sleep on that,' I said, and
turned my back on him. 'I wonder that *you* can,' cries he, and
locks the door.

"Well, after that, I couldn't. Not very well. That was three weeks
ago. We have had a slow passage through the Java Sea; drifted
about Carimata[9] for ten days. When we anchored here they

7. Narrow passage between the islands
of Sumatra and Java in the East Indies;
the *Sephora* has been heading up from
the Indian Ocean into the Java Sea.
8. After Cain killed his brother Abel,
"the Lord set a mark upon Cain, lest

any finding him should kill him"
(Genesis iv.15).
9. Carimata (or Karimata) Strait, between the islands of Borneo and Billi-
ton, connects the Java Sea with the
South China Sea.

thought, I suppose, it was all right. The nearest land (and that's five miles) is the ship's destination; the consul would soon set about catching me; and there would have been no object in bolting to these islets there. I don't suppose there's a drop of water on them. I don't know how it was, but tonight that steward, after bringing me my supper, went out to let me eat it, and left the door unlocked. And I ate it—all there was, too. After I had finished I strolled out on the quarter-deck. I don't know that I meant to do anything. A breath of fresh air was all I wanted, I believe. Then a sudden temptation came over me. I kicked off my slippers and was in the water before I had made up my mind fairly. Somebody heard the splash and they raised an awful hullabaloo. 'He's gone! Lower the boats! He's committed suicide! No, he's swimming.' Certainly I was swimming. It's not so easy for a swimmer like me to commit suicide by drowning. I landed on the nearest islet before the boat left the ship's side. I heard them pulling about in the dark, hailing, and so on, but after a bit they gave up. Everything quieted down and the anchorage became as still as death. I sat down on a stone and began to think. I felt certain they would start searching for me at daylight. There was no place to hide on those stony things—and if there had been, what would have been the good? But now I was clear of that ship, I was not going back. So after a while I took off all my clothes, tied them up in a bundle with a stone inside, and dropped them in the deep water on the outer side of that islet. That was suicide enough for me. Let them think what they liked, but I didn't mean to drown myself. I meant to swim till I sank—but that's not the same thing. I struck out for another of these little islands, and it was from that one that I first saw your riding light. Something to swim for. I went on easily, and on the way I came upon a flat rock a foot or two above water. In the daytime, I dare say, you might make it out with a glass from your poop. I scrambled up on it and rested myself for a bit. Then I made another start. That last spell must have been over a mile."

His whisper was getting fainter and fainter, and all the time he stared straight out through the porthole, in which there was not even a star to be seen. I had not interrupted him. There was something that made comment impossible in his narrative, or perhaps in himself; a sort of feeling, a quality, which I can't find a name for. And when he ceased, all I found was a futile whisper: "So you swam for our light?"

"Yes—straight for it. It was something to swim for. I couldn't see any stars low down because the coast was in the way, and I couldn't see the land, either. The water was like glass. One might have been swimming in a confounded thousand-feet deep cistern with no place for scrambling out anywhere; but what I didn't like was the notion of swimming round and round like a crazed bullock before I gave out; and as I didn't mean to go back . . . No. Do you see me being hauled back, stark naked, off one of these little islands by the scruff of the neck and fighting like a wild beast? Somebody would have got killed for certain, and I did not want any of that. So I went on. Then your ladder—"

"Why didn't you hail the ship?" I asked, a little louder.

He touched my shoulder lightly. Lazy footsteps came right over our heads and stopped. The second mate had crossed from the other side of the poop and might have been hanging over the rail, for all we knew.

"He couldn't hear us talking—could he?" My double breathed into my very ear, anxiously.

His anxiety was an answer, a sufficient answer, to the question I had put to him. An answer containing all the difficulty of that situation. I closed the porthole quietly, to make sure. A louder word might have been overheard.

"Who's that?" he whispered then.

"My second mate. But I don't know much more of the fellow than you do."

And I told him a little about myself. I had been appointed to take charge while I least expected anything of the sort, not quite a fortnight ago. I didn't know either the ship or the people. Hadn't had the time in port to look about me or size anybody up. And as to the crew, all they knew was that I was appointed to take the ship home. For the rest, I was almost as much of a stranger on board as himself, I said. And at the moment I felt it most acutely. I felt that it would take very little to make me a suspect person in the eyes of the ship's company.

He had turned about meantime; and we, the two strangers in the ship, faced each other in identical attitudes.

"Your ladder—" he murmured, after a silence. "Who'd have thought of finding a ladder hanging over at night in a ship anchored out here! I felt just then a very unpleasant faintness. After the life I've been leading for nine weeks, anybody would have got out of condition. I wasn't capable of swimming round as far as your rudder chains. And, lo and behold! there was a ladder to get hold of. After I gripped it I said to myself, 'What's the good?' When I saw a man's head looking over I thought I would swim away presently and leave him shouting—in whatever language it was. I didn't mind being looked at. I—I liked it. And then you speaking to me so quietly—as if you had expected me—made me hold on a little longer. It had been a confounded lonely time—I don't mean while swimming. I was glad to talk a little to somebody that didn't belong to the *Sephora*. As to asking for the captain, that was a mere impulse. It could have been no use, with all the ship knowing about me and the other people pretty certain to be round here in the morning. I don't know—I wanted to be seen, to talk with somebody, before I went on. I don't know what I would have said. . . . 'Fine night, isn't it?' or something of the sort."

"Do you think they will be round here presently?" I asked with some incredulity.

"Quite likely," he said, faintly.

He looked extremely haggard all of a sudden. His head rolled on his shoulders.

"H'm. We shall see then. Meantime get into that bed," I whispered. "Want help? There."

It was a rather high bed-place with a set of drawers underneath. This amazing swimmer really needed the lift I gave him by seizing his leg. He tumbled in, rolled over on his back, and flung one arm across his eyes. And then, with his face nearly hidden, he must have looked exactly as I used to look in that bed. I gazed upon my other self for a while before drawing across carefully the two green serge curtains which ran on a brass rod. I thought for a moment of pinning them together for greater safety, but I sat down on the couch, and once there I felt unwilling to rise and hunt for a pin. I would do it in a moment. I was extremely tired, in a peculiarly intimate way, by the strain of stealthiness, by the effort of whispering and the general secrecy of this excitement. It was three o'clock by now and I had been on my feet since nine, but I was not sleepy; I could not have gone to sleep. I sat there, fagged out, looking at the curtains, trying to clear my mind of the confused sensation of being in two places at once, and greatly bothered by an exasperating knocking in my head. It was a relief to discover suddenly that it was not in my head at all, but on the outside of the door. Before I could collect myself the words "Come in" were out of my mouth, and the steward entered with a tray, bringing in my morning coffee. I had slept, after all, and I was so frightened that I shouted, "This way! I am here, steward," as though he had been miles away. He put down the tray on the table next the couch and only then said, very quietly, "I can see you are here, sir." I felt him give me a keen look, but I dared not meet his eyes just then. He must have wondered why I had drawn the curtains of my bed before going to sleep on the couch. He went out, hooking the door open as usual.

I heard the crew washing decks above me. I knew I would have been told at once if there had been any wind. Calm, I thought, and I was doubly vexed. Indeed, I felt dual more than ever. The steward reappeared suddenly in the doorway. I jumped up from the couch so quickly that he gave a start.

"What do you want here?"

"Close your port, sir—they are washing decks."

"It is closed," I said, reddening.

"Very well, sir." But he did not move from the doorway and returned my stare in an extraordinary, equivocal manner for a time. Then his eyes wavered, all his expression changed, and in a voice unusually gentle, almost coaxingly:

"May I come in to take the empty cup away, sir?"

"Of course!" I turned my back on him while he popped in and out. Then I unhooked and closed the door and even pushed the bolt. This sort of thing could not go on very long. The cabin was as hot as an oven, too. I took a peep at my double, and discovered that he had not moved, his arm was still over his eyes; but his chest heaved; his hair was wet; his chin glistened with perspiration. I reached over him and opened the port.

"I must show myself on deck," I reflected.

Of course, theoretically, I could do what I liked, with no one to say nay to me within the whole circle of the horizon; but to lock my cabin door and take the key away I did not dare. Directly I put my head out of the companion I saw the group of my two officers, the second mate barefooted, the chief mate in long india-rubber boots, near the break of the poop, and the steward halfway down the poop ladder talking to them eagerly. He happened to catch sight of me and dived, the second ran down on the main deck shouting some order or other, and the chief mate came to meet me, touching his cap.

There was a sort of curiosity in his eye that I did not like. I don't know whether the steward had told them that I was "queer" only, or downright drunk, but I know the man meant to have a good look at me. I watched him coming with a smile which, as he got into point-blank range, took effect and froze his very whiskers. I did not give him time to open his lips.

"Square the yards by lifts and braces before the hands go to breakfast."

It was the first particular order I had given on board that ship; and I stayed on deck to see it executed, too. I had felt the need of asserting myself without loss of time. That sneering young cub got taken down a peg or two on that occasion, and I also seized the opportunity of having a good look at the face of every foremast man as they filed past me to go to the after braces. At breakfast time, eating nothing myself, I presided with such frigid dignity that the two mates were only too glad to escape from the cabin as soon as decency permitted; and all the time the dual working of my mind distracted me almost to the point of insanity. I was constantly watching myself, my secret self, as dependent on my actions as my own personality, sleeping in that bed, behind that door which faced me as I sat at the head of the table. It was very much like being mad, only it was worse because one was aware of it.

I had to shake him for a solid minute, but when at last he

opened his eyes it was in the full possession of his senses, with an inquiring look.

"All's well so far," I whispered. "Now you must vanish into the bathroom."

He did so, as noiseless as a ghost, and I then rang for the steward, and facing him boldly, directed him to tidy up my stateroom while I was having my bath—" and be quick about it." As my tone admitted of no excuses, he said, "Yes, sir," and ran off to fetch his dustpan and brushes. I took a bath and did most of my dressing, splashing, and whistling softly for the steward's edification, while the secret sharer of my life stood drawn up bolt upright in that little space, his face looking very sunken in daylight, his eyelids lowered under the stern, dark line of his eyebrows drawn together by a slight frown.

When I left him there to go back to my room the steward was finishing dusting. I sent for the mate and engaged him in some insignificant conversation. It was, as it were, trifling with the terrific character of his whiskers; but my object was to give him an opportunity for a good look at my cabin. And then I could at last shut, with a clear conscience, the door of my stateroom and get my double back into the recessed part. There was nothing else for it. He had to sit still on a small folding stool, half smothered by the heavy coats hanging there. We listened to the steward going into the bathroom out of the saloon, filling the water bottles there, scrubbing the bath, setting things to rights, whisk, bang, clatter—out again into the saloon—turn the key—click. Such was my scheme for keeping my second self invisible. Nothing better could be contrived under the circumstances. And there we sat; I at my writing desk ready to appear busy with some papers, he behind me, out of sight of the door. It would not have been prudent to talk in daytime; and I could not have stood the excitement of that queer sense of whispering to myself. Now and then, glancing over my shoulder, I saw him far back there, sitting rigidly on the low stool, his bare feet close together, his arms folded, his head hanging on his breast—and perfectly still. Anybody would have taken him for me.

I was fascinated by it myself. Every moment I had to glance over my shoulder. I was looking at him when a voice outside the door said:

"Beg pardon, sir."

"Well!" . . . I kept my eyes on him, and so, when the voice outside the door announced, "There's a ship's boat coming our way, sir," I saw him give a start—the first movement he had made for hours. But he did not raise his bowed head.

"All right. Get the ladder over."

I hesitated. Should I whisper something to him? But what? His immobility seemed to have been never disturbed. What could I tell him he did not know already? . . . Finally I went on deck.

II

The skipper of the *Sephora* had a thin red whisker all round his face, and the sort of complexion that goes with hair of that color; also the particular, rather smeary shade of blue in the eyes. He was not exactly a showy figure; his shoulders were high, his stature but middling—one leg slightly more bandy than the other. He shook hands, looking vaguely around. A spiritless tenacity was his main characteristic, I judged. I behaved with a politeness which seemed to disconcert him. Perhaps he was shy. He mumbled to me as if he were ashamed of what he was saying; gave his name (it was something like Archbold—but at this distance of years I hardly am sure), his ship's name, and a few other particulars of that sort, in the manner of a criminal making a reluctant and doleful confession. He had had terrible weather on the passage out— terrible—terrible—wife aboard, too.

By this time we were seated in the cabin and the steward brought in a tray with a bottle and glasses. "Thanks! No." Never took liquor. Would have some water, though. He drank two tumblerfuls. Terrible thirsty work. Ever since daylight had been exploring the islands round his ship.

"What was that for—fun?" I asked, with an appearance of polite interest.

"No!" He sighed. "Painful duty."

As he persisted in his mumbling and I wanted my double to hear every word, I hit upon the notion of informing him that I regretted to say I was hard of hearing.

"Such a young man, too!" he nodded, keeping his smeary blue, unintelligent eyes fastened upon me. What was the cause of it— some disease? he inquired, without the least sympathy and as if he thought that, if so, I'd got no more than I deserved.

"Yes; disease," I admitted in a cheerful tone which seemed to shock him. But my point was gained, because he had to raise his voice to give me his tale. It is not worth while to record that version. It was just over two months since all this had happened, and he had thought so much about it that he seemed completely muddled as to its bearings, but still immensely impressed.

"What would you think of such a thing happening on board your own ship? I've had the *Sephora* for these fifteen years. I am a well-known shipmaster."

He was densely distressed—and perhaps I should have sympathized with him if I had been able to detach my mental vision from the unsuspected sharer of my cabin as though he were my second self. There he was on the other side of the bulkhead, four or five feet from us, no more, as we sat in the saloon. I looked politely at

Captain Archbold (if that was his name), but it was the other I saw, in a gray sleeping suit, seated on a low stool, his bare feet close together, his arms folded, and every word said between us falling into the ears of his dark head bowed on his chest.

"I have been at sea now, man and boy, for seven-and-thirty years, and I've never heard of such a thing happening in an English ship. And that it should be my ship. Wife on board, too."

I was hardly listening to him.

"Don't you think," I said, "that the heavy sea which, you told me, came aboard just then might have killed the man? I have seen the sheer weight of a sea kill a man very neatly, by simply breaking his neck."

"Good God!" he uttered, impressively, fixing his smeary blue eyes on me. "The sea! No man killed by the sea ever looked like that." He seemed positively scandalized at my suggestion. And as I gazed at him, certainly not prepared for anything original on his part, he advanced his head close to mine and thrust his tongue out at me so suddenly that I couldn't help starting back.

After scoring over my calmness in this graphic way he nodded wisely. If I had seen the sight, he assured me, I would never forget it as long as I lived. The weather was too bad to give the corpse a proper sea burial. So next day at dawn they took it up on the poop, covering its face with a bit of bunting; he read a short prayer, and then, just as it was, in its oilskins and long boots, they launched it amongst those mountainous seas that seemed ready every moment to swallow up the ship herself and the terrified lives on board of her.

"That reefed foresail saved you," I threw in.

"Under God—it did," he exclaimed fervently. "It was by a special mercy, I firmly believe, that it stood some of those hurricane squalls."

"It was the setting of that sail which—" I began.

"God's own hand in it," he interrupted me. "Nothing less could have done it. I don't mind telling you that I hardly dared give the order. It seemed impossible that we could touch anything without losing it, and then our last hope would have been gone."

The terror of that gale was on him yet. I let him go on for a bit, then said, casually—as if returning to a minor subject:

"You were very anxious to give up your mate to the shore people, I believe?"

He was. To the law. His obscure tenacity on that point had in it something incomprehensible and a little awful; something, as it were, mystical, quite apart from his anxiety that he should not be suspected of "countenancing any doings of that sort." Seven-and-thirty virtuous years at sea, of which over twenty of immaculate command, and the last fifteen in the *Sephora*, seemed to have laid him under some pitiless obligation.

"And you know," he went on, groping shamefacedly amongst his feelings, "I did not engage that young fellow. His people had some interest with my owners. I was in a way forced to take him on. He looked very smart, very gentlemanly, and all that. But do you know —I never liked him, somehow. I am a plain man. You see, he wasn't exactly the sort for the chief mate of a ship like the *Sephora*."

I had become so connected in thoughts and impressions with the secret sharer of my cabin that I felt as if I, personally, were being given to understand that I, too, was not the sort that would have done for the chief mate of a ship like the *Sephora*. I had no doubt of it in my mind.

"Not at all the style of man. You understand," he insisted, superfluously, looking hard at me.

I smiled urbanely. He seemed at a loss for a while.

"I suppose I must report a suicide."

"Beg pardon?"

"Sui-cide! That's what I'll have to write to my owners directly I get in."

"Unless you manage to recover him before tomorrow," I assented, dispassionately. . . . "I mean, alive."

He mumbled something which I really did not catch, and I turned my ear to him in a puzzled manner. He fairly bawled:

"The land—I say, the mainland is at least seven miles off my anchorage."

"About that."

My lack of excitement, of curiosity, of surprise, of any sort of pronounced interest, began to arouse his distrust. But except for the felicitous pretense of deafness I had not tried to pretend anything. I had felt utterly incapable of playing the part of ignorance properly, and therefore was afraid to try. It is also certain that he had brought some ready-made suspicions with him, and that he viewed my politeness as a strange and unnatural phenomenon. And yet how else could I have received him? Not heartily! That was impossible for psychological reasons, which I need not state here. My only object was to keep off his inquiries. Surlily? Yes, but surliness might have provoked a point-blank question. From its novelty to him and from its nature, punctilious courtesy was the manner best calculated to restrain the man. But there was the danger of his breaking through my defense bluntly. I could not, I think, have met him by a direct lie, also for psychological (not moral) reasons. If he had only known how afraid I was of his putting my feeling of identity with the other to the test! But, strangely enough—(I thought of it only afterward)—I believe that he was not a little disconcerted by the reverse side of that weird situation, by something in me that reminded him of the man he was seeking—suggested a mysterious similitude to the young fellow he had distrusted and disliked from the first.

However that might have been, the silence was not very prolonged. He took another oblique step.

"I reckon I had no more than a two-mile pull to your ship. Not a bit more."

"And quite enough, too, in this awful heat," I said.

Another pause full of mistrust followed. Necessity, they say, is mother of invention, but fear, too, is not barren of ingenious suggestions. And I was afraid he would ask me point-blank for news of my other self.

"Nice little saloon, isn't it?" I remarked, as if noticing for the first time the way his eyes roamed from one closed door to the other. "And very well fitted out, too. Here, for instance," I continued, reaching over the back of my seat negligently and flinging the door open, "is my bathroom."

He made an eager movement, but hardly gave it a glance. I got up, shut the door of the bathroom, and invited him to have a look round, as if I were very proud of my accommodation. He had to rise and be shown round, but he went through the business without any raptures whatever.

"And now we'll have a look at my stateroom," I declared, in a voice as loud as I dared to make it, crossing the cabin to the starboard side with purposely heavy steps.

He followed me in and gazed around. My intelligent double had vanished. I played my part.

"Very convenient—isn't it?"

"Very nice. Very comf . . ." He didn't finish, and went out brusquely as if to escape from some unrighteous wiles of mine. But it was not to be. I had been too frightened not to feel vengeful; I felt I had him on the run, and I meant to keep him on the run. My polite insistence must have had something menacing in it, because he gave in suddenly. And I did not let him off a single item; mate's room, pantry, storerooms, the very sail locker which was also under the poop—he had to look into them all. When at last I showed him out on the quarter-deck he drew a long, spiritless sigh, and mumbled dismally that he must really be going back to his ship now. I desired my mate, who had joined us, to see to the captain's boat.

The man of whiskers gave a blast on the whistle which he used to wear hanging round his neck, and yelled, "*Sephora's* away!" My double down there in my cabin must have heard, and certainly could not feel more relieved than I. Four fellows came running out from somewhere forward and went over the side, while my own men, appearing on deck too, lined the rail. I escorted my visitor to the gangway ceremoniously, and nearly overdid it. He was a tenacious beast. On the very ladder he lingered, and in that unique, guiltily conscientious manner of sticking to the point:

"I say . . . you . . . you don't think that—"

I covered his voice loudly:

"Certainly not. . . . I am delighted. Good-by."

I had an idea of what he meant to say, and just saved myself by the privilege of defective hearing. He was too shaken generally to insist, but my mate, close witness of that parting, looked mystified and his face took on a thoughtful cast. As I did not want to appear as if I wished to avoid all communication with my officers, he had the opportunity to address me.

"Seems a very nice man. His boat's crew told our chaps a very extraordinary story, if what I am told by the steward is true. I suppose you had it from the captain, sir?"

"Yes. I had a story from the captain."

"A very horrible affair—isn't it, sir?"

"It is."

"Beats all these tales we hear about murders in Yankee ships."

"I don't think it beats them. I don't think it resembles them in the least."

"Bless my soul—you don't say so! But of course I've no ac-quaintance whatever with American ships, not I, so I couldn't go against your knowledge. It's horrible enough for me. . . . But the queerest part is that these fellows seemed to have some idea the man was hidden aboard here. They had really. Did you ever hear of such a thing?"

"Preposterous—isn't it?"

We were walking to and fro athwart the quarter-deck. No one of the crew forward could be seen (the day was Sunday), and the mate pursued:

"There was some little dispute about it. Our chaps took offense. 'As if we would harbor a thing like that,' they said. 'Wouldn't you like to look for him in our coal hole?' Quite a tiff. But they made it up in the end. I suppose he did drown himself. Don't you, sir?"

"I don't suppose anything."

"You have no doubt in the matter, sir?"

"None whatever."

I left him suddenly. I felt I was producing a bad impression, but with my double down there it was most trying to be on deck. And it was almost as trying to be below. Altogether a nerve-trying situa-tion. But on the whole I felt less torn in two when I was with him. There was no one in the whole ship whom I dared take into my confidence. Since the hands had got to know his story, it would have been impossible to pass him off for anyone else, and an ac-cidental discovery was to be dreaded now more than ever. . . .

The steward being engaged in laying the table for dinner, we could talk only with our eyes when I first went down. Later in the afternoon we had a cautious try at whispering. The Sunday quietness of the ship was against us; the stillness of air and water around her was against us; the elements, the men were against us—everything was against us in our secret partnership; time itself—for this could not go on forever. The very trust in Providence was, I suppose, denied to his guilt. Shall I confess that this thought cast me down very much? And as to the chapter of accidents which counts for so much in the book of success, I could only hope that it was closed. For what favorable accident could be expected?

"Did you hear everything?" were my first words as soon as we took up our position side by side, leaning over my bed-place.

He had. And the proof of it was his earnest whisper, "The man told you he hardly dared to give the order."

I understood the reference to be to that saving foresail.

"Yes. He was afraid of it being lost in the setting."

"I assure you he never gave the order. He may think he did, but he never gave it. He stood there with me on the break of the poop after the maintopsail blew away, and whimpered about our last hope—positively whimpered about it and nothing else—and the night coming on! To hear one's skipper go on like that in such weather was enough to drive any fellow out of his mind. It worked me up into a sort of desperation. I just took it into my own hands and went away from him, boiling, and— But what's the use telling you? *You* know! . . . Do you think that if I had not been pretty fierce with them I should have got the men to do anything? Not it! The bosun perhaps? Perhaps! It wasn't a heavy sea—it was a sea gone mad! I suppose the end of the world will be something like that; and a man may have the heart to see it coming once and be done with it—but to have to face it day after day— I don't blame anybody. I was precious little better than the rest. Only—I was an officer of that old coal-wagon, anyhow—"

"I quite understand," I conveyed that sincere assurance into his ear. He was out of breath with whispering; I could hear him pant slightly. It was all very simple. The same strung-up force which had given twenty-four men a chance, at least, for their lives, had, in a sort of recoil, crushed an unworthy mutinous existence.

But I had no leisure to weigh the merits of the matter—footsteps in the saloon, a heavy knock. "There's enough wind to get under way with, sir." Here was the call of a new claim upon my thoughts and even upon my feelings.

"Turn the hands up," I cried through the door. "I'll be on deck directly."

I was going out to make the acquaintance of my ship. Before I left the cabin our eyes met—the eyes of the only two strangers on board. I pointed to the recessed part where the little campstool awaited him and laid my finger on my lips. He made a gesture—somewhat vague—a little mysterious, accompanied by a faint smile, as if of regret.

This is not the place to enlarge upon the sensations of a man who feels for the first time a ship move under his feet to his own independent word. In my case they were not unalloyed. I was not wholly alone with my command; for there was that stranger in my cabin. Or rather, I was not completely and wholly with her. Part of me was absent. That mental feeling of being in two places at once affected me physically as if the mood of secrecy had penetrated my very soul. Before an hour had elapsed since the ship had begun to move, having occasion to ask the mate (he stood by my side) to take a compass bearing of the Pagoda, I caught myself reaching up to his ear in whispers. I say I caught myself, but enough had escaped to startle the man. I can't describe it otherwise than by saying that he shied. A grave, preoccupied manner, as though he were in possession of some perplexing intelligence, did not leave him henceforth. A little later I moved away from the rail to look at the compass with such a stealthy gait that the helmsman noticed it—and I could not help noticing the unusual roundness of his eyes. These are trifling instances, though it's to no commander's advantage to be suspected of ludicrous eccentricities. But I was also more seriously affected. There are to a seaman certain words, gestures, that should in given conditions come as naturally, as instinctively as the winking of a menaced eye. A certain order should spring on to his lips without thinking; a certain sign should get itself made, so to speak, without reflection. But all unconscious alertness had abandoned me. I had to make an effort of will to recall myself back (from the cabin) to the conditions of the moment. I felt that I was appearing an irresolute commander to those people who were watching me more or less critically.

And, besides, there were the scares. On the second day out, for instance, coming off the deck in the afternoon (I had straw slippers on my bare feet) I stopped at the open pantry door and spoke to the steward. He was doing something there with his back to me. At the sound of my voice he nearly jumped out of his skin, as the saying is, and incidentally broke a cup.

"What on earth's the matter with you?" I asked, astonished.

He was extremely confused. "Beg your pardon, sir. I made sure you were in your cabin."

"You see I wasn't."

"No, sir. I could have sworn I had heard you moving in there not a moment ago. It's most extraordinary . . . very sorry, sir."

I passed on with an inward shudder. I was so identified with my secret double that I did not even mention the fact in those scanty, fearful whispers we exchanged. I suppose he had made some slight noise of some kind or other. It would have been miraculous if he hadn't at one time or another. And yet, haggard as he appeared, he looked always perfectly self-controlled, more than calm—almost invulnerable. On my suggestion he remained almost entirely in the bathroom, which, upon the whole, was the safest place. There could be really no shadow of an excuse for anyone ever wanting to go in there, once the steward had done with it. It was a very tiny place. Sometimes he reclined on the floor, his legs bent, his head sustained on one elbow. At others I would find him on the campstool, sitting in his gray sleeping suit and with his cropped dark hair like a patient, unmoved convict. At night I would smuggle him into my bed-place, and we would whisper together, with the regular footfalls of the officer of the watch passing and repassing over our heads. It was an infinitely miserable time. It was lucky that some tins of fine preserves were stowed in a locker in my stateroom; hard bread I could always get hold of; and so he lived on stewed chicken, paté de foie gras, asparagus, cooked oysters, sardines—on all sorts of abominable sham delicacies out of tins. My early morning coffee he always drank; and it was all I dared do for him in that respect.

Every day there was the horrible maneuvering to go through so that my room and then the bathroom should be done in the usual way. I came to hate the sight of the steward, to abhor the voice of that harmless man. I felt that it was he who would bring on the disaster of discovery. It hung like a sword over our heads.

The fourth day out, I think (we were then working down the east side of the Gulf of Siam, tack for tack, in light winds and smooth water)—the fourth day, I say, of this miserable juggling with the unavoidable, as we sat at our evening meal, that man, whose slightest movement I dreaded, after putting down the dishes ran up on deck busily. This could not be dangerous. Presently he came down again; and then it appeared that he had remembered a coat of mine which I had thrown over a rail to dry after having been wetted in a shower which had passed over the ship in the afternoon. Sitting stolidly at the head of the table I became terrified at the sight of the garment on his arm. Of course he made for my door. There was no time to lose.

"Steward," I thundered. My nerves were so shaken that I could not govern my voice and conceal my agitation. This was the sort of thing that made my terrifically whiskered mate tap his forehead with his forefinger. I had detected him using that gesture while talking on deck with a confidential air to the carpenter. It was too far to hear a word, but I had no doubt that this pantomime could only refer to the strange new captain.

"Yes, sir," the pale-faced steward turned resignedly to me. It was this maddening course of being shouted at, checked without rhyme or reason, arbitrarily chased out of my cabin, suddenly called into it, sent flying out of his pantry on incomprehensible errands, that accounted for the growing wretchedness of his expression.

"Where are you going with that coat?"

"To your room, sir."

"Is there another shower coming?"

"I'm sure I don't know, sir. Shall I go up again and see, sir?"

"No! never mind."

My object was attained, as of course my other self in there would have heard everything that passed. During this interlude my two officers never raised their eyes off their respective plates; but the lip of that confounded cub, the second mate, quivered visibly.

I expected the steward to hook my coat on and come out at once. He was very slow about it; but I dominated my nervousness sufficiently not to shout after him. Suddenly I became aware (it could be heard plainly enough) that the fellow for some reason or other was opening the door of the bathroom. It was the end. The place was literally not big enough to swing a cat in. My voice died in my throat and I went stony all over. I expected to hear a yell of surprise and terror, and made a movement, but had not the strength to get on my legs. Everything remained still. Had my second self taken the poor wretch by the throat? I don't know what I would have done next moment if I had not seen the steward come out of my room, close the door, and then stand quietly by the sideboard.

Saved, I thought. But, no! Lost! Gone! He was gone!

I laid my knife and fork down and leaned back in my chair. My head swam. After a while, when sufficiently recovered to speak in a steady voice, I instructed my mate to put the ship round at eight o'clock himself.

"I won't come on deck," I went on. "I think I'll turn in, and unless the wind shifts I don't want to be disturbed before midnight. I feel a bit seedy."

"You did look middling bad a little while ago," the chief mate remarked without showing any great concern.

They both went out, and I stared at the steward clearing the table. There was nothing to be read on that wretched man's face. But why did he avoid my eyes I asked myself. Then I thought I should like to hear the sound of his voice.

"Steward!"

"Sir!" Startled as usual.

"Where did you hang up that coat?"

"In the bathroom, sir." The usual anxious tone. "It's not quite dry yet, sir."

For some time longer I sat in the cuddy. Had my double vanished as he had come? But of his coming there was an explanation, whereas his disappearance would be inexplicable. . . . I went slowly into my dark room, shut the door, lighted the lamp, and for a time dared not turn round. When at last I did I saw him standing bolt upright in the narrow recessed part. It would not be true to say I had a shock, but an irresistible doubt of his bodily existence flitted through my mind. Can it be, I asked myself, that he is not visible to other eyes than mine? It was like being haunted. Motionless, with a grave face, he raised his hands slightly at me in a gesture which meant clearly, "Heavens! what a narrow escape!" Narrow indeed. I think I had come creeping quietly as near insanity as any man who has not actually gone over the border. That gesture restrained me, so to speak.

The mate with the terrific whiskers was now putting the ship on the other tack. In the moment of profound silence which follows upon the hands going to their stations I heard on the poop his raised voice: "Hard alee!" and the distant shout of the order repeated on the maindeck. The sails, in that light breeze, made but a faint fluttering noise. It ceased. The ship was coming round slowly; I held my breath in the renewed stillness of expectation; one wouldn't have thought that there was a single living soul on her decks. A sudden brisk shout, "Mainsail haul!" broke the spell, and in the noisy cries and rush overhead of the men running away with the main brace we two, down in my cabin, came together in our usual position by the bed-place.

He did not wait for my question. "I heard him fumbling here and just managed to squat myself down in the bath," he whispered to me. "The fellow only opened the door and put his arm in to hang the coat up. All the same——"

"I never thought of that," I whispered back, even more appalled than before at the closeness of the shave, and marveling at that something unyielding in his character which was carrying him through so finely. There was no agitation in his whisper. Whoever was being driven distracted, it was not he. He was sane. And the proof of his sanity was continued when he took up the whispering again.

"It would never do for me to come to life again."

It was something that a ghost might have said. But what he was alluding to was his old captain's reluctant admission of the theory of suicide. It would obviously serve his turn—if I had understood at all the view which seemed to govern the unalterable purpose of his action.

"You must maroon me as soon as ever you can get amongst these islands off the Cambodje[1] shore," he went on.

"Maroon you! We are not living in a boy's adventure tale," I protested. His scornful whispering took me up.

1. I.e., Cambodia.

"We aren't indeed! There's nothing of a boy's tale in this. But there's nothing else for it. I want no more. You don't suppose I am afraid of what can be done to me? Prison or gallows or whatever they may please. But you don't see me coming back to explain such things to an old fellow in a wig and twelve respectable tradesmen, do you? What can they know whether I am guilty or not—or of *what* I am guilty, either? That's my affair. What does the Bible say? 'Driven off the face of the earth.'[2] Very well. I am off the face of the earth now. As I came at night so I shall go."

"Impossible!" I murmured. "You can't."

"Can't? . . . Not naked like a soul on the Day of Judgment. I shall freeze on to this sleeping suit. The Last Day is not yet—and . . . you have understood thoroughly. Didn't you?"

I felt suddenly ashamed of myself. I may say truly that I understood—and my hesitation in letting that man swim away from my ship's side had been a mere sham sentiment, a sort of cowardice.

"It can't be done now till next night," I breathed out. "The ship is on the offshore tack and the wind may fail us."

"As long as I know that you understand," he whispered. "But of course you do. It's a great satisfaction to have got somebody to understand. You seem to have been there on purpose." And in the same whisper, as if we two whenever we talked had to say things to each other which were not fit for the world to hear, he added, "It's very wonderful."

We remained side by side talking in our secret way—but sometimes silent or just exchanging a whispered word or two at long intervals. And as usual he stared through the port. A breath of wind came now and again into our faces. The ship might have been moored in dock, so gently and on an even keel she slipped through the water, that did not murmur even at our passage, shadowy and silent like a phantom sea.

At midnight I went on deck, and to my mate's great surprise put the ship round on the other tack. His terrible whiskers flitted round me in silent criticism. I certainly should not have done it if it had been only a question of getting out of that sleepy gulf as quickly as possible. I believe he told the second mate, who relieved him, that it was a great want of judgment. The other only yawned. That intolerable cub shuffled about so sleepily and lolled against the rails in such a slack, improper fashion that I came down on him sharply.

"Aren't you properly awake yet?"

"Yes, sir! I am awake."

"Well, then, be good enough to hold yourself as if you were. And keep a lookout. If there's any current we'll be closing with

2. "And Cain said unto the Lord, ' * * * Behold, thou hast driven me out this day from the face of the earth * * * ' " (Genesis iv.13–14).

some islands before daylight."

The east side of the gulf is fringed with islands, some solitary, others in groups. On the blue background of the high coast they seem to float on silvery patches of calm water, arid and gray, or dark green and rounded like clumps of evergreen bushes, with the larger ones, a mile or two long, showing the outlines of ridges, ribs of gray rock under the dark mantle of matted leafage. Unknown to trade, to travel, almost to geography, the manner of life they harbor is an unsolved secret. There must be villages—settlements of fishermen at least—on the largest of them, and some communication with the world is probably kept up by native craft. But all that forenoon, as we headed for them, fanned along by the faintest of breezes, I saw no sign of man or canoe in the field of the telescope I kept on pointing at the scattered group.

At noon I gave no orders for a change of course, and the mate's whiskers became much concerned and seemed to be offering themselves unduly to my notice. At last I said:

"I am going to stand right in. Quite in—as far as I can take her."

The stare of extreme surprise imparted an air of ferocity also to his eyes, and he looked truly terrific for a moment.

"We're not doing well in the middle of the gulf," I continued, casually. "I am going to look for the land breezes tonight."

"Bless my soul! Do you mean, sir, in the dark amongst the lot of all them islands and reefs and shoals?"

"Well—if there are any regular land breezes at all on this coast one must get close inshore to find them, mustn't one?"

"Bless my soul!" he exclaimed again under his breath. All that afternoon he wore a dreamy, contemplative appearance which in him was a mark of perplexity. After dinner I went into my stateroom as if I meant to take some rest. There we two bent our dark heads over a half-unrolled chart lying on my bed.

"There," I said. "It's got to be Koh-ring. I've been looking at it ever since sunrise. It has got two hills and a low point. It must be inhabited. And on the coast opposite there is what looks like the mouth of a biggish river—with some town, no doubt, not far up. It's the best chance for you that I can see."

"Anything. Koh-ring let it be."

He looked thoughtfully at the chart as if surveying chances and distances from a lofty height—and following with his eyes his own figure wandering on the blank land of Cochin China,[3] and then passing off that piece of paper clean out of sight into uncharted regions. And it was as if the ship had two captains to plan her course for her. I had been so worried and restless running up and down that I had not had the patience to dress that day. I had remained in my sleeping suit, with straw slippers and a soft floppy

3. South of Cambodia, with coast on the Gulf of Siam and the South China Sea.

hat. The closeness of the heat in the gulf had been most oppressive, and the crew were used to see me wandering in that airy attire.

"She will clear the south point as she heads now," I whispered into his ear. "Goodness only knows when, though, but certainly after dark. I'll edge her in to half a mile, as far as I may be able to judge in the dark—"

"Be careful," he murmured, warningly—and I realized suddenly that all my future, the only future for which I was fit, would perhaps go irretrievably to pieces in any mishap to my first command.

I could not stop a moment longer in the room. I motioned him to get out of sight and made my way on the poop. That unplayful cub had the watch. I walked up and down for a while thinking things out, then beckoned him over.

"Send a couple of hands to open the two quarter-deck ports," I said, mildly.

He actually had the impudence, or else so forgot himself in his wonder at such an incomprehensible order, as to repeat:

"Open the quarter-deck ports! What for, sir?"

"The only reason you need concern yourself about is because I tell you to do so. Have them open wide and fastened properly."

He reddened and went off, but I believe made some jeering remark to the carpenter as to the sensible practice of ventilating a ship's quarter-deck. I know he popped into the mate's cabin to impart the fact to him because the whiskers came on deck, as it were by chance, and stole glances at me from below—for signs of lunacy or drunkenness, I suppose.

A little before supper, feeling more restless than ever, I rejoined, for a moment, my second self. And to find him sitting so quietly was surprising, like something against nature, inhuman.

I developed my plan in a hurried whisper.

"I shall stand in as close as I dare and then put her round. I shall presently find means to smuggle you out of here into the sail locker, which communicates with the lobby. But there is an opening, a sort of square for hauling the sails out, which gives straight on the quarter-deck and which is never closed in fine weather, so as to give air to the sails. When the ship's way is deadened in stays and all the hands are aft at the main braces you shall have a clear road to slip out and get overboard through the open quarter-deck port. I've had them both fastened up. Use a rope's end to lower yourself into the water so as to avoid a splash—you know. It could be heard and cause some beastly complication."

He kept silent for a while, then whispered, "I understand."

"I won't be there to see you go," I began with an effort. "The rest . . . I only hope I have understood, too."

"You have. From first to last," and for the first time there seemed to be a faltering, something strained in his whisper. He caught hold of my arm, but the ringing of the supper bell made me start. He didn't, though; he only released his grip.

After supper I didn't come below again till well past eight o'clock. The faint, steady breeze was loaded with dew; and the wet, darkened sails held all there was of propelling power in it. The night, clear and starry, sparkled darkly, and the opaque, lightless patches shifting slowly against the low stars were the drifting islets. On the port bow there was a big one more distant and shadowily imposing by the great space of sky it eclipsed.

On opening the door I had a back view of my very own self looking at a chart. He had come out of the recess and was standing near the table.

"Quite dark enough," I whispered.

He stepped back and leaned against my bed with a level, quiet glance. I sat on the couch. We had nothing to say to each other. Over our heads the officer of the watch moved here and there. Then I heard him move quickly. I knew what that meant. He was making for the companion; and presently his voice was outside my door.

"We are drawing in pretty fast, sir. Land looks rather close."

"Very well," I answered. "I am coming on deck directly."

I waited till he was gone out of the cuddy, then rose. My double moved too. The time had come to exchange our last whispers, for neither of us was ever to hear each other's natural voice.

"Look here!" I opened a drawer and took out three sovereigns. "Take this, anyhow. I've got six and I'd give you the lot, only I must keep a little money to buy some fruit and vegetables for the crew from native boats as we go through Sunda Straits."

He shook his head.

"Take it," I urged him, whispering desperately. "No one can tell what—"

He smiled and slapped meaningly the only pocket of the sleeping jacket. It was not safe, certainly. But I produced a large old silk handkerchief of mine, and tying the three pieces of gold in a corner, pressed it on him. He was touched, I suppose, because he took it at last and tied it quickly round his waist under the jacket, on his bare skin.

Our eyes met; several seconds elapsed, till, our glances still mingled, I extended my hand and turned the lamp out. Then I passed through the cuddy, leaving the door of my room wide open. . . . "Steward!"

He was still lingering in the pantry in the greatness of his zeal, giving a rub-up to a plated cruet stand the last thing before going to bed. Being careful not to wake up the mate, whose room was opposite, I spoke in an undertone.

He looked round anxiously. "Sir!"

"Can you get me a little hot water from the galley?"

"I am afraid, sir, the galley fire's been out for some time now."

"Go and see."

He fled up the stairs.

"Now," I whispered, loudly, into the saloon—too loudly, perhaps, but I was afraid I couldn't make a sound. He was by my side in an instant—the double captain slipped past the stairs—through the tiny dark passage . . . a sliding door. We were in the sail locker, scrambling on our knees over the sails. A sudden thought struck me. I saw myself wandering barefooted, bareheaded, the sun beating on my dark poll. I snatched off my floppy hat and tried hurriedly in the dark to ram it on my other self. He dodged and fended off silently. I wonder what he thought had come to me before he understood and suddenly desisted. Our hands met gropingly, lingered united in a steady, motionless clasp for a second. . . . No word was breathed by either of us when they separated.

I was standing quietly by the pantry door when the steward returned.

"Sorry, sir. Kettle barely warm. Shall I light the spirit lamp?"

"Never mind."

I came out on deck slowly. It was now a matter of conscience to shave the land as close as possible—for now he must go overboard whenever the ship was put in stays. Must! There could be no going back for him. After a moment I walked over to leeward and my heart flew into my mouth at the nearness of the land on the bow. Under any other circumstances I would not have held on a minute longer. The second mate had followed me anxiously.

I looked on till I felt I could command my voice.

"She will weather," I said then in a quiet tone.

"Are you going to try that, sir?" he stammered out incredulously.

I took no notice of him and raised my tone just enough to be heard by the helmsman.

"Keep her good full."

"Good full, sir."

The wind fanned my cheek, the sails slept, the world was silent. The strain of watching the dark loom of the land grow bigger and denser was too much for me. I had shut my eyes—because the ship must go closer. She must! The stillness was intolerable. Were we standing still?

When I opened my eyes the second view started my heart with a thump. The black southern hill of Koh-ring seemed to hang right over the ship like a towering fragment of the everlasting night. On that enormous mass of blackness there was not a gleam to be seen, not a sound to be heard. It was gliding irresistibly toward us and yet seemed already within reach of the hand. I saw the vague figures of the watch grouped in the waist, gazing in awed silence.

"Are you going on, sir?" inquired an unsteady voice at my elbow.

I ignored it. I had to go on.

"Keep her full. Don't check her way. That won't do now," I said warningly.

"I can't see the sails very well," the helmsman answered me, in strange, quavering tones.

Was she close enough? Already she was, I won't say in the shadow of the land, but in the very blackness of it, already swallowed up as it were, gone too close to be recalled, gone from me altogether.

"Give the mate a call," I said to the young man who stood at my elbow still as death. "And turn all hands up."

My tone had a borrowed loudness reverberated from the height of the land. Several voices cried out together: "We are all on deck, sir."

Then stillness again, with the great shadow gliding closer, towering higher, without a light, without a sound. Such a hush had fallen on the ship that she might have been a bark of the dead floating in slowly under the very gate of Erebus.[4]

"My God! Where are we?"

It was the mate moaning at my elbow. He was thunderstruck, and as it were deprived of the moral support of his whiskers. He clapped his hands and absolutely cried out, "Lost!"

"Be quiet," I said sternly.

He lowered his tone, but I saw the shadowy gesture of his despair. "What are we doing here?"

"Looking for the land wind."

He made as if to tear his hair, and addressed me recklessly.

"She will never get out. You have done it, sir. I knew it'd end in something like this. She will never weather, and you are too close now to stay. She'll drift ashore before she's round. O my God!"

I caught his arm as he was raising it to batter his poor devoted head, and shook it violently.

"She's ashore already," he wailed, trying to tear himself away.

"Is she? . . . Keep good full there!"

"Good full, sir," cried the helmsman in a frightened, thin, child-like voice.

I hadn't let go the mate's arm and went on shaking it. "Ready about, do you hear? You go forward"—shake—"and stop there" —shake—"and hold your noise"—shake—"and see these head sheets properly overhauled"—shake, shake—shake.

And all the time I dared not look toward the land lest my heart should fail me. I released my grip at last and he ran forward as if

4. Entry to Hades; place of pitch darkness.

fleeing for dear life.

I wondered what my double there in the sail locker thought of this commotion. He was able to hear everything—and perhaps he was able to understand why, on my conscience, it had to be thus close—no less. My first order "Hard alee!" re-echoed ominously under the towering shadow of Koh-ring as if I had shouted in a mountain gorge. And then I watched the land intently. In that smooth water and light wind it was impossible to feel the ship coming-to. No! I could not feel her. And my second self was making now ready to slip out and lower himself overboard. Perhaps he was gone already . . . ?

The great black mass brooding over our very mastheads began to pivot away from the ship's side silently. And now I forgot the secret stranger ready to depart, and remembered only that I was a total stranger to the ship. I did not know her. Would she do it? How was she to be handled?

I swung the mainyard and waited helplessly. She was perhaps stopped, and her very fate hung in the balance, with the black mass of Koh-ring like the gate of the everlasting night towering over her taffrail.[5] What would she do now? Had she way on her yet? I stepped to the side swiftly, and on the shadowy water I could see nothing except a faint phosphorescent flash revealing the glassy smoothness of the sleeping surface. It was impossible to tell—and I had not learned yet the feel of my ship. Was she moving? What I needed was something easily seen, a piece of paper, which I could throw overboard and watch. I had nothing on me. To run down for it I didn't dare. There was no time. All at once my strained, yearning stare distinguished a white object floating within a yard of the ship's side. White on the black water. A phosphorescent flash passed under it. What was that thing? . . . I recognized my own floppy hat. It must have fallen off his head . . . and he didn't bother. Now I had what I wanted—the saving mark for my eyes. But I hardly thought of my other self, now gone from the ship, to be hidden forever from all friendly faces, to be a fugitive and a vagabond on the earth, with no brand of the curse on his sane forehead to stay a slaying hand . . . too proud to explain.

And I watched the hat—the expression of my sudden pity for his mere flesh. It had been meant to save his homeless head from the dangers of the sun. And now—behold—it was saving the ship, by serving me for a mark to help out the ignorance of my strangeness. Ha! It was drifting forward, warning me just in time that the ship had gathered sternway.

"Shift the helm," I said in a low voice to the seaman standing still like a statue.

5. Rail across the stern.

The man's eyes glistened wildly in the binnacle light as he jumped round to the other side and spun round the wheel.

I walked to the break of the poop. On the overshadowed deck all hands stood by the forebraces waiting for my order. The stars ahead seemed to be gliding from right to left. And all was so still in the world that I heard the quiet remark "She's round," passed in a tone of intense relief between two seamen.

"Let go and haul."

The foreyards ran round with a great noise, amidst cheery cries. And now the frightful whiskers made themselves heard giving various orders. Already the ship was drawing ahead. And I was alone with her. Nothing! no one in the world should stand now between us, throwing a shadow on the way of silent knowledge and mute affection, the perfect communion of a seaman with his first command.

Walking to the taffrail, I was in time to make out, on the very edge of a darkness thrown by a towering black mass like the very gateway of Erebus—yes, I was in time to catch an evanescent glimpse of my white hat left behind to mark the spot where the secret sharer of my cabin and of my thoughts, as though he were my second self, had lowered himself into the water to take his punishment: a free man, a proud swimmer striking out for a new destiny.

1909   1912

WILLIAM BUTLER YEATS
(1865–1939)

1891: Organization of the Rhymers' Club.
1899: Launching of the Irish National Theatre.
1914: *Responsibilities*.
1923: Nobel Prize.
1928: *The Tower*.

William Butler Yeats was born in Sandymount, Dublin. His father's family, of English stock, had been in Ireland for at least 200 years; his mother's, the Pollexfens, hailing originally from Devon, had been for some generations in Sligo, in the west of Ireland. J. B. Yeats, his father, had abandoned the law to take up painting, at which he made a somewhat precarious living. The Yeatses were in London from 1874 until 1883, when they returned to Ireland—to Howth, a few miles from Dublin. On leaving high school in Dublin in 1883 Yeats decided to be an artist, with poetry as his avocation, and attended art school; but he soon left, to concentrate on poetry. His first published poems appeared in the *Dublin University Review* in 1885.

Yeats's father was a religious skeptic, but he believed in the "religion of art." Yeats himself, religious by temperament but unable to believe in Christian orthodoxy, sought all his life for traditions of esoteric thought that would compensate for a lost religion. This search led him to various kinds of mysticism, to folklore, theosophy, spiritualism, and Neo-Platonism—not in any strict chronological order, for he kept returning to and reworking earlier aspects of his thought. In middle life he elaborated a symbolic system of his own, based on a variety of sources, which enabled him to strengthen the pattern and coherence of his poetic imagery. The student of Yeats is constantly coming up against this willful and sometimes baffling esotericism which he cultivated sometimes playfully, sometimes earnestly, sometimes treating it as though it were a body of truths and sometimes as though it were a convenient language of symbols. Modern scholarship has traced most of Yeats's mystical and quasi-mystical ideas to sources that were common to Blake and Shelley and which sometimes go far back into pre-Platonic beliefs and traditions. But his greatness as a poet lies in his ability to communicate the power and significance of his symbols, by the way he expresses and organizes them, even to readers who know nothing of his system.

Yeats's childhood and young manhood were spent between Dublin, London, and Sligo, and each of these places contributed something to his poetic development. In London in the 1890's he met the important poets of the day, and in 1891 was one of the founders of the Rhymers' Club, whose members included Lionel Johnson, Ernest Dowson, and many other characteristic figures of the 90's. Here he acquired ideas of poetry which were vaguely Pre-Raphaelite: he believed, in this early stage of his career, that a poet's language should be dreamy, evocative, and ethereal. From the countryside around Sligo he got something much more vigorous and earthy—a knowledge of the life of the peasantry and of their folklore. In Dublin he was influenced by the currents of Irish nationalism and, while often in disagreement with those who wished to use literature for crude political ends, he nevertheless learned to see his poetry as a contribution to a rejuvenated Irish culture. The three influences of Dublin, London, and Sligo did not develop in chronological order—he was going to and fro between these places throughout his early life—and we sometimes find a poem based on Sligo folklore in the midst of a group of dreamy poems written under the influence of the Rhymers' Club or an echo of Irish nationalist feeling in a lyric otherwise wholly Pre-Raphaelite in tone.

We can distinguish quite clearly, however, the main periods into which Yeats's poetic career falls. He began in the tradition of self-conscious romanticism which he learned from the London poets of the 90's. Spenser and Shelley, and a little later Blake, were also important influences. One of his early verse plays ends with a song:

> The woods of Arcady are dead
> And over is their antique joy;
> Of old the world on dreaming fed;
> Gray Truth is now her painted toy.

About the same time he was writing poems (e.g., *The Stolen Child*) deriving from his Sligo experience, with a quiet precision of natural imagery, country place names, and themes from folklore. A little later—i.e., in the latter part of his first period—Dublin literary circles sent him to Standish O'Grady's *History of Ireland: Heroic Period*, where he found the great stories of the heroic age of Irish history, and to George Sigerson's and Douglas Hyde's translations of Gaelic poetry into "that dialect which gets from Gaelic its syntax and keeps its still partly Tudor vocabulary." Even when he plays with Neo-Platonic ideas, as in *The Rose of the World* (also the product of the latter part of his early period), he can link them with Irish heroic themes and so give a dignity and a *style* to his imagery not normally associated with this sort of poetic dreaminess. Thus the heroic legends of old Ireland and the folk traditions of the modern Irish countryside provided Yeats with a stiffening for his early dreamlike imagery, which is why even his first, "90's" phase is productive of interesting poems. *The Lake Isle of Innisfree*, spoiled for some by overanthologizing, is nevertheless a fine poem of its kind: it is the clarity and control shown in the handling of the imagery which keeps all romantic fuzziness out of it and gives it its haunting quality. In *The Man Who Dreamed of Faeryland* he makes something peculiarly effective out of the contrast between human activities and the strangeness of nature. In *The Madness of King Goll* the disturbing sense of the *otherness* of the natural world drives the king mad. (Such contrasts are common in the early Yeats; in his later poetry he tries to resolve what he called these "antinomies" in inclusive symbols. See, for example, *Crazy Jane Talks to the Bishop*.)

It is important to realize that Yeats had a habit of revising his earlier poems in later printings, tightening up the language and getting rid of the more self-indulgent romantic imagery. The revised versions are found in his *Collected Poems*, which therefore present a somewhat muted picture of his poetic development. For the complete picture one should consult the Variorum Edition edited by Peter Allt and Russell K. Alspach, 1957.

It was Irish nationalism that first sent Yeats in search of a consistently simpler and more popular style. He tells in one of his autobiographical essays how he sought for a style in which to express the elemental facts about Irish life and aspirations. This led him to the concrete image, as did Hyde's translations from Gaelic folk songs, in which "nothing * * * was abstract, nothing worn-out." But other forces were also working on him. He began to feel more and more that his earlier poetic styles could not speak for the whole self. Looking back in 1906, he found that he had mistaken the poetic ideal. "Without knowing it, I had come to care for nothing but impersonal beauty. * * * We should ascend out of common interests, the thoughts of the newspapers, of the market place, but only so far as we can carry the normal, passionate, reasoning self, the personality as a whole." The result of the abandonment of "impersonal beauty," and of the desire to "carry the normal, passionate, reasoning self" into his poetry, is seen in the volumes of collected poems, *In the Seven Woods* (1903) and *The Green Helmet and Other Poems* (1910). *The Folly of Being Comforted*, *Adam's Curse*, and *The Old Men Admiring Themselves* are from the former of these, and one can see immediately how Yeats here combines the colloquial with the formal. This is characteristic of his "second period."

By this time Yeats had met the beautiful actress and violent Irish nationalist Maud Gonne, with whom he was desperately in love for many years, but who persistently refused to marry him. This affair is reflected in many of the poems of his second period, notably *No Second Troy*, published in *The Green Helmet*. He had also met Lady Gregory, Irish writer and promoter of Irish literature, in 1896 and she invited him to spend the following summer at her country house, Coole Park, in Galway. Yeats spent many holidays with Lady Gregory and discovered the attractiveness of the "country house ideal," seeing in an aristocratic life of elegance and leisure in a great house a method of imposing order on chaos and a symbol of the Neo-Platonic dance of life. He expresses this view many times in his poetry—e.g., at the end of *A Prayer for My Daughter*—and it became an important part of Yeats's complex of attitudes. The middle classes, with their Philistine money-grubbing, he detested, and for his ideal characters he looked either below them, to peasants and beggars, or above them, to the aristocracy, for each of these had their own traditions and lived according to them.

It was under Lady Gregory's influence that Yeats became involved in the founding of the Irish National Theatre in 1899. This led to his active participation in problems of play production, which included political problems of censorship, economic problems of paying carpenters and actors, and other aspects of "theater business, management of men." All this had an effect on his style. The reactions of Dublin audiences did not encourage Yeats's trust in popular judgment, and his bitterness with the "Paudeens," middle-class shopkeepers—who seemed to him to be without any dignity, or understanding, or nobility of spirit—produced some of the most effective poems (e.g., *September* 1913 and *To a Shade*) of his third or middle period. This period is best represented by the volume *Responsibilities* (1914), whose title is significant of the change in Yeats's view of the poetic function. Yeats was now becoming more and more of a public figure. In 1922 he was appointed a senator of the recently established Irish Free State and served until 1928, playing an active part not only in promoting the arts but also in general political affairs, in which he supported the views of the Protestant landed class.

Meanwhile Yeats was responding in his own way to the change in poetic taste represented in the poetry and criticism of Ezra Pound and T. S. Eliot immediately before World War I. A gift for epigram had already begun to emerge in his poetry: in the volume entitled *The Wild Swans at Coole* (1919) he has a poem citing Walter Savage Landor (the 19th-century poet who wrote some fine lapidary verse) and John Donne as masters. To the precision, and the combination of colloquial and formal, which he had achieved early in the century, he now added a "metaphysical" as well as an epigrammatic element, and this is seen in the later poems of his third period. He also continued his experiments with different kinds of rhythm. At the same time he was continuing his search for a language of symbols and pursuing his esoteric studies. Yeats married in 1917, and his wife proved so sympathetic to his imaginative needs that the automatic writing which she produced (believed by Yeats to have been dictated by spirits, but apparently faked by Mrs. Yeats to help her husband) gave him the elements of a symbolic system which he later worked out in his book *A Vision* (1925, 1937) and which he used in all sorts of ways in much of his later poetry. The system was both a theory of the movements of history and a theory of the different types of personality, each movement and type being related in various complicated ways to a different phase of the moon. Some of Yeats's poetry is unintelligible without a knowledge of A *Vision;* but the better poems, such as the two on Byzantium, can be appreciated without such knoweldge by the experienced reader who responds sensitively to the patterning of the imagery reinforced by the incantatory effect of the rhythms. Some recent criticism decries attempts by those who are not experts in the background of Yeats's esoteric thought to discuss his poetry and insists that only a detailed knowledge of Yeats's sources can yield his poetic meaning; but while it is true that some particular images do not yield all their significance to whose who are ignorant of the background, it is also true that too literal a paraphase of the symbolism in the light of the sources robs the poems of their power by reducing them to mere exercises in the use of a code.

The Tower (1928) and *The Winding Stair* (1933), from which the poems from *Sailing to Byzantium* through *After Long Silence* have been here selected, represent the mature Yeats at his very best—a realist-symbolist-metaphysical poet with an uncanny power over words. These volumes represent his fourth and greatest period. Here, in his poems of the 1920's and 1930's, winding stairs, spinning tops, "gyres," spirals of all kinds, are important symbols; not only are they connected with Yeats's philosophy of history and of personality, but they also serve as a means of resolving some of those contraries that had arrested him from the beginning. Life is a journey up a spiral staircase; as we grow older we cover the ground we have covered before, only higher up; as we look down the winding stair below us we measure our progress by the number of places where we were but no longer are. The journey is both repetitious and progressive; we go both round and upward. Through symbolic images of this kind Yeats explores the paradoxes of time and change, of growth and identity, of love and age, of life and art, of madness and wisdom.

The Byzantium poems show Yeats trying to escape from the turbulence of life to the calm eternity of art. But in his fifth and final period he returned to the turbulence after (if only partly as a result of) undergoing the Steinach glandular operations in 1934, and his last poems have a controlled yet startling wildness. Yeats's return to life, to "the foul rag-and-bone shop of the heart," is one of the most impressive final phases of any poet's career. "I shall be a sinful man to the end, and think upon my deathbed of all the nights I wasted in my youth," he wrote in old age to a correspondent, and in his very last letter he wrote: "When I try to put all into a phrase I say, 'Man can embody truth but he cannot know it.' * * * The abstract is not life and everywhere draws out its contradictions. You can refute Hegel but not the Saint or the Song of Sixpence." When he died in September, 1939, he left a body of verse which, in variety and power, makes him beyond question the greatest 20th-century poet of the English language.

The Madness of King Goll[1]

I sat on cushioned otter skin:
My word was law from Ith to Emain,
And shook at Inver Amergin [2]
The hearts of the world-troubling seamen,
And drove tumult and war away   5
From girl and boy and man and beast;
The fields grew fatter day by day,
The wild fowl of the air increased;
And every ancient Ollave [3] said,   ·
While he bent down his fading head,   10
'He drive away the Northern cold.'
They will not hush, the leaves a-flutter round me, the
     beech leaves old.

I sat and mused and drank sweet wine;
A herdsman came from inland valleys,
Crying, the pirates drove his swine   15
To fill their dark-beaked hollow galleys.
I called my battle-breaking men
And my loud brazen battle cars
From rolling vale and rivery glen;
And under the blinking of the stars   20
Fell on the pirates by the deep,
And hurled them in the gulph of sleep:
These hands won many a torque of gold.
They will not hush, the leaves a-flutter round me, the
     beech leaves old.

But slowly, as I shouting slew   25
And trampled in the bubbling mire,
In my most secret spirit grew
A whirling and a wandering fire:
I stood: keen stars above me shone,
Around me shone keen eyes of men: 30
I laughed aloud and hurried on
By rocky shore and rushy fen;
I laughed because birds fluttered by,
And starlight gleamed, and clouds flew high,
And rushes waved and waters rolled.   35
They will not hush, the leaves a-flutter round me, the
     beech leaves old.

1. Yeats's first poem to be published in England (in *The Leisure Hour*, September, 1887). Its original title was *King Goll, An Irish Legend*. Like most of Yeats's early poems, the text was later much revised, and it is the revised version that is printed here. (In all cases of revision, we print the version revised by Yeats for his *Collected Poems*.) The legend tells of an ancient Irish king, who went mad and hid himself in a valley near Cork, where all the madmen of Ireland were believed to wish to gather if they were free. Yeats's father painted his son (in the latter's words) "as King Goll, tearing the strings out of a harp, being insane with youth."
2. The ancient Irish place names evoke the old heroic legends of Ireland. Emain, said to have been founded by Queen Macha of the Golden Hair (4th century), was in County Armagh (Armagh-Ard-macha, hill of Macha); it is now Navan Rath.
3. Learned man.

And now I wander in the woods
When summer gluts the golden bees,
Or in autumnal solitudes
Arise the leopard-colored trees;   40
Or when along the wintry strands
The cormorants shiver on their rocks;
I wander on, and wave my hands,
And sing, and shake my heavy locks.
The gray wolf knows me; by one ear   45
I lead along the woodland deer;
The hares run by me growing bold.
*They will not hush, the leaves a-flutter round me, the
    beech leaves old.*

I came upon a little town
That slumbered in the harvest moon,   50
And passed a-tiptoe up and down,
Murmuring, to a fitful tune,
How I have followed, night and day,
A tramping of tremendous feet,
And saw where this old tympan lay   55
Deserted on a doorway seat,
And bore it to the woods with me;
Of some inhuman misery
Our married voices wildly trolled.
*They will not hush, the leaves a-flutter round me, the
    beech leaves old.*   60

I sang how, when day's toil is done,
Orchil shakes out her long dark hair
That hides away the dying sun
And sheds faint odors through the air:
When my hand passed from wire to wire   65
It quenched, with sound like falling dew,
The whirling and the wandering fire;
But lift a mournful ulalu,
For the kind wires are torn and still,
And I must wander wood and hill   70
Through summer's heat and winter's cold.
*They will not hush, the leaves a-flutter round me, the
    beech leaves old.*

                                                    1887, 1888

The Stolen Child

Where dips the rocky highland
Of Sleuth Wood [4] in the lake,
There lies a leafy island

4. This and other places mentioned in
the poem are in County Sligo, in north-
western Ireland, where Yeats spent much
of his childhood.

Where flapping herons wake
The drowsy water rats;
There we've hid our faery vats,
Full of berries
And of reddest stolen cherries.
Come away, O human child!
To the waters and the wild
With a faery, hand in hand,
For the world's more full of weeping than you can understand.

Where the wave of moonlight glosses
The dim gray sands with light,
Far off by furthest Rosses
We foot it all the night,
Weaving olden dances
Mingling hands and mingling glances
Till the moon has taken flight;
To and fro we leap
And chase the frothy bubbles,
While the world is full of troubles
And is anxious in its sleep.
Come away, O human child!
To the waters and the wild
With a faery, hand in hand,
For the world's more full of weeping than you can understand.

Where the wandering water gushes
From the hills above Glen-Car,
In pools among the rushes
That scarce could bathe a star,
We seek for slumbering trout
And whispering in their ears
Give them unquiet dreams;
Leaning softly out
From ferns that drop their tears
Over the young streams.
Come away, O human child!
To the waters and the wild
With a faery, hand in hand,
For the world's more full of weeping than you can understand.

Away with us he's going,
The solemn-eyed:
He'll hear no more the lowing
Of the calves on the warm hillside
Or the kettle on the hob
Sing peace into his breast,
Or see the brown mice bob
Round and round the oatmeal chest.
For he comes, the human child,
To the waters and the wild

With a faery, hand in hand,
From a world more full of weeping than he can understand.

1886, 1889

Down by the Salley Gardens[5]

Down by the salley gardens my love and I did meet;
She passed the salley gardens with little snow-white feet.
She bid me take love easy, as the leaves grow on the tree;
But I, being young and foolish, with her would not agree.

In a field by the river my love and I did stand,   5
And on my leaning shoulder she laid her snow-white hand.
She bid me take life easy, as the grass grows on the weirs;
But I was young and foolish, and now am full of tears.

1889

The Rose of the World[1]

Who dreamed that beauty passes like a dream?
For these red lips, with all their mournful pride,
Mournful that no new wonder may betide,
Troy passed away in one high funeral gleam,
And Usna's children died.[2]   5

We and the laboring world are passing by:
Amid men's souls, that waver and give place
Like the pale waters in their wintry race,
Under the passing stars, foam of the sky,
Lives on this lonely face.   10

Bow down, archangels, in your dim abode:
Before you were, or any hearts to beat,
Weary and kind one lingered by His seat;
He made the world to be a grassy road
Before her wandering feet.   15

1892

5. Originally entitled *An Old Song Re-sung*, with Yeats's footnote: "This is an attempt to reconstruct an old song from three lines imperfectly remembered by an old peasant woman in the village of Ballysodare, Sligo, who often sings them to herself." "Salley" is a variant of "sallow," a species of willow tree.
1. The Platonic Idea of eternal Beauty. "I notice upon reading these poems for the first time for several years that the quality symbolized as The Rose differs from the Intellectual Beauty of Shelley and of Spenser in that I have imagined it as suffering with man and not as something pursued and seen from afar" (Yeats, in 1925).
2. In Old Irish legend, the Ulster warrior Naoise, son of Usna or Usnach (pronounced *Ushna*), carried off the beautiful Deirdre, whom King Conchubar of Ulster had intended to marry, and with his two brothers took her to Scotland. Eventually Conchubar lured the four of them back to Ireland and killed the three brothers.

The Lake Isle of Innisfree[3]

I will arise and go now, and go to Innisfree,
And a small cabin build there, of clay and wattles[4] made:
Nine bean-rows will I have there, a hive for the honeybee,
And live alone in the bee-loud glade.

And I shall have some peace there, for peace comes dropping slow,   5
Dropping from the veils of the morning to where the cricket sings;
There midnight's all a glimmer, and noon a purple glow,
And evening full of the linnet's wings.

I will arise and go now, for always night and day
I hear lake water lapping with low sounds by the shore;   10
While I stand on the roadway, or on the pavements gray,
I hear it in the deep heart's core.

                                        1890, 1892

The Sorrow of Love

The brawling of a sparrow in the eaves,
The brilliant moon and all the milky sky,
And all that famous harmony of leaves,
Had blotted out man's image and his cry.

A girl arose that had red mournful lips   5
And seemed the greatness of the world in tears,
Doomed like Odysseus and the laboring ships
And proud as Priam murdered with his peers;[5]

Arose, and on the instant clamorous eaves,
A climbing moon upon an empty sky,   10
And all that lamentation of the leaves,
Could but compose man's image and his cry.

                                        1892

When You Are Old[6]

When you are old and gray and full of sleep,
And nodding by the fire, take down this book,

3. Island in Lough Gill, County Sligo. "My father had read to me some passage out of [Thoreau's] *Walden*, and I planned to live some day in a cottage on a little island called Innisfree * * * "
4. Stakes interwoven with twigs or branches.
5. Odysseus (whom the Romans called Ulysses), hero of Homer's *Odyssey* which describes how, after having fought in the siege of Troy, he wandered for ten years before reaching his home, the Greek island of Ithaca. Priam was king of Troy at the time of the siege and was killed when the Greeks captured the city.
6. A poem suggested by a sonnet of the 16th-century French poet Pierre de Ronsard; it begins *"Quand vous serez bien vieille, au soir, à la chandelle"* ("When you are old, sitting at evening by candle light"), but ends very differently from Yeats's poem.

And slowly read, and dream of the soft look
Your eyes had once, and of their shadows deep;

How many loved your moments of glad grace,⁵
And loved your beauty with love false or true,
But one man loved the pilgrim soul in you,
And loved the sorrows of your changing face;

And bending down beside the glowing bars,
Murmur, a little sadly, how Love fled¹⁰
And paced upon the mountains overhead
And hid his face amid a crowd of stars.

1892

Who Goes with Fergus?⁷

Who will go drive with Fergus now,
And pierce the deep wood's woven shade,
And dance upon the level shore?
Young man, lift up your russet brow,
And lift your tender eyelids, maid,⁵
And brood on hopes and fear no more.

And no more turn aside and brood
Upon love's bitter mystery;
For Fergus rules the brazen cars,
And rules the shadows of the wood,¹⁰
And the white breast of the dim sea
And all disheveled wandering stars.

1893

The Man Who Dreamed of Faeryland

He stood among a crowd at Dromahair;⁸
His heart hung all upon a silken dress,
And he had known at last some tenderness,
Before earth took him to her stony care;
But when a man poured fish into a pile,⁵
It seemed they raised their little silver heads,
And sang what gold morning or evening sheds
Upon a woven world-forgotten isle
Where people love beside the raveled⁹ seas;

7. Fergus, in Irish heroic legend, "king of the proud Red Branch Kings," gave up his throne voluntarily to Conchubar to learn by dreaming and meditating the bitter wisdom of the poet and philosopher. This poem is quoted by Buck Mulligan in *Ulysses*, and a line of it also comes into Stephen Dedalus' mind.
8. This and other place names in the poem refer to places in County Sligo.
9. Tangled; hence here "turbulent."

That Time can never mar a lover's vows 10
Under that woven changeless roof of boughs:
The singing shook him out of his new ease.

He wandered by the sands of Lissadell;
His mind ran all on money cares and fears,
And he had known at last some prudent years 15
Before they heaped his grave under the hill;
But while he passed before a plashy place,
A lugworm with its gray and muddy mouth
Sang that somewhere to north or west or south
There dwelt a gay, exulting, gentle race 20
Under the golden or the silver skies;
That if a dancer stayed his hungry foot
It seemed the sun and moon were in the fruit:
And at that singing he was no more wise.

He mused beside the well of Scanavin, 25
He mused upon his mockers: without fail
His sudden vengeance were a country tale,
When earthy night had drunk his body in;
But one small knotgrass growing by the pool
Sang where—unnecessary cruel voice— 30
Old silence bids its chosen race rejoice,
Whatever raveled waters rise and fall
Or stormy silver fret the gold of day,
And midnight there enfold them like a fleece
And lover there by lover be at peace. 35
The tale drove his fine angry mood away.

He slept under the hill of Lugnagall;
And might have known at last unhaunted sleep
Under that cold and vapor-turbaned steep,
Now that the earth had taken man and all: 40
Did not the worms that spired about his bones
Proclaim with that unwearied, reedy cry
That God has laid his fingers on the sky,
That from those fingers glittering summer runs
Upon the dancer by the dreamless wave. 45
Why should those lovers that no lovers miss
Dream, until God burn Nature with a kiss?
The man has found no comfort in the grave.

1891, 1892

The Secret Rose[1]

Far-off, most secret, and inviolate Rose,
Enfold me in my hour of hours; where those

1. The Rose is a symbol of beauty (see
"The Rose of the World," below), and
in this poem "this spiritual beauty was
seen as part of Yeats's own belief that
there would be a revelation due to the
creation of Celtic mysteries (and a complete understanding between Yeats and
Maud Gonne)" [A. N. Jeffares]. Yeats

Who sought thee in the Holy Sepulcher,
Or in the wine-vat, dwell beyond the stir
And tumult of defeated dreams; and deep
Among pale eyelids, heavy with the sleep   5
Men have named beauty. Thy great leaves enfold
The ancient beards, the helms of ruby and gold
Of the crowned Magi;[2] and the king whose eyes
Saw the Pierced Hands and Rood of elder rise   10
In Druid vapor and make the torches dim;
Till vain frenzy awoke and he died;[3] and him
Who met Fand walking among flaming dew
By a gray shore where the wind never blew,
And lost the world and Emer for a kiss;[4]   15
And him who drove the gods out of their liss,[5]
And till a hundred morns had flowered red
Feasted, and wept the barrows of his dead;
And the proud dreaming king who flung the crown
And sorrow away, and calling bard and clown   20
Dwelt among wine-stained wanderers in deep woods;[6]
And him who sold tillage, and house, and goods,
And sought through lands and islands numberless years,
Until he found, with laughter and with tears,
A woman of so shining loveliness   25
That men threshed corn at midnight by a tress,
A little stolen tress.[7] I, too, await

reveals how he used his sources in an interesting note: "I find that I have unintentionally changed the old story of Conchubar's death. He did not see the Crucifixion in a vision but was told of it * * * I have imagined Cuchulain meeting Fand 'walking among the flaming dew,' because, I think, of something in Mr. Standish O'Grady's books. [See above, p. 1563.] I have founded the man 'who drove the gods out of their liss,' or fort, upon something I have read about Caoilte after the battle of Gabhra, when almost all his companions were killed, driving the gods out of their liss, * * * I have founded 'the proud dreaming king' upon Fergus, but when I wrote my poem here, and in the song in my early book, 'Who will drive with Fergus now?' I only knew him in Mr. Standish O'Grady, * * * I have founded 'him who sold tillage, and house, and goods,' upon something in 'The Red Pony,' a folk-tale in Mr. Larminie's *West Irish Folk Tales.* A young man 'saw a light before him on the high-road. When he came as far, there was an open box on the road, and a light coming up out of it. He took up the box. There was a lock of hair in it. Presently he had to go to become the servant of a king for his living. There were eleven boys. When they were going out into the stable at ten o'clock, each of them took a light but he. He took no candle at all with

him. Each of them went into his own stable. When he went into his stable he opened the box. He left it in a hole in the wall. The light was great. It was twice as much as in the other stables.' The king hears of it, and makes him show him the box. The king says, 'You must go and bring me the woman to whom the hair belongs.' In the end the young man, and not the king, marries the woman."
2. The Magi are of course the "wise men" from the East who came to do homage to the infant Jesus. Mrs. Yeats told T. R. Henn that the image in lines 7–9 was "perhaps based on Botticelli's 'Adoration of the Magi,' with a Pre-Raphaelite overlay."
3. King Conchubar, in early Christian legend, is said to have died on the day of Christ's crucifixion in a fit of rage at hearing the news. Yeats, as his note explains, makes Conchubar see the crucifixion in a vision raised by the magic of the ancient Celtic priests, or Druids. The "Pierced Hands" are, of course, Christ's, and the "Rood" is the Cross.
4. The ancient Irish hero Cuchulain was seduced by Fand away from his wife Emer.
5. Fort. This is Caoilte, legendary Irish hero and companion of Oisin, son of Finn, poet and warrior.
6. The "proud dreaming king" is Fergus. See Yeats's note.
7. Yeats describes this tale in his note.

The hour of thy great wind of love and hate.
When shall the stars be blown about the sky,
Like the sparks blown out of a smithy, and die?   30
Surely thine hour has come, thy great wind blows,
Far-off, most secret, and inviolate Rose?

                                          1896, 1897

The Folly of Being Comforted

One that is ever kind said yesterday:
"Your well-beloved's hair has threads of gray,
And little shadows come about her eyes;
Time can but make it easier to be wise
Though now it seem impossible, and so   5
All that you need is patience."

                        Heart cries, "No,
I have not a crumb of comfort, not a grain.
Time can but make her beauty over again:
Because of that great nobleness of hers
The fire that stirs about her, when she stirs,   10
Burns but more clearly. O she had not these ways
When all the wild summer was in her gaze."

O heart! O heart! if she'd but turn her head,
You'd know the folly of being comforted.

                                          1902, 1903

Adam's Curse[1]

We sat together at one summer's end,
That beautiful mild woman, your close friend,
And you and I, and talked of poetry.
I said: "A line will take us hours maybe;
Yet if it does not seem a moment's thought,   5
Our stitching and unstitching has been naught.
Better go down upon your marrowbones
And scrub a kitchen pavement, or break stones
Like an old pauper, in all kinds of weather;
For to articulate sweet sounds together   10
Is to work harder than all these, and yet
Be thought an idler by the noisy set
Of bankers, schoolmasters, and clergymen
The martyrs call the world."

---

1. To work for a living was the curse imposed by God upon Adam after the Fall (see Genesis iii.17–19). The poem reflects an incident in Yeats's passionate but hopeless love for the beautiful actress Maud Gonne (see A. N. Jeffares, *W. B. Yeats: Man and Poet*, 1949, pp. 128–29).

And thereupon   15
That beautiful mild woman for whose sake
There's many a one shall find out all heartache
On finding that her voice is sweet and low
Replied: "To be born woman is to know—
Although they do not talk of it at school—   20
That we must labor to be beautiful."

I said: "It's certain there is no fine thing
Since Adam's fall but needs much laboring.
There have been lovers who thought love should be
So much compounded of high courtesy   25
That they would sigh and quote with learned looks
Precedents out of beautiful old books;
Yet now it seems an idle trade enough."

We sat grown quiet at the name of love;
We saw the last embers of daylight die,   30
And in the trembling blue-green of the sky
A moon, worn as if it had been a shell
Washed by time's waters as they rose and fell
About the stars and broke in days and years.

I had a thought for no one's but your ears: 35
That you were beautiful, and that I strove
To love you in the old high way of love;
That it had all seemed happy, and yet we'd grown
As weary-hearted as that hollow moon.

1902, 1903

The Old Men Admiring Themselves in the Water

I heard the old, old men say,
"Everything alters,
And one by one we drop away."
They had hands like claws, and their knees
Were twisted like the old thorn trees   5
By the waters.
I heard the old, old men say,
"All that's beautiful drifts away
Like the waters."

1903

No Second Troy[1]

Why should I blame her that she filled my days
With misery, or that she would of late
Have taught to ignorant men most violent ways,
Or hurled the little streets upon the great,
Had they but courage equal to desire?   5

1. Another poem about Maud Gonne, who was a passionate Irish nationalist, preaching violence to achieve Irish independence (see lines 3–5).

What could have made her peaceful with a mind
That nobleness made simple as a fire,
With beauty like a tightened bow, a kind
That is not natural in an age like this,
Being high and solitary and most stern?   10
Why, what could she have done, being what she is?
Was there another Troy for her to burn?[2]

1910

The Fascination of What's Difficult[3]

The fascination of what's difficult
Has dried the sap out of my veins, and rent
Spontaneous joy and natural content
Out of my heart. There's something ails our colt
That must, as if it had not holy blood   5
Nor on Olympus leaped from cloud to cloud,
Shiver under the lash, strain, sweat and jolt
As though it dragged road-metal. My curse on plays
That have to be set up in fifty ways,
On the day's war with every knave and dolt,   10
Theater business, management of men.
I swear before the dawn comes round again
I'll find the stable and pull out the bolt.

1910

September 1913[4]

What need you, being come to sense,
But fumble in a greasy till
And add the halfpence to the pence
And prayer to shivering prayer, until
You have dried the marrow from the bone?   5
For men were born to pray and save:
Romantic Ireland's dead and gone,
It's with O'Leary[5] in the grave.

Yet they were of a different kind,
The names that stilled your childish play,   10
They have gone about the world like wind,
But little time had they to pray

2. Helen of Troy was, of course, the cause of the destruction of the "first" Troy. The mixture of admiration and bitterness reflected here is characteristic of many of Yeats's poems about Maud Gonne.
3. Written when Yeats was director-manager of the Abbey Theatre. "Subject. To complain of the fascination of what's difficult. It spoils spontaneity and pleasure, and wastes time. Repeat the line ending difficult three times and

rhyme on bolt, exalt, colt, jolt" (Yeats's diary for September, 1909).
4. The poem reflects Yeats's disillusion with the state of the Irish national movement (for independence from Great Britain). Contrast *Easter 1916*, where the heroism of the Easter Rebellion, 1916, has led him to withdraw his criticism.
5. John O'Leary, Irish nationalist of great spirit and integrity who died in 1907.

For whom the hangman's rope was spun,
And what, God help us, could they save?
Romantic Ireland's dead and gone,   15
It's with O'Leary in the grave.

Was it for this the wild geese spread
The gray wing upon every tide;
For this that all that blood was shed,
For this Edward Fitzgerald[6] died,   20
And Robert Emmet and Wolfe Tone,
All that delirium of the brave?
Romantic Ireland's dead and gone,
It's with O'Leary in the grave.

Yet could we turn the years again,   25
And call those exiles as they were
In all their loneliness and pain,
You'd cry, "Some woman's yellow hair
Has maddened every mother's son":
They weighed so lightly what they gave.   30
But let them be, they're dead and gone,
They're with O'Leary in the grave.

                                                     1913

To a Shade[1]

If you have revisited the town, thin Shade,
Whether to look upon your monument
(I wonder if the builder has been paid)
Or happier-thoughted when the day is spent
To drink of that salt breath out of the sea   5
When gray gulls flit about instead of men,
And the gaunt houses put on majesty:
Let these content you and be gone again;
For they are at their old tricks yet.
                                        A man
Of your own passionate serving kind who had brought 10
In his full hands what, had they only known,
Had given their children's children loftier thought,
Sweeter emotion, working in their veins
Like gentle blood, has been driven from the place,
And insult heaped upon him for his pains,   15

6. Lord Edward Fitzgerald (1763–98),
a British officer who, after being dismissed from the army for disloyal activities, joined the United Irishmen (an
Irish nationalist organization), was arrested, and died in prison. Robert Emmet (1778–1803) was also an Irish
patriot, executed for treason after a
heroic career. Theobald Wolfe Tone

(1763–98), one of the chief founders
of the United Irishmen, committed suicide in prison in Dublin.
1. I.e., the spirit of the great Irish
nationalist leader, Charles Stewart Parnell (1846–91). Yeats is here expressing his disgust at the grubby materialism and Philistinism of the Dublin
middle classes.

And for his openhandedness, disgrace;[2]
Your enemy, an old foul mouth, had set
The pack upon him.
                                Go, unquiet wanderer,
And gather the Glasnevin[3] coverlet
About your head till the dust stops your ear,   20
The time for you to taste of that salt breath
And listen at the corners has not come;
You had enough of sorrow before death—
Away, away! You are safer in the tomb.

1913   1913

The Cold Heaven[4]

Suddenly I saw the cold and rook-delighting heaven
That seemed as though ice burned and was but the more ice,
And thereupon imagination and heart were driven
So wild that every casual thought of that and this
Vanished, and left but memories, that should be out of season   5
With the hot blood of youth, of love crossed long ago;
And I took all the blame out of all sense and reason,
Until I cried and trembled and rocked to and fro,
Riddled with light. Ah! when the ghost begins to quicken,[5]
Confusion of the deathbed over, is it sent   10
Out naked on the roads, as the books say, and stricken
By the injustice of the skies for punishment?

1912

The Wild Swans at Coole[1]

The trees are in their autumn beauty,
The woodland paths are dry,
Under the October twilight the water
Mirrors a still sky;
Upon the brimming water among the stones   5
Are nine-and-fifty swans.

2. Sir Hugh Lane, Lady Gregory's nephew, had collected a number of important modern French paintings which he wished to give to the city of Dublin, provided they were permanently housed in a suitable building. Fierce abuse of the paintings and of the proposed design of the gallery in the Dublin nationalist press caused Lane to send the pictures to the London National Gallery. (Lane was drowned on the *Lusitania* in 1915; after years of bitter court dispute over an unwitnessed codicil to his will bequeathing the paintings to Dublin, an arrangement was reached in 1959 for the pictures to hang first in Dublin and then in London, for five years at a time.)
3. The cemetery where Parnell is buried.

4. Yeats told Maud Gonne, in answer to her inquiry, that this poem "was an attempt to describe the feelings aroused in him by the cold and detachedly beautiful winter sky. He felt alone and responsible in that loneliness for all the past mistakes that tortured his peace of mind. It was a momentary intensity of dreamlike perception, where physical surroundings remained fixed clear in the mind, to accentuate the years of thought and reality that passed in review in an instantaneous and yet eternal suspension of time" (A. N. Jeffares).
5. Come alive.
1. I.e., Coole Park, Lady Gregory's country estate, where Yeats was a frequent guest.

The nineteenth autumn has come upon me
Since I first made my count;[2]
I saw, before I had well finished,
All suddenly mount   10
And scatter wheeling in great broken rings
Upon their clamorous wings.

I have looked upon those brilliant creatures,
And now my heart is sore.
All's changed since I, hearing at twilight,   15
The first time on this shore,
The bell-beat of their wings above my head,
Trod with a lighter tread.

Unwearied still, lover by lover,
They paddle in the cold   20
Companionable streams or climb the air;
Their hearts have not grown old;
Passion or conquest, wander where they will,
Attend upon them still.

But now they drift on the still water,   25
Mysterious, beautiful;
Among what rushes will they build,
By what lake's edge or pool
Delight men's eyes when I awake some day
To find they have flown away?

1916   1917

Easter 1916[1]

I have met them at close of day
Coming with vivid faces
From counter or desk among gray
Eighteenth-century houses.
I have passed with a nod of the head   5
Or polite meaningless words,
Or have lingered awhile and said
Polite meaningless words,
And thought before I had done
Of a mocking tale or a gibe   10
To please a companion
Around the fire at the club,
Being certain that they and I
But lived where motley is worn:

2. His first visit had been in 1897 (nineteen years earlier).

1. On Easter Sunday of 1916, Irish nationalists launched a heroic but unsuccessful revolt against the British government; the week of street fighting that followed is known as the Easter Rebellion. As a result, a number of the nationalists were executed: Britain, at war with Germany, was in no mood to tolerate Irish agitation for independence —which was supported, for obvious reasons, by Germany. Yeats knew the chief rebels personally.

All changed, changed utterly: 15
A terrible beauty is born.

That woman's days were spent
In ignorant good will,
Her nights in argument
Until her voice grew shrill. 20
What voice more sweet than hers
When, young and beautiful,
She rode to harriers?[2]
This man had kept a school
And rode our wingéd horse;[3] 25
This other his helper and friend
Was coming into his force;
He might have won fame in the end,
So sensitive his nature seemed,
So daring and sweet his thought. 30
This other man I had dreamed
A drunken, vainglorious lout.[4]
He had done most bitter wrong
To some who are near my heart,
Yet I number him in the song; 35
He, too, has resigned his part
In the casual comedy;
He, too, has been changed in his turn,
Transformed utterly:
A terrible beauty is born. 40

Hearts with one purpose alone
Through summer and winter seem
Enchanted to a stone
To trouble the living stream.
The horse that comes from the road, 45
The rider, the birds that range
From cloud to tumbling cloud,
Minute by minute they change;
A shadow of cloud on the stream
Changes minute by minute; 50
A horse-hoof slides on the brim,
And a horse plashes within it;
The long-legged moorhens dive,
And hens to moorcocks call;
Minute by minute they live: 55
The stone's in the midst of all.

Too long a sacrifice
Can make a stone of the heart.
O when may it suffice?

2. Constance Gore-Booth (afterwards Countess Markiewicz), a member of the Sligo county aristocracy. A gay and beautiful girl, she had annoyed Yeats by becoming an embittered nationalist.
3. Patrick Pearse, who was a schoolmaster, a leader in the movement to restore the Gaelic language in Ireland, and a poet (hence the reference to "our wingéd horse"—Pegasus, the horse of the Muses). "His helper and friend" was Thomas MacDonagh.
4. Major John MacBride. Maud Gonne, to Yeats's great disgust, had married MacBride in 1903, only to be separated from him after two years.

That is Heaven's part, our part   60
To murmur name upon name,
As a mother names her child
When sleep at last has come
On limbs that had run wild.
What is it but nightfall?   65
No, no, not night but death;
Was it needless death after all?
For England may keep faith
For all that is done and said.
We know their dream; enough   70
To know they dreamed and are dead;
And what if excess of love
Bewildered them till they died?
I write it out in a verse—
MacDonagh and MacBride   75
And Connolly[5] and Pearse
Now and in time to be,
Wherever green is worn,
Are changed, changed utterly:
A terrible beauty is born.   80

                                    1916, 1920

On a Political Prisoner[1]

She that but little patience knew,
From childhood on, had now so much
A gray gull lost its fear and flew
Down to her cell and there alit,
And there endured her fingers' touch   5
And from her fingers ate its bit.

Did she in touching that lone wing
Recall the years before her mind
Became a bitter, an abstract thing,
Her thought some popular enmity: 10
Blind and leader of the blind
Drinking the foul ditch where they lie?

When long ago I saw her ride
Under Ben Bulben[2] to the meet,
The beauty of her countryside   15
With all youth's lonely wildness stirred,
She seemed to have grown clean and sweet
Like any rock-bred, sea-borne bird:

Sea-borne, or balanced on the air
When first it sprang out of the nest   20

5. James Connolly, Pearse's partner in
leading the insurrection. Like the other
rebels named here, he was executed by
shooting.
1. Constance Gore-Booth Markiewicz,
who was imprisoned after the Easter

Rebellion. She also figures in *Easter
1916.*
2. Mountain in County Sligo. The Gore-
Booths lived at Lissadell, not far from
Ben Bulben.

Upon some lofty rock to stare
Upon the cloudy canopy,
While under its storm-beaten breast
Cried out the hollows of the sea.

1920, 1921

The Second Coming[1]

Turning and turning in the widening gyre
The falcon cannot hear the falconer;
Things fall apart; the center cannot hold;
Mere anarchy is loosed upon the world,
The blood-dimmed tide is loosed, and everywhere   5
The ceremony of innocence is drowned;
The best lack all conviction, while the worst
Are full of passionate intensity.[2]

Surely some revelation is at hand;   10
Surely the Second Coming is at hand.
The Second Coming! Hardly are those words out
When a vast image out of *Spiritus Mundi*[3]
Troubles my sight: somewhere in sands of the desert
A shape with lion body and the head of a man,
A gaze blank and pitiless as the sun,   15
Is moving its slow thighs, while all about it
Reel shadows of the indignant desert birds.
The darkness drops again; but now I know
That twenty centuries of stony sleep
Were vexed to nightmare by a rocking cradle,[4]   20

1. This poem expresses Yeats's sense of the dissolution of the civilization of his time, the end of one cycle of history and the approach of another. He called each cycle of history a "gyre" (line 1) —literally a circular or spiral turn (Yeats pronounced it with a hard *g*). He imagines a falconer losing control of the falcon which sweeps in ever widening circles around him until it breaks away altogether, and sees this as a symbol of the end of the present gyre of civilization—what he once described as "all our scientific democratic fact-finding heterogeneous civilization." The birth of Christ brought to an end the cycle that had lasted from what Yeats called the "Babylonian mathematical starlight" (2000 B.C.) to the dissolution of Greco-Roman culture. "What if the irrational return?" Yeats asked in his prose work *A Vision.* "What if the circle begin again?" He speculates that "we may be about to accept the most implacable authority the world has known." The new Nativity ("the rough

beast" of lines 21–22) is deliberately mysterious, both terrible and regenerative.
2. Lines 4–8 refer to the Russian Revolution of 1917, seen as a portent, but later Yeats accepted the poem as an unconscious prophecy of the rise of Fascism also. Speaking in 1924, Yeats declared: "It is impossible not to ask oneself to what great task of the nations we have been summoned in this transformed world where there is so much that is obscure and terrible." "The ceremony of innocence" suggests Yeats's view of ritual as the basis of civilized living. Cf. the last stanza of *A Prayer for My Daughter.*
3. The Spirit or Soul of the Universe, with which all individual souls are connected through the "Great Memory," which Yeats held to be a universal subconscious in which the human race preserves its past memories. It is thus a source of symbolic images for the poet.
4. I.e., the cradle of the infant Christ.

And what rough beast, its hour come round at last,
Slouches towards Bethlehem to be born?

1920, 1921

A Prayer for My Daughter[1]

Once more the storm is howling, and half hid
Under this cradle-hood and coverlid
My child sleeps on. There is no obstacle
But Gregory's wood[2] and one bare hill
Whereby the haystack- and roof-leveling wind,   5
Bred on the Atlantic, can be stayed;
And for an hour I have walked and prayed
Because of the great gloom that is in my mind.

I have walked and prayed for this young child an hour
And heard the sea-wind scream upon the tower,   10
And under the arches of the bridge, and scream
In the elms above the flooded stream;
Imagining in excited reverie
That the future years had come,
Dancing to a frenzied drum,   15
Out of the murderous innocence of the sea.[3]

May she be granted beauty and yet not
Beauty to make a stranger's eye distraught,
Or hers before a looking glass, for such,
Being made beautiful overmuch,   20
Consider beauty a sufficient end,
Lose natural kindness and maybe
The heart-revealing intimacy
That chooses right, and never find a friend.

Helen being chosen found life flat and dull   25
And later had much trouble from a fool,[4]
While that great Queen, that rose out of the spray,[5]
Being fatherless could have her way
Yet chose a bandy-leggéd smith for man.
It's certain that fine women eat   30
A crazy salad with their meat
Whereby the Horn of Plenty[6] is undone.

1. Yeats's daughter, christened Anne Butler, was born on February 26, 1919, in the refitted Norman tower of Thoor Ballylee (Ballylee Castle) in Galway, where Yeats lived: it is not far from Coole Park. The wind from the Atlantic roared in constantly (lines 1, 5–6).
2. Originally part of the Gregory estate, which had once also included Thoor Ballylee.
3. A reference to Yeats's visions of the future (cf. *The Second Coming*).

4. Presumably Paris, who carried Helen off from her husband.
5. Venus, wife (in the *Odyssey* and later accounts) of Vulcan, "bandy-legged" god of fire and forge (line 29).
6. The traditional image of the "Horn of Plenty" is generally associated by Yeats not only with abundance of the good things of the earth but also with the good life, conceived to be based on order and elegance (see concluding lines).

In courtesy I'd have her chiefly learned;
Hearts are not had as a gift but hearts are earned
By those that are not entirely beautiful;   35
Yet many, that have played the fool
For beauty's very self, has charm made wise,
And many a poor man that has roved,
Loved and thought himself beloved,
From a glad kindness cannot take his eyes.   40

May she become a flourishing hidden tree
That all her thoughts may like the linnet[7] be,
And have no business but dispensing round
Their magnanimities of sound,
Nor but in merriment begin a chase,   45
Nor but in merriment a quarrel.
O may she live like some green laurel
Rooted in one dear perpetual place.

My mind, because the minds that I have loved,
The sort of beauty that I have approved,   50
Prosper but little, has dried up of late,
Yet knows that to be choked with hate
May well be of all evil chances chief.
If there's no hatred in a mind
Assault and battery of the wind   55
Can never tear the linnet from the leaf.

An intellectual hatred is the worst,
So let her think opinions are accursed.
Have I not seen the loveliest woman born[8]
Out of the mouth of Plenty's horn,   60
Because of her opinionated mind
Barter that horn and every good
By quiet natures understood
For an old bellows full of angry wind?

Considering that, all hatred driven hence,   65
The soul recovers radical innocence
And learns at last that it is self-delighting,
Self-appeasing, self-affrighting,
And that its own sweet will is Heaven's will;
She can, though every face should scowl   70
And every windy quarter howl
Or every bellows burst, be happy still.

And may her bridegroom bring her to a house
Where all's accustomed, ceremonious;
For arrogance and hatred are the wares   75
Peddled in the thoroughfares.
How but in custom and in ceremony
Are innocence and beauty born?

7. A small European songbird.   8. Maud Gonne.

Ceremony's a name for the rich horn,
And custom for the spreading laurel tree.   80
June, 1919   1919, 1921

Sailing to Byzantium[1]

1

That is no country for old men. The young
In one another's arms, birds in the trees
—Those dying generations—at their song,
The salmon-falls, the mackerel-crowded seas,
Fish, flesh, or fowl, commend all summer long   5
Whatever is begotten, born, and dies.
Caught in that sensual music all neglect
Monuments of unaging intellect.

2

An aged man is but a paltry thing,
A tattered coat upon a stick, unless   10
Soul clap its hands and sing, and louder sing
For every tatter in its mortal dress,
Nor is there singing school but studying
Monuments of its own magnificence;
And therefore I have sailed the seas and come   15
To the holy city of Byzantium.

3

O sages standing in God's holy fire
As in the gold mosaic of a wall,[2]
Come from the holy fire, perne in a gyre,[3]
And be the singing-masters of my soul.   20
Consume my heart away; sick with desire

1. This poem should be read together with *Byzantium*. Byzantium had become for Yeats the symbol of art or artifice as opposed to the natural world of biological activity, and as he grew older he turned away from the sensual world of growth and change to the timeless world of art (though he returned to the sensual world later on). He wrote in *A Vision:* "I think that if I could be given a month of antiquity and leave to spend it where I chose, I would spend it in Byzantium [modern Istanbul] a little before Justinian opened St. Sophia and closed the Academy of Plato [i.e., ca. A.D. 535]. * * * I think that in early Byzantium, maybe never before or since in recorded history, religious, aesthetic, and practical life were one, that architects and artificers * * * spoke to the multitude in gold and silver. The painter, the mosaic worker, the worker in gold and silver, the illuminator of sacred books were almost impersonal, almost perhaps without the consciousness of individual design, absorbed in their subject matter and that the vision of a whole people." In his old age, the poet repudiates the world of biological change (of birth, growth, and death), putting behind him images of breeding and sensuality to turn to "monuments of unaging intellect," in a world of art and artifice outside of time. The theme of this poem, though not the treatment, is similar to that of Keats's *Ode on a Grecian Urn.* Note that the stanza form is *ottava rima,* used with great originality in the placing of pauses.

2. Like the mosaic figures on the walls of the Church of Hagia Sophia ("Holy Wisdom") in Byzantium.

3. I.e., whirl round in a spiral motion. "Perne" (or "pirn") is literally a bobbin, reel, or spool, on which something is wound. It became a favorite word of Yeats's, used as a verb meaning "to spin round"; he associated the spinning with the spinning of fate. Here he asks the saints on the wall to descend in this symbolic spinning motion and help him to enter into their state.

And fastened to a dying animal
It knows not what it is; and gather me
Into the artifice of eternity.

4

Once out of nature I shall never take   25
My bodily form from any natural thing,
But such a form as Grecian goldsmiths make
Of hammered gold and gold enameling
To keep a drowsy Emperor awake;[4]
Or set upon a golden bough to sing   30
To lords and ladies of Byzantium
Of what is past, or passing, or to come.

1927   1927

Leda and the Swan[1]

A sudden blow: the great wings beating still
Above the staggering girl, her thighs caressed
By the dark webs, her nape caught in his bill,
He holds her helpless breast upon his breast.

How can those terrified vague fingers push   5
The feathered glory from her loosening thighs?
And how can body, laid in that white rush,
But feel the strange heart beating where it lies?

A shudder in the loins engenders there
The broken wall, the burning roof and tower[2]   10
And Agamemnon dead.
                              Being so caught up,
So mastered by the brute blood of the air,
Did she put on his knowledge with his power
Before the indifferent beak could let her drop?

1923   1924, 1928

4. "I have read somewhere," Yeats wrote, "that in the Emperor's palace at Byzantium was a tree made of gold and silver, and artificial birds that sang." Cf. also Hans Christian Andersen's *Emperor's Nightingale*, which may have been in Yeats's mind at the time.
1. In Greek mythology Zeus visited Leda in the form of a swan. As a result of the union Leda gave birth to Helen and to Clytemnestra (wife of Agamemnon). Yeats saw Zeus's visit to Leda as an "annunciation," marking the beginning of Greek civilization: "I imagine the annunciation that founded Greece as made to Leda, remembering that they showed in a Spartan temple, strung up to the roof as a holy relic, an unhatched egg of hers, and that from one of her eggs came love and from the other war" (*A Vision*). In the original Cuala Press edition Yeats noted: "I wrote *Leda and the Swan* because the editor of a political review asked me for a poem. I thought, 'After the individualist, demagogic movement, founded by Hobbes and popularized by the Encyclopedists and the French Revolution, we have a soil so exhausted that it cannot grow that crop again for centuries.' Then I thought, 'Nothing is now possible but some movement from above preceded by some violent annunciation.' My fancy began to play with Leda and the Swan for metaphor, and I began this poem; but as I wrote, bird and lady took such possession of the scene that all politics went out of it, and my friend tells me that his 'conservative readers would misunderstand the poem.'" Note that this poem is in sonnet form; the placing of the pauses gives it a rhetorical pattern not normally associated with the sonnet.
2. I.e., the destruction of Troy, caused by Helen's elopement with the Trojan Paris. Agamemnon was murdered by his wife Clytemnestra, the other daughter of Leda and the Swan.

Among School Children

1

I walk through the long schoolroom questioning;
A kind old nun in a white hood replies;
The children learn to cipher and to sing,
To study reading-books and history,
To cut and sew, be neat in everything   5
In the best modern way—the children's eyes
In momentary wonder stare upon
A sixty-year-old smiling public man.

2

I dream of a Ledaean body,[1] bent
Above a sinking fire, a tale that she   10
Told of a harsh reproof, or trivial event
That changed some childish day to tragedy—
Told, and it seemed that our two natures blent
Into a sphere from youthful sympathy,
Or else, to alter Plato's parable,   15
Into the yolk and white of the one shell.[2]

3

And thinking of that fit of grief or rage
I look upon one child or t'other there
And wonder if she stood so at that age—
For even daughters of the swan can share   20
Something of every paddler's heritage—
And had that color upon cheek or hair,
And thereupon my heart is driven wild:
She stands before me as a living child.

4

Her present image floats into the mind—   25
Did Quattrocento[3] finger fashion it
Hollow of cheek as though it drank the wind
And took a mess of shadows for its meat?
And I though never of Ledaean kind
Had pretty plumage once—enough of that,   30
Better to smile on all that smile, and show
There is a comfortable kind of old scarecrow.

5

What youthful mother, a shape upon her lap
Honey of generation had betrayed,

---

1. "Ledaean": adjective from "Leda," meaning "like Helen of Troy" (Leda's daughter). The reference is to Maud Gonne (as also in lines 19–28).
2. In Plato's *Symposium* Aristophanes explains Love by supposing that "the primeval man was round and had four hands and four feet, back and sides forming a circle, one head with two faces," and was subsequently divided into two. "After the division, the two parts of man, each desiring his other half, came together, and threw their arms about one another eager to grow into one." The fact that Helen was born from an egg (as the daughter of Leda and the Swan) suggests Yeats's image for such a union.
3. 15th-century; a reference to Italian painters of the period, especially Botticelli (ca. 1444–1510).

And that must sleep, shriek, struggle to escape   35
As recollection or the drug decide,[4]
Would think her son, did she but see that shape
With sixty or more winters on its head,
A compensation for the pang of his birth,
Or the uncertainty of his setting forth?   40

6

Plato thought nature but a spume that plays
Upon a ghostly paradigm of things;
Solider Aristotle played the taws
Upon the bottom of a king of kings;[5]
World-famous golden-thighed Pythagoras[6]   45
Fingered upon a fiddle-stick or strings
What a star sang and careless Muses heard:
Old clothes upon old sticks to scare a bird.[7]

7

Both nuns and mothers worship images,[8]
But those the candles light are not as those   50
That animate a mother's reveries,
But keep a marble or a bronze repose.
And yet they too break hearts—O Presences
That passion, piety, or affection knows,
And that all heavenly glory symbolize—   55
O self-born mockers of man's enterprise;

8

Labor is blossoming or dancing where
The body is not bruised to pleasure soul,
Nor beauty born out of its own despair,
Nor blear-eyed wisdom out of midnight oil.   60
O chestnut tree, great-rooted blossomer,
Are you the leaf, the blossom, or the bole?
O body swayed to music, O brightening glance,
How can we know the dancer from the dance?[9]

1927

4. "I have taken the 'honey of generation' from Porphyry's essay on 'The Cave of the Nymphs,' but find no warrant in Porphyry for considering it the 'drug' that destroys the 'recollection' of prenatal freedom" [Yeats's note]. Porphyry was a Neo-Platonic philosopher of the 3rd century A.D. "Honey of generation," by blotting out the memory of prenatal happiness, "betrays" an infant to be born into this world. The infant will either "sleep" or "struggle to escape" (from this world) depending on whether the drug works or the recollection of blissful prenatal life overcomes the oblivion caused by the drug.
5. Plato thought nature was a mere appearance ("spume") veiling the ultimate spiritual and mathematical reality ("ghostly paradigm"); Aristotle was "solider" in that he believed that form really inhered in the matter of nature, and thus that nature itself had reality.

Aristotle was tutor to Alexander the Great, and disciplined him by applying the "taws" or strap.
6. Greek philosopher (early 6th century B.C.), interested in mathematics and the mathematical study of acoustics and music; his disciples, the Pythagoreans, developed a mystical philosophy of numerical relations and united the notions of astronomical and mathematical relations in the theory of the music of the spheres. Pythagoreans regarded their master with veneration as a god with a golden thigh.
7. A contemptuous description of the philosophies of Plato, Aristotle, and Pythagoras.
8. Nuns worship images of Christ or the Virgin; mothers worship their own inward images of their children.
9. Yeats's view of life as a cosmic dance, in which every human faculty joins harmoniously. The individual be-

A Dialogue of Self and Soul[1]

1

MY SOUL. I summon to the winding ancient stair;
    Set all your mind upon the steep ascent,
    Upon the broken, crumbling battlement,
    Upon the breathless starlit air,
    Upon the star that marks the hidden pole;   5
    Fix every wandering thought upon
    That quarter where all thought is done:
    Who can distinguish darkness from the soul?

MY SELF. The consecrated blade upon my knees
    Is Sato's ancient blade,[2] still as it was,   10
    Still razor-keen, still like a looking glass
    Unspotted by the centuries;
    That flowering, silken, old embroidery, torn
    From some court lady's dress and round
    The wooden scabbard bound and wound,   15
    Can, tattered, still protect, faded adorn.

MY SOUL. Why should the imagination of a man
    Long past his prime remember things that are
    Emblematical of love and war?
    Think of ancestral night that can,   20
    If but imagination scorn the earth
    And intellect its wandering
    To this and that and t'other thing,
    Deliver from the crime of death and birth.

MY SELF. Montashigi, third of his family, fashioned it   25
    Five hundred years ago, about it lie
    Flowers from I know not what embroidery—
    Heart's purple—and all these I set
    For emblems of the day against the tower
    Emblematical of the night,   30
    And claim as by a soldier's right
    A charter to commit the crime once more.

comes involved in the process, as the dancer becomes part of the dance. Yeats relates the idea of the cosmic dance to his views of ritual, elegance, and order (cf. "the ceremony of innocence" in *The Second Coming* and the end of *Prayer for my Daughter*), and sees it as a means of reconciling the conflicting opposites of ordinary life.

1. Yeats here debates two opposing claims: the soul's summons to wisdom, resignation from an active life, the spiritual ascent—symbolized by the winding stair, a symbol similar to that of Byzantium—against the summons to the life of action and passion, symbolized by the sword of the second stanza and championed by the "Self."

2. A Japanese called Sato had given Yeats a sword, telling him that it was a symbol of life and that its silk-embroidered sheath was a symbol of beauty. Thus the sword in its scabbard is "emblematical of love and war" (line 19) and represents the "day," as opposed to the "night" represented by the tower and the winding stair (lines 29–30).

MY SOUL. Such fullness in that quarter overflows
  And falls into the basin of the mind
  That man is stricken deaf and dumb and blind,   35
  For intellect no longer knows
  Is from the *Ought*, or *Knower* from the *Known*—
  That is to say, ascends to Heaven;
  Only the dead can be forgiven;
  But when I think of that my tongue's a stone.   40

2

MY SELF. A living man is blind and drinks his drop.
  What matter if the ditches are impure?
  What matter if I live it all once more?
  Endure that toil of growing up;
  The ignominy of boyhood; the distress   45
  Of boyhood changing into man;
  The unfinished man and his pain
  Brought face to face with his own clumsiness;

  The finished man among his enemies?—
  How in the name of Heaven can he escape   50
  That defiling and disfigured shape
  The mirror of malicious eyes
  Casts upon his eyes until at last
  He thinks that shape must be his shape?
  And what's the good of an escape   55
  If honor find him in the wintry blast?

  I am content to live it all again
  And yet again, if it be life to pitch
  Into the frog-spawn of a blind man's ditch,
  A blind man battering blind men;   60
  Or into that most fecund ditch of all,
  The folly that man does
  Or must suffer, if he woos
  A proud woman not kindred of his soul.

  I am content to follow to its source   65
  Every event in action or in thought;
  Measure the lot; forgive myself the lot!
  When such as I cast out remorse
  So great a sweetness flows into the breast
  We must laugh and we must sing,   70
  We are blest by everything,
  Everything we look upon is blest.

1929

For Anne Gregory

  "Never shall a young man,
    Thrown into despair
  By those great honey-colored

Ramparts at your ear,
Love you for yourself alone   5
And not your yellow hair."

"But I can get a hair-dye
And set such color there,
Brown, or black, or carrot,
That young men in despair   10
May love me for myself alone
And not my yellow hair."

"I heard an old religious man
But yesternight declare
That he had found a text to prove   15
That only God, my dear,
Could love you for yourself alone
And not your yellow hair."

1931, 1932

Byzantium[1]

The unpurged images of day recede;
The Emperor's drunken soldiery are abed;
Night resonance recedes, night-walkers' song
After great cathedral gong;
A starlit or a moonlit dome[2] disdains   5

1. The world of artifice and eternity to which Yeats journeyed in *Sailing to Byzantium* is now seen also as the world of death and spiritual purification from the "mire or blood" of life. As the poem opens, the "unpurged images of day" and then "night resonance" recede after the sounding of the gong at midnight (symbolic of the summons to death)—i.e., images of both the conscious (day) mind and the subconscious (night) mind depart, leaving the self in the hushed starlight or moonlight, purged of the "mere complexities" of flesh-and-blood life. This purified self "disdains" the confusion and murkiness of the unpurified self. In the second stanza the soul, released from what Yeats once called "the strain one upon another of opposites" of ordinary life, sees his spirit-guide leading him to the world of changelessness and purity. He hails this guide (a mediating figure between man, image, and shade) because he is now far enough beyond life to be able to do so. The third stanza shows the poet in the midst of the death-world of artifice and eternity, admiring the golden artifacts which, "in glory of changeless metal" (line 22), scorn the "complexities" and impurities of earthly creatures. In the next stanza the poet sees purgatorial fires burning away the "complexities" of bodily life; yet, unlike earthly flame which consumes as it burns, this flame "cannot singe a sleeve" (line 32). Finally, the poet finds himself no longer clearly in the world of pure spirit: he is pulled back by the tug of human emotion. He sees the smithies of the metalworkers buttressing the city against the dark tides of impurity and lust, while the dance of eternal life on the cold marble floor similarly helps to stem the flood (these are Platonic and Neo-Platonic images). But art and artifice cannot succeed in repelling the sensual life that beats against the city walls: in the end, human images break through and "beget" yet further images (cf. *Sailing to Byzantium*, in which he wanted to escape from "whatever is begotten, born, and dies"). The poem concludes on a note of human passion, "that dolphin-torn, that gong-tormented sea." In this instance, the gong is calling the poet back to life, not from life to death. He has discovered that art is nourished by life and in the end leads back to it. Yeats himself said that this poem was written "to warm myself back to life" after a serious illness.

2. "Starlit" and "moonlit" had a special symbolic significance for Yeats, as part of his theory of history and personality

All that man is,
All mere complexities,
The fury and the mire of human veins.

Before me floats an image, man or shade,
Shade more than man, more image than a shade;   10
For Hades' bobbin bound in mummy-cloth
May unwind the winding path;[3]
A mouth that has no moisture and no breath
Breathless mouths may summon;
I hail the superhuman;   15
I call it death-in-life and life-in-death.

Miracle, bird or golden handiwork,
More miracle than bird or handiwork,
Planted on the starlit golden bough,[4]
Can like the cocks of Hades crow,   20
Or, by the moon embittered, scorn aloud
In glory of changeless metal
Common bird or petal
And all complexities of mire or blood.

At midnight on the Emperor's pavement flit   25
Flames that no faggot feeds, nor steel has lit,
Nor storm disturbs, flames begotten of flame,
Where blood-begotten spirits come
And all complexities of fury leave,
Dying into a dance,   30
An agony of trance,
An agony of flame[5] that cannot singe a sleeve.

Astraddle on the dolphin's mire and blood,[6]
Spirit after spirit! The smithies break the flood,

in terms of the phases of the moon (in *A Vision*). The first phase—that of the dark of the moon, when only the stars shine—is the phase when "body is completely absorbed in its supernatural environment." The fifteenth phase—the full moon—is the phase of complete subjectivity, where the mind is "completely absorbed by being." Thus both phases are states of *being:* they reject the complexities of the world of *becoming* and change.

In the Cuala Press edition of 1932, "disdains" is printed as "distains" (i.e., discolors, pollutes); all subsequent printings, however, read "disdains." It has been argued that the first reading must be correct, but it makes less sense, and Yeats never corrected the "disdains" in later printings.
3. The spool of man's fate, which spins his destiny and which is symbolized by the wrappings around a mummy, may lead man, as it unwinds, to the realm of pure spirit (or up the winding stair, in another of Yeats's favorite images).
4. The "starlit golden bough" is part of the death-world of artifice and eter-

nity; it is opposed to a real, living bough, which would be lighted by the sun or the moon (cf. note 2). The bough is also associated with the mystical tree of the esoteric Hebrew doctrine of the cabala, in whose branches "the birds lodge and build their nests; that is, the souls or angels have their place." The "cocks of Hades" are the birds standing outside time whose crowing proclaims the cycles of rebirth to mortal beings: the golden birds of art, who live in the same tree, are similarly eternal.
5. The "agony of flame" was suggested to Yeats by a Japanese *Nō* play, *Motomezulka*, wherein a young girl suffers from perpetual burning, which is a sense of her own guilt. A priest tells her that the flames will cease if she no longer believes in their reality; she finds herself incapable of disbelief, however, and the play ends in "the dance of her agony."
6. The dolphin, in ancient art, was a symbol of the soul in transit from one state to another. Mounted on its back, the poet here is able to ride over the

The golden smithies of the Emperor!   35
Marbles of the dancing floor
Break bitter furies of complexity,
Those images that yet
Fresh images beget,
That dolphin-torn, that gong-tormented sea.   40

1930   1932

Crazy Jane Talks with the Bishop[1]

I met the Bishop on the road
And much said he and I.
"Those breasts are flat and fallen now,
Those veins must soon be dry;
Live in a heavenly mansion,   5
Not in some foul sty."

"Fair and foul are near of kin,
And fair needs foul," I cried.
"My friends are gone, but that's a truth
Nor grave nor bed denied,   10
Learned in bodily lowliness
And in the heart's pride.

"A woman can be proud and stiff
When on love intent;
But Love has pitched his mansion in   15
The place of excrement;
For nothing can be sole or whole
That has not been rent."

1932

After Long Silence

Speech after long silence; it is right,
All other lovers being estranged or dead,
Unfriendly lamplight hid under its shade,
The curtains drawn upon unfriendly night,
That we descant and yet again descant   5
Upon the supreme theme of Art and Song:
Bodily decrepitude is wisdom; young
We loved each other and were ignorant.

1932

sea of human passions—except that the
dolphin itself is made of "mire or
blood."
1. One of a series of poems dealing
with the paradox that wisdom may reside with fools and beggars (such as
Jane) rather than with the respectable
representatives of orthodoxy (such as
the Bishop). This poem also deals with
a favorite Yeatsian theme, the resolution of opposites, of what he called
elsewhere "all those antinomies / Of
day and night."

Lapis Lazuli[1]

(FOR HARRY CLIFTON)

I have heard that hysterical women say
They are sick of the palette and fiddle bow,
Of poets that are always gay,
For everybody knows or else should know
That if nothing drastic is done   5
Aeroplane and Zeppelin will come out,
Pitch like King Billy[2] bomb-balls in
Until the town lie beaten flat.

All perform their tragic play,
There struts Hamlet, there is Lear,   10
That's Ophelia, that Cordelia;
Yet they, should the last scene be there,
The great stage curtain about to drop,
If worthy their prominent part in the play,
Do not break up their lines to weep.   15
They know that Hamlet and Lear are gay;
Gaiety transfiguring all that dread.
All men have aimed at, found and lost;
Black out; Heaven blazing into the head:
Tragedy wrought to its uttermost.   20
Though Hamlet rambles and Lear rages,
And all the drop-scenes drop at once
Upon a hundred thousand stages,
It cannot grow by an inch or an ounce.

On their own feet they came, or on shipboard,   25
Camel-back, horse-back, ass-back, mule-back,
Old civilizations put to the sword.
Then they and their wisdom went to rack:
No handiwork of Callimachus,[3]
Who handled marble as if it were bronze,   30

1. A deep blue stone. "I notice that you have much lapis lazuli; someone has sent me a present of a great piece carved by some Chinese sculptor into the semblance of a mountain with temple, trees, paths, and an ascetic and pupil about to climb the mountain. Ascetic, pupil, hard stone, eternal theme of the sensual east. The heroic cry in the midst of despair. But no, I am wrong, the east has its solutions always and therefore knows nothing of tragedy. It is we, not the east, that must raise the heroic cry" (Yeats to Dorothy Wellesley, July 6, 1935).
2. King William III (William of Orange), who defeated the army of King James II at the Battle of the Boyne in 1690.
3. Greek sculptor (5th century B.C.), supposedly the originator of the Corinthian column and of the use of the running drill to imitate folds in drapery in statues. Yeats wrote of him: "With Callimachus pure Ionic revives again * * * and upon the only example of his work known to us, a marble chair, a Persian is represented, and may one not discover a Persian symbol in that bronze lamp, shaped like a palm * * * ? But he was an archaistic workman, and those who set him to work brought back public life to an older form" (*A Vision*).

Made draperies that seemed to rise
When sea wind swept the corner, stands;
His long lamp chimney shaped like the stem
Of a slender palm, stood but a day;
All things fall and are built again,   35
And those that build them again are gay.

Two Chinamen, behind them a third,
Are carved in lapis lazuli,
Over them flies a long-legged bird,
A symbol of longevity;   40
The third, doubtless a servingman,
Carries a musical instrument.

Every discoloration of the stone,
Every accidental crack or dent,
Seems a watercourse or an avalanche,   45
Or lofty slope where it still snows
Though doubtless plum or cherry branch
Sweetens the little halfway house
Those Chinamen climb towards, and I
Delight to imagine them seated there;   50
There, on the mountain and the sky,
On all the tragic scene they stare.
One asks for mournful melodies;
Accomplished fingers begin to play.
Their eyes mid many wrinkles, their eyes,   55
Their ancient, glittering eyes, are gay.

                                                          1938

Long-legged Fly[1]

That civilization may not sink,
Its great battle lost,
Quiet the dog, tether the pony
To a distant post;
Our master Caesar is in the tent   5
Where the maps are spread,
His eyes fixed upon nothing,
A hand under his head.
Like a long-legged fly upon the stream
His mind moves upon silence.   10

1. The first stanza shows Caesar planning one of his history-making campaigns: any disturbing noise now will
alter the course of civilization. In the
next stanza Helen of Troy as a child
practices a part: the future of Troy
and of the ancient world depends
on her being allowed to train herself to
be a woman. Finally, Michelangelo
works in the Sistine Chapel in Rome: he
must be undisturbed if his art is to be
unspoiled, so that it can give to future
generations of "girls at puberty" their
first disturbing thoughts of men.

That the topless towers[2] be burnt
And men recall that face,
Move most gently if move you must
In this lonely place.
She thinks, part woman, three parts a child,   15
That nobody looks; her feet
Practice a tinker shuffle
Picked up on a street.
Like a long-legged fly upon the stream
Her mind moves upon silence.   20

That girls at puberty may find
The first Adam in their thought,
Shut the door of the Pope's chapel,
Keep those children out.
There on that scaffolding reclines   25
Michael Angelo.
With no more sound than the mice make
His hand moves to and fro.
Like a long-legged fly upon the stream
His mind moves upon silence.   30

1939

The Circus Animals' Desertion[1]

1

I sought a theme and sought for it in vain,
I sought it daily for six weeks or so.
Maybe at last, being but a broken man,
I must be satisfied with my heart, although
Winter and summer till old age began   5
My circus animals were all on show,
Those stilted boys, that burnished chariot,
Lion and woman[2] and the Lord knows what.

2

What can I but enumerate old themes?
First that sea-rider Oisin[3] led by the nose   10
Through three enchanted islands, allegorical dreams,
Vain gaiety, vain battle, vain repose,
Themes of the embittered heart, or so it seems,
That might adorn old songs or courtly shows;

2. Of Troy. Cf. "Was this the face that launched a thousand ships / And burnt the topless towers of Ilium?" (Marlowe, *Dr. Faustus*).
1. Yeats in old age looks back on some of the main themes of his poems and plays as circus animals that have now deserted him, leaving him with only the refuse of his human passions.
2. Cf. "On the gray rock of Cashel I suddenly saw / A Sphinx with **woman** breast and lion paw * * * " (Yeats, *The Double Vision of Michael Robartes*).
3. Pronounced *Ushéen.* Hero of an Old Irish legend, he was beguiled by a fairy woman to the fairy world and returned 150 years later to find his friends dead and Ireland Christian. Subject of an early long poem by Yeats (1889).

But what cared I that set him on to ride,   15
I, starved for the bosom of his faery bride?

And then a counter-truth filled out its play,
The Countess Cathleen was the name I gave it;
She, pity-crazed, had given her soul away,
But masterful Heaven had intervened to save it.[4]   20
I thought my dear must her own soul destroy,
So did fanaticism and hate enslave it,
And this brought forth a dream and soon enough
This dream itself had all my thought and love.

And when the Fool and Blind Man stole the bread   25
Cuchulain fought the ungovernable sea;[5]
Heart-mysteries there, and yet when all is said
It was the dream itself enchanted me:
Character isolated by a deed
To engross the present and dominate memory.   30
Players and painted stage took all my love,
And not those things that they were emblems of.

3
Those masterful images because complete
Grew in pure mind, but out of what began?
A mound of refuse or the sweepings of a street,   35
Old kettles, old bottles, and a broken can,
Old iron, old bones, old rags, that raving slut
Who keeps the till. Now that my ladder's gone,
I must lie down where all the ladders start,
In the foul rag-and-bone shop of the heart.   40

1939

Under Ben Bulben[1]

1
Swear by what the sages spoke
Round the Mareotic Lake[2]

4. Title of an early Yeats play (1892) about an Irish countess who, although she sold her soul to the devil to get food for the starving people, goes to Heaven anyway, for God looks "on the motive, not the deed."
5. In Yeats's play *On Baile's Strand* (1904), where he probes for symbolic meanings in an old Irish legend.
1. One of Yeats's last poems, ending with the epitaph he wrote for himself. He wished to be buried in the churchyard of the village of Drumcliff, which lies "under Ben Bulben," mountain in County Sligo. Although he died on the French Riviera, his body was later brought back and buried at Drumcliff.

2. Lake Mareotis, bordering the city of Alexandria where a school of Neo-Pythagorean philosophers flourished in the 1st century A.D. By Lake Mareotis also flourished (3rd century A.D.) the Christian Neo-Platonists, in whom Yeats was much interested. The lake is mentioned in Shelley's poem *The Witch of Atlas*, a poem which Yeats admired and interpreted in his own way, seeing the Witch as a symbol of timeless, absolute beauty; hence what she "knew" and "spoke"; and what "set the cocks a-crow" can be related to the "miracle" that "can like the cocks of Hades crow" in *Byzantium*.

That the Witch of Atlas knew,
Spoke and set the cocks a-crow.

Swear by those horsemen, by those women   5
Complexion and form prove superhuman,[3]
That pale, long-visaged company
That air in immortality
Completeness of their passions won;
Now they ride the wintry dawn   10
Where Ben Bulben sets the scene.

Here's the gist of what they mean.

2

Many times man lives and dies
Between his two eternities,
That of race and that of soul,   15
And ancient Ireland knew it all.
Whether man die in his bed
Or the rifle knocks him dead,
A brief parting from those dear
Is the worst man has to fear.   20
Though gravediggers' toil is long,
Sharp their spades, their muscles strong,
They but thrust their buried men
Back in the human mind again.

3

You that Mitchel's prayer have heard,   25
"Send war in our time, O Lord!"[4]
Know that when all words are said
And a man is fighting mad,
Something drops from eyes long blind,
He completes his partial mind,   30
For an instant stands at ease,
Laughs aloud, his heart at peace.
Even the wisest man grows tense
With some sort of violence
Before he can accomplish fate,   35
Know his work or choose his mate.

4

Poet and sculptor, do the work,
Nor let the modish painter shirk
What his great forefathers did,
Bring the soul of man to God,   40
Make him fill the cradles right.

Measurement began our might:
Forms a stark Egyptian thought,

3. The *sidhe* or fairy folk, who were believed to ride through the countryside near Ben Bulben. The gist of Yeats's thought here is: "Swear by those who speak superhuman, eternal truths." These truths are summed up in the second section of the poem: man has an afterlife both in the future of his individual soul and in the memory he leaves behind on earth.
4. John Mitchel, an Irish patriot imprisoned for his activities, wrote in his *Jail Journal*: "Give us war in our time, O Lord!"

Forms that gentler Phidias wrought.[5]
Michael Angelo left a proof   45
On the Sistine Chapel roof,
Where but half-awakened Adam
Can disturb globe-trotting Madam
Till her bowels are in heat,[6]
Proof that there's a purpose set   50
Before the secret working mind:
Profane perfection of mankind.

Quattrocento[7] put in paint
On backgrounds for a God or Saint
Gardens where a soul's at ease;   55
Where everything that meets the eye,
Flowers and grass and cloudless sky,
Resemble forms that are or seem
When sleepers wake and yet still dream,
And when it's vanished still declare,   60
With only bed and bedstead there,
That heavens had opened.
                              Gyres run on;
When that greater dream had gone
Calvert and Wilson, Blake and Claude,[8]
Prepared a rest for the people of God,   65
Palmer's phrase, but after that
Confusion fell upon our thought.

                    5
Irish poets, learn your trade,
Sing whatever is well made,
Scorn the sort now growing up   70
All out of shape from toe to top,
Their unremembering hearts and heads
Base-born products of base beds.
Sing the peasantry, and then
Hard-riding country gentlemen,   75
The holiness of monks, and after
Porter-drinkers' randy laughter;
Sing the lords and ladies gay
That were beaten into the clay
Through seven heroic centuries;   80

5. Greek sculptor (5th century B.C.), generally thought to have raised the classical ideal in art to its highest culmination. Yeats here itemizes steps in his history of knowledge and the arts, beginning with Babylonian mathematics ("measurement"), through "stark Egyptian thought," to the Renaissance of Michelangelo. Each of these steps is related to Yeats's cyclical theory of history.
6. Cf. *Long-Legged Fly*, stanza 3.
7. 15th-century Italian art.
8. Works by the five artists mentioned in lines 64–66 all provided images for Yeats's poetry: Edward Calvert, 19th-century wood-engraver; Richard Wilson, 18th-century landscape painter; William Blake, "one of the great mythmakers and mask-makers"; Claude Lorrain, 17th-century landscape painter; and (in line 66) Samuel Palmer, 19th-century landscape painter and etcher, one of whose works was "The Lonely Tower." Calvert, Blake, and Palmer knew each other and shared a view of the holiness of art. (See T. R. Henn, *The Lonely Tower*, 1950.)

Cast your mind on other days
That we in coming days may be
Still the indomitable Irishry.

6

Under bare Ben Bulben's head
In Drumcliff churchyard Yeats is laid.   85
An ancestor was rector there
Long years ago, a church stands near,
By the road an ancient cross.
No marble, no conventional phrase;
On limestone quarried near the spot   90
By his command these words are cut:
  Cast a cold eye
  On life, on death.
  Horseman, pass by!

September 4, 1938   1939

From Reveries over Childhood and Youth[1]
[*The Yeats Family*]

Some six miles off towards Ben Bulben and beyond the Channel,[2] as we call the tidal river between Sligo and the Rosses, and on top of a hill there was a little square two-storied house covered with creepers and looking out upon a garden where the box borders were larger than any I had ever seen, and where I saw for the first time the crimson steak of the gladiolus and awaited its blossom with excitement. Under one gable a dark thicket of small trees made a shut-in mysterious place, where one played and believed that something was going to happen. My great-aunt Micky lived there. Micky was not her right name for she was Mary Yeats and her father had been my great-grandfather, John Yeats, who had been Rector of Drumcliffe, a few miles further off, and died in 1847. She was a spare, high-colored, elderly woman and had the oldest-looking cat I had ever seen, for its hair had grown into matted locks of yellowy white. She farmed and had one old manservant, but could not have farmed at all, had not neighboring farmers helped to gather in the crops, in return for the loan of her farm implements and "out of respect for the family," for as Johnny Mac-Gurk, the Sligo barber said to me, "The Yeatses were always very respectable." She was full of family history; all her dinner knives were pointed like daggers through much cleaning, and there was a little

---

1. Yeats wrote a variety of autobiographical essays between 1914 and 1928: these were originally published separately and later collected as *The Autobiography of W. B. Yeats* (1936, 1953). The selections given here are from *Reveries over Childhood and* *Youth,* first published in 1915, and *The Trembling of the Veil,* first published in 1922.
2. Yeats's favorite County Sligo landscape. Cf. the places named in *The Stolen Child.*

James the First cream-jug with the Yeats motto and crest, and on her dining-room mantelpiece a beautiful silver cup that had belonged to my great-great-grandfather, who had married a certain Mary Butler. It had upon it the Butler crest and had been already old at the date 1534, when the initials of some bride and bridegroom were engraved under the lip. All its history for generations was rolled up inside it upon a piece of paper yellow with age, until some caller took the paper to light his pipe.

Another family of Yeats, a widow and her two children on whom I called sometimes with my grandmother, lived near in a long low cottage, and owned a very fierce turkey cock that did battle with their visitors; and some miles away lived the secretary to the Grand Jury and Land Agent, my great-uncle Mat Yeats and his big family of boys and girls; but I think it was only in later years that I came to know them well. I do not think any of these liked the Pollexfens, who were well off and seemed to them purse-proud, whereas they themselves had come down in the world. I remember them as very well-bred and very religious in the Evangelical way and thinking a good deal of Aunt Micky's old histories. There had been among our ancestors a King's County soldier, one of Marlborough's[3] generals, and when his nephew came to dine he gave him boiled pork, and when the nephew said he disliked boiled pork he had asked him to dine again and promised him something he would like better. However, he gave him boiled pork again and the nephew took the hint in silence. The other day as I was coming home from America, I met one of his descendants whose family has not another discoverable link with ours, and he too knew the boiled pork story and nothing else. We have the General's portrait, and he looks very fine in his armor and his long curly wig, and underneath it, after his name, are many honors that have left no tradition among us. Were we country people, we could have summarized his life in a legend. Other ancestors or great-uncles bore a part in Irish history; one saved the life of Sarsfield[4] at the battle of Sedgemoor; another, taken prisoner by King James's army, owed his to Sarsfield's gratitude; another, a century later, roused the gentlemen of Meath[5] against some local Jacquère,[6] and was shot dead upon a county road, and yet another "chased the United Irishmen[7] for a fortnight, fell into their hands and was hanged." The notorious

3. John Churchill, Duke of Marlborough (1650–1722), English general in the War of the Spanish Succession (1702–13).
4. Patrick Sarsfield (d. 1693), Irish Jacobite general who served in the battle of Sedgemoor (1685) when the Duke of Monmouth, illegitimate son of Charles II who was claiming the throne from his uncle James II, was defeated and captured.
5. Maritime county in province of Lein-

ster, in the east of Ireland.
6. Peasant revolutionary. The "Jacquerie" was a peasants' revolt (1358) against the nobles in northern France (the term derived from *Jacques Bonhomme*, the nobility's contemptuous name for a peasant).
7. Irish society founded 1791 by Theobald Wolfe Tone which later was influential in causing the Irish rebellion of 1798.

Major Sirr, who arrested Lord Edward Fitzgerald[8] and gave him the bullet wound he died of in the jail, was godfather to several of my great-great-grandfather's children; while to make a balance, my great-grandfather had been Robert Emmett's[9] friend and was suspected and imprisoned though but for a few hours. One great-uncle fell at New Orleans in 1813, while another, who became Governor of Penang,[1] led the forlorn hope at the taking of Rangoon, and even in the last generation of all there had been lives of some power and pleasure. An old man who had entertained many famous people, in his eighteenth-century house, where battlement and tower showed the influence of Horace Walpole,[2] had but lately, after losing all his money, drowned himself, first taking off his rings and chain and watch as became a collector of many beautiful things; and once to remind us of more passionate life, a gunboat put into Rosses, commanded by the illegitimate son of some great-uncle or other. Now that I can look at their miniatures, turning them over to find the name of soldier, or lawyer, or Castle official,[3] and wondering if they cared for good books or good music, I am delighted with all that joins my life to those who had power in Ireland or with those anywhere that were good servants and poor bargainers, but I cared nothing as a child for Micky's tales. I could see my grandfather's ships come up the bay or the river, and his sailors treated me with deference, and a ship's carpenter made and mended my toy boats and I thought that nobody could be so important as my grandfather. Perhaps, too, it is only now that I can value those more gentle natures so unlike his passion and violence. An old Sligo priest has told me how my great-grandfather John Yeats always went into his kitchen rattling the keys, so much did he fear finding some one doing wrong, and of a speech of his when the agent of the great landowner of his parish brought him from cottage to cottage to bid the women send their children to the Protestant school. All promised till they came to one who cried, "Child of mine will never darken your door." "Thank you, my woman," he said, "you are the first honest woman I have met today." My uncle, Mat Yeats, the Land Agent, had once waited up every night for a week to catch some boys who stole his apples and when he caught them had given them sixpence and told them not to do it again. Perhaps it is only fancy or the softening touch of the miniaturist that makes me discover in their faces some courtesy and much gentleness. Two eighteenth-century faces interest me the

8. British officer (1763–98) who, after dismissal from the army for disloyal activities, joined the United Irishmen. Cf. *September 1913*, lines 19–22.

9. 1778–1803; Irish patriot, hanged at Dublin for treason.

1. Island in Malaya. Rangoon, capital of Burma, was taken by the British in 1824.

2. The 18th-century English author whose pseudo-Gothic house, Strawberry Hill, much influenced subsequent "Gothic" architecture in England and elsewhere.

3. I.e., official at Dublin Castle, where the Viceroy (representing the British Crown) lived with his staff before Irish independence was achieved in 1922.

most, one that of a great-great-grandfather, for both have under their powdered curling wigs a half-feminine charm, and as I look at them I discover a something clumsy and heavy in myself. Yet it was a Yeats who spoke the only eulogy that turns my head: "We have ideas and no passions, but by marriage with a Pollexfen we have given a tongue to the sea cliffs."

Among the miniatures there is a larger picture, an admirable drawing by I know not what master, that is too harsh and merry for its company. He was a connection and close friend of my great-grandmother Corbet, and though we spoke of him as "Uncle Beattie" in our childhood, no blood relation. My great-grandmother who died at ninety-three had many memories of him. He was the friend of Goldsmith and was accustomed to boast, clergyman though he was, that he belonged to a hunt club of which every member but himself had been hanged or transported for treason, and that it was not possible to ask him a question he could not reply to with a perfectly appropriate blasphemy or indecency.

[An Irish Literature]

From these debates, from O'Leary's[4] conversation, and from the Irish books he lent or gave me has come all I have set my hand to since. I had begun to know a great deal about the Irish poets who had written in English. I read with excitement books I should find unreadable today, and found romance in lives that had neither wit nor adventure. I did not deceive myself, I knew how often they wrote a cold and abstract language, and yet I who had never wanted to see the houses where Keats and Shelley lived would ask everybody what sort of place Inchedony was, because Callanan[5] had named after it a bad poem in the manner of *Childe Harold*. Walking home from a debate, I remember saying to some college student, "Ireland cannot put from her the habits learned from her old military civilization and from a church that prays in Latin. Those popular poets have not touched her heart, her poetry when it comes will be distinguished and lonely." O'Leary had once said to me, "Neither Ireland nor England knows the good from the bad in any art, but Ireland unlike England does not hate the good when it is pointed out to her." I began to plot and scheme how one might seal with the right image the soft wax before it began to harden. I had noticed that Irish Catholics among whom had been born so many political martyrs had not the good taste, the household courtesy and decency of the Protestant Ireland I had known, yet Protestant Ireland seemed to think of nothing but getting on in the world. I thought we might bring the halves together if we

4. John O'Leary (d. 1907), an Irish nationalist, for whom Yeats had great respect. Cf. *September 1913* ("Romantic Ireland's dead and gone, / It's with O'Leary in the grave").
5. Jeremiah John Callanan, Anglo-Irish poet, published *The Recluse of Inchedony and Other Poems* in 1830.

had a national literature that made Ireland beautiful in the memory, and yet had been freed from provincialism by an exacting criticism, an European pose.

1915

From The Trembling of the Veil
[*London and Pre-Raphaelitism*]

At the end of the 'eighties my father and mother, my brother and sisters and myself, all newly arrived from Dublin, were settled in Bedford Park in a red-brick house with several mantelpieces of wood, copied from marble mantelpieces designed by the brothers Adam,[1] a balcony and a little garden shadowed by a great horse-chestnut tree. Years before we had lived there, when the crooked ostentatiously picturesque streets with great trees casting great shadows had been a new enthusiasm: the Pre-Raphaelite movement at last affecting life. But now exaggerated criticism had taken the place of enthusiasm, the tiled roofs, the first in modern London, were said to leak, which they did not, and the drains to be bad, though that was no longer true; and I imagine that houses were cheap. I remember feeling disappointed because the co-operative stores, with their little seventeenth-century panes, had lost the romance I saw there when I passed them still unfinished on my way to school; and because the public-house, called The Tabard after Chaucer's Inn, was so plainly a common public-house; and because the great sign of a trumpeter designed by Rooke, the Pre-Raphaelite artist, had been freshened by some inferior hand. The big red-brick church had never pleased me, and I was accustomed, when I saw the wooden balustrade that ran along the slanting edge of the roof where nobody ever walked or could walk, to remember the opinion of some architect friend of my father's, that it had been put there to keep the birds from falling off. Still, however, it had some village characters and helped us to feel not wholly lost in the metropolis. I no longer went to church as a regular habit, but go I sometimes did, for one Sunday morning I saw these words painted on a board in the porch: "The congregation are requested to kneel during prayers; the kneelers are afterwards to be hung upon pegs provided for the purpose." In front of every seat hung a little cushion and these cushions were called "kneelers." Presently the joke ran through the community, where there were many artists who considered religion at best an unimportant accessory to good architecture and who disliked that particular church.

---

1. James and Robert, 18th-century Scottish architects and furniture designers who successfully adapted ancient Roman style in their work in England and Scotland.

I could not understand where the charm had gone that I had felt, when as a schoolboy of twelve or thirteen I had played among the unfinished houses, once leaving the marks of my two hands, blacked by a fall among some paint, upon a white balustrade.

Yet I was in all things Pre-Raphaelite. When I was fifteen or sixteen my father had told me about Rossetti and Blake and given me their poetry to read; and once at Liverpool on my way to Sligo I had seen Dante's *Dream* in the gallery there, a picture painted when Rossetti had lost his dramatic power and today not very pleasing to me, and its color, its people, its romantic architecture had blotted all other pictures away. It was a perpetual bewilderment that when my father, moved perhaps by some memory of his youth, chose some theme from poetic tradition, he would soon weary and leave it unfinished. I had seen the change coming bit by bit and its defense elaborated by young men fresh from the Paris art schools. "We must paint what is in front of us," or "A man must be of his own time," they would say, and if I spoke of Blake or Rossetti they would point out his bad drawing and tell me to admire Carolus Duran and Bastien-Lepage.[2] Then, too, they were very ignorant men; they read nothing, for nothing mattered but "knowing how to paint," being in reaction against a generation that seemed to have wasted its time upon so many things. I thought myself alone in hating these young men, their contempt for the past, their monopoly of the future, but in a few months I was to discover others of my own age, who thought as I did, for it is not true that youth looks before it with the mechanical gaze of a well-drilled soldier. Its quarrel is not with the past, but with the present, where its elders are so obviously powerful and no cause seems lost if it seem to threaten that power. Does cultivated youth ever really love the future, where the eye can discover no persecuted Royalty hidden among oak leaves,[3] though from it certainly does come so much proletarian rhetoric?

I was unlike others of my generation in one thing only. I am very religious, and deprived by Huxley and Tyndall,[4] whom I detested, of the simple-minded religion of my childhood, I had made a new religion, almost an infallible church of poetic tradition, of a fardel[5] of stories, and of personages, and of emotions, inseparable from their first expression, passed on from generation to generation by poets and painters with some help from philosophers and theologians. I wished for a world where I could discover this tradition

2. Carolus Duran (1837–1917) and Jules Bastien-Lepage (1848–84), French painters.
3. Charles II, after the decisive defeat of his father Charles I by the Parliamentarians at Naseby in 1645, hid in an oak tree before escaping abroad.
4. Thomas Henry Huxley (1825–95),

biologist and popularizer of Darwin's ideas; John Tyndall (1820–93), physicist and active propagandist for science and materialism.
5. Bundle. This archaic word suggests Yeats's poetic attitude at the stage in his life which he is describing.

perpetually, and not in pictures and in poems only, but in tiles round the chimney piece and in the hangings that kept out the draft. I had even created a dogma: "Because those imaginary people are created out of the deepest instinct of man, to be his measure and his norm, whatever I can imagine those mouths speaking may be the nearest I can go to truth." When I listened they seemed always to speak of one thing only: they, their loves, every incident of their lives, were steeped in the supernatural. Could even Titian's "Ariosto"[6] that I loved beyond other portraits have its grave look, as if waiting for some perfect final event, if the painters before Titian had not learned portraiture, while painting into the corner of compositions full of saints and Madonnas, their kneeling patrons? At seventeen years old I was already an old-fashioned brass cannon full of shot, and nothing had kept me from going off but a doubt as to my capacity to shoot straight.

[Oscar Wilde]

My first meeting with Oscar Wilde was an astonishment. I never before heard a man talking with perfect sentences, as if he had written them all overnight with labor and yet all spontaneous. There was present that night at Henley's,[7] by right of propinquity or of accident, a man full of the secret spite of dullness, who interrupted from time to time, and always to check or disorder thought; and I noticed with what mastery he was foiled and thrown. I noticed, too, that the impression of artificiality that I think all Wilde's listeners have recorded came from the perfect rounding of the sentences and from the deliberation that made it possible. That very impression helped him, as the effect of meter, or of the antithetical prose of the seventeenth century, which is itself a true meter, helped its writers, for he could pass without incongruity from some unforeseen, swift stroke of wit to elaborate reverie. I heard him say a few nights later: "Give me *The Winter's Tale*, 'Daffodils that come before the swallow dare' but not *King Lear*. What is *King Lear* but poor life staggering in the fog?" and the slow, carefully modulated cadence sounded natural to my ears. That first night he praised Walter Pater's *Studies in the History of the Renaissance*: "It is my golden book; I never travel anywhere without it; but it is the very flower of decadence: the last trumpet should have sounded the moment it was written." "But," said the dull man, "would you not have given us time to read it?" "Oh no," was the retort, "there would have been plenty of time afterwards—in either world." I think he seemed to us, baffled as we were by youth, or by infirmity, a triumphant figure, and to some of us a figure from another age,

6. Titian (ca. 1477–1576), a Venetian painter, was thought to have painted a portrait of Lodovico Ariosto, the Italian poet and author of *Orlando Furioso*. The painting is now described simply as "Portrait of a Man."
7. William Ernest Henley (1849–1903), poet, critic, and editor.

an audacious Italian fifteenth-century figure. A few weeks before I had heard one of my father's friends, an official in a publishing firm that had employed both Wilde and Henley as editors, blaming Henley who was "no use except under control" and praising Wilde, "so indolent but such a genius"; and now the firm became the topic of our talk. "How often do you go to the office?" said Henley. "I used to go three times a week," said Wilde, "for an hour a day but I have since struck off one of the days." "My God," said Henley, "I went five times a week for five hours a day and when I wanted to strike off a day they had a special committee meeting." "Furthermore," was Wilde's answer, "I never answered their letters. I have known men come to London full of bright prospects and seen them complete wrecks in a few months through a habit of answering letters." He too knew how to keep our elders in their place, and his method was plainly the more successful, for Henley had been dismissed. "No he is not an aesthete," Henley commented later, being somewhat embarrassed by Wilde's Pre-Raphaelite entanglement; "one soon finds that he is a scholar and a gentleman." And when I dined with Wilde a few days afterwards he began at once, "I had to strain every nerve to equal that man at all"; and I was too loyal to speak my thought: "You and not he said all the brilliant things." He like the rest of us had felt the strain of an intensity that seemed to hold life at the point of drama. He had said on that first meeting, "The basis of literary friendship is mixing the poisoned bowl"; and for a few weeks Henley and he became close friends till, the astonishment of their meeting over, diversity of character and ambition pushed them apart, and, with half the cavern helping, Henley began mixing the poisoned bowl for Wilde. Yet Henley never wholly lost that first admiration, for after Wilde's downfall he said to me: "Why did he do it? I told my lads to attack him and yet we might have fought under his banner."

[The Handiwork of Art]

Though I went to Sligo every summer, I was compelled to live out of Ireland the greater part of every year, and was but keeping my mind upon what I knew must be the subject matter of my poetry. I believed that if Morris[8] had set his stories amid the scenery of his own Wales, for I knew him to be of Welsh extraction and supposed wrongly that he had spent his childhood there, that if Shelley had nailed his *Prometheus*,[9] or some equal symbol, upon some Welsh or Scottish rock, their art would have entered more intimately, more microscopically, as it were, into our thought and given perhaps to modern poetry a breadth and stability like that

---

8. William Morris (1834–96), the poet, painter, and socialist.

9. A reference to Shelley's lyrical drama, *Prometheus Unbound*.

of ancient poetry. The statues of Mausolus and Artemisia[1] at the British Museum, private, half-animal, half-divine figures, all unlike the Grecian athletes and Egyptian kings in their near neighborhood, that stand in the middle of the crowd's applause, or sit above measuring it out unpersuadable justice, became to me, now or later, images of an unpremeditated joyous energy, that neither I nor any other man, racked by doubt and inquiry, can achieve; and that yet, if once achieved, might seem to men and women of Connemara or of Galway their very soul. In our study of that ruined tomb raised by a queen to her dead lover, and finished by the unpaid labor of great sculptors, after her death from grief, or so runs the tale, we cannot distinguish the handiwork of Scopas from that of Praxiteles,[2] and I wanted to create once more an art where the artist's handiwork would hide as under those half-anonymous chisels or as we find it in some old Scots ballads, or in some twelfth- or thirteenth-century Arthurian Romance. That handiwork assured, I had martyred no man for modeling his own image upon Pallas Athena's buckler; for I took great pleasure in certain allusions to the singer's life, one finds in old romances and ballads, and thought his presence there all the more poignant because we discover it half lost, like portly Chaucer, behind his own maunciple and pardoner upon the Canterbury roads. Wolfram von Eschenbach,[3] singing his German Parsifal, broke off some description of a famished city to remember that in his own house at home the very mice lacked food, and what old ballad singer was it who claimed to have fought by day in the very battle he sang by night? So masterful indeed was that instinct that when the minstrel knew not who his poet was, he must needs make up a man: "When any stranger asks who is the sweetest of singers, answer with one voice: 'A blind man; he dwells upon rocky Chios;[4] his songs shall be the most beautiful forever.'" Elaborate modern psychology sounds egotistical, I thought, when it speaks in the first person, but not those simple emotions which resemble the more, the more powerful they are, everybody's emotion, and I was soon to write many poems where an always personal emotion was woven into a general pattern of myth and symbol. When the Fenian poet[5] says that his heart has grown cold and callous—"For thy hapless fate, dear Ireland, and sorrows of my own"—he but follows tradition and if he does not move us deeply, it is because he has no sensuous musical vocabulary

1. Mausolus, king of Caria (in Asia Minor) in 4th century B.C. He married his sister Artemisia, who after his death built the famous monument named after him, the Mausoleum; a Greek statue of Mausolus and other sculptures from the Mausoleum is in the British Museum.
2. Greek sculptor of late 5th and early 4th century B.C. Scopas was a Greek sculptor of the 4th century B.C. who

went to Halicarnassus to superintend the sculpture of the Mausoleum (see previous note).
3. German poet of late 12th and early 13th century, who wrote the epic poem *Parzival.*
4. Greek island in the Aegean—one of the seven places which claimed Homer as its son.
5. I.e., a poet of Irish nationalism.

that comes at need, without compelling him to sedentary toil and so driving him out from his fellows. I thought to create that sensuous, musical vocabulary, and not for myself only, but that I might leave it to later Irish poets, much as a medieval Japanese painter left his style as an inheritance to his family, and I was careful to use a traditional manner and matter, yet changed by that toil, impelled by my share in Cain's curse,[6] by all that sterile modern complication, by my "originality," as the newspapers call it, did something altogether different. Morris set out to make a revolution that the persons of his *Well at the World's End* or his *Waters of the Wondrous Isles*, always, to my mind, in the likeness of Artemisia and her man, might walk his native scenery; and I, that my native scenery might find imaginary inhabitants, half-planned a new method and a new culture. My mind began drifting vaguely towards that doctrine of "the mask" which has convinced me that every passionate man (I have nothing to do with mechanist, or philanthropist, or man whose eyes have no preference) is, as it were, linked with another age, historical or imaginary, where alone he finds images that rouse his energy. Napoleon was never of his own time, as the naturalistic writers and painters bid all men be, but had some Roman emperor's image in his head and some condottiere's[7] blood in his heart; and when he crowned that head at Rome with his own hands he had covered, as may be seen from David's[8] painting, his hesitation with that emperor's old suit.

[The Origin of The Lake Isle of Innisfree]

I had various women friends on whom I would call towards five o'clock mainly to discuss my thoughts that I could not bring to a man without meeting some competing thought, but partly because their tea and toast saved my pennies for the bus ride home; but with women, apart from their intimate exchanges of thought, I was timid and abashed. I was sitting on a seat in front of the British Museum feeding pigeons when a couple of girls sat near and began enticing my pigeons away, laughing and whispering to one another, and I looked straight in front of me, very indignant, and presently went into the Museum without turning my head towards them. Since then I have often wondered if they were pretty or merely very young. Sometimes I told myself very adventurous love stories with myself for hero, and at other times I planned out a life of lonely austerity, and at other times mixed the ideals and planned a life of lonely austerity mitigated by periodical lapses. I had still

6. The curse imposed on Cain for killing his brother was to be "a fugitive and a vagabond" (Genesis iv.12). Yeats seems to be thinking of the curse imposed on *Adam*, that he should have to work (Genesis iii.19).
7. Mercenary soldier (14th- and 15th-century Italy)—usually hired as a leader with a band of his followers.
8. Jacques Louis David (1748–1825), French historical painter, court painter to Napoleon: he painted a picture of Napoleon's coronation.

the ambition, formed in Sligo in my teens, of living in imitation of Thoreau on Innisfree, a little island in Lough Gill,[9] and when walking through Fleet Street very homesick I heard a little tinkle of water and saw a fountain in a shop window which balanced a little ball upon its jet, and began to remember lake water. From the sudden remembrance came my poem *Innisfree*, my first lyric with anything in its rhythm of my own music. I had begun to loosen rhythm as an escape from rhetoric and from that emotion of the crowd that rhetoric brings, but I only understood vaguely and occasionally that I must for my special purpose use nothing but the common syntax. A couple of years later I would not have written that first line with its conventional archaism—"Arise and go"—nor the inversion in the last stanza. * * *

[The Rhymers' Club]

I had already met most of the poets of my generation. I had said, soon after the publication of *The Wanderings of Usheen*,[1] to the editor of a series of shilling reprints, who had set me to compile tales of the Irish fairies, "I am growing jealous of other poets and we will all grow jealous of each other unless we know each other and so feel a share in each other's triumph." He was a Welshman, lately a mining engineer, Ernest Rhys,[2] a writer of Welsh translations and original poems, that have often moved me greatly though I can think of no one else who has read them. He was perhaps a dozen years older than myself and through his work as editor knew everybody who would compile a book for seven or eight pounds. Between us we founded The Rhymers' Club, which for some years was to meet every night in an upper room with a sanded floor in an ancient eating-house in the Strand called The Cheshire Cheese. Lionel Johnson, Ernest Dowson, Victor Plarr, Ernest Radford, John Davidson, Richard le Gallienne, T. W. Rolleston, Selwyn Image, Edwin Ellis, and John Todhunter came constantly for a time, Arthur Symons and Herbert Horne, less constantly, while William Watson joined but never came and Francis Thompson[3] came once but never joined; and sometimes if we met in a private house, which we did occasionally, Oscar Wilde came. It had been useless to invite him to The Cheshire Cheese for he hated Bohemia. "Olive Schreiner,"[4] he said once to me, "is staying in the East End because that is the only place where people do not wear masks upon their faces, but I have told her that I live in the West

9. See *The Lake Isle of Innisfree,* above, and the note on it.
1. An early long poem by Yeats (1889). Yeats later spelled the name of the hero "Oisin."
2. 1859–1946; Welsh writer and editor; original editor of Everyman's Library.
3. The names here are of poets and writers of the 90's who were fellow members with Yeats of the Rhymers' Club. Francis Thompson (1859–1907), who "never joined," was the author of *The Hound of Heaven.*
4. South African novelist, author of *The Story of an African Farm* (1883).

End because nothing in life interests me but the mask."

We read our poems to one another and talked criticism and drank a little wine. I sometimes say when I speak of the club, "We had such and such ideas, such and such a quarrel with the great Victorians, we set before us such and such aims," as though we had many philosophical ideas. I say this because I am ashamed to admit that I had these ideas and that whenever I began to talk of them a gloomy silence fell upon the room. A young Irish poet, who wrote excellently but had the worst manners, was to say a few years later, "You do not talk like a poet, you talk like a man of letters," and if all the Rhymers had not been polite, if most of them had not been to Oxford or Cambridge, the greater number would have said the same thing. I was full of thought, often very abstract thought, longing all the while to be full of images, because I had gone to the art school instead of a university. Yet even if I had gone to a university, and learned all the classical foundations of English literature and English culture, all that great erudition which once accepted frees the mind from restlessness, I should have had to give up my Irish subject matter, or attempt to found a new tradition. Lacking sufficient recognized precedent I must needs find out some reason for all I did. * * *

1922

JAMES JOYCE
(1882–1941)

1915: *Dubliners.*
1916: *A Portrait of the Artist as a Young Man.*
1922: *Ulysses.*
1939: *Finnegans Wake.*

James Joyce was born in Dublin, son of a talented but feckless father who is accurately described by Stephen Dedalus in *A Portrait of the Artist as a Young Man* as a man who had in his time been "a medical student, an oarsman, a tenor, an amateur actor, a shouting politician, a small landlord, a small investor, a drinker, a good fellow, a storyteller, somebody's secretary, something in a distillery, a tax-gatherer, a bankrupt, and at present a praiser of his own past." The elder Joyce drifted steadily down the financial and social scale, his family moving from house to house, each one less genteel and more shabby than the previous. James Joyce's whole education was Catholic, from the age of 6 to the age of 9 at Clongowes Wood College, and from 11 to 16 at Belvedere College, Dublin. Both were Jesuit institutions, and were normal roads to the priesthood. He then studied modern languages at University College, Dublin.

From a comparatively early age Joyce regarded himself as a rebel against the shabbiness and Philistinism of Dublin. In his early youth he was very religious, but in his last year at Belvedere he began to reject his Catholic faith in favor of a literary mission which he saw as involving rebellion and exile. He refused to play any part in the nationalist or other popular activities of his fellow students, and created some stir by his outspoken articles, one of which, on the Norwegian playwright Henrik Ibsen, appeared in the *Fortnightly Review* for April, 1900. He taught himself Norwegian to be able to read Ibsen and to write to him. When an article by Joyce, significantly entitled *The Day of the Rabblement*, was refused, on instructions of the faculty adviser, by the student magazine that had commissioned it, he had it printed privately. By 1902, when he received his B.A. degree, he was already committed to a career as exile and writer. For Joyce, as for his character Stephen Dedalus, the latter implied the former. To preserve his integrity, to avoid involvement in popular sentimentalities and dishonesties, and above all to be able to re-create with both total understanding and total objectivity the Dublin life he knew so well, he felt that he had to go abroad.

Joyce went to Paris after graduation, was recalled to Dublin by his mother's fatal illness, had a short spell there as a schoolteacher, then returned to the Continent in 1904 to teach English at Trieste and then at Zurich. He took with him Nora Barnacle, an uneducated Galway girl with no interest in literature; her native vivacity and peasant wit charmed Joyce, and the two lived in devoted companionship until Joyce's death, though they were not married until 1931. In 1920 Joyce settled in Paris, where he lived until December, 1940, when the war forced him to take refuge in Switzerland; he died in Zurich a few weeks later.

Proud, obstinate, absolutely convinced of his genius, given to fits of sudden gaiety and of sudden silence, Joyce was not always an easy person to get on with, yet he never lacked friends and throughout his 36 years on the Continent was always the center of a literary circle. Life was hard at first. At Trieste he had very little money, and he did not improve matters by drinking heavily, a habit checked somewhat by his brother Stanislaus who came out from Dublin to act (as Stanislaus put it much later) as his "brother's keeper." His financial position was much improved by the patronage of Mrs. Harold McCormick (Edith Rockefeller), who provided him with a monthly stipend from March, 1917, until September, 1919, when they quarreled, apparently because Joyce refused to submit to psychoanalysis by Carl Jung, who had been heavily endowed by Mrs. McCormick. The New York lawyer and art patron John Quinn, steered in Joyce's direction by Ezra Pound, also helped Joyce financially in 1917. A more permanent benefactor was the English feminist and editor Harriet Shaw Weaver, who not only subsidized Joyce generously from 1917 to the end of his life, but occupied herself indefatigably with arrangements for publishing his work.

Joyce's almost life-long exile from his native Ireland has something paradoxical about it. No writer has ever been more soaked in Dublin, its atmosphere, its history, its topography; in spite of doing most of his writing in Trieste, Zurich, and Paris, he wrote only and always about Dublin. He devised ways of expanding his accounts of Dublin, however, so that they became microcosms, small-scale models, of all human life, of all history and all geography. Indeed that was his life's work: to write about Dublin in such a way that he was writing about all of human experience.

Joyce began his career by writing a series of stories etching with extraordinary clarity aspects of Dublin life. But these stories—published as Dubliners in 1915—are more than sharp realistic sketches. In each, the detail is so chosen and organized that carefully interacting symbolic meanings are set up, and as a result Dubliners is a book about man's fate as well as a series of sketches of Dublin. (Araby, for example, is meticulously accurate in every physical detail, yet it is also a symbolic story about the relation between dreams and reality.) Further, the stories are presented in a particular order so that new meanings arise from the relation between them.

This was Joyce's first phase: he had to come directly to terms with the life he had rejected, to see it for what it was and for what it meant. Next, he had to come to terms with the meaning of his own development as a man dedicated to writing. He did this by weaving his autobiography into a novel so finely chiseled and carefully organized, so stripped of everything superfluous, that each word contributes to the presentation of the theme: the parallel movement toward art and toward exile. A part of Joyce's first draft has been posthumously published under the original title of Stephen Hero (1944): a comparison between it and the final version which Joyce gave to the world, A Portrait of the Artist as a Young Man (1916), will show how carefully Joyce reworked and compressed his material for maximum effect. The Portrait is not literally true as autobiography, though it has many autobiographical elements; but it is representatively true not only of Joyce but of the relation between the artist and society in the modern world.

In the Portrait Stephen worked out a theory of art which considers that art moves from the lyrical form—which is the simplest, the personal expression of an instant of emotion—through the narrative form—no longer purely personal—to the dramatic—the highest and most perfect form, where "the artist, like the God of creation, remains within or behind or beyond or above his handiwork, invisible, refined out of existence, indifferent, paring his fingernails." This view of art, which involves the objectivity, even the exile, of the artist (even though the artist uses only the materials provided for him by his own life) is related to that held by the poets of the 90's. More widely, it is related to the rejection by the artist of the ordinary world of middleclass values and activities which we see equally, though in different ways, in Matthew Arnold's war against the Philistines and in the concept (very un-Arnoldian) of the artist as bohemian. Joyce's career belongs to that long chapter in the history of the arts in Western civilization which begins with the artist's declaring his independence and ends with his feeling his inevitable "alienation." But if Joyce was alienated, as in certain ways he clearly was, he made his alienation serve his art: the kinds of writing represented by Ulysses and Finnegans Wake represent the most consummate craftsmanship put at the service of a humanely comic vision of all life. Some (though surprisingly few) of Joyce's innovations in organization and style have been imitated by other writers, but these books are, and will probably remain, unique in our literature. They are not freaks or historical oddities, but serious and exciting works.

From the beginning Joyce had trouble with the Philistines. Publication of *Dubliners* was held up for many years while he fought with both English and Irish publishers about certain words and phrases which they wished to eliminate. (It was the former who finally published the book.) His masterpiece *Ulysses* was banned in both Britain and America on its first appearance in 1922, its earlier serialization in the *Little Review* (March 1918–December 1920) having had to stop abruptly when the U.S. Post Office brought a charge of obscenity against it. Fortunately, Judge Woolsey's history-making decision in favor of *Ulysses* in the United States District Court on December 6, 1933, resulted in the lifting of the ban and the free circulation of the work first in America and soon afterwards in Britain.

ULYSSES

Ulysses is an account of one day in the lives of citizens of Dublin in the year 1904: it is thus the description of a limited number of events involving a limited number of people in a limited environment. Yet Joyce's ambition—which took him seven years to realize—is to make his action into a microcosm of all human experience. The events are not therefore told on a single level; the story is presented in such a manner that depth and implication are given to them and they become symbolic of the activity of Man in the World. The most obvious of the devices which Joyce employs in order to make clear the microcosmic aspect of his story is the parallel with Homer's *Odyssey*: every episode in *Ulysses* corresponds in some way to an episode in the *Odyssey*. Joyce regarded Homer's Ulysses as the most "complete" man in literature, a man who is shown in all his aspects—both coward and hero, cautious and reckless, weak and strong, husband and lover, father and son, sublime and ridiculous; so he makes his hero, Leopold Bloom, an Irish Jew, into a modern Ulysses, and by so doing helps to make him Everyman and to make Dublin the world.

The book opens at eight o'clock on the morning of June 16, 1904. Stephen Dedalus (the same character we saw in the *Portrait*, but this is two years after our last glimpse of him there) had been summoned back to Dublin by his mother's fatal illness and now lives in an old military tower on the shore with Buck Mulligan, a rollicking medical student, and an Englishman called Haines. In the first three episodes of *Ulysses*, which concentrate on Stephen, he is built up as an aloof, uncompromising artist, rejecting all advances by representatives of the normal world, the incomplete man, to be contrasted later with the complete Leopold Bloom, who is much more "normal" and conciliatory. After tracing Stephen through his early-morning activities and learning the main currents of his mind, we go, in the fourth episode, to the home of Bloom. We follow closely his every activity: attending a funeral, transacting his business, eating his lunch, walking through the Dublin streets, worrying about his wife's infidelity with Blazes Boylan—and at each point the contents of his mind, including retrospect and anticipation, are presented to the reader, until all his past history is revealed. Finally, Bloom and Stephen, who have just been missing each other all day, get together. By this time it is late, and Stephen, who has been drinking with some medical students, is the worse for liquor. Bloom, moved by a paternal feeling towards Stephen (his own son had died in infancy and in a symbolic way Stephen takes his place), follows him during subsequent adventures in the role of protector. The climax of the book comes when Stephen, far gone in drink, and Bloom, worn out with fatigue, succumb to a series of hallucinations where their subconscious and unconscious come to the surface in dramatic form and their whole personalities are revealed with a completeness and a frankness unique in literature. Then Bloom takes the unresponsive Stephen home and gives him a meal. After Stephen's departure Bloom retires to bed—it is now 2 A.M. on June 17—while his wife Molly, representing the principles of sex and reproduction on which all human life is based, closes the book with a long monologue in which her experiences as woman are remembered.

On the level of realistic description, *Ulysses* pulses with life and can be enjoyed for its evocation of early 20th-century Dublin. On the level of psychological exploration, it gives a profound and moving presentation of the personality and consciousness of Leopold Bloom and (to a lesser extent) Stephen Dedalus. On the level of style, it exhibits the most fascinating linguistic virtuosity. On a deeper symbolic level, the novel explores the paradoxes of human loneliness and sociability (for Bloom is both Jew and Dubliner, both exile and citizen, just as all men are in a sense both exiles and citizens), and it explores the problems posed by the relations between parent and child, between the generations, and between the sexes. At the same time, through its use of themes from Homer, Dante, and Shakespeare, from literature, philosophy, and history, the book weaves a subtle pattern of allusion and suggestion which illuminates many aspects of human experience. The more one reads *Ulysses* the more one finds in it, but at the same time one does not need to probe into the symbolic meaning in order to relish both its literary artistry and its human feeling. At the forefront stands Leopold Bloom, from one point of view a frustrated and confused outsider in the society in which he moves, from another a champion of kindness and justice whose humane curiosity about his fellows redeems him from mere vulgarity and gives the book its positive human foundation.

Readers who come to *Ulysses* with expectations about the way the story is to be presented derived from their reading of Victorian novels or even of such 20th-century novelists as Conrad and Lawrence will find much that is at first puzzling. Joyce presents the consciousness of his characters directly, without any explanatory comment which tells the reader whose consciousness is being rendered (this is the "stream-of-consciousness" method). He may move, in the same paragraph and without any sign that he is making such a transition, from a description of a character's action—e.g., Stephen walking along the shore or Bloom entering a restaurant—to an evocation of the character's mental response to this action. That response is always multiple: it derives partly from the character's immediate situation and partly from the whole complex of attitudes which his past history has created in him. To suggest this multiplicity, Joyce may vary his style, from the flippant to the serious or from a realistic description to a suggestive set of images which indicate what might be called the general tone of the character's consciousness. Past and present mingle in the texture of the prose because they mingle in the texture of consciousness; and this mingling can be indicated by puns, by sudden breaks into a new kind of style or a new kind of subject matter, or by some other device for keeping the reader constantly in sight of the shifting, kaleidoscopic nature of human awareness. With a little experience, the reader learns to follow the implications of Joyce's shifts in manner and content—even to follow that at first sight bewildering passage in the "Proteus" episode where Stephen does not go to visit his uncle and aunt but, passing the road that leads to their house, imagines the kind of conversation that would take place in his home *if* he had gone to visit his uncle and had then returned home and reported that he had done so. *Ulysses* must not be approached as though it were a novel written in a traditional manner; all preconceptions must be set aside and we must follow wherever the author leads us and let the language tell us what it has to say without our troubling whether language is being used "properly" or not.

<h3 style="text-align:center">FINNEGANS WAKE</h3>

Joyce's last work, *Finnegans Wake*, was published in 1939; it took more than fourteen years to write, and Joyce considered it his masterpiece. In *Ulysses* he had made the symbolic aspect of the novel at least as important as the realistic aspect, but in *Finnegans Wake* he gave up realism altogether. This vast story of a symbolic Irishman's cosmic dream develops by enormous reverberating puns a continuous expansion of meaning, the elements in the puns deriving from every conceivable source in history, literature, mythology, and Joyce's personal experience. The whole book being (on one level at least) a dream, Joyce invents his own dream language in which words are combined, distorted, created by fitting together bits of other words, used with several different meanings at once, often drawn from several different languages at once, and fused in all sorts of ways to achieve whole clusters of meaning simultaneously. In fact, so many echoing suggestions can be found in every word or phrase that a full annotation of even a few pages would require a large book. It has taken the co-operative work of a number of devoted readers to make clear the complex interactions of the multiple puns and pun-clusters through which the ideas are projected, and every rereading reveals new meanings. It is true that many readers find the efforts of explication demanded by *Finnegans Wake* too arduous; some, indeed, feel that the law of diminishing returns has now begun to operate, and that the effort of both author and reader is disproportionate. Nevertheless, the book has great beauty and fascination even for the casual reader. Students are advised to read aloud—or to listen to the record of Joyce reading aloud—the extract printed in this anthology, in order to appreciate the degree to which the rhythms of the prose assist in conveying the meaning.

To an even greater extent than *Ulysses*, *Finnegans Wake* aims at embracing all of human history. The title is from an Irish-American ballad about Tom Finnegan, a hod carrier who falls off a ladder when drunk and is apparently killed, but who revives when during the "wake" (the watch by the dead body) someone spills whiskey on him. The theme of death and resurrection, of cycles of change coming round in the course of history, is central to *Finnegans Wake*, which derives one of its main principles of organization from the cyclical theory of history put forward in 1725 by the Italian philosopher Giambattista Vico. Vico held that history passes through four phases: the divine or theocratic, when people are governed by their awe of the supernatural; the aristocratic (the "heroic age" reflected in Homer and in *Beowulf*); the democratic and individualistic; and the final stage of chaos, a fall into confusion which startles man back into supernatural reverence and starts the process once again. Joyce, like Yeats, saw his own generation as in the final stage awaiting the shock that will bring man back to the first.

A mere account of the narrative line of *Finnegans Wake* cannot, of course, give any idea of the content of the work. If one explains that it opens with Finnegan's fall, then introduces his successor Humphrey Chimpden Earwicker, who is Everyman, and whose dream constitutes the novel; that he is presented as having guilt feelings about an indecency he committed (or may have committed) in Phoenix Park, Dublin; that his wife Anna Livia Plurabelle or ALP (who is also Eve, Iseult, Ireland, the River Liffey) changes her role just as he does; that he has two sons Shem and Shaun (or Jerry and Kevin), who represent introvert and extrovert, artist and practical man, creator and popularizer, and symbolize this basic dichotomy in human nature by all kinds of metamorphoses; and if one adds that, in the four books into which *Finnegans Wake* is divided (after Vico's pattern), actions comic or grotesque or sad or tender or desperate or passionate or terribly ordinary (and very often several of these things at the same time) take place with all the shifting meanings of a dream, so that characters change into others or into inanimate objects and the setting keeps shifting—if we explain all this, we still have said very little about what makes *Finnegans Wake* what it is. The dreamer, whose initials HCE indicate his universality ("Here Comes Everybody"), is at the same time a particular person, who keeps a pub in Chapelizod, a Dublin suburb on the River Liffey near Phoenix Park. His mysterious misdemeanor in Phoenix Park is in a sense Original Sin: Earwicker is Adam as well as a primeval giant, the Hill of Howth, the Great Parent ("Haveth Childers Everywhere" is another expansion of HCE), and Man in History. Other characters who flit and change through the book, such as the Twelve Customers (who are also twelve jurymen and public opinion) and the Four Old Men (who are also judges, the authors of the four Gospels, and the four elements), help to weave the texture of multiple significance so characteristic of the work. But always it is the punning language, extending significance downwards—rather than the plot, developing it lengthwise—that bears the main load of meaning.

Araby[1]

North Richmond Street, being blind, was a quiet street except at the hour when the Christian Brothers' School set the boys free.[2]

1. The third of the fifteen stories in *Dubliners*. This tale of the frustrated quest for beauty in the midst of drabness is both meticulously realistic in its handling of details of Dublin life and the Dublin scene and highly symbolic in that almost every image and incident suggests some particular aspect of the theme (e.g., the suggestion of the Holy Grail in the image of the chalice, mentioned in the fifth paragraph). Joyce was drawing on his own childhood

An uninhabited house of two storeys stood at the blind end, detached from its neighbours in a square ground. The other houses of the street, conscious of decent lives within them, gazed at one another with brown imperturbable faces.

The former tenant of our house, a priest, had died in the back drawing-room. Air, musty from having been long enclosed, hung in all the rooms, and the waste room behind the kitchen was littered with old useless papers. Among these I found a few paper-covered books, the pages of which were curled and damp: *The Abbot,* by Walter Scott, *The Devout Communicant* and *The Memoirs of Vidocq.*[3] I liked the last best because its leaves were yellow. The wild garden behind the house contained a central apple-tree and a few straggling bushes under one of which I found the late tenant's rusty bicycle-pump. He had been a very charitable priest; in his will he had left all his money to institutions and the furniture of his house to his sister.

When the short days of winter came dusk fell before we had well eaten our dinners. When we met in the street the houses had grown sombre. The space of sky above us was the colour of ever-changing violet and towards it the lamps of the street lifted their feeble lanterns. The cold air stung us and we played till our bodies glowed. Our shouts echoed in the silent street. The career of our play brought us through the dark muddy lanes behind the houses where we ran the gauntlet of the rough tribes from the cottages, to the back doors of the dark dripping gardens where odours arose from the ashpits, to the dark odorous stables where a coachman smoothed and combed the horse or shook music from the buckled harness. When we returned to the street light from the kitchen windows had filled the areas. If my uncle was seen turning the corner we hid in the shadow until we had seen him safely housed. Or if Mangan's sister came out on the doorstep to call her brother in to his tea we watched her from our shadow peer up and down the street. We waited to see whether she would remain or go in and, if she remained, we left our shadow and walked up to Mangan's steps resignedly. She was waiting for us, her figure defined by the light from the half-opened door. Her brother always teased her before he obeyed and I stood by the railings looking at

recollections, and the uncle in the story is a reminiscence of Joyce's father. But in all the stories in *Dubliners* dealing with childhood, the child lives not with his parents but with an uncle and aunt —a symbol of that isolation and lack of proper relation between "consubstantial" ("in the flesh") parents and children which is a major theme in Joyce's work.

2. The Joyce family moved to 17 North Richmond Street, Dublin, in 1894, and Joyce had earlier briefly attended the Christian Brothers' school a few doors away (The Christian Brothers are a Catholic religious community). The details of the house described here correspond exactly to those of No. 17.

3. François Eugène Vidocq (1775–1857) had an extraordinary career as soldier, thief, chief of the French detective force, and private detective. *The Abbot* is a historical novel dealing with Mary Queen of Scots, *The Devout Communicant* a Catholic religious manual.

her. Her dress swung as she moved her body and the soft rope of her hair tossed from side to side.

Every morning I lay on the floor in the front parlour watching her door. The blind was pulled down to within an inch of the sash so that I could not be seen. When she came out on the doorstep my heart leaped. I ran to the hall, seized my books and followed her. I kept her brown figure always in my eye and, when we came near the point at which our ways diverged, I quickened my pace and passed her. This happened morning after morning. I had never spoken to her, except for a few casual words, and yet her name was like a summons to all my foolish blood.

Her image accompanied me even in places the most hostile to romance. On Saturday evenings when my aunt went marketing I had to go to carry some of the parcels. We walked through the flaring streets, jostled by drunken men and bargaining women, amid the curses of labourers, the shrill litanies of shop-boys who stood on guard by the barrels of pigs' cheeks, the nasal chanting of street-singers, who sang a *come-all-you*[4] about O'Donovan Rossa, or a ballad about the troubles in our native land. These noises converged in a single sensation of life for me: I imagined that I bore my chalice safely through a throng of foes. Her name sprang to my lips at moments in strange prayers and praises which I myself did not understand. My eyes were often full of tears (I could not tell why) and at times a flood from my heart seemed to pour itself out into my bosom. I thought little of the future. I did not know whether I would ever speak to her or not or, if I spoke to her, how I could tell her of my confused adoration. But my body was like a harp and her words and gestures were like fingers running upon the wires.

One evening I went into the back drawing-room in which the priest had died. It was a dark rainy evening and there was no sound in the house. Through one of the broken panes I heard the rain impinge upon the earth, the fine incessant needles of water playing in the sodden beds. Some distant lamp or lighted window gleamed below me. I was thankful that I could see so little. All my senses seemed to desire to veil themselves and, feeling that I was about to slip from them, I pressed the palms of my hands together until they trembled, murmuring: "O love! O love!" many times.

At last she spoke to me. When she addressed the first words to me I was so confused that I did not know what to answer. She asked me was I going to *Araby*.[5] I forgot whether I answered yes

4. Street ballad, so called from its opening words. This one was about the 19th-century Irish nationalist Jeremiah Donovan, popularly known as O'Donovan Rossa.

5. The bazaar, described by its "official catalogue" as a "Grand Oriental Fête," was actually held in Dublin on May 14–19, 1894.

or no. It would be a splendid bazaar, she said she would love to go.
"And why can't you?" I asked.

While she spoke she turned a silver bracelet round and round
her wrist. She could not go, she said, because there would be a retreat[6] that week in her convent. Her brother and two other boys
were fighting for their caps and I was alone at the railings. She
held one of the spikes, bowing her head towards me. The light
from the lamp opposite our door caught the white curve of her
neck, lit up her hair that rested there and, falling, lit up the hand
upon the railing. It fell over one side of her dress and caught
the white border of a petticoat, just visible as she stood at ease.

"It's well for you," she said.

"If I go," I said, "I will bring you something."

What innumerable follies laid waste my waking and sleeping
thoughts after that evening! I wished to annihilate the tedious
intervening days. I chafed against the work of school. At night
in my bedroom and by day in the classroom her image came between me and the page I strove to read. The syllables of the word
Araby were called to me through the silence in which my soul
luxuriated and cast an Eastern enchantment over me. I asked for
leave to go to the bazaar on Saturday night. My aunt was surprised
and hoped it was not some Freemason affair.[7] I answered few questions in class. I watched my master's face pass from amiability to
sternness; he hoped I was not beginning to idle. I could not call
my wandering thoughts together. I had hardly any patience with
the serious work of life which, now that it stood between me and
my desire, seemed to me child's play, ugly monotonous child's play.

On Saturday morning I reminded my uncle that I wished to go
to the bazaar in the evening. He was fussing at the hallstand, looking for the hat-brush, and answered me curtly:

"Yes, boy, I know."

As he was in the hall I could not go into the front parlour and
lie at the window. I left the house in bad humour and walked
slowly towards the school. The air was pitilessly raw and already
my heart misgave me.

When I came home to dinner my uncle had not yet been home.
Still it was early. I sat staring at the clock for some time and, when
its ticking began to irritate me, I left the room. I mounted the staircase and gained the upper part of the house. The high cold empty
gloomy rooms liberated me and I went from room to room singing. From the front window I saw my companions playing below
in the street. Their cries reached me weakened and indistinct and,
leaning my forehead against the cool glass, I looked over at the

6. Period of seclusion from ordinary activities devoted to religious exercises;
"her convent" is, of course, her convent
school.

7. His aunt shares her church's distrust of the Freemasons, an old European secret society, reputedly anti-Catholic.

dark house where she lived. I may have stood there for an hour, seeing nothing but the brown-clad figure cast by my imagination, touched discreetly by the lamplight at the curved neck, at the hand upon the railings and at the border below the dress.

When I came downstairs again I found Mrs. Mercer sitting at the fire. She was an old garrulous woman, a pawnbroker's widow, who collected used stamps for some pious purpose. I had to endure the gossip of the tea-table. The meal was prolonged beyond an hour and still my uncle did not come. Mrs. Mercer stood up to go: she was sorry she couldn't wait any longer, but it was after eight o'clock and she did not like to be out late, as the night air was bad for her. When she had gone I began to walk up and down the room, clenching my fists. My aunt said:

"I'm afraid you may put off your bazaar for this night of Our Lord."

At nine o'clock I heard my uncle's latchkey in the halldoor. I heard him talking to himself and heard the hallstand rocking when it had received the weight of his overcoat. I could interpret these signs. When he was midway through his dinner I asked him to give me the money to go to the bazaar. He had forgotten.

"The people are in bed and after their first sleep now," he said.

I did not smile. My aunt said to him energetically:

"Can't you give him the money and let him go? You've kept him late enough as it is."

My uncle said he was very sorry he had forgotten. He said he believed in the old saying: "All work and no play makes Jack a dull boy." He asked me where I was going and, when I had told him a second time he asked me did I know *The Arab's Farewell to his Steed*.[8] When I left the kitchen he was about to recite the opening lines of the piece to my aunt.

I held a florin tightly in my hand as I strode down Buckingham Street towards the station. The sight of the streets thronged with buyers and glaring with gas recalled to me the purpose of my journey. I took my seat in a third-class carriage of a deserted train. After an intolerable delay the train moved out of the station slowly. It crept onward among ruinous houses and over the twinkling river. At Westland Row Station a crowd of people pressed to the carriage doors; but the porters moved them back, saying that it was a special train for the bazaar. I remained alone in the bare carriage. In a few minutes the train drew up beside an improvised wooden platform. I passed out on to the road and saw by the lighted dial of a clock that it was ten minutes to ten. In front of me was a large building which displayed the magical name.

I could not find any sixpenny entrance and, fearing that the bazaar would be closed, I passed in quickly through a turnstile,

8. Once-popular sentimental poem by Caroline Norton.

handing a shilling to a weary-looking man. I found myself in a big hall girdled at half its height by a gallery. Nearly all the stalls were closed and the greater part of the hall was in darkness. I recognised a silence like that which pervades a church after a service. I walked into the centre of the bazaar timidly. A few people were gathered about the stalls which were still open. Before a curtain, over which the words *Café Chantant*[9] were written in coloured lamps, two men were counting money on a salver. I listened to the fall of the coins.

Remembering with difficulty why I had come I went over to one of the stalls and examined porcelain vases and flowered tea-sets. At the door of the stall a young lady was talking and laughing with two young gentlemen. I remarked their English accents and listened vaguely to their conversation.

"O, I never said such a thing!"

"O, but you did!"

"O, but I didn't!"

"Didn't she say that?"

"Yes. I heard her."

"O, there's a . . . fib!"

Observing me the young lady came over and asked me did I wish to buy anything. The tone of her voice was not encouraging; she seemed to have spoken to me out of a sense of duty. I looked humbly at the great jars that stood like eastern guards at either side of the dark entrance to the stall and murmured:

"No, thank you."

The young lady changed the position of one of the vases and went back to the two young men. They began to talk of the same subject. Once or twice the young lady glanced at me over her shoulder.

I lingered before her stall, though I knew my stay was useless, to make my interest in her wares seem the more real. Then I turned away slowly and walked down the middle of the bazaar. I allowed the two pennies to fall against the sixpence in my pocket. I heard a voice call from one end of the gallery that the light was out. The upper part of the hall was now completely dark.

Gazing up into the darkness I saw myself as a creature driven and derided by vanity; and my eyes burned with anguish and anger.

1905   1914

9. Literally "singing café" (café providing musical entertainment, popular early in this century).

From A Portrait of the Artist as a Young Man[1]
[The Interview with the Director]

The director stood in the embrasure of the window, his back to the light, leaning an elbow on the brown crossblind, and, as he spoke and smiled, slowly dangling and looping the cord of the other blind, Stephen stood before him, following for a moment with his eyes the waning of the long summer daylight above the roofs or the slow deft movements of the priestly fingers. The priest's face was in total shadow, but the waning daylight from behind him touched the deeply grooved temples and the curves of the skull. Stephen followed also with his ears the accents and intervals of the priest's voice as he spoke gravely and cordially of indifferent themes, the vacation which had just ended, the colleges of the order abroad, the transference of masters. The grave and cordial voice went on easily with its tale, and in the pauses Stephen felt bound to set it on again with respectful questions. He knew that the tale was a prelude and his mind waited for the sequel. Ever since the message of summons had come for him from the director his mind had struggled to find the meaning of the message; and during the long restless time he had sat in the college parlour waiting for the director to come in his eyes had wandered from one

1. *A Portrait of the Artist as a Young Man* is the story of the development of Stephen Dedalus from earliest childhood until his full realization of his destiny as artist and of the implications of that destiny. There is a considerable amount of autobiography in the book, but it is far from straight autobiography. Everything is organized to show the parallel development of artist and exile: for Joyce, the writer can only achieve the objectivity proper to an artist by totally withdrawing from all implication in the life of the community from which he is to draw his material. In the novel Stephen rejects one by one his home, his religion, his country, growing ever more aloof and independent, exclaiming *"Non serviam"* ("I will not serve") to all the representatives of orthodoxy and convention, and even to the claims of friendship and personal affection. Stephen the artist comes into being at the moment when he has successfully resisted the temptation to enter the Jesuit order: he suddenly realizes that he is born to dwell apart, to look objectively on the world of men and record their doings with the artist's disinterested craftsmanship. He might well have become a priest, but the choice lay only between priest and artist, between "the

power of the keys, the power to bind and loose from sin," and the artist's godlike power to re-create the world with the word. That is why Stephen's rejection of the call to join the Jesuit order preludes the climax of the *Portrait* (which comes at the end of the second extract here printed). The first extract shows Stephen's response to that call, and the second shows him shortly afterwards experiencing his first true aesthetic vision as he looks at the girl standing with kilted skirts in the water and sees her without the desire either to possess or to convert but with the artist's joy in the presence of her reality.

As so often, Joyce in this book combines meticulous realism of detail with a persistent symbolism. The hero's name, for example, is itself symbolic. Stephen was the first Christian martyr, and in Greek mythology Daedalus was the first craftsman (or artist: the Greeks had one word for both), who made the labyrinth for King Minos at Crete; later, when Minos turned against him, he made himself wings and escaped by flying across the sea—symbol for Joyce of the artist's flight into necessary exile. The name "Daedalus" means "cunning craftsman": the artist for Joyce was both martyr and pioneer craftsman.

sober picture to another around the walls and his mind wandered from one guess to another until the meaning of the summons had almost become clear. Then, just as he was wishing that some unforeseen cause might prevent the director from coming, he had heard the handle of the door turning and the swish of a soutane.[2]

The director had begun to speak of the Dominican and Franciscan orders and of the friendship between Saint Thomas and Saint Bonaventure.[3] The Capuchin dress, he thought, was rather too . . .

Stephen's face gave back the priest's indulgent smile and, not being anxious to give an opinion, he made a slight dubitative movement with his lips.

—I believe, continued the director, that there is some talk now among the Capuchins themselves of doing away with it and following the example of the other Franciscans.

—I suppose they would retain it in the cloisters? said Stephen.

—O, certainly, said the director. For the cloister it is all right, but for the street I really think it would be better to do away with, don't you?

—It must be troublesome, I imagine?

—Of course it is, of course. Just imagine when I was in Belgium I used to see them out cycling in all kinds of weather with this thing up about their knees! It was really ridiculous. *Les jupes,*[4] they call them in Belgium.

The vowel was so modified as to be indistinct.

—What do they call them?

—*Les jupes.*

—O!

Stephen smiled again in answer to the smile which he could not see on the priest's shadowed face, its image or spectre only passing rapidly across his mind as the low discreet accent fell upon his ear. He gazed calmly before him at the waning sky, glad of the cool of the evening and the faint yellow glow which hid the tiny flame kindling upon his cheek.

The names of articles of dress worn by women or of certain soft and delicate stuffs used in their making brought always to his mind a delicate and sinful perfume. As a boy he had imagined the reins by which horses are driven as slender silken bands and it shocked him to feel at Stradbrooke the greasy leather of harness. It had shocked him, too, when he had felt for the first time beneath his tremulous fingers the brittle texture of a woman's stocking for, retaining nothing of all he read save that which seemed to him an

2. Cassock.
3. St. Bonaventure, Italian Scholastic philosopher (known as "the seraphic doctor"), became general of the Franciscan order in 1256; his contemporary, St. Thomas Aquinas (*doctor angelicus,* or "the angelic doctor"), lead-

ing Scholastic philosopher, was a member of the Dominican order. The Capuchins were a special order of Franciscans, so called from the long pointed "capuche," or hood, which they wore.
4. Skirts.

echo or a prophecy of his own state, it was only amid softworded phrases or within rosesoft stuffs that he dared to conceive of the soul or body of a woman moving with tender life.

But the phrase on the priest's lips was disingenuous for he knew that a priest should not speak lightly on that theme. The phrase had been spoken lightly with design and he felt that his face was being searched by the eyes in the shadow. Whatever he had heard or read of the craft of jesuits he had put aside frankly as not borne out by his own experience. His masters, even when they had not attracted him, had seemed to him always intelligent and serious priests, athletic and highspirited prefects. He thought of them as men who washed their bodies briskly with cold water and wore clean cold linen. During all the years he had lived among them in Clongowes[5] and in Belvedere he had received only two pandies[6] and, though these had been dealt him in the wrong, he knew that he had often escaped punishment. During all those years he had never heard from any of his masters a flippant word: it was they who had taught him christian doctrine and urged him to live a good life and, when he had fallen into grievous sin, it was they who had led him back to grace. Their presence had made him diffident of himself when he was a muff in Clongowes and it had made him diffident of himself also while he had held his equivocal position in Belvedere. A constant sense of this had remained with him up to the last year of his school life. He had never once disobeyed or allowed turbulent companions to seduce him from his habit of quiet obedience: and, even when he doubted some statement of a master, he had never presumed to doubt openly. Lately some of their judgments had sounded a little childish in his ears and had made him feel a regret and pity as thought he were slowly passing out of an accustomed world and were hearing its language for the last time. One day when some boys had gathered round a priest under the shed near the chapel, he heard the priest say:

—I believe that Lord Macaulay was a man who probably never committed a mortal sin in his life, that is to say, a deliberate mortal sin.[7]

Some of the boys had then asked the priest if Victor Hugo were not the greatest French writer. The priest had answered that Victor Hugo had never written half so well when he had turned against the church as he had written when he was a catholic.

—But there are many eminent French critics, said the priest, who consider that even Victor Hugo, great as he certainly was, had not so pure a French style as Louis Veuillot.[8]

---

5. The Jesuit school which Stephen (and the young Joyce) attended before going to Belvedere College.
6. Hard blows on the palm of the hand (for punishment).

7. The life of the Whig historian Thomas Babington Macaulay (1800–59) was noted for its purity.
8. A 19th-century French journalist and leader of the French "Ultramon-

The tiny flame which the priest's allusion had kindled upon Stephen's cheek had sunk down again and his eyes were still fixed calmly on the colourless sky. But an unresting doubt flew hither and thither before his· mind. Masked memories passed quickly before him: he recognised scenes and persons yet he was conscious that he had failed to perceive some vital circumstance in them. He saw himself walking about the grounds watching the sports in Clongowes and eating slim jim out of his cricket-cap. Some jesuits were walking round the cycletrack in the company of ladies. The echoes of certain expressions used in Clongowes sounded in remote caves of his mind.

His ears were listening to these distant echoes amid the silence of the parlour when he became aware that the priest was addressing him in a different voice.

—I sent for you today, Stephen, because I wished to speak to you on a very important subject

—Yes, sir.

—Have you ever felt that you had a vocation?

Stephen parted his lips to answer yes and then withheld the word suddenly. The priest waited for the answer and added:

—I mean have you ever felt within yourself, in your soul, a desire to join the order. Think.

—I have sometimes thought of it, said Stephen.

The priest let the blindcord fall to one side and, uniting his hands, leaned his chin gravely upon them, communing with himself.

—In a college like this, he said at length, there is one boy or perhaps two or three boys whom God calls to the religious life. Such a boy is marked off from his companions by his piety, by the good example he shows to others. He is looked up to by them; he is chosen perhaps as prefect by his fellow sodalists. And you, Stephen, have been such a boy in this college, prefect of Our Blessed Lady's sodality.[9] Perhaps you are the boy in this college whom God designs to call to Himself.

A strong note of pride reinforcing the gravity of the priest's voice made Stephen's heart quicken in response. —To receive that call, Stephen, said the priest, is the greatest honour that the Almighty God can bestow upon a man. No king or emperor on this earth has the power of the priest of God. No angel or archangel in heaven, no saint, not even the Blessed Virgin herself has the power of a priest of God: the power of the keys, the power to bind and to loose from sin, the power of exorcism, the power to cast out from the creatures of God the evil spirits that have power over them, the power, the authority, to make the great God of Heaven come down

tanes" (who supported the Pope's claim to be spiritual head of the church everywhere).

9. A religious fellowship.

upon the altar and take the form of bread and wine. What an awful power, Stephen!

A flame began to flutter again on Stephen's cheek as he heard in this proud address an echo of his own proud musings. How often had he seen himself as a priest wielding calmly and humbly the awful power of which angels and saints stood in reverence! His soul had loved to muse in secret on this desire. He had seen himself, a young and silentmannered priest, entering a confessional swiftly, ascending the altarsteps, incensing, genuflecting, accomplishing the vague acts of the priesthood which pleased him by reason of their semblance of reality and of their distance from it. In that dim life which he had lived through in his musings he had assumed the voices and gestures which he had noted with various priests. He had bent his knee sideways like such a one, he had shaken the thurible[1] only slightly like such a one, his chasuble[2] had swung open like that of such another as he turned to the altar again after having blessed the people. And above all it had pleased him to fill the second place in those dim scenes of his imagining. He shrank from the dignity of celebrant because it displeased him to imagine that all the vague pomp should end in his own person or that the ritual should assign to him so clear and final an office. He longed for the minor sacred offices, to be vested with the tunicle of subdeacon at high mass, to stand aloof from the altar, forgotten by the people, his shoulders covered with a humeral veil,[3] holding the paten within its folds or, when the sacrifice had been accomplished, to stand as deacon in a dalmatic of cloth of gold on the step below the celebrant, his hands joined and his face towards the people, and sing the chant, *Ite missa est.*[4] If ever he had seen himself celebrant it was as in the pictures of the mass in his child's massbook, in a church without worshippers, save for the angel of the sacrifice, at a bare altar and served by an acolyte scarcely more boyish than himself. In vague sacrificial or sacramental acts alone his will seemed drawn to go forth to encounter reality: and it was partly the absence of an appointed rite which had always constrained him to inaction whether he had allowed silence to cover his anger or pride or had suffered only an embrace he longed to give.

He listened in reverent silence now to the priest's appeal and through the words he heard even more distinctly a voice bidding him approach, offering him secret knowledge and secret power. He would know then what was the sin of Simon Magus[5] and what the

---

1. Censer (container in which incense is burned).
2. Sleeveless outer garment worn by celebrant at Mass.
3. Veil covering the shoulders. "Paten": plate on which bread is placed in celebration of the Eucharist (Holy Communion).

4. "Go; it is sent forth." The traditional formula of dismissal at the end of the Mass.
5. The Simon who offered money in order to be given the power of laying on of hands possessed by the apostles (see Acts viii.18–19).

sin against the Holy Ghost for which there was no forgiveness. He would know obscure things, hidden from others, from those who were conceived and born children of wrath. He would know the sins, the sinful longings and sinful thoughts and sinful acts, of others, hearing them murmured into his ears in the confessional under the shame of a darkened chapel by the lips of women and of girls: but rendered immune mysteriously at his ordination by the imposition of hands his soul would pass again uncontaminated to the white peace of the altar. No touch of sin would linger upon the hands with which he would elevate and break the host; no touch of sin would linger on his lips in prayer to make him eat and drink damnation to himself not discerning the body of the Lord. He would hold his secret knowledge and secret power, being as sinless as the innocent: and he would be a priest for ever according to the order of Melchisedec.[6]

—I will offer up my mass tomorrow morning, said the director, that Almighty God may reveal to you His holy will. And let you, Stephen, make a novena[7] to your holy patron saint, the first martyr who is very powerful with God, that God may enlighten your mind. But you must be quite sure, Stephen, that you have a vocation because it would be terrible if you found afterwards that you had none. Once a priest always a priest, remember. Your catechism tells you that the sacrament of Holy Orders is one of those which can be received only once because it imprints on the soul an indelible spiritual mark which can never be effaced. It is before you must weigh well, not after. It is a solemn question, Stephen, because on it may depend the salvation of your eternal soul. But we will pray to God together.

He held open the heavy hall door and gave his hand as if already to a companion in the spiritual life. Stephen passed out on to the wide platform above the steps and was conscious of the caress of mild evening air. Towards Findlater's church a quartette of young men were striding along with linked arms, swaying their heads and stepping to the agile melody of their leader's concertina. The music passed in an instant, as the first bars of sudden music always did, over the fantastic fabrics of his mind, dissolving them painlessly and noiselessly as a sudden wave dissolves the sandbuilt turrets of children. Smiling at the trivial air he raised his eyes to the priest's face and, seeing in it a mirthless reflection of the sunken day, detached his hand slowly which had acquiesced faintly in that companionship.

As he descended the steps the impression which effaced his troubled selfcommunion was that of a mirthless mask reflecting a sunken

---

6. "Thou art a priest forever after the order of Melchisedec" (Hebrews v.6). Cf. Genesis xiv.18: "And Melchizedek king of Salem brought forth bread and wine: and he was the priest of the most high God."

7. Devotion consisting of prayers on nine consecutive days.

day from the threshold of the college. The shadow, then, of the life of the college passed gravely over his consciousness. It was a grave and ordered and passionless life that awaited him, a life without material cares. He wondered how he would pass the first night in the novitiate and with what dismay he would wake the first morning in the dormitory. The troubling odour of the long corridors of Clongowes came back to him and he heard the discreet murmur of the burning gasflames. At once from every part of his being unrest began to irradiate. A feverish quickening of his pulses followed and a din of meaningless words drove his reasoned thoughts hither and thither confusedly. His lungs dilated and sank as if he were inhaling a warm moist unsustaining air, and he smelt again the moist warm air which hung in the bath in Clongowes above the sluggish turfcoloured water.

Some instinct, waking at these memories, stronger than education or piety quickened within him at every near approach to that life, an instinct subtle and hostile, and armed him against acquiescence. The chill and order of the life repelled him. He saw himself rising in the cold of the morning and filing down with the others to early mass and trying vainly to struggle with his prayers against the fainting sickness of his stomach. He saw himself sitting at dinner with the community of a college. What, then, had become of that deeprooted shyness of his which had made him loth to eat or drink under a strange roof? What had come of the pride of his spirit which had always made him conceive himself as a being apart in every order?

The Reverend Stephen Dedalus, S. J.[8]

His name in that new life leaped into characters before his eyes and to it there followed a mental sensation of an undefined face or colour of a face. The colour faded and became strong like a changing glow of pallid brick red. Was it the raw reddish glow he had so often seen on wintry mornings on the shaven gills of the priests? The face was eyeless and sourfavoured and devout, shot with pink tinges of suffocated anger. Was it not a mental spectre of the face of one of the jesuits whom some of the boys called Lantern Jaws and others Foxy Campbell?

He was passing at that moment before the jesuit house in Gardiner Street, and wondered vaguely which window would be his if he ever joined the order. Then he wondered at the vagueness of his wonder, at the remoteness of his soul from what he had hitherto imagined her sanctuary, at the frail hold which so many years of order and obedience had of him when once a definite and irrevocable act of his threatened to end for ever, in time and in eternity, his freedom. The voice of the director urging upon him the proud claims of the church and the mystery and power of the priestly

8. Society of Jesus (the Jesuit order).

office repeated itself idly in his memory. His soul was not there to hear and greet it and he knew now that the exhortation he had listened to had already fallen into an idle formal tale. He would never swing the thurible before the tabernacle as priest. His destiny was to be elusive of social or religious orders. The wisdom of the priest's appeal did not touch him to the quick. He was destined to learn his own wisdom apart from others or to learn the wisdom of others himself wandering among the snares of the world.

The snares of the world were its ways of sin. He would fall. He had not yet fallen but he would fall silently, in an instant. Not to fall was too hard, too hard: and he felt the silent lapse of his soul, as it would be at some instant to come, falling, falling, but not yet fallen, still unfallen, but about to fall.

[*The Walk on the Shore*]

He could wait no longer.

From the door of Byron's publichouse to the gate of Clontarf Chapel, from the gate of Clontarf Chapel to the door of Byron's publichouse, and then back again to the chapel and then back again to the publichouse he had paced slowly at first, planting his steps scrupulously in the spaces of the patchwork of the footpath, then timing their fall to the fall of verses. A full hour had passed since his father had gone in with Dan Crosby, the tutor, to find out for him something about the university. For a full hour he had paced up and down, waiting: but he could wait no longer.

He set off abruptly for the Bull,[9] walking rapidly lest his father's shrill whistle might call him back; and in a few moments he had rounded the curve at the police barrack and was safe.

Yes, his mother was hostile to the idea, as he had read from her listless silence. Yet her mistrust pricked him more keenly than his father's pride and he thought coldly how he had watched the faith which was fading down in his soul aging and strengthening in her eyes. A dim antagonism gathered force within him and darkened his mind as a cloud against her disloyalty: and when it passed, cloudlike, leaving his mind serene and dutiful towards her again, he was made aware dimly and without regret of a first noiseless sundering of their lives.

The university! So he had passed beyond the challenge of the sentries who had stood as guardians of his boyhood and had sought to keep him among them that he might be subject to them and serve their ends. Pride after satisfaction uplifted him like long slow waves. The end he had been born to serve yet did not see had led him to escape by an unseen path: and now it beckoned to him once more and a new adventure was about to be opened to him.

9. The places and buildings referred to in this extract are all in Dublin. The Bull is a long tongue of land by the sea, fortified to form a protecting sea wall.

It seemed to him that he heard notes of fitful music leaping up wards a tone and downwards a diminished fourth, upwards a tone and downwards a major third, like triple-branching flames leaping fitfully, flame after flame, out of a midnight wood. It was an elfin prelude, endless and formless; and, as it grew wilder and faster, the flames leaping out of time, he seemed to hear from under the boughs and grasses wild creatures racing, their feet pattering like rain upon the leaves. Their feet passed in pattering tumult over his mind, the feet of hares and rabbits, the feet of harts and hinds and antelopes, until he heard them no more and remembered only a proud cadence from Newman:[1]—

—Whose feet are as the feet of harts and underneath the ever-lasting arms.

The pride of that dim image brought back to his mind the dignity of the office he had refused. All through his boyhood he had mused upon that which he had so often thought to be his destiny and when the moment had come for him to obey the call he had turned aside, obeying a wayward instinct. Now time lay between: the oils of ordination would never anoint his body. He had refused. Why?

He turned seaward from the road at Dollymount and as he passed on to the thin wooden bridge he felt the planks shaking with the tramp of heavily shod feet. A squad of Christian Brothers was on its way back from the Bull and had begun to pass, two by two, across the bridge. Soon the whole bridge was trembling and resounding. The uncouth faces passed him two by two, stained yellow or red or livid by the sea, and as he strove to look at them with ease and indifference, a faint stain of personal shame and commiseration rose to his own face. Angry with himself he tried to hide his face from their eyes by gazing down sideways into the shallow swirling water under the bridge but he still saw a reflection therein of their topheavy silk hats, and humble tapelike collars and loosely hanging clerical clothes.

—Brother Hickey.

Brother Quaid.

Brother MacArdle.

Brother Keogh.

Their piety would be like their names, like their faces, like their clothes; and it was idle for him to tell himself that their humble and contrite hearts,[2] it might be, paid a far richer tribute of devotion than his had ever been, a gift tenfold more acceptable than his elaborate adoration. It was idle for him to move himself to be generous towards them, to tell himself that if he ever came to their gates, stripped of his pride, beaten and in beggar's weeds, that they

1. John Henry Cardinal Newman.
2. "The sacrifices of God are a broken spirit: a broken and a contrite heart,
O God, thou wilt not despise" (Psalms li.17).

would be generous towards him, loving him as themselves. Idle and embittering, finally, to argue, against his own dispassionate certitude, that the commandment of love bade us not to love our neighbour as ourselves with the same amount and intensity of love but to love him as ourselves with the same kind of love.

He drew forth a phrase from his treasure and spoke it softly to himself:

—A day of dappled seaborne clouds.—

The phrase and the day and the scene harmonised in a chord. Words. Was it their colours? He allowed them to glow and fade, hue after hue: sunrise gold, the russet and green of apple orchards, azure of waves, the greyfringed fleece of clouds. No, it was not their colours: it was the poise and balance of the period itself. Did he then love the rhythmic rise and fall of words better than their associations of legend and colour? Or was it that, being as weak of sight as he was shy of mind, he drew less pleasure from the reflection of the glowing sensible world through the prism of a language manycoloured and richly storied than from the contemplation of an inner world of individual emotions mirrored perfectly in a lucid supple periodic prose?

He passed from the trembling bridge on to firm land again. At that instant, as it seemed to him, the air was chilled; and looking askance towards the water he saw a flying squall darkening and crisping suddenly the tide. A faint click at his heart, a faint throb in his throat told him once more of how his flesh dreaded the cold infra-human odour of the sea: yet he did not strike across the downs on his left but held straight on along the spine of rocks that pointed against the river's mouth.

A veiled sunlight lit up faintly the grey sheet of water where the river was embayed. In the distance along the course of the slow-flowing Liffey slender masts flecked the sky and, more distant still, the dim fabric of the city lay prone in haze. Like a scene on some vague arras, old as man's weariness, the image of the seventh city of Christendom was visible to him across the timeless air, no older nor more weary nor less patient of subjection than in the days of the thingmote.[3]

Disheartened, he raised his eyes towards the slowdrifting clouds, dappled and seaborne. They were voyaging across the deserts of the sky, a host of nomads on the march, voyaging high over Ireland, westward bound. The Europe they had come from lay out there beyond the Irish Sea, Europe of strange tongues and valleyed and woodbegirt and citadelled and of entrenched and marshalled races. He heard a confused music within him as of memories and names which he was almost conscious of but could not capture even for

3. Ancient Scandinavian public assembly; Dublin, "the seventh city of Christendom," was settled and ruled by the Danes in the 9th and 10th centuries.

an instant; then the music seemed to recede, to recede, to recede: and from each receding trail of nebulous music there fell always one long-drawn calling note, piercing like a star the dusk of silence. Again! Again! Again! A voice from beyond the world was calling.

—Hello, Stephanos!

—Here comes The Dedalus!

—Ao! . . . Eh, give it over, Dwyer, I'm telling you or I'll give you a stuff in the kisser for yourself. . . . Ao!

—Good man, Towser! Duck him!

—Come along, Dedalus! Bous Stephanoumenos![4] Bous Stephaneforos!

—Duck him! Guzzle him now, Towser!

—Help! Help! . . . Ao!

He recognised their speech collectively before he distinguished their faces. The mere sight of that medley of wet nakedness chilled him to the bone. Their bodies, corpsewhite or suffused with a pallid golden light or rawly tanned by the suns, gleamed with the wet of the sea. Their divingstone, poised on its rude supports and rocking under their plunges, and the rough-hewn stones of the sloping breakwater over which they scrambled in their horseplay, gleamed with cold wet lustre. The towels with which they smacked their bodies were heavy with cold seawater: and drenched with cold brine was their matted hair.

He stood still in deference to their calls and parried their banter with easy words. How characterless they looked: Shuley without his deep unbuttoned collar, Ennis without his scarlet belt with the snaky clasp, and Connolly without his Norfolk coat with the flap-less sidepockets! It was a pain to see them and a sword-like pain to see the signs of adolescence that made repellent their pitiable nakedness. Perhaps they had taken refuge in number and noise from the secret dread in their souls. But he, apart from them and in silence, remembered in what dread he stood of the mystery of his own body.

—Stephanos Dedalos! Bous Stephanoumenos! Bous Stephaneforos!

Their banter was not new to him and now it flattered his mild proud sovereignty. Now, as never before, his strange name seemed to him a prophecy. So timeless seemed the grey warm air, so fluid and impersonal his own mood, that all ages were as one to him. A moment before the ghost of the ancient kingdom of the Danes had looked forth through the vesture of the hazewrapped city. Now, at the name of the fabulous artificer,[5] he seemed to hear the noise of dim waves and to see a winged form flying above the waves and

---

4. Greek, "garlanded ox." "Stephanos" is the Greek for "crown," and sacrificial animals were crowned with garlands. "Bous Stephaneforos" means similarly "crown-bearing (or garland-bearing) ox."

5. The Greek craftsman Daedalus: see introductory note to *A Portrait*.

slowly climbing the air. What did it mean? Was it a quaint device opening a page of some medieval book of prophecies and symbols, a hawklike man flying sunward above the sea, a prophecy of the end he had been born to serve and had been following through the mists of childhood and boyhood, a symbol of the artist forging anew in his workshop out of the sluggish matter of the earth a new soaring impalpable imperishable being?

His heart trembled; his breath came faster and a wild spirit passed over his limbs as though he were soaring sunward. His heart trembled in an ecstasy of fear and his soul was in flight. His soul was soaring in an air beyond the world and the body he knew was purified in a breath and delivered of incertitude and made radiant and commingled with the element of the spirit. An ecstasy of flight made radiant his eyes and wild his breath and tremulous and wild and radiant his windswept limbs.

—One! Two! . . . Look out!

—O, Cripes, I'm drownded!

—One! Two! Three and away!

—The next! The next!

—One! . . . Uk!

—Stephaneforos!

His throat ached with a desire to cry aloud, the cry of a hawk or eagle on high, to cry piercingly of his deliverance to the winds. This was the call of life to his soul not the dull gross voice of the world of duties and despair, not the inhuman voice that had called him to the pale service of the altar. An instant of wild flight had delivered him and the cry of triumph which his lips withheld cleft his brain.

—Stephaneforos!

What were they now but the cerements shaken from the body of death—the fear he had walked in night and day, the incertitude that had ringed him round, the shame that had abased him within and without—cerements, the linens of the grave?

His soul had arisen from the grave of boyhood, spurning her graveclothes. Yes! Yes! Yes! He would create proudly out of the freedom and power of his soul, as the great artificer whose name he bore, a living thing, new and soaring and beautiful, impalpable, imperishable.

He started up nervously from the stoneblock for he could no longer quench the flame in his blood. He felt his cheeks aflame and his throat throbbing with song. There was a lust of wandering in his feet that burned to set out for the ends of the earth. On! On! his heart seemed to cry. Evening would deepen above the sea, night fall upon the plains, dawn glimmer before the wanderer and show him strange fields and hills and faces. Where?

He looked northward towards Howth. The sea had fallen below

the line of seawrack on the shallow side of the breakwater and already the tide was running out fast along the foreshore. Already one long oval bank of sand lay warm and dry amid the wavelets. Here and there warm isles of sand gleamed above the shallow tides and about the isles and around the long bank and amid the shallow currents of the beach were lightclad figures, wading and delving.

In a few moments he was barefoot, his stockings folded in his pockets, and his canvas shoes dangling by their knotted laces over his shoulders and, picking a pointed salteaten stick out of the jetsam among the rocks, he clambered down the slope of the breakwater.

There was a long rivulet in the strand and, as he waded slowly up its course, he wondered at the endless drift of seaweed. Emerald and black and russet and olive, it moved beneath the current, swaying and turning. The water of the rivulet was dark with endless drift and mirrored the highdrifting clouds. The clouds were drifting above him silently and silently the seatangle was drifting below him; and the grey warm air was still: and a new wild life was singing in his veins.

Where was his boyhood now? Where was the soul that had hung back from her destiny, to brood alone upon the shame of her wounds and in her house of squalor and subterfuge to queen it in faded cerements and in wreaths that withered at the touch? Or where was he?

He was alone. He was unheeded, happy, and near to the wild heart of life. He was alone and young and wilful and wildhearted, alone amid a waste of wild air and brackish waters and the seaharvest of shells and tangle and veiled grey sunlight and gayclad lightclad figures of children and girls and voices childish and girlish in the air.

A girl stood before him in midstream, alone and still, gazing out to sea. She seemed like one whom magic had changed into the likeness of a strange and beautiful seabird. Her long slender bare legs were delicate as a crane's and pure save where an emerald trail of seaweed had fashioned itself as a sign upon the flesh. Her thighs, fuller and softhued as ivory, were bared almost to the hips where the white fringes of her drawers were like feathering of soft white down. Her slateblue skirts were kilted boldly about her waist and dovetailed behind her. Her bosom was as a bird's, soft and slight, slight and soft as the breast of some darkplumaged dove. But her long fair hair was girlish: and girlish, and touched with the wonder of mortal beauty, her face.

She was alone and still, gazing out to sea; and when she felt his presence and the worship of his eyes her eyes turned to him in quiet sufferance of his gaze, without shame or wantonness. Long, long she suffered his gaze and then quietly withdrew her eyes from his and bent them towards the stream, gently stirring the water with her foot hither and thither. The first faint noise of gently moving water broke the silence, low and faint and whispering, faint as the bells of sleep; hither and thither, hither and thither: and a faint flame trembled on her cheek.

—Heavenly God! cried Stephen's soul, in an outburst of profane joy.

He turned away from her suddenly and set off across the strand. His cheeks were aflame; his body was aglow; his limbs were trembling. On and on and on and on he strode, far out over the sands, singing wildly to the sea, crying to greet the advent of the life that had cried to him.

Her image had passed into his soul for ever and no word had broken the holy silence of his ecstasy. Her eyes had called him and his soul had leaped at the call. To live, to err, to fall, to triumph, to recreate life out of life! A wild angel had appeared to him, the angel of mortal youth and beauty, an envoy from the fair courts of life, to throw open before him in an instant of ecstasy the gates of all the ways of error and glory. On and on and on and on!

He halted suddenly and heard his heart in the silence. How far had he walked? What hour was it?

There was no human figure near him nor any sound borne to him over the air. But the tide was near the turn and already the day was on the wane. He turned landward and ran towards the shore and, running up the sloping beach, reckless of the sharp shingle, found a sandy nook amid a ring of tufted sandknolls and lay down there that the peace and silence of the evening might still the riot of his blood.

He felt above him the vast indifferent dome and the calm processes of the heavenly bodies; and the earth beneath him, the earth that had borne him, had taken him to her breast.

He closed his eyes in the languor of sleep. His eyelids trembled as if they felt the vast cyclic movement of the earth and her watchers, trembled as if they felt the strange light of some new world. His soul was swooning into some new world, fantastic, dim, uncertain as under sea, traversed by cloudy shapes and beings. A world, a glimmer, or a flower? Glimmering and trembling, trembling and unfolding, a breaking light, an opening flower, it spread in endless succession to itself, breaking in full crimson and unfolding and fading to palest rose, leaf by leaf and wave of light by wave of light, flooding all the heavens with its soft flushes, every flush deeper than other.

Evening had fallen when he woke and the sand and arid grasses of his bed glowed no longer. He rose slowly and, recalling the rapture of his sleep, sighed at its joy.

He climbed to the crest of the sandhill and gazed about him. Evening had fallen. A rim of the young moon cleft the pale waste of sky like the rim of a silver hoop embedded in grey sand; and the tide was flowing in fast to the land with a low whisper of her waves, islanding a few last figures in distant pools.

1904–14   1916

From Ulysses

[*Proteus*]¹

Ineluctable modality of the visible: at least that if no more, thought through my eyes.² Signatures of all things I am here to read, seaspawn and seawrack, the nearing tide, that rusty boot. Snot-green, bluesilver, rust: coloured signs. Limits of the diaphane.³ But

1. "Proteus" is so titled because of the deliberate analogies that exist between it and the description of Proteus in *Odyssey* IV. (Joyce did not title any of the episodes in *Ulysses*, but the names are his; he used them in correspondence and in talk with friends.)

In Homer's *Odyssey*, Proteus is the changing sea god who continually alters his shape: when Telemachus, the son of Ulysses, asks Menelaus for help in finding his father, Menelaus tells him that he encountered Proteus by the seashore on the island of Pharos "in front of Egypt," and that, by holding on to him while he changed from one shape to another, he was able to force him to tell what had happened to Ulysses and the other Greek heroes of the Trojan war. In Joyce's narrative, Stephen Dedalus (who, like Homer's Telemachus, is looking for a father, but not in the literal "consubstantial" sense) is walking by the Dublin shore alone, "along Sandymount strand," speculating on the shifting shapes of things and the possibility of knowing truth by mere appearances.

First Stephen meditates on the "modality of the visible" and on the mystical notion that God writes his signature on all His works; then on the "modality of the audible," closing his eyes and trying to know reality simply through the sense of hearing. As he continues his walk, the people and objects he sees mingle in his thoughts with memories of his past relations with his family, of his schooldays, his residence in Paris whence he was recalled by his mother's fatal illness, his feel-ing of guilt about his mother's death (he had refused to kneel down and pray at her bedside, since he considered it would be a betrayal of his integrity as an unbeliever), and a variety of speculations about life and reality often derived from mystical works he had read "in the stagnant bay of Marsh's library" (in Dublin). This episode gives the reader a profound awareness of the nature of Stephen's sensibility and the contents of his conscious and subconscious mind and also sets going themes to be developed later in other episodes of *Ulysses*. The highly theoretical, inquiring, musing, speculating mind of Stephen is in sharp contrast to the practical, humane, sensual, concrete imagination of the book's real hero, Leopold Bloom, but there are also significant parallels between the streams of consciousness of the two. Some of the more important themes which emerge in Stephen's reverie are pointed out in footnotes.

The text given here has been collated with the Odyssey Press edition of *Ulysses* (1932), which is accepted as the "definitive standard edition."

2. I.e., the sense of sight provides an unavoidable way ("ineluctable modality") of knowing reality, the knowledge thus provided being a kind of "thought through [the] eyes." The phrase "signature of all things" comes from the German mystic Jakob Böhme, (1575–1624).

3. Transparency. Stephen is speculating on Aristotle's view of perception as developed in his *De Anima*.

he adds: in bodies. Then he was aware of them bodies before of them coloured. How? By knocking his sconce against them. sure. Go easy. Bald he was and a millionaire, *maestro di color che sanno.*[4] Limit of the diaphane in. Why in? Diaphane, adiaphane.[5] If you can put your five fingers through it, it is a gate, if not a door. Shut your eyes and see.

Stephen closed his eyes to hear his boots crush crackling wrack and shells. You are walking through it howsomever. I am, a stride at a time. A very short space of time through very short times of space. Five, six: the *nacheinander.*[6] Exactly: and that is the ineluctable modality of the audible. Open your eyes. No. Jesus! If I fell over a cliff that beetles o'er his base,[7] fell through the *nebeneinander* ineluctably. I am getting on nicely in the dark. My ash sword hangs at my side. Tap with it: they do.[8] My two feet in his boots are at the end of his legs, *nebeneinander.* Sounds solid: made by the mallet of *Los Demiurgos.*[9] Am I walking into eternity along Sandymount strand? Crush, crack, crik, crick. Wild sea money. Dominie[1] Deasy kens them a'.

> *Won't you come to Sandymount,*
> *Madeline the mare?*

Rhythm begins, you see. I hear. A catalectic tetrameter[2] of iambs marching. No, agallop: *deline the mare.*

Open your eyes now. I will. One moment. Has all vanished since? If I open and am for ever in the black adiaphane. *Basta!*[3] I will see

---

4. There was a tradition that Aristotle was bald, with thin legs, small eyes, and a lisp. Aristotle is also traditionally supposed to have inherited considerable wealth and to have been presented with a fortune by his former pupil Alexander the Great. The Italian phrase is Dante's description of Aristotle in the *Inferno,* and means "the master of them that know."
5. What is not transparent (opposite of "diaphane").
6. "After one another." Stephen, with eyes shut, is now sensing reality through the sense of sound only: unlike sight, sound falls on the sense of hearing in chronological sequence, one sound after another.
7. "What if it tempt you toward the flood, my lord, / Or to the dreadful summit of the cliff / That beetles o'er his base into the sea * * * " (*Hamlet* I.iv.69–71). *"Nebeneinander":* beside one another.
8. Stephen is still walking with his eyes shut, tapping with his "ash sword" (the walking stick of ash wood he a¹ways carried), as "they" (i.e., blind

people) do. "His boots": Buck Mulligan's. Stephen, lacking boots of his own, had borrowed a castoff pair of Mulligan's.
9. The Demiurge, supernatural being who made the world in subordination to God. The mystical notion of the Demiurge who created the world haunts Stephen's mind; it is the Demiurge who writes his signature on created objects and whose mallet fashioned them. The world, sensed by the ear only, "sounds solid," as though made by the Demiurge's hammer.
1. Schoolmaster. Mr. Deasy was the headmaster of the school where Stephen taught (the previous episode has shown Stephen teaching). "Kens them a'": knows them all; Stephen is putting Deasy into a mock-Scottish folk song.
2. The first of the two lines of popular verse which have come into Stephen's head consists metrically of four iambic feet ("tetrameter") with the unstressed syllable of the first iamb missing ("catalectic").
3. Italian, "Enough!"

if I can see.

See now. There all the time without you: and ever shall be, world without end.

They came down the steps from Leahy's terrace prudently, *Frauenzimmer*:[4] and down the shelving shore flabbily their splayed feet sinking in the silted sand. Like me, like Algy,[5] coming down to our mighty mother. Number one swung lourdily[6] her midwife's bag, the other's gamp poked in the beach. From the liberties, out for the day. Mrs. Florence MacCabe,[7] relict of the late Patk Mac-Cabe, deeply lamented, of Bride Street. One of her sisterhood lugged me squealing into life. Creation from nothing. What has she in the bag? A misbirth with a trailing navelcord, hushed in ruddy wool. The cords of all link back, strandentwining cable of all flesh. That is why mystic monks. Will you be as gods? Gaze in your omphalos. Hello. Kinch here. Put me on to Edenville. Aleph, alpha: nought, nought, one.[8]

Spouse and helpmate of Adam Kadmon:[9] Heva, naked Eve. She had no navel. Gaze. Belly without blemish, bulging big, a buckler of taut vellum, no, whiteheaped corn, orient and immortal, standing from everlasting to everlasting.[1] Womb of sin.

Wombed in sin darkness I was too, made not begotten. By them, the man with my voice and my eyes and a ghostwoman with ashes on her breath.[2] They clasped and sundered, did the coupler's will. From before the ages He willed me and now may not will me away

---

4. "Midwives": Stephen sees them coming from Leahy's Terrace, which runs by the beach.
5. Algernon Charles Swinburne, who wrote: "I will go back to the great sweet mother, / Mother and lover of men, the sea. I will go down to her, I and none other * * * " (*The Triumph of Time*).
6. Heavily (coined by Stephen from the French *lourd*). Stephen, like Joyce, had studied modern languages at University College, Dublin, and his preoccupation with words and languages is part of his character as potential literary artist. "Gamp": umbrella; and perhaps reference to Mrs. Gamp, the nurse in Dickens' *Martin Chuzzlewit*.
7. Stephen imagines the first midwife is called Mrs. MacCabe. "Relict": widow.
8. Stephen is speculating on the mystical significance of the navel cord, seeing it as linking the generations, the combined navel cords stretching back to Adam and Eve. A mystic gazed in his *omphalos* (navel) to make contact with the first man. Stephen thinks of himself ("Kinch," his nickname) calling up Adam in "Edenville" through his navel,

using the line of linked navel cords as a telephone line. Adam's telephone number, "Aleph, alpha: nought, nought, one," begins with the first letters of the Hebrew and of the Greek alphabet to suggest the great primeval number.
9. "Adam the Beginner," so called in Hebrew cabalistic literature of the Middle Ages; "Heva" is Hebrew for Eve. Because she was not born in the regular way, but created from Adam's rib, she had no navel.
1. Stephen is led, through reflection on Eve's navel-less "belly without blemish," to a recollection of the description of the original Eden (Paradise) by Thomas Traherne (ca. 1637–74), from whose prose *Centuries of Meditation* he quotes: "The corn was orient and immortal wheat, which should never be reaped, nor was ever sown. I thought it had stood from everlasting to everlasting. * * * " But immediately afterwards Stephen reflects that such language is inappropriate to Eve's body, as hers was the "womb of sin"—i.e., she first ate the fatal apple and brought forth sin.
2. Stephen is haunted by thoughts of his mother in this guise.

or ever. A *lex eterna*[3] stays about Him. Is that then the divine substance wherein Father and Son are consubstantial? Where is poor dear Arius[4] to try conclusions? Warring his life long on the contransmagnificandjewbangtantiality.[5] Illstarred heresiarch.[6] In a Greek watercloset he breathed his last: euthanasia. With beaded mitre and with crozier, stalled upon his throne, widower of a widowed see, with upstiffed omophorion, with clotted hinderparts.

Airs romped around him, nipping and eager airs. They are coming, waves. The whitemaned seahorses, champing, brightwindbridled, the steeds of Mananaan.[7]

I mustn't forget his letter for the press. And after? The Ship, half twelve. By the way go easy with that money like a good young imbecile. Yes, I must.[8]

His pace slackened. Here. Am I going to Aunt Sara's or not? My consubstantial father's voice. Did you see anything of your artist brother Stephen lately? No? Sure he's not down in Strasburg terrace with his aunt Sally? Couldn't he fly a bit higher than that, eh? And and and and tell us Stephen, how is uncle Si? O weeping God, the things I married into. De boys up in de hayloft. The drunken little costdrawer and his brother, the cornet player. Highly respectable gondoliers. And skeweyed Walter sirring his father, no less. Sir. Yes, sir. No, sir. Jesus wept: and no wonder, by Christ.[9]

I pull the wheezy bell of their shuttered cottage: and wait. They take me for a dun, peer out from a coign of vantage.[1]

—It's Stephen, sir.

3. Eternal law. God's eternal law, Stephen reflects, willed his birth from the beginning. He then goes on to speculate on the nature of the divine substance and whether God the Father and God the Son are of the same substance ("consubstantial").

4. 3rd-century theologian who "tried conclusions" on this matter, maintaining that Christ was less divine than God (Arius' views were condemned as heretical by the Council of Nicaea in 325).

5. Ironic "portmanteau word" made up of terms connected with the Arian controversy—"consubstantial," "transubstantial" (of a substance that changes into another)—and with the facts of Christ's nature (e.g., "Jew"; Jesus was a Jew, as Leopold Bloom in a later episode reminds an anti-Semitic Irishman).

6. Arch-heretic. Arius died suddenly in Constantinople in 336. He was never a bishop, and Stephen's image of him at the moment of death in full episcopal attire seems to combine recollections of other early "heresiarchs." In an earlier reverie Stephen had conjured up in his mind "a horde of heresies fleeing with mitres awry." These heretics are connected in Stephen's mind with argument about the relation between God the Father and God the Son and so

with the problem of the true nature of paternity, which haunts him constantly.

7. Mananaan MacLir, Celtic sea god; his steeds are the "white horses" (still the name in Britain for the white foam on top of waves).

8. Mr. Deasy had given Stephen a letter to the press to be taken to the newspaper office. After that he has an appointment with Mulligan at The Ship, a tavern. "That money" is Mr. Deasy's last payment to him.

9. Stephen has been wondering whether to call on his uncle and aunt, Richie and Sara Goulding. He imagines his father interrogating him about the visit as if he had gone, and then pictures his cousins asking after his father, Simon Dedalus (his cousins' "uncle Si"). Simon Dedalus is contemptuous of his wife's relations (Sara Goulding is his wife's sister). Stephen knows that any mention of them will bring on the familiar abuse of "the things I married into"—at best "highly respectable gondoliers" (from Gilbert and Sullivan's opera *The Gondoliers*). The scene that follows is also Stephen's purely imaginary picture of what the visit would be like.

1. Favorable corner.

—Let him in. Let Stephen in.

A bolt drawn back and Walter welcomes me.

—We thought you were someone else.

In his broad bed nuncle Richie, pillowed and blanketed, extends over the hillock of his knees a sturdy forearm. Clean chested. He has washed the upper moiety.

—Morrow, nephew.

He lays aside the lapboard whereon he drafts his bills of costs for the eyes of Master Goff and Master Shapland Tandy, filing consents and common searches and a writ of *Duces Tecum.*[2] A bogoak frame over his bald head: Wilde's *Requiescat.*[3] The drone of his misleading whistle brings Walter back.

—Yes, sir?

—Malt[4] for Richie and Stephen, tell mother. Where is she?

—Bathing Crissie, sir.

Papa's little bedpal. Lump of love.

—No, uncle Richie. . .

—Call me Richie. Damn your lithia water. It lowers. Whusky!

—Uncle Richie, really. . .

—Sit down or by the law Harry I'll knock you down.

Walter squints vainly for a chair.

—He has nothing to sit down on, sir.

—He has nowhere to put it, you mug. Bring in our Chippendale chair. Would you like a bite of something? None of your damned lawdeedaw air here; the rich of a rasher fried with a herring? Sure? So much the better. We have nothing in the house but backache pills.

All'erta![5]

He drones bars of Ferrando's *aria di sortita.* The grandest number, Stephen, in the whole opera. Listen.

His tuneful whistle sounds again, finely shaded, with rushes of the air, his fists bigdrumming on his padded knees.

This wind is sweeter.

Houses of decay, mine, his and all. You told the Clongowes gentry you had an uncle a judge and an uncle a general in the army.[6] Come out of them, Stephen. Beauty is not there. Nor in the stagnant bay of Marsh's library where you read the fading prophecies of Joachim Abbas.[7] For whom? The hundredheaded

2. "You shall take with you": opening words of search warrant. Goulding was a law clerk with Messrs. Goff and Tandy.

3. Poem by Oscar Wilde.

4. Whisky.

5. "Look out!" The first words of the *aria di sortita* (aria of a singer's entrance) sung by Ferrando, captain of the guard, in Verdi's opera *Il Trovatore.*

6. Stephen, reflecting on the steady social decline of his family, is remembering that, while at school at Clongowes Wood College, he had pretended to have important relations.

7. Abbot Joachim of Floris (the monastery of San Giovanni in Fiore, Italy), 12th-century mystic and theologian, whose prophetic work *Expositio in Apocalypsin* Stephen (i.e., Joyce) had read in Marsh's Library.

rabble of the cathedral close.[8] A hater of his kind ran from them to the wood of madness, his mane foaming in the moon, his eyeballs stars. Houyhnhnm, horsenostrilled.[9] The oval equine faces, Temple, Buck Mulligan, Foxy Campbell. Lantern jaws. Abbas father,[1] furious dean, what offence laid fire to their brains? Paff! *Descende, calve, ut ne nimium decalveris.*[2] A garland of grey hair on his comminated head see him me clambering down to the footpace (*descende*), clutching a monstrance, basiliskeyed. Get down, bald poll! A choir gives back menace and echo, assisting about the altar's horns, the snorted Latin of jackpriests moving burly in their albs, tonsured and oiled and gelded, fat with the fat of kidneys of wheat.

And at the same instant perhaps a priest round the corner is elevating it. Dringdring! And two streets off another locking it into a pyx.[3] Dringadring! And in a ladychapel another taking housel all to his own cheek. Dringdring! Down, up, forward, back. Dan Occam[4] thought of that, invincible doctor. A misty English morning the imp hypostasis tickled his brain. Bringing his host down and kneeling he heard twine with his second bell the first bell in the transept (he is lifting his) and, rising, heard (now I am lifting) their two bells (he is kneeling) twang in diphthong.

Cousin Stephen, you will never be a saint.[5] Isle of saints.[6] You were awfully holy, weren't you? You prayed to the Blessed Virgin that you might not have a red nose. You prayed to the devil in Serpentine avenue that the fubsy widow in front might lift her clothes still more from the wet street. *O si, certo!*[7] Sell your soul for that, do, dyed rags pinned round a squaw. More tell me, more still! On the top of the Howth tram alone crying to the rain: *naked women!* What about that, eh?

What about what? What else were they invented for?

8. I.e., the precinct of a cathedral (Marsh's Library is in the close of St. Patrick's Cathedral).
9. St. Patrick's Close has recalled Jonathan Swift (who was Dean of St. Patrick's). Stephen remembers Swift's misanthropy (he was "a hater of his kind") and his creation of the Houyhnhnms (noble horses) in Book IV of *Gulliver's Travels.* Then he thinks of people he knew who have horse-faces.
1. "Abbas" means literally "father."
2. "Go down, bald-head, lest you become even balder." This sentence, from Joachim's *Concordia* of the Old and New Testaments, is based on the mocking cry of the children to the prophet Elisha (II Kings ii.23: "Go up, thou bald head"); Joachim saw Elisha as a forerunner of St. Benedict—both had shaven or baldish heads. Stephen imagines the "comminated" (i.e., threatened) head of Joachim descending, clutching a "monstrance" (receptacle in which the consecrated host is exposed for adoration), in the midst of a nightmare church service.
3. Vessel in which the Host (consecrated bread or wafer) is kept. Stephen is imagining such a service, with himself officiating (he almost became a priest).
4. William of Occam or Ockham ("Dan" means "master"), 14th-century English theologian, who held that the individual thing is the reality and its name, the universal, an abstraction; he was concerned with "hypostasis"—the essential part of a thing as distinct from its attributes.
5. A parody of the words of Dryden to his distant relative Swift: "Cousin, you will never make a poet."
6. Ireland was called *"insula sanctorum,"* ("isle of saints") in the Middle Ages.
7. "Oh yes, certainly!"

Reading two pages apiece of seven books every night, eh? I was young. You bowed to yourself in the mirror, stepping forward to applause earnestly, striking face. Hurray for the Goddamned idiot! Hray! No-one saw: tell no-one. Books you were going to write with letters for titles. Have you read his F? O yes, but I prefer Q. Yes, but W is wonderful. O yes, W. Remember your epiphanies[8] on green oval leaves, deeply deep, copies to be sent if you died to all the great libraries of the world, including Alexandria? Someone was to read them there after a few thousand years, a mahamanvantara.[9] Pico della Mirandola like. Ay, very like a whale.[1] When one reads these strange pages of one long gone one feels that one is at one with one who once. . .

The grainy sand had gone from under his feet. His boots trod again a damp crackling mast, razorshells, squeaking pebbles, that on the unnumbered pebbles beats, wood sieved by the shipworm, lost Armáda. Unwholesome sandflats waited to suck his treading soles, breathing upward sewage breath. He coasted them, walking warily. A porterbottle stood up, stogged to its waist, in the cakey sand dough. A sentinel: isle of dreadful thirst.[2] Broken hoops on the shore; at the land a maze of dark cunning nets; farther away chalkscrawled backdoors and on the higher beach a dryingline with two crucified shirts. Ringsend: wigwams of brown steersmen and master mariners. Human shells.

He halted. I have passed the way to aunt Sara's. Am I not going there? Seems not. No-one about. He turned northeast and crossed the firmer sand towards the Pigeonhouse.[3]

—*Qui vous a mis dans cette fichue position?*

—*C'est le pigeon, Joseph.*

8. Joyce's own term for the prose poems he wrote as a young man. An epiphany, he said, was the sudden "revelation of the whatness of a thing" —of a gesture, a phrase, or a thought which he had experienced; he attempted to express, in the writing, the moment at which "the soul of the commonest object * * * seems to us radiant." Stephen's recollection of early and exotic literary ambitions is drawn directly from Joyce's own ambitions at the same age.
9. Cycle of change and recurrence, in Indian mystical thought. It is connected in Stephen's mind with the constant ebb and flow of the sea by which he is walking. Pico della Mirandola was a 15th-century mystical philosopher; his *Heptaplus* is a mystical account of the creation, much influenced by Jewish cabalistic thought.
1. Polonius to Hamlet (*Hamlet* III.ii.399) with reference to the changing shape of a cloud. The Protean theme of constant change, of ebb and flow, and of metempsychosis (i.e., trans-

migration of souls: a major theme in *Ulysses*), is working in Stephen's mind. The following sentence is a parody of an elegant, condescending modern essay on Pico or some other early mystic.
2. The atmosphere of the sandflats reminds Stephen of a desert island where men die of thirst. (The island of Pharos, where Menelaus found Proteus, was an "island of dreadful hunger.")
3. The Pigeon house in Ringsend, an old structure built on a breakwater in Dublin Bay and which in the course of time has served a great variety of purposes, suggests to Stephen the Dove which is the symbol of the Holy Spirit, and this in turn suggests an irreverent dialogue (supposedly between Joseph and Mary when Mary is found to be pregnant: "Who has got you into this wretched condition?" "It was the pigeon [i.e., the Holy Dove], Joseph"). This he had picked up in Paris from the blasphemous M. Léo Taxil, whose book *La Vie de Jésus* ("The Life of Jesus") is mentioned in the next paragraph.

Patrice, home on furlough, lapped warm milk with me in the bar MacMahon. Son of the wild goose, Kevin Egan of Paris. My father's a bird, he lapped the sweet *lait chaud* with pink young tongue, plump bunny's face. Lap, *lapin*. He hopes to win in the *gros lots*. About the nature of women he read in Michelet. But he must send me *La Vie de Jésus* by M. Léo Taxil. Lent it to his friend.[4]

—*C'est tordant, vous savez. Moi je suis socialiste. Je ne crois pas en l'existence de Dieu. Faut pas le dire à mon père.*

—*Il croit?*

—*Mon père, oui.*

Schluss. He laps.[5]

My Latin quarter hat. God, we simply must dress the character. I want puce gloves. You were a student, weren't you? Of what in the other devil's name? Paysayenn. P. C. N., you know: *physiques, chimiques et naturelles.*[6] Aha. Eating your groatsworth of *mou en civet*, fleshpots of Egypt, elbowed by belching cabmen. Just say in the most natural tone: when I was in Paris, *boul' Mich',*[7] I used to. Yes, used to carry punched tickets to prove an alibi if they arrested you for murder somewhere. Justice. On the night of the seventeenth of February 1904 the prisoner was seen by two witnesses. Other fellow did it: other me. Hat, tie, overcoat, nose. *Lui, c'est moi.*[8] You seem to have enjoyed yourself.

Proudly walking. Whom were you trying to walk like? Forget: a dispossessed. With mother's money order, eight shillings, the banging door of the post office slammed in your face by the usher. Hunger toothache. *Encore deux minutes.* Look clock. Must get. *Fermé.* Hired dog! Shoot him to bloody bits with a bang shotgun, bits man spattered walls all brass buttons. Bits all khrrrrklak in place clack back. Not hurt? O, that's all right. Shake hands. See what I meant, see? O, that's all right. Shake a shake. O, that's all only all right.[9]

4. Stephen had first met Léo Taxil through Patrice, the son of "Kevin Egan of Paris," who in real life was the exiled nationalist Joseph Casey. The phrase "my father's a bird" comes from *The Song of the Cheerful Jesus,* a blasphemous poem by Buck Mulligan (actually Oliver Gogarty, who really wrote the poem); Stephen recalls Patrice reciting it as he drank warm milk (*"lait chaud"*), lapping it like a *"lapin"* ("rabbit"), and expressing the hope that he would win something substantial in the French national lottery (*gros lot:* "first prize"). Jules Michelet (1798–1874) was a French historian.
5. Conversation between Stephen and Patrice: "It's screamingly funny, you know. I'm a socialist myself. I don't believe in the existence of God. Mustn't tell my father." "He is a believer?"

"My father, yes." "*Schluss*": end.
6. I.e., the faculty of physics, chemistry, and biology at the École de Médecine in Paris, where Stephen, like Joyce, took a premedical course for a short time. The faculty was popularly known as "P. C. N." (pronounced "Paysayenn"). *"Mou en civet":* stew.
7. Popular Parisian abbreviation for the Boulevard Saint Michel.
8. "He is me"—a parody of Louis XIV's remark, *"L'état c'est moi"* ("I am the state").
9. A recollection of the occasion when, desperate for money, Stephen had received a money order for eight shillings from his mother. Afflicted with both hunger and toothache, he had gone to cash it at the post office—which was closed, even though, as he expostulated with the man at the door, there were still two minutes (*"encore deux min-*

You were going to do wonders, what? Missionary to Europe after fiery Columbanus.[1] Fiacre and Scotus on their creepystools in heaven spilt from their pintpots, loudlatinlaughing: *Euge! Euge!*[2] Pretending to speak broken English as you dragged your valise, porter threepence, across the slimy pier at Newhaven. *Comment?* Rich booty you brought back; *Le tutu*, five tattered numbers of *Pantalon Blanc et Culotte Rouge*,[3] a blue French telegram, curiosity to show:

—Mother dying come home father.[4]

The aunt thinks you killed your mother. That's why she won't.[5]

> *Then here's a health to Mulligan's aunt*
> *And I'll tell you the reason why.*
> *She always kept things decent in*
> *The Hannigan famileye.*

His feet marched in sudden proud rhythm over the sand furrows, along by the boulders of the south wall. He stared at them proudly, piled stone mammoth skulls. Gold light on sea, on sand, on boulders. The sun is there, the slender trees, the lemon houses.

Paris rawly waking, crude sunlight on her lemon streets. Moist pith of farls[6] of bread, the froggreen wormwood, her matin incense, court the air. Belluomo rises from the bed of his wife's lover's wife, the kerchiefed housewife is astir, a saucer of acetic acid in her hands. In Rodot's Yvonne and Madeleine newmake their tumbled beauties, shattering with gold teeth *chaussons* of pastry, their mouths yellowed with the *pus* of *flan breton*.[7] Faces of Paris men go by, their wellpleased pleasers, curled conquistadores.[8]

Noon slumbers. Kevin Egan rolls gunpowder cigarettes through fingers smeared with printer's ink,[9] sipping his green fairy as Patrice his white. About us gobblers fork spiced beans down their gullets. *Un demi setier!*[1] A jet of coffee steam from the burnished caldron. She serves me at his beck. *Il est irlandais. Hollandais? Non fromage. Deux irlandais, nous, Irlande, vous savez? Ah oui!*[2] She thought you wanted a cheese *hollandais*. Your postprandial, do you know

---

utes") until the official closing time. In his retrospective rage he imagines himself shooting the "hired dog" to bits, and then in a revulsion of feeling has a mental reconciliation with him.
1. 6th-century Irish missionary on the Continent. Fiacre was a 6th-century Irish saint. Duns Scotus (ca. 1265–1308): Scholastic theologian and philosopher. "Creepystools": low stools.
2. "Well done!"
3. Like the preceding name, name of French popular periodical.
4. This telegram was actually received by Joyce in Paris.
5. Stephen recalls Buck Mulligan's telling him that his (Mulligan's) aunt disapproved of Stephen because, by refusing to pray at his dying mother's bedside, he had hastened her death.

Stephen then tries to laugh away his feeling of guilt by quoting mentally a (slightly parodied) verse of a popular song.
6. Thin circular cakes.
7. Memories of a restaurant in Paris: "*chaussons*" are pastry turnovers; "*flan breton*" is a pastry filled with custard.
8. Conquerors (Spanish).
9. Egan (i.e., Joseph Casey) became a typesetter for the Parisian edition of the *New York Herald*.
1. Abusive Parisian slang for a liquid measure (about one fourth of a liter) —here, presumably, of wine or beer.
2. "He is Irish. Dutch? Not cheese. We are two Irishmen, Ireland, you understand? Oh, yes!"

that word? Postprandial. There was a fellow I knew once in Barcelona, queer fellow, used to call it his postprandial. Well: *slainte!*[3] Around the slabbed tables the tangle of wined breaths and grumbling gorges. His breath hangs over our saucestained plates, the green fairy's fang thrusting between his lips. Of Ireland, the Dalcassions, of hopes, conspiracies, of Arthur Griffith now.[4] To yoke me as his yokefellow, our crimes our common cause. You're your father's son. I know the voice. His fustian shirt, sanguineflowered, trembles its Spanish tassels at his secrets. M. Drumont,[5] famous journalist, Drumont, know what he called queen Victoria? Old hag with the yellow teeth. *Vieille ogresse* with the *dents jaunes.* Maud Gonne, beautiful woman, *La Patrie*, M. Millevoye, Félix Faure,[6] know how he died? Licentious men. The froeken, *bonne à tout faire,*[7] who rubs male nakedness in the bath at Upsala. *Moi faire*, she said. *Tous les messieurs.*[8] Not this *Monsieur*, I said. Most licentious custom. Bath a most private thing. I wouldn't let my brother, not even my own brother, most lascivious thing. Green eyes, I see you. Fang, I feel. Lascivious people.

The blue fuse burns deadly between hands and burns clear. Loose tobacco shreds catch fire: a flame and acrid smoke light our corner. Raw facebones under his peep of day boy's hat. How the head centre got away, authentic version. Got up as a young bride, man, veil, orangeblossoms, drove out the road to Malahide. Did, faith. Of lost leaders, the betrayed, wild escapes. Disguises, clutched at, gone, not here.[9]

Spurned lover. I was a strapping young gossoon[1] at that time, I tell you, I'll show you my likeness one day. I was, faith. Lover, for her love he prowled with colonel Richard Burke, tanist[2] of his sept, under the walls of Clerkenwell[3] and, crouching, saw a flame of vengeance hurl them upward in the fog. Shattered glass and toppling masonry. In gay Paree he hides, Egan of Paris, unsought by any save by me. Making his day's stations, the dingy printingcase, his three taverns, the Montmartre lair he sleeps short night in, rue de la Goutte-d'Or, damascened with flyblown faces of the

3. Gaelic, "Your health!"
4. Two extremes of Irish history: from the Dalcassian line came the early kings of Munster (from A.D. 300 on); Arthur Griffith (1872–1922) was an Irish revolutionary leader, founder of the Sinn Fein ("We Ourselves") movement.
5. Édouard Drumont (1844–1917), French politician and bitter anti-Semite.
6. Maud Gonne, the beautiful actress and violent Irish nationalist whom Yeats loved; *"La Patrie"*: the Fatherland; Charles Millevoye (1782–1816), French poet; Félix Faure, 19th-century French statesman.
7. Maid-of-all-work (French, translat-

ing the preceding Swedish word).
8. "I do all the gentlemen" (in broken French).
9. Another Protean theme of change. Egan had told Stephen of his cousin James Stephens' escape from prison disguised as a bride (Stephens was really the cousin of Casey, the original of Egan in this episode).
1. Boy.
2. Successor-apparent to a Celtic chief. "Sept": clan.
3. District in east central London. Stephen is recalling Egan's conversation about the Fenian violence in London which necessitated his fleeing to France.

gone. Loveless, landless, wifeless. She is quite nicey comfy without
her outcast man,[4] madame, in rue Gît-le-Coeur, canary and two
buck lodgers. Peachy cheeks, a zebra skirt, frisky as a young thing's.
Spurned and undespairing. Tell Pat[5] you saw me, won't you? I
wanted to get poor Pat a job one time. *Mon fils*, soldier of France.
I taught him to sing. *The boys of Kilkenny are stout roaring blades.*
Know that old lay? I taught Patrice that. Old Kilkenny:[6] saint
Canice, Strongbow's castle on the Nore. Goes like this. O, O. He
takes me, Napper Tandy,[7] by the hand.

> O, O the boys of
> Kilkenny. . .

Weak wasting hand on mine. They have forgotten Kevin Egan,
not he them. Remembering thee, O Sion.[8]

He had come nearer the edge of the sea and wet sand slapped
his boots. The new air greeted him, harping in wild nerves, wind
of wild air of seeds of brightness. Here, I am not walking out to
the Kish lightship, am I? He stood suddenly, his feet beginning to
sink slowly in the quaking soil. Turn back.

Turning, he scanned the shore south, his feet sinking again slowly
in new sockets. The cold domed room of the tower[9] waits. Through
the barbicans[1] the shafts of light are moving ever, slowly ever as
my feet are sinking, creeping duskward over the dial floor. Blue
dusk, nightfall, deep blue night. In the darkness of the dome they
wait, their pushedback chairs, my obelisk valise, around a board of
abandoned platters. Who to clear it? He has the key.[2] I will not
sleep there when this night comes. A shut door of a silent tower
entombing their blind bodies, the panthersahib and his pointer.[3]
Call: no answer. He lifted his feet up from the suck and turned
back by the mole of boulders. Take all, keep all. My soul walks
with me, form of forms. So in the moon's midwatches I pace the
path above the rocks, in sable silvered, hearing Elsinore's tempting
flood.[4]

4. I.e., Egan's wife, who is "quite nicey
comfy" in the metaphorical "rue Gît-le-
Cœur" (i.e., the street where the heart
lies dead) back home in Ireland.
5. Patrice, Egan's son.
6. Kilkenny is called after the Irish
St. Canice (its Irish name is Cill Chain-
nigh), on the river Nore, where Strongbow (the second Earl of Pembroke, who
invaded Ireland in the 12th century),
had his stronghold.
7. James Napper Tandy (1740–1803),
Irish revolutionary, hero of the song
The Wearing of the Green.
8. Cf. Psalm cxxxvii.1 (in the King
James Bible): "we wept, when we remembered Zion." But "Zion" in the
Douay (Roman Catholic) Bible, is
spelled "Sion," and the Book of Common Prayer has "When we remembered
thee, O Sion."

9. Where Stephen lived with Buck Mulligan.
1. Outworks of a castle.
2. In the preceding episode, Mulligan
asked for and got the key of the tower
from Stephen.
3. I.e., Mulligan and the Englishman
Haines, who live with Stephen in the
tower. Stephen thinks of them as calling for him in vain, since he has decided not to return.
4. Cf. *Hamlet* I.ii.242, where the ghost
of Hamlet's murdered father is described as having a beard of "sable
silver'd." Allusions to *Hamlet* occur
often in *Ulysses;* in a later episode
Stephen expounds the theory that
Shakespeare is to be identified, not
with Hamlet himself, but with his betrayed father.

The flood is following me. I can watch it flow past from here. Get back then by the Poolbeg road to the strand there. He climbed over the sedge and eely oarweeds and sat on a stool of rock, resting his ashplant in a grike.

A bloated carcass of a dog lay lolled on bladderwrack. Before him the gunwale of a boat, sunk in sand. *Un coche ensablé.*[5] Louis Veuillot called Gautier's prose. These heavy sands are language tide and wind have silted here. And there, the stoneheaps of dead builders, a warren of weasel rats. Hide gold there. Try it. You have some. Sands and stones. Heavy of the past. Sir Lout's toys. Mind you don't get one bang on the ear. I'm the bloody well gigant rolls all them bloody well boulders, bones for my steppingstones. Feefaw-fum. I zmells de bloodz oldz an Iridzman.[6]

A point, live dog, grew into sight running across the sweep of sand. Lord, is he going to attack me? Respect his liberty. You will not be master of others or their slave. I have my stick. Sit tight. From farther away, walking shoreward across from the crested tide, figures, two. The two maries. They have tucked it safe among the bulrushes. Peekaboo. I see you. No, the dog. He is running back to them. Who?

Galleys of the Lochlanns[7] ran here to beach, in quest of prey, their bloodbeaked prows riding low on a molten pewter surf. Dane vikings, torcs of tomahawks aglitter on their breasts when Malachi wore the collar of gold. A school of turlehide whales stranded in hot noon, spouting, hobbling in the shallows. Then from the starving cagework city a horde of jerkined dwarfs, my people, with flayers' knives, running, scaling, hacking in green blubbery whalemeat. Famine, plague and slaughters. Their blood is in me, their lusts my waves. I moved among them on the frozen Liffey, that I, a changeling, among the spluttering resin fires. I spoke to no-one: none to me.

The dog's bark ran towards him, stopped, ran back.[8] Dog of my enemy. I just simply stood pale, silent, bayed about. *Terribilia meditans.*[9] A primrose doublet, fortune's knave, smiled on my fear. For that are you pining, the bark of their applause? Pretenders: live their lives. The Bruce's brother, Thomas Fitzgerald, silken knight, Perkin Warbeck, York's false scion, in breeches of silk of whiterose ivory, wonder of a day, and Lambert Simnel, with a tail

5. "A coach embedded in the sand." Louis Veuillot was a 19th-century French journalist; Théophile Gautier, a 19th-century French poet, novelist, and critic.
6. Stephen is thinking of the boulders on the shore as the work of a large but clumsy giant ("Sir Lout"). "They [Sir Lout and his family] were giants right enough * * * My Sir Lout has rocks in his mouth instead of teeth. He articulates badly" (Joyce to Frank Budgen, reported in Budgen's *James*

Joyce and the Making of Ulysses, 1934).
7. Scandinavians (Gaelic). Stephen is meditating on the Vikings who settled Dublin; it was here that they came ashore, he thinks.
8. The dog in this and subsequent paragraphs keeps changing in appearance; he "is the mummer among beasts—the Protean animal" (Joyce to Budgen). Joyce himself was afraid of dogs.
9. "Meditating **terrible things.**"

of nans and sutlers, a scullion crowned.[1] All kings' sons. Paradise of pretenders then and now. He saved men from drowning[2] and you shake at a cur's yelping. But the courtiers who mocked Guido in Or san Michele were in their own house. House of . . . We don't want any of your medieval abstrusiosities. Would you do what he did? A boat would be near, a lifebuoy. *Natürlich*,[3] put there for you. Would you or would you not? The man that was drowned nine days ago off Maiden's rock. They are waiting for him now. The truth, spit it out. I would want to. I would try. I am not a strong swimmer. Water cold soft. When I put my face into it in the basin at Clongowes. Can't see! Who's behind me? Out quickly, quickly! Do you see the tide flowing quickly in on all sides, sheeting the lows of sands quickly, shellcocoacoloured? If I had land under my feet. I want his life still to be his, mine to be mine. A drowning man. His human eyes scream to me out of horror of his death. I . . . With him together down . . . I could not save her.[4] Waters: bitter death: lost.

A woman and a man. I see her skirties. Pinned up, I bet.

Their dog ambled about a bank of dwindling sand, trotting, sniffing on all sides. Looking for something lost in a past life. Suddenly he made off like a bounding hare, ears flung back, chasing the shadow of a lowskimming gull. The man's shrieked whistle struck his limp ears. He turned, bounded back, came nearer, trotted on twinkling shanks. On a field tenney a buck, trippant, proper, unattired.[5] At the lacefringe of the tide he halted with stiff forehoofs, seawardpointed ears. His snout lifted barked at the wavenoise, herds of seamorse. They serpented towards his feet, curling, unfurling many crests, every ninth, breaking, plashing, from far, from farther out, waves and waves.

Cocklepickers.[6] They waded a little way in the water and, stooping, soused their bags, and, lifting them again, waded out. The dog yelped running to them, reared up and pawed them, dropping on all fours, again reared up at them with mute bearish fawning. Unheeded he kept by them as they came towards the drier sand, a rag of wolf's tongue redpanting from his jaws. His speckled body ambled ahead of them and then loped off at a calf's gallop. The carcass lay on his path. He stopped, sniffed, stalked round it,

---

1. Stephen is meditating on pretenders (i.e., false claimants): the names here are those of pretenders who have figured in English history. This is the Proteus theme again—disguises and changes.
2. Mulligan had saved a man from drowning.
3. Of course.
4. A man had been drowned off the coast, and his body had not yet been recovered. As Stephen thinks of the horror of drowning he recalls once again his mother's death.
5. At this point in its constantly changing appearance the dog looks like a heraldic animal and is described in the language of heraldry; the sentence "On a field * * * unattired" means: "On an orange-brown (tawny) background, a buck, tripping, in natural colors, without horns."
6. Stephen recognizes the man and woman on the beach as gypsy cocklepickers (cockles are edible shellfish, like mussels).

brother, nosing closer, went round it, sniffling rapidly like a dog all over the dead dog's bedraggled fell. Dogskull, dogsniff, eyes on the ground, moves to one great goal. Ah, poor dogsbody. Here lies poor dogsbody's body.

—Tatters! Out of that, you mongrel.

The cry brought him skulking back to his master and a blunt bootless kick sent him unscathed across a spit of sand, crouched in flight. He slunk back in a curve. Doesn't see me. Along by the edge of the mole he lolloped, dawdled, smelt a rock and from under a cocked hindleg pissed against it. He trotted forward and, lifting his hindleg, pissed quick short at an unsmelt rock. The simple pleasures of the poor. His hindpaws then scattered sand: then his forepaws dabbled and delved. Something he buried there, his grandmother.[7] He rooted in the sand, dabbling, delving and stopped to listen to the air, scraped up the sand again with a fury of his claws, soon ceasing, a pard,[8] a panther, got in spousebreach,[9] vulturing the dead.

After he woke me up last night same dream or was it? Wait. Open hallway. Street of harlots. Remember. Haroun al Raschid.[1] I am almosting it. That man led me, spoke. I was not afraid. The melon he had he held against my face. Smiled: creamfruit smell. That was the rule, said. In. Come. Red carpet spread. You will see who.

Shouldering their bags they trudged, the red Egyptians.[2] His blued feet out of turnedup trousers slapped the clammy sand, a dull brick muffler strangling his unshaven neck. With woman steps she followed: the ruffian and his strolling mort.[3] Spoils slung at her back. Loose sand and shellgrit crusted her bare feet. About her windraw face her hair trailed. Behind her lord his helpmate, bing awast, to Romeville.[4] When night hides her body's flaws calling under her brown shawl from an archway where dogs have mired. Her fancyman is treating two Royal Dublins in O'Loughlin's of Blackpitts. Buss her, wap in rogue's rum lingo, for, O, my dimber wapping dell.[5] A shefiend's whiteness under her rancid rags. Fumbally's lane that night: the tanyard smells.

---

7. Reference to a joke Stephen had made to his pupils in school that morning about "the fox burying his grandmother under a hollybush." This has many symbolic reverberations throughout *Ulysses*. The buried grandmother suggests Stephen's mother, the Church, and Ireland (the "Poor Old Woman"), while the hollybush, evergreen tree of life, represents resurrection in which, in spite of his religious disbelief, Stephen is much interested and about which (as about metempsychosis) he is continually brooding.

8. Leopard or panther.

9. I.e., begotten in adultery.

1. Stephen's dream of the famous Caliph of Baghdad, of the "street of harlots," and of his meeting a man with a melon, foreshadows his meeting later in the day with Leopold Bloom and his visit to the brothel area of Dublin.

2. I.e., gypsies. As Stephen watches the gypsy cockle-pickers with their dog he imagines their vagabond life and recalls fragments of gypsy speech and of thieves' slang.

3. Gypsies' "freewoman" (i.e., a harlot). "Spoils": the association gypsy-Egyptian reminds Stephen of the Israelites "spoiling the Egyptians" in Exodus xii.36.

4. Go away to London.

5. 17th-century thieves' slang—"buss":

> White thy fambles, red thy gan
> And thy quarrons dainty is.
> Couch a hogshead with me then.
> In the darkmans clip and kiss.[6]

Morose delectation Aquinas tunbelly calls this, *frate porcospino*.[7]
Unfallen Adam rode and not rutted. Call away let him:[8] *thy quarrons dainty is*. Language no whit worse than his. Monkwords, mary-
beads jabber on their girdles: roguewords, tough nuggets patter in
their pockets.

Passing now.

A side-eye at my Hamlet hat. If I were suddenly naked here as
I sit? I am not. Across the sands of all the world, followed by the
sun's flaming sword, to the west, trekking to evening lands. She
trudges, schlepps, trains, drags, trascines her load.[9] A tide westering, moondrawn, in her wake. Tides, myriadislanded, within her,
blood not mine, *oinopa ponton*,[1] a winedark sea. Behold the handmaid of the moon. In sleep the wet sign calls her hour, bids her
rise. Bridebed, childbed, bed of death, ghostcandled.[2] *Omnis caro
ad te veniet*. He comes, pale vampire, through storm his eyes, his
bat sails bloodying the sea, mouth to her mouth's kiss.[3]

Here. Put a pin in that chap, will you? My tablets.[4] Mouth to
her kiss. No. Must be two of em. Glue 'em well. Mouth to her
mouth's kiss.

His lips lipped and mouthed fleshless lips of air: mouth to her
womb. Oomb, allwombing tomb.[5] His mouth moulded issuing
breath, unspeeched: ooeeehah: roar of cataractic planets, globed,
blazing, roaring wayawayawayawayawayaway. Paper. The bank-
notes, blast them. Old Deasy's letter. Here. Thanking you for hospitality tear the blank end off. Turning his back to the sun he bent
over far to a table of rock and scribbled words.[6] That's twice I forgot to take slips from the library counter.

His shadow lay over the rocks as he bent, ending. Why not endless till the farthest star? Darkly they are there behind this light,

kiss; "wap": copulate with; "rum":
good; "dimber": pretty; "wapping
dell": whore.
6. More thieves' slang: "fambles":
hands; "gan": mouth; "quarrons":
body; "couch a hogshead": come to bed;
"darkmans": night; "clip": kiss. These
four lines and some of the phrases in
the preceding paragraph are quoted
from a song of the period, *The Rogue's
Delight in Praise of His Strolling Mort*
(cf. note 3).
7. "Brother porcupine" (Italian), a reference to the fat ("tunbelly") but
prickly philosopher, St. Thomas Aquinas.
8. The gypsy is calling his dog.
9. All words suggesting moving or dragging. " 'I like that crescendo of verbs,'
he [Joyce] said. 'The irresistible tug
of the tides' " (Budgen).

1. "Winedark sea" (Homer).
2. He is thinking of his mother again.
The Latin (from the burial service)
means: "All flesh will come to thee."
3. Death comes like the Flying Dutchman in a phantom ship to give the fatal
kiss.
4. Cf. Hamlet I.v.107: "My tablets!"
5. Stephen's consciousness here can be
illuminated with reference to Blake's
poem *The Gates of Paradise*, which
concludes: "The door of death I open
found / And the worm weaving in the
ground: / Thou'rt my mother from the
womb, / Wife, sister, daughter, to the
tomb * * * " Cf. also "the earth that's
nature's mother is her tomb. / What
is her burying ground that is her womb
* * * " (*Romeo and Juliet*, II.iii.9–10).
6. Stephen tears off the blank end of
Mr. Deasy's letter to the press and

darkness shining in the brightness, delta of Cassiopeia, worlds. Me sits there with his augur's rod of ash, in borrowed sandals, by day beside a livid sea, unbeheld, in violet night walking beneath a reign of uncouth stars.[7] I throw this ended shadow from me, manshape ineluctable, call it back. Endless, would it be mine, form of my form? Who watches me here? Who ever anywhere will read these written words? Signs on a white field. Somewhere to someone in your flutiest voice. The good bishop of Cloyne[8] took the veil of the temple out of his shovel hat: veil of space with coloured emblems hatched on its field. Hold hard. Coloured on a flat: yes, that's right. Flat I see, then think distance, near, far, flat I see, east, back. Ah, see now. Falls back suddenly, frozen in stereoscope. Click does the trick. You find my words dark. Darkness is in our souls, do you not think? Flutier. Our souls, shamewounded by our sins, cling to us yet more, a woman to her lover clinging, the more the more.

She trusts me, her hand gentle, the longlashed eyes. Now where the blue hell am I bringing her beyond the veil?[9] Into the ineluctable modality of the ineluctable visuality. She, she, she. What she? The virgin at Hodges Figgis' window on Monday looking in for one of the alphabet books you were going to write. Keen glance you gave her. Wrist through the braided jess of her sunshade. She lives in Leeson park, with a grief and kickshaws, a lady of letters. Talk that to some else, Stevie: a pickmeup. Bet she wears those curse of God stays suspenders and yellow stockings, darned with lumpy wool. Talk about apple dumplings, *piuttosto.*[1] Where are your wits?

Touch me. Soft eyes. Soft soft soft hand. I am lonely here. O, touch me soon, now. What is that word known to all men? I am quiet here alone. Sad too. Touch, touch me.

He lay back at full stretch over the sharp rocks, cramming the scribbled note and pencil into a pocket, his hat tilted down on his eyes. That is Kevin Egan's movement I made nodding for his nap, sabbath sleep. *Et vidit Deus. Et erant valde bona.*[2] Alo! *Bonjour,* welcome as the flowers in May. Under its leaf he watched through peacocktwittering lashes the southing sun. I am caught in this burn-

---

writes a poem that will be quoted later in the novel.

7. He imagines himself as the constellation Cassiopeia, supposed to represent the wife of Cepheus (an Ethiopian king) seated in a chair and holding up her arms. His ash walking stick he thinks of as an "augur's [Roman soothsayer's] rod of ash."

8. George Berkeley, Bishop of Cloyne (in Ireland), 1685-1753, who argued that the external world has no objective reality but exists only in the mind of the perceiver. Stephen (as at the opening of this episode) is experimenting again with ways of sensing reality.

9. "She" is Psyche, the soul, whom he is bringing from "beyond the veil." But from metaphysical speculations on reality and the soul Stephen is led (by the Psyche association) to think of "the virgin at Hodges Figgis' window."

1. Rather, sooner.

2. Connecting two phrases from the Vulgate: "And God saw" (Genesis i.4) and "And they were very good" (Genesis i.31).

ing scene. Pan's hour, the faunal noon. Among gumheavy serpent-
plants, milkoozing fruits, where on the tawny waters leaves lie wide.
Pain is far.

And no more turn aside and brood.[3]

His gaze brooded on his broadtoed boots, a buck's castoffs
nebeneinander. He counted the creases of rucked leather wherein
another's foot had nested warm. The foot that beat the ground
in tripudium, foot I dislove. But you were delighted when Esther
Osvalt's shoe went on you: girl I knew in Paris. *Tiens, quel petit
pied!*[4] Staunch friend, a brother soul: Wilde's love that dare not
speak its name. He now will leave me. And the blame? As I am.
As I am. All or not at all.

In long lassoes from the Cock lake the water flowed full, covering greengoldenly lagoons of sand, rising, flowing. My ashplant will
float away. I shall wait. No, they will pass on, passing chafing
against the low rocks, swirling, passing. Better get this job over
quick. Listen: a fourworded wavespeech: seesoo, hrss, rsseeiss ooos.
Vehement breath of waters amid seasnakes, rearing horses, rocks.
In cups of rocks it slops: flop, slop, slap: bounded in barrels. And,
spent, its speech ceases. It flows purling, widely flowing, floating
foampool, flower unfurling.

Under the upswelling tide he saw the writhing weeds lift languidly and sway reluctant arms, hising up their petticoats,[5] in
whispering water swaying and upturning coy silver fronds. Day by
day: night by night: lifted, flooded and let fall. Lord, they are
weary: and, whispered to, they sigh. Saint Ambrose heard it, sigh
of leaves and waves, waiting, awaiting the fullness of their times,
diebus ac noctibus iniurias patiens ingemiscit.[6] To no end gathered:
vainly then released, forth flowing, wending back: loom of the
moon. Weary too in sight of lovers, lascivious men, a naked woman
shining in her courts, she draws a toil of waters.

Five fathoms out there. Full fathom five thy father lies.[7] At once
he said. Found drowned. High water at Dublin bar. Driving before it a loose drift of rubble, fanshoals of fishes, silly shells. A
corpse rising saltwhite from the undertow, bobbing landward, a
pace a pace a porpoise. There he is. Hook it quick. Sunk though
he be beneath the watery floor. We have him. Easy now.

3. The first line of the second (and last) stanza of Yeats's poem *Who Goes with Fergus,* which is often in Stephen's mind. The line expresses for him the mood of noontide stillness and of lotos-eating in a lush oriental scene which overcomes him momentarily when he realizes that it is 12 o'clock, the hour of the Greek nature god Pan, "faunal noon." This oriental lotos-eating theme, which is associated also with Bloom, is important in the *Ulysses.*
4. "Look, what a little foot!"
5. A phrase from a vulgar song sung by Mulligan earlier that morning.
6. "Night and day he patiently groaned forth his wrongs" (St. Ambrose).
7. The theme of the drowned man is important in this episode (cf. the drowned sailor in Eliot's *Waste Land*). This line is from Ariel's song in *The Tempest* (I.ii.396).

Bag of corpsegas sopping in foul brine. A quiver of minnows, fat of a spongy titbit, flash though the slits of his buttoned trouserfly. God becomes man becomes fish becomes barnacle goose becomes featherbed mountain. Dead breaths I living breathe, tread dead dust, devour a urinous offal from all dead. Hauled stark over the gunwale he breathes upward the stench of his green grave, his leprous nosehole snoring to the sun.

A seachange this, brown eyes saltblue. Seadeath, mildest of all deaths known to man. Old Father Ocean. *Prix de Paris:*[8] beware of imitations. Just you give it a fair trial. We enjoyed ourselves immensely.

Come. I thirst. Clouding over. No black clouds anywhere, are there?[9] Thunderstorm. Allbright he falls, proud lightning of the intellect, *Lucifer, dico, qui nescit occasum.*[1] No. My cockle hat and staff and his my sandal shoon.[2] Where? To evening lands. Evening will find itself.

He took the hilt of his ashplant, lunging with it softly, dallying still. Yes, evening will find itself in me, without me. All days make their end. By the way next when is it? Tuesday will be the longest day. Of all the glad new year, mother,[3] the rum tum tiddledy tum. Lawn Tennyson, gentleman poet. *Già.*[4] For the old hag with the yellow teeth. And Monsieur Drumont, gentleman journalist. *Già.* My teeth are very bad. Why, I wonder? Feel. That one is going too. Shells. Ought I go to a dentist, I wonder, with what money? That one. Toothless Kinch, the superman. Why is that, I wonder, or does it mean something perhaps?

My handkerchief. He threw it. I remember. Did I not take it up?

His hand groped vainly in his pockets. No, I didn't. Better buy one.

He laid the dry snot picked from his nostril on a ledge of rock, carefully. For the rest let look who will.

Behind. Perhaps there is someone.

He turned his face over a shoulder, rere regardant.[5] Moving

8. "Prize of Paris"; the reference is probably to the Paris Exposition of 1889, where prizes were awarded in various categories of food, etc.: the prize-winning commodities bear the seal of the prize on the label (hence, "beware of imitations"). Stephen mentally awards the prize to death by drowning. "Seachange" is from Ariel's song, once more.
9. Stephen is looking up to make sure the sky does not threaten a thunderstorm; like Joyce, he hates thunder.
1. Thunder and lightning recall the Fall of Lucifer, "Lucifer, I say, who knows not his fall."
2. From Ophelia's mad song (*Hamlet*, IV.v.23–26): "How should I your true-love know / From another one? / By his cockle hat and staff, / And his sandal shoon." Ophelia, too, was drowned.
3. "You must wake and call me early, call me early, mother dear; / Tomorrow 'ill be the happiest time of all the glad New Year * * * " From *The May Queen* by Alfred, Lord Tennyson ("Lawn Tennyson").
4. Of course!
5. Looking behind him (heraldic terminology). Stephen, as we leave him sitting by the shore, is described in a highly stylized, heraldic language, as though he had himself become a work of art.

through the air high spars of a threemaster, her sails brailed up on the crosstrees,[6] homing, upstream, silently moving, a silent ship.

[*Lestrygonians*][1]

Pineapple rock, lemon platt, butter scotch. A sugarsticky girl shovelling scoopfuls of creams for a christian brother. Some school treat. Bad for their tummies. Lozenge and comfit manu-facturer to His Majesty the King. God. Save. Our. Sitting on his throne, sucking red jujubes white.

A sombre Y. M. C. A. young man, watchful among the warm sweet fumes of Graham Lemon's, placed a throwaway in a hand of Mr Bloom.

Heart to heart talks.

Bloo . . . Me? No.

Blood of the Lamb.[2]

His slow feet walked him riverward, reading. Are you saved? All are washed in the blood of the lamb. God wants blood victim. Birth, hymen, martyr, war, foundation of a building, sacrifice, kidney burntoffering, druid's altars. Elijah is coming. Dr John Alex-

---

6. When Budgen pointed out to Joyce that "crosstrees" was not the proper nautical term for the spars to which the sails are bent, Joyce thanked him but added: "But the word 'crosstrees' is essential. It comes in later on and I can't change it. After all, a yard is also a crosstree for the onlooking land-lubber." Joyce later uses "crosstree" in a reference to the crucifixion of Christ, so that the suggestion here is of Ste-phen as both artist and martyr (as his name implies). But the ship is also a real ship, which actually arrived in Dublin on June 16, 1904.

1. It is lunch time in Dublin and Leo-pold Bloom, as he walks through the city in no great hurry (for he likes to linger and watch what goes on around him), thinks of food. The Lestrygonians in Book X of the *Odyssey* are canni-bals, and throughout this episode there are suggestions of the slaughter of liv-ing creatures for food, or of food as something disgusting, which make some-what tenuous contact with Homer's de-scription of the cannibals spearing Ulysses' men for food; the parallel is not, however, profound or very impor-tant. What is most important about this episode is that it shows us Bloom's consciousness responding to the sights and sounds of Dublin. His humane curi-osity, his desire to learn and to im-prove the human lot, his sympathetic concern for Mrs. Breen and Mrs. Pure-foy, his feeding the gulls, his recollec-tions of a happier time when his daugh-ter was a baby and his relations with his wife Molly were thoroughly satis-factory, his interest in opera, his con-tinuous shying away from thoughts of his wife's rendezvous with the dashing Blazes Boylan—all this helps to build up his character in depth and to differ-entiate him sharply from Stephen. Un-like Stephen, Bloom's interest in lan-guage is confined to simple puns and translations, his interest in poetry is obvious and sentimental; his interest in the nature of reality takes the form of half-forgotten fragments of science remaining in his mind from schooldays. Everything about him is concrete, prac-tical, sensual, and middlebrow or low-brow, as distinct from the abstract, theoretical, esoteric speculations of Ste-phen in the "Proteus" episode. For ex-ample, when Stephen saw seagulls, he speculated on Daedalus and on flying as a symbol of the artist going into exile; when Bloom sees them, he thinks they must be hungry and buys a bun to feed them. There are parallels be-tween their two streams of conscious-ness. Bloom's thoughts, in a sense, in-clude Stephen's, but in a popularized and even vulgarized form.

The text of this selection has also been collated with the Odyssey Press edition of 1932.

2. Bloom has been handed a religious leaflet ("throwaway") containing the phrase "Blood of the Lamb." He at first mistakes "Blood" for "Bloom."

ander Dowie, restorer of the church in Zion, is coming.[3]

> *Is coming! Is coming!! Is coming!!!*
> *All heartily welcome.*

Paying game. Torry and Alexander last year. Polygamy. His wife will put the stopper on that. Where was that ad some Birmingham firm the luminous crucifix? Our Saviour. Wake up in the dead of night and see him on the wall, hanging. Pepper's ghost idea. Iron nails ran in.

Phosphorous it must be done with. If you leave a bit of codfish for instance. I could see the bluey silver over it. Night I went down to the pantry in the kitchen. Don't like all the smells in it waiting to rush out. What was it she wanted?[4] The Malaga raisins. Thinking of Spain. Before Rudy[5] was born. The phosphorescence, that bluey greeny. Very good for the brain.

From Butler's monument house corner he glanced along Bachelor's walk. Dedalus' daughter there still outside Dillon's auctionrooms. Must be selling off some old furniture. Knew her eyes at once from the father. Lobbing about waiting for him. Home always breaks up when the mother goes. Fifteen children he had. Birth every year almost. That's in their theology or the priest won't give the poor woman the confession, the absolution. Increase and multiply. Did you ever hear such an idea? Eat you out of house and home. No families themselves to feed. Living on the fat of the land. Their butteries and larders. I'd like to see them do the black fast Yom Kippur.[6] Crossbuns. One meal and a collation for fear he'd collapse on the altar. A housekeeper of one of those fellows if you could pick it out of her. Never pick it out of her. Like getting L s. d.[7] out of him. Does himself well. No guests. All for number one. Watching his water. Bring your own bread and butter. His reverence. Mum's the word.

Good Lord, that poor child's dress is in flitters. Underfed she looks too. Potatoes and marge, marge and potatoes. It's after they feel it. Proof of the pudding. Undermines the constitution.

As he set foot on O'Connell bridge a puffball of smoke plumed up from the parapet. Brewery barge with export stout. England. Sea air sours it, I heard. Be interesting some day get a pass through Hancock to see the brewery. Regular world in itself. Vats of porter, wonderful. Rats get in too. Drink themselves bloated as big as a collie floating. Dead drunk on the porter. Drink till they puke again

---

3. Dowie was a Scottish-American evangelist who established the "Christian Catholic Apostolic Church in Zion" (i.e., Zion City, Illinois) in 1901.
4. "She" is Bloom's wife Molly, born in Gibraltar.
5. Their son, who had died in infancy eleven years before.
6. Jewish Day of Atonement.
7. I.e., cash: £, s., d. are the abbreviations, respectively, for pounds, shillings, and pence.

like christians. Imagine drinking that! Rats: vats. Well of course if we knew all the things.

Looking down he saw flapping strongly, wheeling between the gaunt quay walls, gulls. Rough weather outside. If I threw myself down? Reuben J's son must have swallowed a good bellyful of that sewage.[8] One and eightpence too much. Hhhhm. It's the droll way he comes out with the things. Knows how to tell a story too.

They wheeled lower. Looking for grub. Wait.

He threw down among them a crumpled paper ball. Elijah thirtytwo feet per sec is com.[9] Not a bit. The ball bobbed unheeded on the wake of swells, floated under by the bridge piers. Not such damn fools. Also the day I threw that stale cake out of the Erin's King picked it up in the wake fifty yards astern. Live by their wits. They wheeled, flapping.

> *The hungry famished gull*
> *Flaps o'er the waters dull.*

That is how poets write, the similar sounds. But then Shakespeare has no rhymes: blank verse. The flow of the language it is. The thoughts. Solemn.

> *Hamlet, I am thy father's spirit*
> *Doomed for a certain time to walk the earth.*[1]

—Two apples a penny! Two for a penny!

His gaze passed over the glazed apples serried on her stand. Australians they must be this time of year. Shiny peels: polishes them up with a rag or a handkerchief.

Wait. Those poor birds.

He halted again and bought from the old applewoman two Banbury cakes for a penny and broke the brittle paste and threw its fragments down into the Liffey. See that? The gulls swooped silently two, then all, from their heights, pouncing on prey. Gone. Every morsel.

Aware of their greed and cunning he shook the powdery crumb from his hands. They never expected that. Manna.[2] Live on fishy flesh they have to, all sea birds, gulls, seagoose. Swans from Anna

---

8. Reuben J. Dodd, Dublin solicitor (lawyer), whose son had been rescued from the Liffey River by a man to whom Reuben J. had given two shillings as a reward—"one and eightpence too much," as Simon Dedalus had remarked to Bloom earlier that morning when they were discussing the incident. It is Dedalus' comment that Bloom is thinking of in the following sentences.

9. I.e., Elijah is coming, accelerating at the rate of 32 feet per second per second, the acceleration rate of falling bodies. ("Elijah is coming" is the legend on the handbill Bloom is tossing away)

1. *Hamlet* I.v.9–10 (slightly misquoted).

2. The divine food (small, round, and white) which the children of Israel ate in the wilderness (Exodus xvi.14–15).

Liffey[3] swim down here sometimes to preen themselves. No accounting for tastes. Wonder what kind is swanmeat. Robinson Crusoe had to live on them.

They wheeled, flapping weakly. I'm not going to throw any more. Penny quite enough. Lot of thanks I get. Not even a caw. They spread foot and mouth disease too. If you cram a turkey, say, on chestnut meal it tastes like that. Eat pig like pig. But then why is it that saltwater fish are not salty? How is that?

His eyes sought answer from the river and saw a rowboat rock at anchor on the treacly swells lazily its plastered board.

Kino's
11/–
Trousers.[4]

Good idea that. Wonder if he pays rent to the corporation. How can you own water really? It's always flowing in a stream, never the same, which in the stream of life we trace. Because life is a stream. All kinds of places are good for ads. That quack doctor for the clap used to be stuck up in all the greenhouses. Never see it now. Strictly confidential. Dr Hy Franks. Didn't cost him a red like Maginni the dancing master self advertisement. Got fellows to stick them up or stick them up himself for that matter on the q. t. running in to loosen a button. Fly by night. Just the place too. POST NO BILLS. POST NO PILLS. Some chap with a dose burning him. If he. . .

O!

Eh?

No . . . No.

No, no. I don't believe it. He wouldn't surely?

No, no.[5]

Mr Bloom moved forward raising his troubled eyes. Think no more about that. After one. Timeball on the ballast office is down. Dunsink time. Fascinating little book that is of Sir Robert Ball's.[6] Parallax. I never exactly understood. There's a priest. Could ask

---

3. The Liffey flows from the Wicklow Mountains northeast and east to Dublin Bay.
4. I.e., eleven shillings ("11/–") for Kino's Trousers. Bloom is a canvasser for advertisements: he receives commissions from newspapers for getting tradesmen to place advertisements with them.
5. Blazes Boylan, flashy philanderer, is due to call on Molly Bloom that afternoon, to discuss the program of a concert which he is managing for her (Molly is a singer). Bloom knows that Boylan and his wife will commit adultery together. Here it suddenly occurs to him that Boylan might give Molly

a "dose" of venereal disease, but he puts the thought from him as incredible.
6. The "timeball on the ballastoffice" registers the official time of the observatory at Dunsink. Noticing that the timeball is down, which means that it is after 1 o'clock, Bloom is reminded of the observatory, then of the Irish astronomer Sir Robert Ball's popular book on astronomy, *The Story of the Heavens* (1886), and of the astronomical term "parallax" he found in the book but which he "never exactly understood."

him. Par it's Greek: parallel, parallax. Met him pikehoses[7] she
called it till I told her about the transmigration. O rocks!

Mr Bloom smiled O rocks at two windows of the ballast office.
She's right after all. Only big words for ordinary things on account
of the sound. She's not exactly witty. Can be rude too. Blurt out
what I was thinking. Still I don't know. She used to say Ben Dollard had a base barreltone voice. He has legs like barrels and you'd
think he was singing into a barrel. Now, isn't that wit? They used
to call him big Ben. Not half as witty as calling him base barreltone. Appetite like an albatross. Get outside of a baron of beef.
Powerful man he was at storing away number one Bass.[8] Barrel of
Bass. See? It all works out.

A procession of whitesmocked men marched slowly towards him
along the gutter, scarlet sashes across their boards. Bargains. Like
that priest they are this morning: we have sinned: we have suffered.
He read the scarlet letters on their five tall white hats: H. E. L. Y. S.
Wisdom Hely's. Y lagging behind drew a chunk of bread from
under his foreboard, crammed it into his mouth and munched as
he walked. Our staple food. Three bob a day, walking along the
gutters, street after street. Just keep skin and bone together, bread
and skilly. They are not Boyl: no: M'Glade's men. Doesn't bring
in any business either. I suggested to him about a transparent show
cart with two smart girls sitting inside writing letters, copybooks,
envelopes, blotting paper. I bet that would have caught on. Smart
girls writing something catch the eye at once. Everyone dying to
know what she's writing. Get twenty of them round you if you
stare at nothing. Have a finger in the pie. Women too. Curiosity.
Pillar of salt. Wouldn't have it of course because he didn't think
of it himself first. Or the inkbottle I suggested with a false stain
of black celluloid. His ideas for ads like Plumtree's potted under
the obituaries, cold meat department. You can't lick 'em. What?
Our envelopes. Hello! Jones, where are you going? Can't stop,
Robinson, I am hastening to purchase the only reliable inkeraser
Kansell, sold by Hely's Ltd, 85 Dame Street. Well out of that ruck
I am. Devil of a job it was collecting accounts of those convents.
Tranquilla convent. That was a nice nun there, really sweet face.
Wimple suited her small head. Sister? Sister? I am sure she was
crossed in love by her eyes. Very hard to bargain with that sort of
woman. I disturbed her at her devotions that morning. But glad
to communicate with the outside world. Our great day, she said.

---

7. Molly's way of pronouncing "metempsychosis." When Bloom had explained metempsychosis to her that
morning, she had exclaimed "O rocks"
at the pretentious term. He now mentally repeats "O rocks!" at the thought
of the word "parallax."
8. A popular British beer.

Feast of Our Lady of Mount Carmel. Sweet name too: caramel. She knew, I think she knew by the way she. If she had married she would have changed. I suppose they really were short of money. Fried everything in the best butter all the same. No lard for them. My heart's broke eating dripping. They like buttering themselves in an out. Molly tasting it, her veil up. Sister? Pat Claffey, the pawnbroker's daughter. It was a nun they say invented barbed wire.

He crossed Westmoreland street when apostrophe S had plodded by. Rover cycleshop. Those races are on today. How long ago is that? Year Phil Gilligan died. We were in Lombard street west. Wait, was in Thom's. Got the job in Wisdom Hely's year we married. Six years. Ten years ago: ninetyfour he died, yes that's right, the big fire at Arnott's. Val Dillon was lord mayor. The Glencree dinner. Alderman Robert O'Reilly emptying the port into his soup before the flag fell, Bobbob lapping it for the inner alderman. Couldn't hear what the band played. For what we have already received may the Lord make us. Milly[9] was a kiddy then. Molly had that elephantgrey dress with the braided frogs. Mantailored with selfcovered buttons. She didn't like it because I sprained my ankle first day she wore choir picnic at the Sugarloaf. As if that. Old Goodwin's tall hat done up with some sticky stuff. Flies' picnic too. Never put a dress on her back like it. Fitted her like a glove, shoulder and hips. Just beginning to plump it out well. Rabbit pie we had that day. People looking after her.

Happy. Happier then. Snug little room that was with the red wallpaper, Dockrell's, one and ninepence a dozen. Milly's tubbing night. American soap I bought: elderflower. Cosy smell of her bathwater. Funny she looked soaped all over. Shapely too. Now photography.[1] Poor papa's daguerreotype atelier he told me of. Hereditary taste.

He walked along the curbstone.

Stream of life. What was the name of that priestlylooking chap was always squinting in when he passed? Weak eyes, woman. Stopped in Citron's saint Kevin's parade. Pen something. Pendennis? My memory is getting. Pen . . . ? of course it's years ago. Noise of the trams probably. Well, if he couldn't remember the dayfather's name that he sees every day.

Bartell d'Arcy was the tenor, just coming out then. Seeing her home after practice. Conceited fellow with his waxedup moustache. Gave her that song *Winds that blow from the south.*

Windy night that was I went to fetch her there was that lodge meeting on about those lottery tickets after Goodwin's concert in the supper room or oakroom of the mansion house. He and I be-

---

9. Bloom's 15-year-old daughter.   1. Milly is working at a photographer's.

hind. Sheet of her music blew out of my hand against the high school railings. Lucky it didn't. Thing like that spoils the effect of a night for her. Professor Goodwin linking her in front. Shaky on his pins, poor old sot. His farewell concerts. Positively last appearance on any stage. May be for months and may be for never. Remember her laughing at the wind, her blizzard collar up. Corner of Harcourt road remember that gust? Brrfoo! Blew up all her skirts and her boa nearly smothered old Goodwin. She did get flushed in the wind. Remember when we got home raking up the fire and frying up those pieces of lap of mutton for her supper with the Chutney sauce she liked. And the mulled rum. Could see her in the bedroom from the hearth unclamping the busk of her stays. White.

Swish and soft flop her stays made on the bed. Always warm from her. Always liked to let herself out. Sitting there after till near two, taking out her hairpins. Milly tucked up in beddyhouse. Happy. Happy. That was the night. . .

—O, Mr Bloom, how do you do?

—O, how do you do, Mrs Breen?[2]

—No use complaining. How is Molly those times? Haven't seen her for ages.

—In the pink, Mr Bloom said gaily, Milly has a position down in Mullingar, you know.

—Go away! Isn't that grand for her?

—Yes, in a photographer's there. Getting on like a house on fire. How are all your charges?

—All on the baker's list, Mrs Breen said.

How many has she? No other in sight.

—You're in black I see. You have no. . .

—No, Mr Bloom said. I have just come from a funeral.

Going to crop up all day, I foresee. Who's dead, when and what did he die of? Turn up like a bad penny.

—O dear me, Mrs Breen said, I hope it wasn't any near relation.

May as well get her sympathy.

—Dignam, Mr Bloom said. An old friend of mine. He died quite suddenly, poor fellow. Heart trouble, I believe. Funeral was this morning.

> Your funeral's tomorrow
> While you're coming through the rye.
> Diddlediddle dumdum
> Diddlediddle. . .

—Sad to lose the old friends, Mrs Breen's woman eyes said melancholily.

Now that's quite enough about that. Just quietly: husband.

2. Mrs. Breen had been an old sweetheart of Bloom's.

—And your lord and master?

Mrs Breen turned up her two large eyes. Hasn't lost them anyhow.

—O, don't be talking, she said. He's a caution to rattlesnakes. He's in there now with his lawbooks finding out the law of libel. He has me heartscalded. Wait till I show you.

Hot mockturtle vapour and steam of newbaked jampuffs rolypoly poured out from Harrison's. The heavy noonreek tickled the top of Mr Bloom's gullet. Want to make good pastry, butter, best flour, Demerara sugar, or they'd taste it with the hot tea. Or is it from her? A barefoot arab stood over the grating, breathing in the fumes. Deaden the gnaw of hunger that way. Pleasure or pain is it? Penny dinner. Knife and fork chained to the table.

Opening her handbag, chipped leather, hatpin: ought to have a guard on those things. Stick it in a chap's eye in the tram. Rummaging. Open. Money. Please take one. Devils if they lose sixpence. Raise Cain. Husband barging. Where's the ten shillings I gave you on Monday? Are you feeding your little brother's family? Soiled handkerchief: medicinebottle. Pastille that was fell. What is she? . . .

—There must be a new moon out, she said. He's always bad then.[3] Do you know what he did last night?

Her hand ceased to rummage. Her eyes fixed themselves on him, wide in alarm, yet smiling.

—What? Mr Bloom asked.

Let her speak. Look straight in her eyes. I believe you. Trust me.

—Woke me up in the night, she said. Dream he had, a nightmare.

Indiges.

—Said the ace of spades[4] was walking up the stairs.

—The ace of spades! Mr Bloom said.

She took a folded postcard from her handbag.

—Read that, she said. He got it this morning.

—What is it? Mr Bloom asked, taking the card. U. P.?

—U. P.: up, she said. Someone taking a rise out of him. It's a great shame for them whoever he is.

—Indeed it is, Mr Bloom said.

She took back the card, sighing.

—And now he's going round to Mr Menton's office. He's going to take an action for ten thousand pounds, he says.

She folded the card into her untidy bag and snapped the catch.

Same blue serge dress she had two years ago, the nap bleaching. Seen its best days. Wispish hair over her ears. And that dowdy

3. Mr. Breen is mentally disturbed.   4. Symbol of death.

toque, three old grapes to take the harm out of it. Shabby genteel.
She used to be a tasty dresser. Lines round her mouth. Only a year
or so older than Molly.

See the eye that woman gave her, passing. Cruel. The unfair sex.

He looked still at her, holding back behind his look his discontent. Pungent mockturtle oxtail mulligatawny. I'm hungry too.
Flakes of pastry on the gusset of her dress: daub of sugary flour
stuck to her cheek. Rhubarb tart with liberal fillings, rich fruit interior. Josie Powell that was. In Luke Doyle's long ago, Dolphin's
Barn, the charades. U. P.: up.

Change the subject.

—Do you ever see anything of Mrs Beaufoy, Mr Bloom asked.

—Mina Purefoy? she said.

Philip Beaufoy I was thinking. Playgoer's club.[5] Matcham often
thinks of the masterstroke. Did I pull the chain? Yes. The last
act.

—Yes.

—I just called to ask on the way in is she over it. She's in the
lying-in hospital in Holles street. Dr Horne got her in. She's three
days bad now.

—O, Mr Bloom said. I'm sorry to hear that.

—Yes, Mrs Breen said. And a houseful of kids at home. It's a
very stiff birth, the nurse told me.

—O, Mr Bloom said.

His heavy pitying gaze absorbed her news. His tongue clacked in
compassion. Dth! Dth!

—I'm sorry to hear that, he said. Poor thing! Three days! That's
terrible for her.

Mrs Breen nodded.

—She was taken bad on the Tuesday. . .

Mr Bloom touched her funnybone gently, warning her.

—Mind! Let this man pass.

A bony form strode along the curbstone from the river, staring
with a rapt gaze into the sunlight through a heavy stringed glass.
Tight as a skullpiece a tiny hat gripped his head. From his arm a
folded dustcoat, a stick and an umbrella dangled to his stride.

—Watch him, Mr Bloom said. He always walks outside the
lampposts. Watch!

—Who is he if it's a fair question, Mrs. Breen asked. Is he dotty?

—His name is Cashel Boyle O'Connor Fitzmaurice Tisdall Far-
rell, Mr Bloom said, smiling. Watch!

5. Bloom is thinking of the story *Matcham's Masterstroke*, by "Mr. Philip Beaufoy, Playgoers' club, Lon-don," which he had read in the toilet that morning. He then mentally quotes the opening sentence.

—He has enough of them, she said. Denis will be like that one of these days.

She broke off suddenly.

—There he is, she said. I must go after him. Goodbye. Remember me to Molly, won't you?

—I will, Mr Bloom said.

He watched her dodge through passers towards the shopfronts. Denis Breen in skimpy frockcoat and blue canvas shoes shuffled out of Harrison's hugging two heavy tomes to his ribs. Blown in from the bay. Like old times. He suffered her to overtake him without surprise and thrust his dull grey beard towards her, his loose jaw wagging as he spoke earnestly.

Meshuggah.[6] Off his chump.

Mr Bloom walked on again easily, seeing ahead of him in sunlight the tight skullpiece, the dangling stick, umbrella, dustcoat. Going the two days. Watch him! Out he goes again. One way of getting on in the world. And that other old mosey lunatic in those duds. Hard time she must have with him.

U. P.: up. I'll take my oath that's Alf Bergan or Richie Goulding. Wrote it for a lark in the Scotch house, I bet anything. Round to Menton's office. His oyster eyes staring at the postcard. Be a feast for the gods.

He passed the *Irish Times*. There might be other answers lying there. Like to answer them all. Good system for criminals. Code. At their lunch now. Clerk with the glasses there doesn't know me. O, leave them there to simmer. Enough bother wading through fortyfour of them. Wanted smart lady typist to aid gentleman in literary work. I called you naughty darling because I do not like that other world. Please tell me what is the meaning. Please tell me what perfume does your wife.[7] Tell me who made the world. The way they spring those questions on you. And the other one Lizzie Twigg. My literary efforts have had the good fortune to meet with the approval of the eminent poet A. E. (Mr Geo Russell).[7a] No time to do her hair drinking sloppy tea with a book of poetry.

Best paper by long chalks for a small ad. Got the provinces now. Cook and general, exc cuisine, housemaid kept. Wanted live man for spirit counter. Resp girl (R. C.) wishes to hear of post in fruit or pork shop. James Carlisle made that. Six and a half per cent

6. Yiddish, "mad."
7. Bloom is mentally quoting a letter written to him by the typist Martha Clifford, with whom he is carrying on a purely epistolary love affair (she had misspelled "word" as "world": "I do not like that other *world*"). Lizzie Twigg was one of the other typists who had answered his advertisement for a

secretary "to aid gentleman in literary work" (Bloom's pretext for beginning such an affair).
7a. A. E. (George Russell, 1867–1935), the Irish poet mentioned as a reference by Lizzie Twigg when she answered Bloom's advertisement, is later encountered by Bloom with a woman who Bloom speculates might be Lizzie.

dividend. Made a big deal on Coates's shares. Ca'canny. Cunning old Scotch hunks. All the toady news. Our gracious and popular vicereine.[8] Bought the *Irish Field* now. Lady Mountcashel has quite recovered after her confinement and rode out with the Ward Union staghounds at the enlargement yesterday at Rathoath. Uneatable fox. Pothunters too. Fear injects juices make it tender enough for them. Riding astride. Sit her horse like a man. Weightcarrying huntress. No sidesaddle or pillion for her, not for Joe. First to the meet and in at the death. Strong as a brood mare some of those horsey women. Swagger around livery stables. Toss off a glass of brandy neat while you'd say knife. That one at the Grosvenor this morning. Up with her on the car: wishwish. Stonewall or fivebarred gate put her mount to it. Think that pugnosed driver did it out of spite. Who is this she was like? O yes! Mrs Miriam Dandrade that sold me her old wraps and black underclothes in the Shelbourne hotel. Divorced Spanish American. Didn't take a feather out of her my handling them. As if I was her clotheshorse. Saw her in the viceregal party when Stubbs the park ranger got me in with Whelan of the *Express*. Scavenging what the quality left. High tea. Mayonnaise I poured on the plums thinking it was custard. Her ears ought to have tingled for a few weeks after. Want to be a bull for her. Born courtesan. No nursery work for her, thanks.

Poor Mrs Purefoy! Methodist husband. Method in his madness. Saffron bun and milk and soda lunch in the educational dairy. Eating with a stopwatch, thirtytwo chews to the minute. Still his muttonchop whiskers grew. Supposed to be well connected. Theodore's cousin in Dublin Castle. One tony relative in every family. Hardy annuals he presents her with. Saw him out at the Three Jolly Topers marching along bareheaded and his eldest boy carrying one in a marketnet. The squallers. Poor thing! Then having to give the breast year after year all hours of the night. Selfish those t.t's are. Dog in the manger. Only one lump of sugar in my tea, if you please.

He stood at Fleet street crossing. Luncheon interval a six penny at Rowe's? Must look up that ad in the national library.[9] An eightpenny in the Burton. Better. On my way.

He walked on past Bolton's Westmoreland house. Tea. Tea. Tea. I forgot to tap Tom Kernan.[1]

Sss. Dth, dth, dth! Three days imagine groaning on a bed with a vinegared handkerchief round her forehead, her belly swollen out!

8. Wife of the Viceroy, who represented the British Crown in Ireland; Bloom is thinking of the society column in the *Irish Times*.
9. Bloom's goal, on his walk through Dublin, is the National Library, where he wants to look up an advertisement in a back number of the *Kilkenny People*.
1. A Dublin tea merchant and friend of Bloom's, whom Bloom had earlier intended to ask ("tap") for some tea.

Phew! Dreadful simply! Child's head too big: forceps. Doubled up inside her trying to butt its way out blindly, groping for the way out. Kill me that would. Lucky Molly got over hers lightly. They ought to invent something to stop that. Life with hard labour. Twilight-sleep idea: queen Victoria was given that. Nine she had. A good layer. Old woman that lived in a shoe she had so many children. Suppose he was consumptive. Time someone thought about it instead of gassing about the what was it the pensive bosom of the silver effulgence. Flapdoodle to feed fools on. They could easily have big establishments. Whole thing quite painless out of all the taxes give every child born five quid at compound interest up to twentyone, five per cent is a hundred shillings and five tiresome pounds, multiply by twenty decimal system, encourage people to put by money save hundred and ten and a bit twentyone years want to work it out on paper come to a tidy sum, more than you think.

Not stillborn of course. They are not even registered. Trouble for nothing.

Funny sight two of them together, their bellies out. Molly and Mrs Moisel. Mothers' meeting. Phthisis retires for the time being, then returns. How flat they look after all of a sudden! Peaceful eyes. Weight off their minds. Old Mrs Thornton was a jolly old soul. All my babies, she said. The spoon of pap in her mouth before she fed them. O, that's nyumyum. Got her hand crushed by old Tom Wall's son. His first bow to the public. Head like a prize pumpkin. Snuffy Dr Murren. People knocking them up at all hours. For God's sake doctor. Wife in her throes. Then keep them waiting months for their fee. To attendance on your wife. No gratitude in people. Humane doctors, most of them.

Before the huge high door of the Irish house of parliament a flock of pigeons flew. Their little frolic after meals. Who will we do it on? I pick the fellow in black. Here goes. Here's good luck. Must be thrilling from the air. Apjohn, myself and Owen Goldberg up in the trees near Goose green playing the monkeys. Mackerel they called me.

A squad of constables debouched from College street, marching in Indian file. Goose step. Foodheated faces, sweating helmets, patting their truncheons. After their feed with a good load of fat soup under their belts. Policeman's lot is oft a happy one. They split up into groups and scattered, saluting towards their beats. Let out to graze. Best moment to attack one in pudding time. A punch in his dinner. A squad of others, marching irregularly, rounded Trinity railings, making for the station. Bound for their troughs. Prepare to receive cavalry. Prepare to receive soup.

He crossed under Tommy Moore's roguish finger. They did right to put him up over a urinal: meeting of the waters.[2] Ought to be places for women. Running into cakeshops. Settle my hat straight. *There is not in this wide world a vallee.* Great song of Julia Morkan's. Kept her voice up to the very last. Pupil of Michael Balfe's wasn't she?

He gazed after the last broad tunic. Nasty customers to tackle. Jack Power could a tale unfold: father a G man. If a fellow gave them trouble being lagged they let him have it hot and heavy in the bridewell.[3] Can't blame them after all with the job they have especially the young hornies. That horse policeman the day Joe Chamberlain was given his degree in Trinity he got a run for his money.[4] My word he did! His horse's hoofs clattering after us down Abbey street. Luck I had the presence of mind to dive into Manning's or I was souped. He did come a wallop, by George. Must have cracked his skull on the cobblestones. I oughtn't to have got myself swept along with those medicals. And the Trinity jibs[5] in their mortarboards. Looking for trouble. Still I got to know that young Dixon who dressed that sting for me in the Mater and now he's in Holles street where Mrs Purefoy. Wheels within wheels. Police whistle in my ears still. All skedaddled. Why he fixed on me. Give me in charge. Right here it began.

—Up the Boers!

—Three cheers for De Wet![6]

—We'll hang Joe Chamberlain on a sourapple tree.

Silly billies: mob of young cubs yelling their guts out. Vinegar hill. The Butter exchange band. Few years time half of them magistrates and civil servants. War comes on: into the army helterskelter: same fellows used to whether on the scaffold high.

Never know who you're talking to. Corney Kelleher he has Harvey Duff in his eye. Like that Peter or Denis or James Carey that blew the gaff on the invincibles. Member of the corporation too. Egging raw youths on to get in the know. All the time drawing secret service pay from the castle.[7] Drop him like a hot potato. Why those plain clothes men are always courting slaveys. Easily twig a man used to uniform. Squarepushing up against a backdoor. Maul her a bit. Then the next thing on the menu. And who is the gentleman does be visiting there? Was the young master saying anything? Peeping Tom through the keyhole. Decoy duck. Hotblooded young student fooling round her fat arms ironing.

---

2. *The Meeting of the Waters* was a famous poem by the much-loved Irish poet Thomas Moore (1779–1852) whose statue Bloom now passes.
3. Prison.
4. When Joseph Chamberlain, the British Colonial Secretary, came to Dublin to receive an honorary degree from Trinity College, a group of medical students rioted against him and against the Boer War.
5. Trinity College students.
6. Boer general.
7. I.e., from the British government, whose representative lived at Dublin Castle.

—Are those yours, Mary?

—I don't wear such things. . . Stop or I'll tell the missus on you. Out half the night.

—There are great times coming, Mary. Wait till you see.

—Ah, get along with your great times coming.

Barmaids too. Tobacco shopgirls.

James Stephens'[8] idea was the best. He knew them. Circles of ten so that a fellow couldn't round on more than his own ring. Sinn Fein.[9] Back out you get the knife. Hidden hand. Stay in. The firing squad. Turnkey's daughter got him out of Richmond, off from Lusk. Putting up in the Buckingham Palace hotel under their very noses. Garibaldi.[1]

You must have a certain fascination: Parnell.[2] Arthur Griffith is a squareheaded fellow but he has no go in him for the mob. Want to gas about our lovely land. Gammon and spinach. Dublin Bakery Company's tearoom. Debating societies. That republicanism is the best form of government. That the language question should take precedence of the economic question. Have your daughters invei- gling them to your house. Stuff them up with meat and drink. Michaelmas goose. Here's a good lump of thyme seasoning under the apron for you. Have another quart of goosegrease before it gets too cold. Halffed enthusiastists. Penny roll and a walk with the band. No grace for the carver. The thought that the other chap pays best sauce in the world. Make themselves thoroughly at home. Shove us over those apricots, meaning peaches. The not far distant day. Home Rule sun rising up in the northwest.[3]

His smile faded as he walked, a heavy cloud hiding the sun slowly, shadowing Trinity's surly front. Trams passed one another, ingoing, outgoing, clanging. Useless words. Things go on same; day after day: squads of police marching out, back: trams in, out. Those two loonies mooching about. Dignam carted off. Mina Purefoy swollen belly on a bed groaning to have a child tugged out of her. One born every second somewhere. Other dying every second. Since I fed the birds five minutes. Three hundred kicked the bucket. Other three hundred born, washing the blood off, all are washed in the blood of the lamb, bawling maaaaaa.

Cityful passing away, other cityful coming, passing away too: other coming on, passing on. Houses, lines of houses, streets, miles

---

8. Irish nationalist revolutionary.
9. Irish revolutionary movement; the Gaelic words mean "We Ourselves."
1. Bloom is thinking of a variety of nationalist conspirators who escaped from danger, among them the 19th-cen- tury Italian patriot and general Giu- seppe Garibaldi.

2. Charles Stewart Parnell (1846–91), Irish nationalist political leader. Arthur Griffith was founder of the Sinn Fein.
3. Reference to Arthur Griffith's com- ment on the *Freeman* masthead, which showed the sun rising in the northwest from behind the bank of Ireland. Bloom has a *Freeman* in his pocket.

of pavements, piledup bricks, stones. Changing hands. This owner, that. Landlord never dies they say. Other steps into his shoes when he gets his notice to quit. They buy the place up with gold and still they have all the gold. Swindle in it somewhere. Piled up in cities, worn away age after age. Pyramids in sand. Built on bread and onions. Slaves Chinese wall. Babylon. Big stones left. Round towers. Rest rubble, sprawling suburbs, jerrybuilt, Kerwan's mushroom houses, built of breeze. Shelter for the night.

No one is anything.

This is the very worst hour of the day. Vitality. Dull, gloomy: hate this hour. Feel as if I had been eaten and spewed.

Provost's house. The reverend Dr Salmon: tinned salmon. Well tinned in there. Wouldn't live in it if they paid me. Hope they have liver and bacon today. Nature abhors a vacuum.

The sun freed itself slowly and lit glints of light among the silver ware in Walter Sexton's window opposite by which John Howard Parnell[4] passed, unseeing.

There he is: the brother. Image of him. Haunting face. Now that's a coincidence. Course hundreds of times you think of a person and don't meet him. Like a man walking in his sleep. No-one knows him. Must be a corporation meeting today. They say he never put on the city marshal's uniform since he got the job. Charley Boulger used to come out on his high horse, cocked hat, puffed, powdered and shaved. Look at the woebegone walk of him. Eaten a bad egg. Poached eyes on ghost. I have a pain. Great man's brother: his brother's brother. He'd look nice on the city charger. Drop into the D. B. C. probably for his coffee, play chess there. His brother used men as pawns. Let them all go to pot. Afraid to pass a remark on him. Freeze them up with that eye of his. That's the fascination: the name. All a bit touched. Mad Fanny and his other sister Mrs Dickinson driving about with scarlet harness. Bolt upright like surgeon M'Ardle. Still David Sheehy beat him for south Meath. Apply for the Chiltern Hundreds and retire into public life. The patriot's banquet. Eating orangepeels in the park. Simon Dedalus said when they put him in parliament that Parnell would come back from the grave and lead him out of the House of Commons by the arm.

—Of the twoheaded octopus, one of whose heads is the head upon which the ends of the world have forgotten to come while the other speaks with a Scotch accent. The tentacles. . .

They passed from behind Mr Bloom along the curbstone. Beard and bicycle. Young woman.

And there he is too. Now that's really a coincidence: secondtime. Coming events cast their shadows before. With the approval of the

4. C. S. Parnell's brother.

eminent poet Mr Geo Russell.[5] That might be Lizzie Twigg with him. A. E.: what does that mean? Initials perhaps. Albert Edward, Arthur Edmund, Alphonsus Eb Ed El Esquire. What was he saying? The ends of the world with a Scotch accent. Tentacles: octopus. Something occult: symbolism. Holding forth. She's taking it all in. Not saying a word. To aid gentleman in literary work.

His eyes followed the high figure in homespun, beard and bicycle, a listening woman at his side. Coming from the vegetarian. Only weggebobbles and fruit. Don't eat a beefsteak. If you do the eyes of that cow will pursue you through all eternity. They say it's healthier. Wind and watery though. Tried it. Keep you on the run all day. Bad as a bloater. Dreams all night. Why do they call that thing they gave me nutsteak? Nutarians. Fruitarians. To give you the idea you are eating rumpsteak. Absurd. Salty too. They cook in soda. Keep you sitting by the tap all night.

Her stockings are loose over her ankles. I detest that: so tasteless. Those literary ethereal people they are all. Dreamy, cloudy, symbolistic. Esthetes they are. I wouldn't be surprised if it was that kind of food you see produces the like waves of the brain the poetical. For example one of those policemen sweating Irish stew into their shirts; you couldn't squeeze a line of poetry out of him. Don't know what poetry is even. Must be in a certain mood.

> *The dreamy cloudy gull*
> *Waves o'er the waters dull.*

He crossed at Nassau street corner and stood before the window of Yeates and Son, pricing the field glasses. Or will I drop into old Harris's and have a chat with young Sinclair? Wellmannered fellow. Probably at his lunch. Must get those old glasses of mine set right. Gœrz lenses, six guineas. Germans making their way everywhere. Sell on easy terms to capture trade. Undercutting. Might chance on a pair in the railway lost property office. Astonishing the things people leave behind them in trains and cloak rooms. What do they be thinking about? Women too. Incredible. Last year travelling to Ennis had to pick up that farmer's daughter's bag and hand it to her at Limerick junction. Unclaimed money too. There's a little watch up there on the roof of the bank to test those glasses by.

His lids came down on the lower rims of his irides. Can't see it. If you imagine it's there you can almost see it. Can't see it.

He faced about and, standing between the awnings, held out his right hand at arm's length towards the sun. Wanted to try that often. Yes: completely. The tip of his little finger blotted out the

5. Bloom wonders whether the woman with A.E. might be Lizzie Twigg and then goes on to speculate on the meaning of "A.E." and on Russell's mystical ideas.

sun's disk. Must be the focus where the rays cross. If I had black glasses. Interesting. There was a lot of talk about those sunspots when we were in Lombard street west. Terrific explosions they are. There will be a total eclipse this year: autumn some time.

Now that I come to think of it, that ball falls at Greenwich time. It's the clock is worked by an electric wire from Dunsink. Must go out there some first Saturday of the month. If I could get an introduction to professor Joly or learn up something about his family. That would do to: man always feels complimented. Flattery where least expected. Nobleman proud to be descended from some king's mistress. His foremother. Lay it on with a trowel. Cap in hand goes through the land. Not go in and blurt out what you know you're not to: what's parallax? Show this gentleman the door.

Ah.

His hand fell again to his side.

Never know anything about it. Waste of time. Gasballs spinning about, crossing each other, passing. Same old dingdong always. Gas, then solid, then world, then cold, then dead shell drifting around, frozen rock like that pineapple rock. The moon. Must be a new moon out, she said. I believe there is.

He went on by la Maison Claire.

Wait. The full moon was the night we were Sunday fortnight exactly there is a new moon. Walking down by the Tolka. Not bad for a Fairview moon. She was humming: The young May moon she's beaming, love. He other side of her. Elbow, arm. He. Glowworm's la-amp is gleaming, love. Touch. Fingers. Asking. Answer. Yes.

Stop. Stop. If it was it was.[6] Must.

Mr Bloom, quick breathing, slowlier walking, passed Adam court.

With a deep quiet relief, his eyes took note: this is street here middle of the day Bob Doran's bottle shoulders. On his annual bend, M'Coy said. They drink in order to say or do something or *cherchez la femme*.[7] Up in the Coombe with chummies and streetwalkers and then the rest of the year as sober as a judge.

Yes. Thought so. Sloping into the Empire. Gone. Plain soda would do him good. Where Pat Kinsella had his Harp theater before Whitbread ran the Queen's.[8] Broth of a boy. Dion Boucicault business with his harvestmoon face in a poky bonnet. Three Purty Maids from School. How time flies eh? Showing long red pantaloons under his skirts. Drinkers, drinking, laughed spluttering, their drink against their breath. More power, Pat. Coarse red: fun for drunkards: guffaw and smoke. Take off that white hat. His parboiled eyes. Where is he now? Beggar somewhere. The harp that

---

6. Bloom is thinking again of his wife's infidelities.

7. "Look for the woman" (in the case).

8. The Queen's Theatre. Dion Boucicault was an Irish-born American dramatist, manager, and actor.

once did starve us all.[9]

I was happier then. Or was that I? Or am I now I? Twentyeight I was. She twentythree when we left Lombard street west something changed. Could never like it again after Rudy. Can't bring back time. Like holding water in your hand. Would you go back to then? Just beginning then. Would you? Are you not happy in your home, you poor little naughty boy? Wants to sew on buttons for me. I must answer. Write it in the library.

Grafton street gay with housed awnings lured his senses. Muslin prints silk, dames and dowagers, jingle of harnesses, hoofthuds lowringing in the baking causeway. Thick feet that woman has in the white stockings. Hope the rain mucks them up on her. Country bred chawbacon. All the beef to the heels were in. Always gives a woman clumsy feet. Molly looks out of plumb.

He passed, dallying, the windows of Brown Thomas, silk mercers. Cascades of ribbons. Flimsy China silks. A tilted urn poured from its mouth a flood of bloodhued poplin: lustrous blood. The huguenots brought that here. *La causa è santa!*[1] Tara tara. Great chorus that. Tara. Must be washed in rainwater. Meyerbeer. Tara: bom bom bom.

Pincushions. I'm a long time threatening to buy one. Stick them all over the place. Needles in window curtains.

He bared slightly his left forearm. Scrape: nearly gone. Not today anyhow. Must go back for that lotion. For her birthday perhaps. Junejuly augseptember eighth. Nearly three months off. Then she mightn't like it. Women won't pick up pins. Say it cuts lo.

Gleaming silks, petticoats on slim brass rails, rays of flat silk stockings.

Useless to go back. Had to be. Tell me all.

High voices. Sunwarm silk. Jingling harnesses. All for a woman, home and houses, silk webs, silver, rich fruits, spicy from Jaffa. Agendath Netaim.[2] Wealth of the world.

A warm human plumpness settled down on his brain. His brain yielded. Perfume of embraces all him assailed. With hungered flesh obscurely, he mutely craved to adore:

Duke street. Here we are. Must eat. The Burton. Feel better then.

He turned Combridge's corner, still pursued. Jingling hoofthuds. Perfumed bodies, warm, full. All kissed, yielded: in deep summer fields, tangled pressed grass, in trickling hallways of tenements, along sofas, creaking beds.

9. A reference to the lack of financial success of the Harp Theatre through a punning reworking (almost worthy of Stephen Dedalus) of Tom Moore's famous *Harp That Once Through Tara's Halls*.
1. "The cause is sacred," chorus from Meyerbeer's opera *Les Huguenots*, which Bloom is recalling. The Huguenots were 16th- and 17th-century French Protestants, many of whom fled to Britain to escape persecution.
2. "Planters' Company" (Hebrew). Bloom recalls a leaflet advertising an early Zionist settlement which he had seen that morning and is still carrying in his pocket.

—Jack, love!

—Darling!

—Kiss me, Reggy!

—My boy!

—Love![3]

His heart astir he pushed in the door of the Burton restaurant. Stink gripped his trembling breath: pungent meatjuice, slop of greens. See the animals feed.

Men, men, men.

Perched on high stools by the bar, hats shoved back, at the tables calling for more bread no charge, swilling, wolfing gobfuls of sloppy food, their eyes bulging, wiping wetted moustaches. A pallid suetfaced young man polished his tumbler knife fork and spoon with his napkin. New set of microbes. A man with an infant's saucestained napkin tucked round him shovelled gurgling soup down his gullet. A man spitting back on his plate: halfmasticated gristle: no teeth to chewchewchew it. Chump chop from the grill. Bolting to get it over. Sad booser's eyes. Bitten off more than he can chew. Am I like that? See ourselves as others see us. Hungry man is an angry man. Working tooth and jaw. Don't! O! A bone! That last pagan king of Ireland Cormac in the schoolpoem choked himself at Sletty southward of the Boyne.[4] Wonder what he was eating. Something galoptious. Saint Patrick converted him to Christianity. Couldn't swallow it all however.

—Roast beef and cabbage.

—One stew.

Smells of men. His gorge rose. Spaton sawdust, sweetish warmish cigarette smoke, reek of plug, spilt beer, men's beery piss, the stale of ferment.

Couldn't eat a morsel here. Fellow sharpening knife and fork, to eat all before him, old chap picking his tootles. Slight spasm, full, chewing the cud. Before and after. Grace after meals. Look on this picture then on that. Scoffing up stewgravy with sopping sippets of bread. Lick it off the plate, man! Get out of this.

He gazed round the stooled and tabled eaters, tightening the wings of his nose.

—Two stouts here.

—One corned and cabbage.

That fellow ramming a knifeful of cabbage down as if his life depended on it. Good stroke. Give me the fidgets to look. Safer to eat from his three hands. Tear it limb from limb. Second nature to

---

3. Sensual images are leading Bloom to imagine love scenes from a sentimental novel. The cannibal Lestrygonians had used "the handsome daughter of Lestrygonian Antiphates" as a decoy to lure Ulysses' men to her father, and Bloom is drawn by his sensual and sexual imagination to enter Burton's restaurant —only to be disgusted by the grossness of the atmosphere.

4. Bloom is recalling a "schoolpoem" about a legendary incident in Irish history.

him. Born with a silver knife in his mouth. That's witty, I think. Or no. Silver means born rich. Born with a knife. But then the allusion is lost.

An illgirt server gathered sticky clattering plates. Rock, the bailiff, standing at the bar blew the foamy crown from his tankard. Well up: it splashed yellow near his boot. A diner, knife and fork upright, elbows on table, ready for a second helping stared towards the food-lift across his stained square of newspaper. Other chap telling him something with his mouth full. Sympathetic listener. Table talk. I munched hum un thu Unchster Bunk un Munchday. Ha? Did you, faith?

Mr Bloom raised two fingers doubtfully to his lips. His eyes said.

—Not here. Don't see him.[5]

Out. I hate dirty eaters.

He backed towards the door. Get a light snack in Davy Byrne's. Stopgap. Keep me going. Had a good breakfast.

—Roast and mashed here.

—Pint of stout.

Every fellow for his own, tooth and nail. Gulp. Grub. Gulp. Gobstuff.

He came out into clearer air and turned back towards Grafton street. Eat or be eaten. Kill! Kill!

Suppose that communal kitchen years to come perhaps. All trotting down with porringers and tommycans to be filled. Devour contents in the street. John Howard Parnell example the provost of Trinity every mother's son don't talk of your provosts and provost of Trinity women and children, cabmen, priests, parsons, field-marshals, archbishops. From Ailesbury road, Clyde road, artisan's dwellings north Dublin union, lord mayor in his gingerbread coach, old queen in a bathchair. My plate's empty. After you with our in-corporated drinkingcup. Like sir Philip Crampton's fountain. Rub off the microbes with your handkerchief. Next chap rubs on a new batch with his. Father O'Flynn would make hares of them all. Have rows all the same. All for number one. Children fighting for the scrapings of the pot. Want a soup pot as big as the Phoenix Park. Harpooning flitches and hindquarters out of it. Hate people all around you. City Arms hotel *table d'hôte* she called it. Soup, joint and sweet. Never know whose thoughts you're chewing. Then who'd wash up all the plates and forks? Might be all feeding on tabloids that time. Teeth getting worse and worse.

After all there's a lot in that vegetarian fine flavour of things from the earth garlic, of course, it stinks Italian organgrinders crisp of onions, mushrooms truffles. Pain to animal too. Pluck and draw fowl. Wretched brutes there at the cattlemarket waiting for the

5. He pretends he is looking for someone he cannot see, so that he has an excuse to leave without eating.

poleaxe to split their skulls open. Moo. Poor trembling calves.
Meh. Staggering bob. Bubble and squeak. Butchers' buckets wobble
lights. Give us that brisket off the hook. Plup. Rawhead and bloody
bones. Flayed glasseyed sheep hung from their haunches, sheep-
snouts bloodypapered sniveling nosejam on sawdust. Top and
lashers going out. Don't maul them pieces, young one.

Hot fresh blood they prescribe for decline. Blood always needed.
Insidious. Lick it up, smoking hot, thick sugary. Famished ghosts.

Ah, I'm hungry.

He entered Davy Byrne's. Moral pub. He doesn't chat. Stands a
drink now and then. But in leapyear once in four. Cashed a cheque
for me once.

What will I take now? He drew his watch. Let me see now.
Shandygaff?

—Hello, Bloom! Nosey Flynn said from his nook.

—Hello, Flynn.

—How's things?

—Tiptop . . . Let me see. I'll take a glass of burgundy and . . .
let me see.

Sardines on the shelves. Almost taste them by looking. Sandwich?
Ham and his descendants mustered and bred there. Potted meats.
What is home without Plumtree's potted meat? Incomplete. What
a stupid ad! Under the obituary notices they stuck it. All up a
plumtree. Dignam's potted meat. Cannibals would with lemon and
rice. White missionary too salty. Like pickled pork. Except the
chief consumes the parts of honour. Ought to be tough from exercise. His wives in a row to watch the effect. *There was a right royal
old nigger. Who ate or something the somethings of the reverend
Mr MacTrigger.* With it an abode of bliss. Lord knows what concoction. Cauls mouldy tripes windpipes faked and minced up. Puzzle find the meat. Kosher. No meat and milk together. Hygiene that
was what they call now. Yom kippur fast spring cleaning of inside.
Peace and war depend on some fellow's digestion. Religions. Christmas turkeys and geese. Slaughter of innocents. Eat, drink and be
merry. Then casual wards full after. Heads bandaged. Cheese di-
gests all but itself. Mighty cheese.

—Have you a cheese sandwich?

—Yes, sir.

Like a few olives too if they had them. Italian I prefer. Good
glass of burgundy; take away that. Lubricate. A nice salad, cool as
a cucumber. Tom Kernan can dress. Puts gusto into it. Pure olive
oil. Milly served me that cutlet with a sprig of parsley. Take one
Spanish onion. God made food, the devil the cooks. Devilled crab.

—Wife well?

—Quite well, thanks . . . A cheese sandwich, then. Gorgon-
zola, have you?

—Yes, sir.

Nosey Flynn sipped his grog.

—Doing any singing those times?

Look at his mouth. Could whistle in his own ear. Flap ears to match. Music. Knows as much about it as my coachman. Still better tell him. Does no harm. Free ad.

—She's engaged for a big tour end of this month. You may have heard perhaps.

—No. O, that's the style. Who's getting it up?

The curate[6] served.

—How much is that?

—Seven d., sir . . . Thank you, sir.

Mr Bloom cut his sandwich into slender strips. *Mr MacTrigger.* Easier than the dreamy creamy stuff. *His five hundred wives. Had the time of their lives.*

—Mustard, sir?

—Thank you.

He studded under each lifted strip yellow blobs. *Their lives.* I have it. *It grew bigger and bigger and bigger.*

—Getting it up? he said. Well, it's like a company idea, you see. Part shares and part profits.

—Ay, now I remember, Nosey Flynn said, putting his hand in his pocket to scratch his groin. Who is this was telling me? Isn't Blazes Boylan mixed up in it?

A warm shock of air heat of mustard haunched on Mr Bloom's heart. He raised his eyes and met the stare of a bilious clock. Two. Pub clock five minutes fast. Time going on. Hands moving. Two. Not yet.[7]

His midriff yearned then upward, sank within him, yearned more longly, longingly.

Wine.

He smellsipped the cordial juice and, bidding his throat strongly to speed it, set his wineglass delicately down.

—Yes, he said. He's the organiser in point of fact.

No fear. No brains.

Nosey Flynn snuffed and scratched. Flea having a good square meal.

—He had a good slice of luck, Jack Mooney was telling me, over that boxing match Myler Keogh won again that soldier in the Portobello barracks. By God, he had the little kipper down in the county Carlow he was telling me. . . .

Hope that dewdrop doesn't come down into his glass. No, snuffled it up.

—For near a month, man, before it came off. Sucking duck eggs

---

6. Bartender.

7. I.e., not yet time for Boylan to visit Molly.

by God till further orders. Keep him off the boose, see? O, by God, Blazes is a hairy chap.

Davy Byrne came forward from the hindbar in tuckstitched shirt sleeves, cleaning his lips with two wipes of his napkin. Herring's blush. Whose smile upon each feature plays with such and such replete. Too much fat on the parsnips.

—And here's himself and pepper on him, Nosey Flynn said. Can you give us a good one for the Gold cup?

—I'm off that, Mr Flynn, Davy Byrne answered. I never put anything on a horse.

—You're right there, Nosey Flynn said.

Mr. Bloom ate his strips of sandwich, fresh clean bread, with relish of disgust, pungent mustard, the feety savour of green cheese. Sips of his·wine soothed his palate. Not logwood that. Tastes fuller this weather with the chill off.

Nice quiet bar. Nice piece of wood in that counter. Nicely planed. Like the way it curves there.

—I wouldn't do anything at all in that line, Davy Byrne said. It ruined many a man the same horses.

Vintners' sweepstake. Licensed for the sale of beer, wine and spirits for consumption on the premises. Heads I win tails you lose.

—True for you, Nosey Flynn said. Unless you're in the know. There's no straight sport going now. Lenehan gets some good ones. He's giving Sceptre today. Zinfandel's the favourite, lord Howard de Walden's, won at Epsom. Morny Cannon is riding him. I could have got seven to one against Saint Amant a fortnight before.

—That so? Davy Byrne said. . . .

He went towards the window and, taking up the petty cash book, scanned its pages.

—I could, faith, Nosey Flynn said snuffling. That was a rare bit of horseflesh. Saint Frusquin was her sire. She won in a thunderstorm, Rothschild's filly, with wadding in her ears. Blue jacket and yellow cap. Bad luck to big Ben Dollard and his John O'Gaunt. He put me off it. Ay.

He drank resignedly from his tumbler, running his fingers down the flutes.

—Ay, he said, sighing.

Mr Bloom, champing standing, looked upon his sigh. Nosey numskull. Will I tell him that horse Lenehan?[8] He knows already. Better let him forget. Go and lose more. Fool and his money. Dewdrop coming down again. Cold nose he'd have kissing a woman. Still they might like. Prickly beards they like. Dog's cold noses. Old Mrs. Riordan with the rumbling stomach's Skye terrier in the City Arms hotel. Molly fondling him in her lap. O the big doggybow-

8. Bloom is wondering whether to pass on a tip from Lenehan, who wrote for the racing paper *Sport*.

wowsywowsy!

Wine soaked and softened rolled pith of bread mustard a moment mawkish cheese. Nice wine it is. Taste it better because I'm not thirsty. Bath of course does that. Just a bite or two. Then about six o'clock I can. Six, six. Time will be gone then. She. . .

Mild fire of wine kindled his veins. I wanted that badly. Felt so off colour. His eyes unhungrily saw shelves of tins, sardines, gaudy lobster's claws. All the odd things people pick up for food. Out of shells, periwinkles with a pin, off trees, snails out of the ground the French eat, out of the sea with bait on a hook. Silly fish learn nothing in a thousand years. If you didn't know risky putting anything into your mouth. Poisonous berries. Johnny Magories. Roundness you think good. Gaudy colour warns you off. One fellow told another and so on. Try it on the dog first. Led on by the smell or the look. Tempting fruit. Ice cones. Cream. Instinct. Orangegroves for instance. Need artificial irrigation. Bleibtreustrasse.[9] Yes but what about oysters. Unsightly like a clot of phlegm. Filthy shells. Devil to open them too. Who found them out? Garbage, sewage they feed on. Fizz and Red bank oysters. Effect on the sexual. Aphrodis. He was in the Red bank this morning. Was he oyster old fish at table. Perhaps he young flesh in bed. No. June has no ar no oysters. But there are people like tainted game. Jugged hare. First catch your hare. Chinese eating eggs fifty years old, blue and green again. Dinner of thirty courses. Each dish harmless might mix inside. Idea for a poison mystery. That archduke Leopold was it. No. Yes, or was it Otto one of those Habsburgs? Or who was it used to eat the scruff off his own head? Cheapest lunch in town. Of course, aristocrats. Then the others copy to be in the fashion. Milly too rock oil and flour. Raw pastry I like myself. Half the catch ·of oysters they throw back in the sea to keep up the price. Cheap. No one would buy. Caviare. Do the grand. Hock in green glasses. Swell blowout. Lady this. Powdered bosom pearls. The *élite*. *Crème de la crème*.[1] They want special dishes to pretend they're. Hermit with a platter of pulse keep down the stings of the flesh. Know me come eat with me. Royal sturgeon. High sheriff, Coffey, the butcher, right to venisons of the forest from his ex.[2] Send him back the half of a cow. Spread I saw down in the Master of the Rolls' kitchen area. Whitehatted *chef* like a rabbi. Combustible duck. Curly cabbage *à la duchesse de Parme*. Just as well to write it on the bill of fare so you can know what you've eaten too many drugs spoil the broth. I know it myself. Dosing it with Edward's desiccated soup. Geese stuffed silly for them. Lobsters boiled alive. Do ptake some

9. The Berlin street which contained the offices of the "Planters' Company."
1. "Cream of the cream" (i.e., the very best, socially).
2. All sturgeon caught in or off Britain were the property of the king, according to the ancient traditional rights to certain kinds of fish or game. Bloom goes on to imagine a Dublin butcher having a "right to venisons of the forest from his ex[cellency]"—i.e., the Viceroy.

ptarmigan. Wouldn't mind being a waiter in a swell hotel. Tips, evening dress, halfnaked ladies. May I tempt you to a little more filleted lemon sole, miss Dubedat? Yes, do bedad. And she did bedad. Huguenot name I expect that. A miss Dubedat lived in Killiney I remember. *Du, de la,* French. Still it's the same fish, perhaps old Micky Hanlon of Moore street ripped the guts out of making money, hand over fist, finger in fishes' gills, can't write his name on a cheque, think he was painting the landscape with his mouth twisted. Moooikill A Aitcha Ha. Ignorant as a kish of brogues,[3] worth fifty thousand pounds.

Stuck on the pane two flies buzzed, stuck.

Glowing wine on his palate lingered swallowed. Crushing in the winepress grapes of Burgundy. Sun's heat it is. Seems to a secret touch telling me memory. Touched his sense moistened remembered. Hidden under wild ferns on Howth. Below us bay sleeping sky. No sound. The sky. The bay purple by the Lion's head. Green by Drumleck. Yellowgreen towards Sutton. Fields of undersea, the lines faint brown in grass, buried cities. Pillowed on my coat she had her hair, earwigs in the heather scrub my hand under her nape, you'll toss me all. O wonder! Coolsoft with ointments her hand touched me, caressed: her eyes upon me did not turn away. Ravished over her I lay, full lips full open, kissed her mouth. Yum. Softly she gave me in my mouth the seedcake warm and chewed. Mawkish pulp her mouth had mumbled sweet and sour with spittle. Joy: I ate it: joy. Young life, her lips that gave me pouting. Soft, warm, sticky gumjelly lips. Flowers her eyes were, take me, willing eyes. Pebbles fell. She lay still. A goat. No-one. High on Ben Howth rhododendrons a nannygoat walking surefooted, dropping currants. Screened under ferns she laughed warmfolded. Wildly I lay on her, kissed her; eyes, her lips, her stretched neck, beating, woman's breasts full in her blouse of nun's veiling, fat nipples upright. Hot I tongued her. She kissed me. I was kissed. All yielding she tossed my hair. Kissed, she kissed me.[4]

Me. And me now.

Stuck, the flies buzzed.

His downcast eyes followed the silent veining of the oaken slab. Beauty: it curves: curves are beauty. Shapely goddesses, Venus, Juno: curves the world admires. Can see them library museum standing in the round hall, naked goddesses. Aids to digestion. They don't care what man looks. All to see. Never speaking, I mean to

---

3. A basket of shoes.
4. Bloom is remembering when he first proposed to Molly, on the Hill of Howth, near Dublin. Molly also recalls this in the final "Penelope" episode, which is her soliloquy: " * * * we were lying on the rhododendrons on Howth head in the grey tweed suit and his straw hat the day I got him to propose to me yes * * * my God after that long kiss I near lost my breath * * * I saw he understood or felt what a woman is and I knew I could always get round him and I gave him all the pleasure I could leading him on * * * "

say to fellows like Flynn. Suppose she did Pygmalion and Galatea[5] what would she say first? Mortal! Put you in your proper place. Quaffing nectar at mess with gods, golden dishes, all ambrosial. Not like a tanner lunch we have, boiled mutton, carrots and turnips, bottle of Allsop. Nectar, imagine it drinking electricity: god's food. Lovely forms of woman sculped Junonian. Immortal lovely. And we stuffing food in one hole and out behind: food, chyle, blood, dung, earth, food: have to feed it like stoking an engine. They have no. Never looked. I'll look today. Keeper won't see. Bend down let something fall see if she.

Dribbling a quiet message from his bladder came to go to do not to do there to do. A man and ready he drained his glass to the lees and walked, to men too they gave themselves, manly conscious, lay with men lovers, a youth enjoyed her, to the yard.

When the sound of his boots had ceased Davy Byrne said from his book:

—What is this he is? Isn't he in the insurance line?

—He's out of that long ago, Nosey Flynn said. He does canvassing for the *Freeman*.

—I know him well to see, Davy Byrne said. Is he in trouble?

—Trouble? Nosey Flynn said. Not that I heard of. Why?

—I noticed he was in mourning.

—Was he? Nosey Flynn said. So he was, faith. I asked him how was all at home. You're right, by God. So he was.

—I never broach the subject, Davy Byrne said humanely, if I see a gentleman is in trouble that way. It only brings it up fresh in their minds.

—It's not the wife anyhow, Nosey Flynn said. I met him the day before yesterday and he coming out of that Irish farm dairy John Wyse Nolan's wife has in Henry street with a jar of cream in his hand taking it home to his better half. She's well nourished, I tell you. Plovers on toast.

—And is he doing for the *Freeman?* Davy Byrne said.

Nosey Flynn pursed his lips.

—He doesn't buy cream on the ads he picks up. You can make bacon of that.

—How so? Davy Byrne asked, coming from his book.

Nosey Flynn made swift passes in the air with juggling fingers. He winked.

—He's in the craft,[6] he said.

—Do you tell me so? Davy Byrne said.

—Very much so, Nosey Flynn said. Ancient free and accepted

5. Pygmalion was the sculptor whose statue of Galatea came alive.
6. I.e., in the "free and accepted order" of Freemasons, one of the oldest European secret societies; it was not in good repute in predominantly Roman Catholic countries like Ireland.

order. Light, life and love, by God. They give him a leg up. I was told that by a, well, I won't say who.

—Is that a fact?

—O, it's a fine order, Nosey Flynn said. They stick to you when you're down. I know a fellow was trying to get into it, but they're as close as damn it. By God they did right to keep the women out of it.

Davy Byrne smiledyawnednodded all in one:

—Iiiiiichaaaaaaach!

—There was one woman, Nosey Flynn said, hid herself in a clock to find out what they do be doing. But be damned but they smelt her out and swore her in on the spot a master mason. That was one of the Saint Legers of Doneraile.

Davy Byrne, sated after his yawn, said with tearwashed eyes:

—And is that a fact? Decent quiet man he is. I often saw him in here and I never once saw him, you know, over the line.

—God Almighty couldn't make him drunk, Nosey Flynn said firmly. Slips off when the fun gets too hot. Didn't you see him look at his watch? Ah, you weren't there. If you ask him to have a drink first thing he does he outs with the watch to see what he ought to imbibe. Declare to God he does.

—There are some like that, Davy Byrne said. He's a safe man, I'd say.

—He's not too bad, Nosey Flynn said, snuffling it up. He has been known to put his hand down too to help a fellow. Give the devil his due. O, Bloom has his good points. But there's one thing he'll never do.

His hand scrawled a dry pen signature beside his grog.

—I know, Davy Byrne said.

—Nothing in black and white, Nosey Flynn said.

Paddy Leonard and Bantam Lyons came in. Tom Rochford followed, a plaining hand on his claret waistcoat.

—Day, Mr. Byrne.

—Day, gentlemen.

They paused at the counter.

—Who's standing? Paddy Leonard asked.

—I'm sitting anyhow, Nosey Flynn answered.

—Well, what'll it be? Paddy Leonard asked.

—I'll take a stone ginger, Bantam Lyons said.

—How much? Paddy Leonard cried. Since when, for God's sake? What's yours, Tom?

—How is the main drainage? Nosey Flynn asked, sipping.

For answer Tom Rochford pressed his hand to his breastbone and hiccupped.

—Would I trouble you for a glass of fresh water, Mr Byrne? he said.

—Certainly, sir.

Paddy Leonard eyed his alemates.

—Lord love a duck, he said, look at what I'm standing drinks to! Cold water and gingerpop! Two fellows that would suck whisky off a sore leg. He has some bloody horse up his sleeve for the Gold cup. A dead snip.

—Zinfandel is it? Nosey Flynn asked.

Tom Rochford spilt powder from a twisted paper into the water set before him.

—That cursed dyspepsia, he said before drinking.

—Breadsoda is very good, Davy Byrne said.

Tom Rochford nodded and drank.

—Is it Zinfandel?

—Say nothing, Bantam Lyons winked. I'm going to plunge five bob on my own.

—Tell us if you're worth your salt and be damned to you, Paddy Leonard said. Who gave it to you?

Mr Bloom on his way out raised three fingers in greeting.

—So long, Nosey Flynn said.

The others turned.

—That's the man now that gave it to me, Bantam Lyons whispered.

—Prrwht! Paddy Leonard said with scorn. Mr Byrne, sir, we'll take two of your small Jamesons after that and a. . .

—Stone ginger, Davy Byrne added civilly.

—Ay, Paddy Leonard said. A suckingbottle for the baby.

Mr Bloom walked towards Dawson street, his tongue brushing his teeth smooth. Something green it would have to be: spinach say. Then with those Röntgen rays searchlight you could.

At Duke lane a ravenous terrier choked up a sick knuckly cud on the cobble stones and lapped it with new zest. Surfeit. Returned with thanks having fully digested the contents. First sweet then savoury. Mr Bloom coasted warily. Ruminants. His second course. Their upper jaw they move. Wonder if Tom Rochford will do anything with that invention of his. Wasting time explaining it to Flynn's mouth. Lean people long mouths. Ought to be a hall or a place where inventors could go in and invent free. Course then you'd have all the cranks pestering.

He hummed, prolonging in solemn echo, the closes of the bars:

> *Don Giovanni, a cenar teco*
> *M'invitasti.*[8]

8. Since Molly is a singer, Bloom is familiar with opera. Here he recalls the song sung by the Commendatore's statue in Mozart's *Don Giovanni*, and translates accurately the Italian words he quotes, except for *"teco"* ("with you"). This opera supplies some of the key themes in *Ulysses,* and the famous duet between Don Giovanni and Zerlina, *"Là ci darèm la mano"* ("There we will join hands"), haunts Bloom's mind continually throughout the day. It is on the program of Molly's concert which she is discussing with Boylan that after-

Feel better. Burgundy. Good pick me up. Who distilled first? Some chap in the blues. Dutch courage. That *Kilkenny People* in the national library now I must.

Bare clean closestools, waiting, in the window of William Miller, plumber, turned back his thoughts. They could: and watch it all the way down, swallow a pin sometimes come out of the ribs years after, tour round the body, changing biliary duct, spleen squirting liver, gastric juice coils of intestines like pipes. But the poor buffer would have to stand all the time with his insides entrails on show. Science.

—*A cenar teco*.

What does that *teco* mean? Tonight perhaps.

> *Don Giovanni, thou hast me invited*
> *To come to supper tonight,*
> *The rum the rumdum.*

Doesn't go properly.

Keyes: two months if I get Nannetti[9] to. That'll be two pounds ten, about two pounds eight. Three Hynes owes me. Two eleven. Presscott's ad. Two fifteen. Five guineas about. On the pig's back.

Could buy one of those silk petticoats for Molly, colour of her new garters.

Today. Today. Not think.[1]

Tour the south then. What about English watering places? Brighton, Margate. Piers by moonlight. Her voice floating out. Those lovely sideside girls. Against John Long's a drowsing loafer lounged in heavy thought, gnawing a crusted knuckle. Handy man wants job. Small wages. Will eat anything.

Mr Bloom turned at Gray's confectioner's window of unbought tarts and passed the reverend Thomas Connellan's bookstore. *Why I left the church of Rome?* Bird's Nest. Women run him. They say they used to give pauper children soup to change to protestants in the time of the potato blight. Society over the way papa went to for the conversion of poor jews. Same bait. Why we left the church of Rome?

A blind stripling stood tapping the curbstone with his slender cane. No tram in sight. Wants to cross.

—Do you want to cross? Mr Bloom asked.

The blind stripling did not answer. His wall face frowned weakly. He moved his head uncertainly.

—You're in Dawson street, Mr Bloom said. Molesworth street is opposite. Do you want to cross? There's nothing in the way.

---

noon, and Bloom associates it with her adultery with Boylan.
9. Proofreader and business manager of the *Freeman's Journal*, and in charge of the advertising Bloom is trying to get for the paper. If he will add a complimentary reference to Keyes, a grocer, in a gossip column, Keyes promises to renew his advertisement, which means a commission for Bloom.
1. I.e., of Molly and Boylan.

The cane moved out trembling to the left. Mr Bloom's eye followed its line and saw again the dyeworks' van drawn up before Drago's. Where I saw his brilliantined hair just when I was. Horse drooping. Driver in John Long's. Slaking his drouth.

—There's a van there, Mr Bloom said, but it's not moving. I'll see you across. Do you want to go to Molesworth street?

—Yes, the stripling answered. South Frederick street.

—Come, Mr Bloom said.

He touched the thin elbow gently: then took the limp seeing hand to guide it forward.

Say something to him. Better not do the condescending. They mistrust what you tell them. Pass a common remark.

—The rain kept off.

No answer.

Stains on his coat. Slobbers his food, I suppose. Tastes all different for him. Have to be spoonfed first. Like a child's hand his hand. Like Milly's was. Sensitive. Sizing me up I daresay from my hand. Wonder if he has a name. Van. Keep his cane clear of the horse's legs tired drudge get his doze. That's right. Clear. Behind a bull: in front of a horse.

—Thanks, sir.

Knows I'm a man. Voice.

—Right now? First turn to the left.

The blind stripling tapped the curbstone and went on his way, drawing his cane back, feeling again.

Mr Bloom walked behind the eyeless feet, a flatcut suit of herringbone tweed. Poor young fellow! How on earth did he know that van was there? Must have felt it. See things in their foreheads perhaps. Kind of sense of volume. Weight would he feel it if something was removed. Feel a gap. Queer idea of Dublin he must have, tapping his way round by the stones. Could he walk in a beeline if he hadn't that cane? Bloodless pious face like a fellow going in to be a priest.

Penrose! That was that chap's name.

Look at all the things they can learn to do. Read with their fingers. Tune pianos. Or we are surprised they have any brains. Why we think a deformed person or a hunchback clever if he says something we might say. Of course the other senses are more. Embroider. Plait baskets. People ought to help. Work basket I could buy Molly's birthday. Hates sewing. Might take an objection. Dark men they call them.

Sense of smell must be stronger too. Smells on all sides bunched together. Each person too. Then the spring, the summer: smells. Tastes. They say you can't taste wines with your eyes shut or a cold in the head. Also smoke in the dark they say get no pleasure.

And with a woman, for instance. More shameless not seeing.

That girl passing the Stewart institution, head in the air. Look at me. I have them all on. Must be strange not to see her. Kind of a form in his mind's eye. The voice temperature when he touches her with fingers must almost see the lines, the curves. His hands on her hair, for instance. Say it was black for instance. Good. We call it black. Then passing over her white skin. Different feel perhaps. Feeling of white.

Postoffice. Must answer.[2] Fag today. Send her a postal order two shillings half a crown. Accept my little present. Stationer's just here too. Wait. Think over it.

With a gentle finger he felt ever so slowly the hair combed back above his ears. Again. Fibres of fine fine straw. Then gently his finger felt the skin of his right cheek. Downy hair there too. Not smooth enough. The belly is the smoothest. No-one about. There he goes into Frederick street. Perhaps to Levenston's dancing academy piano. Might be settling my braces.

Walking by Doran's public house he slid his hand between waistcoat and trousers and, pulling aside his shirt gently, felt a slack fold of his belly. But I know it's whiteyellow. Want to try in the dark to see.

He withdrew his hand and pulled his dress to.

Poor fellow! Quite a boy. Terrible. Really terrible. What dreams would he have, not seeing. Life a dream for him. Where is the justice being born that way. All those women and children excursion beanfeast burned and drowned in New York.[3] Holocaust. Karma they call that transmigration for sins you did in a past life the reincarnation met him pikehoses.[4] Dear, dear, dear. Pity of course: but somehow you can't cotton on to them someway.

Sir Frederick Falkiner going into the freemasons' hall. Solemn as Troy. After his good lunch in Earlsfort terrace. Old legal cronies cracking a magnum. Tales of the bench and assizes and annals of the bluecoat school.[5] I sentenced him to ten years. I suppose he'd turn up his nose at that stuff I drank. Vintage wine for them, the year marked on a dusty bottle. Has his own ideas of justice in the recorder's court. Wellmeaning old man. Police chargesheets crammed with cases get their percentage manufacturing crime. Sends them to the rightabout. The devil on moneylenders. Gave Reuben J. a great strawcalling. Now he's really what they call a dirty jew. Power those judges have. Crusty old topers in wigs. Bear with a sore paw. And may the Lord have mercy on your soul.

Hello, placard. Mirus bazaar. His excellency the lord lieuten-

---

2. Martha Clifford's letter.
3. This terrible disaster on an excursion steamer on the Hudson took place on June 15, 1904, and was reported in the Dublin papers on June 16.
4. I.e., metempsychosis: Bloom is remembering again their morning conversation on this subject, when Molly exclaimed "O rocks!"
5. Sir Frederick Falkiner wrote the history of the "bluecoat school" in Oxmantown, Dublin. The Dublin "bluecoat school" was founded by Charles II for poor children.

ant. Sixteenth today it is. In aid of funds for Mercer's **hospital**.
The Messiah was first given for that. Yes. Handel. What about
going out there. Ballsbridge. Drop in on Keyes. No use sticking
to him like a leech. Wear out my welcome. Sure to know someone
on the gate.

Mr Bloom came to Kildare street. First I must. Library.

Straw hat in sunlight. Tan shoes. Turnedup trousers. It is. It is.[6]

His heart quopped softly. To the right. Museum. Goddesses. He
swerved to the right.

Is it? Almost certain. Won't look. Wine in my face. Why did
I? Too heady. Yes, it is. The walk. Not see. Not see. Get on.

Making for the museum gate with long windy strides he lifted
his eyes. Handsome building. Sir Thomas Deane designed. Not
following me?

Didn't see me perhaps. Light in his eyes.

The flutter of his breath came forth in short sighs. Quick. Cold
statues: quiet there. Safe in a minute.

No, didn't see me. After two. Just at the gate.

My heart!

His eyes beating looked steadfastly at cream curves of stone.
Sir Thomas Deane was the Greek architecture.

Look for something I.

His hasty hand went quick into a pocket, took out, read unfolded
Agendath Netaim. Where did I?

Busy looking for.

He thrust back quickly Agendath.

Afternoon she said.

I am looking for that. Yes, that. Try all pockets. Handker. *Freeman*. Where did I? Ah, yes. Trousers. Purse. Potato. Where did I?
Hurry. Walk quietly. Moment more. My heart.

His hand looking for the where did I put found in his hip pocket
soap lotion have to call tepid paper stuck. Ah, soap there! Yes.
Gate.[7]

Safe!

1914–21   1922

6. Bloom catches a glimpse of Boylan
and tries to avoid an encounter.

7. Anxious to avoid Boylan, Bloom pretends to admire the architecture of the
Museum and National Library building,
and then pretends to be looking for
something in his pockets, where he finds
the "Agendath Netaim" leaflet. He continues to search desperately in his pockets to avoid looking up and seeing
Boylan, discovers the potato he carries
as a remedy against rheumatism and
a cake of soap he had bought that
morning (the soap reminds him that
he must call at the chemist's to collect
a face lotion he had ordered for Molly).
At last he goes through the National
Library gate and feels safe.

From Finnegans Wake[1]

From *Anna Livia Plurabelle*

* * * Well, you know or don't you kennet[2] or haven't I told you every telling has a taling and that's the he and the she of it. Look, look, the dusk is growing! My branches lofty are taking root. And my cold cher's[3] gone ashley. Fieluhr?[4] Filou! What age is at? It saon[5] is late. 'Tis endless now senne[6] eye or erewone[7] last saw Waterhouse's clogh.[8] They took it asunder, I hurd thum sigh. When will they reassemble it? O, my back, my back, my bach![9] I'd want to go to Aches-les-Pains.[10] Pingpong! There's the Belle for Sexaloitez![11] And Concepta de Send-us-pray! Pang! Wring out the clothes! Wring in the dew![12] Godavari,[13] vert the showers! And

1. Because the meanings in *Finnegans Wake* are developed not by action but by language—a great network of multiple puns that echo themes back and forth throughout the book—the careful reading of a single passage, even out of context, will convey more than any summary of the "plot" (some discussion of the general plan of the work is given in the Joyce introduction). The particular passage selected here was one of Joyce's favorites, and there exists a phonograph recording of it made by himself. It consists of the closing pages of the eighth chapter of Book I; the chapter was published separately as *Anna Livia Plurabelle* in 1928 and 1930, although the finished book omits this title.

The entire chapter is a dialogue, and the scene is the river Liffey: two washerwomen are washing in public the dirty linen of HCE and ALP (the "hero" and "heroine"; see the Joyce introduction), and gossiping as they work. As this excerpt opens, it is growing dark; things become gradually less and less distinct, so that the washerwomen cannot be sure what the objects seen in the dusk really are. As it grows darker, the river becomes wider (we get nearer its mouth) and the wind rises, so that the women have more and more difficulty hearing each other. At last, as night falls, they become part of the landscape, an elm tree and a stone on the river bank. Toward the end of the dialogue they ask to hear a tale of Shem and Shaun (HCE's two sons), and this question points the way to Book II, which opens with the two boys (metamorphosed for the moment into Glugg and Chuff) playing in front of the tavern in the evening.

A complete annotation of even this brief passage is, of course, a physical impossibility in this anthology. The notes that are provided are intended to indicate the nature of what Joyce does with language and to enable the reader

to see what is going on. But there are all sorts of suggestions built up in the language that are not referred to in the notes: each reader will find some for himself.

2. Ken it ("know it") + Kennet (river in England). Rivers in *Finnegans Wake* symbolize the flow of life, and thousands of river names are suggested throughout the book in allusive pun-combinations, as here.

3. Cold cheer (i.e., cold comfort) + cold chair + (perhaps) culture. "Gone ashley": gone to ashes. Going to ashes suggests the fiery death and rebirth of the mythical phoenix: from the ashes of the dead phoenix rises a new one. Modern culture, which can provide only cold cheer, is in the state of decay, the "going to ashes," which precedes the stage of rebirth into a new cultural cycle (according to Giambattista Vico's cyclical theory of history, which is important to *Finnegans Wake*). "Gone ashley" also means "turned into an ash tree" (i.e., it is so cold that the speaker feels herself turning into a tree).

4. *Viel Uhr?* (German, "What's the time?") "Filou": pickpocket, thief (French). The question echoes so as to suggest that time is a thief.

5. Soon + Saône (river in France).

6. Since + Senne (river in Belgium).

7. E'er a one + *Erewhon* (novel by Samuel Butler—"Nowhere" spelled backwards).

8. Clock or bell (Irish) + the name of an Irish river.

9. Brook (German) + dear (Welsh).

10. Cf. Aix-les-Bains, France.

11. *Sex* (Latin, "six") + *laüten* (German, "to ring [the bells]"). The Angelus bell is rung every six hours.

12. Cf. "Ring out the old, ring in the new" (Tennyson, *In Memoriam*).

13. God of Eire; also the name of a river in India. "Vert": avert + *vert* (French, "green"), for "the showers" make grass green.

grant thaya grace! Aman. Will we spread them here now? Ay, we will. Flip! Spread on your bank and I'll spread mine on mine. Flep! It's what I'm doing. Spread! It's churning chill. Der went[14] is rising. I'll lay a few stones on the hostel sheets. A man and his bride embraced between them. Else I'd have sprinkled and folded them only. And I'll tie my butcher's apron here. It's suety yet. The strollers will pass it by. Six shifts, ten kerchiefs, nine to hold to the fire and this for the code,[15] the convent napkins, twelve, one baby's shawl. Good mother Jossiph[16] knows, she said. Whose head? Mutter snores? Deataceas![17] Wharnow are alle her childer, say? In kingdome gone or power to come or gloria be to them farther? Allalivial, allalluvial![18] Some here, more no more, more again lost alla stranger.[19] I've heard tell that same brooch of the Shannons[20] was married into a family in Spain. And all the Dunders de Dunnes[21] in Markland's[22] Vineland beyond Brendan's herring pool[23] takes number nine in yangsee's[24] hats. And one of Biddy's[25] beads went bobbing till she rounded up lost histereve[26] with a marigold and a cobbler's candle in a side strain of a main drain of a manzinahurries[27] off Bachelor's Walk. But all that's left to the last of the Meaghers[28] in the loup of the years prefixed and between is one kneebuckle and two hooks in the front. Do you tell me that now? I do in troth. Orara por Orbe and poor Las Animas![29]

14. *Der Wind* (German, "the wind") + Derwent (river in England).
15. Cold + code (i.e., the code in which the book is written). The numbers in this sentence have special meanings indicated in other episodes.
16. Joseph + *joss* (pidgin English, "God") + gossip (which derives from *god-sib*, Middle English, "godparent").
17. Latin, "Goddess, may you be silent!" Dea Tacita, in Roman mythology, is the name sometimes given to Acca Laurentia, mistress of Hercules and foster-mother of Romulus and Remus.
18. Multiple punning—Anna Livia + all alive + *la lluvia* (Spanish, "rain") + alluvial—suggesting the mother-river-fertility associations of ALP. At least two other meanings are also present: All alive O! (street cry of shellfish vendors) + Alleluia (Vulgate Latin form of "Hallelujah").
19. Cf. *à l'étranger* (French, "abroad").
20. Ornament and branch of the Shannons (family and river).
21. The form of the name suggests an aristocratic Anglo-Norman family. "Dunder" suggests thunder; *dun* is an Irish word meaning "hill," "fort on a hill."
22. Borderland + land of the mark (i.e., land of money, or America; "Vineland" or Vinland was the Norse name for America). Both King Mark of Cornwall (a character in the Tristan and

Iseult story) and Mark of the Gospels are primary symbolic characters in *Finnegans Wake*.
23. The Atlantic Ocean; St. Brendan was an Irish monk who sailed out into the Atlantic to find the terrestrial paradise.
24. Yankees' + Yangtze (river in China). The de Dunnes have swollen heads now that they have emigrated to America.
25. Diminutive form of the name Bridget; St. Brigid (or Bridget) is a patron saint of Ireland. "Biddy" is also a term for an Irish maidservant.
26. Yester eve (last night) + eve of history. The sentence may be paraphrased: "Irish history got lost when she went off in a side branch of the main Roman Catholic Church, and Biddy (i.e., Ireland) landed herself in the dirt." There are also Freudian implications here.
27. Man's in a hurry + Manzanares (river in Spain).
28. Thomas Francis Meagher, Irish patriot and revolutionary, who was transported to Van Diemen's Land in 1849 and escaped to America in 1852. "Loup": loop + *loup* (French, "wolf" and also "solitary man"). Cf. Wolfe Tone, the ill-fated Irish revolutionist.
29. *Ora pro nobis* (Latin, "pray for us") + Orara (river in New South Wales) + *pro orbe* (Latin, "for the world") + Orbe (river in France). "Las Animas": souls (Spanish); also

Ussa, Ulla, we're umbas[30] all! Mezha, didn't you hear it a deluge
of times, ufer[31] and ufer, respund to spond?[32] You deed, you deed!
I need, I need! It's that irrawaddyng[33] I've stoke in my aars. It all
but husheth the lethest zswound. Oronoko![34] What's your trouble?
Is that the great Finnleader[35] himself in his joakimono on his statue
riding the high horse there forehengist?[36] Father of Otters,[37] it is
himself! Yonne there! Isset that? On Fallareen Common? You're
thinking of Astley's Amphitheayter where the bobby restrained you
making sugarstuck pouts to the ghostwhite horse of the Peppers.[38]
Throw the cobwebs from your eyes, woman, and spread your washing proper! It's well I know your sort of slop. Flap! Ireland sober
is Ireland stiff. Lord help you, Maria, full of grease, the load is
with me! Your prayers. I sonht zo![39] Madammangut! Were you
lifting your elbow, tell us, glazy cheeks, in Conway's Carrigacurra
canteen? Was I what, hobbledyhips?[40] Flop! Your rere gait's creak-
orheuman bitts your butts disagrees.[41] Amn't I up since the damp
dawn, marthared mary allacook, with Corrigan's pulse and varicoarse
veins, my pramaxle smashed, Alice Jane in decline and my oneeyed
mongrel twice run over, soaking and bleaching boiler rags, and
sweating cold, a widow like me, for to deck my tennis champion
son, the laundryman with the lavandier flannels? You won your
limpopo[42] limp fron the husky[43] hussars when Collars and Cuffs
was heir to the town and your slur gave the stink to Carlow.[44] Holy
Scamander,[45] I sar it again! Near the golden falls. Icis on us! Seints
of light! Zezere![46] Subdue your noise, you hamble creature! What

the name of a river in Colorado. The
entire sentence may be read: "Pray for
us and for all souls."
30. *Umbra* (Latin, "shade") + Umba
(river in Africa). "Ussa," "Ulla," and
"Mezha" are also river names; each
contains a number of other meanings.
31. Bank (of river).
32. *Spund* (German, "bung").
33. A multiple pun: Irrawady (river in
Burma) + irritating + wadding. This
and the following sentence may be
paraphrased: "It's that wadding I've
stuck in my ears. It hushes the least
sound."
34. *Oroonoko* (novel by Mrs. Aphra
Behn about a "noble savage," published
ca. 1678).
35. Fionn mac Cumhail (Finn Mac-
Cool), legendary hero of ancient Ireland. "Joakimono": i.e., comic kimono;
joki is the Finnish word for river; the
name Joachim is perhaps also implied.
36. Hengist was the Jute invader of
England (with Horsa), ca. 449; he
founded the kingdom of Kent.
37. Father of Waters (i.e., the Mis-
sissippi) + Father of Orders (i.e., Saint
Patrick).
38. Philip Astley's Royal Amphithea-
tre was a famous late 18th-century English circus, specializing in trained
horses; "Pepper's Ghost" was a popular circus act. One of the washerwomen
has been reproving the other, who
thought she saw the great Finn himself riding his high horse, by telling her
that once before she had to be restrained by a policeman for making
"sugarstuck pouts" at a circus horse.
39. I thought so + Izontzo (river in
Italy).
40. Hobbledehoy + wobbly hips.
41. The sentence is a punning discussion of her hard work and ailments.
The first four words may also be read:
"Your rear get (i.e., your last child) is
Greek or Roman."
42. Name of a river in south Africa.
43. Cf. *uisge* (Gaelic, "whisky," but
literally, "water [of life]").
44. I.e., "You got a slur on your reputation carrying on with soldiers in the
Age of Elegance, and the scandal was
all over Ireland" (ALP is being addressed, and some of her many lovers
are mentioned). "Carlow" is a county
in Ireland.
45. River near Troy, famous in classical legend. "I sar": I saw + Isar (river
in Germany).
46. See there + Zezere (river in Portugal).

is it but a blackburry growth or the dwyergray ass them four old codgers[47] owns. Are you meanam[48] Tarpey and Lyons and Gregory? I meyne now, thank all, the four of them, and the roar of them, that draves[49] that stray in the mist and old Johnny MacDougal along with them. Is that the Poolbeg flasher beyant,[50] pharphar, or a fireboat coasting nyar[51] the Kishtna or a glow I behold within a hedge or my Garry come back from the Indes? Wait till the honeying of the lune,[52] love! Die eve, little eve, die![53] We see that wonder in your eye. We'll meet again, we'll part once more. The spot I'll seek if the hour you'll find. My chart shines high where the blue milk's upset. Forgivemequick, I'm going! Bubye! And you, pluck your watch, forgetmenot. Your evenlode.[54] So save to jurna's[55] end! My sights are swimming thicker on me by the shadows to this place. I sow[56] home slowly now by own way, moyvalley way. Towy[57] I too, rathmine.

Ah, but she was the queer old skeowsha anyhow, Anna Livia, trinkettoes! And sure he was the quare old buntz too, Dear Dirty Dumpling,[58] foostherfather of fingalls[59] and dottergills. Gammer and gaffer we're all their gangsters. Hadn't he seven dams to wive him? And every dam had her seven crutches. And every crutch had its seven hues.[60] And each hue had a differing cry. Sudds[61] for me and supper for you and the doctor's bill for Joe John. Befor! Bifur![62] He married his markets, cheap by foul, I know, like any Etrurian

---

47. The Four Old Men, who represent, among other things, the authors of the Gospels and the four elements.
48. Meaning + Menam (river in Thailand). The precise connotations of the three proper names that follow escape the present annotator.
49. Drives + Drave (river in Hungary).
50. I.e., the Poolbeg Lighthouse beyond (this lighthouse is in Dublin Bay); "pharphar": far far + Pharphar (river in Damascus) + *pharos* (Greek, "lighthouse").
51. Near + Nyar (river in India). "Kishtna": Kish (city in ancient Mesopotamia, traditionally the ruling city after the Flood) + Krishna (Hindu god of joy) + Kistna (river in India) + the Kish lightship (in Dublin Bay).
52. Loon (Scottish, "boy") + *luna* (Latin, "moon"). "Honeying of the lune": honeymoon, etc.
53. This sentence suggests traditional lovers' prayers for the day to die and night to come, and it also recalls the death of "little Eva" in *Uncle Tom's Cabin*. The sentences that follow are echoes of popular songs.
54. Evening load + Evenlode (river in England).
55. Journey + Jurna (river in Brazil).
56. Sow (river in England).
57. Name of a river in Wales. Moy is

the name of an Irish river; and Moyvalley and Rathmine are names of Dublin suburbs.
58. "Dumpling" suggests Humpty Dumpty, whose fall is one of the many involved in the vastly symbolic fall of Finnegan. The phrase "Dear Dirty Dublin" occurs in *Ulysses*.
59. A pun-cluster: Fine Gael (the United Ireland Party) + fine Gaels + Fingal (river in Tasmania) + *Fingal* (the poem by James Macpherson, supposedly a translation from the Gaelic original of Ossian, an ancient Gaelic poet and son of Fingal—who is the same as Fionn mac Cumhail or Finn MacCool).
60. Colors of the rainbow (suggested a few lines later by "pinky limony creamy" and "turkiss indienne mauves"). In these sentences Joyce is punningly parodying the nursery rhyme, "As I was going to St. Ives / I met a man with seven wives * * * "
61. Suds (slang term for beer) + soap-suds + sudd (the floating vegetable matter which often obstructs navigation on the White Nile).
62. Bifurcated creature! This image of man as a forked being suggests HCE (cf. "*Etrurian Catholic Heathen*"). HCE's marital history, in his role as the Great Parent or generator, is one of the themes in this passage.

Catholic Heathen, in their pinky limony creamy birnies[63] and their turkiss indienne mauves. But at milkidmass[64] who was the spouse? Then all that was was fair. Tys Elvenland![65] Teems of times and happy returns. The seim anew.[66] Ordovico[67] or viricordo. Anna was, Livia is, Plurabelle's to be. Northmen's thing made southfolk's place but howmulty plurators made eachone in person?[68] Latin me that, my trinity scholard, out of eure sanscreed into oure eryan![69] *Hircus Civis Eblanensis!*[70] He had buckgoat paps on him, soft ones for orphans. Ho,[71] Lord! Twins of his bosom. Lord save us! And ho! Hey? What all men. Hot? His tittering daughters of. Whawk?

Can't hear with the waters of. The chittering waters of. Flittering bats, fieldmice bawk talk. Ho! Are you not gone ahome? What Thom Malone? Can't hear with bawk of bats, all thim liffeying waters of. Ho, talk save us! My foos won't moos.[72] I feel as old as yonder elm. A tale told of Shaun or Shem? All Livia's daughtersons. Dark hawks hear us. Night! Night! My ho head halls. I feel as heavy as yonder stone. Tell me of John or Shaun? Who were Shem and Shaun the living sons or daughters of? Night now! Tell me, tell me, tell me, elm! Night night! Telmetale of stem or stone.[73] Beside the rivering waters of, hitherandthithering waters of. Night!

1923–38   1939

63. Coats of mail.
64. Milking time + Michaelmas (September 29).
65. 'Tis the land of Elves + Tys Elv (Norway).
66. The same again + Seim (river in Ireland).
67. The Ordovices were an ancient British tribe in northern Wales, and Ordovician is a term for a geological period. "Ordovico" is also a pun on Vico and his order of historical phases. Joyce is here suggesting the cyclical nature of things: the marital history of HCE is the history of ever-renewing life ("the seim anew"), and HCE's bride is Everywoman, past, present, and future ("Anna was, Livia is, Plurabelle's to be"). "Viricordo" is another verbal twist to Vico and his cycles, suggesting his *ricorso* ("recurrence," i.e., the 4th stage of the cycle which brings back the 1st), as well as overtones from the Latin *vir* (man) and *cor* (heart): the heart of man beats on, through all phases of civilization.
68. This sentence may be paraphrased: "The assembly of the Norsemen made the South-folk's place (i.e., as the Vikings settled Dublin), but how many marital pluralists (the word 'plurators'

suggests men who had many wives or mistresses) went into the making of each of us?" The question is another link with the theme of HCE as the Great Parent.
69. I.e., out of your Sanskrit into your Aryan. "Sanscreed" has further punning meanings: *sans* screed (without script) + *sans* creed (without faith). Thus the phrase can read: "out of your illiteracy or faithlessness into Irish" (Eire-an). The greatest skeptic must pause in reverence before the endless flow of life, represented by Irish history.
70. Latin, "The Goat-Citizen of Dublin!" The goat is the symbol of lust and so of fecundity; "*Eblanensis*" is the adjective form of Eblana, the name given by the 3rd-century Alexandrian geographer Ptolemy to what may have been the site of the modern Dublin.
71. Chinese, "river."
72. Move + *Moos* (German, "moss"). Her foot ("foos") won't move; it is also turning to moss.
73. Stone and elm tree are important symbols in *Finnegans Wake*. Signifying permanence and change, time and space, mercy and justice, they undergo many changes of symbolic meaning throughout the book.

D. H. LAWRENCE
(1885–1930)

1912: Gives up school teaching for literature.
1915: *The Rainbow*, first of the "new" novels.

David Herbert Lawrence was born in the Midland mining village of East-wood, Nottinghamshire. His father was a miner; his mother, better edu-cated than her husband and self-consciously genteel, fought all her married life to lift her children out of the working class. Lawrence was aware from an early age of the struggle between his parents; he was very much on his mother's side during his childhood, resenting his father's coarse and sometimes drunken behavior and allying himself with his mother's deli-cacy and refinement. After the death of an elder brother he became the center of his mother's emotional life and played in his own relation to her a loving and protective role. His mother's claims on him kept frustrating his relationships with girls, and the personal problems and conflicts that re-sulted are presented in his first really distinguished novel, *Sons and Lovers* (1913), where, against a background of paternal coarseness and vitality conflicting with maternal refinement and gentility, he sets the theme of the demanding mother who has given up the prospect of achieving a true emotional life with her husband and turns to her sons with a stultifying and possessive love. Many years later Lawrence came to feel that he had misjudged his father, whose coarseness represented after all a genuine vitality and some wholeness of personality, even if these qualities were im-poverished and distorted by the civilization in which he lived.

Spurred on by his mother, Lawrence escaped through education from the mining world of his father. He won a scholarship to Nottingham high school and later, after working first as a clerk and then as an elementary school teacher (1902–6), studied for two years at Nottingham University College, where he obtained his teacher's certificate in 1908. Meanwhile he was reading on his own a great deal of literature and some philosophy and was working on his first novel, encouraged (as he was in all his early writing) by Jessie Chambers, the "Miriam" of *Sons and Lovers*. His first published work was a group of poems which appeared in the *English Review* for November, 1909. The following February the same periodical pub-lished his first short story. He was now regarded in London literary circles as a promising young writer; his first novel, *The White Peacock* (1910), was received with respect. From 1908 to 1912 he taught school in Croydon, a southern suburb of London, but he gave this up after falling in love with Frieda von Richthofen, the German wife of a Professor of French at Nottingham. They went to Germany together and married in 1914, after Frieda had been divorced by her first husband.

Abroad with Frieda, Lawrence finished *Sons and Lovers*, the autobiographical novel at which he had been working off and on for years. The war brought them back to England, where Frieda's German origins and Lawrence's fierce objection to the war gave him trouble with the authorities. More and more—especially after the banning of his next novel, *The Rainbow*, in 1915—Lawrence came to feel that the forces of modern civilization were arrayed against him. As soon as he could leave England after the war he sought refuge in Italy, Australia, Mexico, then again in Italy, and finally in the south of France, often desperately ill, restlessly searching for an ideal, or at least a tolerable, community in which to live. He died of tuberculosis in the south of France on the 2nd of March, 1930, at the early age of 44.

Shortly before his death he had written:

> Give me the moon at my feet
> Put my feet upon the crescent, like a Lord!
> O let my ankles be bathed in moonlight, that I may go
> sure and moon-shod, cool and bright-footed
> towards my goal.
>
> For the sun is hostile, now
> his face is like the red lion . . .

In these elemental images he invoked his end, a gesture at once heroic and desperate. It was typical of him to symbolize his passing with reference to the sun and moon, for Lawrence was at home with such cosmic images as no other English writer except Blake has ever been; he was at home, one might say, with the universe, with all that is deep-rooted and elemental in man and nature, and at constant war with the mechanical and artificial, with the constraints and hypocrisies that civilization imposes on man's fundamental self. His most characteristic writings are essentially a record in symbolic terms of his explorations of human individuality and of all that hindered it and all that might fulfill it, whether in the natural world or in the world of other individuals.

This is not what the English novel is generally supposed to do, and Lawrence, with new things to say and a new way of using the novel form, was not easily or quickly appreciated. His early novels, *The White Peacock*, *The Trespasser*, and even the original and impressive *Sons and Lovers*, were more conventional in style and treatment; they aroused contemporary interest and even acclaim, and it appeared that he might be on his way to becoming one of the acknowledged and popular Georgian novelists. But with the publication of *The Rainbow* in 1915 the true, original Lawrence first emerged clearly, and the critics turned away in bewilderment and condemnation. *The Rainbow* was suppressed as indecent a month after its publication, and the war between Lawrence and the world of timid convention was on. The rest of his life, during which he produced about a dozen more novels and many poems, short stories, sketches, and miscellaneous articles, was, in his own words, "a savage enough pilgrimage," marked by incessant struggle and by moments of frustration and despair. Lawrence was one of those artists who had to create the taste by which he could be appreciated. He had no gift for explaining his attitude and literary technique in simple expository prose. He could explain himself only by performing, by operating in his own way as an artist, letting the work of art speak with its own voice and pulse with its own life. When he tried to talk *about* his ideas, instead of projecting them symbolically in art, he was often irritatingly and vaguely rhetorical. "Sense of truth," "supreme impulse" are phrases characteristic of Lawrence's belief in intuition, in the dark forces of the inner self, that must not be allowed to be swamped by the rational faculties but must be brought into a harmonious relation with them. It was a point of view—or rather, a perception, a passionate insight—which could not be convincingly expressed in argument, but demanded direct projection in art.

The genteel culture of Lawrence's mother came more and more to represent death for Lawrence. In much of his later work, and especially in some of his short stories, he sets the deadening restrictiveness of middle-class conventional living against the forces of liberation that are often represented by an outsider—a peasant, a gypsy, a working man, a primitive of some kind, someone free by circumstance or personal effort. The recurring theme of his short stories—which contain some of his best work—is the distortion of love by possessiveness or gentility or a false romanticism or a false conception of the life of the artist, and the achievement of a living relation between a man and a woman against the pressure of class-feeling or tradition or habit or prejudice.

His two masterpieces, *The Rainbow* and *Women in Love* (both of which developed out of what was originally conceived as a single novel to be called *The Sisters*), are to be read as symbolic and dramatic poems in prose. In these novels Lawrence probes with both subtlety and power into various aspects of relationship—the relationship between man and his environment, the relationship between the generations, the relationship between man and woman, the relationship between instinct and intellect, and above all the proper basis for the marriage relationship as he conceived it. He is concerned too with the impact of modern industrial civilization on human sensibility, and finds many ways, at once realistic and symbolic, of projecting this. At the very opening of *The Rainbow*, where Lawrence is dealing with the family history of the Brangwens, whose annals he is about to tell, he makes clear even by the rhythms of his prose, as well as by his tone and imagery, that this is not to be a chronicle family novel like Galsworthy's *Forsyte Saga*.

The Rainbow is built on sets of human relationships, both horizontal and vertical. Thus we first see the marriage of Tom Brangwen with the Polish widow Lydia Lensky; then Tom's relationship with his step-daughter Anna; then Anna's relationship with her husband Will; then Will's relationship with his daughters Ursula and Gudrun; and so on. The truth of emotional detail in the presentation of these developing relationships is rendered with extraordinary force and subtlety. A fine example is in the extract below, which shows Tom Brangwen comforting his little step-daughter Anna.

In the relationship of Anna and Will in marriage we begin to find the true Laurentian doctrine that marriage is a fight and at the same time, if properly realized, a means of mystic knowledge through the awareness by one partner (in ultimate intimacy) of the essential *otherness* of the other. After the amorous luxury and mutual discovery of the first few days of marriage, Anna suddenly turns into the brisk housewife and sends the bewildered Will out of doors while she sets about her housework. Lawrence's view of marriage as a struggle derived from his own relationship with his strong-minded German-born wife Frieda. There are more and bitterer lovers' quarrels in Lawrence's novels than anywhere else in English literature. Lawrence's "crockery-throwing" view of love could become tedious, except that, as he presents it, it is bound up with the deepest rhythms and most profound instincts of the man-woman relationship. It is even more strong in *Women in Love*, which deals with Ursula and Gudrun Brangwen and their search for an adequate love relationship. The novel is, however, very much more than the traditional love quest, the developing relationships of Ursula and Rupert Birkin on the one hand and Gudrun and Gerald Crich on the other.

In Rupert there is more than a little of Lawrence himself, yet Lawrence is still able occasionally to laugh at him. Gerald, coldly handsome son of a powerful Midland mineowner, accumulates for himself, as the novel progresses, all the deadening and distorting effects of modern industrial civilization. Lawrence does not simply make Gerald's behavior inadequate or offensive; he is able to invent for his characters actions which while wholly realistic on the surface, or social level, are at the same time profoundly symbolic. This symbolism does not always come off, but when it does the effect is remarkable, as in a scene where Gerald forces his terrified mare to stand by the railway line while a shunting train hisses and clanks back and forth, or in the extraordinary scene with the rabbit (reprinted below). The novel as a whole reveals a deep sense of English provincial life, in which—in spite of all Lawrence's wanderings abroad and of the foreign setting of many of his novels—his sensibility was really deeply rooted, much as George Eliot's was. His intimacy with the English scene, especially with provincial middle-class and working-class patterns of thought and feeling and the relation between them, is revealed again and again in the short stories, notably in "Fanny and Annie," "Daughters of the Vicar," "The Fox," "The Christening," and "Tickets Please."

In *The Rainbow* and *Women in Love*, then, Lawrence is developing a radically new kind of novel in which he explores kinds of human relationships with a combination of uncanny psychological precision and intense poetic feeling. They have an acute surface realism, a sharp sense of time and place, and brilliant topographical detail, and at the same time their high poetic symbolism, both of the total pattern of action and of incidents and objects within it, establishes a rhythm of meaning that is missed by those who read the novels with the conventional categories of "plot" and "characters" in mind. His next novel, *Aaron's Rod* (1922), is more uneven; in it Lawrence, employing many of his own experiences, explores problems of human relations under the question of moral and political leadership, which for a time obsessed him. He was concerned with the struggle for leadership in marriage as well as in politics. Two other novels on the theme of leadership, *Kangaroo* (1923), set in Australia, and *The Plumed Serpent* (1926), set in Mexico, similarly uneven, show him trying to give symbolic fictional form to his own problems and preoccupations. But *Kangaroo* in particular has its moments of uncanny perceptiveness, and it is extraordinary how Lawrence, drawing on his experiences during a short stay in Australia, was able to get beneath the skin of the country and evoke so much of the essential reality of both place and people.

It is hard to think of another English novelist whose best and most characteristic work makes such a disquieting assault on our normal patterns of thought and feeling. It is not simply that Lawrence is a rebel against convention—many writers have been that—or that his views are startling, though they sometimes are. It is rather that the whole response to life, and in particular to the problems posed by human relationships, that emerges from his novels and stories seems to come so profoundly from the deepest recesses of his being and therefore assault the deepest recesses of *our* being, that the challenge seems to go beyond that which is normally asserted by a work of art. It is difficult to escape the challenge; to make any attempt to respond fully to what he is saying is to be drawn into his world, forced to share his vision.

Although there are complex critical reasons for the posthumous triumph of this writer who was so much reviled in his lifetime, there is also a simple and striking reason that must not be forgotten. Lawrence had vision; he had a poetic sense of life, he had a keen ear and a piercing eye for every kind of vitality and color and sound in the world, for landscape, be it of England or Italy or New Mexico; for the individuality and concreteness of things in nature, and for the individuality and concreteness of people. His travel sketches are as impressive in their way as his novels; he seizes both on the symbolic incident and on the concrete reality, and each is interpreted in terms of the other. He looked at the world freshly, with his own eyes, avoiding formulas and clichés; and he forged for himself a kind of utterance which, at his best, was able to convey powerfully and vividly what his fresh original vision showed him. This kind of originality has its drawbacks; he was sometimes shrill, sometimes repetitive, sometimes almost hysterical; some scenes in his novels are murky with unachieved symbolism or splutter with unresolved passion. But the great Lawrence remains.

This restless pilgrim with his uncanny perceptions into the depths of physical things, with his uncompromising honesty and originality in his view of men and the world, cannot be dismissed as merely a great eccentric. Nor is he a great prophet. He is essentially an artist; it is his *rendering* of life in his art, not his preaching about life's meaning, that matters.

Odor of Chrysanthemums

I

The small locomotive engine, Number 4, came clanking, stumbling down from Selston with seven full wagons. It appeared round the corner with loud threats of speed, but the colt that it startled from among the gorse,[1] which still flickered indistinctly in the raw afternoon, out-distanced it at a canter. A woman, walking up the railway line to Underwood, drew back into the hedge, held her basket aside, and watched the footplate of the engine advancing. The trucks[2] thumped heavily past, one by one, with slow inevitable movement, as she stood insignificantly trapped between the jolting black wagons and the hedge; then they curved away towards the coppice[3] where the withered oak leaves dropped noiselessly, while the birds, pulling at the scarlet hips beside the track, made off into the dusk that had already crept into the spinney.[4] In the open, the smoke from the engine sank and cleaved to the rough grass. The fields were dreary and forsaken, and in the marshy strip that led to the whimsey,[5] a reedy pit pond, the fowls had already abandoned their run among the alders, to roost in the tarred fowl house. The pit bank loomed up beyond the pond, flames like red sores licking its ashy sides, in the afternoon's stagnant light. Just beyond rose the tapering chimneys and the clumsy black headstocks of Brinsley Colliery.[6] The two wheels were spinning fast up against the sky, and the winding engine rapped out its little spasms. The miners were being turned up.

The engine whistled as it came into the wide bay of railway lines beside the colliery, where rows of trucks stood in harbor.

Miners, single, trailing, and in groups, passed like shadows diverging home. At the edge of the ribbed level of sidings squat a low cottage, three steps down from the cinder track. A large bony vine clutched at the house, as if to claw down the tiled roof. Round the bricked yard grew a few wintry primroses. Beyond, the long garden sloped down to a bush-covered brook course. There were some twiggy apple trees, winter-crack trees, and ragged cabbages. Beside the path hung disheveled pink chrysanthemums, like pink cloths hung on bushes. A woman came stooping out of the felt-covered fowl house, halfway down the garden. She closed and

---

1. Also known as furze or whin, a prickly bush with yellow flowers common on heaths, moors, and hillsides all over Britain.
2. Open freight cars.
3. A wood of small trees or shrubs.

4. Copse, thicket.
5. Machine for raising ore or water from a mine.
6. Coal mine; "headstocks" support revolving parts of a machine.

padlocked the door, then drew herself erect, having brushed some bits from her white apron.

She was a tall woman of imperious mien, handsome, with definite black eyebrows. Her smooth black hair was parted exactly. For a few moments she stood steadily watching the miners as they passed along the railway: then she turned towards the brook course. Her face was calm and set, her mouth was closed with disillusionment. After a moment she called:

"John!" There was no answer. She waited, and then said distinctly:

"Where are you?"

"Here!" replied a child's sulky voice from among the bushes. The woman looked piercingly through the dusk.

"Are you at that brook?" she asked sternly.

For answer the child showed himself before the raspberry canes that rose like whips. He was a small, sturdy boy of five. He stood quite still, defiantly.

"Oh!" said the mother, conciliated. "I thought you were down at that wet brook—and you remember what I told you——"

The boy did not move or answer.

"Come, come on in," she said more gently, "it's getting dark. There's your grandfather's engine coming down the line!"

The lad advanced slowly, with resentful, taciturn movement. He was dressed in trousers and waistcoat of cloth that was too thick and hard for the size of the garments. They were evidently cut down from a man's clothes.

As they went slowly towards the house he tore at the ragged wisps of chrysanthemums and dropped the petals in handfuls among the path.

"Don't do that—it does look nasty," said his mother. He refrained, and she, suddenly pitiful, broke off a twig with three or four wan flowers and held them against her face. When mother and son reached the yard her hand hesitated, and instead of laying the flower aside, she pushed it in her apron-band. The mother and son stood at the foot of the three steps looking across the bay of lines at the passing home of the miners. The trundle of the small train was imminent. Suddenly the engine loomed past the house and came to a stop opposite the gate.

The engine-driver, a short man with round gray beard, leaned out of the cab high above the woman.

"Have you got a cup of tea?" he said in a cheery, hearty fashion.

It was her father. She went in, saying she would mash.[7] Directly,

---

7. Infuse the tea, i.e., let it stand after pouring boiling water over the tea leaves in order to gain strength.

she returned.

"I didn't come to see you on Sunday," began the little gray-bearded man.

"I didn't expect you," said his daughter.

The engine driver winced; then, reassuming his cheery, airy manner, he said:

"Oh, have you heard then? Well, and what do you think——?"

"I think it is soon enough," she replied.

At her brief censure the little man made an impatient gesture, and said coaxingly, yet with dangerous coldness:

"Well, what's a man to do? It's no sort of life for a man of my years, to sit at my own hearth like a stranger. And if I'm going to marry again it may as well be soon as late—what does it matter to anybody?"

The woman did not reply, but turned and went into the house. The man in the engine-cab stood assertive, till she returned with a cup of tea and a piece of bread and butter on a plate. She went up the steps and stood near the footplate of the hissing engine.

"You needn't 'a' brought me bread an' butter," said her father. "But a cup of tea"—he sipped appreciatively—"it's very nice." He sipped for a moment or two, then: "I hear as Walter's got another bout on," he said.

"When hasn't he?" said the woman bitterly.

"I heerd tell of him in the Lord Nelson braggin' as he was going to spend that b—— afore he went: half a sovereign that was."

"When?" asked the woman.

"A' Sat'day night—I know that's true."

"Very likely," she laughed bitterly. "He gives me twenty-three shillings."

"Aye, it's a nice thing, when a man can do nothing with his money but make a beast of himself!" said the gray-whiskered man. The woman turned her head away. Her father swallowed the last of his tea and handed her the cup.

"Aye," he sighed, wiping his mouth. "It's a settler,[8] it is——"

He put his hand on the lever. The little engine strained and groaned, and the train rumbled towards the crossing. The woman again looked across the metals. Darkness was settling over the spaces of the railway and trucks: the miners, in gray somber groups, were still passing home. The winding engine pulsed hurriedly, with brief pauses. Elizabeth Bates looked at the dreary flow of men, then she went indoors. Her husband did not come.

The kitchen was small and full of firelight; red coals piled glowing up the chimney mouth. All the life of the room seemed in the

8. Crushing (or final) blow.

white, warm hearth and the steel fender reflecting the red fire. The cloth was laid for tea; cups glinted in the shadows. At the back, where the lowest stairs protruded into the room, the boy sat struggling with a knife and a piece of white wood. He was almost hidden in the shadow. It was half-past four. They had but to await the father's coming to begin tea. As the mother watched her son's sullen little struggle with the wood, she saw herself in his silence and pertinacity; she saw the father in her child's indifference to all but himself. She seemed to be occupied by her husband. He had probably gone past his home, slunk past his own door, to drink before he came in, while his dinner spoiled and wasted in waiting. She glanced at the clock, then took the potatoes to strain them in the yard. The garden and fields beyond the brook were closed in uncertain darkness. When she rose with the saucepan, leaving the drain steaming into the night behind her, she saw the yellow lamps were lit along the high road that went up the hill away beyond the space of the railway lines and the field.

Then again she watched the men trooping home, fewer now and fewer.

Indoors the fire was sinking and the room was dark red. The woman put her saucepan on the hob, and set a batter pudding near the mouth of the oven. Then she stood unmoving. Directly, gratefully, came quick young steps to the door. Someone hung on the latch a moment, then a little girl entered and began pulling off her outdoor things, dragging a mass of curls, just ripening from gold to brown, over her eyes with her hat.

Her mother chid her for coming late from school, and said she would have to keep her at home the dark winter days.

"Why, mother, it's hardly a bit dark yet. The lamp's not lighted, and my father's not home."

"No, he isn't. But it's a quarter to five! Did you see anything of him?"

The child became serious. She looked at her mother with large, wistful blue eyes.

"No, mother, I've never seen him. Why? Has he come up an' gone past, to Old Brinsley? He hasn't, mother, 'cos I never saw him."

"He'd watch that," said the mother bitterly, "he'd take care as you didn't see him. But you may depend upon it, he's seated in the Prince o' Wales. He wouldn't be this late."

The girl looked at her mother piteously.

"Let's have our teas, mother, should we?" said she.

The mother called John to table. She opened the door once more and looked out across the darkness of the lines. All was deserted:

she could not hear the winding-engines.

"Perhaps," she said to herself, "he's stopped to get some ripping [9] done."

They sat down to tea. John, at the end of the table near the door, was almost lost in the darkness. Their faces were hidden from each other. The girl crouched against the fender slowly moving a thick piece of bread before the fire. The lad, his face a dusky mark on the shadow, sat watching her who was transfigured in the red glow.

"I do think it's beautiful to look in the fire," said the child.

"Do you?" said her mother. "Why?"

"It's so red, and full of little caves—and it feels so nice, and you can fair smell it."

"It'll want mending directly," replied her mother, "and then if your father comes he'll carry on and say there never is a fire when a man comes home sweating from the pit. A public house is always warm enough."

There was silence till the boy said complainingly: "Make haste, our Annie."

"Well, I am doing! I can't make the fire do it no faster, can I?"

"She keeps wafflin' it about so's to make 'er slow," grumbled the boy.

"Don't have such an evil imagination, child," replied the mother.

Soon the room was busy in the darkness with the crisp sound of crunching. The mother ate very little. She drank her tea determinedly, and sat thinking. When she rose her anger was evident in the stern unbending of her head. She looked at the pudding in the fender, and broke out:

"It is a scandalous thing as a man can't even come home to his dinner! If it's crozzled up to a cinder I don't see why I should care. Past his very door he goes to get to a public house, and here I sit with his dinner waiting for him——"

She went out. As she dropped piece after piece of coal on the red fire, the shadows fell on the walls, till the room was almost in total darkness.

"I canna see," grumbled the invisible John. In spite of herself, the mother laughed.

"You know the way to your mouth," she said. She set the dustpan outside the door. When she came again like a shadow on the hearth, the lad repeated, complaining sulkily:

"I canna see."

"Good gracious!" cried the mother irritably, "you're as bad as your father if it's a bit dusk!"

9. Taking out or cutting away coal or stone (a mining and quarrying term).

Nevertheless, she took a paper spill from a sheaf on the mantel-piece and proceeded to light the lamp that hung from the ceiling in the middle of the room. As she reached up, her figure displayed itself just rounding with maternity.

"Oh, mother——!" exclaimed the girl.

"What?" said the woman, suspended in the act of putting the lamp glass over the flame. The copper reflector shone handsomely on her, as she stood with uplifted arm, turning to face her daughter.

"You've got a flower in your apron!" said the child, in a little rapture at this unusual event.

"Goodness me!" exclaimed the woman, relieved. "One would think the house was afire." She replaced the glass and waited a moment before turning up the wick. A pale shadow was seen floating vaguely on the floor.

"Let me smell!" said the child, still rapturously, coming forward and putting her face to her mother's waist.

"Go along, silly!" said the mother, turning up the lamp. The light revealed their suspense so that the woman felt it almost unbearable. Annie was still bending at her waist. Irritably, the mother took the flowers out from her apron band.

"Oh, mother—don't take them out!" Annie cried, catching her hand and trying to replace the sprig.

"Such nonsense!" said the mother, turning away. The child put the pale chrysanthemums to her lips, murmuring:

"Don't they smell beautiful!"

Her mother gave a short laugh.

"No," she said, "not to me. It was chrysanthemums when I married him, and chrysanthemums when you were born, and the first time they ever brought him home drunk, he'd got brown chrysanthemums in his buttonhole."

She looked at the children. Their eyes and their parted lips were wondering. The mother sat rocking in silence for some time. Then she looked at the clock.

"Twenty minutes to six!" In a tone of fine bitter carelessness she continued: "Eh, he'll not come now till they bring him. There he'll stick! But he needn't come rolling in here in his pit dirt, for *I* won't wash him. He can lie on the floor——Eh, what a fool I've been, what a fool! And this is what I came here for, to this dirty hole, rats and all, for him to slink past his very door. Twice last week—he's begun now——"

She silenced herself, and rose to clear the table.

While for an hour or more the children played, subduedly intent, fertile of imagination, united in fear of the mother's wrath, and in dread of their father's home-coming, Mrs. Bates sat in her rocking chair making a "singlet" of thick cream-colored flannel, which gave a dull wounded sound as she tore off the gray edge. She worked at her sewing with energy, listening to the children, and her anger wearied itself, lay down to rest, opening its eyes from time to time and steadily watching, its ears raised to listen. Sometimes even her anger quailed and shrank, and the mother suspended her sewing, tracing the footsteps that thudded along the sleepers outside; she would lift her head sharply to bid the children "hush," but she recovered herself in time, and the footsteps went past the gate, and the children were not flung out of their play-world.

But at last Annie sighed, and gave in. She glanced at her wagon of slippers, and loathed the game. She turned plaintively to her mother.

"Mother!"—but she was inarticulate.

John crept out like a frog from under the sofa. His mother glanced up.

"Yes," she said, "just look at those shirt-sleeves!"

The boy held them out to survey them, saying nothing. Then somebody called in a hoarse voice away down the line, and suspense bristled in the room, till two people had gone by outside, talking.

"It is time for bed," said the mother.

"My father hasn't come," wailed Annie plaintively. But her mother was primed with courage.

"Never mind. They'll bring him when he does come—like a log." She meant there would be no scene. "And he may sleep on the floor till he wakes himself. I know he'll not go to work tomorrow after this!"

The children had their hands and faces wiped with a flannel. They were very quiet. When they had put on their nightdresses, they said their prayers, the boy mumbling. The mother looked down at them, at the brown silken bush of intertwining curls in the nape of the girl's neck, at the little black head of the lad, and her heart burst with anger at their father, who caused all three such distress. The children hid their faces in her skirts for comfort.

When Mrs. Bates came down, the room was strangely empty, with a tension of expectancy. She took up her sewing and stitched for some time without raising her head. Meantime her anger was tinged with fear.

II

The clock struck eight and she rose suddenly, dropping her sewing on her chair. She went to the stair-foot door, opened it, listening. Then she went out, locking the door behind her.

Something scuffled in the yard, and she started, though she knew it was only the rats with which the place was over-run. The night was very dark. In the great bay of railway lines, bulked with trucks, there was no trace of light, only away back she could see a few yellow lamps at the pit top, and the red smear of the burning pit bank on the night. She hurried along the edge of the track, then, crossing the converging lines, came to the stile by the white gates, whence she emerged on the road. Then the fear which had led her shrank. People were walking up to New Brinsley; she saw the lights in the houses; twenty yards farther on were the broad windows of the Prince of Wales, very warm and bright, and the loud voices of men could be heard distinctly. What a fool she had been to imagine that anything had happened to him! He was merely drinking over there at the Prince of Wales. She faltered. She had never yet been to fetch him, and she never would go. So she continued her walk towards the long straggling line of houses, standing back on the highway. She entered a passage between the dwellings.

"Mr. Rigley?—Yes! Did you want him? No, he's not in at this minute."

The raw-boned woman leaned forward from her dark scullery and peered at the other, upon whom fell a dim light through the blind of the kitchen window.

"Is it Mrs. Bates?" she asked in a tone tinged with respect.

"Yes. I wondered if your Master was at home. Mine hasn't come yet."

"'Asn't 'e! Oh, Jack's been 'ome an' 'ad 'is dinner an' gone out. 'E's just gone for 'alf an hour afore bedtime. Did you call at the Prince of Wales?"

"No——"

"No, you didn't like——! It's not very nice." The other woman was indulgent. There was an awkward pause. "Jack never said nothink about—about your Master," she said.

"No!—I expect he's stuck in there!"

Elizabeth Bates said this bitterly, and with recklessness. She knew that the woman across the yard was standing at her door listening, but she did not care. As she turned:

"Stop a minute! I'll just go an' ask Jack if 'e knows anythink," said Mrs. Rigley.

"Oh no—I wouldn't like to put——!"

"Yes, I will, if you'll just step inside an' see as th' childer doesn't come downstairs and set theirselves afire."

Elizabeth Bates, murmuring a remonstrance, stepped inside. The other woman apologized for the state of the room.

The kitchen needed apology. There were little frocks and trousers and childish undergarments on the squab and on the floor, and a litter of playthings everywhere. On the black American cloth [1] of the table were pieces of bread and cake, crusts, slops, and a teapot with cold tea.

"Eh, ours is just as bad," said Elizabeth Bates, looking at the woman, not at the house. Mrs. Rigley put a shawl over her head and hurried out, saying:

"I shanna be a minute."

The other sat, noting with faint disapproval the general untidiness of the room. Then she fell to counting the shoes of various sizes scattered over the floor. There were twelve. She sighed and said to herself: "No wonder!"—glancing at the litter. There came the scratching of two pairs of feet on the yard, and the Rigleys entered. Elizabeth Bates rose. Rigley was a big man, with very large bones. His head looked particularly bony. Across his temple was a blue scar, caused by a wound got in the pit, a wound in which the coal dust remained blue like tattooing.

" 'Asna 'e come whoam yit?" asked the man, without any form of greeting, but with deference and sympathy. "I couldna say wheer he is—'e's non ower theer!"—he jerked his head to signify the Prince of Wales.

" 'E's 'appen gone up to th' Yew," said Mrs. Rigley.

There was another pause. Rigley had evidently something to get off his mind:

"Ah left 'im finishin' a stint," he began. "Loose-all [2] 'ad bin gone about ten minutes when we com'n away, an' I shouted: 'Are ter comin', Walt?' an' 'e said: 'Go on, Ah shanna be but a'ef a minnit,' so we com'n ter th' bottom, me an' Bowers, thinkin' as 'e wor just behint, an' 'ud come up i' th' next bantle [3]——".

He stood perplexed, as if answering a charge of deserting his mate. Elizabeth Bates, now again certain of disaster, hastened to reassure him:

"I expect 'e's gone up to th' Yew Tree, as you say. It's not the first time. I've fretted myself into a fever before now. He'll come home when they carry him."

"Ay, isn't it too bad!" deplored the other woman.

"I'll just step up to Dick's an' see if 'e *is* theer," offered the man, afraid of appearing alarmed, afraid of taking liberties.

"Oh, I wouldn't think of bothering you that far," said Elizabeth Bates, with emphasis, but he knew she was glad of his offer.

As they stumbled up the entry, Elizabeth Bates heard Rigley's wife run across the yard and open her neighbor's door. At this, suddenly all the blood in her body seemed to switch away from her

1. Oilcloth.
2. Signal for end of work.
3. Group.

heart.

"Mind!" warned Rigley. "Ah've said many a time as Ah'd fill up them ruts in this entry, sumb'dy 'll be breakin' their legs yit."

She recovered herself and walked quickly along with the miner.

"I don't like leaving the children in bed, and nobody in the house," she said.

"No, you dunna!" he replied courteously. They were soon at the gate of the cottage.

"Well, I shanna be many minnits. Dunna you be frettin' now, 'e'll be all right," said the butty.[4]

"Thank you very much, Mr. Rigley," she replied.

"You're welcome!" he stammered, moving away. "I shanna be many minnits."

The house was quiet. Elizabeth Bates took off her hat and shawl, and rolled back the rug. When she had finished, she sat down. It was a few minutes past nine. She was startled by the rapid chuff of the winding engine at the pit, and the sharp whirr of the brakes on the rope as it descended. Again she felt the painful sweep of her blood, and she put her hand to her side, saying aloud: "Good gracious!—it's only the nine o'clock deputy[5] going down," rebuking herself.

She sat still, listening. Half an hour of this, and she was wearied out.

"What am I working myself up like this for?" she said pitiably to herself, "I s'll only be doing myself some damage."

She took out her sewing again.

At a quarter to ten there were footsteps. One person! She watched for the door to open. It was an elderly woman, in a black bonnet and a black woolen shawl—his mother. She was about sixty years old, pale, with blue eyes, and her face all wrinkled and lamentable. She shut the door and turned to her daughter-in-law peevishly.

"Eh, Lizzie, whatever shall we do, whatever shall we do!" she cried.

Elizabeth drew back a little, sharply.

"What is it, mother?" she said.

The elder woman seated herself on the sofa.

"I don't know, child, I can't tell you!"—she shook her head slowly. Elizabeth sat watching her, anxious and vexed.

"I don't know," replied the grandmother, sighing very deeply. "There's no end to my troubles, there isn't. The things I've gone through, I'm sure it's enough——!" She wept without wiping her

4. Workmate (cf. "buddy").   5. Minor coal-mine official.

eyes, the tears running.

"But, mother," interrupted Elizabeth, "what do you mean? What is it?"

The grandmother slowly wiped her eyes. The fountains of her tears were stopped by Elizabeth's directness. She wiped her eyes slowly.

"Poor child! Eh, you poor thing!" she moaned. "I don't know what we're going to do, I don't—and you as you are—it's a thing, it is indeed!"

Elizabeth waited.

"Is he dead?" she asked, and at the words her heart swung violently, though she felt a slight flush of shame at the ultimate extravagance of the question. Her words sufficiently frightened the old lady, almost brought her to herself.

"Don't say so, Elizabeth! We'll hope it's not as bad as that; no, may the Lord spare us that, Elizabeth. Jack Rigley came just as I was sittin' down to a glass afore going to bed, an' 'e said: ' 'Appen you'll go down th' line, Mrs. Bates. Walt's had an accident. 'Appen you'll go an' sit wi' 'er till we can get him home.' I hadn't time to ask him a word afore he was gone. An' I put my bonnet on an' come straight down, Lizzie. I thought to myself: 'Eh, that poor blessed child, if anybody should come an' tell her of a sudden, there's no knowin' what'll 'appen to 'er.' You mustn't let it upset you, Lizzie —or you know what to expect. How long is it, six months—or is it five, Lizzie? Ay!"—the old woman shook her head—"time slips on, it slips on! Ay!"

Elizabeth's thoughts were busy elsewhere. If he was killed— would she be able to manage on the little pension and what she could earn?—she counted up rapidly. If he was hurt—they wouldn't take him to the hospital—how tiresome he would be to nurse!—but perhaps she'd be able to get him away from the drink and his hateful ways. She would—while he was ill. The tears offered to come to her eyes at the picture. But what sentimental luxury was this she was beginning? She turned to consider the children. At any rate she was absolutely necessary for them. They were her business.

"Ay!" repeated the old woman, "it seems but a week or two since he brought me his first wages. Ay—he was a good lad, Elizabeth, he was, in his way. I don't know why he got to be such a trouble, I don't. He was a happy lad at home, only full of spirits. But there's no mistake he's been a handful of trouble, he has! I hope the Lord'll spare him to mend his ways. I hope so, I hope so. You've had a sight o' trouble with him, Elizabeth, you have indeed. But he was a jolly enough lad wi' me, he was, I can assure you. I don't know how it is. . . ."

The old woman continued to muse aloud, a monotonous irritating sound, while Elizabeth thought concentratedly, startled once, when she heard the winding engine chuff quickly, and the brakes skirr with a shriek. Then she heard the engine more slowly, and the brakes made no sound. The old woman did not notice. Elizabeth waited in suspense. The mother-in-law talked, with lapses into silence.

"But he wasn't your son, Lizzie, an' it makes a difference. Whatever he was, I remember him when he was little, an' I learned to understand him and to make allowances. You've got to make allowances for them——"

It was half-past ten, and the old woman was saying: "But it's trouble from beginning to end; you're never too old for trouble, never too old for that——" when the gate banged back, and there were heavy feet on the steps.

"I'll go, Lizzie, let me go," cried the old woman, rising. But Elizabeth was at the door. It was a man in pit clothes.

"They're bringin' 'im, Missis," he said. Elizabeth's heart halted a moment. Then it surged on again, almost suffocating her. "Is he—is it bad?" she asked.

The man turned away, looking at the darkness:

"The doctor says 'e'd been dead hours. 'E saw 'im i' th' lamp-cabin."

The old woman, who stood just behind Elizabeth, dropped into a chair, and folded her hands, crying: "Oh, my boy, my boy!"

"Hush!" said Elizabeth, with a sharp twitch of a frown. "Be still, mother, don't waken th' children: I wouldn't have them down for anything!"

The old woman moaned softly, rocking herself. The man was drawing away. Elizabeth took a step forward.

"How was it?" she asked.

"Well, I couldn't say for sure," the man replied, very ill at ease. "'E wor finishin' a stint an' th' butties 'ad gone, an' a lot o' stuff come down atop 'n 'im."

"And crushed him?" cried the widow, with a shudder.

"No," said the man, "it fell at th' back of 'im. 'E wor under th' face an' it niver touched 'im. It shut 'im in. It seems 'e wor smothered."

Elizabeth shrank back. She heard the old woman behind her cry:

"What?—what did 'e say it was?"

The man replied, more loudly: "'E wor smothered!"

Then the old woman wailed aloud, and this relieved Elizabeth.

"Oh, mother," she said, putting her hand on the old woman, "don't waken th' children, don't waken th' children."

She wept a little, unknowing, while the old mother rocked herself and moaned. Elizabeth remembered that they were bringing him home, and she must be ready. "They'll lay him in the parlor," she said to herself, standing a moment pale and perplexed.

Then she lighted a candle and went into the tiny room. The air was cold and damp, but she could not make a fire, there was no fireplace. She set down the candle and looked round. The candlelight glittered on the luster-glasses, on the two vases that held some of the pink chrysanthemums, and on the dark mahogany. There was a cold, deathly smell of chrysanthemums in the room. Elizabeth stood looking at the flowers. She turned away, and calculated whether there would be room to lay him on the floor, between the couch and the chiffonier. She pushed the chairs aside. There would be room to lay him down and to step round him. Then she fetched the old red tablecloth, and another old cloth, spreading them down to save her bit of carpet. She shivered on leaving the parlor; so, from the dresser drawer she took a clean shirt and put it at the fire to air. All the time her mother-in-law was rocking herself in the chair and moaning.

"You'll have to move from there, mother," said Elizabeth. "They'll be bringing him in. Come in the rocker."

The old mother rose mechanically, and seated herself by the fire, continuing to lament. Elizabeth went into the pantry for another candle, and there, in the little penthouse under the naked tiles, she heard them coming. She stood still in the pantry doorway, listening. She heard them pass the end of the house, and come awkwardly down the three steps, a jumble of shuffling footsteps and muttering voices. The old woman was silent. The men were in the yard.

Then Elizabeth heard Matthews, the manager of the pit, say: "You go in first, Jim. Mind!"

The door came open, and the two women saw a collier backing into the room, holding one end of a stretcher, on which they could see the nailed pit boots of the dead man. The two carriers halted, the man at the head stooping to the lintel of the door.

"Wheer will you have him?" asked the manager, a short, white-bearded man.

Elizabeth roused herself and came from the pantry carrying the unlighted candle.

"In the parlor," she said.

"In there, Jim!" pointed the manager, and the carriers backed round into the tiny room. The coat with which they had covered the body fell off as they awkwardly turned through the two doorways, and the women saw their man, naked to the waist, lying stripped for work. The old woman began to moan in a low voice of horror.

"Lay th' stretcher at th' side," snapped the manager, "an' put 'im on th' cloths. Mind now, mind! Look you now——!"

One of the men had knocked off a vase of chrysanthemums. He stared awkwardly, then they set down the stretcher. Elizabeth did not look at her husband. As soon as she could get in the room, she went and picked up the broken vase and the flowers.

"Wait a minute!" she said.

The three men waited in silence while she mopped up the water with a duster.

"Eh, what a job, what a job, to be sure!" the manager was saying, rubbing his brow with trouble and perplexity. "Never knew such a thing in my life, never! He'd no business to ha' been left. I never knew such a thing in my life! Fell over him clean as a whistle, an' shut him in. Not four foot of space, there wasn't— yet it scarce bruised him."

He looked down at the dead man, lying prone, half naked, all grimed with coal dust.

" ' 'Sphyxiated', the doctor said. It *is* the most terrible job I've ever known. Seems as if it was done o' purpose. Clean over him, an' shut 'im in, like a mouse-trap"—he made a sharp, descending gesture with his hand.

The colliers standing by jerked aside their heads in hopeless comment.

The horror of the thing bristled upon them all.

Then they heard the girl's voice upstairs calling shrilly: "Mother, mother—who is it? Mother, who is it?"

Elizabeth hurried to the foot of the stairs and opened the door:

"Go to sleep!" she commanded sharply. "What are you shouting about? Go to sleep at once—there's nothing——"

Then she began to mount the stairs. They could hear her on the boards, and on the plaster floor of the little bedroom. They could hear her distinctly:

"What's the matter now?—what's the matter with you, silly thing?"—her voice was much agitated, with an unreal gentleness.

"I thought it was some men come," said the plaintive voice of the child. "Has he come?"

"Yes, they've brought him. There's nothing to make a fuss about. Go to sleep now, like a good child."

They could hear her voice in the bedroom, they waited whilst she covered the children under the bedclothes.

"Is he drunk?" asked the girl, timidly, faintly.

"No! No—he's not! He—he's asleep."

"Is he asleep downstairs?"

"Yes—and don't make a noise."

There was silence for a moment, then the men heard the frightened child again:

"What's that noise?"

"It's nothing, I tell you, what are you bothering for?"

The noise was the grandmother moaning. She was oblivious of everything, sitting on her chair rocking and moaning. The manager put his hand on her arm and bade her "Sh—sh!!"

The old woman opened her eyes and looked at him. She was shocked by this interruption, and seemed to wonder.

"What time is it?" the plaintive thin voice of the child, sinking back unhappily into sleep, asked this last question.

"Ten o'clock," answered the mother more softly. Then she must have bent down and kissed the children.

Matthews beckoned to the men to come away. They put on their caps and took up the stretcher. Stepping over the body, they tiptoed out of the house. None of them spoke till they were far from the wakeful children.

When Elizabeth came down she found her mother alone on the parlor floor, leaning over the dead man, the tears dropping on him.

"We must lay him out," the wife said. She put on the kettle, then returning knelt at the feet, and began to unfasten the knotted leather laces. The room was clammy and dim with only one candle, so that she had to bend her face almost to the floor. At last she got off the heavy boots and put them away.

"You must help me now," she whispered to the old woman. Together they stripped the man.

When they arose, saw him lying in the naïve dignity of death, the woman stood arrested in fear and respect. For a few moments they remained still, looking down, the old mother whimpering. Elizabeth felt countermanded. She saw him, how utterly inviolable he lay in himself. She had nothing to do with him. She could not accept it. Stooping, she laid her hand on him, in claim. He was still warm, for the mine was hot where he had died. His mother had his face between her hands, and was murmuring incoherently. The old tears fell in succession as drops from wet leaves; the mother was not weeping, merely her tears flowed. Elizabeth embraced the body of her husband, with cheek and lips. She seemed to be listening, inquiring, trying to get some connection. But she could not. She was driven away. He was impregnable.

She rose, went into the kitchen, where she poured warm water into a bowl, brought soap and flannel and a soft towel. "I must wash him," she said.

Then the old mother rose stiffly, and watched Elizabeth as she carefully washed his face, carefully brushing his big blond moustache from his mouth with the flannel. She was afraid with a bottomless fear, so she ministered to him. The old woman, jealous, said:

"Let me wipe him!"—and she kneeled on the other side drying slowly as Elizabeth washed, her big black bonnet sometimes brushing the dark head of her daughter-in-law. They worked thus in silence for a long time. They never forgot it was death, and the touch of the man's dead body gave them strange emotions, different in each of the women; a great dread possessed them both, the mother felt the lie was given to her womb, she was denied; the wife felt the utter isolation of the human soul, the child within her was a weight apart from her.

At last it was finished. He was a man of handsome body, and his face showed no traces of drink. He was blond, full fleshed, with fine limbs. But he was dead.

"Bless him," whispered his mother, looking always at his face, and speaking out of sheer terror. "Dear lad—bless him!" She spoke in a faint, sibilant ecstasy of fear and mother love.

Elizabeth sank down again to the floor, and put her face against his neck, and trembled and shuddered. But she had to draw away again. He was dead, and her living flesh had no place against his. A great dread and weariness held her: she was so unavailing. Her life was gone like this.

"White as milk he is, clear as a twelve-month baby, bless him, the darling!" the old mother murmured to herself. "Not a mark on him, clear and clean and white, beautiful as ever a child was made," she murmured with pride. Elizabeth kept her face hidden.

"He went peaceful, Lizzie—peaceful as sleep. Isn't he beautiful, the lamb? Ay—he must ha' made his peace, Lizzie. 'Appen he made it all right, Lizzie, shut in there. He'd have time. He wouldn't look like this if he hadn't made his peace. The lamb, the dear lamb. Eh, but he had a hearty laugh. I loved to hear it. He had the heartiest laugh, Lizzie, as a lad——"

Elizabeth looked up. The man's mouth was fallen back, slightly open under the cover of the moustache. The eyes, half shut, did not show glazed in the obscurity. Life with its smoky burning gone from him, had left him apart and utterly alien to her. And she knew what a stranger he was to her. In her womb was ice of fear, because of this separate stranger with whom she had been living as one flesh. Was this what it all meant—utter, intact separateness, obscured by heat of living? In dread she turned her face away. The fact was too deadly. There had been nothing between them, and yet they had come together, exchanging their nakedness repeatedly. Each time he had taken her, they had been two isolated beings, far apart as now. He was no more responsible than she. The child was like ice in her womb. For as she looked at the dead man, her mind, cold and detached, said clearly: "Who am I? What have I been doing? I have been fighting a husband who did not exist. *He* existed all the time. What wrong have I done? What was that I have been living with? There lies the reality, this man." And her soul died in her for fear: she knew she had never seen him, he had never seen her, they had met in the dark and had fought in the dark, not knowing whom they met or whom they fought. And now she saw, and turned silent in seeing. For she had been wrong. She had said he was something he was not; she had felt familiar with him. Whereas he was apart all the while, living as she never lived, feeling as she never felt.

In fear and shame she looked at his naked body, that she had known falsely. And he was the father of her children. Her soul was torn from her body and stood apart. She looked at his naked body and was ashamed, as if she had denied it. After all, it was itself. It seemed awful to her. She looked at his face, and she turned her own face to the wall. For his look was other than hers, his way was not her way. She had denied him what he was—she saw it now. She had refused him as himself. And this had been her life, and his life. She was grateful to death, which restored the truth. And she knew she was not dead.

And all the while her heart was bursting with grief and pity for him. What had he suffered? What stretch of horror for this helpless man! She was rigid with agony. She had not been able to help him. He had been cruelly injured, this naked man, this other being, and she could make no reparation. There were the children—but the children belonged to life. This dead man had nothing to do with them. He and she were only channels through which life had flowed to issue in the children. She was a mother—but how awful she knew it now to have been a wife. And he, dead now, how awful he must have felt it to be a husband. She felt that in the next world he would be a stranger to her. If they met there, in the beyond, they would only be ashamed of what had been before. The children had come, for some mysterious reason, out of both of them. But the children did not unite them. Now he was dead, she knew how eternally he was apart from her, how eternally he had nothing more to do with her. She saw this episode of her life closed. They had denied each other in life. Now he had withdrawn. An anguish came over her. It was finished then: it had become hopeless between them long before he died. Yet he had been her husband. But how little!

"Have you got his shirt, 'Lizabeth?"

Elizabeth turned without answering, though she strove to weep and behave as her mother-in-law expected. But she could not, she was silenced. She went into the kitchen and returned with the garment.

"It is aired," she said, grasping the cotton shirt here and there to try. She was almost ashamed to handle him; what right had she or anyone to lay hands on him; but her touch was humble on his body. It was hard work to clothe him. He was so heavy and inert. A terrible dread gripped her all the while: that he could be so heavy and utterly inert, unresponsive, apart. The horror of the distance between them was almost too much for her—it was so infinite a gap she must look across.

At last it was finished. They covered him with a sheet and left him lying, with his face bound. And she fastened the door of the little parlor, lest the children should see what was lying there. Then, with peace sunk heavy on her heart, she went about making tidy the kitchen. She knew she submitted to life, which was her immediate master. But from death, her ultimate master, she winced with fear and shame.

1911, 1914

The Horse Dealer's Daughter

"Well, Mabel, and what are you going to do with yourself?" asked Joe, with foolish flippancy. He felt quite safe himself. Without listening for an answer, he turned aside, worked a grain of tobacco to the tip of his tongue, and spat it out. He did not care about anything, since he felt safe himself.

The three brothers and the sister sat round the desolate breakfast-table, attempting some sort of desultory consultation. The morning's post had given the final tap to the family fortunes, and all was over. The dreary dining-room itself, with its heavy mahogany furniture, looked as if it were waiting to be done away with.

But the consultation amounted to nothing. There was a strange air of ineffectuality about the three men, as they sprawled at table, smoking and reflecting vaguely on their own condition. The girl was alone, a rather short, sullen-looking young woman of twenty-seven. She did not share the same life as her brothers. She would have been good-looking, save for the impressive fixity of her face, "bull-dog," as her brothers called it.

There was a confused tramping of horses' feet outside. The three men all sprawled round in their chairs to watch. Beyond the dark holly bushes that separated the strip of lawn from the high-road, they could see a cavalcade of shire horses swinging out of their own yard, being taken for exercise. This was the last time. These were the last horses that would go through their hands. The young men watched with critical, callous look. They were all frightened at the collapse of their lives, and the sense of disaster in which they were involved left them no inner freedom.

Yet they were three fine, well-set fellows enough. Joe, the eldest, was a man of thirty-three, broad and handsome in a hot, flushed way. His face was red, he twisted his black moustache over a thick finger, his eyes were shallow and restless. He had a sensual way of uncovering his teeth when he laughed, and his bearing was stupid. Now he watched the horses with a glazed look of helplessness in his eyes, a certain stupor of downfall.

The great draught horses swung past. They were tied head to tail, four of them, and they heaved along to where a lane branched off from the highroad, planting their great hoofs floutingly in the fine black mud, swinging their great rounded haunches sumptu-ously, and trotting a few sudden steps as they were led into the lane, round the corner. Every movement showed a massive, slumbrous strength, and a stupidity which held them in subjec-tion. The groom at the head looked back, jerking the leading rope. And the cavalcade moved out of sight up the lane, the tail of the last horse, bobbed up tight and stiff, held out taut from the swinging great haunches as they rocked behind the hedges in a motion-like sleep.

Joe watched with glazed hopeless eyes. The horses were almost like his own body to him. He felt he was done for now. Luckily he was engaged to a woman as old as himself, and therefore her father, who was steward of a neighboring estate, would provide him with a job. He would marry and go into harness. His life was over, he would be a subject animal now.

He turned uneasily aside, the retreating steps of the horses echoing in his ears. Then, with foolish restlessness, he reached for the scraps of bacon rind from the plates, and making a faint whistling sound, flung them to the terrier that lay against the fender. He watched the dog swallow them, and waited till the creature looked into his eyes. Then a faint grin came on his face, and in a high, foolish voice he said:

"You won't get much more bacon, shall you, you little b——?"

The dog faintly and dismally wagged its tail, then lowered its haunches, circled round, and lay down again.

There was another helpless silence at the table. Joe sprawled uneasily in his seat, not willing to go till the family conclave was dissolved. Fred Henry, the second brother, was erect, clean-limbed, alert. He had watched the passing of the horses with more *sang froid*. If he was an animal, like Joe, he was an animal which controls, not one which is controlled. He was master of any horse, and he carried himself with a well-tempered air of mastery. But he was not master of the situations of life. He pushed his coarse brown moustache upwards, off his lip, and glanced irritably at his sister, who sat impassive and inscrutable.

"You'll go and stop with Lucy for a bit, shan't you?" he asked. The girl did not answer.

"I don't see what else you can do," persisted Fred Henry.

"Go as a skivvy," [1] Joe interpolated laconically.

The girl did not move a muscle.

"If I was her, I should go in for training for a nurse," said Malcolm, the youngest of them all. He was the baby of the family, a young man of twenty-two, with a fresh, jaunty *museau*.[2]

But Mabel did not take any notice of him. They had talked at her and round her for so many years, that she hardly heard them at all.

The marble clock on the mantelpiece softly chimed the half-hour, the dog rose uneasily from the hearth-rug and looked at the party at the breakfast-table. But still they sat on an ineffectual conclave.

"Oh, all right," said Joe suddenly, apropos of nothing. "I'll get a move on."

He pushed back his chair, straddled his knees with a downward jerk, to get them free, in horsey fashion, and went to the fire. Still he did not go out of the room; he was curious to know what the others would do or say. He began to charge his pipe, looking down at the dog and saying in a high, affected voice:

"Going wi' me? Going wi' me are ter? Tha'rt goin' further than tha counts on just now, dost hear?"

The dog faintly wagged his tail, the man stuck out his jaw and covered his pipe with his hands, and puffed intently, losing himself in the tobacco, looking down all the while at the dog with an absent brown eye. The dog looked up at him in mournful distrust. Joe stood with his knees stuck out, in real horsey fashion.

"Have you had a letter from Lucy?" Fred Henry asked of his sister.

1. Servant girl.   2. Face (French slang).

"Last week," came the neutral reply.

"And what does she say?"

There was no answer.

"Does she *ask* you to go and stop there?" persisted Fred Henry.

"She says I can if I like."

"Well, then, you'd better. Tell her you'll come on Monday." This was received in silence.

"That's what you'll do then, is it?" said Fred Henry, in some exasperation.

But she made no answer. There was a silence of futility and irritation in the room. Malcolm grinned fatuously.

"You'll have to make up your mind between now and next Wednesday," said Joe loudly, "or else find yourself lodgings on the curbstone."

The face of the young woman darkened, but she sat on immutable.

"Here's Jack Ferguson!" exclaimed Malcolm, who was looking aimlessly out of the window.

"Where?" exclaimed Joe loudly.

"Just gone past."

"Coming in?"

Malcolm craned his neck to see the gate.

"Yes," he said.

There was a silence. Mabel sat on like one condemned, at the head of the table. Then a whistle was heard from the kitchen. The dog got up and barked sharply. Joe opened the door and shouted:

"Come on."

After a moment a young man entered. He was muffled up in overcoat and a purple woolen scarf, and his tweed cap, which he did not remove, was pulled down on his head. He was of medium height, his face was rather long and pale, his eyes looked tired.

"Hello, Jack! Well, Jack!" exclaimed Malcolm and Joe. Fred Henry merely said: "Jack."

"What's doing?" asked the newcomer, evidently addressing Fred Henry.

"Same. We've got to be out by Wednesday. Got a cold?"

"I have—got it bad, too."

"Why don't you stop in?"

"*Me* stop in? When I can't stand on my legs, perhaps I shall have a chance." The young man spoke huskily. He had a slight Scotch accent.

"It's a knockout, isn't it," said Joe, boisterously, "if a doctor goes round croaking with a cold. Looks bad for the patients, doesn't it?"

The young doctor looked at him slowly.

"Anything the matter with *you*, then?" he asked sarcastically.

"Not as I know of. Damn your eyes, I hope not. Why?"

"I thought you were very concerned about the patients, wondered if you might be one yourself."

"Damn it, no, I've never been patient to no flaming doctor, and hope I never shall be," returned Joe.

At this point Mabel rose from the table, and they all seemed to become aware of her existence. She began putting the dishes together. The young doctor looked at her, but did not address her. He had not greeted her. She went out of the room with the tray, her face impassive and unchanged.

"When are you off then, all of you?" asked the doctor.

"I'm catching the eleven-forty," replied Malcolm. "Are you goin' down wi' th' trap, Joe?"

"Yes, I've told you I'm going down wi' th' trap, haven't I?"

"We'd better be getting her in then. So long, Jack, if I don't see you before I go," said Malcolm, shaking hands.

He went out, followed by Joe, who seemed to have his tail between his legs.

"Well, this is the devil's own," exclaimed the doctor, when he was left alone with Fred Henry. "Going before Wednesday, are you?"

"That's the orders," replied the other.

"Where, to Northampton?"

"That's it."

"The devil!" exclaimed Ferguson, with quiet chagrin.

And there was silence between the two.

"All settled up, are you?" asked Ferguson.

"About."

There was another pause.

"Well, I shall miss yer, Freddy, boy," said the young doctor.

"And I shall miss thee, Jack," returned the other.

"Miss you like hell," mused the doctor.

Fred Henry turned aside. There was nothing to say. Mabel came in again, to finish clearing the table.

"What are *you* going to do, then, Miss Pervin?" asked Ferguson. "Going to your sister's, are you?"

Mabel looked at him with her steady, dangerous eyes, that always made him uncomfortable, unsettling his superficial ease.

"No," she said.

"Well, what in the name of fortune *are* you going to do? Say what you mean to do," cried Fred Henry, with futile intensity.

But she only averted her head, and continued her work. She folded the white table cloth, and put on the chenille cloth.

"The sulkiest bitch that ever trod!" muttered her brother.

But she finished her task with perfectly impassive face, the young doctor watching her interestedly all the while. Then she went out.

Fred Henry stared after her, clenching his lips, his blue eyes fixing in sharp antagonism, as he made a grimace of sour exasperation.

"You could bray her into bits, and that's all you'd get out of her," he said, in a small, narrowed tone.

The doctor smiled faintly.

"What's she *going* to do, then?" he asked.

"Strike me if *I* know!" returned the other.

There was a pause. Then the doctor stirred.

"I'll be seeing you tonight, shall I?" he said to his friend.

"Ay—where's it to be? Are we going over to Jessdale?"

"I don't know. I've got such a cold on me. I'll come round to the Moon and Stars, anyway."

"Let Lizzie and May miss their night for once, eh?"

"That's it—if I feel as I do now."

"All's one——"

The two young men went through the passage and down to the back door together. The house was large, but it was servantless now, and desolate. At the back was a small bricked house yard and beyond that a big square, graveled fine and red, and having stables on two sides. Sloping, dank, winter-dark fields stretched away on the open sides.

But the stables were empty. Joseph Pervin, the father of the family, had been a man of no education, who had become a fairly large horse dealer. The stables had been full of horses, there was a great turmoil and come-and-go of horses and of dealers and grooms. Then the kitchen was full of servants. But of late things had declined. The old man had married a second time, to retrieve his fortunes. Now he was dead and everything was gone to the dogs, there was nothing but debt and threatening.

For months, Mabel had been servantless in the big house, keeping the home together in penury for her ineffectual brothers. She had kept house for ten years. But previously it was with unstinted means. Then, however brutal and coarse everything was, the sense of money had kept her proud, confident. The men might be foul-mouthed, the women in the kitchen might have had reputations, her brothers might have illegitimate children.

But so long as there was money, the girl felt herself established, and brutally proud, reserved.

No company came to the house, save dealers and coarse men. Mabel had no associates of her own sex, after her sister went away. But she did not mind. She went regularly to church, she attended to her father. And she lived in the memory of her mother, who had died when she was fourteen, and whom she had loved. She had loved her father, too, in a different way, depending upon him, and feeling secure in him, until at the age of fifty-four, he married again. And then she had set hard against him. Now he had died and left them all hopelessly in debt.

She had suffered badly during the period of poverty. Nothing, however, could shake the curious, sullen, animal pride that dominated each member of the family. Now, for Mabel, the end had come. Still she would not cast about her. She would follow her own way just the same. She would always hold the keys of her own situation. Mindless and persistent, she endured from day to day. Why should she think? Why should she answer anybody? It was enough that this was the end, and there was no way out. She need not pass any more darkly along the main street of the small town, avoiding every eye. She need not demean herself any more, going into the shops and buying the cheapest food. This was at an end. She thought of nobody, not even of herself. Mindless and persistent, she seemed in a sort of ecstasy to be coming nearer to her fulfilment, her own glorification, approaching her dead mother, who was glorified.

In the afternoon, she took a little bag, with shears and sponge and a small scrubbing-brush, and went out. It was a gray, wintry day, with saddened, dark green fields and an atmosphere blackened by the smoke of foundries not far off. She went quickly, darkly along the causeway, heeding nobody, through the town to the churchyard.

There she always felt secure, as if no one could see her, although as a matter of fact she was exposed to the stare of everyone who passed along under the churchyard wall. Nevertheless, once under the shadow of the great looming church, among the graves, she felt immune from the world, reserved within the thick churchyard wall as in another country.

Carefully she clipped the grass from the grave, and arranged the pinky-white, small chrysanthemums in the tin cross. When this was done, she took an empty jar from a neighboring grave, brought water, and carefully, most scrupulously sponged the marble head-stone and the coping-stone.

It gave her sincere satisfaction to do this. She felt in immediate contact with the world of her mother. She took minute pains, went through the park in a state bordering on pure happiness, as if in performing this task she came into a subtle, intimate con- nection with her mother. For the life she followed here in the world was far less real than the world of death she inherited from her mother.

The doctor's house was just by the church. Ferguson, being a mere hired assistant, was slave to the countryside. As he hurried now to attend to the out-patients in the surgery, glancing across the graveyard with his quick eye, he saw the girl at her task at the grave. She seemed so intent and remote, it was like looking into another world. Some mystical element was touched in him. He slowed down as he walked, watching her as if spellbound.

She lifted her eyes, feeling him looking. Their eyes met. And each looked again at once, each feeling, in some way, found out by the other. He lifted his cap and passed on down the road. There remained distinct in his consciousness, like a vision, the memory of her face, lifted from the tombstone in the churchyard, and looking at him with slow, large, portentous eyes. It *was* por- tentous, her face. It seemed to mesmerize him. There was a heavy power in her eyes which laid hold of his whole being, as if he had drunk some powerful drug. He had been feeling weak and done before. Now the life came back into him, he felt delivered from his own fretted, daily self.

He finished his duties at the surgery as quickly as might be, hastily filling up the bottles of the waiting people with cheap drugs. Then, in perpetual haste, he set off again to visit several cases in another part of his round, before tea-time. At all times he preferred to walk if he could, but particularly when he was not well. He fancied the motion restored him.

The afternoon was falling. It was gray, deadened, and wintry, with a slow, moist, heavy coldness sinking in and deadening all the faculties. But why should he think or notice? He hastily climbed the hill and turned across the dark green fields, following the black cinder-track. In the distance, across a shallow dip in the country, the small town was clustered like smouldering ash, a tower, a spire, a heap of low, raw, extinct houses. And on the nearest fringe of the town, sloping into the dip, was Oldmeadow, the Pervins' house. He could see the stables and the outbuildings distinctly, as they lay towards him on the slope. Well, he would not go there many more times! Another resource would be lost to him, another place gone: the only company he cared for in the alien, ugly little town he was losing. Nothing but work, drudgery, constant hastening from dwelling to dwelling among the colliers and the iron-workers. It wore him out, but at the same time he had a craving for it. It was a stimulant to him to be in the homes of the working people, moving, as it were, through the innermost body of their life. His nerves were excited and gratified. He could come so near, into the very lives of the rough, inarticulate, powerfully emotional men and women. He grumbled, he said he hated the hellish hole. But as a matter of fact it excited him, the contact with the rough, strongly-feeling people was a stimulant applied direct to his nerves.

Below Oldmeadow, in the green, shallow, soddened hollow of fields, lay a square, deep pond. Roving across the landscape, the doctor's quick eye detected a figure in black passing through the gate of the field, down towards the pond. He looked again. It would be Mabel Pervin. His mind suddenly became alive and attentive.

Why was she going down there? He pulled up on the path on the slope above, and stood staring. He could just make sure of the small black figure moving in the hollow of the failing day. He seemed to see her in the midst of such obscurity, that he was like a clairvoyant, seeing rather with the mind's eye than with ordinary sight. Yet he could see her positively enough, whilst he kept his eye attentive. He felt, if he looked away from her, in the thick, ugly falling dusk, he would lose her altogether.

He followed her minutely as she moved, direct and intent, like something transmitted rather than stirring in voluntary activity, straight down the field towards the pond. There she stood on the bank for a moment. She never raised her head. Then she waded slowly into the water.

He stood motionless as the small black figure walked slowly and deliberately towards the center of the pond, very slowly, gradually moving deeper into the motionless water, and still moving forward as the water got up to her breast. Then he could see her no more in the dusk of the dead afternoon.

"There!" he exclaimed. "Would you believe it?"

And he hastened straight down, running over the wet, soddened fields, pushing through the hedges, down into the depression of callous wintry obscurity. It took him several minutes to come to the pond. He stood on the bank, breathing heavily. He could see nothing. His eyes seemed to penetrate the dead water. Yes, perhaps that was the dark shadow of her black clothing beneath the surface of the water.

He slowly ventured into the pond. The bottom was deep, soft clay, he sank in, and the water clasped dead cold round his legs. As he stirred he could smell the cold, rotten clay that fouled up into the water. It was objectionable in his lungs. Still, repelled and yet not heeding, he moved deeper into the pond. The cold water rose over his thighs, over his loins, upon his abdomen. The lower part of his body was all sunk in the hideous cold element. And the bottom was so deeply soft and uncertain, he was afraid of pitching with his mouth underneath. He could not swim, and was afraid.

He crouched a little, spreading his hands under the water and moving them round, trying to feel for her. The dead cold pond swayed upon his chest. He moved again, a little deeper, and again, with his hands underneath, he felt all around under the water. And he touched her clothing. But it evaded his fingers. He made a desperate effort to grasp it.

And so doing he lost his balance and went under, horribly, suffocating in the foul earthy water, struggling madly for a few moments. At last, after what seemed an eternity, he got his footing, rose again into the air and looked around. He gasped, and knew he was in the world. Then he looked at the water. She had risen near him. He grasped her clothing, and drawing her nearer, turned to take his way to land again.

He went very slowly, carefully, absorbed in the slow progress. He rose higher, climbing out of the pond. The water was now only about his legs; he was thankful, full of relief to be out of the clutches of the pond. He lifted her and staggered on to the bank, out of the horror of wet, gray clay.

He laid her down on the bank. She was quite unconscious and running with water. He made the water come from her mouth, he worked to restore her. He did not have to work very long before he could feel the breathing begin again in her; she was breathing naturally. He worked a little longer. He could feel her live beneath his hands; she was coming back. He wiped her face, wrapped her in his overcoat, looked round into the dim, dark gray world, then lifted her and staggered down the bank and across the fields.

It seemed an unthinkably long way, and his burden so heavy he felt he would never get to the house. But at last he was in the stable yard, and then in the house yard. He opened the door and went into the house. In the kitchen he laid her down on the hearth-rug and called. The house was empty. But the fire was burning in the grate.

Then again he kneeled to attend to her. She was breathing regularly, her eyes were wide open and as if conscious, but there seemed something missing in her look. She was conscious in herself, but unconscious of her surroundings.

He ran upstairs, took blankets from a bed, and put them before the fire to warm. Then he removed her saturated, earthy-smelling clothing, rubbed her dry with a towel, and wrapped her naked in the blankets. Then he went into the dining room, to look for spirits. There was a little whisky. He drank a gulp himself, and put some into her mouth.

The effect was instantaneous. She looked full into his face, as if she had been seeing him for some time, and yet had only just become conscious of him.

"Dr. Ferguson?" she said.

"What?" he answered.

He was divesting himself of his coat, intending to find some dry clothing upstairs. He could not bear the smell of the dead, clayey water, and he was mortally afraid for his own health.

"What did I do?" she asked.

"Walked into the pond," he replied. He had begun to shudder like one sick, and could hardly attend to her. Her eyes remained full on him, he seemed to be going dark in his mind, looking back at her helplessly. The shuddering became quieter in him, his life came back to him, dark and unknowing, but strong again.

"Was I out of my mind?" she asked, while her eyes were fixed on him all the time.

"Maybe, for the moment," he replied. He felt quiet, because his strength had come back. The strange fretful strain had left him.

"Am I out of my mind now?" she asked.

"Are you?" he reflected a moment. "No," he answered truthfully. "I don't see that you are." He turned his face aside. He was afraid now, because he felt dazed, and felt dimly that her power was stronger than his, in this issue. And she continued to look at him fixedly all the time. "Can you tell me where I shall find some dry things to put on?" he asked.

"Did you dive into the pond for me?" she asked.

"No," he answered. "I walked in. But I went in overhead as well."

There was silence for a moment. He hesitated. He very much wanted to go upstairs to get into dry clothing. But there was another desire in him. And she seemed to hold him. His will seemed to have gone to sleep, and left him, standing there slack before her. But he felt warm inside himself. He did not shudder at all, though his clothes were sodden on him.

"Why did you?" she asked.

"Because I didn't want you to do such a foolish thing," he said.

"It wasn't foolish," she said, still gazing at him as she lay on the floor, with a sofa cushion under her head. "It was the right thing to do. I knew best, then."

"I'll go and shift these wet things," he said. But still he had not the power to move out of her presence, until she sent him. It was as if she had the life of his body in her hands, and he could not extricate himself. Or perhaps he did not want to.

Suddenly she sat up. Then she became aware of her own immediate condition. She felt the blankets about her, she knew her own limbs. For a moment it seemed as if her reason were going. She looked round, with wild eye, as if seeking something. He stood still with fear. She saw her clothing lying scattered.

"Who undressed me?" she asked, her eyes resting full and inevitable on his face.

"I did," he replied, "to bring you round."

For some moments she sat and gazed at him awfully, her lips parted.

"Do you love me, then?" she asked.

He only stood and stared at her, fascinated. His soul seemed to melt.

She shuffled forward on her knees, and put her arms round him, round his legs, as he stood there, pressing her breasts against his knees and thighs, clutching him with strange, convulsive certainty, pressing his thighs against her, drawing him to her face, her throat, as she looked up at him with flaring, humble eyes of transfiguration, triumphant in first possession.

"You love me," she murmured, in strange transport, yearning and triumphant and confident. "You love me. I know you love me, I know."

And she was passionately kissing his knees, through the wet clothing, passionately and indiscriminately kissing his knees, his legs, as if unaware of everything.

He looked down at the tangled wet hair, the wild, bare, animal shoulders. He was amazed, bewildered, and afraid. He had never thought of loving her. He had never wanted to love her. When he rescued her and restored her, he was a doctor, and she was a patient. He had had no single personal thought of her. Nay, this introduction of the personal element was very distasteful to him, a violation of his professional honor. It was horrible to have her there embracing his knees. It was horrible. He revolted from it, violently. And yet—and yet—he had not the power to break away.

She looked at him again, with the same supplication of powerful love, and that same transcendent, frightening light of triumph. In view of the delicate flame which seemed to come from her face like a light, he was powerless. And yet he had never intended to love her. He had never intended. And something stubborn in him could not give way.

"You love me," she repeated, in a murmur of deep, rhapsodic assurance. "You love me."

Her hands were drawing him, drawing him down to her. He was afraid, even a little horrified. For he had, really, no intention of loving her. Yet her hands were drawing him towards her. He put out his hand quickly to steady himself, and grasped her bare shoulder. A flame seemed to burn the hand that grasped her soft shoulder. He had no intention of loving her: his whole will was against his yielding. It was horrible. And yet wonderful was the touch of her shoulders, beautiful the shining of her face. Was she perhaps mad? He had a horror of yielding to her. Yet something in him ached also.

He had been staring away at the door, away from her. But his hand remained on her shoulder. She had gone suddenly very still. He looked down at her. Her eyes were now wide with fear, with doubt, the light was dying from her face, a shadow of terrible grayness was returning. He could not bear the touch of her eyes' question upon him, and the look of death behind the question.

With an inward groan he gave way, and let his heart yield towards her. A sudden gentle smile came on his face. And her eyes, which never left his face, slowly, slowly filled with tears. He watched the strange water rise in her eyes, like some slow fountain coming up. And his heart seemed to burn and melt away in his breast.

He could not bear to look at her any more. He dropped on his knees and caught her head with his arms and pressed her face against his throat. She was very still. His heart, which seemed to have broken, was burning with a kind of agony in his breast. And he felt her slow, hot tears wetting his throat. But he could not move.

He felt the hot tears wet his neck and the hollows of his neck, and he remained motionless, suspended through one of man's eternities. Only now it had become indispensable to him to have her face pressed close to him; he could never let her go again. He could never let her head go away from the close clutch of his arm. He wanted to remain like that for ever, with his heart hurting him in a pain that was also life to him. Without knowing, he was looking down on her damp, soft brown hair.

Then, as it were suddenly, he smelt the horried stagnant smell of that water. And at the same moment she drew away from him and looked at him. Her eyes were wistful and unfathomable. He was afraid of them, and he fell to kissing her, not knowing what he was doing. He wanted her eyes not to have that terrible, wistful, unfathomable look.

When she turned her face to him again, a faint delicate flush was glowing, and there was again dawning that terrible shining of joy in her eyes, which really terrified him, and yet which he now wanted to see, because he feared the look of doubt still more.

"You love me?" she said, rather faltering.

"Yes." The word cost him a painful effort. Not because it wasn't true. But because it was too newly true, the *saying* seemed to tear open again his newly torn heart. And he hardly wanted it to be true, even now.

She lifted her face to him, and he bent forward and kissed her on the mouth, gently, with the one kiss that is an eternal pledge. And as he kissed her his heart strained again in his breast. He never intended to love her. But now it was over. He had crossed over the gulf to her, and all that he had left behind had shriveled and become void.

After the kiss, her eyes again slowly filled with tears. She sat still, away from him, with her face drooped aside, and her hands folded in her lap. The tears fell very slowly. There was complete silence. He too sat there motionless and silent on the hearth rug. The strange pain of his heart that was broken seemed to consume him. That he should love her? That this was love! That he should be ripped open in this way! Him, a doctor! How they would all jeer if they knew! It was agony to him to think they might know.

In the curious naked pain of the thought he looked again to her. She was sitting there drooped into a muse. He saw a tear fall, and his heart flared hot. He saw for the first time that one of her shoulders was quite uncovered, one arm bare, he could see one of her small breasts; dimly, because it had become almost dark in the room.

"Why are you crying?" he asked, in an altered voice.

She looked up at him, and behind her tears the consciousness of her situation for the first time brought a dark look of shame to her eyes.

"I'm not crying, really," she said, watching him, half frightened.

He reached his hand, and softly closed it on her bare arm.

"I love you! I love you!" he said in a soft, low vibrating voice, unlike himself.

She shrank, and dropped her head. The soft, penetrating grip of his hand on her arm distressed her. She looked up at him.

"I want to go," she said. "I want to go and get you some dry things."

"Why?" he said. "I'm all right."

"But I want to go," she said. "And I want you to change your things."

He released her arm, and she wrapped herself in the blanket, looking at him, rather frightened. And still she did not rise.

"Kiss me," she said wistfully.

He kissed her, but briefly, half in anger.

Then, after a second, she rose nervously, all mixed up in the blanket. He watched her in her confusion as she tried to extricate herself and wrap herself up so that she could walk. He watched her relentlessly, as she knew. And as she went, the blanket trailing, and as he saw a glimpse of her feet and her white leg, he tried to remember her as she was when he had wrapped her in the blanket. But then he didn't want to remember, because she had been nothing to him then, and his nature revolted from remembering her as she was when she was nothing to him.

A tumbling muffled noise from within the dark house startled him. Then he heard her voice: "There are clothes." He rose and went to the foot of the stairs, and gathered up the garments she had thrown down. Then he came back to the fire, to rub himself down and dress. He grinned at his own appearance when he had finished.

The fire was sinking, so he put on coal. The house was now quite dark, save for the light of a street-lamp that shone in faintly from beyond the holly trees. He lit the gas with matches he found on the mantelpiece. Then he emptied the pockets of his own clothes, and threw all his wet things in a heap into the scullery. After which he gathered up her sodden clothes, gently, and put them in a separate heap on the copper-top in the scullery.

It was six o'clock on the clock. His own watch had stopped. He ought to go back to the surgery. He waited, and still she did not come down. So he went to the foot of the stairs and called:

"I shall have to go."

Almost immediately he heard her coming down. She had on her best dress of black voile, and her hair was tidy, but still damp. She looked at him—and in spite of herself, smiled.

"I don't like you in those clothes," she said.

"Do I look a sight?" he answered.

They were shy of one another.

"I'll make you some tea," she said.

"No, I must go."

"Must you?" And she looked at him again with the wide, strained, doubtful eyes. And again, from the pain of his breast, he knew how he loved her. He went and bent to kiss her, gently, passionately, with his heart's painful kiss.

"And my hair smells so horrible," she murmured in distraction. "And I'm so awful, I'm so awful! Oh no, I'm too awful." And she broke into bitter, heart-broken sobbing. "You can't want to love me, I'm horrible."

"Don't be silly, don't be silly," he said, trying to comfort her, kissing her, holding her in his arms. "I want you, I want to marry you, we're going to be married, quickly, quickly—tomorrow if I can."

But she only sobbed terribly, and cried:

"I feel awful. I feel awful. I feel I'm horrible to you."

"No, I want you, I want you," was all he answered, blindly, with that terrible intonation which frightened her almost more than her horror lest he should *not* want her.

1922

From The Rainbow

From *Chapter II. They Live at the Marsh* [1]

One afternoon, the pains began, Mrs. Brangwen was put to bed, the midwife came. Night fell, the shutters were closed, Brangwen came in to tea, to the loaf and the pewter teapot, the child, silent and quivering, playing with glass beads, the house, empty, it seemed, or exposed to the winter night, as if it had no walls.

Sometimes there sounded, long and remote in the house, vibrating through everything, the moaning cry of a woman in labor. Brangwen, sitting downstairs, was divided. His lower, deeper self was with her, bound to her, suffering. But the big shell of his body remembered the sound of owls that used to fly round the farmstead when he was a boy. He was back in his youth, a boy, haunted by the sound of the owls, waking up his brother to speak to him. And his mind drifted away to the birds, their solemn, dignified faces, their flight so soft and broad-winged. And then to the birds his brother had shot, fluffy, dust-colored, dead heaps of softness with faces absurdly asleep. It was a queer thing, a dead owl.

He lifted his cup to his lips, he watched the child with the beads. But his mind was occupied with owls, and the atmosphere of his boyhood, with his brothers and sisters. Elsewhere, fundamental, he was with his wife in labor, the child was being brought forth out of their one flesh. He and she, one flesh, out of which life must be put forth. The rent was not in his body, but it was of his body. On her the blows fell, but the quiver ran through to him, to his last fiber. She must be torn asunder for life to come forth, yet still they were one flesh, and still, from further back, the life came out of him to her, and still he was the unbroken that has the broken rock in its arms, their flesh was one rock from which the life gushed, out of her who was smitten and rent, from him who quivered and yielded.

He went upstairs to her. As he came to the bedside she spoke to him in Polish.

1. Tom Brangwen, a Nottinghamshire farmer, married Lydia Lensky, widow of a Polish émigré doctor. Anna is Lydia's child by her first marriage. The scene is Marsh Farm, a few miles south of East- wood, where Lawrence was born, and just across the Nottinghamshire-Derbyshire border from the town of Ilkeston where Lawrence trained as a teacher. Lydia is about to have her first child by Tom.

"Is it very bad?" he asked.

She looked at him, and oh, the weariness to her, of the effort to understand another language, the weariness of hearing him, attending to him, making out who he was, as he stood there fair-bearded and alien, looking at her. She knew something of him, of his eyes. But she could not grasp him. She closed her eyes.

He turned away, white to the gills.

"It's not so very bad," said the midwife.

He knew he was a strain on his wife. He went downstairs.

The child glanced up at him, frightened.

"I want my mother," she quavered.

"Ay, but she's badly," he said mildly, unheeding.

She looked at him with lost, frightened eyes.

"Has she got a headache?"

"No—she's going to have a baby."

The child looked round. He was unaware of her. She was alone again in terror.

"I want my mother," came the cry of panic.

"Let Tilly undress you," he said. "You're tired."

There was another silence. Again came the cry of labor.

"I want my mother," rang automatically from the wincing, panic-stricken child, that felt cut off and lost in a horror of desolation.

Tilly came forward, her heart wrung.

"Come an' let me undress her then, pet lamb," she crooned. "You s'll have your mother in th' mornin', don't you fret, my duckie; never mind, angel."

But Anna stood upon the sofa, her back to the wall.

"I want my mother," she cried, her little face quivering, and the great tears of childish, utter anguish falling.

"She's poorly, my lamb, she's poorly tonight, but she'll be better by mornin'. Oh, don't cry, don't cry, love, she doesn't want you to cry, precious little heart, no, she doesn't."

Tilly took gently hold of the child's skirts. Anna snatched back her dress, and cried, in a little hysteria:

"No, you're not to undress me—I want my mother,"—and her child's face was running with grief and tears, her body shaken.

"Oh, but let Tilly undress you. Let Tilly undress you, who loves you, don't be wilful tonight. Mother's poorly, she doesn't want you to cry."

The child sobbed distractedly, she could not hear.

"I want my mother," she wept.

"When you're undressed, you s'll go up to see your mother—when you're undressed, pet, when you've let Tilly undress you, when you're a little jewel in your nightie, love. Oh, don't you cry, don't you——"

Brangwen sat stiff in his chair. He felt his brain going tighter. He crossed over the room, aware only of the maddening sobbing.

"Don't make a noise," he said.

And a new fear shook the child from the sound of his voice. She cried mechanically, her eyes looking watchful through her tears, in terror, alert to what might happen.

"I want—my—mother," quavered the sobbing, blind voice.

A shiver of irritation went over the man's limbs. It was the utter, persistent unreason, the maddening blindness of the voice and the crying.

"You must come and be undressed," he said, in a quiet voice that was thin with anger.

And he reached his hand and grasped her. He felt her body catch in a convulsive sob. But he too was blind, and intent, irritated into mechanical action. He began to unfasten her little apron. She would have shrunk from him, but could not. So her small body remained in his grasp, while he fumbled at the little buttons and tapes, unthinking, intent, unaware of anything but the irritation of her. Her body was held taut and resistant, he pushed off the little dress and the petticoats, revealing the white arms. She kept stiff, overpowered, violated, he went on with his task. And all the while she sobbed, choking:

"I want my mother."

He was unheedingly silent, his face stiff. The child was now incapable of understanding, she had become a little, mechanical thing of fixed will. She wept, her body convulsed, her voice repeating the same cry.

"Eh, dear o' me!" cried Tilly, becoming distracted herself. Brangwen, slow, clumsy, blind, intent, got off all the little garments, and stood the child naked in its shift upon the sofa.

"Where's her nightie?" he asked.

Tilly brought it, and he put it on her. Anna did not move her limbs to his desire. He had to push them into place. She stood, with fixed, blind will, resistant, a small, convulsed, unchangeable thing weeping ever and repeating the same phrase. He lifted one foot after the other, pulled off slippers and socks. She was ready.

"Do you want a drink?" he asked.

She did not change. Unheeding, uncaring, she stood on the sofa, standing back, alone, her hands shut and half lifted, her face, all tears, raised and blind. And through the sobbing and choking came the broken:

"I—want—my—mother."

"Do you want a drink?" he said again.

There was no answer. He lifted the stiff, denying body between his hands. Its stiff blindness made a flash of rage go through him. He would like to break it.

He set the child on his knee, and sat again in his chair beside the fire, the wet, sobbing, inarticulate noise going on near his ear, the child sitting stiff, not yielding to him or anything, not aware.

A new degree of anger came over him. What did it all matter? What did it matter if the mother talked Polish and cried in labor, if this child were stiff with resistance, and crying? Why take it to heart? Let the mother cry in labor, let the child cry in resistance, since they would do so. Why should he fight against it, why resist? Let it be, if it were so. Let them be as they were, if they insisted.

And in a daze he sat, offering no fight. The child cried on, the minutes ticked away, a sort of torpor was on him.

It was some little time before he came to, and turned to attend to the child. He was shocked by her little wet, blinded face. A bit dazed, he pushed back the wet hair. Like a living statue of grief, her blind face cried on.

"Nay," he said, "not as bad as that. It's not as bad as that, Anna, my child. Come, what are you crying for so much? Come, stop now, it'll make you sick. I wipe you dry, don't wet your face any more. Don't cry any more wet tears, don't, it's better not to. Don't cry—it's not so bad as all that. Hush now, hush—let it be enough."

His voice was queer and distant and calm. He looked at the child. She was beside herself now. He wanted her to stop, he wanted it all to stop, to become natural.

"Come," he said, rising to turn away, "we'll go an' supper-up the beast."

He took a big shawl, folded her round, and went out into the kitchen for a lantern.

"You're never taking the child out, of a night like this," said Tilly.

"Ay, it'll quieten her," he answered.

It was raining. The child was suddenly still, shocked, finding the rain on its face, the darkness.

"We'll just give the cows their something-to-eat, afore they go to bed," Brangwen was saying to her, holding her close and sure.

There was a trickling of water into the butt, a burst of raindrops sputtering on to her shawl, and the light of the lantern swinging, flashing on a wet pavement and the base of a wet wall. Otherwise it was black darkness: one breathed darkness.

He opened the doors, upper and lower, and they entered into the high, dry barn, that smelled warm even if it were not warm. He hung the lantern on the nail and shut the door. They were in another world now. The light shed softly on the timbered barn, on the whitewashed walls, and the great heap of hay; instruments cast their shadows largely, a ladder rose to the dark arch of a loft. Outside there was the driving rain, inside, the softly illuminated stillness and calmness of the barn.

Holding the child on one arm, he set about preparing the food for the cows, filling a pan with chopped hay and brewer's grains and a little meal. The child, all wonder, watched what he did. A new being was created in her for the new conditions. Sometimes, a little spasm, eddying from the bygone storm of sobbing, shook her small body. Her eyes were wide and wondering, pathetic. She was silent, quite still.

In a sort of dream, his heart sunk to the bottom, leaving the surface of him still, quite still, he rose with the panful of food, carefully balancing the child on one arm, the pan in the other hand. The silky fringe of the shawl swayed softly, grains and hay trickled to the floor; he went along a dimly lit passage behind the mangers, where the horns of the cows pricked out of the obscurity. The child shrank, he balanced stiffly, rested the pan on the manger wall, and tipped out the food, half to this cow, half to the next. There was a noise of chains running, as the cows lifted or dropped their heads sharply; then a contented, soothing sound, a long snuffing as the beasts ate in silence.

The journey had to be performed several times. There was the rhythmic sound of the shovel in the barn, then the man returned walking stiffly between the two weights, the face of the child peering out from the shawl. Then the next time, as he stooped, she freed her arm and put it round his neck, clinging soft and warm, making all easier.

The beasts fed, he dropped the pan and sat down on a box, to arrange the child.

"Will the cows go to sleep now?" she said, catching her breath as she spoke.

"Yes."

"Will they eat all their stuff up first?"

"Yes. Hark at them."

And the two sat still listening to the snuffing and breathing of cows feeding in the sheds communicating with this small barn. The lantern shed a soft, steady light from one wall. All outside was still in the rain. He looked down at the silky folds of the paisley shawl. It reminded him of his mother. She used to go to church in it. He was back again in the old irresponsibility and security, a boy at home.

The two sat very quiet. His mind, in a sort of trance, seemed to become more and more vague. He held the child close to him. A quivering little shudder, re-echoing from her sobbing, went down her limbs. He held her closer. Gradually she relaxed, the eyelids began to sink over her dark, watchful eyes. As she sank to sleep, his mind became blank.

When he came to, as if from sleep, he seemed to be sitting in a timeless stillness. What was he listening for? He seemed to be listening for some sound a long way off, from beyond life. He remembered his wife. He must go back to her. The child was asleep, the eyelids not quite shut, showing a slight film of black pupil between. Why did she not shut her eyes? Her mouth was also a little open.

He rose quickly and went back to the house.

"Is she asleep?" whispered Tilly.

He nodded. The servant woman came to look at the child who slept in the shawl, with cheeks flushed hot and red, and a whiteness, a wanness round the eyes.

"God-a-mercy!" whispered Tilly, shaking her head.

He pushed off his boots and went upstairs with the child. He became aware of the anxiety grasped tight at his heart, because of his wife. But he remained still. The house was silent save for the wind outside, and the noisy trickling and splattering of water in the water butts. There was a slit of light under his wife's door.

He put the child into bed wrapped as she was in the shawl, for the sheets would be cold. Then he was afraid that she might not be able to move her arms, so he loosened her. The black eyes opened, rested on him vacantly, sank shut again. He covered her up. The last little quiver from the sobbing shook her breathing.

This was his room, the room he had had before he married. It was familiar. He remembered what it was to be a young man, untouched.

He remained suspended. The child slept, pushing her small fists from the shawl. He could tell the woman her child was asleep. But he must go to the other landing. He started. There was the sound of the owls—the moaning of the woman. What an uncanny sound! It was not human—at least to a man.

He went down to her room, entering softly. She was lying still, with eyes shut, pale, tired. His heart leapt, fearing she was dead. Yet he knew perfectly well she was not. He saw the way her hair went loose over her temples, her mouth was shut with suffering in a sort of grin. She was beautiful to him—but it was not human. He had a dread of her as she lay there. What had she to do with him? She was other than himself.

Something made him go and touch her fingers that were still grasped on the sheet. Her brown-gray eyes opened and looked at him. She did not know him as himself. But she knew him as the man. She looked at him as a woman in childbirth looks at the man who begot the child in her: an impersonal look, in the extreme hour, female to male. Her eyes closed again. A great, scalding peace went over him, burning his heart and his entrails, passing off into the infinite.

When her pains began afresh, tearing her, he turned aside, and could not look. But his heart in torture was at peace, his bowels were glad. He went downstairs, and to the door, outside, lifted his face to the rain, and felt the darkness striking unseen and steadily upon him.

The swift, unseen threshing of the night upon him silenced him and he was overcome. He turned away indoors, humbly. There was the infinite world, eternal, unchanging, as well as the world of life.

1912–14   1915

From Women in Love

Chapter XVIII. Rabbit[1]

Gudrun knew that it was a critical thing for her to go to Shortlands. She knew it was equivalent to accepting Gerald Crich as a lover. And though she hung back, disliking the condition, yet she knew she would go on. She equivocated. She said to herself, in torment recalling the blow and the kiss, "After all, what is it? What is a kiss? What even is a blow? It is an instant, vanished at once. I can go to Shortlands just for a time, before I go away, if only to see what it is like." For she had an insatiable curiosity to see and to know everything.

She also wanted to know what Winifred was really like. Having heard the child calling from the steamer in the night, she felt some mysterious connection with her.

Gudrun talked with the father in the library. Then he sent for his daughter. She came accompanied by Mademoiselle.

"Winnie, this is Miss Brangwen, who will be so kind as to help you with your drawing and making models of your animals," said the father.

The child looked at Gudrun for a moment with interest, before she came forward, and with face averted offered her hand. There was a complete *sang froid* and indifference under Winifred's childish reserve, a certain irresponsible callousness.

"How do you do?" said the child, not lifting her face.

"How do you do?" said Gudrun.

Then Winifred stood aside, and Gudrun was introduced to Mademoiselle.

1. Anna (of *The Rainbow*) eventually married her stepfather's nephew Will Brangwen. *Women in Love* is largely the story of Anna and Will's two daughters Ursula and Gudrun and their attempts to establish successful relationships with their lovers Rupert Birkin and Gerald Crich respectively. As this chapter opens Gudrun, on the brink of a serious love affair with Gerald, has accepted an invitation from Gerald's father to stay at Shortlands, the Criches' luxurious home, in order to tutor Gerald's younger sister Winifred.

"You have a fine day for your walk," said Mademoiselle, in a bright manner.

"*Quite* fine," said Gudrun.

Winifred was watching from her distance. She was as if amused, but rather unsure as yet what this new person was like. She saw so many new persons, and so few who became real to her. Mademoiselle was of no count whatever, the child merely put up with her, calmly and easily, accepting her little authority with faint scorn, compliant out of childish arrogance of indifference.

"Well, Winifred," said the father, "aren't you glad Miss Brangwen has come? She makes animals and birds in wood and in clay, that the people in London write about in the papers, praising them to the skies."

Winifred smiled slightly.

"Who told you, Daddie?" she asked.

"Who told me? Hermione told me, and Rupert Birkin."

"Do you know them?" Winifred asked of Gudrun, turning to her with faint challenge.

"Yes," said Gudrun.

Winifred readjusted herself a little. She had been ready to accept Gudrun as a sort of servant. Now she saw it was on terms of friendship they were intended to meet. She was rather glad. She had so many half inferiors, whom she tolerated with perfect good-humor.

Gudrun was very calm. She also did not take these things very seriously. A new occasion was mostly spectacular to her. However, Winifred was a detached, ironic child, she would never attach herself. Gudrun liked her and was intrigued by her. The first meetings went off with a certain humiliating clumsiness. Neither Winifred nor her instructress had any social grace.

Soon, however, they met in a kind of make-believe world. Winifred did not notice human beings unless they were like herself, playful and slightly mocking. She would accept nothing but the world of amusement, and the serious people of her life were the animals she had for pets. On those she lavished, almost ironically, her affection and her companionship. To the rest of the human scheme she submitted with a faint bored indifference.

She had a Pekinese dog called Looloo, which she loved.

"Let us draw Looloo," said Gudrun, "and see if we can get his Looliness, shall we?"

"Darling!" cried Winifred, rushing to the dog, that sat with contemplative sadness on the hearth, and kissing its bulging brow. "Darling one, will you be drawn? Shall its mummy draw its portrait?" Then she chuckled gleefully, and turning to Gudrun, said: "Oh, let's!"

They proceeded to get pencils and paper, and were ready.

"Beautifullest," cried Winifred, hugging the dog, "sit still while its mummy draws its beautiful portrait." The dog looked up at her with grievous resignation in its large, prominent eyes. She kissed it fervently, and said: "I wonder what mine will be like. It's sure to be awful."

As she sketched she chuckled to herself, and cried out at times: "Oh, darling, you're so beautiful!"

And again chuckling, she rushed to embrace the dog, in penitence, as if she were doing him some subtle injury. He sat all the time with the resignation and fretfulness of ages on his dark velvety face. She drew slowly, with a wicked concentration in her eyes, her head on one side, an intense stillness over her. She was as if working the spell of some enchantment. Suddenly she had finished. She looked at the dog, and then at her drawing, and then cried, with real grief for the dog, and at the same time with wicked exultation:

"My beautiful, why did they?"

She took her paper to the dog, and held it under his nose. He turned his head aside as in chagrin and mortification, and she impulsively kissed his velvety bulging forehead.

"'S a Loolie, 's a little Loozie! Look at his portrait, darling, look at his portrait, that his mother has done of him." She looked at her paper and chuckled. Then, kissing the dog once more, she rose and came gravely to Gudrun, offering her the paper.

It was a grotesque little diagram of a grotesque little animal, so wicked and so comical, a slow smile came over Gudrun's face, unconsciously. And at her side Winifred chuckled with glee, and said: "It isn't like him, is it? He's much lovelier than that. He's *so* beautiful—mmm, Looloo, my sweet darling." And she flew off to embrace the chagrined little dog. He looked up at her with reproachful, saturnine eyes, vanquished in his extreme agedness of being. Then she flew back to her drawing, and chuckled with satisfaction.

"It isn't like him, is it?" she said to Gudrun.

"Yes, it's very like him," Gudrun replied.

The child treasured her drawing, carried it about with her, and showed it, with a silent embarrassment, to everybody.

"Look," she said, thrusting the paper into her father's hand.

"Why, that's Looloo!" he exclaimed. And he looked down in surprise, hearing the almost inhuman chuckle of the child at his side.

Gerald was away from home when Gudrun first came to Shortlands. But the first morning he came back he watched for her. It was a sunny, soft morning, and he lingered in the garden paths, looking at the flowers that had come out during his absence. He was clean and fit as ever, shaven, his fair hair scrupulously parted at the side, bright in the sunshine, his short, fair moustache closely clipped, his eyes with their humorous kind twinkle, which was so deceptive. He was dressed in black, his clothes sat well on his well-nourished body. Yet as he lingered before the flower-beds in the morning sunshine, there was a certain isolation, a fear about him, as of something wanting.

Gudrun came up quickly, unseen. She was dressed in blue, with woolen yellow stockings, like the Bluecoat boys.[2] He glanced up in surprise. Her stockings always disconcerted him, the pale-yellow stockings and the heavy, heavy black shoes. Winifred, who had been playing about the garden with Mademoiselle and the dogs, came flitting towards Gudrun. The child wore a dress of black-and-white stripes. Her hair was rather short, cut round and hanging level in her neck.

"We're going to do Bismarck, aren't we?" she said, linking her hand through Gudrun's arm.

"Yes, we're going to do Bismarck. Do you want to?"

"Oh yes—oh, I do! I want most awfully to do Bismarck. He looks *so* splendid this morning, so *fierce*. He's almost as big as a lion." And the child chuckled sardonically at her own hyperbole. "He's a real king, he really is."

"Bonjour, Mademoiselle," said the little French governess, wavering up with a slight bow, a bow of the sort that Gudrun loathed, insolent.

"Winifred veut tant faire le portrait de Bismarck——! Oh, mais toute la matinée—'We will do Bismarck this morning!'—Bismarck, Bismarck, toujours Bismarck! C'est un lapin, n'est-ce pas, mademoiselle?"

"Oui, c'est un grand lapin blanc et noir. Vous ne l'avez pas vu?" said Gudrun in her good, but rather heavy French.

"Non, mademoiselle, Winifred n'a jamais voulu me le faire voir. Tant de fois je le lui ai demandé, 'Qu'est ce donc que ce Bismarck, Winifred?' Mais elle n'a pas voulu me le dire. Son Bismarck, c'était un mystère."

"Oui, c'est un mystère, vraiment un mystère! Miss Brangwen, say that Bismarck is a mystery," cried Winifred.

"Bismarck is a mystery, Bismarck, c'est un mystère, der Bismarck, er ist ein Wunder," said Gudrun, in mocking incantation.

"Ja, er ist ein Wunder," repeated Winifred, with odd seriousness, under which lay a wicked chuckle.

"Ist er auch ein Wunder?" came the slightly insolent sneering of Mademoiselle.

"Doch!" said Winifred briefly, indifferent.

"Doch ist er nicht ein König. Beesmarck, he was not a king,

2. The boys at Christ's Hospital (a secondary school) wear a traditional uniform of blue gowns and yellow stockings.

2540 · *D. H. Lawrence*

Winifred, as you have said. He was only—il n'était que chancelier."

"Qu'est ce qu'un chancelier?"[3] said Winifred, with slightly contemptuous indifference.

"A chancelier is a chancellor, and a chancellor is, I believe, a sort of judge," said Gerald, coming up and shaking hands with Gudrun. "You'll have made a song of Bismarck soon," said he.

Mademoiselle waited, and discreetly made her inclination, and her greeting.

"So they wouldn't let you see Bismarck, Mademoiselle?" he said.

"Non, Monsieur."

"Ay, very mean of them. What are you going to do to him, Miss Brangwen? I want him sent to the kitchen and cooked."

"Oh no," cried Winifred.

"We're going to draw him," said Gudrun.

"Draw him and quarter him and dish him up," he said, being purposely fatuous.

"Oh no," cried Winifred with emphasis, chuckling.

Gudrun detected the tang of mockery in him, and she looked up and smiled into his face. He felt his nerves caressed. Their eyes met in knowledge.

"How do you like Shortlands?" he asked.

"Oh, very much," she said, with nonchalance.

"Glad you do. Have you noticed these flowers?"

He led her along the path. She followed intently. Winifred came, and the governess lingered in the rear. They stopped before some veined salpiglossis flowers.

"Aren't they wonderful?" she cried, looking at them absorbedly. Strange how her reverential, almost ecstatic admiration of the flowers caressed his nerves. She stooped down, and touched the trumpets, with infinitely fine and delicate-touching finger tips. It filled him with ease to see her. When she rose, her eyes, hot with the beauty of the flowers, looked into his.

"What are they?" she asked.

"Sort of petunia, I suppose," he answered. "I don't really know them."

"They are quite strangers to me," she said.

They stood together in a false intimacy, a nervous contact. And he was in love with her.

She was aware of Mademoiselle standing near, like a little

---

3. "Winifred wants so much to do a portrait of Bismarck——! Oh, but all morning * * * Bismarck, Bismarck, always Bismarck! He's a rabbit, isn't he, mademoiselle?" "Yes, he's a big white-and-black rabbit. Haven't you seen him?" * * * "No, mademoiselle, Winifred has never wanted to have me see him. I've so often asked her, 'What is this Bismarck, then, Winifred?' But she wouldn't tell me. Her Bismarck remained a mystery." "Yes, he's a mystery, truly a mystery! * * *" "Bismarck is a mystery, Bismarck is a mystery, Bismarck is a marvel," * * * "Yes, he is a marvel," * * * "Is he a marvel, too?" * * * "Indeed!" * * * "But he is not a king * * *—he was only chancellor." "What is a chancellor?"

French beetle, observant and calculating. She moved away with Winifred, saying they would go to find Bismarck.

Gerald watched them go, looking all the while at the soft, full, still body of Gudrun, in its silky cashmere. How silky and rich and soft her body must be. An excess of appreciation came over his mind, she was the all-desirable, the all-beautiful. He wanted only to come to her, nothing more. He was only this, this being that should come to her, and be given to her.

At the same time he was finely and acutely aware of Mademoiselle's neat, brittle finality of form. She was like some elegant beetle with thin ankles, perched on her high heels, her glossy black dress perfectly correct, her dark hair done high and admirably. How repulsive her completeness and her finality was! He loathed her.

Yet he did admire her. She was perfectly correct. And it did rather annoy him, that Gudrun came dressed in startling colors, like a macaw, when the family was in mourning. Like a macaw she was! He watched the lingering way she took her feet from the ground. And her ankles were pale yellow, and her dress a deep blue. Yet it pleased him. It pleased him very much. He felt the challenge in her very attire—she challenged the whole world. And he smiled as to the note of a trumpet.

Gudrun and Winifred went through the house to the back, where were the stables and the outbuildings. Everywhere was still and deserted. Mr. Crich had gone out for a short drive, the stableman had just led round Gerald's horse. The two girls went to the hutch that stood in a corner, and looked at the great black-and-white rabbit.

"Isn't he beautiful! Oh, do look at him listening! Doesn't he look silly!" she laughed quickly, then added: "Oh, do let's do him listening, do let us, he listens with so much of himself;—don't you, darling Bismarck?"

"Can we take him out?" said Gudrun.

"He's very strong. He really is extremely strong." She looked at Gudrun, her head on one side, in odd calculating mistrust.

"But we'll try, shall we?"

"Yes, if you like. But he's a fearful kicker!"

They took the key to unlock the door. The rabbit exploded in a wild rush round the hutch.

"He scratches most awfully sometimes," cried Winifred in excitement. "Oh, do look at him, isn't he wonderful!" The rabbit tore round the hutch in a flurry. "Bismarck!" cried the child, in rousing excitement. "How *dreadful* you are! You are beastly." Winifred looked up at Gudrun with some misgiving in her wild excitement. Gudrun smiled sardonically with her mouth. Winifred made a strange crooning noise of unaccountable excitement. "Now he's still!" she cried, seeing the rabbit settled down in a far corner of the hutch. "Shall we take him now?" she whispered excitedly, mysteriously, looking up at Gudrun and edging very close. "Shall we get him now?——" she chuckled wickedly to herself.

They unlocked the door of the hutch. Gudrun thrust in her arm and seized the great, lusty rabbit as it crouched still, she grasped its long ears. It set its four feet flat, and thrust back. There was a long scraping sound as it was hauled forward, and in another instant it was in mid-air, lunging wildly, its body flying like a spring coiled and released, as it lashed out, suspended from the ears. Gudrun held the black-and-white tempest at arms' length, averting her face. But the rabbit was magically strong, it was all she could do to keep her grasp. She almost lost her presence of mind.

"Bismarck, Bismarck, you are behaving terribly," said Winifred in a rather frightened voice. "Oh, do put him down, he's beastly."

Gudrun stood for a moment astounded by the thunderstorm that had sprung into being in her grip. Then her color came up, a heavy rage came over her like a cloud. She stood shaken as a house in a storm, and utterly overcome. Her heart was arrested with fury at the mindlessness and the bestial stupidity of this struggle, her wrists were badly scored by the claws of the beast, a heavy cruelty welled up in her.

Gerald came round as she was trying to capture the flying rabbit under her arm. He saw, with subtle recognition, her sullen passion of cruelty.

"You should let one of the men do that for you," he said, hurrying up.

"Oh, he's *so* horrid!" cried Winifred, almost frantic.

He held out his nervous, sinewy hand and took the rabbit by the ears from Gudrun.

"It's most *fearfully* strong," she cried in a high voice, like the crying of a seagull, strange and vindictive.

The rabbit made itself into a ball in the air and lashed out, flinging itself into a bow. It really seemed demoniacal. Gudrun saw Gerald's body tighten, saw a sharp blindness come into his eyes.

"I know these beggars of old," he said.

The long, demon-like beast lashed out again, spread on the air as if it were flying, looking something like a dragon, then closing up again, inconceivably powerful and explosive. The man's body, strung to its efforts, vibrated strongly. Then a sudden sharp, white-edged wrath came up in him. Swift as lightning he drew back and brought his free hand down like a hawk on the neck of the rabbit. Simultaneously, there came the unearthly abhorrent scream of a rabbit in the fear of death. It made one immense writhe, tore his wrists and his sleeves in a final convulsion, all its belly flashed white in a whirlwind of paws, and then he had slung it round and had it under his arm, fast. It cowered and skulked. His face was gleaming with a smile.

"You wouldn't think there was all that force in a rabbit," he said, looking at Gudrun. And he saw her eyes black as night in her pallid face, she looked almost unearthly. The scream of the rabbit, after the violent tussle, seemed to have torn the veil of her consciousness. He looked at her, and the whitish, electric gleam in his face intensified.

"I don't really like him," Winifred was crooning. "I don't care for him as I do for Loozie. He's hateful really."

A smile twisted Gudrun's face as she recovered. She knew she was revealed.

"Don't they make the most fearful noise when they scream?" she cried, the high note in her voice like a seagull's cry.

"Abominable," he said.

"He shouldn't be so silly when he has to be taken out," Winifred was saying, putting out her hand and touching the rabbit tentatively, as it skulked under his arm, motionless as if it were dead.

"He's not dead, is he, Gerald?" she asked.

"No, he ought to be," he said.

"Yes, he ought!" cried the child, with a sudden flush of amusement. And she touched the rabbit with more confidence. "His heart is beating so fast. Isn't he funny? He really is."

"Where do you want him?" asked Gerald.

"In the little green court," she said.

Gudrun looked at Gerald with strange, darkened eyes, strained with underworld knowledge, almost supplicating, like those of a creature which is at his mercy, yet which is his ultimate victor. He did not know what to say to her. He felt the mutual hellish recognition. And he felt he ought to say something to cover it. He had the power of lightning in his nerves, she seemed like a soft recipient of his magical, hideous white fire. He was unconfident, he had qualms of fear.

"Did he hurt you?" he asked.

"No," she said.

"He's an insensible beast," he said, turning his face away.

They came to the little court, which was shut in by old red walls in whose crevices wallflowers were growing. The grass was soft and fine and old, a level floor carpeting the court, the sky was blue overhead. Gerald tossed the rabbit down. It crouched still and would not move. Gudrun watched it with faint horror.

"Why doesn't it move?" she cried.

"It's skulking," he said.

She looked up at him, and a slight sinister smile contracted her white face.

"Isn't it a *fool!*" she cried. "Isn't it a sickening *fool?*" The vindictive mockery in her voice made his brain quiver. Glancing up at him, into his eyes, she revealed again the mocking, white-cruel recognition. There was a league between them, abhorrent to them both. They were implicated with each other in abhorrent mysteries.

"How many scratches have you?" he asked, showing his hard forearm, white and hard and torn in red gashes.

"How really vile!" she cried, flushing with a sinister vision. "Mine is nothing."

She lifted her arm and showed a deep red score down the silken white flesh.

"What a devil!" he exclaimed. But it was as if he had had knowledge of her in the long red rent of her forearm, so silken and soft. He did not want to touch her. He would have to make himself touch her, deliberately. The long, shallow red rip seemed torn across his own brain, tearing the surface of his ultimate consciousness, letting through the forever unconscious, unthinkable red ether of the beyond, the obscene beyond.

"It doesn't hurt you very much, does it?" he asked, solicitous.

"Not at all," she cried.

And suddenly the rabbit, which had been crouching as if it were a flower, so still and soft, suddenly burst into life. Round and round the court it went, as if shot from a gun, round and round like a furry meteorite, in a tense hard circle that seemed to bind their brains. They all stood in amazement, smiling uncannily, as if the rabbit were obeying some unknown incantation. Round and round it flew, on the grass under the old red walls like a storm.

And then quite suddenly it settled down, hobbled among the grass, and sat considering, its nose twitching like a bit of fluff in the wind. After having considered for a few minutes, a soft bunch with a black, open eye, which perhaps was looking at them, perhaps was not, it hobbled calmly forward and began to nibble the grass with that mean motion of a rabbit's quick eating.

"It's mad," said Gudrun. "It is most decidedly mad."

He laughed.

"The question is," he said, "what is madness? I don't suppose it is rabbit-mad."

"Don't you think it is?" she asked.

"No. That's what it is to be a rabbit."

There was a queer, faint, obscene smile over his face. She looked at him and saw him, and knew that he was initiate as she was initiate. This thwarted her, and contravened her, for the moment.

"God be praised we aren't rabbits," she said in a high, shrill voice.

The smile intensified a little on his face.

"Not rabbits?" he said, looking at her fixedly.

Slowly her face relaxed into a smile of obscene recognition.

"Ah, Gerald," she said in a strong, slow, almost manlike way. "—All that, and more." Her eyes looked up at him with shocking nonchalance.

He felt again as if she had hit him across the face—or rather as if she had torn him across the breast, dully, finally. He turned aside.

"Eat, eat, my darling!" Winifred was softly conjuring the rabbit, and creeping forward to touch it. It hobbled away from her. "Let its mother stroke its fur then, darling, because it is so mysterious——"

1916   1920

From Etruscan Places

Tarquinia[1]

In Cerveteri there is nowhere to sleep, so the only thing to do is to go back to Rome, or forwards to Cività Vecchia. The bus landed us at the station of Palo at about five o'clock: in the midst of nowhere: to meet the Rome train. But we were going on to Tarquinia, not back to Rome, so we must wait two hours, till seven.

In the distance we could see the concrete villas and new houses of what was evidently Ladispoli, a seaside place, some two miles away. So we set off to walk to Ladispoli, on the flat sea road. On the left, in the wood that forms part of the great park, the nightingales had already begun to whistle, and looking over the wall one could see many little rose-colored cyclamens glowing on the earth in the evening light.

We walked on, and the Rome train came surging round the bend. It misses Ladispoli, whose two miles of branch line runs only in the hot bathing months. As we neared the first ugly villas on the road the ancient wagonette drawn by the ancient white horse, both

---

1. Long before 1927, when Lawrence made his Etruscan journey with his American friend Earl Brewster, he had been interested in the Etruscans and their art. The Etruscans were the most important of the pre-Roman inhabitants of Italy; they spread out from their original territory (modern Tuscany, region in Central Italy) to dominate about a third of Italy, but were in their turn conquered by the Romans. Scholars are still uncertain about the precise identity of the Etruscans, and inscriptions in their language have never been deciphered. Of their twelve cities, Lawrence visited and describes Caere (modern Cervetri, Cerveteri), Tarquinii (later Corneto Tarquinia, now Tarquinia), Vulci (modern Volci), Volaterrae (modern Volterra). Tarquinia is some fifty miles northwest of Rome, up the Italian west coast, and the Italian towns mentioned by Lawrence in this essay are in this area of Italy: Cività Vecchia is north of Rome, about half way between Rome and Tarquinia, on the coast.

looking sun-bitten almost to ghostliness, clattered past. It just beat us.

Ladispoli is one of those ugly little places on the Roman coast, consisting of new concrete villas, new concrete hotels, kiosks, and bathing establishments; bareness and non-existence for ten months in the year, seething solid with fleshy bathers in July and August. Now it was deserted, quite deserted, save for two or three officials and four wild children.

B. and I lay on the gray-black lava sand, by the flat, low sea, over which the sky, gray and shapeless, emitted a flat, wan evening light. Little waves curled green out of the sea's dark grayness, from the curious low flatness of the water. It is a peculiarly forlorn coast, the sea peculiarly flat and sunken, lifeless-looking, the land as if it had given its last gasp, and was now forever inert.

Yet this is the Tyrrhenian sea of the Etruscans, where their shipping spread sharp sails, and beat the sea with slave-oars, roving in from Greece and Sicily, Sicily of the Greek tyrants; from Cumae, the city of the old Greek colony of Campania, where the province of Naples now is; and from Elba, where the Etruscans mined their iron ore. The Etruscans sailed the seas. They are even said to have come by sea, from Lydia in Asia Minor, at some date far back in the dim mists before the eighth century B.C. But that a whole people, even a whole host, sailed in the tiny ships of those days, all at once, to people a sparsely peopled central Italy, seems hard to imagine. Probably ships did come—even before Ulysses. Probably men landed on the strange flat coast, and made camps, and then treated with the natives. Whether the newcomers were Lydians or Hittites with hair curled in a roll behind, or men from Mycenae or Crete, who knows. Perhaps men of all these sorts came, in batches. For in Homeric days a restlessness seems to have possessed the Mediterranean basin, and ancient races began shaking ships like seeds over the sea. More people than Greeks, or Hellenes, or Indo-Germanic groups, were on the move.[2]

2. Lawrence is casting his mind's eye over the Tyrrhenian Sea, which is that very roughly circular area of the Mediterranean bounded on the east by the west coast of Italy, on the south by Sicily, and on the west by the islands of Sardinia and Corsica, with the little island of Elba lying between Corsica and the Italian mainland. On this sea the Etruscans plied their trade, sailing south to Sicily, which had been colonized by Greece from the 8th century B.C. and where in the 5th and 6th centuries B.C., under the Greek tyrants Hippocrates of Gela, Gelon, and Hieron, Greek civilization in Sicily reached its peak. The Greeks colonized not only Sicily but part of the mainland of Italy, notably the fertile region of Campania (lying be- tween the Appenines and the Tyrrhenian Sea) with its city of Cumae, the first Greek colony in Italy. Etruscan forces in Campania were crushed by the forces of Cumae, aided by those of the Greek Sicilian colony Syracuse, in 474 B.C. Lawrence then extends his vision further east, where he speculates the Etruscans might have come from—perhaps from Lydia, the territory in Asia Minor which dominated trade routes both eastward to the Orient and westward to Greece and Italy, a great entrepot of trade in the ancient Mediterranean world, a pioneer in music, and the first state to use coined money. The Hittites were an ancient people in Asia Minor (c. 2000 to 1200 B.C.). Mycenae is one of the most ancient of Greek cities some fourteen miles south-

But whatever little ships were run ashore on the soft, deep, gray-black volcanic sand of this coast, three thousand years ago, and earlier, their mariners certainly did not find those hills inland empty of people. If the Lydians or Hittites pulled up their long little two-eyed ships on to the beach, and made a camp behind a bank, in shelter from the wet strong wind, what natives came down curiously to look at them? For natives there were, of that we may be certain. Even before the fall of Troy, before even Athens was dreamed of, there were natives here. And they had huts on the hills, thatched huts in clumsy groups most probably; with patches of grain, and flocks of goats and probably cattle. Probably it was like coming on an old Irish village, or a village in the Scottish Hebrides in Prince Charlie's day,[3] to come upon a village of these Italian aborigines, by the Tyrrhenian sea, three thousand years ago. But by the time Etruscan history starts in Caere, some eight centuries B.C., there was certainly more than a village on the hill. There was a native city, of that we may be sure; and a busy spinning of linen and beating of gold, long before the Regolini-Galassi tomb was built.[4]

However that may be, somebody came, and somebody was already here, of that we may be certain, and, in the first place, none of them were Greeks or Hellenes. It was the days before Rome rose up: probably when the first comers arrived it was the days even before Homer. The newcomers, whether they were few or many, seem to have come from the east, Asia Minor or Crete or Cyprus. They were, we must feel, of an old, primitive Mediterranean and Asiatic or Aegean stock. The twilight of the beginning of our history was the nightfall of some previous history, which will never be written. Pelasgian is but a shadow-word.[5] But Hittite and Minoan, Lydian, Carian, Etruscan, these words emerge from shadow, and perhaps from one and the same great shadow come the peoples to whom the names belong.

---

west of Corinth. Crete is the Mediterranean island (southeast of Greece and southwest of Asia Minor) colonized by Greeks after an earlier flourishing Bronze Age culture. It was a great center of commerce. Lawrence's history is perhaps vague here, as he imagines ancient peoples migrating across the Mediterranean. The phrase "Homeric days" can have little specific meaning, for the Homeric poems deal with the siege of Troy (mid-13th century B.C.) but are the result of centuries of oral poetry composed, recited and transmitted by later professional bards living in a very different civilization from that of Troy and its age, and were finally written down in a third and still more different phase of civilization some time between the late 9th and early 7th centuries B.C. The Hellenes are the ancient Greeks. Indo-Germanic (more usually, Indo-European) is not a term for a race, but for a group of languages (which include the Greek, Italic, Celtic, Germanic, and Slavic).

3. Prince Charles Edward led his unsuccessful Jacobite rebellion in 1745.

4. The most important of the ancient Etruscan tombs in the necropolis in the hill to the northwest of Caere (Cervetri), dating from around the mid-7th century B.C. The name comes from the tomb's discoverers.

5. Pelasgians are mentioned by Homer as Trojan allies "from afar," and the name came to be used by the Greeks to denote the aboriginal inhabitants of Greece. All accounts of the Pelasgians which we have are legendary and modern scholars have come to no certain conclusion about their identity.

The Etruscan civilization seems a shoot, perhaps the last, from the prehistoric Mediterranean world, and the Etruscans, newcomers and aborigines alike, probably belonged to that ancient world, though they were of different nations and levels of culture. Later, of course, the Greeks exerted a great influence. But that is another matter.

Whatever happened, the newcomers in ancient central Italy found many natives flourishing in possession of the land. These aboriginals, now ridiculously called Villanovans, were neither wiped out nor suppressed. Probably they welcomed the strangers, whose pulse was not hostile to their own. Probably the more highly developed religion of the newcomers was not hostile to the primitive religion of the aborigines; no doubt the two religions had the same root. Probably the aborigines formed willingly a sort of religious aristocracy from the newcomers; the Italians might almost do the same today. And so the Etruscan world arose. But it took centuries to arise. Etruria was not a colony, it was a slowly developed country.

There was never an Etruscan nation: only, in historical times, a great league of tribes or nations using the Etruscan language and the Etruscan script—at least officially—and uniting in their religious feeling and observances. The Etruscan alphabet seems to have been borrowed from the old Greeks, apparently from the Chalcidians of Cumae—the Greek colony just north of where Naples now is. But the Etruscan language is not akin to any of the Greek dialects, nor, apparently, to the Italic. But we don't know. It is probably to a great extent the language of the old aboriginals of southern Etruria, just as the religion is in all probability basically aboriginal, belonging to some vast old religion of the prehistoric world. From the shadow of the prehistoric world emerge dying religions that have not yet invented gods or goddesses, but live by the mystery of the elemental powers in the Universe, the complex vitalities of what we feebly call Nature. And the Etruscan religion was certainly one of these. The gods and goddesses don't seem to have emerged in any sharp definiteness.

But it is not for me to make assertions. Only, that which half emerges from the dim background of time is strangely stirring; and after having read all the learned suggestions, most of them contradicting one another; and then having looked sensitively at the tombs and the Etruscan things that are left, one must accept one's own resultant feeling.

Ships came along this low, inconspicuous sea, coming up from the Near East, we should imagine, even in the days of Solomon—even, maybe, in the days of Abraham.[6] And they kept on coming.

6. The age of the Old Testament patriarchs cannot be certainly dated: probably between the 18th and 16th centuries B.C. (the second quarter of the 2nd millennium B.C.). King Solomon reigned over Israel in the 10th century B.C.

As the light of history dawns and brightens, we see them winging along with their white or scarlet sails. Then, as the Greeks came crowding into colonies in Italy, and the Phoenicians began to exploit the western Mediterranean, we begin to hear of the silent Etruscans, and to see them.

Just north of here Caere founded a port called Pyrgi, and we know that the Greek vessels flocked in, with vases and stuffs and colonists coming from Hellas or from Magna Graecia, and that Phoenician ships came rowing sharply, over from Sardinia, up from Carthage, round from Tyre and Sidon; while the Etruscans had their own fleets, built of timber from the mountains, caulked with pitch from northern Volterra, fitted with sails from Tarquinia, filled with wheat from the bountiful plains, or with the famous Etruscan articles of bronze and iron, which they carried away to Corinth or to Athens or to the ports of Asia Minor. We know of the great and finally disastrous sea-battles with the Phoenicians and the tyrant of Syracuse. And we know that the Etruscans, all except those of Caere, became ruthless pirates, almost like the Moors and the Barbary corsairs later on. This was part of their viciousness, a great annoyance to their loving and harmless neighbors, the law-abiding Romans—who believed in the supreme law of conquest.

However, all this is long ago. The very coast has changed since then. The smitten sea has sunk and fallen back, and weary land has emerged when, apparently, it didn't want to, and the flowers of the coastline are miserable bathing places such as Ladispoli and seaside Ostia, desecration put upon desolation, to the triumphant trump of the mosquito.

The wind blew flat and almost chill from the darkening sea, the dead waves lifted small bits of pure green out of the leaden grayness, under the leaden sky. We got up from the dark gray but soft sand, and went back along the road to the station, peered at by the few people and officials who were holding the place together till the next bathers came.

At the station there was general desertedness. But our things still lay untouched in a dark corner of the buffet, and the man gave us a decent little meal of cold meats and wine and oranges. It was already night. The train came rushing in, punctually.

It is an hour or more to Città Vecchia, which is a port of not much importance, except that from here the regular steamer sails to Sardinia. We gave our things to a friendly old porter, and told him to take us to the nearest hotel. It was night, very dark as we emerged from the station.

And a fellow came furtively shouldering up to me.

"You are foreigners, aren't you?"

"Yes."

"What nationality?"

"English."

"You have your permission to reside in Italy—or your passport?"

"My passport I have—what do you want?"

"I want to look at your passport."

"It's in the valise! And why? Why is this?"

"This is a port, and we must examine the papers of foreigners."

"And why? Genoa is a port, and no one dreams of asking for papers."

I was furious. He made no answer. I told the porter to go on to the hotel, and the fellow furtively followed at our side, half-a-pace to the rear, in the mongrel way these spy-louts have.

In the hotel I asked for a room and registered, and then the fellow asked again for my passport. I wanted to know why he demanded it, what he meant by accosting me outside the station as if I was a criminal, what he meant by insulting us with his requests, when in any other town in Italy one went unquestioned—and so forth, in considerable rage.

He did not reply, but obstinately looked as though he would be venomous if he could. He peered at the passport—though I doubt if he could make head or tail of it—asked where we were going, peered at B.'s passport, half excused himself in a whining, disgusting sort of fashion, and disappeared into the night. A real lout.

I was furious. Supposing I had not been carrying my passport— and usually I don't dream of carrying it—what amount of trouble would that lout have made me! Probably I should have spent the night in prison, and been bullied by half-a-dozen low bullies.

Those poor rats at Ladispoli had seen me and B. go to the sea and sit on the sand for half-an-hour, then go back to the train. And this was enough to rouse their suspicions, I imagine, so they telegraphed to Città Vecchia. Why are officials always fools? Even when there is no war on? What could they imagine we were doing?

The hotel manager, propitious, said there was a very interesting museum in Città Vecchia, and wouldn't we stay the next day and see it. "Ah!" I replied. "But all it contains is Roman stuff, and we don't want to look at that." It was malice on my part, because the present regime considers itself purely ancient Roman. The man looked at me scared, and I grinned at him. "But what do they mean," I said, "behaving like this to a simple traveler, in a country where foreigners are invited to travel!" "Ah!" said the porter softly and soothingly. "It is the Roman province. You will have no more of it when you leave the Provincia di Roma." And when the Italians give the soft answer to turn away wrath, the wrath somehow turns away.

We walked for an hour in the dull street of Città Vecchia. There

seemed so much suspicion, one would have thought there were
several wars on. The hotel manager asked if we were staying. We
said we were leaving by the eight-o'clock train in the morning, for
Tarquinia.

And, sure enough, we left by the eight-o'clock train. Tarquinia is
only one station from Cività Vecchia—about twenty minutes over
the flat Maremma country, with the sea on the left, and the green
wheat growing luxuriantly, the asphodel sticking up its spikes.

We soon saw Tarquinia, its towers pricking up like antennae on
the side of a low bluff of a hill, some few miles inland from the sea.
And this was once the metropolis of Etruria, chief city of the great
Etruscan League. But it died like all the other Etruscan cities, and
had a more or less medieval rebirth, with a new name. Dante knew
it, as it was known for centuries, as Corneto—Corgnetum or Corne-
tium—and forgotten was its Etruscan past. Then there was a feeble
sort of wakening to remembrance a hundred years ago, and the
town got Tarquinia tacked on to its Corneto: Corneto-Tarquinia.
The Fascist regime,[7] however, glorying in the Italian origins of
Italy, has now struck out the Corneto, so the town is once more,
simply, Tarquinia. As you come up in the motor-bus from the station you see the great black letters, on a white ground, painted on
the wall by the city gateway: *Tarquinia.* So the wheel of revolution
turns. There stands the Etruscan word—Latinized Etruscan—beside the medieval gate, put up by the Fascist power to name and
unname.

But the Fascists, who consider themselves in all things Roman,
Roman of the Caesars, heirs of Empire and world power, are beside
the mark restoring the rags of dignity to Etruscan places. For of all
the Italian people that ever lived, the Etruscans were surely the
least Roman. Just as, of all the people that ever rose up in Italy, the
Romans of ancient Rome were surely the most un-Italian, judging
from the natives of today.

Tarquinia is only about three miles from the sea. The omnibus
soon runs one up, charges through the widened gateway, swirls
round in the empty space inside the gateway, and is finished. We
descend in the bare place, which seems to expect nothing. On the
left is a beautiful stone palazzo—on the right is a café, upon the
low ramparts above the gate. The man of the *Dazio,* the town customs, looks to see if anybody has brought foodstuffs into the town
—but it is a mere glance. I ask him for the hotel. He says: "Do you
mean to sleep?" I say I do. Then he tells a small boy to carry my
bag and take us to Gentile's.

Nowhere is far off, in these small wall-girdled cities. In the warm
April morning the stony little town seems half asleep. As a matter

7. A right-wing totalitarian system of   Benito Mussolini in 1922 and surviving
government established in Italy by   there until his overthrow in 1943.

of fact, most of the inhabitants are out in the fields, and won't come in through the gates again till evening. The slight sense of deserted-ness is everywhere—even in the inn, when we have climbed up the stairs to it, for the ground floor does not belong. A little lad in long trousers, who would seem to be only twelve years old but who has the air of a mature man, confronts us with his chest out. We ask for rooms. He eyes us, darts away for the key, and leads us off upstairs another flight, shouting to a young girl, who acts as chambermaid, to follow on. He shows us two small rooms, opening off a big, desert sort of general assembly room common in this kind of inn. "And you won't be lonely," he says briskly, "because you can talk to one another through the wall. *Toh! Lina!*" He lifts his finger and listens. "*Eh!*" comes through the wall, like an echo, with startling nearness and clearness. "*Fai presto!*" says Albertino. "*È pronto!*" comes the voice of Lina. "*Ecco!*" says Albertino to us.[8] "You hear!" We cer-tainly did. The partition wall must have been butter muslin. And Albertino was delighted, having reassured us we should not feel lonely nor frightened in the night.

He was, in fact, the most manly and fatherly little hotel manager I have ever known, and he ran the whole place. He was in reality fourteen years old, but stunted. From five in the morning till ten at night he was on the go, never ceasing, and with a queer, abrupt, sideways-darting alacrity that must have wasted a great deal of energy. The father and mother were in the background—quite young and pleasant. But they didn't seem to exert themselves. Albertino did it all. How Dickens would have loved him! But Dickens would not have seen the queer wistfulness, and trustful-ness, and courage in the boy. He was absolutely unsuspicious of us strangers. People must be rather human and decent in Tarquinia, even the commercial travelers: who, presumably, are chiefly buyers of agricultural produce, and sellers of agricultural implements and so forth.

We sallied out, back to the space by the gate, and drank coffee at one of the tin tables outside. Beyond the wall there were a few new villas—the land dropped green and quick, to the strip of coast plain and the indistinct, faintly gleaming sea, which seemed some-how not like a sea at all.

I was thinking, if this were still an Etruscan city, there would still be this cleared space just inside the gate. But instead of a rather forlorn vacant lot it would be a sacred clearing, with a little temple to keep it alert.

Myself, I like to think of the little wooden temples of the early Greeks and of the Etruscans: small, dainty, fragile, and evanescent as flowers. We have reached the stage when we are weary of huge

---

8. "Hey, Lina!" "What!" "Hurry up!"   "Right away!" "There you are!"

stone erections, and we begin to realize that it is better to keep life fluid and changing than to try to hold it fast down in heavy monuments. Burdens on the face of the earth are man's ponderous erections.

The Etruscans made small temples, like little houses with pointed roofs, entirely of wood. But then, outside, they had friezes and cornices and crests of terra cotta, so that the upper part of the temple would seem almost made of earthenware, terra-cotta plaques fitted neatly, and alive with freely modeled painted figures in relief, gay dancing creatures, rows of ducks, round faces like the sun, and faces grinning and putting out a big tongue, all vivid and fresh and unimposing. The whole thing small and dainty in proportion, and fresh, somehow charming instead of impressive. There seems to have been in the Etruscan instinct a real desire to preserve the natural humor of life. And that is a task surely more worthy, and even much more difficult in the long run, than conquering the world or sacrificing the self or saving the immortal soul.

Why has mankind had such a craving to be imposed upon? Why this lust after imposing creeds, imposing deeds, imposing buildings, imposing language, imposing works of art? The thing becomes an imposition and a weariness at last. Give us things that are alive and flexible, which won't last too long and become an obstruction and a weariness. Even Michelangelo becomes at last a lump and a burden and a bore. It is so hard to see past him.

Across the space from the café is the Palazzo Vitelleschi, a charming building, now a national museum—so the marble slab says. But the heavy doors are shut. The place opens at ten, a man says. It is nine-thirty. We wander up the steep but not very long street, to the top.

And the top is a fragment of public garden, and a look-out. Two old men are sitting in the sun, under a tree. We walk to the parapet, and suddenly are looking into one of the most delightful landscapes I have ever seen: as it were, into the very virginity of hilly green country. It is all wheat—green and soft and swooping, swooping down and up, and glowing with green newness, and no houses. Down goes the declivity below us, then swerving the curve and up again, to the neighboring hill that faces in all its greenness and long-running immaculateness. Beyond, the hills ripple away to the mountains, and far in the distance stands a round peak, that seems to have an enchanted city on its summit.

Such a pure, uprising, unsullied country, in the greenness of wheat on an April morning!—and the queer complication of hills! There seems nothing of the modern world here—no houses, no contrivances, only a sort of fair wonder and stillness, an openness which has not been violated.

The hill opposite is like a distinct companion. The near end is quite steep and wild, with evergreen oaks and scrub, and specks of black-and-white cattle on the slopes of common. But the long crest is green again with wheat, running and drooping to the south. And immediately one feels: that hill has a soul, it has a meaning.

Lying thus opposite to Tarquinia's long hill, a companion across a suave little swing of valley, one feels at once that, if this is the hill where the living Tarquinians had their gay wooden houses, then that is the hill where the dead lie buried and quick, as seeds, in their painted houses underground. The two hills are as inseparable as life and death, even now, on the sunny, green-filled April morning with the breeze blowing in from the sea. And the land beyond seems as mysterious and fresh as if it were still the morning of Time.

But B. wants to go back to the Palazzo Vitelleschi: it will be open now. Down the street we go, and sure enough the big doors are open, several officials are in the shadowy courtyard entrance. They salute us in the Fascist manner: *alla Romana!* Why don't they discover the Etruscan salute, and salute us *all'Etrusca!* But they are perfectly courteous and friendly. We go into the court-yard of the palace.

The museum is exceedingly interesting and delightful, to anyone who is even a bit aware of the Etruscans. It contains a great number of things found at Tarquinia, and important things.

If only we would realize it, and not tear things from their settings. Museums anyhow are wrong. But if one must have museums, let them be small, and above all, let them be local. Splendid as the Etruscan museum is in Florence, how much happier one is in the museum at Tarquinia, where all the things are Tarquinian, and at least have some association with one another, and form some sort of *organic* whole.

In the entrance room from the cortile [9] lie a few of the long sar-cophagi in which the nobles were buried. It seems as if the primi-tive inhabitants of this part of Italy always burned their dead, and then put the ashes in a jar, sometimes covering the jar with the dead man's helmet, sometimes with a shallow dish for a lid, and then laid the urn with its ashes in a little round grave like a little well. This is called the Villanovan way of burial, in the well-tomb.

The newcomers to the country, however, apparently buried their dead whole. Here, at Tarquinia, you may still see the hills where the well-tombs of the aboriginal inhabitants are discovered, with the urns containing the ashes inside. Then come the graves where the dead were buried unburned, graves very much like those of today. But tombs of the same period with cinerary urns are found

9. Courtyard.

near to, or in connection. So that the new people and the old apparently lived side by side in harmony, from very early days, and the two modes of burial continued side by side, for centuries, long before the painted tombs were made.

At Tarquinia, however, the main practice seems to have been, at least from the seventh century on, that the nobles were buried in the great sarcophagi, or laid out on biers, and placed in chamber-tombs, while the slaves apparently were cremated, their ashes laid in urns, and the urns often placed in the family tomb, where the stone coffins of the masters rested. The common people, on the other hand, were apparently sometimes cremated, sometimes buried in graves very much like our graves of today, though the sides were lined with stone. The mass of the common people was mixed in race, and the bulk of them were probably serf-peasants, with many half-free artisans. These must have followed their own desire in the matter of burial: some had graves, many must have been cremated, their ashes saved in an urn or jar which takes up little room in a poor man's burial place. Probably even the less important members of the noble families were cremated, and their remains placed in the vases, which became more beautiful as the connection with Greece grew more extensive.

It is a relief to think that even the slaves—and the luxurious Etruscans had many, in historical times—had their remains decently stored in jars and laid in a sacred place. Apparently the "vicious Etruscans" had nothing comparable to the vast dead-pits which lay outside Rome, beside the great highway, in which the bodies of slaves were promiscuously flung.

It is all a question of sensitiveness. Brute force and overbearing may make a terrific effect. But in the end, that which lives lives by delicate sensitiveness. If it were a question of brute force, not a single human baby would survive for a fortnight. It is the grass of the field, most frail of all things, that supports all life all the time. But for the green grass, no empire would rise, no man would eat bread: for grain is grass; and Hercules or Napoleon or Henry Ford would alike be denied existence.

Brute force crushes many plants. Yet the plants rise again. The Pyramids will not last a moment compared with the daisy. And before Buddha or Jesus spoke the nightingale sang, and long after the words of Jesus and Buddha are gone into oblivion the nightingale still will sing. Because it is neither preaching nor teaching nor commanding nor urging. It is just singing. And in the beginning was not a Word, but a chirrup.

Because a fool kills a nightingale with a stone, is he therefore greater than the nightingale? Because the Roman took the life out of the Etruscan, was he therefore greater than the Etruscan? Not he! Rome fell, and the Roman phenomenon with it. Italy today is far more Etruscan in its pulse than Roman: and will always be so. The Etruscan element is like the grass of the field and the sprouting of corn, in Italy: it will always be so. Why try to revert to the Latin-Roman mechanism and suppression?

In the open room upon the courtyard of the Palazzo Vitelleschi lie a few sarcophagi of stone, with the effigies carved on top, something as the dead crusaders in English churches. And here, in Tarquinia, the effigies are more like crusaders than usual, for some lie flat on their backs, and have a dog at their feet; whereas usually the carved figure of the dead rears up as if alive, from the lid of the tomb, resting upon one elbow, and gazing out proudly, sternly. If it is a man, his body is exposed to just below the navel, and he holds in his hand the sacred *patera*, or *mundum*, the round saucer with the raised knob in the center, which represents the round germ of heaven and earth. It stands for the plasm, also, of the living cell, with its nucleus, which is the indivisible God of the beginning, and which remains alive and unbroken to the end, the eternal quick of all things, which yet divides and subdivides, so that it becomes the sun of the firmament and the lotus of the waters under the earth, and the rose of all existence upon the earth; and the sun maintains its own quick, unbroken for ever; and there is a living quick of the sea, and of all the waters; and every living created thing has its own unfailing quick. So within each man is the quick of him, when he is a baby, and when he is old, the same quick; some spark, some unborn and undying vivid life-electron. And this is what is symbolized in the *patera*, which may be made to flower like a rose or like the sun, but which remains the same, the germ central within the living plasm.

And this *patera*, this symbol, is almost invariably found in the hand of a dead man. But if the dead is a woman her dress falls in soft gathers from her throat, she wears splendid jewelry, and she holds in her hand not the *mundum*, but the mirror, the box of essence, the pomegranate, some symbols of her reflected nature, or of her woman's quality. But she, too, is given a proud, haughty look, as is the man: for she belongs to the sacred families that rule and that read the signs.

These sarcophagi and effigies here all belong to the centuries of the Etruscan decline, after there had been long intercourse with the Greeks, and perhaps most of them were made after the conquest of Etruria by the Romans. So that we do not look for fresh, spontaneous works of art, any more than we do in modern memorial stones. The funerary arts are always more or less commercial. The rich man orders his sarcophagus while he is still alive, and the monument carver makes the work more or less elaborate, according to the price. The figure is supposed to be a portrait of the man who orders it, so we see well enough what the later Etruscans look like. In the third and second centuries B.C., at the fag end of their existence as a people, they look very like the Romans of the same day, whose busts we know so well. And often they are given the tiresomely haughty air of people who are no longer rulers indeed, only by virtue of wealth.

Yet, even when the Etruscan art is Romanized and spoilt, there still flickers in it a certain naturalness and feeling. The Etruscan *Lucumones*, or prince-magistrates, were in the first place religious seers, governors in religion, then magistrates; then princes. They were not aristocrats in the Germanic sense, nor even patricians in the Roman. They were first and foremost leaders in the sacred mysteries, then magistrates, then men of family and wealth. So there is always a touch of vital life, of life-significance. And you may look through modern funerary sculpture in vain for anything so good even as the Sarcophagus of the Magistrate, with his written scroll spread before him, his strong, alert old face gazing sternly out, the necklace of office round his neck, the ring of rank on his finger. So he lies, in the museum at Tarquinia. His robe leaves him naked to the hip, and his body lies soft and slack, with the soft effect of relaxed flesh the Etruscan artists render so well, and which is so difficult. On the sculptured side of the sarcophagus the two death dealers wield the hammer of death, the winged figures wait for the soul, and will not be persuaded away. Beautiful it is, with the easy simplicity of life. But it is late in date. Probably this old Etruscan magistrate is already an official under Roman authority: for he does not hold the sacred *mundum*, the dish, he has only the written scroll, probably of laws. As if he were no longer the religious lord or Lucumo. Though possibly, in this case, the dead man was not one of the Lucumones anyhow.

Upstairs in the museum are many vases, from the ancient crude pottery of the Villanovans to the early black ware decorated in scratches, or undecorated, called *bucchero*, and on the painted bowls and dishes and amphoras which came from Corinth or Athens, or to those painted pots made by the Etruscans themselves more or less after the Greek patterns. These may or may not be interesting: the Etruscans are not at their best, painting dishes. Yet they must have loved them. In the early days these great jars and bowls, and smaller mixing bowls, and drinking cups and pitchers, and flat wine cups formed a valuable part of the household treasure. In very early times the Etruscans must have sailed their ships to Corinth and to Athens, taking perhaps wheat and honey, wax and bronze ware, iron and gold, and coming back with these precious jars, and stuffs, essences, perfumes and spice. And jars brought from overseas for the sake of their painted beauty must have been household treasures.

But then the Etruscans made pottery of their own, and by the thousand they imitated the Greek vases. So that there must have been millions of beautiful jars in Etruria. Already in the first century B.C. there was a passion among the Romans for collecting Greek and Etruscan painted jars from the Etruscans, particularly from the Etruscan tombs: jars and the little bronze votive figures and statuettes, the *sigilla Tyrrhena*[1] of the Roman luxury. And when the tombs were first robbed, for gold and silver treasure, hundreds of fine jars must have been thrown over and smashed. Because even now, when a part-rifled tomb is discovered and opened, the fragments of smashed vases lie around.

As it is, however, the museums are full of vases. If one looks for the Greek form of elegance and convention, those elegant "still-unravished brides of quietness," one is disappointed. But get over the strange desire we have for elegant convention, and the vases and dishes of the Etruscans, especially many of the black bucchero ware, begin to open out like strange flowers, black flowers with all the softness and the rebellion of life against convention, or red-and-black flowers painted with amusing free, bold designs. It is there nearly always in Etruscan things, the naturalness verging on the commonplace, but usually missing it, and often achieving an originality so free and bold, and so fresh, that we, who love convention and things "reduced to a norm," call it a bastard art, and commonplace.

It is useless to look in Etruscan things for "uplift." If you want uplift, go to the Greek and the Gothic. If you want mass, go to the Roman. But if you love the odd spontaneous forms that are never to be standardized, go to the Etruscans. In the fascinating little Palazzo Vitelleschi one could spend many an hour, but for the fact that the very fullness of museums makes one rush through them.

1932

Why the Novel Matters

We have curious ideas of ourselves. We think of ourselves as a body with a spirit in it, or a body with a soul in it, or a body with a mind in it. *Mens sana in corpore sano.* The years drink up the wine, and at last throw the bottle away, the body, of course, being the bottle.

It is a funny sort of superstition. Why should I look at my hand, as it so cleverly writes these words, and decide that it is a mere nothing compared to the mind that directs it? Is there really any

---

1. Tyrrhenian statuettes.

huge difference between my hand and my brain? Or my mind? My hand is alive, it flickers with a life of its own. It meets all the strange universe in touch, and learns a vast number of things, and knows a vast number of things. My hand, as it writes these words, slips gaily along, jumps like a grasshopper to dot an *i*, feels the table rather cold, gets a little bored if I write too long, has its own rudiments of thought, and is just as much *me* as is my brain, my mind, or my soul. Why should I imagine that there is a *me* which is more *me* than my hand is? Since my hand is absolutely alive, me alive.

Whereas, of course, as far as I am concerned, my pen isn't alive at all. My pen *isn't me* alive. Me alive ends at my finger tips.

Whatever is me alive is me. Every tiny bit of my hands is alive, every little freckle and hair and fold of skin. And whatever is me alive is me. Only my fingernails, those ten little weapons between me and an inanimate universe, they cross the mysterious Rubicon [1] between me alive and things like my pen, which are not alive, in my own sense.

So, seeing my hand is all alive, and me alive, wherein is it just a bottle, or a jug, or a tin can, or a vessel of clay, or any of the rest of that nonsense? True, if I cut it it will bleed, like a can of cherries. But then the skin that is cut, and the veins that bleed, and the bones that should never be seen, they are all just as alive as the blood that flows. So the tin can business, or vessel of clay, is just bunk.

And that's what you learn, when you're a novelist. And that's what you are very liable *not* to know, if you're a parson, or a philosopher, or a scientist, or a stupid person. If you're a parson, you talk about souls in heaven. If you're a novelist, you know that paradise is in the palm of your hand, and on the end of your nose, because both are alive; and alive, and man alive, which is more than you can say, for certain, of paradise. Paradise is after life, and I for one am not keen on anything that is *after* life. If you are a philosopher, you talk about infinity, and the pure spirit which knows all things. But if you pick up a novel, you realize immediately that infinity is just a handle to this self-same jug of a body of mine; while as for knowing, if I find my finger in the fire, I know that fire burns, with a knowledge so emphatic and vital, it leaves Nirvana merely a conjecture. Oh, yes, my body, me alive, *knows*, and knows intensely. And as for the sum of all knowledge, it can't be anything more than an accumulation of all the things I know in the body, and you, dear reader, know in the body.

1. When Julius Caesar crossed the River Rubicon (near Rimini, Italy) in 49 B.C., in defiance of the Senate's orders, this indicated his intention of advancing against Pompey and thus involving the country in civil war. Hence to "cross the Rubicon" means to take an important and irrevocable decision.

These damned philosophers, they talk as if they suddenly went off in steam, and were then much more important than they are when they're in their shirts. It is nonsense. Every man, philosopher included, ends in his own finger tips. That's the end of his man alive. As for the words and thoughts and sighs and aspirations that fly from him, they are so many tremulations in the ether, and not alive at all. But if the tremulations reach another man alive, he may receive them into his life, and his life may take on a new color, like a chameleon creeping from a brown rock on to a green leaf. All very well and good. It still doesn't alter the fact that the so-called spirit, the message or teaching of the philosopher or the saint, isn't alive at all, but just a tremulation upon the ether, like a radio message. All this spirit stuff is just tremulations upon the ether. If you, as man alive, quiver from the tremulation of the ether into new life, that is because you are man alive, and you take sustenance and stimulation into your alive man in a myriad ways. But to say that the message, or the spirit which is communicated to you, is more important than your living body, is nonsense. You might as well say that the potato at dinner was more important.

Nothing is important but life. And for myself, I can absolutely see life nowhere but in the living. Life with a capital L is only man alive. Even a cabbage in the rain is cabbage alive. All things that are alive are amazing. And all things that are dead are subsidiary to the living. Better a live dog than a dead lion. But better a live lion than a live dog. *C'est la vie!*

It seems impossible to get a saint, or a philosopher, or a scientist, to stick to this simple truth. They are all, in a sense, renegades. The saint wishes to offer himself up as spiritual food for the multitude. Even Francis of Assisi turns himself into a sort of angel-cake, of which anyone may take a slice. But an angel-cake is rather less than man alive. And poor St. Francis might well apologize to his body, when he is dying: "Oh, pardon me, my body, the wrong I did you through the years!" It was no wafer, for others to eat.

The philosopher, on the other hand, because he can think, decides that nothing but thoughts matter. It is as if a rabbit, because he can make little pills, should decide that nothing but little pills matter. As for the scientist, he has absolutely no use for me so long as I am man alive. To the scientist, I am dead. He puts under the microscope a bit of dead me, and calls it me. He takes me to pieces, and says first one piece, and then another piece, is me. My heart, my liver, my stomach have all been scientifically me, according to the scientist; and nowadays I am either a brain, or nerves, or glands, or something more up-to-date in the tissue line.

Now I absolutely flatly deny that I am a soul, or a body, or a mind, or an intelligence, or a brain, or a nervous system, or a bunch of glands, or any of the rest of these bits of me. The whole is greater than the part. And therefore, I, who am man alive, am greater than my soul, or spirit, or body, or mind, or consciousness, or anything else that is merely a part of me. I am a man, and alive. I am man alive, and as long as I can, I intend to go on being man alive.

For this reason I am a novelist. And being a novelist, I consider myself superior to the saint, the scientist, the philosopher, and the poet, who are all great masters of different bits of man alive, but never get the whole hog.

The novel is the one bright book of life. Books are not life. They are only tremulations on the ether. But the novel as a tremulation can make the whole man alive tremble. Which is more than poetry, philosophy, science, or any other book-tremulation can do.

The novel is the book of life. In this sense, the Bible is a great confused novel. You may say, it is about God. But it is really about man alive. Adam, Eve, Sarai, Abraham, Isaac, Jacob, Samuel, David, Bath-Sheba, Ruth, Esther, Solomon, Job, Isaiah, Jesus, Mark, Judas, Paul, Peter: what is it but man alive, from start to finish? Man alive, not mere bits. Even the Lord is another man alive, in a burning bush, throwing the tablets of stone at Moses's head.

I do hope you begin to get my idea, why the novel is supremely important, as a tremulation on the ether. Plato makes the perfect ideal being tremble in me. But that's only a bit of me. Perfection is only a bit, in the strange make-up of man alive. The Sermon on the Mount makes the selfless spirit of me quiver. But that, too, is only a bit of me. The Ten Commandments set the old Adam shivering in me, warning me that I am a thief and a murderer, unless I watch it. But even the old Adam is only a bit of me.

I very much like all these bits of me to be set trembling with life and the wisdom of life. But I do ask that the whole of me shall tremble in its wholeness, some time or other.

And this, of course, must happen in me, living.

But as far as it can happen from a communication, it can only happen when a whole novel communicates itself to me. The Bible —but *all* the Bible—and Homer, and Shakespeare: these are the supreme old novels. These are all things to all men. Which means that in their wholeness they affect the whole man alive, which is the man himself, beyond any part of him. They set the whole tree trembling with a new access of life, they do not just stimulate growth in one direction.

I don't want to grow in any one direction any more. And, if I can help it, I don't want to stimulate anybody else into some particular direction. A particular direction ends in a *cul-de-sac*. We're in a *cul-de-sac* at present.

I don't believe in any dazzling revelation, or in any supreme

Word. "The grass withereth, the flower fadeth, but the Word of the Lord shall stand for ever." That's the kind of stuff we've drugged ourselves with. As a matter of fact, the grass withereth, but comes up all the greener for that reason, after the rains. The flower fadeth, and therefore the bud opens. But the Word of the Lord, being man-uttered and a mere vibration on the ether, becomes staler and staler, more and more boring, till at last we turn a deaf ear and it ceases to exist, far more finally than any withered grass. It is grass that renews its youth like the eagle, not any Word.

We should ask for no absolutes, or absolute. Once and for all and for ever, let us have done with the ugly imperialism of any absolute. There is no absolute good, there is nothing absolutely right. All things flow and change, and even change is not absolute. The whole is a strange assembly of apparently incongruous parts, slipping past one another.

Me, man alive, I am a very curious assembly of incongruous parts. My yea! of today is oddly different from my yea! of yesterday. My tears of tomorrow will have nothing to do with my tears of a year ago. If the one I love remains unchanged and unchanging, I shall cease to love her. It is only because she changes and startles me into change and defies my inertia, and is herself staggered in her inertia by my changing, that I can continue to love her. If she stayed put, I might as well love the pepper pot.

In all this change, I maintain a certain integrity. But woe betide me if I try to put my finger on it. If I say of myself, I am this, I am that!—then, if I stick to it, I turn into a stupid fixed thing like a lamp-post. I shall never know wherein lies my integrity, my individuality, my me. I *can* never know it. It is useless to talk about my ego. That only means that I have made up an *idea* of myself, and that I am trying to cut myself out to pattern. Which is no good. You can cut your cloth to fit your coat, but you can't clip bits off your living body, to trim it down to your idea. True, you can put yourself into ideal corsets. But even in ideal corsets, fashions change.

Let us learn from the novel. In the novel, the characters can do nothing but *live*. If they keep on being good, according to pattern, or bad, according to pattern, or even volatile, according to pattern, they cease to live, and the novel falls dead. A character in a novel has got to live, or it is nothing.

We, likewise, in life have got to live, or we are nothing.

What we mean by living is, of course, just as indescribable as what we mean by *being*. Men get ideas into their heads, of what they mean by Life, and they proceed to cut life out to pattern. Sometimes they go into the desert to seek God, sometimes they go into the desert to seek cash, sometimes it is wine, woman, and song, and again it is water, political reform, and votes. You never know what it will be next: from killing your neighbor with hideous bombs and gas that tears the lungs, to supporting a Foundlings Home and preaching infinite Love, and being co-respondent in a divorce.

In all this wild welter, we need some sort of guide. It's no good inventing Thou Shalt Nots!

What then? Turn truly, honorably to the novel, and see wherein you are man alive, and wherein you are dead man in life. You may love a woman as man alive, and you may be making love to a woman as sheer dead man in life. You may eat your dinner as man alive, or as a mere masticating corpse. As man alive you may have shot at your enemy. But as a ghastly simulacrum of life you may be firing bombs into men who are neither your enemies. nor your friends, but just things you are dead to. Which is criminal, when the things happen to be alive.

To be alive, to be man alive, to be whole man alive: that is the point. And at its best, the novel, and the novel supremely, can help you. It can help you not to be dead man in life. So much of a man walks about dead and a carcass in the street and house, today: so much of women is merely dead. Like a pianoforte with half the notes mute.

But the novel you can see, plainly, when the man goes dead, the woman goes inert. You can develop an instinct for life, if you will, instead of a theory of right and wrong, good and bad.

In life, there is right and wrong, good and bad, all the time. But what is right in one case is wrong in another. And in the novel you see one man becoming a corpse, because of his so-called goodness, another going dead because of his so-called wickedness. Right and wrong is an instinct: but an instinct of the whole consciousness in a man, bodily, mental, spiritual at once. And only in the novel are *all* things given full play, or at least, they may be given full play, when we realize that life itself, and not inert safety, is the reason for living. For out of the full play of all things emerges the only thing that is anything, the wholeness of a man, the wholeness of a woman, man alive, and live woman.

1936

Piano

Softly, in the dusk, a woman is singing to me;
Taking me back down the vista of years, till I see
A child sitting under the piano, in the boom of the tingling
 strings
And pressing the small, poised feet of a mother who smiles
 as she sings.

In spite of myself, the insidious mastery of song
Betrays me back, till the heart of me weeps to belong
To the old Sunday evenings at home, with winter outside
And hymns in the cozy parlor, the tinkling piano our guide.

So now it is vain for the singer to burst into clamor
With the great black piano appassionato. The glamor
Of childish days is upon me, my manhood is cast
Down in the flood of remembrance, I weep like a child for the
    past.

1918

Bavarian Gentians

Not every man has gentians in his house
in Soft September, at slow, Sad Michaelmas.

Bavarian gentians, big and dark, only dark
darkening the daytime torchlike with the smoking blueness of
    Pluto's gloom,[1]
ribbed and torchlike, with their blaze of darkness spread blue   5
down flattening into points, flattened under the sweep of white day
torch-flower of the blue-smoking darkness, Pluto's dark-blue daze,
black lamps from the halls of Dis, burning dark blue,
giving off darkness, blue darkness, as Demeter's pale lamps give off
    light,
lead me then, lead me the way.   10

Reach me a gentian, give me a torch
let me guide myself with the blue, forked torch of this flower
down the darker and darker stairs, where blue is darkened on blue-
    ness.
even where Persephone[2] goes, just now, from the frosted September
to the sightless realm where darkness was awake upon the dark   15
and Persephone herself is but a voice
or a darkness invisible enfolded in the deeper dark
of the arms Plutonic, and pierced with the passion of dense gloom,
among the splendor of torches of darkness, shedding darkness on
    the lost bride and her groom.

1923

---

1. Pluto was god of the underworld in classical mythology; he was also called "Dis" (line 8).
2. Bride of Pluto, who abducted her from the earth, and daughter of Demeter, goddess of the fruits of the earth (line 14). She was allowed to return to earth every spring but had to descend again to Hades in the autumn, "the frosted September." Demeter and Persephone were central figures in ancient fertility myths, where Persephone's annual descent and return were linked with the death and rebirth of vegetation.

Snake

A snake came to my water trough
On a hot, hot day, and I in pajamas for the heat,
To drink there.

In the deep, strange-scented shade of the great dark carob tree
I came down the steps with my pitcher   5
And must wait, must stand and wait, for there he was at the trough
  before me.

He reached down from a fissure in the earth-wall in the gloom
And trailed his yellow-brown slackness soft-bellied down, over the
  edge of the stone trough
And rested his throat upon the stone bottom,
And where the water had dripped from the tap, in a small clear-
  ness,   10
He sipped with his straight mouth,
Softly drank through his straight gums, into his slack long body,
Silently.

Someone was before me at my water trough,
And I, like a second-comer, waiting.   15

He lifted his head from his drinking, as cattle do,
And looked at me vaguely, as drinking cattle do,
And flickered his two-forked tongue from his lips, and mused a
  moment,
And stooped and drank a little more,
Being earth-brown, earth-golden from the burning bowels of the
  earth   20
On the day of Sicilian July, with Etna smoking.

The voice of my education said to me
He must be killed,
For in Sicily the black black snakes are innocent, the gold are veno-
  mous.

And voices in me said, If you were a man   25
You would take a stick and break him now, and finish him off.

But must I confess how I liked him,
How glad I was he had come like a guest in quiet, to drink at my
  water trough
And depart peaceful, pacified, and thankless
Into the burning bowels of this earth?   30

Was it cowardice, that I dared not kill him?
Was it perversity, that I longed to talk to him?
Was it humility, to feel so honored?
I felt so honored.

And yet those voices: 35
If you were not afraid, you would kill him!

And truly I was afraid, I was most afraid,
But even so, honored still more
That he should seek my hospitality
From out the dark door of the secret earth.   40

He drank enough
And lifted his head, dreamily, as one who has drunken,
And flickered his tongue like a forked night on the air, so black,
Seeming to lick his lips,
And looked around like a god, unseeing, into the air,   45
And slowly turned his head,
And slowly, very slowly, as if thrice adream
Proceeded to draw his slow length curving round
And climb the broken bank of my wall-face.

And as he put his head into that dreadful hole,   50
And as he slowly drew up, snake-easing his shoulders, and entered
      further,
A sort of horror, a sort of protest against his withdrawing into that
      horrid black hole,
Deliberately going into the blackness, and slowly drawing himself
      after,
Overcame me now his back was turned.

I looked round, I put down my pitcher,   55
I picked up a clumsy log
And threw it at the water trough with a clatter.

I think it did not hit him;
But suddenly that part of him that was left behind convulsed in un-
      dignified haste,
Writhed like lightning, and was gone   60
Into the black hole, the earth-lipped fissure in the wall-front
At which, in the intense still noon, I stared with fascination.

And immediately I regretted it.
I thought how paltry, how vulgar, what a mean act!
I despised myself and the voices of my accursed human education. 65

And I thought of the albatross,[1]
And I wished he would come back, my snake.

For he seemed to me again like a king,
Like a king in exile, uncrowned in the underworld,
Now due to be crowned again.   70

And so, I missed my chance with one of the lords
Of life.
And I have something to expiate:
A pettiness.

                                                            1923

1. Coleridge's *Ancient Mariner*.

The Ship of Death

1

Now it is autumn and the falling fruit
and the long journey towards oblivion.

The apples falling like great drops of dew
to bruise themselves an exit from themselves.

And it is time to go, to bid farewell
to one's own self, and find an exit
from the fallen self.

2

Have you built your ship of death, O have you?
O build your ship of death, for you will need it.

The grim frost is at hand, when the apples will fall
thick, almost thundrous, on the hardened earth.

And death is on the air like a smell of ashes!
Ah! can't you smell it?

And in the bruised body, the frightened soul
finds itself shrinking, wincing from the cold
that blows upon it through the orifices.

3

And can a man his own quietus make
with a bare bodkin?

With daggers, bodkins, bullets, man can make
a bruise or break of exit for his life;
but is that a quietus, O tell me, is it quietus?

Surely not so! for how could murder, even self-murder
ever a quietus make?

4

O let us talk of quiet that we know,
that we can know, the deep and lovely quiet
of a strong heart at peace!

How can we this, our own quietus, make?

5

Build then the ship of death, for you must take
the longest journey, to oblivion.

And die the death, the long and painful death
that lies between the old self and the new.

Already our bodies are fallen, bruised, badly bruised,
already our souls are oozing through the exit
of the cruel bruise.

Already the dark and endless ocean of the end
is washing in through the breaches of our wounds,
already the flood is upon us.

Oh build your ship of death, your little ark
and furnish it with food, with little cakes, and wine
for the dark flight down oblivion.   40

6

Piecemeal the body dies, and the timid soul
has her footing washed away, as the dark flood rises.

We are dying, we are dying, we are all of us dying
and nothing will stay the death-flood rising within us
and soon it will rise on the world, on the outside world.   45

We are dying, we are dying, piecemeal our bodies are
        dying
and our strength leaves us,
and our soul cowers naked in the dark rain over the flood,
cowering in the last branches of the tree of our life.

7

We are dying, we are dying, so all we can do   50
is now to be willing to die, and to build the ship
of death to carry the soul on the longest journey.

A little ship, with oars and food
and little dishes, and all accoutrements
fitting and ready for the departing soul.   55

Now launch the small ship, now as the body dies
and life departs, launch out, the fragile soul
in the fragile ship of courage, the ark of faith
with its store of food and little cooking pans
and change of clothes,
upon the flood's back waste   60
upon the waters of the end
upon the sea of death, where still we sail
darkly, for we cannot steer, and have no port.

There is no port, there is nowhere to go   65
only the deepening blackness darkening still
blacker upon the soundless, ungurgling flood
darkness at one with darkness, up and down
and sideways utterly dark, so there is no direction any
        more
and the little ship is there; yet she is gone.   70
She is not seen, for there is nothing to see her by.
She is gone! gone! and yet
somewhere she is there.
Nowhere!

8

And everything is gone, the body is gone   75
completely under, gone, entirely gone.
The upper darkness is heavy as the lower,
between them the little ship
is gone
It is the end, it is oblivion.

9
And yet out of eternity a thread   80
separates itself on the blackness,
a horizontal thread
that fumes a little with pallor upon the dark.

Is it illusion? or does the pallor fume
A little higher?
Ah wait, wait, for there's the dawn,   85
the cruel dawn of coming back to life
out of oblivion

Wait, wait, the little ship
drifting, beneath the deathly ashy gray
of a flood-dawn.   90

Wait, wait! even so, a flush of yellow
and strangely, O chilled wan soul, a flush of rose.

A flush of rose, and the whole thing starts again.

10
The flood subsides, and the body, like a worn sea-shell
emerges strange and lovely.   95
And the little ship wings home, faltering and lapsing
on the pink flood,
and the frail soul steps out, into her house again
filling the heart with peace.

Swings the heart renewed with peace   100
even of oblivion.

Oh build your ship of death, oh build it!
for you will need it.
For the voyage of oblivion awaits you.

1929–30   1933

T. S. ELIOT
(1888–1965)

1915: Settles in London.
1917: *Prufrock and Other Observations.*
1922: *The Waste Land.*
1927: Becomes British subject; confirmed in Anglican Church.
1944: *Four Quartets.*

Thomas Stearns Eliot was born in St. Louis, Missouri, of New England stock. He entered Harvard in 1906, and was influenced there by the anti-romanticism of Irving Babbitt and the philosophical and critical interests of George Santayana, as well as by the enthusiasm that prevailed in certain Harvard circles for Elizabethan and Jacobean literature, the Italian Renaissance, and Indian mystical philosophy. His philosophical studies included intensive work on the English idealist philosopher F. H. Bradley, on whom he eventually wrote his Harvard dissertation. (Bradley's emphasis on the private nature of individual experience, "a circle enclosed on the outside," had considerable influence on the private imagery of Eliot's poetry and on the view of the relation between the individual and other individuals reflected in much of his poetry.) Later Eliot studied literature and philosophy in France and Germany, before going to England shortly after the outbreak of World War I in 1914. He studied Greek philosophy at Oxford, taught school in London, and then obtained a position with Lloyd's Bank which he held until 1925, when he joined the London publishing firm of Faber and Gwyer, becoming a director when the firm became Faber and Faber in 1929.

Eliot started writing literary and philosophical reviews soon after settling in London. He wrote for the *Athenaeum* and the *Times Literary Supplement*, among other periodicals, and was assistant editor of the *Egoist* from 1917 to 1919. In 1922 he founded the influential quarterly, the *Criterion*, which he edited until it ceased publication in 1939. His poetry first appeared in 1915, when *The Love Song of J. Alfred Prufrock* was printed in *Poetry* magazine (Chicago) and a few other short poems were published in the short-lived periodical, *Blast*. His first published collection of poems was *Prufrock and Other Observations*, 1917; two other small collections followed in 1919 and 1920; in 1922 *The Waste Land* appeared, first in the *Criterion* in October, then in the *Dial* (in America) in November, and finally in book form. *Poems 1909–25* (1925) collected these earlier poems. Meanwhile he was also publishing collections of his critical essays, notably *The Sacred Wood* in 1920 and *Homage to John Dryden* in 1924. *For Lancelot Andrewes* followed in 1928 and in 1932 he included most of these earlier essays with some new ones in *Selected Essays*. Eliot became a British subject and joined the Church of England in 1927.

"Our civilization comprehends great variety and complexity, and this variety and complexity, playing upon a refined sensibility, must produce various and complex results. The poet must become more and more comprehensive, more allusive, more indirect, in order to force, to dislocate if necessary, language into his meaning." This remark, from Eliot's essay on *The Metaphysical Poets* (1921), gives one clue to his poetic method from *Prufrock* through *The Waste Land*. In the attenuated romantic tradition of the Georgian poets who were active when he settled in London, in their quietly meditative pastoralism, faded exoticism, or self-consciously realistic descriptions of urban life, he saw an exhausted poetic mode being employed, with no verbal excitement or original craftsmanship. He sought to make poetry more subtle, more suggestive, and at the same time more precise. He had learned from the Imagists the necessity of clear and precise images, and he learned, too, from T. E. Hulme and from his early supporter and adviser Ezra Pound to fear romantic softness and to regard the poetic medium rather than the poet's personality as the important factor. At the same time, the "hard dry" images advocated by Hulme were not enough for him; he wanted wit, allusiveness, irony. He saw in the metaphysical poets how wit and passion could be combined, and he saw in the French Symbolists how an image could be both absolutely precise in what it referred to physically and at the same time endlessly suggestive in the meanings it set up because of its relationship to other images. The combination of precision, symbolic suggestion, and ironic mockery in the poetry of the late 19th-century French poet Jules Laforgue attracted and influenced him, and he was influenced too by other 19th-century French poets: by Théophile Gautier's artful carving of impersonal shapes of meaning; by Charles Baudelaire's strangely evocative explorations of the symbolic suggestions of objects and images; by the Symbolist poets Paul Verlaine, Arthur Rimbaud, and Stéphane Mallarmé. He also found in the Jacobean dramatists a flexible blank verse with overtones of colloquial movement: Middleton, Tourneur, Webster, and others, taught him as much—in the way of verse movement, imagery, the counterpointing of the accent of conversation and the note of terror—as either the metaphysicals or the French Symbolists.

Hulme's protests against the romantic concept of poetry fitted in well enough with what Eliot had learned from Irving Babbitt at Harvard; yet for all his severity with such poets as Shelley, for all his conscious cultivation of a classical viewpoint and his insistence on order and discipline rather than on mere self-expression in art, one side of Eliot's poetic genius is, in one sense of the word, romantic. The Symbolist influence on his imagery, his interest in the evocative and the suggestive, such lines as "And fiddled whisper music on those strings / And bats with baby faces in the violet light / Whistled, and beat their wings," and such recurring images as the hyacinth girl and the rose garden, all show what could be called a romantic element in his poetry. But it is combined with a dry ironic allusiveness, a play of wit, and a colloquial element, which are not normally found in poets of the romantic tradition.

Eliot's real novelty—and the cause of much bewilderment when his poems first appeared—was his deliberate elimination of all merely connective and transitional passages, his building up of the total pattern of meaning through the immediate juxtaposition of images without overt explanation of what they are doing, together with his use of oblique references to other works of literature (some of them quite obscure to most contemporary readers). *Prufrock* presents a symbolic landscape where the meaning emerges from the mutual interaction of the images, and that meaning is enlarged by echoes, often ironic, of Hesiod and Dante and Shakespeare. *The Waste Land* is a series of scenes and images with no author's voice intervening to tell us where we are, but with the implications developed through multiple contrasts and through analogies with older literary works often referred to in a distorted quotation or half-concealed allusion. Further, the works referred to are not necessarily works which are central in the Western literary tradition: besides Dante and Shakespeare there are pre-Socratic philosophers, minor (as well as major) 17th-century poets and dramatists, works of anthropology, history, and philosophy, and other echoes of the poet's private reading. In a culture where there is no longer any assurance on the part of the poet that his public has a common cultural heritage, a common knowledge of works of the past, Eliot felt it necessary to build up his own body of references. It is this which marks the difference between Eliot's use of earlier literature and, say, Milton's. Both poets are difficult to the modern reader, who needs editorial assistance in recognizing and understanding many of the allusions—but Milton was drawing on a body of knowledge common to educated men in his day. Nevertheless, this aspect of Eliot can be exaggerated: the fact remains that the nature of his imagery together with the movement of his verse generally succeed in setting the tone he requires, in establishing the area of meaning to be developed, so that even a reader ignorant of most of the literary allusions can often get the "feel" of the poem and achieve some understanding of what it says.

Eliot's early poetry, until at least the middle 1920's, is mostly concerned in one way or another with the Waste Land, with aspects of the decay of culture in the modern Western world. After his formal acceptance of Anglican Christianity we find a penitential note in much of his verse, a note of quiet searching for spiritual peace, with considerable allusion to Biblical, liturgical, and mystical religious literature and to Dante. *Ash Wednesday* (1930), a poem in six parts, much less fiercely concentrated in style than the earlier poetry, explores with gentle insistence a mood both penitential and questioning. The so-called "Ariel" poems (the title is accidental, and has nothing to do with their form or content) present or explore aspects of religious doubt or discovery or revelation, sometimes, as in *Marina*, using a purely secular imagery and sometimes, as in *Journey of the Magi*, drawing on Biblical incident. In *Four Quartets* (of which the first, *Burnt Norton*, appeared in the *Collected Poems* of 1935, though all four were not completed until 1943, when they were published together) Eliot further explored essentially religious moods, dealing with the relation between time and eternity and the cultivation of that selfless passivity which can yield the moment of timeless revelation in the midst of time. The mocking irony, the savage humor, the deliberately startling juxtaposition of the sordid and the romantic, give way in these later poems to a quieter poetic idiom, often still complexly allusive but never deliberately shocking.

Eliot's criticism was the criticism of a practicing poet who worked out in relation to his reading of older literature what he needed to hold and to admire. He lent the growing weight of his authority to that shift in literary taste that replaced Milton by Donne as the great 17th-century English poet, and replaced Tennyson in the 19th century by Hopkins. His often-quoted description of the late 17th-century "dissociation of sensibility"— keeping wit and passion in separate compartments—which he saw as determining the course of English poetry throughout the 18th and 19th centuries, is both a contribution to the rewriting of English literary history and an explanation of what he was aiming at in his own poetry: the re-establishment of that *unified* sensibility he found in Donne and other early 17th-century poets and dramatists. His view of tradition, his dislike of the poetic exploitation of the author's own personality, his advocacy of what he called "orthodoxy," made him suspicious of what he considered eccentric geniuses such as Blake and D. H. Lawrence. On the other side, his dislike of the grandiloquent and his insistence on complexity and on the mingling of the formal with the conversational made him distrustful of the influence of Milton on English poetry. He considered himself "classicist in literature, royalist in politics, and Anglo-Catholic in religion" (*For Lancelot Andrewes*, 1928), in favor of order against chaos, tradition against eccentricity, authority against rampant individualism; yet his own poetry is in many respects untraditional and certainly highly individual in tone. His conservative and even authoritarian habit of mind has alienated some who admire—and some whose own poetry has been much influenced by—his poetry.

Eliot's plays have all been, directly or indirectly, on religious themes. *Murder in the Cathedral* (1935) deals with the murder of Archbishop Thomas à Becket in an appropriately ritual manner, with much use of a chorus and with the central speech in the form of a sermon by the archbishop in his cathedral shortly before his murder. *The Family Reunion* (1939) deals with the problem of guilt and redemption in a modern upper-class English family; it makes a deliberate attempt to combine choric devices from Greek tragedy with a poetic idiom subdued to the accents of drawing-room conversation. In his three later plays, all written in the 1950's, *The Cocktail Party*, *The Confidential Clerk*, and *The Elder Statesman*, he achieved popular success by casting a serious religious theme in the form of a sophisticated modern social comedy, using a verse that is so conversational in movement that when spoken in the theater it does not sound like verse at all.

Critics differ on the degree to which Eliot succeeded in his last plays in combining box-office success with dramatic effectiveness. But there is no disagreement on his importance as one of the great renovators of the English poetic dialect, whose influence on a whole generation of poets, critics, and intellectuals generally was enormous. His range as a poet is limited, and his interest in the great middle ground of human experience (as distinct from the extremes of saint and sinner) deficient: but when in 1948 he was awarded the rare honor of the Order of Merit by King George VI and also gained the Nobel Prize in literature, his positive qualities were widely and fully recognized—his poetic cunning, his fine craftsmanship, his original accent, his historical and representative importance as *the* poet of the modern Symbolist-metaphysical tradition.

The Love Song of J. Alfred Prufrock[1]

S'io credesse che mia risposta fosse
A persona che mai tornasse al mondo,
Questa fiamma staria senza piu scosse.
Ma perciocche giammai di questo fondo
Non torno vivo alcun, s'i'odo il vero,
Senza tema d'infamia ti rispondo.[2]

Let us go then, you and I,
When the evening is spread out against the sky
Like a patient etherized[3] upon a table;
Let us go, through certain half-deserted streets,
The muttering retreats   5
Of restless nights in one-night cheap hotels
And sawdust restaurants with oyster shells:
Streets that follow like a tedious argument
Of insidious intent
To lead you to an overwhelming question . . .   10
Oh, do not ask, "What is it?"
Let us go and make our visit.

In the room the women come and go
Talking of Michelangelo.

The yellow fog that rubs its back upon the windowpanes,   15
The yellow smoke that rubs its muzzle on the windowpanes
Licked its tongue into the corners of the evening,
Lingered upon the pools that stand in drains,
Let fall upon its back the soot that falls from chimneys,
Slipped by the terrace, made a sudden leap,   20

1. A dramatic monologue in which the speaker builds up a mood of social futility and inadequacy through the thoughts and images which haunt his consciousness and by means of the symbolic landscape in which he moves. The title implies an ironic contrast between the romantic suggestions of "love song" and the dully prosaic name, "J. Alfred Prufrock." The quotation from Dante's *Inferno* which stands at the head of the poem adds to this contrast a note of profound hopelessness. Prufrock himself, middle-aged and unhappy, is not really at home in the society in which he is condemned to live; he is aware of the futility of such visits as he is paying, of his own awkwardness and maladjustment, and his self-conscious response to the demands made on him. He is haunted not only by a knowledge of the pettiness and triviality of this world, but also by a sense of his own sexual inadequacy and a feeling that once, somewhere, he had had a vision of a life more real and

more beautiful, but that he has long since strayed from that reality to the artificial and barren existence in which he now suffocates. The lost dreamworld was paradoxically the only real world, man's true element, and out of it he drowns.
2. "If I thought that my reply would be to one who would ever return to the world, this flame would stay without further movement; but since none has ever returned alive from this depth, if what I hear is true, I answer you without fear of infamy." Dante, *Inferno* XXVII.61–66. Guido da Montefeltro, shut up in his flame (the punishment given to false counselors), tells the shame of his evil life to Dante because he believes Dante will never return to earth to report it.
3. A contrast is perhaps here implied between "ether" as the free sky or the heavens and the word's medical connotations—helplessness, disease, the elimination of consciousness and personality.

And seeing that it was a soft October night,
Curled once about the house, and fell asleep.

And indeed there will be time[4]
For the yellow smoke that slides along the street,
Rubbing its back upon the windowpanes;   25
There will be time, there will be time
To prepare a face to meet the faces that you meet;
There will be time to murder and create,
And time for all the works and days of hands[5]
That lift and drop a question on your plate;   30
Time for you and time for me,
And time yet for a hundred indecisions,
And for a hundred visions and revisions,
Before the taking of a toast and tea.

In the room the women come and go   35
Talking of Michelangelo.

And indeed there will be time
To wonder, "Do I dare?" and, "Do I dare?"
Time to turn back and descend the stair,
With a bald spot in the middle of my hair—   40
(They will say: "How his hair is growing thin!")
My morning coat, my collar mounting firmly to the chin,
My necktie rich and modest, but asserted by a simple pin—
(They will say: "But how his arms and legs are thin!")
Do I dare   45
Disturb the universe?
In a minute there is time
For decisions and revisions which a minute will reverse.

For I have known them all already, known them all—
Have known the evenings, mornings, afternoons,   50
I have measured out my life with coffee spoons;
I know the voices dying with a dying fall[6]
Beneath the music from a farther room.
    So how should I presume?

And I have known the eyes already, known them all—   55
The eyes that fix you in a formulated phrase,
And when I am formulated, sprawling on a pin,
When I am pinned and wriggling on the wall,
Then how should I begin
To spit out all the butt-ends of my days and ways?   60
    And how should I presume?

And I have known the arms already, known them all—
Arms that are braceleted and white and bare

4. Cf. Andrew **Marvell**'s *To His Coy Mistress:* "Had we but world enough and time * * * "
5. *Works and Days* is a poem about the farming year by Hesiod, Greek poet of 8th century B.C. Eliot's contrast is between useful agricultural labor and the futile "works and days of hands" engaged in meaningless social gesturing.
6. Ironic recollection of Orsino's speech in *Twelfth Night* (I.i.4): "That strain again! It had a dying fall."

(But in the lamplight, downed with light brown hair!)
Is it perfume from a dress 65
That makes me so digress?
Arms that lie along a table, or wrap about a shawl.
    And should I then presume?
    And how should I begin?

.   .   .   .   .

Shall I say, I have gone at dusk through narrow streets 70
And watched the smoke that rises from the pipes
Of lonely men in shirt-sleeves, leaning out of windows? . . .

I should have been a pair of ragged claws
Scuttling across the floors of silent seas.[7]

.   .   .   .   .

And the afternoon, the evening, sleeps so peacefully! 75
Smoothed by long fingers,
Asleep . . . tired . . . or it malingers,
Stretched on the floor, here beside you and me.
Should I, after tea and cakes and ices,
Have the strength to force the moment to its crisis? 80
But though I have wept and fasted, wept and prayed,
Though I have seen my head (grown slightly bald) brought in upon
    a platter,[8]
I am no prophet—and here's no great matter;
I have seen the moment of my greatness flicker,
And I have seen the eternal Footman hold my coat, and snicker, 85
And in short, I was afraid.

And would it have been worth it, after all,
After the cups, the marmalade, the tea,
Among the porcelain, among some talk of you and me,
Would it have been worth while, 90
To have bitten off the matter with a smile,
To have squeezed the universe into a ball
To roll it toward some overwhelming question,
To say: "I am Lazarus,[9] come from the dead,
Come back to tell you all, I shall tell you all"— 95
If one, settling a pillow by her head,
    Should say: "That is not what I meant at all.
    That is not it, at all."

And would it have been worth it, after all,
Would it have been worth while,
After the sunsets and the dooryards and the sprinkled streets, 100

7. I.e., he would have been better as a
crab on the ocean bed. Perhaps, too, the
motion of a crab suggests futility and
growing old; cf. *Hamlet* II.ii.205–6:
"for you yourself, sir, should be old as
I am, if, like a crab, you could go backward."
8. Like that of John the Baptist. See
Mark vi.17–28 and Matthew xiv.3–11.
9. Cf. Luke xvi.19–31 and John xi.1–
44.

After the novels, after the teacups, after the skirts that trail along
    the floor—
And this, and so much more?—
It is impossible to say just what I mean!
But as if a magic lantern threw the nerves in patterns on a
    screen: 105
Would it have been worth while
If one, settling a pillow or throwing off a shawl,
And turning toward the window, should say:
    "That is not it at all,
    That is not what I meant, at all."   110

       · · · · ·

No! I am not Prince Hamlet, nor was meant to be;
Am an attendant lord, one that will do
To swell a progress,[1] start a scene or two,
Advise the prince; no doubt, an easy tool,
Deferential, glad to be of use,   115
Politic, cautious, and meticulous;
Full of high sentence,[2] but a bit obtuse;
At times, indeed, almost ridiculous—
Almost, at times, the Fool.

I grow old . . . I grow old . . .   120
I shall wear the bottoms of my trousers rolled.

Shall I part my hair behind? Do I dare to eat a peach?
I shall wear white flannel trousers, and walk upon the beach.
I have heard the mermaids singing, each to each.

I do not think that they will sing to me.   125

I have seen them riding seaward on the waves
Combing the white hair of the waves blown back
When the wind blows the water white and black.

We have lingered in the chambers of the sea
By sea-girls wreathed with seaweed red and brown   130
Till human voices wake us, and we drown.
1910–11   1915, 1917

From Landscapes[3]
Rannoch, by Glencoe[4]

Here the crow starves, here the patient stag
Breeds for the rifle. Between the soft moor

1. In the Elizabethan sense of a state journey made by a royal or noble person. Elizabethan plays sometimes showed such "progresses" crossing the stage.
2. In its older meanings, "opinions," "sententiousness."
3. Under this title Eliot grouped five short poems, each dealing with a specific place. The last two are reprinted here.
4. In Scotland.

And the soft sky, scarcely room
To leap or soar. Substance crumbles, in the thin air
Moon cold or moon hot. The road winds in   5
Listlessness of ancient war
Languor of broken steel,
Clamor of confused wrong, apt
In silence. Memory is strong
Beyond the bone. Pride snapped,   10
Shadow of pride is long, in the long pass
No concurrence of bone.

Cape Ann[5]

O quick quick quick, quick hear the song sparrow,
Swamp sparrow, fox sparrow, vesper sparrow
At dawn and dusk. Follow the dance
Of the goldfinch at noon. Leave to chance
The Blackburnian warbler, the shy one. Hail   5
With shrill whistle the note of the quail, the bobwhite
Dodging by baybush. Follow the feet
Of the walker, the water thrush. Follow the flight
Of the dancing arrow, the purple martin. Greet
In silence the bullbat. All are delectable. Sweet sweet sweet   10
But resign this land at the end, resign it
To its true owner, the tough one, the sea gull.
The palaver is finished.

1933–34   1936

Sweeney Among the Nightingales[1]

ὤμοι, πέπληγμαι καιρίαν πληγὴν ἔσω.[2]

Apeneck Sweeney spreads his knees
Letting his arms hang down to laugh,
The zebra stripes along his jaw
Swelling to maculate[3] giraffe.

5. On the northern coast of Massachusetts, not far from the New Hampshire border; a wilderness area in the middle of the cape is inhabited by the birds Eliot here describes.

1. This poem shows Eliot's characteristic method of presenting his meaning through multiple parallels and contrasts. Lust, cruelty, and violence have always existed in the world; but in heroic periods of history they have sprung from grand passions of love or hate and have later been embodied in meaningful myths. The nightingale, in Greek myth, was the symbol of the transformation of human lust into art: Philomela, having been ravished and had her tongue cut out by her sister's husband Tereus, was turned into a nightingale and sings eternally. The horrors of Agamemnon's murder are similarly subsumed in the search for and achievement of divine justice (cf. Aeschylus' dramatic trilogy, the *Oresteia*). But the shabby animality of Sweeney and his drunken lady friend (significantly anonymous), frolicking lewdly in a restaurant, is unrelieved by any such transmutation. In Sweeney's world violence is limited to overturning a coffee cup and tearing at grapes, and lust has become only a "gambit," easily "declined."

2. "Alas, I am struck with a mortal blow within" (Aeschylus, *Agamemnon*, line 1343). The voice of Agamemnon heard crying out from the palace as he is murdered by his wife Clytemnestra.

3. Spotted, stained.

The circles of the stormy moon 5
Slide westward toward the River Plate,[4]
Death and the Raven drift above
And Sweeney guards the hornéd gate.[5]

Gloomy Orion and the Dog
Are veiled;[6] and hushed the shrunken seas; 10
The person in the Spanish cape
Tries to sit on Sweeney's knees

Slips and pulls the tablecloth
Overturns a coffee cup,
Reorganized upon the floor 15
She yawns and draws a stocking up;

The silent man in mocha brown
Sprawls at the window sill and gapes;
The waiter brings in oranges
Bananas figs and hothouse grapes; 20

The silent vertebrate in brown
Contracts and concentrates, withdraws;
Rachel *née* Rabinovitch
Tears at the grapes with murderous paws;

She and the lady in the cape 25
Are suspect, thought to be in league;
Therefore the man with heavy eyes
Declines the gambit, shows fatigue,

Leaves the room and reappears
Outside the window, leaning in, 30
Branches of wistaria
Circumscribe a golden grin;

The host with someone indistinct
Converses at the door apart,
The nightingales are singing near 35
The Convent of the Sacred Heart,

And sang within the bloody wood
When Agamemnon cried aloud,[7]
And let their liquid siftings fall
To stain the stiff dishonored shroud. 40

1918, 1919

4. Estuary on South American coast between Argentina and Uruguay, formed by the Uruguay and Paraná rivers.
5. The gates of horn, in Hades, through which true dreams come to the upper world.
6. "Orion" and the "Dog" are the constellations. For Sweeney and his friend, the gate of vision is blocked and the great mythmaking constellations are "veiled."
7. Agamemnon was not murdered in a "bloody wood," but in his bath. Eliot is here telescoping Agamemnon's murder with the wood where Philomela was ravished and also with the "bloody wood" of Nemi, where, in ancient times, the old priest was slain by his successor (as described in the first chapter of Sir James Frazer's *Golden Bough*). The great myths of regeneration represented by this ritual slaying are meaningless for Sweeney and his friends, as are the song of the nightingales and the spiritual reality represented by the Convent of the Sacred Heart.

Whispers of Immortality[1]

Webster[2] was much possessed by death
And saw the skull beneath the skin;
And breastless creatures under ground
Leaned backward with a lipless grin.

Daffodil bulbs instead of balls   5
Stared from the sockets of the eyes!
He knew that thought clings round dead limbs
Tightening its lusts and luxuries.

Donne,[3] I suppose, was such another
Who found no substitute for sense,   10
To seize and clutch and penetrate;
Expert beyond experience,

He knew the anguish of the marrow
The ague of the skeleton;
No contact possible to flesh   15
Allayed the fever of the bone.

      .   .   .

Grishkin is nice: her Russian eye
Is underlined for emphasis;
Uncorseted, her friendly bust
Gives promise of pneumatic bliss.   20

The couched Brazilian jaguar
Compels the scampering marmoset
With subtle effluence of cat;
Grishkin has a maisonette;

The sleek Brazilian jaguar   25
Does not in its arboreal gloom
Distil so rank a feline smell
As Grishkin in a drawing room.

And even the Abstract Entities
Circumambulate her charm;   30
But our lot crawls between dry ribs
To keep our metaphysics warm

1918, 1919

1. The effects are here again achieved by contrasts and parallels. The Elizabethan and Jacobean poets and dramatists were obsessed by death and suffered the anguish of those for whom all knowledge comes through the senses but who know that the senses, doomed to decay, cannot satisfy the ultimate long-ings. By contrast Grishkin, high-class prostitute, is wholly committed to the flesh, like an animal; even abstract philosophy is seduced by her charms.
2. John Webster, Jacobean dramatist, author of *The Duchess of Malfi* and *The White Devil.*
3. The poet John Donne (1572–1631).

The Waste Land is a poem about spiritual dryness, about the kind of existence in which no regenerating belief gives significance and value to men's daily activities, sex brings no fruitfulness, and death heralds no resurrection. Eliot himself gives one of the main clues to the theme and structure of the poem in a general note, in which he stated that "not only the title, but the plan and a good deal of the symbolism of the poem were suggested by Miss Jessie L. Weston's book on the Grail legend: *From Ritual to Romance*" (1920). He further acknowledged a general indebtedness to Sir James Frazer's *Golden Bough* (12 volumes, 1890–1915), "especially the two volumes *Adonis, Attis, Osiris*," in which Frazer deals with ancient vegetation myths and fertility ceremonies. Miss Weston's study, drawing on material from Frazer and other anthropologists, traced the relationship of these myths and rituals to Christianity and most especially to the legend of the Holy Grail. She found an archetypal fertility myth in the story of the Fisher King whose death, infirmity, or impotence (there are many forms of the myth) brought drought and desolation to the land and failure of the power to reproduce themselves among both men and beasts. This symbolic Waste Land can be revived only if a "questing knight" goes to the Chapel Perilous, situated in the heart of it, and there asks certain ritual questions about the Grail (or Cup) and the Lance— originally fertility symbols, female and male respectively. The proper asking of these questions revives the king and restores fertility to the land. The relation of this original Grail myth to fertility cults and rituals found in many different civilizations, and represented by stories of a dying god who is later resurrected (e.g., Tammuz, Adonis, Attis), shows their common origin in a response to the cyclical movement of the seasons, with vegetation dying in winter to be resurrected again in the spring. Christianity, according to Miss Weston, gave its own spiritual meaning to the myth; it "did not hesitate to utilize the already existing medium of instruction, but boldly identified the Deity of Vegetation, regarded as Life Principle, with the God of the Christian Faith." The Fisher King is related to the use of the fish symbol in early Christianity. Miss Weston states "with certainty that the Fish is a Life symbol of immemorial antiquity, and that the title of Fisher has, from the earliest ages, been associated with the Deities who were held to be specially connected with the origin and preservation of Life." Eliot, following Miss Weston, thus uses a great variety of mythological and religious material, both occidental and oriental, in order to paint a symbolic picture of the modern Waste Land and the need for regeneration. Eliot's use of anthropological material must not blind us to his stress on the religious consolation available to those who live in the inferno of modern life. The terror of that life—its loneliness, emptiness, and irrational apprehensions—as well as its misuse of sexuality are vividly presented, but the poem ends with a benediction. Another significant general source for the poem is the composer Richard Wagner, some of whose operas (*Götterdämmerung* ["Twilight of the Gods"], *Parsifal, Rheingold*, and *Tristan and Isolde*) are drawn on.

When the poem was first published in book form in 1922, Eliot added a series of notes identifying some of his sources or suggesting relationships between various images or allusions; these notes are quoted in the present editor's footnotes to the poem.

The Waste Land

"Nam Sibyllam quidem Cumis ego ipse oculis meis vidi in ampulla pendere, et cum illi pueri dicerent: Σίβυλλα τί θέλεις; respondebat illa: ἀποθανεῖν θέλω."[1]

FOR EZRA POUND[2]

il miglior fabbro

I. The Burial of the Dead[3]

April is the cruelest month, breeding
Lilacs out of the dead land, mixing
Memory and desire, stirring
Dull roots with spring rain.
Winter kept us warm, covering   5
Earth in forgetful snow, feeding
A little life with dried tubers.
Summer surprised us, coming over the Starnbergersee[4]
With a shower of rain; we stopped in the colonnade,
And went on in sunlight, into the Hofgarten,[5]   10
And drank coffee, and talked for an hour.
Bin gar keine Russin, stamm' aus Litauen, echt deutsch.[6]
And when we were children, staying at the archduke's,

1. From the *Satyricon* of Petronius (1st century A.D.): "For once I myself saw with my own eyes the Sibyl at Cumae hanging in a cage, and when the boys said to her 'Sibyl, what do you want?' she replied, 'I want to die.' " The Cumaean Sibyl was the most famous of the Sibyls, the prophetic old women of Greek mythology: she guided Aeneas through Hades in the *Aeneid*. She had been granted immortality by Apollo, but since she forgot to ask for perpetual youth, she shrank into withered old age and her authority declined. Cf. other prophets in the poem: Madame Sosostris and Tiresias.
2. Ezra Pound (1885–), the American expatriate poet who was a key figure in the modern movement in poetry, helped Eliot with the final revisions. "*Il miglior fabbro*" (i.e., the better craftsman) was a tribute originally paid to the Provencal poet Arnaut Daniel in Dante's *Purgatorio* XXVI.117.
3. The title comes from the Anglican burial service. April is the cruelest month because it brings no true renewal but instead tortures us with vain recollections. The seasons as they are here described do not form part of a living cycle; the people whose chatter we hear in international holiday resorts do not wish a really new life, and April is thus cruel in another sense because it suggests resurrection to those who do

not wish it. With a sudden shift in tone the voice becomes suggestive of the prophet Ezekiel announcing the dryness and hopeless fragmentation of civilization; then this voice gives way to songs of romantic passion and memories of lost opportunities for love. We next see the mysteries of ancient religion transformed into fashionable fortune-telling by a fake Egyptian clairvoyante; the elemental symbols of the ancient Tarot pack of cards have degenerated into a trickster's patter (but still immensely evocative, and with each character in the pack related to themes to be developed later in the poem). Then the vision changes to a more direct picture of modern civilization: Baudelaire's Paris, modern London, Dante's Limbo, all three seen as really the same; the feverish speaker turns the great resurrection ritual into a mad and sinister question about gardening; and the author rounds on the reader to insist that he see himself in the same situation.
4. Lake near Munich. The scene in this and the following eight lines was suggested by Countess Marie Larisch, *My Past* as a means of evoking European decadence before World War I.
5. Public park in Munich, with a zoo and cafés.
6. "I am not Russian at all; I come from Lithuania, a true German."

My cousin's, he took me out on a sled,
And I was frightened. He said, Marie, 15
Marie, hold on tight. And down we went.
In the mountains, there you feel free.
I read, much of the night, and go south in the winter.

What are the roots that clutch, what branches grow
Out of this stony rubbish? Son of man,[7] 20
You cannot say, or guess, for you know only
A heap of broken images, where the sun beats,
And the dead tree gives no shelter, the cricket no relief,[8]
And the dry stone no sound of water. Only
There is shadow under this red rock,[9] 25
(Come in under the shadow of this red rock),
And I will show you something different from either
Your shadow at morning striding behind you
Or your shadow at evening rising to meet you;
I will show you fear in a handful of dust. 30
    Frisch weht der Wind
    Der Heimat zu
    Mein Irisch Kind,
    Wo weilest du?[1]
"You gave me hyacinths first a year ago; 35
They called me the hyacinth girl."
—Yet when we came back, late, from the Hyacinth garden,
Yours arms full, and your hair wet, I could not
Speak, and my eyes failed, I was neither
Living nor dead, and I knew nothing, 40
Looking into the heart of light, the silence.
Oed' und leer das Meer.[2]

Madame Sosostris,[3] famous clairvoyante,
Had a bad cold, nevertheless
Is known to be the wisest woman in Europe, 45

---

7. "Cf. Ezekiel II, i" [Eliot's note].
Here God is addressing Ezekiel, "Son
of man." God continues, "stand upon
thy feet, and I will speak unto thee."
8. "Cf. Ecclesiastes XII, v" [Eliot's
note]. The verse cited by Eliot is part
of the Preacher's picture of the desolation of old age, "when they shall
be afraid of that which is high, and
fears shall be in the way, and the almond tree shall flourish, and the grasshopper shall be a burden, and desire
shall fail * * *."
9. Cf. Isaiah xxxii.2: the "righteous
king" "shall be * * * as rivers of
water in a dry place, as the shadow of
a great rock in a weary land."
1. "V. *Tristan und Isolde*, I, verses
5–8" [Eliot's note]. In Wagner's opera,
a sailor recalls the girl he has left be-

hind: "Fresh blows the wind to the
homeland; my Irish child, where are
you waiting?"
2. "Id. III, verse 24" [Eliot's note].
In Act III of *Tristan und Isolde*, Tristan lies dying. He is waiting for Isolde
to come to him from Cornwall, but a
shepherd, appointed to watch for her
sail, can only report, "Waste and empty
is the sea."
3. A mock Egyptian name (suggested
to Eliot by "Sesostris, the Sorceress of
Ecbatana," the name assumed by a
character in Aldous Huxley's novel
Crome Yellow who dresses up as a
gypsy to tell fortunes at a fair). The
anticlimactic effect of "had a bad
cold" is deliberate; it is intended to be
ironic and debunking.

With a wicked pack of cards.[4] Here, said she,
Is your card, the drowned Phoenician Sailor,[5]
(Those are pearls that were his eyes. Look!)
Here is Belladonna, the Lady of the Rocks,[6]
The lady of situations.
Here is the man with three staves,[7] and here the Wheel,   50
And here is the one-eyed merchant,[8] and this card,
Which is blank, is something he carries on his back,
Which I am forbidden to see. I do not find
The Hanged Man.[9] Fear death by water.   55
I see crowds of people, walking round in a ring.
Thank you. If you see dear Mrs. Equitone,
Tell her I bring the horoscope myself:
One must be so careful these days.

4. I.e., the Tarot deck of cards. The four suits of the Tarot pack, discussed by Jessie Weston in *From Ritual to Romance*, are the cup, lance, sword, and dish—the life symbols found in the Grail story. Miss Weston noted that "today the Tarot has fallen somewhat into disrepute, being principally used for purposes of divination." Some of the cards mentioned in lines 46–56 are discussed by Eliot in his note to this passage: "I am not familiar with the exact constitution of the Tarot pack of cards, from which I have obviously departed to suit my own convenience. The Hanged Man, a member of the traditional pack, fits my purpose in two ways: because he is associated in my mind with the Hanged God of Frazer, and because I associate him with the hooded figure in the passage of the disciples to Emmaus in Part V. The Phoenician Sailor and the Merchant appear later; also the 'crowds of people,' and Death by Water is executed in Part IV. The Man with Three Staves (an authentic member of the Tarot pack) I associate, quite arbitrarily, with the Fisher King himself."

5. See Part IV. Phlebas the Phoenician and Mr. Eugenides, the Smyrna merchant—both of whom appear later in the poem—are different phases of the same symbolic character, here identified as the "Phoenician Sailor." Mr. Eugenides exports "currants" (line 210); the drowned Phlebas floats in the "current" (line 315). The line that follows is from Shakespeare's *Tempest* (I.ii.398), Ariel's song to the shipwrecked Ferdinand, who was "sitting on a bank / Weeping again the King my father's wrack," when "this music crept by me on the waters." The song is about the supposed drowning of Ferdinand's father, Alonso. *The Waste Land* contains many references to *The Tempest:* the supposed drowning of Alonso and Ferdinand is regarded as their purification by water, and the

"sea change" suffered by Alonso typifies, from one point of view, suffering transmuted into art (Eliot was impressed by the ritual element in Shakespeare's last plays). Ferdinand is also associated with Phlebas and Mr. Eugenides and therefore with the "drowned Phoenician Sailor." Drowning and sea change are both, of course, the work of water. Symbol of purification, baptism, refreshment, and growth, water plays diverse roles in the poem.

6. "Belladonna": beautiful lady. The word also suggests Madonna (the Virgin Mary) and therefore the Madonna of the Rocks (as in Leonardo da Vinci's painting); the rocks symbolize the Church. But there are other rocks—the rocks of dryness, of the Waste Land (e.g., lines 331 ff.). Belladonna is also an eye-cosmetic and a poison—the "deadly" nightshade. In the next line, the woman-figure of the Virgin becomes "the lady of situations," foreshadowing the neurasthenic lady of intrigue in Part II.

7. Life-force symbol, associated by Eliot with the Fisher King. The "Wheel" is the wheel of fortune, whose turning represents the reversals of human life.

8. Mr. Eugenides, "one-eyed" because the figure is in profile on the card and also as a suggestion of evil or crookedness. The mysterious burden on his back may be the mysteries of the fertility cults which, Miss Weston emphasizes, Phoenician merchants carried throughout the Mediterranean, or simply "the burthen of the mystery," "the heavy and the weary weight / Of all this unintelligible world" in Wordsworth's *Tintern Abbey.*

9. On his card in the Tarot pack he is shown hanging from one foot from a T-shaped cross. He symbolizes the self-sacrifice of the fertility god who is killed in order that his resurrection may bring fertility once again to land and people.

Unreal City,[1]   60
Under the brown fog of a winter dawn,
A crowd flowed over London Bridge, so many,[2]
I had not thought death had undone so many.
Sighs, short and infrequent, were exhaled,[3]
And each man fixed his eyes before his feet.   65
Flowed up the hill and down King William Street,
To where Saint Mary Woolnoth kept the hours
With a dead sound on the final stroke of nine.[4]
There I saw one I knew, and stopped him, crying: "Stetson![5]
You who were with me in the ships at Mylae![6]   70
That corpse you planted last year in your garden,
Has it begun to sprout?[7] Will it bloom this year?
Or has the sudden frost disturbed its bed?
Oh keep the Dog far hence, that's friend to men,
Or with his nails he'll dig it up again![8]   75
You! hypocrite lecteur!—mon semblable—mon frère!"[9]

---

1. "Cf. Baudelaire: *'Fourmillante cité,*
cité pleine de rêves, / Où le spectre en
plein jour raccroche le passant' [Eli-
ot's note]. The lines are quoted from
Les Sept Vieillards ("The Seven Old
Men") by Charles Baudelaire (1821–
67); it is poem XCIII of *Les Fleurs du
Mal* ("The Flowers of Evil"). The lines
may be translated: "Swarming city, city
full of dreams, / Where the specter in
broad daylight accosts the passerby."
2. "Cf. Inferno III, 55–57 * * * "
[Eliot's note]. The note goes on to
quote Dante's lines, which may be translated: "So long a train of people, /
that I should never have believed /
That death had undone so many."
Dante, just outside the gate of Hell,
has seen "the wretched souls of those
who lived without disgrace and without
praise." In his essay on Baudelaire
Eliot argued that in a sense it was
better to be positively evil than to be
neither good nor evil.
3. "Cf. Inferno IV, 25–27 * * * "
[Eliot's note]. In Limbo, the first circle of Hell, Dante has found the virtuous heathen, who lived before Christianity and are therefore eternally unable
to achieve their desire of seeing God.
Dante's lines, cited by Eliot, mean:
"Here, so far as I could tell by listening, / there was no lamentation except
sighs, / which caused the eternal air to
tremble."
4. "A phenomenon which I have often
noticed" [Eliot's note]. St. Mary Woolnoth is a church in the "City" of London (the financial district); the crowd
is flowing across London Bridge to work
in the City.
5. Presumably representing the "aver-

age businessman."
6. The battle of Mylae (260 B.C.) in
the First Punic War, which, like World
War I, was fought for economic reasons.
7. A distortion of the ritual death of
the fertility god.
8. "Cf. the Dirge in Webster's *White
Devil*" [Eliot's note]. In the play by
John Webster (d. 1625), the dirge,
sung by Cornelia, has the lines: "But
keep the wolf far thence, that's foe to
men, / For with his nails he'll dig them
up again." Eliot makes the "wolf" into
a "Dog," which is not a "foe" but a
"friend" to man. The image may be
intended to suggest the ultimate degeneration of the fertility ritual, where
the dying god is something buried in a
suburban back garden to be dug up
again by a friendly dog. There may be
a reference to Sirius, the Dog Star,
which is important in Egyptian mythology as heralding the fertilizing floods
of the Nile (this is discussed by Miss
Weston). But most important in this
passage is the feverish nightmare atmosphere which it develops.
9. "V. Baudelaire, Preface to *Fleurs du
Mal*" [Eliot's note]. The passage is the
last line of the introductory poem *Au
Lecteur* ("To the Reader") in Baudelaire's *Fleurs du Mal;* it may be translated: "Hypocrite reader!—my likeness
—my brother!" *Au Lecteur* describes
man as sunk in stupidity, sin, and evil;
but the worst in "each man's foul me-
nagerie of sin" is Boredom, the *"mons-
tre délicat"*—"You know him, reader * * * " Like Baudelaire, Eliot is
here shocking the reader into full participation in the poem.

II. A Game of Chess[1]

The Chair she sat in, like a burnished throne,[2]
Glowed on the marble, where the glass
Held up by standards wrought with fruited vines
From which a golden Cupidon peeped out   80
(Another hid his eyes behind his wing)
Doubled the flames of sevenbranched candelabra
Reflecting light upon the table as
The glitter of her jewels rose to meet it,
From satin cases poured in rich profusion;   85
In vials of ivory and colored glass
Unstoppered, lurked her strange synthetic perfumes,
Unguent, powdered, or liquid—troubled, confused
And drowned the sense in odors; stirred by the air
That freshened from the window, these ascended   90
In fattening the prolonged candle flames,
Flung their smoke into the laquearia,[3]
Stirring the pattern on the coffered ceiling.
Huge sea-wood fed with copper
Burned green and orange, framed by the colored stone,   95
In which sad light a carvéd dolphin swam.
Above the antique mantel was displayed
As though a window gave upon the sylvan scene[4]
The change of Philomel,[5] by the barbarous king

1. The title suggests two plays by Thomas Middleton (1570–1627): *A Game at Chess* and, more significantly, *Women Beware Women*, which has a scene in which a mother-in-law is distracted by a game of chess while her daughter-in-law is seduced: every move in the chess game represents a move in the seduction. Section II opens with a bored woman of leisure sitting before her dressing table in an atmosphere where the ornaments, the perfumes, the sheer excess of objects stifle the senses, while works of art emphasize the distinction between grandeur and futility. The neurasthenia and mounting hysteria revealed by the dialogue (or anterior monologue, or the remarks in quotation marks may be spoken by the lady and those not in quotation marks may represent her husband's unspoken answers) and the degeneration of culture through parody and jazzing up of lines from Shakespeare culminate in the meaningless yet terrifying "knock." This at once becomes the barman's knock on the counter as he calls closing time, and thus the scene changes to the lower end of the social scale, with women talking in a pub about methods of abortion—another aspect of that sterility and misuse of sex which help to make up the modern Waste Land.
2. "Cf. *Antony and Cleopatra*, II, ii, 1. 190" [Eliot's note]. In Shakespeare's play, Enobarbus' famous description of the first meeting of Antony and Cleopatra begins, "The barge she sat in, / like a burnish'd throne, / Burn'd on the water. * * * " Eliot's language in the opening lines of Part II is full of ironic distortions of Enobarbus' speech.
3. "Laquearia. V. *Aeneid*, I, 726 * * * " [Eliot's note]. *Laquearia* means "a paneled ceiling," and Eliot's note quotes the passage in the *Aeneid* which was his source for the word. The passage may be translated: "Blazing torches hang from the gold-paneled ceiling [*laquearibus aureis*], and torches conquer the night with flames." Virgil is here describing the banquet given by Dido, queen of Carthage, for Aeneas, with whom she fell in love. (Carthage is the scene of more "unholy loves" later in the poem; cf. line 307 and Eliot's note on it.)
4. "Sylvan scene. V. Milton, *Paradise Lost*, IV, 140" [Eliot's note]. The phrase is part of the first description of Eden, which we see through Satan's eyes.
5. "V. Ovid, *Metamorphoses*, VI, Philomela" [Eliot's note]. The note is a reference to Ovid's version of the Greek myth of the rape of Philomela by "the barbarous king" Tereus, husband of her sister Procne. Philomela was transformed into a nightingale. Eliot's note for line 100 refers ahead to his elaboration of the nightingale's song.

So rudely forced; yet there the nightingale 100
Filled all the desert with inviolable voice
And still she cried, and still the world pursues,
"Jug Jug"[6] to dirty ears.
And other withered stumps of time
Were told upon the walls; staring forms 105
Leaned out, leaning, hushing the room enclosed.
Footsteps shuffled on the stair.
Under the firelight, under the brush, her hair
Spread out in fiery points
Glowed into words, then would be savagely still. 110

"My nerves are bad tonight. Yes, bad. Stay with me.
Speak to me. Why do you never speak. Speak.
    What are you thinking of? What thinking? What?
I never know what you are thinking. Think."

I think we are in rats' alley[7] 115
Where the dead men lost their bones.

"What is that noise?"
                    The wind under the door.[8]
"What is that noise now? What is the wind doing?"
                    Nothing again nothing. 120
                                "Do
You know nothing? Do you see nothing? Do you remember
Nothing?"

    I remember
Those are pearls that were his eyes. 125
"Are you alive, or not? Is there nothing in your head?"
                                        But

O O O O that Shakespeherian Rag—
It's so elegant
So intelligent 130
"What shall I do now? What shall I do?"
"I shall rush out as I am, and walk the street
With my hair down, so. What shall we do tomorrow?
What shall we ever do?"
                    The hot water at ten. 135
And if it rains, a closed car at four.
And we shall play a game of chess,[1]
Pressing lidless eyes and waiting for a knock upon the door.

When Lil's husband got demobbed,[2] I said—
I didn't mince my words, I said to her myself, 140

6. Conventional representation of nightingale's song in Elizabethan poetry. The tragic myth has become degraded into a dirty story.
7. "Cf. Part III, l. 195" [Eliot's note].
8. "Cf. Webster: 'Is the wind in that door still?'" [Eliot's note]. The line cited in the note is from John Webster's *The Devil's Law Case* (III.ii.162).
1. "Cf. the game of chess in Middleton's *Women Beware Women*" [Eliot's note]. The significance of this chess game is discussed in note 1 for this section.
2. British slang for "demobilized" (discharged from the army).

HURRY UP PLEASE ITS TIME[3]
Now Albert's coming back, make yourself a bit smart.
He'll want to know what you done with that money he gave you
To get yourself some teeth. He did, I was there.
You have them all out, Lil, and get a nice set,   145
He said, I swear, I can't bear to look at you.
And no more can't I, I said, and think of poor Albert,
He's been in the army four years, he wants a good time,
And if you don't give it him, there's others will, I said.
Oh is there, she said. Something o' that, I said.   150
Then I'll know who to thank, she said, and give me a straight look.
HURRY UP PLEASE ITS TIME
If you don't like it you can get on with it, I said.
Others can pick and choose if you can't.
But if Albert makes off, it won't be for lack of telling.   155
You ought to be ashamed, I said, to look so antique.
(And her only thirty-one.)
I can't help it, she said, pulling a long face,
It's them pills I took, to bring it off, she said.
(She's had five already, and nearly died of young George.)   160
The chemist[4] said it would be all right, but I've never been the
    same.
You *are* a proper fool, I said.
Well, if Albert won't leave you alone, there it is, I said,
What you get married for if you don't want children?
HURRY UP PLEASE ITS TIME   165
Well, that Sunday Albert was home, they had a hot gammon,[5]
And they asked me in to dinner, to get the beauty of it hot—
HURRY UP PLEASE ITS TIME
HURRY UP PLEASE ITS TIME
Goonight Bill. Goonight Lou. Goonight May. Goonight.   170
Ta ta. Goonight. Goonight.
Good night, ladies, good night, sweet ladies, good night, good night.[6]

III. The Fire Sermon[7]

The river's tent is broken: the last fingers of leaf
Clutch and sink into the wet bank. The wind

3. The traditional call of the British bartender at closing time.
4. Druggist.
5. Ham or bacon.
6. Cf. the mad Ophelia's departing words (*Hamlet* IV.v.72). Ophelia, too, met "death by water."
7. Just as water both purifies and drowns, so fire both purges and destroys: in this part, the roles of fire are emphasized. The Fire Sermon itself was preached by the Buddha against the fires of lust and other passions which destroy men and prevent their regeneration. The section opens with an autumn scene on the Thames, which is made increasingly sinister by such devices as ironic references to or distortions of famous passages in literature and the mocking equation of noble rituals of the past with modern trivialities and obscenities. We turn briefly to Mr. Eugenides, degenerate descendant of the Syrian merchants who had once spread the fertility cults throughout the Mediterranean, and then to the deliberately horrible scene of modern lust, sex without meaning. Seductions on the Thames, old and new, with parodic echoes of Wagner, Shakespeare, and Dante, lead to a further expression of the sense of nothingness and meaninglessness that characterizes the modern Waste Land, and the section ends with the Occidental St. Augustine echoing the Oriental Buddha in a call for the renunciation of lust.

Crosses the brown land, unheard. The nymphs are departed.   175
Sweet Thames, run softly, till I end my song.[8]
The river bears no empty bottles, sandwich papers,
Silk handkerchiefs, cardboard boxes, cigarette ends
Or other testimony of summer nights. The nymphs are departed.
And their friends, the loitering heirs of city directors;   180
Departed, have left no addresses.
By the waters of Leman I sat down and wept . . .[9]
Sweet Thames, run softly till I end my song,
Sweet Thames, run softly, for I speak not loud or long.
But at my back in a cold blast I hear[1]   185
The rattle of the bones, and chuckle spread from ear to ear.
A rat crept softly through the vegetation
Dragging its slimy belly on the bank
While I was fishing[2] in the dull canal
On a winter evening round behind the gashouse   190
Musing upon the king my brother's wreck[3]
And on the king my father's death before him.
White bodies naked on the low damp ground
And bones cast in a little low dry garret,
Rattled by the rat's foot only, year to year.   195
But at my back from time to time I hear[4]
The sound of horns and motors, which shall bring
Sweeney to Mrs. Porter in the spring.[5]
O the moon shone bright on Mrs. Porter
And on her daughter   200
They wash their feet in soda water[6]
Et Ô ces voix d'enfants, chantant dans la coupole![7]

8. "V. Spenser, *Prothalamion*" [Eliot's note]. Eliot's line is the refrain from Spenser's marriage song, which is also set by the Thames in London—but a very different Thames from the modern littered river.

9. Cf. Psalms cxxxvii.1, in which the exiled Hebrews mourn for their homeland: "By the rivers of Babylon, there we sat down, yea, we wept, when we remembered Zion." Lake Leman is another name for Lake Geneva; Eliot wrote *The Waste Land* in Lausanne, by that lake. The common noun "leman" is an archaic word meaning, in the bad sense, an illicit sweetheart or mistress; hence "the waters of Leman" become associated with the fires of lust.

1. An ironic distortion of Andrew Marvell's famous lines from *To His Coy Mistress:* "But at my back I always hear / Time's wingéd chariot hurrying near * * *" Cf. line 196.

2. To fish is to seek eternity and salvation (cf. the Fisher King), but this activity is now degraded and dirtied.

3. "Cf. *The Tempest*, I, ii" [Eliot's note]. See line 48.

4. "Cf. Marvell, *To His Coy Mistress*" [Eliot's note].

5. "Cf. Day, *Parliament of Bees:* 'When of the sudden, listening, you shall hear, / A noise of horns and hunting, which shall bring / Actaeon to Diana in the spring, / Where all shall see her naked skin . . .' " [Eliot's note]. Actaeon was changed to a stag and hunted to death after he saw Diana, the goddess of chastity, bathing with her nymphs. In parodying the poem by John Day (1574–ca. 1640), Eliot is implying that Actaeon's fate indicates a very different set of values from those represented by the association of Sweeney and Mrs. Porter.

6. "I do not know the origin of the ballad from which these lines are taken: it was reported to me from Sydney, Australia" [Eliot's note]. One of the less vulgar versions of the song, which was popular among Australian troops in World War I, went as follows: "O the moon shines bright on Mrs. Porter / And on the daughter / Of Mrs. Porter. / They wash their feet in soda water / And so they oughter / To keep them clean."

7. "V. Verlaine, *Parsifal*" [Eliot's note]. The line is translated, "And O those children's voices singing in the dome!" Verlaine's sonnet describes Parsifal, the questing knight, resisting all

Twit twit twit
Jug jug jug jug jug jug
So rudely forc'd.
Tereu[8]   205

Unreal City
Under the brown fog of a winter noon
Mr. Eugenides, the Smyrna[9] merchant
Unshaven, with a pocket full of currants
C.i.f.[1] London: documents at sight,   210
Asked me in demotic French[2]
To luncheon at the Cannon Street Hotel[3]
Followed by a weekend at the Metropole.

At the violet hour, when the eyes and back   215
Turn upward from the desk, when the human engine waits
Like a taxi throbbing waiting,
I Tiresias,[4] though blind, throbbing between two lives,
Old man with wrinkled female breasts, can see
At the violet hour, the evening hour that strives
Homeward, and brings the sailor home from sea,[5]   220
The typist home at teatime, clears her breakfast, lights

sensual temptations to keep himself
pure for the Grail; Wagner's *Parsifal*
had his feet washed before entering the
castle of the Grail.

8. "Tereu" is a reference to Tereus,
who "rudely forc'd" Philomela; it was
also one of the conventional words for
a nightingale's song in Elizabethan poetry. Cf. the song from John Lyly's
Alexander and Campaspe (1564): "Oh,
'tis the ravished nightingale. / *Jug, jug,
jug, jug, tereu!* she cries," and lines
100 ff.

9. Seaport in western Turkey; here associated with Carthage and the ancient
Phoenician and Syrian merchants (unlike those of modern Smyrna), who
spread the old mystery cults. The sort
of cult spread by Mr. Eugenides is indicated by his suggestion of "a weekend at the Metropole" (a luxury hotel
at Brighton).

1. "The currants were quoted at a price
'carriage and insurance free to London';
and the Bill of Lading etc. were to be
handed to the buyer upon payment of
the sight draft" [Eliot's note].

2. Popular, vulgar French.

3. By the station which was then chief
terminus for travelers to the continent;
hence, a favorite meeting place for
businessmen going or coming from
abroad.

4. "Tiresias, although a mere spectator and not indeed a 'character,' is yet
the most important personage in the
poem, uniting all the rest. Just as the
one-eyed merchant, seller of currants,
melts into the Phoenician Sailor, and
the latter is not wholly distinct from
Ferdinand Prince of Naples, so all the
women are one woman, and the two

sexes meet in Tiresias. What Tiresias
sees, in fact, is the substance of the
poem. The whole passage from Ovid is
of great anthropological interest
* * * " [Eliot's note]. The note then
quotes the Latin text of Ovid's *Metamorphoses* which tells the story of
Tiresias' change of sex. The Latin may
be translated: "[The story goes that
once Jove, having drunk a great deal,]
jested with Juno. He said, 'Your pleasure in love is really greater than that
enjoyed by men.' She denied it; so
they decided to seek the opinion of the
wise Tiresias, for he knew both aspects
of love. For once, with a blow of his
staff, he had committed violence on two
huge snakes as they copulated in the
green forest; and—wonderful to tell—
was turned from a man into a woman
and thus spent seven years. In the
eighth year he saw the same snakes
again and said: 'If a blow struck at
you is so powerful that it changes the
sex of the giver, I will now strike at
you again.' With these words he struck
the snakes, and his former shape was
restored to him and he became as he
had been born. So he was appointed
arbitrator in the playful quarrel, and
supported Jove's statement. It is said
that Saturnia [i.e., Juno] was quite
disproportionately upset, and condemned the arbitrator to perpetual
blindness. But the almighty father (for
no god may undo what has been done
by another god), in return for the sight
that was taken away, gave him the
power to know the future and so
lightened the penalty paid by the honor."

5. "This may not appear as exact as
Sappho's lines, but I had in mind the

Her stove, and lays out food in tins.
Out of the window perilously spread
Her drying combinations touched by the sun's last rays.[5a]   225
On the divan are piled (at night her bed)
Stockings, slippers, camisoles, and stays.
I Tiresias, old man with wrinkled dugs
Perceived the scene, and foretold the rest—
I too awaited the expected guest.   230
He, the young man carbuncular,[6] arrives,
A small house agent's clerk, with one bold stare,
One of the low on whom assurance sits
As a silk hat on a Bradford[7] millionaire.
The time is now propitious, as he guesses,   235
The meal is ended, she is bored and tired,
Endeavors to engage her in caresses
Which still are unreproved, if undesired.
Flushed and decided, he assaults at once;
Exploring hands encounter no defense;   240
His vanity requires no response,
And makes a welcome of indifference.
(And I Tiresias have foresuffered all
Enacted on this same divan or bed;
I who have sat by Thebes[8] below the wall   245
And walked among the lowest of the dead.)
Bestows one final patronizing kiss,
And gropes his way, finding the stairs unlit . . .

She turns and looks a moment in the glass,
Hardly aware of her departed lover;   250
Her brain allows one half-formed thought to pass;
"Well now that's done: and I'm glad it's over."
When lovely woman stoops to folly and
Paces about her room again, alone,
She smoothes her hair with automatic hand,   255
And puts a record on the gramophone.[9]

"This music crept by me upon the waters"[1]
And along the Strand, up Queen Victoria Street.

'longshore' or 'dory' fisherman, who returns at nightfall" [Eliot's note]. Sappho's poem addressed Hesperus, the evening star, as the star that brings everyone home from work to evening rest; her
poem is here distorted by Eliot. There
is also an echo of Robert Louis Stevenson's *Requiem* in line 221 ("Home is
the sailor, home from sea").
5a. The present editor has been informed
that this and the preceding line constitute a "great allusion" to Keats's lines
"Charmed magic casements, opening on
the foam/ Of perilous seas, in faery lands
forlorn" (*Ode to a Nightingale*, lines
69–70) but he remains skeptical. It is,
however, certainly a powerful antiromantic image.
6. Pimply.

7. A Yorkshire woolen-manufacturing
town, where many rapid fortunes were
made in World War I.
8. Tiresias lived in Thebes for many
generations, where he witnessed the
tragic fates of Oedipus and Creon; he
prophesied in the market place by the
wall of Thebes.
9. "V. Goldsmith, the song in *The Vicar
of Wakefield*" [Eliot's note]. Olivia, a
character in Oliver Goldsmith's novel,
sings the following song when she returns to the place where she was seduced: "When lovely woman stoops to
folly / And finds too late that men betray / What charm can soothe her melancholy, / What art can wash her guilt
away? / The only art her guilt to
cover, / To hide her shame from every

O City city, I can sometimes hear
Beside a public bar in Lower Thames Street,   260
The pleasant whining of a mandolin
And a clatter and a chatter from within
Where fishmen lounge at noon: where the walls
Of Magnus Martyr hold
Inexplicable splendor of Ionian white and gold.[2]   265

    The river sweats[3]
    Oil and tar
    The barges drift
    With the turning tide
    Red sails   270
    Wide
    To leeward, swing on the heavy spar.
    The barges wash
    Drifting logs
    Down Greenwich reach   275
    Past the Isle of Dogs.[4]
          Weialala leia
          Wallala leialala

    Elizabeth and Leicester[5]
    Beating oars
    The stern was formed   280
    A gilded shell
    Red and gold
    The brisk swell
    Rippled both shores
    Southwest wind   285
    Carried down stream
    The peal of bells

eye, / To give repentance to her lover / And wring his bosom—is to die."
1. "V. *The Tempest*, as above" [Eliot's note]. Cf. line 48. (The line is from Ferdinand's speech, continuing after "weeping again the King my father's wrack.")
2. "The interior of St. Magnus Martyr is to my mind one of the finest among [Sir Christopher] Wren's interiors. * * * " [Eliot's note]. In these lines, the "pleasant" music, the "fishmen" resting after labor, and the splendor of the church interior all suggest a world of true values, where work and relaxation are both real and take place in a context of religious meaning. It is but a momentary glimpse of an almost lost world.
3. "The Song of the (three) Thames-daughters begins here. From line 292 to 306 inclusive they speak in turn. V. *Götterdämmerung*, III, i: the Rhine-daughters" [Eliot's note]. The Thames-daughters, both old and new, reflect a barren world of shabbiness and lust. Eliot parallels them with the Rhine-maidens in Wagner's opera *Die Götter-*

dämmerung ("The Twilight of the Gods") who lament that, with the gold of the Nibelungs stolen, the beauty of the river is gone. The refrain in lines 277–78 is borrowed from Wagner.
4. Greenwich is a borough in London on the south side of the Thames; opposite is the Isle of Dogs (a peninsula): Eliot presumably intends a reference to the earlier theme of the Dog.
5. The fruitless love of Queen Elizabeth and the Earl of Leicester (Sir Robert Dudley) is recalled in Eliot's note: "V. [J. A.] Froude, *Elizabeth*, Vol. I, ch. iv, letter of De Quadra to Philip of Spain: 'In the afternoon we were in a barge, watching the games on the river. (The queen) was alone with Lord Robert and myself on the poop, when they began to talk nonsense, and went so far that Lord Robert at last said, as I was on the spot there was no reason why they should not be married if the queen pleased.' " Even these two great figures from the 16th century represent no past glory and no contrast to present sordidness. (Queen Elizabeth was born in the old Green-

White towers
> Weialala leia   290
> Wallala leialala

"Trams and dusty trees.
Highbury bore me. Richmond and Kew
Undid me.[6] By Richmond I raised my knees
Supine on the floor of a narrow canoe."   295

"My feet are at Moorgate,[7] and my heart
Under my feet. After the event
He wept. He promised 'a new start.'
I made no comment. What should I resent?"

"On Margate[8] Sands.   300
I can connect
Nothing with nothing.
The broken fingernails of dirty hands.
My people humble people who expect
Nothing."   305
> la la

To Carthage then I came[9]

Burning burning burning burning[1]
O Lord Thou pluckest me out[2]
O Lord Thou pluckest   310

burning

IV. Death by Water[3]

Phlebas the Phoenician, a fortnight dead,
Forgot the cry of gulls, and the deep sea swell

wich House, by the river, where Greenwich Hospital now stands.)
6. "Cf. *Purgatorio*, V, 133 * * * "
[Eliot's note]. The *Purgatorio* lines,
which Eliot here parodies, may be
translated: "Remember me, who am La
Pia. / Siena made me, Maremma undid
me." Highbury is a residential London
suburb; Richmond is a pleasant part of
London westward up the Thames, with
boating and riverside hotels; Kew, adjoining Richmond, has the famous Kew
Gardens.
7. Slum area in east London.
8. Popular seaside resort on Thames
estuary.
9. "V. St. Augustine's *Confessions:* 'to
Carthage then I came, where a caldron
of unholy loves sang all about mine
ears'" [Eliot's note]. The passage
from the *Confessions* quoted here occurs in St. Augustine's account of his
youthful life of lust. Cf. line 92 and
its note.
1. "The complete text of the Buddha's
Fire Sermon (which corresponds in importance to the Sermon on the Mount)
from which these words are taken, will
be found translated in the late Henry

Clarke Warren's *Buddhism in Translation* (Harvard Oriental Series).
* * * " [Eliot's note]. In the sermon, the Buddha instructs his priests
that all things "are on fire. * * * The
eye * * * is on fire; forms are on
fire; eye-consciousness is on fire; impressions received by the eye are on
fire; and whatever sensation, pleasant,
unpleasant, or indifferent, originates in
dependence on impressions received by
the eye, that also is on fire. And with
what are these on fire? With the fire
of passion, say I, with the fire of hatred,
with the fire of infatuation * * * "
For Christ's Sermon on the Mount see
Matthew v-vii.
2. "From St. Augustine's *Confessions*
again. The collocation of these two
representatives of eastern and western
asceticism, as the culmination of this
part of the poem, is not an accident"
[Eliot's note]. Cf. also Zechariah iii.2,
where God, rebuking Satan, speaks of
Joshua the high priest as "a brand
plucked out of the fire."
3. This section has been interpreted in
two ways: either it signifies death by
water without resurrection (water *mis-*

And the profit and loss.

                A current under sea   315
Picked his bones in whispers. As he rose and fell
He passed the stages of his age and youth
Entering the whirlpool.
                Gentile or Jew
O you who turn the wheel and look to windward,   320
Consider Phlebas, who was once handsome and tall as you.

V. *What the Thunder Said*[4]

After the torchlight red on sweaty faces
After the frosty silence in the gardens
After the agony in stony places
The shouting and the crying   325
Prison and palace and reverberation
Of thunder of spring over distant mountains
He who was living is now dead[5]
We who were living are now dying
With a little patience   330

Here is no water but only rock
Rock and no water and the sandy road
The road winding above among the mountains
Which are mountains of rock without water
If there were water we should stop and drink   335
Amongst the rock one cannot stop or think
Sweat is dry and feet are in the sand
If there were only water amongst the rock
Dead mountain mouth of carious teeth that cannot spit
Here one can neither stand nor lie nor sit   340

used), or it symbolizes the sacrificial death which precedes rebirth. It is true that Phlebas is purged of his commercial interests and vanities when he suffers a sea change, and Miss Weston tells of the annual casting into the sea at Alexandria of an effigy of the head of Adonis—to be taken out after seven days by jubilant celebrators of the cult. The majority of interpreters, however, see Phlebas' drowning as a death by water which brings no resurrection, although there is a strange sense of peace in the death. Cf. line 47 and its note.
4. "In the first part of Part V three themes are employed: the journey to Emmaus, the approach to the Chapel Perilous (see Miss Weston's book), and the present decay of eastern Europe" [Eliot's note]. The journey to Emmaus (see line 360 and its note) is a significant feature in the story of Christ, and in this section the Waste Land is more clearly related to that story. Christ is associated with the slain fertility god, but there is still no resurrection. The rocky landscape is described with a new and agonizing intensity until everything breaks down in

hallucination in which visions of the decay of the great cities of Western civilization give way to nightmare images of horror. Then the scene changes to the Chapel Perilous in the midst of the Waste Land: it seems empty and derelict and apparently the quest has been in vain. But suddenly the cock crows, the lightning flashes, and the fertilizing rain falls. The thunder peals and gives its message of salvation in terms of Oriental wisdom, the Sanskrit words for "Give, Sympathize, Control." But we are too timidly prudent to give properly, too shut in within our own individualities to be able to sympathize properly, and we can more easily respond to control than exercise it. Salvation remains problematical.
5. These lines, containing allusions to Christ's imprisonment and trial, and to Gethsemane and Golgotha, suggest the hopeless days between Good Friday and Easter, between the Crucifixion and the Resurrection—associated with the death of the Fisher King and the moment of despair in the Waste Land when regeneration seems impossible.

There is not even silence in the mountains
But dry sterile thunder without rain
There is not even solitude in the mountains
But red sullen faces sneer and snarl
From doors of mudcracked houses   345
     If there were water

And no rock
If there were rock
And also water
And water   350
A spring
A pool among the rock
If there were the sound of water only
Not the cicada[6]
And dry grass singing   355
But sound of water over a rock
Where the hermit thrush[7] sings in the pine trees
Drip drop drip drop drop drop drop
But there is no water

Who is the third who walks always beside you?[8]   360
When I count, there are only you and I together
But when I look ahead up the white road
There is always another one walking beside you
Gliding wrapped in a brown mantle, hooded
I do not know whether a man or a woman   365
—But who is that on the other side of you?

What is that sound high in the air[9]
Murmur of maternal lamentation
Who are those hooded hordes swarming
Over endless plains, stumbling in cracked earth   370
Ringed by the flat horizon only
What is the city over the mountains
Cracks and reforms[1] and bursts in the violet air
Falling towers

6. Grasshopper. Cf. the prophecy of Ecclesiastes, "the grasshopper shall be a burden, and desire shall fail * * * " (and cf. also line 23 and its note).
7. "This is * * * the hermit thrush which I have heard in Quebec County. * * * Its 'water-dripping song' is justly celebrated" [Eliot's note].
8. "The following lines were stimulated by the account of one of the Antarctic expeditions (I forget which, but I think one of Shackleton's): it was related that the party of explorers, at the extremity of their strength, had the constant delusion that there was *one more member* than could actually be counted" [Eliot's note]. This reminiscence is associated with the journey of Christ's disciples to Emmaus given in Luke xxiv.13–16: "And it came to pass, that, while they communed together and reasoned, Jesus himself drew near, and went with them. But their eyes were holden that they should not know him."

9. Eliot's note for lines 367–77 is: "Cf. Herman Hesse, *Blick ins Chaos* ["A Glimpse into Chaos"] * * * " The note then quotes a passage from the German text, which is translated: "Already half of Europe, already at least half of Eastern Europe, on the way to Chaos, drives drunk in sacred infatuation along the edge of the precipice, sings drunkenly, as though hymn singing, as Dmitri Karamazov [in Dostoyevski's *Brothers Karamazov*] sang. The offended bourgeois laughs at the songs; the saint and the seer hear them with tears."
1. Used ironically.

Jerusalem Athens Alexandria   375
Vienna London
Unreal

A woman drew her long black hair out tight
And fiddled whisper music on those strings
And bats with baby faces in the violet light   380
Whistled, and beat their wings
And crawled head downward down a blackened wall
And upside down in air were towers
Tolling reminiscent bells, that kept the hours
And voices singing out of empty cisterns and exhausted wells.   385

In this decayed hole among the mountains
In the faint moonlight, the grass is singing
Over the tumbled graves, about the chapel
There is the empty chapel, only the wind's home.[2]
It has no windows, and the door swings,   390
Dry bones can harm no one.
Only a cock stood on the rooftree
Co co rico co co rico[3]
In a flash of lightning. Then a damp gust
Bringing rain   395

Ganga[4] was sunken, and the limp leaves
Waited for rain, while the black clouds
Gathered far distant, over Himavant.[5]
The jungle crouched, humped in silence.
Then spoke the thunder
DA[6]   400
Datta: what have we given?
My friend, blood shaking my heart
The awful daring of a moment's surrender
Which an age of prudence can never retract
By this, and this only, we have existed   405
Which is not to be found in our obituaries
Or in memories draped by the beneficent spider[7]
Or under seals broken by the lean solicitor

2. Suggesting the moment of near despair before the Chapel Perilous, when
the questing knight sees nothing there
but decay. This illusion of nothingness
is the knight's final test.
3. The crowing of the cock signals the
departure of ghosts and evil spirits.
Cf. *Hamlet* I.i.157 ff.
4. The river Ganges.
5. I.e., snowy mountain; the name of
a peak in the Himalayas.
6. "'Datta,   dayadhvam,   damyata'
(Give, sympathize, control). The fable
of the meaning of the Thunder is found
in the *Brihadaranyaka—Upanishad*, 5,
1. * * * " [Eliot's note]. The Hindu
fable referred to is that of gods, men,
and demons each in turn asking of

their father Prajapati, "Speak to us,
O Lord." To each he replied with the
one syllable *"DA,"* and each group interpreted it in a different way: *"Datta,"*
to give alms; *"Dayadhvam,"* to have
compassion; *"Damyata,"* to practice
self-control. The fable concludes, "This
is what the divine voice, the Thunder,
repeats when he says: *DA, DA, DA:*
'Control yourselves; give alms; be compassionate.' Therefore one should practice these three things: self-control,
alms-giving, and compassion."
7. "Cf. Webster, *The White Devil*, V,
vi: ' . . . they'll remarry / Ere the
worm pierce your winding-sheet, ere
the spider / Make a thin curtain for
your epitaphs'" [Eliot's note].

In our empty rooms   410
D A
Dayadhvam: I have heard the key[8]
Turn in the door once and turn once only
We think of the key, each in his prison
Thinking of the key, each confirms a prison   415
Only at nightfall, ethereal rumours
Revive for a moment a broken Coriolanus[9]
D A
Damyata: The boat responded
Gaily, to the hand expert with sail and oar   420
The sea was calm, your heart would have responded
Gaily, when invited, beating obedient
To controlling hands

                         I sat upon the shore
Fishing,[1] with the arid plain behind me   425
Shall I at least set my lands in order?[2]
London Bridge is falling down falling down falling down[3]
Poi s'ascose nel foco che gli affina[4]
Quando fiam uti chelidon[5]—O swallow swallow

8. "Cf. *Inferno,* XXXIII, 46 * * * "
[Eliot's note]. In this passage from
the *Inferno* Ugolino recalls his imprisonment in the tower with his children,
where they starved to death: "And I
heard below the door of the horrible
tower being locked up." Eliot implies
that we cannot obey the command to
sympathize because we are imprisoned
within the circle of our own egotism.
Eliot's note for this line goes on to
quote F. H. Bradley, *Appearance and
Reality,* p. 346, as follows: " 'My external sensations are no less private
to myself than are my thoughts or my
feelings. In either case my experience
falls within my own circle, a circle
closed on the outside; and, with all its
elements alike, every sphere is opaque
to the others which surround it. . . .
In brief, regarded as an existence which
appears in a soul, the whole world for
each is peculiar and private to that
soul.' "
9. Coriolanus, who acted out of pride
rather than duty, is an obvious example of a man locked in the prison of
his own self. He led the enemy against
his native city out of injured pride
(cf. Shakespeare's *Coriolanus*).
1. "V. Weston: *From Ritual to Romance;* chapter on the Fisher King"
[Eliot's note].
2. The inclusive "I," who sits in the
symbolic act of fishing (seeking salvation, regeneration, eternity) with the
Waste Land behind him, wonders how
far he can order his affairs. There is
a note of subdued hope or at least of
determination in these lines. The "at
least" suggests a reasonable minimum
of achievement.

3. One of the later lines of this nursery
rhyme is: "Take the key and lock her
up, my fair lady."
4. "V. *Purgatorio,* XXVI, 148 * * * "
[Eliot's note]. The note goes on to
quote lines 145–48 of the *Purgatorio,*
in which Arnaut Daniel, the Provençal
poet, addresses Dante: " 'Now I pray
you, by that virtue which guides you
to the summit of the stairway, be mindful in due time of my pain.' " Then
(in the line Eliot quotes here) "he
hid himself in the fire which refines
them." The purgatorial vision of refining fire—as distinct from the fires
of lust—represents one of the hopeful
fragments shored up by the seeker for
regeneration and order.
5. "V. *Pervigilium Veneris.* Cf. Philomela in Parts II and III" [Eliot's
note]. The Latin phrase in the text
means, "When shall I be as the swallow?" It comes from the *Pervigilium
Veneris* ("Vigil of Venus"), an anonymous late Latin poem combining a
hymn to Venus with a description of
spring. In the last two stanzas of the
Pervigilium occurs a recollection of the
Tereus-Procne-Philomela myth (except
that in this version the swallow is identified with Philomela); the anonymous
poet's mood changes to one of sadness,
combined with hope for renewal: "The
maid of Tereus sings under the poplar
shade, so that you would think musical
trills of love came from her mouth and
not a sister's complaint of a barbarous
husband. * * * She sings, we are silent. When will my spring come? When
shall I be as the swallow that I may
cease to be silent? I have lost the Muse
in silence, and Apollo regards me not

Le Prince d'Aquitaine à la tour abolie[6]   430
These fragments I have shored against my ruins[7]
Why then Ile fit you. Hieronymo's mad againe.[8]
Datta. Dayadhvam. Damyata.
           Shantih   shantih   shantih[9]

1921   1922

Journey of the Magi[1]

"A cold coming we had of it,
Just the worst time of the year
For a journey, and such a long journey:
The ways deep and the weather sharp,
The very dead of winter."[2]   5
And the camels galled, sore-footed, refractory,
Lying down in the melting snow.
There were times we regretted
The summer palaces on slopes, the terraces,
And the silken girls bringing sherbet.
Then the camel men cursing and grumbling   10
And running away, and wanting their liquor and women,
And the night-fires going out, and the lack of shelters,
And the cities hostile and the towns unfriendly
And the villages dirty and charging high prices: 15
A hard time we had of it.

* * * " For "O swallow swallow" cf. Swinburne's *Itylus*, which begins, "Swallow, my sister, O sister swallow, / How can thine heart be full of spring?" and Tennyson's lyric in *The Princess:* "O Swallow, Swallow, flying, flying south * * * "

6. "V. Gerard de Nerval, Sonnet *El Desdichado*" [Eliot's note]. The French line may be translated, "The Prince of Aquitaine in the ruined tower." One of the cards in the Tarot pack is "the tower struck by lightning." The ruined tower is symbolic of a decayed tradition.

7. This may refer to the whole poem —fragments assembled by the poet in the attempt to come to terms with his situation.

8. "V. Kyd's *Spanish Tragedy*" [Eliot's note]. Subtitled "Hieronymo's Mad Againe," Kyd's play (1594) is an early example of the Elizabethan tragedy of revenge. Hieronymo, driven mad by the murder of his son, has his revenge when he is asked to write a court entertainment. He replies, "Why then Ile fit you!" (i.e., accommodate you), and assigns the parts in the entertainment so that, in the course of the action, his son's murderers are killed.

9. "Shantih. Repeated as here, a formal ending to an Upanishad. 'The Peace which passeth understanding' is our equivalent to this word" [Eliot's note]. The Upanishads are poetic dialogues on Hindu metaphysics, written after the Vedas, the ancient Hindu scriptures, and in part commenting on them. The fact that the benediction is in a language so foreign to Western tradition may indicate that the solution is willed, not achieved. The fragments with which the poem ends seem like a desperate attempt at ordering chaos, but it breaks down in madness ("Hieronymo's mad againe"). We end with the threefold message repeated and the benediction uttered; but the issue remains in doubt.

1. One of the three wise men who came from the east to Jerusalem to do homage to the infant Jesus (Matthew ii.1–12) is recalling in old age the meaning of the experience.

2. Adapted from a passage in a Nativity sermon by the 17th-century divine Lancelot Andrewes: "A cold coming they had of it at this time of the year, just the worst time of the year to take a journey, and specially a long journey in. The ways deep, the weather sharp, the days short, the sun farthest off, *in solstitio brumali*, 'the very dead of winter.'"

At the end we preferred to travel all night,
Sleeping in snatches,
With the voices singing in our ears, saying
That this was all folly.   20

Then at dawn we came down to a temperate valley,
Wet, below the snow line, smelling of vegetation;
With a running stream and a water mill beating the darkness,
And three trees on the low sky,
And an old white horse galloped away in the meadow.[3]   25
Then we came to a tavern with vine-leaves over the lintel,
Six hands at an open door dicing for pieces of silver,[4]
And feet kicking the empty wineskins.
But there was no information, and so we continued
And arrived at evening, not a moment too soon   30
Finding the place; it was (you may say) satisfactory.

All this was a long time ago, I remember,
And I would do it again, but set down
This set down
This: were we led all that way for   35
Birth or Death? There was a Birth, certainly,
We had evidence and no doubt. I had seen birth and death,
But had thought they were different; this Birth was
Hard and bitter agony for us, like Death, our death.
We returned to our places, these Kingdoms,   40
But no longer at ease here, in the old dispensation,
With an alien people clutching their gods.
I should be glad of another death.

1927

Marina[1]

Quis hic locus, quae regio, quae mundi plaga?[2]

What seas what shores what gray rocks and what islands
What water lapping the bow

3. A series of images of freshness and renewal, combined with anticipations of disaster. The "three trees on the low sky" suggest the three crosses, with Christ crucified on the center one; the men dicing for pieces of silver suggest the soldiers dicing for Christ's garments and Judas' betrayal of him for thirty pieces of silver.
4. "Why, for all of us, out of all that we have heard, seen, felt, in a lifetime, do certain images recur, charged with emotion, rather than others? * * * six ruffians seen through an open window playing cards at night at a small French railway junction where there was a water mill" (Eliot, *The Use of*

Poetry and the Use of Criticism).
1. Marina is Pericles' daughter in Shakespeare's play *Pericles Prince of Tyre*: she was born at sea, lost to her father, then as a young woman found by him again. This poem evokes the mood of hushed wonder with which Pericles rediscovered his daughter, who had almost miraculously preserved her innocence and virtue through harrowing experiences. The situation is of course symbolic: a mood is established of regeneration, of escape from lust into love and from violence and confusion into peace. The symbolic boat on which the reunion takes place was originally made by the speaker, but for

And scent of pine and the woodthrush singing through the fog
What images return
O my daughter.   5

Those who sharpen the tooth of the dog, meaning
Death
Those who glitter with the glory of the hummingbird, meaning
Death
Those who sit in the sty of contentment, meaning   10
Death
Those who suffer the ecstasy of the animals, meaning
Death

Are become unsubstantial, reduced by a wind,
A breath of pine, and the woodsong fog   15
By this grace dissolved in place

What is this face, less clear and clearer
The pulse in the arm, less strong and stronger—
Given or lent? more distant than stars and nearer than the eye

Whispers and small laughter between leaves and hurrying feet 20
Under sleep, where all the waters meet.

Bowsprit cracked with ice and paint cracked with heat.
I made this, I have forgotten
And remember.
The rigging weak and the canvas rotten   25
Between one June and another September.
Made this unknowing, half conscious, unknown, my own.
The garboard strake[3] leaks, the seams need calking.
This form, this face, this life
Living to live in a world of time beyond me; let me   30
Resign my life for this life, my speech for that unspoken,
The awakened, lips parted, the hope, the new ships.

What seas what shores what granite islands towards my timbers
And woodthrush calling through the fog
My daughter.   35

                                                              1930

a purpose he cannot remember; it is battered and frail; but it serves its purpose, having led him to this moment of grace, dedication, and new hope. One must not be too literal in pressing a meaning on each of the images: this is the most delicately evocative of all Eliot's poems.

2. "What place is this, what country, what region of the world?" Spoken by Hercules on regaining sanity after having killed his children in his madness, in Seneca's play *Hercules Furens* ("The Mad Hercules"). This is a situation contrary to the one evoked in the poem. Eliot once wrote to a correspondent that he wished to achieve a "crisscross" between the scenes in the Senecan and the Shakespearean plays. He appears to be making that association between birth and death which he uses so often (as in *The Waste Land* and *Journey of the Magi*).

3. The planking nearest to the boat's keel—hence its most vital spot.

From FOUR QUARTETS
Little Gidding[1]

I

Midwinter spring is its own season
Sempiternal[2] though sodden towards sundown,
Suspended in time, between pole and tropic.
When the short day is brightest, with frost and fire,
The brief sun flames the ice, on pond and ditches, 5
In windless cold that is the heart's heat,
Reflecting in a watery mirror
A glare that is blindness in the early afternoon.
And glow more intense than blaze of branch, or brazier,
Stirs the dumb spirit: no wind, but pentecostal fire[3] 10
In the dark time of the year. Between melting and freezing

1. This is the fourth of Eliot's *Four Quartets,* four related poems each divided into five "movements" in a manner reminiscent of the structure of a quartet or a sonata and each dealing with some aspect of the relation of time and eternity, the meaning of history, the achievement of the moment of timeless insight. Though the *Four Quartets* constitute a unified sequence, they were each written separately and can be read as individual poems. "*Little Gidding* can be understood by itself, without reference to the preceding poems, which it yet so beautifully completes" (Helen Gardner). Each of the four is named after a place. Little Gidding is a village in Huntingdonshire where in 1625 Nicholas Ferrar established an Anglican religious community; it was broken up in 1647, toward the end of the Civil War, by the victorious Puritans; the chapel, however, was rebuilt in the 19th century and still exists. The poet recalls a midwinter visit to the chapel; he evokes the scene and uses it for a starting point for a meditation on England's past and present, on the possibility of redemption through purgation. Eliot wrote the poem in 1942, when he was a fire-watcher during World War II, and he looks back at the history and meaning of Little Gidding from his own war experience in order to project its present significance.

The first section or movement is itself in three parts of which the first sets the scene and the season, the second asserts the significance of this place at any season, and the third reminds us of the original purpose of the community and suggests what these dead can communicate to us now, to achieve "the intersection of the timeless moment." The second movement is much more lyrical in tone, and broods over change and decay. It then changes to a Dan-

tesque verse form (suggesting Dante's *terza rima,* but unrhymed) in which the poet describes himself walking at dawn after an air raid and encountering a "dead master" returned temporarily from Purgatory. (The scene also recalls Dante's meeting his own dead master Brunetto Latini in Hell.) The spirit talks of the relation between past and present, their common concern with language, and the slow and difficult progress toward purgation; he disappears when the All Clear sounds. The third movement broods over the uses of memory and attitudes toward history; recalls that the combatants in that earlier war are now "folded in a single party"; concedes that one cannot revive lost causes; and suggests that in detachment and in the view of past suffering as purgation a sense of peace and of renewal might be achieved. The short lyrical fourth movement elaborates the notion of purgation (the dove of peace has become the bombing plane), sees fire as purgative as well as destructive, and emphasizes the dual nature of love and the alternative of the two kinds of fire. The final movement accepts the movements of history and sees history as "a pattern of timeless moments," so that here at this moment in Little Gidding "while the light fails / On a winter afternoon, in a secluded chapel / History is now and England." The poet now sees the rose of life and the yew tree of death interpenetrating at each moment and ends with a vision of suffering and love, the fire and the rose, as one.
2. Eternal, everlasting.
3. On the Pentecost day after the death and resurrection of Christ, there appeared to His apostles "cloven tongues like as of fire * * * And they were all filled with the Holy Ghost" (Acts ii).

The soul's sap quivers. There is no earth smell
Or smell of living thing. This is the springtime
But not in time's covenant. Now the hedgerow
Is blanched for an hour with transitory blossom 15
Of snow, a bloom more sudden
Than that of summer, neither budding nor fading,
Not in the scheme of generation.
Where is the summer, the unimaginable
Zero summer? 20

        If you came this way,
Taking the route you would be likely to take
From the place you would be likely to come from,
If you came this way in may time, you would find the hedges
White again, in May, with voluptuary sweetness. 25
It would be the same at the end of the journey,
If you came at night like a broken king,[4]
If you came by day not knowing what you came for,
It would be the same, when you leave the rough road
And turn behind the pigsty to the dull façade 30
And the tombstone. And what you thought you came for
Is only a shell, a husk of meaning
From which the purpose breaks only when it is fulfilled
If at all. Either you had no purpose
Or the purpose is beyond the end you figured 35
And is altered in fulfillment. There are other places
Which also are the world's end, some at the sea jaws,
Or over a dark lake, in a desert or a city—
But this is the nearest, in place and time,
Now and in England. 40

        If you came this way,
Taking any route, starting from anywhere,
At any time or at any season,
It would always be the same: you would have to put off
Sense and notion. You are not here to verify, 45
Instruct yourself, or inform curiosity
Or carry report. You are here to kneel
Where prayer has been valid. And prayer is more
Than an order of words, the conscious occupation
Of the praying mind, or the sound of the voice praying. 50
And what the dead had no speech for, when living,
They can tell you, being dead: the communication
Of the dead is tongued with fire beyond the language of the living.
Here, the intersection of the timeless moment
Is England and nowhere. Never and always. 55

              II

Ash on an old man's sleeve
Is all the ash the burnt roses leave.

4. I.e., Charles I. King Charles visited Ferrar's community more than once, and is said to have paid his last visit in secret after his final defeat in the Civil War.

Dust in the air suspended
Marks the place where a story ended.
Dust inbreathed was a house—   60
The wall, the wainscot, and the mouse.
The death of hope and despair,
  This is the death of air.[5]

There are flood and drouth
Over the eyes and in the mouth,   65
Dead water and dead sand
Contending for the upper hand.
The parched eviscerate soil
Gapes at the vanity of toil,
Laughs without mirth.   70
  This is the death of earth.

Water and fire succeed
The town, the pasture, and the weed.
Water and fire deride
The sacrifice that we denied.   75
Water and fire shall rot
The marred foundations we forgot,
Of sanctuary and choir.
  This is the death of water and fire.

In the uncertain hour before the morning   80
 Near the ending of interminable night
 At the recurrent end of the unending
After the dark dove with the flickering tongue
 Had passed below the horizon of his homing
 While the dead leaves still rattled on like tin   85
Over the asphalt where no other sound was
 Between three districts whence the smoke arose
 I met one walking, loitering and hurried
As if blown towards me like the metal leaves
 Before the urban dawn wind unresisting.   90
 And as I fixed upon the down-turned face
That pointed scrutiny with which we challenge
 The first-met stranger in the waning dusk
 I caught the sudden look of some dead master
Whom I had known, forgotten, half recalled   95
 Both one and many; in the brown baked features
 The eyes of a familiar compound ghost[6]
Both intimate and unidentifiable.

5. "The death of air," like that of "earth" and of "water and fire" in the succeeding stanzas, recalls the theory of the creative strife of the four elements propounded by Heraclitus (Greek philosopher of 4th and 5th centuries B.C.): "Fire lives in the death of air; air lives in the death of fire; water lives in the death of earth; and earth lives in the death of water." But at this point in the poem, unlike Heraclitus' theory, death is not intermingled with life.
6. Cf. Shakespeare, *Sonnet* LXXXVI, line 9: "that affable familiar ghost." W. B. Yeats is the "dead master" who is an important part of this "compound ghost."

So I assumed a double part,[7] and cried
    And heard another's voice cry: "What! are *you* here?"   100
Although we were not. I was still the same,
    Knowing myself yet being someone other—
    And he a face still forming; yet the words sufficed
To compel the recognition they preceded.
    And so, compliant to the common wind,   105
    Too strange to each other for misunderstanding,
In concord at this intersection time
    Of meeting nowhere, no before and after,
    We trod the pavement in a dead patrol.
I said: "The wonder that I feel is easy,   110
    Yet ease is cause of wonder. Therefore speak:
    I may not comprehend, may not remember."
And he: "I am not eager to rehearse
    My thought and theory which you have forgotten.
    These things have served their purpose: let them be.   115
So with your own, and pray they be forgiven
    By others, as I pray you to forgive
    Both bad and good. Last season's fruit is eaten
And the fullfed beast shall kick the empty pail.
    For last year's words belong to last year's language   120
    And next year's words await another voice.
But, as the passage now presents no hindrance
    To the spirit unappeased and peregrine[8]
    Between two worlds become much like each other,
So I find words I never thought to speak   125
    In streets I never thought I should revisit
    When I left my body on a distant shore.
Since our concern was speech, and speech impelled us
    To purify the dialect of the tribe[9]
    And urge the mind to aftersight and foresight,   130
Let me disclose the gifts reserved for age
    To set a crown upon your lifetime's effort.
    First, the cold friction of expiring sense
Without enchantment, offering no promise
    But bitter tastelessness of shadow fruit   135
    As body and soul begin to fall asunder.
Second, the conscious impotence of rage
    At human folly, and the laceration
    Of laughter at what ceases to amuse.
And last, the rending pain of re-enactment   140
    Of all that you have done, and been; the shame
    Of motives late revealed, and the awareness
Of things ill done and done to others' harm

---

7. Two interpretations have been suggested: either the poet assumes the part of Dante as he accosted people in Hell or Purgatory, or else he assumes the part of his own other self.
8. Foreign, coming from abroad.
9. A rendering of the line "*Donner un sens plus pur aux mots de la tribu*" in Stéphane Mallarmé's sonnet *Le Tombeau d'Edgar Poe* ("The Tomb of Edgar Poe"). There are many less direct literary echoes in this passage, some recalling Milton, some various Jacobean dramatists, some Dante.

Which once you took for exercise of virtue.
Then fools' approval strings, and honor stains.   145
From wrong to wrong the exasperated spirit
  Proceeds, unless restored by that refining fire[1]
  Where you must move in measure, like a dancer."
The day was breaking. In the disfigured street
  He left me, with a kind of valediction,   150
  And faded on the blowing of the horn.[2]

III

There are three conditions which often look alike
Yet differ completely, flourish in the same hedgerow:
Attachment to self and to things and to persons, detachment
From self and from things and from persons; and, growing between
    them, indifference   155
Which resembles the others as death resembles life,
Being between two lives—unflowering, between
The live and the dead nettle. This is the use of memory:
For liberation—not less of love but expanding
Of love beyond desire, and so liberation   160
From the future as well as the past. Thus, love of a country
Begins as attachment to our own field of action
And comes to find that action of little importance
Though never indifferent. History may be servitude,
History may be freedom. See, now they vanish,   165
The faces and places, with the self which, as it could, loved them,
To become renewed, transfigured, in another pattern.

Sin is Behovely, but
All shall be well, and
All manner of things shall be well.[3]   170
If I think, again, of this place,
And of people, not wholly commendable,
Of no immediate kin or kindness,
But some of peculiar genius,
All touched by a common genius,   175
United in the strife which divided them;
If I think of a king at nightfall,[4]

---

1. Cf. *The Waste Land*, line 428 and its note.
2. Cf. *Hamlet*, I.ii.157. "It faded on the crowing of the cock." The horn is the All Clear signal after an air raid (the dialogue has taken place between the dropping of the last bomb and the sounding of the All Clear). Eliot called the section which ends with this line "the nearest equivalent to a canto of the *Inferno* or *Purgatorio*" that he could achieve, and spoke of his intention to present "a parallel, by means of contrast, between the *Inferno* and the *Purgatorio* * * * and a hallucinated scene after an air raid."
3. A quotation from the 14th-century English mystic, Dame Juliana of Norwich: "Sin is behovabil [inevitable], but all shall be well and all shall be well and all manner of thing shall be well." It is the accent of genuine mystical experience and authority that Eliot wishes to convey in using Dame Juliana's words. The thought expressed—that in spite of sin or even through sin all shall be well—is a variation of the "fortunate fall" (*felix culpa*) idea found in Milton and elsewhere.
4. Charles I. He died "on the scaffold" in 1649, while his principal advisers, Archbishop Laud and Thomas Wentworth, Earl of Strafford, were both executed earlier by the victorious Parliamentary forces. Eliot is here meditating on the English Civil War and refusing to take sides, for history subsumes both sides. The war becomes a symbol of purgation through suffering. Cf. conclusion of this section.

Of three men, and more, on the scaffold
And a few who died forgotten
In other places, here and abroad,   180
And of one who died blind and quiet[4a]
Why should we celebrate
These dead men more than the dying?
It is not to ring the bell backward
Nor is it an incantation   185
To summon the specter of a Rose.
We cannot revive old factions
We cannot restore old policies
Or follow an antique drum.
These men, and those who opposed them   190
And those whom they opposed
Accept the constitution of silence
And are folded in a single party.
Whatever we inherit from the fortunate
We have taken from the defeated   195
What they had to leave us—a symbol:
A symbol perfected in death.
And all shall be well and
All manner of thing shall be well
By the purification of the motive   200
In the ground of our beseeching.

IV

The dove descending breaks the air
With flame of incandescent terror
Of which the tongues declare
The one discharge from sin and error.   205
The only hope, or else despair
   Lies in the choice of pyre or pyre—
   To be redeemed from fire by fire.

Who then devised the torment? Love.
Love is the unfamiliar Name   210
Behind the hands that wove
The intolerable shirt of flame[5]
Which human power cannot remove.
   We only live, only suspire
   Consumed by either fire or fire.   215

V

What we call the beginning is often the end
And to make an end is to make a beginning.
The end is where we start from. And every phrase
And sentence that is right (where every word is at home,
Taking its place to support the others,   220
The word neither diffident nor ostentatious,

4a. Milton.
5. Out of love for her husband Hercules, Deianira gave him the poisoned shirt of Nessus. She had been told that it would increase his love for her, but instead it so corroded his flesh that in his agony he mounted a funeral pyre and burned himself to death.

An easy commerce of the old and the new,
The common word exact without vulgarity,
The formal word precise but not pedantic,
The complete consort[6] dancing together)   225
Every phrase and every sentence is an end and a beginning,
Every poem an epitaph. And any action
Is a step to the block, to the fire, down the sea's throat
Or to an illegible stone: and that is where we start.
We die with the dying: 230
See, they depart, and we go with them.
We are born with the dead:
See, they return, and bring us with them.
The moment of the rose and the moment of the yew tree
Are of equal duration. A people without history   235
Is not redeemed from time, for history is a pattern
Of timeless moments. So, while the light fails
On a winter's afternoon, in a secluded chapel
History is now and England.
With the drawing of this Love and the voice of this Calling[7]   240

We shall not cease from exploration
And the end of all our exploring
Will be to arrive where we started
And know the place for the first time.
Through the unknown, remembered gate   245
When the last of earth left to discover
Is that which was the beginning;
At the source of the longest river
The voice of the hidden waterfall
And the children in the apple tree   250
Not known, because not looked for
But heard, half-heard, in the stillness
Between two waves of the sea.[8]
Quick now, here, now, always—
A condition of complete simplicity   255
(Costing not less than everything)
And all shall be well and
All manner of thing shall be well
When the tongues of flame are in-folded
Into the crowned knot of fire   260
And the fire and the rose are one.

1942   1942, 1943

---

6. The word means both "company" and "harmony of sounds."
7. This line is from an anonymous 14th-century mystical work, the *Cloud of Unknowing*.
8. The voice of the children in the apple tree symbolizes the sudden moment of insight. Cf. the conclusion to

Burnt Norton (the first of the *Four Quartets*), where the laughter of the children in the garden has a like meaning: "Sudden in a shaft of sunlight / Even while the dust moves / There rises the hidden laughter / Of children in the foliage / Quick now, here, now, always * * * "

Tradition and the Individual Talent[1]

I

In English writing we seldom speak of tradition, though we occasionally apply its name in deploring its absence. We cannot refer to "the tradition" or to "a tradition"; at most, we employ the adjective in saying that the poetry of So-and-so is "traditional" or even "too traditional." Seldom, perhaps, does the word appear except in a phrase of censure. If otherwise, it is vaguely approbative, with the implication, as to the work approved, of some pleasing archaeological reconstruction. You can hardly make the word agreeable to English ears without this comfortable reference to the reassuring science of archaeology.

Certainly the word is not likely to appear in our appreciations of living or dead writers. Every nation, every race, has not only its own creative, but its own critical turn of mind; and is even more oblivious of the shortcomings and limitations of its critical habits than of those of its creative genius. We know, or think we know, from the enormous mass of critical writing that has appeared in the French language the critical method or habit of the French; we only conclude (we are such unconscious people) that the French are "more critical" than we, and sometimes even plume ourselves a little with the fact, as if the French were the less spontaneous. Perhaps they are; but we might remind ourselves that criticism is as inevitable as breathing, and that we should be none the worse for articulating what passes in our minds when we read a book and feel an emotion about it, for criticizing our own minds in their work of criticism. One of the facts that might come to light in this process is our tendency to insist, when we praise a poet, upon those aspects of his work in which he least resembles anyone else. In these aspects or parts of his work we pretend to find what is individual, what is the peculiar essence of the man. We dwell with satisfaction upon the poet's difference from his predecessors, especially his immediate predecessors; we endeavor to find something that can be isolated in order to be enjoyed. Whereas if we approach a poet without this prejudice we shall often find that not only the best, but the most individual parts of his work may be those in which the dead poets, his ancestors, assert their immortality most vigorously. And I do not mean the impressionable period of adolescence, but the period of full maturity.

Yet if the only form of tradition, of handing down, consisted in

1. First published in the *Egoist* (1919) and later collected in *The Sacred Wood* (1920), this essay is one of Eliot's most influential pieces of criticism.

following the ways of the immediate generation before us in a blind or timid adherence to its successes, "tradition" should positively be discouraged. We have seen many such simple currents soon lost in the sand; and novelty is better than repetition. Tradition is a matter of much wider significance. It cannot be inherited, and if you want it you must obtain it by great labor. It involves, in the first place, the historical sense, which we may call nearly indispensable to any one who would continue to be a poet beyond his twenty-fifth year; and the historical sense involves a perception, not only of the pastness of the past, but of its presence; the historical sense compels a man to write not merely with his own generation in his bones, but with a feeling that the whole of the literature of Europe from Homer and within it the whole of the literature of his own country has a simultaneous existence and composes a simultaneous order. This historical sense, which is a sense of the timeless as well as of the temporal and of the timeless and of the temporal together, is what makes a writer traditional. And it is at the same time what makes a writer most acutely conscious of his place in time, of his own contemporaneity.

No poet, no artist of any art, has his complete meaning alone. His significance, his appreciation is the appreciation of his relation to the dead poets and artists. You cannot value him alone; you must set him, for contrast and comparison, among the dead. I mean this as a principle of aesthetic, not merely historical, criticism. The necessity that he shall conform, that he shall cohere, is not one-sided; what happens when a new work of art is created is something that happens simultaneously to all the works of art which preceded it. The existing monuments form an ideal order among themselves, which is modified by the introduction of the new (the really new) work of art among them. The existing order is complete before the new work arrives; for order to persist after the supervention of novelty, the *whole* existing order must be, if ever so slightly, altered; and so the relations, proportions, values of each work of art toward the whole are readjusted; and this is conformity between the old and the new. Whoever has approved this idea of order, of the form of European, of English literature will not find it preposterous that the past should be altered by the present as much as the present is directed by the past. And the poet who is aware of this will be aware of great difficulties and responsibilities.

In a peculiar sense he will be aware also that he must inevitably be judged by the standards of the past. I say judged, not amputated, by them; not judged to be as good as, or worse or better than, the dead; and certainly not judged by the canons of dead critics. It is a judgment, a comparison, in which two things are measured by each other. To conform merely would be for the new work not really to conform at all; it would not be new, and would therefore not be a work of art. And we do not quite say that the new is more valuable because it fits in; but its fitting in is a test of its value—a test, it is true, which can only be slowly and cautiously applied, for we are none of us infallible judges of conformity. We say: it appears to conform, and is perhaps individual, or it appears individual, and may conform; but we are hardly likely to find that it is one and not the other.

To proceed to a more intelligible exposition of the relation of the poet to the past: he can neither take the past as a lump, an indiscriminate bolus,[2] nor can he form himself wholly on one or two private admirations, nor can he form himself wholly upon one preferred period. The first course is inadmissible, the second is an important experience of youth, and the third is a pleasant and highly desirable supplement. The poet must be very conscious of the main current, which does not at all flow invariably through the most distinguished reputations. He must be quite aware of the obvious fact that art never improves, but that the material of art is never quite the same. He must be aware that the mind of Europe— the mind of his own country—a mind which he learns in time to be much more important than his own private mind—is a mind which changes, and that this change is a development which abandons nothing en route, which does not superannuate either Shakespeare, or Homer, or the rock drawing of the Magdalenian[3] draftsmen. That this development, refinement perhaps, complication certainly, is not, from the point of view of the artist, any improvement. Perhaps not even an improvement from the point of view of the psychologist or not to the extent which we imagine; perhaps only in the end based upon a complication in economics and machinery. But the difference between the present and the past is that the conscious present is an awareness of the past in a way and to an extent which the past's awareness of itself cannot show.

Someone said: "The dead writers are remote from us because we *know* so much more than they did." Precisely, and they are that which we know.

I am alive to a usual objection to what is clearly part of my program for the métier of poetry. The objection is that the doctrine requires a ridiculous amount of erudition (pedantry), a claim which can be rejected by appeal to the lives of poets in any pantheon. It will even be affirmed that much learning deadens or perverts poetic sensibility. While, however, we persist in believing that a poet ought to know as much as will not encroach upon his necessary receptivity and necessary laziness, it is not desirable to confine knowledge to whatever can be put into a useful shape for examinations, drawing rooms, or the still more pretentious modes of pub-

2. A round mass of anything: a large pill.
3. The most advanced culture of the European Paleolithic period (from discoveries at La Madeleine, France).

licity. Some can absorb knowledge, the more tardy must sweat for it. Shakespeare acquired more essential history from Plutarch[4] than most men could from the whole British Museum. What is to be insisted upon is that the poet must develop or procure the consciousness of the past and that he should continue to develop this consciousness throughout his career.

What happens is a continual surrender of himself as he is at the moment to something which is more valuable. The progress of an artist is a continual self-sacrifice, a continual extinction of personality.

There remains to define this process of depersonalization and its relation to the sense of tradition. It is in this depersonalization that art may be said to approach the condition of science. I, therefore, invite you to consider, as a suggestive analogy, the action which takes place when a bit of finely filiated[5] platinum is introduced into a chamber containing oxygen and sulphur dioxide.

II

Honest criticism and sensitive appreciation are directed not upon the poet but upon the poetry. If we attend to the confused cries of the newspaper critics and the *susurrus*[6] of popular repetition that follows, we shall hear the names of poets in great numbers; if we seek not Blue-book[7] knowledge but the enjoyment of poetry, and ask for a poem, we shall seldom find it. I have tried to point out the importance of the relation of the poem to other poems by other authors, and suggested the conception of poetry as a living whole of all the poetry that has ever been written. The other aspect of this Impersonal theory of poetry is the relation of the poem to its author. And I hinted, by an analogy, that the mind of the mature poet differs from that of the immature one not precisely in any valuation of "personality," not being necessarily more interesting, or having "more to say," but rather by being a more finely perfected medium in which special, or very varied, feelings are at liberty to enter into new combinations.

The analogy was that of the catalyst.[8] When the two gases previously mentioned are mixed in the presence of a filament of platinum, they form sulphurous acid. This combination takes place only if the platinum is present; nevertheless the newly formed acid contains no trace of platinum, and the platinum itself is apparently unaffected; has remained inert, neutral, and unchanged. The mind of the poet is the shred of platinum. It may partly or exclusively operate upon the experience of the man himself; but, the more perfect the artist, the more completely separate in him will be the

4. Greek biographer (1st century A.D.) of Greek and Roman celebrities, from whose work Shakespeare drew the plots of his Roman plays.
5. Drawn out like a thread.
6. Murmuring, buzzing.

7. British official government publication.
8. Substance that triggers a chemical change without itself being affected by the reaction.

man who suffers and the mind which creates; the more perfectly will the mind digest and transmute the passions which are its material.

The experience, you will notice, the elements which enter the presence of the transforming catalyst, are of two kinds: emotions and feelings. The effect of a work of art upon the person who enjoys it is an experience different in kind from any experience not of art. It may be formed out of one emotion, or may be a combination of several; and various feelings, inhering for the writer in particular words or phrases or images, may be added to compose the final result. Or great poetry may be made without the direct use of any emotion whatever: composed out of feelings solely. Canto XV of the *Inferno* (Brunetto Latini)[9] is a working up of the emotion evident in the situation; but the effect, though single as that of any work of art, is obtained by considerable complexity of detail. The last quatrain gives an image, a feeling attaching to an image, which "came," which did not develop simply out of what precedes, but which was probably in suspension in the poet's mind until the proper combination arrived for it to add itself to.[1] The poet's mind is in fact a receptacle for seizing and storing up numberless feelings, phrases, images, which remain there until all the particles which can unite to form a new compound are present together.

If you compare several representative passages of the greatest poetry you see how great is the variety of types of combination, and also how completely any semi-ethical criterion of "sublimity" misses the mark. For it is not the "greatness," the intensity, of the emotions, the components, but the intensity of the artistic process, the pressure, so to speak, under which the fusion takes place, that counts. The episode of Paolo and Francesca[2] employs a definite emotion, but the intensity of the poetry is something quite different from whatever intensity in the supposed experience it may give the impression of. It is no more intense, furthermore, than Canto XXVI,[3] the voyage of Ulysses, which has not the direct dependence upon an emotion. Great variety is possible in the process of transmutation of emotion: the murder of Agamemnon,[4] or the agony of Othello, gives an artistic effect apparently closer to a possible

9. Dante meets in Hell his old master Brunetto Latini, suffering eternal punishment for unnatural lust, yet still loved and admired by Dante, who addresses him with affectionate courtesy. It is one of the most moving passages in the *Inferno*.
1. Dante's strange interview with Brunetto is over, and Brunetto moves off to continue his punishment: "Then he turned round, and seemed like one of those / Who run for the green cloth [in the footrace] at Verona / In the

field; and he seemed among them / Not the loser but the winner."
2. Illicit lovers whom Dante meets in the second circle of Hell (*Inferno* V) and at whose punishment and sorrows he swoons with pity.
3. Of the *Inferno*. Ulysses, suffering in Hell for "false counseling," tells Dante of his final voyage.
4. By his wife Clytemnestra; the central action of Aeschylus' play *Agamemnon*.

original than the scenes from Dante. In the *Agamemnon*, the artistic emotion approximates to the emotion of an actual spectator; in *Othello* to the emotion of the protagonist himself. But the difference between art and the event is always absolute; the combination which is the murder of Agamemnon is probably as complex as that which is the voyage of Ulysses. In either case there has been a fusion of elements. The ode of Keats contains a number of feelings which have nothing particular to do with the nightingale, but which the nightingale, partly, perhaps, because of its attractive name, and partly because of its reputation, served to bring together.

The point of view which I am struggling to attack is perhaps related to the metaphysical theory of the substantial unity of the soul: for my meaning is, that the poet has, not a "personality" to express, but a particular medium, which is only a medium and not a personality, in which impressions and experiences combine in peculiar and unexpected ways. Impressions and experiences which are important for the man may take no place in the poetry, and those which become important in the poetry may play quite a negligible part in the man, the personality.

I will quote a passage which is unfamiliar enough to be regarded with fresh attention in the light—or darkness—of these observations:

> And now methinks I could e'en chide myself
> For doting on her beauty, though her death
> Shall be revenged after no common action.
> Does the silkworm expend her yellow labors
> For thee? For thee does she undo herself?
> Are lordships sold to maintain ladyships
> For the poor benefit of a bewildering minute?
> Why does yon fellow falsify highways,
> And put his life between the judge's lips,
> To refine such a thing—keeps horse and men
> To beat their valors for her? . . .[5]

In this passage (as is evident if it is taken in its context) there is a combination of positive and negative emotions: an intensely strong attraction toward beauty and an equally intense fascination by the ugliness which is contrasted with it and which destroys it. This balance of contrasted emotion is in the dramatic situation to which the speech is pertinent, but that situation alone is inadequate to it. This is, so to speak, the structural emotion, provided by the drama. But the whole effect, the dominant tone, is due to the fact that a number of floating feelings, having an affinity to this emotion by no means superficially evident, have combined with it to give us a new art emotion.

It is not in his personal emotions, the emotions provoked by par-

5. From Cyril Tourneur's *The Revenger's Tragedy* (1607), III.iv.

ticular events in his life, that the poet is in any way remarkable or interesting. His particular emotions may be simple, or crude, or flat. The emotion in his poetry will be a very complex thing, but not with the complexity of the emotions of people who have very complex or unusual emotions in life. One error, in fact, of eccentricity in poetry is to seek for new human emotions to express; and in this search for novelty in the wrong place it discovers the perverse. The business of the poet is not to find new emotions, but to use the ordinary ones and, in working them up into poetry, to express feelings which are not in actual emotions at all. And emotions which he has never experienced will serve his turn as well as those familiar to him. Consequently, we must believe that "emotion recollected in tranquility"[6] is an inexact formula. For it is neither emotion, nor recollection, nor, without distortion of meaning, tranquility. It is a concentration, and a new thing resulting from the concentration, of a very great number of experiences which to the practical and active person would not seem to be experiences at all; it is a concentration which does not happen consciously or of deliberation. These experiences are not "recollected," and they finally unite in an atmosphere which is "tranquil" only in that it is a passive attending upon the event. Of course this is not quite the whole story. There is a great deal, in the writing of poetry, which must be conscious and deliberate. In fact, the bad poet is usually unconscious where he ought to be conscious, and conscious where he ought to be unconscious. Both errors tend to make him "personal." Poetry is not a turning loose of emotion, but an escape from emotion; it is not the expression of personality, but an escape from personality. But, of course, only those who have personality and emotions know what it means to want to escape from these things.

III

ὁ δὲ νοῦς ἴσως Θειότερόν τι χαὶ ἀπαθές ἐστιν.[7]

This essay proposes to halt at the frontier of metaphysics or mysticism, and confine itself to such practical conclusions as can be applied by the responsible person interested in poetry. To divert interest from the poet to the poetry is a laudable aim: for it would conduce to a juster estimation of actual poetry, good and bad. There are many people who appreciate the expression of sincere emotion in verse, and there is a smaller number of people who can appreciate technical excellence. But very few know when there is an expression of *significant* emotion, emotion which has its life in the poem and not in the history of the poet. The emotion of art is impersonal. And the poet cannot reach this impersonality with-

6. Wordsworth, Preface to *Lyrical Ballads*, 2nd edition (1800). Wordsworth said that poetry "takes its origin from emotion recollected in tranquility."

7. "The mind is doubtless something more divine and unimpressionable." Aristotle, *De Anima* ("On the Soul"), I.4.

out surrendering himself wholly to the work to be done. And he is not likely to know what is to be done unless he lives in what is not merely the present, but the present moment of the past, unless he is conscious, not of what is dead, but of what is already living.

1919, 1920

The Metaphysical Poets

By collecting these poems[1] from the work of a generation more often named than read, and more often read than profitably studied, Professor Grierson has rendered a service of some importance. Certainly the reader will meet with many poems already preserved in other anthologies, at the same time that he discovers poems such as those of Aurelian Townshend or Lord Herbert of Cherbury here included. But the function of such an anthology as this is neither that of Professor Saintsbury's admirable edition of Caroline poets nor that of the *Oxford Book of English Verse*. Mr. Grierson's book is in itself a piece of criticism and a provocation of criticism; and we think that he was right in including so many poems of Donne, elsewhere (though not in many editions) accessible, as documents in the case of "metaphysical poetry." The phrase has long done duty as a term of abuse or as the label of a quaint and pleasant taste. The question is to what extent the so-called metaphysicals formed a school (in our own time we should say a "movement"), and how far this so-called school or movement is a digression from the main current.

Not only is it extremely difficult to define metaphysical poetry, but difficult to decide what poets practice it and in which of their verses. The poetry of Donne (to whom Marvell and Bishop King are sometimes nearer than any of the other authors) is late Elizabethan, its feeling often very close to that of Chapman. The "courtly" poetry is derivative from Jonson, who borrowed liberally from the Latin; it expires in the next century with the sentiment and witticism of Prior. There is finally the devotional verse of Herbert, Vaughan, and Crashaw (echoed long after by Christina Rossetti and Francis Thompson); Crashaw, sometimes more profound and less sectarian than the others, has a quality which returns through the Elizabethan period to the early Italians. It is difficult to find any precise use of metaphor, simile, or other conceit, which is common to all the poets and at the same time important enough as an element of style to isolate these poets as a group. Donne, and

---

1. *Metaphysical Lyrics and Poems of the Seventeenth Century:* Donne to Butler. Selected and edited, with an Essay, by Herbert J. C. Grierson (1921). Eliot's essay was originally a review of this book in the London *Times Literary Supplement*.

often Cowley, employ a device which is sometimes considered characteristically "metaphysical"; the elaboration (contrasted with the condensation) of a figure of speech to the farthest stage to which ingenuity can carry it. Thus Cowley develops the commonplace comparison of the world to a chessboard through long stanzas (*To Destiny*), and Donne, with more grace, in A *Valediction*,[2] the comparison of two lovers to a pair of compasses. But elsewhere we find, instead of the mere explication of the content of a comparison, a development by rapid association of thought which requires considerable agility on the part of the reader.

> On a round ball
> A workman that hath copies by, can lay
> An Europe, Afrique, and an Asia,
> And quickly make that which was nothing, all;
> So doth each tear,
> Which thee doth wear,
> A globe, yea world, by that impression grow,
> Till thy tears mixed with mine do overflow
> This world; by waters sent from thee, my heaven dissolvéd so.[3]

Here we find at least two connections which are not implicit in the first figure, but are forced upon it by the poet: from the geographer's globe to the tear, and the tear to the deluge. On the other hand, some of Donne's most successful and characteristic effects are secured by brief words and sudden contrasts:

> A bracelet of bright hair about the bone,[4]

where the most powerful effect is produced by the sudden contrast of associations of "bright hair" and of "bone." This telescoping of images and multiplied associations is characteristic of the phrase of some of the dramatists of the period which Donne knew: not to mention Shakespeare, it is frequent in Middleton, Webster, and Tourneur, and is one of the sources of the vitality of their language.

Johnson, who employed the term "metaphysical poets," apparently having Donne, Cleveland, and Cowley chiefly in mind, remarks of them that "the most heterogeneous ideas are yoked by violence together."[5] The force of this impeachment lies in the failure of the conjunction, the fact that often the ideas are yoked but not united; and if we are to judge of styles of poetry by their abuse, enough examples may be found in Cleveland to justify Johnson's condemnation. But a degree of heterogeneity of material compelled into unity by the operation of the poet's mind is omnipresent in poetry. We need not select for illustration such a line as:

2. I.e., *A Valediction: Forbidding Mourning.*
3. Donne's *A Valediction: Of Weeping,* lines 10–18.
4. *The Reliure,* line 6.
5. See Samuel Johnson's *Life of Cowley.*

Notre âme est un trois-mâts cherchant son Icarie;[6]

we may find it in some of the best lines of Johnson himself (*The Vanity of Human Wishes*):

> His fate was destined to a barren strand,
> A petty fortress, and a dubious hand;
> He left a name at which the world grew pale,
> To point a moral, or adorn a tale.

where the effect is due to a contrast of ideas, different in degree but the same in principle, as that which Johnson mildly reprehended. And in one of the finest poems of the age (a poem which could not have been written in any other age), the *Exequy* of Bishop King, the extended comparison is used with perfect success: the idea and the simile become one, in the passage in which the Bishop illustrates his impatience to see his dead wife, under the figure of a journey:

> Stay for me there; I will not fail
> To meet thee in that hollow Vale.
> And think not much of my delay;
> I am already on the way,
> And follow thee with all the speed
> Desire can make, or sorrows breed.
> Each minute is a short degree,
> And ev'ry hour a step towards thee.
> At night when I betake to rest,
> Next morn I rise nearer my West
> Of life, almost by eight hours sail,
> Than when sleep breathed his drowsy gale. . . .
> But hark! My pulse, like a soft drum
> Beats my approach, tells Thee I come;
> And slow howe'er my marches be,
> I shall at last sit down by Thee.

(In the last few lines there is that effect of terror which is several times attained by one of Bishop King's admirers, Edgar Poe.) Again, we may justly take these quatrains from Lord Herbert's Ode,[7] stanzas which would, we think, be immediately pronounced to be of the metaphysical school:

> So when from hence we shall be gone,
> And be no more, nor you, nor I,
> As one another's mystery,
> Each shall be both, yet both but one.

---

6. "Our soul is a three-masted ship searching for her Icarie"; a line from Charles Baudelaire's poem, *Le Voyage* (Icarie is an imaginary utopia in *Voyage en Icarie,* 1840, a novel by the French socialist Etienne Cabet).

7. Lord Herbert of Cherbury (1583–1648), brother of George Herbert. The "Ode" is his *Ode upon a Question moved, whether Love should continue forever?*

This said, in her uplifted face,
   Her eyes, which did that beauty crown,
   Were like two stars, that having faln down,
Look up again to find their place:

While such a moveless silent peace
   Did seize on their becalmèd sense,
   One would have thought some influence
Their ravished spirits did possess.

There is nothing in these lines (with the possible exception of the stars, a simile not at once grasped, but lovely and justified) which fits Johnson's general observations on the metaphysical poets in his essay on Cowley. A good deal resides in the richness of association which is at the same time borrowed from and given to the word "becalmed"; but the meaning is clear, the language simple and elegant. It is to be observed that the language of these poets is as a rule simple and pure; in the verse of George Herbert this simplicity is carried as far as it can go—a simplicity emulated without success by numerous modern poets. The *structure* of the sentences, on the other hand, is sometimes far from simple, but this is not a vice; it is a fidelity to thought and feeling. The effect, at its best, is far less artificial than that of an ode by Gray. And as this fidelity induces variety of thought and feeling, so it induces variety of music. We doubt whether, in the eighteenth century, could be found two poems in nominally the same meter, so dissimilar as Marvell's *Coy Mistress* and Crashaw's *Saint Teresa*; the one producing an effect of great speed by the use of short syllables, and the other an ecclesiastical solemnity by the use of long ones:

Love, thou art absolute sole lord
   Of life and death.

If so shrewd and sensitive (though so limited) a critic as Johnson failed to define metaphysical poetry by its faults, it is worth while to inquire whether we may not have more success by adopting the opposite method: by assuming that the poets of the seventeenth century (up to the Revolution[8]) were the direct and normal development of the precedent age; and, without prejudicing their case by the adjective "metaphysical," consider whether their virtue was not something permanently valuable, which subsequently disappeared, but ought not to have disappeared. Johnson has hit, perhaps by accident, on one of their peculiarities, when he observes that "their attempts were always analytic"; he would not agree that, after the dissociation, they put the material together again in a new unity.

It is certain that the dramatic verse of the later Elizabethan and early Jacobean poets expresses a degree of development of sensibil-

8. Of 1688; when James II was replaced by William and Mary.

ity which is not found in any of the prose, good as it often is. If we except Marlowe, a man of prodigious intelligence, these dramatists were directly or indirectly (it is at least a tenable theory) affected by Montaigne. Even if we except also Jonson and Chapman, these two were probably erudite, and were notably men who incorporated their erudition into their sensibility: their mode of feeling was directly and freshly altered by their reading and thought. In Chapman especially there is a direct sensuous apprehension of thought, or a recreation of thought into feeling, which is exactly what we find in Donne:

> in this one thing, all the discipline
> Of manners and of manhood is contained;
> A man to join himself with th' Universe
> In his main sway, and make in all things fit
> One with that All, and go on, round as it;
> Not plucking from the whole his wretched part,
> And into straits, or into nought revert,
> Wishing the complete Universe might be
> Subject to such a rag of it as he;
> But to consider great Necessity.[9]

We compare this with some modern passage:

> No, when the fight begins within himself,
> A man's worth something. God stoops o'er his head,
> Satan looks up between his feet—both tug—
> He's left, himself, i' the middle; the soul wakes
> And grows. Prolong that battle through his life![1]

It is perhaps somewhat less fair, though very tempting (as both poets are concerned with the perpetuation of love by offspring), to compare with the stanzas already quoted from Lord Herbert's Ode the following from Tennyson:

> One walked between his wife and child,
> With measured footfall firm and mild,
> And now and then he gravely smiled.
> The prudent partner of his blood
> Leaned on him, faithful, gentle, good,
> Wearing the rose of womanhood.
> And in their double love secure,
> The little maiden walked demure,
> Pacing with downward eyelids pure.
> These three made unity so sweet,
> My frozen heart began to beat,
> Remembering its ancient heat.[2]

9. From *The Revenge of Bussy d'Ambois* (IV.i.137–46).
1. Robert Browning's *Bishop Blou-*
gram's Apology, lines 693–97.
2. Tennyson's *The Two Voices*, lines 412–23.

The difference is not a simple difference of degree between poets. It is something which had happened to the mind of England between the time of Donne or Lord Herbert of Cherbury and the time of Tennyson and Browning; it is the difference between the intellectual poet and the reflective poet. Tennyson and Browning are poets, and they think; but they do not feel their thought as immediately as the odor of a rose. A thought to Donne was an experience; it modified his sensibility. When a poet's mind is perfectly equipped for its work, it is constantly amalgamating disparate experience; the ordinary man's experience is chaotic, irregular, fragmentary. The latter falls in love, or reads Spinoza, and these two experiences have nothing to do with each other, or with the noise of the typewriter or the smell of cooking; in the mind of the poet these experiences are always forming new wholes.

We may express the difference by the following theory: The poets of the seventeenth century, the successors of the dramatists of the sixteenth, possessed a mechanism of sensibility which could devour any kind of experience. They are simple, artificial, difficult, or fantastic, as their predecessors were; no less nor more than Dante, Guido Cavalcanti, Guinicelli, or Cino.[3] In the seventeenth century a dissociation of sensibility set in, from which we have never recovered; and this dissociation, as is natural, was aggravated by the influence of the two most powerful poets of the century, Milton and Dryden. Each of these men performed certain poetic functions so magnificently well that the magnitude of the effect concealed the absence of others. The language went on and in some respects improved; the best verse of Collins, Gray, Johnson, and even Goldsmith satisfies some of our fastidious demands better than that of Donne or Marvell or King. But while the language became more refined, the feeling became more crude. The feeling, the sensibility, expressed in the *Country Churchyard* (to say nothing of Tennyson and Browning) is cruder than that in the *Coy Mistress*.

The second effect of the influence of Milton and Dryden followed from the first, and was therefore slow in manifestation. The sentimental age began early in the eighteenth century, and continued. The poets revolted against the ratiocinative, the descriptive; they thought and felt by fits, unbalanced; they reflected. In one or two passages of Shelley's *Triumph of Life*, in the second *Hyperion*, there are traces of a struggle toward unification of sensibility. But Keats and Shelley died, and Tennyson and Browning ruminated.

After this brief exposition of a theory—too brief, perhaps, to

3. These last three poets, all of whom lived in the 13th century, were members of the Tuscan school of lyric love poets (Guido Guinicelli was hailed by Dante in the *Purgatorio* as "father of Italian poets"; Cino da Pistoia was a friend of Dante and Petrarch).

carry conviction—we may ask, what would have been the fate of the "metaphysical" had the current of poetry descended in a direct line from them, as it descended in a direct line to them? They would not, certainly, be classified as metaphysical. The possible interests of a poet are unlimited; the more intelligent he is the better; the more intelligent he is the more likely that he will have interests: our only condition is that he turn them into poetry, and not merely meditate on them poetically. A philosophical theory which has entered into poetry is established, for its truth or falsity in one sense ceases to matter, and its truth in another sense is proved. The poets in question have, like other poets, various faults. But they were, at best, engaged in the task of trying to find the verbal equivalent for states of mind and feeling. And this means both that they are more mature, and that they wear better, than later poets of certainly not less literary ability.

It is not a permanent necessity that poets should be interested in philosophy, or in any other subject. We can only say that it appears likely that poets in our civilization, as it exists at present, must be *difficult*. Our civilization comprehends great variety and complexity, and this variety and complexity, playing upon a refined sensibility, must produce various and complex results. The poet must become more and more comprehensive, more allusive, more indirect, in order to force, to dislocate if necessary, language into his meaning. (A brilliant and extreme statement of this view, with which it is not requisite to associate oneself, is that of M. Jean Epstein, *La Poésie d'aujourd'hui*.[4]) Hence we get something which looks very much like the conceit—we get, in fact, a method curiously similar to that of the "metaphysical poets," similar also in its use of obscure words and of simple phrasing.

> O géraniums diaphanes, guerroyeurs sortilèges,
> Sacrilèges monomanes!
> Emballages, dévergondages, douches! O pressoirs
> Des vendanges des grands soirs!
> Layettes aux abois,
> Thyrses au fond des bois!
> Transfusions, représailles,
> Relevailles, compresses et l'éternal potion,
> Angélus! n'en pouvoir plus
> De débâcles nuptiales! de débâcles nuptiales![5]

4. "Poetry of Today."
5. "O transparent geraniums, warrior incantations, / Monomaniac sacrileges! / Packing materials, shamelessnesses, shower baths! O wine presses / Of great evening vintages! / Hard-pressed baby linen, / Thyrsis in the depths of the woods! / Transfusions, reprisals, / Churchings, compresses, and the eternal potion, / Angelus! no longer to be borne [are] / Catastrophic marriages! catastrophic marriages!" This passage is from *Derniers vers X* ("Last Poems," 1890), by Jules Laforgue (1860–87). Eliot oddly sees a similarity between this kind of hysterical free association and the strictly ordered imagery of the metaphysicals. But it is the combination of "obscure words and simple phrasing" that strikes him in both.

The same poet could write also simply:

> *Elle est bien loin, elle pleure,*
> *Le grand vent se lamente aussi . . .*[6]

Jules Laforgue, and Tristan Corbière[7] in many of his poems, are nearer to the "school of Donne" than any modern English poet. But poets more classical than they have the same essential quality of transmuting ideas into sensations, of transforming an observation into a state of mind.

> *Pour l'enfant, amoureux de cartes et d'estampes,*
> *L'univers est égal à son vaste appétit.*
> *Ah, que le monde est grand à la clarté des lampes!*
> *Aux yeux du souvenir que le monde est petit!*[8]

In French literature the great master of the seventeenth century —Racine—and the great master of the nineteenth—Baudelaire— are in some ways more like each other than they are like any one else. The greatest two masters of diction are also the greatest two psychologists, the most curious explorers of the soul. It is interesting to speculate whether it is not a misfortune that two of the greatest masters of diction in our language, Milton and Dryden, triumph with a dazzling disregard of the soul. If we continued to produce Miltons and Drydens it might not so much matter, but as things are it is a pity that English poetry has remained so incomplete. Those who object to the "artificiality" of Milton or Dryden sometimes tell us to "look into our hearts and write." But that is not looking deep enough; Racine or Donne looked into a good deal more than the heart. One must look into the cerebral cortex, the nervous system, and the digestive tracts.

May we not conclude, then, that Donne, Crashaw, Vaughan, Herbert and Lord Herbert, Marvell, King, Cowley at his best, are in the direct current of English poetry, and that their faults should be reprimanded by this standard rather than coddled by antiquarian affection? They have been enough praised in terms which are implicit limitations because they are "metaphysical" or "witty," "quaint" or "obscure," though at their best they have not these attributes more than other serious poets. On the other hand, we must not reject the criticism of Johnson (a dangerous person to disagree with) without having mastered it, without having assimilated the Johnsonian canons of taste. In reading the celebrated passage in his essay on Cowley we must remember that by wit he clearly means something more serious than we usually mean today;

6. "She is far away, she weeps, / The great wind mourns also." From *Derniers vers XI, Sur une défunte* ("On a Dead Woman").
7. 1845–75; also a French Symbolist poet.

8. From Baudelaire's *Le Voyage:* "For the child, in love with maps and prints, / The universe matches his vast appetite. / Ah, how big the world is by lamplight! How small the world is to the eyes of memory!"

in his criticism of their versification we must remember in what a
narrow discipline he was trained, but also how well trained; we
must remember that Johnson tortures chiefly the chief offenders,
Cowley and Cleveland. It would be a fruitful work, and one requiring a substantial book, to break up the classification of Johnson (for there has been none since) and exhibit these poets in all
their difference of kind and of degree, from the massive music of
Donne to the faint, pleasing tinkle of Aurelian Townshend—whose
Dialogue Between a Pilgrim and Time is one of the few regrettable
omissions from the excellent anthology of Professor Grierson.

1921

Ulysses, Order, and Myth

Mr. Joyce's book has been out long enough for no more general
expression of praise, or expostulation with its detractors, to be
necessary; and it has not been out long enough for any attempt at a
complete measurement of its place and significance to be possible.
All that one can usefully do at this time, and it is a great deal to do,
for such a book, is to elucidate any aspect of the book—and the
number of aspects is indefinite—which has not yet been fixed. I
hold this book to be the most important expression which the
present age has found; it is a book to which we are all indebted,
and from which none of us can escape. These are postulates for anything that I have to say about it, and I have no wish to waste the
reader's time by elaborating my eulogies; it has given me all the
surprise, delight, and terror that I can require, and I will leave it
at that.

Amongst all the criticisms I have seen of the book, I have seen
nothing—unless we except, in its way, M. Valéry Larbaud's[1] valuable paper which is rather an Introduction than a criticism—which
seemed to me to appreciate the significance of the method employed—the parallel to the Odyssey, and the use of appropriate
styles and symbols to each division. Yet one might expect this to be
the first peculiarity to attract attention; but it has been treated as
an amusing dodge, or scaffolding erected by the author for the purpose of disposing his realistic tale, of no interest in the completed
structure. The criticism which Mr. Aldington[2] directed upon
Ulysses several years ago seems to me to fail by this oversight—but,
as Mr. Aldington wrote before the complete work had appeared,
fails more honorably than the attempts of those who had the
whole book before them. Mr. Aldington treated Mr. Joyce as a

1. French writer (1881–1957) important in the modern movement, translator
of *Ulysses*.
2. Richard Aldington (1892–   ), English poet, novelist, and critic.

prophet of chaos; and wailed at the flood of Dadaism [3] which his prescient eye saw bursting forth at the tap of the magician's rod. Of course, the influence which Mr. Joyce's book may have is from my point of view irrelevance. A very great book may have a very bad influence indeed; and a mediocre book may be in the event most salutary. The next generation is responsible for its own soul; a man of genius is responsible to his peers, not to a studio-full of uneducated and undisciplined coxcombs. Still, Mr. Aldington's apathetic solicitude for the half-witted seems to me to carry implications about the nature of the book itself to which I cannot assent; and this is the important issue. He finds the book, if I understand him, to be an invitation to chaos, and an expression of feelings which are perverse, partial, and a distortion of reality. But unless I quote Mr. Aldington's words I am likely to falsify. "I say, moreover," he says,[4] "that when Mr. Joyce, with his marvelous gifts, uses them to disgust us with mankind, he is doing something which is false and a libel on humanity." It is somewhat similar to the opinion of the urbane Thackeray upon Swift. "As for the moral, I think it horrible, shameful, unmanly, blasphemous; and giant and great as this Dean is, I say we should hoot him." (This, of the conclusion of the Voyage to the Houyhnhnms—which seems to me one of the greatest triumphs that the human soul has ever achieved.)—It is true that Thackeray later pays Swift one of the finest tributes that a man has ever given or received: "So great a man he seems to me that thinking of him is like thinking of an empire falling." (And Mr. Aldington, in his time, is almost equally generous.)

Whether it is possible to libel humanity (in distinction to libel in the usual sense, which is libeling an individual or a group in contrast with the rest of humanity) is a question for philosophical societies to discuss; but of course if *Ulysses* were a "libel" it would simply be a forged document, a powerless fraud, which would never have extracted from Mr. Aldington a moment's attention. I do not wish to linger over this point: the interesting question is that begged by Mr. Aldington when he refers to Mr. Joyce's "great *undisciplined* talent."

I think that Mr. Aldington and I are more or less agreed as to what we want in principle, and agreed to call it classicism. It is because of this agreement that I have chosen Mr. Aldington to attack on the present issue. We are agreed as to what we want, but not as to how to get it, or as to what contemporary writing exhibits

---

3. Dadaism, founded in Zurich, Switzerland, during World War I, aimed at showing contempt for all traditional aesthetic and moral values and bourgeois institutions by random, illogical, spontaneous reflection (both in literature and in the visual arts) of the casual happenings of experience. The language was often deliberately infantile. Surrealism developed from one wing of the Dadaist movement.
4. *English Review*, April, 1921 [Eliot's note].

a tendency in that direction. We agree, I hope, that "classicism" is not an alternative to "romanticism," as of political parties, Conservative and Liberal, Republican and Democrat, on a "turn-the-rascals-out" platform. It is a goal toward which all good literature strives, so far as it is good, according to the possibilities of its place and time. One can be "classical," in a sense, by turning away from nine-tenths of the material which lies at hand, and selecting only mummified stuff from a museum—like some contemporary writers, about whom one could say some nasty things in this connection, if it were worth while (Mr. Aldington is not one of them). Or one can be classical in tendency by doing the best one can with the material at hand. The confusion springs from the fact that the term is applied to literature and to the whole complex of interests and modes of behavior and society of which literature is a part; and it has not the same bearing in both applications. It is much easier to be a classicist in literary criticism than in creative art—because in criticism you are responsible only for what you want, and in creation you are responsible for what you can do with material which you must simply accept. And in this material I include the emotions and feelings of the writer himself, which, for that writer, are simply material which he must accept—not virtues to be enlarged or vices to be diminished. The question, then, about Mr. Joyce, is: how much living material does he deal with, and how does he deal with it: deal with, not as a legislator or exhorter, but as an artist?

It is here that Mr. Joyce's parallel use of the Odyssey has a great importance. It has the importance of a scientific discovery. No one else has built a novel upon such a foundation before: it has never before been necessary. I am not begging the question in calling *Ulysses* a "novel"; and if you call it an epic it will not matter. If it is not a novel, that is simply because the novel is a form which will no longer serve; it is because the novel, instead of being a form, was simply the expression of an age which had not sufficiently lost all form to feel the need of something stricter. Mr. Joyce has written one novel—*The Portrait*; Mr. Wyndham Lewis has written one novel—*Tarr* [5]. I do not suppose that either of them will ever write another "novel." The novel ended with Flaubert and with James. It is, I think, because Mr. Joyce and Mr. Lewis, being "in advance" of their time, felt a conscious or probably unconscious dissatisfaction with the form, that their novels are more formless than those of a dozen clever writers who

5. First novel (1918) of Percy Wyndham Lewis (1884–1957), English novelist, poet, critic, painter, who denounced his contemporaries' interest in the flux of time and the stream of consciousness and advocated "conceptual quality, hard exact outline, grand architectural propor-tion." A strong satirical novel, *Tarr* is in a way the antithesis of *Ulysses* in its rejection of interior monologue and of submergence in the drift of time and consciousness. Edwin Muir once called Lewis "the hair of the dog that bit Lawrence and Joyce."

are unaware of its obsolescence.

In using the myth, in manipulating a continuous parallel between contemporaneity and antiquity, Mr. Joyce is pursuing a method which others must pursue after him. They will not be imitators, any more than the scientist who uses the discoveries of an Einstein in pursuing his own, independent, further investigations. It is simply a way of controlling, of ordering, of giving a shape and a significance to the immense panorama of futility and anarchy which is contemporary history. It is a method already adumbrated by Mr. Yeats, and of the need for which I believe Mr. Yeats to have been the first contemporary to be conscious. It is a method for which the horoscope is auspicious. Psychology (such as it is, and whether our reaction to it be comic or serious), ethnology, and *The Golden Bough* have concurred to make possible what was impossible even a few years ago. Instead of narrative method, we may now use the mythical method. It is, I seriously believe, a step toward making the modern world possible for art, toward that order and form which Mr. Aldington so earnestly desires. And only those who have won their own discipline in secret and without aid, in a world which offers very little assistance to that end, can be of any use in furthering this advance.

1923, 1948

Yeats[1]

The generations of poetry in our age seem to cover a span of about twenty years. I do not mean that the best work of any poet is limited to twenty years: I mean that it is about that length of time before a new school or style of poetry appears. By the time, that is to say, that a man is fifty, he has behind him a kind of poetry written by men of seventy, and before him another kind written by men of thirty. That is my position at present, and if I live another twenty years I shall expect to see still another younger school of poetry. One's relation to Yeats, however, does not fit into this scheme. When I was a young man at the university, in America, just beginning to write verse, Yeats was already a considerable figure in the world of poetry, and his early period was well defined. I cannot remember that his poetry at that stage made any deep impression upon me. A very young man, who is himself stirred to write, is not primarily critical or even widely appreciative. He is looking for masters who will elicit his consciousness of what he wants to say himself, of the kind of poetry that is in him to write. The taste of an adolescent writer is intense, but narrow: it is determined by personal needs. The kind of poetry that I needed, to teach me the use

1. The first annual Yeats Lecture, delivered to the Friends of the Irish Academy at the Abbey Theatre, Dublin, in 1940.

of my own voice, did not exist in English at all; it was only to be found in French. For this reason the poetry of the young Yeats hardly existed for me until after my enthusiasm had been won by the poetry of the older Yeats; and by that time—I mean, from 1919 on—my own course of evolution was already determined. Hence, I find myself regarding him, from one point of view, as a contemporary and not a predecessor; and from another point of view, I can share the feelings of younger men, who came to know and admire him by that work from 1919 on, which was produced while they were adolescent.

Certainly, for the younger poets of England and America, I am sure that their admiration for Yeats's poetry has been wholly good. His idiom was too different for there to be any danger of imitation, his opinions too different to flatter and confirm their prejudices. It was good for them to have the spectacle of an un-questionably great living poet, whose style they were not tempted to echo and whose ideas opposed those in vogue among them. You will not see, in their writing, more than passing evidences of the impression he made, but the work, and the man himself as poet, have been of the greatest significance to them for all that. This may seem to contradict what I have been saying about the kind of poetry that a young poet chooses to admire. But I am really talking about something different. Yeats would not have this influence had he not become a great poet; but the influence of which I speak is due to the figure of the poet himself, to the integrity of his passion for his art and his craft which provided such an impulse for his extraordinary development. When he visited London he liked to meet and talk to younger poets. People have sometimes spoken of him as arrogant and overbearing. I never found him so; in his conversations with a younger writer I always felt that he offered terms of equalty, as to a fellow worker, a practitioner of the same mistery.[2] It was, I think, that, unlike many writers, he cared more for poetry than for his own reputation as a poet or his picture of himself as a poet. Art was greater than the artist: and this feeling he communicated to others; which was why younger men were never ill at ease in his company.

This, I am sure, was part of the secret of his ability, after be-coming unquestionably the master, to remain always a contempor-ary. Another is the continual development of which I have spoken. This has become almost a commonplace of criticism of his work. But while it is often mentioned, its causes and its nature have not been often analyzed. One reason, of course, was simply con-centration and hard work. And behind that is character: I mean

---

2. The original spelling of a word later confused with "mystery" (of different origin and meaning); it means an art, skill, or craft with the implication that the practitioners belong to a closed corporation.

the special character of the artist as artist—that is, the force of character by which Dickens, having exhausted his first inspiration, was able in middle age to proceed to such a masterpiece, so different from his early work, as *Bleak House*. It is difficult and unwise to generalize about ways of composition—so many men, so many ways—but it is my experience that toward middle age a man has three choices: to stop writing altogether, to repeat himself with perhaps an increasing skill of virtuosity, or by taking thought to adapt himself to middle age and find a different way of working. Why are the later long poems of Browning and Swinburne mostly unread? It is, I think, because one gets the essential Browning or Swinburne entire in earlier poems; and in the later, one is reminded of the early freshness which they lack, without being made aware of any compensating new qualities. When a man is engaged in work of abstract thought—if there is such a thing as wholly abstract thought outside of the mathematical sciences—his mind can mature, while his emotions either remain the same or only atrophy, and it will not matter. But maturing as a poet means maturing as the whole man, experiencing new emotions appropriate to one's age, and with the same intensity as the emotions of youth.

One form, a perfect form, of development is that of Shakespeare, one of the few poets whose work of maturity is just as exciting as that of their early manhood. There is, I think, a difference between the development of Shakespeare and Yeats, which makes the latter case still more curious. With Shakespeare, one sees a slow, continuous development of mastery of his craft of verse, and the poetry of middle age seems implicit in that of early maturity. After the first few verbal exercises you say of each piece of work: "This is the perfect expression of the sensibility of that stage of his development." That a poet should develop at all, that he should find something new to say, and say it equally well, in middle age, has always something miraculous about it. But in the case of Yeats the kind of development seems to me different. I do not want to give the impression that I regard his earlier and his later work almost as if they had been written by two different men. Returning to his earlier poems after making a close acquaintance with the later, one sees, to begin with, that in technique there was a slow and continuous development of what is always the same medium and idiom. And when I say development, I do not mean that many of the early poems, for what they are, are not as beautifully written as they could be. There are some, such as *Who Goes with Fergus?*, which are as perfect of their kind as anything in the language. But the best, and the best known of them, have this limitation: that they are as satisfactory in isolation, as "anthology pieces," as they are in the context of his other poems of the same period.

I am obviously using the term "anthology piece" in a rather special sense. In any anthology, you find some poems which give you complete satisfaction and delight in themselves, such that you are hardly curious who wrote them, hardly want to look further into the work of that poet. There are others, not necessarily so perfect or complete, which make you irresistibly curious to know more of that poet through his other work. Naturally, this distinction applies only to short poems, those in which a man has been able to put only a part of his mind, if it is a mind of any size. With some such you feel at once that the man who wrote them must have had a great deal more to say, in different contexts, of equal interest. Now among all the poems in Yeats's earlier volumes I find only in a line here or there, that sense of a unique personality which makes one sit up in excitement and eagerness to learn more about the author's mind and feelings. The intensity of Yeats's own emotional experience hardly appears. We have sufficient evidence of the intensity of experience of his youth, but it is from the retrospections in some of his later work that we have our evidence.

I have, in early essays, extolled what I called impersonality in art, and it may seem that, in giving as a reason for the superiority of Yeats's later work the greater expression of personality in it, I am contradicting myself. It may be that I expressed myself badly, or that I had only an adolescent grasp of that idea—as I can never bear to re-read my own prose writings, I am willing to leave the point unsettled—but I think now, at least, that the truth of the matter is as follows. There are two forms of impersonality: that which is natural to the mere skillful craftsman, and that which is more and more achieved by the maturing artist. The first is that of what I have called the "anthology piece," of a lyric by Lovelace or Suckling, or of Campion,[3] a finer poet than either. The second impersonality is that of the poet who, out of intense and personal experience, is able to express a general truth; retaining all the particularity of his experience, to make of it a general symbol. And the strange thing is that Yeats, having been a great craftsman in the first kind, became a great poet in the second. It is not that he became a different man, for, as I have hinted, one feels sure that the intense experience of youth had been lived through—and indeed, without this early experience he could never have attained anything of the wisdom which appears in his later writing. But he had to wait for a later maturity to find expression of early experience; and this makes him, I think, a unique and especially interesting poet.

3. Thomas Campion (1567–1619), poet and musician, known for his song lyrics. Richard Lovelace (1618–58) and Sir John Suckling (1609–42) were Cavalier poets of considerable charm and limited range. All three are best known for a few individual poems.

Consider the early poem which is in every anthology, *When you are old and gray and full of sleep*, or *A Dream of Death* in the same volume of 1893. They are beautiful poems, but only craftsman's work, because one does not feel present in them the particularity which must provide the material for the general truth. By the time of the volume of 1904 there is a development visible in a very lovely poem, *The Folly of Being Comforted*, and in *Adam's Curse*; something is coming through, and in beginning to speak as a particular man he is beginning to speak for man. This is clearer still in the poem *Peace*, in the 1910 volume. But it is not fully evinced until the volume of 1914, in the violent and terrible epistle dedicatory of *Responsibilities*, with the great lines

> *Pardon that for a barren passion's sake,*
> *Although I have come close on forty-nine. . . .*[4]

And the naming of his age in the poem is significant. More than half a lifetime to arrive at this freedom of speech. It is a triumph.

There was much also for Yeats to work out of himself, even in technique. To be a younger member of a group of poets, none of them certainly of anything like his stature, but further developed in their limited path, may arrest for a time a man's development of idiom. Then again, the weight of the pre-Raphaelite prestige must have been tremendous. The Yeats of the Celtic twilight—who seems to me to have been more the Yeats of the pre-Raphaelite twilight—uses Celtic folklore almost as William Morris uses Scandinavian folklore. His longer narrative poems bear the mark of Morris. Indeed, in the pre-Raphaelite phase, Yeats is by no means the least of the pre-Raphaelites. I may be mistaken, but the play, *The Shadowy Waters*, seems to me one of the most perfect expressions of the vague enchanted beauty of that school: yet it strikes me—this may be an impertinence on my part—as the western seas described through the back window of a house in Kensington,[5] an Irish myth for the Kelmscott Press; and when I try to visualize the speakers in the play, they have the great dim, dreamy eyes of the knights and ladies of Burne-Jones.[6] I think the phase in which he treated Irish legend in the manner of Rossetti or Morris is a phase of confusion. He did not master this legend until he made it a vehicle for his own creation of character—not, really, until he began to write the *Plays for Dancers*.[7] The point is, that in becoming more Irish, not

---

4. Lines 19 and 20 of this 22-line poem.
5. This genteel residential section of West London is contrasted with the romantic vision supposedly seen from its windows. The Kelmscott Press was founded in 1890 by William Morris to bring back good design to printing.

6. Sir Edward Coley Burne-Jones (1833–1898), pre-Raphaelite painter.
7. The first of these, *At the Hawk's Well*, was performed in March 1916. Two volumes of *Plays for Dancers* were published, the first in 1919 and the second (containing this play) in 1921.

in subject matter but in expression, he became at the same time universal.

The points that I particularly wish to make about Yeats's development are two. The first, on which I have already touched, is that to have accomplished what Yeats did in the middle and later years is a great and permanent example—which poets-to-come should study with reverence—of what I have called Character of the Artist: a kind of moral, as well as intellectual, excellence. The second point, which follows naturally after what I have said in criticism of the lack of complete emotional expression in his early work, is that Yeats is preeminently the poet of middle age. By this I am far from meaning that he is a poet only for middle-aged readers: the attitude towards him of younger poets who write in English, the world over, is enough evidence to the contrary. Now, in theory, there is no reason why a poet's inspiration or material should fail, in middle age or at any time before senility. For a man who is capable of experience finds himself in a different world in every decade of his life; as he sees it with different eyes, the material of his art is continually renewed. But in fact, very few poets have shown this capacity of adaptation to the years. It requires, indeed, an exceptional honesty and courage to face the change. Most men either cling to the experiences of youth, so that their writing becomes an insincere mimicry of their earlier work, or they leave their passion behind, and write only from the head, with a hollow and wasted virtuosity. There is another and even worse temptation: that of becoming dignified, of becoming public figures with only a public existence—coatracks hung with decorations and distinctions, doing, saying, and even thinking and feeling only what they believe the public expects of them. Yeats was not that kind of poet: and it is, perhaps, a reason why young men should find his later poetry more acceptable than older men easily can. For the young man can see him as a poet who in his work remained in the best sense always young, who even in one sense became young as he aged. But the old, unless they are stirred to something of the honesty with oneself expressed in the poetry, will be shocked by such a revelation of what a man really is and remains. They will refuse to believe that *they* are like that.

> *You think it horrible that lust and rage*
> *Should dance attendance upon my old age;*
> *They were not such a plague when I was young:*
> *What else have I to spur me into song?* [8]

These lines are very impressive and not very pleasant, and the

8. These four lines are a complete poem, "The Spur," first published in *The Lon-* *don Mercury,* March 1938, and then in *Last Poems and Plays,* 1940.

sentiment has recently been criticized by an English critic whom I generally respect. But I think he misread them. I do not read them as a personal confession of a man who differed from other men, but of a man who was essentially the same as most other men; the only difference is in the greater clarity, honesty and vigor. To what honest man, old enough, can these sentiments be entirely alien? They can be subdued and disciplined by religion, but who can say that they are dead? Only those to whom the maxim of La Rochefoucauld applies: "Quand les vices nous quittent, nous nous flattons de la créance que c'est nous qui les quittons." [9] The tragedy of Yeats's epigram is all in the last line.

Similarly, the play *Purgatory* [1] is not very pleasant, either. There are aspects of it which I do not like myself. I wish he had not given it this title, because I cannot accept a purgatory in which there is no hint, or at least no emphasis upon Purgation. But, apart from the extraordinary theatrical skill with which he has put so much action within the compass of a very short scene of but little movement, the play gives a masterly exposition of the emotions of an old man. I think that the epigram I have just quoted seems to me just as much to be taken in a dramatic sense as the play *Purgatory*. The lyric poet—and Yeats was always lyric, even when dramatic—can speak for every man, or for men very different from himself; but to do this he must for the moment be able to identify himself with every man or other men; and it is only his imaginative power of becoming this that deceives some readers into thinking that he is speaking for and of himself alone—especially when they prefer not to be implicated.

I do not wish to emphasize this aspect only of Yeats's poetry of age. I would call attention to the beautiful poem in *The Winding Stair*, in memory of Eva Gore-Booth and Con Markiewicz,[2] in which the picture at the beginning, of:

> *Two girls in silk kimonos, both*
> *Beautiful, one a gazelle,*

gets great intensity from the shock of the later line;

> *When withered, old and skeleton gaunt,*

and also to *Coole Park*, beginning

> *I meditate upon a swallow's flight,*
> *Upon an aged woman and her house.*

9. "When our vices abandon us, we flatter ourselves with the belief that it is we who are abandoning them."
1. 1938.

2. Two sisters of the Sligo county aristocracy. Eva was a poetess. See *Easter 1916*, note 2.

In such poems one feels that the most lively and desirable emotions of youth have been preserved to receive their full and due expression in retrospect. For the interesting feelings of age are not just different feelings; they are feelings into which the feelings of youth are integrated.

Yeats's development in his dramatic poetry is as interesting as that in his lyrical poetry. I have spoken of him as having been a lyric poet—in a sense in which I should not think of myself, for instance, as lyric; and by this I mean rather a certain kind of selection of emotion rather than particular metrical forms. But there is no reason why a lyric poet should not also be a dramatic poet; and to me Yeats is the type of lyrical dramatist. It took him many years to evolve the dramatic form suited to his genius. When he first began to write plays, poetic drama meant plays written in blank verse. Now, blank verse has been a dead meter for a long time. It would be outside of my frame to go into all the reasons for that now: but it is obvious that a form which was handled so supremely well by Shakespeare has its disadvantages. If you are writing a play of the same type as Shakespeare's, the reminiscence is oppressive; if you are writing a play of a different type, it is distracting. Furthermore, as Shakespeare is so much greater than any dramatist who has followed him, blank verse can hardly be dissociated from the life of the sixteenth and seventeenth centuries: it can hardly catch the rhythms with which English is spoken nowadays. I think that if anything like regular blank verse is ever to be reestablished, it can be after a long departure from it, during the course of which it will have liberated itself from period associations. At the time of Yeats's early plays it was not possible to use anything else for a poetry play: that is not criticism of Yeats himself, but an assertion that changes in verse forms come at one moment and not at another. His early verse-plays, including the *Green Helmet*, which is written in a kind of irregular rhymed fourteener, have a good deal of beauty in them, and, at least, they are the best verse-plays written in their time. And even in these, one notices some development of irregularity in the metric. Yeats did not quite invent a new meter, but the blank verse of his later plays shows a great advance toward one; and what is most astonishing is the virtual abandonment of blank verse meter in *Purgatory*. One device used with great success in some of the later plays is the lyrical choral interlude. But another, and important, cause of improvement is the gradual purging out of poetical ornament. This, perhaps, is the most painful part of the labor, so far as the versification goes, of the modern poet who tries to write a play in verse. The course of improvement is toward a greater and greater starkness. The beautiful line for its own sake is a luxury dangerous even for the poet who has made himself a virtuoso of the technique of the theater. What is necessary is a beauty which shall not be in the line or the isolable passage, but woven into the dramatic texture itself; so that you can hardly say whether the lines give grandeur to the drama, or whether it is the drama which turns the words into poetry. (One of the most thrilling lines in *King Lear* is the simple:

Never, never, never, never, never [3]

but, apart from a knowledge of the context, how can you say that it is poetry, or even competent verse?) Yeats's purification of his verse becomes much more evident in the four *Plays for Dancers* and in the two in the posthumous volume: those, in fact, in which he had found his right and final dramatic form.

It is in the first three of the *Plays for Dancers*, also, that he shows the internal, as contrasted with the external, way of handling Irish myth of which I have spoken earlier. In the earlier plays, as in the earlier poems, about legendary heroes and heroines, I feel that the characters are treated, with the respect that we pay to legend, as creatures of a different world from ours. In the later plays they are universal men and women. I should, perhaps, not include *The Dreaming of the Bones* [4] quite in this category, because Dermont and Devorgilla are characters from modern history, not figures of pre-history; but I would remark in support of what I have been saying that in this play these two lovers have something of the universality of Dante's Paolo and Francesca, and this the younger Yeats could not have given them. So with the Cuchulain of *The Hawk's Well*, [5] the Cuchulain, Emer and Eithne of *The Only Jealousy of Emer*; [6] the myth is not presented for its own sake, but as a vehicle for a situation of universal meaning.

I see at this point that I may have given the impression, contrary to my desire and my belief, that the poetry and the plays of Yeats's earlier period can be ignored in favor of his later work. You cannot divide the work of a great poet so sharply as that. Where there is the continuity of such a positive personality and such a single purpose, the later work cannot be understood, or properly enjoyed, without a study and appreciation of the earlier; and the later work again reflects light upon the earlier, and shows us beauty and significance not before perceived. We have also to take account of the historical conditions. As I have said above, Yeats was born into the end of a literary movement, and an English movement at that: only those who have toiled with

---

3. *Lear*, V. 3. 308.
4. Written 1917, first published in *Two Plays for Dancers*, 1919.

5. See footnote 7 above.
6. Written 1917–1918, first published in *Four Plays for Dancers*, 1921.

language know the labor and constancy required to free oneself from such influences—yet, on the other hand, once we are familiar with the older voice, we can hear its individual tones even in his earliest published verse. In my own time of youth there seemed to be no immediate great powers of poetry either to help or to hinder, either to learn from or to rebel against, yet I can understand the difficulty of the other situation, and the magnitude of the task. With the verse-play, on the other hand, the situation is reversed, because Yeats had nothing, and we have had Yeats. He started writing plays at a time when the prose-play of contemporary life seemed triumphant, with an infinite future stretching before it, when the comedy of light farce dealt only with certain privileged strata of metropolitan life; and when the serious play tended to be an ephemeral tract on some transient social problem. We can begin to see now that even the imperfect early attempts he made are probably more permanent literature than the plays of Shaw; and that his dramatic work as a whole may prove a stronger defense against the successful urban Shaftesbury Avenue [7] vulgarity which he opposed as stoutly as they. Just as, from the beginning, he made and thought his poetry in terms of speech and not in terms of print, so in the drama he always meant to write plays to be played and not merely to be read. He cared, I think, more for the theater as an organ for the expression of the consciousness of a people, than as a means to his own fame or achievement; and I am convinced that it is only if you serve it in this spirit that you can hope to accomplish anything worth doing with it. Of course, he had some great advantages, the recital of which does not rob him of any of his glory: his colleagues, a people with a natural and unspoiled gift for speech and for acting. It is impossible to disentangle what he did for the Irish theater from what the Irish theater did for him. From this point of advantage, the idea of the poetic drama was kept alive when everywhere else it had been driven underground. I do not know where our debt to him as a dramatist ends—and in time, it will not end until that drama itself ends. In his occasional writings on dramatic topics he has asserted certain principles to which we must hold fast: such as the primacy of the poet over the actor, and of the actor over the scene-painter; and the principle that the theater, while it need not be concerned only with "the people" in the narrow Russian sense, must be for the people; that to be permanent it must concern itself with fundamental situations. Born into a world in which the doctrine of "Art for Art's sake" was generally accepted, and living on into one in which art has been asked to be instrumental to social purposes, he

7. London theater district, thus signifying the commercial theater.

held firmly to the right view which is between these, though not in any way a compromise between them, and showed that an artist, by serving his art with entire integrity, is at the same time rendering the greatest service he can to his own nation and to the whole world.

To be able to praise, it is not necessary to feel complete agreement; and I do not dissimulate the fact that there are aspects of Yeats's thought and feeling which to myself are unsympathetic. I say this only to indicate the limits which I have set to my criticism. The questions of difference, objection and protest arise in the field of doctrine, and these are vital questions. I have been concerned only with the poet and dramatist, so far as these can be isolated. In the long run they cannot be wholly isolated. A full and elaborate examination of the total work of Yeats must some day be undertaken; perhaps it will need a longer perspective. There are some poets whose poetry can be considered more or less in isolation, for experience and delight. There are others whose poetry, though giving equally experience and delight, has a larger historical importance. Yeats was one of the latter: he was one of those few whose history is the history of their own time, who are a part of the consciousness of an age which cannot be understood without them. This is a very high position to assign to him: but I believe that it is one which is secure.

1940, 1957

Selected Bibliographies

THE MIDDLE AGES

Beowulf

The best critical essay of *Beowulf* remains J. R. R. Tolkien's Gollancz lecture, *Beowulf, the Monsters, and the Critics*, 1937. The most exhaustive scholarly discussion is R. W. Chambers' *Beowulf: An Introduction to the Study of the Poem*, 3rd edition, with a supplement by C. L. Wrenn, 1959. W. W. Lawrence's *Beowulf and the Epic Tradition*, 1928, is still of value. Recent works by Dorothy Whitelock, *The Audience of Beowulf*, 1958, A. C. Brodeur, *The Art of Beowulf*, 1959, and Kenneth Sisam, *The Structure of Beowulf*, 1965, mingle fine general criticism with some highly specialized discussion.

Geoffrey Chaucer

The standard edition of Chaucer's writing is F. N. Robinson's *The Complete Works of Chaucer*, 2nd edition, 1957. The present editor's anthology of Chaucer's poetry, from which are taken the selections printed here, is helpful to the nonspecialist, as is A. C. Baugh's *Chaucer's Major Poetry*, 1963. Vivid presentations of Chaucer in the background of 14th-century England are found in Marchette Chute's *Geoffrey Chaucer of England*,‡ 1946, and D. S. Brewer's *Chaucer and His Time*, 1963. The raw material for Chaucer's biography is contained in *Chaucer Life-Records*, edited by M. M. Crow and C. C. Olson, 1966. For a succinct account of the sources and literary background of Chaucer's works, see R. D. French's *A Chaucer Handbook*, 2nd edition, 1947; a complete reproduction of the known sources of the *Canterbury Tales* is contained in the scholarly compendium *Sources and Analogues of Chaucer's Canterbury Tales*, edited by W. F. Bryan and Germaine Dempster, 1941, 1958. Muriel Bowden, *A Commentary on the General Prologue to the Canterbury Tales*, 1948, provides a wealth of background information on the individual Canterbury pilgrims. For literary criticism, all the following works contain stimulating material: P. F. Baum, *Chaucer: A Critical Appreciation*, 1958; H. S. Bennett, *Chaucer and the Fifteenth Century*, 1947; D. S. Brewer, *Chaucer*, 1953; B. H. Bronson, *In Search of Chaucer*,‡ 1960; G. K. Chesterton, *Chaucer*, 1932; Nevill Coghill, *The Poet Chaucer*, 1949, and *Geoffrey Chaucer*, 1956; H. S. Corsa, *Chaucer, Poet of Mirth and Morality*, 1964; T. W. Craik, *The Comic Tales of Chaucer*, 1964; W. C. Curry, *Chaucer and the Medieval Sciences*,‡ rev., 1960; Germaine Dempster, *Dramatic Irony in Chaucer*, 1932; Maurice Hussey, A. C. Spearing, and James Winny, *An Introduction to Chaucer*,‡ 1965; G. L. Kittredge, *Chaucer and His Poetry*, 1915; W. W. Lawrence, *Chaucer and the Canterbury Tales*, 1950; Emile Legouis, *Goeffrey Chaucer*, 1913; J. L. Lowes, *Geoffrey Chaucer and the Development of His Genius*, 1934; R. M. Lumiansky, *Of Sondry Folk*, 1955; Kemp Malone, *Chapters on Chaucer*, 1951; J. M. Manly, *Some New Light on Chaucer*, 1926; Charles Muscatine, *Chaucer and the French Tradition*,‡ 1957; H. R. Patch, *On Rereading Chaucer*, 1939; R. O. Payne, *The Key of Remembrance*, 1963; Raymond Preston, *Chaucer*, 1952; R. K. Root, *The Poetry of Chaucer*, 2nd edition, 1922; P. V. D. Shelly, *The Living Chaucer*, 1940; John Speirs, *Chaucer the Maker*, 1951; and J. S. P. Tatlock, *The Mind and Art of Chaucer*, 1950. D. W. Robertson's *A Preface to Chaucer*, 1962, is a most learned, stimulating, doctrinaire, and controversial introduction to the reading of Chaucer. The following are collections of critical essays by various writers: *Discussions of the Canterbury Tales*,‡ edited by C. J. Owen, 1961; *Chaucer Criticism: The Canterbury Tales*,‡ edited by R. J. Schoeck and J. Taylor, 1960; and *Chaucer: Modern Essays in Criticism*,‡ edited by E. C. Wagenknecht, 1959. See the prefatory remarks to Chaucer's poems in Robinson's edition and the editor's commentary in his anthology.

The standard bibliographies are E. P. Hammond, *Chaucer: A Bibliographical Manual*, 1908; D. D. Griffith, *Bibliography of Chaucer*, 1955; and W. R. Craw-ford, *Bibliography of Chaucer 1954–63*, 1967. See also Caroline Spurgeon's *Five Hundred Years of Chaucer Criticism and Allusion, 1357–1900*, 1925.

THE SIXTEENTH CENTURY

Edmund Spenser

The Works of Edmund Spenser: A Variorum Edition, edited by Edwin Greenlaw, C. G. Osgood, F. M. Padelford, and Ray Heffner, 10 vols., 1932–49, summarizes modern scholarly knowledge. A one-volume edition is *The Poetical Works*,‡ edited by J. C. Smith and E. de Selincourt for the Oxford Standard Authors, 1912.

A good introduction for the student is H. S. V. Jones, *A Spenser Handbook*, 1930. Critical works of importance are A. Kent Hieatt, *Short Time's Endless Monument: The Symbolism of the Numbers in Edmund Spenser's Epithalamion*, 1960; Alastair Fowler, *Spenser and the Numbers of Time*, 1964; Graham Hough, *A. Preface to The Faerie Queene*,‡ 1962; Pauline Parker, *The Allegory of The Faerie Queene*, 1960; Paul E. McLane, *Spenser's Shepheardes Calender*, 1961; Robert Ellrodt, *Neoplatonism in the Poetry of Spenser*, 1960; William Nelson, *The Poetry of Edmund Spenser*,‡ 1963; William Nelson, ed., *Form and Convention in the Poetry of Edmund Spenser*, 1961; Kathleen Williams, *Spenser's Faerie Queene: World of Glass*, 1966; C. S. Lewis, *The Allegory of Love*,‡ 1936, and *English Literature in the Sixteenth Century*, 1954; J. W. Bennett, *The Evolution of "The Faerie Queene,"* Chicago, 1942; L. Bradner, *Edmund Spenser and "The Faerie Queene,"* Chicago, 1948; and A. C. Hamilton, *The Structure of Allegory in The Faerie Queene*, 1961.

William Shakespeare

On *1 Henry IV* see *The Variorum Shakespeare, Henry the Fourth Part One*, ed. S. B. Hemmingway, 1936; G. B. Evans, "Supplement to Henry IV. Part I" *Shakespeare Quarterly*, VII (1956), 3; John Dover Wilson, *The Fortunes of Falstaff*,‡ 1944; F. P. Wilson, *Marlowe and the Early Shakespeare*, 1953;

Irving Ribner, *The English History Play in the Age of Shakespeare*, 1957; L. B. Campbell, *Shakespeare's "Histories,"* 1947; H. Levin, "Falstaff Uncolted," *Modern Language Notes*, LXI (1946), 305–10; E. M. W. Tillyard, *Shakespeare's History Plays*,‡ 1946.

There are many editions of the sonnets, ranging from the convenient paperback Signet edition, 1964, with an introduction by W. H. Auden, to the two-volume *New Variorum* edited by Hyder E. Rollins, 1944. Commentary is extensive and much of it worthless, but sensible guidance may be found in Tucker Brooke's edition, 1936, which attempts a rearrangement; Edward Hubler, *The Sense of Shakespeare's Sonnets*,‡ 1952; J. B. Leishman, *Themes and Variations in Shakespeare's Sonnets*,‡ 1961; *The Riddle of Shakespeare's Sonnets: Essays by Edward Hubler, Northrop Frye, Leslie Fiedler, Stephen Spender and R. P. Blackmur*, 1962; and Hilton Landry, *Interpretations in Shakespeare's Sonnets*, 1963.

The poems have been edited by Hyder E. Rollins in the *New Variorum* edition, 1938. More manageable are the recent editions by F. T. Prince, 1960, and J. C. Maxwell, 1966. William H. Matchett has published *The Phoenix and the Turtle*, 1965. G. Wilson Knight's *The Mutual Flame*, 1955, discusses the sonnets and *The Phoenix and the Turtle*.

The standard scholarly authority on the life and works is E. K. Chambers, *William Shakespeare, A Study of Facts and Problems*, 1930. A well-written and dependable biography for the student and general reader is Marchette Chute, *Shakespeare of London*,‡ 1949. A scrupulously objective account is G. E. Bentley's *Shakespeare: A Biographical Handbook*, 1961. Bibliographies of Shakespearean studies appear in the periodical *Shakespeare Quarterly*.

THE SEVENTEENTH CENTURY

John Donne

For nearly fifty years the standard edition of Donne's poems was that in two volumes by Sir Herbert J. C. Grierson, 1912. In 1952 Miss Helen Gardner re-edited the *Divine Poems* and in 1965 added a volume of *Elegies and the Songs and Sonnets*. These new editions alter the text of some poems in some particulars on the basis of new manuscript evidence and offer to redate many of them. It is by no means clear that the text is always improved by the new

readings or that the new dating will hold up; one can only say many questions remain open. Under the editorship of G. R. Potter and Evelyn Simpson, a new edition of Donne's *Sermons* has been issued, 10 vols., 1953–59. *A Complete Poetry and Selected Prose*, under the editorship of John Hayward, 1929, is handy and handsome.

All biographies are based more or less directly on Walton's *Life*; the best one currently available is still Sir Edmund Grosse's *Life and Letters of John*

Donne, 1899. E. S. LeComte's recent biography, *Grace to a Witty Sinner,* 1965, is more popular in character.

T. S. Eliot's essays on Donne, the metaphysical poets, and the 17th century have been remarkably influential. They include an essay on "The Metaphysical Poets," originally a review of Grierson's anthology of *Metaphysical Lyrics and Poems* ‡ but reprinted as an independent essay in *Homage to John Dryden,* 1924, in Eliot's *Selected Essays,* 1932, and elsewhere. Eliot also took another, not quite congruent, view of the poet in *A Garland for John Donne,* edited by Theodore Spencer, 1931. Other collections of critical essays have been prepared by Helen Gardner,‡ 1962, and Frank Kermode, 1962.

Pierre Legouis' *Donne the Craftsman,* 1928, was an interesting early study; more recently Arnold Stein has offered close scrutinies of *John Donne's Lyrics,* 1962, and Joan Webber in *Contrary Music,* 1963, has analyzed Donne's prose style. J. B. Leishman, in *The Monarch of Wit: An Analytical and Comparative Study of the Poetry of John Donne,*‡ 1951 and 1959, provides an analytic survey. Rosemond Tuve's *Elizabethan and Metaphysical Imagery,*‡ 1947, offered a revolutionary, conservative view of Donne's imagery; and Leonard Unger, in *Donne's Poetry and Modern Criticism,* 1950, undertook to survey the whole troubled field. The standard bibliography of Donne, first published by Geoffrey Keynes in 1914, was revised in 1932 and again in 1958.

Ben Jonson

The standard edition of Jonson's works is that of C. H. Herford and Percy and Evelyn Simpson, published by the Clarendon Press in eleven volumes, 1925–52. This edition is meticulous in reproducing the old spellings, and typographically it is very elegant; but to find one's way around in it takes some practice. Of earlier editions, the handiest and most correct (though the text has been modernized) is that of W. Gifford, 9 vols., 1875.

Because Jonson's work falls into several different categories, general introductory accounts of the whole man are few. G. Gregory Smith did a biography for the English Men of Letters series, 1919, and a recent popular life is that of Marchette Chute, *Ben Jonson of Westminster,*‡ 1953. A. C. Swinburne wrote a characteristically acute and enthusiastic *Study of Ben Jonson,* 1889, and Maurice Castelain a weighty *Ben Jonson, l'homme et l'oeuvre,* 1907; both these books, though long out of date, retain the power to instruct and interest.

Special studies of the masques generally, and of Jonson's masques in particular, have been written by Enid Welsford, *The Court Masque,* 1927, Allardyce Nicoll, *Stuart Masques and the Renaissance Stage,* 1937, and Stephen Orgel, *The Jonsonian Masque,* 1965. Wesley Trimpi has written a good account of *Ben Jonson's Poems,* 1962; and C. F. Wheeler has studied *Classical Mythology in the Plays, Masques, and Poems of Ben Jonson,* 1938. There are of course many studies of Jonson as a dramatist, the comedies and satires having received particular attention. Jonas Barish has edited *Ben Jonson,*‡ 1963, a collection of critical essays. In 1938 S. A. Tannenbaum published a *Concise Bibliography* of Jonson, and in 1947 added a Supplement to it.

John Milton

Despite occasional textual eccentricities, the opulent Columbia Milton, a complete edition of poetry and prose, 18 vols., 1931–38, is widely accepted as standard; controversy continues over details, however, and anyone interested may consult Harris Fletcher's 4-volume facsimile edition of the *Poetical Works,* 1943–48, Miss Helen Darbishire's radical re-editing of the poetry, 1952–55, and the currently appearing Yale edition of the *Prose Works,* for a spectrum of editorial procedures and principles. Of the annotated editions of *Paradise Lost,* A. W. Verity's text, 1910, is probably still the least cumbersome and the most sensible.

The definitive, monumental biography of Milton is that of David Masson, 7 vols., 1859–94, rev. 1881–96; Sir Walter Raleigh's *Milton,* 1900, is handier to use, less pontifical in tone, and still relevant, though much disputed. Harris Fletcher's *Intellectual Development of John Milton,* 1956–61, 2 vols. projected for several volumes, promises to be in its way as encyclopaedic as Masson. While it takes no account at all of Milton the rebel (in fact, denies his existence), C. S. Lewis's *Preface to Paradise Lost,*‡ 1942, rev., 1960, is bright, persuasive, and enormously useful as a first approach. It may be corrected by A. J. A. Waldock's *Paradise Lost and Its Critics* ‡ 1947; B. Rajan's *Paradise Lost and the 17-Century Reader,* 1947; and G. W. Whiting, *Milton's Literary Milieu,* 1939. E. M. W. Tillyard's handbook, *Milton,* 1930, 1949, is in some ways more acute in setting forth the outstanding problems than J. H. Hanford's *Milton Handbook* 4th edition, 1946. David Daiches, under the short, sufficient title of *Milton,*‡ 1961, offers a general introductory survey of the poet's accomplishment; and the beginning student is likely to profit as well, by Marjorie H. Nicolson's *John Milton, a Reader's Guide to his Poetry,*‡ 1963. Collections of critical essays have been edited by A. E. Barker, 1965, and Louis L. Martz, 1966; the latter has also done an informative thematic study of *The Paradise Within,*‡ 1964, which includes discussions of Vaughan and Traherne as well as of Milton.

Specialized studies are beyond enumeration; only a scattering of the most useful can be named here. Robert Bridges has written the best account of *Milton's Prosody*, 2nd edition, 1921; Maurice Kelley has shown the intimate relation of Milton's theology, as expressed in the treatise *On Christian Doctrine* with his views in *Paradise Lost*, in *This Great Argument*, 1941; Malcolm M. Ross, *Poetry and Dogma*, 1954, suggests some of the theological complexities behind Milton's problems with incarnation; F. T. Prince has traced *The Italian Element in Milton's Verse*, 1954; and Theodore Banks has studied *Milton's Imagery*, 1950. An important study of *Samson Agonistes* is that of F. Michael Krouse, *Milton's Samson and the Christian Tradition*, 1949. Douglas Bush, in a series of lectures published as *Paradise Lost in Our Time*, 1945, has defended Milton against his New Critical enemies, and sometimes against his friends. D. H. Stevens did the basic bibliography, a *Reference Guide to Milton from 1800 to the Present Day*, 1930; it was supplemented by Harris Fletcher in *Contributions to a Milton Bibliography*, 1931.

But the bibliographers seem to have been falling far behind the current terrifying spate of books and articles on Milton.

Francis Bacon

The big edition of Bacon is *The Works*, 15 vols., edited by Spedding, Ellis, and Heath, 1860–64. Among the biographical introductions may be recommended that done for the English Men of Letters series by R. W. Church, 1884, and two more recent ones, *Francis Bacon: A Biography*, by Mary Sturt, 1932, and *Bacon*, by Charles Williams, 1933. Christopher Hill's *Intellectual Origins of the English Revolution*, 1965, demonstrates most tellingly the existence of a popular scientific tradition, in the vernacular, which lent body and popular support to Bacon's magisterial scientific dicta. An old-fashioned but still interesting book is *Francis Bacon of Verulaam* by Kuno Fischer, translated from the German and published in 1857. Two specialized studies of particular interest are F. H. Anderson's *The Philosophy of Francis Bacon*, 1948, and K. R. Wallace, *Francis Bacon on Communication & Rhetoric*, 1943.

THE RESTORATION AND THE EIGHTEENTH CENTURY

John Dryden

In 1961 appeared the long-awaited *Life of John Dryden* by Charles E. Ward. Also useful are George Saintsbury's brief *Dryden*, 1881, or the excellent biographical sketch in George R. Noyes' edition of the *Poetical Works*, 2nd edition, 1950. The only edition of the *Works* is the unsatisfactory one in 18 volumes by Sir Walter Scott and George Saintsbury, 1882–93. Of a new edition of the *Works*, begun under the general editorship of the late Edward N. Hooker and carried on under H. T. Swedenberg, Jr., three volumes have appeared: Vol. I, E. N. Hooker adn H. T. Swedenberg, Jr., eds. *Poems, 1649–1680*, 1956; Vol. VIII, J. H. Smith and D. MacMillan, eds., 1962, and Vol. IX, J. Loftis and V. A. Dearing, eds., 1966, each contain three plays. A bibliography of work on Dryden is Samuel H. Monk, *John Dryden: A List of Critical Studies—1895 to 1948*, 1950. The poems have been edited by James Kinsley, 4 vols., 1958. The best (but not complete) edition of the *Essays* is W. P. Ker's, 1900.

The best extended critical study of Dryden's poetry is Mark Van Doren's *The Poetry of John Dryden*, 1920, reissued in 1946 as *John Dryden: A Study of His Poetry* ‡. A. W. Verral's *Lectures of Dryden*, 1914, is valuable, as are T. S. Eliot's two studies, *Homage to John Dryden*, 1924, and *John Dryden*

the Poet, the Dramatist, the Critic, 1932. Arthur H. Hoffman's *John Dryden's Imagery*, 1962, is relevant not only to Dryden but also to Augustan poetry in general. Louis I. Bredvold's *The Intellectual Milieu of John Dryden*,‡ 1934, remains a valuable study of Dryden's philosophical, political, and religious ideas although some of its conclusions have been questioned in recent years, notably in Thomas H. Fujimura, "Dryden's *Religio Laici*: An Anglican Poem," *Publication of the Modern Language Association*, LXXVI (1961), 205–217. John C. Aden in *The Critical Opinions of John Dryden, A Dictionary*, 1963, brings together Dryden's critical ideas under convenient headings.

Jonathan Swift

Biographers have found it difficult to write of Swift without advancing some special and private thesis about his character and personal life. Sir Henry Craik's *Life of Jonathan Swift*, 2 vols., 1882, has the advantage of being freer from moral prejudice than any other 19th-century biography of Swift, and the even greater advantage of having been written before the Freudians began to psychoanalyze the Dean. Carl Van Doren's *Swift*, 1930, is readable; and a more recent study, Irvin Ehrenpreis's *The Personality of Jonathan Swift*,

1958, is full of good things as well as of a certain amount of ingenious and not wholly convincing theorizing. Ehrenpreis has so far published two excellent volumes of a three-volume biography: *Mr. Swift and His Contemporaries*, 1962, and *Dr. Swift*, 1968. The standard edition of the poems is by Sir Harold Williams, 3 vols., 1937, rev., 1958. Joseph Horrell's edition of the *Collected Poems*, 2 vols., The Muses' Library, 1958, is less expensive than Williams' and almost, but not entirely, relies on the canon and text established by Williams in his edition. Herbert Davis's edition of the prose works in 14 volumes, published over a period of years, is now all but complete, Swift's *Correspondence* has been edited by F. Elrington Ball, 6 vols., 1910–14; and by Sir Harold Williams, 5 vols., 1963–65. Distinguished editions of other works are Herbert Davis's *The Drapier's Letters*, 1935; Harold Williams' *Journal to Stella*, 1948; A. C. Guthkelch and D. Nichol Smith, *A Tale of a Tub*, 2nd edition, 1958; and Frank H. Ellis, *A Discourse of the Contests and Dissentions Between the Nobles and the Commons in Athens and Rome*, 1967. Useful bibliographies have been provided by Arthur H. Scouten in his edition of H. Teerink's *A Bibliography of the Writings of Jonathan Swift*, 1963, Louis A. Landa and James E. Tobin, *Jonathan Swift: A List of Critical Studies Published from 1895 to 1945*, 1945, and James J. Stathis, *A Bibliography of Swift Studies, 1945–65*, 1967.

Critical studies long and short abound. The student should find especially helpful Ricardo Quintana's *The Mind and Art of Jonathan Swift*, 1936, and *Swift: an Introduction*,‡ 1955. Arthur E. Case's *Four Essays on Gulliver's Travels*, 1945, and Maurice Johnson's *The Sin of Wit: Jonathan Swift as a Poet*, 1950, are useful special studies. Most of Herbert Davis's excellent critical pieces on Swift have been brought together in *Jonathan Swift, Essays on his Satire and Other Studies*,‡ 1964; in recent years there have appeared a number of paperbound collections of important essays, particularly those on *Gulliver's Travels*. Milton Voight has summarized the movements in Swift studies in *Swift and the Twentieth Century*, 1964.

Alexander Pope

There is no reliable complete edition of all of Pope's works. Defective though it is in many respects, the Victorian edition in 10 volumes by Elwin and Courthope, 1871–89, must still be consulted, though with caution. The excellent Twickenham Edition of the poems, a co-operative undertaking by several scholars (the general editor is John Butt), is now complete in 6 volumes (except for the volumes that will contain the translation of Homer, which are in preparation) and in a convenient single volume with selected notes ‡. Revised editions of individual volumes have appeared from time to time. The introductory and critical materials and the notes are most valuable. Only one volume of Norman Ault's edition of *The Prose Works*, 1936, was published before the editor's death.

No sound biography of Pope exists. George Sherburn's *Early Career of Alexander Pope*, 1934, is authoritative, but unfortunately it does not study the poet's life beyond about 1726. It is an essential book, for it corrects many misinterpretations and distortions of Pope's character and motives that mar earlier biographies. Edith Sitwell's biography ‡ is sentimental; earlier lives were marred by prejudice or misunderstanding. Ault's *New Light on Pope*, 1949, makes important miscellaneous contributions to Pope's biography. Sherburn's edition of the *Correspondence*, 1956, 5 vols., is standard, though it should be supplemented by his publication of some further letters in the *Review of English studies*, new. ser., IX (1958), 388–406. R. H. Griffith, *Alexander Pope: A Bibliography*, 1962, is a 2-volume listing of Pope's writings.

The best detailed critical study of the poems is Geoffrey Tillotson's *On the Poetry of Pope*, 2nd edition, 1950; and the same author's *Pope and Human Nature*, 1958, throws light on a difficult subject. Austen Warren's *Alexander Pope as Critic and Humanist*, 1929, though somewhat dated, is still useful. Much information is gathered up in Robert W. Rogers' *The Major Satires of Alexander Pope*, 1955. Reuben A. Brower's *Alexander Pope: The Poetry of Allusion*, 1959, is an enlightening study of Pope's lifelong habit of felicitous quotation from and adaptation of phrases, images, and ideas from earlier European poets, especially, though not exclusively, from the poets of classical antiquity. Maynard Mack, ed. *Essential Articles for the Study of Alexander Pope*, 1964, conveniently brings together a number of short studies.

Samuel Johnson

Others among Johnson's friends besides Boswell wrote of him: notably, Mrs. Hester Lynch Thrale Piozzi, whose *Anecdotes* appeared in 1786; Sir John Hawkins, whose *Life* was published in 1787 and reissued in 1961, edited and abridged by Bertram H. Davis; and Fanny Burney (Mme D'Arblay), from whose diary the Johnsonian passages are found most conveniently in C. B. Tinker's *Dr. Johnson and Fanny Burney*, 1911. James L. Clifford's *Young Sam Johnson*,‡ 1955, is a thorough study of Johnson's early life and a necessary supplement to Boswell's rather sketchy account of Johnson's life before their meeting in 1763. The poems were admirably edited by David Nichol Smith and E. L. McAdam, 1941. The first volume of the new Yale Edition of the *Works*, "Diaries, Prayers, and Annals," edited by E. L. McAdam and Donald and Mary Hyde, was published in 1958; it was followed by Vol. II, W. J. Bate, J. M. Bullitt, L. F. Powell, eds. *The Idler* and *The Adventurer*, 1963; and Vol. VI, E. L. McAdam with George Milne, eds. *Poems*, 1964. R. W. Chapman's edition of the letters, 3 vols., 1952, is authoritative. James L. Clifford, *Johnsonian Studies, 1887–1950. A Survey and Bibliography*, 1951, and J. L. Clifford and O. J. Greene, *Johnsonian Bibliography 1950–1960, A Supplement*, in *Johnsonian Studies* (Cairo), 1962, will soon be brought up to date in a more convenient form.

Some interesting modern studies of Johnson are W. C. B. Watkins' three essays in *Perilous Balance: The Tragic Genius of Swift, Johnson, and Sterne*, 1939; B. H. Bronson's "Johnson Agonistes," 1944 (reissued in *Johnson Agonistes and Other Essays*, 1965); W. J. Bate's *The Achievement of Samuel Johnson*, 1955; W. K. Wimsatt, Jr., *The Prose Style of Samuel Johnson*,‡ 1941; Donald J. Greene's *The Politics of Samuel Johnson*, 1960; and Arieh Sachs' *Passionate Intelligence: Imagination and Reason in the Work of Samuel Johnson*, 1967. *Johnson, Boswell, and Their Circle*, 1965, and Donald J. Greene, ed. *Samuel Johnson, A Collection of Critical Essays*,‡ 1965, bring together short studies by various hands. Aspects of Johnson's criticism are treated in Joseph E. Brown's *The Critical Opinions of Samuel Johnson*, 1926; Jean Hagstrum's *Samuel Johnson's Literary Criticism*, 1952; and Arthur Sherbo's *Samuel Johnson, Editor of Shakespeare*, 1956. Johnson's interesting notes to Shakespeare's comedies, histories, and seven of the tragedies have been reprinted by the Augustan Reprint Society in its publications Nos. 59, 60, 65, 66, 71, 72, 73. G. B. Hill's edition of the *Lives of the Poets*, 1905, has been recently reprinted.

James Boswell

A vast amount has been written about Boswell, much now outmoded by the discovery within the last quarter of a century of Boswell's private papers. Most of this outdated material is now simply ill informed, prejudiced, and worthless. Frederick A. Pottle's *James Boswell, The Earlier Years, 1740–1769*, 1966, makes good use of the private papers. C. B. Tinker's lively and percipient *Young Boswell*, 1922, is useful. Frederick A. Pottle's *The Literary Career of James Boswell*, 1929, was the first attempt to establish the canon of Boswell's writings. The *Letters*, edited by C. B. Tinker, 2 vols., 1924, will have to be supplemented by the recently recovered correspondence, of which one volume has been published: Ralph S. Walker, ed. *The Correspondence of James Boswell and John Johnston of Grange*, 1966. The *Private Papers of James Boswell from Malahide Castle*, edited by Geoffrey Scott and F. A. Pottle, 18 vols., 1928–34, made available the first of Boswell's papers to be discovered. Volumes of the trade edition of the *Journals*, under the general editorship of F. A. Pottle, appear regularly. The *Journal of a Tour to the Hebrides* has been edited, as first published, by R. W. Chapman, 1924; and, as originally written, by Frederick A. Pottle, 1936. The introductory material and illustrative notes in these volumes and the Malahide papers are of great value. Anthony E. Brown has provided a useful bibliography in "Boswellian Studies: A Bibliography," *Cairo Studies in English*, 1963–66.

A wise and sympathetic brief study of Boswell is B. H. Bronson's "Boswell's Boswell," in *Johnson and Boswell*,‡ 1944. *Johnson, Boswell, and Their Circle: Essays Presented to L. F. Powell*, 1965, is a valuable collection. The best edition of the *Life* is L. F. Powell's revised and enlarged edition of the earlier edition by G. B. Hill, 6 vols., 1934–50. A helpful guide through the *Life* is J. L. Smith-Dampier's *Who's Who in Boswell?*, 1935. Mention should perhaps be made of Thomas Babington Macaulay's brilliantly paradoxical, highly prejudiced account of Boswell in his review in 1831 of Croker's edition of the *Life of Johnson*. It blackened Boswell's reputation for nearly a century and its influence is still alive. It is easily available in any of the numerous printings of Macaulay's *Critical and Historical Essays*.

THE ROMANTIC PERIOD

William Blake

The beautifully printed *The Complete Writings of William Blake*, edited by Geoffrey Keynes, 1957, has now been replaced as the scholar's edition by *The Poetry and Prose of William Blake*, edited by David Erdman and Harold Bloom, 1965, which includes painstaking textual notes and brief commentaries on many of the poems. There is a good *Life of William Blake* by Mona Wilson, 1927, rev., 1948; but the first full account, Alexander Gilchrist's *The Life of William Blake*, which appeared in 1863, is a charming work which has been a source-book for all later biographers, and is available (expertly edited and supplemented by Ruthven Todd) in Everyman's Library, 1945.

The modern era of the scholarly explication of Blake symbolism was begun by S. Foster Damon's trail-blazing *William Blake: His Philosophy and Symbols*, 1924; the same scholar has also published an extremely helpful *Blake Dictionary: The Ideas and Symbols of William Blake*, 1965. Of more recent books perhaps the most useful are: Northrop Frye's classic analysis of Blake's moral allegory, *Fearful Symmetry*,‡ 1947; Mark Schoer's study emphasizing Blake's characteristic union of political, moral, and religious radicalism, *William Blake: The Politics of Vision*,‡ 1946; David V. Erdman's detailed investigation of the relation of Blake's poetry to the historical events of his time, *Blake: Prophet Against Empire*, 1954; Peter Fisher's incisive exposition of Blake's thought, *The Valley of Vision*, 1961; and Harold Bloom's illuminating commentaries on the individual poems, *Blake's Apocalypse: A Study in Poetic Argument*,‡ 1963. Modern critical essays are collected in *Blake*,‡ edited by Northrop Frye, 1966. H. M. Margoliouth's *William Blake*, 1951, is a concise introduction to the man and his work. Studies emphasizing the poems written before the long "prophetic books" are: Hazard Adams, *William Blake: A Reading of the Shorter Poems*, 1963. Robert F. Gleckner, *The Piper and the Bard*, 1959; and E. D. Hirsch, Jr., *Innocence and Experience: An Introduction to Blake*,‡ 1964. *A Concordance to the Writings of William Blake*, edited by David Erdman, 1967, is an important aid in elucidating his symbolism. Finally, there is a large and growing list of books which reproduce (some of them in splendid color) Blake's etched poems, drawings, and engravings. The excellent *Blake Bibliography*, edited by G. E. Bentley, Jr., and Martin K. Nurmi, 1964, includes an annotated list of all works by and about Blake, as well as Blake's illustrations for the work of others, published reproductions of his drawings, paintings, and engravings, and other Blakeana.

William Wordsworth

Ernest de Selincourt, the great Wordsworth scholar, has edited *The Poetical Works* (with Helen Darbishire), 5 vols., 1940–49; the variorum edition of *The Prelude*, with the texts of 1805 and 1850 on facing pages (revised by Helen Darbishire, 1959); and *The Letters of William and Dorothy Wordsworth*, 6 vols., 1935–39. He has also written the biography of Dorothy Wordsworth, 1933, and edited her *Journals*, 2 vols., 1941. A useful collection of Wordsworth's poems in one volume was edited for Oxford Standard Authors by Thomas Hutchinson and revised by Ernest de Selincourt,‡ 1950. Until recently, the standard biography was George McLean Harper, *William Wordsworth: His Life, Works, and Influence*, 2 vols., 1916, rev., 1929; Mary Moorman's *William Wordsworth*, 2 vols., 1957 and 1965, takes advantage of the greatly expanded scholarship of the last three decades. Edith Batho, *The Later Wordsworth*, 1933, is a detailed study of Wordsworth after 1805. H. M. Margoliouth deals briefly with the relations between two great poets in *Wordsworth and Coleridge, 1795–1835*, 1953.

Walter Raleigh's *Wordsworth*, 1903, H. W. Garrod's *Wordsworth, Lectures and Essays*, 1923, 2nd edition, 1927, Helen Darbishire's *The Poet Wordsworth*,‡ 1950, and Carl Woodring's, *Wordsworth*,‡ 1965, are useful introductions to Wordsworth's poetry. *The Mind of a Poet*, by Raymond D. Havens, 2 vols., 1941, is a detailed study of *The Prelude*; Herbert Lindenberger, *On Wordsworth's Prelude*,‡ 1963, is a more recent and lively exploration of the poem. Various aspects of Wordsworth's thought are discussed in M. M. Rader, *Presiding Ideas in Wordsworth's Poetry*, 1931; Basil Willey, *The Eighteenth Century Background*,‡ 1940; and N. P. Stallknecht, *Strange Seas of Thought*, 2nd ed., 1958. Prominent among the books which attest the growing interest in Wordsworth are John Jones, *The Egotistical Sublime*, 1954, and Geoffrey Hartman's impressive study of *Wordsworth's Poetry, 1787–1814*, 1964. A collection of recent critical essays is available in *Discussions of William Wordsworth*,‡ edited by J. M. Davis, 1964.

Samuel Taylor Coleridge

The *Complete Works*, ed. W. G. T. Shedd, 7 vols., 1853, 1884, though very far from complete, is the most inclusive collection of Coleridge's works; it will be superseded by the edition of Coleridge's writings now in process under the general editorship of Kathleen Coburn. The standard edition of the *Complete Poetical Works* is by E. H. Coleridge, 2 vols., 1912; a one-volume edition of *The Poems* by the same editor is available in Oxford Standard Authors. The most fully annotated edition of *Biographia Literaria* is by John Shawcross, 2 vols., 1907; a good reprint of the critical classic was edited by George Watson in 1956. Thomas Middleton Raysor has edited the fragmentary remains of *Coleridge's Shakespearean Criticism*, 2 vols., 1930, and *Coleridge's Miscellaneous Criticism*, 1936. The definitive edition of Coleridge's *Collected Letters* is now being issued by Earl Leslie Griggs: the first four volumes (covering 1785–1819) were published in 1956–1959. The first two volumes of Coleridge's extraordinary *Notebooks* are available, meticulously edited by Kathleen Coburn, 1957–61.

E. K. Chambers, *Samuel Taylor Coleridge*, 1938, gives a condensed and unsympathetic factual account of Coleridge's life. Lawrence Hanson, *The Life of S. T. Coleridge: The Early Years*, 1938, is an extensive study of the poet's life and writings to 1800; and H. M. Margoliouth has described the most fruitful literary association on record in his *Wordsworth and Coleridge, 1795–1834*, Home University Library, 1953. The best inclusive critique of Coleridge as poet is by Humphry House, *Coleridge*, 1953. *The Road to Xanadu*, 1927, rev.,‡ 1930, by J. L. Lowes, which investigates the sources and composition of *The Ancient Mariner* and *Kubla Khan*, has achieved the status of a critical classic. Recent discussion of Coleridge as philosopher and critic will be found in M. H. Abrams, *The Mirror and the Lamp*,‡ 1953, René Wellek, *A History of Modern Criticism 1750–1950*, Vol. II, 1955, Richard Harter Fogle, *The Idea of Coleridge's Criticism*, 1962, and J. A. Appleyard, *Coleridge's Philosophy of Literature*, 1965.

George Gordon, Lord Byron

The Works of Lord Byron, 1898–1904, contains seven volumes of *Poetry*, edited by Ernest Hartley Coleridge, and six volumes of *Letters and Journals*, edited by Rowland E. Prothero; the latter have been supplemented by *Lord Byron's Correspondence*, 2 vols., 1922, edited by Sir John Murray. There are numerous editions of the collected poems; a well-chosen and annotated selection has been published in two volumes in the Odyssey Press Series: *Don Juan and Other Satiric Poems*, edited by Louis I. Bredvold, 1935, and *Childe Harold's Pilgrimage and Other Romantic Poems*, edited by Samuel C. Chew, 1936. Selections from the letters have been prepared by V. H. Collins, *Lord Byron in His Letters*, 1927, and by R. G. Howarth, *Letters of Lord Byron*, 1933. *His Very Self and Voice*, by Ernest J. Lovell, Jr., 1954, is a compilation of Byron's conversations, and *Byron: A Self-Portrait*, edited by Peter Quennel, 2 vols., 1950, reprints selected letters and the text of his diaries.

The standard biography, a circumstantial and objective narrative, is Leslie A. Marchand's *Byron: A Biography*, 3 vols., 1957. Shorter and very readable lives are Ethel C. Mayne, *Byron*, one-volume edittion, 1924, and Peter Quennell, *Byron*, 1934. Charles Du Bos' *Byron and the Need of Fatality*, trans. E. C. Mayne, 1932, attempts a depth analysis of Byron's temperament. The fascination of Byron the man and the apparent difficulty of saying unobvious things about his poetry have until recently made for a dearth of primarily critical writings about Byron. Among the criticism may be mentioned: William J. Calvert, *Byron: Romantic Paradox*, 1935; G. Wilson Knight's symbolic interpretations and praises of Byron, *The Burning Oracle*, 1939, and *Lord Byron: Christian Virtues*, 1954; E. J. Lovell, Jr., *Byron: The Record of a Quest*, 1950; Paul West, *Byron and the Spoiler's Art*, 1960; Andrew Rutherford, *Byron*, 1961; M. K. Joseph, *Byron, the Poet*, 1964, and L. A. Marchand, *Byron's Poetry: A Critical Introduction*,‡ 1965. *Byron*,‡ 1963, edited by Paul West, is a collection of twentieth-century essays in criticism.

An edition of *Don Juan* which incorporates the changes Byron made in his manuscripts is *Byron's Don Juan*, edited by T. G. Steffan and W. W. Pratt, 4 vols., 1957; the first volume, by Steffan, is a full and revealing commentary on his poem. Other discussions of Byron's masterpiece are: P. G. Trueblood, *The Flowering of Byron's Genius: Studies in Byron's Don Juan*, 1945; and E. F. Boyd, *Byron's Don Juan: A Critical Study*, 1945; and George M. Ridenour, *The Style of "Don Juan,"* 1960.

Percy Bysshe Shelley

The standard collection of Shelley's writings is *The Complete Works*, edited in 10 vols. by Roger Ingpen and Walter E. Peck, 1926–30. The most useful single volume of the poems is in the Oxford Standard Authors, edited by Thomas Hutchinson and reissued in 1933 with Introduction and Notes by Benjamin P. Kurtz. *Shelley's Prose* was collected by David Lee Clark in 1954; and *The Letters* were edited by Frederick L. Jones in 2 vols., 1964.

The classic life is Newman Ivey White's *Shelley*, 2 vols., 1940, which is also available in a condensed single volume under the title *Portrait of Shelley*, 1945. A graceful short biography and appreciation is Edmund Blunden's *Shelley: A Life Story*,‡ 1946. Kenneth Neill Cameron, in *The Young Shelley*,‡ 1950, emphasizes the development of Shelley's radical social and political thinking. C. E. Pulos, *The Deep Truth: A Study of Shelley's Scepticism*,‡ 1954, a valuable corrective of standard views of Shelley, emphasizes the philosophic scepticism at the center of his idealism.

Shelley's Major Poetry,‡ by Carlos Baker, 1948, provides useful analyses of the longer poems which stress their ideational content; Carl H. Grabo, in *A Newton Among Poets*, 1930, and Desmond King-Hele, in *Shelley: His Thought and Work*, 1960, deal with Shelley's conversion of scientific knowledge into poetic imagery. *The Imagery of Keats and Shelley*, 1949, by Richard H. Fogle, is an analysis of the stylistic qualities of Shelley's poetry.

As early as 1900, W. B. Yeats, in "The Philosophy of Shelley's Poetry" (reprinted in *Essays*, 1924), dealt with Shelley as one of the great symbolist poets; the essay reveals the paradoxical position of modern critics who revere Yeats but condemn Shelley, one of Yeats's most important poetic models. Recent treatments of Shelley's symbolic imagery are Peter Butter, *Shelley's Idols of the Cave*, 1954, and Harold Bloom's innovative study, *Shelley's Mythmaking*, 1959, which puts Shelley in the line of the visionary poets whose imaginative processes were instinctively mythopeic. Earl Wasserman's *The Subtler Language*, 1959, includes detailed explications of *Mont Blanc*, *The Sensitive Plant*, and *Adonais*, and his *Shelley's Prometheus Unbound: A Critical Reading*, 1965, extends this close reading to Shelley's masterpiece. Other recent critiques are Milton Wilson, *Shelley's Later Poetry*, 1959, and R. G. Woodman, *The Apocalyptic Tradition in the Poetry of Shelley*, 1964. *Shelley*,‡ ed. George M. Ridenour, 1965, is an anthology of modern critical essays. Shelley's *Prometheus Unbound: A Variorum Edition*, edited by Lawrence J. Zillman, 1959, incorporates variant interpretations of the poem in general and of the details of its text.

John Keats

The two best editions of Keats's poems are Ernest de Selincourt's *Poems*, 5th edition, 1926, and H. W. Garrod's *Poetical Works*,‡ 2nd edition, 1958. Hyder E. Rollins's *The Letters of John Keats*, 2 vols., 1958, has now replaced M. B. Forman's earlier collection of the letters, 4th edition, 1952.

Sir Sidney Colvin's *John Keats*, 1917, and Amy Lowell's *John Keats*, 2 vols., 1925, have now been replaced by W. J. Bate's notable study of the poet's life, writings, and place in the English poetic tradition, *John Keats*,‡ 1963. Two shorter critical biographies, both valuable, are Aileen Ward, *John Keats: The Making of a Poet*,‡ 1963, and Douglas Bush, *John Keats*, 1966. Among the many critical writings on the poet, the following are especially useful: C. D. Thorpe, *The Mind of John Keats*, 1926 (on Keats's thought); M. R. Ridley, *Keats's Craftsmanship*,‡ 1933 (based on the revisions in Keats's manuscripts); W. J. Bate, *The Stylistic Development of Keats*, 1945, 1958; R. H. Fogle, *The Imagery of Keats and Shelley*, 1949 (a fine study of Keats's characteristic diction and figurative language); Earl Wasserman, *The Finer Tone*, 1953 (a close and sometimes oversubtle analysis of the major poems); and E. C. Pettet, *On the Poetry of Keats*, 1957. *Keats*,‡ edited by W. J. Bate, 1964, reprints a number of recent critical essays.

THE VICTORIAN AGE

Thomas Carlyle

The *Works* have been edited by H. D. Traill, 30 vols., 1898–1901, and a 30 volume collection of the *Letters* (edited by C. R. Sanders and others) is in process of being published. C. F. Harrold's edition of *Sartor Resartus* (1937) is helpful concerning Carlyle's debt to German literature, as is Louis Cazamian's *Carlyle*, translated in 1932, concerning his religious background. J. A. Froude's *Thomas Carlyle*, 1882–84, remains, despite its inaccuracies, the standard biography. A reasonable account of his marriage is given by Lawrence and Elizabeth Hanson in their *Necessary Evil: The Life of Jane Welsh Carlyle*, 1952. Emery Neff's *Carlyle and Mill*, 1926, and Eric Bentley's *A Century of Hero-Worship*,‡ 1944, are recommended as studies of Carlyle's thought. John Holloway's *The Victorian Sage*,‡ 1953, includes a chapter analyzing Carlyle's rhetoric. George B. Tennyson's *Sartor Called Resartus*, 1965, is an important critical study. For other discussions see Carlisle Moore's critical bibliography in *The English Romantic Poets and Essayists*, edited by Carolyn and Lawrence Houtchens (Revised edition), 1966.

Alfred, Lord Tennyson

Tennyson's *Works* were edited by his son Hallam, Lord Tennyson, in 9 vols., 1907–8. A readily available one-volume edition was edited by W. J. Rolfe, 1898. Hallam Tennyson's *Alfred Lord Tennyson: A Memoir*, 2 vols., 1897, is a mine of scattered anecdotes and valuable information. The best biography is Sir Charles Tennyson's *Alfred Tennyson*, 1949, Sir Harold Nicolson's *Tennyson*, 1923, a critical study more than a biography, gives a lively but distorted assessment of Tennyson's achievement. Also unsympathetic is Paull F. Baum's *Tennyson Sixty Years After*, 1948. A judicious corrective is supplied by Jerome H. Buckley's *Tennyson: The Growth of a Poet*,‡ 1961, and also by Valerie Pitt's *Tennyson Laureate*, 1962.

Some of the most interesting discussions are in introductory essays to Tennyson's poems by T. S. Eliot, 1936; W. C. DeVane,‡ 1940; W. H. Auden, 1944; H. M. McLuhan,‡ 1956; and Jerome H. Buckley,‡ 1958. Also useful are *A Commentary on Tennyson's "In Memoriam,"* by A. C. Bradley, 1901; *The Formation of Tennyson's Style*, by J. F. A. Pyre, 1921; *The Alien Vision of Victorian Poetry*, by E. D. H. Johnson, 1952; and *Critical Essays on the Poetry of Tennyson*, edited by John Kilham, 1960.

Robert Browning

A variorum edition of Browning's poetry, edited by Roma A. King Jr. and others, is projected to be published in 1969. Meanwhile a standard edition is that edited by F. G. Kenyon, 10 vols., 1912. Also projected is a collection of Browning's letters in 21 vols., to be edited by Philip Kelley and Ronald Hudson. W. Hall Griffin and H. C. Minchin's *The Life of Robert Browning*, 1910, rev., 1938, is the standard biography. It may be compared with Betty Miller's *Robert Browning: A Portrait*, 1952, a lively psychoanalytical study. W. C. DeVane's *A Browning Handbook*, rev., 1955, is a model compilation of factual data concerning each of Browning's poems: sources, composition, and reputation.

The critical assessments in G. K. Chesterton's *Robert Browning*, 1903, are colorfully expressed and often shrewd. Roma A. King, Jr.'s *The Bow and the Lyre*,‡ 1957, contains detailed discussions of some of the principal monologues. Robert Langbaum's *The Poetry of Experience* ‡ is an admirable attempt to relate Browning's monologues to some of the main developments in modern literature. For an understanding of Browning's ideas, W. O. Raymond's *The Infinite Moment*,‡ 1965, is suggestive. Many of the best discussions of Browning's achievement, especially discussions of individual poems, have been conveniently assembled in two collections that rarely overlap each other: *Robert Browning: A Collection of Critical Essays*, edited by Philip Drew,‡ 1966, and *The Browning Critics*,‡ edited by Boyd Litzinger and K. L. Knickerbocker, 1965. The latter collection also includes an extensive bibliography.

Matthew Arnold

The Works, 1903, is an incomplete collection of Arnold's writings; it must be supplemented by later editions such as *The Poetical Works*, edited by C. B. Tinker and H. F. Lowry, 1950, and the elaborately annotated *Poems of Arnold*, edited by Kenneth Allott, 1965; the *Note-Books*, edited by H. F. Lowry, Karl Young, and W. H. Dunn, 1952; and *The Letters of Arnold to * * * Clough*, edited by H. F. Lowry, 1932. Since 1960 several of the projected 10 volumes of Arnold's *Complete Prose Works*, edited by R. H. Super, have been published. For a study of these prose works see William Robbins' *The Ethical Idealism of Matthew Arnold*, 1959.

Lionel Trilling's excellent *Matthew Arnold* ‡ (1949) remains a standard critical and biographical study but see also W. Stacy Johnson's *The Voices of Matthew Arnold*, 1961; Dwight Culler's *Imaginative Reason*, 1966, and G. Robert Stange's *Matthew Arnold: The Poet as Humanist*, 1967. Two useful investigations of Arnold's literary and intellectual background are Leon Gottfried's *Matthew Arnold and the Romantics*, 1963, and Warren D. Anderson's *Matthew Arnold and the Classical Tradition*, 1965. One of the best shorter essays is E. K. Brown's Introduction to *Representative Essays of Arnold*, 1936, and see also Geoffrey and Kathleen Tillotson, *Mid-Victorian Studies*, 1965, pp. 152–238.

John Stuart Mill

Since 1963 several of the projected 20 volumes of the *Collected Works*, edited by F. E. L. Priestly, have been published (including volumes of Mill's letters). A. W. Benn, *The History of English Rationalism in the Nineteenth Century*, 2 vols., 1906. Karl Britton, *John Stuart Mill*, 1953; Emery Neff, *Carlyle and Mill*, 1926; M. St. J. Packe, *The Life of J. S. Mill*, 1954.

THE TWENTIETH CENTURY

Thomas Hardy

Hardy published about a dozen volumes of poetry in his lifetime; of these, the most important are *Wessex Poems and Other Verses*, 1898; *Poems of the Past and Present*, 1902; *Time's Laughingstocks*, 1909; *Satires of Circumstance*, 1914. The *Collected Poems* were issued in one volume in 1932 and have several times been reprinted. There are several collected editions of Hardy's works, notably the Wessex Edition, 21 vols., 1912–14, and the Mellstock Edition, 37 vols., 1919–20.

Hardy of Wessex, by Carl J. Weber, 1940, is the best general account of Hardy's life and work. The two biographical volumes by his wife—*The Early Life of Thomas Hardy*, 1928, and *The Later Years of Thomas Hardy*, 1930—are packed with information, much of it dictated by Hardy himself. *Thomas Hardy*, by Douglas Brown, 1954, is an excellent critical study. "The Shorter Poems of Hardy," by R. P. Blackmur, to be found in Blackmur's *Language as Gesture*, 1952, is one of the finest critical discussions of Hardy's poetry. *Hardy: A Collection of Critical Essays*,‡ edited by A. J. Guerard, 1963, is a useful collection.

Gerard Manley Hopkins

Robert Bridges edited the first (posthumous) edition of Hopkins' poems in 1918; a second edition, with "An Appendix of Additional Poems," appeared with a critical introduction by Charles Williams in 1930; the third edition, adding some further unpublished poems, was edited by W. H. Gardner in 1948 with additional notes and a biographical introduction. This is now the standard edition.

In addition to the poems, Hopkins' letters and parts of his notebooks have been published, and these are of great interest to students of Hopkins' mind and of his poetic techniques: *The Letters of Gerard Manley Hopkins to Robert Bridges* and *The Correspondence of G. M. Hopkins and Richard Watson Dixon*, edited by C. C. Abbott, 2 vols., 1935; *Further Letters of Gerard Manley Hopkins*, edited by C. C. Abbott, 1937, rev., 1956; and *Notebooks and Papers of Gerard Manley Hopkins*, edited by Humphry House, 1937. House has also edited *Journals and Papers*, 1959; the edition was completed by Graham Storey. This, together with *Sermons and Devotional Writings*, edited by Christopher Devlin, 1959, constitutes a revised edition of the *Notebooks and Papers*. A useful selection of Hopkins' poetry and prose is *A Hopkins Reader*,‡ edited by John Pick, 1953.

The most elaborate study of Hopkins is *G. M. Hopkins: A Study of Poetic Idiosyncrasy in Relation to Poetic Tradition*, by W. H. Gardner, 2 vols., 1944, 1949. *Gerard Manley Hopkins*, by the Kenyon Critics, 1945, contains some helpful critical essays, and *The Shaping Vision of Gerard Manley Hopkins*, by Alan Heuser, 1958, is a careful study of the relation of certain of Hopkins' dominating ideas to his poetic theory and practice. *Gerard Manley Hopkins*, by G. F. Lahey, 1930, is a biography, as is *Gerard Manley Hopkins, Priest and Poet*,‡ by J. Pick, 2nd ed., 1966.

George Bernard Shaw

The Collected Works of Bernard Shaw, in the Ayot St. Lawrence Edition, 30 vols., appeared in 1930 ff. Selections of drama are *Nine Plays*, 1931; *Seven Plays*, 1951; and *Selected Plays*, 4 vols. (containing 27 plays), 1948–57. Many of the plays are also available in inexpensive reprints. Selections of his prose include *Bernard Shaw, Selected Prose*, edited by Diarmuid Russell, 1952; *Plays and Players* (drama criticism), edited by A. C. Ward, 1952; and *Shaw on Music*,‡ edited by Eric Bentley, 1955.

Of the many books on Shaw, the best critical study is Eric Bentley's *Bernard Shaw: A Reconsideration*,‡ 1947. Hesketh Pearson's biography, *Shaw: A Full-length Portrait*, was first published in 1942; Pearson added in 1950 *G.B.S.: A Postscript*. The two books are now available in a single volume. Edmund

Wilson's essay, "Shaw at Eighty," in *The Triple Thinkers*,‡ 1938, 1952, is a stimulating discussion of Shaw as thinker and playwright. *G.B.S. 90: Aspects of Shaw's Life and Works*, edited by S. Winsten, 1946, contains essays by a variety of writers. *G. B. Shaw, A Collection of Critical Essays*,‡ edited by R. J. Kaufmann, 1965.

Joseph Conrad

Standard is *The Uniform Edition of the works of Joseph Conrad*, 22 vols., 1923–28, reprinted in 1946 ff, as *The Collected Edition of the Works of Joseph Conrad*. Other collections are the Concord Edition, 22 vols., 1923–28, and the Memorial Edition, 21 vols., 1925.

Two perceptive studies of Conrad are *Conrad the Novelist*,‡ by Albert J. Guerard, 1958, and *Joseph Conrad, Achievement and Decline*, by Thomas Mosher, 1957. *The Portable Conrad*,‡ edited by Morton D. Zabel, 1947, contains a good selection with a helpful introduction (Zabel has also edited *Tales of the East and West*, 1958; *Lord Jim*,‡ *Youth*, and *The Shadow-Line*, all 1959; and, in one volume, *The Shadow-Line*, *Typhoon*, and *The Secret Sharer*, under the title *The Shadow-Line and Two Other Tales*,‡ 1959). *The Conrad Companion*, 1948 (originally published as *The Conrad Reader*, 1946), edited by A. J. Hoppé, contains a large selection from the stories and other writings with a biographical introduction. The discussion of Conrad in *The Great Tradition*,‡ by F. R. Leavis, 1949, is valuable. There is a chapter on Conrad in *The Novel and the Modern World*,‡ by D. Daiches, 2nd edition, 1960, which deals at length with *The Nigger of the "Narcissus," Lord Jim*, and *Nostromo. Joseph Conrad, Life and Letters*, edited by G. Jean-Aubry, 2 vols., 1927; *The Sea Dreamer*, by G. Jean-Aubry, 1957; and *Joseph Conrad*,‡ by Jocelyn Baines, 1960, are biographies. The last is now the standard biography.

William Butler Yeats

In addition to poems and verse plays, Yeats published essays, short stories, and autobiographical writings, and produced editions of William Blake (with Edwin Ellis) and of some poems of Spenser. He also edited the *Oxford Book of Modern Verse. Collected Poems*, Definitive Edition, 1956, and *Collected Plays*, 2nd edition, 1952, collect Yeats's main work into two convenient volumes, while his letters are collected in *The Letters of W. B. Yeats*, edited by Allan Wade, 1954. Yeats's mystical work *A Vision* was first published in 1925; a new, much revised edition appeared in 1937. *Mythologies* was published in 1959. Yeats's autobiographical writings are combined in *The Autobiography of*

W. B. Yeats,‡ 1938 ff. Peter Alt and Russell K. Alspach edited a variorum edition of the *Poems* in 1957.

Three helpful books on Yeats as both man and poet are: *Yeats, the Man and the Masks,*‡ by Richard Ellmann, 1948; *W. B. Yeats, Man and Poet,*‡ by Norman Jeffares, 1949; *The Lonely Tower: Studies in the Poetry of W. B. Yeats*, by T. R. Henn, 1950. *W. B. Yeats,*‡ by Joseph Hone, 1942, 2nd ed., 1962, is a biography. *The Permanence of Yeats,*‡ edited by James Hall and Martin Steinmann, 1950. *Yeats: A Collection of Critical Essays,*‡ edited by John Unterecker, 1963, and *In Excited Reverie*, edited by A. N. Jeffares and K. G. W. Cross, 1965, are three of several useful collections of critical essays on the poet.

James Joyce

Dubliners ‡ is available in various editions. A critical edition of *A Portrait of the Artist as a Young Man,*‡ based on the autograph manuscript, was published in 1964. *Ulysses* ‡ was first published in the United States in 1934; a greatly superior text was published in 1961. *Finnegans Wake* ‡ was published in 1939, and a revised text, incorporating the author's corrections, in 1958. There are three volumes of Joyce's *Letters*, the first edited by Stuart Gilbert, 1957, and the second and third by Richard Ellmann, 1966.

Good general accounts of Joyce's work will be found in *James Joyce,*‡ by Harry Levin, 1941, and *James Joyce,*‡ by William Y. Tindall, 1950. *James Joyce's Ulysses,*‡ by Stuart Gilbert, 1930, rev., 1952, and *James Joyce and the Making of Ulysses,*‡ by Frank Budgen, 1934, 1937, are almost necessary works for the reader of *Ulysses*, as are *A Skeleton Key to Finnegans Wake,*‡ by J. Campbell and H. M. Robinson, 1944, and *The Books at the Wake,*‡ by J. S. Atherton, 1959, for the reader of *Finnegans Wake*. Four chapters in *The Novel and the Modern World,*‡ by David Daiches, 2nd ed., 1960, give a general critical account of Joyce's work. *James Joyce: Two Decades of Criticism*, edited by Seon Givens, 1948, is a useful anthology of criticism. *James Joyce,*‡ by Richard Ellmann, 1959, is the standard biography. *Surface and Symbol,*‡ by Robert M. Adams, 1963, studies the raw material of actual Dublin life in *Ulysses*.

D. H. Lawrence

The standard edition of the collected works is the Phoenix Edition, 1955. *Collected Poems* appeared in 1928 and 1932, *Selected Poems* (selected by Richard Aldington) in 1934, and *Complete Poems*, 3 vols., in 1964. *Studies in Classic American Literature,*‡ was published in 1923.

Lawrence was a highly controversial figure long before his death, and soon after it a spate of books about him by friends, enemies, and acquaintances began to pour from the press. Most of these are one-sided, but his wife's memoir, *Not I, But the Wind . . .* , by Frieda Lawrence, 1934, is an important and moving book. Two critical studies neatly supplement each other, *D. H. Lawrence: Novelist*, by F. R. Leavis, 1955, which is an impassioned argument for Lawrence's supreme greatness, and the much cooler, less "committed," but not unsympathetic *The Dark Sun*, by Graham Hough, 1956, which has a helpful chapter on Lawrence's poetry. *Double Measure*, by George Ford, 1965, is an excellent study of *Women in Love* and *The Rainbow*, and various short stories that illustrate the same themes. The best biography is *The Intelligent Heart,*‡ by Harry T. Moore, 1954; but Lawrence's own *Letters*, ed. by Aldous Huxley, 1932, and much more fully |but| still incompletely by Harry T. Moore in 1962, provide the best introduction to his life.

T. S. Eliot

The fullest one-volume collections of Eliot's poetry are *Collected Poems, 1909–1963*, 1963, and *The Complete Poems and Plays* (including the plays through *The Cocktail Party*), 1952. Some critical essays are in *Selected Essays*, 1932, and *On Poetry and Poets,*‡ 1957.

Among the many books on Eliot, *The Achievement of T. S. Eliot,*‡ by F. O. Matthiessen, rev., 1947, has the enthusiasm of a pioneer work; *T. S. Eliot: A Study of His Writings by Various Hands*, edited by B. Rajan, 1947, and *T. S. Eliot, a Selected Critique,*‡ edited by Leonard Unger, 1948, bring together a variety of critical essays including some helpful explications of *The Waste Land* and *Four Quartets; The Art of T. S. Eliot,*‡ by Helen Gardner, is a perceptive critical study of his poetry; *T. S. Eliot, the Design of his Poetry,*‡ by Elizabeth Drew, 1950, is a systematic chronological survey and explanation; *A Reader's Guide to T. S. Eliot,*‡ by George Williamson, 1953, is thorough and informative in its explanation of obscurities and references; and *T. S. Eliot's Poetry and Plays,*‡ by Grover Smith, Jr., 1956, goes through the poems and plays in an exhaustive and even exhausting manner. The best short critical book on Eliot is *T. S. Eliot*, by Northrop Frye, 1963.

Index

Absalom and Achitophel, 792

Abt Vogler, 2016

"A cold coming we had of it, 2598

Adam scrivain, if evere it thee bifalle, 180

Adam's Curse, 2375

Adonais, 1622

After Long Silence, 2394

Afterthought, 1330

A Gentle Knight was pricking on the plane, 220

Ah, Are You Digging on My Grave?, 2226

Ah, did you once see Shelley plain, 1968

Ah, fading joy, how quickly art thou past!, 791

Ah Sun-Flower, 1226

Air and Angels, 507

Alas, 'tis true I have gone here and there, 398

Alexander's Feast, 833

A little black thing among the snow, 1224

A little onward lend thy guiding hand, 704

All along the valley, stream that flashest white, 1924

All human things are subject to decay, 817

All look and likness caught from earth, 1423

All Nature seems at work. Slugs leave their lair, 1427

A lovely form there sate beside my bed, 1428

Amid the desolation of a city, 1616

Among School Children, 2388

Amoretti, 370

And Did Those Feet, 1250

Andrea del Sarto, 1994

An old, mad, blind, despised, and dying king, 1583

Apeneck Sweeney spreads his knees, 2578

Apparent Failure, 2025

Apparition, The, 499

April is the cruelest month; breeding, 2582

Araby, 2418

Areopagitica, 584

Argument against the Abolishing of Christianity in England, An, 868

Arms and the Man, 2248

Arnold, Matthew, 2030

—A simple Child, 1258

Ask Me No More, 1876

A snake came to my water trough, 2565

Asolando, Epilogue to, 2030

A spirit seems to pass, 2215

As Rochefoucauld his maxims drew, 857

As some fond virgin, whom her mother's care, 1034

A sudden blow: the great wings beating still, 2387

As virtuous men pass mildly away, 502

As, when a tree's cut down, the secret root, 788

At a Solemn Music, 563

At Flores in the Azores Sir Richard Grenville lay, 1928

At Francis Allen's on the Christmas eve, 1855

A thing of beauty is a joy forever, 1676

At the midnight in the silence of the sleep-time, 2030

At the round earth's imagined corners, blow, 519

Author's Apology for Heroic Poetry and Heroic License, The, 847

Autobiography (**Mill**), 2192

Avenge, O Lord, thy slaughtered saints, whose bones, 574

Awake, my St. John! leave all meaner things, 1039

Bacon, Francis, 745

Bait, The, 501

Batter my heart, three-personed God, 520

Bavarian Gentians, 2564

Because you have thrown off your prelate lord, 573

Behold her, single in the field, 1324

Below the thunders of the upper deep, 1843

Beneath these fruit-tree boughs that shed, 1313

Beowulf, 1

Best and brightest, come away!, 1636

Better Part, The, 2074

Binsey Poplars, 2237

Biographia Literaria, 1429

Bishop Orders His Tomb at Saint Praxed's Church, The, 1962

Blake, William, 1210

Blake's Notebook, Poems from, 1249

Blasted with sighs, and surrounded with tears, 498

Blest pair of Sirens, pledges of Heaven's joy, 563

Blow, Blow, Thou Winter Wind, 389

Book of Thel, The, 1230

Book Was Writ of Late Called Tetrachordon, A, 572

Boswell, James, 1151

Boswell on the Grand Tour, 1154

Break, Break, Break, 1867

Break of Day, 507

Bright Star, 1693

Broken Appointment, A, 2214

Browning, Robert, 1947

Buried Life, The, 2042

Busy old fool, unruly sun, 506

But do not let us quarrel any more, 1994

By an Evolutionist, 1944

Byron, George Gordon, Lord, 1454

By the Rushy-fringed Bank, 564

Byzantium, 2392

Caliban upon Setebos, 2008

Calm was the even, and clear was the sky, 791

Camden, most reverend head, to whom I owe, 537
Canonization, The, 497
Canterbury Tales, The, 71
Cape Ann, 2578
Captain or Colonel, or Knight in Arms, 572
Careful observers may foretell the hour, 855
Carlyle, Thomas, 1768
[Carlyle's Portraits of His Contemporaries], 1774
[Carrion Comfort], 2240
Catch not my breath, O clamorous heart, 1922
Channel Firing, 2224
Characteristics, 1784
Charge of the Light Brigade, The, 1920
Chaucer, Geoffrey, 61
Childe Harold's Pilgrimage, 1465
"Childe Roland to the Dark Tower Came," 1972
Chimney Sweeper, The (Songs of Experience), 1224
Chimney Sweeper, The (Songs of Innocence), 1220
Christabel, 1401
Circus Animals' Desertion, The, 2397
Clod & the Pebble, The, 1224
Cloud, The, 1608
Clouds, lingering yet, extend in solid bars, 1329
Cold Heaven, The, 2379
Coleridge, Samuel Taylor, 1378
Coleridge, 2178
Come, dear children, let us away, 2037
Come Down, O Maid, 1877
Come leave the loathéd stage, 545
Come live with me and be my love, 501
Come, My Celia, 543
Come to me in my dreams, and then, 2051
Complaint to His Purse, 180
Composed in the Valley Near Dover, On the Day of Landing, 1328
Composed by the Side of Grasmere Lake, 1329
Composed upon Westminster Bridge, September 3, 1802, 1327
Comrades, leave me here a little, while as yet 'tis early morn, 1867
Comus, Songs from, 564
Condemned to Hope's delusive mine, 1087
Confessions, 2005
Conquest of Granada, II, Epilogue to The, 790
Conrad, Joseph, 2297
Constancy to an Ideal Object, 1428
Convergence of the Twain, The, 2225
"Courage!" he said, and pointed toward the land, 1850
Cowley, 1136
Crazy Jane Talks with the Bishop, 2394
Creep into thy narrow bed, 2075
Crossing the Bar, 1946
Cruelty has a Human Heart, 1229
Cuddie, for shame hold up thy heavye head, 208
Culture and Anarchy, 2109

Darkling Thrush, The, 2216
Darkness, 1463
Dawn, The, 1945
Dear, had the world in its caprice, 1980
Death, be not proud, though some have calléd thee, 520
Dedication (to Idylls of the King), 1924
Defense of Poetry, A, 1656
Dejection: An Ode, 1419
Description of a City Shower, A, 855
Devotions upon Emergent Occasions, 526
Dialogue of Self and Soul, A, 2390
Dirge, A, 1636
Discourse Concerning the Original and Progress of Satire, A, 849
Divine Image, A (Songs of Experience), 1229
Divine Image, The (Songs of Innocence), 1219
Does the Eagle know what is in the pit?, 1230
Don Juan, 1485
Donne, John, 490
Donne, the delight of Phoebus and each Muse, 538
Don't thou 'ear my 'erse's legs, as they canters awaäy?, 1926
Dover Beach, 2061
Down by the Salley Gardens, 2370
Drink to me only with thine eyes, 542
Drummer Hodge, 2215
Dryden, John, 784
Duns Scotus's Oxford, 2238
During Wind and Rain, 2229

Eagle: A Fragment, The, 1874
Earth has not anything to show more fair, 1327
Earth rais'd up her head, 1223
Earth's Answer, 1223
Easter 1916, 2380
Ecstasy, The, 503
Elegiac Stanzas, 1325
Elegy, An, 539
Elegy IV. The Perfume, 512
Elegy to the Memory of an Unfortunate Lady, 1035
Eliot, T. S., 2569
Endymion, 1675
England in 1819, 1583
Eolian Harp, The, 1381
Epigram on Milton, 833
Epilogue to Asolando, 2030
Epistle to Dr. Arbuthnot, 1060
Epistle to Miss Blount, 1034
Epistle to Robert, Earl of Oxford and Mortimer, 1037
Epistle II: To a Lady, 1052
Epitaph, 1429
Epitaph on Elizabeth, L. H., 539
Epithalamion, 374
Essay of Dramatic Poesy, An, 842
Essay on Criticism, An, 1001
Essay on Man, An, 1038
Essays (Bacon), 746
Etruscan Places, 2545
Evening's Love, Song from An, 791
Eve of St. Agnes, The, 1683
Expostulation and Reply, 1261
Extempore Effusion upon the Death of James Hogg, 1331

Fables Ancient and Modern, The Preface to, 850

Faerie Queene, The, 212

Fall of Hyperion, The, 1720

Fanatics have their dreams, wherewith they weave, 1722

Farewell: thou are too dear for my possessing, 395

Farewell, thou child of my right hand, and joy, 538

Farewell, too little, and too lately known, 824

Far-off, most secret, and inviolate Rose, 2373

Fascination of What's Difficult, The, 2377

Father of all! in every age, 1046

Fear death?—to feel the fog in my throat, 2016

Fear No More the Heat o' the Sun, 390

Felix Randal, 2239

Finnegans Wake, 2488

First Satire of the Second Book of Horace Imitated, The, 1048

Five years have passed; five summers, with the length, 1264

Flea, The, 500

Flee fro the prees and dwelle with soothfastnesse, 183

Flower in the Crannied Wall, 1928

Folly of Being Comforted, The, 2375

For Anne Gregory, 2391

For God's sake hold your tongue, and let me love, 497

Forsaken Merman, The, 2037

For the Sexes: The Gates of Paradise, 1248

Four Quartets, 2601

Fra Lippo Lippi, 1981

"Frater Ave atque Vale," 1933

French Revolution, The, 1818

Fresh spring the herald of loves mighty king, 373

Friend of the wise! and teacher of the good!, 1423

From harmony, from heavenly harmony, 831

From low to high doth dissolution climb, 1330

From you have I been absent in the spring, 396

From Wynyard's Gap the livelong day, 2217

Frost at Midnight, 1417

Full Fathom Five, 391

Function of Criticism at the Present Time, The, 2088

Funeral, The, 509

Garden of Love, The, 1226

General Prologue, The, 73

Gentilesse, 182

Glory be to God for dappled things, 2236

Go and catch a falling star, 494

God's Grandeur, 2234

Goethe in Weimar sleeps, and Greece, 2049

Go, for they call you, shepherd from the hill, 2055

Good Friday, 1613. Riding Westward, 517

Good-Morrow, The, 494

Grammarian's Funeral, A, 2002

Green Linnet, The, 1313

Growing Old, 2074

Grow old along with me!, 2020

Gr-r-r—there go, my heart's abhorrence!, 1954

Gulliver's Travels, 878

Gypsy Songs, 541

Had I but plenty of money, money enough and to spare, 1978

Hail to thee, blithe Spirit!, 1610

Half a league, half a league, 1920

Hap, 2212

Happy the man whose wish and care, 1033

Happy ye leaves when as those lilly hands, 370

Hardy, Thomas, 2210

Hark! ah, the nightingale—, 2052

Hear the voice of the Bard!, 1222

He clasps the crag with crooked hands, 1874

Hellas, Choruses from, 1619

Hence loathéd Melancholy, 555

Hence vain deluding Joys, 559

Henry IV, Part 1, 403

Here lies, to each her parents' ruth, 537

Here often, when a child I lay reclined, 1874

Here, on our native soil, we breathe once more, 1328

Here the crow starves, here the patient stag, 2577

He stood among a crowd at Dromahair, 2372

History of Rasselas, Prince of Abyssinia, The, 1094

Hold, are you mad? you damned confounded dog, 789

Holy Sonnets, 518

Holy Thursday (Songs of Experience), 1224

Holy Thursday (Songs of Innocence), 1221

Home-Thoughts, from Abroad, 1961

Home-Thoughts, from the Sea, 1962

Hopkins, Gerard Manley, 2230

Horse Dealer's Daughter, The, 2515

House, 2028

Householder, The, 2027

How changed is here each spot man makes or fills!, 2067

How fevered is the man, who cannot look, 1696

How like a winter hath my absence been, 396

How Soon Hath Time, 571

How sweet I roam'd from field to field, 1215

How They Brought the Good News from Ghent to Aix, 1960

How warm this woodland wild recess!, 1426

Human Abstract, The, 1227

Hurrahing in Harvest, 2237

Hymn of Apollo, 1613

Hymn of Pan, 1614

Hymn to Christ, at the Author's Last Going into Germany, A, 521

Hymn to God My God, in My Sickness, 522

Hymn to God the Father, A, 523
Hymn to Intellectual Beauty, 1577

I am a little world made cunningly, 519
I am poor brother Lippo, by your leave!, 1981
I arise from dreams of thee, 1583
I Askéd a Thief, 1249
I bring fresh showers for the thirsting flowers, 1608
I can love both fair and brown, 496
I caught this morning morning's minion, 2236
I chanced upon a new book yesterday, 2029
Idler No. 31, 1092
I dream of a red-rose tree, 1971
Idylls of the King, 1924
If but some vengeful god would call to me, 2212
If by dull rhymes our English must be chained, 1695
If from the public way you turn your steps, 1298
If, in the month of dark December, 1460
If yet I have not all thy love, 505
If you have revisited the town, thin Shade, 2378
I had a dream, which was not all a dream, 1463
I have done one braver thing, 495
I have heard that hysterical women say, 2395
I have led her home, my love, my only friend, 1922
I have met them at close of day, 2380
I heard a thousand blended notes, 1260
I heard the old, old men say, 2376
I leant upon a coppice gate, 2216
I Look into My Glass, 2214
Il Penseroso, 559
I met a traveler from an antique land, 1579
I met the Bishop on the road, 2394
Impercipient, The, 2212
In a solitude of the sea, 2225
In a Year, 1989
Indian Emperor, Song from *The*, 791
Indian Serenade, The, 1583
Indifferent, The, 496
In Drear-Nighted December, 1681
Infant Sorrow, 1228
In front the awful Alpine track, 2044
In Harmony with Nature, 2036
In Love, If Love Be Love (in *Idylls of the King*), 1926
In Memoriam A. H. H., 1878
In pious times, ere priestcraft did begin, 794
In the Valley of Cauteretz, 1924
In this lone, open glade I lie, 2051
In Time of "The Breaking of Nations," 2229
Introduction (*Songs of Experience*), 1222
Introduction (*Songs of Innocence*), 1218
In what torn ship soever I embark, 521
Inversnaid, 2240
In Xanadu did Kubla Khan, 1400
I said—Then, dearest, since 'tis so, 1991
I sat on cushioned otter skin, 2367
Isolation. To Marguerite, 2040

I sought a theme and sought for it in vain, 2397
I sprang to the stirrup, and Joris, and he, 1960
Is this a holy thing to see, 1224
I summon to the winding ancient stair, 2390
I thought of thee, my partner and my guide, 1330
It Is a Beauteous Evening, 1327
It is an ancient Mariner, 1384
It is the first mild day of March, 1262
It keeps eternal whisperings around, 1675
It little profits that an idle king, 1863
It once might have been, once only, 2006
I Traveled Among Unknown Men, 1283
It Was a Beauty That I Saw, 538
I walk through the long schoolroom questioning, 2388
I Wandered Lonely As a Cloud, 1314
I wander thro' each charter'd street, 1227
I want a hero: an uncommon want, 1487
I was angry with my friend, 1228
I was thy neighbor once, thou rugged Pile!, 1325
I weep for Adonais—he is dead!, 1622
I went to the Garden of Love, 1226
I will arise and go now, and go to Innisfree, 2371
I wonder, by my troth, what thou and I, 494
I wonder do you feel today, 2000
I would to heaven that I were so much clay, 1487

Johnson, Samuel, 1072
Jonson, Ben, 530
Journey of the Magi, 2598
Joyce, James, 2412
June Bracken and Heather, 1945
Just for a handful of silver he left us, 1959

Keats, John, 1669
Kind pity chokes my spleen; brave scorn forbids, 514
Kraken, The, 1843
Kubla Khan, 1399

La Belle Dame sans Merci, 1694
Laboratory, The, 1957
Lady of Shalott, The, 1846
Lake Isle of Innisfree, The, 2371
L'Allegro, 555
Lamb, The, 1219
Lament, A, 1618
Lamia, 1704
Landscapes, 2577
Lantern Out of Doors, The, 2235
Lapis Lazuli, 2395
Last Ride Together, The, 1991
Last Word, The, 2075
Late, my grandson! half the morning have I paced these sandy tracts, 1934
Lausanne, 2215
Lawrence, D. H., 2493
Lawrence, of Virtuous Father Virtuous Son, 574
Lectures on Shakespeare, 1450
Leda and the Swan, 2387
Let man's soul be a sphere, and then, in this, 517

Let Me Enjoy, 2220
Let me not to the marriage of true minds, 398
Let me pour forth, 508
Let Observation, with extensive view, 1076
Letter of the Authors, A, 215
Letters **(Keats):** To Benjamin Bailey, 1736; To George and Georgiana Keats, 1746; To George and Thomas Keats, 1738; To John Hamilton Reynolds, 1740, 1742; To Percy Bysshe Shelley, 1750; To John Taylor, 1741; To Richard Woodhouse, 1745
Let the bird of loudest lay, 401
Let us begin and carry up this corpse, 2002
Let us go then, you and I, 2574
Let us play, and dance, and sing, 546
Life of Samuel Johnson, LL.D., The, 1156
Lift not the painted veil which those who live, 1580
Light flows our war of mocking words, and yet, 2042
Like as the waves make towards the pebbled shore, 394
Like as, to make our appetites more keen, 398
Lines ("Here often, when a child I lay reclined"), 1874
Lines Composed a Few Miles Above Tintern Abbey, 1264
Lines: When the Lamp Is Shattered, 1635
Lines Written in Early Spring, 1260
Lines Written in Kensington Gardens, 2051
Lines Written in the Bay of Lerici, 1638
Literature and Science, 2152
Little Black Boy, The, 1221
Little Gidding, 2601
Little Lamb, who made thee?, 1219
Lives of the Poets, 1136
Locksley Hall, 1867
Locksley Hall Sixty Years After, 1934
Lo I the man, whose Muse whilome did maske, 218
London, 1227
London, 1802, 1328
Long-expected one and twenty, 1088
Long fed on boundless topes, O race of man, 2074
Longing, 2051
Long-legged Fly, 2396
Look at the stars! Look look up at the skies!, 2234
Look in thy glass, and te the face thou viewest, 391
Lost Leader, The, 1959
Lotos-Eaters, The, 1850
Love Among the Ruins, 196
Lover's Infiniteness, 505
Love's Alchemy, 499
"Love seeketh not Itself to ck, The, 1224
Love Song of J. Alfred, 2574
Lucy Gray, 1283
Lycidas, 565
Lyke as a ship tha ough the ocean wyde, 371
Lyrical Ballads, 1

Mac Flecknoe, 817
Madame, ye been of alle beautee shrine, 179
Madness of King Goll, The, 2367
Mad Song, 1216
Man Who Dreamed of Faeryland, The, 2372
Márgarét, are you gríeving, 2239
Mariana, 1844
Marina, 2599
Mark but this flea, and mark in this, 500
Marriage à la Mode, Song from, 792
Marriage of Heaven and Hell, The, 1234
Maud, 1921
Maurice de Guérin, 2107
Meeting at Night, 1965
Memorabilia, 1968
Memorial Verses, 2049
Memory, hither come, 1216
Men call you fayre, and you doe credit it, 373
Men of England, wherefore plow, 1582
Merciless Beauty, 181
Metaphysical Poets, The, 2615
Methought I Saw My Late Espoused Saint, 575
Michael, 1298
Midwinter spring is its own season, 2601
Mill, John Stuart, 2168
Miller's Tale, The, 156
Milton, John, 553
Milton, 1138
Milton! thou shouldst be living at this hour, 1328
Mock on, Mock on, Voltaire, Rousseau, 1250
Modest Proposal, A, 988
Monarch of Gods and Daemons, and all Spirits, 1587
Mont Blanc, 1573
Morning, 1250
Morte d'Arthur, 1855
Most glorious Lord of lyfe, th on his day, 372
Motions and Means, on land a it war, 1331
Move Eastward, Happy Ea rs of
Much have I traveled in gold, 1672 18
Music, when soft voi s
Mutability **(Shelley** 15
Mutability **(Wor wor** ice, 248
Mutual Forgi ess c any cages
My aspens dear he lied in every quelled, 2237
My fir though a drowsy numbness wo d, 1972
My heart ach pains, 170 p, 1315
My Heart through greedy covetize,
My hung
371 ness, 1956
My L s' eyes are nothing like the
My 0
sther bore me in the southern wild,
M 1
mother groand! my father wept, 1228
My pensive Sara! thy soft cheek reclined, 1381
My spirit is too weak, 1675

Neutral Tones, 2213
Never any more, 1989
Never Pain to Tell Thy Love, 1249
"Never shall a young man, 2391
New Atlantis, The, 760
Nigger of the "Narcissus," Preface to The, 2299
Nobly, nobly Cape Saint Vincent to the northwest died away, 1962
No, for I'll save it! Seven years since, 2025
No longer mourn for me when I am dead, 394
No, no, go not to Lethe, neither twist, 1703
Northern Farmer, 1926
No Second Troy, 2376
Not every man has gentians in his house, 2564
Nothing is so beautiful as spring, 2235
Nothing so true as what you once let fall, 1052
Not, I'll not, carrion comfort, Despair, not feast on thee, 2240
Not marble, nor the gilded monuments, 393
Not mine own fears, nor the prophetic soul, 397
Novum Organum, 753
Now it is autumn and the falling fruit, 2567
[No Worst, There Is None], 2241
Now Sleeps the Crimson Petal, 1876
Now that I, tying thy glass mask tightly, 1957
Nun's Priest's Tale, The, 141
Nurse's Song (Songs of Experience), 1225
Nurse's Song (Songs of Innocence), 1220

October, 207
Ode: Intimations of Immortality, 1315
Urn, 1698
ly, 1702
1033
gale, 1700
322
545
696
Ode the 696
Odor Chr ind, 1584
Faceums, 2498
Of ma fitt dis 597
Of Marriage and Sie, and the fruit, 1673
O for ten years tha 748
Of Studies, 72 verwhelm,
Of this worls theatre in 372
ye stay,
Oft I had heard of Lucy Gra
Of Truth, 746
O Goddess! hear these tune bers, wrung, 1696
O golden-tongued Romance with lute!, 1682
Oh, Galuppi, Baldassaro, this is very to find!, 1966
Oh Mistress Mine, 389
Oh, talk not to me of a name great in story, 1567

Oh there is blessing in this gentle breeze, 1337
Oh, thou! in Hellas deemed of heavenly birth, 1465
Oh, to be in England, 1961
Old Fitz, who from your suburb grange, 1933
Old Men Admiring Themselves in the Water, The, 2376
O Lyric Love, 2026
On a Political Prisoner, 2382
Once, and but once found in thy company, 512
Once more the storm is howling, and half hid, 2384
On Donne's Poetry, 1427
One day I wrote her name upon the strand, 373
On either side the river lie, 1846
One that is ever kind said yesterday, 2375
One We Knew, 2222
On Fame, 1696
On First Looking into Chapman's Homer, 1672
On Liberty, 2181
Only a man harrowing clods, 2229
On Man, on Nature, and on Human Life, 1333
On My First Daughter, 537
On My First Son, 538
On Seeing the Elgin Marbles for the First Time, 1675
On Sitting Down to Read King Lear Once Again, 1682
On the Death of Dr. Robert Levet, 1087
On the Late Massacre in Piedmont, 574
On the New Forcers of Conscience Under the Long Parliament, 573
On the Sea, 1675
On the Sonnet, 1695
O quick quick quick, quick hear the song sparrow, 2578
O Rose, thou art sick, 1225
O soft embalmer of the still midnight, 1695
Others abide our question. Thou art free, 2036
O thou, who plumed with strong desire, 1615
O what can ail the, Knight at arms, 1694
O wild West Wid, thou breath of Autumn's being, 184
O world! O life! time!, 1618
Ozymandias, 157

Palladium, 2073
Paradise Lost,
Paradoxes and problems, 524
Pardoner's Prague and Tale, The, 125
Parson's Tale e, 173
iting at Mong, 1966
Phead Pres, 1828
Phan 14
Philo ict, 1428
pho nix 32
Piano the Turtle, The, 401
Pied B
Piping 76
Pity we alleys wild, 1218
Plays Fran ore, 1227
Poems old), ce to, 2246
nce to, 2076

Poetical Sketches, 1215
Poison Tree, A, 1228
Poor soul, the center of my sinful earth, 401
Pope, Alexander, 995
Pope, 1147
Porphyria's Lover, 1953
Portrait of the Artist as a Young Man, A, 2424
Prayer for My Daughter, A, 2384
Prayers and Meditations, 1120
Preface to *Plays Pleasant*, 2246
Preface to *Poems* **(Arnold)**, 2076
Preface to Shakespeare, The, 1125
Preface to *The Nigger of the "Narcissus,"* 2299
Preface to the Second Edition of *Lyrical Ballads*, 1268
Prelude, The, 1336
Princess, Songs from *The*, 1874
Prologue Spoken by Mr. Garrick, 1085
Prometheus Unbound, 1586
Prospice, 2016

Queen and Huntress, 541

Rabbi Ben Ezra, 2020
Rainbow, The, 2530
Rambler No. 5, 1089
Rambler No. 4, 1121
Rannoch, by Glencoe, 2577
Rape of the Lock, The, 1014
Rash Bride, The, 2220
Reason is our soul's left hand, faith her right, 510
Recluse, The, 1333
Recollections of Love, 1426
Red of the Dawn!, 1945
Relic, The, 509
Requiescat, 2053
Resembles life what once was deemed of light, 1423
Resolution and Independence, 1309
Respectability, 1980
Revenge, The, 1928
Reveries over Childhood and Youth, 2401
Rime of the Ancient Mariner, The, 1383
Rintrah roars & shakes his fires in the burdend air, 1235
River, that rollest by the ancient walls, 1566
Roman Virgil, thou that singest, 1931
Rose of the World, The, 2370
Rough wind, that moanest loud, 1636
Round the cape of a sudden came the sea, 1966
Row us out from Desenzano, to your Sirmione row!, 1933
Ruined Cottage, The, 1285

Sabrina Fair, 564
Sailing to Byzantium, 2386
St. Agnes' Eve—Ah, bitter chill it was!, 1683
Saint Peter sat by the celestial gate, 1545
Samson Agonistes, 701
Sartor Resartus, 1795
Satire III, Religion, 514
Savage I was sitting in my house, late, lone, 2027
Scholar Gypsy, The, 2054

Season of mists and mellow fruitfulness, 1735
Second Coming, The, 2383
Secret Rose, The, 2373
Secret Sharer, The, 2329
Secular Masque, The, 838
See the chariot at hand here of Love, 543
September 1913, 2377
Sermon LXXVI **(Donne)**, 529
Set where the upper streams of Simois flow, 2073
Shakespeare, William, 384
Shakespeare, 2036
Shall I compare thee to a summer's day, 392
Shall I sonnet-sing you about myself?, 2028
Shaw, George Bernard, 2242
She came to the village church, 1921
She Dwelt Among the Untrodden Ways, 1281
She Hears the Storm, 2223
She left me at the silent time, 1638
Shelley, Percy Bysshe, 1568
Shepheardes Calender, The, 207
She that but little patience knew, 2382
She told how they used to form for the country dances, 2222
She took the dappled partridge flecked with blood, 1846
She Walks in Beauty, 1461
Ship of Death, The, 2567
Short Song of Congratulation, A, 1088
Show me, dear Christ, Thy spouse so bright and clear, 521
Shut, shut the door, good John! (fatigued, I said), 1061
Sick Rose, The, 1225
Sigh No More Ladies, 388
Silent Voices, The, 1946
Since all that beat about in Nature's range, 1428
Since I am coming to that holy room, 522
Sleep and Poetry, 1673
Slow, Slow, Fresh Fount, 540
Slumber Did My Spirit Seal, A, 1283
Snake, 2565
Soliloquy of the Spanish Cloister, 1954
Solitary Reaper, The, 1324
Some that have deeper digged love's mine than I, 499
Sometimes a lantern moves along the night, 2235
Song for St. Cecilia's Day, A, 831
Song ("Go and catch a falling star"), 494
Song ("How sweet I roam'd from field to field"), 1215
Song ("Memory, hither come"), 1216
Songs of Experience, 1222
Songs of Innocence, 1218
Song: To Celia, 542
Song to the Men of England, 1582
Sonnet ("Lift not the painted veil which those who live"), 1580
Sonnet ("She took the dappled partridge flecked with blood"), 1846
Sonnets **(Shakespeare)**, 391
Sonnets **(Wordsworth)**, 1327
Sorrow of Love, The, 2371
So We'll Go No More A-Roving, 1485
Speech after long silence; it is right, 2394

Spenser, Edmund, 204
Splendor Falls, The, 1875
Spring, 2235
Spring and Fall, 2239
Standing aloof in giant ignorance, 1683
Stanzas for Music, 1462
Stanzas from the Grande Chartreuse, 2062
Stanzas in Memory of the Author of Obermann, 2044
Stanzas to the Po, 1566
Stanzas Written in Dejection, Near Naples, 1580
Stanzas Written on the Road Between Florence and Pisa, 1567
Starlight Night, The, 2234
Steamboats, Viaducts, and Railways, 1331
Stern Daughter of the Voice of God!, 1322
Still to Be Neat, 544
Stolen Child, The, 2368
Stop, Christian passer-by!—Stop, child of God, 1429
Strange Fits of Passion Have I Known, 1280
Strew on her roses, roses, 2053
Strong Son of God, immortal Love, 1879
Study of Poetry, The, 2130
Such were the notes thy once-loved Poet sung, 1037
Suddenly I saw the cold and rook-delighting heaven, 2379
Summer ends now; now, barbarous in beauty, the stooks arise, 2237
Sun Rising, The, 506
Sunset and evening star, 1946
Surprised by Joy, 1329
Swear by what the sages spoke, 2398
Sweeney Among the Nightingales, 2578
Sweet and Low, 1874
Sweet Echo, 564
Sweet love, renew thy force; be it not said, 394
Swift, Jonathan, 852
Swift as a spirit hastening to his task, 1641
Swiftly walk o'er the western wave, 1617

Tables Turned, The, 1262
Take, Oh, Take Those Lips Away, 390
Tears, Idle Tears, 1875
Tell Me Where Is Fancy Bred, 388
Tempest, Prologue to The, 788
Tennyson, Alfred, Lord, 1839
That civilization may not sink, 2396
That is no country for old men. The young, 2386
That night your great guns, unawares, 2224
That's my last Duchess painted on the wall, 1956
That time of year thou mayst in me behold, 395
That with this bright believing band, 2212
The awful shadow of some unseen Power, 1577
The brawling of a sparrow in the eaves, 2371
The cock is crowing, 1308
The everlasting universe of things, 1573
The faery beam upon you, 541

The firste fader and findere of gentilesse, 182
The Frost performs its secret ministry, 1417
The gray sea and the long black land, 1965
The keen stars were twinkling, 1638
The Lord let the house of a brute to the soul of a man, 1944
Thel's Motto, 1230
The rain set early in tonight, 1953
There are (I scarce can think it, but am told), 1048
There Be None of Beauty's Daughters, 1462
There is a Yew Tree, pride of Lorton Vale, 1314
There on the top of the down, 1945
There was a roaring in the wind all night, 1309
There was a time in former years, 2223
There was a time when meadow, grove, and stream, 1317
The sea is calm tonight, 2061
These to His Memory—since he held them dear, 1924
The sleepless Hours who watch me as I lie, 1613
The sun is warm, the sky is clear, 1580
The trees are in their autumn beauty, 2379
The unpurged images of day recede, 2392
The wild winds weep, 1216
The woods decay, the woods decay and fall, 1865
The world is charged with the grandeur of God, 2234
Th' expense of spirit in a waste of shame, 399
They Say That Hope Is Happiness, 1462
They sing their dearest songs, 2229
They that have power to hurt and will do none, 395
They throw in Drummer Hodge, to rest, 2215
They who have best succeeded on the stage, 790
This darksome burn, horseback brown, 2240
This Living Hand, 1736
[Thou Art Indeed Just, Lord], 2241
Thou art not, Penshurst, built to envious show, 532
Thou fair-hair'd angel of the evening, 1215
Though beauty be the mark of praise, 539
Though I Am Young and Cannot Tell, 542
Thou hast made me, and shall Thy work decay?, 518
Thou still unravished bride of quietness, 1698
Thou youngest virgin-daughter of the skies, 825
Three poets, in three distant ages born, 833
Three Years She Grew, 1282
Thrise happie she, that is so well assured, 372
Through Alpine meadows soft-suffused, 2062
Thyrsis, 2067

'Tis better to be vile than vile esteemed, 399

'Tis hard to say, if greater want of skill, 1001

'Tis the middle of night by the castle clock, 1402

'Tis true, 'tis day; what though it be?, 507

Tithonus, 1865

To ———, 1618

To a Friend, 2037

To a Shade, 2378

To a Skylark, 1610

To Autumn, 1735

Toccata of Galuppi's, A, 1966

To draw no envy, Shakespeare, on thy name, 535

To Edward FitzGerald (Browning), 2029

To E. FitzGerald (Tennyson), 1933

To find the Western path, 1250

To His Scribe Adam, 180

To Homer, 1683

To Jane: The Invitation, 1636

To Jane: The Keen Stars Were Twinkling, 1638

To John Donne, 538

To Marguerite—Continued, 2041

To me, fair friend, you never can be old, 397

To Mercy, Pity, Peace, and Love, 1219

To Miss ———, 1084

To My Sister, 1262

To Night, 1617

To Penshurst, 532

To Rosamond, 179

To Sleep, 1695

To the Countess of Bedford, 510

To the Evening Star, 1215

To the Memory of Mr. Oldham, 824

To the Memory of My Beloved Master William Shakespeare, 535

To the Muses, 1217

To the Pious Memory of the Accomplished Young Lady Mrs. Anne Killigrew, 825

To Tirzah, 1229

To Virgil, 1931

Tower of Famine, The, 1616

Towery city and branchy between towers, 2238

To William Camden, 537

To William Wordsworth, 1423

To you, my purs, and to noon other wight, 180

Tradition and the Individual Talent, 2608

Trampwoman's Tragedy, A, 2217

Trembling of the Veil, The, 2405

Triumph of Charis, The, 543

Triumph of Life, The, 1640

Truth, 183

Turning and turning in the widening gyre, 2383

'Twas at the royal feast, for Persia won, 833

'Twas on a Holy Thursday, their innocent faces clean, 1221

'Twas Summer and the sun was mounted high, 1286

Twice or thrice had I loved thee, 507

Twicknam Garden, 498

Two in the Campagna, 2000

Two loves I have of comfort and despair, 400

Two spirits: An Allegory, The, 1615

Tyger, The, 1225

Tyrannic Love, Epilogue to, 789

Ulysses (Joyce), 2438

Ulysses (Tennyson), 1863

Ulysses, Order, and Myth, 2623

Under Ben Bulben, 2398

Undertaking, The, 495

Under the Greenwood Tree, 388

Under the Waterfall, 2227

Universal Prayer, The, 1046

Up at a Villa—Down in the City, 1978

Upon a time, before the faery broods, 1705

Up! up! my friend, and quit your books, 1262

Valediction: Forbidding Mourning, A, 502

Valediction: Of Weeping, A, 508

Vanity of Human Wishes, The, 1076

Vanity, saith the preacher, vanity!, 1962

Verses on the Death of Dr. Swift, 857

Vision of Delight, The, 546

Vision of Judgment, The, 1544

[Vision of The Last Judgment, A], 1251

Walk, The, 2228

Waste Land, The, 2581

We are as clouds that veil the midnight moon, 1573

We Are Seven, 1258

Webster was much possessed by death, 2580

We Christmas-caroled down the Vale, and up the Vale, and round the Vale, 2220

Well! If the bard was weather-wise, who made, 1419

We sat together at one summer's end, 2375

We stood by a pond that winter day, 2213

We were apart; yet, day by day, 2040

Whan that April with his showres soote, 73

What beckoning ghost, along the moonlight shade, 1035

What dire offense from amorous causes springs, 1016

Whate'er is Born of Mortal Birth, 1229

What guyle is this, that those her golden tresses, 371

What is he buzzing in my ears?, 2005

What is it to grow old?, 2074

What Is Life?, 1423

What Is Poetry?, 2170

What need you, being come to sense, 2377

What seas what shores what gray rocks and what islands, 2599

When a Man Hath No Freedom to Fight for at Home, 1567

When by thy scorn, O murderess, I am dead, 499

When Daffodils Begin to Peer, 390

When Daisies Pied, 386

"Whenever I plunge my arm, like this, 2227

When first, descending from the moorlands, 1331
When I Consider How My Light Is Spent, 575
When I do count the clock that tells the time, 392
When I Have Fears, 1682
When, in disgrace with fortune and men's eyes, 393
When in the chronicle of wasted time, 397
When Learning's triumph o'er her barbarous foes, 1085
When my grave is broke up again, 509
When my love swears that she is made of truth, 400
When my mother died I was very young, 1220
When Passion's Trance Is Overpast, 1619
When Stella strikes the tuneful string, 1084
When the Assault Was Intended to the City, 572
When the dumb Hour, clothed in black, 1946
When the lamp is shattered, 1635
When the voices of children are heard on the green (*Songs of Experience*), 1225
When the voices of children are heard on the green (*Songs of Innocence*), 1220
When to the sessions of sweet silent thought, 393
When We Two Parted, 1460
When You Are Old, 2371
Where dips the rocky highland, 2368
Where, like a pillow on a bed, 503
Where the Bee Sucks, There Suck I, 391
Where the quiet-colored end of evening smiles, 1969
Whether on Ida's shady brow, 1217
Whispers of Immortality, 2580
Who dreamed that beauty passes like a dream?, 2370
Whoever comes to shroud me, do not harm, 509
Who Goes with Fergus?, 2372
Who prop, thou ask'st, in these bad days, my mind?, 2037
Who will go drive with Fergus now, 2372
Why Did I Laugh Tonight?, 1693

Why should a foolish marriage vow, 792
Why should I blame her that she filled my days, 2376
Why the Novel Matters, 2558
"Why, William, on that old gray stone, 1261
Wife of Bath's Prologue and Tale, The, 95
Wild Swans at Coole, The, 2379
['Will sprawl, now that the heat of day is best, 2009
Wilt Thou forgive that sin where I begun, 523
Windhover, The, 2236
With blackest moss the flower plots, 1844
With Donne, whose muse on dromedary trots, 1427
Women and Roses, 1971
Women in Love, 2536
Woosel Cock So Black of Hue, The, 387
Wordsworth, William, 1255
Wordsworth, 2118
Work Without Hope, 1427
World Is Too Much with Us, The, 1328
World's Great Age, The, 1620
Worlds on Worlds, 1619
Wouldst thou hear what man can say, 539
Would that the structure brave, the manifold music I build, 2016
Written After Swimming from Sestos to Abydos, 1460
Written in March, 1308
Yeats, William Butler, 2362
Yeats, 2626
Ye learned sisters which have oftentimes, 374
Yes! in the sea of life enisled, 2041
Yet once more, O ye laurels, and once more, 566
Yew Trees, 1314
You Ask Me, Why, Though Ill at Ease, 1855
You did not come, 2214
You did not walk with me, 2228
Youre yën two wol slee me sodeinly, 181
Youth, 2302
Youth and Art, 2006

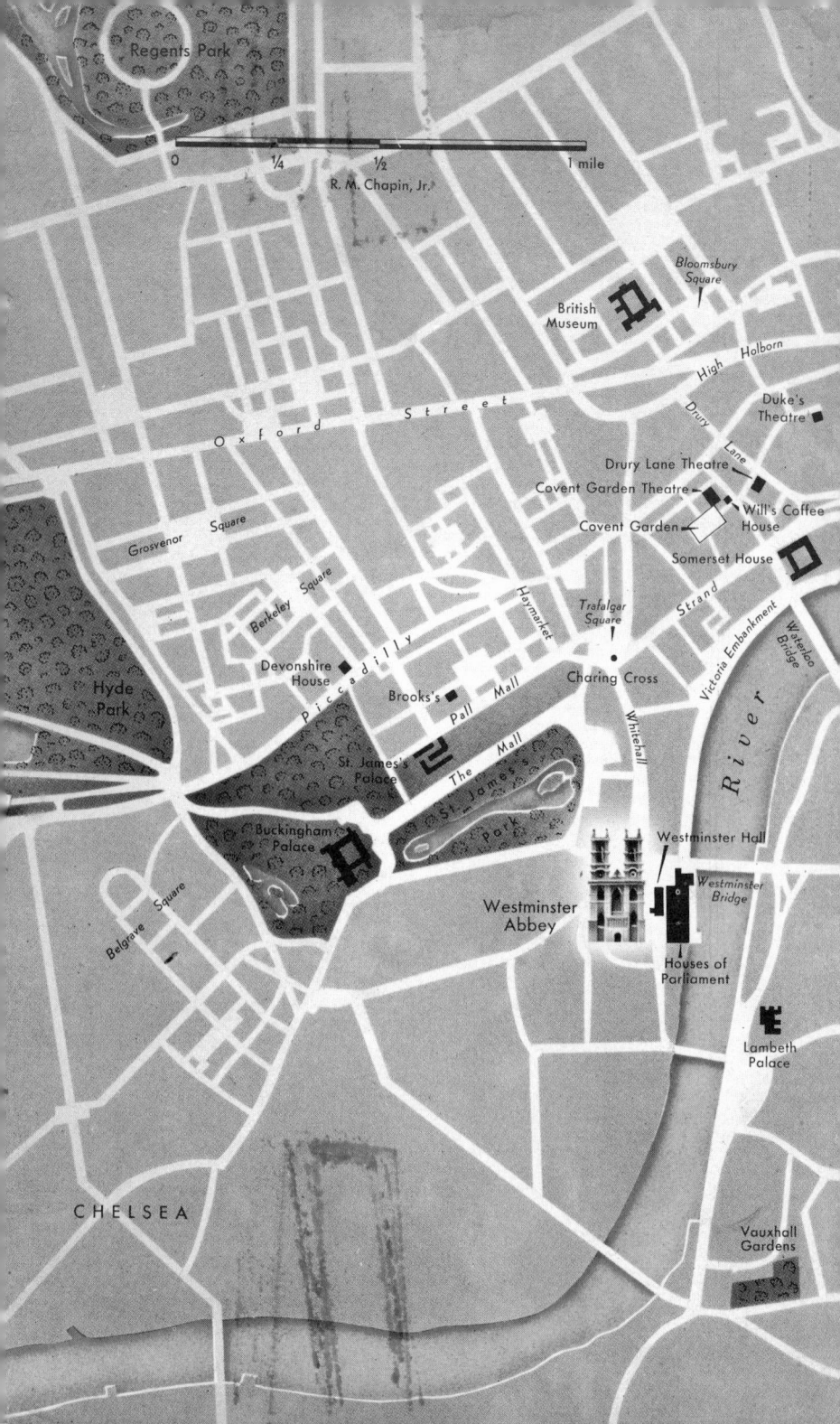